AGE, WEIGHT & DISTANCE TABLE

For use with Chase and Hurdle races

Distance	Age	Jan	Feb	Mar	Apr	May	June
2m	5	12—7	12—7	12—7	12—7	12—7	12—7
	4	11–13	12–0	12–1	12–2	12–3	12–4
2¼m	5	12—7	12—7	12—7	12—7	12—7	12—7
	4	11–12	11–13	12–0	12–1	12–2	12–3
2½m	5	12—7	12—7	12—7	12—7	12—7	12—7
	4	11–11	11–12	11–13	12–0	12–1	12–2
2¾m	5	12—6	12—7	12—7	12—7	12—7	12—7
	4	11–10	11–11	11–12	11–13	12–0	12–1
3m	5	12—6	12—6	12—7	12—7	12—7	12—7
	4	11—8	11–10	11–11	11–12	11–13	12–0

Distance	Age	July	Aug	Sep	Oct	Nov	Dec
2m	5	12—7	12—7	12—7	12—7	12—7	12—7
	4	12—4	12—5	12—5	12—6	12—6	12—7
	3	11—5	11—6	11—8	11—9	11—11	11—12
2¼m	5	12—7	12—7	12—7	12—7	12—7	12—7
	4	12—3	12—4	12—5	12—5	12—6	12—6
	3	11—4	11—5	11—7	11—8	11—9	11—10
2½m	5	12—7	12—7	12—7	12—7	12—7	12—7
	4	12—2	12—3	12—4	12—5	12—6	12—6
	3		11—4	11—6	11—7	11—8	11—9
2¾m	5	12—7	12—7	12—7	12—7	12—7	12—7
	4	12—2	12—3	12—4	12—5	12—5	12—6
	3					11—7	11—8
3m	5	12—7	12—7	12—7	12—7	12—7	12—7
	4	12—1	12—2	12—3	12—4	12—5	12—5
	3				11—5	11—6	11—7

For 6-y-o's and older, use 12-7 in all cases

Note Race distances in the above tables are shown only at ¼-mile intervals. For races of 2m1f use the 2¼-mile table weights; for races of 2m3f use 2½ miles; and so forth. For races over odd distances, the nearest distance shown in the table should be used. Races over distances longer than 3 miles should be treated as 3-mile races.

National Hunt Flat races A separate age, weight & distance table is used for NH Flat races but there is no weight-for-age allowance for 5-y-o's; over 2 miles from January to November the allowance for 4-y-o's is 1 lb less than it is over jumps.

CHASERS &
HURDLERS
2003/04

Price £66.00

A TIMEFORM PUBLICATION

A Timeform Publication

Compiled and produced by

G. Greetham (Director), D. P. Cleary (Editor), M. J. Taylor (Handicapper),
G. J. Cunningham, J. Ingles, M. S. Rigg and E. K. Wilkinson (essays),
P. E. Turner (additional research), S. Hindle (short commentaries),
P. A. Muncaster (short commentaries and proof checking), G. Crowther (proof
checking), M. Hall, D. Holdsworth, W. Muncaster, A-M. Stevens and R. Todd
(production).

CONTENTS

The age, weight and distance table, for use in applying the ratings in races involving horses of different ages, appears on the end paper at the front of the book

Best Mate returns after completing the first hat-trick in the Cheltenham Gold Cup for almost forty years

Chasers & Hurdlers 2003/04

Introduction

'I would sooner fail than not be among the greatest.' Jump racing should hope—for more reasons than one—that the philosophy of John Keats rubs off on the connections of jumping's biggest star **Best Mate** now that the horse has fulfilled expectations with a third victory in the Cheltenham Gold Cup. Best Mate's historic win was the biggest story of the 2003/4 season and the media understandably had a field day. To get a steeplechaser to the Gold Cup fit and well three years in a row, let alone to win it three years in a row, is a remarkable achievement, as even a cursory study of the history of the race will show. For that reason alone Best Mate and his painstakingly single-minded connections deserved the adulation. But to place Best Mate, as some did, above Desert Orchid and some of the other champions of the past thirty years or so—let alone above Arkle, the last horse to win three Gold Cups—can hardly be justified yet on any rational appreciation of his form. The latest Gold Cup which Best Mate won fairly narrowly from 33/1-shot **Sir Rembrandt** and 20/1-shot **Harbour Pilot** was a substandard affair. Best Mate put up his best performance of the season in the Ericsson Chase at Leopardstown, after deviating from what looked likely to develop into a Christmas tradition of tackling the King George VI Chase (won in Best Mate's absence by his veteran stable-companion **Edredon Bleu**). Arkle's astonishing overall record would withstand the hyperbole of a fourth, or even a fifth, Gold Cup win for Best Mate because, at the moment, Best Mate is apparently unlikely ever to face the stiff tasks in handicaps which, time and again, allowed Arkle and Desert Orchid to show just how good they were. Best Mate has made a total of ten appearances in his three Gold Cup-winning seasons and his essay poses questions about how well his present achievements might stand the test of time. A comparison is drawn, not with Arkle, but with another three-time Cheltenham champion, the Champion Hurdle winner See You Then.

Sir Rembrandt (left) and Harbour Pilot push Best Mate all the way

A modern-day record crowd of 70,739 for Grand National day is provided with a thrilling curtain-raiser as Rhinestone Cowboy comes late to beat a high-class field in the Aintree Hurdle

Victories by reigning champions seemed set beforehand to be celebrated more generally at the latest Cheltenham Festival, which was a sell-out on all three days. The winners of all four of the major championships returned to defend their crowns and all four arrived at the Festival in good form. Best Mate was the only one to retain his title, another tribute in itself to his achievement. French-trained hurdler **Baracouda** ran with credit in attempting a third successive victory in the Stayers' Hurdle, but he met his match in **Iris's Gift** who had pushed him close the previous year when still a novice. The staying division also included Iris's Gift's more versatile stable-companion **Rhinestone Cowboy**, winner of the Aintree Hurdle and the Champion Stayers' Hurdle at Punchestown; he put up one of the best performances of the season in a handicap when third under top weight in the Coral Cup at the Festival, showing form at least the equal of that shown by the principals in the Champion Hurdle. The staying division was again stronger than the two-mile division in which the 2003 winner **Rooster Booster** was beaten in the Champion Hurdle by 33/1-shot **Hardy Eustace** who repeated the form when the pair met again in Punchestown's Champion Hurdle, shortly after the end of the British season (the Punchestown Festival is covered in this edition of *Chasers & Hurdlers*, as are some other key events after the close of the British season, though form figures do not appear in the commentaries for technical reasons). The third champion deposed at the Cheltenham Festival was Irish-trained **Moscow Flyer**, who unseated his rider in the Queen Mother Champion Chase. He is an outstanding chaser—the highest-rated horse in this edition of *Chasers & Hurdlers*—and bettered the form of his 2003 Champion Chase win when putting up a cracking performance in the Tingle Creek Chase at Sandown in December, one of five victories in the latest season. Moscow Flyer redeemed

6

himself after Cheltenham when winning at both Aintree (Melling Chase) and Punchestown (Champion Chase).

The Queen Mother Champion Chase was won in fine style by the previous year's Arkle Trophy winner **Azertyuiop** but that performance was 10 lb below his best, a tremendous weight carrying effort when second in the season's top two-mile handicap chase, the Victor Chandler at Ascot in January. This was the equal best performance (with Carvill's Hill's breathtaking victory in the 1991 Welsh National) seen in a handicap over jumps since Desert Orchid's day. The essay on Azertyuiop harks back to the handicap performances of such as Arkle and Desert Orchid and also lists some of the latest season's other notable handicap performances, among them Rooster Booster's outstanding effort when just touched off in the Tote Gold Trophy and Baracouda's win in the Sandown Hurdle. Edredon Bleu and Sir Rembrandt, as well as Rhinestone Cowboy, were others who produced top-class or high-class efforts in handicaps, races which offer more potential than weight-for-age events for finding out just how good the top horses are.

Despite massive prize money—including £348,000 to the winner, £132,000 to the runner-up and £66,000 to the third—and lenient handicapping of the top weights, the latest Grand National attracted very few runners of Gold Cup class and was anything but a vintage renewal. Attendances for the three days of the meeting were, however, a modern-day record and the domestic television audience for British racing's biggest show-piece was the highest since 1998. Records were also set for betting turnover on the National, some sources estimating that it touched £120m for the first time. The essay on Grand National

Two out in the Queen Mother Champion Chase—
Azertyuiop is about to strike for home, while the novice Venn Ottery (right) is still going strikingly well

winner **Amberleigh House**, trained by Ginger McCain who enjoyed Aintree glory with Red Rum, looks at the changes made to the Grand National course and to the conditions of the race since Red Rum's day. Grand National runner-up **Clan Royal**, who had beaten Amberleigh House very narrowly in the Becher Chase over the big National fences in the autumn, was one of two high profile runners-up during the season whose defeats may, partly at least, have been affected by the fact that their jockeys lost their whip.

The other was **Royal Emperor** in the Royal & SunAlliance Chase and his write-up recounts a few other noteworthy historical examples of jockeys losing whips. The result of the SunAlliance was open to different interpretations and left a confused picture among the season's leading staying novices. **Mossy Green** might have won had he not fallen when disputing the lead two out; **Pizzaro** was in front of the eventual winner when brought down at the same fence; **Calling Brave** was still going well when departing four out; and the eventual third **Our Vic**, representing the owner/trainer/jockey combination of David Johnson, Martin Pipe and Tony McCoy, spoiled his chance by failing to settle and making mistakes. And the winner? Well, Irish-trained **Rule Supreme** rewarded his trainer's enterprise by going on to an even greater success, in France's principal hurdle race, the Grande Course de Haies d'Auteuil in June. Rule Supreme's jumping of fences had let him down when he unseated his rider trying to follow up his Cheltenham win in the Mildmay Novices' Chase at Aintree, where Royal Emperor fell and the race went to his stable-companion **Simply Supreme**. The season's two best novices didn't contest either the Royal & SunAlliance or the Mildmay, Our Vic's stable-companion **Therealbandit** being aimed at the Gold Cup instead of the SunAlliance and **Strong Flow** missing the rest of the season after making a tremendous impression when winning the Hennessy Cognac Gold Cup at Newbury and then injuring a knee when winning the Feltham Novices' Chase at Kempton's Christmas meeting.

Among the two-mile novice chasers, **Well Chief** won the Arkle Trophy at Cheltenham and the Maghull Novices' Chase at Aintree for the Johnson/Pipe/McCoy combination. There wasn't much between the top novices at up to two and a half miles, **Hi Cloy** beating Arkle runner-up **Kicking King** in the Powers Gold Cup before himself being beaten by **Lord Sam** in the Ellier Developments Novices' Chase at Punchestown. Well Chief's owner ended the season as champion for the fourth time, Pipe was champion trainer for the fourteenth and McCoy champion jockey for the ninth. McCoy's eventful campaign and his triumph over Richard Johnson (second to McCoy for the seventh season in a row) is outlined in Well Chief's essay, while Martin Pipe's close battle for the trainers' championship with Paul Nicholls is a topic for the entry on **Tiutchev**, the highest-rated horse in the Pipe stable in the latest season. The review of **Tikram** includes an appraisal of Timmy Murphy who will be riding David Johnson's horses next season following McCoy's decision to accept a retainer for another of Pipe's closest challengers, Jonjo O'Neill, who pipped Philip Hobbs for third in the trainers' championship.

The patient O'Neill was only seventh in the trainers' table at the end of October as the jumping programme was hit by an unusually dry autumn. Ludlow, Taunton and Wincanton lost fixtures in October because of hard going, while Exeter, Carlisle and Wetherby had to abandon races on their chase courses because conditions were unsafe. Some of the meetings that went ahead did so with pitifully small fields. Tracks staging summer jumping have to produce going no firmer than good to firm, but the latest season raised worries about jumping in the early-autumn. Extensive watering—the course had to buy in five million gallons—was necessary before Cheltenham's October meeting and before its prestigious Open meeting in November, while below-average rainfall

resulted in Cheltenham's Tripleprint Gold Cup meeting in December having
to be switched from the New course to the Old, on which the Open meeting
had taken place. Changes are in the air for jumping following publication in
November of a blueprint for the sport's future by Racecourse Holdings Trust,
which includes Cheltenham and Aintree and is the biggest investor in jumping
among the various racecourse groupings. The main suggestions are set out in
the essay on **Rigmarole**, one 'absolutely essential' requirement being for
courses to produce going that is 'at least good to firm.'

Timeform's view is that there is a case for starting the core jumps season
later—say at the end of October or in early-November—and ending it a month
later. Field sizes over jumps are at their lowest between August and October
and, all things being equal, suitable going is easier to produce in May (after a
winter's rain) than in October. As outlined in the summary on **Macs Joy**, the
traditional end-of-season programme at Sandown could be switched to the end
of May, extending the media focus over what is already a busy month for
jumping (more jump meetings are staged in May than October). An end-of-May
finish would allow some retiming of valuable races staged in Britain after the
major Festivals at Cheltenham and Aintree, avoiding a clash, for example,
between Sandown's valuable programme and Ireland's major Festival at
Punchestown, and perhaps also allowing Ayr's Scottish National meeting to
be run a little later.

After agreement was reached between racing's governing bodies and the
Office of Fair Trading over an investigation into anti-competitive practices,
the BHB produced *The Modernisation of British Racing*, a document outlining
changes that are to be introduced to meet the OFT's demands. Among them is
the introduction of an element of competition into the fixture list—a key OFT
requirement—and a major say for racecourses in the development of data

Champion jockey Tony McCoy split from champion owner David Johnson
and champion trainer Martin Pipe at the end of the season to join J. P. McManus and Jonjo O'Neill

New high profile owners Graham and Andrea Wylie with one of their big-money purchases Inglis Drever after an impressive victory in the Winter Novices' Hurdle at Sandown

income. Racecourses will continue to control the sale of live pictures, while profits from the sale of data to bookmakers (through a new body British Horseracing Enterprises) will be distributed to racecourses in proportion to the amount of betting revenue generated by their meetings. The need to make jumping commercially appealing for betting was another key recommendation of the Racecourse Holdings Trust blueprint, one that is now enshrined in agreements over picture rights which include cuts in payments to racecourses staging events with fewer than eight runners. All-weather Flat racing has a proven record of producing competitive racing for betting shop and armchair punters and some had feared that, if the OFT's initial ruling had been enforced, a fixture free-for-all would have led to jumping fixtures being lost to all-weather Flat in the winter, which would also have benefited the bookmakers because the all-weather yields a higher betting percentage per runner than jumps racing.

As a result of the proposals in *The Modernisation of British Racing* there will be an overall increase in the number of meetings from 1,341 in 2004 to 1,500 by 2006, virtually all the expansion taking place on the Flat and some of it, no doubt, in the winter when jump racing—though its own numbers are unaffected—will almost certainly account for a smaller proportion of meetings than at present. All-weather racing draws horses away from jumping—there was a decrease in the combined total of jumpers and dual-purpose horses of 8% between 1998 and 2003—and jumping will have to respond. The extended entry on **Isio** includes Timeform's comments on some of the changes proposed, including amendments to the programme of novice chases which currently attract the smallest fields. The BHB might also do well to revisit the report of its Off-Course Betting Development Group in 1997, a subject touched on in the entry on **Starzaan**. The popularity of summer jumping is covered in the essay on **Ballycassidy** but that arm of the sport is not yet strong enough, and does not have a clear enough identity, to stage a 'summer season', one of the BHB's plans being the creation of distinct winter and summer seasons for jumping. An experiment in the mid-'nineties with separate championships for summer jumping proved short lived. There have been some new ideas in jumping in the last couple of seasons which include: attempts to encourage more mares, through the introduction of 50% owners' premiums for British-bred mares and the increase in the mares' allowance to 7 lb in Grade 1 and Grade 2 races (discussed in the write-up on Champion Bumper winner **Total Enjoyment**); and the introduction of junior National Hunt Flat races (covered in the entry on **Secret Ploy**), beginners chases (the only qualification being that a horse has not won a chase) and valuable introductory novice hurdles, the two last-named providing opportunities for better horses.

The first two introductory hurdles were run at Sandown (subsequent Triumph Hurdle runner-up **Chief Yeoman** was the beaten favourite) and at Ayr in mid-November. The latter was won by the Cambridgeshire winner Chivalry, making his debut over hurdles, from another useful Flat recruit Vintage Premium (the progressive **Lingo**, who turned into a very promising hurdler, had also looked set to have his first race over hurdles in the same race). Chivalry was the first winner to carry the colours of Andrea and Graham Wylie. The Tyneside computer millionaire and his wife, whose appetite was whetted by the success the previous season of Lord Transcend (who ran in the name of her beauty salon), purchased several high profile horses off the Flat, and some established jumpers, to set up a string with Howard Johnson. The pick of the Flat recruits was **Inglis Drever**, the season's highest-rated novice hurdler who reportedly lost a shoe when just beaten by **Fundamentalist** in the Royal & SunAlliance Novices' Hurdle at Cheltenham. The Wylies also had another top novice in **Royal Rosa** who fetched a British record for a jumper sold at auction when they paid 340,000 guineas for him at the Doncaster May Sales in 2003. That record lasted just twelve months, until **Garde Champetre**, winner of the Mersey Novices' Hurdle at Aintree, made 530,000 guineas at the same sale, Howard Johnson being among the underbidders this time as the gelding was knocked down to representatives of J. P. McManus. Garde Champetre was fifth in the Supreme Novices' Hurdle at Cheltenham, a race

Garde Champetre fetches 530,000 guineas at the Doncaster May Sales,
a British record for a jumper sold at auction

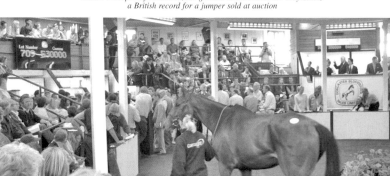

dominated by the Irish-trained pair **Brave Inca** and **War of Attrition**. None of those mentioned put up the sort of performance Iris's Gift or Baracouda recorded as a novice, but that is not to say that they were a substandard bunch. Quite a few can be expected to make their mark in the next season or two. The same probably cannot be said for the leading British- and Irish-trained juveniles, who were all much of a muchness, the season's three top races each won by a different horse, **Made In Japan**, **Al Eile** and **Cherub**, while **Trouble At Bay** and **Power Elite**, the highest-rated juveniles in Britain and Ireland respectively, both recorded below-form efforts in championship events.

The surge in the volume of betting since the abolition of betting tax in October 2001 is well on track to paying a good dividend to the Treasury. The offshore bookmakers are back and the healthy profits returned by the big chains in the most recent financial year have yielded extra corporation tax, in addition to the 15% tax on bookmakers' gross profits that replaced the percentage deduction from turnover imposed on punters. Racing received an unexpected windfall of an extra £10m in payments made to the Levy Board, in spite of the fact that the move to a gross profits tax has made it worthwhile for bookmakers to introduce low-margin betting products, such as fixed-odds betting terminals and video roulette. Bookmakers have come a long way since they were dependent on big events like Cheltenham and the Grand National. Racing now accounts for only just over 60% of off-course betting with bookmakers—though total volume has gone up since the abolition of betting tax—and contributes less than half of total profits. The Tote, whose on-course turnover at the Cheltenham Festival exceeded £10m for the first time, celebrated its seventy-fifth anniversary with a makeover, changing the name of its off-course business to totesport, used for the first time in connection with its flagship sponsorship of the Gold Cup. The business, whose on-course identity became totepool, looks set to be sold to a racing trust, which will continue to plough profits back into racing, but the new names—with their internet-friendly, lower-case letters—acknowledge the fact that, along with the other major chains, totesport now takes bets on a whole range of sports, as well as also deriving profits from the fixed-odds betting terminals and other games in its 450 betting shops. Tote chairman Peter Jones announced a rise in turnover of 61% to almost £1.5bn for the year ending March 31st 2004, with pre-tax profits up from £7.7m to £11.6m. Rival High Street bookmaking chains have argued strongly against the proposed preferential sale (said to be for around £75m, half market value), wanting the totesport shops sold to the highest bidder.

Traditional bookmakers staged a series of much more public attacks on another perceived threat, from the person-to-person on-line betting exchanges. The chief executive of Ladbrokes, Chris Bell, caused a furore when suggesting on BBC2's *Money Programme* that 'at least one race a day, if not more, is being corrupted by the availability of laying horses to lose on betting exchanges.' The claim was widely condemned, the Jockey Club pointing out that Ladbrokes and other bookmakers were supposed to have agreed 'a memorandum of understanding' under which unusual or suspicious betting patterns are reported. 'If Ladbrokes have any evidence of a pattern of so-called fixed races, they should have shared it with the Jockey Club. They have not done so,' said the Jockey Club's executive director Christopher Foster. The bookmakers' hostility to the betting exchanges—also regarded as a danger to the sport's integrity by the BHB—seemed aimed at influencing the Government to increase the regulation of betting exchanges and their customers, particularly high volume layers. In the end, though, the Government seemed to conclude that opposition was largely driven by bookmakers' commercial concerns about the success of the exchanges. Over £50m was traded on Betfair at the latest Cheltenham

Festival, with more than £5m on a single race (the Gold Cup) for the first time. A proposal from a committee of MPs, examining a draft Gambling Bill, that high volume layers—effectively professionals—on the exchanges should be 'made subject to the appropriate levy arrangements' and have their status checked, was rejected by the Government.

Bookmakers and other organisations, including the BHB, had told the committee that the exchanges present an opportunity for those with 'inside information' to profit from the uninformed punter 'by allowing customers to place bets that a particular horse will lose.' The Government decided that, when betting exchange customers bet in a properly regulated environment, they represent no more of a threat to the rest of the betting public, or the integrity of the sport, than customers of traditional bookmakers. All betting exchange customers are registered with the exchanges which work closely with the Jockey Club in identifying any wrong-doing. Two owners were 'warned off'—one for two years, the other for six months—in the latest season after being found guilty of laying their own horses on Betfair in contravention of a rule introduced in September, which also bans trainers and stable staff from behaving similarly. The Jockey Club warned all owners and trainers that their runners would be under scrutiny for irregular betting patterns, such as a horse drifting suspiciously in the betting.

An enlarged Jockey Club security team—with a new head in Paul Scotney—now has greater powers, including being able to examine trainers' telephone and betting records and jockeys' mobile phone records. The Jockey Club launched a series of investigations in the latest season, more often than not prompted by information on betting patterns passed on by exchanges. No case arose but Martin Pipe was asked for details of his phone records around the time that one of his horses Intox flopped in a selling hurdle at Ludlow in the autumn. Nicky Henderson, whose splendid run of success in big Saturday

Allegations of corruption again rocked the sport—Chris Bell, chief executive of Ladbrokes, caused a stir when claiming that betting exchanges were a danger to the sport's integrity; jockey Sean Fox was suspended for 21 days after controversially parting company with his mount in a beginners chase at Fontwell in which there were unusual betting patterns

races is outlined in the entry on **Fondmort**, was questioned—and his jockey Marcus Foley asked to produce his phone records—over the running of Tollbrae in a maiden chase at Leicester in February. Four days earlier, Foley had enjoyed the biggest victory of his career in the Tote Gold Trophy as Henderson extended his fine record in the race with **Geos** whose write-up makes an interesting contrast between Henderson's training methods and those of another trainer who won the race four times (in its days as the Schweppes), Captain Ryan Price.

Rumours circulated in the latest season of criminal collusion with jockeys to lose races, and allegations appeared in the *Racing Post* that there were links between cases involving Tollbrae, a Flat horse Red Lancer (beaten at Wolverhampton in October) and Ice Saint, though the Jockey Club would not comment on the claims. Jockey Mattie Batchelor, whose involvement was first revealed by the *Daily Mail*, did not ride in the Tollbrae or Ice Saint races but admitted being interviewed about the three cases, and to being in phone contact with punter John McCracken on the racedays in question, though he denied any impropriety. Another relatively little-known jockey Sean Fox had been thrust into the national newspaper and TV headlines after collecting a twenty-one-day ban (against which an appeal is pending at the time of writing) when controversially parting company with Ice Saint, who drifted noticeably in the betting in a beginners chase at Fontwell in March. Only four days earlier, conditional jockey Willie Worthington had picked up a fourteen-day ban for making insufficient effort on the narrowly-beaten Wild Power in a handicap hurdle at Taunton—a case *Timeform Perspective* labelled 'as bad a case of its sort seen in a long time.' The Jockey Club reopened investigations into the defeat of Wild Power in July. The Ice Saint and Wild Power incidents followed hot on the heels of some unwelcome coverage for racing after champion Flat jockey Kieren Fallon lost a race at Lingfield when easing up on Ballinger Ridge. Fallon was the subject of far-fetched 'race-fixing' allegations after an investigation by undercover reporters from the *News of The World*. He was banned for twenty-one days after admitting a breach of rule 156 in connection with his riding of Ballinger Ridge but was eventually cleared of being linked in any way with betting patterns on the race. At the time of writing, he still faces a charge of bringing racing into disrepute relating to elements of the *News of The World* story, as does another Flat jockey John Egan. Fallon's solicitor maintained, however, that there were insufficient grounds for conducting the inquiry and threatened High Court action to stop it going ahead.

Trainer Shaun Keightley and jockey Pat McCabe were eventually charged by the Jockey Club over the running of Red Lancer and charges were also brought in another Flat case, that of the Alan Berry-trained Hillside Girl who was pulled up in a minor event at Carlisle in 2003. Senior Flat jockey Gary Carter will also have to answer charges of preventing his mounts from running on their merits in eight races between the beginning of August and the end of September 2003. There were reported to be links in the Carter investigation with punter Christopher Coleman who was banned for two years in January 2003 after being found guilty of seeking to gain betting advantage by accessing privileged information from former jump jockey Barrie Wright. Coleman managed to establish with the Jockey Club that he had no links with the fugitive drug baron Brian Wright (no relation to Barrie Wright) who was 'warned off' indefinitely in December 2002 after being at the centre of a long-running investigation into doping and race-fixing. Among those who admitted being involved with Brian Wright was former jump jockey, now bloodstock agent, Graham Bradley who was banned by the Jockey Club for eight years in 2002 after being found guilty of passing information for reward and other offences. The sentence was reduced by the Jockey Club to five years in 2003 and

Bradley's legal appeal on the grounds that the penalty was disproportionate, and therefore illegal, reached the High Court in late-June, when the Jockey Club announced that 'providing it is not inconsistent with the pending judgement' Bradley's disqualification would be enforced as soon as the judgement in the appeal was given.

Back on the track, the latest jumping season saw the demise of attheraces, the dedicated horseracing channel, though two new channels were launched in May and June, topics touched on in the essay on **Puntal**. Exploiting the overseas market for British racing holds the key to the long-term viability of wall-to-wall domestic coverage, with across-the-board forty-eight-hour declaration of runners arguably essential, as discussed under **Sporazene**. Among the equine casualties in the latest season the saddest loss was that of **Jair du Cochet**, French-trained conqueror of Best Mate in the Peterborough Chase at Huntingdon and second favourite for the Gold Cup when breaking a hind leg on the gallops in March. Other fatalities during the season included: Poliantas who collapsed after finishing second in the Paddy Power Gold Cup; Brother Joe put down after fracturing a shoulder when falling in a novice chase on the same card; Behrajan with a heart attack and Take Control with a broken leg, both in the Tote Classic at Warwick; Shooting Light with a broken leg three fences from home in the Racing Post Chase; and Xenophon suffering a fatal fall in the Irish Grand National.

Shooting Light's owner John Brown, who spent nearly all his working life with bookmakers Hills, rising from 'tea-boy and board marker' to chairman, announced his retirement and his forthright contribution (he was the prime mover in persuading the Government to abolish betting tax) will be missed. Mary Reveley was set to transfer power at one of the North's most successful stables to son Keith by September, after saddling her 2,000th winner when Diamond Sal took the Aintree Bumper on Grand National day. Another Aintree-

Two of the most notable retirements—Norman Williamson hung up his boots on medical advice in the autumn and Mary Reveley, who had her 2,000th winner when Diamond Sal won at Aintree, was set to hand over her trainer's licence to son Keith

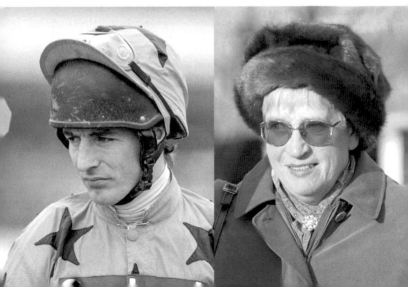

winning trainer Toby Balding, whose career highlights are outlined in the essay on **Accipiter**, has also said he is to retire, handing over to his son-in-law Jonathan Geake in the next season. Nick Gaselee, who trained Party Politics to win the 1992 Grand National, also called it a day, while, among the jockeys, Norman Williamson hung up his boots on medical advice in October. He rode a host of big-race winners including completing a double in 1995 on Master Oats in the Gold Cup and Alderbrook in the Champion Hurdle.

Jump racing also lost the legendary Fred Winter who died in April. His famous ride on Mandarin in the Grand Steeple-Chase de Paris is recalled in the essay on **Kingscliff**. When asked to compare current Gold Cup winners with Arkle, that horse's owner Anne, Duchess of Westminster used to reply 'Ask me again when he's won three.' Sadly, she didn't live to see Best Mate equal Arkle's achievement, passing away in August, aged 88. Another respected figure, Johnny Henderson, father of trainer Nicky, died in December at the age of 83. He was one of the architects of Racecourse Holdings Trust, which had its origins at Cheltenham where, in response to a threatened takeover by property developers, Henderson got together a group of investors to buy the course for £240,000 in 1963; the group set up Racecourse Holdings Trust the following year and, a decade later, handed their shares to the Jockey Club for a nominal sum, ensuring future revenue would be ploughed back into racing.

Winter and Henderson are to be remembered at the Cheltenham Festival. Johnny Henderson is to have his name attached to the Grand Annual Chase on the fourth day of the revamped Cheltenham Festival in 2005. The meeting will start as usual on Tuesday with the traditional opening of the Supreme Novices' Hurdle, the Arkle and the Champion Hurdle. Wednesday will continue to feature the Royal & SunAlliance Novices' Hurdle and Novices' Chase and the Queen Mother Champion Chase, while the centrepiece of Thursday will be the Stayers' Hurdle and a new weight-for-age Grade 2 race with penalties, the Festival Chase—a revamped Cathcart—over two miles five furlongs. The Gold Cup will be run on Friday when the Triumph Hurdle will open proceedings. Among the new races are the Fred Winter Juvenile Handicap over two miles and a cross country chase, both of which will be run on Tuesday. A new novice limited handicap chase over two miles five furlongs opens the programme on Thursday, and a new novice hurdle over three miles will be run on Friday. The three-mile novice hurdle is close enough in value to the SunAlliance to pose a danger of diluting the quality of that excellent race (as evidenced in the entry on **Comply Or Die**). The hurdling population is significantly bigger than that for chasing and it would make more sense to stage a two-and-a-half-mile intermediate hurdle (juveniles/novices and second-season hurdlers). This could possibly be a handicap. The EBF Novices' Handicap Final, thought in line to be switched from Sandown is not included. It would, of course, have been a good addition to the Festival programme but at the same time have weakened a good Sandown card.

As well as providing a Timeform rating and commentary for every horse that ran over jumps or in bumpers in Britain, *Chasers & Hurdlers* also deals in detail with the pick of the Irish-trained horses not seen out in Britain. A Timeform review of jump racing in France, together with Timeform ratings for all the leading performers, is included for the first time, though some of the most interesting French horses are still given essays, including 'France's Best Mate' **Kotkijet**, the highest-rated four-year-old hurdler in Europe **Maia Eria** and **Cyrlight**, a possible for the next King George VI Chase. As usual, the horses whose names are highlighted in bold in this introduction are among the hundred or so that have essays or extended entries.

September 2004

Moscow Flyer (Barry Geraghty)

CHAMPION JUMPER & BEST TWO-MILE CHASER – RATED AT 183
MOSCOW FLYER
10 b.g. Moscow Society – Meelick Lady (Duky)
Owner Mr Brian Kearney   Trainer Mrs J. Harrington

BEST STAYING CHASER – RATED AT 176+
BEST MATE
9 b.g. Un Desperado – Katday (Miller's Mate)
Owner Mr Jim Lewis   Trainer Miss H. C. Knight

BEST NOVICE CHASER — RATED AT 156p
STRONG FLOW
7 br.g. Over The River – Stormy Skies (Strong Gale)
Owner Mr B. C. Marshall   Trainer P. F. Nicholls

BEST PERFORMANCE IN A HUNTER CHASE – RATED AT 133
EARTHMOVER
13 ch.g. Mister Lord – Clare's Crystal (Tekoah)
Owner Mr R. M. Penny   Trainer P. F. Nicholls

BEST TWO-MILE HURDLER — RATED AT 167
HARDY EUSTACE
7 b.g. Archway – Sterna Star (Corvaro)
Owner Mr Laurence Byrne   Trainer D. T. Hughes

BEST STAYING HURDLER — RATED AT 172
IRIS'S GIFT
7 gr.g. Gunner B – Shirley's Gift (Scallywag)
Owner Mr Robert Lester   Trainer Jonjo O'Neill

BEST NOVICE HURDLER – RATED AT 152
INGLIS DREVER
5 b.g. In The Wings – Cormorant Creek (Gorytus)
Owner Andrea & Graham Wylie   Trainer J. Howard Johnson

BEST JUVENILE HURDLER – RATED AT 143
MAIA ERIA
4 b.f. Volochine – Soldouna (Kaldoun)
Owner Mr J. P. Dubois   Trainer Y. Porzier

BEST BUMPER PERFORMER – RATED AT 122
SECRET PLOY
4 b.g. Deploy – By Line (High Line)
Owner Mr A. M. Carding   Trainer H. Morrison

THE TIMEFORM 'TOP 100'
CHASERS AND HURDLERS

Hurdlers

172	Iris's Gift
171	Baracouda
168+	Rhinestone Cowboy
167	Hardy Eustace
166	Rooster Booster
160	Crystal d'Ainay
158	Intersky Falcon
158	Westender
155	Foreman
153	Rosaker
153	Sacundai
152	Back In Front
152	Inglis Drever
152	Monkerhostin
151	Fota Island
150	Hasty Prince
149	Geos
149	Rule Supreme
149	Sh Boom
149	Solerina
148p	Brave Inca
148	Cornish Rebel
148	Davenport Milenium
148d	In Contrast
147p	Fundamentalist
147	Newmill
147	Royal Rosa
147	Vic Toto
146p	Our Vic
146	Georges Girl
146	Golden Cross
146	The French Furze
145+	Starzaan
145?	Sleep Bal
145§	Holy Orders
145	Kotkijet
145	Tiutchev
144p	Lingo
144	Accipiter
144	Copeland
144	Harchibald
144	Mr Cool
144	Spirit Leader
143	Comply Or Die
143	Limerick Boy
142	Calling Brave
142	Royal Shakespeare
142	Well Chief
142	Yogi
141	Alexanderthegreat
141	Court Shareef
141	Crazy Horse
141	Santenay
141	Spectrometer
140§	Deano's Beeno
140	Batman Senora

140	Mistanoora
140	Saintsaire
140	Tramantano
139p	Unleash
139	Ar Muin Na Muice
139	Benbyas
139	Bold Bishop
139	Garde Champetre
139	Gralmano
139	Sadlers Wings
139	Specular
138p	Cloudy Grey
138+	Thesis
138	Albuhera
138	Battle Warning
138	Contraband
138	Kadoun
138	Scarthy Lad
137p	Rockstown Boy
137	Claymore
137	Tardar
137	The Bajan Bandit
136+	Royal Emperor
136	Aine Dubh
136	Florida Coast
136	Korelo
136	Le Passing
136d	October Mist
136	Paperprophet
136	Perle de Puce
136	Persian Waters
136	Risky Reef

Chasers

183	Moscow Flyer
182	Azertyuiop
176+	Best Mate
171+	Beef Or Salmon
170	Jair du Cochet
169	Edredon Bleu
169	Sir Rembrandt
168	Florida Pearl
168	Harbour Pilot
168	Tiutchev
167	Keen Leader
167	Kotkijet
165	First Gold
165	Isio
164	Le Coudray
163	Behrajan
163	Cenkos
163	Flagship Uberalles
162x	Valley Henry
162	Hand In Hand
162	Rince Ri
161	Fondmort
159	Grey Abbey

159	Le Roi Miguel
158	Hussard Collonges
157p	Kingscliff
157	Bindaree
157	Impek
157	Kadarann
156p	Strong Flow
156	Native Upmanship
155+	Therealbandit
155	Poliantas
154	Irish Hussar
154	Truckers Tavern
154	Turgeonev
153	Marlborough
153	Royal Emperor
152x	Seebald
152	Got One Too
152	Hi Cloy
151	Kicking King
151	Upgrade
150p	Lord Sam
150p	Our Vic
150p	Well Chief
150+	Pizarro
150	Artic Jack
150	Cloudy Bays
150	Mossy Green
150	Shooting Light
149x	Rule Supreme
149	Armaturk
149	Colonel Braxton
149	La Landiere
149	Native Scout
149	Swansea Bay
149	Thisthatandtother
148x	Ballybough Rasher
148	Batman Senora
148	D'Argent
148	Foly Pleasant
148	Jurancon II
148	Venn Ottery
147	Joly Bey
147	Puntal
146	Alcapone
146	Amberleigh House
146	Farmer Jack
146	Go Roger Go
146	Hot Shots
146	Knife Edge
146	Our Armageddon
146	Palarshan
145+	Calling Brave
145+	Tidour
145x	Rathgar Beau
145	Golden Alpha
145	Nil Desperandum
145	Stormez

145	Strong Run	144	Wahiba Sands	142	Ei Ei
144x	Tyneandthyneagain	143p	Cyrlight	142	Fadoudal du Cochet
144	Duke of Buckingham	143?	It Takes Time	142	Gunner Welburn
144	Enrique	143	Glenelly Gale	142	Horus
144	Hedgehunter	143	Lord Noelie	142	Joss Naylor
144	Iris Royal	143	Tikram	142	Mister McGoldrick
144d	Latalomne	142x	Moscow Express	142	Scots Grey
144	Native Jack	142x	Redemption	142	St Pirran
144	Royal Auclair	142§	Arctic Copper		
144	Southern Star	142	Barrow Drive		

THE TIMEFORM TOP JUVENILES, NOVICES, HUNTER CHASERS AND NH FLAT HORSES

Juvenile Hurdlers
143	Maia Eria
136	Kauto Star
135	Trouble At Bay
134p	Made In Japan
134	Cherub
133	Howle Hill
133	Locksmith
133	Power Elite
132	Chief Yeoman
132	Top Strategy
131	Al Eile
129	Analogy
128	Quick
127	King Revo
127	Mondul
126	Essex
126	Imazulutoo
126	Val du Don
125	Royal Katidoki
124p	Definate Spectacle
124	Dalaram
124	My Will
124	Silk Screen

Novice Hurdlers
152	Inglis Drever
148p	Brave Inca
148	Cornish Rebel
147p	Fundamentalist
147	Big Moment
147	Newmill
147	Royal Rosa
147	War of Attrition
144p	Lingo
144	Accipiter
143	Comply Or Die
143	Eric's Charm
143	Grey Report
142	Royal Shakespeare
141	Alexanderthegreat
141	Court Shareef
140	Fleet Street
140	Royal Alphabet
140	Self Defense
140	Strike Back

Novice Chasers
156p	Strong Flow
155+	Therealbandit
153	Royal Emperor
152	Hi Cloy
151	Kicking King
150p	Lord Sam
150p	Our Vic
150p	Well Chief
150+	Pizarro
150	Mossy Green
149x	Rule Supreme
149	Thisthatandtother
148	D'Argent
148	Venn Ottery
147	Puntal
146	Our Armageddon
145+	Calling Brave
145+	Tidour
145	Nil Desperandum
144	Duke of Buckingham
144x	Tyneandthyneagain

National Hunt Flat Horses
122	Secret Ploy
121	Mount Clerigo
118	Total Enjoyment
117	Geill Sli
117	Master Albert
116	Forty Licks
115p	Villon
115	Mr Mcauley
115	Refinement
115	Royal Paradise
114	Augherskea
114	Demarco
114	Knocknabooly
114	Tigerlion
113	Kildare
113	Monteforte
113	Wild Cane Ridge
112	Major Vernon
112	Martinstown
112	Noplanofaction
112	Only Vintage
112	The Posh Paddy
112	Toemac

Hunter Chasers
137	Hermes III*
135	Earthmover
133	Lord Atterbury*
130	Never Compromise
129	Spot Thedifference*
128	Macgeorge
126	Bright Approach
125	County Derry
122	Forest Gunner
120§	General Claremont*
119	General Montcalm
118	Dantie Boy*
118x	Silence Reigns
117d	Bitofamixup
117§	Mullensgrove
116p	Oneminutetofive
116	Abbeytown*
116	Placid Man
115	Gun'N Roses II
115	Sikander A Azam

*NB * indicates best performance achieved in a race other than a hunter chase*

2003/04 STATISTICS

The following tables show the leading owners, trainers, jockeys, sires of winners and horses over jumps in Britain during 2003/04. The prize-money statistics, compiled by *Timeform*, relate to win-money and to first-three prize money. Win money has traditionally been used to decide the trainers' championship, though since 1994 the BHB and the National Trainers' Federation have recognised championships decided by total prize money as determined by the *Racing Post*. The jockeys' championship has traditionally been decided by the number of winners.

OWNERS (1,2,3 earnings)	Horses	Indiv'l Wnrs	Races Won	Runs	%	Stakes £
1 Mr D. A. Johnson	63	24	48	287	16.7	883,350
2 Mr J. P. McManus	81	26	36	264	13.6	772,588
3 Mr Jim Lewis	9	4	8	29	27.5	464,643
4 Sir Robert Ogden	41	17	35	152	23.0	435,321
5 Mr Trevor Hemmings	42	17	31	165	18.7	414,645
6 Halewood International Ltd	16	4	4	70	5.7	380,990
7 Mr J. Hales	8	4	5	28	17.8	247,500
8 Mr C. G. Roach	6	5	13	31	41.9	199,120
9 Mr B. C. Marshall	4	4	8	22	36.3	189,320
10 Mr Laurence Byrne	1	1	1	2	50.0	185,000

OWNERS (by win-money)	Horses	Indiv'l Wnrs	Races Won	Runs	%	Stakes £
1 Mr D. A. Johnson	63	24	48	287	16.7	584,019
2 Mr Jim Lewis	9	4	8	29	27.5	377,019
3 Mr J. P. McManus	81	26	36	264	13.6	369,307
4 Sir Robert Ogden	41	17	35	152	23.0	363,769
5 Halewood International Ltd	16	4	4	70	5.7	358,206
6 Mr Trevor Hemmings	42	17	31	165	18.7	335,366
7 Mr J. Hales	8	4	5	28	17.8	192,734
8 Mr Laurence Byrne	1	1	1	2	50.0	174,000
9 Mr B. C. Marshall	4	4	8	22	36.3	161,932
10 Mr C. G. Roach	6	5	13	31	41.9	149,226

TRAINERS (1,2,3 earnings)	Horses	Indiv'l Wnrs	Races Won	Runs	%	Stakes £
1 M. C. Pipe	236	96	175	1069	16.3	2,263,718
2 P. F. Nicholls	153	73	127	650	19.5	2,078,144
3 Jonjo O'Neill	172	63	102	632	16.1	1,483,091
4 P. J. Hobbs	160	68	121	706	17.1	1,440,312
5 N. J. Henderson	115	56	79	370	21.3	1,145,939
6 Miss Venetia Williams	119	51	89	562	15.8	877,137
7 Miss H. C. Knight	76	30	42	257	16.3	819,486
8 N. A. Twiston-Davies	87	44	79	386	20.4	724,123
9 Mrs S. J. Smith	96	41	69	428	16.1	698,846
10 A. King	73	26	47	260	18.0	475,233
11 J. Howard Johnson	64	24	41	197	20.8	458,952
12 R. C. Guest	72	29	46	401	11.4	412,446

TRAINERS (by win-money)	Horses	Indiv'l Wnrs	Races Won	Runs	%	Stakes £
1 M. C. Pipe	236	96	175	1069	16.3	1,561,863
2 P. F. Nicholls	153	73	127	650	19.5	1,371,722
3 Jonjo O'Neill	172	63	102	632	16.1	1,034,442
4 N. J. Henderson	115	56	79	370	21.3	870,080
5 P. J. Hobbs	160	68	121	706	17.1	811,046
6 Miss H. C. Knight	76	30	42	257	16.3	646,486
7 Miss Venetia Williams	119	51	89	562	15.8	597,172
8 N. A. Twiston-Davies	87	44	79	386	20.4	558,874
9 Mrs S. J. Smith	96	41	69	428	16.1	474,300
10 D. McCain	31	8	8	133	6.0	380,194
11 J. Howard Johnson	64	24	41	197	20.8	350,819
12 A. King	73	26	47	260	18.0	345,988

TRAINERS (with 100+ winners)	Horses	Indiv'l Wnrs	Races Won	2nd	3rd	Runs	%
M. C. Pipe	236	96	175	121	106	1069	16.3
P. F. Nicholls	153	73	127	129	78	650	19.5
P. J. Hobbs	160	68	121	120	81	706	17.1
Jonjo O'Neill	172	63	102	72	50	632	16.1

JOCKEYS (by winners)	1st	2nd	3rd	Unpl	Total Mts	%
1 A. P. McCoy	209	144	111	336	800	26.1
2 R. Johnson	186	158	107	440	891	20.8
3 G. Lee	94	87	68	376	625	15.0
4 A. Dobbin	89	61	45	304	499	17.8
5 A. Thornton	86	68	64	311	529	16.2
6 R. Thornton	73	59	70	319	521	14.0
7 C. Llewellyn	65	48	37	270	420	15.4
8 R. Walsh	62	66	41	125	294	21.0
9 J. Tizzard	61	69	54	286	470	12.9
10 J. Culloty	58	48	49	212	367	15.8
11 T. J. Murphy	57	53	41	260	411	13.8
12 N. Fehily	52	54	41	230	377	13.7

JOCKEYS (1,2,3 earnings of £500,000+)	Races Won	Rides	%	Stakes £
1 A. P. McCoy	209	800	26.1	1,956,037
2 R. Johnson	186	891	20.8	1,884,302
3 R. Walsh	62	294	21.0	1,421,428
4 G. Lee	94	625	15.0	1,310,705
5 J. Culloty	58	367	15.8	1,019,931
6 A. Thornton	86	529	16.2	808,728
7 L. Cooper	45	284	16.1	703,124
8 M. A. Fitzgerald	51	338	15.0	698,643
9 C. Llewellyn	65	420	15.4	681,525
10 R. Thornton	73	521	14.0	655,282
11 T. J. Murphy	57	411	13.8	653,779
12 A. Dobbin	89	499	17.8	637,651
13 B. J. Geraghty	13	76	17.1	621,563
14 J. Tizzard	61	470	12.9	567,992

JOCKEYS (by win-money, £500,000+)	Races Won	Rides	%	Stakes £
1 A. P. McCoy	209	800	26.1	1,401,731
2 R. Johnson	186	891	20.8	1,192,075
3 G. Lee	94	625	15.0	1,064,854
4 R. Walsh	62	294	21.0	989,786

		1st	2nd	3rd	Unpl		
5	J. Culloty	58	367	15.8			765,367
6	A. Thornton	86	529	16.2			540,633
7	C. Llewellyn	65	420	15.4			515,875
8	B. J. Geraghty	13	76	17.1			512,312

CONDITIONAL JOCKEYS		1st	2nd	3rd	Unpl	Total Mts	%
1	J. E. Moore	48	53	42	268	411	11.6
2	S. Thomas	47	48	37	205	337	13.9
3	A. Tinkler	43	17	18	185	263	16.3

AMATEUR RIDERS		1st	2nd	3rd	Unpl	Total Mts	%
1	Mr O. Nelmes	14	12	16	88	130	10.7
2	Mr T. Greenall	12	15	9	74	110	10.9
3	Mr N. Williams	10	11	4	47	72	13.8

SIRES OF WINNERS (1,2,3 earnings of £300,000+)		Races Won	Runs	%	Stakes £
1	Roselier (by Misti IV)	76	650	11.6	811,305
2	Be My Native (by Our Native)	52	425	12.2	688,922
3	Supreme Leader (by Bustino)	60	469	12.7	654,857
4	Un Desperado (by Top Ville)	29	205	14.1	445,749
5	Buckskin (by Yelapa)	7	71	9.8	407,120
6	Mister Lord (by Sir Ivor)	30	204	14.7	361,848
7	Phardante (by Pharly)	47	467	10.0	355,040
8	Garde Royale (by Mill Reef)	18	79	22.7	352,679
9	Strong Gale (by Lord Gayle)	32	192	16.6	339,501
10	Lord Americo (by Lord Gayle)	39	345	11.3	333,987
11	Mandalus (by Mandamus)	28	212	13.2	314,105
12	Alflora (by Niniski)	32	346	9.2	301,172
13	Montelimar (by Alleged)	25	238	10.5	300,202

SIRES OF WINNERS (by win-money)		Indiv'l Horses	Races Wnrs	Won	Stakes £
1	Roselier (by Misti IV)	165	40	76	505,816
2	Supreme Leader (by Bustino)	140	40	60	498,017
3	Be My Native (by Our Native)	130	36	52	426,401
4	Buckskin (by Yelapa)	16	6	7	376,573
5	Un Desperado (by Top Ville)	56	20	29	366,688
6	Strong Gale (by Lord Gayle)	53	20	32	270,896
7	Lord Americo (by Lord Gayle)	91	27	39	232,621
8	Phardante (by Pharly)	113	25	47	218,530
9	Moscow Society (by Nijinsky)	39	13	20	218,168
10	Alflora (by Niniski)	93	24	32	217,669

LEADING HORSES (1,2,3 earnings)		Races Won	Runs	Stakes £
1	Amberleigh House 12 br.g. Buckskin–Chancy Gal	1	6	365,044
2	Azertyuiop 7 b.g. Baby Turk–Temara	2	5	225,300
3	Best Mate 9 b.g. Un Desperado–Katday	1	2	214,000
4	Hardy Eustace 7 b.g. Archway–Sterna Star	1	2	185,000
5	Clan Royal 9 b.g. Chef de Clan II–Allee du Roy	1	2	178,500
6	Rooster Booster 10 gr.g. Riverwise–Came Cottage	1	6	167,300
7	Isio 8 b.g. Silver Rainbow–Swifty	2	4	163,802
8	Rigmarole 6 b.g. Fairy King–Cattermole	6	14	163,479
9	Well Chief 5 ch.g. Night Shift–Wellesiena	4	5	161,921
10	Edredon Bleu 12 b.g. Grand Tresor–Nuit Bleue III	4	4	153,883

EXPLANATORY NOTES

'Chasers & Hurdlers 2003/04' deals individually, in alphabetical sequence, with every horse that ran over the sticks or in National Hunt Flat races in Britain during the 2003/4 season, plus a number of foreign-trained horses that did not race here. For each of these horses is given (1) its age, colour and sex, (2) its breeding and, where this information has not been given in a previous Chasers & Hurdlers or Racehorses Annual, a family outline (3) a form summary giving its Timeform rating—or ratings—at the end of the previous season, followed by the details of all its performances during the past season, (4) a Timeform rating—or ratings—of its merit (which appears in the margin), (5) a Timeform commentary on its racing or general characteristics as a racehorse, with some suggestions, perhaps, regarding its prospects for 2004/5 and (6) the name of the trainer in whose charge it was on the last occasion it ran.

The book is published with a twofold purpose. Firstly, it is intended to have permanent value as a review of the exploits and achievements of the more notable of our chasers and hurdlers in the 2003/4 season. Thus, while the commentaries upon the vast majority of the horses are, of necessity, in note form, the best horses are more critically examined. The text is illustrated by half-tone portraits of the most notable horses (where these are available) and photographs of the major races. Secondly, the book is designed to help the punter to analyse races, and the notes which follow contain instructions for using the data.

TIMEFORM RATINGS

The Timeform Rating of a horse is simply the merit of the horse expressed in pounds and is arrived at by careful examination of its running against other horses using a scale of weight for distance beaten. Timeform maintains a 'running' handicap of all horses in training throughout the season.

THE LEVEL OF THE RATINGS

At the close of each season the ratings of all the horses that have raced are re-examined, and, if necessary, the general level of the handicap is adjusted so that all the ratings are kept at the same standard level from year to year. Some of the ratings may, therefore, be different from those in the final issue of the 2003/4 Timeform Chasing Black Book series.

RATINGS AND WEIGHT-FOR-AGE

The reader has, in the ratings in this book, a universal handicap embracing all the horses in training it is possible to weigh up, ranging from tip-top performers, with ratings from 170 upwards, down to the meanest platers, rated around the 60 mark. All the ratings are at weight-for-age, so that equal ratings mean horses of equal merit. In using Timeform to assess the prospects of various runners, allowance should be made for any difference specified by the Age, Weight and Distance Table at the front.

Steeplechase ratings, preceded by c, should not be confused with hurdle ratings, preceded by h. Where a horse has raced over fences and also over hurdles its ratings as a chaser and hurdler are printed one above the other, the steeplechase rating (c) being placed above the hurdle rating (h).

Thus with REGALITY c157
h143

the top figure, 157, is the rating to be used in steeplechases, and the one below, 143, is for use only in hurdle races. Where a horse has a rating based on its performance in a National Hunt Flat race (usually referred to in the text as a bumper) it is preceded by 'F'. The procedure for making age and weight adjustments to the ratings (i.e. for the calculation of Race Ratings) is as follows:

A.   Horses of the Same Age

If the horses all carry the same weight there are no adjustments to be made, and the horses with the highest ratings have the best chances. If the horses carry different weights, jot down their ratings, and to the rating of each horse add one point for every pound the horse is set to carry less than 12st 7lb, or subtract one point for every pound it has to carry more than 12st 7lb. When the ratings have been adjusted in this way the highest resultant figure indicates the horse with the best chance at the weights.

Example (any distance: any month of the season)

Teucer	5 yrs (11-0) ..	Rating 140 ..	add 21	 161
Kiowa	5 yrs (10-7) ..	Rating 125 ..	add 28	 153
Golden Age	5 yrs (10-4) ..	Rating 120 ..	add 31	 151

Teucer has the best chance, and Golden Age the worst

B.   Horses of Different Ages

In this case, reference must be made to the Age, Weight and Distance Table at the front. Use the Table for steeplechasers and hurdlers alike. Treat each horse separately, and compare the weight it has to carry with the weight prescribed for it in the table, according to the age of the horse, the distance of the race and the month of the year. Then, add one point to the rating for each pound the horse has to carry less than the weight given in the table: or, subtract one point from the rating for every pound it has to carry more than the weight prescribed by the table. The highest resultant figure indicates the horse most favoured by the weights.

Example (2¾m steeplechase in January)

(Table Weights: 8-y-o 12-7; 7-y-o 12-7; 5-y-o 12-6)

Black Book	8 yrs (12-8) ..	Rating 140 ..	subtract 1 ..	139
Pressman	7 yrs (12-3) ..	Rating 132 ..	add 4	136
Copyright	5 yrs (12-7) ..	Rating 150 ..	subtract 1 ..	149

Copyright has the best chance, and Pressman the worst

Example (3m hurdle race in March)

(Table Weights: 9-y-o 12-7; 5-y-o 12-7; 4-y-o 11-11)

Oxer	9 yrs (10-12) ..	Rating 110 ..	add 23 ..	133
Clairval	5 yrs (10-7) ..	Rating 119 ..	add 28	147
Gallette	4 yrs (10-7) ..	Rating 128 ..	add 18 ..	146

Clairval has the best chance, and Oxer the worst

C.   Horses in National Hunt Flat races

The procedure for calculating Race Ratings in National Hunt Flat races is precisely the same as in (A) or (B).

Example (2m N.H. Flat in February)

(Table Weights: 6-y-o 12-7; 5-y-o 12-7; 4-y-o 12-1)

Squall	· 6 yrs (10-12) ..	Rating 88 ..	add 23	111
Lupin	5 yrs (11-3) ..	Rating 97 ..	add 18	115
Chariot	4 yrs (10-9) ..	Rating 84 ..	add 20	104

Lupin has the best chance, and Chariot the worst

The National Hunt Flat ratings are on a scale comparable with that used for hurdlers and chasers. The ratings can therefore be used not only within the context of National Hunt Flat races themselves, but also as an indication of the potential form of such horses in their first few starts over jumps.

JOCKEYSHIP AND RIDERS' ALLOWANCES

For the purposes of rating calculations it should, in general, be assumed that the allowance the rider is able to claim (3 lb, 5 lb, or 7 lb) is nullified by his or her inexperience. Therefore, the *weight adjustments to the ratings should be calculated on the weight allotted by the handicapper, or determined by the conditions of the race,* and no extra addition should be made to a rating because the horse's rider claims an allowance. This is the general routine procedure; but, of course, after the usual adjustments have been made the quality of jockeyship is still an important factor to be considered when deciding between horses with similar chances.

WEIGHING UP A RACE

The ratings tell which horses in a particular race are most favoured by the weights; but complete analysis demands that the racing character of each horse is also studied carefully to see if there is any reason why the horse might be expected not to run up to its rating. It counts for little that a horse is thrown in at the weights if it has no pretensions whatever to staying the distance, or is unable to act on the prevailing going. Suitability of distance and going are no doubt the most important points to be considered, but there are others. For example, the ability of a horse to accommodate itself to the conformation of the track. There is also the matter of a horse's ability and dependability as a jumper and of its temperament: nobody would be in a hurry to take a short price about a horse with whom it is always an even chance whether it will get round or not, or whether it will consent to race.

A few minutes spent checking up on these matters in the commentaries upon the horses concerned will sometimes put a very different complexion on a race from that which is put upon it by the ratings alone. We repeat, therefore, that the correct way to use Timeform, or this annual volume, in the analysis of individual races is, first to use the ratings to discover which horses are most favoured by the weights, and second, to check through the comments on the horse to see what factors other than weight might also affect the outcome of the race.

THE FORM SUMMARIES

The form summaries enclosed in the brackets list each horse's performances in the last season in sequence, showing, for each race, its distance in furlongs, the state of the going and the horse's placing at the finish. Steeplechase form figures are prefixed by the letter 'c' and N.H. Flat race (bumper) form figures by the letter 'F', the others relating to form over hurdles.

The going is symbolised as follows: f–firm, m–good to firm, g–good, d–good to soft/dead, s–soft, v–heavy.

Placings are indicated up to sixth place, by superior figures, an asterisk denoting a win; and superior letters are used to convey what happened to the horse during the race: F–fell (F^3 denotes remounted and finished third); pu–pulled up, ur–unseated rider; bd–brought down; R–refused; rtr–refused to race; su–slipped up; ro–ran out; co–carried out; wd–withdrawn; dis–disqualified.

Thus, [2003/4 h82, F80: 16g 16s* c18g^{pu} 16f^2 c20v^F Apr 10] states that the horse was rated 82 over hurdles and 80 in bumpers at the end of the previous season. In the 2003/4 jumping season the horse ran five times; unplaced in a 2m hurdle race on good going, winning a 2m hurdle race on soft going, being pulled up in a 2¼m steeplechase on good going, running second in a 2m hurdle race on firm going and falling in a 2½m steeplechase on heavy going. Its last race was on April 10th.

Where sale prices are given they are in guineas unless otherwise stated. The prefix IR denotes Irish guineas, IR £ denotes Irish punts, $ refers to American dollars, francs refers to French francs and € indicates the euro. Any other currencies are converted into pounds sterling at the prevailing exchange rate.

THE RATING SYMBOLS

The following symbols, attached to the ratings, are to be interpreted as stated:-

p   likely to improve.

P   capable of *much* better form.

+   the horse may be better than we have rated it.

d   the horse appears to have deteriorated, and might no longer be capable of running to the rating given.

§   unreliable (for temperamental or other reasons).

§§   so temperamentally unsatisfactory as to be not worth a rating.

x   poor jumper.

xx   a very bad jumper, so bad as to be not worth a rating.

?   the horse's rating is suspect or, used without a rating, the horse can't be assessed with confidence or, if used in the in-season Timeform publications, that the horse is out of form.

CHASERS & HURDLERS 2003/04

Horse	Commentary	Rating

ABABOU (FR)   8 ch.g. Synefos (USA) – Racine Carree (FR) (Dom Racine (FR)) **c96**
[2003/4 c73, h–: c25s* c25g^{pu} Mar 28] successful 6 times in points in Britain, including **h–**
in February: easily best effort in hunters when winning novice at Market Rasen in March:
stays 25f: acts on soft going: tried blinkered. *Mrs Lucy Latchford*

ABAJANY   10 b.g. Akarad (FR) – Miss Ivory Coast (USA) (Sir Ivor (USA)) [2003/4 **h59**
h72: 17m³ Aug 25] leggy gelding: poor maiden hurdler: best around 2m with emphasis
on speed: acts on good to firm going: tried visored. *R. J. Baker*

ABALVINO (FR)   10 ch.g. Sillery (USA) – Abalvina (FR) (Abdos) [2003/4 c127, h–: **c119**
c17g c16d^F c16d⁴ c16v³ c16s⁴ c16d c17g² c18g Mar 27] quite good-topped gelding: fairly **h–**
useful handicap chaser: best effort in 2003/4 when third to Kelrev at Uttoxeter in January:
best around 2m: acts on heavy going: wore cheekpieces last 2 starts: tongue tied: usually
enthusiastic front runner. *P. R. Webber*

ABBEYKNOCK BOY (IRE)   7 b. or br.g. Alphabatim (USA) – Haha Dash (IRE) **c–**
(Lord Ha Ha) [2003/4 c73, h67: c24m⁶ May 5] poor maiden hurdler/chaser: won point in **h–**
January: stays 3m: acts on good to soft going: tried visored/tongue tied: none too genuine.
M. F. Harris

ABBEY'S GIRL (IRE)   8 b.m. Elbio – Abbey Trinity (IRE) (Tender King) [2003/4 **h–**
h–: 24s 19d 19g^{pu} Aug 12] ex-Irish mare: of no account: sold out of K. J. Burke's stable
£2,000 Ascot June Sales after reappearance: has worn cheekpieces. *J. D. Frost*

ABBEYTOWN (IRE)   7 ch.g. Over The River (FR) – Call Queen (Callernish) **c116**
[2003/4 c24s c20s c24d² c32g⁵ Mar 17] sturdy gelding: first foal: dam winning pointer:
won twice in points in 2003: progressive form first 4 outings in steeplechases, running
really well despite mistakes when fifth to Native Emperor in valuable amateur novice at
Cheltenham: stays 4m: raced on good ground or softer. *K. Riordan, Ireland*

ABBOTS COURT (IRE)   9 b.g. Hallowed Turf (USA) – Coronea Sea Queen (IRE) **c–**
(Bassompierre) [2003/4 c61: c26m^F Oct 4] big gelding: winning pointer but little show in
steeplechases. *R. H. Alner*

ABERDARE   5 b.m. Overbury (IRE) – Temple Heights (Shirley Heights) [2003/4 F16g **F80**
F16s⁴ F17s F17d Feb 23] 1,200 3-y-o: eighth foal: half-sister to 3 winners, including
winning 2m hurdler Red Crescent (by Red Sunset) and fairly useful 7f winner Smith And
Western (by Factual): dam, fair 2m winner on Flat, half-sister to smart 1¼m performer
Belle Poitrine: easily best effort in bumpers when fourth in mares event at Newcastle in
January. *J. R. Bewley*

ABERNANT LADY   7 gr.m. Absalom – Hosting (Thatching) [2003/4 h–: 22m Jul **h–**
14] no form on Flat or in 2 novice hurdles (lame only outing in 2003/4). *A. G. Newcombe*

ABERTHATCH (FR)   5 b.m. Thatching – Academy Angel (FR) (Royal Academy **h–**
(USA)) [2003/4 h97: 17s^{pu} 16g^{pu} Feb 21] lengthy mare: modest form when placed both
starts over hurdles in 2002/3: off a year, ran as if amiss on reappearance and lame next
time. *M. J. Ryan*

ABIGAIL   4 gr.f. Simply Great (FR) – Stormy Gal (IRE) (Strong Gale) [2003/4 F17g **F–**
Apr 24] first foal: dam unraced, out of useful hurdler up to 2½m Buck Up: well held in
bumper on debut. *T. D. Easterby*

ABILITY   5 b.g. Alflora (IRE) – Beatle Song (Song) [2003/4 16m Apr 13] modest **h–**
maiden on Flat (should stay 1¼m), sold out of C. Brittain's stable £10,000 Ascot October
Sales: showed little on hurdling debut. *S. C. Burrough*

ABLE NATIVE (IRE)   7 b.m. Thatching – Native Joy (IRE) (Be My Native (USA)) **c89**
[2003/4 c89, h96: c20s^{ur} c16g⁵ 20g⁴ 16g* 20v² 16g Jun 22] medium-sized mare: modest **h101**
chaser: fair handicap hurdler: won mares event at Hexham in May: effective at 2m to easy
3m: acts on good to firm and heavy going: wears blinkers/cheekpieces: usually tongue
tied. *R. C. Guest*

ABOU ZULU 4 ch.g. Abou Zouz (USA) – Mary From Dunlow (Nicholas Bill) [2003/4 **h– §** 16f⁴ 17m Oct 10] lengthy gelding: disappointing maiden on Flat: showed more temperament than ability in 2 juvenile hurdles, wearing cheekpieces/blinkers. *H. A. McWilliams*

ABOVE THE CUT (USA) 12 ch.g. Topsider (USA) – Placer Queen (Habitat) **c–** [2003/4 c–, h87: 22g 24m* 27g* 22d⁴ 27g5 Jun 28] small gelding: maiden chaser: fair **h100** handicap hurdler: won at Exeter in May and Newton Abbot in June: lame final start: best at 2¾m+: acts on firm and good to soft going: held up. *C. P. Morlock*

ABRAHAM SMITH 4 b.g. Lord Americo – Alice Smith (Alias Smith (USA)) **F–** [2003/4 F14d⁴ Mar 22] second foal: dam, modest hurdler/maiden chaser, stayed 3m: well-held fourth to Flying Falcon in bumper at Hereford on debut: will be suited by much greater test of stamina. *B. J. Eckley*

ABSOLUTELY HOPEFUL 11 ch.g. Nearly A Hand – Owena Deep (Deep Run) **c– x** [2003/4 c–x, h–: c25d5 Feb 15] angular gelding: poor hurdler/maiden chaser: stays 3¼m: **h–** raced mainly on good going or softer (acts on heavy): blinkered: usually tongue tied: tends to make mistakes over fences: lazy. *Simon Jones*

ABUELOS 5 b.g. Sabrehill (USA) – Miss Oasis (Green Desert (USA)) [2003/4 16vᵖᵘ **h–** Nov 23] half-brother to winning 2m hurdler/chaser Keen Waters (by Keen): poor on Flat (stays 1m), well beaten for T. McGovern in April: showed little on hurdling debut. *S. Dow*

ABZUSON 7 b.g. Abzu – Mellouise (Handsome Sailor) [2003/4 h102, F96: 20d 19dᶠ **h96** 21s6 20d² 20s³ 25d² Mar 22] big gelding: fair novice hurdler: stays 2½m: acts on heavy going. *J. R. Norton*

ACADEMIC GOLD (IRE) 6 ch.g. Royal Academy (USA) – Penultimate (USA) **h–** (Roberto (USA)) [2003/4 16dᵖᵘ Jan 13] good-bodied gelding: half-brother to 2¾m hurdle winner Usk Valley (by Tenby): one-time fair maiden around 1m on Flat for T. D. Barron: showed nothing on hurdling debut. *R. D. Tudor*

ACADEMY BRIEF (IRE) 4 b.g. Brief Truce (USA) – Stylish Academy (IRE) **h73** (Royal Academy (USA)) [2003/4 16gᵖᵘ 17m³ 17g⁴ 17f² Sep 30] modest maiden on Flat (stays 11f): poor juvenile hurdler: acts on firm ground. *J. W. Mullins*

ACAMANI (GER) 7 b.g. Winged Love (IRE) – Adjani (Surumu (GER)) [2003/4 **h–** 21fᵖᵘ Oct 29] smart on Flat (stayed 1¾m), successful twice in Germany at 2/3 yrs, placed once from 5 starts in 2003 for Frau K. Schlick: placed all 3 starts over hurdles in 2002: fatally injured in novice at Cheltenham: stayed 2½m: acted on good to soft ground. *C. Von Der Recke, Germany*

ACCADEMIC (IRE) 7 ch.g. Accordion – Giolla's Bone (Pitpan) [2003/4 h90, F80: **c–** 21gᵖᵘ c20dᶠ Mar 19] angular gelding: showed some ability in bumper and on first of 3 **h–** starts over hurdles: not fluent prior to falling eleventh on chasing debut: should stay beyond 19f. *S. E. H. Sherwood*

ACCELERATION (IRE) 4 b.g. Groom Dancer (USA) – Overdrive (Shirley Heights) **h80 §** [2003/4 16g6 16d 16s5 18v⁴ 16g6 Mar 13] tall gelding: fair on Flat (will prove best at 2m+, has failed to impress with attitude), sold out of Sir Mark Prescott's stable 20,000 gns Newmarket Autumn Sales, successful in March: modest juvenile hurdler: wore cheekpieces/visor last 4 starts: one to treat with caution. *R. Allan*

ACCEPTING 7 b.g. Mtoto – D'Azy (Persian Bold) [2003/4 h89: 21g⁴ 26m* 24g5 **h99** 24mᵖᵘ 24s⁴ 23d5 26g⁴ 26g Mar 17] compact gelding: modest hurdler: won novice handicap at Huntingdon in May: seems suited by 3m+: acts on good to firm and good to soft ground: wore cheekpieces last 4 starts. *J. Mackie*

ACCESS OVERSEAS 7 b.m. Access Ski – Access Advantage (Infantry) [2003/4 **h68** h72: 19d5 19g⁴ 22g6 16d³ 16d 16d Apr 8] rather sparely-made mare: poor hurdler: stays easy 2¾m: acts on firm and good to soft going. *J. D. Frost*

ACCIPITER 5 b.g. Polar Falcon (USA) – Accuracy (Gunner B) [2003/4 F90: **h144** F17s³ F17g* 16d² 22s* 19s* 20s5 20d* 24g* Apr 2] **F104**
　　Thanks to Accipiter, Toby Balding's final visit to the Grand National meeting as a trainer ended on a high note, the gelding's victory in the Martell Cognac Sefton Novices' Hurdle giving him yet another big-race success at a course where he has enjoyed some of his greatest triumphs in a career which began in 1956. Balding, due to hand over the reins in November to his assistant Jonathan Geake, saddled two winners of the National itself, Highland Wedding and Little Polveir, while he won the Aintree Hurdle on five successive occasions, the first of them

with Beech Road before four victories with Morley Street. Beech Road and Morley Street were also Champion Hurdle winners, so when Cool Ground won the 1992 Cheltenham Gold Cup it meant that Balding's name could be added to the list of trainers responsible for the winners of the National, Gold Cup and Champion Hurdle. The only other trainer with a current licence to have completed the treble is Kim Bailey. It would take too long to list all the other important jumps races won by Balding-trained runners, but Morley Street's two Breeders' Cup Chase wins, along with the victories of Kildimo in the Sun Alliance Chase and Decent Fellow in the Sweeps Hurdle, are certainly worthy of mention. Decent Fellow's name reminds us that Balding made his mark on the Flat, too, albeit at a much lower level than his brother Ian, the trainer of Mill Reef, who retired at the end of the 2002 season. Toby Balding won the John Porter Stakes with Decent Fellow, while he landed the Stewards' Cup/Ayr Gold Cup double with Green Ruby. Toby Balding has also been instrumental in the development of a host of well-known riders, Adrian Maguire and Tony McCoy to name but two, as well as making major contributions to the racing industry on the political side—he has been chairman of the National Hunt branch of the National Trainers' Federation for over twenty years. That his wife Caro should have taken exception to Balding's omission from a *Racing Post* list of '100 Racing Greats' is understandable given his achievements.

Accipiter was one of thirteen who lined up for the Sefton Novices' Hurdle, a Grade 1 event run over an extended three miles which had been won twelve months earlier by Iris's Gift. None of the runners in the latest edition could boast form anything like so strong as that of Iris's Gift, but several had already established themselves as smart novices. Best Mate's brother Cornish Rebel started a short-priced favourite and had won both his starts over hurdles including the Challow Novices' Hurdle at Newbury; Grey Report had finished third in the Royal & SunAlliance Novices' Hurdle at Cheltenham on his previous start; while Eric's Charm had finished an excellent second under top weight in a valuable novices handicap at Sandown almost three weeks beforehand, that race won by Control

Martell Cognac Sefton Novices' Hurdle, Aintree—
the progressive Accipiter gets the better of Grey Report at the last

Man who was in opposition again. Accipiter could finish only fifth in the Sandown race, having won novice events at Wincanton and Taunton on his two previous starts, but one week later he gave a much improved performance to win a valuable twenty-runner handicap at Ascot by five lengths from Paperprophet, the manner of the victory suggesting that he would prove well suited by the extra half mile of the Sefton. So it proved. Stamina was at a premium after a strong early pace, and Accipiter, well suited by the way the race unfolded, battled on gamely, despite wandering, to maintain his advantage after making smooth progress from the rear to lead two out, by which time both Cornish Rebel, who had gone in snatches, and Control Man were out of contention, and Eric's Charm was running out of stamina. The front-running Grey Report wasn't to be brushed aside so easily, though, and he pushed Accipiter to the limit as the pair pulled clear, only three quarters of a length separating them at the line. It was probably just an average renewal of the season's biggest prize for three-mile novice hurdlers, and Accipiter will have to improve a good deal further if he is to trouble the leading staying hurdlers in the next season. That said, Accipiter is a thoroughly genuine sort who is going the right way, and there should be more good races to be won with him, be it over hurdles or fences. The sturdy, lengthy Accipiter certainly looks the sort to make a chaser.

Accipiter (b.g. 1999)	Polar Falcon (USA) (b or br 1987)	Nureyev (b 1977)	Northern Dancer / Special
		Marie d'Argonne (ch 1981)	Jefferson / Mohair
	Accuracy (ch 1981)	Gunner B (ch 1973)	Royal Gunner / Sweet Councillor
		Veracious (ch 1973)	Astec / Gospel Truth

Miss B. Swire's "Accipiter"

Accipiter is from a family which has done his owner/breeder Bridget Swire proud, being one of its numerous representatives to have carried Miss Swire's well-known lilac silks to victory over the years. They include his dam Accuracy, who was herself a stayer and a fairly useful one at that, both on the Flat and over hurdles, though she did go the wrong way temperamentally, often whipping round at the start and also refusing to race once, while she didn't always go through with her effort. Accuracy died in 2000 and produced several winners before her last foal Accipiter. They include two mares who did well on the Flat, Star Precision (by Shavian), a useful winner up to thirteen furlongs, and Little Pippin (by Rudimentary), a fairly useful winner over a mile and a half. The latter, closely related to Accipiter, was also a fair winner over hurdles. Their half-brother Brave Tornado (by Dominion) was a fairly useful stayer on the Flat who showed useful form over hurdles, winning seven times at up to three miles. Accipiter's grandam Veracious, a fairly useful performer at a mile and a quarter to two miles, is also responsible for the smart mare So True, who herself produced Bomb Alaska, another smart Flat performer to race in Miss Swire's colours. Accipiter's great grandam Gospel Truth was a useful winner at around a mile and a half. Before embarking on his hurdling career, Accipiter showed progressive form in four bumpers and won the last of them, at Newton Abbot in November. He has been ridden on all his appearances to date by his stable's conditional rider Tom Best, who was seen to particularly good effect on him at Aintree where, because of the value of the race, he was unable to claim his 5-lb allowance. Accuracy acted well in the mud and most of her offspring take after her. Accipiter himself has raced only on good ground or softer, winning twice on soft. *G. B. Balding*

ACCORDING TO BILLY (IRE) 5 b.g. Accordion – Graphic Lady (IRE) (Phardante (FR)) [2003/4 F16s* F16d³ Feb 22] €54,000 3-y-o: second foal: brother to fairly useful bumper winner Gotaknockonthehead: dam, placed in bumper/novice hurdle, from family of Cheltenham Gold Cup winner Garrison Savannah: won bumper at Punchestown on debut in December: better form when 5 lengths third to Sweet Kiln at Naas: will stay beyond 2m. *E. J. O'Grady, Ireland* **F100**

ACCORDION ETOILE (IRE) 5 b.g. Accordion – Royal Thimble (IRE) (Prince Rupert (FR)) [2003/4 F16s* 20m* 16m* 16d⁵ Nov 30] lengthy gelding: second foal: dam fair hurdler around 2m: fair form in bumpers, winning at Clonmel in May: successful first 2 starts over hurdles, in maiden in July and Grade 3 novice at Navan (beat Newmill 1½ lengths) in November: edgy, fifth in Grade 1 won by same horse at Fairyhouse: stays 2½m. *Paul Nolan, Ireland* **h122 F89**

ACCORDION GIRL (IRE) 6 b.m. Accordion – Triple d'Or (Golden Love) [2003/4 F75: F16g⁴ 22gᵖᵘ Jun 21] lengthy, rather unfurnished mare: poor form in 2 bumpers: no show on hurdling debut, jumping poorly. *J. W. Mullins* **h– F73**

ACERTACK (IRE) 7 b.g. Supreme Leader – Ask The Madam (Strong Gale) [2003/4 h66p: c21dᵖᵘ c16g c16gᶠ c20s³ c17s⁵ c24g⁶ c18g² Mar 27] lengthy gelding: poor maiden hurdler/chaser: bred to be suited by 2½m+: raced on good going or softer. *R. Rowe* **c80 h–**

ACES FOUR (IRE) 5 ch.g. Fourstars Allstar (USA) – Special Trix (IRE) (Peacock (FR)) [2003/4 F16v² F16g² F16d⁵ Apr 17] €39,000 4-y-o: medium-sized gelding: second foal: dam unraced sister to useful hurdler/chaser up to 21f Atone and half-sister to useful chaser around 2½m Music Be Magic: fair form when second at Wetherby and Ayr first 2 starts in bumpers: tends to hang left. *W. McKeown* **F96**

ACHILLES WINGS (USA) 8 b.g. Irish River (FR) – Shirley Valentine (Shirley Heights) [2003/4 h109: 20m⁵ 20g⁴ 22g* 22g³ 22d⁵ Dec 26] leggy gelding: fair handicap hurdler: won 5-runner event at Newton Abbot in November: stays easy 2¾m: acts on soft going: wore cheekpieces last 3 starts. *Miss K. M. George* **h109**

ACOUSTIC (IRE) 10 br.g. Orchestra – Rambling Ivy (Mandalus) [2003/4 c90, h–: c24m² c24s³ Mar 19] big, rangy gelding: winning pointer: modest maiden chaser: stays 3m: acts on soft and good to firm ground. *O. Brennan* **c90 h–**

ACQUIRED (IRE) 6 b. or br.m. Presenting – The Scarlet Dragon (Oats) [2003/4 F16m F16m⁵ F16g⁵ Mar 4] fourth foal: dam of little account: modest form last 2 starts in bumpers. *Mrs H. Dalton* **F75**

ACROSS THE WATER   10 b.m. Slip Anchor – Stara (Star Appeal) [2003/4 16m   c–
19d⁶ 19d Mar 15] no form outside points. *G. H. Jones*   h–

ACT IN TIME (IRE)   12 b.g. Actinium (FR) – Anvil Chorus (Levanter) [2003/4 c99,   c107 d
h–: 22g² c22m² c30gᵖᵘ c26d³ c24g⁶ c24g² c24d² c31d Apr 22] good-topped gelding: h90
second run over hurdles when runner-up in amateur novice at Exeter very early in season:
fair chaser: won point in April: stays 29f: acts on heavy and good to firm going: visored
once, wore cheekpieces fourth start: races prominently: hard ride. *T. R. George*

ACTIVE ACCOUNT (USA)   7 b. or br.g. Unaccounted For (USA) – Ameritop   h–
(USA) (Topsider (USA)) [2003/4 h–: 17d May 17] fair on Flat (barely stays 11f): no form
over hurdles. *Mrs H. Dalton*

ACUSHNET   5 b.g. Ezzoud (IRE) – Flitcham (Elegant Air) [2003/4 F18g Apr 22] fifth   F–
foal: half-brother to 6f winner Arlington Lady (by Prince Sabo): dam 13f winner: seemed
green when well held in bumper on debut. *N. B. King*

ACUTEANGLE (IRE)   8 b. or br.m. Cataldi – Sharp Mama VII (Damsire Unreg-   c–
istered) [2003/4 c21gᵘʳ Mar 3] of no account nowadays. *Mrs S. Wall*   h–

ADALIE   10 b.m. Absalom – Allied Newcastle (Crooner) [2003/4 c84, h78: c20sʳᵒ 16v   c93
c19s² 19s c19s* c19d⁶ c19s³ c20dᵖᵘ Apr 21] sturdy mare: winning hurdler: modest   h–
chaser: trained second start by J. Joseph: won novice handicap at Hereford in February:
stays 19f: acts on heavy going: reportedly bled from nose fourth outing. *P. J. Hobbs*

ADALPOUR (IRE)   6 b.g. Kahyasi – Adalya (IRE) (Darshaan) [2003/4 h77: 19d²   h81
17m³ 19dᵖᵘ 16g⁴ Apr 5] modest on Flat (stays 2m): poor maiden hurdler: claimed £5,000
from D. Burchell on reappearance, left D. Lloyd before final start: stays 19f: acts on soft
ground: takes good hold. *C. W. Moore*

ADAMANT APPROACH (IRE)   10 b.g. Mandalus – Crash Approach (Crash   c141
Course) [2003/4 c138p, h–: c16d⁵ c20s 16s⁶ c18d² 17d Mar 18] sturdy gelding: useful   h127
chaser: out of sorts in 2003/4 prior to 2 lengths second to Alcapone in minor event at
Thurles in March: smart hurdler at best: well below that level in Grade 2 at Gowran and
valuable handicap at Cheltenham: best around 2m: acts on heavy going, probably on good
to firm. *W. P. Mullins, Ireland*

ADAMANT JAMES (IRE)   5 b.g. Sri Pekan (USA) – Classic Romance (Cadeaux   h–
Genereux) [2003/4 16vᵖᵘ Nov 23] modest maiden on Flat (seems to stay 1m) for
T. McCarthy: showed nothing on hurdling debut. *S. Dow*

ADARMA (IRE)   6 b.m. Topanoora – Overtime (IRE) (Executive Perk) [2003/4 16d*   h115
16d* 16dᵘʳ 20s⁵ 20d⁵ Apr 11] rangy, rather unfurnished mare: second foal: half-sister to
bumper winner Lost Time (by Glacial Storm): dam, brought down only start over hurdles,
half-sister to smart hurdler/useful chaser up to 3m Time For A Run: won on first of 2
starts in bumpers in 2002/3: fairly useful form over hurdles, winning maiden at Punchestown and minor event at Gowran in November: creditable fifth to McGruders Cross in
Grade 3 novice at Naas fourth start: stays 2½m: raced only on good to soft/soft going.
C. Roche, Ireland

AD ASTRA   5 b.g. Alhijaz – So It Goes (Free State) [2003/4 F17d³ Dec 17] 14,000   F95
3-y-o: leggy gelding: brother to 2 winners, including winning 2m hurdler Thats All Folks
and half-brother to several winners on Flat: dam, 6f winner, half-sister to dam of useful
6f/7f performer Pomfret Lad: third to Wicked Weasel in bumper at Bangor on debut.
M. Bradstock

ADDED DIMENSION (IRE)   13 b.g. Top Ville – Lassalia (Sallust) [2003/4 h–: 16d*   h84
Oct 30] close-coupled gelding: poor handicap hurdler: won weak event at Towcester only
start in 2003/4: stays 21f: acts on any going: effective tongue tied or not. *N. A. Dunger*

ADECCO (IRE)   5 b.g. Eagle Eyed (USA) – Kharaliya (FR) (Doyoun) [2003/4 h96:   h–
20d May 3] useful-looking gelding: fair juvenile hurdler in 2002/3: unlikely to stay 2½m:
tried blinkered: flashes tail under pressure, and temperament under suspicion. *R. C. Guest*

ADELE   4 b.f. Cloudings (IRE) – Sharp Practice (Broadsword (USA)) [2003/4 F16v   F–
F16d Mar 14] leggy filly: first foal: dam well held in bumpers: well beaten in 2 bumpers.
J. G. O'Neill

ADELPHI BOY (IRE)   8 ch.g. Ballad Rock – Toda (Absalom) [2003/4 h95: 16m*   h105
22g² Aug 25] second outing over hurdles, won novice at Perth in June: went lame when
neck second of 3 in similar event at Cartmel. *M. Todhunter*

34

ADELPHIE LASS   4 b.f. Theatrical Charmer – Miss Adventure (Adonijah) [2003/4   **F–**
F12g Nov 12] fifth foal: half-sister to winning 2m hurdler Indy Carr (by Pyramus) and
fair middle-distance stayer Ardleigh Charmer (by Theatrical Charmer): dam 1½m
winner: ninth of 23 in 3-y-o bumper on debut. *M. R. Hoad*

AD HOC (IRE)   10 b.g. Strong Gale – Knockarctic (Quayside) [2003/4 c156+, h140+:   **c141**
c27g⁶ c24s⁶ c29g^F Jan 10] lengthy gelding: useful hurdler: very smart handicap chaser in   **h–**
2002/3: below form in listed events on completed starts in 2003/4: reported in February
to miss remainder of season through injury: effective at 3m to 33f: acts on good to firm
and heavy going. *P. F. Nicholls*

ADIEMUS   6 b.g. Green Desert (USA) – Anodyne (Dominion) [2003/4 16d Nov 29]   **h–**
smart on Flat (stayed 1¼m) for J. Noseda, successful at Nad Al Sheba in February, fatally
injured following month: jumped poorly when last of 10 finishers in novice at Newbury
only start over hurdles. *R. T. Phillips*

ADIYSHA (IRE)   7 b.m. Namaqualand (USA) – Adira (IRE) (Ballad Rock) [2003/4   **h75**
16d⁶ 16f 16m⁶ 16f² 17m² 19m⁵ 17m⁵ 16m⁵ 16g² 16f³ 19m³ Nov 27] ex-Irish mare:
lightly-raced maiden on Flat (stays 8.5f): poor maiden hurdler: left P. Nolan after fourth
start: stays easy 19f: best on good going or firmer (acts on firm): blinkered once.
D. A. Rees

ADJIRAM (IRE)   8 b.g. Be My Guest (USA) – Adjriyna (Top Ville) [2003/4 h65§:   **h59 §**
16d 16g⁶ Mar 10] sturdy gelding: bad maiden hurdler: best around 2m: acts on firm and
good to soft going: ungenuine. *A. W. Carroll*

ADMIRAL PEARY (IRE)   8 b. or br.g. Lord Americo – Arctic Brief (Buckskin   **h100 x**
(FR)) [2003/4 h100, F93: 26m² 27d^{pu} May 16] smallish, close-coupled gelding: fair
handicap hurdler: probably best at 2¾m+: acts on heavy and good to firm going: sketchy
jumper: free-going sort (often forces pace), and no easy ride. *C. R. Egerton*

ADOPTED HERO (IRE)   4 b.g. Sadler's Wells (USA) – Lady Liberty (NZ) (Noble   **h120**
Bijou (USA)) [2003/4 16s³ 16s* 17g⁶ 16g Apr 1] smallish, good-topped gelding: brother
to winning 2m hurdler State Power and half-brother to fairly useful 2½m hurdler Outer
Limit (by Caerleon): useful on Flat (will stay 2m), sold out of J. Gosden's stable 120,000
gns Newmarket Autumn Sales: won juvenile hurdle at Huntingdon in February, beating
Chief Yeoman easily by 2½ lengths: sixth of 18 finishers behind Made In Japan in
Triumph Hurdle at Cheltenham, again jumping fluently and travelling strongly until after
2 out: well below best at Aintree 2 weeks later. *G. L. Moore*

ADRADEE (IRE)   10 b.m. Ajraas (USA) – Miss Tan A Dee (Tanfirion) [2003/4 c–,   **c–**
h72: 16m⁶ 18m⁵ 17m⁶ 19d³ 17g⁵ 22f c21f³ c19g⁵ c16g^{pu} Apr 4] sparely-made mare: poor   **h72**
handicap hurdler nowadays: no worthwhile form over fences: badly amiss final outing:
stays 19f: acts on firm and soft going: effective tongue tied or not. *M. J. Weeden*

ADRONIKUS (IRE)   7 ch.g. Monsun (GER) – Arionette (Lombard (GER)) [2003/4   **h–**
h93: 22m May 9] angular gelding: modest handicap hurdler: seemed to down tools after
being crowded in back straight when tailed off at Wincanton in May: may prove best
short of 3m: acts on good to firm going: blinkered/tongue tied. *D. J. Wintle*

ADVOCATUS (GER)   6 b.g. Law Society (USA) – Aguilas (Konigsstuhl (GER))   **h– §**
[2003/4 h77: 26g 24m^{pu} 26g^{pu} 21g^{pu} 26s 26s Jan 7] good-topped gelding: poor maiden
hurdler: tried blinkered/in cheekpieces: irresolute. *A. G. Hobbs*

ADYTON (GER)   4 b.c. Second Set (IRE) – Alliance (GER) (Milford) [2003/4 16d^{pu}   **h?**
16v* 16v² Mar 24] successful 3 times from 7 starts up to around 1¼m on Flat in Germany
at 3 yrs, including on sand at Neuss in November: pulled up in juvenile at Plumpton on
hurdling debut in December: placed twice in Italy in 2004, winning maiden at Pisa: has
had tongue tied. *M. Hofer, Germany*

AEGEAN   10 b.g. Rock Hopper – Sayulita (Habitat) [2003/4 c114, h–: c25d³ c25g⁶   **c109**
May 22] tall gelding: fair handicap chaser: stays 25f: acts on good to firm and good to soft   **h–**
going: usually sound jumper. *Mrs S. J. Smith*

AEGEAN PIRATE (IRE)   7 b.g. Polykratis – Rusheen Na Corra (IRE) (Burslem)   **F–**
[2003/4 F–: F16m F17m F16f³ Oct 9] no show in bumpers. *C. J. Hemsley*

AEGEAN SUNRISE   6 ch.g. Deploy – Dizzydaisy (Sharpo) [2003/4 21d 20s 16d²   **h90**
18d^{pu} Mar 21] sturdy gelding: modest maiden hurdler, lightly raced: amiss final outing:
best efforts around 2m: raced on good ground or softer. *Jamie Poulton*

AELRED 11 b.g. Ovac (ITY) – Sponsorship (Sparkler) [2003/4 c106, h82: c17g⁴ c20g **c118 ?**
c20g³ c16g* c16d⁵ c20s* c20v⁵ c20v⁵ c20d* c22g⁵ c21g^F Apr 2] sturdy gelding: fairly **h–**
useful handicap chaser: won at Southwell and Newcastle in December and Newcastle
again in February: stays 2½m: acts on heavy and good to firm going: tried in cheekpieces:
has had tongue tied: has won or been placed in 12 of 15 races at Newcastle: usually races
prominently. *R. Johnson*

AERLEON PETE (IRE) 10 b.g. Caerleon (USA) – Bristle (Thatch (USA)) [2003/4 **c–**
c16m^F c20m^{pu} 16g 16m 16g⁵ 22g 19m⁵ Aug 30] smallish ex-Irish gelding: one-time **h95**
useful hurdler: form since 2000/1, including over fences, only when fifth in handicap fifth
start: tried blinkered/in cheekpieces: sometimes tongue tied. *Jonjo O'Neill*

AFADAN (IRE) 6 br.g. Royal Academy (USA) – Afasara (IRE) (Shardari) [2003/4 **h– §**
h106§: 16m⁴ 16d^{pu} Nov 15] sturdy gelding: fairly useful on Flat (stays 1¾m): winning
hurdler: long way below best both starts in 2003/4: raced mainly around 2m: acts on soft
going: tried tongue tied: weak finisher. *J. R. Jenkins*

AFARAD (IRE) 9 b.g. Slip Anchor – Afasara (IRE) (Shardari) [2003/4 20d^{pu} Apr **c–**
21] leggy ex-Irish gelding: one-time useful handicap hurdler: easily won maiden at **h–**
Kilbeggan on chasing debut in early-2001/2: little form since, left C. Roche and off 16
months before only outing in 2003/4: stays 2½m: acts on good to firm and heavy going:
tried tongue tied. *Jonjo O'Neill*

AFEEF (USA) 5 b.g. Dayjur (USA) – Jah (USA) (Relaunch (USA)) [2003/4 17s 17s⁵ **h74**
16m 19g^{pu} Apr 1] good-topped gelding: fair maiden at best on Flat (stays 1m): poor form
over hurdles: has failed to settle. *R. T. Phillips*

A FEW BOB BACK (IRE) 8 b.g. Bob Back (USA) – Kottna (USA) (Lyphard **c97**
(USA)) [2003/4 h112: 20d^F 22s³ 24d c21v³ c23v^{ur} c20d⁴ Mar 11] smallish gelding: fair **h112**
handicap hurdler: modest form both completed outings over fences: stays 25f: acts on
good to firm and soft going, probably on heavy: has won with/without blinkers/cheek-
pieces. *D. Eddy*

AFICIONADO (IRE) 10 b.g. Marju (IRE) – Haneena (Habitat) [2003/4 h–: c19g⁶ **c–**
c19g⁶ c23m³ c21g⁶ Jun 13] of little account nowadays: tried blinkered. *R. Williams* **h–**

A FINE STORY 8 b. or br.g. Le Moss – Kelly's Story (Netherkelly) [2003/4 c24g^{pu} **c–**
Mar 12] first foal: dam winning pointer: maiden pointer: showed nothing in hunter on
steeplechase debut. *H. Hill*

AFISTFULLOFDOLLARS (IRE) 6 b.g. Be My Native (USA) – Myra Gaye **F105**
(Buckskin (FR)) [2003/4 F100p: F16d³ F16d² F16d³ F16s³ F18d* Mar 4] useful bumper
performer: won at Thurles in March: third to Malahide Marina at Leopardstown previous
outing: will stay at least 2½m. *N. Meade, Ireland*

AFRICAN SUNSET (IRE) 4 b.g. Danehill Dancer (IRE) – Nizamiya (Darshaan) **h–**
[2003/4 16d^F 16d 16g^{pu} Mar 6] well beaten in 6f maiden at 2 yrs: showed little in 3
juvenile hurdles, left A. Mullins after second start: joined J. H. Johnson. *J. W. F. Aynsley*

AFRO MAN 6 b.g. Commanche Run – Lady Elle (IRE) (Persian Mews) [2003/4 h95, **h99 p**
F–: 21g* Nov 5] winning Irish pointer: progressive form over hurdles: won novice at
Kempton only start in 2003/4 by 2½ lengths from Castlemore: will stay beyond 21f:
likely to progress further. *C. J. Mann*

AFTER EIGHT (GER) 4 b.c. Sir Felix (FR) – Amrei (Ardross) [2003/4 16f² 16s* **h112**
16s⁴ 16g² Dec 27] compact colt: successful up to 1½m on Flat in Germany in 2003:
fairly useful form in juvenile hurdles (trained first start by C. Von Der Recke): won at
Huntingdon in November by 1½ lengths from Howle Hill: acts on firm and soft ground.
M. F. Harris

AFTER GALWAY (IRE) 8 b.g. Camden Town – Money For Honey (New Brig) **h72**
[2003/4 17s^{ur} 18g 20s^{pu} 16d⁴ Apr 22] poor form over hurdles: has pulled hard.
Miss V. Scott

AFTER ME BOYS 10 b.g. Arzanni – Realm Wood (Precipice Wood) [2003/4 h119: **h120**
20v³ 20s 24g* Mar 6] workmanlike gelding: fairly useful handicap hurdler, lightly raced:
won at Doncaster in March, idling near finish: effective at 2½m to 3m: acts on any going:
reliable. *Mrs S. J. Smith*

AFTER PUCK (IRE) 6 ch.m. Un Desperado (FR) – Domitor's Lass (Domitor (USA)) **h94**
[2003/4 F18d 16g³ 20f 16m² 20f⁴ Jul 13] second foal: dam poor and untrustworthy novice **F–**

hurdler: modest form in bumpers and over hurdles: raced up to 2½m: acts on good to firm going (bumper form on good to soft). *M. Hourigan, Ireland*

AFTER THE BLUE (IRE)   7 b.g. Last Tycoon – Sudden Interest (FR) (Highest   **h–**
Honor (FR)) [2003/4 h89: 20m 1/df⁰ 1/df⁰ 24s⁰ 16d⁰ Apr 12] compact gelding.
winning hurdler: no form in 2003/4: tried visored: usually tongue tied. *K. G. Wingrove*

AFZAL ROSE   4 b.f. Afzal – Fortria Rosie Dawn (Derring Rose) [2003/4 F17g Mar   **F–**
28] first foal: dam won once over fences at 17f, should have stayed 3m: well held in mares
bumper on debut. *M. Scudamore*

AGAIN AN AGAIN (IRE)   8 b.g. Montelimar (USA) – Running Board (IRE) (Deep   **c111**
Run) [2003/4 h100, F86: 18g 24d 20d⁶ c20m c20d⁴ c18d* c22s* c17d² Apr 13] leggy   **h–**
gelding: fair form, out of form early in season: fair form over fences, winning maiden
at Fairyhouse in February and novice at Downpatrick in March: effective at 2m to 2¾m:
acts on firm and soft going: effective blinkered or not: has had tongue tied. *S. Donohoe,
Ireland*

AGAIN JANE   4 ch.f. Then Again – Janie-O (Hittite Glory) [2003/4 F13g F13v⁵ F16s   **F–**
Jan 21] dipped-backed filly: eighth foal: half-sister to winning 3m hurdler Dunroyal Lad
(by Primitive Rising): dam, winning selling hurdler, best at 7f/1m on Flat: well beaten in
bumpers and claimer on Flat. *J. M. Jefferson*

AGILE KING   13 b.g. Rakaposhi King – My Aisling (John de Coombe) [2003/4   **c–**
c26s⁰ Apr 29] modest pointer: successful 3 times in 2003: little impact in novice hunter
chases. *A. J. Tizzard*

AGINCOURT (IRE)   8 b.g. Alphabatim (USA) – Miss Brantridge (Riboboy (USA))   **c96 §**
[2003/4 c85, h66: c25s* c29d⁰ c28d⁰ c24v⁰ Feb 7] workmanlike gelding: modest   **h–**
handicap chaser: easily best effort in 2003/4 when winning conditional jockeys event at
Towcester in November: should stay beyond 25f: raced on good going or softer (acts on
heavy): blinkered once: often gets behind: not one to trust. *John R. Upson*

AGITANDO (IRE)   8 b.g. Tenby – Crown Rose (Dara Monarch) [2003/4 h112x: 16d⁶   **h108 x**
16gᶠ 16m⁵ 16m³ Apr 13] sturdy gelding: fair handicap hurdler: raced around 2m, likely
to stay further: acts on soft and good to firm going: has worn cheekpieces: sketchy
jumper: has found little. *B. De Haan*

A GLASS IN THYNE (IRE)   6 br.g. Glacial Storm (USA) – River Thyne (IRE)   **h106**
(Good Thyne (USA)) [2003/4 19m³ 20d² Jan 10] €17,000 4-y-o: leggy gelding: first foal:
dam unraced half-sister to top-class chaser Native Upmanship: fair form when placed in
novice hurdles at Lingfield and Ascot: will stay beyond 2½m. *B. N. Pollock*

AGNESE   4 ch.f. Abou Zouz (USA) – Efizia (Efisio) [2003/4 F16g F16s Mar 13] second   **F79**
foal: dam 9f/1¼m winner: modest form on second of 2 starts in bumpers. *J. R. Jenkins*

AH YEAH (IRE)   7 b.g. Roselier (FR) – Serena Bay (Furry Glen) [2003/4 F16s⁵ 21d   **c79**
16d 17s⁶ c25g⁵ c25d² c19s⁵ c24gˢᵘ Apr 16] close-coupled gelding: third foal: half-brother   **h85**
to winning pointer by Be My Native: dam unraced: dead-heated in maiden Irish point in   **F85**
2003: fifth in bumper: modest form at best in 3 starts over hurdles: poor form in handicap
chases: stays 25f: raced on good ground or softer: wore cheekpieces last 4 outings: has
found little. *K. C. Bailey*

AIDE DE CAMP (FR)   5 b.g. Saint Preuil (FR) – Baraka de Thaix II (FR) (Olmeto)   **F89**
[2003/4 F17g* Apr 10] fourth foal: half-brother to French middle-distance winners
Intelectuelle (by Montorselli) and Je T'Aime (by Sir Brink): dam, maiden, half-sister to
fairly useful chaser up to 21f Verka de Thaix: won maiden bumper at Newton Abbot on
debut by 3 lengths from Fox John, despite looking inexperienced. *P. F. Nicholls*

AIDEN (IRE)   10 b.g. Supreme Leader – Chevaux-Vapeur (Le Moss) [2003/4 21s   **h–**
25s⁰ 22s⁰ 24g⁰ 25s⁰ Mar 15] sturdy gelding: modest maiden hurdler in 2001/2: no
show on return: tried visored/blinkered: lazy. *Mrs L. Richards*

AIFUNG (IRE)   6 ch.m. Bigstone (IRE) – Palmyra (GER) (Arratos (FR)) [2003/4 F89:   **h81**
20s⁵ 19m⁴ 22m⁵ 21d³ 21g Mar 27] leggy mare: poor hurdler: won mares novice at
Newton Abbot in July: stays 2¾m: best efforts on good going or firmer. *R. H. Buckler*

AINE DUBH (IRE)   7 b.m. Bob Back (USA) – Deep Thyne (IRE) (Good Thyne   **h136**
(USA)) [2003/4 h101: 16g 20d* 22d* 20d 20m⁴ 20d 16s⁴ 20d 21g⁶ 24g³ Apr 1] leggy,
plain mare: useful hurdler: won minor event at Punchestown in May and handicap at
Galway in August: better than ever when sixth to Monkerhostin in Coral Cup and third to

Iris's Gift in Grade 2 at Aintree: needs testing conditions around 2m and stays 3m: acts on soft going: tried tongue tied. *Kevin F. O'Donnell, Ireland*

AIN TECBALET (FR) 6 b.g. Riverquest (FR) – La Chance Au Roy (FR) (Rex Magna (FR)) [2003/4 c?, h87: c19m² c20s² c21s^{pu} c26g² c24s^{pu} c25m⁴ c31d^{pu} Apr 22] medium-sized gelding: maiden hurdler: winning chaser in France: fair form in handicaps in 2003/4: stays 3¼m: acts on soft and good to firm going: tried blinkered: sold to join F. Murphy 15,000 gns Doncaster May Sales. *N. J. Henderson* **c100 h–**

AIR ATTACHE (USA) 9 b.g. Sky Classic (CAN) – Diplomatic Cover (USA) (Roberto (USA)) [2003/4 c113, h–: c20m* May 15] useful hunter chaser: won at Ludlow by 1¾ lengths from Epsilo de La Ronce: stays 21f: acts on firm going (not discredited on good to soft): tongue tied: takes good hold. *K. R. Pearce* **c113 h–**

AIRCON (IRE) 9 ch.g. Moscow Society (USA) – Corrielek (Menelek) [2003/4 c82x, h–: c20g⁴ c21g² c21m² c24d⁴ c21m² c20m⁴ c19m³ c25d Oct 30] good-topped gelding: poor handicap chaser: stays 21f: acts on firm and soft going: usually visored, tried in cheekpieces: sketchy jumper. *R. Dickin* **c82 x h–**

AIR OF CONFUSION 6 b.g. Mr Confusion (IRE) – First Born (Be My Native (USA)) [2003/4 F74: 16g³ 20g^{pu} 17g⁴ 17g* 17m³ Oct 10] medium-sized gelding: modest novice hurdler: won at Bangor in September: raced mainly around 2m: acts on good to firm going. *Mrs K. Walton* **h94**

AISLE 7 b.g. Arazi (USA) – Chancel (USA) (Al Nasr (FR)) [2003/4 16m^{pu} May 27] half-brother to fairly useful hurdler Canada (by Ezzoud), stays 2½m: poor on Flat: showed nothing on hurdling debut. *L. R. James* **h–**

AKARUS (FR) 9 b.g. Labus (FR) – Meris (FR) (Amarko (FR)) [2003/4 c128, h113: c29d^F c29g^{pu} c36d^F Apr 3] fair maiden hurdler: useful handicap chaser: failed to complete in 2003/4, disputing lead and still going well when falling heavily 4 out in Welsh **c135 h–**

National at Chepstow on reappearance: badly hampered when falling sixth (Becher's) in Grand National at Aintree: stays 4¼m: acts on heavy going: effective with/without blinkers. *M. C. Pipe*

AKHTARI (IRE) 4 b.c. In The Wings – Akishka (Nishapour (FR)) [2003/4 16d¹ 16dᶠ **h114 p**
Apr 13] half-brother to 3 winning hurdlers, notably useful Akasian (by Alzao), stays 3m: dam unraced, out of Arc winner Akiyda: fairly useful form when winning 1½m maiden on debut, sold out of J. Oxx's stable 120,000 gns Newmarket Autumn Sales, fourth in 2m minor event in early-April: fourth in juvenile maiden at Down Royal on hurdling debut: stepping up on that effort when falling last in Grade 2 novice won by Royal Alphabet at Fairyhouse, likely to have finished fifth: should improve further. *D. T. Hughes, Ireland*

AKINA (NZ) 13 b.g. Ivory Hunter (USA) – Wairoa Belle (NZ) (Bold Venture (NZ)) **c– x**
[2003/4 c–x, h–x: c25pᵘ c20gᶠ Aug 23] lengthy gelding: winning hurdler in New **h– x**
Zealand: little form outside points in Britain, usually let down by jumping: has worn cheekpieces/blinkers. *B. J. Llewellyn*

ALAARED (USA) 4 b.g. King of Kings (IRE) – Celtic Loot (USA) (Irish River (FR)) **h–**
[2003/4 16gpᵘ 18d⁶ 16g Apr 12] angular gelding: has only one eye and wears eyecover: fairly useful on Flat (stays 1¾m), sold out of J. Dunlop's stable 13,000 gns Newmarket Autumn Sales: little impact in 3 runs over hurdles. *D. R. Gandolfo*

ALABASTER 9 gr.m. Gran Alba (USA) – Last Ditch (Ben Novus) [2003/4 c25m⁴ **c–**
Mar 9] lightly raced and no form over jumps: tried in cheekpieces. *N. J. Hawke* **h–**

ALAGAZAM 6 ch.g. Alhijaz – Maziere (Mazilier (USA)) [2003/4 h–: 23m⁵ 21m 22g **h–**
22mpᵘ Jul 13] compact gelding: signs of only a little ability over hurdles. *B. I. Case*

ALAKDAR (CAN) 10 ch.g. Green Dancer (USA) – Population (General Assembly **c90**
(USA)) [2003/4 c–, h69: 24m c23m* c21d* c26g⁵ c22g³ c22g³ c24dpᵘ Nov 27] good- **h–**
topped gelding: maiden hurdler: modest chaser: won handicap at Worcester and minor event at Newton Abbot in July: stays 3m: acts on firm and soft going: blinkered on reappearance, visored final start. *C. J. Down*

ALAM (USA) 5 b.g. Silver Hawk (USA) – Ghashtah (USA) (Nijinsky (CAN)) [2003/4 **h105**
h104: 17d⁶ 17d⁶ 16d³ 16s⁶ 20v³ 20d Feb 23] sturdy gelding: fair handicap hurdler: should stay easy 2½m: acts on heavy going. *P. Monteith*

ALASIL (USA) 4 b.g. Swain (IRE) – Asl (USA) (Caro) [2003/4 16g 18s⁵ 16d Mar 1] **h87**
strong, compact gelding: fairly useful on Flat (stays 1½m), sold out of J. Dunlop's stable 41,000 gns Newmarket Autumn Sales: modest form at best over hurdles. *Mrs N. Smith*

ALAYZEASS (IRE) 5 b.m. Aahsaylad – In Reverse (IRE) (Cardinal Flower) [2003/4 **F–**
F16d Nov 30] second foal: half-sister to fairly useful hurdler up to 2½m Star of Bethlehem (by Jolly Jake): dam unraced, out of half-sister to useful hurdler up to 21f Don Valentino: well held in bumper on debut. *J. S. Moore*

ALBAMART WOOD 8 gr.g. Gran Alba (USA) – Marty's Round (Martinmas) **c–**
[2003/4 c–: c16mbᵈ May 15] lengthy gelding: no worthwhile form over fences: placed in maiden points in February/March: tried tongue tied. *R. J. Hodges*

ALBANY (IRE) 4 ch.g. Alhaarth (IRE) – Tochar Ban (USA) (Assert) [2003/4 16g* **h115**
16s³ 24d* 22gpᵘ Apr 16] sturdy gelding: fairly useful on Flat (stays 1¾m), sold out of Mrs J. Ramsden's stable 57,000 gns Newmarket Autumn Sales: fairly useful juvenile hurdler: won at Catterick in February and Hexham (novice) in March: best effort when third to King Revo at Haydock in between. *J. Howard Johnson*

ALBA ROSE 5 gr.m. Overbury (IRE) – Belle Rose (IRE) (Roselier (FR)) [2003/4 **F–**
F16g Feb 18] first foal: dam modest hurdler, stayed 3m: showed little in mares bumper on debut. *J. N. R. Billinge*

ALBATROS (FR) 7 b. or br.g. Shining Steel – Abalvina (FR) (Abdos) [2003/4 c125, **c–**
h114: 20g 16f* 16s 16d 16s⁶ 17s⁴ 16s⁵ 20d⁶ Feb 21] angular gelding: fairly useful chaser/ **h120**
handicap hurdler: won over hurdles at Tramore in August: stays 2½m: acts on any going: effective tongue tied or not: consistent. *E. J. O'Grady, Ireland*

ALBERT HOUSE (IRE) 6 ch.g. Carroll House – Action Plan (Creative Plan (USA)) **h98**
[2003/4 F78: 20s⁵ 21gᶠ 20dᶠ 21g 21s⁵ Mar 15] workmanlike gelding: chasing type: modest form over hurdles. *R. H. Alner*

ALBERTINO LAD 7 ch.g. Mystiko (USA) – Siokra (Kris) [2003/4 F91: F16gᶠ 16d³ **h83**
16d⁶ Apr 23] workmanlike gelding: fair form at best in bumpers: better effort over **F74**
hurdles when third in novice at Hexham in December. *L. Lungo*

ALBERT SQUARE (IRE) 7 b.g. Alflora (IRE) – Place Stephanie (IRE) (Hatim (USA)) [2003/4 F79: 17d4 19s 20s4 21dpu Apr 8] sturdy gelding: modest form at best in novice hurdles: will be suited by 3m: raced only on good to soft/soft going. *R. Rowe* **h85**

ALBRIGHTON 9 b.g. Terimon – Bright One (Electric) [2003/4 c–p, h111: 20g c20d* 22d c20spu Mar 14] angular gelding: winning hurdler: fairly useful chaser: won maiden at Kilbeggan in June: best effort when third to Liscannor Lad in valuable novice handicap at Punchestown in late-April: effective at 2½m to 25f: acts on good to firm and good to soft going. *N. Meade, Ireland* **c117 h–**

ALBUHERA (IRE) 6 b.g. Desert Style (IRE) – Morning Welcome (IRE) (Be My Guest (USA)) [2003/4 16m6 17f* 16m* 16f* 16m6 16g2 16d* 17d* 16d5 16g* 16g 16g 16g2 Apr 16] good-topped gelding: smart on Flat (stays 1¼m) at 3 yrs for M. Johnston: missed 2002 (reportedly fractured pedal bone), useful nowadays: useful novice hurdler: successful at Exeter, Chepstow and Cheltenham (handicap) in October, Newbury in November, Taunton in December and Newbury again (quickened in good style to beat Scorned 6 lengths) in February: best effort when short-headed by Self Defense in Grade 2 at Cheltenham sixth start: below form last 3 outings: will prove best around 2m with emphasis on speed: acts on firm and good to soft going: tongue tied: held up. *P. F. Nicholls* **h138**

ALBUNDY (IRE) 5 b.g. Alzao (USA) – Grove Daffodil (IRE) (Salt Dome (USA)) [2003/4 h80: 20gF 18g6 20m3 Jun 20] poor maiden hurdler: should stay beyond 2m: wears cheekpieces: has found little and one to treat with caution. *B. Mactaggart* **h– §**

ALCAPONE (IRE) 10 b.g. Roselier (FR) – Ann's Cap (IRE) (Cardinal Flower) [2003/4 c143, h–: c20g2 c25m5 c20s5 c24d5 c24spu c18d4 c36dpu Apr 3] workmanlike gelding: has had wind operation: smart chaser: won minor event at Thurles in March by 2 lengths from Adamant Approach: prominent to halfway in Grand National at Aintree next time: well below form at Punchestown later in month: has form up to 3m, at least as effective at shorter: acts on good to firm and heavy going: has worn near-side pricker. *M. F. Morris, Ireland* **c146 h–**

ALCATRAS (IRE) 7 b. or br.g. Corrouge (USA) – Kisco (IRE) (Henbit (USA)) [2003/4 h78§: c21g4 c23gF c24s5 c24g2 c24m2 c25g5 c26g Apr 22] workmanlike gelding: little show in novice hurdles (refused to race once): modest novice steeplechaser, has been let down by jumping. *B. J. M. Ryall* **c85 + h– §**

ALCHEMYSTIC (IRE) 4 b.g. In The Wings – Kama Tashoof (Mtoto) [2003/4 16g5 18g* 18s4 19g5 Mar 27] well-made gelding: fairly useful on all-weather, fair on turf on Flat (stays 1½m), sold out of Mrs A. Perrett's stable 15,000 gns Newmarket Autumn Sales: fair form in juvenile hurdles: won at Fontwell in December: stays 19f: has carried head high. *G. L. Moore* **h102**

ALCOPOP 5 b.g. Alderbrook – Albaciyna (Hotfoot) [2003/4 F17g2 F17m3 F16g4 Mar 10] useful-looking gelding: eighth known foal: closely related to fair staying hurdler Ardour Glowing (by Ardross) and half-brother to 2 other winners: dam maiden, from family of very smart 1¼m winners Last Second and Alborada: fair form in bumpers, hanging fire and carrying head awkwardly last 2 starts. *Miss Venetia Williams* **F92**

K2 Recruitment Jane Shouler Birthday Novices' Hurdle, Newbury—
Albuhera (left) makes it six wins for the season;
two other smart Flat performers Scorned and Dictum (right) are in contention at the last

D. J. & F. A. Jackson's "Albuhera"

ALCRIS 5 b. or br.g. Alderbrook – One of Those Days (Soviet Lad (USA)) [2003/4 **F84**
F16g Mar 6] €26,000 3-y-o: first foal: dam unraced half-sister to high-class hurdlers
Anzum, a stayer, and Jazilah, best at 2m: favourite, eighth of 18 in bumper at Doncaster
on debut, taking fierce hold early. *Jonjo O'Neill*

ALDERBURN 5 b.g. Alderbrook – Threewaygirl (Orange Bay) [2003/4 F17m² F16g **F96**
F16d³ Apr 12] fourth foal: dam bumper/2¼m hurdle winner: best effort in bumpers when
third of 18 to Snoopy Loopy at Huntingdon. *H. D. Daly*

ALDIRUOS (IRE) 4 ch.c. Bigstone (IRE) – Ball Cat (FR) (Cricket Ball (USA)) **h69**
[2003/4 16g⁵ 17m⁵ 16m 16dᵖᵘ 17s Apr 6] ex-French colt: first foal: dam Belgian 7f
winner: thrice-raced on Flat at 3 yrs, won 1½m claimer (claimed from J. C. Rouget
€18,000) in April, left Y. Porzier following month: not fluent and only poor form over
hurdles: tried blinkerd/tongue tied: headstrong. *P. J. Hobbs*

ALEEMDAR (IRE) 7 b.g. Doyoun – Aleema (Red God) [2003/4 h108d: 20v 16m **h–**
20mᵖᵘ 16mᵖᵘ 16dᵖᵘ 19gᵖᵘ Mar 10] winning hurdler: no form in 2003/4: claimed from
Miss K. Marks £6,000 second start: best at 2m: acts on soft and good to firm going: tried
blinkered/visored: has had tongue tied. *A. E. Jones*

AL EILE (IRE) 4 b.g. Alzao (USA) – Kilcsem Eile (IRE) (Commanche Run) **h131**
[2003/4 16m* 16g* 16d² 17g 16g* Apr 1]
    For the second year running, a 4-lb penalty theoretically prevented the
Triumph Hurdle winner from completing the double in the Anniversary Hurdle at
Aintree, Al Eile beating Made In Japan by three quarters of a length in April a year
after Spectroscope had failed by a head to overcome Le Duc. While it may

be equitable that Grade 1 winners carry a penalty in Grade 2 contests (the race
conditions for the Anniversary stipulate that the winner of a Class A hurdle be
penalised), the connections of Spectroscope and Made In Japan would both have
been better off had they finished second at Cheltenham and won at Aintree, the
Anniversary being worth over £5,000 more to the winner than the Triumph, the
supposed championship event. There hasn't been much between the two races in
recent years. Since 1995, when Kissair became the third successive Triumph
winner to top the juvenile ratings in *Chasers & Hurdlers*, and excluding 2000/1,
only one Triumph winner, Scolardy, has featured as the best juvenile to race in
Britain and Ireland, compared with two Anniversary Hurdle winners, Deep Water
and Hors La Loi III, and two winners of the Champion Four Year Old Hurdle at
Punchestown, Grimes and Sporazene. The three other top juveniles, Escartefigue,
Grand Seigneur and Trouble At Bay, didn't win any of the three top races. Grade 1
status should not be set in stone and, on the face of it, there is a case for making the
Triumph the Grade 2 event and the Anniversary Hurdle the Grade 1, particularly
given the current prize money differential. At the very least, it would be worth
considering giving Grade 1 status to both and downgrading the mid-season
mis-named Finale at Chepstow, juvenile hurdlers meriting a different programme
to other categories.

   Al Eile's success at Aintree was something of a surprise, which could fairly
be said of his earlier wins. He hardly seemed a likely sort for hurdling judged on his
Flat form—he was no better than fair for Sheena Collins, producing his best effort

over a mile and looking short of stamina for hurdling. Al Eile took well to it though, winning a couple of seven-runner races on his first two starts, at Listowel in September and Cheltenham (when fifth favourite, defeating Web Perceptions) in November, then running with plenty of credit when runner-up to Top Strategy at Leopardstown. Not seen again until the Triumph, nearly three months later, Al Eile went off a well-supported 16/1-chance but only briefly threatened to get into contention, finishing fifteenth of eighteen finishers. He started at 25/1 at Aintree but showed his Triumph effort hadn't done him justice, responding to pressure after having a fair bit to do into the straight, switched to the far rail before the last and getting the better of Made In Japan towards the finish. Al Eile wasn't weighted to confirm placings with Made In Japan on terms 4 lb worse at Punchestown shortly after the end of the British season, but he was disappointing for the second time in the top three juvenile events, coming only ninth of the twelve to complete, nearly fifteen lengths behind close finishers Cherub and Made In Japan.

Al Eile (IRE) (b.g. 2000)	Alzao (USA) (b 1980)	Lyphard (b 1969)	Northern Dancer Goofed
		Lady Rebecca (b 1971)	Sir Ivor Pocahontas II
	Kilcsem Eile (IRE) (b 1989)	Commanche Run (b 1981)	Run The Gantlet Volley
		Senane (ch 1981)	Vitiges Formulate

Al Eile is the fifth foal and only winner out of his dam Kilcsem Eile, who has a long way to go to match the achievements at stud of both the grandam Senane and third dam Formulate. Both produced numerous winners, Senane's including

Mr M. A. Ryan's "Al Eile"

the Bunbury Cup winner Crumpton Hill, those out of Formulate, herself winner of
the 1978 Hoover Fillies Mile, including the 1998 Oaks winner Shahtoush and the
1990 Oaks runner-up Game Plan. At stud, Game Plan has produced a couple of
good performers at up to a mile and a quarter, Strategic and Sobieski. This isn't a
family associated with jumpers and Al Eile may well have his work cut out to
improve the profile much further. He is far from certain to improve for a step up in
trip and may not be easy to place in conditions races or handicaps at around two
miles. Rather leggy in appearance, Al Eile has yet to race on extremes of going,
showing form on good to firm and good to soft (form on soft on Flat). *J. Queally,
Ireland*

ALESSANDRO SEVERO 5 gr.g. Brief Truce (USA) – Altaia (FR) (Sicyos (USA)) **h–**
[2003/4 20m⁴ 17g 24gᵖᵘ Mar 9] fairly useful on all-weather, fair on turf on Flat (stays
1½m): no promise over hurdles, sold out of N. Littmoden's stable 3,400 gns Doncaster
October Sales after debut. *Mrs D. A. Hamer*

ALEXANDER BANQUET (IRE) 11 b.g. Glacial Storm (USA) – Black Nancy **c141**
(Monksfield) [2003/4 c24d⁶ c24s⁶ c24s c24d⁴ c25d² c26g c36dᶠ Apr 3] strong gelding: **h–**
top-class chaser at best: missed 2002/3 reportedly due to suspensory problem and not
the force of old: flattered when fourth to Florida Pearl in Hennessy Cognac Gold Cup at
Leopardstown in February, staying on strongly as leaders tired: soon tailed off in
Cheltenham Gold Cup in March: has twice failed to complete in Grand National at
Aintree, outpaced when falling eighteenth final start: should stay beyond 3¼m: has form
on good to firm going, used to go particularly well on soft/heavy: genuine. *W. P. Mullins,
Ireland*

ALEXANDER MILENIUM (IRE) 8 b.g. Be My Native (USA) – Kissowen **c–**
(Pitpan) [2003/4 c–p, h90p: F16g 16s³ 17gᵖᵘ Nov 21] rangy, good sort: smart bumper **h106**
winner: lightly raced over jumps, third in maiden hurdle at Gowran very early in season, **F–**
final start for W. Mullins: should stay at least 2½m: often shapes as if having problem.
Jonjo O'Neill

ALEXANDER MUSICAL (IRE) 6 b. or br.g. Accordion – Love For Lydia (IRE) **h76**
(Law Society (USA)) [2003/4 F16f F16g 25dᵖᵘ 17g⁴ Apr 1] €15,000 4-y-o: tall, angular **F–**
ex-Irish gelding: third foal: dam, Irish maiden, from family of 1000 Guineas winner
Quick As Lightning: signs of only a little ability in bumpers (left J. G. Burns after reappearance): blinkered, poor form on second of 2 starts over hurdles. *S. T. Lewis*

ALEXANDER PARK (IRE) 7 b.g. Yashgan – Lady Laramie (IRE) (Le Bavard (FR)) **c–**
[2003/4 h–: c21vᵖᵘ 24sᵖᵘ 24sᵖᵘ Feb 22] sturdy gelding: no sign of ability. *John R. Upson* **h–**

ALEXANDERTHEGREAT (IRE) 6 b.g. Supreme Leader – Sandy Jayne **h141**
(IRE) (Royal Fountain) [2003/4 21d* 19d² 24s* 22s³ 23s 25g³ Mar 16]
Alexanderthegreat came within a length and a half of emulating his dam's
half-brother Fissure Seal in winning the staying handicap hurdle at the Cheltenham
Festival. Fissure Seal won what was then the American Express Gold Card Handicap Hurdle Final in the 1992/3 season, one of seven wins during the campaign,
three over hurdles and four, including the big novice handicap at Punchestown,
over fences. Fissure Seal failed to win again over another three seasons' racing,
though he was better than ever when second in the Leopardstown Chase and the
Thyestes at the age of ten. Alexanderthegreat has so far run just in points and over
hurdles and it will be disappointing if he can't add substantially to a tally of three
wins once he goes novice chasing. Alexanderthegreat ran twice in points as a
five-year-old for Richard Barber, winning a maiden on his debut, then finishing
third after jumping left while holding every chance at the last. Following the
familiar path from Barber to Paul Nicholls, Alexanderthegreat won two of his first
three starts over hurdles, novices at Plumpton and Exeter, though his defeat by
Copsale Lad at the latter venue on his second start represents rather better form.
After that it was handicaps, and with them immediate and marked improvement,
despite being thrown in at the deep end, taking on the champion staying hurdler at
Sandown. Even his Macedonian namesake might have blanched at facing Baracouda after such limited experience, though Alexanderthegreat was receiving 25 lb
(still 27 lb more than his mark in the original long handicap). Going to two out, a
shock result looked a possibility and though Alexanderthegreat couldn't sustain his
challenge, also losing second to Yogi close home, to finish two and a half lengths

behind Baracouda was some performance. He couldn't repeat it when taking on Iris's Gift, again from out of the handicap, in a Pertemps qualifier at Haydock just a week later but his performance in the Final itself was his best in six starts over hurdles. Again travelling smoothly, he disputed the lead with G V A Ireland at the last but couldn't get past, both overhauled by Creon close home. Raced on good going or softer, Alexanderthegreat clearly possesses plenty of stamina but he isn't a sluggard. Apart from Fissure Seal, his family isn't a distinguished one, and Alexanderthegreat was bought for just 9,000 guineas in a private sale at the Doncaster May Sales in 2002. He is the third foal and only winner out of his unraced dam Sandy Jayne. *P. F. Nicholls*

ALEXANDRA PARADE (IRE)   7 b.m. Mister Lord (USA) – Ballyanihan (Le Moss) [2003/4 20g⁵ 20s² 22v⁴ 20sᵖᵘ Feb 14] rangy mare: bumper winner: modest form over hurdles: should stay beyond 2½m: acts on soft going. *Mrs J. C. McGregor*   **h88**

ALFA SUNRISE   7 b.g. Alflora (IRE) – Gipsy Dawn (Lighter) [2003/4 F104: 21v⁵ 19m⁶ 20s⁴ 19s² 24g 24gᶠ Mar 10] angular gelding: bumper winner: modest novice hurdler: will prove best at 2½m+: acts on soft going. *R. H. Buckler*   **h96**

ALFIE BRIGHT   6 ch.g. Alflora (IRE) – Candlebright (Lighter) [2003/4 17d 20vᵖᵘ 20sᵖᵘ Apr 21] well-made gelding: third foal: half-brother to winning 2¾m chaser Mount Gay (by Montelimar) and winning 2½m hurdler Toad Hall (by Henbit): dam, fair hurdler/chaser, stayed 2½m: no form over hurdles. *Mrs L. B. Normile*   **h–**

ALFIE (IRE)   6 b.g. Alphabatim (USA) – Brave Bavard (Le Bavard (FR)) [2003/4 17d Oct 29] IR £10,000 3-y-o: sixth foal: half-brother to winning pointer by Supreme Leader: dam unraced: well held in novice hurdle at Sedgefield on debut: sold 2,800 gns Doncaster May Sales. *Miss Lucinda V. Russell*   **h–**

ALFIE PLUNKETT   5 b.g. Mind Games – River of Fortune (IRE) (Lahib (USA)) [2003/4 F16d F16d 17sᵖᵘ 19gᵖᵘ Apr 16] 500 3-y-o, 3,200 4-y-o: first foal: dam 2-y-o 7f seller winner, second only start over hurdles: no sign of ability. *Mrs Jane Galpin*   **h–**
F–

ALFIE'S SUN   5 b.g. Alflora (IRE) – Sun Dante (IRE) (Phardante (FR)) [2003/4 F16d F16s⁵ F16d² Feb 2] big, rangy gelding: third foal: dam unraced half-sister to useful hurdler Chauvinist, out of half-sister to smart hurdler/useful chaser up to 3m Forest Sun: progressive form in bumpers, ½-length second of 17 to Moorlands Return at Kempton: will stay beyond 2m. *D. E. Cantillon*   **F97**

ALFIE TWOFOURTWO (IRE)   8 b.g. Jolly Jake (NZ) – Spin N'Win (Cardinal Flower) [2003/4 20d⁵ c24sᵖᵘ c21sᵖᵘ c25gᵖᵘ 20dᶠᵗʳ 27dᵖᵘ Mar 16] good-topped ex-Irish gelding: first foal: dam, lightly raced in points, half-sister to NH Chase winner Rith Dubh: third in bumper: poor maiden hurdler: sold out of M. Morris's stable 10,000 gns Doncaster May (2002) Sales: pulled up all 3 starts over fences (bled from nose on first): stays 2½m: refused to race in visor last time (wore cheekpieces previous one). *Ferdy Murphy*   **c– §**
h74 §

ALFIE VALENTINE   8 b.g. Alflora (IRE) – My Aisling (John de Coombe) [2003/4 24g 16d 19sᵖᵘ Apr 11] tenth foal: half-brother to winning 2m hurdler Lady Remainder (by Remainder Man) and winning pointer by Rakaposhi King: dam disqualified 2-y-o 7f and 1¼m winner: no show over hurdles. *Mrs P. Ford*   **h–**

ALF LAUREN   6 b.g. Alflora (IRE) – Gokatiego (Huntercombe) [2003/4 F87: F17g Nov 18] won bumper at Bangor on debut in March 2003: well held in similar event 8 months later. *A. King*   **F–**

ALFLORIANO   5 b.g. Alflora (IRE) – Swallowfield (Wattlefield) [2003/4 F16d Mar 11] 4,000 4-y-o: workmanlike gelding: third foal: half-brother to 2m hurdle winner Aerion (by Ardross): dam lightly raced: tailed off in bumper on debut. *O. Sherwood*   **F–**

ALFY RICH   8 b.g. Alflora (IRE) – Weareagrandmother (Prince Tenderfoot (USA)) [2003/4 h77: 22s 24sᵖᵘ 26s 21s⁵ 19vᵇᵈ 17m⁴ 19d³ 17s⁴ 17s 20s⁶ Apr 17] tall gelding: poor handicap hurdler: stays 21f: acts on heavy and good to firm going. *P. M. Rich*   **h76**

ALGARVE   7 b.g. Alflora (IRE) – Garvenish (Balinger) [2003/4 h–, F72: 20d² 20d* 20dᵖᵘ 22s⁴ Jan 10] rangy, useful-looking gelding: type to make a chaser: modest novice hurdler: made all in handicap at Aintree in November: probably stays 2¾m: acts on soft ground. *H. D. Daly*   **h98**

ALGENON (DEN)   4 br.g. Asaasy (USA) – La Natte (FR) (Native Guile (USA)) [2003/4 F16g³ F16d⁵ Mar 28] unfurnished gelding: seventh foal: half-brother to winner up to 1½m Mister Swing (by Kaldoun): dam winner on Flat/around 2m over hurdles: fair form in bumpers, 4 lengths third of 20 to Lord Gale at Haydock on debut. *Ferdy Murphy*   **F95**

ALGYMO   4 b.f. Tamure (IRE) – Red Point (Reference Point) [2003/4 F16s F17g 20d   h–
Apr 21] second foal: dam, poor maiden hurdler, granddaughter of Oaks and St Leger   F–
winner Dunfermline: well held in bumpers and maiden hurdle. *S. C. Burrough*

ALIABAD (IRE)   9 b. or br.g. Doyoun – Alannya (FR) (Relko) [2003/4 20m³ 22g⁴   h74
21m³ 24f³ 22f³ 21s 21m² 26sᵖᵘ 16g 19m⁴ 17m⁴ Mar 9] angular gelding: poor maiden
hurdler: probably stays 3m: acts on firm and good to soft going: tried visored/tongue tied:
has looked hard ride. *J. G. M. O'Shea*

ALIAS (IRE)   6 br.g. Allegoric (USA) – Snowdrifter (Strong Gale) [2003/4 F17f⁴ 20m   c– x
26gᵖᵘ c16dᵖᵘ c23f³ c24d² c23m⁶ c24dᶠ c27s⁵ c24g⁵ c24gᵖᵘ c24d⁶ Mar 28] 7,500 4-y-o: h–
workmanlike gelding: fourth foal: half-brother to winning pointer by Doubletour: dam,   F–
won 2m hurdle, half-sister to fairly useful 2m hurdler Hard As Iron: won 2½m maiden on
completed start in points in 2003, little other sign of ability: usually wears headgear:
sketchy jumper: sold 3,500 gns Doncaster May Sales. *P. T. Dalton*

ALI BRUCE   4 b.g. Cadeaux Genereux – Actualite (Polish Precedent (USA)) [2003/4   F–
F16d Jan 22] 13,000 3-y-o: fourth foal: half-brother to useful 1m and 1¼m winner
Shamrock City (by Rock City) and 7f winners Saltwood (by Mujtahid) and Witness (by
Efisio): dam, French 10.5f winner, from family of Old Vic and High Top: shaped like
non-stayer in bumper at Ludlow on debut. *D. E. Cantillon*

ALICUDI (IRE)   4 b.g. Ali-Royal (IRE) – Nawadder (Kris) [2003/4 16s² 16v* 16d   h111
Apr 12] half-brother to winning hurdler/chaser up to 2½m Yaakum (by Glint of Gold):
fair on Flat (stays 2m) for M. Grassick: best effort in juvenile hurdles when winning
minor event at Fairyhouse in January by 2 lengths from Rocket Ship: raced on going
softer than good. *W. Durkan, Ireland*

ALISA (IRE)   4 b.f. Slip Anchor – Ariadne (GER) (Kings Lake (USA)) [2003/4 F12g   F–
F14g F12m Dec 10] leggy filly: third foal: half-sister to middle-distance winners in
Denmark by Ezzoud and Italy by Vettori: dam, German winner around 1m, out of sister
to dam of 2000 Guineas winner King's Best and Arc winner Urban Sea, dam of top-class
1½m colt Galileo: well held in 3-y-o bumpers: modest form on Flat: tried in cheekpieces.
B. I. Case

ALITTLEMOREACTION   6 b.g. Alflora (IRE) – Ilderton Road (Noalto) [2003/4   h–
F–: 20s 21s 21d Apr 11] unfurnished gelding: no sign of ability. *M. J. Roberts*

ALIZARIN (IRE)   5 b.m. Tagula (IRE) – Persian Empress (IRE) (Persian Bold)   h–
[2003/4 20fᵖᵘ Sep 14] disappointing maiden on Flat: no form in novice hurdle (looked
temperamental) and points. *A. C. Wilson*

ALKA INTERNATIONAL   12 b.g. Northern State (USA) – Cachucha (Gay Fan-   c–
dango (USA)) [2003/4 c95, h?: 16s⁴ 16d 23v⁶ 18sᶠ Feb 9] lengthy gelding: lightly raced   h–
over fences: fair hurdler: stays 21f, at least when conditions aren't testing: acts on heavy
going: blinkered nowadays. *Mrs P. Townsley*

ALL BLEEVABLE   7 b.g. Presidium – Eve's Treasure (Bustino) [2003/4 h72: 16m³   h96
17g⁴ 17m² 17g² 16s⁴ 16g* 16g* 16s³ Mar 19] close-coupled gelding: modest hurdler:
improved form when winning selling handicap at Fakenham in February and novice
handicap at Doncaster in March: best around 2m: acts on good to firm and heavy going:
consistent. *Mrs S. Lamyman*

ALL BUT (IRE)   12 b.g. Roselier (FR) – Cloncunny (Teofane) [2003/4 c20g³ 20s⁵   c67
c27s⁵ c21vᵖᵘ c19gᵖᵘ c28dᵖᵘ c24d³ c25s⁶ Apr 4] good-topped gelding: winning pointer: h–
poor maiden hurdler/steeplechaser: left J. Parkes after fifth start: stays 3½m: acts on
heavy ground: tried blinkered: often tongue tied. *James Clements, Ireland*

ALLEGED AFFAIR (IRE)   7 gr.g. Safety Catch (USA) – Wren's Princess (Wrens   F–
Hill) [2003/4 F80: F16g⁵ Oct 15] tall gelding: twice-raced in bumpers, well held only
outing in 2003/4: will be suited by greater test of stamina. *B. D. Leavy*

ALLEGEDLY RED   5 ch.m. Sabrehill (USA) – Tendency (Ballad Rock) [2003/4   h75
h64: 19f* 20d 17g⁵ 16g⁴ 19gᵖᵘ 16g⁴ Mar 10] poor hurdler: dead-heated in mares maiden
at Catterick in November: stays easy 19f: acts on firm going: tongue tied final outing.
Mrs A. Duffield

ALLEGED SLAVE (IRE)   9 ch.g. Husyan (USA) – Lek Dawn (Menelek) [2003/4   c107
h98: c24sᵖᵘ c22sᵖᵘ c20g³ c19s² c20d² c16d* Apr 12] workmanlike gelding: runner-up on   h–
first of 3 starts over hurdles: fair novice chaser: won handicap at Huntingdon: stays 2½m:
raced on good going or softer (acts on heavy). *A. King*

ALLEGIANCE   9 b.g. Rock Hopper – So Precise (FR) (Balidar) [2003/4 h–: 16g 16s 16s[4] 17s[5] 16s Feb 18] leggy gelding: one-time modest hurdler around 2m: lightly raced and no form since 2000/1: blinkered/visored earlier in career. *P. Wegmann* **h–**

ALLER MOOR (IRE)   13 b.g. Dry Dock – Boggy Peak (Shirley Heights) [2003/4 c105: c25m[pu] c25s[pu] c24s[pu] Dec 29] workmanlike gelding: fairly useful hunter chaser in 2002/3: pulled up all 3 starts back in handicaps: should stay beyond 25f: acts on soft going, seemingly unsuited by firmer than good. *C. J. Gray* **c–**

ALL EYEZ ON ME (IRE)   7 b.g. Torus – Ella Rosa (Le Bavard (FR)) [2003/4 c–x, h–: 24m Jun 18] of no account. *Dr P. Pritchard* **c - x** **h–**

ALLEZ MOUSSON   6 b.g. Hernando (FR) – Rynechra (Blakeney) [2003/4 24s 20d Feb 23] fair on Flat (best at 2m+): well held both starts over hurdles. *A. Bailey* **h79 ?**

ALLEZ SCOTIA   5 ch.m. Minster Son – Allez (Move Off) [2003/4 F16s F16d F16g F17v[3] 16g 24s[3] Apr 21] ninth foal: dam of little account: modest form in bumpers: well beaten in 2 novice hurdles. *R. Nixon* **h67** **F77**

ALLEZ TOUJOURS (IRE)   9 b.g. Castle Keep – Adapan (Pitpan) [2003/4 c–, h71: 20g[pu] 22m[pu] May 29] lengthy gelding: poor maiden hurdler: failed to complete all 3 starts in handicap chases (won point in March): should stay beyond 2m: acts on soft going: blinkered final outing (looked unwilling). *M. Sheppard* **c–** **h–**

ALLFRIENDS   5 b. or br.g. Alflora (IRE) – Three Friends (IRE) (The Parson) [2003/4 F16d F16s Feb 7] first foal: dam modest form in bumpers: well held in 2 bumpers. *H. P. Hogarth* **F–**

ALL HONEY (IRE)   7 ch.m. Fourstars Allstar (USA) – A Bit of Honey (The Parson) [2003/4 c–, h83d: 20d[3] 16g* 16d[F] 16m 22m 16g[5] 16d[5] Nov 27] leggy mare: failed to complete in 2 chases: poor hurdler: won amateur seller at Uttoxeter in May: effective at 2m to 2¾m: acts on heavy going: blinkered once. *Miss K. Marks* **c–** **h71**

ALLIMAC (IRE)   7 b.g. Alphabatim (USA) – Firewood (IRE) (Brush Aside (USA)) [2003/4 c111, h–: c20m[3] c16m[3] c20m[pu] Dec 27] lengthy gelding: fairly useful chaser: stays 2½m: acts on firm going (runner-up in bumper on good to soft): often front runner: has bled from nose, including final outing. *Miss H. C. Knight* **c116** **h–**

ALL IN THE STARS (IRE)   6 ch.g. Fourstars Allstar (USA) – Luton Flyer (Condorcet (FR)) [2003/4 h75: 21v[pu] 20d[4] 24s[ur] 22d[2] 24s[pu] 26s[5] 26g[5] Mar 17] smallish, sturdy gelding: won maiden point in 2003 (subsequently tested positive for morphine): fair handicap hurdler: stays 3¼m: acts on soft going: visored last 2 starts. *D. P. Keane* **h106**

ALL ON MY OWN (USA)   9 ch.g. Unbridled (USA) – Some For All (USA) (One For All (USA)) [2003/4 16g[2] 16s[pu] Dec 19] close-coupled gelding: poor maiden on Flat: well held only outing over fences: bad maiden hurdler: raced mainly around 2m: tried blinkered. *I. W. McInnes* **c–** **h56**

ALLOTROPE (IRE)   9 b.g. Nashwan (USA) – Graphite (USA) (Mr Prospector (USA)) [2003/4 c–, h–: c24s[pu] May 2] leggy gelding: poor handicap hurdler: no worthwhile form in points/2 hunter chases: stays 2¾m: acts on good to firm and heavy going: blinkered last 3 starts. *Lady Susan Brooke* **c–** **h–**

ALL RIGHT FOR TIME   6 b.m. Sula Bula – Penny Falls (Push On) [2003/4 F16d 25s[pu] Dec 20] fourth foal: dam winning hunter chaser: no form in bumper or novice hurdle. *C. C. Bealby* **h–** **F–**

ALL ROCK HARD (NZ)   6 ch.g. Bigstone (IRE) – My Lady Gray (NZ) (Otehi Bay (AUS)) [2003/4 16s[5] 19g[2] 16g[3] 16d 16d 16f[3] 16g Mar 6] New Zealand-bred gelding: successful twice (7f/11f) from 20 starts on Flat in Australasia: modest novice hurdler: stays 19f: acts on firm going: wore cheekpieces/blinkers last 5 starts. *R. C. Guest* **h89**

ALL SEWN UP   12 ch.g. Jazetas – Rose of Bradford (Levanter) [2003/4 c16g[pu] Jun 28] poor maiden pointer. *R. J. Baker* **c–**

ALL SONSILVER (FR)   7 b.g. Son of Silver – All Licette (FR) (Native Guile (USA)) [2003/4 c96, h94: c24s[3] c25s[2] c20s* c24v* c20d[3] c24s[6] Mar 13] useful-looking gelding: won 2 of 3 starts over hurdles: fair handicap chaser: improved in 2003/4, winning at Newcastle in January and February: stays 25f: acts on heavy going: patiently ridden (has idled in front): sold to join P. Kelsall 35,000 gns Doncaster May Sales. *M. Todhunter* **c109** **h–**

ALLSTAR LEADER (IRE)   7 b.g. Fourstars Allstar (USA) – Rugged Leader (Supreme Leader) [2003/4 h–, F88: 18d[5] 16f[2] 24g[2] 20f* 21m[2] Jul 22] leggy gelding: poor **h79**

hurdler: won handicap at Sligo in July: reportedly distressed final start: stays 3m when emphasis is on speed: acts on firm going. *J. J. Lambe, Ireland*

ALL THINGS EQUAL (IRE) 5 b.g. Supreme Leader – Angel's Dream (King's Ride) [2003/4 F16g² F17d Apr 3] lengthy, useful-looking gelding: fifth foal: half-brother to winning pointer by Un Desperado: dam, fair hurdler, stayed 3¼m: won 2½m maiden Irish point on debut in 2003: encouraging head second to Kimono Royal in bumper at Kempton: virtually ran off course on bend into straight in Grade 2 at Aintree. *S. E. H. Sherwood* **F95**

ALLTIME DANCER (IRE) 12 b.g. Waajib – Dance On Lady (Grundy) [2003/4 c–, h–: c24g Mar 12] compact gelding: one-time fairly useful hurdler: winning pointer: poor maiden steeplechaser: stays 3¼m: acts on firm and good to soft going: has won in blinkers. *Mrs C. F. Lambert* **c–** **h–**

ALLUDE (IRE) 5 b.g. Darshaan – Ahliyat (USA) (Irish River (FR)) [2003/4 h113: 16m* 17g* 16g* 16m² Jul 13] strong, lengthy gelding: fair hurdler: won novices at Worcester and Cartmel in May and Perth in June: will stay further than 2m: acts on good to firm and good to soft going: wears cheekpieces. *C. J. Mann* **h104**

ALLUMEE 5 ch.g. Alflora (IRE) – Coire Vannich (Celtic Cone) [2003/4 F16d⁵ F17s⁵ F16g F17g Apr 13] 24,000 4-y-o: sturdy gelding: sixth foal: brother to 2m hurdle winner Flower of Pitcur and half-brother to poor 2m hurdler Dellone (by Gunner B): dam, winning hurdler, stayed 2½m: fairly useful form when fifth of 22 at Newbury on debut, best effort in bumpers. *P. J. Hobbs* **F95**

AL MABROOK (IRE) 9 b.g. Rainbows For Life (CAN) – Sky Lover (Ela-Mana-Mou) [2003/4 h–: 17g² 21g³ 18g 18d⁵ 16s^F 21s⁶ 17v* 19g* 17s* Feb 10] close-coupled gelding: modest handicap hurdler: won last 3 outings, conditional jockeys selling events first 2, at Sedgefield in January and Catterick and Sedgefield in February: stays 21f: acts on any going: tried in cheekpieces/visor. *N. G. Richards* **h89**

ALMANOSO 8 b.m. Teenoso (USA) – Almanot (Remainder Man) [2003/4 h–: 21s^pu 22g³ c20g^pu 26s^pu 22s² 22s^pu 24g Apr 1] bad maiden hurdler: jumped poorly on chasing debut: stays 3¼m: acts on soft going: blinkered last 3 starts: unreliable. *R. Curtis* **c– §** **h58 §**

ALMARAVIDE (GER) 8 ch.g. Orfano (GER) – Allerleirauh (GER) (Espresso) [2003/4 h–: 16d² 20d* 20v³ 21g Mar 17] smallish gelding: fairly useful handicap hurdler, lightly raced: won at Ascot in January by 2½ lengths from Sonevafushi: should stay beyond 2½m: acts on heavy going, not discredited on firm. *M. Bradstock* **h122**

ALMAYDAN 6 b.g. Marju (IRE) – Cunning (Bustino) [2003/4 17g⁴ 19d² 17g* 16g² 17s* Apr 6] strong gelding: fair on Flat (barely stays 2½m): fairly useful novice hurdler: won at Taunton (maiden) in February and Exeter (ran on strongly despite hanging left to beat Lacdoudal 3½ lengths) in April: will stay beyond 19f: raced on good going or softer over hurdles. *R. Lee* **h129**

ALMIER (IRE) 6 gr.g. Phardante (FR) – Stepfaster (Step Together (USA)) [2003/4 F16d⁵ F16s* 20g⁵ 16g Nov 15] small gelding: second foal: brother to bumper winner Pharviva: dam, modest chaser, stayed 27f: fair form in bumpers, won at Listowel in September: little impact over hurdles. *M. Hourigan, Ireland* **h67** **F88**

ALMIRE DU LIA (FR) 6 ch.g. Beyssac (FR) – Lita (FR) (Big John (FR)) [2003/4 h91: 20v c20s³ c20s* c25g³ c20d^pu Apr 23] big gelding: modest hurdler, needed race on reappearance: better over fences, won weak novice at Newcastle in March: good third to Strong Resolve at Kelso 8 days later: stays 25f: acts on firm and soft going: usually wears cheekpieces/visor. *Mrs S. C. Bradburne* **c104** **h–**

ALMNADIA (IRE) 5 b.m. Alhaarth (IRE) – Mnaafa (IRE) (Darshaan) [2003/4 h99: 22f³ 21m 20m 16s 19d⁴ 22g⁶ 21g⁵ 24d⁴ 21m Apr 15] smallish mare: fair handicap hurdler: stays 3m: acts on soft and firm going. *S. Gollings* **h103**

ALMONTASIR (IRE) 6 b.g. Distinctly North (USA) – My Blue (Scenic) [2003/4 F–: F16g May 2] no show in bumpers. *T. P. McGovern* **F–**

ALMOST AN ANGEL (IRE) 14 ch.g. Lancastrian – Ballykytton (Signa Infesta) [2003/4 c25d^pu Apr 30] winning pointer, little form otherwise. *S. T. Lewis* **c–** **h–**

ALPH 7 b.g. Alflora (IRE) – Royal Birthday (St Paddy) [2003/4 16s Feb 19] tall, lengthy, rather sparely-made gelding: tenth foal: half-brother to top-class 2m hurdler Royal Derbi and bumper winner Phal (both by Derrylin) and fairly useful 2m hurdler Ivy Edith (by Blakeney): dam no form on Flat: ran green when seventh of 13 in novice hurdle at Sandown on debut: should improve. *R. Ingram* **h85**

ALPHABETIC   7 ch.g. Alflora (IRE) – Incamelia (St Columbus) [2003/4 F93: 20m³ **h93**
19m³ Dec 10] well-made gelding: placed third in bumpers: modest form when third in
novice hurdles: will stay beyond 2½m. *N. J. Henderson*

ALPHA CENTAURI (IRE)   10 ch.g. Alphabatim (USA) – Darna Glen (Furry Glen) **c–**
[2003/4 c–, h93: c24gᵖᵘ c19sᶠ Mar 20] strong, good-topped gelding: bumper winner: **h–**
completed only once over jumps, including in points. *P. Butler*

ALPHA GIOCONDA (IRE)   7 b.g. Alphabatim (USA) – Rio Dulce (Rio Carmelo **h– p**
(FR)) [2003/4 21gʳᵒ Mar 5] IR £25,000 4-y-o: angular gelding: half-brother to useful
hurdler/winning chaser Rio's King (by King's Ride), stayed 21f, and winning pointer by
Good Thyne: dam won over hurdles/on Flat: green, not far away when running out 4 out
in novice hurdle at Newbury on debut. *N. J. Henderson*

ALPHA GOLD (IRE)   9 ch.g. Alphabatim (USA) – Show M How (Ashmore (FR)) **c– x**
[2003/4 c25gᵖᵘ Apr 3] smallish gelding: winning chaser: lame on first start for 2 years: **h–**
should stay beyond 3m: acts on heavy and good to firm going: not a fluent jumper.
H. D. Daly

ALPHA IMAGE (IRE)   5 b.g. Alphabatim (USA) – Happy Image (Le Moss) **h–**
[2003/4 20sᵖᵘ 24vᵖᵘ Jan 10] 6,000 4-y-o: sixth foal: brother to winning pointer: dam
unraced: showed nothing in novice hurdles at Uttoxeter. *Mrs L. Williamson*

ALPHA LEATHER   13 gr.g. Zambrano – Harvey's Choice (Whistlefield) [2003/4 **c–**
c–, h–: c25dᵘʳ c24m c34vᵖᵘ May 21] tall gelding: no longer of any account: tried visored. **h–**
M. J. Grassick

ALPHA NOBLE (GER)   7 b.g. Lando (GER) – Alpha (GER) (Frontal) [2003/4 **h85**
h90p: 16mᶠ Sep 13] modest form on hurdling debut in 2002/3: would have been in frame
but for falling fatally last in maiden at Worcester. *Miss Venetia Williams*

ALPHA RHYTHM (IRE)   6 b.g. Alphabatim (USA) – Glenn Ard (IRE) (Al Sirat) **h111**
[2003/4 18d⁶ 19s⁵ 16fʳᵒ 16f³ 16m² 19gᵉ 20g⁴ 24m² 24m* 24d 22dᵖᵘ Apr 12] fair hurdler:
won twice in August and novice at Cork in November: stays 3m: acts on good
to firm going. *N. Meade, Ireland*

ALPHA ROMANA (IRE)   10 b.g. Alphabatim (USA) – Stella Romana (Roman **c100 d**
Warrior) [2003/4 c100, h–: c16d* c16gᵉ c20gᵉ c20mᵖᵘ c22dᵖᵘ Apr 7] strong, lengthy **h–**
gelding: fairly useful hunter chaser on his day: won at Cheltenham (second successive
win in race) in April and Hexham (made all) in May: off 9 months, ran poorly last 2
outings: stays 21f: acts on soft and good to firm going. *Mrs S. E. Busby*

ALPHA ROSE   7 ch.m. Inchinor – Philgwyn (Milford) [2003/4 16m² 20s 17g⁵ 16m* **h96**
Oct 9] modest on Flat (best at 1½m/1¾m), sold out of M. Bell's stable 20,000 gns
Newmarket Autumn (2002) Sales: improved effort over hurdles when winning novice
handicap at Huntingdon, left clear at the last: should stay beyond 2m: acts on good to firm
going. *C. R. Egerton*

ALPHASUPREME (IRE)   7 ch.m. Alphabatim (USA) – Railway Rabbit (IRE) **F–**
(Supreme Leader) [2003/4 F74: F17mᵖᵘ May 14] non-thoroughbred mare: poor form on
first of 3 starts in bumpers: saddle slipped at Exeter in May: will stay beyond 2m.
C. J. Down

ALPHAZAR (IRE)   9 br.g. Alphabatim (USA) – Ravaleen (IRE) (Executive Perk) **c112**
[2003/4 20g⁶ 20s³ 19s c20g* c20dᵘʳ c17d* c20sᵖᵘ c20sᵖᵘ Apr 4] first foal: dam unraced **h106**
half-sister to fairly useful hurdler up to 2½m Coralpha: fair hurdler/chaser: won over
fences at Wexford (maiden) in October and Leopardstown (handicap) in December:
should stay beyond 2½m: acts on heavy going. *Anthony Mullins, Ireland*

ALPINE FOX   7 b.g. Risk Me (FR) – Hill Vixen (Goldhill) [2003/4 F16g² F16g* **h116 p**
F16m* F16m² 16d² Nov 30] sturdy gelding: sixth foal: half-brother to 3 winners, **F111**
including 2m chaser Floosy (by Governor General) and 2m selling hurdler That There (by
Oats): dam 1½m winner: useful in bumpers, won at Worcester in May and June: ½-length
second to The Posh Paddy in listed event at Cheltenham: encouraging 11 lengths second
to Grey Report in maiden at Newbury on hurdling debut: sure to improve and win a race
over hurdles. *T. R. George*

ALPINE HIDEAWAY (IRE)   11 b.g. Tirol – Arbour (USA) (Graustark) [2003/4 **c–**
c–, h72: 16m 17g⁴ 17m² 17g* 17m⁴ Aug 30] angular gelding: poor handicap hurdler: **h75**
won seller at Sedgefield in August: raced mainly around 2m: best form on good going
or firmer (acts on firm): tried blinkered/visored, wears cheekpieces nowadays.
J. S. Wainwright

ALPINE PANTHER (IRE)   11 b.g. Tirol – Kentucky Wildcat (Be My Guest (USA))   c–
[2003/4 c–, h–: c33d^{pu} Apr 30] lengthy, angular gelding: one-time useful hurdler/fair   h–
maiden chaser: no form in hunters: blinkered last 2 starts: tried tongue tied. *C. R. Cox*

ALPINE SLAVE   7 ch.g. Alflora (IRE) – Celtic Slave (Celtic Cone) [2003/4 h110:   c105
c20s^{pu} c25d^4 c22s^4 c26s^2 c24d^3 c24g* Apr 18] sturdy gelding: fair hurdler: similar form   h–
over fences, won maiden at Stratford: stays 3¼m: raced on good going or softer (acts on
soft). *N. J. Gifford*

ALRIDA (IRE)   5 b.g. Ali-Royal (IRE) – Ride Bold (USA) (J O Tobin (USA)) [2003/4   h94 p
17d^2 Mar 7] fairly useful on Flat (stays 2m), not at best in 2003, sold out of W. Jarvis'
stable 30,000 gns Newmarket Autumn Sales: 11/2 from 11/1, 10 lengths second to
Valeureux in novice at Market Rasen on hurdling debut, keeping on not knocked about:
will stay further: should improve. *R. A. Fahey*

ALSCOT FOXY LADY (IRE)   7 b.m. Foxhound (USA) – Arena (Sallust) [2003/4   c–
h–: 16g c16m^3 c16m^5 Jul 9] no form over hurdles: probably flattered on chasing debut: h–
blinkered final start. *R. Dickin*

ALSINA   13 b.g. Alias Smith (USA) – Tersina (Lighter) [2003/4 c92: c25d May 3] fair   c–
pointer: easily best effort in hunter chases when second at Hexham in 2002/3: stays 25f.
Peter Innes

ALSKA (FR)   11 b. or br.m. Leading Counsel (USA) – Kolkwitzia (FR) (The Wonder   c94
(FR)) [2003/4 c84, h–: c21s^6 c25m^5 c31f^4 c24d^5 c25m^2 c25g^5 c24g* Apr 16] angular   h–
mare: modest hunter chaser: won at Taunton, leading line having still been well off pace
2 out: probably stays 31f: acts on any going: tried blinkered/visored. *P. L. Southcombe*

ALSTON WONDER MAN (IRE)   9 ch.g. Husyan (USA) – Welsh Thorn (Welsh   h75
Saint) [2003/4 17m* 20g^{pu} Oct 24] eighth foal: half-brother to 2 winning pointers by
Don: dam won on Flat and up to 2½m over hurdles in Ireland: well held in bumper in
2002/3 for W. Flavin: third in maiden Irish point previous month: well backed, won seller
(sold from S. Kirk 7,000 gns) at Market Rasen in August, pulling hard and soon clear:
went lame next time: bred to stay beyond 2m. *Mrs J. R. Buckley*

ALSYATI   6 ch.g. Salse (USA) – Rubbiyati (Cadeaux Genereux) [2003/4 17s 16d 16v^{pu} h79 +
16g* Mar 10] lengthy gelding: modest on Flat (stays 11.5f), sold out of C. Brittain's stable
5,000 gns Newmarket Autumn Sales: first form over hurdles when winning selling
handicap at Chepstow. *D. Burchell*

ALTAREEK (USA)   7 b.g. Alleged (USA) – Black Tulip (FR) (Fabulous Dancer   h94
(USA)) [2003/4 h75: 16g^4 20d^2 21s^2 26s^4 26g 27d^{pu} Apr 23] bumper winner: modest
novice hurdler: stays 3¼m: raced on good going or softer over hurdles (acts on soft):
blinkered. *J. M. Jefferson*

ALTAY   7 b.g. Erins Isle – Aliuska (IRE) (Fijar Tango (FR)) [2003/4 h122+: 16m* 16m^6 h128
16g 16f^2 Feb 29] big, leggy gelding: fairly useful on Flat (stays 13f): has reached similar
level over hurdles, won Swinton Handicap at Haydock in May, holding on gamely to beat
Patsy Veale ½ length: good second of 5 to enterprisingly-ridden Wet Lips in handicap at

Merewood Homes Swinton Handicap Hurdle, Haydock—a thrilling finish with less than four lengths
covering the first six at the line; the winner Altay is mostly hidden by leader Patsy Veale

Musselburgh: probably ideally suited by sharp 2m: acts on firm and good to soft going. *R. A. Fahey*

ALTHREY RULER (IRE) 11 b.g. Phardante (FR) – Keego's Aunt (Tyrant (USA)) **c78** [2003/4 h78: 24m^pu c16m^pu c16u^3 c17g^3 c20m^F Nov 13] angular gelding: has reportedly **h–** been tubed: poor hurdler: similar form over fences, left W. Clay after third outing: stays easy 21f: acts on any going: tried blinkered. *W. M. Brisbourne*

ALTITUDE DANCER (IRE) 4 b.g. Sadler's Wells (USA) – Height of Passion **h89** (Shirley Heights) [2003/4 17m^2 16m^6 16g^3 22s Jan 10] smallish gelding: half-brother to fair 2m hurdler Albuquerque (by Barathea): fair on Flat (will stay beyond 2m), successful in February for P. Blockley: modest form over hurdles: should be suited by further than 2m. *B. Ellison*

AL TOWD (USA) 7 b.g. Kingmambo (USA) – Toujours Elle (USA) (Lyphard **h114** (USA)) [2003/4 16d^6 20s* 20s^4 24d 20s^4 22s^3 22d* Apr 12] sturdy gelding: fair hurdler: won minor event at Clonmel in December and 27-runner handicap at Fairyhouse in April, beating Well Presented 2½ lengths in latter: soon off bridle in handicap at Punchestown 2 weeks later: stays 2¾m: acts on heavy going. *M. Halford, Ireland*

ALVA GLEN (USA) 7 b.g. Gulch (USA) – Domludge (USA) (Lyphard (USA)) **h87 d** [2003/4 17g^ur 20m^3 16m^F 16m 16g 16m^ur 17d 17s Apr 6] smart at best on Flat (stays 1¾m): headstrong and largely disappointing over hurdles. *Miss Venetia Williams*

ALVARO (IRE) 7 ch.g. Priolo (USA) – Gezalle (Shareef Dancer (USA)) [2003/4 c–, **c75** h85: 27g^2 24m^3 22g^5 c23g^4 Aug 23] workmanlike gelding: poor hurdler: thrice-raced **h73** over fences, didn't impress with jumping final outing: stays 27f: acts on good to soft and good to firm going: blinkered once: inconsistent. *D. J. Wintle*

ALVINO 7 b.g. Alflora (IRE) – Rose Ravine (Deep Run) [2003/4 h112p: c20g^2 c17d* **c117** c20g^pu c21m* c20m^4 Apr 23] has reportedly been hobdayed: successful on second of 2 **h–** runs over hurdles in 2002/3: fairly useful form over fences, won novices at Market Rasen in December and Wincanton in March, beating Saint Esteben by 2½ lengths in good style in latter: stays 21f: acts on good to firm and good to soft going: breathing problem third and final outings. *Miss H. C. Knight*

ALWAYS 5 b.g. Dynaformer (USA) – Love And Affection (USA) (Exclusive Era **h115** (USA)) [2003/4 16s^2 16g* 16m* 16g 20d^2 16d^4 20s^4 16v^6 20d^4 Apr 11] leggy gelding: fairly useful on Flat (stays 1½m), sold out of J. Dunlop's stable 35,000 gns Newmarket July (2002) Sales: fairly useful hurdler: won maiden and novice at Roscommon in August, beating Felix The Great by neck in latter: probably stays 2½m: acts on soft and good to firm going: tried blinkered/tongue tied. *N. Meade, Ireland*

ALWAYS BELIEVE (USA) 8 b.g. Carr de Naskra (USA) – Wonder Mar (USA) **h–** (Fire Dancer (USA)) [2003/4 16d^pu Apr 21] one-time useful on Flat (stays 7f) in USA/ UAE, of little account nowadays: sold out of M. Bosley's stable £1,400 Ascot July Sales: tongue tied, no show in novice on hurdling debut. *Mrs P. Ford*

ALWAYS IN DEBT (IRE) 5 b.g. Norwich – Forever In Debt (Pragmatic) [2003/4 **F83** F16s^6 Mar 20] €24,000 3-y-o: first foal: dam maiden pointer: around 16 lengths sixth of 21 to Something Gold in bumper at Ascot on debut, taking while to get hang of things: likely to stay at least 2½m. *P. J. Hobbs*

ALWAYS ON THE LINE 10 gr.g. Arapahos (FR) – Fiona's Waltz (General **c93** Ironside) [2003/4 c26d^F c24g^ur c23m^3 Apr 13] workmanlike gelding: won maiden in Ireland, and also successful 5 times in points in Britain, including in 2004: best effort in hunters when 2¾ lengths third of 4 finishers to Kingston-Banker in novice at Exeter. *R. Barber*

ALWAYS RAINBOWS (IRE) 6 b. or br.g. Rainbows For Life (CAN) – Maura's **c–** Guest (IRE) (Be My Guest (USA)) [2003/4 h117: 16g 22s^pu 16d c16d 20v 16s 17s^5 17d^3 **h92** 19g^2 16d Mar 22] useful-looking gelding: fairly useful hurdler at best, modest in 2003/4: well beaten in maiden chase (bled from nose): should stay 2½m: acts on heavy going: usually wears headgear. *B. S. Rothwell*

ALWAYS SOMETHING (IRE) 7 b.m. Insan (USA) – Lizzie Simms (IRE) **c–** (Phardante (FR)) [2003/4 c20g^6 c21s c25g^5 c32d^pu Mar 18] IR 4,400 3-y-o: ex-Irish mare: first foal: dam unraced: winning pointer: no form in steeplechases, left M. Condon before reappearance: tried blinkered. *Mrs M. Reveley*

ALWAYS WAYWARD 9 br.g. Terimon – Forever Together (Hawaiian Return **c–** (USA)) [2003/4 c16g Dec 16] tall gelding: poor maiden hurdler in 1999/00: well held in **h–**

novice handicap chase on return: stays 2¾m: acts on soft and good to firm going (won bumper on heavy). *Mrs S. Wall*

AMACITA 6 b.m. Shareef Dancer (USA) – Kina (USA) (Bering) [2003/4 h78d: 19m^pu May 26] poor maiden on Flat in 2002: form over hurdles only on debut: tried in visor/cheekpieces/tongue strap. *K. G. Wingrove* h–

AMANDA KASAKOVA 8 ch.m. Kasakov – Manna Green (Bustino) [2003/4 h–: 16d^pu May 3] little sign of ability. *J. R. Norton* h–

AMANDARI (FR) 8 ch.g. Petit Loup (USA) – Baby Sitting (FR) (Son of Silver) [2003/4 h–: 19d 25g^5 24v^pu 21g^6 Apr 12] rather leggy gelding: no worthwhile form over hurdles in Britain, bought out of Mrs K. Walton's stable 2,800 gns Doncaster October Sales: tried in cheekpieces. *J. K. Hunter* h–

AMANPURI (GER) 6 br.g. Fairy King (USA) – Aratika (FR) (Zino) [2003/4 16v^2 17g^F Feb 19] fifth living foal: half-brother to 3 winners on Flat in Germany, including smart performer up to 1¾m Aratikos (by Konigsstuhl): dam, German 9f winner, out of half-sister to Oaks winner Polygamy: won twice on Flat in Germany, poor in Britain: 9 lengths second in maiden at Ballinrobe on hurdling debut: sold out of D. Weld's stable 15,000 gns Newmarket July Sales: well held when falling last in maiden at Taunton: joined P. Blockley. *Miss Gay Kelleway* h98

AMARAKU 5 b.g. Kylian (USA) – Shernborne (Kalaglow) [2003/4 17g^5 24f^6 20g^pu Oct 15] poor maiden on Flat: no aptitude for hurdling. *A. L. Forbes* h–

AMARI (IRE) 9 ch.g. Grand Plaisir (IRE) – Teazle (Quayside) [2003/4 c–, h–: c24d^pu 24m 26s^pu Jan 7] angular gelding: maiden jumper outside points, no form for long time: visored last 2 starts. *A. G. Hobbs* c– h–

AMBER DAWN 5 ch.m. Weld – Scrambird (Dubassoff (USA)) [2003/4 F17m Apr 15] angular mare: fifth foal: sister to fairly useful bumper/21f hurdle winner Red Brook: dam modest novice hurdler/chaser who stayed 3¼m: well held in mares bumper at Cheltenham on debut. *B. J. Llewellyn* F–

AMBER GO GO 7 ch.m. Rudimentary (USA) – Plaything (High Top) [2003/4 h61: 16g^pu c21g^5 21g^F 16g 19g^4 27d^3 Mar 16] lengthy mare: bad hurdler: left K. Hogg after third outing (trained by M. Todhunter second start only): stays 27f. *James Moffatt* c– h52

AMBER GOLD 6 b.m. Tragic Role (USA) – Dark Amber (Formidable (USA)) [2003/4 F–: F17g F16m^5 19d^6 19s^pu Dec 20] leggy, angular mare: little sign of ability. *Mrs S. M. Johnson* h– F–

AMBERLEIGH HOUSE (IRE) 12 br.g. Buckskin (FR) – Chancy Gal (Al Sirat) [2003/4 c135, h104: 23m^3 c24m^4 c27d^2 20s^pu c24g^5 c36d* Apr 3] c146 h105

There will almost certainly never be another Red Rum. His achievements in the Grand National, British racing's biggest showpiece, are unlikely to be surpassed. Red Rum stands alone with three wins and two seconds in five successive appearances, a phenomenal record that stirred the imagination of the general

Martell Cognac Grand National Chase (Handicap), Aintree—
Alexander Banquet on the far side is quickest away of the thirty-nine starters

*The first—Kelami's jockey (striped sleeves) cannot survive interference
as he joins Artic Jack and Luzcadou out of the race*

public. The news of Red Rum's withdrawal through injury on the eve of what would have been his sixth Grand National (for which, at the age of thirteen, he was a short-priced favourite), and the decision that he would not race again, made the front page of every national newspaper in 1978, coverage that was unprecedented. Few racehorses have reached so wide an audience as Red Rum who, along with Arkle and Desert Orchid, dominated a poll conducted in February by the *Racing Post* to find the most popular horse in the history of the sport in Britain and Ireland. Arkle, Desert Orchid and Red Rum—who finished in that order—amassed more than half the votes between them in a poll which showed the popularity of jumping. Jumpers filled six of the top ten places—Istabraq, One Man and Sea Pigeon were also in the top ten—and fifth-placed Brigadier Gerard was the highest Flat racer.

The top horses over jumps stay around much longer than most of their counterparts on the Flat and racegoers and armchair followers get to know them better. But jumping's popularity also owes much to its visual appeal. The Grand National, for example, nearly always provides a striking spectacle. The latest edition drew its biggest domestic television audience (the race is also shown in another 120 countries) since 1998. A total of 10.3m tuned in, 69% of the watching terrestrial audience. Attendances over the three days of Aintree totalled 147,439, including 70,739 on National day, both a modern-day record. Records were also set for betting turnover on the National, sources estimating that turnover on the race reached £120m for the first time, helped by increased telephone and internet betting. The final National under Martell sponsorship certainly delivered the goods with a drama-packed race and a thrilling finish, the winner Amberleigh House trained by veteran Ginger McCain who enjoyed Aintree glory with Red Rum.

The latest Grand National was the last of thirteen—including the void race in 1993—sponsored by Martell and, with the eight preceding editions run under the Seagram banner, also ended a twenty-one-race association with the parent companies, whose support has gone hand in hand with major redevelopment at Aintree which is now enjoying its most successful period in modern times. Canadian-based Seagram's first sponsorship—in Hallo Dandy's year—came at the start of a new era for the world's most famous steeplechase after a long-running saga in which its future at Aintree was threatened. The course was saved after mounting public concern, and a well conducted media campaign, prompted

The fifth—(from right to left) Alexander Banquet, Gunner Welburn, Puntal, Hedgehunter and Alcapone dispute the early running

negotiations between the Jockey Club and the course's owners the Walton Group. Aintree eventually passed into the hands of Racecourse Holdings Trust, a Jockey Club subsidiary, in May 1983 for £3.4m, a little more than the Walton Group had reportedly paid for the course in 1973, the year of Red Rum's first victory. The Walton Group staged the Grand Nationals of 1974 and 1975 but did not excel at racecourse management—much increased admission charges in 1975 resulted in the smallest crowd in living memory, around 9,000—and they made an agreement with Ladbrokes who developed the Grand National meeting with flair from 1976 to 1982, abandoning Flat racing and designing an all-jumping programme to complement the Cheltenham Festival. The Ladbrokes team faced an uphill task at first—the big race itself was run under three different banners during the period—but Aintree did have Red Rum whose exploits in themselves helped considerably to restore the flagging fortunes of the race and, ultimately, to save it as one of racing's greatest assets.

The Grand National is usually a magnificent shop window for the sport, though the course and the fences are not so formidable nowadays as they were in Red Rum's era. Except for a change in the design of the plain fences, which were sloped on the take-off side, and the lowering of the top weight to 12-0—both of which took place in the 'sixties—the course that Red Rum tackled was not significantly different from that around the turn of the century when another great Aintree horse Manifesto ran in eight Grand Nationals, winning twice (the second time under 12-7), finishing third three times (carrying 12-13, 12-8 and 12-3) and failing only once to jump round. He made his final appearance in the race at the age of fifteen.

Continued consideration of ways to reduce the risks and dangers attached to the Grand National have led to more changes since Red Rum's day, starting with the reduction of the safety limit from fifty to forty in 1984 when most of the traditional, largely arbitrary qualifications for Grand National entry were also scrapped. Those at the foot of the original long handicap became liable to compulsory elimination, working up from the lowest weight, and the 1984 National field contained only eight runners who had originally been allotted less than 10-0. There were a record twenty-three finishers. After an outcry over the deaths of two horses at Becher's Brook in the 1989 renewal, a Jockey Club review of Grand National safety led to alterations to the course, most importantly to Becher's, where the ditch was partly filled in and the bank on the landing side regraded to remove the tricky camber. The same review also resulted in further changes to the race conditions, setting a minimum official handicap rating below which horses would

*First Becher's—a melee, caused largely by the riderless Shardam,
puts a quarter of the field out of the race, including 2002 winner Bindaree (left, at the top of his jump);
Amberleigh House is far left, Clan Royal is down on his nose on the inside*

be ineligible for entry. This fluctuated over the first few years between 105 and 120 but has been at 110 since 1998. Since the deaths of three horses in the 1998 National, a Jockey Club panel has had the power to veto any Grand National entry on the basis of its 'suitability for the race', regardless of its BHB mark. No horse is now allowed to take up its entry if it runs after the five-day declaration stage (one of the horses killed in 1998 had fallen in a race over the National fences on the opening day of the meeting). Pre-race veterinary checks have become compulsory for all Grand National runners. A further Jockey Club investigation into five deaths—including two over the National fences—at the big Aintree meeting in 2000 led, among other things, to further modifications to the rather upright plain fences on the National course. They were fitted with a more prominent padded guard rail, with additional spruce above the guard rail to give a more sloping appearance on the take-off side, making them more inviting.

The latest significant change to the Grand National course came when the inside running rail at the Canal Turn was realigned in an attempt to prevent crowding at the fence after mayhem on the first circuit in the sorry National spectacle of 2001. Amberleigh House was one of nine put right out of the race when

*The Chair—Takagi is the only casualty at the course's biggest fence,
which presents no problems for Aintree specialist Amberleigh House (noseband)*

a riderless horse veered sharply across the fence on the take-off side; 150/1-shot Amberleigh House refused after the loose horse collided with him. Amberleigh House, a useful chaser in Ireland, had been purchased earlier that season out of Michael Hourigan's yard but had shown little form since. Amberleigh House failed to recapture his very best form the next season either, but he did win the Becher Chase over the big, unusual National fences in the autumn, credentials which would have given him a virtually-automatic place in the National field in the days before 1984. Some way out of the original handicap, however, he was among twenty-two excluded at the final forty-eight-hour declaration stage. Amberleigh House failed narrowly to 'make the cut' and was among four nominated reserves, but he ran instead—finishing unplaced—in the Topham Chase over a circuit or so of the National fences the day before. His trainer argued vehemently that horses proven over the Aintree fences should be given an inflated mark in the original handicap for the Grand National to ensure a place in the line-up. The so-called 'Aintree factor' was still being taken into account to some extent at the time by the BHB handicapper, though the remodelling of parts of the National course and a slight easing of the fences were thought to have reduced the significance of previous experience.

Amberleigh House improved his good record over the National fences in the 2002/3 season with second place in the Becher Chase and third in the Grand National. After the previous year's controversial elimination of Amberleigh House and also of Gunner Welburn, who had been successful over the big fences in the Fox Hunters', the BHB handicapper was asked by the Aintree executive to give greater credence to form over the National fences. Amberleigh House and Gunner Welburn got into the 2003 National comfortably, Amberleigh House given 8 lb more than he would have carried in a normal handicap. Amberleigh House finished fourteen lengths third to clear-cut winner Monty's Pass, with the always-prominent Gunner Welburn, who failed to see out the marathon trip in the fairly testing conditions, fourth of fourteen finishers.

The running of proven Aintree horses Amberleigh House and Gunner Welburn—Monty's Pass had finished second in a Topham—seemed to justify

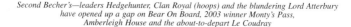

*Second Becher's—leaders Hedgehunter, Clan Royal (hoops) and the blundering Lord Atterbury
have opened up a gap on Bear On Board, 2003 winner Monty's Pass,
Amberleigh House and the about-to-depart Le Coudray*

allowing previous form over the Aintree fences to influence the original handicap (the Aintree executive had submitted a study backing its claims that the 'Aintree factor' remained as strong as ever). Nonetheless, the easing of the National fences appeared to have a bearing on the return, particularly for a time in the 'nineties, of top steeplechasers to the National—the current Gold Cup winner Garrison Savannah, Cool Ground, The Fellow and Master Oats all contested the race. In a move started in 2001, the top weights now receive *relatively* more favourable treatment from the handicapper as a matter of course in the National, than they would away from Aintree. It must be said that the policy hasn't yet proven conspicuously successful, though the fourth, fifth and sixth in the Gold Cup contested the 2002 edition. The BHB handicapper responsible for the National weights, Phil Smith, says controversially that it is his ambition 'that a horse with 11-0 or more wins it.' Lenient handicapping of some of those towards the top of the weights led to twenty-three horses being allotted 11-0 or more in the original handicap for the latest National, including Monty's Pass whose handicap mark went up by 14 lb from the previous year, putting him within 5 lb of original top weight First Gold and within 3 lb of the likes of the similarly leniently-treated Rince Ri and Harbour Pilot, horses of Gold Cup class who would have been set to concede more to Monty's Pass and most of the rest in any other handicap. Although this policy has not so far produced a leniently-treated top-weighted winner, it is hard to see any justification for it. After all, the Grand National was worth nearly £150,000 more to the winner than the Gold Cup, so what greater incentive do connections of good horses need?

First Gold always seemed unlikely to run, but it looked for a time as if Rince Ri would take his chance (Harbour Pilot was withdrawn soon after being promoted to favouritism after coming third in the Gold Cup). With illness ruling out Rince Ri (and another leading Irish contender, the former Irish Grand National winner Timbera), top weight of 11-12 on the day in by no means a vintage National was carried by Le Coudray (in the same ownership as First Gold), who had divided Florida Pearl and Rince Ri in the Hennessy Cognac Gold Cup at Leopardstown in February. Ten of the thirty-nine starters (impressive Eider Chase winner Tyneand-thyneagain was withdrawn too late to be replaced by a reserve) carried 11-0 or more, over half of them having experience over the National fences, including, as well as Monty's Pass, the 2002 winner Bindaree and the 2002 second and fourth

Second Canal Turn—Hedgehunter steers a wider course than his two closest pursuers

What's Up Boys and Kingsmark, neither of whom had shown their form since returning from injury. Most prominent among the top weights in the betting were Bindaree, successful in the Welsh National in December, and Davids Lad, still close up when falling four out in the 2002 National and an absentee in 2003 while serving a forty-two-day ban under schooling in public rules.

Bindaree and Davids Lad were among no fewer than seven 11/1 co-favourites in Ladbrokes ante-post market on the eve of the race, joined by Thyestes Chase winner Hedgehunter (10-12), the runner-up in the Hennessy at Newbury Joss Naylor (10-11), Jurancon II (10-7) who had run away with the Red Square Vodka Gold Cup at Haydock after the publication of the National weights, Clan Royal (10-5) and thorough stayer Bear On Board (10-1), runner-up to Jurancon at Haydock after three successive wins. Clan Royal, one of four eventual 10/1 co-favourites (with Jurancon, Joss Naylor and Bindaree), had two victories to his credit over the National fences, in the Topham at the 2003 National meeting and in the Tote Becher Chase at the November meeting. The National was Clan Royal's first outing since a very game, short head victory over Amberleigh House, the pair a distance clear, in the four-finisher Becher in which Bindaree had been full of running, narrowly in front, when falling at second Valentine's. Amberleigh House, who started at 16/1 for the National, had run twice since the Becher, readily outpaced and pulled up in a handicap hurdle at Haydock on his return to action in mid-February and not discredited when a never-dangerous fifth to Grey Abbey in the Grimthorpe Chase over three miles at Doncaster in early-March.

Considering that the going was on the soft side of good—similar to the previous year—the front runners went off at too strong a pace in the latest National, after a twelve-minute delay at the start. The field became well strung out by halfway. Two of the '11-0 brigade', 80/1-shot Alcapone and 100/1-shot Alexander Banquet (tailed off in the Cheltenham Gold Cup last time) were in the leading group over the early fences. Another of the top weights, front-running Peter Marsh Chase winner Artic Jack, was one of three casualties at the first, while the Pipe-trained and McCoy-ridden Jurancon, pushed along to try to get up near the leaders after missing the break, got only as far as the fourth. A pile-up caused by the riderless Shardam at Becher's—which went some way to restoring its formidable reputation at the latest National meeting—claimed nearly a quarter of the field, most significant among the nine put out of the race being Bindaree who unseated his rider after being badly hampered and crowded out. With Blowing Wind, bidding to get round in the National for a fourth successive time, Akarus, Bounce Back and Montreal also among the casualties, the Pipe stable's seven-strong challenge was reduced after just six fences to the useful but somewhat temperamental novice Puntal and ex-hunter Lord Atterbury. Both were prominent, along with Gunner Welburn and Hedgehunter, the last-named taking over in front after the eighth and keeping up the good gallop. Amberleigh House was in the middle of the field, having swerved to avoid the fallen Jurancon at the fourth and then landed flat-footed after

58

The last—Clan Royal survives a bad mistake . . . . .

scrambling over Becher's. Clan Royal was being given a classic Aintree ride, his jockey 'hunting' him round and keeping close to the inner for most of the first circuit, the partnership kept intact by a splendid recovery after a bad mistake at Becher's, where Clan Royal was down on his nose.

Hedgehunter led over the Chair from Puntal, Lord Atterbury, Alcapone, Gunner Welburn, Alexander Banquet and—starting to take closer order—Clan Royal and Monty's Pass. There were twenty-two still in the race as the field set off into the country for a second time. Alexander Banquet fell at the eighteenth where Gunner Welburn, who made a mistake at the seventeenth and was beginning to fade, was pulled up. Puntal was still moving with uncustomary zest in third when unseating his jockey at the nineteenth, where Joss Naylor, who had never given his supporters much hope, was eventually pulled up a long way adrift. No top weight has triumphed in the National since Red Rum did so for his second and third victories, but Le Coudray still looked set to figure before he fell at second Becher's, his rider yet to make a move. Clan Royal had moved closer, travelling strongly, running down to second Becher's and joined Lord Atterbury and Hedgehunter, the

. . . . . but the fading Hedgehunter is not so lucky,
leaving Lord Atterbury and Amberleigh House to take up the chase

trio clear at Becher's, over half a dozen lengths ahead of Bear On Board and Monty's Pass, with Amberleigh House only sixth. Amberleigh House was still ten lengths behind as the survivors crossed the Melling Road, and he was no closer to the three leaders at the second last where he jumped to the right.

Clan Royal's rider, whose whip had flown out of his hand when his mount made a mistake five out, went for home in earnest from the second last. Clan Royal led over the last by two and a half lengths from Lord Atterbury; Hedgehunter fell when seemingly held in third while Amberleigh House had begun to close perceptibly as the leaders started to tire between the last two fences. Clan Royal's flashing tail was a sign of his distress and, desperately tired, he had to be wrenched to the right after blundering at the last and briefly looking as if he might run off the course, seeming to be heading too straight for a time. The equally exhausted Lord Atterbury was kept to the straightest line for negotiating the elbow, diagonally from the last fence to the finishing rail that passes the Chair fence. The two leaders were locked together rounding the elbow as they began the final run to the line. Amberleigh House's rider reported afterwards that he had resisted an urge to try to go after the leaders any earlier—'There was a strong headwind in the straight and I thought they might come back'—but by the elbow the staying-on Amberleigh House was making up ground hand over fist and the gap had been reduced to two or three lengths. Though out on his feet, Clan Royal rallied gamely to get the better of Lord Atterbury, but the pair were seemingly going up and down on the spot relative to Amberleigh House who kept on relentlessly to deprive Clan Royal of the lead well inside the final furlong. Some drew comparisons afterwards with Red Rum's overhauling of the wandering and exhausted Crisp in 1973, but Crisp had been fifteen in front at the last and the horses involved in the finish of the latest National weren't in anything like the same league as Red Rum and Crisp. Amberleigh House passed the post three lengths in front of the luckless Clan Royal with Lord Atterbury, who required oxygen and a thorough dousing with cold water to revive him after the race, two lengths away in third. The winning time was 9m 20.22sec, just over a second faster than the previous year, but there were some fairly striking differences in the way the two races were run. The leaders in the latest National reached halfway in a time five seconds quicker than 2003, reflecting the strong gallop, and were still seven seconds faster at the second last; from the second last to the line took six seconds longer than the time taken for the same section by Monty's Pass who had his National won from a long way out.

As in the two previous years, concentrating on horses with proven form over the Grand National course paid dividends in the latest edition. There were

The run-in—Amberleigh House overhauls the tiring leaders;
Liam Cooper on Clan Royal has lost his whip

The winning post—Graham Lee celebrates one of the most dramatic National wins in recent memory

eleven finishers, eight of which had either figured prominently in a previous Grand National or had completed the course in other races over the fences. The first three finished a long way clear, Monty's Pass coming fourth, twenty-nine lengths behind Lord Atterbury. Spot Thedifference, who had got round in a Fox Hunters' and was effectively brought down four out in the 2002 National, plodded on for fifth after being virtually tailed off at second Becher's, then came a couple of Aintree veterans, Smarty and Ardent Scout. Smarty was the only other runner to get round without mishap in Red Marauder's National and had also come second (to Amberleigh House) in a Becher Chase; Ardent Scout, winner of a Becher Chase and in the frame in the race on three other occasions, had finally risen enough in the handicap to get into the National for the first time at the age of twelve. Bear On Board didn't keep on so well as expected and managed only eighth, ahead of Kingsmark, The Bunny Boiler and Davids Lad, none of whom was ever a factor. There were no serious injuries to any of the runners, though two jockeys needed hospital treatment.

With Red Rum long departed (he is buried near the Aintree winning post), few, including perhaps the man himself, could have envisaged Ginger McCain's triumphing in the National for a fourth time. 'If the ground stays as it is and he gets the luck, he's nailed on to be in the first five, a clear run and he can be in the first three,' was how he summed up Amberleigh House's chances beforehand. Before Red Rum came along, McCain was a little-known trainer with a small stable behind a car saleroom in a residential part of Southport, his horses doing much of their training on the beach. In 1990 he moved to rural Cheshire to train at Cholmondeley near Malpas but, before Amberleigh House came along, he had acquired something of a reputation as a 'one-horse trainer', though he continued to make personal appearances with Red Rum who enjoyed an active retirement and lived to be thirty. McCain trained over two hundred and twenty winners over jumps between the end of 1976/7 and Amberleigh House's win—including, incidentally, Hallo Dandy who won three times over fences for McCain in the early part of his career before being transferred to Gordon Richards who eventually saddled him to win the 1984 National. McCain's best seasonal tally since the days of Red Rum has been eighteen and he has failed to reach double figures on sixteen occasions. Amberleigh House came into McCain's hands after he was purchased privately, reportedly for 90,000 punts (around £75,000 at the time), by locally-born international vintner John Halewood, who incidentally had another runner in the latest National, French-trained Kelami who unseated his rider when hampered at the first. Halewood bought Amberleigh House on McCain's recommendation, though McCain, who had seen the horse win at Punchestown, apparently thought he had 'done the owner's money' when the horse arrived from Ireland. 'It's the dead of night and I'm standing in my dressing gown and slippers, the ramp of the horsebox is lowered and there is this Godforsaken little horse—no rug, no head collar, its coat standing up like a cork mat—as a simple Englishman, I thought I'd been stitched up,' recalled McCain. Jockey Graham Lee had a struggle to establish himself in the North but, thanks partly to the firepower provided by new owners Graham and Andrea Wylie, he enjoyed his best campaign so far in the latest season, riding ninety-four winners and finishing third in the jockeys' table. He has had two rides in the Grand National, both on Amberleigh House, and among his other headline-making achievements in the latest season was a 55,964/1 four-timer at Wetherby on Charlie Hall Chase day. He also rode the winner of the Scottish Grand National, Grey Abbey, and was the regular jockey of the season's top novice hurdler Inglis Drever.

Amberleigh House is a lengthy individual, though at 15.2 hands he is on the small side for a chaser. He passed through the sale-ring in Ireland for only 1,000 guineas as an unnamed four-year-old and saw a racecourse for the first time at five, finishing down the field in a bumper and a novice hurdle (ridden by one A. P. McCoy) at the end of the 1996/7 season. He got off the mark when winning a bumper at Naas the following autumn and went on to do well over hurdles that season, winning twice and contesting good races including the Supreme Novices' Hurdle at Cheltenham (twelfth at 50/1) and the Jameson Gold Cup Novices' Hurdle at Fairyhouse (second to Unamed). Amberleigh House showed similarly fairly useful form when sent over fences in his third season, the pick of his efforts a third in the Denny Gold Medal Novices' Chase at Leopardstown and a fifth in the Grand Annual on a second appearance at the Cheltenham Festival. He went on to develop into a smart chaser at up to two and a half miles, making a third visit to the Cheltenham Festival to contest the Grand Annual as an eight-year-old, after which he won the Emo Oil Handicap Chase at the Punchestown Festival, the performance that really brought him to the attention of his present trainer. There was some talk that Amberleigh House might be sent over for the Doncaster Sales but, when he wasn't, McCain set up the deal to purchase him privately.

Amberleigh House (IRE) (br.g. 1992)			
	Buckskin (FR) (b 1973)	Yelapa (br 1966)	Mossborough
			Your Point
		Bete A Bon Dieu (b 1964)	Herbager
			Caralline II
	Chancy Gal (bl 1982)	Al Sirat (br 1962)	Double Jay
			Gay Darling
		Art Mistress (b 1969)	Master Owen
			Lady Artist II

Amberleigh House wasn't tried beyond two and a half miles when trained in Ireland but his sire the top-class out-and-out stayer Buckskin, who died in 1995, was well established as a sire of staying chasers. Amberleigh House's dam Chancy Gal was a modest maiden on the Flat and over hurdles but is from a good jumping family, her dam Art Mistress being a sister to the top-class two- to two-and-a-half-mile chaser Artifice, who shrugged off a daunting series of training setbacks to win numerous good handicaps in her career and also finish runner-up in the Queen Mother Champion Chase. Art Mistress didn't enjoy so illustrious a racing career as her brother, or her half-brothers the useful staying chaser Cnoc Dubh, who was placed in an Irish Grand National, or the very popular weight-carrying gelding Bigaroon, winner of the Irish Cesarewitch three times and also successful over hurdles. Their dam Lady Artist II, who gained her only success in a bumper, had a remarkable record as a broodmare, her first twelve foals all winning, Art Mistress being among them. Art Mistress was a fairly useful stayer on the Flat, second to Bigaroon in his third Irish Cesarewitch, and also won over hurdles at up to two and a half miles. The family was in the news again in June when Amberleigh House's unbroken four-year-old half-brother by Dr Massini fetched €130,000, a record price for the Goffs Land Rover Sale. The gelding was knocked down to Amberleigh House's trainer. Apart from Amberleigh House, Chancy Gal has bred only one other winner under rules, The Guarantor (by Executive Perk), who showed fairly useful form when winning two bumpers at Tipperary early in the latest season for

Halewood International Ltd's "Amberleigh House"

Willie Mullins. Amberleigh House occupies the box used by Red Rum in retirement and also had a small tuft of Red Rum's hair sewn into the braid on his bridle in the latest National. Amberleigh House emulated Red Rum by winning the race as a twelve-year-old but he will have to achieve something even Red Rum couldn't if he is returned to Aintree. Not only would success make Amberleigh House the oldest winner of the National since 1923, but it would also give his trainer a fifth win in the race, making him the most successful trainer in the history of the race, surpassing Fred Rimell with whom he now jointly holds the record. The sound-jumping Amberleigh House reportedly came out of the latest National 'without a scratch on him' and his proven record over the Aintree fences—placings in successive Nationals and first or second in the last three runnings of the Becher Chase—makes him well equipped to make a bold bid to further improve his standing in Aintree history. No doubt he'll first be tackling the Becher Chase for a fourth time in November. *D. McCain*

AMBER LILY 12 ch.m. Librate – Just Bluffing (Green Shoon) [2003/4 h–: 17m⁵ 16d⁶ Oct 30] sturdy mare: winning hurdler, no form for long time: tried blinkered. *S. T. Lewis* **h–**

AMBER MOSS 9 ch.g. Phardante (FR) – Queen's Darling (Le Moss) [2003/4 c76§, h–: c25d c20s⁶ c22gᶠ c20gᵖᵘ 20s 27f² 24d c25gᵘʳ 24s² Apr 21] workmanlike gelding: winning hurdler/maiden chaser: stays 27f, at least when emphasis is on speed: tried in cheekpieces: ungenuine. *Mrs C. J. Kerr* **c– §**
h76 §

AMBER STARLIGHT 6 b.m. Binary Star (USA) – Stupid Cupid (Idiot's Delight) [2003/4 16d⁶ Dec 5] unfurnished mare: fourth foal: half-sister to poor chaser Flinders (by Henbit), stays 3¼m: dam, fairly useful hurdler/winning chaser up to 25f, half-sister to useful jumper up to 25f Run Up The Flag: 66/1 and in need of outing, held up and not **h81 p**

knocked about when around 30 lengths sixth to Sixo in novice hurdle at Sandown on debut: should improve. *R. Rowe*

AMBIENCE   7 ch.g. Wolfhound (USA) – Amber Fizz (USA) (Effervescing (USA))   **F–**
[2003/4 F82: F17m Jun 18] modest form at best in bumpers: takes good hold.
M. J. Gingell

AMBIENCE LADY   8 b.m. Batshoof – Upper Caen (High Top) [2003/4 h76, F65:   **c98**
c17g2 c17m3 c20m* c21f2 c21m2 c19g2 c21dpu c20d5 Jan 22] leggy mare: has had a foal: **h–**
poor form over hurdles: modest novice chaser: won handicap at Worcester in November:
likely to prove best up to around 2½m: acts on firm ground (won bumper on soft).
J. W. Mullins

AMBITION ROYAL (FR)   4 ch.g. Cyborg (FR) – Before Royale (FR) (Dauphin du   **F98**
Bourg (FR)) [2003/4 F14g* F16d4 Apr 17] strong, stocky gelding: first foal: dam,
winning hurdler/11.5f winner on Flat, sister to smart hurdler around 2m Blue Royal:
favourite, won 3-y-o bumper at Warwick on debut in November by 2½ lengths from
Golden Measure: left N. Henderson, well held at Ayr and Punchestown in spring.
Mrs L. B. Normile

AMBRY   7 b.g. Machiavellian (USA) – Alkaffeyeh (IRE) (Sadler's Wells (USA))   **h119**
[2003/4 h114§: 17m4 20m* 20m* 20m2 21f4 25g2 25d5 Dec 26] compact gelding: fairly
useful handicap hurdler: won at Bangor in August and Worcester in September: went
with much more zest than on previous 2 starts when good second to Therealbandit in
listed event at Cheltenham: stays 25f: acts on heavy and good to firm going: usually
blinkered/visored up to 2003/4. *Mrs S. J. Smith*

AMBUSHED (IRE)   8 b.g. Indian Ridge – Surprise Move (IRE) (Simply Great (FR))   **c91**
[2003/4 h95: 16g3 16g6 16g* 16g 17g 16d c16g6 c16d4 Mar 18] modest handicap hurdler: **h99**
won at Perth in June: below that form both starts over fences: raced around 2m: acts on
soft and good to firm going. *P. Monteith*

AMERAS (IRE)   6 b.m. Hamas (IRE) – Amerindian (Commanche Run) [2003/4   **h71**
16gpu 16g 16m3 17d6 20g2 18d 24d4 21v5 16v5 20s5 16d2 22d Apr 5] angular mare: fairly
useful maiden (stays 1m) at 3 yrs for W. Mullins, poor on Flat nowadays: poor novice
hurdler: barely stays 3m: acts on heavy going: has had tongue tied: races freely.
Miss S. E. Forster

AMERICANCONNECTION (IRE)   8 b.g. Lord Americo – Ballyea Jacki (Straight   **c–**
Lad) [2003/4 c–, h87: 22f* 25f3 24g5 Nov 4] tall gelding: well held in maiden chase: **h92**
modest hurdler: made all in amateur novice at Exeter in October, just holding on under
very strong pressure (rider suspended): probably stays 25f: acts on firm going. *M. C. Pipe*

AMICELLI (GER)   5 b.g. Goofalik (USA) – Arratonia (GER) (Arratos (FR)) [2003/4   **h106**
16g6 20g3 21g5 Mar 26] useful-looking ex-German gelding: successful 4 times over 1¼m
from 12 starts on Flat at 3/4 yrs for I. Schalter: fair form in novice/maiden hurdles: stays
21f. *C. J. Mann*

AMID THE CHAOS (IRE)   4 ch.c. Nashwan (USA) – Celebrity Style (USA)   **h110**
(Seeking The Gold (USA)) [2003/4 16d 16v3 16v5 16d Feb 18] well-made colt: ran 4
times on Flat in 2003, fairly useful form when eighth in Queen's Vase at Royal Ascot,
won 1¼m maiden next time: fair form when placed in juvenile hurdles at Punchestown
in January (Grade 3) and late-April (blinkered): tongue tied fourth outing. *D. K. Weld,
Ireland*

AMJAD   7 ch.g. Cadeaux Genereux – Babita (Habitat) [2003/4 h87: 16gpu 17g c16g5   **c77 ?**
c16f3 c16m6 c16f3 Oct 25] leggy gelding: modest hurdler, no form since winning   **h–**
conditional jockeys handicap in 2002/3: poor form first 2 starts over fences: best around
2m: acts on firm and good to soft going: pulls hard. *Miss Kate Milligan*

AMMONIAS (GER)   5 b.h. Monsun (GER) – Augreta (GER) (Simply Great (FR))   **h115**
[2003/4 16d4 21g3 21d2 21g Mar 17] good-topped horse: useful on Flat in Germany,
successful 4 times over 1¼m for P. Schiergen: fairly useful form in novice hurdles, 1¼
lengths second of 22 to Dangerously Good in steadily-run event at Kempton: out of depth
final outing: well up to winning a race over hurdles. *C. J. Mann*

AMONG EQUALS   7 b.g. Sadler's Wells (USA) – Epicure's Garden (USA) (Affirmed   **h108**
(USA)) [2003/4 16g 18d2 16g3 Mar 26] angular gelding: fairly useful juvenile hurdler in
2000/1: reportedly suffered overreach on reappearance, only start for R. Phillips: placed
in handicaps 4 months later at Fontwell (reluctant to race) and Newbury: will stay beyond
2¼m: raced on good going or softer (acts on heavy). *C. M. Meade*

AMPLIFI (IRE)   7 b.g. Phardante (FR) – Season's Delight (Idiot's Delight) [2003/4 h100p: 16d^F 19g^4 17g c16s^ur c16g^3 c18g^F c20d c20d^pu 20d Apr 21] medium-sized gelding: novice hurdler, disappointing in 2003/4: generally let down by jumping over fences: should stay 2½m: acts on good to soft going. *P. J. Hobbs*   **c87 x** **h84**

AMPHINA (IRE)   9 b.g. Shardari – Cotton Gale (Strong Gale) [2003/4 ¢17m* c17d^4 c16m^4 c16f^4 c17m* c17g^3 Nov 20] IR 9,800 4-y-o: fifth foal: half-brother to 3 winners by Roselier, including fairly useful hurdler Absolutely Equiname, stayed 25f: dam won 2¾m hurdle in Ireland: twice-raced hurdler: runner-up in 2 maiden Irish points in 2003: poor chaser: bought out of C. McBratney's stable 4,000 gns Doncaster May Sales: won novice handicaps at Bangor in August and Southwell in November: form only around 2m: acts on good to firm going, probably on good to soft: has had tongue tied: tends to finish weakly. *Mrs S. J. Smith*   **c75** **h–**

AMRITSAR   7 ch.g. Indian Ridge – Trying For Gold (USA) (Northern Baby (CAN)) [2003/4 17m^pu 16m^6 16m 16m 16g^2 Jul 31] poor maiden on Flat, sold out of P. Howling's stable 500 gns Doncaster November (2002) Sales: best effort over hurdles when second in seller at Stratford: raced around 2m: tried tongue tied. *K. G. Wingrove*   **h69**

AMUSEMENT   8 ch.g. Mystiko (USA) – Jolies Eaux (Shirley Heights) [2003/4 h71: 17g^pu May 1] leggy gelding: poor maiden hurdler: pulled hard in cheekpieces only start in 2003/4. *D. G. Bridgwater*   **h–**

AMY LEWIS   6 b.m. Sir Harry Lewis (USA) – Trecento (Precious Metal) [2003/4 F16g Feb 28] lengthy, unfurnished mare: first foal: dam, modest hurdler, stayed 2½m: some late headway when around 14 lengths ninth of 20 in bumper at Haydock on debut. *J. Mackie*   **F82**

ANALOGY (IRE)   4 ch.g. Bahhare (USA) – Anna Comnena (IRE) (Shareef Dancer (USA)) [2003/4 18f* 17g^2 16g^6 17g 24d* 22g^2 Apr 22] lengthy gelding: fair on Flat (stays 13f), sold out of Sir Mark Prescott's stable 27,000 gns Doncaster August Sales: useful juvenile hurdler: won at Fontwell in August and Ludlow in April, beating Bay Kenny 5 lengths in novice at latter: stays easy 3m: acts on firm and good to soft ground: blinkered when out of depth fourth start: usually tongue tied. *C. J. Mann*   **h129**

ANALYZE (FR)   6 b.g. Anabaa (USA) – Bramosia (Forzando) [2003/4 16f^3 17f^2 16f^3 16g 16d^pu Dec 6] compact gelding: fairly useful on Flat (best around 1¼m), successful twice in 2003 for M. Channon: modest form at best over hurdles: likely to prove best around 2m: acts on firm going: not a fluent jumper. *B. G. Powell*   **h99**

ANATAR (IRE)   6 b.g. Caerleon (USA) – Anaza (Darshaan) [2003/4 h128: 22g 20d 20d^4 17d 20s 21g 18d^5 Apr 7] leggy gelding: fairly useful handicap hurdler in 2002/3, winning 5 times: below form in 2003/4: will prove best up to 2½m: raced mainly on good going or softer (acts on heavy). *M. C. Pipe*   **h111**

ANDALEER (IRE)   9 b.m. Phardante (FR) – Dunleer Duchess (Our Mirage) [2003/4 c–, c82, h79: 19f^4 c18s^pu Jan 26] poor maiden hurdler, off 17 months before reappearance: poor form on first of 2 starts over fences: acts on firm and good to soft going: tongue tied in 2003/4: takes good hold. *Mrs H. Dalton*   **c–** **h–**

ANDREAS (FR)   4 b.g. Marchand de Sable (USA) – Muscova Dancer (FR) (Muscovite (USA)) [2003/4 16g^3 16g* 17s^3 18g* 18g^3 16d Apr 17] ex-French gelding: second foal: half-brother to cross-country chase winner around 2¾m Art of Fighting (by Marignan): dam maiden: twice-raced on Flat: successful in juvenile hurdles at Divonne-Les-Bains in July and Cagnes-sur-Mer in December: left M. Boudot, last of 10 in steadily-run event at Ayr: raced around 2m on good going or softer. *P. F. Nicholls*   **h?**

ANDREW DOBLE   5 ch.g. Sabrehill (USA) – Verchinina (Star Appeal) [2003/4 h93: 17s^3 17m^pu 19d^4 21d^pu c20g^4 c17m^pu Sep 27] sturdy gelding: poor hurdler: little show in 2 outings over fences (reluctant to line up, saddle slipped final one): likely to prove best around 2m: acts on heavy going: has pulled hard. *Miss Venetia Williams*   **c–** **h87**

ANDROMACHE   5 ch.m. Hector Protector (USA) – South Sea Bubble (IRE) (Bustino) [2003/4 h–: 19f^3 17g 16g^pu 16d 17s^2 16s Jan 16] angular mare: poor maiden hurdler: raced mainly around 2m: acts on soft going: visored last 2 starts. *G. B. Balding*   **h75**

ANDY GIN (FR)   5 b.g. Ski Chief (USA) – Love Love Kate (FR) (Saint Andrews (FR)) [2003/4 h120: 16m 16g^5 16d 16s^pu Feb 20] leggy gelding: won juvenile on hurdling debut in 2002/3: well below that form since: should stay beyond 17f. *P. J. Hobbs*   **h–**

ANDY'S BIRTHDAY (IRE)   13 ch.g. King Luthier – Clonroche Abendego (Pauper) [2003/4 c–, h–: c20s 24s^6 c25d* c25s^4 c24d^6 Mar 24] angular gelding: maiden hurdler: modest handicap chaser: won at Hereford in January: stays 3¼m: acts on heavy going: **c92** **h–**

tried visored, wears cheekpieces nowadays: usually tongue tied: races prominently. *Miss S. J. Wilton*

ANFLORA 7 b.m. Alflora (IRE) – Ancella (Tycoon II) [2003/4 F18f⁴ Aug 18] second **F73** foal: dam useful pointer: winning pointer: fourth of 7 in bumper at Fontwell. *B. J. Llewellyn*

ANGEL DELIGHT 8 gr.m. Seymour Hicks (FR) – Bird's Custard (Birdbrook) **c96** [2003/4 h95: c20d² Dec 15] plain, angular mare: modest hurdler: ran to similar level **h–** when second in handicap at Plumpton on chasing debut, only start in 2003/4: likely to prove best up to 3m: acts on good to firm and good to soft going. *Miss Venetia Williams*

ANGELENA BALLERINA 6 b.m. Roselier (FR) – True Clown (True Song) **c–** [2003/4 h–, F75: 21vᵖᵘ 19s⁶ c25sᶠ Feb 22] leggy mare: no form over hurdles: tongue tied, **h–** fell fatally on chasing debut. *Mrs H. Dalton*

ANGELLO 7 ch.g. Selkirk (USA) – Pomorie (IRE) (Be My Guest (USA)) [2003/4 **h–** 20m May 7] well beaten in bumper and in novice on hurdling debut. *J. A. B. Old*

ANGELS VENTURE 8 ch.g. Unfuwain (USA) – City of Angels (Woodman (USA)) **h114 §** [2003/4 17m³ 17m³ 16d² 16g⁵ 16m⁵ 16f* 16g² 16f² Nov 20] close-coupled gelding: fair handicap hurdler: made all at Wincanton in October: should stay 2½m: acts on firm and good to soft going: visored once (ran well), slowly away when running poorly in cheekpieces fifth start: has had tongue tied: irresolute. *J. R. Jenkins*

ANGIE GOLD 7 b.m. Mesleh – Gold Duchess (Sonnen Gold) [2003/4 h–, F–: 20d⁴ **h–** 17d⁴ May 28] lengthy mare: of little account. *Mrs S. J. Smith*

ANGIOLINI (USA) 7 ch.g. Woodman (USA) – Danse Royale (IRE) (Caerleon **h–** (USA)) [2003/4 h69: 16g 16m 19mᵖᵘ Mar 4] ex-Irish gelding: little form over hurdles: left N. Glynn prior to final outing: tried blinkered: has had tongue tied. *A. E. Jones*

AN GIRSEACH (IRE) 7 b.m. Roselier (FR) – Elfi (IRE) (Le Moss) [2003/4 20m⁴ **h75** 20d Nov 26] IR £7,000 4-y-o: fourth foal: half-sister to bumper winner Belmont Tess (by Castle Keep): dam unraced half-sister to fairly useful staying chaser Pinkpinkfizz, from family of high-class 2m hurdler Supreme Halo: won mares maiden point in Ireland in 2003: better effort in novice hurdles when fourth at Worcester: will be suited by a stiffer test of stamina. *M. C. Pipe*

ANGUILLA 9 b.g. Rudimentary (USA) – More Wise (Ballymore) [2003/4 h66: 21sᵘʳ **h71** 21d 24dᵖᵘ Apr 21] workmanlike gelding: poor maiden hurdler: should be suited by further than 21f. *P. T. Dalton*

ANIMAL MAGIC 4 b.f. Shareef Dancer (USA) – Blessed Lass (HOL) (Good Times **h–** (ITY)) [2003/4 16gᵖᵘ 16g Feb 11] small filly: poor maiden on Flat (should stay 1m), sold out of M. Easterby's stable 750 gns Doncaster September (2002) Sales: showed little in 2 starts over hurdles. *C. J. Down*

ANKLES BACK (IRE) 7 b.g. Seclude (USA) – Pedalo (Legal Tender) [2003/4 c–: **c104** 20sᵖᵘ c23m* c23g* c24gᵖᵘ c21mᵖᵘ Apr 15] close-coupled, workmanlike gelding: pulled **h–** up on hurdling debut: won novice chases at Leicester in December and January: lame fourth start, found nothing final one: will stay beyond 23f: acts on good to firm ground: forces pace: sound jumper in main. *Mrs H. Dalton*

AN MODH DIREACH (IRE) 10 b.g. Don't Forget Me – Gothic Lady (Godswalk **c117** (USA)) [2003/4 16d 16dˢᵘ c18d³ 16s c17s⁶ c17vᵖᵘ Jan 31] tall gelding: winning hurdler/ **h–** chaser: easily best effort in handicaps in 2003/4 when third over fences at Punchestown in November: best around 2m: acts on heavy going, below form all starts on good to firm: blinkered: usually races prominently. *T. M. Walsh, Ireland*

ANNA ALMOST 6 b.m. Tragic Role (USA) – Princess Hotpot (IRE) (King's Ride) **h–** [2003/4 h61: 16gᵖᵘ May 2] poor maiden hurdler: raced around 2m: acts on good to firm ground: tried visored. *T. R. Wall*

ANNABEE 7 gr.m. Norton Challenger – Annaway (New Brig) [2003/4 c23gᵖᵘ c25dᵖᵘ **c–** c24sᶠ 21gᵖᵘ Feb 11] lengthy, workmanlike mare: no form: left Mrs L. Wadham after **h–** reappearance. *B. I. Case*

ANNAGHMORE GALE (IRE) 10 br.g. Strong Gale – Kept In The Dark (Kemal **c– §** (FR)) [2003/4 c61: 16gᵖᵘ c21d Apr 30] rangy ex-Irish gelding: maiden hurdler: fair **h–** chaser in 2002/3: no form in 3 starts for current stable: blinkered once: has had tongue tied: sometimes refuses/reluctant to race. *Miss Sarah George*

ANNA WALHAAN (IRE) 5 b.g. Green Desert (USA) – Queen's Music (USA) **h87** (Dixieland Band (USA)) [2003/4 16m³ 16m 16g⁶ Nov 11] close-coupled gelding: fairly useful on Flat (stays 8.5f), sold out of M. Channon's stable 15,000 gns Newmarket July Sales: modest form at best over hurdles, shaping as though having stamina limitations. *Ian Williams*

ANNEKA LOUISE   10 ch.m. Jendali (USA) – Scotgavotte (FR) (Dunbeath (USA)) [2003/4 c22g^{pu} May 24] fair pointer: little sign of ability otherwise. *R. J. Jackson*   c–
h–

ANNIE BYERS   8 ch.m. Sula Bula – Tuneful Flutter (Orchestra) [2003/4 h76, F91: 20m^3 20m* c20d* c22d^5 c20g^2 22g* Apr 4] rather leggy, useful-looking mare: fair handicap hurdler: won novice events at Leicester (mares) in November and Wincanton in April: fair form over fences, winning novice handicap at Sandown in December: stays 2¾m: acts on good to firm and heavy going. *J. G. Portman*   c105
h91 +

ANNIE DIPPER   9 ch.m. Weld – Honey Dipper (Golden Dipper) [2003/4 c25d^{pu} c26s^5 c24g^2 c22d^5 c21g^2 Apr 10] seventh foal: half-sister to useful hurdler/winning chaser Sonny Hill Lad (by Celtic Cone), stayed 3¼m: dam placed once from 4 starts over hurdles: poor maiden chaser: likely to prove suited by 3m+. *C. J. Gray*   c66

ANNIE FLEETWOOD   6 ch.m. Anshan – Gold Luck (USA) (Slew O' Gold (USA)) [2003/4 h72, F–: 22g^3 24m May 14] poor form over hurdles: remote second in point in March. *C. P. Morlock*   h78

ANNIE GREENLAW   8 b.m. Petoski – Cascabel (Matahawk) [2003/4 16s 16d c16g^3 c17d^F Apr 11] 900 5-y-o: sixth foal: half-sister to winner in Austria by Ballacashtal: dam fair 7f and 1m winner: no sign of ability. *P. R. Hedger*   c–
h–

ANNIES GOLD (IRE)   8 b.m. Spanish Place (USA) – Leventos (Le Moss) [2003/4 h–: 21g^{pu} 20s^{pu} Dec 26] no sign of ability: tried blinkered. *Mrs S. M. Johnson*   h–

ANNIES THEME   6 b.m. Weld – Metannee (The Brianstan) [2003/4 F16g May 2] second live foal: dam, winning hurdler, stayed 21f: failed to complete in 3 points in 2003: well beaten in bumper. *Dr J. R. J. Naylor*   F–

ANNODYCE   6 b.m. Faustus (USA) – Coleford (USA) (Secreto (USA)) [2003/4 h–: 16g 17d Mar 3] signs of only a little ability over hurdles. *Miss Z. C. Davison*   h–

ANNO JUBILO (GER)   7 b. or br.g. Lando (GER) – Anna Maria (GER) (Night Shift (USA)) [2003/4 h116: 16s^6 16d 16d Apr 12] good-topped gelding: fair hurdler: easily best effort in 2003/4 when seventh of 9 in minor event at Fairyhouse final start: raced at 2m: acts on good to soft going. *C. F. Swan, Ireland*   h114

ANNS GIRL   11 br.m. Newski (USA) – Nearly Married (Nearly A Hand) [2003/4 c–, h86: 16g* 16m^3 17m May 29] sturdy mare: poor hurdler: won mares selling handicap at Worcester in May: best form up to 19f: acts on any going: tried visored, blinkered nowadays: often needs plenty of driving. *J. C. Fox*   c–
h79

ANONYMITY   6 ch.g. Exit To Nowhere (USA) – Wind of Roses (USA) (Lomond (USA)) [2003/4 19f 18d^3 20m^2 24g* 24m 21g c16d c18v Apr 21] modest hurdler: won handicap at Listowel in September: well held both starts over fences: stays 3m: acts on good to firm and good to soft ground: usually tongue tied. *G. T. Lynch, Ireland*   c–
h94

ANOTHER BALLY   8 br.g. Neltino – Michele My Belle (Lochnager) [2003/4 c19g^F c17d^3 20d^{pu} Apr 21] third both starts in maiden points in Ireland in 2003: no form in maiden hurdles/chases. *Mrs H. Dalton*   c–
h–

ANOTHER CHANCE   9 b.g. Golden Heights – Lapopie (Deep Run) [2003/4 22s^{pu} c20v^3 c24g^2 c25s^6 c20v^3 20s^5 c20d^6 Apr 23] useful-looking gelding: fair hurdler/chaser: stays 3m: raced on good going or softer (acts on heavy): tried in cheekpieces: races prominently. *J. M. Jefferson*   c100
h109

ANOTHER CLUB ROYAL   5 b.g. Overbury (IRE) – Miss Club Royal (Avocat) [2003/4 16g* 16f^4 19g Mar 5] fifth foal: half-brother to 3 poor jumpers: dam fair staying hurdler/chaser: won weakly-contested novice hurdle at Uttoxeter on debut: well beaten in 2 conditional jockeys novice handicaps: bred to stay well beyond 2m. *D. McCain*   h74

ANOTHER CONQUEST   5 b.m. El Conquistador – Kellys Special (Netherkelly) [2003/4 F16s^5 21d^{pu} 17g^6 Apr 10] rather leggy mare: fourth foal: sister to fairly useful chaser Kellys Conquest, stays 25f, and bumper winner Special Conquest: dam maiden pointer: first sign of ability when sixth in mares maiden hurdle at Newton Abbot. *J. W. Mullins*   h76
F–

ANOTHER COPPER   8 ch.g. Bandmaster (USA) – Letitica (Deep Run) [2003/4 c66, h89?: 27s^6 c21g^F 26m^3 22g^2 24v^{pu} 24s^4 24g^6 24g^4 c20v^{pu} c26g^2 Apr 12] compact gelding: poor chaser: modest maiden hurdler: stays 3¼m: acts on any going: effective   c74 §
h86 §

blinkered or not: often soon off bridle: often let down by jumping over fences: unreliable. *C. J. Down*

ANOTHER DUDE (IRE) 7 br.g. Shardari – Gemma's Fridge (Frigid Aire) [2003/4 **h112** h111: 20d 16d^pu 16d^3 16g* 16d^pu 17d^3 Apr 18] lengthy gelding: type to make a chaser: fair handicap hurdler: won at Musselburgh in February: stays 19f: raced on good going or softer (acts on heavy): ran respectably in blinkers final start. *J. Howard Johnson*

ANOTHER GENERAL (IRE) 9 ch.g. Glacial Storm (USA) – Whats In A Name **c–** (IRE) (Le Moss) [2003/4 c120, h–: c26s^pu c24g^pu c24s^pu c26g^F Mar 1] angular gelding: **h–** fairly useful hurdler/chaser at best: no form in 2003/4: should stay beyond 25f: acts on heavy going. *R. T. Phillips*

ANOTHER GRADUATE (IRE) 6 ch.g. Naheez (USA) – Another Daisy (Major **h–** Point) [2003/4 F–: 17g 20s Dec 19] smallish gelding: tailed off in bumper and novice hurdles. *John R. Upson*

ANOTHER ISLAY 13 b.g. Tobin Lad (USA) – Coincidence Girl (Manacle) [2003/4 **c–** c21s^pu May 2] leggy gelding: winning pointer, little form otherwise: usually blinkered: **h–** has had tongue tied. *K. Robson*

ANOTHER JOKER 9 b.g. Commanche Run – Just For A Laugh (Idiot's Delight) **c107** [2003/4 c–, h–: c19g* c16g^2 21m^6 c16f* c18g^6 c16d^2 c16m^pu Feb 25] lengthy, workman- **h–** like gelding: maiden hurdler: fair chaser: won maiden at Hereford in May and novice at Haydock in October: reportedly struck into final start: stays 19f: possibly best on good going or firmer: bold-jumping front runner. *J. L. Needham*

ANOTHER JUSTICE 8 ch.g. Dolphin Street (FR) – Unheard Melody **c–** (Lomond (USA)) [2003/4 c20g^pu c24f^pu Feb 29] poor pointer. *R. V. Westwood* **h–**

ANOTHER MOOSE (IRE) 9 b.g. Mister Lord (USA) – Moose (IRE) (Royal Foun- **c–** tain) [2003/4 c113, h–: c22s^F c25d^pu 21g^4 23s 24g^F Feb 28] useful-looking gelding: fair **h114** hurdler/maiden chaser: stayed 3¼m: raced on good going or softer (acted on heavy): free-going sort: dead. *Miss E. C. Lavelle*

ANOTHER PROMISE (IRE) 5 b.g. Presenting – Snape (IRE) (Strong Gale) **h90** [2003/4 21g 19g^5 22d^5 Mar 7] third foal: dam never ran: showed some ability in novice hurdles at Market Rasen last 2 starts. *J. A. Supple*

ANOTHER RUM (IRE) 6 b.g. Zaffaran (USA) – Sharp Fashion VII (Damsire Unreg- **h121** istered) [2003/4 F18d^3 22m* 24d 20s^3 24s* 24d^2 22s^6 22g^2 Apr 16] quite good-topped **F84** gelding: brother to bumper winner Bealtaine and half-brother to winning pointer by Jamesmead: dam unraced, from family of top-class 2m to 2½m chaser Katabatic: fair form in bumpers: fairly useful novice hurdler: won at Ayr in November and February: excellent head second to Kivotos in handicap there final start: will stay beyond 3m: acts on good to firm and soft going (bumper form on heavy). *I. A. Duncan, Ireland*

ANSARI (IRE) 7 b.g. Selkirk (USA) – Anaza (Darshaan) [2003/4 16d 20m 20d^5 16s **h111** Dec 14] smallish, leggy gelding: fair handicap hurdler, missed 2002/3: stays 2½m: acts on any going. *Patrick O. Brady, Ireland*

ANSAR (IRE) 8 b.g. Kahyasi – Anaza (Darshaan) [2003/4 c129, h–: c18d^5 c22s^5 Jul **c128** 30] leggy gelding: one-time smart hurdler: fairly useful chaser: fifth of 22 to Nearly A **h–** Moose in Galway Plate in July: will stay 3m: acts on soft and good to firm going. *D. K. Weld, Ireland*

ANSHABIL (IRE) 5 br.g. Anshan – Billeragh Thyne (IRE) (Good Thyne (USA)) **F91** [2003/4 F16g^3 F16d^5 Mar 19] first foal: dam unraced half-sister to very smart 2m to 3m chaser Second Schedual: fair form in bumpers at Ascot and Warwick. *A. King*

ANSWERED PROMISE (FR) 5 gr.g. Highest Honor (FR) – Answered Prayer **h–** (Green Desert (USA)) [2003/4 16s^pu Nov 29] close-coupled gelding: modest on Flat (stays 1¼m): showed little in novice on hurdling debut. *A. W. Carroll*

ANTARTIC PRINCE (IRE) 8 ch.g. Glacial Storm (USA) – Clonea Fog (Laurence **c95** O) [2003/4 c24s^2 Jan 16] IR 4,200 4-y-o: workmanlike ex-Irish gelding: half-brother to fairly useful hunter chaser Ensign Ewart (by Buckskin) and winning pointer by Lapierre: dam lightly raced: fair form at best in bumpers for Miss S. Collins: won maiden Irish point in 2002: bought 17,000 gns Doncaster May (2002) Sales: won point in Britain in 2003: modest form when second of 4 finishers in novice chase at Huntingdon: will stay beyond 3m. *P. J. Hobbs*

ANTIQUE GOLD 10 b.g. Gildoran – Chanelle (The Parson) [2003/4 16g^pu Mar 12] **h–** rangy gelding: fairly useful form when runner-up in novice hurdles in 1999/00: no show either start since. *R. Allan*

Western Pleasure Craddockstown Novices' Chase, Punchestown—
Anxious Moments (nearest camera), Caishill and Golden Row (centre) jump the last

ANTONINE 4 ch.g. Selkirk (USA) – Eversince (USA) (Foolish Pleasure (USA)) **F89**
[2003/4 F16m⁴ Apr 13] IR 85,000Y, 5,000 3-y-o: half-brother to several winners, notably
high-class German middle-distance performer Caitano (by Niniski): dam French 2-y-o
1m winner: around 10 lengths fourth of 14 in conditional jockeys bumper at Chepstow on
debut. *C. J. Mann*

ANTONY EBENEEZER 5 ch.h. Hurricane Sky (AUS) – Captivating (IRE) (Wolf- **h93**
hound (USA)) [2003/4 h83: 16m⁴ 16g* 16m⁴ 16m⁵ 16f⁵ 16m⁵ 16g³ 16g⁵ Apr 18] leggy
horse: modest on Flat (stays 2m): modest handicap hurdler: won at Stratford in July:
raced at 2m: acts on good to firm going, unraced on soft/heavy: usually tongue tied: free-
going sort. *C. R. Dore*

ANXIOUS MOMENTS (IRE) 9 b.g. Supreme Leader – Ms Brooks (IRE) (Lord **c132**
Ha Ha) [2003/4 h–: c16s* c16g^pu c16d* c20d⁵ c17d² c16d^F Mar 7] tall, close-coupled **h–**
gelding: fairly useful hurdler: useful novice chaser: won at Listowel in September and
Punchestown (Grade 2, beat Caishill 4 lengths) in November: fell heavily first final
outing: best at 2m: raced on good going or softer (acts on soft). *C. F. Swan, Ireland*

ANY NEWS 7 ch.g. Karinga Bay – D'Egliere (FR) (Port Etienne (FR)) [2003/4 20m^pu **h–**
17m^pu Jul 18] IR 5,000Y: ex-Irish gelding: second foal: dam unraced half-sister to very
smart French chaser Algan: fair maiden on Flat (stays 9f) at 5 yrs: poor form at best over
hurdles: sold out of W. Mullins' stable 6,500 gns Newmarket Autumn (2002) Sales: has
had tongue tied. *P. A. Blockley*

ANYPORTINASTORM (IRE) 6 b.g. Glacial Storm (USA) – Port Alley (Torus) **F102**
[2003/4 F16d² F16s⁵ F18d² F16d Nov 22] seventh foal: half-brother to winning 2¾m
chaser Pharalley (by Phardante): dam unraced half-sister to useful staying chaser Very
Very Ordinary: fairly useful form in bumpers: best effort when winning at Punchestown
in early-May by 7 lengths from Glacial Moss. *Patrick Mullins, Ireland*

ANZAL (IRE) 6 b.g. Kahyasi – Anazara (USA) (Trempolino (USA)) [2003/4 h76: **h92**
19m* 22m⁵ 20m* 22m^pu 19g^pu 20d^pu Apr 21] small, leggy gelding: has reportedly had
breathing operation: modest handicap hurdler: easily won novices at Exeter in May and
Worcester (conditional jockeys) in June: should stay beyond 2½m: acts on good to soft
and good to firm going: tried blinkered/tongue tied: patiently ridden. *D. R. Gandolfo*

AOIFEROB (IRE) 6 b.g. Commanche Run – Lancana (IRE) (Lancastrian) [2003/4 **c–**
c25d^pu c26s^pu c25g^F Apr 4] IR 12,000 3-y-o: third foal: half-brother to bumper winners
by Supreme Leader and Tanaos: dam lightly-raced hurdler: won maiden Irish point in
2003: showed little in 3 steeplechases: tried visored. *B. G. Powell*

APADI (USA) 8 ch.g. Diesis – Ixtapa (USA) (Chief's Crown (USA)) [2003/4 h89: **c–** §
16g^rtr 17m* 17g³ 16m^d 16g⁵ 16s 16v⁵ c16v⁴ Feb 4] sturdy gelding: modest handicap **h88** §
hurdler: won seller at Market Rasen in June: sold out of M. Chapman's stable 3,600 gns

Doncaster October Sales after next start: distant fourth in novice handicap on chasing debut: barely stays 19f: acts on any going: tried in cheekpieces: usually held up: headstrong: twice refused or very reluctant to race in 2003/4: not one to trust. *R. C. Guest*

A PIECE OF CAKE (IRE) 11 gr.g. Roselier (FR) – Boreen Bro (Boreen (FR)) [2003/4 c139, h–: c25d⁵ c25d⁴ Dec 27] good-topped gelding: useful handicap chaser in 2002/3, well held both starts in 2003/4: needs testing conditions at 2½m and stays 4m: has won on good to firm going, raced mainly on softer (acts on heavy). *Mrs M. Reveley* c– h–

APOLLO THEATRE 6 b.g. Sadler's Wells (USA) – Threatening (Warning) [2003/4 F98: 17v³ 20g⁴ 21g³ Mar 26] useful-looking gelding: fair form when in frame in novice at Fakenham and maiden at Newbury last 2 starts over hurdles: will stay beyond 21f. *R. Rowe* h102

APOLLO VICTORIA (FR) 7 b.g. Sadler's Wells (USA) – Dame Solitaire (CAN) (Halo (USA)) [2003/4 16vᵖᵘ 16d Dec 29] half-brother to Woman's Company (by Law Society), 17f chase winner in France: useful on Flat (probably stays 11.5f at 2/3 yrs for A. O'Brien, tailed off on belated return in March: better effort in novice hurdles when mid-field at Newbury. *B. G. Powell* h98

A POUND DOWN (IRE) 7 b.g. Treasure Hunter – Ann's Queen (IRE) (Rhoman Rule (USA)) [2003/4 c23sᵖᵘ Apr 6] IR £2,400 4-y-o: third foal: dam won around 1½m on Flat/2m over hurdles: won maiden Irish point in 2003: bought 4,000 gns Doncaster January (2004) Sales: possibly went amiss in novice on steeplechasing debut. *N. G. Ayliffe* c–

APPLE JOE 8 b.g. Sula Bula – Hazelwain (Hard Fact) [2003/4 c73, h–: c24g⁵ c25s³ c24d⁶ c26s* c24v² c26g⁴ c24dᵘʳ c24v³ Apr 4] lengthy gelding: no form over hurdles: poor handicap chaser: won amateur event at Plumpton in December: stays 3¼m: acts on heavy going: wore cheekpieces last 5 starts. *A. J. Whiting* c82 h–

APRIL ACE 8 ch.g. First Trump – Champ d'Avril (Northfields (USA)) [2003/4 h–: 17m Mar 9] no form over hurdles. *R. J. Baker* h–

APRIL ALLEGRO (FR) 8 br.g. Doyoun – April Lee (Lyphard (USA)) [2003/4 c78, h123: 24d 22g⁴ 24m 20m c20d³ c22s c25m⁴ c25m Sep 5] compact gelding: fairly useful handicap hurdler, below form in 2003/4: easily best effort over fences (often let down by jumping) when third in maiden at Wexford in July: stays 3m: acts on heavy and good to firm going: tried blinkered: has had tongue tied. *M. Hourigan, Ireland* c97 x h114

APRIL LOUISE 8 b.m. Meqdaam (USA) – California Dreamin (Slip Anchor) [2003/4 h94: 17s⁶ 16f May 10] plain, sparely-made mare: modest handicap hurdler: well below form both starts early in 2003/4: should stay 2½m: yet to race on heavy going, acts on any other: sold 10,000 gns Doncaster November Sales. *T. R. Wall* h–

APRIL MISS (FR) 4 bl.f. Averti (IRE) – Lady of Jakarta (USA) (Procida (USA)) [2003/4 18f⁵ 16g³ 18m² 16m¹ 16g⁶ Nov 11] well held in 4 maidens on Flat for J. Allen: poor juvenile hurdler: visored first start. *Mrs L. Wadham* h74

APRIL SPIRIT 9 b.m. Nomination – Seraphim (FR) (Lashkari) [2003/4 c89, h–: c23m² c21d* c21m⁴ c26g* Sep 12] leggy, sparely-made mare: modest handicap chaser: successful at Southwell in August and September: stays 3¼m: acts on any going. *Mrs S. J. Smith* c92 h–

APRIL TREASURE 9 b.m. Stani (USA) – Eleri (Rolfe (USA)) [2003/4 c58, h–: 20m 20mᵖᵘ 26m⁵ 16mᵖᵘ Sep 13] leggy mare: bad maiden hurdler/chaser: sold £1,700 Ascot October Sales: won point in April. *Mrs P. Ford* c– h–

AQRIBAA (IRE) 6 b. or br.g. Pennekamp (USA) – Karayb (IRE) (Last Tycoon) [2003/4 h62: 16g Nov 15] poor maiden hurdler: raced around 2m on good going or firmer: takes good hold. *A. J. Lockwood* h–

AQUA PURA (GER) 5 b.g. Acatenango (GER) – Actraphane (Shareef Dancer (USA)) [2003/4 h–: 21g 16v³ 24sᵖᵘ 16d⁴ Mar 11] lengthy gelding: no form over hurdles. *B. J. Curley* h–

ARABIAN MOON (IRE) 8 ch.g. Barathea (IRE) – Excellent Alibi (USA) (Exceller (USA)) [2003/4 h126: c20f³* c18f* c21g² 24m 21f⁵ c20sᵖᵘ c24m⁵ 22d⁶ 17d Jan 24] compact gelding: won 2 novice chases in small fields at Fontwell in August: fairly useful handicap hurdler: left S. Dow after fifth start, out of sorts subsequently: stays 3m, at least when conditions aren't testing: acts on firm and good to soft going: tried in cheekpieces/visor: has found little. *M. C. Pipe* c105 d h115 d

ARAF 5 b.g. Millkom – Euphyllia (Superpower) [2003/4 h82: 17mᵖᵘ 16m 17m Jul 17] medium-sized gelding: poor maiden hurdler: raced around 2m. *N. Wilson* h–

ARAGLIN   5 b.g. Sadler's Wells (USA) – River Cara (USA) (Irish River (FR)) [2003/4   **h89**
h–: 19m* 16m³ 20d 21m² 19d⁵ 19d 21d⁶ 21d Apr 12] small, sturdy gelding: modest
hurdler: won maiden at Market Rasen in October: stays 21f: acts on good to firm going:
tried blinkered. *Mrs S. J. Wilton*

ARAWAK PRINCE (IRE)   8 ch.g. College Chapel – Alpine Symphony (Northern   **c–**
Dancer) [2003/4 c87, h87: c17mᶠ Oct 11] leggy gelding: winning hurdler: last of 2   **h–**
finishers on chasing debut, let down by jumping/temperament both other starts over
fences: best around 2m: acts on good to firm going, seemingly not on soft/heavy: usually
visored: races freely: has found little. *G. Prodromou*

ARBIE (CAN)   5 b.g. Mountain Cat (USA) – Empress of Love (USA) (Czaravich   **h–**
(USA)) [2003/4 18mᵖᵘ Sep 23] of no account on Flat nowadays: in cheekpieces, showed
nothing on hurdling debut. *Mrs L. C. Jewell*

ARC EN CIEL   6 b.g. Rainbow Quest (USA) – Nadia Nerina (CAN) (Northern Dancer)   **h–**
[2003/4 h–: 16g Feb 14] lengthy, angular gelding: modest on Flat nowadays (best form
up to 1½m): well held in 2 novice hurdles nearly 2 years apart. *G. L. Moore*

ARCEYE   7 b.g. Weld – Flower of Tintern (Free State) [2003/4 F17m F16s 20dᵖᵘ Mar   **h–**
22] 5,000 4-y-o: fifth foal: half-brother to winning pointer by Seymour Hicks: dam fairly   **F–**
useful up to 1¼m on Flat/winning 2m hurdler: no sign of ability. *M. G. Rimell*

ARCH CAPER (IRE)   7 b.m. Archway (IRE) – African Caper (IRE) (Brush Aside   **F–**
(USA)) [2003/4 F17g May 18] 600 4-y-o: second foal: dam unraced half-sister to fairly
useful chaser up to 2¾m Dictum: well held in bumper on debut. *C. N. Kellett*

ARCHENKO   4 b.g. Weldnaas (USA) – Silverdale Rose (Nomination) [2003/4 F16g   **F–**
Mar 13] 1,500 4-y-o: sixth foal: brother to modest sprinter Dawn Patrol: dam well beaten
both starts at 2 yrs: ninth of 10 in bumper on debut: well beaten in 2 maidens on Flat
following month. *A. Berry*

ARCHIAS (GER)   5 b.g. Darshaan – Arionette (Lombard (GER)) [2003/4 16g 16g   **h91**
16g⁶ 16d 16d Feb 21] ex-German gelding: half-brother to winning 2m hurdler Adronikus
(by Monsun): successful twice up to 1½m from 4 starts on Flat at 3 yrs, last of 8 only start
in 2003 for P. Schiergen: modest form at best over hurdles: has had tongue tied: races
freely. *R. C. Guest*

ARCHIE BABE (IRE)   8 ch.g. Archway (IRE) – Frensham Manor (Le Johnstan)   **h110**
[2003/4 h93: 16d* 16d⁴ 16d² 16s³ Jan 31] angular, workmanlike gelding: fair on Flat
(stays 1½m), successful in April: fair novice hurdler: won at Wetherby in November:
likely to stay beyond 2m: acts on good to soft ground. *J. J. Quinn*

ARCHIRONDEL   6 b.g. Bin Ajwaad (IRE) – Penang Rose (NZ) (Kingdom Bay   **h–**
(NZ)) [2003/4 19d Jan 19] smallish gelding: modest on Flat (stays 11f), sold out of John
Berry's stable 7,800 gns Doncaster October Sales: showed nothing on hurdling debut.
M. D. Hammond

ARCH STANTON (IRE)   6 b.g. Lahib (USA) – Sweet Repose (High Top) [2003/4   **h134**
h124: 16d² 16d* 16s⁵ 18s⁴ 16g⁶ 16d² Apr 12] angular gelding: useful hurdler: won
maiden at Leopardstown in December and novice at Punchestown in late-April: in good
form in between, length second to Dawn Invasion in minor event at Fairyhouse: likely to
stay beyond 2¼m: acts on heavy going. *W. P. Mullins, Ireland*

ARCTIC BLUE   4 b.g. Polar Prince (IRE) – Miss Sarajane (Skyliner) [2003/4 16g Jul   **h–**
26] modest maiden on Flat: tailed off in juvenile on hurdling debut. *J. S. Moore*

ARCTIC BURNER (IRE)   10 b.g. Glacial Storm (USA) – Lucky Appeal (Star   **c– §**
Appeal) [2003/4 16m Jun 18] sturdy gelding: winning hurdler/chaser up to 19f: placed in   **h– §**
points in 2004: sometimes visored/blinkered: ungenuine. *J. C. Tuck*

ARCTIC CHALLENGE (IRE)   10 b.g. Glacial Storm (USA) – Ruckinge Girl   **c124**
(Eborneezer) [2003/4 c119, h–: c21g⁴ c20mᵘʳ c20d³ Dec 20] rather leggy gelding: fairly   **h–**
useful handicap chaser: won at Stratford in May: creditable third to Spring Grove at
Warwick final start: stays 21f: acts on good to firm and heavy going: effective in cheekpieces or without: usually front runner: has found little. *K. R. Burke*

ARCTIC COPPER (IRE)   10 b.g. Montelimar (USA) – Miss Penguin (General   **c142 §**
Assembly (USA)) [2003/4 c142, h–: c16g² c20g⁴ c24f² c20s² c20d c17s c16v⁴ c20s⁴   **h–**
c25d⁴ Feb 21] good-topped gelding: useful chaser: head second to Edredon Bleu in
Grade 2 at Clonmel fourth start: below form subsequently: effective at 2m to 29f: acts on
any going: wears blinkers/cheekpieces: has had tongue tied: usually finds little and not
one to trust. *N. Meade, Ireland*

ARCTIC FANCY (USA) 11 ch.g. Arctic Tern (USA) – Fit And Fancy (USA) (Vaguely Noble) [2003/4 c125, h–: c20s² c19d^{pu} c20g³ c20g c20d⁵ c24d^{ur} Apr 12] good-topped gelding: fairly useful handicap chaser: below form after first outing: barely stays 3m: below form on firm going, acts on any other: usually races prominently: has hung left. *Miss H. C. Knight* **c121 d**
h–

ARCTIC GAMBLE 12 b.g. Arctic Lord – Honey Gamble (Gambling Debt) [2003/4 c97: c25m Apr 13] workmanlike gelding: modest chaser: let down by jumping on return from year off: stays 25f: best efforts on good going or firmer. *L. G. Cottrell* **c–**

ARCTIC GLOW 5 ch.m. Weld – Arctic Mission (The Parson) [2003/4 19d^{pu} 19g 19g Apr 16] sixth foal: dam, poor novice hurdler, half-sister to fairly useful staying hurdler Golden Arctic: no form in 3 novice hurdles. *Mrs H. Pudd* **h–**

ARCTIC KING 11 b.g. Arctic Lord – Dunsilly Bell (London Bells (CAN)) [2003/4 c–, h–: c25d³ Feb 15] rangy gelding: winning pointer: maiden steeplechaser: probably stays 25f: acts on soft going: tried blinkered. *A. M. Lloyd* **c75**
h–

ARCTIC LAGOON (IRE) 5 ch.g. Bering – Lake Pleasant (IRE) (Elegant Air) [2003/4 h78: 16g³ 16g⁵ 20g³ 20g⁶ c21d³ c16d² c20d² c21v^{pu} c16g c19g⁴ c20g² Mar 12] rather leggy gelding: poor maiden hurdler: better form when placed first 3 runs over fences, but no show subsequently: stays 21f: raced mainly on good/good to soft going: visored final start: often tongue tied. *Mrs S. C. Bradburne* **c93**
h78

ARCTIC MOSS (IRE) 5 ch.m. Moscow Society (USA) – Arctic Match (Royal Match) [2003/4 F16g* F16s Mar 13] tall, rather unfurnished mare: seventh foal: half-sister to winning 2m hurdler Ballyanne Supreme (by Supreme Leader): dam lightly-raced maiden: won mares bumper at Musselburgh on debut in February: very much on toes, tailed off in valuable similar event at Sandown. *G. A. Swinbank* **F94**

ARCTIC PLAYBOY 8 b.g. Petoski – Arctic Oats (Oats) [2003/4 h–, F93: 20d 19s Dec 20] angular gelding: well held over hurdles. *Ian Williams* **h–**

ARCTIC RAINBOW (IRE) 6 b.g. King's Ride – Arctic Chatter (Le Bavard (FR)) [2003/4 F17s⁴ 21d⁴ 22s 20s⁴ 16d⁴ Mar 12] €17,000 4-y-o: workmanlike gelding: eleventh foal: brother to winning hurdler around 2m Clooneen and half-brother to winning hurdler/pointer Sound of Jura (by Deep Run), stayed 25f: dam unraced sister to dam of useful chaser up to 21f Garnwin: fourth in bumper on debut: modest form over hurdles: should stay 3m: races freely. *D. B. Feek* **h98**
F81

ARCTIC SKY (IRE) 7 b.g. Arctic Lord – Lake Garden Park (Comedy Star (USA)) [2003/4 h107, F94: c20m* Nov 5] fair hurdler: not fluent when winning match for novice at Kempton on chasing debut: will stay beyond 21f: acts on good to firm going. *N. J. Henderson* **c111**
h–

ARCTIC SPIRIT 9 b.g. Arctic Lord – Dickies Girl (Saxon Farm) [2003/4 c93, h–: 16s³ Apr 11] close-coupled gelding: modest handicap chaser: poor maiden hurdler: barely stays 19f: acts on heavy going, probably not on firmer than good: tried visored: usually races prominently: sometimes makes mistakes. *R. Dickin* **c–**
h74

ARCTIC TIMES (IRE) 8 ch.g. Montelimar (USA) – Miss Penguin (General Assembly (USA)) [2003/4 c98, h–: c24g⁵ c24m* c26d^F Mar 18] good-topped gelding: fair hunter chaser: won at Wexford in May: successful in 3 points in 2004 but failed to complete in valuable hunters at Cheltenham and Punchestown: stays 25f: acts on good to firm and heavy going. *Eugene M. O'Sullivan, Ireland* **c98**
h–

ARDASHIR (FR) 5 b.g. Simon du Desert (FR) – Antea (FR) (Esprit du Nord (USA)) [2003/4 h–: 20g 16d² 17d 20s² 24d 24s* 20m Apr 24] leggy gelding: fairly useful hurdler: much improved when winning handicap at Bangor in April: likely to prove better at 3m than 2½m: acts on soft going, probably on good to firm. *N. A. Twiston-Davies* **h122**

ARDEN HILLS (IRE) 10 b.g. Supreme Leader – Pisa (IRE) (Carlingford Castle) [2003/4 c–, h75: 20m⁶ 22m² 17g⁶ 22g⁵ 22s³ 22g c21s c21g⁴ Apr 10] poor hurdler: little form in steeplechases: should stay 3m: acts on good to firm and heavy going. *J. D. Frost* **c–**
h84

ARDENT SCOUT 12 b.g. Ardross – Vidette (Billion (USA)) [2003/4 c130, h–: c20m⁴ c29g⁴ c24s⁴ c33d c36d c24s Apr 17] rangy gelding: fairly useful handicap chaser: creditable fourth at Wetherby and Haydock first and fourth starts: below form otherwise in 2003/4, remote seventh of 11 finishers to Amberleigh House in Grand National at Aintree sixth outing: stays 4m: acts on good to firm and heavy going: sound jumper. *Mrs S. J. Smith* **c129**
h–

ARM

ARDSTOWN 13 b.m. Ardross – Booterstown (Master Owen) [2003/4 c24s⁶ Jan 23] **c–**
compact mare: one-time fairly useful chaser: well below form in 4 handicaps since
2000/1. *R. F. Knipe*

ARDWELSHIN (FR) 6 b.g. Ajdayt (USA) – Reem Dubai (IRE) (Nashwan (USA)) **h67**
[2003/4 h–: 17d 16dᵖᵘ 16s³ 17gᵖᵘ 17sᵖᵘ Mar 23] workmanlike gelding: form over hurdles
only when third in selling handicap at Stratford in December: blinkered (hung) final start.
C. J. Down

ARGENTO 7 b.g. Weldnaas (USA) – Four M'S (Majestic Maharaj) [2003/4 h113: **c110**
c16mᶠ c16g³ c16f* c17d³ c16dᶠ c19gᵘʳ c17g c17g⁴ Mar 28] leggy gelding: fair hurdler/ **h–**
novice chaser: won over fences at Catterick in November: would also have won at
Newcastle in December but for falling last: raced mainly around 2m: acts on any going:
races prominently. *G. M. Moore*

ARIJAZ 7 b.g. Teenoso (USA) – Zajira (IRE) (Ela-Mana-Mou) [2003/4 F77: F16g 16g **h80**
16gᵖᵘ 20f⁸ 24g³ Mar 13] modest form at best in bumpers: poor hurdler: won novice at **F–**
Musselburgh in February: barely stays 3m: acts on firm going. *Mrs L. B. Normile*

ARIMERO (GER) 4 b.g. Monsun (GER) – Averna (Heraldiste (USA)) [2003/4 16s⁴ **h104**
16s 16g⁶ 16g Apr 1] leggy, useful-looking ex-German gelding: maiden on Flat, in frame
6 times (up to 11f) from 8 starts at 3 yrs for A. Trybhul: fair form over hurdles: free to post
final outing. *C. F. Swan, Ireland*

ARISTOXENE (FR) 4 b.g. Start Fast (FR) – Petite Folie (Salmon Leap (USA)) **h107**
[2003/4 16d* 16d² 16s³ Jan 31] good-topped gelding: type to make a chaser: fifth foal:
half-brother to winning pointer by Murmure: dam winning hurdler around 2m: fair form
in juvenile hurdles: won at Fontainebleau in November on debut: similar form when
placed at Wetherby and Doncaster subsequently: will stay 2½m: joined N. Henderson.
G. Macaire, France

ARJAY 6 b.g. Shaamit (IRE) – Jenny's Call (Petong) [2003/4 16dᵖᵘ Nov 15] fair on Flat **h–**
(stays 1¼m): jumped poorly in novice on hurdling debut. *Andrew Turnell*

ARJAYPEAR (IRE) 5 b.g. Petardia – Lila Pedigo (IRE) (Classic Secret (USA)) **h84**
[2003/4 h–: 16mᵘʳ 16m² 16m² 20f² 19m Sep 10] poor maiden hurdler: stays easy 2½m:
acts on firm going: tried blinkered. *A. King*

ARK ADMIRAL 5 b.g. Inchinor – Kelimutu (Top Ville) [2003/4 17g³ 16g³ Apr 18] **h86**
trained by B. Meehan, useful handicap 1¼m winner at 3 yrs, well below form in 2003: tongue
tied, modest form when third both starts over hurdles. *P. F. Nicholls*

ARLAS (FR) 9 b.g. Northern Fashion (USA) – Ribbon In Her Hair (USA) (Sauce Boat **c–**
(USA)) [2003/4 c26gᵖᵘ c25g⁶ c24g⁶ c23sᵖᵘ Apr 6] close-coupled gelding: useful **h–**
handicap chaser in 2001/2: off 2 years, showed little on return: effective blinkered or not,
visored and tongue tied final start: no easy ride: prone to mistakes. *M. C. Pipe*

ARLEQUIN DE SOU (FR) 10 b.g. Sir Brink (FR) – Colombine (USA) (Empery **c68**
(USA)) [2003/4 c123, h–: c20m⁶ Feb 25] lengthy, useful-looking gelding: fairly useful **h–**
handicap chaser at best: looked to have deteriorated considerably in points/hunter: stays
3m: acts on good to firm and heavy going: blinkered: races prominently: not an easy ride
(has hung markedly left). *Miss Polly Curling*

ARMAGH SOUTH (IRE) 5 ch.g. Topanoora – Mogen (Adonijah) [2003/4 F16d **h79**
20d⁶ 20s 22g 22g Mar 28] €21,000 4-y-o: half-brother to useful bumper winner Arctic Force **F76**
(by Arctic Lord) and winning pointer by Brush Aside: dam unraced half-sister to smart
chaser up to 3m Oregon Trail and smart hurdler up to 2½m Tiananmen Square: ninth of
15 in bumper on debut: poor form on first of 3 starts in novice hurdles. *J. Howard Johnson*

ARMAGUEDON (FR) 6 b.g. Garde Royale – Miss Dundee (FR) (Esprit du Nord **h111 p**
(USA)) [2003/4 F114: 19g² 16g* Mar 12] good-topped gelding: useful form in bumpers:
second to Thosewerethedays in novice at Catterick on hurdling debut: easily made all in
similar event at Ayr 3 months later: may prove best around 2m: has worn crossed
noseband: sure to improve. *L. Lungo*

ARMATURK (FR) 7 ch.g. Baby Turk – Armalita (FR) (Goodland (FR)) [2003/4 **c149**
c144, h–: 24g⁵ c20s⁸ c21d⁴ c16s* c17g² c16m⁶ c16g² c16d⁴ Apr 17] tall, angular gelding: **h–**
winning hurdler: smart chaser: won handicap at Doncaster in January by 11 lengths from
Exit Swinger: good second subsequently to easy winner Azertyuiop in Grade 2 at
Newbury and Tidour in valuable handicap at Aintree, lacklustre efforts on sixth and final

73

starts: has won over 21f, best form at 2m: acts on good to firm and heavy going: usually
tongue tied: usually races with plenty of zest. *P. F. Nicholls*

ARMEN (FR)   7 b.g. Kaldoun (FR) – Anna Edes (FR) (Fabulous Dancer (USA))   **c93**
[2003/4 17g c24g³ c19g² c19dᵖᵘ c19gᶠ Apr 1] workmanlike gelding: useful juvenile   **h–**
hurdler in 2000/1: off 2½ years, tenth of 14 in handicap at Cheltenham on return: modest
form at best over fences, failing to convince with jumping: should stay beyond 2m: raced
on good going or softer (acts on heavy): visored final start. *M. C. Pipe*

ARMS ACROSSTHESEA   5 b.g. Namaqualand (USA) – Zolica (Beveled (USA))   **h–**
[2003/4 h80: 17g May 26] angular gelding: poor maiden hurdler: raced around 2m: acts
on good to firm going: blinkered last 3 starts in 2002/3: joined A. Whillans. *F. P. Murtagh*

AR MUIN NA MUICE (IRE)   8 ch.m. Executive Perk – Raashideah (Dancer's Image   **c118 p**
(USA)) [2003/4 h134+: c24s² c24gᶠ 23s⁵ 25g⁵ Mar 16] good-topped mare: encouraging   **h139**
start over fences when ½-length second to Rum Pointer in novice at Uttoxeter on
reappearance: fell tenth next time: useful hurdler: good fifth of 24 to Creon in Pertemps
Final at Cheltenham final outing: stays 25f: acts on good to firm and soft going: not the
most fluent jumper over hurdles. *Jonjo O'Neill*

A ROMP TOO FAR (IRE)   8 b.g. Eurobus – Saxa Princess (IRE) (Lancastrian)   **c–**
[2003/4 h–: c25dᵖᵘ Feb 12] medium-sized gelding: maiden hurdler: demoted to second   **h–**
after winning maiden point in February: showed nothing in hunter later in month: tried in
cheekpieces. *M. Ranger*

AROSEFORCLARE   8 b.m. Royal Vulcan – Lovelyroseofclare (Torus) [2003/4 h–:   **h–**
21m 22mᵖᵘ 26g⁵ Jul 4] of little account. *Miss K. M. George*

AROUND BEFORE (IRE)   7 ch.g. Be My Native (USA) – Glynn Cross (IRE)   **c105**
(Mister Lord (USA)) [2003/4 c25d⁶ c24dᶠ 20m⁴ 24m 26m² c24d* c26f* c24m² 26m*   **h94 +**
24f* Oct 16] 30,000 4-y-o: third foal: half-brother to winning hurdler/fairly useful chaser
Glin Castle (by Carlingford Castle), stays 3m: dam winning pointer: won maiden point in
2003: trained first 3 starts in 2003/4 by E. Bolger: tongue tied after next outing and much
improved, winning handicap chases at Uttoxeter and Fontwell (novice) in August and
handicap hurdles at Huntingdon and Towcester in October: stays 3¼m: acts on firm and
good to soft going: tried in cheekpieces. *Jonjo O'Neill*

ARRIBILO (GER)   10 b.g. Top Ville – Arborea (GER) (Priamos (GER)) [2003/4 c–, h91§: 17g May 1] good-topped gelding: very stiff task and held when falling 2 out on chasing debut: modest hurdler: needs sharp 2m: acts on soft and good to firm going: tried visored/blinkered: pulls hard, and has carried head high: unreliable. *B. P. J. Baugh*   **c–** **h– §**

ARTEEA (IRE)   5 b.g. Oscar (IRE) – Merric (IRE) (Electric) [2003/4 F16d* Apr 13] €7,500 3-y-o, €31,000 4-y-o: well-made gelding: third foal: dam unraced: won Goffs Land Rover Bumper at Fairyhouse on debut impressively by 3 lengths from The Spoonplayer: only eighth to Geill Sli in Grade 1 bumper at Punchestown later in month. *M. Hourigan, Ireland*   **F99**

ARTE ET LABORE (IRE)   4 b.f. Raphane (USA) – Bouffant (High Top) [2003/4 16d 16f Nov 22] half-sister to winning hurdlers Petrula (by Tagula), at 2½m, and Mutasariff (by Polish Patriot), around 2m: poor maiden on Flat (probably stays 1¼m): well held in 2 juvenile hurdles. *K. A. Ryan*   **h–**

ARTEMESIA   9 b.m. Teenoso (USA) – Annicombe Run (Deep Run) [2003/4 h85: 20m* 22d⁴ c20m² c21m⁴ 21d⁴ 21s Dec 26] smallish mare: modest handicap hurdler: won mares event at Fakenham (third course win) in May: similar form when runner-up in novice at Hexham on chasing debut (stiffish task in handicap next time): effective at 2½m to 3m: acts on good to firm and good to soft going (bumper form on soft). *Ferdy Murphy*   **c89** **h88**

ARTEMISE (FR)   6 b.m. Cyborg (FR) – Articule (FR) (Art Francais (USA)) [2003/4 h71?, F–: 17g² 19d 16d* 16s 16d⁵ Mar 14] leggy mare: modest hurdler: won novice handicap at Wincanton in December: should be suited by 2½m+: raced on good going or softer. *A. King*   **h93**

ART EXPERT (FR)   6 b.g. Pursuit of Love – Celtic Wing (Midyan (USA)) [2003/4 h77: 23d^{pu} 26g^{pu} Jul 4] little sign of ability over hurdles: tried in cheekpieces. *Mrs N. Macauley*   **h–**

Goffs Land Rover Bumper, Fairyhouse—Arteea makes an impressive debut

ARTHUR DALY (IRE)   7 b.g. Lord Americo – Time Talker (IRE) (Stalker) [2003/4   **c92**
20g 20s³ c19m³ 24s² c24fᵇᵈ c22mᶠ c20g³ c28g⁴ c24d c20s³ c25m⁵ Apr 14] winning   **h92**
pointer: modest maiden hurdler/chaser on balance of form: effective at 19f to 3m: acts on
good to firm and heavy going. *D. P. Murphy, Ireland*

ARTHUR PENDRAGON   4 b.g. Botanic (USA) – Blue Room (Gorytus (USA))   **h–**
[2003/4 18sᵖᵘ Jan 26] modest form on first of 2 completed starts on Flat (bred to stay
1¼m) for B. Hills: lost touch after 4 out in juvenile on hurdling debut. *Jonjo O'Neill*

ARTHURS KINGDOM (IRE)   8 b.g. Roi Danzig (USA) – Merrie Moment (IRE)   **c79 §**
(Taufan (USA)) [2003/4 h70§: 27dᵘʳ c27d² c25dᵘʳ c27v⁴ 27dᵖᵘ c25s⁵ c21g Apr 12]   **h– §**
lengthy gelding: poor handicap hurdler: similar form when second in weak amateur
handicap on chasing debut: no form subsequently: stays 27f: acts on good to firm and
heavy going: tried visored, often wears cheekpieces: unreliable. *Miss Kate Milligan*

ARTIC JACK (FR)   8 b.g. Cadoudal (FR) – Si Jamais (FR) (Arctic Tern (USA))   **c150**
[2003/4 c28s* c25d³ c24s* c28m³ c36dᶠ c29dᵖᵘ Apr 12]   **h–**
         Not too long after the demise of stable stalwart The Last Fling, owner
Trevor Hemmings and trainer Sue Smith had another good performer to represent
them in the valuable staying chases around Haydock. Artic Jack had been a useful
novice chaser for Nicky Henderson in 2001/2, winning in small fields at Folkestone
and Ascot, as well as being tried against the best novices at Cheltenham and
Aintree, but he had been off for nineteen months before he made his debut for his
new stable in the Tim Molony Handicap Chase at Haydock on Hennessy day. Artic
Jack is not the first horse to benefit from the move to Craiglands Farm, and he made
light of both his absence and joint top weight to run out an impressive winner of the
eight-runner contest at odds of 16/1, making all and having his rivals in trouble a
long way from home. Only three others completed, the first of them Rugged River
nine lengths behind, with course regular Bobby Grant (who broke a leg) and the
subsequent Irish Grand National winner Granit d'Estruval among those pulled up.
Despite his ability, The Last Fling was all too often prone to errors. Artic Jack, on
the other hand, combined his bold round of jumping with a near-faultless display
over the big Haydock fences, a performance which augured well for his chances in
the track's more valuable handicaps later in the winter. He reportedly got his tongue
over the bridle when a remote third behind Gunner Welburn and Skippers Cleuch in
the Rowland Meyrick Handicap Chase at Wetherby next time, but was on song

Peter Marsh Chase (Limited Handicap), Haydock—Artic Jack brings to an end Kingscliff's winning run

again for the Peter Marsh Chase back at Haydock in January, a race The Last Fling had won four years earlier. Artic Jack showed further improvement with another display of relentless galloping from the front, though he did not get all the credit he might have done in ending the unbeaten record of odds-on Kingscliff, who reportedly pulled muscles. The favourite briefly looked like making a race of it two out, but Artic Jack went clear again on the run-in for a thirteen-length success. You're Agoodun and outsider Ebony Light were left well behind as the only other finishers after Horus had unseated five out. Another 9 lb rise in the handicap meant that Artic Jack had to give 13 lb or more all round in the Red Square Vodka Gold Cup Chase at the same course the following month, another race that The Last Fling had taken four years earlier. Artic Jack looked in great shape and led the field with his usual exhilarating jumping to begin with, but was headed at the thirteenth and ended up finishing a remote third to Jurancon II and Bear On Board.

Artic Jack joined that pair in the Grand National field, one of three runners (from three different yards) in Mr Hemmings' colours attempting to atone for wretched luck that has befallen some of his horses in a race he has set out his stall to win. The Last Fling contested three Nationals, completing only on his first attempt and falling fatally on his final try, while stable-companion Goguenard met with a similar fate in the race a year later. All told, only three of fourteen runners in his colours have completed, all of them well held. Artic Jack had given the impression that he would make a fine sight over the National fences, but he got no further than the first, a typical casualty at a fence which claims its fair share of those who tackle it a little too boldly. All of the Hemmings horses did at least come back safely this time, but there was little change of luck for their owner whose Hedgehunter led for a long way before coming down at the last when a tired third. As for Artic Jack, he was turned out nine days later for the Irish Grand National at Fairyhouse, carrying top weight, but he was pulled up on the second circuit, a serious mistake at the thirteenth effectively sealing his fate.

Artic Jack (FR) (b.g. 1996)	Cadoudal (FR) (br 1979)	Green Dancer (b 1972)	Nijinsky
			Green Valley
		Come To Sea (gr 1971)	Sea Hawk II
			Camarilla
	Si Jamais (FR) (ch 1984)	Arctic Tern (ch 1973)	Sea Bird II
			Bubbling Beauty
		Sigune (ch 1973)	Sheshoon
			Soles

Artic Jack originated with one of France's most successful breeders of jumpers, Madame Georges Vuillard. Jacqueline Vuillard may not be familiar in Britain, but her stud's products have carried her name to success in some big races, the males all named 'Jack' and the females 'Line'. As well as Artic Jack, Mondial Jack was also successful in Britain in the latest season. Or Jack, a triple winner of the Gran Premio di Merano and the Grand Prix de Pau and runner-up in the Grand Steeple-Chase de Paris, and Line Marine, the 2003 Grand Steeple-Chase winner, are two of Madame Vuillard's best representatives. Artic Jack is by France's leading sire of jumpers, Cadoudal, out of a mare whose four wins over jumps included one of Auteuil's most prestigious chases, the Prix des Drags. Si Jamais has bred two other winners, Sibarite (by Pampabird) and Muguette (by Royal Charter), both successful around two miles in the French Provinces, over hurdles and fences respectively. Beyond that, the pedigree is basically a Flat one, though grandam Sigune, third in the Prix de Royaumont, later showed plenty of ability in winning over hurdles and fences. She was a half-sister to the useful Bill O'Gorman-trained two-year-old Stella Matutina, but there is stamina again in the next generation as they were out of a half-sister to the high-class stayer Samos III, winner of the Prix Royal-Oak, runner-up in the Ascot Gold Cup, and also successful in the Prix Gladiateur in the days when it was run over a marathon three miles.

Artic Jack is a big, rangy gelding. He stays three and a half miles and acts on good to firm and heavy going, though all his wins have come on good ground or softer. He is best on galloping tracks, and his bold jumping and front-running style stands him in good stead in the small fields that typically contest Haydock's better chases. *Mrs S. J. Smith*

ARTIC REASON (IRE) 5 b.g. Perugino (USA) – Vendetta Valentino (USA) (Bering) **h89**
[2003/4 16s³ 18mʳᵒ 16g 16s⁴ 19s 16s Apr 22] lengthy, rather sparely-made gelding:

modest maiden hurdler: raced mainly around 2m: acts on soft ground: tried blinkered.
E. McNamara, Ireland

ARUBA DAM (IRE)   6 br.m. Be My Native (USA) – Arumah (Arapaho) [2003/4 F–:   **h68**
F16m³ 16f³ Nov 8] little show in 2 bumpers: poor form when third of 5 in novice on **F–**
hurdling debut. *P. F. Nicholls*

ARZILLO   8 b.g. Forzando – Titania's Dance (IRE) (Fairy King (USA)) [2003/4 16mᶠ **h79**
16gᵘʳ 17gᵖᵘ 16m⁵ 16g⁴ 16m³ Sep 7] poor on Flat (stays 7f): poor novice hurdler: likely to
need sharp 2m: raced on good/good to firm going: has worn cheekpieces. *J. M. Bradley*

ASADOR (FR)   8 ch.g. Kadounor (FR) – Apos (FR) (Baillamont (USA)) [2003/4 **c–**
c131, h–: 17dᶠ 17dᵖᵘ Mar 3] tall, angular gelding: useful hurdler/chaser at best: dropped **h88**
markedly in class, just in front when falling last in selling hurdle at Hereford (claimed
from P. Nicholls £5,000) on reappearance: stays 19f: acts on heavy and good to firm
going: front runner. *A. G. Juckes*

ASCARI   8 br.g. Presidium – Ping Pong (Petong) [2003/4 17g² 16m 17fᵖᵘ 26gᵖᵘ 16d⁶ **c–**
Nov 27] angular gelding: fair on Flat (stays 1½m) in 2002, sold out of W. Jarvis' stable **h74**
4,500 gns Doncaster September (2002) Sales: poor maiden hurdler: held when falling
only start over fences: has pulled hard. *A. L. Forbes*

ASCOOLASICE   6 b.g. Thethingaboutitis (USA) – Frozen Pipe (Majestic Maharaj) **c–**
[2003/4 c24sᵖᵘ Feb 12] first foal: dam winning pointer: showed little in 2 points/hunter
chase. *Miss L. J. Brewer*

ASHFIELD JAKE (IRE)   12 br.g. Jolly Jake (NZ) – Ashfield Rose (Mon Capitaine) **c–**
[2003/4 c–, h–: c16dᵖᵘ c25mᵖᵘ Jun 11] lengthy gelding: no form outside points. **h–**
S. T. Lewis

ASHGAR (USA)   8 ch.g. Bien Bien (USA) – Ardisia (USA) (Affirmed (USA)) [2003/4 **c– §**
c105§, h98§: 26d² 21f² 16m³ 27s 21g⁵ Apr 12] quite good-topped gelding: winning **h83 §**
hurdler/chaser: poor form in 2003/4: barely stays 4m: acts on any going: usually blinkered: has reportedly broken blood vessel: ungenuine. *M. D. Hammond*

ASHGREEN   7 b.g. Afzal – Space Kate (Space King) [2003/4 c21d Apr 30] little form **c90**
in novice hurdles: fair pointer, successful on 3 of 4 completed starts in 2003: ran better **h–**
than result suggests when seventh of 11 finishers to Red Brook Lad in maiden at Cheltenham on hunter chase debut, every chance until 2 out. *S. Turner*

ASHLEYBANK HOUSE (IRE)   7 b.g. Lord Americo – Deep Perk (IRE) (Deep **h108 +**
Run) [2003/4 h85p, F89: 20gᵖᵘ 20d 16s* 24v* 22gᵖᵘ 20dᵘʳ Apr 10] well-made gelding:
fair hurdler: improved efforts when easily winning novice handicaps at Ayr in December
and January: went as if amiss next time: effective at testing 2m to 3m: acts on heavy going
(unraced on firmer than good). *L. Lungo*

ASHLEY BROOK (IRE)   6 ch.g. Magical Wonder (USA) – Seamill (IRE) (Lafon- **h121**
taine (USA)) [2003/4 F110: 17g* 17d² 19s* 19s³ 21m⁵ Apr 14] strong gelding: type to
make a chaser: fairly useful novice hurdler: won at Exeter in November and Taunton
(beat Lotus des Pictons 21 lengths, making virtually all) in December: should stay beyond
19f: acts on soft going, possibly not ideally suited to good to firm final outing. *K. Bishop*

ASHLEY MARSH   6 b.g. Alflora (IRE) – Annapuma (Rakaposhi King) [2003/4 **h–**
19sᵖᵘ 19d 19s 22s 17sᵖᵘ Apr 6] third foal: brother to winning pointer Farlington: dam
unraced: no form over hurdles. *T. R. George*

ASHLEY MUCK   11 b.g. Gunner B – Miss Muck (Balinger) [2003/4 c120§, h–: **c118**
c20m⁴ c20m² c20m³ Jun 18] compact gelding: fairly useful handicap chaser: stays at least **h–**
21f: acts on any going: tried visored/blinkered: has looked ungenuine in past. *M. C. Pipe*

ASHNAYA (FR)   6 b.m. Ashkalani (IRE) – Upend (Main Reef) [2003/4 h81: 16g⁴ **h86**
20g* 21g 20d⁴ Nov 14] modest handicap hurdler: won at Hexham in May: stays 2½m:
raced on good going or softer (acts on soft): tried blinkered, wears cheekpieces
nowadays: not an easy ride: inconsistent. *W. Storey*

ASHSTORM (IRE)   8 ch.g. Glacial Storm (USA) – Sandy Ash (IRE) (Boreen (FR)) **c120**
[2003/4 c24mᵖᵘ c22f⁶ c22d² c25d* c25dᵖᵘ Apr 11] non-thoroughbred gelding: first foal: **h–**
dam unraced: once-raced hurdler: fairly useful handicap chaser: won amateur event at
Punchestown in December by ½ length from Hume Castle: good second in 4m amateur
event at Punchestown in early-May: acts on good to firm and heavy going. *J. E. Kiely,
Ireland*

ASHTAROUTE (USA)   4 b.f. Holy Bull (USA) – Beating The Buzz (IRE) (Bluebird **h–**
(USA)) [2003/4 19d 16g⁶ Mar 10] small filly: modest maiden on Flat: achieved little in 2
novice hurdles. *M. C. Chapman*

ASHTON VALE   5 ch.g. Ashkalani (IRE) – My Valentina (Royal Academy (USA)) [2003/4 h97: 17d^{pu} 17s Dec 26] sturdy gelding: fair juvenile hurdler in 2002/3: sold out of P. Nicholls' stable 4,000 gns Doncaster August Sales: no show both subsequent starts: raced around 2m: acts on firm and good to soft going: tongue tied. *M. A. Barnes*   **h–**

ASHTORETH (IRE)   5 ch.m. Ashkalani (IRE) – Sally Chase (Sallust) [2003/4 h66: 16m^6 1/d^2 16g^3 1/m^{pu} 1/g^6 Jul 28] sturdy mare: poor maiden hurdler: will prove best around 2m: acts on good to firm and heavy going: wore cheekpieces final outing: has pulled hard. *D. McCain*   **h68**

ASHWELL (IRE)   5 gr.g. Anshan – Willshego (Welsh Captain) [2003/4 F16s 19g^4 19g^5 20d^F Mar 22] 9,000 4-y-o: close-coupled gelding: sixth foal: half-brother to 3 winners, including 3m hurdler Sir Ryco (by Lord Americo) and useful bumper winner Fenagh Express (by Buckskin): dam maiden: eighth in bumper on debut: modest form at best in 3 starts over hurdles. *C. C. Bealby*   **h84** **F72**

ASHWICKE GAMBLER   8 b.g. Tout Ensemble – Miss Dollymouse (Nader) [2003/4 22d^{pu} 22m 22g^{pu} Jun 13] first foal: dam never ran: of no account. *J. W. Mullins*   **h–**

ASK FOR LUCK (IRE)   7 b.g. Camden Town – French Thistle (Kemal (FR)) [2003/4 h89, F83: 22g Apr 18] workmanlike gelding: last in Irish point: novice hurdler, modest at best: will stay beyond 3m. *J. G. Portman*   **h75**

ASK ME WHAT (IRE)   7 b.m. Shernazar – Laffan's Bridge (IRE) (Mandalus) [2003/4 h89+, F89: 16g^2 20s^3 16g^5 c20d^{ur} c16s^{ur} Apr 11] modest hurdler: unseated early both starts over fences: stays 21f: acts on good to firm and heavy going: blinkered third outing. *Miss Venetia Williams*   **c–** **h99**

ASK THE GATHERER (IRE)   6 b.g. Be My Native (USA) – Shean Bracken (IRE) (Le Moss) [2003/4 F16g* 20g^3 Dec 9] fourth living foal: dam unraced sister to useful staying jumpers Brackenfield and Brackenheath: won bumper at Wexford on debut in May: left W. J. Burke, 13 lengths behind to Big Moment in novice at Fontwell on hurdling debut: should improve. *P. F. Nicholls*   **h109 p** **F94**

ASKTHEJUDGE (IRE)   5 b.g. Revoque (IRE) – Law Student (Precocious) [2003/4 h111p: 16g* Jul 21] fairly useful up to 1½m on Flat: lightly raced over hurdles (ran out on debut), won maiden at Ballinrobe impressively only start in 2003/4. *Francis Ennis, Ireland*   **h111**

ASLAPOFTHEEURO (IRE)   6 b.g. Eurobus – Slapoftheballot (Ragapan) [2003/4 20m 26m^{pu} 22g 22g 24m Jul 9] second foal: dam, ran once in bumper, from family of smart but ungenuine chaser up to 3m Pimberley Place: successful once (maiden) from 7 starts in Irish points: bought 15,500 gns Doncaster May Sales: no form over hurdles: visored final start. *M. C. Pipe*   **h–**

ASPARAGUS (IRE)   10 b.g. Roselier (FR) – Arctic Bead (IRE) (Le Moss) [2003/4 c120, h–: c20g^4 c16d^{pu} c16v^2 c20s^3 c20d* c24s^4 Apr 17] smallish gelding: winning hurdler: fairly useful handicap chaser: won at Bangor in March by ½ length from Juralan: stays 3m: raced on good going or softer (acts on heavy): tongue tied: usually races prominently: genuine. *M. Sheppard*   **c118** **h–**

ASSESSED (IRE)   10 b.g. Montelimar (USA) – Tax Code (Workboy) [2003/4 c24s^4 Jan 11] tall, angular gelding: winning hurdler/useful novice chaser in 2001/2: off 21 months, distant fourth behind Cloudy Bays in valuable handicap at Leopardstown: needs good test around 2m and stays 3m: raced on good going or softer (acts on heavy). *W. P. Mullins, Ireland*   **c–** **h–**

ASSIGNATION   4 b.g. Compton Place – Hug Me (Shareef Dancer (USA)) [2003/4 17s 16m Feb 21] close-coupled gelding: modest maiden (probably stays 1¼m), sold out of B. R. Millman's stable £1,700 Ascot November Sales: well beaten in 2 novice hurdles. *Miss M. Bragg*   **h–**

ASSOON   5 b.g. Ezzoud (IRE) – Handy Dancer (Green God) [2003/4 F17m^2 F16m* 19m^2 18g^2 Oct 5] half-brother to several winners, including useful 2m hurdlers Roll A Dollar (by Spin of A Coin) and Mersey Beat (by Rock Hopper) and smart 1m to 1½m winner Karinga Bay (by Ardross): dam 1¼m winner: won bumper at Worcester in July: placed in maidens on Flat next 2 starts: better effort in novice hurdles when 1¼ lengths second to Kaparolo at Fontwell: likely to be suited by greater test of stamina. *G. L. Moore*   **h112** **F89**

ASSUMETHEPOSITION (FR)   4 gr.g. Cyborg (FR) – Jeanne Grey (FR) (Fast Topaze (USA)) [2003/4 F16v^4 F17d F16g Mar 6] unfurnished gelding: fifth foal: half-brother to 7.5f winner Jolie Dorothee (by Dear Doctor): dam unraced half-sister to high-   **F80**

class French hurdler up to around 3¼m Isabey: fair form on second of 3 outings in bumpers: will stay beyond 2m. *R. C. Guest*

ASSURED MOVEMENTS (USA) 8 b.g. Northern Flagship (USA) – Love At Dawn (USA) (Grey Dawn II) [2003/4 h90: 19m⁶ 16m Jun 28] lengthy gelding: modest hurdler: below form in sellers early in 2003/4: stays 2¾m: acts on soft and firm going: tried in headgear: tongue tied: has looked none too keen. *Mrs D. A. Hamer* **h–**

ASTAFORT (FR) 5 ch.g. Kendor (FR) – Tres Chic (USA) (Northern Fashion (USA)) [2003/4 h79: 16m⁴ 16g⁴ 18g³ 20d 20s 16s³ Apr 21] good-topped gelding: poor maiden hurdler: stays 1½m: acts on heavy going. *A. C. Whillans* **h81**

ASTLE (IRE) 6 ch.g. Spectrum (IRE) – Very Sophisticated (USA) (Affirmed (USA)) [2003/4 17gᵖᵘ Jun 11] fairly useful at one time on Flat (stays 8.5f), has become very disappointing: showed nothing in novice on hurdling debut. *Mrs N. Macauley* **h–**

ASTON MARA 7 b.g. Bering – Coigach (Niniski (USA)) [2003/4 h86: 20g³ 21m* 19g⁴ 20m⁴ 21m⁴ 19m⁶ 19m⁴ 22mᶠ 22g Feb 10] neat gelding: modest handicap hurdler: won at Huntingdon (seller) in May and Market Rasen in June: lost form after: stays 3m: acts on firm and soft going. *M. A. Buckley* **h96 d**

ASTON (USA) 4 b.g. Bahri (USA) – Halholah (USA) (Secreto (USA)) [2003/4 16g⁴ 16g⁵ 16d⁶ 16d Apr 10] fair maiden on Flat (stays 1½m): modest form in juvenile hurdles, sold out of N. Meade's stable €19,000 Goffs October Sale after debut (blinkered). *C. F. Swan, Ireland* **h92**

ASTORMYDAYISCOMING 6 b.g. Alhaatmi – Valentine Song (Pas de Seul) [2003/4 h79: 16g 16m 20g 19m⁶ 22gᶠ 22gᵖᵘ 26d⁶ 16gᵖᵘ Sep 7] leggy gelding: poor maiden hurdler, no form in 2003/4: should stay 3m: usually wears headgear: tried tongue tied. *G. F. Bridgwater* **h–**

ASTRAL AFFAIR (IRE) 5 br.m. Norwich – Jupiters Jill (Jupiter Pluvius) [2003/4 F16m² F16m⁴ F17d 22sᵖᵘ 25dᵖᵘ Mar 14] unfurnished mare: ninth foal: half-sister to winning chasers up to 2½m I Like It A Lot (by Proverb) and Orchipedzo (by Le Moss): dam never ran: placed on first of 2 starts in maiden Irish points in 2003: modest form at best in bumpers: pulled up both starts over hurdles, saddle slipped on first. *P. A. Pritchard* **h–**
F76

ASTRAL DANCER (IRE) 4 b.g. Fourstars Allstar (USA) – Walk N'Dance (IRE) (Pennine Walk) [2003/4 F17d⁶ Apr 18] 16,000 3-y-o: fourth foal: dam unraced half-sister to fairly useful hurdler up to 3m Bustling Rio: sixth of 13 to Elfkirk in bumper at Carlisle on debut, smooth headway 4f out before fading. *J. Mackie* **F64**

ASTRAL PRINCE 6 ch.g. Efisio – Val d'Erica (Ashmore (FR)) [2003/4 h57: 16g⁵ 17g⁶ c20gᵘʳ c17m⁴ c17d² c17g² c17m⁵ c16d⁶ Apr 12] lengthy gelding: modest and unreliable on Flat: bad maiden hurdler/poor maiden chaser: left A. Crook after fourth start: raced mainly around 2m: acts on soft going: usually wears cheekpieces: has had tongue tied. *Mrs K. Walton* **c67**
h–

ASTRO GLIDE (IRE) 8 ch.m. Star Quest – Polly-Glide (Pollerton) [2003/4 20gᵖᵘ 21vᵖᵘ Jan 13] sturdy, plain mare: fifth foal: half-sister to winning 19f chaser Royal Pot Black (by Royal Fountain): dam winning Irish chaser: showed nothing in 2 races over hurdles. *Mrs L. B. Normile* **h–**

ASTRONAUT 7 b.g. Sri Pekan (USA) – Wild Abandon (USA) (Graustark) [2003/4 16m 16m⁴ 20d* Aug 7] good-topped gelding: poor on Flat in 2003: modest hurdler: won selling handicap (sold to M. Pipe 6,000 gns) at Uttoxeter: stays 2½m: acts on good to firm and good to soft going: tried blinkered: refused to race once. *A. E. Jones* **h96 §**

ATAHUELPA 4 b.g. Hernando (FR) – Certain Story (Known Fact (USA)) [2003/4 16gᶠ 16m² 16mᵖᵘ 16g⁴ Nov 2] leggy gelding: half-brother to fairly useful 2m hurdler Pharly Story (by Pharly): fairly useful on Flat (stays 9f), trained by P. Cole at 3 yrs: would have won juvenile at Stratford on hurdling debut but for falling last: disappointing after, tongue tied final outing: free-going sort. *M. F. Harris* **h108 d**

ATALANTA SURPRISE (IRE) 7 ch.g. Phardante (FR) – Curragh Breeze (Furry Glen) [2003/4 h76, F76: c21g³ 16d c24vᵖᵘ 21d c26gᶠ Mar 10] workmanlike gelding: poor maiden hurdler: let down by jumping/temperament over fences: stays 21f: acts on heavy going. *R. H. Buckler* **c76 §**
h–

ATALYA 7 ch.g. Afzal – Sandy Looks (Music Boy) [2003/4 c76, h96: c16gᵖᵘ c17mᵖᵘ 16m c19d⁵ 17g 16s 16d Mar 24] workmanlike gelding: winning 2m hurdler/maiden chaser, no form in 2003/4. *S. T. Lewis* **c–**
h–

ATHENIAN LAW 7 br.g. Darshaan – Titania's Way (Fairy King (USA)) [2003/4 **h105** h102+: 17f^pu 16m^2 Jul 9] fair handicap hurdler: raced around 2m: acts on soft and good to firm going: sold only 2,300 gns Doncaster August Sales, pulled up in point in 2004. *P. J. Hobbs*

ATHENRY GENT (IRE) 5 ch.g. Fourstars Allstar (USA) – Covette (Master Owen) **h–** [2003/4 25s 16g 20f^5 Feb 29] workmanlike gelding: eighth foal: half-brother to fairly useful hurdler/useful chaser Eskimo Jack (by Glacial Storm), stays 3m: dam, placed in 2m novice hurdles, from family of one-time top-class staying chaser Alexander Banquet: third in maiden Irish point in 2003: well beaten in 3 starts over hurdles. *J. Howard Johnson*

ATHNOWEN (IRE) 12 b.g. Lord Americo – Lady Bluebird (Arapaho) [2003/4 c99§, **c96 §** h–§: c16m c21g^4 c16g^2 c20s* c21s^F c21d^2 c21m^ur c19s^2 c23s^2 Apr 6] sturdy gelding: **h– §** modest handicap chaser: won at Uttoxeter in December: effective at 2m to 3m: acts on soft and good to firm going: visored once: often makes mistakes: refused to race once in 2002/3. *J. R. Payne*

ATLANTIC CROSSING (IRE) 7 b.g. Roselier (FR) – Ocean Mist (IRE) (Crash **c87 x** Course) [2003/4 h99: 20d^pu c20s^2 c20d^ur c20d^F c21v^6 c20s^F 24d 20s 24s Apr 17] leggy, **h–** quite good-topped gelding: winning hurdler: let down by jumping over fences, and no form back over hurdles last 3 starts: should stay beyond 2½m: raced on good going or softer: tried blinkered. *P. Beaumont*

ATLANTIC HAWK 6 b.g. Daar Alzamaan (IRE) – Pyewacket (Belfort (FR)) [2003/4 **h–** F86: 20d^ur 24s^ur Apr 4] well-made gelding: fair form in bumpers: off nearly 12 months, unseated early both starts over hurdles: has pulled hard/shown tendency to hang under pressure. *Ferdy Murphy*

ATLANTIC LADY (GER) 6 br.m. Dashing Blade – Atlantic City (GER) (Medicus **h–** (GER)) [2003/4 h84: 16m 17d Dec 2] leggy mare: poor maiden hurdler. *Mrs N. S. Sharpe*

ATLANTIC RHAPSODY (FR) 7 b.g. Machiavellian (USA) – First Waltz (FR) **c115 §** (Green Dancer (USA)) [2003/4 h121: c16d 16v c20d c17g^2 c18g^2 18s^2 c16d^3 c16s^4 c16s^2 **h116 §** c17s^2 c16s^2 c16d^F Apr 8] leggy gelding: fairly useful hurdler/maiden chaser: best around 2m: acts on heavy going, probably on good to firm: tried blinkered/in cheekpieces: successful only start in tongue strap: patiently ridden: ungenuine. *T. M. Walsh, Ireland*

ATLANTICUS (IRE) 8 b.g. Kings Lake (USA) – Amazonia (GER) (Alpenkonig **c–** (GER)) [2003/4 c88, h73+: c17d c21s^pu c20g^F 16v 20d Mar 11] lengthy, angular gelding: **h–** fair hurdler at best: no form in 2003/4, including in novice chases: sold out of C. Grant's stable 700 gns Doncaster January Sales before final start: stays 2½m: acts on soft going: visored third start: has had tongue tied. *Mrs E. Slack*

ATLASTABOY (IRE) 8 b.g. Phardante (FR) – Corcaigh (Town And Country) [2003/4 **c113** h105, F94: c25d^3 c27s* c23g^pu c32g^ur Mar 17] well-made gelding: fair hurdler: best effort **h–** over fences when winning handicap at Taunton in January by 6 lengths from Bramblehill Duke: will stay beyond 27f: acts on soft going. *T. R. George*

A TOI A MOI (FR) 4 ch.g. Cyborg (FR) – Peperonelle (FR) (Dom Pasquini (FR)) **h105** [2003/4 15g^2 18d^2 16s^4 17d Jan 24] tall, workmanlike ex-French gelding: third foal: dam maiden: runner-up in juvenile hurdles at Clairefontaine and Auteuil for T. Civel: better effort in graded company in Britain when seventh to Mondul in Grade 2 at Cheltenham. *Miss Venetia Williams*

ATOMIC BREEZE (IRE) 10 b. or br.g. Strong Gale – Atomic Lady (Over The River **c64 §** (FR)) [2003/4 c71§, h–: c25g^pu c24m^pu c25m^pu c26m^pu c25m^5 c27m^4 c28f^2 c27d^2 c21g^F **h–** Apr 1] plain gelding: poor chaser: stays 3½m: acts on firm and good to soft going: not a fluent jumper: unreliable. *D. M. Forster*

ATOSKI 10 b.g. Petoski – Culm Valley (Port Corsair) [2003/4 c22m^pu Jun 21] fair **c–** pointer at best: no form over hurdles/in steeplechases, lame only start in 2003/4. **h–** *Mrs H. Dalton*

ATTACK 8 gr.g. Sabrehill (USA) – Butsova (Formidable (USA)) [2003/4 h87, F–: **c–** c16m^3 c21g^3 c21g^pu Feb 20] angular gelding: won 2m novice hurdle in 2002/3: no other **h–** form over jumps, sold out of P. Hobbs's stable 4,800 gns Doncaster November Sales after second start: blinkered once: tongue tied. *Mrs Julie Read*

ATTICUS FINCH (IRE) 7 b.g. Witness Box (USA) – Dramatic Loop (IRE) (Balin- **c95 x** ger) [2003/4 c84, h84: 17g^4 21m^4 16m^2 c20g^5 c19f^3 c20m^3 c25d* c24s^F c20g* c24g^ur **h81** Apr 10] workmanlike gelding: poor hurdler: won intermediate at Southwell in May:

modest handicap chaser: won at Catterick in January and Market Rasen in March: effective at 2m to 25f: acts on firm and good to soft going: free-going sort: often let down by jumping. *M. Stirk*

ATTORNEY GENERAL (IRE) 5 b.g. Sadler's Wells (USA) – Her Ladyship (Polish Precedent (USA)) [2003/4 17g* 16s^F 17d^3 16g^4 Mar 26] medium-sized gelding: fairly useful on Flat (will be suited by 1¾m+), sold out of Sir Michael Stoute's stable 75,000 gns Newmarket Autumn (2002) Sales: won novice at Newton Abbot in November on hurdling debut: better form in handicaps last 2 starts, third to Ela Re in well-contested novice event at Cheltenham and fourth to Dancing Bay at Newbury (awkward head carriage): will stay 2½m. *J. A. B. Old* **h109**

ATUM RE (IRE) 7 br.g. Be My Native (USA) – Collopy's Cross (Pragmatic) [2003/4 h106: c19g^2 c16m^bd c17m* c16m^3 c16d^2 c16g^3 c20m^2 c17s* Apr 17] tall, good-topped gelding: fair hurdler: useful novice chaser: won in small fields at Market Rasen in October and Bangor in April: good efforts when placed in Grade 2 events on 3 of 4 starts in between, 11 lengths second of 5 to Calling Brave at Kempton on last occasion: likely to prove best up to 2½m: acts on soft and good to firm going: sound jumper: free-going sort. *P. R. Webber* **c132 h–**

AUBURN DUKE 4 ch.g. Inchinor – Dakota Girl (Northern State (USA)) [2003/4 F16d^6 Mar 25] third foal: half-brother to modest hurdler Westernmost (by Most Welcome), stays 21f: dam, fair hurdler, stayed 3m: sixth of 11 in falsely-run bumper at Ludlow on debut. *W. Jenks* **F–**

AUBURN SPIRIT 9 ch.g. Teamster – Spirit of Youth (Kind of Hush) [2003/4 c86, h–: 24g^4 c25s^2 c25v^2 c25v^2 c25d c26v* c24s^6 c24g^2 c26g^2 c29d* c29d^4 23s^3 25d^2 Apr 11] tall gelding: poor hurdler: fair handicap chaser: won at Fontwell in January and Warwick (made virtually all) in March: will probably stay beyond 29f: acts on good to firm and heavy going: visored final outing: tough, though sometimes takes plenty of driving. *M. D. I. Usher* **c104 h80**

AUDIOSTREETDOTCOM 7 ch.g. Risk Me (FR) – Ballagarrow Girl (North Stoke) [2003/4 h91§: 22s^F 22g 20s^2 20v^3 c18s^pu 20v^4 21s^5 21g^3 21d c21s^6 c21g^pu Apr 10] lengthy gelding: modest handicap hurdler: showed little in 3 chases: stays 2¾m: raced mainly on good going or softer (acts on heavy), well below form on good to firm going: wears hood and cheekpieces: ungenuine. *G. B. Balding* **c– § h95 §**

AUDITOR 5 b.g. Polish Precedent (USA) – Annaba (IRE) (In The Wings) [2003/4 17g^6 16f^pu 19g^6 16m^5 16v^pu c20d^4 Jan 22] rather sparely-made ex-Irish gelding: fairly useful on Flat (stays 1¾m) at 3 yrs, sold out of J. Oxx's stable £12,500 Ascot June Sales: no form over hurdles or on chasing debut: looked ungenuine in blinkers second start. *S. T. Lewis* **c– h–**

AUDITTY (IRE) 11 b.g. Montelimar (USA) – Tax Code (Workboy) [2003/4 c115d, h–: c16m^F c20g^3 c16m* c16m^2 c17g^3 c20g c22g^pu Nov 16] lengthy gelding: fair handicap chaser: won at Worcester in September: let down by jumping last 2 starts: stays 2½m: very best efforts on good going or firmer (acts on firm). *W. Jenks* **c103 h–**

AUETALER (GER) 10 gr.g. Niniski (USA) – Astica (GER) (Surumu (GER)) [2003/4 16g^4 20m^5 16v 16d 22f^5 20s^6 20m 21g Nov 14] smallish, leggy gelding: winning chaser, but not a fluent jumper of fences: one-time very smart hurdler for M. Pipe: fair form in 2003/4: has won at 2¾m, best form up to 2½m: acts on firm and good to soft going: tried blinkered/visored. *E. McNamara, Ireland* **c– h112**

AUGHERSKEA (IRE) 5 b.g. Oscar (IRE) – Closing Thyne (IRE) (Good Thyne (USA)) [2003/4 F17s^2 F16d* Apr 13] €32,000 3-y-o: well-made gelding: second foal: dam little sign of ability: useful in bumpers: favourite, won 26-runner event at Fairyhouse by 1½ lengths from Justified: better form when 2 lengths third to Geill Sli in Grade 1 at Punchestown 15 days later: likely to stay beyond 2m: interesting prospect for hurdles. *N. Meade, Ireland* **F114**

AUGHMOR RIVER (IRE) 9 b.g. Over The River (FR) – Morego (Way Up North) [2003/4 c25g^pu Mar 28] ex-Irish gelding: fourth foal: brother to fair chaser Family Business, stays 3m: dam unraced: won 2 points in Britain in 2003, placed first 2 starts in 2004: no form in hunter chases. *R. W. Gardiner* **c–**

AULD NICK (IRE) 6 b.g. Old Vic – Grey Tor (Ahonoora) [2003/4 F74: 16d^4 21s^4 19s^5 26s 24g^pu Mar 4] workmanlike gelding: poor form over hurdles: visored final start (raced too freely): has looked none too keen. *M. C. Pipe* **h77**

AULD THYNES SAKE (IRE) 7 b.g. Good Thyne (USA) – La Fairy (IRE) (Lafontaine (USA)) [2003/4 F96: 20d 16m 21g Mar 5] workmanlike gelding: in frame in bumpers: well held in novice/maiden hurdles: should stay at least 2½m. *Mrs Merrita Jones* **h74**

AUNT HILDA 5 b.m. Distant Relative – Aloha Jane (USA) (Hawaii) [2003/4 h67: 16f 16d⁵ 16g 16g 16m⁴ 1/m⁴ 1/t Sep 30] poor maiden hurdler: raced around 2m: acts on firm and good to soft going: usually wears headgear. *M. F. Harris* **h63**

AUNTIE ALBA 6 b.m. Gran Alba (USA) – Auntie Lorna (Uncle Pokey) [2003/4 20vᵖᵘ 16mᵖᵘ May 29] first foal: dam of little account: no sign of ability. *N. J. Pomfret* **h–**

AUNTIE JACHINTA 6 b.m. Governor General – Hopeful Alda (Kambalda) [2003/4 F17s F16g Feb 20] third foal: half-sister to winning hurdler around 2m Fionnuala (by Royal Vulcan): dam, modest hurdler who stayed 21f, half-sister to useful staying chaser Bold Agent: well held in bumpers, hampered at start in second. *J. A. Supple* **F70**

AURAZURE (IRE) 6 gr.g. Roselier (FR) – Siul Currach (Deep Run) [2003/4 F16d⁴ F17s⁴ Feb 17] fourth foal: half-brother to winning 3m chaser Manfred Mann (by Mandalus) and bumper winner Hotters (by Be My Native): dam, second over hurdles, half-sister to Scottish Grand National winner Baronet (by Roselier): fair form when fourth in bumpers at Ludlow and Folkestone: bred to be suited by further. *C. R. Egerton* **F96**

AUTCAESAR AUTNIHIL (IRE) 9 b.g. Supreme Leader – Monagey (Pimpernels Tune) [2003/4 c–, h–: c26vᵖᵘ c23vᶠ May 26] big, angular gelding: no worthwhile form over hurdles/fences: tried visored. *A. G. Juckes* **c–** **h–**

AUTUMN RAIN (USA) 7 br.g. Dynaformer (USA) – Edda (USA) (Ogygian (USA)) [2003/4 h91+: 22gᵖᵘ Nov 4] novice hurdler, modest form at best: reportedly knocked himself only outing in 2003/4: may prove best short of 25f. *D. L. Williams* **h–**

AVADI (IRE) 6 b.g. Un Desperado (FR) – Flamewood (Touching Wood (USA)) [2003/4 F66: F16m⁴ F17d 20s⁶ 24g⁵ 19g⁶ Apr 3] useful-looking gelding: modest form at best in bumpers: best effort over hurdles when fifth in novice amateur event at Chepstow: stays 3m. *Mrs H. Dalton* **h87** **F77**

AVALANCHE (FR) 7 gr.g. Highest Honor (FR) – Fairy Gold (Golden Fleece (USA)) [2003/4 c123, h99: c20g⁶ c19d³ c24g⁴ c20g² c20g³ c20m* 21d³ c20g³ c16d* Apr 17] big, workmanlike gelding: fair maiden hurdler: useful handicap chaser: won at Kempton in February and Ayr in April, second run in 24 hrs when beating Log On Intersky 9 lengths **c141** **h107 +**

Albert Bartlett And Sons Handicap Chase, Ayr—tough and reliable Avalanche routs his four opponents

at latter course: stays 21f: unraced on firm going, acts on any other: races prominently: pulls hard: sound jumper. *J. R. Best*

AVALON BUCK (IRE)   11 b.g. Buckskin (FR) – Lilly's Way (Golden Love) [2003/4 c–x, h–: c23g[6] c24d[6] c26d[2] c26m[pu] 22g[pu] c24m[5] Aug 9] rather sparely-made gelding: winning hurdler: fair chaser on his day: stays 3m: acts on heavy going: blinkered/in cheekpieces last 4 starts: usually races prominently: poor jumper. *Miss Venetia Williams*   **c102 x** **h– x**

AVANTI TIGER (IRE)   5 b. or br.g. Supreme Leader – Reign of Terror (IRE) (Orchestra) [2003/4 F16s 21d Mar 28] €11,000 4-y-o: medium-sized gelding: fourth foal: dam, ran once in points, half-sister to top-class staying chaser Life of A Lord: eighth of 19 in maiden bumper at Huntingdon on debut: well held in maiden there on hurdling debut. *C. C. Bealby*   **h–** **F84**

AVAS DELIGHT (IRE)   6 b.g. Ajraas (USA) – Whothatis (Creative Plan (USA)) [2003/4 F18d F16g[5] F20d[5] 17g 20s 16d 17d[4] 16g* 17g[2] Apr 13] ex-Irish gelding: second foal: dam lightly-raced half-sister to useful chaser up to 2¾m Moon Devil: modest form in bumpers for S. Treacy, including over 2½m: raced mainly at shorter over hurdles, won novice handicap at Wincanton in March. *R. H. Alner*   **h87 +** **F84**

AVEBURY   8 b.g. Fairy King (USA) – Circle of Chalk (FR) (Kris) [2003/4 h89: c16m[2] Apr 28] modest hurdler: similar form when 4 lengths second of 4 in novice at Newcastle on chasing debut: will prove best around 2m: acts on good to firm and good to soft going: best efforts when tongue tied. *G. M. Moore*   **c89** **h–**

AVEC PLAISIR (IRE)   9 ch.g. Grand Plaisir (IRE) – Ballinellard Lady (Fine Blade (USA)) [2003/4 c–, h–: c25g[pu] May 29] good-topped gelding: modest form on second of 2 outings over hurdles: pulled up all starts in steeplechases: won point in April: stays 3m: tried blinkered. *T. R. George*   **c–** **h–**

AVEIRO (IRE)   8 b.g. Darshaan – Avila (Ajdal (USA)) [2003/4 19m[pu] Oct 2] rather leggy gelding: fair on all-weather Flat (stays 2m), successful in January and March (for Miss G. Kelleway): pulled up all 3 runs over hurdles: tried blinkered. *B. G. Powell*   **h–**

AVENEL   12 b.m. Decent Fellow – Mermaid (Furry Glen) [2003/4 c21s[pu] Feb 24] ex-Irish mare: once-raced hurdler: lightly raced in points in Britain, won maiden in 2003: reportedly lame on hunter chase debut. *R. Allan*   **c–** **h–**

AVERSE (USA)   5 b.m. Lord Avie (USA) – Averti (USA) (Known Fact (USA)) [2003/4 F16d[2] F16s Mar 13] 3,000 3-y-o: big, angular mare: third foal: half-sister to 3 winners, including useful 1¼m winner Averted View (by Distant View): dam, 6f and 7f winner, half-sister to very smart performer up to 11f Defensive Play: 3½ lengths second of 18 to First Harmony in mares bumper at Wetherby on debut: possibly unsuited by softer ground in valuable similar event at Sandown 4 months later. *N. G. Richards*   **F88**

AVITTA (IRE)   5 b.m. Pennekamp (USA) – Alinova (USA) (Alleged (USA)) [2003/4 h99: 18g[3] 16g[F] 16d[5] 17d[ur] 16s[2] 16g[3] 16m[6] 16g[2] Apr 16] rangy mare: fair handicap hurdler: likely to prove best around 2m: acts on heavy going: weak finisher. *Miss Venetia Williams*   **h109 §**

AWAY HOME (IRE)   6 ch.g. Carroll House – Mugs Away (Mugatpura) [2003/4 F103: F16s[3] 20s* 20s[2] 20s* 20d[2] Jan 25] workmanlike gelding: will make a chaser: useful in bumpers: good start over hurdles, won maiden at Limerick in December and intermediate at Leopardstown (beating Lordofourown comfortably by 6 lengths) in January: second in Grade 3 novices at Naas (to McGruders Cross) and Leopardstown (beaten 4 lengths by impressive Watson Lake): will stay 3m: acts on soft going: usually tongue tied. *M. J. P. O'Brien, Ireland*   **h122** **F106**

AWESOME WELLS (IRE)   10 b.g. Sadler's Wells (USA) – Shadywood (Habitat) [2003/4 h74: 20s[pu] 16s 16d 16g[3] 24g Apr 1] strong gelding: poor hurdler: stays 2½m: acts on soft going: sometimes tongue tied: inconsistent. *D. J. Wintle*   **h72**

AY CARUMBA   7 b.g. Seymour Hicks (FR) – Aldington Peach (Creetown) [2003/4 F–: 19m[pu] 16g[pu] Nov 19] no sign of ability. *J. F. Panvert*   **h–**

AYE AYE POPEYE (IRE)   6 ch.g. Imperial Frontier (USA) – Boskovice (IRE) (Flash of Steel) [2003/4 h112: 16g* 17g 16d 16d 16d 16d[2] 16d Apr 13] compact gelding: fair hurdler: won novice at Punchestown very early in season: good second at Leopardstown in December: best at 2m: acts on heavy going: tried blinkered: none too consistent. *Mrs J. Harrington, Ireland*   **h114**

AYE SURELY (IRE)   10 b.g. Legal Circles (USA) – Uno Navarro (Raga Navarro
(ITY)) [2003/4 c101d, h89: 24m⁶ 26mᵖᵘ Oct 10] leggy gelding: modest hurdler/
chaser: stays 27f: acts on heavy going: usually blinkered when trained in Ireland.
Mrs A. M. Thorpe

**c–
h–**

AZERTYUIOP (FR)   7 b.g. Baby Turk – Temara (FR) (Rex Magna (FR)) [2003/4
c159p, h–: c17gᵘʳ c16d² c16g² c17g* c16g* Mar 17]

**c182
h–**

The big handicaps offer more potential than weight-for-age championship
events for finding out just how good the top horses are. Desert Orchid, for example,
earned his Timeform rating of 187 not on any of his appearances in the King George
VI Chase (which he won four times), nor in winning the Cheltenham Gold Cup, but
in the Racing Post Handicap at Kempton in February 1990 in which, under a
penalty and carrying 12-3, he won by eight lengths, putting up the finest performance seen over jumps since the halcyon days of Arkle, Flyingbolt and Mill House.
Arkle's performances conceding lumps of weight in handicaps such as the
Leopardstown Chase, the Hennessy and the Whitbread showed far better than his
level-weights Gold Cup-winning performances what he was capable of. Likewise,
Flyingbolt, whose career was dogged by illness and injury, showed when winning
the Massey Ferguson Gold Cup (under 12-6 by fifteen lengths) and the Irish Grand
National (carrying 12-7) that he was almost as good at his best as Arkle. An
objective study of the form-book put those two performances ahead of Flyingbolt's
form when running away with the Champion Two-Mile Chase at the Cheltenham
Festival in the same season (he was also third in the Champion Hurdle the day after
the Champion Chase).

Azertyuiop was the latest winner of the Queen Mother Champion Chase, as
the two-mile championship has come to be known. He won in the style of an
outstanding chaser, jumping well and drawing clear in tremendous fashion, but the
form he showed was 10 lb below his season's best. Azertyuiop's performance in the
Victor Chandler Chase at Ascot in January was the one that earned him his
Timeform rating of 182 and, as such, deserves pride of place in a review of his
campaign. Azertyuiop didn't win the Victor Chandler, the best two-mile handicap
of the season, but in going down by a neck to Isio, to whom he was conceding 19 lb,
he put up—by our reckoning at least—the equal best performance (with Carvill's
Hill's breathtaking display in the 1991 Welsh National) seen in a handicap over
jumps since Desert Orchid's in the Racing Post. Desert Orchid put up several other
really outstanding weight-carrying efforts in handicaps—including victories in the
Whitbread and the Irish Grand National—and he underlined his versatility by

*Queen Mother Memorial Fund Game Spirit Chase, Newbury—Azertyuiop has little trouble
landing the odds; stable-companion Armaturk is still a close second on sufferance three out*

continuing to give brilliant performances at two miles, at which distance he was regarded as a specialist for long enough. In the same season he completed the King George VI Chase/Gold Cup double, he also won the Tingle Creek (then a handicap) by twelve lengths, conceding between 20 lb and 28 lb to four rivals, and the inaugural running of the Victor Chandler, pushed to the limit by the very smart Panto Prince, who was in receipt of 22 lb. Desert Orchid prevailed by a head at Ascot in a driving finish after a tremendous duel with Panto Prince from the home turn, and the latest Victor Chandler also produced an epic.

With 7/2 favourite Azertyuiop carrying top weight of 11-10 at Ascot, only three of the thirteen runners—the others being the previous year's winner Young Devereaux (10-7) and Isio (10-5)—were set to run off their correct marks. Isio had finished third to Azertyuiop in the Arkle Trophy at Cheltenham the previous season and had a 19 lb pull for twelve lengths. Azertyuiop and Isio stretched clear of the Victor Chandler field in the home straight and, in a stirring duel, with very little in it from the second last, the pair produced good jumps at the final fence and answered their riders' every call on the flat. Azertyuiop nosed ahead briefly before just giving best in a pulsating finish, the first two nine lengths clear of third-placed Got One Too who had a further four to spare over fourth-placed Native Scout, an improving Irish handicapper who had finished a good second to Moscow Flyer in a Grade 2 event at Leopardstown on his most recent start. The in-form Hot Shots, 11 lb out of the weights, came fifth. Six of the Victor Chandler runners won next time out, including four of the first five home, and the form looked as solid by the end of the season as it did at the time. If there was another horse in training remotely capable of giving Isio a 19-lb beating over two miles, it could only have been Moscow Flyer. When Moscow Flyer and Isio met later in the season, however, it was at level weights in the Melling Chase over two and a half miles at Aintree where Moscow Flyer, with his ears pricked, beat Isio by six lengths. Immediately after the Victor Chandler, incidentally, Isio was quoted at only 14/1 for the Champion Chase in a market headed by defending champion Moscow Flyer and Azertyuiop.

There was so much discussion in the latest season of the pros and cons of running top-class horses under big weights in handicaps that it is worth recording the view of Azertyuiop's trainer after the Victor Chandler. 'Last year he had soft races and learned little, he was always winning on the bridle. He will have learned more from this than any other race he has had over fences.' The best performances in handicaps in the latest season, after Azertyuiop's, were recorded by Edredon Bleu at Wincanton and Exeter on his first two starts, Rhinestone Cowboy, third under top weight in the Coral Cup, Rooster Booster, a short head second under top

Queen Mother Champion Chase, Cheltenham—Azertyuiop confirms himself an outstanding chaser; runner-up Flagship Uberalles still has Tiutchev (left) and Venn Ottery to pass two out

weight in the Tote Gold Trophy, by Baracouda when conceding lumps of weight all round in the Sandown Hurdle and by Sir Rembrandt when runner-up to Bindaree in the Welsh Grand National. All were top-class efforts, each worth a rating of at least 166. Edredon Bleu subsequently won the King George VI Chase at Kempton, Rhinestone Cowboy went on to win both the Aintree Hurdle and the Champion Stayers' at Punchestown, while Rooster Booster was runner-up in the Champion Hurdle, the Aintree Hurdle and the Emo Oil Champion Hurdle at Punchestown. None of those performances, judged on the bare form, surpassed the handicap efforts of Edredon Bleu, Rhinestone Cowboy and Rooster Booster. Sir Rembrandt had to improve only a little on his Chepstow run to finish runner-up to Best Mate in the Cheltenham Gold Cup. Baracouda bettered his Sandown form when runner-up in the Stayers' Hurdle at Cheltenham, for which the winner Iris's Gift had also been warmed up under top weight in a handicap, carrying 11-12 into second in an eighteen-runner qualifier in the Pertemps Handicap series at Haydock.

Azertyuiop began his second season over fences as the biggest threat to Moscow Flyer's domination of the two-mile scene. Azertyuiop barely put a foot wrong as a novice and looked a magnificent prospect, one worthy of following in the tradition of good Arkle winners in recent times such as Waterloo Boy, Remittance Man, Klairon Davis, Flagship Uballes, Tiutchev and Moscow Flyer himself, all of whom had gone on to win championship events in open company. Azertyuiop's performance in the Arkle had been very similar in merit to Moscow Flyer's in the race the previous year and the first of their two meetings in the latest season, in the Tingle Creek at Sandown in December, was anticipated eagerly. Azertyuiop had lost his unblemished record over fences when slipping and unseating his rider at the first in the Haldon Gold Cup at Exeter and was said by his trainer to be '12 kilos heavy' at Sandown. It is very unusual for a runner from Nicholls' yard to want for fitness but, considering the lack of a satisfactory preparatory outing, it was to Azertyuiop's credit that he produced the level of performance that he did in going down to Moscow Flyer by four lengths in a vintage renewal of the Tingle Creek in which the winner had to better the form he showed when beating Native Upmanship and Cenkos by seven lengths and three in the previous season's Champion Chase. Flagship Uballes was seven lengths behind Azertyuiop in third at Sandown with Azertyuiop beating his own stable-companions Le Roi Miguel and Cenkos, back in fourth and fifth, by over ten lengths.

The second clash between Azertyuiop and Moscow Flyer in the Queen Mother Champion Chase promised to be one of the highlights—potentially *the* highlight—of the Festival meeting. Moscow Flyer was seen out only once between Sandown and Cheltenham—when landing the odds from Native Scout at Leopardstown at Christmas—while Azertyuiop followed up his Victor Chandler performance with a straightforward twelve-length victory from another stable-companion Armaturk in the Queen Mother Memorial Fund Game Spirit Chase at Newbury in February. Moscow Flyer started at 6/5-on at Cheltenham, with Azertyuiop at 15/8 and 14/1 bar in a thoroughly representative field of eight. The big clash failed to materialise, Moscow Flyer parting company with his rider four from home and leaving Azertyuiop to come home nine lengths ahead of the 2002 winner Flagship Uballes (beaten two lengths further than he had been at Sandown), with another ex-Arkle winner Tiutchev a length and a half further away in third and Cenkos, third in the two previous runnings, a creditable fourth. Azertyuiop's performance was one of the best in the race in recent times. He produced a breathtaking round of jumping, going on at the seventh of the twelve fences and quickening magnificently round the turn into the final straight before running on in fine style all the way to the line. It was a major anti-climax that Moscow Flyer failed to complete, leaving the question of which was the better of two outstanding two-mile chasers still unsettled, for the time being at least. If there is anything between Moscow Flyer and Azertyuiop, it surely cannot be much. Among Champion Chase winners of Timeform's experience, only two have earned higher ratings than Moscow Flyer and Azertyuiop. They are Flyingbolt and the 1965 winner the exhilarating Dunkirk who, in an all-too-short career, also carried 12-7 to victory in the Mackeson Gold Cup, then run over two miles and a few yards.

The tall, good-looking Azertyuiop often impresses in the paddock, though he spoiled his appearance by sweating at the start of the Queen Mother Champion

Mr J. Hales's "Azertyuiop"

	Baby Turk (b 1982)	Northern Baby (b 1976)	Northern Dancer / Two Rings
Azertyuiop (FR) (b.g. 1997)		Vieille Villa (b 1974)	Kashmir II / Vieille Demeure
	Temara (FR) (b 1985)	Rex Magna (br 1974)	Right Royal V / Chambre d'Amour
		Charabia (b 1976)	Bazin / Kachabia

Chase. His sire the now-deceased Baby Turk (also the sire of Armaturk) was a very smart performer at up to thirteen and a half furlongs, winner of the Grand Prix de Deauville at that trip, and has sired numerous good winners over jumps in France. Rex Magna, the sire of Azertyuiop's anglo-arab dam Temara, won the Prix Royal-Oak (French St Leger) so there is stamina on both sides of the pedigree. Temara herself won four times at around a mile and a quarter but her best offspring before Azertyuiop was Bipbap (by Dom Pasquini), the best French four-year-old chaser of 1998 who stayed well, his subsequent record including a good third in the Prix La Haye Jousselin over nearly three and a half miles. Judged from remarks made by his trainer, Azertyuiop seems unlikely to be tried again at much beyond two miles over fences. It is worth bearing in mind, however, that his consistent record over hurdles included a creditable fifth, showing smart form, over two and a half in the Aintree Hurdle. The reliable Azertyuiop acts on soft and good to firm going and was not discredited on his only outing on heavy. It bears repeating that he is a fine jumper of fences. *P. F. Nicholls*

AZZEMOUR (FR)   5 ch.g. Morespeed – Tarde (FR) (Kashtan (FR)) [2003/4 F18g⁴   F85 p
Apr 22] fifth foal: brother to outstanding French hurdler/winning chaser Le Sauvignon
and useful staying chaser Montifault: dam unraced: shaped well when 20½ lengths fourth
to Just Classic in bumper at Fontwell on debut, taking good hold in rear and keeping on
not knocked about: sure to improve. *P. F. Nicholls*

B

BABY GEE   10 ch.m. King Among Kings – Market Blues (Porto Bello) [2003/4 h86:   h92
16d³ 16g⁴ 20m⁶ 16g⁶ 21v⁵ 16g⁶ 16s⁶ 16g 18g Mar 28] small mare: modest handicap
hurdler: won at Perth in June and Catterick in January: stays 21f: unraced on firm going,
acts on any other: game and reliable. *D. W. Whillans*

BABY JANE   10 b.m. Old Vic – Sutosky (Great Nephew) [2003/4 20m⁶ 17d^pu 19f 16g⁶   h–
16d^pu Jan 13] sturdy, lengthy mare: third in juvenile hurdle in 1997/8: no form since, has
been to stud: tried in cheekpieces. *R. Johnson*

BABY RUN (FR)   4 b.g. Baby Turk – Run For Laborie (FR) (Lesotho (USA)) [2003/4   F105
F12g³ F13d* F12d² F16g⁵ Feb 14] 32,000 3-y-o: good-topped gelding: third foal:
half-brother to 9f winner Run For More (by Sanglamore): dam 9f winner: fairly useful
form in bumpers, winning at Exeter in December by 1½ lengths from Historic Place:
behind Secret Ploy next 2 starts, beaten ½ length at Cheltenham and 15 lengths when
fifth in Grade 2 at Newbury (hung badly right on bend after stands): front runner.
N. A. Twiston-Davies

BABY SISTER   5 ch.m. King Among Kings – Market Blues (Porto Bello) [2003/4   F87
F16g⁶ F16d² Feb 8] eighth foal: sister to several winners, including fairly useful hurdler
who stayed 2¾m Palacegate King: dam poor maiden: easily better effort in bumpers 7
months apart when ¾-length second to Young Scotton at Musselburgh. *D. W. Whillans*

BACARDI BOY (IRE)   8 b.g. Lord Americo – Little Welly (Little Buskins) [2003/4   c96
h99: c26v³ c26d³ c24s^ur c24g³ c24s⁵ c24d³ Mar 28] sturdy gelding: winning hurdler: h–
modest novice chaser: looked all over winner until losing action second start, folded
dramatically final one: will stay beyond 3¼m: acts on heavy going. *T. R. George*

BACCARAT (IRE)   10 b.g. Bob Back (USA) – Sarahlee (Sayyaf) [2003/4 c88x, h–:   c– x
c25d^pu Feb 15] strong, robust gelding: novice chaser, fair at best: sold out of T. Fitz-   h–
gerald's stable £2,600 Ascot November Sales: pulled up in point/hunter in 2004: stays
21f: acts on heavy going: tongue tied last 2 starts: often let down by jumping. *Lady Susan
Brooke*

BACHELORS PAD   10 b.g. Pursuit of Love – Note Book (Mummy's Pet) [2003/4   h67 §
h67: 16g 19m⁴ 17m³ 17m⁶ 16m⁴ 17m⁵ 16d³ 16s³ 16d^ur 16d 16s 21g Mar 17] lengthy,
angular gelding: poor hurdler: raced mainly around 2m: acts on heavy and good to firm
going: usually wears cheekpieces: lazy: sold £1,200 Ascot April Sales. *Miss S. J. Wilton*

BACHELOR'S TONIC (IRE)   6 b.g. Fayruz – Dance Alone (USA) (Monteverdi)   F–
[2003/4 F16m F16g⁶ F16d³ Nov 13] medium-sized gelding: no worthwhile form in
bumpers, sold out of C. Mann's stable 3,500 gns Doncaster August Sales after reappearance: wears crossed noseband. *K. A. Morgan*

BACKBEAT (IRE)   7 ch.g. Bob Back (USA) – Pinata (Deep Run) [2003/4 h99: c18g^pu   c–
Nov 30] sturdy gelding: modest hurdler: blinkered, jumped badly right in novice handi-   h–
cap on chasing debut, only outing in 2003/4: better around 2½m than shorter, and should
stay further: raced only on good/good to soft going: tends to sweat. *D. R. C. Elsworth*

BACKCRAFT (IRE)   6 b.g. Bob Back (USA) – Bawnanell (Viking (USA)) [2003/4   h115
h115: 17g⁵ 20m² 16m* 16g Jul 3] lengthy gelding: fair handicap hurdler: won easily at
Hexham in June: probably best up to 2½m: has won on heavy going, best form on good to
firm. *L. Lungo*

BACK IN FRONT (IRE)   7 br.g. Bob Back (USA) – Storm Front (IRE) (Strong   h152
Gale) [2003/4 h151p: 16g* 16d² 16m² 16d* 16d⁵ Dec 29] workmanlike gelding: smart
hurdler: won Evening Herald Champion Novices' Hurdle in April 2003 and second to
Quazar in another Grade 1 event 3 days later, both at Punchestown, and Grade 2 Mongey
Communications Morgiana Hurdle (rallied to beat Sacundai 1½ lengths) at same course

in November: bit below best when fifth of 7 to Golden Cross in Grade 1 at Leopardstown, and missed rest of season: has won at 2½m, raced mainly at 2m: acts on heavy going, bumper winner on good to firm. *E. J. O'Grady, Ireland*

BACK IN THE GAME 8 ch.g. Phountzi (USA) – Chasmarella (Yukon Eric (CAN))   **h–**
[2003/4 16g 20v^pu 24g Mar 10] first foal: dam won 2¾m hurdle: no sign of ability. *Miss Z. C. Davison*

BACK ON SONG (IRE) 5 b.m. Bob Back (USA) – No Blues (IRE) (Orchestra)   **h–**
[2003/4 F16g 19g^F 16s 20g Jan 23] €4,600 3-y-o: smallish, workmanlike mare: second   **F–**
foal: dam, maiden hurdler, half-sister to smart staying hurdler Trapper John: no form in bumper or novice hurdles. *J. Howard Johnson*

BACK ON TOP (IRE) 10 b.g. Bob Back (USA) – Top Girl (IRE) (High Top) [2003/4   **c133**
c131, h122: c25d* c22s⁴ 24s 25g c20g^pu c29d^pu Apr 12] good-topped gelding: fairly   **h121**
useful handicap hurdler/useful handicap chaser: won valuable event at Punchestown in May: pulled up in similar contests last 2 starts: should stay beyond 25f: acts on soft going: reportedly had respiratory infection third outing. *J. L. Hassett, Ireland*

BACKSCRATCHER 10 b.g. Backchat (USA) – Tiernee Quintana (Artaius (USA))   **c76 §**
[2003/4 h76: 24m⁴ 24m 24m³ c24g⁶ c20f^pu c24s* c26d c23g c25d⁶ c25d^F c24s^pu Mar 21]   **h70 §**
rather leggy gelding: poor maiden hurdler: form over fences only when winning novice handicap at Uttoxeter in December: stays 3m: acts on good to firm and soft going: tried blinkered: unreliable. *John R. Upson*

BACK TO BEN ALDER (IRE) 7 b. or br.g. Bob Back (USA) – Winter Fox (Martin-   **h113**
mas) [2003/4 F105: 16d* Mar 12] good sort: won bumper impressively on debut: reportedly injured next time: odds on, won novice at Sandown on hurdling debut year later by 1¼ lengths from Nyrche: again not fluent when only ninth of 19 in similar event at Punchestown in late-April. *N. J. Henderson*

BACYAN (IRE) 7 ch.g. Denel (FR) – Naycab (Le Moss) [2003/4 F17m* 24d⁵ 16d³   **h98**
25s² 25g* 24s^pu Feb 14] big gelding: second foal: dam, winning pointer, from family of   **F97**
high-class staying chaser Couldn't Be Better: successful in maiden point in 2003: won bumper at Carlisle in October: modest novice hurdler: won at Catterick in January by 25 lengths, disputing lead when left clear 2 out: suited by 3m+: acted on soft going (bumper win on good to firm): dead. *Mrs A. Hamilton*

BADEN VUGIE (IRE) 7 bl.g. Hamas (IRE) – Bag Lady (Be My Guest (USA))   **c–**
[2003/4 c–, h–: c16d^ur c24d^pu Mar 27] sturdy, lengthy gelding: of little account.   **h–**
S. T. Lewis

BADGER BEER 12 b.g. Town And Country – Panda Pops (Cornuto) [2003/4 c79:   **c92**
c25m² c25m^F Mar 11] workmanlike gelding: fair hunter chaser: stayed 25f: acted on firm and good to soft going: usually tongue tied: dead. *J. W. Dufosee*

BADGERS GLORY 8 b. or gr.g. Neltino – Shedid (St Columbus) [2003/4 c–, h–:   **c–**
c20g⁶ Apr 12] little sign of ability: tried blinkered. *G. P. Enright*   **h–**

BADRINATH (IRE) 10 b.g. Imperial Frontier (USA) – Badedra (Kings Lake (USA))   **h–**
[2003/4 16g^pu Dec 4] modest on Flat: no show in 2 starts over hurdles 3 years apart. *H. J. Collingridge*

BADWORTH GALE (IRE) 10 br.g. Strong Gale – Badsworth Madam (Over The   **c–**
River (FR)) [2003/4 c–: c25g^pu c21d^pu Apr 12] no form in steeplechases. *J. E. Dillon*

BAGANITE (AUS) 5 ch.g. Grand Lodge (USA) – Lady Triscanny (AUS) (Sir Tris-   **h–**
tram) [2003/4 F16v F16s 24g^pu Mar 6] compact gelding: no form in bumpers or novice   **F–**
hurdle. *Jonjo O'Neill*

BAHLINO (IRE) 4 gr.g. Bahhare (USA) – Azulino (IRE) (Bluebird (USA)) [2003/4   **h87**
16g³ 16g⁴ Mar 10] good-topped gelding: fairly useful on Flat (stays 1½m), sold out of W. Jarvis' stable 75,000 gns Newmarket Autumn Sales: faded when in frame in novice hurdles at Catterick, tongue tied second time. *J. Howard Johnson*

BAIE D'ALONG (FR) 5 b.m. Tel Quel (FR) – County Kerry (FR) (Comrade In   **F–**
Arms) [2003/4 F–: F17m^pu Jul 14] no sign of ability in 2 bumpers. *N. J. Hawke*

BAIE DES SINGES 10 b.g. Royal Vulcan – Mikey's Monkey (Monksfield) [2003/4   **c– x**
c17d⁴ c20s⁴ c19s^F c16g c17d⁴ Mar 27] workmanlike gelding: maiden jumper, no form   **h–**
since chasing debut in 2000/1: tried blinkered: sketchy jumper. *M. J. M. Evans*

BAIKALINE (FR) 5 b.m. Cadoudal (FR) – Advantage (FR) (Antheus (USA)) [2003/4 **c–**
16v[6] Jan 10] ex-French mare: third foal: half-sister to 3 winners, including fair hurdler **h–**
around 2m Bolchoi Star (by Baryshnikov): dam, winning 2m hurdler, half-sister to useful
chaser up to 2¾m Applescott: third over 11f on first of 3 starts on Flat: fair maiden
hurdler: pulled up on steeplechase debut: left B. Barbier, well held only start in 2003/4:
raced mainly around 2m: acts on heavy ground. *Ian Williams*

BAILEY CONTRACT 6 b.m. Contract Law (USA) – Megabucks (Buckskin (FR)) **h–**
[2003/4 F17v 17d[ur] Apr 18] second foal: half-sister to fair hurdler Turrill House (by **F–**
Charmer), stays 21f: dam, fairly useful 2m hurdler, sister to dam of smart hurdler Georges
Girl: tailed off in bumper: jumped poorly on hurdling debut. *A. C. Whillans*

BAILEY'S BRO (IRE) 7 br.g. Castle Keep – Boreen Bro (Boreen (FR)) [2003/4 **h–**
h–, F–: 22s[pu] Dec 30] close-coupled gelding: no form in bumper or 2 maiden hurdles.
M. Bradstock

BAILEYS PRIZE (USA) 7 ch.g. Mister Baileys – Mar Mar (USA) (Forever Casting **c–**
(USA)) [2003/4 h91§: c19d 19g 17s 17g Apr 13] medium-sized gelding: maiden hurdler, **h82 §**
modest at best: tailed off on chasing debut: left C. Gray after third outing: stays 19f: acts
on soft going: tried blinkered/visored: ungenuine. *B. J. Llewellyn*

BAILY MIST (IRE) 7 b.m. Zaffaran (USA) – Mixed Blends (The Parson) [2003/4 **c111**
24d 22d[6] 20d 16d 20s* 20s[4] 24s[4] 20d 20s* 20d c20d[ur] c22s* 20d Apr 11] 70,000 4-y-o: **h108**
fifth foal (all by Zaffaran): dam, useful hurdler/chaser who stayed 2½m, half-sister to
dual Whitbread Gold Cup winner Topsham Bay: fair hurdler: won mares races at Punchestown (intermediate) in December and Limerick (minor event) in February: successful
in Grade 3 mares novice at latter course in March on completed start over fences:
effective at 2m to 3m: acts on heavy: tried in cheekpieces. *M. F. Morris, Ireland*

BAJAN GIRL (FR) 4 b.f. Emperor Jones (USA) – Lovely Noor (USA) (Fappiano **F83**
(USA)) [2003/4 F12g F14g[3] F12m Dec 10] leggy, unfurnished filly: eighth foal: half-
sister to several winners, notably one-time very smart chaser Wahiba Sands (by Pharly),
stays 21f, and fairly useful hurdler around 2m Medaille Militaire (by Highest Honor):
dam, won around 1m in USA, out of half-sister to 1980 St Leger winner Light Cavalry
and 1981 1000 Guineas winner Fairy Footsteps: easily best effort in 3-y-o bumpers
(folded very tamely on debut) when third to Ambition Royal at Warwick: visored final
outing. *M. C. Pipe*

BAKERS DOZEN 4 ch.g. Whittingham (IRE) – Blue Empress (Blue Cashmere) **h–**
[2003/4 17m Nov 20] half-brother to fair hurdler Wortley Boy (by Zambrano), stays
2¾m: well held in 2 maidens in 2003 for P. D. Evans: showed nothing on hurdling debut.
T. R. George

BAKIRI (IRE) 6 b.g. Doyoun – Bakiya (USA) (Trempolino (USA)) [2003/4 h–: 22m[5] **h84**
20d 16d 20s 19m* 19g[2] Mar 15] tall gelding: poor hurdler: won selling handicap at
Taunton in March: stays easy 2¾m: best form on good/good to firm going: tried tongue
tied: claimed to join A. Reid £5,000 final start. *R. T. Phillips*

BAK ON BOARD 8 b.g. Sula Bula – Kirstins Pride (Silly Prices) [2003/4 c–, h–: **c–**
c26s[5] Apr 29] workmanlike gelding: little form over hurdles: winning pointer, including **h–**
in 2004: well beaten in novice hunter on steeplechase debut. *Miss L. Gardner*

BAK TO BILL 9 b.g. Nicholas Bill – Kirstins Pride (Silly Prices) [2003/4 h114: 22s[4] **c106**
c23m[ur] 22g[5] c24g[ur] c23g[2] c24s[2] c23g c23s[2] c19s[4] c24g[3] c23d[ur] c24g[2] Apr 18] lengthy **h114**
gelding: fair hurdler/novice chaser: stays 3m: acts on any going: wore cheekpieces last 2
starts: usually ridden by Miss L. Gardner: consistent. *Mrs S. Gardner*

BALAKAR (IRE) 8 b.g. Doyoun – Balaniya (USA) (Diesis) [2003/4 h92: 17g[3] May **h91**
24] leggy gelding: modest hurdler: raced mainly around 2m: acts on soft and good to firm
going: tried tongue tied, including last 2 starts. *M. F. Harris*

BALAPOUR (IRE) 6 b.g. Kahyasi – Balaniya (USA) (Diesis) [2003/4 h127§: 16d **h131**
19s[6] 16s[ur] 16s 16g[4] 17d[4] 16d[4] Apr 12] smallish gelding: useful hurdler: ran well in
County Hurdle (Handicap) at Cheltenham for second successive year when fourth to
Sporazene sixth outing: seems suited by well-run 2m: acts on firm and soft going
(possibly not on heavy): usually tongue tied: difficult to win with. *Patrick O. Brady,
Ireland*

BAL DE NUIT (FR) 5 gr.g. Balleroy (USA) – Eoline (FR) (In Fijar (USA)) [2003/4 **c130**
c117+, h128: c20s[2] c18d* c16g* c16v[3] Jan 24] tall, leggy gelding: has plenty of scope: **h–**
fairly useful form when winning both completed starts over hurdles in Britain: useful
novice chaser: won at Newbury in December and Ascot (3-runner Grade 2, beat Non So

*Victor Chandler Get More Back Lightning Novices' Chase, Ascot—
the grey Bal de Nuit leads Mercato and Non So early on in a weak renewal of this Grade 2 event*

14 lengths) in January: only third of 4 to Kalca Mome at Haydock: best around 2m: acts on good to firm and heavy going. *P. F. Nicholls*

BALINAHINCH CASTLE (IRE)   7 b.g. Good Thyne (USA) – Emerald Flair (Flair Path) [2003/4 h108: 24g^{pu} Sep 24] useful-looking gelding: chasing type: runner-up in maiden point on debut: fair form when winning 2 novice hurdles for J. O'Neill in 2002/3: no form since. *Mrs L. B. Normile*   **h–**

BALISTEROS (FR)   15 b.g. Bad Conduct (USA) – Oldburry (FR) (Fin Bon) [2003/4 c100, h–: c25d^2 c24g* 24g^6 Jun 6] workmanlike gelding: prolific winning pointer, successful in February (twice) and April: first win in hunters since 2000 at Stratford in May: well beaten in handicap hurdle 6 days later: stays 3½m: acts on heavy and good to firm going: ran badly only start in visor: not a straightforward ride. *Mrs B. K. Thomson*   **c100 h–**

BALKIRK   7 ch.g. Selkirk (USA) – Balenare (Pharly (FR)) [2003/4 h79: 16m^{pu} 22g^{pu} 19m^3 17v 19g Dec 18] angular gelding: maiden hurdler: no form in 2003/4: tried blinkered/in cheekpieces: tongue tied after second start. *Mrs H. M. Bridges*   **h–**

BALLA D'AIRE (IRE)   9 b. or br.g. Balla Cove – Silius (Junius (USA)) [2003/4 c–, h–: 16d^6 c21d^2 c23f* c24g^4 Feb 20] leggy gelding: maiden hurdler: poor chaser: won very weak maiden at Leicester in December: stays easy 23f: acts on firm and good to soft going: tried blinkered. *K. F. Clutterbuck*   **c73 h–**

BALLADEER (IRE)   6 b.g. King's Theatre (IRE) – Carousel Music (On Your Mark) [2003/4 h114: 20m^2 22f* 21m^4 21m* 21g 24d^{pu} 24s Apr 17] close-coupled gelding: fair hurdler: won novices at Wincanton in October and Ludlow in November: should stay 3m: acts on firm and soft going: usually races prominently. *Miss H. C. Knight*   **h105**

BALLAD MINSTREL (IRE)   12 gr.g. Ballad Rock – Sashi Woo (Rusticaro (FR))   c–
[2003/4 c–, h–: c21s^{pu} c20d^{pu} Mar 25] tall, good-topped gelding: one-time fairly useful   h–
hurdler/chaser: has deteriorated considerably, though placed first 2 starts in points in
2004: successful with/without blinkers. *Miss J. E. Foster*

BALLARDS BOY (FR)   5 b.g. Sleeping Car (FR) – Anita (FR) (Olmeto) [2003/4 F :   h
16m May 10] well held in bumper and novice hurdle. *N. J. Pomfret*

BALLET-K   10 ch.m. Gunner B – Nicolene (Nice Music) [2003/4 c21g^{pu} c22v^6 c25d*   c97
Jan 1] strong, lengthy mare: one-time useful hurdler: missed 2002/3: best effort in novice   h–
chases when winning at Exeter in 2004: stays 25f: acts on heavy and good to firm going.
C. Roberts

BALL GAMES   6 b.g. Mind Games – Deb's Ball (Glenstal (USA)) [2003/4 h74: 16g   h75 §
17d 17g^4 16m^2 16g^{pu} Dec 3] close-coupled gelding: poor maiden hurdler: raced around
2m: often visored, wore cheekpieces final start: moody. *James Moffatt*

BALLINCLAY KING (IRE)   10 b.g. Asir – Clonroche Artic (Pauper) [2003/4   c135 §
c148, h–: c24d^{pu} c25d^3 c20s c21d^6 c21d c24s^{pu} c32g^{pu} Mar 28] tall, rather leggy gelding: h–
winning hurdler: useful handicap chaser, largely out of sorts in 2003/4: stays 25f: acts on
heavy going: tried in cheekpieces: has broken blood vessels, including final outing: has
been reluctant to race: one to leave alone. *Ferdy Murphy*

BALLINURE BOY (IRE)   11 b.g. Meneval (USA) – Sweet Cahore (General Iron-   c84
side) [2003/4 c101: c23g^4 Mar 12] fairly useful pointer, successful in February: won on
hunter chase debut in 2002, failed to see race out when fourth of 6 at Leicester in March:
should stay beyond 21f. *Mrs S. J. Hickman*

BALLISTIC BOY   7 ch.g. First Trump – Be Discreet (Junius (USA)) [2003/4 22g   h–
22d^{pu} Apr 5] good-topped gelding: fair hurdler in 2001/2 for J. O'Neill: showed nothing
on return. *R. W. Thomson*

BALLOFASOP (IRE)   7 b.g. Shalford (IRE) – Sosalolomome (IRE) (Salse (USA))   h–
[2003/4 F16m F18s 21v^{pu} 21s^{pu} 22d Feb 12] stocky gelding: second foal: dam unraced,   F–
out of sister to top-class hurdler up to 25f French Holly and half-sister to top-class staying
hurdler Deano's Beeno: no sign of ability: tried in blinkers/cheekpieces: has had tongue
tied. *A. J. Whiting*

BALLYAAHBUTT (IRE)   5 b.g. Good Thyne (USA) – Lady Henbit (IRE) (Henbit   F–
(USA)) [2003/4 F16g F16s Jan 6] €26,000 4-y-o: useful-looking gelding: fourth foal:
dam unraced, from family of top-class staying chaser The Dikler: well held in 2 bumpers.
B. G. Powell

BALLYADAM (IRE)   6 b.g. Eve's Error – Rugged View (Rugged Man) [2003/4   F–
F16g Mar 6] €9,000 4-y-o: medium-sized gelding: second known foal: half-brother to
2½m bumper winner Ruff Justice (by Cashel Court): dam lightly raced in bumpers/
points: no form in maiden Irish points and bumper at Newbury. *G. B. Balding*

BALLYALBANY (IRE)   6 b.g. Lord Americo – Raisin Turf (IRE) (Phardante (FR))   h–
[2003/4 F17d^3 F16g F16g 20s Mar 13] IR 15,000 3-y-o: sturdy gelding: second foal: dam,   F84
maiden hurdler who stayed 2¾m, half-sister to useful hurdler/chaser up to 2½m Around
The Horn: regressed after third in bumper at Hereford on debut. *Mrs Susan Nock*

BALLYAMBER (IRE)   9 b.g. Glacial Storm (USA) – El Scarsdale (Furry Glen)   c133
[2003/4 c123, h–: c20d^3 c25d^4 c21s^3 c17d^6 c18d^5 c16s* c17s* c17d^F Apr 11] tall, good   h–
sort: useful chaser: successful in maiden and novice at Punchestown and novice at Navan (beat
Direct Bearing 1½ lengths) in March, and novice at Punchestown (by 20 lengths from
John James) in late-April: effective at 2m to 3m: acts on heavy going, won bumper on
good to firm. *W. P. Mullins, Ireland*

BALLYARDS (IRE)   6 gr.g. Roselier (FR) – Another Partner (Le Bavard (FR))   h–
[2003/4 19g^F 20d 22d 25d^{pu} Mar 22] sturdy gelding: sixth foal: half-brother to 3 winners,
including fairly useful hurdler Will of The People (by Supreme Leader), stays 3m: dam
placed in points: placed in maiden Irish points in 2003: bought 10,000 gns Doncaster May
Sales: signs of only a little ability in 4 novice hurdles: sold 2,500 gns Doncaster May
Sales. *Mrs S. J. Smith*

BALLYBOUGH RASHER (IRE)   9 b.g. Broken Hearted – Chat Her Up (Proverb)   c148 x
[2003/4 c131x, h–: 24m^2 c25m* Nov 1] sturdy gelding: lightly-raced hurdler, best effort   h116
when second to Battle Warning in handicap at Aintree on reappearance: smart chaser:
much improved when 40/1-winner of bet365 Charlie Hall Chase at Wetherby, travelling

bet365 Charlie Hall Chase, Wetherby—
40/1-shot Ballybough Rasher lowers the colours of 2002 winner Marlborough

well held up and leading last, drifting left but beating Marlborough 6 lengths: reported in February to miss remainder of season: effective at 2½m to 4m: acts on soft and good to firm ground: often let down by jumping over fences. *J. Howard Johnson*

BALLYBROPHY (IRE) 9 gr.g. Roselier (FR) – Bavardmore (Le Bavard (FR)) **c124**
[2003/4 c111p, h–: c25d* c28s^pu c24d^pu c24s* c24s c32g^F c33d Apr 17] workmanlike **h–**
gelding: fairly useful handicap chaser: won at Aintree (completed hat-trick) in May and Chepstow in January, showing plenty of resolution after making lot of running when beating Toulouse-Lautrec 6 lengths at latter: stays 29f: acts on heavy going: wore headgear last 5 outings: usually sound jumper. *S. E. H. Sherwood*

BALLYCASSIDY (IRE) 8 br.g. Insan (USA) – Bitofabreeze (IRE) (Callernish) **c140**
[2003/4 c120, h–: c21g* c24m* c20m* c22s c22m* c19m³ c25g* c24g* c24m* **h–**
c24g² c25s^pu Feb 7]
 As the popularity of summer jumping in Britain increases so does the quality of the horses on show at this time of the year—Strong Flow, Therealbandit, Jurancon II and Rigmarole, all of whom developed into smart-or-better performers, were among those winning races in front of large and enthusiastic crowds—and with some very good prize money on offer this trend looks sure to continue. The most valuable event in the summer jumping calendar in Britain, the Tote Scoop6 Summer Plate run at Market Rasen in July, was worth £70,000, with over £40,000 going to the winner. No surprise, then, that this two-and-a-half-mile handicap chase should attract a cracking field of in-form horses, with eight of the fifteen entries successful on their previous starts. This group included Chicuelo, winner of the race twelve months earlier, and a couple of novice chasers in Ballycassidy and Duke of Buckingham, and it was the two novices, both in their second season over fences, who shared favouritism at 11/2 in what looked a very open race. While Chicuelo and Duke of Buckingham failed to run up to their best, Ballycassidy, with wins under his belt at Newton Abbot and Stratford on his first two starts of the

94

season, showed further improvement to complete his hat-trick in good style, soon well in command after being sent on three out and winning with something to spare by six lengths from Ei Ei. The race will provide happy memories for Barry Geraghty, who was partnering Ballycassidy for the first time, but not for Richard Johnson. Johnson, on board Ballycassidy at both Newton Abbot and Stratford, was claimed to ride another prolific novice Brother Joe who fell at the eleventh. Ballycassidy and Johnson were reunited successfully at Market Rasen two months later, and the partnership went on to gain three more victories in novice company before the end of the year, one at Aintree, where he was the only finisher, and two at Newbury. The first of those Newbury victories came in a Grade 2 contest, the Worcester Novices' Chase, in which Ballycassidy showed great determination to hold off the favourite Native Emperor by a head. On his last two starts of the season, Ballycassidy ran close to his best, despite a marked tendency to jump left, when second to Strong Flow in the Grade 1 Feltham Novices' Chase at Kempton, but was then pulled up at Wetherby where he found the soft ground against him, as he had when bidding to follow up his Summer Plate win in Ireland's top summer jumps race, the Galway Plate. Not seen out after February, Ballycassidy has shown his form on good to soft going, but has put up his best performances on good and good to firm.

		Insan (USA) (b 1985)	Our Native (b 1970)	Exclusive Native
Ballycassidy (IRE) (br.g. 1996)				Our Jackie
			Artania (gr 1979)	Ruritania
				Arctic Actress
	Bitofabreeze (IRE) (br 1990)		Callernish (br 1977)	Lord Gayle
				Azurine
			Chake-Chake (b or br 1980)	Goldhill
				Cottstown Breeze

Ballycassidy earned around £120,000 in win and place prize money in the latest season, an excellent return for a horse who cost present connections 24,000

stanjamesuk.com Worcester Novices' Chase, Newbury—
much closer this time as Ballycassidy holds off Native Emperor for the sixth of his seven wins in 2003/4

guineas at the Doncaster May Sales. The winner of a point in Ireland in 2000, Ballycassidy then had had three seasons with Alan King for whom he showed fairly useful form over hurdles, winning four times. He did look a difficult ride—and very much a stayer—at that time, needing plenty of driving, but it has to be said that he has raced with plenty of zest since. Ballycassidy is the second foal of Bitofabreeze, a mare who didn't start racing until after his birth. A modest performer at up to three miles over hurdles, Bitofabreeze gained her sole win in a seventeen-furlong mares' maiden at Tralee. Her dam Chake-Chake, who won twice over hurdles, is a half-sister to the Hennessy Cognac Gold Cup winner Cogent and the very useful staying chaser Another Breeze. Ballycassidy, who was tried in blinkers on his final start over fences in the 2002/3 season, is effective from two and a half miles to twenty-seven furlongs. *P. Bowen*

BALLYCONNELL (IRE) 8 b.g. Insan (USA) – Stormy Skies (Strong Gale) **c121**
[2003/4 20f² c22s² c23g² c20f* c24g^pu c25g⁴ c21d* c24g Mar 16] lengthy, useful-looking **h92**
ex-Irish gelding: first foal: half-brother to winning hurdler/very progressive chaser Strong Flow (by Over The River), stays 3¼m: dam, maiden jumper, half-sister to useful staying chaser Plenty Crack: runner-up only run over hurdles: fairly useful chaser, sold out of D. Weld's stable 21,000 gns Doncaster October Sales after fifth start: first past post in maidens at Tipperary (demoted) and Tralee in August and novice handicap at Cheltenham (only runner not involved in melee 4 out) in January: stays 3m: acts on firm and soft going: sound jumper: has shown signs of temperament. *Miss Venetia Williams*

BALLYCREEN EUPHONY (IRE) 7 b.g. Nearly A Nose (USA) – My Faery Fey **h–**
VII (Damsire Unregistered) [2003/4 17s Apr 6] first foal: dam never ran: no show in novice hurdle on debut. *J. C. Tuck*

BALLYDAVID (IRE) 12 b.g. Lord Americo – Arctic Bavard (Le Bavard (FR)) **c–**
[2003/4 c–, h60: 20m^F May 7] poor maiden hurdler/chaser, very lightly raced since **h–**
1998/9: stayed 21f: acted on good to firm going: tried tongue tied: dead. *G. B. Balding*

96

BALLY GOOD   6 b.g. Alderbrook – Another Debt (Pitpan) [2003/4 F18s aF16g^pu Dec 13] first foal: dam tailed off in 2 bumpers: showed nothing in 2 bumpers. *B. G. Powell* **F–**

BALLYHAND   7 b.g. Nearly A Hand – Ballynora (Ballacashtal (CAN)) [2003/4 F17d F17m^6 Jul 14] sold out of R. Alner's stable £2,700 Ascot June (2002) Sales: first sign of ability in bumpers when sixth at Newton Abbot, racing prominently in steadily-run race. *W. J. Reed* **F76 ?**

BALLYHANNON (IRE)   15 b.g. Strong Gale – Chestnut Fire (Deep Run) [2003/4 c34v^pu May 21] of little account. *Miss J. Froggatt* **c–**
h–

BALLYKETTRAIL (IRE)   8 b.g. Catrail (USA) – Ballykett Lady (USA) (Sir Ivor (USA)) [2003/4 h118: 20d^F 20m^6 20d^pu Apr 22] well-made gelding: will make a chaser: fairly useful hurdler: no form in 3 handicaps in 2003/4: stays 2½m: raced mainly on good going or softer: tried blinkered/in cheekpieces: has had tongue tied. *Jonjo O'Neill* **h–**

BALLY LIRA   12 b.m. Lir – Ballyorney Girl (New Member) [2003/4 c120§, h–§: c32g c25s^pu c24s c26v c26g^3 Mar 10] lengthy, sparely-made mare: handicap chaser: no form in 2003/4: visored once, also tried in cheekpieces: has been ridden in spurs: thoroughly ungenuine. *P. R. Rodford* **c– §**
h– §

BALLY LIR LADY   10 b.m. Lir – Ballyorney Girl (New Member) [2003/4 17g 22g^4 22g^5 20m Aug 2] leggy mare: poor maiden hurdler: likely to stay 3m: acts on good to firm and good to soft going. *S. C. Burrough* **c–**
h66

BALLYLUSKY (IRE)   7 b.g. Lord Americo – Blackbushe Place (IRE) (Buckskin (FR)) [2003/4 c96p, h119: c25d* c24d^F c24d^4 23v* 22s Feb 7] medium-sized, well-made gelding: won novice handicap at Aintree in November on first start over fences for current stable: let down by jumping next 2 outings, also hung right on second occasion: useful handicap hurdler: better than ever when winning at Haydock in January by 19 lengths from His Nibs: lacklustre effort in Grade 3 event at Sandown following month: effective at 2½m to 25f: acts on good to firm and heavy ground: usually front runner over hurdles (held up over fences in 2003/4). *Jonjo O'Neill* **c107 +**
h130

BALLYMENAGH (IRE)   12 br.g. Buckskin (FR) – Breeze Dancer (Torus) [2003/4 c25g^ur Mar 28] good-bodied gelding: maiden hurdler/chaser: winning pointer: stays 25f: acts on good to firm going: not a fluent jumper. *K. E. Robson* **c–**
h–

Timeform Novices' Handicap Chase, Cheltenham—
ex-Irish Ballyconnell (checks) makes the running on his way to winning an eventful race

BALLYNATTIN BLUE (IRE)   11 ch.g. Good Thyne (USA) – Ballynattin Moss (Le   h–
Moss) [2003/4 h102: 20m⁵ 21vᵖᵘ Jan 13] tall gelding: fair handicap hurdler: no show
either start in 2003/4 (reluctant to line up on reappearance): best at 3m+: acts on heavy
going. *J. N. R. Billinge*

BALLYROBERT (IRE)   7 b. or br.g. Bob's Return (IRE) – Line Abreast (High Line)   c103
[2003/4 c80, h82: c16g* c18g* c16g* c21dᶠ c18g⁵ c18gᵘʳ Mar 27] good-bodied gelding: h–
fair chaser: won maiden at Towcester and novice handicap at Newbury in November and
handicap at Ascot in December: jumped poorly last 3 starts: should stay beyond 2¼m:
raced on good going or softer. *N. A. Gaselee*

BALLY'S BAK   6 ch.m. Bob Back (USA) – Whatagale (Strong Gale) [2003/4 h–, F81:   h85
17gᵘʳ 20g³ 24d³ 25s 22vᶠ 24gᵖᵘ 24v 20d Apr 18] sturdy mare: modest maiden hurdler:
stays 3m: acts on heavy going. *Mrs S. J. Smith*

BALLYSTONE (IRE)   11 ch.g. Roselier (FR) – Gusserane Princess (Paddy's Stream)   c115
[2003/4 c120, h115: c30g⁵ c25gᵘʳ 24g⁵ 25g c20d³ c24g⁴ Apr 10] well-made gelding: h104
fairly useful handicap hurdler/chaser: best effort in 2003/4 when fourth to Robbo over
fences at Carlisle: best at 3m+: acts on heavy and good to firm going: visored once,
effective in cheekpieces or not. *L. Lungo*

BALLYVADDY (IRE)   8 gr.g. Roselier (FR) – Bodalmore Kit (Bargello) [2003/4 c–,   c94 p
h110: c24m* 21m* 24g² c23dᵖ Apr 21] sturdy gelding: fairly useful handicap hurdler: h125
much improved, winning at Kempton (second win in race) in October by 1½ lengths
from Supreme Arrow: successful both starts over fences in 2003/4, in novice handicaps
at Ludlow in May and Worcester in April: stays 25f: acts on good to firm and heavy
going: tried visored/in cheekpieces: usually held up: open to further improvement over
fences. *G. B. Balding*

BALLYWALTER (IRE)   8 ch.g. Commanche Run – Call Me Honey (Le Bavard (FR))   c–
[2003/4 h71, F72: c22g c19fᵖᵘ Oct 16] lengthy gelding: winning pointer: poor maiden   h–
hurdler: lame final outing: stays 25f: acts on good to firm ground. *N. A. Gaselee*

BALMORAL QUEEN   4 br.f. Wizard King – Balmoral Princess (Thethingaboutitis   h–
(USA)) [2003/4 F14g 17s 17d 17dᶠ 16sᵖᵘ Apr 11] stocky filly: first foal: dam poor selling   F–
hurdler who stayed 21f: little sign of ability. *D. McCain*

BALOO   8 b.g. Morpeth – Moorland Nell (Neltino) [2003/4 h92: 22g² 27g* 24m⁵   c86
c24m² c24g² c24d³ c22g³ Dec 9] small gelding: fair handicap hurdler: won at Newton   h105
Abbot in June: modest form over fences: stays 27f: best form on good going: effective
tongue tied. *J. D. Frost*

BAMBI DE L'ORME (FR)   5 gr.g. True Brave (USA) – Princesse Ira (FR) (Less Ice)   c116
[2003/4 17s* c17s⁶ c17d³ 17s⁴ c17s² c16d* c16gᶠ³ c19g² Apr 3] tall ex-French gelding: h122
second foal: dam, maiden, sister to fairly useful French hurdler Bambi Less: successful 3
times over hurdles in Provinces, including at Nantes in May: fairly useful novice chaser:
left G. Chaignon, easily won maiden at Newcastle on British debut in February: upsides
Ladalko when falling 2 out (remounted) in 3-runner race at Huntingdon next time: stays
19f: raced on good ground or softer: free-going sort, usually waited with. *Ian Williams*

BANANA RIDGE   6 ch.m. Primitive Rising (USA) – Madison Girl (Last Fandango)   F83
[2003/4 F17m⁴ Jun 21] 1,500 3-y-o: fourth foal: half-sister to 2 winners on Flat, including
useful 6f/7f performer Madly Sharp (by Sharpo): dam winning hurdler, stayed 2½m: won
2½m maiden on completed start in points in 2003: fourth to La Luna in bumper at Market
Rasen. *T. D. Walford*

BANASAN (IRE)   6 b.g. Marju (IRE) – Banaja (IRE) (Sadler's Wells (USA)) [2003/4   c125
h117: 16gᵘʳ 20d³ 16g² 20g* c22s* c17g* c19sᶠ Sep 21] leggy gelding: fairly useful   h120
hurdler: won minor event at Bellewstown in July: successful at Galway first 2 outings
over fences, in maiden later in July and novice (beat Emperors Guest ½ length) in
September: running best race when falling last, though held in third at time, in handicap
won by Broadstone Road at Listowel: effective at 2m to 2¾m: acts on firm and soft going:
blinkered once. *M. J. P. O'Brien, Ireland*

BANDIT BROWN (IRE)   8 b.g. Supreme Leader – Parkroe Lady (IRE) (Deep Run)   c93
[2003/4 c22s² Mar 24] poor form over hurdles in 2001/2: second of 4 finishers in maiden   h–
chase at Towcester on return: stays 2¾m. *P. Winkworth*

BAN DUBH   5 b.m. Syrtos – Hatherley (Deep Run) [2003/4 F16g F17d Mar 27] fifth   F–
foal: half-sister to 4 winners, including winning 21f hurdler Mrs Duf (by Teenoso) and
bumper winner Squire Shandy (by Afzal): dam, poor novice hurdler, stayed 19f: signs of
only a little ability in 2 bumpers. *J. Rudge*

BANGOR ERRIS (IRE) 11 ch.g. Executive Perk – Dawn Infidel (IRE) (Fidel) c–
[2003/4 22gᵖᵘ Jul 31] lengthy gelding: poor handicap chaser in 2001/2: no show in novice h–
hurdle on return: tried visored. *A. J. Chamberlain*

BANJO HILL 10 b.g. Arctic Lord – Just Hannah (Macmillion) [2003/4 c110, h92: c112
c23g* c20m⁶ c24g⁶ c20g⁵ c26g⁴ c23sᵖᵘ Apr 6] lengthy, good-bodied gelding: fair handi- h–
cap chaser: won at Exeter very early in season: stays 23f: acts on firm and good to soft
going: game. *Miss E. C. Lavelle*

BANKER COUNT 12 b.g. Lord Bud – Gilzie Bank (New Brig) [2003/4 c20sᵖᵘ c24s c128
c24dᵖᵘ c24gᶠ c20g² Apr 18] big gelding: smart handicap chaser in 2001/2, no more than h–
fairly useful in 2003/4: stays 25f, at least as effective around 2½m: acts on good to firm
and heavy going: held up: has found little. *Miss Venetia Williams*

BANKERSDRAFT 9 ch.g. Mazaad – Overdraft (Bustino) [2003/4 c64, h–: c24m⁶ c–
May 5] compact gelding: little form in steeplechases: has worn tongue strap/cheekpieces: h–
sold 1,000 gns Doncaster May Sales, poor form in points in 2004. *R. C. Guest*

BANNERET (USA) 11 b.g. Imperial Falcon (CAN) – Dashing Partner (Formidable c§§
(USA)) [2003/4 c§§, h§§: c20mᴿ 17dʳʳ Dec 2] smallish gelding: maiden hurdler: yet to h§§
complete in points/hunter chases: left F. Matthews after reappearance: tried blinkered/
visored: has had tongue tied: thoroughly ungenuine. *K. G. Wingrove*

BANNINGHAM BLAZE 4 b.f. Averti (IRE) – Ma Pavlova (USA) (Irish River (FR)) h80
[2003/4 16g⁴ 16m² 16f² 16f³ 16gᵖᵘ 16sᵖᵘ 16g⁶ 19g⁵ 16g² 20dᵖᵘ Apr 12] compact filly:
half-sister to one-time useful hurdler L'Opera (by Old Vic), stays 2½m: fair on Flat (stays
1½m): poor juvenile hurdler: barely stays 19f: acts on firm going, poor efforts on softer
than good: blinkered final start. *C. R. Dore*

BANSHA BRU (IRE) 4 b.g. Fumo di Londra (IRE) – Pride of Duneane (IRE) (Anita's h–
Prince) [2003/4 F17s 16d Mar 12] unfurnished gelding: first foal: dam never ran: tailed F–
off in bumper and novice hurdle: pulls hard: third on Flat in April. *Miss E. C. Lavelle*

BARABBAS (USA) 5 b.g. Royal Academy (USA) – Kamsi (USA) (Afleet (CAN)) F84
[2003/4 F16f² F16m Feb 21] compact gelding: third foal: dam, French 9f winner,
half-sister to US Grade 1 1¼m winner Vaudeville: second of 5 in bumper at Wincanton
on debut: well held in similar event three months later. *R. F. Johnson Houghton*

BARACOUDA (FR) 9 b.g. Alesso (USA) – Peche Aubar (FR) (Zino) [2003/4 h171
h175: 24d* 25d* 22s* 24g² Mar 18]

A lasting image from the Cheltenham Festival was the sight of an emotional
Francois Doumen, tears in his eyes, pulling at Baracouda's tail in the unsaddling
enclosure after the gelding's failed bid to land a third Stayers' Hurdle. Defeat for
Baracouda was not something with which his connections were used to having to
come to terms, and it says much for his outstanding record in the top staying hurdles
over the last four seasons that this rare reverse should have had such an effect on
his trainer. Since going down to another outstanding French-trained hurdler Le
Sauvignon at Auteuil in the autumn of 2000, Baracouda had been beaten only once
in fifteen starts and three and a half years of competition at the top level prior to the
latest Festival, a magnificent record.

To say that Baracouda 'lost nothing in defeat' at Cheltenham might sound a
little hollow to those closest to him, but the truth was that Baracouda's length and a
half defeat at the hands of Iris's Gift ranks as one of the best performances of his
career. He was simply beaten by another outstanding hurdler, one who had, after
all, gone close to taking Baracouda's crown as a novice in a tremendous renewal
of the same race twelve months earlier. The 2003 Stayers' Hurdle had been widely
regarded as not just the race of the Festival, but one of the best races of recent times,
and if the third protagonist from the year before, Limestone Lad, was not around
again this time, it still provided a fascinating rematch between champion Baracouda and challenger Iris's Gift. Sequels often fail to live up to the original, but
this was one that didn't disappoint. Whilst Iris's Gift had been favourite ahead of
Baracouda in ante-post betting on the Stayers' Hurdle in the autumn, Baracouda
had enjoyed much the smoother preparation through the winter and was sent off
at odds on to become the first to win the stayers' championship three times—a
landmark that he would surely have achieved already but for the loss of the 2001
Festival due to the foot and mouth outbreak. Baracouda ran a typical race, settled
off the pace and hitting something of a 'flat spot' at around halfway. Iris's Gift was

sent for home earlier than he had been the year before, but the result looked all set to be the same as Baracouda came to join issue just after the last. But with the pair now well clear, Baracouda was never quite able to force his head in front as his younger rival pulled out a bit extra in the last hundred yards.

It had looked as though Baracouda might well be going chasing in the latest season, and before his reappearance in the autumn he had been installed as ante-post favourite for the Royal & SunAlliance Chase, and even as a 16/1-chance for the Gold Cup. However, his trainer announced a rethink. 'The horse has schooled over our fences and is ready to switch whenever we feel like it, but for the moment . . . I prefer to stay in the discipline he has mastered so well. He has learned very pleasantly but I don't think I have enough invention to do something different.' Conditions were too firm for Baracouda to attempt a third consecutive winning reappearance in the Ascot Hurdle in November, and he returned instead with a seven-length defeat of old rival Deano's Beeno in the Ballymore Properties Long Distance Hurdle at Newbury the following week. Ridden more handily than usual, Baracouda was soon in command after hitting the front two out and did not have to run anywhere near his best against a rival whose form and enthusiasm were at a low ebb in the latest season.

A month later, Baracouda and Deano's Beeno clashed again in the Cantor Sport Long Walk Hurdle at Ascot. Baracouda was making his fourth consecutive appearance in the race, his third against Deano's Beeno. In 2000, while still a novice, Baracouda made a spectacular British debut in the Long Walk when slamming Deano's Beeno (then at the height of his powers) by fourteen lengths. In Deano's Beeno's absence the following season, Baracouda strolled to a twenty-four length success, but in 2002, with his old rival back again, it had been a different story. Baracouda was sent off at 11/4-on to complete his hat-trick but, after being some twenty lengths behind Deano's Beeno at Swinley Bottom, he bridged the gap to draw upsides on the run-in but was unable to get his head in front and went down by a length. Until the latest Festival, that was Baracouda's only defeat on British soil.

With Iris's Gift still on the sidelines, Baracouda was made the 7/2-on favourite for the six-runner Long Walk, with Deano's Beeno at 7/1 and stable-companion Mr Cool at 10/1. The latter had failed only narrowly to inflict his own surprise defeat on Baracouda in the previous season's Ascot Hurdle, poaching a huge advantage which on that occasion Baracouda had managed to claw back to win by a neck. Tactics were clearly going to be important again, though it was obviously going to play straight into the hands of Thierry Doumen and Baracouda

Ballymore Properties Long Distance Hurdle, Newbury—
Baracouda is far too strong for old rival Deano's Beeno

Cantor Sport Long Walk Hurdle, Ascot—surprise tactics on the Pipe second string Mr Cool (right) cannot prevent Baracouda from recording his third wide-margin win in this race

if the Pipe stable-companions both adopted their usual catch-me-if-you-can tactics, risking cutting each other's throats. Mr Cool was given the task of making the running, while surprisingly Deano's Beeno was ridden to stalk Baracouda, presumably with the intention of beating him for a turn of foot. It seemed an unlikely scenario, and as the Pipe battle-plan disintegrated (Mr Cool was picked off two out, while Deano's Beeno was unable to follow Baracouda's move), Baracouda won with complete authority, drawing thirty lengths clear of the tiring Mr Cool on the run-in to register what was, at least on form, another of his best performances. Deano's Beeno finished another five lengths back in third, with the remainder soundly beaten.

Baracouda made one more appearance before the Festival, unexpectedly in a handicap, the Tote Scoop6 Sandown Hurdle in February. Top-class hurdlers are rarely asked to compete in handicaps nowadays, though Baracouda, who ran off a BHB mark of 170 at Sandown, was the first of several to do so in the weeks that followed, Rooster Booster (166) finishing second in the Tote Gold Trophy, Iris's Gift (167) making his reappearance in a Pertemps Handicap qualifier at Haydock and Rhinestone Cowboy (165) running third in the Coral Cup at Cheltenham. Baracouda's performance at Sandown was a far cry from his only other outing in a handicap. On that occasion, as a five-year-old at Auteuil, he had carried 9-13 to victory, his very first success on what was his third outing over hurdles. At Sandown he shouldered 11-12, with his eight rivals between 1 lb and 26 lb out of the handicap. Baracouda was sent off the 15/8-on favourite and, in the end, did not have to run anywhere near his best, moving up smoothly to lead on the bridle at the last, only to idle markedly on the run-in. The 25/1-shots Yogi and Alexander-thegreat filled the places, two lengths and half a length behind, from 13 lb and 26 lb out of the handicap respectively.

To recap briefly on the tall, leggy Baracouda's pedigree, his sire Alesso was a very smart stayer in France as a three-year-old. His dam Peche Aubar was only an ordinary maiden on the Flat, but she was a half-sister to Salmana, third in the Prix Marcel Boussac, and was out of a useful performer at up to a mile and a quarter in Ireland, Salto Mortale. As well as Baracouda, his dam has produced a Flat winner in France, Kerdrein (by Big John), and her final foal, a brother to Baracouda named Saint Aubar, has won over hurdles in the French Provinces for Guillaume Macaire.

Tote Scoop6 Sandown Hurdle (Handicap)—
a successful sortie into handicap company, holding off Yogi (right) and Alexanderthegreat

Baracouda is one of several top-class jumpers Francois Doumen has handled over the years. 'He's certainly my favourite among the hurdlers I've trained,' he said in the latest season, 'but it's hard to compare him with Ubu, who won every big race in France, or The Fellow, who was two noses away from winning three Cheltenham Gold Cups.' Ubu III actually contested the Stayers' Hurdle himself, promoted to second behind Nomadic Way in 1992, but he had a terrific record at Auteuil, winning the Grande Course de Haies in 1992 and 1993, finishing runner-up in 1994, and then becoming the only horse to win the Grand Steeple-Chase de Paris as well the following year, a race that had a tragic outcome when he collapsed and died after crossing the line. Since being bought privately by J. P. McManus after his first success in the Long Walk Hurdle, Baracouda has been back to Auteuil just once, and then only to take up an alternative engagement following the abandonment of the Cheltenham Festival in 2001. It's hard to believe that Baracouda wouldn't have had at least a couple of Grande Course de Haies to his name by now if connections had wished to take that route with him. Instead, as his trainer puts it, 'In France, he has disappeared off the map.' If Baracouda hasn't got the press he deserves in his own country, his tremendous record doesn't seem to have earned him a particularly exalted place in the affections of the British racing public either. 'In England, it has taken time for him to be appreciated, although I think he is now,' observed his trainer. 'If he'd been a grey, he'd have been a hero much earlier.'

Baracouda (FR) (b.g. 1995)	Alesso (USA) (b 1983)	Alleged (b 1974)	Hoist The Flag Princess Pout
		Leandra (b 1978)	Luthier Ady Endre
	Peche Aubar (FR) (b 1984)	Zino (b 1979)	Welsh Pageant Cyriana
		Salto Mortale (ch 1971)	Hul A Hul Dover Lassie

Perhaps making the staying hurdlers top of the bill on the Thursday of the new-look four-day Cheltenham Festival will raise the profile of a division which has tended to carry less prestige for its champion than those who dominate the best staying chases or the top two-mile hurdles. With no hint of Baracouda's powers diminishing, and his chief rival Iris's Gift set to move on to novice chasing, it looks like Rhinestone Cowboy will now be the main obstacle to Baracouda's dominating the staying hurdles for another season. Both horses are produced late, so they could be involved in some fascinating encounters. That's assuming, of course, that Baracouda isn't switched to fences himself, though it now looks rather late in the day for such a move. Although Baracouda's early successes came in the mud, his performances on good ground at the last two Festivals have shown that he doesn't need soft or heavy. Baracouda is a fluent jumper and has an exceptional turn of foot for a stayer, and, if that goes along with a tendency to come off the bridle mid-race and idle at the finish, those are quirks that his regular partner Thierry Doumen was well used to. Doumen announced his retirement from the saddle in August following a shoulder operation, leaving open the interesting possibility of Tony McCoy, retained by Baracouda's owner, taking over in the next season. *F. Doumen, France*

BARBED BROACH (IRE)   11 b.g. Waajib – Miss Galwegian (Sandford Lad) [2003/4 c21m^{pu} May 21] poor maiden pointer: sold £850 Ascot October Sales. *N. W. Padfield*   c–

BARBIZON (NZ)   10 b.g. Oregon (USA) – Fleece Tum (NZ) (Umteen (NZ)) [2003/4 c85, h–: c24m^{ur} c24m2 May 26] workmanlike gelding: winning hurdler: modest chaser: went lame run-in final start: stays 3m: acts on soft and good to firm going: tongue tied. *B. De Haan*   c90 h–

BARCELONA   7 b.g. Barathea (IRE) – Pipitina (Bustino) [2003/4 h117: 22g* 22m^2 20m^4 18g^5 Dec 9] compact gelding: has reportedly had breathing operation: fair handicap hurdler: won at Fontwell in May: stays 2¾m: acts on firm and soft going: often blinkered/ in cheekpieces: effective tongue tied or not: none too consistent. *G. L. Moore*   h112

BARCHAM AGAIN (IRE)   7 b.g. Aristocracy – Dante's Thatch (IRE) (Phardante (FR)) [2003/4 h91, F–: 22d^5 20g^6 c25s^{ur} c24d 21g^5 26s^6 c20s^3 c19s^3 c25d^F c24g^{pu} c25d* c20v^{pu} Apr 4] good-topped gelding: modest form at best over hurdles: modest chaser (has been let down by jumping): won handicap at Hereford in March: stays 25f: raced on good going or softer: wore cheekpieces after fourth start. *K. C. Bailey*   c93 h81

BARD OF DRUMCOO (IRE)   9 ch.g. Orange Reef – Sporting Houdini (Monseigneur (USA)) [2003/4 c72: c30m^5 May 10] winning pointer, including several times in 2004: poor form in steeplechases. *M. A. Kemp*   c61

BARDON BOY   10 ch.g. Rakaposhi King – Paper Dice (Le Dauphin) [2003/4 c–, h–: c26s^3 c24m^4 c28d^6 May 30] workmanlike gelding: fair pointer/novice hunter chaser: stayed 3¼m: acted on any going: tried blinkered: often let down by jumping: dead. *Mrs Monica Tory*   c92 x h–

BARFLEUR (IRE)   4 b.f. Anshan – Lulu Buck (Buckskin (FR)) [2003/4 F17m Apr 15] €10,000 3-y-o: medium-sized filly: eighth foal: half-sister to winning 2½m chaser Dunowen (by Be My Native) and winning pointer by Phardante: dam unraced half-sister to useful staying chaser Highfrith, from family of high-class 2m chaser I'm A Driver: seventh of 15 in mares bumper at Cheltenham on debut, considerably handled and never nearer: should improve. *Miss E. C. Lavelle*   F82 p

BARITO (GER)   7 b.g. Winged Love (IRE) – Blumme (CHI) (Jadar (CHI)) [2003/4 c113, h–: c21d^6 c22g^2 c19g^9 c25d^5 c20f* c24d^3 c20g^{pu} c21g^F Apr 2] leggy gelding: fairly useful chaser: won at Merano in August and Cheltenham in October, beating Mr Baxter Basics 9 lengths in 8-runner handicap at latter: probably flattered when last of 3 finishers in intermediate won easily by Impek at Sandown: stays 2¾m: acts on soft and firm going. *C. Von Der Recke, Germany*   c122 + h–

BARNARDS GREEN (IRE)   6 ch.g. Florida Son – Pearly Castle (IRE) (Carlingford Castle) [2003/4 F75: 16m^3 17g^6 17g 22g^{pu} c19s c16g^3 c24d^F c19d^{pu} Mar 24] lengthy gelding: poor novice hurdler/chaser: should stay beyond 2m. *R. H. Alner*   c84 ? h–

BARNES GREEN   6 br.g. Teenoso (USA) – Almanot (Remainder Man) [2003/4 F16m May 10] third foal: dam placed in bumper: well held in bumper on debut. *L. Wells*   F–

BARNEY RADETZKY (IRE)   8 b.g. Jurado (USA) – Clarrie (Ballyciptic) [2003/4 c16m^{pu} May 27] IR 8,800 3-y-o: half-brother to 6 winners, including fairly useful chaser No Pain No Gain (by Orchestra), stays 3m: dam winning hurdler: won maiden Irish point in 2003, little sign of ability otherwise: tried tongue tied. *I. A. Duncan, Ireland*   c– h–

BARNEYSIAN 8 b.g. Petoski – Rosemoss (Le Moss) [2003/4 h–: c23mp^u May 10] workmanlike gelding: signs of only a little ability over hurdles: showed nothing on chasing debut. *R. Dickin*   c– h–

BARNEYS LYRIC 4 ch.g. Hector Protector (USA) – Anchorage (IRE) (Slip Anchor) [2003/4 17g^{ur} 17g* 16g* 16f^3 16g^3 16s^6 24s^3 27d^4 Apr 23] angular gelding: fair form in 1½m maidens on Flat for R. Charlton: fairly useful juvenile hurdler: made all at Bangor and Perth in September: stays 3m: acts on soft going. *N. A. Twiston-Davies*   h115

BARNEYS REFLECTION 4 b.g. Petoski – Annaberg (IRE) (Tirol) [2003/4 F13v 21d 21d^6 Mar 28] first foal: dam, 6f winner at 2 yrs and later successful in Sweden, half-sister to useful 2m hurdler Have Merci: first sign of ability when sixth of 17 in maiden hurdle at Huntingdon. *Mrs L. Wadham*   h77 F–

BARON ALLFOURS 12 gr.g. Baron Blakeney – Georgian Quickstep (Dubassoff (USA)) [2003/4 c–, h–: c24m c26g^{pu} c24m^3 c26g^2 c22m* c20f^2 Aug 25] poor chaser: won maiden at Fontwell in August: lame next time: acts on firm and good to soft going: sometimes weak finisher. *Miss Z. C. Davison*   c77 h–

BARON ARON (IRE) 9 br.g. Lord Americo – Eleika (Camden Town) [2003/4 16d* c20g^F c17d* c16m^{pu} c17d^3 c20s^{pu} c16m c16d^5 c17d^F c16s^F Mar 24] good-topped gelding: half-brother to winning pointer by Roselier: dam behind in 3 Irish bumpers: modest hurdler: won handicap at Clonmel in June: similar form when winning maiden chase at Ballinrobe in July, final outing for D. Hassett: showed little subsequently: raced mainly around 2m: acts on heavy going: blinkered last 4 starts. *B. N. Pollock*   c96 d h96

BARON BLITZKRIEG 6 b.g. Sir Harry Lewis (USA) – Steel Typhoon (General Ironside) [2003/4 F16d^5 20d^6 16v^{pu} Dec 15] sixth foal: half-brother to fairly useful hurdler Personal Assurance (by Un Desperado), stays 2¾m, and staying hurdler/chaser Tactix (by Nearly A Hand): dam, behind in bumper, sister to very smart 2m to 2½m chaser Blitzkrieg: unseated in point on debut in 2003: fifth in bumper: no show in 2 novice hurdles. *Jonjo O'Neill*   h– F74

BARON'S PHARAOH (IRE) 9 b.g. Phardante (FR) – Katomi (Monksfield) [2003/4 20d^{pu} 16d 19d^{pu} Dec 28] quite good-topped gelding: successful both starts over hurdles in 2001/2: signs of retaining ability only on final start: should stay beyond 19f: raced on good going or softer. *A. W. Carroll*   h79

BARONS PHARJAN (IRE) 7 b.g. Phardante (FR) – Widden Fields (Shy Groom (USA)) [2003/4 22d^{pu} 19d^{pu} 19g c20d^{pu} Mar 15] tall gelding: third foal: dam 2m hurdle winner: no sign of ability. *A. W. Carroll*   c– h–

BARON STEANE (IRE) 5 b.g. Lord Americo – Lottosprite (IRE) (Sandalay (IRE)) [2003/4 F16d^4 F16d^5 Apr 12] useful-looking gelding: fourth foal: half-brother to useful chaser Winning Dream (by Hollow Hand), stays 29f: dam unraced: better effort in bumpers when fourth at Chepstow. *Lady Connell*   F83

BARON WINDRUSH 6 b.g. Alderbrook – Dame Scarlet (Blakeney) [2003/4 F–: 20s^6 22d* 25d* 22g^3 Apr 22] tall gelding: fairly useful novice hurdler: won at Market Rasen (conditional jockeys) and Wetherby in March: good third to True Lover in stronger contest at Fontwell: stays 25f: acts on good to soft going: type to progress further when going over fences. *N. A. Twiston-Davies*   h118

BARRACAT (IRE) 7 b.g. Good Thyne (USA) – Helens Fashion (IRE) (Over The River (FR)) [2003/4 F96: 17s^{pu} Feb 17] won bumper on debut in early-2002/3: jumped badly from halfway in novice hurdle nearly 2 years later. *B. W. Hills*   h–

BARRACK BUSTER 5 b.m. Bigstone (IRE) – Tarkhana (IRE) (Dancing Brave (USA)) [2003/4 16g^3 16s^4 16m* 19f* 20d Apr 11] sparely-made mare: modest maiden on Flat (stays 2m): fair hurdler: won mares maiden and mares novice at Kilbeggan in August, impressive when beating Fiddlers Bar 20 lengths in latter: creditable fourth to Stashedaway in mares listed event at Punchestown in early-May: should stay beyond 19f: seems best on going firmer than good. *Martin Brassil, Ireland*   h114

BARREN LANDS 9 b.g. Green Desert (USA) – Current Raiser (Filiberto (USA)) [2003/4 c116, h116: 21g 20d^{pu} Mar 20] compact gelding: fairly useful handicap hurdler/chaser: off 14 months, shaped as if retaining much of his ability over hurdles at Newbury on reappearance: beaten long way out in competitive event at Ascot just 2 weeks later: stays 19f: acts on soft and good to firm going. *K. Bishop*   c– h–

BARRESBO 10 br.g. Barrys Gamble – Bo' Babbity (Strong Gale) [2003/4 h115: 24g^{pu} 22d^3 22g 20d 16d Dec 6] sturdy gelding: fair handicap hurdler: form in 2003/4 only when   h114

third at Cartmel in May: stays 2¾m: raced mainly on good going or softer (acts on heavy).
A. C. Whillans

BARRONS PIKE   5 ch.g. Jumbo Hirt (USA) – Bromley Rose (Rubor) [2003/4 F16s **F—**
F16g Dec 20] ninth foal. half-brother to fairly useful 2m hurdler Little Bromley (by
Riberetto) and winning 3m hurdler Chabrimal Minster (by Minster Son): dam unraced:
well held in 2 bumpers. *F. S. Storey*

BARROSA   5 b.m. Sabrehill (USA) – Shehana (USA) (The Minstrel (CAN)) [2003/4 **h61**
h–: 16f⁶ 17g³ 16f⁴ 19m⁵ Nov 27] poor maiden on Flat (best efforts at 6f): poor maiden
hurdler: sold £3,700 Ascot December Sales, resold £1,350 Ascot April Sales. *Miss
K. M. George*

BARROW DRIVE   8 b.g. Gunner B – Fille de Soleil (Sunyboy) [2003/4 c140+, h–: **c142**
c20g^F c25m³ c24f³ c26g⁶ c22s* c20s² c18d⁴ c20g c20s⁴ Mar 27] sturdy gelding: useful **h—**
chaser: won minor event at Tramore in January by 11 lengths from Ceoil Agus Craic: ¾
length second to Rathgar Beach in Grade 3 Red Mills Chase at Gowran following month
(awarded race on technical grounds): best at 2½m+: probably acts on any going: tongue
tied: usually races prominently: tough and consistent. *Anthony Mullins, Ireland*

BARROW (SWI)   7 br.g. Caerleon (USA) – Bestow (Shirley Heights) [2003/4 h86: **h—**
23m^pu May 7] angular gelding: winning hurdler: broke down only start in 2003/4: will
stay 3m: acts on soft and good to firm going. *Ferdy Murphy*

BARRY ISLAND   5 b.g. Turtle Island (IRE) – Pine Ridge (High Top) [2003/4 16d^pu **h—**
Nov 29] leggy gelding: half-brother to fair hurdler Stylus (by Sharpo), stayed 19f: fairly
useful on Flat (will stay at least 1½m), successful in January: behind when blundering
and pulled up 2 out in well-contested novice at Newbury (bled from nose) on hurdling
debut. *D. R. C. Elsworth*

BARTLET   5 b.g. Infantry – Deviji (Mansingh (USA)) [2003/4 F16g May 21] sturdy **F—**
gelding: sixth foal (all by Infantry): dam unraced: completely tailed off in bumper on
debut. *M. A. Allen*

BARTON   11 ch.g. Port Etienne (FR) – Peanuts (FR) (Mistigri) [2003/4 c136, h–: c20m² **c139**
Nov 1] tall, lengthy gelding: one of the best novice chasers in 2001/2: tore ligament in **h—**
foot and below best after, though useful form when neck second to Turgeonev in handicap
at Wetherby in November: stayed 25f: acted on heavy and good to firm going: dead.
T. D. Easterby

BARTON BANDIT   8 ch.g. Sula Bula – Yamrah (Milford) [2003/4 c76, h–: c23m^pu **c—**
c20m Aug 2] medium-sized gelding: winning pointer: poor maiden chaser: let down by **h—**
jumping in handicaps in 2003/4: usually tongue tied. *J. M. Bradley*

BARTON BARON (IRE)   6 b.g. Phardante (FR) – Boolavogue (IRE) (Torus) [2003/4 **h—**
F–: 20d^pu 16d 16s 17d Feb 15] big, well-made gelding: signs of only a little ability.
D. P. Keane

BARTON BOG (IRE)   10 gr.g. Roselier (FR) – Al's Niece (Al Sirat) [2003/4 c–§, **c— §**
h–§: c24d^pu c25v⁵ c24s³ c23m³ c24g^pu c24d^pu Mar 27] workmanlike gelding: of no **h— §**
account nowadays: left J. Cornwall prior to final start: sometimes blinkered: ungenuine.
M. J. M. Evans

BARTON DANTE   7 b.m. Phardante (FR) – Cindie Girl (Orchestra) [2003/4 h104: **h104**
20d⁴ 20g² May 24] tall mare: fair handicap hurdler: stays 21f: acts on good to firm
and heavy going: has had tongue tied: often makes mistakes/looks no easy ride.
M. W. Easterby

BARTON GATE   6 b.g. Rock Hopper – Ruth's River (Young Man (FR)) [2003/4 h–, **h100**
F78: 16d^pu 19d⁴ 16s* 16s* 16d³ 17d⁶ Mar 27] tall, close-coupled gelding: has scope:
modest hurdler: won 2 handicaps at Uttoxeter (first conditional jockeys novice) in
December: best efforts at 2m: acts on soft going: tried blinkered, visored last 5 outings.
D. P. Keane

BARTON HILL   7 b.g. Nicholas Bill – Home From The Hill (IRE) (Jareer (USA)) **h90**
[2003/4 h95, F80: 19g* 24v⁵ 20v 20s⁶ Mar 20] leggy gelding: modest hurdler: won
maiden at Market Rasen in December: probably stays 3m: acts on heavy going.
T. D. Easterby

BARTON MAY   5 ch.m. Midnight Legend – Yamrah (Milford) [2003/4 19s 20s⁵ 20v⁴ **h82**
22d³ 23s Apr 4] lengthy mare: sixth foal: half-sister to fairly useful 2m hurdler Capricorn
Princess (by Nicholas Bill) and winning pointer by Sula Bula: dam successful up to 11.5f
on Flat: poor novice hurdler: stays 2¾m: tongue tied last 2 starts. *D. P. Keane*

BARTON NIC 11 b.g. Nicholas Bill – Dutch Majesty (Homing) [2003/4 c66+, h95: 20s* 22v^{pu} 16d* 18s^4 20v^F 20s 17d c16d* c20v^4 Apr 4] workmanlike gelding: fair handicap hurdler: won at Bangor (seller) in May and Plumpton in December: lightly raced over fences, took advantage of mark much lower than over hurdles in conditional jockeys handicap at Chepstow in March: won at 3m, better at shorter: acts on heavy going: wears blinkers/cheekpieces. *D. P. Keane* **c78 +** **h111**

BARTON SANDS (IRE) 7 b.g. Tenby – Hetty Green (Bay Express) [2003/4 17g^{pu} 16m 16d^{pu} 17m Mar 9] formerly useful on Flat (barely stays 1½m), fair nowadays: no show in 4 starts over hurdles: visored and tongue tied after debut. *M. C. Pipe* **h–**

BARTON SUN (IRE) 5 b.g. Indian Ridge – Sun Screen (Caerleon (USA)) [2003/4 F16v F16d Apr 21] IR 70,000Y: good-topped gelding: third foal: half-brother to smart hurdler/chaser up to 2½m Hill Society (by Law Society): dam maiden half-sister to 1000 Guineas and Oaks winner Mysterious: well held in 2 bumpers. *R. N. Bevis* **F–**

BASIL 11 br.g. Lighter – Thrupence (Royal Highway) [2003/4 c78, h–: c24g^{ur} c25d^{pu} c24m^R c26d^F c29s* c26s^{pu} Jan 19] tall gelding: no form over hurdles: poor handicap chaser: won at Plumpton in January: largely let down by jumping otherwise: stays 29f: best efforts on going softer than good (acts on heavy). *R. H. Buckler* **c79 x** **h–**

BASINET 6 b.g. Alzao (USA) – Valiancy (Grundy) [2003/4 17g^2 17g^F 17g^3 Sep 30] half-brother to winning hurdler Jarrwah (by Niniski), stayed 3m: fair on Flat (stays 9f): shaped with promise first 2 starts over hurdles: likely to prove best at sharp 2m. *J. J. Quinn* **h91**

BASSANO (USA) 10 b.g. Alwasmi (USA) – Marittima (USA) (L'Emigrant (USA)) [2003/4 c–, h–: c23m^2 c26g^{pu} c21d^5 c30m^{bd} c23g^3 c20m^6 Sep 7] stocky, lengthy gelding: poor maiden chaser: stays 23f: acts on heavy and good to firm going: has found little: tongue tied last 2 starts. *S. C. Burrough* **c68** **h–**

BASSEY (IRE) 11 b.g. Be My Native (USA) – Evergreen Lady (Smartset) [2003/4 c24s^F Feb 12] leggy, useful-looking gelding: modest hurdler in 2000/1: left N. Henderson, fell third in hunter chase on return: tried blinkered. *Miss Fiona-Jane Hatfield* **c–** **h–**

BATH HOUSE BOY (IRE) 11 b.g. Don't Forget Me – Domiciliate (Kings Lake (USA)) [2003/4 24m^{pu} 26m^3 c25m^{pu} 24m^3 Oct 11] compact gelding: maiden chaser: poor hurdler: stays 3m: acts on soft and firm going: tried blinkered: often let down by jumping over fences: often races lazily. *Mrs P. Bickerton* **c– x** **h76**

BATHSHEBA 5 b.m. Overbury (IRE) – Winnow (Oats) [2003/4 F–: 16s 17g 19d Mar 15] rather unfurnished mare: no sign of ability. *K. Bishop* **h–**

BATHWICK ANNIE 8 ch.m. Sula Bula – Lily Mab (FR) (Prince Mab (FR)) [2003/4 h95: 20d^6 c24s* c22d* c20g* c22s^{pu} Mar 28] workmanlike mare: modest maiden hurdler: much better in novice chases, won handicaps at Huntingdon and Newbury (beat Full On 6 lengths) in December and mares event at Market Rasen (by 1¾ lengths from Annie Byers) in February: reportedly distressed in Grade 3 mares contest at Limerick final start: will stay beyond 3m: acts on soft going: bold-jumping front runner, though has tendency to go right. *D. P. Keane* **c120** **h87**

BATMAN SENORA (FR) 8 b.g. Chamberlin (FR) – Cartza (FR) (Carmarthen (FR)) [2003/4 c152, h123: 20s^2 c29s^2 c22d c27s* c24d^F Dec 28] **c148** **h140**

    Batman Senora's win in a Group 1 chase at Auteuil in November, against a number of the leading French chasers and worth nearly £85,000 to the winner, probably didn't get the attention it deserved in the British press. That wasn't surprising, given that the winner is hardly a household name in Britain after just one appearance here, but his achievement at Auteuil was a noteworthy one for a British stable. Despite the excellent prize money on offer at France's premier jumping track, runners from the British Isles there are few and far between, especially in chases, where the varied nature of the obstacles is presumably the main deterrent. Consequently, Batman Senora is one of only a handful of British- or Irish-trained horses to have distinguished themselves over fences at Auteuil. A couple who did early in the twentieth century were the Grand National winners Jerry M and Troytown who went to Aintree as winners of the Grand Steeple-Chase de Paris in 1910 and 1919 respectively. The most celebrated British-trained winner at Auteuil must be Mandarin, the 1962 Grand Steeple-Chase winner, whose remarkable success after his bit broke in the early stages was recalled in obituaries on his rider Fred Winter who died in April. Since Mandarin, and until the latest season, the best

effort among those to have challenged from Britain or Ireland for France's biggest jumping prize came from Captain Christy who was runner-up in 1975. Tied Cottage has been among those who have tried and failed since, though he did win a lesser chase at Auteuil in 1978.

Batman Senora's win came in the Prix La Haye Jousselin, the chase second in importance only to the Grand Steeple-Chase and run over just a furlong and a half shorter. Despite years of experience around Auteuil—he won his first chase there as a four-year-old—Batman Senora has a *bête noire* among the track's varied obstacles in the form of the riviere des tribunes, the big water jump in front of the stands which has to be jumped twice in both the Grand Steeple-Chase and the Prix La Haye Jousselin. This takes a lot more jumping than the standard water jump on a British track, needing to be met to gain enough momentum to clear the spread of more than five metres. Batman Senora regularly stutters into this fence, almost giving the impression that he is about to refuse, and, more often than not, lands with his hind legs in the water. So far at least, though, he has negotiated it without mishap. To prove the point that this isn't a fence to be trifled with, it claimed the long odds-on favourite Kotkijet, normally as fine a jumper as you'll see around Auteuil, on the first circuit of the Prix La Haye Jousselin. His departure made Batman Senora's task all the easier in what was quite an eventful race all round. Another casualty was the previous year's winner Sunny Flight, who ran straight into the rail ditch and fence in the back straight and deposited his rider on top of it. Batman Senora, an habitual front runner, led his remaining rivals a merry dance and hung on gamely in the straight, looking tired approaching the final hurdle but holding on to win by a length and a half from another experienced campaigner Rougenoir.

Batman Senora's debut for Ian Williams' stable had been a winning one in a novice hurdle at Bangor in April 2003. He had been entered in that month's Grand National, but his first main target for his new yard was a second crack at the Grand Steeple-Chase the following month. He had been promoted to second on the disqualification of Double Car in the 2002 renewal when under the care of Patrick Rago. After a preparatory run over hurdles at Auteuil in the Prix Jean Granel in early-May, finishing second, Batman Senora was runner-up again in the Grand Steeple-Chase, but this time on his own merits. He had seen off most of his rivals by the home turn but was passed by the mare Line Marine going to the last and just held on for second, ten lengths behind the winner. That performance earned Batman Senora favouritism for the Prix des Drags, effectively a consolation event for the Grand Steeple-Chase, but he seemed not to be over his exertions from three weeks earlier and came in last of the seven finishers. Batman Senora was clearly a fresher horse when making his next appearance in the Prix La Haye Jousselin five months later. He then took on Best Mate and company in the Ericsson Chase at Leopardstown in December but wasn't up to the task, tailed off when falling at the last.

After the end of the latest season in Britain, Batman Senora made a third attempt on the Grand Steeple-Chase. Kept fresh again, his only run beforehand coming in the Prix Jean Granel once more (now with listed status), which he won. Batman Senora managed only sixth in the Grand Steeple-Chase though, behind the impressive winner Kotkijet. Batman Senora effectively surrendered his lead to that rival with another hesitant jump at the water at the start of the final circuit.

Mr G. Polinski's "Batman Senora"

Batman Senora (FR) (b.g. 1996)	Chamberlin (FR) (b 1978)	Green Dancer (b 1972)	Nijinsky
			Green Valley
		On The Wing (b 1970)	Tanerko
			Nellie Fleet
	Cartza (FR) (b 1977)	Carmarthen (ch 1964)	Devon
			Kuwait
		Tzara (b 1973)	Night And Day
			Midnight Moon

Batman Senora is the only winner produced by his dam in a lengthy stud career, though one of his half-sisters is responsible for the Imperial Cup winner Korelo. Batman Senora's dam Cartza ran just the twice on the Flat but was a half-sister to the good jumpers Vaquero, winner of the Grand Prix de Pau, and Bokaro, a smart hurdler who won races in Britain, France, Italy and the States with Charlie Brooks. Grandam Tzara, placed in France as a two-year-old, was a sister to the high-class French horse El Toro who was best at a mile. The rangy Batman Senora stays well, and, as a regular at Auteuil, has encountered little other than soft or heavy conditions, though it was good to firm when he won at Bangor. He is usually blinkered nowadays and is genuine. His chances of winning more good races at Auteuil will depend very much on the presence or absence of Kotkijet, and perhaps on whether his aversion to the water jump becomes something more serious. *Ian Williams*

BATON CHARGE (IRE)   6 b.g. Gildoran – Frizzball (IRE) (Orchestra) [2003/4   **c88**
F18d⁶ F16v c24g⁴ c20g² c19gᵖᵘ Apr 1] IR £13,000 3-y-o: rangy, angular gelding: second   **F–**
foal: dam twice-raced in bumpers: won maiden Irish point in 2003: form otherwise only
when second of 3 finishers to Mondial Jack in novice chase at Kempton in March: trained
by Lady A. Maxwell first start in bumpers. *T. R. George*

BATOUTOFTHEBLUE   11 br.g. Batshoof – Action Belle (Auction Ring (USA))   **c–**
[2003/4 h–: c26dᵘʳ May 28] quite good-topped gelding: one-time fair hurdler: twice   **h–**
runner-up in points: will stay beyond 25f: acts on good to firm going: has hung/carried
head awkwardly under pressure. *K. Robson*

BATSWING   9 b.g. Batshoof – Magic Milly (Simply Great (FR)) [2003/4 c121, h–:   **c121 d**
c16d³ c17g² c21g² c16m⁴ c20mᵖᵘ c16m⁶ c16mᵖᵘ 19g⁵ 16d 16d 16d 16g Feb 18] lengthy   **h101**
gelding: fairly useful hurdler/chaser at best: out of form after fourth start: barely stays
21f: acts on good to firm and heavy going: tried in blinkers/cheekpieces: has had tongue
tied: difficult ride. *B. Ellison*

BATTLE LINE   5 b.g. Brief Truce (USA) – Forest Heights (Slip Anchor) [2003/4 h–:   **h87**
16m⁶ 20s² 20m 18m³ 21g Nov 14] compact gelding: modest and unreliable maiden on
Flat (stays 1½m): modest maiden hurdler: stays 2½m: acts on soft and good to firm going.
E. McNamara, Ireland

BATTLE WARNING   9 b.g. Warning – Royal Ballet (IRE) (Sadler's Wells (USA))   **h138**
[2003/4 h109: 24m* 24s* 25d* Dec 12] angular gelding: useful hurdler: much improved
in 2003/4, unbeaten in handicaps at Aintree in October, Ascot in November and Cheltenham in December, beating Imperial de Thaix ½ length at last-named: stays 25f: acts on
soft and good to firm going: blinkered once: has raced lazily. *P. Bowen*

BATTO   4 b.g. Slip Anchor – Frog (Akarad (FR)) [2003/4 16d 21s⁴ 20d⁵ Feb 23] modest   **h80**
maiden on Flat (should stay at least 1¾m) for W. Haggas: poor form over hurdles.
G. M. Moore

BAY CASTER   11 b.g. Gunner B – Marina Bird (Julio Mariner) [2003/4 21gᵖᵘ 21gᵖᵘ   **h–**
Mar 26] sturdy, workmanlike gelding: won bumper on debut in 1998 for C. Egerton:
showed nothing in 2 races over hurdles on return. *P. R. Webber*

Pertemps Handicap Hurdle (Qualifier), Cheltenham—
Battle Warning makes it three wins from as many starts in 2003/4 for his resurgent stable

BAY KENNY 6 b.g. Karinga Bay – Erica Superba (Langton Heath) [2003/4 F16g⁴ **h117** F17g⁶ F17m* 20d⁴ 22s⁶ 21d* 24g⁴ 24d² Apr 8] well-made gelding: chasing type: seventh **F93** foal: half-brother to several winners, including fair staying chaser Lord Seamus (by Arctic Lord): dam, winning chaser, half-sister to very smart chaser The Tsarevich: best effort in bumpers when winning maiden at Hereford in November: fair novice hurdler: won at Plumpton in March: good second to Analogy at Ludlow: will prove best at 3m+: yet to race on extremes of going. *K. C. Bailey*

BAY MAGIC (IRE) 11 b.g. Ela-Mana-Mou – Come In (Be My Guest (USA)) [2003/4 **c–** c90, h87: 24dᵘʳ 24g² 24dᵖᵘ 22m³ 23d 20s³ c25s Jan 16] plain gelding: poor maiden **h77** hurdler: modest chaser: below form only run over fences in 2003/4: effective at 2½m to 25f: acts on heavy and good to firm going: usually wears headgear: has been let down by jumping over fences. *Miss Lucinda V. Russell*

BAY MAID 6 b.m. Karinga Bay – Maid To Match (Matching Pair) [2003/4 F18f³ Aug **F74** 18] best effort in bumpers (trained in 2001/2 by P. Webber) when third at Fontwell. *Lady Connell*

BDELLIUM 6 b.m. Royal Vulcan – Kelly's Logic (Netherkelly) [2003/4 F–: 16g⁶ 21g **c92 ?** 16vᵖᵘ 21s⁶ 21s⁶ c20g³ c22dᵖᵘ Mar 21] sturdy mare: little sign of ability over hurdles: **h–** probably flattered on first of 2 starts in mares novice chases. *B. I. Case*

BEACHCOMBER 9 b.g. Kuwait Beach (USA) – Miss Rupert (Solar Topic) [2003/4 **c–** c24sᶠ c24dʳᵒ Apr 8] 1,700 4-y-o, 2,500 6-y-o: third foal: dam unraced: lightly raced in points, won maiden in March: failed to complete in 2 hunters. *J. Groucott*

BEACHCOMBER BAY (IRE) 9 ch.g. Un Desperado (FR) – Beachcomber Lass **c135** (Day Is Done) [2003/4 c130, h99+: c18d* c16d⁴ c24dᵖᵘ c17s⁵ c20s³ c20sᶠ c18d⁵ c16s⁵ **h–** c20s⁶ c17d Apr 11] lengthy gelding: useful chaser: won novice at Punchestown in May: good efforts in graded events fourth and fifth starts, below form subsequently: stays 2½m: raced on good going or softer (acts on heavy): tried blinkered: sold 15,000 gns Doncaster May Sales. *N. Meade, Ireland*

BEACON OF LIGHT (IRE) 6 b.m. Lake Coniston (IRE) – Deydarika (IRE) (Kah- **h75** yasi) [2003/4 17g⁶ 20d⁶ 21d* 19g⁶ 21v⁶ 23v 24d 21d² Mar 16] smallish mare: little form on Flat: poor hurdler: won seller at Sedgefield in November: stays 21f: acts on good to soft ground: usually wears cheekpieces. *Ferdy Murphy*

BEAMISH PRINCE 5 ch.g. Bijou d'Inde – Unconditional Love (IRE) (Polish Patriot **h85** (USA)) [2003/4 16d⁴ 16g⁶ 16g⁶ 17s⁵ 16gᶠ Mar 10] leggy gelding: fair but probably ungenuine on Flat (may prove best around 1¼m), claimed from M. Johnston £6,000 in July: modest form over hurdles: raced around 2m. *G. M. Moore*

BEARAWAY (IRE) 7 b.g. Fourstars Allstar (USA) – Cruiseaway (Torus) [2003/4 **h96** F16m⁵ F17m* F16g² 16m* 16g³ 17g⁴ 16f* 16f⁵ Oct 29] fifth foal: half-brother to fair 2m **F101** hurdler Justaway (by Mill Fontaine): dam unraced, from family of smart chaser up to 25f Sparky Gayle and high-class chaser around 2½m Golden Freeze: third once from 3 starts in maiden Irish points: best effort in bumpers when winning maiden at Southwell in June: modest novice hurdler: won at Worcester in July and Towcester (simple task) in October: will stay beyond 17f: raced on good going or firmer: wore cheekpieces/tongue tied final start. *Mrs H. Dalton*

BEARE NECESSITIES (IRE) 5 ch.g. Presenting – Lady Laburnum (Carlingford **h88 p** Castle) [2003/4 17g Nov 21] €34,000 3-y-o: fifth foal: dam lightly-raced half-sister to top-class 2m chaser Waterloo Boy: seventh of 16 in novice hurdle at Exeter on debut: will stay 2½m: should do better. *A. Ennis*

BEAR ON BOARD (IRE) 9 b.g. Black Monday – Under The River (Over The River **c130** (FR)) [2003/4 c115, h–: c26sᵖᵘ c24s* c30d* c33d* c28m² c36d Apr 3] well-made geld- **h–** ing: useful handicap chaser: best form around 2m: successful at Haydock in November, Bangor (beat Harlov by ½ length) in December and Cheltenham (by 2 lengths from Fasgo) in January: creditable second to Jurancon II in very valuable event at Haydock in February: remote eighth of 11 finishers to Amberleigh House in Grand National at Aintree: thorough stayer: acts on good to firm and heavy going: game and reliable. *A. King*

BEASLEY 5 b.g. First Trump – Le Shuttle (Presidium) [2003/4 h77: 17m⁵ 17g⁴ 20d⁶ **h73 x** 20m⁵ Aug 16] poor maiden hurdler: best form around 2m: acts on any going: tried in headgear: sketchy jumper: sold £1,300 Ascot October Sales: won point in April. *D. McCain*

BEAT THE BANK (IRE) 9 b. or br.g. Good Thyne (USA) – Must Clear (Al Sirat) **c–** [2003/4 c24sᵘʳ c23s³ c24gᵖᵘ c23dᵖᵘ Apr 21] 13,000 4-y-o: lengthy, useful-looking gelding: third foal: dam unraced, out of sister to very smart jumper at 2m to 3m Chinrullah: won maiden point in 2001: no form in steeplechases: looked temperamental in cheekpieces third start. *O. Sherwood*

BEAT THE HEAT (IRE) 6 b.g. Salse (USA) – Summer Trysting (USA) (Alleged (USA)) [2003/4 h104: 16m* 16g⁴ 16d² 16s³ 16d³ 16sᵖᵘ Maᵢ 13] angular gelding: fairly useful on Flat (stays 1½m): of similar standard over hurdles: won maiden at Aintree in October and handicap at Kelso in November: good efforts in handicaps third to fifth starts: will stay beyond 17f: acts on good to firm and heavy going: tried blinkered: held up. *Jedd O'Keeffe*   **h115**

BEAT THE RETREAT 9 b.g. Terimon – Carpet Slippers (Daring March) [2003/4 c90, h85: c19gᵘʳ c20m³ May 26] medium-sized gelding: fair form at best in novice hurdles: second in 3-runner novice on chasing debut: no show both starts early in 2003/4, and little impact in points subsequently: probably stays 2½m: acts on good to soft ground, probably on good to firm: inconsistent. *A. King*   **c–** **h–**

BEAU ARTISTE 4 ch.g. Peintre Celebre (USA) – Belle Esprit (Warning) [2003/4 16g² 17g² Apr 12] fair but ungenuine maiden on Flat (stays 1½m), sold out of J. O'Keeffe's stable 16,000 gns Newmarket Autumn Sales: modest form when second both starts over hurdles. *J. Howard Johnson*   **h94**

BEAU BRUN (FR) 8 b. or br.g. Cadoudal (FR) – Atakaia (FR) (Ataxerxes (GER)) [2003/4 h–: c23gᵖᵘ May 2] lengthy gelding: of little account. *G. B. Balding*   **c–** **h–**

BEAUCHAMP GIGI (IRE) 6 b.m. Bob Back (USA) – Beauchamp Grace (Ardross) [2003/4 F16f* F16g⁴ Feb 18] €15,000 4-y-o: third foal: dam, useful hurdler/fair chaser up to 3m, half-sister to very smart middle-distance stayer Beauchamp Hero: easily won bumper at Cork on debut in October: sold out of J. Kiely's stable 200,000 gns Doncaster November Sales: again favourite, 3¾ lengths fourth to Arctic Moss in mares event at Musselburgh. *J. Howard Johnson*   **F97**

BEAUCHAMP MAGIC 9 b.g. Northern Park (USA) – Beauchamp Buzz (High Top) [2003/4 h–: c16gᵖᵘ Jan 9] lengthy gelding: no worthwhile form over jumps, sold out of K. Burke's stable 400 gns Ascot August Sales prior to chasing debut (bled from nose): tried blinkered/tongue tied. *K. G. Wingrove*   **c–** **h–**

BEAUCHAMP Q 5 b.g. Inchinor – Beauchamp Buzz (High Top) [2003/4 F16g⁴ F16v F16d F16g Mar 6] leggy gelding: eighth foal: half-brother to useful middle-distance stayer Beauchamp Jade (by Kalaglow) and temperamental 1½m to 2m winner Beauchamp Magic (by Northern Park): dam, stayed 1m, half-sister to very smart middle-distance stayer Beauchamp Hero and useful hurdler up to 3m Beauchamp Grace: fourth to The Muratti at Warwick on debut, easily best effort in bumpers: wore cheekpieces final start. *A. P. Jones*   **F90**

Miles Gosling Handicap Chase, Cheltenham—an unusually tight finish to a long-distance event, with Bear On Board (centre) coming out on top from Fasgo (No.4)

BEAUCHAMP QUEST 5 b.g. Pharly (FR) – Beauchamp Kate (Petoski) [2003/4 **F–**
F17g Apr 10] second foal: half-brother to fair but ungenuine Beauchamp Ribbon (by
Vettori), stays 11.7f: dam, disappointing maiden, half-sister to useful middle-distance
stayer Beauchamp Jade, out of half-sister to very smart 1½m winner Beauchamp Hero:
tailed off in bumper on debut. *A. P. Jones*

BEAU CHASSEUR (FR) 6 ch.g. Cyborg (FR) – Safari Girl (FR) (Faraway Son **c–**
(USA)) [2003/4 16m 17gpu 16g 17spu Jan 22] workmanlike ex-French gelding: **h–**
ninth foal: half-brother to 5 winners, including chasers by Ti King and Dom Pasquini:
dam maiden, from family of useful hurdler/chaser Saint Preuil: successful over fences at
Durtal and Dieppe in 2002/3 for G. Macaire: maiden hurdler: no form in Britain, sold out
of N. Richards' stable 5,000 gns Doncaster August Sales after second start. *P. Winkworth*

BEAU COUP 7 b.g. Toulon – Energance (IRE) (Salmon Leap (USA)) [2003/4 21g⁴ **h76**
21d⁵ 20dur 20s⁵ 17s⁵ 24spu 22s⁵ 22gpu Apr 4] poor maiden hurdler: stays 2¾m: raced on
good going or softer. *John R. Upson*

BEAUFORT COUNTY (IRE) 7 b.g. Torus – Afternoon Tea (IRE) (Decent Fellow) **F102**
[2003/4 F18g² F16s³ F16s⁵ Dec 26] second foal: dam unraced half-sister to useful chaser
up to 25f On The Other Hand, from family of top-class staying chaser Righthand Man:
fairly useful form when placed first 2 starts in bumpers, third to Blazing Liss at Navan on
second occasion. *N. Meade, Ireland*

BEAU JAKE (IRE) 9 b.g. Jolly Jake (NZ) – Cool Mary (Beau Charmeur (FR)) **c–**
[2003/4 c97?, h–: 24mᶠ May 7] poor maiden jumper: probably stays 3¼m: acts on soft **h–**
going (bumper form on good to firm): sold 4,000 gns Doncaster May Sales, runner-up in
point in 2004. *N. M. Babbage*

BEAULY (IRE) 9 b.g. Beau Sher – Woodland Theory (Sheer Grit) [2003/4 h63: 21m⁵ **h79**
19g⁴ 16g* 17d⁵ Dec 17] good-topped gelding: fell in maiden point in 2002: poor handicap
hurdler: well backed, improved form when winning conditional jockeys event at Warwick in December: likely to prove best around 2m: acts on firm and good to soft going,
possibly unsuited by softer: front runner. *J. G. M. O'Shea*

BEAUSEJOUR (USA) 6 ch.m. Diesis – Libeccio (NZ) (Danzatore (CAN)) [2003/4 **h86**
h70: 16g³ 16m⁶ 18m⁴ 16g 16m* 16m⁴ 16m⁵ 18s⁴ 16g⁵ 19g² 19g⁶ Apr 18] smallish mare:
modest hurdler: won novice claimer at Worcester in June: left B. Powell after eighth
outing: likely to prove best up to 19f: acts on good to firm going, possibly not on soft:
wore cheekpieces fifth to eighth outings: jumps none too fluently. *J. Gallagher*

BEAUSHERAM (IRE) 10 b.g. Beau Sher – Rock of Sence (Swan's Rock) [2003/4 **c125**
c25d⁵ c24sᶠ c25spu c22s² c22d⁴ c20d* c20s⁴ c20s⁴ c20spu c22s c21g⁴ c24s⁶ c22dᶠ Apr **h–**
12] rangy gelding: winning hurdler: fairly useful chaser: best effort when winning maiden
at Navan in November by 3 lengths from Hi Cloy: stayed 25f: acted on soft and good to
firm going: effective blinkered or not: dead. *J. M. Kiernan, Ireland*

BEAU SUPREME (IRE) 7 b.g. Supreme Leader – Miss Sabreur (Avocat) [2003/4 **h102**
21g² 21g³ 21g⁴ 22g Apr 18] type to make a chaser: fourth foal: half-brother to winning
pointer by Buckskin: dam winning pointer: placed all 4 starts in maiden points in 2003:
fair form over hurdles: stays 21f. *C. J. Down*

BEAU TORERO (IRE) 6 gr.g. True Brave (USA) – Brave Lola (FR) (Dom Pasquini **c–**
(FR)) [2003/4 c75, h–, F92: 16m³ 19m* 16d² Dec 26] lengthy gelding: poor form only **h86**
outing over fences: modest hurdler: won novice handicap at Taunton in November, soon
clear: stays easy 19f: acts on good to firm and good to soft going. *B. N. Pollock*

BEAVER LODGE (IRE) 7 gr.g. Grand Lodge (USA) – Thistlewood (Kalamoun) **c96**
[2003/4 h114: 19g³ c20g² c23m² c23d³ c20gpu Sep 13] workmanlike gelding: fair handi- **h111**
cap hurdler: modest form in novice chases: sold out of C. Mann's stable 25,000 gns
Doncaster August Sales after third start: lame final one: stays 23f: acts on good to firm
and heavy going. *B. P. J. Baugh*

BEBE BLEU (IRE) 8 b.m. Terimon – Fu's Lady (Netherkelly) [2003/4 20spu 22mur **h– x**
May 29] runner-up in bumper on debut: no form over jumps, including points. *M. C. Pipe*

BE BOP BENTLEY 9 br.g. Arms And The Man – Playful Touch (Lepanto (GER)) **c–**
[2003/4 c16g c24gur Apr 18] of no account. *P. Maskill*

BED BUG (FR) 6 b.g. Double Bed (FR) – Cotation (FR) (Recitation (USA)) [2003/4 **h102**
h99, F93: 20g² 16g⁴ 21g³ 19dpu 16g⁶ Mar 7] tall, leggy gelding: fair handicap hurdler:
stays 21f: acts on good to firm going. *N. J. Henderson*

BEDFORD LEADER 6 b.m. Bedford (USA) – Neladar (Ardar) [2003/4 F–: 22m **h83**
26m⁵ 16v² 21v⁶ 24s³ 24g Feb 19] seemingly poor form when placed over hurdles,
possibly flattered both times. *A. P. Jones*

BEE AN BEE (IRE) 7 b.g. Phardante (FR) – Portia's Delight (IRE) (The Parson) **c125**
[2003/4 h110: c24d* c24d² c25gᶠ c25s* c25s⁴ c24g* c24sᵘʳ Apr 17] well-made gelding: **h–**
fair hurdler: better over fences, won novice at Uttoxeter (very easily) in November and
handicaps at Folkestone in January and Newbury (idled after leading last when beating
Desailly ½ length) in March: will stay beyond 25f: raced on good going or softer (acts on
heavy): tried visored. *T. R. George*

BEECHBROOK GALE (IRE) 8 b.g. Toulon – Swan Upping (Lord Gayle (USA)) **c–**
[2003/4 c–: c21g⁵ 24mᵖᵘ Oct 26] lengthy gelding: little form. *John R. Upson* **h–**

BEECHCOURT 7 b.g. Son Pardo – Calametta (Oats) [2003/4 h110, F–: 18d³ 16s* **h111**
16s Jan 11] tall gelding: has reportedly had wind operation: fair hurdler: easily won
maiden at Cork in January: raced around 2m on good to soft/soft going: has hung left.
M. J. P. O'Brien, Ireland

BEECHWOOD 6 b.g. Fraam – Standard Rose (Ile de Bourbon (USA)) [2003/4 F95: **h76**
16dᵖᵘ 17d⁵ 17s 16g Mar 25] lengthy gelding: fairly useful in bumpers in 2002/3: poor
form at best over hurdles: needs emphasis on speed at 2m: sold £6,800 Cheltenham April
Sales. *Miss H. C. Knight*

BEEDULUP 9 br.g. Perpendicular – Biloela (Nicholas Bill) [2003/4 c–, h75: 22g 21g⁵ **c69**
22m 27d c20m² c20m⁵ c20fᵘʳ Oct 9] leggy gelding: poor hurdler/maiden chaser: stayed **h73**
2¾m: acted on good to firm and good to soft going: tried in cheekpieces/visor: dead.
P. Wegmann

BEEF OR SALMON (IRE) 8 ch.g. Cajetano (USA) – Farinella (IRE) (Salmon **c171 +**
Leap (USA)) [2003/4 c165p, h–: c20s³ c20d* c16d* c24d³ c26g⁴ Mar 18] **h–**
 The longer the search for another Irish-trained Gold Cup winner goes on,
the more the spotlight falls on Beef Or Salmon. Irish horses have fallen on hard
times in the Gold Cup since a golden spell in the 'sixties and 'seventies. Arkle's
three consecutive victories between 1964 and 1966 were followed by another for
the same stable through Fort Leney in 1968. L'Escargot's double in 1970 and 1971
preceded the victory of the mare Glencaraig Lady. Captain Christy and Ten Up
kept the ball rolling in 1974 and 1975, while Davy Lad's success in 1977 meant
Irish-trained horses had won ten of the last fourteen renewals. Things have gone
downhill since. Tied Cottage's success in 1980 was expunged when he failed a dope
test. Dawn Run and Imperial Call sparked some of the most raucous celebrations
seen at the Festival when winning in 1986 and 1996 respectively, but a tally of two
Gold Cups from the last twenty-six renewals represents a long time between drinks
for a racing nation which values Cheltenham success above all else.
 Whether Beef Or Salmon can end the drought with a victory at Cheltenham
depends to a large extent on two factors. The first—Best Mate's continued
wellbeing—is one Beef Or Salmon's connections can do precious little about. But
the second, Beef Or Salmon's sometimes-haphazard jumping, is one his experienced trainer feels he is finally getting to grips with. Michael Hourigan now
believes that a third fence fall when second favourite for the 2003 Gold Cup left
Beef Or Salmon with muscle damage in his hindquarters which hindered his
progress on and off for the best part of twelve months. That being so, Beef Or
Salmon did well to win two valuable chases before Christmas. He fared even better
after a comprehensive defeat by Best Mate in the Ericsson Chase, following a Gold
Cup fourth with an impressive success in the Punchestown Heineken Gold Cup. All
in all, it was another fine season for arguably Ireland's best staying chaser, yet there
remains a nagging doubt about whether he will ever be able to beat Best Mate.
 First things first, though. For the second year running, Beef Or Salmon
made his reappearance in the Clonmel Oil Chase in November. Twelve months
earlier, pitched in for his chasing debut, he made the most of a hefty weight
allowance from Sackville. This time, having missed an intended outing on the Flat
at Leopardstown, Beef Or Salmon was receiving 4 lb from the rejuvenated Edredon
Bleu. It looked like being enough as he quickened to challenge his front-running
rival at the last, but some sluggish earlier jumps were followed by a much more
serious mistake at the last. The blunder almost certainly cost him victory and,

although his odds were cut for the Gold Cup, it was clear there were still questions to be answered. An eloquent response came with a much more fluent performance in the John Durkan Memorial Punchestown Chase. The Punchestown Chase hasn't always lived up to its Grade 1 billing, but, with dual previous winner Native Upmanship joined by Tiutchev, Rince Ri and Le Coudray, the latest renewal looked well up to scratch. Native Upmanship, having missed his intended prep race, was the first to crack four out as lack of condition began to tell. Tiutchev proved much tougher and would have run right up to his best without a late error. However, Beef Or Salmon, odds on as at Clonmel, reaped the benefit of a far more polished round of jumping and was already beginning to assert when Tiutchev belted the last. His Gold Cup odds were cut again (to around 11/2) after he quickened three and a half lengths clear. Despite some sketchy jumping back at two miles, Beef Or Salmon repeated his 2002 success in the O'Connell Warehousing Hilly Way Chase at Cork the following weekend and connections headed into Christmas in justifiably positive mood.

Then came the announcement that Best Mate's Christmas target was to be the Ericsson at Leopardstown as opposed to the King George at Kempton. If the news came as an unpleasant surprise to Hourigan he did his best to mask it. 'I'm not worried that he's coming over to take us on and there was never any question of us dodging him,' he said. 'Sunday should tell us plenty.' The expected showdown never looked like materialising. Best Mate went off at odds on, Beef Or Salmon starting at 2/1 to land the showpiece of the four-day meeting for the second year running. Beef Or Salmon was, however, jumping ponderously well before he hit the fourth last and looked third best from a long way out, finally beaten nine lengths and four behind Best Mate and Le Coudray. Beef Or Salmon's rider reported that the horse had gurgled during the race, while the stable later added that mucus was found in Beef Or Salmon's lungs. Connections faced the added worry of Beef Or Salmon's recurring muscular problems during the run-up to the Hennessy Cognac Gold Cup back at Leopardstown in February. Four days before the race, the physio treating Beef Or Salmon advised that a bid for the Hennessy would place Beef Or Salmon's presence in the Gold Cup in jeopardy. The warning was heeded and

John Durkan Memorial Punchestown Chase—
Beef Or Salmon (right) is poised to pounce on the leader Tiutchev

Punchestown Heineken Gold Cup—
2003 winner First Gold is no match for Ireland's leading staying chaser

patience was rewarded when Beef Or Salmon returned from a break with two of the best performances of his career.

Racecourse gallops at Thurles and Cork and a schooling session at Limerick paved the way for Beef Or Salmon's return to Cheltenham, where he was sent off at 10/1, the subject of far less publicity than a year earlier. Beef Or Salmon came right back to his best, though his performance was somewhat out of character in that he struggled to go the pace for much of the final circuit. Careful jumping left him with plenty to do four out, but he stayed on strongly in the straight and was still gaining steadily as he passed the post three and a half lengths behind Best Mate in fourth. Hourigan reported afterwards that Beef Or Salmon had been 'a cripple at Christmas'. There was no Best Mate to contend with at Punchestown in April, but the Gold Cup third Harbour Pilot and the previous year's Punchestown Gold Cup winner First Gold were in the line-up. Beef Or Salmon, who was featured on RTE television skipping nimbly through a dressage class as part of his big race preparations, showed he was clearly back on top of his game, showing the best form of his career under a typically confident Murphy ride, jumping safely then showing a telling turn of foot between the last two fences and beating Harbour Pilot by four lengths with something in hand. Murphy waxed lyrical about Beef Or Salmon's 'quick and accurate' jumping, while Hourigan ruminated on what might have happened had Beef Or Salmon been in the same form on Gold Cup day. The Championship Chase at Down Royal, a race bypassed in 2003, is the likely spring-board for a campaign which will again almost certainly involve the big prizes at Leopardstown and Punchestown, as well as the Gold Cup.

Beef Or Salmon's pedigree, such as it is, was analysed in the preceding edition of *Chasers & Hurdlers*. To recap, Beef Or Salmon's sire Cajetano was useful on the Flat and over hurdles and, after being retired to stud in Ireland in 1993, was eventually sold to Sardinia. Beef Or Salmon is the fourth foal and first notable performer out of the once-raced Farinella. Since producing him, she has foaled a Saddlers' Hall filly who made 52,000 guineas as a three-year-old but has yet to run, while a visit to Carroll House produced Our House, who failed to progress after a promising hurdling debut for Martin Pipe during the latest season.

Beef Or Salmon (IRE) (ch.g. 1996)	Cajetano (USA) (b 1986)	Run The Gantlet (b 1968)	Tom Rolfe
			First Feather
		Intensive (1979)	Sir Wiggle
			Flying Legs
	Farinella (IRE) (ch 1988)	Salmon Leap (ch 1980)	Northern Dancer
			Fish-Bar
		Boldella (b 1977)	Bold Lad
			Ardelle

A strong gelding, Beef Or Salmon is versatile as regards distance. He has now won good races at two miles to twenty-five furlongs over fences and saw out the extra two furlongs in the Gold Cup thoroughly. Another plus point from the latest season was that Beef Or Salmon proved soft ground is by no means a prerequisite for him. The ground was good for both the Gold Cup and the Punchestown Gold Cup, though whether Beef Or Salmon would be able to produce his best on going firmer than good remains unproven. One thing which isn't open to doubt is that Beef Or Salmon has the ability to win more good races. A record of four Grade 1 victories and three other graded wins from just eleven outings over fences makes impressive reading. Beef Or Salmon's turn of foot should continue to be a

Mr B. J. Craig's "Beef Or Salmon"

potent weapon in small fields when the early pace is steady. But the Cheltenham Gold Cup places much stiffer demands on a chaser. As well as jumping slowly on occasions, it should be noted that Beef Or Salmon also lost momentum by going sharply right at the downhill fences on both circuits at Cheltenham. Beef Or Salmon is certainly young enough to win a Gold Cup and is probably good enough to win an average one. Whether his jumping has improved enough remains the most pertinent question. *M. Hourigan, Ireland*

BEEFY NOVA 12 ch.g. Ra Nova – Cherry Sip (Nearly A Hand) [2003/4 c78x, h–: c21m² c21g⁶ c23m⁶ c22g⁵ c24d⁵ c22g² c21d³ c22s* c24g* c24g⁴ Mar 17] workmanlike gelding: poor handicap chaser: won amateur events at Fontwell in February and Huntingdon in March: stays 3m: acts on good to firm and heavy going. *G. H. Yardley* **c75 h–**

BEEHIVE LAD 10 b.g. Then Again – Steel Typhoon (General Ironside) [2003/4 20s 16g c17g³ May 24] lengthy, sparely-made gelding: poor maiden hurdler, lightly raced: hasn't convinced with jumping over fences, including when third in weak novice handicap at Cartmel: raced mainly around 2m: acts on soft and good to firm going: sold 800 gns Doncaster August Sales. *R. Ford* **c77 h–**

BEEN HERE BEFORE 4 ch.g. Fearless Action (USA) – Mistral Magic (Crofter (USA)) [2003/4 F16g F16s Apr 4] sixth foal: half-brother to 2 winning pointers: dam lightly-raced daughter of Ribblesdale third Hunting Cap: tailed off in bumpers. *D. W. Barker* **F–**

BEETLE BUG 4 br.f. Robellino (USA) – Special Beat (Bustino) [2003/4 16s⁵ 19d⁵ 17dᵘʳ 19gᵖᵘ 16d⁵ Apr 12] poor maiden on Flat (barely stays 2m), sold out of J. Portman's stable 1,400 gns Doncaster October Sales: little form over hurdles: tongue tied after debut. *A. M. Hales* **h52**

BE FAIR 6 br.g. Blushing Flame (USA) – Tokyo (Mtoto) [2003/4 F114: 16m* 16m* 21g* Nov 2] well-made gelding: will make a chaser: useful bumper performer: landed odds in novice events at Huntingdon first 3 starts over hurdles, challenging when left clear 2 out and beat The Indispensable 6 lengths on return from 5-month absence third occasion: off another 6 months, under 4 lengths fourth of 8 to Sadlers Wings in Grade 1 at Punchestown in late-April, keeping on: stays 21f: has awkward head carriage: may do better yet. *D. E. Cantillon* **h122**

BEFORE DARK (IRE) 6 b.g. Phardante (FR) – Menebeans (IRE) (Duky) [2003/4 F16s² F17s³ F16g F16g Feb 28] sturdy gelding: fourth foal: half-brother to winning pointer/2m hurdler Dalcassian Buck (by Buckskin): dam unraced half-sister to fairly useful staying hurdler/chaser Menebuck: fairly useful form when placed in bumpers at Huntingdon and Exeter: will stay 2½m. *Mrs H. Dalton* **F101**

BEFORE THE MAST (IRE) 7 br.g. Broken Hearted – Kings Reserve (King's Ride) [2003/4 F93: F16m* 17dᵖᵘ 16d³ Dec 6] rangy, rather sparely-made gelding: useful form in bumpers: off a year, made all at Huntingdon in October despite hanging left under pressure: disappointing in 2 outings over hurdles: has been early to post: needs to settle better. *Noel T. Chance* **h76 F105**

BEGSY'S BULLET 9 b.m. Primitive Rising (USA) – Seeker's Sister (Ashmore (FR)) [2003/4 c74, h77: c20s⁴ c21vᵖᵘ 20s³ c20sᵖᵘ 21s* Jan 16] compact mare: winning chaser, failed to complete over fences in 2003/4: modest hurdler: improved form when winning conditional jockeys handicap at Huntingdon: will stay beyond 21f: raced only on soft/heavy going. *D. McCain* **c– h91**

BEHAN 5 ch.g. Rainbows For Life (CAN) – With Finesse (Be My Guest (USA)) [2003/4 16g 16m Nov 24] small gelding: poor on Flat (best form up to 1¼m): blinkered, no show in 2 races over hurdles. *A. Crook* **h–**

BEHAVINGBADLY (IRE) 9 b.g. Lord Americo – Audrey's Turn (Strong Gale) [2003/4 c110x, h–: c25sᵘʳ c30gꟳ 20d c26d c31d* Apr 22] good-topped gelding: winning hurdler: fair handicap chaser: 25/1, returned to form when winning 16-runner event at Perth: stays 31f: raced on good going or softer (acts on heavy): often let down by jumping. *A. Parker* **c105 x h–**

BEHRAJAN (IRE) 9 b. or br.g. Arazi (USA) – Behera (Mill Reef (USA)) [2003/4 c168, h–: c24s² c29gꟳ Jan 10] big, angular gelding: very smart hurdler/top-class chaser, successful on 11 of 29 starts, including 2003 Pillar Property Chase: creditable second, clear of remainder, to Horus in listed handicap at Ascot (won race in 2002) on reappearance: fell fatally at Warwick following month: should have stayed beyond 3¼m: acted on heavy and good to firm going: raced prominently: was prone to the odd mistake: game. *H. D. Daly* **c163 h–**

BEHZAD (IRE) 5 b.g. Kahyasi – Behriya (IRE) (Kenmare (FR)) [2003/4 F84: 16g³ **h86**
17g³ 20g² 20g² 20mᵖᵘ Jul 16] sturdy gelding: modest novice hurdler: reportedly distressed final outing: will stay beyond 2½m. *D. McCain*

BEKSTAR 9 b.m. Nicholas Bill – Murex (Royalty) [2003/4 h97d: 17g⁵ 19d⁶ 18s Dec **h–**
31] lengthy, rather sparely-made mare: modest handicap hurdler at best: well below form
in 2003/4: stays 2¾m: acts on firm and good to soft going. *J. C. Tuck*

BELALCAZAR 5 b.g. El Conquistador – Ruby Celebration (New Member) [2003/4 **F–**
F17g Apr 10] fifth foal: dam, maiden, sister to winning hunter What's Yours and half-
sister to several winning pointers: well held in bumper on debut. *Miss I. E. Craig*

BELCARO (GER) 5 b.g. Dashing Blade – Bella Carolina (GER) (Surumu (GER)) **h96**
[2003/4 16g⁶ 17g* 16g³ Apr 12] rather leggy gelding: successful 4 times up to around
1½m from 12 starts on Flat in Germany at 4 yrs for I. Schalter: won maiden hurdle at
Taunton in April: again favourite, similar form when third to I D Technology in novice at
Plumpton: raced around 2m on good ground. *C. J. Mann*

BELFAST BOY (IRE) 6 b.g. Forest Wind (USA) – Abadila (IRE) (Shernazar) **h–**
[2003/4 16g²⁰ 20f⁴ Aug 24] third foal: dam twice-raced half-sister to smart French
hurdler Chinese Gordon: little sign of ability, left J. Clements after second outing.
P. J. Flynn, Ireland

BELISARIO (IRE) 10 b. or br.g. Distinctly North (USA) – Bold Kate (Bold Lad **c122**
(IRE)) [2003/4 c108, h–: c24s* Mar 13] big, leggy gelding: fairly useful handicap chaser, **h–**
lightly raced: off a year, showed himself better than ever when winning at Newcastle by 8
lengths from King's Bounty: better around 3m than shorter: acts on heavy and good to
firm going. *M. W. Easterby*

BELLA BAMBINA 4 b.f. Turtle Island (IRE) – Lady Eurolink (Kala Shikari) [2003/4 **h75 §**
16f³ 16m⁶ 16s² Jan 14] poor maiden on Flat (best effort at 1¼m) for J. Dunlop: poor form
in juvenile hurdles, looking less than keen last 2 starts: visored first 2. *M. C. Pipe*

BELLACACCIA (IRE) 8 ch.m. Beau Sher – Game Gambler (IRE) (Long Pond) **h84**
[2003/4 h79: 24m* Apr 28] small, sparely-made mare: poor hurdler: won minor event at
Newcastle: stays 3m: acts on good to firm going. *C. W. Thornton*

BELLA CASTANA 4 ch.f. Efisio – Simple Logic (Aragon) [2003/4 16gᵘʳ Nov 30] **h–**
leggy, close-coupled filly: well held in maidens on Flat: tried to refuse and unseated
fourth in juvenile on hurdling debut: sold 1,600 gns Doncaster January Sales. *A. Charlton*

BELLA LIANA (IRE) 4 b.f. Sesaro (USA) – Bella Galiana (ITY) (Don Roberto **F–**
(USA)) [2003/4 F13g Nov 30] third foal: half-sister to Italian 6f to 11f winner Rischio
Totale (by Love The Groom): dam unraced: well beaten in bumper on debut. *J. Parkes*

BELLA MARY 9 b.m. Derrylin – Pro-Token (Proverb) [2003/4 h92?: c20s⁵ c21g³ **c70**
c22m³ c24fᵖᵘ c20sᵖᵘ c25sᶠ 16s⁵ 22d 21g 26d Mar 28] workmanlike mare: poor maiden **h63**
hurdler/chaser: stays at least 21f: acts on soft going. *C. T. Pogson*

BELLA PAVLINA 6 ch.m. Sure Blade (USA) – Pab's Choice (Telsmoss) [2003/4 **h–**
16gᶠ 16mᵖᵘ May 7] fair on Flat (stays 1½m), much improved and successful 5 times in
2004 for W. M. Brisbourne: failed to complete in 2 starts over hurdles. *M. Todhunter*

BELLAPORT GIRL 6 b.m. Supreme Leader – Derry Nell (Derrylin) [2003/4 F17m **F–**
F16m F18f Aug 18] first foal: dam unraced, from family of Champion Hurdle winners
Morley Street and Granville Again: well held in 3 bumpers. *Dr J. R. J. Naylor*

BELLEFLEUR 7 b.m. Alflora (IRE) – Isabeau (Law Society (USA)) [2003/4 h75: **c–**
17g⁶ 21dᶠ 23d c24sᵖᵘ 16dᵖᵘ Jan 13] sturdy mare: poor maiden hurdler: visored, no show **h–**
on chasing debut: has looked none too genuine. *J. M. Jefferson*

BELLINO EMPRESARIO (IRE) 6 b.g. Robellino (USA) – The Last Empress **h69**
(IRE) (Last Tycoon) [2003/4 h–: 16g 17g 16m 19mᵖᵘ Nov 20] angular gelding: little show
over hurdles: pulls hard. *B. Llewellyn*

BELL LANE LAD (IRE) 7 b.g. Wakashan – Busti Lass (IRE) (Bustineto) [2003/4 **h103**
h79, F77: 22d* 22v⁴ 20d² Dec 19] useful-looking gelding: type to make a chaser: fair
handicap hurdler: changed stables and improved in 2003/4, won at Uttoxeter in November and 7 lengths second to Master Trix at Ascot: will stay beyond 2¾m: acts on good to
firm and good to soft going, possibly not on heavy. *A. King*

BELL TEX (IRE) 12 br.g. Orchestra – Lyngard (Balliol) [2003/4 h–: 16m 17d 16m⁵ **h–**
Jun 18] poor novice hurdler, lightly raced: stays 2½m: acts on good to firm going.
J. C. Fox

BELL TOR (IRE) 7 b.m. King's Ride – Shannon Juliette (Julio Mariner) [2003/4 **h83 §** h78: 21s⁵ 21g² 22g Dec 9] lengthy mare: modest maiden hurdler: will stay 3m: acts on heavy going: temperamental. *D. R. Gandolfo*

BEL OMBRE (FR) 4 b.g. Nikos – Danse du Soleil (FR) (Morespeed) [2003/4 F18gᵖᵘ **F–** Apr 22] 38,000 3-y-o: second foal: half-brother to winning 2m hurdler Danse Neige (by Welkin): dam 9f winner: went lame in bumper on debut. *O. Sherwood*

BELSKI 11 br.g. Arctic Lord – Bellekino (Relkino) [2003/4 c97: c22g³ c23g* c23g³ **c105** c25v* c24gᵖᵘ c23d* c25mᵖᵘ Apr 13] fair chaser: won novice in December and handicaps in February and March, all at Exeter: ran as if amiss fifth and final starts: will stay beyond 25f: unraced on firm going, acts on any other. *C. L. Tizzard*

BELUGA (IRE) 5 gr.g. John French – Mesena (Pals Passage) [2003/4 aF16g³ F16s **F85** Feb 20] good-topped gelding: half-brother to several winners, including fair staying chaser Master Gleason (by Gleason): dam unraced: much better effort in bumpers when third on polytrack at Lingfield on debut, dictating pace. *M. Pitman*

BELVENTO (IRE) 12 b.g. Strong Gale – Salufair (Salluceva) [2003/4 c99§, h–: **c99 §** c26g⁵ c25f² c22m⁴ Jun 21] good sort: modest chaser: successful in points in March and **h–** April: stays 3¼m: best efforts on good/good to firm going: inconsistent. *N. J. Gifford*

BE MERRY (IRE) 5 ch.m. Broken Hearted – Charlies Rising (IRE) (Rising) [2003/4 **F83** F16g⁶ Mar 13] first foal: dam unraced: 7 lengths sixth of 10 in bumper at Ayr on debut. *I. A. Gault, Ireland*

BE MY ADELINA (IRE) 6 b.m. Be My Native (USA) – Adelinas Leader (IRE) **F92** (Supreme Leader) [2003/4 F88: F17d* May 17] fair form in mares bumpers, won at Bangor by 9 lengths from No More Money: will stay 2½m. *P. F. Nicholls*

BE MY BELLE (IRE) 8 b.m. Be My Native (USA) – Boreen Belle (Boreen (FR)) **c139** [2003/4 c133, h–: c24f⁴ c26gᵖᵘ 24d² c24s² c24s⁵ c24d⁶ Feb 8] strong mare: useful **h129** hurdler/chaser: won Thyestes Handicap Chase in 2003: twice runner-up at Leopardstown in 2003/4, behind Sacundai in Grade 2 hurdle and Cloudy Bays in valuable handicap chase: better around 3m than shorter: went well on soft/heavy going (tailed off on firm): often made running: retired. *S. J. Treacy, Ireland*

BE MY BETTER HALF (IRE) 9 b.g. Be My Native (USA) – The Mrs (Mandalus) **c114** [2003/4 c114, h–: c25d³ c20s³ c18vᶠ Apr 21] fair chaser, lightly raced: should stay **h–** beyond 2¾m: acts on heavy going. *A. L. T. Moore, Ireland*

BE MY DESTINY (IRE) 7 b.g. Be My Native (USA) – Miss Cali (Young Man (FR)) **c121** [2003/4 h110: c17vᶠ c18d² c16g³ c20g⁶ c24g* c24gᶠ Mar 6] tall gelding: fair hurdler: **h–** fairly useful chaser: very much on toes, improved form when winning novice at Newbury in February, going well 3 lengths behind Mister Banjo when left clear 3 out: likely to prove better at 3m than shorter: raced on good ground or softer (acts on heavy). *M. Pitman*

BE MY DREAM (IRE) 9 b.g. Be My Native (USA) – Dream Toi (Carlburg) [2003/4 **c91** c110d, h–: c25g³ c24m May 29] tall gelding: fair hunter chaser: won point in March: **h–** suited by 3m+: acts on heavy going: wore visor/cheekpieces in 2003/4. *R. J. Webb*

BE MY FRIEND (IRE) 8 ch.g. Be My Native (USA) – Miss Lamb (Relkino) [2003/4 **c–** h106+: c20gᶠ 16sᵖᵘ Nov 22] lightly-raced winning hurdler: fell seventh in novice on **h–** chasing debut: should stay beyond 17f. *Mrs H. Dalton*

BE MY MANAGER (IRE) 9 b.g. Be My Native (USA) – Fahy Quay (Quayside) **c136** [2003/4 c124, h–: c24m* c20d⁴ c20gᵖᵘ 22gᵖᵘ Mar 12] tall gelding: has reportedly had leg **h–** trouble: useful handicap chaser: back to best in 2003/4, winning at Perth in September and Wetherby (beat Hunters Tweed by length) in December: easy to back, amiss at Kempton (lame) and Ayr (over hurdles, bled from nose) last 2 starts: stays 3m: acts on any going. *M. Todhunter*

BE MY OWN (IRE) 8 b.g. Lord Americo – No Slow (King's Ride) [2003/4 22s 22gᵖᵘ **h61** 16gᶠ 20d² 22gᵘʳ Apr 18] poor maiden hurdler: stays 2½m: acts on soft and good to firm ground. *R. H. Buckler*

BE MY VALENTINE (IRE) 6 b.m. Be My Native (USA) – Valantonia (IRE) (Over **h–** The River (FR)) [2003/4 F16g⁴ F16d 21v Jan 13] neat mare: fourth foal: half-sister to **F81** winning 3¾m hurdler Bison King (by King's Ride): dam unraced half-sister to Champion Hurdle winners Morley Street and Granville Again: better effort in bumpers when fourth in mares event at Ludlow: failed to settle when ninth of 11 finishers in mares novice at Sedgefield on hurdling debut. *C. R. Egerton*

BENBECULA (IRE) 7 b.g. Glacial Storm (USA) – Lough View (Radical) [2003/4 **c107**
h114+: c22v[pu] c21d[3] c24g[2] c20d[F] Mar 11] rangy, angular gelding: fair maiden hurdler/ **h–**
chaser: fell fatally at Carlisle: stayed 3m: raced on good going or softer (acted on heavy):
visored last 5 starts. *P. R. Webber*

BENBOW 7 ch.g. Gunner B – Juno Away (Strong Gale) [2003/4 h?, F–: 26g[pu] May 1] **h–**
poor form over hurdles: placed in points in 2004. *F. Jordan*

BEN BRITTEN 5 ch.g. Sabrehill (USA) – Golden Panda (Music Boy) [2003/4 17d **h–**
Apr 10] half-brother to winning hurdler/chaser Decoded (by Deploy), stays 3¼m: well
beaten in 2 starts around 7f at 2 yrs for J. Wainwright: not knocked about when seventh of
16 to Flownaway in novice at Carlisle on hurdling debut: may do better. *N. G. Richards*

BENBYAS 7 b.g. Rambo Dancer (CAN) – Light The Way (Nicholas Bill) [2003/4 **h139**
h134: 16d[5] 16s 16v* 16g 17d[6] 16d[2] Apr 17] medium-sized gelding: fairly useful on Flat,
won twice in April: useful handicap hurdler: won at Uttoxeter in January by 10 lengths
from Talarive, eased run-in: contested valuable events after, excellent 5 lengths second to
Copeland in limited handicap at Ayr: best around 2m: raced mainly on good going or
softer (acts on heavy): rare poor effort when sweating and on toes second start: usually
forces pace: superb jumper: most genuine and reliable. *D. Carroll*

BENEFIT 10 b.g. Primitive Rising (USA) – Sobriquet (Roan Rocket) [2003/4 c77, **c72**
h81: 21s c21s[pu] c21s 23g[4] 24d[5] c25d[3] Mar 22] small, lengthy gelding: poor handicap **h84**
hurdler/novice chaser: probably stays 25f: raced on good going or softer (acts on heavy).
Miss L. C. Siddall

BEN EWAR 10 b.g. Old Vic – Sunset Reef (Mill Reef (USA)) [2003/4 h111: 16g[4] **h109 §**
20m[ur] 16g[6] 16v[pu] 16g[2] 18d Apr 7] leggy, angular gelding: fair handicap hurdler: stays
2½m: probably acts on any going: tried tongue tied: has broken blood vessels: unreliable.
K. O. Cunningham-Brown

BEN FROM KETTON 9 b.g. Cruise Missile – Saucy Girl (Saucy Kit) [2003/4 c25d **c–**
May 3] fair pointer: no show in 2 hunters. *S. J. Robinson*

BENGAL BOY 8 b.g. Gildoran – Bengal Lady (Celtic Cone) [2003/4 c86x, h91: **c75 x**
c20s[ur] c20m[pu] c16g[4] 22m c21g[3] c21g[pu] Aug 8] good-topped gelding: poor handicap **h–**
chaser/maiden hurdler: probably stays 21f: acts on good to firm and heavy going:
blinkered last 2 outings: tried tongue tied: often let down by jumping over fences: sold
3,200 gns Doncaster October Sales, won point in March. *P. Beaumont*

BENJAMIN BUCKRAM (IRE) 5 b.g. Topanoora – Red Bit (IRE) (Henbit (USA)) **F–**
[2003/4 F16g Feb 21] €50,000 3-y-o: fifth foal: half-brother to bumper winners Ard
Solus (by Supreme Leader) and The Beeches (by Be My Native): dam unraced half-sister
to top-class 2m to 2½m chaser Waterloo Boy: pulled hard when tenth of 16 to The
Thunderer in bumper at Ascot on debut. *C. R. Egerton*

BENJAMIN (IRE) 6 b.g. Night Shift (USA) – Best Academy (USA) (Roberto **h–**
(USA)) [2003/4 h–: 17f 16m Oct 6] smallish gelding: poor maiden on Flat (stays 1m): no
worthwhile form over hurdles: tongue tied. *Jane Southcombe*

BENJI 13 ch.g. High Kicker (USA) – Snap Tin (Jimmy Reppin) [2003/4 c16m[pu] c20g[3] **c85 §**
c17g[pu] c18f[3] c19m* c20m[pu] Sep 23] lengthy, angular gelding: modest handicap chaser, **h–**
off 3 years before reappearance: won at Hereford in September, idling after left clear 2
out: presumably amiss later in month: stays 21f: acts on firm and good to soft going: tried
blinkered, not since 1997/8: ungenuine. *R. Ingram*

BEN MORE 6 b.g. Seymour Hicks (FR) – Stac-Pollaidh (Tina's Pet) [2003/4 h70, **h70**
F82: 22f[pu] 20g[3] 19g[3] 16g 16d[5] 21g[2] 22g[3] 20d[pu] Apr 7] rather unfurnished gelding: poor
maiden hurdler: claimed from J. King £6,000 sixth outing: probably stays 2¾m: acts on
firm and good to soft going (unraced on soft/heavy). *Miss K. Marks*

BENNANABAA 5 b.g. Anabaa (USA) – Arc Empress Jane (IRE) (Rainbow Quest **F–**
(USA)) [2003/4 F16m[6] Oct 22] 1,200F, 5,000Y: fourth foal: half-brother to fairly useful
2m hurdler Rob Leach (by Robellino) and 1½m to 2m winner Manzoni (by Warrshan):
dam unraced: pulled hard when tailed off in bumper on debut: little form on Flat.
S. C. Burrough

BENNIE'S PRIDE (IRE) 8 b.g. Welsh Term – Mugs Away (Mugatpura) [2003/4 **c120**
c103, h103, F92: c25g c19s[2] c19d* c21g[F] Feb 29] well-made gelding: winning hurdler: **h–**
fairly useful handicap chaser, left E. O'Grady after first outing: won listed event at
Leopardstown in January by 2 lengths from Fiery Ring: should stay beyond 2¾m: acts on
good to firm and heavy going. *M. J. P. O'Brien, Ireland*

BENO (IRE) 5 b.g. Ridgewood Ben – Future Romance (Distant Relative) [2003/4 F16m F16s F16d F17v 16g^pu Apr 5] angular gelding: third foal: half-brother to winning Flat stayer Regency Red (by Dolphin Street): dam unraced: no sign of ability. *Mrs H. O. Graham* **h–** **F–**

BENOVA BOY 12 ch.g. Ra Nova – Alithorne (Kinglet) [2003/4 c24m c23m^5 c23m^3 c24g^3 c21m^F c24g^4 c26d^3 c23g^6 Aug 23] lengthy gelding: winning pointer: poor maiden steeplechaser: stays 3m: acts on firm and good to soft going: wears headgear. *S. J. Gilmore* **c60**

BENRAJAH (IRE) 7 b.g. Lord Americo – Andy's Fancy (IRE) (Andretti) [2003/4 h105: c21m^F c25f* c26g^2 c25g* c20d^4 c24g^2 c22g^3 c20g^6 Apr 3] well-made gelding: winning hurdler: fair chaser: won 3-runner novice at Kelso in October and handicap at Catterick in December: good efforts when placed: stays 3¼m: acts on good to soft going (second in bumper on soft), simple task on firm: races prominently. *M. Todhunter* **c112** **h–**

BENSON (IRE) 9 b. or br.g. Hawkstone (IRE) – Erin St Helen (IRE) (Seclude (USA)) [2003/4 c103, h–: c25d c20d^F c24d^pu Apr 8] workmanlike gelding: winning chaser: well beaten on completed start in hunters in 2003/4: best efforts around 2½m on good going: sketchy jumper. *J. W. Mullins* **c–** **h–**

BENTYHEATH LANE 7 b.g. Puissance – Eye Sight (Roscoe Blake) [2003/4 h65: 16d^4 16g 16m 16m^3 17m^2 17m 16m^5 17m c16f^6 Oct 23] poor maiden hurdler: last of 6 in novice on chasing debut: raced mainly around 2m: acts on good to firm going. *M. Mullineaux* **c–** **h71**

BENVOLIO 7 br.g. Cidrax (FR) – Miss Capulet (Commanche Run) [2003/4 c–, h–: c26s^pu 26m^pu 22m Aug 30] smallish gelding: of little account: left C. Kellett after first outing: wore cheekpieces next time. *P. L. Clinton* **c–** **h–**

BE OFF WITH YOU 5 b.m. Nalchik (USA) – Tilstock Maid (Rolfe (USA)) [2003/4 F16m F16g Aug 23] fourth foal: sister to 2m hurdle winner Warminghamsharpish: dam unraced: well beaten in 2 bumpers. *B. R. Foster* **F–**

BERENGARIO (IRE) 4 b.g. Mark of Esteem (IRE) – Ivrea (Sadler's Wells (USA)) [2003/4 F12g 16s 17s 16d 17d^3 16g 16g^6 Mar 25] sixth foal: half-brother to 3 winners, including fairly useful 1994 2-y-o 7f winner who stayed 1¼m Hedera (by Woodman): dam, 7f winner at 2 yrs and second in Ribblesdale Stakes, half-sister to Oaks d'Italia winner Ivyanna: sold unraced out of D. Loder's stable £4,400 Ascot April (2003) Sales: well held in bumper on debut: poor form over hurdles: tried blinkered. *S. C. Burrough* **h67** **F–**

BERGAMO 8 b.g. Robellino (USA) – Pretty Thing (Star Appeal) [2003/4 h104d: 20v^4 24g 21d^2 21d^3 16d^2 17d^2 19g^5 16g^2 21g^3 Apr 12] small gelding: modest hurdler: stays 21f: acts on soft and good to firm going: tried visored/in cheekpieces, usually blinkered: no battler. *B. Ellison* **h95 §**

BERING GIFTS (IRE) 9 b.g. Bering – Bobbysoxer (Valiyar) [2003/4 c102§, h113§: c21d Apr 12] workmanlike gelding: fair handicap hurdler: fair hunter chaser, tailed off at Fakenham after year's absence: stays easy 21f: acts on firm going: needs waiting tactics: temperamental. *Mrs T. J. Hill* **c– §** **h– §**

BERKELEY HALL 7 b.m. Saddlers' Hall (IRE) – Serious Affair (Valiyar) [2003/4 h82?: 16d^2 16g^6 20m^pu Aug 16] modest on Flat (stays 1m): poor form over hurdles, lame final start: likely to prove best at 2m: tried in cheekpieces. *R. Lee* **h77**

BERLIN BLUE 11 b.g. Belmez (USA) – Blue Brocade (Reform) [2003/4 c125, h–: c24m^6 c32m^6 Jun 29] compact gelding: winning hurdler: fairly useful handicap chaser, below form both starts early in 2003/4: stays 4m: acts on good to firm and good to soft going: usually sound jumper. *R. M. Stronge* **c–** **h–**

BERMAHO (IRE) 4 b.g. Desert Story (IRE) – Shydico (IRE) (Nordico (USA)) [2003/4 16g* 16f^5 16d^6 16s^pu 16d^3 16d Dec 26] half-brother to winning 2m hurdler Treasure Cove (by Treasure Kay): fairly useful on Flat (stays 1m): fairly useful juvenile hurdler: won maiden at Roscommon in August: tried in cheekpieces/blinkers: races prominently. *G. M. Lyons, Ireland* **h111**

BERMUDA (IRE) 5 b.g. Sadler's Wells (USA) – Sequel (IRE) (Law Society (USA)) [2003/4 F16m F17g^5 16s^pu 16s^pu 20d^pu 24s 22d Feb 12] 355,000F: sturdy gelding: sixth foal (all by Sadler's Wells): brother to 2 winners, notably useful Irish 7f to 1¾m winner Family Tradition: dam maiden half-sister to outstanding broodmare Slightly Dangerous and to dam of Rainbow Quest: sold unraced out of A. O'Brien's stable 10,000 gns Newmarket Autumn (2002) Sales: modest form in bumpers, sold out of W. Jenks's stable 3,700 gns Doncaster May Sales after debut: little show over hurdles: tried in cheekpieces/blinkers. *G. F. Edwards* **h–** **F80**

BERNARDON (GER) 8 b.g. Suave Dancer (USA) – Bejaria (GER) (Konigsstuhl **h118**
(GER)) [2003/4 h131§: 16g^pu 16s^4 16s^pu 16d^4 18g^3 16m^6 Apr 13] close-coupled gelding:
one-time useful hurdler for M. Pipe: best effort in handicaps in 2003/4 when sixth to
River City in well-contested event at Chepstow (wore cheekpieces): will prove best
around 2m: acts on soft and good to firm going: tried visored: takes good hold (saddle
slipped first/third starts). *R. C. Guest*

BERNINI (IRE) 4 b.g. Grand Lodge (USA) – Alsahah (IRE) (Unfuwain (USA)) **h102**
[2003/4 16s^3 16s^5 17d^3 19g Mar 27] good-topped gelding: trained by M. Bell, won 1½m
maiden on all-weather in 2003, no comparable form on turf: regressed in juvenile hurdles
after third at Newbury on debut: should stay further than 2m. *N. J. Henderson*

BERRINGTON (NZ) 7 b.g. Fort Prospect (USA) – Calamity (NZ) (Bally Royal) **h–**
[2003/4 h–: 16g^pu May 21] tall gelding: no sign of ability. *A. J. Deakin*

BERRYWHITE (IRE) 6 ch.g. Barathea (IRE) – Berryville (USA) (Hatchet Man **h–**
(USA)) [2003/4 19g^pu 17s Feb 11] ex-German gelding: successful at 1¼m and 11f at
4 yrs on Flat, placed 4 times in 2003 for U. Stoltefuss: bled both starts over hurdles.
C. Grant

BERTIE ARMS 4 b.f. Cloudings (IRE) – Pugilistic (Hard Fought) [2003/4 F16s Apr **F–**
12] half-sister to 3 winners by Gunner B, including fair hurdler/chaser up to 2¾m Gunner
Marc: dam unraced half-sister to smart 2m hurdler Jobroke: seventh of 13 finishers in
mares bumper on debut. *J. M. Jefferson*

BERTIEBANOO (IRE) 6 ch.g. Be My Native (USA) – Gemeleks Gem (IRE) (Car- **h114**
lingford Castle) [2003/4 F17s 21v* 24s^5 25d^2 24s Apr 17] €52,000 4-y-o: workmanlike **F83**
gelding: second foal: dam lightly-raced half-sister to one-time useful chaser up to 21f
Pete The Parson: seventh in bumper on debut: fair form in novice hurdles: found plenty
when winning at Plumpton in November: stays 25f: acts on heavy going. *P. J. Hobbs*

BERTIE O'TOOLE 10 b.g. Jendali (USA) – Young Mary (Young Generation) **c–**
[2003/4 20v 24s 24d^pu c21d^ur Mar 30] winning pointer: no form over hurdles: disputing **h–**
lead when unseating tenth in handicap on steeplechase debut: tongue tied last 3 starts.
Mrs R. L. Elliot

BESEIGED (USA) 7 ch.g. Cadeaux Genereux – Munnaya (USA) (Nijinsky (CAN)) **h107**
[2003/4 h105p, F96: 16m* 16g* 16g^pu 16s 16g Feb 18] workmanlike gelding: successful
first 4 starts over hurdles, including handicaps at Kelso (conditional jockeys) and Perth
(intermediate) in May: no form in 3 runs after 5½-month absence: stays 19f, at least when
conditions aren't testing: acts on good to firm and good to soft going. *R. A. Fahey*

BESSIE BUNTER 8 b.m. Rakaposhi King – Black H'Penny (Town And Country) **h–**
[2003/4 h83d: 24v May 21] poor maden hurdler: won point in January: bred to be suited
by 2½m+: raced on soft/heavy going. *J. A. B. Old*

BEST MATE (IRE) 9 b.g. Un Desperado (FR) – Katday (FR) (Miller's Mate) **c176 +**
[2003/4 c182, h–: c20s^2 c24d* c26g* Mar 18] **h–**
 And so the expected came to pass: Best Mate kept his date with destiny
and joined Golden Miller, Cottage Rake and Arkle as a three-time winner of the
Cheltenham Gold Cup. Such is his superiority among the current crop of staying
chasers and, touch wood, so strong is his constitution that he may yet surpass
Cottage Rake and Arkle in winning a fourth Gold Cup or even join Golden Miller
in winning a fifth. After his latest success in March, Best Mate was quoted at no
longer than 5/2 to win again in 2005 and at just 12/1 to win both then and in
2006. 'Immortal' screamed the front page of the next day's *Racing Post*, a word
which can, of course, often be heard followed by invisible. How appropriate. Best
Mate was, frustratingly, notable by his absence for much of the season and wasn't
required to show himself any better than he had in either of his previous Gold Cup
campaigns. He was seen in action just twice in the first part of the winter, not at all
between Christmas and the Festival and was back in cotton wool even before the
last torn-up betting ticket had been swept up at Prestbury Park. Best Mate's latest
Gold Cup, all told a substandard affair, at least had the novelty of being in the
balance until very late in the race. His best performance of the season came in the
Ericsson Chase at Leopardstown at Christmas, when he put up a display which has
had no equal by a chaser in Ireland for at least a decade. Best Mate also suffered a
defeat, just his third in thirteen starts over fences, when going down to Jair du
Cochet on his reappearance in the Peterborough Chase at Huntingdon.

The Peterborough Chase had been the occasion of Best Mate's successful reappearance in 2002/3, and the possibility of defeat was not generally being seriously considered before the latest running. Although Best Mate's last public appearance, not counting a stable open day, had been when winning his second Gold Cup in stunning fashion by ten lengths in March, he had made a winning start to each of his four previous campaigns. Trainer Henrietta Knight was in unusually confident mood. 'There's no excuse—Best Mate is one hundred percent ready'. It didn't appear that way in the paddock beforehand. Best Mate looked as if the run might well be needed to bring him to a peak and it was evident quite early in the race that he wasn't quite in top form. His jumping wasn't up to its usual standard and, when main rival Jair du Cochet quickened turning into the straight, Best Mate was unable to respond, going down by eight lengths, conceding 5 lb to the winner. While the outcome was painted as a disaster in some quarters—Best Mate didn't run within a stone of his best—he was barely eased at all in betting on the Gold Cup and, in truth, remained much the most likely winner of both that race and the King George VI Chase at Kempton. Jair du Cochet had been a high-class hurdler and, in 2002/3, a smart and unexposed novice chaser, so the result was nowhere near so bad as it appeared to some. In mitigation, connections pinpointed the rain-softened ground as the main cause of defeat. 'Bottomless and very slippy' was the trainer's view. It seemed to be overlooked that Best Mate had won a King George on soft ground and a Grade 1 novice chase on heavy.

Unlike the previous season, when several alternative options came and went, Huntingdon had been the chosen venue for Best Mate's reappearance from an early stage. It was generally assumed that the next step would be a third successive appearance in the King George. Although Best Mate's performances in that race hadn't been marked by the authority of his wins in the Gold Cup, he had beaten Marlborough by a length and a half in 2002 and it's at least arguable that, ridden more for stamina, he might have beaten Florida Pearl in 2001. Apart from the Gold Cup, the King George is the most important race of the season for three-mile chasers, but it eventually became clear that connections were considering another option, the Ericsson at Leopardstown. Although in theory races of the same status, the Ericsson lacks the history and prestige of the King George and in 2003 the win prize-money was £20,000 greater at Kempton. That the Leopardstown race was even being considered seemed to offend some, in Britain at least, but after a month of umming and erring ('I would be sad about him not running at Kempton for the public . . .') it was decided to go to Ireland. A brave move at the time by connections, who looked sure to be slated if things didn't go to plan, but, in one regard, the pressure was off on the day, as forty-eight hours previously the same team had landed the King George with their 'substitute' Edredon Bleu.

Ericsson Chase, Leopardstown—Best Mate bounces back from his Huntingdon reverse

The Ericsson might have been a stronger race than it turned out—Keen Leader and Harbour Pilot were among late absentees—but in Beef Or Salmon there was a challenger with serious claims to Best Mate's crown. Despite home support for the pretender, Best Mate went off at odds on with Beef Or Salmon 2/1 and the rest, headed by Rince Ri, Le Coudray and Colonel Braxton, at 11/1 or longer. Turned out in fantastic shape, Best Mate was an altogether different proposition compared to Huntingdon, and he was imperious in victory. It would be hard to find a better example of precision jumping than Best Mate's that day and it was evident, well before he quickened away two out, that it would take something altogether exceptional to prevent a Best Mate victory. Le Coudray took second, nine lengths back, with Beef Or Salmon, later found to have mucus in his lungs, four lengths further away in third and the rest well beaten. Le Coudray's subsequent effort in the Hennessy behind Florida Pearl suggested the form of the Ericson wasn't quite so good as it looked on the day, but it is hard to bring to mind a better one in Ireland since Desert Orchid won the Irish National in 1990. Miss Knight was justifiably jubilant: 'The past month has been hell, trying to decide between this race and the King George and all the stick we've got about restricting the number of races Best Mate runs in. He's silenced his critics today.' Best Mate's presence at Leopardstown boosted the crowd to nearly 20,000, 5,500 up on the previous year.

Bookmakers took the opportunity to shorten Best Mate for the Gold Cup after his win in Ireland, though at that stage there appeared to be several plausible challengers. Jair du Cochet's stock had dipped with a dismal display behind Edredon Bleu at Kempton but Kingscliff and Keen Leader, to name two, couldn't yet be dismissed on the grounds they weren't good enough. Best Mate's trainer herself, presciently, said before Christmas: 'There are at least five pretenders but they have all got to be there on the day in March. No-one appreciates how difficult that is.' While Best Mate was kept ticking over, the pretenders mostly came up short of the standard set by Best Mate's performances at Cheltenham and Leopardstown. Kingscliff was beaten in the Peter Marsh at Haydock, the Pillar at Cheltenham rehabilitated Jair du Cochet but dented the ambitions of Sir Rembrandt and left punters in the dark about how good the novice Therealbandit might be, Keen Leader flopped in the AON at Newbury and Beef Or Salmon sat out the Hennessy which went to Florida Pearl. Best Mate, having been 5/4 for Cheltenham after the Ericsson, was no better than a 6/4-on chance after the AON. Jair du Cochet was the only other to figure at single-figure odds, with Kingscliff next in the betting. In the month between then and Cheltenham, both Jair du Cochet, fatally so, and Kingscliff were ruled out by injury, along with Florida Pearl. Of the thirteen that figured at 33/1 or shorter for the Gold Cup in ante-post betting in early-November, only five made the line-up at Cheltenham. Available at 10/1 in November, Beef Or Salmon went off the same odds at Cheltenham, while First Gold, third to Edredon Bleu at Kempton, was two points longer. Having been 25/1 back in the autumn, Keen Leader and 2003 runner-up Truckers Tavern were sent off at shorter odds, 10/1 and 22/1 respectively, more by virtue of their presence than by virtue of outstanding overall form. All told, only ten went to post for the totesport Cheltenham Gold Cup, the smallest field since 1996 and the joint-second smallest since 1975. Therealbandit, having just his fourth start over fences, provided some opposition to Best Mate in the betting, sent off 15/2 second favourite. Irish Hussar, whose form in finishing second in the AON looked nowhere near good enough, went off at 16/1, with the previous year's third Harbour Pilot at 20/1, Sir Rembrandt, an unexpected runner after a setback through injury, at 33/1 and Alexander Banquet at 80/1 completing the field. Best Mate was 11/8-on.

The 2004 Cheltenham Gold Cup was a thrilling race, run at a generally searching gallop. Harbour Pilot and First Gold were well away and, after the former hit the second fence, First Gold set the pace. The field was soon quite well spread out and by the top of the hill first time, with First Gold clear, Irish Hussar was already off the bridle, Alexander Banquet well behind and Beef Or Salmon also well off the pace. Best Mate had settled comfortably in fifth and was again jumping like clockwork. As First Gold was briefly given a breather, the field closed up passing the winning post with a circuit to go, but he soon stretched again, leaving Irish Hussar and Truckers Tavern toiling. Keen Leader was the next to feel the pinch, after a mistake at the third ditch, and Therealbandit folded soon after. By

totesport Cheltenham Gold Cup Chase—not much in it at the third last between (from left to right) Sir Rembrandt, Harbour Pilot, First Gold and Best Mate

four out, only four mattered: First Gold, still leading but now narrowly, Harbour Pilot, the improving Sir Rembrandt and Best Mate. At that stage it looked more a question of how far Best Mate might win by, but as the quartet came down the hill another question, which hadn't often sprung to mind in Best Mate's Gold Cup runs, came up. Might he, perhaps, after all be beaten? At the third last Best Mate was tucked in on the rails and turning for home the situation was beginning to look critical, as he was hemmed in by Paul Carberry on Harbour Pilot. Culloty managed to extricate Best Mate and he quickened to lead two out as First Gold dropped away. Even then victory wasn't looking secured. Harbour Pilot continued to press and still held every chance at the last, while on the flat Sir Rembrandt rallied wide. At the line, Best Mate was all out to hold Sir Rembrandt by half a length with Harbour Pilot a length and a quarter further back in third. Beef Or Salmon, who had been eight lengths down and flat out three out, closed all too late, in fourth, with First Gold fifth and a distance back to the remaining three finishers.

This was emphatically not a vintage Gold Cup and in form terms Best Mate's performance was, barring his defeat by Jair du Cochet, about his worst since he lost his novice status. Since Norton's Coin in 1990, only one Gold Cup-winning performance rates as low as Best Mate's in 2004. Still, in the aftermath of the Gold Cup, the echo of history drowned out almost everything else. Immortality is too metaphysical a concept but, leaving aside the merits of individual performances, three wins in the Cheltenham Gold Cup has to qualify as one of the great equine achievements. After all, Arkle (1964-1966) and Golden Miller (1932-1936) are indisputably two of the greatest names in the history of National Hunt racing. Cottage Rake (1948-1950) is rather less well known. Randall and Morris in *A Century of Champions* rated him the twentieth best chaser between 1900-1999 on a figure equivalent to a Timeform rating of 177. Cottage Rake's wins came at a time when the Gold Cup was evolving from being regarded as not much more than a Grand National trial into the premier championship event it is today. One of the first great horses to be trained by Vincent O'Brien, Cottage Rake gained relatively narrow wins in 1948 and 1949 and reserved his most impressive performance for the 1950 running. John Welcome, in *The Cheltenham Gold Cup*, writes somewhat disparagingly about the race ('If the Gold Cup is ever dull, this one was') but the dullness sprang from Cottage Rake's superiority. His main opponent was Finnure, who had beaten him three quarters of a length when receiving 11 lb in the 1949 King George VI Chase, but there was never much chance of the placings being confirmed. As the *Bloodstock Breeders' Review* put it: 'Without being asked for a

*Early on the run-in and Best Mate is on his way to an historic third Gold Cup,
though he is still being pressed by Harbour Pilot (noseband) and Sir Rembrandt . . . . .*

serious effort he cantered home ten lengths ahead of Finnure . . . to all intents and
purposes Cottage Rake was in a class by himself.' Rather like Best Mate, Cottage
Rake's jumping was a great asset, as was his speed. He gained a couple of notable
wins away from Cheltenham, in the 1948 King George and in the Emblem Chase at
Manchester where he beat the subsequent Gold Cup winner Silver Fame. Unlike
Golden Miller or Arkle, Cottage Rake failed to make an impact in handicaps, lack
of stature being offered as a reason for this. After the 1948 Gold Cup, Cottage Rake
failed when conceding three stone to Hamstar in the Irish Grand National; two
years later, carrying 12-7, he started at evens in the same race but could finish
only fourth.

Quite how high history, as opposed to the next day's headline writers, will
place Best Mate in the pantheon of great steeplechasers remains to be seen. At the
time of writing, there isn't really enough evidence to go on and, if his trainer has her
way, there may well not be a lot more as the seasons progress. While further Gold
Cup successes have an obvious attraction, it is hard to understand the apparent lack
of desire on the part of connections to test a little further just how good Best Mate
is. Owner Jim Lewis, both at Leopardstown and talking to the crowd when interviewed after the Gold Cup, expressed the wish to take Best Mate to Punchestown
for the Punchestown Gold Cup at the end of April. After presumably brief discussion with the training team, this option was immediately ruled out. As Miss Knight
put it:'He's been to Ireland. He has had the toughest race of his life. There is limited
mileage in any horse. I am trying to get the best out of this horse not trying
to compare him to Arkle. I am not saying that Baracouda or Rooster Booster lost
for this reason, but both ran in handicaps. We do not want the same to happen to
Best Mate.' Whatever might have cost Rooster Booster the Champion Hurdle it
emphatically wasn't any ill effects from his race at Newbury—over a month had
elapsed since—and Baracouda was surely just beaten by a better horse in Iris's Gift,
who in any case went into the Stayers' Hurdle on the back of a defeat under top
weight in a handicap. Knight failed to mention the winner of the Champion Chase
Azertyuiop, who had produced the best handicap performance of recent years in
narrow defeat under top weight in the Victor Chandler two months previously. It is
also worth mentioning in this context Rhinestone Cowboy, whose third place under
top weight in the Coral Cup proved no bar to his winning the Aintree Hurdle and
the Champion Stayers' Hurdle at Punchestown. No one is arguing that Best Mate
should be running week in week out, carrying top weight in the Welsh National one
day then catching the boat to Ireland for the Ericsson the next. If his constitution
demanded it, then campaigning Best Mate as sparingly as he has been to date would
make perfect sense. According to his trainer, Best Mate tends to run up light when
he is fully fit and never carries any excess fat over his rib cage. 'If Best Mate were
to run as often as many of the journalists suggest,' she said, 'there would be nothing
left of him when it really mattered. He would end up looking like a hat rack.' That
said, there is nothing in Best Mate's racing record to support the notion of a fragile
creature whose appearances need to be eked out so sparingly. Best Mate isn't a
prospective stallion whose reputation needs protecting to ensure profitability in his
future career, he's a gelding whose only function is to race. There is no shame

involved in being beaten in a handicap and there is scant evidence that it harms a good horse's long-term prospects either.

Best Mate's second and most recent appearance in a handicap came when beaten by Wahiba Sands at Ascot in November 2001, the first of his defeats over fences. Do not expect to see Best Mate in another handicap as things stand. His next campaign is due to begin not at Huntingdon, following defeat in the latest Peterborough Chase, but in a contest tailor made for him at Exeter in November. This will have Grade 2 status, carry considerable prize money and create a lot of interest, but it's no criticism of a fine track to say that this event should not be taking place. There are races enough within the pattern already for the small pool of top chasers, without creating one specifically for one horse whose trainer regards none of the others as ideal (the Charlie Hall at Wetherby, the Peterborough, the Hennessy at Newbury, the Edward Hanmer at Haydock, the Rehearsal at Chepstow, the Haldon Gold Cup at Exeter, the Tingle Creek at Sandown, the transferred Desert Orchid at Aintree, the Tommy Whittle at Haydock, the James Nicholson at Down Royal and the Punchestown Chase, to name a few). Perhaps Best Mate isn't at his most effective at distances short of three miles, or on soft or heavy ground, or on a sharp track, but there is no evidence in the form-book to suggest he can't give something like his running under any combination of those conditions. He has even run well on good to firm, though whether he'll get the chance to tackle such conditions again must be doubted and could, ironically, put paid to plans for his reappearance. The ground at the equivalent Exeter meeting in 2003 was good to firm in places, so presumably a dry autumn could deter connections, meaning the race is only likely to attract a couple of the better horses who might otherwise run in the following week's Hennessy at Newbury. What will a campaign, even if completed without blemish, of a customised race at Exeter, the successor to the Ericsson and a fourth Cheltenham Gold Cup prove unless another chaser of Best Mate's ability emerges among his rivals? History invites tiresome references to Arkle, a subject on which plenty was said in *Chasers & Hurdlers 2002/03*. There is no need to rehearse again those arguments. Best Mate bears closer comparison with another three-time winner of one of Cheltenham's great races See You Then. See You Then won the Champion Hurdle in 1985, 1986 and 1987 but fragile legs severely restricted his appearances. He was prepared for a fourth tilt at the title in 1988 but fractured his off hind at Wincanton on his reappearance a month before Cheltenham. Summing up his career, *Chasers & Hurdlers 1987/88* said: 'though his place among his contemporaries was long and widely recognised and his place in the history of the sport is assured, he failed to capture the public's imagination in the way his recent predecessors Dawn Run, Sea Pigeon, Monksfield and Night Nurse did. There are two obvious reasons for this. Firstly, See You Then raced in an era when the standard among hurdlers was generally regarded, rightly, as not

. . . . . Best Mate is pushed all the way to the line by Sir Rembrandt

outstanding and the races for the Champion Hurdle were arguably less competitive than some in recent years . . . Secondly, See You Then raced so little.' Anyone who has seen Desert Orchid on his many public appearances since he was retired, or who remembers the affection felt for Red Rum in similar circumstances, will know the warmth with which the true greats of the sport are regarded. Will cheers ring out quite so resoundingly down the years for Best Mate?

Best Mate (IRE) (b.g. 1995)	Un Desperado (FR) (b 1983)	Top Ville (b 1976)	High Top / Sega Ville
		White Lightning (gr 1970)	Baldric II / Rough Sea
	Katday (FR) (br 1987)	Miller's Mate (b 1982)	Mill Reef / Primatie
		Kanara (b 1973)	Hauban / Alika

Best Mate is a big, rangy gelding who usually impresses in appearance. His breeding has been comprehensively covered in previous Annuals, though the record of his remarkable dam Katday is fully discussed in the essay in this Annual on Cornish Rebel. Despite reservations about the campaigning of Best Mate, it is impossible not to be impressed by the way Henrietta Knight, with husband Terry Biddlecombe, has produced Best Mate spot on for each of his Gold Cup appearances. Miss Knight has a public image almost of a latter-day Margaret Rutherford, one she helps along the way in interviews. Talking to Donald McRae in *The Guardian*, for example, she said: 'I only ever wear that outfit on Gold Cup day now, so there will be a quiver of trepidation when I dig it out again. Let's hope the moths have not got to it. I would be devastated if I couldn't wear the blue suit and pearl

Mr Jim Lewis' "Best Mate"

necklace at Cheltenham.' In a 'Gold Cup Countdown' column in *The Daily Telegraph* in the latest season, she wrote: 'On the home front, my amaryllis on the kitchen window sill is bursting into flower on the right day and the lucky ladybirds have again appeared in my bathroom. All I need now is to see a load of straw on my way to the races', A touching picture of dottiness, one which perhaps doesn't fit quite so well with the trainer's reaction to celebrations in the winner's enclosure at Cheltenham. Greeted by Jim Lewis and his entourage singing the Best Mate song, Knight joined the likes of Kenneth Tynan and Johnny Rotten among those who have used on live television what was once the most shocking word in the English language. We've heard the singing and, frankly, don't blame her. *Miss H. C. Knight*

BEST WAIT (IRE) 7 b.m. Insan (USA) – Greek Melody (IRE) (Trojan Fort) [2003/4 h109: c17g³ 16g² 16s⁴ 17sF 16s 16d⁵ 16s⁶ 16d⁵ 16d² c20s⁵ 16s⁶ c16d² c18d² c20dF Mar 17] fairly useful handicap hurdler: left P. Nicholls, would have won at Killarney in July but for falling last: fair form over fences: raced mainly around 2m: acts on soft and good to firm going (won bumper on firm): wore cheekpieces last 6 outings: tongue tied: held up: has pulled hard/found little. *T. Hogan, Ireland* **c104 h116**

BEST WORLD (FR) 4 b.g. Lost World (IRE) – Katevana (FR) (Cadoudal (FR)) [2003/4 16g⁵ 16s 16s Mar 6] leggy, plain gelding: sixth foal: half-brother to smart hurdler/useful chaser Katarino, stays 3m, and fair hurdler around 2m Karolina (both by Pistolet Bleu): dam unraced, from family of Katko and Kotkijet: well held in 3 juvenile hurdles. *Paul John Gilligan, Ireland* **h–**

BESUTO (IRE) 7 br.g. Fourstars Allstar (USA) – Mabbots Own (Royal Trip) [2003/4 h–, F77: 16mpu 22gpu Apr 18] no form over hurdles. *D. D. Scott* **h–**

BE SWIFT 5 ch.g. Millkom – Conwy (Rock City) [2003/4 19m⁶ Oct 2] modest maiden at best on Flat: looked irresolute when tailed off in novice on hurdling debut. *A. J. Chamberlain* **h–**

BETABATIM (IRE) 9 b.g. Alphabatim (USA) – Lucy Platter (FR) (Record Token) [2003/4 c–, h88: c16gpu Nov 19] modest hurdler: hasn't completed in 3 races over fences: should stay beyond 2m: acts on good to firm and good to soft going. *J. E. Brockbank* **c– h–**

BE THE TOPS (IRE) 6 br.g. Topanoora – Be The One (IRE) (Supreme Leader) [2003/4 20v⁵ 20g³ 20g* 22m* c24dpu 22d c31dpu Apr 22] first foal: dam poor half-sister to fairly useful hurdler up to 2½m More of It: won only start in Irish points in 2002: modest form over hurdles: won maiden at Perth (idled) in June and novice at Cartmel (not fluent/hung fire) in July: went with little zest on 3 starts after 8-month absence, particularly over fences: should stay 3m: acts on good to firm and heavy going: wore cheekpieces/blinkers last 4 outings: not one to trust (almost ran out second start). *Jonjo O'Neill* **c– § h97 §**

BETHILDA 8 br.m. Joligeneration – Woodland Firefly (Mins Baby) [2003/4 22g⁵ Aug 12] poor maiden pointer: well beaten on hurdling debut. *C. J. Down* **h–**

BETTER DAYS (IRE) 8 b.g. Supreme Leader – Kilkilrun (Deep Run) [2003/4 c–, h–: c21m* c20sF c16d³ c20d* c20s⁵ c24gpu c21g c20g⁵ c20d³ Apr 17] useful-looking gelding: fairly useful novice chaser: won at Southwell in November and Haydock in December: generally well below best after, on consecutive days last 2 starts: stays 21f: acts on soft and good to firm ground: usually a front runner. *Mrs S. J. Smith* **c125 h–**

BETTER MOMENT (IRE) 7 b.g. Turtle Island (IRE) – Snoozeandyoulose (IRE) (Scenic) [2003/4 c84, h90: 17g 16m⁴ 17g* 20d² 19g³ 17m* Aug 25] smallish gelding: poor form only run over fences: modest hurdler: won sellers at Southwell in July and August: best around 2m: acts on firm and soft going: tried blinkered, visored nowadays: tried tongue tied: often looks none too keen. *M. C. Pipe* **c– § h98 §**

BETTERTHEDEVILUNO 5 b.g. Hector Protector (USA) – Aquaglow (Caerleon (USA)) [2003/4 17dpu Mar 15] third of 5 in 7f seller at 2 yrs: looked wayward in seller on hurdling debut. *D. McCain* **h–**

BETTER THINK AGAIN (IRE) 10 b.g. Brush Aside (USA) – Ride The Rapids (Bulldozer) [2003/4 24d³ 24d 24m⁵ 21g³ 24s² Dec 14] rangy gelding: fairly useful form on last of 3 starts over fences: fair handicap hurdler: left D. Kelly after third start: stays 3¼m: acts on good to firm and heavy going: visored once over fences (let down by jumping). *Mrs Edwina Finn, Ireland* **c– h108**

BETTER THYNE (IRE) 8 ch.g. Good Thyne (USA) – Cailin Cainnteach (Le Bavard (FR)) [2003/4 c111, h102: c25v³d Dec 15] strong gelding: fair handicap hurdler: failed to **c102 h–**

complete but showed plenty of promise first 2 starts over fences: disqualified from third after taking wrong course in amateur handicap at Towcester, only outing in 2003/4: best at 3m+: acts on heavy going. *V. R. A. Dartnall*

BETTERWARE BOY   4 ch.g. Barathea (IRE) – Crystal Drop (Cadeaux Genereux)   **h–**
[2003/4 16s 17d 17s Jan 20] workmanlike gelding: fair form in 1¼m maidens, sold out of Mrs A. Perrett's stable £4,500 Ascot October Sales: well held in 3 juvenile hurdles. *P. M. Phelan*

BE UPSTANDING   9 ch.g. Hubbly Bubbly (USA) – Two Travellers (Deep Run)   **c101 §**
[2003/4 c112, h93: c25gur c24d5 c25s2 c24d3 c25sur c27sF c22s3 Mar 7] big gelding: fair   **h–**
handicap chaser: stays at least 25f: acts on heavy going: wore cheekpieces last 3 starts: often let down by jumping/temperament. *Ferdy Murphy*

BEWLEYS BERRY (IRE)   6 ch.g. Shernazar – Approach The Dawn (IRE) (Orches-   **F99 P**
tra) [2003/4 F18s* Apr 7] €28,000 4-y-o: brother to winning 2¼m hurdler Logical Approach and half-brother to winning 2½m chaser Majestic Approach (by Mandalus): dam unraced half-sister to useful chaser up to 3m Wise Approach: successful last 3 starts in points: odds on, won bumper at Gowran impressively, quickly going clear when shaken up: joined J. H. Johnson: good prospect. *J. A. Berry, Ireland*

BEXLEY (IRE)   6 b.g. Torus – Regency Charm (IRE) (Prince Regent (FR)) [2003/4   **h–**
F16v F16s4 20d 20d6 20dpu Apr 10] rangy gelding: second foal: dam, lightly raced in   **F83**
points, half-sister to Sun Alliance Hurdle second Torboy: modest form on second of 2 starts in bumpers: well held in novice and maiden hurdles: sold 7,000 gns Doncaster May Sales. *C. Grant*

BEYOND BORDERS (USA)   6 b.g. Pleasant Colony (USA) – Welcome Proposal   **h90 §**
(Be My Guest (USA)) [2003/4 h89§: 16g 19g3 16d 16s3 17d 16d4 18d3 19g5 22g Apr 24] compact gelding: modest maiden hurdler: best form around 2m: probably acts on any going: tried blinkered: unenthusiastic. *S. Gollings*

BEYOND CONTROL (IRE)   9 b.g. Supreme Leader – Bucktina (Buckskin (FR))   **c–**
[2003/4 c–, h120: 25d4 22m Feb 21] strong, useful-looking gelding: fair form only   **h129 ?**
completed outing in steeplechases (let down by jumping otherwise): fairly useful hurdler: very stiff task, distant fourth of 6 to Baracouda in Grade 1 at Ascot on reappearance: stays 3¼m: acts on heavy going, possibly unsuited by good to firm. *C. L. Tizzard*

BEYOND THE POLE (USA)   6 b.g. Ghazi (USA) – North of Sunset (USA)   **h–**
(Northern Baby (CAN)) [2003/4 16s 22spu 16s Jan 19] fair on Flat (stays 2m), successful twice in February: showed little in 3 outings over hurdles: tried tongue tied. *B. R. Johnson*

BEYONDTHEREALM   6 b.g. Morpeth – Workamiracle (Teamwork) [2003/4 F16s   **h93**
F18v 16d5 Mar 24] medium-sized gelding: third foal: dam once-raced daughter of useful   **F89**
staying chaser Armagnac Princess: won 2½m maiden on first of 2 starts in points in 2003: better effort in bumpers when never-dangerous seventh of 14 to Noplanofaction in Grade 2 at Chepstow on debut: 100/1, 11¼ lengths fifth to Jonanaud in novice there on hurdling debut: will stay beyond 2m. *J. D. Frost*

BHANOYI (IRE)   5 ch.g. Perugino (USA) – Bourgeonette (Mummy's Pet) [2003/4   **h–**
16m May 29] half-brother to fair hurdler Silks Domino (by Dominion), stayed 25f: of little account on Flat: well beaten on hurdling debut. *P. S. McEntee*

BICYCLE THIEF (IRE)   11 b.g. Archway (USA) – Push Bike (Ballad Rock) [2003/4   **c– x**
c109, h–: c24dF c24gF 24s Apr 17] smallish gelding: fair handicap hurdler/chaser: fell   **h–**
early both starts over fences in 2003/4, well held on return to hurdles: stays 3m: acts on heavy going: tried blinkered: has failed to impress with attitude. *Miss Venetia Williams*

BID FOR FAME (USA)   7 b. or br.g. Quest For Fame – Shroud (USA) (Vaguely   **h112**
Noble) [2003/4 h98: 16g3 16m* 20m3 25g4 20g3 Nov 21] leggy gelding: useful on Flat (stays 2m), successful in December for N. Tinkler: fair hurdler: easily landed odds in novice at Uttoxeter in October: should stay 3m: acts on good to firm going: has jumped none too fluently. *N. J. Henderson*

BID SPOTTER (IRE)   5 b.g. Eagle Eyed (USA) – Bebe Auction (IRE) (Auction   **h71**
Ring (USA)) [2003/4 16g 20dpu 20d4 16s2 16spu 17dpu 21d Apr 12] stocky gelding: half-brother to winning 21f hurdler Magenko (by Forest Wind): modest on Flat (stays 1½m): poor novice hurdler. *Mrs Lucinda Featherstone*

BIG ATOLL (NZ)   12 b.g. Coral Reef (FR) – Medamac (NZ) (Yipp) [2003/4 17g Jun   **c–**
13] rangy gelding: twice-raced maiden chaser: one-time fairly useful 2m hurdler: very   **h–**
lightly raced nowadays and little sign of retaining ability: best efforts when blinkered. *Miss C. Dyson*

BIG BONE (FR)   4 b.g. Zayyani – Bone Crasher (FR) (Cadoudal (FR)) [2003/4 F16g3   **F94**
F17d5 F16s* Mar 13] third foal: half-brother to winning 25f chaser Good Bone (by

Perrault): dam no sign of ability: progressive form in bumpers, won at Newcastle by 1¾ lengths from Raven's Last: will stay beyond 2m: sold 41,000 gns Doncaster May Sales. *T. P. Tate*

BIG MAX   9 b.g. Rakaposhi King – Edwina's Dawn (Space King) [2003/4 c92, h–: c21g⁴ c26g⁵ c19s² c20g⁴ 19v* 21d² 19g⁵ 22gᵖᵘ Apr 18] modest hurdler/maiden chaser: won handicap at Exeter in February: stays 3m: unraced on firm going, acts on any other. *Miss K. M. George*   **c90 h98**

BIG MOMENT   6 ch.g. Be My Guest (USA) – Petralona (USA) (Alleged (USA)) [2003/4 16v* 20g* 21d² 20g³ 21g⁵ Mar 17]   **h147**
    The line credited to the late Fred Winter about the four courses in Britain beginning with 'F'—Fakenham, Folkestone, Fontwell and effing Plumpton—may still hold true for the current generation of jump jockeys. The overall standard of racing at Plumpton, a sharp, roller coaster track, is about as low as it gets. In recent seasons, however, the track has attracted a better standard of novice and in 2003/4 quite a few subsequently useful performers met with success there, Comply Or Die, Alexanderthegreat, Non So, Tidour and Grey Report among them. Grey Report and Comply Or Die went on to finish third and fourth in the Royal & SunAlliance Hurdle at the Cheltenham Festival and the fifth home that day Big Moment was another Plumpton novice winner. He made a successful debut over hurdles at the track in November, defeating the subsequent Grade 2 winner Garde Champetre, and went on to win an ordinary novice at Fontwell the following month. Big Moment failed to win again but his performance next time wasn't far off the best by a novice hurdler all season. It came in the Grade 1 Challow Hurdle at Newbury and saw Big Moment finish a long way clear of useful performers Grey Report, Control

R. Doel, A. Black, Dr J. Howells & D. Broad's "Big Moment"

Man and Mon Villez. The trouble was he was half a length behind Cornish Rebel, caught close home after leading travelling well after three out. Big Moment couldn't quite match that effort in two subsequent runs, possibly less emphasis on stamina on less testing ground finding him out. He finished third behind Starzaan and Vic Toto when favourite for the National Spirit at Fontwell and just under nine lengths behind Fundamentalist at Cheltenham. Big Moment is likely to be suited by three miles and, while he is unlikely to be up to Stayers' Hurdle class, he has the ability to win a good race or two. Seven weeks after Cheltenham, Big Moment finished third in the Chester Cup, running as well as he ever has on the Flat, which encourages hopes of further progress when he is returned to hurdling in the autumn. His sound jumping is also likely to be an asset.

Big Moment isn't much of a hurdler on looks, being smallish and leggy, which may be why he cost just 28,000 guineas at the Newmarket Autumn (2002) Sales after showing useful form at three and four years on the Flat when with Barry Hills. He comes from a family noted for middle-distance stayers. His dam Petralona was listed-placed in France and is a sister to the Park Hill Stakes winner Eva Luna, herself dam of the St Leger winner Brian Boru. The grandam Media Luna was placed in the Oaks, as was her half-sister Suni. Other smart Flat performers in the family include the Kentucky Oaks winner Flute, the Ebor runner-up Media Star and the Copo de Oro de San Sebastian winner King Cobra. *Mrs A. J. Perrett*

BIG PERKS (IRE) 12 ch.g. Executive Perk – Secret Ocean (Most Secret) [2003/4 c17g Oct 11] tall, angular gelding: maiden hurdler/chaser, fair on balance of form: off 2 years, last of 7 in handicap chase at Bangor: raced mainly around 2m: acts on soft and good to firm going: below form when tongue tied. *P. T. Dalton* — c– h–

BIG QUICK (IRE) 9 ch.g. Glacial Storm (USA) – Furryvale (Furry Glen) [2003/4 h98: 22mᵖᵘ May 26] modest handicap hurdler, poor effort only start in 2003/4: best at 3m+: unraced on heavy going, acts on any other. *L. Wells* — h–

BIG ROB (IRE) 5 b.g. Bob Back (USA) – Native Shore (IRE) (Be My Native (USA)) [2003/4 F16s⁵ 16s⁶ 21gᵖᵘ Mar 5] 60,000 4-y-o: tall, good-topped gelding: first foal: dam, fairly useful hurdler up to 21f, sister to fairly useful hurdler/chaser around 2½m Native Recruit: fifth of 12 in bumper at Huntingdon on debut: better effort in novice hurdles when sixth of 13 at Sandown: should stay beyond 2m. *B. G. Powell* — h85 F87

BIG SMOKE (IRE) 4 gr.g. Perugino (USA) – Lightning Bug (Prince Bee) [2003/4 16d 16g 16s Mar 20] fairly useful on Flat (stays 1¼m), sold out of B. Meehan's stable 18,000 gns Newmarket Autumn Sales: tailed off all 3 starts over hurdles. *J. Howard Johnson* — h–

BIG STAR (IRE) 7 ro.g. Fourstars Allstar (USA) – Dame Blakeney (IRE) (Blakeney) [2003/4 F–: F16g 16g 17d⁵ Apr 18] well held in bumpers (for J. Haldane) and novice hurdles. *M. A. Barnes* — h– F–

BIG TREE (FR) 6 ch.g. Apple Tree (FR) – Maria Cara (FR) (Trepan (FR)) [2003/4 F17m⁵ F17m² 22mᵖᵘ 16g 18s Jan 16] tall, unfurnished gelding: tenth foal: half-brother to 7 winners, including fairly useful 2m hurdler Zetho (by Lesotho): dam winning hurdler/chaser up to around 2½m in France: better effort in bumpers at Carlisle when second to Bacyan: no form in novice hurdles. *J. M. Jefferson* — h– F95

BIG WHEEL 9 ch.g. Mujtahid (USA) – Numuthej (USA) (Nureyev (USA)) [2003/4 c87, h99: 16g⁴ 20g³ 17m² 16f* 16f* Oct 18] angular gelding: modest form on completed start over fences: fair handicap hurdler: better than ever when winning 5-runner events at Kelso in October: effective at 2m, barely stays 21f: acts on firm and soft going: tried blinkered. *N. G. Richards* — c– h108

BIGWIG (IRE) 11 ch.g. Thatching – Sabaah (USA) (Nureyev (USA)) [2003/4 h83§: 22m* 21m³ 22d Jun 9] rather sparely-made gelding: poor handicap hurdler: won at Wincanton in May: stays 2¾m: acts on any going: tried visored, blinkered nowadays: has won 5 times at Plumpton: often less than keen, and not one to trust. *G. L. Moore* — h77 §

BILIVERDIN (IRE) 10 b.g. Bob Back (USA) – Straw Beret (USA) (Chief's Crown (USA)) [2003/4 c17g⁶ c19d⁴ c23s* c20m* Apr 23] big, close-coupled gelding: winning hurdler: useful chaser: won novices at Exeter in March and April (beat below-par Supreme Prince 14 lengths) and Sandown (handicap, all out after blundering last when beating Jahash by neck in 4-runner event) later in April: stays 23f, effective at much shorter: acts on soft and good to firm going (won bumper on heavy): has had jumping problems in the past. *G. B. Balding* — c129 h–

BILL BROWN 6 b.g. North Briton – Dickies Girl (Saxon Farm) [2003/4 F16g 16s 16g 17mᵖᵘ Apr 15] leggy gelding: second foal: half-brother to modest chaser Arctic Spirit (by Arctic Lord), stays 19f: dam poor sister to fairly useful staying hurdler Desperate: no form in bumper and novice hurdles. *R. Dickin* **h–** **F–**

BILLESEY (IRE) 6 b.g. King's Ride – Rose Runner (IRE) (Roselier (FR)) [2003/4 F16d* Mar 21] second foal: dam unraced: 4/1 from 8/1, won 14-runner bumper at Stratford on debut by 1¼ lengths from Peggy's Prince. *S. E. H. Sherwood* **F89**

BILL HAZE 8 ch.g. Romany Rye – Brilliant Haze VII (Damsire Unregistered) [2003/4 c24mᵖᵘ Apr 13] half-brother to winning pointers by Zero Watt and Krisinsky: poor maiden pointer: blinkered, no show on hunter chase debut. *P. Dando* **c–**

BILLIE JOHN (IRE) 9 ch.g. Boyne Valley – Lovestream (Sandy Creek) [2003/4 h94: c17g* c16m³ c16mᶠ c16m* c17m⁴ c17f⁴ 17m³ Oct 25] modest hurdler: better over fences: won weakly-contested novice at Kelso very early in season and 4-runner handicap at Sedgefield in July: best around 2m: raced on good going or firmer (acts on firm): takes strong hold, and usually races prominently: consistent. *Mrs K. Walton* **c108** **h93**

BILL ME UP (IRE) 8 b.g. Shardari – Little Credit (Little Buskins) [2003/4 c19s² Apr 6] ex-Irish gelding: half-brother to several winners, including one-time fairly useful chaser Minister For Fun (by The Parson), stays 3m: dam winning pointer: won maiden point in 2002, showed little otherwise in Ireland: sold out of Mrs D. Love's stable 8,000 gns (privately) Doncaster August (2002) Sales: prolific winner in points in Britain: fast-finishing neck second to Mouseski in hunter at Exeter: will stay 3m: acts on soft going. *J. Heard* **c99** **h–**

BILL OWEN 8 ch.g. Nicholas Bill – Pollys Owen (Master Owen) [2003/4 c–: c25gᵖᵘ c18f* Aug 22] medium-sized gelding: poor form in steeplechases: made most when winning 4-finisher handicap at Fontwell: should stay beyond 2¼m. *D. P. Keane* **c80**

BILL'S ECHO 5 br.g. Double Eclipse (IRE) – Bit On Edge (Henbit (USA)) [2003/4 F75: 19g³ 16d⁶ 16vᶠ 20d⁶ 19g⁴ 17g³ c16dᶠ Mar 28] leggy gelding: modest maiden hurdler: running good first race over fences when falling last in novice handicap at Huntingdon: stays 19f: acts on good to soft going: has found life difficult. *R. C. Guest* **c98** **h97**

BILLY BALLBREAKER (IRE) 8 b.g. Good Thyne (USA) – Droichead Dhamhile (IRE) (The Parson) [2003/4 h64: 22g 22d³ 22f⁵ 24m³ c26g⁶ c24s 24s² 24s 24g Mar 9] leggy gelding: hasn't impressed with jumping and/or attitude over fences: modest maiden hurdler: stays 3m: acts on soft going: visored last 3 outings: has bled from nose: races freely. *C. L. Tizzard* **c–** **h86**

BILLY BONNIE (IRE) 7 ch.g. Anshan – Sinology (Rainbow Quest (USA)) [2003/4 h124: 24s 24v 20d⁵ 22d⁵ Apr 12] medium-sized gelding: fairly useful handicap hurdler: should stay 3m: raced on going softer than good (acts on heavy): tried tongue tied. *N. Meade, Ireland* **h116**

BILLY BRICK 6 b.g. Nalchik (USA) – Tilstock Maid (Rolfe (USA)) [2003/4 F16m 20mᵖᵘ Aug 16] third foal: brother to 2m hurdle winner Warminghamsharpish: dam unraced: no show in bumper and maiden hurdle. *B. R. Foster* **h–** **F–**

BILLY TWO RIVERS (IRE) 5 ch.g. Woodborough (USA) – Good Visibility (IRE) (Electric) [2003/4 16g 16s 20d 16g⁶ 20dᵖᵘ Apr 23] well held on Flat at 3 yrs for R. Fisher: little form over hurdles. *D. R. MacLeod* **h74**

BILLYVODDAN (IRE) 5 b.g. Accordion – Derryclare (Pollerton) [2003/4 F17d F16s³ 16d³ 20s⁶ 16g³ Mar 6] €90,000 3-y-o: lengthy, workmanlike gelding: seventh foal: dam unraced, out of half-sister to smart chaser Comeragh King and useful staying chaser Seskin Bridge: better effort in bumpers when third to Northaw Lad in maiden at Uttoxeter: modest form in novice hurdles: will prove better around 2½m than shorter. *H. D. Daly* **h99** **F92**

BILLYWILL (IRE) 10 b. or br.g. Topanoora – Sandy Maid (Sandy Creek) [2003/4 c18dᵖᵘ c21gᵖᵘ c21d² c19s* c20s² c16s³ c32gᵖᵘ Mar 17] lengthy ex-Irish gelding: maiden hurdler: modest chaser: left V. Bowens after reappearance: won handicap at Hereford in December: should stay beyond 21f: acts on heavy going: tried in cheekpieces: tongue tied last 5 starts. *J. W. Mullins* **c98** **h–**

BINDAREE (IRE) 10 ch.g. Roselier (FR) – Flowing Tide (Main Reef) [2003/4 c138, h–: c27dᶠ c26d² c29d* c29g⁶ c36dᵘʳ Apr 3] **c157** **h–**

The 2002 Martell Grand National winner Bindaree has managed to complete the course only once in four visits to Aintree since, finishing a remote sixth in the same event a year later after being left with too much to do following a mistake at Becher's on the first circuit. Bindaree, through no fault of his own, got

Coral Welsh National (Handicap Chase), Chepstow—
Bindaree (right) gamely holds off Sir Rembrandt for his first win since the 2002 Grand National

no further than the same fence in the latest edition, unseating his rider when badly hampered in the melee there; while he fell at the second in the 2002 Becher Chase and at second Valentine's, when holding a narrow lead and still full of running in the latest renewal of that race. Away from Aintree, Bindaree's jumping hasn't given too much cause for concern, and in a couple of appearances at Chepstow in December he showed himself better than ever, finishing runner-up to Sir Rembrandt in the Rehearsal Chase then winning the Coral Welsh National by half a length from the same horse. Bindaree hadn't been able to get Sir Rembrandt off the bridle in the Rehearsal, and he looked to have it all on to turn the tables in the Welsh National, even with an 8-lb pull in the weights. Sir Rembrandt was sent off favourite at 2/1, with Bindaree at 10/1 in a race which attracted twelve other runners, four of them trained by Martin Pipe. The only challenger from Ireland, Hedgehunter, who had finished fourth in the Hennessy Cognac Gold Cup on his previous start, was second favourite at 7/2. Conditions weren't quite so testing as they often can be for this event, run over a distance just short of three and three quarter miles, but it still provided a thorough test of stamina, the field soon becoming well strung out. Bindaree, prominent from the off, was under pressure in fourth place turning for home, Kings Mistral, Sir Rembrandt and Akarus the ones ahead of him. The complexion of the race changed markedly early in the straight. Sir Rembrandt, having just taken a narrow lead, forfeited it when blundering five out, while both Akarus, who still looked to be travelling well, and Kings Mistral came down at the next, the pair disputing the lead at the time. Now Sir Rembrandt was in front again, pressed by Hedgehunter who had gradually worked his way into contention, and Bindaree. Whereas the second-named flattered to deceive, Bindaree found plenty as he and Sir Rembrandt began to pull well clear and, staying on gamely, Bindaree gained the upper hand on the run-in to win by half a length. Bindaree thus emulated his former stable-companion Earth Summit in completing the Grand National/ Welsh National double. At Warwick two weeks after the Welsh National, Bindaree ran as though he hadn't fully recovered from his efforts and was a distant third when falling at the last, remounted to finish sixth.

Bindaree is the last of three foals produced by the unraced Flowing Tide, the others being the winning pointer Keep Flowing (by Castle Keep) and a hurdler of little account named Tidal Race (by Homo Sapien). Flowing Tide was bred for the Flat and comes from a stout family developed by owner-breeder Dick Hollingsworth whose mares have produced a string of high-class horses down the years. Bindaree's great grandam Ripeck, who stayed a mile and a half, is the dam of Oaks winner Bireme among others; his grandam Helm won at a mile and a quarter and stayed a mile and a half, but did not enhance the family name at stud. Bindaree, who needs at least three miles and stays four and a half, hasn't raced on firm going but

Mr H. R. Mould's "Bindaree"

			Misti IV	Medium
	Roselier (FR)		(br 1958)	Mist
	(gr 1973)	Peace Rose	Fastnet Rock
Bindaree (IRE)			(gr 1959)	La Paix
(ch.g. 1994)		Main Reef	Mill Reef
	Flowing Tide		(ch 1976)	Lovely Light
	(ch 1985)	Helm	Royal Palace
			(ch 1973)	Ripeck

acts on any other. He was blinkered on his last three outings in 2000/1, including when finishing a creditable fourth in the John Hughes Trophy on his first attempt at the National fences. *N. A. Twiston-Davies*

BINDY BONDY 7 b.m. Beveled (USA) – Rockmount Rose (Proverb) [2003/4 h–, F70: 20g 16m⁵ 17m 16m⁶ Aug 8] smallish mare: no form over hurdles: sold £1,000 Ascot October Sales. *J. R. Best*   **h–**

BINNY BAY 8 b.m. Karinga Bay – Binny Grove (Sunyboy) [2003/4 c77, h85: c19m⁴ c20d* c20m⁴ c20mᵖᵘ c25sᵖᵘ c21s c20m⁵ Mar 4] leggy mare: modest hurdler: poor chaser: benefited from rivals' mishaps when winning novice handicap at Perth in July: no form after struck into fourth start: stays 21f: acts on good to firm and heavy going: blinkered last 2 starts: effective tongue tied or not: not one to trust. *D. McCain*   **c77 §**
h– §

BINT ST JAMES 9 b.m. Shareef Dancer (USA) – St James's Antigua (IRE) (Law Society (USA)) [2003/4 h–: 20vᵖᵘ 17g Mar 28] winning selling hurdler, no form for long time: tried visored. *W Clay*   **h–**

BIRCHALL BELLE (IRE)   6 b.m. Presenting – Queenford Belle (Celtic Cone)   **F67**
[2003/4 F–: F16g⁶ F16sᵖᵘ Dec 26] poor form in bumpers: lame final start. *P. D. Evans*

BIRDWATCH   6 b.g. Minshaanshu Amad (USA) – Eider (Niniski (USA)) [2003/4   **h– p**
F16m⁶ F16s³ F16v² F16s³ 20g⁵ Apr 16] 10,500 4-y-o: sturdy gelding: ninth foal: half-   **F93**
brother to useful hurdler/fairly useful chaser Ledgendry Line, stays 25f, and useful
hurdler/chaser up to 25f Foundry Lane (both by Mtoto): dam fair 2-y-o 9f winner: fair
form in bumpers: soon struggling after mistake fifth in novice at Ayr on hurdling debut:
should be suited by further than 2m: should do better over hurdles. *Mrs M. Reveley*

BIRKDALE (IRE)   13 gr.g. Roselier (FR) – Clonroche Lady (Charlottesvilles Flyer)   **c–**
[2003/4 24d³ c25d⁶ c25sᵖᵘ c26dᵖᵘ Mar 11] smallish, good-topped gelding: one-time smart   **h97**
hurdler/useful chaser: modest form over hurdles on return from 20-month absence:
showed little in 3 starts back over fences: stays 25f: acts on heavy going, possibly
unsuited by good to firm: tried tongue tied: usually races up with pace. *Ferdy Murphy*

BIRTH OF THE BLUES   8 ch.g. Efisio – Great Steps (Vaigly Great) [2003/4 h–:   **h–**
16g Nov 19] angular gelding: modest on Flat (stays 13f), successful in April: no form
over hurdles. *A. Charlton*

BISHOP'S BLADE   7 b.g. Sure Blade (USA) – Myrtilla (Beldale Flutter (USA))   **h–**
[2003/4 h–: 20g⁴ Oct 5] blinkered, well beaten both starts over hurdles. *E. Retter*

BISHOP'S BRIDGE (IRE)   6 b.g. Norwich – River Swell (IRE) (Over The River   **F98**
(FR)) [2003/4 F74: F16g² F16d³ F16d Apr 21] tall gelding: best effort in bumpers (fairly
useful form) when short-head second to Toemac at Kempton on reappearance: likely to
stay beyond 2m: has hung right (also found little final start). *Andrew Turnell*

BISON KING (IRE)   7 b.g. King's Ride – Valantonia (IRE) (Over The River (FR))   **h105**
[2003/4 F98: 20d³ 20d³ 26s* 24g⁵ 24d³ 24s Mar 20] big, rangy gelding: chasing type: fair
hurdler: won novice at Huntingdon in December by 5 lengths from Montemoss: good
length third to Glen Warrior in handicap at Bangor: stays 3¼m: raced on good going or
softer: races prominently. *C. R. Egerton*

BISQUET-DE-BOUCHE   10 ch.m. Most Welcome – Larive (Blakeney) [2003/4 c–,   **c–**
h–: 24g⁴ 27d⁶ 22m³ May 29] sparely-made mare: poor handicap hurdler: stays 25f: acts   **h66**
on good to firm and good to soft going. *A. W. Carroll*

BIT OF A BROAD   7 b.m. Tudor Diver – Broad Appeal (Star Appeal) [2003/4 F16g   **h–**
24mᵖᵘ 20mᵖᵘ Jun 20] first foal: dam modest 1m winner: no sign of ability. *R. Shiels*   **F–**

BITOFAMIXUP (IRE)   13 br.g. Strong Gale – Geeaway (Gala Performance) [2003/4   **c117 d**
c–, h–: c25f* c28g* c26gᵖᵘ c24dꟳ c21gᵖᵘ Apr 1] tall, rangy gelding: one-time useful   **h–**
chaser: back to something like best in points (3 wins) and hunter chases in 2003, winning
at Folkestone and Stratford (Intrum Justitia Cup, beat Bright Approach ½ length), both in
May: failed to complete all 3 starts in steeplechases later in season: stays 3½m: acts on
firm and soft going: tried blinkered: often tongue tied. *M. J. Roberts*

BIT OF A SNOB   13 b.g. St Columbus – Classey (Dubassoff (USA)) [2003/4 c–, h–:   **c67**
c21dᵖᵘ c19m c19m³ c18g² c16mꟳ 16dᵖᵘ c20g Feb 18] leggy gelding: winning 2m hurdler/   **h–**
chaser, retains only a little ability: acts on soft and firm going: sometimes blinkered: front
runner. *J. S. King*

BIT O' GOLD   6 b.g. Henbit (USA) – Run of Gold (Deep Run) [2003/4 F–: 16g Apr   **h–**
30] no sign of ability. *Mrs K. B. Mactaggart*

BIT O MAGIC (IRE)   12 ch.g. Henbit (USA) – Arpal Magic (Master Owen) [2003/4   **c99**
c98, h–: c22m³ c17gꟳ c20mꟳ Jun 14] workmanlike gelding: modest handicap chaser: fell   **h–**
fatally at Hexham: stayed easy 2¾m: acted on firm and soft going: tried blinkered. *Ferdy
Murphy*

BIT O'SPEED (IRE)   13 b.g. Henbit (USA) – Speedy Debbie (Pollerton) [2003/4 c92,   **c–**
h–: c20fᵖᵘ May 10] rangy gelding: fair chaser at best: stayed 3m: acted on firm and good   **h–**
to soft going: dead. *Mrs S. Richardson*

BITTER SWEET   8 gr.m. Deploy – Julia Flyte (Drone (USA)) [2003/4 h98: 16f³ 17f²   **h92**
16m⁵ Oct 10] sparely-made mare: modest on Flat (best around 1¼m nowadays), won
twice in 2003: modest handicap hurdler: raced around 2m: unraced on heavy going,
probably acts on any other: sold 4,200 gns Doncaster November Sales. *J. L. Spearing*

BLACK APALACHI (IRE)   5 b.g. Old Vic – Hattons Dream (IRE) (Be My Native   **F96 p**
(USA)) [2003/4 16s* Jan 15] €48,000 3-y-o: first foal: dam unraced half-sister to useful
hurdler up to 21f Erintante and fairly useful chaser up to 25f Delgany Royal: won maiden

bumper at Down Royal on debut, beating Accordingly by 8 lengths with something in hand: will stay beyond 2m: sure to improve. *P. J. Rothwell, Ireland*

BLACKBERRY WAY   10 ch.m. Almoojid – Prickly Path (Royal Match) [2003/4 c87, h–: c21g[pu] c20d c25m[3] c22g[3] c24s[pu] Apr 17] tall mare: winning pointer: best effort in hunter chases when third to easy winner Silence Reigns at Newbury fourth outing: stays 25f: acts on soft and good to firm going: tongue tied last 2 starts. *Ms Louise Cullen*   **c91 h–**

BLACK BOB (IRE)   7 b.g. Good Thyne (USA) – Midsummer Blends (IRE) (Duky) [2003/4 20s[pu] 20d 20s[pu] Feb 14] IR 12,000 3-y-o: big, lengthy gelding: sixth foal: half-brother to winning 3m chaser Harry Hotspur (by Celio Rufo): dam unraced half-sister to smart staying chaser Topsham Bay and useful staying hurdler/chaser Mixed Blends: no form in 3 novice hurdles. *J. S. Haldane*   **h–**

BLACK BULLET (NZ)   11 br.g. Silver Pistol (AUS) – Monte d'Oro (NZ) (Cache of Gold (USA)) [2003/4 c116, h–: c16d[F] May 2] tall, angular gelding: fairly useful handicap chaser: fell sixth at Punchestown in May: stays 2½m: acts on good to firm and heavy going: has been early to post: has bled from nose: races prominently. *Mrs J. Candlish*   **c– h–**

BLACK CHURCH LAD (IRE)   8 gr.g. Ashmolean (USA) – Petit Guest (Northern Guest (USA)) [2003/4 18g[2] 20g* 16d[2] 16g[3] 20d 20d[4] 24d[pu] 20v 20d 16g Mar 15] leggy gelding: placed both starts in Irish points in 2001: fair handicap hurdler: won at Killarney in May: out of form last 4 starts: stays 2½m: acts on soft ground: has worn cheekpieces. *M. Hourigan, Ireland*   **h104**

BLACKCHURCH LASS (IRE)   6 b.m. Taum Go Leor (IRE) – Melons Lady (IRE) (The Noble Player (USA)) [2003/4 21g[4] 18m[5] c19m[F] c20f[4] Oct 9] small, angular mare: of little account: tried tongue tied. *Evan Williams*   **c– h–**

BLACKCHURCH MIST (IRE)   7 b.m. Erins Isle – Diandra (Shardari) [2003/4 h102, F81: 21f* 21m[5] 22m[2] 22g[4] 21d[3] 20g* c21g* c22m[2] c21m[pu] 24g c20g[5] 22d[pu] Mar 12] angular mare: fair handicap hurdler: won at Warwick in May and Worcester in August: successful chasing debut in novice at Stratford in September: disappointing after, jumped badly in cheekpieces eleventh start: should stay 3m: acts on firm and good to soft going: tongue tied: often front runner. *B. W. Duke*   **c106 h109**

BLACK COLLAR   5 br.m. Bob's Return (IRE) – Rosemoss (Le Moss) [2003/4 F17g[6] Apr 24] 3,000 (privately) 4-y-o: fifth foal: dam placed in bumpers/novice hurdle: won both starts in points in 2004: around 12 lengths sixth of 15 in bumper at Market Rasen: will be suited by greater emphasis on stamina: sold to join K. Bailey 41,000 gns Doncaster May Sales. *T. D. Walford*   **F77**

BLACKCOUNTRY LAD   9 b.g. Henbit (USA) – Cupids Bower (Owen Dudley) [2003/4 h–: 20m Jun 29] good-topped gelding: no sign of ability. *A. P. James*   **h–**

BLACK DE BESSY (FR)   6 b.g. Perrault – Emerald City (Top Ville) [2003/4 17d[3] 19g[5] c18m* 19d* c19d[2] c20g[4] c20s[2] c20s[3] 19g c18d[4] c19g[3] c18d* c22g[3] Apr 22] ex-French gelding: fourth foal: dam unraced half-sister to smart sprinter Glifahda: fair hurdler: successful twice in Provinces, including at Vichy in August: won over fences at Aix-Les-Bains in July: left G. Blasco, fair form in Britain last 3 starts: won 5-runner novice at Fontwell in April: stays 2¾m: acts on soft and good to firm ground. *D. R. C. Elsworth*   **c111 h?**

BLACKERGREEN   5 b.g. Zaffaran (USA) – Ballinderry Moss (Le Moss) [2003/4 F16d[2] Apr 23] 5,000 3-y-o: second foal: dam ran once over hurdles: shaped quite well when 16 lengths second of 16 to Eggmount in bumper at Perth on debut, left with plenty to do after being badly hampered early on: will stay beyond 2m. *Mrs M. Reveley*   **F93 +**

BLACK FROST (IRE)   8 ch.g. Glacial Storm (USA) – Black Tulip (Pals Passage) [2003/4 h116: c22g* c20d[4] c19s[4] c22m* c25g[F] c20g[ur] Apr 3] sturdy gelding: fairly useful hurdler: similar form over fences, won novices at Haydock in November and February (best effort, beat Burundi by 1½ lengths in handicap): let down by jumping last 2 starts: stays 2¾m: acts on good to firm and heavy going: none too reliable. *Mrs S. J. Smith*   **c120 h–**

BLACKIES ALL (USA)   6 b.g. Hazaam (USA) – Alljess (USA) (Tom Rolfe) [2003/4 20g 24d[3] 24s 24s 22g* Mar 28] ex-Irish gelding: little form on Flat: fair hurdler: left A. Lee, improved form when winning 17-runner handicap at Market Rasen: stays 3m: raced on good ground or softer: tried blinkered. *W. M. Brisbourne*   **h99**

BLACK LEGEND (IRE)   5 b.g. Marju (IRE) – Lamping (Warning) [2003/4 17d 21g 16g[6] Mar 4] angular gelding: modest maiden on Flat (should stay 1½m) in Ireland at 3 yrs for C. O'Brien: best effort in novice hurdles when sixth of 12 at Ludlow: tongue tied last 2 starts. *R. Lee*   **h85**

BLACK LEOPARD (IRE) 5 b. or br.g. Presenting – Glen Laura (Kambalda) [2003/4 h–
17d Apr 18] sixth foal: dam unraced, from family of smart staying chaser Zeta's Lad:
pulled up in maiden point on debut: never near to challenge in novice hurdle. *P. D. Niven*

BLACK MARQUESS (IRE) 7 b.g. Great Marquess – Kitty Wren (Warpath) h–
[2003/4 F19d F16m⁶ F16s F16s 16g⁴ Apr 16] half-brother to fairly useful hurdler/chaser F–
The Villager (by Zaffaran), stays 25f: dam, winning selling hurdler who stayed 2½m,
sister to smart hurdler up to 2½m Path of Peace and half-sister to useful staying hurdler
Road To Mandalay: no form in bumpers (hung badly left second start) or novice hurdle.
I. A. Duncan, Ireland

BLACKOUT (IRE) 9 b.g. Black Monday – Fine Bess (Fine Blade (USA)) [2003/4 c–
c–, h–: c25d³ c24mᵖᵘ c20sᵖᵘ c25vᶠ c25g⁴ c25gᵖᵘ c25gᵖᵘ Apr 5] poor maiden hurdler/ h–
chaser: stays 25f. *J. Barclay*

BLACK SAINT 7 br.g. Perpendicular – Fool's Errand (Milford) [2003/4 16sᵖᵘ 19sᶠ h–
Apr 11] good-bodied gelding: little sign of ability: tried tongue tied. *P. Wegmann*

BLACK SMOKE 7 gr.g. Ala Hounak – Korean Citizen (IRE) (Mister Lord c94
(USA)) [2003/4 20v 20s c24d² c23g² c24d* Apr 18] second foal: dam, winning pointer, h–
half-sister to 1991 Foxhunters winner Lovely Citizen: well beaten in 2 maiden points and
2 novice hurdles: modest form in steeplechases, won 3-finisher maiden hunter at Carlisle:
stays 3m: acts on good to soft going. *R. C. Guest*

BLACK STRIPE LADY 6 b.m. Karinga Bay – Garvenish (Balinger) [2003/4 F65: h–
F16d 21v Jan 13] useful-looking mare: poor form on first of 3 starts in bumpers for F–
M. Todhunter: showed little on hurdling debut. *R. Ford*

BLACK SWAN (IRE) 4 b.g. Nashwan (USA) – Sea Spray (IRE) (Royal Academy h–
(USA)) [2003/4 16g⁶ 17m 16g 16d Mar 19] lengthy gelding: well held on Flat and over
hurdles. *G. A. Ham*

BLAIRGOWRIE (IRE) 5 b.g. Supreme Leader – Parsons Term (IRE) (The Parson) F98
[2003/4 F17d² Apr 18] 30,000 4-y-o: fourth foal: half-brother to Irish point winner
Huncheon Siss (by Phardante): dam, fair hurdler up to 3m, half-sister to fairly useful 2m
to 2½m hurdler Blasket Run: 18 lengths second to impressive Villon in bumper at Carlisle
on debut, clear of rest. *J. Howard Johnson*

BLAKENEY COAST (IRE) 7 b.g. Satco (FR) – Up To More Trix (IRE) (Torus) c98
[2003/4 c80, h–: c20m* c20g³ c17mᵘʳ 24m⁵ c17m* c17g* Oct 6] good sort: lightly raced h80
over hurdles: modest chaser: won novice handicaps at Wetherby (match) in May and
Plumpton in September (first run after being sold out of Mrs M. Reveley's stable 10,000
gns Doncaster August Sales) and October (fortunate): stays 2½m: acts on good to firm
ground: front runner. *C. L. Tizzard*

BLAKES ROAD (IRE) 7 b. or br.g. Be My Native (USA) – Joyau (IRE) (Roselier F–
(FR)) [2003/4 F16g F16g⁶ Aug 23] first foal: dam unraced sister to Grand National
winner Royal Athlete, from good jumping family: well held in bumpers: third in point in
April. *Miss Venetia Williams*

BLANC C'EST BLANC (FR) 7 ch.g. Royal Charter – Tamilda (FR) (Rose Laurel) h112
[2003/4 F18d* 16d* 16m³ 20m* 20m⁵ 18s⁴ Nov 29] strong, lengthy gelding: will make a F99
chaser: brother to fairly useful chasers Tiraldo, stays 25f, and Tacolino, stays 2½m: dam
unraced half-sister to smart French hurdler Talego: won bumper at Galway in July: fair
hurdler: easily won maiden there in September and novice at Fairyhouse (beat Kelly's
Craft 2½ lengths) in October: will stay beyond 2½m: acts on soft and good to firm going.
A. L. T. Moore, Ireland

BLANK CANVAS (IRE) 6 b.g. Presenting – Strong Cloth (IRE) (Strong Gale) F76
[2003/4 F17d⁶ F16g Mar 27] 24,000 4-y-o: useful-looking gelding: first foal: dam
unraced half-sister to fairly useful staying chaser Parahandy: modest form in bumpers:
will stay 2½m. *K. C. Bailey*

BLASKET SOUND (IRE) 12 b.g. Lancastrian – June's Friend (Laurence O) [2003/4 c–
c–§, h86§: 27d⁴ 24v⁵ 24s* 22s⁴ 26d³ Mar 22] rather sparely-made gelding: modest h91
hurdler: won handicap at Uttoxeter in December: stays 27f: acts on good to firm and
heavy going: tried blinkered. *D. J. Wintle*

BLAU GRAU (GER) 7 b.g. Neshad (USA) – Belle Orfana (GER) (Orfano (GER)) h60
[2003/4 16m⁴ 16g⁵ Dec 11] ex-German gelding: successful 5 times up to 8.5f on Flat,
including on British debut in early-2003 (claimed from H. Hiller 6,000 gns), below form
subsequently for R. Wilman/P. Blockley: shaped like non-stayer both starts over hurdles.
K. A. Morgan

BLAZEAWAY (USA) 4 b. or br.g. Hansel (USA) – Alessia's Song (USA) (Air h71
Forbes Won (USA)) [2003/4 17m² 16g⁵ 17dᵖᵘ 17g 16dᵖᵘ Apr 21] angular gelding: fair

maiden on Flat (stays 1¼m) for M. Johnston: poor juvenile hurdler: blinkered last 2 starts: has failed to impress with attitude. *R. S. Brookhouse*

BLAZING BATMAN   11 ch.g. Shaab – Cottage Blaze (Sunyboy) [2003/4 c67, h81: 23g², 24m c26g³ c26d¹ c26g⁰ᵘ 27f⁵ e22f⁰ᵐ c26ᵤᵤ³ c23ᵤᵤ⁵ c28f³ c23t* c26m³ c25m² c24m² c26d⁵ c25v³ c16s³ c17g⁵ c24s² c21g Apr 2] sturdy gelding: maiden hurdler: fair handicap chaser: won match at Exeter in October: good end to season, second of 3 finishers to Finbar's Revenge at Stratford in March: stays 29f: acts on any going: blinkered once (pulled up): has broken blood vessels/looked unenthusiastic. *Dr P. Pritchard*   **c100 h67**

BLAZING FIDDLE (IRE)   5 b.g. Anshan – Second Violin (IRE) (Cataldi) [2003/4 F16d Apr 23] €30,000 4-y-o: first foal: dam unraced half-sister to dam of top-class staying chaser Rince Ri: always behind in bumper on debut. *J. M. Jefferson*   **F–**

BLAZING GUNS (IRE)   5 ch.g. Un Desperado (FR) – Quefort (Quayside) [2003/4 F16d⁶ F16d Feb 2] very tall, leggy gelding: twelfth foal: brother to useful 2m hurdler Unarmed and half-brother to winning 3m hurdler Tricias Pride (by Broken Hearted) and winning pointer Fresh Ice (by Aristocracy): dam unraced: fair form in bumpers at Newbury and Kempton: will stay 2½m. *Miss H. C. Knight*   **F87**

BLAZING HILLS   8 ch.g. Shaab – Cottage Blaze (Sunyboy) [2003/4 c25v⁴ᵈ c25d⁶ c24g⁵ c29dᵘʳ Mar 19] good-bodied gelding: modest chaser in 2001/2 for K. Bailey: shaped as if retaining most of his ability in handicaps first 3 starts in 2003/4: will stay beyond 3¼m: acts on firm going: blinkered last 6 starts: sometimes makes mistakes. *P. T. Dalton*   **c81 h–**

BLAZING LISS (IRE)   5 b.m. Supreme Leader – Liss de Paor (IRE) (Phardante (FR)) [2003/4 F100p: F16d* F16m* F16s* F16gᶠ Mar 17] small, stocky mare: useful bumper   **F109**

Mrs N. Flynn's "Blazing Liss"

performer: won at Punchestown in May, Galway in October and Navan (made all and not fully extended to beat Mr Murphy 3½ lengths) in December: good 1½ lengths second to Geill Sli in Grade 1 at Punchestown in late-April: held up, still going well when clipping heels and falling 6f out in Champion Bumper at Cheltenham: bred to stay at least 2½m. *J. E. Kiely, Ireland*

BLAZING SADDLES (IRE) 5 b.g. Sadler's Wells (USA) – Dalawara (IRE) (Top Ville) [2003/4 h71: 16g 16s 16s 19g 26m^pu Mar 9] disappointing maiden on Flat, sold out of P. Hedger's stable £2,300 Ascot July Sales: little sign of ability over hurdles: wears cheekpieces. *Mrs J. Candlish*   h–

BLENCATHRA 5 b.m. Midnight Legend – April City (Lidhame) [2003/4 F17g Mar 28] third foal: half-sister to 2000 2-y-o 5f winner Bowfell (by Alflora): dam won over hurdles at 2m and also on Flat at 9.7f: well beaten in mares bumper on debut. *C. Smith*   F–

BLEU SUPERBE (FR) 9 b.g. Epervier Bleu – Brett's Dream (FR) (Pharly (FR)) [2003/4 c136, h–: c17g^pu c16m* c16s³ c16g⁶ c16s³ c16m³ c16g^pu c16d^F Apr 17] rather sparely-made gelding: useful handicap chaser: returned to form (pulled up previous 4 starts) when winning 6-runner event at Ascot in November by 5 lengths from Hot Shots: creditable efforts next 3 outings: ideally suited by 2m: acts on good to firm and heavy going: tried tongue tied: races prominently: often let down by jumping. *Miss Venetia Williams*   c138 x   h–

BLIND SMART (IRE) 6 br.g. Phardante (FR) – Smart Chick (True Song) [2003/4 F17m F17m Jun 11] fifth known foal: half-brother to modest staying chaser Old Cavalier (by Idiot's Delight) and winning 2¾m hurdler Drum Majorette (by Infantry): dam, placed over hurdles, half-sister to smart staying chaser Smart Tar: well held in bumpers. *M. F. Harris*   F–

BLOOD SUB (IRE) 7 b.g. Roselier (FR) – Clearwater Glen (Furry Glen) [2003/4 h106P, F95: c20s^F c20s^pu Dec 13] medium-sized gelding: won second of 2 outings over hurdles in 2003/4: failed to complete in novice chases at Haydock (fell 5 out) and Cheltenham (valuable sales race, pulled up after badly hampered twelfth), still raced comfortably each time: will prove suited by further than 2½m: remains a horse of some potential. *Jonjo O'Neill*   c– p   h–

BLOSSOM WHISPERS 7 b.m. Ezzoud (IRE) – Springs Welcome (Blakeney) [2003/4 h70§: 27s⁴ 24g⁶ 22g 22s Feb 9] smallish mare: ungenuine maiden hurdler: sold out of Mrs M. Reveley's stable 2,000 gns Doncaster May Sales after first outing: tried cheekpieces/blinkers. *N. G. Ayliffe*   h– §

BLOWING AWAY (IRE) 10 b. or br.m. Last Tycoon – Taken By Force (Persian Bold) [2003/4 c–, h55: 16g c16m^F May 29] bad handicap hurdler: no show over fences: probably stays 3m: acts on firm and soft going: tried visored/tongue tied. *Julian Poulton*   c–   h–

BLOWING WIND (FR) 11 b. or br.g. Fabulous Dancer (USA) – Bassita (Bustino) [2003/4 c120, h–: c20g⁴ c19g c24s^R c36d^R c20m Apr 23] lengthy gelding: one-time smart handicap chaser, on the downgrade: best form up to 25f: acts on heavy and good to firm going: tried blinkered, not since 1998/9. *M. C. Pipe*   c117   h–

BLOW ME DOWN 5 b.m. Overbury (IRE) – Chinook's Daughter (IRE) (Strong Gale) [2003/4 F18f⁵ F17m F17m F16m⁶ 16v^pu 16s 16s 21g^pu Feb 25] leggy mare: first foal: dam, poor novice hurdler, half-sister to fairly useful staying chaser Highfrith: little sign of ability. *F. Jordan*   h–   F73

BLUE AMERICO (IRE) 6 br.g. Lord Americo – Princess Menelek (Menelek) [2003/4 F77+: 17g³ 16d⁵ 17s* 19g⁶ 16m² 16g³ Apr 4] useful-looking gelding: type to make a chaser: fair novice hurdler: won at Taunton in February: best form around 2m: acts on soft and good to firm going: takes good hold. *P. F. Nicholls*   h111

BLUE AWAY (IRE) 6 b. or br.g. Blues Traveller (IRE) – Lomond Heights (IRE) (Lomond (USA)) [2003/4 20g* 21m* 22d Apr 12] lengthy gelding: fairly useful on Flat (stays 2m): improved efforts over hurdles when winning handicaps at Punchestown in late-April and Cheltenham (intermediate) in November: heavily backed and visored, beat Mr Ed a neck at latter: not discredited in blinkers final outing: stays 21f: yet to race on firm going, acts on any other: held up. *P. Hughes, Ireland*   h112

BLUE BAR 6 gr.m. Norton Challenger – Royal Scarlet (Royal Fountain) [2003/4 17d 16d^pu 24s^F 22g^pu 24s^pu Apr 21] fifth foal: half-sister to 3 winners, including modest hurdler Captaintwothousand (by Milieu): dam poor novice hurdler: completed once from 3 starts in maiden points in 2003: no form over hurdles. *Mrs R. L. Elliot*   h–

BLUE BROOK   5 ch.g. Alderbrook – Connaught's Pride (Hubbly Bubbly (USA)) **F68**
[2003/4 F16v F16m Mar 11] useful-looking gelding: first foal: dam, poor hurdler who
stayed 2¾m, half-sister to smart chaser up to 3m Mr Moonraker: poor form in bumpers.
Mrs S. D, Williams

BLUE BUSINESS   6 br.g. Roselier (FR) – Miss Redlands (Dubassoff (USA)) [2003/4 **h100**
F16m² 20d 22d³ 24m² 22g³ Apr 18] 72,000 3-y-o: unfurnished gelding: sixth foal: half- **F85**
brother to several winners, notably top-class staying chaser See More Business (by
Seymour Hicks): dam of little account: second in bumper on debut: fair form in novice
hurdles: stays 3m. *P. F. Nicholls*

BLUE BUSTER   4 b.g. Young Buster (IRE) – Lazybird Blue (IRE) (Bluebird (USA)) **F86**
[2003/4 F17d⁶ Mar 11] tall, good sort: third foal: half-brother to Strong Presence (by
Anshan), winner up to 9f here and in Hong Kong: dam unraced: 16¼ lengths sixth of 18
to Sobraon in bumper at Carlisle on debut. *M. W. Easterby*

BLUE CANYON (IRE)   6 b.g. Phardante (FR) – Miss Gosling (Prince Bee) [2003/4 **h80**
F79: 20g 20d^pu 21d⁴ Mar 25] strong, lengthy gelding: first form in novice hurdles when
around 30 lengths fourth of 7 finishers to Hunting Yuppie at Ludlow, racing freely: tongue
tied second start. *B. De Haan*

BLUE CASCADE (IRE)   5 b.g. Royal Academy (USA) – Blaine (USA) (Lyphard's **h–**
Wish (FR)) [2003/4 17m^pu 16f^pu Oct 9] modest maiden on Flat (stays 1¼m), sold out of
S. Dow's stable £1,400 Ascot June (2002) Sales: tongue tied, no show in 2 selling hurdles.
G. E. Jones

BLUE CIRCLE   4 b.c. Whittingham (IRE) – Reshift (Night Shift (USA)) [2003/4 16s^pu **h–**
Dec 20] sturdy, close-coupled colt: poor maiden on Flat (stays 6f): no show on hurdling
debut. *M. Mullineaux*

BLUE CORRIG (IRE)   4 gr.g. Darnay – Myristica (IRE) (Doyoun) [2003/4 16g³ **h108**
16m* 16d 16s 16d⁵ 16v⁴ 16d Feb 21] useful middle-distance stayer on Flat: fair juvenile
hurdler: won maiden at Fairyhouse in October: disappointing subsequently: tried blink-
ered/in cheekpieces: usually finds little. *Joseph Crowley, Ireland*

BLUE DANCE   5 b.g. Danzig Connection (USA) – Blues Player (Jaazeiro (USA)) **h– p**
[2003/4 20d⁶ Apr 21] half-brother to several winners, including 9f and 1¼m winner Your
Most Welcome (by Most Welcome) and 2m hurdle winner Blue Orleans (by Dancing
Spree): dam 2m winner: signs of ability in maiden hurdle at Worcester on debut, getting
behind after ponderous jumps early but improving to dispute lead into straight before
tiring 3 out. *N. A. Twiston-Davies*

BLUE DERBY (IRE)   6 b.g. Supreme Leader – Minigirls Niece (IRE) (Strong Gale) **h109**
[2003/4 F87: 22g⁶ 17g 17d⁴ 19d⁵ 19s⁶ 22g⁵ Apr 18] fair novice hurdler: won at Exeter in
December: left P. Hobbs before final start (tongue tied): stays 2¾m: acts on good to soft
going (won bumper on firm): often looks lazy. *Ms Bridget Nicholls*

BLUE ENDEAVOUR (IRE)   6 b.g. Endeavour (USA) – Jingle Bells (FR) (In The **h104**
Mood (FR)) [2003/4 F86: F17m⁴ 19g⁵ 17s⁴ 22g³ Apr 13] good-topped gelding: fair form **F87**
in bumpers: best effort in novice hurdles at Exeter when fourth to Almaydan: should be
suited by further than 17f. *P. F. Nicholls*

BLUE ETTE (IRE)   4 b.g. Blues Traveller (IRE) – Princess Roxanne (Prince Tender- **F–**
foot (USA)) [2003/4 F16g F17d Mar 27] quite good-topped gelding: fifth foal: brother
to winning sprinter in Italy: dam effective from 1m to 1½m: well held in bumpers.
G. A. Swinbank

BLUEGRASS BEAU   4 ch.g. Bluegrass Prince (IRE) – Blushing Belle (Local Suitor **h–**
(USA)) [2003/4 18m⁴ Sep 23] fair on Flat (should stay at least 1¼m), generally out of
form in 2003: tailed-off last of 4 finishers in juvenile at Fontwell on hurdling debut.
B. G. Powell

BLUE HAWK (IRE)   7 ch.g. Prince of Birds (USA) – Classic Queen (IRE) (Classic **h93**
Secret (USA)) [2003/4 16g* 17g³ Oct 27] angular gelding: modest hurdler: won seller at
Uttoxeter in September on return from long absence: likely to stay beyond 17f: acts on
firm going: forces pace. *Miss L. V. Davis*

BLUE (IRE)   8 b.h. Bluebird (USA) – Watership (USA) (Foolish Pleasure (USA)) **c113**
[2003/4 16g 20m³ 22d c25f* c20f² c21m⁴ c20f⁴ c20d⁶ Nov 23] fair hurdler/chaser: won **h109**
maiden chase at Kilbeggan in August: good efforts next 2 starts, poor ones last 2:
probably stays 25f: acts on firm going: tried blinkered. *N. Meade, Ireland*

BLUE IRISH (IRE)   13 gr.g. Roselier (FR) – Grannie No (Brave Invader (USA)) **c97 x**
[2003/4 c–, h84: c25g^pu c30g² c26m^pu Jul 17] workmanlike gelding: shows traces of **h–**

stringhalt: poor maiden hurdler: modest handicap chaser: broke down final start: stays 27f: acts on heavy going: usually wears blinkers/cheekpieces: sketchy jumper of fences. *Ferdy Murphy*

BLUE JAR   6 b.g. Royal Abjar (USA) – Artist's Glory (Rarity) [2003/4 h–: 17s^{pu} 16m May 5] of no account. *M. Mullineaux*   h–

BLUE LEADER (IRE)   5 b.g. Cadeaux Genereux – Blue Duster (USA) (Danzig (USA)) [2003/4 h–: 16g* 18g^5 16g* Mar 17] tall gelding: won poor handicap hurdler: won conditional jockeys seller at Fakenham in October and ladies event at Huntingdon in March: will prove best at 2m: wore cheekpieces second start. *G. Brown*   h82

BLUE LIZARD (IRE)   7 b.g. Roselier (FR) – Rathsallagh Tartan (Strong Gale) [2003/4 F16d F16s 20s^{pu} Apr 17] good-bodied gelding: poor form on first of 2 starts over hurdles: showed little in novice chase after 11-month absence. *Ferdy Murphy*   c–
h–

BLUE MAINE (IRE)   7 b.m. Doubletour (USA) – Bluejama (Windjammer (USA)) [2003/4 F16d F16s 20s^{pu} Apr 17] IR £20,000 3-y-o: ninth foal: half-sister to fair hurdler/winning hunter chaser Cabin Hill (by Roselier), stayed 25f: dam winning Irish hurdler: won maiden on last of 4 starts in points in 2003: no form in bumpers or novice hurdle. *R. A. Curran, Ireland*   h–
F–

BLUE MORNING   6 b.m. Balnibarbi – Bad Start (USA) (Bold Bidder) [2003/4 F–: F16g 16g^6 16m 16v^{pu} Feb 5] unfurnished mare: little sign of ability. *Mrs J. C. McGregor*   h–
F–

BLUE ORLEANS   6 b.g. Dancing Spree (USA) – Blues Player (Jaazeiro (USA)) [2003/4 16g^{pu} Jun 27] leggy gelding: won juvenile on hurdling debut in 2001/2: lightly raced and no form since, including in points. *R. Brotherton*   h–

BLUE PLANET (IRE)   6 b.g. Bluebird (USA) – Millie Musique (Miller's Mate) [2003/4 h92+: 22v^{pu} 20s Dec 31] workmanlike gelding: modest form at best over hurdles: stays 21f: acts on soft going: tongue tied second start. *P. G. Murphy*   h79

BLUE RIDE (IRE)   7 b.m. King's Ride – Charmere's Beauty (IRE) (Phardante (FR)) [2003/4 h129: 22f^2 25g^5 Nov 15] lengthy, rather sparely-made mare: fairly useful hurdler: probably stays 25f: acts on firm and good to soft going, probably on soft: has her quirks. *P. F. Nicholls*   h125

BLUE ROMANCE (IRE)   6 b.m. Bob Back (USA) – Double Symphony (IRE) (Orchestra) [2003/4 F16f* 16d^F 21d^5 Jan 9] €80,000 4-y-o: first foal: dam useful hurdler/chaser, stayed 21f: odds on, won 5-runner bumper at Wincanton on debut in November: tongue tied, 14¾ lengths fifth of 18 in maiden at Ludlow on completed start over hurdles. *P. F. Nicholls*   h80
F80

BLUE RONDO (IRE)   4 b.g. Hernando (FR) – Blueberry Walk (Green Desert (USA)) [2003/4 16s^R Feb 18] modest maiden on Flat (stays 1¼m), sold out of R. Charlton's stable 17,000 gns Newmarket July Sales: showed much more temperament than ability in juvenile on hurdling debut. *Ian Williams*   h– §

BLUE SAVANNA   4 ch.g. Bluegrass Prince (IRE) – Dusk In Daytona (Beveled (USA)) [2003/4 16g^5 17m^2 16g^d 17d^5 Mar 15] leggy gelding: modest on Flat (stays 1½m), successful in March: form over hurdles only when second to easy winner Triumph of Dubai in juvenile seller at Taunton, racing freely in front: wore blinkers/cheekpieces after debut. *J. G. Portman*   h75

BLUE SHANNON (IRE)   6 b.m. Be My Native (USA) – Shannon Foam (Le Bavard (FR)) [2003/4 F80: 20g 16f^{pu} Nov 8] leggy mare: second of 4 in bumper on debut: has shown little since, including over hurdles. *Ms Bridget Nicholls*   h–

BLUES STORY (FR)   6 b.g. Pistolet Bleu (IRE) – Herbe Sucree (FR) (Tiffauges) [2003/4 h–, F75: 16g^5 20m 20d^4 17d c16g c20d^{pu} Mar 10] lengthy gelding: modest maiden hurdler: sold out of P. Webber's stable 15,000 gns Doncaster May Sales after reappearance: well held on completed start over fences: stays 2½m: acts on good to soft going. *R. Ford*   c–
h96 d

BLUE STREAK (IRE)   7 ch.g. Bluebird (USA) – Fleet Amour (USA) (Afleet (CAN)) [2003/4 h97: 18f 16m* 16m^2 16v^3 18s^5 21s 21g Apr 12] angular gelding: modest hurdler: won claimer at Plumpton in October for second successive year: well held in handicaps there last 2 starts, looking none too keen first time: raced mainly around 2m: acts on good to firm and heavy going: wore eyeshields/blinkers last 6 outings. *G. L. Moore*   h97

BLUE VENTURE (IRE)   4 ch.g. Alhaarth (IRE) – September Tide (IRE) (Thatching) [2003/4 17m* 17g^{pu} Sep 13] lengthy gelding: fair maiden at best on Flat at 2 yrs: won   h86 juvenile at Market Rasen on hurdling debut: most disappointing at Bangor 2 months later: likely to need sharp 2m. *P. C. Haslam*

BLUE YONDER 4 b.f. Terimon – Areal (IRE) (Roselier (FR)) [2003/4 F16d Feb 2] **F–** unfurnished filly: second foal: dam ran twice: showed nothing in bumper on debut. *Mrs N. S. Sharpe*

BLUNHAM 4 b.g. Danzig Connection (USA) – Relatively Sharp (Sharpen Up) **h–** [2003/4 16g Mar 10] leggy gelding: modest on Flat (stays 1m): well held in seller on hurdling debut. *M. C. Chapman*

BLUNHAM HILL (IRE) 6 ch.g. Over The River (FR) – Bronach (Beau Charmeur **c97** (FR)) [2003/4 h91: 20g 21v² 21vᵖᵘ 23s² 20s⁴ c25s³ c22s* Mar 24] quite good-topped **h95** gelding: modest maiden hurdler: similar form in 2 maiden chases at Towcester, winning 4-finisher event: will stay beyond 25f: acts on heavy going. *John R. Upson*

BLUSHING BULL 5 b.g. Makbul – Blush (Gildoran) [2003/4 F16v² F16g F16d² **F107** Mar 24] good-topped gelding: first foal: dam, 11.6f winner, half-sister to fairly useful 2m hurdler Woodurather: useful form when runner-up in bumpers at Uttoxeter (beaten neck by Mount Clerigo) and Chepstow (tended to hang left). *P. F. Nicholls*

BLUSHING PRINCE (IRE) 6 b.g. Priolo (USA) – Eliade (IRE) (Flash of Steel) **h85** [2003/4 17f² 16f* 16g² 21m³ Nov 24] unreliable on Flat (stays 10.8f), better on all-weather than turf: modest form over hurdles: won maiden at Wetherby in October: likely to prove best at 2m: tongue tied: sold 800 gns Doncaster May Sales. *Mrs L. Stubbs*

BLYTH BROOK 12 b.g. Meadowbrook – The Bean-Goose (King Sitric) [2003/4 **c105** c105x, h–: c20m* c20g* c20gᵖᵘ c24g* c21gᵖᵘ c21gᶠ Apr 1] leggy gelding: fairly useful **h–** hunter chaser: won at Newcastle and Perth (both novices) early in season and Mussel-burgh (beat Son of Anshan 6 lengths) in February: effective at 2½m to 27f: acts on good to firm going, probably on good to soft: has been let down by jumping (fell Becher's in Fox Hunters' at Aintree). *W. T. Reed*

BOARDROOM DANCER (IRE) 7 b.g. Executive Perk – Dancing Course (IRE) **c88** (Crash Course) [2003/4 h–, F71: 24sᵖᵘ c25d³ c24g* Dec 5] lengthy, workmanlike geld- **h–** ing: first form over jumps when easily winning poor 3-runner maiden chase at Southwell: stays 3m. *D. J. Caro*

BOARDWALK KNIGHT (IRE) 7 b.g. Shardari – Takhyira (Vayrann) [2003/4 h90: **c–** c16g Aug 8] ex-Irish gelding: modest hurdler: no show on chasing debut: raced at 2m on **h–** good going or softer (acts on soft). *M. Todhunter*

BOATER 10 b.g. Batshoof – Velvet Beret (IRE) (Dominion) [2003/4 h102§: 16m 17m **h– §** 22g Jun 11] sturdy gelding: fair handicap hurdler, no form since reappearance in 2002/3: stays 19f: acts on any going: usually blinkered: carries head high/has found little, and not one to rely on. *R. J. Baker*

BOBALONG (IRE) 7 b.g. Bob's Return (IRE) – Northern Wind (Northfields (USA)) **h104 ?** [2003/4 F72: 20d 22s⁶ 22sᵖᵘ 24s* 25dᵖᵘ 24gᵖᵘ Mar 26] workmanlike gelding: form over hurdles only when making all in slowly-run maiden at Chepstow in January: stays 3m: acts on soft going: tongue tied final outing. *C. P. Morlock*

BOBANVI 6 b.m. Timeless Times (USA) – Bobanlyn (IRE) (Dance of Life (USA)) **h71 §** [2003/4 h67§: 27s³ 20d 22g* 21m⁵ 20m⁴ 22g⁴ 24g⁵ 25dᵖᵘ Dec 27] smallish mare: poor hurdler: won conditional jockeys selling handicap at Cartmel in August: stays 2¾m: acts on soft going: wears headgear: sometimes looks less than keen, and not one to trust. *J. S. Wainwright*

BOB AR AGHAIDH (IRE) 8 b.g. Bob Back (USA) – Shuil Ar Aghaidh (The Parson) **h114** [2003/4 h106: 20d* 19sᶠ 21sᵖᵘ 20s 22gᶠ Apr 13] sturdy gelding: left A. Lidderdale, improved effort over hurdles when winning novice at Uttoxeter in November: every chance when falling twice afterwards, ran poorly both starts in between: stays at least 2½m: acts on heavy going. *C. Tinkler*

BOBAYARO (IRE) 8 b.g. Bob Back (USA) – Instanter (Morston (FR)) [2003/4 c109, **c121** h104: c23g* c24m* c24dᶠ Jul 2] tall gelding: fair hurdler: fairly useful chaser: won **h–** novices at Wetherby in May and Perth in June: poised to challenge when falling heavily 5 out in handicap at Perth: stays 25f: acts on soft and good to firm going: blinkered once in bumpers: usually sound jumper. *N. G. Richards*

BOBBIE JAMES (IRE) 8 ch.g. Roselier (FR) – Brown Forest (Brave Invader (USA)) **h–** [2003/4 F–: 21fᵖᵘ May 10] workmanlike gelding: no sign of ability in bumpers or novice hurdle. *J. Mackie*

BOB

BOBBI ROSE RED 7 ch.m. Bob Back (USA) – Lady Rosanna (Kind of Hush) [2003/4 **c64** h70?, F–: 24s⁴ 20d³ 16g⁴ 22d⁵ 21vᵖᵘ 22s 20v⁶ c19g⁵ Feb 6] lengthy, sparely-made mare: **h72** poor maiden hurdler: well beaten in novice on chasing debut: effective at 2m, probably stays 25f: acts on good to soft going. *P. T. Dalton*

BOB BOB BOBBIN 5 gr.g. Bob Back (USA) – Absalom's Lady (Absalom) [2003/4 **F109** F16s² F16g⁴ Feb 14] 15,000 4-y-o: tall, leggy gelding: first foal: dam, very smart hurdler/winning chaser, stayed 3m: useful form in 2 Grade 2 bumpers, 4 lengths second of 14 to Noplanofaction at Chepstow and 9 lengths fourth of 24 to Secret Ploy at Newbury: will stay beyond 2m. *C. L. Tizzard*

BOBBY BLAKENEY 9 gr.g. Baron Blakeney – Coming Out (Fair Season) [2003/4 **h–** h–: 22d 20mᵖᵘ Jun 1] no form in points or novice hurdles. *Miss L. V. Davis*

BOBBY DAZZLER 5 b.g. Bob's Return (IRE) – Preachers Popsy (The Parson) **h109** [2003/4 F17d 20d⁵ 21d 21g² 20s* Apr 21] €33,000 3-y-o: good-topped gelding: fifth **F–** foal: half-brother to 21f hurdle winner Silk Vestments (by Rakaposhi King) and fairly useful bumper winner Scarlet Poppy (by Petoski): dam, maiden, out of half-sister to useful chasers around 3m Colonel Heather and Fudge Delight: well held in bumper on debut: fair form over hurdles: won maiden at Perth by 2 lengths from Your A Gassman: likely to stay beyond 21f: acts on soft going. *N. A. Twiston-Davies*

BOBBY GRANT 13 ch.g. Gunner B – Goldaw (Gala Performance) [2003/4 c134, h–: **c–** c28sᵖᵘ Nov 29] close-coupled gelding: high-class chaser at best: stayed 25f: raced on **h–** good going or softer (acted on heavy): dead. *P. Beaumont*

BOB JUSTICE (IRE) 8 b.g. Bob Back (USA) – Bramdean (Niniski (USA)) [2003/4 **c–** c123, h–: 24d⁴ 19s² 16s³ 16d⁵ Apr 12] rather leggy gelding: fairly useful chaser: useful **h133** hurdler: good efforts when third to Georges Girl in Grade 2 at Gowran in February and fifth to Rhinestone Cowboy in Grade 1 at Punchestown in late-April: effective at 2m to easy 3m: acts on heavy going. *T. M. Walsh, Ireland*

BOB LE GAOTH (IRE) 8 br.g. Bob Back (USA) – Shuil Le Gaoth (IRE) (Strong **h94** Gale) [2003/4 h–: 22v³ 20s 22sᵖᵘ Mar 23] useful bumper winner: very lightly raced over hurdles: modest form when considerately-handled third in novice at Fontwell on reappearance: ran badly both subsequent starts: will stay 3m: raced on going softer than good. *C. Tinkler*

BOBOSH 8 b.g. Devil's Jump – Jane Craig (Rapid Pass) [2003/4 h90: 16s⁶ Apr 11] **h–** leggy gelding: modest hurdler: off 17 months, below form in handicap only start in 2003/4: stays 21f: acts on soft and good to firm going: visored once (tried to run out): usually front runner. *R. Dickin*

BOBSBEST (IRE) 8 b.g. Lashkari – Bobs (Warpath) [2003/4 c–, h75: 21m² 20m² **c–** c22m⁶ 20m³ 24f⁴ 24m⁵ 22dᵇᵈ 19s⁵ 20s⁵ 24g⁴ Mar 4] small, angular gelding: failed to con- **h84** vince with jumping over fences (fell when visored): poor handicap hurdler: left R. Dickin after fifth start: stays 3m: acts on good to firm going, probably on soft. *R. J. Price*

BOB'S BUSTER 8 b.g. Bob's Return (IRE) – Saltina (Bustino) [2003/4 c85, h85: 17s **c103** c16g* c16d⁴ c16d* c16s* c16s³ c17s* c16v² c16s³ c17s³ c16d³ c16d⁶ Apr 22] sturdy **h–** gelding: winning hurdler: improved chaser in 2003/4, winning handicaps at Hexham (novice) in November, Doncaster and Sedgefield in December and Kelso (idled) in Jan-uary: raced around 2m: acts on heavy and good to firm going: wore cheekpieces last 8 starts: held up: headstrong: consistent. *R. Johnson*

BOB'S GONE (IRE) 6 ch.g. Eurobus – Bob's Girl (IRE) (Bob Back (USA)) [2003/4 **h104** h92: 22g* 24vᵖᵘ Nov 29] fair hurdler: won handicap at Stratford in July: ran as if amiss only subsequent start: stays 2¾m: acts on good to firm and soft going: joined N. Richards. *R. J. Smith*

BOBSLEIGH 5 b.g. Robellino (USA) – Do Run Run (Commanche Run) [2003/4 17s² **h111** 20s² 16s* 20s⁶ 22g⁴ Feb 22] angular gelding: fairly useful on Flat (stays 2½m): fair novice hurdler: won at Plumpton in January: will stay beyond 2¾m: acts on soft ground. *Mrs A. J. Perrett*

BOB'S SHERIE 5 b.m. Bob's Return (IRE) – Sheraton Girl (Mon Tresor) [2003/4 **h–** 20sꟳ 21d 16s⁵ 16sᵖᵘ 17m 17d Mar 27] sturdy mare: no sign of ability. *W. M. Brisbourne*

BOB'S TEMPTATION 5 br.g. Bob's Return (IRE) – Temptation (IRE) (Clearly **F–** Bust) [2003/4 F17d Mar 27] 5,000 4-y-o: first foal: dam unraced: tailed-off last in bumper on debut. *A. J. Wilson*

144

BOB'S THE BUSINESS (IRE)   10 b.g. Bob Back (USA) – Kiora (Camden Town) **c101**
[2003/4 c25s* c29d^{pu} Mar 14] fair pointer: won maiden at Towcester on steeplechasing
debut: ran poorly in handicap following month: should stay beyond 25f. *Ian Williams*

BOB THE PILER   8 b.g. Jendali (USA) – Laxay (Laxton) [2003/4 h18p: 20g^4 17d* **h111**
16v* 20v 16s^2 20s Apr 4] medium-sized gelding: fair hurdler: improved efforts when
winning novice at Carlisle in November and handicap at Newcastle in January: stays
2½m: raced on good going or softer (acts on heavy). *N. G. Richards*

BODFARI CREEK   7 ch.g. In The Wings – Cormorant Creek (Gorytus (USA)) **h112**
[2003/4 h91: 16m^2 20m^2 24m* 24m* 22f* 24m^4 20m^3 Sep 13] fair maiden: won maiden
at Worcester in June and novices at Worcester in July and Fontwell in August: sold out of
P. Webber's stable 20,000 gns Doncaster August Sales before final win: stays 3m: raced
mainly on good going or firmer (acts on firm): consistent. *J. G. Portman*

BODFARI ROSE   5 ch.m. Indian Ridge – Royale Rose (FR) (Bering) [2003/4 h87: **h86**
17d^2 17s^2 16m^3 16m^2 20d^6 20g^{pu} Sep 13] modest maiden hurdler: raced mainly around
2m, below form over 2½m last 2 starts: acts on soft and good to firm going: tried
blinkered, wore cheekpieces in 2003/4. *A. Bailey*

BODFARI SIGNET   8 ch.g. King's Signet (USA) – Darakah (Doulab (USA)) [2003/4 **h107**
h96: 20g^{pu} 20m^5 20g^4 20g^3 22f^4 22f* 22g^4 20m^2 24g^4 16d^2 16g^2 16f^3 18g 20d Apr 10]
leggy gelding: fair handicap hurdler: won at Kelso in October: effective at 2m to easy 3m:
acts on firm and soft going: tried in headgear: usually waited with. *Mrs S. C. Bradburne*

BOGIE BOGEY   4 b.f. Royal Applause – Classic Colleen (IRE) (Sadler's Wells **F–**
(USA)) [2003/4 F12g F12m^{pu} Dec 10] quite good-topped filly: third foal: half-sister to
Classic Millennium (by Midyan), fair up to 1¾m, and 1¼m winner Sculptor (by Salse):
dam, maiden who stayed 1¾m, half-sister to very smart miler Alhijaz: no sign of ability
in two 3-y-o bumpers. *G. B. Balding*

BOHEMIAN BOY (IRE)   6 gr.g. Roselier (FR) – Right Hand (Oats) [2003/4 22s^5 **h116**
22s^2 21s^2 Jan 19] fifth foal: half-brother to winning pointer by Royal Fountain: dam
unraced, from family of top-class staying chaser Righthand Man: won maiden hurdle at
Folkestone on debut in December: runner-up in novices there and at Plumpton: likely to
be at least as effective at 3m. *M. Pitman*

BOHEMIAN SPIRIT (IRE)   6 b.g. Eagle Eyed (USA) – Tuesday Morning (Sadler's **c104**
Wells (USA)) [2003/4 c24s^{ur} c21g* c20d^{pu} c21d* Apr 12] fairly useful hunter chaser:
won at Ayr in March and Fakenham in April: stays 21f. *M. J. Brown*

BOHILL LAD (IRE)   10 b.g. Contract Law (USA) – La Sass (Sassafras (FR)) [2003/4 **c–**
c116, h111: 16g 17m^4 20m^5 17f^6 Sep 30] lengthy gelding: fairly useful handicap chaser: **h108**
fair handicap hurdler: best effort in 2003/4 when fourth at Newton Abbot second start:
best form up to 19f: acted on firm and soft going: blinkered twice: dead. *J. D. Frost*

BOING BOING (IRE)   4 b.g. King's Theatre (IRE) – Limerick Princess (IRE) (Polish **h97**
Patriot (USA)) [2003/4 16m* 16f^{pu} 17d^3 16s^5 16d 16g Apr 18] sturdy gelding: modest on
Flat (stays 1m), sold from J. Hills 8,500 gns after winning seller in September: won
juvenile at Stratford in October on hurdling debut: generally below that form subsequently: needs sharp 2m. *Miss S. J. Wilton*

BOLD ACTION (IRE)   13 b.g. Denel (FR) – Loughan-Na-Curry (No Argument) **c– §**
[2003/4 c24g^{pu} May 12] workmanlike gelding: winning hurdler/chaser: stays 4m: has **h–**
won on good to firm going, goes well on heavy: effective blinkered or not: inconsistent.
Jon Trice-Rolph

BOLD AFFAIR   5 ch.g. Bold Arrangement – So Curious (Gildoran) [2003/4 F16m **F–**
F16g Mar 7] leggy gelding: first foal: dam never ran: showed nothing in 2 bumpers.
Mrs L. Williamson

BOLD BISHOP (IRE)   7 b.g. Religiously (USA) – Ladybojangles (IRE) (Buckskin **h139**
(FR)) [2003/4 F117: 16d^2 17d* 20s^2 16s* 16s* 16s^2 16g^6 Apr 2] rangy gelding: smart
bumper performer (blinkered final outing): useful novice hurdler: easily won at Market
Rasen and Stratford in December and Sandown (by 3 lengths from Simoun) in February:
best effort when 4 lengths second to Scorned in valuable handicap at Sandown in March,
leading on bridle 2 out but not finding quite so much as winner: should stay 2½m: acts on
soft and good to firm going: type to do well in novice chases in 2004/5. *Jonjo O'Neill*

BOLD CARDOWAN (IRE)   8 br.g. Persian Bold – Moving Trend (IRE) (Be My **c–**
Guest (USA)) [2003/4 c–, h88: 24m^3 24m 22m^6 Jul 17] small gelding: jumped poorly and **h83**
reportedly had breathing problem on chasing debut: poor hurdler: stays 3m: acts on good
to firm and heavy going: tends to carry head high: inconsistent. *John Berry*

BOLD CENTURY 7 b.g. Casteddu – Bold Green (FR) (Green Dancer (USA)) [2003/4 **h–**
17gF Nov 5] modest on Flat (stays 13f) at 4 yrs for T. J. Naughton: well held when falling
last in novice on hurdling debut. *S. C. Burrough*

BOLD CLASSIC (IRE) 11 b.g. Persian Bold – Bay Street (Grundy) [2003/4 c25s5 **c93 ?**
c25g5 c25s2 c27g3 Apr 16] close-coupled gelding: winning hurdler/chaser, modest form **h–**
over fences in 2003/4: stays 27f: acts on heavy and good to firm going. *C. Grant*

BOLD HUNTER 10 b.g. Polish Precedent (USA) – Pumpona (USA) (Sharpen Up) **c–**
[2003/4 c74, h–: 16dur 17d 16v2 16s 16s 19d Mar 11] sturdy gelding: poor chaser: form **h63**
returned to hurdling in 2003/4 only when second in selling handicap at Towcester in December: stays easy 21f: acts on any going: tried blinkered, not since 2000/1. *M. J. M. Evans*

BOLD JOGGER (IRE) 7 b.g. Persian Bold – Mouette (FR) (Fabulous Dancer (USA)) **h–**
[2003/4 h–: 20g 24mpu Jun 7] good-topped gelding: no worthwhile form over hurdles.
M. J. Gingell

BOLD KING (FR) 9 gr.g. Turgeon (USA) – Vanila Fudge (USA) (Bold Bidder) **c106 §**
[2003/4 c106§, h105§: c24s2 c28d4 c32m c25d6 c25mpu Mar 4] tall gelding: fair hurdler/ **h– §**
chaser: laboured efforts after reappearance: sold out of I. Williams' stable 5,500 gns
Doncaster November Sales after third outing: barely stays 3¼m: acts on firm and soft
going: tried visored, wore cheekpieces final start: not one to trust. *Paul Morris*

BOLD MOMENTO 5 b.g. Never So Bold – Native of Huppel (IRE) (Be My Native **F–**
(USA)) [2003/4 F–: F17m Jun 21] well held in 2 bumpers. *B. De Haan*

BOLD NAVIGATOR 14 b.g. Lighter – Drummond Lass (Peacock (FR)) [2003/4 **c89**
c94: c30dur c27s* c27s5 c26dpu Mar 11] modest chaser, lightly raced: won handicap at
Sedgefield in December: stays 27f: acts on soft going. *A. M. Crow*

BOLD STATEMENT 12 ch.g. Kris – Bold Fantasy (Bold Lad (IRE)) [2003/4 c–x, **c87 x**
h–: c25g2 c24g4 c24d3 May 30] strong, workmanlike gelding: fair pointer/hunter chaser **h–**
nowadays: stays 25f: acts on any going: wears cheekpieces: has tongue tied: sketchy
jumper: sold £2,700 Ascot October Sales. *S. Flook*

BOLD TACTICS (IRE) 8 br.g. Jurado (USA) – Bold Lyndsey (Be My Native (USA)) **c96**
[2003/4 c99: c21d2 c21g2 c19s2 c16g4 Apr 3] fair pointer/hunter chaser: left F. Hutsby
after second start: won point in March: may prove best around 2½m: acts on soft going.
Mrs P. Grainger

BOLEYKNOWSBEST (IRE) 6 b.g. Camden Town – Barrys Best (IRE) (King **h116**
Luthier) [2003/4 h97*, F102: F18m 16d2 18d3 16d2 16s2 16v3 16d* 16d6 Apr 13] fairly **F–**
useful form at best in bumpers: fairly useful hurdler: won maiden at Thurles in February
and 28-runner handicap at Punchestown (dead-heated with Kelly's Craft) in late-April:
raced around 2m: acts on heavy going. *R. P. Burns, Ireland*

BOLSHIE BARON 15 b.g. Baron Blakeney – Contrary Lady (Conwyn) [2003/4 **c62 x**
c84x, h–: c30m4 c25m6 Jun 11] small, sturdy gelding: winning pointer: poor maiden **h–**
steeplechaser: left H. Wheeler after reappearance: stays 31f: acts on good to firm and
good to soft going: tried blinkered: tongue tied: often makes mistakes. *B. N. Doran*

BOLSHOI BALLET 6 b.g. Dancing Spree (USA) – Broom Isle (Damister (USA)) **h99**
[2003/4 h95: 20v4 16m* 16g2 16g 19d 16d5 Dec 27] quite good-topped gelding: fair on
Flat (probably stays 2m): modest handicap hurdler: won at Haydock in November: should
stay 2½m: acts on good to firm and heavy going: wore cheekpieces last 5 starts. *J. Mackie*

BOLTON BARRIE (IRE) 6 b.g. Broken Hearted – Ballyduggan Queen (IRE) (King **c–**
Luthier) [2003/4 F89: 16g 17g5 20g3 16m 20m* 25f* 16fbd c16f6pu 19d3 20d6 24g2 Jan 7] **h94**
sturdy gelding: modest handicap hurdler: won novices at Carlisle and Wetherby in
October: soon struggling on chasing debut: stays 25f: acts on firm and good to soft going:
ran poorly only start in cheekpieces. *R. C. Guest*

BOLTON CASTLE 7 b.g. Royal Fountain – Elegant Mary (Grey Ghost) [2003/4 **F–**
F16g Dec 20] fourth foal: dam winning 2m hurdler: soundly beaten in bumper on debut.
G. A. Harker

BOLTON FOREST (IRE) 11 b.g. Be My Native (USA) – Tickenor Wood (Le **c–**
Bavard (FR)) [2003/4 c–, h–: c20vpu Mar 21] tall gelding: winning hurdler/chaser: **h–**
showed nothing only start since 2002: tried tongue tied. *Miss S. E. Forster*

BOMBA CHARGER 12 b.g. Prince of Peace – Lady Guinevere (Tormento) [2003/4 **c–**
c90, h–: c33dpu Apr 30] fair pointer/hunter chaser: raced too freely in blinkers at Chelten- **h–**
ham in April: won point following month: should stay beyond 3¼m. *Mrs R. Welch*

BOND DIAMOND 7 gr.g. Prince Sabo – Alsiba (Northfields (USA)) [2003/4 16m **h–**
Jul 16] half-brother to winning 2m hurdler Sharriba (by Sharrood): fairly useful on Flat
(stays 1¼m): not fluent and hampered fourth when well held in novice on hurdling debut:
sold 17,000 gns Newmarket Autumn Sales, resold 3,200 gns Doncaster May Sales.
P. R. Webber

BONEYARROW (IRE) 8 ch.g. Over The River (FR) – Apicat (Buckskin (FR)) **c136**
[2003/4 c123p, h–: c17s* c20s* c21d⁴ c20d² Feb 22] sturdy gelding: one-time useful **h–**
hurdler: similar standard over fences: won maiden at Clonmel in December and novice at
Gowran in January: good efforts in frame behind Pizarro and Jim in graded novices at
Leopardstown and Naas respectively: bred to stay 3m+: raced on good going or softer
(acts on heavy): consistent. *W. P. Mullins, Ireland*

BONFIRE NIGHT (IRE) 8 b.m. Air Display (USA) – Smokey Path (IRE) (Scally- **c54 x**
wag) [2003/4 F–: 16g 22d 16d⁴ 21g c16f³ c25d c20s c16s³ Mar 24] workmanlike mare: **h66**
poor form over hurdles: failed to convince with jumping in handicap chases: likely to
prove best short of 25f. *R. Dickin*

BONITO 6 ch.g. Pivotal – Bonita (Primo Dominie) [2003/4 16g⁶ Nov 1] modest on **h69**
Flat (stays 1m): sixth of 12 in novice seller at Kelso on hurdling debut. *P. C. Haslam*

BONNET'S PIECES 5 b.m. Alderbrook – Chichell's Hurst (Oats) [2003/4 F17s 20s **h–**
19gᵖᵘ 16sᵖᵘ Feb 19] medium-sized mare: third foal: dam, winning hurdler/chaser, stayed **F–**
25f: no sign of ability. *Mrs P. Sly*

BONNIE FLORA 8 b.m. Then Again – My Minnie (Kind of Hush) [2003/4 17s 19sᵖᵘ **h–**
16s 22g 17gF Apr 13] modest on Flat (stays 1½m) at 5 yrs, only poor in 2002 for
K. Bishop: signs of only a little ability over hurdles. *J. W. Mullins*

BONNIE PARKER (IRE) 5 b.m. Un Desperado (FR) – Strong Gara (IRE) (Strong **h95 ?**
Gale) [2003/4 F17d F16g⁵ 21s 27g 21vᵖ 20g⁶ 22d⁵ 21dᵘʳ 24sᵖᵘ 24sᵖᵘ Apr 21] small, **F76**
leggy mare: second foal: half-sister to bumper winner Get With It (by Presenting): dam
unraced, from family of high-class staying chaser Cahervillahow: won mares novice
hurdle at Sedgefield in January: no comparable form: stays 21f: acts on heavy going:
sometimes none too fluent. *Ferdy Murphy*

BONNY BOY (IRE) 9 b.g. Bustino – Dingle Bay (Petingo) [2003/4 c–§, h–§: c26dᵖᵘ **c– §**
26mᵖᵘ c24vⁿ c25g c26gᵖᵘ c28d⁶ Mar 21] sturdy gelding: winning pointer: little form **h–**
otherwise: usually visored/in cheekpieces: tried tongue tied: ungenuine. *D. A. Rees*

BONNYBRIDGE (IRE) 7 ch.m. Zaffaran (USA) – Oralee (Prominer) [2003/4 c–, **c–**
h–, F68: c22g⁴ c20m c20g c23f⁶ c21s⁶ c18d c20d Mar 17] winning pointer, little form **h–**
otherwise: usually blinkered. *Liam Lennon, Ireland*

BONNY BUSONA 4 b.f. Abou Zouz (USA) – La Busona (IRE) (Broken Hearted) **F71**
[2003/4 F13g aF16g⁴ Apr 4] £1,500 3-y-o: second foal: dam, Italian 7.5f winner at
2 yrs, out of half-sister to Gran Criterium second Akeem: poor form in 2 bumpers.
K. F. Clutterbuck

BONNY GREY 6 gr.m. Seymour Hicks (FR) – Sky Wave (Idiot's Delight) [2003/4 **F88**
F16gᵘʳ F16d* Apr 21] 1,200 4-y-o: third foal: dam tailed off in bumper: stumbled and
unseated in bumper on debut: fair form when winning similar event at Worcester, staying
on strongly having got detached. *P. D. Evans*

BONNY GROVE 4 b.g. Bonny Scot (IRE) – Binny Grove (Sunyboy) [2003/4 F13v **F–**
Dec 15] sixth foal: half-brother to winning hurdler/chaser Binny Bay (by Karinga Bay),
stays 21f, and bumper winner Dorans Grove (by Gildoran): dam bumper winner/poor
novice hurdler: showed little in 3-y-o bumper on debut. *G. A. Harker*

BONNYJO (FR) 5 br.g. Cyborg (FR) – Argument Facile (FR) (Argument (FR)) **F79**
[2003/4 F18s⁴ F16d Apr 12] 18,000 4-y-o: rather leggy gelding: second foal: half-brother
to 17f hurdle winner Le Rodriguais (by Kadalko): dam, placed twice at 1¼m on Flat,
half-sister to smart French hurdler Lake Powell: better effort in bumpers when fourth at
Plumpton on debut. *P. R. Webber*

BONUS BRIDGE (IRE) 9 b.g. Executive Perk – Corivia (Over The River (FR)) **c128**
[2003/4 c116, h–: c23g³ c20m² c20m² c16d* c16g* c16s³ c16g⁴ c17sᵖᵘ Apr 17] tall **h–**
gelding: winning hurdler: fairly useful novice chaser: won in small fields at Chepstow
in November and Ludlow in January: best effort when fourth to Well Chief in Grade 1 at
Aintree: stays 2½m: acts on soft and good to firm going: races prominently: has wandered
under pressure/finished weakly. *H. D. Daly*

BONUS TRIX (IRE) 8 b.g. Executive Perk – Black Trix (Peacock (FR)) [2003/4 **h85**
h90: 20d⁶ 19d⁴ Dec 5] good topped gelding: modest maiden hurdler: breathing problem

both starts in 2003/4, left A. Lidderdale after reappearance (tongue tied): should stay at least 2½m. *C. Tinkler*

BOOBEE (IRE)   8 b.g. Mister Lord (USA) – Who's She (Tall Noble (USA)) [2003/4   **h78**
20g 24g^{pu} Feb 13] IR 30,000 4-y-o: strong gelding: chasing type: half-brother to 2
winning pointers by Henbit: dam, maiden pointer, half-sister to smart chaser up to 21f
Stormy Passage: ninth of 10 in novice hurdle on debut: showed nothing next time: sold
1,000 gns Doncaster May Sales. *P. M. Phelan*

BOOGY WOOGY   8 ch.g. Rock Hopper – Primulette (Mummy's Pet) [2003/4 c91§,   **c– §**
h–§: c25s^{pu} Feb 7] leggy, lengthy gelding: winning hurdler/maiden chaser: stays 25f: acts   **h– §**
on soft and good to firm going: blinkered: ungenuine. *Robert Bowling*

BOOKS LAW   6 b.g. Contract Law (USA) – In A Whirl (USA) (Island Whirl (USA))   **h–**
[2003/4 h–: 20m^{pu} Aug 2] no show in 3 races over hurdles: tried in cheekpieces.
Mrs D. A. Hamer

BOOK'S WAY   8 br.g. Afzal – In A Whirl (USA) (Island Whirl (USA)) [2003/4 c–,   **c–**
h–: 16m 22g 22g 21m³ 26m² 24m* 22f⁴ 23m^{ur} 24d⁴ 24g c20m⁵ c27s^{pu} c24g^{pu} 21g 24d   **h65**
Apr 21] sparely-made gelding: poor hurdler, left Mrs D. Hamer after second start: won
very weak novice at Hexham in October: no form in steeplechases: stays 3¼m: acts on
firm going: tried visored/in cheekpieces. *D. W. Thompson*

BOOKS WHIRL   7 b.m. Henbit (USA) – In A Whirl (USA) (Island Whirl (USA))   **h–**
[2003/4 20m^{pu} Jul 23] little sign of ability in varied company: sold £4,200 Ascot October
Sales. *Mrs D. A. Hamer*

BOOM OR BUST (IRE)   5 ch.g. Entrepreneur – Classic Affair (USA) (Trempolino   **h81**
(USA)) [2003/4 h81: 16m^F 17g⁴ 16s³ 16d 17d⁵ 16g⁴ Apr 18] angular gelding: poor
maiden hurdler: raced around 2m: acts on soft and good to firm going: tried blinkered,
sometimes wears cheekpieces: not a straightforward ride. *Miss K. M. George*

BOON COMPANION   5 b.g. Sure Blade (USA) – Pea Green (Try My Best (USA))   **h64**
[2003/4 20g 20g⁵ 20d^{pu} Nov 27] medium-sized gelding: well held on Flat: poor form on
second of 3 starts over hurdles: may prove best short of 2½m. *John Berry*

BOOZY DOUZ   4 ch.f. Abou Zouz (USA) – Ackcontent (USA) (Key To Content   **h–**
(USA)) [2003/4 16m^{pu} 16g 17m⁴ 16m Dec 10] no form on Flat or over hurdles.
H. S. Howe

BORDER BANDIT (IRE)   5 b.g. Shahanndeh – Mwanamio (Sole Mio (USA))   **F82**
[2003/4 F16m⁴ F16m³ F17d F16d^{pu} Apr 23] 13,000 (privately) 4-y-o: half-brother to
several winners, including smart hurdler/useful chaser Padre Mio (by The Parson), stayed
3m: dam, winning 2m hurdler, from family of very smart 2m hurdler Mwanadike: modest
form in bumpers: broke down final start. *A. Crook*

BORDER BURN   10 ch.g. Safawan – Burning Ryme (Rymer) [2003/4 c85: c26g⁴   **c65**
May 18] workmanlike gelding: poor maiden steeplechaser: probably stays 3¼m: tried
blinkered. *M. J. Gingell*

BORDER FARMER (IRE)   11 b.g. Riverhead (USA) – Double Figures (FR)   **c– x**
(Double Form) [2003/4 c–, h–: c25d⁶ c25g^{ur} c31f^{pu} c23m⁵ Jun 18] modest pointer: often   **h–**
let down by jumping in steeplechases. *Mrs S. Richardson*

BORDER GLEN   8 b.g. Selkirk (USA) – Sulitelma (USA) (The Minstrel (CAN))   **h–**
[2003/4 h–: 19m^{pu} May 26] compact, plain gelding: no form over hurdles: tried blinkered/
visored. *P. Wegmann*

BORDER LIGHT   11 ch.g. Lighter – Border Cherry (Deep Run) [2003/4 c–: c25m⁶   **c78**
May 15] lengthy gelding: modest pointer/maiden hunter chaser (often none too fluent):
stays 3¼m: acts on soft and good to firm going: sold £2,000 Ascot February Sales.
H. J. Manners

BORDER STAR (IRE)   7 b.g. Parthian Springs – Tengello (Bargello) [2003/4 h86:   **c–**
c17g^{pu} 17d⁶ 17d⁶ 19d 23s^{pu} 27s 22d⁴ Jun 24] lengthy gelding: no show on chasing   **h78**
debut: poor handicap hurdler: stays 2¾m: acts on soft and good to firm going: in cheek-
pieces/blinkers after reappearance: tried tongue tied. *J. M. Jefferson*

BORDER TALE   4 b.g. Selkirk (USA) – Likely Story (IRE) (Night Shift (USA))   **h108**
[2003/4 17g³ 16m* 16g^{pu} 16s^{pu} 16g³ 16s 17g Mar 18] sturdy gelding: fairly useful on Flat
(stays 12.3f): fair juvenile hurdler: won at Haydock in November: best effort when third
to Tusk at Kempton fifth start: acts on good to firm ground, possibly not on soft.
C. Weedon

BOREHILL JOKER   8 ch.g. Pure Melody (USA) – Queen Matilda (Castle Keep) **c79**
[2003/4 c–, h99: c19g³ c16d c16v⁴ c16m⁵ c16g⁵ c19vᵖᵘ c19d c19gᵖᵘ 16s⁵ Apr 11] sparely- **h82**
made gelding: poor handicap hurdler/maiden chaser: barely stays 2½m: raced mainly on
good going or softer (acts on heavy): tried blinkered; tongue tied: often makes running.
E. Haddock

BORING GORING (IRE)   10 b.g. Aristocracy – Coolrusk (IRE) (Millfontaine) **c82 x**
[2003/4 c89x, h–: c25m² c25gᶠ 24sᵖᵘ 22g Feb 22] rangy gelding: poor hurdler/maiden **h–**
chaser: stays 25f: acts on soft and good to firm ground: tongue tied: sketchy jumper.
Miss A. M. Newton-Smith

BORN LEADER (IRE)   6 b.g. Supreme Leader – Real Lace (Kampala) [2003/4 **h88**
F17d⁶ F16s² 16v 21g³ 21g Mar 26] IR £35,000 3-y-o, 46,000 4-y-o: tall, lengthy gelding: **F95**
sixth foal: half-brother to modest hurdler Native of Kerry (by Be My Native), stays 2½m:
dam, 1m winner, half-sister to useful filly up to 1m Lady Eileen: fairly useful form when
neck second to Premium First in maiden bumper at Wetherby: seemingly best effort over
hurdles when ninth of 20 in maiden at Newbury final start. *A. King*

BORORA   5 gr.g. Shareef Dancer (USA) – Bustling Nelly (Bustino) [2003/4 h–p: 17mᶠ **h101**
16m⁵ 17m* 16g³ 17dᶠ 17d² 16d⁶ Mar 21] close-coupled gelding: fair hurdler: won novice
handicap at Hereford in October: will prove best around 2m: acts on good to firm and
good to soft ground: got loose before final start. *R. Lee*

BORO SOVEREIGN (IRE)   11 b.g. King's Ride – Boro Penny (Normandy) [2003/4 **c95 d**
c21dᵖᵘ c24s⁴ c25sᵖᵘ c20g⁶ c19sᵘʳ c20dᵖᵘ Apr 8] lengthy gelding: one-time fairly useful **h–**
hurdler: modest handicap chaser: form in 2003/4 only when fourth at Chepstow in
January: stays 3m: acts on soft and good to firm going: sometimes finds little/runs as if
amiss. *M. Scudamore*

BORZOV (IRE)   11 ch.g. Kefaah (USA) – Esquire Lady (Be My Guest (USA)) [2003/4 **c92**
c24gᵖᵘ c25fᵖᵘ c25m* c24f Aug 24] maiden hurdler: modest handicap chaser: form in **h–**
2003/4 only when winning at Market Rasen in August: stays 25f: best on good going or
firmer: has been let down by jumping. *T. J. Taaffe, Ireland*

BOSHAM MILL   6 ch.g. Nashwan (USA) – Mill On The Floss (Mill Reef (USA)) **h118**
[2003/4 20m* 22m⁴ 20g² 24m* 25g* 25sᵖᵘ Dec 13] leggy gelding: smart but untrustworthy stayer over hurdles, sold out of G. Wragg's stable 25,000 gns Newmarket Autumn
(2002) Sales: successful 3 of 6 starts over hurdles (left I. Williams after second outing), in
novices at Chepstow in May and Carlisle (hard held) in October and handicap at Kempton
in November, heavily eased when beating Veneguera by 4 lengths at last-named: stays
25f: acts on good to firm going (reportedly lost action on soft final outing): blinkered
third start (looked less than hearty closing stages). *Jonjo O'Neill*

BOSPHORUS   5 b.g. Polish Precedent (USA) – Ancara (Dancing Brave (USA)) **h–**
[2003/4 F–: 16f³ 20m⁴ Oct 22] modest on Flat (may prove best at 1½m/1¾m), successful
in April: well held in 2 novice hurdles, visored on second occasion. *D. G. Bridgwater*

BOSS MAN (IRE)   4 b.g. Entrepreneur – Triste Oeil (USA) (Raise A Cup (USA)) **h–**
[2003/4 17m Aug 1] half-brother to modest 2m hurdler Secret Gift (by Cadeaux Genereux): temperamental maiden on Flat: well held in juvenile on hurdling debut: sold 900
gns Doncaster October Sales. *T. D. Easterby*

BOSS ROYAL   7 ch.g. Afzal – Born Bossy (Eborneezer) [2003/4 c69x, h–: c19s c16g **c78 x**
c19s³ c18sᵖᵘ c16d c16g⁶ Apr 18] workmanlike gelding: winning hurdler: poor form over **h–**
fences: stays 2½m, at least when conditions aren't testing: acts on soft and good to firm
going: usually tongue tied: races prominently: often let down by jumping over fences.
G. A. Ham

BOSS TWEED (IRE)   7 b.g. Persian Bold – Betty Kenwood (Dominion) [2003/4 **h88**
h82+: 16g 16m³ 16g³ 16gᵖᵘ Aug 16] modest maiden hurdler: raced at 2m: acts on good to
firm going: tongue tied. *B. Mactaggart*

BOSTON LASS   7 br.m. Terimon – Larksmore (Royal Fountain) [2003/4 c72, h63: **c72**
c21s² c22gᵖᵘ c26g² c22sᵖᵘ c27sᶠ c20d⁵ c24s⁶ c22s⁵ Mar 24] close-coupled mare: poor **h–**
maiden hurdler/chaser: seems to stay 27f: acts on heavy and good to firm going: sometimes wears cheekpieces. *R. D. E. Woodhouse*

BOSUNS MATE   11 ch.g. Yachtsman (USA) – Langton Lass (Nearly A Hand) [2003/4 **c95 x**
c107x, h–: c28gᵖᵘ c22sᵘʳ c20d³ c26dᵘʳ c24g⁵ Apr 1] useful-looking gelding: fair pointer/ **h–**
hunter chaser: suited by 3m+: acts on heavy and good to firm going: effective visored/
blinkered or not, wore cheekpieces final start: often forces pace: usually let down by
jumping. *M. Keighley*

BOSWORTH BOY 6 b.g. Deploy – Krill (Kris) [2003/4 h–: 20m⁴ Aug 16] good-topped gelding: placed once from 3 starts in bumpers: soundly beaten both outings over hurdles. *J. Gallagher* **h–**

BOSWORTH DIXIE (IRE) 4 b.f. Turtle Island (IRE) – Alice En Ballade (Tap On Wood) [2003/4 16mᵖᵘ Oct 4] medium-sized filly: signs of only a little ability in maidens on Flat for R. Hollinshead/J. Gallagher: temperamental display on hurdling debut: sold £2,000 Ascot November Sales. *Miss J. S. Davis* **h–**

BOSWORTH GYPSY (IRE) 6 b.m. Aahsaylad – Googly (Sunley Builds) [2003/4 F16s⁵ F16v Jan 10] 5,200 4-y-o: second foal: dam fairly useful hurdler/winning chaser who stayed 3m, also fair up to 2¼m on Flat: better effort in bumpers at Uttoxeter when fifth on debut. *J. Gallagher* **F78**

BOULTA (IRE) 10 ch.g. Commanche Run – Boulta View (Beau Chapeau) [2003/4 c90: c20m⁶ c25g² c24s⁴ c25g⁴ Apr 5] fair maiden hunter chaser: stays 25f: acts on good to firm ground: wears cheekpieces: has had tongue tied. *Mrs Clare Moore* **c92**

BOUNCE AGAIN (FR) 4 b.g. Jeune Homme (USA) – Lattaquie (FR) (Fast Topaze (USA)) [2003/4 F18s³ F17d Mar 27] fifth foal: half-brother to one-time smart hurdler/very smart chaser Bounce Back (by Trempolino), stays 29f, and 13f winner Hep To The Jive (by Bahri): dam winner around 1½m in France: soon off bridle when showing modest form in 2 bumpers. *M. C. Pipe* **F81**

BOUNCE BACK (USA) 8 ch.g. Trempolino (USA) – Lattaquie (FR) (Fast Topaze (USA)) [2003/4 c143, h–: c29d³ c29dᵖᵘ c36dᶠ c29m Apr 24] tall gelding: smart hurdler/very smart chaser in 2001/2, long way below best since: stays 29f: acts on heavy and good to firm going: tried blinkered/visored: makes mistakes: often soon off bridle. *M. C. Pipe* **c128 x** **h–**

BOUND 6 b.g. Kris – Tender Moment (IRE) (Caerleon (USA)) [2003/4 h113: 17dᶠ 16s* 17g³ 17d² 17d 20g Apr 1] tall gelding: will make a chaser: fairly useful handicap hurdler: won at Huntingdon in December: good efforts when third to Demi Beau and second to Idaho d'Ox at Cheltenham next 2 starts: will prove best around 2m: acts on soft and good to firm going: sometimes tongue tied: races freely: has found little. *Mrs L. Wadham* **h127**

BOUNDARY HOUSE 6 ch.g. Alflora (IRE) – Preacher's Gem (The Parson) [2003/4 F16d F16d 19gᵖᵘ Apr 3] 30,000 4-y-o: leggy, sparely-made gelding: seventh foal: half-brother to fairly useful hurdler/winning chaser Joliver (by Strong Gale), stayed 3¼m, and winning staying hurdler Kind Cleric (by Supreme Leader): dam, modest 2½m hurdler, half-sister to good hunter Rolls Rambler and Eider Chase winner David's Duky: better effort in bumpers when seventh at Kempton second start: no encouragement on hurdling debut. *J. A. B. Old* **h–** **F87**

BOURBON MANHATTAN 6 b.g. Alflora (IRE) – Vanina II (FR) (Italic (FR)) [2003/4 F111: 16d* 16v² 16d³ 16m² 16g 20g* Apr 16] rangy, useful-looking gelding: type to make a chaser: useful bumper performer: useful form in novice hurdles: won at Aintree (by 11 lengths from Bold Bishop) in November and Ayr (beat Mount Karinga 5 lengths) in April: best efforts when neck second to Fool On The Hill at Wincanton and eighth of 19 to Brave Inca in Supreme Novices' Hurdle at Cheltenham (not fluent) fourth and fifth outings: will prove at least as effective at 2½m as shorter: acts on good to firm and soft going, below form on heavy: reportedly returned lame when jumping sloppily third outing. *A. King* **h134**

BOURGEOIS 7 ch.g. Sanglamore (USA) – Bourbon Girl (Ile de Bourbon (USA)) [2003/4 20s 16g* 16vᵖᵘ 16g² Mar 10] compact gelding: half-brother to fair hurdler Bourbon Dynasty (by Rainbow Quest), stays 2¾m: stout stayer on Flat (stays 19f): fair form over hurdles: won novice at Catterick in January: should stay 2½m: reportedly distressed third outing. *T. D. Easterby* **h103**

BOWCLIFFE COURT (IRE) 12 b.g. Slip Anchor – Res Nova (USA) (Blushing Groom (FR)) [2003/4 h–: 16m Jun 28] sparely-made gelding: veteran 2m hurdler, retains little ability: tried tongue tied. *G. H. Jones* **h–**

BOWD LANE JOE 5 gr.g. Mazaad – Race To The Rhythm (Deep Run) [2003/4 16d 20d³ 16d Jan 19] tall, unfurnished gelding: second foal: dam poor novice staying hurdler: well held over hurdles. *A. W. Carroll* **h–**

BOWFELL 6 b.m. Alflora (IRE) – April City (Lidhame) [2003/4 21g 17g Apr 24] of no account nowadays: tried blinkered/visored. *M. E. Sowersby* **h–**

BOWLEAZE (IRE) 5 br.g. Right Win (IRE) – Mrs Cullen (Over The River (FR)) [2003/4 F101: 17g⁴ Nov 18] created good impression when winning bumper at Exeter on **h94**

debut in 2002/3: fourth to Control Man in novice hurdle at Newton Abbot only start in 2003/4. *R. H. Alner*

BOWLES PATROL (IRE) 12 gr.g. Roselier (FR) – Another Dud (Le Bavard (FR)) [2003/4 c90, h : c25g⁶ May 1] leggy gelding: modest handicap chaser: showed little only start in 2003/4: stays 27f: acts on good to firm and heavy going. *John R. Upson*
c–
h–

BOWLING BEAUTY 6 bl.m. Alderbrook – Bowling Fort (Bowling Pin) [2003/4 F72: 17d May 28] signs of a little ability in bumper in 2002/3: showed nothing in mares novice selling hurdle 2 months later. *Miss S. E. Forster*
h–

BOW SPRIT 4 ch.g. Fleetwood (IRE) – Longwood Lady (Rudimentary (USA)) [2003/4 17dᵖᵘ Nov 28] modest maiden on Flat (stays 1m) for M. Channon: no show in juvenile on hurdling debut. *B. G. Powell*
h–

BOW STRADA 7 ch.g. Rainbow Quest (USA) – La Strada (Niniski (USA)) [2003/4 c128, h131: 21g 24gᵇᵈ 24mᵖᵘ Apr 15] angular, close-coupled gelding: fairly useful chaser: useful hurdler: no show in handicaps in 2003/4: stays 21f: acts on firm and good to soft going. *P. J. Hobbs*
c–
h–

BOX BUILDER 7 ch.g. Fraam – Ena Olley (Le Moss) [2003/4 c–, h104: 24g⁵ Mar 6] close-coupled gelding: has reportedly had breathing operation: no encouragement either start over fences: fair hurdler: creditable fifth in handicap at Doncaster only start in 2003/4: stays 3m: acts on firm and good to soft going: tongue tied for former stable. *H. Morrison*
c–
h104

BOXER'S DOUBLE 7 b.g. Petoski – Grayrose Double (Celtic Cone) [2003/4 c–, h–: 22m 17g⁴ c20m³ c19gᵖᵘ Nov 21] lengthy gelding: bad maiden hurdler/chaser: tried in headgear. *G. A. Ham*
c–
h–

BOX OF TRICKS (IRE) 4 ch.g. Barathea (IRE) – Chocolate Box (Most Welcome) [2003/4 aF16g⁴ Apr 4] IR 38,000Y, 1,800 3-y-o: first foal: dam 13f winner, sister to very smart performer up to 2m Arctic Owl, a good family: tongue tied, well held in bumper on debut. *Mrs B. E. Matthews*
F–

BOYNE BANKS (IRE) 9 ch.g. Boyne Valley – Pallatess (Pall Mall) [2003/4 c79, h–: c25gᵖᵘ May 1] winning pointer, including in March: little form in steeplechases: tried blinkered. *N. A. Twiston-Davies*
c–
h–

BOY'S HURRAH (IRE) 8 b.g. Phardante (FR) – Gorryelm (Arctic Slave) [2003/4 c24g* c20f² c32gᵖᵘ Mar 17] strong gelding: half-brother to several winners, including fairly useful 2½m to 3m chaser Strong Deel (by Strong Gale): dam maiden: successful 4 times in Irish points: fair form in bumpers in 2002 for J. A. Berry, winning 2½m event at Listowel: bought 20,000 gns Doncaster November Sales: won novice at Musselburgh on chasing debut in January: stiff task final outing: stays 3m: acts on firm going. *J. Howard Johnson*
c106

BRACEY RUN (IRE) 14 b.g. The Parson – Outdoor Ivy (Deep Run) [2003/4 c–x, h101: 21g³ 20m Jun 1] good-bodied gelding: modest handicap hurdler: should stay beyond 21f: acts on good to firm and heavy going: visored (ran in snatches) once: has found little. *A. J. Lidderdale*
c– x
h96

BRACHVOGEL (GER) 10 gr.g. Val Des Pres (FR) – Bastei (GER) (Authi) [2003/4 c19g² Apr 1] sturdy gelding: modest maiden hurdler: off 2 years, second of 5 finishers in weak novice at Taunton on chasing debut only start in 2003/4: stays 19f: acts on soft and good to firm ground: formerly tongue tied. *J. D. Frost*
c92
h–

BRACKENHEATH (IRE) 13 b.g. Le Moss – Stable Lass (Golden Love) [2003/4 c86x, h–: c25f⁴ May 21] sturdy gelding: fair pointer/hunter chaser nowadays: stays 27f: acts on heavy going, probably on good to firm: effective with or without blinkers: often let down by jumping. *Mrs D. M. Grissell*
c90 x
h–

BRACKEN RUN (IRE) 10 b.g. Commanche Run – Stable Lass (Golden Love) [2003/4 24sᵖᵘ 20mᵖᵘ Jun 1] ex-Irish gelding: no sign of ability: sold 800 gns Doncaster August Sales. *D. Pearson*
h–

BRACKNEY BOY (IRE) 10 b.g. Zaffaran (USA) – Donard Lily (Master Buck) [2003/4 c–x, h–: 24d 24d² 24m² May 27] didn't take to chasing: modest hurdler: stays 3m: acts on good to firm and soft going: blinkered in 2003/4. *I. A. Duncan, Ireland*
c– x
h90

BRAD 6 b.g. Deploy – Celia Brady (Last Tycoon) [2003/4 F92: F17m⁵ 20d⁶ 18sᵖᵘ c20dᵘʳ Mar 15] lengthy gelding: fair form in bumpers: poor form on first of 2 starts in novice hurdles: unseated second on chasing debut: should be suited by further than 17f. *P. R. Webber*
c–
h70
F85

BRADFORD BRIDGE 11 ch.m. Cruise Missile – Opt Out (Spartan General) [2003/4   **c–**
c21s^{pu} Apr 29] runner-up twice in points: showed nothing on steeplechase debut.
W. S. Kittow

BRADLEY MY BOY (IRE) 8 ch.g. Treasure Hunter – Clonaslee Baby (Konigssee)   **c–**
[2003/4 c–, h78: 16g 16f Sep 14] behind when falling last on chasing debut: little form   **h–**
over hurdles: has had tongue tied. *Mrs A. M. Naughton*

BRADY BOYS (USA) 7 b.g. Cozzene (USA) – Elvia (USA) (Roberto (USA)) [2003/4   **c81**
h76: 20m 20f² 16m⁵ c20m⁴ c19d c16m² c19g⁴ Apr 3] poor hurdler/novice chaser: **h76**
probably stays 2½m: acts on any going: tried visored. *J. G. M. O'Shea*

BRAEBURN 9 b.g. Petoski – Great Granny Smith (Fine Blue) [2003/4 c93?: c19s^{pu}   **c82**
c20g⁶ c23g⁴ Jan 27] poor maiden chaser, lightly raced: stays 3m: acts on soft going.
R. T. Phillips

BRAES OF MAR 14 b.g. Bustino – Barbella (Barolo) [2003/4 c24g Mar 12] tall   **c–**
gelding: one-time fair chaser: well held in hunter on return: tried blinkered. *Bob McEwen*   **h–**

BRAMBLEHILL DUKE (IRE) 12 b.g. Kambalda – Scat-Cat (Furry Glen) [2003/4   **c113 x**
c130x, h–: c25d^{pu} c24d⁶ c26d^{pu} c24s³ c27s² c26v⁵ c28d c36d^R Apr 3] medium-sized   **h–**
gelding: fair handicap chaser: stays 27f: acts on good to firm and heavy going: often takes
strong hold: often let down by jumping: none too consistent. *Miss Venetia Williams*

BRAMLYNN BROOK (FR) 6 ch.g. Apple Tree (FR) – Sainte Lys (FR) (Don Rober-   **h104**
to (USA)) [2003/4 F97: F18s* 21v* 20s² 21s² 20s⁶ Mar 13] big, lengthy gelding: chasing   **F103**
type: fairly useful in bumpers, made all in maiden at Plumpton in November: fair
hurdler: won novice at Towcester later in month: will stay 3m: raced only on soft/heavy
going over hurdles. *Miss Venetia Williams*

BRANDESTON RON (IRE) 5 b.g. Presenting – Boolavogue (IRE) (Torus) [2003/4   **h–**
F16g F16g 22g^{pu} Apr 18] workmanlike gelding: has scope: third foal: dam lightly-raced   **F–**
sister to useful staying chaser Flashthecash: no form in bumpers or novice hurdle. *Jonjo
O'Neill*

BRANDSBY STRIPE 9 ch.g. Nomadic Way (USA) – I'm Fine (Fitzwilliam (USA))   **c70**
[2003/4 h67: c17s* c20s^{pu} c25d^{pu} c16g^{ur} c16g⁶ c24g^{pu} c20d⁴ c20d^{pu} 21g Apr 12] poor   **h–**
form over hurdles: fortunate to win novice handicap at Bangor in May on chasing debut:
little show subsequently: should stay beyond 17f: acts on soft going: tried blinkered/in
cheekpieces. *P. Beaumont*

BRANDY WINE (IRE) 6 b.g. Roselier (FR) – Sakonnet (IRE) (Mandalus) [2003/4   **h–**
F16v⁶ 20v Jan 24] 46,000 4-y-o: rangy gelding: first foal: dam unraced half-sister to   **F83**
smart staying chaser Seven Towers: sixth of 12 in bumper on debut: still looked in need
of race when well held in novice hurdle week later. *L. Lungo*

BRANSTON NELL 5 b.m. Classic Cliche (IRE) – Indefinite Article (IRE) (Indian   **h–**
Ridge) [2003/4 20g^{pu} Mar 6] poor on Flat (stays easy 2m): showed nothing on hurdling
debut. *C. R. Dore*

BRANSTON TIGER 5 b.h. Mark of Esteem (IRE) – Tuxford Hideaway (Cawston's   **h–**
Clown) [2003/4 16d⁵ Dec 1] half-brother to fairly useful hurdler/fair chaser around 2m
Barnburgh Boy (by Shalford): fairly useful on Flat (stays 7f) for J. Given: well held in
maiden on hurdling debut: likely to have stamina limitations. *G. A. Swinbank*

BRASSIE 5 b.g. Celtic Swing – Gong (Bustino) [2003/4 F16s* F16d² F16g Mar 17]   **F104**
leggy, lengthy gelding: fourth foal: half-brother to fairly useful 6.8f and 1¼m winner
Ecstasy (by Pursuit of Love) and fairly useful bumper/middle-distance winner Order (by
Deploy): dam, 1¼m winner who stayed 1½m, half-sister to smart middle-distance stayer
Waterfield and smart sprinter Gaelic Storm: fairly useful bumper performer: won at
Uttoxeter on debut in December by 10 lengths from Phar Far Away: easily better subse-
quent effort (stiff task final start) when second of 18 to Demarco at Ludlow. *R. M. Beckett*

BRASSIS HILL (IRE) 13 b.g. Marktingo – Mystery Woman (Tula Rocket) [2003/4   **c58**
c67, h–: c21m⁵ May 21] bad maiden chaser: stays 21f: acts on firm and soft going: tried   **h–**
blinkered: formerly tongue tied. *Mrs D. M. Grissell*

BRATHAY MAJIC 10 ch.m. Totem (USA) – Roches Roost (Pauper) [2003/4 20d^{pu}   **h–**
Mar 11] lightly-raced mare, seemingly of little account. *W. S. Coltherd*

BRAVE CARADOC (IRE) 6 b.g. Un Desperado (FR) – Drivers Bureau (Proverb)   **h90**
[2003/4 F79: 20g 20s⁶ 21d⁶ 25s^{pu} 23s² 24d⁵ Apr 21] tall, rather unfurnished gelding:
modest form over hurdles: should be suited by 3m+: acts on soft going. *G. L. Moore*

BRAVE DANE (IRE) 6 b.g. Danehill (USA) – Nuriva (USA) (Woodman (USA)) **h92 +**
[2003/4 17d^{ur} 16d Jan 10] long-backed gelding: fairly useful on Flat (stays 11.7f),
successful 3 times in 2004 by end of March: poor form over hurdles: running best race in
amateur novice handicap at Hereford when hampered and unseated run-in: likely to prove
best around 2m. *A. W. Carroll*

BRAVE EAGLE (IRE) 9 gr.g. Roselier (FR) – Pil Eagle (FR) (Piling (USA)) [2003/4 **c– p**
24s* 24s* 24d* 22s⁵ Mar 14] won point on debut in 2000: no form in steeplechases **h124**
(capable of better): progressive hurdler, won handicaps at Limerick in December and
Punchestown and Naas (completed 4-timer) in February: will stay beyond 3m: raced on
good going or softer (acts on heavy). *Patrick G. Kelly, Ireland*

BRAVE EFFECT (IRE) 8 br.g. Bravefoot – Crupney Lass (Ardoon) [2003/4 h86: **c90**
20d^{bd} 22d^{pu} c16f² c20m^{pu} 17m⁴ Oct 10] well-made gelding: modest hurdler: poor form **h93**
on steeplechasing debut, badly let down by jumping next time: stays 2½m: acts on firm
and good to soft going: tried tongue tied: has finished weakly. *M. Todhunter*

BRAVE INCA (IRE) 6 b.g. Good Thyne (USA) – Wigwam Mam (IRE) (Com- **h148 p**
manche Run) [2003/4 h79p, F117: 20d* 16s* 18s* 16g* Mar 16]
Horses are not machines. They have neither motors nor engines, they do not
have tanks that empty or accelerators for jockeys to press. They emphatically do
not have a cruising speed. Describing the actions of a horse using such mechanical
terms is every bit as misleading as crediting it with human qualities. Were it as
predictable as the most finely-tuned Formula One car, a racehorse would be a far
duller creature, though it would, admittedly, sometimes be less frustrating. Why
some horses fail to achieve all that they might can sometimes be explained in terms
of temperament or physical infirmities. Gradual improvement can be similarly
rationalised: greater maturity, increased fitness, a training regime better suited to
the individual needs of a horse. But, explaining how a horse suddenly improves out
of all recognition, turns overnight from, as some might say, a Minardi to a Ferrari,
can be all but impossible.
Take Brave Inca. When he lined up for a bumper at Fairyhouse in March
2003, as what passes for a rank outsider in such a contest in Ireland, he had run
four times over hurdles, showing no better than poor form, and most recently had
been beaten nearly thirty-five lengths off a mark of 91 when a 20/1-chance on his
handicap bow. He won that bumper by twenty lengths, confirmed himself one of
the best performers in that sphere in Ireland at Navan three weeks later and returned
to hurdling in the latest campaign to reel off a string of five victories, ending with
three Grade 1 successes which showed him the best two-mile novice around. Other
than experience bringing fluency to his jumping, it's hard to see just where the

*Letheby & Christopher Supreme Novices' Hurdle, Cheltenham—Ireland's recent stranglehold
on the Festival opener is secure at the last, with Brave Inca (left) and War of Attrition pulling clear*

Evening Herald Champion Novices' Hurdle, Punchestown—Brave Inca's battling qualities are again in evidence as he rallies between Royal Shakespeare (noseband) and Royal Alphabet

dramatic and sudden improvement came from. Not that that mattered much to punters—Brave Inca was sent off favourite for all bar one of those five wins and in landing the Letheby & Christopher Supreme Novices' Hurdle at Cheltenham in March he gave followers of the Irish-trained 'banker' in the Festival opener their third successive flying start, Like-A-Butterfly and Back In Front having delivered the goods in the two previous years. The latest was not a vintage renewal of the Supreme Novices'. A couple of major contenders, both good ex-Flat horses, were missing, the ante-post favourite Lingo withdrawn days before the race and Sadlers Wings switched to the Royal & SunAlliance Hurdle. That race could have been an option for Brave Inca, as could the Coral Cup, in which he looked the pick of the weights, but connections opted for the Supreme Novices', not due to the shorter trip but because of fears of drying ground: Brave Inca hadn't raced on anything less testing than good to soft and there was some doubt whether he would be at the Festival at all. The pick of the eighteen lining up against Brave Inca at Cheltenham looked to be Albuhera and the mares Mariah Rollins and Perle de Puce, but none of that trio ran up to their best. In a race which was more steadily run than usual, Brave Inca's main threat came from another Irish-trained challenger, the unconsidered War of Attrition. Travelling well close to the pace, Brave Inca quickened ahead after two out with War of Attrition, who had come from further back to lead, also going well, and they had a thrilling duel in the straight, Brave Inca getting on top close home to win by a neck, the pair seven lengths clear of the third Fleet Street. Back In Front's win the year before had set the tone for the meeting, so far as the fate of the favourites went, and if that wasn't anything like the same story in 2004, there was one feature of the 2004 Supreme Novices' which, in contrast to 2003, pleasingly repeated itself. Twelve months previously the starts at the Festival mostly brought deserved criticism for the officials, but in 2004 the starts were an object lesson in how the job should be done, virtually every race getting under way with the minimum of fuss.

Brave Inca's other races in 2003/4 took place in Ireland. He had two outings in handicaps before Christmas, still looking to have something to learn about jumping when winning over two and a half miles at Fairyhouse, but much more assured when beating another dramatic improver Georges Girl four lengths at Navan two weeks later, after both had been produced on the bridle at the last. After that, Brave Inca was due to go for the Pierse at Leopardstown, for which he would have started at short odds, but a setback ruled him out and he wasn't seen again until early-February, when he took on the cream of Ireland's novices in the renamed Deloitte (where Touche has gone is one for the Gardai) Novices' Hurdle at Leopardstown. Newmill and Mariah Rollins, who had filled the first two placings, though not in the same order, in the Royal Bond and the Future Champions, looked the form pick, although the very well-regarded Watson Lake started odds on. Brave Inca, at 13/2, was fourth choice in a field of seven but came out best, doing well to overcome a fluff at the second last, just as the pace was picking up, and going on to defeat Newmill by three quarters of a length.

Brave Inca's wins in the Deloitte Novices' and Supreme Novices' were closely run things, but not quite so close as in the Evening Herald Champion Novices' Hurdle at Punchestown shortly after the end of the British season. Although neither Newmill nor War of Attrition was in the field, if anything the Champion Novices' was the strongest of the three events. The unbeaten Royal Shakespeare and Royal Alphabet, winners of graded events at Aintree and Fairyhouse respectively, as well as such promising sorts as Rockstown Boy and Dawn Invasion, made it a worthy 'decider' for the top novice honours. It looked a cracking race in anticipation and didn't disappoint, providing one of the most memorable hurdle races of the year. In a race run at a stronger pace than either the Deloitte or the Supreme, Brave Inca again travelled strongly but so too did Royal Shakespeare and Royal Alphabet. After Royal Alphabet had had to give best, going to the last, a formidable tussle ensued, with Brave Inca getting his nose in front after the last and holding on all out by a short head. Royal Alphabet took third ahead of Rockstown Boy with a nine-length gap to the fifth. Connections of the first three all expressed the view afterwards that their charges would probably be given a campaign culminating in the 2005 Champion Hurdle, and, if they progress as hoped, could

Novices Syndicate's "Brave Inca"

add depth to the rather thin ranks of the top two-mile hurdlers. Brave Inca has regularly given the impression that he would be more effective at around two and a half miles than two, though clearly it's hard to argue with his record at the trip, while his trainer's and rider's view that he is better on ground softer than good is also hard to justify on form. He had no problem going the pace at Punchestown and his jumping seems generally more assured, so Brave Inca has plenty going for him as a prospective Champion Hurdle candidate.

Brave Inca (IRE) (b.g. 1998)	Good Thyne (USA) (br 1977)	Herbager (b 1956)	Vandale II
			Flagette
		Foreseer (b or br 1969)	Round Table
			Regal Gleam
	Wigwam Mam (IRE) (ch 1993)	Commanche Run (b 1981)	Run The Gantlet
			Volley
		Rozifer (ch 1978)	Lucifer
			Rozeen

Brave Inca is more of a chaser than a hurdler on looks—he's a strong sort—though his sire Good Thyne's good hurdlers have generally outshone his chasers. Brave Inca's family, until he came along, has been dominated by one name, Merry Gale, who is out of a half-sister to Brave Inca's grandam Rozifer. Merry Gale was a top-class and versatile chaser in his prime who twice won the Punchestown Chase and once the Martell Cup. Rozifer is the only one of the dams on the bottom line of Brave Inca's pedigree to race, and was successful over hurdles and fences. She produced a bumper winner and a winning pointer, while the third dam Rozeen produced six similarly minor winners. Brave Inca is the first foal of the unraced Wigwam Mam. Brave Inca was bought for just 14,000 punts at the 2001 Land Rover Sale and has proved a similar bargain to the year-older Hardy Eustace, who went for 21,000 punts a little earlier in the day. *Colm A. Murphy, Ireland*

BRAVE KNIGHT 7 b.g. Presidium – Agnes Jane (Sweet Monday) [2003/4 c?, h–: 17m⁶ c24g² Nov 2] leggy gelding: little form over jumps: sold £7,500 Ascot December Sales. *N. Bycroft* — **c– h–**

BRAVE LORD (IRE) 7 ch.g. Mister Lord (USA) – Artic Squaw (IRE) (Buckskin (FR)) [2003/4 F83: 24g* 17d 20sᵖᵘ Mar 28] strong, lengthy gelding: chasing type: convincingly won intermediate at Perth in May on hurdling debut: form in novices after only when second to Snowy at Kelso: likely to prove best at 3m+. *L. Lungo* — **h85**

BRAVE PILGRIM (IRE) 7 b.g. Bravefoot – Abi's Dream (Paddy's Stream) [2003/4 F18g* Nov 27] half-brother to winning hurdler/chaser Master Crusader (by Mandalus), stayed 3¼m: dam showed no sign of ability: won bumper at Thurles on debut by 1½ lengths from Beaufort County. *Mrs Jonah Wragg, Ireland* — **F103**

BRAVE SPIRIT (FR) 6 b.g. Legend of France (USA) – Guerre Ou Paix (FR) (Comrade In Arms) [2003/4 h–, F–: 17g⁵ 17g 16s c20sᶠ c25gᵖᵘ c24g² Mar 17] rather leggy gelding: poor form over hurdles/fences: stays 3m: tried in cheekpieces: has made mistakes over fences. *Ian Williams* — **c76 h78 ?**

BRAVE THOUGHT (IRE) 9 b.g. Commanche Run – Bristol Fairy (Smartset) [2003/4 h118: c16dᶠ c16s² c16s⁴ c16v* c20s⁴ c17g⁵ c20v² c20d² Apr 23] sturdy gelding: fairly useful hurdler: bought out of M. Purcell's stable €35,000 Goffs June Sale: fair novice chaser: won weak event at Ayr in January: better form when runner-up last 2 starts: stays 2½m: raced mainly on going softer than good (acts on heavy): not a straightforward ride. *P. Monteith* — **c104 h–**

BRAVURA 6 ch.g. Never So Bold – Sylvan Song (Song) [2003/4 16m⁴ May 29] half-brother to 2 winners over jumps: fair on polytrack on Flat (best at 1m to 1¼m, usually blinkered): in cheekpieces, modest form when fourth to very easy winner Be Fair in novice at Huntingdon on hurdling debut. *G. L. Moore* — **h89**

BRAZIL (IRE) 6 b.g. Germany (USA) – Alberta Rose (IRE) (Phardante (FR)) [2003/4 h–, F69: 16mᶠ 16mᵖᵘ 19s c16d c16dᵘʳ c16gᶠ Mar 3] little sign of ability: has flashed tail under pressure. *T. R. George* — **c– h–**

BREAKING BREEZE (IRE) 9 b.g. Mandalus – Knockacool Breeze (Buckskin (FR)) [2003/4 c104, h–: c18gᵖᵘ Apr 22] winning hurdler: fair chaser: little encouragement on return from 19-month lay-off: barely stays 21f: acts on soft and good to firm going: free-going sort. *J. S. King* — **c– h–**

BREATHOFFRESHAIR (IRE) 7 ch.g. Fresh Breeze (USA) – Carl Louise (Invited (USA)) [2003/4 F16m 20s^{pu} Dec 19] second foal: dam, maiden pointer, ran once over hurdles: showed nothing in bumper (for C. Price) and novice hurdle. *J. Gallagher* **h–** **F—**

BREATHTAKING VIEW (USA) 8 b.g. Country Pine (USA) – Lituya Bay (USA) (Empery (USA)) [2003/4 h74: 16m 19g* 17g* 17m^5 19g^6 16m^5 19m^2 16g^3 Oct 24] leggy gelding: modest handicap hurdler: will probably prove best up to 2½m: raced mainly on good/good to firm going: tried in cheekpieces: ran well when tongue tied final start. *G. Prodromou* **h86**

BREEMA DONNA 6 b.m. Sir Harry Lewis (USA) – Donna del Lago (Kings Lake (USA)) [2003/4 F17m^6 Sep 10] first foal: dam, fair but none too trustworthy staying chaser, half-sister to fairly useful staying chaser Drum Battle: never a factor in maiden bumper on debut. *R. Dickin* **F—**

BREEZE HOME 8 b.g. Homo Sapien – Poppy's Pride (Uncle Pokey) [2003/4 16m^6 19m 17f* 16g* Dec 11] modest hurdler, off nearly 2 years prior to reappearance: much improved when winning conditional jockeys handicap at Market Rasen in October and novice claimer at Ludlow in December: likely to prove best around 2m: raced on good going or firmer (acts on firm). *Ian Williams* **h92**

BREEZER 4 b.g. Forzando – Lady Lacey (Kampala) [2003/4 16m^4 18s 16g 16d Mar 28] angular gelding: brother to winning 2m hurdler Lord Fernando: fair maiden on Flat (stays 1m): best effort in juvenile hurdles when fourth to Trouble At Bay at Wincanton: will prove best at 2m: ran badly in visor final start. *G. B. Balding* **h91**

BREEZY WARRIOR (IRE) 5 b.g. Commanche Run – Another Crash (Crash Course) [2003/4 F16m^4 F17g^6 F17d^4 19g^{pu} 19d^{pu} 20s^{pu} Jan 6] 5,000 4-y-o: useful-looking gelding: eleventh foal: half-brother to winning 23f hurdler Johnstons Buck (by Buckskin): dam unraced: modest form on last of 3 starts in bumpers: no show over hurdles: tried in cheekpieces. *E. W. Tuer* **h–** **F82**

BREGOGUE (IRE) 10 ch.g. Alphabatim (USA) – Sandra's Joy (Pollerton) [2003/4 c113, h–: c22s^{pu} c17f^4 c23m^6 c20v^3 c17d c16f^3 c20d Apr 10] plain gelding: fairly useful handicap chaser: effective at 2m to 3m: acts on any going: none too consistent. *Ms Helen Mary O'Keeffe, Ireland* **c115** **h–**

BREKNEN LE NOIR (FR) 6 b.g. Pelder (IRE) – Roziyna (Reform) [2003/4 16g^2 16g^3 16v^4 16v* 16s 20d^{pu} 17s^2 20s* Apr 17] good-topped gelding: smart on Flat, successful 7 times up to 1½m in France, including at 4 yrs for Mme C. Barbe: fair hurdler: won handicap at Ascot in January and novice at Bangor: stays 2½m: acts on heavy going (yet to race on firmer than good): blinkered last 5 starts: front runner: jumps none too fluently (went markedly left seventh outing). *P. J. Hobbs* **h113**

BRERETON (IRE) 8 b.g. Be My Native (USA) – Society News (Law Society (USA)) [2003/4 h90: 21m^6 c21g* c21d^4 c24g^F Jun 12] useful-looking gelding: modest novice hurdler: won handicap at Fakenham impressively on chasing debut in May: sold out of N. Henderson's stable 25,000 gns Doncaster Sales later in month: let down by jumping both subsequent starts, visored final one: should stay beyond 21f. *M. C. Pipe* **c104** **h85**

BRESSBEE (USA) 6 ch.g. Twining (USA) – Bressay (USA) (Nureyev (USA)) [2003/4 16m^3 Oct 18] smallish, leggy gelding: fairly useful at best on all-weather Flat (stays 11f), successful in March: visored, failed to settle when 15 lengths third to Fleet Street in maiden at Stratford on hurdling debut: sold to join N. Littmoden £10,500 Ascot December Sales. *J. W. Unett* **h88**

BREVITY 9 b.g. Tenby – Rive (USA) (Riverman (USA)) [2003/4 16m Sep 27] useful at best on Flat (stays 7f), on downgrade: pulled hard when well held in novice on hurdling debut: most unlikely to stay 2m: sold 3,600 gns Doncaster October Sales. *J. M. Bradley* **h–**

BREWSTER (IRE) 7 b.g. Roselier (FR) – Aelia Paetina (Buckskin (FR)) [2003/4 h106, F100: 23s^4 25g 21m^3 Apr 14] rather leggy gelding: useful hurdler: much improved in 2003/4, in frame in handicap at Haydock (35 lb out of weights) and quite valuable novice won by Copsale Lad at Cheltenham: likely to prove better around 3m than shorter: acts on good to firm and heavy going: sure to win races over hurdles. *Ian Williams* **h130**

BRIAN JAMES 10 ch.g. River God (USA) – Rose Orchard (Rouser) [2003/4 c–§, h80§: c25g^{pu} 26g^{pu} May 26] sturdy gelding: little show in 3 starts over fences: poor handicap hurdler: stays 27f: raced on good going or softer (acts on heavy): tried in blinkers/cheekpieces: ungenuine. *F. P. Murtagh* **c– §** **h– §**

BRIAR (CZE) 5 b.g. House Rules (USA) – Bright Angel (AUT) (Antuco (GER)) [2003/4 h91+: 26m^6 24s Jan 14] leggy, close-coupled gelding: modest hurdler as a juve- **h81**

nile: below form in 2 handicaps in 2003/4: stays 2½m: acts on heavy going, well below best on good to firm: wore eyeshields on reappearance, usually in cheekpieces. *M. Pitman*

BRIAR ROSE (IRE) 9 gr.m. Roselier (FR) – Born Lucky (Deep Run) [2003/4 c–, h–: c24mpu c25g5 c25g4 c30d* c25d c25v* c33d c26dpu Mar 11] lengthy mare: poor chaser: won handicaps at Newcastle in November and Kelso in February: suited by 3m+: acts on heavy going. *N. M. L. Ewart* **c85** **h–**

BRIARY BOY (IRE) 12 ch.g. Mister Lord (USA) – Aprolon Princess (IRE) (Duky) [2003/4 c26sur Apr 29] fair pointer in 2003: has failed to complete in 3 steeplechases. *Miss M. Taylor* **c–** **h–**

BRIC A BRAC 7 ch.m. Minster Son – Greenhill's Girl (Radetzky) [2003/4 h–: 20d6 16g 17d 16gpu 17m Jul 17] small mare: of no account. *W. G. Young* **h–**

BRIDGEND BLUE (IRE) 8 b.g. Up And At 'em – Sperrin Mist (Camden Town) [2003/4 h–: 20m6 16m5 Oct 3] bad maiden hurdler: tried blinkered/tongue tied. *J. S. Hubbuck* **h–**

BRIEF CONTACT (IRE) 6 b.g. Brief Truce (USA) – Incommunicado (IRE) (Sadler's Wells (USA)) [2003/4 16vpu Dec 15] leggy gelding: maiden on Flat: lightly raced over hurdles, modest form at best: blinkered. *Jamie Poulton* **h–**

BRIERY MEC 9 b.g. Ron's Victory (USA) – Briery Fille (Sayyaf) [2003/4 16g Mar 17] no form on Flat since 2002: showed nothing on belated hurdling debut. *H. J. Collingridge* **h–**

BRIGADE CHARGE (USA) 9 b.g. Affirmed (USA) – Fairy Footsteps (Mill Reef (USA)) [2003/4 c116+, h–: c17g6 c20dpu c20gpu 21g Mar 5] well-made gelding: fairly useful handicap chaser: left C. Roche, no form in 2003/4, including back over hurdles (wore cheekpieces): should stay beyond 19f: acts on good to firm and heavy ground: blinkered (sour display) third start. *Jonjo O'Neill* **c–** **h–**

BRIGADIER DU BOIS (FR) 5 gr.g. Apeldoorn (FR) – Artic Night (FR) (Kaldoun (FR)) [2003/4 h–: 16g 16vpu 16s3 Feb 18] lengthy gelding: poor novice hurdler: tried blinkered/tongue tied. *Mrs L. Wadham* **h82**

BRIGANTE GIRL (IRE) 6 b.m. Old Vic – Strong Winds (IRE) (Strong Gale) [2003/4 F87: F17g6 Oct 11] lengthy, unfurnished mare: fair form at best in bumpers: will stay beyond 2m. *N. G. Richards* **F76**

BRIGHT APPROACH (IRE) 11 gr.g. Roselier (FR) – Dysart Lady (King's Ride) [2003/4 c126: c33dur c31f* c28g2 c25dpu c26d c26m* Apr 15] smallish gelding: smart hunter chaser: successful at Folkestone in May and Cheltenham in April, back to best to beat Macgeorge 2 lengths at latter: stays 33f: acts on firm and good to soft going. *J. G. Cann* **c126**

BRIGHT EAGLE (IRE) 4 ch.g. Eagle Eyed (USA) – Lumiere (USA) (Northjet) [2003/4 17g Mar 28] half-brother to smart bumper winner Geill Sli (by Charente River): modest maiden on Flat (stays 1¾m) for C. Wall: raced freely when well held in juvenile on hurdling debut. *R. Lee* **h–**

BRIGHT GREEN 5 b.g. Green Desert (USA) – Shining High (Shirley Heights) [2003/4 16d5 16v* 16d 17g4 Apr 10] second foal: dam 2m winner on Flat: fairly useful on Flat (stays 1¼m), sold out of E. Dunlop's stable 26,000 gns Newmarket Autumn (2002) Sales, showed nothing in 2 starts in 2003: modest form over hurdles: won novice at Chepstow in February: raced around 2m on good going or softer (acts on heavy). *J. A. B. Old* **h98**

BRIGHT NOVEMBER 13 b.g. Niniski (USA) – Brigata (Brigadier Gerard) [2003/4 c–, h–: c21d4 Apr 30] tall, leggy gelding: fairly useful chaser at best, well-held fourth in hunter at Cheltenham in April: stays 2½m: acts on soft and good to firm going: 6 of 7 wins on right-handed tracks: usually front runner: sometimes let down by jumping. *D. Fortt* **c83 +** **h–**

BRIGHT STEEL (IRE) 7 gr.g. Roselier (FR) – Ikeathy (Be Friendly) [2003/4 h–: 17m5 22g4 25dpu Dec 27] rather leggy gelding: no worthwhile form: sold 3,200 gns Doncaster January Sales. *A. Parker* **h–**

BRIGHT TIMES AHEAD (IRE) 6 ch.m. Rainbows For Life (CAN) – Just A Second (Jimsun) [2003/4 F16g F16d Mar 24] third foal: half-sister to winner up to 10.5f in Italy by Soviet Lad: dam, maiden hurdler/chaser, suited by test of stamina: well held in 2 bumpers, badly left on debut. *C. J. Drewe* **F–**

BRILLIANTRIO 6 ch.m. Selkirk (USA) – Loucoum (FR) (Iron Duke (FR)) [2003/4 16dpu 17m 16g Nov 11] half-sister to 3 winners over jumps: fair on Flat (stays 1¼m), sold **h–**

from J. O'Shea 7,000 gns after winning seller in June: no form over hurdles: tongue tied second start: pulls hard. *M. C. Chapman*

BRILLYANT DANCER 6 b.m. Environment Friend – Brillyant Glen (IRE) (Glenstal (USA)) [2003/4 17d⁵ 16v Jan 21] third foal: dam, of little account, half-sister to useful Irish hurdler/chaser up to 2½m Isthatafact: poor maiden on Flat (stays 1¼m): well beaten in novice and maiden hurdles. *Mrs A. Duffield* — h–

BRINGONTHECLOWNS (IRE) 5 b.g. Entrepreneur – Circus Maid (IRE) (High Top) [2003/4 16g* 16s 16f³ 16f 16g² 16mᶠ Dec 4] angular gelding: useful on Flat (stays 1m): fair hurdler: won maiden at Wexford in June: left A. Mullins after fourth outing: likely to prove best at sharp 2m: acts on any going: tongue tied last 2 starts. *M. F. Harris* — h106

BRIOS BOY 4 ch.g. My Best Valentine – Rose Elegance (Bairn (USA)) [2003/4 16dᵘʳ 16f⁵ 16g 16dᵖᵘ Dec 12] leggy gelding: well beaten on Flat: little show over hurdles, including in seller: tried in blinkers/cheekpieces: races freely. *G. A. Harker* — h–

BROADBROOK LASS 10 ch.m. Broadsword (USA) – Netherbrook Lass (Netherkelly) [2003/4 c101: c24dᵖᵘ c20d⁴ Apr 24] has had 2 foals: fair chaser: off a year and tongue tied, below best in 2 starts in April: stays 3m: acts on good to firm and heavy ground: front runner: tail flasher. *Mrs H. Dalton* — c86

BROADGATE FLYER (IRE) 10 b.g. Silver Kite (USA) – Fabulous Pet (Somethingfabulous (USA)) [2003/4 c89, h76: c24m* c22g⁵ c24s³ c24g* c24g⁴ c16m⁴ c24dᵖᵘ c24m³ c25f* c25f⁴ Oct 18] medium-sized gelding: winning hurdler: modest handicap chaser: won at Newcastle, Perth and Kelso in first half of season, left in front run-in after Executive Games took wrong course at last-named: distressed final start: stays 25f: acts on firm going, not on soft/heavy: blinkered once (jumped poorly): tongue tied. *Miss Lucinda V. Russell* — c93 h–

BROADSTONE ROAD (IRE) 7 ch.g. Magical Wonder (USA) – Administer (Damister (USA)) [2003/4 c16d⁵ c20s³ c17v⁴ c20f* c22s c21f³ 19f² 22f⁴ 20s c19s* c20f* c22m* c20gᵖᵘ Nov 15] workmanlike gelding: second foal: dam 1½m winner on Flat: fair hurdler: fairly useful chaser: won novice at Navan in June and handicaps at Listowel in September and Cork and Galway (beat Gothic Lord 5 lengths) in October: ran badly in novice at Cheltenham final start: stays 2¾m: acts on firm and soft ground. *Paul John Gilligan, Ireland* — c117 h113

BROADWAY BAY 6 b.g. Karinga Bay – Brownscroft (Dubassoff (USA)) [2003/4 F16g F16d F16d 17g 24m Mar 4] first foal: dam poor maiden pointer: no sign of ability: tongue tied. *G. A. Ham* — h– F–

BROCHRUA (IRE) 4 b.f. Hernando (FR) – Severine (USA) (Trempolino (USA)) [2003/4 16s 19d⁶ 17g⁶ Apr 16] ex-Irish filly: poor maiden up to 13f on Flat at 3 yrs for R. Donohoe: poor form over hurdles. *J. D. Frost* — h63

BROCKTON MIST (IRE) 9 ch.g. Mister Lord (USA) – Glens Princess (Prince Hansel) [2003/4 c119, h100: c23g² May 21] strong, lengthy gelding: fair hurdler: better form over fences, though sometimes let down by jumping: should stay beyond 3m: acts on good to firm and good to soft going: sold 18,000 gns Doncaster May (2003) Sales. *P. J. Hobbs* — c110 h–

BROCTUNE MELODY 5 b. or br.g. Merdon Melody – Eider (Niniski (USA)) [2003/4 F17m F16s F16g⁶ Jan 24] workmanlike gelding: tenth foal: half-brother to useful hurdler/fairly useful chaser Ledgendry Line, stays 25f, and useful hurdler/chaser up to 25f Foundry Lane (both by Mtoto): dam fair 2-y-o 9f winner: modest form in bumpers. *Mrs M. Reveley* — F83

BROGUESTOWN BREEZE (IRE) 11 b.g. Montelimar (USA) – Spin A Coin (Torus) [2003/4 c91, h–: c20d⁵ c21dᶠ c22s c25d c25g⁶ c24g⁶ c28d⁵ c26g Apr 12] workmanlike gelding: winning chaser, little sign of retaining ability in 2003/4: tried in cheekpieces. *R. Dean* — c– h–

BROKEN DREAM (IRE) 7 b.g. Broken Hearted – A Little Further (Mandalus) [2003/4 c100, h–: c21g c22s⁵ c20g⁴ c24dᵘʳ c26g³ c23d⁵ Apr 21] maiden hurdler/chaser, sold out of Miss H. Knight's stable £7,200 Ascot December Sales after reappearance: modest form at best over fences in 2003/4: stays 2¼m: acts on heavy going (unraced on firmer than good). *P. R. Rodford* — c94 h–

BROMLEY ABBEY 6 ch.m. Minster Son – Little Bromley (Riberetto) [2003/4 F16d F16m⁶ Nov 6] lengthy mare: second foal: dam fairly useful 2m hurdler: little show in 2 bumpers. *R. Ford* — F–

BRONCO STYLE (IRE) 6 ch.g. Executive Perk – Name A Reason (IRE) (Buckskin (FR)) [2003/4 F17g F16m Sep 14] €1,200 4-y-o: second foal: dam unraced: well beaten in 2 bumpers: sold £2,000 Ascot October Sales. *C. J. Gray* **F—**

BRONHALLOW 11 b.g. Belmez (USA) – Grey Twig (Godswalk (USA)) [2003/4 c83, h–: c23g^pu c25g c21d² c24g* c21m^pu Jul 13] angular gelding: winning hurdler: modest novice chaser: won weak event at Stratford in June: probably acts on any going: usually visored/blinkered: tongue tied. *Mrs Barbara Waring* **c86 h—**

BRONZESMITH 8 b.g. Greensmith – Bronze Age (Celtic Cone) [2003/4 c112x, h–: c21s^ur c23g⁴ c20g⁵ c16m² c17g^pu c19d^bd c19d⁴ c19s^pu Jan 22] lengthy gelding: fair maiden chaser, often let down by jumping: seems suited by well-run 2m: acts on soft and good to firm going (bumper form on heavy): tried tongue tied: weak finisher. *B. J. M. Ryall* **c106 § h—**

BROOKLANDS LAD 7 b.g. North Col – Sancal (Whistlefield) [2003/4 h87, F85: 22m³ 20m^pu 22g c17g⁶ c20m⁵ Dec 18] workmanlike gelding: poor maiden hurdler: poor form both outings over fences: should stay beyond 19f: tongue tied last 2 outings. *J. W. Mullins* **c75 h78**

BROOKLYN BREEZE (IRE) 7 b. or br.g. Be My Native (USA) – Moss Gale (Strong Gale) [2003/4 h127p, F99: c20d* Nov 27] useful-looking gelding: unbeaten in 3 novice hurdles in 2002/3: won novice at Carlisle on chasing debut most impressively by 25 lengths from Simply Supreme, jumping well and pulling clear after leading before 4 out: stays 3m: unraced on extremes of going: seemed sure to improve and win plenty more races, but wasn't seen out again. *L. Lungo* **c131 p h—**

BROOKLYN BROWNIE (IRE) 5 b.g. Presenting – In The Brownies (IRE) (Lafontaine (USA)) [2003/4 F16g F16m* F16g F17v Mar 21] €41,000 3-y-o: good-bodied gelding: third foal: half-brother to winning pointer by Good Thyne: dam unraced: fair form in bumpers, won at Hexham in June: likely to be suited by 2½m+: possibly unsuited by heavy going. *J. M. Jefferson* **F90**

BROOKLYN'S GOLD (USA) 9 b.g. Seeking The Gold (USA) – Brooklyn's Dance (FR) (Shirley Heights) [2003/4 h124: 16m 16m c16s² 16g⁵ c16g⁶ 16g⁶ 16g Mar 15] close-coupled, quite good-topped gelding: fairly useful hurdler: very stiff task (acted as pacemaker) and probably flattered in Christmas Hurdle at Kempton fourth start: better effort over fences when 14 lengths second to Kalca Mome in 5-runner novice at Hereford: raced around 2m: has won on soft going, best form on good/good to firm. *Ian Williams* **c102 h114**

BROOKS 8 b.g. Minster Son – Melody Moon (Philip of Spain) [2003/4 c19g^F c21d^pu c20d⁴ c19g⁵ Apr 3] twice-raced in points in 2002, winning 2/1 maiden: modest form over fences: likely to prove best around 2m: free-going sort. *John R. Upson* **c93**

BROOKSIE 9 b.g. Efisio – Elkie Brooks (Relkino) [2003/4 h100: 20m 16f⁴ 16m^pu 19s 19s 16s⁵ 17m 19d⁵ 19g⁴ 17g^pu Apr 10] angular gelding: poor handicap hurdler nowadays: barely stays 2¾m: acts on any going: visored/blinkered: has had tongue tied: has found little. *Miss K. M. George* **h76**

BROOK STREET 7 b.g. Cruise Missile – Sweet Spice (Native Bazaar) [2003/4 h66, F77: 21v³ 21s⁴ Jan 4] workmanlike gelding: poor form over hurdles: will stay 3m: has looked hard ride. *C. L. Tizzard* **h69**

BROOKSY DOVE 6 ch.g. Alderbrook – Coney Dove (Celtic Cone) [2003/4 17s^pu 25d^pu Mar 14] third foal: half-brother to winning 2½m hurdler Scratch The Dove (by Henbit): dam, 21f hurdle winner, half-sister to 1994 Champion Hurdle winner Flakey Dove: showed nothing in 2 novice hurdles. *A. E. Price* **h—**

BROOM CLOSE (IRE) 10 b.g. Yashgan – Pick Nine (Tumble Wind (USA)) [2003/4 c87?, h78: 24m c21g^pu c21g^pu May 26] lengthy gelding: poor hurdler: novice chaser: no form in 2003/4: stays 2½m: acts on heavy going: tried in cheekpieces. *R. Johnson* **c— h—**

BROOMERS HILL (IRE) 4 b.g. Sadler's Wells (USA) – Bella Vitessa (IRE) (Thatching) [2003/4 F12s² F13v⁴ F16g Mar 27] sturdy gelding: fourth foal: half-brother to fairly useful 1999 2-y-o 6f winner Bella Bellisimo (by Alzao) and fairly useful 7f/1m winner Ros The Boss (by Danehill): dam, non form, half-sister to high-class 2m hurdler Kingsmill: well-backed favourite, 9 lengths second to Locksmith in 3-y-o event at Ascot, easily best effort in bumpers. *L. A. Dace* **F81**

BROPHYS SONNET (IRE) 9 b. or br.m. Homo Sapien – Shanna Golden (IRE) (Le Bavard (FR)) [2003/4 16m May 27] IR 500 3-y-o: first foal: dam ran once in bumper: maiden pointer: no show on hurdling debut. *I. A. Duncan, Ireland* **h—**

*Enter The £1 Million Tote Ten To Follow Rising Stars Novices' Chase, Chepstow—
the ill-fated Brother Joe claims the last of his seven chase wins in a match with Puntal*

BROTHER JOE (NZ) 10 ch.g. Hula Town (NZ) – Olivia Rose (NZ) (Travolta (FR)) **c137**
[2003/4 h154§: c23m² c16m* c21m* c20mF c21g* c20m* c19m* c21g* c19g* c20gF **h– §**
Nov 15] smallish gelding: smart on his day over hurdles but not one to trust: successful on
7 of 10 starts over fences, in novices at Worcester, Uttoxeter, Newton Abbot, Huntingdon,
Chepstow (2) and Fakenham between June and November: easily beat sole rival Puntal in
Grade 2 at Chepstow for final win: fell fatally at Cheltenham: stayed 25f, was effective at
much shorter: acted on any going: blinkered once: free-going sort: not a fluent jumper.
P. J. Hobbs

BROTHER TED 7 b.g. Henbit (USA) – Will Be Wanton (Palm Track) [2003/4 F–: **h–**
20g⁶ Jun 12] leggy gelding: little sign of ability: tried tongue tied. *J. K. Cresswell*

BROUGHTON KNOWS 7 b.g. Most Welcome – Broughtons Pet (IRE) (Cyrano de **h73**
Bergerac) [2003/4 16m⁴ 16g⁵ May 30] modest on Flat (stays 2m, often looks quirky),
successful first 4 starts in 2004: poor form both outings over hurdles, jumped badly
second time. *W. J. Musson*

BROUGHTONS MILL 9 gr.g. Ron's Victory (USA) – Sandra's Desire (Grey Desire) **h53**
[2003/4 16m 16d 16s 16s² 17g⁶ 16d⁴ Apr 12] close-coupled gelding: poor maiden on Flat:
bad form over hurdles: raced around 2m: wore cheekpieces last 2 starts. *J. A. Supple*

BROWN BEN 10 b.g. General Gambul – City Sunset (Sunyboy) [2003/4 c20mF c21g³ **c–**
c26m⁴ c16d⁴ c16d Dec 2] tall gelding: first foal: dam maiden pointer: little sign of ability
over fences: sold £1,020 Ascot February Sales. *D. P. Keane*

BROWN CHIEFTAIN (IRE)   11 b.g. Meneval (USA) – Brown Trout (IRE) (Beau   c–
Charmeur (FR)) [2003/4 c–: c26mpu May 29] fair pointer, successful twice in 2003: no
form in steeplechases: tried blinkered. *A. W. G. Geering*

BROWN ESQUIRE   13 b.g. Broadleaf – Ana Brown (Souvran) [2003/4 c–, h–:   c–
c25mpu Mar 4] lengthy gelding: winning pointer: pulled up both starts in hunter chases   h–
since 2002: stays 3m: acts on good to firm going. *Miss G. Dewhurst*

BROWNEYES BLUE (IRE)   6 b.g. Satco (FR) – Bawnard Lady (Ragapan) [2003/4   F71
F16v F16s F16d5 Apr 23] sixth foal: half-brother to winning Irish pointer by Spanish
Place: dam, won 2m hurdle in Ireland, out of half-sister to top-class hurdler/chaser Dawn
Run: well held in bumpers. *D. R. MacLeod*

BROWN FLYER   7 gr.g. Baron Blakeney – Brown Veil (Don't Look) [2003/4 20d6   h–
17s 20d Mar 22] brother to modest pointer Brown Robber: dam winning hurdler/fair
staying chaser: showed little in 3 outings over hurdles. *H. D. Daly*

BROWNINGS EXPRESS   5 b.g. Elmaamul (USA) – Chushan Venture (Pursuit of   h–
Love) [2003/4 F16d F16g 24spu Apr 4] sturdy gelding: first foal: dam unraced, out of   F–
half-sister to 2000 Guineas winner Tirol: showed little in bumpers or novice hurdle.
M. W. Easterby

BROWN TEDDY   7 b.g. Afzal – Quadrapol (Pollerton) [2003/4 h95, F73: 19g* Dec   h104
3] lengthy gelding: fair hurdler: looked open to further improvement after winning
conditional jockeys handicap at Catterick, but wasn't seen out again: should stay at least
2½m. *R. Ford*

BRUERN (IRE)   7 b.g. Aahsaylad – Bob's Girl (IRE) (Bob Back (USA)) [2003/4 F–:   h–
F16d 16s Jan 16] quite good-topped gelding: well held in bumpers and novice hurdle.   F–
Mrs Mary Hambro

BRUNSTON CASTLE   4 b.g. Hector Protector (USA) – Villella (Sadler's Wells   h–
(USA)) [2003/4 19vpu Feb 2] half-brother to 2½m hurdle winner Ennoble (by Highest
Honor): modest on Flat (likely to stay 1¾m): tongue tied, no show on hurdling debut.
B. R. Millman

BRUSH A KING   9 b.g. Derrylin – Colonial Princess (Roscoe Blake) [2003/4 h83:   c–
21g2 25g2 26m* 25m 26s6 c26g3 c20f4 16s 25g 23g5 Feb 20] plain gelding: tailed off both   h89
starts over fences: modest handicap hurdler: won at Southwell in June: stays 3¼m: acts
on good to firm going, probably on heavy: tried blinkered: claimer ridden: inconsistent.
C. T. Pogson

BRUSH THE ARK   10 b.m. Brush Aside (USA) – Expensive Lark (Sir Lark) [2003/4   h83
h83: 19d 17d3 21g Mar 27] small, lengthy mare: poor maiden hurdler: effective at 2m to
3¼m: raced on good going or softer (acts on soft). *J. S. Smith*

BRUTHUINNE (IRE)   9 ch.g. Vaquillo (USA) – Portane Miss (Salluceva) [2003/4   c– §
c102, h–: c20gpu c23mpu Jun 1] strong gelding: fair chaser: disappointing both starts early   h–
in 2003/4, reluctant to race second time: won 3-runner point in March: stays easy 3¼m:
acts on soft and good to firm going: often front runner: one to treat with caution.
B. G. Powell

BUADHACH (IRE)   8 b.g. Petoski – Viking Rocket (Viking (USA)) [2003/4 c–§,   c– §
h–§: c16dF Apr 30] lengthy, angular gelding: poor and temperamental hurdler in 2001/2:   h– §
little show in 2 hunter chases: should stay beyond 2½m: acts on good to soft going
(bumper form on firm): tried tongue tied. *M. A. Hill*

BUALADHBOS (IRE)   5 b.g. Royal Applause – Goodnight Girl (IRE) (Alzao (USA))   h–
[2003/4 h–: 16g 22mpu Jul 13] workmanlike gelding: maiden on Flat: no form in 3 starts
over hurdles. *F. Jordan*

BUBBA BOY (IRE)   4 b. or br.g. Anshan – Royal Patrol (IRE) (Phardante (FR))   F91
[2003/4 F17g2 Apr 13] third foal: dam lightly raced: would have won bumper at Exeter
on debut but for running green, beaten ½ length by Gaelic Music. *M. C. Pipe*

BUBBLE BOY (IRE)   5 ch.g. Hubbly Bubbly (USA) – Cool Charm (Beau Charmeur   F83
(FR)) [2003/4 F17g5 Apr 13] third foal: half-brother to winning pointer by Lanfranco:
dam, winning pointer, from family of Pizarro: 9 lengths fifth of 15 to Gaelic Music in
bumper at Exeter on debut. *B. G. Powell*

BUBBLE BROOK   6 b.g. Alderbrook – Leinster Girl (Don) [2003/4 F16g May 21]   F–
£1,000 4-y-o: workmanlike gelding: second foal: dam unraced: tailed off in bumper on
debut. *H. J. Manners*

*Doncaster Bloodstock Sales Future Champions Novices' Chase, Cheltenham—
the lightly-raced Buckby Lane pulls clear of Isard III (grey) and Simply Supreme*

BUBBLE UP (IRE)   5 b.m. Nicolotte – Mousseux (IRE) (Jareer (USA)) [2003/4 16d³   **h74**
16m^F Sep 7] fair maiden up to 1m on Flat: poor form both starts over hurdles: tried tongue
tied: dead. *J. G. Portman*

BUCKBY LANE   8 b.g. Nomadic Way (USA) – Buckby Folly (Netherkelly) [2003/4   **c131 p**
h119+: c20g² c20s* Dec 13] tall, useful-looking gelding: fairly useful hurdler: second   **h–**
start over fences, won valuable sales novice at Cheltenham by 13 lengths from Isard III,
jumping more fluently than on debut and quickening away 2 out: should stay 3m: acts on
soft and good to firm going: looked sure to progress further over fences, but wasn't seen
out again. *P. R. Webber*

BUCKLAND KNIGHT (IRE)   8 b. or br.g. Commanche Run – Myra Gaye (Buck-   **c114 ?**
skin (FR)) [2003/4 h–: c25m^{ur} c26d^F c25s^F c24s^F Apr 17] lengthy gelding: winning   **h–**
hurdler: fell/unseated all 4 outings in hunter chases, running easily best race at Warwick
second outing, falling at last when 8 lengths behind winner Macgeorge: stays 3¼m: acts
on heavy going: blinkered last 3 starts in 2002/3. *Mrs Laura J. Young*

BUCKLAND LAD (IRE)   13 ch.g. Phardante (FR) – Belcraig (Foggy Bell) [2003/4   **c88**
c21m* c24g May 31] sparely-made gelding: one-time fairly useful handicap chaser: has   **h–**
deteriorated considerably, but dead-heated with Shu Gaa in weak hunter at Folkestone in
May: stays 3m: acts on good to firm and heavy going. *Mrs D. M. Grissell*

BUCKSKIN LAD (IRE)   9 b. or br.g. Buckskin (FR) – Loverush (Golden Love)   **h–**
[2003/4 h83: 24s^{pu} 26s^{pu} Jan 7] poor hurdler: broke down final start: stays 3¼m: acts on
soft going: tried in cheekpieces. *Mrs N. S. Sharpe*

BUDDY GIRIE   11 b.g. Lord Bud – Hatsu-Girie (Ascertain (USA)) [2003/4 c90, h–:   **c91**
c21s² c26g² c28d⁵ May 30] fair hunter chaser: stays 27f: acts on soft going. *P. Cornforth*   **h–**

BUDE   5 gr.g. Environment Friend – Gay Da Cheen (IRE) (Tenby) [2003/4 h82: 21m   **c–**
16m³ 16g⁴ 16d* 19m 17g⁵ c17g^{ur} c16m³ c20m^{pu} 24g³ Mar 4] angular gelding: modest   **h85 §**
handicap hurdler: won at Uttoxeter in August: distant last of 3 in novice at Warwick, let
down by jumping both other starts over fences: stays easy 3m: acts on good to firm and
good to soft going: effective blinkered/in cheekpieces or not: usually races prominently:
not one to trust. *S. A. Brookshaw*

BULA'S QUEST   5 b.g. Sula Bula – Dinkies Quest (Sergeant Drummer (USA)) [2003/4   **F95**
F17m* F16m³ Sep 14] second foal: dam winning pointer: fair form in bumpers, won at
Newton Abbot on debut in August by 2½ lengths from Dalawan. *L. G. Cottrell*

BULGARIA MOON   4 ch.g. Groom Dancer (USA) – Gai Bulga (Kris) [2003/4 17g   **h–**
Aug 23] half-brother to 5-y-o Chivalry (by Mark of Esteem): little form on Flat: bled
from nose when tailed off on hurdling debut. *C. Grant*

BUNGEE JUMPER   14 b.g. Idiot's Delight – Catherine Bridge (Pitpan) [2003/4 c–§,   **c102**
h–§: c16m^{bd} c16m* c16g⁵ c17m³ c17m* Aug 9] sturdy gelding: winning hurdler: fair   **h–**

handicap chaser: won at Uttoxeter (made all) in June and Stratford: best around 2m: acts on firm going: tried blinkered/in cheekpieces: has found little. *B. D. Leavy*

BUNKUM   6 b.g. Robellino (USA) – Spinning Mouse (Bustino) [2003/4 h115: 20d[5] **c107** 20s[6] c19d[4] c16s[5] c24s[F] c21d[2] c19g[pu] Apr 3] good-topped gelding: fair hurdler: best effort **h107** over fences when fifth to Simply Gifted in handicap at Chepstow: should stay beyond 2½m: acts on heavy ground. *R. Lee*

BUNRATTY'S SOLE (IRE)   6 br.g. Phardante (FR) – Bucks Gift (IRE) (Buckley) **c–** [2003/4 c24s[6] Apr 12] €11,500 4-y-o: third foal: half-brother to fairly useful hurdler Millcroft Seaspray (by Good Thyne), stays 3m: dam unraced: winning pointer, including in March: in cheekpieces, well beaten in hunter chase at Fakenham. *N. M. Bloom*

BURDENS BOY   8 b.g. Alflora (IRE) – Dalbeattie (Phardante (FR)) [2003/4 19g[F] Feb **h92 +** 19] smallish gelding: won on first of 2 starts over hurdles in 2001/2: off over 2 years, travelled well long way and fourth when fell last in handicap at Taunton: should stay at least 2½m: raced on good going or softer. *H. D. Daly*

BURDENS GIRL   7 ch.m. Alflora (IRE) – Dalbeattie (Phardante (FR)) [2003/4 h–, **h101** F–: 19g[pu] 21g[2] 21d[6] 17d* 17g* Apr 3] fair hurdler: much improved when winning handicaps at Taunton (novice) in March and Hereford (made all to win with something in hand) in April: should be as effective at 2½m as 2m: raced mainly on good/good to soft ground. *H. D. Daly*

BURLEY DON CARLOS   8 b.g. Neltino – Burley Bianca (Kinglet) [2003/4 c25g[ur] **c–** Apr 4] fair pointer, won 3-runner race in April: unseated ninth on hunter chase debut at Wincanton. *D. Pipe*

BURNING GOLD   6 b.g. Gildoran – Regan (USA) (Lear Fan (USA)) [2003/4 21v[pu] **h–** 19d[pu] Jan 1] first foal: dam winning hurdler/fair chaser up to 25f: third on completed start in maiden points in 2003: bought 4,000 gns Doncaster August Sales: no show in 2 novice hurdles. *Mrs S. D. Williams*

BURNING SHORE (IRE)   4 b.f. Desert King (IRE) – Gerante (USA) (Private **h85** Account (USA)) [2003/4 16m[3] 16m[3] 16d[2] 17g[2] 20g[5] 23d[3] Apr 12] IR 7,000Y: fifth foal: half-sister to 3 winners, including useful 1999 2-y-o 7f winner Chez Cherie (by Wolfhound): dam, ran once in France, out of half-sister to smart French 1¼m winner Glity: modest juvenile hurdler: stays 23f. *Mrs L. Wadham*

BURNING TRUTH (USA)   10 ch.g. Known Fact (USA) – Galega (Sure Blade **c113** (USA)) [2003/4 h107: 16m[4] 19g[4] c16m[2] c16m[2] c16m[2] c17m[3] c16m[F] c16m[2] c19m[2] c20f* **h111** Oct 9] good-topped gelding: fair hurdler/chaser: easily landed odds in 5-runner maiden chase at Ludlow (lame) in October: stays 2½m: acts on firm going: reliable. *M. Sheppard*

BURNT COPPER (IRE)   4 b.g. College Chapel – Try My Rosie (Try My Best (USA)) **h81** [2003/4 16m[3] 16m[5] 17d[pu] 16d[5] Dec 15] smallish gelding: half-brother to winning 2m hurdler Tanimbar (by Persian Bold): fair maiden on Flat (stays 1½m): poor form in juvenile hurdles. *J. R. Best*

BURNTOAKBOY   6 b.g. Sir Harry Lewis (USA) – Sainte Martine (Martinmas) **h113** [2003/4 F17s* F20d[4] F16s[5] 24s 20s[6] 16s* 20d[4] Apr 12] leggy, unfurnished **F95** gelding: second foal: dam winning chaser up to 23f: won at Killarney in July on first of 3 starts in bumpers: fair form over hurdles, won maiden at Punchestown in March: good efforts after when in frame in minor event at Fairyhouse and novice (sixth to Arch Stanton) at Punchestown: stays 2½m: acts on soft going. *N. Nelson, Ireland*

BURNT OUT (IRE)   5 ch.m. Anshan – Lantern Lover (Be My Native (USA)) [2003/4 **h110** F18d[5] F16f[4] F16d[4] F16d[4] F16d[6] F18d[3] 20s* 24d 20s[3] Apr 11] €9,500 3-y-o: **F85** unfurnished mare: half-sister to 5 winners in Germany, including listed hurdle winner Louis (by Ordos): dam bumper winner: fair form in bumpers: fair hurdler: easily won mares maiden at Down Royal in January: best effort when third to G V A Ireland in novice at Punchestown in early-May: stays 3m: acts on soft and good to firm going. *J. A. O'Connell, Ireland*

BURUNDI (IRE)   10 b.g. Danehill (USA) – Sofala (Home Guard (USA)) [2003/4 c94, **c110** h118: c20m[2] c20g[3] c17g* c20m[2] c20g[3] c22m[2] c20g[2] c22g[4] Mar 26] tall gelding: fairly **h–** useful handicap hurdler: fair novice chaser: won at Stratford in July: stays 2¾m: acts on soft and good to firm going, possibly not on heavy: fell only run in blinkers: held up: consistent. *A. W. Carroll*

BURWOOD BREEZE (IRE)   8 b.g. Fresh Breeze (USA) – Shuil Le Cheile (Quay- **c110** side) [2003/4 c98, h–: c24m[2] c24g[2] c24s[F] c23d[2] c24d[2] c24s[ro] c24g[3] c24d* c24m[2] Apr 13] **h–** workmanlike gelding: fair chaser: comfortably won novice at Bangor in March: good second to Felix Darby in handicap at Chepstow final start: stays 3m: acts on soft and good to firm going: patiently ridden: ran out sixth outing: consistent. *T. R. George*

BUS 9 ch.g. Weld – Roaring Breeze (Roaring Riva) [2003/4 c90?, h–: c17g⁴ c16g⁵ Aug 4] angular gelding: poor hurdler/novice chaser: raced mainly around 2m: acts on good to firm ground: has had tongue tied. *Mrs L. Williamson* — c–, h–

BUSH HILL BANDIT (IRE) 9 b. or br.g. Executive Perk – Baby Isle (Menelek) [2003/4 c92, h–: c24m³ c28d³ᵈ c76g⁵ c24s⁵ Apr 12] fair hunter chaser: barely stays 3½m: acts on good to firm going, probably on soft. *Mrs Anne-Marie Hays* — c92, h–

BUSHIDO (IRE) 5 br.g. Brief Truce (USA) – Pheopotstown (Henbit (USA)) [2003/4 h108: 17d⁶ 17d 19d² 16d⁵ 19d* 19s³ 20dᵖᵘ 20s Apr 4] small gelding: fair handicap hurdler: won 16-runner event at Catterick in January: stays 19f: acts on soft going: tends to hang left, and has gone in snatches. *Mrs S. J. Smith* — h112

BUSH PARK (IRE) 9 b.g. Be My Native (USA) – By All Means (Pitpan) [2003/4 c117?, h–: c23g⁵ c24s⁵ c21m⁵ 24f² 25m² c20s² c19d* c22m² c24d³ c21d⁴ c21mᵖᵘ c24gᵖᵘ Mar 6] strong, lengthy gelding: modest handicap chaser: fair handicap chaser: won at Chepstow in November: lacklustre efforts last 3 starts: effective at 2½m to 25f: acts on any going: tried blinkered/visored: effective tongue tied or not: one to treat with caution. *R. H. Alner* — c109 §, h99

BUSINESS CLASS (NZ) 12 b.g. Accountant (NZ) – Fury's Princess (NZ) (Our Kungfu (NZ)) [2003/4 c104, h–: 21g c21g c16g² c22f⁴ c20m⁴ c20m* c20f³ c20g³ c24g² c22g⁵ c20gᵘʳ c21g⁵ c20d² Apr 24] lengthy gelding: lightly raced over fences: modest handicap chaser: won 3-runner race at Leicester in November: best form at 2½m/2¾m: acts on firm and good to soft going: tried in cheekpieces: sold 4,200 gns Doncaster May Sales. *Mrs M. Reveley* — c98, h–

BUSINESS TRAVELLER (IRE) 4 ch.g. Titus Livius (FR) – Dancing Venus (Pursuit of Love) [2003/4 16sᵘʳ 16s 16g⁵ 16d⁴ 19g* 22g Apr 18] first foal: dam, fair Irish 2m hurdler, half-sister to fairly useful 2m hurdler Shining Edge: poor maiden on Flat (stays 2m) for G. A. Swinbank: modest form over hurdles, won juvenile handicap at Newbury in March easily by 3½ lengths from Glencoyle: should stay beyond 19f (all but fell final start). *R. J. Price* — h98

BUSMAN (IRE) 15 ch.g. Be My Guest (USA) – Cistus (Sun Prince) [2003/4 c25gᵖᵘ May 1] close-coupled, sparely-made gelding: one-time fair hunter chaser. *K. R. Pearce* — c–, h–

BUSTER BUTTONS 12 b.g. Lord Bud – Lady Buttons (New Brig) [2003/4 26dᵖᵘ May 28] winning pointer, failed to complete in 2 starts in 2003: no show on hurdling debut. *R. E. Barr* — h–

BUSTER CLYDE (IRE) 7 b.g. Bustomi – The Red Mare (Sagaro) [2003/4 F–: 20d Nov 2] well held in bumper and novice hurdle. *J. R. Bewley* — h–

BUSTER (IRE) 5 ch.g. Presenting – Chez Georges (Welsh Saint) [2003/4 F16s 16g 21dᵖᵘ Mar 28] €42,000 3-y-o, €35,000 (privately) 4-y-o: fifth foal: half-brother to fairly useful hurdler/winning chaser The Extra Man (by Sayaarr), stays 3m, and winning 3m chaser Kaikoura Girl (by Desse Zenny): dam ran twice: showed nothing in bumper and 2 maiden hurdles. *M. J. Ryan* — h–, F–

BUSTISU 7 b.m. Rakaposhi King – Tasmin Gayle (IRE) (Strong Gale) [2003/4 F71: 16vᵖᵘ 16m 16d 21d³ Mar 1] poor form in bumpers and over hurdles: stays 21f: difficult ride (has hung right). *D. J. Wintle* — h71

BUSTLING RIO (IRE) 8 b.g. Up And At 'em – Une Venitienne (FR) (Green Dancer (USA)) [2003/4 c–, h–: 20d 19g 20d⁶ Mar 11] good-topped gelding: successful on 2 of 3 starts over fences: fairly useful hurdler at best: long way below form in 2003/4: stays 3m: acts on heavy and good to firm going: usually held up. *P. C. Haslam* — c–, h–

BUSTYERBUBBLE 4 b.f. Sri Pekan (USA) – South Sea Bubble (IRE) (Bustino) [2003/4 16sᵖᵘ Nov 18] no show in seller on Flat and over hurdles. *C. N. Kellett* — h–

BUTLEIGH ROSE 9 ch.m. Nicholas Bill – Mistress McKenzie (Deep Run) [2003/4 c19mᶠ May 14] no form over hurdles: maiden pointer: in rear when fell sixth in novice hunter chase. *Miss N. Stephens* — c–, h–

BUTTRESS 5 b.h. Zamindar (USA) – Furnish (Green Desert (USA)) [2003/4 F16g³ F16g² F16d Mar 22] 10,000 3-y-o, 800 4-y-o: strong horse: first foal: dam, 5f winner who stayed 7f, out of half-sister to Derby winner Quest For Fame: fair form when placed in bumpers: will prove best at sharp 2m. *M. W. Easterby* — F89

BUZ KIRI (USA) 6 b.g. Gulch (USA) – White Corners (USA) (Caro) [2003/4 h71: **h80**
20g⁴ 20m⁴ 24m 16g 16g² 16d² 16d² 16d Dec 12] compact gelding: modest on Flat (stays
2m), successful in February and March: poor maiden hurdler: stays 2½m: acts on good to
firm and good to soft going: has had tongue tied. *A. W. Carroll*

BUZYBAKSON (IRE) 7 b. or br.g. Bob Back (USA) – Middle Verde (USA) (Sham **c103**
(USA)) [2003/4 h101, F83: 17g^pu c20d⁵ c20s⁴ c24s^pu c20g c24s² c24g⁵ c25s⁴ c25g^pu Apr **h–**
2] leggy gelding: winning hurdler: fair novice chaser: stays 3m: acts on heavy going:
hasn't convinced with jumping over fences. *J. R. Cornwall*

BY DEFINITION (IRE) 6 gr. or b.m. Definite Article – Miss Goodbody (Castle **h–**
Keep) [2003/4 h–: 16m^pu 16m 16m 16d Dec 26] of little account, left J. M. Bradley after
second start: has worn cheekpieces/blinkers. *J. C. Tuck*

BYGONE 6 b.g. Past Glories – Meltonby (Sayf El Arab (USA)) [2003/4 F84: F17s⁶ **F84**
F17g Apr 24] modest form in bumpers. *J. Hetherton*

BYLAND 4 b.g. Danzig (USA) – Coxwold (USA) (Cox's Ridge (USA)) [2003/4 **F87**
aF16g² Apr 4] £5,000 3-y-o: third foal: dam, successful up to 11f and placed in Grade 1
company in USA, half-sister to useful miler Magical Strike: 1¾ lengths second to Lin
d'Estruval in bumper on polytrack at Lingfield on debut. *K. A. Morgan*

BYRON LAMB 7 b.g. Rambo Dancer (CAN) – Caroline Lamb (Hotfoot) [2003/4 **c131**
c126p, h–: c16d² c19g⁴ c20v^ur c20g^pu Mar 17] leggy gelding: useful handicap chaser: **h–**
best effort when ¾-length second to Sir Storm in 5-runner event at Wetherby: probably
best short of 2½m when conditions are testing: raced on good going or softer (acts on
heavy): reliable: sold 31,000 gns Doncaster May Sales. *N. G. Richards*

BYWELL BEAU (IRE) 5 b.g. Lord Americo – Early Dalus (IRE) (Mandalus) **F92**
[2003/4 F16d⁴ F16d³ Apr 23] 12,000 4-y-o: sturdy gelding: third foal: half-brother to
useful staying chaser Rugged River (by Over The River): dam unraced: better effort in
bumpers when third to Eggmount at Perth: will stay beyond 2m. *J. I. A. Charlton*

C

CABALLE (USA) 7 ch.m. Opening Verse (USA) – Attirance (FR) (Crowned Prince **h–**
(USA)) [2003/4 h99d: 21g May 18] workmanlike mare: modest hurdler: fractured
pelvis only outing in 2003/4: should stay 2½m: acts on heavy going: tried blinkered.
Dr P. Pritchard

CABARET QUEST 8 ch.g. Pursuit of Love – Cabaret Artiste (Shareef Dancer (USA)) **c–**
[2003/4 c–, h–: 16g c16g⁶ c16m^ur Jun 28] good-topped gelding: little form over jumps: **h–**
tried tongue tied/in cheekpieces: dead. *R. C. Guest*

CABER (IRE) 4 b.g. Celtic Swing – Arusha (IRE) (Dance of Life (USA)) [2003/4 **h80**
F16d 20d² Apr 21] sixth foal: half-brother to useful bumper winner Armageddon (by **F–**
Deploy): dam, 2-y-o 1m winner, half-sister to 2000 Guineas winner Don't Forget Me:
favourite when well held in bumper: 14 lengths second to Celtic Boy in maiden at
Worcester on hurdling debut, tiring after 3 out: will probably prove best around 2m.
O. Sherwood

CABILLE (FR) 12 ch.g. Lesotho (USA) – Ironique (FR) (Riverman (USA)) [2003/4 **c–**
c–, h–: c23g^pu 22d^pu 20m^pu c23m^pu Jul 9] workmanlike gelding: no longer of any account: **h–**
often wears headgear. *H. G. Owen*

CADOU ROYAL (FR) 8 b.g. Cadoudal (FR) – Leonie Des Champs (FR) (Crystal **c127**
Palace (FR)) [2003/4 c118, h–: 16d c20s* c17s* c20s^pu 19d³ Mar 7] good-topped gelding: **h109**
fair handicap hurdler: fairly useful handicap chaser: won at Navan in December and
January, beating Backdoor Champion 2 lengths on latter occasion: stays 2½m: raced on
going softer than good (acts on heavy): has found little. *A. L. T. Moore, Ireland*

CADRILLON (FR) 14 br.g. Le Pontet (FR) – Jenvraie (FR) (Night And Day) [2003/4 **c80**
c86, h–: c25d³ May 22] smallish, sparely-made gelding: modest hunter chaser: stays **h–**
3¾m: acts on soft going: sometimes blinkered, wore cheekpieces only start in 2003/4.
Miss J. E. Foster

CAESAREAN HUNTER (USA) 5 ch.g. Jade Hunter (USA) – Grey Fay (USA) **h–**
(Grey Dawn II) [2003/4 17s 16d 16g Apr 12] fairly useful on all-weather, fair on turf on
Flat (stays 2m), sold out of S. Kirk's stable 31,000 gns Newmarket Autumn Sales: no
form in 3 novice hurdles. *R. T. Phillips*

CAESAR'S PALACE (GER) 7 ch.g. Lomitas – Caraveine (FR) (Nikos) [2003/4 **h101**
h118d: 24g⁴ 22d⁵ 20g 24g⁴ 24m² 24m³ 24g³ 24v³ 24d³ 22g² 24s⁶ 27d² Apr 23]

CAL

workmanlike gelding: fair handicap hurdler: most consistent without winning in 2003/4: stays 27f: unraced on firm going, acts on any other: effective with or without headgear: has looked hard ride in past. *Miss Lucinda V. Russell*

CAGED TIGER 5 b.g. Classic Cliche (IRE) – Run Tiger (IRE) (Commanche Run) [2003/4 F17d⁴ Mar 11] well-made gelding: first foal. dam unraced, out of sister to high-class 2m chaser Young Snugfit: 15¼ lengths fourth of 18 to Sobraon in bumper at Carlisle on debut: sold only 1,300 gns Doncaster May Sales. *T. P. Tate*   F89

CAHER SOCIETY (IRE) 12 ch.g. Moscow Society (USA) – Dame's Delight (Bally-moss) [2003/4 c94x, h–: c24g⁵ c24dᵘʳ c20d³ c16g³ Apr 3] lengthy gelding: fair hunter chaser: stays 3m: acts on heavy going: sketchy jumper. *Paul Morris*   c83 x h–

CAIMIN'S CAPER (IRE) 6 gr.g. Norwich – Dj Rose (IRE) (Dominion) [2003/4 F16s²ᵈ F16v⁶ 16d 16s 16s* 16v* 16s* 16d* Apr 10] good-topped gelding: second foal: dam unraced sister to fairly useful hurdler up to 3m Suir Venture: fair form on first of 2 starts in bumpers: progressive hurdler: successful in maiden and novice at Tramore in January, novice handicap at Wexford in March and maiden at Cork in April: creditable third of 29 to Supreme Being in handicap at Punchestown later in April: stays 2½m: acts on heavy going. *J. T. R. Dreaper, Ireland*   h123 F86

CAISHILL (IRE) 5 b. or bg.g. Dolphin Street (FR) – Pretonic (Precocious) [2003/4 h119: 16g 20f² 24g² c24m⁴ c19mᵘʳ c22gᶠ 16m⁴ c16m* c16d² c24g⁴ c16d³ c17d⁴ c19s⁴ c20s c21g³ c20s⁶ c17s³ c18v³ Apr 21] useful-looking gelding: fair hurdler: fairly useful novice chaser: won maiden at Thurles in November: very best form at 2m: probably acts on any going: blinkered after eleventh start: tough. *Joseph Crowley, Ireland*   c117 h108

CAITLAND 5 b.m. Puissance – Lorlanne (Bustino) [2003/4 16g Sep 25] poor and ungenuine maiden on Flat (stays 1m): showed nothing on hurdling debut. *R. Allan*   h–

CAITRIONA'S CHOICE (IRE) 13 b.g. Carmelite House (USA) – Muligatawny (Malacate (USA)) [2003/4 c109, h–: c16g⁵ c16s* c17d² c16m² c16m⁵ c17g⁴ c16mᵖᵘ c16d² c16s³ c16dᵖᵘ c17s c16v⁶ c16d c16sᵖᵘ Mar 20] tall gelding: fairly useful handicap chaser: won at Perth in May: generally out of form after next 2 outings: raced mainly around 2m: acts on any going: effective tongue tied or not: held up: has taken little interest: inconsistent. *P. Monteith*   c117 d h–

CAKE IT EASY (IRE) 4 ch.f. Kendor (FR) – Diese Memory (USA) (Diesis) [2003/4 16d Apr 17] fair on Flat (stays 1½m), won second of 2 starts in 2003 for M. Johnston: 66/1, 21½ lengths seventh of 10 to Dalaram in steadily-run juvenile at Ayr on hurdling debut. *Mrs M. Reveley*   h92

CALAMINT 5 gr.g. Kaldoun (FR) – Coigach (Niniski (USA)) [2003/4 h–: 17gᵖᵘ May 1] no form over hurdles or in points: sold £800 Ascot June Sales. *K. C. Bailey*   h–

CALAMINTHA 4 b.f. Mtoto – Calendula (Be My Guest (USA)) [2003/4 17d* 18g² 16s* 22d 16gᶠ Mar 15] medium-sized filly: fair on Flat, wide-margin winner of 1¾m seller in October (sold from R. Beckett 13,200 gns): of similar merit over hurdles, odds on when winning juvenile at Bangor in November and mares novice at Leicester (made all) in January: should stay beyond 2¼m: acts on soft ground: visored last 3 starts: not a fluent jumper: has shown signs of temperament. *M. C. Pipe*   h107

CALATAGAN (IRE) 5 ch.g. Danzig Connection (USA) – Calachuchi (Martinmas) [2003/4 h109: 17d* 17d³ 16d 16g⁶ 16d⁶ 16g* Mar 15] fairly useful handicap hurdler: won at Sedgefield in November (made all) and Stratford (beat Mobasher by 5 lengths) in March: likely to prove best at 2m: acts on good to soft ground: successful on Flat in April. *J. M. Jefferson*   h117

CALCOT FLYER 6 br.g. Anshan – Lady Catcher (Free Boy) [2003/4 F80: 22d⁴ 26g⁵ 24g Feb 13] rather unfurnished gelding: poor form first 2 starts in novice hurdles: likely to prove best at 3m+. *A. King*   h84

CALDAMUS 12 gr.g. Scallywag – Portodamus (Porto Bello) [2003/4 c98, h–: c25mᵖᵘ Mar 11] workmanlike gelding: fair hunter chaser: ran as if amiss in March, won point fol-lowing month: stays 25f: acts on good to soft going: usually front runner. *Miss S. Waugh*   c– h–

CALDER RIVER 6 b.m. Alderbrook – Calametta (Oats) [2003/4 F16gᵇᵈ F17d³ F20m F17g⁵ 16d⁶ 16d 16d⁶ 24d⁶ 20d 24dᶠ Feb 22] €40,000 4-y-o: lengthy, angular mare: half-sister to several winners, including fairly useful staying chaser Skillwise (by Buckley) and fair 2m hurdler Beechcourt (by Son Pardo): dam, Irish maiden, half-sister to good hurdlers William Crump and Tomintoul: modest form in bumpers and over hurdles: stayed 3m: acted on good to soft going: tongue tied last 6 starts: dead. *Mrs Sandra McCarthy, Ireland*   h99 F80

CALIFORNIA SON (IRE) 8 ch.g. Lycius (USA) – Madame Nureyev (USA) (Nureyev (USA)) [2003/4 17g³ 17g 19g³ 16g³ c16g² c16v³ c16m⁴ Mar 2] sturdy gelding: c? h?

167

half-brother to 2 poor hurdlers: poor maiden at 3/4 yrs in Britain for C. Popham, subsequently successful up to 21f in Scandinavia, including at 6 yrs: placed over hurdles and on chasing debut at Taby in October: showed little in maiden chases at Wetherby and Leicester. *Ms K. Stenefeldt, Sweden*

CALIWAG (IRE)   8 b.g. Lahib (USA) – Mitsubishi Style (Try My Best (USA))   c–
[2003/4 c–, h–: c16f5 c20g3 c17m4 c24m4 Oct 18] lengthy gelding: little form over   h–
hurdles or fences: blinkered final start: tried tongue tied. *Jamie Poulton*

CALLING BRAVE (IRE)   8 ch.g. Bob Back (USA) – Queenie Kelly (The Parson)   c145 +
[2003/4 h125: 24d* c25g* c20d* c20m* c24gur Mar 17]   h142
    For the second year running Nicky Henderson drew a blank at the Chelten-
ham Festival, a meeting where he has enjoyed considerable success over the years.
It might have been a different story, though, if Calling Brave hadn't unseated his
rider four out in the Royal & SunAlliance Chase, disputing third and still travelling
well at the time having jumped soundly enough until then. It was the third time
Calling Brave had returned empty handed from the Festival. In 2002 he came
eighth to Pizarro in the Champion Bumper, and the following year trailed home last
of eighteen finishers behind Hardy Eustace in the Royal & SunAlliance Novices'
Hurdle.
    Whereas Calling Brave was one of the outsiders on his first two appear-
ances at Cheltenham—he had a record of one win from three starts in bumpers and
two from five in novice hurdles going into those races—only three of the runners in
the Royal & SunAlliance Chase started at odds shorter than Calling Brave, who had
won all three of his starts over fences. Calling Brave did have one more run over
hurdles before embarking on his chasing career in a maiden at Folkestone in
December, showing improved form to win a handicap at Aintree in November in
very good style by five lengths from Sh Boom. The latter's stable-companion
Drombeag was the only one seriously backed to beat Calling Brave at Folkestone,
but Calling Brave landed the odds readily enough despite a mixed round of
jumping, having too much speed for Drombeag in the latter stages. Calling Brave
faced only two opponents on his next start, in a novice chase at Sandown, and again
started at odds on. Although second favourite Mister Banjo failed to give his

*racingpostpix.co.uk Pendil Novices' Chase, Kempton—
Calling Brave is a willing partner for stand-in jockey Tony McCoy*

running, Patricksnineteenth ensured that the favourite didn't have matters all his own way, Calling Brave living up to the second part of his name as he gained the upper hand close home to win by three quarters of a length.

Calling Brave's final appearance before Cheltenham should have been in a novice chase on the first day of Kempton's two-day February meeting, but when that fixture was abandoned because of frost Calling Brave was switched to the Grade 2 racingpostpix.co.uk Pendil Novices' Chase on the second day, a race worth more than twice as much to the winner. The Pendil rarely attracts a field of any size and only four lined up against Calling Brave, although all four were winning chasers who had shown at least fairly useful form. With his usual rider Mick Fitzgerald on the injured list, Tony McCoy came in for the mount on Calling Brave and he made sure that the stamina of two of the gelding's main rivals Atum Re and Santenay, both of whom were stepping up in trip, was tested fully, setting the pace and really forcing matters after halfway. Calling Brave's jumping, apart from a mistake four out, was more fluent than it had been at Sandown, and he stayed on much too well for Atum Re and Santenay, who were the only others still in contention in the second half of the race, winning by eleven lengths.

		Bob Back (USA) (br 1981)	Roberto (b 1969)	Hail To Reason
Calling Brave (IRE) (ch.g. 1996)				Bramalea
			Toter Back (ch 1967)	Carry Back
				Romantic Miss
		Queenie Kelly (b 1986)	The Parson (b 1968)	Aureole
				Bracey Bridge
			Saucy Society (b 1967)	Choral Society
				Saucy Vic

Sir Robert Ogden's "Calling Brave"

Calling Brave is the seventh foal of the unraced Queenie Kelly, whose previous produce include the smart staying chaser Ottowa (by Roselier), who was leading when falling at the tenth on his attempt to win the Royal & SunAlliance Chase, and the smart bumper performer Queens Harbour (by Brush Aside), the latter a former stable-companion of Calling Brave. The next dam Saucy Society won on the Flat and over hurdles and is a half-sister to the smart Irish hurdler Troyswood. Saucy Society is also the grandam of the useful jumper Frickley. Calling Brave, a well-made gelding who acts on soft and good to firm going, has shown himself effective at two and a half miles, though ultimately he is likely to prove best at three miles or over even further. Calling Brave's departure in the SunAlliance may well turn out a blessing in disguise so far as his prospects in handicaps are concerned. The three and a quarter miles of Newbury's Hennessy Gold Cup certainly won't be a problem for him, and he could well be a leading candidate for that race in the next season. *N. J. Henderson*

CALLMECOZMO (IRE) 6 ch.g. Zaffaran (USA) – Call Me Connie (IRE) (Combine Harvester) [2003/4 F16d* Mar 24] first live foal: dam, winning Irish pointer, sister to fairly useful 2m hurdler Combine Call: looked good prospect when winning bumper at Chepstow on debut, making all to beat Blushing Bull 2 lengths, pair clear. *P. R. Webber* **F105**

CALL ME JACK (IRE) 8 b.g. Lord Americo – Tawney Rose (Targogan) [2003/4 c91, h89: 16d⁴ c16d⁴ c16vᵖᵘ c19gᶠ c16gᶠ c16g³ c16gᵘʳ c17g² c16sᵘʳ c17d⁵ Apr 24] rangy gelding: modest handicap hurdler/novice chaser: raced mainly around 2m: acts on heavy going: usually tongue tied: often front runner: often let down by jumping over fences. *J. Hetherton* **c87 x** **h90**

CALL ME SONIC 8 b.g. Henbit (USA) – Call-Me-Dinky (Mart Lane) [2003/4 c–, h82: c21mᵖᵘ May 9] novice hurdler: no form in steeplechases, won twice in points in March: sold 2,500 gns Doncaster May Sales. *R. H. Alner* **c–** **h–**

CALL OF THE WILD 4 ch.g. Wolfhound (USA) – Biba (IRE) (Superlative) [2003/4 16s⁶ 16gᶠ Feb 6] lengthy gelding: modest maiden on Flat (stays 9f): signs of ability in juvenile hurdles at Doncaster and Catterick (fell 2 out). *R. A. Fahey* **h78**

CALLOW LAKE (IRE) 4 b.g. Bahhare (USA) – Sharayif (IRE) (Green Desert (USA)) [2003/4 16d* 16d⁴ 16s³ 16d* Mar 31] fairly useful on Flat (stays 17f): of similar merit over hurdles: won twice at Clonmel, juvenile in November and minor event (beat Michael Mor 3½ lengths) in March: likely to stay beyond 2m. *D. Wachman, Ireland* **h120**

CALL THE MARK (IRE) 5 b.g. Goldmark (USA) – Shalerina (USA) (Shalford (IRE)) [2003/4 16m 16g 16mᵖᵘ Jun 28] poor maiden on Flat (stays 1m): little show over hurdles, including in seller: sold 700 gns Doncaster August Sales. *C. N. Kellett* **h–**

CAL MAC 5 b.g. Botanic (USA) – Shifting Mist (Night Shift (USA)) [2003/4 16s 16s 16dᵇᵈ 20s 17g³ Apr 24] fairly useful but ungenuine on Flat (stays 8.5f), sold out of H. Morrison's stable 7,000 gns Newmarket Autumn Sales: first form over hurdles when third in selling handicap at Market Rasen: will prove best around 2m. *J. G. Carr, Ireland* **h84**

CALON LAN (IRE) 13 b.g. Bustineto – Cherish (Bargello) [2003/4 c88§, h–: c16m c16mᵖᵘ c19m³ c20m⁶ c19d⁵ c24gᵖᵘ Jan 9] fair hurdler/chaser at best, retains little ability: tried blinkered: temperamental. *R. Williams* **c66 §** **h–**

CALVADOS (USA) 5 b.g. Seattle Slew (USA) – A Votre Sante (USA) (Irish River (FR)) [2003/4 c18g c22dᶠ 16s 16s⁵ 16v² 20d⁵ c16m² Mar 2] fair maiden on Flat: modest form over hurdles: runner-up in point in 2003: best effort in steeplechases when 12 lengths second of 4 to Master Rex in maiden at Leicester, jumping less than fluently: stays 2½m. *John A. Quinn, Ireland* **c78** **h92**

CALVIC (IRE) 6 ch.g. Old Vic – Calishee (IRE) (Callernish) [2003/4 F16f⁶ 20g⁶ 21v⁴ 21v³ 20s Feb 7] unfurnished gelding: second foal: half-brother to 2½m bumper/point winner Calithyne (by Good Thyne): dam winning pointer: brought down last in Irish point in 2003: sixth of 12 in bumper at Cheltenham: fair form over hurdles: won novice at Towcester in November: will stay 3m: acts on heavy going. *T. R. George* **h100**

CAMADERRY (IRE) 6 ch.g. Dr Devious (IRE) – Rathvindon (Realm) [2003/4 h83: 17s 16g 17gᵖᵘ Mar 28] sturdy gelding: maiden hurdler: no form in 2003/4. *Mrs A. M. Naughton* **h–**

CAMARADERIE 8 b.g. Most Welcome – Secret Valentine (Wollow) [2003/4 h83§: 20g⁶ 16m c17gᵘʳ Mar 28] winning hurdler, well beaten in 2003/4: unseated second on chasing debut: raced mainly around 2m: acts on good to firm and good to soft going: effective blinkered or not: unreliable. *A. G. Juckes* **c– §** **h– §**

CAMDENATION (IRE) 8 b.g. Camden Town – Out The Nav (IRE) (Over The River (FR)) [2003/4 h93: 21g4 Apr 12] modest hurdler: not discredited on return from 14-month lay-off: likely to stay 3m: acts on soft going. *N. J. Gifford* **h84**

CAMDEN TANNER (IRE) 8 b.g. Camden Town – Poor Elsie (Crash Course) [2003/4 h128+: c17d* c16dF c20s2 c21d c16d2 c20s* c17s Mar 27] good-topped gelding: fairly useful hurdler: similar level over fences, won at Tipperary (minor event) in May and Punchestown (novice, beat Marcus du Berlais by length) in March: running creditably when falling last final outing (remounted): effective at 2m to 3m: acts on heavy ground: patiently ridden (hung fire third start): consistent. *Robert Tyner, Ireland* **c125 h–**

CAMERON BRIDGE (IRE) 8 b.g. Camden Town – Arctic Raheen (Over The River (FR)) [2003/4 c114x, h102: c19m9 c20m* c16s5 c20g6 20d6 c20gF c20m5 Apr 23] useful-looking gelding: fair hurdler: fairly useful handicap chaser: won at Chepstow in October and Kempton (by 4 lengths from Janiture) in November: below form over fences after: stays 2½m: acts on soft and good to firm going. *P. J. Hobbs* **c129 h108**

CAMERON JACK 9 b.g. Elmaamul (USA) – Ile de Reine (Ile de Bourbon (USA)) [2003/4 c75x, h–: c20g 20m3 26g* 26m* 27g3 22dpu Apr 5] lengthy, angular gelding: usually let down by jumping over fences: modest hurdler: won weak maiden and novice handicap at Southwell in July: stays 3¼m: acts on good to firm and heavy going: has flashed tail under pressure. *Miss Kate Milligan* **c– x h92**

CAMITROV (FR) 14 b.g. Sharken (FR) – Emitrovna (FR) (Buisson d'Or) [2003/4 c79, h–: c20g5 c20dpu Mar 25] leggy gelding: one-time smart chaser: not easy to train and no sign of retaining ability in 2004. *D. Line* **c– h–**

CAMPAIGN TRAIL (IRE) 6 b.g. Sadler's Wells (USA) – Campestral (USA) (Alleged (USA)) [2003/4 h127p: 24d* 25d* 25d2 Jan 10] good-topped gelding: useful handicap hurdler, lightly raced: won at Bangor (sweating) and Wetherby (got up close home to beat His Nibs by neck) in December: creditable second to Mistanoora at Warwick following month: stays 25f: acts on soft going: patiently ridden. *Jonjo O'Neill* **h134**

CAMP HILL 10 gr.g. Ra Nova – Baytino (Neltino) [2003/4 c93, h–: c16d6 c22gpu 17d c20spu c24spu c25v5 c20s* c26d6 c20v* c20g c26dpu Apr 18] angular gelding: maiden hurdler: poor chaser: won from out of handicap at Carlisle in February and March: barely stays testing 25f: best on soft/heavy going: inconsistent. *J. S. Haldane* **c85 § h–**

CAMROSS 8 b.g. Teenoso (USA) – Arizona Belle (Arab Chieftain) [2003/4 21v* 24s6 Feb 22] poor hurdler: off 21 months, won novice handicap at Towcester in December: stays 3m: raced on good going or softer (acts on heavy): refused at first once in 2001/2. *J. C. Fox* **h84**

CANADA 6 b.g. Ezzoud (IRE) – Chancel (USA) (Al Nasr (FR)) [2003/4 h124: 22m* Jul 19] leggy gelding: useful on Flat (stays 1½m): useful handicap hurdler: soon clear and maintained good gallop when winning at Market Rasen by 20 lengths from Blackchurch Mist: will stay 3m: acts on good to firm and heavy going. *M. C. Pipe* **h135**

Rocom Handicap Hurdle, Wetherby—Campaign Trail (No.6) shades the verdict over His Nibs

CANADA ROAD (IRE) 6 b.g. Great Marquess – New Technique (FR) (Formidable (USA)) [2003/4 F81: F17d F16m 21v^pu 17s Feb 6] little sign of ability. *R. J. Smith*   **h–**
F–

CANADIANE (FR) 9 ch.m. Nikos – Carmonera (FR) (Carmont (FR)) [2003/4 c117, h116: c20g⁶ c21m² c20m⁴ c17m⁴ c21g⁴ c20m c20s⁴ c16g* c20d c19s³ Feb 3] sparely-made mare: fairly useful handicap hurdler: fair handicap chaser: fortunate to win 4-runner race at Chepstow in November: best up to around 21f: acts on firm and soft going: tried in cheekpieces, visored last 3 starts: ungenuine. *M. C. Pipe*   **c112 §**
h– §

CANAL END (IRE) 7 b.g. Montelimar (USA) – Miss Cripps (IRE) (Lafontaine (USA)) [2003/4 h85: 22m⁴ 24m⁵ 22g Jun 21] modest maiden hurdler: stays 3m: acts on good to firm going. *Jonjo O'Neill*   **h91**

CANATRICE (IRE) 4 gr.f. Brief Truce (USA) – Cantata (IRE) (Saddlers' Hall (IRE)) [2003/4 16m⁴ 16g³ 16s^pu 21d 20g 17m⁴ Apr 14] good-topped filly: modest on Flat (stays 1½m), successful in August for B. Johnson: modest juvenile hurdler: best efforts around 2m: wears cheekpieces: swished tail on debut. *T. D. McCarthy*   **h81**

CA NA TRONA (IRE) 5 b.g. Accordion – Sterna Star (Corvaro (USA)) [2003/4 F16d 16g⁵ 21g⁴ 24g Mar 26] good-topped gelding: sixth foal: half-brother to Champion Hurdle winner Hardy Eustace (by Archway), stays 21f: dam, 1½m winner, out of half-sister to Star Appeal: ninth of 19 in bumper at Newbury on debut: modest form over hurdles, 18½ lengths fourth of 19 to Fountain Hill in novice at same course: should stay beyond 21f: sold 16,500 gns Doncaster May Sales. *N. J. Henderson*   **h96**
F80

CANCUN CARIBE (IRE) 7 ch.g. Port Lucaya – Miss Tuko (Good Times (ITY)) [2003/4 h90: 16d* Apr 11] won 2 of 4 starts over hurdles: left J. Frost and off 13 months, further improvement when making most in minor event at Plumpton, quickening clear between last 2: likely to prove best around 2m. *Evan Williams*   **h97 +**

CANDARLI (IRE) 8 ch.g. Polish Precedent (USA) – Calounia (IRE) (Pharly (FR)) [2003/4 h114: 16s⁵ 16m⁶ 16d⁴ 16d³ 16g 16d⁶ Apr 8] rather sparely-made gelding: fair handicap hurdler: raced at 2m: acts on good to soft going, probably on good to firm. *D. R. Gandolfo*   **h104**

CANDELLO 6 b.m. Supreme Leader – Oubava (FR) (Groom Dancer (USA)) [2003/4 F16g* Mar 4] third known foal: half-sister to French middle-distance winner Belle Oubava (by Linamix): dam, French middle-distance winner, half-sister to useful French hurdler Grand Patron and fairly useful hurdler/chaser around 2½m Litchanine: 6/5-on, won mares bumper at Ludlow on debut by 2 lengths from Polyanthus Jones, pair clear: likely to improve. *N. J. Henderson*   **F98 p**

CANE BRAKE (IRE) 5 b.g. Sadler's Wells (USA) – Be My Hope (IRE) (Be My Native (USA)) [2003/4 16d⁵ 16d³ 18d² 20s* 16s³ Feb 1] third foal: dam useful hurdler around 2m: best effort over hurdles (fairly useful form) when winning maiden at Fairyhouse in January by 7 lengths from Lasquini du Moulin: stays 2½m: raced only on soft/good to soft going. *D. Wachman, Ireland*   **h115**

CA NE FAIT RIEN (IRE) 8 gr.g. Denel (FR) – Fairytale-Ending (Sweet Story) [2003/4 F82: 20g Oct 11] modest in bumpers: tailed off on Flat debut and in novice hurdle. *N. M. Babbage*   **h–**

CANNY CHIFTANE 8 b.g. Be My Chief (USA) – Prudence (Grundy) [2003/4 h–§: 20d 20v^pu 20d^pu 20g 20v^pu 22s^pu 21g Mar 17] stocky gelding: winning hurdler, no longer of any account: usually blinkered/visored: ungenuine. *Miss C. J. E. Caroe*   **h– §**

CANNY SCOT 7 b.g. Slip Anchor – Pomade (Luthier) [2003/4 18m² 16m 22g* 22g* Nov 21] leggy ex-Irish gelding: brother to fairly useful winner up to 13.3f Spikenard and half-brother to 2 winners, including winning 2½m hurdler Pomatum (by General Assembly): dam disqualified 9f winner on sole outing: modest form in bumpers: upped in trip and improved form over hurdles last 2 starts, won handicaps at Newton Abbot (ladies) and Exeter (novice): will stay 3m. *R. Curtis*   **h85**

CANON BARNEY (IRE) 9 b. or br.g. Salluceva – Debbies Candy (Candy Cane) [2003/4 c111x, h–: 20d c24d^pu c24s 24d^F 24s⁵ Mar 20] sturdy gelding: fair hurdler/chaser: stays 3¼m: raced on going softer than good: wore cheekpieces last 2 starts: poor jumper of fences. *Jonjo O'Neill*   **c– x**
h101

CANON MCCARTHY (IRE) 8 ch.g. Be My Native (USA) – Archetype (Over The River (FR)) [2003/4 c81, h–: c24g³ c25v³ c23s^pu Jan 20] tall gelding: has run tubed: poor maiden hurdler/chaser: lame final start: stays 25f: acts on soft ground: has had tongue tied. *S. T. Lewis*   **c–**
h–

CANSALRUN (IRE) 5 b.m. Anshan – Monamandy (IRE) (Mandalus) [2003/4 F17d⁶ F17m² F16m⁴ 17g 21sᵖᵘ 20g⁵ Dec 9] €3,100 3-y-o: rather unfurnished mare: third foal: dam, winning pointer, from family of high-class staying chaser Simon Legree: modest form in bumpers: best effort over hurdles when fifth to Big Moment in novice at Fontwell. *J. W. Mullins*
h81
F76

CANTARINHO 6 b.g. Alderbrook – Hot Hostess (Silly Season) [2003/4 c72: c24s* Apr 12] successful twice in points in 2004 prior to winning hunter chase at Fakenham by 14 lengths from Courage Under Fire: stays 3m: acts on soft going. *D. J. Kemp*
c110

CAN'T BE SCRABBLE 11 b.g. Gargoor – Scribble Along (Supergrey) [2003/4 c–: 24m² 20m² 22m* 22gᵖᵘ 22f⁴ 19g⁴ 24m⁴ Sep 7] winning pointer: fell early in hunter chase: modest novice hurdler: made all at Stratford in July: may prove best up to 2¾m: acts on good to firm going: has looked less than straightforward (amateur ridden). *C. J. Down*
c– §
h89 §

CANTERBURY JACK (IRE) 7 b.g. Supreme Leader – Crest of The Hill (Prince Regent (FR)) [2003/4 h101: c23gᵖᵘ Mar 12] fair form at best over hurdles: left M. Pipe, won twice in points in February: jumped poorly and looked temperamental in hunter chase at Leicester: will stay beyond 3m: tried visored. *D. Pipe*
c– §
h–

CANTORIS 4 b.g. Unfuwain (USA) – Choir Mistress (Chief Singer) [2003/4 16sᵖᵘ 16m 16g 21g 17s⁵ 19g⁶ Apr 16] close-coupled gelding: tried tubed: modest maiden on Flat (probably stays 1½m), sold out of M. Johnston's stable 4,000 gns Doncaster October Sales: no form over hurdles: blinkered last 2 starts: tried tongue tied. *C. L. Popham*
h–

CANTYS BRIG (IRE) 7 gr.g. Roselier (FR) – Call Catherine (IRE) (Strong Gale) [2003/4 h–, F–: 20v 24d⁶ 24v 19sᵖᵘ Apr 11] little sign of ability. *Miss L. C. Siddall*
h–

CAPACOOSTIC 7 ch.m. Savahra Sound – Cocked Hat Girl (Ballacashtal (CAN)) [2003/4: 16mᵖᵘ Jun 18] no form in claiming hurdles: sold £800 Ascot July Sales, third in point in April. *A. G. Juckes*
h–

CAP CLASSIQUE 5 b.g. Classic Cliche (IRE) – Champenoise (Forzando) [2003/4 F16m F16g⁴ F17m* Sep 10] fourth foal: half-brother to 3 winners on Flat, including fairly useful 5f winner Dreams Desire (by Mind Games): dam 1m winner: modest form in bumpers, won maiden at Hereford: wears eyeshields and not straightforward ride. *Simon Earle*
F83

CAPE CANAVERAL (IRE) 5 b.g. Sadler's Wells (USA) – Emmaline (USA) (Affirmed (USA)) [2003/4 h114d: 20g⁹ 19s³ 20s 20s Feb 7] rangy, good sort: fair hurdler: made hard work of landing odds in maiden at Fontwell in November: looked unenthusiastic after: stays 2½m: raced mainly on good going or softer: one to be wary of. *G. L. Moore*
h100 §

CAPE COAST 7 b.g. Common Grounds – Strike It Rich (FR) (Rheingold) [2003/4 19mᶠ 16f 16m Oct 18] smallish gelding: poor on Flat (stays 7f): little worthwhile form in selling hurdles: sold 900 gns Doncaster November Sales. *P. D. Evans*
h–

CAPE STORMER (IRE) 9 b.g. Be My Native (USA) – My Sunny South (Strong Gale) [2003/4 c119, h110: c20d⁴ c20g* c21g Apr 1] workmanlike gelding: fair hurdler: fairly useful chaser: won hunter at Leicester in March by 20 lengths from Guignol du Cochet: not especially fluent when well held in Fox Hunters' at Aintree: seems best short of 3m: raced mainly on good going or firmer: reliable. *Mrs C. M. Gorman*
c114
h–

CAP IN HAND 12 ch.g. Nearly A Hand – Beringa Bee (Sunley Builds) [2003/4 h–: 16g 20g⁵ May 22] leggy, lengthy gelding: veteran hurdler, retains little ability. *Mrs S. J. Smith*
h–

CAPPADRUMMIN (IRE) 7 ch.g. Bob Back (USA) – Out And About (Orchestra) [2003/4 h100: 20g 16s⁴ Jan 8] rather leggy gelding: bumper winner: fair form over hurdles, lightly raced: bred to stay beyond 2m: sold 4,800 gns Doncaster May Sales. *N. J. Henderson*
h101

CAPRICCIO (IRE) 7 gr.g. Robellino (USA) – Yamamah (Siberian Express (USA)) [2003/4 24g⁶ Sep 24] maiden on Flat: winning hurdler, lightly raced: should be suited by further than 17f: acts on heavy going: blinkered once. *Mrs S. C. Bradburne*
h–

CAPRICORN PRINCESS 10 b.m. Nicholas Bill – Yamrah (Milford) [2003/4 h114: 16d 20m³ c21m² c17m⁴ Oct 11] angular mare: fair handicap hurdler: poor form on 2 starts over fences, reportedly lame second time: best form around 2m: acts on good to firm and good to soft going: tried tongue tied: front runner. *B. D. Leavy*
c80
h107

CAPRIOLO (IRE) 8 ch.g. Priolo (USA) – Carroll's Canyon (IRE) (Hatim (USA)) [2003/4 h97§: 20g² 18m² 22g⁴ 20m⁵ 20m² 20d 18s³ 20v⁴ 18s⁶ 19d 21g Apr 12] sturdy gelding: modest hurdler: barely stays 2¾m: acts on good to firm and heavy going: tried blinkered, wears cheekpieces nowadays: irresolute. *P. G. Murphy*
h97 §

CAP

CAPTAIN CLOONEY (IRE) 11 b.g. Supreme Leader – Capincur Lady (Over The River (FR)) [2003/4 c81, h–: c26s² c29s⁶ c26s c25dᵖᵘ c26g⁴ c24dᵖᵘ c21g⁵ Apr 10] poor handicap chaser, shows his form only occasionally: stays 3¼m: raced on good going or softer (acts on heavy). *N. R. Mitchell* — **c80 d** **h–**

CAPTAIN CORELLI 7 b.g. Weld – Deaconess (The Parson) [2003/4 F16s⁴ 20d⁶ 16g² Mar 6] good-topped gelding: fairly useful form in bumpers: off 20 months, 17 lengths fourth to Noplanofaction in Grade 2 at Chepstow: easily better effort in novice hurdles when second to comfortable winner Rooster's Reunion at Huntingdon: bred to be suited by much further than 2m. *M. Pitman* — **h97** **F96**

CAPTAIN DARLING (IRE) 4 b.g. Pennekamp (USA) – Gale Warning (IRE) (Last Tycoon) [2003/4 16g⁵ Nov 2] fair on Flat (barely stays 1¼m): never a factor in juvenile maiden at Huntingdon on hurdling debut. *R. M. H. Cowell* — **h–**

CAPTAIN FLINDERS (IRE) 7 b.g. Satco (FR) – Auburn Queen (Kinglet) [2003/4 F96: 17g⁵ 21d³ Feb 2] rangy gelding: will make a chaser: better effort in bumpers in 2002/3 for C. Mann when second at Huntingdon: showed promise both starts in novice hurdles, third of 22 to Dangerously Good in steadily-run event at Kempton: will stay beyond 21f: open to improvement and sure to win a race. *Miss H. C. Knight* — **h109 p**

CAPTAIN GINGER 4 ch.g. Muhtarram (USA) – Brand (Shareef Dancer (USA)) [2003/4 16sᵖᵘ Jan 14] half-brother to fair 2m hurdler Brandy Snap (by Broadsword) and bumper winner Cherry Brandy (by Elmaamul): fair on Flat (stays easy 1m): raced freely and showed little on hurdling debut. *H. Morrison* — **h–**

CAPTAIN HARDY (IRE) 4 b.g. Victory Note (USA) – Airey Fairy (IRE) (Alzao (USA)) [2003/4 16s 18s⁶ 16s 17d² 16g* Apr 18] close-coupled gelding: useful on Flat (stays 1¼m), successful twice in 2003, sold out of S. Kirk's stable 16,000 gns Newmarket Autumn Sales: improved efforts over hurdles last 2 starts, won conditional jockeys handicap at Wincanton: raced around 2m on good ground or softer. *G. Brown* — **h88**

CAPTAIN JAKE 9 b.g. Phardante (FR) – Cherry Crest (Pollerton) [2003/4 c–, h–: c24gᵘʳ c25g² c25gᵖᵘ c25vᵖᵘ Dec 26] big gelding: twice-raced hurdler: form over fences only when second in very weak novice handicap at Folkestone: wore cheekpieces last 3 starts. *M. Appleby* — **c80 ?** **h–**

CAPTAIN MADUCK (IRE) 6 b.g. Distinctly North (USA) – Avril's Choice (Montelimar (USA)) [2003/4 F16s F16d Dec 29] €10,000 4-y-o: tall gelding: fourth foal: brother to 1m winner in Denmark and half-brother to Irish 1¼m winner Ballylennon Mist (by Digamist): dam lightly-raced half-sister to smart performer up to 1¼m Trevita: tailed off in bumpers. *M. Pitman* — **F–**

CAPTAIN MOONLIGHT (IRE) 8 b.g. Religiously (USA) – Next Adventure (IRE) (Denel (FR)) [2003/4 c17sᵘʳ c16s³ c17s c20s c20s³ c24d⁴ c24s* c24d* c24d⁴ c20vᵖᵘ Apr 17] compact gelding: useful at one time over hurdles: fair chaser: won handicaps at Wexford and Limerick within 5 days in March: stays 3m: raced on going softer than good (acts on heavy). *T. J. O'Mara, Ireland* — **c111** **h–**

CAPTAIN MURPHY (IRE) 6 b.g. Executive Perk – Laura Daisy (Buckskin (FR)) [2003/4 F16s F16s⁴ F16s² F16d² Apr 17] €6,000 4-y-o: tall, unfurnished gelding: second foal: half-brother to modest hurdler Iceberge (by Glacial Storm), from point: fairly useful form in bumpers, no match for impressive Dunnet Head at Ayr final start. *J. I. A. Charlton* — **F96**

CAPTAIN O'NEILL 10 b.g. Welsh Captain – The Last Tune (Gunner B) [2003/4 c85, h81: 20sᵖᵘ 20m² 24mᵖᵘ c20m c20m² c25mᵖᵘ c25mᵖᵘ c19mᵖᵘ 20sᵖᵘ Nov 29] lengthy, angular gelding: has been tubed: poor handicap hurdler/maiden chaser: stays 3m: acts on any going: tried visored: sketchy jumper: unreliable. *A. W. Carroll* — **c– x** **h85 d**

CAPTAIN RAWLINGS 5 ch.g. Lancastrian – Coombesbury Lane (Torus) [2003/4 F16d 19gᶠ 16g 22g Apr 18] first foal: dam, modest hurdler, stayed 3m: well held in bumper and over hurdles. *H. D. Daly* — **h–** **F–**

CAPTAIN ROBIN (IRE) 10 b.g. Supreme Leader – Gentle Madam (Camden Town) [2003/4 h80: 22g May 21] well-made gelding: bumper winner: lightly raced and poor form at best over hurdles: should prove best at 2½m+. *N. A. Twiston-Davies* — **h–**

CAPTAIN RON (IRE) 8 b.g. Marju (IRE) – Callas Star (Chief Singer) [2003/4 c–, h–: c21gᵖᵘ 19v 21gᵖᵘ 22m Mar 11] leggy gelding: no form outside points, left S. Lloyd after reappearance. *Mrs S. M. Johnson* — **c–** **h–**

CAPTAIN'S LEAP (IRE) 8 ch.g. Grand Plaisir (IRE) – Ballingowan Star (Le Moss) **h81**
[2003/4 h80p: 16s[pu] 16s[6] 17s 24d[4] 20s[pu] Apr 4] sturdy gelding: poor form over hurdles:
will prove better at 3m than shorter. *L. Lungo*

CAPTAIN SMOOTHY 4 b.g. Charmer – The Lady Captain (Neltino) [2003/4 F12g[6] **F84**
F13g[6] F12d Jan 1] unfurnished gelding: first foal: dam bumper winner: modest form in
3-y-o bumpers first 2 starts. *M. J. Gingell*

CAPTAINS TABLE 11 b.g. Welsh Captain – Wensum Girl (Ballymoss) [2003/4 c116: **c–**
c20m Nov 19] workmanlike gelding: fairly useful chaser: prominent until blundering 5
out in handicap at Kempton, only outing in 2003/4: should stay 2½m: acts on good to firm
and good to soft going. *R. Dickin*

CAPTAIN SUNSHINE (IRE) 6 ch.g. Bob Back (USA) – Elite (Lord Gayle (USA)) **F109**
[2003/4 F16d[2] F19d* Apr 10] €44,000 4-y-o: lengthy gelding: brother to winner in Italy:
dam won at 1¼m: favourite, won 22-runner bumper at Cork comfortably in April, beating Breach of Trust 2 lengths: improved again when 4 lengths third to Major Vernon at
Punchestown later in month, nearest at finish: looks sort to make an impact over hurdles.
N. Meade, Ireland

CAPTAIN'S WALK 8 b.g. Seymour Hicks (FR) – Mayina (Idiot's Delight) [2003/4 **h–**
h–: 24m[pu] May 14] well beaten only completed outing over hurdles: dead. *P. Bowen*

CAPTAINTWOTHOUSAND 9 b.g. Milieu – Royal Scarlet (Royal Fountain) **c–**
[2003/4 c92, h–: 19g[6] c24d[4] c21v[5] c16d[ur] c16v[5] c22s[pu] c21d[ur] 22g[pu] Mar 28] good-topped **h–**
gelding: modest hurdler/novice chaser, well below best in 2003/4: stays 19f: acts on
heavy going: blinkered final start: tried tongue tied. *C. W. Fairhurst*

CAPTAIN VALIANT (IRE) 6 b.g. Supreme Leader – Anna Valley (Gleason **F–**
(USA)) [2003/4 F92: F16m May 5] fair form when placed in bumpers, well held only
start in 2003/4: bred to be suited by 2½m+. *G. B. Balding*

CAPTAIN ZINZAN (NZ) 9 b.g. Zabeel (NZ) – Lady Springfield (NZ) (Sharivari **c–**
(USA)) [2003/4 c96, h92: 22m[2] 21m* 20m* 20m* Jun 28] leggy gelding: modest maiden **h121**
chaser: fairly useful handicap hurdler: in good form early in 2003/4, winning at Huntingdon and Worcester (2): completed hat-trick at latter in impressive fashion by 5 lengths
from Wagner: stays 2¾m when emphasis is on speed: acts on good to firm going: held up.
L. A. Dace

CAPT PUGWASH 6 ch.g. Karinga Bay – Spire Belle (Final Straw) [2003/4 F16m[2] **F86**
Nov 8] first foal: dam lightly-raced maiden pointer: going on well at finish when 2½
lengths second to Cooldine King in bumper at Sandown on debut. *B. W. Hills*

CARACCIOLA (GER) 7 b.g. Lando (GER) – Capitolina (FR) (Empery (USA)) **c141**
[2003/4 h123: 16m* 16m[2] c16d[2] c16g* c16g[2] c16g Mar 16] leggy gelding: useful **h131 +**
hurdler: won handicap at Sandown in November: good second to Rigmarole in valuable

Jobs@Pertemps Wayward Lad Novices' Chase, Kempton—
Caracciola (left) lowers the colours of Arkle favourite Thisthatandtother

Mr P. J. D. Pottinger's "Caracciola"

similar event at Cheltenham 8 days later: made very promising start over fences, winning 3-runner novice events at Haydock (by 4 lengths from Our Armageddon) and Kempton (beat Thisthatandtother 3½ lengths, again jumping soundly) in December: reportedly returned lame when beaten by Palua at Kempton, never going well when last of 8 finishers in Grade 1 novice at Cheltenham: raced at 2m: acts on good to firm and good to soft going. *N. J. Henderson*

CARAPUCE (FR) 5 ch.g. Bigstone (IRE) – Treasure City (FR) (Moulin) [2003/4 h87: 16g 20g* 20g* 24d³ 17s* 24gᵖᵘ Apr 2] good-topped ex-French gelding: fairly useful hurdler, much improved in 2003/4: won novice handicaps in small fields at Ayr and Hexham within 5 days in November and novice at Carlisle (left well clear when main rival Dileer fell last when upsides) in February: stiff task, tailed off when pulled up 2 out in Grade 1 novice at Aintree: effective around 2m to 3m: raced on good going or softer (acts on soft): wore cheekpieces on debut. *L. Lungo*   **h122**

CARBONADO 10 b.g. Anshan – Virevoite (Shareef Dancer (USA)) [2003/4 c99, h–: c25d² c20m⁶ c24g⁴ c25m⁴ c24dᵖᵘ Mar 15] well-made gelding: fair hunter chaser: stays 25f: acts on soft and good to firm going: tongue tied: none too reliable. *H. R. Tuck*   **c97** **h–**

CARBURY CROSS (IRE) 10 b. or br.g. Mandalus – Brickey Gazette (Fine Blade (USA)) [2003/4 c148§, h–: c21m² c27gᵖᵘ c27dᵘʳ c29d⁴ c33dᶠ c29gᵖᵘ Jan 10] smallish, close-coupled gelding: one-time very smart chaser, generally disappointing since 2001/2: should stay beyond 3¼m: best form on good/good to firm going (ran poorly on heavy): has won with/without blinkers: ungenuine. *Jonjo O'Neill*   **c138 d** **h–**

CARDENAS (GER) 5 b. or br.g. Acatenango (GER) – Cocorna (Night Shift (USA)) [2003/4 17d² 16d* 20g* 16g⁴ 20g Apr 1] leggy gelding: successful 3 times up to 1¾m on Flat in Germany in 2003: useful form over hurdles: won novice at Newbury in December and Group 1 Gran Corsa Siepi di Roma in February: left M. Hofer, fourth to Brave Inca in Supreme Novices' Hurdle at Cheltenham and seventh to Garde Champetre in Grade 2   **h138**

novice at Aintree, hanging left both times, particularly at latter after meeting trouble on home turn: stays 2½m. *C. R. Egerton*

CARDINAL MARK (IRE) 10 b.g. Ardross – Sister of Gold (The Parson) [2003/4 c82 c88, h–: 25f⁴ c21v³ c20s⁶ 24d² 20d¹ c21d* Mar 30] leggy gelding: modest hurdler; poor h94 handicap chaser: won at Sedgefield despite interference at last: effective around 2½m to 3¼m: acts on any going: tried blinkered: not a fluent jumper of fences. *Mrs S. J. Smith*

CARDINGTON 5 b.g. Saddlers' Hall (IRE) – Passionelle (Nashwan (USA)) [2003/4 h98 p F17m⁵ F17m⁴ F17m³ 16d⁴ 17d² Apr 18] lengthy gelding: has scope: first foal: dam F95 twice-raced half-sister to smart performer up to 1½m Precede and smart stayer Warm Feeling: progressive form in bumpers: showed promise in 2 novice hurdles 5 months apart, jumping and hanging right but pulling clear of rest when second to Lucky Duck at Carlisle: remains open to improvement. *Mrs S. J. Smith*

CAREW 8 b.g. Minster Son – The White Lion (Flying Tyke) [2003/4 h–: c17m² c21g⁵ c76 c26m² c21g³ Sep 30] leggy gelding: no form in novice hurdles: runner-up twice in weak h– novice chases early in 2003/4. *C. Grant*

CAREW LAD 8 b.g. Arzanni – Miss Skindles (Taufan (USA)) [2003/4 F77: 24m⁶ Jun h– 28] won maiden point in 2003: well held on hurdling debut. *Mrs D. A. Hamer*

CAREYSVILLE (IRE) 13 b.g. Carmelite House (USA) – Kavali (Blakeney) c– [2003/4 c104, h–: c26v⁴ May 26] tall gelding: fair chaser, lightly raced nowadays: stays h– 3¼m: acts on good to firm and heavy going. *Miss Venetia Williams*

CARIBBEAN COVE (IRE) 6 gr.g. Norwich – Peaceful Rose (Roselier (FR)) c– [2003/4 h99p, F73: 21f* c21gᶠ c20gᵖᵘ 19s⁵ 20s³ 21g 24sᵖᵘ Apr 17] close-coupled geld- h100 ing: landed odds in novice hurdle at Warwick in May: form after only when third to Foly Pleasant in handicap at Haydock: ran as if amiss last 2 outings: failed to complete in 2 novice chases: should stay 3m: acts on firm and soft going: sold to join R. Guest 25,000 gns Doncaster May Sales. *Miss H. C. Knight*

CARIBBEAN LAD (IRE) 8 ch.g. Denel (FR) – Daisy Star (Star Appeal) [2003/4 h– 22gᵖᵘ 17dᵖᵘ 24gᵖᵘ Nov 30] no form over hurdles. *J. R. Turner*

CARIBBEAN MAN 4 b.g. Hector Protector (USA) – Caribbean Star (Soviet Star h84 (USA)) [2003/4 16m³ 17m⁶ 16s⁴ 16d² Jan 13] sturdy gelding: fair form on debut, ran as if amiss all 3 subsequent starts on Flat, sold out of Sir Michael Stoute's stable £6,800 Ascot August Sales: modest form over hurdles: tried in cheekpieces final start: has looked hard ride. *B. J. Llewellyn*

CARIBBEAN SUN (IRE) 4 b.c. Grand Lodge (USA) – Carranita (IRE) (Anita's h– Prince) [2003/4 16sᵖᵘ Dec 20] close-coupled colt: well held on Flat: no show on hurdling debut. *B. Palling*

CARIBEAN DREAM 9 ch.m. Afzal – Lovelek (Golden Love) [2003/4 h–: 20sᵖᵘ h– May 22] unseated in point in 2000: no show in 2 novice hurdles 3 years later. *G. E. Jones*

CARLESIMO (IRE) 6 b. or br.g. Erins Isle – Diamond Display (IRE) (Shardari) h113 [2003/4 h121: 16d 17f⁶ Aug 26] fairly useful hurdler at best: fair form when midfield in 2 handicaps in 2003/4: raced around 2m: acts on any going. *N. Meade, Ireland*

CARLOTTA 7 b.m. Carlingford Castle – Baryta (Nishapour (FR)) [2003/4 F16v⁶ 18s h– 16dᵖᵘ 21sᵖᵘ Mar 15] second foal: dam ran once in bumper: sixth of 13 in bumper on debut: F64 no form over hurdles. *N. J. Gifford*

CARLOVENT (FR) 9 b.g. Cadoudal (FR) – Carlaya (FR) (Carmarthen (FR)) [2003/4 c– x c–x, h133x: 23m 25d 22d³ 20d⁵ 22s⁶ 25gᵖᵘ 24g 20m Apr 24] angular gelding: reportedly h112 x blind in one eye: useful hurdler, well below best in 2003/4: races mainly around 3m nowadays: acts on heavy and good to firm going (looked ill at ease on firm): blinkered once, visored nowadays: sketchy jumper: ungenuine. *M. C. Pipe*

CARLTON CRACKER 12 b.g. Primitive Rising (USA) – Miss Cracker Jack c– (Ancient Monro) [2003/4 c22vᵖᵘ Nov 29] big gelding: winning chaser in 2001/2: pulled h– hard only subsequent outing: stays 25f: acts on good to soft ground. *C. N. Kellett*

CARLUCCIOS QUEST 6 b.g. Terimon – Jindabyne (Good Times (ITY)) [2003/4 F– F17g Oct 27] first foal: dam of little account: showed nothing in bumper on debut. *Mrs H. Dalton*

CARLY BAY 6 b.m. Carlton (GER) – Polly Minor (Sunley Builds) [2003/4 h94, F79: h105 16vᶠ 18g⁴ 24gᵖᵘ 16s² 21s³ 16dᵖᵘ Mar 1] useful-looking mare: fair handicap hurdler: lame final start: probably stays 21f: raced on good going or softer (acts on heavy): hung badly left fifth outing. *G. P. Enright*

CARLYS QUEST 10 ch.g. Primo Dominie – Tuppy (USA) (Sharpen Up) [2003/4 **h104 +** 23s³ 21d 20d⁴ Apr 18] leggy gelding: useful at one time on Flat, well held only start in 2002: fair novice hurdler for J. Neville in 1998/9: best effort on return when eye-catching fourth in novice handicap at Carlisle: stays 2½m: acts on soft going: visored/blinkered: tongue tied in 2003/4. *Ferdy Murphy*

CARMELITE (IRE) 9 ch.g. Good Thyne (USA) – Monks Lass (IRE) (Monksfield) **c–** [2003/4 16gᵖᵘ Nov 30] sturdy ex-Irish gelding: fairly useful hurdler/chaser at best for Mrs **h–** J. Harrington: reportedly had breathing problem only outing in 2003/4: stays 2½m: acts on heavy going: tried tongue tied: often jumps poorly. *Mrs S. Wall*

CARNACRACK 10 b.g. Le Coq d'Or – Carney (New Brig) [2003/4 c87: c22g⁶ c24g⁴ **c88** c26m* c25f³ c25f² c28g³ c27d³ c25d⁶ Jan 15] modest handicap chaser: won at Cartmel in July: suited by 3m+: acts on any going: usually wears cheekpieces: races prominently: amateur ridden. *Miss S. E. Forster*

CARNANEY GIRL 6 ch.m. Primitive Rising (USA) – Mossberry Fair (Mossberry) **c–** [2003/4 16dᵖᵘ 17gᵖᵘ 16m 17mʳᵗʳ 16m 21fᵖᵘ c16sᶠ Feb 3] angular mare: seventh foal: half- **h– §** sister to winning hurdler/fair 2m chaser Pegasus Bay (by Tina's Pet) and winning pointer by Infantry: dam winning hurdler: has shown more temperament than ability. *A. E. Jones*

CARNEYS CROSS (IRE) 6 b.g. Kahyasi – Cityjet (IRE) (Orchestra) [2003/4 **c113** c24gᵘʳ c17s² c22v* c20s⁵ c21d c24d³ c20sᵖᵘ Apr 4] stocky gelding: first foal: dam **h–** lightly-raced half-sister to high-class staying chaser Toby Tobias: fair hurdler/chaser: won maiden over fences at Limerick in December: will stay beyond 3m: raced on good going or softer (acts on heavy). *S. J. Treacy, Ireland*

CARNOUSTIE (USA) 6 gr.m. Ezzoud (IRE) – Sarba (USA) (Persepolis (FR)) **h91 §** [2003/4 h91§: 26m² 22g⁵ 20s 19gᵖᵘ Mar 15] modest hurdler: stays 3¼m: acts on good to firm and good to soft going: wears cheekpieces/blinkers: not one to rely on. *R. T. Phillips*

CARN RIVERS (IRE) 9 ch.g. Over The River (FR) – Carnowen (Deep Run) [2003/4 **h–** 20g⁶ 17g³ Oct 11] 8,000 4-y-o, 2,500 6-y-o: angular gelding: fourth foal: half-brother to winning pointer by Spin of A Coin: dam unplaced in bumpers/points: apparently better effort over hurdles when third of 4 in novice at Bangor, probably flattered after setting slow pace. *Mrs S. J. Smith*

CAROLINA (FR) 7 b.m. Baby Turk – Record High (FR) (High Top) [2003/4 20d⁴ **h117** 16v* 16d² 16v³ Jul 20] fifth foal: half-sister to fairly useful French hurdler Klakos (by Nikos) and prolific 9f to 13f winner Top Price (by Synefos): dam ran 3 times: fair maiden on Flat (stays 2m): fairly useful hurdler: won mares minor event at Sligo in June: best around 2m: raced only on going softer than good over hurdles. *W. P. Mullins, Ireland*

CAROLINE'S ROSE 6 bl. or br.m. Fraam – Just Rosie (Sula Bula) [2003/4 F–: 17m **h63** 19mᵖᵘ 17g⁵ 16m⁶ 16f³ 16d⁵ 16m⁶ 16g⁶ Dec 11] signs of only a little ability over hurdles: has had tongue tied. *A. P. Jones*

CAROUBIER (IRE) 4 ch.g. Woodborough (USA) – Patsy Grimes (Beveled (USA)) **h96** [2003/4 17g⁴ 16m⁵ 16m* 17d⁵ Nov 28] leggy gelding: fairly useful on Flat (stays 11f), successful 5 times in 2003 and twice in 2004 for various trainers: easily best effort in juvenile hurdles when making all at Warwick in November: will prove best with emphasis on speed around 2m: blinkered last 2 starts. *Ian Williams*

CARPENTERS BOY 4 b.g. Nomination – Jolly Girl (Jolly Me) [2003/4 F16g F17d **F81** Mar 27] eighth foal: half-brother to winning pointer by Afzal: dam ran twice: second and better effort in bumpers when mid-field in 18-runner event at Bangor. *Mrs A. M. Thorpe*

CARRAIG BROL (IRE) 10 b.g. Cataldi – Davy's Hall (Weavers' Hall) [2003/4 **c–** c25gᵖᵘ c20vᵖᵘ c16sᵖᵘ Apr 4] dead maiden pointer: tried in cheekpieces. *W. S. Coltherd*

CARRIAGE RIDE (IRE) 6 b.g. Tidaro (USA) – Casakurali (Gleason (USA)) **h86** [2003/4 h–: 20m 18s 17sᵖᵘ 20s² 20d Apr 18] angular gelding: modest novice hurdler: will probably stay beyond 2½m: acts on soft going. *N. G. Richards*

CARRICK TROOP (IRE) 11 gr.g. Roselier (FR) – Over The Pond (IRE) (Over The **c119 +** River (FR)) [2003/4 c118: c17g⁶ c20g² c17g* Nov 29] tall gelding: fairly useful handicap chaser: won strongly-run event at Newbury by ¾ length from Tango Royal, pair well clear: has won at 27f but best up to 2½m: acts on good to firm and heavy going: usually sound jumper: held up, and suited by well-run race. *Mrs M. Reveley*

CARRIGAFOYLE 9 b.g. Young Senor (USA) – Miss Skindles (Taufan (USA)) **h72** [2003/4 h87: 20m³ 21m May 29] sturdy gelding: poor maiden hurdler: sold 4,600 gns Doncaster August Sales. *O. Brennan*

CARRIG BOY (IRE) 14 ch.g. Long Pond – Shining Brightly (Giolla Mear) [2003/4 **c88**
c20d* May 16] fair pointer, lightly raced: won novice hunter at Stratford, coming from
long way off pace in well-run race: stays 2½m: acts on good to soft going. *I. Anderson*

CARROLL'S GOLD (IRE) 6 br.g. Carroll House – Missfethard On Sea (Deep Run) **h73**
[2003/4 F91: 16m² 16mᶠ Aug 8] poor form when second in novice at Uttoxeter on
hurdling debut: fell fatally at Worcester. *E. L. James*

CARRYONHARRY (IRE) 10 ch.g. Roselier (FR) – Bluebell Avenue (Boreen Beag) **c114 x**
[2003/4 c128x, h–: c24g⁶ c24s⁴ c33d c30g c33d c29m Apr 24] leggy gelding: fairly useful **h–**
handicap chaser at best, just fair form in 2003/4: stays 3m: acts on good to firm and heavy
going: usually visored: often let down by jumping. *M. C. Pipe*

CASAYANA 4 b.f. Sir Harry Lewis (USA) – Five And Four (IRE) (Green Desert **h–**
(USA)) [2003/4 F16s 17gᵖᵘ Feb 10] fourth foal: dam, no sign of ability, half-sister to **F–**
smart staying hurdler Burgoyne: showed nothing in bumper or juvenile hurdle.
D. McCain

CASE OF POTEEN (IRE) 8 b. or br.m. Witness Box (USA) – On The Hooch (Over **c82**
The River (FR)) [2003/4 h82: 24d² 25d⁴ 20g* Feb 8] medium-sized mare: modest **h95**
hurdler: won mares novice at Musselburgh in January: sixth of 8 finishers in novice there
on chasing debut: stays 3m: acts on heavy going. *Mrs S. C. Bradburne*

CASH CONVERTER (IRE) 6 ch.g. Houmayoun (FR) – Golden Symphony (Le **F95**
Moss) [2003/4 F18d³ F20g² Sep 17] IR £15,500 3-y-o: fifth foal: half-brother to winning
hurdler/fair chaser Ennel Boy (by Torus), stays 27f: dam unraced, from family of
top-class chaser Leap Frog: progressive form in 3 bumpers, placed both starts in 2003/4:
joined R. Phillips. *E. U. Hales, Ireland*

CASHEL DANCER 5 b.m. Bishop of Cashel – Dancing Debut (Polar Falcon (USA)) **h86**
[2003/4 h77: 19g* 17m³ 20m* 19g⁴ 19m³ 17m³ 20m² 16g 21g⁶ 16d³ 21d Apr 8] lengthy,
angular mare: modest novice hurdler: won weak mares event at Uttoxeter in June:
awarded similar race at Hereford in May on technical grounds: stays 2½m: acts on good
to firm and good to soft ground: has been let down by jumping. *S. A. Brookshaw*

CASH 'N' CREDIT 6 b.m. Homo Sapien – Not Enough (Balinger) [2003/4 h68: **c74**
c16m* c16m⁴ c17d⁵ c16d c20g c19d c25m² c25d⁵ c20d⁴ Apr 21] leggy mare: poor form **h–**
over hurdles: similar form over fences, won novice handicap at Worcester in June: stays
25f: acts on good to firm going: tried in cheekpieces. *R. Dickin*

CASH RETURN 5 b.m. Bob's Return (IRE) – We're In The Money (Billion (USA)) **h–**
[2003/4 h–, F–: 20gᵘʳ 24m⁵ 20g Mar 8] lengthy mare: signs of only a little ability over
hurdles. *B. G. Powell*

CASSIA HEIGHTS 9 b.g. Montelimar (USA) – Cloncoose (IRE) (Remainder Man) **c116**
[2003/4 c105, h–: c24g² c22f* c21d⁴ c31g² c24d³ c24dᵖᵘ c24m² c21g* Apr 2] tall geld- **h–**
ing: fairly useful handicap chaser: won at Haydock (made most) in October and Aintree

*Martell Cognac Topham Chase (Handicap), Aintree—outsider Cassia Heights (spots) overhauls
leader Scotmail Boy to provide trainer Steve Brookshaw with a fourth winner over the National fences*

in April, beat Longshanks a length in Martell Cognac Topham Chase on latter course: stays 31f: acts on soft and firm going: tongue tied: has run well sweating: sound jumper. *S. A. Brookshaw*

CASTANET 5 b.m. Pennekamp (USA) – Addaya (IRE) (Persian Bold) [2003/4 h81: **h84** 16g⁶ 16d 17s⁵ 21d⁵ 21g³ 16g⁴ 21d Apr 8] lengthy mare: poor maiden hurdler: stays 21f: acts on firm and soft going. *A. E. Price*

CASTLEBOY (IRE) 6 b.g. King's Ride – Bissie's Jayla (Zambrano) [2003/4 F16s **F–** Feb 20] €32,000 4-y-o: lengthy gelding: fifth foal: dam unraced half-sister to top-class staying chaser Docklands Express: showed some ability when well held in bumper at Sandown on debut. *P. J. Hobbs*

CASTLEBRIDGE 7 b.g. Batshoof – Super Sisters (AUS) (Call Report (USA)) **h– §** [2003/4 h–: 16dᵖᵘ Nov 13] leggy gelding: signs of only a little ability over hurdles: usually visored/blinkered: ungenuine. *K. R. Burke*

CASTLEDIVA 7 ch.m. Carlingford Castle – Bivadell (Bivouac) [2003/4 23s Apr 4] **h–** fourth foal: dam maiden pointer: maiden pointer: tailed off in mares novice on hurdling debut. *B. N. Pollock*

CASTLE FOLLY (IRE) 12 b.g. Carlingford Castle – Air Plane (Arratos (FR)) **c–** [2003/4 c97: c22v c18s c16d Mar 24] modest chaser: tailed off in 3 handicaps on return from 15-month absence: stays 3¼m, at least when conditions aren't testing: acts on good to firm going: usually blinkered. *J. White*

CASTLEFORD (IRE) 6 b.g. Be My Native (USA) – Commanche Bay (IRE) (Com- **c89** manche Run) [2003/4 F96: 24g³ 21g 19g 22d c24d³ 22s³ 26g³ Apr 3] medium-sized **h85** gelding: modest novice hurdler: similar form when third in novice handicap at Sandown on chasing debut: looks very much a stayer: acts on soft ground. *P. J. Hobbs*

CASTLE HATIM 6 b.m. Hatim (USA) – Castle Fountain (Royal Fountain) [2003/4 **h–** F16m F16g 24sᵖᵘ 22gᵖᵘ Mar 28] second foal: dam unraced: no sign of ability. *W. Amos* **F–**

CASTLEMORE (IRE) 6 b.g. Be My Native (USA) – Parsonetta (The Parson) **h97** [2003/4 F95: F16m² 21g² 20d⁵ 20d 21d³ Mar 25] unfurnished gelding: in frame all 3 **F88** starts in bumpers: modest form in novice hurdles: will stay beyond 21f. *P. J. Hobbs*

CASTLE PRINCE (IRE) 10 b.g. Homo Sapien – Lisaleen Lady (Miner's Lamp) **c121 ?** [2003/4 c111, h–: c16f⁴ c16m³ c17g⁵ c16f⁵ c16d⁶ c16g⁴ Apr 18] tall gelding: fair chaser, **h–** often flattered in face of stiff tasks, including on second and third outings: best around 2m: acts on firm and soft going: held up: tricky ride. *R. J. Hodges*

CASTLE RICHARD (IRE) 7 gr.g. Sexton Blake – Miss McCormick (IRE) (Roselier **c103** (FR)) [2003/4 h110, F76: c20g² c25d² c20dᶠ c21sᵘʳ 25g 20d 20d³ Apr 10] sturdy, close- **h100** coupled gelding: runner-up on completed starts over fences, fair form on first occasion: fair hurdler: should stay 3m: raced on good going or softer (acts on heavy): blinkered sixth start. *G. M. Moore*

CASTLE RING 5 b.g. Sri Pekan (USA) – Understudy (In The Wings) [2003/4 17g³ **h87** Nov 20] modest on Flat (stays 1½m): third in amateur novice at Market Rasen on hurdl- ing debut. *R. Hollinshead*

CASTLE RIVER (USA) 5 b.g. Irish River (FR) – Castellina (USA) (Danzig Connec- **h94** tion (USA)) [2003/4 h–: 16m² 16f* 16m⁴ 16f 16g⁴ 16gᵖᵘ Nov 19] close-coupled gelding: modest on Flat (stays 1¼m): modest hurdler: won steadily-run novice at Towcester in October: will prove best around 2m: acts on firm going: joined O. O'Neill. *B. G. Powell*

CASTLESHANE (IRE) 7 b.g. Kris – Ahbab (IRE) (Ajdal (USA)) [2003/4 h130: **h127** 16f³ Nov 8] tall, quite good-topped gelding: will make a chaser: fairly useful hurdler: fit from Flat, creditable third of 4 to Well Chief in limited handicap at Wincanton only start in 2003/4: raced mainly around 2m: acts on firm and good to soft going: blinkered once: free-going front runner. *S. Gollings*

CASTLE WEIR (IRE) 7 b.g. Lord Americo – Alchymya (Cosmo) [2003/4 c24s² **c98** c24d³ c25d⁴ c26dᵖᵘ c24s² Apr 7] IR 2,800 7-y-o: sturdy gelding: second foal: dam winning pointer: winning pointer: fair hunter chaser: out of depth fourth start: stays 25f: acts on soft ground. *W. P. Mullins, Ireland*

CATALPA CARGO (IRE) 10 b.g. Buckskin (FR) – Money For Honey (New Brig) **c128** [2003/4 h115: 20d* c17d* c22s³ c21m* c22d² c20d² Nov 30] big, deep-girthed gelding: **h115** fairly useful hurdler: won minor event at Punchestown in May: useful novice over fences, won maiden at Navan later in May and Grade 3 at Tipperary in October: good second to Satco Express in Grade 3 at Punchestown and Nil Desperandum in Grade 1 at Fairyhouse last 2 starts: effective around 2m and will stay beyond 2¾m: acts on heavy and good to firm going. *C. Roche, Ireland*

CATCHATAN (IRE) 9 b.g. Cataldi – Snowtan (IRE) (Tanfirion) [2003/4 c92, h–: c24g⁴ c23mᵖᵘ c23mᵖᵘ Jul 23] lengthy gelding: modest chaser: out of sorts in 2003/4: usually tongue tied. *P. R. Webber* **c– h–**

CATCH THE PERK (IRE) 7 b.g. Executive Perk – Kilbally Quilty (IRE) (Montelimar (USA)) [2003/4 h–, F86: 16s⁵ 20m c22dᵖᵘ c20m c16gᵖᵘ c20d* Mar 18] medium-sized gelding: in cheekpieces, first worthwhile form over jumps when winning handicap chase at Hexham: stays 2½m. *Miss Lucinda V. Russell* **c74 h–**

CATEEL BAY 6 ch.m. Most Welcome – Calachuchi (Martinmas) [2003/4 h–: 16m 17d May 28] of little account: sold 1,400 gns Doncaster August Sales. *H. Alexander* **h–**

CATFISH HUNTER 4 b.g. Safawan – Secret Account (Blakeney) [2003/4 F16g Mar 17] third foal: half-brother to winning pointer by Contract Law: dam unraced half-sister to useful 6f/7f performer in Britain/UAE Numbered Account: tailed off in bumper on debut. *Mrs L. P. Baker* **F–**

CATHERINE'S WAY (IRE) 12 b.g. Mandalus – Sharp Approach (Crash Course) [2003/4 c–, h–: c21gᵘʳ Feb 20] compact gelding: veteran chaser, retains little ability. *Martin Ward* **c– h–**

CAUCASIAN (IRE) 6 gr.g. Leading Counsel (USA) – Kemal's Princess (Kemal (FR)) [2003/4 F–: F16m 16d 16s Dec 13] lengthy, rather unfurnished gelding: little sign of ability: bred to need further than 2m. *Ian Williams* **h– F–**

CAVVIES NIECE 6 b.m. Ballet Royal (USA) – Cavisoir (Afzal) [2003/4 h–, F–: 19gᵖᵘ May 1] no show in bumper or 2 hurdles: tried tongue tied. *H. J. Manners* **h– F–**

CAYMANS GIFT 4 ch.g. Cayman Kai (IRE) – Gymcrak Cyrano (IRE) (Cyrano de Bergerac) [2003/4 F16d 16g⁶ 20s⁶ Apr 21] second foal: dam, modest hurdler who stayed 3m, half-sister to one-time useful chaser around 2½m River Wye: no sign of ability in bumper and 2 hurdles (jumped poorly). *A. C. Whillans* **h– F–**

CEANANNAS MOR (IRE) 10 b. or br.g. Strong Gale – Game Sunset (Menelek) [2003/4 c123§, h–: c33gᵖᵘ c23g* c32g* Nov 14] useful-looking gelding: has reportedly had breathing operation: fairly useful handicap chaser: won at Exeter and Cheltenham in November, beating Royal County Buck 2½ lengths on second occasion: stays 4m: acts on soft going, probably on good to firm: sometimes finishes weakly. *N. J. Henderson* **c124 h–**

CEASERS REIGN (IRE) 12 ch.g. Rhoman Rule (USA) – Dora Gayle (Lord Gayle (USA)) [2003/4 c25m⁶ May 9] workmanlike ex-Irish gelding: signs of only a little ability over hurdles: first completion in steeplechases when last of 6 finishers in novice hunter at Wincanton: fair pointer: joined F. Lloyd, in frame twice in April. *T. D. B. Underwood* **c83 h–**

CEDAR 7 gr.g. Absalom – Setai's Palace (Royal Palace) [2003/4 h73: 22dᵖᵘ 16v³ c19sᶠ c20d Mar 15] poor form over hurdles: showed little both starts over fences. *R. Dickin* **c– h73**

CEDAR CHIEF 7 b.g. Saddlers' Hall (IRE) – Dame Ashfield (Grundy) [2003/4 c– §, h–§: c25f⁵ c24d⁶ c24g c19s⁶ Mar 20] stocky gelding: poor hurdler/maiden steeplechaser: won 2 points in April: stays 3m: acts on any going: needs blinkers: hard ride. *K. Tork* **c– § h– §**

CEDAR GREEN 10 br.g. Bustino – Explosiva (USA) (Explodent (USA)) [2003/4 c119: c24sᵖᵘ c30sᵖᵘ c30dᵖᵘ c25v* c24sᵖᵘ c32gᵖᵘ Mar 28] rangy gelding: fair handicap chaser: made all at Wetherby in January: pulled up all other starts since 2002/3, including in cross-country event at Punchestown in late-April: thorough stayer: acts on heavy ground: usually wears blinkers, also tried in cheekpieces: unreliable. *K. C. Bailey* **c113 §**

CEDAR MASTER (IRE) 7 b.g. Soviet Lad (USA) – Samriah (IRE) (Wassl) [2003/4 h94: 16m³ 19m* 22m² Sep 23] modest novice hurdler: left R. O'Sullivan prior to winning at Market Rasen in August: probably stays 2¾m: acts on good to firm going: wears blinkers: tongue tied last 2 starts: not one to trust implicitly. *J. R. Boyle* **h98**

CEDAR RANGERS (USA) 6 b.g. Anabaa (USA) – Chelsea (USA) (Miswaki (USA)) [2003/4 16m 16m⁴ 16m³ 17f³ 16m 19m⁴ 19d³ 18s 16d⁵ Apr 8] angular gelding: modest on Flat (stays 1m), sold out of R. O'Sullivan's stable £1,700 Ascot June Sales: poor maiden hurdler: stays 19f: acts on firm and good to soft going: races freely. *G. F. Edwards* **h72**

CEEAWAYHOME 5 b.g. Nomadic Way (USA) – Dame Scarlet (Blakeney) [2003/4 F16d* F16s⁴ Feb 7] €11,000 3-y-o: half-brother to 3 winners, including fairly useful 2m hurdler/winning hunter Good Glow (by Jalmood) and progressive hurdler Baron Windrush (by Alderbrook), stays 25f: dam unraced sister to Sun Alliance Hurdle winner Fealty: won bumper at Naas on debut in November in good style by 2 lengths from Geill **F100**

Sli: again favourite, failed to improve as expected when 4½ lengths fourth to No Complications there next time. *J. E. Kiely, Ireland*

CELEBRATION TOWN (IRE)   7 b. or br.g. Case Law – Battle Queen (Kind of Hush) [2003/4 h80: 16d² 16m⁶ 16m* 16g 16m* 16m³ 16g³ 16g Apr 5] modest hurdler: won handicaps at Hexham in June and Haydock (conditional jockeys) in October: will prove best at 2m: acts on good to firm and good to soft going: has refused/been reluctant to line up. *N. G. Richards*   **h97**

CELESTIAL GOLD (IRE)   6 br.g. Persian Mews – What A Queen (King's Ride) [2003/4 c22s* c24g³ c24s³ c32g² c25m* Apr 14] tall gelding: seventh foal: half-brother to bumper winner Trimmer Wonder (by Celio Rufo): dam unraced, out of half-sister to top-class staying chaser L'Escargot: won 3 out of 4 starts in points in 2003: useful novice chaser: won in small fields at Towcester in November and Cheltenham (beat L'Aventure 1¼ lengths) in April: best effort when 1¾ lengths second to Native Emperor in valuable amateur event at Cheltenham in March: stays 4m: acts on soft and good to firm going. *M. C. Pipe*   **c133**

CELESTIAL HEIGHTS (IRE)   5 b.g. Fourstars Allstar (USA) – Aon Dochas (IRE) (Strong Gale) [2003/4 aF16g⁴ Dec 13] €20,000 3-y-o, 22,000 4-y-o: second foal: dam, won 2m chase, half-sister to smart chaser up to 21f Native Charm and useful 2½m chaser Sir Dante: fourth to Ruby Too in bumper on polytrack at Lingfield on debut. *O. Sherwood*   **F82**

CELESTIAL LIGHT (IRE)   7 b.m. Archway (IRE) – Lady Heather (Tirol) [2003/4 F16s⁵ F16d² F20g⁴ F19m⁶ F16s⁴ F18g² 20d² 16s* 20s* Jan 18] IR £3,500 4-y-o: half-sister to winners on Flat by Common Grounds and Astronef: dam unraced: fairly useful in bumpers: fair hurdler: won mares maiden at Tramore in December and handicap at Fairyhouse in January: stays 2½m: acts on soft going. *D. T. Hughes, Ireland*   **h110 F96**

April Novices' Chase, Cheltenham—
Celestial Gold lands the odds from L'Aventure (diamonds) and Dear Deal (right)

CELIBATE (IRE)   13 ch.g. Shy Groom (USA) – Dance Alone (USA) (Monteverdi) **c–** [2003/4 c124, h–: c24d Feb 2] sparely-made gelding: one-time smart chaser: soundly **h–** beaten in handicap at Kempton only start in 2003/4: stayed 21f: acted on any going: tried blinkered: usually raced prominently: sound jumper: reportedly retired. *C. J. Mann*

CELIOSO (IRE)   7 b.g. Celio Rufo – Bettons Rose (Roselier (FR)) [2003/4 h80: c25d^F **c122** 22d c22m⁵ c21g* c24g² c20m² c21d* c28g* c30g² Jan 24] lengthy gelding: winning **h–** hurdler: fairly useful chaser: won novices at Sedgefield in September and November and handicap at Market Rasen in December: improved again when second to Harlov in handicap at Catterick final start: best form at 3½m+: acts on good to firm and good to soft going. *Mrs S. J. Smith*

CELTA VIGO (IRE)   6 b.m. Executive Perk – Alice Freyne (IRE) (Lancastrian) **h–** [2003/4 F16g 16s^{ro} 27s^{pu} Dec 26] first foal: dam twice-raced half-sister to top-class 2m to **F–** 25f hurdler Aonoch: no sign of ability in bumper and 2 novice hurdles. *Mrs L. B. Normile*

CELTIC ACTION   11 b.g. Fearless Action (USA) – Llanon (Owen Dudley) [2003/4 **h–** 20d^{pu} Nov 26] fourth foal: half-brother to winning 21f chaser Cader Idris (by St Columbus): dam well beaten on Flat at 2 yrs: showed nothing on very belated debut. *D. R. Wellicome*

CELTIC BLAZE (IRE)   5 b.m. Charente River (IRE) – Firdaunt (Tanfirion) [2003/4 **h95 §** h88: 17d 16d² 16d⁴ 21v⁴ 16d 16d⁶ 16d⁶ Mar 18] small, sturdy mare: modest maiden hurdler: should stay beyond 2m: raced on good ground or softer over hurdles: wore cheekpieces last 2 starts: unreliable. *B. S. Rothwell*

CELTIC BOY (IRE)   6 b.g. Arctic Lord – Laugh Away (Furry Glen) [2003/4 F16d⁶ **h91** 24d⁶ 20d* Apr 21] €22,000 4-y-o: fifth foal: half-brother to 2½m chase winner Keep **F71** Smiling (by Broken Hearted) and winning pointer by John French: dam won at 2m on Flat: placed in maiden points in 2003: sixth in bumper: second start over hurdles when winning maiden at Worcester: should stay beyond 2½m. *P. Bowen*

CELTIC DUKE   12 b.g. Strong Gale – Celtic Cygnet (Celtic Cone) [2003/4 c96, h–: **c92** c24m* c25d⁴ c24s⁴ Apr 12] sturdy gelding: fair hunter chaser: won at Fakenham in May: **h–** won points in February and March: stays 3½m: acts on firm and good to soft going (possibly not on heavy): jumps safely. *J. M. Turner*

CELTIC FLOW   6 b.m. Primitive Rising (USA) – Celtic Lane (Welsh Captain) [2003/4 **c63** h–, F–: 21s⁵ 16m 21d⁵ 17v⁶ 19g⁶ c25g² 24d⁵ c26d^F Apr 18] leggy mare: poor maiden **h64** hurdler: similar form on completed start over fences: stays 25f: acts on good to soft going: tried blinkered. *C. R. Wilson*

CELTIC LEGEND (FR)   5 br.g. Celtic Swing – Another Legend (USA) (Lyphard's **c71** Wish (FR)) [2003/4 h76: 16g 20d 25d⁶ c16g² c19g Mar 5] tall, leggy gelding: poor **h–** maiden hurdler: similar form on first of 2 starts over fences, though carried head high and hung right under pressure: form only around 2m: raced only on good/good to soft going: tried tongue tied. *Mrs M. Reveley*

CELTIC MAJOR (IRE)   6 br.g. Roselier (FR) – Dun Oengus (IRE) (Strong Gale) **h94** [2003/4 F18s² F16v⁵ 16v 16s⁵ Feb 20] €74,000 4-y-o: second foal: dam, **F100** 2½m hurdle winner, half-sister to dam of smart 2m to 2½m chaser Strong Run: second to Bramlynn Brook in maiden at Plumpton on debut, better effort in bumpers: seemed to show modest form on second of 2 starts in novice hurdles: will be suited by 2½m+. *Jonjo O'Neill*

CELTIC PRIDE (IRE)   9 gr.g. Roselier (FR) – Grannie No (Brave Invader (USA)) **c99** [2003/4 c–, h–: c23m³ c23m³ c23g^{ur} c23m³ c26v⁴ May 21] tall gelding: winning hurdler: didn't really **h–** take to fences, apparently best effort in 2003/4 when third of 4 finishers in novice at Worcester (marked tendency to jump right): should stay beyond 3m: raced mainly on good going or softer (acts well on soft/heavy): sold 2,100 gns Doncaster January Sales. *P. Bowen*

CELTIC RUFFIAN (IRE)   6 b.g. Celio Rufo – Candid Lady (Arctic Lord) [2003/4 **h–** F18m² F17s 20s^{ur} 22v^{pu} 22g 22g^{pu} 27g Apr 22] second foal: half-brother to winning 2m **F70 ?** hurdler Macs-Bet (by King Luthier): dam unraced, out of half-sister to useful hurdler at 2½m+ Motivator: fell in maiden Irish point on debut in 2003: second of 4 in bumper: no subsequent form, mainly over hurdles. *R. Rowe*

CELTIC SON (FR)   5 b.g. Celtic Arms (FR) – For Kicks (FR) (Top Ville) [2003/4 **F101** F16g⁶ F16g⁴ F16g Mar 17] sturdy ex-Irish gelding: half-brother to 3 winners, including fairly useful hurdlers For None (by Sanglamore), stays 2½m, and Sonevafushi (by Ganges), stays 25f: dam half-sister to smart French jumper up to 3m Summit: fairly useful form in bumpers: won at Thurles on debut in 2002/3 for E. McNamara: will stay beyond 2m. *M. C. Pipe*

Queen Elizabeth The Queen Mother Celebration Chase, Sandown—Cenkos repeats his 2002 win

CELTIC STAR (IRE)   6 b.g. Celtic Swing – Recherchee (Rainbow Quest (USA)) [2003/4 h99: 17d^{pu} 20m 20m^3 21f^3 22g^3 17g* c16s^{ur} 16v^{pu} c17d^{pu} c24m^5 Apr 13] lengthy gelding: successful on Flat in July and August: modest handicap hurdler: won at Newton Abbot in November: left N. Williams, little encouragement last 4 starts, 3 in chases: best efforts around 2m: acts on firm and soft going: effective visored or not, also tried in cheekpieces: has hung badly left: one to treat with caution. *Miss K. M. George*   **c– h99 §**

CELTIC TANNER (IRE)   5 b.g. Royal Abjar (USA) – Mills Pride (IRE) (Posen (USA)) [2003/4 F–: 16d 16v^{pu} Dec 15] medium-sized gelding: little sign of ability. *D. J. Wintle*   **h–**

CELTIC TED   6 b.g. Celtic Swing – Careful Dancer (Gorytus (USA)) [2003/4 17g May 24] well held on Flat and in 2 races over hurdles: tried in cheekpieces. *P. Butler*   **h–**

CELTIC VISION (IRE)   8 b.g. Be My Native (USA) – Dream Run (Deep Run) [2003/4 h121: 24m^5 c16m^3 c16m^3 c21g^3 c21g^2 c24d^F c20f^{pu} 16s 25d^{pu} 21g^F 22m 21g 19m Mar 9] rather leggy gelding: let down by jumping and only modest form at best over fences: fairly useful hurdler: no form in 2003/4, left J. O'Neill after eighth start: stays 21f: acts on heavy going: tried in headgear, blinkered last 2 starts: has had tongue tied/suffered breathing problems: patiently ridden. *M. Appleby*   **c96 x h–**

CENKOS (FR)   10 ch.g. Nikos – Vincenza (Grundy) [2003/4 c163, h–: c16f* 16g^6 c16g* c16d^5 c16s^4 c16g^4 c20g^4 c16m* Apr 24] strong, lengthy gelding: winning hurdler: high-class chaser: won minor event at Warwick in May, quite valuable handicap at Cheltenham (made all to beat stable-companion Kadarann 1¼ lengths) in November and valuable minor contest at Sandown (by 1½ lengths from Impek) in April: best around 2m: acts on any going: blinkered once (ran badly): has got on toes: usually a fluent jumper. *P. F. Nicholls*   **c163 h128**

CENTAUR KOMET   6 b.g. Komaite (USA) – Rather Gorgeous (Billion (USA)) [2003/4 F16d Nov 15] 4,400 4-y-o: fourth foal: brother to 13f winner Subadar Major: dam successful at 2½m over hurdles/temperamental 1¾m winner: tongue tied, showed nothing in bumper on debut. *D. McCain*   **F–**

CENTRAL COMMITTEE (IRE) 9 ch.g. Royal Academy (USA) – Idle Chat **h–**
(USA) (Assert) [2003/4 h106: 22g 22g 21d Apr 12] leggy gelding: has had wind operation: fair handicap hurdler: out of sorts in 2003/4: stays 3m: acts on firm and good to soft
going (unproven on softer), blinkered once: formerly tongue tied. *R. T. Phillips*

CENTRAL HOUSE 7 b.g. Alflora (IRE) – Fantasy World (Kemal (FR)) [2003/4 **c140**
h121, F106: 16g⁶ c20d² c17s* c17d* c17d² c16gᵘʳ c20d⁴ Apr 13] **h108**
It's a pity Central House suffered a rare lapse, in the Arkle Trophy at Cheltenham, in his usually excellent jumping as the field cleared the last ditch, four from
home, where he was still full of running up with the leaders. While it's impossible
to be adamant about where Central House would have finished had he not unseated
his rider, the way he was travelling and his other form suggest he could well have
secured third place behind Well Chief and Kicking King. Central House ran four
times over fences before Cheltenham. After being beaten a short head by Nil Desperandum on his debut, he won his next two, a maiden at Fairyhouse and the
Grade 1 Denny Gold Medal Novices' Chase at Leopardstown. He defeated
Anxious Moments by twenty-five lengths in the latter, though things would have
been a lot tighter had market rival Kicking King not fallen two out when holding a
lead of a couple of lengths. Central House wasn't good enough to deny Kicking
King when they met again over the same course and distance next, in the Irish
version of the Arkle, going down by three and a half lengths. He gave the
impression that day that he would be worth another try over two and a half miles
and he lined up at that trip for a fourth successive Grade 1 on his only start after
Cheltenham, in the Powers Gold Cup at Fairyhouse in April. Kicking King was
again in the field along with Nil Desperandum, who also had a Grade 1 win to his
name, but the trio were eclipsed by Hi Cloy. In what was a good field, Central
House finished fourth, essentially not up to the task, rather than lacking in stamina.
Useful in bumpers (second to Hardy Eustace in the Land Rover) before not
really coming up to expectations over hurdles, Central House is tall and leggy in

Denny Gold Medal Novices' Chase, Leopardstown—
Central House has only the riderless In The Forge for company at the last

Mr John F. Kenny's "Central House"

appearance and has come into his own over fences, though it is surprising he is as effective as he is at two miles given his pedigree. He is by Alflora out of Fantasy World, a fair hurdler at up to three miles for Josh Gifford. Fantasy World is out of a sister to the useful Irish jumper Carigeensharragh who was placed in both the Kerry National and the Troytown Chase. Central House, bought for IR £28,000 as a four-year-old, is Fantasy World's second foal. Her third, Central Arch (by Dilum), showed ability in bumpers for Central House's trainer Dessie Hughes in the latest season. Some good chasers have won the Denny Gold Medal Novices' Chase in the last decade, including Klairon Davis, Danoli, Native Upmanship and Moscow Flyer, but the penalty incurred in most conditions races by winning a Grade 1 means Central House will have to improve, coming somewhere near the standard of those horses, to enjoy much success out of novice company. He has been raced mainly on good going or softer, though ran creditably over hurdles on his only outing on good to firm. *D. T. Hughes, Ireland*

CEOIL AGUS CRAIC (IRE)   13 ch.g. Orchestra – Cracked Advice (Cracksman) **c121** [2003/4 c22s^{ur} c22d^5 c24g^3 c22s^2 24v^4 20s c24s^4 Mar 14] workmanlike gelding: fairly **h99** useful chaser: missed 2002/3 but as good as ever on return, placed behind Rockwell Island in listed handicap at Wexford in October and Barrow Drive in minor event at

Tramore in January: stays 3m: acts on heavy going, probably on good to firm: has had tongue tied. *M. G. Holden, Ireland*

CEOL NA SRAIDE (IRE) 5 h m, King's Theatre (IRE) – My Lady's Key (USA) h92
(Key To The Mint (USA)) [2003/4 16g⁶ 16s³ 16m² 16d⁶ 16s⁶ 16d 16gᵘʳ Mar 5] sparsely-made mare: fairly useful on Flat (stays 1½m), some creditable efforts in 2003 for J. Bolger, below form all starts in Britain: modest novice hurdler: will probably stay beyond 2m: acts on soft and good to firm going. *B. S. Rothwell*

CERESFIELD (NZ) 8 br.m. Westminster (NZ) – Audrey Rose (NZ) (Blue Razor c106
(USA)) [2003/4 c–, h89+: c16g* c16m³ c17g² c20g⁵ c20d² c17g² c17m* c17g³ c16m² h–
c16m* c16m⁵ c17f c17m⁶ c17m² c16g⁵ c16g* c16g⁵ c16d⁴ Mar 22] leggy mare: modest maiden hurdler: fair chaser: won novices at Hexham (handicap) in April and Cartmel in July, conditional jockeys handicap at Uttoxeter in September and novice handicap in February: best around 2m: acts on good to firm going: in cheekpieces after fourth start, tongue tied after ninth: front runner/races prominently. *R. C. Guest*

CESARE BORGIA (IRE) 4 ch.c. Dr Devious (IRE) – Prospering (Prince Sabo) h–
[2003/4 16dᵖᵘ 16f⁶ 16gᶠ 16g Jan 15] poor maiden on Flat for A. Berry: little show in juvenile hurdles. *R. Johnson*

C'EST FANTASTIQUE (IRE) 7 b.m. Hernando (FR) – Dolcezza (FR) (Lichine c–
(USA)) [2003/4 16d⁴ 16g* 20v³ 20m* 16d⁵ 20s³ c22dᶠ Feb 25] eighth foal: half-sister to h112
3 winners on Flat: dam unraced close relation of smart French performer up to 10.5f Caprarola: won on Flat in Germany: fair hurdler: won mares maiden at Limerick in June and minor event at Punchestown in October: jumped poorly and well held when falling last in maiden on chasing debut: stays 2½m: acts on soft and good to firm going: tried in cheekpieces: tongue tied last 4 starts. *M. J. P. O'Brien, Ireland*

CETTI'S WARBLER 6 gr.m. Sir Harry Lewis (USA) – Sedge Warbler (Scallywag) h94
[2003/4 F–: 20g 21s³ 16v* 21d³ 22v⁵ 20s⁶ 21gᵖᵘ Mar 27] tall mare: type to make a chaser: modest novice hurdler: 100/1, won at Towcester in December: should stay 3m: acts on heavy going. *Mrs P. Robeson*

CHABRIMAL MINSTER 7 b.g. Minster Son – Bromley Rose (Rubor) [2003/4 h92: h105
24d* Mar 11] leggy gelding: better effort in novice hurdles at Carlisle a year apart when winning by 3½ lengths from Fromragstoriches: stays 3m. *R. Ford*

CHA CHA CHA DANCER 4 ch.g. Groom Dancer (USA) – Amber Fizz (USA) h98 ?
(Effervescing (USA)) [2003/4 17s⁶ 16g 16g³ Mar 28] strong gelding: half-brother to several winners, including modest 2m hurdler Ambidextrous (by Shareef Dancer): twice-raced at 2 yrs, modest form on debut: best effort over hurdles when third in juvenile at Kelso. *G. A. Swinbank*

CHADSWELL (IRE) 11 b.g. Lord Americo – Marita Ann (Crozier) [2003/4 c96, c–
h98: 24g 26g Mag 26] sturdy gelding: modest handicap hurdler/chaser in 2002/3: well h–
below form in 2 hurdles in May, and little impact in points subsequently: thorough stayer: raced mainly on good going or softer (acts on heavy): tried in cheekpieces: has had tongue tied: has gone in snatches. *R. Ford*

CHAIN LINE 14 br.g. Relkino – Housemistress (New Member) [2003/4 c–, h–: 16m⁴ c–
Jun 20] big, rangy gelding: winning hurdler: dead. *J. W. F. Aynsley* h–

CHAKRA 10 gr.g. Mystiko (USA) – Maracuja (USA) (Riverman (USA)) [2003/4 17d h–
16dᵖᵘ 17s Jan 22] winning sprinter, little form on Flat in 2002 for M. Saunders: waste of time over hurdles. *C. J. Gray*

CHALFORD MILL 4 b.g. Blushing Flame (USA) – Crambella (IRE) (Red Sunset) F–
[2003/4 F13v Dec 15] second foal: dam, maiden who stayed 1½m, half-sister to fairly useful 3m chaser Symbol of Success: well held in 3-y-o bumper on debut. *C. W. Thornton*

CHALOM (IRE) 6 b.g. Mujadil (USA) – The Poachers Lady (IRE) (Salmon Leap h78
(USA)) [2003/4 17g 21d 19d 16d⁶ Apr 12] lengthy gelding: half-brother to one-time useful hurdler Pembroke Square (by Tenby), stays 3m: fairly useful but lightly raced on Flat (stays 1m) for B. Meehan: poor form over hurdles: likely to prove best around 2m. *O. Sherwood*

CHAMOSS ROYALE (FR) 4 ch.f. Garde Royale – Chamoss (FR) (Tip Moss (FR)) h119 p
[2003/4 17v* 22g* Mar 25] ex-French filly: second foal: dam, winning chaser around 2¾m, half-sister to useful hurdler/chaser Saint Preuil: unbeaten in 2 starts over hurdles, minor event at Pau in January for J-P. Totain and mares novice at Wincanton: fairly useful form when beating Marjina 8 lengths at latter: likely to improve further. *P. F. Nicholls*

187

Royal British Legion Poppy Appeal Persian War Novices' Hurdle, Chepstow—
Champagne Harry (right) takes advantage of Comply Or Die's mistake at the second last

CHAMPAGNE HARRY 6 b.g. Sir Harry Lewis (USA) – Sparkling Cinders (Nether- **h128**
kelly) [2003/4 h–, F82: 16g⁴ 17g* 20v² 20m* 20g* 24m² 24g* 21f³ 20g* 21m³ 25s³ 24g⁵
24s⁶ 21g 24g³ 24m⁵ Apr 15] workmanlike gelding: will make a chaser: fairly useful
novice hurdler: won at Hereford in May, Worcester and Uttoxeter in June, Perth in September and Chepstow (Grade 2, beat Comply Or Die 5 lengths) in November: creditable
efforts in Grade 1 events at Cheltenham and Aintree and handicap at Cheltenham
(sweating, fifth to Wintertide) last 3 starts: stays 3m: acts on any going: consistent.
N. A. Twiston-Davies.

CHAMPAGNE LIL 7 gr.m. Terimon – Sparkling Cinders (Netherkelly) [2003/4 h85: **c–**
21m* 19m* 20m² 24g² 20m⁴ c25d³ c20s⁴ c19d 22s Apr 6] leggy mare: fair handicap **h105**
hurdler: won at Ludlow (novice) and Hereford (mares) in May: let down by jumping in 3
starts over fences, also took little interest on final one: stays 3m, effective at much shorter:
acts on good to firm and good to soft going, possibly unsuited by soft. *N. A. Twiston-
Davies*

CHAMPAGNE LOU LOU 6 b.m. Supreme Leader – Highfrith (Deep Run) [2003/4 **F–**
F16s⁶ F16v Feb 4] 10,000 4-y-o: leggy, workmanlike mare: sixth foal: half-sister to poor
staying chaser Sniper (by Gunner B): dam fairly useful staying chaser: signs of only a
little ability in 2 bumpers. *A. Parker*

CHAMPAGNE SUNDAE (IRE) 6 b.g. Supreme Leader – Partners In Crime **F81**
(Crofthall) [2003/4 F17s⁶ F17gᵖᵘ Apr 1] 5,000 4-y-o: third foal: dam won around 2m over
hurdles in Ireland: well-held sixth of 8 in bumper at Folkestone on debut: probably amiss
in similar event at Taunton. *P. Winkworth*

CHAMPETRE (FR) 6 b.g. Pursuit of Love – Fermiere (FR) (General Holme (USA)) **h76**
[2003/4 17d³ 17g 16m⁴ Apr 13] ex-French gelding: fairly useful around 1m (stays 1¼m)
on Flat at 2/3 yrs for J-C. Rouget: looked headstrong and just poor form over hurdles
(reluctant to line up last 2 starts): likely to prove best at 2m. *Miss Victoria Roberts*

CHANCE FLIGHT 4 b.f. Busy Flight – Castle Maid (Castle Keep) [2003/4 F16m **F–**
Mar 11] fifth foal: dam 5f winner: well held in bumper on debut. *R. J. Hodges*

CHANCE MEETING 6 b.m. Overbury (IRE) – Pepper Star (IRE) (Salt Dome **h–**
(USA)) [2003/4 F17v⁶ 16s Jan 6] sparely-made mare: fifth foal: half-sister to 1¼m **F–**

winner Gunboat Diplomacy (by Mtoto): dam unraced half-sister to Champion Hurdle winner Kribensis: shaped better than result when well held in mares bumper on debut but trailed throughout in mares novice hurdle. *A. King*

CHANCERS DANTE (IRE)   8 b.g. Phardante (FR) – Own Acre (Linacre) [2003/4 h75: 24g² 24m* c21g³ c16vF c24spu Dec 26] angular gelding: modest hurdler: won handicap at Hexham in May: no form over fences: stays 27f: has form on heavy going, possibly better on good/good to firm: not fluent when blinkered final outing. *Ferdy Murphy*   c–
h92

CHANDELIER   4 ch.g. Sabrehill (USA) – La Noisette (Rock Hopper) [2003/4 16mpu 16d Dec 15] sturdy gelding: modest on Flat (stays 1m): no show in 2 juvenile hurdles, in cheekpieces on second occasion. *M. S. Saunders*   h–

CHANGED TIMES (IRE)   6 br.g. Semillon – Miss Ivy (IRE) (Le Bavard (FR)) [2003/4 c24g² c25dF c27s⁴ c24dpu c16d⁵ Mar 17] €7,500 4-y-o: second foal: dam bumper winner: winning pointer in 2003: poor maiden steeplechaser: effective at 2m to 3m: usually blinkered. *Liam Lennon, Ireland*   c78

CHAN MOVE   12 b.g. Move Off – Kanisa (Chantro) [2003/4 h–: 21spu 20gpu 17d 19g⁶ 22mpu 17m 21mpu Jul 22] leggy gelding: poor maiden hurdler: stays 2½m: acts on soft and good to firm going: tried in cheekpieces, often blinkered. *W. J. Smith*   h–

CHANNAHRLIE (IRE)   10 gr.g. Celio Rufo – Derravarragh Lady (IRE) (Radical) [2003/4 c86, h94: c25f³ c26m* c20m* c24m* c23f* c24d² c23g³ c24mpu Mar 4] tall, angular gelding: modest chaser: had excellent season, winning amateur events at Warwick (handicap), Lingfield (minor contest) and Ludlow (handicap) in November and handicap at Leicester in December: stays 3½m: acts on soft and firm going: usually wears cheekpieces, visored last 3 starts. *R. Dickin*   c99
h–

CHANNEL HIGHLANDER   9 b.g. Jendali (USA) – Young Mary (Young Generation) [2003/4 c16gpu c16g³ 20dpu Nov 14] good-topped gelding: poor maiden hurdler: little show over fences: best around 2m: acts on heavy going: weak finisher, and not to be trusted. *L. Lungo*   c– §
h– §

Mr Gavin MacEchern's "Champagne Harry"

CHANTICLIER 7 b.g. Roselier (FR) – Cherry Crest (Pollerton) [2003/4 h105: 26g³ **h111** 21g² Nov 6] well-made gelding: fair maiden hurdler, lightly raced: should stay beyond 21f. *K. C. Bailey*

CHAPARRO AMARGOSO (IRE) 11 b.g. Ela-Mana-Mou – Champanera (Top **c– x** Ville) [2003/4 c103, h–: c20m c19d^{ur} Mar 22] has stringhalt: fair handicap chaser in **h–** 2002/3 for B. Ellison: signs of retaining only a little ability in points/hunters: seems best at 2m: acts on firm and good to soft ground: visored twice: has had tongue tied: sketchy jumper. *F. L. Matthews*

CHAPEL ROYALE (IRE) 7 gr.g. College Chapel – Merci Royale (Fairy King **h–** (USA)) [2003/4 h79: 17m 16m⁵ Oct 20] leggy gelding: poor maiden hurdler: tongue tied when well held in 2 handicaps in 2003/4: sold 5,000 gns Doncaster August Sales, well below form on Flat in 2004 for Mrs N. Sharpe. *Evan Williams*

CHAPEL TIMES 5 b.g. Supreme Leader – Dippers Daughter (Strong Gale) **F87** [2003/4 F17v³ Mar 21] eighth foal: half-brother to useful 2m chaser Dines (by Phardante) and fairly useful hurdler G V A Ireland (by Beneficial), stays 25f: dam unraced half-sister to smart chaser up to 3m Royal Dipper and useful staying chaser Henry Mann: third to Wild Cane Ridge in bumper at Carlisle on debut. *H. D. Daly*

CHAPELTOWN (IRE) 12 b.g. Denel (FR) – Lady Dunsford (Torus) [2003/4 h–: **c108** 16g c19g* c19m² Apr 13] well-made gelding: useful handicap hurdler at best: won weak **h–** maiden at Taunton on chasing debut: no match for Polar Red in novice at Exeter later in month: stays 19f: acts on soft and good to firm going. *N. J. Henderson*

CHAPTER HOUSE (USA) 5 b.g. Pulpit (USA) – Lilian Bayliss (IRE) (Sadler's **h92** Wells (USA)) [2003/4 16s⁵ 16d^{ur} 20s 20d 16g Apr 5] good-topped gelding: fair on Flat (should stay beyond 1m) at 3 yrs for J. Gosden, sold out of D. Nicholls' stable 20,000 gns Newmarket Autumn Sales after running poorly only start in 2003: fifth to Steppes of Gold in novice at Haydock on hurdling debut: little form subsequently: will prove best around 2m: blinkered final start. *M. W. Easterby*

CHARLATAN (IRE) 6 b.g. Charnwood Forest (IRE) – Taajreh (IRE) (Mtoto) [2003/4 **h–** h–: 16s⁶ 16d Apr 12] of no account. *Mrs C. A. Dunnett*

CHARLIE 6 b.g. Pharly (FR) – Leave It To Lib (Tender King) [2003/4 F16g⁴ F16m⁵ **h–** 17g⁶ Sep 13] IR £4,600 3-y-o, €17,000 4-y-o: second foal: half-brother to useful sprinter **F88** Willhewiz (by Wizard King): dam 7f/1m winner: better effort in bumpers when fourth to Minster Missile in slowly-run event at Kelso on debut: jumped with little fluency when well held in novice on hurdling debut. *N. A. Twiston-Davies*

CHARLIEADAMS (IRE) 14 b.g. Carlingford Castle – Lucy Platter (FR) (Record **c– x** Token) [2003/4 c108x: c24f^{pu} c21g⁶ c25g Apr 5] workmanlike gelding: fair chaser: **h–** improved form for L. Lungo fourth to eighth starts in 2002/3: disappointing back in hunters: stays 3¼m: acts on good to firm and heavy going: sketchy jumper. *J. F. W. Muir*

CHARLIE BUBBLES (IRE) 7 b.g. Un Desperado (FR) – Bounty (IRE) (Cataldi) **h–** [2003/4 F–: 16g 16m Apr 13] well held in bumper and maiden hurdles. *B. De Haan*

CHARLIE CASTALLAN 4 gr.g. Wace (USA) – Castle Cary (Castle Keep) [2003/4 **F–** F16m F16g Mar 25] fourth foal: half-brother to 5f winner Blazing Castle (by Vague Shot): dam 5f winner: well beaten in 2 bumpers. *N. J. Hawke*

CHARLIE CHAPEL 5 b.g. College Chapel – Lightino (Bustino) [2003/4 F16s^{pu} **F89** F16d⁵ F17d Mar 27] sturdy gelding: sixth foal: half-brother to winning hurdler around 2m Alambeat (by Fairy King) and useful performer around 1½m Ligne Gagnante (by Turtle Island): dam maiden half-sister to very smart Italian middle-distance performer Welsh Guide: best effort in bumpers (looked wayward on debut) when eighth of 18 at Bangor final start. *W. M. Brisbourne*

CHARLIE MOON (IRE) 5 gr.g. Moonax (IRE) – Charlottes Lot (Fine Blade (USA)) **F–** [2003/4 F16d Feb 2] useful-looking gelding: third foal: dam, maiden, half-sister to smart 2m hurdler Lady Daisy: well held in bumper on debut. *Jonjo O'Neill*

CHARLIE'S ANGEL 6 gr.m. Rakaposhi King – Dunnohalm (Kalaglow) [2003/4 **c61** F16m⁵ F16m c16d⁵ c20g⁵ Mar 12] £1,100 4-y-o: first foal: dam, bumper winner, half- **h–** sister to good middle-distance stayer Celio Rufo: successful 4 times in points, including **F72** in April: signs of only a little ability otherwise. *P. York*

CHARLIES BRIDE (IRE) 9 b. or br.m. Rich Charlie – Nordic Bride (IRE) (Nordico **h–** (USA)) [2003/4 17d^{pu} 16g Jan 24] fair at one time on Flat: poor form in 2 novice hurdles in 1999/00 for J. O'Neill: tongue tied, showed nothing on return. *M. A. Barnes*

CHARLIES DOUBLE 5 b.g. Double Eclipse (IRE) – Pendil's Niece (Roscoe Blake) F79
[2003/4 F16g aF16g³ Apr 4] 8,000 4-y-o: sixth foal: half-brother to winning hurdler
around 2m Handsome Henry (by Handsome Sailor): dam, winning pointer, from family
of top-class staying chaser Pendil: better effort in bumpers when third to Lin d'Estruval
on polytrack at Lingfield. *J. R. Best*

CHARLIES FUTURE 6 b.g. Democratic (USA) – Faustelerie (Faustus (USA)) c101
[2003/4 h107: 22s³ 22g⁵ c19d⁴ c19s³ c19d³ c19v² Feb 2] tall gelding: fair handicap h105
hurdler: similar form over fences: stays 2¾m: acts on heavy ground. *S. C. Burrough*

CHARLIESMEDARLIN 13 b.g. Macmillion – Top Cover (High Top) [2003/4 c–, c84
h–: c25gᵖᵘ c26gᵖᵘ c21g³ c24g* c21g³ Jun 21] workmanlike gelding: poor handicap chas- h–
er: won at Uttoxeter in June: stays 3m: acts on firm going: visored once: has had tongue
tied. *Mrs Barbara Waring*

CHARLIES MEMORY 5 b.g. Blushing Flame (USA) – Hat Hill (Roan Rocket) h90
[2003/4 F16g F16v⁵ F16g⁵ 20d 16g³ 21d³ Mar 30] good-topped gelding: half-brother F84
to several winners, including winning 2m hurdler Nore Hill (by Town And Country):
dam ran 4 times: modest form in bumpers and novice hurdles: tried tongue tied.
M. W. Easterby

CHARLIE STRONG (IRE) 11 b.g. Strong Gale – The Village Vixen (Buckskin c–
(FR)) [2003/4 c99: c26dᵖᵘ Mar 18] strong gelding: fairly useful hunter chaser: very stiff
task in Foxhunter at Cheltenham: should stay beyond 23f: acts on firm and soft going.
R. Kelvin-Hughes

CHARLIE WHITESTONE 5 b.g. Sovereign Water (FR) – Khatti Hawk (Hittite F–
Glory) [2003/4 F16g F16m Jun 14] 1,400 3-y-o: ninth foal: dam sister to Triumph Hurdle
winner Saxon Farm: well held in 2 bumpers: sold £1,600 Ascot December Sales.
R. D. E. Woodhouse

CHARLOTTE LAMB 4 gr.f. Pharly (FR) – Caroline Lamb (Hotfoot) [2003/4 F13g F–
Nov 30] medium-sized filly: sister to fairly useful hurdler/useful chaser Byron Lamb,
stays 19f, and half-sister to several other winners, including useful hurdler Mr Lamb (by
Deploy): dam, winning hurdler, half-sister to useful 2m hurdler Burns: well beaten in
3-y-o bumper on debut. *Miss S. E. Hall*

CHARLY BOMBER 6 ch.g. Lancastrian – Charlycia (Good Times (ITY)) [2003/4 F–
F17g Apr 10] second foal: dam, modest hurdler, stayed 2½m: tailed off in bumper on
debut. *Miss M. Bragg*

CHARLY JACK 5 b.g. Alderbrook – Reperage (USA) (Key To Content (USA)) F–
[2003/4 F16s Dec 26] €20,000 3-y-o: ninth foal: half-brother to fair staying chaser
Flapjack Lad (by Oats) and winner on Flat in Holland by Fulmar: dam, French 1m winner,
from family of very smart 2m hurdler/chaser Western Rose: showed nothing in bumper
on debut. *Ferdy Murphy*

CHARMING ADMIRAL (IRE) 11 b.g. Shareef Dancer (USA) – Lilac Charm c91 §
(Bustino) [2003/4 c93§, h80§: 20d c25g⁵ c25v³ c20s c24sᵖᵘ Mar 20] sturdy gelding: h– §
winning hurdler: modest handicap chaser: stays 25f: acts on heavy ground: blinkered:
usually races prominently: moody. *Mrs A. Duffield*

CHARM OFFENSIVE 6 b.m. Zieten (USA) – Shoag (USA) (Affirmed (USA)) h79
[2003/4 h72: 22f⁴ 22f³ 24g* 24sᵖᵘ 24d 26s 24g⁶ 22d Mar 21] poor hurdler: won conditional jockeys minor event at Towcester in November: should stay beyond 3m: best
efforts on good going. *C. J. Gray*

CHARMOUTH FOREST 8 ch.g. Lir – Crimson Lady (Crimson Beau) [2003/4 h–
h75: 27sᵖᵘ Apr 29] poor maiden hurdler: tongue tied, breathing problem only outing in
2003/4: barely stays 2¾m: raced on good going or softer. *C. J. Gray*

CHARNWOOD STREET (IRE) 5 b.g. Charnwood Forest (IRE) – La Vigie (King h68 §
of Clubs) [2003/4 h71: 20d 17g 16v⁵ 21sᵖᵘ 24g 20d⁵ 26s⁵ 24g Nov 30] close-coupled
gelding: poor on Flat (stays 2m): poor maiden hurdler: probably stays 3¼m: acts on soft
ground: visored after reappearance: less than keen. *D. Shaw*

CHARTER ROYAL (FR) 9 gr.g. Royal Charter (FR) – Tadjmine (FR) (Tadj (FR)) c– §
[2003/4 c66§, h–§: c16g 21g⁶ 19g c24g⁴ c24gᵖᵘ Feb 8] compact gelding: poor handicap h–
chaser/maiden hurdler: effective at 2m to 3m: acts on good to firm and heavy going: tried
blinkered: unreliable. *A. R. Dicken*

CHASE THE SUNSET (IRE) 6 ch.g. Un Desperado (FR) – Cherry Chase (IRE) h96 +
(Red Sunset) [2003/4 h83§, F–: 16f² 16d⁵ 17g² 17d 20s³ Feb 19] useful-looking gelding:
chasing sort: modest form in novice hurdles: stays 2½m. *Miss H. C. Knight*

CHASING THE BRIDE   11 b.g. Gildoran – Bride (Remainder Man) [2003/4 c24g[5] c25m* c24g* Apr 18] quite good-topped gelding: useful hunter chaser: won at Wincanton in March and Stratford (beat News Flash by 29 lengths) in April: stays 25f: acts on firm and good to soft going: effective tongue tied or not. *Miss A. Goschen*   **c107**

CHATEAU ROSE (IRE)   8 b.g. Roselier (FR) – Claycastle (IRE) (Carlingford Castle) [2003/4 c110, h94: c30s[5] c22m[F] c24d[4] c24s[pu] 20s 24m[4] 22s[4] Mar 23] compact gelding: fair handicap chaser: modest maiden hurdler: likely to prove best at 3m+: unraced on firm going, acts on any other: tried blinkered. *N. A. Gaselee*   **c112 h94**

CHATER FLAIR   7 b.g. Efisio – Native Flair (Be My Native (USA)) [2003/4 h93: 16d[F] 19d[ur] 20g 26d[pu] Mar 22] maiden hurdler: showed little in 2003/4: should prove best at 2½m+: tried visored. *D. Burchell*   **h—**

CHAUVINIST (IRE)   9 b.g. Roselier (FR) – Sacajawea (Tanfirion) [2003/4 h139: c16d[3] Dec 6] smallish, leggy, plain gelding: useful hurdler in 2002/3: third of 6 finishers to impressive Thisthatandtother in Grade 2 novice chase at Sandown only start in 2003/4: effective at 2m, should be at least as good around 2½m: raced on good going or softer (very best effort on heavy): usually on toes: likely to improve over fences. *N. J. Henderson*   **c121 p h—**

CHEEKY BOY DANNY   6 ch.g. Formidable (USA) – Moments Joy (Adonijah) [2003/4 F16d F17d Apr 18] seventh foal: half-brother to winner in Hong Kong by Squill: dam, maiden who probably stayed 1½m, half-sister to top-class 2m to 2½m hurdler Flown: well held in 2 bumpers. *R. D. E. Woodhouse*   **F—**

CHEERY MARTYR   6 b.m. Perpendicular – Kate O'Kirkham (Le Bavard (FR)) [2003/4 F17v F16s[5] 17d[4] Apr 18] fourth foal: half-sister to poor 2m hurdler Percy Beck (by Minster Son): dam bumper winner: signs of ability in bumpers and novice hurdle. *P. Needham*   **h71 F77**

CHELSEA'S DIAMOND   4 b.f. Man Among Men (IRE) – Sharp Thistle (Sharpo) [2003/4 F18g Apr 22] fourth foal: sister to 1m winner Sharp Monkey and half-sister to winner abroad by Kalaglow: dam fairly useful 7f winner: well held in bumper on debut. *J. Akehurst*   **F—**

CHEMICALREACTION   4 b.g. Definite Article – Ewar Snowflake (Snow Chief (USA)) [2003/4 17m[bd] 16m 16f[3] 16g 16g Jan 15] poor maiden on Flat (should stay 1¼m): poor juvenile hurdler: blinkered/visored last 3 starts. *R. A. Fahey*   **h79**

CHEM'S TRUCE (IRE)   7 b.g. Brief Truce (USA) – In The Rigging (USA) (Topsider (USA)) [2003/4 h104: 17g[pu] 16m[3] 17m[2] 16g[2] 16s[4] 17g[6] 16s[5] 16g Mar 6] leggy, close-coupled gelding: fair handicap hurdler: likely to prove best around 2m: acts on soft and good to firm going. *Miss Venetia Williams*   **h111**

CHERGAN (IRE)   11 b.g. Yashgan – Cherry Bright (IRE) (Miner's Lamp) [2003/4 c115, h–: c20g[3] c21m[F] c25f* c20g[5] c16m[2] c16d[4] c24m[2] c19g* c21g c16d[5] Apr 22] lengthy gelding: fairly useful handicap chaser: won at Kelso in October and Doncaster in March: effective at 2m to easy 25f: acts on any going: has won/been placed on 14 of 15 starts at Musselburgh: usually very sound jumper (well held both starts over National fences at Aintree). *Mrs S. C. Bradburne*   **c123 h—**

CHEROKEE BAY   4 b.f. Primo Dominie – Me Cherokee (Persian Bold) [2003/4 16s[5] 16d[3] 19d[2] 16g[4] 18g[2] Apr 22] modest on Flat (stays 1¼m), sold out of J. Osborne's stable 6,000 gns Newmarket Autumn Sales: of similar standard over hurdles: likely to prove best around 2m. *G. L. Moore*   **h93**

CHEROKEE RUN (IRE)   10 b.g. Commanche Run – Hampton Grange (Boreen (FR)) [2003/4 c25m[4] c25m* c28d[pu] c25d[pu] Feb 12] sturdy gelding: fair pointer: best effort in hunters when winning at Wincanton in May: stays 25f: acts on good to firm going. *A. J. Tizzard*   **c89**

CHERRY GOLD   10 b.g. Rakaposhi King – Merry Cherry (Deep Run) [2003/4 c108: c24m* 22g[3] 24m* c26m[4] 24m[3] c25m[4] c24d[ur] c24m* Apr 13] fairly useful hunter chaser: won at Chepstow early and late in season, on latter occasion in same race for second successive year: easily best effort in novice hurdles when winning at Market Rasen in August: should stay beyond 3m: acts on good to firm going: wore cheekpieces last 2 starts: front runner: tends to make mistakes. *Evan Williams*   **c105 x h93**

CHERRY QUEEN   6 ch.m. Royal Vulcan – Cherry Sip (Nearly A Hand) [2003/4 F16f F16d 20s[pu] Dec 11] angular mare: sixth foal: half-sister to one-time fair chaser Beefy Nova (by Ra Nova), stays 3m: dam pulled up in 2 points: no sign of ability, virtually refused to race second start: sold 500 gns Doncaster January Sales. *C. N. Kellett*   **h— F—**

CHERRY RED (IRE)   5 b.m. Un Desperado (FR) – Island Crest (Jupiter Island)   **F101 p**
[2003/4 F18s* Mar 14] first foal: dam unraced half-sister to fairly useful 2½m chaser Rowington: won 19-runner bumper at Cork impressively on debut by 9 lengths from Brutto Facie: useful prospect. *J. E. Kiely, Ireland*

CHERUB (GER)   4 b.g. Winged Love (IRE) – Chalkidiki (GER) (Nebos (GER))   **h134**
[2003/4 16g⁴ 16s² 17g⁴ 16g Apr 1]

Another shuffling of the cards, among a substandard crop of juvenile hurdlers, and it was Cherub who came to the top in the Colm McEvoy Auctioneers Champion Four Year Old Hurdle at Punchestown. It was Cherub's third meeting with both Made In Japan and Al Eile, the former having fared best of the trio when winning the Triumph Hurdle at Cheltenham and the latter emerging the winner when they next met in the Anniversary Hurdle at Aintree. Of his two races at the earlier Festivals, Cherub ran much his better race at Cheltenham, finishing just over three lengths fourth behind Made In Japan and seeing out the race really well considering he had taken a strong hold on the heels of the leaders early on. In a more steadily-run race at Aintree, Cherub's tendency to race freely seemed to take more of a toll and he managed only ninth.

As well as the first two from Aintree, Al Eile and Made In Japan, the next three home from the Anniversary Hurdle, My Will, Tarque and Nopekan, were among Cherub's opponents at Punchestown, as was the Irish-trained Triumph Hurdle third Top Strategy. Two more Irish horses headed the betting, Power Elite, who had been third to older novices at Fairyhouse the time before, and Essex, winner of both his starts. With such a field, the race promised to bring some sort of order to the juvenile ranks, but it failed to do so after no more than a fair pace resulted in a muddling race. Cherub looked in good shape beforehand and returned to form, taking a good hold again but leading just after the final flight. He was all out to hold on by a short head from the rallying Made In Japan, with a length back to Essex in third and little more than five lengths covering the first half dozen. Power Elite and Al Eile were among those who finished well held. It was a second win in the race in three years for the combination of trainer Jonjo O'Neill and jockey Tony Dobbin after Quazar's win in 2002. Cherub had had very little hurdling experience before being pitched in against the top juveniles at Cheltenham,

Colm McEvoy Auctioneers Champion Four Year Old Hurdle, Punchestown—
Cherub (right) reverses Cheltenham placings with Made In Japan (stripes)

Aintree and Punchestown. He made his debut just two months before the Triumph when finishing an encouraging fourth to Tusk at Kempton and showed improvement when second to the same rival (who went on to start second favourite for the Triumph) at Sandown three weeks later.

Cherub has what has come to be a fairly typical profile for a German import in that he showed useful form over middle distances in his country of birth. Trained by Andreas Schutz, his only win came in a national listed race at Munich as a two-year-old over a mile but he kept good company at three, finishing tenth in the Deutsches Derby. Like Cherub, his sire Winged Love gained his biggest success in Ireland, winning the Derby there. The Andre Fabre-trained Winged Love ran at the Curragh in a change to original plans to run him in the Deutsches Derby, though Germany was where he began his stud career before moving to Northern Ireland where he now stands as a jumps sire. His other German-bred winners in Britain in the latest season included the fairly useful chaser Barito and the progressive hurdler True Lover. Cherub's dam Chalkidiki, a winner at up to a mile and placed in listed company, produced three other useful winners in Germany before Cherub, the most notable being his brother Cheirokratie, Germany's top two-year-old in 2000 who didn't really train on. Cherub's grandam Charline is an unraced half-sister to the grandam of a couple of notable performers. One is Camp David, a smart stayer who was a rare German runner in the Gold Cup at Ascot in 1997, and the other is Caracciola, another useful import from Germany to make his mark in Britain in the latest season.

Atlantic Joinery Limited's "Cherub"

Cherub (GER) (b.g. 2000)	Winged Love (IRE) (b 1992)	In The Wings (b 1986)	Sadler's Wells High Hawk
		J'Ai Deux Amours (b 1986)	Top Ville Pollenka
	Chalkidiki (GER) (ro 1989)	Nebos (b 1976)	Caro Nostrana
		Charline (b 1980)	Pentathlon Clementina

The compact Cherub has raced only at around two miles and looks likely to prove best at that trip, for the time being at least. He has raced mainly on good ground over hurdles, but his win on the Flat came on heavy. Cherub has had his tongue tied over hurdles (except for his debut) and was blinkered once on the Flat. As he didn't get off the mark until after the end of the season in Britain, Cherub is in the unusual position for a leading juvenile hurdler of still being eligible for novice events in 2004/5. *Jonjo O'Neill*

CHESTER PARK   6 ch.g. King's Signet (USA) – Good Skills (Bustino) [2003/4 F–: F17m Jul 14] well beaten in bumpers and maiden on Flat. *K. Bishop*   **F–**

CHEVALIER ERRANT (IRE)   11 b. or br.g. Strong Gale – Luminous Run (Deep Run) [2003/4 c125d, h–: c20g^F c22g^3 c19g^4 c20g^F Mar 12] tall, good sort: fair handicap chaser: probably stays easy 3m: acts on good to firm and heavy going. *M. Todhunter*   **c109 h–**

CHEVET GIRL (IRE)   9 ch.m. Roselier (FR) – Vulcash (IRE) (Callernish) [2003/4 c97p, h106: 17m c16m^F 16d^5 16d^4 Dec 13] plain mare: fell both starts over fences: fair handicap hurdler: best around 2m: acts on good to firm and good to soft going: free-going front runner. *J. Howard Johnson*   **c– h101**

CHEYENNE CHIEF   5 b.g. Be My Chief (USA) – Cartuccia (IRE) (Doyoun) [2003/4 h96: 16d May 3] leggy gelding: winning hurdler, has gone the wrong way temperamentally: should stay 2½m+: acts on good to soft going, probably on good to firm: best efforts without blinkers/cheekpieces: tried tongue tied. *G. M. Moore*   **h– §**

CHICA BONITA   5 ch.m. Blushing Flame (USA) – Lutine Royal (Formidable (USA)) [2003/4 F17s F16d Mar 19] sixth foal: half-sister to winning hurdler around 2m Zesti (by Charmer) and 1½m winner Sam Peeb (by Keen): dam, lightly-raced maiden, from family of 1000 Guineas winner Fairy Footsteps and St Leger winner Light Cavalry: tailed off in 2 maiden bumpers. *J. E. Long*   **F–**

CHICAGO BREEZE (IRE)   7 b.m. Lord Americo – Anguillita (IRE) (King of Clubs) [2003/4 27d^4 c16d^{ur} c21d^{pu} Mar 30] ex-Irish mare: second foal: half-sister to useful bumper winner Chelsea Bridge (by Over The River): dam, maiden, out of half-sister to useful juvenile hurdlers Seldom Dry and Native Friend: modest form in bumpers: maiden hurdler: little show in 2 starts over fences: stays 2½m. *Ferdy Murphy*   **c– h–**

CHICAGO BULLS (IRE)   6 b.g. Darshaan – Celestial Melody (USA) (The Minstrel (CAN)) [2003/4 h119: 22s^5 21g^2 24s^3 c25d^3 c24s^{ur} c24d^5 c24d^4 24m Apr 15] compact gelding: fairly useful handicap hurdler: won at Towcester in November: around 9 lengths third to impressive Therealbandit in novice at Cheltenham on chasing debut: disappointing over fences after, mistakes and looked hard ride when blinkered seventh outing: stays 25f: acts on heavy going. *A. King*   **c128 h127**

CHICAGO CITY (IRE)   11 br.g. Strong Gale – Orchardstown (Pollerton) [2003/4 c21g^2 c24g c19s^5 c24g^F Apr 18] rangy gelding: one-time fairly useful chaser: off over 2 years, well held in hunters in 2003/4: stays 2¾m: acts on soft and good to firm going. *N. J. Gifford*   **c87 h–**

CHICUELO (FR)   8 b.g. Mansonnien (FR) – Dovapas (FR) (Paseo (FR)) [2003/4 c136, h–: c20m 24m* c24m* c25f^3 c24d^2 24d c21d^4 22s c24m^5 c24g^5 c33d^{pu} Apr 17] compact gelding: useful handicap hurdler/chaser: won over hurdles at Worcester in August and over fences at Ascot (5-runner race, by 6 lengths from Moor Lane) in November: below form last 4 outings: stays easy 25f: probably acts on any going: tried blinkered, visored nowadays: not a fluent jumper of fences: hasn't impressed with attitude. *M. C. Pipe*   **c138 x h130**

CHIEF MOUSE   11 b.g. Be My Chief (USA) – Top Mouse (High Top) [2003/4 c94d, h–: c26d^{pu} c19d^{pu} Mar 22] workmanlike gelding: winning chaser: sold out of B. Leavy's stable £3,100 Ascot February Sales: no show in hunters following month, reportedly lame in first: stays 3m: acts on firm and good to soft going, probably not on soft: tried blinkered/in cheekpieces/tongue tied: moody. *J. E. Price*   **c– § h–**

CHIEF OF JUSTICE   7 b.g. Be My Chief (USA) – Clare Court (Glint of Gold)   **c69**
[2003/4 c20g⁴ c20d Feb 19] medium-sized gelding: formerly fair on Flat (stays 1½m):
mistakes both starts in hunter chases. *Mrs Laura J. Young*

CHIEF SUSPECT (IRE)   12 b.g. Yashgan – Clerihan Miss (Tarqogan) [2003/4 c21m   **c–**
May 21] rangy gelding: no sign of ability outside points (won maiden in 2003). *Michael*   **h–**
Blake

CHIEF WARDANCE   10 ch.g. Profilic – Dolly Wardance (Warpath) [2003/4 c16dᵘʳ   **c–**
c16d⁴ Dec 27] lengthy gelding: one-time fairly useful 2m handicap hurdler, well below   **h–**
best in 2001/2: well beaten on completed outing over fences (finished lame): acts on good
to firm and heavy going. *C. N. Kellett*

CHIEF YEOMAN   4 b.g. Machiavellian (USA) – Step Aloft (Shirley Heights)   **h132**
[2003/4 16m* 16m² 16g⁴ 16s* 16s² 17g² 17m³ Apr 14]
    'No point in worrying about our handicap mark now,' said Chief Yeoman's
trainer after the 40/1-shot had finished an excellent, keeping-on second to Made In
Japan in the Triumph Hurdle at Cheltenham. The leading four-year-old hurdlers
nearly always find it tough going when they first step up to championship company
and Chief Yeoman's prospects in his second season now look none too bright in
handicaps either. That said, he was a generally progressive juvenile and may have a
little more improvement in him yet. His third of five behind Lough Derg when
favourite for quite a valuable contest at Cheltenham in April can be overlooked, as
he ran out of steam in the closing stages after being sent for home in earnest too far
from home. Chief Yeoman, who ran in the Queen's colours, was a useful handicapper on the Flat for Sir Michael Stoute but, with a Lingfield maiden the only win

B. Moore & E. C. Stephens' "Chief Yeoman"

to his name, he was sent up to the Doncaster August Sales and sold for 21,000 guineas. He made his debut over hurdles less than three months later, winning a juvenile maiden hurdle at Kempton. Chief Yeoman's finishing effort (he was tried in headgear on the Flat) when in the frame at Sandown and Newbury on his next two starts, left something to be desired. But he produced an altogether more convincing display to win from Lord of Beauty at Newbury in January and also ran well when second at Huntingdon the following month, facing a stiff task trying to concede 10 lb to Adopted Hero. The close-coupled Chief Yeoman is by the now-deceased Machiavellian who has not had many runners over hurdles. Chief Yeoman's winning dam Step Aloft, a half-sister to smart performers at up to a mile and a quarter Starlet and Unknown Quantity and to the Queen Mother's 1986 Imperial Cup winner Insular, has also bred Bright And Breezy (by Barathea), a winner over seven furlongs in Germany. Chief Yeoman ran on the Flat as though he should stay a mile and a half, and he should stay further than two miles over hurdles. He acts on soft and good to firm going. *Miss Venetia Williams*

CHINA CHASE (IRE) 5 b.g. Anshan – Hannies Girl (IRE) (Invited (USA)) [2003/4 **F68** F16m F16m[6] Mar 11] €12,000 3-y-o: sturdy gelding: second foal: dam, fair chaser around 2m, half-sister to useful 2m to 3m chaser Desert Lord: poor form on second of 2 starts in bumpers at Wincanton. *J. L. Spearing*

CHISM (IRE) 13 br.g. Euphemism – Melody Gayle VII (Damsire Unregistered) **c– §** [2003/4 c33d[pu] Apr 30] workmanlike gelding: one-time fairly useful hunter chaser, little form outside points since 1998/9: tried blinkered/visored/tongue tied: temperamental. *R. J. King*

CHITA'S FLIGHT 4 gr.f. Busy Flight – Chita's Cone (Celtic Cone) [2003/4 F14d[6] **F–** F17g Apr 10] third foal: dam winning pointer: well beaten in bumpers. *S. C. Burrough*

CHIVALRY 5 b.g. Mark of Esteem (IRE) – Gai Bulga (Kris) [2003/4 16g* 16s* 18g[4] **h128** 16g* Apr 16] well-made gelding: useful on Flat (barely stays testing 1¼m), won Cambridgeshire on reappearance in 2003, sold out of Sir Mark Prescott's stable 170,000 gns Newmarket Autumn Sales: won 3 of 4 starts over hurdles, novices at Ayr in November

Dawn Introductory Novices' Hurdle, Ayr—
useful recruits from the Flat Chivalry (left) and Vintage Premium fight out the finish

Andrea & Graham Wylie's "Chivalry"

and April and 17-runner handicap at Kelso in January: blinkered, beat below-form Albuhera by 13 lengths in 4-runner event on final outing: likely to prove best at 2m: room for improvement in his jumping. *J. Howard Johnson*

CHIVES (IRE) 9 b.g. Good Thyne (USA) – Chatty Actress (Le Bavard (FR)) [2003/4 **c–** c166, h–: c24d⁴ c29dᵖᵘ Dec 27] well-made gelding: usually impresses in appearance: **h–** very smart chaser: disappointing both starts in 2003/4: stays 29f: acts on heavy going: usually sound jumper: has broken blood vessels. *Miss H. C. Knight*

CHIVITE (IRE) 5 b.g. Alhaarth (IRE) – Laura Margaret (Persian Bold) [2003/4 h92: **h115** 18g² 20m* 24m³ 20m* 18f² 21g 22d 19d* 17g⁴ 19g* Apr 13] angular gelding: fair hurdler: won maiden at Huntingdon in May, novice at Uttoxeter in July and handicaps at Taunton in December and Exeter (by 3½ lengths from Manly Money) in April: stays 2½m, possibly not 3m: acts on good to firm and good to soft going. *P. J. Hobbs*

CHOCKDEE (FR) 4 b.g. King's Theatre (IRE) – Chagrin d'Amour (IRE) (Last **h113** Tycoon) [2003/4 16g⁵ 16g⁴ 16d Apr 17] useful-looking gelding: fourth foal: half-brother to 3 winners, including smart middle-distance stayer Total Turtle (by Turtle Island): in frame all 5 starts on Flat (stays 1½m) in France for F. Rohaut, showing fairly useful form: sold €125,000 Goffs (France) July Sale: easily best effort in juvenile hurdles (put head in air and failed to run on on debut) when fourth to Trouble At Bay in Grade 2 at Kempton. *P. F. Nicholls*

CHOCOLATE SOLDIER (IRE) 6 ch.g. Mister Lord (USA) – Traditional Lady **h66** (Carlingford Castle) [2003/4 F–: F17m* F16g* 24m⁴ Sep 14] failed to complete in 3 **F101** points: much improved when winning bumpers at Sedgefield in July and Worcester in August: favourite, well-held fourth in maiden at Worcester (finished distressed) on hurdling debut: should stay beyond 2m: blinkered in 2003/4: front runner. *Evan Williams*

198

CIM

CHOCO ROCO 7 b.g. Faustus (USA) – Leilaway (Scallywag) [2003/4 F16d F17s 22s^pu 24g^pu 16d Mar 21] workmanlike gelding: third foal: dam placed over hurdles: no form in bumpers or novice hurdles: has looked wayward. *D. Burchell* — **h– F–**

CHOISTY (IRE) 14 ch.g. Callernish – Rosemount Rose (Ashmore (FR)) [2003/4 c–, h–: c24m^pu c28d^5 c26d^pu c25g^3 Apr 3] close-coupled gelding: one-time fairly useful handicap chaser, modest in 2003/4: stays 29f: acts on soft and good to firm going. *H. E. Haynes* — **c87 h–**

CHRIS AND RYAN (IRE) 6 b.g. Goldmark (USA) – Beautyofthepeace (IRE) (Exactly Sharp (USA)) [2003/4 F–: F16s 17d^pu Mar 27] no sign of ability in bumpers or novice hurdle. *Mrs L. B. Normile* — **h– F–**

CHRISTINAS COTTAGE (IRE) 10 ch.m. Abednego – Inverdonan (Our Mirage) [2003/4 20g May 10] well beaten in bumper in 1999: maiden pointer: well held in maiden hurdle at Hexham. *G. J. McKeever, Ireland* — **h–**

CHRISTMAS TRUCE (IRE) 5 b.g. Brief Truce (USA) – Superflash (Superlative) [2003/4 h83p: 22g^5 16v^3 19d^4 21d^5 21d^6 Apr 12] good-topped gelding: poor maiden hurdler: seems to stay 21f: wore cheekpieces last 3 starts. *Ian Williams* — **h78**

CHRISTON CANE 6 b.g. El Conquistador – Dancing Barefoot (Scallywag) [2003/4 aF16g^6 Apr 4] first foal: dam no sign of ability: poor form when sixth of 14 in bumper on polytrack at Lingfield on debut. *Dr J. R. J. Naylor* — **F74**

CHRISTOPHER 7 gr.g. Arzanni – Forest Nymph (NZ) (Oak Ridge (FR)) [2003/4 h112: 21m^5 20m^3 c19d* c20g^5 Jan 27] close-coupled gelding: fair handicap hurdler: similar form on 2 starts over fences, won maiden at Exeter (beat Madam Flora ½ length) in January: should stay beyond 2½m: acts on any going. *P. J. Hobbs* — **c111 h108**

CHRISTY JNR (IRE) 10 b.g. Andretti – Rare Currency (Rarity) [2003/4 h–: 24d 27s^4 26m^6 c27m^5 c22d^3 c24d^ur c24s^bd c24g 24d 27d^6 Mar 16] lengthy gelding: bad maiden hurdler/chaser. *C. J. Teague* — **c– h–**

CHRISTY SENIOR (IRE) 9 b.g. Erins Isle – Persian Sparkler (Persian Bold) [2003/4 20g^pu 16m^6 17m 17g^3 16g^6 17g^5 18m 18m^pu Sep 20] leggy gelding: no show only run over fences: maiden hurdler: tried blinkered: tongue tied: dead. *J. J. Lambe, Ireland* — **c– h–**

CHRISTY'S PRIDE (IRE) 12 ch.m. Kambalda – Caddy Shack (Precipice Wood) [2003/4 c–, h–: c30g^pu c24s^pu 24g 24s Jan 14] smallish, workmanlike mare: usually let down by jumping over fences: handicap hurdler, well held in 2003/4: stays 3¼m: acts on heavy going. *C. Weedon* — **c– x h–**

CHROMAZONE 7 gr.m. Roselier (FR) – Gold Bash (Golden Love) [2003/4 17g 20s^ur 20m May 26] plain mare: fourth live foal: half-sister to fair hurdler up to 2½m Dorans Way (by Jeu de Paille): dam unraced: no sign of ability. *D. J. Caro* — **h–**

CHURCHTOWN GLEN (IRE) 11 b. or br.g. Be My Native (USA) – Hill Side Glen (Goldhill) [2003/4 c83§, h–: 24g^6 Jun 12] rangy, good-topped gelding: poor handicap hurdler/chaser: stays 3¼m: acts on good to firm and heavy going: tried blinkered/tongue tied: often finds little. *Ian Williams* — **c– § h–**

CHURLISH LAD (IRE) 7 b.g. Commanche Run – Pennyala (Skyliner) [2003/4 F86: F16g F16v F16v 21d^pu Mar 1] bumper winner: in cheekpieces, no show in novice on hurdling debut. *M. Bradstock* — **h– F85**

CIGARILLO (IRE) 6 br.g. Vestris Abu – Rose-Anore (Roselier (FR)) [2003/4 F16m^3 F16m^3 20m 16m^2 19d^pu 19s^3 20g^3 19g* 21d* Mar 30] rather leggy gelding: third both starts in bumpers: fair novice hurdler: won at Newbury (conditional jockeys handicap) and Sedgefield (amateurs) in March: will stay beyond 21f: acts on soft and good to firm going. *Noel T. Chance* — **h104 F89**

CILLAMON 7 b.m. Terimon – Dubacilla (Dubassoff (USA)) [2003/4 F73: F16m^3 May 7] won 3-finisher maiden point in 2003: poor form in 2 bumpers at Chepstow year apart: will be well suited by stiffer test of stamina. *L. G. Cottrell* — **F75**

CILL CHURNAIN (IRE) 11 b.g. Arctic Cider (USA) – The Dozer (IRE) (Bulldozer) [2003/4 c–, h119: 20m^6 c21m* 24m^2 c21m^3 24m* c20g* 24d^3 c25d* 25d^6 Dec 26] small, plain gelding: fairly useful handicap hurdler/chaser: improved further in 2003/4, winning over hurdles at Market Rasen and over fences at Uttoxeter, Aintree (beat Log On Intersky 1½ lengths) and Kelso: stays 25f: acts on heavy and good to firm going: races prominently: genuine and consistent: a credit to connections. *Mrs S. J. Smith* — **c121 h126**

CIMARRONE COVE (IRE) 9 gr.g. Roselier (FR) – Sugarstown (Sassafras (FR)) [2003/4 c113§, h–: c24g^6 c25d^F c20d^pu Mar 25] well-made gelding: fair handicap chaser — **c79 § h–**

in 2002/3: off over a year, well beaten on completed start in hunters, left D. Easterby after second outing: should stay beyond 3¼m: acts on heavy going: tried blinkered/visored: unreliable. *M. W. Easterby*

CINNAMON CLUB 12 b.m. Derrylin – Cinnamon Run (Deep Run) [2003/4 c–, h–: c24m⁵ May 10] workmanlike mare: winning 2m hurdler: fair pointer, successful all 4 completed starts in 2003: no form in 2 hunter chases (weakened quickly over 3m): acts on good to soft ground: tried blinkered/tongue tied. *Mrs Ruth Hayter*
c–
h–

CINNAMON LINE 8 ch.g. Derrylin – Cinnamon Run (Deep Run) [2003/4 h98: 24gᶠ 22g⁴ Apr 10] tall, good sort: type to make a chaser: modest maiden hurdler, off a year before reappearance: stays 3m: raced on good going or softer (acts on heavy): has bled from nose. *R. H. Alner*
h97

CINTRA RUBY (IRE) 6 b.m. Phardante (FR) – Ardfallon (IRE) (Supreme Leader) [2003/4 17g 16g³ 16dᵖᵘ 17sᵖᵘ 16d 16g⁶ Feb 11] €3,000 4-y-o: leggy, sparely-made mare: fourth foal: dam, fourth in bumper, from family of useful chasers Bells Life and Indian Tonic, both of whom stayed at least 3m: pulled up in 2 points in 2003: poor form over hurdles: bred to stay 2½m. *W. K. Goldsworthy*
h78

CIONN MHALANNA (IRE) 6 b.g. Corrouge (USA) – Pennyland (Le Bavard (FR)) [2003/4 F83: F16g 19g⁶ 20s 20s 24d⁴ 24sᵖᵘ Apr 4] modest form in bumpers: well held in novice hurdles. *P. Beaumont*
h80 ?
F–

CIRCLE OF WOLVES 6 ch.g. Wolfhound (USA) – Misty Halo (High Top) [2003/4 h90: 23m³ 20g³ 20m⁴ 22gᵖᵘ 22m 21m³ 21s* 20d³ 22d 21g Apr 12] close-coupled gelding: modest hurdler: won conditional jockeys handicap at Plumpton in November: stays 21f: acts on soft and good to firm going: tried in cheekpieces. *M. J. Gingell*
h87

CIRCUMSTANCE 6 ch.m. Beveled (USA) – Instant Pleasure (Bairn (USA)) [2003/4 h–: 17mᵖᵘ May 26] no aptitude for hurdling. *R. Dickin*
h–

CIRCUS MAXIMUS (USA) 7 b.g. Pleasant Colony (USA) – Crockadore (USA) (Nijinsky (CAN)) [2003/4 h110: c24m* 20d* c24sᵖᵘ c16s² Apr 11] compact ex-Irish gelding: fair on Flat (stays 2m): fair hurdler: won claimer at Leicester in January: unconvincing when winning 2-finisher novice at Huntingdon on chasing debut in October: unwilling display final start: stays 3m: acts on good to firm and heavy going: usually blinkered: unreliable. *Ian Williams*
c106 §
h109 §

CISCO 6 b.g. Shambo – School Run (Deep Run) [2003/4 h–: 22g⁶ Mar 28] well-made gelding: poor maiden hurdler: tried blinkered: sold 3,000 gns Doncaster November Sales. *B. Mactaggart*
h–

CITA VERDA (FR) 6 b.m. Take Risks (FR) – Mossita (FR) (Tip Moss (FR)) [2003/4 h116+: 16m⁶ 16s³ 16g³ 16d³ 16s⁶ Dec 20] well-made mare: chasing type: fairly useful handicap hurdler: best efforts around 2m: acts on good to firm and heavy going: free-going sort: genuine. *P. Monteith*
h119

CITIMAN (AUS) 7 b.g. Citidancer – Taimian (NZ) (Taipan) [2003/4 21g Feb 11] compact gelding: successful twice around 1¼m from 25 starts on Flat in New Zealand: showed little on hurdling debut. *A. J. Whitehead*
h–

CITY FLYER 7 br.g. Night Shift (USA) – Al Guswa (Shernazar) [2003/4 16mᵘʳ 16m May 26] medium-sized gelding: poor on Flat in 2003: lightly raced and well held over hurdles. *Miss J. Feilden*
h67

CITY GENT 10 b.g. Primitive Rising (USA) – Classy Lassy (Class Distinction) [2003/4 c86, h–: c16g² c17gᵖᵘ May 24] well-made gelding: maiden hurdler: modest chaser: best efforts around 2m: acts on good to firm and heavy going: tried blinkered/in cheekpieces: has had tongue tied: sometimes let down by jumping. *N. Wilson*
c88
h–

CITY REACH 8 b.g. Petong – Azola (IRE) (Alzao (USA)) [2003/4 h–: 16g 17g⁴ 16m 17dᵖᵘ Jul 27] workmanlike gelding: no worthwhile form over hurdles: usually tongue tied. *Miss M. Bragg*
h–

CLANDESTINO (FR) 5 b.g. General Holme (USA) – Corolina (USA) (Nashua) [2003/4 F16d F17mᵖᵘ F17g F16d Apr 17] 4,200 3-y-o: half-brother to several winners in France on Flat/over jumps, including very smart performer up to 10.5f Bint Alnasr (by Al Nasr), dam of leading hurdler in USA Al Skywalker: dam never ran: no show in bumpers. *Mrs K. Walton*
F–

CLAN LAW (IRE) 6 b.g. Danehill (USA) – My-O-My (IRE) (Waajib) [2003/4 F16d Apr 23] 8,500 3-y-o: third foal: half-brother to useful 2001 2-y-o 5f winner Lord Merlin (by Turtle Island) and 1m winner in Italy by Foxhound: dam, useful 5f winner, out of
F–

half-sister to useful Irish 5f to 7f performer Title Roll: well held in bumper on debut.
Mrs L. B. Normile

CLAN ROYAL (FR) 9 b.g. Chef de Clan II (FR) – Allee du Roy (FR) (Rex Magna **c139**
(FR)) [2003/4 c123, h–: c27d* c36d² Apr 3] **h–**

What do the following have in common—Tim Hyde, Jimmy Brogan, Dick
Francis, John Lawrence (later Lord Oaksey), John Kenneally, Ron Barry, Richard
Pitman, Ridley Lamb, Phil Tuck, Chris Grant, Guy Landau, Chris Grant (for a
second time), Mark Pitman, Adrian Maguire, David Bridgwater, Richard Johnson
and Liam Cooper? They have all glimpsed Aintree glory after leading at the last or
early on the run-in in a Grand National, only for history to be snatched from their
grasp on the four-hundred-and-ninety-four-yard run from the final fence to the
winning post. The horses involved were Prince Regent (carrying 12-5 in the first
post-war National), First of The Dandies, Devon Loch (who famously came down
on the run-in in 1956), Carrickbeg, Purple Silk, Sandy Sprite, Crisp (caught by Red
Rum after being fifteen clear at the last), Sebastian V, Mr Snugfit, Young Driver,
Lean Ar Aghaidh, Durham Edition, Garrison Savannah (attempting to emulate
Golden Miller's still unique feat by adding the National to his same-season Gold
Cup win), Moorcroft Boy, Encore Un Peu, What's Up Boys and Clan Royal.

Clan Royal didn't look so much in command at the last as some of the others
mentioned, but his defeat aroused more controversy than most. A blunder five out
(where the rider lost his whip) and a failure to take the most direct route after the
last may have cost Clan Royal the race, but until misfortune overtook him the horse
was given a classic Aintree ride by stable jockey Cooper, who took only three
mounts all season for a trainer other than Jonjo O'Neill. Cooper, who has a record
of three wins and a second from six rides over the National fences, is a good
horseman and followed the adage 'Hunt round on the first circuit and ride a race on
the second.' Sticking close to the inner most of the way and collecting Clan Royal
splendidly after a mistake had the horse on his nose at first Becher's, Cooper spent
a good part of the second circuit trying to steady the exuberant Clan Royal after

Tote Becher Chase (Handicap), Aintree—Clan Royal edges out fellow course specialist
Amberleigh House (noseband) in a stirring dress rehearsal for the National

Mr J. P. McManus' "Clan Royal"

making ground in eye-catching style to join the leading group on the run down to second Becher's. Clan Royal was clear with Lord Atterbury and Hedgehunter from Becher's and the trio were still ten in front of eventual winner Amberleigh House crossing the Melling Road. Cooper sent Clan Royal for home in earnest after the second last, using the flat of his hand on his mount's rump to try to galvanise him. They led at the last by two and a half lengths from Lord Atterbury, with Hedge-hunter falling when looking held in third. But Clan Royal and Lord Atterbury were both desperately weary—Clan Royal's flashing tail a sign of his distress—and Clan Royal blundered his way through the fence. Exhausted and seemingly floundering, Clan Royal at first took the wrong line on the run-in, keeping straight instead of heading diagonally towards the elbow where the finishing rail passes the Chair. Cooper had to yank hard on the reins to get Clan Royal back on course, but the advantage had been lost and Lord Atterbury was level rounding the elbow. Clan Royal edged past Lord Atterbury again but had nothing left when Amberleigh House came at him inside the final furlong. Clan Royal went down by three lengths, prompting a debate about whether the extra yards travelled on the run-in, and the momentum lost, cost him the race. If Clan Royal was an unlucky loser, there was no hint of sourness from his trainer, who was the first to hug and congratulate Amber-leigh House's trainer on his fourth Grand National success. Clan Royal was one of four runners in the latest National carrying the McManus colours. By a quirk of fate, O'Neill rode three times for McCain in the National without success, in his days as a jockey. The owner, whose previous best in a National was third in 1992 with Laura's Beau, was also sporting in defeat, expressing the view that, if Clan Royal lost the National for any reason, it was by racing too freely, particularly early on the second circuit.

Back in November, when Clan Royal had last been seen out, he and Amberleigh House had met in the Tote Becher Chase over the National fences. The placings were the other way round, Clan Royal prevailing by a short head after he and Amberleigh House became locked in a rare battle from the second last, Cooper's efforts on this occasion earning him a two-day ban for excessive use of the whip. The Becher—in which the Chair was omitted because of the low sun—was Clan Royal's second win over the National fences, following his success in the Topham at the 2003 Grand National meeting. Clan Royal is described by his trainer as a 'big, awkward type that you wouldn't think was an Aintree horse' and has had plenty of problems jumping over conventional fences, but he scarcely put a foot wrong in the Topham or the Becher and seems to relish tackling the big, unusual fences. He reportedly returned from the National with a hind leg injury but, all being well, will be back at Aintree for another meeting with Amberleigh House in the Becher Chase before a second crack at the National. He is very much one for the shortlist.

Clan Royal (FR) (b.g. 1995)	Chef de Clan II (FR) (ch 1990)	Cyborg (ch 1982)	Arctic Tern
			Cadair
		Charabia (b 1976)	Bazin
			Kachabia
	Allee du Roy (FR) (b 1982)	Rex Magna (br 1974)	Right Royal V
			Chambre d'Amour
		Alliance (br 1965)	Alcide
			Synaldo

Clan Royal began his racing career in Ireland, developing into a fairly useful handicap chaser for Arthur Moore before being transferred to his present trainer before the 2002/3 season. He is French bred, from the first crop of the selle francais stallion Chef de Clan II, a winner four times in the French Provinces at around a mile and a half and a half-brother to the dam of top-class two-mile chaser Azertyuiop. Clan Royal's dam the unraced Allee du Roy has bred four other winners, Reine Lucia (by Northern Treat), Allee du Port (by Port Etienne)—both successful on the Flat and over hurdles—the fairly useful hurdler/chaser at around two miles Roboratif (by Robore), and Turgeon Royale (by Turgeon), fair over hurdles and fences. One of Allee du Roy's half-sisters is the dam of the smart chaser up to twenty-one furlongs Manhattan Castle and the useful French and American jumper Le Ronceray. Clan Royal's grandam Alliance was a half-sister to Irish Oaks runner-up Lastarria and Poule d'Essai des Pouliches runner-up Suvannee. Clan Royal acts on soft and good to firm going. As has already been said, his jumping away from Aintree has sometimes been less than fluent. *Jonjo O'Neill*

CLARENDON (IRE) 8 ch.g. Forest Wind (USA) – Sparkish (IRE) (Persian Bold) [2003/4 h113: 17g² c16gF Jun 21] sturdy gelding: fair hurdler at best: tended to jump right but still just in front when fell last in novice won by Idaho d'Ox at Newton Abbot on chasing debut: raced around 2m: acts on good to firm and heavy going: found little on reappearance. *P. J. Hobbs* — c87 h95

CLASSICAL BEN 6 ch.g. Most Welcome – Stoproveritate (Scorpio (FR)) [2003/4 F91: F16g³ F16d* 19g⁴ Feb 6] lengthy gelding: fairly useful form in bumpers, successful twice, including at Catterick in January: around 16 lengths fourth to easy winner Meggies Gamble in novice event here on hurdling debut, still going well when blundering 3 out: should do better. *R. A. Fahey* — h84 p F99

CLASSIC CALVADOS (FR) 5 b.g. Thatching – Mountain Stage (IRE) (Pennine Walk) [2003/4 16dpu 16g 17d⁴ Apr 10] modest maiden on Flat (should stay 1m) at 3 yrs for Mrs J. Ramsden: tongue tied, first form in 3 novice hurdles when fourth to easy winner Flownaway at Carlisle. *P. D. Niven* — h79

CLASSIC CAPERS 5 ch.g. Classic Cliche (IRE) – Jobiska (Dunbeath (USA)) [2003/4 F16s* F16s⁵ F17d⁴ Apr 18] 12,000 3-y-o: seventh foal: half-brother to several winners, including fairly useful sprinter Mile High (by Puissance): dam lightly-raced half-sister to useful miler Joligeneration: fairly useful form in bumpers, won at Ayr on debut in February. *J. M. Jefferson* — F99

CLASSIC CHINA 7 ch.m. Karinga Bay – Chanelle (The Parson) [2003/4 F88: 23m* 22vF 22d⁵ 24g⁶ 23s⁵ Apr 4] rather leggy mare: poor novice hurdler: won mares event at Lingfield in November: should stay 3m: tried in cheekpieces in bumpers. *J. W. Mullins* — h85

CLA

CLASSIC CONKERS (IRE) 10 b.g. Conquering Hero (USA) – Erck (Sun Prince) **h74**
[2003/4 h84: 20m 24m^F Jun 18] poor maiden hurdler: likely to stay 3m: acts on heavy going: amateur ridden. *Miss J. Feilden*

CLASSIC LASH (IRE) 8 b.g. Classic Cheer (IRE) – Khaiylasha (IRE) (Kahyasi) **c99**
[2003/4 c95, h81: c21s^3 c20m^4 c20m^2 c20g^F c20d^3 Jul 2] poor handicap hurdler: modest **h—**
handicap chaser: stays 3m: acts on firm and soft going: blinkered once (below form). *P. Needham*

CLASSIC LIN (FR) 4 gr.f. Linamix (FR) – Classic Storm (Belfort (FR)) [2003/4 **F—**
F16s Jan 10] leggy, sparely-made filly: fourth foal: dam, fair 5f/6f winner, out of smart middle-distance filly Lady Tamara: tailed off in bumper and 1½m event on Flat. *A. Berry*

CLASSIC NATIVE (IRE) 6 b. or br.g. Be My Native (USA) – Thats Irish (Furry **h110**
Glen) [2003/4 F116: 20d^2 20s^4 19g^6 24d^5 Mar 10] tall, good sort: smart bumper performer: only fair form over hurdles, including on handicap debut: will prove best at 3m+: strong-galloping sort. *Jonjo O'Neill*

CLASSIC QUARTET 4 b.f. Classic Cliche (IRE) – Carolside (Music Maestro) **h79**
[2003/4 16g^2 Sep 7] half-sister to winning 2m hurdler Otto E Mezzo (by Persian Bold): modest form on Flat: in cheekpieces, head second to Maunby Rocker in juvenile maiden at Uttoxeter on hurdling debut. *Mrs L. Williamson*

CLASSIC REVIVAL 6 ch.g. Elmaamul (USA) – Sweet Revival (Claude Monet **h—**
(USA)) [2003/4 F16m 19m^{pu} 20m^{pu} Nov 9] 500 3-y-o: brother to useful 2002 2-y-o 7.5f **F—**
winner Sweet Return, later Grade 1 1¼m winner in USA, and half-brother to fairly useful but inconsistent 6f (at 2 yrs) to 1¼m winner Sweet Reward (by Beveled): dam 1¼m winner: no form, including in points. *Mrs A. Price*

CLASSIC ROCK 5 b.g. Classic Cliche (IRE) – Ruby Vision (IRE) (Vision (USA)) **h73**
[2003/4 F74: 19m* 22g^{pu} Apr 4] lengthy gelding: poor form when winning 5-runner novice at Hereford (unseated and bolted before start) on hurdling debut in March: dropped right away in novice handicap next time: bred to stay beyond 19f. *J. W. Unett*

CLASSIC RUBY 4 b.f. Classic Cliche (IRE) – Burmese Ruby (Good Times (ITY)) **F—**
[2003/4 F16d Mar 10] 4,800 3-y-o: sixth foal: half-sister to 2½m chase winner Precious Island (by Jupiter Island): dam dual bumper winner: tenth of 19 in maiden bumper on debut. *M. R. Bosley*

CLASSIFY 5 b.g. Classic Cliche (IRE) – Slmaat (Sharpo) [2003/4 F91: 17s^F 18d^3 22g^5 **h108**
Apr 22] placed in bumpers: fair form in novice hurdles: should stay 2½m+. *P. F. Nicholls*

CLASSI MAUREEN 4 ch.f. Among Men (USA) – Hi-Hannah (Red Sunset) [2003/4 **h—**
17g 17g Apr 16] poor form over 6f at 2 yrs for J. M. Bradley: tailed off both starts over hurdles. *Mrs S. M. Johnson*

CLASS OF NINETYTWO (IRE) 15 b.g. Lancastrian – Lothian Lassie (Precipice **c—**
Wood) [2003/4 c99, h—: c24g^4 May 17] workmanlike gelding: fair pointer/hunter chaser, **h—**
tailed off at Bangor in May: stays 4¼m: acts on soft and good to firm going: has had tongue tied. *S. Wynne*

CLASSY CLARE 6 b.m. Nicholas Bill – Clare's Choice (Pragmatic) [2003/4 h—: **h—**
16m^{pu} Jun 1] no form. *J. M. Bradley*

CLASSY CLARENCE (IRE) 7 ch.g. Un Desperado (FR) – Winscarlet North (Gar- **h64**
land Knight) [2003/4 F—: 22s^5 22s 24g 22d^{pu} 26d Mar 28] sturdy gelding: poor maiden hurdler: tried blinkered. *C. Tinkler*

CLAUDE GREENGRASS 8 ch.g. Shalford (IRE) – Rainbow Brite (BEL) (Captain's **c91 p**
Treasure) [2003/4 h96: 17d* c18g 16d^{bd} 17d 16g^{bd} 16m^{pu} Apr 13] sturdy gelding: fair **h105**
handicap hurdler: won at Carlisle in November: never on terms when seventh of 11 in novice handicap at Newbury on chasing debut (should improve): raced mainly around 2m on good going or softer (acts on heavy): probably best in blinkers: not a fluent jumper. *Jonjo O'Neill*

CLAYDON CAVALIER 5 b.g. Regal Embers (IRE) – Marsdale (Royal Palace) **F—**
[2003/4 F16d Mar 28] second foal: dam of little account: well held in bumper on debut. *J. R. Jenkins*

CLAYLORD (IRE) 10 b.g. Lord Americo – Princess Seal (Prince Tenderfoot (USA)) **h—**
[2003/4 16g^{pu} Mar 10] sturdy gelding: little sign of ability, very lightly raced. *Mrs L. B. Normile*

CLAYMORE (IRE) 8 b.g. Broadsword (USA) – Mazza (Mazilier (USA)) [2003/4 **c133**
c132, h—: 19g* c20g^2 c19d^F 20v* 20g^2 21g 24g^{bd} 22g^5 Apr 16] leggy, lengthy gelding: **h137**

204

useful handicap chaser: good second to Redemption at Newbury, mistakes 3 out and last: running well when fell heavily 2 out at Chepstow next time: similar standard over hurdles, successful in handicaps at Exeter in November and Wetherby (beat Kivotos 1½ lengths) in January: effective at 2m to 3m: acts on heavy going: usually races prominently: reliable. *O. Sherwood*

CLAYPHENTO   6 b.m. Lyphento (USA) – Canny Member (New Member) [2003/4   **h–**
17g 17m^F 17g^{pu} Jun 3] sixth foal: dam unraced half-sister to fairly useful staying chaser Giddycan: no sign of ability: tried blinkered. *R. H. Alner*

CLEAR DAWN (IRE)   9 b.g. Clearly Bust – Cobra Queen (Dawn Review) [2003/4   **c102**
c102, h–: c24g c24g^4 c22d^3 c24m* c25s^{pu} c22v^{ur} c21s^3 Apr 12] well-made gelding: fair   **h–**
handicap chaser: back to best when winning at Musselburgh in December, making most: stays 3m: unraced on firm going, acts on any other: prone to odd mistake. *J. M. Jefferson*

CLEOPATRAS THERAPY (IRE)   7 b.g. Gone Fishin – Nec Precario (Krayyan)   **h88 ?**
[2003/4 F94: F16m^5 20s^{pu} 20v^{pu} 19g^4 20d^4 20d 24s Apr 17] leggy, good-topped gelding: **F–**
bumper winner: in frame twice over hurdles, though possibly flattered in steadily-run races and no form otherwise in 2003/4. *T. H. Caldwell*

CLETTWR GIRL (IRE)   6 gr.m. Roselier (FR) – Spring Bavard (Le Bavard (FR))   **F–**
[2003/4 F16m Jul 23] first foal: dam winning pointer: well behind in bumper on debut. *K. R. Pearce*

CLEVER THYNE (IRE)   7 b.g. Good Thyne (USA) – Clever Milly (Precipice   **c–**
Wood) [2003/4 c–p, h98: 26g* May 1] medium-sized gelding: fell only start over fences: **h99**
modest hurdler: won maiden at Hereford: stays 3¼m: raced on good going or softer: has had tongue tied. *H. D. Daly*

CLEYMOR HOUSE (IRE)   6 ch.g. Duky – Deise Lady (Le Bavard (FR)) [2003/4   **c59**
h–: 20d c21d^4 c21s^5 c20s c24g Mar 6] lengthy gelding: well held over hurdles: bad novice   **h–**
chaser: has looked hard ride. *John R. Upson*

CLICHY   4 b.f. Classic Cliche (IRE) – Kentucky Tears (USA) (Cougar (CHI)) [2003/4   **F82**
F16s^3 F16g F17v^6 Mar 21] ninth foal: half-sister to winning hurdler around 2m Noble Colours (by Distinctly North) and 2 winners on Flat: dam unraced: best effort in bumpers when third in mares event at Newcastle: sold 3,000 gns Doncaster May Sales. *M. Dods*

CLIFTON MIST   8 gr.m. Lyphento (USA) – Brave Maiden (Three Legs) [2003/4 h83:   **h87**
16g^4 19m^2 16g^3 19d^4 17s^4 24d^4 Feb 2] lengthy, angular mare: modest handicap hurdler: effective at 2m to 3m: acts on any going: often takes strong hold: consistent. *H. S. Howe*

CLINGSTONE   8 b.m. Henbit (USA) – Linen Leaf (Bold Owl) [2003/4 h84: c16g^4 **c89**
c16m^6 Nov 20] modest form over hurdles/fences, often runs as if amiss: bred to stay at   **h–**
least 2½m: acts on good to soft going. *T. R. George*

CLIQUEY   5 b.g. Muhtarram (USA) – Meet Again (Lomond (USA)) [2003/4 16m^3 **h88**
20g^{pu} 20g^2 19m^4 16s^4 16m* 16m^3 17d^{pu} 19g* 16g Apr 18] fair at best on Flat (stays 1m) at 3 yrs for J. Osborne: modest hurdler: won sellers at Leicester (for O. Sherwood, sold £3,100 Ascot December Sales) in November and Stratford (tongue tied, sold from B. Llewellyn 5,600 gns) in March: stays 19f: acts on good to firm going: effective blinkered or not. *R. H. Buckler*

CLODOALD (FR)   7 b.g. Beaudelaire (USA) – Mint Stick (FR) (Tropular) [2003/4   **c– §**
c–§, h106§: c20g^{pu} c17g^{pu} c22m^{pu} c21g c19m^5 22g Mar 28] leggy gelding: fair hurdler at   **h– §**
best: no form in 2003/4, including over fences: left M. Pipe before final start: stays 2½m: acts on good to firm and heavy going: often visored: usually tongue tied: ungenuine. *A. Crook*

CLONMEL'S MINELLA (IRE)   13 b.g. Strong Gale – Martones Chance (Golden   **c116**
Love) [2003/4 c105, h–: c25g^4 c25g^2 c20d^2 c22d^3 c20f^6 c22d^4 c19s^3 c24m^{su} Oct 12]   **h–**
medium-sized gelding: fairly useful chaser: broke leg at Limerick: probably stayed 4m, effective at much shorter: acted on any going: effective blinkered or not. *M. Hourigan, Ireland*

CLONROCHE VINYLS (IRE)   9 ch.m. Rashar (USA) – Clonroche Beggar (Pauper)   **h84**
[2003/4 h78: 20d^5 24s^2 24v^3 24d^F Dec 17] lengthy mare: bumper winner: poor maiden hurdler: stays 3m: raced on good going or softer (acts on heavy). *Ferdy Murphy*

CLOONE EXPRESS   5 ch.g. Polar Falcon (USA) – Simple Logic (Aragon) [2003/4   **h–**
16d^{pu} Mar 1] modest form on second of 3 starts on Flat at 2 yrs for N. Callaghan: breathing problem on hurdling debut (tongue tied). *Mrs L. C. Jewell*

CLOONE RIVER (IRE) 8 b. or br.g. Un Desperado (FR) – Grangemills (Strong **h121** Gale) [2003/4 h118: 16d² Jul 31] fairly useful on Flat (stays 1½m), successful in August and September: fairly useful hurdler: good ¾-length second to Sabadilla in 21-runner Guinness Galway Hurdle: best form at 2m: acts on firm and soft ground. *Paul Nolan, Ireland*

CLOONLOO ANNIE 5 ch.m. Be My Chief (USA) – Don't Be Late (Pollerton) **h–** [2003/4 F16g F16s 16vᵖᵘ Jan 21] fifth foal: dam, fairly useful chaser, stayed 3¼m: no **F–** show in bumpers/maiden hurdle. *M. Todhunter*

CLOTH OF GOLD 7 b.g. Barathea (IRE) – Bustinetta (Bustino) [2003/4 h120: 22s **h–** Apr 6] lightly raced on Flat (maiden) and over hurdles: fairly useful form when winning handicap at Newton Abbot in early-2002/3: always behind on far more testing ground on belated return: will stay 3m: acts on good to firm going. *Lady Herries*

CLOUDING OVER 4 gr.f. Cloudings (IRE) – Wellwotdouthink (Rymer) [2003/4 **F67** F16d⁶ F16s Apr 12] third foal: half-sister to bumper winner No Chance (by St Ninian): dam bumper/novice hurdle winner: poor form on first of 2 starts in mares bumpers. *Mrs M. Reveley*

CLOUDY BAY BOY 6 gr.g. Petoski – Smoke (Rusticaro (FR)) [2003/4 c16gᶠ Apr 3] **c–** fourth foal: dam poor 2m novice hurdler/1½m winner on Flat: won maiden point in 2003: weakening after helping force pace when falling 2 out in hunter chase at Hereford. *Mrs Caroline Bailey*

CLOUDY BAYS (IRE) 7 ch.g. Hubbly Bubbly (USA) – Bellteen (Beau Charm- **c150** eur (FR)) [2003/4 c110x, h89x, F–: c22s⁵ c20d c17f³ c18f⁵ c20v* c20f² c24gᵘʳ **h105** 20m⁴ c24d* c24s* c24d⁵ Feb 8]

Fourteen runs in 2002/3 brought two successes for Cloudy Bays, in a maiden hurdle at Wexford and a maiden chase at Listowel, and he appeared in *Chasers & Hurdlers 2002/03* with ratings of 110x over fences and 89x over hurdles. 'Often let down by his jumping' appeared to sum him up admirably. He hardly

Pierse Contracting Troytown Handicap Chase, Navan—
Cloudy Bays produces an impressive front-running performance

Pierse Leopardstown Handicap Chase—another all-the-way success off a much higher handicap mark

seemed a likely candidate for an essay one year on, let alone a horse that on his final start would line up for one of Ireland's top chases, the Hennessy at Leopardstown, given a fairly good chance by some and sent off at 6/1. Cloudy Bays was, in truth, taking a rather bigger step up in class than the market implied and he finished a remote fifth to Florida Pearl but, between the end of 2002/3 and his appearance in the Hennessy, Cloudy Bays improved out of all recognition, becoming a three-stone better horse over a period of seven months.

Cloudy Bays' improvement didn't begin immediately the new season opened. He had four outings in handicap chases before June was out and only once finished within ten lengths of the winner, when third to King Carew over seventeen furlongs at Cork. His next two runs showed the first signs of improvement, both in his form and his jumping, and he won the first of them, a handicap over two and a half miles on unseasonably heavy ground at Tipperary in July, the race already well won when he blundered two out. It wasn't, though, until his next appearance, in the Kerry National at Listowel and a first outing over fences at three miles, that Cloudy Bays really began to reveal his true colours. His tendency to error cost him once again, as he blundered and unseated his rider two out, but he had run his field ragged to that point, employing the catch-me-if-you-can tactics which would bring two major handicaps later in the season.

Cloudy Bays had a short break after Listowel, returning nearly two months later to run much his best race over hurdles. That proved an ideal prep for the Pierse Contracting Troytown Handicap Chase at Navan. The Troytown is one of Ireland's principal handicaps, named after the celebrated Irish chaser who won the 1919 Grand Steeple-Chase de Paris as a six-year-old, less than six months after his debut, and the 1920 Grand National, under 11-9 and reportedly very easily. Troytown didn't, though, get a chance to build on these achievements, as he broke a leg in a fall back at Auteuil in the summer. The Troytown Chase was first contested in 1937 and has been won by some famous horses over the years but it had never before attracted a field as large as nineteen, nor can it often have been won in such

207

devastating fashion as it was by Cloudy Bays. The eighteen others simply never saw him. He was twenty lengths clear in no time at all and that was where he stayed, those behind toiling in vain to close a long way from home. Cloudy Bays won by twenty-five lengths from Star Clipper. The runner-up wasn't seen out again but plenty of the others were and they did little to suggest the winner was anything other than much improved. In any case, Cloudy Bays confirmed it himself with another bold-jumping, pillar-to-post display, off a mark 16 lb higher, in the Pierse Leopardstown Chase in January. Eight took him on this time but they made as much of an impact as the eighteen had at Navan. Be My Belle got closest but Cloudy Bays was still fourteen lengths clear and looking well on top at the line.

Cloudy Bays (IRE) (ch.g. 1997)	Hubbly Bubbly (USA) (ch 1985)	Mr Prospector (b 1970)	Raise A Native
			Gold Digger
		Din (ro 1974)	Drone
			Durga
	Bellteen (ch 1986)	Beau Charmeur (b 1968)	Le Fabuleux
			Cymbale
		Coolteen (b 1962)	Vulgan
			Ding Dong Day

Cloudy Bays was spoken of as a possible for the National Hunt Handicap at Cheltenham but wasn't seen out after the Hennessy. His form is a bit short of the standard required for top conditions races, and big handicaps may continue to offer him his best opportunities. With a tendency to make the odd blunder, he possibly isn't an ideal candidate to emulate Troytown at Aintree. Cloudy Bays is though likely to stay beyond three miles, having seen the trip out well on soft going at Leopardstown. His stamina presumably comes from his dam, as his sire Hubbly Bubbly was a smart American sprinter. Cloudy Bays' unraced dam Bellteen is by the strong staying influence Beau Charmeur and there is plenty of stamina in her family as well. Cloudy Bays is her fourth foal, the three previous ones including the fair pointer Noluckmate (by Satco) and the maiden Wild Day (by Ikdam), who finished fifth in the 2002 Champion INH Flat at Punchestown. The grandam Coolteen produced two winners outside points, including the Midlands National second The Songwriter, and she is also the grandam of the Ulster National winner Teal Bridge. Cloudy Bays' third dam Ding Dong Day also features as the third dam of Pizarro. The rather leggy Cloudy Bays acts on any going, though may prove best on good or softer. He has had his tongue tied, though not in 2003/4, and, having worn blinkers on three starts from his final one in 2002/3, has worn cheekpieces subsequently, except when without any headgear at all at Listowel. *C. Byrnes, Ireland*

CLOUDY BLUES (IRE) 6 ro.g. Glacial Storm (USA) – Chataka Blues (IRE) **F—** (Sexton Blake) [2003/4 F16d Dec 29] 15,000 4-y-o: first foal: dam unraced: well beaten in bumper at Newbury on debut. *R. H. Buckler*

CLOUDY CREEK (IRE) 10 gr.g. Roselier (FR) – Jacob's Creek (IRE) (Buckskin **c73** (FR)) [2003/4 c110?, h—: c25d³ c24dᵖᵘ Mar 15] strong, well-made gelding: winning **h—** hurdler: novice steeplechaser, well held on completed start in hunters in 2003/4: should stay beyond 3m: acts on soft going. *Miss E. Leppard*

CLOUDY GREY (IRE) 7 gr.g. Roselier (FR) – Dear Limousin (Pollerton) **h138 p** [2003/4 F115: 16d* Jan 10]
Cloudy Grey was restricted to just one appearance over hurdles in 2003/4 but he made the most of it, showing useful form in winning a novice at Ascot on Victor Chandler day. He met with an injury soon after but, provided he makes a full recovery, seems sure to make up for lost time in 2004/5, and hopefully Iris's Gift won't be the only big grey making an impact in novice chases. Cloudy Grey created a good impression in bumpers in 2002/3, winning twice and finishing second to Cornish Rebel in the Grade 2 Challow Hurdle at Newbury in February. With connections keen to give the Champion Bumper a miss (his trainer feared the experience might be too much), it was nearly a year before Cloudy Grey was seen on the racecourse again. A setback in the autumn delayed Cloudy Grey's hurdling debut and, when he appeared at Ascot in January, he looked as if the race would do him good, a factor reflected in his drifting in the betting. Sent off third favourite in

a field in which a quartet had already shown fairly useful form, though the rest looked to have little going for them, Cloudy Grey set off in front and by the second last had only Le Passing posing a threat; belying his somewhat burly appearance, Cloudy Grey quickened readily before the final flight and won by six lengths from Le Passing with a further seven to the third Dangerously Good. The runner-up went on to finish second in a Grade 2 novice at Wetherby, the third won his next two and three others in the field that ran subsequently also did their bit to uphold the form. Cloudy Grey looked set to play a significant role in good novice events as the spring advanced but in February it was announced that he had fractured a fetlock in a racecourse gallop and would be out for the rest of the season. He subsequently had the fracture screwed. Cloudy Grey's pedigree was detailed in last year's Annual, though his year-younger sister Tap The Barrel has since shown a little ability in bumpers and over hurdles for Michael Hourigan in Ireland. Cloudy Grey is bred to stay three miles but is clearly anything but a one-paced sluggard. He has raced on good going or softer. *Miss E. C. Lavelle*

CLOUNTIES HILL (IRE)   7 b.g. Simply Great (FR) – Pass Thurn (Trimmingham)   **h120**
[2003/4 16s* 20s⁴ 19d⁵ 22d⁸ 22s⁴ 20d⁴ 22s 22sᶠ Mar 27] 13,000 4-y-o: big, rangy gelding: third foal: dam dual bumper winner: fairly useful novice hurdler: won at Galway (maiden) in July and Punchestown in November: later fourth in 2 Grade 3 events: better at 2½m/2¾m than shorter: raced on good to soft/soft going: was effective with/without cheekpieces/tongue strap: dead. *W. P. Mullins, Ireland*

CLOWNFISH   10 b.g. Silly Prices – Sea Sand (Sousa) [2003/4 c24gᵘʳ c22gᵖᵘ Nov 1]   **c–**
tall gelding: poor maiden chaser, no sign of retaining ability. *A. R. Dicken*   **h–**

CLUB ROYAL   7 b.g. Alflora (IRE) – Miss Club Royal (Avocat) [2003/4 h76: 21s*   **c75**
21sᵖᵘ c20g³ c20g⁴ c27mᵖᵘ 24gᵖᵘ c16d¹ c21sᵖᵘ c24fᵘʳ Feb 29] good-topped gelding: poor   **h78**
hurdler: won weak maiden at Sedgefield in May: similar form on completed starts over fences: bred to stay beyond 21f: acts on soft going: raced freely in blinkers final start. *D. McCain*

COACHMAN (IRE)   6 b.g. King's Ride – Royal Shares (IRE) (Royal Fountain)   **h–**
[2003/4 F–: 17d⁵ 20g 19g 25dᵖᵘ 17vᵖᵘ 17gᵇᵈ Apr 24] rather leggy gelding: no sign of ability. *A. J. Lockwood*

COASTGUARD (IRE)   10 b.g. Satco (FR) – Godlike (Godswalk (USA)) [2003/4   **c81 x**
c85x, h–: c21m⁴ 22m³ 22d c25g⁶ c20m⁵ c22gᵖᵘ 20vᵖᵘ Mar 21] compact gelding: modest   **h87**
handicap hurdler/chaser: left C. Mann and no form after third start: should stay beyond 3m: acts on good to firm and heavy going: wears blinkers/cheekpieces: sketchy jumper. *D. Pearson*

COBBET (CHR)   8 b.g. Favoured Nations (IRE) – Creace (CZE) (Sirano (CZE))   **c121**
[2003/4 c120, h–: c17m* c16g* c20m⁵ c17m⁴ c18g³ c16m⁴ Apr 15] leggy gelding: **h–**
winning hurdler: fairly useful chaser: easily landed odds in novices at Kelso in May and Perth (completing hat-trick) in June: creditable efforts all 4 starts back in handicaps: barely stays 21f: acts on firm and good to soft going: genuine and consistent. *T. R. George*

COBRECES   6 b.g. Environment Friend – Oleada (IRE) (Tirol) [2003/4 c120+, h112+:   **c112 §**
c19d⁵ c20g⁶ c24s c24m⁶ c20d² c24g⁵ Apr 1] tall, useful-looking gelding: winning   **h–**
hurdler: handicap chaser, generally disappointing in 2003/4: stays 2½m: unraced on firm going, acts on any other: blinkered last 3 starts, tongue tied last 2: one to treat with caution. *P. F. Nicholls*

COCKATOO RIDGE   7 ch.g. Riverwise (USA) – Came Cottage (Nearly A Hand)   **h98**
[2003/4 F90: 16d 19g 22d⁴ 24g⁴ 21g⁶ 22gᵖᵘ Apr 18] sturdy gelding: modest novice hurdler: stays 3m: acts on good to soft going (won bumper on firm). *N. R. Mitchell*

COCK OF THE ROOST (IRE)   7 b.g. Executive Perk – Sly Maid (Rapid River)   **c–**
[2003/4 h–, F–: 20mᵖᵘ 17m c16m⁴ c21gᵖᵘ c20mᵖᵘ c19mᵖᵘ c19gᵖᵘ Nov 4] lengthy gelding: **h–**
of little account: tried blinkered/tongue tied. *S. T. Lewis*

COCTAIL LADY (IRE)   4 ch.f. Piccolo – Last Ambition (IRE) (Cadeaux Genereux)   **h86**
[2003/4 16g* 16m⁶ 18fᵖᵘ 16m⁴ 16f⁶ 16m⁴ 16sᵖᵘ Dec 13] sparely-made filly: modest maiden on Flat (stays easy 7f) at 2 yrs, well held in 2003: modest juvenile hurdler: 100/1, won 14-runner event at Stratford in July: likely to need emphasis on speed at 2m: raced mainly on good going or firmer: tongue tied final start. *B. W. Duke*

CODE SIGN (USA)   5 b.g. Gulch (USA) – Karasavina (IRE) (Sadler's Wells (USA))   **h96**
[2003/4 h63+: 16m* 17m⁵ 16m² 18f³ 19mᵖᵘ Sep 10] leggy gelding: modest novice hurdler: improved form when winning handicap at Worcester in May: blinkered first time, lame final start: should stay beyond 2¼m: acts on firm going. *P. J. Hobbs*

CODY 5 ch.g. Zilzal (USA) – Ibtihaj (USA) (Raja Baba (USA)) [2003/4 h–: 16g 16d **h79**
17d⁴ 19d² 24s 16d⁴ 22sᶠ 17g⁶ 21gᶠ 16g 19d⁴ 24g² 22g 24dᵖᵘ Apr 21] close-coupled
gelding: poor maiden hurdler: stays 3m: acts on good to soft going: effective visored or
not: tried tongue tied. *G. A. Ham*

CODYS CASTLE 12 b.g. Ascendant – Hurricane Lizzie (Kalimnos) [2003/4 c16g **c–**
Mar 12] ex-Irish gelding: little sign of ability, including in points: tried blinkered. *Mrs* **h–**
E. M. Collinson

COERCION (IRE) 6 b.g. Ilium – Nicholas Ferry (Floriferous) [2003/4 F16d F17d **h–**
F16s 17d Apr 18] seventh foal: brother to fairly useful chaser Scotmail Lad and fair **F–**
hurdler Sea Ferry, both effective up to 3m: dam ran in 3 Irish points: no form in bumpers
or novice hurdle. *R. F. Fisher*

COLCA CANYON (IRE) 7 b.g. Un Desperado (FR) – Golden Flats (Sonnen Gold) **c137**
[2003/4 F16g* 16m* 16g* c16f² c19m* c16sᵘʳ c21m² c17d³ c16g⁵ c17d² Apr 11] big, **h113 p**
lengthy gelding: brother to fair 2m hurdle winner Come Alive and a thoroughly tempera- **F96**
mental maiden hurdler and half-brother to winning 2m to 2½m hurdler Coast Along (by
Satco): dam modest sprinter: successful first 3 starts in 2003/4, in bumper at Ballinrobe,
maiden hurdle at Navan and novice hurdle at Limerick, all in July: improved good deal
further when switched to fences, winning maiden at Listowel in September: useful efforts
when third to Kicking King in Grade 1 novice at Leopardstown and length second to
Fadoudal du Cochet in valuable handicap at Fairyhouse: in narrow lead when fell 2 out in
another Grade 1 novice at Punchestown in late-April: best around 2m: acts on soft and
good to firm going. *Mrs J. Harrington, Ireland*

COLCA'S DATE 5 br.m. Sovereign Water (FR) – Rabdanna (Rabdan) [2003/4 F16s **h–**
16g Mar 17] small mare: second foal: dam lightly-raced half-sister to high-class hurdler **F–**
Floyd: well beaten in bumper and maiden hurdle. *J. Gallagher*

Mr Philip F. Myerscough's "Colca Canyon"

COLD CLASS (IRE) 11 b.g. Glacial Storm (USA) – Cameo Class (Roi Guillaume h–
(FR)) [2003/4 24m 21g^pu Jul 4] lightly-raced novice hurdler: no form in handicaps in
2003/4: should stay 3m. *Miss A. M. Newton-Smith*

COLD COMFORT 12 b.g. Arctic Lord – Main Brand (Main Reef) [2003/4 h–x: h– x
16m^pu Jun 28] error-prone novice hurdler, very lightly raced. *I. R. Brown*

COLD ENCOUNTER (IRE) 9 ch.g. Polar Falcon (USA) – Scene Galante (FR) c92 d
(Sicyos (USA)) [2003/4 c21m^5 24m c28f^pu c24g* c24m* c26g* c25d^2 c24s^pu c25d^4 h63
c24s^pu c26g Apr 22] lengthy, angular gelding: maiden hurdler: modest handicap chaser:
made all at Bangor in October and in small fields at Kempton and Fontwell in November:
out of form after: stays 3¼m: acts on firm and good to soft going: tried blinkered/visored.
R. M. Stronge

COLEHAM 6 b.m. Saddlers' Hall (IRE) – Katie Scarlett (Lochnager) [2003/4 F91: F–
F17d May 17] fair bumper winner: off 11 months before soundly beaten only run in
2003/4: has wandered under pressure. *W. M. Brisbourne*

COLESHILL LAD 4 br.g. Wizard King – Hallowed Ground (IRE) (Godswalk (USA)) h–
[2003/4 F12s 16g 16s^5 17s 16s^pu Mar 15] medium-sized gelding: first foal: dam, modest F–
sprint maiden, half-sister to smart 2m to 2½m hurdler Bank View: more sign of temperament than ability: left M. Scudamore after fourth start. *J. Joseph*

COLLECTIVE DREAM 9 b.g. North Col – Toumanova (High Line) [2003/4 h–: h– x
27s^pu 21s 20d^pu 16s^F 19d^F Mar 11] deep-girthed gelding: no form over hurdles: makes
mistakes. *R. Curtis*

COLLEGE CITY (IRE) 5 b.g. College Chapel – Polish Crack (IRE) (Polish Patriot h68
(USA)) [2003/4 h78: 16d^6 16m 16m Sep 14] poor hurdler: stays 19f: acts on soft going:
tried in cheekpieces. *R. C. Guest*

COLLEGE CRACKER 6 b.m. Environment Friend – Primo Panache (Primo F–
Dominie) [2003/4 F16d F16s Dec 26] first foal: dam no form: well beaten in 2 bumpers.
J. F. Coupland

COLLIER COUNTY (IRE) 9 ch.g. Be My Native (USA) – Deep Kitty (IRE) (Deep h118
Run) [2003/4 17s^4 19s* 22s* Feb 5] fairly useful hurdler, very lightly raced: successful in
maiden at Naas in January and novice at Clonmel (stayed on well to beat Like A Bee 2
lengths) in February: likely to stay 3m: raced on going softer than good. *E. J. O'Grady,
Ireland*

COLLIER HILL 6 ch.g. Dr Devious (IRE) – Polar Queen (Polish Precedent (USA)) h114
[2003/4 16d^h 16d^2 16g^3 18g^6 Mar 6] sturdy gelding: useful on Flat (stays easy 2m): won
maiden at Kelso on hurdling debut in December: failed to progress: should stay beyond
2m. *G. A. Swinbank*

COLLIERS COURT 7 b.g. Puget (USA) – Rag Time Belle (Raga Navarro (ITY)) h–
[2003/4 F74: 20s^pu Apr 17] poor form on first of 3 starts in bumpers in 2002/3: pulled
much too hard in novice hurdle. *Mrs L. Williamson*

COLLIERS QUAY (IRE) 8 b.g. Warcraft (USA) – Francois's Crumpet (IRE) (Strong h–
Gale) [2003/4 h106, F–: 22s^pu Apr 6] fair hurdler: off 15 months, no show in handicap
only start in 2003/4: stays 3¼m: acts on soft and good to firm going: has had tongue tied.
Miss Venetia Williams

COLNEL RAYBURN (IRE) 8 b.g. Un Desperado (FR) – Super Boreen (Boreen c123 +
(FR)) [2003/4 h114: c20d^4 c20s* c24d^5 c20s^4 c20d^4 c24s* c29d^F Apr 12] tall gelding: h–
fair hurdler: fairly useful novice chaser: won at Navan in December and March (quite
valuable handicap, beat Rose Perk 3 lengths): in cheekpieces, still travelling strongly
when falling fourteenth in Irish Grand National at Fairyhouse: likely to stay beyond 3m:
acts well on soft/heavy going: held up: has his quirks. *Paul Nolan, Ireland*

COLNE VALLEY AMY 7 b.m. Mizoram (USA) – Panchellita (USA) (Pancho Villa h–
(USA)) [2003/4 17s^pu 16d 16s^6 Mar 15] poor on Flat (stays 1¼m): little show in novice
hurdles: joined Mrs S. Smith. *G. L. Moore*

COLNSIDE BROOK 5 br.m. Sovereign Water (FR) – Armagnac Messenger (Pony h89 p
Express) [2003/4 F16m^2 20s 22g^4 Apr 18] quite good-topped mare: sixth foal: half-sister F85
to winning 2m hurdler Colnside Bonnie (by Afzal) and 2 winning pointers: dam winning
pointer: neck second to Zaffre in mares bumper at Warwick on debut: not knocked about
in 2 novice hurdles, much better effort when fourth to El Vaquero at Wincanton: should
improve again. *B. G. Powell*

COLOMBIAN GREEN (IRE) 10 b.g. Sadler's Wells (USA) – Sharaya (USA) c80 §
(Youth (USA)) [2003/4 c107§, h114§: c16m c19d^4 c25g^4 Apr 4] useful-looking gelding: h– §

fair handicap hurdler: largely disappointing over fences: left D. Gandolfo after second start, in frame in point and novice hunter subsequently: stays easy 21f: raced mainly on good going or softer (acts on heavy): often weak finisher and not one to trust. *P. Greenwood*

COLONEL BLAZER 12 b.g. Jupiter Island – Glen Dancer (Furry Glen) [2003/4 c25d[pu] Feb 15] sparely-made gelding: fair pointer nowadays: showed little on hunter chase debut: probably stays 27f: acts on firm and good to soft going: usually blinkered/in cheekpieces: not to be trusted. *Miss Elaine Bywater* — c– § h–

COLONEL BRADLEY (IRE) 10 b.g. Un Desperado (FR) – Dora Frost (Stradavinsky) [2003/4 c20d* c20g* c20f* c24g⁴ c29d[pu] Apr 12] tall gelding: fair handicap hurdler: much improved chaser in 2003/4, won maiden at Wexford in July and handicaps at Tipperary (idled) and Tralee in August: off 7 months, let down by jumping in valuable handicaps at Fairyhouse and Punchestown in April: should stay 3m: acts on firm and good to soft going. *C. F. Swan, Ireland* — c114 h–

COLONEL BRAXTON (IRE) 9 b.g. Buckskin (FR) – Light The Lamp (Miner's Lamp) [2003/4 c156, h–: c24d⁴ Dec 28] well-made gelding: very smart chaser in 2002/3: ran as if race was needed when respectable fourth to Best Mate in Grade 1 at Leopardstown only outing in 2003/4: successful around 2m, should stay 3¼m: raced on good going or softer (acts on heavy): usually races up with pace. *D. T. Hughes, Ireland* — c149 h–

COLONEL BROWN (IRE) 8 b.g. Scenic – Musical Smoke (IRE) (Orchestra) [2003/4 c–, h–: c16g[F] 20g 16m Jun 18] sturdy gelding: winning chaser: of little account nowadays: tried blinkered: sometimes tongue tied. *A. G. Hobbs* — c– h–

COLONEL FRANK 7 b.g. Toulon – Fit For Firing (FR) (In Fijar (USA)) [2003/4 h113p, F90: 19g⁵ c24m² c20v* Jan 12] useful-looking gelding: fair hurdler: encouraging start over fences when beaten a neck by Ballycassidy in match for novice at Newbury: simple task in 3-runner maiden at Fontwell month later, again jumping well: stays 3m: unraced on firm going, acts on any other: often front runner. *B. G. Powell* — c128 h–

COLONEL KURTZ (USA) 6 b.g. Slip Anchor – Rustaka (USA) (Riverman (USA)) [2003/4 h–: 26g[pu] May 1] poor maiden on Flat: pulled up both starts over hurdles. *J. S. King* — h–

COLONIAL RULE (USA) 7 b.g. Pleasant Colony (USA) – Musicale (USA) (The Minstrel (CAN)) [2003/4 h83§: 22g⁶ 24d⁴ c20m⁶ 20v⁴ Jan 10] close-coupled gelding: poor hurdler: soon dropped himself out on chasing debut: stays 3¼m: acts on heavy going: tried blinkered/visored: has had tongue tied: moody. *Mrs L. B. Normile* — c– § h74 §

COLONIAL SUNSET (IRE) 10 b.g. Lancastrian – Thai Nang (Tap On Wood) [2003/4 c103, h70: c23m[pu] c26s² c17v³ Nov 23] rather sparely-made gelding: winning hurdler: fair novice chaser in 2002/3 for Dr P. Pritchard: out of sorts in 2003/4: stays 21f: acts on heavy going: tried blinkered/in cheekpieces: has had tongue tied. *A. J. Whiting* — c– h–

COLONNADE 5 b.m. Blushing Flame (USA) – White Palace (Shirley Heights) [2003/4 20g⁴ 16d Dec 1] modest maiden on Flat (stays 2m): poor form in 2 maiden hurdles. *C. Grant* — h77

COLORADO FALLS (IRE) 6 b.g. Nashwan (USA) – Ballet Shoes (IRE) (Ela-Mana-Mou) [2003/4 h103: 16s³ 18v⁵ 17d² Feb 23] leggy gelding: fairly useful on Flat (probably stays 15f): fair handicap hurdler: should stay beyond 17f: acts on soft ground. *P. Monteith* — h111

COLOURFUL LIFE (IRE) 8 ch.g. Rainbows For Life (CAN) – Rasmara (Kalaglow) [2003/4 c–x, h121: 16m 20d 20s 20d⁵ 20g³ 20g⁴ 24m² Apr 15] big, lengthy gelding: fairly useful handicap hurdler: at least respectable efforts all starts in 2003/4, fourth of 23 to Zibeline in listed race at Aintree and second to Wintertide at Cheltenham on last 2: stays 3m: acts on good to firm and heavy going: tried in cheekpieces: usually held up, and tends to carry head awkwardly under pressure: consistent. *Mrs M. Reveley* — c– x h118

COLQUHOUN 10 b.g. Rakaposhi King – Red Rambler (Rymer) [2003/4 c103, h–: c21g³ c21g³ c21g² c20m² c20m³ Aug 1] good-topped gelding: winning hurdler: fair maiden steeplechaser: won point in March for D. Pipe: possibly best short of 3m: acts on good to soft and good to firm going: often let down by jumping over fences. *T. R. George* — c101 x h–

COLTMINATOR 4 b.c. Robellino (USA) – Darshay (FR) (Darshaan) [2003/4 16d³ 16g⁶ 16s³ 16v Apr 7] won over 7f (at 2 yrs) from 7 starts on Flat in Germany: poor form over hurdles. *Frau E. Mader, Germany* — h78

COLUMBA (IRE) 8 b.g. Lord Americo – Jackson Miss (Condorcet (FR)) [2003/4 h125: 16d⁴ 20m² 16d⁴ 17f 16s 16d⁴ 16s 20d⁶ 20d[F] Feb 28] angular gelding: fairly useful — h123 hurdler: best effort in 2003/4 when fourth to Sabadilla in Galway Hurdle (Handicap) third start: stays 2½m: acts on heavy going: tried blinkered. *D. T. Hughes, Ireland*

COLUMBUS (IRE) 7 b.g. Sadler's Wells (USA) – Northern Script (USA) (Arts And Letters (USA)) [2003/4 h110: 24d² 25g^pu 24d⁵ 25d⁵ 25g² 23g 27d³ Apr 23] angular gelding: fairly useful handicap hurdler: stays 27f: acts on firm and soft going: blinkered/visored: often looks none too keen, but is consistent. *Mrs J. Candlish*   **h117**

COLVADA 8 b.m. North Col – Prevada (Soldier Rose) [2003/4 c–, h–: 21s 22s^pu 21g Mar 17] useful-looking mare: little form over jumps. *Ian Williams*   **c– h–**

COLWAY RITZ 10 b.g. Rudimentary (USA) – Million Heiress (Auction Ring (USA)) [2003/4 20d² Nov 14] lengthy, angular gelding: fair on Flat (stays 1¾m): lightly raced over hurdles, second in handicap at Newcastle only start in 2003/4: stays 2½m, at least as effective at 2m. *W. Storey*   **h83**

COMANCHE WAR PAINT (IRE) 7 b.g. Commanche Run – Galeshula (Strong Gale) [2003/4 c–, h87: 26g⁵ c25m* c23m* c25f² c25f* c25d² c27s⁴ c30g² Mar 9] has reportedly been pinfired: modest form over hurdles: fairly useful chaser: won novices in small fields at Wincanton in May and Worcester in June and handicap at former course in November: stays 3¾m: probably acts on any going. *P. F. Nicholls*   **c121 h92**

COMBE CASTLE 9 gr.g. Carlingford Castle – Silver Cirrus (General Ironside) [2003/4 c–, h–: c24m^pu c21d^ur 24v² 24v^pu 24s^pu 26g Mar 17] lengthy gelding: left K. Bailey and off 7 months after reappearance: sign of ability only when second of 5 finishers in novice hurdle at Towcester in January, making most: tried blinkered/in cheekpieces: sketchy jumper of fences. *N. B. King*   **c– h83 ?**

COMBINED VENTURE (IRE) 8 b.h. Dolphin Street (FR) – Centinela (Caerleon (USA)) [2003/4 h–: 17m c16m⁶ c16m² c20m⁵ c17d^f⁶ Aug 11] sparely-made horse: little form over hurdles: poor novice chaser: form only around 2m: acts on good to firm and good to soft going: has had tongue tied. *P. T. Dalton*   **c69 h–**

COME BYE (IRE) 8 b.g. Star Quest – Boreen Dubh (Boreen (FR)) [2003/4 F18d³ F20v³ F16g⁴ 21v^bd 21d 22s^pu 18s² 17d 17d 21d Mar 28] ex-Irish gelding: third foal: dam placed in points: won maiden point in 2003: fair form in bumpers for W. J. Burke: poor maiden hurdler: stays 2¾m: visored last 2 starts: tongue tied in Britain. *Miss A. M. Newton-Smith*   **h76 F86**

COME IN MOSCOW (IRE) 8 ch.m. Over The River (FR) – Kiria Mou (USA) (To-Agori-Mou) [2003/4 c109, h–: c20g⁵ c20d^pu c22s⁶ 20m⁵ c24d^f c24d 20s⁵ 22d c20d* c24s³ c20d* Apr 10] lengthy, angular mare: modest hurdler: fair chaser: won handicaps at Limerick in February and Cork in April: very stiff task in Grade 1 at Punchestown later in April: stays 3m, effective at much shorter: acts on heavy and good to firm ground. *John Joseph Murphy, Ireland*   **c112 h89**

COME ON BOY 10 ch.g. Henbit (USA) – Miss Rewarde (Andy Rew) [2003/4 c–: c20g^pu c16g^pu Apr 3] maiden pointer: tried blinkered. *Mark Doyle*   **c–**

COME ON GEORGE (IRE) 8 b.g. Barathea (IRE) – Lacovia (USA) (Majestic Light (USA)) [2003/4 c–, h–: c25d^pu Mar 22] angular gelding: no form outside points: makes mistakes. *S. E. H. Sherwood*   **c– x h–**

COMETE DU LAC (FR) 7 b.m. Comte du Bourg (FR) – Line du Nord (FR) (Esprit du Nord (USA)) [2003/4 c120§, h–§: 17g 17g 19m^pu 16g⁵ 21s^pu 19s 16s* 16g 16d 16s^pu Apr 21] leggy mare: winning hurdler/chaser in France: easily best effort in Britain (left M. Hammond after third outing) when winning mares handicap hurdle at Chepstow in January: stays 21f: acts on any going: usually blinkered/visored: unreliable. *Mrs N. Macauley*   **c– § h78 §**

COME THE DAWN 8 b.m. Gunner B – Herald The Dawn (Dubassoff (USA)) [2003/4 19g^pu Apr 3] close-coupled mare: modest form on first of 2 starts in bumpers in 2001/2 for Mrs H. Dalton: lame in maiden hurdle on return. *M. Sheppard*   **h–**

COMFORTABLE CALL 6 ch.g. Nashwan (USA) – High Standard (Kris) [2003/4 h69: 16g⁴ 19g² 20m² 20s* 21g Apr 12] lengthy gelding: poor handicap hurdler: off 9 months, won conditional jockeys seller at Newcastle in March: stays 2½m: acts on soft and good to firm going: tongue tied: often makes mistakes. *H. Alexander*   **h75**

COMMANCHE COURT (IRE) 11 ch.g. Commanche Run – Sorceress (FR) (Fabulous Dancer (USA)) [2003/4 c163, h129: 24g⁵ 24d⁶ c16v c25d^pu Feb 21] lengthy, good sort: one-time very smart hurdler/top-class chaser: well below best in 2003/4: best at 3m+ on good going or softer (acts on heavy): usually held up: usually sound jumper (lost chance with bad mistake when blinkered final outing). *T. M. Walsh, Ireland*   **c– h129**

COM

COMMANCHE GENERAL (IRE) 7 b.g. Commanche Run – Shannon Amber **h–**
(IRE) (Phardante (FR)) [2003/4 h84, F91: 23m^{pu} Nov 11] lengthy, angular gelding: poor
hurdler: jumped badly until start in 2003/4: probably stays 3m: acts on good to soft going,
not discredited on good to firm. *J. F. Panvert*

COMMANCHE HERO (IRE) 11 ch.g. Cardinal Flower – Fair Bavard (Le Bavard **c103**
(FR)) [2003/4 c88, h81: c25g^2 c25g^2 24m^2 c24m* c24g* c25g^5 24m^3 c30s^2 c32g c22d^3 **h90**
Apr 7] workmanlike gelding: modest maiden hurdler: fair handicap chaser: won at Huntingdon in September and Bangor in October: stays 3¾m: acts on heavy and good to firm
going: has found little. *R. J. Price*

COMMANCHE JIM (IRE) 8 b.g. Commanche Run – On A Dream (Balinger) **c113**
[2003/4 c106, h–: c26g^3 c29m^2 c25d^{pu} c27s^5 c26v^3 c29d^6 c26g^4 Apr 10] sturdy gelding: **h–**
winning hurdler: fair handicap chaser: should stay beyond 3¼m: acts on heavy going:
often less than fluent over hurdles but better jumper of fences: lazy: none too consistent.
R. H. Alner

COMMANCHE QUEST (IRE) 8 b.g. Commanche Run – Conna Dodger (IRE) **c101**
(Kemal (FR)) [2003/4 c103, h94: c25d* 24d^2 c25d^3 c25d^4 c25s^2 Jan 16] lengthy gelding: **h96**
modest maiden hurdler: fair chaser: won novice at Hexham in May: stays 25f: acts on
soft going: ran poorly only try in blinkers: sometimes let down by jumping over fences.
Mrs M. Reveley

COMMANCHE SPIRIT (IRE) 10 b.g. Commanche Run – Emmett's Lass (Deep **c–**
Run) [2003/4 c27d^{pu} Mar 16] lengthy gelding: no form in steeplechases. *Mrs Sue Bell*

COMMANCHE SUMMER 10 b.m. Commanche Run – Royal Typhoon (Royal **c– §**
Fountain) [2003/4 c68, h75: 22g^4 24m^2 27g^4 Jun 3] leggy mare: poor maiden hurdler/ **h84 §**
chaser: stays 27f: acts on good to firm and heavy going: not one to trust. *J. D. Frost*

COMMANCHE WIND (IRE) 9 b.g. Commanche Run – Delko (Decent Fellow) **h–**
[2003/4 h99: 22g^5 19g^F 20g^6 Aug 16] lengthy gelding: modest handicap hurdler: below
form in 2003/4: stays 21f: acts on good to firm and good to soft going: tends to jump right.
E. W. Tuer

COMMERCIAL FLYER (IRE) 5 ch.g. Carroll House – Shabra Princess (Buckskin **h96**
(FR)) [2003/4 20s^4 19v^2 16g Feb 11] €25,000 3-y-o: lengthy, angular gelding: fifth
foal: half-brother to smart hurdler/promising chaser up to 3m Our Vic (by Old Vic): dam
maiden chaser: favourite, shaped well when fourth in novice hurdle at Chepstow on
debut, failed to progress. *M. C. Pipe*

COMMONCHERO (IRE) 7 b.g. Desert of Wind (USA) – Douala (GER) (Pentath- **c121**
lon) [2003/4 h109, F104: 16f^2 16d^2 16s* c16d^4 c16s* c17d Jan 25] sparely-made gelding: **h121**
fairly useful hurdler: won handicap at Fairyhouse (tongue tied) in November by ½ length
from Puck Out: badly hampered on chasing debut, readily won maiden at Punchestown
in December: stiff tasks in Grade 1 events at Leopardstown and Punchestown (second of
4 finishers to Say Again) subsequently: raced around 2m: acts on firm and soft going.
M. J. P. O'Brien, Ireland

COMMON GIRL (IRE) 6 gr.m. Roselier (FR) – Rumups Debut (IRE) (Good Thyne **F76**
(USA)) [2003/4 F85: F16s F16g^4 Mar 17] workmanlike mare: in frame twice from 4
starts in bumpers. *O. Brennan*

COMMONWEALTH (IRE) 8 b.g. Common Grounds – Silver Slipper (Indian **h84**
Ridge) [2003/4 17g^4 17d^5 Feb 15] rather sparely-made gelding: one-time fair hurdler:
left K. Morgan/off 18 months, poor form both starts in 2003/4: raced around 2m: acts
on good to firm and good to soft going: usually tongue tied: usually races prominently.
Mrs J. Candlish

COMMON WORLD (USA) 5 ch.h. Spinning World (USA) – Spenderella (FR) **h115**
(Common Grounds) [2003/4 16g^2 16d^5 Apr 12] compact horse: smart at best on Flat
(stays 1¼m) for G. Butler: length second to Nopekan in minor event at Leopardstown on
hurdling debut: better effort subsequently when tenth of 13 to Brave Inca in Grade 1
novice at Punchestown in late-April. *N. Meade, Ireland*

COMPADRE 6 gr.g. Environment Friend – Cardinal Press (Sharrood (USA)) [2003/4 **c88**
h–: 16d^5 16g^4 16m^4 c16d^3 c16g^3 c16d^3 c16g^5 Feb 18] tall gelding: poor form over **h80**
hurdles: modest form over fences: likely to prove best at 2m: acts on good to firm and
good to soft going. *P. Beaumont*

COMPANION 6 b.m. Most Welcome – Benazir (High Top) [2003/4 17s^{pu} Dec 16] **h– §**
sturdy mare: sister to poor hurdler Escort, stays 3m: modest on all-weather Flat (barely
stays 1½m) for Julian Poulton: withdrawn after unruly at start on intended hurdling debut
and showed more temperament than ability in novice at Folkestone (wore cheekpieces).
T. D. McCarthy

214

COMPLETE OUTSIDER 6 b.g. Opera Ghost – Alice Passthorn (Rapid Pass) **h–**
[2003/4 F17f* F16m³ 24g^ur 16d Mar 21] second foal: dam no sign of ability: fair form in **F92**
bumpers, won at Exeter in October: veered left and unseated fifth in novice on hurdling
debut: well held in similar event later in month. *Nick Williams*

COMPLY OR DIE (IRE) 5 b.g. Old Vic – Madam Madcap (Furry Glen) [2003/4 **h143**
16m* 21m* 20g² 25s* 21g⁴ Mar 17]
  Runners in the latest renewal of the Royal & SunAlliance Novices' Hurdle
will have to go some to match the exploits of those that took part in the 2003
running. The winner Hardy Eustace landed the Champion Hurdle in the latest
season while Foreman won the AIG Europe Champion Hurdle, Puntal the Betfred
Gold Cup and Pizarro, Nil Desperandum and Hi Cloy were all successful in
Grade 1 novice events over fences. Throw in Lord Sam, Sh Boom, Calling Brave
and Mossy Green and it's clear the race more than served its purpose as both a
championship event for novice hurdlers and a testing ground for future stars. The
2003 SunAlliance Hurdle was the most strongly contested race of its type all season
and the 2004 version has fair claims to be the same, so close attention should be
paid to those that figured prominently. One runner with every chance of making an
impact in novice chases in 2004/5 is Comply Or Die, who finished an excellent
fourth, beaten under five lengths, behind Fundamentalist at Cheltenham, sticking to
his task really well after coming off the bridle at halfway. Comply Or Die started at
33/1, though his odds reflected as much his position as the stable's second string

Mr D. A. Johnson's "Comply Or Die"

than his chance on form. He had won three of four previous starts over hurdles, novices at Chepstow, Plumpton and Cheltenham between October and December. In the Grade 2 Bristol Novices' Hurdle at Cheltenham Comply Or Die looked well served by the step up to three miles and stayed on gradually to get the better of Phar From Frosty over the last three flights, winning in resolute fashion by three lengths. A blunder two out had cost him his chance on his previous start, when favourite in another Grade 2 novice, at Chepstow, but his jumping was hard to fault on either start at Cheltenham.

Comply Or Die is a non-thoroughbred gelding, by Old Vic and the third foal and first winner out of the unraced Madam Madcap, who herself is a half-sister to the dam of the useful chaser at up to twenty-five furlongs Midland Flame. Comply Or Die shares his third dam Lady Flame with the smart hurdler Flame Creek. Flame Creek was less than convincing over fences early in 2003/4, despite winning all three starts in novice chases, but Comply Or Die can be expected to make a much better fist of things. He has the scope for it, being a tall gelding, if at present rather unfurnished, and it will be no surprise if he is back to claim more of the sponsors' money in the Royal & SunAlliance Chase at the 2005 Festival. Comply Or Die has raced mainly on good/good to firm going, though it was soft when he won at Cheltenham. *M. C. Pipe*

COMPOSTELLO (IRE)   9 ch.g. Erins Isle – Your Mine (Push On) [2003/4 h113: c24f³ c18m* c17mᶠ c16d⁴ c19d⁶ c21g² c16dᵘʳ Mar 7] workmanlike gelding: fair hurdler: fairly useful chaser: easily won maiden at Fairyhouse in October: second to Hi Cloy in novice at Leopardstown in February: stays 21f: acts on good to firm and good to soft going: successful only start in blinkers. *N. Meade, Ireland*   **c118 h–**

COMPTON AVIATOR   8 ch.g. First Trump – Rifada (Ela-Mana-Mou) [2003/4 16m⁵ Oct 22] half-brother to smart hurdler/fairly useful maiden chaser Tiger Groom (by Arazi), stays 2½m, and useful hurdler Rifawan (by Cox's Ridge), stayed 2½m: fair on Flat (stays 1½m): tongue tied, not knocked about as he was left behind when fifth in novice at Chepstow on hurdling debut. *A. W. Carroll*   **h–**

COMPTON CHICK (IRE)   6 b.m. Dolphin Street (FR) – Cecina (Welsh Saint) [2003/4 h97: c20m* c25m⁴ c20m² c26gᵘʳ 22m³ c20m* c23g⁵ c26f³ c25m² c22g⁴ c25m³ c25fᵖᵘ Nov 8] poor maiden hurdler: modest novice chaser: won at Ludlow (mares event) in May and Worcester (handicap) in August: stays easy 3¼m: acts on firm and soft going: wears headgear: tongue tied: hard ride. *J. W. Mullins*   **c90 h79**

COMPTON COMMANDER   6 ch.g. Barathea (IRE) – Triode (USA) (Sharpen Up) [2003/4 16m 16m 16d 16d⁶ 16g⁶ 21d⁴ Apr 8] quite good-topped gelding: fairly useful but ungenuine on Flat (stays 1¾m): only modest form over hurdles: stays 21f: yet to race on extremes of going: visored fifth start: not a straightforward ride. *Ian Williams*   **h87**

COMTE DE CHAMBORD   8 gr.g. Baron Blakeney – Show Rose (Coliseum) [2003/4 20g³ 21m 19g⁶ 16d c20vᵘʳ c21dᵘʳ c20v⁶ Mar 21] medium-sized gelding: modest form at best in bumpers: no form over hurdles or fences (twice unseated). *A. M. Campion*   **c– x h–**

CONCHITA   7 b.m. St Ninian – Carnetto (Le Coq d'Or) [2003/4 F95+: F16d* Apr 28] successful at Hexham twice from 4 starts in bumpers, won easily very early in season. *G. A. Harker*   **F95 +**

CONDOYLE (IRE)   11 b.g. Rare One – Worthy Gale (Strong Gale) [2003/4 c62, h–: c16m Jun 28] lengthy gelding: poor maiden hurdler/steeplechaser, not impressiing with jumping over fences: barely stays 2¾m: acts on good to firm and good to soft ground: tried blinkered: has pulled hard. *R. J. Baker*   **c– x h–**

CONOR'S PRIDE (IRE)   7 ch.g. Phardante (FR) – Surely Madam (Torenaga) [2003/4 F16g 22d 17m³ 16f* 19f³ 17f⁵ 18m 16f⁵ c20m⁶ 16g⁶ 18g 16g Apr 5] ex-Irish gelding: no show in 3 bumpers: modest hurdler: won maiden at Tramore in August: last of 6 in maiden on chasing debut, then sold out of M. Hourigan's stable 2,600 gns Doncaster November Sales: stays easy 19f: best form on firm going. *B. Mactaggart*   **c– h97 F–**

CONQUER (IRE)   9 b.g. Phardante (FR) – Tullow Performance (Gala Performance) [2003/4 c–, h–: c24d² c24sᶠ c22g² c24g c24d² Apr 12] lengthy gelding: fair maiden steeplechaser: stays 25f: acts on good to firm and heavy going. *H. D. Daly*   **c102 h–**

CONROY   5 b.g. Greensmith – Highland Spirit (Scottish Reel) [2003/4 F84: F16m 16m² 16g² 17d³ 16d² Aug 7] leggy gelding: modest form in bumpers: fair form first 2 starts in novice hurdles: raced mainly around 2m. *F. Jordan*   **h100 F76**

CONSTANT HUSBAND 11 gr.g. Le Solaret (FR) – Miss Mirror (Magic Mirror) **c–**
[2003/4 20d[6] May 16] tall, sparely-made gelding: winning chaser: reportedly lame only **h–**
start since 2000. *R. N. Bevis*

CONSTANTINE 4 gr.g. Linamix (FR) – Speremm (IRE) (Sadler's Wells (USA)) **h110**
[2003/4 16m[6] 16d 17s* 16s[4] 16d[3] Mar 28] good-topped gelding: fairly useful on Flat
(should prove best short of 2m), sold out of J. Goldie's stable 26,000 gns Newmarket
Autumn Sales: fair juvenile hurdler: won maiden at Folkestone in January: will stay
beyond 17f: acts on soft going: has shown signs of temperament. *G. L. Moore*

CONTEMPORARY ART 6 b.g. Blushing Flame (USA) – Marie La Rose (FR) **c–**
(Night Shift (USA)) [2003/4 c20g 18g[6] c20m[pu] 20m[pu] 16m[6] Oct 4] ex-French gelding: **h–**
won twice up to 1¼m on Flat, sold out of J. Hammond's stable €12,000 Goffs Arc (2002)
Sale: also successful over hurdles at Lyon Villeurbanne and over fences at Compiegne in
late-2002/3: bought out of T. Trapenard's stable €15,000 Goffs July Sale: no form in
Britain: has pulled hard. *M. C. Pipe*

CONTEMPO SUITE (IRE) 7 b.g. Lord Americo – Kintullagh (Crash Course) **c117**
[2003/4 c22m[F] c18g[4] c22d* c20v* c24s[F] c28v[4] c28d[pu] c22s[F] Mar 21] IR 13,000 3-y-o: **h–**
half-brother to temperamental winning 19f chaser Magellan Bay (by Orchestra): dam
unraced half-sister to top-class 2m chaser Rathgorman: fair hurdler: fairly useful form
over fences, winning maiden at Downpatrick and handicap at Limerick in December:
stays 2¾m: acts on heavy going. *C. F. Swan, Ireland*

CONTINENTAL (IRE) 6 ch.g. Rashar (USA) – Twilight Katie (Stubbs Gazette) **F90**
[2003/4 F16d[2] Mar 19] IR 20,000 3-y-o: ex-Irish gelding: sixth foal: dam Irish bumper
winner: sixth in bumper at Gowran on debut for P. Doyle: better form when ½-length
second to Real Definition in similar event at Warwick 17 months later. *P. J. Hobbs*

CONTRABAND 6 b.g. Red Ransom (USA) – Shortfall (Last Tycoon) [2003/4 16g[3] **h138**
17m* 16m* 16g* 16v[2] 16g 21g 16g[2] 17m* Apr 15] good-topped gelding: useful middle-

Mr D. A. Johnson's "Contraband"

distance stayer on Flat, sold out of W. Haggas' stable 64,000 gns Newmarket Autumn Sales: useful novice hurdler: won at Taunton (maiden) in December and Kempton in December and Cheltenham (beat Self Defense 1¼ lengths) in April: best effort when neck second to Royal Shakespeare in Grade 2 at Aintree earlier in April: likely to prove best around 2m with emphasis on speed (below form on heavy going): free-going front runner: interesting prospect for novice chases in 2004/5. *M. C. Pipe*

CON TRICKS 11 b.g. El Conquistador – Dame Nellie (Dominion) [2003/4 c20d* c22v^F c26d* Dec 31] tall gelding: modest hurdler/chaser: off nearly 2 years before reappearance: won handicap chases at Plumpton and Fontwell (novice) in December: fell first in between: stays 27f: raced on good going or softer (acts on soft): front runner. *J. W. Mullins*
  c99 +
  h–

CONTROL MAN (IRE) 6 ch.g. Glacial Storm (USA) – Got To Fly (IRE) (Kemal (FR)) [2003/4 F118: 17g* 20d³ 21d⁴ 18s* 20s* 24g^{pu} Apr 2] angular gelding: useful novice hurdler: won at Newton Abbot in November, Fontwell in February and Sandown in March: much improved in Grade 3 EBF Sunderlands NH Novices' Handicap Hurdle at last-named, beating Eric's Charm 2½ lengths despite jumping badly left last, also idling: likely to prove best at 2½m+: will prove best on going softer than good (acts on heavy): visored last 2 starts: races prominently: tricky ride. *M. C. Pipe*
  h130

CONUNDRUM (IRE) 6 ch.g. Dr Devious (IRE) – Wasabi (IRE) (Polar Falcon (USA)) [2003/4 17m^{ro} Aug 30] fairly useful on Flat (stays 1½m) in 2002 for P. Harris, no form for D. Chapman: behind when running out fifth on hurdling debut. *A. C. Wilson*
  h–

COOKIES BANK 6 b.g. Broadsword (USA) – Kitty Come Home (Monsanto (FR)) [2003/4 F–: 19s³ 24s^{ur} 17g 22s^{pu} Mar 23] modest form when third in novice at Taunton on hurdling debut: no show subsequently. *Mrs S. D. Williams*
  h89

COOK O'HAWICK (IRE) 7 b.g. King's Ride – Miners Yank (Miner's Lamp) [2003/4 h65p, F69: 16s² 16v⁶ Jan 17] good-topped gelding: poor maiden hurdler: will be suited by 2½m: sold 4,000 gns Doncaster May Sales. *L. Lungo*
  h69

COOLBYTHEPOOL 4 b.g. Bijou d'Inde – Alchi (USA) (Alleged (USA)) [2003/4 16d⁶ Mar 21] half-brother to winning 2m hurdler Pickens (by Theatrical): fairly useful on Flat (stays 13f), sold out of M. Johnston's stable 20,000 gns Newmarket Autumn Sales, and gelded: sixth in novice at Stratford on hurdling debut. *Ian Williams*
  h73

COOL DEGREE (IRE) 6 br.g. Arctic Lord – Ballyfin Maid (IRE) (Boreen (FR)) [2003/4 F85: 22m⁶ Nov 16] leggy gelding: fair form in bumpers in 2002/3: off 7 months, little encouragement in novice on hurdling debut only start in 2003/4: should stay at least 2½m. *Ferdy Murphy*
  h–

European Breeders Fund Sunderlands 'National Hunt' Novices' Handicap Hurdle Final, Sandown—Control Man, visored for the first time, jumps badly left but still beats top weight Eric's Charm

COOLDINE KING (IRE) 5 b.g. Germany (USA) – Tara's Serenade (IRE) (Orchestra) [2003/4 F16m* 19s² 21d³ 16g^F 17g^{pu} Apr 3] €10,000 3-y-o: rather leggy gelding: third foal: dam, lightly-raced hurdler, half-sister to fairly useful hurdler up to 3m Minella Captain: well ridden from front when winning bumper at Sandown on debut in November: modest form when placed on completed starts over hurdles. *P. R. Webber* **h95 F89**

COOLE PRESENCE (IRE) 5 b.m. Presenting – Eleanors Joy (Sheer Grit) [2003/4 20g^{pu} Jan 23] fourth foal: half-sister to fairly useful hunter Coole Abbey (by Viteric), stays 25f: dam, lightly-raced maiden Irish pointer, half-sister to dual Foxhunter winner Fantus: brought down in 4-y-o Irish point on debut in 2003: showed nothing in mares novice hurdle. *R. Johnson* **h–**

COOLERS QUEST 5 b.m. Saddlers' Hall (IRE) – Lucidity (Vision (USA)) [2003/4 16g 16d 19g 16s c16s⁴ c20g⁵ Apr 12] leggy, workmanlike mare: little sign of ability. *P. C. Ritchens* **c– h–**

COOLE SPIRIT (IRE) 11 b.g. All Haste (USA) – Chocolate Biscuit (Biskrah) [2003/4 c127, h–: c29v³ c24g^{pu} Dec 27] small gelding: fairly useful handicap chaser: creditable third of 5 finishers to Jeremy Spider in quite valuable event at Plumpton in November: stays 29f: raced on good going or softer (acts on heavy). *Miss E. C. Lavelle* **c127 h–**

COOLE VENTURE (IRE) 10 b.g. Satco (FR) – Mandavaur (IRE) (Mandalus) [2003/4 c24g³ c28d² May 30] ex-Irish gelding: third foal: half-brother to modest hurdler Freeline Fontaine (by Lafontaine), stays 3m: dam unraced half-sister to fairly useful jumper up to 3m Calmos: twice-raced in bumpers: prolific winning pointer, successful in March and April: placed both starts in hunter chases: stays 3½m well. *Mrs Edward Crow* **c102**

COOLING CASTLE (FR) 8 ch.g. Sanglamore (USA) – Syphaly (USA) (Lyphard (USA)) [2003/4 16g⁵ 17d* 16d 16g 17g⁵ Mar 28] poor hurdler: won selling handicap at Sedgefield in November, idling: raced mainly around 2m: acts on good to soft ground: sold 1,800 gns Doncaster May Sales. *Ronald Thompson* **h80**

COOLING OFF (IRE) 7 b.m. Brief Truce (USA) – Lovers' Parlour (Beldale Flutter (USA)) [2003/4 h86§: 20m³ 26m^{pu} 19g* 16g 21s⁴ Dec 11] sturdy mare: poor hurdler: off 5 months and sweating, won handicap at Warwick in November: stays 2½m: acts on soft and good to firm going: effective visored or not: races prominently: sometimes loses interest. *J. R. Jenkins* **h84 §**

COOL INVESTMENT (IRE) 7 b.g. Prince of Birds (USA) – Superb Investment (IRE) (Hatim (USA)) [2003/4 c115, h101: 20d⁵ c29v^F c29d^{ur} c24d c24s^{pu} 26s c29d^{pu} 26d^{pu} Mar 22] leggy, close-coupled gelding: maiden hurdler: fairly useful handicap chaser: in cheekpieces, broke leg at Hereford: stayed 29f: acted on heavy going: tried tongue tied. *R. M. Stronge* **c124 h94**

COOL MATE (IRE) 6 br.g. Montelimar (USA) – Another Advantage (IRE) (Roselier (FR)) [2003/4 F17g F17m⁶ 20d⁴ 20s^{pu} 20s 16v 17s⁴ Feb 11] IR £20,000 3-y-o: tall gelding: second foal: half-brother to winning 3m hurdler You're The Man (by Lapierre): dam unraced sister to useful staying chaser Ebony Jane: signs of only a little ability. *Mrs Dianne Sayer* **h80 ? F–**

COOL MONTY (IRE) 10 ch.g. Montelimar (USA) – Rose Ground (Over The River (FR)) [2003/4 c98, h–: c17g^{pu} c16s* c16s⁶ c17g* c20m⁴ Feb 28] close-coupled gelding: maiden hurdler: fairly useful chaser: much improved in 2003/4, won handicaps at Huntingdon (conditional jockeys) in December and Market Rasen (beat Lord North 9 lengths) in February: stays 21f: acts on soft and good to firm going: breathing problem third start: best form on right-handed tracks. *A. M. Balding* **c122 h–**

COOLNAHILLA (IRE) 8 gr.g. Roselier (FR) – Reoss (King's Ride) [2003/4 c16d³ c24s³ c24s² c24d² c20d² c20d² c20v* Apr 17] fair handicap chaser: in good form in 2003/4, improved effort when easily beating Jasmin d'Oudairies 20 lengths at Listowel: effective at 2½m to 3m: raced only on going softer than good (acts on heavy): wore cheekpieces at Listowel, blinkered previous 2 starts: consistent. *W. J. Burke, Ireland* **c113 h–**

COOL ROXY 7 b.g. Environment Friend – Roxy River (Ardross) [2003/4 h97: 16g⁶ 16m⁶ 16g* 21g⁵ 22d⁵ 20s³ 23g* 16s* 21m⁵ Apr 14] stocky gelding: fairly useful handicap hurdler: all 5 wins at Fakenham, including in October, February and March: suited by good test at 2m and stays easy 23f: acts on soft and good to firm going: genuine. *A. G. Blackmore* **h119**

COOL SONG 8 ch.g. Michelozzo (USA) – Vi's Delight (New Member) [2003/4 h–, F78: 22g^F 22d c25g* c28d^{pu} Dec 4] strong gelding: little encouragement over hurdles: off over 6 months, won very weak maiden at Market Rasen on chasing debut: reportedly lost action in handicap following month: stays 25f. *D. J. Caro* **c71 h–**

COO

COOL SPICE 7 b.m. Karinga Bay – Cool Run (Deep Run) [2003/4 16m² 16f* 16m³ 16d³ 17d⁵ 19m⁵ 19g* 21m⁶ Apr 15] smallish mare: fairly useful on Flat (stays 13f): fairly useful hurdler: won maiden at Cheltenham in October and handicap at Taunton (much improved when beating Odagh Odyssey by 12 lengths) in April: probably stays 21f: acts on firm and good to soft going: patiently ridden. *P. J. Hobbs* **h119**

COOLTEEN HERO (IRE) 14 b.g. King Luthier – Running Stream (Paddy's Stream) [2003/4 c75: c25gᵖᵘ May 1] tall gelding: poor handicap chaser: placed several times in points in 2004: probably stays 25f: acts on any going: usually races prominently. *R. H. Alner* **c–**

COOMBE GOLD (IRE) 7 b.g. Insan (USA) – Augustaeliza (IRE) (Callernish) [2003/4 21s Nov 3] workmanlike gelding: lightly raced and little sign of ability. *N. J. Gifford* **h–**

COPELAND 9 b.g. Generous (IRE) – Whitehaven (Top Ville) [2003/4 h144+: c17d³ 16s⁴ 16g 17d³ 20g 16d* Apr 17] smallish, sturdy gelding: fair form when third in novice at Plumpton on chasing debut (should do better over fences): useful hurdler: best effort in 2003/4 when winning Samsung Electronics Scottish Champion Hurdle (Limited Handicap) at Ayr by 5 lengths from Benbyas: stays 2½m, raced mainly over shorter: acts on heavy and good to firm going: formerly blinkered, visored nowadays: often races up with pace. *M. C. Pipe* **c101 p** **h144**

COPPEEN CROSS (IRE) 10 b.g. Phardante (FR) – Greek Opal (Furry Glen) [2003/4 c21g⁶ c20g² c22mᵖᵘ c20g⁶ Jul 6] rather leggy gelding: once-raced Irish pointer: poor form over hurdles: poor form in steeplechases: stays 2½m. *O. Brennan* **c77** **h–**

COPPER SHELL 10 ch.g. Beveled (USA) – Luly My Love (Hello Gorgeous (USA)) [2003/4 c80x, h–: c19g⁵ c20d⁴ c24sᵘʳ c21d⁶ c26s⁶ c25d* c24d Mar 24] leggy, plain gelding: maiden hurdler: poor handicap chaser: won at Folkestone in February despite idling: stays 25f: possibly best on going softer than good (acts on heavy) nowadays: wears headgear: tongue tied: often not a fluent jumper. *Miss A. M. Newton-Smith* **c75 x** **h–**

COPPLESTONE (IRE) 8 b.g. Second Set (IRE) – Queen of The Brush (Averof) [2003/4 h77: 16m³ 16g* 17g² 16g⁴ 17m⁴ 17d⁵ 20d 16d 19d 16v 18v⁴ 19g 20vᵖᵘ 17dᵖᵘ Apr 18] modest handicap hurdler: won sellers at Newcastle and Hexham early in season: stays 19f: acts on heavy and good to firm going: wears cheekpieces: comes from off pace, and has failed to impress with finishing effort. *W. Storey* **h94**

COPSALE LAD 7 ch.g. Karinga Bay – Squeaky Cottage (True Song) [2003/4 h97: 19d* 18s³ 20s 21m* Apr 14] strong, lengthy gelding: chasing type: largely progressive form over hurdles: won novices at Exeter (beat Alexanderthegreat 4 lengths) in January **h120 +**

Telectronics Systems 'National Hunt' Auction Novices' Hurdle, Cheltenham—
Copsale Lad holds off the persistent Grey Report (right)

and Cheltenham (quite valuable event, by ½ length from Grey Report despite mistakes) in April: will stay beyond 21f: acts on soft and good to firm going. *N. J. Henderson*

COQ DE MIRANDE (FR)   10 gr.g. Gairloch – Carmonera (FR) (Carmont (FR)) [2003/4 c17f^{rtr} c17g 16m² c16g⁶ c16m⁶ 16m^{rtr} c16m^{pu} Dec 18] ex-Irish gelding: fair hurdler: useful chaser at best: left A. Moore after fifth start: raced around 2m: best efforts on good going or firmer: tried tongue tied: refused to race twice in 2003/4: one to avoid. *Miss K. Marks*   **c102 §** / **h106 §**

COQ HARDI DIAMOND (IRE)   10 b.g. King's Ride – Snoqualmie (Warpath) [2003/4 c115, h–: c24d c24d c28v* c24s^F Mar 14] good sort: fairly useful handicap chaser: better than ever when winning valuable event at Punchestown in February by ¾ length from Rule Supreme, pair clear: stays 3½m well: acts well on heavy going: blinkered last 2 starts: has worn near-side pricker. *N. Meade, Ireland*   **c123** / **h–**

CORALBROOK   4 b.g. Alderbrook – Coral Delight (Idiot's Delight) [2003/4 F16g Mar 17] tenth foal: half-brother to several winning hurdlers, including Kino's Cross (by Relkino), fairly useful at 2m: dam, useful hurdler who stayed 21f, sister to useful 2m to 2¾m chaser Our Fun: showed little in bumper on debut. *Mrs P. Robeson*   **F–**

CORAL ISLAND   10 b.g. Charmer – Misowni (Niniski (USA)) [2003/4 c112, h–: c20g 21s Feb 16] useful-looking gelding: fair handicap chaser: no encouragement either start in 2003/4, in handicap hurdle on second occasion: stays 2¾m: acts on firm and soft going: tried blinkered, not since early-1999/00. *R. M. Stronge*   **c–** / **h–**

CORAZONADO (FR)   4 b.g. Pistolet Bleu (IRE) – Heleda (FR) (Zino) [2003/4 F18g Apr 22] second foal: dam maiden who stayed 11f: well held in bumper on debut. *R. H. York*   **F–**

CORBIE LYNN   7 ch.m. Jumbo Hirt (USA) – Kilkenny Gorge (Deep Run) [2003/4 F17m 16f² 16g³ 22m² 20d 22g* 22g* Mar 28] smallish mare: third known foal: dam poor pointer: well behind in bumper: generally progressive over hurdles, won handicap and novice in March, both at Kelso: stays 2¾m. *W. S. Coltherd*   **h98** / **F–**

CORDILLA (IRE)   6 b.g. Accordion – Tumble Heather (Tumble Wind (USA)) [2003/4 F91: 20s 20s⁵ 20s* 17s* 20g^{pu} Apr 23] big gelding: chasing type: progressive hurdler: won novice at Ayr in December, handicap at Carlisle in February and novice handicap at Perth in April: effective around 2m, shapes as though will stay beyond 2½m: acts on soft going: has shown high head carriage. *N. G. Richards*   **h104 +**

CORE OF SILVER (IRE)   5 b.g. Nucleon (USA) – My Silversmith (IRE) (Cyrano de Bergerac) [2003/4 F–: F17m 16f^{ur} 16g Nov 1] big gelding: showed little in 2 bumpers: signs of a little ability in 2 novice hurdles at Kelso. *P. Monteith*   **h64** / **F–**

CORKAN (IRE)   10 b.g. Torus – Broad Tab (Cantab) [2003/4 c86, h–: c20g c25g c23m^{pu} c26g^{ur} c24g^{ur} Oct 27] rather sparely-made gelding: modest handicap chaser: largely out of sorts in 2003/4: stays 3¼m: acts on good to firm going: wore cheekpieces last 2 outings: usually front runner. *J. Cullinan*   **c85 ?** / **h–**

CORK HARBOUR (FR)   8 ch.g. Grand Lodge (USA) – Irish Sea (Irish River (FR)) [2003/4 h–: 17g^{ur} 17m* Oct 18] best effort over hurdles when easily winning selling handicap at Market Rasen: raced around 2m: acts on good to firm going: blinkered. *P. Bowen*   **h90**

CORLETTO (POL)   7 b.g. Professional (IRE) – Cortesia (POL) (Who Knows) [2003/4 c94, h–: c16d⁵ c16g^{pu} 17d^{pu} Jul 27] good-topped gelding: winning hurdler: modest maiden chaser: below form early in 2003/4: stays 21f: acts on soft and good to firm going: blinkered second start. *T. R. George*   **c82** / **h–**

CORN BUNTING   7 b. or br.m. Teenoso (USA) – Annie Kelly (Oats) [2003/4 17g⁶ Nov 9] fifth in bumper on debut in 2001: pulled up in 2 points in 2003, pulled hard when sixth in mares maiden hurdle at Southwell. *B. N. Pollock*   **h65**

CORNISH GALE (IRE)   10 br.g. Strong Gale – Seanaphobal Lady (Kambalda) [2003/4 c109+, h–: 22m* 16m* 20g² c20g 22m^{ur} c24g^{pu} Mar 6] well-made gelding: fair hurdler: landed odds in 2 novices at Wincanton in May: fairly useful chaser at one time, well below best since 2001/2: stays 2¾m: best efforts on good/good to firm going: has had tongue tied: of suspect temperament. *P. F. Nicholls*   **c–** / **h102**

CORNISH JESTER   5 b.g. Slip Anchor – Fortune's Girl (Ardross) [2003/4 F16s⁶ F16d Apr 21] useful-looking gelding: third foal: half-brother to fairly useful bumper winner Diamond Sal (by Bob Back): dam fair hurdler, stayed 27f: better effort in bumpers when sixth at Huntingdon. *P. J. Hobbs*   **F91**

221

CORNISH REBEL (IRE)   7 br.g. Un Desperado (FR) – Katday (FR) (Miller's   **h148**
Mate) [2003/4 F118: 20d* 21d* 24g Apr 2]

Sheikh Mohammed has owned some top-class racehorses over the years,
but Katday was not one of them. Trained by Alex Pantall, she carried his colours to
success in three small races scattered around the West of France, at La Rochelle-
Chatelaillon, Questembert and Cholet, earning not a great deal more than the
70,000 francs she had cost as a foal. Katday earned a further £600 the following
year, running in the colours of Saeed Manana in a three-race campaign over hurdles
in Ireland with John Fowler. She was sold for 4,000 guineas at the Newmarket
December Sales in 1991. So much for Katday the racehorse. As a broodmare she
has been a different proposition altogether, and there was no better illustration of
that than during a twenty-four-hour period at the end of December when three of
her sons won important prizes. First foal Best Mate won the Grade 1 Ericsson
Chase at Leopardstown just twenty minutes after fourth foal Inexorable landed a
Grade 3 novice hurdle at Limerick, while the following day it was the turn of her
third foal Cornish Rebel to take a Grade 1 event with victory in the Stan James
Challow Hurdle at Newbury. In addition to that clutch of wins, there was also the
winning debut of foal number five, Sidalcea, in a bumper at Punchestown in November, while second foal Inca Trail completed a full set of successes for Katday's
offspring in the latest season when taking a valuable handicap hurdle at Wincanton
in February. There was, of course, the small matter of Best Mate's third Cheltenham
Gold Cup to round off a remarkable winning spree among Katday's foals.

Best Mate has given his younger siblings a lot to live up to, and Cornish
Rebel's name in particular rarely appears in the press without the epithet 'Best
Mate's brother'. Cornish Rebel is always going to be burdened with that tag, and it
was, after all, largely for that reason that he fetched a sale-topping IR £110,000 at
the Derby Sale in 2001 on the back of Best Mate's very promising novice chase
campaign. Cornish Rebel's most impressive racecourse debut, in a Grade 2 bumper
at Newbury in February 2003, did little to dampen expectations, though a disappointing effort followed when second favourite for the Champion Bumper at
Cheltenham. Cornish Rebel's latest campaign, in novice hurdles, took a similar
course, ending on a downbeat note after expectations had been fuelled with another
big-race success at Newbury. Cornish Rebel's rivals in the Challow Hurdle came
from a variety of backgrounds, though, for the most part, they had in common the
fact that they had a lot more racing experience. Distant Prospect and Big Moment
were useful staying handicappers from the Flat, Control Man, like Cornish Rebel,
was another leading performer in bumpers from the previous season, Grey Report
had come from the Irish pointing field, while Mon Villez had already shown useful
form over fences in France. Cornish Rebel started joint favourite with Distant

Stan James Challow Novices' Hurdle, Newbury—
Cornish Rebel (No.3) recovers to edge out Big Moment after losing ground with this last-flight mistake

Mr C. G. Roach's "Cornish Rebel"

Prospect after easily landing the odds in an ordinary novice hurdle at Chepstow a month earlier. Cornish Rebel came out of the Newbury race looking a cracking prospect, still with only four races under his belt. Patiently ridden, he was a couple of lengths down on leader Big Moment after jumping the last less than fluently, but to his credit battled back to force his head in front close home and win by half a length, the pair pulling well clear of Grey Report, who had set the pace, with the remainder soundly beaten.

If Cornish Rebel's season had ended there, we would have had no hesitation in writing him up as a top novice chasing prospect, with the looks—he's a rangy, good-topped gelding—as well as the pedigree to excel over fences. Still not the finished article, chasing could yet easily be the making of Cornish Rebel. He has shown a similar level of ability over hurdles to that shown by Best Mate at the same stage of his career. However, his dismal performance when a short-priced favourite for the Sefton Novices' Hurdle at Aintree is hard to ignore completely and does temper enthusiasm about his prospects in competitive events in the future. Cornish Rebel had missed the Royal & SunAlliance Novices' Hurdle at Cheltenham where conditions were considered not testing enough for him over the trip, but he looked in good shape for the Aintree race run over three furlongs further, his first outing for more than three months. Patiently ridden again, Cornish Rebel never looked like taking a hand, running in snatches and receiving a reminder at the end of the first circuit before seeming to down tools after five out, eventually finishing a tailed-off last of the eight finishers. His trainer has himself described Cornish Rebel as 'quirky' and not the most straightforward to train, and there may be more to Cornish Rebel's tendency to hang left in his early races than simple inexperience.

223

It's also worth mentioning that Katday was blinkered in some of her French races, and she was wearing them for the first time when gaining the first of her wins.

Katday's first three foals, Best Mate, Inca Trail and Cornish Rebel, are all by Un Desperado, while Inexorable and Sidalcea are the results of visits to Roselier and Oscar respectively. Her as-yet unraced offspring are the three-year-old filly Flying Iris (also by Un Desperado), and a two-year-old colt by Pistolet Bleu. As previous essays on Best Mate have pointed out, Katday comes from a family which has produced some excellent horses on the Flat. Her grandam Alika is out of a mare who was also responsible for the top-class pair Abdos, winner of the Grand Criterium, and Dynamiter, a dual winner of the Champion Stakes. More pertinently from a jumping point of view, Katday's half-sisters include a runner-up in the Breeders' Cup Steeplechase, Kalankoe, and a good French chaser, Charlie Turquoise, who finished third in France's most important chase for four-year-olds, the Prix Maurice Gillois.

		Top Ville	High Top
	Un Desperado (FR)	(b 1976)	Sega Ville
	(b 1983)	White Lightning	Baldric II
Cornish Rebel (IRE)		(gr 1970)	Rough Sea
(br.g. 1997)		Miller's Mate	Mill Reef
	Katday (FR)	(b 1982)	Primatie
	(br 1987)	Kanara	Hauban
		(b 1973)	Alika

Katday went through the ring twice more after her racing days in Ireland were over. She was picked up for just IR 1,500 guineas by Irish-based Dutchman Jacques Van't Hart in 1993, her paltry price seemingly a reflection of her breeding record at that time; she had slipped a foal to her first covering and been barren the following year. 'A friend told me that for such small money I couldn't go too far wrong.' explained Mr Van't Hart, who described Katday as 'a lovely mare, very attractive, about 15.3 hands with a lovely head and a good eye.' Having by now produced the foal that was Best Mate (himself sold as a foal for just IR2,500 guineas) but with her future value still to be revealed, Katday was sold on again for IR5,500 guineas in 1996 in foal to Un Desperado. Her buyer this time was Philip Myerscough, owner of Baroda Stud, whose leading novice chaser at the time (and future Arkle winner) Ventana Canyon was by the same sire. It seems a safe bet that Katday's current owner will not want to part with her. *P. F. Nicholls*

CORPORATE PLAYER (IRE) 6 b.g. Zaffaran (USA) – Khazna (Stanford) [2003/4 **h100** F81: 16d* 16s⁵ 18d⁵ Mar 21] useful-looking gelding: fair form in novice hurdles: won at Wincanton in January: should stay beyond 2m: tried tongue tied, best efforts when not. *Noel T. Chance*

CORRAGE (IRE) 7 b.g. Corrouge (USA) – Cora Gold (Goldhill) [2003/4 22d² Jul **h90** 30] left N. Twiston-Davies/off 17 months, much better effort over hurdles when 1½ lengths second to Mystic Forest in maiden at Newton Abbot: likely to be at least as effective over shorter. *R. T. Phillips*

CORRARE (IRE) 7 b.m. Corrouge (USA) – Granig Rarity (Rarity) [2003/4 h61: **h–** 26mᵖᵘ 21s Dec 3] little form over hurdles: tried blinkered. *J. R. Boyle*

CORRIB BOY (IRE) 4 b.g. Flying Spur (AUS) – First Strike (IRE) (Magical Strike **h116 x** (USA)) [2003/4 16g² 16g² 16d³ 16d³ 16g* 16d⁶ 16d² 16s² 20d Apr 11] leggy gelding: half-brother to useful hurdler up to 2½m Strike Back and useful bumper winner Rugged Jacket (both by Bob Back): fair on Flat (stays 13f): fairly useful juvenile hurdler: won maiden at Thurles in December: raced mainly at 2m: acts on soft going: tried blinkered: often makes mistakes. *Joseph Crowley, Ireland*

CORRIB ECLIPSE 5 b.g. Double Eclipse (IRE) – Last Night's Fun (IRE) (Law **F107** Society (USA)) [2003/4 F16m* F16s² F16g F16g Mar 17] compact gelding: first foal: dam, lightly-raced Irish maiden, stayed 1½m: won slowly-run bumper at Worcester on debut in September: better form when second to Refinement in quite valuable race at Ascot and tenth of 24 to Total Enjoyment, nearest finish, in Champion Bumper at Cheltenham final outing: will be suited by further than 2m: won Queen Alexandra Stakes at Ascot on Flat debut in June. *Jamie Poulton*

CORRIB LAD (IRE) 6 b.g. Supreme Leader – Nun So Game (The Parson) [2003/4 **h–** F97: 17g 17d 16s Dec 30] well-made gelding: third in bumper: well held in novice hurdles: has shown signs of temperament. *P. J. Hobbs*

CORRIE MOR (IRE) 9 ch.g. Moscow Society (USA) – Corrie Lough (IRE) (The Parson) [2003/4 c25g² c23mᵖᵘ Apr 13] small gelding: fair pointer: much better effort in hunters when second at Catterick: stays 25f. *Mrs S. E. Busby* — c87 h–

CORRIES WOOD (IRE) 5 b.g. Corrouge (USA) – Ewood Park (Wishing Star) [2003/4 F16g 16g 16f⁴ 21m² 1¹/g³ 18m³ Sep 12] €15,000 3-y-o: sixth foal: half-brother to fairly useful staying hurdler Blackburn (by Roselier) and modest hurdler around 2½m Mr Musicmaker (by Asir): dam, 2½m hurdle winner, out of half-sister to high-class miler Belmont Bay: left D. Murphy after well held in bumper on debut: poor maiden hurdler: probably better around 2½m than shorter: acts on firm going. *J. J. Lambe, Ireland* — h81 F–

CORROBOREE (IRE) 7 b.g. Corrouge (USA) – Laura's Toi (Quayside) [2003/4 h95+: 16g⁶ c20d⁶ Dec 5] leggy, rather sparely-made gelding: fair hurdler: off 12 months, won conditional jockeys handicap at Kempton in November for second year running: finished lame on chasing debut: should stay beyond 2m: raced mainly on good going or softer (acts on heavy). *N. A. Twiston-Davies* — c– h109

COSCOROBA (IRE) 10 ch.m. Shalford (IRE) – Tameeza (USA) (Shahrastani (USA)) [2003/4 20s 17d Mar 30] close-coupled mare: poor maiden 2m hurdler for P. Monteith in 1999/00: no form on return: sketchy jumper. *D. W. Whillans* — h– x

COSI CELESTE (FR) 7 b.g. Apeldoorn (FR) – Lemixikoa (FR) (Mendez (FR)) [2003/4 16g 16s 25dᵖᵘ 19g⁶ Apr 24] good-topped gelding: sixth foal: half-brother to C'Est Extra (by Round Sovereign), winner up to 1¼m on Flat/winning 2m hurdler and winning sprinter Ville de Lumiere (by Art Francais): dam maiden: failed to complete in 2 maiden points in 2003: first form over hurdles when sixth in novice at Market Rasen, possibly flattered in steadily-run race. *John Allen* — h83 ?

COSMIC CASE 9 b.m. Casteddu – La Fontainova (IRE) (Lafontaine (USA)) [2003/4 h100: 20gᶠ 16s* 16g² 16g 16g² 17m³ 20g² 16d 16s 16s 16d 16g Apr 16] angular mare: fair handicap hurdler: third course win when successful at Perth in May: stays 2½m: acts on good to firm and heavy going: effective visored or not: held up: tough and genuine. *J. S. Goldie* — h110

COSMIC FLIGHT (IRE) 8 b.g. Torus – Palatine Lady (Pauper) [2003/4 h–, F70: 19m May 26] rangy gelding: modest in bumpers: no form over hurdles or in points: tried in cheekpieces. *N. M. Babbage* — h–

COSMIC RANGER 6 b.g. Magic Ring (IRE) – Lismore (Relkino) [2003/4 h55: 16m⁴ 16g 17g² 17m c21sᵖᵘ c21vᵖᵘ c16v⁴ c16vᶠ c16d Mar 30] workmanlike gelding: bad maiden hurdler: showed little over fences: raced mainly around 2m: acts on good to firm and heavy going. *H. Alexander* — c– h56

COSMIC SONG 7 b.m. Cosmonaut – Hotaria (Sizzling Melody) [2003/4 h66: 16m⁴ 16g⁶ 19g Jun 11] poor form over hurdles: probably best around 2m. *R. M. Whitaker* — h73

COSMOCRAT 6 b.g. Cosmonaut – Bella Coola (Northern State (USA)) [2003/4 h95: 16d* 16v³ 20s 16mᵖᵘ Apr 13] rangy gelding: modest handicap hurdler: won at Uttoxeter in November: best at 2m: acts on heavy going. *R. M. Stronge* — h98

COSSACK DANCER (IRE) 6 b.g. Moscow Society (USA) – Merry Lesa (Dalesa) [2003/4 F16d⁶ F16s³ F16g Feb 14] €35,000 4-y-o: unfurnished gelding: half-brother to several winners, notably top-class chaser up to 25f Merry Gale (by Strong Gale): dam, 2m maiden hurdle winner/winning pointer, from family of Brave Inca: easily best effort in bumpers when third to Progressive at Huntingdon in December, tending to hang left but keeping on. *M. Bradstock* — F99

COTOPAXI (IRE) 8 b.g. Turtle Island (IRE) – Ullapool (Dominion) [2003/4 h125: 16d 21g* Jan 17] rather leggy gelding: fairly useful handicap hurdler: career-best effort when winning at Kempton by 1¾ lengths from Zero Risk: stays easy 21f: acts on good to firm and heavy going: effective blinkered or not. *Miss Venetia Williams* — h128

COTTAGE HILL 5 b.m. Primitive Rising (USA) – Celtic Lane (Welsh Captain) [2003/4 F16g 19g Apr 24] lengthy mare: second foal: dam poor pointer: well beaten in bumper and novice hurdle. *C. R. Wilson* — h– F–

COTTAM GRANGE 4 b.c. River Falls – Karminski (Pitskelly) [2003/4 16m⁶ 16v⁶ 16g⁴ 16g 24d³ 21d⁴ 20d Apr 18] medium-sized colt: poor maiden on Flat (stays 2m): modest juvenile hurdler: stays 3m: acts on good to soft going. *M. W. Easterby* — h91

COTTY'S ROCK (IRE) 5 ch.g. Beneficial – Its Good Ere (Import) [2003/4 F17d Apr 18] €22,000 4-y-o: half-brother to fair 2m chaser Livin It Up and winning pointer/hunter False Tail (both by Roselier): dam, 1¼m winner, from family of smart 1m to 1¼m performer Mellottie: raced freely when well held in bumper on debut. *J. Howard Johnson* — F–

COUGAR (IRE) 4 b.g. Sadler's Wells (USA) – Pieds de Plume (FR) (Seattle Slew (USA)) [2003/4 16s⁶ 16d 18s⁶ 19g² 19gᵖᵘ Mar 27] well-made gelding: twice-raced on Flat at 2 yrs for A. O'Brien, fairly useful form in 1m maiden on debut: modest form over hurdles: lame final start: stays 19f. *R. Rowe* **h88**

COULD BE CLASS 5 b.m. Gildoran – Olympic Rose (IRE) (Roselier (FR)) [2003/4 F16d aF16g Apr 4] third foal: dam, once-raced, out of half-sister to fairly useful staying chaser Dinny Walsh: showed little in 2 bumpers. *A. Ennis* **F–**

COULD IT BE LEGAL 7 b.g. Roviris – Miss Gaylord (Cavo Doro) [2003/4 F–: 19dᵘʳ 17s 19m Mar 4] workmanlike gelding: no sign of ability. *P. M. Rich* **h–**

COULDN'T BE PHAR (IRE) 7 ch.g. Phardante (FR) – Queenford Belle (Celtic Cone) [2003/4 F–: 16d³ 21vᵖᵘ 19sᵖᵘ Dec 20] well-held third of 7 finishers in novice hurdle at Towcester, only sign of ability: should stay at least 2½m. *D. R. Gandolfo* **h76 ?**

COULTERS CANDY 6 ch.g. Clantime – Heldigvis (Hot Grove) [2003/4 h92?, F90: 16g⁵ 16s³ 16m 20dᵖᵘ Jul 2] runner-up in bumper on debut: poor on balance of form over hurdles: unlikely to stay beyond 2m. *A. C. Whillans* **h78**

COULTHARD (IRE) 11 ch.g. Glenstal (USA) – Royal Aunt (Martinmas) [2003/4 c–§, h109§: 16d³ 16d 16d⁴ 16v 16s⁵ c16d² c16dᵖᵘ Apr 12] angular gelding: fair handicap hurdler, below form after reappearance: maiden chaser: modest form when second of 4 finishers in novice handicap at Huntingdon: best around 2m: acts on heavy going, possibly not on good to firm: has had tongue tied: held up, and best in strongly-run race: irresolute. *Mrs P. Sly* **c95 §** **h102 §**

COUNSEL 9 ch.g. Most Welcome – My Polished Corner (IRE) (Tate Gallery (USA)) [2003/4 20gᵖᵘ 16g 24g⁶ Mar 4] smallish gelding: winning pointer: poor hurdler: no form in 2003/4: stays 2¾m: acts on good to firm going. *J. C. Tuck* **h–**

COUNTASH 5 b.g. Botanic (USA) – Jenny Mere (Brigadier Gerard) [2003/4 F16mˢᵘ F16mᵖᵘ 17sᵖᵘ Feb 6] half-brother to 2½m hurdle winner Kedge Anchor Man (by Bustino): dam poor maiden who stayed 1m: no sign of ability: left A. James after second start. *D. Burchell* **h–** **F–**

COUNTBACK (FR) 5 b.g. Anabaa (USA) – Count Me Out (FR) (Kaldoun (FR)) [2003/4 F78: F17d 16vᵖᵘ 16s 17s 16d² 17g⁵ Apr 24] sturdy gelding: well held in bumpers: poor novice hurdler: raced around 2m: tried blinkered, wore cheekpieces last 2 starts. *C. C. Bealby* **h66** **F–**

COUNT CAMPIONI (IRE) 10 br.g. Brush Aside (USA) – Emerald Flair (Flair Path) [2003/4 24d⁴ 24g³ c26v* Feb 7] lengthy gelding: one-time useful hurdler, off 2½ years before reappearance: in frame in Grade 2 at Newbury and minor event at Cheltenham in 2003/4: fair chaser: won handicap at Chepstow on return to fences by 1½ lengths from Mr Dow Jones: stays 3¼m: acts on heavy and good to firm going: tried blinkered/visored: sometimes looks difficult ride. *M. Pitman* **c110** **h122**

COUNTESS CAMILLA 7 br.m. Bob's Return (IRE) – Forest Pride (IRE) (Be My Native (USA)) [2003/4 F104: 21s³ 16v* 16v² 22v* 20s* 21gᵖᵘ Mar 27] good-topped mare: successful 3 times in novice hurdles, at Towcester in December and in mares events at Haydock in January and Carlisle (4/1-on) in February: weakened quickly in valuable mares novice handicap at Newbury final outing: will stay 3m: acts on heavy ground: has shown tendency to jump right. *K. C. Bailey* **h116**

COUNTESS ELTON (IRE) 4 ch.f. Mukaddamah (USA) – Be Prepared (IRE) (Be My Guest (USA)) [2003/4 16d 16d 16g Dec 3] no longer of any account on Flat: well held in 3 juvenile hurdles: headstrong. *R. E. Barr* **h–**

COUNTESS KIRI 6 b.m. Opera Ghost – Ballagh Countess (King's Ride) [2003/4 F16m⁶ F17g³ F16m⁴ Jun 1] first foal: dam winning hurdler/chaser who stayed 2½m: modest form at best in bumpers: runner-up on first completed start in points. *P. Bowen* **F80**

COUNTESS POINT 6 ch.m. Karinga Bay – Rempstone (Coronash) [2003/4 F16v² F18g* F16s⁴ F17m³ Apr 15] tall mare: second foal: sister to bumper winner Earl's Kitchen: dam poor pointer: fairly useful form in bumpers: made all to beat Kings Bay by ½ length in mares event at Fontwell in February: sweating, good fourth to Marsh Run in valuable similar contest at Sandown: will be suited by 2½m+. *C. L. Tizzard* **F101**

COUNT FOSCO 6 b.g. Alflora (IRE) – Carrikins (Buckskin (FR)) [2003/4 F16d⁵ 20s 16g⁵ Apr 5] third foal: dam, modest hurdler who stayed 2½m, sister to useful hurdler up to 21f Yellow Spring: modest form in bumper on debut: better effort over hurdles when fifth to Lucky Duck in novice at Kelso: should stay beyond 2m. *T. J. Fitzgerald* **h85** **F83**

COU

COUNTING 9 ch.m. Minster Son – Elitist (Keren) [2003/4 24m^pu Jun 28] half-sister to several poor performers, including winning 3m hurdler Kralingen (by Move Off): dam plating-class maiden: showed nothing in novice hurdle on debut. *L. P. Grassick* **h–**

COUNT OSKI 8 b.g. Petoski – Sea Countess (Ercolano (USA)) [2003/4 c93, h–: c24g^5 c24m^ur c24g^3 c24d^3 Apr 12] tall gelding: modest chaser: should stay beyond 3m: best efforts on good/good to soft ground: blinkered third start. *M. J. Ryan* **c93 h–**

COUNTRY KRIS 12 b.g. Town And Country – Mariban (Mummy's Pet) [2003/4 c–, h–: 22d 17s^pu Apr 6] workmanlike gelding: veteran hurdler, no form since 2001/2: tried in headgear. *B. J. M. Ryall* **c– h–**

COUNTRY LAD 4 br.g. Rock City – Northern Line (Camden Town) [2003/4 F16d^pu Mar 11] medium-sized gelding: sixth live foal: half-brother to 5f winner Miss Eliminator (by Komaite) and 7f winner in Germany by Cyrano de Bergerac: dam fairly useful 5f winner: showed nothing in bumper on debut. *Ferdy Murphy* **F–**

COUNTRYSIDE FRIEND 7 ch.g. Sabrehill (USA) – Well Proud (IRE) (Sadler's Wells (USA)) [2003/4 16g^pu 19f^pu 20g Oct 5] beaten easily in match only run on Flat, sold out of M. Pipe's stable 800 gns Newmarket July (2000) Sales: no form over hurdles. *D. L. Williams* **h–**

COUNTRYWIDE STAR (IRE) 6 ch.g. Common Grounds – Silver Slipper (Indian Ridge) [2003/4 h62: 17d^ur 16g 16s^3 16d Apr 12] sturdy gelding: little form: visored in 2003/4. *C. N. Kellett* **h–**

COUNT THE COST (IRE) 5 ch.g. Old Vic – Roseaustin (IRE) (Roselier (FR)) [2003/4 17g^pu 21g^5 20g^2 17d^4 Nov 27] workmanlike gelding: first foal: dam, modest hurdler, stayed 3m: modest form over hurdles: will stay 3m. *J. Wade* **h87**

COUNT TIROL (IRE) 7 b.g. Tirol – Bid High (IRE) (High Estate) [2003/4 19g 22d^pu c19v^pu Feb 2] no form over jumps: tried blinkered. *J. R. Payne* **c– h–**

COUNT TONY 10 ch.g. Keen – Turtle Dove (Gyr (USA)) [2003/4 h–: c23m^pu 20m^pu 20m^4 22g 21d^5 20g^5 22g^8 22g^8 21g^8 20d^6 19s^8 22m^6 Feb 21] close-coupled gelding: no show in novice chase: fairly useful handicap hurdler: left J. Gallagher after fifth start: did very well after, winning at Market Rasen (seller) in November, Fontwell (conditional jockeys) and Kempton in December and Doncaster (best effort, beat Just The Jobe 14 lengths) in January: stays 2¾m: acts on any going: blinkered (ran poorly once), wore cheekpieces last 6 starts. *P. Bowen* **c– h118**

COUNTY CLASSIC 5 b.m. Noble Patriarch – Cumbrian Rhapsody (Sharrood (USA)) [2003/4 F82: F17m^3 F17d* F16d^3 19f^6 16s^4 21v^2 Jan 13] leggy mare: fair form in bumpers, won at Sedgefield in October: modest form in mares novice hurdles: stays 21f: acts on heavy going. *T. D. Easterby* **h91 F91**

COUNTY DERRY 11 b.g. Derrylin – Colonial Princess (Roscoe Blake) [2003/4 c129: c26d^2 c24g^4 c26v* c28g^pu c26g^8 c26d^3 c26m^4 Apr 15] strong gelding: smart hunter chaser: won at Uttoxeter (twice) in May and Fontwell by 4 lengths from Earth-mover) in February: respectable third of 10 finishers to same horse in Foxhunter at Cheltenham: suited by 3m+: has won on good to firm going, probably suited by more testing conditions (acts on heavy): wore cheekpieces last 3 starts: sometimes makes mistakes. *J. R. Scott* **c125**

COUNTY FLYER 11 b.g. Cruise Missile – Random Select (Random Shot) [2003/4 c86, h–: c25g* c24g^pu 22g^3 c24d^pu 22m^3 c24s^3 c23g^pu Jan 27] lengthy, plain gelding: poor maiden hurdler: modest handicap chaser: won at Hereford in May: lame final start: stays 25f: acts on firm and soft going: blinkered once. *J. S. Smith* **c89 h78**

COUNTYKAT (IRE) 4 b.g. Woodborough (USA) – Kitty Kildare (USA) (Seattle Dancer (USA)) [2003/4 16s Dec 20] fairly useful on Flat (stays 1¼m): soon behind after mistake third in juvenile at Warwick on hurdling debut. *K. R. Burke* **h–**

COURAGE UNDER FIRE 9 b.g. Risk Me (FR) – Dreamtime Quest (Blakeney) [2003/4 c114, h–: c25s^F c23g^2 c24g^5 c24s^2 Apr 12] good-topped gelding: fair chaser: stays 3¼m: raced on good going or softer (acts on heavy): blinkered: usually races prominently. *C. C. Bealby* **c109 h–**

COURSING RUN (IRE) 8 ch.g. Glacial Storm (USA) – Let The Hare Run (IRE) (Tale Quale) [2003/4 c109p, h–: c24d* c30d^pu c24s* c24s^6 c29d^pu Mar 14] smallish, angular gelding: winning hurdler: fairly useful handicap chaser: favourite, won at Bangor (idled) in November and Newbury (beat Swincombe 3 lengths) in January: badly let down by jumping in visor first time final start: should stay beyond 3m: raced only on good to soft/soft going. *H. D. Daly* **c119 h–**

COURTCARD 5 b.m. Persian Bold – Hafhafah (Shirley Heights) [2003/4 h–: 16m[F]   **h– §**
17m 19m[pu] 16v[pu] 21s[pu] Jan 16] of little account and temperamental to boot: usually wears
cheekpieces. *Mrs Lucinda Featherstone*

COURT CHAMPAGNE 8 b.m. Batshoof – Fairfield's Breeze (Buckskin (FR))   **h91**
[2003/4 h85: 16m 20v* 19m[pu] May 26] modest handicap hurdler: won at Uttoxeter in
May: ran poorly 5 days later: stays 2½m: acts on any going: wore cheekpieces last 5
starts: inconsistent. *R. J. Price*

COURTELIMORR 4 b.f. Defacto (USA) – Auntie Fay (IRE) (Fayruz) [2003/4 17m[ur]   **h–**
17g 17m[pu] Sep 27] medium-sized filly: bad maiden on Flat: well beaten on completed
start over hurdles: wears blinkers/cheekpieces. *B. S. Rothwell*

COURT EMPEROR 4 b.g. Mtoto – Fairfields Cone (Celtic Cone) [2003/4 F14g   **F–**
F13d F16g F16g Mar 7] fifth foal: half-brother to 3 winners, including useful hurdler up
to 21f Court Shareef (by Shareef Dancer): dam, useful hurdler, stayed 2¾m: well held in
bumpers and maidens on Flat. *R. J. Price*

COURT EMPRESS 7 ch.m. Emperor Fountain – Tudor Sunset (Sunyboy) [2003/4   **h75**
F–: 17g 18g[5] Apr 22] poor form in 2 starts over hurdles: will stay 2½m. *P. D. Purdy*

COURTLEDGE 9 b.g. Unfuwain (USA) – Tremellick (Mummy's Pet) [2003/4 c93,   **c–**
h–: c24g[pu] c21s[pu] c20v[pu] 16d Apr 12] lengthy gelding: maiden hurdler: handicap chaser,   **h–**
no form since early-2002/3: stays 3m: acts on good to firm and heavy going: tried in
cheekpieces/visor. *M. J. Gingell*

COURT LENEY (IRE) 9 b.g. Commanche Run – Dont Call Me Lady (Le Bavard   **c–**
(FR)) [2003/4 26m[3] 20g 24g c29d* c29s[pu] c21s[6] c25d[ur] c24g[pu] 17g 21d[5] Apr 11] winning   **h–**
pointer: little form over hurdles: won 3-runner handicap at Fakenham in November after
he and sole remaining rival had been impeded and refused 5 out: well beaten only other
completed start in steeplechases: tried in cheekpieces. *G. Prodromou*

COURT MUSIC (IRE) 5 b. or br.m. Revoque (IRE) – Lute And Lyre (IRE) (The   **h–**
Noble Player (USA)) [2003/4 17d[pu] Nov 11] half-sister to winning hurdler around 2m in
Austria by Petardia: modest on Flat (stays 7f) at 3 yrs for T. Easterby, poor nowadays: no
show on hurdling debut. *R. E. Barr*

COURT OF JUSTICE (USA) 8 b.g. Alleged (USA) – Captive Island (Northfields   **c76**
(USA)) [2003/4 h97: 20d[5] 16d[4] 16d 16d* 16v 16s[2] c20g[6] Apr 24] leggy, angular gelding: **h106**
fair hurdler: back to near best when winning amateur handicap at Leicester in January:
well-held sixth of 7 finishers in novice at Market Rasen on chasing debut: stays 2½m:
raced on good going or softer (acts on heavy): often wears cheekpieces: has carried head
awkwardly. *K. A. Morgan*

COURT ORDEAL (IRE) 9 ch.g. Kris – In Review (Ela-Mana-Mou) [2003/4 17d[pu]   **c–**
Dec 17] close-coupled gelding: novice chaser: one-time modest handicap hurdler: lame   **h–**
only outing since 2001/2: stays 19f: tried blinkered/visored. *R. N. Bevis*

COURT SHAREEF 9 b.g. Shareef Dancer (USA) – Fairfields Cone (Celtic Cone)   **h141**
[2003/4 16g[2] 17g[2] 16g[2] 20m* 21f[2] 20g[3] 20g[4] 21g[2] 20g[3] 16d[6] Apr 17] compact gelding:
useful on Flat up to 2m: useful hurdler: won handicap at Worcester in September:
improved further, length second of 27 to Monkerhostin from 14 lb out of weights in
valuable handicap at Cheltenham eighth start and around 1½ lengths third to Garde
Champetre in Grade 2 novice at Aintree on ninth: stays 21f: acts on firm going: held up.
R. J. Price

COUSTOU (IRE) 4 b.g. In Command (IRE) – Carranza (IRE) (Lead On Time (USA))   **h–**
[2003/4 16d[ur] Feb 8] fairly useful on Flat (probably stays 1m) for W. Jarvis, stiffish tasks
all 4 starts in 2003: unseated fourth in juvenile on hurdling debut. *A. R. Dicken*

COVENT GARDEN 6 b.g. Sadler's Wells (USA) – Temple Row (Ardross) [2003/4   **h128**
h128p: 22d[3] Dec 6] sturdy gelding: unbeaten in 5 starts over hurdles in 2002/3, in 4
handicaps and Grade 2 at Kelso: did best of those coming from off pace when close third
to Hersov in handicap at Sandown, only outing in 2003/4: effective at 2m to easy 3m: acts
on firm and good to soft going, unraced on soft/heavy. *J. Howard Johnson*

COWBOYBOOTS (IRE) 6 b.g. Lord Americo – Little Welly (Little Buskins)   **c97**
[2003/4 h119: 25d[pu] c20g c20d[F] c22s[bd] 22s[5] 24m Apr 15] well-made gelding: fair   **h109**
hurdler: modest form only completed start over fences: should prove suited by 3m+: acts
on heavy going: has hinted at temperament. *L. Wells*

COXWELL COSSACK 11 ch.g. Gildoran – Stepout (Sagaro) [2003/4 16g[pu] Mar   **c–**
17] sturdy gelding: fair handicap hurdler at best: no show on first start for nearly 2 years: **h–**
fell both outings over fences: stays 2¾m: acts on firm and soft going. *A. M. Campion*

COY LAD (IRE) 7 ch.g. Be My Native (USA) – Don't Tutch Me (The Parson) [2003/4 **h77**
F69: 16g^ur 17d 16d 24g³ Feb 18] useful-looking gelding: fair form at best in bumpers:
poor form over hurdles. *T. J. Fitzgerald*

COYOTE LAKES 5 ch.g. Be My Chief (USA) – Oakbrook Tern (USA) (Arctic Tern **F–**
(USA)) [2003/4 F16s Feb 20] leggy gelding: sixth foal: half-brother to 1m winner Lady
Eil (by Elmaamul): dam French 2-y-o 1m winner: tailed off in bumper on debut. *Mrs
L. C. Jewell*

CRACKING DAWN (IRE) 9 b.g. Be My Native (USA) – Rare Coin (Kemal (FR)) **c–**
[2003/4 c125p, h–: c20g^pu c24d^pu Dec 29] well-made gelding: fair hurdler/chaser, very **h–**
lightly raced: no show in 2 handicaps over fences in 2003/4: will stay beyond 3m.
R. H. Alner

CRACKING WALKER (IRE) 8 ch.g. Rashar (USA) – Futile Walk (Crash Course) **h–**
[2003/4 21d 24g^F 22m^ur Mar 11] shallow-girthed gelding: third in Irish point: form over
hurdles only when found in novice on debut in 2000/1. *G. B. Balding*

CRACK ON CHERYL 10 b.m. Rakaposhi King – Furstin (Furry Glen) [2003/4 **c–**
c19d^pu 26g^F 24g^pu 25s^pu c24g^F Apr 18] winning pointer, of little account otherwise: tried **h–**
blinkered. *V. Y. Gethin*

CRACKRATTLE (IRE) 10 ch.g. Montelimar (USA) – Gaye Le Moss (Le Moss) **c–**
[2003/4 c–: c22g^pu May 24] fair pointer: no form in 4 steeplechases: tried in cheekpieces:
tongue tied. *B. N. Pollock*

CRAFTY MISS (IRE) 5 b. or br.m. Warcraft (USA) – Mrs Rumpole (IRE) (Strong **F–**
Gale) [2003/4 F16g Mar 25] €3,000 3-y-o, 6,200 4-y-o: third foal: dam, bumper winner/
placed over hurdles in Ireland, sister to Triumph Hurdle winner Alone Success: showed
nothing in bumper on debut. *C. J. Down*

CRAFTY MONKEY (IRE) 7 b.g. Warcraft (USA) – Mikey's Monkey (Monksfield) **h–**
[2003/4 F78: 16g 16g 16d 22g^pu Apr 18] good-topped gelding: no form in novice hurdles.
M. Pitman

CRAGG PRINCE (IRE) 5 b.g. Roselier (FR) – Ivory Queen (Teenoso (USA)) **F96**
[2003/4 F16g F17d² Mar 27] 5,600 4-y-o: second foal: dam once-raced in bumpers:
easily better effort in bumpers when 6 lengths second to Pearly Bay at Bangor: will stay
beyond 17f. *Mrs S. J. Smith*

CRAIGMOR 4 br.g. Polar Falcon (USA) – Western Horizon (USA) (Gone West **h–**
(USA)) [2003/4 16g 16d 16m⁵ 16d 16g^d Dec 18] maiden on Flat, tailed off 2 starts in
2004: little form over hurdles. *M. F. Harris*

CRAMOND (IRE) 6 br.g. Lord Americo – Rullahola (Bluerullah) [2003/4 F85?: **F91**
F16g⁴ Jan 23] better effort in bumpers 9 months apart when fourth to Esh Bran Girl at
Musselburgh: will be suited by further than 2m. *A. Parker*

CRANBORNE (IRE) 7 b.m. King's Ride – Random Wind (Random Shot) [2003/4 **h–**
F–: F16m 18s Jan 16] good-topped mare: no sign of ability. *A. H. Mactaggart* **F–**

CRAOBH RUA (IRE) 7 b.g. Lord Americo – Addies Lass (Little Buskins) [2003/4 **h86**
F16m⁵ 16d 20d 16s⁴ 20v 16g⁶ 16g² Apr 18] 13,000 3-y-o: ex-Irish gelding: half-brother **F74**
to fair staying chaser Decent Man (by Derring Rose): dam unraced: poor form in bumpers: modest maiden hurdler: left M. Cunningham after fifth start: should stay beyond 2m:
acts on good to soft ground. *R. H. Alner*

CRARAE JACK 6 gr.g. Gran Alba (USA) – Double Dose (Al Sirat) [2003/4 F–: 19g^F **h–**
24d^pu Mar 11] smallish, leggy gelding: no form in bumpers (tongue tied) or over hurdles.
H. P. Hogarth

CRAZY HORSE (IRE) 11 b.g. Little Bighorn – Our Dorcet (Condorcet (FR)) **c–**
[2003/4 c–, h–: 23m³ 23s^pu 23v^pu 20g Apr 1] smallish, plain gelding: very smart hurdler **h141**
at best: showed himself still capable of useful form when fourth to Persian Waters in
handicap at Haydock in May: off 8 months, no form in 3 subsequent starts (not knocked
about on a couple of occasions): stays easy 23f: acts on good to firm and heavy going:
hard ride (has often found little). *L. Lungo*

CRAZY MAZIE 7 b.m. Risk Me (FR) – Post Impressionist (IRE) (Ahonoora) [2003/4 **h72**
h66: 26m³ 24g^pu 21s² 16s^pu 19d⁴ 23s Apr 4] angular mare: poor maiden hurdler: best form
around 2½m: acts on soft going. *K. A. Morgan*

CREAM CRACKER 6 b.m. Sir Harry Lewis (USA) – Cream By Post (Torus) **F72**
[2003/4 F16m⁵ F14d Mar 22] third foal: sister to useful bumper winner Mister Wellard:

dam, winning hurdler/fair pointer, out of half-sister to useful hurdler/chaser up to 25f Gallaher: poor form on first of 2 outings in bumpers. *Ms Bridget Nicholls*

CREATIVE TIME (IRE) 8 b.g. Houmayoun (FR) – Creative Princess (IRE) (Creative Plan (USA)) [2003/4 c105, h–: c24g⁴ c24dᵖᵘ c24d* c23dᵖᵘ Apr 21] rangy gelding: modest handicap chaser: won at Stratford in March: likely to stay beyond 3m: acts on soft going. *Miss H. C. Knight* **c96 h–**

CREED (IRE) 4 ch.g. Entrepreneur – Ardent Range (IRE) (Archway (IRE)) [2003/4 17m⁴ 16fᵖᵘ Oct 5] workmanlike gelding: modest maiden on Flat (stays 1¾m): poor form when fourth in juvenile at Market Rasen on hurdling debut (reportedly hung): sold out of R. Fahey's stable 5,200 gns Doncaster August Sales: lame second start. *F. P. Murtagh* **h66**

CREGG HOUSE (IRE) 9 ch.g. King Persian – Loyal River (Over The River (FR)) [2003/4 c135§, h114§: 16d c23m c22s c24d c20d³ c20s⁴ Feb 1] tall gelding: winning hurdler, left P. Mullins after reappearance: useful chaser at best: not the force of old, and almost certainly flattered in Grade 3 at Thurles (fourth of 5 to Native Upmanship) final start: effective at 2m to 25f (held when refusing both starts over further): acts on heavy going: tried blinkered/in cheekpieces: has had tongue tied: temperamental. *S. Donohoe, Ireland* **c114 § h– §**

CREON 9 b.g. Saddlers' Hall (IRE) – Creake (Derring-Do) [2003/4 c–x, h120: c22v³ 25d c24d 23vᵖᵘ 20v⁶ 25g* Mar 16] leggy gelding: modest handicap hurdler: in cheekpieces, back to best when winning 24-runner Pertemps Final at Cheltenham, gradually working way into contention and staying on strongly to lead near line and beat G V A Ireland ½ length: stays 3¼m: acts on good to firm and heavy going: tried blinkered/tongue tied: usually held up and often finds little: sketchy jumper of fences. *Jonjo O'Neill* **c90 + h122**

CRESSWELL GOLD 7 b.m. Homo Sapien – Running For Gold (Rymer) [2003/4 h–, F–: 19g 19m⁴ 17dᵘ 22g⁴ 20mᵖᵘ 22m 19m⁵ 19m⁵ Sep 10] winning pointer: no form over hurdles: often wears cheekpieces: tongue tied. *D. A. Rees* **h–**

CRESSWELL KATIE (IRE) 6 b.m. King's Ride – Romantic Rose (IRE) (Strong Gale) [2003/4 16s 24mᵖᵘ Sep 14] IR £2,100 3-y-o: third foal: half-sister to fair hurdler Meggie's Beau (by Good Thyne), stays 2½m: dam placed once in points: no form in 4 maiden hurdles, left P. Doyle before final start. *W. K. Goldsworthy* **h–**

CRESSWELL QUAY 11 ch.g. Bold Fox – Karatina (FR) (Dilettante II) [2003/4 c103, h–: c26d* c26g c24s⁶ c24d⁵ c24sᵖᵘ Apr 17] sturdy gelding: fair handicap chaser: won at Plumpton in December: no form after, left P. Bowen before final start: stays 3¼m: acts on any going: held up. *W. K. Goldsworthy* **c109 h–**

CRIAIRE PRINCESS (IRE) 6 b.m. Tidaro (USA) – Lough Borough (IRE) (Orchestra) [2003/4 F16g³ 22m² 24s² 20d⁶ 24s* 22d* 24s² 22s³ 24d³ 16d* 22s² Mar 27] first foal: dam never ran: placed both runs in bumpers: fair novice hurdler: won at Limerick (maiden) in December, Thurles in January and Limerick (battled on gamely to beat Greenhall Rambler a neck in listed mares event) in March: finds 2m on sharp side and stays 3m: acts on good to firm and heavy going: front runner. *Eugene Cleary, Ireland* **h114 F89**

Pertemps Final (Handicap), Cheltenham—
Timmy Murphy conjures a late run out of 50/1-shot Creon (star on cap, centre)
to beat G V A Ireland (noseband) and Alexanderthegreat (striped sleeves)

CRIMSON DANCER 4 b.f. Groom Dancer (USA) – Crimson Rosella (Polar Falcon (USA)) [2003/4 17m² 16mᵖᵘ 16s² 16g² 17dᵘʳ Mar 22] leggy, angular filly: fairly useful on Flat (stays 1½m), successful 4 times in 2003, sold out of W. Haggas' stable 27,000 gns Newmarket Autumn Sales: fair form over hurdles, runner-up all 3 completed starts: raced around 2m: tongue tied after second start. *Miss S. J. Wilton* **h98**

CRIMSON FLOWER (IRE) 9 ch.m. Soviet Lad (USA) – Crimson Kiss (Hello Gorgeous (USA)) [2003/4 18g* 16d⁵ 16s³ 16d Apr 13] leggy mare: fairly useful handicap hurdler: won at Punchestown very early in season: creditable efforts next 2 starts: stays 2½m: raced mainly on good going or softer (acts on heavy). *J. Morrison, Ireland* **h115**

CRINAN (IRE) 6 ch.g. Carroll House – Esther (Persian Bold) [2003/4 F–: 17d 16v⁴ 16s⁵ 19g Mar 26] sturdy gelding: poor form in novice hurdles: bred to be suited by further than 2m (pulled hard final start). *Mrs P. Sly* **h77 +**

CRISIS (IRE) 8 b.g. Second Set (IRE) – Special Offer (IRE) (Shy Groom (USA)) [2003/4 23d 21d Mar 14] close-coupled gelding: fair handicap hurdler at best: well held in 3 starts since 2000/1: stays 2½m: raced on good going or softer (acts on heavy). *P. T. Dalton* **h–**

CRISTOFORO (IRE) 7 b.g. Perugino (USA) – Red Barons Lady (IRE) (Electric) [2003/4 h–: 17g⁵ 16m* 16g² 16g² Nov 19] lengthy, good-topped gelding: progressive form over hurdles in 2003/4: won novice handicap at Plumpton in October: runner-up both starts after, behind Island Stream in conditional jockeys novice handicap at Kempton final one: will prove best around 2m: acts on good to firm going: successful on Flat in April. *B. J. Curley* **h94**

CRISTOPHE 6 b.g. Kris – Our Shirley (Shirley Heights) [2003/4 h68: 24s⁴ 20m c20mᵖᵘ 22m 17g 22v 19v⁴ 16s 21g 17g 17s⁴ 21d* 24d* Apr 21] lengthy gelding: soon struggling on chasing debut: poor hurdler: sold out of Mrs B. Thomson's stable 5,700 gns Doncaster October Sales after fifth outing: won conditional jockeys handicaps at Plumpton (seller) and Worcester (novice) 10 days apart: stays 3m: acts on heavy going: tried in headgear. *Mrs A. M. Thorpe* **c–
h75**

CROAGHNACREE (IRE) 7 b.m. Mister Lord (USA) – Castle Flame (IRE) (Carlingford Castle) [2003/4 h–, F–: 20dᵖᵘ 20dᵖᵘ 20vᶠ Jan 21] workmanlike mare: no sign of ability. *S. J. Marshall* **h–**

CROCADEE 11 b.g. Rakaposhi King – Raise The Dawn (Rymer) [2003/4 c–, h–: 21g³ 20d⁵ Mar 24] tall, useful-looking gelding: one-time useful hurdler/chaser, very lightly raced nowadays: better effort in handicap hurdles in 2003/4 when third to Gin Palace at Kempton: stays easy 23f: acts on good to firm and heavy going: has run well when sweating: races freely. *Miss Venetia Williams* **c–
h120**

CROC AN OIR (IRE) 7 ch.g. Treasure Hunter – Cool Mary (Beau Charmeur (FR)) [2003/4 c–, F–: 23m⁴ 26g³ c26g* Aug 4] poor form in 2 starts over hurdles: much improved on second outing over fences when winning conditional jockeys handicap at Newton Abbot: stays 3¼m. *Miss Venetia Williams* **c88
h75**

CROC EN BOUCHE (USA) 5 b.g. Broad Brush (USA) – Super Cook (USA) (Best Turn (USA)) [2003/4 F–: F17m May 14] no form in bumpers. *Mrs H. Dalton* **F–**

CROCODILES DEN (IRE) 8 b.g. Alphabatim (USA) – Misty Gold (Arizona Duke) [2003/4 c–, h–: c21gᵖᵘ May 18] placed in maiden Irish points: no form otherwise: tried tongue tied (bled from nose): sold 2,200 gns Doncaster August Sales. *P. A. Blockley* **c–
h–**

CROFT COURT 13 b.g. Crofthall – Queen of Dara (Dara Monarch) [2003/4 c25g⁶ May 1] modest pointer: winning steeplechaser, no form in hunters: stays 3¼m: tried blinkered. *Nick Seal* **c–**

CROIX DE GUERRE (IRE) 4 gr.g. Highest Honor (FR) – Esclava (USA) (Nureyev (USA)) [2003/4 16m² 18s² 14g² 20g² 16s² 18d² Apr 7] tall gelding: half-brother to bumper winner Sento (by Persian Bold): modest and wayward on Flat (stays 1½m), sold out of Sir Mark Prescott's stable 18,000 gns Newmarket Autumn Sales: fair juvenile hurdler, runner-up on 5 of 6 starts: stays 2½m: acts on soft ground: blinkered last 3 outings: doesn't have ideal attitude. *P. J. Hobbs* **h107**

CROKER (IRE) 9 ch.g. Rainbows For Life (CAN) – Almagest (Dike (USA)) [2003/4 h85: 19v c16dᵖᵘ Mar 15] workmanlike gelding: modest handicap hurdler: no show in 2003/4, including on chasing debut: stays 2½m: acts on good to firm and heavy going: tried blinkered/visored: has looked difficult ride. *S. T. Lewis* **c– §
h– §**

CROMER PIER   9 b.g. Reprimand – Fleur du Val (Valiyar) [2003/4 h–: 16g 19m³ 19g 26mᵖᵘ 16vꟳ 17g 16d Jan 22] leggy gelding: winning hurdler, little form since 2000/1: tried visored/blinkered. *G. Fierro*   **h–**

CROMWELL (IRE)   9 b.g. Last Tycoon – Catherine Parr (USA) (Riverman (USA)) [2003/4 c–, h–: 21g c17m⁶ c25m² c27m⁶ c21g⁴ c28f* c24g⁵ c28g⁴ c28d³ c28g⁵ c24s⁶ Jan 21] workmanlike gelding: winning hurdler: modest handicap chaser: in-and-out form in 2003/4, winning at Market Rasen (eighth course success) in October: stays 3½m: acts on any going: usually blinkered: has gone in snatches/jumped none too fluently. *M. C. Chapman*   **c85** **h–**

CRONIN'S BOY   10 b.g. Picea – Honey Plum (Kind of Hush) [2003/4 20d c17sꟳ 16s 20v* Jan 17] sturdy gelding: likely to have finished third but for falling 2 out in maiden at Limerick on chasing debut: fairly useful handicap hurdler: best effort in 2003/4 when winning at Punchestown: stays 2½m: goes well on soft/heavy ground: ran poorly only start in blinkers: has had tongue tied. *E. Sheehy, Ireland*   **c99** **h116**

CROOKED MILE (IRE)   7 b.g. Be My Native (USA) – Extra Mile (Torus) [2003/4 F16g⁴ F16g³ 16f³ 16m³ 19d³ 16s² 16d⁴ 16s* 16s³ 16d Mar 7] IR 22,000 4-y-o: second foal: brother to bumper winner Sonnerschien: dam bumper winner: fairly useful form at best in bumpers: fair hurdler: won maiden at Down Royal very easily in January: raced mainly at 2m: acts on soft going. *J. A. O'Connell, Ireland*   **h113** **F92**

CROOKSTOWN CASTLE (IRE)   6 gr.g. Castle Keep – Moorstown Rose (IRE) (Roselier (FR)) [2003/4 F16g² F16g² 19g⁴ 22v⁵ 21d Feb 2] rangy gelding: has scope: third foal: dam unraced: second to Alpine Fox in bumper at Worcester on debut: seemingly best effort in novice hurdles when tenth of 22 to Dangerously Good in steadily-run event at Kempton. *Noel T. Chance*   **h89** **F95**

CROSBY DANCER   5 b.g. Glory of Dancer – Mary Macblain (Damister (USA)) [2003/4 16sᵖᵘ 17dᵘʳ Apr 10] poor maiden on Flat (stays 1¼m) at 2/3 yrs for John Harris: no show on hurdling debut, unseated first next time. *W. S. Coltherd*   **h–**

CROSBY DON   9 b.g. Alhijaz – Evening Star (Red Sunset) [2003/4 c72?, h–: c16m³ c20g Apr 24] leggy gelding: poor maiden hurdler/chaser: stays 2¾m: acts on firm and soft going. *J. R. Weymes*   **c–** **h–**

CROSBY DONJOHN   7 ch.g. Magic Ring (IRE) – Ovideo (Domynsky) [2003/4 h–: 17m² 17fꟳ Oct 5] smallish gelding: poor and unreliable on Flat (stays 1¼m): little worthwhile form over hurdles, though likely to have finished third but for falling 2 out in conditional jockeys handicap at Market Rasen. *J. R. Weymes*   **h59**

CROSBY ROCKER   6 b.m. Rock Hopper – Mary Macblain (Damister (USA)) [2003/4 19fᵖᵘ Nov 22] of little account on Flat: jumped badly right on hurdling debut: sold £520 Ascot December Sales. *John A. Harris*   **h–**

CROSSBOW CREEK   6 b.g. Lugana Beach – Roxy River (Ardross) [2003/4 F106: F16s⁶ F16d⁶ 16v² 16g* 16d⁴ 16g⁴ Apr 18] rangy gelding: type to make a chaser: fairly useful form in bumpers: confirmed promise of hurdling debut when winning maiden at Ludlow in February by 2 lengths from Easter Present: below form both subsequent starts: raced at 2m. *M. G. Rimell*   **h106** **F99**

CROSS RIVER   9 b.g. Reprimand – River Maiden (USA) (Riverman (USA)) [2003/4 c20gᵖᵘ Mar 12] lengthy, good-topped gelding: no form over hurdles: won twice in points in 2004: no show in maiden hunter chase at Leicester. *Joss Saville*   **c–** **h–**

CROW CREEK (IRE)   6 br.g. Presenting – Rossacrowe Gale (IRE) (Strong Gale) [2003/4 F64: F17g⁵ F16d 24gᵖᵘ 19d 21g 26mᵖᵘ Mar 9] little sign of ability, left B. Doran after reappearance: tried blinkered. *T. P. Walshe*   **h–** **F–**

CROWN AND CUSHION   11 b.g. High Adventure – Soulieana (Manado) [2003/4 c26dᵖᵘ Mar 14] sparely-made gelding: winning hurdler/chaser, no show in hunter in March: stays 3m: acts on soft going: blinkered once. *Mrs Kim Sly*   **c–** **h–**

CROWNFIELD   5 b.g. Blushing Flame (USA) – Chief Island (Be My Chief (USA)) [2003/4 h103: 16mⁿ May 7] workmanlike gelding: improved efforts over hurdles last 2 starts, winning conditional jockeys novice at Wetherby: successful on Flat later in month: should stay beyond 2m. *Mrs M. Reveley*   **h103**

CRUISE LEADER (IRE)   8 b.g. Supreme Leader – Ormskirk Mover (Deep Run) [2003/4 c22dᵘʳ c20d* c20v* Jan 17] good-topped gelding: type to carry condition: fair hurdler for Miss H. Knight in 2000/1: off nearly 3 years before unseating on chasing debut: won both subsequent starts, handicaps at Wetherby in December (novice) and January: jumped well on both occasions, idled when beating Deep Water by neck second   **c120 p** **h–**

time: will stay beyond 2½m: raced on going softer than good (acts on heavy): open to further improvement over fences. *C. Grant*

CRUISE THE FAIRWAY (IRE)   8 b.g. Insan (USA) – Tickhill (General Assembly (USA)) [2003/4 c26g^pu Nov 29] tall gelding: fairly useful hurdler/chaser: lame only owing since 2001/2: stays 3m: acts on heavy going, bumper form on good to firm. *B. G. Powell*   c–
h–

CRUISING ALONG   6 gr.m. Thethingaboutitis (USA) – Cruising On (Cruise Missile) [2003/4 F16s F16d Apr 21] first foal: dam poor maiden winning 2m chaser: refused winning in maiden form on debut: well beaten in 2 bumpers. *P. T. Dalton*   F–

CRUISING CLYDE   5 ch.g. Karinga Bay – Bournel (Sunley Builds) [2003/4 F16s F16m* Feb 21] £2,600 4-y-o: stocky gelding: first foal: dam 2¾m hurdle winner who stayed 3¼m: 66/1, won 18-runner event at Wincanton, making all and keeping on well to beat O'Toole ¾ length, second start in bumpers: sold to join C. Mann 30,000 gns Doncaster May Sales. *E. Retter*   **F95**

CRUMBS   4 b.f. Puissance – Norska (Northfields (USA)) [2003/4 F16d Apr 17] sister to winning hurdler Titus Bramble, stays 2¾m, and half-sister to several other winners, including fairly useful hurdler Eponine (by Sharpo), stays 21f: dam maiden who stayed 1¼m: soundly beaten in bumper on debut. *B. Mactaggart*   F–

CRUNCHY (IRE)   6 ch.g. Common Grounds – Credit Crunch (IRE) (Caerleon (USA)) [2003/4 h93: 16m³ 16g³ 16s^pu 17s^pu 17d 19g³ Apr 24] small gelding: fair on Flat (stays 11f): modest maiden hurdler: stays 19f: acts on good to firm and good to soft going: tried in cheekpieces: usually tongue tied. *B. Ellison*   **h91**

CRUSOE (IRE)   7 b.g. Turtle Island (IRE) – Self Reliance (Never So Bold) [2003/4 h–: 16s^pu Dec 20] fair on Flat (stays 9.4f), successful 5 times on all-weather in 2003: no form over hurdles: tried blinkered/tongue tied. *A. Sadik*   h–

CRYPTOGAM   4 b.f. Zamindar (USA) – Moss (Alzao (USA)) [2003/4 16d 16g Dec 3] half-sister to fair hurdler Javelin (by Generous), stays 2½m: fair maiden at best on Flat (should stay 1¼m), sold out of Mrs A. Perrett's stable 8,500 gns Doncaster August Sales: no encouragement in 2 juvenile hurdles. *M. E. Sowersby*   h–

CRYSTAL BROOK   6 b.m. Alderbrook – Earles-Field (Wolverlife) [2003/4 F17g 16m^pu c16g^pu Apr 3] half-sister to Portland winner Musical Season and 6f/7f winner in Italy (both by Merdon Melody): dam unraced half-sister to smart and very tough 1985 2-y-o Dublin Lad: little sign of ability, including in points: sold out of E. Williams' stable £1,800 Ascot October Sales after second start. *C. Staley*   c–
h–
F–

CRYSTAL D'AINAY (FR)   5 b.g. Saint Preuil (FR) – Guendale (FR) (Cadoudal (FR)) [2003/4 c?, h125: 20d² 21s* 24g² 20d* 24g³ 24g⁴ Apr 1]   c–
h160

'If ifs and buts were candy and nuts, wouldn't it be a Merry Christmas?' The wry old American adage, popularised by the celebrated American Football commentator 'Dandy' Don Meredith, certainly rings true for Crystal d'Ainay, who would begin the 2004/5 season as one of the most exciting novice chase prospects in training were it not for the fact that he has already won a race over fences. That success, which came in a five-runner contest for three-year-olds at Angers in December 2002 for Guillaume Macaire, means he will start the next season in valuable staying hurdles rather than against seasoned chasers. That being so, he will face formidable opposition from Baracouda and Rhinestone Cowboy in top conditions races, while handicaps will be difficult to find given his lofty BHB assessment. But Crystal d'Ainay has already come a long way since joining Alan King and, with time very much on his side, he needs only to stay sound to make his presence felt in more good races.

Crystal d'Ainay's second season with King comprised four races at Cheltenham sandwiched between two at Aintree. The first Cheltenham run, which followed a highly encouraging reappearance behind his stable-companion Mughas in a valuable Aintree handicap, was the Jet UK Relkeel Hurdle in December. King held a close affinity with Relkeel who won two Bula Hurdles during his time as assistant to David Nicholson, and a third barely two weeks after he took over from his former boss at Jackdaws Castle in 1999. Memories were rekindled as Relkeel was paraded before the race. Hopes for the future of a highly promising younger recruit were heightened afterwards, as Crystal d'Ainay travelled strongly from the off and gradually got the better of a rousing finish with Sh Boom to score by a length. The one minor blemish on an otherwise polished performance came when

Byrne Bros Cleeve Hurdle, Cheltenham—Crystal d'Ainay proves too strong for Hardy Eustace

Crystal d'Ainay idled up the hill despite firmish handling from Robert Thornton. It was a trait which manifested itself again, this time to costly effect, in the Spa Hurdle on New Year's Eve. Deano's Beeno stole the headlines with a thoroughly mulish performance which resulted in Tony McCoy being handed a five-day improper riding ban for hitting his mount repeatedly in an attempt to get him to jump off. The incident ensured racing rang out the old year with a spate of damaging headlines suggesting that the champion jockey had struck his mount fifty times. The headlines were swiftly followed by a phone poll on Channel 4 the following day which drew a response from almost 30,000 callers, of which forty-one per cent favoured an increased ban and forty-two per cent thought there should have been no ban at all. Jockey Club PR director John Maxse described McCoy's actions as an incident which 'sent out all the wrong signals'. Meanwhile, Channel 4 pundit John Francome sent out a crystal clear signal as to how he views a large section of his audience, simultaneously doing his prospects of a career in the diplomatic corps precious little good, with the bizarre suggestion that a lot of the voters were 'probably the sort that let their children go off mugging people and don't discipline them at all.' So far as the race itself was concerned, Crystal d'Ainay failed to quicken in the anticipated fashion after cruising upsides Sh Boom before the last; meeting him on terms 4 lb better than in the Relkeel Hurdle, Sh Boom rallied to beat him by a length again. King blamed himself for issuing Thornton with orders to challenge as late as possible, learning a valuable lesson which paid dividends in the Byrne Bros Cleeve Hurdle just over three weeks later.

After failing to justify its status as a championship contest, the Cleeve Hurdle has been downgraded from Grade 1 to Grade 2, at the same time being reduced in distance by a furlong. Ironically, the latest renewal did contain a budding champion in the shape of Hardy Eustace, though he was only just beginning to run into form after a subdued start to the season. All the same, Crystal d'Ainay, ridden by Jimmy McCarthy while Thornton nursed a broken collarbone, put up a fine performance to beat him. Only two mattered once Redemption weakened quickly before the last. Hardy Eustace stuck to his task willingly until eased slightly close home, but Crystal d'Ainay always had the edge and drew three lengths clear despite running a shade lazily again. The next question was whether a step up to three miles would enable Crystal d'Ainay to step up enough to make an impact against Baracouda and Iris's Gift in the bonusprint.com Stayers' Hurdle. Odds of 20/1 were still available after the Cleeve Hurdle but by the big day Crystal d'Ainay was down to 8/1 to buck one of the longest-established trends in jump racing. No five-year-old has won the Stayers' Hurdle. But trends had nothing whatsoever to do with Crystal d'Ainay's defeat at the Festival. Indeed, with Thornton back aboard, he ran the race of his life, unable to live with Iris's Gift and Baracouda but staying on to pull well clear of the remainder in third. Iris's Gift was again in the line-up when Crystal d'Ainay signed off for the season in the Liverpool Hurdle. King summed up his approach to the Aintree race by saying 'I've no expectation of beating Iris's Gift but will be delighted if we get in the money.' In a slowly-run race, which was never likely to play to his strengths, Crystal d'Ainay ran below his Cheltenham form, niggled along to chase the leaders from a long way out before being outpaced from the second last to finish over eight lengths behind the winner in fourth.

Crystal d'Ainay (FR) (b.g. 1999)	Saint Preuil (FR) (gr 1991)	Dom Pasquini (gr 1980)	Rheffic
			Boursonne
		Montecha (br 1972)	Montevideo II
			Chasseresse
	Guendale (FR) (b or br 1992)	Cadoudal (br 1979)	Green Dancer
			Come To Sea
		Rose Sanguine (ch 1982)	Sang Bleu
			Rosa d'Estrees

Precocity is a notable feature in Crystal d'Ainay's pedigree. His sire Saint Preuil was a useful hurdler for Macaire at the age of three and showed similar form

Mr Tony Fisher & Mrs Jeni Fisher's "Crystal d'Ainay"

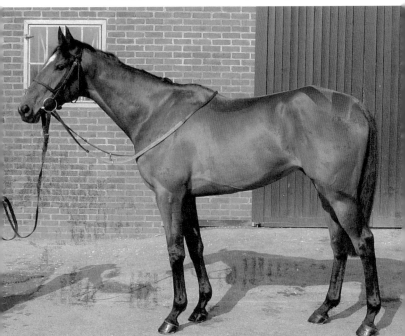

over fences at four. At stud he has also produced My Will, a dual juvenile hurdle winner for Macaire who showed useful form for Paul Nicholls in the latest season, and the useful chaser Royal Atalza. Crystal d'Ainay's dam Guendale, who finished unplaced on the Flat and over hurdles, produced a minor winner over hurdles and fences on her first visit to Saint Preuil. Crystal d'Ainay is her second foal, while a subsequent visit to Dom Alco produced Etoile d'Ainay, a winner over hurdles and fences in the spring of 2004. Crystal d'Ainay is a good-topped gelding who acts on ground ranging from soft to good and has yet to race on going firmer than good. He clearly stays very well but is not short on pace and is likely to prove every bit as effective at two and a half miles as at three. Connections could be forgiven for cursing the fact that success in a low-key affair at Angers denies them the chance to plan a potentially lucrative novice chasing campaign. Yet ifs and buts seem to carry refreshingly little weight with the trainer who takes the view that 'we would probably have had to spend a lot more money to get him had his novice status still been intact.' The West Yorkshire Hurdle at Wetherby in late-October looks a likely starting point for a campaign which will probably involve at least a couple more trips to Cheltenham. Looking further down the line, Crystal d'Ainay should eventually make a fine sight if he jumps as boldly over fences as he does over hurdles. *A. King*

CRYSTAL DANCE (FR)   4 gr.g. Loup Solitaire (USA) – Somptueuse (FR) (Crystal Palace (FR)) [2003/4 17s 17s³ c17d³ c17d 15d 15s c17s⁴ c17s³ 16s 16g⁶ 20d 17g⁶ Apr 12] leggy ex-French gelding: eighth foal: half-brother to winner on Flat by Dancing Spree: dam 1m winner: thrice-raced on Flat: maiden hurdler/chaser, left J-Y. Artu after eighth start: only poor form in Britain: raced mainly around 2m: acts on soft going. *C. Grant*   **c95**
h92

CRYSTAL GIFT   12 b.g. Dominion – Grain Lady (USA) (Greinton) [2003/4 20v⁶ 20v² 20s⁴ 20s² Apr 4] small, sparely-made gelding: fair handicap hurdler, off 22 months prior to reappearance: stays 3m: raced mainly on good going or softer (acts on heavy). *A. C. Whillans*   **h111**

CULBANN (IRE)   5 b.m. Religiously (USA) – Persian Gem (IRE) (Persian Heights) [2003/4 F17m⁴ Apr 15] smallish mare: first foal: dam won Irish point: 6¾ lengths fourth to Golden Odyssey in mares bumper at Cheltenham on debut, nearest finish. *G. A. Harker*   **F86**

CULCABOCK (IRE)   4 b.g. Unfuwain (USA) – Evidently (IRE) (Slip Anchor) [2003/4 16m* 16d³ 16g 18v³ 17s⁴ 16g³ 16g4 16s² Apr 4] leggy gelding: modest on Flat (stays 11f): modest juvenile hurdler: soon in clear lead when successful at Ayr in November: raced around 2m: acts on soft and good to firm going. *P. Monteith*   **h91**

CULLEN ROAD (IRE)   6 b.g. Wakashan – My Wings (Erin's Hope) [2003/4 h63, F87?: 16m³ 17m Jun 21] leggy gelding: poor novice hurdler: tried in cheekpieces. *J. R. Jenkins*   **h63**

CULLIAN   7 b.m. Missed Flight – Diamond Gig (Pitskelly) [2003/4 h91: 22s c16g³ c25dᵖᵘ 20d 20vᵖᵘ 16g² Apr 4] good-topped mare: modest hurdler: sold out of Mrs N. Smith's stable 5,500 gns Doncaster January Sales after fifth outing: better effort over fences when 18 lengths third to Kalca Mome in novice at Newton Abbot: should stay beyond 21f: raced mainly on going softer than good: has won in cheekpieces: tried blinkered/tongue tied. *J. G. M. O'Shea*   **c88**
h92

CUMBRIAN KNIGHT (IRE)   6 b.g. Presenting – Crashrun (Crash Course) [2003/4 h100, F96: 16g⁴ 17g8* 17d² 20d⁴ 16s 16dᵖᵘ 16d 17d² Apr 18] good-topped gelding: fair novice hurdler: odds on, won at Bangor in October: good second to Ebinzayd in handicap at Carlisle final start: stays 2½m: raced mainly on good going or softer (acts on soft). *J. M. Jefferson*   **h109**

CUPLA CAIRDE   4 b.c. Double Eclipse (IRE) – Four-Legged Friend (Aragon) [2003/4 16m⁶ 16d² 16d³ 16s² 16v* 16s² 16s 16g* 16d³ Apr 12] compact colt: modest up to 1½m on Flat: fairly useful juvenile hurdler: won at Punchestown (Grade 3 event, by 1½ lengths from Top Strategy, eased run-in) in January and Stratford in March: good third to Essex at Fairyhouse following month: raced at 2m: acts on heavy going: best efforts when blinkered: usually makes running: consistent. *D. T. Hughes, Ireland*   **h122**

CURIOSITSKI   8 b.m. Petoski – Nosey's Daughter (Song) [2003/4 22m Jul 14] poor form in bumpers: well held all starts over hurdles. *D. A. Rees*   **h–**

CURLY SPENCER (IRE)   10 br.g. Yashgan – Tim's Brief (Avocat) [2003/4 c109, h107: c24gᵖᵘ c20g³ c20v⁴ c22v⁴ c22gᵖᵘ c20v² c24gᵖᵘ c20s³ Apr 21] quite good-topped   **c109**
h–

gelding: winning hurdler: fair handicap chaser: should stay 3m: best efforts on going softer than good (acts on heavy): shaped as if amiss 3 times in 2003/4: sold 10,000 gns Doncaster May Sales. *A. Parker*

CURRAGH GOLD (IRE) 4 b.f. Flying Spur (AUS) – Go Indigo (IRE) (Cyrano de Bergerac) [2003/4 16s 17s 16s 19m² 22gᵖᵘ Apr 10] modest on Flat (should stay 1m): poor form over hurdles: stays easy 19f: acts on good to firm going: blinkered first 2 outings. *Mrs P. N. Dutfield*   **h78**

CURTINS HILL (IRE) 10 b.g. Roi Guillaume (FR) – Kinallen Lady (IRE) (Abednego) [2003/4 h104: c24m³ c20f⁴ c20m³ c18g c23g² c21d² c24d* c22g³ Mar 5] lengthy gelding: fair hurdler: fair handicap chaser: at least as good over fences, best effort when winning novice handicap at Sandown in February by 5 lengths from Running Machine: stays 3m: acts on soft and good to firm going: patiently ridden. *T. R. George*   **c111 h–**

CUSH JEWEL (IRE) 8 b.m. Executive Perk – Shannon Jewel (IRE) (Le Bavard (FR)) [2003/4 20g 24g³ 21m⁴ 26m³ 21f* 24m³ 19d² c26sᶠ 20m² 21m⁵ 19s⁵ 21g Feb 13] leggy mare: first foal: dam unraced half-sister to fairly useful hurdler/chaser up to 25f Indian Scout: won mares maiden point in 2002: fell fourth on steeplechase debut: modest hurdler, left D. Fenton after reappearance: won 3-runner novice handicap at Towcester in October: best efforts around 2½m: acts on firm and good to soft going. *J. G. M. O'Shea*   **c– h91**

CUSP 4 b.f. Pivotal – Bambolona (Bustino) [2003/4 16s 16v⁶ 16gᵘʳ 17d Apr 10] tall filly: half-sister to several winners, including fairly useful chaser up to 2½m Scottish Bambi and fairly useful 2m hurdler Miss Haggis (both by Scottish Reel): well beaten on Flat: poor form over hurdles: running best race when stumbling and unseating after last in juvenile won by Albany at Catterick. *C. W. Thornton*   **h76**

CUTHILL HOPE (IRE) 13 gr.g. Peacock (FR) – Sicilian Princess (Sicilian Prince) [2003/4 c113, h–: c20dᵖᵘ c25s⁴ c25s⁵ c22vᵘʳ Feb 5] good-topped gelding: fair handicap chaser: well below best in 2003/4: stays 25f: acts on heavy going, probably on good to firm: effective visored or not: usually races prominently. *A. C. Whillans*   **c– h–**

CUTTHROAT 4 ch.g. Kris – Could Have Been (Nomination) [2003/4 F16d³ Mar 25] fifth foal: dam unraced half-sister to Prix du Jockey Club winner Polytain: 8 lengths third to State of Play in falsely-run bumper at Ludlow on debut. *T. P. Tate*   **F86**

CUT THROAT JAKE 7 ch.g. Karinga Bay – French Lip (Scorpio (FR)) [2003/4 24mᵖᵘ 26gᵖᵘ 16m 20m 20gᵘʳ Aug 23] seems of no account. *S. J. Gilmore*   **h–**

CUTTHROAT KID (IRE) 14 b.g. Last Tycoon – Get Ahead (Silly Season) [2003/4 21d Apr 11] neat gelding: poor hurdler: stays 3¼m: probably acts on any going: effective blinkered/visored or not. *T. R. Greathead*   **h–**

CYANARA 8 b.m. Jupiter Island – Shamana (Broadsword (USA)) [2003/4 h–: c16m⁵ c21g³ c24g⁵ c20mᶠ c26mᵖᵘ c26m⁵ c26m² c22g⁶ c26g³ c24f⁴ c20m³ c19g³ c19sᵇᵈ c22v² c19s⁵ 24g c22g² c22d³ c20g Apr 3] compact mare: winning hurdler: poor maiden chaser: seems to stay 3¼m: acts on soft and good to firm going. *Dr P. Pritchard*   **c? h–**

CYBELE ERIA (FR) 7 b.m. Johann Quatz (FR) – Money Can't Buy (Thatching) [2003/4 c94, h112§: 16f⁴ 17s⁶ Jan 20] close-coupled mare: winning hurdler/chaser: sold out of N. Henderson's stable 10,000 gns Doncaster May Sales after reappearance: raced around 2m: acts on soft going: weak finisher. *John Allen*   **c– h95 §**

CYBORG DE SOU (FR) 6 b.g. Cyborg (FR) – Moomaw (Akarad (FR)) [2003/4 F16g F16g F16g 16s 16s⁴ 17s² 16s⁶ 16d* Apr 23] IR £15,000 3-y-o, 15,000 4-y-o: ex-Irish gelding: second foal: dam won at 1¼m on Flat and up to 2½m over hurdles in France: showed little in bumpers: modest hurdler, left J. Maxwell after fifth start: won maiden at Perth: bred to stay beyond 2m: acts on soft going. *G. A. Harker*   **h93 F–**

CYBORSUN (FR) 7 ch.g. Cyborg (FR) – Kaprika (FR) (Cadoudal (FR)) [2003/4 c19s* c19d 16s⁵ c17s⁵ Mar 27] well-made gelding: third foal: half-brother to very smart hurdler/smart chaser Geos (by Pistolet Bleu) and winning 17f chaser Daprika (by Epervier Bleu): dam, minor 15f hurdle winner, also 1¼m winner on Flat: fairly useful hurdler/chaser in France: first form in Ireland when winning handicap chase at Naas in January by 1½ lengths from Bennie's Pride: respectable efforts at best subsequently: stays 2½m: acts on heavy going. *A. L. T. Moore, Ireland*   **c119 h99**

CYFOR MALTA (FR) 11 b.g. Cyborg (FR) – Force Nine (FR) (Luthier) [2003/4 c166, h–: c20g⁵ c25d⁶ c20gᵖᵘ c25gᵖᵘ c21m Apr 14] tall, lengthy gelding: top-class chaser on his day, won same valuable handicap at Cheltenham in November in 1998 and 2002 (successful 4 times there in total): long way below best in 2003/4: stayed 25f: acted on soft and good to firm going: tried visored: had tendency to jump left: retired. *M. C. Pipe*   **c– h–**

CYINDIEN (FR)   7 b. or br.g. Cyborg (FR) – Indiana Rose (FR) (Cadoudal (FR)) **c–** [2003/4 h102: 20g³ c22d c20s⁴ 24s⁶ 20g 17g 22g³ Apr 18] rather sparely-made gelding: **h97** well held in handicaps both starts over fences: modest maiden hurdler: stays 25f: raced on good going or softer: signs of temperament when tried in headgear. *Ms Bridget Nicholls*

CYRIUM (IRE)   5 b.g. Woodborough (USA) – Jarmar Moon (Unfuwain (USA)) **F84** [2003/4 F–: F16m⁴ F16g Mar 7] big, rangy gelding: apparently easily best effort in bumpers when fourth of 8 at Ludlow in May: sold out of R. Fisher's stable 18,000 gns Doncaster August Sales: headstrong. *C. J. Mann*

CYRLIGHT (FR)   4 ch.g. Saint Cyrien (FR) – Yellow Light (FR) (Lightning **c143 p** (FR)) [2003/4 16d* c17s* c17d* c17v* c17s* c20s* c20s* Apr 24] **h?**

        Although the chance of crack French chaser Kotkijet running in Britain seems slim, the exciting four-year-old chaser Cyrlight, all being well, will contest the King George VI Chase at Kempton in December. The race conditions regarding age are set to be changed to allow him to take part and though he will need to improve on form against his peers he will receive a handy 13-lb allowance because of his assumed immaturity. In this case, it is some assumption. So far Cyrlight has a perfect record, having won his only start over hurdles and all seven over fences.

Gras Sayove Cinema–Prix Ferdinand Dufaure, Auteuil—the outstanding four-year-old chaser Cyrlight

They haven't been races of limited consequence either. After winning a four-runner event over hurdles at Vichy on his debut in August, Cyrlight won three of the most important three-year-old chases at Auteuil, including the top one, the Group 2 Prix Congress. He then returned there in the spring to win the four graded events for four year old chasers, the Duc d'Anjou, the Fleuret, the Jean Stern and the Group 1 Prix Ferdinand Dufaure. And Cyrlight didn't just win, he slaughtered the opposition, running up a series of winning margins rarely seen at the highest level anywhere. After winning by a length and a half on his chasing bow, Cyrlight recorded victories by ten lengths, six lengths (twice), ten lengths again and eight lengths, usually giving away weight, before he put his twelve rivals to the sword in the Dufaure, winning by fifteen lengths and ten lengths.

No winner of the Dufaure in recent times achieved that level of performance time after time and few have even come close in terms of quality of races won. In 1996, Kizitca won three other graded events, including the Prix La Perichole, which at the time was run before the Dufaure, and finished third in the Jean Stern. In 1994, Parika also won the Fleuret and Duc d'Anjou (and had won the Congress the previous autumn) but fell in the Jean Stern. In 1990, Ucello II won the Jean Stern and the Duc d'Anjou but didn't contest the Fleuret. Neither Kizitca, who never won again, nor Parika, who was off over four years after winning the Dufaure, made much impact subsequently but Ucello II went on to become one of Francois Doumen's celebrated 'three musketeers', along with The Fellow and Ubu III, who all won the Grand Steeple-Chase de Paris among a host of big races. Front-running Cyrlight's quick jumping and exuberant style are reminscient of Ucello, though he has shown a tendency to jump right at mainly left-handed Auteuil, so Kempton might well suit him.

Cyrlight has so far raced at up to two and a half miles and on going softer than good, though he gives the impression he will stay an easy three miles. His sire Saint Cyrien raced only at a mile and nine furlongs but his progeny include the top-class mile-and-a-half performer Epervier Bleu and the smart French jumpers Douze Douze and Sunny Flight. Cyrlight's dam Yellow Light won at a mile and a quarter. Her five previous foals include the useful chaser/fairly useful hurdler Roscoff (by Start Fast), who has raced at up to two and a half miles in France for Cyrlight's trainer. *A. Chaille-Chaille, France*

D

DABARPOUR (IRE)   8 b. or br.g. Alzao (USA) – Dabara (IRE) (Shardari) [2003/4 h101: 16g 20g⁵ 19g⁴ c17s⁴ 17g² 17g⁴ 16m 16m⁶ 16d 16d Feb 8] good-topped gelding: winning hurdler: poor on balance of form in 2003/4: breathing problem on chasing debut: sold out of J. O'Shea's stable 2,000 gns Doncaster October Sales after eighth start: best around 2m: acts on firm and good to soft going: tried in cheekpieces/visor: often tongue tied. *M. A. Barnes*   c–   h90

DABUS   9 b.g. Kris – Licorne (Sadler's Wells (USA)) [2003/4 c–, h91: 16d 19gʳᵗʳ 16dᵘʳ 17g 17m* 17g⁵ Sep 30] medium-sized gelding: fell second only outing over fences: modest hurdler: won selling handicap at Sedgefield in September: barely stays 19f: acts on firm and good to soft going: takes good hold: refused to race second start. *M. C. Chapman*   c–   h89 §

DAD'S ELECT (GER)   5 b.g. Lomitas – Diamond Lake (USA) (Cox's Ridge (USA)) [2003/4 17gʳᵒ c18f² 17g⁴ 16g³ 16s 18v* 20g² 17v* 20s⁵ 16g Apr 2] good-topped ex-German gelding: won over 1½m on Flat at 3 yrs: twice successful over hurdles in Italy for P. Vovcenko, in handicap at Milan in November and minor event at Rome in December: fair form on first of 2 starts in novices in Britain: second at Bad Harzburg on chasing debut in July: stays 2½m: acts on heavy going, probably on firm. *C. J. Mann*   c?   h109

DADS GIFT   6 ch.g. Ajjaj – Lyricist (Averof) [2003/4 F14d² F17g F16m Apr 13] half-brother to several winners, including 25f hurdle winner Rusty Music (by Rustingo): dam unraced: poor form in bumpers. *R. L. Brown*   F69

DADS LAD (IRE)   10 b.g. Supreme Leader – Furryvale (Furry Glen) [2003/4 c86: c26v² c28d* c28gᵖᵘ c24g* c25s³ Jan 20] fair handicap chaser: won at Market Rasen (first outing for 6 months) in December and Ascot in January: thorough stayer: raced on   c100

DAI

good going or softer (acts on heavy): usually blinkered: has looked difficult ride. *Miss Suzy Smith*

DAILY RUN (IRE) 6 b.g. Supreme Leader – Rugged Run (Deep Run) [2003/4 F16s 20v 20d 17d^{pu} Apr 10] fourth foal: half-brother to fair hurdler Poachers Run (by Executive Perk), stays 23f: dam unraced, from family of top-class staying chaser Jodami: no sign of ability. *G. M. Moore*   **h–** **F–**

DAISY DALE 6 gr.m. Terimon – Quetta's Girl (Orchestra) [2003/4 F17m^6 16g^4 16f^2 19m^4 16g Dec 11] signs of only a little ability in bumpers and over hurdles. *K. Bishop*   **h72 ?** **F–**

DAJAZAR (IRE) 8 b.g. Seattle Dancer (USA) – Dajarra (IRE) (Blushing Groom (FR)) [2003/4 c98, h102: 18g^F Apr 30] runner-up in maiden on chasing debut: fair handicap hurdler for P. Rothwell, tailed off both completed starts for current stable: stays 2¾m: acts on any going: usually blinkered in Ireland: has had tongue tied. *Miss V. Scott*   **c–** **h–**

DALARAM (IRE) 4 b.g. Sadler's Wells (USA) – Dalara (IRE) (Doyoun) [2003/4 17d 16d* 16g 16d* Apr 17] medium-sized gelding: useful on Flat (stays 2m), sold out of Sir Michael Stoute's stable 67,000 gns Newmarket Autumn Sales: fairly useful juvenile hurdler: won at Musselburgh (maiden) in February and Ayr in April: improved appreciably when beating Parknasilla 5 lengths at latter: will stay beyond 2m: tongue tied first 3 starts: has worn crossed noseband. *J. Howard Johnson*   **h124**

DALAWAN 5 b.g. Nashwan (USA) – Magdala (IRE) (Sadler's Wells (USA)) [2003/4 F17m^2 Aug 25] second foal: dam unraced half-sister to smart performer up to 2½m Heron Island: second to Bula's Quest in bumper at Newton Abbot on debut: sold 5,000 gns Doncaster May Sales. *A. J. Chamberlain*   **F93**

DALBLAIR (IRE) 5 b.g. Lake Coniston (IRE) – Cartagena Lady (IRE) (Prince Rupert (FR)) [2003/4 16g^3 16g^4 Jan 7] sturdy gelding: fair on Flat (stays 1½m) for J. Glover: modest form when in frame in 2 novice hurdles. *M. Todhunter*   **h88**

DALCASSIAN BUCK (IRE) 10 ch.g. Buckskin (FR) – Menebeans (IRE) (Duky) [2003/4 c69x, h88: c21s^3 c17g^{pu} c21m^6 c24s^2 c25v c21d^3 c24m^{ur} c21g^4 c24g^{pu} Apr 16] workmanlike gelding: winning hurdler: poor maiden chaser: stays 3m: acts on soft going: reported lame final start: often let down by jumping over fences. *C. L. Popham*   **c80 x** **h–**

DALCASSIAN KING (IRE) 11 b.g. King's Ride – Niagara Lass (Prince Hansel) [2003/4 17g^{pu} 16m^{pu} c16m^2 c16d^5 c16d^4 c16m c16d c19s c16g 19m^{pu} c25d^6 c19m c24g^5 Apr 18] tall gelding: winning pointer: poor maiden hurdler/steeplechaser: stays 3m: acts on good to firm and good to soft going: tried blinkered (looked less than keen)/in cheekpieces. *P. Wegmann*   **c75 ?** **h–**

DALE CREEK (IRE) 9 b.g. Mandalus – Typhoon Signal (Aristocracy) [2003/4 c92, h–: c23m^6 c26g^4 c26m^{ur} c19m^{pu} Sep 10] poor chaser: stays 25f: acts on good to soft going, probably on good to firm: often let down by jumping: sold £4,500 Ascot November Sales prior to showing little in points. *R. H. Alner*   **c84 x** **h–**

DALKEYS LAD 4 b.g. Supreme Leader – Dalkey Sound (Crash Course) [2003/4 F16v^3 F16s^3 F17d Mar 11] sturdy gelding: fifth foal: half-brother to fair hurdler This Thyne (by Good Thyne), stays 25f: dam useful staying chaser: best effort in bumpers when third at Ayr second start. *Mrs L. B. Normile*   **F88**

DALLINGTON BROOK 5 b.g. Bluegrass Prince (IRE) – Valetta (Faustus (USA)) [2003/4 F17s F16d Mar 21] workmanlike gelding: third foal: half-brother to winning 19f hurdler Gimco (by Pelder): dam well beaten in maidens: tailed off in 2 bumpers, blinkered on second occasion. *Dr J. R. J. Naylor*   **F–**

DALRIATH 5 b.m. Fraam – Alsiba (Northfields (USA)) [2003/4 16v 17d^F Mar 7] half-sister to winning 2m hurdler Sharriba (by Sharrood): modest maiden on Flat (best around 1m), sold out of P. Flynn's stable 2,500 gns Newmarket Autumn Sales: keeping on in fourth when falling 2 out in novice at Market Rasen, second start over hurdles: will prove best around 2m with emphasis on speed. *M. C. Chapman*   **h82**

DALUS PARK (IRE) 9 b.g. Mandalus – Pollerton Park (Pollerton) [2003/4 c96: c24s^3 c25v* c25v^{pu} c24s^4 c24v^3 c31d^6 Apr 22] good-topped gelding: fair chaser: won handicap at Towcester in January: thorough stayer: acts on heavy going: hung right and carried head high on reappearance. *C. C. Bealby*   **c98**

DALYMACANDOYLELINE (IRE) 8 b.g. Boyne Valley – Gerties Pride (The Parson) [2003/4 c19g^{pu} c22d^F c23f Jun 24] IR 11,000 4-y-o: second foal: dam fairly useful hurdler/chaser, stayed 3m: winning pointer: no form in bumpers or steeplechases: tried blinkered. *N. F. Glynn, Ireland*   **c–**

240

DAMARISCO (FR)   4 b.g. Scribe (IRE) – Blanche Dame (FR) (Saint Cyrien (FR))   **h–**
[2003/4 16g Nov 30] angular ex-French gelding: half-brother to 3 winners over jumps, including fair hurdler around 2m Calhoun and winning hurdler/chaser around 2m Prowler (both by Sheyrann): successful over 11f on Flat for C. Boutin: well held in juvenile on hurdling debut. *P. J. Hobbs*

DAME EDNA (FR)   4 b.f. Octagonal (NZ) – Mohave Desert (USA) (Diesis) [2003/4   **h–**
16d 16sᵖᵘ Jan 4] lightly raced and no sign of ability on Flat or over hurdles. *Miss S. West*

DAME MARGARET   4 ch.f. Elmaamul (USA) – Pomorie (IRE) (Be My Guest   **h–**
(USA)) [2003/4 16g Jan 17] poor maiden on Flat (stays 13f) at 3 yrs for M. Bell: tailed off in juvenile on hurdling debut: sold £650 Ascot February Sales. *J. A. B. Old*

DAMIEN'S CHOICE (IRE)   12 b.g. Erin's Hope – Reenoga (Tug of War) [2003/4   **c99 §**
c106, h–: c17g c16m c16m c16dᴰᴿ 17s c16s c16dʳᵗʳ 16s⁴ 19m⁵ 16d 16g Apr 4] tall gelding: **h79 §**
winning chaser/hurdler, sold out of G. A. Swinbank's stable 6,000 gns Doncaster August Sales after second start: little form subsequently: stays 2½m: acts on soft and good to firm going: has worn visor/cheekpieces, effective without: held up: refused to race seventh start (has been reluctant in past) and not one to trust. *Dr P. Pritchard*

DAMIENS PRIDE (IRE)   14 b.g. Bulldozer – Riopoless (Royal And Regal (USA))   **c89**
[2003/4 c103d: c21d c25m⁴ c26mᴿ May 29] fair hunter chaser: won point in April: stays 3¼m: acts on firm going, possibly unsuited by soft. *Mrs S. J. Batchelor*

DAM THE BREEZE   11 b.g. Ikdam – Cool Breeze (Windjammer (USA)) [2003/4   **c109**
c105, h–: c25mᵖᵘ c24g⁶ 24m* c25mᵖᵘ 26m³ c24m c25m² c21g⁶ Apr 1] lengthy gelding: **h104**
fair hurdler/chaser: won handicaps over fences at Hereford in May and over hurdles at Uttoxeter (conditional jockeys event) in July: prominent long way when sixth of 15 finishers in Fox Hunters' at Aintree final start: stays 3¼m: acts on firm and good to soft going: visored once: often jumps right (reportedly hung right throughout second start): genuine front runner. *Evan Williams*

DAMUS (GER)   10 b.g. Surumu (GER) – Dawn Side (CAN) (Bold Forbes (USA))   **c111 §**
[2003/4 c125d, h110: c20m c19m⁴ c17mᵖᵘ c16m² c16m⁵ 16sᵖᵘ Apr 21] leggy gelding: **h–**
fair hurdler/chaser: left I. Williams after reappearance: sold out of M. Pipe's stable 2,500 gns Doncaster January Sales before final start: stays easy 2½m: acts on any going: tried visored: usually races prominently. *Mrs J. C. McGregor*

DANA ANNE (IRE)   7 ch.m. Abednego – Joyful Rosanna (Kemal (FR)) [2003/4 F16f   **F–**
Sep 14] fourth foal: half-sister to fair chaser Ammieanne (by Zaffaran), stays 2¾m: dam unraced, out of half-sister to fairly useful staying chasers Hume Castle and Clyde Ranger: well behind in bumper on debut. *J. K. Magee, Ireland*

DANABU (IRE)   6 b.g. Un Desperado (FR) – Ishtar Abu (St Chad) [2003/4 F17sᵖᵘ   **F–**
Feb 10] half-brother to several winners, including very smart hurdler Condor Pan (by Condorcet), stayed 2½m: dam Irish 1½m winner: showed nothing in bumper on debut. *C. Grant*

DANAKIL   9 b.g. Warning – Danilova (USA) (Lyphard (USA)) [2003/4 16g⁴ 16g⁴ Nov   **h96**
25] small, compact gelding: fairly useful on Flat (should stay 1¾m): modest form when fourth in 2 novice hurdles: likely to be suited by a greater test of stamina. *S. Dow*

DANCE ALL NIGHT   5 b.g. Suave Dancer (USA) – Lyndseylee (Swing Easy (USA))   **h–**
[2003/4 17dᵘʳ 17d Apr 10] modest maiden at 2 yrs for A. Bailey: well beaten on completed start in novice hurdles. *C. W. Moore*

DANCE IN TUNE   7 ch.g. Mujtahid (USA) – Dancing Prize (IRE) (Sadler's Wells   **c96**
(USA)) [2003/4 h100: 16m⁵ c16m³ May 29] modest hurdler: similar form when third in   **h92**
handicap at Newton Abbot on chasing debut: will prove best around 2m: raced on good going or firmer: sold 1,600 gns Doncaster August Sales. *P. J. Hobbs*

DANCE OF LIFE   5 b.m. Shareef Dancer (USA) – Regan (USA) (Lear Fan (USA))   **h73**
[2003/4 h72+: 17g 17m⁵ 17mᵖᵘ 16gᵖᵘ 16s 17d Mar 27] poor maiden hurdler: raced around   2m: best efforts on good going: tried in cheekpieces, usually wears blinkers: jumps none too fluently. *S. Gollings*

DANCER LIFE (POL)   5 b.h. Professional (IRE) – Dyktatorka (POL) (Kastet   **h110**
(POL)) [2003/4 16mᶠ 16gᶠ 17g 16g* 16g 17g 16dᶠ 16g Mar 7] angular horse: successful 6 times from 6.5f to 1¾m on Flat in Poland, including 4 times in 2002 for A. Walicki, notably in Polish Derby and Polish St Leger: fair form over hurdles, winning novice at Huntingdon in November: likely to stay beyond 2m: blinkered 2 of last 3 starts. *Jonjo O'Neill*

DANCER POLISH (POL)   6 b.g. Professional (IRE) – Doloreska (POL) (Who **h–**
Knows) [2003/4 h89: 16g[pu] 16m[6] 19m[6] 22d[pu] 16m[pu] Dec 10] close-coupled gelding:
winning hurdler: no form in 2003/4: tried blinkered. *A. Sadik*

DANCING BAY   7 b.g. Suave Dancer (USA) – Kabayil (Dancing Brave (USA)) **h127**
[2003/4 h117: 16d[2] 16v[6] 16s 16g* 20g Apr 1] sturdy gelding: fairly useful handicap
hurdler: won at Hexham in December and Newbury in March, by ¾ length from Fenix
at latter course: stays 21f: acts on soft going, unraced on firmer than good: held up.
N. J. Henderson

DANCING DANOLI   4 b.f. Bin Ajwaad (IRE) – Wave Dancer (Dance In Time (CAN)) **F–**
[2003/4 F12m F16v Feb 7] tenth foal: half-sister to winners around 1m by Sharrood and
Jalmood: dam, 11.7f winner, half-sister to smart jumper in Britain/USA Sailors Dance
and very smart stayer Longboat: showed little in 2 bumpers. *M. Wellings*

DANCING DILL   9 b.m. Dancing High – Some Shiela (Remainder Man) [2003/4 **h–**
20d[pu] Jul 2] poor maiden hurdler: soon beaten only outing since early-2001/2. *J. P. Dodds*

DANCING FOSENBY   8 b.g. Terimon – Wave Dancer (Dance In Time (CAN)) **c73 +**
[2003/4 c–, h–: c21f[4] May 21] bad maiden hunter hurdler: left with too much to do when never- **h–**
nearer fourth of 6 finishers in novice hunter chase at Folkestone in May: won points in
March and April: stays 21f: acts on firm going: tried blinkered: races freely. *Miss
P. C. Lownds*

DANCING HILL   5 b.m. Piccolo – Ryewater Dream (Touching Wood (USA)) [2003/4 **h–**
24m 19d Mar 15] half-sister to fair handicap hurdler Touch Closer (by Inchinor), stays 2¾m:
modest on Flat (stays 6f) at 2 yrs for W. Turner, bought £2,000 Ascot June Sales: no form
in 2 runs over hurdles, tongue tied on second occasion. *Mrs E. B. Scott*

DANCING PEARL   6 ch.m. Dancing Spree (USA) – Elegant Rose (Noalto) [2003/4 **h114**
h96: 17d[2] 16g[2] 16d[2] 16g* 16g[4] Apr 16] leggy mare: fair handicap hurdler: won mares
event at Doncaster in March: raced around 2m: acts on soft going, probably on good to
firm: reliable. *C. J. Price*

DANCING PHANTOM   9 b.g. Darshaan – Dancing Prize (IRE) (Sadler's Wells **h92**
(USA)) [2003/4 17d 16d Dec 17] rather leggy gelding: traces of stringhalt: fairly useful
on Flat (stays 13f): won novice on hurdling debut in 1999: very lightly raced and just
modest form since: edgy sort. *James Moffatt*

DANCING TILLY   6 b.m. Dancing Spree (USA) – L'Ancressaan (Dalsaan) [2003/4 **h–**
19f 16g[5] 16g[bd] Dec 11] half-sister to fairly useful hurdler/winning chaser Mr Cospector
(by Cosmonaut), stays 3¼m: poor maiden on Flat (stays 11f): signs of only a little ability
over hurdles, brought down by loose horse final start (wore cheekpieces). *R. A. Fahey*

DAN DE MAN (IRE)   13 br.g. Phardante (FR) – Slave De (Arctic Slave) [2003/4 c68§, **c67 §**
h–§: c20g[F] 20s[6] 16s[4] c21v 17s c21d[3] c19m Apr 13] lengthy gelding: poor handicap **h69 §**
hurdler/chaser: stays 21f: acts on heavy going, probably on good to firm: best held up:
unreliable. *Miss L. C. Siddall*

DANEBANK (IRE)   4 b.g. Danehill (USA) – Snow Bank (IRE) (Law Society (USA)) **h–**
[2003/4 16g Mar 15] brother to fairly useful 2m chaser Apparition: fair maiden on Flat
(stays 1½m), sold out of J. Hills's stable 11,000 gns Newmarket Autumn Sales: well held
in juvenile on hurdling debut. *J. Mackie*

DANGEROUS DAN MCGO (IRE)   6 b.g. Un Desperado (FR) – Sharnad (IRE) **F95**
(Shardari) [2003/4 F16s[4] F16s Mar 20] tall gelding: has scope: first foal: dam unraced
half-sister to fairly useful hurdler Vic Ville: fourth to Royal Paradise in bumper at
Sandown on debut: possibly hadn't got over that race when only ninth of 21 at Ascot:
likely to stay at least 2½m. *M. C. Pipe*

DANGEROUSLY GOOD   6 b.g. Shareef Dancer (USA) – Ecologically Kind **h125**
(Alleged (USA)) [2003/4 h117: 16d[3] 21d* 22g* 20d 21m[2] Apr 14] leggy gelding: fairly
useful hurdler: won novices at Kempton and Fontwell (by 2½ lengths from Jivaty) in
February: good second of 11 to Xellance in handicap at Cheltenham: stays 2¾m: acts
on good to firm and good to soft going: wears headgear: has carried head awkwardly.
G. L. Moore

DANIELS HYMN   9 b.g. Prince Daniel (USA) – French Spirit (FR) (On Your Mark) **c106**
[2003/4 h110: 24d[5] 20g[2] c17s[4] c24d[3] c22d[pu] 20g[3] Jul 2] well-made gelding: fair hurdler: **h113**
similar form on first of 3 starts over fences: stays 21f: acts on good to soft and good to
firm going (won bumper on firm): blinkered last 3 outings. *Miss F. M. Crowley, Ireland*

DANISH DECORUM (IRE)   5 ch.g. Danehill Dancer (IRE) – Dignified Air (FR) **h82**
(Wolver Hollow) [2003/4 19m[6] 16m[4] 17g[6] Nov 5] angular gelding: half-brother to 2

winning chasers, including modest Regal Aura (by Glow), stays 21f: fairly useful at best on Flat (stays 1½m), sold out of C. Cox's stable 9,000 gns Doncaster August Sales: poor form over hurdles. *Evan Williams*

DANNY LEAHY (FR) 4 b.g. Danehill (USA) – Paloma Bay (IRE) (Alzao (USA)) **h83**
[2003/4 16g 20d⁴ 20d Mar 11] leggy gelding: half-brother to one-time useful 2m hurdler Spectroscope (by Spectrum): fair maiden on Flat (stays 1¼m), sold out of J. Given's stable 13,000 gns Newmarket Autumn Sales: poor form over hurdles. *M. D. Hammond*

DANSE SLAVE (FR) 5 b.m. Broadway Flyer (USA) – Snow Girl (FR) (River Mist **h83**
(USA)) [2003/4 h87, F–: 22dᵖᵘ 22dᵖᵘ 19g⁶ Apr 16] poor hurdler: stays 19f: acts on good to firm and good to soft going. *R. H. Alner*

DANS PRIDE (IRE) 6 b.g. Presenting – Mindyourown (IRE) (Town And Country) **F91**
[2003/4 F16v⁴ F16⁴ Feb 21] tall gelding: fourth foal: dam unraced, from family of useful chaser/smart hurdler up to 3m Forest Sun: fourth in 4-y-o maiden Irish point on debut: better effort in bumpers when fourth at Wincanton, second start. *Noel T. Chance*

DANTE CITIZEN (IRE) 6 ch.g. Phardante (FR) – Boreen Citizen (Boreen (FR)) **c98**
[2003/4 17g 16d⁵ 16d⁵ 24s² 22d⁵ 26s c20d³ c24d* c24d⁵ Apr 8] IR £5,000 3-y-o: sturdy **h93**
gelding: fifth foal: brother to fair chaser Pharaway Citizen, stays 3¼m, and half-brother to winning pointers by Henbit and Supreme Leader: dam winning 2m chaser: winning pointer: well beaten in bumper for E. O'Sullivan: modest hurdler: similar form over fences, making all in novice at Ludlow in March: should stay beyond 3m: acts on soft going. *T. R. George*

DANTECO 9 gr.g. Phardante (FR) – Up Cooke (Deep Run) [2003/4 c97, h90: 20g **c86 x**
20mᵖᵘ c21g⁶ c27g³ c27d³ c24m³ Dec 16] big gelding: modest hurdler/chaser: best form **h–**
up to 21f: possibly needs good going or firmer (acts on firm): has worn cheekpieces: headstrong: sketchy jumper. *Miss Kate Milligan*

DANTE'S BANKER (IRE) 8 ch.g. Phardante (FR) – Nancy Myles (The Parson) **c–**
[2003/4 22m⁴ 26m² c25mᶠ Oct 31] angular gelding: third foal: dam useful hurdler **h75**
who stayed 3m: well beaten in bumper: winning pointer in Ireland: bought 2,500 gns Doncaster May Sales: poor form in 2 novice hurdles: badly let down by jumping on steeplechasing debut, but won another point in April. *C. C. Bealby*

DANTE'S BATTLE (IRE) 12 b.g. Phardante (FR) – No Battle (Khalkis) [2003/4 **c– x**
c114x, h113: 17gᵖᵘ 16m 16m 19g* 20m* 17m⁵ 19m³ 19m* c17m⁴ c24m⁴ c21gᵖᵘ Apr 10] **h86**
fairly useful hurdler/chaser at best: nowhere near so good nowadays but successful in selling hurdles at Newton Abbot (handicap) and Huntingdon (conditional jockeys) in August and Stratford in October: ran poorly over fences last 3 starts: stays 21f: acts on good to soft and good to firm going: has reportedly bled from nose: often let down by jumping over fences. *Miss K. Marks*

DANTE'S BROOK (IRE) 10 ch.g. Phardante (FR) – Arborfield Brook (Over The **c67**
River (FR)) [2003/4 c77, h–: c16g⁵ c16gᵖᵘ c17mᵘʳ c17m³ c16g² c16f⁵ Sep 14] strong, **h–**
lengthy gelding: poor maiden steeplechaser: best around 2m: acts on firm going: often tongue tied. *B. Mactaggart*

DANTE'S PORRIDGE (IRE) 8 b.g. Phardante (FR) – Canal Street (Oats) [2003/4 **h93**
16m² Nov 6] workmanlike gelding: first foal: dam twice-raced in bumpers/over hurdles: failed to complete in 2 maiden points in 2003: some promise when second to Don Valentino in 3-finisher novice at Haydock on hurdling debut, travelling best long way. *Mrs S. J. Smith*

DANTES REEF (IRE) 8 b.g. Phardante (FR) – Thousand Flowers (Take A Reef) **c121 p**
[2003/4 h101, F101: 17g² 20d³ c20dᶠ c16s c17s* 20d* 20d³ Mar 20] third and easily best **h123 +**
effort over fences when winning maiden at Navan in February: improved form returned to hurdling when beating Finians Ivy impressively by 4 lengths in handicap at Fairyhouse 12 days later: travelled really strongly long way when good third to Accipiter in competitive handicap at Ascot final start: stays 2½m: acts on heavy going, probably on good to firm: open to further improvement over fences. *A. J. Martin, Ireland*

DANTES VENTURE (IRE) 7 b.g. Phardante (FR) – Fast Adventure (Deep Run) **c83**
[2003/4 h98: 26g² c21m³ 24sᵖᵘ 22g² 24sᵖᵘ 22g⁴ Apr 18] sturdy gelding: jumped poorly **h100**
when third of 5 in novice at Southwell on chasing debut: fair maiden hurdler: stays 3¼m: acts on heavy going: tried visored. *D. J. Caro*

DANTIE BOY (IRE) 8 br.g. Phardante (FR) – Ballybride Gale (IRE) (Strong Gale) **c118**
[2003/4 c101, h110: 19g² 20m⁵ c20g² c20mᶠ c21g² 20m² c24g² Apr 16] lengthy gelding: **h113**
fair hurdler: fairly useful chaser: off 7 months and left P. Hobbs before final start: probably stays 3m: raced mainly on good going or firmer (acts on firm). *A. W. Congdon*

DANZIG FLYER (IRE) 9 b.g. Roi Danzig (USA) – Fenland Express (IRE) (Reason- **h–**
able (FR)) [2003/4 h–: 16g 22m Jun 29] little form over hurdles. *B. D. Leavy*

DANZIG PRINCE 5 b.g. Danzig Connection (USA) – Lovely Greek Lady (Ela-Mana- **h77 ?**
Mou) [2003/4 20m^pu 21m³ 20d² 19m⁴ 20d 16d⁵ 16d 16g^pu Feb 20] half-brother to fairly
useful 2m hurdler Indiana Princess (by Warrshan): no form on Flat: poor novice hurdler:
wore headgear after debut: looked reluctant final outing. *K. A. Morgan*

DAPHNE'S DOLL (IRE) 9 b.m. Polish Patriot (USA) – Helietta (Tyrnavos) [2003/4 **h–**
17g 16m 20s 24g^pu 21d Mar 1] poor on Flat (barely stays 1½m): no form over hurdles.
Dr J. R. J. Naylor

DARAB (POL) 4 ch.g. Alywar (USA) – Damara (POL) (Pyjama Hunt) [2003/4 16g **h–**
Mar 15] ex-Polish gelding: successful 3 times up to 1¼m from 13 starts on Flat for
G. Wroblewski: showed little in juvenile on hurdling debut. *T. R. George*

DARA CAPALL (IRE) 4 b.g. Simply Great (FR) – She's Pretty (Furry Glen) [2003/4 **F84 p**
F16d F16g³ Mar 10] useful-looking gelding: fifth foal: half-brother to fair hurdler Legal
Challenge (by Strong Gale), stays 3m: dam, fairly useful hurdler who stayed 21f,
half-sister to useful chaser up to 2½m Around The Horn: showed promise in bumpers at
Musselburgh and Catterick, running on strongly from well back when 2 lengths third to
The Weaver at latter: got loose at start on debut: capable of better. *Mrs M. Reveley*

DARDANUS 6 ch.g. Komaite (USA) – Dance On A Cloud (USA) (Capote (USA)) **c102**
[2003/4 h103: c20g^F May 21] medium-sized gelding: fair hurdler: tiring in third when **h–**
falling last in handicap at Worcester on chasing debut: probably stays 2½m: acts on good
to firm going: blinkered (ran poorly) once: has gone well forcing pace. *C. J. Mann*

DARENEUR (IRE) 4 ch.f. Entrepreneur – Darayna (IRE) (Shernazar) [2003/4 F12m **F77**
Dec 10] seventh foal: half-sister to smart 1m winner Dear Daughter (by Polish Precedent)
and winners abroad by Caerleon and Suave Dancer: dam, Irish 7f/1m winner, out of very
smart 6f/7f performer Dafayna, herself half-sister to high-class performers Dolpour and
Doyoun: eighth of 14 in 3-y-o fillies bumper at Newbury on debut: well held on Flat in
April. *W. M. Brisbourne*

D'ARGENT (IRE) 7 gr.g. Roselier (FR) – Money Galore (IRE) (Monksfield) **c148**
[2003/4 h–: 22g³ 22g⁵ c26m* c24d* c24g* c25m⁵ c25g^pu Apr 2] **h116 +**
    If the form of the Roscoe Harvey Novices' Chase at Warwick in January
can be taken at face value then the winner D'Argent begins 2004/5 a very well
handicapped horse indeed. D'Argent came home twenty-six lengths ahead of
Tyneandthyneagain after the favourite Royal Emperor had fallen three out. At that
point, D'Argent was still out in front and full of running, four lengths up on Royal
Emperor and going much the better. After being left clear, D'Argent was able to
coast in. Royal Emperor went on to better things, as did Tyneandthyneagain, but

*Roscoe Harvey Memorial Novices' Chase, Warwick—an assured round of jumping gains D'Argent
a third course win; he's pictured leading fellow grey Royal Emperor*

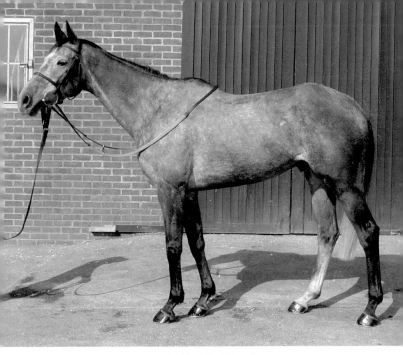

Mr Nigel Bunter's "D'Argent"

D'Argent did not and as a consequence he looks favourably weighted in relation to that pair. A feature of his win that day, as it had been of his earlier successes on the same course on his first two starts over fences, had been his jumping but it let D'Argent down on both his subsequent appearances. He started at 11/10 favourite for a listed event against some useful but exposed rivals at Wincanton in February but was never able to get a clear lead, after jumping far less fluently, and finished fifth of six to Exit Swinger. D'Argent missed the Royal & SunAlliance Chase after that effort and his next appearance came in the Mildmay Novices' Chase at Aintree, for which he started second favourite behind Royal Emperor, who since their previous meeting had gone down narrowly at Cheltenham. D'Argent was again very disappointing, jumping with a lack of confidence and pulled up with a circuit to go. His performances at Wincanton and Aintree take some explaining away but it may be best to forgive D'Argent at least once, for the switch to a sharp, right-handed track may not have suited him at Wincanton, while his stable was out of sorts by the Grand National meeting.

Even if D'Argent's form against Royal Emperor at Warwick flatters him, he's still shown much better form over fences than over hurdles. He's been helped by a step up to three miles or more (he raced at shorter distances over hurdles) but his pedigree also suggests he should be better as a chaser than a hurdler. D'Argent is by Roselier and his grandam is a half-sister to the Cheltenham Gold Cup winner Glencaraig Lady, from the family of the good-class staying chasers Maid of Money and Ten of Spades. D'Argent was bought for IR 26,000 guineas as a three-year-old. A leggy, useful-looking gelding, he has done nearly all his racing on going ranging from good to firm to good to soft, though he was beaten only narrowly on heavy on his hurdling debut. *A. King*

245

DARIOLE (IRE) 8 b.g. Priolo (USA) – Dance Land (IRE) (Nordance (USA)) [2003/4   c110
h129: 20m[6] 16v[5] 22d c20f* 20f[4] c21m[5] 22d Apr 12] fairly useful handicap hurdler: h128
fair form in 2 novice chases, winning at Tralee in August: stays 2½m: acts on any going.
M. Halford, Ireland

DARJEELING (IRE) 5 b.m. Presenting – Afternoon Tea (IRE) (Decent Fellow)   F–
[2003/4 F16s F17s F16g Mar 7] €3,000 4-y-o, resold 7,000 4-y-o: angular mare: third
foal: dam unraced half-sister to useful chaser up to 25f On The Other Hand, from family
of top-class staying chaser Righthand Man: signs of some ability in bumpers, though
headstrong and not a straightforward ride. *Mrs S. Gardner*

DARK ARTIST (IRE) 5 b.g. Perugino (USA) – Black Ivor (USA) (Treasure Kay)   F100
[2003/4 F16f* F16m[4] Oct 5] half-brother to 2 winning 2m hurdlers, including fairly
useful Tequila (by Mystiko): dam unraced: won bumper at Naas on debut in June: fourth
to Euro Leader at Tipperary in October. *J. E. Kiely, Ireland*

DARK BEN (FR) 4 b.g. Solar One (FR) – Reine d'Auteuil (FR) (Cap Martin (FR))   F74
[2003/4 F17v Mar 21] sixth foal: brother to winning 2m hurdler/chaser Arbitraire and
half-brother to 2 other winners: dam unraced half-sister to useful miler Rising Colours:
seventh of 11 in bumper at Carlisle on debut. *Miss Kate Milligan*

DARK CHARACTER 5 b.g. Reprimand – Poyle Jezebelle (Sharpo) [2003/4 F95:   h91
F17g* 16g[R] 19g[3] Dec 3] tall, unfurnished gelding: fairly useful form in bumpers, success-   F99
ful at Bangor on reappearance in October: refused third on hurdling debut and folded
tamely when third in novice at Catterick following month: best treated with caution.
G. A. Swinbank

DARK CRUSADER (IRE) 9 br.g. Cajetano (USA) – Glissade (Furry Glen) [2003/4   c– §
c–§, h–§: 20g c21m[ur] c22d[5] c21s[pu] Dec 26] tall gelding: winning hurdler: of little   h– §
account nowadays: blinkered for both wins, also tried visored: ungenuine. *Miss Lucinda
V. Russell*

DARK DOLORES 6 b.m. Inchinor – Pingin (Corvaro (USA)) [2003/4 16g[ur] 17s[pu]   h–
Dec 16] poor maiden on Flat (stays 1¼m): no form in 2 races over hurdles. *J. R. Boyle*

DARK ISLAND 9 b.g. Silver Season – Isle Maree (Star Appeal) [2003/4 h–: 26m[3]   c–
22f[6] 16g c20g Apr 12] lengthy, rather sparely-made gelding: no sign of ability. *Mrs Mary   h–
A. Meek*

DARK MANDATE (IRE) 6 b. or br.m. Mandalus – Ceoltoir Dubh (Black Minstrel)   c–
[2003/4 h–: 20g[pu] 20s[pu] 20d c16d[pu] c16d[pu] Mar 30] workmanlike mare: no sign of ability.   h–
J. S. Haldane

DARKNESS 5 ch.g. Accordion – Winnowing (IRE) (Strong Gale) [2003/4 F16g[3] Mar   F97
6] tall, lengthy, unfurnished gelding: third live foal: dam, winning hurdler who stayed
2½m, out of half-sister to top-class 2m to 25f hurdler Aonoch: third of 21 to Spirit of New
York in bumper at Newbury on debut. *C. R. Egerton*

DARK ROOM (IRE) 7 b.g. Toulon – Maudlin Bridge (IRE) (Strong Gale) [2003/4   c118
c109: c20g[4] c21d* c24d c33d[pu] c21g[F] Apr 2] lengthy gelding: fairly useful handicap
chaser: improved form when winning betfair.com Grand Sefton Chase at Aintree in

betfair.com Grand Sefton Chase (Handicap), Aintree—
Dark Room (No.9) chases 2003 Fox Hunters' winner Divet Hill over The Chair

November by 3 lengths from Scotmail Boy, still last approaching final fence: no form subsequently: stays 25f: acts on heavy going: jumps none too fluently. *Jonjo O'Neill*

DARK SHADOWS   9 b.g. Machiavellian (USA) – Instant Desire (USA) (Northern Dancer) [2003/4 h94; 20g² 22g⁶ 20g³ 20m⁴ 24d⁷ Nov 14] smallish gelding: modest maiden hurdler: probably stays 3m: acts on good to firm and good to soft going: not a fluent jumper: consistent. *W. Storey*   **h92**

DARK SLANEY (IRE)   9 b.g. Meneval (USA) – Black Valley (IRE) (Good Thyne (USA)) [2003/4 20sᵖᵘ 25s 25gᵖᵘ Jan 24] first foal: half-brother to fairly useful hurdler Macs Valley (by Hubbly Bubbly), stays 2½m: dam, winning pointer, half-sister to useful 2m to 2½m hurdler/chaser Sean Ogue: no form in points or over hurdles. *P. D. Niven*   **h–**

DARK STRANGER (FR)   13 b.g. Iveday (FR) – Abeille Royale (USA) (Turn To Mars (USA)) [2003/4 c24g Mar 16] workmanlike gelding: useful handicap chaser: off 2 years, made running to 4 out when tailed off in valuable event at Cheltenham only outing in 2003/4: stays 29f: acts on any going: blinkered: unreliable. *M. C. Pipe*   **c– §**
h–

DARK THUNDER (IRE)   7 br.g. Religiously (USA) – Culkeern (Master Buck) [2003/4 c26sᵖᵘ 21d 22g³ 21s⁶ Mar 15] IR £1,300 4-y-o: brother to fairly useful hurdler/useful chaser Intelligent, stayed 4¼m, and half-brother to fair chaser up to 3¼m Willchris (by Fidel): dam unraced: no worthwhile form, including in maiden Irish points. *T. P. McGovern*   **c–**
h–

DARK VOCATION (IRE)   4 b.g. College Chapel – Shadia (USA) (Naskra (USA)) [2003/4 16d 16g⁴ 16d³ 16d 16d 16d Apr 12] half-brother to winning hurdler around 2m Executive Choice (by Don't Forget Me): modest maiden on Flat (probably stays 9f): best effort over hurdles when third in juvenile minor event at Leopardstown: well held subsequently: tongue tied. *Frederick John Bowles, Ireland*   **h99**

DARK WHISPER (IRE)   5 b.g. Ali-Royal (IRE) – Bolino Star (IRE) (Stalker) [2003/4 F17g⁴ F17m³ F16m⁵ F16m² Aug 21] €3,800 3-y-o: first foal: dam, useful 2m hurdler, sister to useful 2m hurdler More Dash Thancash: best effort in bumpers when ½-length equal-second to Theatre Groom in 21-runner event at Worcester. *Ian Williams*   **F91**

DARNLEY   7 b. or br.g. Henbit (USA) – Reeling (Relkino) [2003/4 h95, F–: 16s* c16d* c16g⁴ c17g c16d⁴ Apr 22] tall gelding: modest hurdler: won novice at Perth in May: fair form over fences, successful in novice at Newcastle on chasing debut in December: raced around 2m, likely to stay further: acts on soft and good to firm going. *J. N. R. Billinge*   **c100**
h95

DASHING CHARM   5 b.g. Charmer – New Cruiser (Le Solaret (FR)) [2003/4 F16m F16d 21d Apr 12] stocky gelding: first foal: dam well beaten in points: no form in 2 bumpers/maiden hurdle. *C. C. Bealby*   **h–**
F–

DASHING DOLLAR (IRE)   13 b.g. Lord Americo – Cora Swan (Tarqogan) [2003/4 h–: 20mᶠ 22m 16v³ 24s⁶ 19v² 22s 24sᵖᵘ 24gᵖᵘ Apr 1] smallish, workmanlike gelding: poor handicap hurdler nowadays: stays 2¾m: needs good going or softer (acts on heavy): has been mounted on track/reluctant to race: not to be trusted. *J. R. Payne*   **h61 §**

DASHING HOME (IRE)   5 b.g. Lahib (USA) – Dashing Rose (Mashhor Dancer (USA)) [2003/4 h127: 16g⁶ 16d 16m⁴ 16d Apr 13] tall gelding: will make a chaser: useful on Flat up to 1½m, successful in April: fairly useful hurdler: not sure to stay beyond 2m: acts on good to firm and heavy going. *N. Meade, Ireland*   **h119**

DASHING SPUR (IRE)   4 b.g. Flying Spur (AUS) – Glamour Stock (USA) (Marfa (USA)) [2003/4 17dᵖᵘ Nov 17] well held in 2 races at 2 yrs for R. Beckett: no show on hurdling debut. *Miss Victoria Roberts*   **h–**

DASHING STEVE   5 b.g. Danzig Connection (USA) – Blazing Sunset (Blazing Saddles (AUS)) [2003/4 h–: 16mᵖᵘ May 5] bad maiden on Flat (tried visored): no form over hurdles. *Mrs A. M. Thorpe*   **h–**

DATBANDITO (IRE)   5 gr.g. Un Desperado (FR) – Most of All (Absalom) [2003/4 F17d⁵ F16g² F16g⁴ Mar 13] €34,000 3-y-o: quite good-topped gelding: sixth foal: brother to 2½m hurdle winner Eden Royale: dam maiden half-sister to useful 2m hurdler Music Wonder: fair form all 3 starts in bumpers. *L. Lungo*   **F92**

DATITO (IRE)   9 b.g. Over The River (FR) – Crash Call (Crash Course) [2003/4 16d³ Jan 13] tall gelding: bumper winner: off nearly 2 years and only third start over hurdles when third to Parknasilla in novice at Leicester only outing in 2003/4: should be suited by at least 2½m. *R. T. Phillips*   **h102**

DAT MY HORSE (IRE) 10 b.g. All Haste (USA) – Toposki (FR) (Top Ville) [2003/4   **cxx**
cxx, h113: 27g 22m^pu 19g^5 Apr 13] big, workmanlike gelding: not a good walker: badly   **h97**
let down by jumping in steeplechases: winning hurdler, modest form at best in 2003/4:
stays 3¼m: best form on good going: sometimes finishes tamely. *Evan Williams*

DAVENPORT DEMOCRAT (IRE) 6 ch.g. Fourstars Allstar (USA) – Storm Court   **F100**
(IRE) (Glacial Storm (USA)) [2003/4 F105+: F16g^3 Sep 18] tall, rather unfurnished gelding: fairly useful bumper winner: ran well when third, finding little, to Oscar's Advance
at Listowel only start in 2003/4. *W. P. Mullins, Ireland*

DAVENPORT MILENIUM (IRE) 8 b.g. Insan (USA) – Society Belle (Callernish)   **h148**
[2003/4 h149: 20d^4 16s^2 16d^5 16g Mar 16] useful-looking gelding: smart hurdler:
best efforts in 2003/4 when length second to Rigmarole in Bula Hurdle at Cheltenham
and fifth of 8 to Foreman in steadily-run Grade 1 at Leopardstown: last of 13 finishers
in Champion Hurdle at Cheltenham: will stay beyond 2½m: raced on good going and
softer (won bumper on heavy): reportedly underwent wind operation after final start.
W. P. Mullins, Ireland

DAVIDS LAD (IRE) 10 b.g. Yashgan – Cool Nora (IRE) (Lafontaine (USA)) [2003/4   **c138**
c148, h–: c20g^3 c22s^5 c17s^6 c20s^2 c18d^6 c36d Apr 3] strong, lengthy gelding: winning   **h–**
hurdler: smart chaser on his day: best effort in 2003/4 (not at all knocked about most other
starts) when length second to easy winner Native Upmanship in Grade 2 at Thurles in
February: last of 11 finishers in Grand National at Aintree: stays 29f: acts on any going:
usually tongue tied (has reportedly had palate operation): held up: usually sound jumper.
A. J. Martin, Ireland

DAVOSKI 10 b.g. Niniski (USA) – Pamela Peach (Habitat) [2003/4 c148, h–: c20s^pu   **c122**
c19g^5 c17g^3 c16m^3 Apr 15] angular gelding: useful hurdler at one time: smart chaser in   **h–**
2002/3 for Miss V. Williams, just fairly useful form in handicaps on return: successful at
21f, best efforts at 2m: acts on good to firm and heavy going: looked none too keen third
outing: still prone to mistakes. *Ms Bridget Nicholls*

DAWN INVASION (IRE) 5 b.g. Common Grounds – Princess of Zurich (IRE) (Law   **h134**
Society (USA)) [2003/4 16d^F 20d 16s* 16d* Apr 12] useful-looking gelding: smart on
Flat (stays easy 1¾m), sold out of Mrs A. Perrett's stable 65,000 gns Newmarket Autumn
Sales: promising efforts first 2 starts over hurdles: successful in maiden at Cork in March
and minor event at Fairyhouse (useful form when beating Arch Stanton by length) in
April: bit below best when sixth to Brave Inca in Grade 1 novice at Punchestown later in
April. *Anthony Mullins, Ireland*

DAWN'S COGNAC (IRE) 11 b.g. Glacial Storm (USA) – Misty Venture (Foggy   **c– x**
Bell) [2003/4 c–x: c21d c24m^F Apr 13] rangy gelding: fair pointer, successful in February
and March: let down by jumping and no form in steeplechases. *D. Brace*

DAWTON (POL) 6 br.h. Greinton – Da Wega (POL) (Who Knows) [2003/4 16m Dec   **h–**
10] successful 7 times from 19 starts on Flat (up to 1½m) at 3/4 yrs in Poland, left
A. Walicki after runner-up in 13f Group 3 event at Warsaw in September 2002: well held
in maiden on hurdling debut. *T. R. George*

DAY DU ROY (FR) 6 b.g. Ajdayt (USA) – Rose Pomme (FR) (Rose Laurel) [2003/4   **c115**
c?, h?: 17g^2 17g^5 17g^2 20m^* 19d^5 17g^3 c20d^3 c19s^6 20s^3 20g^4 17g^2 c20g* Apr 18] rather   **h110**
leggy gelding: fair handicap hurdler: won at Haydock in November: fairly useful chaser:
improved form when winning handicap at Stratford by 2 lengths from Banker Count:
stays 2½m: acts on soft and good to firm going: tried blinkered/tongue tied: held up, and
usually finds little. *Jonjo O'Neill*

DAYENOO (FR) 4 b.g. Subotica (FR) – La Cenomane (FR) (Master Thatch) [2003/4   **F83**
F17v^2 Mar 21] 8,000 3-y-o: tenth foal: half-brother to several winners on Flat in France:
dam, won up to 1½m in France, half-sister to useful French chaser Pantruche: second to
Neidpath Castle in bumper at Carlisle on debut. *M. W. Easterby*

DAYTIME ARRIVAL (IRE) 6 ch.g. Lucky Guest – Daymer Bay (Lomond (USA))   **h–**
[2003/4 16s^pu 21s^pu Dec 26] ex-Irish gelding: no form on Flat or over hurdles, leaving
W. Flavin before reappearance: blinkered twice. *K. S. Thomas*

DAYTIME DAWN (IRE) 13 b.g. Rashar (USA) – Ard Clos (Ardoon) [2003/4 c–,   **c–**
h–: c16d^pu c21m May 21] one-time useful hunter chaser, retains little ability: tried tongue   **h–**
tied. *R. N. C. Wale*

DAZZLING RIO (IRE) 5 b.g. Ashkalani (IRE) – Dazzling Fire (IRE) (Bluebird   **h87 d**
(USA)) [2003/4 h87: 17m^2 17g^4 21m^2 21g^4 20m^4 16g 16d^pu Dec 12] lengthy gelding:

modest maiden hurdler: stays easy 21f: unraced on extremes of going: bled internally in cheekpieces sixth start. *Miss Kate Milligan*

DD'S GLENALLA (IRE)   7 b.m. Be My Native (USA) – Willowho Pride (Arapaho) [2003/4 F81: 20g² 23m⁶ 21d⁴ 20v⁵ 21d 26m² 21g 24d³ Apr 21] quite good-topped mare: runner-up in Irish point: modest novice hurdler: stays 3¼m: acts on good to firm and good to soft going: of suspect temperament (has flashed tail). *N. A. Twiston-Davies*   **h89**

DEAD-EYED DICK (IRE)   8 b.g. Un Desperado (FR) – Glendale Charmer (Down The Hatch) [2003/4 c89, h–: c24g³ c19g* c19d^F c24v^pu Feb 7] tall gelding: hinted at temperament over hurdles: modest handicap chaser: won at Exeter in November despite hanging left: stays 23f: acts on good to soft going: often runs as though amiss. *Nick Williams*   **c90 h–**

DEADLY DORIS   10 b.m. Ron's Victory (USA) – Camp Chair (Ela-Mana-Mou) [2003/4 h–§: 19s Feb 6] sturdy mare: of no account nowadays: tried blinkered: ungenuine. *N. A. Smith*   **h– §**

DEALER DEL   10 b.g. Deltic (USA) – No Deal (Sharp Deal) [2003/4 c97: c25g* c25m^pu c26g* c25s^F Mar 24] big, rangy gelding: modest chaser: won handicap at Hereford in May and minor event at Newton Abbot in June: stayed 3¼m: acted on good to soft ground: dead. *C. J. Down*   **c97**

DEALER'S CHOICE (IRE)   10 gr.g. Roselier (FR) – Cam Flower VII (Damsire Unregistered) [2003/4 c115, h99: 27s* c24d⁶ c20g^pu c20g* 24d c20d⁶ c20d Apr 8] rather leggy gelding: modest hurdler: won novice at Newton Abbot in April, final start for M. Pitman: fair handicap chaser: won at Ludlow in February: stays 27f: acts on soft going: blinkered once: usually let down by jumping over fences. *Miss Victoria Roberts*   **c111 § h95 §**

DEANO'S BEENO   12 b.g. Far North (CAN) – Sans Dot (Busted) [2003/4 c–, h167d: 23m⁶ 24d² 25d³ 24g⁴ 24g³ 24g Apr 1] leggy gelding: had hobday and tie-back operations: won only outing over fences: top-class hurdler in his prime: no more than useful in 2003/4, looking particularly unenthusiastic last 3 starts: best at 3m+: acted on any going: tried blinkered/visored: fluent-jumping front runner, though usually raced lazily: has been retired. *M. C. Pipe*   **c– h140 §**

DEAR BOY   5 ch.g. Anshan – Kev's Lass (IRE) (Kemal (FR)) [2003/4 21g^pu 16s 16d^pu Dec 12] third foal: dam, won 2m hurdle, half-sister to useful 2m hurdler Impulsive Dream: no sign of ability. *J. A. Supple*   **h–**

DEAR DEAL   11 b.g. Sharp Deal – The Deer Hound (Cash And Carry) [2003/4 c112, h–: c24f^F c24g² c25d⁵ c24s³ c33d⁶ c24d* c24g² c32g⁶ c25m³ Apr 14] lengthy gelding: fairly useful chaser: won novice at Cheltenham in October and handicap at Kempton in February: stays at least 4m: acts on soft and firm going: tried blinkered/tongue tied: consistent. *C. L. Tizzard*   **c122 h–**

DEAR SIR (IRE)   4 ch.g. Among Men (USA) – Deerussa (IRE) (Jareer (USA)) [2003/4 17m 17f³ 16g^pu Nov 30] tall gelding: half-brother to winning hurdler around 2m in Italy by Archway: modest maiden on Flat (stays 13f): easily best effort in juvenile hurdles when winning at Huntingdon in November. *Mrs P. N. Dutfield*   **h84**

DEBANDY BOY   4 b.g. Timeless Times (USA) – Judys Girl (IRE) (Simply Great (FR)) [2003/4 17m^pu 17g^pu Aug 8] sturdy gelding: brother to modest maiden hurdler up to 2¾m Grate Times: little worthwhile form on Flat: no show in 2 juvenile hurdles, in cheekpieces on second occasion. *J. S. Wainwright*   **h–**

DEBATABLE   5 ch.g. Deploy – Questionable (Rainbow Quest (USA)) [2003/4 F16m* Jun 28] third foal: brother to 1998 2-y-o 7f winner Hesitation and fair hurdler/chaser In Question, stays 21f: dam unraced sister to useful French stayer Ecologist and half-sister to dam of St Leger winner Toulon: useful form when winning bumper at Worcester on debut by 6 lengths from Theatre Groom: sold 11,500 gns Doncaster November Sales. *P. R. Webber*   **F105**

DEBBIE   5 b.m. Deploy – Elita (Sharpo) [2003/4 16g⁶ 17g^F Apr 1] fair on Flat (best form around 1¼m), sold out of I. Wood's stable 16,000 gns Newmarket Autumn Sales: sixth in maiden at Huntingdon on hurdling debut: again none too fluent and fading when falling 2 out in similar event at Taunton following month. *B. D. Leavy*   **h85**

DE BLANC (IRE)   4 b.f. Revoque (IRE) – Queen's Share (Main Reef) [2003/4 16g⁵ 16d* Mar 21] good-topped filly: half-sister to fairly useful 2m hurdler/chaser Persian King (by Persian Bold): useful on Flat (stays 11f) in Italy, sold out of A. Renzoni's stable 25,000 gns Newmarket December Sales: shaped quite well when fifth in juvenile at   **h108**

DEB

Newbury on hurdling debut: won similar event at Stratford readily by 3 lengths from Famous Grouse. *Miss Venetia Williams*

DEB'S SON   7 b.g. Minster Son – Deb's Ball (Glenstal (USA)) [2003/4 h80: 24m⁴ 26g 24g⁶ 22g 21d² 24d Dec 17] sparely-made gelding: poor hurdler: stays 27f: acts on good to firm and heavy going: wears visor/cheekpieces: not a fluent jumper: unreliable. *James Moffatt*   **h83 §**

DECENT BOND (IRE)   7 b.g. Witness Box (USA) – Decent Skin (IRE) (Buckskin (FR)) [2003/4 c25gᵘʳ Apr 5] £7,000 5-y-o: third foal: dam unraced: fair pointer, successful in March and April (twice): mistakes prior to unseating fifth on hunter chase debut. *V. Thompson*   **c–**

DECENT ROSE (IRE)   6 ch.m. Roselier (FR) – Decent Banker (Decent Fellow) [2003/4 F16m⁵ F16d 18sᵖᵘ 20dᵖᵘ Apr 10] second foal: dam unraced daughter of smart staying chaser Money Boat: fifth in bumper at Hexham on debut: disappointing subsequently, including over hurdles. *J. I. A. Charlton*   **h–**   **F75**

DECODED   8 ch.g. Deploy – Golden Panda (Music Boy) [2003/4 c83, h–: c25gᶠ c27gᵘʳ c26d⁵ Apr 23] compact gelding: poor chaser: little show in point/hunters in 2004: stays 3¼m: acts on good to firm and heavy going: often wears cheekpieces. *Mrs Sarah L. Dent*   **c–**   **h–**

DECO STAR (IRE)   5 b.g. Dolphin Street (FR) – Ecco Mi (IRE) (Priolo (USA)) [2003/4 17d 19dᵖᵘ 17d⁴ Mar 15] modest on Flat (stays 1½m), sold out of I. Wood's stable 5,500 gns Doncaster March Sales: no form over hurdles: visored and tongue tied last 2 outings. *C. J. Gray*   **h–**

DEE DEE BEA   6 b.m. Bustino – Dante's Delight (Idiot's Delight) [2003/4 F17g Oct 11] 4,200 5-y-o: workmanlike mare: second foal: dam lightly-raced 2m maiden jumper: tailed off in mares bumper on debut. *L. Wells*   **F–**

DEEPASTHEOCEAN   5 b.h. Kris – Dance On A Cloud (USA) (Capote (USA)) [2003/4 F16s F16m⁴ F16g 20fᵖᵘ 16d Apr 23] second foal: half-brother to 2¼m hurdle winner Dardanus (by Komaite): dam, 2-y-o 7f winner who probably stayed 9f, out of US Grade 1 9f winner (at 5 yrs) Sharp Dance: fourth in bumper at Musselburgh in December: no form otherwise, including over hurdles: has pulled hard. *M. D. Hammond*   **h–**   **F80**

DEEP KING (IRE)   9 b. or br.g. King's Ride – Splendid Run (Deep Run) [2003/4 c99d: c21dᵖᵘ c16d⁴ c20mᵖᵘ c18g³ Apr 22] lengthy gelding: modest chaser: stays 23f: acts on firm going: has had tongue tied (including when successful): often let down by jumping. *J. W. Mullins*   **c85**

DEEP QUEST   5 b.g. El Conquistador – Ten Deep (Deep Run) [2003/4 17d Dec 11] fourth foal: dam, poor novice hurdler, barely stayed 3m: always behind in novice hurdle on debut. *S. C. Burrough*   **h–**

DEEP RETURN (IRE)   7 b.g. Bob's Return (IRE) – Parsons Honour (IRE) (The Parson) [2003/4 F18g* 18d* 22s³ 20s³ 20d Apr 11] first foal: dam unraced half-sister to useful hurdler/chaser up to 25f Coq Hardi Affair: won bumper at Downpatrick on debut in November: fairly useful novice hurdler: won at Gowran (maiden) in December and Sligo in late-April: improved effort when second to G V A Ireland at Punchestown in early-May: effective at 2m to 3m: acts on heavy and good to firm ground. *N. Meade, Ireland*   **h121**   **F107**

DEEP SIGH   7 b.g. Weld – At Long Last (John French) [2003/4 h–, F77: 21vᵖᵘ 16d 16s² 16s c20dᶠ c18gᴿ 16dᵘʳ Apr 12] good-topped gelding: form over hurdles only when second in conditional jockeys novice handicap at Uttoxeter in December: fell fourth on chasing debut, jumped poorly prior to refusing sixth next time: raced mainly around 2m on going softer than good. *D. R. Gandolfo*   **c– x**   **h73 x**

DEEP WATER (USA)   10 b.g. Diesis – Water Course (USA) (Irish River (FR)) [2003/4 c118, h113: c16s⁴ c22d⁶ c20v² c19g* c22g c24d⁴ Apr 23] leggy gelding: winning hurdler: fairly useful handicap chaser: won at Catterick in February by neck from Noshinannikin: barely stays 2¾m: acts on good to firm and heavy going: visored twice (won on first occasion). *M. D. Hammond*   **c120**   **h–**

DEER DANCER   4 b.g. Tamure (IRE) – Anatomic (Deerhound (USA)) [2003/4 F13d³ F13v³ 17s² 17v* 17s³ Apr 6] second foal: dam, twice-raced, out of half-sister to top-class miler Rousillon: third in two 3-y-o bumpers: progressive form over hurdles, won weak juvenile at Exeter in February prior to good third to Tinoveritas in novice there: will stay beyond 17f: raced only on going softer than good. *J. D. Frost*   **h101**   **F94**

DEER DOLLY (IRE) 7 b.m. Welsh Term – Wild Deer (Royal Buck) [2003/4 h–: 21v^pu c25d^F Dec 1] thrice-raced mare, let down by jumping or temperament all starts: tried in cheekpieces. *P. Butler*   c–
h–

DEEWAAR (IRE) 4 b.g. Ashkalani (IRE) – Chandni (IRE) (Ahonoora) [2003/4 16g Mar 27] lengthy, sparely-made gelding: half-brother to fairly useful 2m hurdler Chanoud (by Ezzoud): modest maiden on Flat (stays 11f) at 3 yrs for J. S. Moore: well beaten in novice on hurdling debut. *J. C. Fox*   h–

DEFENDTHEREALM 13 br.g. Derring Rose – Armagnac Princess (Armagnac Monarch) [2003/4 27d^pu Jul 30] sturdy gelding: winning hurdler/chaser: fair pointer nowadays: stays 3¼m: acts on good to firm and heavy going: tried blinkered. *J. D. Frost*   c–
h–

DEFERLANT (FR) 7 ch.g. Bering – Sail Storm (USA) (Topsider (USA)) [2003/4 c111§, h111§: 17d 21g 18d^5 17g Apr 3] close-coupled gelding: winning chaser: fairly useful handicap hurdler at one time: modest at best in 2003/4, left Mrs H. Dalton after reappearance: stays 21f: acts on soft and good to firm going: visored: tends to race freely/ finish weakly. *K. Bell*   c– §
h96 §

DEFINATE SPECTACLE (IRE) 4 b.g. Spectrum (IRE) – Silver Bubble (USA) (Silver Hawk (USA)) [2003/4 16d^3 16s* 16s^4 16d^2 Apr 12] sturdy gelding: useful on Flat (stays 9f) for K. Prendergast: progressive form over hurdles: won juvenile maiden at Navan in March and juvenile minor event at Punchestown in late-April: well-backed favourite when beating Amid The Chaos 6 lengths at latter: should continue to improve. *N. Meade, Ireland*   h124 p

DEJA VU (IRE) 5 b.g. Lord Americo – Khalkeys Shoon (Green Shoon) [2003/4 17d^5 24d^4 24d 20g^pu Feb 8] €7,000 4-y-o: sturdy gelding: fifth foal: brother to fair hurdler around 2½m The Dark Lord: dam unraced sister to dam of useful chaser up to 2½m Mulkev Prince: much improved when winning novice handicap at Musselburgh in January: lame there month later: stays 2½m. *J. Howard Johnson*   h85

DELAWARE BAY 5 ch.g. Karinga Bay – Galacia (IRE) (Gallic League) [2003/4 h82: 19g^5 22d c19v^3 c19g^pu Mar 9] useful-looking gelding: poor maiden hurdler, off a year before reappearance: never a factor after mistake first on chasing debut, lame next time: likely to prove better around 2½m than shorter: acts on heavy going. *R. H. Alner*   c71
h82

DELGANY ROYAL (IRE) 12 b.g. Denel (FR) – Glen of Erin (Furry Glen) [2003/4 c121, h101: c24g^pu c23g* c26m^pu Apr 15] tall, angular ex-Irish gelding: fairly useful handicap chaser at best: left D. Hughes after reappearance (wore cheekpieces): won point in February and 6-runner hunter at Leicester (made all and jumped well) following month: probably stays 29f: acts on heavy going, possibly not on good to firm. *Mrs Nicola Pollock*   c103
h–

DELICEO (IRE) 11 b.g. Roselier (FR) – Grey's Delight (Decent Fellow) [2003/4 c87§, h–§: c22g^2 c24d^ur c19d* c19s^3 c20d* c20g^3 c20d^4 Mar 25] leggy gelding: maiden hurdler: fair handicap chaser: won at Hereford in December and Ludlow in January: stays 25f: acts on any going: usually held up: unreliable. *M. Sheppard*   c101 §
h– §

DELLONE 12 b.g. Gunner B – Coire Vannich (Celtic Cone) [2003/4 c–x, h67: 16s^6 Feb 16] sturdy gelding: poor handicap hurdler/error-prone maiden chaser: form only around 2m: acts on heavy going. *T. R. George*   c– x
h–

DELPHI 8 ch.g. Grand Lodge (USA) – Euridice (IRE) (Woodman (USA)) [2003/4 h98d: 26m May 29] smallish gelding: modest maiden hurdler: should stay beyond 2½m: acts on soft and good to firm going: tried blinkered/visored: has looked none too keen. *B. G. Powell*   h–

DELPHINE 5 ch.m. Old Vic – Oh So Bright (Celtic Cone) [2003/4 F17m^6 Apr 15] un-furnished mare: third foal: dam, fair hurdler who stayed 2¾m, from family of Hennessy winner Ever Blessed: under 9 lengths sixth of 14 to Golden Odyssey in mares bumper at Cheltenham on debut: bred to need more of a test of stamina. *T. R. George*   F84

DEL TROTTER (IRE) 9 b.g. King Luthier – Arctic Alice (Brave Invader (USA)) [2003/4 c107, h90: 16g^2 c16s^4 19d^4 24v^5 20s Mar 20] fair chaser at best: modest maiden hurdler: stays 19f: acts on heavy going: tried blinkered: has looked tricky ride. *J. Howard Johnson*   c88
h87

DEMARCO (IRE) 6 ch.g. Old Vic – Peas (IRE) (Little Wolf) [2003/4 F16d* F16g^3 F16g Mar 17] medium-sized gelding: first foal: dam unraced half-sister to fairly useful chaser around 2½m Too Plush: pulled up in Irish point in 2003: won bumper at Ludlow in January impressively by 6 lengths from Brassie: better form when 4 lengths third   F114

Mr R. A. Bartlett's "Demarco"

of 24 to Secret Ploy in Grade 2 at Newbury: failed to take eye beforehand when ninth of 24 to Total Enjoyment in Champion Bumper at Cheltenham: will be suited by 2½m+. *N. J. Henderson*

DEMASTA (NZ) 13 ch.g. Northerly Native (USA) – Hit It Gold (AUS) (Hit It Benny (AUS)) [2003/4 c135, h–: c20m^{pu} c16s^3 c16g^F Mar 6] compact gelding: useful chaser at best: sold out of N. Henderson's stable 4,500 gns Doncaster May Sales after reappearance: off 8 months, fair form when third to Monte Cristo in handicap at Fakenham: best around 2m: best efforts on good going or firmer (acts on firm): tried in cheekpieces: bold-jumping front runner. *Ms A. E. Embiricos*   **c112 h–**

DEMI BEAU 6 b.g. Dr Devious (IRE) – Charming Life (NZ) (Sir Tristram) [2003/4 h109: 17g^5 17g* 17d 16d^F Apr 3] tall gelding: useful handicap hurdler: much improved when winning at Cheltenham in December by ¾ length from Perouse: running well when falling last in listed event won by Puck Out at Aintree: raced around 2m: yet to race on extremes of going: prone to dropping out tamely. *C. J. Mann*   **h133**

DEMOPHILOS 6 b.g. Dr Devious (IRE) – Graecia Magna (USA) (Private Account (USA)) [2003/4 16d* 16s^2 Jan 10] tall gelding: half-brother to useful hurdler/fairly useful chaser up to 2½m Theseus (by Danehill) and fairly useful hurdler/chaser up to 2½m Polydamas (by Last Tycoon): smart at best on Flat (stays 1¾m) for Mrs A. Perrett, runner-up in St Leger at Doncaster in 2001: won 4-runner intermediate at Leopardstown in December on hurdling debut by distance: reportedly broke down when 2 lengths second to Pedina in novice at Navan. *D. T. Hughes, Ireland*   **h119**

DEMPSEY (IRE) 6 b.g. Lord Americo – Kyle Cailin (Over The River (FR)) [2003/4 F101: F17m* 17d* 17v* 16g^F 16g* Apr 4] good-topped gelding: type to make a chaser: fairly useful in bumpers, landed odds at Hereford in October: fairly useful novice hurdler: **h121 F104**

successful on first 3 completed starts, at Folkestone in November and December (long odds on) and Wincanton (beat Gaora Bridge 4 lengths) in April: not discredited when ninth in Grade 1 at Punchestown later in April: bred to stay at least 2½m: room for improvement in his jumping but may do better yet. *M. Pitman*

DENBY (IRE)   4 b.g. Sri Pekan (USA) – Latch Key Lady (USA) (Tejano (USA)) [2003/4 F16v 16s⁵ Mar 13] rather unfurnished gelding: third live foal: half-brother to 5f winner Foxkey (by Foxhound): dam lightly-raced maiden: well beaten in bumper and juvenile hurdle. *M. W. Easterby*   **h–**
F–

DENEISES BLOSSOM (IRE)   11 b.m. Beau Sher – Lindabell (Over The River (FR)) [2003/4 c66§, h69§: c27d³ 22d c24d⁵ 17v⁴ 16g Jan 24] angular mare: poor maiden hurdler/steeplechaser, left W. Storey after third outing: stayed 27f: best efforts on going softer than good (acted on heavy): wore cheekpieces final start: usually found little: dead. *G. A. Harker*   **c58 §**
h75 §

DENE VIEW (IRE)   9 br.g. Good Thyne (USA) – The Furnituremaker (Mandalus) [2003/4 c98, h94: 17s c16g⁴ 16s c20g⁵ Jan 23] sturdy gelding: modest handicap hurdler/chaser: stays 21f: acts on good to soft and good to firm going: tried blinkered (ran poorly): ungenuine. *R. A. Fahey*   **c95 §**
h– §

DENNEY'S WELL (IRE)   9 ch.g. Good Thyne (USA) – Julias Well (Golden Love) [2003/4 c82: c20v⁵ c26g⁵ c24d Mar 24] winning pointer: lightly raced and little form in steeplechases: tried blinkered. *R. Ford*   **c–**

DENNIS THE MENNIS (IRE)   5 b.g. Fourstars Allstar (USA) – Farm Approach (Tug of War) [2003/4 F14d F17g F18g Apr 22] €12,000 4-y-o: eleventh foal: half-brother to 3 winners, notably smart staying chaser Feathered Gale (by Strong Gale): dam unraced half-sister to Hennessy winner Approaching: well beaten in bumpers. *Mrs A. M. Thorpe*   **F–**

DENNY ISLAND   8 b.g. Rock Hopper – Bara Peg (Random Shot) [2003/4 16mᵖᵘ 21vᵖᵘ c22gᵖᵘ 19sᵖᵘ Dec 29] third foal: dam modest staying chaser: no sign of ability. *J. W. Mullins*   **c–**
h–

DEOCH AN DORAIS (IRE)   9 b.g. Supreme Leader – General Rain (General Ironside) [2003/4 c98, h–: c17s³ 25gᵖᵘ Nov 19] tall, good sort: modest maiden hurdler/chaser: effective at 2m to 23f: acts on soft going: sometimes let down by jumping over fences: often finds little: sold 6,200 gns Doncaster May Sales. *N. J. Henderson*   **c99 §**
h– §

DEPTFORD (IRE)   4 b.g. Un Desperado (FR) – Katty London (Camden Town) [2003/4 F16s⁶ F16g Mar 27] €44,000 3-y-o: rather unfurnished gelding: fifth foal: half-brother to fair chaser L'Idefix (by Buckskin), stays 25f: dam unraced: very green when sixth of 21 to Royal Paradise in bumper at Sandown on debut: had too much use made of him next time. *P. R. Chamings*   **F88**

DEPUTY LEADER (IRE)   12 b.g. Florida Son – Larne (Giolla Mear) [2003/4 c78, h–: c21s⁶ c20g⁶ c26d⁶ May 28] rangy gelding: winning pointer: little form in steeplechases. *K. Hunter*   **c–**
h–

DEREK TROTTER   5 b.g. Cosmonaut – Cinderella Derek (Hittite Glory) [2003/4 F–: F16m May 7] tailed off in 2 bumpers. *A. D. Smith*   **F–**

DERE STREET   10 b.g. Derring Rose – Jed Again (Cagirama) [2003/4 c25d⁴ May 3] fifth foal: dam maiden pointer: fair pointer, successful in January: fourth in maiden hunter at Hexham. *Mrs R. L. Elliot*   **c73**

DERIVATIVE (IRE)   6 b. or br.g. Erins Isle – Our Hope (Dancing Brave (USA)) [2003/4 h105: 20g* 19g⁵ 21m⁴ 20d⁵ 22d* 21d³ 20v 24g² 25g 24g 24m Apr 15] smallish gelding: fairly useful handicap hurdler: won at Perth in May and Wincanton in December: good efforts when third to Redemption at Cheltenham and second to Joly Bey at Newbury: below form last 3 starts: stays 3m: acts on heavy going: blinkered fourth outing: has jumped less than fluently: lazy. *Miss Venetia Williams*   **h121**

DERRING BRIDGE   14 b.g. Derring Rose – Bridge Ash (Normandy) [2003/4 c–§, h98§: 22g 27g³ 24m² 24m⁵ 24g³ 26m⁵ 23m⁴ 24m⁴ 24d⁵ 24d Dec 17] leggy gelding: winning chaser: fair handicap hurdler: stays 4m: acts on firm and soft going: has had tongue tied: races lazily and needs strong handling: temperamental. *Mrs S. M. Johnson*   **c– §**
h103 §

DERRING DOVE   12 b.g. Derring Rose – Shadey Dove (Deadly Nightshade) [2003/4 c94§, h–: c21dᵖᵘ c24g³ c24gᵖᵘ May 31] angular gelding: fair hunter chaser on his day: stays 3¼m: acts on good to firm and heavy going: unreliable. *H. W. Lavis*   **c– §**
h–

DERRINTOGHER YANK (IRE)   10 b.g. Lord Americo – Glenmalur (Black Minstrel) [2003/4 c115, h–: 21g³ c24dᶠ c25dᶠ Dec 26] rangy gelding: one-time fairly   **c119**
h108

useful hurdler, not discredited on reappearance: similar level of form over fences: would have made frame but for falling last in handicaps at Bangor and Wincanton in 2003/4, running creditably both times: stays 3m: raced mainly on good going or softer: front runner. *S. E. H. Sherwood*

DERRY ANN 8 b.m. Derrylin – Ancat Girl (Politico (USA)) [2003/4 h61, F80: 19g^{pu} 20m^{pu} May 26] workmanlike mare: little form over hurdles: should stay beyond 2m: looked none too keen on reappearance. *G. P. Kelly*   h–

DERRY DICE 8 b.g. Derrylin – Paper Dice (Le Dauphin) [2003/4 h–, F83: 20g 24g² 26s⁶ Dec 20] lengthy gelding: poor novice hurdler: stays 3m: blinkered. *C. T. Pogson*   h79

DERRYQUIN 9 b.g. Lion Cavern (USA) – Top Berry (High Top) [2003/4 h87: 16m^{pu} Aug 25] modest hurdler: went lame only outing in 2003/4: probably needs sharp 2m: raced freely when tried in blinkers. *Miss E. C. Lavelle*   h–

DERVALLOC (IRE) 7 b.g. Zaffaran (USA) – Keeping Company (King's Company) [2003/4 h–, F–: 21s 20d⁶ 21s 22s c22d^{pu} Mar 11] tall gelding: signs of only a little ability: lame on chasing debut (blinkered). *P. Winkworth*   c–
h–

DESAILLY 10 ch.g. Teamster – G W Superstar (Rymer) [2003/4 c119, h–: c24d* c24s² c24g³ c24g² c33d^{pu} Apr 17] strong, lengthy gelding: useful handicap chaser: won at Newbury in December by 7 lengths from Channahrlie: good placed efforts next 3 starts, ½-length second to Bee An Bee at same course fourth outing: never on terms when pulled up in Scottish National at Ayr: best at 2¾m+ (should stay long distances): raced on good going or softer (acts on soft): has finished weakly in past. *G. B. Balding*   c132
h–

DESERT AIR (JPN) 5 ch.g. Desert King (IRE) – Greek Air (IRE) (Ela-Mana-Mou) [2003/4 h117: 16s 16d Apr 3] angular gelding: fairly useful form as juvenile hurdler: tongue tied, below form in handicaps on return from over a year off: will prove best around 2m: raced on good to soft/soft going: visored. *M. C. Pipe*   h108

DESERT SPA (USA) 9 b.g. Sheikh Albadou – Healing Waters (USA) (Temperence Hill (USA)) [2003/4 24g⁵ 19d^{pu} Dec 2] lengthy gelding: poor nowadays on Flat, sold out of A. Reid's stable £1,500 Ascot October Sales: well beaten on completed start over hurdles. *G. E. Jones*   h–

DESERT TRAVELLER (IRE) 6 b.g. Desert Style (IRE) – Cellatica (USA) (Sir Ivor (USA)) [2003/4 h–: 22g^{pu} 24s^{pu} Dec 29] no worthwhile form over hurdles: often blinkered. *R. J. Baker*   h–

DESIGNER LABEL (IRE) 8 ch.g. Insan (USA) – Belle Babillard (IRE) (Le Bavard (FR)) [2003/4 20g⁴ 22g² c25m* Sep 10] strong gelding: modest maiden hurdler, off 19 months before reappearance: won novice handicap at Hereford on chasing debut, jumping soundly and not extended to pull clear 2 out: stays 25f: acts on good to firm and heavy going: looked open to improvement over fences, but wasn't seen out again. *M. Pitman*   c95 +
h87

DESMOND TUTU (IRE) 7 b.g. Be My Native (USA) – Amy Fairy (The Parson) [2003/4 h106, F107: 20m^{pu} Oct 4] workmanlike gelding: fair hurdler: running creditably when breaking down badly before last in handicap at Chepstow: stays 2¾m: successful on firm going, at least as effective on good or softer. *P. F. Nicholls*   h107

DESPERATE MEASURES 8 ch.m. Kasakov – Precious Ballerina (Ballacashtal (CAN)) [2003/4 h63§: c17g⁵ Apr 30] bad maiden hurdler: well beaten in novice on chasing debut: temperamental. *Miss Lucinda V. Russell*   c–
h– §

DESTINO 5 ch.g. Keen – Hanajir (FR) (Cadeaux Genereux) [2003/4 F16m⁶ F16g F16m³ 16g³ 19g Dec 26] 1,400 3-y-o: first foal: dam little form on Flat: modest form in bumpers: little encouragement in 2 starts over hurdles. *Mrs S. J. Smith*   h–
F83

DETONATEUR (FR) 6 b.g. Pistolet Bleu (IRE) – Soviet Princess (IRE) (Soviet Lad (USA)) [2003/4 h105: 17g⁶ 16m Sep 27] leggy gelding: fair maiden hurdler: will prove best up to 19f: acts on heavy going, probably on good to firm: pulled too hard in blinkers on first start. *Ian Williams*   h101

DEUX BONS AMIS 6 b.g. Roselier (FR) – Rippling Melody (Ardross) [2003/4 20d^{pu} 24s Dec 20] third foal: dam unraced: no show in 2 novice hurdles. *P. J. Hobbs*   h–

DEVIL'S PERK (IRE) 6 b.g. Executive Perk – She Devil (Le Moss) [2003/4 20g Sep 24] 9,000 4-y-o: third foal: half-brother to fair hurdler/chaser around 2½m Devil's Run (by Commanche Run): dam winning Irish pointer: showed little in maiden hurdle on debut: won point in April. *J. Wade*   h–

DEVIL'S RUN (IRE)   8 b.g. Commanche Run – She Devil (Le Moss) [2003/4 c111,   **c108** h–: c25g² c23d⁴ c25v⁶ Jan 26] strong gelding: fair handicap chaser: stays 23f: raced on   **h–** good going or softer (probably acts on heavy): reliable. *J. Wade*

DEVIL'S TEARDROP   4 ch.g. Hernando (FR) – River Divine (USA) (Irish River   **h–** (FR)) [2003/4 16g⁴ Apr 18] modest maiden on Flat (should stay 1m), sold out of D. Cosgrove's stable 7,000 gns Newmarket Autumn Sales: jumped with little fluency in novice at Wincanton on hurdling debut. *C. J. Mann*

DEVON MAID   5 ch.m. Fraam – Sharp Dance (Dance of Life (USA)) [2003/4 F16g   **F–** Dec 11] first foal: dam fair 2m hurdler: raced freely when well held in mares bumper on debut: well beaten on Flat later in month. *R. J. Hodges*

DEVON VIEW (IRE)   10 b.g. Jolly Jake (NZ) – Skipaside (Quayside) [2003/4 c132:   **c132** c16s² c20g³ Nov 29] tall gelding: useful handicap chaser: creditable efforts both starts in 2003/4: stays 2½m: unraced on firm going, acts on any other: consistent. *P. F. Nicholls*

DEVOTE   6 b.g. Pennekamp (USA) – Radiant Bride (USA) (Blushing Groom (FR))   **h90** [2003/4 h83: 16m⁵ 16d⁵ 19v⁶ 17g⁴ 17d* 16d⁵ Mar 24] close-coupled gelding: modest hurdler: made all in seller at Taunton in March: stays 19f: acts on heavy going: usually blinkered, tried in cheekpieces: none too easy a ride. *J. D. Frost*

DEWASENTAH (IRE)   5 b.m. Supreme Leader – Our Sioux (IRE) (Jolly Jake (NZ))   **F90** [2003/4 F16s F16s* Apr 4] tall, rather unfurnished mare: third foal: dam unraced half-sister to fairly useful jumper up to 3m Coq Hardi Diamond: second start in bumpers (green on debut), won maiden at Hexham by 1¼ lengths from Serpentine Rock, idling after leading 2f out: will stay beyond 2m. *J. M. Jefferson*

DEXTRA LIGHTING   5 b.g. Then Again – Celtic Dove (Celtic Cone) [2003/4   **h108** F16d⁶ 22s 24sᶠ Jan 23] workmanlike gelding: sixth foal: half-brother to 2¾m hurdle   **F93** winner Solar Dove (by Jupiter Island): dam, modest novice hurdler/1¾m winner on Flat, half-sister to useful chaser up to 25f Dextra Dove, from excellent family: sixth of 22 in bumper at Newbury on debut: second start over hurdles, would have been close second but for falling last in maiden at Chepstow: dead. *C. L. Tizzard*

DIAMANT NOIR   6 b.m. Sir Harry Lewis (USA) – Free Travel (Royalty) [2003/4   **h130** F100: 16g* 16g² 20s² 24g* 24sᶠ 23gᶠ Feb 28] rather unfurnished mare: dual bumper winner: most progressive hurdler: won 2 mares novices at Towcester in November, mares handicap at Kempton in December and Grade 2 skybet.com River Don Novices' Hurdle at Doncaster in January: favourite, very impressive when beating Eva So Charming

skybet.com River Don Novices' Hurdle, Doncaster—the progressive Diamant Noir slams her rivals

27 lengths in 7-runner event at last-named: held in third when fell last in Grade 2 novice at Haydock: stays 3m: acts well on soft going: sweated when below form third outing. *Jonjo O'Neill*

DIAMONDALTERNATIVE (IRE)   9 gr.g. Be My Native (USA) – Dame Blakeney (IRE) (Blakeney) [2003/4 24s³ 22g⁵ 26g* 24m Sep 14] won bumper on debut, subsequently off over 2 years: poor hurdler: won weak maiden at Southwell in July: will prove best at 3m+. *C. R. Egerton*   **h75**

DIAMOND DARREN (IRE)   5 ch.g. Dolphin Street (FR) – Deerussa (IRE) (Jareer (USA)) [2003/4 h81: 22mᵖᵘ 20d 19m⁴ 24d Dec 11] modest hurdler as a juvenile: showed little in 2003/4, sold out of R. Woodhouse's stable £3,300 Ascot June Sales after reappearance: tongue tied last 2 starts. *Miss Victoria Roberts*   **h–**

DIAMOND DAZZLER   6 br.g. Sula Bula – Dancing Diamond (IRE) (Alzao (USA)) [2003/4 F–: F16m 16f⁵ 20m 20vᵖᵘ 16s⁶ Dec 30] leggy, lengthy gelding: no form: tried tongue tied/blinkered: sold £750 Ascot February Sales. *D. P. Keane*   **h–** **F–**

DIAMOND DYNASTY   7 b.g. Son Pardo – Reperage (USA) (Key To Content (USA)) [2003/4 h–: 18g 20gᵖᵘ 18d 20gᶠ 20f Feb 29] workmanlike gelding: of little account: tried blinkered/in cheekpieces. *J. N. R. Billinge*   **h–**

DIAMOND HALL   11 b.g. Lapierre – Willitwin (Majestic Maharaj) [2003/4 c83, h85: c20mᵖᵘ c23gᵘʳ c20m c22d² c19dᵖᵘ Mar 24] good-topped gelding: winning hurdler: poor maiden chaser: barely stays 3m: acts on heavy and good to firm going (won bumper on firm). *R. D. Tudor*   **c–** **h–**

DIAMOND JOSHUA (IRE)   6 b.g. Mujadil (USA) – Elminya (IRE) (Sure Blade (USA)) [2003/4 h102: 20g⁴ 16d 19d 16v 20d 20d Apr 21] smallish gelding: fair hurdler: well below form in 2003/4, left M. Sowersby before final start: stays 2½m: acts on good to soft going: tried blinkered: usually tongue tied. *M. Scudamore*   **h–**

DIAMOND MAXINE (IRE)   4 b.f. Turtle Island (IRE) – Kawther (Tap On Wood) [2003/4 16d* Nov 23] third over 5f at 2 yrs, only form on Flat: won juvenile at Fakenham on hurdling debut by 9 lengths from Burning Shore: not seen out again. *John Berry*   **h94**

DIAMOND MERCHANT   5 ch.g. Vettori (IRE) – Tosca (Be My Guest (USA)) [2003/4 F16s² F18v⁴ F16m Feb 21] angular gelding: second foal: half-brother to 2003 3-y-o 1½m and 13.8f winner Tilla (by Bin Ajwaad): dam unraced daughter of Cheshire and Lancashire Oaks winner Princess Eboli: 4 lengths second to Thistlecraft at Huntingdon, easily best effort in bumpers. *A. King*   **F87**

DIAMOND MICK   4 ch.g. Pivotal – Miss Poll Flinders (Swing Easy (USA)) [2003/4 16d 16s 16g 16s² Apr 11] half-brother to 19f hurdle winner Chilly Lad (by High Kicker): fair maiden on Flat (stays 1¼m) for G. Margarson: modest form over hurdles: usually wears cheekpieces. *R. Johnson*   **h90**

DIAMOND MONROE (IRE)   8 ch.g. Treasure Hunter – Star of Monroe (Derring Rose) [2003/4 h80+: 23m² 24m⁴ 22g² 24m* 24d³ c24s³ c23m⁵ Mar 2] lengthy, angular gelding: modest hurdler: favourite, won handicap at Ludlow in November: not fluent both starts over fences, particularly hesitant when third of 6 finishers in novice at Fakenham: stays 3m: acts on soft and good to firm going. *N. J. Henderson*   **c94** **h96**

DIAMOND ORCHID (IRE)   4 gr.f. Victory Note (USA) – Olivia's Pride (IRE) (Digamist (USA)) [2003/4 16g²ᵈ 16g² 16d Mar 21] modest on Flat (stays 1½m): runner-up at Ludlow (seller, disqualified for taking wrong course) and Stratford first 2 starts in juvenile hurdles, would have won but for mistake last when beaten head by Cupla Cairde at latter: visored last 2 outings. *P. D. Evans*   **h109**

DIAMOND SAL   6 b.m. Bob Back (USA) – Fortune's Girl (Ardross) [2003/4 F100p: F16d² F16s² F16s⁵ F17d* Apr 3] close-coupled mare: 33/1, improved effort in bumpers when winning 15-runner substandard Grade 2 Martell Cognac Champion NH Flat at Aintree, getting on top final 100 yds when beating Young Scotton ½ length: will stay 2½m: sold to join J. H. Johnson 200,000 gns Doncaster May Sales.   **F103**

DIAMONDS WILL DO (IRE)   7 b.m. Bigstone (IRE) – Clear Ability (IRE) (Be My Guest (USA)) [2003/4 h99: 20m* 20g⁵ 20g³ 21g³ 24d 16s Jan 4] rather leggy mare: modest handicap hurdler: won amateur event at Bangor in August: stays 21f (not discredited over 3m): acts on soft and good to firm going: sometimes soon off bridle. *Miss Venetia Williams*   **h97**

DIAMOND VEIN   5 b.g. Green Dancer (USA) – Blushing Sunrise (USA) (Cox's Ridge (USA)) [2003/4 F85: 21sᵖᵘ 20d 24sᵖᵘ Apr 4] bumper winner: no form over hurdles. *S. P. Griffiths*   **h–**

DICEMAN (IRE)   9 b.g. Supreme Leader – Henry's Gamble (IRE) (Carlingford   c122
Castle) [2003/4 c112, h107: c25g^F c25g^4 c20g* c20m^pu c20d* c19d^F c20d^ur Dec 26]   h–
lengthy gelding: fair hurdler: fairly useful handicap chaser: won at Carlisle and Newcastle (beat Dream On Willie 5 lengths) in November: mostly let down by jumping
otherwise in 2003/4: should stay beyond 2½m; raced mainly on good going or softer
(acts on soft). *Mrs S. J. Smith*

DICKENSBURY LAD (FR)   4 b.g. Luchiroverte (IRE) – Voltige de Cotte (FR) (Sau-   h110
moni (FR)) [2003/4 17g* 17d² 16d³ 20s³ Apr 17] 5,000 3-y-o: on weak side at present:
fourth foal: half-brother to middle-distance winner Girl (by Bad Conduct): dam placed up
to 11f on Flat: won juvenile hurdle at Market Rasen in February on debut: upped in trip,
improved form when third to Breknen Le Noir in novice at Bangor: will stay further than
2½m: acts on soft going: room for improvement in his jumping. *N. A. Twiston-Davies*

DICKENS (USA)   4 ch.g. King of Kings (IRE) – Dellagrazia (USA) (Trempolino   h113
(USA)) [2003/4 16g³ 16s 16d² Jan 3] workmanlike gelding: well held in 1m maiden on
debut at 2 yrs, sold out of A. O'Brien's stable 15,000 gns Newmarket July Sales and
gelded: 66/1, easily best effort over hurdles when winning 18-runner juvenile at Sandown
by 1¾ lengths from Mio Caro. *Miss Venetia Williams*

DICKIE LEWIS   6 b.g. Well Beloved – Moneyacre (Veloski) [2003/4 F16m 20m   c–
21d⁴ c22v^pu 26s⁵ c22s⁶ Feb 14] good-bodied gelding: second foal: dam unraced: no form.   h–
D. McCain   F–

DICKINSONS BAY   6 b.m. Arrasas (USA) – Lb's Girl (My Treasure Chest) [2003/4   h–
F17s F18s 19s^pu 18g^pu Apr 22] first foal: dam lightly raced and no form over hurdles: F–
showed nothing in bumpers or maiden hurdles (lame final start): visored last 2 outings.
G. P. Enright

DICK McCARTHY (IRE)   12 b.g. Lancastrian – Waltzing Shoon (Green Shoon)   c– §
[2003/4 c92§, h–: c24g⁴ May 18] medium-sized gelding: modest handicap chaser: h– §
successful in points in March and April: stays 3¼m: acts on any going: tried blinkered
(jumped none too fluently)/in cheekpieces: unreliable. *R. Rowe*

DICK THE TAXI   10 b.g. Karlinsky (USA) – Another Galaxy (IRE) (Anita's Prince)   c101
[2003/4 h113: c16s³ c16s^pu c16d² c16d² c17d* Apr 24] useful-looking gelding: fair   h–
handicap hurdler: best efforts over fences last 2 starts, getting up close home in novice
handicap at Market Rasen: raced around 2m: acts on heavy and good to firm going: held
up, and races freely: jumps fences less than fluently. *R. J. Smith*

DICK TURPIN (USA)   10 br.g. Red Ransom (USA) – Turn To Money (USA) (Turn   h102
To Mars (USA)) [2003/4 h102: 16g* 19g^pu May 24] fair hurdler, off over 3 years before
reappearance in 2002/3: won amateur handicap at Uttoxeter in May: lame 2 weeks later:
effective at 2m to 2½m: acts on soft and good to firm going. *Mrs L. Wadham*

DICTUM (GER)   6 ch.g. Secret 'n Classy (CAN) – Doretta (GER) (Aspros (GER))   h127
[2003/4 16d² 16v* 16g⁴ 16g^pu Mar 16] good-topped ex-German gelding: successful 8
times up to around 11f from 18 starts at 3/4 yrs for H. Remmert, in Group 3 at Frankfurt
on final outing: good start over hurdles, winning novice at Ascot in January by 19 lengths
from Contraband: not so effective after under less testing conditions at Newbury (far from
fluent) and Cheltenham (left impression something amiss in Grade 1): raced at 2m: acts
on heavy going. *Mrs Susan Nock*

Martell Cognac Champion Standard National Hunt Flat, Aintree—
33/1-shot Diamond Sal (left) provides trainer Mary Reveley with her two-thousandth winner in Britain

DIDCOT 5 ch.g. Roselier (FR) – Astromis (IRE) (Torus) [2003/4 F17d F16d Apr 21] **F90**
first foal: dam well beaten in bumper: better effort in bumpers when never-nearer seventh
of 18 to Pearly Bay at Bangor on debut: will be suited by further than 2m. *J. Rudge*

DIDIFON 9 b.g. Zafonic (USA) – Didicoy (USA) (Danzig (USA)) [2003/4 c96, h–: **c101**
c17d⁴ c16m⁶ c21m c16d* Nov 25] compact gelding: winning hurdler: fair chaser: back to **h–**
form when winning handicap at Sedgefield: should stay 2½m: acts on heavy going: tried
blinkered, usually wears cheekpieces nowadays: usually held up. *N. P. McCormack*

DIDN'TSLEEPAWINK (IRE) 8 b.g. Dromod Hill – Kamalee (Kambalda) [2003/4 **c–**
h–: c25gᵖᵘ May 13] compact gelding: mostly well held over hurdles: reportedly had **h–**
breathing problem on chasing debut. *Jonjo O'Neill*

DIE FLEDERMAUS (IRE) 10 b.g. Batshoof – Top Mouse (High Top) [2003/4 **c94 §**
c104§, h–§: c23mʳᵗʳ c21g c20g⁵ c21m³ c24m³ c20g* c23m* c25m² c25fᶠ Oct 16] leggy **h– §**
gelding: modest handicap chaser: won at Worcester in August and September: stays
25f: acts on firm going, probably on soft: occasionally blinkered: often looks ungenuine
(refused to race on reappearance). *D. J. Wintle*

DIEGO GARCIA (IRE) 4 b.g. Sri Pekan (USA) – Chapel Lawn (Generous (IRE)) **h121**
[2003/4 16g⁴ 16v³ 16s² 16d* 16d⁶ Apr 12] rangy gelding: fair form in frame both starts
in maidens (over 1¼m/1½m) on Flat: fairly useful juvenile hurdler: won maiden at
Limerick in February: very good sixth to Cherub in Grade 1 at Punchestown in late-April.
W. P. Mullins, Ireland

DIGGER (IRE) 5 ch.g. Danzig Connection (USA) – Baliana (Midyan (USA)) [2003/4 **h–**
17g Feb 19] fairly useful on all-weather, fair on turf on Flat (stays 2m), successful in
January: well beaten in maiden at Taunton on hurdling debut, soon clear but weakening
quickly after blundering 3 out. *Miss Gay Kelleway*

DIGGING DEEP 8 ch.m. Scorpio (FR) – Two Travellers (Deep Run) [2003/4 21v Jan **h–**
13] good-topped mare: fifth foal: half-sister to winning hurdler/fair chaser Be Upstanding
(by Hubbly Bubbly), stays 25f, and 2½m chase winner Minden Rose (by Lord Bud): dam
unplaced in Irish bumpers: showed little in mares novice hurdle on debut. *Ferdy Murphy*

DIKLERS ROSE (IRE) 5 gr.m. Roselier (FR) – Diklers Run (Deep Run) [2003/4 **F75**
F17v⁴ Mar 21] fifth foal: half-sister to fairly useful chaser up to 3m Catfish Keith and
winning hurdler/fairly useful chaser up to 21f One Nation (both by Be My Native):
dam, maiden, out of unraced half-sister to Cheltenham Gold Cup winner The Dikler:
shaped like a stayer when fourth to Wild Cane Ridge in bumper at Carlisle on debut.
Mrs M. Reveley

DILEER (IRE) 5 b.g. Barathea (IRE) – Stay Sharpe (USA) (Sharpen Up) [2003/4 **h113 +**
17d⁵ 17s² 17sᶠ Feb 11] fairly useful on Flat (stays 1½m), sold out of L. Cumani's stable
30,000 gns Newmarket Autumn Sales: fair form in novice hurdles, upsides winner
Carapuce when falling last at Carlisle: should win similar event. *D. J. Wintle*

DILSAA 7 ch.g. Night Shift (USA) – Llia (Shirley Heights) [2003/4 17m³ 17m³ 17g* **h98**
17g² 17g⁴ 20m* Oct 11] fair on Flat (stays 1¾m), only poor nowadays: modest
novice hurdler: won at Cartmel (maiden) in August and Hexham (pulled hard and just
headed by Lease when left clear last): stays easy 2½m: raced only on good/good to firm
going: has jumped none too fluently. *K. A. Ryan*

DILYS 5 b.m. Efisio – Ramajana (USA) (Shadeed (USA)) [2003/4 17sᵖᵘ Dec 29] fair **h–**
at best on Flat (barely stays 1m), on downgrade: no show in novice on hurdling debut.
W. S. Kittow

DIMITRI (IRE) 7 gr.g. Roselier (FR) – Treidlia (Mandalus) [2003/4 F16s 24v² 24s³ **c– §**
24g c24sᵖᵘ Mar 19] IR £5,000 4-y-o: compact gelding: third foal: brother to very smart **h89 §**
hurdler Classified, stays 3m, and half-brother to winning 2¾m chaser Tourniquet (by **F79**
Torus): dam showed little in bumpers: won maiden Irish point on debut in 2003: tenth of
14 in Grade 2 bumper at Chepstow: modest form when placed over hurdles: detached
by eighth in maiden chase: stays 3m: acts on heavy going: tried blinkered: ungenuine.
S. Gollings

DINARELLI (FR) 5 gr.g. Linamix (FR) – Dixiella (FR) (Fabulous Dancer (USA)) **h87**
[2003/4 17s 17g 16d⁴ 17d 16d⁵ Mar 25] ex-French gelding: half-brother to winning
hurdlers around 2m Diatara and Destin (both by Sillery): successful twice over 1m at 3
yrs on Flat, unplaced in 2003, then left F. Head: seemingly best effort over hurdles when
fourth in maiden at Plumpton: visored first 2 starts. *M. C. Pipe*

DINOFELIS 6 b.g. Rainbow Quest (USA) – Revonda (IRE) (Sadler's Wells (USA)) **h71 §**
[2003/4 h71: 16m³ 16g⁴ 16m⁶ 16m 16f* 16m 16m⁵ 16m Nov 24] leggy gelding: poor

hurdler: won seller at Ludlow in October: raced at 2m: acts on firm ground: wears cheek-pieces: tongue tied once (reportedly hung badly): unreliable. *W. M. Brisbourne*

DINSEY FINNEGAN (IRE) 9 b.g. Fresh Breeze (USA) – Rose of Solway (Derring Rose) [2003/4 c71, h–: c21d⁶ c23g⁶ Mar 12] fair pointer, won in February and April: easily best effort in hunter chases when sixth to Red Brook Lad in maiden at Cheltenham: unlikely to stay much beyond 21f: tried visored, usually wears cheekpieces. *Simon Bloss*   **c86** **h–**

DIONN RIGH (IRE) 9 b.g. Asir – Happy Eliza (Laurence O) [2003/4 c107: c29dᵖᵘ c25s⁴ c24vᵖᵘ c33dᵖᵘ c28dᶠ Mar 30] big, lengthy gelding: fair chaser at best, completed only once in 2003/4: stayed 27f: acted on heavy going: tried in headgear and tongue strap: dead. *J. Howard Johnson*   **c96**

DIONYSIAN (IRE) 5 ch.g. Be My Guest (USA) – Justitia (Dunbeath (USA)) [2003/4 F16d 16d 20g Mar 6] rather leggy gelding: half-brother to several winners, notably high-class hurdler/top-class chaser Bacchanal (by Bob Back), stayed 3m: dam won in Belgium: no sign of ability: sold 600 gns Doncaster May Sales. *R. H. Alner*   **h–** **F–**

DIORAMA (GER) 9 b.m. Bakharoff (USA) – Dosha (FR) (Sharpman) [2003/4 h83: 24fᵖᵘ 21s³ c22g³ c21d⁶ Dec 1] angular mare: poor hurdler: little show in 2 starts over fences: should stay beyond 21f: acts on soft going: tried blinkered/tongue tied. *L. A. Dace*   **c–** **h64**

DIPLOMATIC DAISY (IRE) 5 b.m. Alflora (IRE) – Landa's Counsel (Pragmatic) [2003/4 F24 Mar 24] first foal: dam placed in bumpers: well held in bumper on debut, not knocked about. *D. R. Gandolfo*   **F–**

DIRECT ACCESS (IRE) 9 ch.g. Roselier (FR) – Spanish Flame (IRE) (Spanish Place (USA)) [2003/4 c137, h–: c26gᵖᵘ c25d⁶ c20dᵖᵘ c20d⁴ Feb 21] tall, rangy, angular gelding: useful chaser at best, has generally run as if amiss since reappearance in 2002/3: should stay beyond 25f: acts on heavy going, not discredited on good to firm: tried blinkered: sold to join N. Richards 41,000 gns Doncaster May Sales. *L. Lungo*   **c–** **h–**

DIRECT BEARING (IRE) 7 b.g. Polish Precedent (USA) – Uncertain Affair (IRE) (Darshaan) [2003/4 h132: 16s* c19d* c17d⁵ c21d⁶ c17s² c29dᵖᵘ Apr 12] well-made gelding: useful hurdler, landed odds in minor event at Galway in July: fairly useful novice chaser: impressively won maiden at Leopardstown in December: creditable second to Ballyamber at Navan: joint favourite, badly hampered fifth when pulled up in Irish Grand National at Fairyhouse: stays 19f: acts on heavy going: blinkered once. *D. K. Weld, Ireland*   **c126** **h132**

DIRECT DESCENDANT (IRE) 5 ch.g. Be My Guest (USA) – Prague Spring (Salse (USA)) [2003/4 h83: 17m 21g⁵ 17g³ 16m* 16m² 16g⁴ 17d⁵ Nov 25] workmanlike gelding: poor hurdler: won seller at Hexham in October: best around 2m: raced mainly on good/good to firm going: visored final start. *J. J. Quinn*   **h82**

DIRECT FLIGHT (IRE) 6 ch.g. Dry Dock – Midnight Mistress (Midsummer Night II) [2003/4 F16g* 17g² 20sᵖᵘ 21g⁶ Mar 5] useful-looking gelding: has scope: sixth live foal: half-brother to 3 at least modest hurdlers by Ballacashtal: dam never ran: won bumper at Fakenham in October on debut: modest form at best in novice hurdles: reportedly had breathing problem third outing. *Noel T. Chance*   **h89** **F96**

DIRECTION 6 b.m. Lahib (USA) – Theme (IRE) (Sadler's Wells (USA)) [2003/4 F88: 17d 20d 23s⁴ 26d Mar 28] medium-sized mare: bumper winner: little show over hurdles. *K. A. Morgan*   **h–**

DIRK COVE (IRE) 10 ch.g. Montelimar (USA) – Another Miller (Gala Performance) [2003/4 c100, h–: c24m⁴ c26m² c22g⁴ c30s³ c32g³ c28d c26gᵖᵘ c24d Mar 24] angular gelding: winning hurdler: modest handicap chaser: stays 4m: acts on any going: often blinkered, tried in cheekpieces: uncooperative. *R. Rowe*   **c94 §** **h–**

DISCO KING 10 b.g. Rakaposhi King – Divine Affair (IRE) (The Parson) [2003/4 22mᵖᵘ May 31] no form over hurdles or in points. *O. O'Neill*   **h–**

DISCREET GIRL 5 b.m. Mistertopogigo (IRE) – Pillow Talk (IRE) (Taufan (USA)) [2003/4 F–: 17gᵖᵘ Jul 4] lengthy mare: no form. *Mrs S. Lamyman*   **h–**

DI'S DILEMMA 6 b.m. Teenoso (USA) – Reve En Rose (Revlow) [2003/4 h83: 16g² 16vᶠ 19gᶠ 16s⁴ 21g⁶ 20d⁴ Apr 12] small mare: poor novice hurdler: stays 21f: acts on heavy going. *C. C. Bealby*   **h83**

DISGRACE 4 b.g. Distinctly North (USA) – Ace Girl (Stanford) [2003/4 17g⁴ 16m 16d 17d 16d³ Dec 12] no form on Flat for A. Berry: poor form over hurdles. *Mrs S. J. Smith*   **h80**

DISPOL ROCK (IRE) 8 b.g. Ballad Rock – Havana Moon (Ela-Mana-Mou) [2003/4 h90: 21m Nov 16] angular gelding: winning hurdler: tailed off only outing in   **h–**

2003/4: raced mainly around 2m: acts on heavy going, possibly not on good to firm. *Dr P. Pritchard*

D'ISSAN (IRE) 6 br.g. Commanche Run – Loch Phar (IRE) (Phardante (FR)) [2003/4 F17d Jun 9] IR £3,500 3-y-o: second foal: dam unraced, from family of fairly useful chaser up to 3m Kittinger: well held in bumper on debut. *B. J. M. Ryall*   **F–**

DISTANT PROSPECT (IRE) 7 b.g. Namaqualand (USA) – Ukraine's Affair (USA) (The Minstrel (CAN)) [2003/4 16d² 16m* 21d⁶ 17d⁵ Jan 24] angular gelding: half-brother to modest 2m hurdler Protocol (by Taufan): useful on Flat (stays 2½m): promising ½-length second to Albuhera in novice at Newbury on hurdling debut: again made running when easily winning maiden at same course 11 days later: much better effort after when fifth, staying on strongly, to Idaho d'Ox in handicap at Cheltenham: will prove suited by further than 2m: remains open to improvement granted sufficient test of stamina and should do well in handicaps in 2004/5. *A. M. Balding*   **h120 p**

DISTANT ROMANCE 7 br.m. Phardante (FR) – Rhine Aria (Workboy) [2003/4 h–, F–: 16gᵖᵘ 17v⁵ 16m c16dᵖᵘ Jan 2] probably of little account. *Miss Z. C. Davison*   **c–**   **h–**

DISTANT SKY (USA) 7 ch.g. Distant View (USA) – Nijinsky Star (USA) (Nijinsky (CAN)) [2003/4 h–: 21mᵖᵘ May 5] compact gelding: no worthwhile form over hurdles: dead. *Miss J. S. Davis*   **h–**

DISTANT THUNDER (IRE) 6 b.g. Phardante (FR) – Park Breeze (IRE) (Strong Gale) [2003/4 F97: 17d⁴ 20s* 21dᶠ 23sᵖᵘ 20s* 20g Apr 1] lengthy gelding: fairly useful form over hurdles: won novices at Chepstow (by 7 lengths from Maggies Gamble) in December and Sandown (didn't have to be at best) in March: sweating, ninth of 13 in Grade 2 novice won by Garde Champetre at Aintree: should stay beyond 2½m: raced on good going or softer over hurdles (acts on soft). *R. H. Alner*   **h121**

DISTINCTLY WELL (IRE) 7 b.g. Distinctly North (USA) – Brandywell (Skyliner) [2003/4 h–: 17dᵖᵘ 19sʳᵒ 16s 16g Feb 11] leggy gelding: no form over hurdles, sold out of B. McMahon's stable £3,000 Ascot June Sales before reappearance: resold £850 Ascot April Sales. *M. Sheppard*   **h–**

DIVA DANCER 4 ch.f. Dr Devious (IRE) – Catina (Nureyev (USA)) [2003/4 16g 16g 16sᶜᵒ Apr 4] half-sister to fairly useful hurdler Life of Riley (by Caerleon), stays 3m: well held on Flat: never a threat both completed starts over hurdles. *J. Hetherton*   **h–**

DIVERSITY (IRE) 6 ch.g. Over The River (FR) – Ballymas (Martinmas) [2003/4 20dᶠ 16gᵖᵘ 17d 17d c19sᵘʳ 26g⁴ 26dᵖᵘ Mar 28] ninth foal: brother to poor staying chaser Ballybentragh: dam, maiden on Flat/over hurdles, out of useful Irish hurdler Ballymountain Girl: twice-raced in Irish points, won maiden in 2003: best effort over hurdles when fourth in handicap at Huntingdon: well held when unseating on steeplechasing debut: likely to stay beyond 3¼m: raced on good ground or softer. *Jonjo O'Neill*   **c–**   **h87**

DIVET HILL 10 b.g. Milieu – Bargello's Lady (Bargello) [2003/4 c122, h104: c25m² c21dᵖᵘ 20m⁴ c20sᵖᵘ Dec 20] leggy, quite good-topped gelding: fair hurdler: fairly useful chaser: reportedly struck into himself final start: stays 25f: acts on firm and good to soft going: front runner: usually jumps well: genuine. *Mrs A. Hamilton*   **c122**   **h100**

DIVINE MIST (IRE) 7 br.g. Roselier (FR) – Tate Divinity (IRE) (Tate Gallery (USA)) [2003/4 h–, F83: 24mᵖᵘ Sep 7] lengthy gelding: runner-up in bumper: poor jumper over hurdles and in points. *Jonjo O'Neill*   **h– x**

DIVORCE ACTION (IRE) 8 b.g. Common Grounds – Overdue Reaction (Be My Guest (USA)) [2003/4 c–, h86: 17fᶠ Oct 5] sturdy gelding: well held only outing over fences: modest handicap hurdler: well held when falling last only outing in 2003/4: stays 19f when conditions aren't testing: best form on good going or firmer (acts on firm): has had tongue tied. *S. R. Bowring*   **c–**   **h–**

DIVULGE (USA) 7 b.g. Diesis – Avira (Dancing Brave (USA)) [2003/4 c67, h85: 16g⁴ 16m² 19g⁵ 17m² 16g 17m 16g⁵ Oct 24] leggy gelding: poor form both starts over fences: poor maiden hurdler: best at sharp 2m: acts on soft and good to firm going: wore visor/cheekpieces after reappearance: sketchy jumper: ungenuine: sold 3,000 gns Doncaster May Sales. *A. Crook*   **c– §**   **h81 §**

DIX BAY 9 b.g. Teenoso (USA) – Cooks Lawn (The Parson) [2003/4 c–x, h–: 20vᵖᵘ 16s² 16d⁴ 20d Apr 10] quite good-topped gelding: fair hurdler: form in 2003/4 only when second in claimer at Huntingdon: jumped poorly in 3 novice chases: stays 2½m: acts on soft and good to firm going. *M. W. Easterby*   **c– x**   **h103**

DIXCART VALLEY   8 b.g. Carlingford Castle – Renshaw Wood (Ascertain (USA)) **c–**
[2003/4 c–, h–: c25d⁶ c26gᵖᵘ c24gᵖᵘ c17m³ c21gᵖᵘ Jul 28] quite good-topped gelding: no **h–**
worthwhile form: tried blinkered. *P. Beaumont*

DIXON VARNER (IRE)   14 b.g. Sheer Grit – Raise The Bells (Belfalas) [2003/4 **c–**
c94: c33dᵖᵘ c31fᵖᵘ May 21] workmanlike gelding: one-time leading Irish hunter chaser
for E. Bolger, off 3 years prior to 2002: very much a veteran nowadays, won 3-finisher
point in April. *Mrs D. M. Grissell*

DIZZY LAD (IRE)   8 b.g. Alphabatim (USA) – Court Session (Seymour Hicks (FR)) **h85**
[2003/4 h–: 20m⁶ 22g⁶ 24mᵖᵘ Jul 9] maiden pointer: modest novice hurdler: best effort at
2½m. *J. S. King*

DIZZY'S DREAM (IRE)   6 b.g. Shernazar – Balingale (Balinger) [2003/4 F110: **h115**
22d² 20d² 18d⁵ 16v* 18d³ Feb 25] tall gelding: type to make a chaser: fairly useful novice
hurdler: won maiden 4-finisher at Fairyhouse in January: creditable third after at Limerick and
Punchestown, though rather flattered to deceive behind Arch Stanton at latter in late-
April: effective at 2m to 2¾m: acts on heavy ground. *N. Meade, Ireland*

DIZZY TART (IRE)   5 b.m. Definite Article – Tizzy (Formidable (USA)) [2003/4 **h92**
h89: 16m³ 17m² 22f† Nov 8] leggy, close-coupled mare: modest handicap hurdler: raced
mainly around 2m: acted on firm and good to soft going: dead. *Mrs P. N. Dutfield*

DOBERMAN (IRE)   9 br.g. Dilum (USA) – Switch Blade (IRE) (Robellino (USA)) **c85 §**
[2003/4 h73: 16g⁴ 16g 16g² 16m³ 16m³ 18f* 19m² 20m³ c19m³ c17m³ c20f³ 16f⁴ Oct 26] **h92 §**
poor on Flat: modest hurdler, left W. M. Brisbourne after second outing: won seller at
Fontwell in August: similar form when third all 3 starts over fences: stays 2½m: acts on
soft and firm going: usually visored/blinkered: often looks less than keen under pressure.
P. D. Evans

DOCE VIDA (IRE)   6 b.m. Montelimar (USA) – Miss The Post (Bustino) [2003/4 **h95**
F16g⁵ aF16g* F16g² 16s* 17d 17d² 17s⁶ Apr 6] €45,000 4-y-o: angular mare: second **F95**
foal: dam, 1½m and 2m winner, sister to high-class 2m to 25f hurdler Mysilv: fair form
in bumpers, won on polytrack at Lingfield in November: modest novice hurdler: won
25-runner mares event at Wetherby in January: bred to stay beyond 2m, but isn't lacking
in speed. *A. King*

DOCTOR JOHN   7 ch.g. Handsome Sailor – Bollin Sophie (Efisio) [2003/4 h88: 20d **c–**
c22dᵖᵘ c20dᵖᵘ 20s Jan 27] workmanlike gelding: maiden hurdler: no form in 2003/4, **h–**
including over fences (reportedly broke blood vessel second start): stays 19f: successful
over 2m on Flat in February. *Andrew Turnell*

DOCTORS ORDERS (IRE)   6 b.g. Carroll House – Merapi (Roi Guillaume (FR)) **F100**
[2003/4 F16v² F16s F18d² F19d⁴ F20s³ Apr 22] third foal: half-brother to winning
hurdler Clochmhaoil Castle (by Lord Americo), stays 3m: dam, fairly useful hurdler/
chaser, stayed 21f: fairly useful form in bumpers: best efforts when second to Homer
Wells at Punchestown on debut in January and Afistfullofdollars at Thurles in March.
Michael Cullen, Ireland

DODGER (IRE)   4 b.g. Among Men (USA) – Hazy Image (Ahonoora) [2003/4 18fᵖᵘ **h–**
Aug 25] no form on Flat or in juvenile hurdle. *Jamie Poulton*

DODGER MCCARTNEY   6 ch.g. Karinga Bay – Redgrave Girl (Deep Run) [2003/4 **F90**
F17f² Oct 21] fourth foal: brother to useful hurdler around 2m Grave Doubts: dam fairly
useful 2m hurdler: tongue tied, 2 lengths second of 7 in bumper at Exeter on debut.
K. Bishop

DOE NAL RUA (IRE)   7 b.g. Mister Lord (USA) – Phardante Girl (IRE) (Phardante **c103**
(FR)) [2003/4 h92, F94: 20gʳᵒ 20d 23d⁴ c21d⁵ c25v² c25v³ c22m³ c25g* Mar 10] big, **h85**
rangy gelding: modest maiden hurdler: fair form over fences, winning novice handicap
at Catterick in March: will stay beyond 25f: acts on good to firm and heavy going.
T. D. Easterby

DOESHEKNOW (IRE)   9 b. or br.g. Insan (USA) – Maeves Invader (Brave Invader **c120**
(USA)) [2003/4 c19s² c24m⁴ c22m⁴ c18d Nov 15] fairly useful handicap chaser: easily **h–**
best effort in 2003/4 when second to Broadstone Road at Listowel in September: stays
21f: acts on soft and good to firm going. *P. A. Fahy, Ireland*

DOES IT MATTER   7 b.g. Carlingford Castle – Flopsy Mopsy (Full of Hope) [2003/4 **c–**
h–, F–: 16g c19g⁵ c16m⁶ c16m Jun 11] no sign of ability: headstrong. *P. C. Ritchens* **h–**

DOIGTS D'OR (FR)   9 b.g. Sanglamore (USA) – Doigts de Fee (USA) (L'Emigrant **c88**
(USA)) [2003/4 c85+, h–: c17g⁵ c16m³ c17gᵖᵘ c17dᵖᵘ Aug 11] big, lengthy gelding: **h–**

winning hurdler/modest maiden chaser: lightly raced since 1999/00: best around 2m: acts on soft and good to firm going: headstrong. *P. R. Webber*

DO IT ON DANI   9 br.m. Weld – Dark City (Sweet Monday) [2003/4 h111: 26m⁴ c20mᵖᵘ c26dᵖᵘ 27g⁴ 24m⁴ 24m³ 24f* 21f 24g³ Nov 8] small, leggy mare: jumped badly both starts over fences: fair handicap hurdler: made all at Ludlow in October: suited by 3m+: acts on firm and good to soft going, not on softer. *Mrs A. M. Thorpe*   **c– x** **h111**

DO L'ENFANT D'EAU (FR)   5 ch.g. Minds Music (USA) – L'Eau Sauvage (Saumarez) [2003/4 h130: 16m 16d⁴ 21s⁴ Dec 13] compact gelding: very progressive juvenile hurdler in 2002/3: gradually back to best in 2003/4, fourth of 7 to Crystal d'Ainay in intermediate minor event at Cheltenham final start: stays 21f: raced mainly on good going or softer. *P. J. Hobbs*   **h130**

DOLI CYGNUS   6 gr.m. Bedford (USA) – Damsong (Petong) [2003/4 F84: F16v 21d 16g 16m 19g 22g Apr 10] medium-sized mare: modest form in bumpers: well held over hurdles: wore cheekpieces final start. *E. L. James*   **h–** **F–**

DOLLY BELL (IRE)   6 b.m. Commanche Run – Rosey Park (Boreen (FR)) [2003/4 F16s F16v F16d 17gᵖᵘ Apr 10] 4,100 4-y-o: lengthy mare: third foal: dam unraced sister to useful 3m chaser Glyde Court: well beaten in bumpers and mares maiden hurdle. *J. G. M. O'Shea*   **h–** **F–**

DOLLY DOVE   9 b.m. Gran Alba (USA) – Celtic Dove (Celtic Cone) [2003/4 16s 16s Jan 23] no form. *C. J. Price*   **h–**

DOLMUR (IRE)   4 b. or br.c. Charnwood Forest (IRE) – Kawanin (Generous (IRE)) [2003/4 16d² 16d 16d 16d⁶ 16s² 16s Apr 4] useful on Flat up to 9.4f: fairly useful juvenile hurdler, best effort on debut: wore cheekpieces final start (reportedly distressed). *Anthony Mullins, Ireland*   **h112**

DOLZAGO   4 b.g. Pursuit of Love – Doctor's Glory (USA) (Elmaamul (USA)) [2003/4 17s Jan 20] fair on Flat (stays 13f), sold out of P. Harris' stable 8,000 gns Doncaster November Sales, successful in February: well held in juvenile maiden on hurdling debut. *G. L. Moore*   **h–**

DOM D'ORGEVAL (FR)   4 b.g. Belmez (USA) – Marie d'Orgeval (FR) (Bourbon (FR)) [2003/4 F12g F12s 16m 16s⁶ 17s Jan 7] leggy gelding: half-brother to 3 winners on Flat: dam, French middle-distance winner, half-sister to useful French hurdler Dom Vassal: well held in 3-y-o bumpers/juvenile hurdles. *Nick Williams*   **h–** **F–**

DOMENICO (IRE)   6 b.g. Sadler's Wells – Russian Ballet (USA) (Nijinsky (CAN)) [2003/4 h107: 17d* 20g 17g* 16m² 16f⁶ 16m³ 16m⁵ 19gF 16s Dec 11] good-topped gelding: fair handicap hurdler: won at Southwell in August and September: should stay 2½m: acts on good to firm and heavy going. *J. R. Jenkins*   **h115**

DOMINICAN MONK (IRE)   5 b.g. Lord Americo – Ballybeg Katie (IRE) (Roselier (FR)) [2003/4 F16g³ F16g* F16m⁶ F16d⁴ Mar 28] smallish gelding: first foal: dam unraced sister to top-class chaser The Grey Monk: fairly useful form in bumpers: trained by A. Lidderdale on debut: won at Ludlow in December by ½ length from Green Tango: will stay at least 2½m. *C. Tinkler*   **F102**

DOMINIKUS   7 b.g. Second Set (IRE) – Dolce Vita (GER) (Windwurf (GER)) [2003/4 c105, h–: c16d⁵ c24g³ c20m² c24g* c24g⁴ c26m⁵ Apr 14] leggy gelding: fairly useful handicap chaser: best effort when winning fairly valuable race at Perth in June by 13 lengths from Kaki Crazy: stays 3¼m: acts on firm and good to soft going. *Ferdy Murphy*   **c119** **h–**

DOMQUISTA D'OR   7 b.g. Superpower – Gild The Lily (Ile de Bourbon (USA)) [2003/4 h72: 20s⁶ May 2] leggy, plain gelding: poor maiden hurdler: best form around 2m: acted on soft and good to firm going: twice blinkered: dead. *G. A. Ham*   **h–**

DOM SHADEED   9 b.g. Shadeed (USA) – Fair Dominion (Dominion) [2003/4 h–§: 17m May 14] modest on Flat (should stay 1¾m): little form over hurdles: has refused to race, including both starts in points. *R. J. Baker*   **h– §**

DONADINO (IRE)   11 br.g. Be My Native (USA) – Atteses (Smooth Stepper) [2003/4 c115, h94: c20m⁶ May 10] tall gelding: handicap chaser: well held only start in 2003/4: successful at 21f, very best efforts around 2m: acts on soft and good to firm going. *Jonjo O'Neill*   **c–** **h–**

DONATUS (IRE)   8 b.g. Royal Academy (USA) – La Dame du Lac (USA) (Round Table) [2003/4 h96: 19sᵖᵘ 17s 16dᵖᵘ 16d 16sF 19d 17s⁵ 16g Apr 18] neat gelding: winning hurdler: little form in 2003/4: stays easy 2½m: acts on soft and good to firm going, probably on firm: tried in headgear: often finds little. *Miss K. M. George*   **h62**

DONEGAL SHORE (IRE)   5 b.h. Mujadil (USA) – Distant Shore (IRE) (Jareer   **h61**
(USA)) [2003/4 h–: 16m⁴ 16g 20d⁴ 16m Aug 25] modest on Flat (stays 7f): poor form
over hurdles: has had tongue tied. *Mrs J. Candlish*

DON FAYRUZ (IRE)   12 b.g. Fayruz – Gobolino (Don) [2003/4 16aᵖᵘ Dec 30] lengthy   **h–**
gelding: modest 2m hurdler in 1998/9 for H. Daly: no form in 2 starts over hurdles since
(won on Flat in 2002): tried visored. *B. N. Doran*

DON FERNANDO   5 b.h. Zilzal (USA) – Teulada (USA) (Riverman (USA)) [2003/4   **c109 p**
h131: 17m³ 16m³ c19s² c20g* c21d⁵ Mar 18] leggy horse: useful hurdler: good third in   **h133**
handicaps at Newton Abbot and Chepstow: just fair form over fences, won novice at
Plumpton in March: let down by jumping in Cathcart Chase at Cheltenham final outing:
stays 2½m: acts on soft and good to firm going: remains open to improvement over
fences. *M. C. Pipe*

DON IDO (ARG)   8 b.g. Lazy Boy (ARG) – She's Got You (ARG) (Indalecio (ARG))   **h–**
[2003/4 h77: 16mᵖᵘ 16gᵖᵘ 16dᵖᵘ Dec 12] good-topped gelding: maiden hurdler: no form
in 2003/4: headstrong: has looked temperamental. *J. A. B. Old*

DONIE DOOLEY (IRE)   6 ch.g. Be My Native (USA) – Bridgeofallen (IRE) (Torus)   **h90**
[2003/4 F–: F16d 20vᶠ 16g⁵ 20m* 20s Dec 19] workmanlike gelding: well held both   **F–**
starts in bumpers after 2002: modest hurdler: won maiden at Uttoxeter in June: stays
2½m: acts on good to firm. *P. T. Dalton*

DONNEGALE (IRE)   12 b.g. Strong Gale – Marys Gift (Monksfield) [2003/4 c26d³   **c82 §**
May 28] good sort: winning hurdler/chaser: third in hunter at Cartmel in May: best at   **h–**
3m+: acts on soft and good to firm going: wears headgear: often looks none too keen.
Miss J. E. Foster

DONNY BOWLING   4 b.f. Sesaro (USA) – Breakfast Creek (Hallgate) [2003/4   **h69**
17m⁴ 16fᵖᵘ 16d⁴ 16d 16g⁴ 16gᵖᵘ 16d 17dᵖᵘ 17g⁵ 16s⁴ 17g Apr 24] poor on Flat (stays 1m):
poor juvenile hurdler: will prove best around 2m with emphasis on speed. *M. E. Sowersby*

DONNYBROOK (IRE)   11 ch.g. Riot Helmet – Evening Bun (Baragoi) [2003/4   **c–**
c115, h–: c22mᵖᵘ c20gᵖᵘ c20d⁵ c20d c24dᵖᵘ c24d⁴ c31d Apr 22] tall gelding: winning   **h–**
chaser: largely out of sorts in 2003/4: stays 3m: acts on good to firm and heavy going:
tried blinkered/cheekpieces. *R. D. E. Woodhouse*

DONOVAN (NZ)   5 b.g. Stark South (USA) – Agent Jane (NZ) (Sound Reason (CAN))   **c–**
[2003/4 F16m⁵ F17m F17m⁶ 20m 20sᵖᵘ 16s c16dᵖᵘ 22gᵖᵘ 19g 22d Apr 5] close-coupled   **h76**
New Zealand-bred gelding: modest in bumpers: poor form over hurdles: reportedly had   **F78**
breathing problem on chasing debut: may prove best around 2m: tried in cheekpieces
(looked none too cooperative on first occasion). *R. C. Guest*

DON ROYAL   10 b.g. Rakaposhi King – Donna Farina (Little Buskins) [2003/4 c88:   **c89**
c26s⁴ c21g³ c24d³ c22g⁵ Mar 26] tall gelding: fair pointer: similar form when placed 3
times from 7 starts in hunter chases: probably better around 3m than shorter: acts on good
to soft going. *J. R. Scott*

DON RUBINI   6 b.g. Emarati (USA) – Emerald Ring (Auction Ring (USA)) [2003/4   **c–**
c16dᶠ Apr 30] no form on Flat, in points or hunter chase (tongue tied). *K. Goldsworthy*

DON'T SIOUX ME (IRE)   6 b.g. Sadler's Wells (USA) – Commanche Belle   **h113**
(Shirley Heights) [2003/4 h92: 17g² 19g³ 17g² 16m* 17m⁴ 17m* 17d* 16m⁵ 16m³ 16g
16s 17g⁵ 17d⁶ 16gᶠ 16s² 20g Apr 1] lengthy, angular gelding: fair hurdler: won novices at
Hexham in June and Market Rasen and Southwell in August: stays 19f: acts on good to
firm and soft going: tongue tied after third outing: tends to sweat: free-going front runner:
consistent. *C. R. Dore*

DON VALENTINO (POL)   5 ch.g. Duke Valentino – Dona (POL) (Dakota) [2003/4   **h106**
h–: 16m* 16d⁴ 16d* 18s² 17d Jan 24] tall, close-coupled gelding: fair form over hurdles:
won novice at Haydock in November and conditional jockeys novice handicap at
Doncaster in December: will probably stay 2½m: acts on soft and good to firm going.
T. R. George

DOOBERRY FIRKIN   6 b.m. Presenting – Shipley Bridge (Town And Country)   **h–**
[2003/4 F16f³ F16m⁶ 20d 24s⁶ 19d⁵ 16d Jan 13] 2,000 4-y-o: quite good-topped mare: **F81**
third foal: dam, of little account, from family of top-class staying chaser Righthand Man:
modest form in 2 bumpers: no form over hurdles. *Mrs S. Gardner*

DOOLEY GATE   7 b.g. Petoski – High 'b' (Gunner B) [2003/4 F–: 20sᵖᵘ Dec 26]   **h–**
workmanlike gelding: showed nothing in bumper or novice hurdle. *F. P. Murtagh*

DOONAREE (IRE)   8 b.g. Sadler's Wells (USA) – Rosananti (Blushing Groom   **h120**
(FR)) [2003/4 16v³ 16d³ 18d* 16g⁴ 16m⁵ 20d* 20s⁴ 16s⁴ 20dᶠ 20s⁵ 20g Apr 11] angular
gelding: fairly useful handicap hurdler: won at Galway in August and Punchestown in
November: stays 2½m: acts on heavy going: tongue tied. *T. Hogan, Ireland*

DOOR OF KNOWLEDGE (USA)   4 b.g. Theatrical – Mynador (USA) (Forty Niner   **h83**
(USA)) [2003/4 16m³ 16m⁵ 16g⁴ 16s⁵ 16pᵖᵘ 16g 16d Mar 19] rather leggy, workmanlike gelding: fair on Flat (stays 9f) for D. Weld: modest juvenile hurdler: blinkered
and tongue tied after debut. *M. F. Harris*

DORANS GOLD   10 b.g. Gildoran – Cindie Girl (Orchestra) [2003/4 c125, h–: c20s⁴   **c–**
c20dᶠ 22g⁶ c24sᵘʳ c20dᵖᵘ c24gᵖᵘ Apr 10] lengthy, useful-looking gelding: winning   **h–**
hurdler: fairly useful handicap chaser: no form in 2003/4, sold out of P. Nicholls' stable
10,000 gns Doncaster August Sales after third start: stays 3m: acts on soft and good to
firm going: tried blinkered. *Miss Venetia Williams*

DORANS MAGIC   9 b.g. Gildoran – Mearlin (Giolla Mear) [2003/4 c25g² c26dᶠ Apr   **c102 x**
23] strong, workmanlike gelding: fairly useful hunter chaser: won point in April: stays   **h–**
25f: raced on good going or softer (acts on heavy). *Miss A. Armitage*

DORMY TWO (IRE)   4 b.f. Eagle Eyed (USA) – Tartan Lady (IRE) (Taufan (USA))   **h78**
[2003/4 16d⁵ 16d⁶ 16s³ 17d 17g³ 17g⁵ Apr 12] leggy filly: half-sister to fairly useful
hurdler Lady For Life (by Rainbows For Life), stays 2¾m: lightly-raced maiden on Flat,
sold out of Mrs P. N. Dutfield's stable 3,200 gns Doncaster October Sales: poor juvenile
hurdler: will stay beyond 17f: wore cheekpieces last 2 starts. *J. S. Wainwright*

DOROOSS (IRE)   4 b.g. Charnwood Forest (IRE) – Catherinofaragon (USA) (Chief's   **F80**
Crown (USA)) [2003/4 F16d Mar 19] 26,000F, 100,000Y: third foal: half-brother to fairly
useful 2001 2-y-o 7f winner Lucayan Legacy (by Persian Bold) and winner around 1m
Catstreet (by Catrail): dam unraced half-sister to US Grade 3 8.5f/1¼m winner Gold
Alert: sold unraced out of M. Channon's stable 5,500 gns Newmarket Autumn (2002)
Sales: eighth of 19 in maiden bumper at Warwick on debut. *Ian Williams*

DORSET FERN (IRE)   8 b.m. Tirol – La Duse (Junius (USA)) [2003/4 c–, h66:   **c–**
c22mᵖᵘ 17m Aug 25] lengthy mare: poor maiden hurdler: no show in 2 steeplechases: **h–**
bought out of G. Balding's stable £2,500 Ascot June Sales: tried blinkered: sold £1,300
Ascot October Sales, won point in February. *J. K. Price*

DOTTIE DIGGER (IRE)   5 b.m. Catrail (USA) – Hint-Of-Romance (IRE) (Treasure   **h70**
Kay) [2003/4 h–: 16g⁵ 16g 16g 16g* 16g⁴ 18dᵖᵘ Dec 1] poor hurdler: best effort when
50/1-winner of novice seller at Kelso in November: raced around 2m: has worn cheekpieces, visored in 2003/4. *Miss Lucinda V. Russell*

DOUBLE ACCOUNT (FR)   9 b.g. Sillery (USA) – Fabulous Account (USA) (Priv-   **c–**
ate Account (USA)) [2003/4 c–, h115: 26m* 25d⁵ Dec 12] sturdy gelding: winning   **h115**
chaser: fairly useful handicap hurdler, lightly raced nowadays: won at Huntingdon in
May: creditable fifth at Cheltenham 7 months later: stays 3¼m: probably acts on any
going: blinkered twice, including at Huntingdon. *C. J. Mann*

DOUBLE AGENT   11 ch.g. Niniski (USA) – Rexana (Relko) [2003/4 c–, h–: 22s*   **c–**
23sᵖᵘ 25d⁴ Apr 11] sturdy gelding: maiden chaser: modest hurdler: off 20 months, made   **h91**
all in seller at Folkestone in January: stays 25f: acts on soft and good to firm going: tried
blinkered. *Miss A. M. Newton-Smith*

DOUBLE BLADE   9 b.g. Kris – Sesame (Derrylin) [2003/4 h118: 16d³ 20g² 16g²   **c–**
16g² 17g* 16m* 16m⁵ c16f² c16d³ Dec 20] strong, lengthy gelding: fair hurdler: won   **h108 §**
claimers at Sedgefield (claimed from Mrs M. Reveley £7,000) in September and Plumpton in October: little encouragement in 2 novice chases: best at strongly-run 2m: acts on
firm and good to soft going: unbeaten in 5 starts at Sedgefield: usually held up: carries
head high and not one to trust. *N. Wilson*

DOUBLE BOGEY BLUES (IRE)   8 b.g. Celio Rufo – Belmount Star (IRE) (Good   **c81 x**
Thyne (USA)) [2003/4 c97x, h–: c20vᵖᵘ c24dⁱ c25g Apr 3] angular gelding: poor chaser: **h–**
stays 25f: acts on soft and good to firm going: races prominently: often let down by
jumping. *M. Mullineaux*

DOUBLE BUBBLE (IRE)   6 b. or br.g. Mandalus – Double Talk (Dublin Taxi)   **F–**
[2003/4 F–: F17m Sep 27] no sign of ability in bumpers or points. *C. N. Kellett*

DOUBLE DEAL   5 ch.m. Keen – Close The Deal (Nicholas Bill) [2003/4 F17m F17d⁶   **h82**
F16g³ 16s 16v² 17dᵖᵘ 17d⁵ Apr 10] sixth foal: half-sister to fair hurdler Whatadeal (by   **F71**
Then Again), stays 19f, and 9f to 16.5f winner in Holland by Domynsky: dam, ran only at

2 yrs, stayed 1¼m: poor form in bumpers and over hurdles: likely to stay beyond 2m: acts on heavy ground. *M. W. Easterby*

DOUBLE DESTINY   8 h.g. Anshan – Double Gift (Cragador) [2003/4 h85: 19m⁴ 20mᵖᵘ Jun 7] poor maiden hurdler: stays easy 19f: raced solely on good to firm going: wore cheekpieces in 2003/4. *Miss E. C. Lavelle*   **h85**

DOUBLE DIPLOMACY   8 b.g. State Diplomacy (USA) – Malmo (Free State) [2003/4 h–: c21dᵖᵘ Nov 25] no sign of ability: tried blinkered. *P. Beaumont*   **c–** **h–**

DOUBLE EM   5 b.g. Balnibarbi – Something Speedy (IRE) (Sayf El Arab (USA)) [2003/4 h–: 20vᵖᵘ 16g c24gᶠ 17d Mar 30] no form over hurdles: fell tenth on chasing debut (wore cheekpieces): pulls hard. *D. W. Thompson*   **c–** **h–**

DOUBLE EMBLEM (IRE)   7 ch.m. Weld – Sultry (Sula Bula) [2003/4 F–: F16g Oct 15] lengthy mare: little sign of ability in points and bumpers. *B. R. Foster*   **F–**

DOUBLE HEADER (IRE)   5 b.g. Old Vic – Ballybeggan Lady (IRE) (Le Bavard (FR)) [2003/4 F16g³ F16m Apr 13] 13,000 4-y-o: first foal: dam, winning pointer, half-sister to fairly useful 2m to 3m hurdler Templeroan Prince: better effort in bumpers when third to Rubberdubber at Wincanton: will be suited by greater test of stamina. *Mrs S. D. Williams*   **F95**

DOUBLE HELIX   5 b.g. Marju (IRE) – Totham (Shernazar) [2003/4 16m⁵ 16g 16d 20d⁶ 19g⁴ 19d 20d 17d⁵ 17g 16sᵖᵘ 17g² Apr 24] poor maiden on Flat (best form at 7f): poor novice hurdler: probably best around 2m with emphasis on speed: blinkered/visored last 7 outings: has high head carriage. *M. E. Sowersby*   **h81**

DOUBLE HONOUR (FR)   6 gr.g. Highest Honor (FR) – Silver Cobra (USA) (Silver Hawk (USA)) [2003/4 h123: 20d 20d² 20s² c19d³ c22s* c24g³ c24m* c25g³ c24s* Apr 21] close-coupled gelding: useful hurdler: soon reached similar standard over fences, winning novices at Newbury in January, Taunton (made hard work of straightforward task) in March and Perth (by 14 lengths from eased Whereareyounow) in April: will stay beyond 3m: acts on soft and good to firm going: effective held up or making running: looks tricky ride on occasions, and may benefit from headgear. *P. J. Hobbs*   **c140** **h133**

DOUBLE SCOOP   5 b.g. Double Eclipse (IRE) – Grayrose Double (Celtic Cone) [2003/4 F16d² 20g Dec 9] €35,000 3-y-o: seventh foal: half-brother to bumper winners Grayrose Fleur (by Henbit) and The Muratti (by Alflora): dam, winning hurdler who stayed 3m, out of half-sister to smart 2m to 3m chaser Clear Cut: second of 4 in bumper at Fakenham on debut: well beaten in novice hurdle following month. *B. G. Powell*   **h–** **F87**

DOUBLE SPEY   5 b.g. Atraf – Yankee Special (Bold Lad (IRE)) [2003/4 h94: 26g⁵ Jul 4] workmanlike gelding: modest maiden on Flat (stays 1¾m): modest form on first of 3 starts over hurdles: should stay beyond 2m. *P. C. Haslam*   **h–**

DOUBLE TEE (IRE)   8 br.g. Jurado (USA) – Monkeylane (Monksfield) [2003/4 c–, h–: c24sᵘʳ c21s⁴ c24gᵖᵘ c24m⁶ Mar 4] close-coupled gelding: of little account: tried visored/in cheekpieces. *N. J. Hawke*   **c–** **h–**

DOUBLE TIMER (IRE)   9 ch.g. Doubletour (USA) – Midnightattheoasis (IRE) (King Persian) [2003/4 c–, h–: c20d⁶ Nov 27] medium-sized gelding: progressive form over hurdles in 2001/2: off 22 months, no encouragement on chasing debut only start in 2003/4: stays 3m: acts on soft going. *Jonjo O'Neill*   **c–** **h–**

DOUBLE WHIRL   8 ch.g. Destroyer – Priceless Peril (Silly Prices) [2003/4 22gᵘʳ 20gᵖᵘ 24dᵖᵘ Mar 11] smallish gelding: of no account. *R. Ford*   **h–**

DOUBLE WISH (IRE)   6 b.h. Barathea (IRE) – Love Bateta (IRE) (Caerleon (USA)) [2003/4 h–: 19g 19m 16mᵖᵘ 16mᶠ Jul 23] no worthwhile form over hurdles: tried visored/in cheekpieces: tongue tied. *Miss M. E. Rowland*   **h–**

DOUBLEWOOD (IRE)   6 b.m. Charnwood Forest (IRE) – Double On (IRE) (Doubletour (USA)) [2003/4 F17v F16s⁴ Feb 22] second foal: half-sister to 1m winner Night Rapsody (by Mujtahid): dam, Irish 1m to 1½m winner, from family of useful French chaser Ruggiero and very smart stayer Moonax: well beaten in 2 mares bumpers. *J. A. B. Old*   **F–**

DOUBLE YOU CUBED   10 b.g. Destroyer – Bright Suggestion (Magnate) [2003/4 c–, h–: c25dᵘʳ c25g⁴ c25gᵖᵘ c20d⁶ c25s³ c21vᵖᵘ c25vᵇᵈ 20s² c20g* c16g⁶ c20d² c20dᵖᵘ Apr 23] leggy gelding: poor form over hurdles: modest handicap chaser: won at Ayr in March: stays 2½m: acts on soft ground. *J. S. Goldie*   **c85** **h67**

DOUCEUR DES SONGES (FR)   7 b.m. Art Francais (USA) – Ma Poetesse (FR) (Sorrento (FR)) [2003/4 c–§, h105§: 17g⁵ 16m⁵ 17g⁶ 20m³ 20m* 22f⁴ 18m² 22f⁶ 16m⁶   **c– §** **h87 §**

20g* c18g⁴ 19gᵖᵘ Apr 18] leggy, lengthy mare: maiden chaser: modest hurdler: won claimer at Worcester in August and conditional jockeys seller at Uttoxeter in October: sold out of M. Pipe's stable 4,000 gns Doncaster November Sales before final start: stays 2¾m: acts on any going: effective with visor/cheekpieces or without: ungenuine. *A. L. Forbes*

DOVEDALE   4 b.f. Groom Dancer (USA) – Peetsie (IRE) (Fairy King (USA)) [2003/4 F17m Apr 15] lengthy filly: second foal: dam, fair form in bumpers, half-sister to smart 2m to 3m hurdler Her Honour: better for race, tenth of 15 in mares bumper at Cheltenham (kicked at start and considerably handled) on debut. *Mrs Mary Hambro*   **F77**

DOVETTO   15 ch.g. Riberetto – Shadey Dove (Deadly Nightshade) [2003/4 c–, h–: c24g May 31] sparely-made gelding: poor chaser: stays easy 3m: acts on any going. *A. E. Price*   **c74**
h–

DOWNPOUR (USA)   6 b.g. Torrential (USA) – Juliac (USA) (Accipiter (USA)) [2003/4 h106: 16g* 17d Mar 18] useful-looking gelding: useful hurdler: much improved when winning handicap at Ascot in November by 4 lengths from Going Global: raced freely when well held in valuable handicap at Cheltenham 4 months later: stays 19f: raced on good/good to soft going. *Ian Williams*   **h130**

DOWNTHEREFORDANCIN (IRE)   4 b.g. Groom Dancer (USA) – Merlin's Fancy (Caerleon (USA)) [2003/4 17m² 17mᵘʳ 17g* 18m³ 16f² 20m⁵ 16d² 17d⁵ 16s³ 17s² 20s 16g⁴ 19g 19g⁵ Apr 16] leggy gelding: fair up to 1½m on Flat: fairly useful juvenile hurdler: won at Newton Abbot in September: best form around 2m: acts on firm and soft going: visored prior to last 2 starts: difficult ride: inconsistent. *M. C. Pipe*   **h111 §**

DOWN TO THE WOODS (USA)   6 ch.g. Woodman (USA) – Riviera Wonder (USA) (Batonnier (USA)) [2003/4 16m Sep 17] modest on flat (stays 1¼m): failed to settle and well beaten in maiden on hurdling debut: joined R. Woodhouse. *M. J. Polglase*   **h–**

DRACAENA   7 b.m. State Diplomacy (USA) – Jay-Dee-Jay (Mljet) [2003/4 17d⁶ 19g 21vᵖᵘ 16v⁴ 17d 17d Apr 10] big mare: second foal: dam, modest staying hurdler, out of sister to smart chaser at 2½m+ Straight Jocelyn: no form over hurdles. *P. Beaumont*   **h–**

DRAGON HUNTER (IRE)   9 b.g. Welsh Term – Sahob (Roselier (FR)) [2003/4 c–p, h–: c25dᵖᵘ c24d⁴ c24g c24d² Mar 20] winning hurdler: modest novice chaser: best at 3m+: raced on good ground or softer: has bled from nose. *C. R. Egerton*   **c96**
h–

DRAGON KING   12 b.g. Rakaposhi King – Dunsilly Bell (London Bells (CAN)) [2003/4 c95, h–: c27sˢᵘ c24g² c22m² c22g³ c22g⁵ c26g³ c25d⁵ c25m* c25d* c31gᵖᵘ c28d c27s³ c24g⁵ c28d⁴ Mar 21] sturdy gelding: fair handicap chaser: won at Hereford (amateurs) in November and Folkestone in December: stays 27f: acts on any going: effective in headgear or not: front runner: tends to jump right: tough. *P. Bowen*   **c104**
h–

DRAGON PRINCE   4 b.g. Zamindar (USA) – Nawafell (Kris) [2003/4 16g⁶ Mar 28] fair form in 3 maidens at 2 yrs for M. Jarvis: sold 800 gns Newmarket July Sales: failed to settle when well beaten in juvenile on hurdling debut. *R. C. Guest*   **h–**

DRAGON'S DREAM   6 b.g. Afzal – Another Relation (Relkino) [2003/4 F17m² 19sᵘʳ 24m Mar 4] fourth foal: dam once-raced in points: won second of 2 starts in maiden points in 2003: second in bumper at Newton Abbot: let down by jumping in 2 novice hurdles at Taunton, seventh of 14 on completed outing. *P. F. Nicholls*   **h80**
F86

DRAGUT TORGHOUD (IRE)   8 b.g. Persian Mews – Artist's Jewel (Le Moss) [2003/4 h82+, F77: 21mᵖᵘ May 5] poor form over hurdles: will stay beyond 21f. *N. M. Babbage*   **h–**

DRAKESTONE   13 b.g. Motivate – Lyricist (Averof) [2003/4 c–, h–: 20s² 19m* 17m* 20mᵖᵘ Jun 28] workmanlike gelding: modest hurdler: won seller at Hereford in May and handicap on same course following month: stays 23f: acts on soft and good to firm going: blinkered twice: difficult to keep sound. *R. L. Brown*   **c–**
h91

DRAMA KING   12 b.g. Tragic Role (USA) – Consistent Queen (Queen's Hussar) [2003/4 h76: 20d⁶ May 3] small gelding: poor handicap hurdler: effective at 2m to 2¾m: acts on any going: usually blinkered/visored: inconsistent. *B. J. Llewellyn*   **h– §**

DRAMATIC APPROACH (IRE)   10 b.g. Dry Dock – Gayles Approach (Strong Gale) [2003/4 c23sᶠ Jan 20] well-made gelding: winning pointer in Ireland, fair form when placed in Britain in 2002: fell heavily twelfth in maiden chase. *B. G. Powell*   **c–**
h–

DRAT   5 b.g. Faustus (USA) – Heresy (IRE) (Black Minstrel) [2003/4 F16s⁴ Mar 20] third foal: dam of little account: fourth of 21 in bumper at Ascot on debut, tiring having made headway from well off pace. *R. Mathew*   **F86**

DR CHARLIE 6 ch.g. Dr Devious (IRE) – Miss Toot (Ardross) [2003/4 h98: 20v 20m^{pu} **h97**
22g 19m* 20d^4 19g^5 19s^6 21s^5 21d^{pu} 22g^2 Apr 18] angular gelding: modest handicap
hurdler: sold out of C. Mann's stable 6,500 gns Doncaster May Sales after reappearance
(blinkered): won at Hereford in October: stays 2¾m: acts on good to firm and heavy
going. *Miss C. Dyson*

DR DEDUCTIBLE 12 b.g. Derrylin – Tantrum (Leading Man) [2003/4 c77: c25g* **c88**
c25g^4 c26d^2 May 28] fair hunter chaser, successful at Kelso very early in 2003/4: won
point in March: stays 3¼m: acts on good to soft going: blinkered. *J. E. Brockbank*

DREAM CASTLE (IRE) 10 b.g. Poet's Dream (IRE) – Kerry's Castle (Deep Run) **h74**
[2003/4 16d 20g^5 22g 18d^3 Mar 3] IR 3,400 5-y-o: second foal: dam, maiden, sister to
high-class 2½m to 25f chaser Unguided Missile: poor hurdler: stays 2½m: acts on firm
and soft ground. *Lindsay Woods, Ireland*

DREAM FALCON 4 br.g. Polar Falcon (USA) – Pip's Dream (Glint of Gold) **h102**
[2003/4 16g* 16d^2 17s^3 16s Feb 22] modest maiden on Flat: successful first 2 starts over
hurdles, in juvenile seller (most took wrong course) in December and amateur novice
handicap in January, both at Ludlow: jumped poorly third start, well held at Towcester
final one. *R. J. Hodges*

DREAMING DIVA 5 ch.m. Whittingham (IRE) – Any Dream (IRE) (Shernazar) **h–**
[2003/4 16m^{pu} Dec 10] fair 7f winner at 2 yrs, little form on Flat since: showed nothing
on hurdling debut. *J. C. Fox*

DREAM KING (IRE) 4 b.g. Petardia – Barinia (Corvaro (USA)) [2003/4 18v 16g **h–**
Mar 6] half-brother to winning chaser up to 23f in Czech Republic by Cadeaux Genereux:
little form on Flat, sold out of M. Polglase's stable 700 gns Doncaster October Sales: no
sign of ability over hurdles. *Miss S. E. Forster*

DREAM ON WILLIE (IRE) 7 b.g. Synefos (USA) – Mrs Mahon's Toy (IRE) (Rose- **c102**
lier (FR)) [2003/4 h90: 24d^6 20g^5 c20g^{ur} c21g^2 c20m* c21m^2 c20d^2 c20d^2 c24d^{pu} c21g^2 **h–**
c20d^4 Apr 23] poor maiden hurdler: fair handicap chaser: won novice at Wetherby in
November: best around 2½m: acts on soft and good to firm going: consistent. *E. A. Elliott*

DREAM WITH ME (FR) 7 b.g. Johann Quatz (FR) – Midnight Ride (FR) (Fast **c102**
Topaze (USA)) [2003/4 h125: c20g* c21g^4 c20m^5 c16m^5 c17m^3 c17f^2 Oct 21] sturdy **h–**
gelding: fairly useful hurdler: fair novice chaser: won at Market Rasen in May: stays
2½m: best form over hurdles on good/good to soft going, raced solely on good or firmer
over fences: well below form in blinkers/visor: tongue tied. *M. C. Pipe*

DRIFT AWAY (USA) 4 b.f. Dehere (USA) – Flying Blind (IRE) (Silver Kite (USA)) **h104**
[2003/4 17g^2 17g^5 16m 16g^5 16m* 16s Nov 29] little form on Flat for P. Prendergast:
easily best effort in juvenile hurdles when winning maiden at Down Royal in November:
blinkered third/fourth starts. *J. J. Lambe, Ireland*

DROMBEAG (IRE) 6 b.g. Presenting – Bula Beag (IRE) (Brush Aside (USA)) **c124 p**
[2003/4 F97: c24d^2 c25g^2 c32g^3 Mar 17] big, rangy gelding: won maiden Irish point on
debut in 2002: fairly useful bumper winner: placed all 3 starts in steeplechases, best effort
when third of 13 finishers to Native Emperor in valuable amateur novice at Cheltenham:
stays 4m: probably capable of further improvement and will win races in 2004/5. *Jonjo
O'Neill*

DROMHALE LADY (IRE) 11 gr.m. Roselier (FR) – Miss Minella (Deep Run) **c119**
[2003/4 c22s* 20s^{pu} 24d^6 20d 24s^5 20s^4 22d^4 20s^5 c21g c24s^5 c20s Mar 28] lengthy mare: **h107**
fairly useful handicap chaser: fair handicap hurdler: best effort in 2003/4 when winning
at Killarney in May by 3 lengths from Rheindross: stays 3m: acts on heavy going: tried
blinkered. *M. Hourigan, Ireland*

DROMLEASE EXPRESS (IRE) 6 ch.g. Fourstars Allstar (USA) – Niat Sup- **c110 p**
reme (IRE) (Supreme Leader) [2003/4 20s 16d* 16s* 21g c24d^2 Apr 10] **h138**

Form doesn't work out much better than that of the latest running of the
Pierse Hurdle, the very valuable handicap run at Leopardstown early in January.
Horse after horse came out and ran well, necessitating an ever-higher view to be
taken of the performances of the principals. Mind you, those who followed the
runners blindly in their next races were poorly rewarded: the first to reappear,
tenth-home Cronin's Boy won a handicap six days later at odds of 12/1, but none of
the seventeen others to run before the end of the Irish season won next time out.
Runner-up Macs Joy was first past the post at Leopardstown the following month
but was harshly demoted by the stewards. Notable among the others were the third

Georges Girl, beaten a head in the AIG Europe Champion Hurdle later in the month, and the fifth Arch Stanton who ran very well in the Deloitte Novices' Hurdle behind Brave Inca not long after. Just about the only runner not to boost the form next time was the winner Dromlease Express, but his performance in finishing last of twenty-seven in the Coral Cup at Cheltenham was just too bad to be true and he is likely to be making an impact again in 2004/5.

The Pierse was Dromlease Express' third start in his second season over hurdles. The winner of a two-mile maiden at Gowran from seven outings in his first, he had shown himself on the upgrade by landing a gamble in an eighteen-runner handicap over the same trip at Naas on his previous outing, but had been put up 6 lb for that by the Turf Club handicapper and looked to have no more than an average chance. However, he was again well supported at Leopardstown and, sent off 6/1 joint favourite, can hardly have given his supporters much cause for alarm. Dropped out in rear by his 7-lb claiming rider John Allen, Dromlease Express made good progress two out and was ridden clear after leading at the last, beating the close finishers Macs Joy and Georges Girl three and a half lengths, with no fewer than eleven lengths to the fourth Steel Band. Dromlease Express was completing a notable double for his trainer Charles Byrnes, as Cloudy Bays had won the Leopardstown Chase earlier in the afternoon, the two successes netting prize money of €143,650. One disappointing thing about the Pierse Hurdle was the absence, for the second time in three years, of a British-trained challenge. Although it is seven years since Master Tribe landed what was then The Ladbroke for Jenny Pitman, Geos (second in 2000), Rooster Booster (third in 2001) and Colourful Life (second in 2003) have been placed in the three most recent runnings with British participation and the prize is surely valuable enough to attract more interest in Britain than it does.

Pierse Hurdle (Extended Handicap), Leopardstown—
Dromlease Express takes command at the last from Macs Joy (right) and Georges Girl

Not surprisingly, Dromlease Express faced rather more than a rise of 6 lb for his Pierse Hurdle win, though he was among the market leaders for the Coral Cup when the weights were announced and looked a leading contender, despite the presence of Rhinestone Cowboy resulting in his being 6 lb out of the handicap as well. Nonetheless, only four runners in the handicap started at shorter odds on the day and it was disappointing Dromlease Express couldn't show his form. He would certainly be worth another chance in a good handicap hurdle, though his future may well be over fences. Somewhat surprisingly, he made his debut in a chase at Cork in April, in a three-mile listed event, in which he stayed on to take second on the run-in behind seven-length winner Joueur d'Estruval. The jumping of Dromlease Express could have been better but is sure to improve with experience and he will be winning races over fences.

Dromlease Express (IRE) (ch.g. 1998)	Fourstars Allstar (USA) (b 1988)	Compliance (b 1978)	Northern Dancer / Sex Appeal
		Broadway Joan (ch 1979)	Bold Arian / Courtneys Doll
	Niat Supreme (IRE) (b 1990)	Supreme Leader (b 1982)	Bustino / Princess Zena
		Garry Niat (ch 1982)	Le Bavard / Niatpac

The leggy Dromlease Express comes from the second crop of the very smart American-trained miler Fourstars Allstar, who gained a famous victory for Leo O'Brien in the 1991 Irish Two Thousand Guineas. Dromlease Express is by some way the best of his quite large representation over jumps, though he is also the sire of the smart Flat stayer Jardines Lookout. Dromlease Express' dam Niat Supreme was also trained by an O'Brien—Aidan no less—and showed modest form in winning a bumper at Limerick. Dromlease Express is her second foal, the first his sister Kathella having been only a poor novice hurdler. Niat Supreme is a sister to the fair hurdler at up to three miles Garryduff Supreme and half-sister to a couple of minor winners but it's a fair way back to the last notable name in this family. The third dam Niatpac is out of a sister to the useful chaser Golden Rapper who won the Leopardstown Chase and was leading when falling at second Becher's in Rag Trade's Grand National. Dromlease Express is versatile with regard to trip, having shown form at two miles and three. He has been raced on good going or softer, showing his form only on good to soft and soft. *C. Byrnes, Ireland*

DROM WOOD (IRE) 8 ch.g. Be My Native (USA) – Try Your Case (Proverb) [2003/4 c–, h–: 24m⁶ c20m* c25g⁴ c24g* c30s⁴ c24sᵖᵘ c24s⁵ Dec 29] sturdy, lengthy gelding: maiden hurdler: modest handicap chaser: won at Huntingdon (novice) in May and Chepstow in November: should stay beyond 3m: acts on soft and good to firm going: tongue tied once (won): sold £14,000 Cheltenham April Sales. *T. R. George*   **c92 h–**

DR RAJ 5 ch.g. In The Wings – Tawaaded (IRE) (Nashwan (USA)) [2003/4 F–: F17g 16dᵖᵘ Jan 13] strong, lengthy, dipped-backed gelding: poor form on second of 2 outings in bumpers: tongue tied, weakened quickly after 4 out in novice on hurdling debut: well held in 3 starts on Flat. *B. A. McMahon*   **h– F74**

DR SHARP (IRE) 4 ch.g. Dr Devious (IRE) – Stoned Imaculate (IRE) (Durgam (USA)) [2003/4 18v* 18gᵘʳ 16sᵘʳ 17d² Apr 10] good-topped gelding: fair on Flat (stays 2m): won juvenile at Kelso in February on hurdling debut: similar form only other completed start. *T. P. Tate*   **h97**

DRUIDS CONFEDERACY (IRE) 6 ch.m. Great Marquess – Winsome Blends (IRE) (Zaffaran (USA)) [2003/4 F17v² 16v* 16s 22vᵖᵘ Jan 24] €10,000 3-y-o, €8,500 4-y-o: lengthy, rather leggy mare: second foal: dam, once-raced in points, out of useful hurdler/chaser up to 2½m Mixed Blends, herself half-sister to dual Whitbread Gold Cup winner Topsham Bay: second in mares bumper on debut: won mares novice at Towcester on hurdling debut in December by distance from Countess Camilla: disappointing in similar events at Wetherby and Haydock: should stay beyond 2m. *C. R. Egerton*   **h100 F97**

DRUID'S GLEN (IRE) 8 br.g. Un Desperado (FR) – Fais Vite (USA) (Sharpen Up) [2003/4 c132, h–: c24dᵖᵘ Nov 22] tall, attractive gelding: useful chaser: no chance with winner Kingscliff but set to finish good second when pulled up amiss before last in handicap at Ascot only outing in 2003/4: stays 25f: acts on soft and good to firm going: usually races prominently: not straightforward (has hung/flashed tail). *Jonjo O'Neill*   **c139 h–**

DRU

DRUMDOWNEY LAD (IRE) 5 b.g. Darnay – Alpencrocus (IRE) (Waajib) [2003/4 **c–**
c16d⁵ c16gᵖᵘ Apr 3] €20,000 3-y-o: ex-Irish gelding: third foal: half-brother to winning
sprinter in Italy by Forest Wind: dam ran once in Ireland: well beaten in 2 bumpers for
M. Kinane: won maiden point in Britain in February: no show in steeplechases. *R. H. York*

DRY OLD PARTY (IRE) 5 ch.g. Un Desperado (FR) – The Vine Browne (IRE) **F–**
(Torus) [2003/4 F16g F16s Jan 16] €30,000 4-y-o: has scope: first foal: dam, lightly-
raced maiden, from family of high-class 2m hurdler Deep Idol: well held in 2 bumpers,
showing signs of temperament. *P. Winkworth*

DUAL STAR (IRE) 9 b.g. Warning – Sizes Vary (Be My Guest (USA)) [2003/4 c94, **c90 §**
h83: c17m⁵ c16g⁵ c18f⁴ c16m* c19m³ c17m⁵ c19m⁵ c17g⁶ c16d c16m³ c18gᵖᵘ c19g⁵ Apr **h–**
16] sparely-made gelding: modest handicap chaser: won at Huntingdon in August: left
P. Hobbs after next start and little show subsequently: stays 19f: acts on soft and good to
firm going: tried blinkered: usually tongue tied: has gone in snatches. *L. Waring*

DUBAI SEVEN STARS 6 ch.m. Suave Dancer (USA) – Her Honour (Teenoso **h89 §**
(USA)) [2003/4 h126§: 24d 19d* 22dᵖᵘ 20d⁵ 24s 19g Apr 1] leggy mare: fairly useful
hurdler in 2002/3: nowhere near best in 2003/4, though won seller at Taunton in December: stays 3m: raced on good going or softer (acts on soft): visored: unreliable. *M. C. Pipe*

DUCHAMP (USA) 7 b.g. Pine Bluff (USA) – Higher Learning (USA) (Fappiano **c123**
(USA)) [2003/4 c122, h–: c20m² c21m* c20gᵖᵘ Oct 26] tall, leggy gelding: fairly useful **h–**
handicap chaser: good efforts at Stratford first 2 starts, beating strong-finishing Carbury
Cross a head on second occasion: lifeless effort at Aintree 8 days later: stays 21f: acts on
good to firm and heavy ground: effective visored or not: front runner. *A. M. Balding*

DUKE OF BRITTANY (FR) 5 b.g. Rifapour (IRE) – Fox Trot V (FR) (Abdonski **h76 ?**
(FR)) [2003/4 F17m 16g² 27s⁶ 16g 24g⁶ Feb 18] smallish gelding: first foal: dam un- **F–**
raced: form only when second in novice hurdle at Hexham in November. *Mrs M. Reveley*

DUKE OF BUCKINGHAM (IRE) 8 b.g. Phardante (FR) – Deselby's Choice **c144**
(Crash Course) [2003/4 c102: c16f* c16m* c20m c16g* c17f² c16f² c16gʷᵒ c16m*
c16m* c16g⁶ c16m⁴ Apr 24] lengthy, good sort: useful chaser: had excellent season,
winning novices at Warwick and Huntingdon in May, Perth in August and Kempton in
November, and handicap at Warwick in December: walked over in handicap at Folke-
stone in November: excellent fourth in face of stiff task to Cenkos in valuable contest at
Sandown final start: best at 2m: acts on firm going: usually front runner: sound jumper.
P. R. Webber

DUKE OF EARL (IRE) 5 ch.g. Ali-Royal (IRE) – Faye (Monsanto (FR)) [2003/4 **h124**
h119: 16m* Oct 4] small, leggy gelding: fairly useful hurdler: fit from Flat, won handicap
at Chepstow only start in 2003/4, brought with well-timed run to beat Unleash 1¾
lengths: will stay beyond 17f: acts on good to firm and heavy ground. *S. Kirk*

DUN AN DORAS (IRE) 8 b.g. Glacial Storm – Doorslammer (Avocat) **c99**
[2003/4 h93: 27s⁴ 22g* 22d² 19m² 19g* c19d² c21g³ c20f* c19g⁵ c19dᵖᵘ Mar 23] leggy **h99**
gelding: modest hurdler: won maiden in June and novice in September, both at Newton
Abbot: similar form over fences, landing odds in maiden at Leicester in December: stays
2¾m: acts on any going. *J. D. Frost*

DUNBAY 10 b.g. Dunbeath (USA) – Lekuti (Le Coq d'Or) [2003/4 c16dᶠ c24mᵖᵘ May **c–**
7] poor pointer. *Mrs Peter Shaw*

DUNCLIFFE 7 b.g. Executive Perk – Ida Melba (Idiot's Delight) [2003/4 c19d⁴ c24v² **c92**
Apr 4] first foal: dam unraced, from family of high-class hurdler/very smart chaser up to
2½m Dramatist: won maiden point in 2003: modest form in frame in 2 steeplechases.
R. H. Alner

DUNCRIEVIE GALE 7 gr.g. Gildoran – The Whirlie Weevil (Scallywag) [2003/4 **c75 ?**
h–: c20s² c24sᵘʳ Apr 21] big gelding: lightly raced: off 17 months, got very tired in **h–**
straight when distant second of 4 finishers in novice at Newcastle on chasing debut: badly
hampered and unseated tenth month later: stoutly bred. *Miss Lucinda V. Russell*

DUNDONALD 5 ch.g. Magic Ring (IRE) – Cal Norma's Lady (IRE) (Lyphard's **h–**
Special (USA)) [2003/4 h–: 16g 17mᵖᵘ 16gᵖᵘ Dec 11] strong, workmanlike gelding: poor
on Flat: no form over hurdles: tried tongue tied/in headgear. *M. Appleby*

DUNDRIDGE NATIVE 6 b.m. Be My Native (USA) – Fra Mau (Wolver Hollow) **F74**
[2003/4 F16v⁵ F16m Mar 11] eighth foal: half-sister to useful staying chaser Latent
Talent (by Celtic Cone): dam, fairly useful hurdler, stayed at least 2½m: better effort in
bumpers when fifth at Chepstow on debut. *M. Madgwick*

270

DUNDROD 7 ch.g. Riverwise (USA) – Pallanda (Pablond) [2003/4 F17d 20d⁶ 17dᵖᵘ 16sᵖᵘ Jan 16] 2,000 5-y-o, 3,100 6-y-o: good-topped gelding: third foal: brother to modest chaser Tullons Lane, stays 2¾m: dam winning pointer: little sign of ability. *F. P. Murtagh*   **h–** **F–**

DUNGARVANS CHOICE (IRE) 9 ch.g. Orchestra – Marys Gift (Monksfield) [2003/4 c122, h132: 20d May 3] sturdy, useful-looking gelding: temperamental efforts in 2 novice chases: useful hurdler: running at least respectably when blundering 2 out in handicap won by Haydens Field at Uttoxeter only outing in 2003/4: likely to stay 3m: raced on good going or softer (acts on soft): edgy sort. *N. J. Henderson*   **c–** **h126 ?**

DUNKERRON 7 b.g. Pursuit of Love – Top Berry (High Top) [2003/4 h68: 16m* 16mᵘʳ 16m⁵ 16m 16m⁶ 16f⁴ c17m* c16m⁴ c17g² Nov 21] compact gelding: poor handicap hurdler: won conditional jockeys seller at Huntingdon in May: left J. Joseph, won novice handicap at Plumpton on chasing debut in October: less than fluent both subsequent starts, also looked none too keen final one: best around 2m: acts on good to firm and good to soft going: went off too fast when blinkered. *P. J. Hobbs*   **c82** **h73**

DUNLEA (IRE) 8 b.g. Common Grounds – No Distractions (Tap On Wood) [2003/4 h93: 24m* 21g c20d c19d c17s c17s⁴ c22s c20d⁵ c16sᵖᵘ Apr 4] angular gelding: modest handicap hurdler: won at Hexham in October: form over fences only when fourth in maiden at Fairyhouse: stays easy 3m, effective at much shorter: acts on soft and good to firm going. *J. G. Carr, Ireland*   **c100 ?** **h91**

DUNMANUS BAY (IRE) 7 gr.g. Mandalus – Baby Fane (IRE) (Buckskin (FR)) [2003/4 c–, h86: c19g* c25m c21gᶠ c21g c21gᵖᵘ c21m⁵ 27d⁶ c26g² c26g* c26mᵖᵘ c25dᵖᵘ c24sᵖᵘ Apr 12] lightly-raced hurdler: modest chaser, trained until after fifth start by R. Alner: won weakly-contested handicaps at Exeter very early in season and Newton Abbot (terrific ride by A. McCoy) in September: sold out of M. Pipe's stable 4,000 gns Doncaster October Sales, no show in 2 hunters: stays 3¼m: unraced on extremes of going: usually visored/blinkered: bad jumper, and not one to trust. *Mrs Julie Read*   **c88 x** **h–**

DUNNET HEAD (IRE) 5 ch.g. Shernazar – Kabarda (Relkino) [2003/4 F16d* Apr 17] €34,000 3-y-o: eighth foal: half-brother to winning 2m hurdler Delgany Toulon (by Toulon): dam unraced: won bumper at Ayr impressively on debut by 12 lengths from Captain Murphy, quickening right away when shaken up 2f out: useful prospect. *L. Lungo*   **F108**

DUNNICKS CHANCE 9 b.m. Greensmith – Field Chance (Whistlefield) [2003/4 h65: 19gᵖᵘ 16d⁶ Dec 26] poor maiden hurdler. *F. G. Tucker*   **h–**

DUNNICKS HEAD 8 b.m. Greensmith – Country Magic (National Trust) [2003/4 22dᵖᵘ Feb 12] no show in mares bumper and mares novice hurdle 2 years apart. *F. G. Tucker*   **h–**

DUNNICKS TRUST 6 b.g. Greensmith – Country Magic (National Trust) [2003/4 F–: F16g 19dᵖᵘ 22sᵖᵘ Jan 8] good-bodied gelding: no sign of ability. *F. G. Tucker*   **h–** **F–**

DUNNICKS VIEW 15 b.g. Sula Bula – Country Magic (National Trust) [2003/4 c78, h–: c21m⁵ c24s⁶ c24vᵖᵘ Feb 7] lengthy gelding: veteran handicap chaser, poor form in 2003/4: stays 3¼m: acts on good to firm and heavy going. *F. G. Tucker*   **c72** **h–**

DUNOWEN (IRE) 9 b.g. Be My Native (USA) – Lulu Buck (Buckskin (FR)) [2003/4 c88, h84: 20g⁴ 20d² c21g³ c16s⁵ c20s 22dᵖᵘ Mar 3] lengthy ex-Irish gelding: modest chaser/maiden hurdler: sold out of T. Hyde's stable 21,000 gns Doncaster May Sales after reappearance: stays 21f: raced on good going or softer over jumps (acts on heavy): often blinkered, visored final start: poor jumper of fences. *J. M. P. Eustace*   **c91 x** **h91**

DUNRAVEN 9 b.g. Perpendicular – Politique (Politico (USA)) [2003/4 c80, h76: 16m 16g² 19m⁴ 17m⁴ 16g³ 21g⁵ c16m³ 19g c16g 16s³ 16d⁴ 16s⁴ 16s 16s c16dᵘʳ 16d⁵ Apr 12] workmanlike gelding: poor maiden chaser (jumps poorly): modest handicap hurdler: won seller at Leicester in January, idling: stays 2½m: acts on heavy and good to firm going: tried visored/in cheekpieces: sometimes looks tricky ride. *M. J. Gingell*   **c70 x** **h86**

DUNSEMORE 4 b.f. Prince Daniel (USA) – Admire-A-More (Le Coq d'Or) [2003/4 F16s F16d Apr 23] sixth foal: half-sister to fairly useful hurdler Sillymore (by Silly Prices), stays 2½m: dam, winning hurdler, stayed 2¾m: well held in 2 bumpers. *P. Monteith*   **F–**

DUNSHAUGHLIN (IRE) 7 b.g. Supreme Leader – Russian Gale (IRE) (Strong Gale) [2003/4 F17s⁶ 17s Apr 6] IR 51,000 3-y-o: third foal: brother to useful hurdler/very promising chaser Lord Sam, stays 3m: dam won 3m chase in Ireland: signs of ability in bumper at Newton Abbot and novice hurdle at Exeter nearly 12 months apart: likely to be suited by stiffer test of stamina. *J. A. B. Old*   **h83 p** **F87**

DUNSTER CASTLE   9 ch.g. Carlingford Castle – Gay Edition (New Member)   **c106 +**
[2003/4 c105, h–: c26g* c23m^{pu} c25f^2 c24f^F Oct 28] workmanlike gelding: fair chaser: **h–**
won novice at Fontwell in May: stays 3¼m: acts on soft and firm going: has looked
awkward/found less than expected under pressure. *P. J. Hobbs*

DUNSTON BILL   10 b.g. Sizzling Melody – Fardella (ITY) (Molvedo) [2003/4 c115,   **c107**
h–: c20d^4 c24d^6 c24d^{pu} c24d^3 c24s^3 Apr 17] workmanlike gelding: fair handicap chaser: **h–**
stays 3m: acts on heavy and good to firm going: blinkered. *C. J. Mann*

DUN VICTORY   9 b.g. Destroyer – Dun Gay Lass (Rolfe (USA)) [2003/4 c25g^{pu} Apr   **c–**
5] modest pointer. *Mrs P. Claxton*

DURAID (IRE)   12 ch.g. Irish River (FR) – Fateful Princess (USA) (Vaguely Noble)   **h–**
[2003/4 17m^{pu} Jul 17] workmanlike gelding: one-time fairly useful on Flat: first run over
hurdles since 1999, struck into in maiden at Cartmel. *C. Grant*

DURANTE (IRE)   6 ch.g. Shernazar – Sweet Tune (Welsh Chanter) [2003/4 F16g   **F–**
Mar 27] €30,000 4-y-o: good-bodied gelding: half-brother to fairly useful hurdler/useful
chaser Jenniferjo (by Witness Box), stays 3m: dam ran once: ninth of 18 in bumper at
Newbury on debut. *J. A. B. Old*

DURHAM DANDY   8 b.g. Inchinor – Disco Girl (FR) (Green Dancer (USA)) [2003/4   **c87 d**
c20d^2 c20g c20g^6 c22f^2 c20f^2 c27d^6 Oct 29] angular gelding: winning pointer: poor   **h–**
maiden hurdler/steeplechaser: left Miss J. Foster after second start: probably stays 2¾m:
acts on firm and good to soft going: blinkered 3 times over hurdles, wore cheekpieces in
2003/4. *M. W. Easterby*

DURINGTHENIGHT (IRE)   5 b.g. Namaqualand (USA) – Legend of Spain (USA)   **h–**
(Alleged (USA)) [2003/4 F102: 19f^F Oct 5] fairly useful form in bumpers: fell fatally on
hurdling debut. *G. A. Swinbank*

DURKAR STAR (IRE)   6 b.g. Bin Ajwaad (IRE) – Faith Alone (Safawan) [2003/4   **h–**
16g Jun 12] no sign of ability on Flat or on hurdling debut. *M. C. Chapman*

DUSHAAN   9 ch.g. Anshan – Soon To Be (Hot Spark) [2003/4 h–: 16g c16g^5 17g c16d   **c–**
c21s^{pu} 17v^{pu} Jan 13] good-topped gelding: winning 2m hurdler, no form since 2001: tried   **h–**
blinkered/tongue tied: has looked ungenuine. *Mrs L. B. Normile*

DUSKY LIGHT   6 b.m. Gildoran – Starawak (Star Appeal) [2003/4 h81p, F77: 16d^6 **h77**
17d 20d^5 Apr 7] poor form over hurdles: stays 19f: jumps less than fluently. *P. F. Nicholls*

DUSKY LORD   5 b.g. Lord Americo – Red Dusk (Deep Run) [2003/4 F18g^3 Apr 22]   **F80**
10,000 4-y-o: sixth foal: brother to bumper winner Spud One: dam, poor novice hurdler
who stayed 2½m, sister to high-class 2m to 2½m chaser Deep Sensation: 22 lengths third
of 13 to Itsmyboy in bumper at Fontwell on debut. *N. J. Gifford*

DUSTY BANDIT (IRE)   6 ch.g. Un Desperado (FR) – Marble Miller (IRE) (Mister   **h98**
Lord (USA)) [2003/4 18s^5 19m^3 22g^{pu} Apr 22] sixth foal: brother to fair hurdler/fairly
useful chaser Kymandjen, stays 3m, and half-brother to useful hurdler/fair chaser up to
3m Like A Lion (by Farheen): dam unraced sister to fairly useful staying chaser Folly
Road: best effort in novice hurdles when fifth to Control Man at Fontwell. *P. F. Nicholls*

DUSTY TOO   6 gr.m. Terimon – Princess Florine (USA) (Our Native (USA)) [2003/4   **h112**
h–, F90: 18m* 21m* 20s^3 Jan 26] leggy mare: bumper winner: fair novice hurdler: won
at Fontwell in September and Plumpton (simple task) in October: visored, reportedly
lame when third in mares event back at Fontwell: stays 21f: acts on soft and good to firm
going. *Mrs A. J. Perrett*

DUTCH STAR   5 b.m. Alflora (IRE) – Double Dutch (Nicholas Bill) [2003/4 F16s   **F–**
aF16g Apr 4] seventh foal: sister to useful bumper winner Monteforte and half-sister to
several winners, including fair hurdler up to 2¾m Dutch Dyane (by Midyan): dam useful
stayer: achieved little in 2 bumpers. *G. P. Enright*

DUTSDALE DANCER (IRE)   10 b.g. Commanche Run – Miss Polymer (Doulab   **c–**
(USA)) [2003/4 c124, h–: 20d^{pu} c24d^{pu} 16s 20s^2 c17s^{pu} 16s 20d c20s^{pu} Mar 27] lengthy,   **h121**
rather sparely-made gelding: fairly useful hurdler/chaser: creditable effort in 2003/4 only
when second in listed handicap over hurdles at Navan in January: stays 2½m: acts on any
going: tried blinkered/tongue tied. *A. J. Whelan, Ireland*

DYLAN THE VILLAIN   5 b.g. Overbury (IRE) – Radmore Brandy (Derrylin)   **F–**
[2003/4 F18s F16m F17g Apr 10] second foal: dam winning 2m hurdler: tailed off in
bumpers. *G. A. Ham*

DYNAMIC LIFTER (IRE)   6 ch.g. Be My Native (USA) – Best Trump (Le Bavard   **h93**
(FR)) [2003/4 h84, F75: 24v³ 24g² 27g² 22mᵖᵘ Jul 13] modest novice hurdler: best at
3m+: unraced on firm going, acts on any other: tried blinkered. *Jonjo O'Neill*

DYRICK DAYBREAK (IRE)   5 ch.m. Ali-Royal (IRE) – Lovely Daise (IRE) (Late   **h111 §**
Gallery (USA)) [2003/4 h115. 16g* 16m³ 16dᶠ 16s* 16sʳᵗʳ 16d Mar 17] angular mare: fair
hurdler: won 4-y-o handicap at Listowel in September and 4-y-o minor event at Limerick
(odds on, easily) in December: likely to stay beyond 2m: acts on heavy going: usually
tongue tied: refused to race fifth outing and needs treating with caution. *David A. Kiely,
Ireland*

E

EAGLE EYE BOY   10 b. or br.g. Roscoe Blake – Hayburnwyke (Pretty Form)   **h–**
[2003/4 20m Nov 9] pulled up in maiden point in 2001: tailed off in novice hurdle.
G. F. Bridgwater

EAGLES HIGH (IRE)   5 ch.g. Eagle Eyed (USA) – Bint Al Balad (IRE) (Ahonoora)   **h108 §**
[2003/4 16g⁵ 17g 16d³ 19mʳᵗʳ 20m 16d⁴ 16s⁴ 16d² 20s³ 17s³ 16sᶠ 16s³ 20d³ 19d 16g³ Mar
15] smallish gelding: fairly useful miler on Flat at 3 yrs, sold out of R. Hannon's stable
32,000 gns Newmarket Autumn (2002) Sales, fair form over 1½m+ in 2003: fair hurdler:
stays 2½m: acts on heavy going: has refused/been reluctant to race, and not one to trust.
Patrick O. Brady, Ireland

EAGLET (IRE)   6 b.g. Eagle Eyed (USA) – Justice System (USA) (Criminal Type   **h–**
(USA)) [2003/4 16g 16m⁶ 17gᵘʳ Oct 14] poor maiden on Flat (stays 1m): little show over
hurdles: sold 650 gns Doncaster January Sales. *Miss V. Scott*

EARLSFIELD RAIDER   4 ch.g. Double Trigger (IRE) – Harlequin Walk (IRE)   **h104**
(Pennine Walk) [2003/4 16m* 16s² 16d³ 16s⁴ 16s⁵ 21d* Apr 11] leggy gelding: modest
on Flat (stays 1½m): fair juvenile hurdler: won at Sandown in November and Plumpton
(landed odds with something to spare): will prove at least as effective around 2½m as 2m:
acts on soft and good to firm going: reliable. *G. L. Moore*

EARL SIGURD (IRE)   6 ch.g. High Kicker (USA) – My Kind (Mon Tresor) [2003/4   **h100**
h86+: 17d² 20g⁴ May 24] leggy gelding: modest handicap hurdler: best form around
2m: acts on good to firm and good to soft going: tried in cheekpieces: sold 2,400 gns
Doncaster May Sales. *L. Lungo*

EARLS ROCK   6 b.g. Gunner B – Will Be Wanton (Palm Track) [2003/4 F16m F16g⁴   **h82**
F17g 20d 19g 22g Apr 18] smallish gelding: tenth foal: brother to poor hurdler Dinky   **F68**
Dora, stays 27f, and half-brother to modest 2m chaser The Secret Seven (by Balidar):
dam won 2m selling hurdle: poor form in bumpers: easily best effort over hurdles when
seventh in 2¾m novice at Stratford. *J. K. Cresswell*

EARL TOKEN   8 b.g. Primitive Rising (USA) – Lady Token (Roscoe Blake) [2003/4   **c–**
c–: 24gᵖᵘ Jun 11] maiden pointer: no form in novice chases/hurdle. *R. J. Armson*   **h–**

EARLY EDITION   8 b.g. Primitive Rising (USA) – Ottery News (Pony Express)   **c87**
[2003/4 c–p: 17g⁴ 17d* 20g⁶ 17gᵖᵘ c20sᵖᵘ c20sᵘʳ 20s 21s³ 24vᵖᵘ 17s 19v 22dᶠ c25g*   **h94**
c25gᶠ Apr 2] tall gelding: easily best effort over hurdles when winning novice at Newton
Abbot in July: left O. Carter, first completed start over fences when winning handicap at
Wincanton in March despite bad mistakes 3 out and 2 out: tongue tied, fell heavily second
in Grade 2 novice at Aintree: stays 25f: acts on good to soft going: needs to improve his
jumping over fences: rejoined former stable. *P. F. Nicholls*

EARLY MORNING   9 ch.g. Cruise Missile – Sparkling Tarqua (Never Die Dancing)   **c–**
[2003/4 c23gᵖᵘ c21gᶠ Jun 3] big, lengthy gelding: third on last of 3 starts in maiden points
at 5 yrs: failed to complete in 2 novice chases. *C. J. Down*

EARLY RIVERS   5 b.m. Teenoso (USA) – Cherry Morello (Bargello) [2003/4 F16d   **F–**
F17g Apr 10] half-sister to winning pointer by Lepanto: dam, winning pointer, from
family of useful 2m to 2½m hurdler/chaser Sean Ogue: ran out in point on debut: well
beaten in bumpers. *C. J. Down*

EARLY START   6 ch.m. Husyan (USA) – Gipsy Dawn (Lighter) [2003/4 F98: 16g²   **h111**
Nov 6] lengthy, rather unfurnished mare: fairly useful form in bumpers: well clear of
rest when 4 lengths second to Diamant Noir in mares novice at Towcester on hurdling

debut: seemed sure to progress and win a race over hurdles, but wasn't seen out again. *J. W. Mullins*

EARTH MAN (IRE)   5 b.g. Hamas (IRE) – Rajaura (IRE) (Storm Bird (CAN))   **F93 +**
[2003/4 F16g⁶ F18g² Apr 22] fourth foal: half-brother to fairly useful middle-distance stayer Rajaiyma (by Kahyasi): dam, Irish 1¼m winner, out of smart French middle-distance winner Rajpoura: better effort in bumpers when 8 lengths second to Itsmyboy at Fontwell, edging left. *P. F. Nicholls*

EARTHMOVER (IRE)   13 ch.g. Mister Lord (USA) – Clare's Crystal (Tekoah)   **c135**
[2003/4 c136, h–: c26d* c24g* c28gᵖᵘ c26g² c26d* c26m³ Apr 15]   **h–**
        Sending veterans hunter chasing after distinguished careers isn't always popular. There was disquiet in some quarters when fourteen-year-old Dorans Pride, winner of the Stayers' Hurdle and twice third in the Gold Cup, was brought out of retirement for a seventh run at the Cheltenham Festival in the 2003 Foxhunter. Dorans Pride broke a leg in a fall and had to be put down, prompting much criticism towards his trainer Michael Hourigan for keeping him going past his prime. Feelings were altogether different after thirteen-year-old Earthmover won his second Christie's Foxhunter, his success in March coming six years after his first victory in the race. Earthmover was the top hunter chaser in 1998 when, trained by Richard Barber, he dominated the Foxhunter, winning by eighteen lengths. Transferred to his present trainer afterwards, Earthmover developed into a smart handicap chaser, paying his way over the next few seasons without ever quite fulfilling the highest expectations held for him. He was fifth in a Hennessy and third in a Welsh National, but was prone to mistakes and twice departed early in the Grand National. Returned to hunter chasing as a twelve-year-old, Earthmover did very well, winning six out of eight in 2003 and suffering his only defeats when let down by his jumping when fourth in the Foxhunter and when finishing distressed on his final start, in the Champion Hunters' Chase at Stratford in May.
        Earthmover was one of half a dozen or so hunter chasers in his stable in the latest season and, aimed again at the Foxhunter, he reappeared at Fontwell in late-February. His lack of a recent outing may have contributed to his defeat by County Derry, who had already been placed in a couple of points. Earthmover stripped fitter at Cheltenham where he took his place in a maximum field of twenty-four for the most prestigious hunter chase in the calendar. There had been doubts over the participation of 3/1 favourite Lord Atterbury, an exciting prospect whose preparation had gone far from smoothly since victory in a point in January. Next in the betting were the Irish-trained pair Never Compromise (9/2) and Spot Thedifference (8/1), who had finished first and second respectively in the main Foxhunter trial in Ireland, the Raymond Smith Memorial Hunters Chase at Leopardstown on Hennessy Cognac Gold Cup day. Lord Atterbury's stable-companion Oneminutetofive, who had looked a horse with a bright future when winning four of his five points, started at 12/1, with Earthmover among four horses on 14/1. As usual, there was a wide range of ability on view, with ten of the Foxhunter runners starting at odds ranging from 50/1 to 200/1, and the field was soon well strung out. No more than half a dozen were still in contention at the top of the hill and, after being held up for a change, Earthmover, given a fine ride by his regular partner

Christie's Foxhunter Chase Challenge Cup, Cheltenham—
1998 winner Earthmover rolls back the years to win from leading Irish hunter Never Compromise (centre)

Mr R. M. Penny's "Earthmover"

nowadays Rilly Goschen, stayed on stoutly after being sent to the front five out and rallied gamely when joined at the last by Never Compromise. Earthmover stretched away up the final climb to the finish to win by four lengths; County Derry came twelve lengths behind Never Compromise in third, with a further six back to fourth-placed Oneminutetofive, and a disappointing Lord Atterbury among those pulled up. Earthmover was possibly feeling the effects of his race in the Foxhunter when a beaten favourite, making a couple of mistakes, behind the 2003 Foxhunter runner-up Bright Approach (only seventh in the latest running) back at Cheltenham in April.

			Sir Ivor	Sir Gaylord
	Mister Lord (USA)		(b 1965)	Attica
	(b 1979)		Forest Friend	Linacre
Earthmover (IRE)			(bl 1966)	Belle Sauvage
(ch.g. 1991)			Tekoah	Great White Way
	Clare's Crystal		(br 1970)	Tatelka
	(b or br 1979)		Barbara's Dream	Continuation
			(b 1970)	Mary Makebelieve

The rangy Earthmover, a 7,500-guinea purchase as an unraced four-year-old at the Doncaster May Sales, was almost certainly bought on looks. His dam Clare's Crystal was a poor maiden pointer in Ireland, while his grandam Barbara's Dream, who gained her only win in a Dundalk maiden over a mile and three quarters, produced only minor jumping winners. The game Earthmover was recording the twenty-fourth victory, including seven in points, of his varied career in the latest Foxhunter and, though still prone to mistakes, there is every reason to think he will chalk up a few more wins before retirement. He is best at three miles plus and acts on any going. *P. F. Nicholls*

EAR TO THE GROUND (IRE) 11 gr.m. Roselier (FR) – Shanagale VII (Damsire **c–**
Unregistered) [2003/4 c20mᵖᵘ 20g³ 21g 20dᵇᵈ 24d² 22s Dec 27] winning hurdler/chaser, **h94**
modest form over hurdles in 2003/4: stays 3m: acts on firm and soft going: tried in
blinkers, wears cheekpieces nowadays. *P. J. Rothwell, Ireland*

EASIBROOK JANE 6 b.m. Alderbrook – Relatively Easy (Relkino) [2003/4 h89, **h109**
F72: 21v* 19s* 21d⁶ 21g 21m⁶ Apr 14] tall mare: type to make a chaser: fair novice
hurdler: won at Plumpton in November and Lingfield (left in front 4 out, beat Cooldine
King 13 lengths) in December: will stay 3m: acts on good to firm and heavy going.
C. L. Tizzard

EASTERNKING 5 ch.m. Sabrehill (USA) – Kshessinskaya (Hadeer) [2003/4 h73§: **h73 §**
24f⁴ 24g 17g Mar 28] smallish mare: little form on Flat: poor maiden hurdler: lame
final start: stays 3m: acts on firm and good to soft going: has worn cheekpieces, visored
nowadays: hard ride. *J. S. Wainwright*

EASTERN POINT 10 b.m. Buckskin (FR) – Deep Creek (Deep Run) [2003/4 c21f³ **c94**
c28d c20g c21m⁴ c23m³ c20mᵖᵘ c21g² c23g* Mar 12] successful twice in points in
February: best effort in steeplechases when winning maiden hunter at Leicester: stays
23f: has shown signs of temperament. *P. York*

EASTERN TRIBUTE (USA) 8 b.g. Affirmed (USA) – Mia Duchessa (USA) **c105**
(Nijinsky (CAN)) [2003/4 h112: c16dᵘʳ c21sᵖᵘ c21v² c16s* c20dᵖᵘ c16sᵖᵘ c20sᵖᵘ Apr 21] **h–**
sturdy gelding: fair handicap hurdler: won novice chase at Newcastle in January: failed to
complete four other starts over fences, twice reportedly bled: barely stays 2¾m: raced on
good going or softer (acts on heavy). *A. C. Whillans*

EASTER PRESENT (IRE) 5 br.g. Presenting – Spring Fiddler (IRE) (Fidel) **h104**
[2003/4 F96: F16d⁴ F17s* 16s² 16g² Feb 11] useful-looking gelding: fairly useful form in **F100**
bumpers, easily landed odds in weak race at Hereford in December: runner-up both starts
over hurdles, in novice at Huntingdon and maiden at Ludlow (beaten 2 lengths by
Crossbow Creek): will stay beyond 2m. *Miss H. C. Knight*

EAST HILL (IRE) 8 b.g. Satco (FR) – Sharmalyne (FR) (Melyno) [2003/4 h99: 18g³ **h107**
20g* 21s⁴ 21g 22f² 19d² 20d 20s 21g⁵ 18s Jan 26] workmanlike gelding: chasing type:
fair handicap hurdler: won at Bangor in October: likely to stay 3m: acts on good to firm
and good to soft going, possibly not on soft. *G. B. Balding*

EAST LAWYER (FR) 5 b.g. Homme de Loi (IRE) – East Riding (FR) (Fabulous **h116 d**
Dancer (USA)) [2003/4 18s* 20gᵖᵘ 20sᵖᵘ 16v⁶ Feb 7] good-topped gelding: sixth foal:
half-brother to 1½m winner Eastern Lily (by Caerwent): dam, winning hurdler/chaser
around 2m, half-sister to useful French hurdler/chaser Nordet: thrice-raced on Flat:
fair form over hurdles in France, won 20-runner 4-y-o handicap at Auteuil in May on
final outing for M. Rolland: poor form at best in Britain, running as if amiss first 2
starts: should stay 2½m: raced mainly on soft/heavy going: tried blinkered/tongue tied.
P. F. Nicholls

EAST TYCOON (IRE) 5 ch.g. Bigstone (IRE) – Princesse Sharpo (USA) (Trempo- **h121**
lino (USA)) [2003/4 h121p: 20d⁶ 16d Dec 6] tall, angular gelding: fairly useful hurdler:
shaped well when sixth to Mughas in handicap at Aintree on reappearance, travelling
strongly long way and not given hard time once held: ran poorly at Sandown 2 weeks
later: may prove best around 2m: successful with or without blinkers. *Jonjo O'Neill*

EASTWELL MANOR 6 b.g. Dancing Spree (USA) – Kinchenjunga (Darshaan) **h–**
[2003/4 h72?: 17m May 29] poor form over hurdles: pulled hard when blinkered on
debut. *Miss M. Bragg*

EASTWELL VIOLET 4 b.f. Danzig Connection (USA) – Kinchenjunga (Darshaan) **h–**
[2003/4 17d Nov 17] half-sister to fairly useful hurdler Eastwell Hall (by Saddlers' Hall),
stays 2½m: poor maiden on Flat (should stay beyond 1½m) for S. Dow: tailed off on
hurdling debut. *R. T. Phillips*

EASY RIDER (IRE) 4 b.g. Blues Traveller (IRE) – Curie Express (IRE) (Fayruz) **h75 +**
[2003/4 17g³ 16mF 16d⁵ Jan 10] modest on Flat in Britain: tongue tied, poor form on
hurdling debut: sold out of E. James's stable 6,700 gns Newmarket Autumn Sales: fifth in
4-y-o event at Cagnes-sur-Mer in January: won over 1½m on Flat there later in month.
Mme R. W. Allen, France

EASY SQUEEZY 7 b.g. Alflora (IRE) – Easy Horse (FR) (Carmarthen (FR)) [2003/4 **c– x**
h62, F85: 22d³ 26m⁶ 26m⁶ 20m⁶ c23mᵖᵘ c23mF c24gᵖᵘ 24gF Aug 23] poor novice **h83 §**
hurdler: let down by jumping over fences: should stay at least 3m: acts on good to soft
going: blinkered last 4 starts. *N. A. Twiston-Davies*

EASY TIGER (FR)   6 ch.g. Sillery (USA) – Extreme Dream (FR) (Zino) [2003/4   h–
F67: 16s^{pu} Dec 26] poor form on second of 2 starts in bumpers for N. Henderson: fatally
injured on hurdling debut. *Jonjo O'Neill*

EAU DE COLOGNE   12 b.g. Persian Bold – No More Rosies (Warpath) [2003/4   c122
c134, h–: c25g^4 c24f^3 c27d^{ur} c24g Mar 27] good-topped gelding: useful handicap chaser: h–
below form in 2003/4, jumped badly left second start: stays 25f: acts on any going: wears
headgear. *B. G. Powell*

EAU PURE (FR)   7 b.m. Epervier Bleu – Eau de Nuit (Kings Lake (USA)) [2003/4   c–
17g^{pu} 16v^4 20m 23m^4 16v^{pu} 19s 17s 18g^4 19d* 17d^3 23s^2 21g^{ur} 20d^4 Apr 21] winning   h100
chaser in France: modest hurdler: left B. Pearce and much improved after seventh start,
won amateur handicap at Fontwell and conditional jockeys handicap at Towcester within
4 days in March: best effort when second to Lisa du Chenet in mares novice at Lingfield
in April: stays 23f well: acts on soft ground: tried in cheekpieces. *G. L. Moore*

EAU SO SLOE   13 b.g. Baron Blakeney – Final Attraction (Jalmood (USA)) [2003/4   c–
c–, h–: c24m^{pu} May 29] compact gelding: of no account: usually blinkered.   h–
F. L. Matthews

EBINZAYD (IRE)   8 b.g. Tenby – Sharakawa (IRE) (Darshaan) [2003/4 c–, h118:   c–
18g* 16s 20d 20g^{pu} 17d* Apr 18] angular gelding: fairly useful handicap hurdler: won at   h122
Kelso in first week of season and Carlisle in last, at latter by 3 lengths from Cumbrian
Knight: stays 2½m: acts on any ground. *L. Lungo*

EBITDA (IRE)   6 b.g. Executive Perk – Ursula's Choice (Cracksman) [2003/4 F16m   F–
F16m May 15] IR 20,000 3-y-o, 19,000 4-y-o: half-brother to several winners, including
useful hurdler/fairly useful chaser Bucks-Choice (by Buckskin), stayed 21f: dam won
maiden hurdle: failed to complete in 4 maiden points in 2003: well held in 2 bumpers,
reportedly lame in second. *Miss K. Marks*

EBONY LIGHT (IRE)   8 br.g. Buckskin (FR) – Amelioras Daughter (General Iron-   c126
side) [2003/4 c115, h99: c20g^3 c26g* c29d^{pu} c24s^4 c24v^{pu} c28m^4 c32g^{pu} c24g^6 Apr 10]   h–
tall gelding: modest hurdler: fairly useful handicap chaser: won 5-runner race at Carlisle
in November by 13 lengths from Lisdante: generally below form after: effective at 2½m
to 27f: acts on good to firm and heavy going: sound jumper. *D. McCain*

ECCENTRICITY   6 b.m. Emarati (USA) – Lady Electric (Electric) [2003/4 17s^3 16s^5 h80
Feb 16] half-sister to winning pointer by Never So Bold: well held in 2 races at 2 yrs for
R. Hodges: completed once from 4 starts in maiden points in 2002: better effort in novice
hurdles when third to easy winner Misty Dancer at Taunton. *A. King*

ECHO DU LAC (FR)   8 b.g. Matahawk – Love Dream (FR) (Platonic Love) [2003/4   c106
c110, h–: c24g c24d^2 c25g^{pu} c26g^{pu} Apr 10] sturdy gelding: has reportedly had breathing   h–
operation: fair handicap chaser: ran poorly last 2 starts: stays 3m: acts on heavy going:
often tongue tied: jumps none too fluently: hard ride: sold only 2,800 gns Doncaster May
Sales. *A. King*

ECHO'S OF DAWN (IRE)   12 ch.g. Duky – Nicenames (IRE) (Decent Fellow)   c–
[2003/4 c113: c24d^{pu} c24g c24s^{pu} Mar 21] tall gelding: handicap chaser, has lost his form:
stays 3m. *John R. Upson*

EDE'IFF   7 b.m. Tragic Role (USA) – Flying Amy (Norwick (USA)) [2003/4 h87: 16m^3 c104
16g^5 18s^6 c16g^4 c16g^2 c16s^5 c20m* c16g^2 Apr 4] leggy mare: modest hurdler: better over   h89
fences, left in front twelfth when winning mares novice at Ludlow in March: stays easy
2½m: acts on firm and good going: tongue tied: takes good hold. *W. G. M. Turner*

EDE'S   4 ch.g. Bijou d'Inde – Ballagarrow Girl (North Stoke) [2003/4 16m^2 16s* 16g   h86
Apr 12] half-brother to 3 winning hurdlers, including Audiostreetdotcomm (by Risk Me),
stays 2¾m: poor maiden on Flat, lightly raced: modest form over hurdles: fortunate to
win claimer at Plumpton in March, remote third when clear leader fell 2 out: should stay
beyond 2m: acts on soft and good to firm ground. *W. G. M. Turner*

EDGAR GINK (IRE)   10 ch.g. Step Together (USA) – Turbo Run (Deep Run) [2003/4   c71 +
c95, h–: c21d Apr 30] lengthy gelding: fair hunter chaser, well held at Cheltenham early   h–
in season: stays 25f: acts on firm going: has had tongue tied. *L. Corcoran*

EDGEMOOR PRINCESS   6 b.m. Broadsword (USA) – Stubbin Moor (Kinglet)   F–
[2003/4 F16g F16d F16d Apr 21] sister to fairly useful chaser Edgemoor Prince, stayed 3m,
and half-sister to fair hurdler up to 3m River Ness (by Buckskin): dam unraced: well held
in 2 bumpers. *R. J. Armson*

EDGINSWELL LASS   6 b.m. Morpeth – Oribi Gorge (IRE) (Heraldiste (USA))   h–
[2003/4 F–: 17g 22d Mar 3] sturdy mare: no sign of ability. *Ian Williams*

EDIPO RE   12 b.g. Slip Anchor – Lady Barrister (Law Society (USA)) [2003/4 c16g⁶   c–
16m Jul 23] smallish, angular gelding: modest hurdler at best: no form in point and hunter   h–
chase for B. R. Summers: should stay 2½m: acts on good to firm going. *Ian Williams*

EDITION FRANCAISE (FR)   6 ch.g. Garde Royale – Bull Finch Aulmes (FR)   h–
(Rose Laurel) [2003/4 21fᵖᵘ Oct 29] second foal: half-brother to 11.5f and 13f winner
Izmir Aulmes (by Art Francais): dam fairly useful around 2m over fences in France: ran
twice in points in Ireland in 2003, won maiden on completed start: sustained leg injury on
hurdling debut. *P. F. Nicholls*

EDMO HEIGHTS   8 ch.g. Keen – Bodham (Bustino) [2003/4 h116+: 16m 16d* 16m   c103
17m³ c17g³ c16v* c19g³ c17g⁶ c16s* Mar 13] smallish, leggy gelding: fairly useful   h124
handicap hurdler: won at Aintree in May: fair novice chaser: won at Wetherby (maiden)
in January and Newcastle (left in front 2 out): stays 19f: acts on good to firm and heavy
going: races prominently: genuine. *T. D. Easterby*

EDMO YEWKAY (IRE)   4 b. or br.g. Sri Pekan (USA) – Mannequin (IRE) (In The   h115
Wings) [2003/4 16d⁶ 16d* 16s² 16d⁴ 16s* 16s⁴ 17gᵖᵘ Mar 18] useful-looking gelding:
fairly useful at best on Flat at 2 yrs: fairly useful juvenile hurdler: won at Newcastle in
November and Doncaster in January: suited by good test at trip when beating Emerging
Star a length at latter: will be suited by further than 2m: acts on soft going. *T. D. Easterby*

EDREDON BLEU (FR)   12 b.g. Grand Tresor (FR) – Nuit Bleue III (FR) (Le   c169
Pontet (FR)) [2003/4 c167, h–: c21f* c17g* c20s* c24g* c21d* Feb 12]   h–
When the legendary radio broadcaster Alistair Cooke was given a dinner by
the BBC for his eightieth birthday in 1988, he had already presented around 2,000
editions of *Letter from America*, a series scheduled in March 1946 to last just three
months. 'I have worked out that it will be the year 2006 when I deliver my 3000th,'
Cooke told the assembled guests, '. . . but, looking round the room, I'm not sure
how many of you are going to make it!' Cooke's eventual tally was a staggering
2,869, the final *Letter from America* broadcast on February 20th, 2004, a month
before Cooke died in New York at the age of ninety-five. Cooke defied conventional ideas of what a working span should be and his fifteen-minute 'talks', as he
used to call them, established a record for the world's longest-running speech radio
programme.

When it comes to defying both age and convention, jump racing provided a
few notable examples of its own in the latest season. Perhaps the most remarkable
was that of Edredon Bleu, a veteran chaser whose career in recent years had tended
to be overshadowed by that of his illustrious stable-companion Best Mate. Edredon
Bleu had been a star in his own right in his middle years when earning a thoroughly
justified reputation as one of the most exciting chasers in training. A front runner
whose best performances were marked by spectacularly quick, bold jumping, he
became a standing dish in the best two-mile chases and made a habit of being
involved in races with strong claims to the title 'race of the season'. Among them
were the Queen Mother Champion Chase in 2000 and the substitute championship
race staged at Sandown when Cheltenham was abandoned in 2001, both of which
Edredon Bleu won very gamely. Edredon Bleu's speed and accuracy over the
fences was an object lesson in how much jumping counts, especially in top two-
mile chases. Old age had, however, seemed to be catching up with him and he didn't
look quite the force of old either in 2001/2 or in 2002/3, turning in uncharacteristically moody displays on occasions. Edredon Bleu proved just as effective forcing
the pace at two and a half miles as at two—he made the Peterborough Chase at
Huntingdon his own with four consecutive wins—but three miles seemed too far.
He was one of a fairly long line of horses with top-class form at two miles and two
and a half (Deep Sensation and Flagship Uberalles other notable examples) to be
given the chance to test their stamina in the King George VI Chase, but he failed to
get home in the 2000 renewal.

Any idea that Edredon Bleu was past his prime was dispelled by an excellent campaign in the latest season, one which saw him win five out of five including
the Pertemps King George VI Chase at Kempton, a race which brought him well
and truly out of Best Mate's shadow at the time. It was the stable's decision to
switch Best Mate to the Ericsson Chase at Leopardstown, where the going was
easier than at Kempton, which gave Edredon Bleu an unexpected second crack at
the King George VI Chase. He arrived at Kempton as the winner of all three of his

starts in the current season, beginning with an all-the-way, wide-margin victory in track-record time on firm going in the Fieldspring Desert Orchid Chase at the end of October, the bright spot on an otherwise forgettable twenty-one-horse card at Wincanton which had had to abandon its opening fixture of the season because of hard going. Turned out at Exeter nine days after the Desert Orchid Chase, Edredon Bleu defied top weight for the second year running in the William Hill Haldon Gold Cup, like the Desert Orchid a fairly valuable limited handicap (Edredon Bleu avoided a penalty because race conditions limited the top weight to 11-10). The Haldon Gold Cup lost much of its interest when Arkle winner Azertyuiop slipped and unseated his rider at the first. Edredon Bleu made all, keeping on well to win by two and a half lengths from Wahiba Sands who was in receipt of 20 lb. The form was on a par with that shown by Edredon Bleu in the race twelve months earlier, form which he hadn't maintained subsequently, a couple of successes at Wincanton coming in races in which he didn't have to run anywhere near his best to win.

One interesting postscript to the latest Haldon Gold Cup, which is run over two miles, one and a half furlongs, was the announcement from his trainer that Edredon Bleu wouldn't be going back to two miles, whatever happens.' Edredon Bleu did appear for the Queen Mother Champion Chase in March, but it was to lead the pre-race parade. Edredon Bleu had been denied the opportunity of a fifth win in the Peterborough Chase the previous year when assignments were swapped with Best Mate after the going was considered too firm for Best Mate in the Haldon Gold Cup. Edredon Bleu stood by for a time as a possible substitute for Best Mate in the event of firm going for the latest Peterborough, but, in the end, Edredon Bleu's third appearance of the season came two days before Huntingdon, sent to Ireland for the Grade 2 Clonmel Oil Chase on soft going over two and a half miles. Edredon Bleu isn't at his best on soft and heavy going but he jumped well and battled on in splendid fashion to win by a head from Arctic Copper, though the pair would have been beaten by odds-on Beef Or Salmon had he not ruined his chance with a bad mistake at the last. Edredon Bleu's form at Clonmel was some way below that shown at Wincanton and Exeter.

William Hill Haldon Gold Cup Chase (Limited Handicap), Exeter—
Edredon Bleu emerges from the fog for a second successive win in the race

At the time of the 2002 King George VI Chase, there was much talk of doing away with Kempton's jumping track. Providing Kempton's owners Race-course Holdings Trust with a venue to stage all-weather Flat racing was a priority for the grouping and the location was regarded as ideal for the premier all-weather track in London. Confirmation that jumping at Kempton was not being sacrificed came in November when plans were unveiled to switch jumping to the Flat turf course when the proposed all-weather track is eventually built, as planned, on the existing jumps course. The existing Flat circuit is closer to the crowd than the jumps track and the solution may well enhance jumping at Kempton, as well as providing a state-of-the-art, floodlit all-weather track for Flat racing. Best Mate's Christmas target hinged on the state of the ground at Kempton which connections eventually decided contained too many firm patches; they pointed out that Best Mate had been jarred up after his defeat in the race by Florida Pearl under similar conditions in 2001, suffering from sore shins and muscular problems in a shoulder which had taken six weeks to clear up. So, just five days short of his official twelfth birthday, Edredon Bleu got a second chance. He was a 25/1-shot in a twelve-strong field in which the betting was dominated by the French-trained pair Jair du Cochet (conqueror of Best Mate in the Peterborough) and the 2000 winner First Gold. It wasn't a vintage line-up, the improving handicapper Swansea Bay starting third favourite after a run of four consecutive victories. The previous year's King George runner-up Marlborough and the previous year's Cheltenham Gold Cup fourth Valley Henry were the only others from the ranks of the established leading staying chasers, while there were doubts over the stamina of a number of the other high-class runners, including dual Ascot Chase winner Tiutchev and the winner of the Paddy Power Gold Cup, Fondmort. Conditions gave the likes of Edredon Bleu, Tiutchev and Fondmort virtually as good a chance as they are likely to get to last out the trip in a King George, and all three were still in contention at the third last, as was the Tingle Creek fourth Le Roi Miguel who was just beginning to feel the pinch when making a mistake at the fence (he was in fifth when falling at the last). Jair du Cochet, never travelling smoothly after a couple of mistakes early on, had already

Clonmel Oil Chase, Clonmel—
Beef Or Salmon's bad mistake at the last hands the race to the British raider

Pertemps King George VI Chase, Kempton—Who needs Best Mate?
'Super-sub' Edredon Bleu sees the trip out well to beat Tiutchev and First Gold (hoops)

been pulled up when behind, while Valley Henry had departed, still moving well, at the thirteenth. Edredon Bleu had set off in customary pillar-to-post style but First Gold had deprived him of the lead six from home and was still in front on the home turn. Showing tremendous resolution, Edredon Bleu battled his way back to regain the lead at the second last and held on to win by a length and a quarter and a length from Tiutchev, who had every chance in the straight, and First Gold; Fondmort was five lengths further away in fourth, with a gap of twenty-four lengths to fifth-placed Marlborough.

Edredon Bleu ran only once after the turn of the year, putting in an exhibition round to land odds of 5/1-on in the Betfair Chase at Wincanton in February. His trainer cited a perceived difficulty in finding other races for him, the conclusion seemingly having been reached that Edredon Bleu now needs a right-handed track (despite the fact that he has won twice at the Cheltenham Festival, successful in the Grand Annual there as well as the Champion Chase). With both Cheltenham and Aintree (Melling Chase) therefore ruled out, and connections reluctant to consider Punchestown after the end of the British season, right-handed Perth pointed out the open £30,000-added, three-mile Press & Journal Handicap at their Festival meeting in April. This got the thumbs down because Edredon Bleu, with 11-12, would have had to give away 26 lb to the likely handful that might take him on (the Aintree Fox Hunter winner Forest Gunner carried top weight on the day, running off a BHB mark of 129). Let's hope Edredon Bleu, who goes well fresh, is still as good as ever when he returns in the autumn.

Edredon Bleu (FR) (b.g. 1992)	Grand Tresor (FR) (b 1981)	Grandchant (b 1973)	Grandier II	Singing Queen
		Clef du Tresor (b 1975)	Timmy My Boy	Clef Royale
	Nuit Bleue III (FR) (b 1979)	Le Pontet (br 1965)	Success	Arielle
		Etoile Bleue (b 1970)	Urf	Nuit Bleue

The useful-looking Edredon Bleu was bred and raced in France—winning over eleven furlongs on the Flat and five races from seven starts over jumps—before joining his current stable in the middle of the 1996/7 season. Although regarded for nearly the whole of his career as best at two miles to two and a half, Edredon Bleu does have influences for stamina in his pedigree. His sire Grand Tresor finished in the frame in the fifteen-furlong Prix de Lutece and his victories over hurdles included the Grande Course de Haies de Printemps over around two and a half miles. Edredon Bleu's dam Nuit Bleue III was a winning chaser by Le Pontet, himself winner of the three-mile Grande Course de Haies d'Auteuil. She was twice a winner at Auteuil and good enough to finish second in one of the big handicaps there. Her only other foal, Auteuil Bleu (by Mister Jack) won a thirteen-furlong race for non-thoroughbreds. Nuit Bleue III is half-sister to another decent French chaser Regence Bleu. Her dam Etoile Bleu, who also won over jumps, was out of a selle francais mare but by an anglo-arab stallion Urf, so, both Nuit Bleue III and Edredon Bleu appear as (ac) rather than (sf) in the French non-thoroughbred

Mr Jim Lewis' "Edredon Bleu"

stud book. Edredon Bleu, who wears a tongue strap in his races, is best on going ranging from firm to good to soft and he stays three miles when conditions aren't testing. With the exception of one or two aforementioned displays of moodiness, Edredon Bleu has been as game and consistent a racehorse as you could find, a favourite with the public and a credit to his stable. He has come a long way since Richard Dunwoody pulled him up in a handicap chase—his third race in Britain— on Scottish Grand National day in 1997 and afterwards issued forth on Edredon Bleu's shortcomings. His parting shot to the trainer on that occasion was reportedly: 'And what's more, he can't jump.' Edredon Bleu showed nothing like his true form at first in Britain but, once fully acclimatized, it wasn't long before he was handing out jumping lessons to his opponents. Even in his advancing years, Edredon Bleu in full flight remains one of the finest sights in racing. *Miss H. C. Knight*

EFFECTUAL   11 b.g. Efisio – Moharabuiee (Pas de Seul) [2003/4 c105p, h124: 22s⁴ 27dᵖᵘ Apr 23] compact gelding: won novice on second of 2 outings over fences in 2002/3: one-time smart hurdler: fairly useful form when fourth of 19 to Noble Baron in handicap at Exeter on belated reappearance: ran poorly at Perth later in month: stays 3¼m: acts on any going: sometimes swishes tail. *Miss Venetia Williams*   **c–ht115**

EFFIE GRAY   5 b.m. Sri Pekan (USA) – Rose Bouquet (General Assembly (USA)) [2003/4 h–: 17g³ 17g⁶ 16g 20gᵖᵘ 16d Mar 21] maiden on Flat, fair at best: form over hurdles only when third in mares novice at Sedgefield: sold out of P. Monteith's stable 1,200 gns Doncaster October Sales after fourth outing: tried in cheekpieces. *P. R. Johnson*   **h74**

282

EFFUSIVE 11 b.g. Phardante (FR) – Bubbling (Tremblant) [2003/4 c–, h–: c16f⁴ c17s⁶ c16g⁴ c21mᵘʳ Jul 13] useful-looking gelding: one-time fairly useful handicap hurdler: seemed to be running easily best race over fences when unseating last (remounted) in novice won by Flame Creek at Bangor second start, raced mainly around 2m: acts on firm and good to soft going. *Jonjo O'Neill* — **c103 ? h–**

EGGMOUNT (IRE) 6 b.g. Riberetto – Brigade Leader (IRE) (Supreme Leader) [2003/4 F16d* Apr 23] first foal: dam winning Irish pointer: won maiden on first of 2 starts in Irish points in 2004: favourite, created good impression when easily winning bumper at Perth, by no means fully extended to beat Blackergreen 16 lengths. *T. R. George* — **F109**

EGYPT POINT (IRE) 7 b.g. Jurado (USA) – Cherry Jubilee (Le Bavard (FR)) [2003/4 h–: 24d Apr 8] lengthy gelding: well held in bumper and 2 novice hurdles. *D. G. Bridgwater* — **h80**

EHAB (IRE) 5 b.g. Cadeaux Genereux – Dernier Cri (Slip Anchor) [2003/4 16d 17s⁴ 16d 16g Mar 7] tall gelding: half-brother to winning hurdler around 2½m Karajan (by Fairy King): fair at best on Flat (stays 1¼m), sold out of P. Makin's stable 7,500 gns Newmarket Autumn Sales: poor maiden hurdler. *G. L. Moore* — **h80**

EI EI 9 b.g. North Briton – Branitska (Mummy's Pet) [2003/4 c133, h108: c16f³ c20d* c17g⁸ 19g⁴ 17m² 16g c20m² 16g² 19m⁴ 17g* 19m³ 16f⁴ 16m⁴ c20g³ 20g c20s c19g² c16s⁴ c16g⁶ c16g⁵ c20m³ Apr 23] sturdy gelding: fair handicap hurdler, made all at Cartmel in August: useful handicap chaser: won at Wetherby and Stratford in May: placed in valuable events at Market Rasen and Cheltenham seventh and fourteenth outings: stays 2½m: acts on firm and soft going: headstrong front runner who jumps boldly: outstandingly tough and genuine. *M. C. Chapman* — **c142 h114**

EIGHT (IRE) 8 ch.g. Thatching – Up To You (Sallust) [2003/4 h–: 16g³ 19d Dec 5] compact gelding: modest on Flat (stays 1¾m): poor form over hurdles. *C. G. Cox* — **h74**

EISENHOWER (IRE) 5 b.g. Erins Isle – Lyphard Abu (Lyphard's Special (USA)) [2003/4 17s 20s c25gᵖᵘ Apr 5] second foal: dam, successful up to 13f on Flat, sister to useful 2m hurdler Vestris Abu and half-sister to very smart hurdler up to 2½m Condor Pan: placed twice from 3 starts in maiden Irish points in 2003: bought 12,000 gns Doncaster May Sales: no form in novice hurdles/maiden chase: tried blinkered. *J. Wade* — **c– h–**

ELA AGORI MOU (IRE) 7 ch.g. Ela-Mana-Mou – La Courant (USA) (Little Current (USA)) [2003/4 20dᵖᵘ 16d⁶ 16d⁵ 20g⁴ 24g⁶ 20d³ Feb 8] leggy gelding: poor form over hurdles: stays 2½m: usually wears cheekpieces. *D. Eddy* — **h79**

ELA D'ARGENT (IRE) 5 b.m. Ela-Mana-Mou – Petite-D-Argent (Noalto) [2003/4 h99: 17g⁴ 16dᵖᵘ Dec 27] sparely-made mare: fair on Flat (stays 13f): modest hurdler: claimed out of M. Pipe's stable £12,000 on reappearance, ran badly nearly 6 months later: will prove best at 2m: acts on good to firm going. *Miss K. Marks* — **h89**

ELA JAY 5 b.m. Double Eclipse (IRE) – Papirusa (IRE) (Pennine Walk) [2003/4 h–: 17g³ 21s⁶ 16g² Jan 17] medium-sized mare: modest maiden on Flat (stays 2¼m): fair form over hurdles: won mares novice at Folkestone in November: generally poor efforts after: should stay beyond 17f: joined M. Rimell. *H. Morrison* — **h104**

ELA LA SENZA (IRE) 7 b.g. Lord Americo – Diamond Glow (Kalaglow) [2003/4 h77x: 16m⁵ 20g³ 20m* 22g² 24m 20g* 22m² 21m³ c19d 26gᵖᵘ Apr 3] modest handicap hurdler: won at Worcester in June and Perth (amateurs) in September: well held in handicap on chasing debut: stays 2¾m: acts on good to firm going: sketchy jumper. *N. A. Twiston-Davies* — **c– h99 x**

ELA RE 5 ch.g. Sabrehill (USA) – Lucia Tarditi (FR) (Crystal Glitters (USA)) [2003/4 h102: 17g³ 17g* 17m⁶ 17m³ 16g⁴ 17f³ 17d* 21g Feb 28] sparely-made gelding: fair hurdler: won maiden in May and novice in June, both at Market Rasen, and novice handicap at Cheltenham in January: 33/1, improved when beating Pardishar short head in well-contested event at last-named: likely to prove best around 2m: acts on good to soft and good to firm going: takes strong hold, and patiently ridden. *C. R. Dore* — **h107**

EL BANDITO (IRE) 10 ch.g. Un Desperado (FR) – Red Marble (Le Bavard (FR)) [2003/4 c99+, h–: c22g² c19dᵖᵘ c16d⁴ c20g* c19g² c18g* c20m Apr 23] well-made gelding: fair handicap chaser: won at Leicester in February and Newbury in March: stays 2¾m: acts on good to soft going (bumper winner on firm): has reportedly broken blood vessels. *R. Lee* — **c106 h–**

EL BLADE 7 b.g. Dashing Blade – Elisha (GER) (Konigsstuhl (GER)) [2003/4 c19d⁴ c19d⁵ c19sF Jan 22] leggy gelding: fair hurdler in 2001/2: similar form when fifth in maiden at Hereford on second start over fences: stays 19f: acts on soft going. *B. G. Powell* — **c114 h–**

EL CORDOBES (IRE)   13 b.g. Torus – Queens Tricks (Le Bavard (FR)) [2003/4
c95, h–: c21g³ c17g³ c21g⁴ c21d⁴ c24m⁵ 20f² c24g* c24d* 19dᵖᵘ c25dᵖᵘ c22g⁶ c24gᶠ Feb
20] lengthy gelding: lightly raced over hurdles: modest handicap chaser: won twice at
Fakenham (fourth course success second time) in autumn: no form after: stays easy 3m,
effective over much shorter: acts on firm and soft going: front runner. *Mrs J. R. Buckley*
c90
h72

EL DON   12 b.g. High Kicker (USA) – Madam Gerard (Brigadier Gerard) [2003/4 c–x,
h–: c21s⁵ Apr 29] tall gelding: let down by jumping over fences: veteran hurdler, no
longer of much account: tried blinkered. *B. Scriven*
c– x
h–

ELECTRIC NELLIE   7 gr.m. Neltino – Alternation (FR) (Electric) [2003/4 F73:
20s⁶ 19dᵖᵘ 16g⁵ Feb 21] sturdy mare: no form in novice hurdles, failing to impress with
jumping. *J. F. Panvert*
h– x

ELECTRIQUE (IRE)   4 b.g. Elmaamul (USA) – Majmu (USA) (Al Nasr (FR))
[2003/4 16dᶠ Feb 8] fairly useful on Flat (stays 1¼m), successful in September: close
second but held when fell at the last in juvenile maiden at Musselburgh won by Dalaram
on hurdling debut, taking strong hold early: likely to prove best with emphasis on speed
around 2m: should do better. *J. A. Osborne*
h103 p

ELEGANT ACCORD (IRE)   6 b.m. Accordion – Swan Bridge (IRE) (Supreme
Leader) [2003/4 F17d F16d Apr 21] €18,000 4-y-o: first foal: dam unraced half-sister to
useful staying chaser Samlee: showed little in 2 bumpers. *Mrs P. Ford*
F–

ELEGANT CLUTTER (IRE)   6 b.g. Petorius – Mountain Hop (IRE) (Tirol)
[2003/4 h–: 22g 17g* Oct 27] modest hurdler: 50/1, first form for long time when winning
conditional jockeys novice handicap at Bangor: may prove best around 2m: tried tongue
tied. *R. N. Bevis*
h85

ELENAS RIVER (IRE)   8 br.g. Over The River (FR) – Elenas Beauty (Tarqogan)
[2003/4 c111, h105: c26g² c24m² c24d* c25g* Apr 18] rather sparely-made gelding: fair
hurdler: fairly useful novice chaser: left Miss H. Knight after reappearance: won at Ascot
(maiden, by 18 lengths from Dragon Hunter) in March and April (3-runner race), jumping
soundly in front both times: stays 3¼m: acts on firm and soft going. *P. J. Hobbs*
c116
h–

ELFEET BAY (IRE)   9 b.g. Yashgan – Marjoram (Warpath) [2003/4 h–: c17s⁴ c17s⁵
c17g² c16g⁴ c16m⁵ c16g⁵ c16m⁵ c17mᶜᵒ Jul 17] poor maiden hurdler/chaser: should stay beyond
17f: acts on soft going: tried blinkered, wore cheekpieces last 3 starts. *Mrs L. Williamson*
c73
h–

ELFKIRK (IRE)   5 b.m. Zaffaran (USA) – Winter Sunset (Celio Rufo) [2003/4 F17d*
Apr 18] €4,200 4-y-o: second foal: dam, Irish maiden hurdler, half-sister to fairly useful
chaser up to 3¼m Strong Paladin, out of half-sister to Irish National winner Garoupe:
won bumper at Carlisle on debut by 2 lengths from Lofty Leader, travelling easily to lead
4f out: bred to be suited by further. *J. I. A. Charlton*
F88

ELGAR   7 ch.g. Alflora (IRE) – School Run (Deep Run) [2003/4 h–: 22d³ 17g³ c18gᵖᵘ
c19v* 20sᵖᵘ c20g⁵ c24dᶠ Apr 12] big, strong gelding: maiden hurdler: easily best effort
over fences when winning handicap at Towcester in December: stays 2¾m: acts on heavy
going: tongue tied twice, including at Towcester. *M. Scudamore*
c104
h87

EL GIZA (USA)   6 ch.g. Cozzene (USA) – Gazayil (USA) (Irish River (FR)) [2003/4
16m Apr 13] poor maiden on Flat: always behind in maiden hurdle. *J. M. Bradley*
h–

EL GRAN HOMBRE (USA)   8 ch.g. El Gran Senor (USA) – Conquistress (USA)
(Conquistador Cielo (USA)) [2003/4 17gᵖᵘ Aug 25] lightly raced and no form over
hurdles: tried tongue tied: pulls hard. *Miss Kariana Key*
h–

ELHEBA (IRE)   5 b. or br.g. Elbio – Fireheba (ITY) (Fire of Life (USA)) [2003/4
19v⁵ 17g⁵ 16d⁵ 17d 21dʳᵗʳ 17g* Apr 3] fair on Flat (stays 9.4f): modest hurdler: won seller
at Hereford, patiently ridden in strongly-run race: likely to prove best around 2m: tried
blinkered: refused to race fifth start. *C. J. Down*
h98 §

EL HOMBRE   6 b.g. Afzal – Dunsilly Bell (London Bells (CAN)) [2003/4 F82: 17g
17d³ 20gᵖᵘ 16s⁶ c20s⁴ c20m³ c24gᶠ Mar 17] unfurnished gelding: poor form over hurdles:
similar form over fences: fell fatally at Huntingdon: would have stayed 3m: acted on good
to firm and soft going. *C. C. Bealby*
c72
h79

EL HOMBRE DEL RIO (IRE)   7 ch.g. Over The River (FR) – Hug In A Fog (IRE)
(Strong Gale) [2003/4 h104: c26v² c26m³ c24dᶠ c23gᵖᵘ c24s³ c24d⁶ c28d* c24v² Apr 4]
rangy gelding: fair maiden hurdler/novice chaser: won handicap at Fontwell in March,
idling run-in: stays 3½m: unraced on firm going, acts on any other: has got on edge: often
looks hard ride (may benefit from headgear). *R. H. Alner*
c108
h–

ELIIPOP   6 b.g. First Trump – Hasty Key (USA) (Key To The Mint (USA)) [2003/4   h–
16g^{pu} Jul 31] angular gelding: modest maiden on Flat (stays 1½m): no form in 3 races
over hurdles. *R. J. Price*

ELJAY'S BOY   6 b.g. Sir Harry Lewis (USA) – Woodland Flower (Furry Glen) [2003/4   h85
F91: 21v^4 19s 18v^F 22m^4 16g^3 17g Apr 3] tall, useful-looking gelding: poor novice hurdler: probably stays 2¾m: blinkered last 2 starts: has looked difficult ride. *P. F. Nicholls*

ELLABURY   5 b.m. Overbury (IRE) – Kayella (Fine Blade (USA)) [2003/4 F16m   F–
F16m Nov 3] sixth foal by thoroughbred stallion: half-sister to fairly useful chaser around
2m Fine Harvest and winning pointer Just Ben (both by Oats): dam plating-class maiden:
well held in 2 bumpers. *R. Dickin*

ELLA FALLS (IRE)   9 ch.m. Dancing Dissident (USA) – Over Swing (FR) (Saint   c76
Cyrien (FR)) [2003/4 24m^3 c20g^3 24m^3 19s^5 Jan 7] poor on Flat and over jumps: stays   h80
3m: acts on good to firm and to good going, possibly not on soft. *Mrs H. Dalton*

ELLAMINE   10 b.m. Warrshan (USA) – Anhaar (Ela-Mana-Mou) [2003/4 c–, h95:   c–
19m^2 May 26] sparely-made mare: modest handicap hurdler: effective at 2m to 2¾m: acts   h85
on firm and good to soft going, possibly not on softer: ran creditably when visored: often
tongue tied. *M. C. Pipe*

ELLE ROSEADOR   5 b.m. El Conquistador – The Hon Rose (Baron Blakeney)   F–
[2003/4 F85: F17g^4 Nov 4] fair form in bumpers in 2002/3, tailed off on return.
M. Madgwick

ELLE ROYAL (IRE)   5 br.m. Ali-Royal (IRE) – Silvretta (IRE) (Tirol) [2003/4 h–:   h65
16m^5 16m Jun 18] small, sparely-made mare: disappointing maiden on Flat: poor form
over hurdles: raced around 2m. *T. P. McGovern*

ELLO OLLIE (IRE)   9 b.g. Roselier (FR) – Kayanna (Torenaga) [2003/4 c–x, h89:   c– x
20s 24d^6 24d 24d^{pu} Apr 21] close-coupled gelding: winning chaser: novice hurdler, poor   h77
nowadays: stays 3¼m: raced on good going or softer (acts on soft): effective blinkered or
not: makes mistakes over fences. *Andrew Turnell*

ELLWAY PROSPECT   4 ch.f. Pivotal – Littlemisstrouble (USA) (My Gallant (USA))   h78
[2003/4 16d^5 21d^6 16s^3 21d^4 26d^6 22g^6 Apr 18] half-sister to one-time useful hurdler/
fairly useful chaser Polar Prospect (by Polar Falcon), stays 2½m: generally well held on
Flat for G. Butler: poor juvenile hurdler: stays 2¾m. *Miss I. E. Craig*

EL NOMBRE   5 b.g. El Conquistador – Worth Matravers (National Trust) [2003/4 F16g   F–
Mar 25] fifth foal: half-brother to modest hurdler/winning hunter Mouseski (by Petoski),
stays 19f: dam poor maiden hurdler: showed nothing in bumper on debut. *R. J. Hodges*

EL PEDRO   5 b.g. Piccolo – Standard Rose (Ile de Bourbon (USA)) [2003/4 h83: 16m   h–
Oct 9] leggy, lengthy gelding: modest on Flat (stays easy 1½m): well held over hurdles.
M. R. Channon

EL PENYON   7 b.g. Rock Hopper – Capel Lass (The Brianstan) [2003/4 F–: 17m^5 h–
17d^{pu} Nov 17] no sign of ability: tried tongue tied: sold £1,100 Ascot December Sales.
J. W. Mullins

ELTRINGHAM   4 b.f. Milieu – Whosgotsillyssense (Pragmatic) [2003/4 F17d Apr   F–
18] second foal: dam unraced: well beaten in bumper on debut. *C. R. Wilson*

ELUNA   6 ch.m. Unfuwain (USA) – Elisha (GER) (Konigsstuhl (GER)) [2003/4 c83p,   c–
h115: c20v^{pu} 23s^{pu} Feb 14] lengthy, sparely-made mare: disappointing hurdler: little form   h–
in novice chases: stays easy 21f: acts on good to firm and heavy going: tongue tied 2 of
last 3 starts (has reportedly had breathing problems): edgy sort. *Ian Williams*

EL VAQUERO (IRE)   6 ch.g. Un Desperado (FR) – Marble Fontaine (Lafontaine   h125
(USA)) [2003/4 F98: 17d^3 16s^3 16s^2 20s^F 22g* Apr 18] rangy gelding: will make a
chaser: fairly useful novice hurdler: travelling strongly when falling 3 out in valuable
handicap at Sandown: won at Wincanton following month by 1½ lengths from Red Devil
Robert: will prove best at 2½m+: acts on soft going. *Miss H. C. Knight*

ELVERA   6 b.m. Elmaamul (USA) – Bewitch (Idiot's Delight) [2003/4 F–: F17m Sep   F–
10] little form in 3 bumpers. *J. M. Bradley*

ELVIS   11 b.g. Southern Music – Tyqueen (Tycoon II) [2003/4 c–, h87+: 16g 17s^4 17s^6 c–
18s^3 16g^{bd} Mar 10] strong, lengthy gelding: handicap hurdler, modest at best: beaten around   h81
2m: acted on firm and soft going: tried blinkered/visored: headstrong: dead. *L. Wells*

ELVIS REIGNS   8 b.g. Rock City – Free Rein (Sagaro) [2003/4 c97, h–: c16m c17d^3 c94
May 28] sturdy gelding: modest chaser: stays 2½m: acts on any going: tried blinkered/in   h–
cheekpieces: inconsistent: of suspect temperament. *M. D. Hammond*

ELVIS RETURNS   6 b.g. Alhaatmi – Buckmist Blue (IRE) (Buckskin (FR)) [2003/4 **h99 p**
F16s⁶ F16s 22d² Mar 7] first foal: dam poor bumper performer: sixth to Fairy Skin Maker **F82**
in maiden at Ayr, better effort in bumpers: upped in trip, encouraging start over hurdles
when second to Baron Windrush in conditional jockeys novice at Market Rasen, pair
clear: entitled to improve. *J. M. Jefferson*

EMANATE   6 ch.g. Nicholas Bill – Sleepline Princess (Royal Palace) [2003/4 F17m⁶ **F81**
F16m F16m² Mar 11] rangy, rather unfurnished gelding: half-brother to very smart 2m to
2½m chaser Rockforce (by Rock City) and fairly useful 2m hurdler Sleepline Royale (by
Buzzards Bay): dam fair 6f winner at 2 yrs, became thoroughly temperamental: modest
form in bumpers: didn't look cooperative second start. *P. F. Nicholls*

EMANIC (FR)   4 b.g. Video Rock (FR) – Una Volta (FR) (Toujours Pret (USA)) **h115**
[2003/4 16s* 16d³ 16s⁴ 16g³ 16d³ Apr 17] leggy, useful-looking gelding: fifth foal: half-
brother to 3 winners, notably winning hurdler/useful chaser Japhet (by Perrault), stays
3m: dam winning cross-country chaser: won 2 of 3 starts up to 1½m on Flat in French
Provinces at 3 yrs for G. Macaire: fairly useful juvenile hurdler: won 22-runner event at
Warwick in December impressively by 6 lengths from Edmo Yewkay: best subsequent
effort (found little next 3 starts) when good 9 lengths third to Dalaram at Ayr: bred to stay
at least 2½m: raced on good going or softer: patiently ridden: sold to join P. Nicholls
80,000 gns Doncaster May Sales. *A. King*

EMARATI'S IMAGE   6 b.g. Emarati (USA) – Choir's Image (Lochnager) [2003/4 **h–**
16vᵖᵘ Nov 23] poor on Flat (best at 5f/6f), sold out of J. O'Reilly's stable 2,000 gns
Doncaster August Sales: little prospect of staying over hurdles: sold £3,450 Ascot April
Sales. *R. M. Stronge*

EMBER DAYS   5 gr.m. Reprimand – Evening Falls (Beveled (USA)) [2003/4 16mᵖᵘ **h–**
17d Mar 7] angular mare: fair on Flat (stays 1¼m): well beaten on completed start in
novice hurdles. *J. L. Spearing*

EMBER KING   6 b.g. Regal Embers (IRE) – Innocent Princess (NZ) (Full On Aces **F–**
(AUS)) [2003/4 F16m Aug 2] second foal: dam fair staying hurdler: poor form in maiden
points in 2003: blinkered, tailed off in bumper. *A. P. James*

EMENCEE   7 b.g. Lucky Wednesday – Nattfari (Tyrnavos) [2003/4 F16m⁶ F16m⁴ **h–**
F16m 16m 16g³ Nov 7] sparely-made gelding: modest in bumpers: possibly amiss when **F81**
third in very weak novice hurdle at Uttoxeter. *A. Bailey*

EMERALD EXPRESS   5 b.m. Bigstone (IRE) – Nashkara (Shirley Heights) [2003/4 **F87**
F17g³ F17v F17s³ F16s Mar 13] 15,000 4-y-o: lengthy, angular mare: ninth foal: half-
sister to several winners, including useful hurdler Nahrawali (by Khayasi), stayed 2½m,
and 2m hurdler Marrakech (by Barathea), also useful up to 1½m on Flat: dam, Irish 1½m
winner, half-sister to Arkle Chase winner Champleve and useful French chaser Nimrouz:
fair form when third in bumpers. *P. R. Webber*

EMERALD GREEN (GER)   5 br.g. Goofalik (USA) – Elaine (GER) (Alkalde **h–**
(GER)) [2003/4 16d 16v 16vᵖᵘ 16sᵖᵘ Mar 19] successful once (at 3 yrs) over 9f from 15
starts on Flat in Germany, unplaced in 2003 then left F. Breuss: no show over hurdles,
visored final start. *M. J. Gingell*

EMERALD MIST (IRE)   5 b.m. Sacrament – Jade's Gem (Sulaafah (USA)) [2003/4 **h57**
h61: 19g 21m 20m Jul 16] bad maiden hurdler: probably stays 21f: acts on good to firm
going: won point in April. *G. B. Balding*

EMERGING STAR (IRE)   4 b.g. Desert Style (IRE) – Feather Star (Soviet Star **h108**
(USA)) [2003/4 16m³ 16d² 16dF 19d³ 16s² 16s⁵ Feb 14] smallish gelding: fair on Flat
(stayed 1¼m): fair juvenile hurdler: barely stayed 19f: acted on soft going, probably on
good to firm: dead. *G. M. Moore*

EMILY DEE   5 b.m. Classic Cliche (IRE) – Alpi Dora (Valiyar) [2003/4 16m⁶ 16mᵖᵘ **h–**
Oct 18] sparely-made mare: poor maiden on Flat (should stay 1½m): no sign of ability
over hurdles. *J. M. Bradley*

EMMA'S DREAM   5 ch.m. Karinga Bay – Some Dream (Vitiges (FR)) [2003/4 F17g **F–**
Apr 10] 2,000 (privately) 4-y-o: fourth foal: half-sister to 5f winner Some Dust (by King's
Signet): dam winning 17f hurdler: pulled up in point: well beaten in bumper. *P. F. Nicholls*

EMOTIONAL ARTICLE (IRE)   4 ch.g. Definite Article – Cairo Lady (IRE) **F103**
(Persian Bold) [2003/4 F16v³ F16d* Feb 19] second foal: dam well held both starts on
Flat: better effort in bumpers when winning at Thurles by 4½ lengths from Detonante.
T. J. Taaffe, Ireland

Paddy Fitzpatrick Memorial Novices' Chase, Leopardstown—
Emotional Moment gives further proof that he's far from an accomplished jumper over fences

EMOTIONAL MOMENT (IRE)   7 b.g. Religiously (USA) – Rosceen Bui (IRE)   **c131**
(Phardante (FR)) [2003/4 h140: c22d5 c16g* c24dF c21s* c24sur 16s5 21g5 24g Apr 2]   **h135**
leggy gelding: useful novice chaser: successful in maiden at Thurles in December and
Grade 3 Paddy Fitzpatrick Memorial Novices' Chase at Leopardstown (beat Stashedaway 2½ lengths) in January: generally let down by jumping otherwise over fences:
useful hurdler: creditable fifth to Georges Girl in Grade 2 at Gowran and Monkerhostin
in Coral Cup (Handicap) at Cheltenham: stays 3m: raced on good going or softer (acts on
heavy): tough and consistent. *T. J. Taaffe, Ireland*

EMPEROR ROSCOE   9 b.g. Roscoe Blake – Royal Celt (Celtic Cone) [2003/4   **c–**
c24dpu May 30] fair pointer, successful twice in 2003: no show in hunter chase at Stratford. *A. A. Day*

EMPEROR ROSS (IRE)   9 b. or br.g. Roselier (FR) – Gilded Empress (Menelek)   **c114**
[2003/4 c122+, h–: 20m* c24g3 24g* 24m3 Aug 3] useful-looking gelding: has reportedly   **h114**
had 3 wind operations: fairly useful chaser: successful over hurdles in novice handicap at
Hexham in May and novice at Perth (11/2-on, needed strong driving) in July: found little
both other starts in 2003/4: will stay beyond 27f: acts on good to firm and good to soft
going: tongue tied: usually jumps well. *N. G. Richards*

EMPERORS GUEST   6 b.g. Emperor Jones (USA) – Intimate Guest (Be My Guest   **c127**
(USA)) [2003/4 h118: c17d* c20fur c17g2 c16s2 c18d5 c16s4 c20d5 c16d* c16g5 Apr 3]   **h–**
tall gelding: fairly useful hurdler: made good start over fences, won maiden at Galway in
August and novice at Naas (made all, beat Camden Tanner 8 lengths) in March: 50/1,
creditable fifth of 10 to Well Chief in Grade 2 novice at Aintree: well held in similar

287

contest at Punchestown later in April: raced mainly around 2m: acts on heavy going: tried in cheekpieces. *Patrick Mullins, Ireland*

EMPEROR'S MAGIC (IRE) 13 ch.g. Over The River (FR) – Sengirrefcha (Re-formed Character) [2003/4 c119, h–: c22m c25d² c24s* May 22] lengthy gelding: fairly useful handicap chaser: won at Bangor by 2 lengths from Bold King: effective at 2½m to 25f: acts on good to firm and heavy going: wears cheekpieces/visor: effective tongue tied or not: patiently ridden. *R. C. Guest* **c119 h–**

EMPEROR'S MONARCH 5 ch.g. Emperor Fountain – Shalta (FR) (Targowice (USA)) [2003/4 F16g² F17g F17d Mar 11] leggy gelding: half-brother to fair maiden hurdler up to 21f Fine Sir (by Shardari) and to 2 winners in France, including 1990 2-y-o 1m winner Shotkar (by The Wonder): dam, French 9f winner, half-sister to good French hurdler up to 25f Shafoun: best effort in bumpers when 9 lengths second to What Do'in at Perth. *J. Wade* **F88**

EMPHATIC (IRE) 9 ch.g. Ela-Mana-Mou – Sally Rose (Sallust) [2003/4 h102: 24gᶠ 26s² 24d* 24d² 24g⁵ 26g 24s³ Apr 17] small gelding: fair handicap hurdler: won at Taunton in December: stays 3¼m: acts on heavy and good to firm going: blinkered/visored: races prominently: lazy. *J. G. Portman* **h107**

EMPRESS OF CHINA (IRE) 5 br.m. Anshan – Suggia (Alzao (USA)) [2003/4 F18s F16m aF16g Dec 13] 14,500 4-y-o: eighth foal: half-sister to several winners, including fairly useful hurdler/chaser Fullopep (by Dunbeath), stays 3m: dam lightly-raced half-sister to useful 2m hurdler/chaser Antinous and to dam of top-class staying chaser Simply Dashing: no form in bumpers: blinkered final outing. *Miss Suzy Smith* **F–**

EM'S GUY 6 b.g. Royal Fountain – Gaelic Empress (Regular Guy) [2003/4 F16d 20dᵖᵘ 22gᵖᵘ Mar 28] lengthy gelding: fourth foal: dam winning pointer: showed nothing in bumper or novice hurdles. *A. Parker* **h– F–**

EM'S ROYALTY 7 b.g. Royal Fountain – Gaelic Empress (Regular Guy) [2003/4 h100p: 24d³ Nov 28] modest form when third in novice and maiden hurdles at Ayr nearly 10 months apart. *A. Parker* **h98**

ENCORE CADOUDAL (FR) 6 b.g. Cadoudal (FR) – Maousse (FR) (Labus (FR)) [2003/4 h101: 16d⁴ 16s² 16s* 16v⁴ Feb 5] leggy gelding: fair hurdler: good neck second to Ashleybank House in novice handicap at Ayr: easily won novice at Kelso 3 weeks later: will prove best around 2m: acts on soft going: likely to prove best held up: sold to join H. Hogarth 32,000 gns Doncaster May Sales. *P. Monteith* **h113**

END OF AN ERROR 5 b.m. Charmer – Needwood Poppy (Rolfe (USA)) [2003/4 h67: 23m⁶ 23g⁶ 17m 24g* 17m⁴ 21g* 24g² 24g* 24m⁶ 24m 20d* 25f³ 27s 26gᶠ 22g Mar 28] small, leggy mare: modest handicap hurdler: won at Market Rasen (seller, sold from M. Chapman 5,400 gns) and Sedgefield (novice) in July, Perth in September and Newcastle (dead-heated with Simlet) in November: stays 25f: acts on firm and good to soft going: gets behind, and not a straightforward ride. *Mrs E. Slack* **h93**

EN EL EM FLYER 9 b.g. Seymour Hicks (FR) – Sound 'n' Rhythm (Tudor Rhythm) [2003/4 h67: 19d⁵ c25g* c26s⁴ c24s⁶ c25dᵖᵘ Feb 17] poor maiden hurdler: won 2-finisher novice handicap at Folkestone in November, only form over fences (not a fluent jumper): stays 25f: acts on heavy going. *R. Curtis* **c68 h–**

ENHANCER 6 b.g. Zafonic (USA) – Ypha (USA) (Lyphard (USA)) [2003/4 F103+: F17d Apr 3] good-topped gelding: fairly useful form when successful first 3 starts in bumpers for G. A. Swinbank: well beaten in Grade 2 at Aintree only start in 2003/4. *Mrs L. C. Jewell* **F–**

ENITSAG (FR) 5 ch.g. Pistolet Bleu (IRE) – Rosala (FR) (Lashkari) [2003/4 h104, F93: F16² 16g² 16g⁵ 17g⁶ 18f³ 17m* c21sᶠ c21s* c21d⁴ Apr 12] leggy gelding: fair hurdler: looked none too keen when winning very weak seller at Hereford (sold from M. Pipe 6,400 gns) in September: fair form in hunter chases: won at Fakenham in March: stays 21f: acts on soft going, probably on good to firm: wore headgear first 6 starts: sketchy jumper. *S. Flook* **c93 h101 §**

ENNEL BOY (IRE) 11 ch.g. Torus – Golden Symphony (Le Moss) [2003/4 c–, h106: c17g² c21d* c21g² 25g Nov 15] close-coupled gelding: fair hurdler/chaser: won novice handicap chase at Stratford in May: stays 27f, effective at much shorter: acts on firm and good to soft going: ran well in cheekpieces third start. *N. M. Babbage* **c112 h–**

ENRIQUE (GER) 9 ch.g. Niniski (USA) – Eicidora (GER) (Surumu (GER)) [2003/4 c–, h–: c25m* c32mᵖᵘ 24m⁶ 24m² 24g* c24fᶠ c27gᵖᵘ Nov 15] tall gelding: fairly useful handicap hurdler: made all at Uttoxeter in September: useful handicap chaser: won at **c144 h124 x**

Ludlow in May and Carlisle (by 18 lengths from Nosam) in October: jumped poorly in listed event at Cheltenham final outing: stays 33f when conditions aren't testing: has won on soft going, best form on good ground or firmer (acts on firm): tried blinkered (well held): often sketchy jumper of fences: no easy ride. *P, J Hobbs*

ENSEMBLE 4 b.g. Polish Precedent (USA) – Full Orchestra (Shirley Heights) [2003/4 **h–** 17mᵖᵘ Jul 19] good-topped gelding: of no account on Flat: showed more temperament than ability in juvenile on hurdling debut. *M. W. Easterby*

ENTERTAINER (IRE) 8 b.g. Be My Guest (USA) – Green Wings (General Assem- **c–** bly (USA)) [2003/4 c–, h109: 22g³ 22g 22s 20d³ 22g 20d 20d Apr 22] good-topped **h101** gelding: has reportedly had surgery for sinus problem: well held both starts over fences: fair handicap hurdler: probably stays 2¾m: acts on soft and good to firm going: tried blinkered: of suspect temperament. *A. R. Dicken*

ENTREE (FR) 5 b.m. Ela-Mana-Mou – Easter Baby (Derrylin) [2003/4 F87: F16g³ **F87** May 21] medium-sized mare: fair form in bumpers: blinkered, third to Alpine Fox at Worcester only outing in 2003/4. *P. D. Cundell*

ENVIOUS 5 ch.g. Hernando (FR) – Prima Verde (Leading Counsel (USA)) [2003/4 **h79** h67: 16g 20g⁴ 20d³ 17m² 21g² 16g⁶ 16f* Sep 14] good-topped gelding: poor hurdler: won novice handicap at Hexham in September: stays 21f: acts on firm and good to soft ground: wore cheekpieces last 4 outings. *R. Allan*

ENVIRONMENT AUDIT 5 ch.g. Kris – Bold And Beautiful (Bold Lad (IRE)) **h–** [2003/4 h88: 16d Mar 14] good-topped gelding: bad mover: modest juvenile hurdler in 2002/3: fit from Flat, little encouragement only run in 2003/4: will stay beyond 2m: acts on soft ground. *J. R. Jenkins*

ENZO DE BAUNE (FR) 7 b.g. En Calcat (FR) – Pure Moon (FR) (Pure Flight (USA)) **c114** [2003/4 c98: c22m⁴ c16d³ c22d⁵ c20sᶠ c20g⁴ c16g* c20f* c18g² c20m² Apr 23] good- topped gelding: fair handicap chaser: won at Leicester (conditional jockeys) in January and Musselburgh in February: effective at 2m to 21f: acts on soft and firm going: tried blinkered: races freely: usually makes running: tends to jump right. *G. A. Harker*

EPICURE (FR) 7 b. or br.g. Northern Crystal – L'Epicurienne (FR) (Rex Magna **h88** (FR)) [2003/4 h114d: 20v⁵ 16g⁴ 21g 17f⁵ Sep 30] fair hurdler at best, well below form since fourth start in 2002/3: stays 2½m: acts on soft and good to firm going: visored last 3 outings. *M. C. Pipe*

EPITRE (FR) 7 b.g. Common Grounds – Epistolienne (Law Society (USA)) [2003/4 **h73** h–: 19s⁴ Apr 11] leggy gelding: smart at one time on Flat: off 14 months, first sign of ability over hurdles when fourth of 6 finishers in maiden at Towcester: tried visored. *M. F. Harris*

EPSILO DE LA RONCE (FR) 12 b. or br.g. Le Riverain (FR) – India Rosa (FR) **c105** (Carnaval) [2003/4 c107, h–: c21d³ c20mᶠ c24g⁴ c24g³ c21g Apr 1] medium-sized **h–** gelding: fairly useful hunter chaser: won at Warwick (for second successive year) in May: sold out of S. Flook's stable £9,000 Ascot October Sales after fourth start: ideally suited by around 2½m: acts on any going: blinkered once: has found little and suited by well-run race. *Major General C. A. Ramsay*

EQUAL BALANCE 6 ch.g. Pivotal – Thatcher's Era (IRE) (Never So Bold) [2003/4 **h–** h–: 19gᵖᵘ Nov 25] rather leggy gelding: no form over hurdles. *C. J. Hemsley*

ERCON (IRE) 6 ch.g. Thatching – Certain Impression (USA) (Forli (ARG)) [2003/4 **h–** h–, F68: 22dᵖᵘ Jul 30] workmanlike gelding: no form over hurdles: sold £1,500 Ascot October Sales, fifth in point in April. *L. Waring*

ERIC'S CHARM (FR) 6 b.g. Nikos – Ladoun (FR) (Kaldoun (FR)) [2003/4 **h143** F113+: 19m* 19d* 16d³ 21d² 21g* 20s² 24g⁴ Apr 2]
The surprisingly poor subsequent record of winners of the Grade 2 bumper at Aintree's Grand National fixture wasn't improved by the exploits over hurdles of 2003 victor Classic Native. High hopes were held for him but he failed to win any of his four starts over hurdles in 2003/4 and showed no better than fair form. His lack of success, though, disguises the excellent overall achievements of the 2003 field: of the nineteen finishers, no fewer than fourteen won at least once in 2003/4, an achievement which looks even more impressive when it is considered that three of the five others managed just three runs between them. Nine have shown at least fairly useful form, among the pick of them the useful novice chaser Patricks-nineteenth and Tighten Your Belt who won twice from three starts over hurdles.

M. St Quinton & P. Deal's "Eric's Charm"

Such as El Vacquero, Ashley Brook and Armaguedon have the potential to build on their achievements so far, and the class of 2003 could yet go some way towards matching the previous year's, when those behind the winner included Iris's Gift, Thisthatandtother and Simply Supreme.

The best form shown over jumps by those behind Classic Native came from the fifth home Eric's Charm, who was one of the season's better novice hurdlers, winning three times, putting up useful performances when placed in a couple of Grade 2 events but running his best race when second in a novice handicap at Sandown. In failing by two and a half lengths to concede 15 lb to Control Man, fifteen lengths clear of the third, in the highly-competitive Final of the excellent European Breeders Fund series, Eric's Charm showed form which would have been good enough to get him in the frame in the following week's Royal & SunAlliance Hurdle. The strength of the Sandown form was shown subsequently, with no fewer than seven of those behind the first two going on to run well next time, but neither Eric's Charm nor Control Man ran up to their best on their only subsequent start, in the Grade 1 Sefton Novices' Hurdle at Aintree. Eric's Charm, on terms 15 lb better, fared much the better of the pair, but he became very tired in the closing stages and ended up nearly twenty lengths behind the winner, the Sandown fifth Accipiter. The longer trip offers a possible explanation for a below-par effort, but it may just be he was past his best for the season. Eric's Charm runs as if more of a stayer than his half-brother Monkerhostin (by Shining Steel), who showed he stays an easy three miles when winning the Rendlesham Hurdle at Kempton in February, and he will be worth another chance at the trip. Further details of this family can be found in the essay on Monkerhostin.

Eric's Charm (FR) (b.g. 1998)	Nikos (br 1981)	Nonoalco (b 1971)	Nearctic
			Seximee
		No No Nanette (ro 1973)	Sovereign Path
			Nuclea
	Ladoun (FR) (b 1985)	Kaldoun (gr 1975)	Caro
			Katana
		Puntarella (ch 1971)	Dhaudevi
			Punta Ala

Eric's Charm's wins earlier in the season had all been gained at odds on, at Lingfield and Hereford in the autumn, then at Kempton in February, half an hour before the Rendlesham. All three wins were gained very easily, the last after second favourite Widemouth Bay had run as if amiss, and at the time the form of none of them looked to compare with his efforts in defeat, though the subsequent efforts of Kempton runner-up Bobby Dazzler, coupled with analysis of the time, suggest that effort was a good deal better than it looked on the day. Between Hereford and Kempton, Eric's Charm ran with plenty of credit behind Perle de Puce and Lingo in the Kennel Gate Novices' Hurdle at Ascot and Inglis Drever in the Leamington Novices' Hurdle at Warwick. Eric's Charm made the running in his first five races over hurdles and raced prominently in the other two. He won on good to firm going at Lingfield, acts on soft and has yet to race on extremes. Bought for 40,000 guineas at the Doncaster May Sales in 2002, Eric's Charm is a tall, angular gelding in appearance and an exuberant sort. He has plenty to recommend him as a novice chase prospect in 2004/5. *O. Sherwood*

ERIN ALLEY (IRE) 11 ch.g. Be My Native (USA) – Cousin Flo (True Song) [2003/4 c74, h–: c20s^{pu} c16s^4 c16d^4 Mar 19] sparely-made gelding: poor handicap chaser: stays 21f: acts on heavy going. *D. J. Wintle*   **c71 h–**

ERINS LASS (IRE) 7 b.m. Erins Isle – Amative (Beau Charmeur (FR)) [2003/4 h71: 16m^3 20d 17m* 17g^2 19g 17m* 17m^4 16f^2 16f^{ur} 16g^5 17g Apr 3] rather leggy, workmanlike mare: modest hurdler: won novice handicap in June and mares novice in August, both at Market Rasen: stays 19f: acts on firm and good to soft going: wore cheekpieces final start. *R. Dickin*   **h85**

ERISKAY (IRE) 8 b.g. Montelimar (USA) – Little Peach (Ragapan) [2003/4 21v 20v^{pu} Jan 26] strong gelding: fair hurdler in 2001/2: below form both starts on return: stays 2¾m: raced on good going or softer. *L. Lungo*   **h–**

ERNEST WILLIAM (IRE) 12 b. or br.g. Phardante (FR) – Minerstown (IRE) (Miner's Lamp) [2003/4 c98, h96: 21m 21m^2 24m^{pu} Sep 14] well-made gelding: modest hurdler/chaser nowadays: lame final start: stays 2¾m: acts on good to firm and heavy going: tried in cheekpieces. *J. A. Supple*   **c– h96**

ERRIS EXPRESS (IRE) 6 ch.g. Definite Article – Postie (Sharpo) [2003/4 h–, F–: 17v 16v^{pu} c20s^6 c24g^F c20g c24g^3 c20d^{pu} c16s^3 Apr 11] lengthy gelding: little worthwhile form: visored last 3 starts. *J. R. Jenkins*   **c70 ? h–**

ERRO CODIGO 9 b.g. Formidable (USA) – Home Wrecker (DEN) (Affiliation Order (USA)) [2003/4 h55: 16g 17g^4 20m^5 17m 17g^6 17g^F Aug 25] small, sturdy gelding: bad maiden hurdler. *F. P. Murtagh*   **h–**

ERROL 5 ch.g. Dancing Spree (USA) – Primo Panache (Primo Dominie) [2003/4 16s^6 16g 16v Jan 26] compact gelding: poor maiden on Flat: no worthwhile form over hurdles. *J. F. Coupland*   **h–**

ESCORT 8 b.g. Most Welcome – Benazir (High Top) [2003/4 h78: 16d 17g Mar 28] sturdy gelding: poor hurdler: off 19 months, well beaten both starts in 2003/4: stays 3m: acts on good to firm and heavy going: usually visored in 2002/3. *W. Clay*   **h–**

ESENDI 9 b.g. Buckley – Cagaleena (Cagirama) [2003/4 c–, h–: c24g^3 Oct 27] tall, leggy gelding: lightly-raced maiden hurdler/chaser: stays 3m: acts on soft going: sold 8,000 gns Doncaster November Sales, won point in January. *Miss Venetia Williams*   **c91 h–**

ESENIN 5 b.g. Danehill (USA) – Boojum (Mujtahid (USA)) [2003/4 16m^{pu} Jun 18] most disappointing on Flat: no show on hurdling debut. *D. G. Bridgwater*   **h–**

ESH BRAN GIRL (IRE) 4 b.f. Shahrastani (USA) – Logstown (IRE) (Keen) [2003/4 F13g F16g* F16g^{rtr} F16g Mar 10] unfurnished filly: third foal: dam fair 2m hurdler/useful over middle distances on Flat: easily best effort in bumpers when winning at   **F86**

Musselburgh in January, idling: collided with rail as tape was released next time: sold 5,000 gns Doncaster May Sales. *D. W. Thompson*

ESHBRAN LAD 7 b.g. Golden Lahab (USA) – Lansdowne Lady (Orange Bay) [2003/4 F84: 19g³ Nov 20] leggy gelding: better effort in bumpers in 2002/3 for R. C. Guest when fifth at Wetherby on debut: third to Rakalackey in novice at Market Rasen on hurdling debut only outing in 2003/4, shaping like a stayer. *N. J. Henderson* **h101**

ESHER COMMON (IRE) 6 b.g. Common Grounds – Alsahah (IRE) (Unfuwain (USA)) [2003/4 h78: 16gᵖᵘ May 2] fairly useful at one time on Flat: just poor form over hurdles: tongue tied both starts in 2002/3: headstrong. *A. E. Price* **h–**

ESKIMO PIE (IRE) 5 ch.g. Glacial Storm (USA) – Arctic Verb (Proverb) [2003/4 F17s² F16g⁵ Mar 6] 30,000 4-y-o: seventh foal: half-brother to useful chaser Certainly Strong, stayed 2½m, and high-class chaser up to 25f Speaker Weatherill (both by Strong Gale): dam winning Irish pointer: fairly useful chaser Southerly Buster: fairly useful form when ½-length second to Moonstream in bumper at Folkestone on debut: took strong hold when fifth to Reel Missile in similar event at Doncaster. *C. C. Bealby* **F97**

ESKLEYBROOK 11 b.g. Arzanni – Crystal Run VII (Damsire Unregistered) [2003/4 c145, h–: c16f⁵ c16d c20sᵖᵘ c19g c19g c16g c16m c16mᵖᵘ Apr 24] tall gelding: smart chaser on his day: well below best in 2003/4, trained first 3 starts by N. Twiston-Davies: best around 2m: acts on soft and good to firm going: tried blinkered/in cheekpieces: best making running/racing prominently: often reluctant to race: one to avoid. *V. Y. Gethin* **c120 §**
h–

ESPERADO (IRE) 8 br.m. Un Desperado (FR) – Latin Guest (Be My Guest (USA)) [2003/4 22g* 22d* Jun 9] ex-Irish mare: half-sister to fair 2m hurdler Aquinas and 1m/9f winner Desert Excuse (both by Ahonoora): dam once-raced half-sister to very smart staying 2-y-o Sandy Creek: modest form at best in bumpers for D. Dorgan: won 3 Irish points in 2003: improved form over hurdles when winning 2 handicaps at Newton Abbot in June (first of a novice): will stay beyond 2¾m: tried blinkered. *T. R. George* **h96**

ESPERE D'OR 7 b.g. Golden Heights – Drummer's Dream (IRE) (Drumalis) [2003/4 17dᵖᵘ 16mʳᵒ 16f 16m 16gᵘʳ 16d Nov 27] more temperament than ability: trained by T. Wall on hurdling debut: has had tongue tied. *M. Wellings* **h– §**

ESP HILL 6 ch.m. Moscow Society (USA) – Heatheridge (IRE) (Carlingford Castle) [2003/4 F62: F16d³ 16g⁴ 24dᵖᵘ 16sᵖᵘ Jan 6] poor in bumpers: no show over hurdles: joined J. Billinge. *L. Lungo* **h–**
F62

ESPRIT DE COTTE (FR) 12 b.g. Lute Antique (FR) – Rafale de Cotte (FR) (Italic (FR)) [2003/4 c82, h–: c24gᵖᵘ c20d Feb 19] round-barrelled gelding: type to carry condition: useful chaser at best: a light of other days, though won point in April: stays 25f: acts on soft going: sometimes blinkered. *R. Gurney* **c–**
h–

ESSAY BABY (FR) 4 b.f. Saumarez – Easter Baby (Derrylin) [2003/4 16g Feb 13] leggy filly: half-sister to 2m winner Kintbury (by Kylian): dam winning 2m hurdler: modest maiden on Flat (stays easy 1½m): seventh of 13 in juvenile at Kempton on hurdling debut. *P. D. Cundell* **h73**

ESSEX BIRD 5 b.m. Primitive Rising (USA) – L'Hawaienne (USA) (Hawaii) [2003/4 F17g⁶ 22g 17g Apr 10] 3,000 3-y-o: half-sister to winning 2m hurdler Green's Fine Art (by Kind of Hush): dam twice-raced on Flat: well held in bumper and in 2 mares events over hurdles. *Mrs S. D. Williams* **h–**
F–

ESSEX (IRE) 4 b.g. Sadler's Wells (USA) – Knight's Baroness (Rainbow Quest (USA)) [2003/4 16d* 16d* Apr 12] leggy, angular gelding: fair form on Flat up to 1½m, sold out of Sir Michael Stoute's stable 8,000 gns Newmarket Autumn Sales: successful at Down Royal (maiden) and Fairyhouse (beat Definate Spectacle 5 lengths) first 2 starts in juvenile hurdles: good third to Cherub in Grade 1 at Punchestown in late-April: wore cheekpieces after hurdling debut. *M. J. P. O'Brien, Ireland* **h126**

ESTERS BOY 6 b.g. Sure Blade (USA) – Moheli (Ardross) [2003/4 h73, F70: 20mᵘʳ 22gᵖᵘ Apr 22] unfurnished gelding: thrice-raced over fences, failed to complete in 2003/4. *P. G. Murphy* **h–**

ETERNAL NIGHT (FR) 8 b.g. Night Shift (USA) – Echoes of Eternity (USA) (Cougar (CHI)) [2003/4 c20gᵖᵘ c20dᵖᵘ 16g 16dᵖᵘ Mar 21] good-topped gelding: one-time fairly useful hurdler: fair maiden chaser: bought out of N. Meade's stable 15,000 gns Doncaster October (2002) Sales: no show in 2003/4 after reappearance (still to be asked for effort when slipping badly 4 out): best form around 2m on good going or softer (acts on heavy): blinkered final start: has had tongue tied. *C. J. Mann* **c?**
h–

292

ETHAN SNOWFLAKE   5 b.g. Weld – Snow Child (Mandrake Major) [2003/4 16s^{pu} **h71**
17d^3 Mar 3] sixth foal: brother to winner up to 1¾m in Jersey: dam 6f winner at 2 yrs and
later successful numerous times in Jersey: better effort over hurdles when third in seller
at Folkestone. *John Berry*

EURADREAM (IRE)   6 ch.g. Eurobus – Its All A Dream (Le Moss) [2003/4 18v^4 **h101**
17s^4 16d 16g^2 19s* Apr 11] sixth foal: half-brother to winning hurdler/chaser around 2m
Captain Tandy (by Boyne Valley): dam unraced half-sister to very smart staying hurdler
Pleasure Shared: progressive form over hurdles: won maiden at Towcester by 22 lengths
from The Bar Maid: will stay 3m: acts on soft going. *N. A. Gaselee*

EUROALLSTAR (IRE)   6 gr.g. Roselier (FR) – Pharleng (IRE) (Phardante (FR)) **h–**
[2003/4 F16s F16v 20d 16d Apr 10] first foal: dam, maiden pointer, half-sister to useful **F–**
but ungenuine chaser up to 3m Montana Glen: no sign of ability, including in point.
C. A. McBratney, Ireland

EURO AMERICAN (GER)   4 b.g. Snurge – Egyptale (Crystal Glitters (USA)) **h–**
[2003/4 16g^6 16d^{pu} Jan 10] successful once over 9f (for A. Kleinkorres) from 7 starts on
Flat in 2003: sixth of 10 in juvenile at Rome on hurdling debut: lost place turning for
home in similar event at Warwick: joined B. Powell. *M. Hofer, Germany*

EURO BLEU (FR)   6 b.g. Franc Bleu Argent (USA) – Princess Card (FR) (Gift Card **h108**
(FR)) [2003/4 h?: 20d^2 20v^3 May 21] useful-looking gelding: fair hurdler: stays 2½m:
acts on heavy ground. *Mrs L. Wadham*

EURO FALCON   7 b.h. Polar Falcon (USA) – Sarabah (IRE) (Ela-Mana-Mou) **h87 p**
[2003/4 20g^2 17s^6 Feb 3] lengthy, sparely-made horse: brother to fair 2m hurdler Ice:
successful 11 times up to 1½m on Flat in Germany and Slovakia, showing useful form:
modest form in novice company over hurdles, second to Wintertide at Worcester in
August and sixth to Simoun at Taunton in February: likely to prove best at 2m: probably
still capable of better. *C. Von Der Recke, Germany*

EURO IMPORT   6 ch.g. Imp Society (USA) – Upper Club (IRE) (Taufan (USA)) **h75**
[2003/4 17d^6 Nov 27] sturdy gelding: lightly raced and well held in maidens on Flat:
travelled well long way when sixth in novice at Carlisle on hurdling debut. *P. D. Niven*

EURO LEADER (IRE)   6 b.g. Supreme Leader – Noreaster (IRE) (Nordance (USA)) **h120**
[2003/4 F20g* F16m* F17d^5 16d^2 18v^2 16v^2 16g 20d^{su} Apr 12] IR £30,000 3-y-o: rather **F108**
unfurnished gelding: first foal: dam winning 2m hurdler: won bumpers at Listowel in
September and Tipperary in October: fairly useful novice hurdler: won maiden at Cork
in December: best effort when second to Kahuna in Grade 2 at Punchestown sixth start:
may prove best around 2½m: acts on heavy ground, won bumper on good to firm.
W. P. Mullins, Ireland

EUROLINK ROOSTER   6 b.g. Turtle Island (IRE) – Eurolink Virago (Charmer) **h112**
[2003/4 16m 22g^F 16d^5 16s^3 16s^4 16d^2 18d^F Mar 4] fairly useful on Flat (stays 1¼m): fair
maiden hurdler: would have won at Thurles in March but for falling last: will prove best
around 2m: acts on good to soft going: makes running. *T. G. McCourt, Ireland*

EUROPA   8 b.g. Jupiter Island – Dublin Ferry (Celtic Cone) [2003/4 c144, h–: c16s^3 **c125**
c20g^{pu} 16g Mar 26] big, well-made gelding: useful handicap chaser in 2002/3: well below **h–**
best in 2003/4, including back over hurdles: should stay beyond 2½m: acts on heavy
going, probably on good to firm. *T. P. Tate*

EURYALUS (IRE)   6 ch.g. Presenting – New Talent (The Parson) [2003/4 F16v **h–**
F17d^6 20d 21d Mar 30] €18,000 4-y-o: sturdy gelding: seventh foal: half-brother to **F83**
winning hurdler around 2m Harvest Storm (by Strong Gale) and poor hurdler/chaser
Leitrim Cottage (by Yashgan), stays 3½m: dam placed in bumper: proved headstrong in
bumpers and 2 starts over hurdles, generally well held. *R. F. Fisher*

EVA SO CHARMING   6 ch.g. Karinga Bay – Charming Gale (Strong Gale) [2003/4 **h109**
21g^3 21v^2 22s^3 23s* 24s^2 24g^{pu} 24d^3 Apr 8] strong gelding: will make a chaser: first foal:
dam, modest chaser who stayed 25f, half-sister to smart staying chaser Hanakham: won
2½m maiden on last of 3 starts in points in 2003: fair hurdler: won amateur maiden at
Fakenham in January: will stay beyond 3m: best form on soft going. *Miss H. C. Knight*

EVENING CHORUS (USA)   9 b.g. Shadeed (USA) – Evening Air (USA) (J O Tobin **c–**
(USA)) [2003/4 24m^{pu} 21f^{pu} 22g^{pu} Nov 20] sparely-made gelding: winning hurdler: **h–**
showed nothing in 2003/4: tried blinkered/visored: formerly tongue tied. *P. Wegmann*

EVEN MORE (IRE)   9 b.g. Husyan (USA) – Milan Moss (Le Moss) [2003/4 c98: **c104**
c25m^4 c23m^{ur} c24m* c24m* c23f^2 c25d^5 c24g^6 c30g^6 c25g^2 c25m^2 Apr 13] workmanlike
gelding: fair chaser: won 2 weak novices at Kempton (first a handicap) in November:

barely stays 3¾m: acts on good to firm and good to soft going, unraced on soft/heavy. *R. H. Alner*

EVER PRESENT (IRE) 6 ch.g. Presenting – My Grand Rose (IRE) (Executive Perk) **h108**
[2003/4 h117, F90: 20m⁵ Nov 1] unfurnished gelding: fairly useful hurdler in 2002/3: ran as if needing race only start in 2003/4: should be better suited by 2½m than 2m: acts on soft going. *A. King*

EVERREADY 6 b.g. Afzal – Sister Shot (Celtic Cone) [2003/4 F94: 16d 17d⁶ 16sᵖᵘ **h85**
21g 19vᶠ Feb 2] tall gelding: has scope: modest novice hurdler: stays 21f: free-going sort: joined M. Quinlan. *P. J. Hobbs*

EVIYRN (IRE) 8 b.g. In The Wings – Evrana (USA) (Nureyev (USA)) [2003/4 h–§: **h71 §**
16d² 16s⁴ 21s 19d³ Mar 11] medium-sized gelding: poor handicap hurdler: stays 2½m: acts on heavy going: sometimes visored/wears cheekpieces: irresolute. *J. R. Jenkins*

EVOLUTION (IRE) 7 b.m. Phardante (FR) – Cape Breeze (IRE) (Strong Gale) **h–**
[2003/4 h–: 26m⁴ 20m 23gᵖᵘ 16gᵖᵘ Jun 12] poor maiden hurdler: tried blinkered. *M. J. Gingell*

EWE BEAUTY (FR) 4 b.f. Phantom Breeze – Baie de Chalamont (FR) (Balsamo **F–**
(FR)) [2003/4 F16g F16s Apr 4] leggy filly: second foal: dam winning chaser up to 21f: showed little in 2 bumpers. *Ferdy Murphy*

EXACT (FR) 12 ch.g. Beyssac (FR) – Valse de Sienne (FR) (Petit Montmorency **c78 §**
(USA)) [2003/4 c70, h–: c25g⁴ Apr 30] lengthy gelding: modest pointer/hunter chaser **h–**
nowadays: stays 3m: acts on soft and good to firm going: formerly blinkered: has had tongue tied: temperamental. *Mrs R. L. Elliot*

EXCELLENT VIBES (IRE) 6 b.g. Doyoun – Hawait Al Barr (Green Desert **h84**
(USA)) [2003/4 h–, F–: 19g 19m⁵ 24g* 24mᵖᵘ 24m⁵ 26m² 26m² 24m* 22f* 21f³ 23m⁶
22g⁶ Nov 21] poor hurdler: won handicaps at Uttoxeter in June and Worcester and Exeter (amateurs) in September: looked less than keen last 3 starts: stays 3¼m: acts on firm going: tried visored. *N. A. Twiston-Davies*

EXECUTIVE DECISION (IRE) 10 ch.g. Classic Music (USA) – Bengala (FR) **c105 §**
(Hard To Beat) [2003/4 c116§, h107§: c20mᵖᵘ 16s² c17s⁵ c16s⁴ 16v⁵ c16d⁶ c16gᵘʳ c16d³ **h106 §**
c18g⁴ c16m Apr 15] rangy gelding: has had wind operation: fair handicap hurdler/chaser: best around 2m: acts on heavy and good to firm going: blinkered/visored: held up: usually finds little, and not one to trust. *Mrs L. Wadham*

EXECUTIVE DIRECTOR (IRE) 8 ch.g. Executive Perk – What Side (General **c102**
Ironside) [2003/4 c16d c24s⁵ c18fᶠ c18f³ c22g c17m* c20f³ c24sᶠ Jan 31] tall ex-Irish **h–**
gelding: half-brother to winning hurdler/useful staying chaser Gunther McBride (by Glacial Storm): dam disqualified maiden hurdle winner: winning pointer: fair maiden hurdler: fair chaser: won maiden at Gowran in October: left M. Cullen before final start: best form around 2m: acts on good to firm and heavy going: effective tongue tied or not. *Miss Venetia Williams*

EXECUTIVE GAMES (IRE) 7 b. or br.m. Executive Perk – Scrahans Touch **c85**
(Skyliner) [2003/4 c18f c20g c22d⁵ c16f⁶ c22g c25f⁴ c22g⁵ Nov 1] first foal: dam ran 4 **h–**
times: maiden hurdler/winning pointer: modest maiden steeplechaser: length up when taking wrong course run-in in handicap at Kelso sixth start (continued): stays 25f: acts on firm and good to soft ground: tried tongue tied. *Paul John Gilligan, Ireland*

EXECUTIVE OFFICE (IRE) 11 bl.g. Executive Perk – Lilly's Pride (IRE) (Long **c–**
Pond) [2003/4 c86, h–: c26gᵖᵘ c24mᵖᵘ 24sᵖᵘ Feb 22] leggy gelding: maiden hurdler/ **h–**
winning chaser, no form in 2003/4. *S. T. Lewis*

EXECUTIVE PARK (IRE) 8 br.g. Executive Perk – Brave Park (Brave Invader **c104**
(USA)) [2003/4 c24s* c20dᶠ May 16] ninth foal: dam bumper winner: runner-up on last of 4 starts in maiden Irish points in 2002: won novice at Bangor on hunter chase debut in May impressively by 5 lengths from Major Snowball: narrow lead when falling 2 out at Stratford: stays 3m: acts on soft going. *C. R. Egerton*

EXECUTIVE ROSEANN (IRE) 8 ch.m. Executive Perk – Dazzling Roseann **h–**
(Black Minstrel) [2003/4 21dᵖᵘ Dec 29] workmanlike mare: fourth foal: dam winning pointer: finally got off mark in Irish points in mares maiden in April 2003: well held in bumper for E. Barrett: showed nothing on hurdling debut. *B. G. Powell*

EXHIBIT (IRE) 6 b.g. Royal Academy (USA) – Juno Madonna (IRE) (Sadler's Wells **h–**
(USA)) [2003/4 h–: 17m⁶ 17g 17d⁵ Jul 27] no worthwhile form over hurdles. *N. J. Hawke*

Country Gentlemen's Association Chase, Wincanton—Exit Swinger touches off stable-companion Royal Auclair (noseband) to record his first win in over two years

EXILE 7 b.g. Emperor Jones (USA) – Silver Venture (USA) (Silver Hawk (USA)) [2003/4 16s³ 18g 16s* 16d⁴ 16s* Dec 31] fairly useful on Flat (stays 13f): fair novice hurdler: won at Clonmel (maiden) and Tramore in December: better form when fourth to Green Belt Flyer at Gowran in between: raced around 2m on good going or softer. *Andrew Lee, Ireland* **h114**

EXISTENTIAL (FR) 9 b.g. Exit To Nowhere (USA) – Lyceana (USA) (Super Concorde (USA)) [2003/4 c113, h–: 25g³ 22d⁴ 22d⁶ c24sᵖᵘ 24s⁴ c24g³ c26g⁶ Mar 1] lengthy gelding: modest maiden hurdler: fair handicap chaser: stays 3m: acts on good to firm and heavy going: tried blinkered: often finds little and best treated with caution. *P. F. Nicholls* **c107 §** **h93 §**

EXIT SWINGER (FR) 9 b.g. Exit To Nowhere (USA) – Morganella (FR) (D'Arras (FR)) [2003/4 c142, h–: c21f² c20g⁶ c16s² c21d² c25m* c20g Mar 6] angular gelding: useful chaser: didn't have to be at best to win listed race at Wincanton in February by ½ length from Royal Auclair: stays 25f, at least when emphasis is on speed: acts on good to firm and heavy going: usually held up. *P. F. Nicholls* **c139** **h–**

EXIT TO WAVE (FR) 8 ch.g. Exit To Nowhere (USA) – Hereke (Blakeney) [2003/4 c141, h–: c24d³ c25d⁵ c24d³ c24s³ c28m⁶ c36dᵖᵘ c33d Apr 17] small, strong gelding: has reportedly had breathing operations: useful handicap chaser: best efforts in 2003/4 when third, behind Kings Mistral at Sandown on final occasion: stays 3m: acts on heavy going, seemingly not on firmer than good: blinkered once: effective tongue tied or not. *P. F. Nicholls* **c135** **h–**

EXODOUS (ARG) 8 ch.g. Equalize (USA) – Empire Glory (ARG) (Good Manners (USA)) [2003/4 h95: 20d* 24m² 21g⁴ 16g⁵ 17s² Apr 6] angular gelding: modest hurdler: won weak novice at Uttoxeter in August: needs good test around 2m, should stay beyond 2½m: acts on soft ground. *J. A. B. Old* **h93**

EXOTIC DANCER (FR) 4 b.c. Turgeon (USA) – Northine (FR) (Northern Treat (USA)) [2003/4 15d* 15s* Oct 28] seventh foal: half-brother to several winners, including smart chaser up to around 2¾m Pasquane (by Dom Pasquini): dam, winning hurdler around 2m, out of half-sister to good French chaser around 2¾m Moncourt: runner-up over 1½m only start on Flat: won both starts in juvenile hurdles at Auteuil in October, showing fairly useful form: joined J. O'Neill. *M. Rolland, France* **h119**

EXPENSIVE FOLLY (IRE) 6 b.g. Satco (FR) – Tarasandy (IRE) (Arapahos (FR)) [2003/4 F16d F16g Mar 6] leggy gelding: fourth foal: brother to 3m hurdle winner Brigadier Brown: dam unraced: well held in 2 bumpers. *Mrs A. J. Hamilton-Fairley* **F–**

EXPLODE 7 b.g. Zafonic (USA) – Didicoy (USA) (Danzig (USA)) [2003/4 16g^pu Mar 27] brother to winning 2m hurdler/chaser Didifon: useful on Flat (stays 1¼m) at 3 yrs, modest nowadays: showed nothing on hurdling debut. *Miss L. C. Siddall* **h–**

EXPRESS LILY 5 b.m. Environment Friend – Jaydeeglen (Bay Express) [2003/4 F16f F16g Nov 7] third foal: half-sister to useful bumper/2½m hurdle winner Patriarch Express (by Noble Patriarch): dam maiden half-sister to useful chaser up to 25f Armagret: tailed off in 2 bumpers. *G. A. Harker* **F–**

EXSTOTO 7 b.g. Mtoto – Stoproveritate (Scorpio (FR)) [2003/4 h110: 20m^F 24g² c24d* c24g² Mar 5] angular gelding: fair handicap hurdler: won novice at Newcastle on chasing debut in November: good second in similar event at Doncaster: stays 3m: acts on firm and soft going (pulled up only run on heavy): genuine: open to improvement over fences. *R. A. Fahey* **c112 p** **h109**

EXTRA CACHE (NZ) 11 br.g. Cache of Gold (USA) – Gizmo (NZ) (Jubilee Wine (USA)) [2003/4 c109, h–: c20g c20v⁶ c20g c19g c21s² c20g c21s⁴ Apr 12] leggy gelding: fair chaser in 2002/3: disappointing in handicaps in 2003/4: stays 21f: acts on any going: tried in cheekpieces: usually a sound jumper. *O. Brennan* **c93** **h–**

EXTRA JACK (FR) 12 b.g. Neustrien (FR) – Union Jack III (FR) (Mister Jack (FR)) [2003/4 c133, h–: c20s* May 2] tall gelding: twice-raced over hurdles (winner on first occasion): fairly useful handicap chaser: won at Bangor in May by 2½ lengths from Arctic Fancy: best around 2½m: raced on good going or softer (acts on heavy): blinkered: often forces pace but also effective ridden more patiently: sold 15,000 gns Doncaster May Sales, won point in April. *P. F. Nicholls* **c124** **h–**

EXTRA PROUD 10 ch.g. Dancing High – Spring Onion (King Sitric) [2003/4 c111, h–: c22m c22g c21g⁵ 22f² c22g⁴ c20m Dec 16] winning hurdler/chaser: below best in 2003/4: should stay 3m: acts on soft and good to firm going, probably on firm: tongue tied: sometimes let down by jumping. *W. Amos* **c84** **h93**

EXTREMIST (USA) 5 b.g. Dynaformer (USA) – Strumming (IRE) (Ballad Rock) [2003/4 17d³ 16d³ 16d³ 19s^pu 19s^pu Apr 11] useful-looking gelding: fairly useful on Flat (stays 1½m), sold out of R. Hannon's stable 18,000 gns Newmarket Autumn (2002) Sales: best effort over hurdles when third of 5 finishers in novice at Uttoxeter second start. *K. C. Bailey* **h85**

EYE OF THE TIGER (IRE) 8 ch.g. Regular Guy – Banner Lady (Milan) [2003/4 h102: c24d^pu c21d² c21d^F c17s³ c16s⁵ c24s^F c20g^F Mar 12] fair hurdler/maiden chaser: should have stayed 2½m: acted on soft going: dead. *S. A. Kirk, Ireland* **c103** **h–**

EYES TO THE RIGHT (IRE) 5 ch.g. Eagle Eyed (USA) – Capable Kate (IRE) (Alzao (USA)) [2003/4 h68: 16m 16g^pu 17m⁶ 18m⁴ 17m 16f 16g⁶ Oct 24] leggy gelding: maiden hurdler: showed very little in 2003/4. *A. J. Chamberlain* **h–**

EYZE (IRE) 8 b.g. Lord Americo – Another Raheen (IRE) (Sandalay (IRE)) [2003/4 c–, h86d: 22m² 22g³ 22f² 22f² 24m² 22g³ c25g* c20d c20m* c25g^ur c24g^pu c33d^F Apr 17] modest maiden hurdler: fair form over fences: won novices at Kelso in November and Musselburgh in December: stays 25f: acts on firm and good to soft going: front runner. *B. Mactaggart* **c104** **h92**

EZZ ELKHEIL 5 b.g. Bering – Numidie (FR) (Baillamont (USA)) [2003/4 16g^ur Mar 7] medium-sized gelding: fairly useful on Flat (stays easy 2m): unseated first on hurdling debut. *J. R. Jenkins* **h–**

F

FABLED HISTORIAN (IRE) 4 b.g. Titus Livius (FR) – Princess Raisa (Indian King (USA)) [2003/4 16d^pu 16s^pu Jan 23] ex-Irish gelding: modest form on last of 3 starts on Flat for Miss I. Oakes: no show in 2 races over hurdles. *M. J. Coombe* **h–**

FABLE (USA) 8 b.h. Hansel (USA) – Aragon (Raconteur (USA)) [2003/4 c73, h120: c17f² c20g* c21f* c19s⁴ c16m c20m* c24g⁶ c21d³ c17d⁶ Apr 13] strong gelding: carries condition: useful hurdler at one time: fair chaser: won maiden at Kilbeggan in July, novice at Cork in August and handicap at Fairyhouse in October: stays 21f: acts on firm and soft going: tongue tied. *N. Meade, Ireland* **c111** **h–**

FABREZAN (FR) 5 b.g. Nikos – Fabulous Secret (FR) (Fabulous Dancer (USA)) [2003/4 h93: 17g⁴ 20m^w 22g^pu 22f² 19f³ 24g² 26s^w 21s* 21s* 22d Mar 12] smallish **h117**

gelding: fairly useful hurdler: won novice at Worcester in July, novice claimer at Hereford (claimed from N. Williams £6,000) in January and handicaps at Plumpton later in January and February: stays 3¼m: acts on firm and soft going. *B. J. Llewellyn*

FACE THE LIMELIGHT (IRE)   5 b.g. Quest For Fame – Miss Boniface (Tap On Wood) [2003/4 16g^F 16g Jan 15] fair on Flat (stays 11.6f), sold out of H. Morrison's stable 10,000 gns Newmarket Autumn Sales: showed little in 2 novice hurdles. *Jedd O'Keeffe*   h–

FACTOR FIFTEEN   5 gr.g. Hector Protector (USA) – Catch The Sun (Kalaglow) [2003/4 16m^2 16s 16g^2 16f^2 c16g^{ur} Mar 10] angular gelding: fairly useful on Flat (stays 1½m), sold out of E. Dunlop's stable 48,000 gns Newmarket Autumn Sales: fair novice hurdler: unseated third in maiden chase: likely to prove best around 2m: tried in cheekpieces (tended to carry head high): temperament under suspicion. *J. Howard Johnson*   c– h106

FADALKO (FR)   11 b.g. Cadoudal (FR) – Kalliste (FR) (Calicot (FR)) [2003/4 c151d, h–: 20v^4 Jan 31] good-topped gelding: usually looks very well: has been pin-fired near fore: top-class chaser at best: left P. Nicholls and first run over hurdles since 1998/9, distant fourth in handicap at Ayr: best up to 21f: ran poorly on firm going, acts on any other: blinkered once: usually sound jumper. *M. Todhunter*   c– h114

FADDAD (USA)   8 b.g. Irish River (FR) – Miss Mistletoes (IRE) (The Minstrel (CAN)) [2003/4 h90?: 16s 22s 16s^4 17d Mar 3] angular gelding: poor maiden hurdler: raced mainly around 2m: acts on soft going. *D. C. O'Brien*   h61

FADOUDAL DU COCHET (FR)   11 b.g. Cadoudal (FR) – Eau de Vie (FR) (Dhaudevi (FR)) [2003/4 c138, h–: 16s c16v^3 c16d^F c17d* Apr 11] well-made gelding: winning hurdler: useful chaser: won valuable handicap at Fairyhouse in April by length from Colca Canyon: raced mainly around 2m, only on good going or softer (acts on heavy): wore cheekpieces third start. *A. L. T. Moore, Ireland*   c142 h–

FAILTE (IRE)   6 b.g. Most Welcome – Esh Sham (USA) (Damascus (USA)) [2003/4 17s^F Jan 22] lightly raced and little form on Flat: pulled hard and well held when falling 2 out in novice on hurdling debut. *L. A. Dace*   h–

FAIR CHARMEUR (IRE)   10 ch.m. Buckskin (FR) – Beau Croft Lass (Beau Charmeur (FR)) [2003/4 c24m^4 Apr 13] fair pointer, successful in March: poor form on hunter chase debut. *R. R. Smedley*   c67

FAIR ENOUGH (IRE)   9 b.m. Phardante (FR) – Woodford Princess (Menelek) [2003/4 h75: c23m^4 c24g^{pu} c23g^{pu} 21d 22s^3 22g 22d^3 Mar 3] strong mare: no form over fences: poor maiden hurdler: stays 27f: acts on firm and soft going. *R. Rowe*   c– h76

FAIRFIELDS LAD (IRE)   5 b.g. Norwich – Fahoora (IRE) (Orchestra) [2003/4 24d^{pu} 17d^{pu} Apr 18] leggy gelding: third foal: dam, lightly raced in points, half-sister to one-time useful chaser up to 25f Monnaie Forte: showed nothing in 2 novice hurdles. *J. Howard Johnson*   h–

FAIRLAND (IRE)   5 b.g. Blues Traveller (IRE) – Massive Powder (Caerleon (USA)) [2003/4 16s^6 16g 20m^6 16g^{pu} 16f 18g 16s 21d^{pu} Apr 11] ex-Irish gelding: modest maiden up to 1½m on Flat: poor maiden hurdler: left J. Crowley before final start: tried blinkered/tongue tied. *S. Dow*   h79

FAIRLY SMART   5 b.m. Good Thyne (USA) – Smart Chick (True Song) [2003/4 17d 19g Apr 3] sixth foal: half-sister to modest staying chaser Old Cavalier (by Idiot's Delight) and winning 2¾m hurdler Drum Majorette (by Infantry): dam, placed over hurdles, half-sister to smart staying chaser Smart Tar: well held in 2 races over hurdles. *M. F. Harris*   h–

FAIRMORNING (IRE)   5 b.g. Ridgewood Ben – The Bratpack (IRE) (Mister Majestic) [2003/4 20g^4 16m^{bd} 16g Dec 4] poor maiden on Flat (stays 2m): poor form over hurdles. *J. W. Unett*   h84

FAIR PROSPECT   8 b.g. Sir Harry Lewis (USA) – Fair Sara (McIndoe) [2003/4 h109+: 23d* 25g^2 24d^3 c22g* Dec 9] useful-looking gelding: fair hurdler: won novice at Wetherby in May: won maiden at Fontwell on chasing debut by 13 lengths from The Lyme Volunteer: stays 3m: yet to race on extremes of going: should improve over fences. *P. F. Nicholls*   c110 p h112

FAIR QUESTION (IRE)   6 b.g. Rainbow Quest (USA) – Fair of The Furze (Ela-Mana-Mou) [2003/4 h100: 16d^5 21d* Mar 28] leggy gelding: fair hurdler: upped in trip, best effort when winning maiden at Huntingdon easily by 14 lengths from Smithlyn: stays 21f: acts on good to soft going. *Miss Venetia Williams*   h107

FAI

FAIRTOTO 8 b.g. Mtoto – Fairy Feet (Sadler's Wells (USA)) [2003/4 h–: 21g 24m 22m⁵ 21f³ 22g² 21g 20g* 21s² c19d⁶ c24dᵖᵘ c19d c20m Mar 2] good-topped gelding: has been tubed: poor hurdler: won selling handicap at Leicester in December: little form over fences: should stay beyond 2¾m: acts on firm and soft going: effective blinkered/tongue tied or not: very reluctant to race final start. *D. J. Wintle* — **c–** **h82**

FAIR WIND (IRE) 12 b.g. Strong Gale – Corcomroe (Busted) [2003/4 c113d: c25m⁵ c25s* Apr 11] workmanlike gelding: fair hunter chaser nowadays: successful in point in March prior to winning at Towcester: stays 3¼m: acts on heavy going: tried blinkered: usually held up. *Mrs H. Bartlett* — **c96**

FAIR WIZARD (IRE) 5 b. or br.g. Distinctly North (USA) – Richmond Lillie (Fairbairn) [2003/4 16gᵖᵘ Nov 15] 1,300 4-y-o: lengthy gelding: half-brother to Irish 1½m winner Richmond Lodge (by Sesaro) and 4 winners in Italy and Belgium: dam Irish maiden half-sister to Cheveley Park and Irish 1000 Guineas runner-up Millingdale Lillie: seemed to go badly amiss on debut. *R. Nixon* — **h–**

FAIRWOOD HEART (IRE) 7 b. or br.g. Broken Hearted – Bowery Lass (IRE) (Abednego) [2003/4 h119: 24d⁴ c24f⁵ c16g⁴ c20s² 24s⁶ Jan 11] workmanlike gelding: fairly useful handicap hurdler: good fourth at Navan in May: fair form at best over fences: stays 3m: acts on soft going (won bumper on good to firm). *P. J. Rothwell, Ireland* — **c109** **h121**

FAIRWOOD PRESENT (IRE) 6 ch.g. Presenting – Lady's Wager (Girandole) [2003/4 F16g 20s 20m* 20d³ 16m³ 16m⁵ 20g* 20m² 21m² 20s⁵ 20d³ Apr 11] tall, quite good-topped gelding: half-brother to 4 minor winners: dam unraced: dual bumper winner: won on Flat in June: fairly useful novice hurdler: won at Tramore (maiden) in May and Bangor in October: best subsequent effort when second to Jollyolly at Cheltenham ninth start: likely to stay beyond 21f: acts on good to firm and good to soft going, bumper winner on heavy. *P. J. Rothwell, Ireland* — **h124** **F92**

FAIRY HOUSE (FR) 8 b.g. Tel Quel (FR) – Ceiling (Thatch (USA)) [2003/4 16m 16f 16f³ Jul 11] IR £900 5-y-o: half-brother to fair hurdler/winning chaser Nessfield (by Tumble Wind), stayed 3¼m: 1m winner at 2 yrs in France: poor maiden hurdler: raced around 2m: acts on firm going: has had tongue tied. *S. McParlan, Ireland* — **h62**

FAIRY LOCH 5 b.m. Sure Blade (USA) – Tremloch (Tremblant) [2003/4 18g 16m Oct 18] leggy mare: no sign of ability. *J. W. Mullins* — **h–**

FAIRY SKIN MAKER (IRE) 6 ch.g. Nomadic Way (USA) – Malvern Madam (Reesh) [2003/4 F17g² F17d² F16m⁴ F16s* 20s 16d 16v 20d 17g* 20s 16g* 16s⁶ Apr 21] 2,200 5-y-o: plain gelding: second foal: dam poor maiden hurdler: fairly useful in bumpers, made all at Ayr in November: modest novice hurdler: won handicaps at Sedgefield in March and Kelso in April, idling both times: best form over hurdles around 2m on good ground. *G. A. Harker* — **h97** **F96**

FALCHION 9 b.g. Broadsword (USA) – Fastlass (Celtic Cone) [2003/4 c107, h96: c20dᵖᵘ c21s² c25sᵘʳ 20v² 23s² 20d⁴ c20d c24v²ᶠ 27d⁶ Mar 30] quite good-topped gelding: fair handicap hurdler/maiden chaser: stays 23f: raced mainly on going softer than good (acts on heavy): tongue tied. *J. R. Bewley* — **c105 ?** **h100**

FALCON DU COTEAU (FR) 11 b. or br.g. Apeldoorn (FR) – Ifrika (FR) (Bamako III) [2003/4 c112, h–: c24g⁴ c34m⁴ c20s³ c30sᵖᵘ Nov 22] small gelding: fair handicap chaser: stays 3m: acts on heavy going: sometimes blinkered (including for all wins) but effective when not. *C. J. Mann* — **c109** **h–**

FAMFONI (FR) 11 b.g. Pamponi (FR) – India Rosa (FR) (Carnaval) [2003/4 c122x, h96: c24gᵖᵘ c24sᵖᵘ c24dᵖᵘ Mar 24] quite good-topped gelding: winning hurdler: fairly useful chaser on his day: no form in 2003/4: stays 31f: acts on any going: sometimes wears headgear: far from fluent jumper of conventional fences: has looked less than keen. *K. C. Bailey* — **c– x** **h–**

FAMILIE FOOTSTEPS 10 b.g. Primitive Rising (USA) – Ramilie (Rambah) [2003/4 h–: c16dᵖᵘ Jul 2] good-topped gelding: fair hurdler at best: off 14 months prior to showing little on chasing debut. *G. A. Swinbank* — **c–** **h–**

FAMILY VENTURE (IRE) 7 br.g. Montelimar (USA) – Well Honey (Al Sirat) [2003/4 h97: c21d³ c21d³ c21m* c24m⁴ Dec 16] modest hurdler: fair form over fences, won maiden at Sedgefield in October and novice handicap at Ayr in November: effective around 2½m to 3m: acts on good to firm and good to soft going: tongue tied. *Ferdy Murphy* — **c105** **h–**

FAMOUS GROUSE 4 b.g. Selkirk (USA) – Shoot Clear (Bay Express) [2003/4 16g 16d² 16g Apr 12] useful-looking gelding: smart on Flat (should stay beyond 1¼m), sold — **h107**

out of R. Charlton's stable 90,000 gns Newmarket Autumn Sales: easily best effort in juvenile hurdles when second to De Blanc at Stratford in March. *C. J. Mann*

FANDANGO DE CHASSY (FR)   11 b.g. Brezzo (FR) – Laita de Mercurey (FR) (Dom Luc (FR)) [2003/4 c96, h101: 26m⁵ May 5] good-topped gelding: fair hurdler/modest chaser: tailed off in handicap over hurdles only start in 2003/4: thorough stayer: ideally suited by ground softer than good (acts on heavy): blinkered once, wears cheekpieces/visor nowadays: has had tongue tied. *Mrs L. Wadham* c–
h–

FANION DE NOURRY (FR)   11 ch.g. Bad Conduct (USA) – Ottomane (FR) (Quart de Vin (FR)) [2003/4 c–, h–: c25gᵖᵘ c25dᵖᵘ c25s³ Apr 11] workmanlike gelding: useful hunter chaser at best: largely disappointing since 2000: stays 4¼m: acts on good to firm going. *E. Haddock* c75
h–

FANNY BY GASLIGHT   6 b.m. Opera Ghost – Highly Inflammable (USA) (Wind And Wuthering (USA)) [2003/4 F16m Jun 1] third foal: dam lightly-raced maiden hurdler: no form in points/bumper: sold £1,500 Ascot June Sales. *J. W. Mullins* F–

FANTASTIC ARTS (FR)   4 b.g. Royal Applause – Magic Arts (IRE) (Fairy King (USA)) [2003/4 16gᶠ 16s⁴ 16g² 16s⁶ Feb 14] rather leggy, close-coupled gelding: half-brother to middle-distance winners by Ski Chief and Homme de Loi: dam 1m and 1¼m winner: successful 5 times from 9f to 15f on Flat in France, claimed from Mme J. L. Rossi after final win: easily best effort in juvenile hurdles when neck second to Tusk at Kempton in January. *Miss Venetia Williams* h104

FANTASTIC CHAMPION (IRE)   5 b.g. Entrepreneur – Reine Mathilde (USA) (Vaguely Noble) [2003/4 h120: 16m⁴ 19g² 20g⁴ 20v⁴ 17d 20g* 22g⁴ Apr 22] strong, close-coupled gelding: fairly useful hurdler: won maiden at Fontwell in March: will stay 3m: acts on good to soft going: tried blinkered (ran poorly): failed to impress with attitude fourth outing. *Mrs L. Wadham* h117

FANTASTICO (IRE)   4 b.f. Bahhare (USA) – Minatina (IRE) (Ela-Mana-Mou) [2003/4 16g³ 16d² 16d 16g 20s Mar 20] fair on Flat (stays 2m), successful in August for S. Kirk: best effort over hurdles when second in juvenile at Newcastle in November. *Mrs K. Walton* h82

FARAWAY JOHN (IRE)   6 b.g. Farhaan – Indiana Dancer (Hallgate) [2003/4 h–: 16sᵖᵘ Nov 3] no show in 2 novice hurdles, raced freely in visor on second occasion. *G. P. Enright* h–

FAR BRIDGE (IRE)   9 ch.g. Phardante (FR) – Droichidin (Good Thyne (USA)) [2003/4 c–, h–: c16fᶠ May 10] strong, workmanlike gelding: little sign of ability. *P. Wegmann* c–
h–

FARCEUR (FR)   5 b. or br.g. Anabaa (USA) – Fabulous Account (USA) (Private Account (USA)) [2003/4 19s² 16fᶠ Oct 16] leggy gelding: half-brother to winning hurdler/chaser Double Account (by Sillery), stays 3¼m: maiden on Flat: thrice-raced over fences: modest form over hurdles, left J. Bertran de Balanda after reappearance: reportedly lame on British debut: stays 19f: acts on good to soft going: tried blinkered. *M. C. Pipe* c–
h99

FAR DAWN (USA)   11 b.g. Sunshine Forever (USA) – Dawn's Reality (USA) (In Reality) [2003/4 c98, h–: c24gᶠ c24gᵖᵘ c25m⁶ Aug 3] strong, workmanlike gelding: one-time fairly useful but temperamental hurdler: won weak novice chase in 2002/3: badly let down by jumping in handicaps in 2003/4: stays 3m: acts on good to firm and good to soft going: tried blinkered/tongue tied. *J. Gallagher* c–
h–

FARD DU MOULIN MAS (FR)   11 b. or br.g. Morespeed – Soiree d'Ex (FR) (Kashtan (FR)) [2003/4 c–, h–: 22d 20d 23d 24gᵖᵘ 22d⁴ 22sᵖᵘ Apr 6] good-topped gelding: modest hurdler/chaser nowadays: stays 3m: acts on soft going. *M. E. D. Francis* c–
h94

FARE DEALING (IRE)   11 b.g. Tremblant – Charming Whisper (Deep Run) [2003/4 c89, h95: 22g⁵ c21d² 20d c16gᶠ Dec 5] leggy gelding: modest hurdler/maiden chaser: below form in 2003/4: effective at 2m to 2¾m: probably acts on any going: seems to go well with forcing tactics. *M. J. Gingell* c80
h–

FAREWELL CHILD   7 b.m. Afzal – Bye Bye Baby (FR) (Baby Turk) [2003/4 aF16g 21sᵖᵘ 24g⁵ Dec 5] first foal: dam 2m winner: no sign of ability. *Miss Suzy Smith* h–
F–

FAR GLEN (IRE)   9 b.g. Phardante (FR) – Asigh Glen (Furry Glen) [2003/4 c104, h68§: c24dᵖᵘ Mar 10] big, angular gelding: maiden hurdler/steeplechaser: winning pointer: stays 27f: best efforts on good/good to firm going: has had tongue tied: races freely: inconsistent. *P. H. Morris* c–
h– §

FAR

FAR HORIZON (IRE) 10 b.g. Phardante (FR) – Polly Puttens (Pollerton) [2003/4 h123: c16g⁵ Jan 13] lengthy, useful-looking gelding: lightly raced: fairly useful hurdler: fifth to Keltic Bard in novice at Leicester on chasing debut, only start in 2003/4: better around 2½m than 2m: raced on good going or softer (acts on heavy). *N. J. Henderson*   **c101 h–**

FARINEL 8 b.g. In The Wings – Dame de L'Oise (USA) (Riverman (USA)) [2003/4 c94, h125d: c20g⁴ c20s⁶ c23g³ 22d c17d⁴ c24d⁶ c24s³ c25d* Apr 11] good-topped gelding: fairly useful handicap hurdler at best: fair chaser: won handicap at Fairyhouse in April: stays 25f: acts on soft and good to firm going: tried blinkered. *A. L. T. Moore, Ireland*   **c109 h–**

FARINGTON LODGE (IRE) 6 b.g. Simply Great (FR) – Lodge Party (IRE) (Strong Gale) [2003/4 F71: 20d⁵ 23d⁵ 20v⁴ 24gᵖᵘ 24sᵖᵘ Apr 21] leggy gelding: poor novice hurdler: stays 23f: sold 6,500 gns Doncaster May Sales. *C. Grant*   **h76**

FARLINGTON 7 b.g. Alflora (IRE) – Annapuma (Rakaposhi King) [2003/4 c21d² c21s² c19g² c24g³ Feb 8] tall gelding: second foal: dam unraced: won maiden point in 2003: fair novice steeplechaser: effective at 19f to 3m: acts on soft going. *J. Howard Johnson*   **c104**

FARMER JACK 8 b.g. Alflora (IRE) – Cheryls Pet (IRE) (General Ironside) [2003/4 c143, h–: c19dᵖᵘ c16g c16s* c20g c20g Mar 17] workmanlike gelding: smart chaser: easily best effort in handicaps in 2003/4 when winning at Sandown in February, all out to beat Palarshan ½ length: badly let down by jumping final start: stays 2½m: acts on soft going (won plumper on firm). *P. J. Hobbs*   **c146 h–**

FARMER JOSH 10 b.g. Dancing High – Millie Duffer (Furry Glen) [2003/4 c–, h–: 21mᵘʳ c22mᵘʳ 20d⁵ 25m³ Nov 3] of little account: tried blinkered. *Miss L. V. Davis*   **c– x h–**

FARNAHEEZVIEW (IRE) 6 b.g. Naheez (USA) – Sweet View (King's Ride) [2003/4 F18s² 22s⁴ 24g⁴ 24g² 25d³ Mar 19] compact gelding: fifth foal: half-brother to 19f chase winner Wellie (by Aristocracy) and winning pointer by Tidaro: dam unraced: won maiden Irish point on debut in 2003: bought 20,000 gns Doncaster May Sales: runner-up in bumper: best effort over hurdles when neck second to Whitford Don in novice at Newbury in March, looking thorough stayer. *O. Sherwood*   **h109 F92**

FARNANDO (IRE) 10 b.g. Zaffaran (USA) – Kasperova (He Loves Me) [2003/4 c21gᶠ Apr 1] workmanlike gelding: winning chaser for J. F. O'Shea)/pointer in Ireland: fell Becher's in Fox Hunters' at Aintree: should stay beyond 2½m: acts on heavy going, probably on good to firm: tried blinkered. *S. G. Parkyn*   **c– h–**

FARNE ISLE 5 ch.m. Midnight Legend – Biloela (Nicholas Bill) [2003/4 F91: 16g⁴ 16g⁴ 19f⁴ 16s⁶ 16v⁴ 16d⁵ 17g³ Apr 12] smallish, sparely-made mare: modest novice hurdler: bred to stay 2½m+: wore cheekpieces final outing, tongue tied previous one. *G. A. Harker*   **h87**

FAROUK (IRE) 6 b.g. Fourstars Allstar (USA) – Clontinty Queen (Laurence O) [2003/4 F16d Mar 24] 15,000 4-y-o: half-brother to several winners, including fairly useful staying chaser Tom Bir (by Deep Run): dam unraced half-sister to fairly useful hurdler How Brave: well held in bumper on debut. *Mrs S. D. Williams*   **F–**

FAR PAVILIONS 5 b.g. Halling (USA) – Flambera (FR) (Akarad (FR)) [2003/4 h129: 16m* May 7] useful-looking gelding: fairly useful on Flat: fairly useful hurdler: successful 5 of 6 starts, not hard pressed to beat Sun Bird by 6 lengths, making most, in intermediate at Kelso in May: not seen out again: likely to prove best at 2m: acts on good to firm and good to soft ground. *G. A. Swinbank*   **h118**

FAR TO FALL (IRE) 6 br.g. Phardante (FR) – Fall About (Comedy Star (USA)) [2003/4 20s 24g⁵ Mar 6] rangy gelding: will make a chaser: seventh foal: half-brother to fair hurdler around 2½m Briery Ann (by Anshan): dam, 1½m winner, half-sister to useful staying hurdler/chaser Ultra Flutter: completed once from 3 starts in maiden points in 2003: improved markedly on debut effort over hurdles when fifth to Whitford Don in novice at Newbury, going well long way: likely to improve again. *H. D. Daly*   **h107 p**

FAR TWO FRIENDLY 5 ch.m. Environment Friend – Four Friends (Quayside) [2003/4 F16g Mar 4] fifth foal: dam, winning hurdler/chaser up to 3m in Ireland, half-sister to useful jumpers Book of Gold and Gratification: showed nothing in mares bumper on debut. *Ms Deborah J. Evans*   **F–**

FASGO (IRE) 9 b.g. Montelimar (USA) – Action Plan (Creative Plan (USA)) [2003/4 c114, h–: c26g* c29v² c29d² c33d² c33dᵖᵘ c29m Apr 24] tall, leggy gelding: handicap chaser: improved into useful performer in 2003/4 (reportedly operated on for breathing problem before reappearance), won at Newton Abbot in November: good efforts when runner-up next 3 starts, behind Kings Mistral at Sandown (listed event) and Bear On   **c130 h–**

300

Board at Cheltenham last 2 occasions: stays 33f: acts on heavy going, below form on good to firm: blinkered once: has idled/gone in snatches. *P. F. Nicholls*

FASHION HOUSE   8 b.m. Homo Sapien – High Heels (IRE) (Supreme Leader) [2003/4 c89+, h73; c21g^{pu} c26m^{f1} c24f^b c23g³ c20m³ Mar 4] poor form over hurdles: poor chaser: won 2-runner novice handicap at Ludlow in October: probably stays 3¼m: acts on firm going: has finished weakly. *S. Pike*   **c83 h—**

FASHIONS MONTY (IRE)   8 ch.m. Montelimar (USA) – Fashions Side (Quayside) [2003/4 c25d^{pu} c27v^{pu} c25d c27s* c25g⁴ c24s⁵ c25s² Apr 11] sturdy ex-Irish mare: fifth foal: half-sister to useful 2m hurdler Buckside (by Buckskin): dam fair jumper up to 3m: modest hurdler: similar form over fences, won handicap at Sedgefield in February: stays 27f: acts on heavy ground: usually tongue tied: front runner. *Ferdy Murphy*   **c87 h—**

FASHIONS MYSTIQUE (IRE)   6 b.m. Religiously (USA) – Fashions Side (Quayside) [2003/4 F16s F16s Mar 13] sixth foal: half-sister to useful 2m hurdler Buckside (by Buckskin) and winning hurdler/chaser Fashions Monty (by Montelimar), stays 27f: dam fair jumper up to 3m: tailed off in 2 bumpers. *Ferdy Murphy*   **F—**

FASTER SWEEP (IRE)   7 ch.g. Phardante (FR) – Sweeping Brush (IRE) (Brush Aside (USA)) [2003/4 c25g² Apr 30] first foal: dam unraced half-sister to Maryland Hunt Cup winner Young Dubliner: maiden pointer: easily best form when second in hunter at Kelso. *W. T. Reed*   **c87**

FAST KING (FR)   6 b.g. Housamix (FR) – Fast Girl (FR) (Gay Minstrel (FR)) [2003/4 c—, h97: c19g⁴ 20m³ 17m^{pu} Aug 25] leggy gelding: no show on completed start in novice chases: modest hurdler: sold out of P. Hobbs's stable 5,200 gns Doncaster May Sales and reportedly lame both subsequent starts: stays 19f: acts on soft going: usually blinkered, not in 2003/4: no easy ride: inconsistent. *Dr P. Pritchard*   **c— h—**

FAST MIX (FR)   5 gr.g. Linamix (FR) – Fascinating Hill (FR) (Danehill (USA)) [2003/4 h101: 16m^{pu} 17g 17s⁴ 19g² 16d* 19g^F 16g 17g^{pu} 19g² Apr 16] angular gelding: fair handicap hurdler: won at Plumpton in March: stays 19f: probably acts on any going: visored last 6 outings: sketchy jumper: none too reliable. *M. C. Pipe*   **h114**

FAST TRACK (IRE)   7 b.g. Doyoun – Manntika (Kalamoun) [2003/4 16m^F May 5] sparely-made gelding: fairly useful on Flat (stayed 9.4f) for R. Hannon: only poor form over hurdles: dead. *N. R. Mitchell*   **h—**

FATA ALBERTINA (IRE)   8 b.m. Ela-Mana-Mou – Quiet Awakening (USA) (Secreto (USA)) [2003/4 16m 18g² 18d* 19m² 16f 20f³ 20s 20m* 22m^{pu} Oct 27] medium-sized mare: fairly useful handicap hurdler: won at Wexford in July and Tipperary in October: stayed 2½m: acted on firm and soft going: dead. *W. M. Sheehy, Ireland*   **h118**

FATALISTE (FR)   10 b.g. Nikos – Faracha (FR) (Kenmare (FR)) [2003/4 16m 16m^{4d} 16m⁶ 16m 16m 16g⁶ c20m² c20f³ Aug 22] leggy, lightly-made gelding: useful hurdler at best: signs of retaining only a little ability in 2003/4, including over fences last 2 starts: raced mainly around 2m: acts on soft and good to firm going: tried in cheekpieces/visor. *B. A. Pearce*   **c66 h—**

FATEHALKHAIR (IRE)   12 ch.g. Kris – Midway Lady (USA) (Alleged (USA)) [2003/4 c126, h115: 17g⁶ Apr 12] sparely-made gelding: fairly useful handicap hurdler/chaser: well below form over hurdles only start in 2003/4: stays easy 3½m: acts on any going: all 13 jumps wins at Sedgefield. *B. Ellison*   **c— h—**

FATHER ABRAHAM (IRE)   6 b.g. Idris (IRE) – Mothers Blessing (Wolver Hollow) [2003/4 20s* 21g⁵ 20d⁶ 20s^{pu} c22s^{pu} c16d c20g⁶ Mar 12] useful-looking gelding: brother to 1m winner in Italy and half-brother to several winners, notably Premio Regina Elena winner Treasure Hope: dam middle-distance maiden: best effort when winning maiden hurdle at Gowran in May: sold out of N. Meade's stable 38,000 gns Doncaster Sales later in month: disappointing subsequently, including over fences (blinkered): stays 2½m: acts on soft going: possibly temperamental. *J. Akehurst*   **c— h103 d**

FATHER ANDY (IRE)   11 ch.g. Executive Perk – Twinkle Sunset (Deep Run) [2003/4 c21g^F Apr 1] workmanlike ex-Irish gelding: fair hunter chaser for M. Hourigan: winning pointer in Britain in February: close up when falling Becher's in Fox Hunters' at Aintree: stays 25f: acts on good to firm and heavy going: has had tongue tied: consistent. *R. A. Wernham*   **c— h—**

FATHER BOB   7 gr.g. Bold Fox – Annie Bee (Rusticaro (FR)) [2003/4 19g^{pu} 17d^{pu} c19g^F 19g^{pu} Feb 6] seventh foal: brother to winning hurdler/chaser Silver Minx, stays 25f: dam won at 2m over hurdles: no sign of ability: trained by B. Rothwell on debut. *P. D. Niven*   **c— h—**

FATHER D (IRE) 9 b.g. Mister Lord (USA) – Abrahams Cross (IRE) (Bustomi) [2003/4 h87: 18g 24m 20m c18g^F Mar 27] rangy gelding: modest handicap hurdler: well held in 3 starts early in season: shaped encouragingly in novice handicap chase at Newbury prior to falling 3 out: stays 19f: acts on good to firm and heavy going: headstrong. *R. H. Buckler*   **c– p**
  h–

FATHER MULCAHY 8 b.g. Safawan – Constant Delight (Never So Bold) [2003/4 c–, h–: 20d^{pu} c23v^2 c16f^5 c16g^{pu} c22m* c22g^4 c20s^{pu} Dec 26] workmanlike gelding: maiden hurdler: poor chaser: gifted very weak novice at Haydock (finished lame) in November: seems to stay 2¾m: acts on heavy going, probably on good to firm: tried blinkered, visored last 3 starts: has had tongue tied. *D. McCain*   **c68**
  h–

FATHEROFTHEBRIDE (IRE) 8 gr.g. Roselier (FR) – Trendy Princess (Strong Gale) [2003/4 F20m^6 F17g* F20m^2 F16d^2 F20d* 20g* 20m^5 24m^4 22d^3 24s^{pu} Jan 18] half-brother to fair hurdler Prince Dante (by Phardante), stays 2¾m, and poor 2m hurdler Trendy Auctioneer (by Mazaad): dam unraced: fell in point on debut: useful form in bumpers, winning at Bellewstown (maiden) in July and Galway in September: fair form over hurdles, winning maiden at Listowel later in September: blinkered, signs of temperament last 3 starts: likely to prove best at 3m+. *Joseph Crowley, Ireland*   **h108**
  F105

FATHER PADDY 9 ch.g. Minster Son – Sister Claire (Quayside) [2003/4 c90, h97: c21g^2 Apr 12] good-topped gelding: modest maiden hurdler: similar form both starts over fences: stays 21f: acts on good to firm going, bumper form on soft. *T. J. Fitzgerald*   **c87**
  h–

FATHER RECTOR (IRE) 15 b.g. The Parson – Mwanamio (Sole Mio (USA)) [2003/4 c105, h–: c25m^3 c22g^4 May 24] angular gelding: fair hunter chaser: stays 25f: acts on any going: has looked none too keen. *Mrs F. E. Needham*   **c95**
  h–

FATHOM 6 ch.g. Zafonic (USA) – River Lullaby (USA) (Riverman (USA)) [2003/4 F71: 16m^{pu} Jun 5] sturdy gelding: little sign of ability. *Mrs L. B. Normile*   **h–**

FATTAAN (IRE) 4 b.g. Danehill (USA) – Bintalshaati (Kris) [2003/4 17g^5 17f* 16f^4 Oct 16] modest maiden on Flat (stays 1¼m), sold out of M. Tregoning's stable 6,500 gns Newmarket July Sales: poor form in juvenile hurdles: pulled hard when winning very weak maiden at Exeter in September: claimed by J. O'Shea £5,000 final start. *P. J. Hobbs*   **h74**

FAUNTLEROY (IRE) 5 b.g. Lord Americo – Ballyroe Ann (IRE) (Over The River (FR)) [2003/4 F17s F16s 16s 19g 20g Feb 20] €1,000 3-y-o: lengthy gelding: second foal: dam lightly raced in points: no sign of ability. *J. A. Supple*   **h–**
  F–

FAVOURED OPTION (IRE) 9 ch.g. Glacial Storm (USA) – Hot House Flower (Derring Rose) [2003/4 c113, h–: c25m^2 c23m^3 c24m^5 c22v^4 Nov 29] strong gelding: fair handicap chaser: stays 29f: acts on heavy and good to firm going: often makes mistakes: consistent. *Ian Williams*   **c113**
  h–

FAVOURITE SON (FR) 6 gr.g. Linamix (FR) – Hot Favourite (FR) (Fast Topaze (USA)) [2003/4 16s^2 16d* 20f* Jul 11] won 4 times up to 13f on Flat in France for J-C Rouget: fair hurdler: won minor events at Kilbeggan in June and Wexford in July: stays 2½m: acts on firm and soft going. *E. J. O'Grady, Ireland*   **h115**

FAYRWAY RHYTHM (IRE) 7 b.g. Fayruz – The Way She Moves (North Stoke) [2003/4 h–§: c16d^6 c17g^5 c16s^3 c20d^2 Apr 18] modest hurdler/novice chaser: barely stays 2½m: acts on soft and good to firm going: blinkered/visored: has been tongue tied: ungenuine. *Ian Emmerson*   **c89 §**
  h– §

FAYS TWO (IRE) 6 b.m. Binary Star (USA) – Claudette (Claude Monet (USA)) [2003/4 F16m F17d Apr 18] fourth foal: dam of little account: showed little in 2 bumpers. *A. Robson*   **F–**

FEANOR 6 b.m. Presidium – Nouvelle Cuisine (Yawa) [2003/4 h–: 16m^2 16g^5 17g 17m* 16m^3 17m* 17d^2 17g^5 16d^4 c20g^{pu} 16g 16g Feb 18] leggy mare: showed little on chasing debut: modest handicap hurdler: won at Southwell in June and July: raced around 2m: acts on soft and good to firm going. *Mrs S. A. Watt*   **c–**
  h98

FEAR SIUIL (IRE) 11 b.g. Strong Gale – Astral River (Over The River (FR)) [2003/4 c110, h–: c16d^{pu} c20m c20m^3 c21d^{pu} c21g* c24g* c20m* c24f c20m^3 c20g Apr 18] lengthy gelding: fairly useful handicap chaser: better than ever in 2003/4, winning at Newton Abbot in August and Stratford in September and October: stays 3m: acts on good to firm and good to soft going, probably on firm: tongue tied: reportedly broke blood vessel eighth start. *Nick Williams*   **c120**
  h–

FEELING FIZZICAL 6 b.g. Feelings (FR) – Stepdaughter (Relkino) [2003/4 h–: 24m Oct 25] no form over hurdles. *Mrs J. C. McGregor*   **h–**

Gala Casinos Daily Record Mares' Only Handicap Hurdle, Ayr—
a back-to-form Feel The Pride claims her sixth win of a very productive campaign

FEELING GRAND (IRE)   12 b. or br.g. Naheez (USA) – Tourney's Girl (Yankee Gold) [2003/4 c16g^{pu} May 14] workmanlike ex-Irish gelding: fairly useful chaser at best: sold out of H. de Bromhead's stable 1,000 gns Doncaster October (2002) Sales: no form in handicap or in points since. *Mrs Richard Arthur*   **c–**
h–

FEEL THE PRIDE (IRE)   8 b.m. Persian Bold – Nordic Pride (Horage) [2003/4 h96p: 16g* 16g* 17m* 16f³ 16g* 16d* 16d^{pu} 16g² 18g 16g* 20m^{ur} Apr 24] leggy mare: reportedly fractured cannon bone prior to reappearance: fairly useful hurdler: won maiden at Uttoxeter and novice at Stratford in June, novice at Market Rasen in July and mares handicaps at Haydock and Ayr in November and Ayr in April: beat Avitta 1¼ lengths for final success: raced mainly around 2m: acts on firm and good to soft going, unraced on softer: blinkered after fourth outing: usually patiently ridden. *Jonjo O'Neill*   **h125**

FEIZOR (IRE)   4 ch.f. Titus Livius (FR) – Blues Queen (Lahib (USA)) [2003/4 17m⁴ Aug 16] poor and ungenuine maiden on Flat (stays 1¼m): looked less than straightforward when remote fourth in juvenile at Bangor on hurdling debut: sold 1,800 gns Doncaster October Sales. *R. F. Fisher*   **h–**

FELIX DARBY (IRE)   9 b.g. Buckskin (FR) – Cool Anne (Orchardist) [2003/4 c86, h82: c25m^{pu} c23v^R c24g² c25v⁴ c26s⁴ c24d³ c24m* Apr 13] workmanlike gelding: poor maiden hurdler: modest chaser: won handicap at Chepstow: thorough stayer: acts on soft and good to firm going: often makes mistakes. *Mrs G. Harvey*   **c87**
h–

FELIX (IRE)   8 b.g. Religiously (USA) – Knock Bantiarna (Abednego) [2003/4 c23m^{pu} 22m² 26g^{pu} 22g³ 22m⁶ 24m² 22g⁴ 22g⁴ 22m⁶ c19s c24d^{pu} 19m Mar 4] first foal: dam unraced: won maiden Irish point in 2002: bought 3,400 gns Doncaster January (2003) Sales: poor maiden hurdler: no form in steeplechases: suited by 2¾m+: acts on good to firm going: wore blinkers/cheekpieces after steeplechasing debut. *Miss K. M. George*   **c–**
h80

FELIXRDOTCOM   8 ch.g. Gran Alba (USA) – Golden Curd (FR) (Nice Havrais (USA)) [2003/4 16v^{pu} 18d 23d⁴ Apr 12] sturdy gelding: fair maiden hurdler in 2001/2: modest form at best on return: stays 23f: raced on good going or softer. *N. J. Gifford*   **h87**

FELIX THE GREAT (IRE)   6 b. or br.g. Hamas (IRE) – Sonya's Pearl (IRE) (Conquering Hero (USA)) [2003/4 F16d 16d³ 16g* 16m² 16g* 16m² 16d Apr 13] third foal: half-brother to prolific Italian winner up to 7f Bictor (by Great Commotion): dam unraced, from family of useful 2m hurdler Pollerton: once-raced on Flat: fairly useful bumper winner: fairly useful 2m hurdler: won novice at Wexford in June and minor event at Listowel in September: acts on good to firm and soft ground. *M. Halford, Ireland*   **h118**
F—

FELLOW SHIP   4 b.g. Elmaamul (USA) – Genoa (Zafonic (USA)) [2003/4 16m^F 16g 18s Jan 26] leggy gelding: fairly useful but ungenuine on Flat (stays 11f), claimed out of G. Butler's stable in September: showed little in juvenile hurdles: tongue tied last 2 starts. *P. Butler*   **h–**

FELONY (IRE)   9 ch.g. Pharly (FR) – Scales of Justice (Final Straw) [2003/4 h–: 16d⁴ 24s^{pu} 19m 16g 21d Mar 19] compact gelding: winning 19f hurdler: retains little ability: tried in cheekpieces: tongue tied: has looked temperamental. *L. P. Grassick*   **h–**

FENCOTE GOLD   4 ch.g. Bob's Return (IRE) – Goldaw (Gala Performance) [2003/4 F16d⁶ Feb 8] 16,500 3-y-o: half-brother to several winners, notably high-class staying chaser Bobby Grant (by Gunner B): dam, placed in Irish hurdles, half-sister to fairly   **F83**

useful 2m to 2½m chaser Boreen Daw: sixth in bumper at Musselburgh on debut. *P. Beaumont*

FENCOTE (IRE)   7 b.g. Norwich – Primrose Forest (Menelek) [2003/4 18s^F 19g^{ur}   **h87**
20d 16g⁴ Apr 5] 19,000 4-y-o: good-topped gelding: chasing type: eighth foal: half-brother to fairly useful 2m hurdler Joking Aside (by Brush Aside): dam, ran in bumpers/points, half-sister to useful chaser up to 2½m Malya Mal: dropped in trip, best effort over hurdles when fourth in novice at Kelso. *P. Beaumont*

FEN GYPSY   6 b.g. Nashwan (USA) – Didicoy (USA) (Danzig (USA)) [2003/4 h–:   **h–**
16d^{pu} Nov 15] lengthy gelding: fair on Flat (stays 1¼m): no form over hurdles: tongue tied both starts in 2002/3. *P. D. Evans*

FENIX (GER)   5 b.g. Lavirco (GER) – Frille (FR) (Shareef Dancer (USA)) [2003/4   **h122**
16d⁴ 16v⁴ 17s* 16s³ 16g² 20s² Apr 17] good-topped ex-German gelding: successful twice up to around 11f from 6 starts on Flat, including in 2003 for S. Stokes: fairly useful hurdler: won novice at Folkestone in February: best efforts when placed in handicaps at Sandown (third to Scorned in valuable event) and Newbury (¾-length second to Dancing Bay) next 2 starts: should prove at least as effective at 2½m as 2m: raced on good ground or softer (acts on soft). *Mrs L. Wadham*

FENNEY SPRING   4 b.f. Polish Precedent (USA) – Sliprail (USA) (Our Native   **F89**
(USA)) [2003/4 F16d⁴ F16g² F16d* Mar 14] 2,500 3-y-o: seventh foal: half-sister to fairly useful Irish 9f winner Super Whizz (by Belmez) and winner in Saudi Arabia by Mtoto: dam, 1¼m winner, half-sister to useful 2m to 3m chaser Copernicus: fair form in bumpers, well backed when winning 21-runner mares event at Warwick by head from Kohinor. *W. Jenks*

FERGAL THE PILER   5 b.g. Jendali (USA) – Dorado Beach (Lugana Beach)   **h–**
[2003/4 16g 20s Apr 21] first foal: dam, 7f winner, half-sister to fairly useful staying chaser Drum Battle: showed nothing in 2 races over hurdles. *N. G. Richards*

FERIMON   5 br.g. Terimon – Rhyming Moppet (Rymer) [2003/4 F16s* Jan 16] sturdy   **F106**
gelding: second foal: dam winning pointer: won bumper at Huntingdon on debut by 2½ lengths from Vingis Park: likely to stay at least 2½m. *H. D. Daly*

FERN LORD (IRE)   7 ch.h. Mister Lord (USA) – Deep Fern (Deep Run) [2003/4   **c102**
h115p: c22v³ c22s^{pu} c25s^F c22m^F Feb 28] big horse: progressive form in novice hurdles   **h–**
in 2002/3: promising third in novice at Towcester on steeplechasing debut on reappearance: failed to complete subsequently: will stay beyond 3m. *Jonjo O'Neill*

FEY MACHA (IRE)   9 b.m. Phardante (FR) – West Lodge (Deep Run) [2003/4 h110:   **c– p**
20m 24d⁶ 20f⁴ 22f 20m 24m* 20m⁵ 24m c20s^F Nov 20] strong, lengthy, good sort: fair   **h113**
hurdler: won handicap at Gowran in October: fell first on chasing debut: stays 3m: acts on firm ground (bumper winner on good to soft). *Paul A. Roche, Ireland*

FIDALUS (IRE)   11 b.g. Mandalus – Fifi L'Amour (Fair Turn) [2003/4 c24d^F c22s⁵   **c–**
c20v c19m^{pu} Apr 13] leggy ex-Irish gelding: winning hurdler/chaser: left H. de Brom-   **h–**
head/off over 2 years before reappearance, long way below best in 2003/4: stays 3m: acts on heavy and good to firm going: tried blinkered. *R. C. Guest*

FIDDLERS CREEK (IRE)   5 b.g. Danehill (USA) – Mythical Creek (USA) (Pleasant   **h78**
Tap (USA)) [2003/4 17s⁵ 16f⁵ Feb 29] modest on Flat nowadays (stays 1½m): poor form both starts over hurdles. *R. Allan*

FIELDING'S HAY (IRE)   8 b.m. Supreme Leader – Kates Fling (USA) (Quiet Fling   **c89**
(USA)) [2003/4 c89, h–: c24m* c22s* c25g⁴ c31d^{pu} Apr 22] good-topped mare: modest   **h–**
handicap chaser: won at Huntingdon in May and Towcester (mares event) in March: jumped badly final start: stays 3¼m: acts on soft and good to firm going: tried visored. *Mrs J. Candlish*

FIELDINGS SOCIETY (IRE)   5 ch.g. Moscow Society (USA) – Lone Trail (IRE)   **F–**
(Strong Gale) [2003/4 F17m Oct 10] 8,200 4-y-o: workmanlike gelding: first foal: dam lightly raced in points: looked badly in need of experience when well beaten in bumper on debut. *Mrs J. Candlish*

FIELD MARSHAL (IRE)   6 b.g. Supreme Leader – Strong Serenade (IRE) (Strong   **h112**
Gale) [2003/4 F16g² F16d* 16d 18d² 20s Jan 18] IR £29,000 3-y-o: well-made gelding: **F110**
third foal: brother to useful hurdler/fairly useful chaser Supreme Prince, stays 3m, and 17f hurdle winner Supreme Serenade, and half-brother to 3m hurdle winner That's The Story (by Montelimar): dam 2m hurdle winner: useful form in bumpers, winning at Punchestown in November: fair form over hurdles: reportedly lame final start. *E. J. O'Grady, Ireland*

FIELD OF BLUE 5 b.g. Shambo – Flashing Silks (Kind of Hush) [2003/4 F16s F16g 19s^{pu} Apr 4] has scope: first foal: dam of little account: no form in bumpers or maiden hurdle. *P. Winkworth* **h–** **F–**

FIELDS OF HOME (IRE) 6 b.m. Synefus (USA) – Homefield Girl (IRE) (Rahotep (FR)) [2003/4 c22s² c21s* c24s^F Apr 21] tall, leggy mare: second foal: dam never ran: won maiden Irish point on debut in 2002: much better effort on completed outings in mares novice chases when winning at Sedgefield in February by 10 lengths from Noisetine, idling late on (flashed tail under pressure): likely to stay beyond 21f. *J. Howard Johnson* **c113**

FIER GOUMIER (FR) 9 b.g. Chef de Clan II (FR) – Azilal (FR) (Rex Magna (FR)) [2003/4 c–, h–: c16m⁶ c21m² c24m^{pu} c21m^{pu} Oct 11] leggy gelding: fair handicap chaser: form since 2001/2 only when second at Uttoxeter in September: stays 21f: acts on firm going: tongue tied last 3 appearances, blinkered/in cheekpieces last 2: moody. *Jonjo O'Neill* **c101 §** **h–**

FIERY CREEK 7 ch.m. Moscow Society (USA) – Deep Creek (Deep Run) [2003/4 h–, F–: 21v^{pu} 22s 17s⁴ 16s Jan 16] big, workmanlike mare: poor maiden hurdler: form only around 2m: raced only on soft/heavy going over hurdles. *D. J. Wintle* **h67**

FIERY PEACE 7 ch.g. Tina's Pet – Burning Mirage (Pamroy) [2003/4 h76: 19m² 16m³ 16m⁴ c17m² c16g³ c16m² c16m* c16d* Mar 28] good-topped gelding: modest maiden hurdler: fair chaser: won handicaps at Ludlow in December and Huntingdon (novice) in March: stays 19f: acts on good to firm and good to soft ground. *H. D. Daly* **c111** **h91**

FIERY RING (IRE) 9 b.g. Torus – Kakemona (Kambalda) [2003/4 c124+, h–: c16d² c20d c20m c17m² c16f⁴ c19d c16m⁴ c17s³ c19d² c16v⁶ c17d* c16s³ c17d Apr 11] strong, well-made gelding: fairly useful chaser: made all in handicap at Fairyhouse in February: good third to Junior Fontaine in similar event at Punchestown in late-April: stays easy 2½m: probably acts on any going: has had tongue tied: front runner. *J. R. H. Fowler, Ireland* **c126** **h–**

FIFTEEN REDS 9 b.g. Jumbo Hirt (USA) – Dominance (Dominion) [2003/4 h84: 24g⁵ 27s³ 24m 26m c21m⁶ 24d 24g Jan 7] leggy gelding: poor hurdler: well held after second start, including in novice on chasing debut: stays 27f: acts on firm and soft going: tried visored: none too reliable (ran out once). *J. C. Haynes* **c–** **h74**

FIFTH GENERATION (IRE) 14 b.g. Bulldozer – Fragrant's Last (Little Buskins) [2003/4 c–, h91: 16m⁶ 19m 22d⁴ 20m^F 19m⁵ 16m⁴ 20d⁵ 16s 16s⁵ 16s⁵ 16m⁵ 16g 18d⁶ 16d⁶ Apr 12] workmanlike gelding: veteran hurdler/chaser: stays 3¼m: seems to act on any going: tried blinkered: front runner. *Dr P. Pritchard* **c–** **h–**

FIFTY FRANKS (IRE) 5 b.h. Oscar (IRE) – Deny's Run (IRE) (Commanche Run) [2003/4 F16s⁵ F16g⁴ F16s² 22d 20d⁴ Apr 10] €4,700 3-y-o: workmanlike horse: first foal: dam once-raced half-sister to useful staying chaser Take The Stand: fair form in bumpers: poor form both starts over hurdles. *M. D. Hammond* **h76** **F86**

FIGARO DU ROCHER (FR) 4 ch.g. Beyssac (FR) – Fabinou (FR) (Cavan) [2003/4 17g* 17m² 16g 16m² 16m² 16g 17g 19g 17m⁵ 17g² 17s² 17g⁵ Apr 13] smallish gelding: seventh foal: brother to very smart staying chaser Banjo and half-brother to winning hurdler in France by Tadj: dam, unplaced over jumps, out of French middle-distance and jumping winner: fair juvenile hurdler: trained by J. Barbe, won at Vire in June: acts on soft and good to firm going: visored after third start, also tongue tied last 2. *M. C. Pipe* **h97**

FIGAWIN 9 b.g. Rudimentary (USA) – Dear Person (Rainbow Quest (USA)) [2003/4 c–, h–: c24g* Feb 20] leggy gelding: modest handicap chaser: returned from lengthy absence to win at Fakenham, very confidently ridden by amateur and leading line: stays 3m: acts on soft and good to firm going. *P. A. Blockley* **c91** **h–**

FIGHTING CHANCE (IRE) 4 b.g. Germany (USA) – Una Juna (IRE) (Good Thyne (USA)) [2003/4 F16g³ Mar 27] rangy gelding: second foal: half-brother to useful 2m hurdler War of Attrition (by Presenting): dam, once-raced in points, sister to fairly useful staying chaser Max Pride: promising 5¾ lengths third to River Trapper in bumper at Newbury on debut, travelling well long way. *R. H. Alner* **F88 +**

FIGHTING TIMES 12 b.g. Good Times (ITY) – Duellist (Town Crier) [2003/4 c21v^{pu} May 26] leggy gelding: winning hurdler/chaser: of little account nowadays: usually visored. *Miss K. Marks* **c–** **h–**

FILLE DETENTE 4 ch.f. Double Trigger (IRE) – Matoaka (Be My Chief (USA)) [2003/4 F12g F12m F16g⁴ Feb 20] plain filly: first foal: dam, won around 1m, half-sister to one-time smart 7f/1m performer Calcutta: signs of ability in bumpers. *Mrs P. Sly* **F81**

FILS A PAPA (FR) 5 b.g. Double Bed (FR) – Syvanie (FR) (Sicyos (USA)) [2003/4 **h113** 18s* 18v 19s³ 18s 21g Dec 26] leggy gelding: second foal: dam, middle-distance winner in France, half-sister to very smart French hurdler up to 25f Bedava: modest maiden on Flat: better over hurdles, won minor event at Enghien in October: contested handicaps subsequently, well held on British debut final start: will stay 21f: raced mainly on soft/heavy going. *F. Doumen, France*

FILSCOT 12 b.g. Scottish Reel – Fililode (Mossberry) [2003/4 c101, h–: c23g⁵ c24d³ **c90** Apr 8] compact gelding: modest chaser: stays 25f: acts on firm and soft going: tried **h–** blinkered/visored, all wins when not: none too consistent. *Mrs S. S. Harbour*

FINAL COMMAND 7 ch.g. Gildoran – Fine Fettle (Final Straw) [2003/4 20sᵖᵘ 17s **h–** Apr 6] strong, lengthy gelding: runner-up in bumper on debut in late-2001/2: little promise in 2 novice hurdles on return. *J. C. Tuck*

FINAL DANCER 9 b.g. Ski Dancer – Final Flirtation (Clear Run) [2003/4 20m Aug **h–** 2] failed to complete in points: struck into when well held in novice on hurdling debut. *N. A. Twiston-Davies*

FINAL DEAL (IRE) 5 b.g. Rashar (USA) – Cute Boro (IRE) (Borovoe) [2003/4 **h–** 21gˢᵘ Feb 11] medium-sized gelding: first foal: dam never ran: well beaten in maiden Irish points in 2003: slipped up on hurdling debut. *C. J. Down*

FINAL LAP 8 b.g. Batshoof – Lap of Honour (Final Straw) [2003/4 h67: 17g 16m **h–** 17m 20mᵖᵘ 16gᵖᵘ 22gᵖᵘ 16m 22gᵖᵘ 16d 16s Dec 30] smallish gelding: winning selling hurdler, showed very little in 2003/4: tried visored/blinkered: has taken little interest. *S. T. Lewis*

FINAL PROJECT (IRE) 12 ch.g. Project Manager – Tower Belle (Tower Walk) **c–** [2003/4 c21mᵖᵘ May 21] one-time fairly useful hurdler/fair chaser for D. Wachman: no **h–** form in points and hunter in Britain in 2003: stays 2¾m: acts on firm and soft going. *Mrs G. Drury*

FINAL VIEW (FR) 5 b.g. Distant View (USA) – Unafurtivalagrima (USA) (Quest For **h–** Fame) [2003/4 h–: 26gᵖᵘ Nov 9] lightly raced on Flat: no show in 2 races over hurdles. *N. P. Littmoden*

FINBAR'S LAW 7 b.g. Contract Law (USA) – De Valera (Faustus (USA)) [2003/4 **c–** h82: 20d² 20g 24m⁵ c16vᶠ 17s⁴ 16s Apr 11] modest hurdler: fell third on chasing debut: **h94** stays at least 2½m: acts on good to soft going, probably on good to firm: tongue tied: races freely. *R. Johnson*

FINBAR'S REVENGE 9 b.g. Gildoran – Grotto Princess (Pollerton) [2003/4 c24sᵖᵘ **c100** c24gᶠ c24s* c23dᵖᵘ Apr 21] lengthy gelding: fair chaser, missed 2002/3: won handicap at **h–** Stratford in March: stays 3m: acts on soft and good to firm going: has been blinkered, including last 3 starts: inconsistent. *S. E. H. Sherwood*

FIN BEC (FR) 11 b.g. Tip Moss (FR) – Tourbrune (FR) (Pamponi (FR)) [2003/4 **c119** c101x, h–: c22g* c28g* c24dᵖᵘ Dec 29] strong, lengthy gelding: fairly useful handicap **h–** chaser: won at Towcester and Market Rasen in November: stays 3½m: acts on any going: usually blinkered, has worn cheekpieces: front runner: often let down by jumping. *A. P. Jones*

FINCHES LANE (IRE) 10 b.g. Le Bavard (FR) – Alice Mann (Mandalus) [2003/4 **h–** 19s 22gᵖᵘ Apr 18] third in a point: lightly-raced maiden hurdler: showed nothing in 2003/4 after 2 years off: tried tongue tied. *Miss Victoria Roberts*

FIND ME ANOTHER (IRE) 8 b.g. Shardari – Naujwan Too (Kafu) [2003/4 c20g² **c87** Mar 12] IR 2,200 4-y-o: second foal: dam modest maiden hurdler up to 2½m: winning pointer, including in April: second in maiden hunter at Leicester on steeplechasing debut. *Mrs Caroline Bailey*

FIND THE KING (IRE) 6 b.g. King's Theatre (IRE) – Undiscovered (Tap On **c116** Wood) [2003/4 h122: 17g c20g² c17d² c21f* c21m³ Oct 5] good-topped gelding: fairly **h–** useful hurdler/chaser: fortunate to win maiden chase at Cork in August: much better form when third to Catalpa Cargo in Grade 3 novice at Tipperary: stays 21f: acts on soft and good to firm going: usually tongue tied: has been led in. *E. J. O'Grady, Ireland*

FINE AND DANDY (IRE) 8 b.g. Roselier (FR) – Hawthorn Dandy (Deep Run) **c80** [2003/4 c21f² May 21] leggy gelding: maiden hurdler: modest pointer, successful in **h–** March: similar form when second in novice at Folkestone on hunter chase debut. *J. M. Turner*

FINE FRENZY (IRE) 4 b.f. Great Commotion (USA) – Fine Project (IRE) (Project **h76** Manager) [2003/4 16m³ 16mᵘʳ 16sᵖᵘ Dec 19] modest on Flat (stays 7f), sold out of

J. Hills's stable 2,400 gns Doncaster October Sales: poor form on first of 3 starts over hurdles: saddle reportedly slipped second outing: looked tricky ride final one. *Miss S. J. Wilton*

FINELY TUNED (IRE) 5 b.g. Lord Americo – Gusserane Princess (Paddy's Stream) [2003/4 F16d³ F16g F16g⁵ Mar 7] useful-looking gelding: half-brother to fairly useful hurdler/chaser Mr Pickpocket (by Roselier), stays 3¼m, and fairly useful hunter chaser Overheard (by Over The River): dam, maiden, from family of top-class hunter chaser Eliogarty: fairly useful form at best in bumpers, fifth to Toemac at Kempton final start: bred to be suited by 2½m+. *M. Pitman* **F95**

FINE TIMES 10 b.g. Timeless Times (USA) – Marfen (Lochnager) [2003/4 c–, h–: c24mᶠ May 7] compact gelding: fair hunter chaser: stays 25f: tongue tied. *Milson Robinson* **c– h–**

FINIANS IVY (IRE) 9 b.g. Orchestra – Rambling Ivy (Mandalus) [2003/4 c18d* c25s² c17d⁵ c24sᵖᵘ c19s³ c19d 20d² Feb 28] IR 5,000 4-y-o: deep-girthed gelding: fifth foal: brother to fair 2½m hurdler Flying Fiddler and winning pointer Acoustic: dam placed in Irish bumpers: fairly useful handicap chaser: won novice at Punchestown very early in season: fair handicap hurdler: stays 25f: acts on heavy going. *A. J. Martin, Ireland* **c119 h101**

FINZI (IRE) 6 b.g. Zaffaran (USA) – Sporting Talent (IRE) (Seymour Hicks (FR)) [2003/4 F–: 21f⁵ 26s³ 24v⁵ 23v³ 24d 26d⁵ Mar 22] good-topped gelding: poor novice hurdler: stays 3¼m: probably acts on any going. *M. Scudamore* **h78**

FIOLINO (FR) 11 b.g. Bayolidaan (FR) – Vellea (FR) (Cap Martin (FR)) [2003/4 c–, h–: 24g³ c22gᵖᵘ c25gᵖᵘ May 24] rather leggy gelding: winning chaser: poor maiden hurdler: suited by 3m+: acts on heavy and good to firm going: tried blinkered: sold 1,900 gns Doncaster October Sales. *M. W. Easterby* **c– h82**

FIONN MAC CUMAILL (IRE) 5 ch.g. Sabrehill (USA) – North Gale (Oats) [2003/4 F16g Mar 6] first foal: dam unraced: tailed off in bumper on debut. *J. J. Quinn* **F–**

FIONNULA'S RAINBOW (IRE) 9 ch.m. Rainbows For Life (CAN) – Bon Retour (Sallust) [2003/4 c–§, h84§: 16mᵖᵘ 24mᵖᵘ Aug 1] close-coupled mare: winning hurdler/chaser, showed little in 2003/4: tried blinkered: moody. *S. T. Lewis* **c– § h– §**

FIORI 8 b.g. Anshan – Fen Princess (IRE) (Trojan Fen) [2003/4 c117, h–: c16m* c20m² Jun 21] close-coupled gelding: impresses in appearance: fairly useful chaser: kept on gamely to beat Caitriona's Choice a length in handicap at Hexham on reappearance: good second to Tacolino in similar event at Market Rasen week later: stays 2½m: acts on good to firm and heavy going: usually races prominently: jumps soundly. *P. C. Haslam* **c122 h–**

FIREAWAY 10 b.g. Infantry – Handymouse (Nearly A Hand) [2003/4 c95, h–: c20gᵘʳ c17g³ Mar 28] winning hurdler: no better then modest form on completed starts over fences: should be suited by 2½m: acts on firm and soft going: has hung and jumped left. *O. Brennan* **c82 h–**

FIREBALL MACNAMARA (IRE) 8 b.g. Lord Americo – Glint of Baron (Glint of Gold) [2003/4 c116, h–: 20m Jun 28] useful-looking gelding: fairly useful chaser: fair hurdler: seventh of 8 finishers in handicap at Worcester only start in 2003/4: effective at 2m to 2¾m: acts on firm and soft going. *M. Pitman* **c– h107**

FIRE MOUNTAIN 6 b.g. North Col – Emma Wright (Skyliner) [2003/4 F16m F18g Apr 22] £1,000 4-y-o: angular gelding: sixth foal: half-brother to modest hurdler True Mission (by True Song): dam never ran: well held in 2 bumpers. *C. L. Tizzard* **F–**

FIRE RANGER 8 ch.m. Presidium – Regal Flame (Royalty) [2003/4 h–p, F82: 17g⁴ 19d⁶ 16s⁶ 19s³ 17d 19g⁴ Mar 9] poor maiden hurdler: will stay beyond 19f: raced on good going or softer over hurdles (acts on soft), bumper form on good to firm. *J. D. Frost* **h82**

FIRESIDE LEGEND (IRE) 5 b.g. College Chapel – Miss Sandman (Manacle) [2003/4 h67: 20g May 5] leggy gelding: poor hurdler: usually blinkered: has had tongue tied: temperamental. *Miss M. P. Bryant* **h– §**

FIRESTONE (GER) 7 b.g. Dictator's Song (USA) – Fatinizza (IRE) (Niniski (USA)) [2003/4 h93: 16m³ 16d² 16g Jun 22] leggy gelding: modest handicap hurdler: been placed around 2m: acts on good to firm and heavy going: sometimes tongue tied: has been slowly away. *A. W. Carroll* **h93**

FIROZI 5 b.m. Forzando – Lambast (Relkino) [2003/4 16m² 16g³ 16s Jan 6] smallish mare: half-sister to fair hurdler Angie Marinie (by Sabrehill), stays 2½m: modest on Flat (stays 1¼m): poor form in novice hurdles: will prove best at sharp 2m. *R. A. Fahey* **h80**

FIRST ADARE (IRE) 4 ch.g. Un Desperado (FR) – First Mistake (Posse (USA)) h–
[2003/4 F16d 16s^{pu} 16g Mar 28] fifth foal: brother to useful chaser Peccadillo, stays 3m: F–
dam plating-class maiden: no worthwhile form in bumper or juvenile hurdles. *Miss
Lucinda V. Russell*

FIRST BALLOT (IRE) 8 b.g. Perugino (USA) – Election Special (Chief Singer) h130
[2003/4 16m^2 16f^3 Oct 15] tall, leggy gelding: useful on Flat (stays 2½m): useful
handicap hurdler: good placed efforts both starts in 2003/4, third to Gimmick at Wetherby
on second occasion: should prove at least as effective at 2½m as 2m: acts on firm and soft
going: usually forces pace. *D. R. C. Elsworth*

FIRST BASE 5 ch.g. First Trump – Rose Music (Luthier) [2003/4 h76: 17g May 26] h–
poor maiden on Flat and over hurdles: tried in cheekpieces. *R. E. Barr*

FIRST BOY (GER) 5 b.h. Bering – First Smile (Surumu (GER)) [2003/4 16d^2 Mar h102
24] ex-German horse: successful twice over 1¼m from 11 starts on Flat for P. Rau,
including in 2003: 66/1, 1¾ lengths second to Jonanaud in novice at Chepstow on
hurdling debut, raced freely: not certain to stay much beyond 2m. *D. J. Wintle*

FIRST DYNASTY (USA) 4 br. or b.c. Danzig (USA) – Willow Runner (USA) h91
(Alydar (USA)) [2003/4 16m^3 Dec 10] flat on Flat (stays 9.4f), sold out of A. O'Brien's
stable 16,000 gns Newmarket Autumn Sales, successful in April: third in juvenile at
Newbury on hurdling debut. *Miss S. J. Wilton*

FIRST FLIGHT 8 br.g. Neltino – The Beginning (Goldhill) [2003/4 c–p, h–: c20d^3 c114
c22s^2 c24d^3 Feb 2] close-coupled gelding: fair maiden hurdler/chaser: stays 3m: acts on h–
soft going. *K. C. Bailey*

FIRSTFLOR 5 b.m. Alflora (IRE) – First Crack (Scallywag) [2003/4 F16f* F16m^3 F93
F16s^3 F16g^5 Mar 17] rather leggy mare: first foal: dam, fair hurdler, stayed 3m: fair form
in bumpers, won at Towcester on debut in October. *F. Jordan*

FIRST GOLD (FR) 11 b.g. Shafoun (FR) – Nuit d'Or II (FR) (Pot d'Or (FR)) c165
[2003/4 c171, h–: c25g^{pu} 19v^5 c24g^3 c26g^5 c25g^2 Apr 1] tall gelding: winning hurdler: h121 +
top-class chaser: placed behind Edredon Bleu in King George VI Chase at Kempton and
Tiutchev in Martell Cognac Cup at Aintree (has twice won race): also ran creditably
when attempting repeat win in Punchestown Heineken Gold Cup in Late-April, third to
impressive Beef Or Salmon: stays 29f: raced on good going or softer (acts on heavy):
blinkered over fences nowadays: sound-jumping front runner. *F. Doumen, France*

FIRST GREY 5 gr.m. Environment Friend – Myrtilla (Beldale Flutter (USA)) [2003/4 h73
F79: 16d 16s 16v 20d 20s Mar 20] tall, long-backed mare: poor maiden hurdler: raced
mainly around 2m, only on going softer than good. *E. W. Tuer*

FIRST HARMONY 5 ch.m. First Trump – Enchanting Melody (Chief Singer) [2003/4 F99
F16f* F16d* F16g^2 F16s^6 F17d Apr 3] workmanlike mare: fourth foal: half-sister to
7.5f winner Nunthorpe (by Mystiko) and 9f winner in Italy by Petoski: dam maiden,
should have stayed 1m: fairly useful form in bumpers: won at Hexham in September
and Wetherby (mares) in November: creditable efforts subsequently, seventh of 15 to
Diamond Sal in Grade 2 at Aintree: will stay beyond 17f. *M. Brittain*

FIRST LOVE 8 br.g. Bustino – First Romance (Royalty) [2003/4 c130+, h–: c24g* c113
c19g^{pu} c24d^{pu} Mar 13] good sort: fairly useful chaser: won intermediate at Perth in May: h–
off 8 months, poor efforts in handicaps at Ascot and Sandown (jumped none too fluently)
last 2 starts: stays 3m: raced on good going or softer (acts on heavy): free-going sort,
probably best allowed to stride on: usually sound jumper. *N. J. Henderson*

FIRST OFFICER (USA) 7 b.g. Lear Fan (USA) – Trampoli (USA) (Trempolino c88 d
(USA)) [2003/4 c83, h87: c26g* c24m^{pu} c26m^F c25g^2 c24g^{pu} c25d^{pu} c26g^{pu} Mar 10] h–
well-made gelding: modest maiden hurdler: modest chaser: won handicap at Southwell
in May: no form after: stays 3¼m: acts on good to soft and good to firm going: usually
blinkered, wore cheekpieces final start: has gone in snatches. *C. C. Bealby*

FIRST THOUGHT 6 b.m. Primitive Rising (USA) – Precis (Pitpan) [2003/4 F16m h68
F17m F16g 21s 24v^{pu} 19v^{pu} 19g 22g^6 Mar 25] second known foal: dam, out of smart F65
staying chaser Ottery News, won 17f hurdle: poor form in bumpers and novice hurdles:
should stay 3m. *O. J. Carter*

FIRST TRUTH 7 b.g. Rudimentary (USA) – Pursuit of Truth (USA) (Irish River h–
(FR)) [2003/4 h100: 16g Jun 6] smallish gelding: fair hurdler: off a year, below form only
start in 2003/4: raced around 2m on good going or softer (acts on soft). *Mrs H. Dalton*

FISHERMAN JACK 9 b.g. Carlingford Castle – Troublewithjack (Sulaafah (USA)) **c–**
[2003/4 c24s⁴ c25dᵖᵘ Mar 11] smallish gelding: winning pointer, including in March: no
form in 2 hunter chases. *John Burton*

FISHKI'S LAD 9 b.g. Casteddu – Fishki (Niniski (USA)) [2003/4 c–, h99: 24g⁶ 24m⁵ **c–**
23m* 22g⁵ 25f⁶ 24d⁵ Dec 1 /] leggy, lengthy gelding: modest handicap hurdler: won at **h97**
Haydock in October: stays 3m: acts on heavy and good to firm going: effective with or
without headgear: has looked ungenuine. *E. W. Tuer*

FITTLEWORTH (IRE) 4 gr.f. Bijou d'Inde – Remany (Bellypha) [2003/4 16m Oct **h–**
25] stocky filly: dam half-sister to useful 2m hurdler Lemhill: poor maiden on Flat (stays
11f): tailed off in juvenile maiden on hurdling debut. *W. G. M. Turner*

FITZ THE BILL (IRE) 4 b.f. Mon Tresor – In The Sky (IRE) (Imp Society (USA)) **h–**
[2003/4 16sᶠ 16s 16sᵖᵘ Mar 19] poor maiden on Flat: no form over hurdles. *N. B. King*

FIVE PENCE 8 b.g. Henbit (USA) – Le Saule d'Or (Sonnen Gold) [2003/4 h–: 16d² **h95**
20d² 20s 22g Apr 4] leggy gelding: maiden hurdler, runner-up in novices first 2 starts in
2003/4. *R. T. Phillips*

FIZZY POP 5 b.m. Robellino (USA) – Maria Isabella (FR) (Young Generation) [2003/4 **F–**
F17m F16d F16s Mar 13] half-sister to several winners, including fairly useful hurdler
around 2m Rain In Spain (by Unfuwain): dam, French maiden, half-sister to smart French
sprinter Titus Livius: showed more temperament than ability in bumpers: wore cheekpieces second start. *W. S. Cunningham*

FLAGSHIP UBERALLES (IRE) 10 br.g. Accordion – Fourth Degree (Oats) **c163**
[2003/4 c164, h–: c16g* c16d³ c16d² c16g² c20gᵖᵘ Apr 2] rangy gelding: high-class **h–**
chaser: left clear by departure of Moscow Flyer 2 out when winning Grade 1 BMW Chase
at Punchestown in April 2003: creditable placed efforts behind same horse in Tingle
Creek Chase at Sandown and Azertyuiop in Champion Chase at Cheltenham second and
fourth starts: form only at 2m: acts on soft going, below form all starts on good to firm:

Mr J. P. McManus' "Flagship Uberalles"

well held only run in blinkers: usually sound jumper: carries head high: none too consistent (tends to be best fresh). *P. J. Hobbs*

FLAHIVE'S FIRST   10 ch.g. Interrex (CAN) – Striking Image (IRE) (Flash of Steel) [2003/4 c90, h–: c16g² c17d* c16m² c20m² c21d³ c16d³ c17m* c16m³ c20m⁴ c19m² c16m² c16g² c16f⁴ c19d⁴ c16mᵖᵘ c16dᶠ 16d c16dᵖᵘ Apr 22] sparely-made gelding: winning hurdler: fair handicap chaser: last 4 wins at Cartmel, including in May and August: stays 21f: acts on soft and good to firm going. *D. Burchell*   **c109**
h–

FLAKE   4 ch.g. Zilzal (USA) – Impatiente (USA) (Vaguely Noble) [2003/4 16m³ 17d² 16d² 16s⁵ 16s Mar 20] smallish, close-coupled gelding: half-brother to 2¼m hurdle winner in France by Sadler's Wells: fair on Flat at 2 yrs, well held in 3 starts in 2003: progressive form when placed first 3 starts in juvenile hurdles: well held under more testing conditions last 2: will prove best with emphasis on speed at 2m: pulls hard. *Mrs S. J. Smith*   **h103**

FLAME CREEK (IRE)   8 b.g. Shardari – Sheila's Pet (IRE) (Welsh Term) [2003/4 h154: c17s* c20g* c16f* 16s⁴ 16d³ 16d⁶ Jan 25] tall, leggy gelding: failed to convince with jumping when easily landing odds in novice chases in small fields at Bangor and Wetherby in May and Kelso in October: smart hurdler: creditable efforts when fourth to Rigmarole in slowly-run Bula Hurdle at Cheltenham and third to Golden Cross in Grade 1 at Leopardstown: will prove at least as effective at 2½m as 2m: raced mainly on good going or softer (acts on heavy). *Noel T. Chance*   **c114 p**
h149

FLAMENCA (USA)   5 b.m. Diesis – Highland Ceilidh (IRE) (Scottish Reel) [2003/4 h81§: 16g 16m³ 16g 20m⁶ 21v 20gᵖᵘ Jan 23] sturdy mare: poor maiden hurdler: left R. Allan after fourth start: form only around 2m: acts on good to firm and good to soft going: sometimes visored/in cheekpieces: tongue tied final start: unreliable. *Mrs L. B. Normile*   **h76 §**

FLAME PHOENIX (USA)   5 b.g. Quest For Fame – Kingscote (Kings Lake (USA)) [2003/4 F16m* 16g 17s 16g⁵ Mar 7] sturdy gelding: closely related to Poule d'Essai des Poulains second Rainbow Corner (by Rainbow Quest) and half-brother to several winners, including smart 6f/7f performer Welcome Friend (by Kingmambo): dam won Lowther Stakes: bought unraced out of Mme C. Head-Maarek's stable 42,000 gns New-market Autumn Sales: won bumper at Ludlow on debut in May: best effort over hurdles when fifth of 17 to Lacdoudal in novice at Kempton: will prove best at 2m. *P. R. Webber*   **h107**
F97

FLAMING CHEEK   6 b.g. Blushing Flame (USA) – Rueful Lady (Streetfighter) [2003/4 h76, F83: 16g 17g³ 16g⁵ 16d* 20s⁶ 16s³ 16s³ 21m Apr 14] good-topped gelding: modest hurdler: won novice handicap at Fakenham in November: best effort when third at Towcester seventh outing: should stay beyond 2m: raced mainly on good going or softer (acts on soft). *A. G. Blackmore*   **h94**

FLAMING HECK   7 b.g. Dancing High – Heckley Spark (Electric) [2003/4 F70: 20s 18sᵖᵘ 20v⁴ 20s 16d³ Apr 22] poor novice hurdler: stays 2½m: acts on heavy going. *Mrs L. B. Normile*   **h83**

FLAMINION WAY (IRE)   8 br.g. Good Thyne (USA) – Rose Fointin VII (Damsire Unregistered) [2003/4 24s⁶ Jan 23] first foal: dam never ran: looked in need of experience when well held in maiden hurdle on debut. *Miss Venetia Williams*   **h–**

FLASHANT   9 ch.g. Henbit (USA) – La Furze (Winden) [2003/4 h–: c24g⁵ c23dᵖᵘ Apr 21] lengthy gelding: winning hurdler: no form for long time, including over fences: tried blinkered. *A. W. Carroll*   **c–**
h–

FLASH GORDON   10 ch.g. Gildoran – Florence May (Grange Melody) [2003/4 c93: c16m c20g* c19m² c20m³ c20mᵖᵘ Jul 13] tall gelding: fair handicap chaser, lightly raced: won at Bangor in May: probably stays easy 3m: acts on firm going: front runner. *Mrs S. Richardson*   **c106**

FLASH HENRY   7 b.g. Executive Perk – Running Valley (Buckskin (FR)) [2003/4 F16v 17sᵖᵘ Feb 6] fifth foal: dam of little account: no show in bumper or novice hurdle. *J. L. Needham*   **h–**
F–

FLAT STANLEY   5 b.g. Celtic Swing – Cool Grey (Absalom) [2003/4 h–: 17g May 26] modest maiden on Flat: showed nothing both starts over hurdles: placed in points in March. *R. Bastiman*   **h–**

FLAT TOP   13 b.g. Blakeney – New Edition (Great Nephew) [2003/4 c102, h–: c24dᵖᵘ c25g² c27g⁴ Apr 12] small, sturdy gelding: veteran chaser, several mistakes when 27 lengths second of 4 finishers to Lancastrian Jet in hunter at Market Rasen: stays 3¼m: acts on heavy going, probably on good to firm: blinkered once. *David M. Easterby*   **c85**
h–

Mr W. H. Ponsonby's "Fleet Street"

FLECTHEFAWNA (IRE) 8 b.g. Glacial Storm (USA) – Lady Sperrin (Abednego) **c86**
[2003/4 h91, F–: c24s⁶ c25d⁶ c24dᵘʳ c24d⁴ Feb 20] lengthy gelding: modest form only **h–**
start over hurdles: best effort over fences when fourth in novice handicap at Sandown:
stays 3m: acts on soft going. *L. A. Dace*

FLEET STREET 5 ch.g. Wolfhound (USA) – Farmer's Pet (Sharrood (USA)) **h140**
[2003/4 16m* 16d³ 17s* 16g³ 16g³ Apr 2] leggy gelding: half-brother to winning 2m
hurdlers Never Can Tell (by Emarati) and Tusk (by Fleetwood): fairly useful on Flat,
successful at 6.5f (at 2 yrs) and 7f in Germany for H-J. Groschel: useful hurdler: won
maiden at Stratford in October and novice at Taunton in January: best efforts in graded
events last 2 starts, running particularly well when 7 lengths third of 19 to Brave Inca in
Supreme Novices' Hurdle at Cheltenham: likely to prove best around 2m: acts on soft
and good to firm going. *N. J. Henderson*

FLEETWOOD FOREST 4 b.g. Fleetwood (IRE) – Louise Moillon (Mansingh **F90**
(USA)) [2003/4 F16m³ F16s Mar 20] 15,000 3-y-o: unfurnished gelding: half-brother to
several winners, including fair hurdler Tarra (by Batshoof), stays 3m: dam, 2-y-o 5f
winner/winning jumper, half-sister to smart staying hurdler Sporting Mariner: green, 2
lengths third of 18 to Cruising Clyde in bumper at Wincanton on debut: well held under
much more testing conditions at Ascot. *A. King*

FLEMMING (USA) 7 ch.g. Green Dancer (USA) – La Groupie (FR) (Groom Dancer **h–**
(USA)) [2003/4 h–: 20d 21m 26s Jan 7] no form over hurdles: tried in headgear/tongue
strap: sold £1,000 Ascot February Sales. *A. G. Juckes*

FLEURENKA 6 br.m. Alflora (IRE) – Tochenka (Fine Blue) [2003/4 F16s F16d **F–**
Apr 21] third foal: dam fairly useful staying chaser: showed nothing in 2 bumpers.
D. G. Bridgwater

FLICK EM OFF 4 b.f. Turtle Island (IRE) – Spark (IRE) (Flash of Steel) [2003/4   **F–**
F13v F16d Apr 21] fourth foal: dam, 2-y-o 6f winner, stayed 10.4f: showed nothing in 2
bumpers: trained on debut by J. Pickering. *J. M. Bradley*

FLIGHT COMMAND 6 ch.g. Gunner B – Wing On (Quayside) [2003/4 F103p: **h105**
F16s⁶ 18s³ 20v⁴ 20d⁵ 22g² 20s² Apr 17] big, good-topped gelding: chasing sort: bumper   **F86**
winner: fair novice hurdler: will stay 3m: raced on good going or softer (acts on soft).
P. Beaumont

FLIGHT TO TUSCANY 6 b.m. Bonny Scot (IRE) – Tuscan Butterfly (Beldale   **h–**
Flutter (USA)) [2003/4 h–: 16m 20m⁵ 18m⁶ Sep 23] poor maiden on Flat: well held over
hurdles: tried blinkered/in cheekpieces: sold 2,900 gns Doncaster October Sales.
J. M. Bradley

FLIGHT WEST (IRE) 5 gr.g. Norwich – Bee In The Rose (IRE) (Roselier (FR))   **F90**
[2003/4 F16dʳᵒ F16v F17s Feb 10] good-topped gelding: second foal: dam unraced
half-sister to useful staying chaser Stay On Tracks: in narrow lead when hanging left and
running out early in straight in bumper at Catterick on debut: well held both subsequent
starts. *J. Wade*

FLIGHTY LEADER (IRE) 12 b.g. Supreme Leader – Flighty Ann (The Parson)   **c–**
[2003/4 c–, h–: 24mᵖᵘ 24g 20g⁵ 20m⁴ Jun 20] smallish, lengthy gelding: bad hurdler: **h61**
stays 3¼m: acts on good to firm and heavy going: visored in 2003/4: has looked reluctant.
P. Spottiswood

FLINDERS 9 b.m. Henbit (USA) – Stupid Cupid (Idiot's Delight) [2003/4 c78, h–:   **c82**
c25gᵖᵘ c24m⁴ c25m⁴ c24d* c25d³ c26vꟳ c25dᵖᵘ c25g c26g* Apr 22] leggy mare: poor   **h–**
handicap chaser: won at Fakenham in November and Fontwell (made all) in April: stays
3¼m: acts on firm and good to soft going: inconsistent. *R. Rowe*

FLINDERS CHASE 9 gr.g. Terimon – Proverbial Rose (Proverb) [2003/4 c102§, h–:   **c119**
c17g* c18g³ c20s² c18sᵘʳ c21d⁴ c20d* c16dᵖᵘ c21g⁴ Apr 22] workmanlike gelding: fairly   **h–**
useful chaser: improved in 2003/4, won novice handicap at Exeter in November and
4-runner novice at Sandown in February: 66/1, ran well when 2½ lengths fourth of 14
finishers to Cassia Heights in Topham Chase (Handicap) at Aintree final start: has form
up to 3m: raced on good going or softer (acts on heavy): consistent. *C. J. Mann*

FLITE OF ARABY 7 b.g. Green Desert (USA) – Allegedly Blue (USA) (Alleged   **c–**
(USA)) [2003/4 h–: 16gᵖᵘ c16gᴿ 17m Oct 2] sturdy gelding: no form over jumps: left   **h–**
N. Hawke after second start. *R. J. Price*

FLOOD'S FANCY 11 gr.m. Then Again – Port Na Blath (On Your Mark) [2003/4 h–:   **h–**
24sᵖᵘ May 2] sparely-made mare: of little account nowadays: tried blinkered/tongue tied.
B. R. Foster

FLORA MUCK 8 b.m. Alflora (IRE) – Muckertoo (Sagaro) [2003/4 c–, h79: c25m³   **c76 x**
c26m* c25f² c24g³ c25vꟳ c22s³ c25sᵘʳ Apr 11] tall mare: poor hurdler/chaser: raced   **h–**
exclusively over fences in 2003/4, won conditional jockeys handicap at Uttoxeter in
October: best at 3m+: acts on heavy and good to firm going: often let down by jumping.
N. A. Twiston-Davies

FLORANZ 8 br.m. Afzal – Tuesday Member (New Member) [2003/4 20sᵖᵘ 22m³   **h67**
22gᵖᵘ 19g³ 22g⁴ Oct 5] poor maiden hurdler: stays 2¾m: acts on good to firm going.
Mrs M. Evans

FLORA POSTE 8 ch.m. Alflora (IRE) – Preachers Popsy (The Parson) [2003/4 h–:   **c–**
22dᵖᵘ c20mᶜᵒ c25dᵘʳ c24g⁶ Apr 16] sturdy mare: of little account. *J. C. Tuck*   **h–**

FLORENZAR (IRE) 6 b.m. Inzar (USA) – Nurse Tyra (USA) (Dr Blum (USA))   **h65**
[2003/4 h–: 16m³ 16gᵘʳ 16sᵖᵘ 19g⁶ 16dᵖᵘ Apr 8] angular mare: modest maiden on Flat
(stays 11.5f), claimed from Miss S. West £6,000 in August: form over hurdles only when
third in seller at Ludlow: visored after. *P. D. Evans*

FLORIDA COAST (IRE) 9 b.g. Florida Son – Deep Peace (Deep Run) [2003/4   **h136**
h121?: 18d² 20d 22d² 24d³ 20d² 20s³ 24dᵖᵘ 22d* Feb 28] smallish, sturdy gelding: useful
hurdler: easily landed odds in 5-runner minor event at Fairyhouse, making virtually all:
placed behind stable-companion Solerina in Hatton's Grace Hurdle at Fairyhouse and
Grade 3 at Navan fifth and sixth starts: placed twice on Flat prior to creditable sixth to
Rhinestone Cowboy in Grade 1 at Punchestown in late-April: best at 2½m+: acts on
heavy going. *James Bowe, Ireland*

FLORIDA DREAM (IRE) 5 b.g. Florida Son – Ice Pearl (Flatbush) [2003/4 F16d   **h75**
F16s 16g 17s Apr 6] €100,000 4-y-o: well-made gelding: eighth foal: brother to top-class   **F–**
staying chaser Florida Pearl: dam unraced, out of half-sister to useful staying chaser

Iceman: signs of ability only when seventh in maiden at Huntingdon on hurdling debut.
Ms Bridget Nicholls

FLORIDA (IRE)   6 b.m. Sri Pekan (USA) – Florinda (CAN) (Vice Regent (CAN))   h58 §
[2003/4 h–: 21m⁴ 19f² Oct 16] poor on Flat (stays 2m): bad hurdler: looked far from keen
when second in very weak selling handicap at Towcester. *I. A. Wood*

FLORIDA PEARL (IRE)   12 b.g. Florida Son – Ice Pearl (Flatbush) [2003/4   c168
c156: c25g⁵ c17s* c24d* Feb 8]
        It proved to be his swansong, and it was a glorious one rather than a lament.
Florida Pearl returned unexpectedly in the New Year to add two further graded
successes to his impressive tally, including an unprecedented fourth win in the
Hennessy Cognac Gold Cup at Leopardstown. For the sixth season in seven over
fences he showed top-class form and, while a setback ruled him out of a seventh
consecutive appearance at the Cheltenham Festival, his connections did not call
time on his illustrious career until well after the season was over (he was reported
in April as a possible for Punchestown, though failed to meet the engagement). As
he had looked just about as good as ever when winning at Leopardstown, there had
seemed some grounds for optimism that he could be back on the racecourse later in
the year for one last hurrah. But he was officially retired at the end of July, making
a final appearance before racing on Galway Hurdle day.
        Florida Pearl's return in January, for his first outing since trailing home in
the Punchestown Gold Cup the previous April, was unexpected for two reasons: it
came after a setback in the autumn had been reported as likely to keep him out till
the spring and it came over two miles and a furlong, a trip around a mile short of
the distances of the vast majority of his races over fences. The Grade 3 Normans
Grove Chase at Fairyhouse featured only one chaser near the merit of Florida Pearl,
another not noted for his performances at two miles, Rince Ri, and they held sway
over the specialists in the field, Florida Pearl giving his rivals a jumping lesson out
in front and showing all the old zest which had been missing from his performances
the previous season. He beat Rince Ri two lengths but the proximity of others meant
the form wasn't much better than the best of his efforts in the 2002/3 campaign, so,
for all the style of the performance, when he lined up at Leopardstown three weeks
later he still had quite a bit to prove. So much so, that he started at longer odds
than Rince Ri, fourth favourite in a field of seven at 5/1, behind the favourite Le
Coudray, runner-up to Best Mate in the Ericsson, and the Cheltenham Gold Cup
third Harbour Pilot, making his return to fences, as well as Rince Ri. Florida Pearl
was only a point shorter than the smart handicapper Cloudy Bays, who was taking
a big step up in class. As at Fairyhouse, Florida Pearl's excellent jumping laid the

Normans Grove Chase, Fairyhouse—an exhibition round from Florida Pearl back over a shorter trip

Hennessy Cognac Gold Cup, Leopardstown—
Florida Pearl evades the riderless Harbour Pilot for an historic fourth win in this race

foundations for his performance, a particularly fine leap three out taking him clear with Harbour Pilot after he had travelled strongly and gone on at the twelfth. A close race looked on the cards, with the pair still on the bridle, when Harbour Pilot lost his rider two out. That left Florida Pearl clear and, after being six lengths up when impeded by the riderless horse at the last fence, he was ridden out to defeat Le Coudray by three lengths with Rince Ri a further six back in third. It is impossible to say with confidence what the result would have been had Harbour Pilot completed and it's a pity the pair weren't able to meet again at Cheltenham. At both Fairyhouse and Leopardstown, Florida Pearl was given considerable assistance from Richard Johnson, who had last been on board during the 2000/1 season. Johnson rode Florida Pearl as well as any of the top jockeys who have partnered him in his long career, though Adrian Maguire rode a fine race on him, never having sat on the horse before, to win the 2001 King George VI Chase at Kempton.

Florida Pearl (IRE) (b.g. 1992)	Florida Son (b 1979)	Busted (b 1963)	Crepello / Sans Le Sou
		Peach Stone (b 1968)	Mourne / La Melba
	Ice Pearl (b 1984)	Flatbush (b 1963)	Dumbarnie / Golden Pride
		Ice Blossom (b 1969)	Spartan General / Arctic Pearl

The strong, well-made Florida Pearl has been one of the finest Irish-trained chasers of the last thirty years, as well as just about the most durable, even if his failure to win the Cheltenham Gold Cup—he had Festival wins in the Champion Bumper and the Royal & SunAlliance Chase—unfairly prejudiced some against him. He stayed three and a quarter miles and acted on heavy going, though less testing conditions probably suited him ideally during the latter part of his career. His pedigree has been fully covered in previous Annuals, though a brother and sister made their debuts during the latest campaign: the €100,000-purchase Florida Dream showed signs of only a little ability for Bridget Nicholls, while the topically-named 2000 filly Florida Recount finished last of twenty-eight finishers in a bumper at the 2004 Punchestown Festival. *W. P. Mullins, Ireland*

FLORIDA RAIN (IRE) 8 b.g. Florida Son – Ameretto (Stetchworth (USA)) [2003/4   **h102 +** h111p: 16d[6] Dec 6] big, rangy gelding: lightly raced: won novice hurdle in 2002/3:

shaped much better than distance beaten suggests in handicap at Wetherby only subsequent outing: will be suited by 2½m+: capable of better, though clearly difficult to train. *Mrs M. Reveley*

FLORRIES SON   9 b.g. Minster Son – Florrie Palmer (Deadly Nightshade) [2003/4 **c108** h121: c20g* c25gF c24m² c25gF c20v* c20s⁵ c16s⁴ Apr 4] tall gelding: fairly useful **h–** hurdler: won novice at Hexham impressively on chasing debut very early in season: generally let down by jumping/went as if amiss subsequently, left with very simple task in novice at Newcastle in February: stays 25f: acts on good to firm going, probably on heavy. *M. Todhunter*

FLOWER BREEZE (USA)   4 ch.f. Rahy (USA) – Now Showing (USA) (Golden **h70** Act (USA)) [2003/4 17g⁶ Aug 8] modest maiden on Flat, sold out of M. Channon's stable 6,500 gns Newmarket Autumn Sales: poor form on hurdling debut. *M. W. Easterby*

FLOWER OF PITCUR   7 b.g. Alflora (IRE) – Coire Vannich (Celtic Cone) [2003/4 **h97** F93: 20gᵖᵘ 19s⁶ 19d⁴ 17d* 19g 16g⁴ Mar 25] angular gelding: bumper winner: modest hurdler: won novice handicap at Hereford in February: will prove best around 2m. *T. R. George*

FLOWING RIVER (IRE)   6 ch.g. Over The River (FR) – Minature Miss (Move **F75** Off) [2003/4 F16d⁶ F16d Feb 8] ninth foal: half-brother to fair hurdler The Mickletonian (by K-Battery), stayed 21f: dam, winning hurdler, stayed 3¼m: poor form in bumpers: bred to need much greater test of stamina. *D. Eddy*

FLOWNAWAY   5 b.g. Polar Falcon (USA) – No More Rosies (Warpath) [2003/4 16gF **h104 p** 17d* Apr 10] half-brother to several winners over jumps, including useful chasers at 2½m+ Beachy Head (by Damister) and Eau de Cologne (by Persian Bold) and fairly useful hurdler up to 2½m Only A Rose (by Glint of Gold): useful on Flat (stays 2m), successful 3 times in 2003 for W. Jarvis: odds on both starts in novice hurdles, would have won at Musselburgh (jumped right) but for falling 2 out and beat Dr Sharp hard held by 2 lengths having pulled hard at Carlisle 3 months later: will stay beyond 17f: open to plenty of improvement. *J. Howard Johnson*

FLUFF 'N' PUFF   10 ch.g. Nicholas Bill – Puff Puff (All Systems Go) [2003/4 c95, **c89** h–: c16m⁴ c21g⁴ c21d⁴ c24g² c20d² c20s* c24m³ c24d⁴ Mar 15] strong gelding: modest **h–** handicap chaser: won 18-runner event at Huntingdon in February, coaxed home after travelling best: poor efforts both subsequent starts: stays 3m: acts on good to firm and heavy going: blinkered once, wore cheekpieces last 4 starts: usually races prominently. *J. S. King*

FLUR NA H ALBA   5 b.g. Atraf – Tyrian Belle (Enchantment) [2003/4 16g Mar 10] **h–** strong gelding: fairly useful but unreliable on Flat (stays 1m) for I. Semple: jumped poorly when tailed off on hurdling debut. *J. M. Jefferson*

FLURRY   5 gr.m. Terimon – Queen's Favourite (Sunyboy) [2003/4 F16g Mar 7] 3,500 **F–** 4-y-o: angular mare: fourth foal: dam no sign of ability: backward, showed little in bumper on debut. *C. J. Down*

FLYAWAY ROSE   4 b.f. Busy Flight – Flaming Rose (IRE) (Roselier (FR)) [2003/4 **F–** F18g Apr 22] third foal: half-sister to winning 2½m hurdler Megalex (by Karinga Bay): dam no sign of ability: well held in bumper on debut. *Miss I. E. Craig*

FLYING BOLD (IRE)   9 ch.g. Persian Bold – Princess Reema (USA) (Affirmed **h–** (USA)) [2003/4 h76: 22m May 29] angular gelding: poor hurdler: stays 2¾m: acts on any going: tried blinkered: has looked difficult ride. *N. G. Ayliffe*

FLYING DRUID (FR)   4 b.g. Celtic Swing – Sky Bibi (FR) (Sky Lawyer (FR)) **F86** [2003/4 F16d³ Mar 19] seventh foal: half-brother to 3 winners, including winning hurdler/fairly useful chaser Sky Warrior (by Warrshan), stays 21f: dam maiden: 66/1, 2½ lengths third of 19 to Real Definition in maiden bumper at Warwick on debut. *Evan Williams*

FLYING FALCON   5 b.g. Polar Falcon (USA) – Lemon Balm (High Top) [2003/4 **F105** F17g³ F16s⁶ F16m* F14d* F17d Apr 3] good-topped gelding: half-brother to 3 winners, including 1994 2-y-o 7f winner Quintus Decimus (by Nordico): dam, showed a little ability over hurdles, out of half-sister to useful 2m hurdler The Clown: made all in bumpers at Wincanton and Hereford in March, useful performance when beating Dads Gift 26 lengths at latter: well held in Grade 2 at Aintree. *Miss Venetia Williams*

FLYING FIDDLER (IRE)   13 ch.g. Orchestra – Rambling Ivy (Mandalus) [2003/4 **c–** 21mᵖᵘ May 10] angular gelding: lightly raced over fences: modest handicap hurdler in **h–** 1999/00: lame only second outing since: usually blinkered. *Mrs L. P. Baker*

FLYING FIRST (IRE) 9 b.g. Executive Perk – Rule The Waves (Deep Run) [2003/4 **h–**
h–: 16mᵖᵘ 16m May 26] lengthy, shallow-girthed gelding: no form over hurdles.
T. D. McCarthy

FLYING FUSELIER 5 ch.g. Gunner B – Wing On (Quayside) [2003/4 F16g Mar **F–**
27] 40,000 4-y-o: sturdy gelding: brother to useful 2m jumper Crack On and half-brother
to several other winners, including fairly useful 2m hurdler/chaser Captain Khedive (by
Deep Run) and fair staying hurdler Richmond Lady (by Broadsword): dam never ran:
well held in bumper on debut. *P. J. Hobbs*

FLYING INSTRUCTOR 14 gr.g. Neltino – Flying Mistress (Lear Jet) [2003/4 c20m⁵ **c131**
c23mᵖᵘ c26m³ c23m* Aug 8] workmanlike gelding: has had wind operation: missed **h–**
2002/3: still a useful handicap chaser, won 4-runner event at Worcester: stays 3¼m when
conditions aren't testing: acts on any going: races prominently: jumps soundly: genuine.
P. R. Webber

FLYING LYRIC (IRE) 6 b.g. Definite Article – Lyric Junction (IRE) (Classic Secret **h94**
(USA)) [2003/4 16m 20s⁴ 16d³ 17d Jan 24] leggy gelding: fairly useful on Flat (probably
stays 2m) at 3 yrs for S. Woods: modest form in novice hurdles: stays 2½m. *A. King*

FLYING SPIRIT (IRE) 5 b.g. Flying Spur (AUS) – All Laughter (Vision (USA)) **h119**
[2003/4 h76: 18f* 19m² 18mᵘʳ 16m* 16m² Oct 29] fair on Flat (stays 1½m): fairly useful
hurdler: won novices at Fontwell in August and Plumpton (odds on) in September: no
match for Albuhera when good second in handicap at Cheltenham final start: stays 19f:
acts on firm going. *G. L. Moore*

FLYING TRIX (IRE) 8 b.g. Lord Americo – Bannow Drive (IRE) (Miner's Lamp) **c100**
[2003/4 c22vᵖᵘ c20s c23g⁵ c24g* c26m* Apr 14] sturdy gelding: fair chaser, off nearly 2 **h–**
years before reappearance: won handicaps at Kempton (novice) in March and Cheltenham (beat Midnight Gunner ½ length): stays 3¼m: acts on good to firm and heavy going:
not a straightforward ride. *M. Pitman*

FLYING WANDA 4 b.f. Alzao (USA) – Royal York (Bustino) [2003/4 16s⁴ 16gᵘʳ 16g **h75**
Mar 5] smallish filly: useful on Flat (stays 1¾m) for J. Noseda: only poor form over
hurdles, not impressing with jumping or attitude. *P. F. Nicholls*

FLY KICKER 7 ch.g. High Kicker (USA) – Double Birthday (Cavo Doro) [2003/4 **h97**
h67: 16m 16g² 16g 16g² 17g³ 16f² 16g 17g⁴ 16m* 16g* 17d⁵ Nov 25] modest hurdler:
won handicaps at Wetherby in October (intermediate) and November (novice): best
around 2m: acts on firm going: wears cheekpieces. *W. Storey*

FLYOFF (IRE) 7 b.g. Mtoto – Flyleaf (FR) (Persian Bold) [2003/4 h–: 16m⁴ 16g 16d⁴ **h71 §**
20d 16s⁶ 16g 16gᵖᵘ Feb 20] smallish gelding: modest on Flat (stays 1½m), won twice in
2003: poor maiden hurdler, reluctant at start last 2 outings: raced mainly around 2m: acts
on good to firm and good to soft going: wore eyeshields on reappearance, visored after:
best left alone. *K. A. Morgan*

FLYOVER 7 b.m. Presidium – Flash-By (Ilium) [2003/4 h66: 16d³ 16m⁴ 24m⁶ Jul 9] **h66**
poor maiden hurdler: raced mainly around 2m: acts on good to firm and good to soft
going. *J. C. Fox*

FNAN 8 b.g. Generous (IRE) – Rafha (Kris) [2003/4 c115, h131+: 24g⁴ c22sᵖᵘ c23m* **c122**
c23g c22s c20f⁴ c22d⁶ Sep 10] small, strong gelding: useful hurdler: fairly useful handi- **h131**
cap chaser: won at Tipperary in July by 3½ lengths from Goldstreet: stays easy 3m: acts
on firm and good to soft going: effective tongue tied or not. *N. Meade, Ireland*

FOLLOW THE BEAR 6 ch.g. Weld – Run Lady Run (General Ironside) [2003/4 **F88**
F16g F16g⁵ Mar 27] tall gelding: chasing type: sixth foal: half-brother to winning pointer
by Roselier: dam placed in points: better effort in bumpers when fifth of 18 to River
Trapper at Newbury: hung left on bends at Huntingdon on debut: likely to stay well.
D. R. Gandolfo

FOLLOW THE FLOW (IRE) 8 ch.g. Over The River (FR) – October Lady (Lucifer **c90 d**
(USA)) [2003/4 c–: c26v⁵ c26v³ c26d² c25d⁴ c25v⁵ᵈ c25d c26s c25sᵘʳ c29d⁶ c25s² c25sᵘʳ
c26g⁵ Apr 12] lengthy gelding: modest maiden chaser, well below form after fourth start:
suited by 3m+: acts on heavy going: races prominently. *P. A. Pritchard*

FOLLOW THE TREND (IRE) 10 br.g. Beau Sher – Newgate Princess (Prince **c84 §**
Regent (FR)) [2003/4 c94, h–: c20sᵖᵘ c20sᵖᵘ c21d² c21s³ c25dᵖᵘ c24d³ c19s⁴ c26gᵖᵘ Apr **h–**
12] smallish gelding: poor chaser: barely stays 3m: acts on heavy going, possibly not on
good to firm: tried blinkered, wears cheekpieces/visor nowadays: usually races prominently: not to be trusted. *Miss A. M. Newton-Smith*

FOLLY ROAD (IRE) 14 b.g. Mister Lord (USA) – Lady Can (Cantab) [2003/4 **c– §**
c95§, h–§: c29d Mar 19] big, rangy gelding: fair hunter chaser in 2002/3: unseated in **h– §**

point in January, tailed off back in handicap: acts on heavy and good to firm going: successful with or without visor, also tried in blinkers/cheekpieces: not one to trust. *D. L. Williams*

FOLY PLEASANT (FR) 10 ch.g. Vaguely Pleasant (FR) – Jeffologie (FR) (Jefferson) **c148**
[2003/4 c158, h–: c20s^{pu} c21d^3 20v 20s* 21g Mar 17] sturdy gelding: smart chaser, raced **h124**
mainly at Cheltenham since 2000/1: creditable third to Whereareyounow in fairly
valuable event there in January: fairly useful handicap hurdler: won 16-runner event at
Haydock in February, staying on well to beat Master Ride 1¾ lengths: barely stays 25f
under testing conditions: acts on heavy and good to firm going: tongue tied: edgy sort:
sound jumper: genuine: sold to join Miss K. Marks 100,000 gns Doncaster May Sales.
Miss H. C. Knight

FONDMORT (FR) 8 b.g. Cyborg (FR) – Hansie (FR) (Sukawa (FR)) [2003/4 **c161**
c154, h–: c20g* c24g^4 c19s^{F5} c20g^3 c25g^4 c21m^F Apr 14] **h–**
    Nicky Henderson proved to be in a league of his own in the latest season
when it came to winning those big handicaps which illuminate Saturdays throughout the winter months. Fondmort set the ball rolling in the Paddy Power Gold Cup,
a race known as the Thomas Pink Gold Cup in the three previous seasons; and his
victory was followed by those of Iris Royal in the First National Gold Cup and
Tripleprint Gold Cup, Isio in the Victor Chandler Chase and Vodafone Gold Cup,
Geos in the Tote Gold Trophy and Marlborough in the Racing Post Chase. It is
worth mentioning that Henderson's success in big Saturday races wasn't restricted
to the jumps season, either. From a handful of runners on the Flat in 2003, Henderson won the Cesarewitch with the very smart hurdler Landing Light, an unfortunate
absentee in the latest jumps season after injuring a tendon.
    Fondmort made his reappearance in the Paddy Power Gold Cup over two
and a half miles at Cheltenham, a course where he had run his three best races the
previous season, winning the Tripleprint Gold Cup and finishing second in both the
Mildmay of Flete and the Silver Trophy Chase. The last two races had been won by

Paddy Power Gold Cup Chase (Handicap), Cheltenham—
a second big handicap win at the track for Fondmort, who pulls clear of the ill-fated Poliantas

Mr W. J. Brown's "Fondmort"

Young Spartacus and Poliantas respectively, and this pair were two of just eight who lined up against Fondmort in the Paddy Power, a race which usually attracts a double-figure field. Cyfor Malta, who had won the race twice, including in the previous season when chased home by Poliantas, was also in opposition, set to carry top weight. He and It Takes Time were attempting to give their trainer Martin Pipe a fourth consecutive victory in the contest. Fondmort started favourite at 3/1, with Poliantas at 7/2 and It Takes Time at 4/1 next in the betting. As expected, the complete outsider Ei Ei set a good pace, though he was ignored to some degree and held the lead until after four out, where Poliantas went on. By this time the patiently-ridden Fondmort had moved into third, still travelling well, and he was one of six still in contention going to the next. That had been reduced to just two at the second last, where Fondmort joined Poliantas in the lead and both It Takes Time and sole Irish challenger Risk Accessor, who was travelling at least as well as the winner, fell, hampering Young Spartacus who looked held and leaving the weakening Ei Ei in a remote third. Fondmort soon took the measure of Poliantas and ran on well to win by eight lengths from that horse, who sadly collapsed and died after the race.

Fondmort's connections might have been expected to go for a second Tripleprint Gold Cup, but they passed that over in favour of a tilt at the King George VI Chase even though Fondmort faced a much stiffer task taking on some high-class performers at level weights over a trip, three miles, which he had seemed not to stay on his only previous attempt. In finishing fourth to Edredon Bleu, beaten seven and a quarter lengths, Fondmort ran up to his best though he gave the impression that he didn't quite get home, fading before the last. Fondmort also finished fourth, running a bit below form, in the twenty-five furlong Martell Cup at Aintree in April, though his performance in that suggested he might not have recovered fully from his exertions in the Mildmay of Flete at Cheltenham just over two weeks earlier, when a good third to Tikram. On both of his other starts in the latest season, Fondmort was let down by his jumping. In the Grade 1 Ascot Chase he was held in third when falling at the last; and in the Silver Trophy at Cheltenham on his final outing he fell two out when looking set to finish no better than fourth.

		Arctic Tern	Sea Bird II
	Cyborg (FR)	(ch 1973)	Bubbling Beauty
	(ch 1982)	Cadair	Sadair
Fondmort (FR)		(b 1970)	Blarney Castle
(b.g. 1996)		Sukawa	Sodium
	Hansie (FR)	(br 1969)	Serge de Nimes
	(b 1985)	Hobanty	Hauban
		(b 1970)	Hayati

The rather leggy Fondmort is the fifth reported foal of Hansie, her only other one to have raced being Pinceloup (by Mont Basile) who has been placed over hurdles in France. Hansie won an amateur riders' race in the Provinces over a mile and three quarters and is out of a half-sister to Ex-Libris, winner of the Group 2 Prix du Conseil Municipal at Longchamp. Fondmort, who acts on good to firm and heavy going, was tried in blinkers over hurdles in France, where he began his career in the 1999/00 season. He ended the latest season running off a mark 11 lb higher than the one he started on, and is going to find it difficult if attempting to win either the Paddy Power or the Tripleprint again. At least there will be a suitable non-handicap race for him at the next Cheltenham Festival, with a two-and-a-half-mile conditions chase one of those due to be added to the programme when the meeting expands to four days. *N. J. Henderson*

FONTANESI (IRE)   4 b.g. Sadler's Wells (USA) – Northern Script (USA) (Arts And Letters (USA)) [2003/4 17g* 16g³ 21g 18d* 17g* Apr 16] smallish, sparely-made gelding: brother to fair hurdlers Columbus, stays 25f, and Legible, stays 2½m: twice-raced on Flat, fairly useful form when winning 1¼m maiden in May, left A. O'Brien and gelded: fairly useful hurdler: won maiden at Taunton in February and novice at Fontwell (beat Croix de Guerre by length) and juvenile at Taunton (travelled better in visor first time) in April: should stay 2½m: raced on good/good to soft ground. *M. C. Pipe*   **h115**

FOOL ON THE HILL   7 b.g. Reprimand – Stock Hill Lass (Air Trooper) [2003/4 16d² 16d² 17s⁵ 16m* 16g² 16g⁴ Apr 2] rather leggy gelding: fairly useful on Flat (stays 1½m), sold out of L. G. Cottrell's stable 20,000 gns Doncaster November Sales: fairly useful novice hurdler: won at Wincanton in February by neck from Bourbon Manhattan: good 6 lengths fourth of 12 to Royal Shakespeare in Grade 2 at Aintree: raced around 2m: acts on good to firm and good to soft going (none too fluent and showed signs of temperament on soft). *P. J. Hobbs*   **h129**

FOOTBALL CRAZY (IRE)   5 b.g. Mujadil (USA) – Schonbein (IRE) (Persian Heights) [2003/4 h68p: 16d² 17s⁴ 16m⁴ 19m² 19g⁴ Apr 13] sturdy, lengthy gelding: useful on Flat (stays 1½m), sold out of S. Gollings' stable 11,000 gns Doncaster November Sales: fair novice hurdler: stays 19f: acts on good to firm going: usually wears cheekpieces/blinkers: has looked hard ride. *P. Bowen*   **h113**

FORAGER   5 ch.g. Faustus (USA) – Jolimo (Fortissimo) [2003/4 F16m* May 26] angular gelding: half-brother to several winning hurdlers, notably very smart 2-miler Osric (by Radetzky): dam won from 1½m to 2¼m: won bumper at Huntingdon on debut by 1¾ lengths from Without A Doubt. *M. J. Ryan*   **F93**

FORBEARING (IRE)   7 b.g. Bering – For Example (USA) (Northern Baby (CAN)) [2003/4 16d³ 16d⁴ 25sᵖᵘ 17s* 16d⁴ 17d 16s* 16g* 16g 19g 16g Apr 16] angular gelding: fairly useful on Flat (stays 1½m), claimed from Sir Mark Prescott £15,000 in August: fair handicap hurdler: won at Taunton in December, Leicester in February and Chepstow in March: best around 2m: acts on soft going: visored last 5 outings: takes good hold. *M. C. Pipe*   **h105**

FORCE TWELVE (IRE)   6 b.g. Magical Wonder (USA) – Gale Force Nine (Strong Gale) [2003/4 16g 22m 22d⁶ 20f³ 18g c21d⁵ c20g² c26d³ Dec 31] €12,000 4-y-o: fourth foal: dam, lightly raced on Flat, half-sister to dam of useful staying chaser Sister Stephanie and useful hurdler who stayed 3m The Carrig Rua: little form over hurdles: **c71**
  h56

poor form when placed over fences, jumped poorly and went with little zest in blinkers on first occasion: stays 3¼m: wore cheekpieces third start. *P. R. Hedger*

FORDINGBRIDGE (USA)   4 b.g. Diesis – Souffle (Zafonic (USA)) [2003/4 F16g⁶   **F88**
F16g Mar 27] angular gelding: first foal: dam, useful stayer on Flat, half-sister to very smart performer up to 1½m Grape Tree Road and smart stayers Red Route and Windsor Castle: looked a stayer when never-nearer sixth of 21 to Spirit of New York, easily better effort in bumpers at Newbury. *P. J. Hobbs*

FOREMAN (GER)   6 ch.g. Monsun (GER) – Fleurie (GER) (Dashing Blade)   **h155**
[2003/4 h143: 18s* 19sᶠ 16g⁴ 16d* 16g⁴ 20d Apr 3]
Foreman provided owner J. P. McManus with his sixth win in the AIG Europe Champion Hurdle in the last seven years, following Istabraq's domination of the race from 1998 to 2001 and Like-A-Butterfly's victory over Limestone Lad in a thrilling finish in 2003. Although Ireland's most prestigious hurdling prize, the 2004 edition featured none of the leading contenders for the Champion Hurdle at Cheltenham, and an unsatisfactory affair failed to strengthen the Champion Hurdle claims of those (all bar outsider Georges Girl) who held an entry at Cheltenham. Foreman had run well on his previous outing, blinkered for the first time, when fourth behind Intersky Falcon, Rooster Booster and Sporazene in the Christmas Hurdle at Kempton, though he had looked in need of more of a test of stamina. Davenport Milenium had also run in Britain last time out, finishing second in the Bula at Cheltenham, while the three others ahead of Foreman in the Leopardstown betting has fought out the finish at long odds in the December Festival Hurdle at the track's Christmas meeting, on that occasion Golden Cross beating Spirit Leader (sent off favourite this time) and British-trained Flame Creek. In a tactical affair which saw the field of eight still tightly grouped rounding the home turn, it was J. P. McManus' other runner Fota Island who was still in front jumping the last, but he was soon headed as Foreman came from just off the pace to get the better of the patiently-ridden Georges Girl, holding on for firm handling to win by a head. Fota Island was a length and a half back in third, just ahead of Spirit Leader and Davenport Milenium.
Foreman was sent on to Cheltenham for the Champion Hurdle where he went off the fourth favourite, having been well backed down to 10/1. He ran another good race, improving a little on his Leopardstown form, and kept on to be beaten just over ten lengths into fourth behind Hardy Eustace. He had filled the same position (after being promoted a place) behind the same rival in the Royal & SunAlliance Novices' Hurdle at the Festival twelve months earlier. The return to further in the Aintree Hurdle for his next start had looked likely to suit Foreman, but he ran below his best in seventh in another muddling race, getting caught out when the pace finally quickened in the straight.
Foreman's last four starts (he was blinkered for each of them) showed he was up to taking on the best hurdlers in the British Isles, crowning an interesting career which started in Germany with Christian von Der Recke. He showed useful form on the Flat, being placed in listed races, beaten a short head in the Austrian Derby, and even contesting the Group 1 Grosser Preis von Baden. Over hurdles, Foreman made a successful debut under Tony McCoy as a four-year-old when sent over for a maiden at Folkestone, though it was a more important contest for Foreman than might be imagined, as it effectively decided his future over hurdles. 'I offered Foreman to Martin Pipe before he won at Folkestone,' explained von Der Recke, 'but Tony McCoy didn't like him. So I brought him back to Germany, Thierry Doumen came here, fell in love with the horse and took him home for the same price.' At this stage, Thierry Doumen was associated with Foreman as his rider only—he was in the saddle at Baden Baden on his final start for von Der Recke—and under his father's care Foreman was placed in good company at Auteuil, including when second in the top four-year-old hurdle of the autumn in France, the Prix Renaud du Vivier. When Doumen junior took out a licence later that season, Foreman was one of the three horses he started out with, and he gave him his first winner in Britain when successful in a novice hurdle, appropriately enough, at Kempton. The same track had also been the venue for Doumen senior's first success in Britain with Nupsala in the 1987 King George VI Chase. The Doumen/McManus connection had already been established with First Gold and

AIG Europe Champion Hurdle, Leopardstown—a blood-splattered Thierry Doumen boots home Foreman (blinkers) to beat Georges Girl (right), Fota Island and Spirit Leader (noseband)

Baracouda, and when Foreman reappeared in the latest season, he too had passed into the ownership of McManus. Before his run at Kempton at Christmas, he had two outings at Enghien in November, winning a listed event first time up, and was then in the process of running a good race in the track's most important hurdle of the year, the Group 3 Prix Leopold d'Orsetti, when falling at the last.

Foreman is by the very smart mile-and-a-half performer Monsun who has sired a number of good horses on the Flat in Germany. His most successful exports to Britain over jumps have been Samon and Saitensohn. Foreman's dam Fleurie won three times as a two-year-old, over six and seven furlongs, and has produced another useful winner on the Flat in Fleur (by Perugino), successful at up to a mile, including in listed company. Fleurie's brother Faberger was a smart miler whose biggest success came in Italy's Group 1 Premio Vittorio di Capua. Their dam, Friedrichslust, was an unraced daughter of Friedrichsruh, a winner of Germany's equivalent of the Oaks, the eleven-furlong Preis der Diana. Although this is a German family, one branch of it has done well for the Cheveley Park Stud in Britain. Blessed Event, a half-sister to Foreman's grandam, was a smart filly who reached the frame in the Ribblesdale, Yorkshire Oaks and Champion Stakes. She is the dam of the Great Voltigeur winner Sacrament and grandam of the smart filly at a mile and a quarter Chorist.

Foreman (GER) (ch.g. 1998)	Monsun (GER) (br 1990)	Konigsstuhl (br 1976)	Dschingis Khan
			Konigskronung
		Mosella (b 1985)	Surumu
			Monasia
	Fleurie (GER) (ch 1993)	Dashing Blade (b 1987)	Elegant Air
			Sharp Castan
		Friedrichslust (b 1989)	Caerleon
			Friedrichsruh

The lengthy, angular Foreman generally impresses in appearance, and looked in superb shape at Leopardstown. Although his biggest success to date has come at two miles, all his other wins have been over further (up to twenty-one furlongs) and he should stay further still. He has yet to race on firm ground but acts on any other. Foreman has got Thierry Doumen's fledgling training career off to a fine start and, as he has no immediate plans to switch to training full time, Foreman should give him further success in the saddle as well, although the owner now has a claim on Tony McCoy. *T. Doumen, France*

FOREST BELL (IRE) 6 b.m. Glacial Storm (USA) – Tiverton Castle (IRE) (Supreme Leader) [2003/4 F16s F16v 17g Apr 10] 4,100 4-y-o: rangy mare: first foal: dam unraced, from family of very smart chasers at 2½m+ Comeragh King and Seskin Bridge: tailed off in bumpers/maiden hurdle. *J. G. M. O'Shea* **h–** **F–**

FOREST DANTE (IRE) 11 ch.g. Phardante (FR) – Mossy Mistress (IRE) (Le Moss) [2003/4 c83, h–: c26m² c24g* Dec 5] big, lengthy gelding: modest handicap chaser: idled when winning 5-runner race at Southwell: stays 3¼m: acts on good to firm and heavy going: blinkered once, also tried in cheekpieces (including at Southwell): sometimes let down by jumping. *F. Kirby* **c96** **h–**

FOREST GREEN FLYER 8 b.m. Syrtos – Bolton Flyer (Aragon) [2003/4 h69§: 17gᵖᵘ 16m 17g 20d⁴ Apr 7] angular mare: bad hurdler: stays 2½m: acts on heavy going: tried blinkered/visored: has had tongue tied: unreliable. *O. O'Neill* **h56 §**

FOREST GUNNER 10 ch.g. Gunner B – Gouly Duff (Party Mink) [2003/4 c117, h–: c26g³ c21g* c24d⁵ Apr 23] leggy gelding: winning hurdler: better over fences: improved form when winning 25-runner Martell Cognac Fox Hunters' at Aintree in April, leading from seventh and beating Sikander A Azam 8 lengths: taken on for lead and made mistakes in handicap at Perth final start: stays 3m: raced mainly on good going or softer (acts on soft): usually sound jumper: front runner/races prominently: amateur ridden for all but one of wins. *R. Ford* **c122** **h–**

FOREST HEATH (IRE) 7 gr.g. Common Grounds – Caroline Lady (JPN) (Caro) [2003/4 h84: 16g⁵ May 21] medium-sized gelding: temperamental on Flat, and only poor nowadays: of similar merit over hurdles: tried tongue tied. *H. J. Collingridge* **h79**

FOREST IVORY (NZ) 13 ch.g. Ivory Hunter (USA) – Fair And Square (NZ) (Crown Lease) [2003/4 c–, h101?: 26g³ 27g⁴ 24g³ 27d³ 24g⁴ 22g³ 24mᵖᵘ 24d 24s⁴ 24g⁶ 19v⁴ 24g⁴ 20g 22d² 26d⁵ 24m Apr 15] leggy gelding: veteran handicap hurdler, modest nowadays: stays 4¼m: has form on good to firm going, raced mainly on softer (acts on heavy): tried blinkered/visored: usually soon off bridle. *Dr P. Pritchard* **c–** **h87**

Martell Cognac Fox Hunters' Chase, Aintree—
Forest Gunner leads the field at Becher's, which claims five of his rivals

FOREST MAZE   8 b.m. Arzanni – Forest Nymph (NZ) (Oak Ridge (FR)) [2003/4   **h64**
21g 22d⁴ 19d 23s 24dᵖᵘ Apr 21] leggy mare: won maiden point in 2003: poor form over
hurdles. *A. J. Whiting*

FOREST TUNE (IRE)   6 b.g. Charnwood Forest (IRE) – Swift Chorus (Music Boy)   **h106**
[2003/4 h108: 16s⁴ 16g⁴ 16s 17d³ 17d Apr 18] tall, angular gelding: fair handicap hurdler:
raced around 2m: acts on good to firm going. *B. Hanbury*

FOREVER DREAM   6 b.g. Afzal – Quadrapol (Pollerton) [2003/4 F96: 16g* 19m²   **h110**
17g⁶ 17d 16m³ 16g* 16d² Apr 8] useful-looking gelding: fair hurdler: won novice at
Kempton in November and handicap at Wincanton in March: good second to Smart
Savannah in handicap at Ludlow final start: stays 19f: acts on good to firm and good to
soft going: has shown signs of temperament. *P. J. Hobbs*

FOREVER EYESOFBLUE   7 b.g. Leading Counsel (USA) – Forever Silver (IRE)   **h82 +**
(Roselier (FR)) [2003/4 20s⁵ 18s 25g³ 22g 24v 24s* Apr 21] lengthy gelding: first foal:
dam, poor novice hurdler, out of sister to top-class staying chaser Righthand Man: poor
form over hurdles, improved effort when winning amateur handicap at Perth by 15
lengths: stays 3m: acts on soft going. *A. Parker*

FOREVER MY LORD   6 b.g. Be My Chief (USA) – In Love Again (IRE) (Prince   **h83**
Rupert (FR)) [2003/4 16m⁵ 16d⁵ 16d Mar 28] modest on Flat (stays 2m): poor form in
novice company over hurdles. *J. R. Best*

FOREVER NOBLE (IRE)   11 b.g. Forzando – Pagan Queen (Vaguely Noble)   **c– x**
[2003/4 c–x, h–: c25g⁴ c22gᵖᵘ 20m⁴ 24dᵖᵘ Jul 2] sparely-made gelding: winning hurdler/   **h–**
chaser, no form early in 2003/4: tried blinkered/in cheekpieces: sketchy jumper. *R. Allan*

FOREVER POSH   7 b.m. Rakaposhi King – B Final (Gunner B) [2003/4 F–: F17g   **F–**
Oct 11] leggy mare: well beaten in 2 mares bumpers: sold £850 Ascot February Sales.
Mrs S. M. Johnson

FOREVER WAYWOOD   5 ch.g. Rakaposhi King – I'm Fine (Fitzwilliam (USA))   **F–**
[2003/4 F17d Apr 18] fourth foal: half-brother to winning 17f chaser Brandsby Stripe (by
Nomadic Way): dam winning 2m hurdler: well held in bumper on debut. *P. Beaumont*

FORK LIGHTNING (IRE)   8 gr.g. Roselier (FR) – Park Breeze (IRE) (Strong   **c140 +**
Gale) [2003/4 h117: c23g³ c25d* c24sᵘʳ c24g² c25d* c24g* Mar 16]   **h–**
    It didn't take trainer Alan King quite so long to break his Cheltenham
Festival duck as it did his former boss David Nicholson. Nicholson started training
in the late-'sixties but had to wait until 1986 before Solar Cloud at 40/1 got him off
the mark in the Triumph Hurdle and Charter Party doubled the score later the

William Hill National Hunt Handicap Chase, Cheltenham—
novice Fork Lightning holds off the renewed challenge of Shardam

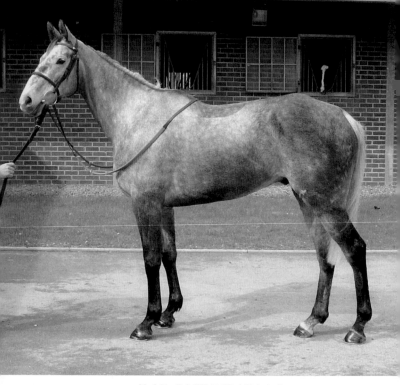

Mr & Mrs F. C. Welch's "Fork Lightning"

same afternoon in the National Hunt Handicap. King, for many years Nicholson's assistant before training briefly in his own right at Jackdaws Castle then moving to Barbury Castle, managed just one placing from nineteen Festival runners prior to 2004, Toto Toscato's third in the 2000 Royal & SunAlliance Chase. However, Fork Lightning, King's third runner on the first day of the 2004 meeting, landed the latest National Hunt Handicap, now sponsored by William Hill, at odds of 7/1. Fork Lightning's presence in the National Hunt Handicap represented a realistic assessment of his ability. He could have run in the Royal & SunAlliance Chase but his form didn't look quite good enough for that, while the eleven-runner field for the handicap was not, in truth, a strong one. Fork Lightning was one of few with any potential to improve and it needed only a return to more fluent jumping and a little improvement for him to beat Shardam by two lengths, with nine lengths back to Royal Auclair. Fork Lightning, surprisingly the first novice to win the race since Jomon in 1972, wasn't seen out again. Apart from Royal Auclair, who was just touched off in the Betfred Gold Cup on the last day of the season, none of the others to run subsequently did anything for the form and Fork Lightning may find things tough in handicaps in 2004/5 unless he can improve further, though he can be expected to be suited by longer distances than twenty-five furlongs, the furthest he has run over so far.

Prior to Cheltenham, Fork Lightning had been kept to novice events below graded level. He won twice from five starts, at Hereford in December on his second and Wincanton in February on his fifth, in the latter surviving mistakes to beat Silver Birch by half a length. His more notable efforts, however, came in defeat between his wins. He was most unfortunate not to follow up his Hereford success at Stratford, set to beat the subsequent National Hunt Chase winner Native Emperor when losing all momentum by sprawling two out (held when unseated rider after being hampered at the last), and he lost little in defeat to Lord Sam at Kempton, going down by a length and a quarter in receipt of 3 lb.

	Roselier (FR) (b 1973)	Misti IV (br 1958)	Medium Mist
Fork Lightning (IRE) (gr.g. 1996)		Peace Rose (gr 1959)	Fastnet Rock La Paix
	Park Breeze (IRE) (b or br 1988)	Strong Gale (br 1975)	Lord Gayle Sterntau
		Park Delight (ch 1974)	Saint Denys Lover's Delight

Fork Lightning, a workmanlike gelding, had shown fairly useful form over hurdles in 2002/3, winning on soft and good to firm going, but was always likely to come into his own over fences. He is by the pre-eminent sire of staying chasers Roselier, the leading sire overall in Britain in 2003/4, judged by win prize-money, 1,2,3 prize-money and number of wins, out of a mare by the dominant sire of the 'nineties Strong Gale. Fork Lightning's dam Park Breeze comes from a long line of unraced mares, the most recent to appear on a racecourse being the sixth dam Senta who ran for the then-Lord Carnarvon on the Flat on the eve of the First World War. More recently, there aren't many winners in the family, though there are a couple of useful staying chasers in Rain Lover, out of the third dam Lover's Delight, who raced for Neville Crump in the early-'seventies, and Park Breeze's brother Risk of Thunder, the peerless cross country performer who won seven successive runnings of the La Touche Cup at Punchestown. Park Breeze has produced two winners apart from Fork Lightning, Moving Earth (by Brush Aside), a fairly useful but temperamental chaser at around two and a half miles, and Distant Thunder (by Phardante), a fairly useful two-and-a-half-mile hurdle winner. *A. King*

FORLORN HOPE   7 b.g. Tragic Role (USA) – Rum N Raisin (Rakaposhi King) [2003/4 h–: 16m^F May 5] no form in 3 starts over hurdles: tried tongue tied. *B. D. Leavy*   **h–**

FORMAL BID (USA)   7 b. or br.g. Dynaformer (USA) – Fantastic Bid (USA) (Auction Ring (USA)) [2003/4 h115: 20g^3 c16g^2 c22g^F Nov 16] medium-sized gelding: fairly useful hurdler: second of 4 in maiden at Towcester on completed outing over fences: stayed 2½m: raced on good going or softer (acted on heavy): patiently ridden: reliable: dead. *C. C. Bealby*   **c83 h120**

FORMAL CLICHE   5 b.g. Classic Cliche (IRE) – Formal Affair (Rousillon (USA)) [2003/4 F16d F16d F16d Apr 17] 36,000 3-y-o: tall, useful-looking gelding: third foal: dam, winning 2m hurdler, half-sister to high-class hurdlers Anzum, a stayer, and Jazilah, best at 2m: well held in bumpers. *Mrs M. Reveley*   **F–**

FORONLYMO   5 b.g. Forzando – Polish Descent (IRE) (Danehill (USA)) [2003/4 17s^{pu} 16g Mar 10] sturdy gelding: fair on all-weather on Flat (stays 1m) at 3 yrs for K. Burke: no show both starts over hurdles. *P. Beaumont*   **h–**

FORRESTFIELD (IRE)   10 b.g. Toca Madera – Interj (Salmon Leap (USA)) [2003/4 c18d^3 c17v^5 c16d 19d^5 c18f* c16m* c16m^2 c16m^5 c17d^6 c17d Apr 13] rangy gelding: maiden hurdler: fair chaser: won maiden in September and handicap in October, both at Punchestown: raced mainly around 2m: acts on firm and soft going. *J. E. Mulhern, Ireland*   **c109 h92**

FORREST TRIBE (IRE)   11 b. or br.g. Be My Native (USA) – Island Bridge (Mandalus) [2003/4 c89§, h–§: c24g c20s c24g^4 c25d^F Mar 22] tall, lengthy gelding: poor handicap chaser nowadays: stays 3½m: acts on good to firm and heavy going: blinkered: has worn tongue strap: irresolute. *W. Jenks*   **c70 § h– §**

FORT SAUMAREZ   5 b.g. Magic Ring (IRE) – Rocquaine Bay (Morston (FR)) [2003/4 17s^{pu} 16g Mar 7] leggy gelding: second foal: dam, 1½m winner, half-sister to fairly useful staying hurdler/chaser The Quads: no form on Flat or in 2 novice hurdles: tried blinkered/tongue tied. *G. L. Moore*   **h–**

FOR

FORTUNATE DAVE (USA) 5 b.g. Lear Fan (USA) – Lady Ameriflora (USA) (Lord **h101**
Avie (USA)) [2003/4 h101: 20m³ 20d 24dᵖᵘ 20g² Mar 6] angular gelding: fair hurdler:
stays 2½m: acts on soft and good to firm going: visored third start: sold 3,200 gns
Doncaster May Sales. *Ian Williams*

FORTUNE ISLAND (IRE) 5 b.g. Turtle Island (IRE) – Blue Kestrel (IRE) (Bluebird **h97**
(USA)) [2003/4 h111p: 16dᵖᵘ 21g 16g 19g⁶ Mar 9] leggy gelding: fairly useful stayer on
Flat: winning hurdler, little impact in handicaps (visored) in 2003/4: should stay 2½m:
raced on good/good to soft going. *M. C. Pipe*

FORTUNE POINT (IRE) 6 ch.g. Cadeaux Genereux – Mountains of Mist (IRE) **h93**
(Shirley Heights) [2003/4 16s³ 16g⁵ 16s³ 16vᵖᵘ Dec 15] angular gelding: modest maiden
hurdler: raced at 2m: acts on soft ground: successful on Flat in February. *A. W. Carroll*

FORTUNE'S FOOL 5 b.g. Zilzal (USA) – Peryllys (Warning) [2003/4 h65: 17d⁶ **h67**
Nov 11] poor form over hurdles: headstrong. *I. A. Brown*

FORTY LICKS (IRE) 7 b.g. Supreme Leader – Bridevalley (Deep Run) [2003/4 **F116**
F18g³ F20s* F20d* F16s* Feb 15]
'As nice and as good a horse as I've seen in a long time,' was trainer Edward
O'Grady's verdict on Forty Licks after the horse's third win from four starts in
bumpers, at Navan in February, which is high praise given Back In Front and
Pizarro are among his current string and he has over thirty years experience of
training good-quality jumpers. However, Forty Licks' level of form in bumpers
suggests such an opinion won't be far wide of the mark and it will be no surprise
if he develops into a leading contender for the Royal & SunAlliance Hurdle at
Cheltenham come March. Indeed, he was entered for that race in 2004, and, had he
taken up either of his entries over hurdles the week after Navan, he could conceiv-
ably have made the line-up. As it was, he was put away for the season. He wasn't
qualified to run in the Champion Bumper at Cheltenham on grounds of age and
wasn't entered for the Grade 1 at Punchestown, when two miles on good ground
might, in any case, have provided an insufficient test of stamina for him.

Camlin (Pro-Am) INH Flat, Navan—the seven-year-old Forty Licks (left)
beats Homer Wells to cement his position as one of Ireland's best bumper performers

Forty Licks had made his debut at his trainer's local track Thurles at the end of November, running a highly promising third, and within barely a month had won twice over two and a half miles: he landed the odds at Clonmel by ten lengths from Insan Express, then followed up in style by the same margin at Leopardstown. Only six lined up that day but in galloping on really strongly to beat Petertheknot, conceding that rival 7 lb, with the remainder trailing in at wide margins, Forty Licks put up not far off the best bumper performance seen in Ireland all season. At Navan seven weeks later Forty Licks had only a length to spare over Homer Wells but, under regular rider Mr J. P. Magnier, he looked as if he had something in hand, and, in any case a drop to two miles in a steadily-run race wasn't exactly playing to his strengths.

Forty Licks (IRE) (b.g. 1997)	Supreme Leader (b 1982)	Bustino (b 1971)	Busted / Ship Yard
		Princess Zena (b 1975)	Habitat / Guiding Light
	Bridevalley (b 1985)	Deep Run (ch 1966)	Pampered King / Trial By Fire
		Arctic Cut (b or br 1972)	Arctic Slave / Flaming Cut

The useful-looking Forty Licks was very well bought at just IR £1,700 as a four-year-old, the fourth-cheapest of all the three- and four-year-old stores by Supreme Leader sold in 2001. He did not have a lot to recommend him on breeding. His lightly-raced dam Bridevalley has produced two winning pointers from three previous foals, Run Monty (by Montelimar) and the useful Thats Dedication (by Zaffaran) while the unraced grandam Arctic Cut produced four winners, including the fairly useful chaser up to three miles Master Vincents and the fair hurdler at two and a half miles or more Dan Raise. Another of Arctic Cut's progeny is the dam of Stay In Touch, who finished second to Earthmover in the 1998 Foxhunter Chase. More remotely, this is the family of a couple of more celebrated horses, the third dam Flaming Cut being the grandam of the high-class hurdler Herbert United and a half-sister to the dam of outstanding chaser Captain Christy. *E. J. O'Grady, Ireland*

FORUM CHRIS (IRE) 7 ch.g. Trempolino (USA) – Memory Green (USA) (Green Forest (USA)) [2003/4 h112: 20g c16d³ c16vᶠ Jan 26] sturdy gelding: unbeaten in 3 starts over hurdles early in 2002/3, well held after helping set strong pace in handicap on reappearance: modest form when third of 4 to Mister McGoldrick in maiden at Wetherby on completed start over fences: will stay 3m: acts on soft and good to firm going: front runner: tail swisher. *Mrs S. J. Smith*   **c92 h–**

FOR YOUR EARS ONLY (IRE) 8 b.g. Be My Native (USA) – Sister Ida (Bustino) [2003/4 h–p, F91: c16m³ 17d 16v³ 17s² 16g⁴ 16g³ 20d³ Apr 23] rangy gelding: poor maiden hurdler: stays 2½m: acts on soft going (bumper form on good to firm): held up. *A. Parker*   **c– h77**

FORZACURITY 5 ch.g. Forzando – Nice Lady (Connaught) [2003/4 h77: 17g* 16m² 16s³ 17s 16d 17s⁵ 16v³ 17d* 16s⁶ Feb 22] leggy gelding: modest hurdler: won seller at Newton Abbot in November (claimed from J. Spearing £6,000 next start) and handicap at Hereford in February: raced around 2m: acts on good to firm and heavy ground: tried in cheekpieces. *D. Burchell*   **h97**

FORZA GLORY 5 ch.m. Forzando – Glory Isle (Hittite Glory) [2003/4 h76: 18f³ Aug 22] small mare: half-sister to fair hurdler/winning chaser Blasket Hero (by Kalaglow), stayed 27f: maiden on Flat: poor maiden hurdler: will prove best around 2m: races freely. *Miss B. Sanders*   **h76**

FOSFORITO (FR) 6 b.g. Zieten (USA) – Bardouine (USA) (Northern Baby (CAN)) [2003/4 17d⁵ 16m⁵ Jun 5] successful over 1m on Flat in Spain at 4 yrs for F. Bedouret: in cheekpieces, poor form on second of 2 outings in novice hurdles. *R. C. Guest*   **h76**

FOTA ISLAND (IRE) 8 b.g. Supreme Leader – Mary Kate Finn (Saher) [2003/4 c116p, h127: 16g³ 20dᶠ 16d³ 16d³ 16g⁶ Mar 16] big, good sort: let down by jumping 2 of 3 runs over fences: much improved over hurdles after turn of year, smart performances in Grade 1 events at Leopardstown (under 2 lengths third to Foreman) in January, Cheltenham (13½ lengths sixth to Hardy Eustace in Champion Hurdle) in March and   **c– h151**

Mr John P. McManus' "Fota Island"

Punchestown (4 lengths third to Hardy Eustace) in late-April: stays 2½m: acts on heavy going: effective making running or ridden more patiently. *M. F. Morris, Ireland*

FOUNTAIN BANK (IRE)   11 b.g. Lafontaine (USA) – Clogrecon Lass (Raise You Ten) [2003/4 c96, h83: c21g^{pu} 21m^5 22m* 22m^4 24m 22f^{pu} Aug 22] good-topped gelding: winning chaser: modest handicap hurdler: won conditional jockeys event at Uttoxeter in June: stayed 3m: best form on good going or firmer: usually wore headgear: dead. *M. J. Gingell*   **c–** **h95 §**

FOUNTAIN HILL (IRE)   5 b.g. King's Theatre (IRE) – Highest Land (FR) (Highest Honor (FR)) [2003/4 F17m* F17d^3 17g^2 21g* 24g^2 Mar 26] €8,000 3-y-o: has scope: first foal: dam, 1½m winner in France, from family of high-class 6f to 8.5f performer Lit de Justice and good middle-distance colts Colonel Collins and Commander Collins: fair form in bumpers, won steadily-run event at Exeter in May: progressed well over hurdles as upped in trip, winning 19-runner novice at Newbury in March by 1½ lengths from Grey Report then length second (well clear) of 15 to Tom's Prize in similar event at same course: better suited by 3m than shorter: may improve further. *P. F. Nicholls*   **h126** **F94**

FOUNTAIN STREET (IRE)   11 b.g. Sharp Charter – Maylands (Windjammer (USA)) [2003/4 c16m^6 c20g^4 c24m^{pu} c20m^3 c25s^{pu} c20d^{pu} Mar 25] unreliable pointer: little form in steeplechases. *Mrs T. R. Kinsey*   **c–** **§**

FOURBOYSTOY (IRE)   5 ch.g. Roselier (FR) – Little Twig (IRE) (Good Thyne (USA)) [2003/4 F16g F16d Mar 22] lengthy gelding: first foal: dam thrice-raced in bumpers: well held in bumpers. *C. C. Bealby*   **F–**

FOUR CANDLES   4 b.f. Perpendicular – Skyers Tryer (Lugana Beach) [2003/4 16f^{pu} Oct 9] first foal: dam 2-y-o 5f winner: showed nothing in juvenile maiden hurdle on debut. *B. P. J. Baugh*   **h–**

FOURSTARGALE (IRE) 7 ch.m. Fourstars Allstar (USA) – Sea Gale (IRE) (Strong Gale) [2003/4 F16f F18s* F16s F18s* 16d Mar 17] first foal: dam useful hurdler/fairly useful chaser around 2m: fairly useful bumper performer: won at Limerick in December and February, clear throughout when beating Chicago Vic 9 lengths on latter occasion: well held in listed mares novice on hurdling debut: should do better. *Mrs M. C. O'Connor, Ireland*
h– p F102

FOUR TO WIN (IRE) 8 b.g. Tremblant – Ballybeg Rose (IRE) (Roselier (FR)) [2003/4 c–, h–: c19g⁵ c16f³ c16mᶠ May 26] rangy gelding: error-prone maiden chaser: blinkered/visored: dead. *Miss Jacqueline S. Doyle*
c– x h–

FOXES FANDANGO 7 br.g. Munjarid – The Pride of Pokey (Uncle Pokey) [2003/4 h–, F80?: 16m Dec 10] big gelding: little show in bumper or maiden hurdles. *N. A. Gaselee*
h–

FOXHALL LADY 7 gr.m. Lyphento (USA) – Carmel (Malaspina) [2003/4 h–, F–: 16dᵖᵘ 22sᵖᵘ Mar 23] no sign of ability. *J. C. Tuck*
h–

FOXIES LAD 13 b.g. Then Again – Arctic Sands (Riboboy (USA)) [2003/4 c79, h–: c19g⁵ c25g May 13] strong, lengthy gelding: novice hurdler: poor chaser: stays 21f: acts on heavy going: tried blinkered: often fails to impress with jumping. *C. J. Gray*
c64 x h–

FOX IN THE BOX 7 b. or gr.g. Supreme Leader – Charlotte Gray (Rolfe (USA)) [2003/4 h96: c24g* c24m* Apr 13] strong gelding: modest hurdler: unbeaten in 2 starts over fences, winning maiden at Uttoxeter in November and novice at Chepstow: fair form when beating Luneray 8 lengths at latter, again jumping soundly and pulling clear run-in despite edging right: will stay beyond 3m: acts on soft and good to firm ground: open to further improvement over fences. *R. H. Alner*
c113 p h–

FOX JOHN 5 b.g. Ballet Royal (USA) – Muskerry Miss (IRE) (Bishop of Orange) [2003/4 F16d⁵ F17g⁴ F17g² F18g⁶ Mar 22] second foal: dam winning Irish pointer: fair form in bumpers: will stay 2½m. *H. J. Manners*
F86

FOXMEADE DANCER 6 b.g. Lyphento (USA) – Georgian Quickstep (Dubassoff (USA)) [2003/4 h–, F–: 19g⁵ 17f⁶ 22g* 22gᵖᵘ 19dᵖᵘ 22s⁴ c16sᵖᵘ 22gᵖᵘ c19mᵖᵘ Apr 13] good-topped gelding: poor hurdler: won selling handicap at Folkestone in November: little form after, including over fences: stays 2¾m: acts on soft going. *P. C. Ritchens*
c– h65

FOXTON BROOK (IRE) 5 br.g. Presenting – Martins Times (IRE) (Bulldozer) [2003/4 F16g⁶ Mar 7] €111,000 3-y-o: sturdy gelding: fifth foal: half-brother to Irish 2½m hurdle winner Camden Times (by Camden Town): dam unraced half-sister to useful 2m to 3m hurdler/chaser Belsir: 11/8-on, sixth of 18 to Toemac in bumper at Kempton on debut: stiff task when well held in Grade 1 at Punchestown in late-April. *N. J. Henderson*
F89

FOXTROTROMEOYANKEE 4 b.g. Tragic Role (USA) – Hope Chest (Kris) [2003/4 17dᵖᵘ 18g⁴ 16sᵖᵘ Jan 14] modest maiden on all-weather on Flat (stays 1¼m): no form in juvenile hurdles. *L. A. Dace*
h–

FOXY ROYALE 8 b.g. Bold Fox – Celtic Royale (Celtic Cone) [2003/4 c19dᶠ Mar 22] won maiden point in 2002: fell heavily second in hunter chase. *Mrs A. Price*
c– h–

FOXY TRIX 5 b.m. Mind Games – Hill Vixen (Goldhill) [2003/4 F17v F16g Dec 11] half-sister to several winners, including useful bumper performer Alpine Fox (by Risk Me) and 2m chaser Floosy (by Governor General): dam, 1½m winner, out of half-sister to useful 2m to 3m chaser Ostrich Duck: well held in 2 mares bumpers and in maiden on Flat. *T. R. George*
F–

FRAGRANT ROSE 8 b.m. Alflora (IRE) – Levantine Rose (Levanter) [2003/4 h104: c20s³ c19d⁶ 16g 19m⁶ May 9] leggy mare: fair hurdler, well beaten in handicaps last 2 starts: failed to convince with jumping both outings over fences: stays 2½m: acts on soft going. *Miss H. C. Knight*
c89 h–

FRAMLINGHAM 9 gr.g. Out of Hand – Sugar Hall (Weatherbird) [2003/4 20s 26sᵖᵘ 24s 19g Mar 5] 2,500 6-y-o, resold 2,000 6-y-o: workmanlike gelding: fourth reported foal: dam winning pointer: little show over hurdles: wore cheekpieces second start. *B. J. Llewellyn*
h–

FRANCIES FANCY (IRE) 7 b.h. Imperial Frontier (USA) – Cheeky Maid (IRE) (Bob Back (USA)) [2003/4 20g⁵ Aug 16] one-time fairly useful 2m hurdler: found little in handicap at Perth, only outing since 2001/2: acts on soft going. *J. J. Lambe, Ireland*
h–

FRANCINES-BOY (IRE) 8 b.g. Namaqualand (USA) – Nancy Drew (Sexton Blake) [2003/4 c95, h–: c16d c20m² c19d c20s² c19s⁶ Jan 4] sturdy gelding: fair handicap chaser: stays 21f: acts on good to firm and heavy going: tried blinkered. *C. Roche, Ireland*
c111 h–

FRANCIS BAY (USA) 9 b.g. Alleged (USA) – Montage (USA) (Alydar (USA)) [2003/4 20g Feb 28] good-topped ex-Irish gelding: fairly useful handicap hurdler/chaser at best for D. Weld: ran as if needing race on first outing for nearly 2 years: stays 2¾m: unraced on firm going, acts on any other: usually blinkered. *Mrs S. J. Smith* **c–** **h95 +**

FRANCKEN (ITY) 5 ro.g. Petit Loup (USA) – Filicaia (Sallust) [2003/4 19gᵖᵘ 21dⁿ Mar 30] poor maiden on Flat for E. Incisa: well held on completed start over hurdles. *Lady Susan Watson* **h67**

FRANCOLINO (FR) 11 b.g. Useful (FR) – Quintefeuille II (FR) (Kashtan (FR)) [2003/4 c–§, h–§: 24mᵖᵘ c23m⁶ c23m³ c26g⁴ c26g² Oct 6] well-made gelding: maiden hurdler: winning chaser: poor nowadays: stays 3¼m: wears cheekpieces (has been tried in blinkers): ungenuine. *N. A. Gaselee* **c71 §** **h– §**

FRANKIE ANSON 7 b.g. Anshan – Smilingatstrangers (Macmillion) [2003/4 h79, F89] 24m⁴ c25m 24m c27mᵖᵘ Jul 22] leggy gelding: poor handicap hurdler: beaten long way out completed outing over fences: stayed 3m: acted on good to firm ground: dead. *M. D. Hammond* **c–** **h79**

FRANKINCENSE (IRE) 8 gr.g. Paris House – Mistral Wood (USA) (Far North (CAN)) [2003/4 h89: 16g⁵ 21s 19g³ 27s⁴ 24dᵖᵘ 27d³ 21g Apr 12] leggy gelding: modest handicap hurdler: barely stays testing 27f: acts on heavy going: races prominently. *A. J. Lockwood* **h85**

FRAZERS FORTUNE 4 ch.g. Environment Friend – Safidar (Roan Rocket) [2003/4 16fᵖᵘ Oct 16] half-brother to poor 2m hurdler Quick Silver Boy (by Kalaglow): well held on Flat: pulled very hard and soon adrift on hurdling debut. *G. Brown* **h–**

FREDDY CRYSTAL (FR) 5 b.g. Northern Crystal – Native Times (FR) (Faraway Times (USA)) [2003/4 c17gᶠ Dec 5] ex-French gelding: half-brother to several winners, including one-time useful chaser up to 2½m Hartley (by Saint Andrews): dam winning hurdler around 2m: thrice-raced on Flat: fair form in 3-y-o hurdles: fairly useful form on second of 2 starts in 4-y-o chases: left S. Kalley, in touch when falling 4 out in novice at Exeter on British debut: raced around 2m, mainly on soft ground. *P. J. Hobbs* **c–** **h–**

FREDERIC FOREVER (IRE) 6 b.g. Exit To Nowhere (USA) – Sarooh's Love (USA) (Nureyev (USA)) [2003/4 h112: 16g⁵ 17g c20g⁵ c19g c20d c24g⁴ Apr 16] compact gelding: fair 2m handicap hurdler: only poor form over fences: acts on soft and good to firm going: blinkered (ran poorly) once: often looks irresolute. *P. J. Hobbs* **c74** **h109**

FRED'S IN THE KNOW 9 ch.g. Interrex (CAN) – Lady Vynz (Whitstead) [2003/4 c112p, h113: 20s⁵ 16s⁴ c20vᶠ c19g³ c20sᵘʳ c17sᵖᵘ 24sᵖᵘ 20s Apr 4] tall gelding: fairly useful handicap hurdler/chaser: creditable efforts in 2003/4 only on second and fourth starts: stays 21f: acts on heavy going: held up. *N. Waggott* **c117** **h116**

FREEDOM BAY 4 b.g. Slip Anchor – Bobbie Dee (Blakeney) [2003/4 17m³ Nov 20] poor maiden up to 1¾m on Flat: well-beaten third to Trouble At Bay in juvenile at Hereford on hurdling debut. *Mrs P. N. Dutfield* **h81**

FREEDOM FIGHTER 13 b.g. Fearless Action (USA) – Zuleika Hill (Yellow River) [2003/4 c–§: c25d⁴ Mar 11] sturdy gelding: fair hunter chaser: won points in February, March and April: best at 3m+: acts on soft and good to firm going: unreliable. *Mrs Rosemary Gasson* **c90 §**

FREEDOM NOW (IRE) 6 b.g. Sadler's Wells (USA) – Free At Last (Shirley Heights) [2003/4 16d 25gᶠ 16s⁵ Feb 7] close-coupled gelding: fairly useful on Flat (stays 1½m), sold out of J. Hills's stable 13,000 gns Newmarket Autumn Sales: running best race over hurdles when falling 2 out in novice at Catterick in January: didn't jump with any fluency in Grade 2 novice final start. *M. D. Hammond* **h89**

FREE RETURN (IRE) 9 ch.g. Magical Wonder (USA) – Free Reserve (USA) (Tom Rolfe) [2003/4 c98, h102: c16mᵖᵘ 19g⁴ Nov 12] modest form at best over fences: modest handicap hurdler: stays 2¾m: acts on firm and good to soft going, probably on soft. *Noel T. Chance* **c–** **h96**

FREE STRIKE (NZ) 7 ch.g. Straight Strike (USA) – Ansellia (NZ) (Nassipour (USA)) [2003/4 20s 21dᵖᵘ 16g Mar 7] leggy, plain gelding: first sign of ability in novice hurdles when seventh of 17 at Kempton final start, though dictated pace and possibly flattered. *P. Mitchell* **h93 ?**

FREESTYLER (IRE) 12 b. or br.g. Phardante (FR) – Financial Burden (Mandalus) [2003/4 c20mᴿ Aug 1] temperamental winning pointer/maiden hurdler/steeplechaser: tongue tied. *B. P. J. Baugh* **c– §** **h–**

FREE TO RUN (IRE)   10 b.g. Satco (FR) – Lady Oats (Oats) [2003/4 c99: c23m³ **c103**
24m^{pu} c24d² c23m² c24f³ c28g³ c24g² c25s⁴ c25s³ c26d⁵ c28d* Mar 30] workmanlike **h–**
gelding: maiden hurdler: fair handicap chaser: won at Sedgefield in March: stays 3½m:
acts on soft and firm going: sound jumper: genuine. *Mrs S. J. Smith*

FREETOWN (IRE)   8 b.g. Shirley Heights – Pageantry (Welsh Pageant) [2003/4 c–, **c–**
h–: 25d^{pu} 23v⁴ 25g Mar 16] tall, leggy gelding: successful once from 2 outings over **h114**
fences: smart handicap hurdler in 2001/2: well below form on return from long absence
in 2003/4: stays 25f: raced mainly on good going or softer (acts on heavy), probably
unsuited by firm. *L. Lungo*

FREE WILLIE (IRE)   4 b.g. Ridgewood Ben – Dance In The Wings (In The Wings) **h–**
[2003/4 16s^{pu} 17s 16d Jan 17] big, workmanlike gelding: fourth foal (all by Ridgewood
Ben): dam unraced, out of smart 1982 2-y-o 6f and 1m winner Dancing Meg: little show
in 3 starts over hurdles: visored. *M. C. Pipe*

FREINDLYPERSUASION   4 b.c. Shambo – Sea Sky (Oats) [2003/4 F13g F17d **F–**
Apr 18] good-topped colt: third foal: dam winning pointer: well beaten in 2 bumpers.
Mrs A. Duffield

FRENCH DIRECTION (IRE)   5 ch.g. John French – Shelikesitstraight (IRE) **h74**
(Rising) [2003/4 21m⁴ 16d 16m 18s⁵ 16g 19g^{ur} Apr 16] first foal: dam never ran: fell in
maiden Irish point on debut in 2003: poor form over hurdles. *R. Rowe*

FRENCH ENVOY (FR)   5 bl.g. Cadoudal (FR) – Miss Merry (FR) (Pedege (FR)) **F85**
[2003/4 F16g⁴ F16d³ Apr 21] third foal: dam, 2m hurdle winner, half-sister to useful
French chaser up to 23f Riverston: in frame in bumpers at Stratford and Worcester. *Ian
Williams*

FRENCH EXECUTIVE (IRE)   9 br.g. Beau Sher – Executive Move (IRE) (Execu- **c113 §**
tive Perk) [2003/4 c114§, h–§: c24s^{pu} c28m* c24g³ c25m⁵ c28d^{pu} c26g* c26m Apr 14] **h– §**
lengthy, angular gelding: winning hurdler: fair handicap chaser: had breathing operation
after reappearance (tongue tied): won at Stratford in October and Plumpton (amateurs) in
March: generally let down by jumping otherwise in 2003/4: stays 3½m: acts on any
going: tried blinkered: often looks none too keen. *P. F. Nicholls*

FRENCH HORN   7 b.g. Fraam – Runcina (Runnett) [2003/4 17s Dec 16] half-brother **h–**
to poor hurdler Paulton (by Lugana Beach), stays 2¾m: modest on Flat (stayed 1¼m):
well held in novice on hurdling debut: dead. *M. J. Ryan*

FRENCH MANNEQUIN (IRE)   5 gr.m. Key of Luck (USA) – Paris Model (IRE) **h97**
(Thatching) [2003/4 h92: 18g⁴ 16f⁶ 17m³ 17m³ 16g⁴ 16m 16m² 16m² 19s⁴ 17s³ 16g*
16g⁵ Mar 5] angular mare: modest handicap hurdler: won mares event at Ludlow in
February: best around 2m: acts on soft and good to firm going: front runner.
Mrs A. J. Hamilton-Fairley

FRENCH TUNE (FR)   6 ch.g. Green Tune (USA) – Guerre de Troie (Risk Me (FR)) **h91**
[2003/4 h–: 17g³ 17g⁶ Aug 25] form over hurdles only when third in novice at Sedgefield
in August: should be suited by further than 17f. *Miss S. E. Hall*

FRENTZEN   7 b.g. Golden Heights – Milly Black (IRE) (Double Schwartz) [2003/4 **c82**
h76: 24m 26m³ 27g c23m² Jul 9] workmanlike gelding: poor maiden hurdler: similar **h77**
form when second in handicap at Worcester on chasing debut: stays 27f: acts on firm
going: has had tongue tied: has looked unwilling. *Miss E. C. Lavelle*

FRESH RUN (FR)   5 b.g. Kadalko (FR) – Tatifly (FR) (Saumon (FR)) [2003/4 16d **h–**
20d 22g^{pu} Feb 22] well-made gelding: chasing type: sixth foal: half-brother to winning
hurdler/cross-country chaser Jecyfly (by Cyborg): dam won up to around 1½m on Flat:
no sign of ability over hurdles, broke down final start. *A. Ennis*

FRETEVAL (FR)   7 b.g. Valanjou (FR) – La Beaumont (FR) (Hellios (USA)) [2003/4 **c90 d**
c93+, h–: c24s³ c20d^{pu} c20s⁵ c20g² c21d^{ur} c23g c23g⁶ c19d³ c19g² c20d² c20g Mar 28] **h–**
good-bodied gelding: fair hunter chaser: poor on balance in handicaps: barely stays
testing 3m: acts on soft going. *S. J. Gilmore*

FREYA ALEX   5 b.m. Makbul – Crissem (IRE) (Thatching) [2003/4 17d* 16m⁶ Jun **h87**
14] modest on Flat (stays 1½m): easily won weak mares novice seller at Cartmel in May
on hurdling debut: only sixth in mares novice at Hexham next time: sold to join
Mrs S. Smith 3,400 gns Doncaster May Sales. *G. M. Moore*

FREYDIS (IRE)   6 b.m. Supreme Leader – Lulu Buck (Buckskin (FR)) [2003/4 F75: **F75**
F16m⁵ F17s⁶ Jan 20] tall mare: modest in bumpers. *S. Gollings*

331

FRIAR PETER 7 b.g. Petoski – Misty Lough (Deep Run) [2003/4 F16g^{pu} 22s^{pu} 24s^{pu} c24g^{ur} c24m^{co} Mar 4] lengthy gelding: eighth foal: dam no sign of ability: looks of no account. *B. G. Powell*

c–
h–
F–

FRIAR WADDON 11 b.g. Pablond – Looking Swell (Simbir) [2003/4 c103x, h–: c21d^{pu} Apr 30] tall gelding: fairly useful pointer, successful in March and April: badly let down by jumping last 3 starts in hunters: stays 23f: acts on good to firm going. *K. Cumings*

c– x
h–

FRIEDHELMO (GER) 8 ch.g. Dashing Blade – Fox For Gold (Glint of Gold) [2003/4 c108, h–: 17g^4 16g^4 16d* 16s^{pu} Mar 13] strong, lengthy gelding: fair hurdler/ chaser: best effort when winning handicap over hurdles at Musselburgh in February: best around 2m: acts on soft and good to firm going: has been tongue tied, not in 2003/4: sketchy jumper of fences: has shaped as if amiss more than once: sold 5,000 gns Doncaster May Sales. *R. A. Fahey*

c–
h112

FRIENDLY FELLOW 5 gr.g. Environment Friend – Good Fetch (Siberian Express (USA)) [2003/4 F16m^5 16s^4 17d^6 19g^3 17s 22g^5 Apr 10] rangy, unfurnished gelding: third foal: dam, 2m juvenile selling hurdle winner: fifth in listed bumper at Cheltenham on debut: modest form over hurdles: stays 2¾m. *M. C. Pipe*

h87
F87

FRIENDLY REQUEST 5 b.m. Environment Friend – Who Tells Jan (Royal Fountain) [2003/4 h–: 19d 16g^6 17d^{pu} 16g 21d^{pu} Apr 8] little sign of ability over hurdles. *Mrs P. Ford*

h–

FRIEND'S AMIGO (IRE) 7 b.g. Accordion – Lady Sipash (Erin's Hope) [2003/4 h120: 16m^3 c17s^5 Dec 7] big, well-made gelding: fairly useful hurdler: creditable third to Khetaam in minor event at Tipperary on reappearance: chasing type but didn't impress with jumping in maiden at Clonmel on debut over fences (should do better): should stay beyond 2m: acts on heavy and good to firm going. *P. M. J. Doyle, Ireland*

c107 p
h121

FRIGHTENING FRED 7 ch.g. Almoojid – Very Bold (Never So Bold) [2003/4 F16m^4 Nov 13] third foal: half-brother to fairly useful Pavement Gates (by Bishop of Cashel), stays 1½m, and Rainbow King (by Puissance), winner in Italy up to 11f: dam 5f winner: tailed off in bumper on debut. *W. M. Brisbourne*

F–

FRILEUX ROYAL (FR) 11 br.g. Sarpedon (FR) – La Frileuse (FR) (El Toro (FR)) [2003/4 c§§, h–§: c24g^R Jun 12] sturdy gelding: winning hurdler/cross-country chaser/ pointer: tried blinkered/visored: thoroughly temperamental (has refused several times over fences). *B. N. Pollock*

c§§
h– §

FRIXOS (IRE) 4 ch.g. Barathea (IRE) – Local Lass (Local Suitor (USA)) [2003/4 16m^5 16f^{pu} 16f 16m^5 16g^{pu} Dec 18] good-topped gelding: trained by P. Cole, fairly useful on all-weather, modest on turf on Flat (stays 1½m): poor juvenile hurdler: blinkered second start: ungenuine. *M. Scudamore*

h75 §

FROM DAWN TO DUSK 5 b.g. Afzal – Herald The Dawn (Dubassoff (USA)) [2003/4 F16m* Apr 13] fourteenth foal: half-brother to fairly useful 2m hurdler Three Scholars and winning 3m hurdler King of Arms (both by Rakaposhi King): dam unraced, from family of Dawn Run: fairly useful form when winning conditional jockeys bumper at Chepstow by 1¼ lengths from The Sawyer. *P. J. Hobbs*

F100

FROMRAGSTORICHES (IRE) 8 b.g. Supreme Leader – Family Birthday (Sandalay (IRE)) [2003/4 20d^2 20d^2 24d^2 24s^4 Apr 4] good-topped gelding: fourth foal: half-brother to winning pointer by Lancastrian: dam, lightly raced in points, from family of very smart staying chaser Lucisis: fair form in novice hurdles, runner-up first 3 starts: stays 3m: raced only on soft/good to soft going. *Mrs S. J. Smith*

h102

FROM THIS MOMENT (IRE) 6 b.g. Parthian Springs – Swatter (IRE) (Over The River (FR)) [2003/4 22g^{pu} 24g^{pu} Mar 26] rather unfurnished gelding: second foal: dam unraced: won maiden Irish point on debut in 2003: pulled up in novice company over hurdles, lame on second occasion. *P. F. Nicholls*

h–

FRONTIER 7 b.g. Indian Ridge – Adatiya (IRE) (Shardari) [2003/4 17s^4 16d^2 17s^3 16g^{bd} Mar 15] medium-sized gelding: fairly useful on Flat (stays 1¼m): fair novice hurdler: likely to prove best around 2m: tongue tied. *B. J. Llewellyn*

h105

FRONTIS 7 ch.g. Be My Chief (USA) – Heavy Rock (IRE) (Ballad Rock) [2003/4 20s^5 c21s^{pu} c24g^2 Feb 18] big, strong, lengthy gelding: no worthwhile form over hurdles: visored, jumped better than on chasing debut when second in handicap at Musselburgh final start: stays 3m. *T. J. Fitzgerald*

c77
h–

FRONT RANK (IRE) 4 b.c. Sadler's Wells (USA) – Alignment (IRE) (Alzao (USA)) [2003/4 16g 16s 16d^5 Mar 1] fair maiden on Flat (should stay 1¾m), sold out of Sir

h92 p

332

Michael Stoute's stable 23,000 gns Newmarket Autumn Sales: not given hard time in 3 starts over hurdles, modest form at best: blinkered first 2 starts: remains open to improvement. *K. C. Bailey*

FROSTY JAK   6 b.g. Morpeth – Allied Newcastle (Crooner) [2003/4 F16s F16d 24s 17s 20g Mar 8] leggy gelding: third foal: half-brother to winning hurdler/chaser Adalie (by Absalom), stays 19f: dam winning hurdler/useful chaser, successful up to 25f: probably flattered on second of 2 starts in bumpers: no form over hurdles. *J. D. Frost*   **h** **F–**

FROSTY RUN (IRE)   6 b.g. Commanche Run – Here To-Day (King's Equity) [2003/4 F80: F16m² 19g⁴ 23sᵖᵘ 17g Feb 19] better effort in bumpers when second at Haydock in November: poor form in maiden hurdles: should stay beyond 19f. *Mrs H. Dalton*   **h80** **F86**

FROZEN ASSETS (IRE)   7 br.g. Shardari – Frost Bound (Hawaiian Return (USA)) [2003/4 F17s 20d 21d 20g Feb 20] useful-looking gelding: fifth in bumper on debut in 2001/2: no form in 2003/4, including over hurdles. *M. Pitman*   **h–** **F–**

FRUIT DEFENDU (FR)   7 b.g. Exit To Nowhere (USA) – Pauvresse (FR) (Home Guard (USA)) [2003/4 17g⁶ 16dᵖᵘ 19s² 17g 16d² Mar 24] good-topped gelding: fairly useful hurdler in 2001/2 for N. Meade: missed 2002/3, reportedly with leg trouble, and only modest form in 2003/4: stays 19f: acts on heavy going: usually blinkered: tongue tied: jumps none too fluently: ungenuine. *P. F. Nicholls*   **h89 §**

FRYS NO FOOL   14 b.g. Idiot's Delight – Scotch And Ice (Balinger) [2003/4 c21d Apr 30] workmanlike gelding: veteran chaser, lightly raced and no sign of retaining ability since 1997/8. *Mrs J. Butler*   **c–** **h–**

FRYUP BOOSTER   7 ch.g. Bollin William – Comedy Imp (Import) [2003/4 h–: 17mᶠ Oct 18] leggy gelding: no show over hurdles: has had tongue tied. *P. T. Midgley*   **h–**

FRYUP SATELLITE   13 br.g. Leading Star – Comedy Imp (Import) [2003/4 c94, h–: c24g⁵ c26d⁴ May 28] good-topped gelding: winning pointer: modest maiden hunter chaser: stays 25f: acts on good to soft and good to firm going. *J. S. Swindells*   **c81** **h–**

FULGERE (IRE)   6 b.g. Old Vic – Moppet's Last (Pitpan) [2003/4 F16v⁵ 20s⁴ Jan 10] 32,000 4-y-o: eighth foal: half-brother to fair chaser up to 21f Crackling Frost (by Green Shoon) and Irish 19f hurdle winner Red Red Red (by Be My Native): dam, maiden pointer, half-sister to useful chaser around 2½m Nickle Moppet: fifth in bumper at Towcester on debut: soon had plenty to do when fourth in novice hurdle at Haydock: will stay beyond 2½m: will do better over hurdles. *K. C. Bailey*   **h– p** **F70**

FULLARDS   6 b.g. Alderbrook – Milly Kelly (Murrayfield) [2003/4 h–: 22d 20d 21vᵖᵘ 19s² 22s⁴ 21s⁵ 22g³ 23g² 26g* 23d Apr 12] sturdy gelding: fair handicap hurdler: won at Haydock (novice) in January and Huntingdon in March: stays 3¼m: raced on good going or softer (acts on soft). *Mrs P. Sly*   **h102**

FULL ENGLISH   5 b.m. Perugino (USA) – Grown At Rowan (Gabitat) [2003/4 F16f 16dᵘʳ Jan 13] fourth foal: half-sister to moody 7f winner Twoforten (by Robellino) and Irish 1¼m winner Wild Zing (by Jupiter Island): dam fair 7f winner: well beaten in 2 races on Flat: showed nothing in bumper, unseated after third on hurdling debut. *A. P. Jones*   **h–** **F–**

FULL HOUSE (IRE)   5 br.g. King's Theatre (IRE) – Nirvavita (FR) (Highest Honor (FR)) [2003/4 16s⁶ 16d³ 21g⁶ 16g* 16g³ 17m³ Apr 15] leggy gelding: fair on the Flat (stays 1¾m): fair form over hurdles: won handicap at Ascot in February: best efforts around 2m: acts on good to soft and good to firm ground. *P. R. Webber*   **h109**

FULL IRISH (IRE)   8 ch.g. Rashar (USA) – Ross Gale (Strong Gale) [2003/4 h126: c16d* c20s² c20sᶠ c16g² c16d* Apr 22] sturdy gelding: fairly useful handicap hurdler: took very well to chasing, winning maiden at Hexham in December and novice at Perth (simple task) in April: particularly good effort when 1¼ lengths second to Mister McGoldrick in novice at Ayr fourth start: stays 21f: raced on good ground or softer (acts on heavy). *L. Lungo*   **c131** **h–**

FULL MINTY   9 br.g. Phardante (FR) – Jouvencelle (Rusticaro (FR)) [2003/4 c108, h–: c20g* c22g² Nov 16] fair hurdler in 2000/1: lightly raced over fences, won novice at Bangor in September: laboured display when second of 4 finishers in similar event at Haydock 2 months later: should stay 3m: acts on soft and good to firm going. *N. A. Twiston-Davies*   **c113** **h–**

FULL OF MICHEL (FR)   5 gr.g. Michel Georges – Quinte Royale (FR) (Kaldoun (FR)) [2003/4 17d³ Nov 17] ninth foal: half-brother to 1½m winner Ahyla (by Holst): dam unraced: thrice-raced over fences in France, winning claimer at Auteuil in October 2002 for J-M. Baudrelle: not fluent when third in novice hurdle at Folkestone on British debut. *N. J. Henderson*   **c–** **h89**

Vodafone Handicap Hurdle, Newbury—
a fine front-running performance from the much improved Fundamental

FULL ON   7 b.g. Le Moss – Flighty Dove (Cruise Missile) [2003/4 h91, F90: 21v[4] c22d[2] c19d[2] c20g[3] Mar 12] useful-looking gelding: modest form at best over hurdles: fair novice chaser: stays 2¾m: raced on good going or softer. *A. M. Hales*   **c100 h81**

FULLOPEP   10 b.g. Dunbeath (USA) – Suggia (Alzao (USA)) [2003/4 c–, h–: c24m[4] May 29] sturdy gelding: one-time fairly useful handicap chaser: winning pointer, jumped markedly left when fourth in hunter at Huntingdon in May: stays 3m: acts on good to firm and good to soft going. *Paul Morris*   **c91 h–**

FULL TIME (IRE)   5 b.g. Bigstone (IRE) – Oiche Mhaith (Night Shift (USA)) [2003/4 16d Dec 1] lightly-raced maiden on Flat: well held in maiden on hurdling debut: joined N. Waggott. *G. A. Swinbank*   **h–**

FULWELL HILL   6 b.m. Anshan – Finkin (Fine Blue) [2003/4 F69: F17d[6] May 17] lengthy mare: chasing type: poor form in 2 bumpers, shaping like a stayer. *Ian Williams*   **F73**

FUNDAMENTAL   5 ch.g. Rudimentary (USA) – I'll Try (Try My Best (USA)) [2003/4 h95: 16m 16m[2] 16m[4] 20s* 16g* 16d[2] Apr 3] leggy gelding: fairly useful handicap hurdler: improved form last 3 starts, winning at Leicester in January and Newbury (galloped on strongly when beating Gone Far 4 lengths) in March: again made running when second to Puck Out in listed contest at Aintree: stays 2½m: acts on soft and good to firm going. *Jonjo O'Neill*   **h124**

FUNDAMENTALIST (IRE)   6 b.g. Supreme Leader – Run For Shelter (Strong Gale) [2003/4 24g* 23g[2] 21g* Mar 17]   **h147 p**
   'Buyer beware' is the maxim best suited to any purchase made during a night in the pub. Customers who take the plunge after a drink or two are seldom surprised when the designer watch bought for a song turns out to be by Steptoe & Son rather than Dolce & Gabbana. Fortunately, there is an exception to every rule, and Fundamentalist's owners seem to have secured a Rolex for the price of a Timex based on his thrilling success in the Royal & SunAlliance Novices' Hurdle. Having arrived at the Gloucestershire yard of Nigel Twiston-Davies in November, Fundamentalist was still without an owner towards the end of January. Several potential buyers passed on him before Felicity Griffin and Carolyn Pennell made

him their first venture into ownership after meeting Twiston-Davies in the Hollow Bottom Pub at Guiting Power. By early-February they were looking forward to the debut of a gelding who was very much an unknown quantity, allowing that he had won three points in Ireland. In early-March they had a live Cheltenham contender on their hands; and a couple of weeks later they were pondering the future of one of the brightest jumping prospects on either side of the Irish Sea.

Fundamentalist made his hurdling debut in a novice over three miles at Kempton in February when he was sent off 7/2 favourite in a field containing a clutch of previous winners. Fundamentalist won with plenty in hand. 'He's very classy and I should think he'll go to Cheltenham,' said Twiston-Davies. Two weeks on, a plan to test his Cheltenham credentials against Garde Champetre and Very Optimistic in the Sidney Banks Memorial Novices' Hurdle at Huntingdon was lost to the weather. A contingency plan saw him contest the Red Square Vodka Prestige Novices' Hurdle at Haydock forty-eight hours later and, despite being beaten, Fundamentalist enhanced his reputation considerably. The conditions of the race forced him to concede 4 lb to Royal Rosa, who had chased home the smart Sh Boom in a Grade 2 contest in January. Strong in the market again, Fundamentalist travelled smoothly under restraint and looked to be moving much better than Royal Rosa (whose owner had paid top whack for his Rolex) as he loomed up on his outside early in the straight, but inexperience showed as he edged into the winner after the last, and he went down by half a length. It's probably as well that Twiston-Davies has had 'only one cross word in eighteen years' with his stable-jockey Carl Llewellyn. A relationship built on less solid foundations might have resulted in an inquest into why the veteran rider didn't switch his whip from his right hand to his left when things got tight.

With Istabraq, Danoli, French Holly, Barton and Hardy Eustace on its roll of honour, no novice event over hurdles in the calendar has a more impressive recent history than the Royal & SunAlliance Hurdle. The Challow Hurdle winner Cornish Rebel was a notable absentee from the latest renewal, yet there seems no reason to suspect it was much below its usual high standard. Inglis Drever lined up with the best form after his runaway win in Grade 2 company at Warwick and led the market at 7/4, followed by Sadlers Wings and Very Optimistic on 9/2 and Big Moment on 11/1. Fundamentalist was sent off at 12/1 over the shortest trip he had encountered under rules, but it was clear when he joined the leaders with ears pricked soon after halfway that he was travelling well within himself. Most of the fancied contenders were towards the end of the main pack as Grey Report jumped the third last with a narrow advantage over Fundamentalist and Inglis Drever. Fundamentalist outpaced Inglis Drever as his rider struck for home after the next, but he had to withstand a strong rally from that horse in the home straight. Fundamentalist made a mistake and jumped left at the final flight and Inglis Drever closed to his quarters fifty yards out, but Fundamentalist kept on under pressure and

Royal & SunAlliance Novices' Hurdle, Cheltenham—
Fundamentalist takes over at the second last from the blundering Grey Report,
with (from left to right) Sadlers Wings, Inglis Drever and Big Moment all close up

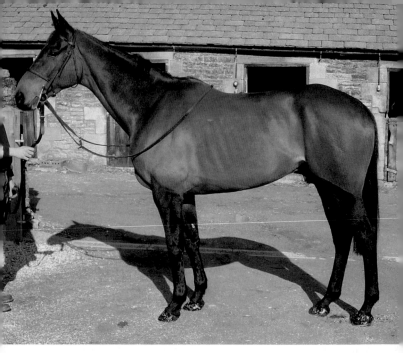

Gripen's "Fundamentalist"

held off his rival by half a length at the line. A trip to Aintree for the Sefton Hurdle two weeks later was bypassed because Fundamentalist was felt to be slightly below par, but the subsequent efforts of Inglis Drever, Grey Report and Sadlers Wings upheld the Royal & SunAlliance form. In any case, Fundamentalist's future has as much to do with his potential as his bare performance at Cheltenham. Fundamentalist improved considerably with each of his outings over hurdles and, though no final decision had been reached as to whether he goes chasing at the time of writing, he appeals as the sort to scale even greater heights over fences.

Fundamentalist has the physique and pedigree to make a fine chaser. A well-made gelding who stood out in the paddock on all his three starts, he is a half-brother to three winners over fences, the fairly useful Wilde Music (by Orchestra), who stayed twenty-three furlongs, and La Brigantine (by Montelimar) and Run For Cover (by Lafontaine), both fair winners around two miles (La Brigantine later went the wrong way). The dam Run For Shelter was a poor maiden on the racecourse but, as a Strong Gale half-sister to the outstanding two-mile chaser Badsworth Boy, it should come as no surprise to see her produce an exceptional horse at stud. Run For Shelter is half-sister to four other winners, the best of them the fairly useful hurdler Hangover. She is also half-sister to the dam of Our Bid, who won the Grade 1 bumper at Punchestown in 1999. Fundamentalist's sire Supreme Leader continues to occupy a place among the elite of jumping sires and added another Festival success with Rule Supreme in the Royal & SunAlliance Chase little more than half an hour after Fundamentalist's win. Keen Leader, Simply Supreme and Lord Sam also enhanced Supreme Leader's reputation as a sire of chasers, while Fota Island represented him with credit in the best company over hurdles.

		Bustino	Busted
	Supreme Leader	(b 1971)	Ship Yard
	(b 1982)	Princess Zena	Habitat
Fundamentalist (IRE)		(b 1975)	Guiding Light
(b.g. 1998)		Strong Gale	Lord Gayle
	Run For Shelter	(br 1975)	Sterntau
	(b 1983)	Falcade	Falcon
		(b 1971)	Perpelia

Twiston-Davies, who famously declined a BBC interview with Desmond Lynam after winning the Grand National with Earth Summit in 1998, is seldom one to waste words for the sake of creating newsprint. 'I know who I am and there's no need to read about it in the papers,' was one of his quotes in an interview during the build-up to the latest National. Another in the same feature related to the satisfaction he has gained from 'building the business up from nothing by saying nothing.' After a spell in the doldrums and thoughts of retirement prior to Bindaree's National win in 2002, business took a marked turn for the better at Grange Hill Farm in the latest season. Twiston-Davies was back in the top ten of the trainers' table with seventy-nine winners, more than for the two previous seasons put together, and a strike rate bettered among that group only by Nicky Henderson. And, contrary to some impressions, Twiston-Davies is not always averse to public speaking. His speech whilst accepting Fundamentalist's award as champion novice hurdler at the British Horseracing Board's 2004 jump racing awards in May was typically short and to the point. 'I'm going to bore you all by saying that I'm retiring again,' he said. 'I've had less trouble with Fundamentalists than George Bush and Tony Blair, so I'm going into politics.' With a horse as rich in promise as Fundamentalist under his care, the chances of Twiston-Davies swapping the horsebox for the ballot box can be safely discounted. Most people would cast their vote for Iris's Gift to lead the way among the novice chasers in the coming season. Rightly so, but it may not be a landslide verdict come next spring if Fundamentalist maintains the rate of progress which marked his novice hurdling campaign. *N. A. Twiston-Davies*

FUNNY GENIE (FR) 11 b.g. Genereux Genie – Sauteuse de Retz (FR) (Funny Hobby) [2003/4 c–, h–: c16gpu c16m 16m Jun 5] angular gelding: no longer of any account: blinkered/visored. *Miss H. M. Irving* — c– h–

FUSION OF TUNES 6 b.m. Mr Confusion (IRE) – Daleria (Darshaan) [2003/4 F16d⁴ F16s 17d Apr 18] rather unfurnished mare: second foal: dam, 11f winner, out of sister to Lancashire Oaks winner Andaleeb: better effort in bumpers when fourth in mares event at Newcastle on debut: well held in novice on hurdling debut. *Mrs K. Walton* — h– F70

G

GABLA (NZ) 8 b.g. Prince of Praise (NZ) – Dynataine (NZ) (Centaine (AUS)) [2003/4 16g³ 16m³ 17m² 17g² 16g³ 17m* 20f³ 16f c16d⁶ 16d Apr 8] leggy New Zealand-bred gelding: successful 11 times up to 1¼m from 32 starts in Australasia: modest hurdler: won conditional jockeys handicap at Carlisle in October: never threatened in handicap on chasing debut: raced mainly around 2m (beaten long way out over 2½m): acts on good to firm going: wore cheekpieces 4 of last 5 outings. *R. C. Guest* — c– h97

GABLESEA 10 b.g. Beveled (USA) – Me Spede (Valiyar) [2003/4 16dpu May 16] tall gelding: no show over hurdles: tried visored. *B. P. J. Baugh* — h–

GABOR 5 b.g. Danzig Connection (USA) – Kiomi (Niniski (USA)) [2003/4 h102: 18g⁵ 16m⁴ 16g* 16s⁶ Nov 22] good-topped gelding: fair handicap hurdler: won at Huntingdon in November: will prove best around 2m: acts on good to firm going (not fluent and well below form on soft): wore eyeshields last 3 outings, blinkers last 2. *G. L. Moore* — h109

GAELIC FLIGHT (IRE) 6 b. or br.g. Norwich – Ash Dame (IRE) (Strong Gale) [2003/4 F16s F16g* Mar 15] rangy gelding: second foal: half-brother to fairly useful Irish chaser up to 25f Mystic Lord (by Roselier): dam ran twice: much better effort in bumpers when making all at Stratford by 8 lengths from Troodos Valley. *Noel T. Chance* — F100

GAE

GAELIC LORD (IRE) 9 b.g. Mister Lord (USA) – Mum's Eyes (Al Sirat) [2003/4   c– x
c21d^{pu} c24m Mar 4] sturdy gelding: lightly raced and little sign of ability: tried in   h–
cheekpieces: poor jumper of fences. *D. R. C. Elsworth*

GAELIC MUSIC (IRE) 5 b.g. Accordion – Cuilin Bui (IRE) (Kemal (FR)) [2003/4   F92
F17g* Apr 13] €20,000 4-y-o: fourth foal: half-brother to fair hurdlers up to 21f King
Harald and Prince Madoc (both by King's Ride): dam, fairly useful hurdler who stayed
3m, half-sister to useful staying hurdler Crank Shaft: won bumper at Exeter on debut by
½ length from Bubba Boy. *M. Bradstock*

GAELIC PROBE (IRE) 10 b.g. Roi Danzig (USA) – Scottish Gaelic (USA) (High-   c–
land Park (USA)) [2003/4 17g^{pu} c24g^{pu} 20g⁵ 17s^{pu} 17g⁴ Dec 26] good-bodied gelding: no   h60
worthwhile form over fences: poor maiden hurdler: best around 2m: acts on heavy going:
tried visored. *R. M. H. Cowell*

GALA DU MOULIN MAS (FR) 10 b.g. Le Riverain (FR) – Soiree d'Ex (FR) (Kash-   c–
tan (FR)) [2003/4 c73, h–: c16g^{pu} 24m^R Jul 16] rangy gelding: maiden hurdler/winning   h–
chaser: no show either start in 2003/4: tried in cheekpieces/blinkers. *M. E. D. Francis*

GALA FESTIVAL (IRE) 5 b.m. Supreme Leader – Noon Performance (Strong Gale)   F72
[2003/4 F17m F16d F16m⁴ F17g Apr 10] tall mare: eighth foal: half-sister to fair hurdler/
fairly useful chaser up to 3m Native Performance (by Be My Native): dam unraced sister
to fairly useful jumpers up to 3m Executive Options and Festival Dreams: poor form in
bumpers. *Mrs P. N. Dutfield*

GALANT EYE (IRE) 5 ch.g. Eagle Eyed (USA) – Galandria (Sharpo) [2003/4 h80:   h91
20m^{pu} 20m 19d* 19g* 19g Apr 1] compact gelding: modest hurdler: won conditional
jockeys novice handicap and novice at Exeter in December: stays 19f: acts on good to
firm and good to soft going. *R. J. Baker*

GALANT MOSS (FR) 10 br.g. Tip Moss (FR) – Tchela (FR) (Le Nain Jaune (FR))   c?
[2003/4 c120, h156d: 21s c19d^F c21g* c19d² c25d Sep 28] leggy gelding: fairly useful   h132
chaser, often let down by jumping: won minor event at La-Roche-Posay in July: very
smart hurdler at best: left M. Pipe after reappearance: barely stays 25f: acts on any going:
tried blinkered/visored: has idled, and best held up. *C. Aubert, France*

GALA PERFORMANCE (USA) 6 b.g. Theatrical – Claxton's Slew (USA) (Seattle   h– x
Slew (USA)) [2003/4 h94, F90: 17m^F Aug 1] useful-looking gelding: caught the eye in
novice on hurdling debut in 2002/3 but disappointing all 3 starts in similar events since,
jumping badly on return: tongue tied in bumpers. *Jonjo O'Neill*

GALAPIAT DU MESNIL (FR) 10 b.g. Sarpedon (FR) – Polka de Montrin (FR)   c94
(Danoso) [2003/4 c132d, h–: c33g² c25d² Feb 17] leggy, angular gelding: useful chaser at   h–
best: mostly disappointing since early-2002/3, including over hurdles: left P. Nicholls and
off over 9 months, second in hunter at Folkestone: stays 31f: acts on good to firm and
heavy going: usually races prominently: sound jumper. *R. T. Phillips*

GALAXY FALLON 6 b.m. Dancing Spree (USA) – No Comebacks (Last Tycoon)   h–
[2003/4 19g^{pu} Mar 5] no form on Flat or on hurdling debut. *M. Dods*

GALAXY SAM (USA) 5 ch.g. Royal Academy – Istiska (FR) (Irish River   h96
(FR)) [2003/4 h74: 22s* 22g 24g⁶ Mar 26] tall gelding: modest hurdler: won conditional
jockeys handicap at Fontwell in January: will stay beyond 3m. *N. J. Gifford*

GALEAWAY (IRE) 10 b.g. Strong Gale – Geeaway (Gala Performance) [2003/4 c73,   c–
h–: c24g c24g^{ur} Mar 12] tall, angular gelding: won point in February: poor chaser: stays   h–
3¼m: acts on firm going: blinkered once: has had tongue tied. *Mrs D. M. Grissell*

GALEN (IRE) 13 br.g. Roselier (FR) – Gaye Le Moss (Le Moss) [2003/4 20d c24g³   c64
c25d^F c24s c20s c25d³ c24s³ Mar 20] compact gelding: winning hurdler: poor handicap   h–
chaser: stays 3¾m: acts on heavy and good to firm going: effective blinkered or not: often
needs plenty of driving. *Mrs S. J. Smith*

GALEY RIVER (USA) 5 ch.g. Irish River (FR) – Carefree Kate (USA) (Lyphard   h81
(USA)) [2003/4 16g⁴ Mar 17] modest on Flat (stays 1¼m): fourth in maiden at Huntingdon on hurdling debut. *J. J. Sheehan*

GALILEO (POL) 8 b.g. Jape (USA) – Goldika (POL) (Dakota) [2003/4 h–: 20g 21g   h134 §
24g⁶ 24m Apr 15] workmanlike gelding: made excellent start to hurdling career when
winning both starts in 2001/2, including Royal & SunAlliance Novices' Hurdle at Cheltenham: reportedly injured sesamoid and well held most outings since, though showed
useful form when sixth to His Nibs in valuable handicap at Aintree in April: stays 3m:
acts on soft ground: visored on reappearance, blinkered at Aintree. *T. R. George*

338

GALLANT BOY (IRE) 5 ch.g. Grand Lodge (USA) – Damerela (IRE) (Alzao (USA)) [2003/4 16m⁴ Aug 8] fairly useful on Flat (stays 1½m): tongue tied, not fluent and soundly beaten in maiden on hurdling debut. *P. D. Evans*   **h–**

GALLANT HERO 5 b.g. Rainbow Quest (USA) – Gay Gallanta (USA) (Woodman (USA)) [2003/4 16mᶠ 17mᶠ Nov 27] smallish gelding: useful on Flat (stays 1½m) for Sir Michael Stoute: fair form in 2 maiden hurdles: needs to improve his jumping. *P. J. Hobbs*   **h105**

GALLIK DAWN 6 ch.g. Anshan – Sticky Money (Relkino) [2003/4 F–: F16g 24m³ 20d 25sᵖᵘ 26sᵖᵘ 16g 19d² 21d Apr 8] sturdy gelding: poor maiden hurdler: should stay 2½m: acts on good to soft going. *A. Hollingsworth*   **h72** **F–**

GALLIUM 7 gr.m. Terimon – Genie Spirit (Nishapour (FR)) [2003/4 h–, F–: 16s 19sᵖᵘ c20mᶠ Mar 4] no sign of ability. *M. Scudamore*   **c–** **h–**

GALTEE VIEW (IRE) 6 b.g. Namaqualand (USA) – Miss Dolly (IRE) (Alzao (USA)) [2003/4 F16f³ F16m³ F18f³ F16g³ F16f* 20m³ 16m* 17m⁴ 24g⁴ 16g⁶ 16s 20d⁵ 16d 20s Jan 18] useful-looking gelding: first foal: half-brother to winner up to 11f in Italy by Titus Livius: dam unraced: fair form in bumpers, successful at Tramore in August: modest hurdler: won maiden at Clonmel in September: effective at 2m to 3m: acts on good to firm ground (won bumper on firm): tongue tied second outing. *C. Roche, Ireland*   **h99** **F92**

GALWAYBAY STAN (IRE) 6 b.g. Safety Catch (USA) – Crook Lady (Croghan Hill) [2003/4 F96: 24sᵖᵘ 22sᵖᵘ 22s³ 24v* Jan 9] winning pointer: modest form in novice hurdles, won at Towcester (tongue tied, reportedly struck into himself): stays 3m: acts on heavy going. *L. Wells*   **h94**

GAMBLERS DREAM (IRE) 7 b.g. Executive Perk – Tinkers Lady (Sheer Grit) [2003/4 16gᵖᵘ 16m Apr 13] ex-Irish gelding: second foal: half-brother to winning 3m hurdler Ojays Alibi (by Witness Box): dam placed in maiden Irish points: won maiden Irish point in 2003: modest form on second of 2 starts in bumpers in 2002/3 for J. O'Callaghan: no form in 2 races over hurdles, finishing distressed on first occasion. *P. J. Hobbs*   **h–**

GAME GUNNER 12 b.g. Gunner B – The Waiting Game (Cruise Missile) [2003/4 c–: c25d* c24g* c26dᵖᵘ Mar 18] big, rangy gelding: useful hunter chaser: won at Cheltenham very early in season and Ludlow in February: didn't run much of a race in Foxhunter at Cheltenham: stays 25f: acts on good to firm and good to soft going. *Miss B. Lewis*   **c111**

GAMEKEEPER 8 ch.g. Mujtahid (USA) – High Tern (High Line) [2003/4 20mˢᵘ 20f² 16d* 16d* 16m³ 20m³ Oct 27] half-brother to winning 2½m selling hurdler Sooty Tern (by Wassl): fairly useful at best on Flat (stays 2m): fairly useful hurdler: won maiden in August and handicap in September, both at Galway: best effort when third to Statim in novice there back at 2½m in October: acts on firm and good to soft going: effective blinkered or not. *P. Hughes, Ireland*   **h117**

GAME ON (IRE) 8 b.g. Terimon – Nun So Game (The Parson) [2003/4 c–, h–: c16m² c17g⁴ c17g³ c17m² c20g² Oct 6] modest novice chaser: stays 2½m: acts on soft and good to firm ground: tried tongue tied: races freely: none too consistent. *B. N. Pollock*   **c90** **h–**

GANDON 7 ch.g. Hernando (FR) – Severine (USA) (Trempolino (USA)) [2003/4 h72: 19g⁵ 17g 20m³ 21g³ 16d Mar 14] poor maiden hurdler: left P. Murphy before final start: stays 2½m: probably acts on any going: tried visored/tongue tied. *A. E. Jones*   **h74**

GAN EAGLA (IRE) 5 b.g. Paris House – Mafiosa (Miami Springs) [2003/4 16g³ 17s 17g⁴ 17d³ 16gᵖᵘ Apr 18] angular gelding: half-brother to poor hurdler Dallachio (by Shernazar), stays 2¾m: fair maiden on Flat (stays 1¼m), sold out of J. Bolger's stable 13,000 gns Newmarket July Sales: modest form over hurdles: likely to prove best at 2m with emphasis on speed. *Miss Venetia Williams*   **h91**

GANGSTERS R US (IRE) 8 br.g. Treasure Hunter – Our Mare Mick (Choral Society) [2003/4 c74, h91: c16g² c25d c21v⁴ c20g* c24g* c24f* c24g Apr 10] tall gelding: winning hurdler: fair chaser: successful in handicaps at Musselburgh in January and February (2): stays easy 3m: acts on any going: has cocked jaw/hung. *A. Parker*   **c104** **h–**

GAORA BRIDGE (IRE) 6 b.g. Warcraft (USA) – Miss Good Night (Buckskin (FR)) [2003/4 20d 16s⁴ 16g³ 16g² Apr 4] IR £7,500 3-y-o: rather unfurnished gelding: seventh foal: half-brother to modest hurdler/fair chaser Lord 'N' Master (by Lord Americo), stays 3m: dam, placed in bumper, half-sister to useful 2m chaser Cottage Run: won 4-y-o maiden Irish point on debut in 2002: fair form over hurdles: should be suited by 2½m+. *C. J. Mann*   **h102**

GARDE BIEN   7 br.g. Afzal – May Lady (Deep Run) [2003/4 c20d^{pu} c16d^2 c19g^{pu} **c78**
c16g^4 c19g^F c16d^6 Mar 30] 33,000 5-y-o: lengthy gelding: fifth foal: dam winning
pointer: runner-up in 2½m maiden point on debut in 2002: poor on balance of form in
steeplechases: bled from nose third start. *Ferdy Murphy*

GARDE CHAMPETRE (FR)   5 b.g. Garde Royale – Clementine Fleurie (FR)   **h139**
(Lionel (FR)) [2003/4 16v^2 17d* 16d^2 16s^2 16g^5 20g* Apr 1]
    Horses in the Million In Mind colours came up trumps again, with two
useful novice hurdlers among those who ran for the latest partnership, Mon Villez
and Garde Champetre. Mon Villez won three races for Nicky Henderson, including
the Grade 2 Rossington Main Novices' Hurdle at Wetherby, while Garde Champetre, just the better of the pair, won twice for Paul Nicholls, notably the Grade 2
Martell Cognac Makro Mersey Novices' Hurdle at Aintree. Not for the first time,
however, the achievements of a Million In Mind horse on the track were subsequently overshadowed by the record-breaking activity he provoked in the sales
ring. At the dispersal of the Million In Mind horses at Doncaster in May, Mon Villez
was sold for 100,000 guineas (and the fairly useful juvenile Emanic, another of
their draft, fetched 80,000 guineas) but it was Garde Champetre who made the
headlines, breaking the record for a jumper at auction when knocked down for
530,000 guineas. This was the fourth record-breaking sale of a Million In Mind
horse after Mysilv in 1994, Mister Banjo in 2000 and Royal Rosa who had fetched
340,000 guineas twelve months earlier. Royal Rosa's new trainer Howard Johnson
was among those bidding for Garde Champetre, as was Paul Nicholls, keen to keep
the gelding in his yard, but when the hammer fell it was to a bid from the representatives of J. P. McManus.
    Garde Champetre was trying two and a half miles for the first time in the
Mersey Novices' Hurdle at Aintree, a trip that looked sure to suit him, and he
started second favourite behind the short-priced Inglis Drever, runner-up in the
Royal & SunAlliance Novices' Hurdle. The unbeaten Monet's Garden was the only
other member of the field at single-figure odds, with the longer-priced horses
including another Cheltenham runner-up, the Coral Cup second Court Shareef.
A steady pace for much of the way made it an unsatisfactory contest and, with the
field still bunched turning for home, the favourite met trouble which almost
certainly cost him the race. At the same stage of the contest, Garde Champetre was
briefly tapped for foot as the pace increased, but he responded to pressure to lead
two out and kept on well to win by a length and a quarter from Monet's Garden,
with Court Shareef a close third and Inglis Drever (giving the winner 8 lb) beaten
just under two lengths back in fourth. In the end, Garde Champetre had not needed
to improve on some good earlier efforts in top company.

*Martell Cognac Makro Mersey Novices' Hurdle, Aintree—Garde Champetre leads from the grey
Monet's Garden and the fading Strike Back (noseband); unlucky-in-running Inglis Drever is also in shot*

Million In Mind Partnership's "Garde Champetre"

Garde Champetre started off at a modest enough level, running into what turned out to be a smart opponent in Big Moment on his British debut and first start over hurdles at Plumpton, and then justified favouritism narrowly but gamely in another novice at Bangor in December. Garde Champetre's early races had featured some less than fluent jumping, and he was still far from the finished article when upped markedly in class for the Tolworth Hurdle at Sandown, where a length and a half defeat by Lingo represented much better form. Not surprisingly, Garde Champetre proved no match for Rhinestone Cowboy in the Agfa Hurdle back at Sandown next time, but that second was a good effort, and so was his staying-on fifth to Brave Inca in the Supreme Novices' Hurdle at Cheltenham where two miles on good ground looked an insufficient test of his stamina. Garde Champetre finished best of all having been off the bridle at halfway and behind three out.

Garde Champetre began his career in France with Guillaume Macaire and won three of his four races as a four-year-old, all of them Flat contests at around a mile and a half restricted to non-thoroughbreds. He won at Royan La Palmyre (Macaire's local track), Compiegne and Pornichet and was beaten a neck for his only defeat. Garde Champetre shares his sire Garde Royale with the afore-mentioned Royal Rosa, as well as the useful chasers from the latest season, Iris Royal and Royal Auclair. Garde Champetre's dam, Clementine Fleurie, managed only a fourth place over hurdles but her record at stud makes much better reading. She has had eight winners, from as many foals to race, who between them have won seventy-five races. Chief contributors to that total have been Un Chouia (by Faucon Noir) and Chou Farci (by Le Gregol), winners of twenty-three and twenty-one races

341

respectively, mainly cross-country events. Garde Champetre apart, the pick of his dam's winners is Choum (also by Faucon Noir), a useful winner both over hurdles and fences at Auteuil at up to two and three quarter miles for Guillaume Macaire. Clementine Fleurie is by the dual Grand Prix de Deauville winner and Arc third Lionel out of an unraced anglo-arab mare.

Garde Champetre (FR) (b.g. 1999)	Garde Royale (br 1980)	Mill Reef (b 1968)	Never Bend
			Milan Mill
		Royal Way (gr 1969)	Sicambre
			Right Away
	Clementine Fleurie (FR) (ch 1979)	Lionel (ch 1963)	Herbager
			La Strada
		Fleur de Saintes (ch 1969)	Thalian
			Saintes Fleur

Garde Champetre is a tall, close-coupled gelding who usually impresses in appearance. Raced only on good going or softer, he should prove better at two and a half miles than two and will stay further. However well he does in novice chases, he is unlikely to come close to repaying his purchase price, though that's not to say he won't win good races over fences for his new connections. He is due to join Jonjo O'Neill. *P. F. Nicholls*

GARDEN FEATURE 6 b.m. Minster Son – Super Fountain (Royal Fountain) [2003/4 h–, F76: 27s 21v⁵ 24vᵖᵘ 24d 21d* 21d⁵ Mar 30] workmanlike mare: poor novice hurdler: won weak mares event at Sedgefield in March: should stay at least 3m. *J. B. Walton* **h84**

GARDEN PARTY II (FR) 10 br.g. Argument (FR) – Betty Royale (FR) (Royal Charter (FR)) [2003/4 c84d, h–: c20s² c16m⁵ c21m⁴ c20d⁴ c21sᵖᵘ c24g⁴ c24g⁵ c24g⁴ c17g⁴ c16g⁴ c16d c16d⁵ Apr 22] strong gelding: poor maiden chaser: effective around 2m to 3m: acts on heavy and good to firm going. *Mrs J. C. McGregor* **c72 h–**

GARDOR (FR) 6 b.g. Kendor (FR) – Garboesque (Priolo (USA)) [2003/4 h–: 16g² 16gᶠ 17gᵖᵘ Jul 6] modest maiden hurdler: raced around 2m on good going or softer: tongue tied. *T. J. Fitzgerald* **h90**

GARETHSON (IRE) 13 b.g. Cataldi – Tartan Sash (Crofter (USA)) [2003/4 c85, h–: c21sᵖᵘ Apr 29] good-bodied gelding: winning novice chaser: probably stays 3m: acts on good to firm and heavy going: sometimes let down by jumping: sold £1,650 Ascot June Sales. *O. W. King* **c– h–**

GARGOYLE GIRL 7 b.m. Be My Chief (USA) – May Hills Legacy (IRE) (Be My Guest (USA)) [2003/4 h82: 16g² 16m⁴ 18d⁴ 16s⁴ 19d⁴ 22g⁵ Mar 12] good-topped mare: modest handicap hurdler: won at Doncaster in January: seems to stay 2¾m: acts on good to firm and good to soft going: wore visor/cheekpieces last 3 starts. *J. S. Goldie* **h88**

GAROLSA (FR) 10 b.g. Rivelago (FR) – Rols du Chatelier (FR) (Diaghilev) [2003/4 c85, h–: c26v* c24s⁵ c29s⁵ c24sᶠ c25sᵖᵘ c24g⁶ c24d* c24v⁴ c25g² Apr 18] useful-looking gelding: fair chaser: won novice at Plumpton in November and handicap at Chepstow in March: probably stays 29f: acts on good to firm and heavy going: tried in headgear: often tongue tied: bled from nose second outing: sketchy jumper. *C. L. Tizzard* **c107 h–**

GARRAHEEN PRINCESS (IRE) 6 b.m. Shernazar – Money Incinerator (Laurence O) [2003/4 16m⁵ 22g Nov 21] ex-Irish mare: seventh foal: half-sister to fairly useful hurdler around 2m Unknown Soldier (by Supreme Leader): dam lightly-raced maiden: signs of only a little ability over hurdles (trained by P. Fahy in 2003/4): tried in cheekpieces. *B. J. Llewellyn* **h–**

GARRUTH (IRE) 10 gr.g. Good Thyne (USA) – Lady Sipash (Erin's Hope) [2003/4 c117§, h–: c25d²ᵈ c25d⁴ Mar 23] medium-sized gelding: has had wind operation: fairly useful chaser at best: better effort in hunters when second at Wincanton, though lost weight cloth after 3 out and disqualified: best at 3m+: successful on good to firm going, best form on more testing ground (acts on heavy): has won with/without blinkers: tried tongue tied: not a fluent jumper of fences: lazy. *R. Barber* **c107 § h–**

GARRYSPILLANE (IRE) 12 b.g. Royal Fountain – Lucylet (Kinglet) [2003/4 c24s⁴ May 2] close-coupled gelding: fairly useful hunter chaser: off more than a year, distant fourth at Bangor: stays 3½m: acts on good to firm going. *P. Jones* **c79 + h–**

GARVIVONNIAN (IRE) 9 b.g. Spanish Place (USA) – Garvivonne (Belfalas) [2003/4 c126, h118: c20g* 19s c20v c22sᵖᵘ c24g c20s⁶ c20d⁶ c24d c20s² c18d c24s² c29d Apr 12] rather leggy gelding: fairly useful hurdler/chaser: won minor event over fences at Killarney in May: one of best subsequent efforts when second to Native Jack in listed **c129 h–**

handicap at Cork in March: stays 3m (didn't see out 29f in Irish Grand National at Fairy-house): acts on good to firm and heavy going. *Edward P. Mitchell, Ireland*

GARW VALLEY   5 h m Mtoto – Morgannwg (IRE) (Simply Great (FR)) [2003/4   **h80**
16m^{ur} 17m^{ur} 16g^3 16m^4 16m^{pu} 16m^4 16m^4 17d^5 Dec 2] light-framed mare. sister to 17f hurdle winner Welsh Dream and half-sister to fair 2m hurdler Penybont (by Unfuwain): dam half-sister to one-time useful hurdler General Cloney: fair maiden at best on Flat (should stay 1¾m): poor maiden hurdler: raced around 2m: acts on good to firm going. *Miss J. Feilden*

GARY'S PIMPERNEL   5 b.g. Shaddad (USA) – Pennine Star (IRE) (Pennine Walk)   **h83 +**
[2003/4 F97: F16g^2 F16d^2 16s^3 16d^5 Apr 23] fairly useful in bumpers, runner-up all 3   **F99**
starts after debut win: just poor form both starts over hurdles, probably found stamina stretched under testing conditions on first occasion. *M. W. Easterby*

GASTORNIS   6 ch.g. Primitive Rising (USA) – Meggies Dene (Apollo Eight) [2003/4   **h–**
h113p, F97: 24m^{pu} Oct 26] lengthy, angular gelding: fair hurdler: ran as though in need of race only outing in 2003/4: will prove best at 2½m+: tongue tied. *M. W. Easterby*

GATE EXPECTATIONS   6 b.m. Alflora (IRE) – Dorazine (Kalaglow) [2003/4 h–,   **h73**
F–: 16m^4 Sep 7] signs of ability only when fourth in weakly-contested maiden hurdle at Worcester: has worn cheekpieces. *R. J. Price*

GATEJUMPER (IRE)   6 b.g. Zaffaran (USA) – Nelly Don (Shackleton) [2003/4 F–:   **h93**
20v^3 21s* 20s 21d 22g Apr 18] leggy gelding: left clear 2 out when winning novice hurdle at Plumpton in January: well below form subsequently: bred to stay 3m+. *R. H. Alner*

GATHERING STORM (IRE)   6 gr.g. Roselier (FR) – Queen of The Rock (IRE)   **h–**
(The Parson) [2003/4 F17s F16s^2 F16s^3 20s 24g Mar 6] €68,000 4-y-o: good-topped   **F94**
gelding: fourth foal: half-brother to winning pointer by Be My Native: dam, placed in bumper, half-sister to very smart chasers at 2½m+ Comeragh King and Seskin Bridge: fair form when placed in bumpers at Huntingdon: well held in 2 races over hurdles, very badly hampered on first occasion: should be suited by 2½m+. *P. R. Hedger*

GATORADE (NZ)   12 ch.g. Dahar (USA) – Ribena (NZ) (Battle-Waggon) [2003/4   **c105**
c106, h103: c21m* c21g* Jul 28] leggy gelding: winning hurdler: fair chaser: back to   **h–**
form to win handicaps at Southwell and Sedgefield in July: stays easy 3m: acts on firm and good to soft going: wears cheekpieces: has broken blood vessels: held up. *R. C. Guest*

GATSBY (IRE)   8 gr.g. Roselier (FR) – Burren Gale (IRE) (Strong Gale) [2003/4   **c100**
c24m^2 c24s* Feb 12] lengthy gelding: modest form on first of 2 starts in novice hurdles: **h–**
made good start in hunter chases, winning at Huntingdon despite idling: will stay beyond 3m: acts on good to firm and soft going. *J. Groucott*

GAUCHO   7 b.g. Rambo Dancer (CAN) – Sioux Be It (Warpath) [2003/4 c19g^{ur} c16s^2 **c86**
c16v^2 c16v c16d^5 c16d^2 Mar 30] strong, compact gelding: won maiden point in 2003: no   **h–**
form over hurdles: modest novice chaser: unproven beyond 2m: raced mainly on good going or softer (acts on heavy): wears cheekpieces. *Miss T. Jackson*

GAULTIER GALE (IRE)   10 b.g. Ajraas (USA) – David's Pleasure (Welsh Saint)   **c–**
[2003/4 c–, h–: c24g^4 c24f^{pu} Feb 29] rather leggy gelding: won 2 points in March, little   **h–**
form in steeplechases since very early in 2001/2: stays 21f: acts on any going: tried visored/blinkered. *Ms J. M. Findlay*

GAY CLOWN   10 b.m. Petoski – Gay Edition (New Member) [2003/4 c20m^F Jun 7]   **c–**
lightly raced and signs of only a little ability over hurdles: off more than 3 years, fell third   **h–**
on chasing debut. *P. J. Hobbs*

GAYE DREAM   6 b.g. Gildoran – Gaye Fame (Ardross) [2003/4 F91: 20g^F 20d^{pu} **h–**
16m^6 21v^4 17d 16d Mar 14] lengthy, angular gelding: little worthwhile form over hurdles: has shown signs of temperament. *M. Scudamore*

GAYE TRIGGER   6 ch.g. Karinga Bay – Gaye Memory (Buckskin (FR)) [2003/4   **h101**
17g^6 19g^3 20s^3 Apr 17] seventh foal: half-brother to 21f hurdle winner Gaye Fame (by Ardross): dam, dual bumper winner and runner-up only outing over hurdles, sister to very smart staying chaser Black Humour, and half-sister to top-class 2m to 3m hurdler Gaye Brief and very smart staying jumper Gaye Chance: progressive form over hurdles (trained by Miss H. Knight on debut), third in novice at Bangor final start: will stay 3m. *J. L. Spearing*

GAY KINDERSLEY (IRE)   6 ch.g. Roselier (FR) – Ramble Bramble (Random Shot)   **h–**
[2003/4 F16d^4 F16g F16g 20s Mar 13] tall, useful-looking gelding: brother to smart staying   **F90**
chaser Seven Towers and half-brother to modest hurdler Pharrambling (by Phardante), stays 3m: dam twice-raced half-sister to very smart staying chaser Deep Bramble: much

better effort in bumpers when fourth to The Rising Moon at Newbury on debut: tailed off in novice on hurdling debut: bred to be suited by at least 2½m. *Mrs M. Reveley*

GAYLE ABATED (IRE)   5 b.g. Moscow Society (USA) – Hurricane Girl (IRE)   **F99**
(Strong Gale) [2003/4 F16s* F16g Mar 17] rangy gelding: fourth foal: half-brother to fairly useful hurdler who stays 3m Strong Project (by Project Manager) and winning pointer by Good Thyne: dam ran once over hurdles after birth of second foal: won bumper at Fairyhouse on debut in January: better form when twelfth of 24 to Total Enjoyment in Champion Bumper at Cheltenham: likely to prove a stayer. *W. P. Mullins, Ireland*

GAY OSCAR (IRE)   5 b. or br.g. Oscar (IRE) – Deep Inthought (IRE) (Warcraft   **F91**
(USA)) [2003/4 F16d² F17d⁴ Apr 18] first foal: dam never ran: second to Rebel Rhythm in bumper at Wetherby on debut: probably unsuited by steady pace when fourth in similar event at Carlisle next time. *Mrs K. Walton*

GAZEILA   5 b.m. Makbul – Liberatrice (FR) (Assert) [2003/4 h–: 16f May 10] small,   **h–**
leggy mare: well beaten over hurdles: sold £650 Ascot June Sales. *J. J. Bridger*

GAZUMP (FR)   6 b.g. Iris Noir (FR) – Viva Sacree (FR) (Maiymad) [2003/4 F88: 17d   **h80**
19d 20s 21d⁵ Apr 8] rangy gelding: poor form in novice hurdles: stays 21f: raced on good going or softer. *N. A. Twiston-Davies*

GEBORA (FR)   5 ch.g. Villez (USA) – Sitapanoki (FR) (Houston (FR)) [2003/4 F97:   **h100**
17m* 17sᵗʳ 17m² 16g⁴ 20m⁴ 21g⁶ 19m* 25d 18s 18s⁵ 19g 19d⁶ 19g⁴ Apr 16] fair novice hurdler: won at Exeter in May and Taunton (handicap) in November: barely stays 21f: best form on good to firm going (won bumper on soft): visored last 5 starts. *M. C. Pipe*

GEE AKER MALAYO (IRE)   8 b.g. Phardante (FR) – Flying Silver (Master Buck)   **h76**
[2003/4 24g⁴ 20sᵖᵘ 20d⁵ Mar 22] strong, lengthy gelding: fair in bumpers in late-2001/2: poor form over hurdles on return. *R. T. Phillips*

GEE BEE BOY   10 ch.g. Beveled (USA) – Blue And White (Busted) [2003/4 c–§,   **c– §**
h–§: 16mᵖᵘ Sep 13] compact gelding: no longer of any account: tried visored/tongue tied: **h– §**
ungenuine. *G. F. Bridgwater*

GEILL SLI (IRE)   6 b.g. Charente River (IRE) – Lumiere (USA) (Northjet)   **F117**
[2003/4 F16d⁴ F16d² F16d* F16s³ F16d* Apr 11]
      In hindsight, it paid to take notice of Noel Meade's entries for the Champion Bumper at Cheltenham, made at the start of March. There were just two of them: Augherskea and Geill Sli. Neither at that stage looked to have quite the credentials required, though Augherskea had made a promising start when runner-up on his debut the previous month. As it turned out, neither ran at Cheltenham but both went on to win at Fairyhouse's Easter meeting and then, shortly after the end of the British season, finished first and third in the Paddy Power Champion INH Flat race at the Punchestown Festival. The market and riding plans suggested that Augherskea was the more fancied of the pair, starting at 13/2 against 11/1 for Geill Sli and

Paddy Power Champion INH Flat, Punchestown—
Geill Sli (second right) and Blazing Liss (right) are about to overhaul leader Tigerlion

ridden by stable amateur Niall 'Slippers' Madden (the son of 'Boots', naturally). However, it was Geill Sli who came out on top after a stable one-two looked a possibility, the pair challenging the leader Tigerlion in the straight before Geill Sli asserted in the final furlong. He won by a length and a half from the favourite Blazing Liss who rallied to deprive Augherskea of second by three quarters of a length, Tigerlion clear of the rest in fourth. This wasn't a vintage renewal of Ireland's top bumper by any means, though Geill Sli's performance was just about good enough to have made the first three in a substandard renewal of the Champion Bumper at Cheltenham. It also represented quite a bit of improvement on his previous form. Geill Sli had won twice from six previous starts in bumpers, getting off the mark and putting up a fairly useful effort at Naas in November and improving on that when winning a well-contested winners-of-three at Fairyhouse all out by three quarters of a length and half a length from the mares Mrs Wallensky and Sweet Kiln. After his Naas win, Geill Sli was reportedly likely to be sent over hurdles next time, so connections were well rewarded for their change of mind. As usual with a bumper horse of his ability, Geill Sli will only have to be reasonably proficient at jumping to win a race over hurdles, though he can be expected to do rather better than that.

Geill Sli (IRE) (b.g. 1998)	Charente River (IRE) (b 1992)	Sadler's Wells (b 1981)	Northern Dancer / Fairy Bridge
		Fruition (b 1978)	Rheingold / Welsh Flame
	Lumiere (USA) (ch 1983)	Northjet (ch 1977)	Northfields / Jellatina
		Attirance (ch 1978)	Crowned Prince / Arosa

The good-topped Geill Sli doesn't exactly have the pedigree of a top jumping prospect. Virtually all the notable horses in his family are Flat performers, while it was difficult to know what to expect of his sire Charente River, from whose first crop he comes. Charente River is certainly bred to make a mark on the Flat, being by Sadler's Wells, a brother to the Breeders' Cup Turf winner Northern Spur, closely related to the high-class stayer Kneller and half-brother to the smart stayer and fairly useful staying hurdler Great Marquess. However, he ran only once, at four years, finishing third in a mile-and-three-quarter maiden at Tipperary, and was sold for just 8,000 guineas at the Newmarket December (1996) Sales. The three dams on the bottom line of Geill Sli's pedigree all won on the Flat in France. His dam Lumiere, a nine-and-a-half-furlong winner at four, has three other winners to her name, the useful Italian sprinter Bella Michela (by Superpower), Angel Love (by Chief Singer), a fair maiden in Britain, with form at up to two and a quarter miles, who was later a listed winner over much, much shorter in Scandanavia, and Kennett Square (by Mansooj), a maiden hurdler who on his only start in a point beat Fiftysevenchannels. The grandam Attirance was a listed winner over a mile and produced six winners on the Flat, notably the useful Irish filly Attractive Crown. The most notable of third dam Arosa's nine winners is the very smart colt at up to ten furlongs Arokar. Arosa is also the grandam of a handful of useful-or-better middle-distance performers, among them the John Porter Stakes winner Spout. Geill Sli is likely to stay two and a half miles when he goes over hurdles. He has raced on good going or softer, though it may be significant that he has been well held on both starts on soft. *N. Meade, Ireland*

GEMI BED (FR)   9 b.g. Double Bed (FR) – Gemia (FR) (King of Macedon) [2003/4 h90: 17d c16m³ c16g c17d* c20d⁴ Apr 11] modest on Flat (stays 2m): poor maiden hurdler: form over fences only when winning handicap at Plumpton in March: moody effort final outing: should stay beyond 17f: acts on good to firm and good to soft going: blinkered. *G. L. Moore*   **c89 § h71**

GEMINEYE LORD (IRE)   7 b.g. Mister Lord (USA) – Mum's Eyes (Al Sirat) [2003/4 h–, F–: 20gᵖᵘ 20d 24gᶠ 25g⁶ Jan 24] rangy gelding: poor form in novice hurdles: needs to jump better. *Mrs S. J. Smith*   **h81**

GEMINI DANCER   5 b.g. Glory of Dancer – Lamloum (IRE) (Vacarme (USA)) [2003/4 F16m F16g 16g⁵ Apr 18] 3,600 4-y-o: second foal: half-brother to 9f and 1¼m winner Anastasia's Shadow (by Theatrical Charmer): dam, fourth over 6f in France, out   **h– F72**

of Irish Oaks winner Olwyn: signs of ability on second of 2 starts in bumpers: well held in novice on hurdling debut. *C. L. Tizzard*

GEMINI GUEST (IRE) 8 ch.g. Waajib – Aldhabyih (General Assembly (USA)) **h112**
[2003/4 16g* 17g5 16d 16g 16m5 22m2 Oct 27] half-brother to winning 17f hurdler Binlaboon (by Polish Precedent): fair hurdler: won novice at Sligo very early in season: effective at 2m to 2¾m: acts on soft and good to firm going. *P. Hughes, Ireland*

GEMSTER 6 b.m. Alflora (IRE) – Gemmabel (True Song) [2003/4 F16g 16d 25spu **h61**
24s6 24g4 Feb 19] angular mare: second foal: dam unraced: well held in bumper: poor **F—**
form over hurdles: stays 3m: raced on good going or softer. *A. Hollingsworth*

GENERAL 7 b.g. Cadeaux Genereux – Bareilly (USA) (Lyphard (USA)) [2003/4 h119: **c100 §**
c17vpu c16v2 c17s4 c16v2 c19s4 Feb 22] good-topped gelding: fairly useful handicap **h—**
hurdler: just fair form over fences, looking moody: best around 2m: raced on good going
or softer (acts well on heavy): blinkered last 4 outings: often front runner: fairly useful on
Flat, sold to join N. Littmoden 8,500 gns after winning seller in March. *Mrs N. Smith*

GENERAL CLAREMONT (IRE) 11 gr.g. Strong Gale – Kasam (General Ironside) **c120 §**
[2003/4 c122, h–: c24m3 c28d2 c32m4 c22d2 c26m3 26m* 25m3 c21gbd Apr 1] workman- **h97 §**
like gelding: fairly useful handicap chaser: first win over hurdles when successful in
novice at Southwell in October: stays 4m: acts on soft and firm going: tried blinkered:
weak finisher. *P. F. Nicholls*

GENERAL CLONEY (IRE) 8 ch.g. Simply Great (FR) – Kitty's Sister (Bustino) **h124**
[2003/4 20s 16d 16s4 16dbd 16g 16d Apr 13] sturdy gelding: fairly useful handicap
hurdler nowadays, off 2½ years before reappearance: stays easy 2¾m: acts on any going.
S. Donohoe, Ireland

GENERAL CUSTER (IRE) 10 b.g. Buckskin (FR) – Cottage Theme (Brave Invader **c—**
(USA)) [2003/4 c25vF 26s3 25g2 26g5 c24gpu Apr 18] rangy gelding: poor maiden **h74**
hurdler: claimed from Evan Williams £3,000 second start: won 3 points in 2003: failed to
complete both outings in steeplechases in 2003/4: stays 3¼m: best efforts on heavy
going: tried blinkered. *F. M. Barton*

GENERAL DUROC (IRE) 8 ch.g. Un Desperado (FR) – Satula (Deep Run) [2003/4 **h114**
h117+, F83: 24dpu 20s4 24d3 24s* 27d Apr 23] well-made gelding: type to make a chaser:
fair handicap hurdler: won at Newcastle in March: should stay beyond 3m: raced on good
ground or softer over hurdles: genuine. *R. T. Phillips*

GENERAL GOSSIP (IRE) 8 b. or br.g. Supreme Leader – Sno-Sleigh (Bargello) **c— p**
[2003/4 h100: 22d2 25d* c24sur 26g Mar 6] sturdy gelding: modest hurdler: won novice **h93**
handicap at Wetherby in December: still to be asked for effort when unseating thirteenth
in handicap at Ascot on chasing debut: stays 25f: raced on good ground or softer: tried
tongue tied. *R. T. Phillips*

GENERAL MONTCALM (IRE) 6 b.g. Roselier (FR) – Pamela's Princess (Black **c119**
Minstrel) [2003/4 c24s2 c24s* c25d2 c24s* c25d3 Apr 13] IR £39,000 3-y-o, resold IR
£38,000 3-y-o: good-topped gelding: fifth foal: half-brother to fair hurdler Melton Made
(by Strong Gale), stayed 21f: dam once-raced half-sister to top-class hurdler/chaser who
stayed 25f Bradbury Star: winning pointer: progressive form first 4 starts in hunters in
2003/4: won at Thurles in February and Gowran in April, beating Castle Weir 25 lengths
at latter: looked likely winner until unseating last in Champion Hunters Chase at Punchestown in late-April: stays 25f: acts on soft ground. *E. J. O'Grady, Ireland*

GENERAL TANTRUM (IRE) 7 b.g. Ilium – Barna Havna (Crash Course) [2003/4 **c—**
h–: c20ddpu Mar 14] strong, lengthy gelding: little sign of ability: tried in cheekpieces. **h—**
A. Ennis

GENERAL WOLFE 15 ch.g. Rolfe (USA) – Pillbox (Spartan General) [2003/4 **c103**
c106, h–: c23v2 May 26] rangy gelding: shows traces of stringhalt: one-time high-class **h—**
chaser: still capable of fair form early in 2003/4, second to Mr Dow Jones in hunter at
Uttoxeter: stays 31f: acts on heavy going. *T. W. Dennis*

GENEROSITY 9 ch.h. Generous (IRE) – Pageantry (Welsh Pageant) [2003/4 16d3 **h90 ?**
16g Jun 12] smart on Flat (probably stays 2¾m) at 4 yrs: very lightly raced over hurdles,
seemingly modest former form when third of 5 in novice at Aintree: should be suited by further
than 2m. *Dr P. Pritchard*

GENEROUS WAYS 9 ch.g. Generous (IRE) – Clara Bow (USA) (Coastal (USA)) **c—**
[2003/4 h90: 16mpu 17gpu 16g 16g3 c16g c16g 16g 17g3 17s Mar 23] sturdy gelding: poor **h82**
hurdler: well held both starts over fences: should stay beyond 2m: acts on good to firm
going: tongue tied: none too reliable. *R. Lee*

GENSCHER 8 b.g. Cadeaux Genereux – Marienbad (FR) (Darshaan) [2003/4 18g c17d^F c20m^{pu} c16g^{pu} c16g^F 22g^{pu} 16g Apr 5] winning hurdler/novice chaser, no form in 2003/4: raced mainly around 2m: acts on firm and soft going: tried in cheekpieces: has had tongue tied: weak finisher. *R. Allan* — **c–** **h–**

GENTLE BEAU 6 b.g. Homo Sapien – Tapua Taranata (IRE) (Mandalus) [2003/4 F98: F17s^4 F17m^2 17g^F 21v^6 16d^6 16g* 19g^5 Mar 9] quite good-topped gelding: fairly useful form in bumpers: fair novice hurdler: won at Ludlow in February: stays 19f. *P. J. Hobbs* — **h102** **r95**

GENUINE ARTICLE (IRE) 8 ch.g. Insan (USA) – Rosemount Rose (Ashmore (FR)) [2003/4 c17m^2 c19m* c19d^{ur} c20g^{pu} c19s^F Jan 31] sturdy gelding: fair hurdler in 2001/2: off course over 2 years and second start over fences, made all in 3-runner maiden at Ascot in November: let down by jumping all 3 subsequent outings: best form up to 19f: acts on firm and good to soft going. *M. Pitman* — **c115** **h–**

GEOGRAPHY (IRE) 4 ch.g. Definite Article – Classic Ring (IRE) (Auction Ring (USA)) [2003/4 16m^4 16f^6 16g^6 17d Nov 17] modest maiden on Flat, sold out of P. Cole's stable 7,000 gns Newmarket July Sales: little show in juvenile hurdles, including a claimer: wears cheekpieces/visor: tried tongue tied. *P. Butler* — **h–**

GEORDIES EXPRESS 12 b.g. Tina's Pet – Maestroes Beauty (Music Maestro) [2003/4 c110: c22s^4 c24f^4 c26d^{ur} c25g^2 c25g Apr 5] leggy, lengthy gelding: fairly useful hunter chaser on his day: stays 27f: probably acts on any going. *G. T. Bewley* — **c102**

GEORGE BLEST 6 ch.g. Safawan – Praise The Lord (Lord Gayle (USA)) [2003/4 F18v F18s Feb 16] 13,000 3-y-o: sixth foal: half-brother to useful hurdler/chaser Whip Hand (by Bob Back), stayed 2½m, bumper winner Mickey Croke (by Alflora) and fair staying chaser Greenwich (by Handsome Sailor): dam Irish maiden: no show in 2 bumpers. *P. Winkworth* — **F–**

GEORGE ROMNEY (USA) 5 b.g. Distant View (USA) – Polish Socialite (USA) (Polish Navy (USA)) [2003/4 16d Mar 1] disappointing maiden on Flat: tongue tied, well beaten in maiden on hurdling debut. *Miss L. J. Sheen* — **h–**

GEORGES GIRL (IRE) 6 b.m. Montelimar (USA) – Keshia (Buckskin (FR)) [2003/4 16s^2 16s^3 16d^2 16s* Feb 14] — **h146**

It's a pity for connections of Georges Girl that the Irish authorities chose not to follow the British Horseracing Board's lead and increase the allowance for mares from 5 lb to 7 lb in Grade 1 races over jumps. The extra 2 lb would, in theory, have made all the difference in the AIG Europe Champion Hurdle at Leopardstown in January, in which Georges Girl went down by just a head to Foreman, belying odds of 25/1. In a muddling contest which developed into a sprint, Georges Girl's performance was greatly to her credit, as she was asked to come from the back of

Red Mills Trial Hurdle, Gowran—
the much improved Georges Girl (near side) just gets the better of Hardy Eustace

Mr Glenn W. D. Martin's "Georges Girl"

the field and just failed after holding every chance at the last. Foreman went on to finish fourth in the Champion Hurdle at Cheltenham and the Leopardstown third Fota Island a good sixth, but Georges Girl's connections hadn't entered her for the Champion, her trainer stating that he would rather wait until 2005. British racegoers might have had a chance to see her in the flesh in the Tote Gold Trophy at Newbury nearly three weeks after Leopardstown, where she would have looked well treated, even from 11 lb out of the handicap, with the weights calculated before the AIG Europe. Georges Girl was an intended runner at the five-day stage but connections decided the ground wouldn't be ideal and she was sent instead for the Grade 2 Red Mills Trial Hurdle at Gowran. This wasn't nearly so valuable a race as the Newbury one but there looked to be just one strong opponent in a field of nine, Hardy Eustace, and he was having to give Georges Girl 13 lb. It proved just enough to tip the balance, Georges Girl nosing ahead towards the finish after Hardy Eustace, without the blinkers he was to wear at Cheltenham, had forced the pace. She won by a short head but, with just ten lengths back to the third, the useful Bob Justice, Georges Girl didn't have to run to her Leopardstown form.

Despite improving the best part of three stone on her 2002/3 form, Georges Girl's win at Gowran proved to be her only one of the season. She faced what was clearly a near-impossible task first time out, trying to give the race-fit Brave Inca 13 lb in a handicap at Navan, running a highly promising race in going down by four lengths after both had travelled on the bridle to the last. A planned outing in a handicap at Leopardstown at Christmas had to be dropped due to the cough but Georges Girl was back there for the Pierse Hurdle a couple of weeks later. She had been an impressive winner of the supporting two-mile handicap on the card the previous year and was well backed at 7/1 to land a race second in value only to the Galway Hurdle among handicap hurdles in Ireland. Turning in, Georges Girl looked all over the winner, travelling every bit as smoothly as she had at Navan but she didn't find so much as Dromlease Express and lost second to Macs Joy near the finish. There were eleven lengths back to the fourth in what proved, in form terms, as strong a handicap hurdle as was run all season. After Gowran, Georges Girl wasn't seen again until she made her Flat debut, in a mile-and-three-quarter minor event at Tipperary. This amateur riders contest was virtually a prep race for horses due to run at the Punchestown Festival, the eight among the first nine home that ran subsequently all appearing over jumps, five of them in Grade 1 races at the Festival. Georges Girl finished second, splitting the stable-companions Solerina and Florida Coast, and faced the winner again at Punchestown (after the end of the British season), in the Emo Oil Champion Hurdle. Fota Island and Hardy Eustace were in the field too, along with Rooster Booster, but Georges Girl looked to have prospects of a place. However, her best efforts have come on good to soft going or softer and she left the strong impression the ground was against her and beat only one home, finishing around seventeen lengths behind Hardy Eustace. Underfoot conditions are likely to dictate plans for Georges Girl in 2004/5.

		Alleged	Hoist The Flag
	Montelimar (USA)	(b 1974)	Princess Pout
	(b 1981)	L'Extravagante	Le Fabuleux
Georges Girl (IRE)		(br 1973)	Fanfreleuche
(b.m. 1998)		Buckskin	Yelapa
	Keshia	(b 1973)	Bete A Bon Dieu
	(ch 1986)	Floater	Brave Invader
		(b 1976)	Lovely Linan

The leggy Georges Girl has raced just once beyond two miles but is bred to stay further, being by Montelimar out of a Buckskin mare. She is the only winner so far out of the dam Keshia, though Aren't We Lucky (by Project Manager) was fair at best and was placed ten times over hurdles and fences at up to twenty-five furlongs. Keshia won on the Flat at up to a mile and a half and is sister or half-sister to three winning hurdlers, the fairly useful two-milers Megabucks and Over The Seas, the latter dam of the useful French hurdler Walk On Seas, and Retinospora, who was also useful over middle distances on the Flat in Italy. The grandam Floater ran just twice in bumpers but her dam Lovely Linan, who was unraced, was still pretty successful at stud, her seven winners including a couple of fairly useful Flat performers, notably Spin of A Coin, who won the Bessborough at Royal Ascot and the Grote Preis der Nederlanden among other races for Ryan Price. *F. Flood, Ireland*

GEORGE STREET (IRE)   6 b.g. Danehill (USA) – Sweet Justice (Law Society (USA)) [2003/4 h–: 20m Aug 8] compact gelding: no form over hurdles. *M. C. Pipe*   **h–**

GEORGIAS GIFT   9 b.g. Genuine Gift (CAN) – Georgias Fancy (Montreal Boy) [2003/4 h–: 16f^pu 20d^pu Mar 11] no show in 3 starts over hurdles: tried tongue tied. *A. M. Crow*   **h–**

GEORGIC BLAZE   10 b.g. Petoski – Pooka (Dominion) [2003/4 c–, h61x: 20d² 20m⁴ May 7] sparely-made gelding: unseated second both starts over fences: poor hurdler: stays 2½m: acts on good to firm and good to soft ground: not a fluent jumper. *G. A. Ham*   **c–** **h63 x**

GEOS (FR)   9 b. or br.g. Pistolet Bleu (IRE) – Kaprika (FR) (Cadoudal (FR)) [2003/4 c152, h147: 16d² 16g* 16g^pu 16m Apr 23]   **c–** **h149**

With twenty-five runners, and the reigning Champion Hurdler heading both the weights and the betting, the latest Tote Gold Trophy was a vintage renewal, proving every bit as competitive in the running as it looked beforehand, as befits the season's most valuable handicap hurdle. In a very strongly-run affair, as many as eight horses still held a chance at the final flight. Top weight Rooster Booster led them over it, looking the likeliest winner, closely attended by the in-form Monkerhostin and the Ladbroke third Saintsaire. Second favourite Sporazene and the previous season's Champion Hurdle runner-up Westender were bang there too, and right on their heels came Saintsaire's stable-companion, the 2000 winner

Geos, beginning to close from off the pace. Rooster Booster was a little untidy at the last but still looked as if he would win for most of the run-in until Geos came with a strong late burst from amongst a pack of pursuers to get up in the very last stride. The winning margin was a short head, with Monkerhostin third, the strong-finishing pair Mughas and Quazar fourth and fifth, and Westender completing the first six home, all of them covered by a couple of lengths or so. The contrast from Geos's first win in the Tote Gold Trophy could not have been greater. Then a five-year-old and relatively unexposed over hurdles, despite good efforts in valuable events at Sandown and Leopardstown beforehand, Geos had won another competitive-looking renewal of the Tote Gold Trophy in scarcely-believable fashion. He had been one of only two horses who ever looked like winning in the straight, and his winning margin of ten lengths was the widest for more than twenty years.

In the four years between his Tote Gold Trophy wins, the handicapper had had ample opportunity to establish Geos's merits and he was one of the most exposed horses in the line-up for the latest edition, as well as one of the senior runners (although a year junior to Rooster Booster). It was his first appearance in a handicap since the 1999/00 season, having spent most of the intervening period competing in top company over both hurdles and fences. Highlights included winning both the Bula Hurdle and Christmas Hurdle late in 2000, finishing fourth in the 2002 Champion Hurdle, and filling the same position in the following season's Champion Chase after gaining his only win over British fences in the Castleford Chase at Wetherby. Geos had had just one outing in the latest season prior to Newbury, finishing second to The French Furze in the 'Fighting Fifth' Hurdle at Newcastle.

Geos's debut in Britain had been a successful one under the then 7 lb-claiming amateur Marcus Foley. More than four years later, Geos gave Foley the biggest win of his career so far at Newbury, whilst stable-jockey Mick Fitzgerald was sidelined through injury. Fitzgerald had partnered Geos in 2000, as well as Nicky Henderson's other Tote Gold Trophy winners, Sharpical in 1998 and Landing Light (who also beat Rooster Booster into second) in 2001. Four wins in seven runnings is an outstanding training record in such a competitive handicap. 'It's a very lucky race [for me] but I don't know why,' commented the trainer afterwards. 'It's not as though I'm as good at laying out horses for handicaps.' Henderson's campaigning of horses in handicaps met with considerable success in big races in the latest season in particular, his methods contrasting with the approach of the man whose record of four Gold Trophy wins Henderson has now equalled.

Tote Gold Trophy Hurdle (Handicap), Newbury—2000 winner Geos
tracks top weight Rooster Booster (checked cap) before collaring him in the dying strides;
also close up are eventual third Monkerhostin (right) and the fading Saintsaire (striped cap)

Thurloe Finsbury's "Geos"

Captain Ryan Price was a master at 'laying one out' and his record of four wins in the first five runnings of the then Schweppes-sponsored Gold Trophy was as controversial as it was remarkable. Rosyth had been placed just once from five starts earlier in the season when adding the 1964 Schweppes (beating subsequent Champion Hurdle winner Salmon Spray) to his win in the inaugural running (against forty rivals at Aintree) the previous year, a result which led to Price having his licence withdrawn for the remainder of that season, as well as jockey Josh Gifford being suspended. Le Vermontois won the stable a third Schweppes in 1966, but the authorities took a dim view again after Hill House showed considerable improvement when winning by twelve lengths the following season. That victory came just a week after he had finished only fourth in a lesser race at Sandown. A protracted inquiry ensued (extending to 171 days!), but the case was finally dismissed after no reason could be established for Hill House's dramatic improvement. Tests revealed a high concentration of the steroid hormone cortisol in the horse's system, but there was nothing to suggest that he had not produced it naturally. Geos, incidentally, became the first horse since Rosyth to win the race twice.

The stud record of Kaprika has continued to flourish since she produced Geos as her first foal. Kaprika's next winner was Cyborsun (by Cyborg), a fairly useful hurdler in France, before winning over fences at Naas for Arthur Moore in the latest season. Daprika (by Epervier Bleu) won on the Flat and over fences (as a four-year-old at Enghien) in France before showing just fair form in a couple of novice hurdles for Nicky Henderson in 2002/3; she was sold for 80,000 guineas at Tattersalls in December. The best of Geos's siblings so far is Kapgarde (by Garde Royale), now standing at stud alongside his maternal grandsire Cadoudal. The Guillaume Macaire-trained Kapgarde showed useful form over hurdles at Auteuil, winning a Group 3 event for four-year-olds and showing better form still in three runs over fences later that year, finishing a close second in the Group 1 Prix Ferdinand Dufaure. Kaprika herself won over eleven furlongs on the Flat and over two miles over hurdles in France and is a sister to Lord Dal, formerly a useful hurdler and fairly useful chaser at up to three miles in Ireland.

		Pistolet Bleu (IRE) (b 1988)	Top Ville (b 1976)	High Top / Sega Ville
Geos (FR) (b. or br.g. 1995)			Pampa Bella (ch 1981)	Armos / Kendie
	Kaprika (FR) (b 1989)	Cadoudal (br 1979)	Green Dancer / Come To Sea
		Lady Corteira (ch 1981)	Carvin / Nadrusa

Geos is a smallish, strong gelding. He is not an obvious chaser on looks but his form when last seen over fences in Britain (he ran solely over hurdles in the latest campaign) is on a par with what he has shown over hurdles. He stays two and a half miles, at least when the emphasis is on speed, and acts on heavy ground, though probably not on good to firm. Geos ran twice after the Tote Gold Trophy but ran poorly both times, being pulled up in the Champion Hurdle and then beating only one home in the Concept Hurdle at Sandown. Geos ended his two previous campaigns with poor efforts only to bounce back the following season, so he could yet play a part in good company again in 2004/5. *N. J. Henderson*

GERALDO (IRE) 7 b.g. Lycius (USA) – Floralia (Auction Ring (USA)) [2003/4 c24gpu c25s 17gpu c23mpu Jul 23] ex-Irish gelding: half-brother to 2m hurdle winner Henry Afrika (by Mujadil): dam, maiden hurdler, half-sister to useful 2m hurdler Carlito Brigante: fair maiden on Flat (stays 1m) at 3 yrs: winning pointer: little form over hurdles/in steeplechases, left S. Gannon after second start: tried tongue tied: sold €4,000 Goffs October Sale. *Noel T. Chance* c– h–

GERI ROULETTE 6 b.m. Perpendicular – Clashfern (Smackover) [2003/4 16s 21vpu 16v* 20sF 17dur Apr 10] good-topped mare: modest on Flat (stays 15f) for E. Alston: easily best effort over hurdles when winning 20-runner mares maiden at Newcastle in January: let down by jumping both subsequent starts: should stay beyond 2m: acts on heavy going. *M. Todhunter* h89

GERRARD (IRE) 6 b.g. Jurado (USA) – Vienna Waltz (IRE) (Orchestra) [2003/4 F16s F16d F17s4 21gpu 21g Mar 26] lengthy gelding: first foal: dam, Irish maiden hurdler, half-sister to temperamental 2m to 2½m hurdle winner Counterpunch: best effort in bumpers (has looked temperamental) when fourth at Exeter: no encouragement in 2 runs over hurdles. *Mrs A. Barclay* h– F84

GETAWAY GIRL 6 b.m. Perpendicular – Viowen (IRE) (Denel (FR)) [2003/4 F16s Apr 12] second reported foal: dam of little account over hurdles: tailed off in mares bumper on debut. *O. Brennan* F–

GETINBYBUTONLYJUST 5 b.g. King's Ride – Madame President (IRE) (Supreme Leader) [2003/4 F16g6 20s6 20v Feb 4] first foal: dam, modest hurdler, stayed 21f: achieved little in bumper and novice hurdles. *Mrs Dianne Sayer* h– F–

GET THE POINT 10 b.g. Sadler's Wells (USA) – Tolmi (Great Nephew) [2003/4 c–, h–: c16mpu c16s* c16g5 c22v3 c21s* c17d2 Apr 24] compact gelding: modest chaser: left R. Stronge after reappearance: won handicaps at Towcester in November and Folkestone in January: stays 2¾m, effective at much shorter: acts on good to firm and heavy going: wore cheekpieces last 2 starts: tried tongue tied. *G. Brown* c93 h–

GET UP AND GO GO (IRE) 7 ch.g. Mister Lord (USA) – Monadante (IRE) (Phardante (FR)) [2003/4 F–: 21d Apr 12] well-made gelding: well held in bumper on debut: better for race, seventh of 18 to Gracilis in maiden hurdle at Huntingdon 18 months later: should do better. *K. C. Bailey* h90 p

GHADAMES (FR) 10 b.g. Synefos (USA) – Ouargla (FR) (Armos) [2003/4 c120d, h–: c20m6 c21g2 c20mpu c20gF 20v* 17s5 Feb 11] fair handicap chaser: sold out of W. M. Brisbourne's stable 3,000 gns Doncaster August Sales after reappearance: first c110 h97

start over hurdles for over 3 years, won conditional jockeys selling handicap at Newcastle in January: best around 2½m: acts on any going: has broken blood vessels, including third outing: goes well fresh. *M. Todhunter*

GHOST MOON 9 b.g. Cadeaux Genereux – Sickle Moon (Shirley Heights) [2003/4 c65x, h–; c20m^{ur} Jun 7] no form over hurdles: poor-jumping novice chaser. *R. J. Hodges* — **c– x h–**

GHOST RIDER (IRE) 7 br.g. Good Thyne (USA) – Pit Runner (Deep Run) [2003/4 F16g^4 20s 18s^4 16v^2 16d Feb 21] IR 36,000 3-y-o: fourth foal: dam, 2m hurdle winner, half-sister to fairly useful chaser around 2½m Visible Difference, out of half-sister to high-class 2m to 2½m chaser Travado: fourth of 17 in bumper at Perth (finished distressed): also travelled comfortably long way when showing progressive form first 3 starts over hurdles: ran as if amiss final start: raced on going softer than good. *L. Lungo* — **h98 F89**

GHUTAH 10 ch.g. Lycius (USA) – Barada (USA) (Damascus (USA)) [2003/4 c91, h87: c16m^4 c16m^4 c16d^{pu} 17g^5 16m^5 16m Aug 8] leggy gelding: modest chaser: poor hurdler: ideally suited by around 2m: best form on good to firm/firm going: blinkered once: best held up: sold £2,300 Ascot December Sales. *Mrs A. M. Thorpe* — **c86 h74**

GIDEON PUTNAM (IRE) 6 b. or br.g. Good Thyne (USA) – Penthouse Pearl (Green Shoon) [2003/4 F16m* F16f^2 24g^6 20s^5 20d^4 Dec 27] 7,500 4-y-o: lengthy, angular gelding: second foal: half-brother to winning pointer by Phardante: dam 2m hurdle winner: won bumper at Chepstow on debut in October: better form when second to New Mischief at Cheltenham: best effort in novice hurdles (badly let down by jumping first time) when fifth to Mon Villez at Uttoxeter: should stay 3m. *Jonjo O'Neill* — **h94 F103**

GIELGUD 7 b.g. Faustus (USA) – Shirl (Shirley Heights) [2003/4 h99: 20m* 21m^3 c22g^2 c24g^{pu} c20g^3 c24g^{pu} c22m^F c24g^{pu} Mar 16] strong, sturdy gelding: modest hurdler: landed odds in 5-runner novice at Wetherby in May: fair form only 2 completed starts over fences: stays 2¾m: acts on soft and good to firm going: usually tongue tied (has reportedly suffered breathing problems): joined N. Twiston-Davies. *P. R. Webber* — **c111 d h93**

GIFTNEYEV (FR) 5 b. or br.g. Goldneyev (USA) – Girl's Gift (FR) (Gairloch) [2003/4 h–: 18g^F May 5] little encouragement in 2 starts over hurdles, tongue tied on second. *C. P. Morlock* — **h–**

GIGS BOUNTY 6 ch.g. Weld – City's Sister (Maystreak) [2003/4 F82: F16g^6 16g* 21s* 20d^2 21s Dec 13] rather unfurnished gelding: modest form at best in bumpers: progressive first 3 starts over hurdles, won novices at Uttoxeter in October and Plumpton in November: stays 21f: acts on soft going. *M. Pitman* — **h109 F68**

GIGS GAMBIT (IRE) 7 ch.g. Hubbly Bubbly (USA) – Music Slipper (Orchestra) [2003/4 c–, h85: c26m* c22g* c26m^3 c24m^{pu} c26d^{pu} Dec 31] well-made gelding: modest form in novice hurdles: won first 2 completed starts over fences, novice handicaps at Fontwell in September and October: disappointing after: stays 3¼m: acts on soft and good to firm going: wore cheekpieces final start. *M. Pitman* — **c100 h–**

GILBERT WHITE 11 b.g. Little Wolf – Caribs Love (Caliban) [2003/4 h–: 16m^6 16m^{pu} Jun 18] rather sparely-made gelding: little form over hurdles. *R. Lee* — **h–**

GILDED ALLY 4 b.g. Gildoran – Allyfair (Scallywag) [2003/4 F16m F17g Apr 1] third foal: dam, modest novice hurdler, stayed well: well held in 2 bumpers. *Mrs S. Gardner* — **F–**

GILFOOT BREEZE (IRE) 7 b.g. Forest Wind (USA) – Ma Bella Luna (Jalmood (USA)) [2003/4 h75: 16m^3 16g^3 17g^5 16f^3 17g^4 18d^2 16s^3 20v^3 Jan 21] compact gelding: poor maiden hurdler: best around 2m: acts on good to firm and good to soft going: tongue tied third outing. *A. Robson* — **h75**

GILLESPIE (IRE) 5 b.g. Persian Bold – Share The Vision (Vision (USA)) [2003/4 F16m F17m^5 21f^5 Oct 8] eighth foal: brother to one-time fairly useful performer Homelife, stays 2m, and half-brother to 3 winners: dam unraced, out of half-sister to Oaks winner Pia: poor form in 2 bumpers: tailed off in seller on hurdling debut. *D. G. Bridgwater* — **h– F74 ?**

GILL THE TILL (IRE) 5 ch.m. Anshan – Bilander (High Line) [2003/4 h–: 22g 22g^5 Nov 5] little form over hurdles. *R. J. Baker* — **h–**

GILOU 8 b.m. Midyan (USA) – Lunagraphe (USA) (Time For A Change (USA)) [2003/4 h77: 21g^3 22m^5 20f* 16m* 16g Apr 5] modest hurdler: won handicap in September and mares novice in October, both at Hexham: effective at 2m to 3m: raced mainly on good to firm/firm going. *C. W. Fairhurst* — **h86**

GIMME SHELTER (IRE) 10 ch.m. Glacial Storm (USA) – Glen Dieu (Furry Glen) [2003/4 c98, h73: 20d c30d[F] c27v[pu] 24v c28d[6] c26d[pu] c32d[4] Mar 18] lengthy, sparely-made mare: winning hurdler: poor handicap chaser, generally let down by jumping in 2003/4: suited by thorough test of stamina: acts on heavy going. *S. J. Marshall* — c82 x h–

GIMMICK (FR) 10 b.g. Chamberlin (FR) – Jaida (FR) (Alfaro) [2003/4 c106, h104: 20m[2] 16f* 16m 16g Nov 30] good-topped gelding: fair form over fences (needs to brush up his jumping): fairly useful handicap hurdler: back to near best when winning at Wetherby in October by 2½ lengths from Rigmarole: effective at 2m to 2½m: acts on any going: blinkered once. *Jonjo O'Neill* — c– h116

GIN 4 b.f. Abou Zouz (USA) – Skedaddle (Formidable (USA)) [2003/4 17g 16g[pu] Sep 24] poor form at 2 yrs for M. W. Easterby: showed nothing in juvenile hurdles. *J. Wade* — h–

GIN AND TERIMONIC 6 gr.m. Terimon – Genie Spirit (Nishapour (FR)) [2003/4 F70: F18s[4] Nov 3] poor form when fourth in 2 bumpers. *P. Winkworth* — F70

GINGERBREAD HOUSE (IRE) 6 b.g. Old Vic – Furun (IRE) (Deep Run) [2003/4 20d* 20g[4] Apr 16] €14,000 4-y-o: lengthy gelding: second foal: dam unraced sister to fairly useful hurdler up to 3m Granville Guest: won twice in Irish points in 2003: favourite, won maiden at Wetherby on hurdling debut in March by 6 lengths from Terre de Java, made most: similar form when fourth of 6 to Bourbon Manhattan in novice at Ayr: will stay 3m. *R. T. Phillips* — h113

GINGERBREAD MAN 9 ch.g. Derrylin – Red Rambler (Rymer) [2003/4 c–, h–: c16g[pu] May 10] good-topped gelding: of little account: tried tongue tied. *J. A. Moore* — c– h–

GINGER FOLLY (IRE) 6 ch.m. General Monash (USA) – Lapland Lights (USA) (Northern Prospect (USA)) [2003/4 F16m[6] Oct 4] plain mare: third foal: dam fair 6f winner: showed nothing in bumper on debut. *P. Butler* — F–

GINGERSLOOKINGREAT (IRE) 5 ch.g. Ashkalani (IRE) – Just An Illusion (IRE) (Shernazar) [2003/4 F17g[4] May 18] first foal: dam fair 2m to 2½m hurdler: tongue tied, 18¼ lengths fourth to Your A Gassman in bumper at Southwell on debut. *O. Brennan* — F86

GINGKO 7 b.g. Pursuit of Love – Arboretum (IRE) (Green Desert (USA)) [2003/4 h88: 17g 16s[3] Dec 20] well-made gelding: fair on Flat (stays 1½m), successful in January: modest novice hurdler: raced around 2m on good going or softer. *P. R. Webber* — h87

GINNER MORRIS 9 b.g. Emarati (USA) – Just Run (IRE) (Runnett) [2003/4 h67: 16d 16g[3] Dec 3] smallish, deep-girthed gelding: poor maiden hurdler: unlikely to stay much beyond 2m: acts on soft ground. *J. Hetherton* — h66

GIN PALACE (IRE) 6 gr.g. King's Theatre (IRE) – Ikala (Lashkari) [2003/4 h120: 21g* 16s[5] 20g 20m[3] Apr 24] good-topped gelding: fairly useful handicap hurdler: won at Kempton in February by ¾ length from Narwhal: creditable efforts at Sandown after when fifth to Scorned in valuable event and third to Korelo: stays 21f: acts on soft and good to firm going: sometimes looks unwilling. *G. L. Moore* — h125

GINSKI 8 b.g. Petoski – Upham Lass (Sula Bula) [2003/4 h–: 22m[pu] 21s[pu] 26g[pu] Apr 3] rather dipped-backed gelding: of little account: sometimes tongue tied. *C. J. Drewe* — h–

GIOCOMO (IRE) 6 ch.g. Indian Ridge – Karri Valley (USA) (Storm Bird (CAN)) [2003/4 h128: c16g* c17d[ur] c19g* c20v[pu] Jan 31] sturdy gelding: fairly useful hurdler (hasn't looked most straightforward of rides): successful both completed starts over fences, in 4-runner maiden at Hexham in November and novice at Catterick in January: stays 2½m: raced on good going or softer (acts on soft): blinkered once: patiently ridden: joined F. Murtagh. *R. A. Fahey* — c110 h–

GIOLLA DE (IRE) 5 b.g. Glacial Storm (USA) – Deep Inagh (Deep Run) [2003/4 F16s[4] F16d[2] F16d[6] Apr 13] fourth foal: half-brother to fairly useful hurdler/fair chaser The Culdee (by Phardante), stays 25f: dam, useful 2m hurdler, from family of top-class 2m to 3m chaser Lough Inagh: fairly useful form in bumpers, 2½ lengths second to Green Peach at Naas in March. *F. Flood, Ireland* — F102

GIORGIO (IRE) 6 b.g. Presenting – Billys Pet (Le Moss) [2003/4 h84: 17g[4] 19s[pu] Dec 20] eighth foal: half-brother to useful hurdler/chaser Ashwell Boy, stays 25f, and fair hurdler up to 2½m Macaw-Bay (both by Strong Gale): dam unraced: 8½ lengths fourth to Attorney General in novice hurdle at Newton Abbot on debut: ran as if amiss next time. *P. J. Hobbs* — h84

GIPSY CRICKETER 8 b.g. Anshan – Tinkers Fairy (Myjinski (USA)) [2003/4 c79, h–: c16m[5] c16m[5] May 26] leggy, sparely-made gelding: poor handicap chaser: won point — c76 h–

in April: stays 2½m: seems suited by good going or firmer (acts on firm): has had tongue tied: headstrong: has been reluctant at start. *D. J. Caro*

GIPSY WOOD   8 gr.m. Rakaposhi King – Silva Linda (Precipice Wood) [2003/4 h–: 16m 17g⁶ 20g 20mᵖᵘ Jun 14] no form over hurdles. *P. Beaumont*   **h–**

GIULIANI   4 b.g. Sadler's Wells (USA) – Anka Germania (Malinowski (USA)) [2003/4 16g 20d⁶ Mar 11] useful-looking gelding: fairly useful on Flat (will stay at least 1¾m), sold out of L. Cumani's stable 40,000 gns Newmarket Autumn Sales: better effort over hurdles when sixth to Monet's Garden in novice at Carlisle, held up and keeping on not knocked about: should improve again. *J. Howard Johnson*   **h83 p**

GIUST IN TEMP (IRE)   5 b.h. Polish Precedent (USA) – Blue Stricks (Bluebird (USA)) [2003/4 16m 16m⁴ 16m² 16g Oct 30] sparely-made horse: poor maiden on Flat (stays 9.4f): best effort over hurdles when second in seller at Stratford: will prove best at 2m. *P. W. Hiatt*   **h79**

GIVE OVER (IRE)   11 b.g. Lord Americo – Romany River (Over The River (FR)) [2003/4 c133, h133: c24g 24m Oct 11] compact gelding: useful hurdler/chaser in 2002/3, below best in 2003/4: stays 29f: best efforts on going softer than good (acts on heavy): tried in cheekpieces: effective held up or ridden prominently. *E. U. Hales, Ireland*   **c–**
h118

GIVERNY (GER)   6 ro.m. Sternkoenig (IRE) – Georgia O'Keeffe (GER) (Helikon (GER)) [2003/4 15g⁶ 15g³ 16g² 17s Dec 16] successful 3 times up to 11f on Flat at 3 yrs, placed on plenty of occasions since: placed over hurdles at Hoppegarten (handicap) and Milan (minor event) in autumn: well beaten in novice at Folkestone. *Frau A. Bertram, Germany*   **h?**

GLACIAL DANCER (IRE)   11 b.g. Glacial Storm (USA) – Castleblagh (General Ironside) [2003/1 c26gᵖᵘ c21s⁴ c25gᵘʳ Mar 28] lengthy gelding: winning hunter/pointer: well held in hunter on completed start in steeplechases in 2003/4: stays 3m: raced on good going or softer (acts on heavy). *Mrs E. J. Clark*   **c77**
h–

GLACIAL DELIGHT (IRE)   5 b.g. Glacial Storm (USA) – Annagh Delight (Saint Denys) [2003/4 F17g Apr 13] eleventh foal: half-brother to winning pointer by Never Got A Chance: dam never ran: ran 3 times in Irish points in 2004, won maiden in January on completed start: eighth of 15 in bumper at Exeter. *Miss E. C. Lavelle*   **F81**

GLACIAL EVENING (IRE)   8 b. or br.g. Glacial Storm (USA) – Cold Evening (IRE) (Strong Gale) [2003/4 h–, F–: 20m⁴ 17f³ 20m² 22m² 22d⁴ 24s* 23s* 22m Feb 21] sturdy gelding: modest hurdler: much improved when winning handicaps at Newbury (21-runner conditional jockeys event) in January and Wetherby (beat Falchion 12 lengths) in February: will stay beyond 3m: best form on soft ground. *R. H. Buckler*   **h99**

GLACIAL RIVER (IRE)   11 ch.g. Glacial Storm (USA) – Lucky Trout (Beau Charmeur (FR)) [2003/4 c91, h–: c24gᵖᵘ c24gᵖᵘ Apr 18] lengthy gelding: modest maiden chaser, off 15 months before reappearance: hampered by loose horse next time: stays 29f: acts on soft and good to firm going. *D. J. Caro*   **c–**
h–

GLACIAL SUNSET (IRE)   9 b.g. Glacial Storm (USA) – Twinkle Sunset (Deep Run) [2003/4 h115+: 21gᵇᵈ 24g 20m Apr 24] workmanlike gelding: fairly useful hurdler: much higher in weights in 2003/4, ran creditably in quite valuable handicap won by Korelo at Sandown final outing: stays 3¼m: acts on firm and good to soft going. *C. Tinkler*   **h118**

GLACIAL TRIAL (IRE)   11 b.m. Glacial Storm (USA) – Protrial (Proverb) [2003/4 c103: c24g* c28g⁴ May 31] fairly useful hunter chaser: led close home when winning at Bangor in May: 50/1, creditable fourth to Bitofamixup in valuable event at Stratford: stays 3½m. *P. Jones*   **c106**

GLADIATORIAL (IRE)   12 b.g. Mazaad – Arena (Sallust) [2003/4 c19sᵖᵘ Apr 6] fair pointer, won 2-runner race in April: let down by jumping in hunter earlier in month: stays 3m: acts on soft and good to firm going (bumper winner on heavy): tried visored/tongue tied. *Mrs Frances Bishop*   **c–**
h–

GLADIE   9 ch.m. Arzanni – Palm Lady (Palm Track) [2003/4 20m⁶ Aug 2] first foal: dam no sign of ability: sixth of 12 in novice hurdle at Worcester on belated debut. *Mrs S. M. Johnson*   **h–**

GLADSTONE SPIRIT (IRE)   4 b.g. Woodborough (USA) – Alpencrocus (IRE) (Waajib) [2003/4 16g³ 16g 16gᵘʳ 17dF Mar 30] smallish gelding: modest form on Flat at 2 yrs for J. Glover: poor form on hurdling debut, well held only other completed start. *G. M. Moore*   **h75**

GLADTOKNOWYOU (IRE) 11 ch.g. Over The River (FR) – Jonsemma (IRE) **c108**
(Denel (FR)) [2003/4 c98: c21s* c24d⁶ c21mᵖᵘ Feb 21] lengthy gelding: lightly raced:
fair chaser: won on reappearance for second successive season, in handicap at Wincanton
in January: ran poorly there final outing: stays 2¾m: acts on soft going. *R. Rowe*

GLADYS AYLWARD 4 b.f. Polar Falcon (USA) – Versami (USA) (Riverman (USA)) **h–**
[2003/4 16f Nov 22] claimed £6,000 from T. Easterby after successful over 7f in June, no
form on Flat since: well held in juvenile claimer (blinkered) on hurdling debut: sold 1,400
gns Doncaster March Sales. *A. Crook*

GLAMOUR GIRL 8 b.m. Lord Americo – Money Galore (IRE) (Monksfield) [2003/4 **h–**
h–: 22m May 29] compact mare: signs of only a little ability. *F. Jordan*

GLANDORE MOON 5 br.g. Presenting – My Gonny (IRE) (Mandalus) [2003/4 F16s **F–**
Mar 20] first foal: dam winning Irish pointer: well held in bumper on debut. *N. J. Gifford*

GLANMERIN (IRE) 13 b.g. Lomond (USA) – Abalvina (FR) (Abdos) [2003/4 c88, **c71 §**
h–: c20g⁶ c21gᵘʳ c21mᵖᵘ c24gᵘʳ c25v³ c19vᶠ c20s³ c24gᵖᵘ c21gᵖᵘ Apr 10] leggy gelding: **h–**
poor handicap chaser: stays 2½m: acts on good to firm and easy going (won on good to firm on Flat):
tried tongue tied earlier in career: ungenuine. *R. Lee*

GLASHEDY ROCK (IRE) 7 b.g. Shernazar – Classical Lady (IRE) (Orchestra) **h–**
[2003/4 h89: 22gᵖᵘ Oct 30] lengthy gelding: won maiden Irish point in 2002: maiden
hurdler, pulled up possibly amiss only start in 2003/4: likely to stay 3m. *Miss H. C. Knight*

GLASS BREAKER 10 b.g. Infantry – Bottle Basher (Le Soleil) [2003/4 c–: c30mᵖᵘ **c–**
May 10] poor pointer: tried blinkered. *Mrs Debby Ewing*

GLASS NOTE (IRE) 6 b.m. Spectrum (IRE) – Alice En Ballade (Tap On Wood) **h–**
[2003/4 19gᵖᵘ 17gᵖᵘ 20m 17m⁶ 21gᵖᵘ 16mᵖᵘ 16fʳᵒ 16m⁶ 20m³ 16vᶠ 16vᵘʳ 16s⁶ 19v 16sᵖᵘ
20sᵖᵘ Apr 17] leggy mare: fair at best on Flat (stays 13f), sold out of T. Stack's stable
€16,000 Goffs February (2003) Sale: no form over hurdles: tried blinkered/tongue tied:
headstrong. *S. T. Lewis*

GLASSON HOUSE (IRE) 5 b.m. Supreme Leader – Nasowas (IRE) (Cardinal **F81**
Flower) [2003/4 F16m² F16m⁴ Aug 2] first foal: dam, maiden hurdler, from family of
top-class 2m to 2½m hurdler Beech Road: modest form when in frame in bumpers at
Worcester: joined R. Phillips. *P. D. Evans*

GLENBURN (IRE) 6 br.g. Dr Devious (IRE) – Edwina (IRE) (Caerleon (USA)) **c– §**
[2003/4 h–: 16g 16m⁵ 16g⁶ 16g c17dʳᵒ 16g Feb 18] no form over hurdles: ran out sixth on **h– §**
chasing debut: tongue tied: refused to race March 12. *Miss Lucinda V. Russell*

GLENCOYLE (IRE) 4 b.g. In The Wings – Lucky State (USA) (State Dinner (USA)) **h109**
[2003/4 16g² 16d* 19g² Mar 27] smallish gelding: fairly useful on Flat (stays 2m), sold
out of A. Stewart's stable 40,000 gns Newmarket Autumn Sales: fair form over hurdles,
won maiden at Plumpton in March: hung badly left under pressure when second to easy
winner Business Traveller in juvenile handicap at Newbury: will be suited by 2½m+.
N. J. Henderson

GLENDAMAH (IRE) 7 b.g. Mukaddamah (USA) – Sea Glen (IRE) (Glenstal (USA)) **h69**
[2003/4 h79: 17s⁵ 20g⁶ May 24] poor hurdler: in frame in points in March and April: stays
easy 21f: acts on good to firm and good to soft ground. *J. R. Weymes*

GLENDEVON GREY 5 gr.g. Karinga Bay – Sandy Etna (IRE) (Sandalay (IRE)) **h–**
[2003/4 F17d F16s 24s Feb 14] workmanlike gelding: first foal: dam maiden pointer: **F–**
well beaten in 2 bumpers and novice hurdle. *G. M. Moore*

GLENELLY GALE (IRE) 10 b. or br.g. Strong Gale – Smart Fashion (Carlburg) **c143**
[2003/4 c127, h–: c17g³ c17d c20f³ c24m² c24f* c16m² 16d⁶ c18d³ c25g c16m Apr 24] **h103**
big, lengthy gelding: winning hurdler: useful chaser: much improved when winning
4-runner Grade 1 James Nicholson Wine Merchant Champion Chase at Down Royal in
November by ¾ length from Arctic Copper: creditable efforts when placed after, third of
7 to Alcapone in minor event at Thurles: stiff tasks last 2 outings: effective at 2m to easy
3m: acts on any going. *A. L. T. Moore, Ireland*

GLENFARCLAS BOY (IRE) 8 b.g. Montelimar (USA) – Fairy Blaze (IRE) (Good **c97 §**
Thyne (USA)) [2003/4 c90, h–: c24g c20s* c20m⁵ c20s* c20sᵖᵘ c16s c20gᶠ c20g² c20sᶠ **h–**
Apr 21] good-topped gelding: modest chaser: won minor events at Perth (fortunate) in
May and Ayr in December: stays 21f: acts on soft and good to firm going: wore cheek-
pieces last 3 starts: often let down by jumping: inconsistent. *Miss Lucinda V. Russell*

GLENGARRA (IRE) 7 ch.g. Phardante (FR) – Glengarra Princess (Cardinal Flower) **h82**
[2003/4 20g 20d³ 16v⁵ 18sᵖᵘ 22g Apr 10] deep-girthed gelding: second foal: dam,
winning hurdler/pointer who stayed 2½m, out of half-sister to smart chaser up to 2¾m
Villierstown: completed once from 3 starts in maiden points in 2003: poor novice hurdler:
looked none too keen fourth start: stays 2½m. *D. R. Gandolfo*

GLENHAVEN BOY (IRE) 6 br.g. Satco (FR) – Dunabell Lady (Garda's Revenge **h–**
(USA)) [2003/4 24gᵖᵘ Nov 21] IR £18,000 3-y-o, €36,000 4-y-o: seventh foal: half-
brother to winning pointer by Farhaan: dam twice-raced on Flat: won maiden on second
of 2 starts in Irish points in 2003: bought 59,000 gns Doncaster May Sales: not fluent and
left well behind when pace increased in novice hurdle at Ascot. *K. C. Bailey*

GLENHAVEN NUGGET (IRE) 8 br.g. Supreme Leader – Jasmine Melody (Jas- **c114**
mine Star) [2003/4 h122: 16d⁵ c19m² Sep 15] sturdy gelding: fairly useful hurdler: odds **h–**
on, made mistakes and found little when second to Colca Canyon in maiden at Listowel
on chasing debut: should stay 2½m: acts on soft going, probably on good to firm: tried
tongue tied in bumpers: not a fluent jumper or a straightforward ride. *E. J. O'Grady,
Ireland*

GLENMOSS TARA (IRE) 6 b.m. Zaffaran (USA) – Majestic Run (Deep Run) **h122**
[2003/4 h122+: 16d² 21s⁵ Dec 13] lengthy, workmanlike mare: has reportedly had minor
wind operation: fairly useful hurdler: creditable second to Feel The Pride in mares
handicap at Ayr on reappearance: stiffish task when well held in intermediate minor event
at Cheltenham (breathing problem) next time: will stay beyond 21f: acts on soft and good
to firm going: tends to idle: tail swisher. *N. G. Richards*

GLENOGUE (IRE) 6 b.m. Hushang (IRE) – Glenamal (Kemal (FR)) [2003/4 16v⁴ **h98**
22s³ 16v³ 19d² 21g⁴ 24s² Apr 21] has scope: third foal: half-sister to winning pointer by
Febrino: dam winning pointer: won maiden Irish point in 2003: modest form over hurdles: 5 lb out of handicap when fourth to Kentford Grebe in valuable mares handicap at
Newbury: probably stays 3m: raced on good going or softer (acts on heavy). *K. C. Bailey*

Mr Frank Bradley's "Glenelly Gale"

GLEN WARRIOR 8 b.g. Michelozzo (USA) – Mascara VII (Damsire Unregistered) **h118**
[2003/4 h98p: 22s* 24g² 22d 21s³ 24d* 24d² Mar 27] tall gelding: chasing type: fairly
useful handicap hurdler: progressive sort, won at Newton Abbot early in season and
Bangor in March: best effort when short-head second to Limerick Leader at latter course
final start: likely to prove best at 3m+: raced on good going or softer: patiently ridden:
reliable. *J. S. Smith*

GLIMPSE OF GLORY 4 b.g. Makbul – Bright-One (Electric) [2003/4 16m 16d **h–**
Nov 14] good-topped gelding: half-brother to fairly useful hurdler/chaser Albrighton (by
Terimon), stays 25f, and 2¾m hurdle winner Mill-Dot (by Petoski): dam winning 2m
hurdler: no form on Flat or in 2 juvenile hurdles. *C. W. Thornton*

GLINGER (IRE) 11 b.g. Remainder Man – Harilla (Sir Herbert) [2003/4 c102, h–: **c104**
20d² 22m² c20g* Aug 16] workmanlike gelding: modest maiden hurdler: fair chaser: **h91**
successful on 3 of last 4 starts over fences, including when making all in 4-runner handicap at Perth: stays 2¾m: acts on good to firm and good to soft going: sound jumper.
N. G. Richards

GLOAMING 6 b.m. Celtic Swing – Kandavu (Safawan) [2003/4 17g⁵ 16mᵖᵘ Oct 18] **h–**
angular mare: one-time fair 6f winner on Flat, poor and unreliable in 2003: no show in 2
starts over hurdles. *J. Gallagher*

GLOBAL CHALLENGE (IRE) 5 b.g. Sadler's Wells (USA) – Middle Prospect **h104 §**
(USA) (Mr Prospector (USA)) [2003/4 16d³ 20s³ 16v 20s 25d⁵ 21d⁴ Apr 12] sturdy
gelding: useful 1½m winner on Flat, lightly raced, for Sir Michael Stoute: fair novice
hurdler: stays 2½m: tried blinkered/tongue tied: temperamental. *Jonjo O'Neill*

GLOBE STAR (IRE) 5 b.m. Germany (USA) – Chaparette (Chaparly (FR)) [2003/4 **F–**
F16g F16d Apr 23] third foal: dam never ran: well held in bumpers. *F. P. Murtagh*

GLORIOUS WELCOME 6 b.g. Past Glories – Rest And Welcome (Town And **h–**
Country) [2003/4 h–: 24s 19v 26gᵖᵘ 21gᵖᵘ Apr 12] sparely-made gelding: of no account:
visored: often tongue tied. *Jane Southcombe*

GLORY OF LOVE 9 b.g. Belmez (USA) – Princess Lieven (Royal Palace) [2003/4 **h–**
22g Nov 4] lengthy gelding: maiden hurdler, very lightly raced: tried visored. *J. A. Supple*

GLORY STOREY (IRE) 10 b.g. Tremblant – Boule de Soie (The Parson) [2003/4 **c–**
c99, h–: 24sᵖᵘ Dec 29] useful-looking gelding: modest handicap chaser for K. Bailey: no **h–**
show back over hurdles only outing in 2003/4: better at 3m than shorter: acts on soft and
good to firm going. *B. J. Llewellyn*

GLORY TRAIL (IRE) 10 b.g. Supreme Leader – Death Or Glory (Hasdrubal) **c–**
[2003/4 c–, h–: c26fᶠ May 21] winning pointer, lightly raced and largely out of sorts since **h–**
2002. *Mrs D. M. Grissell*

GLOSTER GUNNER 5 ch.g. Gunner B – Blue Empress (Blue Cashmere) [2003/4 **h–**
F17s 16v 19g⁶ Mar 6] half-brother to several winners, including fair hurdler Wortley Boy **F–**
(by Zambrano), stays 2¾m, and 1m and 1¼m winner Miami Blues (by Palm Track): dam
showed no ability: tailed off in bumper and novice hurdles. *Dr P. Pritchard*

GLOWING EMBER 4 b.f. Blushing Flame (USA) – California Dreamin (Slip **F–**
Anchor) [2003/4 F12g Nov 12] third foal: half-sister to winning 2m hurdler April Louise
(by Meqdaam) and 2003 2-y-o 1¼m winner Soulacroix (by Kylian): dam, of little
account, closely related to useful performer up to 14.6f Mischief out of useful sprinter
Misguided: well beaten in 3-y-o bumper on debut. *T. R. Wall*

GLYNN DINGLE (IRE) 11 b.g. Millfontaine – Banner Lady (Milan) [2003/4 c100+, **c127**
h–: c24g* c20d* c24gᶠ c22s³ c20g² c24gᵘʳ c24m⁴ c18d c24d 20d Apr 12] workmanlike **h96**
gelding: lightly raced over hurdles: fairly useful handicap chaser: won at Down Royal
and Punchestown early in season: good efforts when placed in Galway Plate and at Perth,
back to near best when seventh in valuable race at Punchestown in late-April: stays 3m:
acts on soft ground: often makes mistakes. *A. J. Martin, Ireland*

GOBLET OF FIRE (USA) 5 b.g. Green Desert (USA) – Laurentine (USA) (Private **h99**
Account (USA)) [2003/4 16s³ 16m⁵ 17s⁵ 16v³ Jan 31] good-topped gelding: smart on
all-weather, useful on turf on Flat (stays 10.5f), good efforts when placed in 2003 for
B. Meehan: modest form when third in novice hurdles at Ascot, reluctant under pressure
on debut: likely to prove best around 2m: blinkered third outing, tongue tied on second:
races freely. *P. F. Nicholls*

GOL

GODFATHER (IRE) 6 ch.g. Insan (USA) – Lady Letitia (Le Bavard (FR)) [2003/4 **h–**
F–: F16m 16g^{pu} Nov 19] tall gelding: no form in bumpers or novice hurdle. *M. Pitman* **F—**

GODS TOKEN 6 gr.g. Gods Solution – Pro-Token (Proverb) [2003/4 F99: 16d² 16s* **h115**
16g⁴ 16g⁴ Apr 12] good-topped gelding: fair form in novice hurdles: won at Sandown in
February by ¾ length from El Vaquero: disappointing last 2 starts: will stay beyond 17f:
acts on soft going (won bumper on good to firm). *Miss Venetia Williams*

GOFAGOLD 9 ch.g. Tina's Pet – Golden Della (Glint of Gold) [2003/4 c92, h87: 20g⁴ **c83**
16s⁵ c16g c16v⁵ c16s³ c16d³ c16s³ c20g⁶ Apr 10] well-made gelding: poor novice **h82**
hurdler/chaser: should stay 2½m: raced on good going or softer (acts on heavy): prone to
odd mistake. *A. C. Whillans*

GO FOR BUST 5 b.g. Sabrehill (USA) – Butsova (Formidable (USA)) [2003/4 F16g **F83**
F17g⁶ Apr 13] €23,000 3-y-o, €40,000 4-y-o: compact gelding: brother to winning 2m
hurdlers Attack and Sabre Butt and half-brother to 3 winners, including fairly useful 11f
winner Bustinetta (by Bustino): dam, 6f winner, half-sister to Derby runner-up Terimon:
modest form both starts in bumpers. *N. J. Henderson*

GOHH 8 ch.g. Alflora (IRE) – Lavenham's Last (Rymer) [2003/4 c96, h93: c16d^F **c99**
c17s^{pu} c17d^{pu} Apr 24] tall, angular gelding: modest hurdler: similar form over fences: **h—**
running good race when falling 3 out in maiden at Newcastle on reappearance: lacklustre
efforts after: should stay at least 2½m: raced on good going or softer (acts on heavy):
usually tongue tied prior to 2003/4. *M. W. Easterby*

GOING GLOBAL (IRE) 7 ch.g. Bob Back (USA) – Ukraine Girl (Targowice (USA)) **h116**
[2003/4: 16g² 18g² 20d³ 20v² 21s Jan 19] strong, compact gelding: has reportedly had
soft palate operation: fairly useful handicap hurdler: improved in 2003/4, placed first 4
starts, let down by jumping when tried in cheekpieces final outing: stays 21f: raced on
good going or softer (acts on heavy): has had tongue tied. *G. L. Moore*

GOING SOLO 8 ch.m. Sula Bula – Little Beaver (Privy Seal) [2003/4 h–, F–: 20m^{pu} **h–**
Jun 1] medium-sized mare: won maiden point in 2003, no other form: pulled hard when **F—**
tried in blinkers. *Mrs S. Gardner*

GOLA CHER (IRE) 10 b.g. Beau Sher – Owen Money (Master Owen) [2003/4 **c131**
c131, h–: c28s³ Nov 29] rangy gelding: useful handicap chaser: typically hard work when **h—**
third of 4 finishers behind impressive Artic Jack at Haydock, only outing in 2003/4: stays
3½m: raced on good going or softer (acts on heavy): tried in blinkers/cheekpieces. lazy.
A. King

GOLA SUPREME (IRE) 9 gr.g. Supreme Leader – Coal Burn (King Sitric) [2003/4 **c—**
c112, h–: c22d^{pu} 24s* 24s^{pu} 22s^{pu} Apr 6] workmanlike gelding: lightly raced: often runs **h109**
as if amiss, but has won 2 of 5 starts over hurdles, including 16-runner handicap at Taun-
ton in February: similar form only completed outing in steeplechases: will stay beyond
3m: acts on heavy going. *R. Lee*

GOLD AGAIN (IRE) 6 b.g. Old Vic – Thomastown Girl (Tekoah) [2003/4 F16s **F75**
F17g⁵ Apr 10] €35,000 4-y-o: lengthy gelding: half-brother to several winners, including
fairly useful 2m hurdler/winning chaser Doran's Town Lad (by Tumble Gold) and fairly
useful hurdler/smart chaser Hi Cloy (by Be My Native), best form around 2½m: dam,
bumper winner, half-sister to 1982 Champion Hurdle winner For Auction: fifth to Honan
in maiden bumper at Newton Abbot. *Noel T. Chance*

GOLDAMIE (IRE) 5 ch.m. Zaffaran (USA) – Keeping Company (King's Company) **h–**
[2003/4 F16s⁶ F17s⁴ 19d 23s Apr 4] sister to one-time useful but ungenuine staying **F79**
hurdler/chaser Browjoshy and half-sister to winner in Austria by Kampala: dam, Irish
middle-distance winner, half-sister to smart 2m hurdler/useful chaser Pearlstone: modest
form in bumpers: well held in mares novice hurdles: should be suited by 3m. *M. Scudamore*

GOLDBROOK 6 b.g. Alderbrook – Miss Marigold (Norwick (USA)) [2003/4 h98: **h118**
16g³ 16m* 17g* 20d³ 16d* 16g 16s⁴ 16g Mar 26] good-topped gelding: fairly useful
hurdler: had good season, won novice at Wincanton in May and handicaps at Exeter in
December and Wincanton in January: good efforts in valuable handicaps next 2 starts,
20 lb wrong at weights when thirteenth to Geos at Newbury and fourth to Scorned at
Sandown: should prove as effective at 2½m as 2m: unraced on firm going, acts on any
other: usually held up. *R. J. Hodges*

GOLDEN ALPHA (IRE) 10 b.g. Alphabatim (USA) – Gina's Love (Golden Love) **c145**
[2003/4 c150, h–: c16m⁵ 16g c16m² c16g c16d³ Apr 17] well-made gelding: winning **h—**
hurdler: smart handicap chaser: creditable second to stable-companion Upgrade at Hay-

359

dock: below form behind Tidour at Aintree and Avalanche at Ayr last 2 starts: best around 2m: acts on firm and soft going (bumper winner on heavy): tried visored: front runner: has found little/looked less than keen. *M. C. Pipe*

GOLDEN AMBER (IRE)   5 ch.g. Glacial Storm (USA) – Rigton Angle (Sit In The Corner (USA)) [2003/4 16vᵖᵘ 19s⁵ Apr 11] half-brother to winning pointer by Strong Gale: dam of little account: showed little both starts over hurdles. *John R. Upson*   **h–**

GOLDEN ARUBA   5 ch.g. Golden Lahab (USA) – Clover Girl (Spin of A Coin) [2003/4 21dᶠ 16dᵖᵘ Dec 12] no form on Flat and in 2 selling hurdles: tried in cheekpieces (looked temperamental). *B. Ellison*   **h–**

GOLDEN BAY   5 ch.m. Karinga Bay – Goldenswift (IRE) (Meneval (USA)) [2003/4 F16g⁴ F17s² F18s* F16s Mar 13] medium-sized mare: first foal: dam, fair hurdler/chaser, stayed 3m: fair form in bumpers, won at Plumpton in February by 8 lengths from Phar Out Phavorite: will stay 2½m+. *G. B. Balding*   **F88**

GOLDEN CHIMES (USA)   9 ch.g. Woodman (USA) – Russian Ballet (USA) (Nijinsky (CAN)) [2003/4 c88, h–: c25g* Mar 10] quite good-topped gelding: winning hurdler: fair hunter chaser: readily won 6-runner race at Catterick by 12 lengths from Corrie Mor: followed up in point over 3 weeks later: stays easy 25f: acts on firm going, probably on soft: tried tongue tied. *G. Tuer*   **c100 h–**

GOLDEN COIN   8 ch.g. St Ninian – Legal Coin (Official) [2003/4 h74, F102: 20s³ Dec 26] strong gelding: fairly useful bumper winner: only poor form over hurdles: stays 2½m: raced on good going or softer (acts on soft). *W. M. Brisbourne*   **h79**

GOLDEN CROSS (IRE)   5 b.g. Goldmark (USA) – Fordes Cross (Ya Zaman (USA)) [2003/4 h130p: 16g³ 16d* 16d 16g Mar 16]   **h146**
   As shock results go, they don't come much bigger than that of the Bewleys Hotels December Festival Hurdle, which took place at Leopardstown's Christmas meeting. No sooner had the winner Golden Cross passed the post than many in attendance were scouring their racecards for information about a horse who, despite there being only seven contenders, probably hadn't entered their calculations beforehand. After all, the ten previous renewals of the race produced an average winner's starting price of just over 2/1. In a race which also featured Flame Creek, Hardy Eustace, Solerina and Spirit Leader, attention centred on the first two in the market, Rhinestone Cowboy and Back In Front, who at the time were favourite and third favourite respectively in the ante-post betting for the Champion Hurdle. Golden Cross, at 66/1, was the complete outsider for the Festival Hurdle, a race which, despite Grade 1 status and win prize money of €52,000, was viewed chiefly

Bewleys Hotels December Festival Hurdle, Leopardstown—
66/1-shot Golden Cross (left) finds more than the eventual third Flame Creek

as a Champion Hurdle trial. The outcome resulted in a major overhaul of the market on the Champion, with Golden Cross himself introduced into the betting at as low as 14/1.

Golden Cross was making his first appearance over hurdles for almost eight months at Leopardstown, although he had shown his well-being when running creditably over two miles on the Flat in October and November, on the last occasion when tried in cheekpieces. He had been Ireland's leading juvenile hurdler in 2002/3, winning a couple of Grade 3 events as well as finishing third behind Spectroscope and Well Chief in the Triumph Hurdle at Cheltenham, and behind Sporazone and Spectroscope in the Champion Four Year Old Hurdle at Punchestown, the last-named event coming shortly after the end of the British season. At that stage Golden Cross was shaping as though he would be well suited by a step up to two and a half miles or more, so it seemed highly unlikely that he would make the substantial improvement required to shake up his six older rivals over two miles at Leopardstown, especially as the race was taking place on the sharper inner hurdles track. As things turned out, Golden Cross didn't need to improve so much as expected, several of his rivals failing to give their running, including Rhinestone Cowboy and Back In Front. It still required a smart performance to win, though, and to his credit Golden Cross, wearing cheekpieces for the first time over hurdles, produced one under his claiming rider Adrian Lane, who was unable to draw his 3-lb allowance because of the status of the race. Solerina, stepping down in trip, set a good pace which served Golden Cross well. The latter made his effort after three out, led on the run-in and stayed on well to hold strong-finishing Spirit Leader by a length and a half with Flame Creek three quarters of a length further back in third. Last to finish was Hardy Eustace who easily turned the tables on Golden Cross in the Champion Hurdle. Golden Cross was sent off at 40/1 after beating only one home in the much more steadily-run eight-runner AIG Europe Champion Hurdle at Leopardstown on his only outing between the December Festival Hurdle and Cheltenham. Golden Cross did return to form at Cheltenham—with Paul Carberry replacing the injured Lane—but had his limitations at two miles exposed, at least when conditions aren't testing. Golden Cross took time to respond, having been niggled at by the fifth, but kept on well after two out to finish seventh of fourteen, almost twenty lengths behind Hardy Eustace. It surely won't be much longer before Golden Cross is given the opportunity to show what he can do over longer distances, and, if he turns up at the next Cheltenham Festival, it may well be for the Stayers' Hurdle over three miles. He should have the necessary stamina for that.

Golden Cross (IRE) (b.g. 1999)	Goldmark (USA) (b 1992)	Lyphard (b 1969)	Northern Dancer
			Goofed
		Gold Rose (b 1987)	Noblequest
			Gold Bird
	Fordes Cross (b 1987)	Ya Zaman (b 1977)	Gallant Man
			Irish Exchange
		Regal Splendour (b 1971)	Sovereign Path
			Madame Caroline

Golden Cross, a winner of three handicaps at up to a mile and a half on the Flat as a three-year-old, is the sixth foal of the unraced Fordes Cross. His dam has produced five other winners on the Flat, the best of them the useful Irish mare She's Our Girl (by Royal Abjar), who stays an easy mile and a half. Golden Cross's grandam Regal Splendour won over six furlongs, while his great grandam Madame Caroline was successful twice at around a mile and a quarter in Ireland. Madame Caroline is the fourth dam of the 1994 Irish Two Thousand Guineas winner Turtle Island, as well as being a half-sister to a runner-up in that race, Turbo Jet, and a runner-up in the Newmarket original, Faberge. The close-coupled Golden Cross has raced only on good ground or softer. He also wore cheekpieces on both of his starts after the Festival Hurdle. *M. Halford, Ireland*

GOLDEN CRUSADER   7 b.g. Gildoran – Pusey Street (Native Bazaar) [2003/4   **h98 ?** h72: 16m² May 5] tall gelding: maiden hurdler: seemingly much improved when second of 12 to River Pirate in intermediate at Ludlow, making most: suited by emphasis on speed at 2m: pulls hard. *J. W. Mullins*

GOLDEN DAWN 7 gr.g. Gran Alba (USA) – Golden Curd (FR) (Nice Havrais (USA)) [2003/4 c–, h–: c16m^{pu} Sep 7] strong, good-bodied gelding: little worthwhile form. *B. D. Leavy* c– h–

GOLDEN FIELDS (IRE) 4 b.f. Definite Article – Quickstep Queen (FR) (Pampabird) [2003/4 16g^6 16g^{4d} 16g 20v^3 16d Feb 8] rather leggy filly: modest on Flat (stays 11f), sold from A. Jarvis 4,800 gns after winning seller in July: little form over hurdles: visored first 3 starts. *A. P. Jones* h–

GOLDEN FLIGHT (FR) 5 b.g. Saint Cyrien (FR) – Sunday Flight (FR) (Johnny O'Day (USA)) [2003/4 h115: c17d^2 c17s* c20s* c20s* c21d^{ur} Jan 1] leggy, useful-looking gelding: fairly useful hurdler: better over fences, won 4-y-o events at Auteuil in September and November (2): looked held in third when unseating 5 out in novice at Cheltenham final start: likely to prove better at 2½m+ than shorter: acts on heavy going. *G. Macaire, France* c128 h–

GOLDEN HAZE 7 ch.m. Safawan – Hazel Hill (Abednego) [2003/4 F–: 21s^3 21s^5 24s^2 24m^{rtr} 20m Jun 14] chunky mare: poor maiden hurdler: refused to race fourth start: sold 3,000 gns Doncaster October Sales. *J. R. Bewley* h62 §

GOLDEN HOST 10 ch.g. Roman Warrior – Prominent Princess (Prominer) [2003/4 20g^{pu} Aug 23] sturdy gelding: no form over hurdles or in maiden points. *R. J. Smith* h–

GOLDEN LAW 6 b.m. Gildoran – Sister-In-Law (Legal Tender) [2003/4 F16g^3 F17g Mar 28] fifth foal: half-sister to fair hurdler up to 21f Tisho (by Sir Harry Lewis): dam, novice hurdler who stayed 2¾m, from family of high-class 2½m chaser Townley Stone and 1991 Grand National third Auntie Dot: easily better effort in mares bumpers when third at Ludlow on debut. *P. R. Webber* F82

GOLDEN LEGEND (IRE) 7 b.g. Last Tycoon – Adjalisa (IRE) (Darshaan) [2003/4 h–: 16m^{pu} May 26] leggy gelding: no form over hurdles: has had tongue tied. *R. J. Price* h–

GOLDEN MEASURE 4 b.g. Rainbow Quest (USA) – Dawna (Polish Precedent (USA)) [2003/4 F14g^2 Nov 25] 22,000 3-y-o: good-topped gelding: third foal: dam, useful 1m winner, half-sister to smart French middle-distance performer Ordinance: 2½ lengths second to Ambition Royal in 3-y-o bumper at Warwick on debut. *G. A. Swinbank* F95

GOLDEN OAK (IRE) 4 b.g. Goldmark (USA) – Embroidery (Lords (USA)) [2003/4 F17v^2 Mar 21] half-brother to useful 2m hurdler Embellished (by Scenic) and to 2 winners on Flat: dam middle-distance maiden: 3½ lengths second to Wild Cane Ridge, pair clear, in bumper at Carlisle on debut. *R. A. Fahey* F98

GOLDEN ODYSSEY (IRE) 4 ch.f. Barathea (IRE) – Opus One (Slip Anchor) [2003/4 F13g* F16g^2 F17g* F17m* Apr 15] unfurnished filly: fourth foal: half-sister to modest hurdler Sun King (by Zilzal), stays 2½m: dam, 1¾m winner, half-sister to high-

Lady Rebecca Mares' Only Standard Open National Hunt Flat, Cheltenham—favourite Golden Odyssey sees off Leroy's Sister to make it three wins from four starts

class hurdler/smart chaser up to 2½m Squire Silk: progressive form in bumpers: won at Doncaster in November, Market Rasen in March and Cheltenham in April, last 2 mares events: beat Leroy's Sister by ¾ length for final success. *Mrs M. Reveley*

GOLDEN OLDIE (IRE)   6 b.g. Old Vic – Misty Gold (Arizona Duke) [2003/4 F16d   F–
F16g Feb 28] third foal: half-brother to winning pointer by Boreen: dam, lightly raced on
Flat, sister to dam of top-class 2m to 3m hurdler/chaser Danoli: well held in 2 bumpers
and on Flat debut in March. *D. Flood*

GOLDEN ORION (IRE)   9 ch.g. Phardante (FR) – Raise The Bells (Belfalas) [2003/4   h76
h86: 22g⁵ Nov 1] leggy gelding: maiden hurdler: lame both starts since 2001/2: stays 3m:
raced on good going or softer. *Mrs J. C. McGregor*

GOLDEN RAMBLER (IRE)   8 b.g. Roselier (FR) – Goldiyana (FR) (Glint of Gold)   h103 +
[2003/4 20g 24d 20g Apr 1] good-topped gelding: took very well to hurdling in 2001/2,
winning 2 of 3 races: best effort in handicaps on return when seventh of 10 finishers to
Limerick Leader at Bangor second start: should prove better suited by 3m than shorter:
raced on good going or softer. *Jonjo O'Neill*

GOLDEN REWARD (SAF)   6 ro.g. Goldmark (SAF) – Enticement (SAF) (Capture   h94 p
Him (USA)) [2003/4 17s⁴ Feb 3] angular gelding: won 6 times at 7f/1m on Flat in South
Africa: fourth to Blue Americo in steadily-run novice at Taunton on hurdling debut,
taking good hold and making couple of mistakes: should improve. *Miss Venetia Williams*

GOLDEN ROD   7 ch.g. Rainbows For Life (CAN) – Noble Form (Double Form)   c76 §
[2003/4 h82: 21m³ 23g³ c21m³ c24g⁴ c24m⁴ 16d⁵ c21dᶜᵒ c21sᵖᵘ Jan 21] sturdy gelding: h85 §
modest hurdler: poor form over fences, has had jumping problems: possibly best around
2½m: acts on good to firm going: tried in cheekpieces, including for win: difficult ride
and not one to trust. *K. C. Bailey*

GOLDEN ROW (IRE)   10 b.g. Ore – Guelder Rose (Trimmingham) [2003/4 c17d²   c131
c17v³ c17f* c17g c17s* c16f* c16g² c17m* c16d³ Nov 16] tall, useful-looking gelding: h–
useful hurdler in 2001/2: useful novice chaser: won at Tipperary in June, Galway in July,
Cork (by 25 lengths from Colca Canyon) in August and Galway again (idled) in October:
stays 2½m: acts on soft and firm going: tongue tied last 6 starts in 2001/2: doesn't always
impress with finishing effort. *E. J. O'Grady, Ireland*

GOLDEN SNOOPY (IRE)   7 ch.g. Insan (USA) – Lovely Snoopy (IRE) (Phardante   F75
(FR)) [2003/4 F16g⁵ Aug 23] IR 28,000 3-y-o, 31,000 4-y-o: sixth foal: half-brother to 3
winners, including fairly useful hurdler/chaser Royal Snoopy (by Royal Fountain), stays
27f, and bumper winner Snoopy Loopy (by Old Vic): dam unraced half-sister to Aintree
Bumper winner Black Mocassin, out of useful Irish hurdler Lovely Bio: fifth to Chocolate
Soldier in bumper at Worcester on debut: joined T. Caldwell. *H. D. Daly*

GOLDEN STORM (IRE)   7 ch.g. Magical Wonder (USA) – Independent Woman   c127
(IRE) (Carmelite House (USA)) [2003/4 c120, h–: c24d⁴ c29s² c24s² c24d c28v⁵ c21g²   h–
c24s⁶ c29d³ Apr 12] smallish, rather leggy gelding: fairly useful handicap chaser: good
efforts in 2003/4 when placed, third to Granit d'Estruval in Irish Grand National at Fairyhouse in April: stays 29f: acts on heavy going: effectual blinkered or not. *Joseph Crowley,
Ireland*

GOLDEN TAMESIS   7 b.g. Golden Heights – Escribana (Main Reef) [2003/4 F16g   h–
21g 25d 22g Apr 18] first foal: dam, modest hurdler, stayed 25f: well held in bumper and   F–
novice hurdles. *R. Dickin*

GOLDEN THUNDERBOLT (FR)   11 b.g. Persian Bold – Carmita (Caerleon (USA))   c–
[2003/4 c–, h86d: 17g 22mᵖᵘ 19g⁵ 16gᶠ 19gᵖᵘ 20sᵖᵘ 17d² 16d* Apr 12] small gelding: h76
poor handicap hurdler: won seller at Fakenham (has good record there), reportedly
finishing lame: effective at 2m to 3m: acts on any going: visored once: has had tongue
tied: often makes running: has looked irresolute. *H. Alexander*

GOLDEN THYNE (IRE)   10 ch.g. Alphabatim (USA) – Droichidin (Good Thyne   h–
(USA)) [2003/4 h–: 23mᵖᵘ May 7] no show in 2 novice hurdles. *Ms A. E. Embiricos*

GOLDERS GREEN   7 b.g. Gildoran – Mayfair Minx (St Columbus) [2003/4 F18s   h–
F17s⁴ 25sᵖᵘ 23sᵖᵘ 19sᵖᵘ Apr 11] strong gelding: no form: blinkered (raced freely) final   F–
start: sold 1,400 gns Doncaster May Sales. *M. G. Rimell*

GOLDHORN (IRE)   9 b.g. Little Bighorn – Stylish Gold (IRE) (Tumble Gold)   h–
[2003/4 19g Mar 5] medium-sized gelding: won on first of 3 starts in bumpers in 1999/00:
well held in novice hurdle on return. *O. Brennan*

GOL

GOLD MENELEK (IRE) 5 ch.g. Goldmark (USA) – Newlands Cross (Mandalus) **h62**
[2003/4 F–: F16m F16m 21m² 22g⁴ Oct 30] well held in bumpers: poor form both starts **F–**
over hurdles. *T. P. McGovern*

GOLD NATIVE (IRE) 6 br.g. Be My Native (USA) – Goldiyana (FR) (Glint of Gold) **h70**
[2003/4 F83: 17s 20s 24s⁵ Apr 4] modest form when in frame in 2 bumpers in 2002/3:
poor form in novice hurdles. *B. Ellison*

GOLDSEAM (GER) 5 gr.g. Neshad (USA) – Goldkatze (GER) (Czaravich (USA)) **h–**
[2003/4 16dᵖᵘ Jan 8] 7f winner in Germany at 2 yrs, placed 5 times at 3 yrs (unplaced both
starts in 2003): well held in juvenile at Enghien on hurdling debut in March 2002 for
Mme P. Gehm: little show in novice at Wincanton. *C. J. Mann*

GOLDSTREET (IRE) 7 b.g. Dolphin Street (FR) – Up To You (Sallust) [2003/4 **c121**
c121, h–: c18d⁴ 20d² c24f² c23m² c20m⁴ c22s Jul 30] good-topped gelding: fairly useful **h121**
hurdler/chaser: stays easy 3m: acts on any going: often blinkered: consistent. *Joseph
Crowley, Ireland*

GOLD SUMMERLAND (HOL) 6 b.m. Learn By Heart (USA) – Sabara Raaphorst **h–**
(HOL) (Glint of Gold) [2003/4 16m Dec 10] successful 7 times on Flat in Holland/
Germany, including up to 7f in 2002, placed 3 times in 2003 for J. Pubben: soundly beaten
in mares novice on hurdling debut (breathing problem). *C. J. Mann*

GOLFAGENT 6 b.g. Kris – Alusha (Soviet Star (USA)) [2003/4 h99§: 24m³ 27g 21g **h96 §**
24g² 24m² 22d 19sᵖᵘ 17g* 19d* 17gᵖᵘ Apr 10] small, close-coupled gelding: modest
hurdler: won seller in February and handicap in March, both at Taunton: effective around
2m to 3m: acts on soft and good to firm going: visored seventh start: tongue tied: refused
to race: unreliable. *Miss K. Marks*

GOLLINGER 8 b.g. St Ninian – Edith Rose (Cheval) [2003/4 c21s⁵ c20g³ c26gᵖᵘ May **c78**
26] modest maiden pointer/hunter chaser: stays 2½m. *R. D. E. Woodhouse*

GOLLUM (IRE) 4 b.g. Spectrum (IRE) – Rigobertha (IRE) (Nordico (USA)) [2003/4 **F100**
F16v² F16g⁴ F16s* Mar 14] smallish gelding: fourth foal: brother to 1½m winner Brave
Harvey: dam, fair 2-y-o 7f winner, half-sister to smart middle-distance filly Ballykett
Nancy: best effort in bumpers when winning at Cork by length from Ginandit: sixth to
Geill Sli in Grade 1 at Punchestown in late-April. *E. Griffin, Ireland*

GOLLYHOTT (IRE) 9 b.g. Roselier (FR) – Liffey Lady (Camden Town) [2003/4 **c–**
21s⁵ c20dᵖᵘ Mar 10] tall gelding: lightly raced and no worthwhile form over jumps: tried **h–**
blinkered: jumps none too fluently: has twice refused to go to post: sold 2,500 gns
Doncaster May Sales. *M. F. Harris*

GOLLY (IRE) 8 b.g. Toulon – Tor-Na-Grena (Torus) [2003/4 F–: c16g³ c22f* c17m² **c97**
c21gᶠ⁴ c23gᵖᵘ c20m³ 16d² c18g³ c20dᵘʳ c19g* Apr 16] angular gelding: modest form **h89**
only start over hurdles: modest chaser: won weak maiden at Market Rasen in October and
handicap at Taunton in April: stays 2¾m: acts on firm and good to soft going: has looked
difficult ride (headstrong). *D. L. Williams*

GONDOLA (AUS) 8 b.g. Air de France (USA) – Idyllic (AUS) (Clear Choice (USA)) **h83**
[2003/4 16g² 16mᶠ Sep 7] successful 3 times up to 9.5f from 29 starts on Flat in Australia:
second in novice at Worcester on hurdling debut: fell fatally next time. *S. E. H. Sherwood*

GONE BONKERS (IRE) 9 b.g. Lord Americo – Lady Harrier (Some Hawk) [2003/4 **h–**
h–: 21mᵖᵘ 16dᵖᵘ Jan 19] good-topped gelding: no sign of ability. *A. M. Campion*

GONE FAR (USA) 7 b.g. Gone West (USA) – Vallee Dansante (USA) (Lyphard **h124**
(USA)) [2003/4 h120p: 16mᶠ 17g 17d 16g² 16sᵖᵘ 20g 21m Apr 14] leggy gelding: fairly
useful hurdler: should stay beyond 17f: acts on soft going: visored last 5 starts. *M. C. Pipe*

GONE TOO FAR 6 b.g. Reprimand – Blue Nile (IRE) (Bluebird (USA)) [2003/4 **h109**
20g⁵ 16m* 16m² 16g² 17m* 16g* 16g 19d³ 20m⁵ 16s⁶ Feb 12] lengthy, angular gelding:
fair hurdler: won amateur novice handicap at Hexham in May, conditional jockeys
handicap at Sedgefield in July and novice handicap at Cheltenham in November: sold out
of M. Dods's stable 18,000 gns Doncaster August Sales before final win: stays 19f: acts
on firm and good to soft going: blinkered/visored after reappearance. *M. C. Pipe*

GO NOMADIC 10 br.g. Nomadic Way (USA) – Dreamago (Sir Mago) [2003/4 c97: **c97**
c25d³ c27d² c25g³ c27g² c26d³ Apr 23] lengthy gelding: fair hunter chaser: won point in
March: stays 31f: acts on heavy going (below best on good to firm): usually tongue tied:
consistent. *D. G. Atkinson*

GOODANDPLENTY 6 b.g. Sovereign Water (FR) – Our Wilma (Master Willie) [2003/4 F16m F16v⁴ F16s 22g Mar 28] first foal: dam, lightly-raced maiden, half-sister to fairly useful 2m hurdler Top Wave and useful 5f/6f winner Flying Squaw: seemingly best effort in bumpers at Ayr when seventh on debut, always well placed: well beaten in novice on hurdling debut. *Mrs J. C. McGregor*
h–
F91 ?

GOOD BONE (FR) 7 b.g. Perrault – Bone Crasher (FR) (Cadoudal (FR)) [2003/4 c21g³ c23f² c20v³ c18s⁵ c25d² c25g* c26g⁶ Apr 12] first foal: half-brother to bumper winner Big Bone (by Zayyani): dam, well beaten on Flat, pulled up only start over hurdles: runner-up on completed start in Irish points in 2003: poor chaser: won handicap at Folkestone in March, idling: stays 25f: acts on good to soft going. *L. Wells*
c83

GOOD BOOK (IRE) 6 b.g. Good Thyne (USA) – Book of Rules (IRE) (Phardante (FR)) [2003/4 F16g⁵ 21g^bd 24m Mar 4] 22,000 4-y-o: useful-looking gelding: chasing type: second foal: half-brother to smart hurdler/chaser Rule Supreme (by Supreme Leader), stays 29f: dam unraced half-sister to useful staying jumpers Scribbler and Sarsfield The Man: poor form in bumper on debut: jumped poorly in 2 races over hurdles, reportedly hung left in cheekpieces final start. *M. Bradstock*
h–
F69

GOOD BOY (FR) 10 b.g. Cadoudal (FR) – Cazeres (FR) (Goodland (FR)) [2003/4 c21d⁵ c24m* May 29] successful over hurdles and fences in France: much better effort in hunter chases when winning at Huntingdon: stays 3m: acts on good to firm and heavy going: tried blinkered. *R. S. Elwell*
c99
h–

GOODBYE GOLDSTONE 8 b.g. Mtoto – Shareehan (Dancing Brave (USA)) [2003/4 h–: 17d^F Oct 29] leggy, sparely-made gelding: lightly raced and little form over hurdles: has worn cheekpieces. *B. Ellison*
h–

GOODBYE MRS CHIPS 5 ch.m. Zilzal (USA) – Happydrome (Ahonoora) [2003/4 h–: 16m⁵ 16g Mar 12] modest maiden at best on Flat: no worthwhile form over hurdles: tongue tied. *Mrs L. B. Normile*
h–

GOOD DEBATE (IRE) 6 b.g. Glacial Storm (USA) – Drachma (Netherkelly) [2003/4 F20g 22g 16d 20s 16v³ 16s 19s² 20s 24s^F Mar 14] €800 4-y-o: fourth foal: dam winning pointer: well held in bumper: poor novice hurdler: stays 19f: acts on heavy going: blinkered last 3 starts. *Paul John Gilligan, Ireland*
h69
F–

GOODENOUGH STAR 4 b.f. Stronz (IRE) – Goodenough Girl (Mac's Imp (USA)) [2003/4 17m^pu Nov 27] poor maiden on Flat: showed nothing on hurdling debut. *J. S. King*
h–

GOOD EVANS ABOVE 7 br.m. Tragic Role (USA) – Dark Amber (Formidable (USA)) [2003/4 16m^pu 16g^pu Sep 7] modest maiden sprinter at 2 yrs for P. D. Evans: no form in 2 starts over hurdles, lame on second occasion. *Mrs S. M. Johnson*
h–

GOOD FORM (IRE) 4 b.g. Danetime (IRE) – Faapette (Runnett) [2003/4 17g^ur 17g^pu Sep 13] half-brother to fair 2m hurdler Bank Statement (by Don't Forget Me) and 2m hurdle winner Premier Leap (by Salmon Leap): poor maiden on Flat (stays 1m): failed to complete in 2 juvenile hurdles. *Miss K. M. George*
h–

GOOD HEART (IRE) 9 ch.g. Be My Native (USA) – Johnstown Love (IRE) (Golden Love) [2003/4 c70, h–: 26g 21g^pu 22g⁶ May 24] sturdy, lengthy gelding: poor maiden hurdler/chaser: possibly best up to 2½m: raced mainly on good going or softer: tried visored/in cheekpieces: has had tongue tied. *T. H. Caldwell*
c–
h–

GOOD LORD LOUIS (IRE) 6 b.g. Presenting – Ash Queen (IRE) (Altountash) [2003/4 17g² 16s⁵ 19s⁶ 19g 21g^pu 21d Apr 8] angular gelding: second foal: dam unraced: modest form over hurdles: should stay beyond 19f: raced on good going or softer: bled internally fifth start. *P. J. Hobbs*
h90

GOOD LORD MURPHY (IRE) 12 br.g. Montelimar (USA) – Semiwild (USA) (Rumbo (USA)) [2003/4 c–§, h90§: 26g^pu 25g 24s 23s 24s⁵ c16s c26v⁶ c30g 26d² 24g⁵ 21m 19g Apr 18] tall gelding: veteran hurdler/chaser, poor and unreliable nowadays: stays 27f: acts on heavy going: tried blinkered/in cheekpieces: ungenuine. *Dr P. Pritchard*
c– §
h84 §

GOODLY NEWS (IRE) 8 b.g. Project Manager – Nordic Relation (IRE) (Nordico (USA)) [2003/4 16g 16m^pu c20m^pu 16g Jul 31] compact gelding: fair maiden on Flat (stays 1m) at 3/4 yrs for J. Bolger: signs of only a little ability over jumps, trained by D. Hassett prior to reappearance: tried visored/tongue tied. *A. W. Carroll*
c–
h–

GOOD OUTLOOK (IRE) 5 b.g. Lord Americo – I'll Say She Is (Ashmore (FR)) [2003/4 17g^F 16s⁶ 19s c22g^F c24g^F c20m* c24g² c20d^pu c19g^F Apr 16] €18,000 3-y-o: sturdy gelding: seventh foal: half-brother to 2m hurdle winner Tax Exempt (by Be My
c89
h75

Native) and 2½m bumper winner Five Alive O (by Alphabatim): dam placed in point: pulled up in 4-y-o 2½m maiden Irish point in 2003: poor form on completed starts in novice hurdles, hanging badly and looking difficult ride: first completed outing over fences when easily winning novice handicap at Leicester in March: bled from nose next 2 starts, and again ran as if amiss final outing: should stay 3m: acts on good to firm going: raced mainly on right-handed courses. *M. C. Pipe*

GOOD POTENTIAL (IRE) 8 b.g. Petardia – Steel Duchess (IRE) (Yashgan) [2003/4 c–, h–§: 16g 22d³ 26m⁴ 22g* 20m 21dᵖᵘ 22f³ 20g* 16d Mar 14] no form in 2 runs over fences: modest handicap hurdler: won at Newton Abbot in June and Bangor in September: ideally suited by 2½m/2¾m: acts on any going: tried blinkered/in cheekpieces: usually tongue tied: not one to rely on. *D. J. Wintle*
c–
h90 §

GOOD SAMARITAN (IRE) 5 ch.g. Insan (USA) – Ballymave (IRE) (Jareer (USA)) [2003/4 F16s Dec 20] €35,000 3-y-o: good-topped gelding: first foal: dam unraced: travelled well long way when seventh to impressive Refinement in bumper at Ascot on debut. *M. Pitman*
F94

GOOD SANTE 5 b.m. Deploy – Kumzar (Hotfoot) [2003/4 F16s F16g Mar 4] 600 3-y-o: fifth living foal: sister to modest winner up to 1¾m Blue Street: dam maiden half-sister to smart performers Osario, at 6f/7f, and Only Yours, at 1m: well beaten in 2 mares bumpers. *M. Scudamore*
F–

GOOD SHUIL (IRE) 9 b.g. Good Thyne (USA) – Shuil Run (Deep Run) [2003/4 c135, h–: c27dᵖᵘ Nov 23] good sort: winning hurdler: useful chaser: no encouragement in 2 races over National fences since leading T. Taaffe: stays 27f: raced on good going or softer (acts on heavy). *C. J. Mann*
c–
h–

GOOD THYNE GUY (IRE) 9 b.g. Good Thyne (USA) – Mourne Trix (Golden Love) [2003/4 24vᵖᵘ 22g² 19d⁶ 24s c22sᵖᵘ 23sᶠ Apr 4] quite good-topped gelding: placed all 3 completed starts in points in 2003: poor hurdler: lightly raced and has achieved little in steeplechases (has been let down by jumping): stays 2¾m: acts on heavy going: tongue tied final start. *C. L. Tizzard*
c–
h84

GOOD THYNE JOHNNY (IRE) 10 b.g. Good Thyne (USA) – Wiasma (Ashmore (FR)) [2003/4 h84: 24s⁵ 21s 22g 20s 16d³ Apr 12] angular gelding: poor handicap hurdler: probably stays 3¼m: acts on soft going, no form on firmer than good: has had tongue tied: takes good hold and usually makes running. *Mrs J. Candlish*
h72

GOOD TIME BOBBY 7 b.g. Primitive Rising (USA) – Goodreda (Good Times (ITY)) [2003/4 h–: 20m Apr 28] small gelding: signs of only a little ability. *G. A. Swinbank*
h–

GOODTIME GEORGE (IRE) 11 b.g. Strong Gale – Game Sunset (Menelek) [2003/4 c–, h–: c22g* c25dᵖᵘ Dec 12] strong gelding: useful hurdler in 1998/9: third outing over fences when winning novice at Newbury: fatally injured month later: stayed 3m: acted on good to firm and heavy going. *M. Pitman*
c112
h–

GOODTIMELADY (IRE) 10 b. or br.m. Good Thyne (USA) – Peppardstownlady (Gleason (USA)) [2003/4 19s⁶ 24g² 26dᵖᵘ 27gᵖᵘ Apr 22] tall mare: modest hurdler, off 2 years before reappearance: looks a thorough stayer: acts on heavy going: tried blinkered. *D. G. Bridgwater*
c–
h91

GOOD TIME MELODY (IRE) 11 b.g. Good Thyne (USA) – Raashideah (Dancer's Image (USA)) [2003/4 c25d³ c20d c26d* Apr 7] sturdy, lengthy gelding: fairly useful hunter chaser nowadays: won at Fontwell by 2 lengths from Ronans Choice: should stay beyond 3¼m: acts on good to firm and heavy going: blinkered twice (won first time): takes plenty of driving. *J. W. Mullins*
c101 §
h–

GOOD TIMING 6 bl.g. Timeless Times (USA) – Fort Vally (Belfort (FR)) [2003/4 h–: 16m 16dᵖᵘ 16m⁶ 17g⁶ Dec 26] sparely-made gelding: poor maiden on Flat: no show over hurdles: pulls hard. *J. Hetherton*
h–

GOOD VINTAGE (IRE) 9 b.g. Lashkari – Furry Hope (Furry Glen) [2003/4 c113, h99: c25g c25m³ c22d c24mᵖᵘ c22f* c28g² c27dᵖᵘ c28dᵖᵘ c29dᴿ Apr 12] workmanlike gelding: fairly useful handicap chaser: won at Cork in October: good second to Montayral in valuable event there next time: long way below form all 3 subsequent starts: stays 3½m: acts on any going: tried blinkered/in cheekpieces. *N. Meade, Ireland*
c119
h–

GOODWOOD PROMISE 5 b.g. Primo Dominie – Noble Destiny (Dancing Brave (USA)) [2003/4 16m Nov 24] poor sprint maiden on Flat: well held in seller on hurdling debut: unlikely to stay 2m. *N. E. Berry*
h–

GOODYS (IRE) 5 ch.g. Good Thyne (USA) – Katie Baggage (IRE) (Brush Aside (USA)) [2003/4 F17f⁵ Oct 5] first foal: dam unraced: badly in need of experience when last of 5 in bumper on debut. *G. Prodromou* **F—**

GO ON JACK 6 ch.g. Saint Keyne – Swift Messenger (Giolla Mear) [2003/4 F16g F17d F17m⁴ F16m Jul 23] 3,100 4-y-o. unfurnished gelding: seventh foal: half-brother to fairly useful staying chaser Hermes Harvest (by Oats): dam, winning hurdler/chaser, stayed well: poor form in bumpers. *G. Fierro* **F72**

GORDON HIGHLANDER 5 b.m. Master Willie – No Chili (Glint of Gold) [2003/4 F79: 20gᵖᵘ 20sᵖᵘ Dec 11] lengthy mare: modest form in bumpers: no show in 2 starts over hurdles. *Mrs P. Robeson* **h—**

GORDONS FRIEND 6 ch.g. Clantime – Auntie Fay (IRE) (Fayruz) [2003/4 17m Jul 17] poor and inconsistent up to 1m on Flat: no show in maiden on hurdling debut. *B. S. Rothwell* **h—**

GORDY'S JOY 4 b.f. Cloudings (IRE) – Beatle Song (Song) [2003/4 17m 16g 16d 16s 17d 16g Apr 18] lengthy, workmanlike filly: no sign of ability: tried blinkered. *G. A. Ham* **h—**

GO ROGER GO (IRE) 12 b.g. Phardante (FR) – Tonto's Girl (Strong Gale) [2003/4 c141, h–: 16d⁶ c20g* c22s c19s² c20g* Oct 9] rangy, good sort: winning hurdler: smart chaser: won minor event at Killarney in July and Grade 3 National Lottery Agent Champion Chase at Gowran (by 3 lengths from Alcapone) in October: probably best up to 21f: acts on good to firm and heavy going. *E. J. O'Grady, Ireland* **c146 h—**

GORTMORE MEWS (IRE) 10 b.g. Persian Mews – Flat Out (Random Shot) [2003/4 c–x, h–: c20m³ c20g⁴ c25dᶠ Jan 15] angular gelding: one-time fairly useful hurdler: modest handicap chaser, lightly raced since 2001/2: stays 2½m: acts on any going: tried blinkered: often let down by jumping over fences: sold 3,500 gns Doncaster May Sales. *Ferdy Murphy* **c94 x h—**

GOSPEL SONG 12 ch.g. King Among Kings – Market Blues (Porto Bello) [2003/4 h85: 16g⁶ 16g² 20g³ 16m 19vᵖᵘ 16v* 16v² 18v⁶ Feb 5] small gelding: modest handicap hurdler: won conditional jockeys event at Wetherby in January: stays 2½m: acts on heavy going: tried tongue tied: free-going sort. *A. C. Whillans* **h86**

GOSS 7 gr.g. Linamix (FR) – Guillem (USA) (Nijinsky (CAN)) [2003/4 16g c16dᵘʳ c16d² c17v* c17m* 16v² c17s⁵ c17sᶠ 16s 16d⁶ Apr 12] tall gelding: fair novice chaser: won maiden at Ballinrobe in June and minor event at Tipperary in July: fairly useful hurdler: best effort in 2003/4 when second to Risk Accessor in minor event at Tipperary later in July: likely to prove best around 2m: acts on good to firm and heavy going: has had tongue tied: looked none too keen final start. *M. J. P. O'Brien, Ireland* **c112 h125**

GOSS HAWK (NZ) 4 br.g. Senor Pete (USA) – Stapleton Row (NZ) (Long Row) [2003/4 F16d Mar 25] New Zealand-bred gelding: seventh in steadily-run bumper at Ludlow on debut. *W. Jenks* **F—**

GOTAKNOCKONTHEHEAD (IRE) 6 b.m. Accordion – Graphic Lady (IRE) (Phardante (FR)) [2003/4 F16g* F17g² 16m⁵ 16m⁶ 24sˢᵘ 16d⁵ 20s Mar 6] IR £3,200 3-y-o: rather unfurnished mare: first foal: dam, placed in bumper and maiden hurdle, from family of Cheltenham Gold Cup winner Garrison Savannah: failed to complete in 2 points: fairly useful form in bumpers: won at Sligo in April: just poor form over hurdles: slipped up in blinkers fifth start (final one for P. Rothwell): wore cheekpieces final outing. *M. Aherne, Ireland* **h83 F95**

GOT ALOT ON (USA) 6 b. or br.g. Charnwood Forest (IRE) – Fleety Belle (GER) (Assert) [2003/4 h72: 17d⁶ 17gᵖᵘ 17dᵖᵘ Jul 27] good-topped gelding: poor maiden hurdler: last of 4 finishers on second of 2 starts in points in 2004. *Miss M. Bragg* **h—**

GOTHAM ABBEY (IRE) 7 gr.m. Gothland (FR) – Abbeyside (Paddy's Stream) [2003/4 h–: 17g³ 16d 19g⁶ Aug 12] leggy mare: signs of only a little ability over hurdles, left B. Llewellyn prior to final start. *Mrs D. A. Hamer* **h—**

GOTHAM (IRE) 7 gr.g. Gothland (FR) – Inchriver (IRE) (Over The River (FR)) [2003/4 h101p: c16s⁴ Dec 19] lengthy gelding: lightly raced: winning hurdler: off 14 months, similar form on chasing debut when fourth to Tidour in maiden at Uttoxeter: should be suited by further than 2m: acts on soft and good to firm going. *R. H. Alner* **c101 h—**

GOTHIC BAY 4 b.g. Gothenberg (IRE) – Greyhill Lady (Grey Desire) [2003/4 16m Nov 6] lengthy gelding: little sign of ability on Flat or on hurdling debut (jumped badly right). *M. W. Easterby* **h—**

Jenny Mould Memorial Handicap Chase, Cheltenham—
stable second string Got One Too is about to be left clear by the fall of Santenay (hoops) two out

GOT ONE TOO (FR)   7 ch.g. Green Tune (USA) – Gloria Mundi (FR) (Saint Cyrien (FR)) [2003/4 c131, h–: c16s* c16s⁵ c16g³ c16d c16m³ Apr 24] strong gelding: developed into smart chaser in 2003/4, winning handicap at Cheltenham in December by 18 lengths from Tysou: good efforts subsequently when third to Isio in valuable handicap at Ascot and Cenkos in valuable minor event at Sandown (led in): will stay 2½m: acts on good to firm and heavy going: usually races up with pace: usually sound jumper. *N. J. Henderson*   **c152 h–**

GOTTABE   11 ch.g. Gunner B – Topsy Bee (Be Friendly) [2003/4 c113, h–: c24s⁴ c20d⁴ c26m³ c23d³ c24d* c24s³ Jan 31] workmanlike gelding: fairly useful handicap chaser: won at Doncaster in January by 20 lengths from Montpelier: good third to Tyneandthyne-again in listed event there later in month: stays 3¼m: acts on heavy and good to firm going: has had tongue tied: effective held up or ridden prominently. *Mrs S. J. Smith*   **c122 h–**

GOVAMIX   6 gr.g. Linamix (FR) – Segovia (Groom Dancer (USA)) [2003/4 F109: 16s* 16vᶠ Feb 1] good sort: useful bumper performer: won 13f maiden on Flat in May: won maiden at Fairyhouse very easily on hurdling debut in January: still to be asked for effort when falling 4 out in Grade 2 at Punchestown: dead. *D. K. Weld, Ireland*   **h113**

GOVERNOR DANIEL   13 b.g. Governor General – Princess Semele (Imperial Fling (USA)) [2003/4 c102, h101: 17g* c19mᵖᵘ 16m* 17g² 20m² 18f² 16m³ 16m* 18g* 21s* Dec 11] sturdy gelding: veteran hurdler/chaser, prolific winner over the years, still capable of fair form over hurdles in 2003: won conditional jockeys claimer at Newton Abbot and seller at Worcester in June, amateur handicap at Towcester in October, and claimers at Fontwell in November and Huntingdon in December: stays easy 21f: acts on firm and soft going: has had tongue tied: usually races prominently: sometimes let down by jumping over fences: tough and consistent. *Ian Williams*   **c– h101**

GO WHITE LIGHTNING (IRE)   9 gr.g. Zaffaran (USA) – Rosy Posy (IRE) (Roselier (FR)) [2003/4 c109, h–: c26vᵖᵘ c22s² c26s³ c32g Mar 17] leggy gelding: twice-raced hurdler: fair maiden chaser: should stay 4m: acts on soft going (won bumpers on good to firm and heavy): free-going front runner: often shapes as if amiss. *M. Bradstock*   **c101 h–**

GRACEFUL DANCER 7 b.m. Old Vic – Its My Turn (Palm Track) [2003/4 h92, F65: 24v 26s 24s c24s³ c25spu 24g⁵ Feb 19] good-topped mare: winning hurdler: poor form on completed outing over fences: stays 3½m: raced only on good going or softer: blinkered (looked unwilling) once, visored since. *C. P. Morlock* — c77 h78

GRACILIS (IRE) 7 b.g. Caerleon (USA) – Grace Note (FR) (Top Ville) [2003/4 17dᶠ 21d* Apr 12] sturdy gelding: fairly useful on Flat (stays 21f): confirmed promise of hurdling debut when winning maiden at Huntingdon by 4 lengths from Mickey Croke, edging right and swishing tail after 2 out: will stay beyond 21f. *G. A. Swinbank* — h110

GRADY 5 ch.g. Bluegrass Prince (IRE) – Lady Sabina (Bairn (USA)) [2003/4 h–: 16m 16g⁶ Oct 30] close-coupled gelding: poor maiden on Flat: no show over hurdles: tried in cheekpieces: sold to join W. M. Brisbourne £1,500 Ascot November Sales. *Miss Jacqueline S. Doyle* — h–

GRALMANO (IRE) 9 b.g. Scenic – Llangollen (IRE) (Caerleon (USA)) [2003/4 c126p, h135: 16m⁴ 25m* 25g⁶ 24g Mar 18] sturdy gelding: successful both starts in novice chases: useful hurdler: won Grade 2 West Yorkshire Hurdle at Wetherby in November by 3 lengths from Royal Emperor: very stiff task final start: stays 25f with emphasis on speed: acts on firm and soft going: tough and genuine. *K. A. Ryan* — c– h139

GRAND AMBITION (USA) 8 b.g. Lear Fan (USA) – Longing To Dance (USA) (Nureyev (USA)) [2003/4 c78, h–: c21mᶠ c21gpu 17g 16m 16g c21g³ Feb 20] poor chaser/maiden hurdler: no form in 2003/4: stays 21f: acts on soft and good to firm going: tried blinkered. *Mrs P. Sly* — c– h–

GRAND CANYON (IRE) 11 b.g. Gallic Heir – Kay Kelly (Pitskelly) [2003/4 c21dpu Apr 30] lengthy gelding: winning pointer: usually let down by jumping in steeplechases: tried blinkered/visored. *Mrs J. Shirley* — c– x h–

GRANDE BRETAGNE (FR) 5 b.g. Legend of France (USA) – L'Epicurienne (FR) (Rex Magna (FR)) [2003/4 F16g 16d 16dpu Mar 28] good-topped gelding: seventh foal: half-brother to several winners, notably useful hurdler/fairly useful chaser L'Epicurien (by Chef de Clan II), stays 21f: dam 9f and 11.5f winner in French Provinces: showed little in bumper and 2 novice hurdles: tongue tied final start. *Ian Williams* — h– F–

GRANDE CREOLE (FR) 5 b.g. Byzantium (FR) – Sclos (FR) (Direct Flight) [2003/4 F18s⁴ F17g³ Apr 1] ninth foal: half-brother to several winners, including fairly useful jumper up to 21f Bleu A L'Ame and fairly useful hurdler Glucose (both by Double Bed), stays 19f: dam, winner on Flat/over fences in France, half-sister to smart French chasers Nucladeno and Nourylande: in frame in bumpers at Fontwell and Taunton (unseated and ran loose before start). *P. F. Nicholls* — F88

John Smith's West Yorkshire Hurdle, Wetherby—Gralmano defeats favourite Royal Emperor to complete a 55,964/1 four-timer on the card for jockey Graham Lee

GRANDEE LINE   9 gr.g. Gran Alba (USA) – Judys Line (Capricorn Line) [2003/4   **c92** c16v³ c22g⁴ c21sᶠ c24vᵖᵘ Apr 4] sturdy gelding: lightly raced: winning hurdler: off 22   **h–** months, third of 4 in novice at Chepstow on chasing debut: failed to repeat effort: should be suited by 2½m+: probably acts on any going. *R. H. Alner*

GRANDE JETE (SAF)   7 ch.g. Jallad (USA) – Corps de Ballet (SAF) (Truely Nure-   **h114** yev (USA)) [2003/4 17d³ 16d* 16v⁵ Jan 31] rather leggy gelding: useful on Flat, success- ful 7 times up to 1¼m in South Africa, including in Group 1 Cape of Good Hope Derby at Kenilworth at 4 yrs for M. de Kock: confirmed debut promise over hurdles when easily landing odds in novice at Wincanton in January: will prove best around 2m with emphasis on speed (jumped sloppily and reportedly lame when well beaten on heavy going). *N. J. Henderson*

GRAND FINALE (IRE)   7 b.h. Sadler's Wells (USA) – Final Figure (USA) (Super   **h122** Concorde (USA)) [2003/4 h91p: 16g* 17g³ 16d* 16s* 16s 16g⁵ Mar 26] compact horse: fairly useful hurdler: won maiden at Worcester in May, novice at Sandown in November and conditional jockeys handicap at Sandown in February: will stay 2½m: acts on soft going. *Miss Venetia Williams*

GRAND GOUSIER (FR)   10 b.g. Perrault – Tartifume II (FR) (Mistigri) [2003/4   **c–** c98, h–: c24gᵖᵘ Feb 11] good-topped gelding: modest handicap chaser in 2002/3: no form   **h–** in points or hunter in 2004: probably stays 3m: acts on heavy going, not fluent only outing on firm. *G. C. Evans*

GRAND LASS (IRE)   5 b.m. Grand Lodge (USA) – Siskin (IRE) (Royal Academy   **h–** (USA)) [2003/4 17d Mar 27] modest on Flat (should stay 1¾m), successful in February (claimed from T. D. Barron £5,000): in cheekpieces, well beaten in mares claimer on hurdling debut. *A. Sadik*

GRAND OPINION (IRE)   5 b.g. Grand Plaisir (IRE) – Cousin Rose (Track Spare)   **F–** [2003/4 F16g F16m Feb 21] good-topped gelding: eighth foal: dam lightly-raced maiden: mid-field in 2 bumpers. *B. W. Duke*

GRAND PRAIRIE (SWE)   8 b.g. Prairie – Platonica (ITY) (Primo Dominie) [2003/4   **h88** h–: 16s⁵ 16s² 17d* 16gᶠ 19g⁶ 16g⁵ Apr 12] sturdy gelding: modest hurdler: won condi- tional jockeys novice handicap at Folkestone in March: likely to prove best around 2m: acts on good to soft ground. *G. L. Moore*

GRAND PROMPT   5 ch.g. Grand Lodge (USA) – Prompting (Primo Dominie)   **h91 §** [2003/4 h99: 16g⁵ 20g* 19m 21m⁵ 19g³ 20m⁴ 22vᵖᵘ 20dᵖᵘ Jan 13] angular gelding: modest hurdler: won novice at Fakenham in May: sold out of Mrs L. Wadham's stable 7,800 gns Doncaster August Sales after fifth start, left B. Johnson before final one: stays 2½m: best form on good going or firmer: usually wears headgear, effective without: unreliable. *Miss L. J. Sheen*

GRAND SLAM (IRE)   9 b.g. Second Set (IRE) – Lady In The Park (IRE) (Last   **c85 §** Tycoon) [2003/4 c86§, h–§: c16s⁶ c20d³ Apr 18] good-bodied gelding: handicap hurdler: **h– §** modest novice chaser: stays 2½m: acts on firm and good to soft going: often takes little interest. *A. C. Whillans*

GRANGEWICK FLIGHT   10 b.g. Lighter – Feathery (Le Coq d'Or) [2003/4 c105:   **c94 §** c24g³ c20d² c20gᵖᵘ c21d⁵ c20d c20d⁴ c22g³ c20g³ c20d³ c20g⁴ c21gᵇᵈ c20dᵘʳ Apr 24] workmanlike gelding: modest handicap chaser: stays 3m: acts on heavy going: effective in cheekpieces/blinkers or not: sometimes let down by jumping: unreliable. *N. Wilson*

GRANIT D'ESTRUVAL (FR)   10 b.g. Quart de Vin (FR) – Jalousie (FR) (Block-   **c133** haus) [2003/4 c–, h–: c27dᵘʳ c28sᵖᵘ c30g³ c33d⁴ c29d* c33dᶠ Apr 17]   **h–**
      Irish-trained horses have had a good run of success in the Grand National at Aintree of late, but Granit d'Estruval's victory in the Powers Gold Label-sponsored Irish Grand National was the first by a British-trained horse in the Fairyhouse race since Mudahim in 1997. Desert Orchid and Omerta had also won Irish Nationals for British stables in the early-'nineties, Rhyme 'N' Reason did so in 1985 (three years before winning at Aintree) and a couple more, Jerpoint and Don Sancho, had won consecutive runnings back in the 'twenties. The latest Irish National winner may have been British-based, but he was bred in France and had both an Irish-born rider and trainer in Brian Harding and Ferdy Murphy respectively. Murphy has made successful raids back across the Irish Sea before, landing the Champion Stayers' Hurdle at the Punchestown Festival with Paddy's Return in 1997 and the Kerry National with Mac's Supreme in 2000. Granit d'Estruval's success was all the more welcome for a yard which had endured a disappointing campaign, with

less than half the number of wins that it had notched up during its best-ever season as recently as 2001/2.

Granit d'Estruval's season mirrored the form of his yard as a whole. He had been restricted to just one outing in the previous campaign, when having to undergo keyhole surgery on a chipped joint. He then failed to complete on his first two outings on his return, at Aintree (not taking to the big fences in the Becher Chase) and Haydock. A third place at Catterick and fourth to Tyneandthyneagain in the Eider Chase at Newcastle showed Granit d'Estruval retained a fair amount of ability, but they were not performances which suggested he would be up to winning a race as competitive as the Irish National, for which he started at 33/1.

With twenty-eight runners, the Irish National attracted its largest field for twenty years, short on quality at the top of the handicap but wide open, with the joint favourites the novice Direct Bearing and the progressive Hume Castle sharing favouritism at 9/1, while others prominent in the betting included the 2003 winner Timbera (forced to miss Aintree after scoping badly), the Cheltenham Foxhunter runner-up Never Compromise, the former Coral Cup winner Xenophon, the dual Grade 3 novice winner Satco Express and Native Jack, an early faller in the race the year before who was fresh from a good win at Cork. The only other British-trained runner was top weight Artic Jack, a first-fence casualty at Aintree nine days earlier. Granit d'Estruval, 5 lb wrong, was among those out of the handicap. Kept to the inside throughout, Granit d'Estruval was always going well and jumped to the front five out where long-time leader What Odds made a mistake. Granit d'Estruval kept on well, edging left under pressure after the last but just managing to hold off the novice Marcus du Berlais by half a length, with another lightly-weighted outsider Golden Storm taking third. Native Jack and Timbera were not far away in fourth and fifth, but a feature of the race was the small number of finishers. Only ten completed, with both the joint favourites being pulled up and the nine fallers including Never Compromise, who went at the first, and Xenophon who was one of two fatalities.

Immediately after the race, when he reportedly showed signs of distress, Granit d'Estruval was ruled out of the Scottish National on the grounds that the race came too soon and that the left-handed track would not suit him. However, Granit d'Estruval came out of the Irish National well and, with the going softening at Ayr,

Powers Gold Label Irish Grand National (Handicap), Fairyhouse—
outsiders Granit d'Estruval and Marcus du Berlais (grey) stage a grandstand finish

connections had a change of heart which almost landed them a second National within a week. Granit d'Estruval pulled clear with the leader Grey Abbey in the straight and was upsides when crashing out at the final fence. No horse has yet won both the Scottish and the Irish Grand National, let alone in the same season.

		Devon	Worden II
	Quart de Vin (FR)	(ch 1958)	Sees
	(b 1972)	Quartelette	Tantieme
Granit d'Estruval (FR)		(b 1963)	Quaker Girl
(b.g. 1994)		Blockhaus	Relic
	Jalousie (FR)	(ch 1953)	Belle Princesse
	(b 1975)	Ukase	Night And Day
		(b 1964)	Joie de La Balance

The tall, useful-looking Granit d'Estruval was sold for 26,000 guineas in the breeze-up section of the Doncaster November Sales as an unraced three-year-old. His sire Quart de Vin crops up in the pedigrees of several well-known French-bred staying chasers, including as the sire of the top-class pair Ucello II and Val d'Alene and as sire of the dam of Gloria Victis and Hussard Collonges. Granit d'Estruval's dam Jalousie has produced numerous winners besides him, including another 'National' winner in the latest season, Igloo d'Estruval (by Garde Royale) who won the Southern National at Fontwell. Jalousie's other winners include a brother to Granit d'Estruval in France named Beaujolais, a winner over fences and in cross-country chases. Much the best of her offspring is the top-class chaser Sabre d'Estruval (by Mistigri) who twice finished runner-up in the Grand Steeple-Chase de Paris—beaten by The Fellow on the second occasion—and won France's most valuable and prestigious handicap chase, the Prix du President de la Republique. Keeping the National theme going, that race is sometimes referred to as the 'French

Mr W. J. Gott's "Granit d'Estruval"

Grand National', though value and prestige apart, it hardly merits that description, being run over the regular Auteuil fences at a distance of less than three miles. As well as being dam of Granit d'Estruval, Jalousie is the grandam of a couple more winners in Britain in the latest season, including the fairly useful chaser Jaloux d'Estruval. Jalousie is out of a winning half sister to the great grandam of the very smart chaser Impek.

Granit d'Estruval is a thorough stayer who has raced only on good ground or softer and acts on heavy. He is a genuine sort, and while his efforts at Fairyhouse and Ayr might have put him on the shortlists of a few for the Grand National itself in 2005, he would have to jump the big fences better than he did in the Becher Chase, in which he unseated at the tenth. That could prove academic, however, as he would probably need to show further improvement in the interim and rise further in the weights to qualify for the National field. *Ferdy Murphy*

GRANITE STEPS   8 gr.g. Gran Alba (USA) – Pablena (Pablond) [2003/4 c100?, h–: 20v* 20d² Apr 10] lengthy gelding: lightly raced and little form over fences: fair handicap hurdler: better than ever in 2003/4, winning at Carlisle in March: good second there following month: stays 25f: raced on going softer than good (acts on heavy). *N. G. Richards*   c–
h110

GRANNY ANNIE   5 b.m. Minster Son – Castle Fountain (Royal Fountain) [2003/4 20dᵘʳ Apr 10] third foal: dam unraced: unseated after jinking badly right after fifth in novice hurdle on debut. *W. Amos*   h–

GRANNY KELLYS TART (IRE)   6 ch.g. Old Vic – Le Idol (Le Bavard (FR)) [2003/4 F18f* F16s² F16gʳᵒ Mar 17] IR £8,200 3-y-o: smallish, angular gelding: half-brother to fairly useful hurdler Myfavouritemartian (by Strong Gale), stayed 2¾m: dam twice-raced half-sister to top-class 2m hurdler Deep Idol: progressive form first 3 starts in bumpers: won at Wexford in July: short-head second to Sweet Kiln (pair well clear) at Navan in March: hung left under pressure and well held when running out around 3f out in Champion Bumper at Cheltenham. *W. P. Mullins, Ireland*   F108

GRANRICH   4 ch.f. Alflora (IRE) – Weareagrandmother (Prince Tenderfoot (USA)) [2003/4 F12s⁶ F13d 17vᶠ Feb 2] leggy filly: sixth foal: sister to 21f hurdle winner Alfy Rich and half-sister to modest hurdle winner Granny Rich (by Ardross), stays 2½m: dam winning hurdler/winner up to 12.5f on Flat: no show in bumpers and juvenile hurdle. *P. M. Rich*   h–
F–

GRANTIE BOY (IRE)   5 b.g. Nashwan (USA) – Radiant (USA) (Foolish Pleasure (USA)) [2003/4 F17m F16m Aug 2] half-brother to several winners, including useful sprinter Poolesta (by Hero's Honor), later Grade 3 8.5f winner in USA, and smart performer up to 1½m Desert Fox (by Sadler's Wells): dam, won around 6f in USA, half-sister to high-class middle-distance stayer Gold And Ivory: tailed off both starts in bumpers (bled from nose on debut): no form in points subsequently. *W. M. Brisbourne*   F–

GRAPHIC APPROACH (IRE)   6 b.g. King's Ride – Sharp Approach (Crash Course) [2003/4 F17d* 20s* 19sᶠ 16s³ Feb 19] strong, lengthy ex-Irish gelding: fourth foal: half-brother to fairly useful chaser up to 2¾m Catherine's Way (by Mandalus): dam, winning hurdler/pointer, half-sister to Irish National winner Feathered Gale, from family of very smart staying chaser Approaching: third start in bumpers (previously trained by E. Hales) when winning at Hereford in December: fairly useful form in novice hurdles, won at Wetherby in January: running creditably when falling last at Taunton later in month: likely to prove better at 2½m than 2m: acts on soft going: type to do well in novice chases in 2004/5. *C. R. Egerton*   h125
F103

GRAPHIC DESIGNER (IRE)   15 b.g. Sheer Grit – Kates Princess (Pitpan) [2003/4 c21m⁵ May 21] strong, lengthy gelding: modest pointer: no form in steeplechases, usually let down by jumping. *J. J. Hazeltine*   c–
h–

GRATE DEEL (IRE)   14 ch.g. The Parson – Cahernane Girl (Bargello) [2003/4 c103, h–: c30g c26mᵖᵘ c26m⁶ c25m³ c27m* Sep 5] smallish, strong gelding: modest handicap chaser: won at Sedgefield in September: best at 3m+: acts on soft and good to firm going: tried blinkered, not for long time. *Mrs S. J. Smith*   c94
h–

GRATOMI (IRE)   14 b.g. Bustomi – Granny Grumble (Politico (USA)) [2003/4 c20fᶠ⁴ c24m³ May 29] workmanlike gelding: veteran chaser: stays 23f: acts on any going: usually races up with pace: often let down by jumping. *Mrs A. E. Lee*   c91 ?
h–

GRATTAN LODGE (IRE)   7 gr.g. Roselier (FR) – Shallow Run (Deep Run) [2003/4 h111: c21v* c20vᶠ c24s* c25g⁴ c24g* Apr 10] good-topped gelding: progressive hurdler   c114
h–

in 2002/3: good start over fences, won novices at Sedgefield in January and Carlisle in March and April: likely to stay long distances: acts on heavy going. *J. Howard Johnson*

GRAVE DOUBTS 8 ch.g. Karinga Bay – Redgrave Girl (Deep Run) [2003/4 h121: 20d 16d* 16m³ 17d Mar 18] good-topped gelding: useful hurdler: won handicap at Wincanton in February by 6 lengths from Nathos: good third to Rigmarole in Kingwell Hurdle there later in month: raced mainly around 2m: acts on firm and good to soft going: tongue tied. *K. Bishop* — **h132**

GRAY'S EULOGY 6 b.g. Presenting – Gray's Ellergy (Oats) [2003/4 h79: 21s⁶ 21vᵘʳ 21vᵖᵘ 24sᵖᵘ 26g⁵ Mar 6] sturdy gelding: poor form on completed outings over hurdles: bred to stay well. *D. R. Gandolfo* — **h72**

GRAYSLAKE (IRE) 8 b.g. King's Ride – Castlegrace (IRE) (Kemal (FR)) [2003/4 h86: c20s⁴ c25sᵘʳ Jan 16] modest form over hurdles in 2002/3, and on completed start in handicap chases: stays 3m: acts on soft going: wore cheekpieces final outing. *K. C. Bailey* — **c96 h–**

GREAT AS GOLD (IRE) 5 b.g. Goldmark (USA) – Great Land (USA) (Friend's Choice (USA)) [2003/4 h94: 16m* 24d* 23d* 24d² 25d 20d Feb 21] fairly useful hurdler: won maiden at Hexham in May and novices at Newcastle in November and Wetherby in December: best effort when short-head second to Wildfield Rufo in handicap at Newcastle later in December: stays 3m: yet to race on extremes of going over hurdles: wears cheekpieces. *B. Ellison* — **h119**

GREAT BENEFIT (IRE) 5 ch.g. Beneficial – That's Lucy (IRE) (Henbit (USA)) [2003/4 F16d Mar 21] €20,000 4-y-o: first foal: dam, Irish maiden hurdler, half-sister to fairly useful hurdler/chaser Duhallow Lodge: showed little in bumper on debut. *Miss H. C. Knight* — **F–**

GREAT CRUSADER 12 ch.g. Deploy – Shannon Princess (Connaught) [2003/4 c–, h111: 27d⁵ c25d² c24gᶠ 24sᵖᵘ 24s 22g⁶ 22d⁵ 26g⁶ 27g Apr 22] small, sturdy gelding: fair handicap hurdler: well below form after reappearance: let down by jumping and only modest form over fences: suited by 3m+: raced mainly on good going or softer (acts on heavy). *M. J. Hogan* — **c87 h111 d**

GREAT HOPPER 9 b.m. Rock Hopper – Spun Gold (Thatch (USA)) [2003/4 16g Jul 3] no worthwhile form on Flat or over hurdles. *F. Watson* — **h–**

GREAT JUBILEE (IRE) 6 ch.g. Beneficial – Red Donna (Don) [2003/4 20m³ Oct 22] IR £22,000 3-y-o: half-brother to 3 winners, including useful bumper performer/fair hurdler up to 2¾m Scarlet Emperor (by Supreme Leader): dam unraced half-sister to smart Flat stayer Alto Volante and useful Irish hurdler Lovely Bio: looked in need of experience when third of 4 in novice at Chepstow on hurdling debut: won points in January and March: will be suited by further than 2½m. *M. C. Pipe* — **h88**

GREAT OAKS 10 b.g. Sylvan Express – Springdale Hall (USA) (Bates Motel (USA)) [2003/4 h85: 20g³ 20m⁶ 16m³ c17gᵖᵘ c20m⁴ 16g⁴ 20g 17sᵖᵘ Apr 6] lengthy gelding: jumped poorly both outings over fences: poor maiden hurdler: sold out of J. M. Jefferson's stable 3,000 gns Doncaster August Sales after fifth start: should stay beyond 2½m: acts on good to firm and heavy going: has pulled hard. *Miss Z. C. Davison* — **c79 x h75**

GREAT OVATION (FR) 5 ch.m. Boston Two Step (USA) – Baldiloa (No Lute (FR)) [2003/4 h80?: 16g⁶ 16s Dec 20] lengthy mare: poor form over hurdles: raced around 2m: has had tongue tied. *R. T. Phillips* — **h83**

GREAT RISK 8 b.m. Risk Me (FR) – Vaisigano (USA) (Vaguely Noble) [2003/4 c24dᶠ Apr 12] sixth foal: sister to Craine Decune, winner up to around 1½m in Holland: dam once-raced, out of very smart 7f to 10.5f winner Votre Altesse: backward, fell first in novice chase on debut. *G. R. Pewter* — **c–**

GREAT TRAVEL (FR) 5 b.g. Great Palm (USA) – Travel Free (Be My Guest (USA)) [2003/4 17g² 16g³ c16fᶠ 16m³ c16s* c16d* c16g² c16d⁴ c18d⁴ Apr 7] good-topped gelding: half-brother to winning hurdler/chaser around 2m King's Travel (by Balleroy): fairly useful on Flat, successful twice around 1¼m at 3 yrs: fair form over hurdles: won 4-y-o event at Nancy in 2002/3 for J. Bertran de Balanda: similar form over fences, winning handicaps at Folkestone (novice) in January and Sandown (idled) in February: likely to prove best at 2m: acts on soft going: has proved troublesome at start/reluctant to race. *P. F. Nicholls* — **c110 h104**

GRECIAN STAR 12 b.g. Crested Lark – Grecian Lace (Spartan General) [2003/4 c100: c30m⁶ c31fᵘʳ May 21] strong, deep-girthed gelding: fair hunter chaser: won at Huntingdon in May: stays 33f: acts on firm and good to soft going. *G. J. Tarry* — **c90**

GREENACRES BOY 9 b.g. Roscoe Blake – Deep Goddess (Deep Run) [2003/4 h–: 20m^{pu} 20g^{pu} 16m 17m 17g 16m 17g^{pu} c17m^F c20m^{ur} c17d^{pu} Nov 28] of no account: tried blinkered/in cheekpieces. *M. Mullineaux* **c– h–**

GREEN ADMIRAL 5 b.g. Slip Anchor – Jade Mistress (Damister (USA)) [2003/4 f77. 16g 17d 19g⁵ 22s 17g³ Mar 16] smallish gelding: poor maiden hurdler: probably stays 19f: has hung/carried head awkwardly. *J. J. Quinn* **h73**

GREENBACK (BEL) 13 b.g. Absalom – Batalya (BEL) (Boulou) [2003/4 c–, h98: 20m 22g 18f⁵ 26s^{pu} 21s⁵ Dec 11] smallish, angular gelding: winning hurdler/chaser: no sign of retaining ability. *J. Joseph* **c– h–**

GREEN BELT FLYER (IRE) 6 b.g. Leading Counsel (USA) – Current Liability (Caribo) [2003/4 20s⁶ 16v* 16m² 16m³ 20d⁵ 16d* 16d⁶ 16v³ 16d* 16d⁴ Apr 13] €20,000 4-y-o: useful-looking gelding: half-brother to useful chaser Lucky Bay (by Convinced), stays 25f: dam unraced half-sister to fairly useful 2m hurdler Healy's Pub: fairly useful novice hurdler: won at Ballinrobe (maiden) in June, Gowran in December and Naas in February, beating Francys Fancy 2 lengths in handicap for final success: best at 2m: acts on good to firm and heavy going: reportedly had lung infection seventh start. *Mrs J. Harrington, Ireland* **h125**

GREENBOROUGH (IRE) 6 b.g. Dr Devious (IRE) – Port Isaac (USA) (Seattle Song (USA)) [2003/4 h–: 20s^{pu} 19s^{pu} 21g 17m⁶ 19d⁵ Mar 22] no form over hurdles: wore cheekpieces last 3 starts. *Mrs P. Ford* **h–**

GREEN DEBATE (USA) 4 b.g. Green Dancer (USA) – Verbal Style (USA) (Verbatim (USA)) [2003/4 F16g* Apr 11] fifth foal: half-brother to 3 winners in North America: dam, won in USA, daughter of smart performer up to 1m Impressive Style: won bumper at Cork on debut by length from Detonante. *Miss F. M. Crowley, Ireland* **F99**

GREENFIELD (IRE) 6 ch.g. Pleasant Tap (USA) – No Review (USA) (Nodouble (USA)) [2003/4 h109: 16d 19s³ 20s⁴ 16d 21d 19g* Apr 18] good-topped gelding: fair hurdler: won handicap at Stratford despite jumping none too fluently: will possibly prove best up to 2½m: raced on good going or softer (acts on soft): blinkered last 3 starts. *R. T. Phillips* **h109**

GREENFIRE (FR) 6 ch.g. Ashkalani (IRE) – Greenvera (USA) (Riverman (USA)) [2003/4 F–: F16g³ 16g 22f⁶ 22f⁵ Oct 18] form only when third in bumper at Perth, allowed to dictate and almost certainly flattered: has had tongue tied. *Mrs Dianne Sayer* **h– F84 ?**

GREEN GAMBLE 4 gr.g. Environment Friend – Gemma's Wager (IRE) (Phardante (FR)) [2003/4 F12g 18v 16s⁶ 18d⁴ 16d Apr 11] first foal: dam won 21f chase: tailed off in bumper on debut: best effort over hurdles when 25¾ lengths fourth in novice at Fontwell. *D. B. Feek* **h86 ? F–**

GREEN GO (GER) 6 ch.g. Secret 'n Classy (CAN) – Green Fee (GER) (Windwurf (GER)) [2003/4 c–, h88: 19m² 20m^{pu} 22m 20m⁴ 17d⁵ 20m³ c21g* c26m* c24g^F c20f^{pu} c20m^{pu} Nov 1] modest hurdler/chaser: won maiden and novice over fences at Cartmel within 3 days in August: stays easy 3¼m, at least as effective at shorter: raced mainly on good going or firmer: has shaped as if amiss more than once (broke blood vessel on chasing debut): front runner. *A. Sadik* **c87 h88**

GREENHALL RAMBLER (IRE) 5 ch.m. Anshan – Gentle Pressure (Sharpo) [2003/4 F18g 16v² 16g⁵ 16g⁴ 20d 16s⁶ 18d* 16d² 20d* Apr 11] half-sister to fair hurdler up to 2½m Ballyhyland (by Supreme Leader): dam unraced: modest form on first of 2 starts in bumpers: improved efforts over hurdles late in season, winning mares novice at Downpatrick in March and Grade 3 mares novice at Limerick (by 1½ lengths from Burnt Out) in April: excellent second to Stashedaway in listed mares event at Punchestown in early-May: stays 2½m: acts on good to firm and good to soft going. *P. A. Fahy, Ireland* **h115 F–**

GREENHOPE (IRE) 6 b.g. Definite Article – Unbidden Melody (USA) (Chieftain) [2003/4 h–: 16g* 16g³ 17d 16d⁴ Apr 3] leggy, useful-looking gelding: fairly useful handicap hurdler: sustained overreach only outing in 2002/3: improved form on return, making all at Kempton in December: respectable efforts when in frame after valuable events at same course (third to Limerick Boy) and Aintree (fourth to Puck Out) in April: stays 2½m: acts on good to firm and good to soft going: usually races up with pace. *N. J. Henderson* **h129**

GREEN ICENI 5 br.g. Greensmith – Boadicea's Chariot (Commanche Run) [2003/4 F88: F17s* 19s 16s³ Jan 16] lengthy, rather unfurnished gelding: progressive form in bumpers, won at Folkestone in November: poor form in 2 novice hurdles: should be suited by further than 17f. *J. R. Best* **h83 F101**

GREEN IDEAL 6 b.g. Mark of Esteem (IRE) – Emerald (USA) (El Gran Senor (USA)) [2003/4 h122: c20f^F c17d^4 c16s^2 c21s^{ur} c16s^3 c16d^2 c20d^{pu} c16d^{pu} Apr 22] compact gelding: fairly useful hurdler in 2002/3 for N. Henderson: novice chaser, fair form at best but has gone the wrong way temperamentally: probably stays 21f, at least as effective at 2m: acts on soft going: tried tongue tied. *Ferdy Murphy* — **c108 §** **h–**

GREENKEYS (AUS) 10 b.g. Bonhomie (USA) – Cindy Doll (AUS) (Cindy's Son) [2003/4 c–, h–: c17s^F c21g^{ur} 17m 20d^4 20m^4 21m^4 c24g^F c20m^6 c26g^6 Aug 4] compact gelding: bad maiden hurdler/chaser: stays 2½m: wears cheekpieces: has jumping problems: sold 1,000 gns Doncaster August Sales, won point in January. *R. C. Guest* — **c– x** **h53**

GREEN 'N' GOLD 4 b.f. Cloudings (IRE) – Fishki (Niniski (USA)) [2003/4 17s 17d^5 21d^3 Mar 30] half-sister to modest hurdler Fishki's Lad (by Casteddu), stays 3m: fair on Flat (stays 2¼m), successful in April: progressive form over hurdles, caught the eye when never-nearer third to Cigarillo in amateur novice at Sedgefield: will stay beyond 21f: open to further improvement. *M. D. Hammond* — **h87 p**

GREEN PEACH (IRE) 6 b.g. Norwich – Larry's Peach (Laurence O) [2003/4 F16d* F16d Apr 11] €28,000 4-y-o: good-topped gelding: half-brother to winning 25f hurdler Native Peach (by Be My Native) and bumper winner Sweep The Peach (by Brush Aside): dam, winning hurdler/chaser who stayed 3m, half-sister to dam of top-class chaser Toby Tobias: odds on, quickened well from rear to win 18-runner bumper at Naas on debut in March: better effort after when fifth to Geill Sli in Grade 1 at Punchestown in late-April. *W. P. Mullins, Ireland* — **F107**

GREENSMITH LANE 8 br.g. Greensmith – Handy Lane (Nearly A Hand) [2003/4 h73: 20m 17m^6 19g^5 17g 18m^8 20g* 16s* 16d^5 16g* 19g Apr 16] modest hurdler: sold out of N. Hawke's stable £3,000 Ascot June Sales prior to reappearance: much improved after, winning selling handicap at Fontwell and novice claimers there and at Plumpton (claimed from B. Llewellyn £5,000) in autumn and handicap at Wincanton in April after only run for Mrs L. Jewell: stays 2½m: acts on soft and good to firm going: wore cheekpieces last 7 outings. *G. B. Balding* — **h96**

GREEN SMOKE 8 gr.g. Green Adventure (USA) – Smoke (Rusticaro (FR)) [2003/4 c86, h–: c20m^{pu} c22g^{pu} Jun 11] novice hurdler/chaser: modest form at best over fences, pulled up sharply as if amiss final start: stays 2¾m: acts on heavy going: wore cheekpieces last 3 starts. *J. M. Jefferson* — **c–** **h–**

GREEN TANGO 5 br.g. Greensmith – Furry Dance (USA) (Nureyev (USA)) [2003/4 F16g^3 F16d* F16g^2 16s* 16g* 16g 16d* Apr 21] 9,000 3-y-o: good-topped gelding: half-brother to fairly useful 2m hurdler Nuvellino (by Robellino): dam once-raced close relation of smart Flat performer/winning hurdler Florid: fairly useful form in bumpers, won at Uttoxeter in November: successful on 3 of 4 starts over hurdles, in novices at Huntingdon in January, Ludlow (by 3½ lengths from King Solomon) in March and Worcester: on toes when well beaten in Grade 2 novice at Aintree: raced at 2m on good going or softer: looks to have a good attitude, and may be capable of better still. *H. D. Daly* — **h122 +** **F103**

GREENWICH 10 br.g. Handsome Sailor – Praise The Lord (Lord Gayle (USA)) [2003/4 c26s^{pu} c25d^3 Feb 17] tall gelding: prolific winner in points in 2002: fairly useful hunter chaser at best: better effort in handicaps in 2003/4 when third to Copper Shell at Folkestone: best at 3m+: acts on good to firm going: often front runner. *M. Scudamore* — **c88** **h–**

GREGORIAN (IRE) 7 b.g. Foxhound (USA) – East River (FR) (Arctic Tern (USA)) [2003/4 16m* 19g^{pu} 17m^5 17g^3 16g^{pu} 16m^3 16m^4 16d* 16d* 16d^3 16d Apr 8] neat gelding: half-brother to winning hurdler/chaser Charlie Chang (by Don't Forget Me), stays 3m: won maiden at Tramore only completed start over fences: modest hurdler: sold out of P. Rothwell's stable 5,000 gns Doncaster November (2002) Sales: won sellers at Ludlow (conditional jockeys) in May, Leicester in December and Ludlow (made most) in January: claimed from J. O'Shea £6,000 penultimate start, reclaimed final one: raced mainly around 2m: acts on good to firm and heavy going: has run as if amiss on several occasions. *R. Flint* — **c–** **h96**

GREGORIO (FR) 10 b.g. Passing Sale (FR) – Apside (FR) (Mistigri) [2003/4 c120, h97: c20d c20s^{bd} c19s c22s c20s^4 c21g 22s Mar 27] maiden hurdler: handicap chaser: best effort in 2003/4 when seventh of 12 to Cyborsun at Naas third start: stays 2½m: acts on good to firm and heavy going: tried blinkered: none too consistent. *Mrs S. A. Bramall, Ireland* — **c114** **h–**

GREGORY PECKORY (IRE) 6 b. or br.g. Teamster – Vill Alba (IRE) (Cataldi) [2003/4 F16g^2 F17d 16f^4 Oct 16] IR £1,700 3-y-o, 3,000 4-y-o: close-coupled gelding: first foal: dam, placed in point, half-sister to fairly useful hurdlers up to 2¾m Coolerin — **h83 ?** **F83**

Boy and Gangabal: much better effort in bumpers when second to Mister Flint at Worcester: fourth of 7 in steadily-run novice at Towcester on hurdling debut: likely to benefit from greater test of stamina. *N. A. Twiston-Davies*

GREY ABBEY (IRE) 10 gr.g. Nestor – Tacovaon (Avocat) [2003/4 c143, h : 20d⁶ 25g* c24g* c33d⁰ Apr 17]   **c159 h116**

Course specialist Grey Abbey's sixth win at Ayr from ten starts (he also lost a further win there on technical grounds) was easily the most important of his career, earning connections just under £70,000 from his win in the Gala Casinos Daily Record Scottish Grand National. As well as being the venue for his first wins over both hurdles and fences, the Scottish track had also seen Grey Abbey's biggest previous success when landing the Future Champion Novices' Chase on Scottish National day in 2001. A year later, he had had his first crack at the track's showpiece event when a close fourth to Take Control in one of the most dramatic finishes to a Scottish National. There was a huge field of twenty-eight for the latest renewal, with Grey Abbey heading the weights on 11-12. No horse had carried more weight to victory since Red Rum followed up the second of his wins at Aintree thirty years earlier. There were four horses in the field who had contested the Grand National a fortnight beforehand, sixth-placed Smarty the only one of them who had completed. The novices Native Emperor and Simply Supreme shared favouritism on 7/1, just ahead of the latter's stable-companion Tipsy Mouse, winner of Kelso's Scottish Borders National, who was backed down from 12/1 to 15/2. The in-form Desailly was a 9/1-chance, with Grey Abbey on 12/1 along with the previous season's runner-up Stormez.

None of the market leaders ever looked like threatening Grey Abbey who galloped his rivals into the ground, leading from the off in his usual style and jumping well throughout. With Simply Supreme a faller at the first and Native Emperor one of the first beaten, most of Grey Abbey's remaining pursuers lost touch on the final circuit. Approaching the straight for the final time, only the previous year's fourth Kerry Lads, another course regular, and Granit d'Estruval, winner of the Irish National just five days earlier, were within striking distance of Grey Abbey who was showing no signs of tiring. The leader's most anxious moment came when he had to be steered rather sharply round the dolled-off second-last fence, allowing Granit d'Estruval, by that point the only conceivable danger, to draw upsides. Jumping the last together, that danger was removed when Granit d'Estruval crashed out, leaving Grey Abbey to come home a distance clear (actually by thirty-seven lengths on the scale used by the BHB) of Kerry Lads. The Fulke Walwyn Kim Muir winner Maximize plugged on for third ahead of Tipsy Mouse, with only nine finishing and the majority of the field pulled up. Grey Abbey's win completed a National double for his rider Graham Lee who had also partnered Amberleigh House at Aintree. Ironically, Grey Abbey's regular jockey until the latest season had been Granit d'Estruval's rider at Ayr, Brian Harding.

Gala Casinos Daily Record Scottish Grand National Handicap Chase, Ayr—Grey Abbey is left clear by Granit d'Estruval's last-fence fall and maintains his excellent record at the track

Grey Abbey began the latest season with a new stable, having moved across the Pennines to Howard Johnson from Barry Murtagh for whom he had already established a fine record. He had reportedly undergone treatment for a fibrillating heart before his reappearance and was returning from almost a year's absence when finishing last of six in the Cleeve Hurdle at Cheltenham in January. Kept to hurdles, but with his sights lowered to a handicap at Catterick, Grey Abbey won there the following month before returning over fences for the Grimthorpe Chase at Doncaster in March. He was not the only front runner in the field, but rallied splendidly when the lead was taken off him to beat Royal Auclair by ten lengths. Amberleigh House used the same race to warm up for Aintree, finishing a well-held fifth.

It will not come as too much of a surprise to learn that Grey Abbey is related to another popular grey chaser trained in the North who had similar attributes and style of racing to Grey Abbey in The Grey Monk. Their respective dams are half-sisters. The Grey Monk, a top-class chaser in his prime, never contested a Scottish National (he was third in the Irish version) but he too had a good record at Ayr, winning all three of his starts there. Grey Abbey has two sisters who have won in points, while his half-brother Mister Dave's (by Bluffer) was a fair winner over fences in the latest season. None of the mares on the bottom line of Grey Abbey's pedigree ever ran. His sire Nestor was a fairly useful staying handicapper on the Flat and was second in the Northumberland Plate. Nestor has had very small crops (Grey Abbey was one of just three reported foals by him in 1994) and consequently minimal success besides Grey Abbey.

		Nishapour (gr 1975)	Zeddaan
	Nestor		Alama
	(gr 1980)	Meadow Rhapsody (ch 1967)	Ragusa
Grey Abbey (IRE)			Meadow Music
(gr.g. 1994)		Avocat (ch 1969)	Relko
	Tacovaon		Pourparler
	(ch 1985)	No Hunting (b 1971)	No Time
			Hunter's Hut

The lengthy Grey Abbey was bought for 12,000 guineas at Doncaster as an unraced four-year-old. He stays four miles plus (though doesn't necessarily need that severe a test of stamina) and acts on heavy ground and good to firm. He had a wind operation earlier in his career and has had his tongue tied, though not in the latest season. A bold-jumping front runner, Grey Abbey is a genuine sort who put up his best effort at Ayr, showing very smart form. He is reportedly to be aimed at the Grand National itself in 2005, and he should put up a bold show at Aintree if taking his chance, as he is reminiscent of another all-the-way winner of the Scottish National, Sebastian V, who put up an exhibition round of jumping when just pipped by Lucius in the 1978 Grand National. If not, there's always the Scottish version again. *J. Howard Johnson*

GREY BROTHER   6 gr.g. Morpeth – Pigeon Loft (IRE) (Bellypha) [2003/4 h111p, F90: 19g³ Mar 9] sturdy gelding: fairly useful form when winning maiden hurdle at Exeter in 2002/3: off a year, encouraging third to Rydon Lane in handicap at same course: will stay at least 3m: remains open to improvement. *J. D. Frost*   **h117 p**

GREY CISEAUX (IRE)   9 gr.g. Mujtahid (USA) – Inisfail (Persian Bold) [2003/4 c87, h–: c21m² 22m² c21m² c25mᵖᵘ 27f² 21m² c24m* c25f⁴ c25g Mar 10] angular gelding: poor hurdler/chaser: won weakly-contested maiden chase at Stratford in October: stays 27f: acts on firm going: effective in blinkers/cheekpieces or without: temperamental. *A. E. Jones*   **c79 §** **h75 §**

GREY REPORT (IRE)   7 gr.g. Roselier (FR) – Busters Lodge (Antwerp City) [2003/4 16d* 16d* 21d³ 18v* 21s* 21g² 21g³ 24g² 21m² Apr 14]   **h143**
    Judged on what he had achieved up to the time of his purchase at the Doncaster August Sales, Grey Report looked by no means cheap at 20,000 guineas, but by the end of the season it wasn't in doubt that connections had picked up a bargain. Grey Report was trained up to the sale by Darragh Brennan in Ireland, where he made all in points at Lingstown and Camolin, after showing modest form at best in three bumpers. Presumably Grey Report did not give the impression with his new stable that there was a great deal better to come. He started at 50/1 on his hurdling debut in a well-contested maiden at Newbury at the end of November when he won easily, making all at a good pace and running on well to beat Alpine Fox by eleven lengths. The same tactics were used when Grey Report went on to land the odds in novices at Cheltenham in December and Fontwell and Plumpton in January. Grey Report's only defeat in his first five outings over hurdles came in the Grade 1 Challow Hurdle at Newbury in late-December, when he went down by half a length and sixteen lengths to Cornish Rebel and Big Moment, having again gone off quickly. Grey Report did not win again after mid-January, but later perform-

European Breeders Fund 'National Hunt' Novices' Hurdle (Qualifier), Cheltenham—
the ultra-game Grey Report proves too strong for Mount Karinga

ances marked him out as one of the season's leading staying novices. He enjoyed the longest break of his campaign before his next run, in a novice at Newbury where, on his first run on ground firmer than good to soft, he failed only by a length and a half to hold Fountain Hill, to whom he was giving 10 lb, with the rest strung out behind. A 25/1 chance for the Royal & SunAlliance at Cheltenham twelve days later, Grey Report soon established a clear lead and, though the field came back at him early on the final circuit, it wasn't until he made a mistake two out that he was passed. Grey Report finished third, beaten half a length and four lengths by Fundamentalist and Inglis Drever, but still turning around the Challow form with Big Moment, who was back in fifth. Grey Report also defeated Challow winner Cornish Rebel when distinguishing himself upped to three miles in the Sefton at Aintree where, after helping set a strong pace, he looked held when tackled by the winner Accipiter three out, but rallied splendidly to go down only by three quarters of a length, with Cornish Rebel the last of the eight to finish. Grey Report never ran a bad race all season, and underlined that he is as tough as he is consistent when, just twelve days after his gruelling race at Aintree, he turned in another cracking effort to finish half a length second to Copsale Lad, to whom he was giving 22 lb, in a novice event at Cheltenham, typically rallying gamely once collared at the last.

Grey Report (IRE) (gr.g. 1997)	Roselier (FR) (gr 1973)	Misti IV (br 1958)	Medium
			Mist
		Peace Rose (gr 1959)	Fastnet Rock
			La Paix
	Busters Lodge (b 1984)	Antwerp City (b 1973)	Klairon
			Term Time
		Corun (b 1973)	Ribocco
			Running Cedar

Mrs D. A. La Trobe's "Grey Report"

Grey Report is out of the lightly-raced pointer Busters Lodge and a brother to the temperamental staying hurdler/chaser The Merry Mason, as well as a half-brother to Port Na Son (by Over The River), a fair chaser at up to twenty-five furlongs in Ireland. Grey Report coped surprisingly well with two miles for a son of Roselier, but three miles or more is likely to suit him ideally, and he is proven on all ground except firm, on which he has yet to race. He has not always hurdled with fluency and has shown a tendency to jump left, particularly when under pressure. It should be mentioned that before his runs in bumpers in Ireland, he twice ran out in points. Though he could be said to be bred for it, Grey Report is not an obvious chaser on looks, being a compact sort, and it would come as no surprise to see him kept to hurdling, at least in the short term. A BHB handicap mark of 146 looks a perfectly reasonable assessment of his form, and the valuable three-and-a-quarter-mile handicap at the Open Meeting at Cheltenham in November appeals as a likely early-season target. Whichever route is chosen for him, this genuine front runner should pay his way again in 2004/5. *P. J. Hobbs*

GREY SAMURAI 4 gr.g. Gothenberg (IRE) – Royal Rebeka (Grey Desire) [2003/4 F17g Apr 24] 7,200Y: third foal: half-brother to 6f winner Grey Cossack (by Kasakov): dam, no sign of ability, out of half-sister to useful 2m to 2¾m hurdler Roberty Lea: well beaten in bumper on debut. *P. T. Midgley* — **F—**

GREY SHARK (IRE) 5 gr.g. Roselier (FR) – Sharkezan (IRE) (Double Schwartz) [2003/4 F16s 16s 16v 17d Mar 27] 1,800 4-y-o: fourth foal: dam unraced: signs of only a little ability in bumper/over hurdles: will be suited by 2½m+. *D. P. Keane* — **h70 ?** / **F—**

GREYTON (IRE) 11 gr.g. Zaffaran (USA) – Rosy Posy (IRE) (Roselier (FR)) [2003/4 c—, h—: c24g^pu Feb 13] useful-looking gelding: winning chaser, very lightly raced nowadays. *L. A. Dace* — **c—** / **h—**

GREYWELL (IRE) 7 b. or br.g. Camden Town – Bellalma (Belfalas) [2003/4 20g^pu c17g^F c18g³ c17s³ c20s³ c21s⁴ c20v³ c16s* c17s^F Mar 27] compact gelding: fair hurdler: similar form over fences, winning maiden at Wexford in March: stays 2½m: acts on heavy going: in cheekpieces and tongue tied last 2 starts. *Miss Elizabeth Doyle, Ireland* — **c110** / **h—**

GRIFFENS BROOK 4 b.g. Alderbrook – Ima Delight (Idiot's Delight) [2003/4 F16d Mar 22] second foal: dam, fair hurdler, stayed 2¾m: well held in bumper on debut. *Mrs P. Sly* — **F—**

GRIFFIN'S LEGACY 5 b.g. Wace (USA) – Griffin's Girl (Bairn (USA)) [2003/4 F18v Jan 12] first foal: dam poor maiden on Flat/over hurdles: showed nothing in bumper on debut. *N. G. Ayliffe* — **F—**

GRIMES 11 b.g. Reprimand – Diva Madonna (Chief Singer) [2003/4 16d c17g* Aug 7] tall, imposing gelding: top-class hurdler in 2001/2: eased once headed 3 out in Galway Hurdle on return: useful chaser: simple task in minor event at Tipperary, not seen out again: stays 2¾m, effective at much shorter: best efforts on good/good to firm going: often none too fluent over fences. *C. Roche, Ireland* — **c120 +** / **h—**

GRIMSHAW (USA) 9 ch.g. St Jovite (USA) – Loa (USA) (Hawaii) [2003/4 20d⁴ 19m* 19m^F 20m⁵ 16d^F c19s^F 16g^pu Feb 11] rather sparely-made gelding: no form over fences: one-time fair handicap hurdler, left T. J. O'Mara before reappearance: won conditional jockeys event at Hereford in September: well held only completed start after: stays 21f: acts on good to firm and heavy going: tried blinkered/in cheekpieces: has had tongue tied. *Mrs D. A. Hamer* — **c—** / **h85**

GRIZZLY ACTIVEWEAR (IRE) 10 ch.g. Camden Town – Boro Cent (Little Buskins) [2003/4 22g⁶ 22d³ 21s 22g⁶ Mar 28] leggy gelding: winning Irish pointer: modest hurdler, left G. M. Moore and off 18 months before reappearance: best at 2¾m+: acts on soft and good to firm going: none too consistent. *B. D. Leavy* — **h91**

GRIZZLY GOLFWEAR (IRE) 10 b.g. Commanche Run – Dunwellan (Tekoah) [2003/4 c93, h—: c24m³ c28d³ c24g^pu Feb 11] lengthy gelding: winning pointer: fair hunter chaser: probably stays 3½m: acts on good to firm and soft going. *Mrs S. E. Hughes* — **c91** / **h—**

GROOVEJET 5 b.g. Emperor Jones (USA) – Sir Hollow (USA) (Sir Ivor (USA)) [2003/4 h—: 18m^pu May 26] leggy gelding: no form in 2 starts over hurdles or in points: tried visored. *J. R. Jenkins* — **h—**

GROUND BALL (IRE) 7 b. or br.g. Bob's Return (IRE) – Bettyhill (Ardross) [2003/4 c125, h110: c18d² 20g³ 16d* c16d³ c22s^F c18d* c16d² c16g Apr 1] well-made gelding: fairly useful hurdler: won minor event at Punchestown in November: useful — **c137** / **h121**

chaser: easily landed odds in minor event at Thurles in January: best effort when 2½ lengths second of 14 finishers to St Pirran in valuable handicap at Cheltenham: needs good test at 2m and likely to stay 2¾m: acts on heavy going: reliable. *C. F. Swan, Ireland*

GROUND BREAKER 4 b.g. Emperor Jones (USA) – Startino (Bustino) [2003/4 F16g⁴ F17g⁵ Apr 24] half-brother to several winners, including poor chaser Advance East (by Polish Precedent) and fairly useful hunter Stoney Valley (by Caerleon), both of whom stay 21f; dam, 1m and 1½m winner, also third in Park Hill Stakes: better effort in bumpers when fourth of 18 to Reel Missile at Doncaster. *M. W. Easterby* **F92**

GROUP ONE'S HOPE 8 b.m. Absalom – Hopeful Waters (Forlorn River) [2003/4 c–, h–: 16m c17g⁵ᵖᵘ c16mᵖᵘ 19f⁴ 17gᵘʳ 16gᵖᵘ Nov 6] of no account: tried visored. *A. W. Carroll* **c–** **h–**

GROUSE HALL 10 ch.g. Primitive Rising (USA) – Em-Kay-Em (Slim Jim) [2003/4 c85, h–: c20g² Oct 15] workmanlike gelding: poor novice hurdler/chaser, very lightly raced nowadays: folded dramatically after being left long way clear 4 out in novice handicap chase at Uttoxeter, only outing in 2003/4: stays 25f: acts on soft going. *M. Todhunter* **c71** **h–**

GROUSE MOOR (USA) 5 b.g. Distant View (USA) – Caithness (USA) (Roberto (USA)) [2003/4 F88: F17s⁵ 16d⁵ 16d⁵ 18s 17dᵖᵘ Mar 3] sturdy gelding: fair form at best in bumpers: regressive form over hurdles, ran as if amiss when tongue tied final outing: should stay beyond 2m. *P. Winkworth* **h96** **F69**

GROVE JULIET (IRE) 5 ch.m. Moscow Society (USA) – Cloona Lady (IRE) (Duky) [2003/4 F16d Mar 21] 3,000 4-y-o: third foal: dam, winning pointer, half-sister to fairly useful 3m hurdler/chaser Leamhog: well beaten in bumper on debut. *B. G. Powell* **F–**

GUARD DUTY 7 b.g. Deploy – Hymne d'Amour (USA) (Dixieland Band (USA)) [2003/4 h123§: c20s² c24g* c26s³ c24m² c32gᵖᵘ c24g⁶ c22g⁶ Apr 22] leggy gelding: fairly useful handicap hurdler in 2002/3: disappointing over fences, unimpressive when landing odds in novice at Taunton in December: stays 25f: acts on heavy going: visored last 4 outings: tongue tied: ungenuine. *M. C. Pipe* **c103 §** **h– §**

GUARDED SECRET 7 ch.g. Mystiko (USA) – Fen Dance (IRE) (Trojan Fen) [2003/4 16d⁴ 17d⁴ 16d⁵ 16v⁴ Jan 26] leggy gelding: fair on Flat (stays 1½m), below form in 2003: fair form over hurdles, won novice at Uttoxeter on debut in November: free-going front runner. *J. Mackie* **h108**

GUDLAGE (USA) 8 b.g. Gulch (USA) – Triple Kiss (Shareef Dancer (USA)) [2003/4 c–, h105] 16m Aug 2] workmanlike gelding: 2m handicap hurdler, very lightly raced nowadays: less than fluent only start over fences: raced mainly on good/good to soft going over jumps: tongue tied. *M. W. Easterby* **c–** **h94**

GUE AU LOUP (FR) 10 gr.g. Royal Charter (FR) – Arche d'Alliance (FR) (Pamponi (FR)) [2003/4 c90, h–: c17m* Jul 19] tall gelding: modest handicap chaser: won at Market Rasen on only outing in 2003/4: stays 2½m: acts on soft and good to firm going: often front runner. *B. Ellison* **c93** **h–**

GUIGNOL DU COCHET (FR) 10 ch.g. Secret of Success – Pasquita (FR) (Bourbon (FR)) [2003/4 c87, h–: c16g⁴ c22s⁵ c20m² c20g² c19s⁴ c20d⁵ c24d* Apr 8] tall gelding: modest chaser: sold out of Mrs L. Richards' stable £6,000 Ascot November Sales after reappearance: won second of 2 starts in points in 2004: best effort in hunters when winning at Ludlow by 4 lengths from Act In Time: stays easy 3m: acts on soft and good to firm going: tried blinkered/visored/tongue tied earlier in career. *S. Flook* **c98** **h–**

GUILSBOROUGH GORSE 9 b.g. Past Glories – Buckby Folly (Netherkelly) [2003/4 c93: c24m³ c25g³ c22g⁵ c23m c24g² c24f* Mar 12] lengthy gelding: modest chaser: favourite, won hunter at Musselburgh in February: stays 25f: has form on soft going, races mainly on good or firmer nowadays (acts on firm): tried blinkered/in cheekpieces. *T. D. Walford* **c96**

GUILT 4 b.c. Mark of Esteem (IRE) – Guillem (USA) (Nijinsky (CAN)) [2003/4 16s 16d* 17d 16s⁵ Feb 8] tall colt: half-brother to useful 2m hurdler/winning chaser Goss (by Linamix) and fair hurdler/chaser Guilder (by Groom Dancer), stayed 2½m: fairly useful middle-distance maiden on Flat, lightly raced, sold out of P. Bary's stable 38,000 gns Newmarket July Sales: best effort in juvenile hurdles when winning at Leopardstown in December: ran as if amiss next time, found little final start: tongue tied after debut. *D. T. Hughes, Ireland* **h113**

GULABILL 5 b.g. Safawan – Gulsha (Glint of Gold) [2003/4 F16s Mar 20] fifth foal: half-brother to fair hurdler/fairly useful chaser Gulshan (by Batshoof), stays 3m: dam, fairly useful hurdler up to 2½m, half-sister to smart 2m hurdler/winning chaser Bold Boss **F76**

and smart 1¼m performer Beau Sher: eleventh of 21 to Something Gold in bumper at Ascot on debut. *N. A. Twiston-Davies*

GULLIBLE GUY   12 b.g. Domynsky – Halmaseta (Lochnager) [2003/4 c20m Apr 28] medium-sized gelding: maiden hurdler: little sign of retaining ability in points/novice hunter chase in 2003: blinkered once. *George R. Moscrop*   c–
h–

GULLIVERS TRAVELS   5 ch.g. Un Desperado (FR) – Drivers Bureau (Proverb) [2003/4 F16g F16g Mar 27] lengthy gelding: has scope: seventh foal: brother to fair hurdler/chaser The Kew Tour, stays 25f, and half-brother to winning pointer by Town And Country: dam ran once: more signs of temperament than ability in bumpers. *G. L. Moore*   F–

GUMLEY GALE   9 b.g. Greensmith – Clodaigh Gale (Strong Gale) [2003/4 h108: 19d 17s 22d⁴ 24d 19g⁴ 22g⁵ Apr 18] sturdy gelding: handicap hurdler, modest form at best in 2003/4: stays 2¾m: acts on good to firm and good to soft going, seemingly not on softer: has looked hard ride. *K. Bishop*   h90

GUMPTION   6 b.g. Muhtarram (USA) – Dancing Spirit (IRE) (Ahonoora) [2003/4 h112: 24sᵖᵘ 20g⁴ 20mᵖᵘ Nov 8] fairly useful but ungenuine maiden on Flat (should stay 2m) for J. Dunlop: second in 3m novice on hurdling debut: most disappointing in 2003/4, lame final outing. *K. C. Bailey*   h85

GUNNA BE KING   10 b.g. Rakaposhi King – Gunna Be Precious (Gunner B) [2003/4 c25dᶠ May 3] modest pointer, successful twice in 2002: fell heavily on hunter chase debut. *Mrs S. Robinson*   c–
h–

GUNNERBE POSH   10 ch.g. Rakaposhi King – Triggered (Gunner B) [2003/4 c–, h71: c23g⁴ c21g⁴ c22m Jun 21] poor novice hurdler/chaser: placed in points in 2004: stays easy 21f: raced mainly on good/good to soft going: usually amateur ridden/races freely. *B. G. Powell*   c66
h–

GUNNER DREAM   8 b.g. Gunner B – Star Route (Owen Dudley) [2003/4 c–: c25dᵖᵘ c25d c25g³ c24sᵖᵘ Feb 11] sturdy, workmanlike gelding: no form in steeplechases. *C. Grant*   c–

GUNNER ROYAL   6 b.g. Gunner B – Loadplan Lass (Nicholas Bill) [2003/4 17d⁵ 24d 20sᵖᵘ Mar 13] good-topped gelding: eighth foal: half-brother to fair 2m hurdler Hill Farm Blues (by Mon Tresor): dam, maiden, half-sister to useful hurdler/winning chaser Strathline: signs of ability in novice hurdles only on debut. *J. Wade*   h–

GUNNER WELBURN   12 ch.g. Gunner B – Vedra (IRE) (Carlingford Castle) [2003/4 c136: c20gᵖᵘ c25d* c29gᵖᵘ c24d* c36dᵖᵘ Apr 3] strong, lengthy gelding: useful chaser: won Rowland Meyrick Handicap at Wetherby (by 4 lengths from Skippers Cleuch) in December and Royal Artillery Gold Cup at Sandown (by 7 lengths from Mercato) in February: pulled up all other starts in 2003/4, didn't go with customary zest in Grand National at Aintree (previously had good record over the fences): best form up to 3¼m: acts on heavy going (below form only outing on good to firm): usually sound jumper. *A. M. Balding*   c142

skybet.com Rowland Meyrick Handicap Chase, Wetherby—
Gunner Welburn (noseband) gets the better of a gruelling duel with Skippers Cleuch

GUN'N ROSES II (FR)   10 gr.g. Royal Charter (FR) – Offenbach II (FR) (Ermitage (FR)) [2003/4 c136x, h–: c22s* c21g³ Apr 1] rangy gelding: useful handicap chaser, trained in 2002/3 by T. Easterby: off over 11 months, won hunter at Haydock in February by 13 lengths from Torduff Express: joint favourite, several mistakes when 15 lengths third of 25 to Forest Gunner in Fox Hunters' at Aintree: stays 3m: raced mainly on good going or softer (acts on heavy): blinkered last 3 starts: front runner: often let down by jumping. *D. P. Keane*   c115 h–

GUNSON HIGHT   7 b.g. Be My Chief (USA) – Glas Y Dorlan (Sexton Blake) [2003/4 h–, F–: 16g* 19g 20s Feb 14] form only when 50/1-winner of 5-runner novice hurdle at Hexham in November: tongue tied then and next start. *M. Todhunter*   h78 ?

GUNTHER MCBRIDE (IRE)   9 b.g. Glacial Storm (USA) – What Side (General Ironside) [2003/4 c140, h119+: c25f² c26g^pu c26g⁴ c24m² c25g⁵ Apr 2] good-topped gelding: fairly useful hurdler: useful handicap chaser: creditable efforts in frame 3 of 5 starts in 2003/4 (badly hampered first on second outing), placed in race for third time when 4 lengths second to Marlborough in Racing Post Chase at Kempton: far from fluent when fifth to Lord of The River at Aintree: stays 33f: acts on any going: races prominently: game and consistent. *P. J. Hobbs*   c132 h–

GURU   6 b.g. Slip Anchor – Ower (IRE) (Lomond (USA)) [2003/4 h101: 16g⁵ Nov 30] leggy gelding: fair handicap hurdler: ran well only outing in 2003/4: probably best around 2m: acts on soft and good to firm going. *G. L. Moore*   h110

GUS BERRY (IRE)   11 ch.g. Montelimar (USA) – Eurolink Sea Baby (Deep Run) [2003/4 c81, h–: c27d⁴ Mar 16] smallish, angular gelding: poor chaser: stays 27f: raced on good going or softer (acts on heavy): often blinkered prior to 2002/3: has had tongue tied. *Mrs Alison Christmas*   c73 h–

GUS DES BOIS (FR)   10 ch.g. Lampon (FR) – Fiacina (FR) (Fiasco) [2003/4 c108, h–: c19d^ur c19d c20s³ c17s⁵ c18s² c19s³ c19g³ c24g⁴ c24m⁶ Apr 13] strong gelding: once-raced hurdler: modest handicap chaser: stays 3m, effective at much shorter: acts on heavy going: visored/blinkered: usually front runner: ungenuine. *R. H. Alner*   c99 § h–

GUTHRIE (IRE)   6 ch.g. Mister Lord (USA) – Nephin Far (IRE) (Phardante (FR)) [2003/4 F16g F17g³ Apr 10] IR £36,000 3-y-o: leggy, unfurnished gelding: first foal: dam, winning pointer, half-sister to fairly useful hurdler/chaser at 2½m+ Badger's Wood and fairly useful 2m hurdler Khan Kicker: better effort in bumpers when 16½ lengths third to Honan in maiden at Newton Abbot: will stay at least 2½m. *A. King*   F87

G V A IRELAND (IRE)   6 b.g. Beneficial – Dippers Daughter (Strong Gale) [2003/4 h102, F102: 20s 20d² 20d⁵ 24s* 24d³ 20s* 24s² 25g² 20d⁵ Apr 11] quite good-topped gelding: fairly useful hurdler: won handicaps at Navan and Punchestown in December and novice at Punchestown in early-May: very good efforts in handicaps when beaten head by Royal All Star at Leopardstown and ½ length by Creon in 24-runner Pertemps Final at Cheltenham seventh and eighth outings: needs good test at 2½m and stays 25f: acts on heavy going. *F. Flood, Ireland*   h127

GWEN   5 ch.m. Beveled (USA) – Taffidale (Welsh Pageant) [2003/4 F–: F16d Mar 14] tailed off in bumpers. *B. L. Lay*   F–

GWENS GIRL   4 b.f. Wizard King – Russian Project (IRE) (Project Manager) [2003/4 F14g F13v F16s Jan 6] lengthy filly: first foal: dam 1¼m winner: no form in 3 bumpers. *M. Wellings*   F–

GWYLAN   9 b.g. Crested Lark – Flopsy Mopsy (Full of Hope) [2003/4 16v^F 21d^pu 18v c20g^F 19g^pu Apr 16] no sign of ability. *J. S. King*   c– h–

H

HAAFEL (USA)   7 ch.g. Diesis – Dish Dash (Bustino) [2003/4 h100: c20m³ c18f² Aug 25] angular gelding: fair on Flat (stays 2m): fair hurdler: similar form in 2 novice chases in small fields: stays 21f: acts on firm and good to soft going, possibly unsuited by softer: tried blinkered. *G. L. Moore*   c97 h–

HACKBALLS CROSS (IRE)   5 b.m. Ashkalani (IRE) – Masalika (IRE) (Kahyasi) [2003/4 F17d F17m⁶ F16m F17m Sep 27] first foal: dam, French 9f winner, half-sister to one-time useful hurdler up to 21f Masalarian: modest form at best in bumpers. *O. Brennan*   F76

HADATH (IRE)   7 br.g. Mujtahid (USA) – Al Sylah (Nureyev (USA)) [2003/4 16m⁵   h–
Nov 9] fair on Flat (stays 1m), left R. Osborne in August: well held over hurdles: tried
blinkered. *B. G. Powell*

HADAWAY LAD   12 ch.g. Meadowbrook – Little Swinburn (Apollo Eight) [2003/4   c–
c–, h–: c25dᶠ c20g⁵ May 24] winning pointer, little form otherwise: tried blinkered.   h–
K. Waters

HADEQA   8 ch.g. Hadeer – Heavenly Queen (Scottish Reel) [2003/4 c20gᵘʳ May 15]   c– x
compact gelding: winning hurdler: little form since 1999, including in points: has had   h–
tongue tied. *M. J. Brown*

HADES DE SIENNE (FR)   9 b.g. Concorde Jr (USA) – Aube de Sienne (FR) (Cupids   c98
Dew) [2003/4 c101, h–: c22m c24gᵖᵘ c28g² c30dᵘʳ c25s³ c20s c28d³ c32d³ Mar 18] work-   h–
manlike gelding: modest handicap chaser: stays 4m: acts on heavy going:
tried visored/in cheekpieces: sold 5,000 gns Doncaster May Sales. *A. Parker*

HADITOVSKI   8 b.g. Hatim (USA) – Grand Occasion (Great Nephew) [2003/4 h122:   c110
c16s⁶ c17g* c16mᵖᵘ c16g* c16dᶠ c20d⁴ Mar 27] compact gelding: fairly useful handicap   h–
hurdler: fair form over fences: won novices in small fields at Market Rasen in December
and Huntingdon in March, extremely fortunate when left clear by falls of 2 other rivals 2
out at latter: stays 2½m: goes well on ground softer than good: visored: usually ridden up
with pace. *J. Mackie*

HA HA HA   6 b.g. Sure Blade (USA) – Crownego (Abednego) [2003/4 F17m⁵ 20d⁵   h–
17g 24mᵖᵘ Oct 26] third foal: dam poor maiden pointer: fifth of 10 in maiden bumper   F–
on debut: no form in 3 novice hurdles, left J. Jenkins before final start: tried visored/in
cheekpieces. *K. F. Clutterbuck*

HAIKAL   7 b.g. Owington – Magic Milly (Simply Great (FR)) [2003/4 h–: 17m 19g²   h81
22f² 24m⁴ 22f 19f⁴ 22g² 16v² 17d³ 24s³ 21g Apr 12] strong, workmanlike gelding: poor
hurdler: effective at testing 2m to 3m: acts on any going: tried blinkered. *R. H. Buckler*

HAILE SELASSIE   4 b.g. Awesome – Lady of The Realm (Prince Daniel (USA))   h90
[2003/4 16s 17d⁶ 17d⁴ Mar 22] close-coupled gelding: fair up to 1½m on Flat (has hinted
at temperament), sold out of B. Hills's stable 15,000 gns Newmarket Autumn Sales: best
effort in juvenile hurdles (modest form) when fourth to Sharp Rigging at Hereford: likely
to prove best at 2m. *W. Jenks*

HAIL STONE (IRE)   9 b.g. Glacial Storm (USA) – Rockmount (IRE) (Cidrax (FR))   c–
[2003/4 c24mᶠ Apr 13] ex-Irish gelding: winning pointer, little form othrewise: tried   h–
blinkered. *Miss K. A. Williams*

HAILSTORM (IRE)   11 ch.g. Glacial Storm (USA) – Sindys Gale (Strong Gale)   c65 x
[2003/4 c83x, h–: c25g c25g² c25g³ c23mᵘʳ c25mᵖᵘ Aug 3] smallish, angular gelding: poor   h–
handicap chaser: stays 25f: acts on soft and good to firm going: usually makes mistakes.
Miss Lucinda V. Russell

HAIL THE KING (USA)   4 gr.g. Allied Forces (USA) – Hail Kris (USA) (Kris S   h90
(USA)) [2003/4 16f⁴ 16g 16gᵖᵘ 16g 16g³ Apr 12] leggy gelding: poor maiden on Flat:
modest juvenile hurdler: sold out of R. Beckett's stable 4,000 gns Doncaster November
Sales after debut: will prove best at 2m: takes good hold. *R. M. Carson*

HAKAM (USA)   5 ch.g. Woodman (USA) – Haniya (IRE) (Caerleon (USA)) [2003/4   h–
16m Jun 18] maiden on Flat (stays 1¾m), modest in 2003: well held in novice claimer on
hurdling debut. *John Berry*

HAKIM (NZ)   10 ch.g. Half Iced (USA) – Topitup (NZ) (Little Brown Jug (NZ))   c100
[2003/4 h84: c20m³ c17d* Aug 11] sturdy gelding: poor maiden hurdler: second start   h–
over fences, jumped well when making all in novice handicap at Southwell: barely stays
2½m: acts on soft and good to firm going: tends to race freely. *J. L. Spearing*

HALE BOPP (GER)   7 b.h. Monsun (GER) – Heatherland (FR) (Be My Guest (USA))   h?
[2003/4 h111: 20s³ 16g Nov 30] sturdy horse: useful at best on Flat (stays 1½m) in Germany: fair hurdler: third in minor event at Munich in November: well held in handicap at
Newbury next time: stays 2½m: acts on heavy ground. *Frau E. Mader, Germany*

HALEXY (FR)   9 b.g. Iron Duke (FR) – Tartifume II (FR) (Mistigri) [2003/4 c126, h–:   c119
c20m⁵ Nov 1] tall, good sort: fairly useful chaser in 2002/3 for Miss V. Williams: weaken-   h–
ed markedly last when last of 5 finishers in handicap at Wetherby, only outing in 2003/4:
has won at 3m, best form over shorter: raced mainly on good going or softer: bold jumper
who races with plenty of zest. *Jonjo O'Neill*

HALF AN HOUR   7 b.g. Alflora (IRE) – Country Mistress (Town And Country)   c–
[2003/4 h100: c20sᵖᵘ c22d c23g Jan 13] well-made gelding: fair hurdler: well held on   h–

completed start over fences: stays 2¾m: acts on firm and good to soft going (won bumper on soft). *A. King*

HALF BARRELL (IRE) 12 br.g. Lord Americo – Araybeam VII (Damsire Unregistered) [2003/4 c114, h–: c20v⁵ c17d* c22d c19sᵖᵘ 24m 22m⁵ c28gᵖᵘ Nov 9] winning hurdler: fairly useful handicap chaser: easily best effort in 2003/4 when winning at Galway (fourth course success) in August: effective around 2m and stays 3m well: acts on heavy going: inconsistent. *V. T. O'Brien, Ireland* **c117 h–**

HALLAND 6 ch.g. Halling (USA) – Northshiel (Northfields (USA)) [2003/4 17g² Apr 1] useful winner up to 1¼m on Flat at 3 yrs, very lightly raced since: encouraging start over hurdles when second to Belcaro in maiden at Taunton, travelling easily under restraint long way. *N. P. Littmoden* **h93 p**

HALLEM HALL 7 ch.g. Little Wolf – Oneninefive (Sayyaf) [2003/4 F16s Dec 27] third foal: dam won 21f selling hurdle: tailed off in Grade 2 bumper at Chepstow on debut. *Mrs E. B. Scott* **F–**

HALLRULE (IRE) 10 ch.g. Be My Native (USA) – Phantom Thistle (Deep Run) [2003/4 c16gᵖᵘ c25gᵖᵘ c24mᵖᵘ c25s* c26d* Apr 18] sturdy gelding: poor chaser: off 3 years before reappearance, left Mrs J. Oliver after third outing: did very well after, winning 2 of 3 starts in points and handicaps (visored) at Hexham (amateur seller) and Carlisle in April: stays 3¼m: acts on soft going. *Miss P. Robson* **c74 h–**

HALL'S MILL (IRE) 15 ch.g. Buckskin (FR) – Grainne Geal (General Ironside) [2003/4 c95+: c21d* Apr 30] workmanlike gelding: fairly useful hunter chaser: as good as ever in 2003, winning 15-runner event at Cheltenham, despite being hampered last: stays 3m: acts on good to firm and good to soft going: sometimes let down by jumping: genuine. *Miss S. Waugh* **c103**

HALLYARDS GAEL (IRE) 10 br.g. Strong Gale – Secret Ocean (Most Secret) [2003/4 c124, h–: c25gᵘʳ c24g* 24g² 22g* c20g³ Nov 15] strong, lengthy gelding: fairly useful handicap chaser/fair handicap hurdler: won over fences at Perth (beat Burwood Breeze ½ length, pair distance clear) in May and over hurdles at Kelso in November: would probably also have won but for being let down by jumping first and third starts: stays 3m: acts on good to soft going: has worn cheekpieces, including last 4 starts: has reportedly had breathing problems. *L. Lungo* **c129 h112**

HAMADEENAH 6 ch.m. Alhijaz – Mahbob Dancer (FR) (Groom Dancer (USA)) [2003/4 h91: 16g⁴ 17m² 17d⁴ 18f⁴ Aug 22] leggy mare: modest hurdler: best around 2m: acts on soft and good to firm going. *D. McCain* **h87**

HAMBLETON JO 4 ch.g. Bijou d'Inde – Elegant Rose (Noalto) [2003/4 16g⁶ 16g 20dᵖᵘ 17d 17g Apr 12] half-brother to winning hurdlers around 2m Ben Bowden (by Sharrood) and Dancing Pearl (by Dancing Spree): poor maiden at 2 yrs for J. Weymes: no show over hurdles. *F. P. Murtagh* **h–**

HAMISH G 7 ch.g. Sure Blade (USA) – Horton Line (High Line) [2003/4 16g 17g⁶ May 13] closely related to fair hurdler up to 2½m Linea-G (by Keen) and half-brother to winning hurdler Sarsta Grai (by Blakeney), stayed 3m: modest form on Flat, lightly raced: better effort over hurdles when sixth of 13 in novice at Hereford. *John Berry* **h72**

HAMMOCK (IRE) 6 b. or br.g. Hamas (IRE) – Sure Victory (IRE) (Stalker) [2003/4 h–: 19fᵖᵘ Oct 16] sturdy gelding: temperamental maiden on Flat: no form over hurdles: tried in cheekpieces. *M. J. Gingell* **h–**

HAM STONE 6 b.g. Picea – Blushing Belle (Local Suitor (USA)) [2003/4 19g 19s Dec 29] good-bodied gelding: well beaten in bumper and novice hurdles. *B. J. M. Ryall* **h–**

HANBRIN ROSE 7 gr.m. Lancastrian – Rymolbreese (Rymer) [2003/4 h72, F–: 22d 20m³ 17g 19g 16d c16g⁶ c20m⁵ c20dᵖᵘ c24g⁵ Apr 16] leggy mare: poor maiden hurdler/chaser: probably stays 3m: acts on good to firm and good to soft going. *R. Dickin* **c71 h65**

HANDA ISLAND (USA) 5 b.g. Pleasant Colony (USA) – Remote (USA) (Seattle Slew (USA)) [2003/4 19d⁵ Dec 12] useful on Flat (stays 2m) at 3 yrs, sold out of H. Cecil's stable 13,000 gns Newmarket Autumn (2002) Sales: off 13 months, fifth to Samby in novice at Doncaster on hurdling debut, disputing or leading for much of way. *C. J. Mann* **h84**

HAND INN HAND 8 b.g. Alflora (IRE) – Deep Line (Deep Run) [2003/4 c141p, h–: 20d³ c20sᵇᵈ c20g² c21dᶠ c19s* c20g⁴ c25g² Apr 1] **c162 h134 +**

Ginger McCain was in typically feisty mood after winning his latest Grand National with Amberleigh House. The Irish and the French felt the rough edge of his tongue as he held forth, as did women trainers, the 'unposed people' who attend Royal Ascot and the 'country types in tweeds' who go to Cheltenham. Most of the flak seemed to be delivered with tongue at least partly in cheek, yet McCain was deadly serious when he argued that any trainer who needs to call on a third party to teach a horse to jump should hand in his licence. Any man who has trained four National winners is plainly entitled to a hearing on the subject of jumping capability. However, times change. Specialist coaches are called on to help refine the techniques of athletes in almost every professional sport nowadays and, when the most gifted pupil in a class of fifty begins to lose his way due to a single recurring flaw, it would be a poor teacher who dismissed the idea of outside assistance. Henry Daly took advantage of it in January by instructing Hand Inn Hand's box driver to make a slight detour on his way to Ascot races. It involved a visit to the Oxfordshire base of the renowned equestrian coach Yogi Breisner for a twenty-minute session jumping a range of around twenty varied obstacles in the indoor school. Last minute cramming is nearly always of limited use when working towards a major test. Not so in this case, however, as Hand Inn Hand went into the 'exam room' a few hours later and emerged with honours, landing the Servo Computer Services' Ascot Chase.

By Grade 1 standards, the Ascot Chase has had a chequered recent history, with wins for proven top-class chasers such as One Man, Martha's Son and Teeton Mill countered by success for relatively lesser lights like Rockforce and Tresor de Mai. The latest renewal, though lacking an outstanding candidate, had some depth thanks to the presence of Tiutchev, Le Roi Miguel and Fondmort. King George runner-up Tiutchev was bidding to add to his 2001 and 2003 Ascot Chase wins, Fondmort lined up after following his Paddy Power Gold Cup win with fourth in the King George, while Le Roi Miguel was stepping back to what was expected to be a more suitable distance after falling when tired in the King George. Impek, See You Sometime and recent French import Royal Atalza made up a seven-runner field for a prize worth almost £60,000 to the winner. Hand Inn Hand attracted plenty of support and was sent off at 15/2 after being available at 11/1 in the morning. For once, those who backed him never had much cause for alarm. The early gallop was no more than fair and he was clearly going best when he quickened into the lead three out. On this occasion, it was the jumping of others which suffered under pressure. Tiutchev, in trouble well before the home turn, seemed booked for fourth when he fell two out, while Fondmort was held in third when coming down at the last. Impek posed the only threat to Hand Inn Hand who stayed on strongly until idling on the run-in to win by four lengths. See You Sometime and Le Roi Miguel were a distance and the same back in third and fourth, with the remounted Fondmort the only other finisher.

Granted a little luck and more fluent jumping, Hand Inn Hand might have won at least two, possibly all three, of his runs over fences prior to Ascot. He made several minor errors before being brought down at the tenth, still travelling strongly, in the Tripleprint Gold Cup at Cheltenham in December, when, in retro-

Servo Computer Services' Ascot Chase—
Hand Inn Hand is in command two out from Impek and Fondmort (right)

spect, handicapped to go very close off a BHB mark of 145. For a long way in a handicap at Kempton over Christmas, Hand Inn Hand looked set to win without breaking sweat—and would almost certainly have won decisively had his regular rider Mark Bradburne sent him on further from home—but he went down by a short head to Scots Grey after losing momentum with clumsy jumps at the final three fences. Then he hit the deck four out in the Ladbroke Trophy at Cheltenham when still travelling well within himself. Two outings in the spring went a long way to confirming that Hand Inn Hand's Ascot performance didn't flatter him. However, they also revived concerns about his ability to jump consistently well over demanding fences. Mistakes at the first and again five out off a BHB mark of 159 in the Vodafone Gold Cup at Newbury in March contributed to a slightly below-par effort, though, in plugging on for fourth behind Isio, Hand Inn Hand fared best of those held up in one of the most competitive handicaps of the season. Stepping up in distance for the Martell Cognac Cup at Aintree in April, Hand Inn Hand finished an excellent third behind the revitalised Tiutchev and First Gold; there were no excuses, save perhaps that Hand Inn Hand would have been a shade closer but for a mistake at the last and one or two lesser errors earlier on.

With Best Mate seemingly headed elsewhere, the Peterborough Chase at Huntingdon could prove a suitable early target for Hand Inn Hand in the next season when the King George could also figure on his agenda. With several potential rivals getting on in years, he could yet develop into an interesting dark horse for that race. Meanwhile, it would be folly to discount the possibility of Hand Inn Hand's winning another valuable prize over hurdles. The form of his close third behind Mughas and Crystal d'Ainay in a handicap hurdle at Aintree on his reappearance in November worked out extremely well and, given that the Coral Cup was mooted as a Cheltenham option, connections seem well aware that his mark over hurdles is upwards of 20 lb lower than his end-of-season BHB chase mark.

		Niniski	Nijinsky
	Alflora (IRE)	(b 1976)	Virginia Hills
	(b 1989)	Adrana	Bold Lad
Hand Inn Hand		(ch 1980)	Le Melody
(b.g. 1996)		Deep Run	Pampered King
	Deep Line	(ch 1966)	Trial By Fire
	(b 1985)	High Board	High Line
		(b 1977)	Matchboard

A close-coupled, workmanlike gelding, Hand Inn Hand takes his name from the Hand Inn, a North Wales hotel and shooting lodge run by his owner-breeder Patrick Burling. His pedigree was outlined in the last *Chasers & Hurdlers* and there is little to add other than that his sister Hand Inn Glove has yet to see a racecourse at the age of seven. Hand Inn Hand has yet to race on firm ground but acts on any other and, although he can take a good hold, he showed at Aintree that he is just as effective at around three miles as he is over two and a half. His prospects of winning more good races look bright. They will be brighter still if his unusually low jumping style can be refined into one which allows a little more margin for error. *H. D. Daly*

HANDSHAKE 4 ch.g. Most Welcome – Lady Day (FR) (Lightning (FR)) [2003/4 16d 16d^{pu} Nov 29] half-brother to winning 2m hurdler Ticker (by Timeless Times): poor maiden on Flat (should stay 1¼m): no show in 2 juvenile hurdles. *W. McKeown* — **h–**

HANDY BOY 9 b.g. Arzanni – Handymouse (Nearly A Hand) [2003/4 c24s^F Feb 12] won point in 2002: fell eighth in hunter chase on return. *M. J. Jackson* — **c–**

HANDYMAN (IRE) 10 b.g. Hollow Hand – Shady Ahan (Mon Capitaine) [2003/4 c126, h–: c23g² c22g³ c25g Dec 18] leggy gelding: fairly useful handicap chaser: stays 3¼m: acts on heavy and good to firm going: reliable. *P. J. Hobbs* — **c123 h–**

HANDY MONEY 7 b.g. Imperial Frontier (USA) – Cryptic Gold (Glint of Gold) [2003/4 h107, F80: 19g* 16m Nov 1] workmanlike gelding: fairly useful hurdler: won handicap at Market Rasen in May: travelled comfortably up with pace long way in similar event at Ascot 5 months later: stays 19f: acts on heavy going. *M. J. Ryan* — **h115**

HANK DANDY 7 ch.m. Bandmaster (USA) – Junior Lancaster (Dubassoff (USA)) [2003/4 F16m⁵ 21s^{pu} Nov 18] third foal: dam lightly raced and no sign of ability: showed nothing in bumper or novice hurdle. *Mrs G. Harvey* — **h– F–**

HANLEY (IRE) 8 b.g. Lashkari – Midnight Gale (IRE) (Tumble Wind (USA)) [2003/4 **h–** F16v 22mᵖᵘ 20mᵖᵘ Aug 25] ex-Irish gelding: second foal: dam maiden: placed once in **F—** bumpers, left D. Hughes after reappearance: maiden hurdler, showed little in 2003/4: blinkered/tongue tied final start. *B. N. Pollock*

HANORLA (IRE) 5 ch.g. Danehill Dancer (IRE) – Aubretia (USA) (Hatchet Man **h113** (USA)) [2003/4 16d² 16d³ 20g² 20v* 16g² Sep 16] half-brother to fair hurdler up to 21f Welsh Lad (by Welsh Term) and winning hurdler/chaser who stays 25f See More Perks (by Executive Perk): fairly useful on Flat (stays 2m): fair hurdler: won minor event at Tipperary in July: stays 2½m: acts on heavy going: consistent. *Joseph Crowley, Ireland*

HANOVER SQUARE 8 b.g. Le Moss – Hilly-Down Lass (Deep Run) [2003/4 c98, **c84** h–: c24mᵘʳ c25g⁵ c28dᵖᵘ c25dᵖᵘ 24s³ 24s³ 24s³ 26s* 24s 26d² Mar 28] workmanlike geld- **h93** ing: maiden chaser: modest handicap hurdler: won at Huntingdon in February: thorough stayer: raced mainly on going softer than good (acts on soft): not a fluent jumper of fences. *N. A. Twiston-Davies*

HAPPICAT (IRE) 9 gr.g. Cataldi – Gladonia (Godswalk (USA)) [2003/4 c–, h109: **c—** 19gᵖᵘ 16gᵖᵘ Jun 27] good-topped gelding: one-time fair hurdler: no show either outing **h—** after 11-month absence: well held all 3 starts over fences: best around 2m: acts on firm going, probably unsuited by soft. *P. R. Webber*

HAPPY CHANGE (GER) 10 ch.g. Surumu (GER) – Happy Gini (USA) (Ginistrelli **c88 x** (USA)) [2003/4 c80, h–: c19g² c21g⁶ c21dᵖᵘ c22g Jul 6] good-topped gelding: winning **h—** hurdler: modest maiden chaser: stays 19f (beaten long way out over further last 3 starts): acts on good to soft going: not a fluent jumper: races freely. *Ian Williams*

HAPPY DAYS 9 b.g. Primitive Rising (USA) – Miami Dolphin (Derrylin) [2003/4 **h78** h78: 20d² 22g⁴ 22g Aug 23] leggy gelding: poor maiden hurdler: lame final outing: stays 2¾m: acts on heavy going: below form both starts in visor. *James Moffatt*

HAPPY HUSSAR (IRE) 11 b.g. Balinger – Merry Mirth (Menelek) [2003/4 c73x, **c— x** h89: 27g⁶ 27g⁶ 16m⁵ 26m² 26mᵖᵘ 19f* 24g 24d 25d 22g³ 19d³ 20g 25d Apr 11] work- **h89** manlike gelding: has stringhalt: winning chaser: modest handicap hurdler: won 4-runner event at Exeter in October: stays 3¼m: acts on any going: has broken blood vessels: sketchy jumper of fences. *Dr P. Pritchard*

HARAPOUR (FR) 6 b.g. Valanour (IRE) – Haratiyna (Top Ville) [2003/4 17s 22v² **h118** 19v* 20v 20d² Mar 24] useful-looking gelding: fairly useful hurdler, off nearly 2 years before reappearance: easily landed odds in novice at Exeter in February: much better form when 3 lengths second to Legal Lunch in handicap at Chepstow final start: stays 2¾m: raced on going softer than good (acts on heavy): has looked temperamental. *P. F. Nicholls*

HARBEN (FR) 5 ch.g. Luchiroverte (IRE) – Dixia (FR) (Altayan) [2003/4 F16g F17m **F—** Oct 10] rather leggy gelding: first foal: dam, twice-raced over hurdles, half-sister to 2 winners, including hurdler/chaser up to 2½m Anita, also successful at 9.5f: signs of only a little ability in 2 bumpers. *M. Todhunter*

HARBOUR PILOT (IRE) 9 b.g. Be My Native (USA) – Las-Cancellas (Monks- **c168** field) [2003/4 c164, h–: 24d c24dᵘʳ c26g³ Mar 18] **h—**

    For those who habitually see their glass half empty, Harbour Pilot has been frustrating over the last two years. Conversely, for those who prefer to see their glass half full, he has been a force in the best company without receiving the rewards his efforts have merited. The 'half empty' brigade can point to a sequence of ten consecutive defeats since Harbour Pilot recorded an emphatic victory over Truckers Tavern and Youlneverwalkalone in the Dr P. J. Moriarty Novices' Chase at Leopardstown in February 2002. To advance the case, it could be added that he has thrown away at least two major prizes because of clumsy jumping. The case for the defence of Harbour Pilot, however, is not difficult to argue. Reaching a place in the Cheltenham Gold Cup (twice), an Ericsson Chase and versions of the Hennessy Gold Cup at both Newbury and Leopardstown is hardly the record of an under-achiever. The glass is far from being half empty for connections either: they have pocketed well over £100,000 in place money since Harbour Pilot's last win. At the age of nine, Harbour Pilot should maintain his form for at least another season or two.

    His trainer is adamant that Harbour Pilot goes particularly well fresh, but the fact that he lined up for the Hennessy Cognac Gold Cup at Leopardstown in February with only one run in eleven months was not intentional. A spell of school-

Kays Syndicate's "Harbour Pilot"

ing over poles with former international show jumper Con Power and a run in a
handicap hurdle at Navan in November had been meant to lay the foundations for a
tilt at Best Mate and Beef Or Salmon in the Ericsson Chase at Leopardstown over
Christmas until the stable shut up shop briefly because of sickness in the yard. More
place money was probably the best Harbour Pilot could have hoped for behind
Best Mate in the Ericsson, and by the time he lined up for a second attempt at the
Hennessy it had been two years since his win in the Moriarty. Harbour Pilot had
finished third behind Beef Or Salmon in the previous year's Hennessy, with no
excuses save that he might have shaded Colonel Braxton for second but for minor
mistakes at two of the last three fences. In the latest Hennessy, looking in tremendous shape after an eleven-week break and sent off the 7/2 second favourite, Harbour
Pilot was upsides Florida Pearl, going every bit as well, on the run to the second
last. There, he produced what one writer described as 'Harbour Pilot's party piece'.
His rider Paul Carberry's description was that 'he just put down on me and there
was no way back.' Either way, Harbour Pilot's exit left Florida Pearl to keep on too
well for the 15/8 favourite Le Coudray.

Carberry's analysis of the performance included the view that 'Harbour
Pilot had never jumped as well . . . I hadn't gone for him and we know he stays well,
so I definitely think we would have won.' Definitely was overstating the case, but
Harbour Pilot had confirmed himself a top-class chaser and odds of 40/1 for the
Gold Cup offered immediately after the Hennessy underestimated his chance by a
fair margin. Come the day he was down to 20/1 and gave his followers a thrilling
run for their money. What's more, he did so with a performance in stark contrast to
his Gold Cup effort of twelve months earlier when he had been run off his feet

before staying on strongly to pass tiring rivals for third. Twelve months on, he looked a much more polished performer. As usual, there was a significant error to report, but, after surviving a blunder at the second, he jumped fluently in second behind First Gold before challenging for the lead three out, his jockey Carberry hemming Best Mate against the inside rail. Two out Harbour Pilot was upsides Best Mate and even at the last was still pressing hard. Harbour Pilot kept on to record the best performance of his career with a close third to Best Mate and Sir Rembrandt.

Harbour Pilot (IRE) (b.g. 1995)	Be My Native (USA) (br 1979)	Our Native (b or br 1970)	Exclusive Native Our Jackie
		Witchy Woman (ch 1972)	Strate Stuff Witchy Norma
	Las-Cancellas (b 1984)	Monksfield (b 1972)	Gala Performance Regina
		Synarria (br 1977)	Guillaume Tell Spinning Jenny

Full details of the rangy Harbour Pilot's pedigree were outlined in previous editions of *Chasers & Hurdlers*. Suffice to say that his year-older half-brother Manolito (by Mandalus) won a poor handicap chase in the latest season, while his seven-year-old half-brother Metal Detector (by Treasure Hunter) graduated to fences and won a couple of uncompetitive events in novice company at around three miles. Meanwhile, a four-year-old half-sister to Harbour Pilot by Houmayoun made €40,000 at the Derby Sales in June. As for Harbour Pilot, it seems clear that a combination of blinkers, a test of stamina and good going or softer show him to best advantage. His programme for the next season is unlikely to differ much from the last two and, provided his jumping does not let him down, he will continue knocking at the door in good races. Interestingly, Carberry, who has excelled more than once at Aintree, has suggested that Harbour Pilot could be the ideal type for the Grand National. Hills made him 10/1 favourite for Aintree in the immediate aftermath of his Gold Cup run. Connections, however, soon came down in favour of Punchestown in late-April, where, after drifting in the market for the Heineken Gold Cup, Harbour Pilot tended to jump left and finished a creditable second to Beef Or Salmon. 'Now his jumping has come together it might be wrong to risk frightening him,' was his trainer's justification for the decision to bypass Aintree. Some would see that as a 'glass half empty' approach. Others, with good reason, would view it as a sensible one. Harbour Pilot needs to eliminate his tendency to take the odd fence by the roots before he can be considered ideal National material. Even the 'half full' brigade might take a little convincing that he can do that. *N. Meade, Ireland*

HARBOUR POINT (IRE) 8 b.g. Glacial Storm (USA) – Forest Jem (Croghan Hill) **h86**
[2003/4 h74, F94: 21m 20g² 20d² Nov 15] lengthy gelding: bumper winner: modest maiden hurdler: should be suited by further than 2½m. *D. J. Caro*

HARBOUR ROCK (IRE) 5 b.g. Midhish – Annie's Glen (IRE) (Glenstal (USA)) **F73**
[2003/4 F16s F16d Jan 22] compact gelding: fourth foal: dam unraced: signs of ability on first of 2 outings in bumpers. *T. J. Wintle*

HARCHIBALD (FR) 5 b.g. Perugino (USA) – Dame d'Harvard (USA) (Quest For **h144** Fame) [2003/4 h124: 16g⁴ 16m⁴ 16g⁸ 17d⁵ Mar 18] rather leggy, useful-looking gelding: has reportedly had wind operation: useful hurdler: won 4-y-o event at Punchestown very early in season and handicap at Leopardstown (beat King Carew by 5 lengths in good style) in February: excelled himself when fourth to Hardy Eustace in Grade 1 at Punchestown in late-April: raced around 2m: acts on heavy and good to firm ground: has had tongue tied: carries head high, and has failed to go through with effort more than once (including when fifth in County Hurdle at Cheltenham). *N. Meade, Ireland*

HARDI DE CHALAMONT (FR) 9 gr.g. Royal Charter (FR) – Naita II (FR) (Dom **c72 x** Luc (FR)) [2003/4 c–, h83: 16g³ 24g⁵ c24d⁴ c22gᶠ 24s Dec 26] leggy gelding: poor **h76** hurdler/chaser: sold out of A. Parker's stable 3,000 gns Doncaster May Sales after reappearance: effective at 2m to 3m: acts on soft and good to firm going: visored most starts in 2002/3, wore cheekpieces on reappearance: often let down by jumping over fences. *Mrs J. Candlish*

HARDIMAN (IRE) 11 ch.g. Phardante (FR) – Mention of Money (Le Bavard (FR)) **c100 §** [2003/4 c24g⁴ c26g³ c29vᵖᵘ c32g⁵ c24dᵖᵘ c29dᵖᵘ Mar 14] workmanlike gelding: fair **h–**

handicap chaser: left C. Roche and off over 14 months before reappearance: probably stays 4m: acts on firm and soft going: has gone in snatches: unreliable. *Jonjo O'Neill*

HARDING 13 b.g. Dowsing (USA) – Orange Hill (High Top) [2003/4 c25d^F Feb 17] well-made gelding: one-time fair hurdler/chaser: winning pointer, well-held second twice in March: stays 3m: acts on heavy going. *Mrs Jenny Gordon*　c–　h–

HARD WINTER (IRE) 7 b.g. Arctic Lord – Lucycello (Monksfield) [2003/4 F16d F18m F16d F20s³ F18d 20d² 22s² 24v* 24v⁵ 22s* 20d Apr 11] sixth foal: half-brother to fairly useful chaser Phar From A Fiddle (by Phardante), stays 25f, and winning 2¾m hurdler Kaiser Sosa (by Welsh Term): dam, placed twice in points, half-sister to high-class 2m chaser Wolf of Badenoch: fair form in bumpers: progressed into fairly useful hurdler, winning maiden at Punchestown in January and novice at Navan in March: tended to jump left when running poorly final start: stays 3m: acts on heavy going. *D. T. Hughes, Ireland*　h116　F89

HARDY BREEZE (IRE) 13 b.g. Henbit (USA) – Chake-Chake (Goldhill) [2003/4 c72, h–: c26g^{pu} Oct 6] poor chaser/maiden hurdler: stays 3¼m: acts on heavy and good to firm going. *Miss A. M. Newton-Smith*　c–　h–

HARDY DUCKETT (IRE) 5 br.g. Key of Luck (USA) – Bramdean (Niniski (USA)) [2003/4 h110, F96: F16d⁵ F16d² 16d² 20s³ 16s* 20d⁴ 16d³ Mar 7] fairly useful in bumpers, second to Total Enjoyment at Fairyhouse in December: of similar merit over hurdles, won maiden at Naas in February by 25 lengths: good second to Arch Stanton in novice at Punchestown in late-April: stays 2½m: acts on soft going. *D. T. Hughes, Ireland*　h121　F101

HARDY EUSTACE (IRE) 7 b.g. Archway (IRE) – Sterna Star (Corvaro (USA)) [2003/4 h149: 20m² 16d 20d² 16s² 16g* Mar 16]　h167

'He's in the Stayers' which looks as if it is going to be a very hot race and it's possible he might run in the Champion Hurdle instead.' The view expressed by Hardy Eustace's trainer before the Cleeve Hurdle at Cheltenham in January was an unusual, but merited, compliment to the top staying hurdlers. The standard of Stayers' Hurdle contestants has historically been some way below that in the Champion Hurdle, but, in each of the last three seasons, the principals in the Stayers' Hurdle have ended the campaign with higher Timeform ratings than their

Smurfit Champion Hurdle Challenge Trophy, Cheltenham—
front runner Hardy Eustace stretches his field on the home turn, stalked by the grey Rooster Booster,
with Fota Island and the blinkered pair Intersky Falcon (striped sleeves) and Foreman next

. . . . . Rooster Booster heads Hardy Eustace briefly at the last but the 33/1-shot finds plenty on the run-in

counterparts in the Champion Hurdle. At the time, the choice for Hardy Eustace's connections between the two championship events at the Cheltenham Festival seemed largely academic—the Coral Cup was also considered—as the horse still had a bit to prove before he could be considered a serious candidate for either race. Quoted at 66/1 for the Champion Hurdle towards the end of January, Hardy Eustace returned to something like his best—without forcing a radical reshaping of any Festival betting—in the Cleeve Hurdle when beaten three lengths by Crystal d'Ainay (subsequently third in the Stayers').

The Cleeve Hurdle was Hardy Eustace's first visit to Cheltenham since winning the previous season's Royal & SunAlliance Novices' Hurdle. The twenty-one-furlong championship event for novices has a roll of honour that resounds with major names, including Danoli, Istabraq and French Holly to name but three of the winners in the last ten editions. The 2003 renewal won by Hardy Eustace was the most strongly contested event of its type all season, but Hardy Eustace hadn't looked like living up to the achievements of the most notable of his predecessors. He was warmed up on the Flat—winning a two-mile maiden at Navan in October—before suffering an eight-length defeat at 4/1-on in the two-and-a-half-mile Lismullen Hurdle on the same course in early-November. Niggled along some way from home, Hardy Eustace never looked like pegging back the winner Rosaker and wasn't knocked about when clearly held. Reportedly suffering from sore shins afterwards, Hardy Eustace wasn't seen again until Christmas when he reverted to two miles for the December Festival Hurdle at Leopardstown. He was off the bridle early on and never out of last place in a field of seven, giving the impression that a return to two and a half miles plus would benefit him. The view seemed to be borne out in the Cleeve Hurdle in which Hardy Eustace was always prominent and drew clear after two out with the winner. Connections gave the impression at first that they might reconsider and take on Baracouda and Iris's Gift in the Stayers' Hurdle. But Hardy Eustace ran his Festival preparatory race in a Champion Hurdle trial, the Red Mills Trial Hurdle at Gowran in mid-February, and ran well, giving weight all round, to finish a short-head second to Georges Girl, runner-up in the AIG Europe Champion Hurdle.

Although back to form, Hardy Eustace was sent off at 33/1 in the Smurfit Champion Hurdle, in which he wore blinkers for the first time, 'to help sharpen him up,' according to his trainer. There has been a shortage of really good two-mile hurdlers since Istabraq's retirement but the latest Champion Hurdle field was

Emo Oil Champion Hurdle, Punchestown—Hardy Eustace confirms Cheltenham placings

representative of the best two-milers around. It contained four of the first five in the previous year's renewal, the winner Rooster Booster, runner-up Westender, fourth-placed Self Defense and fifth-placed Intersky Falcon. The winners of most of the major recognised 'trials' were in the line-up, notably, in betting order, the Bula Hurdle and Kingwell Hurdle winner Rigmarole, the Christmas Hurdle winner Intersky Falcon and the winner of the AIG Europe Champion Hurdle, Foreman. But the market was dominated by Rooster Booster, seven-length winner of the Champion Hurdle Trial at Haydock in January and a superb second under top weight in the Tote Gold Trophy at Newbury. He was the first of three defending champions brought back to earth at the latest Festival—the others being Moscow Flyer (Queen Mother Champion Chase) and Baracouda (Stayers' Hurdle)—but his backers must have entertained expectations of a smooth victory as the Champion Hurdle leaders quickened going down the hill approaching the home turn. The front-running tactics employed on Hardy Eustace at Gowran were repeated at Cheltenham, his rider dictating an early pace which was fair at best and wasn't quickened in earnest until three out. Although an end-to-end gallop would have suited Rooster Booster, everything still seemed to be going to plan as he landed upsides Hardy Eustace at the last, apparently going the better. But Conor O'Dwyer on Hardy Eustace had kept something in reserve and, though Rooster Booster was in front for a stride or two, Hardy Eustace ran on much too stoutly for him and, kept up to his work, stretched five lengths clear on the run-in to become the fourth longest-priced winner in the history of the race. Kirriemuir and Beech Road won at 50/1 in 1965 and 1989 respectively, while For Auction was 40/1 in 1982. Third in the latest Champion Hurdle was the patiently-ridden Intersky Falcon, keeping on well, a further four lengths behind Rooster Booster, without being able to make an impression. Foreman was a length and a quarter further away in fourth, just ahead of Westender, with the AIG Europe Champion Hurdle third Fota Island in sixth. The performances of Foreman and Fota Island made the form of that race and, indirectly, Hardy Eustace's form against Georges Girl, look better than it had at the time. Hardy Eustace's Champion Hurdle effort nonetheless represented a marked improvement on his previous form.

Front-running tactics aren't straightforward to execute, particularly round Cheltenham with its turns and gradients and, most importantly, its uphill finish. Night Nurse in 1976 and Make A Stand in 1997 are the two most recent Champion Hurdle winners to make all (apparently Blaris, in the four-runner inaugural event in 1927, and Victor Norman in 1936 are the only others to have done so). Conor O'Dwyer, who had a Gold Cup success on Imperial Call, deserved the plaudits he received for a tactically-astute ride on Hardy Eustace, though memories of the late Kieran Kelly, who rode the horse to victory in the Royal & SunAlliance Novices' Hurdle, dominated the post-race briefings. Kelly was killed in a fall at Kilbeggan in August and two months later Irish racing suffered another sad loss when Flat apprentice Sean Cleary suffered severe head injuries in a fall at Galway. They were the first racecourse deaths in Britain and Ireland since those of English amateur Trevor Radford in October 2000 and English jump jockey Richard Davis in 1996. The Champion Hurdle victory of Hardy Eustace and the Irish Grand National

victory of Timbera have provided Dessie Hughes with the most high profile victories of his training career; as a jockey, he was also one of the elite band to have won
the Champion Hurdle (Monksfield) and the Gold Cup (Davy Lad). Laurence
Byrne, owner of Hardy Eustace, reportedly named him after a land owner (and
member of the Irish National Hunt Steeplechase Committee) in County Carlow
where he comes from. Oliver Hardy Eustace-Duckett is also the source of the name
for Byrne's fairly useful five-year-old hurdler Hardy Duckett and another five-
year-old Hardy Oliver who are also trained by Hughes.

Any thoughts that Hardy Eustace might have been flattered by the Champ-
ion Hurdle result were dispelled in the Emo Oil Champion Hurdle at Punchestown
in late-April, shortly after the end of the British season. Another meeting with
Rooster Booster in the Aintree Hurdle over two and a half miles was ruled out by
Hardy Eustace's connections because of the closeness of Aintree to Cheltenham—
there was only a two-week gap—but they had no intention of ducking a rematch.
Rooster Booster did contest the Aintree Hurdle, finishing second to Rhinestone
Cowboy, before going on to the Emo Oil Champion Hurdle for which he started
favourite at 13/8, with Hardy Eustace second best at 3/1 in a field of nine. Again
blinkered, Hardy Eustace didn't need to lead from the start—the pace was good—
but, after getting several reminders around halfway, he was in front at the third last
and found plenty under pressure in the straight, for most of which Rooster Booster
again looked well poised, tracking Hardy Eustace on the bridle. Hardy Eustace
jumped the last the better, getting away more quickly then Rooster Booster, and
was ridden out to beat his rival by a length. Third-placed Fota Island finished closer
to the first two—three lengths behind Rooster Booster—than he had at Cheltenham
and, with the County Hurdle fifth Harchibald also close up, the view that could be

Mr Laurence Byrne's "Hardy Eustace"

taken of the form was limited. There was no doubt, however, that Hardy Eustace beat Rooster Booster on merit, as he did at Cheltenham, and was fully deserving of the title of the season's top two-mile hurdler. He will again be a force to be reckoned with in the next Champion Hurdle, for which he was quoted at 10/1 in ante-post lists after the latest Festival. Victory in the Emo Oil Champion Hurdle took Hardy Eustace's career record to six wins from fifteen starts, following his eventual disqualification in January from a maiden hurdle at Punchestown in November 2002, after which a dope test revealed traces of a prohibited substance.

Hardy Eustace (IRE) (b.g. 1997)	Archway (IRE) (ch 1988)	Thatching (b 1975)	Thatch
			Abella
		Rose of Jericho (b 1984)	Alleged
			Rose Red
	Sterna Star (b or br 1984)	Corvaro (b 1977)	Vaguely Noble
			Delmora
		Star Girl (b 1973)	Sovereign Gleam
			Sterna

The good-topped Hardy Eustace is by the smart sprinter Archway, himself a son of a top sprinter in Thatching. Archway was, however, out of Rose of Jericho, also dam of the Derby winner Dr Devious, and Archway's stud career has featured winners over a variety of distances, including a number of notable middle-distance performers on the Flat in Australia. Hardy Eustace, from Archway's final Irish crop, is out of Sterna Star who won a mile-and-a-half ladies race at Tralee as a four-year-old, her only victory. Sterna Star hasn't yet bred another winner but her unbroken three-year-old by Accordion was offered at the 2004 Derby Sale and fetched €160,000 (representing a considerable profit on the sum he fetched as a yearling). Hardy Eustace's once-raced grandam Star Girl bred nine winners, including the useful Flat performer Star Spartan and Star Player, a fairly useful stayer on the Flat and a winner three times over hurdles, his performances including a second in the Imperial Cup. More instantly recognisable is the name of Hardy Eustace's great grandam Sterna, the dam of Prix de l'Arc de Triomphe winner Star Appeal and also the grandam of Strong Gale, the predominant jumps sire of the 'nineties. Hardy Eustace has shown his best form at two miles and has won up to twenty-one furlongs. The going was good to firm for his maiden win on the Flat and he has shown form over hurdles on going ranging from good to heavy. His two best efforts have been in blinkers. *D. T. Hughes, Ireland*

HAREM SCAREM (IRE) 13 b.g. Lord Americo – River Rescue (Over The River (FR)) [2003/4 c84, h–: 16g⁶ c20g⁴ c20s⁵ c24g⁶ c19g³ c20d c16d^pu c17g³ Apr 12] tall, workmanlike gelding: winning hurdler: poor handicap chaser, little form in 2003/4: stays 21f: acts on heavy going: tried in blinkers. *Mrs L. Williamson* **c61 h–**

HAREWOOD END 6 b.g. Bin Ajwaad (IRE) – Tasseled (USA) (Tate Gallery (USA)) [2003/4 16m 16m 17g^ur 17d 16g Dec 3] no longer of much account on Flat: no form over hurdles: tried in cheekpieces/tongue tied: sold 1,700 gns Doncaster January Sales. *A. Crook* **h–**

HARFDECENT 13 b.g. Primitive Rising (USA) – Grand Queen (Grand Conde (FR)) [2003/4 c106x, h–: c20m^pu Jun 7] small, sparely-made gelding: veteran chaser: won point in 2003, no form in 2004: stays 25f: acts on soft and good to firm going: has had tongue tied: often let down by jumping. *A. G. Hobbs* **c– x h–**

HARIK 10 ch.g. Persian Bold – Yaqut (USA) (Northern Dancer) [2003/4 c111, h–: c21m⁴ c20m⁶ c17g⁶ c20m⁶ c16f² c17s² c16m⁴ c18s* c16d c16g^ur c16g c18g² Apr 22] workmanlike gelding: fair handicap chaser: won at Fontwell in February: stays 2½m: acts on any going: has won in visor, usually blinkered: tongue tied. *G. L. Moore* **c107 h–**

HARLEY 6 ch.g. Alderbrook – Chichell's Hurst (Oats) [2003/4 F16g 20d^F 16s 19g^pu 20d Mar 22] sturdy gelding: second foal: dam, winning hurdler/chaser, stayed 25f: no form. *Mrs P. Sly* **h– F–**

HARLOV (FR) 9 ch.g. Garde Royale – Paulownia (FR) (Montevideo) [2003/4 c99, h–: c30d² c30g* c33d⁵ Feb 21] well-made gelding: fair handicap chaser: improved further when winning at Catterick in January: stays 3¾m: acts on heavy going: blinkered once, wore cheekpieces last 4 starts: reliable. *A. Parker* **c110 h–**

HARMONY HALL 10 ch.g. Music Boy – Fleeting Affair (Hotfoot) [2003/4 h–: 16m* **h102**
16m* 16m 16m Sep 14] sturdy gelding: modest on Flat (probably best at 7f/1m): fair
hurdler: won handicaps at Worcester in July and August: soundly beaten last 2 starts.
raced at 2m: acts on good to firm and good to soft going: sold 5,400 gns Doncaster
October Sales. *J. M. Bradley*

HARNAGE (IRE) 9 b.g. Mujadil (USA) – Wilderness (Martinmas) [2003/4 c21gᵖᵘ **c–**
Aug 12] leggy, close-coupled gelding: poor form over hurdles in 2000/1: third in maiden **h–**
points in 2003: no show on steeplechase debut. *Jean-Rene Auvray*

HARPOON HARRY (IRE) 7 ch.g. Alphabatim (USA) – Procastrian (IRE) (Lan- **h95**
castrian) [2003/4 20s⁴ Mar 13] IR £17,000 4-y-o: fourth foal: brother to winning pointer:
dam unraced, from family of high-class staying chaser By The Way: fourth of 19 to Kasthari in novice hurdle at Newcastle on debut, patiently ridden and travelling comfortably
long way: bred to stay beyond 2½m. *K. C. Bailey*

HARRINGAY 4 b.f. Sir Harry Lewis (USA) – Tamergale (IRE) (Strong Gale) [2003/4 **F85 p**
F16g* Mar 6] second foal: dam, temperamental but 19f hurdle winner, half-sister to
useful 2m hurdler Family Way, from family of high-class 2m hurdler Fredcoteri: 6/4-on,
won mares bumper at Huntingdon on debut by ½ length from Simply Mystic: likely to
improve. *Miss H. C. Knight*

HARRIS BAY 5 b.g. Karinga Bay – Harristown Lady (Muscatite) [2003/4 F16d* **F106**
F16d³ Feb 2] €48,000 4-y-o: rangy gelding: first foal: dam, winning hurdler/fairly useful
chaser, stayed 3¼m: won bumper at Ludlow on debut in January by 1½ lengths from Lord
Killeshanra: improved form when third to Itsa Legend in similar event at Kempton: will
be suited by further: type to make his mark over hurdles. *Miss H. C. Knight*

HARROVIAN 7 b.g. Deploy – Homeoftheclassics (Tate Gallery (USA)) [2003/4 h88: **h74 +**
22g³ Mar 28] modest form at best in 3 novice hurdles: left F. Murphy and off 16 months
before reappearance: should stay 3m: may still do better. *Miss P. Robson*

HARRY B 5 b.g. Midyan (USA) – Vilcabamba (USA) (Green Dancer (USA)) [2003/4 **h72**
h91: 17dᵖᵘ 24dᵖᵘ 19d³ Feb 15] maiden hurdler, poor form in 2003/4: looked none too
hearty in cheekpieces final start. *R. J. Price*

HARRY BRIDGES 5 ch.g. Weld – Northern Quay (Quayside) [2003/4 F16g Feb 28] **F–**
quite good-topped gelding: second foal: dam winning pointer: burly, well beaten in bumper on debut. *R. Lee*

HARRY COLLINS 6 ch.g. Sir Harry Lewis (USA) – Run Fast For Gold (Deep Run) **h85**
[2003/4 h–, F76: 20d⁴ 24v³ 22s² 22g² Apr 24] workmanlike gelding: modest novice
hurdler: stays 3m: acts on heavy going: tongue tied on reappearance. *B. I. Case*

HARRYCONE LEWIS 6 b.g. Sir Harry Lewis (USA) – Rosie Cone (Celtic Cone) **c110**
[2003/4 h90: 22d 21v⁵ 25s⁶ 25s c24s* c24sᵖᵘ c24g* c22g³ Mar 26] disappointing maiden **h–**
hurdler: won 2 of 4 starts in novice chases, at Fakenham in January and February: stays
3m: raced on good going or softer (acts on soft). *Mrs P. Sly*

HARRY HOTSPUR (IRE) 11 gr.g. Celio Rufo – Midsummer Blends (IRE) (Duky) **c–**
[2003/4 c25mᵖᵘ Mar 4] big, rangy gelding: poor chaser: stays 3¼m: acts on soft and good **h–**
to firm going: best form in blinkers/visor. *G. C. Evans*

HARRY'S ACE 6 b.g. Phountzi (USA) – Throw In Your Hand (Niniski (USA)) **h–**
[2003/4 F–: F17m³ 20m Jul 9] seemingly easily best effort in bumpers when third in **F87**
steadily-run event at Exeter: well beaten in novice on hurdling debut. *Mrs Merrita Jones*

HARRY'S DREAM 7 b.g. Alflora (IRE) – Cheryls Pet (IRE) (General Ironside) **c109**
[2003/4 h93: 20d³ c21m* c20g⁴ c21s² c22g* c23s Apr 6] leggy, workmanlike gelding: **h93**
modest maiden hurdler: fair chaser: won handicaps at Wincanton in December and Newbury (novice) in March: stays 2¾m: acts on soft and good to firm going. *P. J. Hobbs*

HARRY'S GAME 7 gr.g. Emperor Jones (USA) – Lady Shikari (Kala Shikari) [2003/4 **h74**
16g⁶ May 21] sturdy ex-Irish gelding: fairly useful 6f winner at 2 yrs, modest on Flat
nowadays: better effort in novice company over hurdles when distant sixth at Worcester:
tongue tied on debut. *A. P. Jones*

HARRY THE EAR (IRE) 6 b.g. Definite Article – Kilboy Concorde (African Sky) **h115**
[2003/4 h110: 16g 16g* 16F³ 16d³ 16g² 20m Oct 5] unfurnished gelding: fairly useful
handicap hurdler: won at Naas in August: best at 2m, possibly on good going or firmer:
tongue tied. *M. Halford, Ireland*

HARRY THE HOOVER (IRE) 4 b.g. Fayruz – Mitsubishi Style (Try My Best **h–**
(USA)) [2003/4 16gpu 16d Nov 23] sturdy gelding: fairly useful 6f winner at 2 yrs, well
held in 2003: showed nothing in 2 juvenile hurdles. *M. J. Gingell*

HARRY THE HORSE 6 b.g. Sir Harry Lewis (USA) – Miss Optimist (Relkino) **h–**
[2003/4 h–: 24gpu 17s Apr 6] workmanlike gelding: no form in 3 novice hurdles. *Miss
E. C. Lavelle*

HARTEST ROSE 5 b.m. Komaite (USA) – Plough Hill (North Briton) [2003/4 F87: **h–**
F16m3 F16m 16m6 Jun 20] compact mare: fair bumper winner: visored, well tailed off in **F87**
novice on hurdling debut. *D. E. Cantillon*

HARVIS (FR) 9 b.g. Djarvis (FR) – Tirana (FR) (Over) [2003/4 c123, h114: c20spu **c109 §**
c22g5 c19d5 c24dpu c18s3 c16s6 c16d3 c20m c16d5 c20d5 Mar 25] smallish, angular geld- **h–**
ing: winning hurdler: fairly useful handicap chaser in 2002/3: below best in 2003/4, left
Miss V. Williams and off 7 months after reappearance: effective at 2m to easy 3m: acts on
heavy and good to firm going: often fails to impress with jumping/attitude. *G. B. Balding*

HASANPOUR (IRE) 4 b.g. Dr Devious (IRE) – Hasainiya (IRE) (Top Ville) [2003/4 **h98**
16s* 16s 17gpu Mar 18] good-topped gelding: lightly raced on Flat, useful form when
winning over 13f in September: sold out of Sir Michael Stoute's stable 150,000 gns
Newmarket Autumn Sales: easily accounted for modest opposition when making all in
minor event at Cork on hurdling debut in January: reportedly suffering from respiratory
infection when well held in Grade 2 at Leopardstown next time, weakened quickly after
mistake 3 out in Grade 1 at Cheltenham final start. *C. F. Swan, Ireland*

HAS SCORED (IRE) 6 b.g. Sadler's Wells (USA) – City Ex (Ardross) [2003/4 20s **h–**
Dec 19] sturdy gelding: seventh foal: half-brother to several winners on Flat, including
smart 1m to 1¼m performer Petit Poucet (by Fairy King) and French 12.5f winner
Bengale Lancer (by Sarhoob): dam French 1½m winner: backward, well beaten in novice
hurdle on debut. *Ferdy Murphy*

HASTATE 9 b.g. Persian Bold – Gisarne (USA) (Diesis) [2003/4 c24gpu Mar 5] com- **c–**
pact gelding: fairly useful hunter chaser in 2002: soon behind on return: stays 2¾m: acts **h–**
on soft and good to firm going: tried tongue tied earlier in career: tends to find little.
N. M. Lampard

HASTENER 10 ch.m. Crested Lark – Spartella (Spartan General) [2003/4 c25dpu Apr **c–**
30] poor pointer. *J. L. Barnett*

HASTY PRINCE 6 ch.g. Halling (USA) – Sister Sophie (USA) (Effervescing (USA)) **h150**
[2003/4 h125p: 20g* 16m3 16s3 16s2 16g 16g 24g5 16m* Apr 23] leggy, sparely-made
gelding: progressed into smart hurdler, winning Tote Silver Trophy Handicap at Chepstow in November and steadily-run minor event at Sandown in April, beating Rigmarole

Concept Hurdle, Sandown—
stable second string Hasty Prince wins a muddling race from Rigmarole (right) and Westender (blinkers)

F. F. Racing Services Partnership III's "Hasty Prince"

10 lengths at latter course: best effort in between when second to Rooster Booster in Grade 2 at Haydock in January: stays 2½m: acts on soft and good to firm going: effective held up or ridden prominently. *Jonjo O'Neill*

HATCH GATE   11 gr.g. Lighter – Yankee Silver (Yankee Gold) [2003/4 c68: c24m* **c79** c28d[pu] May 30] won novice hunter chase at Huntingdon in May: refused to race in point in January, won following month: stays 3m: acts on good to firm going. *P. York*

HATSNALL   6 b.g. Mtoto – Anna of Brunswick (Rainbow Quest (USA)) [2003/4 **c–** c73, h86: 22d[6] 19g 16d 21d[4] 21d[5] Apr 12] good-topped gelding: twice-raced chaser: **h79** poor maiden hurdler: stays 21f: acts on heavy going, probably on good to firm. *Miss C. J. E. Caroe*

HATTERAS (FR)   5 b.g. Octagonal (NZ) – Hylandra (USA) (Bering) [2003/4 17s[2] **h97** 17d[4] 18d[5] Apr 7] has reportedly had breathing operation: half-brother to winning French chaser around 2m Hilaire (by Sillery): fairly useful maiden on Flat (stays 1½m) for H. Van de Poele: runner-up at Compiegne in May on last of 3 starts in 4-y-o hurdles for Y. Fouin: modest form in novices both outings in Britain. *P. F. Nicholls*

HAUT CERCY (FR)   9 b.g. Roi de Rome (USA) – Mamoussia (FR) (Laniste) [2003/4 **c139** c139, h–: c25d[2] c24g c29m[pu] Apr 24] leggy gelding: useful handicap chaser: good second **h–** to impressive Kingscliff at Cheltenham on reappearance: ran poorly both starts subsequently (reportedly injured final one): better around 3m than shorter (possibly failed to stay 4m): has won on soft going, best form on good/good to soft. *H. D. Daly*

HAVANTADOUBT (IRE)   4 ch.f. Desert King (IRE) – Batiba (USA) (Time For A **h–** Change (USA)) [2003/4 16s Jan 21] fair on Flat (barely stays 1½m), sold out of

J. Portman's stable 7,000 gns Doncaster November Sales: tailed-off last of 7 finishers in fillies juvenile on hurdling debut. *M. R. Bosley*

HAVE-NO-DOUBT (IRE)   10 b.g. Glacial Storm (USA) – Lady Kas (Pollerton) [2003/4 20v⁶ 22s 19dᵖᵘ 26sᵖᵘ Feb 12] lengthy gelding: winning pointer: second in maiden hunter chase in 2002: no form over hurdles on return. *L. A. Dace*   **c–**
h–

HAVETWOTAKETWO (IRE)   10 b.g. Phardante (FR) – Arctic Tartan (Deep Run) [2003/4 c–x, h–: c25gᵘʳ c27dᵖᵘ c25gᶠ Apr 5] winning pointer: little other form: has had tongue tied. *Michael Smith*   **c– x**
h–

HAVING A PARTY   6 b.m. Dancing High – Lady Manello (Mandrake Major) [2003/4 F16d⁴ F16v³ F16v* F16s Mar 13] sturdy mare: fifth foal: half-sister to fair pointer Clay-walls (by Meadowbrook): dam, placed over hurdles, half-sister to fairly useful chasers up to 25f Sword Beach and Divet Hill: well beaten in 2 maiden points in 2003: bought 2,000 gns Doncaster May Sales: best effort in bumpers when beating Countess Point by head, pair clear, at Chepstow in February. *J. Mackie*   **F95**

HAWAADEJ (IRE)   7 b.g. Barathea (IRE) – Lover's Rose (King Emperor (USA)) [2003/4 F18d F16g c17f⁶ 20m 16m⁵ 16d c16f c20m 20s c21g⁴ c20gᵘʳ c24g c22sᵖᵘ Dec 26] 95,000F, 100,000Y, 9,000 2-y-o: half-brother to several winners, notably Cheveley Park winner and Poule d'Essai des Pouliches runner-up Pass The Peace (by Alzao): dam, 9f winner, half-sister to very smart middle-distance stayer Swell Fellow: little sign of ability. *N. F. Glynn, Ireland*   **c–**
h–
F–

HAWADETH   9 ch.g. Machiavellian (USA) – Ghzaalh (USA) (Northern Dancer) [2003/4 h125: 20g 16g² 16g⁵ 16g³ 17d² 20m Apr 24] compact gelding: useful handicap hurdler: excellent effort from 13 lb out of weights when ½-length second of 23 to Spora-zene in County Hurdle at Cheltenham fifth start: stays 2½m, at least when emphasis on speed: unraced on firm going, acts on any other: tried blinkered, wore cheekpieces last 2 outings: consistent, though a hard ride (often soon off bridle and gets behind). *V. R. A. Dartnall*   **h133**

HAWICK   7 b.g. Toulon – Slave's Bangle (Prince Rheingold) [2003/4 F99: F16g² F16g⁵ 20sᵘʳ Dec 26] fairly useful form in bumpers: jumped awkwardly and unseated third on hurdling debut. *D. W. Whillans*   **h–**
F99

HAWKES RUN   6 b.g. Hernando (FR) – Wise Speculation (USA) (Mr Prospector (USA)) [2003/4 h117: 24m³ 22g⁵ 20m 22m⁶ Jul 19] close-coupled gelding: poor walker: fairly useful handicap hurdler: creditable effort in 2003/4 only when third at Worcester in May: dismounted after line final start: barely stays 3m: acts on soft and good to firm going: blinkered once, wore cheekpieces in 2003/4: has looked ungenuine. *C. J. Mann*   **h115 d**

HAWK'S LANDING (IRE)   7 gr.g. Peacock (FR) – Lady Cheyenne (Stanford) [2003/4 F104: 22g* 21v² 21d² 19d² c16sᶠ c21d* c32gᶠ Mar 17] well-made gelding: fairly useful novice hurdler: won maiden at Stratford in October: second start over fences, won maiden at Folkestone in February: well beaten when falling fatally last in valuable amateur event at Cheltenham: stayed 2¾m: raced on good going or softer (acted on heavy). *Jonjo O'Neill*   **c125**
h117

HAWTHORN   8 ch.g. Primo Dominie – Starr Danias (USA) (Sensitive Prince (USA)) [2003/4 h–: c22gᶠ Mar 26] tall gelding: very lightly-raced maiden hurdler/chaser. *B. J. Clarke*   **c–**
h–

HAWTHORN PRINCE (IRE)   9 ch.g. Black Monday – Goose Loose (Dual) [2003/4 c–, h–, F84: 23m* 23g* 22mᵖᵘ 24m³ 20g⁵ Dec 5] successful in 2 points in 2003: fair hurd-ler: won 2 novices at Fakenham (second a handicap) in May: stays 23f: acts on good to firm going: blinkered last 4 outings in 2002/3, looking far from resolute on final occasion. *Mrs P. Sly*   **h105**

HAYAAIN   11 b.g. Shirley Heights – Littlefield (Bay Express) [2003/4 c–, h102: 24d² 24dᵖᵘ 24g 18v 27d Apr 23] good-topped gelding: modest hurdler nowadays: stays 3¼m: acts on good to firm and good to soft going: blinkered twice: has looked ungenuine. *N. W. Alexander*   **c–**
h87

HAYBURN VAULTS   6 b.m. Bettergeton – Agdistis (Petoski) [2003/4 F–: F17s 17d Mar 10] well held in bumpers and mares novice hurdle. *Mrs S. J. Smith*   **h–**
F–

HAY DANCE   13 b.g. Shareef Dancer (USA) – Hay Reef (Mill Reef (USA)) [2003/4 c88, h–: c20mᵖᵘ May 10] good-topped gelding: veteran hunter chaser: stays 2½m: acts on good to firm and good to soft going: held up. *J. Ibbott*   **c–**
h–

HAYDENS FIELD   10 b.g. Bedford (USA) – Releta (Relkino) [2003/4 h123: 20d* 20d Nov 23] angular gelding: fairly useful handicap hurdler: won at Uttoxeter in May: **h120**

tailed off at Aintree only other start in 2003/4: stays 25f: raced on good going or softer (acts on heavy). *P. M. Rich*

HAYLEY'S PEARL   5 b.m. Nomadic Way (USA) – Pacific Girl (IRE) (Emmson) [2003/4 F16d F11/s F16s 22g^{pu} 17g Apr 3] first known foal: dam poor maiden on Flat: no sign of ability. *Mrs P. Ford*   **h–**
F–

HAYSTACKS (IRE)   8 b.g. Contract Law (USA) – Florissa (FR) (Persepolis (FR)) [2003/4 22d* 22m^5 25f* 24d^6 Dec 20] leggy gelding: modest handicap hurdler: won at Cartmel in May and Catterick (finished lame) in November: stays 25f: acts on firm and good to soft going: usually visored, wore cheekpieces last 2 starts: has carried head awkwardly and found little. *James Moffatt*   **h99 §**

HAYTON BOY   10 ch.g. Gypsy Castle – Young Christine VII (Damsire Unregistered) [2003/4 h–: 24d^{pu} Mar 18] no sign of ability in 4 starts over hurdles: tried tongue tied. *S. G. Chadwick*   **h–**

HAZEL FLIGHT   4 ch.f. Hazaaf (USA) – Sapphire Flight (Scallywag) [2003/4 F17g Apr 10] third foal: dam of little account: little encouragement in bumper on debut. *Miss M. Bragg*   **F–**

HAZELJACK   9 b.g. Sula Bula – Hazelwain (Hard Fact) [2003/4 20g 21g 26v^4 20g^{ur} 20d^6 21d c25v^{pu} 20g^3 21d^4 Mar 18] tall gelding: maiden hurdler/chaser: probably flattered when appearing to show fair form over fences last 2 starts, though would have won novice handicap at Ludlow in December but for unseating last: should stay beyond 2½m: acts on good to soft going. *A. J. Whiting*   **c109 ?**
h–

HAZEL REILLY (IRE)   13 b.m. Mister Lord (USA) – Vickies Gold (Golden Love) [2003/4 c94: c25m^2 May 7] smallish, lengthy, angular mare: fair hunter chaser: stays 31f: acts on heavy going: reliable. *Mrs Sarah L. Dent*   **c94**

HAZY MORN   5 gr.m. Cyrano de Bergerac – Hazy Kay (IRE) (Treasure Kay) [2003/4 16s^F 17m^{pu} Nov 27] poor maiden on Flat: failed to complete both starts over hurdles. *R. J. Hodges*   **h–**

HEARTACHE   7 b.g. Jurado (USA) – Heresy (IRE) (Black Minstrel) [2003/4 h80?: 19d 19d^6 c17d^2 c16s^F Apr 11] tall gelding: signs of only a little ability over hurdles: neck second to Rodber in novice at Bangor on chasing debut: fell eighth next time: has worn cheekpieces. *R. Mathew*   **c91**
h–

HEARTBREAKER (IRE)   4 b.g. In Command (IRE) – No Hard Feelings (IRE) (Alzao (USA)) [2003/4 17g^5 Aug 8] soundly beaten in 4 starts on Flat: fifth in juvenile at Sedgefield on hurdling debut. *M. W. Easterby*   **h78**

HEART MIDOLTIAN (FR)   7 gr.g. Royal Charter – Pride of Queen (FR) (Saint Henri) [2003/4 c126p, h115: c20g* 20m^3 c22s^{pu} 20f^6 c25d^5 c21g c21g^{ur} c29d^F Apr 12] medium-sized, long-necked gelding: has reportedly had wind operation: fairly useful hurdler/chaser: won Grade 3 novice at Punchestown very early in season: generally well held off stiff marks in handicaps subsequently: stays 2¾m: acts on firm and soft going: usually tongue tied. *S. Neville, Ireland*   **c126**
h120

HEARTOFMIDLOTHIAN (IRE)   5 ch.g. Anshan – Random Wind (Random Shot) [2003/4 F16d Mar 28] 12,500 3-y-o: fifth foal: half-brother to fairly useful bumper winner Random Native (by Be My Native): dam, winning hurdler/poor novice chaser who stayed 2½m, half-sister to useful chaser up to 2½m Time For Gold and to dam of high-class chaser up to 25f Sackville: eighth of 15 in bumper at Huntingdon on debut. *K. C. Bailey*   **F76**

HEATHERJACK   7 b.m. Nalchik (USA) – Healaughs Pride (Healaugh Fox) [2003/4 F–: 16g May 22] well beaten in bumper and maiden hurdle. *B. Mactaggart*   **h–**

HEATHYARDS FRIEND   5 b.g. Forest Wind (USA) – Heathyards Lady (USA) (Mining (USA)) [2003/4 h76: 16g 16g Sep 7] leggy gelding: poor hurdler: raced around 2m on good/good to soft going: sold £1,600 Ascot October Sales. *R. Hollinshead*   **h69**

HEATHYARDS GUEST (IRE)   6 ch.g. Be My Guest (USA) – Noble Nadia (Thatching) [2003/4 h69: 16m Apr 28] workmanlike gelding: poor maiden hurdler: raced mainly around 2m: acts on good to firm and good to soft going: tried in cheekpieces/blinkers: jumps none too fluently. *Mrs K. Walton*   **h–**

HEATHYARDS SWING   6 b.g. Celtic Swing – Butsova (Formidable (USA)) [2003/4 16d^6 16g^4 16v 22g 16g Apr 5] half-brother to winning 2m hurdlers Attack and Sabre Butt (both by Sabrehill): modest and ungenuine on Flat (barely stays 1½m), sold out of   **h81**

R. Hollinshead's stable £2,300 Ascot July Sales: poor form over hurdles: wears cheek-pieces. *James Moffatt*

HEATHY GORE   5 ch.m. Environment Friend – Hazel Hill (Abednego) [2003/4 F16s   **F–**
Dec 19] third foal: dam winning pointer: tailed off in bumper on debut. *J. K. Cresswell*

HEAVEN IS ABOVE (IRE)   9 b.g. Hymns On High – Great Supper (Slippered)   **c–**
[2003/4 c24m^{pu} Mar 4] winning hunter chaser in Ireland: no show in point or hunter chase   **h–**
in Britain: stays 3m: acts on good to firm ground. *Mrs S. J. Hickman*

HEAVENLY HILL   7 b.m. Nomadic Way (USA) – Tees Gazette Girl (Kalaglow) [2003/4 F85: 20g 20m^5 Jun 1] strong mare: fair at best in bumpers: no show in 2 novice   **h–**
hurdles. *M. J. Gingell*

HEAVENLY KING   6 b.g. Homo Sapien – Chapel Hill (IRE) (The Parson) [2003/4   **h72**
h–, F73: 19m^2 24m Jun 18] quite good-topped gelding: form over hurdles only when
second in novice handicap at Exeter in May: stays 19f: blinkered in 2003/4. *P. Bowen*

HEAVENLY PLEASURE (IRE)   5 b.m. Presenting – Galynn (IRE) (Strong Gale)   **F76 ?**
[2003/4 F16m F16d^6 Apr 21] third foal: dam unraced, out of half-sister to useful 2m
hurdler Hansel Rag: apparently better effort in bumpers when sixth at Worcester.
C. Roberts

HECKLEY CLARE GLEN   6 b.m. Dancing High – Heckley Spark (Electric)   **F88**
[2003/4 F16d* F16s Jan 21] 6,000 4-y-o: third foal: dam lightly-raced maiden: won
mares bumper at Newcastle on debut: soundly beaten in similar event there 2 months
later: sold 10,000 gns Doncaster May Sales. *N. G. Richards*

HEDGEHUNTER (IRE)   8 b.g. Montelimar (USA) – Aberedw (IRE) (Caerwent)   **c144**
[2003/4 F16d* F16s Jan 21] c25g^2 c26g^4 c29d^3 c24s* c36d^F Apr 3]   **h–**
   Irish hopes of winning a fourth Grand National in six years were hit when
leading contenders Timbera, the ante-post favourite, and the high-class Rince Ri
had to drop out at the eleventh hour. In their absence, the pick of the Irish looked to
be the Goulding Thyestes Chase winner Hedgehunter, a sound jumper with a good
record in the big handicaps. Hedgehunter was an impressive eight-length winner at
Gowran, where much more use was made of him than when in the frame earlier in
the season in the Hennessy Cognac Gold Cup at Newbury (fourth to Strong Flow)
and the Coral Welsh National (third to Bindaree). Hedgehunter had shown a tend-

Goulding Thyestes Handicap Chase, Gowran—
Hedgehunter benefits from a change to front-running tactics

ency in some of his races to hang right and find less than expected under pressure. Allowed to bowl along, he jumped really well in the Thyestes Chase, was clear at halfway and finished well on top after seeing off the only danger—eventual runner-up I'vehadit—some way from home. Front-running tactics were adopted again on Hedgehunter at Aintree, where he jumped boldly and really took to the big, unusual fences. He led from the eighth, setting a strong pace, was only headed two out and would have made the frame had he not come down at the last, the first fall of his career. Hedgehunter would clearly be worth his place in the field again another year.

Hedgehunter (IRE) (b.g. 1996)	Montelimar (USA) (b 1981)	Alleged (b 1974)	Hoist The Flag / Princess Pout
		L'Extravagante (br 1973)	Le Fabuleux / Fanfreluche
	Aberedw (IRE) (b 1990)	Caerwent (b 1985)	Caerleon / Marwell
		Secret Hideaway (b 1983)	Key To The Mint / Turning Bold

The useful-looking Hedgehunter, who often sweats in the preliminaries, also made all when winning the National Trial at Punchestown in the 2002/3 season, the only other steeplechase he has won, for his previous owner Niall Quaid. Bought by Trevor Hemmings after that race, Hedgehunter was travelling like a winner when blundering two out, and all but unseating his rider, in the four-mile National Hunt Chase at the Cheltenham Festival on his first start in the Hemmings

Mr Trevor Hemmings' "Hedgehunter"

colours. A good type for long distance chases, Hedgehunter is by Montelimar, whose progeny include a couple of others that have done well over the National fences, notably the 2003 Grand National winner Monty's Pass (fourth in the latest running) and Cassia Heights who won the Topham Chase at the latest Grand National meeting. Hedgehunter is the first foal of Aberedw, a modest maiden on the Flat and over hurdles for Aidan O'Brien, who was also represented on the race-course in the latest season by Hedgehunter's fair six-year-old brother Merlyn's Monty, winner of a two-and-a-half-mile maiden hurdle at Cork in January. Hedge-hunter has been raced on good going or softer, and acts on heavy. *W. P. Mullins, Ireland*

HEEMANELA (IRE) 9 b.g. Classic Secret (USA) – Ela Man Hee (Ela-Mana-Mou) [2003/4 16f⁵ 17f² 16f³ 20g² 16m* Oct 10] sparely-made gelding: fairly useful on Flat (stays 1¼m): fair hurdler: best effort when winning handicap at Gowran: best around 2m: acts on firm going. *Mrs S. A. Bramall, Ireland*   **h114**

HEE'S A DANCER 12 b.g. Rambo Dancer (CAN) – Heemee (On Your Mark) [2003/4 c20m^pu May 15] leggy, sparely-made gelding: fair hunter chaser: reportedly lame only outing in 2003/4: stays 3m: acts on firm and good to soft going: usually races up with pace. *R. W. J. Willcox*   **c– h–**

HEHASALIFE (IRE) 7 b.g. Safety Catch (USA) – America River (IRE) (Lord Americo) [2003/4 20d 24g² 24f³ 24m² 20g² 20g* 20d c17m⁶ c22g* 20s² 20m⁶ c20f² 20m⁴ c20g³ c20g^ur c20g⁴ Apr 24] tall, shallow-girthed gelding: first foal: dam unraced: won maiden Irish point on debut in 2002: fair hurdler: won maiden at Limerick in July: similar form over fences, winning maiden at Galway in September: sold out of M. Hourigan's stable 25,000 gns Doncaster November Sales: best effort when third in handicap at Kempton in March: stays 3m: acts on firm and soft ground: effective with/without blinkers. *Mrs H. Dalton*   **c112 h103**

HEIDI III (FR) 9 b.g. Bayolidaan (FR) – Irlandaise (FR) (Or de Chine) [2003/4 c123, h–: c24d² c20d³ c24s⁴ Apr 17] close-coupled gelding: useful chaser at best, fair form in 2003/4: stays 25f: acts on good to firm and heavy going: wears cheekpieces: races prominently: genuine. *Mrs L. Williamson*   **c112 h–**

HEKTIKOS 4 ch.g. Hector Protector (USA) – Green Danube (USA) (Irish River (FR)) [2003/4 16d 16s^ur Mar 15] little form on Flat: no show in 2 races over hurdles. *S. Dow*   **h–**

HELDERBERG (USA) 4 b.f. Diesis – Banissa (USA) (Lear Fan (USA)) [2003/4 16s 16g 16g Mar 15] strong filly: fair on Flat (stays 11f), sold out of C. Brittain's stable 11,500 gns Newmarket October Sales: showed nothing in 3 juvenile hurdles. *B. S. Rothwell*   **h–**

HELIXIR DU THEIL (FR) 9 ch.g. Aelan Hapi (USA) – Manolette (FR) (Signani (FR)) [2003/4 c97, h95: c19m³ c26g* c32g^pu Dec 5] workmanlike gelding: maiden hurdler: modest chaser: won novice handicap at Newton Abbot in November: reportedly lame following month: suited by 3m+: acts on soft and good to firm going: in cheekpieces in 2003/4. *R. H. Buckler*   **c88 h–**

HELLO BABY 4 b.g. Jumbo Hirt (USA) – Silver Flyer (Silver Season) [2003/4 F16g⁶ F16d³ F17d² F17d⁵ Apr 18] leggy gelding: second foal: dam never ran: fair form in bumpers, second at Carlisle in March: will be well suited by greater test of stamina. *A. C. Whillans*   **F91**

HELLO DEE 6 b.m. Alflora (IRE) – Donna Farina (Little Buskins) [2003/4 F85: 20m³ 22m^pu Oct 4] placed in mares bumpers in 2002/3: third in novice at Worcester on hurdling debut: looked one to be wary of next time: has high head carriage: sold 800 gns Doncaster November Sales. *Jonjo O'Neill*   **h78**

HELL-OF-A-SHINDY (IRE) 10 b.g. Phardante (FR) – Tonto's Girl (Strong Gale) [2003/4 c107, h–: c24g⁵ 20g³ Oct 5] sturdy gelding: fair handicap chaser: never a factor at Stratford on reappearance: poor form in 2 runs over hurdles: stays 3m: acts on any going: has had tongue tied: held up. *Jonjo O'Neill*   **c– h78**

HELL OF A TIME (IRE) 7 b.g. Phardante (FR) – Ticking Over (IRE) (Decent Fellow) [2003/4 F16g F16m⁵ 24g^pu Nov 8] IR 7,000 4-y-o: workmanlike ex-Irish gelding: third foal: brother to fair hurdler Westmoreland, stays 3m: dam ran once in Irish point: signs of ability in bumpers (trained by Miss F. Crowley on debut): in touch when breaking down home turn in maiden at Chepstow on hurdling debut. *Mrs N. S. Sharpe*   **h– F–**

HELLO MRS 6 b.m. Sir Harry Lewis (USA) – Five And Four (IRE) (Green Desert (USA)) [2003/4 F16s F16s F16s Apr 4] 3,000 4-y-o: second foal: dam, no sign of ability, half-sister to smart staying hurdler Burgoyne: well beaten in bumpers. *Mrs S. J. Smith*   **F–**

HELP YOURSELF (IRE)   8 gr.m. Roselier (FR) – Sweet Run (Deep Run) [2003/4   **h71**
h–: 16g 24m³ 20m 20dᶠ 16fʳᵒ 22d³ 24g⁵ Jan 23] smallish, plain mare: poor maiden
hurdler: stays 3m: acts on good to firm and good to soft going. *L. Lungo*

HELVETIUS   8 b.g. In The Wings – Hejraan (USA) (Alydar (USA)) [2003/4 c104, h–:   **c97**
c25g c22m⁵ c25mᵖᵘ c25s⁴ c21mᵖᵘ 22g⁵ c23m* c26g³ c24m Apr 13] leggy gelding: **h89**
modest handicap hurdler/chaser: won over fences at Leicester in March: stays 3¼m: acts
on any going: has worn cheekpieces/blinkers. *P. C. Ritchens*

HEMSWORTHY   9 ch.g. North Col – Look Back (Country Retreat) [2003/4 h–: 27s³   **h85**
22d Jun 9] tall, lengthy gelding: lightly raced and modest form at best over hurdles.
Miss M. Bragg

HENBRIDGE   8 ch.m. Henbit (USA) – Celtic Bridge (Celtic Cone) [2003/4 h–: 16g   **h64**
17g³ 17gᵖᵘ 20m³ 16g 20m³ Aug 8] poor maiden hurdler: likely to have proved best short
of 2½m: acted on good to firm going: wasn't straightforward (reluctant to line up fourth
start): dead. *Mrs S. M. Johnson*

HENRIANJAMES   9 b.g. Tina's Pet – Real Claire (Dreams To Reality (USA)) [2003/4   **c113**
c101, h87: c16m* c17gᶠ c17f c17g² c16m c17g* c16d⁴ c16g³ 16d Apr 21] strong gelding: **h–**
maiden hurdler: fair handicap chaser: won at Wetherby in May and Market Rasen (4 ran)
in November: raced around 2m: acts on firm and good to soft going: patiently ridden.
Mrs M. Reveley

HENRIETTA (IRE)   6 b.m. Hushang (IRE) – Jennie's First (Idiot's Delight) [2003/4   **h97**
16g* 21s* 16d³ 21d 19g* 21g Mar 27] workmanlike mare: likely to make a chaser: fourth
foal: half-sister to smart chaser up to 3¼m Horus (by Teenoso) and winning pointer by
Rakaposhi King: dam unraced daughter of useful hurdler/chaser up to 3m Jennie Pat: ran
twice in points in 2003, winning maiden on completed start: modest novice hurdler: won
mares events at Towcester (2) in November and Exeter (made all) in March: stays 21f:
acts on soft going. *M. C. Pipe*

HENRY PEARSON (USA)   6 ch.g. Distant View (USA) – Lady Ellen (USA) (Explo-   **h76**
sive Bid (USA)) [2003/4 h79: 20g⁶ 17d 25dᵖᵘ 17v³ 17s³ Feb 10] workmanlike gelding:
poor maiden hurdler: form only around 2m: acts on good to firm and heavy going:
blinkered last 2 starts: often tongue tied. *H. P. Hogarth*

HENRY'S HAPPINESS   5 b.m. Bob's Return (IRE) – Irish Mint (Dusky Boy)   **h72**
[2003/4 F17v aF16g 16s 16s 18s 22m² 20s Apr 17] rather leggy mare: ninth foal: half-   **F–**
sister to modest staying jumpers Father Fortune (by The Parson) and Sorbiere (by Deep
Run): dam, poor novice hurdler/chaser, half-sister to Grand National winner Corbiere:
well held in bumpers: worthwhile form over hurdles only when second in novice handicap at Wincanton: stays 2¾m: acts on good to firm going. *C. P. Morlock*

HENRY THE GREAT (IRE)   5 b.g. Alderbrook – Country Style (Town And Country)   **h–**
[2003/4 25sᵖᵘ Dec 20] €10,500 3-y-o: first foal: dam, winning pointer, half-sister to
high-class staying chaser Earth Summit: showed nothing in novice hurdle on debut.
N. A. Twiston-Davies

HERACLES   8 b.g. Unfuwain (USA) – La Masse (High Top) [2003/4 c112, h112: 22d   **c102**
22sᵖᵘ c26m⁶ Apr 14] leggy gelding: winning hurdler: fair chaser: stays 23f: acts on soft   **h–**
and good to firm going: blinkered final start: often jumps none too fluently. *R. H. Buckler*

HERACLITEAN FIRE (IRE)   7 b.g. Norwich – Mazovia (FR) (Taufan (USA))   **c99**
[2003/4 h90, F78: 22d² 19s 20dᵖᵘ 17m c17d³ c16f⁶ c17gᶠ c17m⁵ c16g* c18g⁶ c17d¹⁴ Dec   **h90**
26] workmanlike gelding: modest maiden hurdler: best effort over fences when winning
handicap at Down Royal in November: effective at 2m to 2¾m: acts on soft going:
blinkered fourth start (ran moody race): none too consistent. *J. J. Lambe, Ireland*

HERCULES MORSE (IRE)   8 b.g. Spanish Place (USA) – Pragownia (Pragmatic)   **c85 x**
[2003/4 20v⁵ c25dᶠ 22s c25g² c26d³ c24gᵘʳ Apr 16] IR 5,800 3-y-o: third foal: dam   **h–**
lightly raced in points: in frame in Irish points in 2002: poor form over hurdles: modest
form when second in handicap chase at Folkestone in March, let down by jumping over
fences otherwise: stays 25f. *D. B. Feek*

HERE COMES HARRY   8 ch.g. Sunley Builds – Coole Dolly Day (Arctic Lord)   **h76**
[2003/4 22d⁴ 19mᵖᵘ 22fᵖᵘ 22m* 21g³ Dec 11] 5,000 3-y-o: first foal: dam unraced: poor
novice hurdler: won handicap at Wincanton in December: will stay 3m: acts on good to
firm going. *C. J. Down*

HERE COMES HENRY   10 ch.g. Dortino – Epryana (English Prince) [2003/4 c105x: **c92 x**
c24d⁵ c26d³ c29s c24sᵖᵘ Feb 3] sturdy gelding: modest handicap chaser: no show in novice   **h–**

on hurdling debut: probably best at 3m+: acts on heavy going: tried blinkered/in cheek-pieces: usually let down by jumping. *R. H. Alner*

HERECOMESPAPIN (IRE)   7 b.m. Naheez (USA) – Bold Kim (King's Ride) [2003/4 F17m² F16m 20m⁴ 19d⁵ 17g⁶ Apr 1] IR 4,200 3-y-o: third live foal: dam, maiden hurdler, sister to useful staying chaser Camelot Knight and half-sister to useful chaser up to 3¼m Bold Argument: won mares maiden on first of 5 starts in Irish points in 2003: bought 2,600 gns Doncaster May Sales: much better effort in bumpers when second at Southwell: poor form over hurdles. *D. J. Wintle*   **h64** **F86**

HERECOMESTANLEY   5 b.g. Missed Flight – Moonspell (Batshoof) [2003/4 F–: F18m³ F17d 16sᵖᵘ Dec 30] good-topped gelding: little sign of ability. *M. F. Harris*   **h–** **F–**

HERES HARRY   4 b.c. Most Welcome – Nahla (Wassl) [2003/4 F16g Mar 15] second foal: dam, fairly useful bumper winner, half-sister to one-time very smart hurdler/smart chaser Blowing Wind, best up to 25f: well held in bumper on debut. *Miss Jacqueline S. Doyle*   **F–**

HERE'S JOHNNY (IRE)   5 ch.g. Presenting – Treble Base (IRE) (Orchestra) [2003/4 F16d³ F16s² F16g* Mar 17] useful-looking gelding: seventh foal: half-brother to 2¾m chase winner Woodchester (by Buckskin): dam unraced: fairly useful form in bumpers: placed at Newbury (third to Red Ruffles) and Sandown (second to Royal Paradise) prior to winning at Huntingdon. *V. R. A. Dartnall*   **F102**

HERMES III (FR)   9 b.g. Quart de Vin (FR) – Queenly (FR) (Pot d'Or (FR)) [2003/4 c141, h116+: c24s³ c20d² c21gᵇᵈ c26d* Apr 23] useful-looking gelding: winning hurdler: useful chaser at best, left N. Henderson after reappearance: won hunter at Perth in April: stays 3¼m: raced on good going or softer (acts on soft). *M. W. Easterby*   **c137** **h–**

HERNANDITA   6 b.m. Hernando (FR) – Dara Dee (Dara Monarch) [2003/4 h–: 18s⁴ 16g⁵ 16g⁴ Mar 25] small, leggy mare: modest handicap hurdler: should stay beyond 2m: acts on heavy going: visored (raced too freely) once: not an easy ride. *Miss E. C. Lavelle*   **h98**

HEROIC (IRE)   8 b.g. War Hero – Happy Patter (Pitpan) [2003/4 c17s³ c24d² c20d⁴ c25d* Dec 13] third foal: brother to winning pointer: dam never ran: fair hurdler/chaser: won maiden chase at Fairyhouse: effective around 2m to 25f: acts on soft ground. *C. F. Swan, Ireland*   **c113** **h–**

HEROICUS (NZ)   7 ch.g. Heroicity (AUS) – Glenford (NZ) (Sackford (USA)) [2003/4 h–: c16g c16fᶠ Sep 14] no form over jumps: headstrong. *F. Kirby*   **c–** **h–**

HERON'S GHYLL (IRE)   7 b.g. Simply Great (FR) – Leisure Centre (IRE) (Tanfirion) [2003/4 F99: F17s 20m⁵ 17d² 21g⁵ 17g* 16s² 17d 20s² 19m* 20d Mar 20] smallish, workmanlike gelding: has reportedly had wind operation: bumper winner: fair novice hurdler: won at Cheltenham (handicap) in December and Taunton in March: stays 2½m: acts on good to firm and soft going. *Miss Venetia Williams*   **h112** **F76**

HER ROYAL HIGHNESS   7 b. or br.m. Rock City – Dutch Princess (Royalty) [2003/4 F16s Dec 26] lengthy mare: well held in bumpers nearly 2 years apart. *P. S. McEntee*   **F–**

HERSOV (IRE)   8 gr.g. Roselier (FR) – Higher Again (IRE) (Strong Gale) [2003/4 c115, h–: 22d* c33d⁴ c24s c33dᵖᵘ Apr 17] rangy gelding: fairly useful form over hurdles, won handicap at Sandown in December: similar form over fences, best effort in handicaps in 2003/4 when fourth to Bear On Board at Cheltenham: stays 33f: acts on soft ground: tried blinkered: sold 40,000 gns Doncaster May Sales. *N. J. Henderson*   **c125** **h125**

HE'S A LEADER (IRE)   5 b.g. Supreme Leader – Raise The Bells (Belfalas) [2003/4 F16d 22sᵖᵘ 24g 19s⁵ Apr 11] €28,000 3-y-o: unfurnished gelding: ninth foal: half-brother to smart hunter Dixon Varner (by Sheer Grit): dam, bumper winner, half-sister to smart 2½m to 3m chaser Raise An Argument and useful staying hurdler Treasure Again: well held in bumper on debut: signs of ability on last of 3 starts over hurdles, not fluent previously. *M. C. Pipe*   **h–** **F–**

HESCONDIDO (FR)   9 gr.g. Dadarissime (FR) – Vahine de Prairie (FR) (Brezzo (FR)) [2003/4 c20g⁵ c20sᵘʳ c20m⁶ c24dᵖᵘ Mar 13] good-topped gelding: useful handicap chaser in 2001/2: no form in 2003/4: blinkered once: poor jumper. *Miss Venetia Williams*   **c– x** **h–**

HE'S MY UNCLE   9 ch.g. Phardante (FR) – Red Dusk (Deep Run) [2003/4 h–: 22m⁵ 20gᵖᵘ May 24] strong gelding: no form. *Mrs J. K. M. Oliver*   **h–**

HESSAC (FR)   9 b.g. Beyssac (FR) – Chic Lilie (FR) (Olmeto) [2003/4 c26g⁵ May 26] winning pointer: fifth in maiden hunter chase at Cartmel. *Ernie Fenwick*   **c79**

HE'S THE BIZ (FR) 5 b.g. Nikos – Irun (FR) (Son of Silver) [2003/4 h72?, F–: 17dᵖᵘ **h90** 20m* 22g³ 24m* 24d⁴ 24gᵖᵘ 22dᵖᵘ Mar 21] good-topped gelding: modest handicap hurdler: won at Worcester in August (amateur novice) and November: stays 3m: acts on good to firm and good to soft ground: sometimes flashes tail. *Nick Williams*

HE'S THE BOSS (IRE) 7 b.g. Supreme Leader – Attykee (IRE) (Le Moss) [2003/4 **h125** F116: 20g* 21sᶠ 21d³ 20s⁵ Feb 14] workmanlike gelding: smart bumper performer: fairly useful form in novice hurdles: won at Ascot in November: third to Inglis Drever in Grade 2 at Warwick: probably went amiss final start, weakening quickly run-in (dismounted after line): will stay beyond 21f: raced on good going or softer. *R. H. Buckler*

HE'S THE GUV'NOR (IRE) 5 b.g. Supreme Leader – Love The Lord (IRE) (Mister **h–** Lord (USA)) [2003/4 F16d F16g F16g⁶ 19s⁴ Apr 4] €62,000 3-y-o: workmanlike geld- **F88** ing: first foal: dam winning hurdler/useful chaser who stayed 25f: seemingly best effort in bumpers when mid-field in Grade 2 at Newbury second start: tailed off in maiden on hurdling debut. *R. H. Buckler*

HETLAND HILL 8 ch.g. Secret Appeal – Mohibbah (USA) (Conquistador Cielo **h–** (USA)) [2003/4 F86: 16mᵖᵘ 17d 19gᵖᵘ Nov 20] travelled comfortably long way both starts in bumpers: no form in 3 novice hurdles. *L. Lungo*

HEVER GOLF GLORY 10 b.g. Efisio – Zaius (Artaius (USA)) [2003/4 h–: 16m⁴ **h60** 16m 19g 17m⁶ 22m⁴ 21mᵖᵘ Jul 18] sturdy gelding: poor maiden hurdler: best at 2m: acts on good to firm going. *C. N. Kellett*

HEVERGOLF PRINCESS (IRE) 9 ch.m. Petardia – High Profile (High Top) **h–** [2003/4 17g 17g 17dᵖᵘ Apr 10] half-sister to winning 2m hurdler Kindergarten Boy (by Mon Tresor): 7f winner at 3 yrs, no show on Flat in 1999: no form over hurdles. *B. Bousfield*

HEY BOY (IRE) 5 b.g. Courtship – Make Me An Island (Creative Plan (USA)) **F87** [2003/4 F16s³ Mar 20] €5,000 3-y-o, 26,000 4-y-o: fourth foal: dam won over hurdles and fences up to 2½m in Ireland: won last of 3 starts in maiden Irish points in 2003: third to Something Gold in bumper at Ascot, looking a stayer. *C. J. Mann*

HEYNESTOWN PRIDE (IRE) 7 ch.m. Zaffaran (USA) – Mayobridge (Our Mir- **h72** age) [2003/4 h–, F–: 21s 16m² 16vᵖᵘ Jan 21] form over hurdles only when second in mares novice at Hexham in June: seems best around 2m with emphasis on speed: free-going sort. *N. G. Richards*

HEY REF (IRE) 7 b.g. King's Ride – Jeanarie (Reformed Character) [2003/4 h114p, **c107** F101: c16s³ c16vᵘʳ 20g⁶ 20dᵖᵘ Apr 10] good-bodied gelding: winning hurdler: third in **h105** maiden at Uttoxeter on completed start over fences: probably stayed 2½m: acted on soft going: dead. *Jonjo O'Neill*

HICKERTHRIFTCASTLE 5 ch.g. Carlingford Castle – Sun Sprite (Morston (FR)) **h–** [2003/4 F16g 20g 17g Apr 3] first foal: dam unraced half-sister to useful 2m hurdler **F–** Faraway Lad: little show in bumper or over hurdles. *C. C. Bealby*

HICKLETON CLUB 6 b.g. Aragon – Honest Opinion (Free State) [2003/4 F–: **h–** F16m F16d 16f 16g Mar 12] no form: won't stay 2m. *R. M. Clark* **F–**

HICKLETON DREAM 7 b.m. Rambo Dancer (CAN) – Elegant Approach (Prince **h76** Ragusa) [2003/4 16m³ 19rᵀ³ Nov 22] poor maiden on Flat (stays 1¾m): similar form when third both starts over hurdles: sold 1,000 gns Doncaster January Sales. *G. A. Swinbank*

HI CLOY (IRE) 7 b.g. Be My Native (USA) – Thomastown Girl (Tekoah) [2003/4 **c152** h120+, F106: 20d⁵ c20d² c20d⁶ c16d² c20s* c24d³ c19s³ c21d³ c21g* c24d* c20d* **h120** Apr 13]

'There are sure to be races to be won with him and he looks one to follow.' So said *Timeform Perspective* after Hi Cloy had finished second on his debut over fences in a maiden chase at Navan in November. Another six runs and eleven weeks later and anyone who kept faith with him was rather worse off than when they started: Hi Cloy won just one of his first seven races over fences, the Grade 2 Guinness Greenmount Novices' Chase at Limerick in December when he justified short-priced favouritism in a substandard six-runner field, ridden out after idling to beat Stashedaway by a length and a half. High Cloy didn't always produce as much as seemed likely in a finish, though he was highly tried on occasions. Three runs came in more strongly-contested Grade 1 novices and he acquitted himself well in two of them (his chance lost when he was hampered in the other), finishing third to Pizarro at Leopardstown in both the William Neville, two days after Limerick, and

the Dr P. J. Moriarty, in early-February on his seventh start. Hi Cloy was beaten a head and two and a half lengths in the latter and would have finished closer had he not been brought to a stop as the runner-up Mossy Green hung into him near the line. It was, though, Hi Cloy's best effort to that point and he hardly looked back after it, winning his next three races and running an excellent race in defeat at Punchestown shortly after the end of the British season. Hi Cloy's progress was such that he ended the campaign rated the best novice chaser trained in Ireland.

The first two victories of Hi Cloy's hat-trick came in races in small fields. He was entitled to win on form and started odds on each time, scoring impressively both at Leopardstown and in a listed event at Limerick. Back in Grade 1 company, the Powers Gold Cup at Fairyhouse promised to be an altogether more demanding task. The Powers Gold Cup can sometimes be a weak race for a supposed championship event but the charge certainly couldn't be levelled at the latest renewal, three of the five others to line up having won a race of similar standing and another looking as if he would have done so but for falling on his previous start. The favourite Kicking King had won the Arkle at Leopardstown as well as finishing second in the Cheltenham version, Nil Desperandum had won the Drinmore over course and distance back in November but had been off through injury since, while Central House landed the Denny Gold Medal at Leopardstown. Mossy Green, still in front when falling two out in the Royal & SunAlliance Chase, had twice finished in front of Hi Cloy and, along with the others mentioned, figured ahead of him in the betting. In truth, Hi Cloy's previous form suggested he had the fifth-best chance in the race. With Mossy Green out of the contest before it began in earnest, a duel developed in the straight between Hi Cloy and Kicking King. Both had travelled strongly held up and Kicking King went on two out. But Hi Cloy was waiting to pounce and, even though he jumped the last around a length down and less well than the leader, Hi Cloy was able to find a good turn of foot to go past Kicking King close home, winning by half a length. The pair finished six lengths clear of Nil Desperandum and there's little reason to think the runner-up wasn't somewhere close to his best.

Hi Cloy's next engagement was due to be the following day, at the inaugural bloodstock sale held at Cheltenham's April meeting, and he'd surely have been the highest-priced lot, but connections chose not to send him. Instead, Hi Cloy was aimed at Punchestown. Rather than drop back to two miles for the Grade 1 Swordlestown Cup and take on Kicking King again, connections opted for the Grade 3 Ellier Developments Novices' Chase over Hi Cloy's optimum trip of two and a half miles. This was a lower graded contest and only four went to post, but they included a formidable opponent in the shape of Lord Sam, who in addition was receiving 2 lb. Although upsides on the bridle at the last, Hi Cloy once more found less than seemed likely, admittedly after being bumped, and went down by a neck. Judged on his efforts in the spring, as he is, it's easy to think that Hi Cloy might have won more of his races. He sometimes looked to be set plenty to do, but his better performances suggest such tactics are necessary. In that regard, he was well handled by Timmy Murphy, who presumably won't be available to ride him in 2004/5. His trainer suggested, after the Fairyhouse win when a trip to the sales seemed likely, that Hi Cloy would be a good sort for well-run handicaps. A race such as the Paddy Power Gold Cup at Cheltenham could well be a good starting point in the autumn. Although most of Hi Cloy's appearances came in single-figure fields, his jumping looks good enough to stand the demands of such a contest.

Hi Cloy (IRE) (b.g. 1997)	Be My Native (USA) (br 1979)	Our Native (b or br 1970)	Exclusive Native / Our Jackie
		Witchy Woman (ch 1972)	Strate Stuff / Witchy Norma
	Thomastown Girl (b 1980)	Tekoah (br 1970)	Great White Way / Tatelka
		Wrong Decision (br 1969)	No Argument / Tourina

Mrs S. McCloy's "Hi Cloy"

Hi Cloy, already the winner of a point, won over hurdles and showed apparently useful form when fourth to Solerina and Hardy Eustace in a Grade 1 novice in 2002/3 but, bearing in mind his stable and his appearance—he's rangy and well made—he always seemed likely to be rather better over fences. Hi Cloy is the tenth foal and easily the best performer out of the bumper winner Thomastown Girl, though she has bred four other winners, including the fairly useful two-mile hurdler and winning chaser Doran's Town Lad (by Tumble Gold). Hi Cloy isn't yet as good as the pick of his grandam Wrong Decision's offspring, as she produced the 1982 Champion Hurdle winner For Auction, who also had enough stamina to finish third in the Grande Course de Haies d'Auteuil. Hi Cloy, on the other hand, is likely to prove best short of three miles. He has been raced only on ground ranging from good to very soft. *M. Hourigan, Ireland*

HIDDEN BOUNTY (IRE) 8 b.g. Generous (IRE) – Sought Out (IRE) (Rainbow Quest (USA)) [2003/4 20m³ 24g* 22s* 23sᶠ 20d* 25gᵖᵘ Mar 16] lengthy, rather leggy gelding: progressive handicap hurdler: won at Ayr and Haydock in November and Newcastle (beat Undeniable a neck) in February: will prove best at 3m+: acts on soft and good to firm going: reportedly had irregular heartbeat final outing: patiently ridden: carries head awkwardly under pressure but seems genuine. *Mrs M. Reveley* **h124**

HIDDEN DEPTH 5 b.g. Classic Cliche (IRE) – Rochestown Lass (Deep Run) [2003/4 F16v F16s Jan 16] lengthy, very unfurnished gelding: fourth foal: half-brother to winning hurdler/chaser Madam Mosso (by Le Moss), stays 3¼m: dam fair staying hurdler: tailed off in 2 bumpers. *P. T. Dalton* **F–**

HIDDEN EXIT 8 b.m. Landyap (USA) – Queen of The Nile (Hittite Glory) [2003/4 h–, F–: 17g 17g 20m² 20m Aug 16] leggy mare: bad maiden hurdler: stays 2½m: sold £1,600 Ascot October Sales. *Mrs L. Williamson* **h52**

HIDDEN PEARL (IRE) 8 b.g. Posen (USA) – Cockney Miss (Camden Town) [2003/4 h60: c21m⁶ c16g⁴ c20mᵖᵘ c25g⁵ Mar 10] big gelding: poor maiden hurdler/chaser: left J. Supple after third start: stays 23f: acts on soft going: has worn cheekpieces, looked reluctant in blinkers. *R. A. Mills* **c–** **h–**

HIDDEN SMILE (USA) 7 b.m. Twilight Agenda (USA) – Smooth Edge (USA) (Meadowlake (USA)) [2003/4 h–: 16m⁴ 16g⁶ 16m² 17m 16m² 17g Apr 3] tall mare: poor maiden hurdler: raced around 2m: yet to race on extremes of going. *F. Jordan* **h77**

HIDDEN VALLEY 12 b.g. St Columbus – Leven Valley (Ragstone) [2003/4 c107, h–: c21d² c21g³ Aug 12] leggy gelding: winning hurdler: fair handicap chaser: stays 2¾m: acts on good to firm going, best efforts on soft/heavy: has won 4 times at Exeter. *J. D. Frost* **c107** **h–**

HIERS DE BROUAGE (FR) 9 b.g. Neustrien (FR) – Thalandrezienne (FR) (Le Correzien (FR)) [2003/4 c105, h–: c20g³ c19d³ c21d² c24sᵖᵘ c21m³ c21m³ c24m⁴ᵈ Apr 13] tall, rangy gelding: fair handicap chaser: barely stays 3m: acts on soft and good to firm going: wore cheekpieces last 3 appearances. *J. G. Portman* **c105** **h–**

HI FI 6 b.g. Homo Sapien – Baroness Orkzy (Baron Blakeney) [2003/4 h81, F81: 20d³ 19d² 20s 19gᶠ 17s* 17s* 20d⁶ Apr 12] leggy gelding: fair hurdler: won handicaps at Exeter in March and April (conditional jockeys): stays 2½m: acts on soft ground. *Ian Williams* **h109**

HIGH ACTION (USA) 4 ch.g. Theatrical – Secret Imperatrice (USA) (Secretariat (USA)) [2003/4 16s 16d 16s Jan 14] sturdy gelding: useful on Flat (likely to stay 1¾m, raced on good going or firmer), sold out of Sir Michael Stoute's stable 52,000 gns Newmarket Autumn Sales: well held in juvenile hurdles, all on going softer than good. *Ian Williams* **h72**

HIGHBANK 12 b.g. Puissance – Highland Daisy (He Loves Me) [2003/4 c–§, h87§: 16g 19g Jun 11] workmanlike gelding: winning chaser/hurdler: well held in 2 selling handicap hurdles in 2003/4: stays 21f: acts on firm and soft going: effective with or without blinkers, below form when visored: ungenuine. *Mrs M. Reveley* **c– §** **h– §**

HIGH BIRD HUMPHREY 5 ch.g. Nomadic Way (USA) – Miss Kewmill (Billion (USA)) [2003/4 F18s⁶ F17d Mar 27] fifth foal: half-brother to winning 3m chaser Kingsthorpe and fair pointer Rising Sap (both by Brotherly): dam modest novice hurdler: mid-field in 2 bumpers. *P. R. Webber* **F81**

HIGH CLASS PET   4 b.f. Petong – What A Pet (Mummy's Pet) [2003/4 F16v F16g   **F–**
Feb 18] sister to 3 winners, notably smart performer up to 1m Petardia, and half-sister to
winner in France: dam French 1m winner: no sign of ability in 2 bumpers. *F. P. Murtagh*

HIGH COTTON (IRE)   9 gr.g. Ala Hounak – Planalife (Beau Charmeur (FR))   **c112 §**
[2003/4 c119§, h–: c22g³ c24gᵖᵘ c25v⁴ c28d² c20d² c25dᶠ Apr 17] useful-looking geld-   **h–**
ing: fair maiden chaser: left D. Elsworth after second start: suited by 3m+: raced on good
going or softer (acts on heavy): tried blinkered: ungenuine. *Mrs M. Reveley*

HIGHCROFT BOY   9 gr.g. Silver Owl – Caroline Ranger (Pony Express) [2003/4   **c–**
c89, h102: c25mᵖᵘ c21gᵖᵘ Jun 3] winning hurdler: runner-up in novice on chasing debut: **h–**
no form in 2003/4, including in points: should stay at least 3m: acts on firm going.
P. J. Hobbs

HIGH DIVA   5 b.m. Piccolo – Gifted (Shareef Dancer (USA)) [2003/4 17sᵖᵘ Dec 16]   **h–**
half-sister to useful 2m hurdler Abbot (by Bishop of Cashel): poor maiden on Flat (stays
1¼m): failed to settle in novice on hurdling debut: joined J. Best. *B. R. Johnson*

HIGH DRAMA   7 b.g. In The Wings – Maestrale (Top Ville) [2003/4 h104: 22g*   **h102**
24mᵖᵘ May 15] fair hurdler: won handicap at Exeter very early in season: stays 2¾m: acts
on firm going. *P. Bowen*

HIGHEST OFFER   5 b.g. Puissance – Scoffera (Scottish Reel) [2003/4 F16g F16s   **F–**
F17d Apr 18] 800 4-y-o: third foal: half-brother to 2003 2-y-o 5f winner Are You There
(by Presidium): dam 2m hurdle winner: signs of only a little ability in 3 bumpers.
W. S. Coltherd

HIGH EXPECTATIONS (IRE)   9 ch.g. Over The River (FR) – Andy's Fancy (IRE)   **c83**
(Andretti) [2003/4 c83: c25dᵖᵘ c19g⁴ c25g² c25gᵖᵘ c25gᵖᵘ c20dᵖᵘ Apr 18] poor chaser:
stays 25f: yet to race on extremes of going. *J. S. Haldane*

HIGHFIELD'S CLOVER   5 b.g. Petoski – Dipped In Clover (Golden Dipper)   **c–**
[2003/4 c21gᵖᵘ Mar 3] third foal: half-brother to winning pointer by Teenoso: dam
winning pointer: not fluent in maiden hunter chase on debut: runner-up in point following
month. *Mrs Jenny Gordon*

HIGH JINKS   9 b.g. High Estate – Waffling (Lomond (USA)) [2003/4 26s⁴ Jan 7]   **h74**
poor on Flat (stays 2m): second start over hurdles when fourth in novice claimer at
Hereford, possibly finding stamina stretched. *R. N. Bevis*

HIGHLAND BRIG   8 b.g. Homo Sapien – Birniebrig (New Brig) [2003/4 c25g⁵ Apr   **c71**
5] fair pointer, twice runner-up in March: last of 5 finishers in novice at Kelso on hunter
chase debut, not fluent. *Tim Butt*

HIGHLAND ISLAND   8 b.m. Jupiter Island – Close Call (Nearly A Hand) [2003/4   **c–**
27d³ c16d 27sᵖᵘ c27sᵖᵘ c24gᵖᵘ Feb 18] second foal: dam never ran: little sign of ability   **h76 ?**
outside points: tongue tied. *Mrs R. L. Elliot*

HIGHLAND REEL   7 ch.g. Selkirk (USA) – Taj Victory (Final Straw) [2003/4 17d⁴   **h85**
17s Dec 29] fairly useful but unreliable on Flat (stays 1¼m): poor form in 2 novice
hurdles, jumped badly second time. *D. R. C. Elsworth*

HIGHLAND ROSE (IRE)   8 b.m. Roselier (FR) – Carrick Grinder (Sheer Grit)   **c–**
[2003/4 c–, h91: 20m⁵ 16v² Aug 26] workmanlike mare: poor hurdler: pulled up in   **h79**
novice chase: successful 3 times in points in 2004: stays at least 2½m: acts on heavy
going. *Ms A. E. Embiricos*

HIGHLAND TRACKER (IRE)   9 ch.g. Indian Ridge – Track Twenty Nine (IRE)   **c–**
(Standaan (FR)) [2003/4 21d* 24g⁶ Nov 30] close-coupled gelding: modest hurdler/   **h87**
chaser: left F. Murphy and off nearly 2½ years, won handicap hurdle at Sedgefield in
October: below form month later: stays 2¾m: acts on soft and good to firm going.
Miss M. E. Rowland

HIGH PADDY   5 b.g. Master Willie – Ivy Edith (Blakeney) [2003/4 h90: 16d⁴ 16s³   **h89**
Mar 15] lengthy, rather sparely-made gelding: modest form in 3 starts over hurdles:
should stay 2½m. *R. Ingram*

HIGH POWERED (GER)   5 b.m. So Factual (USA) – High Habit (Slip Anchor)   **h–**
[2003/4 20gᵖᵘ May 18] maiden on Flat, well held in 2003: pulled hard on hurdling debut.
J. A. Moore

HIGH PRIESTESS (IRE)   5 b.m. Priolo (USA) – Boss Lady (IRE) (Last Tycoon)   **h110 p**
[2003/4 16d³ Dec 27] first foal: dam fairly useful on Flat up to 10.5f: generally progressive on Flat, winning at 1½m/1¾m: encouraging third to Waterlily in maiden at
Leopardstown on hurdling debut: should improve. *M. J. P. O'Brien, Ireland*

HIGH RANK 5 b.g. Emperor Jones (USA) – Hotel Street (USA) (Alleged (USA)) [2003/4 F16g 16g⁴ 21g² 19s 20s 20s⁶ 22d³ 21d² 22d⁵ Mar 21] close-coupled gelding: half-brother to several winners, including smart 2m to 3¼m hurdler Generosa (by Generous): dam lightly-raced 1½m winner: modest form on first of 3 starts in Irish bumpers: sold out of R. Osborne's stable 10,000 gns Doncaster May Sales after reappearance: fair hurdler: improved effort when second of 22 to Storm Prince in handicap at Warwick eighth outing: stays 21f: tongue tied last 3 starts. *J. Mackie* **h105 F–**

HIGH REEF (FR) 6 b.m. Shareef Dancer (USA) – Debate (High Line) [2003/4 16f* 16s² 16m³ Aug 18] successful 3 times up to 10.5f on Flat in French Provinces for F. Rohaut: fair form over hurdles: won maiden at Sligo in July: better form when placed in minor event at Galway and novice at Roscommon: will prove best at sharp 2m. *C. F. Swan, Ireland* **h112**

HIGH ROCKER 6 b.g. First Trump – Wild Abandon (USA) (Graustark) [2003/4 F91: 16mᵖᵘ 22mᵖᵘ 19m 22g 26mᵖᵘ Jul 18] compact gelding: no form over hurdles: tried tongue tied. *M. C. Pipe* **h–**

HIGH SUN 8 b.g. High Estate – Clyde Goddess (IRE) (Scottish Reel) [2003/4 h–: 24sᶠ 19g 20mᵖᵘ May 26] angular gelding: no form over hurdles. *Mrs A. M. Thorpe* **h–**

HIGH TECH MADE (FR) 4 br.g. Nononito (FR) – Home Made (FR) (Appiani II) [2003/4 F16s* Jan 11] half-brother to several winners, including useful chaser up to 25f Gue Made (by Guenole): dam, won from 7f (at 2 yrs) to 2½m on Flat, from family of good French stayers Pompon Rouge and Le Chouan: won 4-y-o maiden bumper at Leopardstown on debut by 1½ lengths from Pixie Dust: bred to stay at least 2½m. *E. U. Hales, Ireland* **F103**

HIGH TOWER 7 b.g. Lycius (USA) – Sedova (USA) (Nijinsky (CAN)) [2003/4 18g c20d⁴ 16g⁵ 16s⁵ c16dᶠ Jan 19] close-coupled gelding: brother to fairly useful chaser up to 25f Dovaly: fair on Flat (stayed 1¾m): modest on balance over hurdles: fourth in maiden at Kilbeggan on chasing debut: sold out of M. O'Brien's stable 7,000 gns Doncaster August Sales: likely to have stayed beyond 2½m: acted on heavy going: tried blinkered/tongue tied: dead. *A. M. Hales* **c98 h88**

HIGHWAY ROBBERY 7 b.g. Un Desperado (FR) – Drivers Bureau (Proverb) [2003/4 h–, F85: 16m⁵ 22d⁶ 22d⁶ c25d⁵ 24d 21d⁶ c24gᶠ Apr 18] modest form over hurdles/fences: sold out of Miss E. Lavelle's stable 8,500 gns Doncaster January Sales: little show in 3 subsequent starts: bred to be suited by further than 2m: yet to race on extremes of going. *Mrs J. Candlish* **c89 h94**

HI LILY 8 b.m. Jupiter Island – By Line (High Line) [2003/4 c81, h85: c21m³ 16d 18g Apr 22] tall mare: poor hurdler/chaser: sold out of C. Bealby's stable 8,000 gns Doncaster May Sales after reappearance: stays 21f: unraced on firm going, acts on any other. *Miss Z. C. Davison* **c79 h–**

HILL CHARM 6 ch.m. Minster Son – Snarry Hill (Vitiges (FR)) [2003/4 h–, F–: 17d 19g 25s Jan 6] little sign of ability. *Mrs S. J. Smith* **h–**

HILL FARM CLASSIC 4 ch.g. Meqdaam (USA) – Wing of Freedom (Troy) [2003/4 17dᵖᵘ 16gᵖᵘ Dec 18] no form on Flat or in juvenile hurdles: tried blinkered. *M. Wellings* **h–**

HILL FORTS HENRY 6 ch.g. Karinga Bay – Maggie Tee (Lepanto (GER)) [2003/4 h–, F67: 22d⁶ 24m 22f² 22g² 22m⁵ Dec 4] poor maiden hurdler: should stay 3m: acts on firm going. *J. W. Mullins* **h79**

HILL PORT (IRE) 7 ch.g. Port Lucaya – Minstrelsdaughter (Black Minstrel) [2003/4 24d 20d 16d³ 20m⁶ 27g* 16s³ Feb 8] leggy gelding: twice-raced chaser: fair hurdler nowadays: won handicap at Sedgefield in July: effective at 2m to 27f: acts on heavy going: usually blinkered prior to 2003/4: ungenuine. *J. J. Lambe, Ireland* **c– § h114 §**

HILLS OF RAKAPOSHI 5 ch.m. Rakaposhi King – Hilly Path (Brave Invader (USA)) [2003/4 F16d F16s⁶ F16d 20dᶠ 18g 20dᶠ Apr 22] medium-sized mare: seventh foal: half-sister to fair staying hurdler Bridal Path (by Teenoso): dam poor novice hurdler: no form in bumpers or novice hurdles. *R. Fielder* **h– F–**

HILLS OF VIEW 6 b.g. Sea Raven (IRE) – Hardwick Sun (Dieu Soleil) [2003/4 F16v 20d 16d Apr 23] big, lengthy gelding: half-brother to several winners, including fairly useful staying hurdler/chaser Portonia (by Ascertain): dam winning hurdler: no form in bumper or 2 starts over hurdles. *J. M. Jefferson* **h– F–**

HILLTIME (IRE) 4 b.g. Danetime (IRE) – Ceannanas (IRE) (Magical Wonder (USA)) [2003/4 17g* 17g² 16g* Sep 6] angular gelding: modest maiden at 2 yrs: won **h102**

juvenile hurdles at Sedgefield in August and Stratford in September, well held by Atahuelpa when left clear last at latter and all out to hold on: will prove best at 2m with emphasis on speed. *J. J. Quinn*

HILLTOP HARRY (IRE) 7 b.g. Commanche Run – Whats In A Name (IRE) (Le Moss) [2003/4 h84, F82: 21d Apr 12] sturdy gelding: won maiden Irish point in 2002: poor form in 3 starts over hurdles, dismounted after line on return from 13 months off. *Lady Connell*　**h–**

HILL TRACK 10 b.g. Royal Match – Win Green Hill (National Trust) [2003/4 c22dpu 20s c21vpu 17gpu 17d* c21gpu Apr 12] good-topped gelding: lightly raced: left C. Teague after third start: 100/1, first form when winning conditional jockeys selling handicap hurdle at Sedgefield in March: pulled up all 3 starts over fences: wore cheekpieces/tongue strap fourth outing. *R. Johnson*　**c–**　**h61 +**

HILL TRAIL 9 ch.g. Royal Match – Win Green Hill (National Trust) [2003/4 c19dpu Mar 22] sturdy gelding: won maiden point in 2003: lightly raced and no form otherwise: tried tongue tied. *R. K. Bliss*　**c–**　**h–**

HIMALAYAN HEIGHTS 9 ch.g. North Col – Chestertons Choice (Country Retreat) [2003/4 c20dpu May 16] poor maiden pointer. *Mrs J. Marles*　**c–**

HIM OF DISTINCTION 5 br.g. Rainbow Quest (USA) – Air of Distinction (IRE) (Distinctly North (USA)) [2003/4 17s6 21d3 Mar 28] compact gelding: fairly useful on Flat (barely stays 1½m), lightly raced, for J. Dunlop: better effort over hurdles when sixth in steadily-run novice at Taunton: will prove best around 2m. *R. T. Phillips*　**h87**

HINT OF MAGIC 7 b.g. Magic Ring (IRE) – Thames Glow (Kalaglow) [2003/4 h–: 16m Jun 18] good-topped gelding: no form in selling hurdles. *H. W. Lavis*　**h–**

HI PAL (IRE) 7 b.g. Phardante (FR) – Bright Princess (IRE) (Deep Run) [2003/4 c24spu Mar 19] third foal: dam ran once in bumper: won last of 4 starts in maiden Irish points in 2002: bought 8,500 gns Doncaster November (2002) Sales: no show in maiden chase. *C. C. Bealby*　**c–**

HIP POCKET (IRE) 8 b.g. Ela-Mana-Mou – Ebony And Ivory (IRE) (Bob Back (USA)) [2003/4 h114: 16d5 20s5 24d4 c24m* Oct 8] close-coupled gelding: fair hurdler: won maiden at Downpatrick on chasing debut: stays 3m: acts on soft and good to firm going: tried blinkered: sold 15,000 gns Doncaster October Sales. *D. K. Weld, Ireland*　**c116**　**h111**

HIRAPOUR (IRE) 8 b.g. Kahyasi – Himaya (IRE) (Mouktar) [2003/4 h130: 20d* 22g* 19m* 19m2 20m* Apr 16] workmanlike gelding: useful hurdler: successful last 5 starts in Britain, including in novice at Aintree and 3-runner intermediate at Kelso in May: left I. Williams, won 2 of 3 outings in USA, at Pine Mountain in November and Grade 1 event at Keeneland in April: stays 2¾m: acts on good to firm and good to soft going. *P. D. Fout, USA*　**h130**

HIRAYNA 5 b.m. Doyoun – Himaya (IRE) (Mouktar) [2003/4 F–: F16g* F17m2 F16g4 16m4 Oct 11] leggy mare: fair form in bumpers, won at Perth in July: not fluent and well beaten on hurdling debut: has raced freely. *W. M. Brisbourne*　**h–**　**F86**

HIRED GUN (IRE) 5 b.g. Needle Gun (IRE) – Monahullen Rose (IRE) (Fayruz) [2003/4 F14d F17g Apr 10] first foal: dam never ran: well beaten in 2 bumpers. *V. R. A. Dartnall*　**F–**

HIRT LODGE 13 ch.g. Jumbo Hirt (USA) – Holly Lodge (Rubor) [2003/4 h90: 26gpu c16d Dec 17] winning hurdler: well beaten on chasing debut: tried in cheekpieces. *J. E. Dixon*　**c–**　**h–**

HI RUDOLF 9 b.g. Ballet Royal (USA) – Hi Darlin' (Prince de Galles) [2003/4 c86, h–: c25dpu c24g3 c18g4 Apr 22] small gelding: poor chaser/maiden hurdler: stays 25f: acts on soft and good to firm going. *H. J. Manners*　**c80**　**h–**

HIRVINE (FR) 6 ch.g. Snurge – Guadanella (FR) (Guadanini (FR)) [2003/4 h80: 16d* 17s* 22v* 25dur 24d* Feb 12] good-topped gelding: modest maiden on Flat (stays 2m): unbeaten in 4 completed outings over hurdles in 2003/4, winning novices at Hexham and Sedgefield prior to being sold out of T. Tate's stable 14,000 gns Doncaster October Sales, and handicaps after at Folkestone and Kempton: fairly useful form when beating Willie John Daly 2½ lengths in 16-runner event at last-named: will stay beyond 3m: raced on going softer than good over hurdles (acts on heavy): open to further improvement granted a sufficient test of stamina, could also do well over fences. *P. Bowen*　**h123 p**

Martell Cognac Somerfield Handicap Hurdle, Aintree—
a chance ride for Joe Tizzard as His Nibs records his third win of 2003/4

HISAR (IRE) 11 br.g. Doyoun – Himaya (IRE) (Mouktar) [2003/4 c–, h–: c16m c16m^{pu} c16g^5 c16g c17g^{pu} c17g^4 c18f^2 c20f^3 c19m^{pu} c20m^5 c17m^4 c16s^5 c16m^{ur} c16s^6 Dec 26] leggy gelding: one-time fairly useful handicap chaser, only poor nowadays: best around 2m: acts on firm and soft going: tried blinkered: often tongue tied in 2003/4. *P. C. Ritchens* — **c69 h–**

HIS NIBS (IRE) 7 b.g. Alflora (IRE) – Mrs Jennifer (River Knight (FR)) [2003/4 h112: c25d^R 23m* 22g* 25d^4 25d^2 25d^4 23v^2 22m^5 25g^4 24g* Apr 2] medium-sized gelding: useful handicap hurdler: won at Lingfield and Market Rasen in November and Aintree in April, best effort when beating Keepatem 2 lengths in valuable 20-runner event at last-named: stays 25f: acts on good to firm and heavy going: consistent. *Miss Venetia Williams* — **c– h131**

HIS SONG (IRE) 11 ch.g. Accordion – Pampered Finch VII (Damsire Unregistered) [2003/4 c–, h122: 22d 24s^5 21g 20s^5 c24d^{pu} Apr 12] strong gelding: one-time useful chaser/smart hurdler: just fair form over hurdles in 2003/4 (found little second/third outings) and little show back over fences final start: stays 3m: best form on good going or softer (acts on heavy): blinkered once: has had tongue tied. *N. J. Henderson* — **c– h113 d**

HISTORIC (IRE) 8 b.g. Sadler's Wells (USA) – Urjwan (USA) (Seattle Slew (USA)) [2003/4 c19d^{pu} c19d^2 c23v* c24g^5 c24d^4 Apr 12] good-topped gelding: impresses in appearance: smart hurdler in 2001/2: second start over fences (reportedly bled from nose on debut), 1¼ lengths second to Mondial Jack in maiden at Hereford: didn't need to repeat that form to win similar event at Exeter in February and novice at Huntingdon (again jumped soundly, beat Conquer by 5 lengths with something in hand): outclassed in Grade 1 novice at Cheltenham in between: stays 25f: acts on heavy going: tried blinkered: races prominently. *T. R. George* — **c124 h–**

HISTORIC PLACE (USA) 4 b.g. Dynaformer (USA) – Captive Island (Northfields (USA)) [2003/4 F13d^2 F12d^3 F16v* F17d^5 Apr 3] medium-sized gelding: half-brother to several winners, notably very smart staying hurdler Rubhahunish (by Darshaan): dam French 6f and 1m winner: sold unraced out of J. Gosden's stable 5,500 gns Newmarket Autumn (2002) Sales: fairly useful form in bumpers: won at Ascot in January by length from Senor Sedona, hampering runner-up 1f out: around 6 lengths fifth of 15 to Diamond Sal in Grade 2 at Aintree. *G. B. Balding* — **F103**

HIT AND RUN (FR) 9 ch.g. River Mist (USA) – La Dunanerie (FR) (Guadanini (FR)) [2003/4 c114+, h–: c16d^{bd} c16m Apr 15] leggy gelding: one-time smart hurdler: fairly useful over fences: brought down ninth on return from 19-month absence, ran poorly next time: best around 2m: has won on good to firm going, best efforts on good or softer (acts — **c– h–**

on soft): usually blinkered/visored, has won when not: usually forces pace: tends to jump right over fences. *M. C. Pipe*

HITCHHIKER   10 b.g. Picea – Lady Lax (Henbit (USA)) [2003/4 c67x, h–: 21m[pu] May 29] plain gelding: winning hurdler/chaser, retains little ability: tried blinkered: poor jumper. *R. Ford*   **c– x h–**

HI TECH   5 b.g. Polar Falcon (USA) – Just Speculation (IRE) (Ahonoora) [2003/4 h69: 16s[5] 24g[5] 24g[4] 16g Apr 18] smallish, angular gelding: modest maiden hurdler: stays 3m. *Dr P. Pritchard*   **h93**

HIT ROYAL (FR)   9 ch.g. Montorselli – Valse Royale (FR) (Cap Martin (FR)) [2003/4 c106, h–: c20m* c20m[6] c19d[2] c24d[6] Apr 12] workmanlike gelding: fair handicap chaser: won at Huntingdon in September: no form after, let down by jumping next 2 starts: successful at 3m, best form over shorter: acts on good to firm and heavy going. *P. R. Webber*   **c106 x h–**

HIT THE NET (IRE)   7 b. or br.h. Be My Native (USA) – Thetravellinglady (IRE) (Callernish) [2003/4 F104: 16d* 20s* Dec 27] good sort: fairly useful form in bumpers: successful both starts over hurdles, in maiden at Gowran in November and minor event at Limerick (beat Oliverjohn 10 lengths) in December: likely to stay beyond 2½m: will progress again. *T. Stack, Ireland*   **h123 p**

HOBART JUNCTION (IRE)   9 ch.g. Classic Secret (USA) – Art Duo (Artaius (USA)) [2003/4 h67: 17g 22m[6] 21m 22m Jun 29] lengthy gelding: poor hurdler: little form since early-2001/2: stays 19f: acts on firm and good to soft going: tried blinkered. *J. A. T. de Giles*   **h–**

HOBGOBLIN   11 ch.g. Fearless Action (USA) – Swallow This (Town Crier) [2003/4 16m 16g[4] May 15] lightly-raced maiden pointer: showed nothing in 2 starts over hurdles. *H. H. G. Owen*   **h–**

HODGSON'S CHOICE (IRE)   5 b.m. Fourstars Allstar (USA) – Waterland Lady (Strong Gale) [2003/4 F16g[5] 16g[pu] Mar 17] fifth foal: half-sister to winning hunter chaser Huncheon Paddy (by Bob's Return): dam runner-up in Irish bumper from 2 starts: modest form on first of 2 outings in bumpers. *M. J. Ryan*   **h– F79**

HOH INVADER (IRE)   12 b.g. Accordion – Newgate Fairy (Flair Path) [2003/4 c–, h87: 16g May 10] tall, good sort: maiden on Flat: one-time fairly useful hurdler/chaser, very much on downgrade: stays 2½m, at least when conditions aren't testing: acts on firm and soft going: tried blinkered/tongue tied: has found little: sold 2,000 gns Doncaster October Sales. *Mrs A. Duffield*   **c– h–**

HOH TEL (IRE)   10 ch.g. Montelimar (USA) – Party Dancer (Be My Guest (USA)) [2003/4 c84x, h–: c25d[2] May 3] lengthy gelding: fair pointer: better effort in hunters when second in maiden at Hexham: stays 25f: acts on soft and good to firm going: usually wears headgear: has gone in snatches: makes mistakes. *G. F. White*   **c90 x h–**

HOH VISS   4 b.g. Rudimentary (USA) – Now And Forever (IRE) (Kris) [2003/4 16s 18s[2] 16s[3] Feb 19] workmanlike gelding: fair maiden on Flat (stays 11.7f) for S. Kirk: progressive form in juvenile hurdles, made mistakes when 6 lengths third of 7 to Made In Japan at Sandown: will stay beyond 2¼m: well up to winning a race. *C. J. Mann*   **h120**

HOLLAND PARK (IRE)   7 gr.g. Roselier (FR) – Bluebell Avenue (Boreen Beag) [2003/4 h99: 19d* 18s[2] 20s[3] 24s[2] Apr 17] workmanlike gelding: type to make a chaser: progressive over hurdles: won novice at Exeter in January by 2 lengths from Hawk's Landing: upped in trip, fairly useful form when 5 lengths second to Ardashir in 17-runner handicap at Bangor, clear of rest: likely to prove better at 3m than shorter: raced on going softer than good: reliable: may do better still. *Mrs S. D. Williams*   **h121**

HOLLOA AWAY (IRE)   12 b.g. Red Sunset – Lili Bengam (Welsh Saint) [2003/4 c–, h–: 22g[pu] 22m[5] 20m[5] Jul 16] sturdy gelding: bad handicap hurdler: stays 2¾m: acts on soft and good to firm going: tried blinkered. *J. A. T. de Giles*   **c– h57**

HOLLOWS MILL   8 b.g. Rudimentary (USA) – Strawberry Song (Final Straw) [2003/4 h86, F–: 16d[2] 16g[6] 16m[3] 16g[6] 17m 16g[3] 16f[5] 17m[F] 17d[3] 17d[2] 17d[2] 20m* 16s 16d 17d[F] 20v[pu] 17d[4] Apr 18] workmanlike gelding: modest handicap hurdler: won at Musselburgh in December: stays 2½m with emphasis on stamina: acts on firm and good to soft going: patiently ridden: has finished weakly. *F. P. Murtagh*   **h92**

HOLLOWS MIST   6 b.g. Missed Flight – Joyfulness (FR) (Cure The Blues (USA)) [2003/4 F17g[3] 16d[pu] 16v[6] 17s[6] 16g[2] 16g[6] Apr 5] 6,000 5-y-o: fourth foal: dam winning 2m hurdler: third in bumper at Sedgefield on debut: modest form over hurdles: should stay 2½m: tongue tied last 4 outings. *F. P. Murtagh*   **h89 F84**

HOLLY ROSE 5 b.m. Charnwood Forest (IRE) – Divina Luna (Dowsing (USA)) **h–**
[2003/4 16m Aug 25] fair but temperamental on Flat (stays 1¼m), successful twice in
2003: in cheekpieces, well held in maiden on hurdling debut. *D. E. Cantillon*

HOLLYWEST (FR) 4 ch.g. Sillery (USA) – Hollywood Trick (USA) (Caro) [2003/4 **h84**
16f⁵ 16m 16d³ 16m 19g⁴ 17g⁴ 16s³ Apr 11] well held in 2 maidens at 2 yrs, sold out
of R. Beckett's stable 1,800 gns Doncaster August Sales after withdrawn start on intended
2003 reappearance: poor juvenile hurdler on balance: acts on soft going: ran creditably
when blinkered final outing: races prominently. *M. E. Sowersby*

HOLY ORDERS (IRE) 7 b.g. Unblest – Shadowglow (Shaadi (USA)) [2003/4 **h145 §**
h144+: 24g⁴ 21s 20d 24g⁵ 24g⁶ Apr 1] compact gelding: smart on Flat (stays 2m): useful
hurdler on his day: won Grade 1 Ballymore Properties Champion Stayers Hurdle at
Punchestown in May, well-held fourth in stronger renewal year later: seemed to run
creditably over 3m behind Iris's Gift at Cheltenham and Aintree, though never dangerous
both times: stays 3m: has won on heavy, probably suited by less testing ground (acts on
good to firm): blinkered: sometimes takes little interest, and not one to rely on.
W. P. Mullins, Ireland

HOMBRE 9 ch.g. Shernazar – Delray Jet (USA) (Northjet) [2003/4 c76, h–: c22g⁴ **c85**
c20s⁵ c21v⁶ c16s² c16s⁵ Mar 20] leggy gelding: poor handicap chaser: effective at 2m to **h–**
3m: acts on any going: tried blinkered. *M. D. Hammond*

HOME AGAIN (IRE) 10 b.g. Homo Sapien – Texarkana (IRE) (Furry Glen) [2003/4 **c76**
c25m³ c19d^pu Mar 22] fair pointer, won in April: better effort in hunter chases at Hereford
when third of 5 to Minella Storm. *E. W. Morris*

HOMEBRED BUDDY 5 ch.g. Environment Friend – Royal Brush (King of Spain) **h–**
[2003/4 F16d 18v 16d^pu 21d^pu Apr 11] lengthy, rather unfurnished gelding: third foal: **F—**
half-brother to winning 3m hurdler Prince des Galles (by Prince des Coeurs): dam, ran
once on Flat, no form over hurdles: of no account. *G. P. Enright*

HOME JAMES (IRE) 7 b.g. Commanche Run – Take Me Home (Amoristic (USA)) **h114**
[2003/4 h116+: 24d⁶ Dec 17] sturdy gelding: fairly useful hurdler: respectable effort in
competitive handicap at Bangor only outing in 2003/4: probably stays 3m: raced on good
going or softer (acts on heavy). *A. King*

HOMELEIGH MOONCOIN 9 ch.g. Jamesmead – Super Sol (Rolfe (USA)) **h115**
[2003/4 h107: 24d⁴ 22d² 24d^pu 24d^pu 25g Mar 16] angular gelding: fairly useful hurdler: little impact in
handicaps last 2 starts: stays 3¼m: acts on good to soft going. *Mrs L. Wadham*

HOME MADE 6 b.g. Homo Sapien – Inch Maid (Le Moss) [2003/4 F–: 20m⁴ c22m^F3 **c77 x**
c24m² c20d^pu c24d^F c20d² c24m⁴ c24d^pu Mar 25] tall gelding: well held in novice hurdle: **h–**
probably flattered when in frame in steeplechases at Ludlow: let down by jumping
otherwise. *S. A. Brookshaw*

HOMER (IRE) 7 b.g. Sadler's Wells (USA) – Gravieres (FR) (Saint Estephe (FR)) **h–**
[2003/4 h98: 18m^pu 17g⁶ Jun 3] winning hurdler: largely out of form since 2001/2: stays
2½m: acts on soft and good to firm going: tongue tied. *M. C. Pipe*

HOMER WELLS (IRE) 6 b.g. Arctic Cider (USA) – Run And Shine (Deep Run) **h–**
[2003/4 F16d⁴ F16v* F16s² F16d² 16d Apr 8] fourth foal: half-brother to winning 2m **F108**
hurdler Phardante Girl (by Phardante): dam unplaced in varied company: useful form in
bumpers, won at Punchestown in January: best effort when length second of 9 to Forty
Licks at Navan third outing: very disappointing when favourite in maiden at Thurles on
hurdling debut. *W. P. Mullins, Ireland*

HOMME DE FER 12 b.g. Arctic Lord – Florence May (Grange Melody) [2003/4 **c99**
c112, h–: c25m⁴ c21g^F4 c23g³ Mar 12] medium-sized gelding: fair handicap chaser in **h–**
2002/3: sold out of K. Bailey's stable 12,500 gns Doncaster May Sales after reappearance: won points in February and April: better effort in hunters in between when third of
6 to Delgany Royal at Leicester: stays 25f: acts on any going, races mainly on good or
firmer nowadays. *N. M. Bloom*

HONAN (IRE) 5 b.g. College Chapel – Medical Times (IRE) (Auction Ring (USA)) **F103**
[2003/4 F16g F16d⁶ F17g* Apr 10] ex-Irish gelding: fourth foal: half-brother to winner
up to 1m in Italy by Scenic: dam unraced: progressive in bumpers, left J. J. Murphy after
second start: favourite, fairly useful form when winning 16-runner maiden at Newton
Abbot by 3½ lengths from Lord Killeshanra, pair clear: likely to prove best around 2m.
M. C. Pipe

HONEST ENDEAVOUR 5 b.g. Alflora (IRE) – Isabeau (Law Society (USA)) **F68**
[2003/4 F16g⁵ F16g F16g Mar 10] well-made gelding: third foal: dam, fair hurdler,
stayed 3¼m: little impact in bumpers. *J. M. Jefferson*

HONEST YER HONOUR (IRE)   8 b.g. Witness Box (USA) – Castle Duchess **h120** (Abednego) [2003/4 16g⁵ 20d² 18d* 19sᶠ 20d⁴ 20d³ Apr 12] sturdy gelding: fairly useful bumper winner: has progressed to similar level over hurdles, impressive when winning handicap at Leopardstown in December: good fourth to Kadoun in similar event at Fairyhouse: stays 2½m: acts on soft going. *R. J. Osborne, Ireland*

HONEYBOURNE   5 b.m. Sri Pekan (USA) – Peetsie (IRE) (Fairy King (USA)) **F—** [2003/4 F16m Jun 1] first foal: dam, fair form in bumpers, half-sister to smart hurdler Her Honour, effective at 2m and stayed well: well held in bumper on debut: modest form when runner-up over 7f on Flat: sold 800 gns Newmarket December Sales. *Mrs Mary Hambro*

HONEY'S GIFT   5 b.m. Terimon – Honeycroft (Crofter (USA)) [2003/4 h79: 16v³ **h86** 16m 18s³ 16s² 20s 16d³ 16s² 16spᵘ Apr 11] modest maiden hurdler: should stay 2½m: acts on heavy ground, probably on good to firm. *G. G. Margarson*

HONEYSTREET (IRE)   4 b.f. Woodborough (USA) – Ring of Kerry (IRE) (Kenmare **h76** (FR)) [2003/4 17m⁴ Nov 20] modest on Flat (stays 1m), successful twice in 2003 for J. S. Moore: took good hold when around 31 lengths fourth to Trouble At Bay in juvenile at Hereford on hurdling debut. *J. D. Frost*

HONNEUR FONTENAIL (FR)   5 ch.g. Tel Quel (FR) – Fontanalia (FR) (Rex **c65** Magna (FR)) [2003/4 h–, F–: 19g⁵ 21vpᵘ c20gᵘʳ c19d c22gˢᵘ c24gˢᵘ Apr 16] angular geld- **h—** ing: jumped poorly when winning weak maiden chase at Fontwell in March: little sign of ability otherwise. *N. J. Hawke*

HO PANG YAU   6 b. or br.g. Pivotal – La Cabrilla (Carwhite) [2003/4 16m 16s 16vpᵘ **h—** 16g 17d Mar 30] close-coupled gelding: half-brother to one-time high-class hurdler/ winning chaser Teaatral (by Saddlers' Hall), stays 3m, and fairly useful hurdler/chaser Mister RM (by Dominion), stayed 2½m: modest 7f winner on Flat at 4 yrs: no form over hurdles, trained first 3 starts by Miss L. Perratt. *Mrs R. L. Elliot*

HOPBINE   8 ch.m. Gildoran – Haraka Sasa (Town And Country) [2003/4 h106: 19g⁴ **h106** 22d* 20v 24d⁶ Mar 7] small, sturdy mare: fair handicap hurdler: easily best effort in 2003/4 when winning at Wincanton in January: should be suited by 3m: acts on heavy going. *J. L. Spearing*

HOPE DIAMOND (IRE)   6 ch.g. Bigstone (IRE) – Mujtahida (IRE) (Mujtahid **c—** (USA)) [2003/4 16d 17m 20m³ 16g 20m⁶ Oct 10] sturdy ex-Irish gelding: first foal: **h—** dam 13f winner: no form, trained until after reappearance by C. McCarthy: tried visored. *Mrs J. Candlish*

HOPEFUL CHANCE (IRE)   7 b.g. Machiavellian (USA) – Don't Rush (USA) **c77** (Alleged (USA)) [2003/4 18g⁵ 18d 16s* 21vpᵘ 16v c16dpᵘ c16d⁴ c21g Apr 12] close- **h85** coupled gelding: modest handicap hurdler: won at Newcastle in December: poor form over fences: stays 2½m: raced on good going or softer (acts on soft): usually tongue tied: inconsistent. *J. R. Turner*

HOPESARISING   5 b.g. Primitive Rising (USA) – Super Brush (IRE) (Brush Aside **h87** (USA)) [2003/4 F16g F16v 16g 19g⁴ 22g⁵ Apr 18] workmanlike gelding: second foal: **F—** dam little sign of ability: well held in bumpers: upped further in trip, modest form when fifth of 14 in novice hurdle at Stratford. *P. R. Johnson*

HOPE SOUND (IRE)   4 b.g. Turtle Island (IRE) – Lucky Pick (Auction Ring (USA)) **h98** [2003/4 16d² 16s³ 16s⁴ 16d 16s⁵ 17g⁴ Apr 12] sturdy gelding: fair form on first of 3 starts in 1¼m maidens on Flat, sold out of J. Noseda's stable 13,000 gns Newmarket Autumn Sales: fair juvenile hurdler: raced around 2m. *B. Ellison*

HOPING   6 b.m. Kris – Shimmering (IRE) (Royal Academy (USA)) [2003/4 20m **h70** 16vpᵘ 16m⁶ 19g⁵ 22m⁴ Aug 30] poor novice hurdler: stays 2¾m: acts on good to firm ground. *A. W. Carroll*

HOPPERTREE   8 b.g. Rock Hopper – Snow Tree (Welsh Pageant) [2003/4 h–: 17dpᵘ **c—** c22sᶠ c24gᵘʳ Feb 11] medium-sized gelding: fair form in bumpers, hinting at tempera- **h—** ment: yet to complete over hurdles or fences. *R. S. Brookhouse*

HORCOTT BAY   4 b.f. Thowra (FR) – Armagnac Messenger (Pony Express) [2003/4 **F—** F17g Apr 10] seventh foal: half-sister to winning 2m hurdler Colnside Bonnie (by Afzal) and 2 winning pointers: dam winning pointer: tailed off in bumper on debut. *M. G. Rimell*

HORIZON (FR)   7 ch.g. Arctic Tern (USA) – Furtchella (FR) (Dancing Spree (USA)) **c—** [2003/4 c–, h–: 17gpᵘ 20m c20vpᵘ c17gpᵘ Apr 12] rather leggy gelding: fair maiden **h—** hurdler/winning chaser in France: no form in Britain. *P. C. Ritchens*

HORNBILL 6 b.g. Sir Harry Lewis (USA) – Tangara (Town Crier) [2003/4 h–: 16d⁶ 19g⁶˙ 22m 16s c20sᵖᵘ c20mᵖᵘ Mar 2] lengthy, workmanlike gelding: bad maiden hurdler: no show both starts over fences (jumped sketchily when tried in blinkers). *Mrs P. Robeson* — **c–** **h56**

HORNER ROCKS (IRE) 8 b.g. Phardante (FR) – Horner Water (IRE) (Over The River (FR)) [2003/4 h109: 20g² c17sᶠ c22d c20d² 20d⁴ c17s* 20s 22s 22d Apr 12] smallish gelding: fair hurdler/chaser: won maiden over fences at Limerick in December: should stay beyond 2½m: acts on heavy going, well held only start on good to firm. *M. Hourigan, Ireland* — **c108** **h111**

HORRIFIED 10 b.g. Deltic (USA) – Parlet (Kinglet) [2003/4 c24dᵖᵘ Mar 15] winning pointer: blinkered, little show in novice hunter at Stratford. *Mrs Janet Ackner* — **c–**

HORS CONCOURS (NZ) 6 b.g. Starjo (NZ) – Lana (NZ) (Tristrams Heritage (NZ)) [2003/4 F16g May 21] tall, unfurnished gelding: tailed off in bumper on debut: showed scarcely more in points. *R. C. Guest* — **F–**

HORS LA LOI (FR) 8 ch.g. Exit To Nowhere (USA) – Kernia (IRE) (Raise A Cup (USA)) [2003/4 h110: 16d² 16m 16g³ 16m* 17m 16g c17m* 16d Apr 8] close-coupled gelding: fairly useful handicap hurdler: better than ever when winning at Stratford in July: jumped better as race progressed when winning 4-runner maiden there on only start over fences: raced around 2m: acts on good to firm and heavy going. *Ian Williams* — **c101 p** **h115**

HORUS (IRE) 9 b.g. Teenoso (USA) – Jennie's First (Idiot's Delight) [2003/4 c138: c24d² c24s* c24sᵘʳ c21d⁶ c24g⁵ c24mᵘʳ c24gᵖᵘ Mar 16] good-topped gelding: useful handicap chaser: won cantorsport.co.uk Silver Cup at Ascot in December by 1½ lengths from Behrajan: running best race after when unseating 2 out in valuable event at Kempton in February won by Marlborough: effective at 2½m to easy 3¼m: acts on soft and good to firm going: pulled too hard when visored: held up. *M. C. Pipe* — **c142**

HOT AIR (IRE) 6 b.g. Air Display (USA) – Lyraisa (Tumble Wind (USA)) [2003/4 F16g F17d F16d⁵ Mar 22] €5,700 4-y-o: lengthy gelding: seventh foal: half-brother to modest chaser Kilbyrne King (by Phardante), stays 2½m: dam once-raced half-sister to smart 2m chaser Abbey Glen: tongue tied, modest form on last of 3 outings in bumpers, allowed to establish clear lead. *J. I. A. Charlton* — **F76**

HOTELIERS' DREAM 6 b.m. Reprimand – Pride of Britain (CAN) (Linkage (USA)) [2003/4 h–: 16g 16g Jul 31] no form: tried visored. *W. S. Kittow* — **h–**

cantorsport.co.uk Silver Cup Handicap Chase, Ascot—
Horus (right) makes his lighter weight tell in a stirring battle with 2002 winner Behrajan

Cantor Mobile Handicap Chase, Ascot—
Hot Shots (left) gains his second course-and-distance win over Upgrade in as many months

HOT GIRL 6 b.m. State Diplomacy (USA) – Hundred Islands (Hotfoot) [2003/4 F17m   F–
F16d[6] F16s Jan 6] plain mare: second foal: dam, poor maiden, stayed 1½m: no form in 3
bumpers. *S. P. Griffiths*

HOT PLUNGE 8 b.g. Bustino – Royal Seal (Privy Seal) [2003/4 c20d c20m[3] c16g[4]   c83
c19s[6] Apr 6] good-topped gelding: winning pointer: best effort in hunters when third to   h–
Phoenix Flyer at Ludlow: stays 2½m: acts on good to firm going. *Mrs J. P. Lomax*

HOT PRODUXION (USA) 5 ch.g. Tabasco Cat (USA) – Princess Harriet (USA)   h103 §
(Mt Livermore (USA)) [2003/4 h100: 20d 20m[3] 20g[2] 22s 20s[2] 21g 21d Mar 14] compact
gelding: fair maiden hurdler: stays 2½m: acts on soft and good to firm going: tried visor-
ed/in cheekpieces: not a fluent jumper or an easy ride (has wandered under pressure).
J. Mackie

HOT SHOTS (FR) 9 b.g. Passing Sale (FR) – Uguette IV (FR) (Chamberlin (FR))   c146
[2003/4 c–, h117: 16g 16m[2] c16m* c16m[2] c16s* c16g[5] 16m* 16s c16m[5] Apr 24] good-   h131
topped gelding: smart handicap chaser: much improved in 2003/4, winning at Ascot in
November (listed event) and December (8 lb out of weights, led near line when beating
Upgrade ½ length): 11 lb out of weights, good fifth to Isio in valuable event at same
course sixth start: took advantage of lower mark over hurdles when beating Blue Americo
impressively by 5 lengths in handicap at Wincanton in March: raced mainly around 2m:
acts on good to firm and heavy going. *M. Pitman*

HOTTERS (IRE) 9 b.g. Be My Native (USA) – Siul Currach (Deep Run) [2003/4   c–
c84, h–: c21s[5] c25s[ur] c32d[pu] 21g[pu] Apr 12] maiden hurdler/chaser, no form in 2003/4:   h–
usually wears headgear: sold 1,300 gns Doncaster May Sales. *J. R. Norton*

HOT WELD 5 b.g. Weld – Deb's Ball (Glenstal (USA)) [2003/4 F99p: 23d[4] 23d[bd]   h97
21d[5] Apr 12] sturdy gelding: runner-up in bumper on debut: best effort over hurdles when
fifth to Gracilis in maiden at Huntingdon, off bridle early and nearest finish: should stay
3m. *Ferdy Murphy*

HOUGHTON BAY (IRE) 9 b.g. Camden Town – Royal Bavard (Le Bavard (FR))   c99
[2003/4 c19d[3] c24d[3] c24d 22d[6] Mar 12] workmanlike gelding: one-time fairly useful   h100
hurdler, missed 2002/3: modest form when placed over fences: stays 3m: acts on good to
firm and heavy going: tried in blinkers/cheekpieces. *J. G. Portman*

HOULIHANS CHOICE 7 ch.g. Norton Challenger – Model Lady (Le Bavard (FR))   h– §
[2003/4 F–: F17s 19s 26s 21s[6] 24s Jan 20] has shown more temperament than ability: F–
tried visored. *B. G. Powell*

HOUSEPARTY (IRE) 6 b. or br.g. Grand Lodge (USA) – Special Display (Welsh   h104
Pageant) [2003/4 h–: 16m[3] 16f[2] 16g 16s[pu] Dec 13] well-made gelding: fairly useful on
Flat at 3 yrs, well held 3 starts since: 11 lengths third to Comply Or Die in novice hurdle
at Chepstow on reappearance: failed to repeat that form, weakening quickly final outing.
J. A. B. Old

HOUSE WARMER (IRE) 5 ch.g. Carroll House – Under The Duvet (IRE) (Brush   h–
Aside (USA)) [2003/4 19s[pu] 24g 20d[pu] Apr 7] €44,000 3-y-o: sturdy gelding: third foal:

dam unraced half-sister to very smart staying hurdler Pleasure Shared: no form in novice hurdles: tried tongue tied. *A. Ennis*

HOWABOYS QUEST (USA) 7 b.g. Quest For Fame – Doctor Black (USA) (Family Doctor (USA)) [2003/4 c–, h66: 22m* 22g⁵ 22m* 20f² c25m² 27d³ 24gᵖᵘ Jan 7] poor handicap hurdler: won seller at Cartmel in July and novice at Market Rasen in August: second start over fences, remote second in weak maiden at Hexham: stays 2¾m: acts on firm and good to soft going, possibly not on heavy: usually wore headgear in 2003/4, ran best race without. *Ferdy Murphy*   **c64 h80**

HOW BURN 11 b.g. Meadowbrook – Kinkell (Netherkelly) [2003/4 c24dᵖᵘ Apr 18] modest pointer: no show in maiden hunter. *Mrs V. S. Jackson*   **c–**

HOWDYDOODY (IRE) 8 b.g. Hawkstone (IRE) – Larry's Law (IRE) (Law Society (USA)) [2003/4 h108: 22g c25d² c25s* c25d Jan 17] lengthy gelding: fair hurdler: favourite, confirmed promise of steeplechasing debut when winning strongly-run handicap at Wincanton in January: blinkered, ran poorly in similar event there 9 days later: will be suited by 3½m+: acts on soft and good to firm going: tongue tied: hard ride, usually soon off bridle. *P. F. Nicholls*   **c118 h100**

HOW GREAT THOU ART 8 b.g. Almoojid – Mamamere (Tres Gate) [2003/4 h68, F83: 22m⁴ 22g² Jun 13] big, lengthy gelding: poor maiden hurdler: stays 2¾m: acts on good to firm going: has raced freely. *R. J. Baker*   **h74**

HOW IS THE LORD (IRE) 8 b.g. Lord Americo – Joaney How (Crash Course) [2003/4 20m² Jul 9] 3,000 4-y-o: second foal: dam bumper winner: won maiden on last of 7 starts in Irish points in 2003: 1¼ lengths second of 17 to Slyboots in novice at Worcester on hurdling debut: likely to stay further. *C. J. Down*   **h87**

HOWLE HILL (IRE) 4 b.g. Ali-Royal (IRE) – Grandeur And Grace (USA) (Septieme Ciel (USA)) [2003/4 16m* 16s² 16d* 17d⁴ 17g⁵ 16g Apr 1] leggy gelding: smart on Flat (stays 1¼m), successful in July: useful juvenile hurdler: won listed event at Wetherby   **h133**

J. E. Brown, R. Benton, R. Devereux, R. A. Lucas' "Howle Hill"

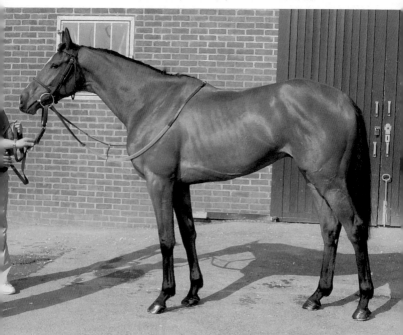

in November and 16-runner novice at Wincanton (odds on, by 3 lengths from Dictum) in January: respectable efforts in graded events at Cheltenham next 2 starts, quickening to lead between last 2 but fading run-in when 7½ lengths fifth of 18 finishers to Made In Japan in Triumph Hurdle: well below best at Aintree 2 weeks later: will prove best with emphasis on speed at 2m: has worn crossed noseband. has sweated. *A. King*

HOW RAN ON (IRE)   13 br.g. Mandalus – Kelly's Bridge (Netherkelly) [2003/4 c76x, h–: c16m⁶ c17g⁴ c1bgᵖᵘ c16g* c16m² c18fᵖᵘ c16m³ c16m⁵ c19m⁶ c16m⁵ Nov 3] poor handicap chaser: won at Newton Abbot in June: stays 21f: acts on any going: tried in cheekpieces/tongue tied: front runner: often let down by jumping. *Mrs L. Williamson*   **c76 x** **h–**

HOWRWENOW (IRE)   6 b.g. Commanche Run – Maythefifth (Hardboy) [2003/4 h101: 24s* c23gᶠ c26m² c24s² 24g² 24d³ Apr 22] good-topped gelding: fairly useful novice hurdler: won at Bangor (idled markedly run-in) in May: best effort when second to impressive Fundamentalist at Kempton: similar form both completed starts in novice chases, beaten 6 lengths by Native Emperor at Warwick on second occasion: best at 3m+: acts on soft and good to firm going. *Miss H. C. Knight*   **c114** **h116**

HOWSHAM LAD   5 b.g. Perpendicular – Sherwood Hope (Eborneezer) [2003/4 F16g Feb 28] smallish gelding: second foal: dam winning pointer: soon struggling in bumper on debut. *G. P. Kelly*   **F–**

HOWYA MATEY (IRE)   7 ch.g. Treasure Hunter – Clonaslee Baby (Konigssee) [2003/4 24m 20m 22m⁵ Jul 13] brother to bumper winner Bradley My Boy and half-brother to several winners, including 1½m performer Classical Influence (by Monksfield): dam never ran: won maiden on completed start in Irish points in 2003, runner-up in Britain in March: no form in novice hurdles: sold 1,000 gns Doncaster May Sales. *M. C. Pipe*   **h–**

HUGE HEART (NZ)   8 b.g. T V Heart Throb (USA) – Christmas Lady (NZ) (Palm Beach (FR)) [2003/4 h–: 20sᵖᵘ c20mᵘʳ Jun 20] stocky gelding: no form over hurdles: left R. Bevis, unseated eighth on chasing debut. *Miss Lucinda V. Russell*   **c–** **h–**

HUGHIE   9 ch.g. Super Sunrise – Clarilaw (White Speck) [2003/4 c21gᵘʳ Mar 12] fourth foal: dam poor maiden pointer: tailed off when unseated eighth in hunter chase at Ayr. *J. S. Haldane*   **c–**

HUGO   8 b.h. Golden Heights – Just Lynn (Legend of France (USA)) [2003/4 17m⁶ May 26] second foal: dam ran twice at 2 yrs: tailed off in novice hurdle on debut. *D. J. Caro*   **h–**

HUGO DE GREZ (FR)   9 b.g. Useful (FR) – Piqua Des Gres (FR) (Waylay) [2003/4 c136, h93+: c25d⁴ c25d⁵ c25gᵖᵘ c24dᵖᵘ Apr 23] close-coupled gelding: winning hurdler: useful handicap chaser in 2002/3: respectable fourth to Cill Churnain at Kelso on reappearance, badly out of sorts after: needs thorough test at 2½m and should stay beyond 3½m: acts well on heavy going: effective tongue tied or not: sound jumper: has won 6 times at Carlisle. *A. Parker*   **c127 d** **h–**

HUGO DE PERRO (FR)   9 b.g. Perrault – Fontaine Aux Faons (FR) (Nadjar (FR)) [2003/4 c–x, h128§: 23m³ 22g* 20mʳᵗʳ 24d⁵ 20sʳᵗʳ 16s c25sᶠ 20d⁶ 20d* 20s⁴ 22gʳᵗʳ Apr 16] leggy gelding: useful hurdler on his day: won handicap at Kelso in May and conditional jockeys claimer at Carlisle in March: winning chaser but usually let down by jumping over fences: stays 3m: acts on heavy and good to firm going: has refused to race 4 times: thoroughly untrustworthy. *P. Monteith*   **c– x** **h131 §**

HUIC HOLLOA (IRE)   8 b.g. Denel (FR) – Buckalgo (IRE) (Buckskin (FR)) [2003/4 h–: 26g 20m⁶ 20m⁶ Jun 29] lengthy gelding: signs of just a little ability over hurdles: sold £5,500 Ascot August Sales: pulled up in 2 points. *J. A. T. de Giles*   **h–**

HUISH (IRE)   13 br.g. Orchestra – Lysandars Lady (Saulingo) [2003/4 h–: 21mᵖᵘ 19gᵖᵘ Jun 11] lightly-raced maiden hurdler. *Mrs N. Macauley*   **h–**

HUKA LODGE (IRE)   7 ch.g. Roselier (FR) – Derrella (Derrylin) [2003/4 h69: 20d⁶ 23dᶠ 25dᵘʳ 24d* 20s² 20dᵖᵘ Apr 23] fair hurdler: won conditional jockeys handicap at Newcastle in February: improved again when second in novice handicap there following month: saddle slipped final outing: stays 3m: raced on going softer than good. *L. Lungo*   **h100**

HULYSSE ROYAL (FR)   9 ch.g. Garde Royale – Ulysse Moriniere (FR) (Mbaiki (FR)) [2003/4 20v 20s 20gᵖᵘ 24s 20m 24d 22] sturdy gelding: useful hurdler at best: off over 2½ years, no form in handicaps in 2003/4, in cheekpieces last 3 outings: stays easy 23f: acts on soft and good to firm going. *O. Sherwood*   **h–**

HUME CASTLE (IRE)   8 b.g. Religiously (USA) – Clyde Avenue (Peacock (FR)) [2003/4 c25g c24g⁵ c22d c24g c25d² c24dʰ c24d c25s* c28vᵖᵘ c21g* c29dᵖᵘ Apr 12] 6,600 4-y-o: useful-looking gelding: tenth foal: half-brother to 4 winners, including   **c128** **h–**

fairly useful staying chaser/winning hurdler Clyde Ranger (by Kemal). dam unraced: winning hurdler: fairly useful handicap chaser: won at Thurles in December, Fairyhouse in January and Leopardstown (listed race, beat Golden Storm by length) in February: very good third to Wotsitooya in valuable event at Punchestown in late-April: should stay beyond 25f: acts on heavy going: has had tongue tied, including at Punchestown. *Mrs J. Harrington, Ireland*

HUMID CLIMATE   4 ch.g. Desert King (IRE) – Pontoon (Zafonic (USA)) [2003/4   **h103** 16s 16g² 16g² 16gᵖᵘ Apr 1] strong, good-bodied gelding: fairly useful 1¼m winner on Flat, sold out of Mrs A. Perrett's stable 14,000 gns Newmarket Autumn Sales: easily best effort over hurdles when second in juvenile at Catterick second start: bled from nose final outing: has had been early to post. *R. A. Fahey*

HUMMING   7 b.g. Bluebird (USA) – Risanda (Kris) [2003/4 h77: 20m⁵ Jul 23] leggy   **h–** gelding: poor form over hurdles, lightly raced: should stay at least 2½m: tried tongue tied. *Miss M. E. Rowland*

HUNCHEON SISS (IRE)   7 b.m. Phardante (FR) – Parsons Term (IRE) (The Parson)   **h–** [2003/4 24dᵖᵘ Mar 11] good-topped ex-Irish mare: second foal: dam, fair hurdler, stayed 3m: won maiden Irish point in 2001: modest maiden hurdler in 2001/2: off 2 years and left I. Ferguson, pulled up quickly after 4 out in novice at Carlisle: stays 2½m: raced on good to soft/soft ground over hurdles: usually tongue tied. *J. Howard Johnson*

HUNTERS CREEK (IRE)   10 b.g. Persian Mews – Creek's Sister (King's Ride)   **c111 x** [2003/4 c111, h95: c20g⁵ 20d³ 19fᶠ c20d⁵ c19g⁵ c19g Mar 6] leggy gelding: modest   **h93** maiden hurdler: fair handicap chaser: would have won at Catterick in November but for falling last: well below form after: stays 2¾m: acts on soft and firm going: often let down by jumping over fences. *Mrs M. Reveley*

HUNTERS TWEED   8 ch.g. Nashwan (USA) – Zorette (USA) (Zilzal (USA)) [2003/4   **c138** c124, h–: c25g⁶ c20d* c20d² c21d* c24mᵖᵘ c20gᵖᵘ c25g Apr 2] leggy gelding: useful   **h–** handicap chaser: won at Wetherby in December and Cheltenham in January, beating Kelrev 8 lengths in Ladbroke Trophy Chase at latter: good second to Be My Manager at Wetherby in between, poor efforts last 3 starts: stays 25f: acts on heavy and good to firm going: usually races prominently: sound jumper. *P. Beaumont*

HUNTERS WOOD (IRE)   9 gr.g. Wood Chanter – Barnmeen Lass (IRE) (Flori-   **c–** ferous) [2003/4 c–, h–: c23gᵖᵘ c25mᵖᵘ Jun 11] lengthy, rather sparely-made gelding: no   **h–** form over hurdles or fences: tried blinkered. *R. J. Baker*

Ladbroke Trophy Chase (Handicap), Cheltenham—northern raider Hunters Tweed (left) outstays Kelrev

HUNTING YUPPIE (IRE) 7 ch.g. Treasure Hunter – Super Yuppie (Belfalas) **h108**
[2003/4 20s⁶ 21d* 20s⁴ Apr 17] robust gelding: will make a chaser: first foal: dam maiden
Irish pointer: in frame twice from 4 starts in maiden points in Ireland in 2003: confirmed
debut promise over hurdles when winning novice at Ludlow in March by 7 lengths from
Jivaty: rather laboured when fourth of 5 finishers to Kadoun in similar event at Bangor:
will be suited by 3m. *N. A. Twiston-Davies*

HURLERS CROSS (IRE) 6 b.g. Jurado (USA) – Maid of Music (IRE) (Orchestra) **c83**
[2003/4 24g⁴ c22f³ 24g⁴ 22s 26g⁵ 26m⁴ c26d* c24dᵖᵘ Mar 28] first foal: dam unraced, out **h72**
of good-class staying chaser Maid of Money: won second of 2 starts in Irish points in
2003: bought 28,000 gns Doncaster May Sales: left J. O'Neill after second outing: poor
maiden hurdler: easily best effort over fences when winning novice handicap at Plumpton
in March, left in front 3 out: stays 3¼m: tried blinkered. *M. Appleby*

HURRICANE BAY 8 ch.g. Karinga Bay – Clodaigh Gale (Strong Gale) [2003/4 c–, **c82**
h76: c24m⁴ c25g* c26m⁴ c25m⁴ c23g² c23m c25m⁵ 25f² 20m⁴ c28gᵖᵘ c25g⁴ Nov 19] **h71**
maiden hurdler: poor handicap chaser: won at Wetherby in May: below best last 6 starts,
left J. O'Neill after first of them: stays 3¼m: acts on good to firm going: tried blinkered/
in cheekpieces: tongue tied last 4 outings. *P. D. Niven*

HURRICANE DIPPER (IRE) 6 b.g. Glacial Storm (USA) – Minnies Dipper (Royal **h–**
Captive) [2003/4 h–, F–: 19m⁵ 17v⁴ 17s³ 16s 21s Mar 15] tall gelding: signs of only a
little ability over hurdles. *Miss A. M. Newton-Smith*

HURRICANE KATIE 5 ch.m. Dolphin Street (FR) – Hurricane Dancer (IRE) **h–**
(Nabeel Dancer (USA)) [2003/4 F17m⁴ 24m⁴ Oct 3] 2,200Y: second foal: dam 7f winner **F–**
at 2 yrs: no show in bumper or novice hurdle (mistakes). *N. Wilson*

HURRICANE LAMP 13 b.g. Derrylin – Lampstone (Ragstone) [2003/4 c136x, h–: **c93 x**
c25d⁴ c25m⁶ c24d Apr 12] rangy gelding: one-time useful chaser, very much on down- **h–**
grade: stays 3m: acts on soft and good to firm going: usually held up: sketchy jumper.
A. King

HUSKY (POL) 6 b.g. Special Power – Hallo Bambina (POL) (Neman (POL)) [2003/4 **h79**
16m² 16g⁶ 17d⁴ 17m 16mᶠ 16g² 16d Nov 23] successful 3 times on Flat in Poland, modest
in Britain, successful over 1¼m in April: poor hurdler: will prove best at sharp 2m: acts
on good to firm going: wears cheekpieces: front runner. *R. M. H. Cowell*

HUSSARD COLLONGES (FR) 9 b.g. Video Rock (FR) – Ariane Collonges (FR) **c158**
(Quart de Vin (FR)) [2003/4 c167, h–: c25gᶠ c24g² c24d³ c25dᶠ Dec 27] useful-looking **h–**
gelding: impresses in appearance: high-class chaser in 2002/3: not at best at Haydock
both completed starts in 2003/4, beaten 5 lengths by Swansea Bay in 3-runner Grade 2 on
first occasion: fell heavily 6 out in listed handicap at Wetherby (reportedly cracked
pelvis) final outing: will stay beyond 3¼m: raced on good going or softer (acts on heavy):
races prominently. *P. Beaumont*

HUSSARD (FR) 9 b.g. Concorde Jr (USA) – Cerise de Totes (FR) (Champ Libre (FR)) **c–**
[2003/4 c24sᵖᵘ Dec 13] good-bodied gelding: winning hurdler/chaser, often shapes as if **h–**
something amiss: stays 3m: acts on heavy going: tried blinkered. *O. Sherwood*

HUTCH 6 b.g. Rock Hopper – Polly's Teahouse (Shack (USA)) [2003/4 17dᵖᵘ 20sᵖᵘ **h92**
17d³ 16d⁶ Apr 22] lengthy gelding: modest form on Flat at 3 yrs for J. Bethell: form in
novice hurdles only when third to King Solomon at Bangor. *P. Beaumont*

HUW THE NEWS 5 b.g. Primo Dominie – Martha Stevens (USA) (Super Concorde **h–**
(USA)) [2003/4 F16m F17m 17dᵖᵘ 19dᵖᵘ Jan 1] ninth foal: half-brother to fair hurdler/ **F–**
chaser Sound of Cheers (by Zilzal), stays 21f, and 11f winner Hester Stanhope (by
Lomond): dam, Nell Gwyn winner, out of CCA Oaks winner, Megazine: no sign of
ability. *C. L. Popham*

HUXLEY (IRE) 5 b.g. Danehill Dancer (IRE) – Biddy Mulligan (Ballad Rock) [2003/4 **h85**
17g Feb 19] ex-Irish gelding: fairly useful on Flat (best form at 7f/1m) at 4 yrs for
P. Roche, well held in 2004 for M. Quinlan: failed to settle when seventh in maiden at
Taunton on hurdling debut. *P. J. Hobbs*

HYLIA 5 ch.m. Sir Harry Lewis (USA) – Lady Stock (Crofter (USA)) [2003/4 F16g⁶ **h78**
F17g 21g⁵ 21g* 19sᵖᵘ Jan 7] unfurnished mare: sixth foal: half-sister to poor 2m hurdler **F78**
Auk (by Absalom): dam 7f winner who stayed 1¼m: mid-field in 2 bumpers: poor form
over hurdles, made all in mares novice at Ludlow in December: stays 21f. *Mrs P. Robeson*

HYPOTHESIS (IRE) 7 b.g. Sadler's Wells (USA) – Surmise (USA) (Alleged (USA)) **h–**
[2003/4 20d Aug 7] runner-up in point in 2003: little form over hurdles: tried blinkered/
visored/tongue tied. *Ian Williams*

IAC

I

IACACIA (FR) 8 b. or br.g. Silver Rainbow – Palencia (FR) (Taj Dewan) [2003/4 c–, **c95** h–: 22g⁵ 20g⁴ 17g⁴ c21m² c16g³ c17m³ c20g c16d Feb 15] small, sparely-made gelding: **h85** modest handicap chaser/maiden hurdler: sold out of Miss V. Williams' stable 4,700 gns Doncaster November Sales before final outing: stays 2¾m: acts on soft and good to firm going: blinkered (none too fluent and found little) seventh start. *E. Haddock*

IADORA 9 br.m. Gildoran – Combe Hill (Crozier) [2003/4 c66, h–: c20sᵖᵘ May 3] **c–** rather leggy mare: poor maiden hurdler/steeplechaser: won point in April: seems to stay **h–** 25f: acts on heavy going. *J. A. B. Old*

IAMBE DE LA SEE (FR) 8 b.m. Useful (FR) – Reine Mati (SWI) (Matahawk) **h97** [2003/4 17g³ 16d 16v⁶ 16g⁴ 16g 17d* Mar 27] useful-looking mare: modest hurdler, off 2½ years prior to reappearance: favourite, won mares claimer at Bangor: raced around 2m on good going or softer (acts on heavy): races freely. *N. J. Henderson*

IBAL (FR) 8 b.g. Balsamo (FR) – Quart d'Hekla (FR) (Quart de Vin (FR)) [2003/4 **c–** c136, h–: c19d⁴ c16d c16s⁵ c16dᵖᵘ Mar 18] big gelding: useful chaser in 2002/3: no form **h–** in handicaps in 2003/4: best form up to 2½m (finished very tired when winning at 3¼m): raced on good going or softer (acts well on heavy): usually front runner. *Mrs N. Smith*

IBERUS (GER) 6 b.g. Monsun (GER) – Iberica (GER) (Green Dancer (USA)) [2003/4 **h–** h100?: 16g 16sᵖᵘ Mar 19] angular gelding: useful at best on Flat: disappointing maiden hurdler: tried in cheekpieces/visor. *S. Gollings*

IBIN ST JAMES 10 b.g. Salse (USA) – St James's Antigua (IRE) (Law Society **c99** (USA)) [2003/4 c98, h–: c28d² Dec 4] sturdy gelding: modest chaser: ran well but **h–** showed signs of temperament only outing in 2003/4: stays 29f: acts on soft going: has worn blinkers, including last 4 starts. *M. Bradstock*

IBIS ROCHELAIS (FR) 8 b.g. Passing Sale (FR) – Ta Rochelaise (FR) (Carmont **c125** (FR)) [2003/4 c125, h–: c24d³ c24d³ c24g³ Mar 16] big, lengthy gelding: fairly useful handicap **h–** chaser: better for reappearance, creditable 10 lengths third of 10 finishers to Maximize in valuable amateur event at Cheltenham (placed in race for second successive year): stays 3m: acts on soft going: has reportedly broken blood vessels: sound jumper nowadays. *A. Ennis*

I CAN IMAGINE (IRE) 9 b.m. Husyan (USA) – Cyn Alley (The Parson) [2003/4 **c117** c117, h105: c29s⁴ 24d³ c24d c28vᵖᵘ c28d³ c24s 22s Mar 27] angular mare: fairly useful **h105** handicap chaser: fair maiden hurdler: stays 29f: raced on good going or softer (acts on heavy): tried blinkered: tongue tied. *Robert Tyner, Ireland*

ICARE D'OUDAIRIES (FR) 8 ch.g. Port Etienne (FR) – Vellea (FR) (Cap Martin **h105** (FR)) [2003/4 h–: 21g⁴ 24s² 24d² 20d 16d⁵ 20v⁵ 16s Feb 20] workmanlike gelding: will make a chaser: fair handicap hurdler: won conditional jockeys event at Cheltenham in November: best at 2½m+: acts on heavy going: visored final outing. *C. L. Tizzard*

ICE AND FIRE 5 b.g. Cadeaux Genereux – Tanz (IRE) (Sadler's Wells (USA)) **h–** [2003/4 16dᵘʳ 16g 17d Mar 27] medium-sized gelding: half-brother to useful hurdler/smart chaser Tarxien (by Kendor), stays 3m: modest maiden on Flat (stays 1¼m) for G. Barnett: well held both completed outings over hurdles. *B. D. Leavy*

ICE COOL LAD (IRE) 10 b.g. Glacial Storm (USA) – My Serena (No Argument) **c87** [2003/4 c76, h–: c26g² c28d⁵ c24g² c24g² c28d² c26gᵖᵘ Apr 22] sturdy gelding: modest **h–** handicap chaser: stays 3½m: acts on heavy going: blinkered once: all 3 wins at Fontwell. *R. Rowe*

ICE CRYSTAL 7 b.g. Slip Anchor – Crystal Fountain (Great Nephew) [2003/4 h106: **h–** 20s 20v⁶ 21s Jan 19] leggy gelding: fair handicap hurdler, no form in 2003/4: should be suited by 3m: acts on heavy going: sold £2,200 Ascot April Sales. *S. Woodman*

ICE CUBE 8 b.g. Rakaposhi King – Arctic Rymes (Rymer) [2003/4 c–, h64: 19d c24dᶠ **c–** c25m⁵ 26s c25vᶠ c24gᵖᵘ Feb 20] close-coupled gelding: winning chaser, no longer of any **h–** account: tried blinkered/in cheekpieces/tongue tied. *Mrs L. Williamson*

ICE GREEN PEARL 6 b.m. Green Ruby (USA) – Ice Moon (Ballymoss) [2003/4 **F–** F16d Jan 22] seventh foal: dam, maiden hurdler/pointer, from family of top-class chaser Florida Pearl: well held in bumper on debut. *M. G. Rimell*

ICELANDIC SPRING 12 ch.g. Derrylin – Snow Time (Deep Run) [2003/4 c83: **c83** c25m⁴ c26g³ May 26] modest hunter chaser: stays 3¼m: acts on good to firm going: blinkered last 4 starts. *J. E. Brockbank*

ICE RAIN (IRE)   4 gr.g. Zaffaran (USA) – Turbet Lass (IRE) (Carlingford Castle)   F–
[2003/4 F16d F17d Apr 18] strong, lengthy gelding: second foal: dam Irish maiden
hurdler: well held in bumpers: sold 4,000 gns Doncaster May Sales. *T. P. Tate*

ICE SAINT   9 gr.g. Ballacashtal (CAN) – Sylvan Song (Song) [2003/4 h82: c22gur Mar   c–
8] good-topped gelding: winning pointer: poor hurdler: weak 4/1-shot, pulled hard and   h–
unseated ninth (rider banned for making insufficient effort to stay on board) in maiden at
Fontwell on steeplechasing debut: should stay 3m: acts on heavy and good to firm going.
M. J. Gingell

ICHI BEAU (IRE)   10 b.g. Convinced – May As Well (Kemal (FR)) [2003/4 c124,   c123
h99: c20d4 c16g3 17g2 20m2 20m* 17g* c20mbd 17g4 c20m4 c20g c16m3 c16d* c16gur   h116
16d c16d6 16d Apr 13] sturdy, deep-bodied gelding: fairly useful handicap chaser: won at
Aintree in November by length from Caitriona's Choice: fairly useful hurdler: simple
tasks when winning novices at Hexham in June and Southwell in July: left F. Murphy
before final outing: barely stays 2½m: acts on heavy and good to firm going: tried in
cheekpieces: usually tongue tied: effective held up or making running: bold jumper of
fences, though inclined to make odd mistake. *A. J. Martin, Ireland*

ICKFORD OKEY   12 b.g. Broadsword (USA) – Running Kiss (Deep Run) [2003/4   c– x
c89, h–: c21dur c25gpu May 13] big, rangy gelding: fair hunter chaser: usually fails to   h–
impress with attitude and/or jumping: stays 3m: acts on good to soft and good to firm
going: tried blinkered. *Mrs S. S. Harbour*

ICONIC   10 b.g. Reprimand – Miami Melody (Miami Springs) [2003/4 c–, h–: c21gpu   c–
Mar 3] novice hurdler/chaser. *Trevor Crawford*   h–

ICY BLAST (IRE)   5 b.g. Glacial Storm (USA) – Fair Lisselan (IRE) (Kemal (FR))   F94
[2003/4 F16s* F16g6 Mar 27] rangy gelding: second foal: dam, winning 2m hurdler/
chaser, half-sister to useful 2½m chaser Gnome's Tycoon: won 12-runner bumper at
Wetherby on debut in February by 8 lengths from Fifty Franks: bit below that form when
sixth of 18 to River Trapper at Newbury. *P. R. Webber*

ICY RIVER (IRE)   7 ch.g. Over The River (FR) – Icy Lou (Bluerullah) [2003/4 h73p,   h100
F80: 20m2 20m3 20d* 20dpu Dec 26] strong, lengthy gelding: fair form over hurdles:
favourite, won novice handicap at Carlisle in November: ran as if amiss next time: will
stay 3m: acts on good to firm and good to soft going. *Mrs M. Reveley*

IDAHO D'OX (FR)   8 b.g. Bad Conduct (USA) – Queseda (FR) (Quart de Vin (FR))   c126
[2003/4 c–, h128: c17g* c17g* c16g* c17g* c20gpu 16d 17g 16g6 17d* 16s 17d 16dpu   h123
16m5 20m5 Apr 24] sparely-made gelding: fairly useful chaser/handicap hurdler:
successful over fences early in season in novice at Exeter, intermediate at Bangor, novice
at Newton Abbot and handicap at Southwell: also won over hurdles at Cheltenham in
January: has won at 2¾m, best form over shorter: acts on any going: used to be blinkered/
visored (not in 2003/4): has failed to impress with attitude over hurdles. *M. C. Pipe*

*Western Daily Press Handicap Hurdle, Cheltenham—outsider Idaho d'Ox (left) enjoys the run of the race
as he beats Bound (hooped cap) and Mambo (right); Avitta is about to unseat*

IDBURY (IRE) 6 b.g. Zaffaran (USA) – Delcarrow (Roi Guillaume (FR)) [2003/4 F–: **h–**
24g[4] Nov 21] strong, good-topped gelding: well held in bumpers and novice hurdle: sold
2,500 gns Doncaster May Sales. *N. A. Twiston-Davies*

IDEAL DE L'ILE (FR) 8 ch.g. Aelan Hapi (USA) – Ad Vitam Eternam (FR) (Cap **c91 ?**
Martin (FR)) [2003/4 c25g[5] c24g Jan 9] angular gelding: twice-raced hurdler in 2001/2: **h–**
won last of 3 starts in maiden points in 2003: seemed to show modest form, despite
several serious mistakes when fifth in maiden at Folkestone on first of 2 starts in
steeplechases. *R. T. Phillips*

IDEAL DU BOIS BEURY (FR) 8 b. or br.g. Useful (FR) – Pampa Star (FR) (Pampa- **c94**
bird) [2003/4 c104, h–: c20m[4] c17g[2] c16g[5] c20d[3] c25d[6] c16g[6] 20v 16g 16f[4] 20g[6] Mar 13] **h–**
leggy gelding: modest maiden chaser: fairly useful hurdler at best: well held in handicaps
last 4 starts: stays 2½m: acts on heavy going, probably on firm: tried visored: held up.
P. Monteith

IDEALKO (FR) 8 b.g. Kadalko (FR) – Belfaster (FR) (Royal Charter (FR)) [2003/4 **c101**
c101, h90: c20d[2] c18m[2] c20d[4] c20m[2] c20g[6] Apr 18] leggy gelding: modest maiden **h–**
hurdler: fair handicap chaser: stays 2½m: acts on soft and good to firm going: reliable.
Ian Williams

IDEAS MAN (IRE) 8 b.g. Executive Perk – Emmodee (Bowling Pin) [2003/4 c–, h–: **c–**
c17g[5] c17m[pu] Jun 18] tall, sparely-made gelding: no worthwhile form over hurdles or **h–**
fences: blinkered once (pulled hard): not a fluent jumper. *D. McCain*

IDIOME (FR) 8 b.g. Djarvis (FR) – Asterie L'Ermitage (FR) (Hamster (FR)) [2003/4 **c114**
c19d[2] c16s* c17s[2] c19d[3] c19g[3] c25d[4] Apr 17] leggy gelding: fairly useful hurdler: missed **h–**
2002/3: fair chaser: won maiden at Hereford in February: stays 2½m: yet to race on firm
going, acts on any other. *Mrs L. C. Taylor*

IDLEWILD (IRE) 9 br.g. Phardante (FR) – Delia Murphy (Golden Love) [2003/4 c–, **c– §**
h–: c16m[R] 26g[pu] May 18] bad maiden pointer: tried blinkered: ungenuine. *M. J. Polglase* **h– §**

IDOLE FIRST (IRE) 5 b.g. Flemensfirth (USA) – Sharon Doll (IRE) (Shahrastani **h114**
(USA)) [2003/4 19g* 20g[3] 20v[2] 19g* Apr 24] smallish, angular gelding: successful 4
times up to 13.5f on Flat in France for R. Chotard: fair novice hurdler: won at Stratford in
July and Market Rasen in April: will stay beyond 2½m: acts on heavy going: jumps none
too fluently. *Miss Venetia Williams*

I D TECHNOLOGY (IRE) 8 ch.g. Commanche Run – Lady Geeno (IRE) (Cheval) **h102**
[2003/4 16d 18d[ur] 16g* Apr 12] rangy ex-Irish gelding: third foal: dam unraced sister to
smart chaser/useful hurdler up to 3m Toureen Prince: modest form first 2 starts in
bumpers, then left S. Mahon and off 3 years: easily best effort in novice hurdles when
winning at Plumpton: should stay at least 2½m. *G. L. Moore*

IFNI DU LUC (FR) 8 b. or br.m. Chamberlin (FR) – Acca du Luc (FR) (Djarvis (FR)) **c129**
[2003/4 c133, h–: c20g* c24g Mar 27] leggy mare: fairly useful handicap chaser: off 10 **h–**
months, won at Kempton in March by 4 lengths from Sir Toby: weakened tamely 4 out
when well held at Newbury 3 weeks later: barely stays testing 3m: acts on heavy going:
has run creditably when sweating. *N. J. Henderson*

IFRANE BALIMA (FR) 8 ch.g. Video Rock (FR) – Balima Des Saccart (FR) (Quart **c90**
de Vin (FR)) [2003/4 h90: 17g[pu] 19s 19d[pu] c16m[3] c16d Mar 22] rather leggy gelding: **h–**
modest hurdler, below form first 3 starts: better effort over fences when third in minor
event at Leicester: raced mainly around 2m: acts on soft and good to firm going: visored
third outing: has pulled hard/hung right. *J. C. Tuck*

IFTIKHAR (USA) 5 b.g. Storm Cat (USA) – Muhbubh (USA) (Blushing Groom **F82**
(FR)) [2003/4 F96: F16m F17m F16g[4] Jul 3] second in bumper at Ludlow on debut in
late-2002/3: below that form in similar events in 2003/4: modest form on Flat subsequently: has had tongue tied. *W. M. Brisbourne*

IGLOO D'ESTRUVAL (FR) 8 br.g. Garde Royale – Jalousie (FR) (Blockhaus) **c113 x**
[2003/4 23m[3] 23m[3] 22d[3] c28d* c27s[F] 24s[5] c30g c23s[5] Apr 6] lengthy, useful-looking gelding: **h95 §**
modest maiden hurdler (ran moody race fifth start): fair handicap chaser: won Tote
Trifecta Southern National at Fontwell in December by 11 lengths from Kildorragh: stays
3¾m: acts on good to soft going: tried blinkered, usually visored: often let down by
jumping over fences: none too consistent. *Mrs L. C. Taylor*

I GOT RHYTHM 6 gr.m. Lycius (USA) – Eurythmic (Pharly (FR)) [2003/4 h97: **h96**
17g[5] 16g[2] 16d[4] 16d[3] 19d 16s[6] Feb 7] sparely-made mare: modest handicap hurdler: likely
to be suited by 2½m+: acts on good to firm and good to soft going. *Mrs M. Reveley*

I HEAR THUNDER (IRE)   6 b.g. Montelimar (USA) – Carrigeen Gala (Strong **c99**
Gale) [2003/4 F–: 19s 20s⁵ 19s³ 20s c20d² 22g Apr 10] lengthy gelding: poor novice **h79**
hurdler: much better from when second in maiden at Stratford on chasing debut: stays
2½m: raced on good going or softer. *R. H. Buckler*

IJIKA (FR)   8 ch.g. Aelan Hapi (USA) – Belle Des Airs (FR) (Saumon (FR)) [2003/4 **c–**
c–, h–: 20g May 21] rather leggy gelding: modest maiden hurdler in 2001/2: no form **h–**
since, including over fences: sold 4,400 gns Doncaster August Sales. *H. D. Daly*

IKRENEL ROYAL (FR)   8 b.g. Bricassar (USA) – Kreneldore (FR) (Trenel) [2003/4 **c–**
c115, h–: c24dᵖᵘ c20d⁴ Dec 12] winning hurdler/chaser, lightly raced: long way below **h–**
best in handicap chases since 2000/1: stays 2½m: acts on heavy going. *N. J. Henderson*

ILABON (FR)   8 ch.g. Secret Haunt (USA) – Ahuille (FR) (Haltea (FR)) [2003/4 **h114**
h120: 20s² 16s 24g 16m* 16d⁴ Apr 21] angular gelding: fair hurdler: easily landed odds
in maiden at Chepstow in April: should stay beyond 2½m: acts on soft and good to firm
going: visored last 2 starts. *M. C. Pipe*

IL'ATHOU (FR)   8 b.g. Lute Antique (FR) – Va Thou Line (FR) (El Badr) [2003/4 **c–**
c145, h–: c20gᵖᵘ 20m⁶ c21g c24sᶠ Apr 17] tall, rather leggy gelding: winning hurdler, found **h98**
little second start: useful handicap chaser in 2002/3, out of sorts in 2003/4: stays 2½m:
acts on heavy going: tends to get on toes and sometimes sweats: bold-jumping front
runner who races freely. *S. E. H. Sherwood*

IL CAPITANO   7 ch.g. Be My Chief (USA) – Taza (Persian Bold) [2003/4 c127, **c126**
h119+: 24m* c21g³ c20mᶠ c20m³ 19fᵖᵘ Aug 28] leggy gelding: useful handicap hurdler: **h130**
better than ever when winning at Ludlow in May by head from Pure Fun: fairly useful
handicap chaser: creditable third of 15 to Ballycassidy in valuable race at Market Rasen
in July: first start after leaving P. Nicholls, jumped poorly and well behind when pulled
up before last in Grade 1 hurdle at Saratoga in August: effective at 19f to 27f: best efforts
on good going or firmer: tough and consistent. *P. F. Nicholls*

IL CAVALIERE   9 b.g. Mtoto – Kalmia (Miller's Mate) [2003/4 h121: 24mᵖᵘ 22g³ **h121 x**
22d⁶ 21g² 21gᵘʳ 21g 24g⁶ 20d Mar 20] sturdy gelding: fairly useful handicap hurdler: best
efforts in 2003/4 when placed at Market Rasen and Kempton: stays 2¾m: acts on firm
and good to soft going: usually held up: tends to make mistakes. *Mrs M. Reveley*

ILE DE LIBRATE   10 b.g. Librate – Little Missile (Ile de Bourbon (USA)) [2003/4 **c90**
c98?, h–: c28d³ May 30] leggy gelding: winning hurdler: modest chaser: numerous **h–**
mistakes when third in handicap at Stratford only outing in 2003/4: probably stays 3½m:
acts on soft and firm going: has had tongue tied. *R. J. O'Sullivan*

ILE DE PARIS (FR)   5 b.g. Cadoudal (FR) – Sweet Beauty (FR) (Tip Moss (FR)) **h98**
[2003/4 17g² 19v² 24g Mar 9] third foal: half-brother to winning 17f hurdler Beauty Rose
(by Rose Laurel): dam unraced half-sister to very smart hurdler/smart staying chaser
Sweet Duke: runner-up first 2 starts in novice hurdles, better effort when beaten 12
lengths by Control Man at Newton Abbot on debut: odds on, found little final start: bred
to stay beyond 17f. *P. J. Hobbs*

ILE DE RE (IRE)   7 gr.m. Roselier (FR) – Kam Slave (Kambalda) [2003/4 22mᵖᵘ **h–**
May 29] sixth foal: half-sister to 2m hurdle winner Drum A Deal (by Lafontaine): dam
winning hurdler: temperamental winning pointer: showed nothing on hurdling debut.
B. G. Powell

ILE DISTINCT (IRE)   10 b.g. Dancing Dissident (USA) – Golden Sunlight (Ile de **c68**
Bourbon (USA)) [2003/4 c–, h–: c24mᵖᵘ c25g⁵ 24m 24m c16d³ᵈ c17g⁴ c18m³ Sep 23] **h–**
angular gelding: has been tubed: poor maiden hurdler/chaser: seems best around 2m: acts
on firm and good to soft going: has been let down by jumping. *K. R. Pearce*

ILE MICHEL   7 b.g. Machiavellian (USA) – Circe's Isle (Be My Guest (USA)) [2003/4 **h97**
16m² 16m 19g³ 16d 16g² Feb 11] smallish gelding: half-brother to winning 2½m hurdler
Flint Knapper (by Kris): useful on Flat (stays 9f), successful 4 times in 2003 (claimed
from Lady Herries £20,000 in September): modest form over hurdles: claimed by
J. O'Shea £6,000 final start: likely to prove best around 2m. *M. C. Pipe*

I'LLEVEIT TOU (IRE)   8 b.g. King Luthier – Shady Jumbo (Callernish) [2003/4 **h93**
F81: 20g 22s⁴ 21g 24dᶠ 20s 22d⁴ 26gᵘʳ 26d⁶ Mar 28] leggy gelding: modest novice
hurdler: stays 3¼m: raced on good going or softer. *R. Rowe*

I'LL FLY   4 ch.g. Polar Falcon (USA) – I'll Try (Try My Best (USA)) [2003/4 16sᵖᵘ **h78**
16g⁵ Mar 17] brother to high-class 2m hurdler Intersky Falcon and smart 7f/1m winner
John Ferneley and half-brother to several winners, including fairly useful hurdlers
Fundamental (by Rudimentary), stays 2½m, and Steel Mirror (by Slip Anchor), stayed

3m: dam 2-y-o 5f winner: better effort over hurdles when fifth in maiden at Huntingdon: well held on Flat debut in April. *J. R. Fanshawe*

ILLICIUM (IRE) 5 b.m. Fourstars Allstar (USA) – Sweet Mignonette (Tina's Pet) **F80** [2003/4 F16s⁶ F16d F16g³ F17g⁴ Mar 28] third foal: half-sister to fairly useful bumper winner Reseda (by Rock Hopper): dam, fairly useful 2m hurdler, half-sister to useful 2m hurdler Cardinal Flower: modest form last 2 starts in bumpers: well held on Flat in April. *Mrs M. Reveley*

ILLINEYLAD (IRE) 10 b.g. Whitehall Bridge – Illiney Girl (Lochnager) [2003/4 **c66** c72, h–: c22m c23m² c23g* c24g⁹ᵖᵘ Sep 13] sparely-made gelding: poor chaser: won **h–** novice handicap at Worcester in August: lame final start: stays 25f: acts on good to firm and good to soft going: visored once: has broken blood vessel. *Mrs N. S. Sharpe*

ILOVETURTLE (IRE) 4 b.g. Turtle Island (IRE) – Gan Ainm (IRE) (Mujadil **h86** (USA)) [2003/4 16s 16s⁶ 17d⁶ 17g² Mar 28] tall, leggy gelding: modest on Flat (stays 1½m): of similar standard over hurdles: pulled hard second start. *M. C. Chapman*

IMAGINAIRE (USA) 9 b.g. Quest For Fame – Hail The Dancer (USA) (Green **c101** Dancer (USA)) [2003/4 c104, h–: c17s⁴ c16s² c19g c18g Mar 27] angular gelding: fair **h–** handicap chaser: effective at 2m to 23f: acts on heavy going, possibly unsuited by good to firm: has had tongue tied: sometimes finds little: jumps well. *Miss Venetia Williams*

IMAGO II (FR) 8 b.g. Chamberlin (FR) – Pensee d'Amour (FR) (Porto Rafti (FR)) **c–** [2003/4 c101, h–: c20m⁶ Jun 7] tall gelding: mostly poor form over hurdles and fences: **h–** runner-up in point in April: tried blinkered. *Jonjo O'Neill*

IMAZULUTOO (IRE) 4 b.c. Marju (IRE) – Zapata (IRE) (Thatching) [2003/4 16g³ **h126** 16g* 16g* 16s* Nov 29] fairly useful at best up to 1m on Flat: successful all 3 starts after hurdling debut, in juveniles at Tipperary (maiden), Gowran and Fairyhouse: beat Top Strategy shade comfortably by 1½ lengths in Grade 3 for final win. *Mrs J. Harrington, Ireland*

I'M DREAMING (IRE) 10 ch.g. White Christmas – Suffolk Bells (London Bells **c89** (CAN)) [2003/4 c89: c21d⁵ c24mᵖᵘ c24dᵖᵘ Mar 15] medium-sized gelding: winning pointer: fair maiden hunter chaser: best around 2½m: acts on heavy going: has had tongue tied: sometimes let down by jumping. *Andrew J. Martin*

I'M FOR WAITING 8 ch.g. Democratic (USA) – Faustelerie (Faustus (USA)) **h78** [2003/4 h72: 19g² 19d⁴ 21s⁴ 22s² 22s 21d 22g³ Apr 24] small gelding: poor handicap hurdler: stays 2¾m: acts on heavy going: blinkered once. *John Allen*

IMMOLA (FR) 8 b. or br.g. Quart de Vin (FR) – Jessica (FR) (Laniste) [2003/4 h106p, **h–** F76: 20dᵖᵘ 20sᵖᵘ Feb 14] tall, useful-looking gelding: chasing type: lightly-raced winning hurdler: no show in 2003/4: races freely. *Miss E. C. Lavelle*

I MOVE EARTH 7 b.m. Bandmaster (USA) – Lady of Milton (Old Jocus) [2003/4 **h–** 22gᵖᵘ Apr 13] lengthy mare: pulled up both starts in novice hurdles, off over 2 years before reappearance. *C. J. Down*

IMPEK (FR) 8 b.g. Lute Antique (FR) – Attualita (FR) (Master Thatch) [2003/4 c152, **c157** h–: c16d² c24d* c24s⁵ c21dᵘʳ c19s² c21d³ c16m² Apr 24] rather leggy gelding: smart **h–** chaser: easily won 3-finisher intermediate at Sandown in December: best efforts subsequently when second to Hand Inn Hand in Grade 1 at Ascot and Cenkos in valuable minor event at Sandown: effective at 2m to easy 3m: acts on soft and good to firm going: disappointing when tried in blinkers: edgy sort, has given trouble at start: patiently ridden: jumps well. *Miss H. C. Knight*

IMPERATIVE (USA) 4 ch.c. Woodman (USA) – Wandesta (Nashwan (USA)) **h88** [2003/4 16g² 16g 17dᵖᵘ 16d⁴ Jan 9] fairly useful maiden on Flat (stays 1½m) in France, sold out of Mme C. Head-Maarek's stable 22,000 gns Newmarket July Sales: runner-up in juvenile maiden at Huntingdon on hurdling debut: below that form subsequently, left J. Unett before final outing: modest form back on Flat for Miss G. Kelleway. *Ian Williams*

IMPERIAL DE THAIX (FR) 8 b.g. Roi de Rome (USA) – Soiree d'Ete (FR) **c113** (Prove It Baby (USA)) [2003/4 c126d, h117d: c23g 22d 25d² c26g² c24s c26g³ 25g c24g **h115** c26g² c26mᵖᵘ c29m Apr 24] leggy, close-coupled gelding: fair handicap hurdler/chaser, on long losing run: stays 3¼m: acts on heavy and good to firm going: visored last 4 starts: usually tongue tied: has been let down by jumping. *M. C. Pipe*

IMPERIAL DREAM (IRE) 6 b.g. Roselier (FR) – Royal Nora (IRE) (Dromod **h89** Hill) [2003/4 F92: 17dᵘʳ 19g² 22sᵖᵘ 22g³ Apr 4] has scope: modest novice hurdler: should be suited by 2½m+. *Miss H. C. Knight*

IMPERIAL ISLAND (FR)   5 b.g. Exit To Nowhere (USA) – Imperial Prospect   F–
(USA) (Imperial Falcon (CAN)) [2003/4 F16v Jan 31] unfurnished gelding: second foal:
dam, ran once on Flat and in bumper, from very good US family: failed to settle when
well beaten in bumper on debut. *J. J. Sheehan*

IMPERIAL LINE (IRE)   10 ch.g. Mac's Imp (USA) – Ellaline (Corvaro (USA))   c–
[2003/4 c89?, h–: c25gᵖᵘ c21g Apr 1] tall gelding: winning hunter chaser: stays 3¼m: h–
acts on good to firm and good to soft going: tongue tied. *H. L. Thompson*

IMPERIAL MAN (IRE)   9 b.g. Mandalus – The Foalicule (Imperial Fling (USA))   c–
[2003/4 c–, h–: 20dᵖᵘ 17dᵘʳ 20g⁴ 24d⁴ Nov 14] winning pointer: little form over hurdles   h–
or in steeplechases, left P. Spottiswood after reappearance: tried blinkered/tongue tied.
R. Johnson

IMPERIAL ROCKET (USA)   7 b. or br.g. Northern Flagship (USA) – Starsawhirl   h87
(USA) (Star de Naskra (USA)) [2003/4 16g⁵ 18mᵖᵘ 16m⁶ 16m² 16g³ Jul 31] strong,
lengthy gelding: modest handicap hurdler: not certain to stay much beyond 2¼m: acts on
good to firm going: tried in cheekpieces. *Mrs A. L. M. King*

IMPERIAL SHO   5 ch.g. Royal Abjar (USA) – Magnetic Point (USA) (Bering)   h–
[2003/4 F–: 20f Feb 29] strong gelding: little sign of ability in bumper and novice hurdle.
J. R. Weymes

IMPERIOUS WAY (GR)   8 b.g. Wadood (USA) – Pringipessa (GR) (Flash N Thunder   h–
(USA)) [2003/4 16gᵖᵘ 18f⁵ Aug 22] won 6 times up to 1¾m from 61 starts in Greece: no
encouragement in 2 novice hurdles. *P. R. Chamings*

IMPERO   6 b.g. Emperor Jones (USA) – Fight Right (FR) (Crystal Glitters (USA))   h62
[2003/4 h–: 16m 16g 21g⁵ 24g 25f⁴ 16g 22g² 21d Mar 19] medium-sized gelding: poor
maiden hurdler: sold out of R. Armson's stable 2,000 gns Doncaster August Sales after
third start: stays 2¾m: tried visored. *W. Clay*

IMPERTIO   10 b.g. Primitive Rising (USA) – Silly Beggar (Silly Prices) [2003/4   c99 §
c105§, h–§: c25d³ c24v⁴ c22v³ c23g⁴ Feb 18] strong gelding: modest handicap chaser: h– §
stays 3½m: acts on good to firm and heavy going: has won with/without blinkers: jumps
soundly in main: weak finisher. *P. Beaumont*

IMPINDA (IRE)   5 b.m. Idris (IRE) – Last Finale (USA) (Stop The Music (USA))   h85
[2003/4 F81: 16g² 16d⁴ 16m³ 20gᵇᵈ Jan 7] smallish mare: modest maiden on Flat: similar
form over hurdles: raced mainly at 2m: unraced on extremes of going: dead. *P. Monteith*

ABN Amro Cross-Product Clearing Chase (Intermediate), Sandown—
Impek has no problems with the longer trip in a small field

IMP

IMPISH JUDE 6 b.m. Imp Society (USA) – Miss Nanna (Vayrann) [2003/4 h86: 16d⁵ **h91**
16g* 16s² 16d⁴ 20v⁶ 16g² 18dᶠ 17d⁶ Apr 18] rather leggy mare: modest handicap hurdler:
won at Leicester in December: best around 2m: raced on good going or softer (acts on
soft). *J. Mackie*

IMPORTANT BOY (ARG) 7 ch.g. Equalize (USA) – Important Girl (ARG) (Candy **h–**
Stripes (USA)) [2003/4 h77: 16mᵖᵘ 17m³ 17d 17gᵖᵘ 16m 17sᵖᵘ 16g Apr 18] little form
over hurdles: tried visored. *D. D. Scott*

IMPS WAY 9 br.m. Nomadic Way (USA) – Dalton's Delight (Wonderful Surprise) **c73**
[2003/4 c24s³ c25gᵘʳ c25g³ Mar 28] leggy mare: fair pointer, successful 3 times in 2004:
failed to repeat form in steeplechases: stays 3m. *Mrs T. Corrigan-Clark*

I'M THE MAN 13 ro.g. Say Primula – Vinovia (Ribston) [2003/4 c105§, h–§: c25g **c– §**
Apr 5] workmanlike gelding: veteran staying chaser: well held in hunter only start in **h– §**
2003/4: acts on any going: inconsistent. *Mrs S. H. Shirley-Beavan*

I'M THINKING SO (IRE) 6 b.g. Roselier (FR) – Arctic Alice (Brave Invader **c–**
(USA)) [2003/4 19s 16d⁶ 16d 20s c23dᵖᵘ Mar 23] €45,000 4-y-o: rather leggy gelding: **h85**
brother to winning staying hurdlers Eimearf Banjo and Roseaustin and half-brother to
several winners, including fair hurdler up to 2½m Alices Run (by Deep Run): dam won
twice in bumpers: tenth of 23 in bumper on debut in 2002/3 for D. Hughes: modest form
on first of 4 starts in novice hurdles: showed little on chasing debut: should stay beyond
19f: blinkered (didn't look straightforward) fourth start. *P. J. Hobbs*

IMTIHAN (IRE) 5 ch.h. Unfuwain (USA) – Azyaa (Kris) [2003/4 20s 16d 16m⁵ 17m* **h112**
16d* 22d* 16d⁵ Apr 17] compact horse: half-brother to fairly useful hurdler Samsaam
(by Sadler's Wells), stays 2½m, and fairly useful hunter up to 3m Shafi (by Reference
Point): fairly useful on Flat (will probably stay 1¾m) at 3 yrs for B. Hills, well held in
2003: progressive form over hurdles, winning handicaps at Taunton (conditional
jockeys), Towcester and Stratford (novice), all in March: stays 2¾m: acts on good to firm
and good to soft ground. *S. C. Burrough*

I'M YOUR MAN 5 gr.g. Bigstone (IRE) – Snowgirl (IRE) (Mazaad) [2003/4 F16g⁵ **F79**
F16m⁵ Dec 16] fourth foal: dam, 5f/6f winner, out of half-sister to high-class sprinter
Petong: fifth in 2 bumpers, modest form at Musselburgh on second occasion: took strong
hold on debut. *Mrs Dianne Sayer*

IN ACCORD 5 ch.g. Accordion – Henry's True Love (Random Shot) [2003/4 F16g⁵ **F96**
Feb 28] good-bodied gelding: tenth foal: half-brother to several winners, including useful
staying chaser Sail By The Stars (by Celtic Cone): dam, third in 2½m selling hurdle, half-
sister to dam of top-class 2½m chaser Dublin Flyer: carrying condition when fifth to Lord
Gale in bumper at Haydock on debut. *H. D. Daly*

INAGH ROAD (IRE) 9 b.g. Broken Hearted – Fiodoir (Weavers' Hall) [2003/4 17g **h79 ?**
16mᵘʳ 16m³ 16mᵖᵘ 17m⁶ 16m Sep 7] good-topped gelding: little worthwhile form over
hurdles: tried blinkered/in cheekpieces: has had tongue tied: has looked temperamental:
sold £2,000 Ascot October Sales, won point in February. *B. N. Pollock*

INAKI (FR) 7 b.g. Dounba (FR) – Incredule (FR) (Concertino (FR)) [2003/4 c103, h–: **c104**
c20s³ c17s* Jan 4] leggy, useful-looking gelding: fair handicap chaser: won at Plumpton **h–**
in January: stays 21f: raced on good going or softer (acts on heavy): effective blinkered/
visored or not. *P. Winkworth*

INCA MOON 4 b.f. Sheikh Albadou – Incatinka (Inca Chief (USA)) [2003/4 16mᵖᵘ **h–**
Nov 3] leggy filly: modest maiden on Flat (stays 1m): made mistakes in juvenile on
hurdling debut. *R. Brotherton*

INCA TRAIL (IRE) 8 br.g. Un Desperado (FR) – Katday (FR) (Miller's Mate) **c96**
[2003/4 h128, F110: c16g² c20sᵖᵘ 22m* 21g 20g Apr 1] tall, good sort: has had breathing **h131**
operation: runner-up on first of 2 starts in novice chases at Huntingdon: useful hurdler:
won handicap at Wincanton in February by 1¾ lengths from Mount Karinga, idling:
well beaten in competitive handicaps at Cheltenham and Aintree last 2 starts, running as
though amiss: will stay 3m: acts on good to firm and soft going: tongue tied last 3 outings:
sold 30,000 gns Doncaster May Sales. *Miss H. C. Knight*

INCH' ALLAH (FR) 8 b.g. Royal Charter (FR) – Cadoudaline (FR) (Cadoudal (FR)) **h95 ?**
[2003/4 17g⁵ 20g⁴ 20sᵖᵘ 16s⁶ Dec 26] first foal: dam won 3 times up to 13f on Flat in
France: sixth in bumper at Leopardstown on debut in December 2001 for C. McCarthy:
easily best effort over hurdles when fourth in novice at Haydock, possibly flattered.
Mrs J. Candlish

INCHING CLOSER 7 b.g. Inchinor – Maiyaasah (Kris) [2003/4 h145: c22s² c24d* **c121**
c23vᵖᵘ 23s 25g Mar 16] tall, leggy gelding: has reportedly had wind operation: smart **h–**

hurdler: short-head second to Celestial Gold in novice at Towcester on chasing debut: then sold out of J. O'Neill's stable 150,000 gns Doncaster November Sales: simple task in similar event at Newcastle following month: disappointing subsequently, back over hurdles last 2 starts: best at 2½m+ (stays 27f)ᵖᵘ acts on soft going: blinkered second to fourth outings. *J. Howard Johnson*

INCHINNAN   7 b.m. Inchinor – Westering (Auction Ring (USA)) [2003/4 16m⁴ 16g³ 16g 16s³ 16d⁵ Feb 12] close-coupled mare: fair on Flat (stays 10.5f): modest maiden hurdler: likely to prove best around 2m: acts on soft going: joined J. Moffatt. *C. Weedon* **h93**

INCH ISLAND (IRE)   4 b.g. Turtle Island (IRE) – Persian Light (IRE) (Persian Heights) [2003/4 16mᶠ 16g 16s² 16gᵖᵘ Mar 6] sturdy gelding: fair on Flat (barely stays 9f): easily best effort over hurdles when second in novice at Kelso, pulling hard in front: withdrawn after refusing to line up fourth intended start. *J. J. Quinn* **h86**

IN CONTRAST (IRE)   8 b. or br.g. Be My Native (USA) – Ballinamona Lady (IRE) (Le Bavard (FR)) [2003/4 h149: 16m³ c17dᵖᵘ 20g⁵ 17d 16d⁵ Apr 3] leggy gelding: smart hurdler: creditable third to Altay in Swinton Hurdle at Haydock in May: pulled up lame after first on chasing debut later in month and below form back over hurdles after 9 months off: effective at 2m to 21f: acts on good to firm and good to soft going (well held on heavy in bumpers): hangs left under pressure: held up and suited by truly-run race: sometimes makes mistakes. *P. J. Hobbs* **c–** **h148 d**

INDEED (IRE)   9 ch.g. Camden Town – Pamrina (Pamroy) [2003/4 c117, h–: c25dᶠ c24sᶠ 22m 22d 20m⁶ Apr 24] strong gelding: winning hurdler/maiden chaser: form in 2003/4 only when sixth to Korelo in handicap hurdle at Sandown (tongue tied) in April: should stay beyond 2½m: acts on good to firm and good to soft going: usually let down by jumping over fences. *N. J. Gifford* **c– x** **h109**

INDEED TO GOODNESS (IRE)   9 b.m. Welsh Term – Clare's Sheen (Choral Society) [2003/4 c99, h99: c22v² 24s³ c24s⁴ c24s c26g⁵ c20d⁶ Apr 8] tall mare: fair hurdler/chaser: stays 3¼m: acts well on soft/heavy going: sometimes let down by jumping over fences. *J. W. Mullins* **c113** **h102**

IN DEMAND   13 b.g. Nomination – Romantic Saga (Prince Tenderfoot (USA)) [2003/4 c20m Apr 28] winning hurdler: no form in 3 hunter chases: won point in March: should stay beyond 2½m: acts on good to firm going. *Alan Balmer* **c–** **h–**

INDESTRUCTIBLE (FR)   5 b.g. Hero's Honor (USA) – Money Bag (FR) (Badayoun) [2003/4 F16sᶠ 22vᵖᵘ 19m Mar 4] sixth foal: half-brother to winners up to around 1¼m Pourquoi Pleurer (by Art Francais) and Africadieu (by Holst): dam won at 9f on Flat and 17f over hurdles in France: no sign of ability. *M. Bradstock* **h–** **F–**

INDIAN BEAT   7 ch.g. Indian Ridge – Rappa Tap Tap (FR) (Tap On Wood) [2003/4 h–: 17g⁵ 16gᵖᵘ 16m 16m⁴ 17f³ 19f⁴ 19d 21m³ 19m² 19d⁵ Dec 11] poor maiden hurdler: stays easy 19f: acts on firm and good to soft going: tried blinkered: has looked none too keen. *C. L. Popham* **h70**

INDIAN CHANCE   10 b.g. Teenoso (USA) – Icy Miss (Random Shot) [2003/4 c115, h–: c24d⁴ c25m* c25d* Dec 26] useful-looking gelding: fairly useful handicap chaser: won twice at Wincanton in December: stays 25f: acts on good to firm and heavy going: usually sound jumper. *Dr J. R. J. Naylor* **c116** **h–**

INDIAN CHASE   7 b.g. Terimon – Icy Gunner (Gunner B) [2003/4 F17m F16m F18f² F17g³ 17gᵖᵘ 21vᵖᵘ 22sᵖᵘ c23gᶠ c20mᴿ 22g Mar 8] lengthy gelding: first foal: dam unraced half-sister to fairly useful chasers up to 25f Indian Chance and Indian Gunner: modest form in bumpers: no show over hurdles or fences: runner-up on Flat in April. *Dr J. R. J. Naylor* **c– §** **h–** **F83**

INDIAN LABURNUM (IRE)   7 b.g. Alphabatim (USA) – St Cristoph (The Parson) [2003/4 21vᵖᵘ c24d⁵ c24s⁴ c25d⁴ c25d² c25s⁴ Apr 11] IR 16,000 3-y-o: sturdy gelding: second foal: brother to winning 2½m hurdler Rolling Tide: dam dual bumper winner: runner-up twice in maiden Irish points in 2003: bought 6,000 gns Doncaster May Sales: not knocked about on hurdling debut: poor form in steeplechases, not jumping well: stays 25f: raced only on going softer than good. *C. C. Bealby* **c82 x** **h–**

INDIAN SCOUT (IRE)   9 b.g. Phardante (FR) – Kemchee (Kemal (FR)) [2003/4 c123, h–: c25g³ c20sᶠ c20dᵖᵘ Mar 27] rangy, good sort: fairly useful chaser: easily best effort in handicaps in 2003/4 when third to Keiran at Wetherby on reappearance: stays 25f, at least as effective at shorter: raced on good going or softer (acts on heavy): bold-jumping front runner. *B. De Haan* **c124** **h–**

INDIAN SOLITAIRE (IRE)   5 b.g. Bigstone (IRE) – Terrama Sioux (Relkino) [2003/4 16g⁵ 17d³ 16d⁵ 16d 16v⁴ 17s² Feb 10] leggy gelding: half-brother to 2m hurdle **h94**

winner Go Native (by Be My Native): fairly useful on Flat (stays 1¾m): modest form in novice hurdles: raced around 2m on good ground or softer. *R. A. Fahey*

INDIAN STAR (GER) 6 b.g. Sternkoenig (IRE) – Indian Night (GER) (Windwurf (GER)) [2003/4 h88+: 19g 17g³ 17g⁶ 17d 16g 17s Dec 29] leggy gelding: poor hurdler: stays 19f. *J. C. Tuck* **h80**

INDIAN SUN 7 ch.g. Indian Ridge – Star Tulip (Night Shift (USA)) [2003/4 h71: 17g 19g 16m⁶ 16m 22mᵖᵘ 16s² 16d² 16d⁵ 19s⁵ 16g⁵ 16d* 17g* 19g Apr 18] compact gelding: fair hurdler: won seller at Chepstow (sold from R. Brown 4,000 gns) in March and handicap at Newton Abbot in April: best around 2m: acts on good to firm and heavy going: blinkered once: usually tongue tied but effective when not. *Mrs A. M. Thorpe* **h100**

INDIAN VENTURE (IRE) 10 b.g. Commanche Run – Believe It Or Not (Quayside) [2003/4 c102, h–: c16g² May 14] lengthy, angular gelding: fair chaser: good second in handicap at Perth only outing in 2003/4: stays easy 2½m: yet to race on extremes of going: carries head high. *N. G. Richards* **c111 h–**

INDIAN VICEROY 11 b.g. Lord Bud – Poppadom (Rapid River) [2003/4 c–, h–: c16sᶠ c19dᵖᵘ Dec 2] workmanlike gelding: poor chaser, little form since 2000/1: blinkered once. *R. T. Phillips* **c– h–**

INDIEN DU BOULAY (FR) 8 ch.g. Chef de Clan II (FR) – Radesgirl (FR) (Radetzky Marsch (USA)) [2003/4 c110§, h–§: c22mᵖᵘ c24gᵖᵘ c24f⁵ c24g³ c25g⁴ Apr 5] leggy gelding: modest chaser: left P. Monteith after second start, won point in February: stays 3m: acts on good to firm and heavy going: tried in headgear: ungenuine. *Major General C. A. Ramsay* **c89 § h– §**

INDIGO BEACH (IRE) 8 b.g. Rainbows For Life (CAN) – Sandy Maid (Sandy Creek) [2003/4 h84: 17mᵖᵘ 16gᵖᵘ Oct 30] good-topped gelding: poor hurdler: left P. McEntee, no show either start in 2003/4: stays easy 21f: acts on good to firm and good to soft going: tried tongue tied, including for last 2 wins: headstrong front runner. *G. J. Smith* **h– §**

INDISCRET (FR) 8 b.g. Garde Royale – Please (FR) (Le Pontet (FR)) [2003/4 c75x, h–: c21m⁵ c26m² Nov 25] medium-sized gelding: poor handicap chaser: finished lame when good second at Warwick: stays 3¼m: acts on good to firm and good to soft going: usually a poor jumper. *F. Jordan* **c75 x h–**

INDOUX (FR) 8 b.g. Useful (FR) – Pin'hup (FR) (Signani (FR)) [2003/4 h86§: c26gᶠ c23gᵖᵘ c19s⁴ c25d⁵ c26s 24s⁶ 24sᵖᵘ 19gᵖᵘ 22mᶠ Mar 11] leggy gelding: poor hurdler/maiden chaser: probably stays 25f: acts on any going: tried blinkered: unreliable. *R. J. Hodges* **c72 § h75 §**

INDULGENT WAY (IRE) 13 gr.g. Roselier (FR) – Glenmore Lady (Stetchworth (USA)) [2003/4 c26s⁶ c21d c22s Feb 9] of no account nowadays: tried blinkered. *A. P. Jones* **c– h–**

INDY MOOD 5 ch.g. Endoli (USA) – Amanta (IRE) (Electric) [2003/4 F16m F16s⁵ F16g* F16v⁶ Jan 24] workmanlike gelding: second foal: dam unraced: best effort in bumpers when winning at Newcastle in December by head from Gary's Pimpernel, pair well clear: will be suited by further than 2m. *Mrs H. O. Graham* **F92**

INEXORABLE (IRE) 6 br.g. Roselier (FR) – Katday (FR) (Miller's Mate) [2003/4 F16d⁴ 22g⁵ 24d* 22s* 24s* 20d² Feb 22] 185,000 4-y-o: fourth foal: half-brother to 4 winners, notably Best Mate and smart hurdler Cornish Rebel (both by Un Desperado): dam won around 11f on Flat in France/placed over hurdles in Ireland: winning pointer: fourth in bumper: winning useful form over hurdles, winning novices at Cork and Limerick in December (both Grade 3 events) and Fairyhouse in January, beating Criaire Princess 12 lengths at last-named: further improvement when 4½ lengths second to easy winner Newmill in Grade 2 at Naas final start: will prove ideally suited by thorough test of stamina: acts on soft going: open to further improvement. *D. Wachman, Ireland* **h129 p F90**

IN EXTREMIS II (FR) 8 b.g. Useful (FR) – Princesa Real (FR) (Garde Royale) [2003/4 c–, h86: c25gᵖᵘ c20g² c20mᵖᵘ c27m c16g c20mᵖᵘ c21g⁴ c21m³ 21g⁴ 17mᵖᵘ Oct 10] close-coupled gelding: winning hurdler: temperamental maiden chaser: stayed 25f: acted on good to firm and good to soft going: wore headgear after reappearance: tried tongue tied: dead. *G. M. Moore* **c86 § h–**

INFAMELIA 8 b.m. Infantry – Incamelia (St Columbus) [2003/4 h–: c24dᵖᵘ Mar 15] winning pointer, lightly raced and little form otherwise: tried blinkered/visored. *Miss Tessa Clark* **c– h–**

INFINITE RISK 5 gr.g. Vettori (IRE) – Dolly Bevan (Another Realm) [2003/4 h–: 16m⁵ 16m 17gᵖᵘ Jun 3] bad 2m maiden hurdler: has worn cheekpieces. *N. J. Hawke* **h59**

INFLUENCE PEDLER   11 b.g. Keen – La Vie En Primrose (Henbit (USA)) [2003/4   **c–** c95, h–: c24g⁶ 24g Apr 1] smallish, well-made gelding: winning hurdler/chaser: showed   **h–** nothing in 2003/4: has had tongue tied. *Miss K. M. George*

IN FOR THE CRAIC (IRE)   5 b.g. Our Emblem (USA) – Lucky State (USA) (State   **h–** Dinner (USA)) [2003/4 18mᶠ May 26] half-brother to winning 2m hurdler Glencoyle (by In The Wings): modest on Flat (stayed 1½m): distant third when falling 4 out in 4-y-o novice at Fontwell on hurdling debut: dead. *P. Butler*

INFRASONIQUE (FR)   8 b.g. Teresio – Quatalina III (FR) (Chateau du Diable (FR))   **c116 d** [2003/4 c130, h–: c24s⁵ c24s⁶ c24d⁴ c24g⁴ c24s⁴ c25g⁶ Apr 3] good-topped gelding: **h–** fairly useful handicap chaser, generally disappointing in 2003/4: stays easy 25f: acts on heavy and good to firm going: tried in cheekpieces, visored last 2 starts: sound jumper. *Mrs L. C. Taylor*

INGENU (FR)   8 b.g. Royal Charter (FR) – Una Volta (FR) (Toujours Pret (USA))   **c–** [2003/4 c–, h99: c23g c25m May 14] rather leggy gelding: winning hurdler/chaser: stays   **h–** 21f: acts on good to firm and heavy going: sold to join P. Wegmann £18,000 Ascot June Sales. *R. H. Alner*

INGLEWOOD   4 ch.g. Fleetwood (IRE) – Preening (Persian Bold) [2003/4 17g⁴   **h87** 17m* 16s 18vᵖᵘ 19g 27d 21g Apr 12] poor maiden on Flat: best effort over hurdles when fortunate winner of juvenile at Bangor in August. *C. W. Thornton*

INGLIS DREVER   5 b.g. In The Wings – Cormorant Creek (Gorytus (USA))   **h152** [2003/4 20d* 20d* 21d* 21g² 20g⁴ Apr 1]

    The best performance in a novice hurdle during the 2003/4 season was produced not at one of the big spring Festivals but at Warwick on a cold afternoon in January. It came from Inglis Drever, subsequently beaten at Cheltenham and Aintree but a young hurdler who remains the sort to make his mark in open company. Inglis Drever lined up for the Grade 2 Pertemps Novices' Hurdle at Warwick with two impressive hurdling wins under his belt, representing an owner and trainer who were increasingly in the news. Inglis Drever's first success came at Aintree in November, when he cruised into contention early in the straight and sprinted clear, despite jumping left, to beat some promising novices. Post-race quotes suggested another small race might be sought as a springboard to something better, but connections later opted for the Grade 2 William Hill Winter Novices' Hurdle at Sandown in December. The Champion Hurdle fourth Self Defense, fresh

William Hill Winter Novices' Hurdle, Sandown—
Inglis Drever is well clear at the last and confirms himself a very smart performer

from a narrow success in a Grade 2 novice event at Cheltenham, promised a stern examination. Smart bumper performer Control Man added depth after an easy win on his hurdling debut at Newton Abbot. Inglis Drever again produced a telling turn of foot between the last two flights, earning a 20/1 quote for the Champion Hurdle after quickening seven lengths clear of Self Defense as the pair drew away from the rest.

The fact that Inglis Drever carried the colours of the Newcastle-based software tycoon Graham Wylie and his wife Andrea struck an immediate chord with the racing media. Wylie had predictably been dubbed jump racing's counterpart to the Chelsea chairman Roman Abramovich after a series of high profile purchases, while Inglis Drever's colourful trainer Howard Johnson added to the interest by referring to Inglis Drever as

'the Boeing 747'. The Warwick performance went some way towards confirming that Inglis Drever was destined to fly high over hurdles. Sent off at 15/8-on in a field of six, Inglis Drever jumped soundly overall, as Eric's Charm set a true gallop, and had no trouble keeping up when the leader tried to stretch him on the final circuit. As at Sandown, Inglis Drever came back on the bridle after being shaken up briefly on the home turn. From two out the winning distance was the only matter to be resolved, and Inglis Drever passed the post seventeen lengths clear of a weary Eric's Charm. The runner-up subsequently bolted up at Kempton before

Pertemps Leamington Novices' Hurdle, Warwick—an impressive third win

finishing an excellent second off a BHB mark of 135 in the EBF Final at Sandown. Inglis Drever's trainer suffers from tinnitus in his left ear, after being kicked while worming a cow in 1996, and used his condition as a handy reason for keeping his counsel when pressed as to whether Inglis Drever would have a tilt at the Champion Hurdle.

As Cheltenham drew nearer, it became clear that Inglis Drever would only take his chance against the top two milers if the ground came up soft. It didn't, and he contested the Royal & SunAlliance Novices' Hurdle, sent off 7/4 favourite in a field of fifteen. Five of the last nine favourites had obliged in the race. Inglis Drever was attempting to join a select club made up of Danoli, Istabraq, Barton, French Holly and Monsignor, but it was clear with a circuit to run, when he was being pushed along, that it wasn't going to be plain sailing. Things looked up as he challenged Grey Report and Fundamentalist three out, but a clumsy jump at the next cost valuable momentum. To his credit, Inglis Drever rallied strongly to get within a couple of lengths of Fundamentalist at the last and continued to eat into the deficit up the hill. A tendency to edge left into the whip cost him, though, as he went down by half a length. Inglis Drever returned without his off-fore shoe, which could account for his tendency to wander, and Johnson's immediate reaction was to express relief as having missed the Champion and to suggest that the '747' would need three weeks to recover from such a tough race. In the event, he was back on the runway again two weeks later for the Mersey Novices' Hurdle at Aintree. Once again he was heavily backed and once again he was beaten, though this time he seemed very unlucky. Looking extremely well and on his toes, Inglis Drever, conceding 5 lb or more to all bar one of his twelve rivals, took a good hold under restraint in a race run at a sedate gallop but became hemmed in on the inside rail as the pace increased on the final bend. Inglis Drever finished strongly after taking a while to get fully opened out and was beaten less than two lengths into fourth behind Garde Champetre.

Cheltenham and Aintree were not the first occasions that Inglis Drever's followers were left to rue what might have been. Two handicap wins on the Flat for Sir Mark Prescott in June 2003 saw him the subject of an ante-post gamble for the

Ebor Handicap. He 'missed the cut' for the York race by six and, after landing the odds in another Newmarket handicap, lack of stamina seemed to find him out in the Cesarewitch. It was after the Cesarewitch defeat that Inglis Drever's previous owner Piers Pottinger decided to send him to the sales rather than keep him to go jumping with Nicky Henderson. Wylie paid 110,000 guineas, which looks very sound business now, and the investment ought to yield more dividends in the next few seasons. Inglis Drever's pedigree contains an interesting blend of good horses from the Flat and over jumps. His sire In The Wings is responsible for the very smart hurdlers Landing Light and Westender from a relatively small number of jumpers. The dam Cormorant Creek was a fair winner over ten furlongs and is a half-sister to the 1983 Champion Stakes winner Cormorant Wood, herself dam of the very smart middle-distance horse Rock Hopper, while the second dam Quarry Wood also produced River Ceiriog, who romped home at 40/1 for Henderson in the 1986 Supreme Novices' Hurdle.

Inglis Drever (b.g. 1999)	In The Wings (b 1986)	Sadler's Wells (b 1981)	Northern Dancer / Fairy Bridge
		High Hawk (b 1980)	Shirley Heights / Sunbittern
	Cormorant Creek (b 1987)	Gorytus (b 1980)	Nijinky / Glad Rags
		Quarry Wood (b 1968)	Super Sam / Phrygia

Inglis Drever, named after a noted Scottish heraldic artist (and Pottinger's uncle), is a sturdy, close-coupled gelding who acts on good to soft ground and handled firmer conditions well on the Flat. He clearly stays two miles five furlongs, though is not short of speed, the 'Fighting Fifth' Hurdle at Newcastle appealing as

Andrea & Graham Wylie's "Inglis Drever"

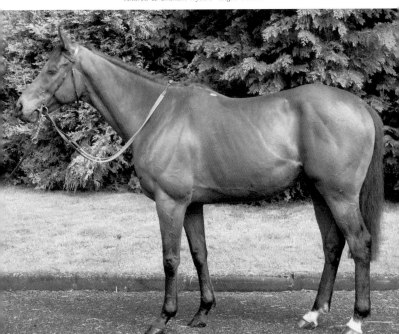

a suitable race in which to assess his championship credentials further. Whatever Inglis Drever's ideal trip turns out to be, his owners seem intent on building one of the most powerful teams of jumpers ever seen in the North. Royal Rosa, Valley Henry and Lord Transcend are all due to represent them at a high level over fences in the next season, while another burst of spending at Doncaster's May Sales in 2004 saw them lay out a total of 350,000 guineas for bumper winners Diamond Sal and Rogues Gallery, not to mention 185,000 guineas for a store horse. A personal fortune estimated at around £175m means Wylie can well afford to take a relaxed attitude to racing as a hobby, which Johnson summed up neatly after Inglis Drever's Sandown win. 'If Graham can come up every fortnight with 3 lb of carrots for the horses, he's happy,' he said. With over forty horses now housed at Johnson's yard at Crook, the Wylie carrot bill has risen considerably since then. However, despite visiting the winner's enclosure with several Flat horses in 2004, the Wylies and Johnson remain committed to producing good hurdlers and chasers. 'We're in this for the jumping,' said Johnson. 'I've told Graham the Flat's only for girls and their hats.' *J. Howard Johnson*

IN GOOD FAITH   12 b.g. Beveled (USA) – Dulcidene (Behistoun) [2003/4 c–, h102d: 17s⁶ 17g* 16m⁵ 16m³ 17g 22m⁴ 17g² 17g⁴ 21m* 21g⁶ 20d⁴ 17d⁴ 21s⁵ 19d³ 16g² 19g 19g 17d 21g Apr 12] leggy gelding: maiden chaser: poor handicap hurdler nowadays: won seller at Cartmel in May and conditional jockeys event at Sedgefield in September: stays easy 21f: acts on any going: has worn cheekpieces. *R. E. Barr*   **c–** **h81**

IN GOOD TIME   5 b.g. Classic Cliche (IRE) – Primum Tempus (Primo Dominie) [2003/4 17m⁴ 16dᵖᵘ Dec 17] lengthy gelding: has scope: well held on Flat, sold out of E. Alston's stable 2,800 gns Doncaster August (2002) Sales: poor form on first of 2 starts in novice hurdles: lame next time. *Mrs S. J. Smith*   **h69**

INIGO JONES (IRE)   8 b.g. Alzao (USA) – Kindjal (Kris) [2003/4 c–, h98: 16g⁵ 16s³ c16g⁴ c16d* c16g* c16g* Apr 18] close-coupled gelding: fair hurdler at best: similar form over fences when winning handicaps at Hereford in March and Wincanton (2) in April, first 2 novices: raced mainly around 2m: acts on heavy and good to firm going: used to be blinkered/headstrap front runner, but more patiently ridden after reappearance. *G. Brown*   **c103** **h84**

INIS CARA (IRE)   12 b.g. Carlingford Castle – Good Sailing (Scorpio (FR)) [2003/4 c85, h–: c24mᵖᵘ Apr 13] good-topped gelding: formerly useful chaser: placed several times in points in 2004 but showed little in hunter at Chepstow. *G. W. Thomas*   **c–** **h–**

INITIATE   6 ch.g. North Col – Silver Fig (True Song) [2003/4 F17m³ Oct 2] first foal: dam winning pointer: third in bumper at Hereford on debut. *J. L. Spearing*   **F78**

INITIATIVE   8 ch.g. Arazi (USA) – Dance Quest (FR) (Green Dancer (USA)) [2003/4 h91: 16m c21gᵖᵘ c16g³ c16m³ Sep 24] smallish gelding: modest handicap hurdler: similar form on second start over fences: best around 2m: acts on soft and good to firm going. *J. Hetherton*   **c88** **h–**

INJUN   5 ch.g. Efisio – Lassoo (Caerleon (USA)) [2003/4 h–: 22s⁵ 16sᵖᵘ 17d⁴ Mar 3] compact gelding: no worthwhile form over hurdles: tried in cheekpieces: tongue tied: ungenuine. *Miss A. M. Newton-Smith*   **h– §**

INJUNEAR (IRE)   6 ch.g. Executive Perk – Chancy Gale (IRE) (Strong Gale) [2003/4 21d⁴ Apr 11] second foal: dam never ran: looked green when fourth in novice hurdle at Plumpton on debut: should improve. *T. P. McGovern*   **h78 p**

INLAND RUN (IRE)   8 b.g. Insan (USA) – Anns Run (Deep Run) [2003/4 21d Feb 2] well-made ex-Irish gelding: third foal: brother to winning 3m chaser Kick For Touch: dam, winning pointer, from family of useful 3m chaser Kilkilwell: modest form in 2 bumpers in June 2001 for M. J. O'Keeffe: ninth of 22 in steadily-run novice hurdle at Kempton on return, failing to settle: bred to stay at least 3m. *R. T. Phillips*   **h92**

INN ANTIQUE (FR)   8 b.g. Lute Antique (FR) – Taghera (FR) (Toujours Pret (USA)) [2003/4 c–, h116§: 20dᵖᵘ 16d c20g⁵ c20g Mar 17] tall gelding: fairly useful hurdler at best: useful handicap chaser (often let down by jumping): ran well when seventh of 16 to Tikram in valuable event at Cheltenham final start: stays 2½m: acts on any going: often finds little. *Ferdy Murphy*   **c130** **h108**

INNER SANCTUM (IRE)   7 ch.g. Bob's Return (IRE) – Princess Wager (Pollerton) [2003/4 h79, F82: 21gᶠ 24gᵖᵘ 20d⁶ Apr 7] sparely-made gelding: poor form on hurdling debut: showed nothing in 2003/4. *Miss Venetia Williams*   **h–**

INN FROM THE COLD (IRE) 8 ch.g. Glacial Storm (USA) – Silver Apollo h–
(General Ironside) [2003/4 h–: 22d Dec 1] strong gelding: little sign of ability. *L. Lungo*

INNOCENT BYSTANDER 5 ch.g. Rudimentary (USA) – Right To The Top (Nash F
wan (USA)) [2003/4 F17d Oct 29] 18,000 3-y-o. second foal: half-brother to useful 7f to
1m winner Convent Girl (by Bishop of Cashel): dam unraced, out of smart 7f to 8.5f filly
Aim For The Top: showed little in bumper on debut. *J. M. Jefferson*

INNOVATE (IRE) 12 b.m. Posen (USA) – Innate (Be My Native (USA)) [2003/4 c–
c81d, h–: c25g May 24] handicap chaser: well held only start in 2003/4: stays 3¼m: acts h–
on firm and good to soft going: tried in cheekpieces: tongue tied: races prominently: not
an easy ride. *Miss Lucinda V. Russell*

INNOX (FR) 8 b.g. Lute Antique (FR) – Savane III (FR) (Quart de Vin (FR)) [2003/4 c136
c134: c19s^{pu} c21s c23s³ c24d² c24g^F c23s^F Apr 18] good-topped gelding: useful chaser:
good placed efforts in handicaps at Auteuil in October and Sandown in February: prob-
ably stays 27f: acts on heavy going: effective blinkered or not: none too consistent.
F. Doumen, France

INSHARANN (FR) 5 b.g. Sheyrann – My Last Chance (FR) (Tiffauges) [2003/4 F–: F–
F16g Mar 15] lame in bumper on debut in 2002/3: showed little in similar event
11 months later. *N. J. Henderson*

INSURRECTION (IRE) 7 b.g. Un Desperado (FR) – Ballycahan Girl (Bargello) h–
[2003/4 F16g 20g 16d 22g Apr 13] IR £14,000 4-y-o: ex-Irish gelding: seventh foal: F–
half-brother to modest chaser Step In Line (by Step Together), stays 3¼m: dam lightly-
raced maiden: runner-up once from 4 starts in maiden points: well beaten in bumper (for
K. Burke) and in 3 races over hurdles. *J. D. Frost*

IN TECHNICOLOR (IRE) 5 b.g. Germany (USA) – Light Argument (IRE) (Tale F100
Quale) [2003/4 F16d³ F16d Apr 13] first foal: dam, fair hunter chaser, half-sister to useful
staying chaser Knight Oil and useful hurdler up to 2¾m Vazon Bay: better effort in
bumpers when third to Green Peach at Naas in March. *A. L. T. Moore, Ireland*

INTELLIGENT (IRE) 8 b.g. Religiously (USA) – Culkeern (Master Buck) [2003/4 c–
c138, h118: c20s c24d^F Dec 5] good-topped gelding: fairly useful hurdler: useful chaser: h–
won Midlands National in 2002/3: fell fatally at Sandown: effective at 2½m given test
and stayed 4¼m: raced on good going or softer (acted on heavy): blinkered once.
Mrs J. Harrington, Ireland

INTENSITY 8 b.g. Bigstone (IRE) – Brillante (FR) (Green Dancer (USA)) [2003/4 h92 +
16d 16f⁵ 21g⁸ 24g* Dec 5] lengthy ex-Irish gelding: fair on Flat (stays 1¾m): modest
hurdler: sold out of R. Osborne's stable €7,000 Goffs October Sale: won twice at
Southwell, handicap in November and novice in December: may prove best short of 3m:
acts on good to soft going: has had tongue tied: sold 8,000 gns Doncaster May Sales.
P. A. Blockley

INTERDIT (FR) 8 b. or br.g. Shafoun (FR) – Solaine (FR) (Pot d'Or (FR)) [2003/4 c110
c109, h97: c25g³ c28d^{pu} c25g^{pu} c28g* c25g* c24d^F c30d c25s³ 21v c30g⁵ c22v* c25s⁶ h–
c30g c32g⁴ c24g^{pu} Apr 10] leggy gelding: winning hurdler: fair handicap chaser: won at
Kelso and Ayr in November and Kelso again in February: below best subsequently,
reluctant to race on one occasion: stays 4m: acts on any going: effective blinkered or not:
usually races prominently. *Mrs B. K. Thomson*

INTERSKY FALCON 7 ch.g. Polar Falcon (USA) – I'll Try (Try My Best (USA)) h158
[2003/4 h161: 16m* 16d³ 16g* 16m² 16g³ 20d⁴ 16m⁵ Apr 23]
There are few better among the established two-mile hurdle championship
contenders than Intersky Falcon who had another successful campaign, winning the
John James McManus Memorial Hurdle at Tipperary and the Jobs@Pertemps City
Christmas Hurdle at Kempton, both for the second year running. He also improved
his placing in the Champion Hurdle, from fifth the previous year to third in the
latest renewal. That said, Intersky Falcon's campaign also included some unexpected reverses, including when beaten at odds on in the 'Fighting Fifth' Hurdle
(another race he'd won in 2002/3) and in the Kingwell Hurdle, after the latter being
found to have trouble with his breathing. Intersky Falcon was fitted with a tongue
strap in his races after the Kingwell—the first of them in the Champion Hurdle—
and had surgery after the end of the season in an effort to cure the wind problem.
There is a dearth of high-class two-mile hurdlers at present and Intersky Falcon,
who hasn't a physique that makes him an obvious novice chasing candidate, will be
following a now-familiar programme again in the next season.

*Jobs@Pertemps City Christmas Hurdle, Kempton—a change of tactics suits the
waited-with Intersky Falcon as he defeats the greys Rooster Booster and Sporazene (noseband)*

Among Intersky Falcon's biggest assets are his fine jumping and an equally
fine turn of foot. Front-running tactics, which made an asset of his quick and
accurate jumping, were replaced by much more patient tactics for Intersky Falcon's
most important objectives in the latest season. After making all in the McManus
Memorial Hurdle and winning unchallenged from a not-fully-wound-up Back In
Front, Intersky Falcon managed only third in the 'Fighting Fifth' after leading four
out and cruising clear entering the straight, probably paying the price for striking
for home in earnest too soon, faltering going to the last and finding little off the
bridle. A change of tactics followed in the Christmas Hurdle in which Intersky
Falcon was able to demonstrate the effectiveness of his turn of foot in a muddling
race which turned into a test of speed. Held up, he took over at the second last and
soon quickened into a winning lead, coming home two and a half lengths clear of
Rooster Booster, whose intended pacemaker Brooklyn's Gold had been virtually
ignored. Sporazene and Foreman filled third and fourth at Kempton where the
winner recorded a performance very near to his best.

After failing to settle and being readily outpointed by Rigmarole in the
Kingwell Hurdle at Wincanton in February, Intersky Falcon was pushed out from
second favourite (behind Rooster Booster) for the Cheltenham championship to a
longest-priced 12/1. He started 8/1 third favourite on the day, behind Rooster Booster and Rigmarole, and was held up in rear, in complete contrast to the previous year
when he had had little left once headed after two out. Still travelling noticeably well
after the third last, Intersky Falcon wasn't asked for his effort in the latest renewal
until the home straight and could make little impression on Hardy Eustace and
Rooster Booster, eventually beaten five lengths and four in a field representative
of the best two-milers around. Intersky Falcon was tried at two and a half miles in
the Aintree Hurdle, the first time he had raced beyond the minimum trip since his
novice days. He ran well too, showing himself fully effective at the trip, at least
when conditions aren't testing. Again proving somewhat intractable when held up
early on, Intersky Falcon moved through to lead on the bridle two out and was
eventually beaten only three quarters of a length, half a length and the same behind
his stable-companion Rhinestone Cowboy, Rooster Booster and Champion Hurdle
fifth Westender. Back at two miles later in the month, Intersky Falcon came a
below-form fifth behind another of his stable companions, Hasty Prince, in the
Concept Hurdle at Sandown, his prospects not helped by being dropped out last in

a steadily-run affair in which he looked dangerous only briefly, early in the home straight.

Intersky Falcon (ch.g. 1997)	Polar Falcon (USA) (b or br 1987)	Nureyev (b 1977)	Northern Dancer
			Special
		Marie d' Argonne (ch 1981)	Jefferson
			Mohair
	I'll Try (ch 1982)	Try My Best (b 1975)	Northern Dancer
			Sex Appeal
		Polifontaine (br 1976)	Bold Lad
			Mortefontaine

Like the Champion Hurdle winner Hardy Eustace, the leggy Intersky Falcon is by a sire who made his name as a sprinter, Polar Falcon. The now-deceased Polar Falcon enjoyed his finest hour on the track when winning the Sprint Cup at Haydock as a four-year-old, though he also won the Lockinge Stakes at a mile; he is probably best known now as the sire of top stallion Pivotal, another sprinter. Intersky Falcon's dam, I'll Try, was also bred for speed and won over five furlongs at Warwick as a two-year-old before later winning in the States. A previous mating with Polar Falcon produced the smart miler John Ferneley, winner of the Lincoln and second in the Royal Hunt Cup. I'll Try has bred several other winners and was also represented on the course in the latest season by the fairly useful hurdler at up to two and a half miles Fundamental (by Rudimentary) who was also in training at Jackdaws Castle. Another brother, four-year-old I'll Fly, showed only poor form in two starts over hurdles for James Fanshawe in the latest season. The fairly useful hurdler/chaser Steel Mirror (by Slip Anchor), who stayed twenty-five furlongs, is another of I'll Try's offspring. Intersky Falcon's performance in the Aintree Hurdle gives his connections a wider choice of targets to aim at in the next season. The

interskyracing.com & Mrs Jonjo O'Neill's "Intersky Falcon"

blinkered Intersky Falcon is not particularly beholden to the state of the ground either, having shown his form on going ranging from firm to soft (yet to race on heavy). *Jonjo O'Neill*

INTERSKY NATIVE (IRE)   8 ch.g. Be My Native (USA) – Creative Music (Creative Plan (USA)) [2003/4 h79: 24m² c25g 24m⁴ 20d² Apr 18] well-made gelding: let down by jumping on chasing debut: poor maiden hurdler: left N. Richards and off 10 months before final start: stays 3m: acts on good to firm and good to soft going: tried in cheekpieces (found little): temperament under suspicion. *J. Howard Johnson*   **c–**
h84

INTERSKY SOVEREIGN (IRE)   6 b.g. Aristocracy – Queen's Prize (Random Shot) [2003/4 h–: 24d³ 25sᴾᵘ Jan 6] unfurnished gelding: poor form on second of 3 starts over hurdles. *J. Howard Johnson*   **h65**

IN THE CLOUDS   4 b.g. Cloudings (IRE) – Tread Carefully (Sharpo) [2003/4 16sᴾᵘ Dec 20] fifth foal: dam, maiden who stayed 1m, half-sister to Champion Hurdle winner and high-class stayer Royal Gait: no form on Flat at 2 yrs: showed nothing on hurdling debut. *T. D. Easterby*   **h–**

IN THE FORGE   7 ch.g. Zilzal (USA) – Harir (Kris) [2003/4 h143: 16d³ c16dᶠ c16dᵘʳ c16d c17dᶠ Dec 26] tall gelding: progressed into useful hurdler: failed to complete 3 of 4 starts over fences, would have been fourth at worst but for unseating last in Grade 2 novice won by Anxious Moments at Punchestown: likely to prove best around 2m: acts on soft going, below form only outing on firmer than good: tongue tied. *M. Halford, Ireland*   **c125**
h–

IN THE FRAME (IRE)   5 b.g. Definite Article – Victorian Flower (Tate Gallery (USA)) [2003/4 16gᶠ 16mᴾᵘ 17s² 16g³ 16m 17s⁶ 16g* Apr 18] rather leggy gelding: fairly useful on Flat (stays 9f) at 3 yrs, sold out of R. Hannon's stable 21,000 gns Newmarket Autumn (2002) Sales: fair novice hurdler: improved form when winning at Wincanton, eased when beating New Mischief 20 lengths: raced around 2m: acts on soft going. *P. J. Hobbs*   **h108**

IN THE PARK (IRE)   7 gr.g. Roselier (FR) – Gay Seeker (Status Seeker) [2003/4 F17v* 22sᴾᵘ Dec 30] IR 18,000 3-y-o, IR £18,000 4-y-o: leggy gelding: half-brother to winning 2m hurdler My Native Girl (by Be My Native) and to 2 winning pointers: dam, winning 2m hurdler, half-sister to top-class 2m hurdler Browne's Gazette: won bumper at Killarney in May on debut: left Miss F. Crowley, disappointing favourite in maiden on hurdling debut, off bridle some way out. *Jonjo O'Neill*   **h–**
F87

IN THE ROUGH (IRE)   13 b.g. Strong Gale – Cherrydawn (Pollerton) [2003/4 c–x, h103: c24s⁵ May 3] lengthy gelding: fair handicap hurdler/chaser: stays 29f: raced on good going or softer (acts on heavy): has looked less than keen: sketchy jumper of fences. *J. A. B. Old*   **c101 x**
h–

IN THE STARS (IRE)   6 ch.g. Definite Article – Astronomer Lady (IRE) (Montekin) [2003/4 16d⁴ 17m² 17s⁵ 16d⁶ c16d⁴ c17d³ Apr 11] modest maiden on Flat (stays easy 13f): modest form over hurdles: easily better effort over fences when fourth of 7 in novice handicap at Hereford, not always fluent: likely to prove best at 2m: wore visor/cheekpieces last 3 starts. *P. R. Webber*   **c87**
h88

INTO BATTLE   10 b.g. Daring March – Mischievous Miss (Niniski (USA)) [2003/4 17s 19gᶠ Mar 10] lengthy gelding: poor handicap hurdler in 2001/2: showed nothing on completed start on return: stays 21f: acts on good to soft going: has had tongue tied. *J. J. Quinn*   **h–**

INTO THE BLACK (IRE)   13 ch.g. Over The River (FR) – Legal Fortune (Cash And Courage) [2003/4 c25dᴾᵘ Apr 30] rather sparely-made gelding: modest novice chaser in early-2000/1: no show in hunter only subsequent outing: tried blinkered. *S. Lloyd*   **c–**
h–

INTO THE SHADOWS   4 ch.f. Safawan – Shadows of Silver (Carwhite) [2003/4 F12g² F12m² F12d⁵ F16d² Apr 12] angular filly: third foal: half-sister to fair 2m hurdler Out of The Shadows (by Rock Hopper): dam, bumper winner/fairly useful 1¾m winner on Flat, ran once over hurdles: fairly useful form in bumpers: ¾-length second of 18 to Snoopy Loopy at Huntingdon final start, well clear of rest: third over 1m on Flat debut 8 days later. *Mrs M. Reveley*   **F101**

INTOX III (FR)   8 ch.g. Garde Royale – Naftane (FR) (Trac) [2003/4 h105d: 17g* 16g³ 16m⁵ c16g⁴ c16g 16f Oct 9] compact gelding: looked one to avoid both starts over fences: fair hurdler: won handicap at Newton Abbot in June: reportedly injured tendon final outing: best around 2m: acts on any going: best in visor: tongue tied. *M. C. Pipe*   **c– §**
h105

INTREPID MOGAL 7 b.g. Terimon – Padrigal (Paddy's Stream) [2003/4 h75: c26v² c24g⁴ c26g* c25g⁶ c23g c25v⁴ c26vᵖᵘ c32gᵖᵘ c25g Apr 3] workmanlike gelding: maiden hurdler: modest chaser: won novice at Doncaster in November, gifted race by rivals' jumping errors: little form after, mostly in handicaps: stays 3¼m: acts on heavy going: races prominently: has bled from nose. *N. J. Pomfret* **c97 h–**

IN TUNE 4 b.g. Distinctly North (USA) – Lingering (Kind of Hush) [2003/4 16sᵖᵘ Mar 19] modest maiden on Flat (best at 7f/1m), sold out of P. Mitchell's stable 2,700 gns Newmarket February Sales: badly hampered fourth on hurdling debut. *S. C. Burrough* **h–**

INTYMCGINTY (IRE) 7 b.g. Port Lucaya – Mother Tongue (Montelimar (USA)) [2003/4 h95, F90: 21s³ 21m⁵ 24g Mar 26] rangy gelding: modest novice hurdler: stays 3m: acts on soft going: not a fluent jumper: sold 4,500 gns Doncaster May Sales. *Noel T. Chance* **h92 x**

INVESTMENT FORCE (IRE) 6 b.g. Imperial Frontier (USA) – Superb Investment (IRE) (Hatim (USA)) [2003/4 16m² 17g* 16m 16gᵘʳ Nov 15] sturdy gelding: half-brother to fairly useful chaser Cool Investment (by Prince of Birds), stays 3m: modest on Flat (stays 1m), successful in July, sold out of M. Johnston's stable 5,000 gns Doncaster August Sales: won novice hurdle at Southwell in September: much stiffer task when soundly beaten in handicap next time: will prove best at 2m: sold £3,000 Cheltenham April Sales. *C. J. Mann* **h97**

INVESTOR RELATIONS (IRE) 6 b.g. Goldmark (USA) – Debach Delight (Great Nephew) [2003/4 h86: 17gᵖᵘ 16m⁵ 16m⁶ 17g 16f⁵ c17mᶠ Nov 9] angular gelding: modest handicap hurdler: in touch when fell heavily 5 out in weakly-contested novice handicap at Southwell on chasing debut: will prove best around 2m: acts on firm and soft going. *N. J. Hawke* **c– h90**

INVIRAMENTAL 8 b.g. Pursuit of Love – Corn Futures (Nomination) [2003/4 24gᵖᵘ 16mᵖᵘ Apr 13] maiden hurdler, off nearly 3 years before reappearance: best around 2m with emphasis on speed: headstrong. *R. Williams* **h–**

INVITADO (IRE) 5 ch.g. Be My Guest (USA) – Lady Dulcinea (ARG) (General (FR)) [2003/4 h–: 16m² 20g⁶ 17m 17m⁴ 17m³ 17m 17m⁴ Oct 18] little form on Flat: poor novice hurdler: raced mainly around 2m: acts on good to firm going: visored (failed to settle) second start: often tongue tied. *T. J. Fitzgerald* **h66**

INVITATION 6 b.g. Bin Ajwaad (IRE) – On Request (IRE) (Be My Guest (USA)) [2003/4 16d⁶ 17s 16g 16g⁵ Mar 6] leggy gelding: half-brother to winning 2¾m hurdler Jay Bee Ell (by Pursuit of Love): fairly useful on Flat (stays around 1¼m): modest novice hurdler: unlikely to stay much beyond 2m: not a straightforward ride. *A. Charlton* **h93**

IOGA (FR) 8 b. or br.g. Video Rock (FR) – Valentia (FR) (Brezzo (FR)) [2003/4 c–, h–: c21d c21s⁵ c24m⁶ Apr 13] ex-French gelding: little form in Britain. *John Allen* **c– h–**

IORANA (FR) 8 ch.g. Marignan (USA) – Fareham (FR) (Fast Topaze (USA)) [2003/4 c117, h107: 16g² 19g* 20g⁴ 20m⁵ Jun 5] leggy gelding: fairly useful chaser in 2002/3: fair hurdler: won seller (sold from M. Pipe 7,750 gns) at Hereford in May: ran poorly both subsequent starts: effective at 2m to easy 2½m: acts on any going: has looked none too keen. *Miss K. Marks* **c– h109**

IRANOO (IRE) 7 b.g. Persian Bold – Rose of Summer (IRE) (Taufan (USA)) [2003/4 16g 17s 16g 17d⁵ Mar 30] bad novice hurdler: should stay beyond 2m: acts on firm going: often tongue tied. *R. Allan* **h55**

IRBEE 12 b.g. Gunner B – Cupids Bower (Owen Dudley) [2003/4 c106§, h–§: c21s* c16g⁴ c23v³ c26m⁶ c20d⁵ c26d⁶ c21gᵘʳ Apr 1] tall, well-made gelding: fairly useful hunter chaser nowadays: won handicap at Newton Abbot very early in season: effective at 2½m to 3¼m: acts on good to firm and heavy going: blinkered: irresolute. *P. F. Nicholls* **c110 § h– §**

IRELAND'S EYE (IRE) 9 b.g. Shareef Dancer (USA) – So Romantic (IRE) (Teenoso (USA)) [2003/4 h100: 20d* 23sᵘʳ 20s 24d 20v 20s³ Apr 4] small gelding: poor maiden on Flat: fair handicap hurdler: won at Hexham in May: little form after: should stay beyond 2½m: raced on going softer than good (acts on heavy). *J. R. Norton* **h101 d**

IRENE KATE 5 b.m. Bob's Return (IRE) – Shean Deas (Le Moss) [2003/4 F17v aF16g⁵ Dec 13] 7,000 4-y-o: third foal: dam, fair pointer, out of half-sister to smart 2½m chaser Winter Rain: poor form on second of 2 outings in bumpers: should be suited by stiffer test of stamina. *P. R. Webber* **F66**

IRILUT (FR) 8 br.g. Lute Antique (FR) – Patchourie (FR) (Taj Dewan) [2003/4 c24sᵖᵘ Feb 12] 8,500 4-y-o: sixth foal: brother to winning chaser around 2½m Jourie: dam, won cross-country chase around 2¾m, half-sister to useful staying hurdler Rositary: fair **c–**

pointer, won 3 of 4 starts in 2003: in cheekpieces, didn't look straightforward in hunter chase at Huntingdon. *R. Waley-Cohen*

IRISH BLESSING (USA)   7 b.g. Ghazi (USA) – Win For Leah (USA) (His Majesty (USA)) [2003/4 h–: 23mᵖᵘ 20v 20dᵖᵘ 20g⁴ 21g³ Mar 17] smallish gelding: poor novice hurdler: stays 21f: tried in blinkers/cheekpieces. *F. Jordan*   **h63**

IRISH DISTINCTION (IRE)   6 b.g. Distinctly North (USA) – Shane's Girl (IRE) (Marktingo) [2003/4 h69: 17s³ 16m* 16m* 16g* 17d² 16m⁴ 16m² 16g 17g³ Apr 3] leggy gelding: fair handicap hurdler: most progressive, winning at Chepstow (novice), Wincanton and Wetherby in May: ran well when placed after: best around 2m: acts on good to firm and good to soft going: headstrong. *T. R. George*   **h102**

IRISH FASHION (USA)   9 ch.g. Nashwan (USA) – L'Irlandaise (USA) (Irish River (FR)) [2003/4 c–, h–: 20mᵖᵘ Oct 4] sturdy gelding: fair handicap hurdler in 2001/2: no show on return from year off: well beaten only outing over fences: best around 2m: acts on soft going. *A. J. Whiting*   **c–**
h–

IRISH FLIGHT (IRE)   7 ch.g. Duky – Arewehavingfunyet (Green Shoon) [2003/4 F16s⁴ F16s 16s² Jan 19] IR 12,500 3-y-o: workmanlike gelding: fifth foal: half-brother to fair chaser Ballyvalogue (by Air Display), stays 3m: dam lightly raced in bumpers: fair form in 2 bumpers: 1¼ lengths second to Bobsleigh in novice at Plumpton on hurdling debut: bred to be suited by further than 2m: should improve. *Noel T. Chance*   **h90 p**
F89

IRISH GOLD (IRE)   9 b.g. Good Thyne (USA) – Ardfallon (IRE) (Supreme Leader) [2003/4 h–: c16v⁵ c19dᵖᵘ Jan 1] very lightly raced and signs of only a little ability, lame final outing. *P. Winkworth*   **c–**
h–

IRISH GROUSE (IRE)   5 b.g. Anshan – Another Grouse (Pragmatic) [2003/4 F17d Dec 17] €50,000 4-y-o: chasing type: first foal: dam fairly useful staying chaser: 7/1 from 14/1, well beaten in bumper at Bangor on debut. *Miss H. C. Knight*   **F–**

IRISH HUSSAR (IRE)   8 b.g. Supreme Leader – Shuil Ard (Quayside) [2003/4 c152p, h–: c26gᵖᵘ c24g² c26gᵖᵘ Mar 18] tall, useful-looking gelding: winning hurdler: smart chaser: ¾-length second to Shooting Light in Grade 2 at Newbury, staying on after being unable to quicken 3 out: let down by jumping both other outings in 2003/4, reportedly returned with sore shins after reappearance in valuable handicap at Newbury in November, stiff task in Cheltenham Gold Cup final start: should stay beyond 25f: raced on good going or softer (won bumper on heavy). *N. J. Henderson*   **c154**
h–

IRISHKAWA BELLEVUE (FR)   6 b. or br.g. Irish Prospector (FR) – Strakawa (FR) (Sukawa (FR)) [2003/4 h–, F89: 20m³ 22g⁵ 27d⁵ 27f³ 22m* 20m² 22g² 22dᵖᵘ 22d* 22g* Apr 18] workmanlike hurdler: won at Fontwell in September and March and Wincanton (made all) in April: stays 2¾m: acts on good to firm and good to soft going: usually blinkered, ran poorly only start in cheekpieces. *Jean-Rene Auvray*   **h99**

IRISHMAN (IRE)   10 b.g. Bob Back (USA) – Future Tense (USA) (Pretense) [2003/4 c86d, h84d: c24mᶠ c21m³ c24d⁴ c26mᵖᵘ c23g* Jan 27] lengthy, workmanlike gelding: poor handicap chaser: 5 lb out of weights, won 17-runner event at Leicester: stays 3m: acts on firm and good to soft ground: tried blinkered/in cheekpieces. *Miss I. E. Craig*   **c74**
h–

IRISH PLEASURE (IRE)   8 b. or br.g. Grand Plaisir (IRE) – Killegney (Reformed Character) [2003/4 20gᵖᵘ 22f⁴ Oct 5] deep-girthed gelding: novice hurdler, little show both outings after 18-month lay-off: should stay beyond 19f. *P. Monteith*   **h62**

IRISH PRINCE (IRE)   8 b.g. Fresh Breeze (USA) – Kilivarig (Crozier) [2003/4 h–, F–: 21g 16d² 16d⁶ 16sᵖᵘ 16g 22gᵖᵘ Mar 8] sturdy gelding: poor maiden hurdler, left D. Shaw before final outing: usually visored: pulls hard: has looked none too keen. *J. G. M. O'Shea*   **h71 §**

IRISH RAIDER (NZ)   10 b.g. Epidaurus (USA) – On The Move (AUS) (Bending Away (USA)) [2003/4 16g 17g May 24] no form in 3 runs over hurdles. *J. L. Spearing*   **h–**

IRISH SEA (USA)   11 b.g. Zilzal (USA) – Dunkellin (USA) (Irish River (FR)) [2003/4 c91, h–: c21s⁴ c16gᶠ c24g⁶ c20gᵖᵘ c21dᵖᵘ 20m³ 21m Aug 25] neat gelding: fair hunter chaser, left S. Flook after third start: poor hurdler: stays 3m, effective at much shorter: acts on any going: blinkered once, wore cheekpieces last 2 starts: often let down by jumping: sold £2,800 Ascot October Sales. *A. E. Price*   **c91 x**
h82

IRISHTOWN LEADER (IRE)   6 b.g. Supreme Leader – Glamorous Gale (Strong Gale) [2003/4 21vᵖᵘ 25sᵖᵘ Jan 6] sixth foal: brother to bumper winner Glamorous Leader and half-brother to 2m hurdle winner Phar Breeze (by Phardante): dam, winning hurdler/chaser, stayed 2½m: no show in 2 outings over hurdles. *Miss M. E. Rowland*   **h–**

IRIS ROYAL (FR)   8 b.g. Garde Royale – Tchela (FR) (Le Nain Jaune (FR))   **c144**
[2003/4 c130, h–: c20m* c19d* c20s* c21dᵖᵘ c21d² Mar 18]   **h–**

The First National Gold Cup and the Tripleprint Gold Cup, two of the most
valuable handicaps in the autumn, were won by Iris Royal, the first horse to complete the double since Kings Fountain in 1991/2. The only other horse to win both
races in the same season was Flyingbolt in 1965/6, when the First National was a
conditions event run over two miles, known as the Black & White Whisky Gold
Cup. Pendil won the Black & White Whisky in 1972/3 and the Massey-Ferguson
Gold Cup (as the Tripleprint was then known) the following season, while, more
recently, Nordance Prince won the First National and finished second in the Tripleprint in 1999/2000. The Tsarevich, in 1983/4, was another to win at Ascot and
finish runner-up at Cheltenham.

The First National, which averaged only seven runners in fifteen runnings
in its former guise, had its distance extended to two and a half miles and was turned
into a limited handicap for first- and second-season chasers in 1981/2, sponsors the
Tote (who dropped out after just one season) believing this would attract more
runners and therefore make for a more attractive ante-post market. But the race has
been struggling for runners again in recent seasons, with only a quartet lining up
in both 2000 and 2001, and only six (in a replacement race at Wincanton) in 2002.
The latest renewal cut up badly from an excellent five-day entry, and Iris Royal
faced just four opponents on the day, Le Roi Miguel, Tarxien, Farmer Jack and Ibal.
Iris Royal was the only member of the field with the benefit of a recent run, having
landed the odds comfortably by eight lengths from Wise King in a four-runner
handicap at Sandown earlier in November, though in truth he was left with only that
horse to beat, after Mersey Beat unseated at the tenth and Zafarabad turned in a
moody effort. Racing from a mark 9 lb higher at Ascot, Iris Royal was sent off the
outsider at 13/2, and looked in trouble briefly when the pace increased at the
eleventh. However, with market leaders Tarxien and Farmer Jack blundering away

First National Gold Cup Chase (Limited Intermediate Handicap), Ascot—
Iris Royal proves too strong for Le Roi Miguel (almost hidden)

Tripleprint Gold Cup (Handicap Chase), Cheltenham—
Iris Royal leads two out with runner-up Risk Accessor (left) yet to make his move;
also in the picture are third Telemoss (right) and the about-to-fall Redemption

their chances, and pacesetter Ibal weakening as if the race was needed, the race boiled down to just Iris Royal and Le Roi Miguel from three out. The latter looked to be going the better of the pair at that point, but Marcus Foley on Iris Royal seized the initiative, rousting him into the lead, and Iris Royal kept on well to win ridden out by a length and three quarters from Le Roi Miguel, who was giving him 20 lb.

While the First National had another disappointingly small turnout, the Tripleprint Gold Cup at Cheltenham in mid-December attracted its largest ever field. Hand Inn Hand started favourite at 7/2, followed by Telemoss at 5/1, with Iris Royal, raised 5 lb to a BHB mark of 142, next at 7/1. The seventeen runners eventually got under way after an unbelievably fussy display from the starter. The pace was good and, with the ground soft, it made for a thorough test at the two-and-a-half-mile trip. Hand Inn Hand had already made several mistakes when brought down at the tenth by the crashing fall of narrow leader Indian Scout. It Takes Time took it up two fences later, but couldn't quicken from the second last, at which point Iris Royal and Telemoss both moved up to dispute the lead on the bridle. Iris Royal quickened clear soon after and, with Telemoss fading, the final challenge was delivered by the confidently-ridden Risk Accessor before Iris Royal found extra on the run-in to win by a head. The first two finished thirteen lengths clear of Telemoss, who was all out to hold off Royal Auclair for third, with the remaining seven finishers well strung out. Iris Royal recorded a performance bordering on smart to complete his hat-trick, but a further 11 lb rise in the weights left him with a stiff task when he next appeared in the Unicoin Homes Chase at Cheltenham on New Year's Day, and he was being niggled at to stay in touch when badly hampered and pulled up four out. Iris Royal had just one more run, when second to Our Armageddon in the Cathcart at the Festival, matching his Tripleprint form in going down by two and a half lengths, despite being off the bridle from an early stage and producing an uncharacteristically sketchy round of jumping. A proposed challenge for the world's richest jumps race, the Nakayama Grand Jump was shelved as a result, and the event went off without representation from either Britain or Ireland.

IRI

Iris Royal (FR) (b.g. 1996)	Garde Royale (br 1980)	Mill Reef (b 1968)	Never Bend / Milan Mill
		Royal Way (gr 1969)	Sicambre / Right Away
	Tchela (FR) (b 1985)	Le Nain Jaune (ch 1979)	Pharly / Lady Berry
		Chailly (b 1968)	Tryptic / Haliade

Iris Royal's dam Tchela was placed at around two miles over jumps in France and has produced two other winners by Garde Royale, the useful Ma Royale, who was second in the top four-year-old hurdle at Auteuil shortly after the end of the British season, and Lisa du Chenet, who showed fair form when successful in a couple of mares novice hurdles over two and a half miles and twenty-three furlongs in 2003/4. Iris Royal is also a half-brother to five other winners, notably Galant Moss (by Tip Moss), a very smart hurdler and useful chaser at up to twenty-five furlongs. Iris Royal was useful over timber before embarking on his chasing career in 2002/3, when he won twice over three miles from six starts in novices. He is on the small side for a chaser, but is a sound jumper in general and has shown his form on both firm and heavy going. The Paddy Power Gold Cup at Cheltenham's Open meeting would seem a logical starting point for Iris Royal's next campaign, but he could well prove vulnerable to more progressive types in handicap chases from now on. *N. J. Henderson*

IRIS'S GIFT 7 gr.g. Gunner B – Shirley's Gift (Scallywag) [2003/4 h172: 23s² 24g* 24g* Apr 1] **h172**

Having established himself as a champion over hurdles, Iris's Gift is to have his attentions turned to steeplechasing. Enough examples spring to mind attesting to the difficulties of making the transition from top-class hurdler to top-class chaser. But there are grounds for optimism with Iris's Gift who, in appearance, is very much most people's idea of the top-class, weight-carrying chaser. His jumping technique over hurdles improved immeasurably with experience and his trainer reports that he has schooled well over fences at home. He used to be such a poor jumper of hurdles—'he wouldn't go near them at first and demolished a few when he did'—that he was actually put over fences at home before embarking on his hurdling career. Iris's Gift's forte is stamina and the three and a quarter miles of the Cheltenham Gold Cup will suit him admirably, always providing, of course, that he progresses satisfactorily and gets that far up the steeplechasing ladder. At the moment, the prospects of his attaining the standard required to succeed novice chasing look excellent. His career change is one that should be anticipated with relish.

Iris's Gift graduated straight from novice events to open championship company in his first season over hurdles, showing top-class form when second to Baracouda in the Stayers' Hurdle at the 2003 Cheltenham Festival on only his sixth start over hurdles, and his first outside novice company. Although he had won five out of five up to then, Iris's Gift's performance against Baracouda still came as a real eye-opener. In one of the most memorable horse-races of recent times, Iris's Gift still looked to be travelling best as the leaders rounded the home turn. There was little between Baracouda, Iris's Gift and Irish-trained Limestone Lad going to the last, and, in a pulsating finish, Baracouda held off Iris's Gift by three quarters of a length. Iris's Gift rounded off that campaign by romping home in Britain's top three-mile novice event, the Sefton Hurdle at Aintree. With reports that Baracouda was set to be switched to fences, Iris's Gift looked, at the time, to have the latest season's top staying hurdles at his mercy. Connections weren't seriously tempted to send Iris's Gift chasing straight away as it had 'taken a good while to get him jumping hurdles.' But very little went to plan at first. Baracouda remained over hurdles, for one thing, and, worse still, Iris's Gift encountered training troubles after an unseasonably dry autumn had delayed his reappearance. By the turn of the year, the situation was looking anything but encouraging, Baracouda having landed the odds in the Long Distance Hurdle at Newbury and the Long Walk Hurdle at Ascot, while Iris's Gift remained confined to Jackdaws Castle with a series of 'niggling problems'. His trainer announced in January: 'Iris's Gift isn't fit yet and I don't

bonusprint.com Stayers' Hurdle, Cheltenham—
Iris's Gift reverses 2003 placings with Baracouda in another splendid renewal

rule out going to the Cheltenham Festival without a preparatory run.' Speculation towards the end of the month that stable-companion Rhinestone Cowboy was being considered as a Stayers' Hurdle possible added further to worries about Iris's Gift's well-being.

The stable did manage to get a run into Iris's Gift before the bonusprint.com Stayers' Hurdle, though talk of a possible further outing in the Rendlesham Hurdle at the end of February came to nothing with the likelihood of firmish going at Kempton. Iris's Gift's pre-Cheltenham appearance came under top weight of 11-12 in a qualifier for the Pertemps Handicap Hurdle. Considering his ten-month absence and the fact that he was conceding the best part of two stone all round in a field of eighteen, Iris's Gift's creditable second to stable-companion Tardar showed that he was probably on course for the Stayers', though his performance, strictly on the book, was nearly a stone below his best. By coincidence, Baracouda had carried top weight the week before in the Sandown Hurdle, frightening off much of the opposition, with the remaining runners all out of the handicap; his winning performance was worth a rating somewhat higher than the one Iris's Gift achieved at Haydock. The rematch between Baracouda and Iris's Gift in the Stayers' Hurdle lived right up to its billing, though, on the day, there seemed more confidence behind the heavily-backed, 11/8-on Baracouda, bidding for his third successive win in the race, than there was behind Iris's Gift who was sent off at 9/2, after opening at 4/1 and touching 5/1 on course. The progressive Cleeve Hurdle winner Crystal d'Ainay started third favourite at 8/1, with Iris's Gift's stable-companion Sh Boom and the Irish mare Solerina (a stable-companion of the sidelined Limestone Lad) the only others to start at shorter than 33/1 in the ten-strong line-up. Both Iris's Gift and Baracouda confirmed their standing as two of the best hurdlers of recent times, Iris's Gift getting the better of the argument this time. Solerina made the running, but with her stamina still unproven over the trip, the gallop was nowhere near as searching as the one set by Limestone Lad the previous year (Barry Geraghty reportedly told Gary Hutchison, Solerina's rider, before the race: 'Don't go too fast. It won't do you any good and you will just be setting it up for Baracouda.'). Iris's Gift was settled on the heels of Solerina while Baracouda was held up in around sixth. Iris's Gift took it up at the second last, Barry Geraghty sending him for home in earnest soon afterwards, with Baracouda closing on the long run to the final flight as the pair pulled clear. Baracouda was just about upsides after jumping the last but

446

Iris's Gift found more up the stiff climb to the finish and forged ahead again to win by a length and a half, with a further thirteen back to Crystal d'Ainay, who finished the same distance ahead of fourth-placed Solerina. The victory of Iris's Gift after such a troubled preparation reflected great credit on his trainer Jonjo O'Neill, though the rare defeat for Baracouda was a big blow for J. P. McManus, owner of Jackdaws Castle where O'Neill trains. 'Not for the first time, my trainer has beaten me,' McManus said after watching his Baracouda record a performance that would have been more than good enough to win the Stayers' Hurdle in a normal year. O'Neill, incidentally, saddled three for McManus in the previous day's National Hunt Chase, only for the stable's fourth runner Native Emperor to carry off the prize. O'Neill did send out a Festival winner in the McManus colours when Creon popped up at 50/1 in the Pertemps Handicap Hurdle Final, after which his owner quipped 'If it had been 500/1 I wouldn't have backed it!'

The gap between the Cheltenham Festival and the Grand National meeting at Aintree was a little more than a fortnight in the latest season, compared to the more usual three weeks. Only four of the ten Grade 1 winners at the Festival were sent on to Aintree, though, in mitigation, three of the six absentees would have had to have been returned from Ireland. The Irish-trained Royal & SunAlliance Chase winner Rule Supreme unseated his rider at the eighth when sent back for the Mildmay Novices' Chase, but the three other big Cheltenham winners, Iris's Gift, Arkle winner Well Chief and Triumph Hurdle winner Made In Japan all performed well, Iris's Gift and Well Chief adding another valuable success to their record. That pair were the only ones to complete a Cheltenham/Aintree double, though no fewer than eleven of the twenty winners at the Grand National meeting had contested races at the Cheltenham Festival, providing evidence that the effect of Cheltenham exertions on Aintree runners can often be overstated. Iris's Gift faced a straightforward-looking task in the Martell Cognac Laurel Pub Company Liverpool Hurdle, a race transferred from Ascot where it was formerly run as the Long Distance Hurdle. Starting at 7/4-on, he gave a fine display of hurdling but was made to work hard to win by two and a half lengths from one of the season's leading staying

Martell Cognac Laurel Pub Company Liverpool Long Distance Hurdle, Aintree—
novice Royal Rosa provides the grey's sternest opposition in the curtain-raiser to the three-day meeting

novices Royal Rosa, the tempo quickening—after a funereal early pace—when Iris's Gift was sent on after halfway. Aine Dubh, sixth in the Coral Cup at Cheltenham, and Crystal d'Ainay finished third and fourth. Rhinestone Cowboy, third under top weight in the Coral Cup, won the Aintree Hurdle two days after Iris's Gift's success in the Liverpool Hurdle. The pair met for the first time over hurdles —they were second and fifth in the 2002 Champion Bumper—in the Champion Stayers' Hurdle at Punchestown, shortly after the end of the British season. Iris's Gift was sent off at odds on, but he wasn't at his best on the day and, though battling on in his usual game fashion, went down by seven lengths to his stablemate, his jumping not particularly fluent on this occasion.

		Gunner B (ch 1973)	Royal Gunner (ch 1962)	Royal Charger
Iris's Gift (gr.g. 1997)				Levee
			Sweet Councillor (b 1968)	Privy Councillor
				Sugarstick
		Shirley's Gift (gr 1986)	Scallywag (gr 1973)	Sea Hawk II
				Scammell
			Earlsgift (b 1976)	Dusky Boy
				Austrian Girl

The fairytale story of Iris's Gift's origins will probably be re-told numerous times in the seasons to come. When former coal merchant Robert Lester was left a small legacy by his mother, it just covered the purchase price—said by the owner to be 'around £5,000'—of the then-unnamed gelding. He was bought privately by his owner from former jump jockey Reg Crank, having been turned down by a number of trainers, reportedly including Henrietta Knight and Henry Daly. Another who missed him was Richard Ford who said after his success with Forest Gunner in the Fox Hunters' Chase, three races after Iris's Gift's Liverpool Hurdle, that, when he bought Forest Gunner from Crank, Iris's Gift was in the same field. Iris's Gift is

Mr Robert Lester's "Iris's Gift"

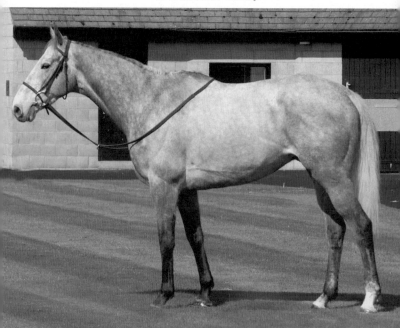

named after the owner's late mother, the sentimental attachment said to be one of the reasons why a reported offer of £1m for the horse was turned down at the start of the latest season. Iris's Gift and Forest Gunner are both by the now-deceased Gunner B whose notable achievements at stud were outlined in last year's essay on Iris's Gift. If Iris's Gift takes after his sire for toughness and gameness, he almost certainly owes his physique to the sire of his dam. The St Leger third Scallywag was a strapping grey, so big that he could not be accommodated in an ordinary starting stall, a special strap being used in place of the rear doors. Shirley's Gift, the dam of Iris's Gift, was unraced, but the grandam Earlsgift was a winning pointer and a half-sister to the top-class hurdler Browne's Gazette out of Austrian Girl, herself an unraced half-sister to the 1961 Ascot Gold Cup winner Pandofell. Earlsgift was originally bought by Reg Crank's father for a reported £1,000 after finishing unplaced in an Irish bumper and coming well behind in four starts there over hurdles; she ran for three seasons in points for the Cranks, her career starting brightly with three successive victories in the space of a little over a fortnight in the 1982 season. Earlsgift won five points in all, needing a stiff test of stamina and being labelled by *Point-to-Pointers and Hunter Chasers* as 'a very shoddy jumper' at the end of her second campaign (in which she failed to win), though the same publication reported the next season that 'she jumped better (generally) than she did . . . and returned to form in consequence.' More details were given about Iris's Gift's family in last year's Annual. The big, workmanlike Iris's Gift, described by his trainer as 'something of a lunatic at home . . . knocking the railings down and galloping over everything', used to hang in some of his early races but is a thoroughly genuine racehorse. He acts on good to firm and heavy going, and will stay beyond twenty-five furlongs, the longest distance he tackled over hurdles. *Jonjo O'Neill*

IRONBRIDGE 9 gr.g. Scallywag – Bahama (Bali Dancer) [2003/4 c20d^F c16m^{pu} Jun 11] of little account, left G. Edwards after reappearance. *M. Mullineaux* — **c–** **h–**

IRON BUCK 11 gr.g. Buckley – Rusty To Reign (General Ironside) [2003/4 c25g^5 c25d^{pu} c22v^{pu} c25v^{pu} c26s^{pu} c24v^{pu} c22d^3 c22s^R c19m Apr 13] plain gelding: won point in 2003: no form in steeplechases. *W. Davies* — **c–**

IRON EXPRESS 8 b.g. Teenoso (USA) – Sylvia Beach (The Parson) [2003/4 c96, h–: c25g^3 c25g^3 c28d^{pu} c26m^2 c21g^2 c25m^{pu} c26m^3 c24g^{pu} c24d^F c25v^2 c22m^{pu} c32d* c28d^5 c31d Apr 22] sparely-made gelding: modest handicap chaser: won at Hexham very early in season and in March: stays 4m: acts on heavy and good to firm going: blinkered seventh start: unreliable. *G. M. Moore* — **c98 §** **h–**

IRON N GOLD 12 b.g. Heights of Gold – Southern Dynasty (Gunner B) [2003/4 c–, h–: c21v* May 26] good-topped gelding: modest handicap chaser: better than ever when gaining third win at Uttoxeter, taken wide and making all: stays 25f: acts on good to firm and heavy going: visored once: often finds little. *B. G. Powell* — **c95** **h–**

IRON WARRIOR (IRE) 4 b.g. Lear Fan (USA) – Robalana (USA) (Wild Again (USA)) [2003/4 16d^{ur} Nov 14] modest maiden on Flat (stays 1½m): unseated early on hurdling debut. *G. M. Moore* — **h–**

IRO ORIGNY (FR) 8 b.g. Saint Cyrien (FR) – Coralline (FR) (Iron Duke (FR)) [2003/4 c§§, h§§: c20g^5 c16m^6 Sep 7] small gelding: poor maiden hurdler/chaser: tongue tied: refused to race last 2 outings in 2002/3: one to leave severely alone. *Miss Venetia Williams* — **c§§** **h§§**

ISAM TOP (FR) 8 b.g. Siam (USA) – Miss Sic Top (FR) (Mister Sic Top (FR)) [2003/4 c–, h101: c16g^6 18s 16d^6 18s^{pu} 18s^F c16g^2 c17d^2 16d 16g^2 Apr 18] compact gelding: winning hurdler, only poor form in 2003/4: poor maiden chaser (makes mistakes): best around 2m: acts on soft and firm going: tried blinkered: usually races prominently: tends to jump right. *M. J. Hogan* — **c68** **h83**

ISARD DU BUARD (FR) 8 b.g. April Night (FR) – Upsala du Buard (FR) (Un Numide (FR)) [2003/4 16s 21d^{pu} Mar 25] bumper winner: no form in 2 novice hurdles after long lay-off. *E. L. James* — **h–**

ISARD III (FR) 8 gr.g. Royal Charter (FR) – Aurore d'Ex (FR) (Mont Basile (FR)) [2003/4 c–p, h127p: c24d^F c20s^2 24m^4 Apr 15] tall, angular gelding: lightly raced: fairly useful form over hurdles and fences: stays 3m: acts on soft and good to firm going: needs to improve jumping over fences. *M. C. Pipe* — **c120** **h115**

ISCA MAIDEN   10 b.m. Full Extent (USA) – Sharp N' Easy (Swing Easy (USA))   c–
[2003/4 c66, h–: 18g⁴ 16v⁵ 19d* 16vᵖᵘ Dec 15] angular mare: maiden chaser: poor   h73
hurdler: won conditional jockeys selling handicap at Market Rasen in December: stays
19f: acts on heavy and good to firm going: inconsistent. *G. Brown*

ISHANDRAZ (GER)   7 gr.g. Mondrian (GER) – Isla Limpia (GER) (Limbo (GER))   h90
[2003/4 h91: 22g² 22mᵖᵘ May 29] modest hurdler: lame final start: stays 25f: acts on good
to firm going: visored in 2003/4: has pulled hard. *M. C. Pipe*

ISIO (FR)   8 b.g. Silver Rainbow – Swifty (FR) (Le Riverain (FR)) [2003/4 c146,   c165
h–: 16d⁵ c16g* c20g* c20g² Apr 2]   h126
        Among the excellent crop of shorter-distance novice chasers in 2002/3,
only Azertyuiop made more of an impression than Isio in their second season over
fences. Indeed, in an average year Isio would have been a contender for a Grade 1
success in the latest season, but faced with two such outstanding chasers as Azertyuiop and Moscow Flyer connections had to content themselves with victories in
two of the season's most valuable handicaps run short of three miles, the Victor
Chandler Chase at Ascot in January and a new and very welcome race, the Vodafone Gold Cup, run over two and a half miles at Newbury ten days before the start
of the Cheltenham Festival. Isio had just two other runs in 2003/4, stepping up to
Grade 1 company at Aintree on his final start when he ran well but was no match
for Moscow Flyer.
        Isio returned to action on Tingle Creek day at Sandown in December but
instead of taking on the crack two-mile chasers, he was in action over hurdles, in an
attempt to take advantage of a much lower mark than he had over fences, in the
valuable William Hill Handicap. Isio ran rather too freely to last home but acquitted
himself well in finishing fifth to Overstrand. The winner failed to win again but Isio
wasn't the only one in the line-up to go on and make an impact later in the season.
Our Vic, Monkerhostin and Starzaan finished second, third and fourth. The Victor
Chandler is the most valuable two-mile handicap chase of the season and the latest
renewal attracted some smart performers, though the presence of Azertyuiop, who
had finished second to Moscow Flyer in the Tingle Creek, meant that only two
others in a field of thirteen were able to race off their proper mark. Isio was one of

Victor Chandler Chase (Handicap), Ascot—
Isio (far side) and top weight Azertyuiop produce one of the best finishes of the season

Vodafone Gold Cup Handicap Chase, Newbury—a new race and another valuable Saturday prize for the Henderson stable, with Isio seeing off the grey Turgeonev

them, set to receive 19 lb after finishing twelve lengths behind Azertyuiop when they were first and third in the previous year's Arkle at Cheltenham. In a thrilling race, one of the most exciting of the whole season, the weight advantage was only just enough to enable Isio to get his head in front in the final strides after Azertyuiop had taken a slight lead early on the run-in. There was a neck in it, with nine lengths back to the winner's stable-companion Got One Too, racing from 2 lb out of the handicap, and the rest well strung out behind. Much of the attention afterwards was, rightly, focussed on the runner-up, who put up one of the best handicap performances of recent years, but Isio had also shown considerable improvement.

Opinions on just how much improvement Isio had shown differed. The BHB handicapper chose to raise his mark only by 6 lb but, by the time Isio went to Newbury for the Vodafone Gold Cup, the form of the Victor Chandler had been franked time and again, four of the field having won in the interim and two others run really well. Isio had previously raced only at around two miles but two and a half proved well within his compass. Jumping and travelling well, Isio quickened to the front at the second last and was soon in no danger, coming home four lengths and six lengths ahead of the outsiders Turgeonev and Seebald. All told, fifteen went to post for the Vodafone Gold Cup, which had prize-money of £100,000 added to stakes, and they included a recent Grade 1 winner in Hand Inn Hand. The Newbury executive, criticised in last year's Annual for the low-key card they staged on the equivalent weekend in 2003, deserves praise for its efforts this time round, providing a good prize as an alternative to Cheltenham for smart horses. Whether it will work quite so well now that, as anticipated, the expanded Festival is to include a valuable Grade 2 weight-for-age chase over two miles five furlongs is another matter.

Overall, the future of jumping looks somewhat brighter than it did at the time of writing of last year's Annual. The BHB has reached a settlement of its investigation by the Office of Fair Trading. Faced with a fixtures free-for-all, the BHB have had plans accepted to introduce a measure of competition into an expanded fixture list in 2006, but, instead of all-weather tracks competing for slots with jumping, both new and existing jumping fixtures will have to remain just that. The BHB, in its report *The Modernisation of British Racing*, couldn't make its support for jumping plainer: 'Jumping remains an integral part of British racing and is extremely popular with spectators and punters.' That was one in the eye for those who favoured a purgative dose of free market economics into the fixture list, something that would have had very serious implications for the overall well-being

451

of National Hunt racing. As it is, under the proposals, National Hunt fixtures will be allowed to be moved between courses, but only in exceptional circumstances between codes. Initially, the number of meetings over jumps will remain as at present, but there is scope for expansion: 'Once further progress has been made in achieving more competitive jump racing, additional BHB jump fixtures will be created.' Building on work done by both the Jump Racing Advisory Panel, formerly the NH Pattern Committee, and a Racecourse Holdings Trust working group which produced a thoughtful and wideranging report on the future of jumping in the autumn, the BHB's report highlights measures to be introduced to make jumping 'more competitive': a restructuring and redefining of the novice chase programme, a refining of the pattern and a reduction in the number of Class B races. The proposals for novice chases, made to JRAP in 2003, provide a recognisable pyramid-type structure and look excellent on paper. There are reservations about the others. It's to be hoped that refining the pattern isn't a euphemism for concentrating big races at a limited number of courses, while reducing the number of Class B races presumably means reducing the number of minor events which serve a useful role but aren't 'bookmaker friendly', attracting small fields and a short-priced favourite. There may be a danger that jumping will follow Flat racing into an ever-more ratings dictated structure. It is far from ideal that the prospects of a horse, unless it is top class, should be dependent almost solely on the assessment of a BHB handicapper. There should be room within the structure for races for non-novices whose conditions aren't based on handicap marks: races restricted to horses that have won just once or twice, or have won races up to a certain value or standard, races with a penalty structure based on prize money won in the last year, are just some of the possibilities.

Sir Peter and Lady Gibbings' "Isio"

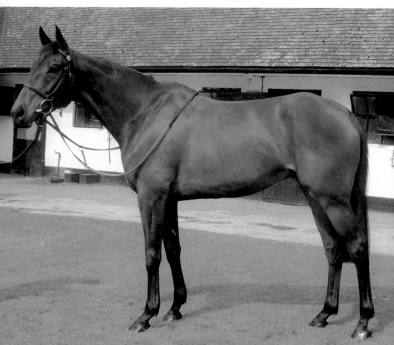

There is clearly less control over the content in those type of races than with a classified stakes, and such events may well produce an odds-on chance or a race with the wrong 'configuration' so far as the bookmakers are concerned. Some of the proposals within *The Modernisation of British Racing* show how clearly the views of the betting industry are being taken into account. The expanded Flat fixture list will be serviced by providing opportunities for those currently being balloted out or eliminated, by restricting most field sizes (both on the Flat and over jumps) to fourteen or twelve depending on the time of year, as well as assuming the recent increases in the number of horses in training and the number of runs per horse will continue at the same or even a slightly accelerated rate. More low-quality, 'Buggins' turn' handicaps, median auction races and bottom-of-the-barrel banded stakes seem likely to be the order of the day. The BHB themselves make clear that the new fixtures will be second rate, as they will have a different name (BHB as opposed to Racecourse fixtures) and 'will effectively be Class B fixtures . . . [with] generally inferior positioning in the Fixture List.' The model behind the reduction in field sizes, to enable this increase in fixtures, is illustrated but the reduction will unfortunately eliminate sixteen-runner handicaps, a type of race where punters are favoured by the general terms of each-way betting. The BHB, the ruling authority of racing, has a duty to represent the interests of all parties involved, which includes the punters. There should not be the slightest suspicion that it is a confederacy of owners and bookmakers.

Isio (FR) (b.g. 1996)	Silver Rainbow (b 1988)	Rainbow Quest (b 1981)	Blushing Groom I Will Follow
		Aryenne (br 1977)	Green Dancer Americaine
	Swifty (FR) (b 1984)	Le Riverain (b 1975)	Riverman Fine
		Miss Fany (ch 1978)	Ermitage Fany Des Saccart

To return to Isio. He held Cheltenham entries, would have had a leading chance in either the Cathcart or the Grand Annual and was around third favourite for the Queen Mother Champion Chase at one time. Connections felt there was little point in taking on Azertyuiop at level weights in the Champion Chase and instead decided to wait for Aintree. Isio started 4/1 second favourite in a field of seven for the Melling Chase and ran up to his handicap form in going down by six lengths to Moscow Flyer. Isio isn't going to be that easy to place in the next season when avoiding Azertyuiop and Moscow Flyer may well be a pre-requisite to another big win. It could, though, be worth thinking about stepping Isio still further up in trip and aiming at the King George in the first part of the winter. The new two miles five furlong chase at the expanded Cheltenham Festival might also be a suitable target later on. The angular Isio is a genuine and consistent sort and a good jumper. He acts on soft and good to firm going. Details of his pedigree were included in last year's Annual, though one of his relations has shown plenty of stamina since: Honore de Beyssac, who is out of a sister to Isio's dam Swifty, won a cross-country chase at Pau in January over three and a half miles. *N. J. Henderson*

ISLAND FAITH (IRE) 7 b. or br.g. Turtle Island (IRE) – Keep The Faith (Furry Glen) [2003/4 h110: c16g* c16d² c20d⁵ c16dᵖᵘ c16s³ Mar 13] strong, compact gelding: fair hurdler: fair novice chaser: won maiden at Carlisle in November: disappointing last 3 starts: best form at 2m: acts on heavy going, possibly unsuited by good to firm: weak finisher. *Ferdy Murphy* **c113 §**
h–

ISLAND FORTRESS 5 ch.m. Infantry – Misty Fort (Menelek) [2003/4 F77: 16g⁵ 16vᵖᵘ 16s⁵ 16g³ 17d³ c17d³ c16g⁵ Apr 4] sturdy mare: modest novice hurdler: similar form when third to Maragun in maiden at Bangor on chasing debut: raced around 2m on good going or softer. *H. D. Daly* **c94**
h89

ISLAND SOUND 7 b.g. Turtle Island (IRE) – Ballet (Sharrood (USA)) [2003/4 c106, h–§: c17d* c16gᵖᵘ 16g² Sep 6] angular gelding: useful on Flat (stays 1½m), successful in July: fair hurdler/chaser: didn't have to be at best to win 5-runner novice chase at Stratford in May: raced around 2m: acts on heavy going: not a fluent jumper of fences: sometimes fails to impress with attitude. *D. R. C. Elsworth* **c93 +**
h115

ISLAND STAR (IRE)   4 b.g. Turtle Island (IRE) – Orthorising (Aragon) [2003/4 16s   h–
16s⁵ Mar 15] disappointing maiden on Flat: well held in juvenile hurdles at Plumpton.
G. P. Enright

ISLANDS THORNS   5 b.g. Thowra (FR) – Holly Hatch (Sulaafah (USA)) [2003/4   h–
F18v F17s 19sᵖᵘ Apr 4] first foal: dam well beaten in bumper: showed nothing in   F–
bumpers/maiden hurdle. *R. H. Alner*

ISLAND STREAM (IRE)   5 b.g. Turtle Island (IRE) – Tilbrook (IRE) (Don't Forget   h103
Me) [2003/4 h99: 16g³ 16m⁶ 20mᵖᵘ 16mᵖᵘ 16m 16g² 16g* 16g* 16gᵘʳ 16s⁵ 16d 17d 19gᵘʳ
16gᵖᵘ 20d⁵ Apr 12] strong gelding: fair hurdler: won handicaps at Uttoxeter and Kempton
(conditional jockeys novice) in November: raced mainly around 2m: acts on heavy going.
J. R. Jenkins

ISLE BE LORD (NZ)   12 b.g. Isle of Man (NZ) – Hi Pico (NZ) (Minnamour) [2003/4   c–
19mᵖᵘ May 26] medium-sized gelding: novice hurdler: no form in steeplechases: tried   h–
blinkered. *B. P. J. Baugh*

ISMAHAAN   5 ch.m. Unfuwain (USA) – River Divine (USA) (Irish River (FR))   F–
[2003/4 F16d aF16gʳᵗʳ F16s⁵ Apr 12] 150,000Y: second foal: dam ran once at 2 yrs: signs
of just a little ability in bumpers: refused to race second start. *M. J. Wallace*

ISOTOP (FR)   8 b.g. Port Etienne (FR) – Clorane (FR) (Rahotep (FR)) [2003/4 24sᶠ   c95
c24g³ c24d² c24v⁴ c24g³ Apr 18] close-coupled gelding: modest maiden hurdler, off   h–
nearly 2 years before reappearance: similar form over fences: stays 3m: raced on good
going or softer (acts on heavy): failed to go through with effort second start. *John Allen*

ISTANBUL (IRE)   5 b.g. Revoque (IRE) – Song of The Glens (Horage) [2003/4 16g   h93 ?
16gʳᵒ 16d⁵ 16g 16g Mar 27] leggy, angular gelding: poor maiden on Flat at 3 yrs for
B. Meehan: fifth of 12 to Albuhera in well-contested novice at Newbury: no comparable
form over hurdles: has worn near-side pricker (ran out second start, reportedly hung on
fourth). *C. J. Mann*

ITALIAN CLOVER   8 b.g. Michelozzo (USA) – National Clover (National Trust)   c–
[2003/4 c24gᵖᵘ c26mᵖᵘ 20m Aug 2] half-brother to top-class chaser Go Ballistic (by   h–
Celtic Cone), stayed 3¼m: dam, very useful pointer, daughter of Welsh Grand National
winner Clover Bud: won twice in points in 2003: no show in 2 steeplechases or novice
hurdle: jumped poorly in blinkers second start. *Mrs H. Dalton*

ITALIAN COUNSEL (IRE)   7 b.g. Leading Counsel (USA) – Mullaghroe (Tarboosh   c–
(USA)) [2003/4 c83, h85: 16mᵘʳ 16m* 16g⁶ 16m* 17m* 19m* 16g 16s 16d Apr 3]   h116
angular gelding: poor maiden chaser: fairly useful handicap hurdler: much improved in
summer, winning twice at both Worcester (including seller) and Market Rasen, beat
Showpiece 7 lengths in valuable event on first occasion at latter course: off 6 months,
well held in competitive races last 3 starts: stays 19f: acts on good to firm going, probably
on heavy: tried in cheekpieces: has had tongue tied: has drifted left. *L. A. Dace*

ITALIAN MIST (FR)   5 b.g. Forzando – Digamist Girl (IRE) (Digamist (USA))   h–
[2003/4 16gᵖᵘ 16m May 29] modest on Flat (barely stays 7f), successful 4 times on
all-weather in 2004: showed nothing in 2 starts over hurdles. *Julian Poulton*

ITCANBEDONE AGAIN (IRE)   5 b.g. Sri Pekan (USA) – Maradata (IRE) (Shar-   h86
dari) [2003/4 h–: 18gᵖᵘ 16m* 17mᵖᵘ Jul 18] fair at best on Flat (barely stays 11f): form
over hurdles only when winning novice handicap at Uttoxeter in June: raced around 2m.
Ian Williams

ITCH   9 b.g. Puissance – Panienka (POL) (Dom Racine (FR)) [2003/4 h64: 16m 16g⁴   h55
16g⁶ May 18] small gelding: bad form over hurdles: barely stays 2m: races freely.
R. Bastiman

ITCHEN MILL   7 b.m. Alflora (IRE) – Treble Chance (Balinger) [2003/4 F78?: 17g⁵   h–
16v⁵ 17g⁶ Jun 21] signs of only a little ability: has pulled hard. *R. H. Alner*

ITCHINTOGO (IRE)   6 b.g. Namaqualand (USA) – Lamp of Phoebus (USA) (Sun-   h–
shine Forever (USA)) [2003/4 F–: F16m⁵ 21s 20g⁴ Nov 10] well held in bumpers and   F–
over hurdles. *L. A. Dace*

I TINA   8 b.m. Lycius (USA) – Tintomara (IRE) (Niniski (USA)) [2003/4 h–: 16g⁴ 16d   h70 §
16m³ 17f 17m⁶ 16g³ 16d* 16s⁴ 16g 17d Mar 27] leggy mare: poor hurdler: won seller at
Chepstow in November: raced mainly around 2m: acts on soft and good to firm going:
visored/blinkered: irresolute. *A. G. Juckes*

ITSABOY   4 b.g. Wizard King – French Project (IRE) (Project Manager) [2003/4 22g⁴   h–
16sᵖᵘ 19sᵖᵘ Apr 4] little form on Flat, none over hurdles. *L. A. Dace*

ITSA LEGEND 5 b.g. Midnight Legend – Onawing Andaprayer (Energist) [2003/4 **F108** F16d* F16g² F16g Mar 17] good-topped gelding: first foal: dam thrice-raced: useful form in bumpers: won 16-runner event at Kempton on debut in February by head from Lord Gale: again looked a stayer when beaten head by Spirit of New York at Newbury and eighth of 24 to Total Enjoyment in Champion Bumper at Cheltenham: will be suited by 2½m+. *A. King*

ITSALF 6 ch.g. Afzal – Sail On Sunday (Sunyboy) [2003/4 F74?: F16g 16d Mar 24] **h–** angular gelding: signs of only a little ability in bumpers: tailed off on hurdling debut. **F–** *J. Rudge*

ITSALLGOINGON 5 b.g. Slip Anchor – Miss Springtime (Bluebird (USA)) [2003/4 **F83** F16g Mar 6] 4,200 4-y-o: third foal: half-brother to 2m hurdle winner My Ace (by Definite Article): dam, 7f/1m winner, became one to treat with caution: ninth of 18 to Reel Missile in bumper at Doncaster on debut. *N. Wilson*

ITS A MYSTERY (IRE) 5 b.m. Idris (IRE) – Blue Infanta (Chief Singer) [2003/4 **h–** 16d⁵ 16g 16s 16dᵘʳ Jan 9] rather leggy mare: no form on Flat or over hurdles. *R. T. Phillips*

ITSASURETHING 4 b.g. Sure Blade (USA) – Ginka (Petoski) [2003/4 F17s F16g **h–** 16d 19s⁶ Apr 4] fourth foal: dam staying maiden: seventh of 9 at Kampton on second of 2 **F–** runs in bumpers, set steady pace and almost certainly flattered: well held both starts over hurdles. *J. W. Mullins*

IT'S A WIZARD 4 b.g. Wizard King – Axed Again (Then Again) [2003/4 16m Nov **h–** 6] modest/temperamental maiden on Flat (stays 7f): last in juvenile on hurdling debut. *M. A. Barnes*

IT'S A WRAP (IRE) 6 b.m. Carroll House – Wraparound Sue (Touch Paper) [2003/4 **h80** F16m 16s² Dec 26] 6,000 4-y-o: eleventh foal: half-sister to modest hurdlers Spoof (by **F–** Good Thyne), stays 27f, and Supreme Music (by Supreme Leader), stays 19f: dam maiden half-sister to smart hurdler/useful chaser up to 25f Pearlstone: failed to complete in 2 points in 2003: well held in bumper: second in seller at Uttoxeter on hurdling debut. *Miss K. Marks*

IT'S BEYOND BELIEF (IRE) 10 b.g. Supreme Leader – Rossacurra (Deep Run) **c100** [2003/4 c114: c26s² c26v⁴ c23sᵖᵘ Apr 6] fair chaser: will stay beyond 3¼m: raced on good going or softer: possibly amiss in blinkers final start. *P. F. Nicholls*

ITSDEDFAST (IRE) 8 ch.g. Lashkari – Amazing Silks (Furry Glen) [2003/4 h–, **h81 x** F95: 17g⁵ 16g⁵ 17g 17d Oct 29] well beaten on Flat: poor novice hurdler: raced mainly around 2m: makes mistakes. *L. Lungo*

IT'S DEFINITE (IRE) 5 b.g. Definite Article – Taoveret (IRE) (Flash of Steel) **h– p** [2003/4 19dᵖᵘ Dec 2] sturdy gelding: fairly useful on Flat (stays 2½m), sold out of A. Jarvis' stable 40,000 gns Doncaster August Sales: lame on hurdling debut. *P. Bowen*

IT'S EJ 6 b.g. Karinga Bay – Merry Marigold (Sonnen Gold) [2003/4 F16s⁶ F16s **F86** F17v⁶ Mar 21] third foal: dam 1¼m winner: sixth in bumper at Wetherby on debut: failed to settle when well held in similar events at Ayr and Carlisle. *Mrs S. J. Smith*

IT'S GOT BUCKLEYS 5 b.g. El Conquistador – Saucey Pup (The Parson) [2003/4 **F–** F16d F17s Feb 17] third foal: dam winning Irish pointer: showed nothing in 2 bumpers. *J. W. Mullins*

ITSGOTTABDUN (IRE) 7 b.g. Foxhound (USA) – Lady Ingrid (Taufan (USA)) **h–** [2003/4 16g 17m 17d 19dᵖᵘ 19d Dec 11] modest 6f winner on Flat at 3 yrs: sold out of A. Reid's stable 1,000 gns Ascot August (2001) Sales: no form over hurdles. *Miss M. Bragg*

ITS GOTTA BE ALFIE (IRE) 9 ch.g. Zaffaran (USA) – Nimbi (Orchestra) [2003/4 **c69 x** c24sᶠ c25d³ c25d⁴ c25dᶠ Mar 22] big gelding: well held over hurdles: poor form over **h–** fences (off 21 months before reappearance): likely to need thorough test of stamina: acts on good to firm and good to soft going: often let down by jumping over fences. *M. Scudamore*

IT'S HARRY 6 b.g. Aragon – Andbracket (Import) [2003/4 F86: F16g³ 17g⁴ 16m³ **h99** 20s³ 20d³ 20s 20d Apr 18] quite good-topped gelding: fair form in bumpers: modest form **F86** in novice hurdles: stays 2½m: acts on soft and good to firm ground. *Mrs S. J. Smith*

IT'S JUST HARRY 7 b.g. Tragic Role (USA) – Nipotina (Simply Great (FR)) [2003/4 **h107 p** 16d³ Mar 12] sturdy gelding: third to Lord Sam in bumper at Newbury on debut: off 2 years, third to Back To Ben Alder in novice at Sandown on hurdling debut: likely to improve. *C. R. Egerton*

IT'S MUSIC (IRE) 5 b.g. Accordion – Leadon Lady (Monksfield) [2003/4 16g⁵ 19s² 18v⁶ c25v² c22m⁶ Feb 28] tall gelding: fourth foal: dam maiden: modest form over hurdles and fences: will prove better at 3m+ than shorter: needs to improve his jumping. *M. C. Pipe* **c93 h93**

ITSMYBOY (IRE) 4 br.g. Frimaire – Hawkfield Lass (IRE) (The Parson) [2003/4 F18g* Apr 22] third foal: dam ran once in Ireland: overcame signs of inexperience to win bumper at Fontwell on debut by 8 lengths from Earth Man. *M. C. Pipe* **F101**

ITSMYTURNNOW (IRE) 9 b.g. Glacial Storm (USA) – Snuggle (Music Boy) [2003/4 c78: c30m³ c26f* c23m⁶ c21g Apr 1] tall gelding: winning pointer: easily best effort in steeplechases when winning novice hunter at Folkestone in May: should stay beyond 3¼m: acts on firm going: has jumped left. *M. J. Roberts* **c92 ?**

IT'S NORMAN 8 b.g. Vantastic – Arrogant Daughter (Aragon) [2003/4 c16gᵖᵘ Mar 12] no sign of ability. *Mrs L. Pomfret* **c– h–**

ITSONLYAGAME 4 b.c. Ali-Royal (IRE) – Mena (Blakeney) [2003/4 16g⁶ Nov 30] angular colt: modest on Flat (stays 11.6f): sixth in juvenile at Newbury on hurdling debut. *R. Ingram* **h73**

ITSONLYME (IRE) 11 b.g. Broken Hearted – Over The Arctic (Over The River (FR)) [2003/4 c119, h–: c25gᵖᵘ c20g² c20d* c20m³ c24g* c20g c24g² c26g⁶ c25d⁶ c24sᵖᵘ c24mᵖᵘ c26mᵖᵘ Apr 14] useful-looking gelding: useful chaser: won intermediate at Wetherby in May and amateur handicap at Cheltenham in November: stays 25f: acts on soft and good to firm going: has found little. *Miss Venetia Williams* **c130 h–**

ITS ONLY POLITE (IRE) 8 b.g. Roselier (FR) – Decent Debbie (Decent Fellow) [2003/4 c91, h–: c24v* Apr 4] workmanlike gelding: progressive form in novice hurdles in 2001/2: left A. Lidderdale and off nearly 15 months, improved form over fences when winning handicap at Lingfield only start in 2003/4, briefly hanging right: should stay beyond 25f: raced on going softer than good (acts on heavy). *C. Tinkler* **c103 + h–**

IT'S RUMOURED 4 ch.g. Fleetwood (IRE) – Etourdie (USA) (Arctic Tern (USA)) [2003/4 16g³ 16m* 16m³ Oct 7] fair form at best on Flat: modest form in juvenile hurdles at Stratford, winning in August. *Jean-Rene Auvray* **h88**

ITS SUNNY 10 ch.m. Sunley Builds – Free To Go (Free State) [2003/4 19f 16g² 17d⁵ 17d³ Mar 27] third foal: dam, lightly-raced maiden on Flat, stayed 1½m well: poor form over hurdles: should stay 2½m. *Mrs S. J. Smith* **h82**

IT'S WALLACE 11 b.g. Bedford (USA) – Rua Batric (Energist) [2003/4 24vᵖᵘ 24s 21s² 20s 21s⁶ 20g* 21d⁶ Mar 19] leggy gelding: little show only outing over fences: fair hurdler, off nearly 2 years before reappearance: won seller at Huntingdon in March: probably stays 3m: acts on good to firm and heavy going: formerly blinkered, tried in cheekpieces: has won 5 times at Plumpton. *Miss S. West* **c– h102**

ITS WALLACE JNR 5 b.g. Bedford (USA) – Built In Heaven (Sunley Builds) [2003/4 h105?: 18g* 21g³ 20v 21g Feb 28] leggy gelding: fair handicap hurdler: won at Fontwell in October: stays 21f: best efforts on good going. *Miss S. West* **h107**

IT TAKES TIME (IRE) 10 b.g. Montelimar (USA) – Dysart Lady (King's Ride) [2003/4 c143+, h156: c20gᶠ c20s⁵ c24gᵖᵘ Dec 26] angular gelding: very smart hurdler, though not a fluent jumper: useful novice chaser in 2002/3: would have run at least creditably but for falling 2 out in valuable handicap won by Fondmort at Cheltenham on reappearance: long way below form in similar event there and King George VI Chase at Kempton (jumped poorly) subsequently: stays 25f: acts on good to firm and heavy going: tends to idle. *M. C. Pipe* **c143 ? h–**

IVANOPH (FR) 8 b.g. Roi de Rome (USA) – Veronique IV (FR) (Mont Basile (FR)) [2003/4 c124, h–: c17d⁶ c17gᵘʳ c17s² c16v c19g³ c20dᵘʳ c24s* Apr 17] tall, sparely-made gelding: has reportedly had breathing operation: winning hurdler: fairly useful handicap chaser: won at Bangor by 3 lengths from Tom's Prize: stays 3m: acts on any going: often finds little: unreliable. *P. F. Nicholls* **c125 § h–**

I'VEHADIT (IRE) 10 ch.g. Treasure Hunter – Had Enough (Hadeer) [2003/4 c135, h–: c20g⁴ 22m³ c20f³ c24d c29s³ 24d⁴ c19s c24s² 20s c24sᵖᵘ Mar 14] lengthy gelding: fairly useful hurdler: useful chaser: creditable second to Hedgehunter in valuable handicap at Gowran in January: reportedly distressed previous outing: stays 29f: ideally suited by going softer than good. *D. T. Hughes, Ireland* **c130 h120**

I'VE NO SAY (IRE) 11 ch.g. Rising – Mon Democrat (Tanfirion) [2003/4 20m c22g² c23m⁴ Jul 23] tall, useful-looking gelding: winning hurdler: modest handicap chaser: off **c93 h–**

over 13 months before reappearance: stays 3m: acts on good to firm and heavy going:
tried visored, wore cheekpieces last 2 outings: has often looked less than keen. *Mrs P. Sly*

IVERAIN (FR)   8 b.g. Le Riverain (FR) – Ursala (FR) (Toujours Pret (USA)) [2003/4   **c122**
c119, h–: c25g² c24m c20g⁴ c20m* c21d c20d⁶ c24dᴿ Dec 29] good-topped gelding: **h–**
fairly useful handicap chaser: left P. Nicholls after second start: won weak race at Haydock in November: stays 25f: acts on good to soft and good to firm going: blinkered once
(well below form). *Sir John Barlow Bt*

IVORSAGOODUN   5 b.m. Piccolo – Malibasta (Auction Ring (USA)) [2003/4 h80:   **h88**
24m⁶ 22g² 17g Apr 13] leggy mare: modest maiden hurdler: off 10 months and left
M. Pipe before final start: seems to stay 3m: acts on good to firm going: tried visored:
probably doesn't have ideal attitude. *N. R. Mitchell*

IVORY BAY   5 b.g. Piccolo – Fantasy Racing (IRE) (Tirol) [2003/4 16g⁶ Nov 12]   **h–**
modest on Flat (probably stays 1¼m): tailed off in novice on hurdling debut: sold 3,000
gns Doncaster November Sales. *J. Hetherton*

IVORY FORT   4 ch.g. Bold Fort – Ivory Girl (IRE) (Sharp Victor (USA)) [2003/4   **F–**
F14d F16m Apr 13] first foal: dam, no sign of ability, half-sister to useful sprinter Cool
Cousin: well held in 2 bumpers, trained by M. Harris on debut. *R. Williams*

IVORY GIRL (IRE)   9 ch.m. Sharp Victor (USA) – Nordic Dance (USA) (Graustark)   **c–**
[2003/4 19gᵖᵘ c20mʳᵒ May 5] no sign of ability on Flat at 2/3 yrs for K. Wingrove: showed   **h–**
nothing in mares novices over hurdles and fences. *R. Williams*

IVORY VENTURE   4 b.f. Reprimand – Julietta Mia (USA) (Woodman (USA))   **h–**
[2003/4 17dᵖᵘ Mar 22] poor on Flat (should stay 6f), sold out of D. Ivory's stable £1,000
Ascot February Sales: soon tailed off on hurdling debut. *I. R. Brown*

IVY HOUSE LAD (IRE)   4 b.g. Presidium – Nice Spice (IRE) (Common Grounds)   **F–**
[2003/4 F16s Feb 7] second foal: dam, little show on Flat, out of half-sister to Middle
Park Stakes winner Mister Majestic and Grand Prix de Paris winner Homme de Loi:
tailed off in bumper and on Flat debut. *I. W. McInnes*

IZNOGOUD (FR)   8 br.g. Shafoun (FR) – Vancia (FR) (Top Dancer (FR)) [2003/4   **c140**
c146x, h–: 25d c26g c24sᵖᵘ c20g* c24m³ c20g² c21gᶠ c29m⁶ Apr 24] tall, leggy gelding: **h–**
has a markedly round action: winning hurdler: useful handicap chaser: back to form when
winning at Kempton in February by 1¼ lengths from Zaffamore: best subsequent effort
when second to Tikram in valuable event at Cheltenham in March: effective at 2½m to
easy 29f: acts on good to firm and heavy going: visored twice (departed early both times).
M. C. Pipe

IZZYKEEN   5 b.g. Keen – Washita (Valiyar) [2003/4 F17g³ Apr 24] 2,600 3-y-o: fifth   **F85**
foal: brother to winner up to 1¾m Los Alamos and half-brother to 1994 2-y-o 7f winner
Last Roundup (by Good Times): dam poor maiden half-sister to high-class middle-
distance stayer Dakota and smart middle-distance stayer Warpath: third to Lockstockandbarrel in bumper at Market Rasen on debut. *Mrs S. J. Smith*

betfair.com Chase (Handicap), Kempton—
Iznogoud (right) challenges the grey Avalanche and wins his first race since his novice days

J

JABIRU (IRE) 11 b. or br.g. Lafontaine (USA) – Country Glen (Furry Glen) [2003/4 **c101** c107, h–: c25m c26m* c25dᵖᵘ c24m³ c22g² c24g³ Apr 16] good-topped gelding: **h–** fairly useful hunter chaser: made all at Newton Abbot in May: won point in February: stays 3½m: best efforts on good going or firmer (acts on firm): often blinkered. *Mrs K. M. Sanderson*

JABOUNE (FR) 7 ch.g. Johann Quatz (FR) – Seasonal Pleasure (USA) (Graustark) **c120** [2003/4 h129: c19g* c16g* c21g² 16m⁴ 16m⁴ c16d⁵ c20d⁴ 16d⁶ 22g Apr 16] compact **h129** gelding: type to carry condition: fairly useful hurdler: good fourth at Ascot and Cheltenham in November: fairly useful novice chaser: won at Hereford and Fakenham in May: stays 19f: acts on good to firm and good to soft going, possibly not on soft: has had tongue tied: genuine and consistent. *A. King*

JABULANI (IRE) 5 b.g. Marju (IRE) – Houwara (IRE) (Darshaan) [2003/4 17d³ **h87** May 28] modest on Flat (stays 9.4f): third in maiden at Cartmel on hurdling debut: likely to prove best around 2m: sold to join Mrs S. Smith 1,500 gns Doncaster May Sales. *G. M. Moore*

JAC AN REE (IRE) 8 b.g. Supreme Leader – Nic An Ree (IRE) (King's Ride) [2003/4 **h87** h–, F90: 21g 21g Mar 26] useful-looking gelding: lightly raced: seemingly easily best effort over hurdles when tenth of 20 in maiden at Newbury final start. *A. King*

JACARADO (IRE) 6 b.g. Jurado (USA) – Lady Mearba (IRE) (Le Bavard (FR)) **h–** [2003/4 F16g 22s 19g 25dᵖᵘ Mar 19] 7,500 4-y-o: good-topped gelding: first foal: dam **F–** unraced: no sign of ability. *R. Dickin*

JACCOUT (FR) 6 b.g. Sheyrann – Jacottiere (FR) (Dom Racine (FR)) [2003/4 **c–** c20mᵖᵘ 16m 22g c20d 16d 20d⁴ 17s⁶ 20v 20s 17d Apr 18] fifth foal: half-brother to 3 **h80** winners on Flat in France: dam 1m winner: fair hurdler/chaser in France: left G. Pannier, only poor form in Britain: stays 2½m: acts on heavy going: tried tongue tied. *R. Johnson*

JACDOR (IRE) 10 b.g. Be My Native (USA) – Bellalma (Belfalas) [2003/4 c–x, **c119** h118: 20d⁶ 20g c24d² c30d c20g⁴ c25v⁵ c24g* c24g* Feb 19] tall gelding: fairly useful **h105** handicap hurdler/chaser: won over fences at Kempton (conditional jockeys) and Taunton in February: stays 25f: acts on good to firm and heavy going: blinkered/visored: has had tongue tied. *R. Dickin*

JACK DASH (IRE) 6 b.g. Teamster – Gathering Moss (Le Moss) [2003/4 F16g⁵ **h–** 22gᵖᵘ Feb 22] €12,000 4-y-o: medium-sized gelding: fourth foal: half-brother to winning **F–** pointer by Roselier: dam winning pointer: little sign of ability in bumper and novice hurdle. *Miss H. C. Knight*

JACK DAWSON (IRE) 7 b.g. Persian Bold – Dream of Jenny (Caerleon (USA)) **h120** [2003/4 h105: 16d³ Apr 3] fairly useful stayer on Flat: lightly-raced winning hurdler: 7 lb out of handicap, improved form when third to Puck Out in listed event at Aintree only outing in 2003/4: should stay beyond 17f: acts on good to firm and good to soft going. *John Berry*

JACK DORAN 4 ch.g. Gildoran – Faustelerie (Faustus (USA)) [2003/4 F12g F14g **F–** F16g Mar 7] unfurnished gelding: fifth foal: half-brother to 2 winning hurdlers by Democratic, including Charlies Future, fair up to 2¾m: dam unraced: showed little in 3 bumpers: saddle slipped second start, pulled hard final one. *J. R. Jenkins*

JACK DURRANCE (IRE) 4 b.g. Polish Precedent (USA) – Atlantic Desire (IRE) **h–** (Ela-Mana-Mou) [2003/4 16d 18s 16g 16d Mar 19] smallish gelding: fair on Flat (will stay 1½m), sold out of M. Johnston's stable 11,000 gns Newmarket Autumn Sales: well beaten in juvenile hurdles. *G. A. Ham*

JACKEM (IRE) 10 b. or br.g. Lord Americo – Laurence Lady (Laurence O) [2003/4 **c– x** c85, h93: c26vᵖᵘ May 21] useful-looking gelding: modest hurdler/novice chaser: stays **h–** 25f: acts on heavy going, probably on good to firm: makes mistakes. *Ian Williams*

JACK FLUSH (IRE) 10 b.g. Broken Hearted – Clubhouse Turn (IRE) (King of Clubs) **h–** [2003/4 17g 17v 16g⁵ 19g 16g 17d Mar 30] leggy gelding: poor hurdler: showed little in 2003/4: often blinkered/visored: usually tongue tied. *M. E. Sowersby*

JACK FULLER (IRE) 7 b.g. Be My Native (USA) – Jacks Sister (IRE) (Entitled) **c94** [2003/4 h75, F84: 20d c16g³ c16d³ c16s² c16m* c16d³ Mar 28] tall gelding: poor maiden **h–** hurdler: modest chaser: won novice handicap at Taunton in March: should be suited by further than 2m: acts on soft and good to firm going: wore cheekpieces on reappearance, visor fourth start and blinkers last 2: looked reluctant final outing. *P. R. Hedger*

JACK HIGH (IRE) 9 br.g. Erdelistan (FR) – Lyntim (Fidel) [2003/4 h127: 20d² 24d 20s c16s^F c21s³ c22s^{ur} c20d⁵ c20s* c17s^F Mar 27] smallish gelding: fairly useful hurdler: fair form over fences, won maiden at Navan in March: needs at least 2½m and will stay beyond 3m: acts well on going softer than good: held up. *T. M. Walsh, Ireland*

**c108
h127**

JACKIE CULLEN (IRE) 7 b.g. Lord Americo – Rose Hand (IRE) (Tarboosh (USA)) [2003/4 F18d F16d² F16m F16d² 16s* c18s⁶ c20d^{ur} c18d⁴ c18d c16d² Apr 8] first foal: dam unraced: fairly useful form in bumpers: fair form on second outing over hurdles when winning maiden at Fairyhouse in November (likely to improve further): fair novice chaser: raced mainly around 2m: acts on soft going. *Mrs J. Harrington, Ireland*

**c103
h106 p
F101**

JACKIE JARVIS (IRE) 7 b.m. Alphabatim (USA) – Miss Brantridge (Riboboy (USA)) [2003/4 c103p: c16g⁵ Mar 12] winning hunter chaser: sold out of P. York's stable £10,000 Ascot June Sales, reluctant to line up at Leicester (refused to race once in bumpers): won point later in month. *J. S. Swindells*

c70 +

JACK MACK 8 b.g. Solway Beleef – Maybella (Quiet Fling (USA)) [2003/4 16m^{pu} Jun 5] fifth foal: dam winning 2m hurdler: pulled up in 2 maiden points in 2002 and in novice hurdle (tongue tied) in June. *M. A. Barnes*

h–

JACK MARTIN (IRE) 7 ch.g. Erins Isle – Rolling Penny (IRE) (Le Moss) [2003/4 F96: F17d⁴ F16v³ 20v^F 21s³ 19g² 20s* 20d² 20g³ Apr 16] leggy gelding: fair in bumpers: progressive hurdler: won novice handicap at Newcastle in March: third to Bourbon Manhattan in novice at Ayr final start: will stay 3m: acts on soft going. *S. Gollings*

**h119
F94**

JACKOFALLTRADES (IRE) 6 b.g. Lord Americo – Wind Chimes (The Parson) [2003/4 h–, F–: 20g^{pu} May 14] little sign of ability. *A. C. Whillans*

h–

JACK OF KILCASH (IRE) 10 br.g. Glacial Storm (USA) – Candora (Cantab) [2003/4 c21f⁶ May 21] fair pointer: last of 6 finishers in novice on hunter chase debut. *Nigel Benstead*

c–

JACK OF SPADES (IRE) 8 b.g. Mister Lord (USA) – Dooney's Daughter (The Parson) [2003/4 c16s c19d^{pu} Jan 7] IR 60,000 3-y-o, 106,000 4-y-o: good-topped gelding: sixth foal: brother to 2 bumper winners, notably very smart 2m to 21f hurdler Monsignor: dam, winning pointer, sister to useful staying hurdler Holy Joe: placed both starts in maiden Irish points in 2002: bought 16,000 gns Doncaster May (2002) Sales: well held on completed outing in maiden chases. *R. Dickin*

c–

JACK POT II (FR) 7 ch.g. Luchiroverte (IRE) – Roxane II (FR) (Signani (FR)) [2003/4 h85, F92: 24d⁴ 21s⁴ 20d⁴ 20d⁵ 24d³ 23v* Jan 26] useful-looking gelding: modest hurdler: improved effort when winning amateur novice at Wetherby: stays 3m: acts on heavy going. *L. Lungo*

h97

JACKS BIRTHDAY (IRE) 6 b.g. Mukaddamah (USA) – High Concept (IRE) (Thatching) [2003/4 h–: 20m^{pu} 20m^{pu} Aug 2] of little account nowadays: tried blinkered. *J. Joseph*

h–

JACKS CRAIC (IRE) 5 b.g. Lord Americo – Boleree (IRE) (Mandalus) [2003/4 F–: F16m² F16d 21s^F 16d³ 16g⁶ Feb 11] good-topped gelding: fair form in bumpers, left C. Weedon after reappearance: modest form over hurdles: should stay 2½m+. *J. L. Spearing*

**h99
F92**

JACKS JEWEL (IRE) 7 b.g. Welsh Term – September Daydream (IRE) (Phardante (FR)) [2003/4 F–: F17g 21g^{pu} 21s³ 24s^{pu} Jan 20] achieved little in bumpers: poor form on second of 3 starts over hurdles. *C. J. Down*

**h81
F–**

JACKSON (FR) 7 b.g. Passing Sale (FR) – Tynia (FR) (Djarvis (FR)) [2003/4 h68?, F–: c25s^{ur} Mar 7] sturdy gelding: signs of only a little ability in bumpers and over hurdles (tongue tied): won points in February, March and April: clear with winner when unseated 5 out in novice hunter chase at Market Rasen. *A. N. Dalton*

**c–
h–**

JACKSONVILLE (FR) 7 b.g. Petit Montmorency (USA) – Quinine Des Aulnes (FR) (Air du Nord (USA)) [2003/4 c87, h–: c25g^{pu} c20s⁵ 24v⁵ c24v⁵ c20d* Apr 23] sturdy gelding: maiden hurdler: modest chaser: off bridle long way out when winning novice handicap at Perth: likely to prove better suited by around 3m than shorter: raced on good going or softer (acts on heavy). *A. Parker*

**c93
h–**

JACK WEIGHELL 5 b.g. Accordion – Magic Bloom (Full of Hope) [2003/4 F–: F17g⁵ F16d 16g 20d 21d 20d Apr 18] good-topped gelding: form in bumpers only when fifth at Sedgefield in October: well held over hurdles. *J. M. Jefferson*

**h–
F82**

JACOB'S WIFE   14 ro.m. Baron Blakeney – Vido (Vimadee) [2003/4 c79, h–: c25g⁴ c20m³ May 15] leggy mare: fair chaser at best: winning pointer: best effort in hunters when third at Ludlow: stays 25f: acts on good to firm and heavy going: blinkered once. *G. L. Edwards*   **c86 h–**

JADE'S TREASURE   5 b.m. Zamindar (USA) – Jade Venture (Never So Bold) [2003/4 F16m⁶ Oct 10] third foal: half-sister to modest hurdler Speed Venture (by Owington), stays 2½m: dam second over 1m to 1¼m on only starts: well held in bumper on debut. *T. Keddy*   **F–**

JAFFA   12 ch.g. Kind of Hush – Sip of Orange (Celtic Cone) [2003/4 c20g* c20g⁵ Mar 28] well-made gelding: fair chaser: off nearly 2 years, won amateur handicap at Leicester in March: best around 2½m: acts on soft going. *Miss J. Wormall*   **c104**

JAHANGIR   5 b.g. Zamindar (USA) – Imperial Jade (Lochnager) [2003/4 16sᵖᵘ Nov 22] compact gelding: modest maiden on Flat (stays 7f): pulled extremely hard in novice on hurdling debut. *B. R. Johnson*   **h–**

JAHASH   6 ch.g. Hernando (FR) – Jalsun (Jalmood (USA)) [2003/4 h118: 24d 20m³ c17f* c19d³ c16s² c16s⁴ c16m² c16g⁴ c20d⁵ c20m² Apr 23] rather leggy gelding: fair hurdler: fairly useful chaser: won novice at Exeter in October: left P. Hobbs after next start: best efforts when fourth to Well Chief in Grade 1 novice at Cheltenham (keeping on late) and second of 4 to Biliverdin in novice handicap at Sandown: effective at 2m to easy 3m: unraced on heavy going, acts on any other. *A. King*   **c128 h111**

JAHIA (NZ)   5 br.m. Jahafil – Lana (NZ) (Tristrams Heritage (NZ)) [2003/4 16g 19gᵖᵘ 16d 16m Oct 9] ran 4 times in New Zealand, winning over 5f and 6f at 3 yrs: little show in 4 races over hurdles and one on Flat in Britain: tongue tied third start. *R. C. Guest*   **h–**

JAIR DU COCHET (FR)   7 b.g. Rahotep (FR) – Dilaure (FR) (Rose Laurel) [2003/4 c150p, h–: 20d² 18v* c20s* c24gᵖᵘ c25d* Jan 24]   **c170 h?**

    The loss of a top-class horse is hard enough to take at any time, but the timing of Jair du Cochet's demise was particularly cruel. Just nine days before the Cheltenham Gold Cup, in which he was expected to line up as the chief threat to Best Mate, Jair du Cochet fractured his off-hind cannon-bone at home in one of his last pieces of work before Cheltenham. The injury was too serious for Jair du Cochet to be saved. His trainer, Guillaume Macaire, announced that neither he, nor his other intended runners at the meeting, would be making the trip to the Festival.

    If Jair du Cochet's loss was the low point of Macaire's season, there had been some notable highs as well. When the French season ended on December 31st, Macaire was crowned champion jumps trainer with a record two hundred and six wins and more than €3 million in prize money. His dominance was overwhelming, due in no small part to a strike rate of 36%. Only one other trainer registered more than a hundred wins and, by way of comparison, Francois Doumen, the only other French trainer of jumpers with a high profile in Britain, trained the winners of just fifteen races over jumps in France in 2003. Macaire's stable jockeys, Jair du Cochet's partner Jacques Ricou and Benoit Gicquel, finished third and fourth respectively in the jockeys' table by number of wins.

    Jair du Cochet's own contribution to the stable's success in France was modest. His outings in the French Provinces in recent seasons were effectively warm-up events for bigger races in Britain where his career had taken root in his days as an outstanding juvenile hurdler. He began the latest season over hurdles, with a second place at Compiegne and a win at Cholet in the autumn, before getting down to the more serious business of taking on Best Mate in the Tote Peterborough Chase at Huntingdon. Macaire had sent out Douze Douze to finish second to Best Mate in the same race the year before. In receipt of 5 lb from the dual Gold Cup winner, Jair du Cochet started second favourite, with Valley Henry and La Landiere the only other credible contenders in a field of six (though one of the no-hopers was Venn Ottery). It turned out to be an unsatisfactory contest, very steadily run in the testing conditions, and there were plenty of possible reasons for the laboured effort which Best Mate turned in on what was his reappearance. But regardless of the odds-on favourite disappointing, Jair du Cochet showed plenty of improvement from his novice form to beat Best Mate and the rest with something in hand, winding up the tempo leaving the back straight and galloping on strongly, even after running down the final fence and giving it a clout. Best Mate was eight lengths back in second, beaten for only the third time over fences.

Among those most impressed by Jair du Cochet's performance was new, big-time owner Graham Wylie who immediately made an offer to buy the horse, seeking an established high-class chaser to add to a string of expensive purchases who were mainly novices. 'We had a jet booked and the money ready,' reported Wylie's trainer Howard Johnson, but the offer was turned down. It was apparently not the last offer made for Jair du Cochet, and it certainly was not the first. More than one bid from Britain to buy Jair du Cochet in his juvenile hurdling season had foundered after he failed to pass the vet.

Guillaume Macaire confessed to being somewhat embarrassed at Jair du Cochet's defeat of Best Mate, describing it as 'regicide'. However, he felt that the better chance of beating Best Mate again would be at Kempton in the King George, rather than at Cheltenham in the Gold Cup. Best Mate's connections opted to go to Leopardstown for the Ericsson Chase instead of Kempton, which left Jair du Cochet to start the 2/1 favourite for the King George. In Best Mate's absence, Jair du Cochet seemed to have an excellent chance. He was proven over the course, his best effort as a novice coming when winning the Feltham Novices' Chase on the same card twelve months earlier. However, things went from bad to worse in the King George, starting with a sluggish jump at the first and effectively ending three fences later when Jair du Cochet blundered badly, all but putting his rider out of the saddle. Never in the race from then on, Jair du Cochet was behind when pulled up four out.

That disappointing effort fuelled speculation in some sections of the media that Ricou would be replaced for Jair du Cochet's next outing, even though his rider had not been the cause of his poor display at Kempton. Despite some eye-catching headlines about a possible change of rider and supposed agonising on the part of his trainer, there seemed little indication that Macaire was ready to ring the changes. 'I have spoken with the owner and he is not very keen to change things,' reported Macaire. 'If I change everything, there will be a disaster.' In any case, Macaire had long since likened the partnership between Ricou and Jair du Cochet to a marriage, and had stressed the point again before the King George. 'They are like husband and wife and you do not tamper with that sort of relationship.'

Tote Peterborough Chase, Huntingdon—Jair du Cochet lowers the colours of a race-rusty Best Mate, with Valley Henry (checked cap) back in third

Pillar Property Chase, Cheltenham—
a final win for the popular French chaser, with 2002 winner Rince Ri the only other finisher

In some eyes, both horse and jockey therefore had something to prove when the pair teamed up again for the Pillar Property Chase at Cheltenham in January. Ricou answered his critics in the best way possible, while Jair du Cochet put his Kempton flop behind him with an impressive display which put him right back in the Gold Cup picture. In the end, he had only the 2002 Pillar winner Rince Ri to beat, doing so by twelve lengths after the runner-up was eased. Moving into the lead at the eighth, Jair du Cochet's jumping was much more fluent than at Kempton, which was more than could be said for some of his rivals. Favourite Therealbandit fell four out when still in contention, while the previous season's Gold Cup runner-up Truckers Tavern went at the next when held in third. The other runners, Valley Henry and Sir Rembrandt, were pulled up. Macaire had mentioned the Cathcart as Jair du Cochet's possible Cheltenham target on the grounds that it would be easier for him to achieve his longed-for first Festival winner in that race than the Gold Cup, but by the time of his accident Jair du Cochet was firmly on course for the big one. What a shame he never made it.

Jair du Cochet (FR) (b.g. 1997)	Rahotep (FR) (b 1978)	Matahawk (br 1972)	Sea Hawk II Carromata
		La Masure (b 1965)	Net Miss Pink
	Dilaure (FR) (b 1984)	Rose Laurel (b 1970)	Klairon Honeysuckle Rose
		Midice (ch 1974)	Dictus Midas

Jair du Cochet was a good-topped gelding who often took the eye in appearance. His pedigree has been covered in previous editions of *Chasers & Hurdlers*. He developed into a top-class chaser in the latest season and will probably be best remembered for his defeat of Best Mate, but he had been a high-class hurdler too and brilliant as a juvenile; his rating of 163 remains the highest given to a juvenile hurdler since *Chasers & Hurdlers* began. Jair du Cochet won thirteen of his twenty-three starts, eight of his wins coming in Britain, and all of his successes gained in the hands of Ricou who rode him on all but two of his starts. Jair du Cochet clearly left a void in his stable, but he left a legacy too. 'It was thanks to Jair du Cochet that I discovered English racing and all the fun that goes with it,' said Macaire. 'He opened up a new world for me.' *G. Macaire, France*

JAKARI (FR)   7 b.g. Apeldoorn (FR) – Tartifume II (FR) (Mistigri) [2003/4 c121, h99: c20m* c19d* c21d⁵ c20s* c20g c21m³ Apr 14] rather leggy gelding: winning hurdler: useful handicap chaser: won at Cheltenham in November, Ascot in December and Ayr (by 5 lengths from Joe Blake) in February: looking very well, creditable third to Seebald in Grade 2 at Cheltenham final start: will stay beyond 21f: acts on soft and good to firm going: races prominently. *H. D. Daly*   **c141 h–**

JAKEAL (IRE)   5 b.g. Eagle Eyed (USA) – Karoi (IRE) (Kafu) [2003/4 17dᵖᵘ Mar 7] half-brother to fairly useful 2m hurdler Stacumny Bridge (by Flying Spur): fair at best on Flat (probably stays 1m): pulled hard in novice on hurdling debut. *R. M. Whitaker*   **h–**

JAKE BLACK (IRE)   4 b.g. Definite Article – Tirhala (IRE) (Chief Singer) [2003/4 16d* 16d⁴ 20d⁴ 16g² Mar 6] fair on Flat (likely to stay 1½m): modest juvenile hurdler: won at Newcastle in November: will prove better at 2m than 2½m: races freely: hung right third start. *J. J. Quinn*   **h94**

JAKE THE JUMPER (IRE)   7 b.g. Jolly Jake (NZ) – Princess Tino (IRE) (Rontino) [2003/4 h86: 24g⁶ 26g² Mar 17] workmanlike gelding: modest maiden hurdler: stays 3¼m: acts on firm and soft going. *Mrs G. Harvey*   **h97**

JALLASTEP (FR)   7 b.g. Boston Two Step (USA) – Balladine (FR) (Rivelago (FR)) [2003/4 h100: 16s 16s 17s³ 22g 20g² 22d⁵ 24s⁵ Apr 21] lengthy, workmanlike gelding: modest handicap hurdler: stays 2¾m: acts on good to firm and good to soft going: wore cheekpieces sixth start. *J. S. Goldie*   **h92**

Derek Hankinson Chase (Handicap), Ascot—Jakari gains the second of three wins in 2003/4

JALONS STAR (IRE) 6 b.g. Eagle Eyed (USA) – Regina St Cyr (IRE) (Doulab **c86**
(USA)) [2003/4 h–: c17d⁴ c19m⁵ c21g² c16m⁴ c16m⁴ c17g³ Jul 26] workmanlike geld- **h–**
ing: winning hurdler: modest form in novice chases: best around 2m: acts on heavy going,
probably on good to firm. *M. Quinn*

JALOUX D'ESTRUVAL (FR) 7 b.g. Kadalko (FR) – Pommette III (FR) (Trac) **c125 x**
[2003/4 c115+, h–: c24s⁴ c23d* c24sF c24sᵘʳ 24s³ c24gF 23s* 24s⁶ Apr 17] tall gelding: **h103 +**
fairly useful handicap chaser: improved effort when winning at Exeter in January: only
fourth start over hurdles when winning handicap at Lingfield in April: stays 25f: raced on
good going or softer (acts on soft): has worn net muzzle: often let down by jumping over
fences. *Mrs L. C. Taylor*

JAMAICAN FLIGHT (USA) 11 b.h. Sunshine Forever (USA) – Kalamona (USA) **h103**
(Hawaii) [2003/4 h105: 19m³ 22m² Oct 18] smallish horse: modest stayer on Flat: fair
handicap hurdler: stays 21f: acts on any going: front runner: has won 7 times at Market
Rasen. *Mrs S. Lamyman*

JAMEROSIER (FR) 7 b.g. The Wonder (FR) – Teuphaine (FR) (Barbotan (FR)) **c113**
[2003/4 c22v² c22s³ Jan 14] strong gelding: fair maiden hurdler/chaser, lightly raced: lik- **h–**
ely to prove better at 3m+ than shorter: raced on going softer than good. *Mrs L. C. Taylor*

JAMIE BROWNE (IRE) 7 ch.g. Sayaarr (USA) – Glowing Embers (Nebbiolo) **c–**
[2003/4 c20m Apr 28] eighth foal: half-brother to winner up to 1¼m Valley of Fire (by
Dancing Brave): dam, Irish 7f and 1¼m winner, half-sister to top-class middle-distance
colt Kalaglow: poor pointer: tongue tied, already held when hanging violently right on
home turn in novice hunter chase at Newcastle. *W. G. Young*

JAMORIN DANCER 9 b.g. Charmer – Geryea (USA) (Desert Wine (USA)) [2003/4 **c84 §**
c77§, h74§: c16g⁵ c16g⁴ c17g² c16m² c17m² c16g² c16m⁵ c17m c17m⁴ c17g³ c16mᵘʳ **h– §**
Sep 7] sturdy gelding: poor handicap chaser: below form after fifth start, sold out of
R. C. Guest's stable 2,800 gns Doncaster August Sales after ninth: raced mainly around
2m: acts on good to firm and good to soft going: tried blinkered, wears cheekpieces
nowadays: irresolute. *S. G. Chadwick*

JANBRE (IRE) 5 br.g. Zaffaran (USA) – Black Gayle (IRE) (Strong Gale) [2003/4 **F96**
F16v² F17s⁵ F18g⁶ Apr 22] €16,000 3-y-o: fourth foal: dam unraced, from family of
one-time top-class staying chaser Alexander Banquet: fairly useful form at Towcester
and Folkestone on first 2 starts in bumpers: will be suited by greater test of stamina.
M. Scudamore

JANDAL 10 ch.g. Arazi (USA) – Littlefield (Bay Express) [2003/4 c–, h–: 17g Apr 13] **c–**
maiden hurdler/chaser. *B. Scriven* **h–**

JANIDOU (FR) 8 b.g. Cadoudal (FR) – Majathen (FR) (Carmarthen (FR)) [2003/4 **c105 §**
h114§: c17s* c16s* 16d c17g⁵ c17m³ c16d³ Nov 22] good-topped gelding: fair handicap **h– §**
hurdler: of similar standard over fences, winning maiden at Kilbeggan in May and novice
at Roscommon in June: bred to stay at least 2½m: acts on heavy going: weak finisher.
A. L. T. Moore, Ireland

JANITURE (FR) 7 gr.m. Turgeon (USA) – Majaway (FR) (Timmy's Way (FR)) **c124**
[2003/4 c124, h–: c20mᵖᵘ c20m² c19d⁵ c16d⁵ c16m Apr 15] lengthy, rather leggy mare: **h–**
has reportedly had breathing operation: fairly useful handicap chaser: easily best effort in
2003/4 (shaped as if amiss more than once) when second to Cameron Bridge at Kempton
in November: stays 21f: probably acts on any going: effective tongue tied or not: has been
let down by jumping: sold 18,000 gns Doncaster May Sales. *P. F. Nicholls*

JANORAMIC (FR) 7 b.g. Panoramic – Victoire V (FR) (Nellio (FR)) [2003/4 c20sᵖᵘ **c–**
16g Apr 18] sturdy gelding: very lightly-raced maiden hurdler/chaser: stays 19f. **h–**
T. J. Fitzgerald

JANOUEIX (IRE) 5 b.g. Desert King (IRE) – Miniver (IRE) (Mujtahid (USA)) **h–**
[2003/4 17gᵖᵘ May 13] poor maiden on Flat (stays 1¼m): failed to settle in novice on
hurdling debut: sold 800 gns Newmarket July Sales. *C. R. Egerton*

JAN'S DREAM (IRE) 10 ch.m. Executive Perk – Aunty Babs (Sexton Blake) **c– x**
[2003/4 c94x, h–: c17sᵘʳ c16gᵘʳ c17gᵖᵘ c16sᵘʳ c17dᵖᵘ c16g Dec 16] good-topped mare: **h–**
winning hurdler/maiden chaser: no form, raced only over fences, in 2003/4: tongue tied:
sketchy jumper. *P. R. Webber*

JANUS DU COCHET (FR) 7 b.g. Rahotep (FR) – Qualite du Cochet (FR) (Illust- **c114 p**
rator (FR)) [2003/4 c21m² c23s* c22s⁴ Feb 14] angular gelding: useful hurdler in 2001/2: **h–**
off 2 years, best effort over fences when winning maiden at Exeter in January: lame
following month: will stay beyond 3m: probably best on good going or softer (acts on
heavy): probably still capable of better over fences. *M. C. Pipe*

JAOKA DU GORD (FR)   7 b.g. Concorde Jr (USA) – Theorie du Cochet (FR)   **c–**
(Franc Ryk) [2003/4 F16d⁴ F16d⁴ c19d c24gᵖᵘ Feb 11] 13,500 4-y-o: good-topped   **F84**
gelding: second known foal: dam placed over jumps in France: modest form in bumpers:
well held in maiden on chasing debut: bled from nose final start. *P. R. Webber*

JARDIN DE BEAULIEU (FR)   7 ch.g. Rough Magic (FR) – Emblem (FR) (Siberian   **c122**
Express (USA)) [2003/4 c103, h–: c20m c18g² c20g* c20g* c20s³ c24gᵖᵘ c20gᵖᵘ Apr 3]   **h–**
well-made gelding: fairly useful handicap chaser: won at Kempton (novices) in December and Warwick (made all) in January: stays 2½m: raced mainly on good going or softer
(acts on soft): wore cheekpieces/blinkers last 4 outings. *Ian Williams*

JARDIN FLEURI (FR)   7 ch.g. Cyborg (FR) – Merry Durgan (FR) (Le Nain Jaune   **c–**
(FR)) [2003/4 17gᵖᵘ 22mᵖᵘ 22d 19f⁵ 21sᵘʳ 19mᵇᵈ 19d 22s² 21g* c19mᵖᵘ Apr 13] first foal: **h86**
dam lightly-raced maiden on Flat: twice-raced over hurdles in France, third in claimer
(claimed out of Y. Porzier's stable 111,000 francs) at Auteuil: off 2 years and modest form
at best in 2003/4, winning seller at Ludlow in February: badly let down by jumping on
chasing debut: stays 2¾m: acts on soft going. *M. C. Pipe*

JAROD (FR)   6 b.g. Scribe (IRE) – Somnambula (IRE) (Petoski) [2003/4 F16d 19m⁶   **h79**
20s 21g 24dᵖᵘ Apr 21] sturdy gelding: first foal: dam won 4 times up to around 1½m on   **F84**
Flat in France: ninth of 16 in bumper on debut: poor form over hurdles: blinkered final
start. *P. J. Hobbs*

JARRO (FR)   8 b.g. Pistolet Bleu (IRE) – Junta (FR) (Cariellor (FR)) [2003/4 c121,   **c–**
h–: c16mᵘʳ Nov 11] workmanlike gelding: fairly useful chaser: tailed off when unseating   **h–**
2 out only start in 2003/4: best around 2m: acts on good to firm and heavy going: free-
going sort: jumps less than fluently. *Miss Venetia Williams*

JASEUR (USA)   11 b.g. Lear Fan (USA) – Spur Wing (USA) (Storm Bird (CAN))   **c–**
[2003/4 c–, h110§: 26m³ 26g⁵ 24m c25gᵖᵘ 24d⁴ 24sᵖᵘ Apr 17] rather leggy gelding: **h105 §**
mistakes both outings over fences: fair handicap hurdler: left G. Barnett after second
start: stays 3¼m: acts on firm and soft going: usually wears headgear: ungenuine.
S. T. Lewis

JASMIN D'OUDAIRIES (FR)   7 b.g. Apeldoorn (FR) – Vellea (FR) (Cap Martin   **c123**
(FR)) [2003/4 c118p, h–: c19d c20s³ c24gᶠ c20s³ c20v² Apr 17] smallish gelding: fairly   **h–**
useful handicap chaser: good third to Prince of Pleasure at Punchestown, better effort
within 3 days in late-April: likely to stay 3m: acts on heavy going. *W. P. Mullins, Ireland*

JASMIN GUICHOIS (FR)   7 ch.g. Dom Alco (FR) – Lady Belle (FR) (Or de Chine)   **c115**
[2003/4 c107, h96: c20d³ c20d* c21m* c24g⁵ c25dᵖᵘ c20g⁵ Apr 24] compact gelding: **h–**
modest hurdler: fairly useful handicap chaser: won at Cheltenham (conditional jockeys)
in December and Wincanton in February: stays 21f: acts on good to firm and heavy going.
Miss Venetia Williams

JASPER ROONEY   5 b.g. Riverwise (USA) – Miss Secret (El Conquistador) [2003/4   **F–**
F16g Mar 25] first foal: dam, novice hurdler, stayed 3m: well beaten in bumper on debut.
C. W. Mitchell

JAUNTY TIMES   4 b.g. Luso – Jaunty June (Primitive Rising (USA)) [2003/4 F16m⁵   **F84**
Apr 13] first foal: dam, modest hurdler, stayed 2¾m: fifth in bumper at Chepstow on
debut. *B. J. Eckley*

JAVA SEA   8 br.g. Warning – Sarah Siddons (FR) (Le Levanstell) [2003/4 c25g⁴ c22d   **c99**
c25vᵖᵘ Jan 26] workmanlike gelding: progressed into fair hurdler in 2001/2: best effort   **h–**
over fences on return when fourth to Calling Brave in maiden at Folkestone, making
mistakes: stays 25f, at least when conditions aren't testing: raced on good going or softer
(probably acts on heavy): races prominently, and usually travels strongly (tends to idle).
Jonjo O'Neill

JAVELIN   8 ch.g. Generous (IRE) – Moss (Alzao (USA)) [2003/4 c16m⁴ c19mᶠ 19m³   **c92**
20m* 19g² 20d⁶ 21gᵖᵘ Dec 26] sturdy, lengthy gelding: modest form on first of 2 starts   **h107**
over fences (needs to jump better): fair handicap hurdler: won at Wetherby in November:
ran as if amiss final start: will stay beyond 2½m: raced mainly on good going or firmer.
Ian Williams

JAVELOT D'OR (FR)   7 b. or br.g. Useful (FR) – Flika d'Or (FR) (Pot d'Or (FR))   **c–**
[2003/4 c–, h–: c20sᶠ c17dᵖᵘ c18sᵖᵘ c18s⁶ c17s⁵ c19sᵖᵘ Mar 24] smallish, lengthy geld-   **h–**
ing: winning jumper in France: no form in Britain. *Miss Venetia Williams*

JAWAH (IRE)   10 br.g. In The Wings – Saving Mercy (Lord Gayle (USA)) [2003/4   **h–**
24mᵖᵘ 20mᵖᵘ 18g Oct 5] sparely-made gelding: fairly useful at best on Flat but thoroughly
ungenuine nowadays: maiden hurdler, no form in 2003/4: tried visored. *H. J. Manners*

JAW

JAWWALA (USA) 5 b.m. Green Dancer (USA) – Fetch N Carry (USA) (Alleged **h84 §**
(USA)) [2003/4 h88§: 16v² 21g² 20m³ 20g² 17gᵖᵘ 19g³ 17sʳᵗʳ 16s 19g⁴ 19s³ Apr 11] leggy
mare: poor maiden hurdler: stays 21f: acts on heavy and good to firm going: usually
wears headgear: has refused/been reluctant to race: one to avoid. *J. R. Jenkins*

JAYBEEDEE 8 b.g. Rudimentary (USA) – Meavy (Kalaglow) [2003/4 h–: 22d 20d **c–**
16d 16v³ 18sᵖᵘ c17d c20g⁵ 16s Apr 11] good-bodied gelding: modest handicap hurdler: **h86**
reportedly finished distressed fifth start (wore cheekpieces): let down by jumping both
starts over fences: best at 2m: raced mainly on going softer than good (acts on heavy):
sold 3,700 gns Doncaster May Sales. *K. C. Bailey*

JAY BEE ELL 7 b.g. Pursuit of Love – On Request (IRE) (Be My Guest (USA)) **h–**
[2003/4 h89+: 21d 22s Apr 6] sturdy gelding: modest hurdler in early-2002/3: little show
on return from lengthy absence: stays easy 2¾m. *A. King*

JAYBEJAY (NZ) 9 b.g. High Ice (USA) – Galaxy Light (NZ) (Balios) [2003/4 c119, **c117 §**
h–: c19d⁴ c25d⁵ c19s² Jan 20] smallish gelding: fairly useful chaser: below best in handi- **h–**
caps in 2003/4: stays 21f: raced mainly on good going or softer: temperamental display in
visor final start: poor jumper: not one to trust. *M. C. Pipe*

JAYED (IRE) 6 b. or br.g. Marju (IRE) – Taqreem (IRE) (Nashwan (USA)) [2003/4 **h77**
h76+: 16m 16m² 16m* 16g³ 17f⁶ 16m⁴ 16g⁴ 16s Dec 30] poor hurdler on balance, flattered when making most to win weakly-contested maiden at Worcester in August: best at
sharp 2m: acts on good to firm going: headstrong front runner. *M. Bradstock*

JAY JAY LASS 4 b.f. Bold Fort – Suelizelle (Carnival Dancer) [2003/4 16mᵖᵘ Oct 4] **h–**
rather sparely-made filly: of little account on Flat for D. Burchell: no show on hurdling
debut. *R. Williams*

JAY MAN (IRE) 14 ch.g. Remainder Man – Pas-De Jay (Pas de Seul) [2003/4 c16gᵘʳ **c–**
c25gᵘʳ Mar 28] sturdy gelding: one-time fair hurdler in Ireland for E. Kearns: runner-up **h–**
in point in 2000: unseated both starts in hunter chases. *Joss Saville*

JAYNEYBEE 6 b.m. Sovereign Water (FR) – Day Return (Electric) [2003/4 F16d **F–**
Apr 28] second foal: dam little promise in 2 hurdles: tailed off in bumper on debut.
R. D. E. Woodhouse

JAZZAAM 5 ch.m. Fraam – Aldwick Colonnade (Kind of Hush) [2003/4 16v⁴ 19s⁴ **h70**
16s⁶ 21d⁵ Mar 1] modest maiden on Flat (stays 1½m): poor form over hurdles.
M. D. I. Usher

JAZZ D'ESTRUVAL (FR) 7 gr.g. Bayolidaan (FR) – Caro d'Estruval (FR) (Caramo **h129**
(FR)) [2003/4 24g* 22s² 25d³ Dec 26] strong, useful-looking gelding: fairly useful
hurdler, lightly raced (reportedly fired prior to reappearance): won handicap at Perth in
May: further improvement when placed in similar events at Haydock and Wetherby (third
to Campaign Trail): stays 25f: raced on good ground or softer. *N. G. Richards*

JAZZ DU FOREZ (FR) 7 b.g. Video Rock (FR) – Ophyr du Forez (FR) (Fin Bon) **c60**
[2003/4 c73, h60: c23g c21g⁵ c26g⁴ c23m⁴ c24s⁵ c25d 21s³ c24g⁴ 27d⁴ c25s⁴ c24g⁴ Apr **h60**
18] smallish gelding: poor maiden hurdler/chaser: stays 25f: acts on heavy and good to
firm going: tried blinkered/in cheekpieces. *John Allen*

JAZZ DUKE 11 ch.g. Rising – Gone (Whistling Wind) [2003/4 c81§, h–§: c26g³ **c81 §**
c26s³ c26d⁵ c26s* Jan 19] leggy gelding: poor chaser: in cheekpieces, won handicap at **h– §**
Plumpton (collapsed and died after race): stayed 27f: raced on good going or softer (acted
on heavy): visored once: moody. *M. J. Weeden*

JAZZ NIGHT 7 b.g. Alhijaz – Hen Night (Mummy's Game) [2003/4 h91: c20dᵖᵘ **c82**
c21g⁶ c16g² c16g* Apr 3] good-topped gelding: modest hunter chaser: won at Hereford: **h–**
best form at 2m on good ground. *Shaun Lycett*

JBALLINGALL 5 b.g. Overbury (IRE) – Sister Delaney (Deep Run) [2003/4 F17d **h–**
20sᵖᵘ Mar 13] seventh foal: dam unraced half-sister to smart staying chaser Father **F–**
Delaney: no sign of ability in bumper and novice hurdle. *N. Wilson*

JEANIE'S LAST 5 b.m. Primitive Rising (USA) – Jean Jeanie (Roman Warrior) **F–**
[2003/4 F16gᵖᵘ F16d F16sᵖᵘ Apr 12] seventh foal: dam poor maiden sprinter: looks of
little account. *C. C. Bealby*

JEEPERS CREEPERS 4 b.g. Wizard King – Dark Amber (Formidable (USA)) **F–**
[2003/4 F12s Nov 22] €5,000 3-y-o: workmanlike gelding: ninth foal: half-brother to
fairly useful Italian middle-distance stayer Di Giacomo (by Bustino): dam, 1m winner at
4 yrs, half-sister to smart middle-distance stayer Rakaposhi King: backward, tailed off in
3-y-o bumper on debut. *Mrs A. M. Thorpe*

JEFERTITI (FR) 7 ch.g. Le Nain Jaune (FR) – Nefertiti (FR) (Tourangeau (FR)) **c102**
[2003/4 c106, h94: c19g² c20m² c20g³ Nov 7] rangy, good sort: maiden hurdler: fair **h–**

466

JET

maiden chaser: possibly amiss final start: stays 2½m: acts on good to firm and heavy going: free-going sort: sold to join Miss L. Russell 20,000 gns Doncaster May Sales. *Miss H. C. Knight*

JEMARO (IRE) 13 b.g. Tidaro (USA) – Jeremique (Sunny Way) [2003/4 c102, h–: c24gᶠ c25m⁵ Mar 4] smallish, good-topped gelding: fairly useful hunter chaser: won point in February: best up to 25f: acts on good to firm and heavy going: usually jumps boldly (though makes the odd mistake) up with pace. *Mrs C. J. Robinson*   **c102** **h–**

JEM'S LAW 5 b.m. Contract Law (USA) – Alnasr Jewel (USA) (Al Nasr (FR)) [2003/4 F16s F16d F16d Mar 21] compact mare: fourth foal: dam unraced: tailed off in 3 bumpers and on Flat debut in April. *J. R. Jenkins*   **F–**

JENAVIVE 4 b.f. Danzig Connection (USA) – Promise Fulfilled (USA) (Bet Twice (USA)) [2003/4 16m 16d⁵ 16d⁶ 16s Jan 23] good-topped filly: modest maiden on Flat (stays 1¾m): poor form in juveniles first 2 starts over hurdles: sold out of T. Easterby's stable 8,000 gns Doncaster November Sales. *N. J. Hawke*   **h74**

JENGA 7 ro.m. Minster Son – Maybe Daisy (Nicholas Bill) [2003/4 h99: 24sᵖᵘ c25s* c22s⁵ c24sᵖᵘ Feb 12] medium-sized mare: successful both outings over hurdles in 2002/3: winning steeplechasing debut in mares handicap at Hereford in December: ran poorly both starts after: stays 25f: raced on going softer than good (acts on heavy): joined O. Sherwood. *K. C. Bailey*   **c105** **h–**

JENNIFERJO (IRE) 7 b. or br.m. Witness Box (USA) – Sweet Tune (Welsh Chanter) [2003/4 c131, h–: c20d⁵ c24s c24d Dec 27] useful chaser: well below form in handicaps in 2003/4: will stay beyond 3m: best on going softer than good (acts on heavy). *P. A. Fahy, Ireland*   **c115** **h–**

JEREMY SPIDER 11 b.g. Nearly A Hand – Lucibella (Comedy Star (USA)) [2003/4 c113, h–: c25g⁵ c29v* c29dᵖᵘ c25sᶠ Jan 8] deep-girthed gelding: fairly useful handicap chaser: won quite valuable event at Plumpton in November by 5 lengths from Fasgo: stays 29f: acts on heavy going: front runner. *C. L. Tizzard*   **c120** **h–**

JERICHO III (FR) 7 b.g. Lute Antique (FR) – La Salamandre (FR) (Pot d'Or (FR)) [2003/4 c107, h–: c16gᵖᵘ c16m 17mᵖᵘ c20dᵖᵘ c21dᵖᵘ c20d³ c20g³ Apr 10] leggy gelding: winning hurdler/chaser: modest form at best in 2003/4: left M. Todhunter after third outing: may prove best short of 2½m: acts on heavy going (bumper winner on good to firm): tried tongue tied/blinkered: pulls hard: prone to mistakes: has had breathing problems. *R. C. Guest*   **c92** **h–**

JEROM DE VINDECY (FR) 7 ch.g. Roi de Rome (USA) – Preves du Forez (FR) (Quart de Vin (FR)) [2003/4 17sᵖᵘ Feb 11] modest hurdler/fair chaser in France for Y. Fouin: well held in novice hurdles in Britain over 2 years apart: tried blinkered. *A. R. Dicken*   **c–** **h–**

JEROPINO (IRE) 6 b.g. Norwich – Guillig Lady (IRE) (Hatim (USA)) [2003/4 20s⁴ 16d 20sᵖᵘ Feb 14] quite good-topped gelding: first foal: dam poor form in Irish bumpers: failed to complete in 2 Irish points in 2003: modest form when fourth in novice at Haydock on hurdling debut: dropped away tamely after making running both subsequent starts. *J. Mackie*   **h94**

JERUFLO (IRE) 9 b.m. Glacial Storm (USA) – Martiness (Martinmas) [2003/4 c80, h–: c21d⁴ c20s⁴ c25vᵖᵘ Dec 26] leggy mare: has reportedly had breathing operation: winning hurdler: poor maiden chaser: should stay beyond 2½m: acts on soft and good to firm going: tongue tied: sold 20,000 gns Doncaster January Sales. *P. R. Webber*   **c75** **h–**

JESPER (FR) 7 b.g. Video Rock (FR) – Belle Des Airs (FR) (Saumon (FR)) [2003/4 17g⁴ May 13] ex-French gelding: third foal: dam, lightly-raced maiden, out of half-sister to smart French chaser Gabion: in frame all 8 starts in non-thoroughbred events up to around 1½m in Provinces for M. Boudot: caught the eye when fourth to Champagne Harry in novice at Hereford on hurdling debut, hampered after fourth and not unduly knocked about after 2 out: bred to stay beyond 2m: seemed likely to do better, but wasn't seen out again. *R. T. Phillips*   **h86**

JESSIE MACDOUGALL 4 br.f. Overbury (IRE) – Miss Crusty (Belfort (FR)) [2003/4 16m⁴ 16d⁶ 16s⁵ Dec 13] smallish filly: modest on Flat (stays 1¼m): poor form over hurdles: trained by P. D. Evans on debut: lame final outing. *Dr P. Pritchard*   **h82**

JE SUIS (IRE) 8 b.m. Le Bavard (FR) – La Tortue (Lafontaine (USA)) [2003/4 h–: 22m Jul 14] angular mare: no form in bumpers or novice hurdles. *B. J. Eckley*   **h–**

JETOWA DU BOIS HUE (FR) 7 b.g. Kadrou (FR) – Vaika (FR) (Cosmopolitan (FR)) [2003/4 c96, h–: c16m* c16m³ c17m³ c16f* Nov 20] lengthy, rather sparely-made   **c107** **h–**

467

gelding: fair handicap chaser: won at Huntingdon in May and Wincanton: let down by jumping both starts in between: raced around 2m: acts on firm and good to soft ground, respectable effort on heavy. *T. R. George*

JEU DE BROOK (FR) 7 b.g. Trebrook – Cabira Des Saccart (FR) (Quart de Vin (FR)) [2003/4 20d c22d c24g⁴ c20gᶠ 16d c22d⁶ c18g* c21d⁵ c20sᵖᵘ 19s⁵ c18s c18s⁶ Apr 8] first foal: dam, twice-raced, out of sister to dam of smart staying hurdler/chaser Tito L'Effronte: maiden hurdler: fairly useful chaser: won maiden at Thurles in November: much improved at Auteuil in spring, won minor event in late-May: stays 2¾m: acts on heavy going: often tongue tied. *F. M. Cottin, France*   **c126 h75**

JEWEL FIGHTER 10 br.m. Good Times (ITY) – Duellist (Town Crier) [2003/4 h52: 16d⁶ 20m² 16g⁶ c16mᶜᵒ c16m⁵ Jul 16] bad maiden hurdler: well held on completed start over fences: stays 2½m: acts on good to firm and good to soft going. *Dr P. Pritchard*   **c– h58**

JEWEL OF INDIA 5 ch.g. Bijou d'Inde – Low Hill (Rousillon (USA)) [2003/4 h83: 16m³ 16m* 16g⁶ 16m⁵ Oct 20] sparely-made gelding: fairly useful on Flat (stays 1¼m): fair hurdler: won maiden at Huntingdon in August and 5-runner novice handicap at Plumpton, jumping more fluently and improved effort at latter: will prove best around 2m with emphasis on speed: acts on good to firm going: sold to join Mrs A. King 11,000 gns Newmarket Autumn Sales. *P. J. Hobbs*   **h103**

JIDIYA (IRE) 5 b.g. Lahib (USA) – Yaqatha (IRE) (Sadler's Wells (USA)) [2003/4 F16m* 19dᵖᵘ 24g⁶ 17d 21d Apr 8] €8,500 4-y-o: lengthy, good-topped ex-Irish gelding: brother to useful middle-distance stayers Rasin and Sarayan and half-brother to another by Machiavellian: dam, 1¼m winner, closely related to high-class middle-distance colt Northern Baby: won bumper at Roscommon on debut in September: fair form in 2 minor events up to 2m on Flat: sold out of J. Kiely's stable 20,000 gns Doncaster November Sales: no worthwhile form over hurdles: likely to prove best short of 3m. *S. Gollings*   **h– F95**

JIMAL 7 b.g. Reprimand – Into The Fire (Dominion) [2003/4 21g 19s 16d⁵ 18g⁶ Mar 8] leggy gelding: maiden hurdler, well held in handicaps in 2003/4. *J. W. Mullins*   **h–**

JIM BELL (IRE) 9 br.g. Supreme Leader – Mightyatom (Black Minstrel) [2003/4 h103: 23d Dec 29] strong gelding: fair handicap hurdler: well held only outing in 2003/4: stays 25f: acts on heavy going: jumps none too fluently. *J. G. M. O'Shea*   **h–**

JIM DORE (IRE) 9 b. or br.g. Mac's Imp (USA) – Secret Assignment (Vitiges (FR)) [2003/4 16dᵖᵘ Apr 21] ex-Irish gelding: little form on Flat: no show both outings over hurdles: fell second in point. *R. Williams*   **h–**

JIM (FR) 7 b.g. Glaieul (USA) – Beautywal (FR) (Magwal (FR)) [2003/4 h117: 20d⁶ 16d c18d* c19s* c24s² c16s² c20d* c20sᶠ Mar 27] lengthy, well-made gelding: fairly useful hurdler: much better over fences, won maiden at Fairyhouse in December and novices at Naas in January and February (beat Boneyarrow 2 lengths in Grade 2 event): likely to prove best around 2½m: acts on heavy going. *J. T. R. Dreaper, Ireland*   **c138 h115**

JIM JAM JOEY (IRE) 11 ch.g. Big Sink Hope (USA) – Ascot Princess (Prince Hansel) [2003/4 c–, h106: 24vᵖᵘ 24s² 24s 24s Mar 20] angular gelding: fair handicap hurdler: form in 2003/4 only when second in conditional jockeys event at Newbury: best at 3m+: acts on heavy going: tried blinkered, including last 3 starts: takes plenty of driving. *Miss Suzy Smith*   **c– h106**

JIMJO 5 ch.g. Up And At 'em – Ushimado (IRE) (Ela-Mana-Mou) [2003/4 F16g F16d Mar 25] fifth foal: half-brother to Irish 5f winner Surprise Me (by Imperial Frontier) and 1m winner in Malaysia by Waajib: dam, fair 2m hurdler/1¼m winner, half-sister to fairly useful hurdler up to 2¾m Moment of Glory: well beaten in bumpers. *W. M. Brisbourne*   **F–**

JIM LAD 4 b.g. Young Ern – Anne's Bank (IRE) (Burslem (IRE)) [2003/4 16m⁴ 16m 16s⁵ 16s² 17g 22g⁶ 17s² 16s⁵ Apr 11] poor maiden on Flat: poor form over hurdles, looked ungenuine final outing: raced mainly around 2m: visored/blinkered last 5 starts. *Dr J. R. J. Naylor*   **h77 §**

JIMMY BLUES 9 b.g. Durgam (USA) – Tibbi Blues (Cure The Blues (USA)) [2003/4 c–, h–: c21g³ c20f c27dᵖᵘ Oct 29] little form over jumps. *Ferdy Murphy*   **c– h–**

JIMMY BOND 5 b.g. Primitive Rising (USA) – Miss Moneypenny (Silly Prices) [2003/4 F16g 20d 20s⁶ 19g 22g 20s⁴ Apr 17] good-topped gelding: first foal: dam ran twice in bumpers: ninth of 13 in bumper on debut: poor form over hurdles: stays 2½m: acts on soft going. *Jedd O'Keeffe*   **h77 F–**

JIMMY JUMBO (IRE) 11 ch.g. Dragon Palace (USA) – Sail On Lady (New Member) [2003/4 c–, h–: c26g⁶ May 26] workmanlike gelding: successful twice in points in 2003: little form in steeplechases. *J. S. Swindells*   **c78 h–**

JIMMYS DUKY (IRE) 6 b.g. Duky – Harvey's Cream (IRE) (Mandalus) [2003/4 h–
20d 27s^{pu} 19g 24d Feb 21] first foal: dam maiden Irish pointer: runner-up on completed
start in maiden Irish points in 2003: no form over hurdles. *D. M. Forster*

JIMMY TENNIS (FR) 7 b. or br.g. Video Rock (FR) – Via Tennise (FR) (Brezzo   c134 x
(FR)) [2003/4 c–x, h–: c19d^{ur} c19d^2 c24d^2 c24s^F c23g* c24m^6 Feb 28] leggy, lengthy   h–
gelding: useful handicap chaser: won at Leicester in February by 10 lengths from
Courage Under Fire: close up when fell 5 out in valuable event at Doncaster time before:
stays 3m: raced mainly on good going or softer (acts on heavy): tried blinkered: often let
down by jumping. *Miss Venetia Williams*

JIMSUE 13 gr.g. Afzal – Gentian (Roan Rocket) [2003/4 16m^{pu} May 5] no sign of   h–
ability only 3 runs, including in point. *B. L. Lay*

JINFUL DU GRAND VAL (FR) 7 b.g. Useful (FR) – Marine (FR) (African Joy)   c–
[2003/4 c20f^6 c25g^{ur} Mar 6] ex-Irish gelding: first foal: dam, maiden chaser, half-sister to
useful 2¾m chase winner Heliophanie and useful hurdler up to 2¾m La Tarasque: well
beaten on completed start in steeplechases when trained by A. Moore: won point in April.
N. W. Alexander

JIVAROS (FR) 7 br.g. Video Rock (FR) – Rives (FR) (Reasonable Choice (USA))   c102
[2003/4 c104p, h–: c28m^F c22v^{pu} c24m^{pu} c25g^4 c24d^5 Apr 12] leggy gelding: fair handi-   h–
cap chaser: stays 25f: acts on good to soft going: keen-going sort, prone to odd error.
H. D. Daly

JIVATY (FR) 7 b.g. Quart de Vin (FR) – Tenacity (FR) (Prove It Baby (USA)) [2003/4   h109
22g^2 21s* 21d^2 Mar 25] 14,500 3-y-o: leggy gelding: third foal: half-brother to winning
chaser Kansas City (by Lute Antique), stays 19f: dam, 1½m winner, from family of
Grande Steeple-Chase de Paris winner Isopani: won last of 4 starts in maiden Irish points
in 2002: fair form in novice hurdles: won at Plumpton in March by 5 lengths from
Jonanaud, jumping left last 2: will stay 3m. *M. C. Pipe*

JIVER (IRE) 5 b.g. Flemensfirth (USA) – Choice Brush (IRE) (Brush Aside (USA))   F84
[2003/4 F16d F16d^4 Mar 25] rather unfurnished gelding: first foal: dam unraced half-
sister to useful hurdler/fairly useful chaser up to 21f Bucks-Choice: modest form in
bumpers at Kempton and Ludlow. *M. Scudamore*

J J BABOO (IRE) 11 b.g. Be My Guest (USA) – Maricica (Ahonoora) [2003/4 c79§,   c– §
h–§: c21g c27g^4 Oct 14] leggy, workmanlike gelding: poor handicap chaser: stays 25f: h– §
tried in headgear: untrustworthy. *Jedd O'Keeffe*

JOCKER DU SAPIN (FR) 7 br.g. Franc Parler – Nymphe Rose (FR) (Rose Laurel)   c90
[2003/4 c16v^4 c16g^5 c17d^6 c16d^2 Mar 24] ex-French gelding: third foal: half-brother to   h–
winning 17f chaser Hunter du Sapin (by Echo de Thurin): dam well beaten on Flat/over
hurdles: unplaced in 6 starts over hurdles at Auteuil at 4 yrs for J. M. Baudrelle: best effort
over fences when second in conditional jockeys handicap at Chepstow: raced around 2m
on good going or softer. *A. J. Whitehead*

JOCKIE WELLS 6 b.g. Primitive Rising (USA) – Princess Maxine (IRE) (Horage)   h–
[2003/4 h–, F–: 16m^6 May 27] well beaten over hurdles: headstrong. *Miss Lucinda
V. Russell*

JODANTE (IRE) 7 ch.g. Phardante (FR) – Crashtown Lucy (Crash Course) [2003/4   c95 p
h83p, F83: 20g^{ur} 20s^{pu} 19d^2 20d 16v^2 16d c16s^2 Apr 4] strong, lengthy gelding: good   h89
mover: modest novice hurdler: encouraging second to The Nomad in novice at Hexham
on chasing debut: should stay further than 2m: raced on good going or softer (acts on
heavy): open to improvement over fences. *P. Beaumont*

JOE BLAKE (IRE) 9 b.g. Jurado (USA) – I've No Idea (Nishapour (FR)) [2003/4   c132
c124: c23d* c20s^2 c28m^{pu} c24d^4 Mar 13] big, workmanlike gelding: useful chaser: won
5-runner handicap at Wetherby in November by 1¼ lengths from Tyneandthyneagain:
improved again when second to Jakari in similar event at Ayr: poor efforts last 2 outings,
making mistakes: stays 3¼m: acts on good to firm and heavy going. *L. Lungo*

JOEBRIGGS 6 b.g. Hatim (USA) – Meadow Brig (Meadowbrook) [2003/4 F16m   F–
Nov 16] second foal: dam unraced: well beaten in bumper on debut. *A. C. Whillans*

JOE COOLEY (IRE) 4 b.g. Accordion – My Miss Molly (IRE) (Entitled) [2003/4   F80 p
F16d^4 Apr 17] €30,000 3-y-o: fifth foal: dam lightly-raced daughter of half-sister to top-
class middle-distance colt Dickens Hill: 3/1, hung off bridle when distant fourth to Wild
Cane Ridge in bumper at Ayr on debut: evidently thought capable of better. *K. A. Ryan*

JOE CULLEN (IRE) 9 ch.g. River Falls – Moycullen (Le Moss) [2003/4 h123:   c88
c17m^2 c16d^F c20m* 17g^6 c16m^2 Oct 26] lengthy gelding: fairly useful hurdler in Ireland: h–

only modest form over fences, won maiden at Market Rasen in August: stays 2½m: acts on good to firm and heavy going. *Ian Williams*

JOE DEANE (IRE) 8 ch.g. Alphabatim (USA) – Craic Go Leor (Deep Run) [2003/4 **c105** c93, h89: c19v² c20s* c24s² c22m⁴ c24s³ Mar 21] strong, lengthy gelding: modest form **h–** on second of 2 starts over hurdles: fair handicap chaser: won at Plumpton in January: stays 3¼m: raced mainly on going softer than good (acts on heavy). *T. R. George*

JOE DI CAPO (IRE) 9 b.g. Phardante (FR) – Supreme Glen (IRE) (Supreme **c82 x** Leader) [2003/4 c95x, h–: c24m⁵ c25gᵖᵘ c30d³ c25d⁵ c24d² c24g⁶ c24s⁴ Jan 21] lengthy, **h–** angular gelding: poor handicap chaser, still a novice: stays 3m: acts on heavy and good to firm going: usually wears headgear: poor jumper: inconsistent: joined T. Easterby. *A. Crook*

JOELY GREEN 7 b.g. Binary Star (USA) – Comedy Lady (Comedy Star (USA)) **h–** [2003/4 h88: 16m May 10] good-topped gelding: modest and unreliable on Flat (probably stays 19f): winning hurdler: blinkered, well beaten in handicap in May. *N. P. Littmoden*

JOE MALONE (IRE) 5 br.g. Rashar (USA) – Bucktina (Buckskin (FR)) [2003/4 **F85** F16d F16s Mar 20] €12,000 3-y-o: rather unfurnished gelding: half-brother to 5 winners, including fairly useful hurdler/fair chaser Beyond Control (by Supreme Leader), stays 3¼m: dam unraced, from family of useful staying chaser Imperial Black: better effort in bumpers when eighth of 16 to Itsa Legend at Kempton on debut. *C. C. Bealby*

JOE PUBLIC (IRE) 6 b.g. Actinium (FR) – Cool Boreen (Boreen (FR)) [2003/4 **h–** F16g 22gᵖᵘ Apr 18] IR £5,000 3-y-o, €8,000 4-y-o: leggy gelding: fifth foal: dam **F–** unraced: no sign of ability in bumper (for F. Murphy) and novice hurdle. *T. P. McGovern*

JOES EDGE (IRE) 7 b. or br.g. Supreme Leader – Right Dark (Buckskin (FR)) **h111** [2003/4 17d² 20s² 20d* 20v 20d⁴ 20s Mar 13] well-made gelding: fair novice hurdler: won at Ascot by 6 lengths from A Glass In Thyne) in January and Carlisle in February: well held in 2 competitive handicaps: will stay beyond 2½m: raced on going softer than good over hurdles: joined F. Murphy. *Miss Venetia Williams*

JOEY TRIBBIANI (IRE) 7 b.g. Foxhound (USA) – Mardi Gras Belle (USA) **c103** (Masked Dancer (USA)) [2003/4 c105, h74: c16d* c17g⁴ c20m⁶ Sep 28] leggy gelding: **h–** novice hurdler: fair handicap chaser: won 4-runner event at Aintree in May: best at 2m: acts on soft and good to firm going. *Ian Williams*

JOFI (IRE) 5 b.g. Shernazar – Giolla Donn (Giolla Mear) [2003/4 F16d Apr 17] **F–** €11,000 4-y-o: half-brother to fairly useful staying chaser Fiveleigh Builds (by Deep Run) and winning pointer by Electric: dam ran once in points: tailed off in bumper on debut. *Miss Lucinda V. Russell*

JOHANN DE VONNAS (FR) 7 b.g. Cadoudal (FR) – Diana de Vonnas (FR) (El **h84** Badr) [2003/4 F86: 20sᵖᵘ 20d³ 22g Apr 22] leggy gelding: off nearly 2 years, poor form in novice hurdles: reportedly had breathing problem final start. *N. J. Henderson*

JOHN JAMES (IRE) 8 b.g. Bravefoot – Glitter Grey (Nishapour (FR)) [2003/4 20d **c122** c18dᶠ c17sᶠ c24s³ c18s* c16g⁶ c20d⁵ Apr 13] angular gelding: second foal: dam, winning **h88** hurdler/fair chaser over 2½m+, half-sister to high-class middle-distance horse Oscar Schindler: fair hurdler: fairly useful novice chaser: made all in maiden at Gowran in February: stiff tasks in Grade 1 events at Cheltenham and Fairyhouse next 2 starts, probably flattered when last of 5 to Hi Cloy at latter: stays 2½m: acts on soft ground (won bumper on good to firm): has worn cheekpieces: front runner. *J. H. Scott, Ireland*

JOHNJOE'S EXPRESS (IRE) 7 gr.g. Moscow Society (USA) – Abigail's Dream **h103** (Kalaglow) [2003/4 F16m² 16s* 18d² 16g⁵ 16m⁶ 16g³ 22s⁵ 20v 18d⁴ 16d Apr 13] work- **F95** manlike gelding: third foal: brother to winning hurdler/chaser who stays 3¾m Misty Ridge: dam, modest hurdler up to 2½m, half-sister to dam of useful chaser at 2½m+ All The Aces and Tolworth Hurdle winner New York Rainbow: fell in point on debut: fair form in bumpers: fair hurdler: won handicap at Galway in July: left M. Hourigan prior to running creditably at Punchestown in late-April: should stay beyond 2¼m: acts on soft and good to firm going. *Mrs J. Harrington, Ireland*

JOHN JORROCKS (FR) 5 br.g. Chamberlin (FR) – Caryatide (FR) (Maiymad) **F72** [2003/4 F16m² F16g Mar 15] third foal: brother to winning 2¾m hurdler Jumpty Dumpty: dam unraced: well held in bumpers. *J. C. Tuck*

JOHNLEGOOD 8 ch.g. Karinga Bay – Dancing Years (USA) (Fred Astaire (USA)) **c–** [2003/4 c92, h102: c20sᵖᵘ Nov 22] workmanlike gelding: winning hurdler: modest **h–** novice chaser: no show only outing in 2003/4: stays 2½m: acts on heavy and good to firm going: sometimes let down by jumping over fences. *G. L. Moore*

JOK

JOHNNY OSCAR   7 b.g. Belmez (USA) – Short Rations (Lorenzaccio) [2003/4   **h93**
17m³ 17d² 17mᵖᵘ Jul 17] fairly useful stayer on Flat, sold out of J. Fanshawe's stable
12,000 gns Newmarket Autumn (2002) Sales: modest form when second in maiden
hurdle at Cartmel: dead. *Miss Venetia Williams*

JOHNNY REB   6 b.g. Danehill (USA) – Dixie Eyes Blazing (USA) (Gone West (USA))   **h66**
[2003/4 16m 17sʳᵒ 17g³ 17g⁶ Apr 24] poor form over hurdles: tongue tied first 3 starts:
headstrong. *Mrs S. J. Smith*

JOHN OLIVER (IRE)   6 gr.g. Lure (USA) – Glitter Grey (Nishapour (FR)) [2003/4   **h117**
F107: 16d⁵ 16d* 16g 16d Apr 12] big, well-made gelding: type to make a chaser: fairly
useful hurdler: won maiden at Leopardstown in January by head from Poachin Again,
idling: stiff task in Grade 1 novice at Cheltenham next time: raced around 2m: acts on
heavy going. *E. J. O'Grady, Ireland*

JOHN RICH   8 b.g. Mesleh – South Lodge (Current Magic) [2003/4 c22f⁴ c22m²   **c68 §**
c25g² c24d² c25dᴿ c25sᵖᵘ 21dʳᵒ 19sᵖᵘ Apr 11] fourth foal: dam unraced: fair pointer,   **h– §**
successful twice in 2003: runner-up in weak novice company over fences: ran out early
on hurdling debut: not one to trust. *M. E. Sowersby*

JOHNS LEGACY   9 gr.g. Almoojid – Flying Joker (Kalaglow) [2003/4 c23mᶠ Apr   **c88 ?**
13] successful both starts in points: keeping on in third when falling 3 out in novice hunter
won by Kingston-Banker at Exeter. *Miss S. E. Robinson*

JOHN STEED (IRE)   7 b.g. Thatching – Trinity Hall (Hallgate) [2003/4 h70: c19g   **c–**
20m 16m 20mᵖᵘ Aug 2] close-coupled gelding: poor hurdler: no form in 2003/4,   **h–**
including on chasing debut: stays 19f: visored final start. *Mrs A. C. Tate*

JOHNSTON'S ART (IRE)   11 b.g. Law Society (USA) – Mirror of Flowers (Artaius   **c– x**
(USA)) [2003/4 c–x, h101§: 24g 20mᵖᵘ 24d* 24m² 27g² 20g⁴ 24g⁵ 22f 27d 20m⁶ Dec 16]   **h98 §**
workmanlike gelding: modest handicap hurdler: won at Perth in July: suited by 3m+: acts
on heavy and good to firm going: blinkered: ungenuine. *Mrs J. C. McGregor*

JOHNSTON'S VILLE (IRE)   11 b.g. Commanche Run – Slavesville (Charlottes-   **c–**
villes Flyer) [2003/4 c25g⁶ May 13] workmanlike gelding: maiden hurdler/steeplechaser,   **h–**
lightly raced: won point in April. *Mrs M. B. Stephens*

JOHN'S TREASURE (IRE)   4 b.g. Entrepreneur – Misallah (IRE) (Shirley Heights)   **h–**
[2003/4 17g Aug 8] tailed off in 7f maiden at 2 yrs for P. Haslam: well held on hurdling
debut. *M. A. Barnes*

JOHN THE MOLE (IRE)   6 ch.g. Glacial Storm (USA) – City Dame (Golden Love)   **c– §**
[2003/4 h79, F84: 20d 25dᵖᵘ c19g c25gᵖᵘ c26d⁶ Apr 18] compact gelding: maiden   **h– §**
hurdler: no form in 2003/4, including over fences: tried in cheekpieces: temperamental.
M. D. Hammond

JOINT ACCOUNT   14 ch.g. Sayyaf – Dancing Clara (Billion (USA)) [2003/4 c124x: **c– x**
c24gᶠ c28d⁶ May 30] plain gelding: veteran staying chaser, very much on downgrade:
acts on firm and soft going: sometimes let down by jumping. *R. Tate*

JOINT AUTHORITY (IRE)   9 b.g. Religiously (USA) – Highway's Last (Royal   **c111**
Highway) [2003/4 h87: c20g⁶ 18g² c21d* c16d² c16s² c20g* c20g² c20gᵘʳ Mar 12]   **h89**
lengthy gelding: modest maiden hurdler: fair chaser: won maiden at Sedgefield in November and handicap at Musselburgh in January: stays 21f: raced on good going or softer
(acts on soft): races prominently: reliable. *L. Lungo*

JOIZEL (FR)   7 b.g. Fill My Hopes (FR) – Anne de Boizel (FR) (Dhausli (FR))   **h–**
[2003/4 20d 24g 24gᵘʳ 22g Apr 10] chunky ex-French gelding: third foal: half-brother to
winning chasers around 2½m by Murmure and Un Numide: dam unraced: won around
11f on Flat at 3 yrs: little show over hurdles, left Y. Fertillet after debut (blinkered).
R. H. Alner

JOJO (FR)   7 ch.g. Dadarissime (FR) – Belle Mome (FR) (Grand Tresor (FR)) [2003/4   **c–**
h–: 16g⁵ c20gᵘʳ 20mᵖᵘ 16m³ 20dᵖᵘ Jul 2] signs of only a little ability, left N. Alexander   **h–**
after second start: sold 1,000 gns Doncaster November Sales. *Miss Lucinda V. Russell*

JOKERS CHARM   13 b.g. Idiot's Delight – By The Lake (Tyrant (USA)) [2003/4 c95,   **c89**
h–: c16mᵖᵘ c21m* c16g⁴ c24gᵖᵘ c16dᵖᵘ Nov 11] workmanlike gelding: maiden hurdler: **h–**
modest handicap chaser: won extremely weak event at Uttoxeter in October: no other
form in 2003/4, lame final outing: has form at 3m, raced mainly over shorter: acts on any
going, except possibly heavy: visored once, blinkered nowadays: tongue tied: sometimes
let down by jumping. *R. C. Guest*

471

Cheltenham Ladies College 150th Anniversary Novices' Hurdle, Cheltenham—
the grey Jollyolly beats Irish raider Fairwood Present to record his sixth win of 2003/4,
also providing Tony McCoy with his hundredth

JOKESMITH (IRE) 6 b.g. Mujadil (USA) – Grinning (IRE) (Bellypha) [2003/4 h–: **h–**
17g^{pu} Sep 30] useful at one time on Flat: went as if amiss both starts over hurdles.
K. A. Ryan

JOLEWIS 6 ch.m. Sir Harry Lewis (USA) – Askwood (IRE) (Gunner B) [2003/4 F16g **F–**
Sep 25] first foal: dam unraced: well held in bumper on debut. *E. W. Tuer*

JOLIKA (FR) 7 b.m. Grand Tresor (FR) – Unika II (FR) (Rolling Bowl (FR)) [2003/4 **h93**
F90: 16g* 16s⁴ 20s* 16d⁴ 20d^{pu} Apr 18] leggy mare: modest form over hurdles: won
intermediate at Perth in May and amateur handicap at Ayr in February: will prove best at
2½m+. *L. Lungo*

JOLI POSH 7 ch.m. Rakaposhi King – Nunswalk (The Parson) [2003/4 F–: 17g Apr **h–**
30] no sign of ability. *R. J. Hodges*

JOLIROSE 9 b.m. Joligeneration – Rose Red City (Relkino) [2003/4 22m^{pu} 22g 22m^{pu} **h–**
19f⁴ Sep 30] of little account. *Miss V. A. Stephens*

JOLI SADDLERS 8 b.m. Saddlers' Hall (IRE) – Vitality (Young Generation) [2003/4 **c–**
24g^{pu} 21d⁶ 21g⁶ c23d^F Apr 21] winning hurdler, off over 2½ years before reappearance: **h–**
well held when falling 3 out on chasing debut: tongue tied last 3 starts. *P. F. Nicholls*

JOLITAN 9 b.g. Joligeneration – Tanber Lass (New Member) [2003/4 c19m^{pu} May **c–**
14] fair pointer, successful in January: blinkered, dropped out after mistake eighth in
novice hunter chase. *P. Greenwood*

JOLLY GIANT (IRE) 8 b.g. Jolly Jake (NZ) – Reve Clair (Deep Run) [2003/4 c104: **c98**
c24s² c30d⁴ c26v^{pu} c24d⁴ Mar 24] tall, useful-looking gelding: modest handicap chaser:
stays 25f: acts on soft going (pulled up both starts on heavy): blinkered last 6 outings:
sometimes let down by jumping: sold 6,000 gns Doncaster May Sales. *P. F. Nicholls*

JOLLY JAKE 10 br.g. Vital Season – Sols Joker (Comedy Star (USA)) [2003/4 c20g⁶ **c64**
Mar 12] modest pointer: sixth of 7 finishers in maiden at Leicester on hunter chase debut.
Miss E. J. Baker

JOLLY JOE (IRE) 7 b.g. Jolly Jake (NZ) – The Bread Robber (Mandalus) [2003/4 **c–**
24s^{pu} c19g⁵ c25m^{pu} Apr 14] big, workmanlike gelding: no sign of ability. *S. T. Lewis* **h–**

JOLLY JOHN (IRE) 13 b.g. Jolly Jake (NZ) – Golden Seekers (Manado) [2003/4 **c–**
c–, h81: 22s⁶ 21d⁴ 24s^{pu} Apr 21] angular gelding: poor maiden hurdler: stays 3m: acts on **h77**
any going: ridden by Mrs C. Mann, usually soon has plenty to do. *C. J. Mann*

472

JOLLY MOONBEAM (IRE)   7 b.m. Jolly Jake (NZ) – Orient Moonbeam (Deep   **c–**
Run) [2003/4 h114, F98: 16g⁵ 17g³ c18gᶠ Nov 19] tall mare: fairly useful hurdler: fell   **h115**
fatally on chasing debut: best around 2m: acted on heavy going. *M. Hourigan, Ireland*

JOLLYOLLY   5 gr.g. Environment Friend – Off The Air (IRE) (Taufan (USA))   **h128**
[2003/4 h93, F–: 18g* 18m² 19m* 19g* 20s 20m* 21f* 21m* 22d² 20gᵖᵘ Feb 22] lengthy
gelding: fairly useful novice hurdler: progressed really well, winning at Fontwell (intermediate), Hereford and Market Rasen early in season, Uttoxeter and Cheltenham (both
handicaps) in October and Cheltenham (beat Fairwood Present 2½ lengths) in November:
stays 21f: acts on firm going, possibly not on softer than good: wore cheekpieces last 7
starts: tough and genuine. *P. Bowen*

JOLLY RED (FR)   7 ch.g. Cyborg (FR) – Orne II (FR) (Beau Fixe) [2003/4 24mᵖᵘ Jun   **h–**
5] won maiden point in 2003: visored, shaped as if amiss on hurdling debut. *M. C. Pipe*

JOLLYSHAU (IRE)   6 b.g. Jolly Jake (NZ) – Escheat (Torus) [2003/4 h77?: 21s 22g⁵   **h78**
19sᵖᵘ 16s 16d⁵ 21g⁵ Apr 12] workmanlike gelding: poor maiden hurdler: stays 21f.
Miss A. M. Newton-Smith

JOLLY SIDE (IRE)   11 b.g. Jolly Jake (NZ) – South Quay Lady (Quayside) [2003/4   **c–**
c100, h86: c16g c17mᵘʳ Aug 9] lengthy gelding: winning chaser: well beaten on com-   **h–**
pleted start in 2003/4: has form up to 2¾m: acts on heavy and good to firm going:
headstrong. *Dr P. Pritchard*

JOLY BEY (FR)   7 ch.g. Beyssac (FR) – Rivolie (FR) (Mistigri) [2003/4 c137, h100p: **c147**
c20g² c19s⁵ 24g* c20g⁵ c21gᶠ Apr 2] tall, angular gelding: useful chaser: 10 lb over-   **h128 p**
weight, shaped really well when fifth to Isio in very valuable handicap at Newbury fourth

Mr David Dunsdon's "Joly Bey"

start: favourite, in front and looked set to win in some style when fell 4 out in Topham Chase (Handicap) at Aintree following month: thrice-raced hurdler, fairly useful form when winning handicap at Newbury in February comfortably by 2 lengths from Deriva-tive, ridden less prominently than usual: stays 25f: raced on good going or softer (acts on heavy): fluent jumper: ridden by Mr D. Dunsdon last 4 starts: capable of further improve-ment over hurdles. *N. J. Gifford*

JONAEM (IRE) 14 b.g. Mazaad – Priors Mistress (Sallust) [2003/4 c69, h66: c27s² 27s⁵ 24d⁶ 22m 27g⁶ Jul 28] compact gelding: poor handicap hurdler/chaser: stays 27f: acts on any going. *Mrs Dianne Sayer* **c60** **h59**

JONALTON (IRE) 5 b.g. Perugino (USA) – Vago Pequeno (IRE) (Posen (USA)) [2003/4 21m* 22g² 20g 19m³ 20m* 24f³ 21mᵖᵘ 21g 22sᶠ 20s 24s² 26g 22g 23dᵖᵘ Apr 12] plain gelding: poor maiden on Flat: modest hurdler: won novice seller at Southwell (easily) in July and handicap at Huntingdon in September: largely poor efforts after: stays 3m: acts on firm and soft going: has had tongue tied. *C. R. Dore* **h99**

JONANAUD 5 b.g. Ballet Royal (USA) – Margaret Modes (Thatching) [2003/4 F76: F16f 16m³ 20d⁵ 16v³ 24vᵖᵘ 24s² 20v* 22d² 21s² 16d* Mar 24] leggy gelding: modest form at best in bumpers: fair hurdler: most progressive, winning handicap in February and novice in March, both at Chepstow: effective at 2m to 3m: acts on heavy ground. *H. J. Manners* **h111** **F71**

JONGLEUR COLLONGES (FR) 7 gr.g. Royal Charter (FR) – Soubrette Collonge (FR) (Saumon (FR)) [2003/4 h97: c24m² Nov 11] useful-looking gelding: modest form over hurdles: odds on, 4 lengths second of 3 finishers in novice at Lingfield on chasing debut: stays 3m: acts on good to firm and heavy going. *R. H. Alner* **c97** **h—**

JONNY'S KICK 4 b.g. Revoque (IRE) – Prudence (Grundy) [2003/4 F16v F16v³ Feb 4] long-backed gelding: half-brother to several winners, including useful 8.5f and 1½m winner Heathyards Rock (by Rock City) and 2 winning selling hurdlers: dam, middle-distance maiden, from family of very smart 1½m winner Catchascatchcan: modest form in bumpers at Wetherby and Newcastle. *T. D. Easterby* **F84**

JORDAN'S RIDGE (IRE) 8 br. or b.g. Indian Ridge – Sadie Jordan (USA) (Hail The Pirates (USA)) [2003/4 c102, h—: c16g* c20m* c20m⁴ c20m* c22g* c25g* c25dᶠ 21v² c20v⁴ c20s⁶ 22g³ 20v Mar 21] sparely-made gelding: fair hurdler: fairly useful handicap chaser: much improved in 2003/4, winning at Hexham (3 times) and Kelso (twice), beating only other finisher Weaver George 1¾ lengths in 4-runner event at latter for final success: stays 25f: has form on heavy going, best efforts on good/good to firm: tried blinkered/tongue tied: has failed to impress with attitude in past. *P. Monteith* **c127** **h102**

JORN DU SOLEIL (FR) 7 ch.g. Murmure (FR) – Ina du Soleil (FR) (Or de Chine) [2003/4 c95, h—: c20m⁶ Sep 25] well-made gelding: type to carry condition: maiden chaser: bought out of M. Hammond's stable 3,000 gns Doncaster August Sales: tailed off only start in 2003/4: has found little. *Mrs J. C. McGregor* **c—** **h—**

JORODAMA KING 10 b.g. Lighter – Princess Hecate (Autre Prince) [2003/4 c71x, h—: c25m⁵ c26m³ c25f² Oct 8] lengthy gelding: poor chaser: left O. Sherwood after reappearance: probably stays 27f: acts on firm and good to soft going: tried blinkered: often let down by jumping: of doubtful temperament. *R. J. Price* **c65 x** **h—**

JOSEPH VERNET (IRE) 7 b. or br.g. Owington – Pizziri (Artaius (USA)) [2003/4 20s⁴ 20d* 24d* 24s⁴ 24v 22d Apr 12] tall, useful-looking gelding: fairly useful hurdler: won handicaps at Punchestown and Leopardstown in December: stays 3m: raced on going softer than good. *Paul Nolan, Ireland* **h119**

JOSHUA'S BAY 6 b.g. Karinga Bay – Bonita Blakeney (Baron Blakeney) [2003/4 h79, F—: 16m² 16m⁴ 21d* 21m³ 21m* 21fᶠ 23m² 20g⁴ 18s* 21g 19g Apr 18] sturdy gelding: fair handicap hurdler: much improved in 2003/4, winning at Southwell in August, Plumpton in October and Fontwell (by 8 lengths from Six of One, clear when jumped markedly left last) in January: stays 23f: acts on any going: consistent. *J. R. Jenkins* **h113**

JOSHUA'S VISION (IRE) 13 b.g. Vision (USA) – Perle's Fashion (Sallust) [2003/4 c—, h—: c24sᵖᵘ Apr 17] workmanlike gelding: winning pointer, little worthwhile form otherwise since 2000: tried visored/in cheekpieces: often tongue tied. *Lady Susan Brooke* **c—** **h—**

JOSS NAYLOR (IRE) 9 b.g. Be My Native (USA) – Sister Ida (Bustino) [2003/4 c146, h—: c26g² c36dᵖᵘ Apr 3] leggy, close-coupled gelding: useful hurdler/chaser: creditable second to impressive Strong Flow in Hennessy Cognac Gold Cup at Newbury on reappearance: never going well and pulled up halfway in Grand National at Aintree 4 months later: should stay beyond 3¼m: acts on heavy going: held up: tends to be on toes. *Jonjo O'Neill* **c142** **h—**

JOUEUR D'ESTRUVAL (FR) 7 gr.g. Perrault – Alrose (FR) (Kalyan (FR)) **c121**
[2003/4 h113: 20d c16g^F c20s c16s^F c17s* c20s^3 c24d* Apr 10] leggy, useful-looking **h108**
gelding: fair hurdler: fairly useful chaser: won maiden at Navan in January and listed
event at Cork in April, easily making all when beating Dromlease Express 7 lengths at
latter: good fifth to Liscannor Lad in valuable novice handicap at Punchestown later in
month, having forced pace and made mistakes: effective at 2m to 25f: acts on soft going:
room for improvement in his jumping. *W. P. Mullins, Ireland*

JOURNEY 11 ch.g. Tina's Pet – Lady Vynz (Whitstead) [2003/4 c–, h–: c22g May 24] **c–**
fair pointer, successful in March: little impact in 3 steeplechases. *Mrs Sarah L. Dent* **h–**

JOY BOX 4 ch.g. Unfuwain (USA) – El Jazirah (Kris) [2003/4 F16g Mar 6] third foal: **F–**
half-brother to useful French middle-distance stayer Mount Elbrus (by Barathea) and 7f
winner Christaleni (by Zilzal): dam unraced sister to Prix de Diane winner Rafha: well
held in bumper at Doncaster on debut. *T. D. Easterby*

JOYCE BEL (FR) 11 b.g. Rose Laurel – Jeanne de Laval (FR) (Gairloch) [2003/4 **c–**
c89, h–: c22g Jul 6] modest handicap chaser, well held only start in 2003/4: stays 3m, **h–**
effective at much shorter: acts on heavy and good to firm going: has worn cheekpieces.
Mrs H. Dalton

JOYE DES ILES (FR) 7 b.g. Mont Basile (FR) – Titjana (FR) (Quart de Vin (FR)) **c–**
[2003/4 c22s^3 c26m^4 c24d^6 c26v^5 c25d^{pu} Feb 17] ex-French gelding: fourth foal: dam **h–**
unraced: pulled up both starts over hurdles: won 2½m maiden on last of 4 outings in
points in 2003: little form in steeplechases in Britain: blinkered. *B. G. Powell*

JOYEUX ROYAL (FR) 7 b.g. Cyborg (FR) – Samba du Cochet (FR) (Tanlas (FR)) **c–**
[2003/4 c114, h–: c20s^{pu} 16m 24s* 24d 27g Apr 22] tall gelding: has had breathing **h102**
operation: fair hurdler/chaser: form in 2003/4 only when winning handicap hurdle at
Chepstow in December: stays 3m: acts on soft and good to firm going: tried blinkered/
tongue tied: has been let down by jumping over fences. *P. F. Nicholls*

JOYFUL PRINCESS 4 b.f. Gildoran – Joyful Pabs (Pablond) [2003/4 F13d F12d **h–**
17v^{pu} Feb 2] lengthy, unfurnished filly: second foal: dam no sign of ability: has shown **F–**
nothing herself. *C. J. Down*

JR-KAY (IRE) 14 ch.g. Tremblant – Promising Very VII (Damsire Unregistered) **c101**
[2003/4 c25d* May 22] fairly useful hunter chaser: won 6-runner event at Wetherby
by 6 lengths from Balisteros: stays 3¼m: acts on good to firm and good to soft going.
Miss A. Armitage

JUBBA'S JESTER (USA) 5 b.g. St Jovite (USA) – Wisecrack (USA) (Secretariat **h–**
(USA) [2003/4 aF16g F16d 19s^{pu} 26s^{pu} Dec 26] 14,500 4-y-o: tall gelding: half- **F–**
brother to winners in USA and France: dam lightly raced in USA: little sign of ability.
B. G. Powell

JUDAIC WAYS 10 b.g. Rudimentary (USA) – Judeah (Great Nephew) [2003/4 c96, **c96**
h–: c23m^{pu} c24m^F Nov 24] lengthy gelding: modest handicap chaser: almost upsides **h–**
winner when falling last at Ludlow (successful there 3 times) in November: stays 3m:
acts on firm and soft going: has shaped as if amiss more than once: prone to the odd bad
mistake. *H. D. Daly*

JUDES LAW 6 gr.m. Contract Law (USA) – Linen Thread (Broxted) [2003/4 F–: **h–**
F17d 17s^{pu} Jan 22] no form, including on Flat: left S. Burrough after reappearance. **F–**
P. R. Rodford

JUDGE JIM 7 b.g. Contract Law (USA) – My Moody Girl (IRE) (Alzao (USA)) **h–**
[2003/4 16m 17m^5 20m Jun 28] rather leggy gelding: tailed off all starts over hurdles:
tried blinkered: sold £1,100 Ascot July Sales. *Mrs S. D. Williams*

JUDICIOUS NORMAN (IRE) 13 br.g. Strong Gale – Smart Fashion (Carlburg) **c74**
[2003/4 c24m^3 c21m^3 May 21] rangy gelding: poor chaser: won maiden point in 2003: **h–**
stays 3m: has had tongue tied. *Miss Katherine Self*

JUDY GALE (IRE) 6 bl.m. Glacial Storm (USA) – Gale Choice (IRE) (Strong Gale) **h–**
[2003/4 h–, F–: 22d^6 Mar 3] no form in bumper or novice hurdles. *J. Gallagher*

JUG OF PUNCH (IRE) 5 ch.g. In The Wings – Mysistra (FR) (Machiavellian (USA)) **h77**
[2003/4 16d 16g^3 16g 21d^3 Apr 8] ex-Irish gelding: 1½m winner on Flat: poor form over
hurdles: stays 21f. *S. T. Lewis*

JULANDI 5 ch.m. Southern Music – Dull'un (True Song) [2003/4 F16m^4 F16f F16m^6 **F79 ?**
Nov 9] first foal: dam unraced: probably flattered when fourth in slowly-run bumper at
Worcester: well held 2 other starts. *B. N. Doran*

JULIA'S CHOICE 5 ch.m. Elmaamul (USA) – Daarat Alayaam (IRE) (Reference **h72**
Point) [2003/4 h72, F–: 16g^{pu} 16m^6 16m^2 23m^3 26s^{pu} Dec 26] leggy mare: poor maiden
hurdler: stays 23f: acts on soft and good to firm going. *J. R. Jenkins*

JULIES BOY (IRE) 7 b.g. Toulon – Chickmo (IRE) (Seclude (USA)) [2003/4 h88, **c86**
F70: 22m^{pu} 24d^{pu} c19s^5 26s^{pu} c24d^2 26d Mar 28] sturdy gelding: novice hurdler/chaser, **h72**
modest form on a couple of occasions: stays 3m: acts on good to soft going. *T. R. George*

JULIE'S LEADER (IRE) 10 b.g. Supreme Leader – Parkavoureen (Deep Run) **c112**
[2003/4 c–, h109: 24m* 27g^2 c26g* Jun 28] workmanlike gelding: fair hurdler, complet- **h112**
ing hat-trick when winning amateur handicap at Chepstow in May: fair chaser: won weak
handicap at Newton Abbot in June: stays 27f: unraced on firm going, acts on any other.
P. F. Nicholls

JUMBO'S DREAM 13 b.g. Jumbo Hirt (USA) – Joyful Star (Rubor) [2003/4 c–, h–: **c74**
24m 24g 24m^6 24g c20m^3 c26m^3 c26m^4 c27m^5 c20g^F c25g^2 c27d* c27s^2 c26d^{pu} c20d^4 **h–**
c28d^{pu} c26d^3 Apr 18] deep-girthed gelding: winning hurdler: poor chaser: won weakly-
contested amateur handicap at Sedgefield in November: stays 27f: unraced on firm going,
acts on any other: tried blinkered, usually wears cheekpieces. *J. E. Dixon*

JUMPTY DUMPTY (FR) 7 b.g. Chamberlin (FR) – Caryatide (FR) (Maiymad) **c–**
[2003/4 c–, h84: 22d^{pu} 19s 18s^{pu} Feb 9] tall gelding: poor hurdler, often runs as if amiss: **h–**
stays 2¾m: acts on firm and soft going. *J. C. Tuck*

JUNE'S RIVER (IRE) 11 ch.g. Over The River (FR) – June Bug (Welsh Saint) **c96 x**
[2003/4 c105x, h–: 20d^4 c20g^4 c20d^{lF} c17s c20s^2 c16g^4 c20s^4 c20d^6 Feb 23] rather leggy **h–**
gelding: first start over hurdles since 1998 when well held on reappearance: modest
handicap chaser: stays 2½m: raced on good going or softer (acts on heavy): held up: often
let down by jumping: unreliable: sold 1,600 gns Doncaster May Sales. *Mrs M. Reveley*

JUNGLE FRESH 11 b.g. Rambo Dancer (CAN) – Report 'em (USA) (Staff Writer **c–**
(USA)) [2003/4 c20f^5 May 10] winning pointer, pulled up all 4 starts in 2003: no show in **h–**
2 hunter chases: tried tongue tied. *M. Rodda*

JUNGLE JINKS (IRE) 9 b.g. Proud Panther (FR) – Three Ladies (Menelek) [2003/4 **c123**
c132+, h–: c25g^{bd} c25m^4 c26g^{pu} c25d^{pu} c25v^3 c24s^2 c28d^4 c32g^5 Mar 28] smallish, **h–**
workmanlike gelding: fairly useful chaser: second to Mr Cospector at Haydock, though
generally disappointing in handicaps in 2003/4: should stay 3½m: acts on heavy going.
G. M. Moore

JUNGLE RUMBLER 5 b.m. Charnwood Forest (IRE) – Blueberry Walk (Green **h–**
Desert (USA)) [2003/4 h–: 17g^6 16g^F Dec 6] no form over hurdles: tried visored.
P. Winkworth

JUNGLI (IRE) 11 b.g. Be My Native (USA) – Simple Mind (Decent Fellow) [2003/4 **c–**
c142?, h–: c16d^F c16m Apr 15] lengthy gelding: useful handicap chaser: very lightly **h–**
raced nowadays, well below best on completed start in 2003/4: stays 2½m: acts on good
to firm and heavy going: usually races up with pace. *P. R. Webber*

JUNIOR FONTAINE (FR) 7 b.g. Silver Rainbow – Blanche Fontaine (FR) (Oakland **c120**
(FR)) [2003/4 h118: 16d c17m* c16s^3 c16s^6 c16s^6 c22s^3 Mar 21] workmanlike gelding: **h–**
fairly useful handicap hurdler: won maiden at Ballinrobe on chasing debut in August:
easily best subsequent effort when winning handicap at Punchestown in late-April by 3½
lengths from Rodber: should stay beyond 17f: acts on any going. *A. L. T. Moore, Ireland*

JUPITER'S FANCY 9 ch.m. Jupiter Island – Joe's Fancy (Apollo Eight) [2003/4 c–, **c65**
h–: c20m^3 17m c21g c26d^4 c21s^6 Feb 24] tall gelding: poor form in steeplechases: left A. Kirtley after **h–**
reappearance, D. Barker before final start. *M. V. Coglan*

JUPON VERT (FR) 7 b.g. Lights Out (FR) – Danse Verte (FR) (Brezzo (FR)) [2003/4 **c95**
c88, h94: 19m c16d c16f^2 c16m* c19g^2 c16s^4 c16d^2 c16m^4 c20d^2 c20d^3 c19g^2 c16g^2 Apr **h–**
18] leggy gelding: winning hurdler: modest handicap chaser: left P. Nicholls after second
start: won at Warwick in November: stays 2½m: acts on soft and firm ground: effective
tongue tied or not: consistent. *R. J. Hodges*

JURADO EXPRESS (IRE) 8 b.g. Jurado (USA) – Express Film (Ashmore (FR)) **c119**
[2003/4 c117, h96: c16d^5 c17d^4 c18d^2 c20s^F c16s^2 c16g Apr 1] workmanlike gelding: **h–**
modest hurdler: fairly useful chaser: good efforts in 2003/4 when second, behind Over
The First in listed handicap at Punchestown fifth start: raced mainly around 2m: acts on
soft going. *A. L. T. Moore, Ireland*

JURALAN (IRE) 9 b.g. Jurado (USA) – Boylan (Buckskin (FR)) [2003/4 c122, h–: **c126**
16d^2 c20s^5 19g^4 c20d^2 c20g^4 Apr 16] tall, good sort: fairly useful chaser: good efforts last **h103**
2 starts, fourth to Simply Gifted in handicap at Ayr: lightly raced over hurdles, won

novice at Doncaster in March by 1¼ lengths from Your A Gassman: stays 21f: raced mostly on good/good to soft going over jumps. *H. P. Hogarth*

JURANCON II (FR) 7 b.g. Scooter Bleu (IRE) Volniste (FR) (Olmeto) [2003/4 c118p, h125: c32m* c29v⁴ c29d⁵ c29g² c28m* c36dᶠ Apr 3]   **c148 h–**

    Days after Tony McCoy's ninth attempt to win the Grand National ended in failure, Ladbrokes opened a book on whether he would ever be successful in the race, pricing him up at 11/8-on never to win the National, rating him an even-money chance to win it. If McCoy does fail to win the National before hanging up his boots, one person who won't be in a position to pick on him is Jonjo O'Neill, to whom the responsibility has passed of providing McCoy—the new stable jockey at Jackdaws Castle—with the ammunition. O'Neill failed to complete on all eight of his National rides, the first on Glenkiln in 1973, a winner over the fences who, in preference to Red Rum, carried the first colours of their owner Noel le Mare. The furthest O'Neill got was the second Canal Turn on Sir Garnet in 1977 when, according to O'Neill, he was knocked clean out of the saddle by another horse. O'Neill twice rode the favourite in the race. In 1978 he was on former winner Rag Trade, who broke down badly and was put down shortly afterwards, while in 1979 he rode that year's Gold Cup winner Alverton, who was going like a winner when falling fatally at second Becher's. O'Neill did manage to conquer the fences as a jockey when partnering Clear Cut to success in the 1974 Topham Chase but the National course has proved rather kinder to him as a trainer, thanks particularly to the exploits of Clan Royal.

    Some have pointed to McCoy's aggressive style of riding as being the reason behind his lack of success in the National, but he too has ridden successfully in the Topham (or the John Hughes Trophy as it was known). Cyfor Malta, as a five-year-old having only his seventh run over fences, ran out one of the easiest winners ever seen over the National fences when taking the 1998 renewal, while Northern Starlight, on whom McCoy won in 2000, was surely one of the smallest horses ever to win over the National fences. Like O'Neill, McCoy has partnered a horse which has fallen fatally at second Becher's in the National. The horse in

Britannia Building Society English Summer National (Handicap), Uttoxeter—
Jurancon II on his way to a much improved performance on just his third start over fences

Red Square Vodka Gold Cup Chase (Handicap), Haydock—a red-letter day for conditional jockey Joey Elliott as Jurancon II puts himself firmly in the Grand National picture

question, Eudipe in 1999, is one of four horses with whom McCoy has parted company in the National, his others being Chatam, his first ride in the race, who fell at the twelfth in 1995, Challenger du Luc, a first-fence faller in 1998, and Dark Stranger, who was sent off favourite in 2000 on the strength of a win in the Mildmay of Flete at the Festival, only to unseat McCoy at the third. McCoy has completed the course twice, both times on Blowing Wind, who was badly hampered by a loose horse at the nineteenth in 2001 before being remounted and finishing third and, then, as favourite in 2002 (like Dark Stranger on the strength of a win in the Mild-may of Flete), completed without mishap to fill the same position, albeit nearly a distance behind the winner. All of McCoy's National rides have been trained so far by Martin Pipe, except for Paul Nicholls' well-fancied Deep Bramble, who was staying on in seventh when breaking down going to two out in 1996. McCoy's 2003 mount Iris Bleu also broke down, this time after a mistake at the Chair. In the latest renewal, Jurancon II was widely thought of as providing McCoy with his best chance so far of winning the race, and he was sent off co-favourite at 10/1. How-ever, Jurancon was also the least experienced of McCoy's National mounts—the National was only the seven-year-old's eighth run over fences—and it showed, as he missed the break and was being ridden along in mid-division when falling at the fourth. Jurancon had indeed, however, looked an ideal type for the race, and he will be one to consider another year, though he almost certainly won't be partnered by McCoy, now that owner David Johnson has a new retained jockey.

Jurancon placed himself in the Grand National picture when putting up a smart performance to run away with the Red Square Vodka Gold Cup at Haydock at the end of February. Unseasonably firmish ground led to several withdrawals in a race worth just under £70,000 to the winner, and very few of the ten runners managed to get into things, among them joint favourites Joe Blake and World Wide Web. Artic Jack made the early running at a good pace, jumping in exhilarating fashion, but Jurancon stayed with him under 5-lb conditional Joey Elliot, and took over at the thirteenth. The patiently-ridden Bear On Board stayed on in vain pursuit in the straight, but could make no further impression as Jurancon galloped on strongly to beat Bear On Board by fifteen lengths, with Artic Jack twenty-one lengths further back in third, the winner knocking eighteen seconds off the course record, set by Rubstic in 1975.

Strangely, given that Jurancon was his choice from Pipe's seven-strong National challenge, McCoy had ridden him just once since his novice hurdling days. Rodi Greene rode Jurancon when he first showed himself effective on good to firm ground back in June in winning the Summer National at Uttoxeter, the second most valuable race of the summer in Britain and one which the same connections had won with the similarly inexperienced Stormez the year before. The Summer National was also hit by non-runners, not to mention the fact that Ackzo collapsed and died even before the race got under way, and it was far from a strong affair for the money on offer, with four of the thirteen runners out of the handicap and others out of form. The pace was good and the majority were in trouble with a circuit to go. The only pair in the field that could be described as unexposed, Jurancon and Take The Stand, were disputing the lead travelling well five out, where the latter fell. Jurancon responded really well to a typically strong ride from Greene (who earned a suspension for using his whip with excessive frequency) to win by half a length from the staying-on Spot Thedifference, with stable-companion Take Control four lengths back in third. Jurancon's best effort in

Mr D. A. Johnson's "Jurancon II"

between his wins at Uttoxeter and Haydock came when three and a half lengths second to Southern Star, from 3 lb out of the weights, in the Tote Classic Chase at Warwick, a race marred by the deaths of both Behrajan and Take Control. Jurancon was let down by his jumping somewhat when a well-held fourth in the Sussex National at Plumpton five months after Uttoxeter, and when a distant last of five finishers to Bindaree in the Welsh National at Chepstow in December, when he was off the bridle with over a circuit to go.

Jurancon II (FR) (b.g. 1997)	Scooter Bleu (IRE) (b 1988)	Commanche Run (b 1981)	Run The Gantlet
			Volley
		Seneca (b 1973)	Chaparral
			Schonbrunn
	Volniste (FR) (ch 1987)	Olmeto (b 1972)	Val de Loir
			Vivara
		Ianiste (b 1974)	Laniste
			Ritournelle II

The tall, leggy Jurancon II is by the little-known yet well-bred Scooter Bleu, a half-brother to Sagace and Simply Great, who won once from just three starts on the Flat, and finished third in the Group 3 Prix du Lys. Jurancon's selle francais dam, Volniste, was successful in a non-thoroughbred race on the Flat at just over eleven furlongs, but failed to win over jumps, while grandam Ianiste ran six times on the Flat without success. Jurancon is the third foal of Volniste, and her only other winner is her fourth, Karakoe (by Gunboat Diplomacy), who was successful over fences and on the Flat in France. Jurancon had four starts on the level in the French Provinces for Thierry Civel, winning once over thirteen furlongs, then showed fairly useful form when successful on three of his nine starts over hurdles for Pipe before his attention was switched to chasing. Jurancon could hardly be labelled consistent. When following his second at Warwick with a win at Haydock, he was stringing a couple of decent efforts together for about the only time in his career. That said, he is very much the type to win more good staying chases. He has yet to race on firm going but acts on any other, and has considerable stamina without being a one-paced plodder. *M. C. Pipe*

JUSTAFANCY   6 b.g. Green Desert (USA) – Justsayno (USA) (Dr Blum (USA)) [2003/4 16m May 7] half-brother to modest 2m hurdler Cipriani Queen (by Seattle Dancer): modest maiden on Flat (likely to prove best at 7f/1m): well held in seller on hurdling debut. *Miss J. Feilden*   h–

JUST ANVIL (IRE)   6 ch.g. Baron Blakeney – Amy Just (IRE) (Bustomi) [2003/4 c20s⁴ c22g⁴ c20s³ c22s Feb 9] second foal: dam unraced: runner-up in 2-finisher maiden Irish point on debut in 2002: bought 10,000 gns Doncaster August (2002) Sales: well beaten in steeplechases. *L. Wells*   c–

JUST ARETHA   8 b.m. Weld – Just Something (Good Times (ITY)) [2003/4 21m 21mᵖᵘ Jul 18] fourth foal: half-sister to fair hurdler up to 2½m Batty's Island (by Town And Country): dam poor maiden on Flat and over hurdles: no show over hurdles or in points, gave trouble at start second outing (has been withdrawn after getting loose). *G. J. Smith*   h–

JUST A TOUCH   8 ch.g. Rakaposhi King – Minim (Rymer) [2003/4 h90: c16d³ c16sᵖᵘ 17s³ c16s⁵ c16dᶠ c16d* Mar 19] workmanlike gelding: modest handicap hurdler: best effort over fences when winning handicap at Warwick (all 3 wins there): barely stays 19f: raced on going softer than good (acts on heavy). *P. Winkworth*   c90 h90

JUST BARNEY BOY   7 b.g. Past Glories – Pablena (Pablond) [2003/4 c–, h–: c24m⁴ c20mᵘʳ c24gᵖᵘ Jul 3] fairly useful pointer, successful in February and March: no form in steeplechases. *R. Nixon*   c– h–

JUST BETH   8 ch.m. Carlingford Castle – One For The Road (Warpath) [2003/4 h64: 24g 27d 20v 24g* 21m² 22g 20m⁵ 24g² 17d² 25dᵖᵘ 16d 17sᵖᵘ 24d² Apr 21] angular mare: poor hurdler: won novice at Market Rasen in June: effective around 2m to 3m: acts on good to firm going, probably on heavy: tried blinkered. *G. Fierro*   h79

JUST BRYAN   5 ch.g. Southern Music – Prospect of Whitby (True Song) [2003/4 F16d Apr 12] medium-sized gelding: first foal: dam of no account: well beaten in bumper on debut. *P. A. Pritchard*   F–

JUST CASSANDRA (IRE)   7 ch.m. Eurobus – Oriental Roo (Amazon) [2003/4 c24s* c24s³ c25d* Apr 13] workmanlike mare: half-sister to 2 winning pointers, includ-   c103 ing winning hurdler/chaser up to 2½m Robin of Sherwood (by Pollerton): dam lightly-raced maiden hurdler: winning pointer, including 3 times in 2004: successful 3 of 4 starts in hunter chases, at Wexford in March and Fairyhouse and Punchestown in April: beat Ace of Spades 4½ lengths in Cox's Cash & Carry Champion Hunters Chase at last-named: stays 25f: acts on soft going. *Mrs Maureen Danagher, Ireland*

JUST CLASSIC 4 gr g. Classic Cliche (IRE) – Misty View (Absalom) [2003/4 F18g* **F106** Apr 22] third foal: dam 7f (at 2 yrs) and 1¼m winner: overcame greenness to win bumper at Funtwell on debut by 11 lengths from Shadow River, leading 4f out and asserting despite hanging right. *M. C. Pipe*

JUST FLORA 8 ch.m. Democratic (USA) – Firgant (USA) (L'Emigrant (USA)) **h–** [2003/4 16g Jun 12] fourth foal: sister to 1½m winner Lord Gizzmo and half-sister to useful but temperamental 2m chaser Nipper Reed (by Celestial Storm): dam ran once: showed little in maiden hurdle on debut. *Miss K. M. George*

JUST FOR FUN (IRE) 6 b.g. Kahyasi – Copper Breeze (IRE) (Strong Gale) [2003/4 **h77 ?** F–: 20g² 16d 24d 24d³ 22d Apr 5] smallish gelding: poor form over hurdles: stays 3m: raced only on good/good to soft going. *Ferdy Murphy*

JUST FOR GER (IRE) 10 b.g. Beau Sher – Reasonar (Reasonable (FR)) [2003/4 **c94** c90, h75: c20spu c17spu c16v* 20s⁶ Feb 14] leggy gelding: poor hurdler: modest handicap **h–** chaser: won at Ayr in January: best form up to 2½m: acts on heavy going, probably on good to firm. *J. S. Goldie*

JUST GOOD FUN (IRE) 10 br.g. Good Thyne (USA) – Killonerry (Croghan Hill) **c–** [2003/4 20v 22d⁵ c22gpu Jul 6] lengthy gelding: fairly useful hurdler in 1999/00: lightly **h98** raced and only modest form at best since, including over fences: stays 3m: acts on soft and good to firm going. *M. Pitman*

JUSTIFIED (IRE) 5 b. or br.g. Leading Counsel (USA) – Monkeylane (Monksfield) **F104 p** [2003/4 F16d² Apr 13] fourth foal: dam, placed several times over hurdles, half-sister to very smart chaser up to 2½m Big Matt: encouraging second to Augherskea in bumper at Fairyhouse on debut: didn't need to improve to win similar event at Sligo easily later in month: remains capable of better. *E. Sheehy, Ireland*

JUST IN DEBT (IRE) 8 b. or br.g. Montelimar (USA) – No Debt (Oats) [2003/4 **c132** c125, h102: c25g 20d³ 24f* 20m² c23g² 22f c24g³ c20s⁵ c28mpu c25g* c36dur c33dpu Apr **h120** 17] useful-looking ex-Irish gelding: fairly useful hurdler: won novice at Kilbeggan in June: useful handicap chaser: left P. Doyle/off 5 months after seventh start: fortunate to win at Ayr in March: stays 25f: acts on soft and firm going. *M. Todhunter*

JUSTIN MAC (IRE) 13 br.g. Satco (FR) – Quantas (Roan Rocket) [2003/4 c111§, **c– §** h–§: c26dR c22g c23mpu Jun 28] good-topped gelding: fair chaser: well below form in **h– §** hunters/handicap in early-2003/4: unproven beyond 21f: acts on good to firm and heavy going: blinkered twice: often finds little: unreliable. *Mrs H. Dalton*

JUSTINO 6 b.g. Bustino – Jupiter's Message (Jupiter Island) [2003/4 19s 18v 16s 19g **h70** 22g⁶ Apr 4] workmanlike gelding: sixth foal: brother to fair hurdler Lord Warford, stays 3m, and half-brother to smart hurdler/high-class chaser up to 3m Bellator (by Simply Great): dam unraced: poor form over hurdles. *G. B. Balding*

JUST IN TIME 9 b.g. Night Shift (USA) – Future Past (USA) (Super Concorde **c–** (USA)) [2003/4 c108, h–: c20mur 19f² 19m* 21f² 20g⁶ 19g⁴ 20g 21m⁴ Apr 14] leggy **h123** gelding: won 3 novice chases in early-2002/3, let down by jumping over fences since: fairly useful handicap hurdler: won at Stratford in October: stays 21f: acts on soft and firm going. *P. J. Hobbs*

JUST JASMINE 12 ch.m. Nicholas Bill – Linguistic (Porto Bello) [2003/4 c140, h–: **c127** c19g⁶ c16m Apr 15] good-topped mare: useful handicap chaser in 2002/3: sixth to **h–** Supreme Catch at Ascot on reappearance: well held at Cheltenham 3 months later: effective at 2m to 21f: acts on any going: goes well for R. Greene: usually held up: usually sound jumper. *K. Bishop*

JUST JED 5 b.g. Presidium – Carrapateira (Gunner B) [2003/4 F16m F16m F16g **h–** 22gpu Mar 28] chunky gelding: second foal: half-brother to fair staying chaser Pink Gin **F–** (by Tickled Pink): dam unraced sister to fairly useful staying chaser Cumrew: no sign of ability. *R. Shiels*

JUSTJIM 12 b.g. Derring Rose – Crystal Run VII (Damsire Unregistered) [2003/4 **c73 §** c92§, h–§: c25dpu c20m⁵ c24d⁵ c24d⁶ Apr 8] sparely-made gelding: winning chaser: poor **h– §** form in hunters in 2003/4: stays 3¼m: acts on soft and good to firm going: tried blinkered/in cheekpieces/tongue tied: unreliable. *Mrs C. Gethin*

JUST KATE 5 b.m. Bob's Return (IRE) – M I Babe (Celtic Cone) [2003/4 F16m³ 16gᵖᵘ 16g⁴ 20d⁵ 21d* Apr 8] third foal: half-sister to winning 3m hurdler Red Rover (by Infantry): dam, winning hurdler/chaser who stayed 19f, half-sister to Grand National winner Red Marauder: third in bumper on debut: best effort over hurdles when winning conditional jockeys novice handicap at Ludlow: will stay 3m: yet to race on extremes of going. *Mrs H. Dalton*   **h81 F81**

JUST LAMBRINI 5 br.m. Overbury (IRE) – Lambrini (IRE) (Buckskin (FR)) [2003/4 F16g⁶ 16mᵖᵘ 16mʳᵒ Dec 10] first foal: dam, poor novice chaser up to 2½m, half-sister to useful but temperamental staying chaser Browjoshy: no sign of ability. *D. McCain*   **h– F–**

JUST MAYBE (IRE) 10 b.g. Glacial Storm (USA) – Purlace (Realm) [2003/4 h122, h–: c26sᵖᵘ 24m 26g² 25g³ Feb 6] good-bodied gelding: fairly useful chaser in 2002/3: modest maiden hurdler: suited by 3m+: acts on heavy going: best in blinkers: tongue tied and ridden in spurs final outing in 2001/2: jumps none too fluently. *Miss Venetia Williams*   **c– x h99**

JUST MIDAS 6 b.g. Merdon Melody – Thabeh (Shareef Dancer (USA)) [2003/4 h–: 22m 16m* 16m* 18f² 17g 19m⁶ Sep 10] leggy, sparely-made gelding: poor hurdler: left N. Smith prior to winning selling handicaps at Uttoxeter in July and Worcester in August: best around 2m: acts on firm going. *M. C. Pipe*   **h83**

JUST MUCKIN AROUND (IRE) 8 gr.g. Celio Rufo – Cousin Muck (IRE) (Henbit (USA)) [2003/4 c75, h–: c21gᶠ c21d² c25fᶠ⁶ c17v⁴ c19g⁴ c17s² c20s² c18s⁵ c20g³ Mar 1] lengthy gelding: modest chaser: won weak handicap at Plumpton in November despite mistakes: stays 21f: acts on heavy going. *R. H. Buckler*   **c88 h–**

JUST MURPHY (IRE) 6 b.g. Namaqualand (USA) – Bui-Doi (IRE) (Dance of Life (USA)) [2003/4 h118: c17g⁸ c16m² c16m* 20gᵖᵘ 17g⁶ Oct 18] leggy gelding: fairly useful hurdler: similar form when winning novice chases at Kelso in May and Worcester (patiently ridden when beating Burning Truth a neck) in July: left N. Henderson before fourth start: stays 2½m: acts on soft and good to firm going: ran poorly tried in cheekpieces: carries head high under pressure. *Janet E. Elliot, USA*   **c120 h–**

JUST REUBEN (IRE) 9 gr.g. Roselier (FR) – Sharp Mama VII (Damsire Unregistered) [2003/4 c–: c21m⁶ c18m⁵ c26d⁴ c25m c21d⁴ c22m³ c20f* c20m² c20m* c20f³ c21m² c20g* c21d⁶ c26v³ c21d⁵ c26g³ c26g⁴ Mar 8] leggy gelding: modest chaser: won handicaps at Fontwell in August, September and December (novice): best form around 2½m: probably acts on any going: tried blinkered/visored. *C. L. Tizzard*   **c89 h–**

JUST RIVA (IRE) 6 ch.m. Roaring Riva – Yankee Trader (Stanford) [2003/4 18d 20s⁶ 24vᵖᵘ 20d² 20s 20dᶠ Apr 10] first foal: dam 7f winner: won maiden point in 2003: poor maiden hurdler: stays 2½m: acts on good to soft going: in cheekpieces second/third outings, blinkered last 4. *C. A. McBratney, Ireland*   **h71**

JUST SAL 8 b.m. Silly Prices – Hanim (IRE) (Hatim (USA)) [2003/4 h77: 16g² 16g 16m⁴ 20gᵖᵘ 17d 17d⁶ 18d 16s 18v 20s³ 20d 16d* 16g² Apr 5] workmanlike mare: modest hurdler: won conditional jockeys mares handicap at Hexham in March: stays 2¾m: acts on heavy going, probably on good to firm going: tried in cheekpieces/blinkers: has shown signs of temperament: none too consistent. *R. Nixon*   **h86**

JUST SERENADE 5 ch.m. Factual (USA) – Thimbalina (Salmon Leap (USA)) [2003/4 h87: 16gᵖᵘ Nov 2] medium-sized mare: modest maiden on Flat (stays 1m): fortunate to win juvenile at Stratford on hurdling debut in 2002/3: in cheekpieces, no show in mares handicap over year later: sold to join T. Walshe 1,700 gns Doncaster November Sales. *M. J. Ryan*   **h–**

JUST SOOTY 9 br.g. Be My Native (USA) – March Fly (Sousa) [2003/4 c–, h–: c20s² c21g* Apr 12] big gelding: poor maiden hurdler: better over fences: second run after 16-month absence, improved form when winning maiden at Sedgefield: stays 21f: acts on soft going, probably on good to firm: takes good hold. *N. G. Richards*   **c100 h–**

JUST STRONG (IRE) 11 b. or br.g. Strong Gale – Just Dont Know (Buckskin (FR)) [2003/4 c92: c25gᵖᵘ c26m² c21gᶠ c21m⁶ c20f⁵ c25m⁴ c27d* c25gᶠ c25g c26d⁵ Apr 18] good-topped gelding: has reportedly been hobdayed: poor handicap chaser: won at Sedgefield in October: stays 27f: acts on good to firm and good to soft going. *Mrs A. M. Naughton*   **c69**

JUST SUPERB 5 ch.g. Superlative – Just Greenwich (Chilibang) [2003/4 h–: 16s* 16d² 17d 16s⁵ 16d* 16d² 16m 19g² Apr 18] smallish gelding: fair handicap hurdler: won at Warwick in December and March, conditional jockeys event on latter occasion: likely to prove best up to 2½m: acts on soft going: usually races prominently. *P. A. Pritchard*   **h100**

JUST THE JOBE   6 gr.g. Roselier (FR) – Radical Lady (Radical) [2003/4 F86: 16d* **h111** 16d 21v^F 19d^3 19s^2 23s^6 22d^F 22g* 24d 20d Apr 10] leggy gelding: fair novice hurdler: won at Hexham in December and Ayr (handicap) in March: should stay 3m: raced on good going or softer over hurdles: wore cheekpieces last 4 starts. *R. C. Guest*

JUSTUPYOURSTREET (IRE)   8 b.g. Dolphin Street (FR) – Sure Flyer (IRE) **h110** (Sure Blade (USA)) [2003/4 20m^pu 16g* 16g^6 16g^5 17d Nov 2] rather leggy gelding: fair handicap hurdler: won at Perth in June: should stay beyond 17f: acts on soft going: tried tongue tied. *Ms Liz Harrison*

JUST WHISKEY (IRE)   11 b.g. Satco (FR) – Illinois Belle (Le Bavard (FR)) **c–** [2003/4 c–, h–: c24m^pu May 5] rangy gelding: lightly raced and no form in steeplechases **h–** since 2001/2 (runner-up in point in 2004): stays 3¼m: acts on soft and firm going: has had tongue tied. *N. A. Twiston-Davies*

K

KABEER   6 ch.g. Unfuwain (USA) – Ta Rib (USA) (Mr Prospector (USA)) [2003/4 **F–** F89: F16d Apr 12] second in bumper on debut in 2002/3 for Julian Poulton: well held in similar event 12 months later. *P. S. McEntee*

KADAM (IRE)   4 b.g. Night Shift (USA) – Kadassa (IRE) (Shardari) [2003/4 16d^5 **h80 p** Mar 21] ex-French gelding: fifth foal: half-brother to very smart chaser around 2m Kadarann (by Bigstone) and fairly useful hurdler Kadara (by Slip Anchor), stays 3m: dam maiden: well beaten in 2 starts over 1¼m at 3 yrs for A. de Royer Dupre: tongue tied, fifth in juvenile at Stratford on hurdling debut: likely to improve for experience. *P. F. Nicholls*

KADARA (IRE)   5 b.m. Slip Anchor – Kadassa (IRE) (Shardari) [2003/4 h111: 20d **h124** 24g^2 16d* 20v^2 23s 24g^5 20d 20m Apr 24] tall, useful-looking mare: will make a chaser: usually looks very well: fairly useful hurdler: won valuable mares handicap at Sandown in January by 1¾ lengths from Dancing Pearl: effective at well-run 2m to 3m: acts on heavy going, probably on good to firm: reportedly unsuited by left-handed track fifth outing. *R. H. Alner*

ladbrokespoker.com Mares' Only Handicap Hurdle, Sandown—
Kadara (left) and Dancing Pearl fight out the finish as Avitta (No.8) flatters to deceive

skybetvegas.com Castleford Chase, Wetherby—Kadarann enjoys a facile success

KADARANN (IRE) 7 b.g. Bigstone (IRE) – Kadassa (IRE) (Shardari) [2003/4 c159, h–: c17g³ c16g² c16d* c17g⁴ c20gᵖᵘ Mar 6] tall, close-coupled gelding: has reportedly had soft palate operation: very smart chaser: placed in handicaps at Exeter (behind Edredon Bleu) and Cheltenham (behind Cenkos) in November: won 3-runner Grade 2 skybetvegas.com Castleford Chase at Wetherby in December by 22 lengths from Flagship Uberalles, distinctly mulish jumping off but pulling clear in straight: well below best in Grade 2 and valuable handicap at Newbury (bled from nose) subsequently: best around 2m: acts on soft and good to firm going: often led in: usually front runner: jumps soundly. *P. F. Nicholls* — c157 h–

KADISKAR (IRE) 6 b.g. Ashkalani (IRE) – Kadissya (USA) (Blushing Groom (FR)) [2003/4 h119+: 16v* 20d* 20d* 20s³ Dec 14] lengthy, useful-looking gelding: fairly useful hurdler: won maiden at Sligo and novice at Cork (by 3 lengths from Rockstown Boy) in June and Grade 3 novice at Navan (by length from Always) in November: creditable placed efforts in graded novices at Navan (third to Newmill) in December and Punchestown (3½ lengths second to Sadlers Wings) in late-April: stays 2½m: acts on heavy going: tongue tied. *C. Roche, Ireland* — h122

KADLASS (FR) 9 b.g. Kadounor (FR) – Brave Lass (Ridan) [2003/4 h89: 17g² 16m May 7] compact gelding: modest hurdler: raced around 2m: acts on good to firm and soft going: game. *Mrs D. A. Hamer* — h89

KADOUKO (FR) 11 br.g. Cadoudal (FR) – Perle Bleue (FR) (Iron Duke (FR)) [2003/4 c99, h–: c16s⁴ c20s⁴ c25vᵖᵘ c16s⁵ c16d c20g² c20d Apr 24] leggy, lengthy gelding: poor handicap chaser: stays 2½m: acts on heavy ground: has had tongue tied: sold (privately) 2,000 gns Doncaster May Sales. *J. R. Cornwall* — c83 h–

KADOUN (FR) 5 gr.g. Sleeping Car (FR) – Dea de Chalamont (FR) (Royal Charter (FR)) [2003/4 c17s* c17d* 17d 19g³ 16g³ 20s* Apr 17] leggy ex-French gelding: second foal: dam winning hurdler/chaser around 2m in France: successful 3 times over fences, including in handicaps at Enghien and Auteuil (final start for H. Billot) early in season: fair hurdler: made all in novice at Bangor in April: stays 2½m: raced on good going or softer (acts on heavy): tried blinkered: tongue tied in Britain (has found little). *H. D. Daly* — c115 h110

KADOUN (IRE) 7 b.g. Doyoun – Kumta (IRE) (Priolo (USA)) [2003/4 c139, h134: c25gᶠ c22s² c16d* c20s 20d* c29d Apr 12] leggy gelding: useful hurdler/chaser: won — c141 h138

Grade 3 Woodlands Park 100 Poplar Square Chase (by ½ length from Rathgan Beau) at Naas in November and handicap hurdle at Fairyhouse in February: effective at 2m to 3m: acts on heavy going, probably on good to firm: sometimes wears headgear, very best form without: formerly none too keen. *M. J. P. O'Brien, Ireland*

KADOUNT (FR)   6 b.g. Oui Account (USA) – Une de Lann (FR) (Spoleto) [2003/4   **h130**
16g⁴ 16s* 16d* 16g 16sᵖᵘ Mar 13] strong, good-bodied gelding: third foal: brother to 13f winner Faccount and half-brother to middle-distance winner Ibos (by Mister Sicy): dam 13f winner: trained by X. L. Le Strang, successful 4 times around 1½m on Flat in French Provinces: won first 3 starts over hurdles, novices at Haydock in November and Plumpton in December and handicap at Leicester (not extended to beat Almaravide 4 lengths) later in December: below best last 2 starts, seeming to lose action on first occasion: raced at 2m on good going or softer. *A. King*

KAFRI D'AIRY (FR)   6 b.m. Sheyrann – Afrika d'Airy (FR) (Marasali) [2003/4 c100,   **c–**
h–: 16gᶠ Apr 12] fair form over fences in France: little encouragement over hurdles in   **h–**
Britain: raced up to 2½m on good ground or softer. *R. T. Phillips*

KAHUNA (IRE)   7 b.g. Mister Lord (USA) – My Baloo (On Your Mark) [2003/4 F109:   **h127**
16m* 16d³ 16d* 16d⁴ 24sᵘʳ 16v* 20d⁵ Mar 4] tall, angular gelding: fairly useful novice hurdler: won at Cork (maiden) in November and Punchestown in December and January (Grade 2, by 7 lengths from Euro Leader): creditable fifth to Brave Inca in Grade 1 at Punchestown in late-April: best at 2m: acts on heavy and good to firm going: front runner: sometimes none too fluent. *E. Sheehy, Ireland*

KAID (IRE)   9 b.g. Alzao (USA) – Very Charming (USA) (Vaguely Noble) [2003/4   **c81 §**
c82§, h91§: 20s⁵ c20m³ c20m⁴ c16d⁶ c20mᵖᵘ c21s³ Mar 21] angular gelding: modest   **h– §**
handicap hurdler: poor maiden chaser: stays 21f: acts on good to firm and heavy going: blinkered/visored once (went in snatches): unreliable. *R. Lee*

KAIKOVRA (IRE)   8 ch.g. Toulon – Drefflane Supreme (Rusticaro (FR)) [2003/4   **h89**
h103: 16g 16g⁴ 19g⁵ 16m 17d⁴ 16m² 17m⁵ 16g³ 16m² 19m* 16f Oct 29] modest hurdler: sold out of N. Chance's stable 11,000 gns Doncaster May Sales after reappearance: finally off mark in weak novice at Hereford in October: stays 19f with emphasis on speed: acts on good to firm going (won bumper on soft): races freely up with pace: sometimes finishes weakly. *M. F. Harris*

KAISER (IRE)   4 b.g. Barathea (IRE) – Emerald Waters (Kings Lake (USA)) [2003/4   **h–**
16gᵖᵘ 16s Jan 23] half-brother to useful hurdlers Persian Waters and Eternal Spring (both by Persian Bold): modest maiden on Flat (stays 1½m) for J. Fanshawe: showed little in 2 juvenile hurdles, visored in claimer on second occasion. *R. T. Phillips*

KAKI CRAZY (FR)   9 b.g. Passing Sale (FR) – Radiante Rose (FR) (Akarad (FR))   **c123 §**
[2003/4 c103§, h–§: 20g⁷ c21m* c24g² c20mᵖᵘ 26m* Aug 25] leggy gelding: fairly   **h125 §**
useful hurdler/chaser: won claiming hurdle at Wetherby and handicap chase at Newton Abbot (final start for M. Hill, trained by J. Frost next outing only) in May, and claiming hurdle at Southwell (claimed £8,000) in August: stays 4m, effective at much shorter: acts on good to firm and heavy going: blinkered/visored: often takes little interest and one to treat with caution. *E. Retter*

KALAMBARI (IRE)   5 b.g. Kahyasi – Kalamba (IRE) (Green Dancer (USA)) [2003/4   **h86 §**
24gᵘʳ 16gᵘʳ 16sᵖᵘ 19sᵘʳ Apr 11] leggy, angular gelding: fairly useful on Flat (stays 15f) at 3 yrs, sold out of Sir Michael Stoute's stable 20,000 gns Newmarket Autumn (2002) Sales: failed to complete all starts over hurdles, unseating after swerving left on 3 occasions: blinkered final start: most temperamental, and one to avoid. *J. Joseph*

KALASARA (IRE)   6 b.g. Darshaan – Kumta (IRE) (Priolo (USA)) [2003/4 16d Dec   **h85**
5] angular gelding: won bumper on debut in April 2002: weakened straight when seventh in novice hurdle at Sandown 20 months later. *C. J. Mann*

KALCA MOME (FR)   6 b.g. En Calcat (FR) – Belle Mome (FR) (Grand Tresor (FR))   **c128**
[2003/4 h123: c16g* c16d² c16s* c20s⁴ c16v* c16m³ c16d* c16g Apr 3] leggy gelding: **h–**
fairly useful hurdler: similar standard over fences: won novices at Newton Abbot in November, Hereford in December, Haydock in January and Sandown (match) in March: best around 2m: acts on heavy and good to firm going. *P. J. Hobbs*

KALIC D'ALM (FR)   6 b.g. Passing Sale (FR) – Bekaa II (FR) (Djarvis (FR)) [2003/4   **h–**
F81: 21vᵖᵘ 19s Dec 13] tall gelding: fifth in bumper on debut: no form since: sold 3,100 gns Doncaster May Sales. *Miss Suzy Smith*

KALI DES OBEAUX (FR)   6 b.m. Panoramic – Alpaga (FR) (Le Pontet (FR))   **c– x**
[2003/4 c100+, h103: c25sᵖᵘ c21sᵖᵘ 22d⁴ 23s³ 20d⁵ Apr 21] compact mare: winning   **h100**
chaser in France: pulled up both starts over fences in Britain, badly let down by jumping

on second occasion: fair maiden hurdler: stays easy 3m: acts on soft and good to firm going. *Mrs L. C. Taylor*

KALIN DE THAIX (FR) 6 ch.g. Agent Bleu (FR) – Une Amie (FR) (Prove It Baby (USA)) [2003/4 16v^pu Jan 26] sturdy ex-French gelding: fourth foal: half-brother to several winners, including smart hurdler/fairly useful chaser up to 2½m Havre de Thaix (by Roi de Rome) and winning 21f chaser Glorieuse de Thaix (by Video Rock): dam won up to around 1¾m on Flat: successful 4 times around 1½m on Flat at 5 yrs in Provinces for C. Diard: showed little in novice hurdle on British debut: sold 6,000 gns Doncaster May Sales. *R. T. Phillips*   h–

KALISKO (FR) 14 b.g. Cadoudal (FR) – Mista (FR) (Misti IV) [2003/4 c24d³ c24d c20s^pu Dec 19] sparely-made gelding: poor chaser: probably stays 25f: acts on heavy and good to firm going. *Miss L. V. Davis*   c64   h–

KALKO DU CHARMIL (FR) 7 b.g. Kadalko (FR) – Licada (FR) (A Tempo (FR)) [2003/4 c–, h–: c20g⁶ c20g^F 22m^pu Jul 13] tall, leggy gelding: no form over hurdles or fences, left G. Macaire before final start. *Ian Williams*   c–   h–

KALLASSOR (FR) 6 b.g. Assessor (IRE) – Balladine (FR) (Rivelago (FR)) [2003/4 h75: c21m^pu 21m^pu May 29] lengthy gelding: poor maiden hurdler: showed nothing on chasing debut: stays 2¾m: acts on firm going: visored last 4 starts in 2002/3, blinkered (looked reluctant) final outing. *P. C. Ritchens*   c–   h–

KALOU (GER) 6 b.g. Law Society (USA) – Kompetenz (IRE) (Be My Guest (USA)) [2003/4 h–: 16s⁴ 16s⁶ Jan 6] good-topped gelding: useful at best on Flat in Germany: poor maiden hurdler: may need sharp 2m. *B. J. Curley*   h71

KALUANA COURT 8 b.m. Batshoof – Fairfields Cone (Celtic Cone) [2003/4 22g^F Jun 27] fairly useful on Flat (stays 17f): lightly raced over hurdles, close third when falling 2 out in novice handicap at Stratford. *R. J. Price*   h80

KALUGA (IRE) 6 ch.m. Tagula (IRE) – Another Baileys (Deploy) [2003/4 h–: 22g c21g⁶ c21d c20v^F c19g⁴ Apr 1] workmanlike mare: poor maiden hurdler: no worthwhile form over fences: stays 2¾m: acts on soft going: tried blinkered. *S. C. Burrough*   c–   h–

KAMILLO (FR) 6 b.g. Agent Bleu (FR) – Detroit III (FR) (Video Rock (FR)) [2003/4 c20g⁶ c20d⁶ c20f* c20g c16s² c20s⁵ c21s* c23s Apr 18] tall, angular gelding: third foal: half-brother to winning cross-country chaser over 2¾m Innsbruck (by Lights Out): dam unraced, from family of top-class French chaser Arenice: maiden hurdler: fair chaser at best in Ireland, winning handicap at Navan in June: much improved back in France, winning minor event at Auteuil in April: best effort when 10 lengths second to Kotkijet in Grand Steeple-Chase de Paris there in late-May, though possibly flattered: stays 29f: acts on soft and firm going: often tongue tied. *F. M. Cottin, France*   c137 ?   h–

KANDJAR D'ALLIER (FR) 6 gr.g. Royal Charter (FR) – Miss Akarad (FR) (Akarad (FR)) [2003/4 c141, h122: c21s* 21f⁴ 20g⁴ 20d c16s^F c16s^pu 16s⁵ c16d c20g Apr 18] leggy gelding: maiden hurdler: useful chaser at best: won valuable handicap at Auteuil in May, then sold privately from J. Bertran de Balanda: long way below best in Britain: stays 21f: acts on heavy going: front runner: sometimes let down by jumping: joined A. King. *M. F. Harris*   c136 d   h94

KANDY FOUR (NZ) 9 ch.g. Zeditave (AUS) – Executive Suite (NZ) (Western Symphony (USA)) [2003/4 c104, h–: c16m May 7] workmanlike gelding: fair chaser: well below form in handicap very early in season: stays 2½m: acts on soft and good to firm going: free-going sort: not always fluent jumper. *P. F. Nicholls*   c–   h–

KANSAS CITY (FR) 6 b.m. Lute Antique (FR) – Tenacity (FR) (Prove It Baby (USA)) [2003/4 c83, h–: 20m³ 24g^pu c19g^ur c16d c20v^pu Apr 4] lengthy mare: winning chaser in France: poor form over fences and hurdles in Britain: stays at least 19f: acts on heavy going, probably on good to firm: has had tongue tied. *M. F. Harris*   c–   h–

KAOLIN DE PERCHE (FR) 6 b.g. Luchiroverte (IRE) – Craven II (FR) (Rhapsodien) [2003/4 h84+: 21v^pu 26s⁵ 24s c25d^pu Mar 22] sturdy gelding: poor maiden hurdler: no show on chasing debut. *C. P. Morlock*   c–   h79

KAPAROLO (USA) 5 ch.g. El Prado (IRE) – Parliament House (USA) (General Assembly (USA)) [2003/4 16m² 18g* 21m² 16m³ 17s³ 22g² 18d* 18d Apr 7] half-brother to fairly useful hurdler Mixsterthetrixster (by Alleged), stays 19f: fair on Flat (stays 14.6f): fairly useful hurdler: won twice at Fontwell, novice in October and handicap in March: stays 2¾m: acts on good to firm and good to soft going. *Mrs A. J. Perrett*   h113

KAPPELHOFF (IRE) 7 b.g. Mukaddamah (USA) – Miss Penguin (General Assembly (USA)) [2003/4 h–: 22g 24m Jul 9] of little account. *Mrs L. Richards*   h–

KAPPILLAN (IRE) 5 b.g. Flemensfirth (USA) – Snuggle (Music Boy) [2003/4 F16v **h–**
F16v 20d Feb 21] sixth foal: half-brother to modest chaser Itsmyturnnow (by Glacial **F—**
Storm), stays 3¼m: dam, won around 2m over hurdles, sister to high-class 2m chaser
Young Snugfit and half-sister to useful jumpers Peanuts Pet, Cashew King, Mr Snugfit
and Half-Brother: little sign of ability in bumpers and novice hurdle. *C. Grant*

KAPSKA (FR) 6 b.g. Silver Rainbow – Chapska (FR) (Le Pontet (FR)) [2003/4 h–: **h–**
21s 25d Apr 11] no sign of ability. *M. J. Roberts*

KARAJAN (IRE) 7 b.g. Fairy King (USA) – Dernier Cri (Slip Anchor) [2003/4 c90, **c94**
h–: c20m⁵ c21g⁴ c24g⁴ c20m² c24g² c20g³ c24gᵖᵘ c20g c20d⁵ Apr 23] angular gelding: **h–**
modest maiden chaser: stays 3m: acts on heavy and good to firm going: prone to breaking
blood vessels. *G. M. Moore*

KARAKUM 5 b.g. Mtoto – Magongo (Be My Chief (USA)) [2003/4 h–: 22gᵖᵘ 16m **h71**
17m² 17m 16f² 16m⁴ 16g³ 16m³ Nov 13] poor maiden hurdler: raced mainly around 2m:
acts on firm going: broke blood vessel final start. *A. J. Chamberlain*

KARATCHI (FR) 6 b. or br.g. Iris Noir (FR) – Eclipse Royale II (FR) (Brezzo (FR)) **h102**
[2003/4 24d* 25dᵖᵘ Mar 22] 26,000 4-y-o: medium-sized gelding: first foal: half-brother
to fair maiden chaser Le Lavandou (by Lights Out): dam unraced: won maiden hurdle at
Ayr on debut: pulled up lame 4 months later: had looked open to improvement. *L. Lungo*

KARIBA DREAM 9 ch.m. Hatim (USA) – Noss Head (New Brig) [2003/4 20gᵖᵘ May **h–**
10] no form in maiden points and maiden hurdle. *W. S. Coltherd*

KARIBEE 4 b.f. Karinga Bay – Jaydeebee (Buckley) [2003/4 F18v 20v⁶ 16s 20dᵖᵘ **h–**
Apr 7] second foal: dam, ran 3 times in bumpers, half-sister to Cheltenham Gold Cup **F—**
winner Master Oats: no show in bumper and novice hurdles. *M. Madgwick*

KARIBLUE 6 ch.m. Imp Society (USA) – Kadastra (FR) (Stradavinsky) [2003/4 F17m **F—**
Nov 20] sixth foal: half-sister to several winners, notably smart 2m chaser Kadastrof (by
Port Etienne): dam French 11f winner: eighth of 15 in bumper at Hereford on debut,
failing to settle and hanging left. *R. Dickin*

KARINGA CITY 7 ch.g. Karinga Bay – Panicaly (Rock City) [2003/4 17s⁵ 21m Apr **h107 ?**
14] smallish gelding: placed both starts in maiden points in 2003: apparently improved
efforts back in novice hurdles (amateur ridden), though possibly flattered. *E. Retter*

KARINGA COIN 6 ch.g. Karinga Bay – Coinridge (Charlie's Pal) [2003/4 F17m **h–**
22sᵖᵘ 19v⁵ 22gᵖᵘ 24gᵖᵘ Mar 9] sturdy gelding: fourth foal: half-brother to winning pointer **F—**
by Baron Blakeney: dam, winning pointer, out of daughter of Grand National winner
Nickel Coin: signs of only a little ability in bumper and over hurdles. *C. J. Down*

KARING KENDA 5 ch.m. Karinga Bay – Song of Kenda (Rolfe (USA)) [2003/4 19gᵘʳ **h–**
22gᵖᵘ Mar 25] first foal: dam, poor maiden hurdler who stayed 2¾m, half-sister to useful
staying chaser Kendal Cavalier: signs of temperament both starts over hurdles. *K. Bishop*

KARISABAN 5 b.g. Hatim (USA) – Swiss Beauty (Ballacashtal (CAN)) [2003/4 F–: **h–**
17dᵖᵘ 16m⁵ Jun 20] no sign of ability: sold to join C. Tizzard 1,300 gns Doncaster August
Sales. *R. Johnson*

KARJU (IRE) 5 b.g. Marju (IRE) – Karmisymixa (FR) (Linamix (FR)) [2003/4 16d³ **h97**
17g² 20g* 16g* Jul 3] ex-Irish gelding: twice-raced on Flat: fair hurdler: won novices at
Perth in June (easily) and July: stays 2½m: acts on soft going. *M. Todhunter*

KARO DE VINDECY (FR) 6 b.g. Mollicone Junior (FR) – Preves du Forez (FR) **c66**
(Quart de Vin (FR)) [2003/4 h68: c17g* c17m⁵ c20m⁴ c21m⁴ c16m⁴ c20d⁴ Apr 18] **h–**
leggy gelding: little form over hurdles: poor chaser: won weak novice handicap at Cartmel in May: stays 2½m: acts on good to firm and good to soft going: tongue tied.
M. D. Hammond

KAROO 6 b.g. Karinga Bay – Cupids Bower (Owen Dudley) [2003/4 F17g Apr 10] **F74**
half-brother to one-time useful chaser Irbee (by Gunner B), stays 3¼m, and modest
chaser Kingsmoor (by Regal Embers), stays 2½m: dam, winning hurdler, stayed 25f:
fourth in point on debut in 2003: seventh in bumper at Newton Abbot. *P. F. Nicholls*

KARYON (IRE) 4 b.f. Presidium – Stealthy (Kind of Hush) [2003/4 16gᵖᵘ 16d⁶ 16g* **h71**
17sᵖᵘ 16g 17g Apr 24] poor maiden on Flat for P. Haslam: form over hurdles only when
winning weak juvenile seller at Catterick in January: wore cheekpieces final start. *Miss
Kate Milligan*

KARZHANG 12 b.g. Rakaposhi King – Smokey Baby (Sagaro) [2003/4 c75, h–: **c–**
c20mᵖᵘ May 15] workmanlike gelding: fair pointer on his day: poor maiden over hurdles **h–**
and in steeplechases: has had tongue tied. *Mrs C. J. Robinson*

KAS

KASHIMO (GER) 5 br.h. Lomitas – Kardia (Mister Rock's (GER)) [2003/4 16g⁴ **h99 p**
Mar 27] good-topped horse: successful 3 times up to 11f on Flat in Germany at 4 yrs for
A. Bolte, fair form in 3 races around 1½m in Britain: shaped encouragingly when fourth
to Self Defense in novice at Newbury on hurdling debut: likely to improve. *G. L. Moore*

KASILIA (FR) 6 b.g. Silver Rainbow – Basilia (FR) (Mont Basile (FR)) [2003/4 **c91**
c21gᵖᵘ c21s³ c21d² Apr 12] third foal: half-brother to 23f cross-country chase winner **h–**
Hippias (by Roi de Rome) and winning French/Swiss chaser up to 21f Ipso Facto (by Le
Riverain): dam maiden: modest maiden hurdler/chaser: placed several times in France,
left Mme I. Pacault after reappearance: runner-up on first of 2 starts in points in Britain in
2004, and placed in 2 hunters at Fakenham: likely to stay 3m: raced on good ground or
softer: usually blinkered in France. *Tim Brown*

KASSEL (USA) 4 ch.g. Swain (IRE) – Gretel (Hansel (USA)) [2003/4 F13v 17g⁴ Feb **h–**
10] €2,500 2-y-o: second foal: dam useful 2-y-o 7f winner who stayed 1m: well held in **F–**
3-y-o bumper and juvenile hurdle. *Ian Williams*

KASTHARI (IRE) 5 gr.g. Vettori (IRE) – Karliyka (IRE) (Last Tycoon) [2003/4 16d³ **h109**
20d* 20s* 24gᵖᵘ Apr 2] tall gelding: smart on Flat (probably best short of 2½m), sold
out of Sir Michael Stoute's stable 95,000 gns Newmarket Autumn Sales: fair form when
winning novice hurdles at Newcastle in February and March: mistakes in Grade 1 novice
at Aintree final start: stays 2½m. *J. Howard Johnson*

KASTINA 5 b.m. Lancastrian – Kit (Green Ruby (USA)) [2003/4 16m 22m³ 20gᵖᵘ **h–**
Aug 23] no sign of ability on Flat or over hurdles. *M. J. Gingell*

KATHAKALI (IRE) 7 b.g. Dancing Dissident (USA) – Shes A Dancer (IRE) (Alzao **h94**
(USA)) [2003/4 h–: 17g 16m* 16m⁵ 16m Sep 14] modest hurdler: won maiden at Wor-
cester in July: will prove best around 2m: acts on good to firm going: wears headgear.
C. J. Bennett

KATHELLA (IRE) 7 b.m. Fourstars Allstar (USA) – Niat Supreme (IRE) (Supreme **h58**
Leader) [2003/4 h–: 22g³ 24g⁴ 22gᵖᵘ Sep 3] bad maiden hurdler: possibly best up to 2¾m.
N. G. Ayliffe

KATIE BUCKERS (IRE) 10 ch.m. Yashgan – Glenkins (Furry Glen) [2003/4 c96d, **c–**
h–: c20s³ May 3] medium-sized mare: winning chaser: out of sorts since very early in **h–**
2002/3: tried in cheekpieces: sold 4,800 gns Doncaster May Sales. *K. C. Bailey*

KATIE SAVAGE 4 b.f. Emperor Jones (USA) – Coax Me Molly (USA) (L'Enjoleur **h–**
(CAN)) [2003/4 16gᵖᵘ 16d 16s⁶ 17dᵘʳ Mar 27] half-sister to 2m hurdle winner Softly
Softly (by Lucky Guest): well beaten in 1¼m maiden on debut: no form over hurdles.
J. Mackie

KATIES DOLPHIN (IRE) 6 ch.m. Dolphin Street (FR) – Kuwah (IRE) (Be My **c–**
Guest (USA)) [2003/4 h77: 21d⁶ 16s⁴ 16g c21sᵖᵘ 19g 21d⁶ 17gᶠ Apr 24] poor maiden **h–**
hurdler: no show in 2003/4, including over fences: tried in cheekpieces: usually tongue
tied. *R. Johnson*

KATIES HERO 6 b.g. Pontevecchio Notte – Kindly Lady (Kind of Hush) [2003/4 F–: **h83**
17g⁵ 20g⁶ 16dᵖᵘ 16g⁵ 17d 17g⁶ Apr 13] poor novice hurdler: probably stays 2½m: tried
blinkered in bumpers. *J. D. Frost*

KATIES TIGHT JEANS 10 b.m. Green Adventure (USA) – Haraka Sasa (Town And **h–**
Country) [2003/4 h–: 17gᵘʳ Jun 28] of little account. *R. E. Peacock*

KATINKA 11 b.m. Rymer – Millymeeta (New Brig) [2003/4 h–: 16gᵖᵘ 20g 20g Jun 22] **h–**
lengthy mare: no form over hurdles: winning pointer, including in February: has had
tongue tied. *A. M. Thomson*

KATMANDU 5 b.g. Sadler's Wells (USA) – Kithanga (IRE) (Darshaan) [2003/4 16s³ **h101**
20v² 20d⁴ 21d* Mar 30] leggy, useful-looking gelding: fairly useful maiden on Flat
(should stay 2m), sold out of L. Cumani's stable 45,000 gns Newmarket Autumn Sales:
blinkered, improved effort over hurdles when winning amateur novice at Sedgefield:
stays 21f: carried head awkwardly second start, wore cheekpieces next time. *J. Howard
Johnson*

KATOOF (USA) 6 b.g. Silver Hawk (USA) – The Caretaker (Caerleon (USA)) [2003/4 **F–**
F16m Nov 8] $500,000Y, 26,000 4-y-o: third foal: brother to St Leger winner Mutafaweq
and half-brother to smart Irish 7f to 1¼m winner Dimitrova (by Swain): dam Irish 7f and
1m winner: tailed off in bumper on debut. *J. A. B. Old*

KATTEGAT 8 b.g. Slip Anchor – Kirsten (Kris) [2003/4 c–, h101: 22gᵖᵘ 22g 16v⁴ **c–**
20m 16d 24s 21sᵘʳ 19d 22d⁶ 25d⁶ 27g* Apr 22] leggy gelding: modest handicap hurdler: **h95**

488

won at Fontwell in April: stays 27f: acts on heavy going: wore blinkers/cheekpieces last 6 starts: not easiest of rides (has carried head awkwardly): usually ridden by Miss L. Bridges. *Mrs H. M. Bridges*

KATY THE DUCK (IRE) 9 br m. Over The River (FR) – Zagliarelle (FR) (Rose Laurel) [2003/4 c–, h69: 16g^F 21g 17d^4 20d Apr 7] angular mare: poor hurdler: probably stays 21f: acts on good to soft going: tried visored. *R. J. Price* **c–** **h61**

KAUSSE DE THAIX (FR) 6 ch.g. Iris Noir (FR) – Etoile de Thaix (FR) (Lute Antique (FR)) [2003/4 F92: c21m^5 c20g^4 Feb 13] useful-looking gelding: fourth on first of 2 starts in bumpers in 2002/3: well held in 2 novice chases, not jumping well. *P. M. Phelan* **c–**

KAUTO STAR (FR) 4 b.g. Village Star (FR) – Kauto Relka (FR) (Port Etienne (FR)) [2003/4 15s* 18s* 18s^F 18s^2 18s^3 18s^5 19s^3 Apr 24] angular gelding: fourth foal: half-brother to winning hurdler/chaser around 2m Kauto Lumen Dei (by Useful): dam unraced: useful hurdler, best effort when winning Prix de Longchamp at Auteuil in late-May easily by 8 lengths from River Charm: also successful there in minor event very early in season and listed race in September, and 10 lengths second to Maia Eria in Group 1 event in November: stays 19f: raced only on soft going: sold privately in June, to race in Britain. *S. Foucher, France* **h136**

KAVI (IRE) 4 ch.g. Perugino (USA) – Premier Leap (IRE) (Salmon Leap (USA)) [2003/4 16g^2 17m* 16m^5 16g^2 17m^3 Sep 27] neat gelding: modest on Flat (stays 1¼m): modest juvenile hurdler: won at Bangor in August: blinkered final start (claimed by S. Earle £5,000). *P. C. Haslam* **h91**

KAY BEE VENTURE 5 ch.m. Karinga Bay – Take The Veil (Monksfield) [2003/4 F17g F17f F17m 19m^{pu} 17d^{ur} 19d^{pu} 26s^{pu} Jan 7] £400 3-y-o: sixth foal: half-sister to fair pointer Flying Veil (by Neltino): dam, showed no aptitude for jumping, half-sister to dam of Grand National winner Party Politics: of no account. *G. F. H. Charles-Jones* **h–** **F–**

KAYSA (GER) 5 b.m. Second Set (IRE) – Kaytiggy (Busted) [2003/4 19g^{pu} 17s^4 16g^F Jun 27] twice-raced on Flat, winning over 7.5f in Italy at 2 yrs: well held on completed start in novice hurdles: tongue tied final outing: joined A. Whiting. *Dr P. Pritchard* **h–**

KAYTASH 5 b.m. Silverdale Knight – Lady Swift (Jalmood (USA)) [2003/4 h–: 17g Oct 14] little sign of ability. *K. W. Hogg, Isle of Man* **h–**

KEDGE ANCHOR MAN 13 b.g. Bustino – Jenny Mere (Brigadier Gerard) [2003/4 c–, h100d: 22g Apr 30] lengthy gelding: winning hurdler: well held in handicap very early in season: stays 23f: raced mainly on good going or softer (acts on soft): races prominently. *N. A. Gaselee* **c–** **h–**

KEEN AND ABLE 4 ch.f. Keen – Four Thyme (Idiot's Delight) [2003/4 F16s F16s Apr 4] lengthy filly: third foal: dam, well beaten in bumper, half-sister to Festival Bumper winner Mucklemeg: signs of only a little ability in 2 bumpers. *N. G. Richards* **F–**

KEEN LEADER (IRE) 8 b.g. Supreme Leader – Keen Gale (IRE) (Strong Gale) [2003/4 c151p, h–: c26d^{ur} c24d* c24g^3 c26g^6 Mar 18] **c167** **h–**
Some of the sheen had rubbed off Keen Leader's reputation by the end of the season—but it would be unwise to write off his championship prospects altogether. Keen Leader's performance in the Tommy Whittle Chase at Haydock in December made him look one of the few genuine threats to Best Mate's dominance of the staying chase division. Turned out quickly after unseating his rider when favourite for the Rehearsal Chase at Chepstow on his reappearance, Keen Leader put in a sound display of jumping at Haydock and galloped on relentlessly, after taking it up three out, to defeat the previous season's Gold Cup runner-up Truckers Tavern by seventeen lengths (seven lengths further than Best Mate had beaten him at Cheltenham). A Christmas clash with Best Mate in the Ericsson Chase at Leopardstown looked on the cards but Keen Leader was a late defector after picking up a flu-like infection. There was then talk for a time of Keen Leader's challenging for the Hennessy Cognac Gold Cup at Leopardstown in early-February but he missed that too, warming up for the Cheltenham Gold Cup nearer home a week later in the AON Chase at Newbury.
The AON Chase is a recognised Gold Cup trial but odds-on Keen Leader failed to enhance his claims, managing only third, closing steadily but unable to peg back the veteran Shooting Light, a 33/1-shot, and another Gold Cup entry Irish Hussar. Conditions at Newbury placed less emphasis on stamina than would have been ideal for Keen Leader and, held up and jumping no more than satisfactorily,

Tommy Whittle Chase, Haydock—Keen Leader gets back on track in impressive fashion

he was always struggling to get on terms in the home straight. Keen Leader's regular jockey Liam Cooper lost the ride in the Gold Cup, replaced by Barry Geraghty who had had the mount in the Tommy Whittle when Cooper was serving a suspension. Starting 10/1 joint-third favourite, Keen Leader was one of the first beaten at Cheltenham, flat out when hitting the fifth last and then left well behind, eventually trailing home sixth of the eight finishers, a distance behind fifth-placed First Gold. It was the third year in a row that hopes of Festival success for Keen Leader had been dashed. He suffered his only defeat as a novice hurdler when falling at the second last, still going well, in the Royal & SunAlliance Hurdle; and he trailed in fifth of six finishers, jumping sketchily, when favourite for the Royal & SunAlliance Chase in 2003. Keen Leader was found to be sick on his return from Cheltenham after the Royal & SunAlliance Chase and, according to his trainer, he 'wasn't right' after the Gold Cup either.

Keen Leader (IRE) (b.g. 1996)	Supreme Leader (b 1982)	Bustino (b 1971)	Busted Ship Yard
		Princess Zena (b 1975)	Guiding Light Habitat
	Keen Gale (IRE) (b 1989)	Strong Gale (br 1975)	Lord Gayle Sterntau
		Keening (b 1969)	Bally Joy Keenogue

Keen Leader wasn't seen out again after the Gold Cup but his running in that race, and his record over fences generally, suggests that he needs ground on the soft side of good to be seen to advantage. He raced only on soft or heavy when creating an excellent impression in his novice hurdling days, but has encountered similarly testing conditions only once as a chaser—when winning the Reynolds-town Chase as a novice by a distance. The tall, angular, rather raw-boned Keen Leader, who is inclined to make the odd mistake over fences, should stay beyond twenty-five furlongs, the longest distance over which he has won so far. Races like the Edward Hanmer Chase and the Tommy Whittle Chase, both at Haydock, appeal as likely pre-Christmas targets in the next season. Connections are also said to be considering a tilt at the Hennessy Cognac Gold Cup at Newbury, another galloping course that should suit the strong-running Keen Leader. A drier than usual autumn in the latest season ruled out the Hennessy which Keen Leader would have been able to tackle off a BHB mark of 156. Although a shade higher in the handicap, he is set to start the 2004/5 season on a fair mark. He has the physique to shoulder big weights in handicaps and should give a good account of himself, granted suitable conditions. Details of Keen Leader's pedigree have been given in the last two Annuals. He is by the now-deceased Supreme Leader who again had a good number of smart or better performers representing him in the latest season, notably Cheltenham Festival winners Fundamentalist and Rule Supreme, the Mildmay Chase winner Simply Supreme and another of the season's leading novice chasers Lord Sam. Keen Leader remains the only winner produced so far by his unraced dam Keen Gale. Racegoers shouldn't be put off Keen Leader in the paddock by his action. He has stringhalt, causing exaggerating bending of a hock, but it doesn't affect his racing performance. Nor does his habit of racing with his tongue hanging out. *Jonjo O'Neill*

KEEN TO THE LAST (FR)   12 ch.g. Keen – Derniere Danse (Gay Mecene (USA)) [2003/4 c99, h–: 21d⁶ c21m* c24g³ c22f³ c20g² c22d* Dec 4] angular gelding: winning hurdler: fair handicap chaser: won at Cartmel in August and Market Rasen in December: stays 25f: acts on any going: visored once. *Mrs S. J. Smith*   **c108 h–**

KEEPATEM (IRE)   8 ch.g. Be My Native (USA) – Ariannrun (Deep Run) [2003/4 h122: 24s³ 25g 24g² Apr 2] workmanlike gelding: chasing type: fairly useful handicap hurdler: good efforts when third to Royal All Star at Leopardstown on reappearance and 2 lengths second to His Nibs in valuable event at Aintree final start: didn't find much when seventh to Creon in Pertemps Final at Cheltenham in between: better around 3m than shorter: raced on good ground or softer (acts on soft). *M. F. Morris, Ireland*   **h126**

KEEPER'S CALL (IRE)   12 b.g. Mandalus – Thistletopper (Le Bavard (FR)) [2003/4 c–: c25dᶠ May 3] good-topped gelding: useful hunter chaser in 1999: on the downgrade. *Mrs V. J. Makin*   **c–**

KEEPERS MEAD (IRE)   6 ch.g. Aahsaylad – Runaway Pilot (Cheval) [2003/4 h68, F89: 24g² 24g* 25s⁶ 24s³ 24g⁵ 22g⁶ Apr 13] useful-looking gelding: type to make a chaser: fair novice hurdler: won at Ascot in November: stays 25f: acts on soft going. *R. H. Alner*   **h107**

KEEP ON RUNNING (FR)   6 ch.g. Beyssac (FR) – Kiruna V (FR) (Thalian) [2003/4 h109: c16mᵖᵘ May 10] lengthy gelding: successful on first of 3 starts in novice hurdles: didn't take to chasing at all in handicap at Worcester very early in season: stays 19f: head-strong. *A. King*   **c– h–**

KEEP SMILING (IRE)   8 b.g. Broken Hearted – Laugh Away (Furry Glen) [2003/4 c109x, h–: 22g³ 19d³ 22d³ c20dᶠ Apr 8] tall, rather sparely-made gelding: successful only completed start in steeplechases: modest maiden hurdler: stays 2¾m: acts on good to soft going: poor jumper. *Miss Venetia Williams*   **c– x h94**

KEEPTHEDREAMALIVE   6 gr.g. Roselier (FR) – Nicklup (Netherkelly) [2003/4 F16s⁵ F17s⁵ F18s³ 21d² Mar 1] €18,000 4-y-o: rather leggy gelding: first foal: dam winning hurdler/fair staying chaser: fairly useful form in bumpers: promising hurdling debut when second to Bay Kenny in novice at Plumpton, travelling strongly long way but kicking for home with third too far out: will stay at least 3m: sure to do better. *R. H. Buckler*   **h103 p F97**

KEEP THE PEACE (IRE)   6 br.g. Petardia – Eiras Mood (Jalmood (USA)) [2003/4 16m Jun 1] fair maiden at best on Flat: well held in novice on hurdling debut: joined K. Wingrove. *D. J. Wintle*   **h–**

KEETCHY (IRE)   5 b.g. Darshaan – Ezana (Ela-Mana-Mou) [2003/4 h87: 19sᵖᵘ 16d Jan 9] modest form on hurdling debut: no show in novice and seller in 2003/4: should be suited by further than 2m. *J. D. Frost*   **h–**

KEIMAR   5 b.g. Syrtos – Crimson Sol (Crimson Beau) [2003/4 F16m F16m 19gᵖᵘ Sep 3] seventh foal: dam poor maiden hurdler: signs of ability on second of 2 starts in bumpers: no show on hurdling debut. *D. G. Bridgwater*   **h– F68**

KEIRAN (IRE)   10 b.g. Be My Native (USA) – Myra Gaye (Buckskin (FR)) [2003/4 c119, h94: c25g* c28sᶠ c28g⁴ c25v* Jan 17] sturdy gelding: fairly useful handicap chaser: won at Wetherby in November and January (by 5 lengths from Wain Mountain): stays at least 25f: acts on good to firm and heavy going: effective blinkered or not. *H. P. Hogarth*   **c127 h–**

KEITHO (IRE)   9 b.g. Niels – Swift Charmer (Beau Charmeur (FR)) [2003/4 c26dᵖᵘ 22g⁴ c21m³ Jul 14] ex-Irish gelding: won 3 times in points in Britain in 2003: poor form on hurdling debut, none in steeplechases: blinkered final start: sold £7,500 Ascot February Sales. *P. F. Nicholls*   **c– h77**

KELAMI (FR)   6 b.g. Lute Antique (FR) – Voltige de Nievre (FR) (Brezzo (FR)) [2003/4 c127, h101: c21s³ c21s⁶ c21s⁵ c24g* c24g⁴ c36dᵘʳ c23s Apr 18] tall gelding: has had soft palate operation: useful chaser: won handicap at Kempton in December by 1½ lengths from Itsonlyme: stays 3m: raced on good going or softer (acts on heavy): tried blinkered (failed to settle)/tongue tied. *F. Doumen, France*   **c130 h–**

KELANTAN   7 b.g. Kris – Surf Bird (Shareef Dancer (USA)) [2003/4 F84: 20vᵘʳ 20g* c16s⁴ c18g⁴ c24s* c23g⁴ c20s³ c22g² c31d⁴ Apr 22] tall gelding: won novice hurdle at Wetherby in May: fair novice chaser: won handicap at Huntingdon in December: stays 3m: acts on soft going: wore cheekpieces last 2 starts. *K. C. Bailey*   **c102 h95**

KELLY PRIDE   7 b.g. Alflora (IRE) – Pearly-B (IRE) (Gunner B) [2003/4 h65: 26d² 20m² 20s⁶ 24d⁵ 25d³ c21v Jan 13] smallish gelding: poor maiden hurdler: well beaten in novice on chasing debut: stays 3¼m: acts on good to firm and good to soft going. *Mrs S. J. Smith*   **c62 h82**

KELLY (SAF)   7 b.g. Ethique (ARG) – Dancing Flower (SAF) (Dancing Champ (USA)) [2003/4 17g³ 16m⁵ Oct 4] medium-sized gelding: useful on Flat, successful 5 times up to 2m in South Africa, including in Group 1 Gold Bowl at Turffontein in 2002 (trained by M. de Kock): not fluent either start in novice hurdles, better effort when fifth at Chepstow: likely to be suited by stiffer test of stamina: reportedly split a pastern. *Miss Venetia Williams*   **h103 +**

KELLY'S CRAFT (IRE)   7 b.g. Warcraft (USA) – Kelly's Bridge (Torus) [2003/4 20gᵖᵘ 16sᵘʳ 16m* 20m² 16d 16d 16d⁴ 16d Apr 13] workmanlike gelding: fairly useful hurdler: won maiden at Punchestown in October and handicap there (dead-heated with Boleyknowsbest, dismounted after line) in late-April: stays 2½m: acts on good to firm and good to soft going: usually tongue tied. *W. P. Mullins, Ireland*   **h115**

KELLYS FABLE   4 b.g. Thowra (FR) – Kellys Special (Netherkelly) [2003/4 F17g⁶ Apr 10] fifth foal: half-brother to fairly useful chaser Kellys Conquest, stays 25f, and bumper winner Special Dream (both by El Conquistador): dam maiden pointer: looked a stayer when sixth in bumper at Newton Abbot on debut. *J. W. Mullins*   **F73**

KELNIK GLORY   8 b.g. Nalchik (USA) – Areal (IRE) (Roselier (FR)) [2003/4 h–: 20m⁴ 22g³ 24m³ Jul 9] poor maiden hurdler: stays 3m: acts on heavy and good to firm going: tried visored/blinkered. *Mrs S. M. Johnson*   **h73**

KELREV (FR)   6 ch.g. Video Rock (FR) – Bellile II (FR) (Brezzo (FR)) [2003/4 c108, h?: c16vᶠ³ c16d⁴ c16v* c21d² 21s² c20g c20g⁴ Mar 17] leggy, angular gelding: winning hurdler: useful handicap chaser: won at Uttoxeter in January by 11 lengths from Asparagus: ran well in valuable events at Cheltenham next and final starts: will prove at least as effective around 2m as 2½m: acts on heavy going: sometimes let down by jumping: has found little. *Miss Venetia Williams*   **c134 h116**

KELTIC BARD   7 b.g. Emperor Jones (USA) – Broughton Singer (IRE) (Common Grounds) [2003/4 h134: c17g² c16s⁵ c16g* c16s² c16g c20g* c20d* Apr 17]   **c139 h–**
 It wasn't only in races over the National fences that loose horses caused mayhem at the latest Grand National meeting at Aintree. The combination of inexperienced horses, amateur riders and a furious gallop led to quite a few early casualties in the novice handicap which immediately followed the National and, after causing problems for the leaders through the race, two riderless horses were still among the group of six in contention going to three out. Keltic Bard, who had typically travelled strongly in rear, had jumped his way into contention by that stage and looked all over the winner at the second last only to encounter the unwelcome attentions of one of the riderless horses after the fence. Keltic Bard lost all momentum, as his rider David Dunsdon checked and switched to avoid being carried out, but he managed to jump the fence and recovered to win going away by five lengths from The Bandit. Fortune also played its part in Keltic Bard's win on his final start,

Ashleybank Investments Future Champion Novices' Chase, Ayr—
Keltic Bard has been left clear by Mister McGoldrick's fall

in the Ashleybank Investments Future Champions Novices' Chase at Ayr later in
April. He would not have won had Mister McGoldrick stood up two out and the
runner-up Thisthatandtother was not at his best, stepping up in trip. The form still
confirmed Keltic Bard a useful chaser. He won by seven lengths, finishing in front
of Thisthatandtother for the second time, the pair having finished fourth and fifth in
the Supreme Novices' Hurdle at the 2003 Cheltenham Festival. That represented
Keltic Bard's best effort in two seasons over hurdles, after being bought out of Sean
Woods's stable for 26,000 guineas at the Newmarket Autumn Sales in 2000. Keltic
Bard had shown fairly useful form at around a mile and a quarter on the Flat as a
three-year-old, when, perversely, he seemed best forcing the pace. Keltic Bard went
to Aintree with one win from five previous starts over fences, in a beginners chase
at Leicester in January. His early form was such that he started a 25/1-chance for
the Arkle at Cheltenham where he failed to run any sort of race, well behind by the
water jump and trailing in seventh of eight finishers. On his form in general and his
Aintree run in particular, Keltic Bard ought to be able to win again in handicap
company—his sound jumping and ability to travel smoothly and finish strongly
will serve him well—and one of the valuable events at around two and a half miles
at Cheltenham could be just the ticket.

The good-topped Keltic Bard isn't bred to stay beyond two and a half miles.
Indeed, there isn't much in the way of stamina in his pedigree at all. His sire
Emperor Jones was a smart miler and isn't a major influence for stamina as a sire,
while his dam Broughton Singer was a modest nine-furlong winner out of a half-
sister to the smart six-furlong and one-mile winner Faustus. Keltic Bard is his
dam's first foal. The second and third are poor but the fourth, Senschal (by Polar
Falcon), was a five-furlong winner at two in 2003. Since his debut over hurdles,
Keltic Bard has raced on good going or softer and acts on soft. *C. J. Mann*

KELTIC BLUE (IRE)   5 b.g. Blues Traveller (IRE) – White Caps (Shirley Heights)   h–
[2003/4 17s Feb 6] eighth foal: brother to winner up to 11f in Italy and half-brother to
winning hurdler/fairly useful chaser Shampooed (by Law Society), stays 2½m: dam
modest maiden from excellent middle-distance family: well held in novice hurdle on
debut. *R. Dickin*

KELTIC HERITAGE (IRE)   10 gr.g. Roselier (FR) – Peek-A-Step (IRE) (Step   c118 d
Together (USA)) [2003/4 c118, h90: 26m⁴ c28m² c24d c24d⁶ c24d⁵ Mar 13] workman-   h82
like gelding: winning hurdler: fairly useful handicap chaser: easily best effort in 2003/4
when second to French Executive at Stratford in October: stays 3½m: acts on soft and
good to firm going: usually tongue tied: sound-jumping front runner. *L. A. Dace*

KELTIC LORD   8 b.g. Arctic Lord – Scarlet Dymond (Rymer) [2003/4 c24dᶠ c19sᵖᵘ   c–
c24gᵖᵘ Apr 16] sparely-made gelding: winning pointer, including in February: no form   h–
otherwise. *Miss S. Waugh*

KELTIC ROCK   5 ch.g. Bigstone (IRE) – Sibley (Northfields (USA)) [2003/4 F16s   F80
F16s Jan 16] tall gelding: tenth foal: half-brother to smart 1m winner Acharne (by Pharly)
and smart French/Spanish 1¼m to 1¾m winner King Cobra (by Ardross): dam French
1¼m winner from good middle-distance staying family: looked a stayer when mid-field
in 2 bumpers. *G. B. Balding*

KEMAL'S COUNCIL (IRE)   8 gr.g. Leading Counsel (USA) – Kemal's Princess   c–
(Kemal (FR)) [2003/4 c117, h–: c24dᵘʳ c25d⁵ c29dᶠ c25sᵖᵘ Jan 6] workmanlike gelding: h–
won first 2 races over fences in 2002/3, no form after: should stay beyond 25f: raced on
good going or softer (acts on heavy): tried blinkered. *Jonjo O'Neill*

KEMPSKI   4 b.g. Petoski – Little Katrina (Little Buskins) [2003/4 F16s⁵ F16s F16s   F72
Apr 4] 2,000 3-y-o: sixth foal: half-brother to winning hurdler/chaser Copperhurst (by
Royal Vulcan), stays 25f, and poor hurdler Chief Chippie (by Mandalus), stays 3m: dam
winning hurdler/chaser who stayed 3m: signs of a little ability first 2 starts in bumpers.
R. Nixon

KENDRA (GER)   5 b.m. Goofalik (USA) – Keniana (IRE) (Sharpo) [2003/4 15g 15g⁵   h70
21s⁴ 16s Feb 16] successful over 1m at 3 yrs, placed over 6.5f on Flat in March: poor form
on first of 2 starts over hurdles in Britain, when fourth in novice claimer at Plumpton:
should be at least as effective over short of 21f. *Frau E. Mader, Germany*

KEN SCOTT (FR)   6 b.g. Kendor (FR) – Scottish Bride (FR) (Owen Dudley) [2003/4   h100
h108: 16s³ 16d⁶ 16d⁶ 21g⁶ 18d³ 17gᵖᵘ Apr 3] good-topped gelding: fair handicap hurdler,
off 10 months (reportedly fractured leg) before reappearance: barely stays 2¼m: raced on
good going or softer (acts on soft). *P. Winkworth*

KENT   9 b.g. Kylian (USA) – Precious Caroline (IRE) (The Noble Player (USA))   h–
[2003/4 20d⁵ May 16] fairly useful on all-weather Flat (stayed 2m), successful 3 times
in 2003: visored, far from fluent when well held in novice on hurdling debut: dead.
P. D. Cundell

KENTFORD BUSY B   10 b.m. Petoski – Busy Mittens (Nearly A Hand) [2003/4 c71,   c–
h–: c25sᵘʳ Apr 11] angular mare: winning hurdler/pointer: not jump well both starts in   h–
hunter chases: stays 2¾m: acts on good to soft going. *Miss S. A. Loggin*

KENTFORD GREBE   5 b.m. Teenoso (USA) – Notinhand (Nearly A Hand) [2003/4   h107
h74, F69: 20g* 21g* 17g⁴ 20s 21g* 21m³ Apr 15] rather unfurnished mare: fair novice
hurdler: won mares events at Bangor in October, Warwick in November and Newbury in
March, EBF Crandon Park Stud Mares NH Novices' Handicap Hurdle at last-named by
1¼ lengths from Material World: improved further when 4 lengths third of 17 to Silver
Charmer in competitive mares handicap at Cheltenham: will stay beyond 21f: best efforts
on good/good to firm going. *J. W. Mullins*

KENTISH WARRIOR (IRE)   6 b.g. Warcraft (USA) – Garden County (Ragapan)   h–
[2003/4 F–: 21vᵖᵘ 20s 22sᵖᵘ Jan 2] workmanlike gelding: no sign of ability: tongue tied.
B. I. Case

KENTUCKY BLUE (IRE)   4 b.g. Revoque (IRE) – Delta Town (USA) (Sanglamore   h118
(USA)) [2003/4 16d* 16dᶠ 16g* 16s⁴ 18g⁵ Mar 6] rangy gelding: fairly useful on Flat
(stays 1½m): fairly useful juvenile hurdler: won at Wetherby (idled markedly) in November and Catterick (made all, beat Humid Climate 1¼ lengths) in February: likely to prove
best around 2m: acts on soft going. *T. D. Easterby*

KEN'TUCKY (FR)   6 b.g. Video Rock (FR) – La Salamandre (FR) (Pot d'Or (FR))   h99
[2003/4 F95: 16m⁴ 21v⁴ 22s 24d⁴ 26g⁸ 24mᵖᵘ Apr 14] leggy gelding: upped in trip, much
improved over hurdles when comfortably winning handicaps at Ludlow in January and

February: reportedly lame final outing: stays 3¼m: acts on good to soft going (bumper form on good to firm). *N. J. Henderson*

KEPI DE KERFELLEC (FR)   6 b.g. Valanjou (FR) – Ulfica (FR) (Quart de Vin   **h69** (FR)) [2003/4 24v^pu 23v^6 17s Feb 11] sturdy ex-French gelding. fifth foal: brother to middle-distance winner James Kerfellec and half-brother to others by The Quiet Bidder and River Majesty: dam 9f winner: won 15f apprentice event at Fontainebleau on Flat debut at 4 yrs for P. Montfort: well held on completed starts in novice hurdles. *M. D. Hammond*

KERCABELLEC (FR)   6 b. or br.g. Useful (FR) – Marie de Geneve (FR) (Nishapour   **h106** (FR)) [2003/4 h101: 16g* 16d^pu 16g^F 16d^6 Mar 28] useful-looking gelding: fair hurdler: won 19-runner novice at Warwick in November: raced at 2m: tongue tied last 2 outings. *N. J. Henderson*

KERRIGAND (FR)   6 gr.g. April Night (FR) – Gouerie (FR) (Cadoudal (FR)) [2003/4   **c125** c102, h120: c23m* c23g* c24m* c24g^5 Jun 22] sturdy, good-bodied gelding: fairly   **h–** useful hurdler/chaser: successful in novice chases at Worcester (2) in May and Uttoxeter (14/1-on in 2-runner race) in June, all by wide margin: numerous mistakes and soon off bridle in fairly valuable handicap at Perth: should stay beyond 3m: acts on good to firm and heavy going: tried blinkered/visored: not easiest of rides. *M. C. Pipe*

KERRYHEAD WINDFARM (IRE)   6 br.g. Bob Back (USA) – Kerryhead Girl   **F101** (IRE) (Be My Native (USA)) [2003/4 F16d^6 F16d^6 F18d^4 F16s* F16d^5 Apr 11] second foal: dam, won bumper and at 1¾m on Flat, half-sister to very smart chaser/useful hurdler up to 2½m Feroda: failed to complete in 2 points in 2003: fairly useful form in bumpers, winning at Navan in March. *M. Hourigan, Ireland*

KERRY LADS (IRE)   9 ch.g. Mister Lord (USA) – Minstrel Top (Black Minstrel)   **c124 x** [2003/4 c126x, h–: c24d^2 c26d^pu c20v^F c28d^5 c24s^pu 24v* c33d^2 Apr 17] workmanlike   **h107** gelding: first run over hurdles for over 2 years, won novice handicap at Carlisle in March: fairly useful handicap chaser: in cheekpieces, made frame in Scottish National at Ayr following month for second year running, weakening straight and left distant second at last behind Grey Abbey: stays 33f: acts on good to firm and heavy going: usually let down by jumping over fences. *Miss Lucinda V. Russell*

KERRY SOLDIER BLUE   15 gr.g. Fine Blue – Kerry Maid (Maestoso) [2003/4 c88:   **c–** c25g^pu May 13] veteran hunter chaser. *D. O. Stephens*

European Breeders Fund Crandon Park Stud Mares'
'National Hunt' Novices' Hurdle Final (Limited Handicap), Newbury—
Kentford Grebe takes the last more fluently than third Supreme Serenade (hooped cap)

KESTICK 9 b.g. Roscoe Blake – Hop The Twig (Full of Hope) [2003/4 c21d³ c19m² **c106** c24m* c24g* Apr 1] fairly useful hunter chaser: favourite, won at Taunton in March and April, always travelling strongly when beating Springfrod 4 lengths on second occasion: won point 11 days later: stays 3m: acts on good to firm and good to soft going. *M. Biddick*

KETTONG (IRE) 4 b.f. Among Men (USA) – Kettenblume (Cagliostro (GER)) **F−** [2003/4 F16s F17d F16s Apr 4] ninth foal: half-sister to winners abroad by Runnett and Cottage Chapel: dam twice-raced half-sister to smart chaser around 2½m Kadi: tailed off in bumpers. *D. W. Barker*

KETY STAR (FR) 6 b.g. Bojador (FR) – Danystar (FR) (Alycos (FR)) [2003/4 h94: **c121** 16m⁴ 22g⁵ c16g³ c16m* c17g* c16m⁴ c16m² c16g* c18m* Dec 10] leggy gelding: **h93** modest maiden hurdler: fairly useful handicap chaser: won at Newton Abbot and Stratford in July, Doncaster in November and Newbury, confirming himself much improved when beating Idealko 9 lengths in 3-runner race at last-named: best around 2m: raced mainly on good/good to firm going. *Miss Venetia Williams*

KEW 5 b.g. Royal Applause – Cutleaf (Kris) [2003/4 h−: 17dᵖᵘ Jul 27] small gelding: **h− x** no form over hurdles: sold out of J. Bridger's stable £2,100 Ascot June Sales: tried in cheekpieces: has pulled hard. *C. L. Popham*

KEW JUMPER (IRE) 5 b.g. Mister Lord (USA) – Pharisee (IRE) (Phardante (FR)) **h91** [2003/4 16sˢᵘ 20s 16g⁵ Mar 6] tall, good-topped gelding: fifth foal: half-brother to winning pointer by Supreme Leader: dam unraced: modest form when fifth in falsely-run novice hurdle at Huntingdon. *Andrew Turnell*

KEWLAKE LANE 6 b.m. Afzal – Sheer Impulse (IRE) (Montelimar (USA)) [2003/4 **F−** F17v Dec 1] first foal: dam, modest novice hurdler who stayed 2¾m, out of useful 2m to 2¾m hurdler Koshear: showed nothing in mares bumper on debut. *R. H. Alner*

KEZ 8 b.g. Polar Falcon (USA) – Briggsmaid (Elegant Air) [2003/4 h74: 16m⁴ May 9] **h87** fairly useful on Flat (stays 1½m) at 6 yrs: modest form at best in 3 novice hurdles: headstrong. *P. R. Webber*

KHALADJISTAN (IRE) 6 br.g. Tirol – Khaladja (IRE) (Akarad (FR)) [2003/4 h86: **c82** c19dᵖᵘ c22v⁵ c19sᵖᵘ 21g‡ 17m* 16dᵖᵘ 17g⁴ c20d* Apr 21] poor hurdler: won novice seller **h83** at Hereford (sold from P. Nicholls 6,500 gns) in March: disappointing over fences prior to winning handicap at Worcester: stays 2½m: acts on good to soft and good to firm going: wore blinkers/cheekpieces last 5 starts: usually tongue tied. *Miss S. J. Wilton*

KHAN KICKER (IRE) 8 b.g. Husyan (USA) – Orient Conquest (Dual) [2003/4 h115: **c109** c21d² c16g² Nov 19] sparely-made gelding: fairly useful hurdler: fair form when runner- **h−** up in maiden chases in small fields: may prove best up to 2½m: acts on soft and good to firm going: tried in cheekpieces. *N. G. Richards*

KHARAK (FR) 5 gr.g. Danehill (USA) – Khariyda (FR) (Shakapour) [2003/4 h98: **h108** 16g⁶ 17d 16d² 16d⁴ 16s⁴ 18v² 20d* 20g³ 24s² 20d⁵ Apr 22] good-bodied gelding: fair handicap hurdler: won at Carlisle in February: good efforts next 2 starts: stays 3m: acts on any going: tried visored/in cheekpieces: reliable. *Mrs S. C. Bradburne*

KHATANI (IRE) 9 b.g. Kahyasi – Khanata (USA) (Riverman (USA)) [2003/4 c119, **c101** h−: c23g c23mᵖᵘ Jun 1] sturdy gelding: winning hurdler: fairly useful handicap chaser: little show in 3 starts in 2003, though runner-up in points year later: actually stayed 21f: raced on good going or firmer (acts on firm): tried tongue tied. *D. R. Gandolfo*

KHAYAL (USA) 10 b.g. Green Dancer (USA) – Look Who's Dancing (USA) (Affirm- **c88 ?** ed (USA)) [2003/4 c−, h−: c19m⁶ c26m² c26g⁴ 24m² c26g⁵ Aug 4] sturdy gelding: **h−** maiden hurdler: best effort in steeplechases when second to Jabiru in 3-finisher hunter at Newton Abbot: stays 3¼m: acts on firm going: tried visored. *C. J. Down*

KHAYSAR (IRE) 6 b.g. Pennekamp (USA) – Khaytada (IRE) (Doyoun) [2003/4 h−: **h96** 16m 16g³ 16g³ 19sᵖᵘ 19dᵖᵘ 16s³ 16d⁵ 17g⁴ 20d² Apr 12] smallish, sturdy gelding: modest handicap hurdler: left Mrs L. Wadham after sixth start: stays 2½m: acts on soft going. *N. B. King*

KHAYYAM (USA) 6 b.g. Affirmed (USA) – True Celebrity (USA) (Lyphard (USA)) **h82** [2003/4 16m 16m³ 16m Jun 28] fairly useful on Flat (probably stays 1½m) at 3 yrs, has deteriorated markedly: poor form in selling/claiming hurdles: tried blinkered. *S. Gollings*

KHETAAM (IRE) 6 b.g. Machiavellian (USA) – Ghassak (IRE) (Persian Bold) **h123** [2003/4 h118: 16g 16m* 16m* Nov 7] lengthy gelding: fairly useful hurdler: won minor event at Tipperary (beat Puck Out ½ length) in October and 2-runner intermediate at Down Royal: stays 2½m, at least as effective around 2m: acts on heavy and good to firm going: stiff task when blinkered. *N. Meade, Ireland*

KICASSO   5 b.g. Environment Friend – Merry Jane (Rymer) [2003/4 F16v F16g Mar **F79 +**
6] rangy gelding with scope: half-brother to winning pointers by Handsome Sailor and
Scorpio: dam, fairly useful hurdler up to 25f, sister to useful 2½m hurdler Merry Junior:
better effort in bumpers when ninth of 21 to Spirit of New York at Newbury second start,
keeping on steadily under sympathetic handling: will stay beyond 2m. *Miss H. C. Knight*

KICKBACK   4 b.g. High Kicker (USA) – Moniques Venture (Midyan (USA)) [2003/4 **h–**
16g^{pu} 16g⁶ Sep 6] of little account on Flat: showed nothing in 2 juvenile hurdles.
B. A. Pearce

KICK FOR TOUCH (IRE)   7 ch.g. Insan (USA) – Anns Run (Deep Run) [2003/4 **c117**
c109, h–: c26g² c24d^F Jan 19] rangy gelding: fairly useful chaser: ran well on completed **h–**
outing in 2003/4: stays 3¼m: acts on good to firm and good to soft ground: sold 34,000
gns Doncaster May Sales. *Miss H. C. Knight*

KICKHAM (IRE)   8 b.g. Supreme Leader – Knocknagow (Buckskin (FR)) [2003/4 **c–**
h117, F106: F16g 16d⁵ 17s* 16d 20g⁵ 16m⁴ c17s c18d⁶ c19d³ Dec 29] tall gelding: use- **h117**
ful bumper winner: fairly useful novice hurdler: won at Cork (maiden) in June, Killarney **F106**
in July and Tipperary (beat Manjor by length) in September: well held in 3 maiden chases:
stays 2½m: acts on soft and good to firm going: has found little. *E. J. O'Grady, Ireland*

KICKING BEAR (IRE)   6 b.g. Little Bighorn – Rongo (IRE) (Tumble Gold) [2003/4 **h–**
h–, F82: F16g Mar 6] rangy gelding: modest form on completed start in bumpers: well held
in 2 novice hurdles a year apart. *R. T. Phillips*

KICKING KING (IRE)   6 b.g. Old Vic – Fairy Blaze (IRE) (Good Thyne (USA)) **c151**
[2003/4 h141p: c16d⁵ c17d^F c16s* c17d* c16g² c20d² Apr 13] **h–**
For a few tantalising moments, one of the more romantic headlines of the
2004 Cheltenham Festival seemed set to come to fruition. Kicking King is trained
by Tom Taaffe, whose father Pat rode Arkle, and he lined up for the race named in
honour of the legendary Irish chaser on the fortieth anniversary of the first of his
three Gold Cup successes. Kicking King jumped the second last upsides Well Chief
and the cheers for another Irish victory, when Well Chief made a mistake at the last,

Baileys Arkle Perpetual Challenge Cup Novices' Chase, Leopardstown—
Kicking King makes up for his mishap in the Denny Gold Medal

grew even louder when Kicking King battled his way to within a neck of his rival early on the run-in. However, Well Chief knuckled down to give McCoy and Pipe their third Arkle success by a length, while Kicking King's connections found themselves in the runner-up spot for the second year running at the Festival. If Taaffe was frustrated at seeing Kicking King follow his second to Back In Front in the 2003 Supreme Novices Hurdle with a second in the Arkle, he didn't show it, turning his thoughts to 2005 and nominating the Gold Cup as a possible target. Whether that is a realistic ambition is another matter, but Kicking King has made a highly encouraging start over fences and should make his mark in good races in the next season.

Kicking King always looked the sort to thrive over fences, though his path to the Arkle was marked by an uncertain start, finishing a remote fifth of six finishers in a Grade 2 novice chase won by Anxious Moments at Punchestown in November, running as though in need of the outing. Kicking King seemed certain to improve appreciably, his sound jumping looking sure to stand him in good stead eventually. And so it did, though not before a tumble in the Denny Gold Medal Novices' Chase at Leopardstown on Boxing Day in the first of four meetings with Central House. Kicking King was a few lengths to the good under Barry Geraghty when his fall two out left Central House to gain a facile success. Geraghty felt that he had 'so much horse under me I would have won by the length of the straight.' Central House's rider Paul Carberry disagreed, though Kicking King was travelling strongly enough to suggest he would have taken plenty of catching had he stood up. Either way, with Anxious Moments beaten twenty-five lengths into second, there was little doubt that Central House and Kicking King were both at least useful. Come the end of the season, any arguments as to the merits of the pair had been settled firmly in favour of Kicking King.

Mr Conor Clarkson's "Kicking King"

Kicking King's second meeting over fences with Central House came after Kicking King had been warmed up in a novice chase at Punchestown where he won by a distance at 7/2-on. All seven runners for the Grade 1 Baileys Arkle Perpetual Challenge Cup in late-January had been entered for the Cheltenham equivalent, and punters at Leopardstown made Kicking King 11/10 favourite, with Central House at 3/1. Kicking King jumped soundly in a truly-run race and moved into the lead travelling strongly after the third last, Central House emerging from the pack to chase him in the straight. Kicking King would have won a shade further than three and a half lengths had he not lost momentum by jumping left at the last. By this stage it was clear that Kicking King would prove just as effective back over a longer trip, his Cheltenham run confirming the view, as did his performance when stepped up to two and a half miles in the Powers Gold Cup in April. A six-strong field at Fairyhouse also included Central House, who had been going well when unseating his rider four out in the Arkle at Cheltenham. Sent off 9/4 favourite, Kicking King was ridden to lead two out but was unable to match Hi Cloy's turn of foot, going down by half a length with Central House well held in fourth. Afterwards, Taaffe reported that Kicking King was probably finished for the season. In the event, however, he was returned to Punchestown shortly after the end of the British season, for the Swordlestown Cup. His form entitled him to his 11/8-on favouritism but he was on his toes beforehand and shaped as if past his best, still a close second but being driven along when brought down by the fall of Colca Canyon two out.

Kicking King (IRE) (b.g. 1998)	Old Vic (b 1986)	Sadler's Wells (b 1981)	Northern Dancer Fairy Bridge
		Cockade (b 1973)	Derring-Do Camenae
	Fairy Blaze (IRE) (b 1991)	Good Thyne (br 1977)	Herbager Foreseer
		Fairy Tree (ch 1970)	Varano Precision Time

A rangy, well-made gelding who usually takes the eye, Kicking King is effective on soft but has yet to race on going firmer than good. Details of his pedigree appeared in last year's *Chasers & Hurdlers*, and there is little to add save that his older half-brother Glenfarclas Boy (by Montelimar) won twice over fences in the latest season while his year-younger sister, named Fairy Dawn, is in training with John Kiely. Contacted after the end of the season, his trainer seemed to have had second thoughts about the Gold Cup but did nominate the John Durkan Memorial Punchestown Chase in December as a likely target before Kicking King is given his chance over three miles. Keeping up a strong gallop is his forte and Kicking King's prospects of staying three miles look bright, though he will need to improve to pose a threat to Beef Or Salmon and Harbour Pilot in races like the former Ericsson Chase. If Kicking King fails to come up to scratch against the best stayers, the revamped Cathcart Chase—to be known as the Festival Chase— over two miles five furlongs would be an obvious Cheltenham Festival alternative. Having reportedly proved tricky when lining up in the past, Kicking King was accompanied by a stable representative at the start before the Arkle, having proved troublesome at Leopardstown. However, Kicking King gave no trouble and has never looked anything other than genuine once racing. Incidentally, his name has nothing to do with either football or the monarchy. His owner's young daughter plumped for Kicking King ahead of tempting alternatives such as Munching Mike and Harry The Hairy Hat Man while using the Letterland reading module. *T. J. Taaffe, Ireland*

KIDITHOU (FR) 6 b.g. Royal Charter (FR) – De Thou (FR) (Trebrook (FR)) [2003/4 **h102** h98p, F95: 16g* 20g* 20g⁴ 27s² 20d² 24d² Mar 18] medium-sized gelding: fair novice hurdler: won twice at Hexham in May: stays 27f: acts on heavy going: jumps none too fluently. *L. Lungo*

KIDS INHERITANCE (IRE) 6 b.g. Presenting – Princess Tino (IRE) (Rontino) **h93** [2003/4 F94: 20g⁴ 16g² 19g⁵ 17s⁴ 16g* Mar 12] good-topped gelding: modest hurdler: won novice handicap at Ayr: probably best short of 2½m: acts on soft going. *J. M. Jefferson*

KIEV (IRE) 4 b.g. Bahhare (USA) – Badrah (USA) (Private Account (USA)) [2003/4 **F76** F16g⁶ F16g aF16g⁵ Apr 4] 92,000F, 170,000Y: leggy gelding: fifth foal: half-brother to

5f/6f winner in Ireland/UAE Moonis and 1999 Irish 2-y-o 6f/7f winner Desert Sky (both useful, by Green Desert): dam, placed once from 2 starts at 1m, half-sister to smart 1¼m performer Husyan: bought out of Sir Michael Stoute's stable 3,200 gns Newmarket July Sales: modest form in bumpers. *D. G. Bridgwater*

KILCASKIN GOLD (IRE)   9 ch.g. Ore – Maypole Gayle (Strong Gale) [2003/4 c–: c25d* c27d^pu Mar 16] winning pointer: form in steeplechases only when winning 16-runner maiden hunter at Hexham in May: should stay beyond 25f: acts on good to soft going: tried blinkered. *R. A. Ross*   **c93**

KILCREGGAN   10 b.g. Landyap (USA) – Lehmans Lot (Oats) [2003/4 22m⁴ 16d 20v^pu 19d^pu 16g^pu Feb 20] leggy gelding: winning 2m hurdler: no form in 2003/4. *Mrs Barbara Waring*   **h–**

KILDARE CHILLER (IRE)   10 b.g. Shahrastani (USA) – Ballycuirke (Taufan (USA)) [2003/4 h99: 20d⁴ 22m⁵ 18g³ Mar 8] leggy gelding: poor handicap hurdler: stays 21f: has won on good to firm going, best efforts on good or softer (acts on heavy): tried in cheekpieces: often gets behind. *P. R. Hedger*   **h83**

KILDARE (IRE)   7 br.g. Supreme Leader – Fairly Deep (Deep Run) [2003/4 F113: F16g³ 19d⁴ 16d² 20s² 20s³ 20d³ 24d⁵ 22s Mar 14] close-coupled gelding: useful bumper performer: fairly useful hurdler: favourite, won 23-runner maiden at Naas in November: better form when placed after, third to Sadlers Wings at Punchestown in late-April: should stay beyond 2½m: acts on soft going: blinkered after sixth start. *D. T. Hughes, Ireland*   **h122** **F113**

KILDEE LASS   5 gr.m. Morpeth – Pigeon Loft (IRE) (Bellypha) [2003/4 F81: 17g⁵ 16m⁵ 16d⁴ 17s⁵ 19g 16d⁴ 17g³ Apr 10] leggy, angular mare: modest hurdler: won mares novice at Wincanton in December: should stay beyond 17f: acts on good to soft going: has pulled hard. *J. D. Frost*   **h87**

KILDORRAGH (IRE)   10 b.g. Glacial Storm (USA) – Take A Dare (Pragmatic) [2003/4 c115: c24s^pu c28d² c24s^R c24v^pu c24g c25s³ c24m⁴ c26g Apr 22] tall, useful-looking gelding: fair handicap chaser: creditable effort in 2003/4 (usually blinkered) only when second to Igloo d'Estruval at Fontwell: stays 3½m: acts on good to firm and heavy going: moody. *L. Wells*   **c113 d**

KILLALA BAY (IRE)   9 b.m. Executive Perk – Killinure Point (Smooth Stepper) [2003/4 c–: c20m³ May 5] no form in 3 starts over fences. *K. C. Bailey*   **c–**

KILLALONGFORD (IRE)   7 b.g. Tenby – Queen Crab (Private Walk) [2003/4 h79: 20m 24m² 24m⁴ 21g² Dec 11] modest maiden hurdler: stays 3m: acts on soft and good to firm going. *Mrs S. M. Johnson*   **h88**

KILLARNEY   6 gr.m. Pursuit of Love – Laune (AUS) (Kenmare (FR)) [2003/4 h66: 17d May 28] sturdy mare: poor maiden hurdler: probably best around 2m: best efforts on good/good to firm going. *Miss Kate Milligan*   **h–**

KILLARNEY PRINCE (IRE)   5 b.g. Lord Americo – Henry Woman (IRE) (Mandalus) [2003/4 F16m³ F16s⁵ F17s Feb 3] 1,800 3-y-o: medium-sized gelding: fifth foal: half-brother to winning pointer by Supreme Leader: dam unraced, out of half-sister to very smart hurdler/useful staying chaser Henry Mann and smart chaser at 2½m+ Royal Dipper: 12 lengths third of 7 in maiden at Ludlow, best effort in bumpers: will stay beyond 2m. *Mrs J. M. Mann*   **F89**

KILLERS FURY (IRE)   5 br.g. Topanoora – Ellen Gail (IRE) (Strong Gale) [2003/4 c24d^F 24g^pu 24g³ Mar 7] €12,000 4-y-o: smallish, rather sparely-made gelding: first foal: dam lightly-raced half-sister to fairly useful hurdler/chaser up to 25f Indian Scout, out of sister to smart chaser at 2½m+ Kissane: won 4-y-o maiden Irish point in 2003: easily best effort in Britain when third to Limerick Leader in novice hurdle at Kempton in March: jumped poorly in novice chase there previous month. *M. C. Pipe*   **c–** **h101**

KILLOUGHTER (IRE)   6 b.g. Magical Wonder (USA) – Miss Bobby Bennett (Kings Lake (USA)) [2003/4 22m^pu May 29] fourth foal: half-brother to winning hurdler Miss B Bennett (by Denel), stayed 3¼m: dam useful hurdler up to 2½m: more signs of temperament than ability in point/novice hurdle (visored). *M. C. Pipe*   **h–**

KILLULTAGH DAWN (IRE)   6 b.m. Phardante (FR) – Rostrevor Lady (Kemal (FR)) [2003/4 F16f F18m 19d⁶ 16d³ 18s 18d⁶ 17s^pu 16d Mar 18] ex-Irish mare: eighth foal: half-sister to several winners, notably useful hurdler/chaser up to 2½m Killultagh Storm (by Mandalus): dam, winning jumper, sister to fairly useful staying chaser Crawford Says: modest form in bumpers: poor maiden hurdler: left M. Hourigan, showed little last 2 starts: stays 19f: acts on heavy ground: tried in cheekpieces. *J. Howard Johnson*   **h82** **F79**

KILLULTAGH STORM (IRE) 10 b.g. Mandalus – Rostrevor Lady (Kemal (FR)) **c140**
[2003/4 c139, h–: c16g³ c20d⁵ 16v⁶ c17d⁵ c24g⁵ c19s* c20g³ c16d⁴ c17d⁴ c16g c17d Apr **h109**
11] strong, lengthy gelding: winning hurdler: useful chaser: made all in minor event at
Listowel in September: generally ran with credit after, including twice at Punchestown in
late-April: effective at 2m to 25f: acts on good to firm and heavy going: ran creditably
only try in blinkers, usually wears cheekpieces nowadays. *W. G. Mullins, Ireland*

KILLULTAGH THUNDER (IRE) 8 b. or br.g. Bravefoot – Rostrevor Lady (Kemal **c109 x**
(FR)) [2003/4 c111, h117: c25g⁶ c24s* c24dᵖᵘ c24sᶠ c28vᵖᵘ 20s 24d 22s 24s³ c29dᶠ Apr **h109**
12] lengthy gelding: fair hurdler/chaser: won maiden chase at Gowran in May: best at
2½m+: acts on heavy going: tried in cheekpieces: often let down by jumping over fences.
W. P. Mullins, Ireland

KILLWILLIE (IRE) 5 b.g. Carroll House – Home In The Glen (Furry Glen) [2003/4 **F90**
F16g⁵ Mar 13] fifth foal: half-brother to fairly useful hurdler Tana River (by Over The
River), stays 2½m, and 2½m bumper winner Forever Friend (by Jurado): dam winning
Irish pointer: 4½ lengths fifth of 10 to Qualitair Pleasure in bumper at Ayr on debut.
J. I. A. Charlton

KILLY BEACH 6 b.g. Kuwait Beach (USA) – Spiritual Lily (Brianston Zipper) **c73**
[2003/4 h81?: c21mᵖᵘ c16d⁶ c21s⁵ c25dᵖᵘ c19m³ Apr 13] leggy gelding: poor maiden **h–**
hurdler/chaser: probably stays 2¾m. *J. W. Mullins*

KILMORE KING (IRE) 7 b.g. Big Sink Hope (USA) – Le Dawn (Le Bavard (FR)) **c70**
[2003/4 c16d⁴ c21g⁴ c21g² c21vᵖᵘ Jan 13] lengthy gelding: second foal: dam unplaced in
bumpers: won maiden on last of 3 starts in Irish points in 2003: bought 3,000 gns
Doncaster May Sales: poor form in steeplechases: stays 21f: tongue tied first 3 starts.
N. Wilson

KILMORE QUAY (IRE) 9 ch.g. Over The River (FR) – Sustenance (Torus) [2003/4 **c90 +**
h–: c25d* c24gᶠ Mar 7] workmanlike gelding: no show in 2 novice hurdles: runner-up 3 **h–**
times in Irish points, including twice in 2003: 10/1 from 33/1, made all and jumped far
more fluently than rivals in 5-runner maiden chase at Towcester in October: fell second
next time: stays 25f. *G. B. Balding*

KILTULAA LAD (IRE) 11 ch.g. Phardante (FR) – Galway Shawl (Cure The Blues **c– x**
(USA)) [2003/4 21m⁵ 21gᵖᵘ 22d 16s 17s 17g² 17s⁶ Apr 6] good-topped gelding: winning **h84**
chaser, though often let down by jumping: form over hurdles in 2003/4 (left D. Williams
after second outing) only when second in selling handicap at Market Rasen: stays easy
2½m: acts on heavy and good to firm going. *J. F. Panvert*

KIMBAMBO (FR) 6 gr.g. Genereux Genie – Contessina (FR) (Mistigri) [2003/4 **h111**
16d* 16d⁶ 16s² 16d⁵ Feb 21] tall gelding: second foal: half-brother to fair hurdler/chaser
Infini (by Le Nain Jaune), stays 2¾m: dam 1½m winner: won maiden hurdle at Kelso
on debut in December: better form last 2 starts: raced at 2m on good to soft/soft going.
N. M. L. Ewart

KIMBERLEY 9 b.g. Shareef Dancer (USA) – Willowbank (Gay Fandango (USA)) **c–**
[2003/4 c–, h117: 24d 24s² 25d Jan 10] compact gelding: winning chaser: fairly useful **h119**
handicap hurdler: stays 3m: raced mainly on good going or softer (acts on heavy): tried
blinkered, usually visored nowadays: formerly tongue tied. *J. G. M. O'Shea*

KIMBO LADY 6 ch.m. Husyan (USA) – Fair Cruise (Cruise Missile) [2003/4 F17s **F–**
Jan 22] 6,000 4-y-o: second foal: dam no sign of ability: well tailed off in bumper on
debut. *R. J. Smith*

KIMDALOO (IRE) 12 b.g. Mandalus – Kimin (Kibenka) [2003/4 c92, h–: c16d* **c92**
c16g³ c20mᵖᵘ May 27] lengthy gelding: modest handicap chaser: won at Hexham in May: **h–**
raced mainly around 2m nowadays: acts on any going: tongue tied. *M. A. Barnes*

KIM FONTAINE (FR) 6 b. or br.g. Silver Rainbow – Blanche Fontaine (FR) **h134**
(Oakland (FR)) [2003/4 F108: F16d* 16d 24d 20d* 22s² 18s⁵ 20dᶠ Mar 4] rather unfurnished gelding: useful form in bumpers, won at Punchestown in May: useful novice
hurdler: won maiden at Leopardstown in December and listed event at Thurles (led near
finish when beating Strike Back by length) in March: best effort when fifth of 7 to Brave
Inca in Grade 1 at Leopardstown in February: stays 2¾m: raced on soft/good to soft going
over hurdles. *W. P. Mullins, Ireland*

KIM FONTENAIL (FR) 4 b.f. Kaldounevees (FR) – Fontanalia (FR) (Rex Magna **h103**
(FR)) [2003/4 F13d⁵ 17s³ 17s³ 19d* 21g⁶ Mar 27] angular filly: sixth foal: half-sister to 3 **F78**
winners, including modest hurdler/fair 2m chaser Soeur Fontenail (by Turgeon) and 2¾m
chase winner Honneur Fontenail (by Tel Quel): dam maiden chaser: fifth of 11 in bumper

on debut: fair form over hurdles: won mares novice at Hereford in February: stays 21f: raced on good going or softer. *N. J. Hawke*

KIMMERIDGE BAY   6 b.m. Karinga Bay – Chanelle (The Parson) [2003/4 F17s F16v 19g Mar 9] eighth foal: sister to winning 23f hurdler Classic China and half-sister to useful hurdler/fair chaser Country Beau (by Town And Country), stays 3m: dam, winning pointer, half-sister to useful hurdler/fairly useful staying chaser Arabian Music: well held in mares bumpers and novice hurdle. *J. W. Mullins*   **h–** **F–**

KIMOE WARRIOR   6 ch.g. Royal Abjar (USA) – Thewaari (USA) (Eskimo (USA)) [2003/4 h75§: 16mF 21m5 17g* 20m5 17mpu 19dpu Mar 15] leggy gelding: poor handicap hurdler: won at Market Rasen in May: best around 2m: acts on any going: usually wears cheekpieces/blinkers: tried tongue tied. *M. Mullineaux*   **h83 §**

KIMONO ROYAL (FR)   6 b. or br.g. Garde Royale – Alizane (FR) (Mourtazam) [2003/4 F16g* F16g4 Mar 27] IR £28,000 3-y-o, 41,000 4-y-o: tall, useful-looking gelding: fourth foal: half-brother to 2 winners by Beyssac, fair hurdler/chaser Gaspairie, stayed 21f, and winning chaser up to 21f Imprevue: dam middle-distance maiden: fairly useful form both starts in bumpers, won 9-runner event at Kempton in February by head from All Things Equal and fourth of 18 to River Trapper at Newbury. *A. King*   **F96**

KIMS PEARL (IRE)   6 b.m. Jurado (USA) – Blushing Pearl (Monksfield) [2003/4 F16d4 Mar 21] fourth foal: dam never ran: under 3 lengths fourth to Billesey in bumper at Stratford on debut. *D. Burchell*   **F81**

KINBURN (IRE)   5 gr.g. Roselier (FR) – Leadaro (IRE) (Supreme Leader) [2003/4 20d 22g4 Mar 28] €66,000 4-y-o: fourth foal: dam unraced half-sister to very smart 2m hurdler Miller Hill and to dam of top-class hurdler Mighty Mogul: poor form at Kelso on second start in novice hurdles. *J. Howard Johnson*   **h65**

KINCORA (IRE)   13 b.g. King Persian – Miss Noora (Ahonoora) [2003/4 c83, h–: c26f4 May 21] angular gelding: fairly useful pointer, won in January: maiden hunter chaser: stays 3m: probably acts on any going. *Ms Lisa Stock*   **c73 h–**

KINDA CRAZY   4 b.g. Petoski – Margaret Modes (Thatching) [2003/4 F16d F17s F16g F16d 17g 19s3 20dpu Apr 21] plain gelding: second foal: half-brother to fair hurdler Jonanaud (by Ballet Royal), effective at 2m to 3m: dam no form on Flat: form only when third of 6 finishers in maiden hurdle at Towcester. *H. J. Manners*   **h84 F–**

KINDLE BALL (FR)   6 gr.m. Kaldounevees (FR) – Scala IV (FR) (Quart de Vin (FR)) [2003/4 F–: F17d5 20m3 16g3 17g* 21g3 16g* 20v3 19d5 21d2 Mar 16] compact mare: better effort in mares bumpers when fifth at Bangor: modest hurdler: won mares maiden in November and mares novice in December, both at Southwell: stays 21f: acts on heavy ground: races prominently. *Miss Venetia Williams*   **h92 F76**

KIND SIR   8 b.g. Generous (IRE) – Noble Conquest (USA) (Vaguely Noble) [2003/4 c107, h–: c20m3 c19d3 c20dpu c16s4 c16g6 c16d5 c16m2 c16m2 c20d* c20d2 c18g* Apr 22] good-topped gelding: fair handicap chaser: jumped better than he often does when winning at Ludlow in March and Fontwell in April: stays easy 2½m: acts on good to firm and heavy going: blinkered once: often forces pace. *A. W. Carroll*   **c104 h–**

KIND WORD (IRE)   11 b. or br.m. Yashgan – Lucifer's Way (Lucifer (USA)) [2003/4 21m4 24v5 20d5 16m 20m2 20fpu Aug 28] angular mare: poor maiden hurdler: stays 3m: acts on good to firm and heavy going: tried blinkered: tongue tied. *C. Wilkinson, Ireland*   **c– h76**

KING BEE (IRE)   7 b.g. Supreme Leader – Honey Come Back (Master Owen) [2003/4 h95: c23g3 c24d2 c24s3 c24d* Mar 28] medium-sized gelding: modest hurdler: fair form over fences: won novice handicap at Huntingdon, making most and finding more for pressure than he sometimes does: stays 3m: acts on heavy ground. *H. D. Daly*   **c109 h–**

KING CAREW (IRE)   6 b.g. Fairy King (USA) – Kareena (Riverman (USA)) [2003/4 c106p, h111: 16g 17g 16g* c17f* 20m c17dF 16d 16m5 c16f2 16d 19s 16dur 16g2 16s3 16d6 Apr 13] useful-looking gelding: useful up to 17f on Flat: fairly useful hurdler/chaser: won minor event over hurdles at Limerick and handicap over fences at Cork in June: good third in handicap hurdle at Punchestown in late-April: raced mainly around 2m: acts on any going: effective with/without blinkers. *M. Hourigan, Ireland*   **c120 h118**

KING COAL (IRE)   5 b. or br.g. Anshan – Lucky Trout (Beau Charmeur (FR)) [2003/4 17vpu 16d Dec 29] sixth foal: half-brother to fair hurdler/fairly useful chaser Supreme Catch (by Supreme Leader), stays 21f: dam, winning pointer, sister to NH Chase winner Smooth Escort: better effort in novice hurdles when tenth of 17 at Newbury. *R. Rowe*   **h95**

KING CREOLE   5 b.g. Slip Anchor – Myrrh (Salse (USA)) [2003/4 16m Oct 4] fair maiden on Flat (stays 1¾m) at 3 yrs, sold out of J. Noseda's stable 11,000 gns Newmarket   **h–**

Autumn Sales, well held in 2003: showed nothing in seller on hurdling debut. *Ian Williams*

KING DARSHAAN   4 b.g. Darshaan – Urchin (IRE) (Fairy King (USA)) [2003/4   h
16m⁵ Nov 8] fair maiden on Flat (stays 1½m): pulled hard when tailed off in juvenile on hurdling debut. *P. R. Hedger*

KING EIDER   5 b. or br.g. Mtoto – Hen Harrier (Polar Falcon (USA)) [2003/4 17s⁴   h108
19d⁶ 16g³ 16m* 16g 16d² Apr 22] smallish gelding: useful on Flat (stays 2m), sold out of J. Dunlop's stable 42,000 gns Newmarket Autumn Sales: fair form over hurdles, made hard work of landing odds in maiden at Wincanton in March: should stay beyond 2m: acts on good to firm and soft going: sold 36,000 gns Doncaster May Sales. *N. J. Henderson*

KINGFISHER EVE (IRE)   6 b.m. Hamas (IRE) – Houwara (IRE) (Darshaan)   h78
[2003/4 20m³ 24d³ Nov 14] workmanlike mare: little form on Flat: placed in small fields both starts over hurdles, swishing tail and looking less than straightforward each time. *C. Grant*

KINGFISHER STAR   9 ch.g. Derrylin – Legata (IRE) (Orchestra) [2003/4 c68: c26fᵖᵘ   c– x
May 21] winning pointer: little impact in 3 novice hunter chases: jumped poorly when blinkered. *S. R. Andrews*

KINGFISHER SUNSET   8 b.g. Alflora (IRE) – Jack It In (Derrylin) [2003/4 F–:   h–
20gᵘʳ Nov 16] good-bodied gelding: little sign of ability in bumpers: unseated first on hurdling debut: sold to join Mrs S. Smith 2,600 gns Doncaster November Sales. *J. G. M. O'Shea*

KING-FOR-LIFE (IRE)   6 ch.g. Rainbows For Life (CAN) – Fair Song (Pitskelly)   h–
[2003/4 h–, F91: 20m Oct 26] tall gelding: fair form in bumpers for G. A. Swinbank: no encouragement in 2 starts over hurdles. *R. Ford*

KING GEORGES (FR)   6 b.g. Kadalko (FR) – Djoumi (FR) (Brezzo (FR)) [2003/4   h100
h86: 22g 25g* 24d 24sꜰ Mar 20] rather leggy gelding: fair handicap hurdler: off over 6 months, improved form when winning at Kempton in November: well held both other completed starts in 2003/4: stays 25f: acts on good to soft ground. *J. C. Tuck*

KING JAMES   7 b.g. Homo Sapien – Bowling Fort (Bowling Pin) [2003/4 19gᵖᵘ   h–
20dᵖᵘ Mar 22] leggy, close-coupled gelding: of little account: usually tongue tied. *J. Mackie*

KINGKOHLER (IRE)   5 b.g. King's Theatre (IRE) – Legit (IRE) (Runnett) [2003/4   h102
h87p: 16d² 16g* 16g* Jan 7] lightly raced on Flat (stays 1½m), successful both starts in 2003: thrice-raced over hurdles, won novice at Musselburgh readily in January by 4 lengths from Beau Artiste: will prove best around 2m. *K. A. Morgan*

KING OF ARMS   6 b.g. Rakaposhi King – Herald The Dawn (Dubassoff (USA))   c73
[2003/4 h–: 24d* 24v⁴ 24gᵖᵘ c21d⁴ 21g⁴ Apr 12] medium-sized gelding: poor handicap   h73
hurdler: won amateur event at Hexham in December: similar form when fourth of 6 finishers in weak handicap at Sedgefield on chasing debut: likely to prove better at 3m than shorter: acts on good to soft going: wore cheekpieces/tongue strap third start: hard ride. *J. Howard Johnson*

KING OF BARBURY (IRE)   7 b.g. Moscow Society (USA) – Aine's Alice (IRE)   h104
(Drumalis) [2003/4 h92: 17d³ 16d 16g⁴ 19g³ Apr 1] sturdy, lengthy gelding: fair hurdler: improved effort (reportedly suffered stress fracture final 2002/3 start) when winning conditional jockeys handicap at Bangor in December: good efforts last 2 starts: stays 19f: raced on good going or softer. *A. King*

KING OF GOTHLAND (IRE)   5 b. or br.g. Gothland (FR) – Rose Deer (Whistling   F97
Deer) [2003/4 F16d F16s⁴ F16g⁴ Feb 28] 16,000 3-y-o: good-topped gelding: half-brother to several winners, including fairly useful hurdler/chaser Dr Bones (by Durgam), stays 3m, and fairly useful 2m hurdler Spirit of Park (by Rashar): dam, lightly raced over jumps in Ireland, out of half-sister to dam of smart staying chaser River Tarquin: progressive form in bumpers, staying-on fourth of 20 to Lord Gale at Haydock final start. *K. C. Bailey*

KING OF MOMMUR (IRE)   9 b.g. Fairy King (USA) – Monoglow (Kalaglow)   c98
[2003/4 c106, h84: c20g⁵ c21mᵖᵘ Sep 7] leggy gelding: modest chaser: stays easy 3m: h–
acts on firm and good to soft going (below form on softer): tried blinkered/in cheekpieces. *B. G. Powell*

KING OF THE ARCTIC (IRE)   6 b.g. Arctic Lord – Ye Little Daisy (Prince Tend-   h102
erfoot (USA)) [2003/4 F16g 20s 20m² 16d* 20s⁴ 16g² 16s⁴ Apr 21] rather unfurnished   F–
ex-Irish gelding: fifth reported foal: dam bumper winner/2m winner on Flat: modest form

in bumpers: fair form over hurdles: left D. Weld and off over 6 months, won novice at Hexham in December: stays 2½m: acts on soft and good to firm going: reportedly suffers breathing problems. *J. Wade*

KING OF THE CASTLE (IRE) 9 b.g. Cataldi – Monashuna (Boreen (FR)) [2003/4 h94: c20d³ c20d⁴ Apr 17] tall gelding: modest hurdler: similar form in face of stiff tasks in 2 novice chases: stays 2½m: acts on firm and good to soft going. *B. Mactaggart*   **c97 h–**

KING OF THE DAWN 13 b.g. Rakaposhi King – Dawn Encounter (Rymer) [2003/4 c84§, h–: c20g c20dᵘʳ c22gᵘʳ Mar 26] angular gelding: poor chaser: left P. Hedger after first outing: won point in April: stays 2¾m: acts on heavy and good to firm going: irresolute. *Mrs Georgina Worsley*   **c– § h–**

KING OF THE FOREST (IRE) 9 b.g. Good Thyne (USA) – Coolbawn Lady (Laurence O) [2003/4 c88: c25g c25dᶠ May 3] lengthy gelding: winning pointer: modest form when second in 2 maiden chases: stayed 25f: tried in cheekpieces: dead. *Miss S. E. Forster*   **c–**

KING OF THE NAUL (IRE) 11 b.g. King's Ride – Glenastar VII (Damsire Unregistered) [2003/4 c20mᵖᵘ May 26] ex-Irish gelding: first known foal: dam never ran: bumper winner: in frame several times in points in Britain in 2002: showed nothing on steeplechasing debut. *C. L. Tizzard*   **c– h–**

KING ON THE RUN (IRE) 11 b.g. King's Ride – Fly Run (Deep Run) [2003/4 c20m⁵ Feb 28] rangy gelding: useful handicap chaser, lightly raced: off 2 years, well held at Kempton only start in 2003/4: stays 3m, at least as effective at 2½m: acts on good to firm and heavy going. *Miss Venetia Williams*   **c– h–**

KING PLATO (IRE) 7 b.g. King's Ride – You Are A Lady (IRE) (Lord Americo) [2003/4 h84: c16d⁴ c20d⁶ c25v⁴ c20sᶠ c20g c20d³ Apr 24] poor hurdler/novice chaser: stays 3m: acts on soft going: jumps fences less than fluently: has shown signs of temperament. *M. D. Hammond*   **c77 h–**

KING PLAYER (IRE) 7 b.g. King's Ride – West Along (Crash Course) [2003/4 F101p: 16dᵖᵘ Nov 30] well-made gelding: chasing type: looked promising when second in bumper at Newbury on debut: appeared to go wrong after rapping third in maiden hurdle there 11 months later. *N. J. Henderson*   **h– p**

KING REVO (IRE) 4 b.g. Revoque (IRE) – Tycoon Aly (IRE) (Last Tycoon) [2003/4 16g* 16d* 16v* 16s* 16g⁶ Apr 1] tall, useful-looking gelding: fairly useful on Flat (stays 1½m): unbeaten first 4 starts over hurdles, won juveniles at Catterick and Wetherby in December, novice at Wetherby in January and juvenile at Haydock (beat My Will a short head in quite valuable event despite carrying head awkwardly) in February: not seen to best advantage when sixth of 18 to Al Eile in Grade 2 juvenile at Aintree, held up in steadily-run contest: raced at 2m on good going or softer: may yet improve further. *P. C. Haslam*   **h127**

KINGS BAY 5 ch.m. Beveled (USA) – Storm of Plenty (Billion (USA)) [2003/4 F17v* F18g² F16s² Mar 13] angular mare: seventh foal: half-sister to fair 2m hurdler Cashaplenty (by Ballacashtal): dam fair 2m hurdler: fairly useful form in mares bumpers, won at Folkestone on debut in December: beaten under length when second to Countess Point at Fontwell and Marsh Run at Sandown (valuable event, again took plenty of time to respond to pressure). *H. Morrison*   **F104**

KING'S BOUNTY 8 b.g. Le Moss – Fit For A King (Royalty) [2003/4 c100, h–: c25g c25gᵘʳ c27s c22g² c24s² c28d³ Mar 30] rangy gelding: fair handicap chaser: stays 3½m: acts on good to firm and heavy going: has looked no easy ride. *T. D. Easterby*   **c104 h–**

KINGS BOY (IRE) 10 ch.g. Be My Native (USA) – Love-In-A-Mist (Paddy's Stream) [2003/4 c21d² Apr 30] good-topped gelding: one-time fairly useful hurdler: of similar standard in points in 2003: tongue tied, second of 15 to Hall's Mill at Cheltenham on hunter chase debut, looking likely winner until slow jump last: should stay beyond 21f: acts on soft and good to firm going: has broken blood vessels. *David M. Easterby*   **c101 h–**

KINGSBRIDGE (IRE) 10 b.g. Cataldi – Rockport Rosa (IRE) (Roselier (FR)) [2003/4 c69, h–: c16g⁴ c26m⁵ c20m³ Aug 16] fair pointer, won in March: maiden hurdler/steeplechaser: effective at 2m to 3¼m: acts on good to firm going: visored once (reportedly distressed): untrustworthy. *M. C. Pipe*   **c67 § h–**

KINGS BROOK 4 br.g. Alderbrook – Kins Token (Relkino) [2003/4 F12d F17s⁶ 16m⁴ 16gᵖᵘ Apr 4] rather unfurnished gelding: fifth foal: dam unraced: better effort in bumpers when sixth at Taunton: fourth to King Eider in maiden at Wincanton on hurdling debut: ran poorly next time, again looking reluctant when driven. *Nick Williams*   **h83 F81**

KINGS CASTLE (IRE)   9 b.g. King's Ride – Kilmana (IRE) (Castle Keep) [2003/4 **c100**
c21g² c24gᵖᵘ 22mᶠ 20dᵖᵘ Mar 20] compact gelding: one-time useful handicap hurdler, **h–**
missed 2002/3: showed little last 2 outings: jumped soundly on chasing debut when
second to impressive Strong Flow in novice at Newton Abbot: lame next time: stays 25f:
acts on good to firm and heavy going. *R. J. Hodges*

KING'S CHAMPION (IRE)   8 b.g. King's Ride – Decent Slave (Decent Fellow) **h93**
[2003/4 20g⁵ Nov 21] rangy gelding: tenth of 18 in bumper on debut: 20 lengths fifth of
10 to He's The Boss in novice hurdle at Ascot 2 years later, running on through beaten
horses. *Mrs Merrita Jones*

KINGSCLIFF (IRE)   7 b.g. Toulon – Pixies Glen (Furry Glen) [2003/4 c137P: **c157 p**
c24d* c25d* c24s² Jan 10]

With the possible exception of the novice Strong Flow, who became the first
horse to win the Hennessy Gold Cup in his first season over fences, no horse was
more talked about as a rising young star of steeplechasing than ex-hunter Kingscliff. Unfortunately, neither Strong Flow nor Kingscliff was able to complete the
campaign, Strong Flow cracking a bone in a knee and missing the second half of
the season and Kingscliff suffering muscular problems which almost certainly
accounted for the only defeat of his most promising career so far. Kingscliff was as
short as 5/1 second favourite for the Cheltenham Gold Cup after Best Mate's
faultless display in the Ericsson Chase at Christmas, by which time Kingscliff had
enhanced his reputation with an amazing victory in a handicap at Ascot on his
reappearance and a very impressive one in another handicap at Cheltenham.
Kingscliff's enforced absence from the Gold Cup was made to look all the more
regrettable when his stable-companion, 33/1-shot Sir Rembrandt, ran Best Mate
to half a length. But to begin with that particularly memorable performance at
Ascot . . .

The history of steeplechasing is littered with remarkable feats of horsemanship in adversity, perhaps the most-often recalled nowadays being Fred Winter's
legendary performance on Mandarin, and that of Tim Brookshaw who rode without
stirrups from second Becher's on runner-up Wyndburgh in the 1959 Grand
National. Some fitting tributes to Fred Winter appeared after his death at the age
of seventy-seven the week after the latest Grand National, a race he won twice
as a jockey and twice as a trainer. He is also the only person to have ridden and
trained winners of the Cheltenham Gold Cup and the Champion Hurdle. Nothing
summed up Winter's place in racing history more succinctly than the fact that—

coral.co.uk Handicap Chase, Ascot—a remarkable performance by ex-hunter Kingscliff and
Andrew Thornton, after the left rein (seen flapping in front of Silver Streak's face) broke early in the race

along with Vincent O'Brien and Lester Piggott—he was the only person on the *Racing Post* birthday list for whom the description 'racing legend' was used. Winter was champion jockey four times and champion trainer eight times, his training career brought to a sudden end in 1987 when he was left paralysed after a stroke (though he continued to hold the licence at Uplands until the summer of 1988). Mandarin was one of the best horses Winter rode and the partnership won both the Cheltenham Gold Cup and the Grand Steeple-Chase de Paris in 1962. The latter victory provided Winter with probably his finest hour. Mandarin's rubber bit broke at the fourth fence and, for the rest of the four-mile, twisting, figure-of-eight course, Winter rode without brakes or steering.

Andrew Thornton's feat of horsemanship on Kingscliff in the coral.co.uk Handicap Chase at Ascot did not come in one of jumping's major races and, for that reason, seems unlikely to rank historically alongside those of Winter and Brookshaw. However, Thornton's ride on the odds-on Kingscliff was nonetheless remarkable. Thornton was left with one rein after Kingscliff's left rein snapped at the third fence. Kingscliff led from that point, jumping the seventeen remaining fences with unerring accuracy, the left rein flapping against his cheek, and he came home seventeen lengths clear of top weight Horus, stretching right away after the third last. The victory preserved Kingscliff's unbeaten record. He won a ten-runner hunter chase at Wincanton, in addition to three points, before starting a well-backed favourite in the Christie's Foxhunter Chase at Cheltenham as a six-year-old. His stable won the Cheltenham Gold Cup with another ex-hunter Cool Dawn, two seasons after that horse ran second in the Foxhunter, and Kingscliff was being talked about as a Gold Cup contender from the moment he won the Foxhunter.

After Kingscliff's Ascot victory on his reappearance, one major bookmaker initially offered odds of 25/1 about him for the 2004 Gold Cup, but his odds were cut quickly in to 16/1. The initial plan had been to wait another season for a Gold Cup challenge but that idea was scrapped when Kingscliff followed up with another eye-catching display in the Tripleprint Chase, a high quality handicap at Cheltenham in December. Kingscliff made light of being raised 18 lb by the BHB handicapper for his Ascot performance, making mincemeat of his six rivals and stretching clear after the second last without needing to be hard ridden to win by six lengths and the same from Haut Cercy and Marlborough. Kingscliff again jumped well in the main, though getting in too close to the last, and there looked to be plenty more improvement to come. Despite still being very inexperienced, he looked a

Tripleprint Chase (Handicap), Cheltenham—no problems with the tack this time as Kingscliff takes the second last more fluently than Exit To Wave (white face) and Marlborough

top-notcher in the making with the potential to pose a threat to Best Mate in the Gold Cup. A further 12 lb rise in his BHB mark meant Kingscliff had to concede weight away all round for the first time in a handicap in the Peter Marsh Chase at Haydock in January. Set to concede between 15 lb and 20 lb to his four rivals, Kingscliff started at 7/4-on. His supporters knew their fate soon after the second last when the bold-jumping front runner Artic Jack began to draw away again after Kingscliff, despite not jumping so well as usual, briefly looked as though he was going to make a race of it. Kingscliff was discovered afterwards to have had a recurrence of muscular problems thought to have been sustained originally in the Ascot race, probably when veering off a true line and colliding with the running rail when the rein broke. He wasn't seen out again.

Kingscliff (IRE) (b.g. 1997)	Toulon (b 1988)	Top Ville (b 1976)	High Top / Sega Ville
		Green Rock (ch 1981)	Mill Reef / Infra Green
	Pixies Glen (b 1985)	Furry Glen (b 1971)	Wolver Hollow / Cleftess
		How Hostile (b 1977)	Tumble Wind / Pixie Hill

The big, rangy Kingscliff will still be only eight when the next Gold Cup is run and, provided he steers clear of illness and injury, should progress again and may well fulfil the highest expectations entertained for him. A Gold Cup involving him, Strong Flow, Best Mate and possibly Iris's Gift is one to dream about. Kingscliff's pedigree was dealt with fully in *Chasers & Hurdlers 2002/03* and the only update is that his year-older half-brother Mister Felix (by Ore) graduated successfully from bumpers to novice hurdling, winning at Doncaster in January. The usually sound-jumping Kingscliff, who stays three and a quarter miles, has yet to race under rules on going firmer than good. *R. H. Alner*

KINGS COMMAND 7 b.g. Henbit (USA) – Country Festival (Town And Country) [2003/4 F90: 16g^{pu} 16m^4 May 15] good-topped gelding: fair form in 2 bumpers: little show in 2 starts over hurdles, breathing problem second time: third in point in January. *A. King* **h–**

KINGSCOTE THUNDER (IRE) 7 b.g. Montelimar (USA) – Sweet Thunder (Le Bavard (FR)) [2003/4 F83: F17g^2 19g^{pu} Sep 3] bumper winner: best effort when second to Material World at Hereford: every chance when going lame after 3 out in novice at Newton Abbot on hurdling debut. *Noel T. Chance* **h– p**
F99

KING'S CREST 6 b.g. Deploy – Classic Beauty (IRE) (Fairy King (USA)) [2003/4 16s^2 16g^3 17s^5 Feb 11] smallish, sturdy gelding: fair on Flat (probably best up to 13f), well held in 2003: best effort in novice hurdles when 1½ lengths second to Travelling Band at Haydock. *R. A. Fahey* **h96**

KINGSDOWN TRIX (IRE) 10 b.g. Contract Law (USA) – Three of Trumps (Tyrnavos) [2003/4 c–§, h86§: 21f^5 19m^{pu} May 26] workmanlike gelding: no form over fences: modest hurdler: stays 27f: acts on soft and good to firm going: tried blinkered: unreliable. *R. Dickin* **c– §**
h– §

KING'S ECHO 6 b.g. Rakaposhi King – Welgenco (Welsh Saint) [2003/4 F75: F16g^4 F16m^3 23d^2 20d 20s^6 22s^{pu} Jan 10] good-topped gelding: barely modest form when in frame all 4 starts in bumpers: form over hurdles only on debut: stays 23f: tried blinkered. *S. Gollings* **h77**
F77

KING'S ENVOY (USA) 5 b.g. Royal Academy (USA) – Island of Silver (USA) (Forty Niner (USA)) [2003/4 h–: 16d^{pu} Dec 1] leggy gelding: no form over hurdles. *Mrs J. C. McGregor* **h–**

KING'S EQUERRY (IRE) 8 b.g. King's Ride – Tiny Tina (Deep Run) [2003/4 24d* 24s 24v^2 24d^5 Feb 22] IR 26,000 4-y-o: third foal: half-brother to modest hurdler Tina Thyne (by Good Thyne), stays 27f: dam maiden, out of half-sister to top-class 2m to 25f hurdler Daring Run: winning pointer: fair hurdler, lightly raced: won handicap at Navan in November: stays 3m: acts on heavy ground. *M. F. Morris, Ireland* **h111**

KINGSFOLD FREDDIE 6 ch.g. Rock City – Kingsfold Flame (No Loiterer) [2003/4 h–, F84: 21f^2 19s c20m^{pu} c21s^{rtr} c17d^4 Apr 11] strong gelding: form over hurdles only when second of 5 in novice at Warwick: no aptitude for chasing: stays 21f: acts on firm **c– §**
h84 §

going: wore visor/cheekpieces in 2003/4: refused to race fourth outing: one to leave alone: sold 2,800 gns Doncaster May Sales. *P. R. Webber*

KINGS HILL LEADER (IRE) 5 b.g. Supreme Leader – Mary Kate Finn (Saher) **F–**
[2003/4 F16v Jan 31] fifth foal: brother to smart hurdler Fota Island, stays 2½m: dam, maiden on Flat/over hurdles, half-sister to smart hurdler up to 3m Castlekellyleader and useful 2m to 2½m hurdler Cailin Supreme (both by Supreme Leader): joint favourite, seventh of 12 in bumper at Ayr on debut. *J. Howard Johnson*

KING SILCA 7 b.g. Emarati (USA) – Silca-Cisa (Hallgate) [2003/4 16m 17m⁵ 16m⁶ **h–**
22g Jun 13] modest on Flat in 2002, sold out of G. L. Moore's stable £1,200 Ascot August Sales: well held over hurdles. *R. Williams*

KINGSLAND TAVERNER 13 ch.g. True Song – Princess Hecate (Autre Prince) **c–**
[2003/4 c86, h–: c25fᵖᵘ c24g⁴ c24mᶠ Jul 13] stocky gelding: maiden jumper, left **h–**
M. Harris after reappearance: stays 3¼m: acts on firm going, probably on good to soft.
A. W. Carroll

KINGS LINEN (IRE) 8 b.g. Persian Mews – Kings Princess (King's Ride) [2003/4 **h72**
h72: 26m² 26m³ Jul 18] poor novice hurdler: stays 3¼m: acts on good to firm going.
B. I. Case

KINGSMARK (IRE) 11 gr.g. Roselier (FR) – Gaye Le Moss (Le Moss) [2003/4 **c–**
c163, h–: c24g³ c24d⁶ c36d Apr 3] smallish gelding: high-class chaser in 2002/3, won **h–**
Edward Hanmer Memorial Chase (Limited Handicap) at Haydock for third year running:
off due to injured tendon later that season, and looked light of other days on return, remote
ninth of 11 finishers in Grand National at Aintree: stays 3¼m: raced mainly on good
going or softer (acts on heavy): sound jumper: patiently ridden. *M. Todhunter*

KING'S MILL (IRE) 7 b.g. Doyoun – Adarika (Kings Lake (USA)) [2003/4 h109: **h–**
20g Sep 24] leggy gelding: useful at best on Flat (suited by 1¼m), well held in 2 starts in
2003: lightly raced over hurdles, fair form at best: jumped poorly only outing in 2003/4:
has broken blood vessel: sold £1,000 Ascot December Sales. *N. A. Graham*

KINGS MISTRAL (IRE) 11 b.g. Strong Gale – Mrs Simpson (Kinglet) [2003/4 **c131**
c113, h–: c29d* c29dᶠ c24v³ c24s* c24g² c29m⁴ Apr 24] rangy gelding: useful chaser: **h–**
better than ever in 2003/4, winning handicaps at Sandown in December and February:

Agfa Diamond Handicap Chase, Sandown—course specialist Kings Mistral gamely holds off Desailly

made all to beat Desailly ½ length for sixth course success on latter occasion: creditable fourth to Puntal in very valuable handicap there: stays 29f: acts on any going: sound-jumping front runner: genuine. *P. R. Chamings*

KINGSMOOR   8 b.g. Regal Embers (IRE) – Cupids Bower (Owen Dudley) [2003/4   **c88** c–, h–: c25d^pu c24m^pu c20m* c25g^pu c20d Apr 21] twice-raced over hurdles: 80/1 and   **h–** 6 lb overweight, form over fences only when winning handicap at Leicester in March: stays 2½m: acts on good to firm going. *K. Bishop*

KING SOLOMON (FR)   5 gr.h. Simon du Desert (FR) – All Square (FR) (Holst   **h118** (USA)) [2003/4 h114: 16g^3 16d* 17s^2 20v^6 16g^2 21g 17d* 16d^bd Apr 3] close-coupled horse: fairly useful hurdler: favourite, won maiden at Chepstow in December and novice at Bangor in March: better form third to fifth outings: stays 2½m: raced on good ground or softer (acts on heavy): tongue tied last 3 starts. *Miss Venetia Williams*

KING'S OPERA (IRE)   6 b.m. King's Theatre (IRE) – Thrifty's Best (Glenstal   **h124** (USA)) [2003/4 h117: 17g^4 17s^4 16d 16g^3 19s^4 16g 22d^F Apr 12] fairly useful hurdler: won handicap at Killarney in May: generally creditable efforts subsequently: stays 19f: acts on soft and good to firm going. *M. J. Grassick, Ireland*

KING'S REIGN (IRE)   8 ch.g. King's Ride – Lena's Reign (Quayside) [2003/4 h–:   **h63** 26m^5 22g^pu Jun 21] lengthy gelding: poor maiden hurdler on balance. *N. A. Twiston-Davies*

KINGS SQUARE   4 b.g. Bal Harbour – Prime Property (IRE) (Tirol) [2003/4 16d 16d   **h–** 16v^pu 16g 24d^pu Mar 18] half-brother to fair 2m hurdlers Property Zone (by Cool Jazz) and Middlethorpe (by Noble Patriarch): little sign of ability on Flat or over hurdles: tried blinkered. *M. W. Easterby*

KINGSTON-BANKER   8 b.g. Teamster – Happy Manda (Mandamus) [2003/4 c102x,   **c104** h–: c24d* c25g* c23m* Apr 13] sturdy gelding: won 2 of 3 starts in points in 2004:   **h–** successful all 3 outings in novice hunters, at Stratford in March and Wincanton and Exeter (beat Tell Tale 2 lengths) in April: stays 25f: acts on any ground: improved jumper. *Mrs S. Alner*

KINGSTON GAME   5 b.g. Mind Games – Valmaranda (USA) (Sir Ivor (USA))   **h–** [2003/4 h–: 16m^pu May 5] of little account on Flat nowadays: no form over hurdles: tried visored. *Miss K. M. George*

KING'S TRAVEL (FR)   8 gr.g. Balleroy (USA) – Travel Free (Be My Guest (USA))   **c85** [2003/4 c–, h79: 17m^6 c17d* c16g^2 Dec 19] tall, angular gelding: poor hurdler: off 6   **h71** months, won novice handicap at Bangor in November on second start over fences: likely to prove best around 2m: raced mainly on good going or softer. *J. D. Frost*

KING SUMMERLAND   7 b.h. Minshaanshu Amad (USA) – Alaskan Princess   **h–** (IRE) (Prince Rupert (FR)) [2003/4 16s^pu 16m 16d 16s Jan 21] leggy horse: successful 8 times up to 1½m on Flat in Holland and Germany, including at Hamburg in July for J. Pubben: no form over hurdles: looking non-stayer. *C. J. Mann*

KINGSWOOD FOX   9 b.g. Bold Fox – Teye (Mummy's Pet) [2003/4 20m^pu Jun 29]   **h–** no sign of ability in points or on hurdling debut. *Mrs A. M. Thorpe*

KINNESCASH (IRE)   11 ch.g. Persian Heights – Gayla Orchestra (Lord Gayle   **h–** (USA)) [2003/4 24m^pu 20v^6 20m 20m^pu 22g^F Sep 6] small, leggy gelding: winning hurdler, little sign of retaining ability. *P. Bowen*

KINNINO   10 b.g. Polish Precedent (USA) – On Tiptoes (Shareef Dancer (USA))   **h–** [2003/4 h66: 16m^5 May 10] small gelding: poor maiden hurdler: raced around 2m: acts on good to firm ground: has worn cheekpieces: races freely. *G. L. Moore*

KIORA BAY   7 b.g. Karinga Bay – Equasion (IRE) (Cyrano de Bergerac) [2003/4 F–:   **F–** F16g 20v^pu Jan 17] rangy gelding: well held in 2 bumpers: showed little in novice on hurdling debut. *P. D. Niven*

KIPLING   8 b.g. Rudimentary (USA) – Sharmood (USA) (Sharpen Up) [2003/4 h86,   **h–** F81: 25s^pu Dec 3] maiden hurdler: showed little only start in 2003/4: stays 27f: raced only on soft/heavy ground. *Miss S. West*

KIPPANOUR (USA)   12 br.g. Alleged (USA) – Innsbruck (General Assembly (USA))   **c– §** [2003/4 c–§, h90§: 27d^pu 27g^5 24g^5 27d^4 26d^4 26m^4 26m^5 26m* 27d* 26s^pu Nov 22]   **h88 §** smallish gelding: winning chaser: modest hurdler: won handicaps at Huntingdon in September and Sedgefield in October: stayed 27f: acted on firm and soft going: usually blinkered/visored: ungenuine: dead. *A. G. Hobbs*

KIRISNIPPA 9 b.g. Beveled (USA) – Kiri Te (Liboi (USA)) [2003/4 h–: 18m⁴ 19m³ **h–** 22f⁴ 19d Oct 30] lengthy gelding: no form over hurdles: tried blinkered. *W. G. M. Turner*

KIRMAR (IRE) 10 b.g. Montelimar (USA) – Winsome Doe (Buckskin (FR)) [2003/4 **c123** c127, h–: c23g* c22s c22d³ Sep 10] tall gelding: fairly useful handicap chaser: won at **h–** Kilbeggan in July: reportedly broke down when creditable third to Wotsitooya in listed event at Galway in September: stays 3m: acts on heavy going (below form on good to firm): has had tongue tied. *P. A. Fahy, Ireland*

KISMET 6 b.m. Tirol – Belamcanda (Belmez (USA)) [2003/4 21sᵖᵘ 17dᵖᵘ 21d Mar 30] **h–** little form on Flat (for E. Incisa) or in 3 starts over hurdles. *Lady Susan Watson*

KISS ME KATE 8 b.m. Aragon – Ingerence (FR) (Akarad (FR)) [2003/4 h74: 23d⁴ **h67** 21s Dec 26] leggy mare: poor handicap hurdler, lightly raced since 2000/1: stays 2½m: acts on heavy and good to firm going. *Mrs P. Robeson*

KITALE (FR) 6 ch.g. Phantom Breeze – Indjaren (FR) (Argument (FR)) [2003/4 **h– §** 20dᵖᵘ 16dʳᵗʳ May 3] second foal: dam maiden: showed nothing on debut: refused to race next time: one to avoid. *Ferdy Murphy*

KITIMAT 7 b.g. Then Again – Quago (New Member) [2003/4 c62, h74: c20f c25m³ **c73** c21m⁶ c20g⁴ c17s⁶ c22vᵛ c18s³ c22s⁴ c20m⁶ c19gᵖᵘ c16s² Mar 24] rangy gelding: poor **h–** chaser: first win in handicap at Fontwell in January: effective at 2m (given a test), barely at 25f: acts on good to firm and heavy going. *R. H. Buckler*

KITSKI (FR) 6 b.g. Perrault – Macyrienne (FR) (Saint Cyrien (FR)) [2003/4 F16g **F101** F17g² Apr 24] unfurnished ex-Irish gelding: second foal: dam unraced: winning pointer: easily won bumper at Cork in 2002/3: sold out of D. Hassett's stable 84,000 gns Doncaster May Sales: blinkered, hung badly when tailed off in Grade 2 at Newbury (bit reportedly slipped) on reappearance: fairly useful form when head second to Lockstock-andbarrel at Market Rasen. *S. Gollings*

KITTENKAT 10 b.m. Riverwise (USA) – Cut Above The Rest (Indiaro) [2003/4 **c94 x** c90x, h–: c26g⁶ c26g⁴ c32g² c30d³ c33dᵖᵘ c25sᵘʳ c23v³ c26s⁶ c30gᵖᵘ c23s⁴ c26gᵘʳ Apr 10] **h–** lengthy, angular mare: modest maiden chaser: out-and-out stayer: acts on heavy going, possibly not on good to firm: sometimes let down by jumping. *N. R. Mitchell*

KITTE OU DOUBLE (FR) 6 b.g. Agent Bleu (FR) – Briffault (FR) (Olmeto) **c113** [2003/4 c21s⁵ 20g 16s³ 21s³ 22g* Feb 10] good-topped ex-French gelding: third foal: **h106** half-brother to winning chaser up to 2¾m Hard Rock (by Video Rock) and winning hurdler around 2m Jeronymo (by Royal Charter): dam unraced, from family of smart chaser up to 23f Ginetta II: fairly useful chaser: left G. Cherel after reappearance: fair hurdler: won handicap at Market Rasen in February: stays 2¾m: acts on heavy ground. *F. Jordan*

KITTY JOHN (IRE) 7 gr.m. Safety Catch (USA) – La Baladina (Modern Dancer) **h77** [2003/4 20m* Nov 9] ex-Irish mare: fifth foal: winning bumper: poor hurdler: left P. Sinnott, won novice at Worcester only outing in 2003/4: stays 2¾m: acts on good to firm and heavy ground. *J. L. Spearing*

KITTYLEE 5 b.m. Bal Harbour – Courtesy Call (Northfields (USA)) [2003/4 16f⁵ **h62** 16g² 16g⁵ 17d⁶ 16d 16s⁵ 20g Mar 6] half-sister to several winners, including fairly useful 2m hurdler/winning chaser Joshua Tree (by Hello Gorgeous): of no account on Flat: poor form over hurdles: joined G. Kelly. *M. A. Buckley*

KITUHWA (USA) 4 br.g. Cherokee Run (USA) – Ruhnke (USA) (Cox's Ridge **h–** (USA)) [2003/4 17g Apr 12] disappointing after debut on Flat, sold out of J. Gosden's stable 4,000 gns Doncaster October Sales: well beaten in juvenile on hurdling debut. *R. Shiels*

KIVOTOS (USA) 6 gr.g. Trempolino (USA) – Authorized Staff (USA) (Relaunch **h123** (USA)) [2003/4 h102: 20g² 22g* 20d⁴ 24d² 25d⁴ 20v² 20d³ 22g* Apr 16] leggy gelding: fairly useful handicap hurdler: won at Kelso in May and Ayr in April, making all to beat Another Rum a head at latter: stays 3m: raced on good going or softer (acts on heavy): genuine. *A. C. Whillans*

KIWI BABE 5 b.m. Karinga Bay – Sunshine Gal (Alto Volante) [2003/4 F17s² 22d* **h93** 19g⁶ Mar 9] 2,000 4-y-o: small, sparely-made mare: half-sister to fair staying hurdler **F90** Weather Wise (by Town And Country) and winning 2m chaser Sunburnt (by Henbit): dam, winning hurdler who stayed 25f, also 1¼m to 2m winner on Flat: second in mares maiden bumper at Folkestone on debut: modest form when winning mares novice at Wincanton on hurdling debut in February: failed to apply herself fully and looked in need of return to further in similar event final start: will stay 3m. *P. F. Nicholls*

KIWI RIVERMAN   4 b.g. Alderbrook – Kiwi Velocity (NZ) (Veloso (NZ)) [2003/4 **F–**
F16s F16m Mar 11] useful-looking gelding: second foal: half-brother to fair hurdler/
winning chaser Manawanui (by Karinga Bay), stays 2½m: dam, fair hurdler/chaser,
suited by test of stamina: well held in 2 bumpers. *C. L. Tizzard*

KJETIL (USA)   4 b.g. King of Kings (IRE) – I Wich (FR) (Kris) [2003/4 16d⁵ 16s⁶ **h105**
16g Feb 28] good sort: useful on Flat in France, successful twice up to around 1½m at 3
yrs, sold out of C. Laffon-Parias' stable €170,000 Goffs Arc Sale: fair form in juvenile
hurdles, but failed to see race out after going well long way all outings and may have a
problem. *P. F. Nicholls*

KLONDIKE CHARGER (USA)   10 b.g. Crafty Prospector (USA) – Forever Wav- **c95 §**
ing (USA) (Hoist The Flag (USA)) [2003/4 c102§, h–: c17g⁵ c22g c26m c24m² c26m* **h–**
c22f* c26g³ c22g³ c21m⁶ c25f³ c28m³ c18g³ Nov 10] leggy gelding: modest handicap
chaser: successful twice at Fontwell in June, stays 3¼m: ideally suited by good going
or firmer: blinkered once: unreliable. *Dr P. Pritchard*

KNIAZ (FR)   6 gr.g. Saint Preuil (FR) – Alberade (FR) (Un Desperado (FR)) [2003/4 **h110**
h111p: 16d⁵ 18s⁶ 16d Apr 13] workmanlike gelding: fair hurdler: returned to form when
fourth in handicap at Punchestown in late-April: may prove best around 2m: acts on soft
going. *A. J. Martin, Ireland*

KNIFE EDGE (USA)   9 b. or br.g. Kris S (USA) – My Turbulent Miss (USA) (My **c146**
Dad George (USA)) [2003/4 c148, h–: c16g⁶ c22s c20d⁶ c16d³ c17d³ c17s⁴ Jan 18] tall **h–**
gelding: smart chaser, last won in February 2002: in cheekpieces, at least respectable
efforts when in frame behind Beef Or Salmon in Grade 2 at Cork, Moscow Flyer in Grade
2 at Leopardstown and Florida Pearl in Grade 3 at Fairyhouse last 3 starts: stays 2½m:
acts on heavy going, possibly not on good to firm. *M. J. P. O'Brien, Ireland*

KNIGHT GENERAL MAC   5 b.g. Presidium – Agnes Jane (Sweet Monday) [2003/4 **h–**
17m Oct 10] angular gelding: well beaten in 2 maidens on Flat at 3 yrs: always behind in
novice on hurdling debut. *N. Bycroft*

KNIGHT OF SILVER   7 gr.g. Presidium – Misty Rocket (Roan Rocket) [2003/4 **c– §**
h66§: 17g 19m 17m* c16g⁵ c16m⁵ Sep 13] sparely-made gelding: poor hurdler: won **h68 §**
claimer at Newton Abbot (claimed from R. Williams £5,000) in August: well held in
novice chases: probably stays 2¾m: acts on soft and good to firm going: tried in
headgear: has been reluctant to race: not to be trusted. *J. D. Frost*

KNIGHTSBRIDGE KING   8 ch.g. Michelozzo (USA) – Shahdjat (IRE) (Vayrann) **h94**
[2003/4 h89§: 17g³ 22mᵖᵘ 16d³ 17d⁶ 16s² 16s* 17d⁶ 19g⁶ 21d 19g⁴ Apr 18] rather
sparely-made gelding: modest hurdler: sold from A. King £6,000 on reappearance: won
selling handicap at Stratford in December: stays 19f: acts on soft and good to firm going:
tried in headgear. *John Allen*

KNIGHTS CROFT   11 b.g. Henbit (USA) – Bright Tiger-Moth (Funny Man) [2003/4 **c–**
c17dᵘʳ Mar 27] first foal: dam never ran: unseated first in maiden chase on belated debut.
S. T. Lewis

KNOCKANARD (IRE)   12 br.g. Executive Perk – Trianqo (Tarqogan) [2003/4 c24sᵖᵘ **c–**
c21sᵖᵘ Apr 12] tall, sparely-made gelding: winning pointer: no form in steeplechases.
M. J. Gingell

KNOCKDOO (IRE)   11 ch.g. Be My Native (USA) – Ashken (Artaius (USA)) [2003/4 **c– §**
c–§, h104§: 24g⁶ 20g² 20m² Aug 16] good-topped gelding: maiden chaser (doesn't jump **h101 §**
fluently): fair hurdler: stays 27f: acts on good to firm and heavy going: visored once: tried
tongue tied. *J. S. Goldie*

KNOCKNABOOLY (IRE)   5 ch.g. John French – Valiyist (IRE) (Valiyar) [2003/4 **F114**
F17s* F16g⁶ Mar 17] strong, good sort: fourth foal: dam, placed once in bumpers,
half-sister to smart chaser who stayed 3m General Idea: useful form first 2 starts in
bumpers, won at Gowran in February by 3 lengths from Augherskea and 11 lengths sixth
of 24 to Total Enjoyment in Champion Bumper at Cheltenham in March: ran as if amiss
in Grade 1 event at Punchestown in late-April: will stay at least 2½m. *W. P. Mullins,
Ireland*

KNOCKRIGG (IRE)   10 ch.g. Commanche Run – Gaiety Lass (Le Moss) [2003/4 c–, **c–**
h77: 17g 16s² 16g² Mar 10] good-bodied gelding: winning chaser: poor handicap hurdler: **h84**
stays 2½m: acts on any going: blinkered once. *Dr P. Pritchard*

KNOCK STAR (IRE)   13 gr.g. Celio Rufo – Star of Monroe (Derring Rose) [2003/4 **c90 ?**
c25m³ c28d⁴ May 30] leggy gelding: form in steeplechases only when third in novice **h–**

hunter at Wincanton in May, making mistakes: won point in April: stays 25f: acts on firm
and good to soft ground: tried blinkered: has had tongue tied. *S. J. Partridge*

KNOCKTOPHER ABBEY   7 ch.g. Pursuit of Love – Kukri (Kris) [2003/4 h97:   **h89 §**
20m 16g 19m⁴ 20sᵖᵘ 20sᵖᵘ 19dᵖᵘ Mar 15] medium-sized gelding: modest hurdler: went
wrong way temperamentally, leaving Miss V. Williams prior to final start: likely to prove
best at 2m: best efforts on good/good to firm going: tried blinkered/visored: free-going
sort. *B. R. Millman*

KNOWN MANEUVER (USA)   6 b.g. Known Fact (USA) – Northern Maneuver   **h–**
(USA) (Al Nasr (FR)) [2003/4 19g⁶ 20sᵖᵘ 19d 20d Mar 22] poor nowadays on Flat (stays
1½m): little show over hurdles: tried blinkered. *M. C. Chapman*

KNOW THYNE (IRE)   10 ch.g. Good Thyne (USA) – Bail Out (Quayside) [2003/4   **h–**
h–: 20mᵖᵘ May 7] lengthy gelding: won bumper on debut in May 2001: little show since,
including in point. *P. T. Dalton*

KOBYLA   6 ch.m. Moscow Society (USA) – Jalmaid (Jalmood (USA)) [2003/4 F16s   **h–**
F16g F16g F16g 21d 25d³ 24sᵖᵘ Apr 4] smallish mare: first foal: dam winning 2½m hurdler/7f   **F–**
and 1m winner on Flat: probably of little account. *H. Alexander*

KOCK DE LA VESVRE (FR)   6 b.g. Sassanian (USA) – Csardas (FR) (Maiymad)   **c132**
[2003/4 c111§, h–: c16g* c20g³ c20m c19d² c21d⁵ c20g c19s* c19gᵖᵘ c24sᵘʳ c24d* Apr   **h–**
23] leggy, lengthy gelding: useful chaser: won intermediate at Perth in May and handi
caps at Towcester in February and Perth in April: best effort when beating Prominent
Profile ½ length in quite valuable event for final win: stays 3m: acts on heavy going: tried
blinkered in France: has been let down by jumping. *Miss Venetia Williams*

KOHINOR   5 b.m. Supreme Leader – Always Shining (Tug of War) [2003/4 F16s³   **F91**
F18s⁵ F16d² Mar 14] smallish, workmanlike mare: eighth foal: half-sister to fair hurdler/
chaser Altapeter (by Mandalus), stayed 25f, and 3m hurdle winner Frosty Light (by
Glacial Storm): dam unraced half-sister to dam of useful chaser up to 3m Mr Strong Gale:
best effort in bumpers when head second to Fenney Spring in mares maiden at Warwick:
bred to stay much further than 2m. *O. Sherwood*

KOLOMA (FR)   6 b. or br.m. Useful (FR) – Cadoudaline (FR) (Cadoudal (FR)) [2003/4   **h–**
F17g F17d 16gᵖᵘ Dec 5] 2,000 5-y-o: third foal: dam won 3 times up to 13f on Flat in   **F–**
France: no sign of ability. *Miss Kate Milligan*

Press & Journal Handicap Chase, Perth—
outsider of eight Kock de La Vesvre benefits from a fine Sam Thomas ride to beat Prominent Profile (No.8)

KOMBINACJA (POL)   6 ch.m. Jape (USA) – Komancza (POL) (Dakota) [2003/4   **h113**
h99+: 16g* 17d* 16f⁴ 16g⁴ 17d 21m² Apr 15] big, lengthy mare: fair hurdler: won
novices at Stratford in May and Newton Abbot in June: stays 21f: acts on firm and good
to soft going. *T. R. George*

KONFUZIUS (GER)   6 h g. Motley (USA) – Katrina (GER) (Windwurf (GER))   **h–**
[2003/4 h58: 17g May 26] bad maiden hurdler: tried in cheekpieces/blinkers. *P. Monteith*

KONKER   8 ch.g. Selkirk (USA) – Helens Dreamgirl (Caerleon (USA)) [2003/4 h113:   **c92**
16g⁴ 17d 16d* 16s c19g² Feb 6] small, compact gelding: fairly useful handicap hurdler: **h118**
won at Wetherby in December: didn't find much when second in novice at Catterick on
chasing debut: best around 2m on going softer than good: usually held up. *Mrs M. Reveley*

KOQUELICOT (FR)   6 ch.g. Video Rock (FR) – Ixia Des Saccarts (FR) (Laniste)   **c121**
[2003/4 20g⁵ 21v³ 16s c20s* c21d* c20d* c24d⁶ c24g* c24s⁵ Apr 17] leggy ex-French   **h98**
gelding: seventh foal: half-brother to 4 winners, including winning chaser up to 21f
Bacanal des Sacart (by Quart de Vin): dam maiden cross-country chaser: trained prior to
2003/4 by G. Cherel: modest form over hurdles: fairly useful chaser: won handicaps at
Uttoxeter (novice) in December, Wincanton in January, Kempton in February and Taunton in April: stays 3m: raced on good ground or softer (acts on heavy): tried blinkered:
jumps soundly. *P. J. Hobbs*

KORAKOR (FR)   10 ch.g. Nikos – Aniflore (FR) (Satingo) [2003/4 c137, h–: c20d³   **c128 d**
c21m³ c20mᶠ c17g c21d⁴ c16d c21gᶠ Apr 2] good-topped gelding: fairly useful handicap   **h–**
chaser: below form after second start: best up to 21f: acts on good to firm and heavy
going. *Ian Williams*

KORELO (FR)   6 b.g. Cadoudal (FR) – Lora du Charmil (FR) (Panoramic) [2003/4   **c124 x**
c126+, h137: c17g⁴ c20m³ c16g³ c16s⁶ c18gᵖᵘ 21g 20g 21m³ 20m* Apr 24] workmanlike   **h136**
gelding: fairly useful chaser, though largely let down by jumping over fences in Britain:
useful handicap hurdler: won quite valuable event at Sandown by length from Xellance:
likely to stay beyond 21f: acts on good to firm and heavy going: poor efforts when
visored. *M. C. Pipe*

KOSMIC LADY   7 b.m. Cosmonaut – Ktolo (Tolomeo) [2003/4 h66: 16m Sep 13]   **h–**
poor maiden 2m hurdler: has had tongue tied. *P. W. Hiatt*

KOSMOS BLEU (FR)   6 ch.g. Franc Bleu Argent (USA) – Fee du Lac (FR) (Cimon)   **h96**
[2003/4 19g² 19dᵘʳ 20sᵖᵘ 21g⁵ Feb 28] tall ex-French gelding: first foal: dam never ran:
12.5f winner on Flat at 4 yrs, sold out of A. Lacombe's stable €12,000 Goffs July Sale:
second in novice hurdle at Exeter on British debut: no form in similar events subsequently: tongue tied final start. *R. H. Alner*

KOTKIJET (FR)   9 b.g. Cadoudal (FR) – Kotkie (Rheffic (FR)) [2003/4 c21s*   **c167**
c22s* c22s* c27sᶠ c22v* 18s* c22s² Apr 12]   **h145**
    A couple of months after Best Mate won his third Cheltenham Gold Cup,
his French counterpart Kotkijet won his second Grand Steeple-Chase de Paris,
three years after his first win in France's most important race over fences. Had
injury not intervened, Kotkijet might himself now have three wins to his name in
the race, maybe even four. The two editions of the Grand Steeple-Chase which
Kotkijet had been forced to sit out were certainly the poorer without him. Neither
the subsequently-disqualified Double Car in 2002, nor the mare Line Marine in
2003, were any better than very smart performers, and both won substandard
renewals. With the other top French-trained chasers of recent seasons, First Gold
and Jair du Cochet, concentrating on British campaigns, there was every chance of
Kotkijet re-establishing himself as the top chaser at Auteuil when he returned after
being kept off the track by tendonitis, assuming of course that he retained the ability
that had won him the 2001 Grand Steeple-Chase as an up-and-coming six-year-old.
    The field for the latest Grand Steeple-Chase was surprisingly large, sixteen
runners the most to go to post since 1986. Though Kotkijet might have been
expected to frighten off much of the opposition, there was good place money on
offer. No fewer than a dozen in the field were aged either six or seven, though the
younger brigade lacked a contender who looked good enough, or progressive
enough, to trouble Kotkijet. The two senior runners, Rougenoir and Urga (a
thirteen-year-old contesting his sixth Grand Steeple), had both seen better days,
while Batman Senora had managed only a place in the two substandard renewals
which Kotkijet had missed. Incidentally, the Ian Williams-trained Batman Senora
contributed to more Anglo-Irish interest in the race than usual. The Irish-trained

Montayral, third in the Betfred Gold Cup last time out, also took part, as did the Francois Cottin-trained Kamillo who had raced in Ireland during his trainer's stint in that country before moving back to France. Jingle Rose had won a selling hurdle for Philip Hobbs when last seen in Britain, but subsequently had made into a useful chaser in France and won Auteuil's most prestigious handicap chase, the Prix du President de La Republique, on his most recent outing.

Despite the large field, Kotkijet was made the 2/1-on favourite on the pari-mutuel and turned in a performance which made the race every bit as one-sided as the betting suggested. He won in typical style too, his rider biding his time on the first circuit before taking up the running heading into the back straight for the final time, jumping fluently. Setting a gallop which gradually left his rivals toiling—only Jerico Vallis was still giving chase turning out of the back straight—Kotkijet stretched clear once in line for home, Thierry Majorcryk checking over his shoulder after the last before celebrating victory well before the winning post, Kotkijet eventually coasting home ten lengths clear. Rank outsiders Kamillo (116/1), Majadal (83/1) and Sun Storm (112/1) reached the frame behind him, but Jerico Vallis, who had looked the second-best horse in the race, fell at the last when an exhausted fourth, paying for the effort of keeping tabs on Kotkijet longer than most.

The Grand Steeple-Chase was Kotkijet's seventh win since his return to action almost twelve months earlier. He had won twice in the summer of 2003, including the listed Prix Rigoletto, and then gained a couple of bigger successes in the autumn in the Group 3 Prix Heros XII and the Group 2 Prix Georges Courtois, winning the latter race in most imposing fashion and with any amount in hand from his stable-companion Turkish Junior. Kotkijet returned in the spring with a win over hurdles and had warmed up for the Grand Steeple-Chase with an easy victory over outsider Princelou, Jerico Vallis and Turkish Junior in the Group 3 Prix Ingre in May.

Even though he dominated the chasing scene at Auteuil in the latest season, there were two occasions when lapses from Kotkijet allowed lesser rivals to profit. The first came in the top chase of the autumn season, the Prix La Haye Jousselin, in which he was bidding for a tenth consecutive success. Normally a fine jumper, the big water jump, the riviere des tribunes, caught him out, Kotkijet suffering the first fall of his career while the race went to Batman Senora. Kotkijet also suffered a

Prix Heros XII, Auteuil—Kotkijet leads narrowly from Kotkita over the last

Gras Savoye Grand Steeple-Chase de Paris, Auteuil—
on his way to a second win in France's biggest race

shock defeat at the hands of his patently inferior stable-companion Turkish Junior in the Prix Murat in April. There were extenuating circumstances though. Kotkijet returned without a shoe and after breaking a blood vessel following a mistake at the wall early in the race. Unable to impose his usual searching gallop as a result, Kotkijet ended up being beaten into second place in a muddling contest in which little more than a couple of lengths covered the first five home.

Three weeks after the Grand Steeple-Chase, Kotkijet attempted an historic double when contesting the Grande Course de Haies d'Auteuil, the 'French Champion Hurdle'. Only three horses had won both the Grand Steeple-Chase and Grande Course de Haies before, most recently Ubu III in the 'nineties. Kotkijet was bidding to be the first to accomplish the feat in the same year, though before 1998 the two races were run closer together than they are currently. Kotkijet ran up to his best hurdling form in finishing third to the Irish-trained Rule Supreme but, with less emphasis on jumping ability, plus a steady pace under less testing conditions than usually prevail at Auteuil, Kotkijet was unable to stretch his rivals, being headed after the last.

Chasing is Kotkijet's game, and the Grand Steeple-Chase will be his main target again in 2005. He is approaching veteran status by French standards and horses as old as ten have a poor record in the race. The ten-year-old El Paso III was awarded the race in 2002 but otherwise no horse older than nine has won since Mandarin in 1962. That said, it is hard to see from where a challenger might emerge to prevent Kotkijet's winning for a third time. The unbeaten Cyrlight could prove a threat, though he has yet to be tested against older rivals or to prove that he stays beyond two and a half miles; it also takes a really good five-year-old to win the Grand Steeple-Chase.

One who did win the race as a five-year-old was the outstanding chaser Katko (by Carmarthen), a half-brother to Kotkijet, who went on to complete a hat-trick of wins in the race. Katko ran in the colours of his breeder, Comte Pierre de Montesson, who turned down what he described as a large offer from the late Daniel Wildenstein after Katko had made a winning debut over hurdles. Relations between Montesson's stud, the Haras des Coudraies, and Daniel Wildenstein remained close, however, and in 1996 Wildenstein bought a batch of the stud's yearlings. Among them was Kotkijet, and so too, incidentally, were three young-sters who went on to make a name for themselves in Britain; Katarino (from the same family as Kotkijet), Geos and Carlovent. In a lengthy stud career, Kotkie, who died in 2002, the dam of Katko and Kotkijet, also produced Kotkito, a brother to Kotkijet, who was a leading chaser as a four-year-old, as well as the useful chaser Kitko and smart hurdler/chaser Kasako (both by Tip Moss). Kotkie was restricted to just six outings over hurdles, but she won four of them, and she had two runs on the Flat, on one occasion finishing second to the future Arc winner Detroit. Kotkie produced just two daughters at stud, both of whom went straight to the paddocks without racing. The elder of the pair, Kakira (also by Cadoudal), has herself already made an excellent start as a broodmare. Her first foal, Kotkita, won six of her first seven starts over hurdles, including the Group 1 event for three-year-olds, the Prix Cambaceres. Kotkita showed useful form over fences in the latest season too, finishing second to her 'uncle' Kotkijet in the Prix Heros XII. On the same card, Kotkita's half-sister Kitka capped a remarkable day for the family when winning the hurdle for three-year-olds.

		Green Dancer	Nijinsky
	Cadoudal (FR)	(b 1972)	Green Valley
	(br 1979)	Come To Sea	Sea Hawk II
Kotkijet (FR)		(gr 1971)	Camarilla
(b.g. 1995)		Rheffic	Traffic
	Kotkie	(b 1968)	Rhenane
	(ch 1977)	Matamine	Tamanar
		(ch 1964)	Ma Zine

Kotkijet has little left to prove at Auteuil, so what are the chances of his racing in Britain? Pretty slim, one would think, reading Alec Wildenstein's comments in *Paris Turf* after the Prix Georges Courtois in November. 'The reason for not wanting Kotkijet to race in England? Quite simply because the English do not

Ecurie Wildenstein's "Kotkijet"

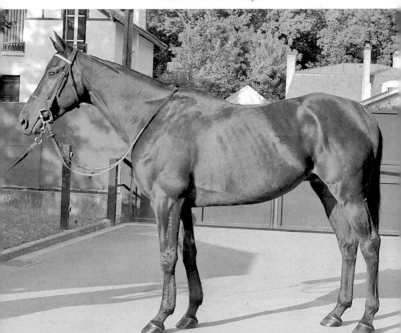

deserve to see such a good jumper over their fences, you can quote me on that.' (The last time a British racecourse had been graced by the presence of a Wildenstein jumper had been in the 1980 Champion Hurdle, in which the dual winner of the Grande Course de Haies Paiute trailed in last of nine runners behind Sea Pigeon.) However, there have been a little more encouraging noises from connections since then. After Kotkijet's return over hurdles in the spring, his trainer, Jean-Paul Gallorini, was quoted in the same paper as saying that an adventure to England at some stage in the future was 'not impossible'. On the same page, an article reported that the trainer had recently attended the Cheltenham Festival and was planning to have runners in Britain in the next season. There was also some encouragement to be gleaned from a larger than usual number of Wildenstein-owned Flat horses contesting races in Britain in the first half of the year. Perhaps the Wildensteins realised that 2004 was the centenary of the signing of the *entente cordiale*, though Alec Wildenstein became embroiled in controversy again on his latest visits to Epsom and Royal Ascot. Of course, even if connections are happy with the idea of letting Kotkijet run in Britain, he presumably would not be risked on ground that was considered too firm. If Kotkijet is not seen out in Britain, racegoers here will not only miss seeing a good jumper, but a most impressive physical specimen too. The almost-black Kotkijet is a lengthy gelding and very powerfully-built—in the words of the French press 'une veritable force de la nature'. He stays twenty-nine furlongs, the longest distance he is ever likely to tackle, and has raced mainly on soft or heavy going. Kotkijet is a top-class chaser, the best at Auteuil by quite some way at present, and he looks sure to win more good races there. *J-P. Gallorini, France*

KOUMBA (FR)   6 b.g. Luchiroverte (IRE) – Agenore (FR) (Le Riverain (FR)) **h71**
[2003/4 h–, F–: 16m 16g³ 20v⁶ May 26] signs of ability (including in points) only when third in amateur selling hurdle at Uttoxeter in May: should stay beyond 2m. *B. N. Pollock*

KOUROS DES OBEAUX (FR)   6 b.g. Grand Tresor (FR) – Valse Des Obeaux (FR) **c86**
(Pot d'Or (FR)) [2003/4 c19d* c19f² c20s⁶ c26sᶠ c26g² c25g³ c23d Mar 23] angular **h–**
ex-French gelding: third foal: half-brother to winning cross-country chaser Helios des Obeaux (by Art Bleu): dam won 2¾m cross-country chase: lightly-raced maiden on Flat: fair maiden hurdler: won 5-y-o non-thoroughbred event at Angers in May on chasing debut, final outing for J. Barbe: modest form at best in Britain: barely stays 3¼m: acts on heavy going (looked ill at ease on firm): tried blinkered, visored last 4 outings: temperament under suspicion. *M. C. Pipe*

KOYAANISQATSI   4 ch.g. Selkirk (USA) – Bogus John (CAN) (Blushing John **h69**
(USA)) [2003/4 16g 16s 16s² 21dᵖᵘ Apr 11] leggy, angular gelding: reluctant to enter stall and well held in 1m maiden only start on Flat: form over hurdles only when second in claimer at Plumpton in March: likely to prove best around 2m. *Jamie Poulton*

KRACH (FR)   6 b.g. Lute Antique (FR) – Voilette (FR) (Brezzo (FR)) [2003/4 h121p: **h120**
24s* Dec 20] very tall gelding: unbeaten in 3 starts on Flat: also showed plenty of ability all 3 starts over hurdles, won 3m novice at Ascot by 10 lengths from Material World: put down after breaking a leg on gallops in February. *F. Doumen, France*

KRACK DE L'ISLE (FR)   6 b.g. Kadalko (FR) – Ceres de L'Isle (FR) (Bad Conduct **h–**
(USA)) [2003/4 h111, F92: 23s Feb 14] lengthy gelding: fair hurdler: stiff task, always behind in handicap only outing in 2003/4: should stay 3m: raced on going softer than good (acts on heavy): sometimes takes strong hold. *A. C. Whillans*

KRISTAL FOREST (IRE)   5 b.g. Charnwood Forest (IRE) – Kristal's Paradise **h68**
(IRE) (Bluebird (USA)) [2003/4 17m³ Jun 18] fair maiden on Flat (stays 12.4f) at 3 yrs for J. Dunlop, well beaten last 5 starts in 2003: third of 6 in intermediate at Southwell on hurdling debut. *Mrs S. Lamyman*

KRISTINEAU   6 ch.m. Cadeaux Genereux – Kantikoy (Alzao (USA)) [2003/4 h–: **h83**
20d⁴ 17d³ 20s⁵ Apr 21] leggy mare: poor maiden hurdler: stays 2½m: tongue tied last 2 starts. *Mrs E. Slack*

KRISTOFFERSEN   4 ch.g. Kris – Towaahi (IRE) (Caerleon (USA)) [2003/4 16g³ **h104 d**
16d 16gᵘʳ 16s 17dᶠ Mar 15] compact gelding: fairly useful on Flat (stays 1½m), sold out of G. Butler's stable 14,000 gns Newmarket Autumn Sales: third in juvenile at Kempton on hurdling debut: failed to repeat that form, claimed £7,400 final start. *R. M. Stronge*

KROISOS (IRE) 6 b.g. Kris – Lydia Maria (Dancing Brave (USA)) [2003/4 h71: 21s[4] **c76** 25s[4] 22g[6] c26s[pu] c24v[pu] c24g c24d[2] c26g* c26g[2] Apr 22] workmanlike gelding: poor **h60** maiden hurdler: similar form over fences, won handicap at Plumpton in April: stays 3¼m: acts on soft going: blinkered last 4 starts. *R. Curtis*

KUNG HEI FAT CHOI (IRE) 9 b.g. Roselier (FR) – Gallant Blade (Fine Blade **c95 x** (USA)) [2003/4 c88x, h–: c25d[pu] c24s* c24g[2] c24g[pu] c24d[3] c25s[pu] Dec 26] modest **h–** handicap chaser: won at Perth (hung badly left run-in) in May: stays 25f: acts on heavy going, probably unsuited by good to firm: usually makes mistakes. *J. S. Goldie*

KUSTOM KIT GRIZZLY (IRE) 9 br.g. Be My Native (USA) – Bridgetown Girl **c–** (Al Sirat) [2003/4 c23g[5] Mar 12] tall gelding: maiden hurdler: fairly useful pointer, **h–** successful in January: no show in maiden hunter chase: stays 3m: acts on good to soft going: tried blinkered/visored. *Mrs F. Kehoe*

KWAHERI 6 b.m. Efisio – Fleeting Affair (Hotfoot) [2003/4 17g Apr 10] half-sister to **h–** 4 winners over jumps, including useful hurdler/fair chaser Rudi Knight (by Rudimentary), stays 21f: fair maiden at 2 yrs, little show on Flat in 2001: well beaten in mares maiden on hurdling debut. *Mrs P. N. Dutfield*

KYLIE TIME (IRE) 7 ch.g. Good Thyne (USA) – Miss Kylogue (IRE) (Lancastrian) **h85** [2003/4 h–, F79: 19g 17d[pu] 16d[3] Apr 23] lengthy gelding: easily best effort over hurdles when third in maiden at Perth: reportedly broke blood vessel time before. *P. Beaumont*

KYLKENNY 9 b.g. Kylian (USA) – Fashion Flow (Balidar) [2003/4 h89p: 16m Dec **h–** 4] good-topped gelding: fairly useful on Flat (stays easy 1½m): lightly raced over hurdles: tongue tied, reportedly had breathing problem only start in 2003/4. *H. Morrison*

KYMANDJEN (IRE) 7 b.g. Un Desperado (FR) – Marble Miller (IRE) (Oats) [2003/4 **c122** 17s 16s[3] c22m* c24d[F] c20d* c24d[2] Dec 27] angular gelding: fifth foal: half-brother to **h108** useful hurdler/fair chaser up to 3m Like A Lion (by Farhaan): dam unraced sister to fairly useful staying chaser Folly Road: twice-raced in points: bumper winner: fair hurdler: successful first 2 completed starts in steeplechases, maiden at Thurles in November and handicap at Punchestown in December: further improvement when second of 28 to World Wide Web in very valuable handicap at Leopardstown later in December, but last of 7 finishers in valuable novice handicap at Punchestown (excitable beforehand) in late-April: stays 3m: acts on good to firm and heavy going. *Paul Nolan, Ireland*

KYMANI PRINCE (IRE) 8 b.g. Shernazar – Best of British (Young Generation) **h71** [2003/4 h100: 16m[5] 16d[F] Dec 1] rather leggy gelding: lightly raced over hurdles, fair form at best: fell fatally at Kelso. *L. Lungo*

KYMBERLYA (FR) 6 ch.g. Esteem Ball (FR) – Catty Douce (FR) (Cadoudal (FR)) **h113** [2003/4 h100: 16v[4] 20m* 20m[su] Jun 18] lengthy, angular gelding: fair form over hurdles: won maiden at Worcester in June: fatally injured there later in month: stayed 2½m: best efforts on good to firm ground: visored last 2 starts. *M. C. Pipe*

KYNANCE COVE 5 b.g. Karinga Bay – Excelled (IRE) (Treasure Kay) [2003/4 **h–** F16m F16m 17s 21g[pu] 20g 16g Apr 18] compact gelding: first foal: dam won around 11f: **F–** no form in bumpers/over hurdles. *C. P. Morlock*

L

LAAZIM AFOOZ 11 b.g. Mtoto – Balwa (USA) (Danzig (USA)) [2003/4 c83, h94: **c–** c27m c26m[3] c27d[5] Oct 29] smallish gelding: winning hurdler/chaser: showed little over **h–** fences in 2003/4: stays 27f: acts on firm and good to soft going (possibly unsuited by soft/ heavy): usually wears cheekpieces: tongue tied: not a fluent jumper of fences. *R. T. Phillips*

LABELTHOU (FR) 5 b.m. Saint Preuil (FR) – Suzy de Thou (FR) (Toujours Pret **h102** (USA)) [2003/4 19s[4] 18d 18s[4] 16g[2] 16d[6] Jan 10] ex-French mare: eighth foal: half-sister to middle-distance winner Helathou (by Video Rock): dam, won up to 11f on Flat, out of half-sister to top-class staying chaser Otage du Perche: twice-raced on Flat: fair form over hurdles: left G. Cherel after third start: raced mainly around 2m. *F. Jordan*

LABULA BAY 10 b.g. Sula Bula – Lady Barunbe (Deep Run) [2003/4 c85, h–: c25d[2] **c101** c23g c24g[3] c23m[3] c26g* c28d[F] c25m* Apr 13] fair handicap chaser: won at Fontwell **h–**

(made all) in March and Exeter in April: stays 3¼m: acts on good to firm and soft going: tried blinkered: has jumped none too fluently: has flashed tail. *B. G. Powell*

LACDOUDAL (FR) 5 gr.g. Cadoudal (FR) – Belfaster (FR) (Royal Charter (FR)) [2003/4 17s^F 16v* 16g* 16g 17s² 17m⁴ Apr 15] smallish, angular gelding: fourth foal: closely related to 2 winners by Kadalko, including fair chaser Idealko, stays 2½m: dam winning chaser up to 19f: 11f winner on Flat: fairly useful novice hurdler: won at Pau (4-y-o event, final outing for F. Nicolle) in December and Kempton (beat Fool On The Hill 4 lengths) in March: found little final start: likely to stay 2½m: raced mainly on good going or softer. *P. J. Hobbs* **h123**

LADALKO (FR) 5 b.g. Kadalko (FR) – Debandade (FR) (Le Pontet (FR)) [2003/4 c16d* c20s^F c16g^{F2} c16g² Mar 25] tall, useful-looking gelding: first foal: half-brother to middle-distance winner Mount Cook (by Gold And Steel): dam winning hurdler/chaser up to 21f in France: once-raced on Flat: fair form when second in 4-y-o event on hurdling debut at Auteuil in 2002/3 for G. Cherel: won maiden at Folkestone impressively on chasing debut in January: let down by jumping subsequently, upsides Bambi de L'Orme when both fell 2 out in novice at Huntingdon third start: should stay beyond 2m. *P. F. Nicholls* **c116 h–**

LADIES FROM LEEDS 5 b.m. Primitive Rising (USA) – Keldholme (Derek H) [2003/4 F16g F16s Feb 7] eighth foal: sister to fair hurdler around 2m Marmaduke Jinks: dam lightly-raced maiden pointer: well held in 2 bumpers. *A. Crook* **F–**

LADYALDER 6 br.m. Alderbrook – Ina's Farewell (Random Shot) [2003/4 F17g^{pu} May 13] 2,300 3-y-o, 5,000 4-y-o: closely related to 2 winners by Ardross, fairly useful hurdler/fair chaser Ardrina, stayed 3¼m, and modest chaser Our Tommy, stays 2½m, and half-sister to 2 winning pointers: dam unraced: showed nothing in bumper on debut. *L. J. Williams* **F–**

LADY ALDERBROOK (IRE) 4 b.f. Alderbrook – Madame President (IRE) (Supreme Leader) [2003/4 F16g aF16g Apr 4] leggy, angular filly: second foal: dam, modest hurdler, stayed 21f: well held in 2 bumpers. *C. J. Down* **F–**

LADY ARNICA 5 b.m. Ezzoud (IRE) – Brand (Shareef Dancer (USA)) [2003/4 h78: 26g^{pu} c22d^{pu} c24d^{pu} Apr 12] lengthy mare: maiden hurdler/chaser, showed nothing in 2003/4. *A. W. Carroll* **c– h–**

LADY AT LEISURE (IRE) 4 ch.f. Dolphin Street (FR) – In A Hurry (FR) (In Fijar (USA)) [2003/4 16v^{pu} 18s^{pu} Jan 26] showed nothing in 2 races over hurdles: won on Flat in April for M. Ryan. *Julian Poulton* **h–**

LADY BARONETTE 7 b.m. Baron Blakeney – Rueful Lady (Streetfighter) [2003/4 c23m^{ur} Apr 13] sixth foal: half-sister to winning hurdler/chaser around 2m Thistle Princess (by Belfort) and winning 2m hurdler Flaming Cheek (by Blushing Flame): dam, winning hurdler, stayed 21f: won maiden point in March: behind when unseating last in novice hunter. *Andrew J. Martin* **c–**

LADY BLAZE 5 ch.m. Alflora (IRE) – Lady Elle (IRE) (Persian Mews) [2003/4 F16g Mar 17] 4,000 3-y-o: second foal: half-sister to 21f hurdle winner Afro Man (by Commanche Run): dam unraced: well beaten in bumper on debut. *Mrs G. Harvey* **F–**

LADY BOB BACK 7 br.m. Bob Back (USA) – Whimbrel (Dara Monarch) [2003/4 h79: 20g⁶ 21v⁴ 24v^{pu} c20g^{ur} c21s^F 24g 17d c21g⁵ Apr 12] lengthy mare: poor maiden hurdler/chaser: should be suited by 3m+: acts on heavy going: tried in cheekpieces/tongue tied: inconsistent, and temperament under suspicion. *M. A. Barnes* **c70 h66**

LADY BOUNCER 6 b.m. Milieu – Superior Maid (Gay Fandango (USA)) [2003/4 F16m^{pu} F16d Mar 14] eighth foal: half-sister to fair 6f winner Dallying (by Dalsaan): dam poor maiden on Flat: ran as if amiss both starts in bumpers, trained on debut by C. Grant. *G. F. Bridgwater* **F–**

LADY BUSTED 9 b.m. Almoojid – Sindos (Busted) [2003/4 16s^{pu} Feb 22] third on first of 2 starts in bumpers in 1999 for J. Neville: showed little in novice hurdle on return. *D. Burchell* **h–**

LADY DYNAMITE 4 b.f. Glacial Storm (USA) – Lady Elle (IRE) (Persian Mews) [2003/4 F16s² F17m Apr 15] leggy filly: third foal: half-sister to 21f hurdle winner Afro Man (by Commanche Run): dam unraced: modest form in mares bumpers at Towcester and Cheltenham, travelling well long way both times: will be suited by more of a test of stamina. *H. D. Daly* **F82**

LAD

LADY FELIX 9 br.m. Batshoof – Volcalmeh (Lidhame) [2003/4 c85, h83+: c23m⁴ May 10] small mare: fair hurdler in 2000/1: modest form both starts in novice chases: better at 3m than shorter: acts on good to firm and good to soft going. *R. H. Alner* **c91 h–**

LADY GLYDE 4 b.f. Inchinor – Happy And Blessed (IRE) (Prince Sabo) [2003/4 16fᵖᵘ Oct 16] poor maiden on Flat (stays 1¼m): showed nothing on hurdling debut. *A. D. Smith* **h–**

LADY GODSON 5 ch.m. Bold Arrangement – Dreamy Desire (Palm Track) [2003/4 F16s F17d Apr 18] half-sister to fair hurdler/chaser Ingletonian (by Doc Marten), stays 2¾m, and ungenuine 1¼m seller winner Ghylldale (by Sweet Monday): dam modest maiden at 2 yrs: well held in 2 bumpers. *B. Mactaggart* **F–**

LADY HARRIET 5 b.m. Sir Harry Lewis (USA) – Forever Together (Hawaiian Return (USA)) [2003/4 F16s F16s 16s* 16d 16gᵖᵘ 16g Apr 18] leggy mare: fifth foal: half-sister to bumper winner Always Wayward (by Terimon): dam well beaten in juvenile hurdle: well held in 2 bumpers: best effort in novice hurdles when winning mares event at Plumpton in February: raced at 2m. *N. J. Gifford* **h86 F–**

LADY HECCLES 5 b.m. Sayaarr (USA) – Rae Un Soleil (Rushmere) [2003/4 F17s Jan 20] first foal: dam no sign of ability: tailed-off last in maiden bumper and 1m maiden on Flat. *M. R. Hoad* **F–**

LADY INCH 6 b.m. Inchinor – Head Turner (My Dad Tom (USA)) [2003/4 h–: 16gᵖᵘ Oct 24] little form on Flat, none over hurdles: tried visored/in cheekpieces. *J. A. Supple* **h–**

LADY IN COMMAND (IRE) 4 b.f. In Command (IRE) – Harmer (IRE) (Alzao (USA)) [2003/4 17mᵖᵘ 17mᵖᵘ Oct 10] workmanlike filly: no form on Flat for R. Beckett: showed more temperament than ability in 2 juvenile hurdles. *Mrs J. Candlish* **h–**

LADY JANAL 6 gr.m. Sir Harry Lewis (USA) – Mrs Dawson (Sharrood (USA)) [2003/4 F16d⁴ 16g 16m 20g⁶ 22d⁶ 24dᶠ 21v³ 20v⁵ 24s 21d³ 21d Mar 30] 3,200 4-y-o: medium-sized mare: fourth foal: dam 1m winner: well-beaten fourth in mares bumper on debut: poor maiden hurdler: stays 21f: raced mainly on good going or softer (acts on heavy). *Miss S. E. Forster* **h69 F–**

LADY LAMBRINI 4 b.f. Overbury (IRE) – Miss Lambrini (Henbit (USA)) [2003/4 F14g Nov 25] leggy filly: first foal: dam modest 2m maiden hurdler: showed little in 3-y-o bumper on debut. *Mrs L. Williamson* **F–**

LADY LAP DANCER 6 b.m. Shareef Dancer (USA) – Jelabna (Jalmood (USA)) [2003/4 h85: 20f⁵ 21fᵖᵘ Oct 8] modest hurdler: bought out of Mrs M. Reveley's stable 1,000 gns Doncaster August Sales: lame final start: will stay beyond 2¾m: acts on heavy going. *R. C. Harper* **h–**

LADY LAUREATE 6 b.m. Sir Harry Lewis (USA) – Cyrillic (Rock City) [2003/4 h110?: 22m² 21g³ 19m² Oct 18] small mare: disappointing maiden over hurdles: failed to impress with attitude all 3 starts in 2003/4: should stay 3m. *G. C. Bravery* **h78 §**

LADY LIGHTHOUSE 6 b.m. Alhijaz – Fairfield's Breeze (Buckskin (FR)) [2003/4 F–: F16m F16gᵖᵘ Dec 11] no form in 3 bumpers. *R. J. Price* **F–**

LADY LOLA (IRE) 6 b.m. Supreme Leader – Regents Prancer (Prince Regent (FR)) [2003/4 F17v⁴ F16d F16s⁶ Apr 12] €10,000 4-y-o: fourth foal: sister to useful bumper winner Supreme Hill: dam, lightly-raced pointer, from family of useful 2m to 2½m chaser Prayukta: signs of only a little ability in mares bumpers: sold 3,000 gns Doncaster May Sales. *C. J. Mann* **F–**

LADY MARANZI 5 b.m. Teenoso (USA) – Maranzi (Jimmy Reppin) [2003/4 16g⁶ 19d Feb 15] 1,500 3-y-o: sixth foal: dam, winning 2½m hurdler/fair 2m chaser, out of half-sister to useful staying jumpers Graphics Solar, Tartan Takeover and Tartan Tyrant: better effort in mares novice hurdles when sixth at Towcester. *Mrs D. A. Hamer* **h73**

LADY MATADOR 5 b.m. El Conquistador – Slashing (Broadsword (USA)) [2003/4 F16v⁵ Jan 9] first foal: dam unraced half-sister to useful hunter chaser Matchplay: showed little in bumper on debut. *Mrs Jane Galpin* **F–**

LADY MERCURY 6 b.m. Rock Hopper – Bellezza (Ardross) [2003/4 h–: 16g⁴ 16f⁶ 19d 16dᵖᵘ 16s Jan 23] leggy mare: of little account: tried blinkered/visored: has had tongue tied. *S. C. Burrough* **h–**

LADY NETBETSPORTS (IRE) 5 b.m. In The Wings – Auntie Maureen (IRE) (Roi Danzig (USA)) [2003/4 h–: 19f* 20d 20g Jan 7] leggy mare: form over hurdles only when **h75**

520

dead-heating in mares maiden at Catterick in November, making running: stays 19f: acts on firm going. *B. S. Rothwell*

LADY OF FORTUNE (IRE) 5 b.m. Sovereign Water (FR) – Needwood Fortune (Tycoon II) [2003/4 F17s* F16n Mar 13] rather unfurnished mare: sixth foal: half-sister to 2 winners by Rolfe, notably top-class hurdler around 2½m Lady Rebecca, and fairly useful bumper winner Brankley Boy (by Afzal): dam unraced sister to useful staying chasers Tartan Takeover and Tartan Tyrant: odds on, won mares bumper at Taunton on debut in January: favourite, quickly beaten 3f out in valuable similar event at Sandown. *N. J. Henderson*   **F93**

LADY OF THE ISLE (IRE) 6 b.m. Aristocracy – Smurfette (Baptism) [2003/4 F16g F16v F16s⁶ 17g Apr 1] IR 18,000 3-y-o: medium-sized mare: sister to fair jumper up to 25f River Unshion and half-sister to fair 2m hurdler Over The Jordan (by Over The River): dam unraced: modest form at best in bumpers, left G. Balding and off 8 months after debut: no show on hurdling debut. *B. D. Leavy*   **h–**   **F78**

LADY RACQUET (IRE) 5 b.m. Glacial Storm (USA) – Kindly Light (IRE) (Supreme Leader) [2003/4 F–: F17s³ F16s F17m⁵ Apr 15] angular mare: modest form in bumpers. *Mrs A. J. Bowlby*   **F84**

LADY SHANAN (IRE) 4 b.f. Anshan – Cothill Lady (IRE) (Orchestra) [2003/4 F16d Mar 25] 5,000 3-y-o: sixth foal: half-sister to winning hurdler Market Scan (by King's Ride), stays 25f, and bumper winner Lesson Well (by Lord Americo): dam unraced, from family of Night Nurse: last of 11 in bumper on debut. *D. A. Rees*   **F–**

LADY SOLRSKI 7 b.m. Petoski – Flaxen Tina (Beau Tudor) [2003/4 h–: c20gᵖᵘ May 24] little sign of ability. *A. C. Whillans*   **c–**   **h–**

LADY STRATAGEM 5 gr.m. Mark of Esteem (IRE) – Grey Angel (Kenmare (FR)) [2003/4 h82d: 20fᵖᵘ 16f⁵ 16m⁶ 16g⁵ 16g⁴ 16s 16g⁶ 19g⁵ Feb 6] close-coupled mare: won juvenile on hurdling debut in 2002/3, little form since: raced mainly at 2m: acts on good to firm going: temperament under suspicion. *E. W. Tuer*   **h62**

LADY WARD (IRE) 6 b.m. Mujadil (USA) – Sans Ceriph (IRE) (Thatching) [2003/4 h87§: 17d⁴ 17g* 17gᵖᵘ 16d 19d 22gᵖᵘ Dec 18] poor hurdler: won amateur selling handicap at Newton Abbot in June: left S. Burrough after next outing: stays 2½m: acts on soft and good to firm going: tried blinkered: ungenuine (often reluctant at start). *P. R. Rodford*   **h77 §**

LADY WEST 4 b.f. The West (USA) – Just Run (IRE) (Runnett) [2003/4 16dᵖᵘ Mar 21] little form on Flat: showed nothing on hurdling debut (tongue tied). *Dr J. R. J. Naylor*   **h–**

LADY WURZEL 5 b.m. Dilum (USA) – Fly The Wind (Windjammer (USA)) [2003/4 F17g 16gᵖᵘ Dec 11] second foal: dam winning staying hurdler/chaser: no sign of ability. *W. S. Kittow*   **h–**   **F–**

LADY ZEPHYR (IRE) 6 b.m. Toulon – Sorimak Gale (IRE) (Strong Gale) [2003/4 F17s³ F16s* Apr 12] fifth foal: half-sister to 2½m hurdle winner Trail Storm (by Supreme Leader): dam unraced: ran 4 times in Irish points, won maiden in January: promising start in mares bumpers, won at Fakenham in April by distance from Maggie Gray. *N. A. Twiston-Davies*   **F106 +**

LAFAYETTE (IRE) 6 b.h. General Monash (USA) – Bezee (Belmez (USA)) [2003/4 h118: 16g³ 17g 16d³ 17f⁴ Aug 26] good-topped horse: fairly useful handicap hurdler: good fourth to Liscahill Hill in listed event at Tralee final outing: raced around 2m: acts on firm and good to soft going. *R. J. Osborne, Ireland*   **h124 +**

LA FOLICHONNE (FR) 5 b.m. Useful (FR) – Allure Folle (FR) (Kenmare (FR)) [2003/4 F16d F16s³ Apr 12] second foal: half-sister to winning chaser up to 19f Baltic Bay (by Caerwent): dam won up to 11f on Flat in France: better effort in bumpers when third in mares event at Fakenham: sold 10,000 gns Doncaster May Sales. *M. C. Banks*   **F74**

LA GANADORA 5 b.m. El Conquistador – Discipline (Roman Warrior) [2003/4 F17s Jan 22] second foal: dam ran once: showed little in mares bumper on debut. *J. White*   **F–**

LAGANSIDE (IRE) 11 b.g. Montelimar (USA) – Ruby Girl (Crash Course) [2003/4 c–§, h–: c25g⁶ c25g⁴ c26dᵖᵘ Apr 23] lengthy gelding: fair chaser at one time: winning pointer, including in March: little show in hunters: stays 3m: unraced on firm going, acts on any other: tried visored: has had tongue tied: unreliable. *J. F. W. Muir*   **c79 §**   **h–**

LAGER DASH 6 b.g. Suave Dancer (USA) – Padelia (Thatching) [2003/4 F–: F17g Oct 27] no show in 2 bumpers. *R. J. Price*   **F–**

LAGGAN BAY (IRE) 4 b.g. Alzao (USA) – Green Lucia (Green Dancer (USA)) [2003/4 16m Dec 10] half-brother to 2 winning hurdlers, notably useful up to 25f Ravens-   **h73**

wood (by Warning): fairly useful on Flat (stays 1½m) for R. Hannon: seventh of 11 in juvenile at Newbury on hurdling debut. *J. C. Fox*

LAGGAN MINSTREL (IRE) 6 b.g. Mark of Esteem (IRE) – Next Episode (USA) h–
(Nijinsky (CAN)) [2003/4 17g^{pu} 16d^{pu} Apr 8] poor on Flat (stays 1m) nowadays: pulled
up in 2 selling hurdles. *B. Llewellyn*

LAGO 6 b.g. Maelstrom Lake – Jugendliebe (IRE) (Persian Bold) [2003/4 16d 17s⁴ h87
22g² 24v⁶ 22d² Apr 5] compact gelding: modest maiden hurdler: missed 2002/3: stays
2¾m: acts on heavy going: wore visor/cheekpieces last 4 starts. *James Moffatt*

LAGO D'ORO 4 b.f. Slip Anchor – Salala (Connaught) [2003/4 F13g⁴ F17s² F16s³ F88
Apr 4] workmanlike filly: eighth foal: half-sister to several winners, including fairly
useful hurdler Mindanao (by Most Welcome), stays 2¾m, and fairly useful hunter My
Nominee (by Nomination), stays 3m: dam, 7f winner, half-sister to smart 2m hurdler Bold
Boss and smart 7f to 1¼m performer Beau Sher: best effort in bumpers when second at
Sedgefield in February: sold 34,000 gns Doncaster May Sales. *Miss J. A. Camacho*

LAGO NAM (FR) 5 gr.g. Cardoun (FR) – Rivalago (FR) (Grey Dawn II) [2003/4 19g h–
19s 16d^{pu} Jan 17] fifth foal: half-brother to winner up to 2½m Riazzino (by Always Fair):
dam runner-up over 11f: no form in 3 novice hurdles. *M. C. Pipe*

LAGOSTA (SAF) 4 ch.g. Fort Wood (USA) – Rose Wine (Chilibang) [2003/4 17g³ h83
17g⁵ 16g² 16f³ 17m⁴ 16g² Nov 2] workmanlike gelding: little form on Flat for W. Haggas:
modest juvenile hurdler: acts on good to firm going. *G. M. Moore*

LAIRD DARA MAC 4 b.c. Presidium – Nishara (Nishapour (FR)) [2003/4 17m⁶ h–
16g⁵ 17g^{pu} Apr 12] angular colt: little sign of ability on Flat or over hurdles. *N. Bycroft*

LAKE 'O' GOLD 5 ch.m. Karinga Bay – Ginka (Petoski) [2003/4 20d⁵ 19f⁶ 20m⁵ h–
24d⁶ Apr 21] modest maiden at best on Flat (stays 13f), sold out of J. Mullins' stable
£1,500 Ascot August Sales: little encouragement over hurdles. *D. W. Thompson*

LAKESIDE LAD 12 b.g. St Columbus – Beyond The Trimm (Trimmingham) c71
[2003/4 c96, h–: c23m^{pu} c21m⁵ c26g³ Aug 4] tall gelding: winning chaser: poor form in h–
handicaps in 2003/4: stays 3¼m: acts on good to firm and good to soft going: has run
creditably in blinkers: refused to race once. *P. A. Blockley*

LALAGUNE (FR) 5 b.m. Kadalko (FR) – Donatella II (FR) (Brezzo (FR)) [2003/4 h109
16d³ 17d⁵ 16v* 16s² 16g^F 22g³ Mar 25] good-topped mare: second foal: half-sister to
2003 3-y-o winner Magloire (by Ragmar): dam, French 1½m winner, out of half-
sister to smart French chaser Gabion: unplaced in 2 outings on Flat in French Provinces
at 3 yrs for E. Augonnet: fair novice hurdler: won mares event at Uttoxeter in January:
effective at 2m to 2¾m: acts on heavy going. *A. King*

LA LANDIERE (FR) 9 b. or br.m. Synefos (USA) – As You Are (FR) (Saint Estephe c149
(FR)) [2003/4 c156, h–: c20s⁴ c24g⁶ c21d³ c21d⁶ Mar 18] rangy mare: one of the leading h–
novice chasers of 2002/3, winning 7 races: easily best effort in 2003/4 when third to
Hunters Tweed in valuable handicap at Cheltenham: stayed easy 3m: acted on soft and
good to firm going: usually raced prominently: sound jumper: died at stud shortly after
being retired. *R. T. Phillips*

LA LUNA (IRE) 7 b.m. Gothland (FR) – Diane's Glen (Furry Glen) [2003/4 F75: h98
F17m* 17m 19f³ 22f* 22f⁵ 20s⁵ Nov 17] best effort in bumpers when winning at Market F84
Rasen in June: modest form over hurdles, easily won conditional jockeys novice at Kelso
in October: stays 2¾m, should be at least as effective at shorter: acts on firm going, poor
efforts on soft. *Noel T. Chance*

LA MAGO 4 b.f. Wizard King – Dancing Dancer (Niniski (USA)) [2003/4 F16d F17v F–
Mar 21] second foal: dam winning hurdler up to 19f: well beaten in bumpers.
F. P. Murtagh

LA MARETTE 6 ch.m. Karinga Bay – Persistent Gunner (Gunner B) [2003/4 h74: h83
19m 16g 16d⁴ 19s⁴ 16s* 19g Apr 18] sturdy mare: poor hurdler: won 19-runner selling
handicap (sold from R. Hodges 9,000 gns) at Towcester in February: should prove as
effective around 2½m as 2m: acts on firm and soft going: tried tongue tied. *John Allen*

LAMBHILL STAKES (IRE) 6 gr.g. King's Ride – Summerhill Express (IRE) h89
(Roselier (FR)) [2003/4 h100, F84: 20g⁴ 25g 24g² 24v⁴ 20s⁵ 23d⁶ Apr 12] rangy, rather
unfurnished gelding: modest maiden hurdler: should stay beyond 3m: raced on good
going or softer over hurdles (acts on heavy): races freely. *J. M. Jefferson*

LAMBRINI BIANCO (IRE) 6 br.g. Roselier (FR) – Darjoy (Darantus) [2003/4 c–
F90: 20v^{pu} 24g c17d⁵ Mar 27] tall gelding: bumper winner: no show in novice hurdles or h–
maiden chase: should be suited by 2½m+. *Mrs L. Williamson*

LAMBRINI GOLD 10 b.g. Gildoran – Fille de Soleil (Sunyboy) [2003/4 c99, h–: 21v^pu c20s^pu c16s^pu c24d^pu Mar 10] big gelding: novice hurdler/winning chaser, pulled up all starts in 2003/4: should stay beyond 2½m: raced on going softer than good (acts on heavy): tried tongue tied/blinkered. *D. McCain* **c–/h–**

LAMBRINI MIST 6 gr.g. Terimon – Miss Fern (Cruise Missile) [2003/4 h–, F–: 20g^pu Jun 22] little sign of ability prior to winning both starts in points in 2004: tried in cheekpieces. *Mrs L. Williamson* **h–**

LAMBRINI PRINCE 10 b.g. Derrylin – Flying Faith (Rymer) [2003/4 c22s^5 c24g c32d^pu c24d^pu c26d^F Apr 11] tall gelding: maiden chaser: no form in 2003/4: stays 3¼m: raced on good going or softer (acts on heavy): tried blinkered. *Mrs L. Williamson* **c–/h–**

LAMP'S RETURN 5 ch.m. Bob's Return (IRE) – Lampstone (Ragstone) [2003/4 F18g^3 Feb 22] unfurnished mare: tenth foal: half-sister to several winners, notably smart 2m chaser Martin's Lamp (by Martinmas) and useful chaser Hurricane Lamp (by Derrylin), stays 3m: dam, novice hurdler/chaser, half-sister to useful 2m hurdler Red Power: clear signs of inexperience when 2¼ lengths third of 8 to Countess Point in mares bumper at Fontwell on debut. *A. King* **F95**

LA MUETTE (IRE) 4 b.f. Charnwood Forest (IRE) – Elton Grove (IRE) (Astronef) [2003/4 16v^pu 16s^pu 16s^5 17d Mar 10] tall filly: fairly useful at best on Flat (stays 1¼m), sold out of Mrs A. Perrett's stable 9,000 gns Doncaster November Sales, has lost her form: poor from over hurdles: will prove best around 2m: possibly not straightforward. *M. Appleby* **h71**

LAMZIG 5 b.g. Danzig Connection (USA) – Lamsonetti (Never So Bold) [2003/4 17g Aug 8] little form on Flat: well held in novice on hurdling debut. *M. Todhunter* **h–**

LANCASHIRE LASS 8 b.m. Lancastrian – Chanelle (The Parson) [2003/4 h55: 22m^2 22g^F 22g 22g^6 21m^ur 24m^3 22g^6 24s c20m^4 Mar 4] poor maiden hurdler: distant fourth of 5 finishers in mares novice at Ludlow on chasing debut: stays 3m: acts on firm going: tried blinkered: possibly best making running: inconsistent. *J. S. King* **c77/h80**

LANCASTRIAN JET (IRE) 13 b.g. Lancastrian – Kilmurray Jet (Le Bavard (FR)) [2003/4 c121: c25d* c25d* c25g* c25s^ur Apr 11] rangy gelding: fairly useful hunter chaser nowadays: favourite, won at Hereford in February and Towcester and Market Rasen in March: stays 4m: acts on heavy going: raced right-handed nowadays: front runner: sound jumper. *H. D. Daly* **c107**

LANCE (IRE) 6 b.g. Old Vic – Gaye Le Moss (Le Moss) [2003/4 F18d* Dec 21] tenth foal: half-brother to 4 winners, notably one-time high-class staying chaser Kingsmark (by Roselier): dam, bumper winner, half-sister to top-class 2m to 3m hurdler Gaye Brief and very smart staying jumper Gaye Chance: won bumper at Thurles on debut by 2½ lengths from Sans Souci Boy. *N. Meade, Ireland* **F100**

LANCIER D'ESTRUVAL (FR) 5 ch.g. Epervier Bleu – Pommette III (FR) (Trac) [2003/4 F16g* F17s 16s 16g 21d^pu Mar 25] ninth foal: half-brother to several winners, including fairly useful chasers around 3m Jaloux d'Estruval (by Kadalko) and Fan d'Estruval (by Quart de Vin) and fair 2m chaser Dame d'Estruval (by Mistigri): dam, winning chaser up to around 3m, half-sister to high-class staying chaser Sabre d'Estruval: won weak bumper at Uttoxeter on debut in October: showed nothing after, including in 3 novice hurdles. *J. C. Tuck* **h–/F75**

LANDESCENT (IRE) 4 b.g. Grand Lodge (USA) – Traumerei (GER) (Surumu (GER)) [2003/4 17g^4 Apr 16] half-brother to fairly useful hurdler Vrin (by Mukaddamah), stays 3m: modest on Flat (stays 1½m), successful twice in 2004: fourth to easy winner Fontanesi in juvenile at Taunton on hurdling debut. *Miss K. M. George* **h73**

LAND ROVER LAD 6 ch.g. Alflora (IRE) – Fililode (Mossberry) [2003/4 F17d F17s 21g 24g^pu 21s^4 23s^pu Apr 4] medium-sized gelding: fifth foal: half-brother to fair hurdler/chaser Filscot (by Scottish Reel), stays 3m, and winning pointer by Rakaposhi King: dam poor maiden hurdler: poor form in bumper on debut: form over hurdles only when fourth in novice at Plumpton: should stay 3m: virtually ran out second start over hurdles. *C. P. Morlock* **h90 ?/F70**

LANGCOURT JESTER 6 ch.m. Royal Vulcan – Singing Clown (True Song) [2003/4 F–: F16m 21g Nov 25] workmanlike mare: little sign of ability. *S. J. Gilmore* **h–/F–**

L'ANGE AU CIEL (FR) 5 b.g. Agent Bleu (FR) – Epopee II (FR) (Comrade In Arms) [2003/4 c17g* Dec 5] second foal: half-brother to 12.5f winner Kape Bleue (by Art Bleu): dam 12.5f winner in France: twice-raced at Pau for J. P. Totain, winning 1½m **c117 p/h–**

event on Flat and 4-y-o hurdle: favourite, maintained unbeaten record in novice chase at Exeter on British debut, responding well to lead close home and beat Keltic Bard a short head: looked sure to improve and win more races, but reportedly chipped a bone and missed rest of season. *P. F. Nicholls*

LANGHAM LAKE   7 b.g. Endoli (USA) – Birbrook Girl (Henricus (ATA)) [2003/4   h–
19v^F 17g^{ro} 24m Mar 4] first foal: dam never ran: no show over hurdles: ran out early second start. *K. Bishop*

LANHEL (FR)   5 ch.g. Boston Two Step (USA) – Umbrella (FR) (Down The River   F84
(FR)) [2003/4 F16s F16g Jan 24] 6,000 4-y-o: workmanlike gelding: third foal: half-brother to French middle-distance winner Iroise III (by Garde Royale): dam won 3 times up to around 1½m on Flat: better effort in bumpers when seventh of 23 to Premium First in maiden at Wetherby, tending to hang left: looked still more of a tricky ride next time. *J. Wade*

LANICENE (FR)   5 b.g. Moon Madness – Ocylla (FR) (Medford (FR)) [2003/4 F16s   F–
Mar 13] fifth foal: half-brother to 21f chase winner Dalecene (by Neustrien): dam, won 2½m cross-country chase: always well behind in bumper on debut. *Ferdy Murphy*

LANMIRE GLEN (IRE)   7 b.g. Jurado (USA) – Cool Glen (Furry Glen) [2003/4   c110
c93, h–: c20v³ c22s⁵ c28d* c28d* c29d^{pu} Apr 12] fair chaser: won handicaps at Limerick   h–
in February and Downpatrick in March: stays 3½m: acts on soft going, bumper form on good to firm. *F. Flood, Ireland*

LANMIRE TOWER (IRE)   10 b.g. Celio Rufo – Lanigans Tower (The Parson)   c– §
[2003/4 c122§, h–: c24d⁵ c32m^{pu} c24g^{pu} c24d^{pu} Apr 12] workmanlike gelding: fairly   h–
useful handicap chaser in 2002/3, has lost his form completely: stays 4m: acts on heavy and good to firm going: tried visored, blinkered nowadays: has jumped markedly right: no easy ride. *S. Gollings*

LANNKARAN (IRE)   11 b.g. Shardari – Lankarana (Auction Ring (USA)) [2003/4   c106
c–, h–: c24d c21s³ c24d⁴ c24d⁴ c24v^{pu} Apr 4] useful-looking gelding: fair handicap   h–
chaser: stays 3m: acts on soft and good to firm going: tried blinkered. *H. D. Daly*

LANOS (POL)   6 ch.g. Special Power – Lubeka (POL) (Milione (FR)) [2003/4 h78:   h84
16d² Apr 11] smallish, angular gelding: fair on Flat: poor form over hurdles: should stay beyond 17f: acts on good to soft and good to firm going: tried blinkered: has had tongue tied: has looked far from keen. *Miss S. West*

LANTERN LAD (IRE)   8 b.g. Yashgan – Lantern Lass (Monksfield) [2003/4 c26s⁵   c–
Dec 3] IR 7,500 4-y-o: ex-Irish gelding: fourth foal: half-brother to winning hurdler/   h–
chaser Party Lad (by King's Ride), stays 25f, and winning pointer by Be My Native: dam fairly useful 2m hurdler/winning chaser: poor maiden hurdler: no form in steeplechases: left M. Hourigan, won maiden point in 2003: bought 1,000 gns Doncaster May Sales: tried blinkered. *R. Ford*

LANTERN LEADER (IRE)   9 b.g. Supreme Leader – Lantern Line (The Parson)   c89
[2003/4 c106, h117: c23f⁴ c22s⁵ c24d 24d^{pu} c25f² c18m 24d* 24d^{pu} c24g⁵ c24g³ c24g⁵   h102
c27s c32d⁶ 18g Mar 28] fairly useful hurdler at best: sold out of M. Hourigan's stable 6,200 gns Doncaster October Sales after sixth outing: won conditional jockeys claimer at Ayr following month: largely disappointing over fences: stays 25f: acts on firm and soft going: effective blinkered or not, also tried in cheekpieces. *Miss Lucinda V. Russell*

LANTY SLEE (IRE)   5 b.g. Supreme Leader – Tell A Tale (Le Bavard (FR)) [2003/4   F71
F16g⁵ Sep 25] €25,000 3-y-o: fourth foal: dam winning hurdler: around 25 lengths fifth of 12 in bumper at Perth on debut: sold 3,500 gns Doncaster November Sales. *N. G. Richards*

LANZLO (FR)   7 b. or br.g. Le Balafre (FR) – L'Eternite (FR) (Cariellor (FR))) [2003/4   h92
h102d: 17g³ 19g² 16g 17m⁶ 20g* 17d⁴ Feb 23] small, angular gelding: modest handicap hurdler: won at Perth in August: stays 2½m: acts on any going. *James Moffatt*

LAOUEN (FR)   6 br.g. Funny Baby (FR) – Olive Noire (FR) (Cadoudal (FR)) [2003/4   h124
h124p, F109: 16m 18g* May 22] leggy gelding: fairly useful form and successful on 5 of 6 starts over hurdles, last win in intermediate at Kelso, doing well to get up to beat Showpiece a neck in tactical affair: will stay 2½m: has won on heavy (in bumper) and good to firm going: reported in mid-October to have met with training setback. *L. Lungo*

LAPADAR (IRE)   5 b. or br.m. Woodborough (USA) – Indescent Blue (Bluebird   h–
(USA)) [2003/4 19d³ 19g 21v^{pu} Jan 13] medium-sized mare: fairly useful at best on

all-weather Flat (stays 1¾m), little form since 3 yrs: well beaten on completed starts over hurdles. *J. R. Weymes*

LA PERROTINE (FR)   4 b.f. Northern Crystal – Haratiyna (Top Ville) [2003/4 F16g² F17g⁶ Mar 28] 54,000 3 y o: seventh foal: half-sister to several winners, including 21f chase winner Harithabad (by Ela-Mana-Mou) and fairly useful hurdler Harapour (by Valanour), stays 2¾m: dam 1m winner: better effort in bumpers when 4 lengths second of 18 to Reel Missile at Doncaster. *J. Howard Johnson*   **F92**

L'ARCHER   6 b.g. Lancastrian – Sailors Joy (Handsome Sailor) [2003/4 F18s⁶ F17s aF16g⁶ 16s 16dᵖᵘ 19g Apr 24] second foal: dam never ran: signs of only a little ability: tongue tied last 4 starts. *A. E. Jessop*   **h–**
F71

LARKHILL JO (IRE)   7 gr.g. Roselier (FR) – Blake's Beauty (Sexton Blake) [2003/4 16d² 16s⁴ 18d⁵ 16d* 16d² 16d 16d* 18d⁵ 16s 16d Apr 10] fairly useful handicap hurdler: won at Galway in August and Punchestown in December: best at 2m: raced mainly on going softer than good (acts on heavy): blinkered once: races prominently. *Brian Nolan, Ireland*   **h115**

LA ROSE   4 b.f. Among Men (USA) – Marie La Rose (FR) (Night Shift (USA)) [2003/4 16m² 16g⁵ 16g² 17d⁵ Mar 27] sturdy filly: half-sister to winning hurdler/chaser around 2m Contemporary Art (by Blushing Flame): poor maiden on Flat (stays easy 1½m): poor form in juvenile hurdles. *J. W. Unett*   **h77**

LARSSARTO (GER)   6 b.h. Lomitas – Lady Shepard (GER) (Shepard (GER)) [2003/4 16d⁴ 24s Feb 3] angular horse: useful on Flat (stays 1¾m), successful 5 times, including at Bad Harzburg in July, Ghlin (on sand) in August and Merano in September: none too fluent when well held in novice hurdles at Wetherby and Taunton. *C. Von Der Recke, Germany*   **h81**

L'ARTISTE BELLEVUE (FR)   5 b.g. Start Fast (FR) – Enus du Manoir (FR) (Le Nain Jaune (FR)) [2003/4 F16g Mar 27] leggy gelding: first foal: dam unraced: well held in bumper at Newbury on debut. *Jean-Rene Auvray*   **F–**

LASCAR DE FERBET (FR)   5 br.g. Sleeping Car (FR) – Belle de Ferbet (FR) (Brezzo (FR)) [2003/4 F17s⁵ F16g³ F17d Mar 27] 20,000 4-y-o: fifth foal: half-brother to winning 2½m hurdler Hakim de Ferbet (by Bad Conduct) and minor 2¼m chase winner Gazoute de Ferbet (by Trebrook): dam unraced half-sister to very smart chaser up to 2½m Ferbet Junior: fair form in bumpers first 2 starts, third to Qualitair Pleasure at Ayr: bolted before start and run best ignored at Bangor 2 weeks later: sold 32,000 gns Doncaster May Sales. *L. Lungo*   **F90**

LASKARI (FR)   5 b.g. Great Palm (USA) – Hatzarie (FR) (Cyborg (FR)) [2003/4 16d Dec 29] first foal: dam unraced, out of half-sister to dam of smart staying hurdler/chaser Tito L'Effronte: trained by S. D. Kalley, thrice-raced on Flat in France, runner-up twice up to 1½m: took strong hold when mid-field in 17-runner novice at Newbury on hurdling debut. *Mrs L. C. Taylor*   **h97**

LASQUINI DU MOULIN (FR)   5 gr.g. Saint Preuil (FR) – Api (FR) (El Badr) [2003/4 F19g² F20d³ 18d⁴ 20s² 20s* 20d² 20s⁴ Mar 14] fourth foal: half-brother to 11.5f winner Isapi du Moulin and 13f winner Kaline du Moulin (both by Royal Charter): dam unraced: won at Naas in August on first of 2 starts in bumpers: fair hurdler: made all in maiden at Clonmel in February: creditable placed efforts in minor events at Down Royal later in month and Punchestown in early-May: raced mainly around 2½m: acts on soft and good to firm going. *W. P. Mullins, Ireland*   **h111**
F91

LAST OF THE GALES (IRE)   10 b.m. Strong Gale – Red Celtic (Celtic Cone) [2003/4 c25m² May 9] has run tubed: successful twice in points in 2003: 1¾ lengths second to Red Brook Lad in novice hunter at Wincanton: stays 25f: acts on good to firm going. *Mrs Caroline Keevil*   **c86**
h–

LAST REBEL (IRE)   5 b.g. Danehill (USA) – La Curamalal (IRE) (Rainbow Quest (USA)) [2003/4 h–: 16g 16dᵖᵘ Apr 11] leggy gelding: no form over hurdles. *R. T. Phillips*   **h–**

LATALOMNE (USA)   10 ch.g. Zilzal (USA) – Sanctuary (Welsh Pageant) [2003/4 c162, h119: c16g⁴ c16f² 17m⁵ c16g³ 16d⁴ c16sᵖᵘ 16g c16d c16g Apr 1] leggy gelding: fairly useful hurdler: useful chaser on balance: has gone wrong way temperamentally, left B. Ellison after sixth outing: stays easy 21f: acts on good to firm and good to soft going, probably on soft: tried blinkered/visored: usually races prominently: joined N. Wilson. *M. C. Pipe*   **c144 d**
h128

LATE CLAIM (USA)   4 ch.g. King of Kings (IRE) – Irish Flare (USA) (Irish River (FR)) [2003/4 16g 16d⁵ 16g* 16g⁴ 16d Mar 28] good-topped gelding: fairly useful on Flat   **h96**

(should stay 1¾m), sold out of B. Hills's stable 23,000 gns Newmarket Autumn Sales: fair juvenile hurdler: won at Kempton in February by head from Glencoyle, final outing for I. Williams: visored second start. *N. J. Henderson*

LATEFA (IRE)   4 ch.f. Among Men (USA) – Kraemer (USA) (Lyphard (USA)) [2003/4 F16g Mar 27] angular filly: half-sister to several winners, including fairly useful 1999 2-y-o 7f winner Dancing Mirage (by Machiavellian) and dam of smart performer in Britain/Hong Kong up to 1½m Housemaster: dam, successful up to 9f in France/USA, half-sister to very smart French miler Shaanxi: last of 18 in bumper at Newbury on debut. *Mrs L. C. Taylor*   **F–**

LATENSAANI   6 b.g. Shaamit (IRE) – Intoxication (Great Nephew) [2003/4 h113: c16m* May 27] leggy gelding: fair hurdler: off 6 months, won novice at Hexham on chasing debut: stays 21f: acts on firm going, possibly not on good to soft. *G. M. Moore*   **c90**
h–

LATITUDE (FR)   5 b.m. Kadalko (FR) – Diyala III (FR) (Quart de Vin (FR)) [2003/4 c18d⁵ c20s* c20d³ c22sᶠ c20s⁶ c19g* c22d* Mar 21] ex-French mare: second foal: half-sister to 2¼m chase winner Jump Out (by Lights Out) and 1½m winner Musique Classique (by Video Rock): dam, maiden jumper, sister to outstanding French chaser Ucello II: 1¼m winner on Flat: fair hurdler/chaser: won 4-y-o chase at Auteuil in June and, after being sold out of T. Civel's stable €60,000 Goffs November Sale, novice chases at Exeter and Fontwell in March: beat Luneray 3 lengths in mares event at last-named: stays 2¾m: acts on soft ground: tried blinkered. *M. C. Pipe*   **c116 +**
h–

LAUDAMUS   6 ch.g. Anshan – Faint Praise (Lepanto (GER)) [2003/4 F18v⁶ Jan 12] fifth foal: half-brother to winning pointer by Lochnager: dam unraced, out of half-sister to very smart staying chaser Special Cargo: sixth of 15 in maiden bumper at Fontwell on debut. *R. H. Alner*   **F69**

LAUDERDALE   8 b.g. Sula Bula – Miss Tullulah (Hubble Bubble) [2003/4 c109, h–: c17g³ c17d⁵ c22g² c20m³ c20d⁴ c17s² c22v² c22g⁴ c24g c31dᵖᵘ Apr 22] good-topped gelding: fair handicap chaser: best at 3m, effective at much shorter: acts on heavy going, possibly not on good to firm: usually front runner. *Miss Lucinda V. Russell*   **c103**
h–

LAUNDMOWER   8 br.g. Perpendicular – Sound Work (Workboy) [2003/4 h–: 21sᵖᵘ 20g² 20g² May 24] poor form over hurdles: stays 2½m: joined R. Bastiman. *Mrs S. J. Smith*   **h79**

LAURAS GIRL   6 b.m. Sir Harry Lewis (USA) – Starlight Wonder (Star Appeal) [2003/4 F17g Mar 28] first foal: dam poor hurdler who stayed 21f: behind in mares bumper on debut. *O. O'Neill*   **F–**

LAURIER D'ESTRUVAL (FR)   5 ch.g. Ragmar (FR) – Grive d'Estruval (FR) (Quart de Vin (FR)) [2003/4 18s² c18g³ 25dᵖᵘ Mar 14] first foal: dam unraced: winner around 1½m on Flat: fair form when runner-up both starts over hurdles in France: third in 4-y-o event at Le Pin Au Haras on chasing debut: left G. Macaire and upped in trip, no show in novice hurdle at Warwick. *S. E. H. Sherwood*   **c?**
h106

L'AVENTURE (FR)   5 b. or br.m. Cyborg (FR) – Amphitrite (FR) (Lazer (FR)) [2003/4 18sᵖᵘ 18d* 18d⁴ c17s² c17s² c19s² c16m² c16gᶠ c20d* c19s* c20s² c24g⁴ c25g² c25m² Apr 14] leggy, angular mare: first foal: dam winning cross-country chaser: fair hurdler: successful 3 times, including in 4-y-o claimer at Auteuil in June (left R. Chotard after next start): fairly useful chaser: left Y. Porzier after seventh outing: won maiden at Ludlow (simple task) and novice at Doncaster (beat Don Fernando 17 lengths) in January: in frame in graded events next 3 starts: stays 25f: acts on good to firm and heavy going: usually blinkered: has had tongue tied: hard ride. *P. F. Nicholls*   **c119**
h107

LA VITA E BELLA (FR)   5 b.m. Le Nain Jaune (FR) – Fontaine Aux Faons (FR) (Nadjar (FR)) [2003/4 F16f⁴ 17s Mar 23] sixth foal: half-sister to 3 winners, including one-time smart hurdler/useful chaser Cadougold (by Cadoudal), stays 3m, and ungenuine but fairly useful hurdler/winning chaser up to 3m Hugo de Perro (by Perrault): dam maiden: showed nothing in bumper (for M. Pipe) or novice selling hurdle. *G. F. H. Charles-Jones*   **h–**
F–

LAWAHIK   10 b.g. Lahib (USA) – Lightning Legacy (USA) (Super Concorde (USA)) [2003/4 h–: 20sᵘʳ May 2] smallish gelding: one-time fairly useful handicap hurdler around 2m: very lightly raced nowadays, no form since 2000/1. *T. H. Caldwell*   **h–**

LAWBOUND (IRE)   6 b.g. Topanoora – Balela (African Sky) [2003/4 F16m Jul 9] half-brother to several winners, including fair 2½m hurdler Bellroi (by Roi Danzig) and fair 2m to 3m hurdler/chaser To-day To-day (by Waajib): dam unraced, from family of very smart middle-distance stayer Top Class: pulled hard after starting slowly when well beaten in bumper on debut. *P. J. Hobbs*   **F–**

LAWMAN 6 b. or br.g. Afzal – Discipline (Roman Warrior) [2003/4 F16g F17s Dec 20] smallish, plain gelding: first live foal: dam ran once: little show in 2 bumpers. *J. White* F–

LAW UNTO HIMSELF 6 b.g. Contract Law (USA) Malacanang (Riboboy (USA)) [2003/4 h–: 19s c19d^F Jan 1] no sign of ability: tried in cheekpieces/blinkers. *N. J. Hawke* c–
h–

LAYASAR 4 br.g. Wizard King – Rasayel (USA) (Bering) [2003/4 F13v^2 F16d^3 F16v Jan 24] second foal: dam fair 1¼m to 1¾m winner, became unreliable: fair form when placed first 2 starts in bumpers. *W. M. Brisbourne* F92

LAZERITO (IRE) 6 b.g. Shernazar – Nemova (IRE) (Cataldi) [2003/4 F16v* 20s* 25d^2 Mar 14] IR 5,800 3-y-o, €11,000 4-y-o, resold €11,500 4-y-o: first foal: dam unraced, from family of useful hurdler who stayed 2½m Tyrolean Dream: successful first 2 starts, in bumper at Towcester in December and maiden hurdle at Folkestone (beat Taffy Dancer 1½ lengths) in February: seemed to find stamina stretched when 10 lengths second to Naunton Brook in novice at Warwick, clear 3 out but tiring in straight: remains likely to do better. *Miss Venetia Williams* h110 p
F97

LAZY BUT LIVELY (IRE) 8 br.g. Supreme Leader – Oriel Dream (Oats) [2003/4 h117: 22s^6 24d c21s* c20v^2 c20g^4 c25v^5 c21d^3 c20v^4 c25g^F c31d^{ur} Apr 22] medium-sized gelding: fairly useful handicap hurdler: fair form first 2 starts over fences, won maiden at Sedgefield in December: largely let down by jumping after: should stay beyond 3m: goes well on soft/heavy going. *R. F. Fisher* c109 x
h117

LAZZAZ 6 b.g. Muhtarram (USA) – Astern (USA) (Polish Navy (USA)) [2003/4 h88: 17g^3 May 1] fair on all-weather Flat (barely stays 1¾m), successful 3 times in 2003: modest novice hurdler: will prove best around 2m. *P. W. Hiatt* h84

LEABURN (IRE) 11 b.g. Tremblant – Conderlea (Scorpio (FR)) [2003/4 c17g^3 c16d* c19s c18g Mar 27] rangy gelding: fairly useful handicap chaser: missed 2002/3 but showed himself nearly as good as ever when winning at Wincanton in December by 1¾ lengths from Nick The Jewel: ran poorly both subsequent starts: best around 2m: acts on heavy going, possibly not good to firm: effective tongue tied or not: has found little. *P. J. Hobbs* c122
h–

LEADAWAY 5 b.g. Supreme Leader – Annicombe Run (Deep Run) [2003/4 F16g 20d 16g Mar 12] fourth foal: half-brother to 3 winners, including modest hurdler/chaser around 2m Workaway (by Alflora): dam, fairly useful hurdler who stayed 3m, half-sister to dam of one-time smart chaser Mr Baxter Basics, stays easy 3m: well beaten in bumper and novice hurdles. *A. Parker* h–
F–

LEADER SUPREME (IRE) 9 b.m. Supreme Leader – Country Daisy VII (Damsire Unregistered) [2003/4 c–, h–: 26m^{pu} May 5] workmanlike mare: little sign of ability: visored only outing (lame) in 2003/4. *J. R. Jenkins* c–
h–

LEADING MAN (IRE) 4 b.g. Old Vic – Cudder Or Shudder (IRE) (The Parson) [2003/4 F16d^4 F16s^4 Feb 14] second foal: dam, poor bumper performer, out of fairly useful 2m hurdler L O Broadway: second and better effort in bumpers when fourth to Classic Capers at Ayr, keeping on well from poor position and still seeming green: will stay beyond 2m. *Ferdy Murphy* F87

LEAD STORY (IRE) 11 br.g. Lead On Time (USA) – Mashmoon (USA) (Habitat) [2003/4 c–§, h–: c21s^{pu} Apr 29] strong gelding: formerly useful hunter chaser on his day, has lost his form: stays 3¼m: acts on soft and good to firm going, probably on firm: tried blinkered: unreliable. *G. Chambers* c– §
h–

LEAGUES (NZ) 9 b.g. Kenfair (NZ) – Hidden Depths (NZ) (Beaufort Sea (USA)) [2003/4 c96x, h–: 17m^4 20m^5 Jun 29] strong, lengthy gelding: poor maiden hurdler: modest form at best over fences (makes mistakes): best efforts at 2m on good going. *M. J. Gingell* c– x
h78

LEAP YEAR LASS 4 ch.f. Fleetwood (IRE) – Lady Phyl (Northiam (USA)) [2003/4 16f^F 16d^5 16d^5 16s^3 16v^5 16d 17d^6 17d^4 17g^{bd} Apr 24] smallish filly: little form on Flat for J. Allen: poor maiden hurdler: raced around 2m: acts on heavy going: has hung/looked unenthusiastic: sketchy jumper. *C. Grant* h71

LEARNED LAD (FR) 6 ch.g. Royal Academy (USA) – Blushing Storm (USA) (Blushing Groom (FR)) [2003/4 h–: 16g Mar 7] workmanlike gelding: fair on Flat (barely stays 1½m): no form in 2 novice hurdles. *Jamie Poulton* h–

LEARN THE LINGO 8 b.g. Teenoso (USA) – Charlotte Gray (Rolfe (USA)) [2003/4 F–: 16d^6 16d^{pu} 17s 16g Mar 10] sturdy gelding: little sign of ability over hurdles: tried tongue tied. *Mrs H. Dalton* h–

LEASE 6 ch.g. Lycius (USA) – Risanda (Kris) [2003/4 20g 16g* 16g 17m* 20m^F Oct **h102**
11] angular gelding: thrice-raced on Flat at 3 yrs, won over 1¼m on debut: fair hurdler:
won seller at Perth (first run after leaving T. Taaffe) in August and novice at Carlisle in
October: would probably have also won novice at Hexham day after second success but
for falling last: stays easy 2½m: acts on good to firm going: tried blinkered/in cheekpieces. *J. G. Carr, Ireland*

LE BIASSAIS (FR) 5 b.g. Passing Sale (FR) – Petite Fanfan (FR) (Black Beauty **F94**
(FR)) [2003/4 F16s F16v* F17d Feb 23] rangy gelding: fourth foal: brother to·winner
around 1½m Gracieux des Pres and half-brother to winning chaser around 2m Horizon
des Pres (by Dearling): dam placed over fences up to 25f: won bumper at Ayr in January
by neck from Birdwatch: again raced freely when disappointing following month.
L. Lungo

LECHE BOTTES (FR) 5 b.g. Sleeping Car (FR) – Gibelotte (FR) (Royal Charter **h104**
(FR)) [2003/4 18s⁵ 20g Apr 1] angular gelding: second foal: dam unraced half-sister to
dam of very smart hurdler up to 2¾m Homme du Jour: in frame up to 13.5f on Flat:
thrice-raced over hurdles in France, fifth in 4-y-o event at Auteuil final start for Mme
I. Pacault: very stiff task and looked none too keen on British debut nearly 10 months
later. *M. C. Pipe*

LECKAMPTON 8 b.m. Bedford (USA) – I'm Unforgettable (Dublin Taxi) [2003/4 **h–**
h–: 26g^{pu} May 1] smallish mare: showed little in bumper and 2 runs over hurdles.
S. E. H. Sherwood

LE COUDRAY (FR) 10 b.g. Phantom Breeze – Mos Lie (FR) (Tip Moss (FR)) **c164**
[2003/4 c142*, h–: c20d⁴ c24d² c24d² c36d^F Apr 3] **h–**
    Four outings in 2003/4 failed to bring a victory for Le Coudray but second
placings in the Ericsson Chase and the Hennessy Cognac Gold Cup at Leopardstown showed that he had made the transition from good novice to top-level
competitor, though perhaps his fall, when going well, at second Becher's in the
Grand National may be his most significant performance with regard to the future.
Becher's was the scene of a dramatic incident in all three races over the National
fences at this year's National meeting. Le Coudray had done well to survive the
chaos there first time round, and he was jumping fluently under a patient ride and
yet to make his move, around a length behind the winner Amberleigh House, when
he departed second time. Second Becher's is a fair way from home and a list of
those going well or in contention, only to fall there, is long, while a list of those to
come back and win the race having departed there is extremely short. Just West Tip
in the last fifty years. That said, the continuing policy of giving lenient marks to
encourage the best horses to run has to work in the favour of such as Le Coudray
eventually and if he is in form and in the line-up again in 2005 he has to be one for
the shortlist.
    Le Coudray's two efforts at Leopardstown were on a par, though prior
expectations meant that the first was generally regarded more positively than the
second. Le Coudray went into the Ericsson on the back of an encouraging reappearance in the Punchestown Chase earlier in December, in which he finished sixteen
lengths fourth to Beef Or Salmon, leaving the impression the run was needed. With
Best Mate in the line-up as well as Beef Or Salmon, Le Coudray was available at
14/1 but managed to split the favourites, moving smoothly into contention three out
but unable to land a blow at Best Mate in the straight. Le Coudray went down by
nine lengths, with Beef Or Salmon, below his best, four lengths behind in third.
With neither Best Mate nor Beef Or Salmon in the line-up for the Hennessy Cognac
Gold Cup, Le Coudray looked to hold a favourite's chance, though that was failing
to anticipate a revitalised Florida Pearl, and Le Coudray, having been left second
two out, could make little impression in the straight, even though the winner was
hampered by the loose Harbour Pilot at the last. Le Coudray's trainer Christy Roche
suggested, after the three-length defeat, that softer ground might have helped—the
going for neither of the Grade 1 events Le Coudray contested was nearly as testing
as it sometimes gets at Leopardstown in the winter—and that may offer the best
chance for Le Coudray to win one of those particular races in 2004/5, though such
conditions will hardly inconvenience the younger pair Beef Or Salmon and Harbour Pilot. Le Coudray wasn't entered for the Cheltenham Gold Cup and though he
finished second in the Stayers' Hurdle in his younger days, the Cheltenham track
and the generally prevailing good or firmer ground probably aren't ideal for him.

Mr John P. McManus' "Le Coudray"

Le Coudray (FR) (b.g. 1994)	Phantom Breeze (b 1986)	Vision (b 1981)	Nijinsky Foreseer
		Ask The Wind (ch 1980)	Run The Gantlet Arburie
	Mos Lie (FR) (b 1989)	Tip Moss (ch 1972)	Luthier Top Twig
		Lestelie (br 1974)	Taj Dewan Leslie

Le Coudray seems sure to be effective over long distances, the step back up to three miles in the latest campaign having suited him. His pedigree has been thoroughly covered in previous Annuals, though one of his relations gained a noteworthy win in 2003/4. Mercato, who is out of a half-sister to Le Coudray's dam Mos Lie, showed more stamina than previously thought likely to land the Grand Military Gold Cup. Le Coudray is a rangy, good-topped gelding. He is effective with or without a tongue strap, though he wore one for all starts in 2003/4. *C. Roche, Ireland*

LE DIAMONT (FR) 5 ch.g. Broadway Flyer (USA) – Lady Diamond (FR) (Diamond **h86** Prospect (USA)) [2003/4 h–, F84: 16m 16m⁴ 21gᵖᵘ Jan 17] angular gelding: best effort over hurdles when fourth to easy winner Distant Prospect in maiden at Newbury: shaped as if amiss next time: should stay beyond 2m: tried tongue tied. *C. P. Morlock*

Mrs J. Stewart's "Le Duc"

LE DUC (FR)   5 b.g. Villez (USA) – Beberova (FR) (Synefos (USA)) [2003/4 h133§: **c138 §**
c16m* c16m⁴ c19sᶠ c16g² 16g c17g* c16g³ c20gᵖᵘ c16g⁴ Apr 16] tall, good-topped **h129 §**
gelding: useful hurdler: useful novice chaser: landed odds at Wetherby (maiden) in October and Kelso (on bridle) in March: best effort when 8 lengths third of 8 finishers to Well
Chief in Arkle Chase at Cheltenham: ran poorly both subsequent starts: raced mainly
around 2m (every chance when fell 2 out over 19f): acts on good to firm and heavy going:
tried blinkered: ungenuine. *P. F. Nicholls*

LEE ANNA   6 ch.m. Karinga Bay – Hachimitsu (Vaigly Great) [2003/4 24mᵖᵘ Mar 4] **h–**
sixth foal: half-sister to winning 2m hurdler Barton Scamp (by Sadeem): dam 6f/7f winner: well beaten on completed outing in maiden points in 2003: showed nothing in novice
hurdle. *R. J. Baker*

LEE'S ROSIE (IRE)   9 b.m. Zaffaran (USA) – Muse of Fire (Laurence O) [2003/4 **c–**
c79+, h–: c25gᵘʳ c28dᵖᵘ May 30] workmanlike mare: won maiden hunter chase at Hex- **h–**
ham in 2002/3, only form over jumps. *Miss Bianca Dunk*

LE FOREZIEN (FR)   5 b.g. Gunboat Diplomacy (FR) – Diane du Forez (FR) (Quart **c108**
de Vin (FR)) [2003/4 c17s c17sᶠ c17g² c17d* c16gᵖᵘ Jan 9] ex-French gelding: first foal: **h–**
dam unraced: placed around 1½m on Flat: modest form over hurdles: best effort over
fences when winning 4-y-o claimer at Auteuil (claimed from T. Civel €19,000) in June:
breathing problem on British debut: raced mainly around 2m on good ground or softer.
C. J. Gray

LEFT BANK (IRE)   8 ch.g. Over The River (FR) – My Friend Fashion (Laurence O) **c84 §**
[2003/4 c79§, h–§: c22gᵖᵘ c25g⁵ c22f² c22gᶠ c19g⁵ c20g² c21d⁵ Mar 30] sturdy gelding: **h– §**

poor handicap chaser: stays 25f: needs good going or firmer: successful with or without headgear: ungenuine. *Mrs M. Reveley*

LE GALLOIS   7 b.g. Deltic (USA)   Safety First (Wassl) [2003/4 F16f aF16g^pu Dec 13] fifth foal: half-brother to 5f winner Wasblest (by Statoblest): dam unraced, from family of top-class performer up to 1½m Celtic Swing: no form in point in 2002 or in 2 bumpers: tongue tied. *D. Brace*   **F—**

LEGAL LUNCH (USA)   9 b.g. Alleged (USA) – Dinner Surprise (USA) (Lyphard (USA)) [2003/4 h103: c19d^pu 24d³ 24d 22s* 22g* 21g² 20d* 24g⁴ Apr 2] smallish, well-made gelding: no encouragement on chasing debut: fairly useful hurdler: won seller (easily) and handicap at Fontwell in February and handicap at Chepstow in March, back to best when beating Harapour 3 lengths, pair clear, at last-named: stays 3m: acts on soft going: tried visored. *W. K. Goldsworthy*   **c—** **h119**

LEGAL STORM (IRE)   12 gr.g. Roselier (FR) – Stormy Waters (Typhoon II) [2003/4 c21g⁵ c23g^F Mar 12] ex-Irish gelding: lightly raced over hurdles: maiden steeplechaser: would have stayed beyond 3m: acted on good to firm and heavy going: dead. *P. York*   **c58** **h—**

LEGATUS (IRE)   7 ch.g. Alphabatim (USA) – Take A Guess (IRE) (Carlingford Castle) [2003/4 c26s² c25d³ Dec 2] IR 14,000 3-y-o, 10,000 4-y-o: sturdy gelding: second foal: dam, placed in point, out of sister to smart staying chaser Aquilifer: successful all 3 completed starts in points: modest form in 2 steeplechases, third to impressive Fork Lightning in novice at Hereford: stays 3¼m: wears visor: likely to do better. *M. C. Pipe*   **c95 p**

LEGGIES LEGACY   13 b.g. Jupiter Island – Hit The Line (Saulingo) [2003/4 c–, h83: 22s 20m May 7] poor handicap hurdler: well beaten both starts early in 2003/4: stays 3m: best on soft/heavy going: blinkered twice (found nothing first time). *J. Gallagher*   **c—** **h—**

LE GRAND ROCHER   7 ch.g. Factual (USA) – Honey Bridge (Crepello) [2003/4 F81: 20d Nov 22] workmanlike gelding: second in bumper at Worcester on debut: never travelling or jumping with any fluency in novice hurdle 18 months later. *Jonjo O'Neill*   **h—**

LE GRIS (GER)   5 gr.g. Neshad (USA) – Lady Pedomade (GER) (Mondrian (GER)) [2003/4 16g 16g 16m² Apr 13] neat gelding: first foal: dam won at 9.5f and 11/2m in Germany: won twice over 1m (at 3 yrs) from 25 starts on Flat in Germany for B. Hellier: best effort over hurdles when second to easy winner Ilabon in maiden at Chepstow. *J. S. Moore*   **h82**

LE GUVNOR   9 br.g. Le Moss – High Heels (IRE) (Supreme Leader) [2003/4 h–: 21g^pu Mar 17] strong gelding: of no account. *G. J. Smith*   **h—**

LEINSTER (IRE)   7 br.g. Supreme Leader – Jennycomequick (Furry Glen) [2003/4 h128f: 20d 16d 20s⁵ Dec 14] good sort: chasing type: useful hurdler: back to best when fifth of 9 to Solerina in Grade 3 at Navan: will stay beyond 2½m: acts on soft ground. *D. T. Hughes, Ireland*   **h135**

LEITH HILL STAR   8 ch.m. Comme L'Etoile – Sunnyday (Sunley Builds) [2003/4 c–, h71: 24m³ 20s* 22v³ 18s* 21s⁴ 21g² 20s* 22d 21m Apr 15] angular mare: fell first only start over fences: modest hurdler: improved in 2003/4, winning mares handicap at Folkestone in November, minor event at Fontwell in December and handicap at Sandown (made all) in February: stays 25f: acts on good to firm and soft going. *M. Scudamore*   **c—** **h95**

LEITRIM ROCK (IRE)   4 b.g. Barathea (IRE) – Kilshanny (Groom Dancer (USA)) [2003/4 17m⁵ Aug 16] modest and ungenuine on Flat (stays 9.4f): none too fluent when well held in juvenile on hurdling debut. *D. W. P. Arbuthnot*   **h—**

LE JOYEUX (FR)   5 br.g. Video Rock (FR) – Agra (FR) (Brezzo (FR)) [2003/4 F16d F16v 22d 25d 21d Apr 12] 18,000 3-y-o: strong gelding: fourth foal: half-brother to winning 21f winner Ici Londres (by Royal Charter): dam, won twice over 1¼m, from family of smart French chaser Gabion and Welsh National winner Edmond: signs of ability in bumpers and over hurdles: tongue tied last 3 starts. *B. I. Case*   **h86 ?** **F—**

LE MINO (FR)   5 b.g. Noblequest (FR) – Minouche (FR) (Fill My Hopes (FR)) [2003/4 16g 25g^pu Jan 24] first foal: dam unraced sister to smart French chaser Kifill and half-sister to smart hurdler/chaser up to 2¾m Douze Douze: no show in 2 novice hurdles. *Ferdy Murphy*   **h—**

LE-MONDE (IRE)   6 br.g. Anabaa (USA) – Alexandra Fair (USA) (Green Dancer (USA)) [2003/4 c97p, h111: 24d c22d² c21g* c20g³ c20v^pu 20s* 19d* 22s 22d Apr 12] angular gelding: best effort over fences when winning maiden at Cork in June: left D. Wachman after fourth start: fairly useful handicap hurdler: won at Naas in March: effective at 19f to 3m: acts on good to firm and heavy going: effective with or without cheekpieces: ran creditably in blinkers (sweating) at Punchestown in late-April. *D. M. Leigh, Ireland*   **c106** **h117**

531

LEO

LEOPHIN DANCER (USA) 6 b.g. Green Dancer (USA) – Happy Gal (FR) (Habitat) **h85**
[2003/4 h72: 16m* 16f³ 16g 16g² 16sᵖᵘ Jan 16] rather leggy gelding: poor on Flat,
successful in April: poor hurdler: won conditional jockeys selling handicap at Worcester
in September: will stay beyond 2m: acts on firm going: has had tongue tied. *P. W. Hiatt*

LE PASSING (FR) 5 b.g. Passing Sale (FR) – Petite Serenade (FR) (Trac) [2003/4 **c–**
16g² 17s* 17s* 16d² 16s² 17d Mar 18] good-topped gelding: seventh foal: half-brother to **h136**
4 winners, including 2½m chase winner Kepi Noir (by Village Star): dam, 10.5f winner,
out of half-sister to dam of useful chaser around 2½m Camitrov: maiden on Flat: in frame
over hurdles and fences at Pau for P. Peltier: progressed into useful novice hurdler in
Britain, winning at Bangor (odds on in 4-y-o event) in May and Taunton in December:
best efforts when second to Cloudy Grey at Ascot and Mon Villez at Wetherby (found
less than seemed likely when beaten 2 lengths in Grade 2): ran as if amiss final outing:
will stay at least 2½m: raced on good going or softer. *P. F. Nicholls*

LE ROCHELAIS (FR) 5 ch.g. Goldneyev (USA) – Olympiade de Brion (FR) (Night **h98**
And Day) [2003/4 16v 16d⁴ 19s³ Apr 4] ex-French gelding: half-brother to several
winners, notably Grande Course de Haies winner Sire Rochelais (by What A Joy) and
very smart chaser Ultra Rochelais (by King's Road): dam never ran: third over 13.5f on
Flat for P. Quinton: eye-catching 6¼ lengths fourth of 16 to Jonanaud in novice at Chepstow: raced freely and tired markedly over longer trip next time: may still do better.
R. H. Alner

LE ROI MIGUEL (FR) 6 b.g. Point of No Return (FR) – Loumir (USA) (Bob's **c159**
Dusty (USA)) [2003/4 c156p, h–: c16d* c19d² c16d⁴ c24gᶠ c19s⁴ c20gᶠ c21m⁶ Apr 14] **h–**
tall, useful-looking gelding: very smart chaser: won Grade 1 novice at Punchestown in
May 2003: good efforts when second to Iris Royal in valuable handicap at Ascot and
fourth to Moscow Flyer in Tingle Creek Chase at Sandown on first 2 runs back later in
year: ran poorly last 2 completed starts, tongue tied on first occasion: stays 19f (weakening when falling last over 3m): raced mainly on good going or softer. *P. F. Nicholls*

LE ROYAL (FR) 5 b.g. Garde Royale – Caucasie (FR) (Djarvis (FR)) [2003/4 20d⁴ **h110**
20s³ 20s* 20v* 20g³ Feb 28] leggy ex-French gelding: second foal: dam, winning 2¼m
chaser in France, out of half-sister to useful chaser around 2½m Camitrov: successful
once from 3 starts around 11f on Flat at 3 yrs for E. Chevalier du Fau: fair form in novice
hurdles, won twice at Haydock in January: raced at 2½m: acts on heavy going.
Mrs M. Reveley

LEROY'S SISTER (FR) 4 b.f. Phantom Breeze – Loumir (USA) (Bob's Dusty **F98**
(USA)) [2003/4 F12m⁶ F18g⁴ F18g⁴ F17m² Apr 15] small, close-coupled filly: lacks scope:
fifth foal: half-sister to fairly useful hurdler/very smart chaser Le Roi Miguel (by Point
of No Return), stays 19f: dam winning hurdler/chaser up to 2½m: fairly useful form in
fillies/mares bumpers, ¾-length second to Golden Odyssey at Cheltenham: tended to
hang left second start. *P. F. Nicholls*

LERUBIS (FR) 5 b.g. Ragmar (FR) – Perle de Saisy (FR) (Italic (FR)) [2003/4 18d⁶ **c98 d**
17d 18s c19s c17v⁴ c20vᵖᵘ 16d 17s 20s⁵ Apr 17] ex-French gelding: seventh foal: half- **h104 d**
brother to 3 winners, including Irish 2m hurdle winner Diamantino (by Altayan): dam
won up to 1½m on Flat: once-raced on Flat: fair maiden hurdler/chaser: left G. Cherel,
poor form in 3 novice hurdles in Britain: tried blinkered. *F. Jordan*

LE SAUVAGE (IRE) 9 b.g. Tirol – Cistus (Sun Prince) [2003/4 h77: 19gᵖᵘ Feb 6] **h–**
leggy gelding: fair hurdler at best, poor nowadays: should stay 3m: acts on heavy going.
D. W. Barker

LESCER'S LAD 7 b.g. Perpendicular – Grange Gracie (Oats) [2003/4 F85: F16g 19g **h69**
20d 16g⁶ 22g⁵ Mar 28] tall, lengthy gelding: modest form at best in bumpers: poor form **F–**
in novice hurdles. *J. Hetherton*

LESDREAM 7 b.g. Morpeth – Lesbet (Hotfoot) [2003/4 h94: 19d* 21s⁴ 22s² Apr 6] **h109**
progressive handicap hurdler: completed hat-trick at Exeter in January on first run for 10
months: 3 lengths second of 19 to Noble Baron at same course in April: will stay 3m: acts
on soft ground. *J. D. Frost*

LESPRIDE 6 b.g. Morpeth – Lesbet (Hotfoot) [2003/4 F17s⁶ F18s 17g Apr 1] second **h–**
foal: brother to progressive hurdler Lesdream, will stay 3m: dam, fair staying hurdler/ **F–**
poor novice chaser: no sign of ability in bumpers and maiden hurdle. *J. D. Frost*

LESSSAIDTHEBETTER (IRE) 7 ch.g. Montelimar (USA) – Urdite (FR) (Con- **c–**
certino (FR)) [2003/4 c26dᵖᵘ c23dᵖᵘ Apr 21] IR 40,000 3-y-o: ex-Irish gelding: half- **h–**
brother to fair hurdler/winning chaser Thunderpoint (by Glacial Storm), stays 3m, and
winning French/Italian jumper Mon Lutteur (by King Luthier): dam, placed at 2 yrs in

France, half-sister to 2 good French jumpers: third on completed start in bumpers: modest form when placed in handicap hurdles in 2002/3: left C. Roche, always behind in 2 handicap chases: stays 2½m: raced on good going or softer. *Jonjo O'Neill*

LESTAT (IRE) 10 b.g. Brush Aside (USA) – Shuilernish (Callernish) [2003/4 c21d Apr 30] fair pointer: never competitive in maiden hunter chase at Cheltenham. *Miss A. Nolan* — c70

LESTER LONGFELLOW 8 b. or br.g. Riverwise (USA) – Cut Above The Rest (Indiaro) [2003/4 h–: c22s^pu c19v^4 c20g^pu Mar 7] tall gelding: lightly raced, signs of only a little ability. *N. R. Mitchell* — c75 ? h–

L'ETANG BLEU (FR) 6 gr.g. Graveron (FR) – Strawberry Jam (FR) (Fill My Hopes (FR)) [2003/4 h91§: c16g^F c16d^pu c16g^3 c20g^ur c16m^6 17f^2 19f^3 16m^3 17g^2 18g^3 c17v^2 c20f^6 c17d^pu 16s 22g 16g^pu c17d^2 c17d^4 Apr 24] leggy gelding: modest hurdler/novice chaser, left M. Pipe after tenth start: effective at 2m to easy 2¾m: acts on any going: often wears headgear/tongue tied: ungenuine. *P. Butler* — c89 § h84 §

LETHEM AIR 6 ch.g. Aragon – Llanddona (Royal Palace) [2003/4 c24d^pu Apr 18] 500 (privately) 3-y-o: half-brother to winning 2¼m hurdler Grey Phoenix (by Petong) and several winners on Flat abroad: dam twice-raced daughter of half-sister to Eclipse winner Canisbay: modest pointer, won maiden in March: raced freely when pulled up on hunter debut. *Tim Butt* — c–

LETITIA'S LOSS (IRE) 6 ch.m. Zaffaran (USA) – Satin Sheen (Abednego) [2003/4 24d^4 27s^* 22v^F Jan 24] plain mare: third foal: dam, winning pointer, half-sister to smart staying chaser Nuaffe: ran 3 times in Irish points in 2003, winning mares maiden on completed start: won novice hurdle at Sedgefield in December: struggling when falling 4 out in mares novice at Haydock month later: stays 27f: acts on soft going. *N. G. Richards* — h90

LET'S CELEBRATE 4 b.g. Groom Dancer (USA) – Shimmer (Bustino) [2003/4 16g^F 16f^F 16m 16g 16g^5 Jan 15] leggy, close-coupled gelding: little form on Flat for C. Brittain: fell on first 2 starts over hurdles, in front when coming down 2 out in maiden at Ludlow on second occasion: achieved little after. *F. Jordan* — h86

LETS GO DUTCH 8 b.m. Nicholas Bill – Dutch Majesty (Homing) [2003/4 h107: 22g Apr 30] workmanlike mare: fair hurdler: lame at Exeter very early in season: will prove best at 3m+: acts on heavy going. *K. Bishop* — h–

LE TURK (FR) 5 b. or br.g. Baby Turk – Valse de Sienne (FR) (Petit Montmorency (USA)) [2003/4 F16v 16m^pu 21g^pu Mar 5] €4,000 4-y-o: good-topped gelding: fourth foal: half-brother to one-time fair hurdler/chaser Exact, stays 3m, and winning chaser around 2½m Heroine de Sienne (both by Beyssac): dam 1m/12.5f winner in France: no sign of ability: sold £1,400 Ascot April Sales. *D. P. Keane* — h– F–

LEVALLOIS (IRE) 8 b.g. Trempolino (USA) – Broken Wave (Bustino) [2003/4 c114, h129: c20m^F c20d 18d Apr 7] smallish gelding: useful hurdler/chaser in France: no form in Britain: stays 21f: acts on heavy going. *P. Winkworth* — c– h–

LEWIS ISLAND (IRE) 5 b.g. Turtle Island (IRE) – Phyllode (Pharly (FR)) [2003/4 h119: 16m c16m^pu 17g 17d 20s^2 19m^* 20d 20d Apr 22] well-made gelding: hesitant first and unseated second on chasing debut: fairly useful handicap hurdler: won at Hereford in March by 2 lengths from Football Crazy: stays 2½m: acts on good to firm and heavy going: usually front runner: not one to rely on: sold 17,000 gns Doncaster May Sales. *N. A. Twiston-Davies* — c– h120 §

LEWS A LADY 6 ch.m. Sir Harry Lewis (USA) – Pretty Gayle (Midland Gayle) [2003/4 F16g Dec 20] third foal: dam fair staying hurdler: tailed off in bumper on debut. *D. Eddy* — F–

LEYAALY 5 ch.m. Night Shift (USA) – Lower The Tone (IRE) (Phone Trick (USA)) [2003/4 16s 16d 23s^pu Apr 4] no sign of ability on Flat or over hurdles. *B. A. Pearce* — h–

LEYLAND COMET (IRE) 6 b. or br.g. Roselier (FR) – Firey Comet (IRE) (Buckskin (FR)) [2003/4 F16g May 15] second foal: dam unraced half-sister to John Hughes Chase winner Joe White: never a factor in bumper on debut. *Ferdy Murphy* — F–

L FOR LEISURE 5 ch.g. Cosmonaut – York Street (USA) (Diamond Shoal) [2003/4 16d^pu Jan 13] half-brother to poor 2m hurdler Coochie (by King of Spain): well beaten in 3 maidens at 2 yrs for W. Turner: no show on hurdling debut. *Julian Poulton* — h–

LIBERMAN (IRE) 6 b.g. Standiford (USA) – Hail To You (USA) (Kirtling) [2003/4 F119: 20m^* 22s^pu 16v^4 19g^5 Feb 19] rather unfurnished gelding: smart bumper performer, won Champion Bumper at Cheltenham in 2002/3: disappointing over hurdles: — h100 x

LIB

7/1-on, typically not fluent and needed firm handling when winning weak maiden at Musselburgh in December: failed to progress in handicaps: should stay beyond 2½m. *M. C. Pipe*

LIBERTHINE (FR) 5 b.m. Chamberlin (FR) – Libertina (FR) (Balsamo (FR)) [2003/4 c107 p c20d* c25g⁴ Apr 2] angular ex-French mare: seventh foal: half-sister to 1m to 11f winner h– Aubisquini (by Dom Pasquini): dam, won 15f hurdle in France, half-sister to very smart hurdler up to 25f Full of Ambition: fairly useful juvenile hurdler in 2002/3, won at Dieppe and Auteuil (twice): left G. Macaire and off 16 months, won maiden at Stratford on chasing debut in March, soon well in control after leading 3 out: blundered fourteenth when tailed-off last of 4 finishers in Grade 2 novice won by Simply Supreme at Aintree: stays 2½m: raced on good ground or softer (acts on soft): open to improvement over fences. *N. J. Henderson*

LIBERTY SEEKER (FR) 5 ch.g. Machiavellian (USA) – Samara (IRE) (Polish h115 Patriot (USA)) [2003/4 17g* 17d* 17d⁶ 16d⁶ 16g⁵ 16g³ Feb 18] good-topped gelding: fair maiden on Flat (stays 1¼m): fair novice hurdler: won at Sedgefield in October and November: best effort when third to Another Dude in handicap at Musselburgh: will prove best around 2m, probably with emphasis on speed: joined P. Niven. *G. A. Swinbank*

LIBRE 4 b.g. Bahamian Bounty – Premier Blues (FR) (Law Society (USA)) [2003/4 h68 16m⁶ 17d 16g Mar 10] leggy gelding: fair on Flat (stays 9f), won in September: favourite, not fluent and failed to settle when sixth of 9 in juvenile at Stratford on hurdling debut: left F. Jordan, always behind in novices at Market Rasen and Catterick (tongue tied): will prove best at 2m with emphasis on speed. *R. C. Guest*

LIES AND PHIBBS (IRE) 6 gr.g. Supreme Leader – Rosy Waters (Roselier (FR)) h– [2003/4 F16s 17s Feb 6] €15,000 4-y-o: smallish ex-Irish gelding: fourth foal: half- F– brother to modest staying hurdlers Foggy (by Merrymount) and Run Sparky (by Commanche Run): dam unraced half-sister to smart staying chaser Johnny Setaside: form in bumpers only when fourth at Down Royal in 2002/3, final start for C. Swan: no show on hurdling debut: joined Mrs S. Smith. *Mrs Barbara Waring*

LIGHTCLIFFE 5 ch.m. Abzu – Iron Lass (Thatch (USA)) [2003/4 F16s Feb 22] F– eighth foal: half-sister to 1993 2-y-o 5f winner Dunedin (by Dunbeath): dam once-raced granddaughter of July Cup winner Merry Madcap: tailed off in bumper on debut. *J. R. Norton*

LIGHT DES MULOTTES (FR) 5 gr.g. Solidoun (FR) – Tango Girl (FR) (Tip Moss h90 x (FR)) [2003/4 F16d F16m* 16g⁴ 17s³ 16g Feb 11] leggy, unfurnished ex-Irish gelding: F99 fourth foal: half-brother to fairly useful 2m hurdler Breeze Girl (by Phantom Breeze) and winning 19f chaser Jazz des Mulottes (by Garde Royale): dam, placed over jumps around 2m in France, half-sister to useful hurdler around 2m Lady Boston: fair form in bumpers: left E. Hales, landed odds in 9-runner event at Worcester in November: modest form over hurdles: will stay beyond 17f: not a fluent jumper. *O. Sherwood*

LIGHTENING RETURNS 5 ch.m. Bob's Return (IRE) – Sally Smith (Alias Smith F– (USA)) [2003/4 F16d Mar 19] second foal: dam, lightly-raced pointer, half-sister to fairly useful staying chasers Calira and Grey Smoke: last of 19 in maiden bumper at Warwick on debut. *S. A. Brookshaw*

LIGHT HEARTED LILY 5 b.m. Deploy – Darling Splodge (Elegant Air) [2003/4 h76 F–: F17m⁵ F16m³ F17m⁶ 21gᵖᵘ 20s⁵ 21dᵖᵘ 20s 22m³ 23d⁵ Apr 12] lengthy mare: signs of F79 ? ability in bumpers: poor form over hurdles: stays 23f: acts on soft and good to firm ground. *R. M. Beckett*

LIGHTIN' JACK (IRE) 6 ch.g. Beneficial – Cillrossanta (IRE) (Mandalus) [2003/4 h91 24g³ Nov 8] rather leggy ex-Irish gelding: third foal: dam winning pointer: runner-up on first of 2 starts in points: fair form at best in bumpers for D. Murphy: travelled smoothly long way when third of 7 in maiden at Chepstow on hurdling debut. *Miss E. C. Lavelle*

LIGHTMOOR LADY 6 b.m. Puget (USA) – Dragon Fire (Dragonara Palace (USA)) F– [2003/4 F–: F16m Jun 1] well held in 2 bumpers. *Mrs L. Williamson*

LIGHTNING QUEST (IRE) 13 b.g. Rainbow Quest (USA) – Rare Roberta (USA) c– (Roberto (USA)) [2003/4 c107, h91: 20d c21s⁴ May 17] tall gelding: modest handicap h– hurdler/fair handicap chaser in first half of 2002/3: well held on return: stays 23f: has won on good to soft going, best form on good or firmer: blinkered once (ran poorly). *Mrs S. J. Smith*

LIGHTNING STAR (USA) 9 b.g. El Gran Senor (USA) – Cuz's Star (USA) (Galaxy c– Libra) [2003/4 c–, h89: 16s 18s⁶ 16s³ 17d² 16g³ 16g⁴ Mar 17] angular gelding: modest h86

534

hurdler: stays 2¾m: probably acts on any going: usually blinkered: none too enthusiastic. *G. L. Moore*

LIGHT ON THE BROOM (IRE)   8 b.g. Aristocracy – Montevelle (IRE) (Monte-   **c110** limar) [2003/4 h109, F96: 16g c22dF c21d⁴ c17sF c18s² c16d* c16d⁴ c20s⁵ Mar 20] fair   **h94** hurdler in 2002/3: similar form over fences, won maiden at Thurles in February: should stay beyond 2¼m: acts on heavy going. *G. Stack, Ireland*

LIGHTS AND MUSIC (IRE)   9 ch.g. Pips Pride – Cut It Fine(USA) (Big Spruce   **c124** (USA)) [2003/4 c22spu c19d c20d³ Dec 7] big, lengthy gelding: fairly useful chaser: **h–** missed 2002/3: easily best effort on return when third to Kymandjen in handicap at Punchestown: stays 2½m: acts on soft going: tongue tied last 2 starts. *N. Meade, Ireland*

LIGHT THE RIVER (IRE)   10 b. or ch.g. Over The River (FR) – Mysterious Light   **c–** (Strong Gale) [2003/4 c25s⁶ Feb 7] leggy gelding: poor chaser in 2001/2: won point in January: hampered twelfth when well held in hunter following month: stays 25f: acts on heavy and good to firm going: blinkered last 5 outings: tongue tied nowadays. *Miss C. Metcalfe*

LIHOU MEL   7 b.m. Pursuit of Love – Lovers Tryst (Castle Keep) [2003/4 F16m May   **F–** 15] fourth reported foal: dam 1¼m winner: seemed to go wrong in bumper on debut. *L. A. Dace*

LIKE A BEE (IRE)   6 b.g. Montelimar (USA) – Dasdilemma (IRE) (Furry Glen)   **h116** [2003/4 F16s* 22s* 24s³ 22s² 20d Apr 12] second foal: dam, well held in bumpers, sister   **F96** to dam of smart 2m to 2½m hurdler Like-A-Butterfly: better effort in bumpers when winning at Clonmel on reappearance in November: third start over hurdles when winning maiden at Navan in January: best effort when second to Collier County in novice at Clonmel in February: stays at least 2¾m: raced on good to soft/soft going. *C. Roche, Ireland*

LIKE A BREEZE   5 bl.m. Bob Back (USA) – Whatagale (Strong Gale) [2003/4 F16v³   **F82** F18gsu Feb 22] rather unfurnished mare: fourth foal: dam, fair chaser, stayed 25f: third of 13 to Having A Party in bumper at Chepstow: well held when slipping up next time. *C. J. Down*

LIKE A LORD (IRE)   6 b. or br.g. Arctic Lord – Likashot (Celtic Cone) [2003/4   **h101** F17m⁵ F16g 20s 20s⁶ 19g³ Mar 5] 5,000 3-y-o, 2,500 4-y-o: angular gelding: second foal: **F73** dam, winning 2m hurdler, sister to top-class 2m to 3m hurdler/chaser Celtic Shot: signs of ability in 2 bumpers: much improved effort when third to Red Ruffles in novice hurdle at Doncaster. *Mrs S. J. Smith*

LIK WOOD POWER (NZ)   7 b.g. Bigstone (IRE) – Lady Paloma (USA) (Clever   **h100** Trick (USA)) [2003/4 16m³ 16mF 21d⁴ 20s² 22d⁶ Mar 3] angular gelding: successful once (over 11f) and placed 9 times from 24 starts on Flat in New Zealand: fair novice hurdler: effective at 2m to 2½m: acts on soft and good to firm going. *R. C. Guest*

LILAC   5 ch.m. Alhijaz – Fairfield's Breeze (Buckskin (FR)) [2003/4 16g 16m 20v 16g*   **h78** 16s⁴ 16g 16g³ 17g³ Apr 13] smallish mare: half-sister to modest hurdler Court Champagne (by Batshoof), stays 2½m: dam won 21f hunter chase: poor hurdler: won conditional jockeys mares handicap at Uttoxeter in June: should stay beyond 17f. *R. J. Price*

LILIUM DE COTTE (FR)   5 b.g. Ragmar (FR) – Vanille de Cotte (FR) (Italic (FR))   **c110 +** [2003/4 h128: c16d* c19spu 17d Mar 18] good-topped gelding: useful juvenile hurdler in   **h–** 2002/3 for G. Macaire: odds on, won maiden at Uttoxeter on chasing debut in November readily by 5 lengths from Polar Red: ran as if amiss both starts after: should stay beyond 17f: raced on good going or softer (acts on heavy). *N. J. Henderson*

LILLEBROR (GER)   6 b.h. Top Waltz (FR) – Lady Soliciti (GER) (Solicitor (FR))   **h–** [2003/4 16g 20spu 16v Jan 26] close-coupled horse: won 5 races on Flat (stays 1½m) in Germany for H. Groschel, largely well held in Britain: no form in 3 novice hurdles. *B. J. Curley*

LILY BROWN   9 br.m. Sula Bula – Lily Mab (FR) (Prince Mab (FR)) [2003/4 c–,   **c–** h–: c20spu May 3] sturdy mare: little form outside points: sold £1,400 Ascot June Sales.   **h–** *D. P. Keane*

LILY SAUNDERS   4 b.fi. Piccolo – Saunders Lass (Hillandale) [2003/4 F17spu F16g   **F–** Mar 4] seventh foal: sister to 2000 2-y-o 6f winner Piccolo Rose and half-sister to 1996 2-y-o 5f winner Saunders Wren (by Handsome Sailor) and winner around 1½m in Italy by Then Again: dam winning 2m hurdler: no show in 2 mares bumpers, looking unwilling on debut. *Mrs N. S. Sharpe*

Tote Scoop6 Lanzarote Hurdle (Handicap), Kempton—Limerick Boy gets the better of Perouse (No.2)

LIMERICK BOY (GER)   6 b.g. Alwuhush (USA) – Limoges (GER) (Konigsstuhl (GER)) [2003/4 h132: 16g² 16dᵖᵘ 16g* 16gᵘʳ 16g 16d 16dᶠ Apr 17] close-coupled gelding: useful hurdler: improved effort when winning Tote Scoop6 Lanzarote Hurdle (Handicap) at Kempton in January, rallying run-in to beat Perouse a neck, pair clear: well beaten on both subsequent completed starts, in Champion Hurdle at Cheltenham and listed handicap at Aintree: should stay beyond 2m: raced only on good/good to soft going. *Miss Venetia Williams*   **h143**

LIMERICK LEADER (IRE)   6 b.g. Supreme Leader – View of The Hills (Croghan Hill) [2003/4 F96: 20g* 20g² 20d² 22s³ 20s⁴ 24g* 24d* 24d⁵ Apr 22] useful-looking gelding: fairly useful hurdler: favourite, won maiden at Perth in September and novice at Kempton and handicap at Bangor (beat Glen Warrior gamely by a short head) in March: will stay beyond 3m: raced on good going or softer: blinkered last 4 starts (has raced lazily): goes well with forcing tactics. *P. J. Hobbs*   **h128**

LIME STONE LASS   7 b.m. General Gambul – Fids VII (Damsire Unregistered) [2003/4 F16f c20mᵖᵘ 19f c25dᵖᵘ Dec 1] fourth foal: dam never ran: no show in varied events. *M. Appleby*   **c–**
h–
F–

LIMON (GER)   5 b.g. Lavirco (GER) – Lohsa (IRE) (Aragon) [2003/4 16g 17g 17f⁶ 16g⁶ 16m⁵ 16d Dec 21] medium-sized gelding: won over 1m at 2 yrs in Germany for P. Rau: poor novice hurdler: raced around 2m: acts on good to firm going: tongue tied after second start. *Ronald O'Leary, Ireland*   **h83**

LINCOLN CROSS (IRE)   9 b.g. Lord Americo – Keen Cross (IRE) (Black Minstrel) [2003/4 h84: 22gᶠ May 5] leggy gelding: poor form over hurdles: stays 2¾m. *O. Sherwood*   **h–**

LINCOLN PLACE (IRE)   9 ch.g. Be My Native (USA) – Miss Lou (Levanter) [2003/4 c104, h96: c20g² c20mᶠ 20m c20m² 19m³ c20dᵖᵘ Dec 12] sturdy gelding: modest maiden hurdler: fair chaser: should stay beyond 2½m: acts on good to firm and good to soft going. *P. J. Hobbs*   **c107**
h89

LINDAJANE (IRE)   12 b.m. Erin's Hope – Tempo Rose (Crash Course) [2003/4 c78, h–: c25g² c20m³ c27dᵖᵘ Nov 11] poor handicap chaser: stays 25f: acts on heavy and good to firm going. *D. W. Whillans*   **c71**
h–

LIN D'ESTRUVAL (FR)   5 b.g. Cadoudal (FR) – Recolte d'Estruval (FR) (Kouban (FR)) [2003/4 F16d⁵ F16g aF16g* Apr 4] tall gelding: fourth foal: half-brother to 11f winner Grain d'Estruval (by Video Rock): dam successful up to 11f on Flat, won around 2m over jumps in France: fair form in bumpers: favourite, won 14-runner event on polytrack at Lingfield by 1¾ lengths from Byland. *C. P. Morlock*   **F92**

LINDSAY (FR)   5 b.g. Chamberlin (FR) – Oliday (FR) (Djarvis (FR)) [2003/4 18g² 16d* 16g² c17g* c17d* c21s² Mar 19] ex-French gelding: eighth foal: brother to 2½m chase winner Johnny's and cross-country chase winner Gladly II and half-brother to one-time fairly useful hurdler/chaser up to 2¾m Folliday (by Sharken): dam, won up to 1¼m on Flat, half-sister to dam of top-class French chaser Oteuil (by Djarvis): 1½m   **c96**
h?

winner on Flat: won 3 of 5 starts over jumps in France, 4-y-o hurdle at Vichy in July and chases at Compiegne in September and October for G. Macaire: favourite, 8 lengths second to Enitsag in hunter at Fakenham on British debut: stays 21f. *G. L. Edwards*

LINE APPLE (FR)   7 ch.m. Apple Tree (FR) – Cackle (USA) (Crow (FR)) [2003/4 c111d, h–: c21s³ c20f² c22m³ May 26] winning hurdler/chaser in France: modest form over fences in 2003/4, left J. Boulter after second outing: stays 2¾m: acts on firm and soft going: has had tongue tied. *P. F. Nicholls*   **c96** **h–**

LINENS FLAME   5 ch.g. Blushing Flame (USA) – Atlantic Air (Air Trooper) [2003/4 16m⁵ May 9] kept on well when fifth of 14 in novice at Wincanton on hurdling debut: improved on Flat in 2004, successful up to around 2m in March and April: likely to improve granted stiffer test of stamina. *B. G. Powell*   **h84**

LINGHAM BRIDESMAID   8 b.m. Minster Son – Lingham Bride (Deep Run) [2003/4 h81: 16g³ 16gᵖᵘ 20d⁴ 21gᵖᵘ Jul 28] small, sparely-made mare: poor maiden hurdler, lame final outing: stays 2½m: acts on good to firm and good to soft going. *Mrs J. C. McGregor*   **h64**

LINGO (IRE)   5 b.g. Poliglote – Sea Ring (FR) (Bering) [2003/4 16d* 16d² 16d* Jan 3]   **h144 p**

An overreach suffered three days before he was due to contest the Supreme Novices' Hurdle at Cheltenham, for which he was the ante-post favourite, resulted in Lingo not only missing that race but also the remainder of the season. However, he will be back in action in 2004/5 and looks sure to build on what was a highly satisfactory start to his hurdling career. Lingo won two of his three starts and showed a level of form which would have seen him go close in the Supreme Novices' Hurdle, even without his making the expected improvement.

Lingo had been most progressive in three seasons' racing on the Flat for Lynda Ramsden's stable, showing smart form when winning the mile-and-a-quarter City And Suburban Stakes at Epsom on his final start before being bought privately by J. P. McManus and sent to his present trainer. Unusually for one trained in Britain, Lingo made his debut over hurdles in Ireland, in a four-year-old minor event at Naas in November. None of his sixteen rivals looked anything special and Lingo landed the odds without too much fuss, jumping fluently and travelling strongly under a patient ride, and ridden to assert in the last hundred yards. Far stronger opposition faced Lingo next time, in the Kennel Gate Novices' Hurdle at Ascot, and he left his Naas form well behind in finishing a length and a quarter second to Perle de Puce, who received 7 lb, beating the likes of Eric's Charm, Self Defense and Albuhera in the process despite Lingo's jumping leaving something to be desired this time. It can be argued that Lingo should have won, as he was alongside the winner going much the better turning in, but Perle du Puce was

ladbrokes.com Tolworth Hurdle, Sandown—Lingo is left with a narrow advantage over Garde Champetre (diamond sleeves) as Perle de Puce falls at the last

allowed to get first run. The pair met again on the same terms three weeks later in the ladbrokes.com Tolworth Hurdle, run at Sandown for the first time since 2000, the abandonment of the three previous Sandown January fixtures having led to the race being transferred to Ascot, Warwick and Wincanton in the respective years. The Tolworth, the first Grade 1 race of the season for two-mile novice hurdlers, attracted just five runners but in terms of quality it was well up to standard. Lingo, who was heavily backed to turn the tables on Perle de Luce and went off favourite at 5/4, was held up and failed to settle, but he did jump more fluently than at Ascot and was travelling best as the pace, dictated by Perle de Puce, increased after three out. The leader was now being pressed by Garde Champetre, but Lingo had his effort delayed until between the last two flights, quickening when shaken up to take a narrow advantage at the last where Perle de Puce, who was flat out, fell. Keeping on well, Lingo went on to beat Garde Champetre by one and a half lengths, the pair clear of third-placed Bourbon Manhattan.

Lingo (IRE) (b.g. 1999)	Poliglote (b 1992)	Sadler's Wells (b 1981)	Northern Dancer
			Fairy Bridge
		Alexandrie (b or br 1980)	Val de L'Orne
			Apachee
	Sea Ring (FR) (b 1990)	Bering (ch 1983)	Arctic Tern
			Beaune
		Blue River (b 1980)	Riverman
			Azurella

Mr John P. McManus' "Lingo"

Lingo, who cost 300,000 francs as a yearling, is from the small first crop of the French-based stallion Poliglote, who did the majority of his racing in France and showed very smart form at up to a mile and a half. Two of Poliglote's five wins came in the Criterium de Saint-Cloud and the Grand Prix d'Evry, while he also finished second to Celtic Swing in the Prix du Jockey-Club. Lingo's dam, Sea Ring, also won in France, over eight and a half furlongs as a three-year-old and ten and a half furlongs at four. Lingo, Sea Ring's third foal, is closely related to her first, the useful French mare Torrealta (by In The Wings) who showed her form over as far as fifteen and a half furlongs; and he is also a half-brother to the fair French hurdler Comandante (by Apple Tree), who gained one of his wins in a two-mile juvenile event at Kempton, and to the 2004 Poule d'Essai des Pouliches winner Torrestrella (by Orpen). The great grandam of Lingo, Azurella, is also the third dam of the 1999 Criterium de Saint-Cloud winner and Prix de Diane third Goldamix. Azurella was a smart middle-distance filly, winner at around a mile and a quarter of the Group 3 Prix de Malleret and Prix de Royaumont. Lingo's grandam Blue River, a seven-furlong winner in France at two who went on to finish third in the Prix d'Aumale, is a half-sister to the Prix de Minerve winner Anitra's Dance, whose successful produce include Solveig, a Group 3 winner over ten and a half furlongs. There is enough stamina in Lingo's pedigree to suggest that he should stay beyond two miles over hurdles, but it is unlikely that he will be asked to tackle further, at least in the short term. The Champion Hurdle, mentioned as a possible target in his first season, will almost certainly be on the agenda in his second, and it would be no great surprise if he improved enough to make his presence felt at that level. The angular Lingo has raced only on good to soft ground over hurdles. His five wins on the Flat were gained on either soft or good to firm ground. *Jonjo O'Neill*

LINK COPPER 15 ch.g. Whistlefield – Letitica (Deep Run) [2003/4 c76, h–: c25m^F May 9] sturdy gelding: one-time fairly useful pointer: modest form both completed starts in hunter chases since 1997. *Mrs E. J. Taplin*

      c–
      h–

LINUS 6 b.g. Bin Ajwaad (IRE) – Land Line (High Line) [2003/4 h86: 19m^su 17d³ 22g³ 22g* 24f^pu 19d 20d² 24s^pu Feb 1] compact gelding: modest hurdler: won seller at Newton Abbot in September: lame final outing: stays 2¾m: acts on heavy going, possibly not on firmer than good: tried in cheekpieces: not one to trust. *C. J. Down*

      h92 §

LION GUEST (IRE) 7 ch.g. Lion Cavern (USA) – Descrescendo (IRE) (Polish Precedent (USA)) [2003/4 h78: 16g⁵ 16m⁴ 20m 20d* 22m⁴ 20g^pu Aug 16] modest hurdler: won novice handicap at Perth in July: running well when going lame there final outing: stays 2½m: acts on good to soft ground. *Mrs S. C. Bradburne*

      h87

LIRFOX (FR) 7 b.m. Foxhound (USA) – Lirfa (USA) (Lear Fan (USA)) [2003/4 h120: c19m* c16m* c17m* c16g³ c16m² c17s⁶ 17v^pu Mar 23] angular mare: fairly useful hurdler: successful first 3 starts in novice chases, landing odds at Hereford in May and and Market Rasen later in June: reluctant to race/let down by jumping next 2 outings, then left M. Pipe: won over hurdles at Saint Malo in late-May: will stay at least 2½m: acts on soft and good to firm going: front runner. *Jack Barbe, France*

      c112
      h?

LIRKIMALONG 11 ch.g. Lir – Kimberley Ann (St Columbus) [2003/4 c24g⁴ Apr 18] modest pointer, won maiden in 2003: well-beaten fourth to Chasing The Bride in hunter at Stratford. *Miss S. Young*

      c–
      h–

LIRSLEFTOVER 12 ch.g. Lir – Full Tan (Dairialatan) [2003/4 c–: c24m⁵ Mar 4] fair pointer, won in March: maiden steeplechaser. *Miss S. Young*

      c72

LIRTA (FR) 5 gr.g. Art Francais (USA) – Sirta (FR) (Le Pontet (FR)) [2003/4 c17s² c17s² c16g⁴ Dec 31] tall, leggy ex-French gelding: fifth foal: half-brother to winning 17f hurdler Harielle II (by Un Numide) and cross-country chaser Ismenie (by Abdonski): dam winning chaser up to 23f: runner-up both starts in 4-y-o hurdles at Pau: fair form over fences: left E. Leenders after second in 4-y-o event at Auteuil: off 7 months, weakened quickly after racing in clear lead until halfway in novice at Cheltenham on British debut: raced around 2m: acts on heavy going. *P. J. Hobbs*

      c108
      h–

LISAAN (IRE) 7 ch.g. Bigstone (IRE) – Linnga (IRE) (Shardari) [2003/4 c109§, h–§: c16g⁴ c18d* c18d² c17s⁴ c19d c22s² c20s⁴ c20v³ Apr 17] workmanlike gelding: winning hurdler: fair handicap chaser: won at Punchestown in November: stays 2¾m: acts on heavy going: effective blinkered or not: often looks unwilling under pressure. *W. Durkan, Ireland*

      c113 §
      h– §

LISA-B (IRE) 7 b.m. Case Law – Nishiki (USA) (Brogan (USA)) [2003/4 h67: 19g c24g^{pu} c26m^{pu} c20m^{pu} Jul 19] of little account: sometimes visored: has worn tongue strap. *D. L. Williams* **c–** **h–**

LISA DU CHENET (FR) 5 b.m. Garde Royale – Tchela (FR) (Le Nain Jaune (FR)) [2003/4 F78: 19s⁵ 20s^s 23s^s 24s^{pu} Apr 21] medium-sized mare: fair form in novice hurdles: won mares events at Fontwell in January and Lingfield (by 4 lengths from Eau Pure with something in hand) in April: should stay 3m: raced only on soft ground over hurdles. *Mrs Susan Nock* **h107**

LISCAHILL HILL (IRE) 13 ch.g. Executive Perk – Carlow Highway (Royal Highway) [2003/4 16g 16d⁴ 16d[*] 16d 16f² 17f[*] 16d² 16g^{pu} 16m^{pu} Oct 10] lengthy gelding: fairly useful handicap hurdler: won at Roscommon in June and Tralee in August: good second to Gamekeeper at Galway in September: well below form both subsequent starts: best around 2m: acts on any going: has had tongue tied. *D. Loughnane, Ireland* **h123**

LISCANNOR LAD (IRE) 6 b.g. Nicolette – Tinerana Memories (IRE) (Don't Forget Me) [2003/4 h119, F90: 20m[*] c18d² c22s^{ur} c18s³ c21g^F c24g⁶ c17d Apr 13] rangy gelding: has scope: fair hurdler: won minor event at Navan in November: fairly useful chaser: improved form when winning valuable novice handicap at Punchestown in late-April by 1½ lengths from Ride The Storm despite carrying head high, coming from off good pace: stays 25f: acts on good to firm and heavy going. *D. T. Hughes, Ireland* **c120** **h105**

LISDANTE (IRE) 11 b.g. Phardante (FR) – Shuil Eile (Deep Run) [2003/4 c114, h–: c20m^{pu} c24g³ c26m[*] c24m^{pu} c26g² Nov 10] sturdy gelding: fair handicap chaser: won 5-runner event at Southwell in August: stays 4m: acts on good to firm and heavy going: tried blinkered: races prominently. *Mrs S. J. Smith* **c110** **h–**

LISLAUGHTIN ABBEY 12 ch.g. Nicholas Bill – Kates Fling (USA) (Quiet Fling (USA)) [2003/4 c95, h–: c23m[*] c21s^{pu} Mar 19] lengthy, sparely-made gelding: fair handicap chaser: won at Worcester in June: stays 3m: acts on any going: has won 5 times at Fakenham. *O. Brennan* **c102** **h–**

Sharp Minds Betfair Novices' Handicap Chase, Punchestown—
jumping errors by fancied runners leave Liscannor Lad (right) to fight it out with Ride The Storm

LISSNABRUCKA (IRE)   6 b.m. Lord Americo – Judy Henry (Orchestra) [2003/4   **h71**
21s⁴ 22vᵖᵘ Jan 24] good-topped mare: ninth foal: half-sister to fair staying hurdler/
winning chaser High Island (by Roselier): dam once-raced half-sister to dam of useful
staying chaser Saxophone: thrice-raced in Irish points in 2003, winning both completed
starts: poor form at Towcester on first of 2 runs in mares novice hurdles. *Jonjo O'Neill*

LITTLE ALFIE (IRE)   7 b.g. Shahanndeh – Debbies Scud (IRE) (Roselier (FR))   **h–**
[2003/4 h62: 19gᵖᵘ Dec 3] strong, sturdy gelding: poor maiden hurdler: raced mainly
around 2m: acts on firm and good to soft going. *B. S. Rothwell*

LITTLE BIG HORSE (IRE)   8 b.g. Little Bighorn – Little Gort (Roselier (FR))   **c109**
[2003/4 h94: c21s³ 23d³ c25s* c25g⁶ c20g* Apr 24] leggy gelding: modest maiden   **h89**
hurdler: fair form over fences, showing much better attitude than previously when
winning novices at Market Rasen in March and April: stays 25f: acts on soft and good to
firm going. *Mrs S. J. Smith*

LITTLE BROWN BEAR (IRE)   10 br.g. Strong Gale – Gladtogetit (Green Shoon)   **c102**
[2003/4 c100, h–: c24g* 24m* 24d⁵ c26mᵖᵘ c24m³ Apr 13] workmanlike gelding: fair   **h78 +**
handicap chaser: won at Fakenham in May: second run over hurdles, made all in weak
novice at Perth following month: stays 3½m: acts on good to firm and good to soft going:
front runner/races prominently: sound jumper. *R. Ford*

LITTLE BUD   10 br.m. Lord Bud – Sindur (Rolfe (USA)) [2003/4 h97: 16m   **h95 §**
21m⁴ 20sᵖᵘ 24g 16s 21d² 18dʳᵗʳ Mar 21] smallish, lengthy mare: modest handicap hurdler:
stays 21f: acts on heavy and good to firm going: tried blinkered: has won 5 times at
Plumpton: reluctant/refused to race last 2 outings: one to treat with caution. *Miss
A. M. Newton-Smith*

LITTLE CHARTRIDGE   6 b.m. Anshan – Auntie Dot (Hallodri (ATA)) [2003/4   **F74**
F16g F17d Mar 27] fourth foal: half-sister to 2½m chase winner Chartridge Hill (by
Crested Lark): dam, useful chaser effective around 2½m and third in 1991 Grand
National, half-sister to high-class chaser Townley Stone: poor form in bumper on debut,
possibly flattered. *P. R. Webber*

LITTLE DAPHNE   6 b.m. Presenting – Glengarra Princess (Cardinal Flower) [2003/4   **h–**
F17m F16m⁴ 22mᵖᵘ Jul 14] third foal: dam, winning pointer/hurdler who stayed 2½m, out   **F74**
of half-sister to smart chaser up to 2¾m Villierstown: third in mares maiden point on
debut: poor form in bumpers: co-favourite, well held in mares novice on hurdling debut.
P. Bowen

LITTLE DOCKER (IRE)   7 b.g. Vettori (IRE) – Fair Maid of Kent (USA) (Diesis)   **c94**
[2003/4 17d 16g³ c20d⁴ c16d² c16d² c16sᶠ c19g⁵ c19g⁵ Jan 24] big, workmanlike geld-   **h97**
ing: winning hurdler, off nearly 2 years before reappearance: modest form over fences:
likely to stay beyond 2½m: acts on good to soft going: needs to jump more fluently over
fences. *T. D. Easterby*

LITTLE ED   6 b.g. Shambo – Edina (IRE) (The Parson) [2003/4 F18s⁵ 17dᵇᵈ 20d² Dec   **h80 ?**
27] first foal: dam, maiden jumper, out of half-sister to smart 2½m chaser Malya Mal: **F73**
poor form in bumper and on completed start over hurdles. *P. R. Webber*

LITTLE ENAM (IRE)   8 gr.g. Un Desperado (FR) – Black Pheasant (IRE) (Sexton   **h–**
Blake) [2003/4 h–, F70: 16vᵖᵘ 16sᵖᵘ Mar 15] no form in novice hurdles. *C. R. Egerton*

LITTLE FARMER   10 b.g. Little Wolf – Sea Farmer (Cantab) [2003/4 c21m* c24g³   **c98**
Mar 5] fairly useful pointer, won in April: won maiden hunter at Folkestone early in   **h–**
season: better form when third to Right To Reply at Newbury: stays 3m: front runner.
Mrs D. M. Grissell

LITTLE FELLA (IRE)   5 b. or br.g. Kahyasi – Copper Breeze (IRE) (Strong Gale)   **h–**
[2003/4 aF16g² 22s Jan 8] €36,000 3-y-o: fourth foal: half-brother to winning pointer by   **F86**
Erins Isle: dam, unraced half-sister to useful staying chaser Sir Leonard: fell first in
maiden Irish point on debut in 2003: 3 lengths second to Ruby Too in bumper on polytrack at Lingfield: not knocked about when well held in novice at Wincanton on hurdling
debut. *B. G. Powell*

LITTLE FLORA   8 ch.m. Alflora (IRE) – Sister's Choice (Lepanto (GER)) [2003/4   **h73**
h85: 20d 16g⁶ 16d Mar 18] compact mare: winning hurdler: little impact in 3 handicaps
in 2003/4: stays 21f: acts on any going: front runner. *Miss V. Scott*

LITTLE HERMAN (IRE)   8 b.g. Mandalus – Kilbricken Bay (Salluceva) [2003/4   **c70**
c–, h70: c26gᵖᵘ c26m³ c23g³ c26g* c26g Apr 12] well-made gelding: novice hurdler: **h–**
poor chaser: won handicap at Chepstow in March: stays 3¼m. *J. A. B. Old*

LITTLE KNOWLEDGE 6 b.m. Terimon – Madam-M (Tina's Pet) [2003/4 F–: F17m Jun 18] well beaten in 2 bumpers over year apart. *N. A. Twiston-Davies*   **F–**

LITTLE LIL 5 ch.m. Sula Bula – Sherzine (Gorytus (USA)) [2003/4 F16d F16d 17g 19g⁵ Apr 16] sixth foal: half-sister to winning 17f hurdler Megazine (by Shaab): dam modest 2m hurdler/1½m winner on Flat: little sign of ability. *J. D. Frost*   **h– F–**

LITTLE LORD LEWIS 5 b.g. Sir Harry Lewis (USA) – Unspoken Prayer (Inca Chief (USA)) [2003/4 F16m⁵ F17m Oct 10] leggy gelding: first live foal: dam poor maiden who stayed 1m: tailed off in 2 bumpers. *Mrs H. O. Graham*   **F–**

LITTLE MICK (IRE) 7 br.g. Mister Lord (USA) – Strong Trump (IRE) (Strong Gale) [2003/4 h–: 16g 20m⁵ Aug 2] lengthy gelding: first form when fifth of 12 in novice hurdle at Worcester: will stay 3m. *J. A. B. Old*   **h74**

LITTLE MISS PRIM 8 b.m. Gildoran – Laced Up (IRE) (The Parson) [2003/4 16dᵖᵘ 22d 21dᵘʳ 24g Mar 26] small mare: little worthwhile form, off over 2 years before reappearance. *J. G. O'Neill*   **h–**

LITTLE MISTER 8 ch.g. Gran Alba (USA) – Chrissytino (Baron Blakeney) [2003/4 h–: 19m² 22mᵖᵘ May 26] of no account: tried blinkered. *N. R. Mitchell*   **h–**

LITTLE ORA (IRE) 7 ch.g. Black Monday – Country Melody (IRE) (Orchestra) [2003/4 16s² 17g⁴ 16g³ 18m³ 16s³ 16s⁶ 18s³ 16s² 16d Feb 22] small, angular gelding: modest handicap hurdler: raced around 2m: acts on heavy and good to firm going. *P. J. Rothwell, Ireland*   **h89**

LITTLE PERSON 5 ch.m. Factual (USA) – Chaleureuse (Final Straw) [2003/4 F17d May 17] half-sister to modest 9f winner Outstanding Talent (by Environment Friend) and winner in Holland by Liboi: dam ran once: tailed off in mares bumper on debut. *G. A. Harker*   **F–**

LITTLE RORT (IRE) 5 b.g. Ali-Royal (IRE) – Florinda (Vice Regent (CAN)) [2003/4 h113: 16g⁴ 16g⁶ 18s* 19s 20s 22s Mar 14] sturdy gelding: fair hurdler: won minor event at Fairyhouse in November: no form after: should stay beyond 2¼m: raced on good ground or softer (acts on heavy): tongue tied. *M. J. Grassick, Ireland*   **h112**

LITTLE ROSS 9 b.g. St Ninian – Little Katrina (Little Buskins) [2003/4 c80, h79: 24g³ 26s c19vᵘ⁴ c22v 16s³ 17d⁴ Mar 3] lengthy gelding: poor maiden hurdler/chaser: effective at 2m, probably at 3m: raced mainly on good going or softer (acts on heavy): tongue tied. *D. B. Feek*   **c– h82**

LITTLE SKY 7 gr.m. Terimon – Brown Coast (Oats) [2003/4 h–, F–: 17gᵖᵘ 16g 26mᵖᵘ Aug 25] little form on Flat, none over hurdles. *D. Mullarkey*   **h–**

LITTLE TASK 6 b.g. Environment Friend – Lucky Thing (Green Desert (USA)) [2003/4 c70, h93d: c17g³ c16mᵘʳ c16g* c16d³ c16g⁶ 17d³ 17g 20f⁴ 26m⁴ Sep 28] small gelding: flattered when winning novice chase at Perth in June: poor handicap hurdler: raced mainly around 2m: acts on firm and good to soft going: tried visored/in cheekpieces. *J. S. Wainwright*   **c97 ? h75**

LITTLE TERN (IRE) 5 b.m. Terimon – Miss Fern (Cruise Missile) [2003/4 F16v⁶ 19dᵖᵘ Feb 15] second foal: dam, winning chaser, stayed 3¼m: no sign of ability in bumper and mares novice hurdle. *R. Dickin*   **h– F–**

LITTLE TOBIAS (IRE) 5 ch.g. Millkom – Barbara Frietchie (IRE) (Try My Best (USA)) [2003/4 h92: 16m 19m⁴ 16d Nov 15] modest on Flat (stays 2m): modest hurdler: stays 19f: acts on firm going: temperamental. *Andrew Turnell*   **h92 §**

LITTLETON AMETHYST (IRE) 5 ch.m. Revoque (IRE) – Sept Roses (USA) (Septieme Ciel (USA)) [2003/4 20mᵖᵘ 16m Dec 10] poor maiden on Flat (barely stays 2m), sold out of T. Naughton's stable 2,500 gns Doncaster May Sales: no form in 2 novice hurdles. *Mrs P. Ford*   **h–**

LITTLETON VALAR (IRE) 4 ch.g. Definite Article – Fresh Look (IRE) (Alzao (USA)) [2003/4 16g⁶ 16g 16f 20s⁵ 17dᵖᵘ Mar 30] poor maiden on Flat (stays 1¼m): little worthwhile form over hurdles: will prove best around 2m. *J. R. Weymes*   **h69**

LITTLETON ZEUS (IRE) 5 ch.g. Woodborough (USA) – La Fandango (IRE) (Taufan (USA)) [2003/4 h–: 20gᵖᵘ 16mᵘʳ May 27] poor maiden over hurdles or in points: tried in cheekpieces. *W. S. Cunningham*   **h–**

LITTLE TUSKA (IRE) 14 gr.g. Step Together (USA) – Peek-A-Boo (Bustino) [2003/4 c70§, h72§: 20m May 7] workmanlike gelding: poor maiden hurdler/handicap chaser: out of sorts since early-2002/3: stays 21f: acts on any going: used to be blinkered: tongue tied: not one to trust. *M. J. M. Evans*   **c– § h– §**

LITTLE VALENTINE (GER)   4 b.c. Gold And Ivory (USA) – Lagoa Feia (GER)   **h86**
(Gimont (GER)) [2003/4 16d⁴ Dec 5] leggy, sparely-made colt: successful once over 1m
from 6 starts on Flat in Germany in 2003: fourth of 6 to Nawow in juvenile at Sandown
on hurdling debut: looks excitable sort. *C. Von Der Recke, Germany*

LITZINSKY   6 b.g. Muhtarram (USA) – Boulevard Girl (Nicholas Bill) [2003/4 20d⁶   **h82**
20s⁶ Mar 13] fair at best on Flat (stays 2¼m well): poor form in 2 novice hurdles at
Newcastle. *C. B. B. Booth*

LIVELY DESSERT (IRE)   11 b.g. Be My Native (USA) – Liffey Travel (Le Bavard   **c–**
(FR)) [2003/4 c95d, h–: 26d⁴ May 28] lengthy gelding: winning chaser/maiden hurdler: **h–**
won point in April: probably stays 4m: acts on good to firm and heavy going: tried
visored/in cheekpieces. *F. P. Murtagh*

LIVELY FELIX   7 b.g. Presidium – Full of Life (Wolverlife) [2003/4 c16m Jun 1]   **c–**
leggy gelding: maiden hurdler: no form since 2000/1, including over fences: tried vis-   **h–**
ored: has had tongue tied: sold £1,000 Ascot December Sales, poor form back on Flat for
D. Arbuthnot. *D. W. P. Arbuthnot*

LIVRET BLEU (FR)   5 b.g. Panoramic – Azur Bleue (FR) (Djarvis (FR)) [2003/4   **c98**
c17s c18s⁶ c17s⁴ c17s⁶ c18s⁶ c17v³ 19s⁶ Jan 14] good-topped ex-French gelding: third   **h79**
foal: half-brother to winning 17f chaser Kepibleu (by Valanjou): dam 1½m winner:
twice-raced on Flat: modest form over fences, claimed from G. Cherel €13,000 after third
in claimer at Auteuil in November: second outing over hurdles, poor form when sixth in
novice at Newbury on British debut: raced mainly around 2m: acts on heavy ground.
A. E. Jessop

LIZZIE BATHWICK (IRE)   5 b.m. Glacial Storm (USA) – Protrial (Proverb)   **h78**
[2003/4 17g⁵ Apr 10] fifth foal: sister to fairly useful hunter chaser Glacial Trial, stays
3½m, and half-sister to fair staying chaser Nativetrial (by Be My Native): dam winning
pointer: fifth in mares maiden hurdle at Newton Abbot on debut: will be suited by 2½m+.
D. P. Keane

LIZZY LAMB   6 b.m. Bustino – Caroline Lamb (Hotfoot) [2003/4 F70: 17m⁵ Aug 30]   **h–**
third in bumper on Flat in 2002/3: off 13 months, fifth of 8 in weakly-contested mares
novice at Market Rasen on hurdling debut. *Miss S. E. Hall*

LIZZYS FIRST   12 b.g. Town And Country – Lizzy Longstocking (Jimsun) [2003/4   **c– x**
c–x, h91: 24m c19d c19g^F Mar 9] workmanlike gelding: modest handicap hurdler: let   **h86**
down by jumping over fences: effective at 19f to 3m: acts on any going: blinkered twice:
none too consistent. *C. J. Down*

LOADED GUN   4 ch.g. Highest Honor (FR) – Woodwardia (USA) (El Gran Senor   **h–**
(USA)) [2003/4 16d⁵ Nov 23] fair maiden at 2 yrs in France for Mme C. Head-Maarek:
well beaten in juvenile on hurdling debut, looking none too keen: sold 2,000 gns
Doncaster March Sales, well held on return to Flat for W. M. Brisbourne. *Miss J. Feilden*

LOAN MAN (IRE)   10 ch.g. Montelimar (USA) – Miss Daisy Dee (Baptism) [2003/4   **c114**
c16d* c20g* c17s⁴ c20f⁵ c21m⁶ c20s^F Mar 14] tall gelding: modest hurdler: fair chaser: **h–**
won maiden at Cork in May and novice at Killarney in July, beating Find The King 4
lengths at latter: stays 2½m: acts on firm and good to soft going: tongue tied. *J. F. O'Shea,
Ireland*

LOBLITE LEADER (IRE)   7 b.g. Tirol – Cyrano Beauty (IRE) (Cyrano de Bergerac)   **h79 +**
[2003/4 h95: 17d⁵ Apr 10] good-topped gelding: modest on Flat (stays 1¾m):
thrice-raced over hurdles, off 14 months before fifth in novice at Carlisle in April.
G. A. Swinbank

LOBUCHE (IRE)   9 b.g. Petardia – Lhotse (IRE) (Shernazar) [2003/4 c–, h–: 16g^pu   **c–**
May 18] small gelding: winning hurdler/maiden chaser: no form since 2001/2: usually   **h–**
tongue tied. *M. C. Chapman*

LOCHBUY JUNIOR (FR)   9 b.g. Saumarez – Chalabiah (Akarad (FR)) [2003/4   **c–**
h104: c21s^pu c19g⁴ Jan 15] rather leggy gelding: winning hurdler: ran as if amiss in 2   **h–**
maiden chases (breathing problem on second occasion): stays 21f: acts on soft going: has
had tongue tied. *M. Todhunter*

LOCHIEDUBS   9 br.g. Cragador – Linn Falls (Royal Fountain) [2003/4 h82: 20d 24d   **c90 x**
27s⁵ c21v^pu c24g⁶ c20s³ c20s* c20g⁶ c20g⁵ c20s^F Apr 21] lengthy gelding: poor maiden   **h–**
hurdler: modest chaser: won novice handicap at Newcastle in March: should stay beyond
2½m: acts on good to firm and heavy going: tried blinkered/in cheekpieces: not a fluent
jumper. *Mrs L. B. Normile*

LOCH NA BPEISC (IRE)   7 b.g. Over The River (FR) – Ballyhire Lady (IRE)   **c61**
(Callernish) [2003/4 h–: c25d^{pu} c24s^{pu} c26d^4 c25d^4 c24v^3 c25s^{pu} Feb 22] stocky gelding: **h–**
poor maiden chaser: badly amiss final start: stays 3m: acts on heavy ground. *P. G. Murphy*

LOCH RED   5 ch.g. Primitive Rising (USA) – Lochcross (Lochnager) [2003/4 F16g   **F–**
Mar 6] second foal: dam poor maiden on Flat: tailed off in bumper on debut.
Mrs A. M. Naughton

LOCH SIDE   6 gr.m. Tina's Pet – Sparkling Time (USA) (Olden Times) [2003/4 F17s^6 **h–**
22d^{pu} 18g^{pu} Apr 22] small, angular mare: half-sister to several winners, including useful   **F80**
hurdler Coworth Park (by Wolver Hollow), stayed 3m, and useful chaser up to 25f
Sparkling Cone (by Celtic Cone): dam ran twice at 2 yrs: sixth of 14 in mares bumper on
debut, looking a stayer: no encouragement either outing over hurdles. *M. Scudamore*

LOCH SOUND   8 b.g. Primitive Rising (USA) – Lochcross (Lochnager) [2003/4 19g   **c–**
c16d^{pu} 16g Apr 5] close-coupled gelding: little sign of ability: tried tongue tied.   **h–**
Mrs A. M. Naughton

LOCK INN   5 b.g. Dolphin Street (FR) – Highest Bid (FR) (Highest Honor (FR))   **h–**
[2003/4 20g^4 20s 22v^4 22s^6 22d 25d Apr 11] poor maiden on Flat (seems to stay 1¾m):
no worthwhile form over hurdles: tried visored. *Miss Z. C. Davison*

LOCKSMITH   4 gr.g. Linamix (FR) – Zenith (Shirley Heights) [2003/4 F12s* F13d^4 **h133**
F12d^4 18s* 17s^2 16g^2 16g Mar 16] angular gelding: fifth foal: half-brother to useful 1¼m   **F100**
winner Spinning Top (by Alzao) and US 7f/9f winner Daytime (by Danehill): dam, 2-y-o
8.5f winner, out of smart miler Soprano: won 3-y-o event at Ascot in November on first
of 3 starts in bumpers: useful form over hurdles: won juvenile at Fontwell in January by
29 lengths from Croix de Guerre: runner-up next 2 starts, good seventh of 19 to Brave
Inca in Supreme Novices' Hurdle at Cheltenham: likely to prove best around 2m: raced
on good going or softer: races prominently. *M. C. Pipe*

LOCKSTOCKANDBARREL (IRE)   5 b.g. Needle Gun (IRE) – Quill Project   **F94**
(IRE) (Project Manager) [2003/4 F17g^4 Apr 24] €20,000 3-y-o: second foal: dam fair 2m
hurdle winner/fairly useful 1¼m winner on Flat: tongue tied, won bumper at Market
Rasen on debut by head from Kitski, pair clear. *M. C. Banks*

LODESTAR (IRE)   7 br.g. Good Thyne (USA) – Let's Compromise (No Argument)   **c107**
[2003/4 c101, h101: 24m* c24g^3 c20m^4 c24g^2 c25d^4 Nov 23] tall gelding: fair hurdler: **h111**
won handicap at Worcester in May: similar form over fences: stays 3¼m: acts on good to
firm and good to soft going. *Ian Williams*

LOFTY LEADER (IRE)   5 b.g. Norwich – Slaney Jazz (Orchestra) [2003/4 F16m   **F91**
F16v^5 F16d F17d^2 Apr 18] €12,000 4-y-o: third foal: half-brother to bumper winner
Oncourse (by Toulon): dam lightly raced in bumpers and points: easily best effort in
bumpers when second to Elfkirk at Carlisle. *W. McKeown*

LOG ON INTERSKY (IRE)   8 ch.g. Insan (USA) – Arctic Mo (IRE) (Mandalus)   **c135**
[2003/4 c122, h90: c17f^3 c20g^2 c16m* c16s c16g^{pu} c16d^2 Apr 17] lengthy gelding: **h–**
has reportedly had wind operation: useful handicap chaser: won at Ayr in November by
7 lengths from Sir Storm: best subsequent effort when respectable second of 4 finishers
to Avalanche there in April: effective at 2m to 21f: acts on firm and soft going: often
tongue tied over hurdles: usually races prominently: usually sound jumper: consistent.
J. Howard Johnson

LOGSDAIL   4 b.g. Polish Precedent (USA) – Logic (Slip Anchor) [2003/4 17g^2 16m^6 **h88 +**
Oct 25] useful-looking gelding: fairly useful on Flat (stays 1m), sold out of Mrs
J. Ramsden's stable 31,000 gns Newmarket July Sales: second in juvenile at Newton
Abbot on hurdling debut, finding little: better than result next time: likely to need sharp
2m: sold to join G. L. Moore 16,000 gns Newmarket Autumn Sales. *P. J. Hobbs*

LOI DE MARTIALE (IRE)   6 br.g. Presenting – Thresa-Anita (IRE) (Over The   **h83**
River (FR)) [2003/4 F87: F16g^3 F17m^3 24d^6 17d Apr 10] good-topped gelding: fair form   **F86**
in bumpers: much better effort in novice hurdles at Carlisle when sixth of 7 finishers:
likely to prove suited by 2½m+. *J. M. Jefferson*

L'OISEAU (FR)   5 br.g. Video Rock (FR) – Roseraie (FR) (Quart de Vin (FR)) [2003/4   **h92**
F16g^2 F17d F17d 16g 20d^3 17d^{pu} 17d^2 Apr 10] leggy gelding: sixth known foal: brother   **F93**
to useful chaser/winning hurdler up to 19f Floridee and half-brother to 2 winners, including cross-country chaser/prolific middle-distance winner Capuccino II (by Pamponi):
dam unraced sister to outstanding French chaser Ucello II, from family of King George
VI Chase winner Nupsala: fair form in bumpers: best efforts in novice hurdles when
placed at Carlisle: stays 2½m: raced only on good/good to soft going. *L. Lungo*

LONE SOLDIER (FR)   8 ch.g. Songlines (FR) – Caring Society (Caerleon (USA)) c–
[2003/4 c–, h–: 17f³ 17m² 17dᵘʳ 16gᵖᵘ 17g 16g 19g* 17gᶠ Mar 28] compact gelding: h79
winning chaser: poor handicap hurdler: won at Catterick in March: stays easy 19f. acts on
firm and soft going: effective tongue tied or not: has found little: inconslstent. *S. B. Clark*

LONESOME DEALER (IRE)   8 b. or br.g. Supreme Leader – Slievenaree (IRE) c–
(Lancastrian) [2003/4 c87, h–: c16gᵖᵘ c17sᶠ 19g³ May 31] maiden chaser: winning 2m h77
hurdler: first form in Britain when third in 19f seller at Hereford (finished lame): acts on
heavy ground: raced freely in visor second start. *B. G. Powell*

LONESOME MAN (IRE)   8 ch.g. Broken Hearted – Carn-Na-Ros (Royal Trip) h95
[2003/4 20d⁶ 20s³ 16g Mar 6] ex-Irish gelding: ninth foal: dam winning pointer: fair form
when placed in maiden hurdles for J. Cosgrave: modest at best in Britain in 2003/4:
should stay beyond 2m: raced on good going or softer (acts on soft). *R. T. Phillips*

LONE STAR (IRE)   12 b.g. Satco (FR) – Masterstown Lucy (Bargello) [2003/4 c–, c–
h–: c24mᵖᵘ May 10] rangy gelding: little form over hurdles or in steeplechases: tried h–
blinkered/tongue tied. *Martin Ward*

LONGMEADOWS BOY (IRE)   4 b.g. Victory Note (USA) – Karoi (IRE) (Kafu) h96
[2003/4 17g* 17gᵖᵘ Sep 13] half-brother to fairly useful 2m hurdler Stacumny Bridge (by
Flying Spur): modest on Flat (stays 1½m): won juvenile at Cartmel on hurdling debut:
possibly amiss following month. *A. Berry*

LONGSHANKS   7 b.g. Broadsword (USA) – Brass Castle (Carlingford Castle) [2003/4 c120 +
c93p, h97: 22d³ 24gᵖᵘ c22g* c20d* c24d* c24d³ c21g² Apr 2] workmanlike gelding: h96 +
modest form over hurdles: won novice at Uttoxeter in May: did very well back over
fences, showing fairly useful form and winning handicaps at Haydock and Ayr (novice)
in November and Haydock in December making all first 2 occasions: good placed efforts
last 2 starts, second to Cassia Heights in Topham Chase (Handicap) at Aintree: stays 3m:
raced on good going or softer: sound jumper. *K. C. Bailey*

LONGSHIP   6 b.g. Saddlers' Hall (IRE) – Main Sail (Blakeney) [2003/4 F16m 17dᵖᵘ h–
May 28] half-brother to fair hurdler up to 2¾m Sailor Boy (by Main Reef) and winning F–
2m hurdler Coble (by Slip Anchor): dam, useful 7f/1m winner, out of half-sister to Oaks
winner Bireme: no sign of ability in bumper or maiden hurdle. *D. McCain*

LONG SHOT   7 b.m. Sir Harry Lewis (USA) – Kovalevskia (Ardross) [2003/4 h93: h102
24m³ 16g* 19g³ 20s² 24g⁵ 17s Jan 20] leggy mare: fair handicap hurdler: made all in
mares event at Huntingdon in November: effective at 2m to 2¾m: acts on soft going: has
flashed tail. *N. J. Henderson*

LONGSTONE BOY (IRE)   12 br.g. Mazaad – Inger-Lea (Record Run) [2003/4 c88: c88
c24m⁵ c20g* c24g³ Apr 1] good-bodied gelding: fair hunter chaser: won point in February and maiden hunter at Leicester in March: stays 3m: acts on firm and good to soft
going. *E. R. Clough*

LONGSTONE LASS   4 b.f. Wizard King – Kamaress (Kampala) [2003/4 F16s⁵ F17s h–
16gᶠ 16gᶠ 16s⁴ Mar 13] unfurnished filly: sixth foal: dam fairly useful up to 1¼m: little F–
sign of ability in bumpers or over hurdles. *W. McKeown*

LONGSTONE LOCH (IRE)   7 b.g. Executive Perk – Lyre-Na-Gcloc (Le Moss) c86 +
[2003/4 h–: 17d⁶ 19s⁶ c19g* Mar 5] lengthy gelding: poor form over hurdles: won h74
handicap at Doncaster on steeplechasing debut: should stay beyond 19f. *C. C. Bealby*

LONG WALK (IRE)   7 b.g. King's Ride – Seanaphobal Lady (Kambalda) [2003/4 c104
20g⁵ c20s³ c21d⁴ c24g* c24g³ c24d* Apr 8] tall, useful-looking gelding: maiden hurdler: h91
fair novice chaser: won at Ludlow in February (maiden) and April: stays 3m: raced on
good going or softer. *H. D. Daly*

LOOK COLLONGES (FR)   5 gr.g. Dom Alco (FR) – Tessy Collonges (FR) (El c119
Badr) [2003/4 c17s² c20s² c16m* c16mᶠ c24d² c21s* Mar 21] good-topped gelding: h–
sixth foal: half-brother to useful chaser Donjuan Collonges (by Trebrook), stayed 3¼m,
and middle-distance winner Idole Collonges (by Brezzo): dam, lightly-raced maiden
chaser, half-sister to dam of high-class staying chaser Baccarat Collonges: modest form
on hurdling debut: fairly useful chaser: won at Warwick (novice) in November and
Auteuil (handicap, by 4 lengths from Karouba) in March: effective at 2m to 3m: acts on
soft and good to firm going. *G. Macaire, France*

LOOKING DEADLY   10 b.m. Neltino – Princess Constanza (Relkino) [2003/4 c63, c–
h63: c17g⁶ 17d May 28] poor maiden hurdler/chaser: raced mainly around 2m: acts on h–
soft going. *F. P. Murtagh*

LOO

LOOKING FORWARD 8 b.g. Primitive Rising (USA) – Gilzie Bank (New Brig) **c98**
[2003/4 c88: c19f* c20s^{pu} c20s^5 c24g^4 c21d* c20d^5 c21g* Apr 12] good-topped gelding:
modest handicap chaser: won at Catterick (idled) in November and Sedgefield in March
and April: stays 21f: acts on firm and good to soft going, possibly unsuited by soft/heavy.
Ferdy Murphy

LOOK SHARPE 13 b.g. Looking Glass – Washburn Flyer (Owen Dudley) [2003/4 **c83**
c83: c20m^2 c24m^4 May 10] modest pointer/maiden hunter chaser: should stay beyond
2½m: raced mainly on good going or firmer. *T. S. Sharpe*

LOOKSHARP LAD (IRE) 6 b.g. Simply Great (FR) – Merry Madness (Raise You **h–**
Ten) [2003/4 F–p: F17d^2 F16g 19g Mar 5] good sort: easily best effort in bumpers when **F95**
second at Bangor in December: well beaten in novice on hurdling debut: should be suited
by further than 17f. *Mrs A. J. Bowlby*

LOOKS LIKE VALUE (IRE) 8 gr.g. Euphemism – Crossdrumrosie (IRE) (Roselier **c–**
(FR)) [2003/4 c–, F–: c19g^{pu} May 13] workmanlike gelding: no form in bumper or
maiden chases: sold 3,500 gns Doncaster May Sales. *K. C. Bailey*

LOOK TO THE FUTURE (IRE) 10 b.g. Roselier (FR) – Toevarro (Raga Navarro **c87**
(ITY)) [2003/4 c–, h94: 22s^3 20v^3 25g c20d^3 c25s^{ur} c21g^4 Apr 12] compact gelding: fair **h100**
maiden hurdler: modest form over fences: stays 2¾m: possibly needs going softer than
good: none too consistent. *Mrs S. J. Smith*

LOOP THE LOUP 8 b.g. Petit Loup (USA) – Mithi Al Gamar (USA) (Blushing **h129**
Groom (FR)) [2003/4 h132: 16m 22g^2 17m 20m^4 20d^5 20s^3 21d^{pu} Jan 1] sturdy gelding:
fairly useful handicap hurdler: at least respectable efforts most starts in 2003/4: needs
good test around 2m, stays 2¾m: acts on soft and good to firm going: effective in
headgear or not: reportedly lost action final outing: consistent but not easy to win with
(often soon off bridle). *Mrs M. Reveley*

LOOPY LINDA (IRE) 6 b.g. Simply Great (FR) – Albane (Shirley Heights) [2003/4 **h–**
h–p, F98: 16v 19g^{pu} Feb 6] leggy gelding: fairly useful in bumpers: no form in 3 novice
hurdles: bled from nose final start: has flashed tail. *T. D. Easterby*

LOOSE NUT 6 b.m. Alflora (IRE) – Emmabella (True Song) [2003/4 F16m 20d^{pu} **h–**
24s^{pu} Jan 23] second foal: dam lightly-raced maiden pointer: no sign of ability. **F–**
A. Hollingsworth

L'ORAGE LADY (IRE) 6 ch.m. Glacial Storm (USA) – Commanche Glen (IRE) **h81**
(Commanche Run) [2003/4 F16m^3 F16m^4 F16g^3 19f* 16g^6 20d Dec 26] 7,500 4-y-o: **F88**
first foal: dam unraced half-sister to 2000 Grand National winner Papillon: fair form in
bumpers: won mares maiden at Catterick in November on hurdling debut: ran poorly final
outing: should prove suited by 2½m+: acts on firm going. *Mrs H. Dalton*

LORAMORE 7 ch.m. Alflora (IRE) – Apsimore (Touching Wood (USA)) [2003/4 h–, **h–**
F74: 16d^5 21d 17g^{pu} Mar 9] no form over hurdles. *J. C. Tuck*

LORD ADPAR 7 b.g. Bold Fox – Emlyn Princess (Julio Mariner) [2003/4 F16m Jun **F–**
28] sixth foal: brother to modest hurdler Gallant Taffy, stays 23f: dam useful hurdler/
winning chaser: soundly beaten in bumper on debut: sold £3,200 Ascot October Sales.
P. Bowen

LORD ALYN (IRE) 6 b.g. Topanoora – Glenstal Priory (Glenstal (USA)) [2003/4 **h76**
F–: F16m^6 F17m^5 F16m* 20m^{pu} 20f^4 16g^6 17m* 17d^{bd} 17v^{pu} Jan 1] useful-looking **F92**
gelding: progressive form in bumpers, won at Worcester in July: poor form when winning
selling handicap hurdle at Hereford in November: ran as if amiss all other starts over
hurdles, lame on second: best efforts around 2m: acts on good to firm going: tongue tied
last 4 outings. *C. R. Egerton*

LORD ATTERBURY (IRE) 8 ch.g. Mister Lord (USA) – Tammyiris (Arapahos **c133**
(FR)) [2003/4 c126p: c33d* c26d^{pu} c36d^3 Apr 3]
　　　　The majority of modern-day Grand National contenders have plenty of
experience over fences, but the latest National was only Lord Atterbury's fifth race
under rules. Furthermore, the National was his first venture outside hunter chases.
Bought for 10,000 guineas at the Doncaster August Sales in 2002 and transferred
from Ireland, where he won only once in six starts in points, the sturdy Lord Atterbury improved by leaps and bounds for David Pipe's pointing yard and was beaten
only once in six completed starts in points and hunter chases in 2003 (one of three
victories in the latter category coming in the novices' hunter over the Mildmay
fences at the Grand National meeting). Lord Atterbury was clearly destined for

Mr D. A. Johnson's "Lord Atterbury"

better things and a switch to father Martin's yard looked on the cards. Pipe senior did not, however, assume control until after the latest Cheltenham Festival at which Lord Atterbury started 3/1 favourite in a maximum field for the Christie's Foxhunter. Lord Atterbury had had a well-documented troubled preparation, after strolling home in the well-contested men's open at the Barbury point in January, and he failed to do himself justice at Cheltenham, well behind when pulled up. It was a very different story in the Grand National a little over two weeks later, Lord Atterbury performing with tremendous credit, considering his lack of experience, to finish third at 40/1 to Amberleigh House and Clan Royal, after being in the first three from halfway and holding every chance until the elbow. Mistakes at second Valentine's and the fifth last marred an otherwise largely competent round of jumping, but the race took its toll, Lord Atterbury being out on his feet in the closing stages and afterwards requiring oxygen (as he had after winning a long-distance hunter chase at Cheltenham very early in the latest season) and a good dousing with water. He ought to be one for the shortlist at Aintree in 2005, provided he has suffered no lasting ill-effects, though it is worth pointing out that he ran poorly, making mistakes, in the Champion Hunters' Chase at Stratford seven weeks after the Grand National. His dam Tammyiris, a winning Irish pointer, reportedly finished some of her races in a distressed condition. Lord Atterbury, a front runner who tackles his fences with zest, has encountered only good and good to soft going so far under rules. *M. C. Pipe*

LORDBERNIEBOUFFANT (IRE)   11 b.g. Denel (FR) – Noon Hunting (Green   c–
Shoon) [2003/4 c–, h125: c26d[4] Apr 7] rather leggy gelding: fairly useful handicap   h–
hurdler/chaser: runner-up in point prior to running poorly in hunter at Fontwell: suited by
3m+: acts on good to firm and heavy going: often sweating/edgy. *David Parker*

LORD BREX (FR)   8 gr.g. Saint Estephe (FR) – Light Moon (FR) (Mendez (FR))   c96 §
[2003/4 h95§: c17s[2] c18g[4] c17s[3] c20m[5] 17g[4] 17m[2] 22g[5] 20g[3] Oct 15] useful-looking   h85 §
gelding: has had breathing operation: one-time useful hurdler: only modest at best nowa-
days, including over fences: claimed £5,000 final outing: stays 2½m: acts on soft and
good to firm going: wears headgear: ungenuine. *J. G. M. O'Shea*

LORD BROADWAY (IRE)   8 b.g. Shardari – Country Course (IRE) (Crash Course)   c96
[2003/4 c80, h–: 26m c24g[4] c25v* c25v*[dis] c25d[3] c30g[pu] c28d[3] c23s[pu] c25m[4] Apr 14]   h–
very tall, angular gelding: maiden hurdler: modest chaser: first past post in conditional
jockeys handicap in November and amateur handicap (disqualified for taking wrong
course) in December, both at Towcester: stays 3½m: unraced on firm going: acts on any
other: tried visored. *N. M. Babbage*

LORD BROCK   5 b.g. Alderbrook – Mariner's Air (Julio Mariner) [2003/4 F14d[3]   F66
Mar 22] third foal: brother to 17f hurdle winner Severn Air: dam, fairly useful hurdler,
stayed 2½m: poor form when third in bumper at Hereford on debut, pulling hard.
N. A. Twiston-Davies

LORD BUCKINGHAM   6 ch.g. Carroll House – Lady Buck (Pollerton) [2003/4   h94
F82: 16m[3] 16d[4] 19m[4] 19g[ur] 17g Apr 13] lengthy gelding: modest novice hurdler: stays
19f: yet to race on extremes of going: has had tongue tied. *N. J. Henderson*

LORD CAPITAINE (IRE)   10 b. or br.g. Mister Lord (USA) – Salvation Sue (Mon   c104
Capitaine) [2003/4 c105: c30g c24v[4] c27s[3] c26d[2] c28d[2] Mar 30] workmanlike gelding:
fair handicap chaser: stays 3½m: acts on soft going: tried blinkered: has had tongue tied:
has won 5 times at Sedgefield: tends to jump right. *J. Howard Johnson*

LORD CASTLE (IRE)   8 ch.g. Mister Lord (USA) – Amandas Castle (IRE) (Carling-   c– x
ford Castle) [2003/4 c21d[pu] c24m[ur] c24m[pu] c24s[pu] Apr 17] soundly beaten in maiden   h–
hurdle: won point in March: jumped badly in hunter chases (left M. Wennington after
third outing): tried visored. *Miss C. Herrington*

LORD CODE (IRE)   6 b.g. Arctic Lord – Tax Code (Workboy) [2003/4 F17g 20d[5]   h85
16d[pu] 24g[pu] 16d Mar 24] €40,000 4-y-o: seventh foal: half-brother to several winners,   F–
including fairly useful hurdler/useful chaser up to 3m Assessed and fair 2m chaser
Auditty (both by Montelimar): dam, winning hurdler, half-sister to dam of useful chaser
up to 3m Springaleak: once-raced in bumpers: modest form on completed starts in novice
hurdles. *R. H. Alner*

LORD DAL (FR)   11 b.g. Cadoudal (FR) – Lady Corteira (FR) (Carvin II) [2003/4 c–,   c–
h–: 16s[5] 20s 22s 16d 17s Mar 23] angular gelding: one-time useful hurdler/fairly useful   h67
chaser, retains little ability: stays 3m: acts on heavy going: tried blinkered, wore
cheekpieces last 2 starts. *A. J. Whitehead*

LORD DILROCK (IRE)   8 ch.g. Lord Americo – Dillrock Damsel (Over The River   h68
(FR)) [2003/4 h–: 16g May 21] strong gelding: third in Irish point in 2000: seocnd and
better effort in novice hurdles a year apart when never-nearer seventh of 17 at Worcester.
Miss G. Browne

LORD DUNDANIEL (IRE)   7 b. or br.g. Arctic Lord – Killoskehan Queen (Dust-   h111
ineto) [2003/4 h87, F–: 20g[2] 20s[3] 20g* 20d 24m[5] Apr 14] smallish gelding: third in
maiden Irish point in 2002: fair hurdler: won novice handicap at Haydock in February:
should stay beyond 2½m: acts on soft going. *B. De Haan*

LORD EARTH (IRE)   6 b.g. Mister Lord (USA) – Mizuna (Ballymore) [2003/4   h95 d
F16m* 24g[4] 20s[5] 24s[5] 21g[3] 22g[pu] 22g[pu] Apr 18] 18,000 4-y-o: tall gelding: sixth foal: F95
half-brother to several winners, including fair chaser Halfpenny Bridge (by Over The
River), stays 3m well: dam, 1¾m winner, half-sister to smart 2m hurdler Raretylo: pulled
up in point on debut: won bumper at Worcester in May: best effort over hurdles when fifth
in novice at Chepstow 2 runs later: stays 2½m: acts on soft and good to firm going:
blinkered final outing. *P. F. Nicholls*

LORD EDWARDS ARMY (IRE)   9 b.g. Warcraft (USA) – Celtic Bombshell (Celtic   c96
Cone) [2003/4 c93, h102: c18d[6] c23f[5] c23g c22d[pu] c21s c25g[4] c21g[F] c25g[2] c27g* Apr   h–
16] strong, lengthy gelding: fair hurdler: modest chaser: sold out of P. Mullins' stable
6,200 gns Doncaster August Sales after fourth start: won hunter at Ayr in April: stays 27f:
acts on firm and soft going: sometimes makes mistakes. *W. T. Reed*

LORD FERNANDO   5 ch.g. Forzando – Lady Lacey (Kampala) [2003/4 h78: 16d⁴   **h79**
16g 17g Nov 18] good-topped gelding: poor handicap hurdler: unlikely to stay much
beyond 17f: acts on soft going: usually visored (wore cheekpieces second outing).
G. B. Balding

LORD GALE (IRE)   6 b.g. Mister Lord (USA) – Dante Gale (IRE) (Phardante (FR))   **F102**
[2003/4 F16s² F16d² F16g* F16g Mar 17] €7,000 4-y-o, resold €11,000 4-y-o: good-
bodied gelding: third foal: half-brother to French winner up to 12.5f Blowing A Gale (by
Moonax): dam ran twice in points, out of half-sister to very smart staying chaser Everett,
from family of smart chaser/high-class hurdler up to 3¼m Cab On Target: fairly useful
form in bumpers: won at Haydock in February by 2½ lengths from Tigers Lair: eleventh
of 24 to Total Enjoyment in Champion Bumper at Cheltenham final start: will be suited
by further than 2m. *N. A. Twiston-Davies*

LORD GEORGE   12 ch.g. Lord Bud – Mini Gazette (London Gazette) [2003/4 c–x: **c– x**
c24g May 31] modest pointer: let down by jumping in hunter chases. *G. C. Evans*

LORD GIZZMO   7 ch.g. Democratic (USA) – Figrant (USA) (L'Emigrant (USA))   **h–**
[2003/4 h–: 16m May 7] close-coupled gelding: modest on Flat (stays 1½m): no form
over hurdles: joined P. Hiatt. *J. Cullinan*

LORD HALFNOTHIN (IRE)   8 b.g. Mandalus – Midnight Seeker (Status Seeker)   **c113**
[2003/4 c22g* c21g* c16f* c21g² Dec 16] third foal: dam placed over jumps in Ireland:
successful twice in Irish points: fourth in bumper for S. Treacy: made all first 3 outings
over fences in Britain, in maiden at Fontwell (jumped right) and novice at Folkestone in
November and novice handicap at Leicester in December: will be suited by 3m: acts on
firm going: jumps soundly. *R. H. Alner*

Red Square Vodka 'Fixed Brush' Novices' Hurdle Final Bonus Race (Handicap), Haydock—
Lord Dundaniel leads Tanners Court to win an ordinary race for the money

LORD HECCLES (IRE) 5 b.g. Supreme Leader – Parsons Law (The Parson) [2003/4 **F91** F16s⁵ F16g F18g Apr 22] 26,000 4-y-o: well-made gelding: sixth foal: half-brother to winning 3m hurdler Parlanca Bay (by Lancastrian): dam, fair hurdler/chaser who stayed 25f, half-sister to dam of one-time top-class staying chaser Marlborough: fifth in bumper at Sandown on debut: well held under less testing conditions subsequently. *G. L. Moore*

LORD JACK (IRE) 8 ch.g. Mister Lord (USA) – Gentle Gill (Pollerton) [2003/4 **c124** c130, h–: c24dᵘʳ c20v² c33d⁶ c24dᵖᵘ Apr 23] angular gelding: fairly useful handicap **h–** chaser: well below best in 2003/4, except when second to Luzcadou at Ayr in January: should stay beyond 3m (failed to stay 33f): probably best on going softer than good (acts on heavy): wore cheekpieces final start: tongue tied: sound jumper: tends to run in snatches. *N. G. Richards*

LORD JAY JAY (IRE) 4 b.g. Lord of Appeal – Mesena (Pals Passage) [2003/4 **F88** F16g⁴ Feb 21] half-brother to several winners, including fair staying chaser Master Gleason (by Gleason): dam unraced: fourth to The Thunderer in bumper at Ascot on debut. *Miss H. C. Knight*

LORD KILLESHANRA (IRE) 5 br.g. Mister Lord (USA) – Killeshandra Lass **F100** (IRE) (King's Ride) [2003/4 F16d² F17s² F17g² Apr 10] 8,200 4-y-o: tall gelding: first live foal: dam, winning pointer, half-sister to dam of dual Foxhunter winner Earthmover: fairly useful form in bumpers, runner-up all 3 starts: will stay at least 2½m. *C. L. Tizzard*

LORD KINSALE (IRE) 11 ch.g. Cidrax (FR) – Wolviston (Wolverlife) [2003/4 **c–** 20g⁶ Oct 5] ex-Irish gelding: very lightly raced and little sign of ability. *D. B. Feek* **h–**

LORD LINGTON (FR) 5 b.g. Bulington (FR) – Tosca de Bussy (FR) (Le Riverain **h101** (FR)) [2003/4 16m⁶ 17s* 16g⁶ 16d⁵ 16g 17g 16m Apr 13] rather leggy gelding: fourth foal: half-brother to fair 2m hurdler Jupiter de Bussy (by Silver Rainbow) and 1½m winner Goliath de Bussy (by Mon Basile): dam winning French 2m chaser, also successful on Flat: ran 5 times up to 12.5f in non-thoroughbred races on Flat in France, successful all 3 starts in 2003 for G. Cherel: fair novice hurdler: won at Folkestone in December: raced around 2m: acts on soft going: blinkered final start. *P. F. Nicholls*

LORD LUKER (IRE) 8 b.g. Lord Americo – Canon's Dream (Le Bavard (FR)) **h77** [2003/4 21d 20s 19gᶠ Apr 3] sturdy gelding: lightly raced and signs of only a little ability. *Miss H. C. Knight*

LORD MAIZEY (IRE) 7 b.g. Mister Lord (USA) – My Maizey (Buckskin (FR)) **c136 p** [2003/4 c108p, F100: c26g⁴ c19d* c19d* Dec 27] big, good-topped gelding: progressive chaser: won 2 handicaps at Chepstow in December: left clear 2 out by fall of Claymore and idled when beating Jimmy Tennis 3½ lengths on second occasion, reportedly knocked hind leg and not seen out again: should stay beyond 19f: raced on good going or softer: races prominently: sound jumper: open to further improvement. *N. A. Twiston-Davies*

LORD MISTRAL 5 b.g. Makbul – South Wind (Tina's Pet) [2003/4 h70: 16m 16g⁶ **h70** May 30] angular gelding: poor maiden hurdler: raced around 2m: acts on good to firm and good to soft going. *Mrs N. S. Sharpe*

LORD MOOSE (IRE) 10 b.g. Mister Lord (USA) – Moose (IRE) (Royal Fountain) **c–** [2003/4 c115, h–: c21dᵖᵘ c24s⁵ c25s⁴ Feb 14] rangy gelding: fairly useful handicap chaser **h–** in 2002/3: well held all 3 starts in 2003/4: reportedly suffering from skin allergy on reappearance, lame final outing: stays 3m: raced on good going or softer (acts on heavy). *H. D. Daly*

LORD NATIVE (IRE) 9 b.g. Be My Native (USA) – Whakapohane (Kampala) **h–** [2003/4 h–: 19g⁵ May 13] rather sparely-made gelding: winning hurdler, very lightly raced: sold 2,800 gns Doncaster May Sales. *N. J. Henderson*

LORD NELLSSON 8 b.g. Arctic Lord – Miss Petronella (Petoski) [2003/4 h89: **c89** c20g⁴ c21m⁴ c20dᶠ c24sᵖᵘ 16g⁴ 16m Mar 11] compact gelding: would have finished **h85** second but for falling last in maiden chase at Ludlow in January: modest maiden hurdler: should stay beyond 21f: acts on soft going: tried in cheekpieces. *J. S. King*

LORD 'N' MASTER (IRE) 8 b.g. Lord Americo – Miss Good Night (Buckskin **c111** (FR)) [2003/4 c107, h90: c23g⁴ c20m⁵ c24d² c24d⁵ c20m³ c24d² c24gᵇᵈ c23sᶠ c29m Apr **h–** 24] useful-looking gelding: fair handicap chaser: stays 3m (stiff task over 29f): acts on soft and good to firm going: often makes mistakes. *R. Rowe*

LORD NOELIE (IRE) 11 b.g. Lord Americo – Leallen (Le Bavard (FR)) [2003/4 **c143** c150, h–: c27g⁵ c25d⁴ c26g* c33dᵖᵘ Apr 17] useful-looking gelding: impresses in appear- **h–**

ance: not a good walker: top-class chaser on his day at one time, useful nowadays: won handicap at Cheltenham in December by 4 lengths from Imperial de Thaix: stays 3¼m well: acts on good to firm and heavy going. *Ms Bridget Nicholls*

LORD NORTH (IRE)   9 b.g. Mister Lord (USA) – Mrs Hegarty (Decent Fellow) [2003/4 c121, h–: c20g c20d⁴ c20m³ c21s⁴ c17g² c16mᵖᵘ Feb 25] rangy gelding: handicap chaser, on the downgrade: stays 2½m: has won on good to firm going, better form on softer (acts on soft): visored 4 of last 5 starts: tongue tied: not one to rely on (often finds little). *P. R. Webber*   **c102 §**
h–

LORD OF BEAUTY (FR)   4 ch.g. Medaaly – Arctic Beauty (USA) (Arctic Tern (USA)) [2003/4 16gᶠ 16g⁴ 16s² 18s³ 16g⁴ 19g³ 16g² Apr 12] leggy, angular gelding: successful at 9f and 1¼m at 2 yrs, in frame twice up to 1½m on Flat at 3 yrs, sold out of H-A. Pantall's stable €40,000 Goffs July Sale: fair juvenile hurdler: stays 19f: raced on good going or softer. *Noel T. Chance*   **h111**

LORD OF ILLUSION (IRE)   7 b.g. Mister Lord (USA) – Jellaride (IRE) (King's Ride) [2003/4 h103: c20mᵘʳ c24d³ Nov 29] tall gelding: fair hurdler: promising steeplechasing debut in novice handicap at Wetherby on reappearance, close third when unseating last: should be suited by 3m: acts on good to firm going, probably on soft. *T. R. George*   **c109**
h–

LORDOFOUROWN (IRE)   6 b.g. Mister Lord (USA) – Twinkling (Star Appeal) [2003/4 F16g* 24mᵖᵘ 16d³ 20s² 20d⁵ Jan 25] IR £9,800 3-y-o: half-brother to winning staying hurdler/chaser Oneofourown (by Varshan): dam winning pointer: winning pointer: won bumper at Roscommon in October: reportedly lame on hurdling debut: fair form subsequently, placed in maiden at Thurles and intermediate at Leopardstown and fifth to Watson Lake in Grade 3 novice at Leopardstown: stays 2½m: acts on soft going. *P. O'Keeffe, Ireland*   **h113**
F99

LORD OF THE BRIDE (IRE)   7 ch.g. Mister Lord (USA) – Carrigan Springs (IRE) (Tale Quale) [2003/4 c21mᵖᵘ c21d⁴ c26m² Aug 25] ex-Irish gelding: second foal: dam lightly-raced maiden: won maiden on last of 4 starts in Irish points in 2003: bought 15,000 gns (privately) Doncaster May Sales: form otherwise only when second in maiden chase at Southwell: tongue tied on reappearance. *M. C. Pipe*   **c71**
h–

LORD OF THE FENS   4 b.g. Danzig Connection (USA) – Zizi (IRE) (Imp Society (USA)) [2003/4 F17g Apr 24] first foal: dam 5f winner: tailed off in bumper on debut. *C. N. Kellett*   **F–**

LORD OF THE HILL (IRE)   9 b.g. Dromod Hill – Telegram Mear (Giolla Mear) [2003/4 c–, h–: c24gᵖᵘ c20g⁴ c19m* c20m* c20f⁵ c16m* c20m* c16d³ c20g⁵ Jan 9] tall gelding: modest chaser: won selling handicap at Hereford and novice handicaps at Huntingdon, Hereford and Ludlow in autumn: will prove best up to 2½m: acts on good to firm going, possibly unsuited by softer than good: tongue tied after second outing: headstrong front runner. *Mrs H. Dalton*   **c98**
h–

LORD OF THE LAND   11 b.g. Lord Bud – Saint Motunde (Tyrant (USA)) [2003/4 c–, h–: 24g 17g² 24g 21m³ 17g² 20g³ c27mᶠ 20g 22f c16m³ c20g² c20g² c25g³ c25sᵖᵘ c20g c25d⁵ 17g* 21gᶠ Apr 12] leggy gelding: modest chaser: poor hurdler: won selling handicap at Market Rasen in March: effective at 2m to 27f: acts on firm and good to soft going (possibly unsuited by soft/heavy): sometimes none too fluent. *Mrs E. Slack*   **c94**
h83

LORD OF THE LOCH (IRE)   13 b. or br.g. Lord Americo – Loughamaire (Brave Invader (USA)) [2003/4 h88: 20d 16s² 16s 19d 20v⁴ 20d⁵ 20s⁴ 16g 21g* Apr 12] leggy, rather plain gelding: has reportedly had tendon trouble: modest handicap hurdler: won seller at Sedgefield: stays 21f: acts on good to firm and heavy going. *W. G. Young*   **h92**

LORD OF THE NORTH (IRE)   7 br.g. Arctic Lord – Ballyfin Maid (IRE) (Boreen (FR)) [2003/4 h66: 19g May 13] poor form over hurdles: won point in April: probably stays 25f. *M. R. Hoad*   **h–**

LORD OF THE PARK (IRE)   7 b.g. Lord Americo – Wind Chimes (The Parson) [2003/4 F17s 16d 17sᶠ 17s 19d 21gᵖᵘ Apr 12] little sign of ability. *John R. Upson*   **h–**
F–

LORD OF THE REALM (IRE)   8 b.g. Mister Lord (USA) – Traditional Lady (Carlingford Castle) [2003/4 c22sᵖᵘ c25dᵖᵘ c19g³ c20dᶠ Mar 19] IR 12,500 4-y-o: rangy gelding: third foal: brother to fairly useful bumper winner Chocolate Soldier: dam unraced: won maiden on last of 3 starts in Irish points in 2003: bought 10,000 gns Doncaster May Sales: little form in 4 steeplechases: tried tongue tied. *K. C. Bailey*   **c73**

Martell Cognac Ember Inns Handicap Chase, Aintree—
the rejuvenated Lord of The River defeats Midland Flame (right)

LORD OF THE RIVER (IRE) 12 br.g. Lord Americo – Well Over (Over The River (FR)) [2003/4 c112, h–: c25s c24g² c24s* c25g* Apr 2] tall, close-coupled gelding: usually looks well: useful handicap chaser: successful at Ascot (by 7 lengths from Tremallt) in March and Aintree (well ridden by P. Carberry, beat Midland Flame 7 lengths in valuable event) in April: stays 25f: has form on good to firm going, raced mainly on good or softer (acts on heavy): sometimes sweats: probably best ridden up with pace: bold jumper. *N. J. Henderson*   **c135** **h–**

LORD OF THE TRACK (IRE) 6 b.g. Eve's Error – Tara's Tribe (Good Thyne (USA)) [2003/4 17d 22g⁶ 22g⁵ 22g 27f* 24gᵘʳ Aug 23] second foal: dam modest 2½m hurdler: successful once from 7 starts in maiden Irish points: bought 11,000 gns Doncaster May Sales: form over hurdles only when winning weakly-contested conditional jockeys selling handicap at Fontwell in August: likely to be best at 3m+: acts on firm ground. *M. C. Pipe*   **h77**

LORD OF THE TURF (IRE) 11 b.g. Supreme Leader – Avida Dancer (Ballymore) [2003/4 c133, h–: c20v² c22s Jul 30] angular gelding: useful handicap chaser: creditable efforts when second to Cloudy Bays at Tipperary and tenth of 22 to Nearly A Moose in Galway Plate: stays 3m: raced on going softer than good (acts on heavy): tried blinkered. *J. Bleahen, Ireland*   **c131** **h–**

LORD OLYMPIA (IRE) 5 b.g. Lord Americo – Mooreshill (IRE) (Le Moss) [2003/4 F17s² F16s⁶ F16d² Mar 11] €38,000 3-y-o: good-topped gelding: fourth foal: brother to fair hurdler Moores Light, stays 2½m: dam unraced half-sister to high-class staying chaser Simon Legree: fairly useful form in bumpers: made running when second to The Sawyer at Towcester final start: will be suited by further. *Miss Venetia Williams*   **F95**

LORD PAT (IRE) 13 ch.g. Mister Lord (USA) – Arianrhod (L'Homme Arme) [2003/4 c65, h72: 19d⁵ 20v⁵ 20s 21g² Apr 12] small gelding: poor form over fences (has had jumping problems): poor handicap hurdler: probably stays 21f: acts on heavy going. *Miss Kate Milligan*   **c–** **h72**

LORD PAYNE (IRE) 6 b.g. Alphabatim (USA) – Clash Boreen (Arapaho) [2003/4 21d³ Apr 12] good-topped gelding: half-brother to winning 3¼m chaser Maxxum Express (by Buckskin): dam lightly-raced novice hurdler: won maiden Irish point on debut in January: encouraging start over hurdles when third to Gracilis in maiden at Huntingdon: will stay beyond 21f: should improve. *M. C. Pipe*   **h100 p**

LORD PERSEUS (IRE) 7 ch.g. Mister Lord (USA) – Greek Empress (Royal Buck) [2003/4 F96: F17g³ 17g⁵ Jun 11] fair bumper winner: well held in novice on hurdling debut. *M. Pitman*   **h–** **F94**

LORD ROCHESTER   8 b.g. Distant Relative – Kentfield (Busted) [2003/4 c95x,   **c– x**
h–: 21m 21gᵖᵘ 17gᵖᵘ 19f* 16m² Oct 26] close-coupled gelding: maiden chaser, usually   **h81**
let down by jumping: poor hurdler nowadays: won very weakly-contested conditional
jockeys selling handicap at Towcester in October: probably stays 3m: acts on firm
going, probably on good to soft: usually blinkered, wore cheekpieces last 2 starts.
K. F. Clutterbuck

LORD RODNEY (IRE)   5 b.g. Hatim (USA) – Howcleuch (Buckskin (FR)) [2003/4   **F84**
F17d³ Apr 18] 6,000 4-y-o: second foal: half-brother to fairly useful bumper winner
Rambling Minster (by Minster Son): dam fair staying chaser: third of 13 in bumper at
Carlisle on debut. *P. Beaumont*

LORD SAM (IRE)   8 b. or br.g. Supreme Leader – Russian Gale (IRE) (Strong   **c150 p**
Gale) [2003/4 h144: c20s* c24s* c24g* Jan 17]   **h–**
          Although Lord Sam didn't always treat fences with any more respect than
he had done hurdles, he not only completed the course in the four chases he
contested but also came out on top in each of them, making his record to date a
remarkable nine wins from ten starts. Lord Sam's only defeat came on his final
start in 2002/3, when he was a promoted third behind Hardy Eustace in the Royal
& SunAlliance Novices' Hurdle at Cheltenham. Lord Sam was a smart novice
hurdler, but he has already shown himself an even better chaser and there is no
reason why he shouldn't continue to progress. He will have to jump more fluently
if he is to maintain his unbeaten run over fences for much longer, though. Much
stiffer tasks await Lord Sam in 2004/5, with the King George VI Chase at Kempton,
a course where he has gained three of his wins, already mentioned as a likely target.
          To be fair to Lord Sam, his jumping technique gave no cause for concern
on his first two appearances in novice chases, at Huntingdon in November and
Lingfield the following month. He won the former by nineteen lengths from Bal de
Nuit, already in command when that horse slipped badly on landing at the last, and
the latter, the Grade 2 December Novices' Chase, by a length and a half from Native
Emperor. That Lord Sam would complete his hat-trick in a five-runner event at
Kempton in January seemed a mere formality, reflected by his starting price of
11/4-on, but on ground much less testing than at Huntingdon and Lingfield he

britishhorseracing.com Novices' Chase, Kempton—Lord Sam maintains his 100% record at the track

Ellier Developments Novices' Chase, Punchestown—
Lord Sam outbattles Hi Cloy (noseband) to gain compensation for missing Cheltenham

jumped slowly on several occasions and needed firmish handling to overcome Fork Lightning who was receiving 3 lb, just a length and a quarter separating the pair at the line. Time was to show Lord Sam had a stiffer task than was first thought. Two months later Fork Lightning proved himself a smart novice when winning the National Hunt Handicap Chase at Cheltenham. Lord Sam should have been contesting the Royal & SunAlliance Chase there, but he was ruled out on the day due to his blood testing below par and missed the remainder of the British season. Thankfully, Lord Sam was back in good health by the time the Punchestown Festival came along at the end of April, and he was sent across for the Grade 3 Ellier Developments Novices' Chase, a two-and-a-half-mile event which attracted three others, all trained in Ireland. It was a race which made up in quality for what it lacked in quantity. While Sum Leader appeared out of his depth, both Hi Cloy and Nil Desperandum had been successful in Grade 1 events and looked sure to provide stiff opposition to Lord Sam, who was very much on his toes in the preliminaries. The race didn't begin to take shape until four out, at which point Sum Leader was joined in the lead by Nil Desperandum, just ahead of Lord Sam as the patiently-ridden Hi Cloy began to take closer order. Lord Sam, who had lost ground when jumping big over the early fences, dropped back to last after a mistake three out but rallied to challenge two out where Sum Leader blundered and lost the lead to Hi Cloy. At the last Lord Sam was upsides Hi Cloy and, after the pair had collided in mid-air, he showed the greater determination to edge ahead on the run-in, winning by a neck. Not for the first time Lord Sam had shown commendable gameness under pressure, and he won't be brushed aside easily when he goes into open company in the next season.

Lord Sam is the second of four foals out of Russian Gale to reach the race-course, and the only one of any note, although Lord Sam's seven-year-old brother

Plain Peeps' "Lord Sam"

Lord Sam (IRE) (b. or br.g. 1996)	Supreme Leader (b 1982)	Bustino (b 1971)	Busted Ship Yard
		Princess Zena (b 1975)	Habitat Guiding Light
	Russian Gale (IRE) (br 1988)	Strong Gale (br 1975)	Lord Gayle Sterntau
		People (br 1983)	Al Sirat Hide Well

Dunshaughlin and five-year-old half-brother Russian Lord (by Topanoora) both appeared for the first time in the latest season and showed ability. Russian Gale, the winner of a three-mile handicap chase at Clonmel, is a daughter of an unraced half-sister to the smart hurdler and Irish Cesarewitch winner Potato Merchant as well as the useful staying hurdler Stag Hill. Lord Sam, a stocky gelding, is effective at two and a half miles to three miles. He has raced only on good ground or softer, and acts on soft. *V. R. A. Dartnall*

LORDS BEST (IRE)   8 b.g. Mister Lord (USA) – Ballinlonig Star (Black Minstrel)   **c118**
[2003/4 h122: c22v^5 c25d* c23v^F Jan 26] workmanlike gelding: fairly useful hurdler: **h–**
similar form over fences, winning maiden at Folkestone in January: well beaten in second
when falling 2 out in novice won by Simply Supreme at Wetherby: will prove best at
3m+: acts on heavy going, probably on good to firm: has drifted/jumped right under
pressure. *A. King*

LORD SEAMUS   9 b.g. Arctic Lord – Erica Superba (Langton Heath) [2003/4 c106, **c102**
h–: c25g^4 c25m^3 c24m^2 c24m^2 c25s^F c25m^3 Apr 13] compact gelding: fair handicap **h–**

chaser: stays 4m: acts on firm and soft going: has worn cheekpieces: often makes mistakes: consistent. *K. C. Bailey*

LORDSTON (IRE) 8 b.g. Mister Lord (USA) – Dawstown (Golden Love) [2003/4 c25d^{pu} c23m^{pu} Apr 13] rangy, good sort: won maiden point in 2002: little show in 2 hunters. *B. G. Powell*
c–
h–

LORD STRICKLAND 11 b.g. Strong Gale – Lady Rag (Ragapan) [2003/4 c109x, h104x: 22g^6 c21m^3 May 29] good-topped gelding: fair handicap hurdler/chaser: stays 3m: acts on soft and firm going: makes mistakes. *P. J. Hobbs*
c95 x
h103 x

LORD THOMAS (IRE) 6 b.g. Grand Lodge (USA) – Noble Rocket (Reprimand) [2003/4 F–: F16g aF16g F16m Feb 21] angular gelding: no form in bumpers. *A. J. Wilson*
F–

LORD TRANSCEND (IRE) 7 gr.g. Aristocracy – Capincur Lady (Over The River (FR)) [2003/4 h148p: c25d* Nov 28] lengthy, angular gelding: smart hurdler, successful on 4 of 5 starts: 5/1-on, made all in maiden at Ayr on chasing debut, jumping quickly and accurately throughout and sauntering clear on final circuit to beat Strong Resolve 17 lengths: stays 25f: raced on good going or softer (acts on heavy): a chaser of considerable potential, though reported in January to have suffered leg injury. *J. Howard Johnson*
c117 P
h–

LORD TRIX (IRE) 5 b.g. Lord Americo – Up To Trix (Over The River (FR)) [2003/4 F16m F16s^5 23v^F 16d^2 Apr 21] €20,000 3-y-o: workmanlike gelding: half-brother to fair staying chaser Hill Trix (by Le Moss) and fair staying hurdler Quickswood (by Yashgan): dam unraced half-sister to useful hurdler/staying chaser Brown Trix: modest form in bumpers: better effort over hurdles when second to Green Tango in novice at Worcester: should be suited by further than 2m. *P. W. Hiatt*
h95
F84

LORD VALNIC (IRE) 8 b.g. Mister Lord (USA) – Any Wonder (Hardboy) [2003/4 c24s^F Feb 12] fair pointer: fell first in hunter chase. *Ms A. E. Embiricos*
c–

LORD VILLE (FR) 5 b.g. Useful (FR) – Triaina (Lancastrian) [2003/4 h98: 16m^2 16m 17g^4 17g 17f^3 Sep 30] leggy gelding: modest handicap hurdler: raced around 2m: acts on firm and good to soft going, ran poorly on heavy. *P. J. Hobbs*
h89

LORD WARFORD 9 b.g. Bustino – Jupiter's Message (Jupiter Island) [2003/4 c–, h–: c21m^4 c21d^3 May 30] sturdy gelding: fair hurdler at best: very disappointing since early-2000/1 (often finds little), including over fences: stays 2¾m: acts on good to soft going: has had tongue tied. *C. L. Popham*
c76
h–

LORD WHO (IRE) 7 b.g. Mister Lord (USA) – Le Bavellen (Le Bavard (FR)) [2003/4 h109, F94: c24s^2 c22d^4 c23g^3 22d^4 c25d^3 c24s* c25d^2 c24s* c24s^2 c24d^2 Mar 17] fair hurdler: fairly useful novice chaser: won at Limerick (maiden) in December and Naas (Grade 2, beat Jim 2 lengths) in January: good second to Satco Express in Grade 3 at Navan and Hi Cloy in listed race at Limerick last 2 starts: will stay beyond 25f: acts on soft going. *P. M. J. Doyle, Ireland*
c124
h109

LORD YORK (IRE) 12 b. or br.g. Strong Gale – Bunkilla (Arctic Slave) [2003/4 c125§, h110§: 20g^2 19m May 31] rangy gelding: fairly useful handicap chaser: fair hurdler: raced around 2m on good going or firmer (acts on firm): usually blinkered/visored: tongue tied once: best forcing pace: unreliable. *Ian Williams*
c– §
h105 §

LORD YOUKY (FR) 10 b.g. Cadoudal (FR) – Lady Corteira (FR) (Carvin II) [2003/4 c20m^3 c24g^3 c23m^{pu} c24m^5 c20g* Dec 11] useful-looking gelding: winning hurdler: fair chaser, missed 2002/3: won novice handicaps at Uttoxeter in November and Ludlow (very fortunate, well held when left clear last): stays 3m: probably acts on any going: often none too fluent. *Ian Williams*
c107
h–

LORENZINO (IRE) 7 ch.g. Thunder Gulch (USA) – Russian Ballet (USA) (Nijinsky (CAN)) [2003/4 h124d: 20g^6 24m^3 c20g^3 c24m* c24m^F c20m^2 c24s^{pu} 22m^{pu} Feb 21] close-coupled gelding: fairly useful handicap hurdler at best, has deteriorated: bled from nose final start: fair form over fences: won weak 4-runner novice at Huntingdon in September: stays easy 3m: acts on firm and soft going: tried tongue tied. *Jonjo O'Neill*
c112
h112

LORGNETTE 10 b.m. Emperor Fountain – Speckyfoureyes (Blue Cashmere) [2003/4 c95, h98: 22d 24s^2 22g^3 26g^2 24s* 24g Apr 2] rather sparely-made mare: fair handicap hurdler: best effort when winning at Ascot in March by 9 lengths from Victory Gunner: novice chaser, hasn't convinced with jumping: stays 3¼m: acts on firm and soft going. *R. H. Alner*
c–
h109

LORIENT EXPRESS (FR) 5 b.g. Sleeping Car (FR) – Envie de Chalamont (FR) (Pamponi (FR)) [2003/4 16f^F 16d^{pu} 16v^5 16s^6 16s^{pu} 16s Feb 20] tall, angular gelding: half-brother to winning 2½m chaser Jockker (by Video Rock): dam unraced: in frame all
h–

3 starts around 1½m on Flat in French Provinces at 3 yrs for L. Manceau: showed little over hurdles. *M. F. Harris*

LORIO DU MISSELOT (FR) 5 gr.g. Dom Alco (FR) – Byrεa (FR) (Quart de Vin (FR)) [2003/4 F16v Jan 17] workmanlike gelding: fourth foal: dam, twice-raced, out of half-sister to smart 23f chase winner Martinet II: well beaten in bumper on debut. *Ferdy Murphy*   **F—**

L'ORPHELIN 9 ch.g. Gildoran – Balula (Balinger) [2003/4 h71: c21s^{pu} c24g^{ur} c19s² c19s^{ur} c19d⁴ c16m⁴ c19d⁴ c26d^{ur} Apr 11] small, rather plain gelding: poor maiden hurdler/chaser: stays 19f: acts on soft and good to firm going: tried visored: makes mistakes over fences. *C. L. Tizzard*   **c81 x** / **h—**

LOSCAR (FR) 5 b.g. General Holme (USA) – Unika II (FR) (Rolling Bowl (FR)) [2003/4 F16s⁶ F17d 17d⁶ Apr 18] fourth foal: half-brother to modest hurdler Jolika (by Grand Tresor), stays 2½m: dam, won over 1¼m in France, out of half-sister to dam of useful chaser around 2½m Camitrov: modest form on first of 2 outings in bumpers: never a factor in novice at Carlisle on hurdling debut. *L. Lungo*   **h—** / **F75**

LOST IN NORMANDY (IRE) 7 b.g. Treasure Hunter – Auntie Honnie (IRE) (Radical) [2003/4 h64, F82: 21m⁶ 26g⁴ 21g c23d^{pu} c20m² c20m c24g* c26m* c24g^{pu} c26s³ 24d Apr 21] lengthy gelding: maiden hurdler: poor handicap chaser: won events in small fields at Bangor (novice) in September and Southwell in October: stays 3¼m: acts on good to firm going: blinkered over fences. *Mrs L. Williamson*   **c76** / **h—**

LOST SOLDIER TWO 4 b.g. Kris – Hejraan (USA) (Alydar (USA)) [2003/4 F13g F16s F16d 16g^{pu} Mar 6] lengthy gelding: fifth foal: half-brother to poor hurdler/modest chaser Helvetius (by In The Wings), stays 23f: dam, lightly-raced maiden, out of smart performer up to 1m Top Socialite, a good US family: bought unraced out of L. Cumani's stable 10,000 gns Newmarket July Sales: no show in bumpers or juvenile hurdle: tried blinkered/in cheekpieces. *R. C. Guest*   **h—** / **F—**

LOST THE PLOT 9 b.m. Lyphento (USA) – La Comedienne (Comedy Star (USA)) [2003/4 h96: c20m² c21g^F c20s c18d Mar 3] tall, leggy mare: modest hurdler: similar form over fences only on first start, left D. Arbuthnot after second: will stay 3m: acts on firm and good to soft going: raced once (shaped as if amiss). *K. Burke, Ireland*   **c99 d** / **h—**

LOS VADOS (GER) 5 b.g. Dashing Blade – La Vega (GER) (Turfkonig (GER)) [2003/4 h72: 16m⁵ 16m⁵ 17m 16g⁶ 20m Nov 8] poor novice hurdler: raced mainly around 2m on good to firm going: dead. *Ian Williams*   **h83**

LOTIER (FR) 6 b.g. Dress Parade – Dame d'Onze Heures (FR) (Noble Cake (USA)) [2003/4 F16d 19s² 16s⁶ 17s* 20s^F Mar 13] well-made gelding: third foal: dam unraced half-sister to very smart staying chaser Gingembre: needed race when seventh in bumper on debut: easily best effort in novice hurdles when winning at Hereford in February by 4 lengths from Locksmith: fell first final outing: will stay 2¾m+. *Mrs L. C. Taylor*   **h118** / **F90**

LOTUS DES PICTONS (FR) 5 b.g. Grand Tresor (FR) – Ballaway (FR) (Djarvis (FR)) [2003/4 c17s c20s⁴ c18s³ c17s⁵ c20s² 16d 19s² 24s* 24g³ 21g* 24g* 20d⁵ 20g⁵ Apr 1] leggy, close-coupled ex-French gelding: second foal: brother to fairly useful hurdler/fair chaser around 2m Kalmist des Pictons: dam unraced sister to dams of good French chasers Otway and Mackay: fair maiden chaser: claimed from B. Secly €19,000 fifth start: fairly useful hurdler: won maiden at Chepstow in January and novices at Ludlow (handicap) and Chepstow (amateurs, easily) in March: good fifth in strongly-contested handicaps at Ascot (behind Accipiter) and Aintree (behind Zibeline) last 2 starts: stays 3m: acts on soft ground: has shown high head carriage. *M. C. Pipe*   **c103** / **h120**

LOU DU MOULIN MAS (FR) 5 b.g. Sassanian (USA) – Houf (FR) (Morespeed) [2003/4 17v 18s¹⁰ 20g² 21g Mar 26] rather leggy gelding: first foal: dam unraced sister to one-time useful hurdler/chaser up to 3m Fard du Moulin Mas: twice-raced on Flat: best effort over hurdles when second in 20-runner 4-y-o event at Auteuil (final outing for T. Trapenard): fair form on second run in novice chases in Britain when head second to Tikram in quite valuable event at Fontwell, making most and jumping fluently: stays 2½m: acts on soft going: tongue tied in Britain. *P. F. Nicholls*   **c112** / **h104**

LOUDY ROWDY (IRE) 13 br.g. Strong Gale – Express Film (Ashmore (FR)) [2003/4 c—, h—: c25g^F c25g⁶ 22f⁴ c25g² c25g^{pu} c22d⁴ c25g⁴ Apr 5] poor maiden hurdler/chaser: stays 25f: visored last 2 starts: has had tongue tied. *Mrs J. K. M. Oliver*   **c68 ?** / **h—**

LOUGHCREW (IRE) 8 ch.g. Good Thyne (USA) – Marys Course (Crash Course) [2003/4 h—: 17d 18v 16g 16s Apr 21] winning hurdler, no form since 2001. *L. Lungo*   **h—**

LOUGH DANTE (IRE) 6 b.g. Phardante (FR) – Shannon Lough (IRE) (Deep Run) **h102**
[2003/4 20s² 20s³ 24g⁴ Feb 21] 10,000 4-y-o: well-made gelding: fourth foal: half-brother to fairly useful 2m hurdler Drumlin (by Glacial Storm): dam once-raced half-sister to useful chaser up to 3m Woodville Star, from family of smart staying jumper Time For A Run: won 2½m maiden point on debut in 2003: best effort in novice hurdles when second to easy winner Very Optimistic at Haydock: should stay 3m. *H. D. Daly*

LOUGH DERG (FR) 4 b.g. Apple Tree (FR) – Asturias (FR) (Pistolet Bleu (IRE)) **h122**
[2003/4 16g* 16d* 17d⁵ 17s² 17m* Apr 14] rather sparely-made gelding: first foal: dam, of little account, half-sister to Grande Course de Haies d'Enghien winner Astronomer: fairly useful juvenile hurdler: won at Newbury (by distance) in November, Warwick in January and Cheltenham, beating Zimbabwe 6 lengths in 5-runner event at last-named: raced around 2m: acts on good to firm and good to soft going. *M. C. Pipe*

LOUGH RYNN (IRE) 6 b.g. Beneficial – Liffey Lady (Camden Town) [2003/4 h–, **h79**
F83: 21g 20dᵖᵘ Jan 10] tall, rather unfurnished gelding: poor form in novice company over hurdles. *H. C. Knight*

LOUIS CSASZAR (IRE) 6 b.g. Arctic Lord – Satlan's Treasure (IRE) (Treasure **h–**
Hunter) [2003/4 F17d 17d Apr 18] €6,500 4-y-o: strong gelding: third foal: dam unraced: **F–**
well held in bumper and novice hurdle. *R. F. Fisher*

LOUISES GLORY (IRE) 9 ch.g. Executive Perk – Ring-Em-All (Decent Fellow) **c76**
[2003/4 c–, h–: c16d⁶ c16s⁵ c16d³ Feb 15] lengthy, angular gelding: poor hurdler/maiden **h–**
chaser: raced mainly around 2m on good ground or softer (acts on heavy): tried blinkered: formerly tongue tied. *D. J. Wintle*

LOUP DU SUD (FR) 5 b.g. Loup Solitaire (USA) – Jetty (FR) (Fabulous Dancer **F–**
(USA)) [2003/4 F16s F16m Mar 11] sturdy gelding: sixth foal: half-brother to 3 winners on Flat, including useful 1¼m winner Fabulous Jet (by Starborough): dam, placed up to 1½m on Flat, sister to smart hurdler up to 2½m Cagney: tailed off in 2 bumpers: sold £2,000 Ascot April Sales. *S. Pike*

LOUP (FR) 5 b.g. Cyborg (FR) – Quintessence III (FR) (El Condor (FR)) [2003/4 16g² **h109**
16d Dec 19] rather sparely-made gelding: ninth foal: brother to high-class staying hurdler/chaser Cyborgo and high-class 2m hurdler Hors La Loi III: dam, 9f winner, placed 3 times over jumps: twice-raced on Flat at 3 yrs for F. Doumen: ½-length second of 17 to Kadount in novice at Haydock on hurdling debut: well held in Grade 2 novice at Ascot: dead. *J. R. Fanshawe*

LOVE KISS (IRE) 9 b.g. Brief Truce (USA) – Pendulina (Prince Tenderfoot (USA)) **h–**
[2003/4 h73: 17dᵖᵘ Nov 25] tall, rather leggy gelding: poor hurdler: best around 2m: raced on good going or softer (acts on soft): usually tongue tied. *M. Dods*

LOVELY LAURA (IRE) 6 ch.m. Port Lucaya – Miss Plum (Ardross) [2003/4 F16sᵖᵘ **F–**
Dec 11] 2,200 5-y-o: third foal: half-sister to poor hurdler Royal Plum (by Inchinor), stays 3¼m: dam, won both starts up to 3m over hurdles/fairly useful out-and-out stayer on Flat, sister to dam of Grade 2 bumper winner Diamond Sal: broke down in bumper on debut. *C. N. Kellett*

LOVELY LULU 6 b.m. Petrizzo – The Green Girls (USA) (Distinctive Pro (USA)) **h–**
[2003/4 F16d 17s Apr 6] leggy mare: first foal: dam twice-raced on Flat: tailed off in **F–**
bumper/novice hurdle. *J. C. Tuck*

LOVE MAIL 6 b.m. Pursuit of Love – Wizardry (Shirley Heights) [2003/4 20vᵖᵘ 22gᵖᵘ **h–**
Apr 22] tall mare: bumper winner: no show in 2 novice hurdles after 2-year absence. *Simon Earle*

LOVERS TALE 6 b.g. Pursuit of Love – Kintail (Kris) [2003/4 h–, F–: 16d⁵ 20m² **c–**
16m⁴ c20mᶠ 19s Jan 22] fell twelfth on chasing debut: poor maiden hurdler: stays 2½m: **h79**
acts on good to firm ground. *H. M. Kavanagh*

LOVE'S DESIGN (IRE) 7 b. or br.g. Pursuit of Love – Cephista (Shirley Heights) **h–**
[2003/4 17m⁵ 16d⁶ Mar 25] modest on Flat (stays 8.5f): pulled hard when well held in seller and claimer over hurdles. *Miss S. J. Wilton*

LOWE GO 4 b.g. First Trump – Hotel California (IRE) (Last Tycoon) [2003/4 17d⁵ **h86**
16s* 16d⁵ 16s 16d 19d² Mar 22] fair maiden on Flat (stays 12.6f): modest hurdler: won juvenile seller (sold from J. Portman 5,800 gns) at Uttoxeter in December: likely to prove best around 2m. *Miss J. S. Davis*

LOWLANDER 5 b.g. Fuji Kiseki (JPN) – Lake Valley (USA) (Mr Prospector (USA)) **h115**
[2003/4 16v 20d 18m* 17f* 20m* 16g⁶ Nov 14] useful on Flat (stays 2m): easily won maiden at Downpatrick and novices at Tralee and Limerick over hurdles in first half of

season: soundly beaten in Grade 2 novice at Cheltenham final outing: will stay beyond 2½m: blinkered after debut. *D. K. Weld, Ireland*

LOYOLA 4 ch.f. New Reputation – Stay With Me Baby (Nicholas Bill) [2003/4 16v^pu 17s^5 16v^4 21d^4 22g^4 18g^6 Apr 22] third foal: dam, 1m winner, half-sister to very smart miler Tellurano: refused to enter stall intended Flat debut: poor form over hurdles: stays 2¾m: acts on heavy going. *Simon Earle* — **h80**

LOY'S LAD (IRE) 8 b.g. Glacial Storm (USA) – Missing Note (Rarity) [2003/4 c16m^4 c25m* c20f^3 c25g^F c25g^2 c24d^F Nov 29] tall, angular ex-Irish gelding: ninth foal: half-brother to several winners, including useful chaser Lord Cyprus (by Ile de Chypre), stayed 3m, and winning 2½m hurdler Lord Rooble (by Jolly Jake): dam poor Irish maiden at 2 yrs: little form in bumpers: well beaten in 2 maiden hurdles, left J. J. Lambe after final start in 2002/3: made most when winning weak maiden chase at Hexham in October by wide margin: seemingly better suited by 3m+ than shorter: tried blinkered: sketchy jumper. *Miss V. Scott* — **c83 x** / **h–**

LOZZY LEE (IRE) 6 b.g. Zaffaran (USA) – Amazing Lee (IRE) (Amazing Bust) [2003/4 F90: 20d^3 19s^F Dec 20] big, good-topped gelding: third to Mount Karinga in novice at Chepstow on hurdling debut after 11-month absence: fell fatally in similar event at Hereford: would have stayed 3m. *M. Scudamore* — **h97**

LUBINAS (IRE) 5 b.g. Grand Lodge (USA) – Liebesgirl (Konigsstuhl (GER)) [2003/4 20d 16v^5 19d^4 26s^F 21d 20d^2 Apr 21] workmanlike gelding: in frame 4 times from 8 starts up to 1½m on Flat in Germany for Frau G. Wenisch: fair novice hurdler: stays 2½m, seemingly not 3¼m: not a fluent jumper. *F. Jordan* — **h101 x**

LUCIFER BLEU (FR) 5 b.g. Kadalko (FR) – Figa Dancer (FR) (Bandinelli (FR)) [2003/4 17s^F 17v* 18s 19s^5 17s^5 19m^2 24m Apr 14] leggy gelding: third foal: dam runner-up in 17f chase in France: fair hurdler: awarded 4-y-o event at Auteuil in May: left G. Cherel after next start: should stay beyond 19f: acts on good to firm and heavy going. *M. C. Pipe* — **h107**

LUCKEN HOWE 5 b.g. Keen – Gilston Lass (Majestic Streak) [2003/4 F17d F17d Apr 18] 12,000 4-y-o: second foal: dam, modest chaser who stayed 3¼m, half-sister to fairly useful 3m chaser Lauderdale Lad: well held in bumpers at Carlisle. *Mrs J. K. M. Oliver* — **F–**

LUCKY ARCHER 11 b.g. North Briton – Preobrajenska (Double Form) [2003/4 17m^5 16g Oct 24] angular gelding: fair on Flat (stays 9f), well below form last 4 starts in 2003: poor maiden hurdler: best at sharp 2m: has had tongue tied. *Ian Williams* — **h70**

LUCKY BAY (IRE) 8 b.g. Convinced – Current Liability (Caribo) [2003/4 c126, h–: c24m^6 c25g^2 c29d^ur c25d^4 Jan 17] well-made gelding: fairly useful chaser: should stay beyond 25f: acts on firm and good to soft going. *Ms Bridget Nicholls* — **c129** / **h–**

LUCKY CATCH (IRE) 6 b.g. Safety Catch (USA) – Lucky Monday (Lucky Wednesday) [2003/4 F74: 23d^ur 24v^pu c16d^F c25g^pu Mar 10] no show in 2 novice hurdles: jumped poorly both starts over fences. *A. Crook* — **c– x** / **h–**

LUCKYCHARM (FR) 5 ch.g. Villez (USA) – Hitifly (FR) (Murmure (FR)) [2003/4 F16g 19g^pu 16m Apr 13] 11,000 4-y-o, resold 5,200 4-y-o: first foal: dam unraced: no form in maiden bumper or hurdles. *R. Dickin* — **h–** / **F–**

LUCKY CLOVER 12 ch.g. Push On – Winning Clover (Winden) [2003/4 c119§, h–§: c33g^pu c25m c26d^pu c26m^pu c24d^3 c26g* c26g^4 c26g^2 c26m^pu c24m^2 c24g^5 Jan 9] well-made gelding: one-time fairly useful chaser, best efforts on cross-country course at Cheltenham: fair form in 2003/4: won handicap at Newton Abbot in August: stays 31f: acts on firm and good to soft going: tried blinkered: temperamental (needs to dominate). *C. L. Tizzard* — **c101 §** / **h– §**

LUCKY DUCK 7 ch.g. Minster Son – Petroc Concert (Tina's Pet) [2003/4 F77: 20s^pu 21s^pu 17s^3 17g^ur 16g* 17d* Apr 18] medium-sized gelding: won novice hurdles at Kelso (jumped right) and Carlisle within a fortnight last 2 starts: fairly useful form when beating Cardington by 12 lengths at latter, soon in long lead and forging clear about 3 out: seems best around 2m: acts on soft going. *Mrs A. Hamilton* — **h116**

LUCKY HEATHER (IRE) 7 b.m. Soviet Lad (USA) – Idrak (Young Generation) [2003/4 h53: 17f^4 16m^6 16g^pu 17m 19d 16g Mar 10] leggy mare: bad maiden hurdler: raced mainly around 2m: acts on firm and good to soft going: tried blinkered. *R. J. Baker* — **h59**

LUCKY JOE (IRE) 11 br.g. Denel (FR) – Breezy Dawn (Kemal (FR)) [2003/4 c70, h71: c25m^pu 26s^pu Dec 20] poor maiden hurdler/steeplechaser: no show in 2003/4 after long absence: stays 3¼m: acts on soft and good to firm going. *J. White* — **c–** / **h–**

LUCKY LARGO (IRE)   4 b. or br.g. Key of Luck (USA) – Lingering Melody (IRE)   **h82**
(Nordico (USA)) [2003/4 17s^pu 16g^6 16s^pu Mar 19] lengthy gelding: fair maiden on Flat
(stays 9f), trained by K. Prendergast at 3 yrs, claimed £6,000 in April: poor form on
completed start over hurdles: possibly unsuited by soft going: blinkered last 2 outings.
S. Gollings

LUCKY LEADER (IRE)   9 b.g. Supreme Leader – Lucky House (Pollerton) [2003/4   **c89 x**
c92?: c23g* c23d^pu c24g^pu c23d^3 c24g^pu Apr 1] lengthy gelding: modest chaser: 4/1 from
14/1, won novice handicap at Exeter in December: stays 23f: raced on good going or
softer: often let down by jumping. *N. R. Mitchell*

LUCKY LEO   4 b.g. Muhtarram (USA) – Wrong Bride (Reprimand) [2003/4 17m^6   **h–**
Jul 19] leggy gelding: fair maiden on Flat (stays 1m): favourite, didn't jump well and
reportedly lost action in juvenile in hurdling debut. *Ian Williams*

LUCKY LUK (FR)   5 b.g. Lights Out (FR) – Citronelle II (FR) (Kedellic (FR))   **F–**
[2003/4 F16d F16m Mar 11] 28,000 3-y-o: compact gelding: second foal: dam, twice-
raced in cross-country chases, half-sister to very smart staying chaser Antonin: well held
in bumpers. *K. C. Bailey*

LUCKY MOSCO   7 b.g. Lucky Wednesday – Gouly Duff (Party Mink) [2003/4 F16m   **F70**
Aug 2] half-brother to fair hurdler/fairly useful chaser Forest Gunner (by Gunner B),
stays 3m, and winning hunter chaser Freddie Fox
(both by Scallywag): dam placed in points: looked a stayer when ninth of 21 in bumper at
Worcester on debut. *Jonjo O'Neill*

LUCKY NOMAD   8 br.g. Nomadic Way (USA) – Daleena (Dalesa) [2003/4 h–: 25f^3   **h56**
Oct 15] medium-sized gelding: upped in trip, bad form when third of 4 in weak novice
handicap hurdle at Wetherby: has worn cheekpieces. *R. Ford*

LUCKY PETE   7 b.g. Lyphento (USA) – Chance's Choice (Pragmatic) [2003/4 F16m   **h63**
22m^6 21g^6 19g^6 24g 22s* 22s 22g 21g^pu Apr 12] leggy, quite good-topped gelding: **F–**
second foal: half-brother to modest hurdler Nick's Choice (by Sula Bula), stays 2¾m:
dam, third in bumper on only start, half-sister to fairly useful staying chaser Spuffington:
poor hurdler: form only when winning selling handicap at Folkestone in January, soon
well clear: stays 2¾m: acts on soft going: wore cheekpieces final outing. *P. J. Jones*

LUCKY SINNA (IRE)   8 b. or br.g. Insan (USA) – Bit of A Chance (Lord Ha Ha)   **c97**
[2003/4 h92: c24s^2 c20g^2 Apr 12] rangy gelding: modest maiden hurdler: left J. Gifford   **h–**
and off 22 months, similar form when second in maiden chases at Fakenham and Plumpton: stays 3m: acts on firm and soft going: has had tongue tied. *B. G. Powell*

LUCKY UNO   8 b.g. Rock City – Free Skip (Free State) [2003/4 16d^pu 16s 17d 20d   **c–**
c20g^pu Apr 24] ungenuine maiden on Flat: no form over jumps. *John A. Harris*   **h–**

LUCY LANCASTER   9 b.m. Elegant Monarch – Lancaster Rose (Canadel II) [2003/4   **h–**
h–: 16m^5 20m^ur 24m Jun 18] no form over hurdles: unseated rider at start second outing.
Miss G. Browne

LUDERE (IRE)   9 ch.g. Desse Zenny (USA) – White Jasmin (Jalmood (USA)) [2003/4   **h80 §**
h91: 24v^pu 22s^3 20d^3 22s^F 21g^6 24g 21d^3 Apr 11] angular gelding: poor hurdler: stays 3m:
acts on any going: blinkered/in cheekpieces last 3 starts: moody. *B. J. Llewellyn*

LUFTIKUS (GER)   7 ch.g. Formidable (USA) – La Paz (GER) (Roi Dagobert) [2003/4   **h80**
h80: 17g 24m^6 24g^2 Aug 23] workmanlike gelding: poor novice hurdler: stays 3m:
looked difficult ride final outing. *A. G. Hobbs*

LUKE AFTER ME (IRE)   4 b.g. Victory Note (USA) – Summit Talk (Head For   **h–**
Heights) [2003/4 16m 16f 16g 16g Jan 15] tall gelding: modest maiden on Flat (stays 7f):
no form in juvenile hurdles, left N. Waggott after third start. *G. A. Swinbank*

LUMACA (IRE)   9 b.g. Riberetto – Broken Mirror (Push On) [2003/4 c66, h–: c25g^pu   **c– x**
May 1] workmanlike gelding: poor handicap hurdler/maiden chaser: best at 3m+: acts on   **h–**
heavy going (bumper form on good to firm): jumps fences none too fluently. *C. Roberts*

LUMYNO (FR)   5 b.g. Lute Antique (FR) – Framboline (FR) (Royal Charter (FR))   **F–**
[2003/4 F16s F17g Apr 1] has scope: first foal: dam, won around 11f on Flat in France,
sister to smart hurdler/useful chaser up to around 2¾m Gatsby IV and half-sister to useful
staying chaser Domaine de Pron: well held in bumpers. *S. E. H. Sherwood*

LUNARDI (IRE)   6 b.g. Indian Ridge – Gold Tear (USA) (Tejano (USA)) [2003/4   **c72**
c72, h–: c20m^3 c21g^4 c20m^ur c25g c24g Mar 12] neat gelding: winning hurdler: poor   **h–**
maiden chaser: probably stays 25f: acts on good to firm and heavy going: tried visored.
D. L. Williams

LUNAR FOX   5 b.m. Roselier (FR) – Leinthall Fox (Deep Run) [2003/4 F17m Apr 15] **F—**
small mare: has no tail: third foal: half-sister to modest hurdler Native Fox (by Be My
Native), stays 2½m: dam poor novice hurdler: well held in mares bumper on debut.
J. L. Needham

LUNAR LEADER (IRE)   4 b.f. Mujadil (USA) – Moon River (FR) (Groom Dancer **h—**
(USA)) [2003/4 16s^pu Jan 21] trained by Mrs L. Stubbs, fair on Flat (stays 1¼m) at 3
yrs, successful 3 times: in cheekpieces, little aptitude for hurdling in fillies juvenile at
Fakenham. *M. J. Gingell*

LUNAR LORD   8 b.g. Elmaamul (USA) – Cache (Bustino) [2003/4 h–: 16s 16g³ 17g⁵ **h89**
Apr 10] leggy gelding: modest handicap hurdler: will stay 2½m: acts on good to soft
going. *D. Burchell*

LUNAR MAXWELL   9 b.g. Dancing High – Pauper Moon (Pauper) [2003/4 c94, h–: **c77**
c23g³ c24d⁴ c24s c24f² Feb 29] rather leggy, close-coupled gelding: winning hurdler: **h—**
novice chaser, poor in 2003/4: stays 3¼m: acts on soft and good to firm going: wore
cheekpieces third start: not an easy ride. *J. I. A. Charlton*

LUNERAY (FR)   5 b.m. Poplar Bluff – Casandre (FR) (Montorselli) [2003/4 18d* **c106**
c19s^F c19s* 16v² c22d² c19g* c24m² Apr 13] ex-French mare: third foal: dam 1¾m **h112**
winner on Flat: once-raced on Flat: fair hurdler/chaser: won mares hurdle at Auteuil in
October and 4-y-o chase at Enghien in November: sold out of T. Civel's stable €95,000
Goffs Sale later in month: successful in novice chase at Hereford in April: stays 2¾m:
acts on soft going, probably on good to firm. *P. F. Nicholls*

LUPIN (FR)   5 b.g. Luchiroverte (IRE) – Amarante II (FR) (Brezzo (FR)) [2003/4 **h96**
h104, F92: 17d 16g 20s^pu 19d⁵ Mar 3] rather unfurnished gelding: winning 2m hurdler:
tongue tied, little impact in handicaps in Britain second and third outings: acts on soft
going. *F. Doumen, France*

LURISTAN (IRE)   4 b.g. Pennekamp (USA) – Linnga (IRE) (Shardari) [2003/4 F14g⁶ **h—**
F12d F16v³ F17s 17v⁵ Feb 2] €7,800 3-y-o: angular gelding: sixth foal: half-brother to **F—**
useful hurdler/winning chaser Lisaan (by Bigstone), stays 2½m, and winning staying
hurdler/chaser Liniyan (by Kahyasi): dam, French winner up to 1½m, from family of top-
class 1½m performers Acamas, Akarad and Akiyda: signs of ability only in bumper on
debut. *S. T. Lewis*

LUSTRAL DU SEUIL (FR)   5 b.g. Sassanian (USA) – Bella Tennise (FR) (Rhap- **h104**
sodien) [2003/4 16g^pu 17s³ 16d² 20s Mar 13] useful-looking gelding: second foal: half-
brother to 2004 3-y-o middle-distance winner Nistabelle (by Lights Out): dam winning
2m chaser: successful twice over 1½m in French Provinces at 4 yrs for M. Boudot: best
effort over hurdles when second to Sindapour in maiden at Plumpton: should stay beyond
2m. *N. J. Henderson*

LUTEUR DES PICTONS (FR)   5 ch.g. Ragmar (FR) – Ezera (FR) (Chamberlin **h—**
(FR)) [2003/4 16g 16s⁵ 17s^pu 16s 22s⁶ 20g^pu Mar 6] good-topped ex-French gelding:
second known foal: dam, winner on Flat, from family of good French chasers Mackay
and Otway: sixth in non-thoroughbred event around 11f at Angers for T. Lerner: signs of
only a little ability over hurdles, left A. Ennis after fourth start. *B. G. Powell*

LUTHELLO (FR)   5 b.g. Marchand de Sable (USA) – Haudello (FR) (Marignan **F84**
(USA)) [2003/4 F16m Nov 16] 46,000 4-y-o: leggy gelding: first foal: dam unraced out
of very smart French hurdler Highello: shaped as if outing was needed when 13 lengths
fourteen of 18 in bumper at Ayr on debut. *J. Howard Johnson*

LUXEMBOURG   5 b.g. Bigstone (IRE) – Princess Borghese (USA) (Nijinsky (CAN)) **h—**
[2003/4 h–, F–: 20d 22d 22s⁴ 26g⁶ Feb 25] lengthy, angular gelding: no form: tried
visored (looked hard ride). *N. A. Twiston-Davies*

LUZCADOU (FR)   11 b.g. Cadoudal (FR) – Luzenia (FR) (Armos) [2003/4 c124, h–: **c119 §**
c21d 20s^F c20d⁵ c20v* c20s⁴ c33d^bd c22g^pu c36d^F c33d^pu Apr 17] good-topped gelding: **h—**
winning hurdler: fairly useful handicap chaser: fortunate to win at Ayr in January, held in
second when Thoseweretheodays fell last: best form around 2½m on soft/heavy going:
blinkered/visored: sometimes let down by jumping: has looked unwilling, including on
second of 2 runs in cross-country races at Punchestown in late-April. *Ferdy Murphy*

LYDFORD CASTLE   10 b.g. Thornberry (USA) – Our Generator (Starch Reduced) **c—**
[2003/4 c24g^pu Apr 1] once-raced over hurdles: winning pointer: blinkered, no show in **h—**
hunter chase. *R. Jarman*

LYNCHAHAUN (IRE)   8 b. or br.g. Good Thyne (USA) – Smart Decision (IRE) (Le **h77**
Moss) [2003/4 h–: 16g 16s⁴ 20g⁴ Jun 6] poor form over hurdles: will stay beyond 2½m.
P. Monteith

LYNPHORD GIRL 13 ch.m. Lyphento (USA) – Woodlands Angel (Levanter) [2003/4 **c89** c75: c19d* c21f² c19g³ c21d⁵ Dec 26] modest chaser: won weak novice at Towcester in October: stays 21f: acts on good to soft going, probably on firm: prone to mistakes. *Dr J. R. J. Naylor*

LYNRICK LADY (IRE) 8 b.m. Un Desperado (FR) – Decent Lady (Decent Fellow) **c94** [2003/4 h94: 24d* 25d 24s⁴ c26sᵖᵘ c26s² Feb 16] tall mare: fair handicap hurdler: won **h106** at Chepstow in November: easily better effort in steeplechases when second in novice at Plumpton: stays 3¼m: acts on heavy going, possibly unsuited by good to firm. *J. G. Portman*

LYNWOOD GOLD 5 b.g. Gold Dust – Beths Wish (Rustingo) [2003/4 F18s 16g **h–** Feb 25] second foal: dam bad maiden hurdler: tailed off in bumper and novice hurdle. **F–** *B. J. Llewellyn*

LYON 4 ch.g. Pivotal – French Gift (Cadeaux Genereux) [2003/4 F17g Apr 13] fourth **F–** foal: half-brother to fairly useful sprinter Whistler (by Selkirk) and 6f winner Stridhana (by Indian Ridge): dam, 2-y-o 6f winner, out of high-class sprinter Soba: well held in bumper on debut. *O. Sherwood*

LYPHARD'S FABLE (USA) 13 b.g. Al Nasr (FR) – Affirmative Fable (USA) **c–** (Affirmed (USA)) [2003/4 c–, h–: c25dᵘʳ Mar 11] compact gelding: winning hurdler/ **h–** maiden chaser: poor pointer nowadays: tried blinkered. *Miss M. Bayliss*

LYPHARITA'S RISK (FR) 9 b.g. Take Risks (FR) – Patissima (FR) (Lightning **c65** (FR)) [2003/4 c20m 16mᵖᵘ c20mᶠ c25mᵖᵘ c19m² c16m* c16m⁵ c20m Dec 18] maiden **h–** hurdler: poor chaser, trained on reappearance by E. Williams: extremely fortunate when winning novice handicap at Ludlow (would have finished last but for both his rivals falling) in November: effective at 2m to easy 3m: probably acts on any going: tried tongue tied: tends to find little. *Mrs M. Evans*

LYRICAL LILY 6 b.m. Alflora (IRE) – Music Interpreter (Kampala) [2003/4 F16d⁵ **F72** Mar 25] 5,000 5-y-o: seventh foal: half-sister to 2¾m hurdle winner Maybe The Business (by Karinga Bay) and fair hunter chaser Mr Collins (by Brush Aside): dam winning 2m hurdler/1¾m winner on Flat: fifth of 11 to State of Play in bumper at Ludlow on debut. *Mrs S. M. Johnson*

LYRICIST'S DREAM 5 b.m. Dreams End – Lyricist (Averof) [2003/4 F16d F16d **F–** Jan 22] half-sister to several winners, including 25f hurdle winner Rusty Music (by Rust-ingo): dam unraced: behind in 2 bumpers at Ludlow. *R. L. Brown*

M

MACANILLO (GER) 6 gr.g. Acatenango (GER) – Midday Girl (GER) (Black Tie **h–** Affair) [2003/4 h–: 16m 16gᵖᵘ Nov 15] good-topped gelding: no form over hurdles. *Ian Williams*

MACEO (GER) 10 ch.g. Acatenango (GER) – Metropolitan Star (USA) (Lyphard **c86 §** (USA)) [2003/4 h109: c17g⁴ c16m² 19m² 16m³ 16g⁶ 16d³ 16s⁶ c16s⁵ 16s⁵ 20g* 16d³ **h110 §** c25gᶠ Apr 5] angular gelding: fair handicap hurdler: won at Ayr in March: little aptitude for chasing: stays 2½m: acts on soft and good to firm going: tried blinkered/in cheek-pieces, including last 3 starts: held up: often looks unenthusiastic. *Mrs M. Reveley*

MACGEORGE (IRE) 14 b.g. Mandalus – Colleen Donn (Le Moss) [2003/4 c130, **c128** h–: c25g* c28gᵖᵘ c22s⁶ c26d* c25d* c26m² Apr 15] lengthy gelding: still a smart hunter **h–** chaser aged 14, making all at Warwick and Exeter (beat The Granby by 27 lengths) in March: also successful at Hereford very early in season: stays 3¼m: acts on good to firm and heavy going: races prominently: bold jumper, makes the odd bad mistake: genuine. *R. Lee*

MACGYVER (NZ) 8 b.g. Jahafil – Corazon (NZ) (Pag-Asa (AUS)) [2003/4 c84, **c67** h86?: c24sᵖᵘ c16g⁶ c19dᵖᵘ Mar 22] medium-sized gelding: winning hurdler: poor maiden **h–** chaser: little form in hunters in 2003/4: best form around 2m on good/good to soft going: headstrong front runner. *M. F. Loggin*

MACHETE MAN 9 b.g. Broadsword (USA) – Ribo Melody (Riboboy (USA)) **c–** [2003/4 c–: 20mᶠ 26mᶠ Jun 11] strong, lengthy gelding: has failed to complete in novice **h–** chases/hurdles: headstrong. *J. A. T. de Giles*

MACH FOUR (IRE) 6 b.g. Bob Back (USA) – Tasmania Star (Captain James) **h86**
[2003/4 F90: 21g^F 20d^{pu} Nov 26] tall gelding: fair in bumpers: keeping on in fourth when
fell heavily 2 out in novice at Kempton on hurdling debut: shaped as if amiss next time.
N. A. Twiston-Davies

MAC HINE (IRE) 7 b.g. Eurobus – Zoe Baird (Aragon) [2003/4 h101, F96: c20m³ **c111 x**
c22d² c20d³ c24g^{pu} c22g* c32g⁶ c25d⁵ Apr 17] tall gelding: novice hurdler: fair novice **h–**
chaser: won handicap at Kelso in March by length from King's Bounty: stays 2¾m
(probably not 4m): acts on good to firm and heavy going: bled from nose fourth start: not
a fluent jumper: has hinted at temperament. *Jonjo O'Neill*

MACHRIHANISH 4 b.g. Groom Dancer (USA) – Goodwood Lass (IRE) (Alzao **h85 §**
(USA)) [2003/4 16g⁴ 16s^{rtr} 16g⁴ 16g^{pu} 17d^{pu} 16g Apr 4] leggy gelding: temperamental
maiden on Flat: poor form over hurdles: refused to race second outing and effectively did
so fourth one, subsequently sold out of Mrs L. Normile's stable £4,000 Ascot February
Sales: one to leave alone. *S. C. Burrough*

MACKENZIE (IRE) 8 b.g. Mandalus – Crinkle Lady (Buckskin (FR)) [2003/4 **h–**
22g^{pu} 16s^{pu} Dec 26] good-topped gelding: lightly-raced maiden hurdler. *Mrs C. J. Kerr*

MACMILLAN 4 b.g. Machiavellian (USA) – Mill On The Floss (Mill Reef (USA)) **h–**
[2003/4 16g^{pu} Sep 7] half-brother to fairly useful hurdler up to 25f Bosham Mill (by
Nashwan), also smart but untrustworthy stayer on Flat: fair maiden on Flat (stays 1½m)
for B. Meehan: didn't impress with attitude on hurdling debut: sold 5,500 gns Newmarket
Autumn Sales. *C. J. Mann*

MACNAMARASBAND (IRE) 15 b.g. Orchestra – Susan Mc Cann (Furry Glen) **c–**
[2003/4 c25g^{pu} May 1] rangy gelding: veteran chaser, little sign of retaining ability in **h–**
2003: tried blinkered. *Mrs P. Chamings*

MACNANCE (IRE) 8 b.m. Mandalus – Colleen Donn (Le Moss) [2003/4 h103: 17s^{pu} **h105**
19m 16g³ 22d⁵ 19s* 17s⁴ 20s⁶ 24d⁶ 20d Apr 21] angular mare: fair handicap hurdler: won
mares event at Hereford in January: stays 3m: acts on good to firm and heavy going.
R. Lee

MACONNOR (IRE) 7 b.g. Religiously (USA) – Door Belle (Fidel) [2003/4 h106p: **c–**
c16v^F 19g Apr 24] rangy gelding: fair form over hurdles, found little final outing: fell **h–**
fourth on debut over fences: bred to stay beyond 2m: pulls hard. *H. D. Daly*

MACREATER 6 b.m. Mazaad – Gold Caste (USA) (Singh (USA)) [2003/4 h73: 20g⁶ **h–**
20g⁶ 19f³ 21s^{pu} 17d 19d 26d^{pu} Mar 28] no worthwhile form over hurdles. *K. A. Morgan*

MACS FLAMINGO (IRE) 4 br.g. Rashar (USA) – Parkality (IRE) (Good Thyne **F102**
(USA)) [2003/4 F16s² Apr 21] first foal: dam unraced: fairly useful form when 2½
lengths second to Nowyouretalking in newcomers bumper at Gowran on debut.
P. A. Fahy, Ireland

MACS JOY (IRE) 5 b.g. Religiously (USA) – Snob's Supreme (IRE) (Supreme **h132 p**
Leader) [2003/4 F16d* F16m³ 16g⁵ 16m² 16d 18d* 16s² 16s² 16s² 16d* Apr 13] **F90**
    The end of the jumps season is a fragmentary mess. What possible sense
does it make to focus all attention on a mixed card at Sandown, hold the last few
races somewhere else, start the next season with a card of no consequence within
twenty-four hours, run a major handicap a week later (for quite a lot of the runners
their last appearance over hurdles until the autumn), and have the season end before
the last major Festival for jumpers takes place in Ireland (which leads to horses,
such as Rule Supreme in 2003/4 and Cherub in 2004/5 being able to run as novices
in Britain but not Ireland by virtue of a win at Punchestown)? The old National Hunt
season was followed by a two-month break in June and July, making it evident
where the start and finish were, but, with thriving summer jumping here to stay,
more thought needs to be given. Moving the end of the season back a week, to a
mixed card at Haydock on Guineas weekend, if anything makes less sense than
where it is now. So here's a more radical suggestion—take the core of the Sandown
card (possibly with the addition of the Haydock race) and run it a month later, as an
all-jumps card, on the last Saturday in May, making that the end of the season.
That should ensure full coverage on television, given that the biggest race on the
corresponding weekend in 2004 was a £50,000 sprint handicap at Musselburgh,
would have the advantage of extending the media focus on jump racing over May
(Kelso and Stratford are among jumps tracks staging valuable and well supported
cards in May) and would move races which now clash with Punchestown to a time

Menolly Homes Handicap Hurdle, Fairyhouse—
the progressive Macs Joy isn't fully extended to beat Tiger Cry (stripes)

when they might attract stronger fields. The end to the season could be followed by a short break, perhaps of a couple of weeks, and the new season could start with a bang with the Summer National at Uttoxeter (worth £75,000 in total prize money in 2004). Given the problems caused by dry weather in the autumn, notably in 2003, when it looked, at one time, touch and go whether the Open meeting at Cheltenham could go ahead, the core jumps season could do with extending at the other end, when suitable ground should be easier to provide. Coping with the change shouldn't be a problem given modern training methods, and Sandown should be able to overcome having to make alterations to its two-day Whitsun Flat fixture.

In terms of dealing with the good horses that ran at Punchestown, it's impossible to remain within the confines of the current British season. Much the same applies to Macs Joy, an Irish-trained novice hurdler whose campaign began when he won a bumper at Tralee on June 2nd and ended eleven months later when winning the aforementioned Haydock race, the Swinton Handicap Hurdle. Early on, Macs Joy looked nothing out of the ordinary, his first five runs over hurdles bringing just a maiden success at Downpatrick. However, once switched to handicaps after the turn of the year, he made marked improvement and there is the prospect of more to come when he returns later in 2004/5. He won twice from four starts and was doubly unfortunate not to add to that tally. At Leopardstown in February, a month after finishing second to Dromlease Express in the Pierse Handicap Hurdle, Macs Joy was clearly the winner on merit when beating Kilbeggan Lad three lengths but was demoted to second for causing interference after the last. Macs Joy looked to have a leading chance in the County Hurdle at Cheltenham but didn't run as his trainer was unwilling to run him 14 lb out of the weights. He then missed Aintree with a 'dirty nose'. Back for Fairyhouse later in April, Macs Joy took advantage of a still lenient-looking mark to win the valuable Menolly Homes Handicap by a length and a half from Tiger Cry. He started 7/2 favourite that day in a field of twenty-seven (only one runner started at longer than 25/1, the starting prices percentage making up at a staggering 183%) and was an even warmer order at Haydock. The Swinton was rather a lop-sided race, with twelve of the nineteen

564

runners out of the handicap, but Macs Joy, himself 4 lb 'wrong', could be called the winner a long way out and put up his best effort to date. The Anglo-Irish Classification, ignoring the official end of the season and taking the performance into account, put Macs Joy on a mark of 144, which is a stiff mark judged on the bare form but may not stop him picking up further wins in competitive handicaps. He reportedly has the William Hill Handicap at Sandown and the Tote Gold Trophy among his targets later in 2004/5. Macs Joy's style of racing, coming with a late run, makes him hard for the handicapper to get to grips with.

Macs Joy (IRE) (b.g. 1999)	Religiously (USA) (b or br 1984)	Alleged (b 1974)	Hoist The Flag
			Princess Pout
		Pas de Nom (b 1968)	Admiral's Voyage
			Petitioner
	Snob's Supreme (IRE) (b 1991)	Supreme Leader (b 1982)	Bustino
			Princess Zena
		Boherash Forest (ch 1982)	Proverb
			In The Forest

Macs Joy has raced at up to two and a quarter miles but should have little trouble staying further. His trainer has handled two of his sire Religiously's other notable offspring—the Midlands National winner Intelligent and the fairly useful chaser at around three miles Hume Castle—while others by Religiously include Emotional Moment, useful up to three miles, and Bold Bishop, a useful novice hurdler raced mainly at two miles so far. There is virtually nothing to record about Macs Joy's family on the distaff side. The three dams at the bottom of his pedigree

Mac's J Racing Syndicate's "Macs Joy"

were unraced. He is the first and only foal of his now-deceased dam Snob's Supreme, who was out of a half-sister to the useful chaser at around two and a half miles Strong Medicine. The third dam In The Forest was a half-sister to the useful hurdler and staying chaser Town Head. Macs Joy is a good-topped gelding and is likely to make at least as good a chaser as a hurdler in due course, though there is more to come over hurdles first. *Mrs J. Harrington, Ireland*

MACY (IRE) 11 ch.g. Sharp Charter – Lumax (Maximilian) [2003/4 c21g⁴ May 12] good-topped gelding: winning pointer: poor maiden steeplechaser: tried visored/in cheekpieces. *Martin Jones* **c–**
h–

MADALYAR (IRE) 5 b.g. Darshaan – Madaniyya (USA) (Shahrastani (USA)) [2003/4 h82: 17m⁴ 17m 20v⁵ c20g Apr 10] angular gelding: poor maiden hurdler: seventh of 17 in handicap at Carlisle on chasing debut: probably stays 2½m. *Jonjo O'Neill* **c73**
h68

MADAM FLORA 7 b.m. Alflora (IRE) – Madam's Choice (New Member) [2003/4 h104: 20s⁴ 16m c19d² 16g³ 21m Apr 15] sparely-made mare: fair hurdler: similar form when ½-length second to Christopher in maiden at Exeter on chasing debut: fective at 2m to 2¾m: acts on soft and good to firm going: front runner: reliable. *M. J. Weeden* **c106**
h106

MADAM MOSSO 8 b.m. Le Moss – Rochestown Lass (Deep Run) [2003/4 c97p, h97: 24m Oct 26] lengthy, workmanlike mare: modest hurdler, below form only outing in 2003/4: won mares novice in 2002/3 on only start over fences: will stay beyond 3¼m: acts on good to firm and heavy going: genuine. *Mrs A. M. Thorpe* **c–**
h–

MADAM'S MAN 8 b.g. Sir Harry Lewis (USA) – Madam-M (Tina's Pet) [2003/4 c104, h100: c21g* c29mF³ c25g³ c30g⁴ c32g Mar 17] rangy gelding: fair hurdler: similar form over fences: won novice handicap at Newton Abbot in November: stays 3¼m: acts on soft and good to firm going. *N. A. Twiston-Davies* **c100**
h–

MADE IN JAPAN (JPN) 4 b.g. Barathea (IRE) – Darrery (Darshaan) [2003/4 16d³ 17s³ 16s* 17g* 16g² Apr 1] **h134 p**

Ireland had eleven, Britain four, France two and Germany, New Zealand and Japan one apiece. Cheltenham Festival winners are bred all over the world nowadays, it seems, and the latest Festival saw success for a particularly cosmopolitan collection of winners. Additionally, the USA, Australia and Poland were represented by horses bred in those countries. There are no prizes for guessing which part of the world the Triumph Hurdle winner Made In Japan hails from, though, as will be seen, his origins are less exotic than his name would suggest.

There were twenty-three runners for the Triumph Hurdle, sponsored by JCB, a slightly smaller field than usual, as a result of a reduced safety limit while the course is made ready for the four-day Festival in 2005. But in other respects it was a fairly typical renewal of the most prestigious race for juvenile hurdlers, with a good pace, some early casualties (three came down at the second flight) and a long-priced winner. The Triumph's reputation for shock results isn't quite what it was, but Made In Japan became the second consecutive 20/1 winner after Spectroscope the year before, which followed Scolardy at 16/1 in 2002. Made In Japan gradually crept into contention after being held up and was poised behind the

JCB Triumph Hurdle, Cheltenham—the five in with a chance at the last are (from left to right) winner Made In Japan, Howle Hill, Cherub, runner-up Chief Yeoman and Top Strategy

leading group turning into the straight. Improving to dispute the lead jumping the last, Made In Japan was driven out up the hill to beat two even longer-odds outsiders, Chief Yeoman and Top Strategy, by two lengths and a neck. Cherub took fourth ahead of Howle Hill, who had looked the winner early in the straight but weakened after the last, while the latter's stable-companion Trouble At Bay proved a disappointing favourite. As his odds at Cheltenham suggested, Made In Japan showed improvement on his earlier form over hurdles in fairly ordinary company. He began with two third places in novices at Wincanton and Taunton. The better of those efforts came on his debut at Wincanton behind Howle Hill. Made In Japan then got off the mark in a juvenile hurdle at Sandown in February when beating the odds-on French import Royal Katidoki by a length.

After Cheltenham, Made In Japan emulated Spectroscope by going on to finish second in the big juvenile hurdles at both Aintree and Punchestown. He could be considered unfortunate not to have completed a clean sweep at all three Festival meetings, being foiled at both Aintree and Punchestown by horses who had finished behind him in the Triumph. In the Anniversary Hurdle at Aintree, Made In Japan was reopposed by six rivals from the Triumph, including Cherub and Howle Hill, but it was Al Eile, well beaten at Cheltenham, who sprung a surprise in beating Made In Japan three quarters of a length. As the Anniversary Hurdle is only a Grade 2 race (despite being worth £10,000 more in total prize money than the Triumph), Made In Japan had to carry a 4-lb penalty for his success at Cheltenham. Taking the weight difference into account, Made In Japan came out the best horse at the

Mr Terry Evans' "Made In Japan"

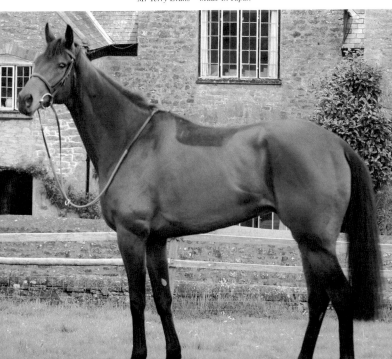

weights, though he probably should still have won in any case, hitting the front plenty soon enough three out and then wandering under pressure once in the lead. In the Champion Four Year Old Hurdle at Punchestown later in April a mistake at the last cost Made In Japan victory. That error lost him the lead, but he rallied strongly all the way to the line before going down by just a short head to the Triumph fourth Cherub.

Made In Japan, bred by Sheikh Mohammed's Darley Stud, was indeed foaled in Japan, where his dam was on secondment, but that's the extent of his connection with the Far East. He is by the high-class miler Barathea, who stands in Ireland, out of the useful Darrery, a winner at mile and a quarter and a mile and a half. As a result of her visit to Japan, where she was covered by Sunday Silence, Darrery produced the Godolphin two-year-old colt Sunday Symphony. Darrery's first foal also started with Godolphin, Al Waffi (by Fairy King) showing useful form as a two-year-old and finishing third in the Gran Criterium. Darrery has also produced a winner in Greece by Green Desert. Made In Japan's grandam Flamenco was a smart filly who did all her racing at up to a mile and gained her biggest win in the Waterford Candelabra Stakes at Goodwood as a two-year-old. She was out of a winning sister to Bold Laddie, a very smart two-year-old sprinter in the States.

Made In Japan (JPN) (b.g. 2000)	Barathea (IRE) (b 1990)	Sadler's Wells (b 1981)	Northern Dancer / Fairy Bridge
		Brocade (b 1981)	Habitat / Canton Silk
	Darrery (b 1990)	Darshaan (br 1981)	Shirley Heights / Delsy
		Flamenco (b 1980)	Dance Spell / Santiago Sweetie

Made In Japan is a tall, useful-looking gelding with scope who must have made plenty of appeal on looks as a potential hurdler when bought off the Flat for 35,000 guineas at the Newmarket Autumn Sales. He had been fairly useful at up to a mile and three quarters for Mikael Magnusson, and had provided his former trainer with his first winner from his very first runner when winning on the polytrack at Lingfield as a two-year-old. Made In Japan was among the best of just an ordinary crop of British and Irish juvenile hurdlers and, rather than taking on older hurdlers in top company from now on, it looks as though Made In Japan will be sent chasing straight away. He has the size to jump fences and, if he jumps the larger obstacles as well as he does hurdles, he should make the grade in novice chases. Made In Japan has raced only at around two miles but will probably stay further. He has yet to race on ground firmer than good over jumps, but acted on firm ground on the Flat. He is held up and tends to wander under pressure. *P. J. Hobbs*

MADEMIST SAM 12 b.g. Lord Bud – Mademist Susie (French Vine) [2003/4 c79, h–: c25gpu Mar 28] workmanlike gelding: winning chaser: placed in points in 2004: stays 3m: acts on soft and good to firm going: has won with/without blinkers. *M. J. Hill*   c– h–

MADGE CARROLL (IRE) 7 b.m. Hollow Hand – Spindle Tree (Laurence O) [2003/4 h86: 20gF 24g2 c25d* c20s* c25gpu 24g3 Feb 19] small, sturdy mare: modest hurdler: fair form over fences, winning mares maiden at Folkestone and mares novice at Huntingdon in December: stays 25f: raced on good going or softer (acts on soft). *T. R. George*   c109 h94

MADIBA 5 b.g. Emperor Jones (USA) – Priluki (Lycius (USA)) [2003/4 h98: 19spu Dec 13] leggy gelding: fair on Flat (stays 2m), successful in January: thrice-raced over hurdles, showed nothing only start in 2003/4. *P. Howling*   h–

MADISON AVENUE (GER) 7 b.g. Mondrian (GER) – Madly Noble (GER) (Irish River (FR)) [2003/4 h99: 20g* May 5] leggy gelding: modest hurdler: not seen out again after winning claimer at Fontwell very early in season: stays 21f: acts on heavy going: tried blinkered. *T. M. Jones*   h88

MADISON DE VONNAS (FR) 4 b.g. Epervier Bleu – Carine de Neuvy (FR) (Shelley (FR)) [2003/4 F16d Apr 12] has scope: dam unraced, out of half-sister to useful staying chaser Jivago de Neuvy: well held in bumper on debut. *Miss E. C. Lavelle*   F–

MADMIDGE 9 b. or br.g. Jendali (USA) – No Rejection (Mummy's Pet) [2003/4 c21dpu Apr 12] fair pointer: successful 3 times in 2004: pulled up in novice hunter chase at Fakenham. *D. J. Kemp*   c–

MAESTRO PLEASE (IRE)   5 b.g. Old Vic – Greek Melody (IRE) (Trojan Fort) **F82**
[2003/4 F16v F16g⁵ Mar 15] rather unfurnished gelding: second foal: half-brother to
fairly useful hurdler around 2m Best Wait (by Insan): dam, 2½m bumper winner, half-
sister to useful hurdler up to 2½m Kiora: better effort in bumpers when fifth of 16 to
Gaelic Flight in maiden at Stratford. *Lady Connell*

MA FURIE (FR)   4 gr.f. Balleroy (USA) – Furie de Carmont (FR) (Carmont (FR)) **h110**
[2003/4 16s* 16g Feb 13] good-topped ex-French filly: half-sister to fairly useful chaser
Lord Carmont (by Goldneyev), probably stays 21f: dam twice-raced, out of half-sister to
top-class staying chaser Otage du Perche: placed twice up to 13f from 3 starts on Flat at 3
yrs: won mares newcomers event at Pau on hurdling debut in January for Mme I. Pacault:
weakened quickly after 3 out in juvenile at Kempton. *Miss H. C. Knight*

MAGALINA (IRE)   5 br.m. Norwich – Pike Review (Dawn Review) [2003/4 F17g⁴ **h80**
16g^pu 16m 16d 24g^pu 19d* 22g Apr 18] €4,000 3-y-o: good-topped mare: third foal: half- **F87**
sister to fairly useful chaser Pancho's Tango (by Arapahos), stayed 3m: dam unraced:
fourth in mares bumper at Bangor on debut: form over hurdles only when 40/1-winner of
mares maiden at Taunton in March, less than fluent at times and wandering markedly
from before 2 out: stays 19f: acts on good to soft going. *D. P. Keane*

MAGENKO (IRE)   7 ch.g. Forest Wind (USA) – Bebe Auction (IRE) (Auction Ring **h77**
(USA)) [2003/4 h–: 20d³ 20d³ 24d² 24g⁵ Feb 4] quite good-topped gelding: poor
handicap hurdler: lame final outing: stays 3m: acts on good to firm and heavy going: tried
blinkered. *F. P. Murtagh*

MAGENTA RISING (IRE)   4 ch.f. College Chapel – Fashion Queen (Chilibang) **h72**
[2003/4 17m 16g 16s⁶ 17m² 16d⁴ Apr 8] small, leggy filly: fair at best on all-weather on
Flat (stays 8.5f), successful in 2003 for P. d'Arcy: poor maiden hurdler: will prove best
around 2m with emphasis on speed. *D. Burchell*

MAGGIE GRAY (IRE)   6 b.m. Erins Isle – Reenoga (Tug of War) [2003/4 F16s F16s² **F76**
Apr 12] fifth foal: sister to one-time fair chaser/winning hurdler Damien's Choice, stays
2½m: dam won over hurdles in Ireland: modest form in 2 bumpers (trained on debut by
G. A. Swinbank), distant second to Lady Zephyr in mares event at Fakenham. *P. D. Niven*

MAGGIES BROTHER   11 b.g. Brotherly (USA) – Sallisses (Pamroy) [2003/4 c96: **c94**
c30m² c34v* c28g^ur c25d⁴ c25d⁵ c25d⁵ Mar 23] workmanlike gelding: fair hunter chaser:
won at Uttoxeter in May: stays 4¼m: acts on good to firm and heavy going. *R. Shail*

MAGICAL BAILIWICK (IRE)   8 ch.g. Magical Wonder (USA) – Alpine Dance **c127**
(USA) (Apalachee (USA)) [2003/4 c–, h–: c16s^f c19s* c25g* c24g* c25d* c24s² c33d³ **h–**
c32g^F Mar 17] leggy, close-coupled gelding: winning hurdler: fairly useful chaser: won
handicaps at Taunton and Cheltenham in December (both novices) and Ludlow and Wincanton in January: good placed efforts behind Tyneandthyneagain in valuable handicaps
at Doncaster and Newcastle last 2 completed starts: stayed 33f: raced mainly on good
going or softer (acted on heavy): blinkered once, visored final outing: tended to race
lazily: dead. *M. C. Pipe*

MAGICAL DAY   5 ch.m. Halling (USA) – Ahla (Unfuwain (USA)) [2003/4 h86: 20m^F **h88 §**
18g⁴ 16m 16m 17m² 16d² 17d* 19t 18s 16d³ 22s^pu 19s Feb 6] leggy mare: modest
hurdler: won seller at Hereford in December: stays 19f: acts on any going: effective with
or without headgear: temperamental. *W. G. M. Turner*

MAGICAL FIELD   6 ch.m. Deploy – Ash Glade (Nashwan (USA)) [2003/4 h85: 19g² **c–**
16s² 20g⁴ c16g^F Mar 10] lengthy mare: modest maiden hurdler: fell fourth on chasing **h91**
debut: likely to prove best around 2m: acts on soft going. *Mrs M. Reveley*

MAGICAL LIAISON (IRE)   6 b.g. Mujtahid (USA) – Instant Affair (USA) (Lyphard **h70**
(USA)) [2003/4 F91: 16d^pu 20s^pu 16s 19m² 21d^pu Mar 25] rather sparely-made gelding:
poor novice hurdler: stays 19f: tried in cheekpieces. *W. Jenks*

MAGICAL WONDERLAND   5 br.m. Thowra (FR) – Alice's Mirror (Magic Mirror) **h68**
[2003/4 F17m* F16m⁵ F17g⁵ 17g⁵ Nov 9] first foal: dam modest and temperamental **F87**
hurdler up to 2½m: won bumper at Hereford on debut in June: better form when fifth in
similar events at Worcester and Bangor: not fluent but not given hard time when fifth in
mares maiden at Southwell on hurdling debut. *B. G. Powell*

MAGIC BENGIE   5 b.g. Magic Ring (IRE) – Zinzi (Song) [2003/4 h–: 20g⁴ 17d^pu **h59**
16g 16g* Jan 24] first form over hurdles when winning selling handicap at Catterick,
making virtually all: tongue tied last 2 starts. *F. Kirby*

MAGIC BOX 6 b.g. Magic Ring (IRE) – Princess Poquito (Hard Fought) [2003/4 h77: 16m² 17m 17gᶠ 17m 17m Oct 18] angular gelding: poor handicap hurdler: best at sharp 2m: acts on good to firm going, probably on good to soft (well below form on soft): wore cheekpieces last 3 starts. *Miss Kate Milligan* **h77**

MAGIC CHARM 6 b.m. Magic Ring (IRE) – Loch Clair (IRE) (Lomond (USA)) [2003/4 h–: 19f⁴ Oct 8] poor on Flat (stays 1½m): well held in 3 starts over hurdles, jumping violently left only one in 2003/4: sold to join J. O'Keeffe 2,000 gns Doncaster March Sales. *A. G. Newcombe* **h– x**

MAGIC COMBINATION (IRE) 11 b.g. Scenic – Etage (Ile de Bourbon (USA)) [2003/4 c–, h120: 16s⁵ 22g⁶ 20dᵖᵘ 20g 20d Apr 10] leggy gelding: useful hurdler at one time, little form in 2003/4: stays 21f: acts on good to firm and heavy going: tried in cheekpieces: usually held up: runner-up on Flat in March. *L. Lungo* **c– h–**

MAGIC DANCER (IRE) 11 b.g. Carefree Dancer (USA) – Giveushope (Whistling Deer) [2003/4 c81d, h–: c27sᵖᵘ c23g Jan 27] lengthy, rather sparely-made gelding: winning hurdler/chaser, retains little ability: tried in headgear. *Capt. J. A. George* **c– h–**

MAGIC DRAGON (FR) 6 ch.g. Cyborg (FR) – Dix Huit Brumaire (FR) (General Assembly (USA)) [2003/4 F88: F16m F16s 20v⁶ 19gᵖᵘ Feb 10] well-made gelding: signs of ability only in bumper on debut: looked less than keen final start. *Mrs M. Reveley* **h– F–**

MAGIC HOUR (IRE) 5 b.g. Weldnaas (USA) – Montohouse (IRE) (Montelimar (USA)) [2003/4 F17d Oct 29] €4,000 4-y-o: second foal: dam ran twice: tailed off in bumper on debut. *W. McKeown* **F–**

MAGICIEN (FR) 8 b.g. Muroto – French Look (FR) (Green River (FR)) [2003/4 c–, h–: c19dᵖᵘ Mar 22] winning pointer, including in April: no form otherwise: has had tongue tied. *Steve Isaac* **c– h–**

MAGIC MISTRAL 6 b.m. Thowra (FR) – Festival of Magic (USA) (Clever Trick (USA)) [2003/4 F17g 16sᵖᵘ 23sᵖᵘ Jan 21] good-topped mare: half-sister to winning hurdler/chaser Afrostar (by Soviet Lad), stays 2½m, and to 2 winners on Flat: dam, 1m winner, half-sister to very smart middle-distance filly Squeak: no sign of ability. *C. C. Bealby* **h– F–**

MAGIC MISTRESS 5 b.m. Magic Ring (IRE) – Sight'n Sound (Chief Singer) [2003/4 19d³ 17g* Apr 10] fairly useful on Flat (stays 1½m), sold out of S. C. Williams' stable 42,000 gns Newmarket Autumn Sales: much better effort over hurdles when winning mares maiden at Newton Abbot comfortably by 10 lengths from Wasted Talent: open to further improvement. *N. J. Henderson* **h117 p**

MAGIC OF SYDNEY (IRE) 8 b.g. Broken Hearted – Chat Her Up (Proverb) [2003/4 c109, h–: c22g⁶ c24d⁵ Dec 29] sturdy gelding: fair chaser: stiff task in 2 handicaps at Newbury in 2003/4: probably stays 25f: acts on good to soft going. *R. Rowe* **c99 h–**

MAGIC RED 4 ch.g. Magic Ring (IRE) – Jacquelina (USA) (Private Account (USA)) [2003/4 16g⁶ 16m² 16s⁶ 16dᵖᵘ Mar 28] workmanlike gelding: half-brother to fairly useful 2m hurdler Eyeballs Out (by Polar Falcon): poor maiden on Flat (seems to stay 1m): best effort in juvenile hurdles when second at Huntingdon (wore cheekpieces) in October: blinkered on debut. *M. J. Ryan* **h82**

MAGIC ROUTE (IRE) 7 b.g. Mr Confusion (IRE) – Another Chapter (Respect) [2003/4 c–, h78: 20mᵖᵘ Oct 25] tall gelding: no show on chasing debut: little form over hurdles: should stay beyond 2m: has worn cheekpieces: sold 5,000 gns Doncaster November Sales, runner-up in point in April. *J. Howard Johnson* **c– h–**

MAGIC TRICK 5 b.g. Magic Ring (IRE) – Les Amis (Alzao (USA)) [2003/4 17m⁵ 16m Aug 25] fair on Flat (probably stays 1m) at 3 yrs for B. Hills, well beaten in 2003: no show in 2 races over hurdles. *Mrs P. N. Dutfield* **h–**

MAGIQUE ETOILE (IRE) 8 b.m. Magical Wonder (USA) – Shes A Dancer (IRE) (Alzao (USA)) [2003/4 c–, h60: 17gᵖᵘ Jun 13] smallish mare: of little account nowadays: tongue tied. *N. J. Hawke* **c– h–**

MAGNEMITE (IRE) 8 b.g. Dromod Hill – Rostoonstown Lass (IRE) (Decent Fellow) [2003/4 c19dᵖᵘ Mar 22] winning pointer: blinkered, no show in hunter on steeplechasing debut. *N. J. Dawe* **c–**

MAGS TWO 7 b.g. Jumbo Hirt (USA) – Welsh Diamond (High Top) [2003/4 h–, F–: 20f⁶ 20g⁵ 20m² 24m⁴ Oct 11] poor novice hurdler: stays 2½m: acts on good to firm going. *Ms Liz Harrison* **h71**

MAHARBAL (FR)   4 b.g. Assessor (IRE) – Cynthia (FR) (Mont Basile (FR)) [2003/4   **h107**
16m* 16g⁵ 18s⁵ Jan 26] good-topped ex-French gelding: third foal: dam middle-distance
winner: sold out of T. Trapenard's stable €45,000 Goffs July Sale after runner-up over
1¼m at Vichy on Flat debut: won juvenile at Newbury on hurdling debut in December:
disappointing in 2 similar events. *N. J. Henderson*

MAIA ERIA (FR)   4 b.f. Volochine (IRE) – Soldouna (FR) (Kaldoun (FR))   **h143**
[2003/4 18s* 18s* 18s* 18s² 18s* 19s* Apr 24]
For the second year running, the highest-rated four-year-old hurdler in
Europe ran solely in France. The Yann Porzier-trained filly Maia Eria produced a
couple of performances at Auteuil in the spring which, had she produced either of
them in the Triumph Hurdle at Cheltenham (for which the going was different),
would have seen her win by a record margin, taking the sex allowance into account.
Although she failed to run up to her best in two outings after the end of the British
season there's no reason to question the merit of her performances in either the Prix
de Pepinvast, in which she beat the useful River Charm fifteen lengths, or in the
Prix Amadou, in which she gave weight and a beating by the same margin to the
British-trained Mondul. Each time she was sent to the front at the start and raced
with characteristic zest, maintaining the gallop all the way to the line. Because of
the nature of the obstacles, the way races tend to be run and variations in ground
conditions, form at Auteuil doesn't always translate exactly to top courses in
Britain and Ireland. There is, however, enough evidence available to be reasonably
confident of the correlation between French and Anglo-Irish form and they should
be reflected, sooner rather than later, in the International Classification over jumps,
with marks published for the top French-raced performers. The handicapper for
France-Galop is listed as being consulted about the assessments of French-trained
horses in the latest Classification, though only those that ran in Britain or Ireland
are included. It can only be for the good of the sport in all three countries and
greater awareness may lead to an increase in the number of challengers from
overseas in each, which would be welcome.
Maia Eria's win in the Amadou was her fifth in six starts. She had gained
three successes in the autumn, all at Auteuil, a newcomers race in September, the

Prix Cambaceres, Auteuil—leading juvenile Maia Eria is well clear

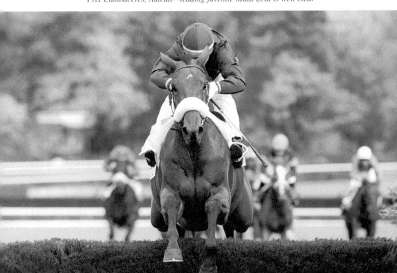

Group 2 Prix Georges de Talhouet-Roy in October and the top three-year-old hurdle, the Group 1 Prix Cambaceres in November. Reopposed by the seven she had beaten in the Group 2 as well as three others, Maia Eria was soon clear and never looked likely to be pegged back, winning by ten lengths from Kauto Star. There was a suspicion she might be flattered given the way the race was run, and there seemed to be some grounds for thinking so after she was beaten six lengths by River Charm in a Group 3 in March. Not a bit of it. Three weeks later Maia Eria showed her true form against River Charm before her superb performance in the Amadou. This time only three of her opponents from the previous race reopposed, including fifth-placed River Charm and Kauto Star.

Maia Eria was the first filly to win the Amadou since Lady Cricket in 1998 (she was also one of only three fillies to win the Cambaceres in the last twenty years). Afterwards, Maia Eria's trainer was lauding her as the best he had trained, which given that he trained the high-class hurdler Royal Chance and the top-class front-running hurdler Marly River was a significant claim. Had Maia Eria's campaign ended there and then, there would have been much to anticipate in the year ahead, but defeats in May and June took some of the gloss off her record. On the first occasion, she could finish only fifth in a race in which Kauto Star, River Charm and Mondul filled the first three places. Maia Eria was later reported as coming into season. She still started even money for the Group 1 Prix Alain du Breil in June, when she met rivals to whom she'd been conceding weight, on weight-for-sex terms, but having established a clear lead and looked to be travelling well to the straight she found little under pressure and could finish only third behind two other fillies, Mesange Royale and Ma Royale. Maia Eria's rider offered no excuses, though her trainer, probably rightly, mentioned the ground, which was a good deal less testing than typical at Auteuil. Maia Eria's first couple of runs in the next season should tell whether such a view is justified.

Maia Eria (FR) (b.f. 2000)	Volochine (IRE) (ch 1991)	Soviet Star (b 1984)	Nureyev
			Veruschka
		Harmless Albatross (b 1985)	Pas de Seul
			North Forland
	Soldouna (FR) (b 1982)	Kaldoun (gr 1975)	Caro
			Katana
		La Sologne (b 1974)	Tanamour
			Telma

The lengthy Maia Eria raced on the Flat, being placed over nine furlongs at two and at a mile and a half at three. She comes from a predominantly Flat-oriented background. Her dam Soldouna was useful over a mile and a half, winning the listed Grand Prix de La Ville de Toulouse, and is a half-sister to the useful middle-distance stayer Solko. Soldouna's seven previous foals include three winners on the Flat, including the durable Amon Quercus (by Shining Steel), still racing at the age of eleven in 2004 and now a winner nine times, with form at up to fifteen furlongs. *Y. Porzier, France*

MAIDEN VOYAGE 6 b.m. Slip Anchor – Elaine Tully (IRE) (Persian Bold) [2003/4 **h105**
h95: 19g*dis 20s* 16m* 20m Jun 28] good-topped mare: fair hurdler: first past post in
mares novices at Hereford (disqualified on technical grounds) and Bangor (despite
idling) in May and Hexham (not at all extended) in June: stays 21f: acts on soft and good
to firm going: visored in 2003/4. *P. R. Webber*

MAID FOR A MONARCH 4 b.f. King's Signet (USA) – Regan (USA) (Lear Fan **h–**
(USA)) [2003/4 16g 17d⁶ 17g 19sᵖᵘ Apr 11] angular filly: little form on Flat, sold out of
J. Given's stable 1,200 gns Newmarket July Sales: no form over hurdles. *Miss J. Feilden*

MAID OF DREAMS (IRE) 7 b.m. Mandalus – Dream of Money (IRE) (Welsh **c113**
Chanter) [2003/4 22g⁵ 22d⁴ 19d³ 20d c18d* c22sᶠ Mar 28] second foal: dam unraced **h95**
half-sister to smart chasers Ten of Spades and Maid of Money: first past post in point:
modest form over hurdles: won mares maiden at Downpatrick impressively on steeplechasing debut: every chance when falling 4 out in Grade 3 mares novice at Limerick later
in month: should stay beyond 19f: acts on good to soft going. *J. R. H. Fowler, Ireland*

MAIDSTONE MAJESTY 7 b.g. Teenoso (USA) – Easby Mosella (Le Moss) **F82**
[2003/4 F17g⁵ May 18] 1,200 4-y-o: fourth foal: dam, failed to complete in 4 points, half-
sister to fairly useful hurdler/chaser up to 3m Sweep Gently: fifth in bumper at Southwell
on debut. *Mrs S. J. Smith*

MAIDSTONE MISTRAL 4 b.g. Slip Anchor – Cayla (Tumble Wind (USA)) [2003/4 **h–** F12g F12s³ 17s³ 17s 17g 17dᵖᵘ 16dᵖᵘ Apr 11] 13,000Y: small, close-coupled gelding: **F82** half-brother to several winners, including sprinters Touch of White (by Song) and Fact-uelle (by Known Fact): dam, no form, out of smart French middle-distance filly Relicia. modest form in 3-y-o bumpers: headstrong and little sign of ability over hurdles. *M. C. Pipe*

MAIDSTONE MONUMENT (IRE) 9 b.g. Jurado (USA) – Loreto Lady (Brave **c106** Invader (USA)) [2003/4 c106, h–: c26dᵖᵘ c24g⁵ c23m* c23m² c23m³ c26m² c26g³ **h90** c26m* c26mᵖᵘ 25m* c26gᵖᵘ c26d² c21g c26mᵖᵘ 27g Apr 22] lengthy gelding: fair chaser: won handicaps at Worcester in July and Plumpton in September: modest hurdler: won handicap at latter course in October: stays 3¼m: acts on good to firm and good to soft going: blinkered once: best on left-handed tracks. *Mrs A. M. Thorpe*

MAIFUL (FR) 4 b.g. Useful (FR) – Shailann (FR) (Gaspard de La Nuit (FR)) [2003/4 **h87** 16s 16m² 17d Mar 27] leggy gelding: second foal: half-brother to 6f to 9f winner La Guilloche (by Esprit du Nord): dam lightly-raced maiden: in frame all 5 starts up to 1½m in non-thoroughbred events on Flat for C. Diard: form over hurdles only when second in maiden at Wincanton in March. *P. F. Nicholls*

MAISEY DOWN 7 b.m. Rakaposhi King – Win Green Hill (National Trust) [2003/4 **h–** F–: F16m⁵ 22d⁶ Feb 12] leggy, plain mare: no sign of ability. *J. A. B. Old* **F–**

MAISIEBEL 6 ch.m. Be My Native (USA) – High 'b' (Gunner B) [2003/4 F–: 20g⁶ **h65** Oct 27] unfurnished mare: well held in 2 bumpers: poor form in mares novice at Bangor on hurdling debut. *R. N. Bevis*

MAITRE DE MUSIQUE (FR) 13 ch.g. Quai Voltaire (USA) – Mativa (FR) **c89 x** (Satingo) [2003/4 c86, h–: c25g³ c30mᵖᵘ c22g⁶ c24d² May 30] tall gelding: fair hunter **h–** chaser nowadays: won point in March: stays 27f: acts on good to firm and heavy going: tongue tied: often makes mistakes: inconsistent. *Mrs F. E. Needham*

MAITRE LEVY (GER) 6 b.g. Monsun (GER) – Meerdunung (EG) (Tauchsport **h90** (EG)) [2003/4 25dᵖᵘ 16d⁶ 17s⁴ 20s Apr 17] ex-German gelding: useful up to 17f on Flat for M. Hofer: modest form over hurdles: tongue tied last 2 outings. *M. C. Pipe*

MAJARIYYA (IRE) 7 ch.m. Lycius (USA) – Madaniyya (USA) (Shahrastani (USA)) **h–** [2003/4 22d 16m 16f Jun 20] modest maiden at best on Flat (stays 1¾m) at 4 yrs, sold out of H. Rogers' stable 1,300 gns Doncaster March (2003) Sales: little form over hurdles: has had tongue tied. *J. K. Magee, Ireland*

MAJED (FR) 8 b.g. Fijar Tango (FR) – Full of Passion (USA) (Blushing Groom (FR)) **c112** [2003/4 c104+, h–: c23m² c26v³ c26d⁴ c25s² c26s* c24g² c23d² c26gᵖᵘ Apr 10] compact **h–** gelding: smart handicap hurdler in 2001/2: fair chaser: bought out of M. Pipe's stable 48,000 gns Doncaster October Sales: won novice at Fontwell in February: stays 3¼m (probably not 4m): acts on good to firm and heavy going: usually blinkered/visored: races prominently: none too consistent. *P. F. Nicholls*

MAJESTIC BAY (IRE) 8 b.g. Unfuwain (USA) – That'll Be The Day (IRE) (That- **c–** ching) [2003/4 c118, h101: 24s Nov 22] sturdy gelding: fairly useful chaser: maiden **h–** hurdler: well held in handicap only start in 2003/4: stays 3m, at least when conditions aren't testing: raced on good going or softer. *J. A. B. Old*

MAJESTIC MOONBEAM (IRE) 6 b.g. Supreme Leader – Magic Moonbeam **c103 ?** (IRE) (Decent Fellow) [2003/4 F97: 22s 16sᵘʳ c17d⁴ 17d 16d Apr 21] won bumper in **h–** 2002/3: fourth at Bangor on completed start in maiden chases, though jumped hesitantly and closed late only as leading trio faltered: well held all 3 runs over hurdles: should be suited by further than 17f. *Jonjo O'Neill*

MAJIC DUST 4 b.g. Wizard King – Fuchu (Jupiter Island) [2003/4 16mᵖᵘ 16gᵖᵘ 16s⁴ **h78** 16s³ 16d⁵ 19g 16g Feb 20] lengthy gelding: well held on Flat: poor form over hurdles: pulled hard in blinkers second start. *J. A. Supple*

MAJLIS (IRE) 7 b.g. Caerleon (USA) – Ploy (Posse (USA)) [2003/4 c–, h–: 16g Jan **c–** 17] strong, well-made gelding: fell fifth on chasing debut: fairly useful hurdler in 2001/2: **h–** badly out of form since, though won on all-weather on Flat in December for R. Cowell: raced around 2m: acts on soft going: blinkered. *T. R. George*

MAJOR BELLE (FR) 5 ch.m. Cyborg (FR) – Mistine Major (FR) (Major Petingo **c–** (FR)) [2003/4 19g⁶ Apr 13] ex-French mare: seventh foal: sister to winning jumper up to **h–** around 2½m Miss Major and half-sister to useful hurdler around 2½m Miss Mansonniene (by Mansonnien): dam won up to 1½m on Flat: winning hurdler/chaser, sold out of P. Boisgontier's stable €18,000 Goffs July Sale: no show in 2 points and a handicap hurdle in Britain: raced mainly around 2m: acts on heavy ground. *M. C. Pipe*

MAJ

MAJOR BENEFIT (IRE) 7 b.g. Executive Perk – Merendas Sister (Pauper) [2003/4   **c112** c67+: c24s² c23vᵖᵘ c22v* c20s² c27s² c32gᵖᵘ Mar 17] strong, workmanlike gelding: fair chaser: left Mrs P. Grainger after second start: won novice at Towcester in December: stays 27f: acts on heavy going. *Miss K. Marks*

MAJOR BLUE 9 ch.g. Scallywag – Town Blues (Charlottown) [2003/4 h90: 16g² 26s*   **h92** 21v² Dec 26] rangy gelding: modest hurdler: won conditional jockeys novice handicap at Hereford in December: finds 2m on sharp side and stays 3¼m: acts on good to firm and heavy ground. *J. G. M. O'Shea*

MAJOR BOB 5 b. or br.g. Syrtos – Miss Pandy (Pitpan) [2003/4 F18s Nov 3] first   **F–** foal: dam lightly raced and no sign of ability: tailed off in bumper on debut. *G. P. Enright*

MAJOR BURNS (IRE) 6 b.g. Aahsaylad – Night Matron (IRE) (Hatim (USA))   **h118** [2003/4 F16g² F18f* F16d⁵ F16m² 16d² 16d² 20s* Apr 21] second foal: dam, showed   **F98** some ability in bumpers, out of half-sister to Night Nurse: fairly useful form in bumpers, winning at Wexford in July: progressed to similar level over hurdles: won maiden at Gowran in April: beaten ½ length by Star of Bethlehem in minor event at Punchestown in early-May: stays 2½m well: acts on soft and good to firm going (bumper win on firm). *W. P. Mullins, Ireland*

MAJOR CATCH (IRE) 5 b.g. Safety Catch (USA) – Inch Tape (Prince Hansel)   **h–** [2003/4 F16s F18v* 18s Feb 9] useful-looking gelding: half-brother to winning 2½m   **F107** hurdler Strong Measure (by Strong Gale) and winning pointer by Paddy's Stream: dam unraced half-sister to dam of top-class staying chaser Righthand Man: stepped up markedly on debut effort when winning bumper at Fontwell in January, coping much the best with extreme conditions: well held in novice hurdle there following month. *N. J. Gifford*

MAJOR DRIVE (IRE) 6 b.g. Sadler's Wells (USA) – Puck's Castle (Shirley Heights)   **h115** [2003/4 h99: 21s² 21v* 23v⁵ 20dᵖᵘ Apr 10] leggy gelding: fairly useful handicap hurdler: bought out of J. H. Johnson's stable 4,000 gns Doncaster October Sales: won over 21f at Sedgefield in January: acted on heavy and good to firm going: dead. *James Moffatt*

MAJOR EURO (IRE) 7 b.g. Lord Americo – Gold Bank (Over The River (FR))   **h111** [2003/4 F86: 20m² 20v³ 20m² 20d 16d⁴ 20s* 21gᶠ 22g Mar 28] good-topped gelding: won maiden Irish point in 2002: fair hurdler: best effort when winning novice handicap at Sandown in February, despite hanging badly left: bred to stay beyond 2½m: acts on soft and good to firm going. *S. J. Gilmore*

MAJORITY VERDICT 8 b.g. Leading Counsel (USA) – Culm Valley (Port Corsair)   **c113** [2003/4 h100p: 22d² 20v* c20s* c20sᶠ Dec 13] rangy gelding: fairly useful form in nov-   **h121** ice hurdles, making all to win at Uttoxeter in May by 6 lengths from Champagne Harry: fortunate to win novice at Haydock on chasing debut, left clear by last-fence fall of Better Days: fell fatally following month: stayed 2¾m: raced on going softer than good (acted on heavy). *H. D. Daly*

MAJOR SHARK (FR) 6 b.g. Saint Preuil (FR) – Cindy Cad (FR) (Cadoudal (FR))   **h90** [2003/4 h85, F83: 16g⁶ 21g² 23d³ 20vᵖᵘ 19m³ 17g 21d³ 22g Apr 24] modest handicap hurdler: should stay 3m: acts on soft and good to firm going: wears cheekpieces: has taken little interest. *Mrs J. Candlish*

MAJORS MISTRESS 5 b.m. Superpower – Polola (Aragon) [2003/4 F16g 16mᵖᵘ   **h–** Jul 16] £520 3-y-o: half-sister to winner up to 13f in Italy by Sayf El Arab: dam third at 5f   **F–** at 2 yrs: no sign of ability, including on Flat. *J. C. Fox*

MAJOR SPECULATION (IRE) 4 b.g. Spectrum (IRE) – Pacific Grove (Persian   **h103** Bold) [2003/4 16g* 17d 16g⁶ 16sᵖᵘ 16gᵇᵈ Apr 18] smallish, leggy gelding: fairly useful on Flat (stays 7f) for G. Butler: won juvenile at Newbury on hurdling debut in November: failed to progress: likely to prove best around 2m with emphasis on speed: visored last 3 starts. *M. C. Pipe*

MAJOR VERNON (IRE) 5 b.g. Flemensfirth (USA) – Rainys Run (Deep Run)   **F112** [2003/4 F16s* F16g Mar 17] sturdy gelding: half-brother to poor chaser Connemara Mist (by Good Thyne), stays 3m: dam bumper winner: successful 2 of 3 starts in bumpers, impressive at Thurles in February and useful form when beating Shiminnie 2 lengths at Punchestown in late-April: only thirteenth of 24 to Total Enjoyment in Champion Bumper at Cheltenham in between. *W. P. Mullins, Ireland*

MAKE HASTE SLOWLY 7 b.g. Terimon – Henry's True Love (Random Shot)   **h99** [2003/4 h102p: 16d³ 16gᵖᵘ Feb 11] rather leggy gelding: placed first 2 starts over hurdles: off a year due to fractured cannon bone before reappearance: will stay beyond 2m. *H. D. Daly*

MAKE IT EASY (IRE) 8 b. or br.g. Alphabatim (USA) – Mammy's Friend (Miner's   **c63** Lamp) [2003/4 c20sᵖᵘ c25g c26dᵖᵘ c20s c25g c28dᵖᵘ c17g² Apr 12] ex-Irish gelding: **h–**

574

second foal: brother to winning pointer: dam won over jumps up to 2½m in Ireland: runner-up once from 6 starts in points: maiden hurdler/chaser: visored, first form when second in selling handicap chase at Plumpton: wore cheekpieces previous 4 outings. *Mrs L. C. Jewell*

MAKE MY HAY   5 b.g. Bluegrass Prince (IRE) – Shashi (IRE) (Shaadi (USA)) [2003/4 16s³ 17d 16g⁶ Apr 12] modest maiden on Flat (stays 1½m): poor form over hurdles, trained by J. White on debut. *J. Gallagher*   **h67 +**

MAKE THE CALL   7 b.m. Syrtos – Dawn Call (Rymer) [2003/4 16vᵖᵘ 21gᵖᵘ 17sᶠ 21d Mar 25] no form. *John Allen*   **h–**

MAKHPIYA PATAHN (IRE)   12 gr.g. Nestor – Our Mare Mick (Choral Society) [2003/4 c–, h–: c26sᵖᵘ c26fᵖᵘ May 21] lengthy gelding: maiden steeplechaser: won point in March: tried in cheekpieces/visor: moody. *J. H. Young*   **c– §**
h–

MAKS PERIL   10 br.g. Makbul – Pink Peril (Mljet) [2003/4 20mᵖᵘ Aug 25] won completed start in points in 2003: no show in seller on hurdling debut. *J. Mackie*   **h–**

MALAHIDE MARINA   5 b.g. Teenoso (USA) – Marina Bird (Julio Mariner) [2003/4 F16s* F16d⁴ Apr 11] useful-looking gelding: seventh foal: half-brother to 3 bumper winners, including 6-y-o Pearly Bay (by Karinga Bay): dam unraced from family of Florida Pearl: useful in bumpers: overcame inexperience to win quite valuable event at Leopardstown on debut in February by length from The Railway Man, wandering badly in front after leading over 1f out: fourth to Geill Sli at Fairyhouse and Major Vernon at Punchestown in late-April. *W. P. Mullins, Ireland*   **F106**

MALBEC (IRE)   7 b.g. Lord Americo – Key-Door (IRE) (Beau Charmeur (FR)) [2003/4 h–: 21s c21g⁴ c29sᶠ Jan 4] of no account: has worn cheekpieces/blinkers. *Miss A. M. Newton-Smith*   **c–**
h–

MALDOUN (IRE)   5 b.g. Kaldoun (FR) – Marzipan (IRE) (Green Desert (USA)) [2003/4 17g³ 16g* 17d³ 16g⁴ 16dᵖᵘ 16g⁶ 16d² 19g Apr 16] ex-French gelding: fairly useful on Flat (stays 1½m) at 3 yrs for R. Gibson: fair hurdler: won maiden at Kelso in May: raced mainly around 2m, only on good/good to soft going: has looked moody. *M. C. Pipe*   **h105**

MALEK (IRE)   8 b.g. Tremblant – Any Offers (Paddy's Stream) [2003/4 c–, h106: c24d³ c25d³ c25sᵖᵘ c25v⁴ c28d* c32gᵖᵘ Mar 28] angular gelding: fair hurdler/chaser, lightly raced: won handicap over fences at Carlisle in February: stays 3½m: raced on good going or softer (acts on heavy): usually let down by jumping over fences. *Mrs M. Reveley*   **c107 x**
h–

MALJIMAR (IRE)   4 b.g. Un Desperado (FR) – Marble Miller (IRE) (Mister Lord (USA)) [2003/4 F16d² Mar 25] eighth foal: brother to fair hurdler/fairly useful chaser Kymandjen, stays 3m, and half-brother to useful hurdler/fair chaser up to 3m Like A Lion (by Farheen): dam unraced sister to one-time fairly useful staying chaser Folly Road: second to State of Play in steadily-run bumper at Ludlow on debut: will probably improve, especially granted more of a test. *Miss H. C. Knight*   **F90 p**

MALLORY   10 b.g. North Col – Veritate (Roman Warrior) [2003/4 h–: 20m* 22m* 20g² 24mᵖᵘ 20d⁴ c25dᶠ c19s⁴ c22g⁴ Feb 10] big, strong gelding: modest hurdler: won novice handicaps at Newcastle in April and Wincanton in May: easily best effort over fences when fourth in 19f novice at Taunton: stays 2¾m: acts on good to firm going, probably on soft. *T. R. George*   **c96**
h96

MALMO BOY (IRE)   5 gr.g. Roselier (FR) – Charming Mo (IRE) (Callernish) [2003/4 F16s 21sᵖᵘ 20d⁵ Apr 21] fourth foal: half-brother to fairly useful bumper winner Northern Native (by Be My Native): dam unraced half-sister to Supreme Novices' Hurdle winner Tourist Attraction: seventh in bumper at Wetherby on debut: no show both starts over hurdles. *Mrs H. Dalton*   **h–**
F68

MALOY (GER)   4 gr.g. Neshad (USA) – Monalind (GER) (Park Romeo) [2003/4 F16d Jan 22] first foal: dam placed once around 6f in Germany: well held in bumper on debut. *P. A. Blockley*   **F–**

MAMBOESQUE (USA)   6 b.g. Miesque's Son (USA) – Brawl (USA) (Fit To Fight (USA)) [2003/4 h77: 20s² 20m² 20sᵖᵘ 20s* Feb 12] leggy gelding: modest handicap hurdler: won at Huntingdon in February: stays 2½m: acts on heavy and good to firm going: tried in cheekpieces, usually visored/blinkered: inconsistent. *J. Mackie*   **h90**

MAMBO (IRE)   6 b.g. Ashkalani (IRE) – Bold Tango (FR) (In Fijar (USA)) [2003/4 16gᶠ 16d* 17d³ 16g Mar 6] tall, leggy gelding: fairly useful novice hurdler: would have made winning reappearance but for falling last at Haydock in November: easily landed   **h118**

odds at Wetherby following month: will probably prove best around 2m: raced on good ground or softer: distressed final outing. *N. J. Henderson*

MAMIDEOS (IRE) 7 br.g. Good Thyne (USA) – Heavenly Artist (IRE) (Heavenly Manna) [2003/4 h97: c22d^F c19d³ c24s² c24g³ c24s* c25g^{pu} Apr 3] lengthy, useful-looking gelding: modest hurdler: fair novice chaser: won maiden at Fakenham in March: stays 3m: raced on good going or softer (acts on soft): tongue tied in 2003/4. *T. R. George*   **c103 h–**

MAN ABOUT TOWN (IRE) 5 b.g. Bob Back (USA) – Pollys Glow (IRE) (Glow (USA)) [2003/4 F16s* F16s³ Feb 15] fourth live foal: half-brother to winning 2m hurdler Daddy's Polly (by Waajib): dam, fairly useful winner up to 1½m, half-sister to Irish 1000 Guineas winner Prince's Polly: won bumper at Fairyhouse impressively on debut in January: failed to improve when third to Forty Licks in similar event at Navan. *T. J. Taaffe, Ireland*   **F97**

MANA-MOU BAY (IRE) 7 b.g. Ela-Mana-Mou – Summerhill (Habitat) [2003/4 h104+: 16m³ 16m² Jun 5] lengthy gelding: fair hurdler: will prove best around 2m: acts on good to firm going: has worn cheekpieces: tends to make mistakes. *B. Ellison*   **h104**

MANAWANUI 6 b.g. Karinga Bay – Kiwi Velocity (NZ) (Veloso (NZ)) [2003/4 h–, F86: 20d³ c16g* c16s* c19s^F c20d^F 17g* Apr 13] sturdy gelding: made good start to chasing career, winning novice handicaps at Folkestone in December and Wetherby in January: returned to hurdling after 2 falls, modest form when winning novice handicap at Exeter in April: stays 2½m: acts on good going. *R. H. Alner*   **c104 h94**

MANBOW (IRE) 6 b.g. Mandalus – Treble Base (IRE) (Orchestra) [2003/4 F–: F16s 20v^{pu} 20d^{pu} Apr 10] very tall gelding: some encouragement on second start in bumpers on reappearance, though again didn't look straightforward: no form in 2 starts over hurdles. *M. D. Hammond*   **h– F81**

MANCHESTER (IRE) 5 b.g. Danehill Dancer (USA) – Lils Fairy (Fairy King (USA)) [2003/4 h–: 17g May 1] angular gelding: no form over hurdles: tried blinkered/tongue tied: sold £1,100 Ascot June Sales. *Miss A. M. Newton-Smith*   **h–**

MANDINGO CHIEF (IRE) 5 b.g. Flying Spur (AUS) – Elizabethan Air (Elegant Air) [2003/4 16d⁶ 20s⁶ 24s⁴ 22s* 24v² 20s^{pu} Apr 4] good-topped gelding: fair maiden on Flat (stays 2¼m) at 3 yrs, sold out of P. d'Arcy's stable 28,000 gns Newmarket Autumn (2002) Sales: modest form over hurdles: won handicap at Folkestone in February: stays 3m: acts on heavy going. *R. T. Phillips*   **h99**

MANDOOB 7 b.g. Zafonic (USA) – Thaidah (CAN) (Vice Regent (CAN)) [2003/4 h–: 16d Dec 15] leggy gelding: fairly useful on Flat (stays 1¾m): lightly raced over hurdles, well held in handicap only start in 2003/4: has had tongue tied. *B. R. Johnson*   **h–**

MANDY'S ROSE (IRE) 8 b. or br.m. Mandalus – Rookery Lady (IRE) (Callernish) [2003/4 h–, F65: 26m* c25g⁴ c21g⁵ Nov 5] lengthy mare: poor form over hurdles: won weakly-contested mares handicap at Huntingdon in May: similar form in 2 starts in steeplechases: stays 3¼m: acts on good to firm going. *T. R. George*   **c72 h67**

MAN FROM DELCARROW (IRE) 7 b.g. Zaffaran (USA) – Delcarrow (Roi Guillaume (FR)) [2003/4 F91: 19g⁴ 22m^{pu} Aug 19] sturdy gelding: fair form on first of 2 outings in bumpers in 2002/3: well held on hurdling debut, second when breaking down run-in in claimer at Stratford next time. *O. Sherwood*   **h78**

MAN FROM HIGHWORTH 5 b.g. Ballet Royal (USA) – Cavisoir (Afzal) [2003/4 F–: F16m⁴ F16v F16d⁵ 16s⁴ 17s 20s 16g³ 16g⁶ 16d* 16g Apr 2] sturdy gelding: fair in bumpers: fair novice hurdler: easily best effort when winning at Stratford in March: best efforts at 2m: acts on good to soft going. *H. J. Manners*   **h104 F93**

MANHATTAN RAINBOW (IRE) 13 b.g. Mandalus – Clara Girl (Fine Blade (USA)) [2003/4 c77: c25g^{pu} Mar 28] lengthy gelding: poor hunter chaser: stays 25f: acts on heavy and good to firm going: tried visored. *Mrs J. M. Hollands*   **c–**

MANHATTAN VIEW (IRE) 5 b.g. Kadeed (IRE) – Haunted For Sure (IRE) (Executive Perk) [2003/4 F16g 20s^{pu} Jan 27] leggy gelding: first foal: dam of little account: no form in bumper or novice hurdle. *B. J. Curley*   **h– F–**

MANHUNTER (IRE) 8 b.g. Mandalus – Pinata (Deep Run) [2003/4 24m^{pu} 22m² 20m² 25m² 22g 24s^F Jan 14] lengthy gelding: modest novice hurdler: stays 25f: acts on good to firm going. *P. Bowen*   **h89**

MANIATIS 7 b.g. Slip Anchor – Tamassos (Dance In Time (CAN)) [2003/4 h106: 16s* 16v^{pu} 16v* 16s⁴ 17d⁴ 16g Apr 18] good sort: useful at best on Flat (stays 1¾m), won in April: modest hurdler: won seller (sold from M. Hammond 8,800 gns) at Uttoxeter in December: raced around 2m: acts on soft going: visored last 2 starts: races prominently. *Mrs J. Candlish*   **h95**

MANIKATO (USA) 10 b.g. Clever Trick (USA) – Pasampsi (USA) (Crow (FR)) **h–**
[2003/4 h–: 18m^{pu} 16d Mar 14] lightly raced and little worthwhile form over hurdles:
sold out of R. Curtis's stable £900 Ascot October Sales after reappearance. *K. G. Wingrove*

MANINGA 8 ch.m. Karinga Bay – Ambeiush (No Rush) [2003/4 h100: 22s 22g 24s^6 **h80**
21s^6 24d 24s^5 25s^{pu} Mar 15] leggy, angular mare: poor handicap hurdler nowadays: stays
21f: raced on good going or softer (acts on soft): tried blinkered. *Mrs L. Richards*

MANJOE (IRE) 6 b.g. Mandalus – Henris Blaze (IRE) (Mont Basile (FR)) [2003/4 **h116**
18g 16f* 24g* 20g^2 20m^{pu} Oct 12] IR 21,000 3-y-o: good-topped gelding: first foal: dam
unraced, out of half-sister to top-class 2m to 3m hurdler/chaser Danoli: fairly useful
bumper winner: similar standard over hurdles, winning maiden at Down Royal in June
and minor event at Cork in July: second to Kickham in novice at Tipperary, lame final
outing: effective at 2m to 3m: acts on firm going, probably on soft. *D. Wachman, Ireland*

MANKIND 13 b.g. Rakaposhi King – Mandarling (Mandalus) [2003/4 c–§, h–§: 22g^{pu} **c– §**
Sep 6] leggy gelding: winning chaser/hurdler: lightly raced nowadays, no form since **h– §**
2001/2: ungenuine. *J. A. T. de Giles*

MANLY MONEY 6 b.g. Homo Sapien – Susie's Money (Seymour Hicks (FR)) **h111**
[2003/4 F17s^5 17d^2 19s* 20d^3 20s^{pu} 19g^2 Apr 13] 10,000 4-y-o: lengthy, rather unfurn- **F91**
ished gelding: fifth foal: half-brother to winning hurdler/modest chaser The Sawdust Kid
(by River God), stays 3¼m: dam unraced: won 2 of 3 starts in points in 2003: fifth in
bumper at Newton Abbot: fair novice hurdler: won at Hereford in December: should stay
beyond 19f: acts on soft going. *P. F. Nicholls*

MAN MURPHY (IRE) 8 b.g. Euphemism – Been About (IRE) (Remainder Man) **c–**
[2003/4 c128, h–: 20v c22v^5 c20d c17s^{pu} Mar 7] sturdy gelding: one-time fairly useful **h–**
hurdler: won 5 of 7 races over fences in 2002/3 for Mrs M. Reveley: out of sorts in
2003/4: should stay beyond 2½m: acts on soft going, possibly amiss only start on good to
firm: tends to idle. *W. McKeown*

MANNERS (IRE) 6 b.g. Topanoora – Maneree (Mandalus) [2003/4 F16m* Nov 6] **F90 P**
quite good-topped gelding: first foal: half-brother to smart bumper performer Refinement
(by Oscar): dam, fair hurdler/chaser, effective at 2m to 3m: landed odds in impressive
style in bumper at Haydock on debut, beating Frosty Run 4 lengths: capable of considerably better. *Jonjo O'Neill*

MANOLITO (IRE) 10 b.g. Mandalus – Las-Cancellas (Monksfield) [2003/4 c76, h–: **c76 x**
c24m^3 c26g^3 c20m^6 c22m* c23m^3 c24m^5 c24g^5 Oct 24] smallish gelding: poor handicap **h–**
chaser: won novice at Market Rasen in June: stays 3¼m, at least when conditions aren't
testing: acts on soft and good to firm going: visored (ran poorly) third start: prone to
mistakes. *B. I. Case*

MAN O'MYSTERY (USA) 7 b.g. Diesis – Eurostorm (USA) (Storm Bird (CAN)) **h132 §**
[2003/4 h128: 16m^{rtr} 16s^{pu} 16g 17d 16d^{pu} 16d^{pu} Apr 17] smallish gelding: useful handicap hurdler: best effort when ninth to Geos in very valuable event at Newbury (9 lb out of
handicap) in February: showed little otherwise in 2003/4: probably best with waiting tactics in with-run races around 2m: acts on good to soft going: temperamental. *P. R. Webber*

MAN ON THE HILL (IRE) 10 b.g. Mandalus – Gipsey Jo (Furry Glen) [2003/4 **c114**
c24d^{pu} c25v^{pu} c20s c20d^2 c19g^5 Mar 6] good-topped gelding: useful novice chaser in **h–**
2001/2: fair form in handicaps on return: stays 3m: acts on good to firm and heavy going:
has had tongue tied: has been attended at start (unseated once): free-going sort: used
to race prominently, but mostly held up in 2003/4. *Ferdy Murphy*

MAN ON THE NILE (IRE) 4 b.g. Snurge – Spirit of The Nile (FR) (Generous **h117**
(IRE)) [2003/4 16g^3 16d* Dec 13] leggy gelding: first foal: dam stayed 2m: twice-raced
on Flat: progressive form in juvenile hurdles, winning well-contested maiden at Fairyhouse in December: sweating, third to Definate Spectacle in minor event at Punchestown
in late-April: will stay beyond 2m. *W. P. Mullins, Ireland*

MANORAM (GER) 5 ch.g. Zinaad – Mayada (USA) (The Minstrel (CAN)) [2003/4 **h85**
h73: 16g^6 20g^{pu} 22g^4 19m^6 24g^5 22d Mar 21] smallish, sparely-made gelding: modest
hurdler: won novice handicap at Worcester in May: poor efforts subsequently (reportedly
broke blood vessel fourth start): should stay beyond 2½m. *Ian Williams*

MANOR DOWN (IRE) 6 b.g. Moscow Society (USA) – Scalp Hunter (IRE) (Com- **h–**
manche Run) [2003/4 h–, F–: 22g^{pu} Apr 30] lengthy, rather unfurnished gelding: no sign
of ability: tried blinkered: has looked temperamental: sold 3,000 gns Doncaster May
(2003) Sales. *P. J. Hobbs*

MANOR STAR 5 b.m. Weld – Call Coup (IRE) (Callernish) [2003/4 F–: F17d 17d **h–**
Nov 28] no form in bumpers or novice hurdle. *B. D. Leavy* **F–**

MANOUBI 5 b.g. Doyoun – Manuetti (IRE) (Sadler's Wells (USA)) [2003/4 20d⁴ 20d³ **h86**
16d Mar 24] good-topped gelding: useful on Flat (stays 1¾m), sold out of Sir Michael
Stoute's stable 52,000 gns Newmarket Autumn Sales: modest form in novice hurdles:
tongue tied, most disappointing final start: joined M. Todhunter. *Jonjo O'Neill*

MANQUE NEUF 5 b.g. Cadeaux Genereux – Flying Squaw (Be My Chief (USA)) **h78**
[2003/4 h–: 18m⁴ 20m⁵ Jul 9] poor form over hurdles. *Mrs L. Richards*

MANSONY (FR) 5 b.g. Mansonnien (FR) – Hairly (FR) (Air de Cour (USA)) [2003/4 **h114**
16d⁵ 16s* 20s 16s* 16d⁴ Feb 22] tall, rather unfurnished ex-French gelding: second foal:
half-brother to winning chaser around 2m Lyfairy (by Lyphard's Wish): dam winning
hurdler around 2m in France: fair hurdler: trained by Y. Fouin in 2002/3: won maiden at
Down Royal in December and minor event at Thurles in February, making all to win
by 3½ lengths from Old Flame at latter: probably best around 2m: acts on soft ground.
A. L. T. Moore, Ireland

MANTEL MINI 5 b.m. Reprimand – Foretell (Tirol) [2003/4 F–: F17v Dec 1] **F–**
lengthy mare: tailed off in 3 bumpers and well beaten in 1m maiden on Flat. *B. A. Pearce*

MANTILLA 7 b.m. Son Pardo – Well Tried (IRE) (Thatching) [2003/4 h73: 16g⁶ 16g² **h113**
16g² 20f* 22m² 21m² 21m* 19f* 20f* 21f* 22f⁶ 21m Apr 15] fair hurdler: left J. Frost
after reappearance: won 5 times in first half of season, handicaps at Fontwell (novice),
Plumpton (seller), Exeter (conditional jockeys seller) and Wetherby and novice at Cheltenham: stays 2¾m: acts on firm and soft going: has been blinkered/visored,
including last 5 starts: has idled. *Ian Williams*

MANTLES PRIDE 9 b.g. Petong – State Romance (Free State) [2003/4 16g 23g⁵ **h–**
16d 17m⁵ Apr 15] smallish gelding: poor on Flat (stays 1½m) nowadays, sold out of
M. Dods's stable 1,800 gns Doncaster November Sales: well held in novice hurdles.
Dr P. Pritchard

MANTLES PRINCE 10 ch.g. Emarati (USA) – Miami Mouse (Miami Springs) **c– §**
[2003/4 c118§, h–§: c36dᵖᵘ Apr 3] sturdy gelding: winning hurdler/chaser, very lightly **h– §**
raced since 2001/2, behind when pulled up halfway in Grand National at Aintree
(visored) only outing in 2003/4: best left alone. *A. G. Juckes*

MANTUSIS (IRE) 9 ch.g. Pursuit of Love – Mana (GER) (Windwurf (GER)) [2003/4 **c88**
c16m³ Jul 9] good-topped gelding: fairly useful hurdler in 2001/2, successful 6 times: **h–**
well-held third in novice chase at Worcester, only outing since: will probably stay 2½m:
acts on good to firm going. *P. J. Hobbs*

MANX ROYAL (FR) 5 b.g. Cyborg (FR) – Badj II (FR) (Tadj (FR)) [2003/4 24gᵖᵘ **h– p**
Apr 2] big, angular gelding, unfurnished at present: third foal: brother to winning 2½m
hurdler Kampala II: dam, maiden, half-sister to 2002 Champion Hurdle winner Hors La
Loi III and high-class hurdler/chaser Cyborgo (both by Cyborg): tailed off when pulled
up 3 out in Grade 1 novice hurdle at Aintree on debut: will do better. *M. C. Pipe*

MANY THANKS 4 b.f. Octagonal (NZ) – Answered Prayer (Green Desert (USA)) **h–**
[2003/4 16gᵘʳ 16gᶠ Mar 10] good-topped filly: fair maiden on Flat (bred to stay 1¼m),
sold out of E. Dunlop's stable 2,500 gns Newmarket December Sales: failed to complete
in 2 races over hurdles. *B. S. Rothwell*

MAPILUT DU MOULIN (FR) 4 b.g. Lute Antique (FR) – Api (FR) (El Badr) **F–**
[2003/4 F17d Mar 11] 8,000 3-y-o: fifth foal: half-brother to 2½m hurdle winner Lasquini
du Moulin (by Saint Preuil) and middle-distance winners Isapi du Moulin and Kaline
du Moulin (both by Royal Charter): dam unraced: tailed off in bumper on debut.
P. A. Blockley

MARABOUT (FR) 7 b.g. Baby Turk – Maria Bethania (FR) (Pharly (FR)) [2003/4 **c–**
c–, h–: c17mᶠ May 7] winning hurdler/maiden chaser: fell fatally in novice chase at **h–**
Kelso: stayed 2½m: acted on heavy going: wore eyecover and eyeshields both starts in
Britain. *Sir John Barlow Bt*

MARAGUN (GER) 8 b.g. General Assembly (USA) – Marcelia (GER) (Priamos **c111**
(GER)) [2003/4 c–p, h119: c17s² 19d⁴ 17g c16sᵖᵘ 17d* c17d* Mar 10] tall gelding: fairly **h97**
useful hurdler at best: modest form in 2003/4, successful in seller at Folkestone in March:
fair form over fences: won maiden at Bangor by 4 lengths from Nev Brown: stays easy
19f: acts on soft and firm going: has been visored, including last 2 outings: tongue tied:
often takes strong hold. *M. C. Pipe*

MARAUD 10 ch.g. Midyan (USA) – Peak Squaw (USA) (Icecapade (USA)) [2003/4 **h89**
h89: 24gᵖᵘ 26g⁴ 26mᵖᵘ 24m* 20m⁴ 25fᶠ 25g⁶ 26g³ 27d Apr 23] smallish gelding: modest
handicap hurdler: left M. Sowersby prior to winning at Carlisle in October: left
R. Hollinshead after sixth outing: suited by 3m+: acts on firm and soft going: tried
blinkered/in cheekpieces: usually front runner. *L. R. James*

MARBLE ARCH   8 b.g. Rock Hopper – Mayfair Minx (St Columbus) [2003/4 h145:   **c– p**
c16mᵖᵘ Nov 19] leggy gelding: very smart hurdler at best: odds on, lame in novice at   **h–**
Kempton on chasing debut: raced mainly around 2m: has won on heavy going, raced
mainly under less testing conditions (acts on good to firm): held up, and travels strongly:
has high head carriage. *H. Morrison*

MARCHENSIS (IRE)   6 ch.g. Great Marquess – Trelissick (Electric) [2003/4 F16g⁵   **F90**
F16m* May 15] 13,000 4-y-o: ninth foal: half-brother to 3 winners on Flat, including fair
6f winner Polruan (by Elmaamul): dam little sign of ability: fair form both starts in
bumpers, won steadily-run event at Ludlow. *O. Sherwood*

MARCHING PREMIER (IRE)   5 ch.g. Zaffaran (USA) – The Marching Lady   **F94**
(IRE) (Archway (IRE)) [2003/4 F16g³ F17d⁶ Mar 27] €22,000 3-y-o: first foal: dam
unraced half-sister to fairly useful chaser up to 25f Marching Marquis: fair form both
starts in bumpers, third to Kimono Royal at Kempton on debut. *Noel T. Chance*

MARCH NORTH   9 b.g. Petoski – Coral Delight (Idiot's Delight) [2003/4 c97, h–:   **c97**
c25gᵖᵘ c24m* May 26] compact gelding: winning hurdler: modest form over fences,   **h–**
making all in intermediate handicap at Huntingdon: stays 3m: acts on soft and good to
firm going, probably on heavy: wears cheekpieces/visor. *Mrs P. Robeson*

MARCUS DU BERLAIS (FR)   7 gr.g. Saint Preuil (FR) – Rosacotte (FR) (Rose   **c129**
Laurel) [2003/4 h128: c16d⁶ c18d⁵ c21d* c21s⁴ c24s⁵ c20s² c29d² Apr 12] fairly useful   **h–**
handicap hurdler: similar form over fences: won maiden at Fairyhouse in January:
excellent ½-length second of 10 finishers to Granit d'Estruval in Irish Grand National
(Handicap) there in April: stays 29f: raced on going softer than good (acts on heavy).
A. L. T. Moore, Ireland

Mr Marcus Beresford's "Marcus du Berlais"

MARCUS WILLIAM (IRE)   7 ch.g. Roselier (FR) – River Swell (IRE) (Over The   **h93**
River (FR)) [2003/4 h106, F80: 20g³ May 5] good-topped gelding: winning hurdler: third
in claimer at Fontwell early in season: fifth in point in January: stays 2½m: acts on heavy
going. *B. G. Powell*

MARDELLO   6 b.m. Supreme Leader – Clonmello (Le Bavard (FR)) [2003/4 F–:   **F87**
F16s* F16g F16g Mar 13] sturdy, useful-looking mare: easily best effort in bumpers when
winning mares event at Haydock on reappearance in January: bred to be suited by 2½m+.
N. J. Henderson

MARDEREIL (IRE)   7 ch.m. Moscow Society (USA) – Slap of The Stick (Weavers'   **h–**
Hall) [2003/4 24s^pu Apr 21] fourth foal: dam, won 2m hurdle, half-sister to dam of useful
chaser up to 19f Dontleavethenest: thrice-raced in Irish points, runner-up on completed
start: led until weakening rapidly before 4 out in mares novice at Perth on hurdling debut:
sold 1,400 gns Doncaster May Sales. *C. J. Mann*

MARGARETS WISH   4 gr.f. Cloudings (IRE) – Gentle Gain (Final Straw) [2003/4   **h69 +**
17d^F 16g³ 16d⁶ Apr 8] poor on Flat (stays 1¼m): similar standard over hurdles. *T. R. Wall*

MARGOULIN (FR)   9 gr.g. Royal Charter (FR) – Marsaude (FR) (Tourangeau (FR))   **c–**
[2003/4 c–, h–: c17g³ c16m⁶ c20s^pu c16s^pu c16g c21d^pu Mar 30] well-made gelding: **h–**
one-time fair hurdler/chaser, retains little ability: sold out of Mrs H. Dalton's stable 7,500
gns Doncaster May Sales after reappearance: has had tongue tied. *Mrs J. C. McGregor*

MARIAH ROLLINS (IRE)   6 b. or br.m. Over The River (FR) – Clonloo Lady   **h133**
(IRE) (Nearly A Nose (USA)) [2003/4 F20d² 16m* 16m* 16d² 16d* 18s³ 16g^ur   **F91**
Mar 16]
        The best was not seen of Mariah Rollins on her only visit to Britain. A
7/1-shot for the Supreme Novices' Hurdle at Cheltenham in March, with only
Brave Inca and Albuhera at shorter odds, Mariah Rollins was a bit edgy beforehand

paddypower.com Future Champions Novices' Hurdle, Leopardstown—
the mare Mariah Rollins takes advantage of a weight pull to reverse placings with Newmill

and raced freely up with the pace, jumping with little fluency, until dropping away after three out, well held when unseating her rider at the last as Brave Inca led the remainder home. In her previous race Mariah Rollins had met Brave Inca on terms slightly worse in a Grade 1 novice event at Leopardstown and finished five and three quarter lengths third to him. Mariah Rollins hadn't looked much out of the ordinary in bumpers, gaining her sole win in a mares race at Thurles on her final outing in 2002/3, but it wasn't long before she showed herself useful over hurdles. She was successful in a maiden at Galway, a listed mares' event at Down Royal and the Grade 2 paddypower.com Future Champions Novice Hurdle at Leopardstown, all before the turn of the year and her only defeat during this period came in a Grade 1 event at Fairyhouse where she finished three quarters of a length second to Newmill. The patiently-ridden Mariah Rollins met Newmill on terms 8 lb better in the Future Champions Hurdle and beat him eight lengths, quickening to lead in the straight and winning with something to spare. The lengthy, narrow Mariah Rollins had a good first season over hurdles, but she is likely to find life much more difficult in her second and it would be no surprise if she had her attentions turned to chasing at some stage. Mariah Rollins is the first foal of Clonloo Lady, who was well held in a bumper on her only start. Clonloo Lady is a half-sister to the winning two-mile hurdler Delgany Toulon and to Dunnet Head, the latter an impressive winner of a bumper at Ayr in April on his only start to date. Mariah Rollins, whose sire Over The River is very much an influence for stamina, hasn't raced beyond two and a quarter miles over hurdles, but she showed her form in bumpers over as far as two and a half and is likely to stay further than that. She acts on soft and good to firm ground. *P. A. Fahy, Ireland*

MARICO (IRE)   11 b.g. Lord Americo – Gilt Course (Crash Course) [2003/4 h76: 19m⁴ 20g² 21f⁵ Oct 9] sturdy gelding: winning pointer: poor maiden hurdler: stayed 2¾m: acted on good to firm going, probably on heavy: visored final start: dead. *Evan Williams*   **h76**

MARIGLIANO (USA)   11 b.g. Riverman (USA) – Mount Holyoke (Golden Fleece (USA)) [2003/4 c100, h96: 16sᵖᵘ 17s³ c16s³ c16s 16d⁶ Mar 11] close-coupled, sparely-made gelding: handicap hurdler/chaser, modest form at best in 2003/4: raced around 2m: acts on good to firm and heavy going: has won with/without cheekpieces. *K. A. Morgan*   **c91 h87**

MARINO WEST (IRE)   9 ch.g. Phardante (FR) – Seanaphobal Lady (Kambalda) [2003/4 c–, h–: c21m³ c29sᵖᵘ c24dᵖᵘ c25sᵖᵘ Apr 11] well-made gelding: winning pointer/hurdler: little show in steeplechases: should stay beyond 2½m: acts on firm going. *N. M. Babbage*   **c– h–**

MARJINA   5 b.m. Classic Cliche (IRE) – Cavina (Ardross) [2003/4 F17v³ F16d⁵ 22d² 22g² Mar 25] big, useful-looking mare: first foal: half-sister to 1½m winner Tomina (by Deploy): dam winning hurdler/2m winner on Flat, half-sister to dam of top-class staying hurdler/chaser Bacchanal: better effort in bumpers when fifth at Newbury in December: runner-up in mares novices at Wincanton on both starts over hurdles: stays 2¾m. *Miss E. C. Lavelle*   **h104 ғ85**

MARKED MAN (IRE)   8 b.g. Grand Plaisir (IRE) – Teazle (Quayside) [2003/4 h99: 17d* 20d 19d⁶ c16s⁶ c19g⁴ c19d* Mar 24] good-topped gelding: fair handicap hurdler: made all at Bangor in May: similar form over fences, winning novice handicap at Chepstow: stays 21f: acts on soft and good to firm going. *R. Lee*   **c103 + h106**

MARK EQUAL   8 b.g. Nicholas Bill – Dissolution (Henbit (USA)) [2003/4 c96, h–: c16g² c19s³ c19g* c20d* c21sᶠ c18d³ c21m⁴ Apr 15] lengthy gelding: fair chaser: improved efforts when easily winning handicaps at Chepstow and Warwick in March: stays 2½m: acts on firm and soft going: tried visored. *M. C. Pipe*   **c110 h–**

MARKET VALUE (IRE)   8 b.g. Montelimar (USA) – Derring Lass (Derring Rose) [2003/4 21mᵖᵘ 17g Jun 28] IR 25,000 4-y-o: sixth foal: brother to winning 17f hurdler Jack Robbo and bumper winner Valiant Melody: dam lightly-raced Irish maiden: little form in varied company: tried visored. *Mrs M. Evans*   **h–**

MARK OF ZORRO (IRE)   4 b.g. Mark of Esteem (IRE) – Sifaara (IRE) (Caerleon (USA)) [2003/4 16g 16d⁶ 16sᵖᵘ 16dᵖᵘ Mar 1] smallish gelding: fairly useful on Flat (stays 1¼m), sold out of R. Hannon's stable 15,000 gns Newmarket Autumn Sales: easily best   **h99**

effort in juvenile hurdles when sixth at Sandown: blinkered last 3 outings, looking less than keen final one (lame). *O. Sherwood*

MARK THE MAN (IRE)   7 b.g. Supreme Leader – Nuala's Pet (Buckskin (FR))   **h116 p**
[2003/4 F110: 16d* 16d³ Dec 27] useful bumper performer in 2002/3: won maiden at Navan on hurdling debut in November very easily despite jumping none too fluently: fairly useful form when third to Mariah Rollins in Grade 2 novice at Leopardstown month later: stays 2½m: likely to progress further. *N. Meade, Ireland*

MARLBOROUGH (IRE)   12 br.g. Strong Gale – Wrekenogan (Tarqogan)   **c153**
[2003/4 c169, h–: c25m² c25d³ c24g⁵ c24m* c24gᵖᵘ c23sᵖᵘ Apr 24]   **h–**
The gods eventually smiled on Ruby Walsh on Saturday February 28th. With his intended mount Montifault scratched from Kempton's feature race, the Racing Post Trophy Chase, Walsh was then booked to ride the favourite Irish Hussar for the Nicky Henderson stable, whose retained jockeys Mick Fitzgerald, Marcus Foley and Andrew Tinkler were all sidelined through injury. However, after the Kempton course had finally been passed fit following overnight frost, Irish Hussar was withdrawn because the ground was considered unsuitable, leaving Walsh once again facing the prospect of being a spectator. Less than two hours before the race was due off, Barry Fenton, set to ride the other Henderson-trained runner Marlborough, was injured in a fall in the Rendlesham Hurdle and Walsh was back in business. Walsh had ridden Marlborough once before, finishing third on him in Newbury's AON Chase two years earlier. This time the partnership was triumphant, leaving Walsh, as well as Fenton, to reflect upon the ups and downs in the life of a National Hunt jockey. Unfortunately for Fenton, he was soon to have further first-hand knowledge of such swings in fortune. He won the Imperial Cup at Sandown two weeks later on Scorned, only to break his leg at Huntingdon four days afterwards when he was unseated in a handicap hurdle. As if to rub salt into the wound, Fenton's intended mount in the next race on the Huntingdon card, The Extra Man, was successful.
There were seven withdrawals from the eighteen declared for the Racing Post Chase at the overnight stage, including the previous year's winner La Land-iere, and as a consequence it wasn't the most competitive renewal of this very valuable event. The weights were headed by Marlborough and Shooting Light, both on 11-12, the latter's weight including a 3-lb penalty for his victory in the AON Chase on his seasonal reappearance. Marlborough himself hadn't won since his first start in the 2002/3 season, when he took the Charlie Hall Chase at Wetherby, though he had put up his best performance two outings later when, over Kempton's three-mile chase course, he was beaten only a length and a half by Best Mate in the King George VI Chase. Six defeats from six starts in the interim, including those in the latest runnings of the Charlie Hall (second to Ballybough Rasher) and King George (remote fifth to Edredon Bleu), resulted in Marlborough's handicap mark falling to 150, the lowest it had been since he'd won off the same one at Cheltenham in December, 2000, over nine months after finishing second to Gloria Victis in the Racing Post Chase. In the latest running of the Racing Post, Marlborough was waited with in mid-field as the 2002 winner Gunther McBride adopted his cust-omary position at the head of affairs, generally setting a good pace. Gunther McBride was still in front turning for home with only five others in contention, the Martin Pipe-trained trio of Iznogoud, Horus and Shooting Light, along with Shar-dam and Marlborough, the last-named pushed along in fifth. Sadly, Shooting Light broke a leg jumping three out, where Horus joined the leader and Marlborough began to work his way into a challenging position. When Horus unseated his rider at the next, holding a very narrow advantage, Marlborough was left in front, quickened clear soon after and was ridden out to win by four lengths from Gunther McBride, who was followed by Iznogoud and Shardam.
Both Marlborough and Shardam were next seen out in the National Hunt Handicap at Cheltenham, which the former had won in 2000. Shardam showed further improvement to finish second, but Marlborough, who was the paddock pick, ran no sort of race, off the bridle in rear before halfway and pulled up six out. Just over a month later, having left Nicky Henderson's stable in the meantime, Marl-borough was pulled up again, this time in a listed event at Auteuil. Predictably,

Racing Post Chase (Handicap), Kempton—Horus' departure two out leaves Marlborough (No.3) to beat 2002 winner Gunther McBride and Iznogoud (right)

given the stage of his career, he failed to adapt to the course and a plan to run him in the Grande Course de Haies came to nothing. It was a disappointing end to Marlborough's seventh season, for the first two of which he had been trained by Tim Forster and then by Henry Daly. Given that he is rising thirteen, retirement surely can't be far off. Marlborough has done sterling service over the years, winning a race over hurdles and ten over fences, topping the £350,000 mark in win and place prize money. His most valuable success, apart from that in the Racing Post Trophy, came in the 2001 Tote Gold Trophy Chase at Sandown, a race also worth £58,000 to the winner. He had two attempts at the Cheltenham Gold Cup, finishing fourth to Best Mate in 2002 but trailing home only eleventh behind that horse the following year, and one tilt at the Grand National, falling at the first when carrying top weight in the 2002 edition.

Marlborough (IRE) (br.g. 1992)	Strong Gale (br 1975)	Lord Gayle (b 1965)	Sir Gaylord
			Sticky Case
		Sterntau (br 1969)	Tamerlane
			Sterna
	Wrekenogan (br 1980)	Tarqogan (br 1960)	Black Tarquin
			Rosyogan
		Wrekalong (ch 1971)	Wrekin Rambler
			Wingalong

Marlborough is a brother to the fair staying chaser Wrekengale and the useful staying hurdler Galeogan, and half-brother to the fair Irish hurdler Cooleogan (by Proverb), the last-named the dam of useful chaser Tullymurry Toff. Their dam Wrekenogan is an unraced daughter of the winning pointer Wrekalong, herself a half-sister to the top-class two-mile hurdler Ekbalco. Marlborough, who stays three and a quarter miles well, acts on good to firm and heavy going. A strong gelding, he was well below form when tried in cheekpieces on his final start in 2002/3. *J. Bertran de Balanda, France*

583

European Breeders Fund/Doncaster Bloodstock Sales Mares' Only Standard Open National Hunt Flat Final, Sandown—rank outsider Marsh Run holds on despite veering left

MARLBOROUGH SOUND   5 b.g. Overbury (IRE) – Dark City (Sweet Monday) [2003/4 F16d⁶ Apr 17] 26,000 4-y-o: seventh foal: half-brother to 3 winners, including fairly useful 2½m hurdler/winning chaser Jessolle (by Scallywag) and fair staying hurdler Do It On Dani (by Weld): dam, well beaten on Flat, half-sister to smart hurdler/useful chaser Better Times Ahead, stayed 3¾m: well beaten in bumper on debut. *N. G. Richards*   **F—**

MARLMONT LAD (IRE)   13 b. or br.g. Homo Sapien – Patricias Choice (Laurence O) [2003/4 c23mᵖᵘ Jul 9] winning pointer: no longer of any account. *Miss G. Browne*   **c—**
h—

MARMADUKE (IRE)   8 ch.g. Perugino (USA) – Sympathy (Precocious) [2003/4 h114: 16m⁴ 16dꟳ Apr 8] good-topped gelding: fair on Flat and over hurdles: should have stayed beyond 17f: acted on good to firm and good to soft going: raced freely/carried head awkwardly: dead. *M. Pitman*   **h103**

MARMADUKE JINKS   10 b.g. Primitive Rising (USA) – Keldholme (Derek H) [2003/4 22g 22g Mar 6] good-topped gelding: winning hurdler: well held in handicaps on return from long lay-off: fell only outing over fences: should stay 2½m: acts on heavy going. *Mrs M. Reveley*   **c—**
h—

MARMALADE MOUNTAIN   9 ch.g. Lochearnhead (USA) – Lady Seville (Orange Bay) [2003/4 c24g⁶ c25sᵖᵘ c24gꟳ c25dᵖᵘ Mar 22] tall, angular gelding: modest pointer: jumped poorly in steeplechases: tried in cheekpieces. *Mrs A. M. Thorpe*   **c– x**

MARON   7 b.g. Puissance – Will Be Bold (Bold Lad (IRE)) [2003/4 16dᵖᵘ Jan 13] poor on Flat (stays 6f): no prospects as a hurdler. *F. Jordan*   **h—**

MARRAKECH (IRE)   7 ch.m. Barathea (IRE) – Nashkara (Shirley Heights) [2003/4 17g² 16s* 16d⁴ 18s 16s Feb 16] lengthy, angular mare: half-sister to useful hurdler Nahrawali (by Kahyasi), stayed 2½m: useful on Flat (should stay beyond 1½m), sold out of P. Harris's stable 16,000 gns Newmarket February (2003) Sales: showed good attitude when winning novice hurdle at Ascot in November: ran poorly last 2 outings: joined W. Musson. *Mrs N. Smith*   **h97**

MARRASIT (IRE)   8 b.m. Zaffaran (USA) – Alligator Crawl (IRE) (Pollerton) [2003/4 c26s⁶ c20g⁵ c25s⁴ Feb 22] first foal: dam placed in point: won twice in Irish points in 2003, awarded maiden on first occasion: bought 12,000 gns Doncaster August Sales: well beaten in 3 steeplechases, looking less than keen second time. *Miss Venetia Williams*   **c—**

MARREL   6 b.g. Shareef Dancer (USA) – Upper Caen (High Top) [2003/4 h64: 20m⁵ 19g² 17g* 16m* 17g* 20m³ 16m³ 22d³ 20dᵖᵘ 17g 16m 20d⁶ Apr 22] poor on Flat (stays 2m): fair hurdler: claimed from S. Keightley £6,000 prior to winning novices at Cartmel in May and Worcester and Newton Abbot in June: stays 2¾m: acts on good to firm and good to soft going: usually visored. *D. Burchell*   **h107**

MARRON PRINCE (FR)   4 ch.g. Cyborg (FR) – Colombine (USA) (Empery (USA)) [2003/4 F16g F18g Apr 22] €12,000 3-y-o: unfurnished gelding: half-brother to several   **F—**

winners, including one-time fairly useful hurdler/chaser Arlequin de Sou (by Sir Brink), stays 3m: dam placed up to 1½m on Flat: showed little in 2 bumpers. *R. Rowe*

MARSHAL BOND 6 b.g. Celtic Swing – Arminda (Blakeney) [2003/4 17d Nov 27] **h–** smallish gelding: no longer of any account on Flat: well held in novice on hurdling debut. *B. Smart*

MARSHAL MURAT (IRE) 8 ch.g. Executive Perk – Magneeto (IRE) (Brush Aside **h–** (USA)) [2003/4 F–: 17d[pu] Dec 17] well-made gelding: lightly raced: no show in novice on hurdling debut may start in 2003/4. *C. R. Egerton*

MARSH RUN 5 b.m. Presenting – Madam Margeaux (IRE) (Ardross) [2003/4 F16f² **F108** F17m* F16g* F16d F16s* Mar 13] 9,000 4-y-o: angular mare: second foal: half-sister to 2m hurdle winner Real Shady (by Bob's Return): dam, tailed off in bumpers, sister to fairly useful staying hurdler Aahsaylad and half-sister to smart sprinter Sartorial: fairly useful form in bumpers, winning maiden at Market Rasen in October and mares events at Hexham in November and Sandown in March, improved effort when winning EBF/ Doncaster Bloodstock Sales Mares Final at last-named gamely by ¾ length from Kings Bay: will stay 2½m. *M. W. Easterby*

MARSHYS MIA 7 b.m. Alflora (IRE) – Woodland Flower (Furry Glen) [2003/4 **F81** F17m² F16m6 F16g5 Oct 24] second foal: half-sister to fair hurdler/fairly useful 2m chaser Stamparland Hill (by Gildoran): dam winning staying hurdler/chaser: modest form in bumpers. *D. Mullarkey*

MARTEENY 9 b.m. Teenoso (USA) – Marejo (Creetown) [2003/4 c25m6 Jun 20] **c62** sturdy mare: maiden hurdler: winning pointer: sixth in novice handicap at Hexham on **h–** steeplechasing debut: stays 25f: acts on good to firm going. *J. B. Walton*

MARTHA REILLY (IRE) 8 ch.m. Rainbows For Life (CAN) – Debach Delight **h82** (Great Nephew) [2003/4 h88: 24g[F] 22d 23s4 Apr 4] sturdy mare: poor handicap hurdler: stays 3m: acts on heavy going, probably on good to firm. *Mrs Barbara Waring*

MARTHA'S BOY (IRE) 13 b.g. Supreme Leader – Madame Martha (Carlingford **c–** Castle) [2003/4 c26d[pu] Apr 7] rangy gelding: created very favourable impression when winning first 3 starts in hunter chases in 1998: pulled up all 5 starts in steeplechases since, though successful twice in points, including in February: stays 25f: acts on soft going: clearly difficult to train. *Mrs Marion Robinson*

MARTHA'S KINSMAN (IRE) 5 b.g. Petoski – Martha's Daughter (Majestic **F100** Maharaj) [2003/4 F16s* F16s Mar 20] first foal: dam, maiden who stayed 2½m, half-sister to top-class chaser up to 21f Martha's Son: won bumper at Huntingdon on debut in December by 6 lengths from Gathering Storm: only eighth at Ascot next time. *H. D. Daly*

MARTIN HOUSE (IRE) 5 b.g. Mujadil (USA) – Dolcezza (FR) (Lichine (USA)) **h85** [2003/4 16g 16v³ 17s 17d6 Apr 10] half-brother to fair hurdler C'Est Fantastique (by Hernando), stays 2½m: fairly useful at one time on Flat (stays 1¼m), sold out of J. Bethell's stable 8,500 gns Newmarket Autumn Sales: easily best effort in novice hurdles when third at Kelso in February: headstrong. *Mrs K. Walton*

MARTIN'S SUNSET 6 ch.g. Royal Academy (USA) – Mainly Sunset (Red Sunset) **h–** [2003/4 18g[F] Oct 5] poor and unreliable on Flat (stays 1½m): well held when falling last in novice on hurdling debut. *W. R. Muir*

MARTINSTOWN (IRE) 5 ch.g. Old Vic – Bella Velutina (Coquelin (USA)) **F112** [2003/4 F16m* F16s* F16g Mar 17]

While it is unusual for the favourite to land the Champion Bumper at the Cheltenham Festival—just two market leaders have been successful in twelve runnings—most of those at the head of the betting have been knocking at the door. Six favourites have finished runner-up, another finished a creditable fourth and only three have flopped. The runners-up, the ill-fated Inca apart, have generally gone on to do well, with Rhinestone Cowboy, Joe Mac, Red Blazer, Heist and Tiananmen Square all proving at least useful over jumps. Strangely though, two of the favourites who flopped (Dawn Leader and Biliverdin) have fared a good deal better than the two winning favourites (the twice-raced maiden hurdler Mucklemeg and the disappointing Liberman). Not that the prospects as a jumper of the latest beaten favourite Martinstown need rely on trends for sustenance: on previous form, looks and pedigree he has got plenty going for him and it will be no surprise if he is back at Cheltenham in March 2005 to put the record straight in one of the novice hurdles.

Martinstown went to Cheltenham unbeaten in two outings the previous autumn, both gained in most impressive fashion. At Naas in October he beat some mediocre rivals but at Fairyhouse the following month he triumphed from a much better field just as convincingly. Runner-up Master Albert was good enough to take third in the Champion Bumper itself, while the third Away Home was a fairly useful novice over hurdles later in the season. The fourth was good enough to win a bumper and the seventh and eighth won over hurdles. Martinstown clearly put up a useful performance with the prospect of more to come. No obvious cause for his Champion Bumper performance came to light. It is possible the less testing ground at Cheltenham told against him (it was soft at Fairyhouse), though his debut win came on good to firm. Martinstown was beaten a long way from home and trailed in fourteenth behind Total Enjoyment. The rangy Martinstown (no relation to Mita Easton's useful staying chaser of the early-'eighties, incidentally) is from a celebrated family, as his dam Bella Velutina is out of In My Time and thus a half-sister to the dual Stayers' Hurdle winner Galmoy, the high-class hurdler and smart chaser Youlneverwalkalone and the Ladbroke winner Dance Beat as well as to the noted broodmare Mursuma. Mursuma's winning progeny include the top-class chaser at up to two and a half miles Direct Route and the smart hurdlers Penny A Day and the aforementioned Joe Mac. Martinstown is by Old Vic and the chances are that he will stay at least two and a half miles. *C. Roche, Ireland*

Moynalvey GFC (Pro-Am) INH Flat, Fairyhouse—Martinstown goes into many a notebook with this smooth win

MARYLAND (IRE) 7 b.m. Executive Perk – Raven Night (IRE) (Mandalus) [2003/4 F87: F16g* F16s Mar 13] workmanlike mare: fair form in mares bumpers: won at Fakenham on reappearance in February: well held in much better company at Sandown, on softer going than previously. *O. Brennan* — **F94**

MARY'S BABY 4 b.f. Magic Ring (IRE) – Everdene (Bustino) [2003/4 17d Nov 17] half-sister to fair 2m hurdler Mark It (by Botanic): fair on Flat (stays 8.3f): likely to have stamina limitations over hurdles, seventh of 10 finishers in juvenile maiden at Folkestone on debut. *Mrs A. J. Perrett* — **h–**

MASALARIAN (IRE) 9 b.g. Doyoun – Masamiyda (Lyphard (USA)) [2003/4 16v c22s⁴ c19s⁴ c24gᵖᵘ Mar 5] well-made ex-Irish gelding: one-time useful hurdler/fairly useful chaser: left A. Moore after third start, won point in April: should stay 2½m: raced on good going or softer (acts on soft): tried blinkered. *Mrs H. M. Bridges* — **c94** **h–**

MA'S CONFUSION 6 b.m. Mr Confusion (IRE) – Spirited Lady VII (Damsire Unregistered) [2003/4 F–: F17mᵖᵘ Jun 21] lengthy mare: no sign of ability in 2 bumpers a year apart. *N. Wilson* — **F–**

MASOURI SANA (IRE) 7 br.m. Broken Hearted – Say Thanks (Thatching) [2003/4 F–: F16s 16sᵖᵘ 19dᵖᵘ Feb 15] tall mare: no sign of ability. *Miss M. E. Rowland* — **h–** **F–**

MASSAC (FR) 5 b.g. Garde Royale – Mirande (FR) (Tiaia (FR)) [2003/4 c17g* 17d² c20g* c20d² 17d² c17s* c20v² c21d² c19s³ Jan 31] good-topped gelding: fourth foal: brother to 2m hurdle winner Messine and half-brother to 3 winners, including fairly useful chaser/winning hurdler around 2¼m Magnus (by Synefos) and fairly useful hurdler/chaser up to 23f Mayence (by Cadoudal): dam won up to 21f over fences in France: won 2 out of 3 starts on Flat (stays 1¾m): fair maiden hurdler: fairly useful chaser: won at Le Lion d'Angers in summer (twice) and Auteuil in October and May (5-y-o non-thoroughbred event): second to Therealbandit in 4-runner novice at Cheltenham eighth start: raced 21f: raced on good going or softer (acts on heavy). *G. Macaire, France* — **c120** **h100 +**

MASSENET (IRE) 9 b.g. Caerleon (USA) – Massawippi (Be My Native (USA)) [2003/4 h–: 16d³ 16d 18s* 22s³ 20s 20v⁶ 20v⁶ 16d⁵ Feb 18] good-topped gelding: fair handicap hurdler: won at Clonmel in December: stays 2¾m: acts on soft ground. *Lindsay Woods, Ireland* — **h106**

MASTER ALBERT (IRE)   6 b.g. Supreme Leader – Mullaun (Deep Run)   **F117**
[2003/4 F16d^{su} F16d* F16s² F16g³ Mar 17]

None the worse for an unfortunate experience at Naas in November on his debut—he slipped up around halfway—Master Albert went on to become one of the season's leading bumper horses and looks very much the sort who will also go on to make his mark over jumps. Master Albert won at Fairyhouse just eleven days after the Naas mishap, bettered that form when chasing home the favourite Martins-town in a stronger contest over the same course a little over two weeks after that and was then off the course until March, reappearing in the Champion Bumper at Cheltenham. Partnered once again by Mr J. P. Magnier, the son of Master Albert's owner and the brother-in-law of the horse's trainer, 50/1-shot Master Albert was the paddock pick in terms of wellbeing and showed further marked improvement in finishing third behind Total Enjoyment and Refinement, beaten two and a half lengths and five lengths, the two in front of him professionally ridden and in receipt of the 7-lb mares allowance. Mr Magnier, who enjoyed tremendous success on Rhinestone Cowboy in the latest season, was found wanting somewhat on Master Albert, didn't shine tactically, or when it came to getting the best out of his mount in the latter stages. Soon held up towards the rear after jumping off near to the front of the twenty-four-runner field, Master Albert finished best of all from an unpromising position three furlongs out, overhauling previous winners Royal Paradise, Mr McAuley, Knocknabooly and Only Vintage in the last furlong or so. Master Albert's display at Cheltenham points towards his staying a fair bit further than two miles, and so does his pedigree. By Supreme Leader, out of Mullaun, a bumper-placed half-sister to the 1994 Festival Bumper winner Mucklemeg, the

Mrs John Magnier's "Master Albert"

well-made Master Albert is a half-brother to the fairly useful jumpers Native Endurance (by Be My Native), who stays twenty-one furlongs, and Total Success (by King's Ride), who stays nineteen furlongs. Master Albert's great grandam Cathy Gale produced, among others, the high-class hunter chaser Gayle Warning and the useful staying hurdler/chaser Deep Gale. *D. Wachman, Ireland*

MASTER BILLYBOY (IRE) 6 b.g. Old Vic – Clonodfoy (Strong Gale) [2003/4 h109p: 22g* 25d 20v 22m³ 20d⁴ Mar 20] leggy gelding: fair handicap hurdler: won at Newton Abbot in November: should be suited by 3m+: acts on good to firm going, probably on heavy: may benefit from headgear. *Mrs S. D. Williams* — **h112**

MASTER BREW 6 b.g. Homo Sapien – Edithmead (IRE) (Shardari) [2003/4 F–: F17s³ 16s 18v⁵ 18s c20mᶠ c24gᵖᵘ c20d³ Apr 21] angular gelding: first form in bumpers when third at Folkestone on reappearance: signs of little ability over hurdles and fences: stays 2½m. *J. R. Best* — **c72**, **h87 ?**, **F83**

MASTER CHIEF (IRE) 10 b. or br.g. Euphemism – Shan's Lass (Mandalus) [2003/4 c17g⁴ c16m³ May 29] poor maiden pointer: tried tongue tied: sold £1,400 Ascot December Sales. *Andrew Turnell* — **c–**

MASTER ELECT (IRE) 7 ch.g. Phardante (FR) – Proud Polly (IRE) (Pollerton) [2003/4 F75: 19d 16s 17gᵖᵘ Apr 3] fifth in bumper on debut in 2002/3 for M. Pitman: off 18 months, little show in 3 races over hurdles. *P. R. Johnson* — **h–**

MASTER FLASH (IRE) 11 ch.g. The Bart (USA) – Continuity Lass (Continuation) [2003/4 c20gᵖᵘ May 24] leggy gelding: poor maiden pointer: tried blinkered/tongue tied. *Andrew Nicholls* — **c–**, **h–**

MASTER FLORIAN (IRE) 7 gr.g. Roselier (FR) – Paddy's Well (Paddy's Stream) [2003/4 h100+: 22d⁴ c23gᵘʳ c23vᵖᵘ c24mᵖᵘ Mar 4] rather sparely-made gelding: fair hurdler: odds on, still to get better of Belski when unseating last in novice at Exeter on steeplechasing debut: went as if amiss both subsequent starts: stays 3m: acts on soft going: tongue tied in 2003/4: not a fluent jumper. *P. F. Nicholls* — **c103**, **h108**

MASTER GATEMAKER 6 b.g. Tragic Role (USA) – Girl At The Gate (Formidable (USA)) [2003/4 h–: 16m 17g 17m* 17g⁶ 17g 16g³ 17m³ 17dᶠ Oct 29] poor hurdler: won seller at Market Rasen (10 lb out of handicap) in August: left R. C. Guest after fifth start: fell fatally at Sedgefield: raced around 2m: acted on good to firm going: often wore cheekpieces/tongue strap: sometimes looked far from keen. *F. P. Murtagh* — **h60**

MASTER GEORGE 7 b.g. Mtoto – Topwinder (USA) (Topsider (USA)) [2003/4 h117: c16g* c23dᶠ c20d Apr 23] close-coupled gelding: fairly useful hurdler: won novice at Newton Abbot in September on chasing debut: well held final start: stays 21f: acts on heavy going: blinkered once. *P. J. Hobbs* — **c96 +**, **h–**

MASTER HENRY (GER) 10 b.g. Mille Balles (FR) – Maribelle (GER) (Windwurf (GER)) [2003/4 c16d³ c16g* c17g³ c16g⁴ c17g* c17g⁶ c17g³ c17m⁴ Oct 18] angular gelding: modest handicap chaser: made all at Perth in July and Cartmel (novice) in August: raced around 2m: acts on good to soft and good to firm going: usually free-going front runner: has hung right under pressure. *Ian Williams* — **c99**, **h–**

MASTER JACKSON 5 b.g. Jendali (USA) – Fardella (ITY) (Molvedo) [2003/4 F16d F17m⁴ 16gᵖᵘ 17d⁴ 19g⁵ 20sᵖᵘ Mar 20] 5,000 3-y-o: half-brother to fairly useful chasers up to 2¾m Dunston Bill (by Sizzling Melody) and Lord of The Sky (by Lord Bud): dam minor 11f winner in France: much better effort in bumpers when fourth at Market Rasen: poor form over hurdles: takes good hold. *T. D. Walford* — **h80**, **F85**

MASTER JED (IRE) 7 br.g. Bob's Return (IRE) – Evan's Love (Master Owen) [2003/4 F84?: 17vᵖᵘ 16d 19m Dec 10] workmanlike gelding: twice-raced in bumpers: no form in 3 novice hurdles. *J. A. B. Old* — **h–**

MASTER JOCK 10 ch.g. Scottish Reel – Mistress Corrado (New Member) [2003/4 c77: c21d⁴ c24g² c24d* c25dᵘʳ c24d⁴ c21g Apr 1] workmanlike gelding: fair hunter chaser: won at Stratford in May and point in March: stays 3m: acts on good to soft going. *P. Jones* — **c92**

MASTER JUBB 6 b.g. Petrizzo – Ziggy's Pearl (USA) (Ziggy's Boy (USA)) [2003/4 F16m F17m 26sᵖᵘ 21dᵖᵘ 16g Feb 11] workmanlike gelding: third foal: dam sprint winner in USA: no sign of ability: tried in headgear. *D. J. Caro* — **h–**, **F–**

MASTER MCNAIR (IRE) 6 br.g. Glacial Storm (USA) – Pollyville (Pollerton) [2003/4 aF16g⁵ 21g⁶ 24g 21gᵖᵘ Mar 5] IR £17,000 3-y-o, 14,000 4-y-o: unfurnished gelding: sixth foal: half-brother to winning 2½m hurdler Cullen Bay (by Supreme Leader) and — **h84**, **F84**

modest 2m hurdler Roses Niece (by Jeu de Paille): dam, placed in bumpers, half-sister to smart staying hurdler Rose Ravine, herself dam of smart staying jumpers Frosty Canyon and Cardinal Red: looked a stayer when fifth in bumper on polytrack at Lingfield on debut: sixth in maiden at Warwick on hurdling debut: failed to settle next time, pulled up and dismounted final start. *P. D. Cundell*

MASTEROFFOXHOUNDS (IRE) 9 br.g. Be My Native (USA) – Sylvia Fox (Deep Run) [2003/4 h117p, F116: c20m* 16f5 Sep 7] smart bumper performer: fit from Flat (won 1¾m maiden), won maiden at Tipperary in July on chasing debut, beating Bassett Tiger ½ length: thrice-raced over hurdles, disappointing in intermediate at Punchestown: stays 2½m: acts on soft and good to firm going: lame final outing in 2002/3: presumably not easy to train. *D. Wachman, Ireland* **c108 h111**

MASTER OF ILLUSION (IRE) 11 ch.g. Castle Keep – Galloping Gold VII (Damsire Unregistered) [2003/4 c109, h–: c24d c26g* c23dpu c24d Jan 19] leggy, sparely-made gelding: fair handicap chaser: easily best effort in 2003/4 when winning at Newton Abbot in November: needs 3m+: acts on any going: usually visored. *R. Lee* **c109 h–**

MASTER PAPA (IRE) 5 br.g. Key of Luck (USA) – Beguine (USA) (Green Dancer (USA)) [2003/4 h117: 16g2 18g4 16m 21m6 16dF 19d 20v 16g* 16g5 16g 16d4 Apr 8] angular gelding: fairly useful hurdler: won at Kempton in March by 10 lengths from Welsh Main: should stay 2½m: acts on good to firm and heavy going. *N. A. Twiston-Davies* **h118**

MASTERPOINT 4 ch.g. Mark of Esteem (IRE) – Baize (Efisio) [2003/4 16d6 17s6 17s Jan 20] sturdy gelding: fairly useful on Flat (stays 1m), claimed from B. Smart £20,000 in August: travelled well long way in juvenile and novice hurdles: will be suited by emphasis on speed at 2m. *R. T. Phillips* **h78**

MASTER REX 9 ch.g. Interrex (CAN) – Whose Lady (USA) (Master Willie) [2003/4 c16dpu c16s5 c16m* c16g* c16mF Apr 15] lengthy gelding: fairly useful hurdler in 2001/2: similar form over fences on return, winning in small fields in March, maiden at Leicester and novice at Wincanton: raced around 2m: has won on soft ground, better form under less testing conditions (acts on firm): refused to line up intended third and final outings. *B. De Haan* **c119 h–**

MASTER RIDE (IRE) 9 b.g. King's Ride – Cahore (Quayside) [2003/4 c103, h103: 19s* c21sF 20s2 22spu Apr 6] fair handicap hurdler: left A. Lidderdale, won at Hereford in December: fair form over fences: stays 23f: raced on good going or softer (acts on heavy). *C. Tinkler* **c109 h113**

MASTER SEBASTIAN 5 ch.g. Kasakov – Anchor Inn (Be My Guest (USA)) [2003/4 F16m2 F16v5 F16d3 Apr 17] 2,800 3-y-o: smallish gelding: sixth foal: closely related to 2 winners by Sabrehill, notably useful hurdler/chaser Mister McGoldrick and half-brother to 2 winners on Flat: dam, 1¼m winner, from good family: fairly useful form in bumpers at Ayr, placed behind Ungaro in November and Dunnet Head in April. *Miss Lucinda V. Russell* **F96**

MASTERS OF WAR (IRE) 7 b.g. Sri Pekan (USA) – Velinowski (Malinowski (USA)) [2003/4 c17g4 c24gF 24v4 20d 20d2 Apr 23] lengthy gelding: half-brother to 17f hurdle winner Tendresse (by Tender King): fairly useful 1¼m winner on Flat for C. O'Brien: poor maiden hurdler, trained prior to reappearance by A. Leahy: let down by jumping both starts over fences, though some promise on debut: stays 2½m: raced on good going or softer. *Jonjo O'Neill* **c83 h81**

MASTER TERN (USA) 9 ch.g. Generous (IRE) – Young Hostess (FR) (Arctic Tern (USA)) [2003/4 c140, h–: c20g c25d c21d c24s 20g c24g c25gpu c24d6 Apr 23] big, leggy gelding: shows traces of stringhalt: has reportedly had wind operation: useful handicap hurdler/chaser at best, well below form in 2003/4: stays 25f: acts on good to firm and heavy going: tried in cheekpieces: patiently ridden: sketchy jumper of fences. *Jonjo O'Neill* **c119 x h119**

MASTER TRIX (IRE) 7 b.g. Lord Americo – Bannow Drive (IRE) (Miner's Lamp) [2003/4 h108: 20d* 24g Apr 2] compact gelding: fairly useful hurdler: much improved when winning handicap at Ascot in December by 7 lengths from Bell Lane Lad: well held in valuable similar event at Aintree: should stay 3m: raced on good going or softer (acts on heavy). *M. Pitman* **h122**

MASTER T (USA) 5 b.g. Trempolino (USA) – Our Little C (USA) (Marquetry (USA)) [2003/4 h102: 16m5 17m5 17m2 16g4 18f2 16mur 16m6 16f5 16fur 16g5 Apr 18] neat gelding: fair handicap hurdler: will prove best around 2m: acts on firm going: tends to find little. *G. L. Moore* **h105**

MASTER WOOD 13 b.g. Wonderful Surprise – Miss Wood (Precipice Wood) [2003/4   **c101**
c112, h–: c25m² c25s² c22s c20v⁶ c27g⁵ Apr 16] sturdy gelding: fair chaser: stays 3¼m: **h–**
acts on heavy going: has won 7 times at Wetherby. *C. Grant*

MATAWA BELLEVUE (FR) 8 b. or br.m. Mister Mat (FR) – Strakawa (FR)   **h–**
(Sukawa (FR)) [2003/4 20sᵖᵘ May 22] third foal: half-sister to winning 2¾m hurdler
Irishkawa Bellevue (by Irish Prospector) and winning cross-country chaser Titou de
Beaulieu (by Gaspard de La Nuit): dam winning cross-country chaser: no show in mares
novice hurdle on debut. *Jean-Rene Auvray*

MATCHBOARD AGAIN (IRE) 6 b.m. Supreme Leader – Avena (Oats) [2003/4   **F–**
F16g Feb 21] first foal: dam, 2m hurdle winner, half-sister to useful hurdler/chaser up to
21f Major Rumpus: well held in bumper on debut. *C. P. Morlock*

MATERIAL WORLD 6 b.m. Karinga Bay – Material Girl (Busted) [2003/4 F103:   **h113**
F17g* 22g² 21s² 24s² 22s 24d³ 22d³ 21g² 21m⁵ Apr 15] sturdy mare: has only one eye   **F103**
(wears eyecover): successful both starts in bumpers, including at Hereford in May: fair
novice hurdler: won at Folkestone in November: stays 3m: acts on soft and good to firm
going: jumps none too fluently: reliable. *Miss Suzy Smith*

MATHMAGICIAN 5 ch.g. Hector Protector (USA) – Inherent Magic (IRE) (Magical   **h–**
Wonder (USA)) [2003/4 17gᵖᵘ May 18] poor maiden on Flat (stays 11f): jumped poorly
and soon behind in intermediate on hurdling debut. *R. F. Marvin*

MATTHEW MUROTO (IRE) 5 b.g. Muroto – Glenmore Star (IRE) (Teofane)   **F77**
[2003/4 F16m³ F16g F18g Apr 22] first foal: dam maiden Irish pointer: modest form in
bumpers. *C. L. Tizzard*

MAUNBY ROCKER 4 ch.g. Sheikh Albadou – Bullion (Sabrehill (USA)) [2003/4   **h90**
17g⁶ 16g* 16g³ 23mᶠ 16f* Nov 22] poor on Flat nowadays: modest form in juvenile
hurdles, winning maiden at Uttoxeter in September and claimer at Catterick in November: likely to prove best over sharp 2m: raced on good going or firmer (acts on firm).
P. C. Haslam

MAUNBY ROLLER (IRE) 5 b.g. Flying Spur (AUS) – Brown Foam (Horage)   **c–**
[2003/4 h–: 17m 17m³ 17m⁵ 17m 16d⁴ 20d* 19d² c21sᵖᵘ 17gᵇᵈ Apr 24] poor hurdler: **h63 §**
won selling handicap at Fakenham in November: no show on chasing debut: stays 2½m:
acts on good to soft going, probably on good to firm: blinkered/visored: ungenuine.
K. A. Morgan

MAUNSELL'S ROAD (IRE) 5 b.g. Desert Style (IRE) – Zara's Birthday (IRE)   **h90**
(Waajib) [2003/4 h85: 24s³ 16d⁵ 16d⁶ 20g⁵ 24g² 20d Apr 18] angular gelding: modest
maiden hurdler: stays easy 3m: best efforts on good going: tried visored. *L. Lungo*

MAXIMINUS 4 b.g. The West (USA) – Candarela (Damister (USA)) [2003/4 16m   **h84 ?**
16g 16m³ Mar 11] tall, good-topped gelding: half-brother to 2½m hurdle winner Mount
Karinga (by Karinga Bay): no form on Flat: seemingly easily best effort over hurdles
when third in maiden at Wincanton, keeping on past beaten horses. *M. Madgwick*

MAXIMIZE (IRE) 10 b.g. Mandalus – Lone Run (Kemal (FR)) [2003/4 c132, h–:   **c139 §**
c25f⁴ c24g² c27dᵖᵘ c33d c24g* c33d³ Apr 17] strong gelding: useful handicap chaser: **h–**
40/1, best effort when winning Fulke Walwyn Kim Muir Challenge Cup at Cheltenham
in March, looking held for much of final circuit but staying on strongly as Merchants
Friend faltered to lead close home: otherwise often looked temperamental in 2003/4:
probably stays 33f: probably acts on any going: visored second/third outings: races prominently: usually sound jumper: one to treat with caution. *M. C. Pipe*

MAXIMUS (IRE) 9 br.g. Un Desperado (FR) – Fais Vite (USA) (Sharpen Up) [2003/4   **c–**
c–, h92: 20sᵖᵘ 22g 19g Apr 1] let down by jumping only outing in steeplechase: winning   **h–**
hurdler, no form in handicaps in 2003/4: stays 2¾m: acts on soft going: tried blinkered:
has had tongue tied: has looked temperamental: sold £2,700 Ascot April Sales.
C. P. Morlock

MAX PRIDE 9 br.g. Good Thyne (USA) – An Bothar Dubh (Strong Gale) [2003/4   **c–**
c115, h104: 24s* c29mᶠ Dec 6] fair handicap hurdler: won at Towcester in November: **h98**
fairly useful handicap chaser: fell fatally at Warwick: thorough stayer: acted on heavy
going: genuine. *R. Dickin*

MAX'S MICRO (IRE) 5 b.g. Inzar (USA) – Guess Who (Be My Guest (USA))   **h–**
[2003/4 h80: 24gᵖᵘ 17g⁶ 16g⁴ Sep 24] poor hurdler: left J. Allen after reappearance: raced
mainly around 2m: acts on heavy going: tried visored/in cheekpieces. *C. Grant*

MAX THE OBSCURE   4 b.g. Cloudings (IRE) – Princess Maxine (IRE) (Horage) **F—**
[2003/4 F16d Apr 23] second foal: dam fair up to 1m on Flat: well held in bumper on debut. *Miss Lucinda V. Russell*

MAYBELLE   9 b.m. Royal Vulcan – Full of Love (Full of Hope) [2003/4 h–: 22g^{pu} **h—**
Apr 30] workmanlike mare: of little account. *J. S. King*

MAYBESEVEN   10 gr.g. Baron Blakeney – Ninth of May (Comedy Star (USA))   **c64**
[2003/4 c64, h–: c23g^5 c25d^5 c24g^{pu} c19s^2 c25s^3 Apr 11] good-topped gelding: poor   **h—**
handicap chaser: stays 3¼m: raced on good going or softer (acts on soft): tried blinkered:
has broken blood vessel: none too consistent. *R. Dickin*

MAYBE SHE WILL   6 b.m. Tudor Diver – Blue Mischief (Precocious) [2003/4 F16d^6 **F82**
F16m* F16g Jan 23] fourth living foal: dam, 6f winner, out of poor sister to Coronation
Cup winner Sea Chimes: best effort in bumpers when winning at Musselburgh in
December. *D. W. Whillans*

MAYB-MAYB   14 ch.g. Gunner B – Mayotte (Little Buskins) [2003/4 c–, h–§: c34v^2 **c—**
c26s^{ur} c25v^2 c29s^{pu} c26s c22g^3 c28d^{pu} Mar 21] tall gelding: winning hurdler: of little   **h—**
account nowadays outside points: wears headgear: formerly tongue tied. *M. Appleby*

MAYERLING   7 b.g. Old Vic – Manon Lescaut (Then Again) [2003/4 h–: 16d^4 19d^6 **c—**
16v^4 24s^2 26s^5 22s c25g^{pu} 24g^6 Apr 1] poor maiden hurdler: jumped slowly and left in   **h70**
handicap on chasing debut: stays 3¼m: acts on soft going. *P. Burgoyne*

MAYSBOYO   6 b.g. Makbul – Maysimp (IRE) (Mac's Imp (USA)) [2003/4 17d^{ur} **h—**
17g^{pu} 16g Jun 12] of no account. *B. P. J. Baugh*

MAZAMET (USA)   11 b.g. Elmaamul (USA) – Miss Mazepah (USA) (Nijinsky   **c—**
(CAN)) [2003/4 16d 17g 21d Apr 8] tall gelding: maiden hurdler/chaser: well held in   **h—**
2003/4: tried visored/blinkered. *O. O'Neill*

MAZILEO   11 b.g. Mazilier (USA) – Embroglio (USA) (Empery (USA)) [2003/4 c121,   **c110**
h–: 24d^{pu} 24g^{pu} c24m c25g^2 Apr 3] workmanlike gelding: winning hurdler/chaser: form   **h—**
in 2003/4 only when second in handicap chase at Hereford (wore cheekpieces), making
much of running: barely stays 25f: acts on firm and soft going: races freely: prone to odd
blunder. *Ian Williams*

MAZURY (USA)   5 b.g. Langfuhr (CAN) – Assurgent (USA) (Damascus (USA))   **h—**
[2003/4 h–: 16m 20g Aug 23] little form over hurdles: twice-raced in points in 2004,
well-held fourth on completed start. *Miss J. S. Davis*

Fulke Walwyn Kim Muir Challenge Cup Handicap Chase (Amateur Riders), Cheltenham—
40/1-shot Maximize reels in long-time leader Merchants Friend (cheekpieces) close home

MAZ

MAZZAREME (IRE) 6 b.g. Supreme Leader – Mazza (Mazilier (USA)) [2003/4 **F94** F17d³ Feb 23] 22,000 4-y-o: fourth foal: half-brother to useful hurdler/chaser Claymore (by Broadsword), stays 3m, and modest 2m hurdler Poulakerry (by Shardari): dam, poor maiden on Flat, half-sister to top-class staying chaser Flashing Steel: shaped well when third to Stagecoachsapphire in bumper at Carlisle on debut. *N. G. Richards*

MAZZINI (IRE) 13 b.g. Celio Rufo – Dontellvi (The Parson) [2003/4 h93: 22sᵖᵘ 27g **h—** Apr 22] useful-looking gelding: veteran hurdler, showed little in 2003/4: stays 2¾m: acts on soft and firm going: has shown signs of temperament. *R. Rowe*

MCCRACKEN (IRE) 8 b.g. Scenic – Sakanda (IRE) (Vayrann) [2003/4 16s 16d 16s* **c98** 16g⁵ c19g* c16s⁵ c24d³ Apr 8] half-brother to winning 2m hurdler Lismeenan (by Be My **h98** Native): dam fair 2m hurdler: modest hurdler nowadays: sold out of N. Meade's stable 12,000 gns Doncaster August (2001) Sales: won claimer (claimed from P. A. Pritchard £6,000) at Huntingdon in February: made all in maiden at Doncaster on chasing debut in March: stays easy 3m: probably acts on any going: wore cheekpieces last 4 starts: usually tongue tied. *R. Ford*

MCCRINKLE (IRE) 7 b.g. Mandalus – Crinkle Lady (Buckskin (FR)) [2003/4 F—: **h—** F16g 20sᵖᵘ 24dᵖᵘ 22g 16d Apr 23] big gelding: of no account. *Mrs C. J. Kerr* **F—**

MCFARLINE (IRE) 8 b.g. Ela-Mana-Mou – Highland Ball (Bold Lad (IRE)) [2003/4 **c—** c—, h—: c16gᵖᵘ c21mᵖᵘ Jul 13] compact gelding: winning hurdler: no longer of any **h—** account: has had tongue tied. *N. J. Hawke*

MCGINTY ALL STARS (IRE) 6 b.m. Fourstars Allstar (USA) – Dowdstown Miss **F—** (Wolver Hollow) [2003/4 F—: F16d Apr 21] no form in bumpers or points. *R. J. Price*

MCGRUDERS CROSS (IRE) 6 b.g. Toulon – Kayanna (Torenaga) [2003/4 F104: **h124** 16m⁵ 22g⁴ 18d* 20s* Jan 4] well-made gelding: fairly useful in bumpers: progressed into fairly useful hurdler, winning maiden at Leopardstown in December and Grade 3 novice at Naas (beat Away Home 2½ lengths) in January: should stay beyond 2½m: acts on soft going: races prominently. *Anthony Mullins, Ireland*

MCMAHON'S BROOK 5 br.g. Alderbrook – McMahon's River (Over The River **F—** (FR)) [2003/4 F14d Mar 22] first foal: dam winning pointer: showed little in bumper on debut. *Mrs N. S. Sharpe*

MCSNAPPY 7 ch.g. Risk Me (FR) – Nannie Annie (Persian Bold) [2003/4 h107: c26dᵘʳ **c103** c24s³ c25sᵖᵘ c26s⁵ c24g* c19d³ c24m⁵ c22g* Apr 22] leggy gelding: maiden hurdler: fair **h—** novice chaser: won at Chepstow (maiden) in March and Fontwell (finished lame) in April: stays 3m: acts on heavy going. *J. W. Mullins*

MEADOWS PRINCE (IRE) 5 b.g. Alzao (USA) – Anita Via (IRE) (Anita's Prince) **F—** [2003/4 F16m Aug 2] second foal: dam unraced: no show in bumper on debut: signs of only a little ability in points. *B. Palling*

MEANDMRSJONES 5 ch.m. Alderbrook – Dunbrody Abbey (Proverb) [2003/4 F16s **F—** F16d Mar 14] third foal: dam, winning 3m chaser, half-sister to fairly useful staying chaser Son of Iris: well beaten in 2 mares bumpers. *J. G. M. O'Shea*

MEASURE UP 5 ch.g. Inchinor – Victoria Blue (Old Vic) [2003/4 16m* Sep 13] **h96** maiden on Flat (stays 9.4f), left M. Bell prior to disappointing in 2003: won maiden at Worcester on hurdling debut, making virtually all: likely to prove best around 2m: sold 7,200 gns Doncaster October Sales. *J. M. Bradley*

MECCA PRINCE (IRE) 9 ch.g. Shalford (IRE) – Fashion Parade (Mount Hagen **c—** (FR)) [2003/4 c24mᵖᵘ May 7] close-coupled gelding: fair pointer: not fluent in novice **h—** hunter chase: tried blinkered. *J. W. Tudor*

MEDALLIST 5 b.g. Danehill (USA) – Obsessive (USA) (Seeking The Gold (USA)) **h73** [2003/4 h73: 17s⁴ 17g⁵ May 26] poor novice hurdler: will prove best around 2m: tried blinkered: changed hands 10,000 gns Doncaster August Sales. *B. Ellison*

MEDELAI 8 b.m. Marju (IRE) – No Islands (Lomond (USA)) [2003/4 h54: 17m⁶ 16f⁴ **c73** c20m* Nov 13] leggy mare: bad maiden hurdler: left long way clear 2 out when winning **h54** maiden at Ludlow on chasing debut: stays 2½m: acts on firm and soft going: blinkered over hurdles: takes strong hold. *A. G. Juckes*

MEDICI (FR) 6 bl.g. Cadoudal (FR) – Marie de Valois (FR) (Moulin) [2003/4 F92: **h—** F16m⁶ 16d Nov 30] leggy gelding: better effort in bumpers when fourth on debut: little **F84** encouragement in maiden on hurdling debut. *Jonjo O'Neill*

592

MEN

MEDKHAN (IRE)   7 ch.g. Lahib (USA) – Safayn (USA) (Lyphard (USA)) [2003/4   **h78**
h–: 17g⁵ 20m 21f⁴ Oct 9] leggy gelding: form over hurdles only when fifth in novice at
Hereford. *F. Jordan*

MEGA CHIC (FR)   4 b.g. Useful (FR) – Pampachic (FR) (Pampabird) [2003/4 17gᵘⁱ   **h–**
16m 16g 17d⁵ Mar 22] third foal: dam, winning 2m hurdler/1½m winner on Flat, half-
sister to dam of useful chaser around 2¾m Turkish Junior and useful hurdler/chaser up to
2¾m Ladykish: twice-raced on Flat at 3 yrs in French Provinces for R. Passelande: no
form over hurdles. *J. C. Tuck*

MEGAZINE   10 b.g. Shaab – Sherzine (Gorytus (USA)) [2003/4 c–, h95: 17mᵖᵘ 17g   **c78**
c17gᶠ Sep 12] modest handicap hurdler: twice-raced chaser, fell fatally at Southwell: **h90**
stayed easy 2¾m: raced mainly on good going or softer (acted on heavy). *J. D. Frost*

MEGGIES GAMBLE (IRE)   7 b.g. Zaffaran (USA) – Glaskerbeg Lady (IRE)   **h123**
(Radical) [2003/4 F94: F16d⁶ 20s² 20v* 19g* 24g⁴ Mar 6] tall gelding: chasing type: **F–**
third on first of 2 starts in bumpers (failed to settle on reappearance): fairly useful form in
novice hurdles, won at Wetherby (soon well clear when beating Moonlit Harbour a
distance) in January and Catterick (again made all and had plenty in hand) in February:
close fourth to Whitford Don in stronger race at Newbury: will stay beyond 3m: raced on
good going or softer (acts on heavy): useful prospect for novice chases. *Miss Venetia
Williams*

MEGGIE'S LAD (IRE)   7 b.g. Beau Sher – Kambaya (IRE) (Kambalda) [2003/4 F96:   **h103**
16d² 19g⁴ 25s³ 24s² 22d⁴ Mar 7] rather sparely-made gelding: fair form over hurdles, best
effort when third to Toon Trooper in novice at Warwick in December: thorough stayer:
acts on soft going. *Miss Venetia Williams*

MELDRUM MEG   4 b.f. Bal Harbour – Strathrusdale (Blazing Saddles (AUS))   **F77**
[2003/4 F16s³ F16d F17g Mar 28] fifth foal: dam twice-raced in bumpers: form in
bumpers only when third at Wetherby on debut. *M. W. Easterby*

MELDRUM STAR (IRE)   7 ch.g. Fourstars Allstar (USA) – Meldrum Lass (Buck-   **h108**
skin (FR)) [2003/4 h86, F73: 22m⁴ 19m² 20g³ 17g³ 20m* 21m³ 19d* 19g² Dec 26] sturdy
gelding: fair handicap hurdler: improved in 2003/4, won at Chepstow in October and
Doncaster in December: likely to be suited by further than 21f: acts on good to firm and
good to soft going. *Mrs S. J. Smith*

MELFORD (IRE)   6 b.g. Presenting – Echo Creek (IRE) (Strong Gale) [2003/4 h–,   **h98**
F86: 19g* 20d 21gᵖᵘ Mar 5] well-made gelding: chasing type: easily best effort when
winning novice hurdle at Exeter in December: should stay beyond 19f. *Miss H. C. Knight*

MELITMA   9 gr.g. Gods Solution – Melsil (Silly Prices) [2003/4 16gᵖᵘ 24dᵖᵘ 21d⁵   **h–**
20gᵖᵘ Apr 16] unseated second in maiden point: no form over hurdles. *R. Nixon*

MELLINO   4 b.f. Robellino (USA) – Krista (Kris) [2003/4 17m⁶ Aug 1] fair maiden   **h–**
up to 1½m on Flat: well held in juvenile on hurdling debut (tried to refuse 2 out): sold
2,500 gns Newmarket Autumn Sales. *T. D. Easterby*

MELODY PRINCESS   11 b.m. Ardross – Letteressie (Alias Smith (USA)) [2003/4   **c–**
c33d⁵ Apr 30] sparely-made mare: modest pointer. *Miss A. Dudley*   **h–**

MELTONIAN   7 ch.g. Past Glories – Meltonby (Sayf El Arab (USA)) [2003/4 h86:   **h84**
20m⁶ 18g⁵ 16m* 16g⁵ 16d⁴ Nov 27] compact gelding: poor hurdler: made all in novice at
Towcester in October: best form up to 21f: acts on good to firm and good to soft going:
visored once. *K. F. Clutterbuck*

MELUSINA (IRE)   4 b.f. Barathea (IRE) – Moon Masquerade (IRE) (Darshaan)   **h89**
[2003/4 18f³ Aug 25] poor maiden on Flat: dam unraced half-sister to Prix du Jockey Club
winner Polytain: third in juvenile at Fontwell on hurdling
debut: sold 10,000 gns Newmarket Autumn Sales. *Mrs A. J. Perrett*

MEMBERS ONLY   5 b.g. Kris – Could Have Been (Nomination) [2003/4 16f⁴ 17s   **h99**
17s² Feb 3] leggy gelding: fourth foal: dam unraced half-sister to Prix du Jockey Club
winner Polytain: second in bumper at Thurles on debut in 2002/3 for J. J. Murphy: best
effort over hurdles when second to Blue Americo in novice at Taunton: lame previous
outing. *M. C. Pipe*

MENDIP MANOR   6 b.g. Rakaposhi King – Broughton Manor (Dubassoff (USA))   **h–**
[2003/4 F–: 20sᵖᵘ 17s 16g 22gᵖᵘ Apr 18] no sign of ability. *S. C. Burrough*

MENDOSINO (GER)   5 b.g. Acatenango (GER) – Maji (Shareef Dancer (USA))   **h95**
[2003/4 16d⁶ 20s³ 21d 18s* 20s 17s 21d Apr 8] leggy ex-German gelding: successful
once over 11f on Flat at 3 yrs for P. Schiergen: modest novice hurdler: won handicap at

593

Fontwell in February, despite carrying head awkwardly: should stay 2½m: raced only on good to soft/soft going: blinkered final outing: has hung. *Miss Venetia Williams*

MENPHIS BEURY (FR) 4 b.g. Art Bleu – Pampa Star (FR) (Pampabird) [2003/4 17s c17v³ 16g^ur 17d³ Mar 22] sturdy ex-French gelding: fourth foal: half-brother to 3 winners, including one-time fairly useful hurdler Ideal du Bois Beury (by Useful), stays 2½m: dam won up to 11f: once-raced over jumps at Pau in December, third in 3-y-o chase on second occasion: left E. Lemartinel, modest form in 2 races over hurdles in Britain: will stay beyond 17f. *H. D. Daly* **c? h96**

MENSCH (IRE) 8 ch.g. Husyan (USA) – Floating Dollar (Master Owen) [2003/4 c78, h–: c26g^pu c24s^pu 26g c24g² Apr 16] poor maiden hurdler/steeplechaser: trained by Mrs S. Johnson on reappearance, P. Morgan next start: won points in January and March: stays 3m: acts on firm going: has worn blinkers/cheekpieces. *Evan Williams* **c73 h–**

MER BIHAN (FR) 4 b.f. Port Lyautey (FR) – Unika II (FR) (Rolling Bowl (FR)) [2003/4 16g^pu 16s 16g⁵ Mar 28] fifth foal: half-sister to modest hurdler Jolika (by Grand Tresor), stays 2½m: dam, won over 1¼m in France, half-sister to dam of useful chaser around 2½m Camitrov: no show in 3 starts over hurdles. *L. Lungo* **h–**

MERCATO (FR) 8 b.g. Mansonnien (FR) – Royal Lie (FR) (Garde Royale) [2003/4 c110, h112: c16g³ c16g³ c16g⁴ c24d² c24g³ c24g* c25g^F c33d^pu Apr 17] tall, good-topped gelding: fair handicap hurdler: fairly useful chaser: best effort when winning Grand Military Gold Cup at Sandown in March by 15 lengths from Kings Mistral, forging clear 2 out: stays 3m: acts on heavy going (won bumper on good to firm): has had tongue tied: usually held up. *J. R. Best* **c123 h–**

MERCHANTS FRIEND (IRE) 9 b.g. Lord Americo – Buck Maid (Buckskin (FR)) [2003/4 c122, h105: c24s* c25g⁴ c26g⁵ c24g^F c25d³ c24s⁵ c24g² c25g^pu Apr 2] good-topped gelding: useful handicap chaser: won at Uttoxeter in May: excellent length second to Maximize in valuable amateur event at Cheltenham in March, jumping much better than usual, long way clear 2 out but tiring run-in and caught close home: should stay beyond 25f: raced mainly on good going or softer (acts on heavy): wore cheekpieces last 5 starts: usually held up: consistent. *C. J. Mann* **c136 x h–**

MERITOCRACY (IRE) 6 b.g. Lahib (USA) – Merry Devil (IRE) (Sadler's Wells (USA)) [2003/4 h–: 17g 16m 16g 16d³ 16d 16g 17g 20g Apr 13] no worthwhile form over hurdles: tried tongue tied. *Miss A. E. Broyd* **h–**

MERLO (IRE) 9 b.g. Supreme Leader – Playwright (Furry Glen) [2003/4 24m^pu 20g^pu Jun 22] winning pointer: no form over hurdles: has had tongue tied. *Mrs L. B. Normile* **h–**

MERRY DAYS (IRE) 4 ch.f. Superlative – Fleur de Tal (Primitive Rising (USA)) [2003/4 F14g F13v Dec 15] leggy filly: second foal: dam, winning 2m hurdler, half-sister to useful winner up to 7f Blakeset: showed little in two 3-y-o bumpers, looking hard ride on second occasion: sold 500 gns (privately) Doncaster January Sales. *N. M. Babbage* **F–**

MERRYLEA-CONFUSED 5 ch.m. Respect – Merry Mermaid (Bairn (USA)) [2003/4 F16m F16g 22g Mar 28] leggy mare: first foal: dam winning hurdler/1½m winner on Flat: little sign of ability: joined Mrs H. Graham. *A. M. Crow* **h– F–**

MERRY MINSTREL (IRE) 11 b.g. Black Minstrel – Merry Lesa (Dalesa) [2003/4 c101: c16g^pu c17m^F Jul 19] tall gelding: winning chaser: stays 3m: acts on good to firm and good to soft going: has high head carriage: sold 5,500 gns Doncaster August Sales, little form in points in 2004. *C. J. Mann* **c–**

MERRY TINA 9 b.m. Tina's Pet – Merry Missus (Bargello) [2003/4 c53, h–: c16g c17g c20g⁵ c17d³ c27s^pu c16s⁵ Apr 4] winning pointer at 2½m, little form otherwise: tried visored. *J. B. Walton* **c64 h–**

MERRYVALE MAN 7 b.g. Rudimentary (USA) – Salu (Ardross) [2003/4 16g² 16g 16s⁴ 17s² 16g 17s⁴ 16g⁵ 16d 16s* 17d^ur 16d* Apr 22] fair at one time on Flat (stays 1¾m): fair novice hurdler: won at Newcastle in March and Perth in April: raced around 2m: acts on soft going: races prominently. *Miss Kariana Key* **h104**

MERSEY BEAT 10 ch.g. Rock Hopper – Handy Dancer (Green God) [2003/4 c112, h–: c20m^ur Nov 8] well-made gelding: one-time useful hurdler: fair chaser: unseated tenth in handicap at Sandown only outing in 2003/4: barely stays 2½m: acts on firm and good to soft going: blinkered twice: has pulled hard. *G. L. Moore* **c– h–**

MERSEY MIRAGE 7 b.g. King's Signet (USA) – Kirriemuir (Lochnager) [2003/4 16d^pu 16g 16s^F 16g⁶ 16s^F Mar 19] on downgrade on Flat: no worthwhile form over hurdles. *R. C. Guest* **h–**

MERYL (FR) 4 ch.g. Garde Royale – Vindhy (FR) (Yelpana (FR)) [2003/4 15d³ 18sᶠ 15s² 17d² 17d³ 18s Apr 12] big, rangy gelding: seventh foal: half-brother to 4 winners, including fair chaser/winning hurdler up to 19f Honey (by Highlanders): dam won several times up to around 1½m on Flat: once-raced on Flat: fairly useful juvenile hurdler: placed twice at Cheltenham in January, behind Trouble At Bay and in Grade 2 behind Mondul: ran poorly at Auteuil in April: well held on chasing debut there following month (should do better): will be suited by greater test of stamina: raced on soft/good to soft going. *G. Macaire, France* **c89 p / h116**

MESSAGE RECU (FR) 8 b.g. Luth Dancer (USA) – High Steppe (Petoski) [2003/4 h110: c16m* c25gᵖᵘ c21d³ c20dᵖᵘ 20dᵖᵘ Mar 24] workmanlike gelding: fair handicap hurdler in 2002/3 for E. O'Grady: form in 2003/4 only when winning very weak maiden chase at Leicester in November: stays 3m: acts on soft going, probably on good to firm. *S. T. Lewis* **c72 / h–**

MESTRE SALA (FR) 9 b.g. Al Nasr (FR) – Light Lida (USA) (Alleged (USA)) [2003/4 c20g³ c20mᶠ c20g* c21d⁴ c24gᵖᵘ Sep 6] lengthy gelding: fairly useful handicap chaser, missed 2002/3: idled briefly when beating Dantie Boy a length at Stratford in June: lame there final start: stays 21f: acts on soft going. *H. D. Daly* **c116 / h–**

METAL DETECTOR (FR) 7 b.g. Treasure Hunter – Las-Cancellas (Monksfield) [2003/4 h112: 20d⁴ 21sᵖᵘ c19d⁵ c24d* c23m* c20g³ c24gᵖᵘ Apr 1] good-topped gelding: fair hurdler: similar form over fences: won maiden at Doncaster (didn't jump well) in January and novice at Leicester (simple task) in March: stays 3m: acts on soft and good to firm going. *K. C. Bailey* **c106 / h112**

METICULOUS 6 gr.g. Eagle Eyed (USA) – Careful (IRE) (Distinctly North (USA)) [2003/4 17mᵖᵘ 17d 16g Mar 10] workmanlike gelding: of little account: tried tongue tied. *M. C. Chapman* **h–**

METICULOUS (USA) 6 b. or br.g. Theatrical – Sha Tha (USA) (Mr Prospector (USA)) [2003/4 h–: 22dᵖᵘ 19mᵖᵘ May 31] good-topped gelding: no form over hurdles: sold £1,550 Ascot December Sales. *Mrs A. M. Thorpe* **h–**

MEVAGISSEY (BEL) 7 b. or br.g. Sula Bula – Fowey (Grand Conde (FR)) [2003/4 F16s Dec 20] workmanlike gelding: dam out of half-sister to very smart miler Poacher's Moon: well tailed off in bumper on debut. *J. R. Boyle* **F–**

MEXICAN PETE 4 b.g. Atraf – Eskimo Nel (IRE) (Shy Groom (USA)) [2003/4 16m* 16m⁴ Nov 1] fairly useful on Flat (stays 1½m): not extended when winning juvenile at Huntingdon on hurdling debut: found less than expected when fourth to Howle Hill in listed juvenile at Wetherby following month. *P. W. Hiatt* **h98**

MEXICAN ROCK 8 b.g. Rock City – Pink Mex (Tickled Pink) [2003/4 16g 17s Apr 6] half-brother to useful hurdler/fairly useful chaser Tragic Hero (by Tragic Role), stays 3m: fairly useful on Flat (stays 7f) at 3 yrs, well beaten since: left R. Guest, well held in 2 novice hurdles. *N. J. Henderson* **h74**

MEXICAN (USA) 5 b.g. Pine Bluff (USA) – Cuando Quiere (USA) (Affirmed (USA)) [2003/4 h89: 16d c16gᶠ c16g* c16v³ c16d⁴ c16dᵖᵘ Apr 22] rather leggy gelding: maiden hurdler: modest chaser: won novice handicap at Catterick in January: raced at 2m: best efforts on good going: has worn cheekpieces over fences: has found little: usually let down by jumping. *M. D. Hammond* **c91 x / h–**

MEZEREON 4 b.f. Alzao (USA) – Blown-Over (Ron's Victory (USA)) [2003/4 16f* 16m² 16gᵖᵘ 16g Apr 1] strong, close-coupled filly: modest on Flat (seems to stay 1½m): won juvenile at Wetherby in October on hurdling debut: better form when second to Howle Hill in listed event at same course following month: disappointing last 2 starts. *D. Carroll* **h102**

MEZZO PRINCESS 12 b.m. Remezzo – Kam Tsin Princess (Prince Regent (FR)) [2003/4 c72, h–: c26d³ Apr 30] poor pointer: tried blinkered. *Mike Lurcock* **c– / h–**

MICE DESIGN (IRE) 7 b.g. Presidium – Diplomatist (Dominion) [2003/4 h–: 19gᵖᵘ 17g Jul 28] modest hurdler in 2001/2: no form since: tried blinkered. *S. B. Clark* **h–**

MICHAEL FINNEGAN (IRE) 11 b. or br.g. Phardante (FR) – Decent Slave (Decent Fellow) [2003/4 c93, h–: c16g 16d 16s Dec 13] sturdy gelding: modest 2m handicap hurdler/maiden chaser, well held in 2003/4: has won on good to firm going, best efforts on softer than good. *Miss L. C. Siddall* **c– / h–**

MICHAEL MOR (IRE) 10 ch.g. Denel (FR) – Oralee (Prominer) [2003/4 c128, h124: c20d² c20v c22s 20d⁶ 16d 19s⁵ 19d 16d² c17d⁶ Apr 11] workmanlike gelding: fairly useful hurdler/chaser: back to near best when sixth to Fadoudal du Cochet in valu- **c128 / h119**

able handicap over fences at Fairyhouse final outing: effective at 2m to 3m: acts on good to firm and heavy going: tried in cheekpieces: held up. *N. Meade, Ireland*

MICHAELS DREAM (IRE) 5 b.g. Spectrum (IRE) – Stormswept (USA) (Storm Bird (CAN)) [2003/4 17d² 16d² 19g² 17s⁴ 20d 16f⁴ 20d Apr 18] modest on Flat (stays 1¾m): modest novice hurdler: best form around 2m: acts on firm and soft going: visored last 3 starts. *J. Hetherton*   **h94**

MICKEY CROKE 7 b.g. Alflora (IRE) – Praise The Lord (Lord Gayle (USA)) [2003/4 F102: 20gᶠ 21d³ 21d 19dᶠ 23vᵖᵘ 21d² Apr 12] rangy, good sort: fair form over hurdles: fell fourth in maiden on chasing debut: will stay 3m: raced on good ground or softer: sold 25,000 gns Doncaster May Sales. *C. R. Egerton*   **c–** **h114**

MICKLOW MINSTER 10 ch.g. Minster Son – Scotto's Regret (Celtic Cone) [2003/4 c–, h–: 24m 26gᵖᵘ c25m c27m² Jul 22] workmanlike gelding: little form over hurdles for long time: modest novice chaser: stays 27f: acts on firm and good to soft ground. *C. Grant*   **c85** **h–**

MICK MURPHY (IRE) 7 b.g. Jurado (USA) – Lee Ford Lady (Kemal (FR)) [2003/4 h–: 17m⁶ 16m 17d⁴ 22g² 23d⁵ 16s 24g c20s c25g⁶ c16s⁴ c21dᶠ Mar 30] big, lengthy gelding: poor maiden hurdler, left Mrs E. Slack after sixth start: showing first form over fences when falling last in handicap at Sedgefield, every chance at time: stays 2¾m: wore cheekpieces/tongue strap last 2 outings. *R. Johnson*   **c70** **h64**

MICKTHECUTAWAY (IRE) 12 b.g. Rontino – Le-Mu-Co (Varano) [2003/4 c–: c25sᵘʳ c24g³ Apr 18] workmanlike gelding: fair pointer nowadays, won in January: well-beaten third at Stratford on completed outing in hunter chases: stays 25f: raced mainly on good going or softer (acts on heavy): usually forces pace. *Daniel Skelton*   **c66** **h–**

MICMAC 6 br.g. Be My Native (USA) – Padykin (Bustino) [2003/4 h–, F–: 17gᵖᵘ Jun 11] no sign of ability. *P. Winkworth*   **h–**

MIDDLEHAM PARK (IRE) 4 b.g. Revoque (IRE) – Snap Crackle Pop (IRE) (Statoblest) [2003/4 16g³ 16g⁵ Mar 13] lengthy gelding: modest maiden around 1m on Flat: better effort in juvenile hurdles when third to Albany at Catterick: will prove best at 2m with emphasis on speed. *P. C. Haslam*   **h82**

MIDDLETHORPE 7 b.g. Noble Patriarch – Prime Property (IRE) (Tirol) [2003/4 h103: 16d⁴ 16d* 16v⁴ 16g² Jan 24] workmanlike gelding: fair on Flat (stays 1¾m), successful in March: fair handicap hurdler: won at Wetherby in December by 2½ lengths from Cumbrian Knight, despite jumping right: good second to Baby Gee at Catterick: best around 2m: raced on good going or softer (acts on heavy): best efforts in blinkers: not a fluent jumper: reliable. *M. W. Easterby*   **h111**

MIDDLEWAY 8 b.g. Milieu – Galway Gal (Proverb) [2003/4 h77?: 20g c25mᵘʳ c24gᵖᵘ 22d⁴ 24g⁵ 24g⁴ c24g⁵ c24g³ c26dᵖᵘ Apr 18] workmanlike gelding: poor hurdler: won handicap at Musselburgh in January: makes mistakes over fences: stays 3m: best efforts on good ground: tried in cheekpieces (including for win). *Miss Kate Milligan*   **c68 x** **h76**

MIDLAND FLAME (IRE) 9 b.g. Un Desperado (FR) – Lathanona (Reformed Character) [2003/4 c128, h–: c20g⁵ c19d⁴ c20g c24g* c25g² c33dᵖᵘ Apr 17] strong, well-made gelding: usually looks very well: useful handicap chaser: back to form when winning at Newbury in March by 2½ lengths from Lord of The River: good second to same horse in quite valuable event at Aintree: stays 25f: best efforts on good going: takes strong hold, and probably best ridden up with pace: usually sound jumper. *Miss H. C. Knight*   **c134** **h–**

MIDLEM MELODY 8 b.m. Syrtos – Singing Hills (Crash Course) [2003/4 c–, h60: 17g c17g² c20f² 20g c16m² c16g³ c16f² c16g* c21m³ c20g* c20d² c16s⁵ c16g* c17s⁴ c20g⁴ c16g³ c16g⁵ c16s⁴ c17g² c20d* Apr 18] medium-sized mare: poor hurdler: modest novice chaser: ran 20 times in 2003/4, winning handicaps at Carlisle and Hexham (mares) in November, Musselburgh in January and Carlisle in April: stays 21f: acts on any going: patiently ridden: has swished tail: tough. *W. S. Coltherd*   **c86** **h–**

MIDNIGHT COUP 8 br.g. First Trump – Anhaar (Ela-Mana-Mou) [2003/4 c70§, h70§: 19g 16m⁴ Jun 18] poor hurdler: lightly raced in steeplechases: won points in January and April: stays 2¾m: acts on firm and soft going: has worn headgear, including last 4 starts: has had tongue tied: ungenuine. *B. G. Powell*   **c– §** **h64 §**

MIDNIGHT CREEK 6 b.g. Tragic Role (USA) – Greek Night Out (IRE) (Ela-Mana-Mou) [2003/4 h99§: 22g² 20d² 24g² 22d² 24dᶠ Mar 27] leggy gelding: fair handicap hurdler: sold out of G. A. Swinbank's stable 12,000 gns Doncaster May Sales after first outing: stays 3m: raced on good going or softer (acts on heavy): tried in cheekpieces/visor: irresolute. *Miss Venetia Williams*   **h104 §**

MIDNIGHT GOLD   4 ch.g. Midnight Legend – Yamrah (Milford) [2003/4 F16d Mar   F–
19] £4,200 3-y-o: seventh foal: half-brother to fairly useful 2m hurdler Capricorn
Princess (by Nicholas Bill) and winning pointer by Sula Bula: dam successful up to 11.5f
on Flat: well held in bumper on debut. *L. P. Grassick*

MIDNIGHT GUNNER   10 b.g. Gunner B – Light Tonight (Lighter) [2003/4 c117+,   c113
h–: c29d6 c24m5 c29d5 c26m2 Apr 14] well-made gelding: fair handicap chaser: best at   h–
3m+: acts on any going: sound jumper: genuine. *A. E. Price*

MIDNIGHT JAZZ (IRE)   14 b.g. Shardari – Round Midnight (Star Appeal) [2003/4   c–
c–, h71: 17gpu 16m Nov 13] good-topped gelding: veteran 2m hurdler: tried blinkered.   h–
J. Harriman

MIDNIGHT ROYAL   9 b.m. Prince Daniel (USA) – Dontella's Girl (Royal Clipper)   h–
[2003/4 16gpu 16g Mar 17] lightly-raced mare: no sign of ability, including in points.
G. R. Pewter

MIDNIGHT SPIRIT   4 b.g. Midnight Legend – West-Hatch-Spirit (Forzando)   F–
[2003/4 F14d F17g Apr 1] first foal: dam once-raced half-sister to useful hurdler up to
2¾m Aspirant Dancer: showed little in bumpers. *S. C. Burrough*

MIDNIGHT TANGO   7 ch.m. Milieu – Whistle Binkie (Slim Jim) [2003/4 h–, F–:   h–
17g 16mpu Oct 3] of no account: tried in cheekpieces: sold 1,200 gns Doncaster October
Sales. *Mrs H. O. Graham*

MID SUMMER LARK (IRE)   8 b.g. Tremblant – Tuney Blade (Fine Blade (USA))   c82
[2003/4 c24d2 Apr 18] maiden pointer: visored, second of 3 finishers to Black Smoke in
maiden hunter chase at Carlisle. *I. McMath*

MID SUSSEX SPIRIT   5 b.g. Environment Friend – Ranyah (USA) (Our Native   F96
(USA)) [2003/4 F16d5 Feb 2] leggy gelding: fifth foal: brother to winning staying chaser
Alfred The Grey: dam 2-y-o 7f winner, became unreliable: around 6 lengths fifth of 16 to
Itsa Legend in bumper at Kempton on debut. *G. L. Moore*

Vodafone Handicap Chase, Newbury—
the sound-jumping Midland Flame bounces back to form

MIDY'S RISK (FR) 7 gr.g. Take Risks (FR) – Martine Midy (FR) (Lashkari) [2003/4 c90, h103: c19d^{pu} Mar 22] lengthy, angular gelding: fair hurdler: little aptitude for chasing: bought out of Mrs N. Smith's stable £5,800 Ascot June Sales: probably stays 21f: acts on heavy going: tried blinkered/in cheekpieces. *Miss S. J. Davies* **c–** **h–**

MI FAVORITA 6 b.m. Piccolo – Mistook (USA) (Phone Trick (USA)) [2003/4 h–: 17s^6 17d^5 17g Jul 28] small mare: no form over hurdles: tried in tongue strap. *Miss Kate Milligan* **h–**

MIGHTY FINE 10 gr.g. Arzanni – Kate Kimberley (Sparkler) [2003/4 c101, h71: c16m^3 17s^2 c21g 21g* Oct 14] rangy gelding: fair chaser: best effort over hurdles when winning handicap at Sedgefield (all 4 successes there): stays 21f: acts on any going. *Mrs E. Slack* **c101** **h92**

MIGHTY GLEN (IRE) 6 br.g. Roselier (FR) – Supreme Glen (IRE) (Supreme Leader) [2003/4 22d^{pu} 19d^{pu} 19g 22g Apr 13] €31,000 4-y-o: sixth foal: half-brother to winning hurdler/maiden chaser Joe di Capo (by Phardante), stays 3m: dam unraced half-sister to high-class 2m hurdler Colonel Yeager: no show in novice hurdles. *A. W. Carroll* **h–**

MIGHTY KILCASH (IRE) 11 ch.g. Black Minstrel – Any Wonder (Hardboy) [2003/4 c–, h92: c30d^6 c28d^{pu} c26v^F Feb 7] big, strong gelding: lightly-raced hurdler/ winning chaser: stays 3¼m: raced on good going or softer (acts on heavy). *Jonjo O'Neill* **c98** **h–**

MIGHTY MAN (IRE) 9 b.g. Mandalus – Mossy Mistress (IRE) (Le Moss) [2003/4 c–, h–: 20d^{pu} Mar 22] smallish, strong gelding: no sign of ability: tried visored. *O. Brennan* **c–** **h–**

MIGHTY MAX 6 b.g. Well Beloved – Jokers High (USA) (Vaguely Noble) [2003/4 h?: 16m 16d Jan 22] little form on Flat or over hurdles: tongue tied. *G. A. Ham* **h–**

MIGHTY MINSTER 7 ch.m. Minster Son – Mighty Fly (Comedy Star (USA)) [2003/4 h85, F78: 20g^F 20m^{pu} 17m^{pu} 17m^{pu} 22g^{pu} May 23] lengthy, sparely-made mare: maiden hurdler: no form in 2003/4, sold out of R. C. Guest's stable 5,000 gns Doncaster May Sales after first outing: tried in cheekpieces: temperamental. *A. E. Jones* **h– §**

MIGHTY MONTEFALCO 8 b.g. Mtoto – Glendera (Glenstal (USA)) [2003/4 c117, h115: c23m^3 24m^5 c20g^4 22s c31g^{pu} Dec 11] workmanlike gelding: has been freeze fired: fairly useful hurdler/chaser: below form after reappearance: should stay beyond 25f: acts on good to firm and good to soft going: tongue tied last 2 outings: sometimes let down by jumping over fences. *Jonjo O'Neill* **c120** **h–**

MIGHTY PIP (IRE) 8 b.g. Pips Pride – Hard To Stop (Hard Fought) [2003/4 16m^3 16m^3 16m Jul 16] ex-Irish gelding: modest on Flat (stays 11f), successful in August: poor 2m maiden hurdler: acts on good to firm and good to soft going. *M. R. Bosley* **h73**

MIGHTY STRONG 10 b.g. Strong Gale – Muffet's Spider (Rymer) [2003/4 c123, h–: c20g^6 c20g* c22g* c22m* c24g^{pu} c20g c20m^{pu} Apr 23] sturdy, lengthy gelding: fairly useful handicap chaser: won at Newbury in November (twice, beating Stars Out Tonight 11 lengths on second occasion) and December: should stay 3m: acts on soft and good to firm going: has bled/had breathing problems in past. *N. J. Henderson* **c128** **h–**

MIGHTY WILLING 7 br.g. Bollin William – Wild Ling (Mufrij) [2003/4 c24s^2 c24d^4 Mar 15] third foal: dam never ran: fair pointer, won twice in 2003: in frame in hunter chases at Huntingdon and Stratford. *Mrs M. R. Sowersby* **c90**

MIGSY MALONE 9 b.m. Afzal – The Dizzy Mole (IRE) (Salluceva) [2003/4 22m May 29] poor maiden pointer in 2002: not fluent when soundly beaten on hurdling debut. *Mrs A. M. Thorpe* **h–**

MIGWELL (FR) 4 b.g. Assessor (IRE) – Uguette IV (FR) (Chamberlin (FR)) [2003/4 18s^3 16s^4 16d 16s^4 16g^F Mar 5] useful-looking ex-French gelding: fifth foal: half-brother to 2 winners by Passing Sale, notably useful hurdler/smart chaser around 2m Hot Shots: dam, won around 2m over fences/around 1½m on Flat, half-sister to good 4-y-o chaser French Kankan: twice-raced on Flat: poor juvenile hurdler, trained first 2 starts by G. Cherel: bled from nose third outing. *D. J. Wintle* **h99**

MIJICO (IRE) 8 b.g. Lord Americo – Mijette (Pauper) [2003/4 c24s^F c25s^{pu} Mar 7] well-made gelding: second in bumper on debut: off nearly 2 years, tired in third when falling last in novice chase at Huntingdon: soon struggling after bad mistake ninth next time: will prove best at 2½m+. *Ferdy Murphy* **c83**

MIKASA (IRE) 4 b.g. Victory Note (USA) – Resiusa (ITY) (Niniski (USA)) [2003/4 16g Jan 15] little form on Flat: no show in juvenile seller on hurdling debut. *R. F. Fisher* **h–**

MIKE SIMMONS 8 b.g. Ballacashtal (CAN) – Lady Crusty (Golden Dipper) [2003/4 **h73** h91§: 24m⁴ 26g⁵ 24g 22m⁶ 22s 22g 20s Apr 17] leggy gelding: poor handicap hurdler: stays 21f: acts on soft going. *L. P. Grassick*

MIKE STAN (IRE) 13 b.g. Rontino – Fair Pirouette (Fair Turn) [2003/4 c–, h–: c21s² **c104** May 17] lengthy gelding: fairly useful handicap chaser in 2000/1: easily better effort after **h–** 2-year absence when second of 4 finishers to Old Hush Wing at Sedgefield: stays 3¼m: acts on soft and good to firm going: makes the odd mistake. *L. Lungo*

MILAN KING (IRE) 11 b.g. King's Ride – Milan Moss (Le Moss) [2003/4 c–, h74d: **c–** 16g⁴ 19g⁴ 17g* 17mᵖᵘ 16mᵖᵘ 17dᶠ Nov 25] lengthy gelding: poor hurdler: ended long **h69 §** losing run in selling handicap at Sedgefield in July: stays 21f: acts on any going: blinkered twice (pulled up both times): unreliable. *A. J. Lockwood*

MILBRIG 8 b.m. Milieu – Meadow Brig (Meadowbrook) [2003/4 h–: 22m⁴ 24gᵖᵘ **h–** May 15] no form over hurdles. *A. C. Whillans*

MILDON (IRE) 8 ch.g. Dolphin Street (FR) – Lycia (Targowice (USA)) [2003/4 h–: **h74** 17m² Sep 5] leggy gelding: poor maiden hurdler, lightly raced: stays 21f: has had tongue tied. *J. R. Weymes*

MILITAIRE (FR) 6 ch.g. Bering – Moon Review (USA) (Irish River (FR)) [2003/4 **c99** c–, h111: c24s³ Apr 12] close-coupled gelding: fair hurdler: won point in March: similar **h–** form when third in hunter chase at Fakenham: stays 3m: acts on heavy going: has had tongue tied. *J. M. Turner*

MILKAT (IRE) 6 b.g. Machiavellian (USA) – Desert Victory (Green Desert (USA)) **h121** [2003/4 h121: 16g 20f² Sep 7] leggy gelding: fairly useful handicap hurdler: good second to Native Performance at Punchestown in September: stays 2½m: acts on any going: blinkered once. *W. P. Mullins, Ireland*

MILLCROFT SEASCAPE (IRE) 5 b.g. Good Thyne (USA) – Dante's Ville (IRE) **F–** (Phardante (FR)) [2003/4 F16g F16d⁴ F16d Mar 25] rather unfurnished gelding: fourth foal: half-brother to smart 2m hurdler Ballyhampshire Boy (by Husyan): dam unraced half-sister to high-class staying chaser By The Way: well held in bumpers. *C. J. Down*

MILLCROFT SEASPRAY (IRE) 8 br.g. Good Thyne (USA) – Bucks Gift (IRE) **c103 ?** (Buckley) [2003/4 c115p, h116: c23g³ c23gᵖᵘ c23vᵖᵘ c24gᵖᵘ c24g⁴ c24mᵖᵘ c25gᵘʳ Apr 4] **h–** fairly useful handicap hurdler: mostly disappointing over fences after reappearance (left R. Alner after second start) though unlucky at Taunton fifth outing, 3 lengths up when slipping on landing 3 out and losing all momentum: will stay beyond 3m: raced mostly on good going or softer (acts on heavy): blinkered last 3 starts, tongue tied last 4. *C. J. Down*

MILLE ET UNE NUITS (FR) 5 b.m. Ecologist – Migre (FR) (Le Gregol (FR)) **F–** [2003/4 F–: F17d May 17] twice-raced in bumpers, hanging markedly both times. *Miss K. Marks*

MILL EMERALD 7 b.m. Old Vic – Milinetta (Milford) [2003/4 c–, h100: 22g⁴ 20v* **c–** 20m⁴ 20sᵖᵘ 20s 22s 24sᵖᵘ 21d Mar 19] small mare: no form in 2 starts over fences: modest **h96 d** hurdler: won valuable selling handicap (for second successive year, sold from Mrs M. Reveley 6,400 gns) at Uttoxeter in May: no form subsequently: stays 2½m: acts on any going: tried in blinkers/cheekpieces: sold 5,000 gns Doncaster May Sales. *Mrs G. Harvey*

MILLENAIRE (FR) 5 b. or br.g. Mister Mat (FR) – Mille Perles (FR) (Kashtan (FR)) **F111** [2003/4 F16v* F16g Mar 17] leggy gelding: fourth foal: dam, winning 2m chaser/middle-distance winner on Flat, half-sister to top-class hurdler/useful chaser Mister Banjo (by Mister Mat): joint-favourite, won bumper at Haydock on debut in January by 1½ lengths from Monteforte, flashing tail and carrying head awkwardly under pressure: again looked temperamental when well held in Champion Bumper at Cheltenham. *Jonjo O'Neill*

MILLENIUM WAY (IRE) 10 ch.g. Ikdam – Fine Drapes (Le Bavard (FR)) [2003/4 **c85** c73, h–: c24m² c21m⁴ May 21] medium-sized gelding: fair hunter chaser: should stay **h–** beyond 3m: acts on any going: blinkered (ran poorly) once. *J. M. Turner*

MILLENNIUM GOLD 9 ch.g. Be My Chief (USA) – Forbearance (Bairn (USA)) **c68 x** [2003/4 c81, h–: c22m³ c21g³ c26m² c24g³ c26g³ c26f² c20f⁶ c24g⁵ Apr 18] winning **h–** pointer: poor maiden steeplechaser, left B. Llewellyn after seventh outing: stays 3¼m: acts on firm and good to soft going: tried blinkered: not a fluent jumper. *M. Frieze*

MILLERSFORD 13 b.g. Meadowbrook – My Seer (Menelek) [2003/4 c92x, h–: c19g⁶ **c– x** 22m⁵ 24v* 22g Jun 28] rangy gelding: modest hurdler/chaser: won handicap over hurdles **h93** at Uttoxeter in May, soon clear under enterprising ride: stays 3¼m: acts on any going: blinkered once: usually makes mistakes over fences. *N. A. Gaselee*

MILLERS MEAD   6 b.g. Sir Harry Lewis (USA) – Childhay Millie (Idiot's Delight)   F–
[2003/4 F16g May 21] unfurnished gelding, looks weak: second foal: dam, modest form
in bumpers, sister to fairly useful chaser up to 21f Sursum Corda: well held in bumper on
debut. *P. F. Nicholls*

MILLERS WAY   6 b.m. Nomadic Way (USA) – Keldholme (Derek H) [2003/4 h–,   c–
F74: c20g Feb 10] big, plain mare: no form in mares novice hurdles or chase. *A. Crook*   h–

MILLIESOME   6 b.m. Milieu – Some Shiela (Remainder Man) [2003/4 F–: F16d   h–
F16m² F16d 16g⁵ Mar 12] modest in bumpers: well held in novice on hurdling debut.   **F80**
J. P. Dodds

MILLIGAN (FR)   9 b.g. Exit To Nowhere (USA) – Madigan Mill (Mill Reef (USA))   h129
[2003/4 h130: 20m⁴ Nov 16] close-coupled gelding: useful hurdler nowadays: left Miss
V. Williams, creditable fourth of 6 to The French Furze in steadily-run handicap at Ayr,
only outing in 2003/4: stays 2½m when emphasis is on speed: acts on soft and good to
firm going, possibly not on heavy: usually patiently ridden. *R. A. Fahey*

MILLKOM ELEGANCE   5 b.m. Millkom – Premier Princess (Hard Fought) [2003/4   h82
h–: 16m 17m² 16m² 17d* 16g 16g Dec 3] poor on Flat (stays 1¼m), won in September:
poor hurdler: won selling handicap at Sedgefield in October, making most: likely to prove
best around 2m: acts on good to firm and good to soft going: blinkered last 3 starts.
K. A. Ryan

MILL LORD (IRE)   11 b.g. Aristocracy – Millflower (Millfontaine) [2003/4 c–, h–:   c–
c19g c18m⁶ May 26] good-bodied gelding: bad maiden steeplechaser: won point in April: h–
often blinkered. *C. J. Drewe*

MILL TOWER   7 b.g. Milieu – Tringa (GER) (Kaiseradler) [2003/4 16m 20sᵖᵘ 24sᵖᵘ   h–
20sᵖᵘ Apr 21] lengthy, workmanlike gelding: no form. *R. Nixon*

MILLYHENRY   13 b.g. White Prince (USA) – Milly's Chance (Mljet) [2003/4 c34vᵖᵘ   c–
May 21] smallish, sturdy gelding: modest pointer nowadays: stays 3½m: acts on heavy
going: blinkered once. *A. J. Tizzard*

MILLYS FILLY   6 b.m. Polish Precedent (USA) – Lemon's Mill (USA) (Roberto   h68
(USA)) [2003/4 h66: 17g³ 20m⁵ 24gᵖᵘ 16g 16mᵖᵘ Oct 4] poor maiden hurdler: claimed
out of O. Sherwood's stable £6,000 second start: stays 2½m: acts on good to firm going:
sold 2,000 gns Doncaster October Sales. *Miss K. Marks*

MILNER BE GOOD   6 b.m. Weld – It Beat All (Laurence O) [2003/4 F17g F16d   F–
F17s Dec 20] lengthy mare: seventh foal: half-sister to 3m hurdle winner Kinnegad Girl
(by Be My Native): dam, bumper winner, half-sister to useful 3m chaser Mr Strong Gale:
no form in bumpers. *Mrs J. Candlish*

MILNER BE GREAT   8 b.g. Weld – Bahama (Bali Dancer) [2003/4 24vᵖᵘ Jan 10]   h–
fourth known foal: dam never ran: showed nothing in novice hurdle on debut: sold 500
gns Doncaster January Sales. *Mrs J. Candlish*

MILORD LESCRIBAA (FR)   4 b.g. Cadoudal (FR) – Mona Lisaa (FR) (Karkour   h114 p
(FR)) [2003/4 16d⁴ 16s* Feb 18] third foal: half-brother to 2¼m hurdle winner Miss
Lescribaa (by Epervier Bleu): dam winning hurdler/chaser up to around 21f in France:
fairly useful form when winning juvenile hurdle at Leicester by 6 lengths from Parknasilla, left clear when runner-up made mistake at the last: carries head slightly awkwardly:
likely to improve further. *M. C. Pipe*

MINDANAO   8 b.m. Most Welcome – Salala (Connaught) [2003/4 h120: 22g* 20m³   h120
16d 18g Mar 28] leggy mare: fairly useful handicap hurdler: easily landed odds in 4-
runner race at Kelso very early in season: well held last 2 starts: stays easy 2¾m: acts on
soft and good to firm going: has been let down by jumping. *L. Lungo*

MINELLA CAPTAIN (IRE)   10 b.g. Phardante (FR) – Last Serenade (Little Busk-   h123
ins) [2003/4 20g 20f* 22d² 22g² 22f* 24g² 20m² 20mF 22m 24m Nov 9] fairly useful
handicap hurdler: progressed well in first half of 2003/4, winning at Tipperary in June
and Tralee (amateurs) in August: excellent second to Fata Albertina at Tipperary in
October, no form subsequently: effective at 2½m to 3m: acts on firm and soft going.
M. Hourigan, Ireland

MINELLA STORM (IRE)   12 b.g. Strong Gale – Maul-More (Deep Run) [2003/4   c87
c81, h–: c25d² c25m* c24m⁵ Apr 13] good-bodied gelding: fair hunter chaser: won   h–
5-runner event at Hereford and point in March: stays 25f: acts on heavy and good to firm
going: has won with/without blinkers. *Miss L. Wilkins*

MINELLY   4 b.f. Defacto (USA) – Lady Liza (Air Trooper) [2003/4 17m⁵ 16gᵖᵘ 16sᵖᵘ   h– §
17g Mar 28] neat filly: poor and temperamental maiden on Flat: well held both completed
outings over hurdles: all but refused at third on third start. *M. E. Sowersby*

MINERS DANCE (IRE)   11 b.g. Miner's Lamp – Prudent Birdie (Lucifer (USA))   c99
[2003/4 c102, h–: c26m⁶ c24g⁴ c30s* c32g* c30d c24g Feb 13] angular gelding: modest   h–
handicap chaser: won at Huntingdon in November and Exeter in December: suited by
thorough test of stamina: acts on heavy going: tried blinkered: hard ride. *B. G. Powell*

MINI CRUISE   14 ch.g. Cruise Missile – Mini Pie (Dike (USA)) [2003/4 c20g⁴   c–
c20g c24g⁵ c24f Feb 29] good-bodied gelding: winning pointer: little other form.   h–
Miss J. Fisher

MINI DARE   7 b.g. Derrylin – Minim (Rymer) [2003/4 h86, F80: c24d² c24sᶠ   c91
c26d² c24d⁴ 26s² 25s⁴ 24d⁴ Apr 21] good-topped gelding: modest novice hurdler/chaser: h87
stays 3¼m: raced on good going or softer (acts on soft): wore cheekpieces final outing.
O. Sherwood

MINI SENSATION (IRE)   11 b.g. Be My Native (USA) – Minorettes Girl (Strong   c–
Gale) [2003/4 c149, h–: 20d 20g c33dᵖᵘ Apr 17] medium-sized gelding: smart handicap   h–
chaser in 2002/3: inadequate trip in handicap hurdles first 2 starts in 2003/4, never on
terms when pulled up in Scottish National at Ayr: suited by thorough test of stamina: acts
well on soft/heavy going: held up: often none too fluent over fences. *Jonjo O'Neill*

MINI STIR   6 b.m. Minster Son – Carat Stick (Gold Rod) [2003/4 F16gᶠ Jul 3] seventh   F–
foal: half-sister to fair chaser Pillaging Pict (by Primitive Rising), stays 3m: dam fair
staying hurdler/chaser: behind when breaking leg in bumper on debut. *J. B. Walton*

MINIVET   9 b.g. Midyan (USA) – Bronzewing (Beldale Flutter (USA)) [2003/4 c–,   c–
h107: 22g 20s² 25g 19g* Mar 5] close-coupled gelding: twice-raced over fences: modest   h94
hurdler: form in 2003/4 only in claimers, winning at Doncaster: effective at 2m to easy
2¾m: acts on soft and good to firm going, possibly not on heavy. *T. D. Easterby*

MINNIE SECRET   5 b.m. Primitive Rising (USA) – Mobile Miss (IRE) (Classic   h–
Secret (USA)) [2003/4 16s⁴ 17dᵘʳ 20dᵖᵘ Mar 22] rather unfurnished mare: first foal: dam,
fair hurdler, stayed 2½m: well beaten on completed outing over hurdles. *B. N. Pollock*

MINORA BLUE   6 b.m. Bob Back (USA) – Minora (Cataldi) [2003/4 F17s⁵   h–
F16g 19g 18dᵖᵘ 19g Apr 16] 70,000 4-y-o: second foal: dam unraced half-sister to high-   F83
class chaser Observe and smart hurdler up to 2½m Minorettes Girl, herself dam of high-
class staying chaser Shotgun Willy: modest form in bumpers: little show over hurdles.
Ms Bridget Nicholls

MINSGILL GLEN   8 b.m. Minster Son – Gilmanscleuch (IRE) (Mandalus) [2003/4   c66
c–, h–: 16m⁴ 16m 20m⁴ 20m c25g⁴ c24g c24d³ c25g⁵ c25g* c26d Apr 18] sturdy mare: h–
little form over hurdles: poor chaser: won very weak maiden at Kelso in April: stays 25f:
yet to race on extremes of going. *Mrs J. K. M. Oliver*

MINSTER ABBI   4 b.f. Minster Son – Elitist (Keren) [2003/4 F17v F17d⁵ Apr 18]   F73
half-sister to several poor performers, including winning 3m hurdler Kralingen (by Move
Off): dam plating-class maiden: poor form in 2 bumpers at Carlisle. *W. Storey*

MINSTER BAY   6 b.g. Minster Son – Melaura Belle (Meldrum) [2003/4 F90: F16g²   h–
16gᵖᵘ Jan 7] fair form when runner-up in bumpers: showed little in novice on hurdling   F90
debut. *W. Storey*

MINSTER BELLE   9 ch.m. Minster Son – Palmahalm (Mandrake Major) [2003/4   c–
c24mᵖᵘ Apr 13] sturdy mare: showed more temperament than ability in bumpers in 2000:
winning pointer: never a factor in hunter chase at Chepstow. *D. W. Barber*

MINSTER BLUE   6 b.m. Minster Son – Elitist (Keren) [2003/4 21vᵖᵘ 20s⁴ 21dᵖᵘ 20d⁵   h–
Apr 10] good-bodied mare: half-sister to several poor performers, including winning 3m
hurdler Kralingen (by Move Off): dam plating-class maiden: little form in novice hurdles.
F. P. Murtagh

MINSTER FAIR   6 b.m. Minster Son – Fair Echo (Quality Fair) [2003/4 h87, F87:   h83
22g⁴ 22d Dec 1] leggy, angular mare: poor maiden hurdler: should be suited by 3m+:
raced on good going or softer (acts on heavy). *A. C. Whillans*

MINSTER GLORY   13 b.g. Minster Son – Rapid Glory (Hittite Glory) [2003/4 c108,   c116
h–: c16m⁴ c17f⁶ c17g* c16m* 17d* 16m* 16f* 19g² 16s⁶ c17s⁶ 17d Apr 18] tall gelding: h103
fairly useful handicap chaser/fair handicap hurdler: won 5 times in little over a month in
autumn, over fences at Bangor and Wetherby and over hurdles (including in conditional

jockeys events) at Carlisle, Leicester and Wincanton: lost form after next outing: stays 19f: acts on soft and firm going: blinkered last 8 starts: races prominently. *M. W. Easterby*

MINSTER MADNESS   9 ch.g. Minster Son – Spring Garden (Silly Prices) [2003/4   **h–**
20g May 24] angular gelding: well held in 3 novice hurdles. *B. Ellison*

MINSTER MEADOW   5 ch.g. Minster Son – Eddies Well (Torus) [2003/4 F16f⁶   **h–**
F17m 20gᵖᵘ 17d Apr 18] tall, unfurnished gelding: second foal: dam, poor chaser who   **F73**
stayed 3m, half-sister to fairly useful chaser up to 3m Frost Bound: well held in bumpers:
no encouragement either start over hurdles. *S. G. Chadwick*

MINSTER MISSILE   6 b.g. Minster Son – Manettia (IRE) (Mandalus) [2003/4 F16g*   **F90**
May 22] first foal: dam, modest hurdler, stayed 27f: hung right under pressure when winning slowly-run bumper at Kelso on debut. *Mrs M. Reveley*

MINSTER PARK   5 b.g. Minster Son – Go Gipsy (Move Off) [2003/4 F16m Aug 2]   **F–**
seventh live foal: half-brother to winning pointer by Silly Prices: dam poor maiden
jumper: never a factor in bumper at Worcester on debut, veering badly right into straight.
S. C. Burrough

MINSTER SHADOW   5 b.g. Minster Son – Polar Belle (Arctic Lord) [2003/4 F16v³   **F94**
F17d⁴ F17d³ Mar 11] 3,500 4-y-o: tall, rather unfurnished gelding: second foal: dam
unraced half-sister to smart chaser up to 3m Mr Moonraker and useful staying hurdler/
chaser Greenhil Tare Away: fair form in bumpers: will stay well beyond 2m. *C. Grant*

MINSTER YORK   10 ch.g. Minster Son – Another Treat (Derring-Do) [2003/4 c120,   **c106** §
h–: c17g 20d⁵ c21g³ c17m² c17g² c17f⁵ c16g² c16m* c16m⁵ c19f⁴ c16g³ Dec 5] smallish,   **h–**
angular gelding: maiden hurdler: fair handicap chaser: won 3-runner event at Towcester
in October: stays easy 21f: probably acts on any going: wore cheekpieces after second
start: tongue tied once: ungenuine. *M. D. Hammond*

MINSTREL HALL   5 b.m. Saddlers' Hall (IRE) – Mindomica (Dominion) [2003/4   **h83**
h82: 17dᵘʳ 16d⁵ 16s 16v 17s⁶ 16g 16g* 16d³ 16g 16g⁵ Apr 16] tall mare: poor hurdler:
won 18-runner seller at Catterick in March, in narrow lead when left clear 2 out: raced
around 2m: acts on soft ground: sometimes tongue tied: whipped round at start sixth
outing. *P. Monteith*

MINT APPROVAL (USA)   5 gr. or ro.g. With Approval (CAN) – Mint Bell (USA)   **h–**
(Key To The Mint (USA)) [2003/4 19s Apr 4] no form on Flat at 2/3 yrs for B. Meehan:
tailed off in maiden on hurdling debut. *Dr P. Pritchard*

MIO CARO (FR)   4 ch.g. Bering – Composition (USA) (Sillery (USA)) [2003/4 16d²   **h111**
16gᵖᵘ 16g³ 17g* Mar 28] good-topped ex-French gelding: successful once over 13.5f
from 4 starts on Flat at 3 yrs for F. Rohaut: fair form first 2 completed starts over hurdles,
second of 18 to Dickens in juvenile at Sandown and third of 17 to Lacdoudal in novice at
Kempton: made hard work landing odds in juvenile at Market Rasen. *Noel T. Chance*

MIOCHE D'ESTRUVAL (FR)   4 bl.g. Lute Antique (FR) – Charme d'Estruval (FR)   **h102**
(Mistigri) [2003/4 16d* 17s* 16s² 16s Mar 20] €40,000 3-y-o: third foal: half-brother to
1½m winner Kart d'Estruval (by Genereaux Genie): dam won 3 times around 1½m: won
juvenile hurdles at Plumpton in December and Exeter (9/2-on, made hard work of beating
Deer Dancer 1¾ lengths) in January: will stay beyond 2m: acts on soft going: visored
third outing: one to have reservations about. *M. C. Pipe*

MIRABAD   5 b.g. Pursuit of Love – Shemaleyah (Lomond (USA)) [2003/4 F16s F16g   **F–**
Jan 23] fifth foal: half-brother to French 1¼m to 1¾m winner No Win No Deal (by Machiavellian): dam, 1¾m winner, half-sister to high-class 2m hurdler Kingsmill: sold unraced
out of A. Stewart's stable 800 gns Newmarket July (2002) Sales: tailed off in 2 bumpers:
sold 1,100 gns Doncaster January Sales. *J. S. Haldane*

MIRANT   5 b.h. Danzig Connection (USA) – Ingerence (FR) (Akarad (FR)) [2003/4   **h116**
h112: 17d* 18m* 17m² 16d⁴ Aug 7] quite good-topped horse: fairly useful hurdler: easily
landed odds in novices at Bangor and Fontwell in May: ran poorly final start: raced
around 2m: unraced on extremes of going: hasn't always looked easiest of rides.
M. C. Pipe

MIRJAN (IRE)   8 b.g. Tenby – Mirana (IRE) (Ela-Mana-Mou) [2003/4 h130§: 16d   **h128** §
24dᵖᵘ 22g³ Apr 16] angular gelding: fairly useful handicap hurdler on his day: in cheekpieces, back to form when very close third to Kivotos at Ayr: stays 2¾m: acts on good to
firm and heavy going: best in headgear nowadays: unreliable. *L. Lungo*

MIRPOUR (IRE)   5 b.g. Turtle Island (IRE) – Mirana (IRE) (Ela-Mana-Mou) [2003/4   **h113**
h118: 16g 20s² 16d* 16m* 17m* 16s⁵ 22d³ 16g⁴ Sep 16] good-topped gelding: fairly
useful hurdler: won novices at Punchestown in May, Navan in June and Bellewstown in

July: creditable efforts all other outings in 2003/4: effective at 2m to 2¾m: acts on good to firm and heavy going: tried in cheekpieces, usually blinkered. *E. Griffin, Ireland*

MISBEHAVIOUR   5 b.g. Tragic Role (USA) – Exotic Forest (Dominion) [2003/4 **h75** h88: 17s* 17g 18g^pu 16v^6 16g^6 16d 22s^6 18d 16d 17g^4 Apr 24] poor handicap hurdler: won 4-runner intermediate at Newton Abbot very early in season: little form after: probably best around 2m: acts on soft going: tried visored, usually wore cheekpieces in 2003/4. *P. Butler*

MISHEAD   6 ch.g. Unfuwain (USA) – Green Jannat (USA) (Alydar (USA)) [2003/4 **h67** h84: 16m 17g^pu 22g^3 19g 17m 17m^3 22g^6 22m^F Aug 30] poor maiden hurdler: probably stays easy 2¾m: acts on good to firm and good to soft going. *M. C. Chapman*

MI SOMBRERO   5 ch.m. Factual (USA) – Rose Elegance (Bairn (USA)) [2003/4 **h–** 17d^pu Mar 27] poor maiden on Flat (stays 7f), sold out of D. Ivory's stable 2,000 gns (privately) Doncaster May Sales: no show in mares claimer on hurdling debut. *Mrs B. E. Matthews*

MISS ARAGONT   5 b.m. Aragon – Uninvited (Be My Guest (USA)) [2003/4 F–: **h–** 17s^pu 17d^pu 19g^pu Jul 6] no sign of ability: tongue tied. *S. G. Chadwick*

MISS BARTON RIDGE   7 b.m. Broadsword (USA) – Yamrah (Milford) [2003/4 **F–** F16m^6 May 7] £3,100 6-y-o: fifth foal: half-sister to fairly useful 2m hurdler Capricorn Princess (by Nicholas Bill): dam successful up to 11.5f on Flat: showed nothing in bumper or in point. *J. M. Bradley*

MISS BIDDY   9 ch.m. Sula Bula – Bickfield Approach (Dubassoff (USA)) [2003/4 **h–** 22m^4 May 29] poor pointer, won maiden in March: well beaten in novice on hurdling debut. *M. S. Saunders*

MISS CHINCHILLA   8 b.m. Perpendicular – Furry Baby (Furry Glen) [2003/4 19g **h97 +** 16g* 21d* 21g Mar 27] compact mare: first foal: dam, fair staying hurdler, out of sister to useful 2m hurdler Another Shot and half-sister to good staying chaser Straight Accord: off 7 months after debut, won selling hurdle (sold from O. Brennan 7,800 gns) at Ludlow in February and mares novice hurdle at Sedgefield (easily) in March: stays 21f: raced only on good/good to soft going. *Miss Venetia Williams*

MISS COLMESNIL (FR)   4 b.f. Dear Doctor (FR) – Princesse Dolly (FR) (The **h98** Wonder (FR)) [2003/4 17g^3 17d^5 15s^5 15s^3 18d^pu Apr 7] ex-French filly: seventh foal: half-sister to winning 2m hurdlers Bally Turk (by Baby Turk) and Super Dika (by Fijar Tango): dam unraced: runner-up twice up to 13f from 4 starts on Flat: third twice in juvenile hurdles: left E. Leenders and off 5 months, no show in novice on British debut. *A. E. Jessop*

MISS COOL   8 b.m. Jupiter Island – Laurel Diver (Celtic Cone) [2003/4 h131: c21g^F **c95** c21m^2 c21d* 25d c19g^ur 24g^6 c20m^F Mar 4] angular mare: useful handicap hurdler at **h–** best, well held in 2003/4: only modest form over fences: had to work hard to win novice at Newton Abbot in July: stayed easy 2¾m: acted on firm and soft going: often visored: dead. *M. C. Pipe*

MISS COSPECTOR   5 ch.m. Emperor Fountain – Gypsy Race (IRE) (Good Thyne **h–** (USA)) [2003/4 F–: F16s F16v^4 F16g 17d 20d^6 Apr 10] leggy, lengthy mare: modest **F82** form in bumpers: never dangerous in novice hurdles, not unduly knocked about second time. *T. H. Caldwell*

MISSED EDITION   6 ch.m. Missed Flight – Exclusive Edition (IRE) (Bob Back **h–** (USA)) [2003/4 17m 16m^pu 19f^pu Oct 5] unfurnished mare: first foal: dam, fair hurdler up to 19f/winning pointer, from family of 1993 Derby third Blues Traveller: no sign of ability. *M. J. Gingell*

MISS EGYPT (IRE)   8 br.m. Alphabatim (USA) – Enchanted Queen (Tender King) **h74** [2003/4 18d^3 20d^2 16g^4 18m^3 18m^4 18m 18m 22g Nov 19] lightly raced on Flat: poor maiden hurdler: stays 2½m: acts on good to firm and good to soft ground: tried blinkered/in cheekpieces. *Lindsay Woods, Ireland*

MISS ELLIE   8 b.m. Elmaamul (USA) – Jussoli (Don) [2003/4 h–: 16d^pu c16g c16s^pu **c–** May 17] workmanlike mare: winning hurdler: no form since 2001/2, including over **h–** fences: stays 3m: acts on good to firm and good to soft going, probably unsuited by softer: has worn cheekpieces. *Mrs C. J. Kerr*

MISS FAHRENHEIT (IRE)   5 b.m. Oscar (IRE) – Gunner B Sharp (Gunner B) **F86** [2003/4 F16s F16g F16g^4 F16d^2 Apr 21] lengthy, angular mare: second foal: closely related to 19f hurdle winner Victory Gunner (by Old Vic): dam unraced sister to useful juvenile hurdler Son of A Gunner: progressive form in bumpers, 1¾ lengths second of 19 to Bonny Grey at Worcester in April: will stay beyond 2m. *C. Roberts*

Bewleys Hotels & EBF National Hunt INH Flat Championship Bumper, Punchestown—
Missindependence (white cap) leads into the straight to pick up a race worth some £6,000 more
than the following day's far superior Champion INH Flat

MISS FOSS 5 b.m. Primitive Rising (USA) – Crammond Brig (New Brig) [2003/4 **F79**
F16g[4] F17g[5] F17m Apr 15] 5,000 3-y-o: tall, unfurnished mare: tenth foal: sister to
bumper winner Jackson's Bay and half-sister to useful 2m to 2½m chaser Easthorpe (by
Sweet Monday): dam fair staying hurdler: modest form first 2 starts in mares bumpers.
R. D. E. Woodhouse

MISSINDEPENDENCE (IRE) 5 b.m. Executive Perk – Bonnies Glory (General **F100**
Ironside) [2003/4 F16s[5] F18d[5d] Mar 3] €2,200 4-y-o: compact mare: third foal: dam win-
ning pointer: easily best effort in bumpers when winning very valuable mares event at
Punchestown in late-April, beating Lovely Present 2 lengths. *C. F. Swan, Ireland*

MISSION TO BE 5 ch.g. Elmaamul (USA) – All The Girls (IRE) (Alzao (USA)) **h86**
[2003/4 F17d[5] 16d[3] 19g[F] 16g[3] Mar 12] third foal: half-brother to 7f winner Ballyjazz (by **F77**
Alhijaz): dam poor maiden stayed 1m: caught the eye when fifth in bumper at Hereford
on debut: modest form over hurdles, not knocked about when third to Armaguedon in
maiden at Ayr final outing: may do better. *Jedd O'Keeffe*

MISS JANICA 6 b.m. Sir Harry Lewis (USA) – Supreme Wonder (IRE) (Supreme **h70**
Leader) [2003/4 h73, F68: 20m[4] Aug 2] poor form over hurdles: will stay 3m. *Miss*
Venetia Williams

MISS JESSICA (IRE) 4 b. or br.f. Woodborough (USA) – Sarah Blue (IRE) (Bob **h–**
Back (USA)) [2003/4 F17s 19m[4] 21d[pu] Apr 12] leggy filly: first foal: dam winning 3m **F–**
hurdler in Ireland: well beaten in bumper: fourth of 5 in very weak novice at Hereford on
hurdling debut: pulled hard when pulled up in maiden next time. *Miss M. E. Rowland*

MISS JOJO (IRE) 4 b. or br.f. Darnay – Rose Tint (IRE) (Salse (USA)) [2003/4 **h–**
16g[pu] Jan 15] little form at 2 yrs: showed nothing in juvenile seller on hurdling debut.
B. S. Rothwell

MISS KOEN (IRE) 5 b.m. Barathea (IRE) – Fanny Blankers (IRE) (Persian Heights) **h–**
[2003/4 h–: 19s[pu] Dec 20] smallish, dipped-backed mare: modest on Flat (stays 1½m)
nowadays, successful in March: little show over hurdles. *D. L. Williams*

MISS LACROIX 9 b.m. Picea – Smartie Lee (Dominion) [2003/4 h73: 20m[2] 21m[6] 22g **h68 §**
24m[2] 22f[5] 19m[pu] 24m 21d[6] Oct 29] compact mare: poor handicap hurdler: stays 3m: acts

604

on good to firm and good to soft going: wears cheekpieces: usually races prominently: unreliable. *R. Hollinshead*

MISS LEHMAN 6 ch.m. Beveled (USA) – Lehmans Lot (Oats) [2003/4 F16d⁵ Apr 28] fourth foal: half-sister to poor hurdler Kilcreggan (by Landyap): dam, placed in bumper, half-sister to smart performer around 9f Mellottie: showed little in bumper or maidens on Flat. *Mrs M. Reveley* **F–**

MISS LEWIS 6 b.m. Sir Harry Lewis (USA) – Teelyna (Teenoso (USA)) [2003/4 F77: F17g F16g 22gᵖᵘ 17g Apr 10] modest form in bumpers in 2002/3: no form since, including over hurdles: tongue tied last 3 starts. *C. J. Down* **h– F–**

MISS LIBRATE 6 b.m. Librate – Hayley's Lass (Royal Boxer) [2003/4 F16d F17s F16s Feb 22] third foal: dam poor novice hurdler: well beaten in bumpers and two 1m maidens on Flat. *J. M. Bradley* **F–**

MISS MAILMIT 7 b.m. Rakaposhi King – Flora Louisa (Rymer) [2003/4 F72: F17d 16g³ 22vᶠ 16g³ 21d⁴ Mar 11] leggy mare: poor form on first of 2 outings in bumpers: running best race over hurdles when falling 2 out in mares novice at Haydock: will stay 3m. *J. A. B. Old* **h87 F–**

MISS MATTIE ROSS 8 b.m. Milieu – Mother Machree (Bing II) [2003/4 h–: 20m⁶ 16g c25vᵘʳ c25g* c25g* c25g* c26dᶠ Apr 23] medium-sized mare: little form over hurdles: much better over fences, won 3 hunters at Kelso in March (2, first a novice) and April (beat Lord Edwards Army 2 lengths): stays 25f. *S. J. Marshall* **c99 h–**

MISS MIA 4 b.f. Merit (IRE) – Alisa Bower (Old Lucky) [2003/4 F17v Mar 21] first foal: dam never ran: well beaten in bumper on debut. *N. Waggott* **F–**

MISS MUFFIN 4 b.f. Contract Law (USA) – Charossa (Ardross) [2003/4 F18g Apr 22] eighth foal: half-sister to winning 2¾m hurdler Phil Sanders (by Arctic Lord): dam, poor maiden on Flat/over hurdles, half-sister to very smart hurdler/useful chaser up to 3m Calapaez: little encouragement in bumper on debut. *Miss B. Sanders* **F–**

MISS O'GRADY (IRE) 12 ch.m. Over The River (FR) – Polar Mistress (IRE) (Strong Gale) [2003/4 c95: c21dᶠ c24m⁴ c19s³ c24g⁴ Apr 1] angular mare: fair pointer/hunter chaser: stays 3¼m: acts on soft and good to firm going: has been let down by jumping: weak finisher (has reportedly broken blood vessels). *Mrs S. Alner* **c92**

MISS PARKER 6 b.m. Saddlers' Hall (IRE) – Quivira (Rainbow Quest (USA)) [2003/4 F17s Jan 20] first foal: dam, won up to around 1½m on Flat, out of sister to very smart miler Noble Minstrel: always well behind in maiden bumper on debut. *M. Wigham* **F–**

MISS PORTCELLO 11 b.m. Bybicello – Port Mallaig (Royal Fountain) [2003/4 c90: c25d² c20gᵖᵘ May 15] fair hunter chaser: will stay beyond 25f: acts on good to firm and good to soft going. *Mrs J. M. Hollands* **c90**

MISS QUICKLY (IRE) 5 b.m. Anshan – Shari Owen (IRE) (Shardari) [2003/4 F16m F17s⁴ 19gᵖᵘ 20d⁵ Apr 7] rather leggy mare: second foal: dam unraced, from family of top-class chaser Strong Promise: better effort in bumpers when fourth to Quid Pro Quo in maiden at Taunton: little show in 2 novice hurdles: should stay at least 2½m. *Miss H. C. Knight* **h– F83**

MISS RIDEAMIGHT 5 b.m. Overbury (IRE) – Nicolynn (Primitive Rising (USA)) [2003/4 F16g⁵ F17s² F16d F17m Apr 15] smallish, lengthy mare: first foal: dam unraced: modest form first 2 starts in bumpers: pulled hard final outing. *B. J. Eckley* **F75**

MISS ROYELLO 7 b.m. Royal Fountain – Lady Manello (Mandrake Major) [2003/4 c21s⁵ c25g³ c25g² c24d³ Apr 18] fourth foal: half-sister to fairly useful bumper winner Having A Party (by Dancing High) and fair pointer Claywalls (by Meadowbrook): dam, placed over hurdles, half-sister to fairly useful chasers at 2½m+ Divet Hill and Sword Beach: won points in February/March: modest form in hunters: stays 25f. *Mrs A. Hamilton* **c80**

MISS SKIPPY 5 b.m. Saddlers' Hall (IRE) – Katie Scarlett (Lochnager) [2003/4 F16d³ F16d Apr 21] sixth foal: sister to bumper winner Coleham and winning 2m hurdler Tara Hall and half-sister to winning 2m hurdler Scarlet Fantasy (by Rudimentary): dam winning 2m hurdler: better effort in bumpers when third at Stratford on debut. *P. D. Evans* **F82**

MISS SUTTON 6 b.m. Formidable (USA) – Saysana (Sayf El Arab (USA)) [2003/4 h–: 16m 17m 17m⁴ 17d 17g 22m Jul 14] no form over hurdles: tried visored. *G. F. H. Charles-Jones* **h–**

MISS TOULON (IRE) 6 b.m. Toulon – Miss Top (IRE) (Tremblant) [2003/4 F16g F16d⁴ F16d F16s* F16s Mar 27] first foal: dam lightly raced and no sign of ability: easily **F101**

best effort in bumpers when winning at Navan in December by 4 lengths from Copper-vega. *Patrick Mullins, Ireland*

MISS TROOPER 4 b.f. Infantry – Mountain Glen (Lochnager) [2003/4 F17g Apr 13] third foal: dam once-raced half-sister to useful staying chaser Honourable Man and Midlands National winner Master Brutus: seventh of 15 in bumper at Exeter on debut. *F. Jordan* **F77**

MISS VETTORI 5 b.m. Vettori (IRE) – Dahlawise (IRE) (Caerleon (USA)) [2003/4 F17m Jul 14] half-sister to several winners up to 9f on Flat: dam fair 2-y-o 6f winner: well held in bumper and 1½m maiden on Flat. *G. L. Moore* **F–**

MISS WIZADORA 9 ch.m. Gildoran – Lizzie The Twig (Precipice Wood) [2003/4 c20s² c21d c20d³ c19sF c20d² Apr 11] poor handicap chaser: should stay 3m: raced on good going or softer (acts on soft): failed to impress with jumping last 3 starts. *Simon Earle* **c75 h–**

MISS WIZZ 4 b.f. Wizard King – Fyas (Sayf El Arab (USA)) [2003/4 16dpu Nov 14] poor on Flat (should stay 1m): no show in juvenile on hurdling debut. *W. Storey* **h–**

MISS WOODPIGEON 8 b.m. Landyap (USA) – Pigeon Loft (IRE) (Bellypha) [2003/4 19s 16s 16g Mar 10] sturdy mare: poor maiden hurdler: stays 19f. *J. D. Frost* **h60**

MISTANOORA 5 b.g. Topanoora – Mistinguett (IRE) (Doyoun) [2003/4 h127: 16f* 20g⁵ 16d 21s⁵ 25d* 22s⁴ 24g² 25g Mar 16] small, leggy gelding: useful hurdler: won handicaps at Cheltenham (conditional jockeys) in October and Warwick (by 3½ lengths from Campaign Trail) in January: respectable efforts when second to Monkerhostin in Grade 2 at Kempton and tenth to Creon in Pertemps Final (Handicap) at Cheltenham last 2 starts: stays 25f well: acts on any going: blinkered: effective held up or ridden prominently. *N. A. Twiston-Davies* **h140**

MISTAWAY 6 b.m. Nomadic Way (USA) – Miss Puck (Tepukei) [2003/4 F–: F16g 19fpu Nov 22] no sign of ability. *I. A. Brown* **h– F–**

MISTER ARJAY (USA) 4 b.c. Mister Baileys – Crystal Stepper (USA) (Fred Astaire (USA)) [2003/4 16d³ 16g³ 16s* 16s* 16d⁴ Apr 17] fairly useful on Flat (stays 1¼m), sold out of G. Butler's stable 14,000 gns Newmarket Autumn Sales: fair juvenile hurdler: won at Fakenham (conditional jockeys maiden) in March and Hexham in April: acts on soft going. *B. Ellison* **h108**

MISTER BANJO (FR) 8 b.g. Mister Mat (FR) – Migre (FR) (Le Gregol (FR)) [2003/4 c20d* c20d³ c24gF c32g c33dpu Apr 17] big, strong, close-coupled gelding: top-class hurdler in 2000/1: reportedly suffered leg problems and off over 2½ years before reappearance: useful form over fences, winning novice at Bangor (by 4 lengths from Patricksnineteenth) in December: leading when falling 3 out in similar race won by Be My Destiny at Newbury in February: likely to prove best at 3m+: best efforts on soft going: possibly ideally suited by left-handed tracks: game. *P. F. Nicholls* **c130 h–**

MISTER BIGTIME (IRE) 10 br.g. Roselier (FR) – Cnoc An Oir (Goldhill) [2003/4 c101, h–: c25s⁵ c24g⁴ Feb 8] well-made gelding: fair maiden chaser: reportedly lame final start: should stay beyond 3m: acts on heavy going. *B. G. Powell* **c100 h–**

MISTER CHISUM 8 b.g. Sabrehill (USA) – Anchor Inn (Be My Guest (USA)) [2003/4 h103: 18g² 16m² 16d⁶ 16gpu 16m² 17gF 16mpu 16m 16f⁴ 17m³ 16f 16g⁴ 16d⁴ 16s 16d 16s² 16v Jan 21] angular gelding: handicap hurdler: left R. Allan after second start, mostly disappointing subsequently: raced around 2m: acts on good to firm going, probably on heavy: temperamental. *Miss Kariana Key* **h103 d**

MISTER CLUB ROYAL 8 b.g. Alflora (IRE) – Miss Club Royal (Avocat) [2003/4 c70, h–: c20gpu c20g* c27dpu c24d⁴ c20m² c20dpu Mar 10] good-topped gelding: poor chaser: won novice handicap at Uttoxeter in October: should stay beyond 2½m: acts on heavy going, probably on good to firm: blinkered fourth start, tongue tied last 2. *D. McCain* **c67 h–**

MISTER DAVE'S (IRE) 9 ch.g. Bluffer – Tacovaon (Avocat) [2003/4 c108, h90: c25g⁴ c23g³ c24g³ c23g* c25dF c24sF c25vur 23s³ 24sF Mar 20] tall, leggy gelding: modest hurdler: fair chaser: won weak novice handicap at Wetherby in November: usually let down by jumping subsequently: stays 27f: acts on heavy and good to firm going: tried to run out second start. *Mrs S. J. Smith* **c105 x h92**

MISTER ERMYN 11 ch.g. Minster Son – Rosana Park (Music Boy) [2003/4 h–§: 21m c16mpu c16mpu Jul 16] tall, sparely-made gelding: winning hurdler: visored/blinkered: temperamental. *L. Montague Hall* **c– § h– §**

MISTER FALCON (FR)   7 b.g. Passing Sale (FR) – Falcon Crest (FR) (Cadoudal   c– §
(FR)) [2003/4 h81§: c21s^bd c19d^5 c21d^pu Apr 12] sparely-made gelding: fair hurdler at   h– §
best: won 2 points in April: no encouragement in hunter chases: stays 27f: acts on soft
and firm ground: used to wear visor: ungenuine. *S. Flook*

MISTER FELIX (IRE)   8 b.g. Ore – Pixies Glen (Furry Glen) [2003/4 h83p, F95:   h118
19d^2 20s 19d* 24g^6 Mar 6] tall gelding: bumper winner: easily best effort over hurdles
when winning novice at Doncaster in January by 3 lengths from Almaydan, making
virtually all: should stay beyond 19f: raced on good going or softer. *Mrs Susan Nock*

MISTER FLINT   6 b.g. Petoski – National Clover (National Trust) [2003/4 F95:   h115
F16d^2 F16g^4 20g^F 20d^4 24s^4 24d^5 16d^2 Apr 23] workmanlike gelding: will make a   F98
chaser: fairly useful in bumpers, won at Worcester in May: would have made winning
debut over hurdles in novice at Haydock in November but for falling 2 out, fairly useful
form when fourth to Inglis Drever in Grade 2 novice at Sandown next time: disappointing
subsequently: should stay beyond 2½m: raced on good going or softer. *P. J. Hobbs*

MISTER FRIDAY (IRE)   7 b. or br.g. Mister Lord (USA) – Rebecca's Storm (IRE)   c104
(Strong Gale) [2003/4 h106: 20m^5 24g^pu c19g^F c24g^pu c20d* c25g^5 c20g^3 Apr 24] leggy   h–
gelding: winning hurdler: fair novice chaser: won maiden at Carlisle in March: stays 27f:
unraced on firm going, acts on any other: visored last 3 starts. *P. D. Niven*

MISTER GRAHAM   9 b.g. Rock Hopper – Celestial Air (Rheingold) [2003/4 c63§,   c– §
h–§: 16m^5 20g^5 19g 26g^4 17g^5 17g 16d^6 c20f^pu 16g^6 Feb 20] strong, lengthy gelding: h– §
maiden hurdler/chaser: no worthwhile form in 2003/4: tried blinkered/visored, usually
wears cheekpieces: has had tongue tied: ungenuine. *K. F. Clutterbuck*

MISTER KINGSTON   13 ch.g. Kinglet – Flaxen Tina (Beau Tudor) [2003/4 c25m^pu   c66
c24g^2 c26m^3 c25f^ur Oct 8] tall, angular gelding: winning pointer: poor maiden steeplechaser: stays 25f: acts on good to soft and good to firm going: blinkered once, usually
visored. *R. Dickin*

MISTERLLANEOUS (IRE)   6 b.g. Mister Lord (USA) – Noras Gale (IRE) (Strong   F92
Gale) [2003/4 F17g^2 May 18] first foal: dam pulled up in Irish point: second to impressive
Your A Gassman in bumper at Southwell on debut: joined S. Bell. *R. Johnson*

MISTER MAGPIE   8 gr.g. Neltino – Magic (Sweet Revenge) [2003/4 c–, h–: c20s^6   c81
c16m^6 c20g^3 c21s^3 c19d c21s* c16d^5 c20d^pu Apr 21] good-topped gelding: poor chaser: h–
won novice handicap at Stratford in March: stays 21f: acts on soft going: blinkered once:
often let down by jumping. *T. R. George*

MISTER MCGOLDRICK   7 b.g. Sabrehill (USA) – Anchor Inn (Be My Guest   c142
(USA)) [2003/4 h132: 16m* c16d^F 16d^6 c16d^3 c16d* c20s* c16m^4 c16g^ur c16g^3   h132
c16g* c20d^F Apr 17]
    Mister McGoldrick was named by his grateful owner in recognition of the
surgeon who carried out a heart by-pass operation on him. If the doctor's post-
operative advice to his patient was to avoid too much excitement in future, then
it went unheeded, because the bold-jumping Mister McGoldrick was sent novice
chasing in the latest season, with all the risks that entails. There were indeed both
ups and downs in Mister McGoldrick's first season over fences, but on the whole
his jumping improved with experience and so did his form, so that by the end of the
season he was even better over fences than he had been over hurdles.
    Mister McGoldrick had progressed into a useful hurdler in 2002/3 and he
returned better than ever over the smaller obstacles with a win in a handicap at
Wetherby on his reappearance in October. A first attempt at chasing ended abruptly
with a first-fence fall at Aintree the following month, and he was returned to
hurdles, presumably as a confidence-booster, in the 'Fighting Fifth' at Newcastle,
though that was aiming a little too highly. Mister McGoldrick's chasing career got
off the ground when he finished third to Full Irish at Hexham, then turned in much
more assured rounds of jumping to defeat three rivals impressively in a beginners
chase at Wetherby in December, following up in a novice at Ayr in February. Full
Irish, odds on to confirm Hexham form, and the useful ex-French hurdler Royaleety, Mister McGoldrick's main rivals at Ayr, both fell, but he would almost
certainly have won anyway. A £20,000 handicap at Haydock against seasoned
chasers was Mister McGoldrick's next race, but he had been harshly treated by the
handicapper and a well-held fourth behind Upgrade represented much his best form
over fences to that point.

Ashleybank Investments Novices' Chase, Ayr—two of the better northern-trained novices, with Mister McGoldrick coming out on top against Full Irish (left)

      That was still only enough to make him a 50/1 outsider when taking on the top two-mile novices in the Arkle at Cheltenham. Mister McGoldrick belied his odds by travelling strongly for a long way up with the good pace, before ultimately weakening and being well held in fourth when blundering and unseating at the last. Mister McGoldrick fulfilled the promise of that run when third to the Arkle winner Well Chief in the Maghull Novices' Chase at Aintree next time. Leading from the sixth, Mister McGoldrick turned in a particularly good round of jumping and seemed to have his rivals in trouble turning into the straight, before being unable to hold off Well Chief and Thisthatandtother in the closing stages. Mister McGoldrick's season ended with mixed fortunes at Ayr's Scottish National meeting. On the Friday he took on five opponents in a two-mile novice worth nearly £10,000 and was rewarded for his good efforts in better company with a win over old rival Full Irish by a length and a quarter. Turned out the following day over half a mile further, Mister McGoldrick looked like collecting over twice as much prize money in the Future Champion Novices' Chase, travelling with typical zest and jumping accurately. However, seven lengths in front at the second last, he stood off too far and came down, leaving Keltic Bard to collect the prize. Had he completed, Mister McGoldrick would have shown his best form over fences so far, and he has been rated accordingly.

Mister McGoldrick (b.g. 1997)	Sabrehill (USA) (ch 1990)	Diesis (ch 1980)	Sharpen Up
			Doubly Sure
		Gypsy Talk (b 1982)	Alleged
			Mazaca
	Anchor Inn (b 1988)	Be My Guest (ch 1974)	Northern Dancer
			What A Treat
		Quiet Harbour (br 1974)	Mill Reef
			Peace

      Mister McGoldrick was a mile-and-a-quarter winner on the Flat for James Given before he was sent jumping, and he comes from a fine family of performers on the level, with the well-known broodmare Peace as his great grandam. The Blue Seal Stakes winner Peace produced several good winners of her own, including Quiet Fling (Coronation Cup), Peacetime (Sandown's Classic Trial) and Inter-mission (Cambridgeshire), as well as appearing in the pedigrees of numerous other good horses, including very smart sprinter Continent, very smart six-furlong to one-mile performer Interval and champion US turf mare Wandesta. Mister

McGoldrick comes from a more modest branch of the family, as his grandam showed no ability in three starts and his dam, Anchor Inn, was only poor. She did, however, win the second of just two career starts on the all-weather at Lingfield, springing a 50/1 shock in a claimer. Anchor Inn, a half sister to the useful French stayer Cutting Reef, has also produced the winning two-mile hurdler Mister Chisum (a brother to Mister McGoldrick), the six- and seven-furlong winner Bargash (by Sharpo) and a nine-furlong winner in Spain by Midyan. The best of Mister McGoldrick's siblings, however, looks like being his close relative the five-year-old Master Sebastian (by Kasakov, a son of Diesis like Mister McGoldrick's sire Sabrehill), who showed fairly useful form in bumpers in the latest season.

The workmanlike Mister McGoldrick stays two and a half miles. A winner twice on heavy ground over hurdles, he had seemed to need going softer than good prior to the latest season, though his win over hurdles at Wetherby and his fourth place at Haydock, both on good to firm ground, showed that to be erroneous. Mister McGoldrick is a free-going, enthusiastic sort who jumps boldly, and, while that may count against him on occasions, it bears repeating that the overall standard of his jumping improved through the season. Mister McGoldrick looks capable of winning a good handicap in 2004/5. *Mrs S. J. Smith*

MISTER MOSS (IRE)   11 b.g. Don Tristan (USA) – Lindas Statement (IRE) (Strong Statement (USA)) [2003/4 c–: c16g³ c22g³ c17m⁵ c20mᵖᵘ Aug 16] winning pointer: modest form in hunters for G. Hanmer first 2 starts: stays 2¾m: bled from nose final outing. *B. P. J. Baugh*   **c84**

MISTER MOUSSAC   5 b.g. Kasakov – Salu (Ardross) [2003/4 16mᵖᵘ 16g⁵ 17g⁶ 24d⁵ 16vᵖᵘ Dec 15] half-brother to 2m hurdle winner Merryvale Man (by Rudimentary): poor maiden on Flat (barely stays 1½m) at 3 yrs for R. Bastiman: showed little over hurdles. *Miss Kariana Key*   **h–**

MISTER MUDDYPAWS   14 b.g. Celtic Cone – Jane's Daughter (Pitpan) [2003/4 c95, h–: c25m³ May 7] lengthy gelding: winning chaser: fair form both starts in hunters: stays 4m: acts on firm and soft going: blinkered twice, successful on first occasion: tends to go in snatches. *C. P. Dennis*   **c95 h–**

MISTER MUSTARD (IRE)   7 b.g. Norwich – Monalma (IRE) (Montekin) [2003/4 F99: 20g² 20s² 17d² 16d⁵ 16m³ Feb 21] quite good-topped gelding: fairly useful novice hurdler: placed 4 of 5 starts, short-head second to Garde Champetre at Bangor on third occasion: stays 2½m: acts on good to firm and good to soft going (won bumper on heavy): has found little. *Ian Williams*   **h115**

MISTER ONE   13 b. or br.g. Buckley – Miss Redlands (Dubassoff (USA)) [2003/4 c–, h–: c30sᵖᵘ c25m² c25g⁴ c23d⁶ c25m³ c30g⁴ c24g c26m Apr 14] lengthy gelding: fairly useful handicap chaser: in-and-out form in 2003/4: stays extreme distances: acts on soft and good to firm going: tried in blinkers/cheekpieces: has had tongue tied: not an easy ride. *C. L. Tizzard*   **c120 h–**

MISTER PEARLY   7 ch.g. Alflora (IRE) – Pearly Dream (Rymer) [2003/4 F17d c18d⁴ c24g³ Jan 17] sturdy gelding: fifth foal: half-brother to 2m hurdle winner Pearlstone (by Teenoso): dam, no sign of ability in novice hurdles, out of half-sister to outstanding 2m chaser Pearlyman: poor maiden pointer: well held in bumper and novice chases: has had tongue tied. *J. W. Mullins*   **c– F–**

MISTER PICKWICK (IRE)   9 b.g. Commanche Run – Buckfast Lass (Buckskin (FR)) [2003/4 c–§, h83§: c20m² 21s⁵ 23s³ 22s⁶ 22gᵖᵘ Apr 18] workmanlike gelding: fair form over fences: poor hurdler: left G. L. Moore before final outing: stays 25f: acts on any going: tried visored/in cheekpieces, usually blinkered: hard ride. *Mrs J. A. Ewer*   **c– § h63 §**

MISTER PUTT (USA)   6 b. or br.g. Mister Baileys – Theresita (GER) (Surumu (GER)) [2003/4 h113: 16g c17dᵘʳ c18d³ c17s⁴ Feb 16] useful-looking gelding: modest hurdler on balance of form: similar form in novice chases: raced mainly around 2m on going softer than good (acts on heavy): blinkered: has had tongue tied. *Mrs N. Smith*   **c90 h–**

MISTER WEBB   7 b.g. Whittingham (IRE) – Ruda (FR) (Free Round (USA)) [2003/4 c–, h65: 20g⁴ 20m³ 23g⁵ 22g* 22g² 22g* Aug 4] little show in 2 races over fences: modest handicap hurdler: won at Newton Abbot in June and August, idling markedly on second occasion: stays 2¾m: acts on good to soft going: visored in 2003/4. *Dr J. R. J. Naylor*   **c– h89**

MISTRESS BANJO   4 b.f. Start Fast (FR) – Temperance (FR) (Beyssac (FR)) [2003/4 F12m³ Dec 10] first foal: dam, maiden, out of half-sister to top-class hurdler/useful   **F93**

chaser Mister Banjo: third to Oscars Vision in 3-y-o fillies bumper at Newbury on debut. *A. King*

MISTRIO 7 gr.h. Linamix (FR) – Mistreat (Gay Mecene (USA)) [2003/4 16d² Mar 28] **h94**
1,100,000 francs Y: half-brother to several winners, including smart performer up to
10.5f Misbegotten (by Baillamont) and fair hurdler/fairly useful chaser up to 21f Married
(by Pursuit of Love): dam, French 1¼m winner, half-sister to dam of very smart middle-
distance colt Mirio: failed to complete in 3 points: second to Musical Stage in novice at
Huntingdon on hurdling debut. *K. C. Bailey*

MISTY CLASS (IRE) 12 gr.g. Roselier (FR) – Toevarro (Raga Navarro (ITY)) **c–**
[2003/4 23s Feb 14] leggy, plain gelding: fairly useful staying hurdler/chaser in 2001/2: **h–**
well held over hurdles only outing since: acts on any ground: blinkered once: sometimes
let down by jumping over fences. *Mrs S. J. Smith*

MISTY DANCER 5 gr.g. Vettori (IRE) – Light Fantastic (Deploy) [2003/4 17s* 17s⁶ **h91 +**
16s^pu 17g^pu Apr 3] fairly useful on Flat (barely stays 1¼m): easily won novice at Taunton
on hurdling debut in January: failed to progress, running as if amiss last 2 starts (tongue
tied final one): likely to prove best at 2m with emphasis on speed. *Miss Venetia Williams*

MISTY FUTURE 6 b.g. Sanglamore (USA) – Star of The Future (USA) (El Gran **c119**
Senor (USA)) [2003/4 h79: 17g⁴ 16m 22d² 22g* 21g⁴ 22g² 19m⁴ c19m² c26m³ c25m* **h92**
c24g⁵ c26m* c25f* c25d² c26g² Nov 30] sturdy gelding: modest hurdler: won novice
handicap at Stratford in June: fairly useful chaser: won maiden at Hereford in October
and handicaps at Plumpton later in month and Wincanton (novice, managed all to win by 5
lengths from Comanche War Paint) in November: stays 3¼m: acts on firm and good to
soft going: blinkered seventh start (finished weakly). *Miss Venetia Williams*

MISTY MEMORY 5 b.m. Alderbrook – Misty Sunset (Le Bavard (FR)) [2003/4 F–: **h–**
F16g F16d F19g Apr 3] no form. *R. F. Knipe* **F–**

MISTY RAMBLE (IRE) 9 b.g. Roselier (FR) – Ramble Bramble (Random Shot) **c86**
[2003/4 c88, h–: c25g² May 10] modest maiden chaser: stays 27f: acts on heavy going: **h–**
tried blinkered: tongue tied: has found less than seemed likely: sold 11,000 gns Doncaster
May (2003) Sales: usually let down by jumping in points in 2004, though successful in
February. *Ferdy Murphy*

MISTY RIDGE (IRE) 9 b.g. Moscow Society (USA) – Abigail's Dream (Kalaglow) **c– x**
[2003/4 c89x, h92x: 19g⁶ c22g⁶ 21g 21d⁴ 22g 16m Sep 13] lengthy, angular gelding: **h– x**
modest hurdler/chaser at best: badly out of sorts in 2003/4: often blinkered: has had
tongue tied: sketchy jumper. *Mrs S. J. Smith*

MITEY PERK (IRE) 5 b.g. Executive Perk – More Dash (IRE) (Strong Gale) **h–**
[2003/4 17d Apr 18] €7,500 3-y-o: fourth foal: half-brother to bumper winner She's Our
Native (by Be My Native): dam, bumper winner/winning pointer, half-sister to fairly
useful chaser up to 25f Royal Jake and fairly useful hurdler up to 3m Aimees Mark: well
beaten in novice hurdle on debut. *J. S. Haldane*

MITHAK (USA) 10 b.g. Silver Hawk (USA) – Kapalua Butterfly (USA) (Stage Door **h– §**
Johnny (USA)) [2003/4 h111: 20s 20v^pu 24d^pu 24s Apr 17] leggy gelding: handicap
hurdler, took little interest in 2003/4. *R. T. Phillips*

MIXED MARRIAGE (IRE) 6 ch.g. Indian Ridge – Marie de Flandre (FR) (Crystal **h–**
Palace (FR)) [2003/4 h102: 20d Apr 21] won maiden on debut over hurdles: bought out
of G. L. Moore's stable £1,300 Ascot December Sales: off over a year, well held in handicap only outing in 2003/4. *Miss Victoria Roberts*

MIXSTERTHETRIXSTER (USA) 8 b.g. Alleged (USA) – Parliament House **c90**
(USA) (General Assembly (USA)) [2003/4 h121: c17s³ Apr 17] tall, angular gelding: **h–**
fairly useful hurdler in 2002/3: off a year, not knocked about when last of 3 finishers
in novice won by Atum Re at Bangor on chasing debut: stays 19f: acts on soft and good
to firm going: keen-going sort (has been early to post): usually races prominently.
Miss T. M. Ide

MIZINKY 4 b.f. El Conquistador – Miss Pimpernel (Blakeney) [2003/4 16g^f 16g 16s⁵ **h72**
16g⁴ 21g⁶ 19m³ 21g Mar 17] small, angular filly: last in 5f claimer on debut at 2 yrs: poor
juvenile hurdler: stays easy 19f: acts on good to firm going. *W. G. M. Turner*

M'LORD 6 b.g. Mister Lord (USA) – Dishcloth (Fury Royal) [2003/4 F16g F16g F17g **F–**
Apr 10] workmanlike gelding: half-brother to fairly useful chaser Parahandy (by Lancastrian), stays 3¼m: dam fairly useful 2m hurdler/winning chaser: unseated first in maiden
point in 2003: no form in bumpers. *G. B. Balding*

MOBASHER (IRE) 5 b.g. Spectrum (IRE) – Danse Royale (IRE) (Caerleon (USA)) **h118**
[2003/4 16d* 16d 16v* 17s² 19g² 16g² Mar 15] leggy gelding: useful on Flat (stays
1¾m), sold out of D. Weld's stable 32,000 gns Newmarket Autumn Sales: fairly useful
novice hurdler: won at Doncaster in December and Towcester in January: good efforts
when runner-up all 3 subsequent starts: stays 19f: raced on good going or softer: carried
head high fifth outing. *Miss Venetia Williams*

MODEM (IRE) 7 b.g. Midhish – Holy Water (Monseigneur (USA)) [2003/4 17dᵘʳ **h82**
17g⁶ 16g⁶ 17g⁴ 17gᵖᵘ 17d² 17m⁴ 16g⁴ 17g² 17m 16m* 16mᵖᵘ 16g⁵ Nov 7] half-brother to
winning hurdler in Jersey: poor on Flat (stayed 1m): of similar ability over hurdles, won
seller at Uttoxeter in October: raced around 2m: acted on good to firm ground: visored
last 8 starts: dead. *D. Shaw*

MODEM (NZ) 10 br.g. Omnicorp (NZ) – Replica (NZ) (Creag-An-Sgor) [2003/4 **c–**
c–, h–: 16dᵖᵘ 21g* 20mᵖᵘ Sep 7] strong, compact gelding: amiss when pulled up both **h118**
starts over fences: fairly useful hurdler: first start since reported wind operation, back
to form to win handicap at Southwell in July, easily beating Vicars Destiny 1¾ lengths:
lame next time: stays 21f: acts on good to firm going: tongue tied on reappearance.
S. E. H. Sherwood

MODULOR (FR) 12 gr.g. Less Ice – Chaumontaise (FR) (Armos) [2003/4 c?, h–: **c–**
22g 19m 17g 22sᵖᵘ 19d 27f⁴ 26d Mar 28] small, plain gelding: one-time fairly useful **h–**
hurdler/useful chaser in France: little form in Britain, sold out of M. Pipe's stable 1,200
gns Doncaster August Sales after third start: stays 21f: probably acts on any going: sometimes wears headgear: has had tongue tied: held up. *L. R. James*

MOFFIED (IRE) 4 b.g. Nashwan (USA) – Del Deya (IRE) (Caerleon (USA)) [2003/4 **F–**
F16d Apr 23] first foal: dam, smart 1¼m performer, out of sister to Oaks winner Unite:
badly hampered early when remote ninth in bumper at Perth on debut. *Mrs L. B. Normile*

MOHAWK BRAVE (IRE) 6 b.g. Be My Native (USA) – Aunty Dawn (IRE) (Strong **h91**
Gale) [2003/4 F86: F16d³ 20dᵘʳ 17d⁶ Dec 26] good sort: fair form in bumpers: upped **F86**
markedly in trip, running best race over hurdles when falling 2 out (held in fifth) in 3¼m
novice at Huntingdon final start. *K. C. Bailey*

MOHERA KING (IRE) 12 b.g. King's Ride – Kilbrien Star (Goldhill) [2003/4 **c– §**
c105§, h–: c20sᵖᵘ Apr 21] sturdy gelding: fair handicap chaser: off 13 months, soon well **h–**
adrift only outing in 2003/4: stays 25f: acts on good to firm and heavy going: often wears
blinkers/cheekpieces. *Ferdy Murphy*

MOLLYCARRSBREKFAST 9 b.g. Presidium – Imperial Flame (Imperial Lantern) **c80**
[2003/4 c–: c24g⁵ c16m c23m⁴ c23m* c24m⁴ Aug 9] fair pointer, successful in May: left
Miss S. Robinson after reappearance, won handicap at Worcester in July: stays 3m: acts
on good to firm going. *K. Bishop*

MOLLY MELLO (GER) 5 ro.m. Big Shuffle (USA) – Manitoba (GER) (Surumu **h–**
(GER)) [2003/4 16vᵖᵘ 20g Jan 23] useful on Flat, successful over 7f on Flat in Germany
for U. Ostmann, including in 2003: failed to impress with attitude in 2 novice hurdles:
probably has stamina limitations: tried blinkered. *M. F. Harris*

MOMENT OF MADNESS (IRE) 6 ch.g. Treasure Hunter – Sip of Orange (Celtic **F90**
Cone) [2003/4 F–: F16d⁴ F16g Feb 28] big, lengthy gelding: chasing type: form in
bumpers only when fourth at Musselburgh on reappearance in February. *T. J. Fitzgerald*

MOMENTOUS JONES 7 b.g. Emperor Jones (USA) – Ivory Moment (USA) (Sir **c–**
Ivor (USA)) [2003/4 c–, h96: 22m 18m⁶ 18m³ 22g⁴ 22g⁵ 18s⁴ 22s⁵ 16s Feb 16] leggy **h81 §**
gelding: pulled up only start over fences: poor hurdler nowadays: stays 2½m: acts on
heavy going: visored once, wore cheekpieces last 3 starts: ungenuine. *M. Madgwick*

MON ARC EN CIEL (FR) 9 b. or br.g. Silver Rainbow – La Bonne Etoile (FR) **h–**
(Margouillat (FR)) [2003/4 16g⁴ 16m 16g Mar 6] tall gelding: little worthwhile form over
hurdles: headstrong. *R. Mathew*

MONARCH'S PURSUIT 10 b.g. Pursuit of Love – Last Detail (Dara Monarch) **c106 §**
[2003/4 c118§, h–: c19g c20d⁵ c17s⁴ Mar 7] rangy, good sort: fairly useful handicap **h–**
chaser in 2002/3, below form in 2003/4: stays 2½m: yet to race on firm going, acts on any
other: usually blinkered: often tongue tied prior to 2002/3: weak finisher. *T. D. Easterby*

MONBONAMI (IRE) 7 b.g. Beau Sher – Hard Riche (Hard Fought) [2003/4 c17vᵖᵘ **c96**
16m 16d c18f⁵ 16g c24d* c24d³ c24d³ c21v² c21s* 21g⁴ Mar 4] sturdy ex-Irish gelding: **h–**
fifth foal: dam unraced: winning pointer: maiden hurdler: left E. Bolger after fourth start:
fair handicap chaser: won at Uttoxeter in November and Fakenham (final outing for
J. O'Neill) in January: stays 3m: acts on heavy ground. *Miss K. Marks*

Wragge & Co Finesse Juvenile Novices' Hurdle, Cheltenham—
Mondul comes out on top from French raider Val du Don (right) in a steadily-run race

MONDEED 7 b.m. Terimon – House Deed (Presidium) [2003/4 F17v³ F20m⁶ F16f **h90** F16f 16m³ 18f² 19g 20f⁵ 24s⁶ 20g² 22m² 16mᵘʳ 16d⁴ 21g⁶ 20g⁶ 21dᶠ 23d* 24dᵖᵘ Apr 21] **F75** smallish mare: first foal: dam unraced: modest in bumpers: modest hurdler: left J. Crowley after twelfth outing: much improved when winning novice handicap at Fakenham in April: stays 23f: acts on firm and good to soft going (bumper form on heavy): effective blinkered or not. *N. B. King*

MONDIAL JACK (FR) 5 ch.g. Apple Tree (FR) – Cackle (USA) (Crow (FR)) **c127** [2003/4 c17vᶠ c17d² 19mᵖᵘ c19d* c20g* c20gᵘʳ c20g* c24gᵖᵘ c25g c20m* Apr 23] **h–** lengthy gelding: twelfth foal: brother to fair hurdler/chaser up to 2¾m Line Apple and half-brother to 6 other winners, notably very smart French staying chaser Grey Jack (by Bikala): dam French 1½m winner: won 4-y-o minor event over hurdles at Pau on debut in 2002/3: fairly useful novice chaser: left C. Aubert after second start: won at Hereford (maiden) in January, Kempton in February and March and handicap at Sandown (led near finish when beating Enzo de Baune ¾ length) in April, jumping much better than on previous 2 starts in last-named: should prove at least as effective at 3m as 2½m: acts on soft and good to firm going. *M. C. Pipe*

MONDUL (GER) 4 b.c. Colon (GER) – Morgenrote (EG) (Aveiro) [2003/4 16g* **h127** 16s* 16s² 17d* 16g⁵ 17g 16d⁶ 19s² Apr 24] leggy colt: trained by C. Von Der Recke, successful 4 times up to around 11f from 10 starts on Flat in Germany in 2003: useful juvenile hurdler: won at Warwick and Lingfield (made all in Grade 2 Summit Junior Hurdle, beating Zimbabwe 12 lengths) in December and Cheltenham (Grade 2 Wragge & Co Finesse Juvenile Novices' Hurdle, by 1¼ lengths from Val du Don) in January: best efforts after when placed in graded events at Auteuil in April and May: appeared to go amiss there in June: stays 19f: possibly suited by going softer than good: has worn off-side pricker: races prominently. *M. F. Harris*

MONET'S GARDEN (IRE) 6 gr.g. Roselier (FR) – Royal Remainder (IRE) **h138** (Remainder Man) [2003/4 F98p: 22g* 20d* 20g² 24d* Apr 22]

In his sixth season as a licensed trainer, Nicky Richards achieved his best results, both by number of wins and prize money totals, and he must now be hoping for a horse who will help bring back the glory days to Greystoke at the top level. Smart hurdler Telemoss looked as though he could be the one to do just that when he won his first three starts over fences in the 2002/3 season, but he has had his problems since and has failed to live up to expectations. The spotlight is now on

Monet's Garden who looks every bit as promising as Telemoss once did. Monet's Garden won a bumper at Ayr on his only start in 2002/3. Having created a very favourable impression in his first season over hurdles, he looks an exciting prospect for novice chases in 2004/5. Off over four months because of a muscular problem after landing the odds in a novice at Kelso in November on his hurdling debut, Monet's Garden repeated the feat in a similar contest at Carlisle on his return and was then stepped up markedly in class. The Grade 2 Mersey Novices' Hurdle at Aintree saw Monet's Garden taking on several other promising individuals, some of whom had acquitted themselves well at the Cheltenham Festival, and though he lost his unbeaten record he came out of the race with considerable credit. Held up and failing to settle in a steadily-run race, Monet's Garden made good progress to dispute the lead in the straight and still have every chance at the last, but he couldn't keep on quite so well as Garde Champetre and was beaten a length and a quarter. On his only subsequent start, Monet's Garden was stepped up to three miles and justified favouritism in another novice event, this time at Perth. With three of his four rivals running well below their best, the race didn't take so much winning as had seemed likely. Even so, there was a lot to like about Monet's Garden's performance. Patiently ridden in a well-run contest, he was travelling best from some way out and was by no means fully extended in pulling clear to win by ten lengths. Monet's Garden, who cost IR £35,000 as a three-year-old, is the first foal of the unraced Royal Remainder. The next dam, also unraced, is a daughter of the useful sprinter Villa Marina. Monet's Garden, raced only on good and good to soft ground to date, isn't short of speed and will prove as effective over two and a half miles as at three. A good-topped chasing type, he has impressed with his jumping of hurdles and should prove equally adept over fences. *N. G. Richards*

MONEY CRAZY (FR)   5 ch.g. Green Tune (USA) – Value For Money (FR) (Highest Honor (FR)) [2003/4 19g 20g 16d⁶ 16s⁶ 17d Mar 3] leggy gelding: second foal: dam French middle-distance winner: well beaten in 2 races on Flat in French Provinces for R. Gibson: showed little over hurdles: blinkered last 2 starts. *Ian Williams*   **h–**

MONEY MAGIC   8 ch.m. Weld – Susie's Money (Seymour Hicks (FR)) [2003/4 c–: c26gᵖᵘ May 26] poor maiden pointer. *Miss S. E. Broadhurst*   **c–**

MONEY MOUNTAIN   7 ch.g. Rakaposhi King – Black H'Penny (Town And Country) [2003/4 F–: 20sᵖᵘ 16vᵖᵘ 22dᵖᵘ 17s Mar 23] workmanlike gelding: no sign of ability: wore cheekpieces final start. *J. A. B. Old*   **h–**

MONGER LANE   8 b.m. Karinga Bay – Grace Moore (Deep Run) [2003/4 h112: c22v* 24g⁶ 24sᵖᵘ Mar 20] tall, good sort: fair handicap hurdler: ran poorly last 2 starts: won match for mares novice at Towcester on chasing debut in January by distance: should be suited by 3m+: seems best on going softer than good: has looked tricky ride, and may benefit from headgear. *K. Bishop*   **c100** **h–**

MONJOYAU (FR)   4 br.g. Pistolet Bleu (IRE) – Ballet Dancer (FR) (Groom Dancer (USA)) [2003/4 16m* 16d⁵ 16s Nov 29] second foal: dam won at 12.5f: useful on Flat up to 1½m for H-A. Pantall: fairly useful form in juvenile hurdles, winning maiden at Galway in October by short head from Raikkonen: better subsequent effort when fifth to Berkeley Note at Punchestown. *E. J. O'Grady, Ireland*   **h113**

MONKERHOSTIN (FR)   7 b.g. Shining Steel – Ladoun (FR) (Kaldoun (FR)) [2003/4 c116, h131: 19g* 16d³ 16s⁴ 21d² 16g³ 24g* 21g* 20d⁶ Apr 3]   **c–** **h152**
Monkerhostin was a different horse in the latest season to the one who had ended the 2002/3 campaign. He had shown a useful level of ability over hurdles, with some good efforts among his performances, but on the whole the negatives had outweighed the positives. He had tended to find little in his races, been tried in a visor and with cheekpieces, had an attempt at reviving his chasing career quickly abandoned, and on his final start was reported to have had a breathing problem. But by the end of the latest season there were only positive things to be said about Monkerhostin. For a start, he was simply a better horse. He ended the season with a hurdles rating 21 lb higher than he had ended the previous campaign. On top of that, Monkerhostin proved most reliable, with a string of good efforts and a win at the Cheltenham Festival, and, having formerly seemed best at around two miles, showed much more versatility and stamina than previously, with good performances at up to three miles.

betfair.com Rendlesham Hurdle, Kempton—Monkerhostin (second left) swoops late to beat Mistanoora (blinkers), Deano's Beeno (diamonds on cap), Mon Villez and Kadara (No.9)

It was probably no coincidence that Monkerhostin's upturn in fortunes came with a change of stables. He had been involved in a pre-season swap with another of his owner's horses, Surprising, who had himself become largely disappointing. Monkerhostin moved from Oliver Sherwood to Philip Hobbs, while Surprising went the other way. It was a switch which brought dividends for all concerned because both horses made successful debuts for their respective new yards in November. Monkerhostin's win came under top weight in a two-mile-three-furlong handicap at Newbury and heralded a succession of good efforts in defeat in some of the most competitive handicaps of the winter. He came third to Overstrand in the William Hill Handicap at Sandown, fourth to Thesis in the Ladbroke at Ascot and was the only one to give Redemption a race when showing improved form upped to two miles five furlongs at Cheltenham on New Year's Day. Off his highest mark yet, Monkerhostin ran another fine race in a vintage renewal of the Tote Gold Trophy at Newbury, travelling well and holding every chance at the last before finishing third, just over a length behind Geos and stable-companion Rooster Booster.

Monkerhostin's rise up the handicap encouraged connections to contest a graded event next, the Rendlesham Hurdle at Kempton in February, though that meant a step up to three miles. Despite the longer trip, on good ground and an easy track, it was speed rather than stamina which proved decisive and Monkerhostin showed a much better turn of foot than his rivals, leading after the last to beat Mistanoora and Deano's Beeno by four lengths and the same, winning with plenty

Coral Cup (Handicap Hurdle), Cheltenham—Monkerhostin and 200/1-shot Court Shareef steal a march on favourite Rhinestone Cowboy (tracking winner)

to spare. The following month, Monkerhostin was returned to handicap company in the Coral Cup at Cheltenham. He was in the minority in the twenty-seven-strong field in being able to race off his proper handicap mark, due to the presence of Rhinestone Cowboy at the top of the weights. Rhinestone Cowboy also headed the betting, with Monkerhostin, the Tote Gold Trophy fourth Mughas and Irish-trained Rosaker the only others on offer at shorter than 10/1 and a third of the field starting at 100/1 or longer. Monkerhostin showed further improvement in beating one of the rank outsiders, Court Shareef, by a length, making rapid headway into contention four out, leading after the second last and finding plenty to hold off the runner up. Rhinestone Cowboy was beaten a total of just over two lengths in third, keeping on strongly after the first two had got away from him, and Mughas completed the frame. Monkerhostin took on Rhinestone Cowboy again, but at level weights, in the Aintree Hurdle on his final start and showed better form still to finish sixth, keeping on after most of the principals made their move on the opposite side of the track in the straight.

Monkerhostin (FR) (b.g. 1997)	Shining Steel (b 1986)	Kris (ch 1976)	Sharpen Up
			Doubly Sure
		Lady Moon (b 1980)	Mill Reef
			Moonlight Night
	Ladoun (FR) (b 1985)	Kaldoun (gr 1975)	Caro
			Katana
		Puntarella (ch 1971)	Dhaudevi
			Punta Ala

Mr M. G. St Quinton's "Monkerhostin"

Monkerhostin is by the very smart miler Shining Steel, winner of the Diomed Stakes for Henry Cecil at three and a Grade 2 event at Hollywood the following year. Like his dam's three previous winners (by Zayyani, L'Emigrant and Petit Loup), Monkerhostin was successful on the Flat in France, and also won over hurdles there before being sent to Britain. More importantly, Monkerhostin is also a half-brother to Eric's Charm (by Nikos) who made into a smart novice hurdler for Oliver Sherwood and Monkerhostin's owner in the latest season, initiating a family double when winning the race before the Rendlesham at Kempton. Both their dam Ladoun and grandam Puntarella won four races on the Flat in France, Ladoun winning at to an extended mile and three quarters and Puntarella at up to thirteen furlongs. Ladoun was also third on her only outing over hurdles and she is a half-sister to the dam of another novice who did well over hurdles in Britain in the latest season, Hirvine.

The lengthy Monkerhostin is effective at two miles to an easy three miles and acts on any going. He races freely and is held up. Monkerhostin is a most reliable gelding nowadays and the form he showed in the latest season reflects plenty of credit on his stable. He had two spells of chasing for his former yard, and, though he won over fences, his jumping generally let him down. However, if that is another department where he has polished up his act, Monkerhostin could prove to be well treated over fences now, given his much higher mark over hurdles. *P. J. Hobbs*

MONKSFORD   5 b.g. Minster Son – Mortify (Prince Sabo) [2003/4 h68+: 16d 17s 17d 16gro 17s5 17sF Apr 6] poor maiden hurdler: raced around 2m on good going or softer: ran out in ladies event fourth start. *B. J. Llewellyn* — **h71 +**

MONNAIE FORTE (IRE)   14 b.g. Strong Gale – Money Run (Deep Run) [2003/4 c21g4 Mar 12] lengthy, good-bodied gelding: veteran chaser, on long losing run: stays 25f: acts on soft and firm going: often sweats: sound jumper. *C. Storey* — **c77 +** **h–**

MONOCKY   9 b.g. Mon Tresor – Solbella (Starch Reduced) [2003/4 20m4 24spu Jan 23] little sign of ability. *Mrs D. A. Hamer* — **h–**

MONOLITH   6 b.g. Bigstone (IRE) – Ancara (Dancing Brave (USA)) [2003/4 h71p: 20g* 20d* 24d3 24d 20d2 Apr 10] compact gelding: much improved efforts over hurdles when winning maiden at Hexham and novice handicap at Bangor in May: good efforts when placed subsequently: stays 3m: raced on good going or softer. *L. Lungo* — **h107 +**

MON PETIT DIAMANT   4 b.f. Hector Protector (USA) – Desert Girl (Green Desert (USA)) [2003/4 16gur 17mpu Aug 1] maiden on Flat, little form in 2003: no form in 2 juvenile hurdles, tongue tied on second occasion: joined M. Polglase. *M. Wigham* — **h–**

MONSAL DALE (IRE)   5 ch.g. Desert King (IRE) – Zanella (IRE) (Nordico (USA)) [2003/4 17m6 16m 20g6 22g5 17s* 16d Jan 13] sturdy gelding: modest on Flat (stays 2m): best effort over hurdles when winning selling handicap at Folkestone in December: well held returned to Flat for N. Berry. *B. J. Llewellyn* — **h70**

MONSIEUR DELAGE   4 b.g. Overbury (IRE) – Sally Ho (Gildoran) [2003/4 F16g5 Mar 10] good-topped gelding: third foal: dam unraced: fifth in bumper at Catterick on debut. *N. Wilson* — **F74**

MONSIEUR MONET (IRE)   5 b.g. Norwich – Sue's A Lady (Le Moss) [2003/4 F16g F16d F20s* Apr 22] useful-looking gelding: half-brother to top-class staying chaser Sir Rembrandt (by Mandalus) and useful hurdler/fairly useful chaser up to 3m Audacter (by Strong Gale): dam Irish bumper winner: won completed start in points: easily best effort in bumpers when winning at Tipperary by 7 lengths from Remember Tom: will stay 3m. *S. Donohoe, Ireland* — **F102**

MONSIEUR POIROT (IRE)   7 b.g. Lapierre – Mallia Miss (IRE) (Executive Perk) [2003/4 h72: 24d 24g3 20m5 24g6 24dpu 16s3 c24g c16v2 c16gpu c20g c16d3 Apr 22] poor maiden hurdler/chaser: stays 3m: acts on heavy going, probably on good to firm: visored 5 of last 6 starts. *Mrs S. C. Bradburne* — **c74** **h74**

MONSIEUR PUNCH (FR)   5 b.g. Beyssac (FR) – Ferlia (FR) (Noir Et Or) [2003/4 18g 21g Dec 6] fourth foal: dam unraced: no show in 2 starts over hurdles. *P. Winkworth* — **h–**

MONSIEUR ROSE (IRE)   8 gr.g. Roselier (FR) – Derring Slipper (Derring Rose) [2003/4 16vF 16s 20s 26d3 27g3 Apr 22] dipped-backed gelding: modest novice hurdler: probably needs 3m+. *N. J. Gifford* — **h88**

MONSIEUR TAGEL (FR)   8 b.g. Tagel (USA) – Miss Zonissa (FR) (Zino) [2003/4   **c– §**
c110§, h106§: 22g 20m⁴ 21f⁶ 21g c20g 19g² 21d³ Mar 19] good-topped gelding: hurdler/   **h106 §**
chaser, on downgrade: stays 2¾m: acts on good to firm and heavy going: blinkered once:
sometimes lets down by jumping over fences: weak finisher and not to be trusted. *Ian
Williams*

MONTAGNETTE   10 ch.m. Gildoran – Deep Crevasse (Rolfe (USA)) [2003/4 h70:   **h67**
24vᵖᵘ 24g⁵ 24vᵖᵘ 24s⁴ 26s⁶ 22s 24g Feb 19] sparely-made mare: poor hurdler: stays 3¼m:
raced on good going or softer (acts on heavy). *M. R. Bosley*

MONTAYRAL (FR)   7 b.g. Lesotho (USA) – Demi Lune de Mars (FR) (Fast (FR))   **c136**
[2003/4 c–, h113: c22d c24gᵖᵘ c24gᵖᵘ c28g* c27g³ c29s 20s³ c25d³ c29d⁶ c29m³ Apr   **h111**
24] leggy gelding: fair hurdler: useful chaser: won quite valuable handicap at Cork in
November: good third to Puntal in very valuable handicap at Sandown in April: very stiff
task when pulled up in Grand Steeple-Chase de Paris in late-May: stays 29f: acts on good
to firm and heavy going. *P. Hughes, Ireland*

MONTEBANK (IRE)   8 b.g. Montelimar (USA) – Lady Glenbank (Tarboosh (USA))   **c–**
[2003/4 c25d⁴ c25g³ c20mᵖᵘ Dec 18] ex-Irish gelding: winning pointer, no form otherwise (trained by A. Kennedy before 2003/4): tried blinkered. *R. T. Phillips*

MONTE CINTO (FR)   4 br.g. Bulington (FR) – Algue Rouge (FR) (Perouges (FR))   **h103**
[2003/4 16s⁶ 16s³ 17v* 16dᶠ 16g Apr 12] ex-French gelding: first foal: dam winning
cross-country chaser: placed up to around 1½m on Flat: thrice-raced in juvenile hurdles
at Pau for T. Trapenard, winning in January: ran poorly final start. *P. F. Nicholls*

MONTE CRISTO (FR)   6 ch.g. Bigstone (IRE) – El Quahirah (FR) (Cadoudal (FR))   **c120**
[2003/4 c105, h108: 18g³ c17m* c20g⁴ c20sᵖᵘ c17s* c16s* c20g c18g⁶ c20g⁵ Apr 18]   **h–**
big, useful-looking gelding: winning hurdler: fairly useful handicap chaser: won at
Stratford in October and December and Fakenham in January: probably stays 2½m: acts
on heavy and good to firm going: effective blinkered/visored or not: none too reliable.
Mrs L. C. Taylor

MONTEFORTE   6 b.g. Alflora (IRE) – Double Dutch (Nicholas Bill) [2003/4 F16v*   **F113**
F16v² Jan 24] 66,000 4-y-o: lengthy, good sort: has reportedly had breathing operation:
sixth foal: half-brother to several winners, including fair hurdler Dutch Dyane (by
Alflora), stays 2¾m: dam useful stayer: won maiden Irish point on debut in 2002: useful
form in bumpers, winning at Towcester by 26 lengths from Riders Revenge and 1½
lengths second to Millenaire at Haydock in January: will stay at least 2½m. *J. A. B. Old*

MONTEL GIRL (IRE)   8 ch.m. Montelimar (USA) – Grassed (Busted) [2003/4 h75,   **h92**
F80: 24m* 27d² 26m⁴ 24m 24s⁵ 21dᶠ 27g⁶ Apr 22] small, angular mare: modest handicap
hurdler: won novice event at Worcester in June: stays 27f: acts on good to firm and good
to soft ground. *T. P. McGovern*

MONTEMOSS (IRE)   7 ch.g. Montelimar (USA) – Gaye Le Moss (Le Moss)   **c97**
[2003/4 h81, F–: 21vᵇᵈ 23d² 26s² c24dᵘʳ c25s² c32g Mar 17] medium-sized gelding: **h97**
modest maiden hurdler: similar form when second in maiden at Towcester on second start
in steeplechases: seemed to take little interest in valuable amateur novice at Cheltenham
final outing: thorough stayer: acts on soft going: sold 25,000 gns Doncaster May Sales.
M. G. Rimell

MONTENEGRO   6 br.g. Terimon – Spartan Sprite (Country Retreat) [2003/4 F16m   **F–**
May 26] workmanlike gelding: third foal: dam, winning chaser, stayed 3¼m: showed
little in bumper on debut: fourth in point in February. *Ferdy Murphy*

MONTE ROSA (IRE)   5 b.m. Supreme Leader – Green Thorn (IRE) (Ovac (ITY))   **F90**
[2003/4 F17g² Mar 28] €7,000 4-y-o: fourth foal: dam unraced: encouraging second to
Golden Odyssey in mares bumper at Market Rasen on debut. *N. G. Richards*

MONTE ROUGE (IRE)   7 ch.g. Montelimar (USA) – Drumdeels Star (IRE) (Le   **h–**
Bavard (FR)) [2003/4 h–: 20d⁶ 25s Jan 6] lengthy gelding: little worthwhile form in 3
starts over hurdles: bred to be suited by 2½m+. *Miss L. C. Siddall*

MONTESINO   5 b.g. Bishop of Cashel – Sutosky (Great Nephew) [2003/4 F84?: F16g   **h84**
17g 17d 16m 16m⁵ 16g² Nov 7] good-bodied gelding: signs of a little ability in 2   **F–**
bumpers: first worthwhile form over hurdles when second in handicap at Uttoxeter (wore
cheekpieces) in November. *R. C. Guest*

MONTESSORI MIO (FR)   5 b.g. Robellino (USA) – Child's Play (USA) (Sharpen   **c77 §**
Up) [2003/4 h99§: 16d² c21g² 21g c21s³ c24d³ c26gᵖᵘ Feb 22] rather angular gelding: **h99 §**
modest hurdler: sold out of Mrs M. Reveley's stable 16,000 gns Doncaster May Sales

after reappearance: didn't really take to fences: best around 2m: acts on good to firm and good to soft going: wears headgear: temperamental. *R. Ford*

MONTEVIDEO   4 b.g. Sadler's Wells (USA) – Montessori (Akarad (FR)) [2003/4 **h106 p** 16s 16s⁴ 16d³ Mar 21] leggy, useful-looking ex-Irish gelding: fairly useful on Flat (stays 2m), sold out of J. Oxx's stable €120,000 Goffs October Sale: better than results suggest first 2 starts over hurdles, improved form after when third in juvenile at Stratford in March and fifth in handicap at Punchestown (heavily-backed favourite) in late-April: will do better over further than 2m. *Jonjo O'Neill*

MONTEZUMA   11 br.m. Beveled (USA) – Miss Kuwait (The Brianstan) [2003/4 **c– x** c65x, h–§: 19s Dec 20] smallish mare: mistakes and signs of only a little ability over **h– §** fences: no form over hurdles: tried blinkered: temperamental. *N. A. Twiston-Davies*

MONTIFAULT (FR)   9 ch.g. Morespeed – Tarde (FR) (Kashtan (FR)) [2003/4 c138, **c127 d** h–: c26g³ c29g⁵ c24sᵖᵘ c24g c21g⁶ Apr 2] lengthy, rather sparely-made gelding: has had **h–** soft palate operation: fairly useful handicap chaser: best effort in 2003/4 when third to Lord Noelie at Cheltenham on reappearance: stays 3¼m: acts on good to firm and heavy going: has had tongue tied: jumps well: not one to rely on. *P. F. Nicholls*

MONTI FLYER   6 b.g. Terimon – Coole Pilate (Celtic Cone) [2003/4 F16m⁴ 21vᵖᵘ **h96** 21d 19s⁴ 23g³ 24g* 26g Apr 3] brother to fair hurdler/winning chaser Pontius, stays 27f, **F89** and half-brother to several above-average jumpers, including smart 3m chaser Lyreen Wonder (by Derrylin) and fairly useful staying chaser It's Himself (by Rakaposhi King): dam unraced sister to high-class 2m hurdler Cruising Altitude: fourth in bumper at Worcester on debut: modest form over hurdles: won handicap at Ludlow in March: stays 3m: raced on good going or softer over hurdles. *P. F. Nicholls*

MONTOSARI   5 ch.g. Persian Bold – Sartigila (Efisio) [2003/4 16d² 16g 16d Jan 10] **h83** strong gelding: modest on Flat (stays 13f): second in maiden at Fakenham on hurdling debut: well held both subsequent starts. *P. Mitchell*

MONTOYA (IRE)   5 b.g. Kylian (USA) – Saborinie (Prince Sabo) [2003/4 h95+: **h101** 16g² 16g³ May 30] close-coupled gelding: fair form over hurdles: will probably prove best around 2m: yet to race on extremes of ground over hurdles. *P. D. Cundell*

MONTPELIER (IRE)   11 b.g. Montelimar – Liscarton (Le Bavard (FR)) **c108 §** [2003/4 c–, h–: c24dᵘʳ c21g⁴ c24d⁴ c24d c24d² c17g⁴ c18g⁵ c16m⁵ Apr 15] rangy gelding: **h–** fair handicap chaser nowadays: probably stays 3m: acts on good to firm and heavy going: blinkered last 4 starts: idles markedly and often finds little. *N. J. Henderson*

MONTREAL (FR)   7 b. or br.g. Chamberlin (FR) – Massada (FR) (Kashtan (FR)) **c116** [2003/4 c130, h–: c25gᶠ c20m⁶ c22m⁴ c21dˢᵘ c24s⁶ c24gᵖᵘ c36dᶠ c24d⁴ Apr 12] leggy **h–** gelding: useful chaser at best: largely out of sorts in 2003/4: stays 25f when conditions aren't testing: acts on any going: tried visored: held up, and has idled/found little: has been let down by jumping. *M. C. Pipe*

MONTU   7 ch.g. Gunner B – Promitto (Roaring Riva) [2003/4 h–, F83?: 17gᶠ 17g 19s **h–** 20sᵖᵘ Feb 12] short-backed gelding: little sign of ability. *Miss K. M. George*

MONTY BE QUICK   8 ch.g. Mon Tresor – Spartiquick (Spartan General) [2003/4 **h–** h68, F–: 17gᵖᵘ 16gᵖᵘ 21sᶠ 20s 16g⁴ Apr 4] leggy gelding: poor maiden hurdler: stays 19f: acts on firm going: has had tongue tied: bled from nose fourth start: has pulled hard. *J. M. Castle*

MONTY FLOOD (IRE)   7 b.g. Camden Town – Clonroche Artic (Pauper) [2003/4 **h–** h–: 24vᵖᵘ Jan 10] rather leggy gelding: no form in 3 novice hurdles: joined Miss M. Rowland. *Ferdy Murphy*

MONTY MINT (IRE)   6 b.g. Broken Hearted – Montetan (IRE) (Montelimar (USA)) **F100** [2003/4 F16d* Feb 28] first foal: dam fair 2m hurdler: improved form in bumpers when winning at Fairyhouse on return from year off, beating Homer Wells 4 lengths. *Thomas Foley, Ireland*

MONTY'S DOUBLE (IRE)   7 b.g. Montelimar (USA) – Macamore Rose (Torus) **c99** [2003/4 h94: c21dᵖᵘ c25s³ c24d⁴ Apr 12] workmanlike gelding: modest form on second **h–** of 2 starts over hurdles: similar form over fences: better around 3m than shorter: acts on soft going. *O. Sherwood*

MONTY'S LASS (IRE)   8 b.m. Montelimar (USA) – Smash N Lass (Crash Course) **c93** [2003/4 c26s* Apr 29] third foal: dam won 2½m chase in Ireland: fair pointer: won novice hunter at Newton Abbot by 1¼ lengths from Legatus. *Mrs S. Prouse*

MONTY'S PASS (IRE) 11 b.g. Montelimar (USA) – Friars Pass (Monksfield) **c135**
[2003/4 c155, h109: 20g⁵ c24g 20s 16d c36d⁴ Apr 3] sturdy gelding: maiden hurdler: **h93**
handicap chaser, easily best effort when winning Martell Cognac Grand National at
Aintree in 2002/3: useful form otherwise, including when remote fourth to Amberleigh
House in latest renewal: stays 4½m: acts on any going: blinkered once (ran poorly): very
sound jumper. *James Joseph Mangan, Ireland*

MONTY'S QUEST (IRE) 9 b.g. Montelimar (USA) – A Bit of Luck (IRE) (Good **c109**
Thyne (USA)) [2003/4 c88, h85: c25d² c24g Apr 10] tall gelding: fair chaser: stays 25f: **h–**
acts on good to soft going, probably on soft. *P. Beaumont*

MONTY'S THEME (IRE) 10 b. or br.g. Montelimar (USA) – Theme Music (Tudor **c62**
Music) [2003/4 c–: c21m² c21gᵘʳ c20m⁴ c19g⁴ c24dᵖᵘ c21dᵘʳ Jan 2] workmanlike
gelding: winning chaser: little form since 2001: tried visored. *P. Wegmann*

MON VILLEZ (FR) 5 ch.g. Villez (USA) – Europa (Legend of France (USA)) **c135**
[2003/4 c134: c20s³ 20v* 20s* 21d⁵ 16s* 24g⁴ 21g Mar 17] tall, angular gelding: useful **h135**
chaser at Auteuil in 2002/3: good third in Group 1 there in May (final start for T. Civel):
useful novice over hurdles in Britain: won at Folkestone (conditional jockeys) and
Uttoxeter in December and Wetherby (Grade 2 Rossington Main Novices' Hurdle, beat
Le Passing 2 lengths) in February: effective at testing 2m to easy 3m: raced on good going
or softer (acts on heavy): sold reportedly to race in USA 100,000 gns Doncaster May
Sales. *N. J. Henderson*

MOODY BLUES (IRE) 10 ch.g. Orchestra – Blue Rainbow (Balinger) [2003/4 c–, **c69**
h78: c26g⁵ c22m⁶ 22m² 22f c24m² Oct 9] medium-sized gelding: poor maiden hurdler/ **h–**
chaser: trained first 2 starts by Miss G. Browne: probably stays 3¼m: acts on soft and
good to firm going: tried blinkered/visored. *A. M. Hales*

MOON 5 br.m. Simply Great (FR) – New Broom (IRE) (Brush Aside (USA)) [2003/4 **F–**
F16d F16g Mar 10] sparely-made mare: second foal: sister to winning 2m hurdler Witch's
Brew: dam, no sign of ability, half-sister to top-class chaser up 25f Simply Dashing (by
Simply Great): well beaten in 2 bumpers. *T. D. Easterby*

Propencity Rossington Main Novices' Hurdle, Wetherby—
Mon Villez (No.5) finds more under pressure than odds-on Le Passing

MOO

MOON COLONY 11 b.g. Top Ville – Honeymooning (USA) (Blushing Groom (FR)) **h86 d**
[2003/4 h90: 16v⁴ 20m⁴ 17f⁴ 21g⁴ 19gᵖᵘ Apr 18] angular gelding: modest hurdler: made
all in handicap at Uttoxeter in May: well below form subsequently: unlikely to stay
beyond 21f: acts on heavy going, probably on good to firm. *A. L. Forbes*

MOON EMPEROR 7 b.g. Emperor Jones (USA) – Sir Hollow (USA) (Sir Ivor **h99**
(USA)) [2003/4 16g⁴ 21g⁵ Mar 5] close-coupled gelding: fairly useful on Flat (stays 2m):
fair hurdler: acts on soft going. *J. R. Jenkins*

MOON GLOW (IRE) 8 b.g. Fayruz – Jarmar Moon (Unfuwain (USA)) [2003/4 c103, **c114**
h–: c16mᵖᵘ c16m* c16m³ c17g³ c16d² c16m³ c20m³ Oct 7] big, strong gelding: fair **h–**
handicap chaser: won at Newton Abbot in May: raced mainly around 2m: acts on firm and
good to soft going: effective blinkered or not: has been taken down early. *J. Gallagher*

MOONLAKE (IRE) 9 b.g. Durgam (USA) – Joyful Prospect (Hello Gorgeous (USA)) **c93**
[2003/4 c16f* c16fᵖᵘ Nov 22] rather leggy gelding: fair handicap hurdler in 2001/2: off **h–**
17 months, won maiden at Hexham on chasing debut: lame 2 months later: best around
2m: acts on soft and firm ground. *Ferdy Murphy*

MOONLIGHT DANCER 6 b.g. Polar Falcon (USA) – Guanhumara (Caerleon **h69**
(USA)) [2003/4 22g 17m 16m² 17d⁶ 22g⁶ 22m 16m Nov 9] fair on Flat (stayed 9f) at 3
yrs, well held in 2002, sold out of K. Burke's stable 1,100 gns Ascot July (2002) Sales:
poor on balance of form over hurdles: tried to refuse second start: dead. *Mrs S. Gardner*

MOONLIGHT GOLD 8 b.g. Jupiter Island – Moonlight Bay (Palm Track) [2003/4 **c–**
20dᵖᵘ 20d⁵ 17d 25dᵖᵘ c19gᵖᵘ Jan 15] brother to 11f winner Moonlight Calypso and 2m **h–**
winner Moonlight Eclipse: dam won 1m seller/juvenile hurdle: no sign of ability (lame
on chasing debut). *J. C. Haynes*

MOONLIGHTING 7 b.m. Lugana Beach – White Flash (Sure Blade (USA)) [2003/4 **c–**
c–, h–: 19mᵖᵘ 19mᵖᵘ Jun 11] no worthwhile form over jumps: tried blinkered/in cheek- **h–**
pieces: tongue tied once. *Mrs N. S. Sharpe*

MOONLITE MAGIC (IRE) 10 br.g. Phardante (FR) – Lucey Allen (Strong Gale) **c– §**
[2003/4 c71§, h–§: 26g May 18] smallish, lengthy gelding: poor hurdler/maiden chaser: **h– §**
stays 27f: acts on heavy ground: usually wears headgear: ungenuine. *Miss Z. C. Davison*

MOONLIT HARBOUR 5 b.g. Bal Harbour – Nuit de Lune (FR) (Crystal Palace **h109**
(FR)) [2003/4 F89: F16m* 17d* 20v² 17s* 20s 17d* Apr 10] medium-sized gelding: **F93**
successful twice in bumpers, including at Hexham in October: fair novice hurdler: won at
Sedgefield later in October and February and Carlisle in April: should stay beyond 17f:
acts on soft and good to firm going. *M. W. Easterby*

MOON MIST 6 gr.m. Accondy (IRE) – Lillies Brig (New Brig) [2003/4 20sᵖᵘ 16s **h–**
16v 24s⁵ 24vᵖᵘ 24sᵖᵘ Apr 21] tall mare: eighth foal: half-sister to winning hurdler/fair
chaser up to 25f Solsgirth (by Ardross): dam fair hunter chaser: little sign of ability.
N. W. Alexander

MOON SPINNER 7 b.m. Elmaamul (USA) – Lunabelle (Idiot's Delight) [2003/4 **h81 §**
h79§: 16m⁶ 16d* 16m³ 16g⁴ Jun 12] leggy mare: poor hurdler: won mares novice seller
at Stratford in May: stays 21f: acts on soft and good to firm going: wore cheekpieces last
3 starts: has had tongue tied: weak finisher and not one to trust. *J. M. Bradley*

MOONSTREAM 4 b.g. Terimon – Lunabelle (Idiot's Delight) [2003/4 F17s* F17s* **F102**
Feb 17] fourth foal: closely related to modest hurdler September Moon (by Bustino),
stays 2¾m, and half-brother to 2 winners, including fairly useful bumper performer

ggbet.com Betting Exchange Standard National Hunt Flat, Exeter—
Moonstream makes a winning debut

Sorrento (by Neltino): dam, winning 2m hurdler/chaser, half-sister to dam of useful hurdler up to 2½m Easter Ross: fairly useful form when winning bumpers at Exeter (beat Quid Pro Quo 1¼ lengths) in January and Folkestone (beat Eskimo Pie ½ length) in February. *N. J. Henderson*

MOONZIE LAIRD (IRE)   6 b. or br.g. Good Thyne (USA) – Sweet Roselier (IRE)   **h68** (Roselier (FR)) [2003/4 F94: 22m⁵ 24vᵖᵘ Jan 10] big, good-topped gelding: won bumper on debut: little impact since, including over hurdles: should stay well beyond 2m. *J. N. R. Billinge*

MOORAMANA   5 ch.g. Alflora (IRE) – Petit Primitive (Primitive Rising (USA))   **F93** [2003/4 F16d⁶ F16s⁴ F17d⁴ Mar 27] first foal: dam winning pointer: fair form when fourth in bumpers at Newcastle and Bangor: will stay beyond 2m. *P. Beaumont*

MOORE'S LAW (USA)   6 b.g. Technology (USA) – Brass Needles (USA) (Twice   **h118** Worthy (USA)) [2003/4 h126: 20m⁵ 20s⁶ 16d³ 20dᶠ Apr 12] leggy gelding: fairly useful hurdler: easily best effort in minor events in 2003/4 when third to Callow Lake at Clonmel: probably stays 21f: acts on good to soft and good to firm going. *M. J. Grassick, Ireland*

MOOR HALL HOPPER   8 gr.g. Rock Hopper – Forgiving (Jellaby) [2003/4 F–:   **c–** c16sᶠ c19dᶠ 17sᵖᵘ Feb 3] workmanlike gelding: no sign of ability. *M. Sheppard*   **h–**

MOORHALL (IRE)   5 b.g. Persian Bold – Never Told (IRE) (Classic Secret (USA))   **h–** [2003/4 h77: 20s 16m May 27] lightly-raced maiden hurdler, no form in 2003/4: tried tongue tied. *J. G. Cosgrave, Ireland*

MOORLAND MONARCH   6 b.g. Morpeth – Moorland Nell (Neltino) [2003/4   **h84** F17s F17m⁴ 19v 17g 24g⁵ 22sᵘʳ 22g⁶ Apr 10] sixth foal: brother to modest hurdler Baloo,   **F89 ?** stays 27f, and half-brother to winning pointer by Teamwork: dam of little account: better effort in bumpers at Newton Abbot when fourth to Bula's Quest: poor novice hurdler: running best race when attempting to run out and unseating last in handicap at Exeter: should stay beyond 2¾m: acts on soft going (bumper form on good to firm). *J. D. Frost*

MOORLANDS RETURN   5 b.g. Bob's Return (IRE) – Sandford Springs (USA)   **F98** (Robellino (USA)) [2003/4 F16d* F16s⁵ Mar 20] big, workmanlike gelding: third foal: half-brother to 2 winners by Then Again, including fairly useful chaser Moorlands Again, stays 4m: dam 11f winner: 33/1, won 17-runner bumper at Kempton on debut in February, showing plenty of resolution to beat Alfie's Sun ½ length: not discredited when fifth of 21 to Something Gold at Ascot: will be suited by further than 2m. *C. L. Tizzard*

MOOR LANE   12 b.g. Primitive Rising (USA) – Navos (Tyrnavos) [2003/4 c125:   **c125** c24m² c27d⁴ c22m³ Dec 10] tall gelding: fairly useful handicap chaser: best effort in 2003/4 when second of 5 to Chicuelo at Ascot, dictating pace: should stay beyond 3m: acts on soft and good to firm going: tried visored: usually races prominently. *A. M. Balding*

MOOR SPIRIT   7 b.g. Nomadic Way (USA) – Navos (Tyrnavos) [2003/4 F74: F17g   **c63** 20sᵖᵘ 25s 25g c21s c19gᶠ c25d⁴ c20dᵘʳ Apr 18] good-topped gelding: poor form in   **h–** bumpers and over fences, none over hurdles: stays 25f: raced on good going or softer: **F–** blinkered last 5 starts. *R. D. E. Woodhouse*

MOOSE MALLOY   7 ch.g. Formidable (USA) – Jolimo (Fortissimo) [2003/4 16s   **h– §** 16gᵖᵘ 16d Apr 12] workmanlike gelding: novice hurdler, little form since debut: usually blinkered, wore cheekpieces final start: ungenuine. *M. J. Ryan*

MORAL JUSTICE (IRE)   11 b.g. Lafontaine (USA) – Proven Right (IRE) (Kemal   **c94** (FR)) [2003/4 c99, h–: c21g⁵ c21g* c20m² c23m³ c22f² c21m⁴ c17fᵖᵘ c20m³ Oct 9] good-   **h–** topped gelding: modest handicap chaser: won at Newton Abbot in June: stays 25f: raced mainly on good going or firmer (acts on firm): tried visored: usually races prominently. *S. J. Gilmore*

MORAL SUPPORT (IRE)   12 ch.g. Zaffaran (USA) – Marians Pride (Pry) [2003/4   **c100 x** c113, h–: c26mᵖᵘ c26g⁵ c32g⁵ c26d⁵ c29s² c25sᵖᵘ Jan 20] angular gelding: formerly   **h–** useful handicap chaser: has deteriorated considerably, though would have won but for bad mistake 2 out at Plumpton penultimate start: stays 3¾m: acts on heavy going: not a fluent jumper: lazy. *J. S. Moore*

MORATORIUM (USA)   9 b.g. El Gran Senor (USA) – Substance (USA) (Diesis)   **h109** [2003/4 h126: 16m 17f 16g Sep 18] close-coupled gelding: fairly useful handicap hurdler at best, lightly raced and well held since reappearance in 2002/3: best around 2m: acts on firm and good to soft going: effective with or without blinkers: has worn tongue strap: takes good hold. *N. Meade, Ireland*

MORCHARD MILL   12 b.g. Out of Hand – Dorothy Jane (He Loves Me) [2003/4   c–
c23m⁴ c26dᵖᵘ 22f³ 26m⁴ Sep 10] no form outside points: tried blinkered/in cheekpieces.   h–
Jean-Rene Auvray

MORELUCK (IRE)   8 b.g. Roselier (FR) – Vulcan Belle (Royal Vulcan) [2003/4   c104
c16d³ c20sᵖᵘ c24g* c25sᵖᵘ c24d² c22g⁵ Apr 22] IR 24,000 3-y-o: good-topped gelding:
first foal: dam, tailed off in bumper, sister to one-time very smart chaser Royal Mountbrowne: won both starts in Irish points: fair novice chaser: won at Musselburgh in
February by 1¼ lengths from Another Chance: likely to prove better at 3m than shorter:
acts on good to soft going: wore cheekpieces final outing: has twice run as if amiss.
K. C. Bailey

MORE RAINBOWS (IRE)   4 b.g. Rainbows For Life (CAN) – Musical Myth (USA)   h113
(Crafty Prospector (USA)) [2003/4 16f* 16f³ 16m² 16g 16dᶠ Apr 13] sparely-made
gelding: fair maiden up to 1½m on Flat: fairly useful juvenile hurdler: successful at
Tramore and Tralee in August: ran well in face of stiff task when seventh in Grade 1 at
Punchestown in late-April: acts on firm ground. *N. Meade, Ireland*

MORLESS   5 b.m. Morpeth – Bush Radio (Hot Grove) [2003/4 h–: 17s 24gᵖᵘ Feb 21]   h–
no sign of ability. *Dr J. R. J. Naylor*

MORNING MELODY   6 b.m. Afzal – Pacific Overture (Southern Music) [2003/4   F–
F–: F16m F16g Aug 23] tailed off in bumpers: tried tongue tied. *Mrs N. S. Sharpe*

MORRIS DANCING (USA)   5 b.g. Rahy (USA) – Summer Dance (Sadler's Wells   h–
(USA)) [2003/4 20sᵖᵘ Apr 17] maiden on Flat, little form since 2 yrs: showed nothing on
hurdling debut. *B. P. J. Baugh*

MORRIS PIPER   11 b.g. Long Leave – Miss Cone (Celtic Cone) [2003/4 c19sᵖᵘ Apr 6]   c– §
sturdy gelding: fair pointer, won first 2 starts in 2004: little impact in hunter chases since
debut, very reluctant to set off at Exeter in April: has had tongue tied. *Mrs R. Partridge*

MORVERN (IRE)   4 ch.g. Titus Livius (FR) – Scotia Rose (Tap On Wood) [2003/4   h–
16g Mar 15] half-brother to one-time fair 2m hurdler Over The Counter (by Persian
Bold): modest maiden on Flat (stays 1¼m): no show in juvenile on hurdling debut.
J. G. Given

MORWICK MILL   10 b.g. Milieu – Charons Daughter (Another River) [2003/4   c–
c26gᵖᵘ May 26] of little account in points: blinkered only start in hunter chases. *S. Waugh*

MOSCOW COURT (IRE)   6 b.g. Moscow Society (USA) – Hogan Stand (Buckskin   h123
(FR)) [2003/4 F16v² F17m² 20f* 22d 22g* 24d⁴ 22s² 20d 20d³ 20dᵖᵘ Apr 11] IR £36,000   F96
3-y-o: fifth foal: half-brother to winning 2m hurdler/chaser My Galliano (by Muharib):
dam winning 2m hurdler: runner-up all 3 starts in bumpers: fairly useful novice hurdler:
won at Cork (maiden) in August and Thurles in November: best efforts when placed in
graded events at Limerick and Naas: stays 3m: probably acts on any going: tried tongue
tied. *Mrs J. Harrington, Ireland*

MOSCOW DANCER (IRE)   7 ch.g. Moscow Society (USA) – Cromhill Lady   h102 +
(Miner's Lamp) [2003/4 h–: 18g* 18d* 16s* Dec 13] big, strong gelding: chasing type:
has reportedly had breathing operation: much improved over hurdles in 2003/4, unbeaten
in 3 starts, winning conditional jockeys handicaps at Kelso and Haydock and amateur
handicap at Kelso in between: stays 2¼m: raced on good ground or softer (acts on soft).
P. Monteith

MOSCOW EXPRESS (IRE)   12 ch.g. Moscow Society (USA) – Corrielek (Mene-   c142 x
lek) [2003/4 c142x, h–: c20g² c20g² c24gᵘʳ c24m⁵ Oct 12] rangy gelding: one-time very   h–
smart chaser: best effort in 2003/4 when second of 5 to Go Roger Go in minor event at
Killarney second start: effective at 2½m to 3¼m: acted on any going: blinkered last 2
starts: effective tongue tied or not: often let down by jumping: reportedly retired.
Miss F. M. Crowley, Ireland

MOSCOW FIELDS (IRE)   6 ch.g. Moscow Society (USA) – Cloverlady (Decent   h80
Fellow) [2003/4 F91: 16g⁴ 19m Dec 10] tall, unfurnished gelding: runner-up in bumper
at Newbury on debut: poor form in 2 novice hurdles, breathing problem second time.
Miss H. C. Knight

MOSCOW FLYER (IRE)   10 b.g. Moscow Society (USA) – Meelick Lady (IRE)   c183
(Duky) [2003/4 c170p, h–: c16gᵘʳ c16m* c16d* c17d* c16gᵘʳ c20g* Apr 2]   h–
    Badsworth Boy, the only horse to win the Queen Mother Champion Chase
three times, won his first sixteen completed steeplechases. The brilliant Moscow
Flyer has now won his first completed fourteen but, if he's not careful, he will be

*William Hill-Tingle Creek Trophy Chase, Sandown—Moscow Flyer emphatically beats
the subsequent Champion Chase first and second Azertyuiop (left) and Flagship Uberalles*

joining Badsworth Boy as one of those champions whose reputation for making
calamitous jumping mistakes was in danger at times of overshadowing his outstanding merit.

Back in the late-'fifties and early-'sixties, Pas Seul earned an equivalent
Timeform rating of 183. He won the Cheltenham Gold Cup as a seven-year-old in
1960 and would have been winning the race for the second time had he not fallen at
the last the previous year when looking all over the winner. Dave Dick, who rode
Pas Seul when he was placed on two other occasions in the Gold Cup and when he
won the 1961 Whitbread under 12-0, reckoned that, but for his sometimes erratic
jumping, he would have been a match in his prime for Arkle and Mill House
(behind whom he finished third in the 1964 Gold Cup at the age of eleven after
being off the course for two years). 'Unfortunately, he used to go straight on sometimes,' said Dick. 'The Aintree fences take a bit of moving but Pas Seul moved the
frame of the twelfth when I rode him in the 1964 National. He pushed the bottom of
the fence out, but still didn't fall ... he never turned over and was on the floor the
other side of the fence with me still on him ... I stepped off and he was sitting there
like a dog—he'd knocked himself out.'

The 'seventies featured the tip-top Captain Christy (Timeform 182), the
most talked-about chaser of his era who inflicted a rare defeat on Pendil in the 1974
King George VI Chase and then beat Bula by thirty lengths in the race the following
year, setting a scorching gallop and beating the course record by more than four
seconds. He was the last novice to win the Gold Cup but his winning performance
in 1974 was marred by a monumental blunder at the last. Captain Christy was
something of a tearaway and, on occasions, gave the impression he was as likely to
plough through the fences as to clear them. He came to grief when almost a fence
clear at the second last in the Wills Premier Chase Final at Haydock.

The late-'eighties and early-'nineties saw another outstanding staying
chaser Carvill's Hill (Timeform 182) sometimes making headlines for the wrong
reasons. Twice a winner of what is now the Hennessy Gold Cup at Leopardstown,
the relentless, long-striding galloper Carvill's Hill also put up one of the finest
weight-carrying performances in Timeform's experience when galloping a good
field into the ground under 11-12 in the Welsh National. But he had a chequered
career, caused at times as much through injury and training troubles as through his
less-than-fluent jumping. He had a tendency to make the occasional unforced error

Paddy Power Dial-A-Bet Chase, Leopardstown—
a bold leap at the last secures a second successive win in the race

and fell at the seventh in the 1989 Cheltenham Gold Cup when attempting to win the race as a novice, frailties in his technique also contributing to his defeat when returning as a short-priced favourite for the 1992 edition in which he was controversially harried from the start by 150/1-shot Golden Freeze.

Badsworth Boy (Timeform 179) was normally an impressively quick jumper but he tended to keep low and brush through the top of his fences, a technique that left little margin for error. He fell four times over fences, unseated his rider twice and was once pulled up after making a very bad mistake. At his best, though, he was in a league of his own among the two-mile chasers around in the first half of the 'eighties and the highest-rated specialist two-miler since the mid-'sixties when the legendary Dunkirk, a very speedy horse by chasing standards and a natural front runner, achieved a Timeform rating of 186. Dunkirk's career was all too short and he was only eight when killed in a fall, running over his wrong trip, against Arkle in the King George VI Chase.

Moscow Flyer, whose perceived jumping deficiencies provided plenty of copy again in the latest season, has unseated his rider on three occasions and fallen twice in his nineteen steeplechases. His splendid winning record would undoubtedly have been improved upon had his jumping not proved fallible, but he has nonetheless taken very high rank among the chasers of Timeform's experience (back to the early-'sixties), his rating of 183 bettered only by Arkle (212), Flyingbolt (210), Mill House (191), Desert Orchid (187), Dunkirk (186) and Burrough Hill Lad (184). Incidentally, those great champions of the 'twenties and 'thirties, Easter Hero and Golden Miller, were rated 190 and 188 respectively in *A Century of Champions*, published by Timeform for John Randall and Tony Morris who extended the handicap to encompass all horses since 1900.

Always physically very much in the mould of a chaser, Moscow Flyer twice got the better, in his hurdling days, of three-times winner of the Champion Hurdle Istabraq, profiting, ironically, from uncharacteristic jumping lapses by Istabraq, in the December Festival Hurdle (which Istabraq wouldn't have won even if he had remained upright) and in the Shell Champion Hurdle. On the latter occasion, in the 2001 edition run at Leopardstown owing to the abandonment of Punchestown, Istabraq had clearly taken Moscow Flyer's measure when he fell at the last, but Moscow Flyer's form on the day was better than that shown by any of the two-mile hurdlers in Britain that season, or in the next. Moscow Flyer met Istabraq on only one other occasion, and was in front when falling himself two out in the AIG Europe Champion Hurdle in 2001. Moscow Flyer would have been good enough to win a Champion Hurdle in an average year and the decision to switch Moscow Flyer to fences in the 2001/2 season, when Istabraq ultimately proved a shadow of his former self, almost certainly—in hindsight—cost Moscow Flyer one or more Grade 1 victories over hurdles (the 2002 Champion Hurdle winner Hors La Loi had the dubious distinction of recording the lowest rating in *Chasers & Hurdlers* of any winner of the race).

A pelvic injury caused Moscow Flyer to miss the Cheltenham Festival as a novice hurdler, but he had the Supreme Novices' winner behind him when winning the Champion Novices' Hurdle at Punchestown. Cheltenham had to be abandoned due to the outbreak of foot and mouth the following year, the season when Moscow Flyer won the December Festival and the Shell Champion Hurdle. He made his first visit to Britain for the 2002 Arkle Trophy, though his record over fences by then included two falls in five starts which hardly instilled confidence before an above-average renewal of the two-mile novice chasers' championship. Starting fourth favourite behind Seebald—after heading the ante-post list for a time earlier in the season—Moscow Flyer jumped immaculately and put up a tremendous performance, achieving the second-highest rating (behind Bobsline) among Arkle winners in a twenty-five-year period. Moscow Flyer added the Swordlestown Cup at Punchestown, not jumping quite so well as at Cheltenham, to end his first season over fences with five wins from seven outings.

Moscow Flyer firmly established himself as the best two-mile chaser in training in his second season over fences, winning the Queen Mother Champion Chase by seven lengths and three from Native Upmanship and Cenkos. He failed to complete the course in Britain's second most important two-mile chase, the Tingle Creek Trophy at Sandown where his regular jockey Barry Geraghty was unseated after a collision with Flagship Uberalles, who stumbled in front of him at the fifth fence. While that exit was entirely excusable, the same could not be said of Moscow Flyer's departure at the second last in the BMW Chase at Punchestown in May (shortly after the start of the latest British season). He hardly took off at all and unseated his rider, leaving the race to Flagship Uberalles who looked as if he was about to become the first opponent to make a race of it with Moscow Flyer during

Martell Cognac Melling Chase, Aintree—
Cheltenham disappointments are banished with a smooth win over Isio

the campaign. Moscow Flyer had survived making a similar hash of the last when winning the Tied Cottage Chase over the same course on his final outing before the Cheltenham Festival.

After a summer's rest, Moscow Flyer returned to action in the Ballymore Homes Fortria Chase at Navan in early-November. Usually held up over fences, Moscow Flyer made the running for a change and quickened after the third last to land the odds from three opponents. Moscow Flyer had previously shown a tendency to idle when in front for too long, but his performance at Navan gave connections more options (Moscow Flyer had never been far away in his hurdle races and had dictated the pace when winning his first Grade 1, the Royal Bond at Fairyhouse). Moscow Flyer's next outing provided a mouth-watering clash with the latest Arkle winner Azertyuiop, who had given a breathtaking display at Cheltenham, matching Moscow Flyer's form in the race. Azertyuiop looked a magnificent prospect and started second favourite at 2/1 behind 6/4-shot Moscow Flyer in the William Hill-Tingle Creek Trophy at Sandown in December. Taking a good hold, Moscow Flyer tracked the leader Cenkos, who was seeking a second successive win in the race, until going on at the ninth of the thirteen fences. The expected stiff challenge from Azertyuiop never really materialised, Moscow Flyer having the race in safe keeping soon after quickening into the lead. Just kept up to his work after the last, Moscow Flyer came home four lengths in front of the strongly-ridden Azertyuiop, with third-placed Flagship Uberalles a further seven lengths back and another of the previous season's leading novices Le Roi Miguel fourth, and Cenkos fifth.

Moscow Flyer bettered his Queen Mother Champion Chase form by 7 lb on the bare result of the Tingle Creek. But the tempo of the race didn't really pick up until the runners were going down the far side (the time for the first third of the race was two seconds slower than for the preceding Grade 2 novice chase over the same distance won by Thisthatandtother). Moscow Flyer and Azertyuiop were still going away from the others as the post was reached and were value on the day—in our view at least—for a fair bit more than the distance they managed to put between themselves and the rest of the Tingle Creek field. Azertyuiop had parted company with his rider at the first on his reappearance and it is arguable that he might not have been quite at his peak at Sandown, though he was beaten fairly and squarely on the day. Azertyuiop put up a cracking performance when second under top weight in the Victor Chandler Chase at Ascot next time, one which made Moscow Flyer's Tingle Creek victory look all the more meritorious.

A second meeting between Moscow Flyer and Azertyuiop took place in the Queen Mother Champion Chase just over three months later, Moscow Flyer completing a straightforward victory in the interim at long odds on in the Paddy Power Dial-a-Bet Chase at Leopardstown's Christmas fixture. Moscow Flyer started at 6/5-on at Cheltenham, with Azertyuiop at 15/8, and was still going very well appro-

Betdaq.com Champion Chase, Punchestown—a fourteenth win from fourteen completed starts over fences; Rathgar Beau (right) prevails in the race for second

aching the fourth last. Moscow Flyer had made a mistake at the fence the previous year and he and Geraghty got it all wrong this time. Moscow Flyer didn't fall, but he belted the fence and gave his rider no chance of staying in the saddle. One of the potential highlights of the Festival—if not potentially *the* highlight—was reduced to a one-horse race. Azertyuiop quickened in tremendous fashion on the home turn and won by nine lengths from Flagship Uberalles. Moscow Flyer's rider reported that his mount had been 'too fresh' and had never really settled into a rhythm. 'He's better off with more racing [he had had a race between Christmas and Cheltenham in the two previous years] ... I had too much horse under me.'

Azertyuiop wasn't seen out again after Cheltenham but Moscow Flyer went on to contest Grade 1 events, as planned (hence his break after Christmas), at both Aintree and Punchestown. He atoned somewhat for his Cheltenham lapse when recording two more impressive victories. His presence in the line-up for the Martell Cognac Melling Chase—over two and a half miles—added spice to what is frequently one of the weakest Grade 1 events of the season. Moscow Flyer settled better than at Cheltenham and jumped well, apart from getting a little too close to the fifth. He went on to win by six lengths after a duel from the third last with the top-class Isio, Moscow Flyer asserting himself between the last two fences and going away on the run-in. Moscow Flyer passed the post ears pricked, with Native Upmanship, winner of the race in the two previous years, a further thirteen lengths behind Isio in third. Back at two miles for the Betdaq.com Champion Chase at Punchestown, shortly after the end of the British season, Moscow Flyer didn't need to run anywhere near his best in a field lacking a British-trained challenger. Leading four out and soon quickening clear, he was always in control and found more than enough, when shaken up, to hold off Rathgar Beau and Strong Run by two lengths and six.

Only three of the seven runners in the Melling Chase—Isio, Native Upmanship and 200/1-shot Strong Magic—had won over two and a half miles or further, and the muddling pace, coupled with the prevailing good going, didn't provide so stiff a test of Moscow Flyer's stamina as it might have done under different circumstances. A crack at the King George VI Chase at Kempton seems to be on the agenda for Moscow Flyer in the next season, though he is unlikely to meet Best Mate there. Moscow Flyer showed his form at two and a half miles over hurdles when second in the Hatton's Grace at Fairyhouse and there is no reason why he shouldn't stay three miles in the King George, given the conditions that usually prevail at Kempton, a flat course which drains well and favours the speedier type of chaser to some degree. Interestingly, in his early days, Moscow Flyer was not thought of by his connections as a prospective two-miler, especially after he failed to show enough speed to win any of his four starts in bumpers.

The strong, lengthy Moscow Flyer usually takes the eye in the paddock and stood out before both the Tingle Creek Trophy and the Queen Mother Champion Chase, looking in magnificent shape at Cheltenham in particular. There is no shortage of stamina in his pedigree. He is by the County Limerick-based Nijinsky stallion Moscow Society, who looked a smart stayer in the making when second in the two-mile Queen's Vase on what turned out to be the last of only three starts. Moscow Flyer's dam Meelick Lady never ran but is by the Prix du Cadran runner-up Duky out of Quiet Life, a winner over hurdles and twice over fences (at up to two and a quarter miles). Quiet Life is from a well-known jumping family, her dam the winning hurdler Brambling being a half-sister to the 1959 Champion Hurdle runner-up Ivy Green, and also to the prolific chasing mare from the 'fifties Bramble Tudor (winner of the Great Yorkshire Chase) and another mare successful over hurdles and fences, Indicate, whose offspring included the Topham and National Hunt Chase winner Artic Ale and the unraced Bardicate who, in turn, bred Green Bramble, Deviner, Polyfemus and Deep Bramble, chasers who were all fairly useful at least, the last-named a high-class performer who won the Ericsson Chase, the Anthony Mildmay, Peter Cazalet Handicap and the Agfa Diamond Chase. Moscow Flyer's achievements and reputation have resulted in some very high prices being paid at the sales for his younger siblings. When his sister—subsequently named Blooming Quick—was sent to the Derby Sale as a three-year-old in 2002 she fetched €215,000, breaking the record for a store filly. Blooming Quick is in training with David Wachman but has yet to race. A yearling half-brother by Luso made €80,000 at Tattersalls Ireland's November Sale in 2003.

Mr Brian Kearney's "Moscow Flyer"

	Moscow Society (USA) (ch 1985)	Nijinsky (b 1967)	Northern Dancer Flaming Page
		Afifa (ch 1974)	Dewan Hooplah
Moscow Flyer (IRE) (b.g. 1994)			
	Meelick Lady (IRE) (b 1988)	Duky (ch 1974)	Midsummer Night II Frondia
		Quiet Life (b 1972)	No Argument Brambling

     Two-mile chasers don't always get the recognition they deserve but, in Moscow Flyer and Azertyuiop, the sport currently has two of the best it has ever seen and should celebrate them while it can. Moscow Flyer is three years older than Azertyuiop so, with much hinging on what happens in the intervening year, it cannot be taken for granted that he will regain the two-mile championship at Cheltenham. No horse has done so since Royal Relief, who won the Champion Chase as an eight-year-old in 1972 and regained the title at the age of ten after coming second the year in between (he also finished second on two other occasions and was once third, making eight appearances in the race in all). Incidentally, the last defending champion to part company with his rider when trying to follow up in the Champion Chase was Lough Inagh who beat Royal Relief in 1975; Lough Inagh, a hot favourite in 1976, barely rose at the open ditch that was then in front of the stands, giving his rider no chance and, ironically, bringing down Royal Relief. Moscow Flyer is a grand sort—tough, genuine and consistent—and his splendid performances in the most recent season made him a deserving recipient of the Timeform Champion Jumper award, just ahead of Azertyuiop and three-times Gold Cup winner Best Mate. Moscow Flyer acts on good to firm and heavy going and has sometimes idled when in front. Much has been said and written on the subject

628

of his jumping but, though fallible, he is mostly fast and accurate. He also has a fine turn of foot. *Mrs J. Harrington, Ireland*

MOSCOW GOLD (IRE)   7 ch.g. Moscow Society (USA) – Vesper Time (The Parson) [2003/4 h–: c17d^F Mar 27] big gelding: bought £4,500 Ascot December Sales: no form: tried blinkered/tongue tied. *A. E. Price*   c–
h–

MOSCOW (IRE)   5 ch.g. Cadeaux Genereux – Madame Nureyev (USA) (Nureyev (USA)) [2003/4 19m^pu Oct 2] half-brother to 2 poor hurdlers: little form on Flat: showed nothing on hurdling debut. *P. D. Evans*   h–

MOSCOW LEADER (IRE)   6 ch.g. Moscow Society (USA) – Catrionas Castle (IRE) (Orchestra) [2003/4 F79: 20m^3 22g* 24m^2 21f^2 24d^3 c25g^F 22d* 20d* c16d^2 c19d c26d^3 c24v* c24d^F Mar 28] sturdy gelding: fair novice hurdler: won at Cartmel in August and handicaps at Kelso and Wetherby in December: similar form over fences: won novice handicap at Carlisle in March: stays 3¼m: acts on any going: wore cheekpieces 6 of last 7 starts. *R. C. Guest*   c105
h102

MOSCOW TRADITION (IRE)   6 b.g. Moscow Society (USA) – Bucks Grove (IRE) (Buckskin (FR)) [2003/4 h95: 17g^3 c20m^ur Sep 23] strong gelding: modest novice hurdler: far from fluent and losing touch when unseating ninth in handicap on chasing debut: placed in points in 2004: stays 21f: acts on heavy going: has shown signs of temperament. *Jonjo O'Neill*   c–
h77

MOSCOW WHISPER (IRE)   7 b.g. Moscow Society (USA) – Native Woodfire (IRE) (Mister Majestic) [2003/4 h105p, F85: 22d* 20m^2 Jun 1] modest form over hurdles: won novice at Stratford in May: will stay 3m. *P. J. Hobbs*   h96

MOSLOB (IRE)   7 b.g. Black Monday – Musical Millie (IRE) (Orchestra) [2003/4 26g^pu 21v^pu c24d^4 Apr 8] IR 600 4-y-o: third foal: half-brother to 3m hunter chase winner The Wipper (by Alphabatim): dam unraced sister to fairly useful chaser up to 2½m Shekels: won maiden Irish point in 2003: no show in 2 starts over hurdles: fourth of 5 finishers in novice at Ludlow on steeplechasing debut. *Miss J. S. Davis*   c–
h–

MOSS CAMPIAN   6 ch.g. Le Moss – Rose Rambler (Scallywag) [2003/4 F18s F17s 22g^pu Apr 22] 2,000 4-y-o: sixth foal: half-brother to 3 winners, including modest staying hurdler/chaser The Snow Burn (by River God): dam unraced sister to fairly useful staying chaser Naughty Future: no form in 2 bumpers and novice hurdle. *L. Wells*   h–
F–

MOSSCOW REALITY   11 ch.m. Le Moss – La Verite (Vitiges (FR)) [2003/4 20s Apr 17] lengthy mare: poor maiden hurdler: should stay 3m. *M. D. McMillan*   h–

MOSS HARVEY   9 ch.g. Le Moss – Wings Ground (Murrayfield) [2003/4 c121, h132: c24d^4 c20d^pu c20s* Apr 21] lengthy gelding: useful hurdler: fairly useful chaser: back to form when winning handicap at Perth by 3 lengths from Xaipete: will stay beyond 25f: raced on good going or softer (acts on heavy): has jumped markedly right over fences. *J. M. Jefferson*   c125
h–

MOSSPAT   5 b.g. Reprimand – Queen And Country (Town And Country) [2003/4 h–: 17d 16g 20d Aug 7] leggy, close-coupled gelding: no form over hurdles: tried in cheekpieces. *W. G. M. Turner*   h–

MOSS RUN (IRE)   10 b.g. Commanche Run – Glenreigh Moss (Le Moss) [2003/4 21s^5 22d^6 22g^3 20s^4 24s^6 23s^6 21d^6 Apr 11] good-bodied gelding: poor handicap hurdler: stays 3m: acts on soft and good to firm ground. *A. E. Jessop*   h76

MOSSY BAY   9 b.g. Phardante (FR) – Mossy Fern (Le Moss) [2003/4 22d^6 Jun 9] winning hurdler: off over 2 years, well held in handicap at Newton Abbot only start in 2003/4: stays 3¼m: raced mainly on good going. *O. Sherwood*   h92

MOSSY GREEN (IRE)   10 b.g. Moscow Society (USA) – Green Ajo (Green Shoon) [2003/4 h127+: c16d* c16d* c17d^4 c21d^2 c24g^F c20d^F Apr 13]   c150
h–

At an age when the majority of jumpers have reached their peak, Mossy Green was shaping as though his best days could still be ahead of him. That's not so surprising given how little racing he has had, and that the latest season was his first over fences. With just seventeen races under his belt, ten-year-old Mossy Green is still relatively inexperienced.

Mossy Green, who had won a maiden point in 2000 and a bumper in 2001, didn't begin his hurdling career until the 2002/3 season, when he showed fairly useful form and won a maiden at Naas from four starts. Mossy Green made a successful debut over fences in a maiden on the same course in November. Left in front at

Greenstar Syndicate's "Mossy Green"

the third, he stayed on very well to account for a good quality field, impressing with his jumping. It was a similar story the following month, in a novice event at Cork, where he again made most and, apart from one peck and a mistake two out, jumped fluently in winning by three quarters of a length from Hi Cloy. Mossy Green was then upped in class and failed to add to those wins, but he did acquit himself well on three of his four starts, the first two in Grade 1 events at Leopardstown, where he finished just over six lengths fourth to Kicking King in the Arkle Novices' Chase and a head second to Pizarro, with Hi Cloy third, in the Dr P. J. Moriarty Novices' Chase. In the latter, the front-running Mossy Green looked to have Pizarro in trouble after two out, but he edged left when ridden on the run-in and was caught close home. Once again Mossy Green jumped fluently, but he was let down by his jumping in his two subsequent races. The first of those came in the three-mile Royal & SunAlliance Chase at the Cheltenham Festival, where twelve months earlier he had finished well held in the Royal & SunAlliance Novices' Hurdle. Mossy Green was untried beyond twenty-one furlongs, but any thoughts that more patient tactics might be adopted in order to conserve his stamina soon disappeared. Mossy Green, a 20/1-chance, raced freely and was allowed to stride on following a mistake at the second and a none-too-fluent jump at the third, and held the advantage until joined by Our Vic going to two out, the pair disputing the lead when Mossy Green, still to be asked for his effort, fell at that fence, bringing down Pizarro. It couldn't be said with confidence that Mossy Green would have stayed, but had he done so he might well have won. As it was, his longer-priced stable-companion Rule Supreme took advantage of the mishaps around him and landed the prize. Mossy Green also fell on his only subsequent start, at the tenth in the Grade 1 Powers Gold Cup at Fairy-

630

house. It's possible his experience at Cheltenham had left his mark, as he hadn't been fluent at many of the previous fences, and this second fall will have done nothing for his confidence. It is to be hoped Mossy Green can recapture the fluency he showed on his first four starts. Provided he does, he could well pick up a good handicap, for he will start the next season on a good mark judged on the form he had seemed on the way to showing at Cheltenham.

Mossy Green (IRE) (b.g. 1994)	Moscow Society (USA) (ch 1985)	Nijinsky (b 1967)	Northern Dancer Flaming Page
		Afifa (ch 1974)	Dewan Hooplah
	Green Ajo (b 1978)	Green Shoon (b 1966)	Sheshoon Chrysoprase
		Ferrajo (b 1971)	Pretendre Elba

The workmanlike Mossy Green was a surprisingly late first foal for his unraced dam Green Ajo. She has continued to prove difficult to get in foal, despite numerous attempts, with just fillies by Teamster in 1999 and Moscow Society in 2001 to show for the effort. Green Ajo is a sister to the fairly useful staying hurdler/ chaser Ferromyn and to the dam of the useful hunter chaser Galway. There is not a lot else to be said about the family. Green Ajo is out of another unraced mare, Ferrajo. The third dam, Elba, was of little account on the racecourse but did produce three minor Flat winners abroad. Mossy Green is effective at two miles and shapes as though he will stay three. He has raced only on good ground or softer and acts on heavy. *W. P. Mullins, Ireland*

MOSTAKBEL (USA)   5 b. or br.g. Saint Ballado (CAN) – Shamlegh (USA) (Flying Paster (USA)) [2003/4 F16m² Jul 9] $160,000F, $430,000Y, 3,500 3-y-o: fourth foal: half-brother to 3 winners abroad: dam winning sprinter in USA: second of 18 to Assoon in bumper at Worcester on debut. *M. D. I. Usher*   **F85**

MOTCOMBE (IRE)   6 ch.m. Carroll House – Cooks Lawn (The Parson) [2003/4 F16g 17g³ 21g⁴ 21d⁵ 16s⁵ 20v² 22s² 22g Apr 10] good-bodied mare: fifth foal: half-sister to fair hurdler Dix Bay (by Teenoso), stays 2½m: dam, staying novice hurdler, half-sister to fairly useful chaser up to 25f Mr Frangipani: eighth in maiden bumper at Worcester on debut: modest novice hurdler: best effort when second of 18 to Noble Baron in handicap at Exeter penultimate outing: will stay 3m: acts on heavy ground: has run well when sweating. *R. H. Alner*   **h90** **F76**

MOTCOMB JAM (IRE)   7 b.g. Frimaire – Flying Flo Jo (USA) (Aloma's Ruler (USA)) [2003/4 h102: c20g³ c19m² c21d* c18g² c21m² Apr 15] rather leggy gelding: fair hurdler: fairly useful chaser: easily won weak novice at Fakenham in November: much better from after when second in novice handicaps at Newbury and Cheltenham: may prove best up to 21f: acts on good to soft and good to firm going. *C. J. Mann*   **c116** **h–**

MOTOWN MELODY (IRE)   6 b.m. Detroit Sam (FR) – Hester Ann (Proverb) [2003/4 F16m² F17m³ F17g² 20g Oct 27] 10,000 4-y-o: sister to fair hurdler/novice chaser Wise Reflection, stays 3m, and half-sister to fairly useful chaser Celtic Giant (by Celtic Cone), stayed 25f, and modest chaser Deependable (by Deep Run), stayed 3¼m: dam, placed up to 3m over hurdles, half-sister to useful 2m/2½m chaser The Dragon Master and useful staying hurdler Spider's Well: fair form when placed all 3 starts in bumpers: never in contention in mares novice on hurdling debut: should be suited by 2½m+. *C. L. Tizzard*   **h–** **F86**

MOULIN RICHE (FR)   4 b.g. Video Rock (FR) – Gintonique (FR) (Royal Charter (FR)) [2003/4 15s² 16s^ro 17g 18s² Apr 21] tall, lengthy gelding: first foal: dam won 4 times up to around 15f on Flat: twice-raced on Flat at 3 yrs, won at 1½m on debut: fairly useful form in juvenile hurdles, seventh of 18 finishers in Triumph Hurdle at Cheltenham, soon off bridle in rear tried in blinkers: travelling strongly when short of room and running out after 3 out at Sandown time before: won listed 4-y-o handicap at Auteuil in early-June: will stay at least 2½m: raced on good going or softer. *F. Doumen, France*   **h118 +**

MOUNSEY CASTLE   7 ch.g. Carlingford Castle – Gay Ticket (New Member) [2003/4 h104+, F89: 22g³ c23m* c24m² c24d³ c24d⁴ c20g* c20g⁵ Apr 3] good-topped gelding: fair hurdler: fairly useful novice chaser: won at Worcester in September and Sandown (handicap) in March, beating Burundi by ¾ length at latter: effective at 2½m to 3m: acts on good to firm and good to soft ground. *P. J. Hobbs*   **c116** **h106**

MOUNTAIN MAN (FR)   6 b.g. Cadoudal (FR) – Montagne Bleue (Legend of   h77
France (USA)) [2003/4 h79, F72: 20d⁴ 21d⁵ Mar 19] lengthy gelding: poor form in 3
starts over hurdles: stays 21f: front runner. *S. E. H. Sherwood*

MOUNTAIN MAYHEM (IRE)   6 br.g. Be My Native (USA) – Arctic Lucy (Lucifer   h–
(USA)) [2003/4 16d Nov 23] workmanlike gelding: half-brother to winning pointers by
Buckskin: dam placed in Irish points: runner-up on last of 3 starts in maiden Irish points
in 2003: tailed off in novice at Aintree on hurdling debut. *Jonjo O'Neill*

MOUNT CLERIGO (IRE)   6 b.g. Supreme Leader – Fair Ava (IRE) (Strong   F121
Gale) [2003/4 F17d* F16v* F16g² Feb 14]
          Having just landed the Ellier Developments Novices' Chase at Punches-
town in April, when Lord Sam battled home ahead of Hi Cloy, it would have been
understandable had trainer Victor Dartnall concentrated solely on the horse who is
currently the star of his small stable. Yet Dartnall also put in a good word for
another Supreme Leader gelding who looks set to make a name for himself over the
next few years. 'I have only eighteen horses and I am very lucky that among them I
have Lord Sam and another really good one in Mount Clerigo, who is bred on the
same lines,' said Dartnall. These are early days to be comparing Mount Clerigo
with Lord Sam, who was among the cream of the crop during his novice hurdling
campaign and is pencilled in for a crack at the King George VI Chase at Kempton
after a similarly promising first season over fences. However, Dartnall's optimism
is built on solid foundations. Few bumper horses in the latest season impressed as
much as Mount Clerigo. Indeed, he showed a higher level of form than Lord Sam
achieved in winning two bumpers in 2002 and, like his stablemate, looks the sort to
come into his own with time and the opportunity to tackle a longer trip.
          Mount Clerigo made his racecourse debut in a valuable bumper at Aintree
in November. With three previous winners and a handful of well-related newcomers from major yards, the sixteen-runner contest looked likely to be a race to
keep an eye on. Perhaps the late support for 20/1-shot Mount Clerigo came from
racegoers who had spent a few minutes assessing the field in the paddock. Mount
Clerigo took the eye much more than most and lived up to the good impression by
racing prominently throughout and galloping on resolutely to beat Supreme's
Legacy by two lengths. The subsequent Carlisle winner Sobraon was well clear of
the remainder in third, while Euro Leader and Salhood, who both went on to show
fairly useful form in novice company over hurdles, were among those who finished
in the ruck.
          Mount Clerigo made a trip to Uttoxeter seven weeks later. Demanding con-
ditions and a sound gallop proved too much for most of a big field, but Mount
Clerigo defied his 7-lb penalty to get the better of a protracted duel with the
newcomer Blushing Bull. Form produced under the gruelling conditions Uttoxeter
tends to provide in mid-winter can prove misleading. However, Mount Clerigo's
performance looked as good as any in a bumper to that point in the season. Though
he lost his unbeaten record next time at Newbury in February, Mount Clerigo
emerged with his reputation considerably enhanced. The AON Standard Open
National Hunt Flat Race, the last race on the Tote Gold Trophy card, has acquired a
reputation as a proving ground for top jumping prospects in recent years.
Monsignor, One Knight, Iris's Gift and Cornish Rebel had all gone on to Grade 1
success over jumps after recent renewals and, with eight individual winners on
show, the latest edition looked well up to scratch. Carrying a double penalty, Mount
Clerigo went off at 9/1 in a field of twenty-four. He was travelling like a winner as
he took up the running early in the straight and kept on after the four-year-old Secret
Ploy swept clear inside the final furlong, going down by four lengths with the
Ludlow winner Demarco a short head away in third and the rest well strung out.
Demarco failed to advertise the form when finishing only ninth in the Champion
Bumper at Cheltenham, but there is little doubt that Secret Ploy and Mount Clerigo
showed a level of form at Newbury at least as good, and probably slightly better,
than Total Enjoyment had to show to win at Cheltenham. Mount Clerigo was
quoted at 16/1 for the Cheltenham race after Newbury but his trainer chose not to
run him, feeling that the demands of the Champion Bumper are too severe for most
young horses.

Mr Stewart Andrew's "Mount Clerigo"

Mount Clerigo (IRE) (b.g. 1998)	Supreme Leader (b 1982)	Bustino (b 1971)	Busted / Ship Yard
		Princess Zena (b 1975)	Habitat / Guiding Light
	Fair Ava (IRE) (b 1989)	Strong Gale (br 1975)	Lord Gayle / Sterntau
		Fair Rullagh (b 1971)	Bluerullah / Fair Reply

   Mount Clerigo is a tall gelding with the scope and pedigree to make a cracking chaser in the longer term. He comes from a family in which stamina is the strong suit, its most notable performer Three Counties, a high-class hunter chaser who won the 1989 Foxhunter Chase at Cheltenham. Three Counties is out of Mount Clerigo's third dam Fair Reply who also produced a pair of fairly useful staying chasers in Kylogue Lady, who numbered the Troytown Chase among her wins, and No Lemon. Another of Fair Reply's offspring Kylogue Daisy is the dam of the Great Yorkshire Chase winner General Command and another fairly useful staying chaser Parsons Boy. One above-average performer in the family to buck the trend of stamina and chasing is Kilbue King, a fairly useful hurdler up to two and a half miles, who shares his grandam Fair Rullagh with Mount Clerigo. Mount Clerigo is the fourth foal and so far only winner out of the unraced Fair Ava. Mount Clerigo handled testing conditions very well at Uttoxeter and seemed fully effective on good ground at Newbury, on both occasions leaving the strong impression that he will be well suited by two and a half miles once he goes jumping. His return to action is eagerly awaited. *V. R. A. Dartnall*

MOUNT COOK (FR)   4 b.g. Gold And Steel (FR) – Debandade (FR) (Le Pontet (FR)) [2003/4 18s⁴ Jan 26] ex-French gelding: second foal: half-brother to fairly useful chaser Ladalko (by Kadalko): dam winning hurdler/chaser up to around 2¾m in France: successful twice up to around 1½m from 3 starts on Flat at 3 yrs for G. Cherel: not knocked about as he tired when 17 lengths fourth to Zimbabwe in juvenile at Fontwell on hurdling debut: should do better. *Mrs H. Dalton*   **h95 p**

MOUNTHOOLEY   8 ch.g. Karinga Bay – Gladys Emmanuel (Idiot's Delight) [2003/4 17d³ Nov 27] strong gelding: modest form at best in novice hurdles, off 19 months before only outing in 2003/4: likely to prove better at 2½m than shorter. *B. Mactaggart*   **h82**

MOUNT KARINGA   6 b.g. Karinga Bay – Candarela (Damister (USA)) [2003/4 F98: 19g⁴ 20d* 16d² 22m² 20s 20g² Apr 16] tall, useful-looking gelding: type to make a chaser: fairly useful hurdler: won novice at Chepstow in November comfortably by 8 lengths from Gigs Bounty: better form when runner-up in novice at Cheltenham (beaten 3½ lengths by Grey Report), handicap at Wincanton (beaten 1¾ lengths by Inca Trail) and novice at Ayr: will stay 3m: acts on good to soft and good to firm going, below form on soft. *P. F. Nicholls*   **h123**

MOUNT PRAGUE (IRE)   10 br.g. Lord Americo – Celtic Duchess (Ya Zaman (USA)) [2003/4 c119, h–: c24g⁶ c20gᶠ c21d² c20s² c18m³ c20m* c20g c20g⁵ c24dᵖᵘ Apr 12] sturdy gelding: fairly useful handicap chaser: won weak event at Leicester in December: stays 3m: acts on good to firm and heavy going: usually wears cheekpieces: usually races right-handed: none too reliable. *K. C. Bailey*   **c117 §**
h–

MOUNTRATH ROCK   7 b.m. Rock Hopper – Point of Law (Law Society (USA)) [2003/4 h73: 22g³ 20f³ Aug 25] small mare: poor and temperamental middle-distance stayer on Flat: poor hurdler: stays 2¾m: acts on firm going: often visored/blinkered: tongue tied: untrustworthy. *Miss B. Sanders*   **h71 §**

MOUNTS BAY   5 ch.m. Karinga Bay – Sweet On Willie (USA) (Master Willie) [2003/4 F17g⁴ F17f⁶ F16m F17g⁵ 17g Apr 10] third foal: dam, winning pointer, sister to useful middle-distance stayers Master Charlie and Willie Conquer: poor form in bumpers: well beaten in mares maiden on hurdling debut: pulls hard. *R. J. Hodges*   **h–**
F75

MOUNTSORREL (IRE)   5 b.g. Charnwood Forest (IRE) – Play The Queen (IRE) (King of Clubs) [2003/4 h–: 16m Jun 28] maiden on Flat, well held in 2003: no form over hurdles: has worn cheekpieces. *T. R. Wall*   **h–**

MOUNT VERNON (IRE)   8 b.g. Darshaan – Chellita (Habitat) [2003/4 h–: 16g 22m May 29] angular gelding: poor maiden hurdler: blinkered and tongue tied on debut. *P. Wegmann*   **h–**

MOUSESKI   10 b.g. Petoski – Worth Matravers (National Trust) [2003/4 c19s* Apr 6] modest hurdler in 2001/2: won 3-runner point in March and confirmed himself much improved when winning 16-runner hunter at Exeter, quickening clear 4 out but tiring late and all out to hold on: stays 19f: acts on soft going. *R. Barber*   **c100**
h–

MOVING EARTH (IRE)   11 b.g. Brush Aside (USA) – Park Breeze (IRE) (Strong Gale) [2003/4 c–§, h103§: c20d² c20m⁵ c24m⁵ 20m* c20mᵖᵘ Nov 16] lengthy gelding: has reportedly had soft palate operation: fairly useful handicap chaser: best effort when second to Ei Ei at Wetherby: successful all 3 completed outings over hurdles, getting up close home to beat Shamsan in handicap at Chepstow in October: best form around 2½m: acts on soft and good to firm going: has had tongue tied: has refused to race several times: one to treat with caution. *A. W. Carroll*   **c124 §**
h107 §

MR ALBERT (IRE)   5 ch.g. Flemensfirth (USA) – Parkroe Lady (IRE) (Deep Run) [2003/4 F17g Apr 24] 11,000 4-y-o: fifth foal: half-brother to winning hurdler around 2m Forest Leader (by Supreme Leader): dam unraced, from family of smart hurdler/chaser at 2½m+ The West Awake: eighth of 15 to Lockstockandbarrel in bumper at Market Rasen on debut. *T. D. Easterby*   **F79**

MR AUCHTERLONIE (IRE)   7 b.g. Mister Lord (USA) – Cahernane Girl (Bargello) [2003/4 F16m⁵ 18s⁵ 24s 22g Mar 28] IR 55,000 3-y-o, 76,000 4-y-o: lengthy gelding: half-brother to several winning staying jumpers, including useful chasers Over The Deel (by Over The River) and Smarty (by Royal Fountain), and useful bumper performer Inca (by Be My Native): dam winning hurdler/chaser in Ireland: fifth of 18 in bumper at Ayr on debut: best effort in novice hurdles when fifth of 19 to Steppes of Gold at Kelso: should be suited by 2½m+. *L. Lungo*   **h90**
F91

MR BANKER 9 b.g. Cashwyn – Flaming Fox (Healaugh Fox) [2003/4 c24g^{pu} c22s^R Mar 24] successful 3 times in points: no show in maiden chases at Chepstow (jumped poorly) and Towcester (behind when refused 3 out). *J. C. Tuck* **c–**

MR BAXTER BASICS 13 b.g. Lighter – Phyll-Tarquin (Tarqogan) [2003/4 c129, h–: c20m* c20d^{pu} c21g^5 c20f^2 c21d^{pu} Nov 22] tall gelding: fairly useful handicap chaser: won at Worcester in May by 2 lengths from Wave Rock, first success for over 3 years: stays easy 3m: acts on any going: makes mistakes: often weak finisher. *Miss Venetia Williams* **c129 x / h–**

MR BEN GUNN 12 ch.g. Newski (USA) – Long John Silvia (Celtic Cone) [2003/4 c90, h78: 20m^6 Aug 8] strong gelding: winning chaser/poor maiden hurdler: won point in April: stays 2½m: acts on firm and good to soft going. *J. D. Frost* **c– / h–**

MR BOO (IRE) 5 b.g. Needle Gun (IRE) – Dasi (Bonne Noel) [2003/4 F16d 16g Apr 12] ninth foal: half-brother to fair staying chaser Johneen (by Strong Gale): dam unraced half-sister to very smart hurdler up to 2½m Minorettes Girl, dam of high-class staying chaser Shotgun Willy, and high-class chaser at 2½m+ Observe: well held in bumper and novice hurdle. *D. B. Feek* **h– / F–**

MR BOSSMAN (IRE) 11 b.g. Jolly Jake (NZ) – Imperial Greeting (Be My Guest (USA)) [2003/4 c122, h–: c22m* c22g^6 c21g^{pu} Apr 2] rangy gelding: fairly useful handicap chaser: won at Kelso in May by 2 lengths from Act In Time: briefly left in lead 4 out when pulled up (reportedly lame) in Topham at Aintree: will stay 3m: acts on soft and good to firm going: tried blinkered, usually wears cheekpieces: often tongue tied. *R. C. Guest* **c123 / h–**

MR BUSBY 11 b.g. La Grange Music – Top-Anna (IRE) (Ela-Mana-Mou) [2003/4 c–, h–: c21g^3 c25g^{pu} c24s^{pu} Apr 17] strong, lengthy gelding: winning hurdler: maiden chaser: bought 1,000 gns Doncaster November Sales: form in hunters in 2004 only when third to Bohemian Spirit at Ayr: stays 21f: acts on good to firm and heavy going. *Michael Smith* **c86 / h–**

MR CAVALLO (IRE) 12 b.g. The Bart (USA) – Mrs Guru (Le Bavard (FR)) [2003/4 c–, h79: 27s^2 26g^6 24g^{pu} 24d^2 27g^4 20f Sep 14] compact gelding: poor handicap hurdler: stays 27f: probably unsuited by heavy going, acts on any other: blinkered once: has looked none too keen: none too consistent. *Miss Lucinda V. Russell* **c– / h76**

MR CHRISTIE 12 b.g. Doulab (USA) – Hi There (High Top) [2003/4 c–§, h84§: c24v 26s^4 24v 26s 27d^{pu} 24d 26d^4 22g Apr 24] sturdy gelding: poor hurdler: needs thorough test of stamina: has form on good to firm going, all wins on softer than good (acts on heavy): tried in headgear: tongue tied: very hard ride, gets behind, and one to steer clear of. *Miss L. C. Siddall* **c§§ / h71 §**

MR COOL 10 b.g. Jupiter Island – Laurel Diver (Celtic Cone) [2003/4 c–, h144: 25d 20g* 25d^2 21d^{pu} 20g Feb 22] workmanlike gelding: useful hurdler: made all in 4-runner Grade 2 PricewaterhouseCoopers Ascot Hurdle in November, beating Quazar a distance: remote second of 6 to Baracouda in Grade 1 at same course following month: ran poorly last 2 outings: probably stays 25f: acts on any going: usually forces pace. *M. C. Pipe* **c– / h144**

MR COONEY (IRE) 10 b.g. Van Der Linden (FR) – Green Orchid (Green Shoon) [2003/4 c25s^{pu} Feb 7] lightly raced in points, winning maiden in 2002: always behind in hunter on only start since. *J. Parkes* **h–**

MR COSPECTOR 7 b.g. Cosmonaut – L'Ancressaan (Dalsaan) [2003/4 c119, h–: 21g^{pu} c25g c20s* c24s* c19s^2 c24g^6 Mar 27] lengthy, angular gelding: winning hurdler: fairly useful chaser: won handicaps at Plumpton in December and Haydock (beat Jungle Jinks 1¾ lengths) in February: effective at 2½m to 3¼m: raced on good going or softer (acts on heavy). *D. L. Williams* **c125 / h–**

MR CUSTARD 12 b.g. Newski (USA) – May Owen (Master Owen) [2003/4 c–: c21s^{pu} Apr 29] workmanlike gelding: fair hunter chaser at best: stays 3m: acts on firm going, pulled up both outings on soft. *Miss L. J. C. Sweeting* **c–**

MR DON (IRE) 5 b.g. Mister Lord (USA) – Paradiso (IRE) (Phardante (FR)) [2003/4 F17g F17s 24s^{pu} 19v^{pu} 19g Mar 5] 4-y-o: second foal: dam unraced: no form in bumpers or over hurdles. *Mrs A. M. Thorpe* **h– / F–**

MR DOW JONES (IRE) 12 b.g. The Bart (USA) – Roseowen (Derring Rose) [2003/4 c110: c21s^5 c25g* c23v* c28g^3 c26m^4 c26v^2 c26g* c24g^6 c29d^2 c26m 27g^2 Apr 22] medium-sized gelding: fair chaser: won hunters at Hereford (fourth course win) and Uttoxeter in 2003 and handicap at Fontwell (by 5 lengths from Kouros des Obeaux) in February: similar form when ½-length second to Kattegat in handicap at Fontwell on hurdling debut: stays 29f: acts on heavy going: tough. *W. K. Goldsworthy* **c113 / h110**

MR ED (IRE) 6 ch.g. In The Wings – Center Moriches (IRE) (Magical Wonder (USA)) **h127 +**
[2003/4 h92: 19f² 20m* 20m* 21m² Nov 16] good-topped gelding: fairly useful on Flat
(stays 2m): fairly useful hurdler: progressed really well, winning novices at Huntingdon
and Aintree (by 8 lengths from Terre de Java) in October: neck second to Blue Away in
intermediate handicap at Cheltenham final start: will stay beyond 21f: acts on firm and
soft going: usually wears cheekpieces: patiently ridden. *P. Bowen*

MR EYE POPPER (IRE) 5 b.g. Sadler's Wells (USA) – Tipperary Tartan (Rarity) **h—**
[2003/4 F16g 21d Apr 12] 10,500 4-y-o: angular gelding: half-brother to several winners, **F—**
including high-class 2m hurdler Destriero (by Ile de Bourbon): dam, won at 1¼m on only
start, half-sister to dam of useful hurdler/chaser up to 3m Palette: well held in bumper and
maiden hurdle (dismounted at finish). *B. D. Leavy*

MR FISHER (IRE) 7 ch.g. Toulon – Parthian Opera (Dalsaan) [2003/4 19m⁵ 25dᵖᵘ **h—**
21dᶠ Mar 30] third foal: half-brother to bumper winner My Hand (by Hollow Hand): dam
unraced, out of half-sister to useful 2m hurdler French Hollow: no form in bumper (for
E. Hales) or 3 novice hurdles. *Miss E. Hill*

MR FLUFFY 7 br.g. Charmer – Hinton Bairn (Balinger) [2003/4 h113p: 24mᵘʳ 21m² **h123**
20mᶠ 21m Apr 14] leggy gelding: fairly useful hurdler: good second to Captain Zinzan in
handicap at Huntingdon: off 9 months, not unduly knocked about final start: likely to stay
3m: acts on good to soft and good to firm going. *P. J. Hobbs*

MR GEORGE 5 b.g. Whittingham (IRE) – Mossalier (Mazilier (USA)) [2003/4 **F—**
F17m Jun 21] 5,000Y: second foal: dam maiden who stayed 7f: refused to settle and hung
left when soundly beaten in bumper on debut. *B. J. Llewellyn*

MR GISBY (USA) 6 b. or br.g. Chief's Crown (USA) – Double Lock (Home Guard **h95**
(USA)) [2003/4 h83: 20g* 19d⁶ 18s 19g³ 19g 20d³ Apr 12] sparely-made gelding: modest
hurdler: won novice at Fakenham in October: stays 2½m: well beaten both starts on soft
ground: visored final outing: front runner/races prominently. *Mrs L. Wadham*

MR HICKMAN (IRE) 7 b.g. Montelimar (USA) – Cabin Glory (The Parson) [2003/4 **c92**
26g⁴ c21d⁴ c23m² c24s⁶ Jan 21] third foal: dam unraced: won maiden point on debut in **h83**
2003: distant fourth to easy winner Tom's Prize in novice at Southwell on hurdling debut:
best effort in novice chases when 1½ lengths second to Ankles Back at Leicester: likely
to prove better around 3m than shorter. *G. Prodromou*

MR HORNBLOWER (IRE) 10 ch.g. Orchestra – Garland (Night Star) [2003/4 **c—**
c16sᵖᵘ c25vᶠ c21sᵖᵘ c20g c26dᵖᵘ Apr 18] medium-sized gelding: modest winner over **h—**
hurdles in 2000/1: no form over fences after 3-year absence. *L. Lungo*

MR JAKE 11 b.g. Safawan – Miss Tealeaf (USA) (Lear Fan (USA)) [2003/4 c21sᵖᵘ **c—**
c25gᵖᵘ Apr 3] big, workmanlike gelding: poor hurdler/chaser: no show in 2 handicaps **h—**
after long lay-off: stays 3m: unraced on heavy going, acts on any other. *H. E. Haynes*

MR KERMIT 13 b.g. Rolfe (USA) – Sea Dart (Air Trooper) [2003/4 c24sᵖᵘ May 2] **c—**
small, sparely-made gelding: fair pointer nowadays, successful in 2003: tailed off by **h—**
halfway in novice hunter: stays 3m: acts on soft going: blinkered once. *Miss J. Froggatt*

MR LAGGAN 9 b.g. Tina's Pet – Galway Gal (Proverb) [2003/4 c72, h–: c25g c20g³ **c80**
c22g² c25m⁴ c24g⁴ c21m⁴ c20f* c20m⁴ c22m² c20m* c20g⁵ Jan 7] workmanlike gelding: **h—**
poor chaser: consistent in 2003/4, winning amateur handicaps at Hexham in September
and Musselburgh in December: stays 25f: acts on soft going, races on firmer nowadays
(acts on firm): has worn cheekpieces. *Miss Kate Milligan*

MR LEAR (USA) 5 b.g. Lear Fan (USA) – Majestic Mae (USA) (Crow (FR)) [2003/4 **h107**
16g 17d 16v* 17s* 16d⁵ Mar 22] sturdy gelding: fair on Flat (stays 13f), successful 3
times in 2003, sold out of T. D. Barron's stable 18,000 gns Newmarket Autumn Sales:
fair form over hurdles: won novice at Kelso and handicap at Sedgefield (showed good
attitude to beat Untidy Daughter 1¾ lengths), both in February: raced around 2m on good
going or softer (acts on heavy). *R. A. Fahey*

MR LEHMAN 7 ch.g. Presidium – Lehmans Lot (Oats) [2003/4 F79: F16m⁶ 16g⁵ **h69**
17gᶠ Apr 3] workmanlike gelding: modest form first 2 starts in bumpers: better effort **F72**
over hurdles when fifth of 18 in seller at Catterick. *Mrs M. Reveley*

MR MAGGET (IRE) 12 gr.g. Salluceva – Linda Dudley (Owen Dudley) [2003/4 **c— x**
c23m⁵ c23mᵖᵘ Jul 16] plain gelding: winning pointer: poor maiden steeplechaser, often **h—**
let down by jumping: tried in cheekpieces/blinkers. *D. P. Keane*

MR MAGNETIC (IRE) 13 b.g. Point North – Miss Ironside (General Ironside) **c— x**
[2003/4 c92x, h–: c24g May 31] medium-sized gelding: fair hunter chaser on his day, not **h—**

at best in 2003: thorough stayer: raced mainly on good going or softer (acts on soft): tried blinkered: sketchy jumper. *Dominic Harvey*

MR MAIIDLO 10 b.g. Rakaposhi King – Fedelm (Celtic Cone) [2003/4 c94§, h–: c25s^{pu} c24s^3 c21g^{pu} Apr 1] leggy, workmanlike gelding: modest chaser: won points in February and March: suited by 3m+: acts on heavy going: blinkered once, effective with or without cheekpieces: has had tongue tied: unreliable. *R. D. E. Woodhouse* **c86 §** **h–**

MR MARKHAM (IRE) 12 b.g. Naheez (USA) – Brighter Gail (Bustineto) [2003/4 c116, h–: 23m 24s^6 c28d Dec 31] workmanlike gelding: has been fired: fairly useful handicap chaser in 2002/3, never a factor at Fontwell on return to fences: better effort over hurdles in 2003/4 when sixth of 7 finishers to Battle Warning in handicap at Ascot: stays 29f: best form on going softer than good (acts on heavy): often blinkered, has been tried in cheekpieces: lazy. *N. J. Gifford* **c–** **h114**

MR MAX (IRE) 11 b.g. Parliament – Aria (Saintly Song) [2003/4 c34v^4 c25s^5 Apr 11] fair form in points in 2002, winning all 3 completed starts: not at best since, well beaten in 2 hunters in 2004. *Miss S. Caton* **c–**

MR MCAULEY (IRE) 6 b.g. Denel (FR) – Dusty Lane (IRE) (Electric) [2003/4 F16d^2 F16d* F16g^5 Mar 17] €30,000 4-y-o: good sort: second foal: brother to winning 3m hurdler World Vision: dam unraced, out of half-sister to top-class 2m to 3m hurdler Aonoch: useful form in bumpers: won at Down Royal in February by 10 lengths from Craanford Mill: looked very well, 10 lengths fifth of 24 to Total Enjoyment in Champion Bumper at Cheltenham: will be suited by more of a test of stamina: useful prospect for novice hurdles. *M. Halford, Ireland* **F115**

MR MCDUCK (IRE) 12 ch.g. Denel (FR) – Coldwater Morning (Laurence O) [2003/4 c–, h–: c21s^3 c22g* May 24] improved performer in points in 2003, and won hunter chase at Market Rasen: stays 2¾m: tried blinkered. *Ms S. Duell* **c91** **h–**

MR MCDUFF (IRE) 8 b.g. Mandalus – Le Glen (Le Bavard (FR)) [2003/4 c–, h88d: c16g^3 c16m^3 c17m^3 c17g^F 16m c17g^4 19f^3 16g^{ur} Oct 24] tall gelding: winning hurdler/ maiden chaser, little form for some time: tried visored: sold 4,500 gns Doncaster November Sales. *M. J. Gingell* **c80 d** **h–**

MR MIDAZ 5 ch.g. Danzig Connection (USA) – Marmy (Midyan (USA)) [2003/4 h83: 17d 17d^4 19d 18v 16g Apr 5] sturdy gelding: poor hurdler: will prove best around 2m: acts on good to soft going. *D. W. Whillans* **h78**

MR MIGHTY (IRE) 8 br.g. Montelimar (USA) – Laurie Belle (Boreen (FR)) [2003/4 c–: c20m c24m May 29] winning Irish pointer: no worthwhile form in hunter chases: tried tongue tied: headstrong. *N. J. Pewter* **c–**

MR MILLER (IRE) 12 b.g. The Bart (USA) – Celtic Connection (Martinmas) [2003/4 c58, h–: c26g^{pu} May 18] tall, sparely-made gelding: bad maiden steeplechaser: thorough stayer: acts on any going: often blinkered. *O. Sherwood* **c–** **h–**

MR MORRISSEY 7 ch.g. Karinga Bay – Barford Lass VII (Damsire Unregistered) [2003/4 24g^{pu} Mar 26] tall gelding: first foal: dam unraced: showed nothing in novice hurdle on debut. *K. Bishop* **h–**

MR MURPHY (IRE) 8 b.g. Un Desperado (FR) – Lady of Eilat (Cut Above) [2003/4 F16s^2 F16s^2 20d^5 16d* Mar 17] half-brother to high-class chaser up to 25f Bertone (by Montelimar) and bumper winner Barny (by Yashgan): dam fair maiden on Flat: fairly useful in bumpers: fair form over hurdles, won maiden at Down Royal in March easily by 10 lengths from Desperado Queen. *J. G. Cosgrave, Ireland* **h110** **F103**

MR MUSIC MAN (IRE) 11 b.g. Accordion – A New Rose (IRE) (Saher) [2003/4 c–, h–: c18g^6 c20d Mar 15] little form over jumps: tried blinkered: has had tongue tied: has looked none too keen. *Mrs G. Harvey* **c–** **h–**

MR NEMO (IRE) 8 b.g. Doubletour (USA) – Snowdrifter (Strong Gale) [2003/4 c27m^3 c20m^{ro} c22m^{pu} c20m^2 c19m^4 c24m^3 c24m^2 c26s^{pu} c25g^F Apr 4] lengthy gelding: third foal: dam won 2m hurdle: winning pointer: poor maiden steeplechaser: stays 27f: acts on good to firm going: tried in cheekpieces: temperamental. *Evan Williams* **c94 §**

MR NO MAN 8 b.g. Cosmonaut – Christmas Show (Petorius) [2003/4 h–: c20s^{pu} c22s^{pu} Mar 7] tall, strong gelding: winning hurdler: lightly raced and no form since 2001, including over fences: should stay at least 2½m: tongue tied last 4 starts. *T. J. Fitzgerald* **c–** **h–**

MR NORM 10 ch.g. Nomadic Way (USA) – Miss Puck (Tepukei) [2003/4 20g^{pu} May 22] poor maiden pointer: showed nothing in claiming hurdle. *I. A. Brown* **h–**

MR PERRY (IRE) 8 br.g. Perugino (USA) – Elegant Tune (USA) (Alysheba (USA))   c–
[2003/4 c–, h–: 16m³ 16m^pu 16m^pu 16g Mar 10] leggy gelding: twice-raced chaser: poor   h77
hurdler: raced mainly around 2m: acts on soft and good to firm going: visored once.
Mrs P. Ford

MR PHIPPS 8 b.g. Shareef Dancer (USA) – Frost In Summer (Busted) [2003/4 h78:   h82
22d⁶ 22s Mar 23] workmanlike gelding: poor form over hurdles: stays 2¾m. *R. T. Phillips*

MR PRESIDENT (GER) 5 b.g. Surako (GER) – Mostly Sure (IRE) (Sure Blade   h99
(USA)) [2003/4 16d³ Mar 24] successful up to 11f on Flat in Germany at 3 and 4 yrs for
U. Stoltefuss: third of 16 to Jonanaud in novice at Chepstow on hurdling debut, every
chance until mistake last. *Miss Venetia Williams*

MR RHUBARB (IRE) 6 ch.g. Shardari – Gale Griffin (IRE) (Strong Gale) [2003/4   h81
F17s F16m⁴ 21d 21d⁵ Mar 1] IR £6,200 3-y-o: angular gelding: first foal: dam winning   F89
pointer: much better effort in bumpers when fourth to Forager at Huntingdon: well held
in novice hurdles at Kempton (failed to settle) and Plumpton. *R. T. Phillips*

MRS BE (IRE) 8 ch.m. Be My Native (USA) – Kilbrack (Perspex) [2003/4 c24g² Feb   c97
11] angular mare: fairly useful pointer, unbeaten in 4 starts in 2003: second to Game
Gunner in hunter chase at Ludlow: will stay beyond 3m. *Mrs O. Cann*

MR SCONES 7 b.g. North Col – Thetford Chase (Relkino) [2003/4 16g May 22]   h–
4,100 4-y-o: seventh foal: dam maiden on Flat and over hurdles: signs of only a little
ability in bumpers and over hurdles. *M. Hourigan, Ireland*

MR SMUDGE 12 ch.g. Fearless Action (USA) – Amerian County (Amerian (USA))   c– §
[2003/4 c89§: c25d^pu c26v⁴ c24g⁶ Mar 12] workmanlike gelding: fair pointer, successful
3 times in 2003: winning hunter chaser, though often fails to impress with attitude: stays
25f: acts on good to firm going: one to treat with caution. *Mrs F. J. Marriott*

MR SNEAKY BOO (IRE) 8 b.g. Little Wolf – Florabalda (Kambalda) [2003/4   c118
c106p, h125: c17d³ c17g² c24f^pu 22d c22f^F Aug 17] lengthy gelding: fairly useful   h–
hurdler: winning chaser, let down by jumping after reappearance: should have stayed
beyond 2½m: acted on soft and good to firm going: tried blinkered: dead. *M. Hourigan,
Ireland*

MRS PHILIP 5 b.m. Puissance – Lightning Legacy (USA) (Super Concorde (USA))   h75
[2003/4 F89: 17m⁴ 19f* 19m² 16d 18g⁴ Mar 8] poor form over hurdles: landed odds in
4-runner mares novice at Exeter in October: stays 19f: raced mainly on good going or
firmer. *P. J. Hobbs*

MR SPLODGE 10 b.g. Gildoran – Ethels Course (Crash Course) [2003/4 c21g⁴ c20g⁴   c75
Mar 12] lengthy, angular gelding: fair pointer, successful in February and April: fourth   h–
both starts in maiden hunter chases: should stay beyond 21f: acts on heavy going.
Mrs T. J. Hill

MRS RITCHIE 7 b.m. Teenoso (USA) – Material Girl (Busted) [2003/4 F74: 19d⁴   h75
Mar 15] poor form in 2 mares bumpers: off nearly 2 years, fourth to Magalina in mares
maiden at Taunton on hurdling debut: will stay beyond 19f. *M. Pitman*

MR STITCH 7 br.g. Lancastrian – Hovian (Hotfoot) [2003/4 c–, h–, F–: c24g^pu 24g^pu   c–
c20m^pu 20d⁶ Nov 14] of no account: tried blinkered. *Mrs L. B. Normile*   h–

MRS WALLENSKY (IRE) 6 gr.m. Roselier (FR) – Shannon Dee (IRE) (Supreme   F104
Leader) [2003/4 F16d* F16s⁴ F16d² Apr 11] second foal: half-sister to winning pointer
by Be My Native: dam lightly-raced half-sister to NH Chase winner Loving Around and
useful hurdlers at 2½m+ Shannon Glen and Verrazano Bridge: won bumper at Clonmel
on debut in December: improved on each subsequent start, ¾-length second to Geill Sli
in well-contested event at Fairyhouse: will be well suited by 2½m+. *W. P. Mullins, Ireland*

MR TIM (IRE) 6 br.g. Naheez (USA) – Ari's Fashion (Aristocracy) [2003/4 F16v   F85
F17d F16s⁴ Apr 4] IR £50,000 3-y-o, 40,000 4-y-o: lengthy, useful-looking gelding: first
foal: dam, lightly-raced maiden, half-sister to dam of useful 2m hurdler Buckside: fair
form in bumpers last 2 starts, seventh to Sobraon at Carlisle and fourth to Dewasentah in
maiden at Hexham. *L. Lungo*

MR WHIZZ 7 ch.g. Manhal – Panienka (POL) (Dom Racine (FR)) [2003/4 16d⁶ 20g^F   h83 +
17g 17g⁶ 16d* Apr 12] rather sparely-made gelding: poor on Flat (stays 1¼m), successful
in January: in cheekpieces, easily best effort over hurdles when winning selling handicap
at Huntingdon in April: will prove best around 2m: acts on good to soft going: tried
tongue tied. *A. P. Jones*

MR WOODENTOP (IRE) 8 b.g. Roselier (FR) – Una's Polly (Pollerton) [2003/4 **c127**
c104p, h120: c24g^2 c24d* c29d^{pu} c22v^F c32g^{pu} c33d^{pu} Apr 17] leggy, close-coupled **h–**
gelding: unbeaten in 4 completed starts over hurdles: improved effort over fences when
winning handicap at Carlisle in November: failed to complete after, mostly in valuable
events: should stay beyond 25f: acts on heavy and good to firm going: has idled. *L. Lungo*

MR WOODLAND 10 br.g. Landyap (USA) – Wood Corner (Sit In The Corner **c112**
(USA)) [2003/4 c110, h–: c21m^{pu} c21m^5 c23g^{ur} Nov 4] quite good-topped gelding: fair **h–**
chaser: creditable effort on completed outing in handicaps in 2003/4: stays 3m: acts on
firm and soft going. *J. D. Frost*

MS TRUDE (IRE) 7 b.m. Montelimar (USA) – Pencil (Crash Course) [2003/4 h–: **c79**
c24m^{pu} c25g^6 c20s^3 c21m^3 c24g* c23g^{ur} c26f^4 17d c20m^F Mar 2] lengthy mare: no form **h–**
over hurdles: poor handicap chaser: made all in novice at Stratford in July: stays 3m: acts
on good to firm going: visored/blinkered last 6 starts. *A. W. Carroll*

MUALLAF (IRE) 12 b.g. Unfuwain (USA) – Honourable Sheba (USA) (Roberto **c– §**
(USA)) [2003/4 h–: 16m^{pu} 17g Jun 11] sturdy gelding: of little account: **h– §**
refused to race final outing. *Mrs A. M. Woodrow*

MUCKLE FLUGGA (IRE) 5 ch.m. Karinga Bay – Dancing Dove (IRE) (Denel **h66**
(FR)) [2003/4 F16d^5 21v 17s 16g Apr 5] rather unfurnished mare: second foal: dam, **F74**
fairly useful hurdler from 2m to 2¾m, half-sister to smart staying chaser Niki Dee: poor
form in mares bumper at Wetherby on debut: well held in 3 starts over hurdles: has pulled
hard. *N. G. Richards*

MUCK SAVAGE 7 b.g. Homo Sapien – Rare Luck (Rare One) [2003/4 h115: c23g* **c123**
c24s^4 c25d^{pu} Jan 1] workmanlike gelding: fair handicap hurdler: fairly useful form when **h–**
winning novice chase at Exeter in November, beating Supreme Prince a length: jumped
right when tailed off in Grade 2 novice next time, lame final outing: stays 3m: raced on
good going or softer (acts on soft). *C. J. Mann*

MUCKY MABEL (IRE) 5 b.m. Grand Plaisir (IRE) – Bolaney Girl (IRE) (Amazing **F–**
Bust) [2003/4 F17d Apr 18] €7,000 4-y-o: first foal: dam, unreliable winning hurdler
around 2m, half-sister to useful chaser up to 3m Nevada Gold: remote seventh, not
knocked about, in bumper at Carlisle on debut. *P. D. Niven*

MUGGY MOSS 6 b.m. Sovereign Water (FR) – Sudberry Lady (IRE) (Commanche **h–**
Run) [2003/4 F16g 20g 22f^5 24d^{pu} 24d 24v^{pu} Jan 31] second foal: dam lightly-raced, out **F–**
of half-sister to smart stayer Tug of War: no sign of ability. *Mrs J. C. McGregor*

MUGHAS (IRE) 5 b.g. Sadler's Wells (USA) – Quest of Passion (FR) (Saumarez) **h143**
[2003/4 h124: 20d 20d* 20d* 21s^3 16g^4 21g^4 24g Apr 2] good-topped gelding: useful
handicap hurdler: much improved in 2003/4, winning at Aintree in November and Chep-

*Freephone Stanley Children In Need Handicap Hurdle, Aintree—Mughas (spotted sleeves)
comes out on top against stable-companion Crystal d'Ainay (centre) and Hand Inn Hand*

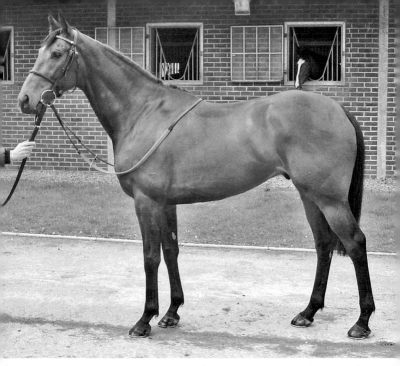

stow (beat Double Honour by 3 lengths) in December: creditable efforts when fourth at Newbury (to Geos in Tote Gold Trophy) and Cheltenham (beaten 4¾ lengths by Monkerhostin in 27-runner Coral Cup): should stay 3m (rather laboured effort final outing): acts on good to firm and heavy going. *A. King*

MUHARIB LADY (IRE)   9 b.m. Muharib (USA) – Brickhill Lady (Le Bavard (FR)) [2003/4 c80, h82: 27d 24m c24d⁵ c26m³ Aug 18] sturdy mare: poor hurdler/chaser, little form early in 2003/4: suited by 3m+: acts on firm and good to soft going. *P. G. Murphy*   **c72**
h–

MUHTADI (IRE)   11 br.g. Marju (IRE) – Moon Parade (Welsh Pageant) [2003/4 c–, h–: 16m 16g³ 17d⁴ Mar 30] workmanlike gelding: poor hurdler: raced mainly around 2m: acts on soft and good to firm going: blinkered. *S. B. Clark*   **c–**
h60

MUHTENBAR   4 b.g. Muhtarram (USA) – Ardenbar (Ardross) [2003/4 F16g Mar 17] first foal: dam winning 21f chaser: eleventh of 20 in bumper at Huntingdon on debut, eased final 1f as if amiss. *J. W. Payne*   **F–**

MULABEE (USA)   5 br.g. Gulch (USA) – Shir Dar (FR) (Lead On Time (USA)) [2003/4 16m 16s⁵ Nov 3] lengthy gelding: fairly useful 7f winner at 2 yrs, little form on Flat since: poor form both outings over hurdles: needs to jump better. *R. T. Phillips*   **h66**

MULAN PRINCESS (IRE)   4 b.f. Mukaddamah (USA) – Notley Park (Wolfhound (USA)) [2003/4 16m⁵ 17gʳᵒ Feb 19] modest on Flat (stays 8.5f): looked headstrong when last of 5 finishers in juvenile at Ascot on hurdling debut: ran out third in seller next time. *S. C. Burrough*   **h–**

MULGA BILL (NZ)   6 br.g. Carolingian (AUS) – Replica (NZ) (Creag-An-Sgor) [2003/4 16g May 22] half-brother to winning hurdler Modem (by Omnicorp), stays 21f: **h–**

unplaced in 4 starts up to 1m on Flat in New Zealand: well held in maiden on hurdling debut. *R. C. Guest*

MULKEV PRINCE (IRE)   13 b.g. Lancastrian – Waltzing Shoon (Green Shoon) [2003/4 c119, h–: c20m² c20f⁴ c16vᵖᵘ c20d⁴ c1/gᵘʳ c21d⁵ c20v⁴ c20g Apr 10] stocky gelding: fair handicap chaser, well below form last 4 starts: stays 2½m: acts on good to firm and heavy going: tried tongue tied: has worn off-side pricker: has won 3 times at Leicester: headstrong front runner, prone to the odd mistake. *D. Pearson*   c110 d
h–

MULLACASH (IRE)   6 b.g. Supreme Leader – The Parson's Line (The Parson) [2003/4 h111, F89: 16g² 20d² c20d⁵ c20d c25d² 18v³ c22s³ c20d² c24s Mar 6] rangy gelding: fair hurdler/maiden chaser: effective at 2m to 25f: acts on heavy going: blinkered last 2 starts. *N. Meade, Ireland*   c103
h110

MULLENSGROVE   10 b.g. Derrylin – Wedding Song (True Song) [2003/4 c99§, h–: c22g² c28g⁵ c24g³ c26g⁴ c25m* c26d c20d* c21gᵘʳ c24d⁵ c24s* Apr 17] good-topped gelding: useful hunter chaser: won at Ludlow (twice) in March and Bangor in April, going clear after 4 out when beating Omni Cosmo Touch 14 lengths at latter: stays 3¼m: acts on soft and good to firm going: has been reluctant to race: inconsistent. *D. Lowe*   c117 §
h–

MULLIGANS FOOL (IRE)   7 ch.m. Torus – Miss Mulligan (Whistling Deer) [2003/4 20gᵘʳ 16f⁴ 16f² 17s 20s 16d³ 17d⁴ Mar 10] angular ex-Irish mare: third foal: half-sister to fair staying hurdler/chaser Mulligan's Boy (by Buckskin): dam, 2¼m hurdle winner/winning stayer on Flat, half-sister to Cheltenham Gold Cup winner Mr Mulligan: third in bumper: modest maiden hurdler: left A. J. Martin after second outing: likely to stay beyond 2½m: acts on any going: wore cheekpieces final start: tried tongue tied. *A. M. Hales*   h87

MULLIGATAWNY (IRE)   10 br.g. Abednego – Mullangale (Strong Gale) [2003/4 h110: c21d³ c24s* Feb 12] lengthy, useful-looking gelding: fair handicap hurdler: much better effort over fences when winning novice handicap at Huntingdon by 2 lengths from Buzybakson, again jumping soundly and left in front 3 out: stays 3m: acts on heavy and good to firm going: still relatively lightly raced, and may do better still. *N. J. Gifford*   c117
h–

MULSANNE   6 b.g. Clantime – Prim Lass (Reprimand) [2003/4 h–: 16gᵖᵘ c16mᵖᵘ Jul 16] of no account: tried blinkered. *P. A. Pritchard*   c–
h–

MULTEEN RIVER (IRE)   8 b.g. Supreme Leader – Blackwater Mist (IRE) (King's Ride) [2003/4 h118p: c17m* c16g* c19d⁴ c16vᶠ c16s c18g⁴ c32g Mar 17] tall, useful-looking gelding: winning hurdler: successful first 2 starts over fences, at Southwell (maiden) in October and Huntingdon (4-runner novice) in November: didn't progress as expected, failing to convince with either jumping or temperament: stays 19f: acts on soft and good to firm going. *Jonjo O'Neill*   c115 x
h–

MULTIGIRL   7 br.m. Ballet Royal (USA) – Last Colours (Afzal) [2003/4 19m 20mᵖᵘ Jun 7] angular mare: no form over hurdles. *H. J. Manners*   h–

MULTI TALENTED (IRE)   8 b.g. Montelimar (USA) – Boro Glen (Furry Glen) [2003/4 c99: c24g⁴ c24m² c24d⁵ c26dᵖᵘ c26v² c24s* c30g⁵ c24s³ c26m c29m Apr 24] tall gelding: fair handicap chaser: won at Ascot in January by 11 lengths from Joe Deane despite mistakes: suited by 3m+: acts on good to firm and heavy going: blinkered last 5 outings: often looks hard ride, though has run well for amateur/conditional jockey. *L. Wells*   c113

MUMARIS (USA)   10 b. or br.g. Capote (USA) – Barakat (Bustino) [2003/4 c102, h–: c16d³ c16m² c16m⁴ c16s² c16d³ c20g⁶ c16v⁴ c20d² c19g⁴ c16s⁶ Mar 20] workmanlike gelding: fair handicap chaser: sold out of M. Campion's stable 5,000 gns Doncaster August Sales after second start: barely stays 2½m: acts on any going: effective in cheekpieces or without: usually sound jumper: has shown signs of temperament. *Miss Lucinda V. Russell*   c100
h–

MUMBLING (IRE)   6 ch.g. Dr Devious (IRE) – Valley Lights (IRE) (Dance of Life (USA)) [2003/4 16m* 17g⁶ 16d⁴ Nov 29] compact gelding: fairly useful on Flat (stays 1¾m), successful in June, sold out of M. Tompkins' stable 14,000 gns Newmarket Autumn Sales: won weak novice at Leicester on hurdling debut in November: better form in much stronger events at Exeter (sixth to Ashley Brook) and Newbury (fourth to Albuhera) later in month: will stay beyond 17f. *B. G. Powell*   h109

MUMUQA (IRE)   12 ch.g. Noalto – Princess Isabella (Divine Gift) [2003/4 c94, h–: c17g⁵ c17mᵖᵘ Aug 9] angular gelding: modest chaser: no show in 2 handicaps in 2003/4: best around 2m: acts on firm and good to soft going: blinkered once: front runner. *B. S. Rothwell*   c–
h–

MUNNY HILL 4 b.g. Golden Heights – More Laughter (Oats) [2003/4 F16d F16m Feb 21] leggy gelding: third foal: dam bad novice hurdler: showed nothing in 2 bumpers. *M. Appleby* **F–**

MUNSTER (IRE) 7 b.g. Zaffaran (USA) – Delway (Fidel) [2003/4 c19d² c17s* c16s³ c16d³ c29d^F Apr 12] IR 100,000 3-y-o: strong, rangy, good sort: fourth foal: dam twice-raced sister to very smart 2m hurdler Fidway: lightly-raced winning hurdler: fair chaser: won maiden at Fairyhouse in January: creditable efforts after when third to True Blue Victory in Grade 2 novice at Navan third start and fourth to Ballyamber in novice at Punchestown in late-April: should stay beyond 19f: acts on soft going: tongue tied. *A. L. T. Moore, Ireland* **c113 h–**

MUNTASIR 4 b.g. Rainbow Quest (USA) – Licorne (Sadler's Wells (USA)) [2003/4 F13d⁶ 16s 17s⁴ 20g⁶ 19g⁴ Mar 27] 320,000Y, 5,200 3-y-o: angular gelding: fifth foal: half-brother to useful 1¼m winner/one-time fair hurdler Dabus (by Kris): dam, fairly useful over middle distances, half-sister to Yorkshire Oaks winner Catchascatchcan: sixth of 11 in bumper on debut: poor form over hurdles: should stay beyond 19f: raced on good going or softer. *P. G. Murphy* **h80 F–**

MUQARRAR (IRE) 5 ch.h. Alhaarth (IRE) – Narjis (USA) (Blushing Groom (FR)) [2003/4 F–: F17m May 24] lengthy horse: well held in bumpers: modest maiden on Flat around 1m. *T. J. Fitzgerald* **F–**

MUQTADI (IRE) 6 b.g. Marju (IRE) – Kadwah (USA) (Mr Prospector (USA)) [2003/4 16m⁵ Oct 18] leggy gelding: modest on Flat (stays easy 1¼m), won in February: failed to settle and found little when fifth in seller at Stratford on hurdling debut: sold to join M. Quinn 4,200 gns Doncaster October Sales. *C. R. Dore* **h63**

MURAT (FR) 4 b.g. Useful (FR) – La Marianne (FR) (Don Roberto (USA)) [2003/4 17s² 17g³ 17g³ Feb 19] second foal: dam, winner around 1½m on Flat in France/in frame up to 2½m over jumps, half-sister to very smart 6f to 1m performer Faraway Times: fair form over hurdles, 5½ lengths third to Almaydan in maiden at Taunton final outing: ran as if amiss time before. *M. C. Pipe* **h102**

MURDINGA 5 br.g. Emperor Jones (USA) – Tintinara (Selkirk (USA)) [2003/4 16g³ 17s^pu 17s^pu 16g⁵ Apr 18] fair maiden on Flat (stays 1¼m), sold out of Lady Herries' stable 11,500 gns Newmarket July Sales: form over hurdles only when third to Optimaite in novice at Leicester. *A. M. Hales* **h94 d**

MURHILL'S PRIDE (IRE) 6 b.g. Great Marquess – Penny's Wishing (Clantime) [2003/4 F16m^ro F17m⁵ F16f² Oct 9] first foal: dam winning sprinter: poor form in bumpers: wore cheekpieces final start: has looked headstrong/wayward. *W. M. Brisbourne* **F70**

MURPHY'S CARDINAL (IRE) 8 b.g. Shernazar – Lady Swinford (Ardross) [2003/4 h128p, F97: c20s* Dec 3] tall gelding: unbeaten in 5 starts, winning bumper and 3 races over hurdles (fairly useful form) in 2002/3: landed odds in novice at Plumpton on chasing debut by 4 lengths from Guard Duty, jumping carefully (showed tendency to go right) but not fully extended: stays 3m: raced on soft/heavy ground: missed rest of season reportedly with pelvic problem but remains sort to do better over fences. *Noel T. Chance* **c118 p h–**

MURPHY'S NAILS (IRE) 7 b.g. Bob's Return (IRE) – Southern Run (Deep Run) [2003/4 F74: 16g⁴ 20m² May 26] lengthy gelding: blinkered, better effort over hurdles when second in maiden at Huntingdon, leading after halfway but hanging left 3 out and headed before last: sold £7,000 Ascot August Sales. *C. R. Egerton* **h96**

MURRAY RIVER (FR) 8 b.g. Esprit du Nord (USA) – Mulika (FR) (Procida (USA)) [2003/4 h125: 23m 20m⁶ c21g⁵ 17g³ 22m* 17m⁴ 22g² 19m² Oct 7] lengthy gelding: little impact on chasing debut: fair hurdler: landed odds in 2-finisher claimer at Stratford in August: stays 2¾m: acts on soft and good to firm ground: tried blinkered, usually visored: tongue tied: irresolute. *M. C. Pipe* **c– h105 §**

MURTAKEZ 4 b.g. Alhaarth (IRE) – Raaqiyya (USA) (Blushing Groom (FR)) [2003/4 16s^pu 17s 16v 16d 16g^F 16g^pu Apr 18] modest form at 2 yrs for M. Tregoning, well held in 2003, sold out of S. Dow's stable £2,500 Ascot October Sales: no aptitude for hurdling: headstrong (withdrawn once after bolting). *S. C. Burrough* **h–**

MURT'S MAN (IRE) 10 b.g. Be My Native (USA) – Autumn Queen (Menelek) [2003/4 c124: 27s c28s⁴ c31g³ c28d c26v Feb 7] good-topped gelding: useful handicap chaser at best: last on all 5 starts in 2003/4, including on hurdling debut (then left P. Nicholls): probably stays 29f: acts on heavy going: tried blinkered/in cheekpieces: ungenuine. *Ms Bridget Nicholls* **c121 § h–**

MURZIM   5 b.g. Salse (USA) – Guilty Secret (IRE) (Kris) [2003/4 16m⁶ Nov 1] fairly   h–
useful on Flat (stays 2m): last of 6 in novice at Ascot on hurdling debut. *J. Gallagher*

MUSALLY   7 ch.g. Muhtarram (USA) – Flourishing (IRE) (Trojan Fen) [2003/4 *c–,*   c76 x
h75; 21m² 26m4 26m4 21m* 24m¹ c20m¹² c20mᵘ² c20mᵖᵘ 20g⁴ 24f³ 20g⁴ 21g² 21d Mar   h90
14] angular gelding: poor form over fences, usually let down by jumping: modest hurdler:
won handicap at Ludlow in May and novice at Southwell in June: best up to 3m: acts on
firm going: usually patiently ridden. *W. Jenks*

MUSCADIN   6 br.g. Shaamit (IRE) – As Mustard (Keen) [2003/4 16g⁶ 20g⁶ 24g 22gᶠ   h–
Sep 6] unfurnished gelding: no worthwhile form over hurdles, sold out of A. Whillans'
stable 2,700 gns Doncaster August Sales after second start: resold 1,000 gns Doncaster
November Sales. *M. J. Gingell*

MUSCATELLI   7 b.m. Perpendicular – Small Money (Altosa Palace) [2003/4 F16g   F–
May 21] sixth foal: dam, winning hurdler/chaser, stayed 3¼m: tailed off in bumper on
debut. *R. D. Wylie*

MUSICAL STAGE (USA)   5 b.g. Theatrical – Changed Tune (USA) (Tunerup   h103
(USA)) [2003/4 16gᶠ 17sᵖᵘ 16d* 16g³ Apr 16] fairly useful on Flat (stays 1½m) as 3 yrs
for D. Weld: 50/1, won 15-runner novice hurdle at Huntingdon in March by 3½ lengths
from Mistrio: 21 lengths third of 4 to Chivalry in similar race at Ayr: raced around 2m:
acts on good to soft going: tongue tied after second outing. *P. R. Webber*

MUSIC TO MY EARS (IRE)   6 ch.g. Phardante (FR) – Evas Charm (Carlburg)   c–
[2003/4 F98: 20m* 19f* 21g⁴ c20fᵖᵘ Oct 29] workmanlike gelding: odds on, won novice   h92
hurdles at Worcester (idled run-in) in September and Market Rasen in October: suffered
hair-line fracture on chasing debut: will stay 3m: successful on firm (easy task) and soft
(in bumper) going. *Jonjo O'Neill*

MUSIMARO (FR)   6 b.g. Solid Illusion (USA) – Musimara (FR) (Margouillat (FR))   h87
[2003/4 h74p, F99: 20m⁵ 21g⁵ 20d 25sᵖᵘ 22s⁴ 20g⁵ 19d* 21d Apr 12] medium-sized
gelding: modest hurdler: won novice seller at Hereford in March, dictating pace: stays
2½m: acts on good to soft and good to firm going: tried blinkered, wore cheekpieces last
4 starts. *O. Sherwood*

MUSKATSTURM (GER)   5 b.g. Lecroix (GER) – Myrthe (GER) (Konigsstuhl   h78
(GER)) [2003/4 h89: 19gᵖᵘ 20d³ 20vᵖᵘ 21dᵖᵘ Mar 14] leggy gelding: poor on balance of
form over hurdles: stays 2½m: blinkered twice. *B. J. Curley*

MUSTANG MOLLY   12 br.m. Soldier Rose – Little 'n' Game (Convolvulus) [2003/4   c–
c80: c16dᵖᵘ c21gᵖᵘ c21sᵖᵘ Mar 19] lengthy, rather sparely-made mare: hunter chaser, has
lost her form: stays easy 3m: acts on firm going, probably on soft. *Andrew J. Martin*

MUST BITE   8 b.g. Bustino – Once Bitten (Brave Invader (USA)) [2003/4 h91: 22g   h113
22d* 22g² 22s⁶ Apr 6] fair handicap hurdler: much improved in 2003/4, winning at
Folkestone and second of 17 to Blackies All at Market Rasen in March: reportedly lame
final outing: stays 2¾m: raced on good going or softer (acts on soft): has flicked tail under
pressure. *Jonjo O'Neill*

MUTABARI (USA)   10 ch.g. Seeking The Gold (USA) – Cagey Exuberance (USA)   h–
(Exuberant (USA)) [2003/4 h62: 17g 16m Jun 18] poor on Flat: lightly raced and little
form over hurdles: tried visored/in cheekpieces. *J. L. Spearing*

MUTADARRA (IRE)   11 ch.g. Mujtahid (USA) – Silver Echo (Caerleon (USA))   c75 §
[2003/4 c–, h88: 16m⁵ 20m c16m 20m⁵ 19d² 18f 17g⁵ 22f⁴ 19fᶠ 16m⁴ 16f² 17g 19mᵘʳ   h86 §
c19g Dec 11] leggy, lengthy gelding: poor handicap hurdler: lightly raced over fences:
effective at 2m to easy 2¾m: acts on firm and good to soft going, possibly not on softer:
tried in cheekpieces: bled from nose final start: often amateur ridden: difficult to win
with. *J. W. Mullins*

MUTAKARRIM   7 ch.g. Mujtahid (USA) – Alyakhh (IRE) (Sadler's Wells (USA))   c114
[2003/4 h128: 16d 20f* 16f* c17mᵘʳ 16m² c16d³ c17dᶠ c16s* Jan 3] sturdy gelding: h127
useful on Flat (stays 1¾m): fairly useful hurdler: landed odds in intermediate events at
Cork and Punchestown in September: fair form over fences, 5 lengths third of 17 to
Mossy Green in strongly-contested maiden at Naas: fortunate to win similar event at
Cork: stays easy 2½m: acts on firm and good to soft going, not at best on softer: usually
blinkered. *D. K. Weld, Ireland*

MUTARED (IRE)   6 b.g. Marju (IRE) – Shahaada (USA) (Private Account (USA))   h–
[2003/4 17gᵖᵘ 16m Sep 27] fairly useful at best on all-weather on Flat (stays 1¼m), has
lost his form: no show either outing over hurdles. *N. P. Littmoden*

643

MUTINEER (IRE) 5 gr.g. Highest Honor (FR) – Miss Amy R (USA) (Deputy **h129**
Minister (CAN)) [2003/4 h128: 16g⁵ 20d 20s 20s⁶ 24s 19s* 24s³ 25g⁶ 22d Apr 12] good-
topped gelding: fairly useful hurdler: won handicap at Naas in January: creditable sixth
of 24 to Creon in valuable handicap at Cheltenham in March: stays 25f: acts on heavy
going: effective with or without blinkers: usually tongue tied. *D. T. Hughes, Ireland*

MVEZO 6 ch.g. Karinga Bay – Queen of The Celts (Celtic Cone) [2003/4 F16d Mar **F82**
19] third foal: dam failed to complete in novice hurdles: ninth of 19 in maiden bumper at
Warwick on debut, weakening closing stages. *Evan Williams*

MY ACE 6 b.m. Definite Article – Miss Springtime (Bluebird (USA)) [2003/4 h–, F83: **h73**
16m 17m 17m⁴ 16m³ 16m* 16f³ 16g² Mar 12] leggy mare: poor hurdler: won novice at
Ludlow in November: sold out of Mrs H. Dalton's stable 4,200 gns Doncaster January
Sales after next outing: raced around 2m: acts on firm going: best efforts over hurdles in
visor/blinkers: tongue tied last 5 outings: has looked none too keen. *James Moffatt*

MY BIG SISTER 5 gr.m. Thethingaboutitis (USA) – My Concordia (Belfort (FR)) **F–**
[2003/4 F17g Mar 28] fifth foal: half-sister to 5f winner Flapdoodle (by Superpower):
dam 1m winner: well beaten in mares bumper on debut. *A. W. Carroll*

MY BOLD BOYO 9 b.g. Never So Bold – My Rosie (Forzando) [2003/4 c–, h98: 22g **c–**
Apr 30] sturdy gelding: once-raced over fences: modest handicap hurdler: all 4 wins at **h–**
Exeter: stays 19f: acts on firm and soft going. *K. Bishop*

MY CARAIDD 8 b.m. Rakaposhi King – Tochenka (Fine Blue) [2003/4 16g Nov 6] **h–**
first foal: dam fairly useful staying chaser: well held in mares novice hurdle at Towcester
on debut. *D. G. Bridgwater*

MYDANTE (IRE) 9 b.m. Phardante (FR) – Carminda (Proverb) [2003/4 h105: c25g⁴ **c74**
c20d⁶ Mar 25] workmanlike mare: fair handicap hurdler: bought £6,000 Ascot November **h–**
Sales: off nearly 2 years, fourth of 6 to Golden Chimes in hunter at Catterick on chasing
debut: always outpaced over inadequate trip next time: stays 27f: acts on soft and firm
going: tried visored: has flashed tail. *S. Flook*

MY GALLIANO (IRE) 8 b.g. Muharib (USA) – Hogan Stand (Buckskin (FR)) **c89**
[2003/4 c86, h94: 16m³ 16m c16s* c16s⁴ 16s⁴ 16g Mar 7] sparely-made gelding: modest **h99**
hurdler/chaser: won handicap over fences at Huntingdon in December: best around 2m:
acts on firm and soft going. *B. G. Powell*

MY GOOD SON (NZ) 9 b.g. The Son (NZ) – Meadow Hall (NZ) (Pikehall (USA)) **c–**
[2003/4 c87, h97: 22m³ Jul 13] rather sparely-made gelding: modest handicap hurdler/ **h94**
chaser: stays 3¼m: acts on any going: effective blinkered or not: tongue tied once (pulled
up). *Ian Williams*

MY LADY LINK (FR) 5 bl.m. Sleeping Car (FR) – Cadoudaline (FR) (Cadoudal **c105**
(FR)) [2003/4 18d² 18d 18s³ 17s 18s 18s³ c17s⁴ c17v* c20d c24gᵘʳ Mar 5] **h105**
ex-French mare: fourth foal: dam won 3 times up to 13f on Flat in France: fair maiden
hurdler: similar form over fences, won claimer (claimed from T. Trapenard €26,000) at
Auteuil in November: showing more than on British debut (though still running below
best) when unseating 2 out in novice at Doncaster: should stay beyond 2¼m: raced
mainly on ground softer than good (acts on heavy). *Miss Venetia Williams*

MY LAST BEAN (IRE) 7 gr.g. Soviet Lad (USA) – Meanz Beanz (High Top) [2003/4 **h107**
16s⁴ 16d⁴ 16g* 16d 16gᵖᵘ Apr 2] lengthy gelding: half-brother to 2 winning hurdlers,
including Bean King (by Ardross), fairly useful around 2m: fair on Flat (stays 13f, usually
blinkered): fair novice hurdler: won 15-runner event at Musselburgh in January by 6
lengths from Factor Fifteen: very stiff task final outing: will stay beyond 2m. *B. Smart*

MY LEGAL EAGLE (IRE) 10 b.g. Law Society (USA) – Majestic Nurse (On Your **h100 +**
Mark) [2003/4 16g* Sep 6] rather sparely-made gelding: fair handicap hurdler: fit
from run on Flat, won 9-runner event at Stratford: should stay 2½m: acts on soft and
good to firm going: in very good form on Flat in 2004, winning 4 times by early-June.
R. J. Price

MY LINE 7 b.g. Perpendicular – My Desire (Grey Desire) [2003/4 h93+: 17m² 17m* **h112**
17d⁴ 17d² 16d⁶ 23d³ 22s² 20d³ 24g* 24m* Apr 14] sturdy gelding: fair hurdler: won
handicap at Carlisle in October and novice handicaps at Ayr in March and Cheltenham in
April: improved form when beating Parsons Legacy ¾ length at last-named, keeping on
strongly to lead close home: will prove best at 3m+: acts on soft and good to firm going:
often looks hard ride, and tried blinkered (including at Ayr): not a fluent jumper: patiently
ridden. *Mrs M. Reveley*

MYLO 6 gr.g. Faustus (USA) – Bellifontaine (FR) (Bellypha) [2003/4 h95, F100: 16g³ 19g² 17m⁴ 20s⁵ Apr 17] compact gelding: modest maiden hurdler: stays 2½m: acts on soft going: blinkered third outing: none too resolute. *Jonjo O'Neill* **h91 §**

MYLO (GER) 5 b.h. Second Set (IRE) – Meerdunung (EG) (Tauchsport (EG)) [2003/4 c18g³ c18d⁴ c16g³ c24dᵖᵘ Feb 2] tall, good-topped horse: in frame at Vittel and Baden-Baden for U. Suter first 2 starts over fences: no form in 2 novice chases at Kempton, jumping badly left (has worn near-side pricker): won at 12.5f on Flat in April for M. Hofer. *C. Von Der Recke, Germany* **c?**

MY MAITE (IRE) 5 b.g. Komaite (USA) – Mena (Blakeney) [2003/4 17s Dec 16] modest on Flat (stays 1½m): tongue tied, tailed off in novice on hurdling debut. *R. Ingram* **h–**

MY MATE WHITEY (IRE) 5 ch.g. Millkom – Imagery (Vision (USA)) [2003/4 h–: 20m May 26] medium-sized gelding: no form. *M. A. Allen* **h–**

MY NATIVE CORK (IRE) 9 b.m. Be My Native (USA) – Autumn Glen (Furry Glen) [2003/4 16d 16gᵖᵘ Jun 6] no form over hurdles: tried tongue tied. *A. J. Martin, Ireland* **h–**

MY PAL VAL (IRE) 4 br.g. Classic Cliche (IRE) – Lessons Lass (IRE) (Doyoun) [2003/4 F14d Mar 22] second foal: dam, fairly useful hurdler who stayed 21f, out of half-sister to dam of top-class staying chaser Behrajan: seventh of 14, not knocked about, to Flying Falcon in bumper at Hereford on debut. *Miss H. C. Knight* **F–**

MY RETREAT (USA) 7 b.g. Hermitage (USA) – My Jessica Ann (USA) (Native Rythm) [2003/4 17s 16v² 16s⁵ 17s 16d Mar 1] modest on Flat (should stay 1¼m), sold out of G. L. Moore's stable £1,500 Ascot October Sales: poor form over hurdles. *R. Fielder* **h83**

MY SHARP GREY 5 gr.m. Tragic Role (USA) – Sharp Anne (Belfort (FR)) [2003/4 17fᵗᵗʳ 16m³ 16g* 16s² 16mᵘʳ 16m* 16g* 16g⁶ 16g 16g⁴ Mar 7] sparely-made mare: modest maiden on Flat (stays 1¼m), claimed from A. Charlton £5,600 in September: modest hurdler: won seller at Stratford in October and, after being claimed from M. Pipe £6,000 fourth start, seller in November and mares handicap in December, both at Ludlow: will prove best at 2m: acts on good to firm going, probably on soft: refused to race on hurdling debut (visored). *J. Gallagher* **h94 +**

MYSON (IRE) 5 ch.g. Accordion – Ah Suzie (IRE) (King's Ride) [2003/4 h97, F79: 18g 21vᵖᵘ c16g⁴ c16d⁵ Jan 2] maiden hurdler: better effort over fences at Folkestone when around 16 lengths fifth to impressive Ladalko in maiden: should be suited by further than 2m. *D. B. Feek* **c83**
 h–

MYSTERI DANCER 6 b.g. Rudimentary (USA) – Mystery Ship (Decoy Boy) [2003/4 h86: 16gᶠ 16m* Aug 9] modest hurdler: improved effort when winning conditional jockeys handicap at Stratford: likely to prove best around 2m. *P. J. Hobbs* **h96**

MYSTERY (GER) 6 br.g. Java Gold (USA) – My Secret (GER) (Secreto (USA)) [2003/4 16g⁶ 16dᵖᵘ 19sᵖᵘ Jan 14] ex-Polish gelding: successful from 1m to 13f on Flat, left D. Kaluba in September 2002: prominent to 2 out when sixth of 7 finishers in steadily-run novice at Leicester on hurdling debut: no show either start after: tried tongue tied. *T. R. George* **h81**

MYSTIC FOREST 5 b.g. Charnwood Forest (IRE) – Mystic Beauty (IRE) (Alzao (USA)) [2003/4 20gᶠ 19g³ 22d* Jul 30] fairly useful on Flat (stays 2m), sold out of B. Meehan's stable 12,000 gns Doncaster May Sales: modest form when landing odds in maiden hurdle at Newton Abbot: will stay 3m: seemed likely to improve further but not seen out again. *C. J. Mann* **h93**

MYSTIC GLEN 5 b.m. Vettori (IRE) – Mystic Memory (Ela-Mana-Mou) [2003/4 F–: F16g⁴ F16d 16g 17d⁶ 16g Apr 5] signs of only a little ability in bumpers and novice hurdles. *P. D. Niven* **h69**
 F77

MYSTIC HILL 13 b.g. Shirley Heights – Nuryana (Nureyev (USA)) [2003/4 h67: 21m² May 29] neat gelding: poor hurdler: stays 2¾m: probably acts on any going. *J. Joseph* **h67**

MYSTIC MAYHEM 5 b.m. Danzig Connection (USA) – Mrs Meyrick (Owen Dudley) [2003/4 F17m Jul 22] third foal: half-sister to fairly useful 5f/6f winner Clan Chief (by Clantime) and a winning pointer by Grey Desire: dam, winning stayer on Flat, lightly-raced novice jumper: tailed off in bumper and maiden on Flat. *R. Bastiman* **F–**

MYSTIC NATIVE (IRE) 11 ch.g. Be My Native (USA) – Mystic River (IRE) (Over The River (FR)) [2003/4 c24g² c24d³ c20vᵖᵘ c20dᵖᵘ 21d Mar 30] successful 3 times in points, including on British debut in 2003: no form otherwise: tried in cheekpieces. *D. Pearson* **c–**
 h–

MYSTIC RIDGE   10 ch.g. Mystiko (USA) – Vallauris (Faustus (USA)) [2003/4 c–, h–: c17s^F c17g^3 May 17] good-bodied gelding: no form over hurdles: poor chaser: would have won novice handicap at Bangor but for falling last when 10 lengths clear: probably best around 2m: acted on soft going: dead. *R. Lee*   **c83 h–**

MYTHICAL KING (IRE)   7 b.g. Fairy King (USA) – Whatcombe (USA) (Alleged (USA)) [2003/4 h117: 16g^5 20d 20m^5 16d^6 20v* 20g^5 20g Apr 1] workmanlike gelding: type to make a chaser: fairly useful handicap hurdler: 33/1, won 14-runner William Hill Handicap at Ascot in January by 4 lengths from Kadara: creditable efforts after behind Paperprophet at Haydock and Zibeline at Aintree: will probably stay beyond 2½m: acts on heavy going, probably on good to firm: patiently ridden. *R. Lee*   **h117**

MYTIMIE (IRE)   9 b.g. Be My Native (USA) – Snoqualmie (Warpath) [2003/4 c105, h–: 20g^pu c25g^3 c26d^4 Apr 23] rangy gelding: fair hurdler/chaser at best: left J. M. Jefferson after reappearance, won 2 points in 2004: showed more stamina than previously when third in hunter at Kelso: stays 25f: acts on heavy and good to firm going: tried in cheekpieces: temperament under suspicion: sold 14,000 gns Doncaster May Sales. *David Parker*   **c91 h–**

MY TRUE LOVE (IRE)   5 b.g. Beneficial – Elfi (IRE) (Le Moss) [2003/4 F84: F17m^5 F16s Dec 20] modest form when fifth on first 2 starts in bumpers, not looking straightforward each time. *R. J. Baker*   **F84**

MYTTON'S QUEST (IRE)   4 ch.g. Grand Lodge (USA) – Fleeting Quest (Rainbow Quest (USA)) [2003/4 17m^6 16g 17g^6 16f^5 17g^5 16m^6 Nov 3] small gelding: maiden on Flat, no form in 2003 for A. Bailey: poor form over hurdles: tongue tied after debut. *Mrs L. Williamson*   **h73**

William Hill Handicap Hurdle, Ascot—
33/1-shot Mythical King is chased home by Kadara (left), Almaravide (white face) and Turtle Soup

Mrs J. Stewart's "My Will"

MY WHISPER (IRE)   5 b.m. Zaffaran (USA) – Floreamus (Quayside) [2003/4 F–: **F–**
F16m May 10] well held in bumpers: won maiden point in April. *A. King*

MY WILL (FR)   4 b.g. Saint Preuil (FR) – Gleep Will (FR) (Laniste) [2003/4 16d* 16s*   **h124**
16s² 16g³ Apr 1] tall, leggy, close-coupled gelding: first foal: dam maiden: successful in
juvenile hurdles at Fontainebleau in October and Enghien in November: left G. Macaire,
much better form when placed in similar events won by King Revo at Haydock and Al
Eile at Aintree (Grade 2): well below form in Grade 1 at Punchestown in late-April: will
be suited by further than 2m: acts on soft going: sort to do well in novice chases in 2004/
5. *P. F. Nicholls*

N

NA CREAGACHA DUBHA (IRE)   6 ch.g. Old Vic – Nova Express (Bonne Noel)   **F105**
[2003/4 F18d² F18s² Feb 5] IR 14,500 3-y-o: half-brother to 3 winners, including 2½m
hurdle winner Good Old Thyne (by Good Thyne): dam, winning 2m hurdler, sister to
useful 2m to 21f hurdler Canute Express and useful 2m hurdler/chaser El-Sid Senior:
runner-up in 2 maiden bumpers, better effort when beaten head by That's An Idea in
20-runner event at Clonmel second time. *N. Meade, Ireland*

NADDERWATER   12 br.g. Arctic Lord – Flying Cherub (Osiris) [2003/4 c23mᵖᵘ   **c–**
20mᵖᵘ Jul 23] very lightly raced, no form over jumps. *Mrs J. G. Retter*   **h–**

NADEEMA (FR)   6 gr.m. Linamix (FR) – Nabagha (FR) (Fabulous Dancer (USA))   **h–**
[2003/4 16sᵖᵘ Feb 18] dam half-sister to useful hurdler Nahrawali, stayed 2½m: 11f
winner at 3 yrs, subsequently sold out of A. de Royer Dupre's stable 120,000 francs: has
shown little in 4 starts over hurdles, left F. Doumen before pulled up in claimer at
Leicester (swished tail constantly before and during race). *B. N. Pollock*

NAFSIKA (USA) 4 b.f. Sky Classic (CAN) – Exotic Beauty (USA) (Java Gold (USA)) [2003/4 16f² 16g^pu 16v^pu 16d^pu 19d 19g^pu Mar 5] poor maiden on Flat (stays 1m) for B. McMahon: form over hurdles only when second in juvenile maiden at Ludlow on debut: sold out of N. Henderson's stable 2,400 gns Doncaster November Sales after next start. *R. C. Harper* **h79**

NAGANO (FR) 6 b.g. Hero's Honor (USA) – Sadinskaya (FR) (Niniski (USA)) [2003/4 20d⁶ Nov 22] medium-sized gelding: successful 3 times up to around 1¼m on Flat: fair maiden hurdler: left J. Bertran de Balanda and off 8 months, weakened quickly when well held in novice at Aintree on British debut. *Ian Williams* **h–**

NAHTHEN LAD (IRE) 15 b.g. Good Thyne (USA) – Current Call (Electrify) [2003/4 c–§, h–: c26d^F Mar 14] tall gelding: fair pointer in 2003: hampered and fell fourth in hunter on return: best short of 3½m: acts on good to firm and heavy going: usually blinkered/visored: often races lazily. *J. A. Danahar* **c– §**
h–

NAILBITER 5 b.g. Night Shift (USA) – Scylla (Rock City) [2003/4 h85, F79: 16m^pu May 26] quite good-topped gelding: modest form over hurdles: lame only outing in 2003/4: probably stays 2½m: tongue tied last 2 starts. *Mrs A. Duffield* **h–**

NAKED FLAME 5 b.g. Blushing Flame (USA) – Final Attraction (Jalmood (USA)) [2003/4 F16s F18g Apr 22] eighth foal: half-brother to several winners, including useful bumper performer Bodfari Queen (by Rudimentary): dam once-raced half-sister to smart 1m to 1¼m performer Gussy Marlowe: behind in bumpers. *A. G. Blackmore* **F–**

NAKED OAT 9 b.g. Imp Society (USA) – Bajina (Dancing Brave (USA)) [2003/4 16d 16s⁵ 17g³ 16d³ Apr 12] leggy gelding: poor form over hurdles: will prove best around 2m. *Mrs L. Wadham* **h72**

NAMELESS WONDER (IRE) 8 b.g. Supreme Leader – Miss Kylogue (IRE) (Lancastrian) [2003/4 h91: 21m 21v³ Jan 13] lengthy gelding: modest maiden hurdler: sold out of N. Henderson's stable 10,500 gns Doncaster May Sales after reappearance: stays 2¾m: acts on heavy going: tried blinkered/visored. *J. Howard Johnson* **h91**

NANDOO 5 b.m. Forzando – Ascend (IRE) (Glint of Gold) [2003/4 21m* 21g² 20f* 16g^pu Oct 30] disappointing maiden on Flat: won weak novice hurdles at Sedgefield in September and Wetherby in October: subsequently sold out of M. Hammond's stable 7,000 gns Doncaster October Sales: wears cheekpieces. *A. G. Juckes* **h82 §**

NARWHAL (IRE) 6 b. or br.g. Naheez (USA) – Well Why (IRE) (The Parson) [2003/4 h99p: 20s* 18v³ 20s* 21g² 20d^pu Mar 20] close-coupled gelding: fairly useful hurdler: won novices at Fontwell (first start for 13 months) in December and Sandown (handicap, beat Ardashir 1¼ lengths) in February: improved again when second to Gin Palace in handicap at Kempton in March: poor effort final outing: should stay 3m: raced on good going or softer (acts on soft). *N. J. Gifford* **h121**

NASHVILLE STAR (USA) 13 ch.g. Star de Naskra (USA) – Mary Davies (Tyrnavos) [2003/4 c–§, h–: c20g c20d² Mar 21] close-coupled gelding: no longer of any account: visored: temperamental. *Miss C. Herrington* **c– §**
h–

NAS NA RIOGH (IRE) 5 b.m. King's Theatre (IRE) – Abstraite (Groom Dancer (USA)) [2003/4 h122: 16g c17g³ 16s³ Feb 7] tall mare: fairly useful juvenile hurdler in 2002/3: better effort in 2003/4 when third in handicap at Wetherby, tending to carry head awkwardly: fair form when third to L'Ange Au Ciel in novice at Exeter on return from 7-month absence on chasing debut (likely to improve): will stay 2½m: probably suited by ground softer than good (acts on heavy). *N. J. Henderson* **c110 p**
h114

NAT GOLD 8 b.g. Push On – April Airs (Grey Mirage) [2003/4 h77: 24m* Jun 5] good-topped gelding: third outing over hurdles, won weak maiden at Uttoxeter by 16 lengths, not fluent and finishing lame. *Mrs D. A. Hamer* **h85**

NATHOS (GER) 7 b.g. Zaizoom (USA) – Nathania (GER) (Athenagoras (GER)) [2003/4 20g² 16d* 16d* 19g² 16d⁴ 16d² 21g⁴ 16s* 20g Apr 1] close-coupled gelding: successful 5 times up to 1¼m in Germany, including twice at 5 yrs for M. Sowa: fairly useful novice hurdler: won at Uttoxeter in November, Sandown (handicap) in December and Plumpton (odds on) in March: best around 2m: raced on good going or softer: usually waited with: consistent. *C. J. Mann* **h121**

NATIAIN (GER) 5 ch.g. Danzig Connection (USA) – Fen Princess (IRE) (Trojan Fen) [2003/4 20d^pu Apr 10] half-brother to useful hurdler/fairly useful chaser Fiori (by Anshan), stays 2½m: well held in 4 races on Flat at 2 and 3 yrs for P. Haslam: pulled up in point and novice hurdle. *W. S. Coltherd* **h–**

NATIVE ALIBI (IRE) 7 b.g. Be My Native (USA) – Perfect Excuse (Certingo)   c77
[2003/4 c–: c25g³ Apr 5] won maiden on first of 3 starts in points in 2004: third
of 5 finishers to Nisbet in maiden at Kelso on hunter chase debut: stays 25f.
Mrs S. H. Shirley-Beavan

NATIVE BEAT (IRE) 9 b.g. Be My Native (USA) – Deeprunonthepound (IRE)   c109
(Deep Run) [2003/4 c106, h–: c24g* c19d³ c18d c20s³ c25s³ c22s* c21g c21gᵘʳ Apr 2]   h–
medium-sized gelding: fair chaser: won cross-country event (third in latest renewal of
race) and handicap at Punchestown, beating Lisaan 3 lengths in latter in February: behind
when hampered and unseated at Becher's in Topham at Aintree: stays 25f: acts on any
going. *J. R. H. Fowler, Ireland*

NATIVE BUCK (IRE) 11 ch.g. Be My Native (USA) – Buckskins Chat (Buckskin   c–
(FR)) [2003/4 c120, h–: c26dᵖᵘ c28dᵖᵘ 23s⁵ 24s Apr 17] leggy gelding: fairly useful   h–
handicap chaser on his day: no form in 2003/4, including over hurdles, left T. George
before final outing: stays 3¾m: acts on heavy going (pulled up only start on firmer than
good): blinkered second outing. *M. F. Harris*

NATIVE COVE (IRE) 12 b.g. Be My Native (USA) – Down All The Coves   c– §
(Athenius) [2003/4 c96§: c26dᵖᵘ Apr 30] fair hunter chaser: lame at Cheltenham very
early in season: stays 31f: acts on soft going: tried visored: unreliable. *E. Haddock*

NATIVE CUNNING 6 b.g. Be My Native (USA) – Icy Miss (Random Shot) [2003/4   h75
F83: F16f⁴ 24g⁵ 22s 21g 22s⁴ 25s* 26g⁶ 25d⁵ Apr 11] big, well-made gelding: chasing   F78
type: modest in bumpers: poor hurdler: well backed and upped in trip, won handicap at
Plumpton in March: suited by good test of stamina: acts on soft ground. *R. H. Buckler*

NATIVE DAISY (IRE) 9 b.m. Be My Native (USA) – Castleblagh (General Ironside)   c–
[2003/4 c–: c25g⁴ c24g⁵ c24f c23f c25f c28d c24dᵖᵒ c24d⁴ Mar 25] workmanlike mare:
winning pointer: little form in steeplechases: wore cheekpieces final start. *K. Burke,
Ireland*

NATIVE DARA (IRE) 11 b.g. Be My Native (USA) – Birchwood (Fordham (USA))   c101 §
[2003/4 20d 18d⁵ c20dᵖᵘ 24s 19s 24v 20s 20d⁶ Feb 28] good-topped gelding: one-time   h115 §
useful hurdler/chaser: best effort in 2003/4 on reappearance: stayed 21f: acted on good
to firm and heavy going: effective blinkered or not: tried tongue tied: unreliable: dead.
N. Meade, Ireland

NATIVE EIRE (IRE) 10 b.g. Be My Native (USA) – Ballyline Dancer (Giolla Mear)   c83
[2003/4 c71, h–: c20g⁶ 20gᵖᵘ c20g* c21v* c20gᵖᵘ Apr 10] tall, angular gelding: winning   h–
hurdler: poor chaser: won handicaps at Wetherby (seller) in November and Sedgefield in
January: stays 21f: raced on good going or softer (acts on heavy). *N. Wilson*

NATIVE EMPEROR 8 br.g. Be My Native (USA) – Fiona's Blue (Crash Course)   c137
[2003/4 h147: c24g² c24s² c24s* c25s² c32g* c33dᵖᵘ Apr 17]   h–
    'Rebranding' is one of the fetishes of the age, generally harmless but seem-
ingly usually expensive, understandably so given the almost giddy level of expert-
ise involved in getting the change of image just perfect. Bookmaking firms have
been indulging quite a bit of late—Fred Done has become Betfred, Stanley Racing
is now Stanleybet and the Tote and Tote Credit have metamorphosed into totepool
and totesport (those internet-friendly lower cases must have been particularly
costly). Along with the last two names go colours not seen in polite society since
the 'sixties. Racing itself has dipped its toe in the rebranding water, with the idea of
redesignating National Hunt racing as British Jumps racing, the reasoning being
that some people are put off the sport, imagining that there is an element of hunting
involved. The mere idea had a predictable effect on people of a certain humour (in
both senses of the word): the perennially choleric spluttered indignantly, the merely
amusing had great fun at the expense of the rebranders. The latter group were aided
by the British Horseracing Board, which didn't seem to know whether or not it
was indeed considering the idea. 'Political correctness', a phrase used only in the
pejorative, was blamed (it had, as ever, 'gone mad'). The idea merited rather more
serious consideration than it got in some quarters. However naive the notion might
seem to those ingrained with the sport, it is all too believable that prospective newcomers are put off National Hunt racing by the name. Changing the brand name to
appeal to a wider public is not throwing out tradition simply for the sake of it, it
might just make commercial sense. In any case, it has to be asked just how widespread is the use of the 'official' name ('Are you stopping for the National Hunt
Flat race?' or 'The National Hunt Meeting is my favourite of the year').

The National Hunt Meeting is, of course, almost universally known as the Cheltenham Festival, so, when the great leap forward comes, perhaps the National Hunt Chase for amateurs can be renamed the Cheltenham Festival Chase, though that title will be in use for a revamped Cathcart at the next Festival. Alternatively, the National Hunt Chase might eventually become known as the Jonjo O'Neill Benefit Chase, as the trainer landed the prize for the third season running in 2004. Native Emperor followed Rith Dubh and Sudden Shock to victory (the trainer had also been successful with Front Line in 1995). Like Sudden Shock, Native Emperor had shown smart form over hurdles, though his chance at Cheltenham was rather more apparent beforehand as he had made a good start over fences, though winning just once, and then fortuitously, from four appearances. Native Emperor looked to hold a leading chance on form after the late withdrawal through injury of ante-post favourite Rosslea. Native Emperor's previous victory had come in a novice chase at Stratford in December, in which one of his rivals, Fork Lightning, had all but fallen when in command two out, bringing another, Howrwenow, to a halt. Better efforts had come from Native Emperor in defeat in Grade 2 novices. He went down by a head to Ballycassidy in the Worcester Novices' Chase at Newbury and by a length and a half to Lord Sam in the December Novices' Chase at Lingfield, receiving weight each time, then found Royal Emperor far too good at level weights in the Towton Novices' Chase at Wetherby. Any of that trio would have been at short odds in the National Hunt Chase, indeed Royal Emperor had just missed out on success in the Royal & SunAlliance Chase earlier in the afternoon. Although Native Emperor would have been up against it in the SunAlliance, the field for the National Hunt Chase was still a strong one compared to those usually gathered under its previous conditions, eighteen of the twenty-two to line up having won over fences. Dropped out in rear, joint-favourite Native Emperor still had it all to do four out but closed relentlessly when asked for his effort and reeled in the enterprisingly-ridden Celestial Gold in the last hundred yards, winning by a length and three quarters. Native Emperor's stable-companion Drombeag was a promising third, and, as he is still a maiden over fences, must be a leading candidate to give his trainer a fourth successive win in 2005.

National Hunt Chase Challenge Cup (Amateur Riders' Novices' Chase), Cheltenham—
ex-professional Robert Widger gets Native Emperor up to beat the enterprisingly-ridden Celestial Gold

J. C., J. R. and S. R. Hitchins' "Native Emperor"

Native Emperor (br.g. 1996)	Be My Native (USA) (br 1979)	Our Native (b or br 1970)	Exclusive Native
			Our Jackie
		Witchy Woman (ch 1972)	Strate Stuff
			Witchy Norma
	Fiona's Blue (b 1982)	Crash Course (b 1971)	Busted
			Lucky Stream
		Bunkilla (b 1972)	Arctic Slave
			Tactina

Both Rith Dubh and Sudden Shock ran just twice, showing little, in the season after their National Hunt Chase win, but Native Emperor has prospects of making more of an impact in handicaps. He followed Sudden Shock in running poorly in the Scottish National a month after his Cheltenham win but he is best forgiven that. The tall, useful-looking Native Emperor is the fifth living foal out of the maiden Fiona's Blue. Her two previous winners have also shown plenty of stamina, Perching (by Strong Gale) being a one-time fair chaser who stays three and a quarter miles, Nupdown Boy (by Orchestra) a three-mile hurdle winner. Fiona's Blue is also dam of Spirit of New York (by Topanoora) who won a bumper for O'Neill's stable on his debut in the latest season. Her final foal, by Bob Back, was sold for €105,000 at the 2003 Derby Sale. Fiona's Blue was half-sister to four useful chasers, none of them noted for their stamina. Deep Heritage was best at around two and a half miles, Lord York at around two, though he won at two and three quarters. Treyford stayed an easy three miles while Dis Train, who was also a useful hurdler and finished second in the Ladbroke, stayed twenty-one furlongs.

651

Their dam, the fair hurdler Bunkilla, was a half-sister to the useful hurdler and smart chaser Tacroy, who won the Thyestes Chase and defeated Royal Bond and Anaglogs Daughter to land the Punchestown Chase. The third dam Tactina was sister to the good Irish chaser Splash who won the 1965 Irish Grand National (when only four took part due to a coughing epidemic) and was third under 12-0 in a more competitive renewal three years later. Native Emperor still has some room for improvement in his jumping but, with just six chases under his belt, progress is still on the cards. He is well suited by a test of stamina and has raced on good going or softer (acts on heavy). *Jonjo O'Neill*

NATIVE GLEN (IRE) 10 b.g. Be My Native (USA) – The Gargle Monster (Furry Glen) [2003/4 c–, h–: c16g[F] May 12] tall gelding: winning 2m hurdler: no form over fences: tongue tied. *S. Lloyd*
c–
h–

NATIVE IVY (IRE) 6 b.g. Be My Native (USA) – Outdoor Ivy (Deep Run) [2003/4 F16d*, 20s³ 20s³ 25d* Mar 19] leggy gelding: fifth foal: brother to fairly useful staying jumpers Monifeth Man and Native King, and half-brother to fair hurdler up to 21f Bracey Run (by The Parson): dam unraced half-sister to useful 2m to 3m chaser Fair Is Fair and useful hurdler up to 21f Killone Abbot: won bumper at Uttoxeter on debut in May for A. Lidderdale: breathing problem on hurdling debut: fair form both outings after, won 15-runner novice at Warwick by length from Bertiebanoo: stays 25f: raced on good to soft/soft going. *C. Tinkler*
h109
F99

NATIVE JACK (IRE) 10 br.g. Be My Native (USA) – Dorrha Daisy (Buckskin (FR)) [2003/4 c128, h119: c20d c24s³ c24s⁴ 20d* c24s* c29d⁴ Apr 12] tall, lengthy gelding: fairly useful hurdler/useful chaser: easily won minor hurdle at Down Royal (made all to win by 9 lengths from Lasquini du Moulin) in February and listed handicap over fences at Cork (second successive win in race, beat Garvivonnian 13 lengths) in March: good fourth of 10 finishers to Granit d'Estruval in Irish Grand National at Fairyhouse final outing: stays 29f: acts on heavy going. *A. L. T. Moore, Ireland*
c144
h126

NATIVE LEGEND (IRE) 9 b.g. Be My Native (USA) – Tickhill (General Assembly (USA)) [2003/4 h99: c24s[F] c20s⁴ c24g³ Apr 10] leggy, angular gelding: modest handicap hurdler: lacklustre efforts on completed starts over fences: stays 3m: unraced on firm going, acts on any other. *Ferdy Murphy*
c–
h–

NATIVE NEW YORKER (IRE) 9 b.g. Be My Native (USA) – Sunbath (Krayyan) [2003/4 h130: 20m Apr 24] rangy gelding: useful handicap hurdler in 2002/3: always behind on return late in 2003/4: should stay 2½m: acts on soft and good to firm going: has had 2 handlers in paddock. *R. Rowe*
h–

NATIVE PEACH (IRE) 9 ch.g. Be My Native (USA) – Larry's Peach (Laurence O) [2003/4 c–, h–: c24g⁶ Jan 10] medium-sized gelding: winning hurdler, lightly raced: little encouragement in 2 outings over fences nearly 10 months apart: will stay beyond 25f: acts on good to firm and good to soft going. *J. A. B. Old*
c–
h–

NATIVE PERFORMANCE (IRE) 9 b.g. Be My Native (USA) – Noon Performance (Strong Gale) [2003/4 c107, h–: c25g⁴ c24g² c24d c25f c23g 24g³ 16m⁶ c24f² 20f* c24g* c24m⁶ᵈ 20m² c26g 22s c29dᵖᵘ Apr 12] tall, useful-looking gelding: fair handicap hurdler/fairly useful handicap chaser: won over hurdles at Punchestown and fences at Listowel (Guinness Kerry National, by neck from River Cora) in September: lost form after twelfth outing: effective at 2½m to easy 3m: acts on firm and soft ground: tried blinkered. *M. Hourigan, Ireland*
c117
h110

NATIVE SCOUT (IRE) 8 b.g. Be My Native (USA) – Carmels Castle (Deep Run) [2003/4 c138, h–: c17d² c17d* c17d² c16g⁴ c16v* c16d² c17d⁴ Apr 11] close-coupled gelding: smart chaser: won handicap at Fairyhouse in November and Grade 3 Byrne Group Tied Cottage Chase at Punchestown (beat Rathgar Beau 8 lengths) in February: creditable efforts most other starts, fourth in valuable handicaps at Ascot and Fairyhouse: should stay 2½m: raced on good going or softer (acts on heavy): tongue tied: consistent. *D. Hassett, Ireland*
c149
h–

NATIVE SESSIONS (IRE) 9 b.g. Be My Native (USA) – Weekly Sessions (Buckskin (FR)) [2003/4 c129, h119: c25gᵖᵘ c29sᵖᵘ c28v c20s² c21g³ Feb 29] good sort: fairly useful handicap chaser: made running and back to form in blinkers last 2 starts, second to Over The First at Navan and third to Hume Castle in listed event at Leopardstown: stays 3m: acts on heavy going: effective tongue tied or not. *N. Meade, Ireland*
c129
h–

NATIVE SPEAKER (IRE) 11 ch.g. Be My Native (USA) – My Wonder (Deep Run) [2003/4 c113, h–: c20gᵖᵘ Mar 28] rangy, useful-looking gelding: winning chaser,
c–
h–

lightly raced (presumably difficult to train): probably best around 2½m: acts on soft going. *P. R. Webber*

NATIVE STAR (IRE)   6 b.g. Be My Native (USA) – Star Chamber (FR) (Tower Walk) [2003/4 F94: 22fᵖᵘ Nov 20] leggy, angular gelding: bumper winner: not fluent and pulled up lame before 2 out on hurdling debut. *P. J. Hobbs*   h–

NATIVE THUNDER (IRE)   9 b.g. Be My Native (USA) – Huntstown Gale (IRE) (Strong Gale) [2003/4 c24sᵖᵘ May 2] big, strong gelding: modest form in novice hurdles in 2001/2: first run since, soon clear but weakened once headed 6 out in novice hunter chase at Bangor: won point in 2004. *Geoffrey Deacon*   c–   h–

NATIVETRIAL (IRE)   9 ch.g. Be My Native (USA) – Protrial (Proverb) [2003/4 c108, h–: c26g² c30dᵖᵘ c26vᵇᵈ c25s⁴ c25v⁴ c33dᵖᵘ Feb 21] sturdy gelding: fair handicap chaser, disappointing after reappearance: stays 33f: acts well on heavy going: tried blinkered/tongue tied: sold £3,800 Cheltenham April Sales. *C. J. Mann*   c103 d   h–

NATIVE UPMANSHIP (IRE)   11 ch.g. Be My Native (USA) – Hi' Upham (Deep Run) [2003/4 c171, h–: c25g³ c20d⁵ c20s* c16d³ c20g³ Apr 2] tall gelding: has stringhalt: top-class chaser at best: on downgrade, though won Grade 2 Maclochlainn Road Markings Limited Kinloch Brae Chase at Thurles (third successive win in race) in February, more forcefully ridden than usual and barely off bridle to beat Davids Lad by length: 19 lengths third of 7 to Moscow Flyer in Melling Chase at Aintree (won previous 2 runnings of race): probably best around 2½m: acts on good to firm and heavy going. *A. L. T. Moore, Ireland*   c156   h–

NATTERJACK (IRE)   6 b.g. Roselier (FR) – Hansel's Lady (IRE) (The Parson) [2003/4 F16d⁶ F16g⁵ F16d Mar 24] €50,000 4-y-o: good-topped gelding: fourth foal: half-brother to winning pointer by Phardante: dam unraced half-sister to Irish Sweeps Hurdle winner Hansel Rag: fair form first 2 starts in bumpers. *A. King*   F90

NATURAL (IRE)   7 b.g. Bigstone (IRE) – You Make Me Real (USA) (Give Me Strength (USA)) [2003/4 h92d: 20d 18d 16s⁶ 16s c16v³ c16s² c20d⁵ c16gᵘʳ c20v⁵ c25gᴿ Apr 5] good-topped gelding: winning hurdler, no form in 2003/4: best effort over fences when second in weak handicap at Carlisle: should stay beyond 2m: acts on soft going: tried blinkered/visored: has looked less than keen. *F. P. Murtagh*   c81   h–

Guinness Kerry National Handicap Chase, Listowel—the departure of Cloudy Bays (cheekpieces) two out lets in Native Performance (left) to edge out the same owner's River Cora

NAUGHTYNELLY'S PET 5 b.g. Balnibarbi – Naughty Nessie (Celtic Cone) F–
[2003/4 F16g F16m Dec 16] third foal: half-brother to 17f hurdle winner Young Lorcan
(by Bay Tern): dam once-raced half-sister to useful staying hurdler House Captain: tailed
off in 2 bumpers. *D. A. Nolan*

NAUNTON BROOK 5 b.g. Alderbrook – Give Me An Answer (True Song) [2003/4 **h103**
F17g⁴ F17d F17d 25d* 24s³ 19g² Apr 24] 15,000 4-y-o: leggy gelding: fourth foal: dam, win- **F85**
ning hurdler/twice-raced steeplechaser, stayed 21f: better effort in bumpers at Bangor
when fourth on debut: fair form over hurdles: won 4-finisher novice at Warwick in March
by 10 lengths from Lazerito: better around 3m than shorter: acts on soft going.
N. A. Twiston-Davies

NAUTICAL 6 ch. or gr.g. Lion Cavern (USA) – Russian Royal (USA) (Nureyev **h–**
(USA)) [2003/4 h86: 17mᵖᵘ 16mᵖᵘ Mar 11] leggy, angular gelding: maiden hurdler: went
as if amiss both starts in 2003/4, 8 months apart, left M. Pipe after first (tongue tied).
A. W. Carroll

NAUTICAL STAR 9 b.g. Slip Anchor – Comic Talent (Pharly (FR)) [2003/4 h–: **h68**
17d² 20g³ 18d 17v⁵ 16g Jan 24] smallish gelding: poor hurdler: should stay beyond 17f:
acts on good to soft going: tried in cheekpieces: inconsistent. *A. C. Whillans*

NAVADO (USA) 5 b.g. Rainbow Quest (USA) – Miznah (IRE) (Sadler's Wells (USA)) **h99**
[2003/4 20s 20s 17d* Mar 7] half-brother to winning 21f hurdler Millions (by Bering):
useful on Flat (stays 1¼m), successful in September, sold out of Sir Michael Stoute's
stable 70,000 gns Newmarket Autumn Sales: first form in 3 novice hurdles (raced on
softer going previously) when winning 18-runner event at Market Rasen by 7 lengths
from Dickensbury Lad, confidently ridden and quickening clear when shaken up after
last. *Jonjo O'Neill*

NAVARONE 10 b.g. Gunner B – Anamasi (Idiot's Delight) [2003/4 c122, h–: c25gᵘʳ **c112**
c24g⁴ c24g c24g c24gᵖᵘ c24d² Mar 15] tall gelding: fair handicap chaser, generally below **h–**
form in 2003/4: stays 3m: acts on good to firm and good to soft going: effective tongue
tied or not: bold-jumping front runner. *Ian Williams*

NAWAMEES (IRE) 6 b.g. Darshaan – Truly Generous (IRE) (Generous (IRE)) **h114**
[2003/4 h117: 16m* 16d⁶ 16g² 16g⁴ 18d³ Apr 7] leggy gelding: fair novice hurdler: won
at Ascot in November by 5 lengths from Optimaite: creditable efforts last 3 starts: should
stay beyond 2¼m: acts on good to firm and good to soft ground. *G. L. Moore*

NAWOW 4 b.g. Blushing Flame (USA) – Fair Test (Fair Season) [2003/4 16d* 16d **h96**
16g⁵ Mar 15] compact gelding: fairly useful on Flat (barely stays 2m): won 6-runner
juvenile at Sandown on hurdling debut in December: well held both starts after, already
poorly placed when hampered sixth final one. *P. D. Cundell*

NDR'S CASH FOR FUN 11 b.g. Ballacashtal (CAN) – Basic Fun (Teenoso (USA)) **h–**
[2003/4 h–: 20d 27s⁶ May 17] workmanlike gelding: winning hurdler, no form since
2001/2: blinkered final start. *A. W. Carroll*

NEARLY A MOOSE (IRE) 8 b.g. Supreme Leader – Miss Tarbow (Tarqogan) **c130**
[2003/4 c120, h–: c20g³ c20d c20d c24f* c22s* Jul 30] compact gelding: useful chaser: **h–**
won minor event at Cork in June and 22-runner Hewlett-Packard Galway Plate (Handicap) in July, beating Kadoun 4 lengths in latter: stays 3m: acts on any going: effective
tongue tied or not: none too consistent. *Patrick Mullins, Ireland*

NEEDWOOD BUCOLIC (IRE) 6 br.g. Charnwood Forest (IRE) – Greek Icon **h–**
(Thatching) [2003/4 20dᵖᵘ 16dF Apr 22] 16,000Y, 1,500 2-y-o: first foal: dam 2-y-o 6f
winner out of half-sister to smart 1½m winner Trakady: won 5f event in Greece at 4 yrs:
shaped like non-stayer both starts over hurdles. *R. Shiels*

NEEDWOOD LION 11 b.g. Rolfe (USA) – Arctic Lion (Arctic Slave) [2003/4 c120, **c–**
h–: c20d⁵ Dec 20] well-made gelding: fairly useful handicap chaser: unable to dominate **h–**
and below form only outing in 2003/4: stays 21f: acts on heavy going, possibly not on
good to firm: free-going sort who usually forces pace: sometimes makes mistakes. *Miss
Venetia Williams*

NEEDWOOD MERLIN 8 b.g. Sizzling Melody – Enchanting Kate (Enchantment) **h–**
[2003/4 h–: 20gᵖᵘ May 10] no show in 3 starts over hurdles. *K. W. Hogg, Isle of Man*

NEEDWOOD SPIRIT 9 b.g. Rolfe (USA) – Needwood Nymph (Bold Owl) [2003/4 **h96**
h99: 20d⁶ 20g 17d⁴ 17d⁴ 16s 16d⁶ 21v Jan 13] close-coupled gelding: modest handicap
hurdler: effective around 2m, should stay beyond 2½m: acts on soft going. *Mrs
A. M. Naughton*

NEGRESKO (FR)   5 gr.g. Great Palm (USA) – Negra (FR) (Tropular) [2003/4 c?, h113: 18g⁵ 17g 17d⁵ 18g⁴ Apr 11] angular gelding: maiden on Flat: fair hurdler: left M. Pipe after reappearance, trained next 2 starts by J. Bertran de Balanda: third in 3-y-o event on chasing debut: raced mainly around 2m: acts on soft and good to firm ground: effective with/without blinkers/visor: temperament under suspicion. *G. Blasco, France*   **c– h102**

NEIDPATH CASTLE   5 b.g. Alflora (IRE) – Pennant Cottage (IRE) (Denel (FR)) [2003/4 F17v* Mar 21] 10,000 3-y-o: second foal: dam winning pointer: won 11-runner bumper at Carlisle on debut by 3 lengths from Dayenoo: will be suited by further. *A. C. Whillans*   **F87**

NELLY MOSER   7 gr.m. Neltino – Boreen's Glory (Boreen (FR)) [2003/4 F76: 19g² 22m⁵ May 29] modest form at best in bumpers: better effort in novice hurdles when third to subsequently-disqualified Maiden Voyage in mares race at Hereford. *Mrs A. J. Hamilton-Fairley*   **h73**

NELSONS NELL (IRE)   8 b.m. Supreme Leader – Lough Neagh Lady (Furry Glen) [2003/4 F18g 22d⁵ 20s³ 18d⁶ 20sᵖᵘ c20d Apr 23] won maiden from 4 starts in Irish points in 2003: once-raced in bumpers: poor maiden hurdler, left G. Young after fourth outing: little show on steeplechasing debut: has pulled hard. *Miss Lucinda V. Russell*   **c– h81 F–**

NEMISTO   10 gr.g. Mystiko (USA) – Nemesia (Mill Reef (USA)) [2003/4 c–, h101: 21f³ 22m* May 29] good-topped gelding: modest hurdler: dropped in class, won selling handicap (sold 5,600 gns) at Newton Abbot in May: stays 2¾m: probably acts on any going: effective tongue tied or not. *R. Lee*   **c– h94**

NEOPHYTE (IRE)   5 gr.g. Broken Hearted – Dunmahon Lady (General Ironside) [2003/4 F17d⁵ Jun 9] €7,800 3-y-o: tenth foal: dam, lightly raced in bumpers/over hurdles, half-sister to dam of very smart chaser up to 25f Second Schedual: fifth of 15 to Woodlands Genpower in bumper at Newton Abbot on debut. *B. De Haan*   **F76**

NEPHITE (NZ)   10 b.g. Star Way – Te Akau Charmer (NZ) (Sir Tristram) [2003/4 c98, h–: c16g⁶ 16g c17d 17m⁵ c17g² 17g c17m⁵ 19g c16d⁴ c16g* 17g c17m³ c17g⁴ c16mᵖᵘ Sep 14] workmanlike gelding: maiden hurdler: fair handicap chaser: back to form when winning at Newton Abbot in August: sold out of R. C. Guest's stable 5,500 gns Doncaster Sales later in month: raced mainly around 2m: acts on good to firm and heavy going: wears headgear: effective tongue tied or not: races prominently: unreliable. *Miss Venetia Williams*   **c102 § h–**

NEPTUNE   8 b.g. Dolphin Street (FR) – Seal Indigo (IRE) (Glenstal (USA)) [2003/4 h75: 19vᵖᵘ Feb 2] lengthy gelding: poor on Flat and over hurdles: should stay beyond 17f: possibly unsuited by heavy going. *J. C. Fox*   **h–**

The Hewlett-Packard Galway Plate (Handicap Chase)—Nearly A Moose holds on to win a typically competitive renewal, with less than twelve lengths covering the first eleven home

NEUTRON (IRE) 7 ch.g. Nucleon (USA) – Balistic Princess (Lomond (USA)) **h114**
[2003/4 h121: 20v Jan 31] angular gelding: fairly useful handicap hurdler: not discredited
only outing in 2003/4: stays 21f: probably acts on any going: tried blinkered, effective
visored or not: has looked difficult ride. *M. C. Pipe*

NEV BROWN (IRE) 8 b. or br.g. Executive Perk – Brandy Hill Girl (Green Shoon) **c114**
[2003/4 21g c16s³ c17d² c16gᵖᵘ Apr 3] IR 18,000 4-y-o: lengthy, workmanlike gelding: **h–**
fourth foal: brother/half-brother to winning pointers: dam unraced, out of half-sister to
useful 2m chaser Cottage Run: tailed off in novice hurdle on belated debut: showed
promise in maidens at Hereford and Bangor first 2 starts over fences, would have won but
for stumbling on landing 2 out at latter: highly tried final outing. *N. A. Twiston-Davies*

NEVEN 5 b.g. Casteddu – Rose Burton (Lucky Wednesday) [2003/4 17d 16d Apr 22] **h–**
fair on Flat (stays 1m), sold out of T. D. Barron's stable 7,000 gns Doncaster January
Sales: no show in 2 novice hurdles: tongue tied on debut. *Miss Lucinda V. Russell*

NEVERBITETHEHAND (IRE) 6 b.g. Aragon – We're Joken (Statoblest) [2003/4 **F–**
F17m F16mʳᵒ Jul 23] second foal: dam, modest sprinter, half-sister to one-time useful
sprinter Friar Tuck: no show in bumper on debut: ran out first bend next time. *R. J. Baker*

NEVER CAN TELL 8 ch.g. Emarati (USA) – Farmer's Pet (Sharrood (USA)) [2003/4 **h86**
h82: 16m* May 5] workmanlike gelding: modest handicap hurdler: not seen out again
after winning at Ludlow very early in season: stays 19f: acts on firm and soft going: has
worn cheekpieces: raced mostly on right-handed tracks. *B. D. Leavy*

NEVER COMPROMISE (IRE) 9 br.g. Glacial Storm (USA) – Banderole (IRE) **c130**
(Roselier (FR)) [2003/4 c22d* c24s* c24d* c26d² c29dᶠ Apr 12] strong gelding: first **h–**
foal: dam unraced half-sister to useful hurdler up to 25f Sip of Orange: maiden hurdler:
developed into smart hunter chaser, winning at Downpatrick and Down Royal in December and Leopardstown (beat Spot Thedifference 1½ lengths) in February: easily best
effort when 4 lengths second of 10 finishers to Earthmover in Foxhunter at Cheltenham:

Mr D. F. Desmond's "Never Compromise"

fell first in Irish Grand National: will stay beyond 3¼m: acts on heavy going: blinkered last 2 starts in 2002/3. *T. M. Walsh, Ireland*

NEVER (FR) 7 b.g. Vettori (IRE) – Neraida (USA) (Giboulee (CAN)) [2003/4 h146· **h117** 16d 16g 16s 16g⁶ Mar 26] tall, sparely-made gelding: smart hurdler in 2002/3: well below best in handicaps in 2003/4, left F. Doumen after reappearance, twice ridden by very inexperienced 10-lb claimer: stays 19f: has won on heavy going, best efforts under less testing conditions. *Jonjo O'Neill*

NEVER IN DEBT 12 ch.g. Nicholas Bill – Deep In Debt (Deep Run) [2003/4 c–, h–: **c–** 20m⁶ 20m Aug 2] workmanlike gelding: maiden steeplechaser: one-time fair hurdler: **h–** retains little ability: tried visored/in cheekpieces. *E. R. Clough*

NEVER MORE (FR) 8 b.g. Sanglamore (USA) – Neraida (Giboulee (CAN)) [2003/4 **c130** c24g² Dec 1] rather leggy gelding: one-time useful hurdler: won on chasing debut in May **h–** 2001: first start since when 4½ lengths second of 6 to Rule Supreme in minor event at Thurles, making much of running: stays 3m: raced on good going or softer (acts on heavy): has found little. *E. J. O'Grady, Ireland*

NEVER PROMISE (FR) 6 b.m. Cadeaux Genereux – Yazeanhaa (USA) (Zilzal **h–** (USA)) [2003/4 17d^pu 16m Nov 6] small mare: poor on Flat nowadays: little show over hurdles, left C. Roberts after reappearance. *D. Loughnane, Ireland*

NEW BIRD (GER) 9 b.g. Bluebird (USA) – Nouvelle Amour (GER) (Esclavo (FR)) **c119** [2003/4 c107, h–: c16d² c16g² c16d* c16m* c17g³ c16m^pu c16m² Apr 15] tall gelding: **h–** has had wind operation: fairly useful handicap chaser: won at Newton Abbot in July and August: off 5½ months, good second of 15 to Tango Royal at Cheltenham final start: best around 2m: acts on heavy and good to firm going: doesn't always look straightforward ride. *Mrs H. Dalton*

NEW CURRENCY (USA) 4 b.g. Touch Gold (USA) – Ceirseach (IRE) (Don't **h112 p** Forget Me) [2003/4 16d⁵ Apr 10] good-topped gelding: fairly useful on Flat (stays 1¼m): stepped up on form of hurdling debut when falling last in juvenile minor event won by Definate Spectacle at Punchestown in late-April, likely to have finished second at worst: should improve further. *J. S. Bolger, Ireland*

NEW DIAMOND 5 ch.g. Bijou d'Inde – Nannie Annie (Persian Bold) [2003/4 19g^pu **h–** 19s^pu Apr 11] half-brother to winning jumpers up to 3m McSnappy and Thanks Keith (both by Risk Me): fair 1m winner at 3 yrs on Flat, well beaten in 2003, sold out of J. Eustace's stable £4,500 Ascot July Sales: no show in 2 maiden hurdles. *Mrs P. Ford*

NEW ERA (IRE) 10 b.g. Distinctly North (USA) – Vaguely Deesse (USA) (Vaguely **c86** Noble) [2003/4 c–, h–: c23d⁵ c24v⁵ Apr 4] workmanlike gelding: fair chaser in 2000/1, **h–** very lightly raced since: stays 3m: acts on good to firm and heavy going. *B. De Haan*

NEW FIELD (IRE) 6 b.g. Supreme Leader – Deep Steel (Deep Run) [2003/4 F16d³ **F102 p** F16d* Feb 21] IR £30,000 3-y-o: fifth foal: half-brother to bumper winner Mister M (by Broken Hearted): dam unraced, from family of Grand National winners Royal Athlete and West Tip: fairly useful from both starts in bumpers, winning 21-runner event at Fairyhouse by 1½ lengths from Be My Leader, kept up to work after looking inexperienced: will stay at least 2½m: promising. *Patrick Mullins, Ireland*

NEWGATE TIMES 5 b.g. Timeless Times (USA) – Newgate Bubbles (Hubbly **F–** Bubbly (USA)) [2003/4 F16d Mar 22] second foal: dam no sign of ability: tailed off in bumper on debut. *N. Wilson*

NEWHALL (IRE) 6 b.m. Shernazar – Graffogue (IRE) (Red Sunset) [2003/4 h127: **h127** 20s⁴ 16s² 16s⁴ 17d Mar 18] smallish, sturdy mare: fairly useful handicap hurdler: best effort in 2003/4 when second to She'll Be Lucky in mares race at Leopardstown: probably stays 2½m: acts on heavy going. *F. Flood, Ireland*

NEWICK PARK 9 gr.g. Chilibang – Quilpee Mai (Pee Mai) [2003/4 c–, h–: c16m* **c101** c18s* c16g² c21m² c20gF Mar 7] good-topped gelding: fair handicap chaser: back to **h–** form in 2003/4, won at Warwick in November and Newbury in January: stays 21f: acts on good to firm and heavy going: has worn cheekpieces. *R. Dickin*

NEWKIDONTHEBLOCK (IRE) 9 b.g. Be My Native (USA) – Jenny's Child **h79** (Crash Course) [2003/4 h70: 16g 16v 16g² 20g³ 16g⁶ Apr 18] tall gelding: poor maiden hurdler, lightly raced: lame final outing: stays 21f: acts on good to firm and good to soft going. *J. R. Jenkins*

NEWLANDS GOLD (IRE) 5 ch.g. Goldmark (SAF) – Persian Polly (Persian Bold) **h130** [2003/4 h120: 16g 16s* 16s 16g³ 22d Apr 12] good-topped gelding: useful handicap hurdler: won at Fairyhouse in January by 6 lengths from Jirlan: best effort when third to

Harchibald at Leopardstown: raced mainly around 2m: acts on heavy going: effective blinkered or not: has looked difficult ride. *M. J. P. O'Brien, Ireland*

NEW LEADER (IRE)   7 b.g. Supreme Leader – Two Spots (Deep Run) [2003/4 h89, F–: 26g 22g[6] c21g c24g[pu] c22d[pu] c20d[F] c25d[ur] c24g Mar 7] angular gelding: novice hurdler, modest form at best: no form over fences: tongue tied last 3 starts. *Mrs L. Richards*   c– h–

NEWMILL (IRE)   6 br.g. Norwich – Lady Kas (Pollerton) [2003/4 F103p: F16m 16g* 16m[2] 16d* 20s* 16d[2] 18s[2] 20d* Feb 22]   h147 F–

'He's a real superstar, but that's his last race of the season. We'll school him over fences now and bring him back in the autumn for his novice chasing season.' It's hardly a conventional policy to miss all of the spring Festival meetings with a novice already proven at Grade 1 level, foregoing the chance of further valuable prizes in the short term in order to play the long game. That though was the plan adopted with the leading Irish novice Newmill and spelt out by trainer Thomas O'Leary after the horse gained his fourth win over hurdles, in the betfair.com Johnstown Novices' Hurdle at Naas in February. The decision revived memories of another six-year-old Irish novice hurdler who was put away after making it four wins over hurdles by February: Carvill's Hill, in 1987/8, missed Cheltenham, where he would have been at short odds for either of the novice hurdles, and was put away with chasing in mind, a decision which had a largely successful outcome. Newmill isn't quite so good a novice over hurdles as was Carvill's Hill, nor would he have had quite the clear-cut chance of that horse had he contested the Supreme Novices', but he would have been a leading contender on form going into the race and wouldn't have needed to improve much to win it. Newmill is an exuberant sort and an excellent jumper of hurdles, with the physique to make a chaser, so there must be every chance, barring injury, that his connections' decision will be well rewarded.

Newmill gained his most notable success over hurdles at Fairyhouse, in the Boylesports Royal Bond Novices' Hurdle in November. He was making his fifth appearance on a racecourse, having won the Goffs Land Rover Bumper at the same course on his debut in 2002/3 and a novice at Wexford on his hurdling debut in October. Most recently he had finished second to Accordion Etoile at Navan, the winner also looking a major contender in the Royal Bond, the pair meeting on the same terms. The two efforts over hurdles had helped erase memories of a wayward effort by Newmill on his reappearance, when he pulled very hard and proved

betfair.com Johnstown Novices' Hurdle, Naas—
Newmill is far too strong for Inexorable (mostly hidden), Moscow Court (noseband) and Hardy Duckett

intractable, virtually pulled up half a mile from home, in a winners' bumper at Tipperary. There was no explanation for that effort but Newmill showed no signs of repeating it after being sent over hurdles. The Royal Bond was a competitive race on paper, with the ten to have run over hurdles successful a total of sixteen times, while the pair making their hurdling debut were both useful in bumpers. Few got into the shake-up after Newmill was sent off into a clear lead. Still with a sizeable advantage two out, he found just enough under pressure to hold off the mare Mariah Rollins by three quarters of a length, with twelve back to the favourite Strike Back in third. It wasn't only the punters who mistakenly preferred Strike Back to Newmill, as Barry Geraghty rode the third, with Garrett Cotter on Newmill, Geraghty having ridden the winner on his first two starts over hurdles. Geraghty didn't make the same mistake again, though punters kept getting it wrong, and it was only at Naas that Newmill finally started favourite in a race.

Newmill didn't have long to rest on his laurels after the Royal Bond. He was out at Navan two weeks later, stepped up to two and a half miles in the Barry & Sandra Kelly Memorial Novices' Hurdle, a Grade 2 and a much weaker race than the Royal Bond, though worth the same with €70,000 prize money. Held up, and thus reverting to earlier tactics, Newmill led on the bridle in the straight and beat Kildare with plenty to spare. Newmill's success over Inexorable in the Johnstown over the same trip on his final start came in similarly easy fashion but, if anything, his two defeats at Leopardstown in between say more about his abilities. He couldn't cope with Mariah Rollins in the Future Champions in December, but was meeting her on terms 8 lb worse than in the Royal Bond and ran as well as could be expected; in the Grade 1 Deloitte Novices' he lost out to Brave Inca by three quarters of a length, seeming to have the race won when quickening two out, but untidy over the final flight and worn down close home. Brave Inca went on to win the Supreme Novices' at Cheltenham.

Newmill (IRE) (br.g. 1998)	Norwich (b 1987)	Top Ville (b 1976)	High Top
			Sega Ville
		Dame Julian (br 1976)	Blakeney
			March Spray
	Lady Kas (b 1984)	Pollerton (b 1974)	Lord Gayle
			Mear-Aille
		Lady Dikler (b 1970)	Even Money
			Coronation Day

The tall, good-topped Newmill is the fifth foal out of Lady Kas, three of the previous ones having won in points, one of them, Ballyknock Lass (by Electric) also winning a bumper. Lady Kas herself won a two-mile maiden hurdle but she is a sister to the fair staying chaser King Kas. Lady Kas is out of the unraced Lady Dikler, who, as the names suggest, is a half-sister to the Cheltenham Gold Cup and King George winner The Dikler, as well as to the useful staying hurdler/chaser Kas, who won the Saddle of Gold Final at Newbury. Newmill isn't a sluggard, far from it, but, despite appearances at Leopardstown, he is likely to prove fully effective in top company at up to two and a half miles. He has yet to race on heavy or firm going but acts on any other. *T. G. O'Leary, Ireland*

NEW MISCHIEF (IRE)   6 b.g. Accordion – Alone Party (IRE) (Phardante (FR)) [2003/4 F77: F16f* F16m³ 16d 16g² Apr 18] big, lengthy gelding: has reportedly had breathing operation: fairly useful form in bumpers at Cheltenham first 2 starts, beating Gideon Putnam 1¾ lengths in October: better effort in novice hurdles when 20 lengths second to In The Frame at Wincanton: has had tongue tied. *Noel T. Chance*   **h87 F98**

NEW PERK (IRE)   6 b.g. Executive Perk – New Chello (IRE) (Orchestra) [2003/4 h81: 21m³ 19g 19m 16m³ 20g³ 20m⁴ 21vᵖᵘ 22sᵇᵈ c20s⁵ c22s⁶ 21d Mar 28] close-coupled gelding: poor maiden hurdler: far from fluent both starts over fences: should stay beyond 2½m: acts on soft and good to firm going: visored final outing. *M. J. Gingell*   **c75 x h81**

NEW RISING   12 b.g. Primitive Rising (USA) – Saucy (Saucy Kit) [2003/4 c92§, h–: c25sᵖᵘ Nov 18] strong, well-made gelding: modest handicap chaser: stays 29f: acts on heavy and good to firm going: usually visored: unreliable. *R. T. Phillips*   **c– § h–**

NEW ROSS (IRE)   12 gr.g. Roselier (FR) – Miss Lucille (Fine Blade (USA)) [2003/4 c–, h–: c26fᵖᵘ May 21] leggy gelding: modest pointer: no form in steeplechases: tried blinkered/visored: sold 2,700 gns Doncaster August Sales. *M. J. Bloom*   **c– h–**

NEWS FLASH (IRE)   12 b.g. Strong Gale – Gale Flash (News Item) [2003/4 c76,   **c78**
h78: 20m c24d^{co} c24g^2 Apr 18] rangy gelding: poor maiden hurdler/chaser, left E. Clough   **h–**
after reappearance: stays 3m: acts on good to soft going, probably on good to firm. *Lady
Susan Brooke*

NEWS MAKER (IRE)   8 b.g. Good Thyne (USA) – Announcement (Laurence O)   **c100**
[2003/4 c119, h–: c24f^4 Oct 28] good-topped gelding: fairly useful chaser: still in con-   **h–**
tention when mistake and hampered 2 out in amateur handicap at Cheltenham, only
outing in 2003/4: stays 3¼m: acts on heavy going: jumps soundly. *Mrs H. Dalton*

NEWSPLAYER (IRE)   8 br.g. Alphabatim (USA) – Another Tycoon (IRE) (Phardante   **c107**
(FR)) [2003/4 h92: 20g c17m^2 c16d* c16g* Oct 14] good sort: modest maiden hurdler: **h–**
quickly better over fences, making all and jumping boldly when easily winning maiden at
Newton Abbot and handicap at Sedgefield: best around 2m: acts on good to soft going
(bumper form on soft): tongue tied after reappearance: races freely. *R. T. Phillips*

NEW TIME (IRE)   5 b.g. Topanoora – Fast Time (IRE) (Be My Native (USA)) [2003/4   **F80**
F16d Apr 21] first foal: dam unraced half-sister to smart hurdler/useful chaser Time For
A Run, stayed 25f: eighth of 19 to Bonny Grey in bumper at Worcester on debut. *Jonjo
O'Neill*

NEWTOWN   5 b.g. Darshaan – Calypso Run (Lycius (USA)) [2003/4 20s^{pu} 17s^{pu} Feb   **h–**
24] second foal: dam once-raced, from very good middle-distance family: twice-raced on
Flat in France at 3 yrs, winning over 1½m at Lyon Parilly for N. Clement: little show in 2
races over hurdles. *M. F. Harris*

NEW VENTURE   5 b.m. Alflora (IRE) – Purple Silk (Belfalas) [2003/4 F16g Nov 7]   **F–**
sixth foal: half-sister to winning hurdler up to 21f Welsh Silk (by Weld): dam, modest
maiden hurdler, stayed 21f: 7/1 from 20/1, well beaten in mares bumper at Hexham on
debut. *W. Storey*

NEXT TO NOTHING (IRE)   7 b.g. Bob's Return (IRE) – Shuil Abhaile (Quayside)   **c107**
[2003/4 h–, F84: 24d^2 25s^{pu} c24d* c24s* c24g^{pu} Apr 10] sturdy gelding: fair form   **h102**
when second in maiden at Ayr on completed start over hurdles: successful first 2 outings
over fences, in 3-runner novice at Carlisle in February and handicap at Newcastle in
March, jumping soundly in front both times: disappointing final start: will stay beyond
3m: raced on good going or softer (acts on soft): sold 25,000 gns Doncaster May Sales.
N. G. Richards

NIAGARA (IRE)   7 b.g. Rainbows For Life (CAN) – Highbrook (USA) (Alphabatim   **c95**
(USA)) [2003/4 h102: 16g^3 20m^2 19g^3 17m^2 c20m* c16f* Oct 8] medium-sized gelding: **h95**
fair on Flat (stays 1½m): modest maiden hurdler: similar form when winning both starts
over fences, maiden at Plumpton and novice at Towcester, both in small fields: stays
2½m: acts on firm going: tried blinkered: front runner/races prominently. *M. H. Tompkins*

NICE GUY EDDIE   5 b.g. Thowra (FR) – Mrs Guyb VII (Damsire Unregistered)   **F–**
[2003/4 F17m Jul 14] first foal: dam never ran: well tailed off in bumper on debut.
N. J. Hawke

NICELY PRESENTED (IRE)   7 b.g. Executive Perk – Minimum Choice (IRE)   **h91**
(Miner's Lamp) [2003/4 F91: 17s^{pu} 20s^{pu} 21g 16d^3 16d^4 Apr 23] workmanlike gelding:
best effort over hurdles when third to Musical Stage in novice at Huntingdon: should stay
beyond 2m. *Jonjo O'Neill*

NICE N SPICEY   7 br.m. Sure Blade (USA) – Dusty Chimes (Foggy Bell) [2003/4   **F–**
F16g F17m F16f^{pu} Oct 16] chunky mare: fifth foal: dam of little account: no better herself. *J. White*

NICE ONE TED (IRE)   8 b.g. Posen (USA) – Arburie (Exbury) [2003/4 h–, F69:   **h–**
24g^{pu} 19d 26s^{pu} Jan 7] lengthy gelding: no form over hurdles: has had tongue tied.
Mrs P. Bickerton

NICHOL FIFTY   10 b.g. Old Vic – Jawaher (IRE) (Dancing Brave (USA)) [2003/4   **h–**
h77: 22g Aug 23] angular gelding: poor on Flat nowadays: lightly-raced winning hurdler:
should stay 2½m: tried tongue tied. *N. Wilson*

NICHO-LINE   7 b.g. Homo Sapien – Littoral (Crash Course) [2003/4 F16m F16m   **F– §**
F16m Sep 14] medium-sized gelding: half-brother to several winners, including one-time
useful chaser Samuel Wilderspin (by Henbit), stays 3¼m: dam, Irish 1½m winner, half-
sister to top-class hurdler Kribensis: showed more temperament than ability in bumpers.
Mrs J. A. Saunders

NICHOLLS CROSS (IRE) 12 b.g. Mandalus – Milan Pride (Northern Guest (USA)) c–
[2003/4 c99, h–: c20m^F Feb 25] rangy ex-Irish gelding: veteran chaser: fell heavily in h–
hunter only start in 2003/4: stays 25f: acts on any going: has found little. *D. McCain Jnr*

NICIARA (IRE) 7 b.g. Soviet Lad (USA) – Verusa (IRE) (Petorius) [2003/4 16s 19g^5 h83
22g^4 Mar 28] medium-sized gelding: winning hurdler around 2m: poor form in 2003/4:
acts on soft and good to firm going. *M. C. Chapman*

NICKEL PLATE 7 b.g. Perpendicular – Tinstone (Nishapour (FR)) [2003/4 F16g^6 h–
21d^{pu} Jan 9] 1,200 3-y-o, £900 5-y-o: third foal: dam maiden 2m hurdler: third in two F–
2½m maiden points in 2003 (took wrong course and disqualified first occasion): no form
in bumper or maiden hurdle. *J. G. M. O'Shea*

NICKEL SUN (IRE) 8 b.g. Phardante (FR) – Deep Green (Deep Run) [2003/4 h117: h117
20d^3 22g^F May 22] sturdy gelding: fairly useful hurdler: fell fatally at Kelso: stayed 2¾m:
acted on good to soft going (won bumper on soft). *Mrs S. J. Smith*

NICKEL SUNTOO (IRE) 7 b.g. Convinced – The Scarlet Dragon (Oats) [2003/4 h81
F88: F17g^6 17g2 20m 20g^5 Aug 23] easily best effort in bumpers on debut: poor form in F74
novice company over hurdles. *Mrs S. J. Smith*

NICK'S CHOICE 8 b.g. Sula Bula – Clare's Choice (Pragmatic) [2003/4 h94: 16m^5 h106
16v* 16d^6 17s^3 Dec 29] compact gelding: fair handicap hurdler: won amateur event at
Plumpton in November: effective at 2m to 2¾m: acts on good to firm and heavy going:
tried blinkered: held up. *D. Burchell*

NICK THE JEWEL 9 b.g. Nicholas Bill – Bijou Georgie (Rhodomantade) [2003/4 c113
c105, h–: c17m* c16g* c16g^3 c16m^3 c16d^2 Dec 26] tall, angular gelding: fair handicap h–
chaser: jumped well when winning at Stratford and Uttoxeter (3-runner race) in October:
best around 2m: acts on soft and good to firm going: front runner. *J. S. King*

NIEMBRO 4 b.g. Victory Note (USA) – Diabaig (Precocious) [2003/4 16m^4 16g^4 16g^3 h90
16m^2 16g* 16s 16g^{pu} 16d 19g^5 Apr 24] poor maiden on Flat (stays 1¼m): modest hurdler:
trained by Mrs L. Pearce first 4 starts: won juvenile at Leicester in December: stays 19f:
acts on good to firm going, possibly not on softer than good. *Mrs T. J. McInnes Skinner*

NIGELLO 12 b.g. El Conquistador – Saffron Poser (Sagaro) [2003/4 c21m^4 c21s^4 19d c79 d
c21^{gur} c19m Apr 13] well-made gelding: one-time fair chaser: sold out of R. Alner's h–
stable £700 Ascot June (2002) Sales: signs of retaining ability only on reappearance:
stays 3m: acts on soft and firm going: blinkered once. *Miss V. A. Stephens*

NIGHT DRIVER (IRE) 5 b.g. Night Shift (USA) – Highshaan (Pistolet Bleu (IRE)) h97
[2003/4 h93: 16g 17m^F 17g^3 17g^5 17s^2 16d^{ur} 16d 16d^{pu} Mar 12] sturdy gelding: modest
maiden hurdler: likely to prove best around 2m: acts on soft and good to firm going:
blinkered (raced too freely) fourth start: joined G. L. Moore. *P. J. Hobbs*

NIGHT FIGHTER (GER) 9 b.g. Dashing Blade – Nouvelle (GER) (Nandino c111
(GER)) [2003/4 c102, h107: c17g^5 c17g* c17m^{pu} Jul 19] sparely-made gelding: fair h–
handicap chaser: best effort when winning at Market Rasen in July: broke down next
time: best around 2m: acts on firm and soft going: often wears cheekpieces: usually
tongue tied. *R. C. Guest*

NIGHT MAIL 4 b.g. Shaamit (IRE) – Penlanfeigan (Abutammam) [2003/4 16d 16g^6 h79
Dec 3] poor maiden on Flat (stays 13.8f): poor form on second of 2 starts in juvenile
hurdles. *M. W. Easterby*

NIGHT MUSIC 7 br.m. Piccolo – Oribi (Top Ville) [2003/4 h67?: 22g^F Apr 30] poor h–
novice hurdler: should stay beyond 19f: acts on soft going: has worn cheekpieces.
G. F. Edwards

NIJWAY 14 b.g. Nijin (USA) – Runaway Girl (FR) (Homeric) [2003/4 c–, h–: c24m c65 ?
c16g^{pu} 22g c21m^{ur} c27m^3 c24m^F c25m^{pu} Oct 3] workmanlike gelding: veteran hurdler/ h–
chaser, little form for long time: has worn eyecover: tongue tied. *M. A. Barnes*

NIL DESPERANDUM (IRE) 7 b.g. Un Desperado (FR) – Still Hoping (Kam- c145
balda) [2003/4 h139, F101: c16d* c20d* c20d* c20d^3 Apr 13] h–
Nil Desperandum is well named, given that he is by Un Desperado out of
Still Hoping, but his owner will no doubt be delighted that the gelding's performances on the racecourse so far make his moniker look most inappropriate. The
winner of a bumper at Roscommon on his debut, in October 2002, Nil Desperandum developed into a useful novice over hurdles later that season, went on to show
even better form over fences in the latest campaign, and looks sure to continue to
do well.

NIL

Nil Desperandum got off the mark over fences at the first time of asking in a maiden at Punchestown in November. He and another chasing debutant, the fairly useful hurdler Central House, had the finish to themselves, with Nil Desperandum staying on strongly to edge ahead near the line. Both horses went on to win Grade 1 novice events before the end of the year, with Central House taking the Denny Gold Medal Chase at Leopardstown and Nil Desperandum the Pierse Group Drinmore Chase at Fairyhouse on his next start. The Drinmore Chase attracted ten runners, and they included the smart novice hurdler Pizarro who had also won his only start over fences and was sent off favourite, with Nil Desperandum next in the betting in what looked quite a good renewal of this prestigious event. Pizarro failed by a long way to give his running, though he would have had his work cut out to cope with Nil Desperandum even if he had done. In a well-run race, the latter again jumped soundly, took the lead after three out, travelling strongly, and soon drew clear without needing to be hard ridden, passing the post with fourteen lengths to spare over his nearest pursuer Catalpa Cargo. It was an eye-catching performance from Nil Desperandum who looked on course for a return visit to the Cheltenham Festival—he had been promoted to sixth in the previous season's Royal & SunAlliance Novices' Hurdle—with the Royal & SunAlliance Chase the obvious race for him. Unfortunately he suffered an overreach in January and was not seen in action again until April. Another Grade 1 event at Fairyhouse, the Powers Gold Cup, was the race chosen for Nil Desperandum's return, and, while not up to winning it, he did acquit himself well in finishing third behind Hi Cloy and Kicking King, one place ahead of Central House. Held up, Nil Desperandum could never quite get on terms with the principals but kept on in the straight to be beaten just over six lengths by the winner. Two weeks later Nil Desperandum ran to a similar level when last of four behind Lord Sam in a Grade 3 novice chase at Punchestown. The emphasis was more on speed than it had been in Nil Desperandum's previous appearances over fences, and he was found wanting when the race began in earnest, a mistake two out finally putting paid to his chance. Nil Desperandum has raced only at two and a half miles over fences, but he won over as far as two and three quarters over hurdles and there is no doubt that a return to further—he will stay at least three miles—will suit him well.

Pierse Group Drinmore Novices' Chase, Fairyhouse—Nil Desperandum gains an impressive success

Mr M. L. Shone's "Nil Desperandum"

Nil Desperandum (IRE) (b.g. 1997)	Un Desperado (FR) (b 1983)	Top Ville (b 1976)	High Top
			Sega Ville
		White Lightning (gr 1970)	Baldric II
			Rough Sea
	Still Hoping (b 1982)	Kambalda (b 1970)	Right Royal V
			Opencast
		Ganston Girl (b 1968)	Vulgan
			Weston Girl

Nil Desperandum is the fifth foal of Still Hoping, whose sole success was gained in a mares maiden point in Ireland. Still Hoping is also the dam of the nine-year-old Irish hurdler Willoughby Joe (by Persian Mews), a winner at up to three miles in the latest season. The next two mares on the bottom line of the pedigree were unraced. Both have produced winning chasers, Nil Desperandum's great grandam Weston Girl being the dam of the fairly useful out-and-out stayer Charley Winking, who won the 1972 National Hunt Chase at Cheltenham and was a brother to Nil Desperandum's grandam Ganston Girl. Weston Girl's half-sister Phrygia is the grandam of the top-class staying chaser Young Hustler. The useful-looking Nil Desperandum has raced only on good going or softer, and he acts on soft. *Miss F. M. Crowley, Ireland*

NIMBUS STRATUS 11 br.g. Welsh Captain – Touching Clouds (Touching Wood (USA)) [2003/4 c–, h–: 22d[pu] 20m[5] Aug 8] lengthy gelding: winning pointer: maiden hurdler, no form for long time: tried blinkered/in cheekpieces. *J. D. Frost*   c–
h–

NINE O THREE (IRE)   15 b.g. Supreme Leader – Grenache (Menelek) [2003/4   h–
h103: 24m⁶ 27g 27gᶠ Jun 28] small gelding: veteran handicap hurdler: well held both
completed starts on return from 10-month absence: stays 27f: probably acts on any going.
Mrs S. D. Williams

NIP ON   10 b.g. Dunbeath (USA) – Popping On (Sonnen Gold) [2003/4 c–, h84: c25dᵖᵘ   c–
c25g c25gᵖᵘ 20f² 27d⁴ Oct 29] poor hurdler: no form in steeplechases: stays 27f: acts on   h79
heavy and good to firm going: tried in blinkers/cheekpieces/tongue tied: sold 1,000 gns
Doncaster January Sales, runner-up in point in April. *J. R. Turner*

NISBET   10 b.g. Lithgie-Brig – Drummond Lass (Peacock (FR)) [2003/4 c81, h77:   c90
c25dᵖᵘ c24m³ c25m c24g³ c25g* c26d² Apr 23] modest chaser, left Miss L. Russell after   h–
fourth start: improved form when winning maiden hunter at Kelso in April: stays 3¼m:
acts on soft and good to firm going: races prominently. *Miss M. Bremner*

NITE FOX (IRE)   5 ch.m. Anshan – New Talent (The Parson) [2003/4 F16g⁶ F16d⁵   F76
Apr 21] eighth foal: half-sister to winning hurdler around 2m Harvest Storm (by Strong
Gale) and poor hurdler/chaser Leitrim Cottage (by Yashgan), stays 3½m: dam placed in
bumper: modest form in bumpers at Huntingdon and Worcester: will stay beyond 2m.
Mrs H. Dalton

NOAFF (IRE)   10 b.g. Mandalus – Good Sailing (Scorpio (FR)) [2003/4 c91+, h–:   c72
c24m³ Apr 13] fair pointer: tongue tied, below best when third in hunter at Chepstow.   h–
John Moore

NO ARGUMENT   5 b.g. Young Ern – As Sharp As (Handsome Sailor) [2003/4 17mᵖᵘ   h–
20dᵖᵘ Nov 21] sturdy gelding: showed nothing in 2 novice hurdles. *C. C. Bealby*

NOBLE AFFAIR   9 b.m. Lancastrian – Abinovian (Ra Nova) [2003/4 c21s⁴ Mar 19]   c–
half-sister to fairly useful pointer Araminta (by Carlingford Castle): fair pointer, successful in January: well beaten in hunter on steeplechase debut. *Mrs L. Pomfret*

NOBLE BARON   8 gr.g. Karinga Bay – Grey Baroness (Baron Blakeney) [2003/4 h79,   c–
F85: c21mᵖᵘ c24sᵖᵘ 22d* 24s⁴ 22s* 22s* Apr 6] workmanlike gelding: failed to complete   h118
both starts in novice chases: much improved returned to hurdles, won handicaps (first 2
novice events) at Exeter in January, March and April: fairly useful form when beating
Lesdream 3 lengths in 19-runner event on final occasion: should stay beyond 2¾m: acts
on soft going. *C. G. Cox*

NOBLE CAESAR (IRE)   6 b. or br.g. Montelimar (USA) – Timely Run (IRE) (Deep   c–
Run) [2003/4 h–: c20dᵖᵘ 16d Dec 17] lengthy gelding: no sign of ability. *M. Todhunter*   h–

NOBLE CALLING (FR)   7 b.h. Caller I D (USA) – Specificity (USA) (Alleged   h93
(USA)) [2003/4 16g⁶ 17d³ 16s 17g⁵ 17m 17s* 17g⁴ 16g³ Apr 18] leggy horse: modest on
Flat (stays easy 1½m): of similar merit over hurdles: easily landed odds in novice seller at
Exeter in March: raced around 2m: acts on soft going, probably on good to firm.
R. J. Hodges

NOBLE COLOURS   11 b.g. Distinctly North (USA) – Kentucky Tears (USA) (Cougar   c–
(CHI)) [2003/4 c16gᵖᵘ c21s⁵ c21dᵖᵘ Apr 12] small gelding: one-time fair hurdler: no form   h–
in points and hunters in 2004: often tongue tied. *Mrs P. J. Ikin*

NOBLE COMIC   13 b.g. Silly Prices – Barony (Ribston) [2003/4 c106, h–: c16m c16d⁶   c92
c21gᵖᵘ c16g² c21gᵖᵘ c16m² c17m c21f⁴ c21f⁴ c16f³ c21mᵖᵘ Dec 4] good-topped gelding: h–
modest handicap chaser: stays 21f: acts on firm and good to soft going, probably not on
softer: folded tamely in cheekpieces fifth outing: has won 5 times at Newton Abbot: races
prominently. *C. L. Tizzard*

NOBLE DEED (IRE)   7 b.g. Lord Americo – Legal Statement (IRE) (Strong State-   h–
ment (USA)) [2003/4 h72: 20sᵖᵘ Feb 19] well-made gelding: chasing type: lightly raced
over hurdles, no encouragement only start in 2003/4. *Miss H. C. Knight*

NOBLEFIR (IRE)   6 b.g. Shernazar – Chrisali (IRE) (Strong Gale) [2003/4 F94: 17d²   h90
20s⁶ 25sᵖᵘ Jan 6] lengthy, well-made gelding: chasing type: won Irish point in 2002:
modest form in novices first 2 starts over hurdles. *L. Lungo*

NOBLE HOUSE   7 ch.g. Gildoran – Trust To Luck (Mandamus) [2003/4 17g⁵ 24m⁶   h93
20d² Nov 14] fifth foal: dam, winning chaser, stayed 2½m: best effort over hurdles when
second to Patriarch Express in novice at Newcastle, again not fluent and no chance with
easy winner after dictating pace: should stay beyond 2½m. *Mrs A. Duffield*

NOBLE HYMN   11 br.g. Arctic Lord – Soraway (Choral Society) [2003/4 c81, h–:   c81
c20m⁴ c25d³ c20g² c27d⁵ Mar 16] close-coupled gelding: modest hunter chaser: stays   h–
25f: acts on good to firm and good to soft going: has had tongue tied. *Mrs C. M. Mulhall*

NOBLE JUSTICE (IRE)   8 b.g. Jurado (USA) – Furry Hope (Furry Glen) [2003/4   **c108** c–, h–: c20s^{pu} c21f* Nov 8] tall gelding: lightly raced: maiden hurdler: fair chaser: first   **h–** form since 2001/2 when winning 4-runner handicap at Wincanton: stays 2¾m: acts on firm going. has had tongue tied. *R. J. Hodges*

NOBLE PHILOSOPHER   4 ch.g. Faustus (USA) – Princess Lucy (Local Suitor   **h–** (USA)) [2003/4 16g^{pu} 16s^{pu} Jan 23] brother to bumper winner Lady Faustus: little form in maidens on Flat: no show in juvenile hurdles: tried blinkered. *R. M. Beckett*

NOBLE PURSUIT (FR)   6 b.g. Pursuit of Love – Pipitina (Bustino) [2003/4 c20g^{pu} **c–** c24g^{pu} Feb 11] sixth foal: half-brother to fair hurdler Barcelona (by Barathea), stays 2¾m, and modest staying chaser Primero (by Lycius): dam fairly useful stayer on Flat: ran once around 1½m in French Provinces at 4 yrs for P. Supple: no show either start over fences: tried tongue tied. *I. R. Brown*

NOBLE SPY (IRE)   10 b.g. Lord Americo – Flashey Blond (Buckskin (FR)) [2003/4   **c–** c–, h–: 21g 20m 24m^{5} Nov 9] good-topped gelding: winning hurdler: well held in hand-   **h–** icaps since 2001/2: no show on chasing debut: stays 25f: tried visored. *Mrs D. A. Hamer*

NOBLE TEVIOT   6 b.g. Lithgie-Brig – Polly Peril (Politico (USA)) [2003/4 F17g   **h–** 17d^{4} 16d 16s 16v^{5} 24d Mar 11] leggy gelding: ninth foal: half-brother to winning staying   **F–** chaser Harden Glen (by Respect): dam never ran: third on first of 2 starts in maiden points in 2003: tailed off in bumper: seemed to show poor form on first of 5 starts over hurdles, though made running and probably flattered. *Miss S. E. Forster*

NOBODY'S FOOL   9 ch.g. St Ninian – Majestic Form (IRE) (Double Schwartz)   **h–** [2003/4 16m^{pu} Jun 5] no sign of ability in 2 runs 4 years apart. *Mrs Dianne Sayer*

NOCKSKY (IRE)   11 b.g. Niniski (USA) – Olivana (GER) (Sparkler) [2003/4 c25g^{pu} **c92** c21g* Apr 10] leggy gelding: one-time useful hurdler/fairly useful chaser: off 2 years   **h–** prior to reappearance, modest form when winning selling handicap at Newton Abbot: stays 3¼m: acts on good to firm and heavy going. *M. C. Pipe*

NO COMPLICATIONS (IRE)   6 b.g. Supreme Leader – Bramble Bird (Montelimar   **F100** (USA)) [2003/4 F16d F16s* Feb 7] half-brother to fairly useful chaser Solvang (by Carlingford Castle), stays 3m: dam unraced half-sister to fairly useful staying chasers Artic Ale and Echo Sounder: easily best effort in bumpers when winning at Naas by ½ length from Tigerlion: will be suited by 2½m. *Paul Nolan, Ireland*

NOD 'N' A WINK   6 b.g. Factual (USA) – Singing Reply (USA) (The Minstrel (CAN))   **F–** [2003/4 F16s Dec 11] angular gelding: second foal: dam, winning hurdler, stayed 2½m: tailed off in bumper and seller on Flat. *C. A. Dwyer*

NOD YA HEAD   8 ch.m. Minster Son – Little Mittens (Little Buskins) [2003/4 F–:   **h66** 17d 16m 20m^{4} 21s 27f^{3} 21d^{4} Mar 16] poor novice hurdler: stays 21f. *R. E. Barr*

NO FEAR (IRE)   8 b.g. Warcraft (USA) – Mandalaw (IRE) (Mandalus) [2003/4 20g^{pu} **h–** May 29] runner-up in bumper on debut: broke leg in novice hurdle over year later. *Mrs S. J. Smith*

NO FINER MAN (IRE)   13 b.g. Lord Americo – Ballaroe Bar (Bargello) [2003/4   **c–** c26g May 26] winning pointer: maiden steeplechaser: stays 2½m. *Miss Angela*   **h–** *Stephenson*

NO FORECAST (IRE)   10 b.g. Executive Perk – Guess Twice (Deep Run) [2003/4   **c108** c109, h–: c24m^{2} c24d^{pu} 24d^{pu} Mar 10] tall gelding: maiden hurdler/winning chaser,   **h–** lightly raced: worn down near finish when second of 3 finishers to Ray Source in handicap over fences at Ascot on reappearance: ran poorly both subsequent starts: stays 3m: acts on good to firm going (won bumper on heavy): difficult to train. *A. M. Hales*

NO GLOATING (IRE)   5 b.g. King's Ride – Arctic Gale (IRE) (Strong Gale) [2003/4   **F–** F16d Apr 17] 16,500 4-y-o: first foal: dam, modest maiden hurdler around 2½m, out of half-sister to smart hurdler/useful chaser Danny Harrold: last of 9 in bumper on debut. *P. D. Niven*

NOISETINE (FR)   6 ch.m. Mansonnien (FR) – Notabilite (FR) (No Pass No Sale)   **c112** [2003/4 h103: c25d^{2} c19s^{2} c22s^{4} c19g* c21s^{2} c20m^{2} c18d^{2} Apr 7] good-topped mare: fair   **h–** handicap hurdler: similar form over fences, won novice at Catterick in February by 17 lengths from Konker: stays 2¾m: acts on good to firm and heavy going: has jumped left. *Miss Venetia Williams*

NO KIDDING   10 b.g. Teenoso (USA) – Vaigly Fine (Vaigly Great) [2003/4 c101, h–:   **c97 x** c16m c20m c16m^{5} c26m c20f^{3} c16m* c20m^{2} c17g^{3} c16g c16s^{5} Dec 26] strong, lengthy   **h–**

gelding: modest handicap chaser: won at Hexham in October: stays 2½m: acts on firm and soft going: sometimes makes mistakes. *J. I. A. Charlton*

NOLIFE (IRE) 8 b.g. Religiously (USA) – Garnerstown Lady (Pitpan) [2003/4 h–: 16mF c20gpu 20g6 20g5 24g4 Jul 3] leggy gelding: little sign of ability outside points. *Miss Lucinda V. Russell*   **c–** **h–**

NOMADIC ICE 7 b.g. Nomadic Way (USA) – Icelolly (Idiot's Delight) [2003/4 25spu 22gpu 19s c24g Apr 18] angular gelding: second foal: dam never ran: no sign of ability. *Mrs G. Harvey*   **c–** **h–**

NOMADIC STAR 9 br.g. Nomadic Way (USA) – Dreamago (Sir Mago) [2003/4 c80: c25d5 c25d6 Mar 23] fair pointer, successful in February: well held in 2 hunters in 2003/4, left D. Atkinson after first: has had tongue tied. *Mrs F. J. Browne*   **c66**

NO MERCY 8 ch.g. Faustus (USA) – Nashville Blues (IRE) (Try My Best (USA)) [2003/4 h79?: 16v 16m 20m2 19g 24m5 20f5 21s6 20d6 Nov 23] angular gelding: poor and unreliable on Flat in 2003: little worthwhile form over hurdles: often wears blinkers/cheekpieces: tried tongue tied. *B. A. Pearce*   **h79 §**

NOMINATE (GER) 4 b.g. Desert King (IRE) – Northern Goddess (Night Shift (USA)) [2003/4 16mpu Sep 27] fair form at best on Flat when trained by P. Cole: lost action on hurdling debut: sold £2,200 Ascot April Sales. *S. T. Lewis*   **h–**

NO MORE MONEY 6 b.m. Alflora (IRE) – Cover Your Money (Precipice Wood) [2003/4 F17d2 F16s4 F17s4 19d4 19g3 Mar 9] useful-looking mare: half-sister to numerous winners, including useful chaser up to 3m Red Striker and Grand National winner Red Marauder (both by Gunner B): dam, fair hurdler/novice chaser, stayed 3m: modest form in bumpers: tongue tied, better effort in mares novice hurdles when third to Henrietta at Exeter: will be suited by further. *Miss H. C. Knight*   **h83** **F85**

NO MUCKIN' ABOUT 9 br.g. Muqadar (USA) – Planet Suite (Space King) [2003/4 c19gpu c16f6 16gpu May 21] workmanlike gelding: of little account and temperamental to boot: tried in cheekpieces. *V. Y. Gethin*   **c– §** **h– §**

NONANTAIS (FR) 7 b.g. Nikos – Sanhia (FR) (Sanhedrin (USA)) [2003/4 h119+, F88: c21d2 c20g3 Mar 7] good-topped gelding: fairly useful hurdler: encouraging second to Hawk's Landing in maiden at Folkestone on chasing debut: failed to jump with any fluency when well-beaten last of 3 finishers in novice at Kempton next time: stays 21f: acts on heavy ground: usually makes running. *M. Bradstock*   **c119** **h–**

NO NAY NEVER (IRE) 9 b.g. Tremblant – Monread (Le Tricolore) [2003/4 h63: 20m c16m4 May 15] little worthwhile form over hurdles: soundly beaten on chasing debut: sold £1,800 Ascot June Sales. *J. W. Mullins*   **c–** **h–**

NONCHALANT (IRE) 6 ch.g. Magical Wonder (USA) – Look Nonchalant (IRE) (Fayruz) [2003/4 h113: c16s3 c24s4 20d5 Feb 28] fair handicap hurdler: similar form both outings over fences: effective at 2m to 3m: acts on soft ground: tried blinkered. *Miss F. M. Crowley, Ireland*   **c113** **h101**

NON SO (FR) 6 b.g. Definite Article – Irish Woman (FR) (Assert) [2003/4 h136: c17d* c17s* c16g2 Jan 10] good-topped gelding: useful handicap hurdler: successful first 2 starts over fences, in novices at Plumpton in December and January (5/2-on, not at all extended to beat Tidour 1¼ lengths), jumping soundly both times: bad mistake seventh when second of 3 to Bal de Nuit in Grade 2 novice at Ascot: will prove best around 2m: raced on good going or softer (acts on soft): usually patiently ridden: free-going sort: remains capable of better over fences. *N. J. Henderson*   **c125 p** **h–**

NON STOP AIMS 6 ch.m. Gunner B – Prevada (Soldier Rose) [2003/4 F16g Mar 17] fifth foal: dam ran once in point: pulled hard when well beaten in bumper on debut. *J. L. Spearing*   **F–**

NON VINTAGE (IRE) 13 ch.g. Shy Groom (USA) – Great Alexandra (Runnett) [2003/4 c–§, h61§: c21m c21gpu c30gpu 17g May 26] workmanlike gelding: winning hurdler/chaser, retains neither ability nor enthusiasm: tried blinkered. *M. C. Chapman*   **c– §** **h– §**

NOPEKAN (IRE) 4 b.g. Sri Pekan (USA) – Giadamar (IRE) (Be My Guest (USA)) [2003/4 16d4 16d2 16s5 16s2 16g* 16g5 16d4 Apr 12] rather leggy, close-coupled gelding: useful on Flat (stays 1¼m): fairly useful juvenile hurdler: won minor event at Leopardstown in February by length from Common World: ran well when fifth to Al Eile in Grade 2 at Aintree next time and to Cherub in Grade 1 at Punchestown in late-April: will prove best at easy 2m: sold to join Miss K. Marks 56,000 gns Doncaster May Sales. *Patrick Mullins, Ireland*   **h122**

NO PICNIC (IRE) 6 ch.g. Be My Native (USA) – Emmagreen (Green Shoon) [2003/4 **h113** h91, F81: 22f³ 20m⁶ 22m⁴ 24g³ 20s² 21v⁴ 24g³ 24g² 24s* 24d² Apr 22] small, leggy gelding: fair novice hurdler: won 17-runner event at Hexham in April by 5 lengths from Schuh Shine: appeared to improve again when second of 5 to Monet's Garden at Perth, though off bridle long way and no chance with easy winner: thorough stayer: acts on good to firm and heavy going. *Mrs S. C. Bradburne*

NOPLANOFACTION (IRE) 7 ch.g. Be My Native (USA) – Creative Music (Crea- **h92** tive Plan (USA)) [2003/4 F16s* 19s² Jan 14] IR 23,000 3-y-o: lengthy gelding: sixth foal: **F112** dam, maiden, half-sister to fairly useful staying hurdler Native Field (by Be My Native): useful form when winning Grade 2 bumper at Chepstow on debut in December by 4 lengths from Bob Bob Bobbin: sustained bad tendon injury when second to impressive Trabolgan in novice at Newbury on hurdling debut: dead. *Jonjo O'Neill*

NORAS LEGACY (IRE) 6 b.m. Old Vic – Balda Girl (IRE) (Mandalus) [2003/4 **h–** F16g F16m 21vᵘʳ 20s⁴ 16g Apr 5] €2,100 4-y-o: smallish mare: third foal: dam unraced: **F–** achieved little in steadily-run bumpers and on both completed starts over hurdles. *Miss Lucinda V. Russell*

NORBERT (IRE) 6 ch.g. Imperial Frontier (USA) – Glowing Reeds (Kalaglow) **h–** [2003/4 F–: 16m May 7] no form, even in points. *M. F. Harris*

NORDANCE PRINCE (IRE) 13 b.g. Nordance (USA) – Shirleys Princess (Sand- **c–** hurst Prince) [2003/4 c130, h–: c19dᵖᵘ c20gᶠ Mar 7] angular gelding: useful handicap **h–** chaser, lightly raced nowadays: failed to complete both starts in 2003/4, though in narrow lead when falling eleventh in handicap at Kempton: stays 2½m: acts on firm and soft going. *Miss Venetia Williams*

NORDIC CREST (IRE) 10 b.g. Danehill (USA) – Feather Glen (Glenstal (USA)) **c–** [2003/4 c–, h–: c26d May 28] sturdy gelding: fair pointer nowadays, successful 3 times **h–** in 2003: tongue tied, well beaten in hunter chase: stays 3m: acts on firm and good to soft going: tried visored. *Mrs C. A. Coward*

NORDIC PRINCE (IRE) 13 b.g. Nordance (USA) – Royal Desire (Royal Match) **c–** [2003/4 c114, h107: 20v* 24d⁶ Mar 27] compact gelding: fair chaser: modest hurdler: **h97** won seller at Uttoxeter in January: effective around 2½m to 3¼m: acts on any going: tried visored. *J. G. M. O'Shea*

NO RETREAT (NZ) 11 b.g. Exattic (USA) – Lerwick (NZ) (Thoreau (FR)) [2003/4 **c98** c24d³ c28dᵖᵘ Mar 30] rangy gelding: fair handicap chaser in 2001/2: well backed, third to **h–** Pharaway Citizen at Bangor on return from nearly 2 years off: ran poorly later in month: probably stays 27f: acts on good to firm and heavy going: sound jumper. *R. T. Phillips*

NORLANDIC (NZ) 12 ch.g. First Norman (USA) – April Snow (NZ) (Icelandic) **c95 x** [2003/4 c100x, h–: c23g c25m* c25dᵖᵘ Mar 23] good-topped gelding: modest handicap **h–** chaser: reportedly finished lame when winning at Exeter in May: left P. Hobbs/fit from points, pulled up in hunter: best form up to 25f: acts on good to firm and heavy going: sketchy jumper. *L. Jefford*

NORMAND DE FER (FR) 7 b.g. Genereux Genie – Xav Wood (FR) (Le Pontet **h82 ?** (FR)) [2003/4 19g⁵ 24g Mar 26] workmanlike gelding: fourth foal: dam once-raced: pulled up in maiden point on debut in 2003: well held in 2 novice hurdles. *John Allen*

NORMANDY SANDS (IRE) 6 b. or br.g. Namaqualand (USA) – Buzz Along **h82 §** (Prince Bee) [2003/4 h–, F78: 24m² 24m³ 26s⁵ 26s³ 24v² 26s⁶ 27s 24v 26g² Apr 3] tall gelding: poor maiden hurdler: thorough stayer: acts on heavy and good to firm going: often wears cheekpieces or visor: lazy and inconsistent. *Mrs J. Candlish*

NORMANIA (NZ) 12 b.g. First Norman (USA) – Brigania (NZ) (Brigand (USA)) **c90** [2003/4 c95, h–: c24d⁵ c22g⁴ c21dᵖᵘ Apr 12] workmanlike gelding: fair hunter chaser: **h–** stays 2¾m: acts on soft and firm going: has had tongue tied. *Miss S. West*

NORTHAW LAD (IRE) 6 ch.g. Executive Perk – Black Tulip (Pals Passage) **h96 p** [2003/4 F88: F18s³ F16g³ F16s* 16g⁴ Feb 11] sturdy gelding: generally progressive in **F98** bumpers, left A. Lidderdale after reappearance: won maiden at Uttoxeter in December by 4 lengths from Lord Gale: fourth of 18 to Crossbow Creek in maiden at Ludlow on hurdling debut, not knocked about: will stay beyond 2m: should improve. *C. Tinkler*

NORTH CROFT 8 b.g. North Street – Sock Jinks (New Member) [2003/4 h–, F–: **h–** 16mᵖᵘ 22gᵖᵘ 17f⁴ 17f⁴ Oct 21] of no account: tried in cheekpieces. *C. J. Gray*

NORTHERN ECHO 7 b.g. Pursuit of Love – Stop Press (USA) (Sharpen Up) [2003/4 **h53 §** h66§: 16d⁶ 16m⁴ 17g 16g⁵ 17g 17m⁶ 16f⁶ 17g⁶ 20m⁵ 17d⁵ Oct 29] compact gelding: bad maiden hurdler: raced mainly around 2m: acts on firm going: tried blinkered/visored, wears cheekpieces nowadays: has worn tongue strap: refused to race once. *K. S. Thomas*

NORTHERN EDITION (IRE)　7 br.g. Good Thyne (USA) – Early Pace (Black Minstrel) [2003/4 c26s* c32g^{pu} Mar 17] 18,500 4-y-o: workmanlike gelding: second foal: dam won point and 2¼m hurdle in Ireland: won 2½m maiden on first of 2 starts in points in 2003: won novice at Plumpton on steeplechasing debut in February by 3½ lengths from Lynrick Lady: stiff task next time: should stay beyond 3¼m: remains likely to improve. *P. F. Nicholls*　**c102 p**

NORTHERN FLASH　10 b.g. Rambo Dancer (CAN) – Spinster (Grundy) [2003/4 c–, h–: c16g^4 c22g c24d^6 c27s c16g^4 c20s^4 c20v^3 c21s c16d^5 c17g^{pu} c20d^{pu} Apr 18] workmanlike gelding: of little account: usually wears headgear: tried tongue tied. *J. C. Haynes*　**c–**　**h–**

NORTHERN MINSTER　5 b.g. Minster Son – Hand On Heart (IRE) (Taufan (USA)) [2003/4 h–, F81: 16g 22f 20d^4 16f* 16s^6 20g^{pu} 16v* 17s 17g 16g^5 Apr 5] poor hurdler: won weak novice handicaps at Catterick in November and Newcastle in February: may prove best around 2m: acts on any going. *F. P. Murtagh*　**h75**

NORTHERN MOTTO　11 b.g. Mtoto – Soulful (FR) (Zino) [2003/4 h70§: c24g^{ur} May 31] neat gelding: poor maiden hurdler: winning pointer: in rear when unseating ninth in hunter at Stratford: stays 25f: acts on any going: tried visored/blinkered: not one to trust. *T. Jewitt*　**c– §**　**h– §**

NORTHERN RAIDER (IRE)　6 b.g. College Chapel – Pepper And Salt (IRE) (Double Schwartz) [2003/4 c71, h–: 24d^{pu} Mar 18] sturdy gelding: won poor race over hurdles in 2001/2: little other sign of ability: tried blinkered. *Miss T. Jackson*　**c–**　**h–**

NORTHERN RAMBLER (IRE)　7 gr.g. Roselier (FR) – Ramble Bramble (Random Shot) [2003/4 h–, F83: 24v^{pu} 23m^3 22g^3 23d 22d^5 c25g^3 Mar 10] quite good-topped gelding: poor novice handicap hurdler: similar form on chasing debut: stays 25f: tried blinkered (numerous mistakes): has looked temperamental. *Mrs M. Reveley*　**c70**　**h76 §**

NORTHERN SHADOWS　5 b.m. Rock Hopper – Shadows of Silver (Carwhite) [2003/4 F16d^3 F16d Apr 12] sturdy mare: second foal: sister to fair 2m hurdler Out of The Shadows: dam, bumper winner/fairly useful 1¾m winner on Flat, ran once over hurdles: better effort in bumpers when 1½ lengths third of 21 to Fenney Spring in mares maiden at Warwick on debut. *Mrs M. Reveley*　**F89**

NORTHERN SVENGALI (IRE)　8 b.g. Distinctly North (USA) – Trilby's Dream (IRE) (Mansooj) [2003/4 16m^6 Dec 16] poor on Flat (stays 7f): tailed off in novice on hurdling debut. *D. A. Nolan*　**h–**

NORTH FACE　7 ch.g. Factual (USA) – Northgate Dancer (Ile de Bourbon (USA)) [2003/4 c–, h–: 16g Jun 6] leggy, lengthy gelding: well held only start over fences: poor hurdler, very lightly raced nowadays: raced around 2m: acts on firm ground, possibly not on softer than good: pulled hard in blinkers. *Miss Lucinda V. Russell*　**c–**　**h–**

NORTH (IRE)　6 br.g. Mukaddamah (USA) – Flamenco (USA) (Dance Spell (USA)) [2003/4 h–: 20s^{pu} Apr 17] no show in 3 novice hurdles. *A. C. Wilson*　**h–**

NORTH OF KALA (IRE)　11 b.g. Distinctly North (USA) – Hi Kala (Kampala) [2003/4 c18m^2 c16d^4 c16m^{pu} Jul 14] sturdy gelding: winning hurdler: fair chaser: would have won handicap at Newton Abbot but for breaking leg 2 out: was best around 2m on good going or firmer. *G. L. Moore*　**c101**　**h–**

NORTH POINT (IRE)　6 b.g. Definite Article – Friendly Song (Song) [2003/4 h109: 16g^5 18d^{pu} 19g Apr 16] smallish, close-coupled gelding: fair 2m hurdler in 2002/3: little impact in 2003/4: acts on good to firm going. *R. Curtis*　**h–**

NORTON SAPPHIRE　5 ch.m. Karinga Bay – Sea of Pearls (IRE) (King's Ride) [2003/4 F16g 17g 21v^{pu} 19g 16s^5 21d 21d^2 Apr 11] 2,000 4-y-o: first foal: dam unraced, out of sister to smart staying chaser Captain Dibble: last of 7 in bumper on debut: first form over hurdles when second in selling handicap at Plumpton: stays 21f. *M. J. Gingell*　**h65**　**F–**

NOSAM　14 b.g. Idiot's Delight – Socher (Anax) [2003/4 c116, h–: c20s^3 c20g^5 c20m^F c24g 22g^6 c21m^6 24m c24m^2 c21g* c25f^2 c25f^3 c24f^2 21d c20d^4 c19g^6 c25g^3 Mar 13] sparely-made, close-coupled gelding: runs occasionally over hurdles: fair handicap chaser: won at Sedgefield in September: effective at 19f to 25f: acts on any going: usually wears cheekpieces nowadays: tongue tied: tough. *R. C. Guest*　**c110**　**h–**

NO SAM NO　6 b.m. Reprimand – Samjamalifran (Blakeney) [2003/4 c–, h73: c25m^5 c24g* c26g^F c26m^{pu} c25d c25d^{pu} c21d^5 c19s c24v^{pu} 24g^6 17g^5 22m^5 Mar 11] leggy mare: poor chaser/maiden hurdler: won maiden over fences at Perth in July: sold out of Mrs　**c73**　**h64**

K. Walton's stable 5,750 gns (privately) Doncaster October Sales before next start: stays 3m: acts on soft going: blinkered last 6 outings. *S. C. Burrough*

NO SHENANIGANS (IRE) 7 h.g. King's Ride – Melarka (Dara Monarch) [2003/4 c106 c16s[3] c16d[2] c16g Apr 3] strong, good sort: useful bumper winner in 2001/2: off nearly 2 years, fair form at best in novice chases, beaten 3 lengths by Kalca Mome in match at Sandown: bred to stay beyond 2m. *N. J. Henderson*

NOSHINANNIKIN 10 ch.g. Anshan – Preziosa (Homing) [2003/4 c116x, h105: 16d[5] c121 x 16d[2] c19g[2] c19g[3] c16d Mar 18] big, strong gelding: fair handicap hurdler: sold out of h110 M. Easterby's stable 4,500 gns Doncaster August Sales after first start: fairly useful handicap chaser: good efforts when placed behind Deep Water at Catterick and Trouble Ahead at Ascot: stays 2½m: acts on soft and good to firm going: tried blinkered: effective tongue tied or not: sketchy jumper of fences. *Mrs S. J. Smith*

NO SMALL PLANS (IRE) 7 br.m. Teamster – Kilmurry Queen (IRE) (Mister Lord h113 (USA)) [2003/4 F18d[3] F20v[2] F16d 20m 22g* 20s[2] 24d[2] 22s[3] 20s[4] 24s[4] 22s[5] 20s[3] Feb 26] F81 third foal: dam, winning pointer, sister to dual Foxhunter winner Earthmover: winning pointer: placed on 2 of 3 starts in bumpers: fair hurdler: won maiden at Downpatrick in November: best efforts on seventh to tenth outings, 3 times in Grade 3 events: stays 3m: acts on soft going. *Gerard Cully, Ireland*

NOSTRADAMUS (USA) 5 b. or br.g. Gone West (USA) – Madam North (CAN) h91 (Halo (USA)) [2003/4 17d[7] 16v[6] 16s 16d Mar 21] good-topped gelding: useful on Flat (stays 1¼m) at 3 yrs for A. O'Brien: modest form on first 2 completed starts over hurdles. *K. Burke, Ireland*

NOTANOTHERDONKEY (IRE) 4 b.g. Zaffaran (USA) – Sporting Talent (IRE) F85 (Seymour Hicks (FR)) [2003/4 F13d F12d F16g[3] Mar 15] tall, unfurnished gelding: third foal (all by Zaffaran): dam unraced half-sister to useful chaser Latent Talent, stayed 25f: best effort in bumpers when third to Gaelic Flight in maiden at Stratford: will stay well beyond 2m. *M. Scudamore*

NOT NOW GEORGE 5 b.g. Sovereign Water (FR) – Threads (Bedford (USA)) h– [2003/4 F–: F16v 17s 20s[F] Feb 14] medium-sized gelding: little sign of ability: sold 1,400 F– gns Doncaster May Sales. *T. H. Caldwell*

NOTSOTINY 8 b.g. Southern Music – Goodbye Roscoe (Roscoe Blake) [2003/4 16m h– 20m[F] 16m[6] 17m Aug 3] second foal: dam of little account: won maiden on completed start in points in 2003: showed nothing over hurdles: tried visored: sold £2,500 Ascot April Sales. *Evan Williams*

NOT TO BE MISSED 6 gr.m. Missed Flight – Petinata (Petong) [2003/4 h82, F81: h68 16g[F] 16g 16g[2] 17m[6] 16m Oct 9] unfurnished mare: poor novice hurdler: likely to prove best around 2m. *R. Dickin*

NOTWHATSHEWANTED (IRE) 7 b.g. Supreme Leader – Wise Nellie (IRE) h– (Brush Aside (USA)) [2003/4 h–, F–: 22m[4] 21d[pu] 21d 22d 22g[5] Apr 13] workmanlike gelding: little worthwhile form over hurdles. *J. W. Mullins*

NOUGHT TO NINETY 6 b.g. Mazaad – Bonnyhill Lass (Royal Fountain) [2003/4 h– 22m[6] May 7] little show in maiden bumper and intermediate hurdle a year apart: won maiden point in April. *C. Grant*

NOUSAYRI (IRE) 9 b.g. Slip Anchor – Noufiyla (Top Ville) [2003/4 c–, h–: c20m[5] c65 May 10] leggy gelding: maiden hurdler: modest form over fences: stays 3m: acts on heavy h– going: has had tongue tied: sold £3,800 Ascot June Sales. *Neil King*

NOUSYR 5 b.m. Syrtos – Noushy (Ahonoora) [2003/4 F17d 16g 16m[pu] Jul 13] fourth h– foal: dam, poor maiden, out of sister to top-class miler Bolkonski: no sign of ability: sold F– £1,400 Ascot August Sales. *D. McCain*

NOVA BEACON 12 b.g. Ra Nova – Ditchling Beacon (High Line) [2003/4 21d Apr h– 12] lengthy gelding: well held in 2 starts over hurdles over 4 years apart. *B. G. Powell*

NOVATARA 12 ch.g. Ra Nova – Asphaltara (Scallywag) [2003/4 c25s[5] c25v[pu] 26s[2] c59 x 26s[2] 26s[3] 26g[3] c26g[3] Apr 12] winning hunter chaser in 2001/2: bad form in handicaps h85 over fences: modest maiden hurdler, left P. Murphy after fourth outing: stays 3¼m: acts on soft and good to firm going: blinkered/visored: often makes mistakes over fences. *B. G. Powell*

NOVEL IDEA (IRE) 6 ch.g. Phardante (FR) – Novelist (Quayside) [2003/4 F16g[6] h– F16s 25s[F] 25d[4] 20d Mar 22] workmanlike gelding: ninth foal: half-brother to winning 3m F77 hurdler/chaser The Writer (by Royal Fountain): dam unraced half-sister to useful staying chasers Book of Kells and Scribbler: won 21f maiden point on debut in 2003: modest form in bumper on first start: little show both completed outings over hurdles. *Mrs H. Dalton*

NOVI SAD (IRE) 6 b.g. Norwich – Shuil Na Gale (Strong Gale) [2003/4 h95, F97: 17s⁵ 16g 16m 25g² Nov 19] workmanlike gelding: modest hurdler: stays 25f: probably acts on soft going: tried in cheekpieces/blinkers: unreliable. *L. Wells* — **h89 §**

NO VISIBILITY (IRE) 9 b.g. Glacial Storm (USA) – Duhallow Lady (IRE) (Torus) [2003/4 c130p, h–: c16m³ c16sᵘʳ c20g³ c20g⁴ c20g⁴ c16d⁴ Mar 18] big, useful-looking gelding: maiden hurdler: useful handicap chaser: generally creditable efforts in 2003/4: stays 2½m: acts on heavy and good to firm going: front runner. *R. H. Alner* — **c130 h–**

NOW AND AGAIN 5 b.g. Shaamit (IRE) – Sweet Allegiance (Alleging (USA)) [2003/4 F17m F16g F16g 19g⁶ 17d 24d Mar 18] 13,000 3-y-o: first foal: dam well beaten in bumpers: signs of only a little ability in bumpers and over hurdles: modest form in maidens on Flat. *M. W. Easterby* — **h– F78**

NOWATOR (POL) 7 ch.g. Jape (USA) – Naradka (POL) (Dakota) [2003/4 h83: 17g* 16d³ 16m 16g⁴ 16mᵖᵘ 16g² 17s Dec 29] close-coupled gelding: fair hurdler: won novice handicap at Hereford in May: may prove best around 2m: acts on good to soft going: takes good hold. *T. R. George* — **h101**

NO WAY HOME (IRE) 6 b.g. Arctic Lord – Soldeu Creek (IRE) (Buckskin (FR)) [2003/4 F16m F16f Jun 30] 1,500 4-y-o, €1,200 5-y-o: first foal: dam unraced sister to smart staying chaser Buckboard Bounce: tailed off in 2 bumpers. *J. K. Magee, Ireland* — **F–**

NOWBYTHEWAY (IRE) 7 b.g. Wakashan – Gilded Empress (Menelek) [2003/4 c16d 23s 21dF Mar 28] 3,000 4-y-o: half-brother to several winners, including useful staying jumper Bishops Island (by The Parson) and fairly useful chaser Emperor Ross (by Roselier), stays 27f: dam, lightly-raced maiden, out of half-sister to high-class 2m chaser Stopped: won maiden Irish point in 2003: no show in maiden chase or hurdles. *J. R. Jenkins* — **c– h–**

NOWELL HOUSE 8 ch.g. Polar Falcon (USA) – Langtry Lady (Pas de Seul) [2003/4 h108: 17d* 16d* 16d Apr 3] smallish, sparely-made gelding: fairly useful on Flat (stays 13f): fairly useful handicap hurdler: improved efforts when winning at Carlisle in February and Wetherby in March, sustained effort to lead close home and beat Petrula a neck at latter: probably best around 2m: raced on ground softer than good over hurdles (acts on heavy). *M. W. Easterby* — **h123**

NOWT 7 b.m. Derrylin – Jolejester (Relkino) [2003/4 h–: 20d⁵ 16g⁵ 17dᵖᵘ 17gᵖᵘ Aug 8] ability matches her name. *D. McCain* — **h–**

NOW THEN SID 5 ch.g. Presidium – Callace (Royal Palace) [2003/4 h87, F82: 20f² 20m 20g* 20g³ 20d⁴ 20g Jan 7] leggy, lightly-made gelding: poor hurdler: made all in 4-runner novice at Hexham in November: stays 2½m: acts on good to firm and good to soft going. *Mrs S. A. Watt* — **h84**

NOWYOURETALKING (IRE) 5 b.g. Oscar (IRE) – Preview Days (IRE) (Supreme Leader) [2003/4 F16s* Apr 21] 21,000 4-y-o: first foal: dam unraced: favourite, won newcomers bumper at Gowran on debut, comfortably by 2½ lengths from Macs Flamingo: will stay beyond 2m: useful prospect. *T. E. Hyde, Ireland* — **F107**

NUCLEAR PROSPECT (IRE) 4 ch.g. Nucleon (USA) – Carraigbyrne (IRE) (Over The River (FR)) [2003/4 16g 16dᵖᵘ 16g⁵ 16g⁴ 16sᵖᵘ Apr 4] lengthy gelding: well held in 2 maidens on Flat: poor juvenile hurdler: probably flattered third outing. *G. M. Moore* — **h68**

NUMBERSIXVALVERDE (IRE) 8 b.g. Broken Hearted – Queens Tricks (Le Bavard (FR)) [2003/4 h119, F91: 16s 20d³ 20s⁵ 22d Apr 12] lengthy gelding: fairly useful hurdler: best effort in 2003/4 when third to Kadoun in handicap at Fairyhouse in February: stays 3m: acts on heavy going. *Martin Brassil, Ireland* — **h117**

NUMITAS (GER) 4 b.c. Lomitas – Narola (GER) (Nebos (GER)) [2003/4 16sᴿ 16g* 20g⁶ Apr 1] useful-looking colt: useful on Flat (stays 2¼m) for Sir Mark Prescott, successful in September: close up when refused out 2 in juvenile at Sandown on hurdling debut: blinkered both starts after, won 22-runner similar event at Newbury in March by neck from Wasted Talent: improved again though made mistakes and looked unwilling after 2 out when sixth of 13 to Garde Champetre in Grade 2 at Aintree: will stay beyond 2½m: of suspect temperament. *P. J. Hobbs* — **h123**

NURSERYMAN (IRE) 7 b.g. Mandalus – The Mighty Midge (Hardgreen (USA)) [2003/4 F–: 20d 20s Dec 19] good-bodied gelding: well held in bumper and novice hurdles. *P. Winkworth* — **h–**

NURZYK (POL) 7 ch.g. Freedom's Choice (USA) – Numeria (POL) (Dakota) [2003/4 h–: 27s* 24v² May 21] smallish gelding: poor form over hurdles: won weak novice handicap at Sedgefield in May: stays 27f: acts on heavy going: jumps none too fluently: sold 8,000 gns Doncaster August Sales. *T. R. George* **h80**

NUTCRACKER LAD (IRE) 6 ch.g. Duky – Allercashin Moon (IRE) (Callernish) [2003/4 F–: 20g 20mᵖᵘ 21vᵖᵘ 17sᵖᵘ 16s 17d 21g* 26dᵖᵘ Mar 28] small, sturdy gelding: form only when winning selling handicap hurdle at Huntingdon in March: visored last 5 starts. *M. J. Gingell* **h62**

NUTTY (IRE) 4 b.f. Sri Pekan (USA) – Mitra (IRE) (Archway (IRE)) [2003/4 21gᵖᵘ Feb 25] no sign of ability on Flat or in selling hurdle. *Mrs S. Gardner* **h–**

NUZUM ROAD MAKERS (IRE) 13 b.g. Lafontaine (USA) – Dark Gold (Raise You Ten) [2003/4 c113, h117: c20g c25s Jan 16] rangy gelding: fairly useful hurdler/fair handicap chaser in 2002/3 for M. Cunningham: off 12 months, no show in 2 handicap chases in 2003/4: stays 25f: acts on good to firm and heavy going: usually blinkered for previous stable: tried tongue tied: not an easy ride. *W. G. Young* **c–** **h–**

NYRCHE (FR) 4 b.g. Medaaly – Thoiry (USA) (Sagace (FR)) [2003/4 15s 15s³ 16s² 16d² Mar 12] leggy ex-French gelding: fourth foal: half-brother to prolific 9f to 1½m winner Pistoiry (by Pistolet Bleu): dam winning hurdler/chaser around 2m: fair form over hurdles: placed at Auteuil and Pau (for A. Lamotte d'Argy) and in novice at Sandown (1¼ lengths second to Back To Ben Alder, might well have won but for mistake last): promising. *A. King* **h115 p**

O

OAKLEY GOLD 6 ch.m. Afzal – Romany Gold (Pauper) [2003/4 F17s Jan 22] first foal: dam of little account over hurdles: 50/1 and amateur ridden, not unduly knocked about when seventh of 14 to Lady of Fortune in mares bumper at Taunton on debut: will probably do better. *S. E. H. Sherwood* **F77 p**

OAKSY 4 b. or br.g. Turtle Island (IRE) – Safe Secret (Seclude (USA)) [2003/4 16dᵖᵘ 16gᵖᵘ Dec 3] good-bodied gelding: well held on Flat, including in seller: sold out of G. Bravery's stable 500 gns Doncaster November (2002) Sales: no show in 2 juvenile hurdles. *I. A. Brown* **h–**

OATIS BROOK 6 b.g. Alderbrook – Lagrimass (Oats) [2003/4 F16g 21d 19mᵖᵘ Mar 4] third known foal: dam ran once: ninth of 21 in bumper on debut: showed nothing in 2 races over hurdles. *Ian Williams* **h–** **F78**

OBOEDIRE (IRE) 11 br.g. Royal Fountain – Another Pride (Golden Love) [2003/4 c–: c25d⁴ c25gᵖᵘ May 29] good-topped gelding: won 4-runner novice in 2001/2, little form otherwise in steeplechases. *Sir John Barlow Bt* **c–**

OCCAM (IRE) 10 ch.g. Sharp Victor (USA) – Monterana (Sallust) [2003/4 c81?, h79: c17g⁴ c17g⁴ c16mᶠ Nov 13] leggy gelding: poor hurdler: maiden chaser: would have won novice handicap at Ludlow but for falling last: raced around 2m: acted on soft and good to firm going: tried in cheekpieces: dead. *A. Bailey* **c– x** **h–**

OCEAN DANCER 7 b.g. Primitive Rising (USA) – Bally Small (Sunyboy) [2003/4 h92, F76: 16m² c17dᶠ c16d* c17g⁴ c16g² Mar 5] tall gelding: modest maiden hurdler: fair chaser: won maiden at Doncaster in December: will stay beyond 19f: acts on good to firm and good to soft going. *P. Beaumont* **c100** **h98**

O CINZA (IRE) 6 gr.g. Norwich – Queenlier (IRE) (Roselier (FR)) [2003/4 F16d 19sᵖᵘ Jan 22] strong, workmanlike gelding: second foal: dam ran twice: showed nothing in bumper and novice hurdle. *Miss H. C. Knight* **h–** **F–**

OCKI 11 gr.g. Octogenarian – Royalty Miss (Royalty) [2003/4 c21mᶠ May 21] lengthy gelding: lightly raced: little sign of ability prior to winning maiden point in 2004. *Mrs M. R. Eagleton* **c–** **h–**

OCKLEY FLYER 5 b.g. Sir Harry Lewis (USA) – Bewails (IRE) (Caerleon (USA)) [2003/4 h–: 19s 18s⁶ 22s 22mᵖᵘ Mar 11] little sign of ability over hurdles: has had tongue tied: has looked uncooperative. *Miss Z. C. Davison* **h–**

OCTOBER MAGIC 5 b.m. Hatim (USA) – Wand of Youth (Mandamus) [2003/4 F16m Dec 16] sixth foal: half-sister to winning pointer by Lancastrian: dam, lightly-raced, out of very smart staying chaser Young Ash Leaf: tailed off in bumper on debut. *A. R. Dicken*   **F–**

OCTOBER MIST (IRE) 10 gr.g. Roselier (FR) – Bonny Joe (Derring Rose) [2003/4 c–, h137: 23m² 20m² 24d⁶ c20d⁵ 20v c19g⁴ c20d⁶ c22g^F 22g⁶ Apr 16] stocky gelding: carries plenty of condition: useful handicap hurdler: generally disappointing after second outing, including back over fences, though won on Flat in April: stays 23f: acts on good to firm and heavy going: wore cheekpieces 3 of last 4 starts: not a fluent jumper of fences. *Mrs M. Reveley*   **c108 h136 d**

ODAGH ODYSSEY (IRE) 10 ch.g. Ikdam – Riverside Willow (Callernish) [2003/4 c124, h–: 22v² 20d⁶ c19g^ur c20g c20g^pu 19g² 21d² Apr 12] sturdy gelding: one-time useful handicap chaser, let down by jumping/shaped as if amiss over fences in 2003/4: fair maiden hurdler: stays 21f: raced on good going or softer (acts on soft). *Miss E. C. Lavelle*   **c– h106**

ODD JOB (IRE) 6 b. or br.g. Jolly Jake (NZ) – Kristellita (FR) (Crystal Palace (FR)) [2003/4 F78: F17m May 14] modest form in bumpers: races freely. *Jonjo O'Neill*   **F82**

ODDLYDODD (IRE) 8 b.g. Tremblant – Poor Times (IRE) (Roselier (FR)) [2003/4 c–, h89: 26m Jun 18] workmanlike gelding: modest handicap hurdler: no form over fences: stays 25f: acts on good to firm and heavy going: tried blinkered. *T. Keddy*   **c– h–**

ODYN DANCER 7 b.m. Minshaanshu Amad (USA) – Themeda (Sure Blade (USA)) [2003/4 20m May 7] poor on Flat (stays 2m), last ran in 2001: hampered first when tailed off on hurdling debut. *M. D. I. Usher*   **h–**

OFF BROADWAY (IRE) 6 b.g. Presenting – Mona Curra Gale (IRE) (Strong Gale) [2003/4 F99: 20g⁶ 21g⁴ 25d^pu 22g Apr 13] rather leggy, close-coupled gelding: best effort in novice hurdles when fourth of 18 to Rakalackey at Ludlow: should stay beyond 21f. *A. King*   **h90**

OFFSHORE (IRE) 11 b.g. Over The River (FR) – Parson's Princess (The Parson) [2003/4 c–: c25d^pu c25d^pu Mar 11] strong gelding: winning pointer: more sign of temperament than ability in steeplechases: tried blinkered. *S. A. Saltmarsh*   **c–**

OFF THE SEAL (NZ) 8 b.g. Imperial Seal – Grand Countess (NZ) (St Puckle) [2003/4 20m⁶ Jul 9] New Zealand-bred gelding: sixth of 17 in novice hurdle at Worcester on debut. *B. G. Powell*   **h68**

O'FLAHERTY'S (IRE) 12 ch.g. Balinger – Deise Lady (Le Bavard (FR)) [2003/4 c–: c20d⁵ c21g c20g^F Mar 12] of little account: tried blinkered. *G. D. Blagbrough*   **c–**

OH BE THE HOKEY (IRE) 6 b.g. Be My Native (USA) – Lucky Perk (IRE) (Executive Perk) [2003/4 F16s^ur F16g² 22d⁴ 18g* 16s⁴ 16s c17s^F c18d* c18v² Apr 21] IR £49,000 3-y-o: second foal: dam, bumper winner, out of useful hurdler up to 2½m Lucky Baloo: best effort in bumpers when second at Roscommon: fair hurdler: won maiden at Thurles in November: better form over fences, won maiden at same course in March: effective at 2m, probably stays 2¾m: raced on good going or softer (acts on heavy). *C. F. Swan, Ireland*   **c115 h108 F97**

OH LORDIE BE (IRE) 6 gr.m. Arctic Lord – Beagan Rose (IRE) (Roselier (FR)) [2003/4 F16v F16d F16d Mar 14] second foal: dam, modest maiden hurdler, stayed 2½m: well beaten in bumpers. *T. P. Walshe*   **F–**

OH SO BRAVE 7 gr.g. Arzanni – Goodbye Roscoe (Roscoe Blake) [2003/4 17g⁵ 16m⁶ 19g⁴ Apr 16] third foal: half-brother to winning pointer by Southern Music: dam of little account: pulled up in 2 points in 2003: poor form over hurdles. *Evan Williams*   **h76**

OH SO POSH 5 b.m. Overbury (IRE) – Sally Ho (Gildoran) [2003/4 F–: F17m⁴ 16g^pu 16d^pu Apr 21] workmanlike mare: little sign of ability: left Mrs A. Thorpe after second outing: tried tongue tied. *B. Llewellyn*   **h– F69 ?**

OH SO ROSIE (IRE) 4 b.f. Danehill Dancer (IRE) – Shinkoh Rose (FR) (Warning) [2003/4 16d³ Nov 23] fair on Flat (stays 1m): well-beaten third of 8 in juvenile at Fakenham on hurdling debut: likely to have stamina problems. *J. S. Moore*   **h63**

OH SO WISLEY 9 b.g. Teenoso (USA) – Easy Horse (FR) (Carmarthen (FR)) [2003/4 c95x, h90: 24g² 21g⁴ 22d 24g^pu Feb 14] smallish gelding: modest form when placed over fences (not fluent): fair handicap hurdler: well-backed favourite, won at Exeter in   **c– x h106**

November: lame final outing: should stay beyond 3m: acts on good to firm and heavy going. *N. A. Twiston-Davies*

OH VLO (FR)   5 b. or br.g. Sassanian (USA) – Lady Christine (FR) (Vayrann) [2003/4 17s 17s⁴ 19s⁶ c17g 18v⁴ 18s³ 16d 20s⁵ 19m³ 19gᵖᵘ Apr 16] rather leggy gelding: half-brother to winning 2m hurdler Le Beuvron (by Morespeed): maiden on Flat: well held on chasing debut: novice hurdler, claimed from J. Bertran de Balanda €18,500 sixth outing: only poor form in Britain: ran as if amiss last 2 starts. *M. C. Pipe*   **c–**
h102 d

OJAYS ALIBI (IRE)   8 b.g. Witness Box (USA) – Tinkers Lady (Sheer Grit) [2003/4 h96, F75: 17dᶠ 19g³ 19d⁴ 16d³ 17s³ 24g* Mar 9] in frame in maiden Irish points: modest hurdler: won novice at Exeter with something in hand: will prove better around 3m than shorter: acts on soft going. *J. D. Frost*   **h99**

OLD BARNS (IRE)   4 b.g. Nucleon (USA) – Surfer Katie (IRE) (Be My Native (USA)) [2003/4 F16g Feb 28] first foal: dam lightly-raced maiden hurdler: 9/1 from 16/1, soundly beaten in bumper at Haydock on debut. *G. A. Swinbank*   **F–**

OLD BEAN (IRE)   8 b.g. Eurobus – Princess Petara (IRE) (Petorius) [2003/4 h–: 16d 21s* 22dᵖᵘ 21gᵖᵘ Apr 12] leggy, angular gelding: fairly useful bumper winner in 2001/2: form over hurdles only when winning novice at Plumpton in January: stays 21f: acts on soft going. *N. J. Henderson*   **h90**

OLD FLAME (IRE)   5 b.g. Oscar (IRE) – Flameing Run (Deep Run) [2003/4 F16f³ F16v³ F16d³ F16d⁵ F18d* 18d⁵ 16s* 16s² 18d* 20d³ 20g Apr 1] lengthy, rather unfurnished gelding: half-brother to useful hurdler/winning chaser up to 3m No Discount (by Be My Native) and fair 2m chaser/winning hurdler Marble Man (by Henbit): dam lightly-raced maiden: fair form in bumpers, won maiden at Downpatrick in December: fairly useful novice hurdler: won at Navan (maiden) in January and Limerick (beat Star of Bethlehem 2½ lengths) in February: hung left under pressure and found less than seemed likely when only ninth of 23 to Zibeline in handicap at Aintree: stays 2½m: raced on good going or softer over hurdles (form in bumpers on firm). *C. F. Swan, Ireland*   **h117**
F92

OLD GOLDEN GREY   7 gr.g. Thethingaboutitis (USA) – Modina April (New Member) [2003/4 F17g F16m 20sᵖᵘ 20sᵖᵘ Jan 10] lengthy gelding: first foal: dam once-raced in points: no sign of ability: tried visored/blinkered. *M. Wellings*   **h–**
F–

OLD HUSH WING (IRE)   11 b.g. Tirol – Saneena (Kris) [2003/4 c–, h98: c25d⁴ c21s* c23mᵖᵘ Jun 28] rather sparely-made gelding: modest hurdler: easily best effort over fences when winning handicap at Sedgefield in May: stays 25f: acts on any going: usually held up. *Mrs S. J. Smith*   **c102**
h–

OLD KING COAL   8 b.g. Miner's Lamp – Mill Shine (Milan) [2003/4 F–: c20mᶠ c16f³ c16g³ c16d⁵ 20vᵖᵘ Jan 21] poor form in steeplechases: went as if amiss on hurdling debut: bred to be suited by further than 2m. *R. Ford*   **c73**
h–

OLD MARSH (IRE)   8 b.g. Grand Lodge (USA) – Lolly Dolly (Alleged (USA)) [2003/4 h117: c19d⁴ c20g² c16s² c16d² c16d⁶ c16g Apr 1] strong gelding: fairly useful hurdler: similar form over fences, neck second to Great Travel in handicap at Sandown fourth start: best around 2m: acts on soft and good to firm going: tried blinkered: effective tongue tied or not: races prominently: prone to mistakes. *Miss Venetia Williams*   **c118**
h–

OLD NOSEY (IRE)   8 b.g. Muharib (USA) – Regent Star (Prince Regent (FR)) [2003/4 h89, F77: 22g² 20m³ 24d³ 22m² 24g* 22m³ 24m⁶ 22f⁵ 20d⁶ Apr 18] poor hurdler: won novice handicap at Perth in August: stays 3m when conditions aren't testing: acts on good to firm and good to soft going: tried blinkered. *B. Mactaggart*   **h84**

OLD OPRY   7 b.g. Old Vic – Tina Rosa (Bustino) [2003/4 h114: c17s² c20sᶠ c18s⁴ Feb 14] good-topped gelding: fair hurdler: similar form both completed starts in maiden chases, second to Central House at Fairyhouse on reappearance: best form around 2m: raced on good going or softer (acts on heavy). *N. Meade, Ireland*   **c112**
h–

OLD ROLLA (IRE)   6 b.g. Old Vic – Criswood (IRE) (Chromite (USA)) [2003/4 h82, F–: c25gᵖᵘ 27s⁴ c25vᶠ c25v⁶ c25g³ c24d⁵ c20dᵖᵘ Apr 18] lengthy gelding: poor maiden hurdler/chaser: stays 27f: raced on good ground or softer (acts on heavy). *C. Grant*   **c82**
h82

OLE GUNNAR (IRE)   12 b.g. Le Bavard (FR) – Rareitess (Rarity) [2003/4 h69: 20d⁴ Apr 21] winning pointer: thrice-raced over hurdles, poor form: should stay beyond 2½m: tried in cheekpieces. *M. S. Wilesmith*   **h–**

OLIMP (POL)   8 ch.g. Saphir (GER) – Olgierda (POL) (Sentyment (POL)) [2003/4 20vᵘʳ 19s⁶ 20sᵘʳ 22s Jan 20] successful 8 times from 1m to 1¼m from 37 starts on Flat in   **h– §**

Poland for M. Janikowski: has shown more temperament than ability over hurdles: tried blinkered. *Miss A. M. Newton-Smith*

OLITHEAGA   9 ch.g. Safawan – Lyaaric (Privy Seal) [2003/4 h–: 22m³ 22g* 19m⁶   **h82** Oct 7] angular gelding: lightly raced over hurdles: unimpressive when landing odds in poor 3-runner maiden at Cartmel in May: left C. Mann, tailed off in seller next time: stays 2¾m: yet to race on extremes of going: wore cheekpieces/blinkers first 2 starts. *N. E. Berry*

OLIVER CROMWELL (IRE)   9 br.g. Mandalus – Gemini Gale (Strong Gale)   **c107** [2003/4 c115, h–: c19s⁵ c25sᵘʳ c24m⁴ c24dᵖᵘ Mar 20] workmanlike gelding: winning   **h–** hurdler: fair form at best over fences, went as if amiss last 2 outings: probably better at 3m than shorter: acts on heavy going: wears cheekpieces/blinkers nowadays: none too genuine. *P. R. Hedger*

OLIVERJOHN (IRE)   7 ch.g. Denel (FR) – Graeme's Gem (Pry) [2003/4 20d 20d   **h114** 19m 20s⁵ 20m 20s² 20d⁵ 20s² 20s² 19s³ 16d 18s⁴ Mar 21] lengthy gelding: half-brother to winning 2¾m hurdler China Gem (by Idiot's Delight): dam, modest novice hurdler up to 2½m, half-sister to useful hurdler Deep Wealth, from family of high-class chaser Fifty Dollars More: fair hurdler: stays 2½m: acts on soft going: tried in cheekpieces. *M. Hourigan, Ireland*

OLIVIER (USA)   6 ch.g. Theatrical – Izara (USA) (Blushing John (USA)) [2003/4   **h89** h101, F78+: 20sᵘʳ 17g⁶ 21d⁵ Mar 14] useful-looking gelding: modest novice hurdler, off over a year before reappearance: should prove as effective at 2m as around 2½m: possibly not straightforward (has hung left). *Miss Venetia Williams*

OLLIE MAGERN   6 b.g. Alderbrook – Outfield (Monksfield) [2003/4 h93+, F–:   **h125** 26g⁴ 27d² 22m* 26m* 22m² 22g* 26m* 25f* 21g 24g⁵ 21m⁶ 24d⁴ Apr 22] smallish gelding: fairly useful novice hurdler: had good season, winning at Stratford in May and July, Hereford (conditional jockeys) in between and Huntingdon (10/1-on in 3-runner race) and Cheltenham in October: best efforts in handicaps next 3 starts: stays 27f: acts on firm and good to soft going: usually makes running. *N. A. Twiston-Davies*

OLNEY LAD   5 b.g. Democratic (USA) – Alipampa (IRE) (Glenstal (USA)) [2003/4   **h114** h82: 16m⁶ 20d* 20d³ 20d* 22m Feb 21] leggy gelding: fair hurdler: won novices at Uttoxeter (handicap) in November and Leicester in December, best effort when beating Limerick Leader by 7 lengths at latter: bled from nose final outing: stays 2½m: acts on good to soft ground (unraced on softer): genuine. *Mrs P. Robeson*

OLYMPIC STORM (IRE)   6 b.g. Glacial Storm (USA) – Philly Athletic (Sit In The   **F–** Corner (USA)) [2003/4 F16dʳᵒ F16d Apr 23] seventh foal: dam modest hurdler up to 3m: won maiden on last of 4 starts in Irish points in 2003: showed more temperament than ability in bumpers. *N. W. Alexander*

OMNI COSMO TOUCH (USA)   8 b.g. Trempolino (USA) – Wooden Pudden   **c103 §** (USA) (Top Ville) [2003/4 c§§, h§§: c21s* c26dᵘʳ c24s² Apr 17] good-topped gelding: **h§§** fair hurdler on his day: won 2 points in 2004 and novice hunter chase at Sedgefield in February: stays 3m: acts on firm and soft going: tried blinkered: usually refuses/reluctant to race: untrustworthy. *Joss Saville*

ON A DEAL   6 b.g. Teenoso (USA) – Gale Spring (IRE) (Strong Gale) [2003/4 F90:   **h90** 22gᵇᵈ 22m² May 9] long-backed gelding: second of 5 to easy winner Cornish Gale in novice at Wincanton on completed outing over hurdles: likely to stay 3m: has looked wayward. *R. J. Hodges*

ON A FULL WAGER   7 b.g. Homo Sapien – Ntombi (Trasi's Son) [2003/4 h–, F78:   **c–** c20gᵖᵘ Mar 12] workmanlike gelding: little sign of ability in varied company.   **h–** *Mrs K. Lawther*

ONASSIS   7 b.g. Roselier (FR) – Jack's The Girl (IRE) (Supreme Leader) [2003/4 h79,   **c–** F79: 24s² 26g⁶ c21g⁶ c26gᵖᵘ Nov 18] sturdy gelding: modest form at best over hurdles: **h88** no encouragement both starts over fences: blinkered. *O. Sherwood*

ONCE SEEN   4 b.g. Celtic Swing – Brief Glimpse (IRE) (Taufan (USA)) [2003/4 16s*   **h97** 16g 16d⁶ 16d Apr 21] close-coupled gelding: fair on Flat (stays 1m), sold out of R. Beckett's stable 18,000 gns Newmarket Autumn Sales: won novice at Plumpton on hurdling debut in February: disappointing after, visored/blinkered last 2 starts. *O. Sherwood*

ONCOURSE (IRE)   8 b.g. Toulon – Slaney Jazz (Orchestra) [2003/4 h–: 16gᵖᵘ 16gᵖᵘ   **h– §** May 21] lengthy gelding: no form over hurdles: reluctant to race final outing. *R. D. Tudor*

ONE A DACKIE 5 b.m. Lord Americo – Oriel Dream (Oats) [2003/4 F73: F16d Apr **F—**
28] well held in bumpers. *Ferdy Murphy*

ONE CORNETTO (IRE) 5 b.g. Eurobus – Costenetta (IRE) (Runnett) [2003/4 **F84**
F16v F18g5 Apr 22] €22,000 4-y-o: lengthy, rather unfurnished gelding: fifth foal: dam
unraced half-sister to fairly useful staying chaser Skillwise: better effort in bumpers when
21¾ lengths fifth to Just Classic at Fontwell. *L. Wells*

ONE DAY (NZ) 6 ch.g. Stark South (USA) – Dragon Pearl (USA) (Ahonoora) **h97**
[2003/4 20d* 24s3 20dpu 20g 24s Mar 20] good-bodied gelding: half-brother to Maguire
(by Casual Lies), smart performer up to 2m on Flat in New Zealand: won novice hurdle at
Carlisle on debut in November: disappointing in handicaps last 2 starts: stays 3m.
R. C. Guest

ONE FIVE EIGHT 5 b.g. Alflora (IRE) – Dark Nightingale (Strong Gale) [2003/4 **h65**
F—: F17m3 F17f* F17g* 20g3 17d Dec 4] fair form in bumpers, successful at Market **F95**
Rasen and Sedgefield in October, making all or most: well held both starts in novice
hurdles. *M. W. Easterby*

ONEFORBERTANDHENRY (IRE) 5 b.g. Rashar (USA) – Roi Vision (Roi Guil- **h64**
laume (FR)) [2003/4 F16m F16s 25g4 Jan 24] tall, rather unfurnished gelding: seventh **F85**
foal: brother to 3m hurdle winner Woman Power: dam unraced: little impact in bumpers
and novice hurdle. *G. M. Moore*

ONE FOR ME 6 br.m. Tragic Role (USA) – Chantallee's Pride (Mansooj) [2003/4 **h108**
h85: 17m6 16gur 18f* 19m3 22g* 19f* 22f* 16m 24g Dec 27] has reportedly had wind
operation: fair handicap hurdler: progressed well in first half of season, winning at Fontwell (twice), Exeter and Wincanton (beat Blue Ride a short head in valuable mares
event): well beaten last 2 outings: stays 2¾m: acts on firm going. *Jean-Rene Auvray*

ONEFOURSEVEN 11 b.g. Jumbo Hirt (USA) – Dominance (Dominion) [2003/4 h–: **h95**
20m4 26g2 21m* 21g* Aug 8] smallish, sturdy gelding: modest hurdler: tongue tied, won
twice at Sedgefield, novice in July and handicap in August: best form up to 21f: acts on
good to firm going. *P. C. Haslam*

ONE KNIGHT (IRE) 8 ch.g. Roselier (FR) – Midnights Daughter (IRE) (Long **c—**
Pond) [2003/4 c150p, h–: c26gF Nov 29] tall gelding: smart novice chaser in 2002/3, **h—**
making all in Royal & SunAlliance Chase at Cheltenham: chipped bone in hock when
falling first in Hennessy Cognac Gold Cup (Handicap) at Newbury and missed rest of
season: will stay beyond 3m: raced on good going or softer (acts on soft): usually front
runner: bold jumper, prone to the odd mistake. *P. J. Hobbs*

ONEMINUTETOFIVE 7 b.g. Neltino – Island Beat (Jupiter Island) [2003/4 c26d4 **c116 p**
Mar 18] 8,500 3-y-o: useful-looking gelding: first foal: dam placed in point: successful
on 5 of 6 starts in points: 12/1, promising 22 lengths fourth of 10 finishers to Earthmover
in Foxhunter at Cheltenham on steeplechasing debut, travelling smoothly long way:
likely to improve and win more races. *D. Pipe*

ONE MORE NATIVE (IRE) 7 ch.g. Be My Native (USA) – Romany Fortune **h—**
(Sunyboy) [2003/4 F85: F17d 16gF Feb 25] angular gelding: modest form first 2 starts in **F—**
bumpers: towards rear when fell 3 out in novice on hurdling debut. *J. L. Needham*

ONE MORE STRIDE 8 gr.g. Beveled (USA) – Gem of Gold (Jellaby) [2003/4 c–, **c—**
h–: 21f2 Oct 9] workmanlike gelding: first form when second of 6 in minor event over **h72**
hurdles at Ludlow: stays 21f: tried blinkered. *Miss Victoria Roberts*

ONE NATION (IRE) 9 br.g. Be My Native (USA) – Diklers Run (Deep Run) **c122**
[2003/4 c–, h110: c19g* c17g5 c19s3 c21d* c20s3 c25gpu Apr 2] big, strong gelding: **h—**
winning hurdler: fairly useful novice chaser: won at Exeter (maiden) in November and
Wincanton (third course win, all out to beat Ruby Gale ½ length in 6-runner event) in
January: seemed to lose confidence after early blunder in Grade 2 at Aintree final start:
stays 21f: acts on heavy going: sold to join R. Brookhouse 60,000 gns Doncaster May
Sales. *Miss H. C. Knight*

ONE NIGHT OUT (IRE) 8 b. or br.g. Jamesmead – Deladeuce (Le Bavard (FR)) **c125**
[2003/4 c122, h–: c22d c17d3 c24s5 c19dF c17d5 22s 22d3 Apr 12] sturdy gelding: fairly **h127**
useful chaser: won maiden in November 2002, subsequently disqualified on technical
grounds: easily best effort in 2003/4 when third in handicap at Fairyhouse: fairly useful
hurdler: good efforts when in frame in competitive handicaps at Fairyhouse and
Punchestown in April: effective around 2m and stays 3m: acts on heavy going, probably
on good to firm. *W. P. Mullins, Ireland*

ONE OF THEM 5 ch.g. Pharly (FR) – Hicklam Millie (Absalom) [2003/4 17s⁶ 17s **h81** 22g 17g Apr 13] neat gelding: half-brother to winning 2½m hurdler Peejay Hobbs (by Alhijaz): successful around 1¼m on Flat at 3 yrs in Germany, placed once from 7 starts in 2003 for B. Hellier: poor form in novice hurdles. *J. S. Moore*

ONEOFTHEMONGOES (IRE) 8 b.g. Ikdam – Miss Hganavak (Abednego) **h67** [2003/4 16d 18d 19s⁵ Apr 4] fifth foal: half-brother to winning 17f hurdler Aslar (by Orange Reef): dam unraced: won maiden Irish point in 2002: bought 500 gns Doncaster August (2002) Sales: well held in 3 starts over hurdles. *Mrs L. C. Jewell*

ONE OF THE NATIVES (IRE) 10 b.g. Be My Native (USA) – Take Me Home **c–** (Amoristic (USA)) [2003/4 c–: c22g Mar 26] lengthy gelding: modest pointer nowadays: no form in 3 starts in steeplechases since 2001/2: tried visored. *Miss J. H. Jenner*

ONE UP (IRE) 6 b.m. Bob Back (USA) – Strong Desire (IRE) (Strong Gale) [2003/4 **h–** h–: 24g May 10] well held over hurdles. *M. Todhunter*

ONEWAY (IRE) 7 b.g. Bob's Return (IRE) – Rendezvous (Lorenzaccio) [2003/4 h94, **c105** F–: c16v³ c20s* c22m⁵ c19dᵖᵘ Mar 24] workmanlike gelding: modest form in novice **h–** hurdles: best effort over fences when winning amateur handicap at Lingfield in December: stays 2½m: raced mainly on going softer than good: has taken strong hold. *M. G. Rimell*

ON LES AURA (IRE) 5 b.g. Germany (USA) – Another Thurn (IRE) (Trimmingham) **h95 +** [2003/4 F17g 19g 22v 19v³ 22d⁶ 22g² Apr 13] first foal: dam maiden Irish pointer: well **F–** held in bumper: modest form in novice hurdles: stays 2¾m. *R. H. Alner*

ONLY FOR GOLD 9 b.g. Presidium – Calvanne Miss (Martinmas) [2003/4 21m⁶ **h–** 16sᵖᵘ 16s Jan 16] poor on Flat (stays 8.5f), sold out of A. Berry's stable 1,000 gns Doncaster October Sales: no show over hurdles. *Dr P. Pritchard*

ONLY ONCE 9 b.g. King's Ride – Rambling Gold (Little Buskins) [2003/4 c117p: **c–** 20s² c33dᵖᵘ Feb 21] rather leggy gelding: very lightly raced: successful both starts over **h91 p** fences in 2002/3: off 11 months, promising hurdling debut when second to stable-companion Paddy The Piper in novice at Ayr: lost touch final circuit in 20-runner Eider Chase at Newcastle week later: stays 27f: acts on heavy going: sold 18,000 gns Doncaster May Sales. *L. Lungo*

ONLY ONE MATTY (IRE) 7 b.g. Satco (FR) – Poundworld (IRE) (Orchestra) **h106** [2003/4 h93: 20d 16s⁴ 24g* 20d² 24g* 24d 22g³ Mar 28] medium-sized gelding: fair hurdler: won handicaps at Musselburgh in January and February, easily making all in novice on latter occasion: stays 3m: acts on soft and good to firm ground: tried blinkered/tongue tied. *Mrs K. Walton*

ONLY VINTAGE (USA) 4 b.g. Diesis – Wild Vintage (USA) (Alysheba (USA)) **F112** [2003/4 F16v⁶ F16d⁴ F16g* F16g Mar 17] 3,700 3-y-o: angular gelding: half-brother to very smart Hong Kong performer up to 1¼m Bullish Luck (by Royal Academy): dam, French 1¼m winner, half-sister to very smart French miler In Extremis and Prix Marcel Boussac winner Juvenia: progressive form in bumpers, winning 16-runner event at Leopardstown in February by 2 lengths from Albert Mooney and 11¾ lengths seventh of 24 to Total Enjoyment in Champion Bumper (failed to settle held up) at Cheltenham. *M. Hourigan, Ireland*

ONLY WALLIS (IRE) 7 b.g. Supreme Leader – Laurdella Lady (Golden Love) **h–** [2003/4 F16s³ 24s⁶ 25d⁶ Mar 19] big, strong gelding: fourth foal: half-brother to 2½m **F101** bumper winner Ballymore Thatch (by Carlingford Castle): dam unraced half-sister to useful chasers Poyntz Pass, best at 2½m, and Solidasarock, best at 3m, from family of Captain Christy: won 2½m maiden point on debut in 2003: bought 10,000 gns Doncaster May Sales: third to impressive Refinement in bumper at Ascot: well held in novice hurdles: should stay at least 2½m. *C. L. Tizzard*

ONLY WORDS (USA) 7 ch.g. Shuailaan (USA) – Conversation Piece (USA) **h91** (Seeking The Gold (USA)) [2003/4 h74: 17s⁶ 16s* 16v² 16v³ 17s³ 17s 19g⁴ Mar 10] workmanlike gelding: modest handicap hurdler: won 21-runner event at Wetherby in January: barely stays 2½m: acts on any going: well below form only run in blinkers: reliable. *A. J. Lockwood*

ONLY YOU 8 b.g. Gildoran – Outfield (Monksfield) [2003/4 h70§, F–: 16g 19v⁶ 19v⁴ **h58 §** Feb 2] leggy, angular gelding: poor maiden hurdler, off 19 months before reappearance: stays 21f: acts on good to firm and good to soft going: weak finisher. *N. A. Twiston-Davies*

ONMYWAYHOME (IRE)   9 br.m. Alphabatim (USA) – Mammy's Friend (Miner's Lamp) [2003/4 c24mpu May 7] won twice in points in 2003: beaten long way out in novice hunter chase at Chepstow. *Mrs Susan Smith*   c– h–

ON THE BONE   12 b.m. Lyphento (USA) – Lydia Languish (Hotfoot) [2003/4 c–: 20v6 c20gF c25s5 c25mF c22s4 c25s6 Apr 11] of no account. *C. N. Kellett*   c– h–

ON THE LUCE   7 b.g. Karinga Bay – Lirchur (Lir) [2003/4 c–, h–: c20m c21d3 c20s4 c24s* c25vpu c20s4 c25d* Mar 22] good-topped gelding: modest chaser, trained by W. T. Reed first outing: won handicaps at Newcastle in January and Wetherby (novice, idled): stays 25f: acts on soft going. *Miss P. Robson*   c89 h–

ON THE MEND (IRE)   11 ch.g. Broken Hearted – Mugs Away (Mugatpura) [2003/4 c117, h113: 20m c22s5 c20g6 c20dpu Mar 25] lengthy gelding: fairly useful hurdler/chaser at best, sold out of M. O'Brien's stable 5,000 gns Doncaster August Sales after second start: no show in 2 hunters in 2004: stays 3m: acts on soft and good to firm going: tried blinkered in bumpers. *Miss S. Balshaw*   c96 h–

ON THE NET (IRE)   6 b.g. Torus – Petted Slave (Orchestra) [2003/4 F18d* F16s F16s* 19s5 Jan 24] fifth foal: brother to winning pointer: dam unraced half-sister to dam of useful chaser at 2½m+ Flashthecash: winning pointer: successful 2 of 3 starts in bumpers, at Tipperary in May and Cork (beat Run My Lord 1½ lengths) in January: fifth to Collier County in maiden at Naas on hurdling debut: likely to improve. *A. M. O'Grady, Ireland*   h84 p F102

ON THE OUTSIDE (IRE)   5 ch.m. Anshan – Kate Fisher (IRE) (Over The River (FR)) [2003/4 F16m5 F16d5 Mar 14] ex-Irish mare: second foal: half-sister to fairly useful bumper winner Word Gets Around (by King's Ride): dam in frame all completed starts over hurdles in Ireland: won mares maiden on second of 2 starts in Irish points in 2003: modest form in bumpers at Cork (for P. Cashman) and Warwick. *S. E. H. Sherwood*   F75

ON THE RUN (IRE)   10 ch.m. Don't Forget Me – Chepstow House (USA) (Northern Baby (CAN)) [2003/4 c81, h79: 18f Aug 18] lengthy, angular mare: poor hurdler/novice chaser: stays 2½m: acts on firm and good to soft going: has had tongue tied. *D. J. Wintle*   c– h–

ON THE VERGE (IRE)   6 ch.g. Alphabatim – Come On Lis (Domynsky) [2003/4 F16g2 F16d* 16vro 16s4 21d 16g Mar 6] workmanlike gelding: second foal: dam unraced: fair form in 2 bumpers at Fakenham, landing odds in 4-runner maiden in November: seemingly best effort over hurdles (ran out on debut) when eighth of 12 finishers in slowly-run novice at Huntingdon final start. *J. R. Jenkins*   h87 ? F94

ONTOS (GER)   8 b. or br.g. Super Abound (USA) – Onestep (GER) (Konigsstuhl (GER)) [2003/4 h116: 16d5 16dpu 16s4 Jan 16] leggy, short-backed gelding: fairly useful hurdler: creditable efforts 2 of 3 starts in 2003/4, fifth to The French Furze in Grade 2 at Newcastle on reappearance for Miss V. Scott: best around 2m: acts on heavy and good to firm going: has finished weakly but is consistent: rejoined former stable. *N. M. L. Ewart*   h114

ONWARDSANDUPWARDS (IRE)   5 b. or br.g. Un Desperado (FR) – Kalifornia Katie (IRE) (Sharp Charter) [2003/4 F89p: 17g2 16d6 22s2 24s2 20s 22gpu Apr 16] tall, useful-looking gelding: will make a chaser: runner-up on 3 of 6 starts over hurdles, ¾ length behind Your So Cool at Taunton final occasion: stays 3m: raced on good going or softer. *P. F. Nicholls*   h119

ONYOURHEADBEIT (IRE)   6 b.g. Glacial Storm (USA) – Family Birthday (Sandalay (IRE)) [2003/4 F17s* 21g Mar 26] IR £10,000 3-y-o: rangy gelding: fifth foal: half-brother to winning pointer by Lancastrian: dam, lightly raced in points, out of half-sister to very smart staying chaser Lucisis: fairly useful form when winning bumper at Sedgefield on debut by 1¾ lengths from Lago d'Oro: eleventh of 20 in maiden at Newbury on hurdling debut following month, tending to hang left under pressure: should do better. *K. C. Bailey*   h86 p F98

ON Y VA (FR)   6 b.g. Goldneyev (USA) – Shakna (FR) (Le Nain Jaune (FR)) [2003/4 18s 19s6 19s2 18s5 20v5 16d Mar 1] leggy ex-French gelding: fifth foal: half-brother to winning hurdlers Shafter (by Hours After), around 2m, and Shkodel (by Goldneyev), up to 19f: dam ran once: placed up to 15f on Flat: last of 6 finishers only start over fences: fairly useful maiden hurdler: left T. Trapenard, ran poorly last 2 starts, bled from nose final one: stays 2½m: raced on good ground or softer (acts on heavy). *R. T. Phillips*   c– h126

OODACHEE   5 b.g. Marju (IRE) – Lady Marguerrite (Blakeney) [2003/4 F100: F17g* 16g3 20m2 20f* 16s5 Mar 27] fair on Flat up to 17f: won at Killarney in May on last of 3 starts in bumpers: fair form over hurdles, won novice at Sligo in July: stays 2½m: acts on firm and soft going. *C. F. Swan, Ireland*   h103 F100

OOS AND AHS 4 b.f. Silver Wizard (USA) – Hot Feet (Marching On) [2003/4 16f^{pu} **h–**
16g Dec 3] well held on Flat: no show in 2 juvenile hurdles, bled from nose on first
occasion. *C. W. Fairhurst*

OPAL'LOU (FR) 8 b.m. Garde Royale – Calligraphie (FR) (R B Chesne) [2003/4   **c– §**
c89§, h–: c21m^{pu} May 9] modest maiden chaser: tongue tied, ran badly in novice hand-   **h–**
icap in May: won point in February: probably stays easy 25f: acts on firm and good to soft
going: weak finisher, and not to be trusted. *P. F. Nicholls*

OPAL RIDGE 7 ch.g. Jupiter Island – The Beginning (Goldhill) [2003/4 F82: c24m^5 **c82 p**
Mar 4] winning pointer: signs of ability when fourth in bumper in 2002/3 and fifth to
Double Honour in novice chase at Taunton on return: should prove suited by further than
2m: likely to improve. *P. R. Webber*

OPERA HALL 4 b.f. Saddlers' Hall (IRE) – Opera Hat (IRE) (Strong Gale) [2003/4   **F86**
F16g^3 F16d^6 Mar 28] first foal: dam very smart chaser at 2m to 3m: third in mares bumper
at Fakenham on debut: only sixth at Huntingdon following month, not knocked about
once held. *H. D. Daly*

OPERASHAAN (IRE) 4 b.g. Darshaan – Comic Opera (IRE) (Royal Academy   **h–**
(USA)) [2003/4 16g Jan 17] maiden on Flat, left T. Clement before seemingly best effort,
over 1¼m in January: jumped poorly when tailed off in juvenile on hurdling debut.
G. L. Moore

OPTIMAITE 7 b.g. Komaite (USA) – Leprechaun Lady (Royal Blend) [2003/4 16m^2 **h110**
16g^4 16g* 16d^6 Jan 13] useful at best on Flat (barely stays 1¾m), only fair in 2003: fair
form over hurdles: won novice at Leicester in December: raced at 2m: acts on good to
firm ground, below form on good to soft (breathing problem) final start: tongue tied.
B. R. Millman

OPTIMISTIC HARRY 5 b.g. Sir Harry Lewis (USA) – Miss Optimist (Relkino)   **h–**
[2003/4 24d 21d^{ur} 19s^{pu} Apr 11] 12,000 4-y-o: close-coupled gelding: second foal: dam,
fairly useful hurdler at 2½m, out of half-sister to smart staying chaser Bold Agent: no
form over hurdles. *P. A. Blockley*

OPTIMISTIC THINKER 10 ch.g. Beveled (USA) – Racemosa (Town Crier)   **c– §**
[2003/4 c–§, h–§: c16g^5 c24d Feb 19] lengthy gelding: has reportedly had soft palate   **h– §**
operation: winning hurdler/chaser around 2m: left T. George after reappearance, no form
in points and amateur event over fences subsequently: tried blinkered/in cheekpieces:
has had tongue tied: often let down by jumping over fences: temperamental.
Miss T. McCurrich

ORACLE DES MOTTES (FR) 5 b.g. Signe Divin (USA) – Daisy Des Mottes (FR)   **h112**
(Abdonski (FR)) [2003/4 h104: 16m^5 16f^2 16d* 17g^3 Dec 18] tall gelding: fair hurdler:
won maiden at Chepstow in December: raced around 2m: acts on soft and firm going: has
failed to impress with attitude. *P. F. Nicholls*

ORAKE PRINCE 5 b.g. Bluegrass Prince (IRE) – Kiri Te (Liboi (USA)) [2003/4 h–:   **h–**
16s^6 16m 17d Dec 2] no form over hurdles. *W. G. M. Turner*

ORANGE ORDER (IRE) 11 ch.g. Generous (IRE) – Fleur d'Oranger (Northfields   **c–**
(USA)) [2003/4 c92, h–: 22d^6 26m^5 Jun 18] leggy, sparely-made gelding: winning   **h81**
hurdler/chaser, on long losing run: stays 21f: acts on any going, though raced mainly on
good or firmer nowadays: successful 5 times at Sedgefield: races prominently: jumps
soundly. *G. M. Moore*

ORANGERIE (IRE) 6 b.g. Darshaan – Fleur d'Oranger (Northfields (USA)) [2003/4   **c–**
h109§: c20m^{ur} May 5] good-topped gelding: fair hurdler: unseated seventh on chasing   **h– §**
debut: effective at 2m to 2¾m: acts on soft and good to firm going: blinkered: tends to
find little. *P. J. Hobbs*

ORANGE TREE LAD 6 b.g. Tragic Role (USA) – Adorable Cherub (USA) (Halo   **h–**
(USA)) [2003/4 h74: 17g^{pu} Aug 25] leggy gelding: poor maiden hurdler: seems best
around 2m: acts on soft going. *D. W. Thompson*

ORAPA 5 b.g. Spectrum (IRE) – African Dance (USA) (El Gran Senor (USA)) [2003/4   **h–**
h–: 19s^{pu} Apr 4] leggy, lengthy gelding: little sign of ability on Flat: no show in 2 outings
over hurdles. *T. D. McCarthy*

ORBICULARIS (IRE) 8 b.g. Supreme Leader – Liffey Travel (Le Bavard (FR))   **h79**
[2003/4 h–: 17s^5 22g* 24s 22s Jan 10] sparely-made gelding: poor hurdler: sold out of
R. Fisher's stable 6,000 gns Doncaster October Sales after reappearance: worthwhile
form only when winning amateur handicap at Exeter in December: stays 2¾m: seems
unsuited by soft going. *Mrs A. M. Thorpe*

ORIENTAL MIST (IRE)   6 gr.g. Balla Cove – Donna Katrina (Kings Lake (USA))   h–
[2003/4 16g[pu] Jun 22] formerly fair on Flat (stays 15f), no form in 2003: little show over hurdles: tried blinkered. *P. Monteith*

ORIENTAL MOON (IRE)   5 ch.m. Spectrum (IRE) – La Grande Cascade (USA)   h–
(Beaudelaire (USA)) [2003/4 16v[pu] 16s 17d³ 16s⁴ 16d Apr 12] modest maiden on Flat (stays 1¼m), little form in 2003 for G. Chung: no form over hurdles. *M. J. Gingell*

ORIENT BAY (IRE)   9 b.g. Commanche Run – East Link (IRE) (Over The River   c61
(FR)) [2003/4 c80?: c25g c25m[pu] c20m² c20m⁴ 26s⁴ 26s 21s 26m³ 21d² Apr 8] strong   h76
gelding: poor maiden hurdler/steeplechaser: stays 3¼m: acts on good to firm and good to soft going: usually wears cheekpieces, blinkered last 2 outings: tongue tied last 5 starts: has jumped poorly/hung under pressure. *M. Sheppard*

ORINOCOVSKY (IRE)   5 ch.g. Grand Lodge (USA) – Brillantina (FR) (Crystal   h82
Glitters (USA)) [2003/4 16d⁵ 19d⁶ 16d[pu] Jan 8] good-topped gelding: fair on Flat (stays 1¾m): best effort over hurdles when fifth in novice at Uttoxeter: went off too quickly in blinkers final start: sold to join N. Littmoden 9,500 gns after successful on Flat in January. *C. R. Egerton*

ORLANDO SUNRISE (IRE)   7 ch.m. Dolphin Street (FR) – Miss Belgravia (USA)   c74 §
(Smarten (USA)) [2003/4 h–: c17m⁴ c17m[F] c20m* c20m[pu] c16f[tr] c20m[ur] c19m[F] Oct 22]   h–
lengthy mare: poor maiden hurdler: similar form over fences: won very weak novice at Worcester in August: stays easy 2½m: acts on good to soft and good to firm going: tried blinkered/visored: races prominently: refused to race fifth outing: one to treat with caution. *R. Dickin*

ORLEANS (IRE)   9 b.g. Scenic – Guest House (What A Guest) [2003/4 c–, h–: c21s⁴   c71
c21s Feb 24] tall gelding: poor pointer/maiden hunter chaser: probably stays 21f: acts on   h–
soft and good to firm going: visored/blinkered: has been reluctant to race (has refused in points). *S. J. Robinson*

ORO STREET (IRE)   8 b.g. Dolphin Street (FR) – Love Unlimited (Dominion)   h83
[2003/4 16m 16g 16m⁵ 16m⁴ 17d² 16m² 16v⁶ 16d³ 25d[pu] 16d 16d Mar 14] workmanlike gelding: one-time fair hurdler: off over 2 years and only poor form in 2003/4: stays 2½m: acts on good to firm and good to soft going: has had tongue tied: has pulled hard/found little. *G. F. Bridgwater*

ORSWELL CREST   10 b.g. Crested Lark – Slave's Bangle (Prince Rheingold)   c111
[2003/4 c105, h–: c24m⁴ c25g³ c24m* c24g⁶ c25m³ c25d[ur] c25g³ Mar 25] lengthy   h–
gelding: fair handicap chaser: made all at Sandown in November: stays 3¼m: acts on soft and good to firm going: usually races up with pace: consistent. *P. J. Hobbs*

ORTHODOX   5 gr.g. Baryshnikov (AUS) – Sancta (So Blessed) [2003/4 16d[pu] Nov   h–
29] good-topped gelding: half-brother to fair hurdler Saint Keyne (by Sadler's Wells), stays 2¾m: fairly useful on Flat (stays 13f): showed little in novice on hurdling debut. *G. L. Moore*

OSCAR BILL (IRE)   5 b.g. Oscar (IRE) – Forecast Rain (IRE) (Phardante (FR))   F84
[2003/4 F16s F17g⁵ Apr 10] stocky gelding: first foal: dam unraced, out of sister to top-class staying chaser Marlborough: signs of ability in 2 bumpers, fifth of 15 in steadily-run event at Newton Abbot. *M. J. Coombe*

OSCAR'S ADVANCE (IRE)   5 b.g. Oscar (IRE) – Banna's Retreat (Vitiges (FR))   F107
[2003/4 F16f F17g* F16g* Sep 18] half-brother to bumper winner Winter Break (by Executive Perk): dam selling hurdler: successful in bumpers at Killarney in July and Listowel in September, useful form when beating Strike Back 3 lengths at latter. *Ms Margaret Mullins, Ireland*

OSCARS VISION (IRE)   4 ch.f. Oscar Schindler (IRE) – Eyelet (IRE) (Satco (FR))   h–
[2003/4 F12m* 16g Dec 27] angular filly: first foal: dam unraced half-sister to Grande   F95
Course de Haies d'Auteuil winner Tongan: 100/1, won 3-y-o fillies bumper at Newbury on debut in December, beating Into The Shadows 1½ lengths: always behind in juvenile hurdle 2 weeks later. *B. W. Duke*

OSCAR THE BOXER (IRE)   5 b.g. Oscar (IRE) – Here She Comes (Deep Run)   F84
[2003/4 F17f² F16g³ F16s F17g Apr 24] 19,000 3-y-o: lengthy, useful-looking gelding: ninth foal: half-brother to useful hurdler/chaser Feathered Leader (by Supreme Leader), stayed 29f: dam poor half-sister to high-class staying chaser Ten Plus: modest form in bumpers: hung badly left third start: will be suited by 2½m+. *J. M. Jefferson*

OSCAR WILDE   12 b.g. Arctic Lord – Topsy Bee (Be Friendly) [2003/4 c–x: c24g   c73 x
Mar 5] tall gelding: winning chaser: well beaten in hunter at Newbury: barely stays 25f: acts on good to soft going: tends to make mistakes. *Mrs S. Alner*

OSO

O SO BOSSY 14 ch.g. Sousa – Bubbling Spirit (Hubble Bubble) [2003/4 c89x: c19m⁵ **c84 x** c24mᶠ Mar 4] fairly useful pointer, successful in February: maiden hunter chaser, usually let down by jumping. *A. W. Congdon*

OSOGLAD 6 b.m. Teenoso (USA) – Gladys Emmanuel (Idiot's Delight) [2003/4 **F78** F17m³ F17m⁵ F17mᵖᵘ Sep 10] second foal: dam modest winning 2m chaser: signs of ability in bumpers, would have been placed at worst but for going lame home turn at Hereford final outing. *Jane Southcombe*

OSO MAGIC 6 b.g. Teenoso (USA) – Scottish Clover (Scottish Reel) [2003/4 16d⁶ **h85** 17d⁶ Apr 10] 6,600 3-y-o: big, lengthy gelding: type to make a chaser: first foal: dam, very useful pointer, half-sister to top-class staying chaser Go Ballistic: pulled hard when sixth in novice hurdle at Wetherby on debut: weakened 2 out when below that form in similar event at Carlisle over 3 months later. *Mrs S. J. Smith*

OSOSHOT 11 b.g. Teenoso (USA) – Duckdown (Blast) [2003/4 h104x: 17g² 22d 23d⁶ **h95** 22d³ 24d⁵ 21d⁴ Mar 14] workmanlike gelding: modest handicap hurdler: stays 23f: acts on soft going: takes strong hold. *A. J. Wilson*

OSSMOSES (IRE) 7 gr.g. Roselier (FR) – Sugarstown (Sassafras (FR)) [2003/4 23d⁴ **c91** c25d³ c25v* c25s⁵ Feb 7] big gelding: sixth foal: brother to fair staying chasers **h86** Cimarrone Cove and Majors Legacy: dam won 2m hurdle in Ireland: fifth in 2½m maiden point in 2003: last of 4 finishers in novice at Wetherby on hurdling debut: modest form in novice chases there subsequently, winning weak event in January: suited by thorough test of stamina. *D. M. Forster*

O'TOOLE (IRE) 5 b.g. Toulon – Legs Burke (IRE) (Buckskin (FR)) [2003/4 F16m² **F94** F16d³ F16m³ Apr 13] lengthy gelding: has scope: first foal: dam unraced, out of half-sister to very smart staying chaser Father Delaney: fair form in bumpers, placed at Wincanton and Chepstow (twice) all 3 starts. *P. J. Hobbs*

OTTOMAN (AUS) 8 br.g. Grand Lodge (USA) – Cushti (AUS) (Gypsy Kingdom **c–** (AUS)) [2003/4 16g³ 16s 19g⁸ 16s 19d 18v c20dᵘʳ Feb 23] leggy, workmanlike gelding: **h85** successful 7 times up to around 13f from 36 starts on Flat in Australia: modest form over hurdles, won maiden at Market Rasen in December: mistake seventh and unseated ninth on chasing debut: stays 19f: raced on good going or softer (acts on heavy). *R. C. Guest*

OUBUS HILL (IRE) 8 b.g. Zaffaran (USA) – Garnerstown Queen (Push On) [2003/4 **c– §** 22g⁶ 24d 20sᵖᵘ c21sᵖᵘ c19g c25vᶠ c20sʳᵒ 27d Mar 16] IR 18,500 4-y-o: strong, work- **h–** manlike gelding: half-brother to winning 2½m hurdler Cabra Towers (by Fidel) and winning pointer by Avocat: dam unraced: little sign of ability: temperamental display final start over fences. *R. F. Fisher*

OUDALMUTEENA (IRE) 9 b.g. Lahib (USA) – Roxy Music (IRE) (Song) [2003/4 **c–** c–, h–§: 21s 22d 22g 24s⁵ 26s 22s² 22s 16s⁶ 19d 24g Apr 1] sturdy gelding: no show only **h70 §** start over fences: poor hurdler: stays 3m: raced mainly on good going or softer (acts on heavy): tried in cheekpieces/visor: ungenuine. *C. J. Gray*

OULTON BROAD 8 b.g. Midyan (USA) – Lady Quachita (USA) (Sovereign Dancer **c–** (USA)) [2003/4 c–, h101: 24g 21d* 16d* Mar 25] sparely-made gelding: fair hurdler: **h101** won claimers at Warwick (claimed from R. Ford £8,000) and Ludlow in March: effective at 2m to 23f: acts on soft and good to firm ground: wears cheekpieces. *F. Jordan*

OUR ARMAGEDDON (NZ) 7 b.g. Sky Chase (NZ) – Monte d'Oro (NZ) (Cache **c146** of Gold (USA)) [2003/4 h118+: c21g² c17g* c20g* c19d* c20d* c16d² c20s* **h–** c16gᵖᵘ c21d* c20g⁴ Apr 3]

Only a handful or so of the hundred or more horses who are the subject of an essay in this edition of *Chasers & Hurdlers* saw racecourse action more often than Our Armageddon. Granted, he only ran half as often as the remarkable Venn Ottery, but a ten-race programme which included six wins, peaking with a Chelt-enham Festival success, provided further proof that a vigorous campaign is not necessarily a barrier to big-race success at the major spring Festivals. Furthermore, Our Armageddon's success at 9/1 in the Cathcart Challenge Cup came just two days after a tilt at the Arkle Trophy had gone badly awry.

Circumstances conspired against Our Armageddon in the Arkle, in which he was forced wide, after being squeezed out at the start, and was pulled up after a bad blunder when struggling at the fourth last. With hindsight, two miles on good ground is probably too sharp a test for Our Armageddon. In the Cathcart he had an

680

North West Racing Club Novices' Chase, Haydock—a typically fluent round of jumping from front runner Our Armageddon who proves too strong for Full Irish

extra five furlongs—on good to soft ground—and only six rivals to beat, instead of the fifteen he had faced forty-eight hours earlier. He had no problem getting to the front in the Cathcart, his jumping fast and fluent from the outset. Four lengths clear with a mile to run, Our Armageddon was still racing with plenty of enthusiasm when the favourite La Landiere threw away what was left of her chance of winning the race for the second year running by slithering on landing over the fourth last. Impek loomed up to challenge at the next, only to produce a characteristically limited response in the home straight, before Iris Royal emerged as a much bigger danger running to the last. Our Armageddon was quick over that fence, despite jumping left, and galloped up the hill with zest to score by two and a half lengths from Iris Royal, becoming the only northern-trained winner at the 2004 Festival.

The Cathcart performance was Our Armageddon's best form of the season and underlined the impression that forcing the pace is the best way to take advantage of his exuberant jumping. However, it would be wrong to assume that he had to leave his previous best form well behind. After finishing second to the ill-fated Brother Joe on his chasing debut at Fakenham in October, Our Armageddon landed the odds with ease in small fields at Kelso and Ayr. Connections considered the First National Gold Cup in November as a possible next objective, only to opt in the end for a four-runner novice chase on the same Ascot card because going for the bigger prize would have meant racing from out of the handicap. Our Armageddon duly justified favouritism, coming home well clear despite showing an alarming tendency to jump left on his first chasing outing on a right-handed track. An equally convincing victory over Silver Knight in the One Man Novices' Chase at Wetherby two weeks later set up Our Armageddon for two runs at Haydock either side of Christmas. On the first, back at two miles, he went down by four lengths to Caracciola in a three-runner race. The fact that he was conceding 8 lb (less his rider's 5-lb allowance) to the progressive Caracciola represented an improved effort, which Our Armageddon confirmed back at two and a half miles in January with an impressive pillar-to-post victory over a useful field headed by Full Irish. Our Armageddon was off the course for over nine weeks until Cheltenham, though he did return to Haydock for a racecourse gallop just over a fortnight before the Arkle. His Cathcart

Cathcart Challenge Cup Chase, Cheltenham—no ill-effects from a run in the Arkle two days earlier as Our Armageddon beats Iris Royal (left) and Impek to record his sixth win of 2003/4

success prompted his trainer to suggest that he would be put away for the season, but he had second thoughts and turned him out at Aintree on Grand National day for a valuable novices' handicap chase confined to amateur riders. Ridden by Dale Jewett and sent off a well-backed 9/4 favourite to give weight all round, Our Armageddon ran just below his Cathcart form. Harried for the lead in a strongly-run race, he jumped a shade less fluently than normal, though, in finishing fourth of fourteen behind Keltic Bard, he did more than enough to confirm that he can make his mark in good handicaps in the next season.

Our Armageddon, who won over a mile from three starts on the Flat in New Zealand, was a progressive novice hurdler in 2002/3 but had the second of his three wins—at Carlisle—expunged when the prohibited substance theobromine was found in his urine sample. Our Armageddon's pedigree isn't entirely unfamiliar to followers of jumping in Britain, as he is a half-brother to Black Bullet (by Silver Pistol), a fairly useful handicap chaser suited by forcing the pace at up to two and a half miles. Black Bullet and Our Armageddon are the only winners from three named foals out of the unraced Monte d'Oro. She in turn is a sister to Saiau Pal, whose six wins at up to a mile and three quarters on the Flat included the Group 2 VRC St Leger and the Group 3 SAJC St Leger in Australia. Our Armageddon's second dam Robyn's Order is a half-sister to Mr Prospector. However, connections have no need to lament the fact that Our Armageddon is a gelding, as the Mr Prospector in question was a seven-furlong winner in Malaysia, not the outstanding American stallion who died in 1999.

Our Armageddon (NZ) (b.g. 1997)	Sky Chase (NZ) (br 1984)	Star Way (ch 1977)	Star Appeal
			New Way
		Vice Reine (br 1977)	Amalgam
			Kind Regards
	Monte d'Oro (NZ) (b 1988)	Cache of Gold (b 1977)	Mr Prospector
			Ever A Madame
		Robyn's Order (br 1975)	Indian Order
			Tiki Time

Our Armageddon is a rather leggy gelding who acts on soft ground and has yet to race on firmer than good over jumps. He has already shown himself effective at up to two miles five furlongs and has prospects of staying three miles. Left-handed tracks may well suit him best, with valuable handicaps like the Paddy Power Gold Cup and the Tripleprint Gold Cup at Cheltenham earmarked as likely

targets for the first half of the 2004/5 season. His bold jumping and durability will
be assets in the next season. His Cathcart success paid a handsome compliment to
trainer Richard Guest, who was saddling his first Festival winner just thirteen
months after taking over the licence at Brancepeth Manor Farm In County Durham
from owner Norman Mason. Guest won the 1989 Champion Hurdle on Beech Road
and the 2001 Grand National on Red Marauder during his days in the saddle and
has firm views about the way his horses should be ridden. But he had no hesitation
in entrusting the ride on Our Armageddon on all his appearances until Aintree in
the latest season to his stable conditional Larry McGrath, who repaid his faith.
R. C. Guest

OUR BEN   5 ch.g. Presenting – Forest Pride (IRE) (Be My Native (USA)) [2003/4
F16d* F16g Mar 17] rather unfurnished gelding: third foal: half-brother to fair hurdler up
to 2¾m Countess Camilla (by Bob's Return): dam modest 2m hurdler: landed odds in
bumper at Limerick on debut in February, staying on strongly to beat Rights of Man 4½
lengths: failed to progress at Cheltenham (Champion Bumper) and Punchestown.
W. P. Mullins, Ireland   **F99**

OUR DREAM (IRE)   5 b.m. Bob Back (USA) – Baybush (Boreen (FR)) [2003/4 F81:
F16d³ 21d² 22v² 20v* Feb 7] strong, compact mare: modest form in 2 mares bumpers:
modest form in mares novice hurdles, easily landed odds at Chepstow: stays 21f: acts on
heavy going: remains open to improvement. *Mrs M. Reveley*   **h97 p / F81**

OUR ETHEL   6 ch.m. Be My Chief (USA) – Annes Gift (Ballymoss) [2003/4 F74:
20m³ May 7] leggy mare: bumper winner: poor form when third in weak novice at
Wetherby on hurdling debut. *Mrs M. Reveley*   **h68**

OUR HOUSE (IRE)   5 ch.g. Carroll House – Farinella (IRE) (Salmon Leap (USA))
[2003/4 19s⁴ 19vᵖᵘ 16g Feb 11] unfurnished gelding: fifth foal: half-brother to top-class
chaser Beef Or Salmon (by Cajetano), stays 3¼m: dam once-raced half-sister to fairly
useful 2m hurdlers Lunulae and Wally Wallensky: best effort over hurdles when fourth in
novice at Taunton on debut: looked hard ride next outing. *M. C. Pipe*   **h87**

OUR IMPERIAL BAY (USA)   5 b.g. Smart Strike (CAN) – Heat Lightning (USA)
(Summer Squall (USA)) [2003/4 h101: 16m⁶ 20dᵖᵘ 20m⁶ 17m⁵ 24m⁵ Sep 14] tall
gelding: poor maiden hurdler: best efforts at 2m: acts on good to firm going: usually
blinkered/visored: has carried head high/found little: won on Flat in March. *R. M. Stronge*   **h79 §**

OUR JOLLY SWAGMAN   9 b.g. Thowra (FR) – Queens Dowry (Dominion) [2003/4
c108, h–: c24m* c28d* c32mᵖᵘ c20m c24s* c33dᵖᵘ Jan 1] sturdy gelding: fairly useful
handicap chaser: won at Chepstow and Stratford in May and Lingfield (beat Tremallt
2½ lengths) in December: lame final start: stays 3½m: acts on good to firm and heavy
going: has worn cheekpieces, usually visored nowadays: has won 4 times at Plumpton.
J. W. Mullins   **c118 / h–**

OUR KEV (IRE)   8 b.g. Be My Native (USA) – Sunbath (Krayyan) [2003/4 h–: c24s²
c21d⁵ c25s⁶ c24g* c24gᵖᵘ Mar 7] tall gelding: maiden hurdler: form in steeplechases only
when winning weak conditional jockeys handicap at Musselburgh in February: stays 3m.
B. G. Powell   **c87 / h–**

OUR LAWMAN   5 b.g. Shareef Dancer (USA) – Motoqua (Mtoto) [2003/4 F16g F17v⁵
17d Apr 18] first foal: dam fairly useful hurdler up to 2½m, out of once-raced half-sister
to Bustino: better effort in bumpers when fifth at Carlisle, always well placed: well beaten
in novice there on hurdling debut. *Mrs S. J. Smith*   **h– / F77 ?**

OUR MAN DENNIS   10 b.g. Arzanni – Pendocks Polly (Grey Steel) [2003/4 16sᵖᵘ
c24m c20d c16d⁵ c19g⁶ c23dᵖᵘ Apr 21] lengthy gelding: poor maiden hurdler/chaser:
probably best around 2m: has shown signs of temperament. *Mrs P. Ford*   **c69 / h–**

OURMAN (IRE)   8 b.g. Good Thyne (USA) – Magic Minstrel (Pitpan) [2003/4 c98,
h–: c25d* c26v² May 21] useful-looking gelding: fair hunter chaser: won at Hexham in
May: likely to prove best at 3m+: raced on good going or softer (acts on heavy): has had
tongue tied: often races up with pace: has raced lazily. *Mrs A. Bell*   **c98 / h–**

OUR MEN   5 b.g. Classic Cliche (IRE) – Praise The Lord (Lord Gayle (USA)) [2003/4
F16d May 3] seventh foal: half-brother to several winners, including useful hurdler/
chaser up to 2½m Whip Hand (by Bob Back) and fairly useful pointer Greenwich (by
Handsome Sailor): dam Irish maiden: ran very wide home turn when eighth of 16 in
bumper at Uttoxeter on debut. *C. R. Egerton*   **F–**

OUR PADDY (IRE)   5 b.g. Ali-Royal (IRE) – Lilting Air (IRE) (Glenstal (USA))   **h–**
[2003/4 16g^pu Oct 30] dam half-sister to dam of smart 2m hurdler Cardinal Hill: modest
on Flat (stays 9f) for P. D. Evans/W. Murphy: raced freely in seller on hurdling debut:
went to UAE. *Mrs L. C. Jewell*

OUR PRIMA DONNA (IRE)   6 ch.m. Be My Native (USA) – Stage Debut (Decent   **h91**
Fellow) [2003/4 20s 21d² 21d³ 22d⁴ 21g Mar 27] €28,000 4-y-o: workmanlike mare:
eighth foal: half-sister to useful chaser up to 27f Hati Roy (by Lafontaine): dam unraced:
modest form over hurdles: likely to be suited by 3m. *Miss H. C. Knight*

OUR TOMMY   11 ch.g. Ardross – Ina's Farewell (Random Shot) [2003/4 c90: c21d⁵   **c75**
c20s⁶ c20v c19m⁵ c20d^pu Apr 21] poor handicap chaser: best short of 3m: raced mainly
on good going or softer (acts on soft): usually races prominently. *A. E. Price*

OUR VIC (IRE)   6 b.g. Old Vic – Shabra Princess (Buckskin (FR)) [2003/4 h140p: **c150 p**
16d² c19v* c24g* c24g³ Mar 17]   **h146 p**
To say the least, there were plenty of room for interpretation of the outcome
after the latest running of the championship event for staying novice chasers, the
Royal & SunAlliance Chase at Cheltenham. Rule Supreme won the race from
Royal Emperor, but the runner-up made a serious mistake at a crucial stage and his
rider shortly after dropped his whip; Mossy Green, still in front, might have won
had he not fallen two out; Pizarro, ahead of the winner at the time, might have won
had he not been brought down at the same fence; there was even a case to be made
for Calling Brave as he was going well when departing four out. It could also be
advanced that, although he completed the course, a series of jumping mistakes by
the favourite Old Vic also put paid to his prospects. It certainly seemed to be a view
taken by the bookmakers, as Our Vic is the shortest-priced of all those who contested the SunAlliance in most ante-post lists for the next Cheltenham Gold Cup.
Until his defeat at Cheltenham, the sky had looked pretty much the limit for
Our Vic. He had been campaigned in a fashion which suggested that either he was
quite fragile or was regarded by connections as somewhat exceptional. His performances and some of the comments made by his connections strongly suggested
the latter. Old Vic won a four-runner four-year-old maiden point in Ireland in March
2002 and was then bought from Tom Costello, the source of many a star chaser over
the years. Our Vic had just three runs over hurdles in 2002/3, winning novices at
Exeter and Taunton and a handicap at Wincanton. He won the handicap, an ordinary
contest otherwise, by a length but the margin could have been considerably wider—
the BHB handicapper raised him 19 lb afterwards—which, coupled with the fact
that Old Vic was quoted at around 25/1 for the 2004 Champion Hurdle, suggested
there was plenty more to come. Trainer Martin Pipe and owner David Johnson were
reportedly far from pleased with the revised mark and Our Vic, who had not been
entered for the novice events at Cheltenham, was put away for the rest of the
season.
When Our Vic returned in the autumn, it was in the William Hill Handicap
Hurdle at Sandown in early-December, a race which Pipe had pretty much made his
own over the years. Carrying joint top weight, Our Vic ran a splendid race, finding
only Overstrand too good and putting up a smart effort. When the weights were
published in January for the Tote Gold Trophy, Our Vic was among the ante-post
market leaders, but by that stage it was clear that, despite the relatively short time
before Cheltenham, he was to begin a novice chase campaign.
Our Vic missed engagements over fences at Cheltenham around New Year
and made his chasing debut in early-February, in a novice event over just under two
and a half miles at Exeter, in which he jumped well and easily landed the odds. A
similarly successful chasing debut twenty-four hours later for his owner's Well
Chief was followed by Our Vic's being stepped up still further in trip for his next
outing. The three-mile Amlin Plus Reynoldstown Novices' Chase at Ascot also
represented quite a step up in class: four of Our Vic's five opponents had won at
least once over fences and Rosslea and Double Honour were proven useful performers. Our Vic dispatched them every bit as authoritatively as he had most of his
other previous challengers. With Timmy Murphy deputising for Tony McCoy, Our
Vic impressed with his jumping, despite a tendency to go left, and won on the bridle
by six lengths from Rosslea. The Arkle, the Cathcart and even the Gold Cup (for

Amlin Plus Reynoldstown Novices' Chase, Ascot—Our Vic puts in a fine leap at an open ditch

which he would have needed to be supplemented) were all still Cheltenham possibilities at this stage, but, in the end, another novice Therealbandit (who had been among the stable's original entries) represented Pipe and Johnson in the Gold Cup, with Our Vic going for the novice event. Well Chief had overcome his lack of chasing experience in the Arkle the previous day but, with plenty of racing on the Flat, he was a different type of horse to Our Vic. Lack of experience was a key factor in Our Vic's defeat in the SunAlliance. Failing to settle and pulling his way up to the leaders at the fourth, Our Vic was left with a definite advantage when Mossy Green fell but his exertions and jumping mistakes told in the straight and, headed at the last, he finished third, beaten just over three lengths by the winner.

Our Vic (IRE) (b.g. 1998)	Old Vic (b 1986)	Sadler's Wells (b 1981)	Northern Dancer / Fairy Bridge
		Cockade (b 1973)	Derring-Do / Camenae
	Shabra Princess (b or br 1983)	Buckskin (b 1973)	Yelapa / Bete A Bon Dieu
		Random View (b or br 1977)	Random Shot / Rising View

'Favourites don't always win' was the trainer's philosophical response to defeat and compensation surely awaits in good measure in 2004/5. Our Vic has already shown himself a smart chaser after just three appearances in novice company and there is the potential for quite a bit more to come. Our Vic is effective at three miles, but it is hard to think that many of his fellow staying novices would have been capable of producing the performance he did over two miles at Sandown. Old Vic is likely to prove just as effective at around two and a half miles and the

Mr D. A. Johnson's "Our Vic"

new Grade 2 race over two miles five furlongs at the Festival may well be an attractive alternative to the Gold Cup, particularly if Therealbandit thrives in the interim. The tall, good-topped Our Vic comes from a non-thoroughbred family in which the better performers of recent times have all been stayers. His grandam Random View, who won a fillies maiden hurdle, is a half-sister to the useful staying hurdler and winning chaser Random View as well as to the dams of the above-average staying jumpers Mr Gossip and Radiation, who was runner-up in an Eider and a Borders National. Our Vic's dam Shabra Princess was a maiden, though she made the frame over both hurdles and fences, and he is her only winner to date. Her fifth and next foal Commercial Flyer (by Carroll House) was in training with Pipe in the latest season and finished in the frame in a couple of novice hurdles. Our Vic has raced on good going or softer, the ground being heavy when he won on his novice chase debut. *M. C. Pipe*

OUTLAW EXPRESS (IRE)   8 b.g. Un Desperado (FR) – Surprise Packet (Torus)   **c66**
[2003/4 c21d[3] c19s c23g c24g[2] c26d[pu] Apr 11] good-topped gelding: well held over   **h–**
hurdles: poor form over fences: stays 3m: tried in cheekpieces, looked none too genuine
both starts in visor: sold 6,500 gns Doncaster May Sales. *P. R. Webber*

OUT OF THE SHADOWS   8 gr.m. Rock Hopper – Shadows of Silver (Carwhite)   **h98**
[2003/4 h107: 16m[5] May 7] strong, lengthy mare: carries condition: should make a
chaser: fair handicap hurdler: saddle slipped/reportedly finished lame only outing in
2003/4: should stay beyond 2m: acts on good to firm and good to soft going: effective in
cheekpieces or not: not the easiest of rides. *Mrs M. Reveley*

OUT OF WESTWOOD   6 ch.m. Out of Hand – Brandy Season (High Season) [2003/4   **F–**
F17m[pu] Aug 25] second foal: dam tailed off in novice hurdles: reportedly lame in bumper
on debut. *Mrs S. Gardner*

OUTSIDE INVESTOR (IRE)   4 b. or br.g. Cadeaux Genereux – Desert Ease (IRE)   **h83**
(Green Desert (USA)) [2003/4 16g⁵ 16g* 16g Jan 23] workmanlike gelding: fairly useful
maiden up to 1¼m on Flat (usually blinkered) for D. Weld: modest form over hurdles first
2 starts, fortunate to win novice at Musselburgh in January; blinkered after debut. sold
30,000 gns Doncaster May Sales. *Ferdy Murphy*

OUTSIDE THE DOOR (IRE)   8 b.g. Husyan (USA) – Twilight Sunset (Deep Run)   **c–**
[2003/4 F20d⁴ F20g⁵ 24gᵖᵘ 20d⁴ 19g⁶ 19g³ c17gᶠ Dec 26] IR 24,000 4-y-o: workman-   **h73**
like ex-Irish gelding: fourth foal: dam twice-raced half-sister to one-time very smart   **F73**
chaser up to 25f Stormyfairweather: won maiden point in 2001: poor form in bumpers
and over hurdles: sold out of A. Moore's stable 7,200 gns Doncaster August Sales after
fourth start: fell eighth on steeplechasing debut: stays 2½m: acts on good to soft going.
Mrs J. R. Buckley

OVER BRIDGE   6 b.g. Overbury (IRE) – Celtic Bridge (Celtic Cone) [2003/4 h–§,   **h78 §**
F79: 19m* 19s⁵ 22sᵇᵈ 19d 19g² 21d Apr 8] smallish, workmanlike gelding: poor hurdler:
won novice handicap at Hereford in November: stays 19f: acts on good to firm going:
ungenuine. *Mrs S. M. Johnson*

OVERBURY AFFAIR   5 b.g. Overbury (IRE) – Dara's Course (IRE) (Crash Course)   **F104 p**
[2003/4 F16d* Dec 26] €38,000 3-y-o: first foal: dam winning pointer: won 29-runner
bumper at Leopardstown on debut by 1½ lengths from Bold As Brass, travelling well
long way and quickening well after initially running green after 2f out: sure to improve.
E. J. O'Grady, Ireland

OVERLORD (IRE)   7 b.g. Lord Americo – Straddler's Hill (IRE) (Torus) [2003/4   **h72**
h66, F–: 20d³ May 16] sturdy gelding: poor form over hurdles: should be suited by 3m+.
B. De Haan

OVERSERVED   5 b. or br.g. Supreme Leader – Divine Comedy (IRE) (Phardante   **h–**
(FR)) [2003/4 18s Jan 16] good-topped gelding: fourth foal: dam, poor form in bumper,
half-sister to useful staying chaser Dakyns Boy: backward, showed some ability when
ninth of 19 in novice hurdle at Kelso on debut. *A. Parker*

OVERSTRAND (IRE)   5 b.g. In The Wings – Vaison La Romaine (Arctic Tern   **h131**
(USA)) [2003/4 h107: 20g* 17g* 17d* 16d* 16s 21g² 21d⁴ 16s Mar 13] lengthy, angular
gelding: useful hurdler: vastly improved form when winning William Hill Handicap at
Sandown in December by 5 lengths from Our Vic: best subsequent effort when second to
Ziggy Zen in novice at Kempton in January: earlier won maiden at Perth in May and
novices at Market Rasen (amateurs) and Carlisle in November: effective at 2m to 21f:
raced on good going or softer: has taken good hold, and usually held up. *Mrs M. Reveley*

William Hill Handicap Hurdle, Sandown—
novice Overstrand takes over at the last from top weight Our Vic (spotted cap) and Monkerhostin

OVER THE CREEK 5 br.g. Over The River (FR) – Solo Girl (IRE) (Le Bavard (FR)) [2003/4 19s[5] 18v[bd] 16d[2] Jan 17] second foal: dam, lightly raced, from family of Grand National winner Rubstic and top-class staying chaser Kildimo: best effort in novice hurdles when ¾-length second to Corporate Player at Wincanton: should prove suited by further than 2m: open to further improvement. *M. C. Pipe*   **h102 p**

OVER THE FIRST (IRE) 9 b. or br.g. Orchestra – Ruby Lodge (Peacock (FR)) [2003/4 c120, h122: c20d[3] c19d c18d[F] 16s[pu] c19s c17s[5] c20s* c21g[6] c16s* c20s[5] Mar 27] rangy gelding: fairly useful hurdler/chaser: won handicaps over fences at Navan in February and Punchestown (listed event, beat Jurado Express 7 lengths) in March: stays 21f: acts on heavy going, possibly not on good to firm: game. *C. F. Swan, Ireland*   **c124** **h–**

OVER THE HILL (IRE) 12 b.g. Over The River (FR) – Joint Equity (Callernish) [2003/4 c–x, h79: c27s[3] c30g[pu] c25m[2] 26m[3] 24g[pu] Jul 6] small gelding: winning hurdler/chaser: left S. Magnier after reappearance: stayed 27f: acted on good to firm and good to soft going: usually blinkered/visored: tried tongue tied: usually let down by jumping over fences: dead. *J. A. Pickering*   **c82 x** **h85**

OVER THE KOHLS (IRE) 6 ch.g. Over The River (FR) – Forever Second (IRE) (Parliament) [2003/4 F16s[pu] Dec 19] first foal: dam unraced: broke down in bumper on debut. *John R. Upson*   **F–**

OVER THE STORM (IRE) 7 b.g. Over The River (FR) – Naas (Ballymore) [2003/4 c121: c24d[3] c25g[2] c24d* Jan 3] workmanlike gelding: fairly useful handicap chaser: good placed efforts first 2 starts and won quite valuable event at Sandown by 2½ lengths from Jimmy Tennis: should stay beyond 25f: raced on good going or softer (acts on soft): genuine. *Miss H. C. Knight*   **c129**

OVERTON ROSE 7 b.m. Cut The Mustard (IRE) – Palmy (USA) (Buckfinder (USA)) [2003/4 F17m 16s Jan 16] fourth foal: dam no worthwhile form on Flat or over hurdles: tailed off in bumper and novice hurdle. *J. R. Bewley*   **h–** **F–**

OVER TO YOU BERT 5 b.g. Overbury (IRE) – Silvers Era (Balidar) [2003/4 F–: 17g[5] Jun 21] modest on Flat (stays 1m): well held in novice on hurdling debut: joined R. Hodges. *Mrs P. N. Dutfield*   **h–**

OVER ZEALOUS (IRE) 12 ch.g. Over The River (FR) – Chatty Di (Le Bavard (FR)) [2003/4 c101+, h–: c30s[3] c29m* c27v[ur] c26g[6] c25d[5] c25s[ur] Apr 11] leggy gelding: modest handicap chaser: fortunate to win at Warwick in December: out of sorts otherwise in 2003/4: thorough stayer: acts on heavy going, probably on good to firm: blinkered/visored: moody. *John R. Upson*   **c91 §** **h– §**

ladbrokes.com Chase (Handicap), Sandown—
a weak race for the money, with Over The Storm beating Jimmy Tennis (No.5) and Exit To Wave

OWEN'S PET (IRE)   10 b.g. Alphabatim (USA) – Ballinlovane (Le Moss) [2003/4 c75
c–, h–: c25g^{pu} c26d^3 Apr 7] lengthy gelding: maiden steeplechaser: better effort in h–
hunters when distant third at Fontwell: stays 3¼m: raced on good going or softer.
Miss S. A. Loggin

OWENWELD   11 ch.g. Weld – Owen Belle (Master Owen) [2003/4 c24m^5 c25m c–
24m^{pu} Jul 9] leggy gelding: poor pointer: no form in handicap chases or hurdle in 2003/4. h–
D. R. Gandolfo

OXIDOR (IRE)   9 br.g. Be My Native (USA) – Euroblend (IRE) (The Parson) [2003/4 h– §
h79§: 24s^{pu} 26s 24s^{pu} 26g Mar 17] close-coupled gelding: handicap hurdler, no form in
2003/4: blinkered/tongue tied: moody. *C. P. Morlock*

OYSTERHAVEN (IRE)   6 b.g. Mister Lord (USA) – Haven's Glory (IRE) (Supreme h98
Leader) [2003/4 F16g 20s* 24g^{pu} Mar 26] €21,000 4-y-o: useful-looking gelding: F82
chasing type: first foal: dam unraced half-sister to smart staying chaser Buck Rogers:
eighth in bumper on debut: won novice at Fontwell on hurdling debut later in December
by length from Bramlynn Brook: appeared to go wrong final start: should stay 3m.
D. P. Keane

OYSTER SHELL (IRE)   7 b.g. Be My Native (USA) – Judys View (King's Ride) h87
[2003/4 h72p: 21g^3 Nov 5] winning Irish pointer: better effort in novice company over
hurdles nearly 9 months apart when third at Kempton. *N. J. Henderson*

P

PAARL ROCK   9 ch.g. Common Grounds – Markievicz (IRE) (Doyoun) [2003/4 17g^5 h66
Apr 1] modest on Flat (stays 2m) in 2001, no form in 2004: second start over hurdles, set
strong pace when distant fifth in maiden at Taunton: will stay beyond 2m: wears headgear. *S. T. Lewis*

PACHINCO   6 ch.g. Bluebird (USA) – Lady Philippa (IRE) (Taufan (USA)) [2003/4 h–
h–: 20g^{pu} 16g 22g^2 22m^6 22g 20g^5 16g^{pu} Nov 16] tall, angular gelding: signs of ability
only when runner-up in weak 2¾m maiden hurdle at Cartmel in May: sold 600 gns
Doncaster November Sales. *J. G. M. O'Shea*

PACIFIC ALLIANCE (IRE)   8 b.g. Fayruz – La Gravotte (FR) (Habitat) [2003/4 h82
h71: 16m^{pu} 17d^5 17m^5 16g* 16d^2 Nov 12] leggy gelding: poor handicap hurdler: first
start after leaving R. Stronge, won at Wexford in October: will prove best around 2m: acts
on good to soft going: tried blinkered: races prominently. *Michael Butler, Ireland*

PACIFIC HIGHWAY (IRE)   5 b.g. Sadler's Wells (USA) – Obeah (Cure The Blues F–
(USA)) [2003/4 F16v F16v F16s Mar 13] half-brother to several winners on Flat, including useful performer up to 13f Panama City (by El Gran Senor): dam 2-y-o 7f winner:
well beaten in 3 bumpers. *Mrs L. B. Normile*

PACIFYC (IRE)   9 b.g. Brief Truce (USA) – Ocean Blue (IRE) (Bluebird (USA)) h– §
[2003/4 h84§: 17g May 24] rather leggy gelding: poor handicap hurdler: off 7 months,
lame only outing in 2003/4: stays 2½m: acts on good to firm and good to soft ground:
tongue tied: ungenuine. *John A. Harris*

PACK LEADER (IRE)   8 b.g. Muharib (USA) – Royal Broderick (IRE) (Lancastrian) c–
[2003/4 h83: c20m^{pu} c20m^{pu} Sep 7] poor form over hurdles: let down by jumping both h–
starts in steeplechases, lame on second occasion: has had tongue tied. *Jonjo O'Neill*

PACO VENTURE (IRE)   9 b.g. Supreme Leader – Ethel's Daughter (Deep Run) c104 §
[2003/4 h109: c24m^F c24m^2 Oct 10] rangy gelding: fair hurdler: runner-up in 2-runner h– §
novice chase: stays 3m: acts on soft and good to firm going: makes mistakes: temperamental. *Miss Venetia Williams*

PADDINGTON GREEN   6 b.g. Primitive Rising (USA) – Mayfair Minx (St Colum- h82
bus) [2003/4 F17d 19s^4 22s^{pu} 17s 19d 22g^2 23d^2 Apr 12] fourth foal: half-brother to very F–
smart 2m hurdler Marble Arch and useful 2m hurdler Tom Paddington (both by Rock
Hopper): dam, fairly useful staying hurdler, half-sister to useful staying chaser Vulgan
Warrior: well held in bumper on debut: poor novice hurdler: likely to stay beyond 23f:
raced on good going or softer: blinkered last 2 starts. *H. Morrison*

PADDY FOR PADDY (IRE)   10 b.g. Mandalus – Lady Rerico (Pamroy) [2003/4 c–
c105: c25d^{pu} Mar 23] fairly useful hunter chaser: won point in February: stays 25f: acts
on soft going. *G. L. Landau*

PADDY MUL   7 ch.h. Democratic (USA) – My Pretty Niece (Great Nephew) [2003/4   h–
16d Dec 1] poor on Flat (stays 2m): tongue tied, little form in novice company over
hurdles. *W. Storey*

PADDY'S PROFILES (IRE)   10 b.g. Euphemism – Dame Niamh (IRE) (Buckskin   h–
(FR)) [2003/4 h–: 20m May 7] lengthy gelding: seems of little account nowadays: tried
visored: sold £1,200 Ascot December Sales. *Miss K. M. George*

PADDY'S THYME (IRE)   8 gr.g. Good Thyne (USA) – Nanny Kehoe (IRE) (Sexton   c–
Blake) [2003/4 c–, h71: c25g^pu Nov 17] workmanlike gelding: poor maiden hurdler: no   h–
form over fences: stays 27f. *B. G. Powell*

PADDY THE DRIVER (IRE)   8 b.g. Grand Plaisir (IRE) – Jude's Hollow (IRE)   h–
(Hollow Hand) [2003/4 h76: 16g 19d^pu Dec 5] maiden hurdler: no show either start in
2003/4. *P. J. Hobbs*

PADDY THE OPTIMIST (IRE)   8 b.g. Leading Counsel (USA) – Erne Duchess   c87
(IRE) (Duky) [2003/4 h74: 16d^4 c20s^3 c26s^pu c24v^pu c25d^3 c20v^pu c19m* c20d^3 Apr 23]   h74
sturdy gelding: poor maiden hurdler: better over fences: won selling handicap (sold from
T. George 7,500 gns) at Chepstow in April: may prove best short of 3m: acts on soft and
good to firm going: blinkered last 4 starts. *D. Burchell*

PADDY THE PIPER (IRE)   7 b.g. Witness Box (USA) – Divine Dibs (Raise You   h134 p
Ten) [2003/4 F101: 16s* 20s* 18g* 18g* Mar 28]
    Paddy The Piper has been able to call the tune in his last six races, and he
may continue to do so in a few more if Len Lungo adopts his usual softly-softly
policy—the Audley Harrison approach according to one of his fellow trainers—
when he sends the gelding over fences in the next season. The winner of bumpers at
Catterick and Wetherby on his last two starts in 2002/3, Paddy The Piper went
unbeaten through his first season over hurdles, quickly developing into a useful
performer. Paddy The Piper's first three victories over hurdles all came in novice
events, two of them at Kelso and one at Ayr in between. He completed the hat-trick
in the Tote Exacta Premier Kelso Hurdle in March, a Grade 2 event in which nine

Tote Exacta Premier Kelso Hurdle (Novices')—
Paddy The Piper puts up a useful performance, chased home by Steppes of Gold (hooped cap)

of the eleven runners were winning hurdlers, with Chivalry, Steppes of Gold and
Tragic Ohio also having won both their starts over timber. Chivalry, who started
favourite, and Tragic Ohio failed to give their running whereas Paddy The Piper
and Steppes of Gold left their previous form behind and had the finish to themselves. Paddy The Piper, still travelling well when taking up the running before two
out, stayed on strongly to win by a length and three quarters. Kelso was also the
venue for Paddy The Piper's final outing of the season. The top weight in an eleven-
runner handicap, he had to work hard to justify favouritism, pushed along to make
headway after four out, going a couple of lengths clear after leading at the last but
all out to hold off Silk Trader, half a length the winning margin. Paddy The Piper, a
quite good-topped gelding who was bought as an unraced three-year-old for IR
26,000 guineas, is stoutly bred and will prove well suited by further than two and a
half miles, the longest distance he has tackled so far. By the smart stayer Witness
Box out of the Raise You Ten mare Divine Dibs, who finished second in a two-mile
hurdle, Paddy The Piper is a half-brother to the fairly useful staying chaser Tell The
Nipper (by Riberetto) and the useful hurdler/chaser Love And Porter (by Sheer
Grit), who stayed twenty-five furlongs. Paddy The Piper has raced only on good
ground or softer. *L. Lungo*

PAGAN DANCE (IRE) 5 b.g. Revoque (IRE) – Ballade d'Ainhoa (FR) (Al Nasr **h115**
(FR)) [2003/4 16d³ 16d Dec 29] good-topped gelding: useful on Flat (stays 14.8f): much
better effort in novice hurdles at Newbury when third to Albuhera in November: raced
freely next time. *Mrs A. J. Perrett*

PAGERMAR (IRE) 10 b. or br.g. Camden Town – Another Coup (Le Patron) [2003/4 **c–**
c24sᵖᵘ May 2] ex-Irish gelding: winning pointer: no form in steeplechases: has had
tongue tied. *Mrs W. D. Sykes*

PAILITAS (GER) 7 b.g. Lomitas – Pradera (GER) (Abary (GER)) [2003/4 h75: 17d **h81**
17m⁵ 16m³ 16m⁴ 16m* 17m³ 17d⁴ Oct 29] rather leggy gelding: poor handicap hurdler:
won at Huntingdon in August: left I. Williams before final start: best at sharp 2m: acts on
good to firm going: headstrong. *G. A. Swinbank*

PAKIEFROMATHLEAGUE (IRE) 6 b.g. Namaqualand (USA) – Krisdaline **h114**
(USA) (Kris S (USA)) [2003/4 16g² Sep 17] fair on Flat (stays 2m): similar standard over
hurdles, best effort when second to Felix The Great in minor event at Listowel only start
in 2003/4: raced at 2m: tried blinkered. *D. T. Hughes, Ireland*

PALACE (FR) 8 b.g. Rahotep (FR) – La Musardiere (FR) (Cadoudal (FR)) [2003/4 **c–**
c23mᵖᵘ Jul 23] signs of only a little ability: tongue tied. *P. F. Nicholls* **h–**

PALAIS (IRE) 9 b.g. Darshaan – Dance Festival (Nureyev (USA)) [2003/4 h79: 26gᵖᵘ **h–**
24g⁶ 22g 19d Dec 4] leggy gelding: poor hurdler: stays 3m: acts on good to firm and good
to soft going: inconsistent. *John A. Harris*

PALARSHAN (FR) 6 b. or br.g. Darshaan – Palavera (FR) (Bikala) [2003/4 c140p, h–: **c146**
c16g c16s² c16d Mar 18] tall, good-topped gelding: smart handicap chaser: best effort **h–**
when second to Farmer Jack at Sandown in February, staying on well despite hanging
right run-in: should stay 2½m: acts on soft and good to firm going. *H. D. Daly*

PALMAC'S PRIDE 4 ch.g. Atraf – Nashwanah (Nashwan (USA)) [2003/4 F12d **F–**
F17sᵖᵘ aF16g Apr 4] workmanlike gelding: third foal: half-brother to 2000 Italian 2-y-o
6f/7f winner Star Eagle (by Eagle Eyed): dam ran twice: showed nothing in bumpers.
M. F. Harris

PALMA (IRE) 6 b. or br.g. Rashar (USA) – Quaybreeze (IRE) (Quayside) [2003/4 **F74**
F18s⁵ Dec 3] IR 6,000 3-y-o, 18,000 4-y-o: first foal: dam unraced: looked inexperienced
when fifth in bumper at Plumpton on debut, going in snatches. *P. R. Webber*

PALOUSE (IRE) 8 gr.g. Toulon – Hop Picker (USA) (Plugged Nickle (USA)) **c90 §**
[2003/4 c16fᵖᵘ c16fᵖᵘ 16f⁶ c20f c18f³ c20m c19d⁶ 18g³ 22dᵖᵘ c16g⁵ Apr 18] tall, leggy **h110 §**
gelding: fair handicap hurdler nowadays: not so good over fences (sketchy jumper): sold
out of P. Rothwell's stable 12,000 gns Newmarket Autumn Sales after fifth start: stays
2½m: acts on firm and good to soft going (possibly unsuited by softer): tried blinkered:
tends to race freely/find little: unreliable. *R. H. Buckler*

PALUA 7 b.g. Sri Pekan (USA) – Reticent Bride (IRE) (Shy Groom (USA)) [2003/4 **c127**
h131: c20g* c25d⁵ c20d⁶ c16g* c16gᵖᵘ c16g⁶ Apr 3] useful-looking gelding: useful **h–**
hurdler at best: fairly useful novice chaser: won at Huntingdon in November and Kemp-

ton in January, beating Caracciola by 1½ lengths at latter (jumped markedly left on occasions): much better effort in Grade 1 events last 2 starts when sixth to Well Chief at Aintree: effective at 2m to 3m: acts on good to firm and heavy ground: has found little. *Miss E. C. Lavelle*

PAMELA ANSHAN 7 b.m. Anshan – Have Form (Haveroid) [2003/4 c95, h–: c16d c19s⁵ c24g* c24mᵖᵘ Mar 4] angular mare: maiden hurdler: modest chaser: won novice at Taunton in February: lame final outing: stays 3m: acts on firm going, probably on soft: often makes running. *S. C. Burrough*   **c95 h–**

PANAMA (IRE) 4 b.g. Peintre Celebre (USA) – Bay Queen (Damister (USA)) [2003/4 16gᵖᵘ Mar 5] leggy gelding: modest maiden on Flat (bred to be suited by 1½m), sold out of M. Bell's stable 1,500 gns Newmarket Autumn Sales: showed nothing in juvenile on hurdling debut, jumping appallingly. *D. R. Wellicome*   **h–**

PANGERAN (USA) 12 b.g. Forty Niner (USA) – Smart Heiress (USA) (Vaguely Noble) [2003/4 c88§, h–: c24m³ c24m⁶ c23m⁶ c20m⁴ c24m⁴ c24m³ c24g² c26m² c24d² c24d³ c26m⁴ Nov 25] leggy gelding: winning chaser, on the downgrade: stays 3¼m: acts on firm and soft going: not a fluent jumper. *N. B. King*   **c86 d h–**

PANMURE (IRE) 8 b.g. Alphabatim (USA) – Serjitak (Saher) [2003/4 c–§, h82§: c16m⁵ c16m* c16f* c16g⁵ Nov 2] good-topped gelding: poor maiden hurdler: modest chaser: improved form when winning minor event at Hexham and novice handicap at Carlisle in October: stays 19f: best efforts on going firmer than good: tried blinkered/tongue tied, not when successful. *P. D. Niven*   **c94 h–**

PANOORAS LORD (IRE)   10 b.g. Topanoora – Ladyship (Windjammer (USA)) [2003/4 h65: c21d⁴ c25sᶠ Mar 7] compact gelding: poor 2m hurdler: left J. Wainwright after chasing debut: showed little in point and hunter subsequently: acts on soft and good to firm going: visored once: has pulled hard. *Martyn Hill*   c– h–

PAPEROUND   6 ch.m. Primitive Rising (USA) – Eye Bee Aitch (Move Off) [2003/4 F16d Apr 28] third foal: sister to fairly useful hurdler/useful chaser Paperising, stays 25f: dam winning selling hurdler: well held in bumper on debut. *N. G. Richards*   F–

PAPERPROPHET   6 b.g. Glory of Dancer – Living Legend (ITY) (Archway (IRE)) [2003/4 h114p, F91: 16s* 20g* 20d² Mar 20] leggy gelding: most progressive handicap hurdler: off a year, won at Ayr in December and Haydock (by 1¼ lengths from Claymore) in February: further improvement when 5 lengths second to Accipiter in strongly-contested event at Ascot: will stay beyond 2½m: acts on soft going. *N. G. Richards*   h136

PAPHIAN BAY   6 b.g. Karinga Bay – Bichette (Lidhame) [2003/4 F–: F17d⁵ 20g* 20d² 26sᵖᵘ Dec 26] rangy gelding: has scope: modest form on second of 2 starts in bumpers: won maiden at Wetherby on hurdling debut in November, jinking before last: should stay beyond 2½m (held when going lame before 3 out over 3¼m). *Ferdy Murphy*   h88 F77

PAPILLON DE IENA (FR)   4 ch.g. Varese (FR) – Belle du Chesne (FR) (R B Chesne) [2003/4 17s³ 18d* 16d Apr 17] €42,000 3-y-o: second foal: dam ran once: easily best effort in novice hurdles when winning at Fontwell in March by 6 lengths from Vingis Park. *M. C. Pipe*   h118

PAPUA   10 ch.g. Green Dancer (USA) – Fairy Tern (Mill Reef (USA)) [2003/4 c18g³ c21g² c21dᵖᵘ c16m* c20f⁴ c16m* c17m³ Oct 18] quite good-topped gelding: fairly useful handicap hurdler in 2001/2: fair chaser: won twice at Uttoxeter, maiden in July and novice in October: lame final outing: best around 2m: acts on firm and good to soft going: often visored/blinkered: tongue tied last 2 starts: carries head awkwardly: unreliable. *J. White*   c112 § h–

PARADE RACER   13 b.g. Derring Rose – Dusky Damsel (Sahib (USA)) [2003/4 c106, h–: c25m* c25gᵖᵘ c24sʳʳʳ c25g c26dᵖᵘ Apr 23] sturdy gelding: fairly useful hunter chaser, won at Kelso in May: largely on downgrade in 2004 (refused to race once), though won 29f point in March: acts on heavy and good to firm going. *Tim Butt*   c104 d h–

PARAHANDY (IRE)   14 b.g. Lancastrian – Dishcloth (Fury Royal) [2003/4 c103: c33dᵖᵘ c25s³ Feb 7] workmanlike gelding: veteran staying chaser: winning pointer, including in March and April: earlier third in hunter at Wetherby: stays 29f: acts on heavy and good to firm going: tried blinkered. *Giles Smyly*   c103

Thyson Technology 10th Anniversary Handicap Hurdle, Haydock—
Paperprophet (left) comes to collar Claymore, winning his fourth race in five starts over hurdles

PARDINI (USA)   5 b.g. Quest For Fame – Noblissima (IRE) (Sadler's Wells (USA))   **h90**
[2003/4 h87p: 22d^F 20g 22g⁶ 23d^{pu} 25s^{pu} 21s⁴ 24s^{pu} 22g² 19g³ Apr 18] angular gelding:
modest novice hurdler: stays 2¾m: acts on good to soft going: tried blinkered.
M. F. Harris

PARDISHAR (IRE)   6 b.g. Kahyasi – Parapa (IRE) (Akarad (FR)) [2003/4 h96: 16s^{pu}   **h115**
18s* 17d² 16s² 16d² 18d⁴ 18d² Apr 7] well-made gelding: fairly useful handicap hurdler:
won at Fontwell in December: improved form when neck second to Stance there final
start: likely to stay 2½m: raced on good going or softer (acts on soft): tongue tied once:
bled from nose on reappearance: has shown signs of temperament. *G. L. Moore*

PARDON WHAT   8 b.g. Theatrical Charmer – Tree Poppy (Rolfe (USA)) [2003/4   **c– x**
c84x, h79x, F95: 20g c26m^F c25g^{pu} 22g⁴ 16s 19g 22g² 25s² 22d⁴ Mar 21] leggy, lengthy   **h77 x**
gelding: winning chaser: poor maiden hurdler: stays 25f well: acts on heavy going: tried
in headgear: usually let down by jumping. *B. G. Powell*

PARISIAN STORM (IRE)   8 b.g. Glacial Storm (USA) – Lost In Paris (Deep Run)   **c96 x**
[2003/4 c22v^{ur} c25d² c23v^{pu} c24s^{pu} c24m⁴ Apr 13] IR 4,100 4-y-o: ex-Irish gelding:
fourth foal: half-brother to winning pointer by Buckskin: dam unraced half-sister to fairly
useful hurdler Beau Pari, stayed 3m: well held in bumper for J. Queally: won both starts
in points in 2003: form in steeplechases only when second in novice at Exeter in January:
mostly let down by jumping otherwise. *Evan Williams*

PARISIENNE GALE (IRE)   5 b.m. Lapierre – Elegant Gale (IRE) (Strong Gale)   **h–**
[2003/4 F16d⁵ F17d 17d^{ur} Mar 10] third foal: dam unraced, out of half-sister to good   **F64**
British/American jumper Inlander: poor form on first of 2 starts in bumpers: unseated
first on hurdling debut. *D. McCain*

PARIS LATINO (FR)   5 b.g. Nikos – Tarbelissima (FR) (Tarbes (FR)) [2003/4 F–:   **h–**
F17m 16f⁴ 16v^{pu} 17d 16d 22s 16g⁶ Apr 18] little sign of ability. *C. L. Tizzard*   **F–**

PARK CITY   5 b.g. Slip Anchor – Cryptal (Persian Bold) [2003/4 h92: 16g³ 16g 18d   **h92**
20d Apr 21] rather leggy gelding: modest handicap hurdler: left P. Hobbs and off 10
months after reappearance: should stay 2½m: acts on soft going: none too consistent.
J. Joseph

PARK LANE BILLIE   4 b.f. Double Eclipse (IRE) – Kathy's Role (Rolfe (USA))   **F–**
[2003/4 F16s F16g Mar 6] unfurnished filly: sixth foal: dam unraced: well beaten in 2
mares bumpers. *J. Mackie*

PARK LANE FREDDIE   6 b.g. Nalchik (USA) – Kathy's Role (Rolfe (USA))   **h82**
[2003/4 h–, F78: 17d⁴ 16m⁶ May 31] leggy gelding: poor form over hurdles: tried tongue
tied. *J. Mackie*

PARKNASILLA   4 b.g. Marju (IRE) – Top Berry (High Top) [2003/4 16d* 16g² 16s²   **h119**
16d² Apr 17] quite good-topped gelding: half-brother to 3 winning jumpers, including
modest 2m hurdler Mr Micky (by Rudimentary): fair on Flat (stays 1½m): fairly useful
juvenile hurdler: won novice at Leicester in January: runner-up all 3 subsequent starts,
beaten 5 lengths by Dalaram in steadily-run event at Ayr on final occasion: acts on soft
going. *M. W. Easterby*

PARK PLACE (IRE)   9 gr.g. Husyan (USA) – Iron Mermaid (General Ironside)   **c–**
[2003/4 c–, h87: 20m^{pu} May 7] workmanlike gelding: not fluent and well beaten only   **h87**
start over fences: modest maiden hurdler: stayed 25f: acted on good to firm and good to
soft going: dead. *J. I. A. Charlton*

PARLOUR GAME   8 br.m. Petoski – Henry's True Love (Random Shot) [2003/4   **c101**
c93, h–: c20s* c24m⁴ c25d* c25s² c24g⁵ c26v^{pu} Feb 7] lengthy, angular mare: fair handi-   **h–**
cap chaser: won at Uttoxeter (mares) in May and Towcester in October: stays 25f: acts on
good to firm and heavy going: has made mistakes. *H. D. Daly*

PAROLE OFFICER   5 b.g. Priolo (USA) – Twosixtythreewest (FR) (Kris) [2003/4   **F–**
F17v Mar 21] fifth foal: half-brother to 7f winner in Germany by Beldale Flutter: dam,
1m winner, half-sister to useful French jumper Exit Sud and useful American jumper
Pelagos: showed nothing in bumper on debut. *J. Wade*

PARSIFAL   5 b.g. Sadler's Wells (USA) – Moss (USA) (Woodman (USA)) [2003/4   **h88**
h–: 17s³ 17g² Sep 30] modest maiden hurdler: headstrong: sold 7,000 gns Doncaster
October Sales, unplaced first 4 starts in points in 2004. *J. Howard Johnson*

PARSON JACK   7 b.g. Bedford (USA) – Scobitora (Thesauros) [2003/4 16v^{pu} Jan 9]   **h–**
third foal: dam unraced: showed little in novice hurdle on debut. *R. Dickin*

PARSON PLOUGHMAN 9 br.g. Riverwise (USA) – Pretty Pantoes (Lepanto **h79**
(GER)) [2003/4 19d 24s 19v[4] 22g Apr 4] plain gelding: form only when fourth in novice
hurdle at Exeter in February, hanging left when weakening run-in. *P. F. Nicholls*

PARSONS LEGACY (IRE) 6 b.g. Leading Counsel (USA) – The Parson's Girl **h111**
(IRE) (The Parson) [2003/4 19g* 21v[pu] 20d* 20s 22m[4] 24s[pu] 24m[2] Apr 14] angular
gelding: second foal: dam well held in bumper: fair novice hurdler: won at Newbury (first
start after leaving W. Flavin) in November and Leicester in December: stays 3m:
has form on heavy going, seems ideally suited by less testing ground (acts on good to firm).
P. J. Hobbs

PARSONS PRIDE (IRE) 8 b.g. Persian Mews – First Prize (IRE) (The Parson) **h92**
[2003/4 h–, F85: 17d 24m* 24m[5] 22f[3] 26m[2] 25f[5] Oct 28] smallish gelding: modest
hurdler: won weak novice at Worcester in September: stays 3¼m: acts on firm ground.
J. W. Tudor

PARTE PRIMA 8 b.g. Perpendicular – Pendle's Secret (Le Johnstan) [2003/4 c21s[ur] **c88**
c21g* c16g[3] c16g[6] Apr 3] blinkered, no show in 2 races over hurdles: fair hunter chaser: **h–**
won maiden at Folkestone in March: will prove best at 2½m+. *Alan Walter*

PARTY ANIMAL (IRE) 12 b.g. Buckskin (FR) – More Chat (Torenaga) [2003/4 c–, **c91**
h–: c25g[3] May 1] rangy gelding: modest chaser, lightly raced: stays 3¼m: raced on good **h–**
going or softer (acts on soft). *K. C. Bailey*

PARTY GAMES (IRE) 7 b.g. King's Ride – Shady Miss (Mandamus) [2003/4 h80, **c–**
F77: 17v[2] 17s[3] 18s[5] 16s[3] c20d[pu] 21s[3] 16g[2] Apr 12] workmanlike gelding: modest maiden **h99**
hurdler: little encouragement on chasing debut: stays 21f: acts on heavy going. *D. B. Feek*

PAS DE SURPRISE 6 b.g. Dancing Spree (USA) – Supreme Rose (Frimley Park) **h–**
[2003/4 16m[pu] Oct 18] sparely-made gelding: modest on Flat (stays 9f): showed little in
maiden on hurdling debut. *P. D. Evans*

PASHA 8 b.m. Ardkinglass – Infanta Maria (King of Spain) [2003/4 16m[pu] May 9] sprint **h–**
maiden on Flat: showed nothing in novice on hurdling debut after 4 years off. *R. J. Baker*

PASSED OUT (IRE) 6 b.g. Shahanndeh – Ah Suzie (IRE) (King's Ride) [2003/4 20g[pu] **h–**
Nov 16] sturdy gelding: second foal: dam never ran: jumped poorly in novice hurdle on
debut. *B. N. Pollock*

PASSENGER OMAR (IRE) 6 b.g. Safety Catch (USA) – Princess Douglas (Bishop **h89**
of Orange) [2003/4 F–: 20m 25d[4] 22g[4] Apr 18] best effort in novice hurdles when fourth
at Stratford final start: tongue tied: refused to race once in 2002/3. *Noel T. Chance*

PASSING WIND (NZ) 10 br.g. Beau Zephyr (AUS) – Miss Row (NZ) (Long Row) **c93 +**
[2003/4 c24g[3] c21d* c20g[F] Jan 9] modest handicap hurdler in 2001/2 for S. Griffiths, **h–**
missed 2002/3: promising third in novice handicap at Bangor on chasing debut: left alone
circuit out in similar event at Fakenham in November: fell second final start: may prove
best short of 3m: probably acts on any going: takes strong hold. *R. C. Guest*

PASS ME BY 5 b.g. Balnibarbi – Errol Emerald (Dom Racine (FR)) [2003/4 F96: 20d[2] **h120**
20g* 20s 20s* 20g 24s 20d Apr 10] tall, angular gelding: fairly useful novice hurdler:
won at Haydock in November and February (stayed on well to beat Special Conquest 1¾
lengths): well held in handicaps last 3 starts: should stay beyond 2½m: raced on good
going or softer. *T. D. Walford*

PATCHES (IRE) 5 b. or br.g. Presenting – Ballykilleen (The Parson) [2003/4 16d[2] **h107**
16d[6] 22d[5] Feb 12] unfurnished gelding: seventh foal: dam unraced: won maiden Irish
point on debut in 2003: best effort over hurdles when ½-length second to King Solomon
(pair well clear) in maiden at Chepstow in December: tongue tied and didn't take the eye
final start. *P. F. Nicholls*

PAT N DEC 5 b.g. Overbury (IRE) – Princess Semele (Imperial Fling (USA)) [2003/4 **F79**
F16g[6] F16d[6] Apr 12] 2,600 4-y-o: workmanlike gelding: seventh foal: half-brother to
fairly useful staying hurdler/chaser Tara-Brogan (by Jupiter Island) and fair hurdler/
chaser up to 21f Governor Daniel (by Governor General): dam fair 2m hurdler/11f winner
on Flat: better effort in bumpers at Huntingdon on debut. *Ian Williams*

PATRIARCH EXPRESS 7 b.g. Noble Patriarch – Jaydeeglen (Bay Express) [2003/4 **h126 +**
F106: 20d* 20s* 21s[6] 18s[2] 19s[6] 18g[3] 24g[5] Apr 2] strong, good sort: fairly useful novice
hurdler: won at Newcastle and Haydock in November: creditable efforts last 2 starts, third
to Paddy The Piper in Grade 2 at Kelso and fifth to Accipiter in Grade 1 at Aintree: likely
to prove best short of 3m: acts on soft ground (won bumper on good to firm). *G. A. Harker*

PATRIARCH (IRE)   8 b.g. Alphabatim (USA) – Strong Language (Formidable **c102 p**
(USA)) [2003/4 h–: c21d³ Feb 17] good sort: fairly useful hurdler in 2000/1: only second **h–**
outing since when third to Hawk's Landing in maiden at Folkestone on chasing debut,
jumping soundly and not unduly knocked about: should stay 3m: acts on heavy and good
to firm going: open to improvement over fences. *M. Pitman*

PATRICKSNINETEENTH (IRE)   7 b.g. Mister Lord (USA) – Many Miracles **c139**
(Le Moss) [2003/4 F101: c20d² c20d² c20s* c24g⁴ Mar 17]
The complexion of the seven-runner Tote Scilly Isles Novices' Chase at
Sandown changed markedly at the eighth of the seventeen fences. What beforehand
had looked a competitive renewal of this Grade 1 event was rendered much less so
when both Ladalko, the favourite, and See You Sometime fell, with Tikram effectively losing whatever chance he had when badly hampered by the latter. With the
leader Puntal downing tools very soon afterwards and One Nation already struggling in rear, the race became virtually a match between Patricksnineteenth and
L'Aventure. Patricksnineteenth had taken the lead at the ninth and quickly established a clear advantage when shaken up at the end of the back straight. He was
never in any danger from thereon, keeping on strongly to win by six lengths. It was
a second success for Patricksnineteenth, the first having come in a bumper at the
same venue twelve months earlier. There was no hurdling career for Patricksnineteenth, who had just two runs over fences before tackling the Scilly Isles, finishing
runner-up to Mister Banjo at Bangor and to Calling Brave at Sandown, where
Mister Banjo finished a remote last of three. Patricksnineteenth made odds-on
Calling Brave work very hard for his victory, not giving best until close home and
going down by just three quarters of a length. On his only run after the Scilly Isles,
Patricksnineteenth was stepped up from two and a half miles to three and ran close
to form in finishing around sixteen lengths fourth to Rule Supreme in the Royal &
SunAlliance Chase at Cheltenham. The performance was a rather flat one, though,
Patricksnineteenth not fluent at times and just plugging on without making any
impression after being hampered two out. It is possible that Patricksnineteenth
requires softer ground than he encountered at Cheltenham, both of his wins being
gained on soft. The well-made Patricksnineteenth, bought as a four-year-old for IR
£32,000, is the fifth living foal out of Many Miracles, an unraced half-sister to the

Tote Scilly Isles Novices' Chase, Sandown—
Patricksnineteenth takes advantage of mishaps to his rivals to land a Grade 1 victory

The Large G & T Partnership's "Patricksnineteenth"

useful staying hurdler Final Run. Many Miracles is responsible for three other winners, the fair two-and-three-quarter-mile chase winner Dunboy Castle (by Carlingford Castle), the two-and-a-half-mile chase winner Phairy Miracles (by Phardante) and the fairly useful staying hurdler and winning chaser Amy Johnson (by Ore). *P. R. Webber.*

PATRIZIO (IRE) 6 ch.g. Erins Isle – Canadian Project (IRE) (Project Manager) **h124**
[2003/4 20g* 20d* 20m* 20d* 20s* Sep 21] leggy gelding: brother to 2m and 2½m hurdle winner Shanesia: 1¼m winner at 3 yrs on Flat: much improved hurdler in first half of 2003/4, unbeaten in 5 starts, intermediate at Wexford and novices at Clonmel, Tipperary (beat Just In Debt 2½ lengths), Galway and Listowel: best at 2½m: acts on soft and good to firm going: blinkered twice in 2002/3. *E. Griffin, Ireland*

PATS FUTURE 5 ch.m. King's Signet (USA) – Bedelia (Mr Fluorocarbon) [2003/4 **h–**
F–: F17f³ F16m 17d 19g Dec 18] smallish mare: signs of ability in bumpers, none in **F82**
novice hurdles. *P. R. Rodford*

PATSY VEALE (IRE) 9 b.g. Accordion – Bermuda Castle (Carlingford Castle) **h124**
[2003/4 h125: 16m² 17f Aug 26] lengthy, angular gelding: fairly useful hurdler: good ½-length second to Altay in Swinton Hurdle (Handicap) at Haydock in May: well held twice on Flat and in valuable handicap hurdle at Tralee subsequently: stays 21f, at least as effective at 2m: acts on firm and soft going. *J. Queally, Ireland*

PATTELLA WOOD (IRE) 6 ch.m. Denel (FR) – West Cove (Quayside) [2003/4 **h–**
19fᵖᵘ 20dᵖᵘ Dec 29] fifth foal: half-sister to 2m chase winner Serenly (by Religiously): dam maiden: well beaten in 2 Irish points in 2002: no show in 2 maiden hurdles. *R. A. Curran, Ireland*

PAULA 4 b.f. Compton Place – Be My Bird (Be My Chief (USA)) [2003/4 F17g Mar 28] fourth foal: half-sister to 7f winner Birdlip Hill (by Prince Sabo) and 1m winner Timeless Chick (by Timeless Times): dam, third at 7f/8.5f at 2 yrs, half-sister to smart performer up to 1¼m Stato One: showed little in mares bumper and 1m maiden on Flat. *M. Dods*　**F–**

PAULA LANE 4 b.f. Factual (USA) – Colfax Classic (Jareer (USA)) [2003/4 16s Dec 20] fair on Flat (stays 1½m): always behind in juvenile on hurdling debut. *R. Curtis*　**h–**

PAULUKE 5 b.m. Bishop of Cashel – Beacon Blaze (Rudimentary (USA)) [2003/4 16m 16g 16d⁵ Dec 6] sturdy mare: modest maiden on Flat (stayed 11f): soundly beaten over hurdles: tried in cheekpieces: dead. *N. J. Hawke*　**h–**

PAVEY ARK (IRE) 6 b.g. King's Ride – Splendid Run (Deep Run) [2003/4 F85: F16g 20d⁶ 17dᵖᵘ 19g⁶ 24dᵖᵘ Mar 11] tall, lengthy gelding: modest form in bumpers: no encouragement in 4 novice hurdles. *James Moffatt*　**h–**

PAVONE QUEST 7 ch.g. Jumbo Hirt (USA) – Gilsan Grey (Grey Ghost) [2003/4 F16g 20vᵖᵘ Jan 17] lengthy gelding: fourth foal: dam winning staying hurdler/chaser: showed little in bumper and novice hurdle, racing freely. *G. M. Moore*　**h–**
F–

PAWN BROKER 7 ch.g. Selkirk (USA) – Dime Bag (High Line) [2003/4 h88p: 16s⁴ 16g³ Dec 26] sturdy gelding: useful on Flat (stays 1½m, tends to find little): best effort over hurdles when third to Contraband in novice at Kempton: raced at 2m: jumps none too fluently. *D. R. C. Elsworth*　**h107**

PAXFORD LADY 7 b.m. Alflora (IRE) – Rakajack (Rakaposhi King) [2003/4 h–: c20s² c21vᵖᵘ c20gᶠ c16d⁵ c16sᶠ c20sᵖᵘ c20sᵖᵘ Jan 21] leggy mare: poor maiden chaser: stays 2½m: acts on soft going: no form in blinkers. *M. F. Harris*　**c79**
h–

PAXFORD TROOPER 10 b.g. Gunner B – Say Shanaz (Tickled Pink) [2003/4 h–: c24dᶠ 21s Dec 26] winning pointer, little other form. *M. F. Harris*　**c–**
h–

PAYFORD BRIDGE 11 br.g. Lighter – Saucy Laura (Crozier) [2003/4 20sᵖᵘ Apr 17] good-topped gelding: of no account. *M. Sheppard*　**c–**
h–

PAY IT FORWARD 6 b.g. Anshan – Kellsboro Kate (Paddy's Stream) [2003/4 h124, F82: 20d³ 20s² 25m⁵ 20d c18dᶠ c20s² c21d Feb 8] well-made gelding: useful hurdler: fifth to Gralmano in Grade 2 at Wetherby in November: best effort over fences when second to Yeoman's Point in maiden at Navan in December: stays 25f when conditions aren't testing: acts on heavy and good to firm going. *Mrs J. Harrington, Ireland*　**c111**
h131

PAYNESTOWN LAD (IRE) 8 b.g. Bravefoot – Athy Lady (Welsh Captain) [2003/4 h86: 21f⁶ 22m 24m⁴ Aug 3] won novice hurdle in 2002/3: little other form: has found little. *Miss C. J. E. Caroe*　**h–**

PC'S EUROCRUISER (IRE) 8 b.g. Fayruz – Kuwait Night (Morston (FR)) [2003/4 h75: 16m 16d⁵ 16g 17gᶠ May 26] compact gelding: poor hurdler: best around 2m on sharp track: acts on soft and good to firm going. *Mrs Dianne Sayer*　**h66**

PEACEMAKER (IRE) 12 br.g. Strong Gale – Gamonda (Gala Performance) [2003/4 c–, h–: c21g² c25g⁶ c23m³ c25f* c21g² c24d⁶ c23g Jan 27] sturdy gelding: poor handicap chaser: won at Towcester in October: stays 25f: acts on firm and soft going: blinkered once: has had tongue tied. *J. R. Cornwall*　**c70**
h–

PEACHY (IRE) 9 b.g. Un Desperado (FR) – Little Peach (Ragapan) [2003/4 19dᵖᵘ Dec 13] leggy gelding: bumper winner: lightly raced over hurdles, no encouragement in handicap only start in 2003/4. *R. T. Phillips*　**h–**

PEAFIELD (IRE) 15 b.g. Torus – La'bavette (Le Bavard (FR)) [2003/4 c26f³ May 21] fairly useful pointer: placed 3 of 4 starts in hunter chases, though appeared to go amiss in novice at Folkestone in May: stays 3¼m: best efforts on good going or firmer. *P. York*　**c78**

PEARLIWHIRL 5 b.m. Alflora (IRE) – Pearlossa (Teenoso (USA)) [2003/4 F73: F17m⁴ 21d 17d⁶ Mar 10] big, lengthy, rather unfurnished mare: much better effort in bumpers when fourth at Hereford on reappearance: poor form in 2 mares novice hurdles. *N. J. Henderson*　**h72**
F87

PEARLY BAY 6 b.m. Karinga Bay – Marina Bird (Julio Mariner) [2003/4 F17d* Mar 27] sixth foal: half-sister to 2 bumper winners: dam unraced half-sister to dam of very smart 2m hurdler/chaser Arctic Kinsman, from family of Florida Pearl: won bumper at Bangor on debut by 6 lengths from Cragg Prince: will stay beyond 17f. *M. G. Rimell*　**F97**

PEASE BLOSSOM (IRE) 5 b.m. Revoque (IRE) – Saneena (Kris) [2003/4 16d² 16g⁵ 16d⁶ 18d⁴ 16s³ 16s 16dᵖᵘ 16s Mar 13] half-sister to fairly useful hurdler up to 21f Old Hush Wing (by Tirol) and winning 2m hurdler Never So Blue (by Never So Bold):　**h90**

modest maiden on Flat (stays 1¾m): modest maiden hurdler: raced around 2m on good ground or softer: tried visored, usually in cheekpieces. *T. G. McCourt, Ireland*

PERRLE RAY 9 br.g Perpendicular – Milly L'Attaque (Military) [2003/4 16m² 21m^pu 17d^F 19g 19g⁵ Dec 3] fourth foal: dam winning pointer: signs of only a little ability in novice hurdles: blinkered last 3 starts. *G. A. Harker* — **h83 ?**

PECCADILLO (IRE) 10 br.g. Un Desperado (FR) – First Mistake (Posse (USA)) [2003/4 c127, h–: c20m² c24f² c24m³ c20m⁵ c24g^ur c20m Feb 28] big, rangy gelding: useful handicap chaser: placed first 3 starts, best effort when second to Swansea Bay in quite valuable event at Kempton on second: stays easy 3m: acts on firm and good to soft going (possibly unsuited by soft): has run well when sweating: usually races prominently: prone to the odd bad run. *R. H. Alner* — **c132 h–**

PEDDARS WAY 5 b.g. Nomadic Way (USA) – Deep Selection (IRE) (Deep Run) [2003/4 F16d Mar 28] 17,500 4-y-o: third foal: half-brother to useful hurdler/chaser Run For Paddy (by Michelozzo), stays 25f: dam no sign of ability: shaped as if badly in need of experience when seventh in bumper at Huntingdon on debut. *A. King* — **F79**

PEDINA (IRE) 6 b.g. Toulon – Bilberry (Nicholas Bill) [2003/4 F18d³ 20d⁵ 24d 16d* 16s* 16v⁴ 16d Apr 13] €32,000 4-y-o: second foal: brother to bumper winner First Day Cover and half-brother to bumper winner Sherberry (by Shernazar): dam, 1¾m winner, half-sister to high-class 2m hurdler Past Glories: fairly useful form in bumpers: progressed to similar level over hurdles, winning maiden at Thurles in December and novice at Navan (by 2 lengths from Demophilos) in January: successful at 2m, should stay further: acts on soft going. *G. M. Lyons, Ireland* — **h121 F96**

PEDLER'S PROFILES 4 br.g. Topanoora – La Vie En Primrose (Henbit (USA)) [2003/4 17g Apr 16] half-brother to 2 winners over jumps, including modest staying chaser/one-time fairly useful hurdler Influence Pedler (by Keen): poor maiden on Flat: well held in juvenile on hurdling debut. *Miss K. M. George* — **h–**

PEEYOUTWO 9 b.g. Golden Heights – Nyika (Town And Country) [2003/4 h–: 20m³ 16m⁶ 16g* 17g² 16g⁴ 16m³ Nov 9] modest hurdler: won novice at Stratford in September: best around 2m: unraced on extremes of ground. *Mrs D. A. Hamer* — **h84**

PEGGY LOU 4 b.f. Washington State (USA) – Rosemary Nalden (Great Commotion (USA)) [2003/4 16m⁵ 16f³ 16m Nov 6] leggy, lengthy filly: modest on Flat (barely stays 2m), successful in June: best effort in juvenile hurdles when third in claimer at Towcester: wore cheekpieces final outing. *B. J. Llewellyn* — **h75**

PEGGY SIOUX (IRE) 7 b.m. Little Bighorn – Gayable (Gay Fandango (USA)) [2003/4 h76p, F82: 20s^pu 21v 16v^pu 20f² 16d Mar 18] sturdy mare: poor maiden hurdler: stays 2½m: probably acts on any going. *J. I. A. Charlton* — **h66**

PEGGY'S PRINCE 6 b.g. Morpeth – Prudent Peggy (Kambalda) [2003/4 F88: F16d² F17g⁶ Apr 10] fair form in bumpers, better effort of 2003/4 when second at Stratford after 11-month absence: will be suited by a greater test of stamina. *J. D. Frost* — **F88**

PEMBROKE SQUARE (IRE) 9 b.g. Tenby – The Poachers Lady (IRE) (Salmon Leap (USA)) [2003/4 c24m^su Nov 11] useful-looking gelding: one-time useful hurdler: fair form in novice chases in 2001/2 for P. Ritchens: slipped up before seventh on return: stayed 3m: acted on soft and good to firm going: effective blinkered/visored or not: usually tongue tied: dead. *Miss E. C. Lavelle* — **c– h–**

PENALTA 8 ch.g. Cosmonaut – Targuette (Targowice (USA)) [2003/4 21m⁴ 20s⁶ Dec 19] poor on Flat (stays 2m): blinkered, better effort over hurdles when sixth in novice at Uttoxeter. *W. M. Brisbourne* — **h90**

PENALTY CLAUSE (IRE) 4 b.g. Namaqualand (USA) – Lady Be Lucky (IRE) (Taufan (USA)) [2003/4 17m³ 16g 16m³ 17m² 16g 16f^F 16d* 21s 16s Feb 12] leggy gelding: poor maiden on Flat: modest hurdler: claimed from G. Prodromou £5,000 fourth start: won seller at Doncaster in December: best at 2m: acts on good to firm and good to soft ground: wore cheekpieces/visor after second outing, also tongue tied last 4: none too consistent. *K. A. Morgan* — **h86**

PENDANT 9 b.g. Warning – Emerald (USA) (El Gran Senor (USA)) [2003/4 c–, h–: c17g⁶ c25m Jun 11] compact gelding: winning hurdler: little form since 1999/00, including over fences: tried visored/blinkered/tongue tied. *Mrs J. Candlish* — **c– h–**

PENDIL'S PRINCESS 5 b.m. Afzal – Pendil's Delight (Scorpio (FR)) [2003/4 F16g⁶ Mar 4] first foal: dam, placed once over hurdles at 3m, out of poor sister to Pendil: sixth in mares bumper at Ludlow on debut. *S. E. H. Sherwood* — **F73**

PENDLE FOREST (IRE)   4 gr.f. Charnwood Forest (IRE) – Pride of Pendle (Grey   **F87 +** Desire) [2003/4 F16s* F16s Feb 14] first foal: dam fair and very durable miler: travelled strongly and quickened clear over 1f out when winning mares bumper at Newcastle on debut by 5 lengths from Diamond Sal: well held at Ayr following month. *R. A. Fahey*

PENDLE HILL   9 gr.g. Roscoe Blake – Pendle Princess (Broxted) [2003/4 c105, h–:   **c–** c24s⁵ Feb 12] useful-looking gelding: fair maiden chaser: won point in January: stays   **h–** 3m: best form on going softer than good (acts on heavy): usually races prominently. *Mrs S. J. Hickman*

PENDRAGON   12 b.g. Bold Fox – Celtic Royale (Celtic Cone) [2003/4 c–: c25dᵖᵘ   **c–** Mar 23] rangy gelding: modest pointer: let down by jumping in hunter chases. *Mrs Sarah Faulks*

PENGUIN BAY   8 b.g. Rock Hopper – Corn Lily (Aragon) [2003/4 c–§, h85§: c16m⁴   **c– §** 16mᵖᵘ May 27] workmanlike gelding: well held over fences: maiden hurdler: form only   **h– §** around 2m: acts on firm going: tried blinkered: ungenuine. *N. Wilson*

PENNANT CASTLE   6 b.g. Alflora (IRE) – Pennant Cottage (IRE) (Denel (FR))   **F–** [2003/4 F17g May 18] first foal: brother to bumper winner Neidpath Castle: dam winning pointer: well held in bumper on debut. *Mrs H. Dalton*

PENNELESS DANCER   5 b.g. Pennekamp (USA) – Villella (Sadler's Wells (USA))   **h–** [2003/4 h–: 17g May 26] maiden on Flat (stays 8.4f): non-stayer over hurdles. *M. E. Sowersby*

PENNEYROSE BAY   5 ch.m. Karinga Bay – Pennethorne Place (Deep Run) [2003/4   **F79** F16d F16v⁶ Feb 7] fourth foal: half-sister to fair hurdler Latimer's Place (by Teenoso), will stay beyond 2½m: dam, bumper winner/maiden hurdler, stayed 2¾m: better effort in bumpers (found little second start) when seventh at Newbury on debut. *G. B. Balding*

PENNILLION   4 b.g. Pennekamp (USA) – Brave Princess (Dancing Brave (USA))   **h–** [2003/4 16sᵖᵘ 16dᵖᵘ Dec 15] €3,000 3-y-o: third foal: dam, 7f winner, half-sister to Supreme Leader: no sign of ability either start over hurdles: sold £1,400 Ascot February Sales. *D. P. Keane*

PENNYAHEI   13 b.m. Malaspina – Pennyazena (Pamroy) [2003/4 c–§, h–§: c24g²   **c106 §** c28gᵖᵘ May 31] angular mare: fairly useful hunter chaser: stays 3¼m: acts on good to   **h– §** firm and heavy going: none too reliable. *S. A. Brookshaw*

PENNY NATIVE (IRE)   12 ch.g. Be My Native (USA) – Penny Maes (Welsh Saint)   **c94** [2003/4 c24f² c21g² c25g Apr 5] sturdy ex-Irish gelding: modest chaser: left A. Moore   **h–** before reappearance: runner-up at Musselburgh (for W. Kerr) and Ayr first 2 starts in hunters: stays 3m: acts on any going: often held up. *Miss J. M. Furness*

PENNY PICTURES (IRE)   5 b.g. Theatrical – Copper Creek (Habitat) [2003/4   **h103** h115p: 16g⁶ 16g 16g⁶ 20g 19g³ Apr 16] small gelding: fair handicap hurdler: seems to stay 19f: acts on soft and good to firm going: races freely. *M. C. Pipe*

PENNY RICH (IRE)   10 br.g. Little Bighorn – Musical Puss (Orchestra) [2003/4 16v   **c– §** c16dᵖᵘ Mar 30] leggy gelding: one-time useful hurdler: left M. Hourigan after reappear-   **h– §** ance: no form in 3 starts over fences: raced around 2m: best efforts on going softer than good: probably needs holding up as long as possible: unreliable. *R. Ford*

PENNY'S CROWN   5 b.m. Reprimand – Two And Sixpence (USA) (Chief's Crown   **h–** (USA)) [2003/4 F17m⁴ F16m² F16f⁵ F17s 19d 22g Mar 25] leggy mare: fifth foal: **F84** half-sister to 2 winners on Flat, including fair 7f performer Sarah's Song (by Warning): dam 17f winner: best effort in bumpers when second at Chepstow in October: left S. Griffiths after third start, H. Kavanagh after fourth: well held in 2 mares events over hurdles. *G. A. Ham*

PENNYS FROM HEAVEN   10 gr.g. Generous (IRE) – Heavenly Cause (USA) (Grey   **h69 §** Dawn II) [2003/4 h83§: 19g 16dᵘʳ 16g 16g³ Apr 18] compact gelding: poor maiden hurdler: best around 2m: acts on soft and good to firm going: tried blinkered: headstrong and irresolute. *Miss T. M. Ide*

PENNY'S LOSS   6 b.m. Primitive Rising (USA) – Lingham Bride (Deep Run) [2003/4   **h–** 20m 22m Jul 14] 1,200 4-y-o: third foal: dam, winning hurdler/chaser who stayed 27f, out of half-sister to very smart staying chaser Everett: no sign of ability in points or novice hurdles. *Evan Williams*

PENRIC   4 b.g. Marju (IRE) – Nafhaat (USA) (Roberto (USA)) [2003/4 16s⁴ 16g⁵ 16s⁴   **h89** 16sᵖᵘ 19g 17g Apr 13] close-coupled gelding: modest maiden on Flat (stays 2m): modest juvenile hurdler: should be suited by further than 17f: acts on soft going: blinkered final start. *C. G. Cox*

PENTHOUSE MINSTREL   10 b. or br.g. Seven Hearts – Pentameron (Heres) [2003/4 c–, h–: c25d³ c19m⁴ c20d³ c28dᵖᵘ c20m⁴ c25fʷᵒ c20f* c25f⁴ c19g² c18gᵖᵘ c21d⁴ c21m⁴ c21d c21g* c21m* Apr 15] lengthy gelding: fair chaser: left Miss N. Stephens after fourth start: walked over in novice at Wincanton: won novice handicap at Cheltenham later in October, amateur handicap at Wincanton in March and novice handicap at Cheltenham in April: effective at 19f to 25f: acts on firm and good to soft going: visored: consistent. *R. J. Hodges*   **c100 h–**

PEPE GALVEZ (SWE)   7 br.g. Mango Express – Mango Sampaquita (SWE) (Colombian Friend (USA)) [2003/4 h126: 19g² Nov 12] sturdy gelding: fairly useful hurdler: creditable second to Monkerhostin in handicap at Newbury, only start in 2003/4: stays 19f: has won on soft going, best efforts on good/good to firm. *Mrs L. C. Taylor*   **h118**

PEPETA   7 b.m. Presidium – Mighty Flash (Rolfe (USA)) [2003/4 c26mᵖᵘ c24m² c20gᵘʳ c21dᵖᵘ c16g³ c19g⁴ Dec 18] leggy mare: probably of little account: has had tongue tied. *D. L. Williams*   **c– h–**

PEPPERSHOT   4 b.g. Vettori (IRE) – No Chili (Glint of Gold) [2003/4 16s³ 17s³ 16s⁵ 16s⁵ 16s Mar 20] workmanlike gelding: half-brother to winning 2½m hurdler Doyenne (by Mystiko): fair maiden on Flat (should be suited by 1½m+), sold out of A. Balding's stable 1,000 gns Newmarket Autumn Sales: modest form in juvenile hurdles: will stay at least 2½m. *G. P. Enright*   **h93**

PEQUENITA   4 b.f. Rudimentary (USA) – Sierra Madrona (USA) (Woodman (USA)) [2003/4 17d⁴ 16g² 16d² 16sᵖᵘ Jan 21] third foal: dam, ungenuine 3m hurdle winner, out of smart 1½m filly Senorita Poquito: fair on Flat (stays 1½m), claimed £10,000 from J. Given in October: won juvenile maiden at Folkestone in November on hurdling debut: runner-up at Newbury and Plumpton next 2 starts, poor effort final one: wore cheekpieces third outing. *G. L. Moore*   **h94**

PER AMORE (IRE)   6 ch.g. General Monash (USA) – Danny's Miracle (Superlative) [2003/4 h116: c17g² c20m* c21g* c21g⁴ c21d³ c17g* 17f² c16fᵖᵘ Oct 28] medium-sized gelding: fair handicap hurdler: fairly useful chaser: won novices at Huntingdon in May and Newton Abbot in June and handicap at Stratford (came off strong pace and possibly flattered) in September: reportedly lost action final start: stays 21f: acts on any going: tried in cheekpieces, blinkered nowadays. *P. J. Hobbs*   **c119 ? h109**

PERANGE (FR)   8 ch.g. Perrault – La Mesange (FR) (Olmeto) [2003/4 c122, h–: c17gᵖᵘ c20mᵖᵘ c19s* c19g⁶ c21mᶠ c20gᵖᵘ Apr 16] close-coupled, workmanlike gelding: fairly useful handicap chaser: won at Taunton in February by 12 lengths from Reiziger: stays 21f: acts on heavy and good to firm going. *P. F. Nicholls*   **c129 h–**

PERCHANCER (IRE)   8 ch.g. Perugino (USA) – Irish Hope (Nishapour (FR)) [2003/4 h–: c16g² c21gᶠ Aug 23] winning hurdler: modest form when second in novice at Sedgefield on completed start over fences: pulled up after saddle slipped in point in April: likely to prove best up to 2½m: acts on heavy going. *P. C. Haslam*   **c88 h–**

PERCHCOURT STEEL (IRE)   8 b.g. Grand Lodge (USA) – Scaravie (IRE) (Drumalis) [2003/4 22sᵖᵘ 19dᵖᵘ Jan 19] lengthy gelding: no sign of ability: tried tongue tied. *A. M. Hales*   **h–**

PERCHING (IRE)   10 b.g. Strong Gale – Fiona's Blue (Crash Course) [2003/4 c70, h–: c22mᵖᵘ May 26] strong gelding: fair chaser in 1999/00: lightly raced and only poor form since: runner-up in point in February: stays 3¼m: acts on good to firm going: has worn cheekpieces. *P. Butler*   **c– h–**

PERCIPIENT   6 b.g. Pennekamp (USA) – Annie Albright (USA) (Verbatim (USA)) [2003/4 F69: 17g 17v⁶ 16d 16s² 16g Mar 6] useful-looking gelding: improved effort over hurdles when second in handicap at Fakenham in January, stumbling badly last when 4 lengths clear: will prove best around 2m: acts on soft going. *D. R. Gandolfo*   **h85**

PERCY BASIL   5 b.g. Petoski – Madam-M (Tina's Pet) [2003/4 F–: F17g 16d Nov 23] leggy, unfurnished gelding: well held in 2 bumpers and a novice hurdle. *Ian Williams*   **h– F–**

PERCY BRAITHWAITE (IRE)   12 b.g. Kahyasi – Nasseem (FR) (Zeddaan) [2003/4 c–, h–: 21mᵖᵘ May 15] small, angular gelding: winning hurdler/chaser: of little account nowadays. *Mrs P. Ford*   **c– h–**

PERCY PARKEEPER   11 b.g. Teenoso (USA) – True Clown (True Song) [2003/4 c122, h–: c24d² c23m⁵ Jun 1] useful-looking gelding: fair handicap chaser: stays 3m: acts on good to firm and heavy going: tried blinkered: best ridden prominently: often makes mistakes. *N. A. Twiston-Davies*   **c110 h–**

PERCY-VERANCE (IRE) 6 ch.g. Dolphin Street (FR) – Sinology (Rainbow Quest   h81
(USA)) [2003/4 17s⁵ Feb 24] compact gelding: runner-up in point in 2003: third race over
hurdles when fifth in novice at Sedgefield: tried tongue tied. *J. J. Quinn*

PERFECT FELLOW 10 b.g. Teamster – G W Supermare (Rymer) [2003/4 c122+,   c127
h–: c20dᵖᵘ c24mᵖᵘ c24d* c24sᵖᵘ Apr 17] smallish, sturdy gelding: fairly useful handicap   h–
chaser, lightly raced: form in 2003/4 only when winning uncompetitive event at Sandown
in March by length from Lord 'N' Master: shaped as if amiss other starts: stays 3m: acts
on good to firm and heavy going. *Miss H. C. Knight*

PERFECT FINISHER 13 b.g. Captain Maverick (USA) – Miss Eutopia (Dunphy)   c–
[2003/4 c20gᵖᵘ Mar 12] poor pointer. *Mrs Jackie Hunt*   h–

PERFECT LIAISON 7 b.g. Alflora (IRE) – Connie's Pet (National Trust) [2003/4   h108 +
F86: 19v* 20s³ Mar 13] tall gelding: won novice at Exeter on hurdling debut in February:
better form when third in similar event at Sandown following month: will stay 3m.
R. H. Alner

PERFECT VENUE (IRE) 11 b.g. Danehill (USA) – Welsh Fantasy (Welsh Pageant)   h– §
[2003/4 16d Nov 27] compact gelding: fairly useful handicap hurdler at best, well beaten
only start since 2001/2: best form around 2m: acts on heavy going: tried blinkered: has
had tongue tied. *A. J. Wilson*

PERHAPS THIS TIME (IRE) 5 b.g. Flemensfirth (USA) – Royal Chapeau (IRE)   F85
(Royal Fountain) [2003/4 F16d⁶ F17g⁴ Apr 10] first foal: dam maiden Irish pointer: better
effort in bumpers when fourth at Newton Abbot: will stay further. *D. P. Keane*

PERIWINKLE LAD (IRE) 7 b.g. Perugino (USA) – Bold Kate (Bold Lad (IRE))   c81 x
[2003/4 c81, h98: 24d c20m³ 22g² 21m⁵ 25g⁵ c22g² 22g² Feb 10] angular ex-Irish   h102
gelding: poor maiden chaser (jumps ponderously): fair handicap hurdler: sold out of
E. McNamara's stable 15,000 gns Doncaster May Sales after reappearance, C. Dwyer's
stable 6,000 gns Doncaster November Sales after sixth start: stays 3m: acts on any going:
tried in blinkers/cheekpieces. *Miss Victoria Roberts*

PERK ALERT (IRE) 10 b.g. Executive Perk – Clondo Blue (IRE) (Miner's Lamp)   c79
[2003/4 c70, h–: c24m² c25gᵖᵘ c24mᵖᵘ May 26] angular gelding: poor handicap chaser: h–
reportedly lame final start: stays 25f: acts on good to firm and good to soft going. *A. King*

PERKYS PRIDE (IRE) 8 b.g. Executive Perk – Josie Mac (Pitpan) [2003/4 h114:   h–
22gᵖᵘ Jun 28] lengthy gelding: useful hurdler at best: in frame both starts in points in
2004 for D. Pipe: stays 2¾m: acts on soft going: tried visored: usually races prominently.
M. C. Pipe

PERLE DE PUCE (FR) 5 b.m. Snurge – Ma Puce (FR) (Tip Moss (FR)) [2003/4   h136
17s² 18v* 18dᵖᵘ 18s 18v³ 19s 18v* 16d* 16d⁶ 16gᵖᵘ 20g Apr 1] lengthy, useful-looking
ex-French mare: fifth foal: half-sister to 3 winners, including useful hurdler/chaser up to
2¾m Reine Elodie (by Cadoudal) and useful French hurdler Le Malemortois (by Phantom Breeze): dam, smart French hurdler up to 25f, out of half-sister to Grande Course de
Haies winner Goodea: 15f winner on Flat: useful novice hurdler: won 4-y-o fillies event
at Auteuil in May, handicap there in November and Grade 2 novice at Ascot (first start
after leaving A. Hosselet, much improved when beating Lingo 1¼ lengths) in December:
just headed by same horse when fell last in Grade 1 novice at Sandown: disappointing last
2 starts, tried in cheekpieces final one after reportedly taking little interest time before:
should stay beyond 2¼m: acts on heavy going. *N. J. Henderson*

PERNICKETY KING 5 b.g. Rakaposhi King – Fussy Lady (Idiot's Delight) [2003/4   F–
F16m F17m Jul 14] third foal: dam, winning hurdler, stayed 2¾m: no sign of ability in
bumpers and (after being sold 1,500 gns Doncaster August Sales) points. *P. J. Hobbs*

PEROUSE 6 ch.g. Alderbrook – Track Angel (Ardoon) [2003/4 h104: 16m 16f⁶ 16s²   h140
16m* 18g⁶ 16d* 17g² 16g² 16m 16dᵖᵘ Apr 17] sturdy gelding: useful handicap hurdler:
much improved when winning at Wincanton, Fontwell and Cheltenham within 9 days in
December: good efforts when runner-up next 2 starts, beaten neck by Limerick Boy in
valuable event at Kempton on latter occasion: bled from nose on reappearance and last 2
outings: raced around 2m: acts on firm and soft going: tongue tied after second outing.
P. F. Nicholls

PERSIAN BROOK 4 b.g. Atraf – Persian Role (Tragic Role (USA)) [2003/4 17mᵖᵘ   h–
Sep 27] no sign of ability in 3 maidens on Flat in 2003: hampered second and soon well
adrift in juvenile seller on hurdling debut. *M. W. Easterby*

PERSIAN KING (IRE) 7 ch.g. Persian Bold – Queen's Share (Main Reef) [2003/4   c115
h110: 16g³ 16m³ c16g⁴ c16m* c16mᶠ Sep 13] good-topped gelding: fairly useful handi   h115

cap hurdler: easily best effort over fences when winning maiden at Worcester in September by 5 lengths from Burning Truth: let down by jumping both other starts: likely to stay beyond 2m: raced mainly on good/good to firm going. *J. A. B. Old*

PERSIAN WATERS (IRE)   8 b.g. Persian Bold – Emerald Waters (Kings Lake (USA)) [2003/4 h124: 23m* May 3] leggy gelding: useful handicap hurdler: best effort when winning Merewood Homes Long Distance Hurdle at Haydock by 6 lengths from October Mist only start in 2003/4: stays 23f: acts on good to firm and good to soft going: reportedly bled from nose once in 2002/3. *J. R. Fanshawe*   **h136**

PERSONAL ASSURANCE   7 b.g. Un Desperado (FR) – Steel Typhoon (General Ironside) [2003/4 h110, F95: 21m* 20m² 22d² 21s⁴ 23s 25g 24gᵖᵘ Apr 2] rangy gelding: fairly useful handicap hurdler: won at Southwell (reluctant at start) in October: at least respectable efforts most subsequent outings: stays 25f: yet to race on firm going, acts on any other. *Jonjo O'Neill*   **h120**

PERSONA PRIDE   10 gr.g. St Enodoc – Le Jour Fortune (Twilight Alley) [2003/4 c–: c24gᵖᵘ Feb 11] angular gelding: modest pointer: little form in steeplechases. *Mrs B. Brown*   **c–**

PERSUETS (IRE)   6 b.m. Gildoran – Furry Queen (Furry Glen) [2003/4 F88: F17d⁴ 17g Jul 28] fair form on first of 2 starts in bumpers: sold out of J. I. A. Charlton's stable 8,600 gns Doncaster May Sales: well held in mares novice on hurdling debut, racing freely. *Ronald Thompson*   **h– F78**

PERTEMPS CINDRELLA   9 ch.m. Almoojid – Cinderella Derek (Hittite Glory) [2003/4 c82, h73: c20sᵖᵘ 24v⁶ May 21] plain, sparely-made mare: poor hurdler/chaser, no form either start very early in season: stays 2¾m: used to act well on ground softer than good: well below form in blinkers/cheekpieces: sold 4,000 gns Doncaster August Sales. *B. D. Leavy*   **c– h–**

PERTEMPS MACHINE   5 b.g. Danzig Connection (USA) – Shamrock Dancer (IRE) (Dance of Life (USA)) [2003/4 h–: 16d 19d 24sᶠ Dec 29] no form. *A. D. Smith*   **h–**

J. Dickson & S. McVie's "Perouse"

PERTEMPS PROFILE 8 b.g. Petoski – Peristyle (Tolomeo) [2003/4 c20s^{pu} c23g c25s⁵ c20d^{pu} Mar 14] smallish, leggy gelding: modest and unreliable handicap hurdler in 2001/2: left A. Streeter and off 20 months, well beaten over fences: usually blinkered/visored. *Ian Williams* **c– h– §**

PERTEMPS SILENUS 6 b.g. Silca Blanka (IRE) – Silvie (Kind of Hush) [2003/4 h–, F–: 17g^F Jun 13] sturdy gelding: of little account: headstrong: dead. *A. D. Smith* **h–**

PERTEMPS SUSIE 8 b.m. Gildoran – Brilliant Future (Welsh Saint) [2003/4 h84: 16f⁵ May 10] lengthy mare: maiden hurdler, poor form only start in 2003/4: stays 19f: acts on firm going, possibly unsuited by soft. *Ian Williams* **h71**

PERTEMPS WIZARD 4 br.g. Silver Wizard (USA) – Peristyle (Tolomeo) [2003/4 16v^{pu} Feb 7] half-brother to winning 2½m hurdler by Petoski: dam winning hurdler: lightly-raced maiden on Flat (should stay 7f+): showed nothing on hurdling debut. *A. D. Smith* **h–**

PERTINO 8 b.g. Terimon – Persian Fountain (IRE) (Persian Heights) [2003/4 c108, h107: c17g⁵ c16m⁴ c16m⁶ 21g⁶ c16s* c16d⁴ c16v c19g⁶ 16g c17g⁵ Apr 5] good-topped gelding: fair handicap hurdler/chaser: won over fences at Ayr in November: stays 2½m: acts on any going: usually wears cheekpieces/blinkers. *J. M. Jefferson* **c111 h–**

PERUVIA (IRE) 4 b.f. Perugino (USA) – Dane's Lane (IRE) (Danehill (USA)) [2003/4 17s 16g 16s^{pu} Mar 20] medium-sized filly: fairly useful on Flat (will prove best short of 1½m), sold out of H. Morrison's stable 13,000 gns Newmarket Autumn Sales: no form in 3 starts over hurdles: likely to prove best with emphasis on speed around 2m: joined R. Beckett. *Mrs A. J. Hamilton-Fairley* **h–**

PERUVIAN PRINCESS 5 gr.m. Missed Flight – Misty View (Absalom) [2003/4 F17m Apr 15] small mare: second foal: dam 7f (at 2 yrs) and 1¼m winner: tailed off in mares bumper on debut. *W. M. Brisbourne* **F–**

PESCETTO LADY (IRE) 6 b.m. Toulon – Glenpatrick Peach (IRE) (Lafontaine (USA)) [2003/4 h100, F87: 16g⁴ 16s⁴ 16f 16g* Sep 18] angular mare: fair hurdler: improved effort when winning handicap at Listowel in September by ¾ length from Harry The Ear: should stay beyond 2m: acts on firm going. *Mrs J. Harrington, Ireland* **h108**

PESSIMISTIC DICK 11 b.g. Derrylin – Tycoon Moon (Tycoon II) [2003/4 c111, h–: c24m⁵ c30g⁴ c32m^{pu} c24m⁵ c26m² c26g* c24f⁵ c27d^{ur} c24g⁵ Dec 5] sturdy gelding: fair handicap chaser: won at Plumpton in October: stays 3¾m: has form on heavy going, races on firmer nowadays (acts on firm): tried blinkered: usually races prominently/jumps soundly. *H. Morrison* **c104 h–**

PETANQUE (IRE) 8 b.g. King's Ride – Phargara (IRE) (Phardante (FR)) [2003/4 h112, F100: 16g⁴ 17g⁴ 16d³ 16s⁴ Jan 31] tall gelding: fairly useful handicap hurdler: good efforts in frame first 3 starts: stays 19f: acts on good to soft going, well held on soft. *N. J. Henderson* **h118**

PETARA (IRE) 9 ch.g. Petardia – Romangoddess (IRE) (Rhoman Rule (USA)) [2003/4 h–: 17g May 24] good-topped gelding: lightly raced and no form over hurdles. *J. S. Wainwright* **h–**

PETERHOUSE 5 b.g. Persian Bold – Run With Pride (Mandrake Major) [2003/4 F16v⁶ 17s^{pu} 17d Apr 10] second foal: half-brother to 2002 2-y-o 6f winner Sigwells Club Boy (by Fayruz): dam ran twice: no show in bumper or 2 novice hurdles. *R. Johnson* **h– F–**

PETER'S IMP (IRE) 9 b.g. Imp Society (USA) – Catherine Clare (Sallust) [2003/4 17g 17g⁵ 17g 17m 22g² 17g* 16f 20g 20m⁶ Oct 25] small, good-bodied gelding: poor hurdler: won selling handicap at Cartmel in August: effective around 2m to 2¾m: best efforts on good going. *A. Berry* **h73**

PETERSON'S CAY (IRE) 6 b.g. Grand Lodge (USA) – Columbian Sand (IRE) (Salmon Leap (USA)) [2003/4 h84, F86: 20m³ 16d 19d* Feb 15] lengthy gelding: poor hurdler: won maiden claimer (claimed to join C. Tizzard £8,000) at Hereford: stays 2½m: acts on good to firm and good to soft going: tried blinkered: temperamental. *Mrs M. Reveley* **h78 §**

PETER'S TWO FUN (FR) 7 b.g. Funambule (USA) – Spinner's Mate (FR) (Miller's Mate) [2003/4 h93§: 16d⁵ 19d^{pu} 16d⁵ c21g³ Apr 10] leggy gelding: winning hurdler, well below best in 2003/4 for J. Flint: poor form on chasing debut: stays 3¼m: acts on firm and soft going: usually visored in 2002/3, folded tamely when blinkered second start: usually front runner: best left alone. *A. S. T. Holdsworth* **c78 h70 §**

PETERTHEKNOT (IRE) 6 ch.g. Beneficial – A Womans Heart (IRE) (Supreme Leader) [2003/4 F16d² F20d² F16v* F16s⁶ 20s² Mar 14] €20,000 4-y-o: first foal: dam lightly-raced maiden: pulled up in point on debut in 2003: fairly useful form in bumpers, winning at Punchestown in January by 5 lengths from Jakers' second to Ulaan Baatar in maiden at Cork on hurdling debut. *Patrick Sinnott, Ireland* **h102**
F98

PETITE MARGOT 5 b.m. Alderbrook – Outfield (Monksfield) [2003/4 F16m F16m⁴ F17m³ F16f* 24m* 25m* 21g* 24d⁴ 24g² 24g³ 21m⁴ 24s* Apr 21] smallish mare: fourth foal: sister to winning staying hurdler Ollie Magern: dam, modest 3m hurdler, from family of high-class 2½m chaser Townley Stone and 1991 Grand National third Auntie Dot: best effort in bumpers (trained on debut by D. Caro) when winning very weak event at Ludlow in October: fairly useful novice hurdler: won at Towcester, Warwick and Ludlow (amateur handicap) before turn of year and mares race at Perth, beating Glenogue by 17 lengths at last-named: will stay beyond 25f: acts on soft and good to firm going (bumper win on firm): reliable. *N. A. Twiston-Davies* **h121**
F83

PETOLINSKI 6 b.g. Petoski – Olnistar (FR) (Balsamo (FR)) [2003/4 h101: c20s⁵ c25d⁴ c26sᵖᵘ c24vᵖᵘ c23d⁴ c23sᵖᵘ Apr 6] winning hurdler: failed to impress with attitude and little worthwhile form over fences: should prove suited by 3m+: acts on soft going: wore cheekpieces last 2 starts: not one to trust. *J. S. King* **c79 §**
h–

PETREA 9 b.m. St Ninian – Polypodium (Politico (USA)) [2003/4 c94, h–: c25d 23d* 25dᵖᵘ 24v* 24d⁶ Mar 18] smallish mare: better effort in hunter chases when third at Stratford in 2002/3: poor handicap hurdler: left W. Burnell, won conditional jockeys events at Wetherby (fortunate) in November and Newcastle in February: stays 3m: acts on heavy going: tried blinkered. *T. D. Walford* **c–**
h80

PETROUGE 8 b.g. Petoski – Red Spider (Red God) [2003/4 c20gᵖᵘ Mar 12] fair pointer, won in April: visored, went with little zest in maiden hunter chase. *Mrs C. J. Robinson* **c–**
h–

PETRULA 5 ch.g. Tagula (IRE) – Bouffant (High Top) [2003/4 17g² 16mᶠ 16d² 20d* 20v⁴ 16d⁵ 17dᵇᵈ 16d² Mar 22] leggy, close-coupled gelding: half-brother to winning hurdler around 2m Mutasarrif (by Polish Patriot): fairly useful on Flat (best form short of 1½m): fairly useful hurdler: won novice handicap at Wetherby in December by 5 lengths from Top of The Left: ran another good race there final start: stays 2½m: acts on heavy going: wore blinkers final outing, cheekpieces previous 4. *K. A. Ryan* **h119**

PETTREE (IRE) 10 ch.g. King Persian – Whackers World (Whistling Deer) [2003/4 c94x, h–: c24m² c28dᵖᵘ c26m* c32m⁵ c26m⁴ c26mᶠ c24gᵖᵘ Oct 11] tall gelding: fair handicap chaser: won at Southwell in June: lame final outing: should stay beyond 3¼m: acts on good to firm and good to soft ground: blinkered once: has got well behind/been let down by jumping. *N. A. Twiston-Davies* **c102**
h–

PETWICK (IRE) 5 b. or br.g. Flemensfirth (USA) – Scottish Minnie (IRE) (Farhaan) [2003/4 aF16g⁴ Nov 11] €20,000 3-y-o: second foal: dam unraced half-sister to fairly useful chaser up to 2½m Scottish Bar: fourth to Doce Vida in bumper on polytrack at Lingfield on debut. *P. G. Murphy* **F84**

PEVERIL PRIDE 6 b.g. Past Glories – Peveril Princess (Town And Country) [2003/4 F16f⁵ 19dᵖᵘ 16d 22dʳᵗʳ 16g 24m³ Mar 4] workmanlike gelding: first foal: dam poor and inconsistent maiden on Flat: last of 5 in bumper on debut: upped in trip, easily best effort over hurdles when third to Willie John Daly in novice at Taunton: refused to race fourth start. *M. J. Weeden* **h98 §**
F–

PEWTER LIGHT (IRE) 7 gr.g. Roselier (FR) – Luminous Light (Cardinal Flower) [2003/4 h–: c25d⁰ c23g³ c25dᵖᵘ c26gᵖᵘ c25d² c25g³ Apr 4] showed little in 3 maiden hurdles: poor novice chaser: stays 25f: acts on good to soft going: tried in cheekpieces. *B. J. M. Ryall* **c79**
h–

PHANTOM HAZE 11 gr.g. Absalom – Caroline Lamb (Hotfoot) [2003/4 c21gᵖᵘ Apr 12] good-topped gelding: maiden hurdler: no show in 2 starts over fences, second after absence of 4½ years: tried blinkered. *J. Parkes* **c–**
h–

PHARAGON (IRE) 6 b.g. Phardante (FR) – Hogan (IRE) (Black Minstrel) [2003/4 h–, F–: 20gᵖᵘ 24sᵖᵘ 24dᵖᵘ c21g c16dᵖᵘ Apr 22] no form. *Mrs C. J. Kerr* **c–**
h–

PHARAWAY CITIZEN (IRE) 9 ch.g. Phardante (FR) – Boreen Citizen (Boreen (FR)) [2003/4 c105, h78+: c27sᵖᵘ c20s⁶ c25dᴿ c24s* c26v⁴ c25s* c24g² c24d* c24g³ c26m³ Apr 14] useful-looking gelding: maiden hurdler: fairly useful handicap chaser: improved jumper and won at Taunton in December, Hereford in February and Bangor in March: good efforts last 2 starts, close third to Flying Trix at Cheltenham final one: stays 3¼m: acts on soft and good to firm going. *T. R. George* **c120**
h–

PHARBEITFROME (IRE) 10 b.g. Phardante (FR) – Asigh Glen (Furry Glen) **c88**
[2003/4 c86, h–: c16d³ c16g² c20m⁵ c16gᶠ c17m* c16m² c17mᵘʳ c16m² c16m³ c16m² **h–**
c17gᵖᵘ c16d² c16g⁵ c16d³ Dec 26] lengthy, workmanlike gelding: modest handicap
chaser: won at Southwell in July: stays 2½m, races mainly over shorter nowadays: unraced on firm going, acts on any other: tongue tied: still prone to odd mistake: consistent.
N. Wilson

PHARBEIT (IRE) 7 b.g. King's Ride – Phargara (IRE) (Phardante (FR)) [2003/4 **h84 §**
h70, F72: 16g 16m² 16m 20mᵘʳ 22dᵖᵘ Jul 30] poor maiden hurdler: should stay beyond
2m: acts on good to firm going: usually blinkered: hard ride: one to avoid. *E. L. James*

PHARCHANCIER 8 gr.g. Pharly (FR) – Lots of Luck (Neltino) [2003/4 16m May **h–**
7] third foal: half-brother to poor 2m hurdler Fortune Hopper (by Rock Hopper): dam 2m
hurdle winner/1m to 1¼m winner on Flat: no show over hurdles on belated debut: sold
2,100 gns Doncaster November Sales. *O. Brennan*

PHAR CITY (IRE) 7 b.g. Phardante (FR) – Aunty Dawn (IRE) (Strong Gale) [2003/4 **c97**
c101, h93, F93: c25gᶠ c23m³ c26gᶠ Apr 10] strong, well-made gelding: modest novice **h–**
hurdler: winning chaser, stiffish task only completed start in 2003/4: stays 21f: acts on
soft and good to firm going. *R. H. Buckler*

PHARDANTE FLYER (IRE) 10 b.g. Phardante (FR) – Shannon Lek (Menelek) **c–**
[2003/4 c–, h–: c17g⁵ May 17] good-topped gelding: one-time useful hurdler: tailed off **h–**
in 2 handicaps in 2002/3: has had jumping problems over fences, reportedly lame at
Bangor in May: should stay 2½m: acts on soft and good to firm going: has shown
tendency to hang. *P. J. Hobbs*

PHAR FAR AWAY 6 b.m. Phardante (FR) – Shannon Juliette (Julio Mariner) [2003/4 **h–**
F16s² 20sᵘʳ 21dᵖᵘ 22g 18gᵖᵘ Apr 22] good-topped mare: third foal: dam, 2¾m hurdle **F88**
winner, half-sister to fairly useful staying chaser Orswell Lad and useful hurdler at 21f
Winston Run: second to Brassie in bumper at Uttoxeter on debut: well beaten but not
knocked about only completed start over hurdles: should be suited by further than 2m.
D. R. Gandolfo

PHAR FROM A FIDDLE (IRE) 8 b. or br.g. Phardante (FR) – Lucycello (Monks- **c116**
field) [2003/4 c121, h–: c23m⁵ c22g* 22f² c24fᵖᵘ c24mᵖᵘ Nov 24] well-made gelding: **h99**
modest maiden hurdler: fairly useful handicap chaser: won 5-runner event at Fontwell in
October, faltering badly close home: reportedly lame final outing: stays 25f: probably
acts on any going: tongue tied: has folded tamely more than once. *P. F. Nicholls*

PHAR FROM FROSTY (IRE) 7 br.g. Phardante (FR) – Cold Evening (IRE) (Strong **h124**
Gale) [2003/4 h90, F92: 20m⁴ 27g³ 24f* 23m* 26g³ 26s* 27d* 25s² Dec 13] useful-
looking gelding: fairly useful hurdler: progressed really well, winning 4 times in October
and November, novice at Market Rasen, conditional jockeys novice handicap at Wetherby, handicap at Huntingdon and novice (simple task) at Sedgefield: further improvement when 3 lengths second to Comply Or Die in Grade 2 novice at Cheltenham: stays
27f: acts on firm and soft going. *C. R. Egerton*

PHAR JEFFEN (IRE) 9 ch.g. Phardante (FR) – Clever Milly (Precipice Wood) **c118 x**
[2003/4 c16f* c16m⁵ c16m² c16dᶠ c16dᵖᵘ c21dᶠ Jan 17] smallish gelding: fairly useful **h–**
chaser: off 19 months, beat sole opponent Harik 1¾ lengths in handicap at Kempton in
October: let down by jumping most starts after: effective at 2m to 2½m: unraced on heavy
going, acts on any other: blinkered final outing: races prominently. *R. J. Hodges*

PHARLY REEF 12 b.g. Pharly (FR) – Hay Reef (Mill Reef (USA)) [2003/4 h98: 16s **h79**
17d 16g 16dᵖᵘ 16g⁵ Apr 4] small gelding: handicap hurdler, little impact in 2003/4: best
around 2m: acts on firm and soft going. *D. Burchell*

PHARLY STAR 10 ch.g. Pharly (FR) – Norapa (Ahonoora) [2003/4 c24m² May 10] **c76**
former eventer: won 2 of 3 starts in points: mixed round of jumping (often went left)
when second of 4 finishers in novice hunter chase at Huntingdon. *Mrs F. M. Midwood*

PHARMISTICE (IRE) 13 b.g. Phardante (FR) – Lucylet (Kinglet) [2003/4 c104, **c–**
h–: c25gᵘʳ c25gᵖᵘ Apr 5] sparely-made gelding: fairly useful hunter chaser at best: **h–**
successful in points in March and April (twice): stays 25f: acts on good to firm going.
Miss N. Stirling

PHAR OUT PHAVORITE (IRE) 5 b.g. Beneficial – Phar From Men (IRE) (Phar- **F96**
dante (FR)) [2003/4 F16d⁴ F18s² F16g Mar 27] €35,000 4-y-o: good-topped gelding: has
plenty of scope: second foal: dam unraced: in frame in bumpers at Kempton (fourth of 16
to Itsa Legend) and Plumpton (hung right into straight): again looked less than straightforward when tailed off final start. *Miss E. C. Lavelle*

PHARPOST (IRE) 9 b.g. Phardante (FR) – Branstown Lady (Deep Run) [2003/4 **c111 §**
c111§, h–: c20m* c20f² c26m³ c20g² c20g² c20f* c24f³ c24g² c24m³ 22g c24m³ c20gᵘ **h99 §**
c21m⁶ Apr 15] lengthy, deep-girthed gelding: lightly-raced winning hurdler: fair chaser:
won weak handicap at Uttoxeter in June and 4-runner novice at Carlisle (left well clear
when Green Ideal fell 2 out) in October: stays 25f: acts on firm and soft going: blinkered
last 2 outings: often finds little. *Miss Venetia Williams*

PHARTODANTE (IRE) 7 b.m. Phardante (FR) – Hennywood (IRE) (Henbit (USA)) **h–**
[2003/4 h–, F–: 20g 20g 21d 22dᵖᵘ 23sᵖᵘ 18g Apr 22] no form: tried in cheekpieces.
Mrs L. C. Jewell

PHASE EIGHT GIRL 8 b.m. Warrshan (USA) – Bugsy's Sister (Aragon) [2003/4 **h67**
h76: 21sᵖᵘ 21sᵖᵘ 22g 26gᵖᵘ 22g⁴ Apr 24] small mare: poor hurdler: best run at 3¼m: acts
on firm going. *J. Hetherton*

PHAZAR 4 b.g. Zamindar (USA) – Ypha (USA) (Lyphard (USA)) [2003/4 F16d Feb **F81**
2] 10,000 3-y-o: well-made gelding: fifth foal: half-brother to useful hurdler/smart chaser
Redemption (by Sanglamore), stays 21f, and useful bumper winner Enhancer (by
Zafonic): dam French 9.5f and 1¼m winner: better for race, ran green when ninth of 17 to
Moorlands Return in bumper at Kempton on debut. *N. J. Hawke*

PHENOMENON 6 b.m. Unfuwain (USA) – Pure (Slip Anchor) [2003/4 16m Dec 10] **h–**
first foal: half-sister to 2003 3-y-o 7f winner Angel Annie (by Alzao): dam unraced sister
to Oaks and St Leger winner User Friendly: mid-field in 18-runner mares novice hurdle
at Leicester on debut. *M. C. Pipe*

PHILDARI (IRE) 8 b.g. Shardari – Philosophical (Welsh Chanter) [2003/4 c91, h104: **c101 §**
c24m² c21g* c24m³ c20mᵖᵘ c20fᶠ c25f³ c21g² c21m⁵ Apr 15] lengthy gelding: maiden **h–**
hurdler: fair chaser: easily won maiden at Southwell in September: stays easy 25f: acts on
soft and firm going: tried in cheekpieces: tongue tied: ungenuine. *P. R. Webber*

PHILIPPA YEATES (IRE) 5 b.m. Hushang (IRE) – Miss Bobby Bennett (Kings **h–**
Lake (USA)) [2003/4 16g 17g 16g Feb 25] medium-sized mare: fifth foal: half-sister to
winning hurdler Miss B Bennett (by Denel), stays 3¼m: dam useful hurdler up to 2½m/
1½m winner on Flat: well held in 3 starts over hurdles. *M. C. Pipe*

PHILOMENA 5 b.m. Bedford (USA) – Mandalay Miss (Mandalus) [2003/4 F16m **F–**
Apr 13] first foal: dam no sign of ability: no show in bumper on debut. *V. R. A. Dartnall*

PHILSON RUN (IRE) 8 b.g. Un Desperado (FR) – Isis (Deep Run) [2003/4 c25d* **c107 p**
Feb 12] strong gelding: fourth foal: dam ran once in bumper: won maiden on second of 2
starts in Irish points in 2003: bought 6,500 gns (privately) Doncaster May Sales: 25/1,
won 5-finisher hunter at Wincanton impressively by 2½ lengths with plenty in hand from
disqualified Garruth, travelling and jumping well throughout: looked open to good deal
of improvement, but reportedly met with setback and not seen out again. *Nick Williams*

Stewart Tory Memorial Trophy Hunters' Chase, Wincanton—
25/1-chance Philson Run looks a smart prospect on his hunter chase debut; the grey Garruth takes second

PHIL THE FENCER 8 gr.g. Neltino – Who's Free (Sit In The Corner (USA)) [2003/4 **h–** 22d Mar 21] lightly-raced maiden hurdler: off 2 years before only start in 2003/4. *John Allen*

PHILTRE (IRE) 10 b.g. Phardante (FR) – Forest Gale (Strong Gale) [2003/4 c–: **c–** c28g[pu] c23m⁵ Jun 28] tall, angular gelding: fairly useful pointer nowadays: no show in valuable hunter and handicap early in 2003/4: stays 3½m: acts on good to firm going: races prominently. *Mrs H. L. Needham*

PHINDA FOREST (IRE) 5 br.m. Charnwood Forest (IRE) – Shatalia (USA) (Shah- **h–** rastani (USA)) [2003/4 h–: 16g 17d⁶ May 28] no form over hurdles: wore cheekpieces in 2003/4. *W. Storey*

PHOENIX PHLYER 10 b.g. Ardross – Brown Coast (Oats) [2003/4 c–, h–: c20m⁵ **c93** c20m* c24m[ur] c20d² c19s⁵ Apr 6] fair hunter chaser: won at Ludlow in February by 9 **h–** lengths from Guignol du Cochet: stays 2½m: acts on soft and good to firm going: tried blinkered/visored, wore cheekpieces last 4 starts: usually races up with pace: none too consistent. *D. Pipe*

PHONE BACK (IRE) 5 b.g. Bob Back (USA) – Will Phone (Buckskin (FR)) [2003/4 **F–** F16g Mar 27] tall gelding: first foal: dam, winning hurdler/fairly useful chaser, stayed 3m: tailed off in bumper at Newbury on debut. *G. L. Moore*

PHOTOGRAPHER (USA) 6 b. or br.g. Mountain Cat (USA) – Clickety Click **h85** (USA) (Sovereign Dancer (USA)) [2003/4 h94: 16d 16d⁴ Dec 26] leggy gelding: modest novice hurdler, lightly raced: not certain to stay beyond 2¼m: acts on soft and good to firm going. *Mrs N. Smith*

PHRED 4 ch.g. Safawan – Phlirty (Pharly (FR)) [2003/4 17s 16g Feb 13] angular **h–** gelding: half-brother to 2m hurdle winner Pheisty (by Faustus): fair on Flat (stays 1m): pulled hard when well held in novice and juvenile hurdles. *R. F. Johnson Houghton*

PHYSICAL GRAFFITI (USA) 7 b.g. Mister Baileys – Gleaming Water (USA) **h87** (Pago Pago) [2003/4 h88: 16d⁵ 16v[pu] 16s[co] 20d 16s Apr 11] compact gelding: modest handicap hurdler, below form after reappearance: stays 19f: acts on heavy going. *J. A. B. Old*

PICQUET OFFICER (IRE) 6 b.g. Safety Catch (USA) – Pitea (Corvaro (USA)) **h–** [2003/4 17g 16f[su] Oct 18] 2,270 (privately) 4-y-o: third foal: dam of little account: ninth of 10 finishers in novice hurdle at Sedgefield on debut: broke leg 4 days later. *Miss S. E. Forster*

PICTURE PALACE 6 ch.g. Salse (USA) – Moviegoer (Pharly (FR)) [2003/4 h95§: **h97** 26g* 21d Apr 12] workmanlike gelding: modest handicap hurdler: won at Southwell in May: stays 3¼m, at least when conditions aren't testing: acts on soft and good to firm going: usually blinkered: has looked temperamental in past. *T. R. George*

PIERPOINT (IRE) 9 ch.g. Archway (IRE) – Lavinia (Habitat) [2003/4 16g 16m[pu] **h–** 16f⁵ 16d Oct 30] poor and unreliable on Flat (stays easy 1m): little form over hurdles, trained first 2 starts by J. M. Bradley. *Mrs A. M. Thorpe*

PIERRE DU FOREZ (FR) 6 ch.g. Sicyos (USA) – Pierre du Luizet (FR) (Fulgus **h– §** (FR)) [2003/4 16d[pu] 19s[pu] 16s 17g[R] 18g[pu] 17s[pu] Mar 23] ex-French gelding: fifth foal: dam won around 1¾m in France: successful over 1¼m on Flat at 3 yrs for J-P. Pelat: no form over hurdles, jumping poorly and/or looking none too keen: visored after debut: one to avoid. *M. C. Pipe*

PIERRE PRECIEUSE 5 ch.m. Bijou d'Inde – Time Or Never (FR) (Dowsing (USA)) **F–** [2003/4 F82: F16g May 15] form in bumpers only on final start in 2002/3: well beaten in 3 starts on Flat: headstrong. *J. S. Goldie*

PIETRO BEMBO (IRE) 10 b.g. Midyan (USA) – Cut No Ice (Great Nephew) **c100** [2003/4 c–, h–: c17d² c17g[pu] c16g⁴ c20m² c24m² c24g⁵ c19m⁴ Sep 10] close-coupled **h–** gelding: winning hurdler: fair novice chaser: best form around 2m: acts on good to firm and heavy going: usually front runner. *P. R. Chamings*

PIETRO VANNUCCI (IRE) 8 b.g. Perugino (USA) – Lady's Bridge (USA) (Sir Ivor **c114 p** (USA)) [2003/4 h: c20d³ c18d³ c16s* Feb 7] lengthy, good sort: useful hurdler in 2001/2: **h–** off nearly 2 years, fair form in maiden chases: won 18-runner event at Naas by ¾ length from Atlantic Rhapsody: will stay beyond 2½m: raced on good going or softer (acts on heavy): has awkward head carriage: better over fences. *N. Meade, Ireland*

PIKESTAFF (USA) 6 ch.g. Diesis – Navarene (USA) (Known Fact (USA)) [2003/4 **h75** h75: 16g* 16g 16f[pu] 20d 16d 17s⁵ 16v 17s Feb 11] small gelding: poor hurdler: won weak maiden at Kelso very early in season: best form around 2m: acts on good to firm going: tongue tied last 5 starts. *M. A. Barnes*

PILCA (FR) 4 ch.g. Pistolet Bleu (IRE) – Caricoe (Baillamont (USA)) [2003/4 15vF 17s⁴ 16g³ 17d* 17d* 16d⁵ 15d* 16f⁴ 16sᵖᵘ 17d⁶ 19g 17m³ 16sᶠ³ Mar 15] small, leggy ex-French gelding: half-brother to winning 2¼m hurdler Epec (by Epervier Bleu): once-raced on Flat: fair juvenile hurdler: won claimers at Dieppe in July, Clairefontaine (claimed from T. Trapenard €10,700) in August and Auteuil (claimed from P. Chevillard €20,000) in September: most unfortunate in similar event at Plumpton (claimed to join Mrs H. Dalton 12,000 gns) final start, 20 lengths clear when falling 2 out (remounted): raced mainly around 2m: acts on soft and good to firm going. *M. C. Pipe* **h103**

PILGRIMS PROGRESS (IRE) 4 b.g. Entrepreneur – Rose Bonbon (FR) (High Top) [2003/4 16d³ 16s³ 16s⁵ 16d⁴ 17d* 19g Mar 27] lengthy gelding: half-brother to poor hurdler Stopwatch (by Lead On Time), stays 21f: fairly useful on Flat (stays 1½m) for T. Stack: fair juvenile hurdler: won amateur maiden at Bangor in March: should stay beyond 17f: acts on good going: ran creditably in blinkers fourth start. *P. J. Hobbs* **h103**

PILLAGING PICT 9 ch.g. Primitive Rising (USA) – Carat Stick (Gold Rod) [2003/4 c114: c25gᵘʳ c25dᵖᵘ c16v⁶ Jan 10] lengthy gelding: fair handicap chaser: well held only completed start in 2003/4: stays 2¾m: raced on good going or softer (acts on soft). *J. B. Walton* **c–**

PILLAR OF FIRE (IRE) 10 gr.g. Roselier (FR) – Cousin Flo (True Song) [2003/4 c–§, h97§: 24m⁴ 21m⁴ c20m² c20g² c24mᵘʳ c20d³ Mar 14] leggy gelding: modest hurdler/ maiden chaser: stays easy 3m: acts on good to firm and good to soft going: visored once: ungenuine. *Ian Williams* **c88 §** **h98 §**

PILLAR TO POST 5 b.g. Bluegrass Prince (IRE) – Parisana (FR) (Gift Card (FR)) [2003/4 F16s F16d Mar 19] good-topped gelding: half-brother to several winners, includ-ing 1991 2-y-o 5f winner Parisien Singer (by Chief Singer) and Irish 11f and 13f winner Swift Cert (by Robellino): dam unraced half-sister to dam of Chief Singer, out of Oaks winner Pia: well held in maiden bumpers. *Ian Williams* **F–**

PILOT'S HARBOUR 8 b.g. Distant Relative – Lillemor (Connaught) [2003/4 c21g⁴ c26mF 27gᵖᵘ 22g 24m⁵ 21g⁴ c20dᵖᵘ Oct 29] winning hurdler: little form in 2003/4 after nearly 2 years off, including over fences: ungenuine. *F. P. Murtagh* **c– §** **h– §**

PIMLICO (IRE) 6 ch.g. Imp Society (USA) – Willow Gale (Strong Gale) [2003/4 F84: 16dᵖᵘ 19m Dec 10] strong gelding: modest form in 2 bumpers in 2002/3: no show in 2 races over hurdles. *B. G. Powell* **h–**

PIN HIGH (IRE) 5 b.g. Needle Gun (IRE) – Eva's Fancy (Distinctly (USA)) [2003/4 F16m⁵ F17d 16s 16g² 22g Apr 13] half-brother to fair hurdler up to 3m Monty's Fancy (by Montelimar) and bumper winner by Good Thyne: dam, won up to 2½m over hurdles, from family of very smart 2m chaser Lord Dorcet: fifth in bumper at Ludlow on debut (saddle slipped next time): easily best effort in novice hurdles when second to Gentle Beau at same course: bred to stay beyond 2m. *Miss H. C. Knight* **h94** **F84**

PINK ECLIPSE 4 b.f. Double Eclipse (IRE) – Caspian Mist (Remainder Man) [2003/4 F13vᵖᵘ F16v F16g Feb 14] leggy filly: third foal: dam, stayed 15f on Flat, won first of 3 starts over hurdles: no show in bumpers: looked very difficult ride on debut. *C. Roberts* **F–**

PINK HARBOUR 6 b.m. Rakaposhi King – Let Me Finish (Chantro) [2003/4 20m⁵ 17g 20g 17d⁴ 16sᵘʳ 17vᵘʳ 19sᵘʳ 21g 27d⁵ Mar 7] lengthy, rather unfurnished mare: third living foal: dam, tailed off in 2 bumpers, half-sister to fairly useful staying chaser River Sirene: no form over hurdles. *D. McCain* **h–**

PINOT NOIR 6 b.g. Saddlers' Hall (IRE) – Go For Red (IRE) (Thatching) [2003/4 17g 16mᵖᵘ Jul 13] fairly useful at best on Flat (stays 1½m), no form since leaving H. Morrison in mid-2002: no show in 2 starts over hurdles: tried in cheekpieces. *G. J. Smith* **h–**

PIPERSLAND 7 b.g. Lir – Celtic Mist (Celtic Cone) [2003/4 19s 19vᵖᵘ Feb 2] third foal: dam unraced, out of useful chaser up to 2¾m Misty Fort: little sign of ability, including in points. *Ms Sue Willcock* **h–**

PIPER'S ROCK (IRE) 13 ch.g. Zaffaran (USA) – Misclaire (Steeple Aston) [2003/4 c25g⁶ Mar 28] workmanlike gelding: winning hurdler/chaser: modest pointer nowadays: made mistakes when tailed off in hunter chase: stays 3¼m: acts on firm and soft going: usually visored. *Miss M. A. Neill* **c–** **h–**

PIP MOSS 9 ch.g. Le Moss – My Aisling (John de Coombe) [2003/4 h76: c24vᵖᵘ Feb 7] lengthy, workmanlike gelding: poor form over hurdles: off 11 months, pulled up in **c–** **h–**

handicap on chasing debut: should stay at least 2½m: raced on ground softer than good. *J. A. B. Old*

PIPSSALIO (SPA)   7 b.g. Pips Pride – Tesalia (SPA) (Finissimo (SPA)) [2003/4 16s³   **h104** 20s⁴ 20d 19s* Apr 4] leggy gelding: poor on Flat (seems to stay 2m) nowadays: fair form over hurdles: won 18-runner maiden at Lingfield by short head from Viciana: stays 2½m: acts on soft going: tongue tied. *Jamie Poulton*

PIRANDELLO DUE   10 b.g. Teenoso (USA) – Bay Girl (Persian Bold) [2003/4 21s   **c– x** 22s c19s⁴ c20sᶠ c24gᵖᵘ Mar 6] sturdy gelding: little form over hurdles or fences (not a   **h–** fluent jumper). *D. P. Keane*

PIRANDELLO (IRE)   6 ch.g. Shalford (IRE) – Scenic Villa (Top Ville) [2003/4   **h120** h103: 16m⁶ 16m² 16g³ 16s* 16s² 16s 17g 16gᶠ Jan 17] rather leggy gelding: fairly useful handicap hurdler: second run within 24 hrs, won at Huntingdon in November: likely to prove best around 2m: acts on soft and good to firm going. *K. C. Bailey*

PISTE BLEU (FR)   4 b.f. Pistolet Bleu (IRE) – Thamissia (FR) (Riverman (USA))   **h66** [2003/4 16f⁶ Oct 9] modest on Flat (stays 1½m), sold out of R. Beckett's stable 3,500 gns Doncaster August Sales: joint favourite, sixth of 9 in juvenile maiden at Ludlow on hurdling debut. *R. Ford*

PISTOL KNIGHT   10 b.g. Jupiter Island – Porchester Run (Deep Run) [2003/4 c21g³   **c71** Mar 3] maiden pointer: third in maiden hunter at Folkestone. *Mrs S. Bowman*

PITMINSTER   6 b.g. Karinga Bay – Eleanora Muse (Idiot's Delight) [2003/4 F17g   **h86** 17s² 17g⁶ Feb 19] 8,000 4-y-o: first foal: dam half-sister to useful hurdler up to 2½m   **F–** Hawthorn Hill Lad, out of half-sister to top-class staying chaser Spanish Steps: failed to complete in 3 points in 2003: never better than mid-division in bumper at Newton Abbot: modest form at Taunton both starts over hurdles, not fluent. *P. F. Nicholls*

PITTSBURGH PHIL (IRE)   7 b.g. Sadler's Wells (USA) – Broadway Joan (USA)   **c118** (Bold Arian (USA)) [2003/4 c17dᵘʳ c17d⁴ c24gᵘʳ Apr 10] leggy gelding: useful hurdler at   **h–** best for M. O'Brien: missed 2002/3: upped markedly in trip, challenging for lead and running easily best race over fences when unseating 2 out in well-contested handicap at Carlisle: likely to stay 3m: raced on good ground or softer. *Jonjo O'Neill*

PIXLEY   4 ch.g. Saxon Farm – Lady Renton (Rolfe (USA)) [2003/4 F17g Apr 13] first   **F–** foal: dam lightly raced and no form on Flat or over hurdles: always behind in bumper on debut. *Mrs P. Bickerton*

PIZARRO (IRE)   7 ch.g. Broken Hearted – Our Swan Lady (Swan's Rock)   **c150 +** [2003/4 h147: 20d⁴ c17g* c20dᵖᵘ c24d* c21d* c24gᵇᵈ Mar 17]   **h–**
        Provided all goes well with Pizarro in the next season, he will surely be turning up at the Cheltenham Festival for the fourth time in succession, with the

William Neville & Sons Novices' Chase, Leopardstown—Pizarro shows himself a smart novice

Gold Cup as his probable target this time around. The three races Pizarro has contested at the fixture so far have all been championship events, and while seeming fortunate to win the Champion Bumper—controversially surviving a stewards' inquiry, after twice impeding runner-up Rhinestone Cowboy—he can be counted unlucky not to have won the Royal & SunAlliance Chase on his latest start. Pizarro was promoted to second behind Hardy Eustace in the Royal & SunAlliance Novices' Hurdle on his other appearance at the Festival. He still has plenty of improvement to make if he is to reach Gold Cup standard but, as a seven-year-old relatively unexposed at distances around three miles, Pizarro should continue to progress. With further experience, he could be an interesting contender, and Cheltenham does seem to bring out the best in him.

Pizarro had four races over fences prior to the Royal & SunAlliance Chase, all in Ireland, and he won three of them. After landing the odds in a maiden at Clonmel in November on his chasing debut, Pizarro gave a lacklustre performance when favourite for the Grade 1 Royal Bond Novices' Chase at Fairyhouse before winning two similar races at Leopardstown. He took the eye in the paddock prior to the William Neville & Sons Novices' Chase in December and jumped much more fluently than at Fairyhouse in winning by nine lengths from the British challenger Rosslea, finding plenty under pressure after leading two out and well in command when drifting right on the run-in. Pizarro again looked very well and didn't have to run quite to that form to follow up in the Dr P. J. Moriarty Novices' Chase, run over twenty-one furlongs in February, shaping as though he would be suited by a return to three miles when winning by a head from Mossy Green. The front-running Mossy Green looked to have Pizarro in trouble two out, but Pizarro kept responding to pressure and produced a strong run from the last to lead close home. Mossy Green was to set Pizarro an even bigger problem in the Royal & SunAlliance Chase, one which he couldn't overcome. Second favourite Pizarro wasn't fluent on a couple of occasions in the back straight and had to be pushed along to make up ground after five out, but he was staying on strongly in fourth, around four lengths behind the leaders Mossy Green and Our Vic, when the former fell and brought Pizarro down at the second last. Pizarro was ahead of the winner Rule Supreme when he departed, and would almost certainly have beaten that horse convincingly.

		Dara Monarch	Realm
	Broken Hearted	(b 1979)	Sardara
	(b 1984)	Smash	Busted
Pizarro (IRE)		(b 1976)	Ash Lawn
(ch.g. 1997)		Swan's Rock	Tyrant
	Our Swan Lady	(b 1977)	Miss Cossie
	(ch 1987)	Our Day	Conte Grande
		(b 1970)	Ding Dong Day

Pizarro is the best jumper sired by Broken Hearted, who died in 2003, though he had another notable winner over fences in the latest season with Ballybough Rasher, who was successful in the Charlie Hall Chase at Wetherby. Pizarro is the only winner to date out of the unraced Our Swan Lady, his six-year-old sister Lady Devondale not having raced since her debut in 2002/3. Our Swan Lady herself is half-sister to four winners, including the fair staying chaser Some Day Soon. The third dam Ding Dong Day, who was unraced, produced three winners, among them another fair staying chaser Day of Wishes. This is a family of stayers, and three miles certainly won't be the limit of Pizarro's stamina. The workmanlike Pizarro acts on heavy going, and he has yet to race on ground firmer than good. *E. J. O'Grady, Ireland*

PLACE ABOVE (IRE)   8 b.g. Alphabatim (USA) – Lucky Pit (Pitpan) [2003/4 h–: 24d 24g c24dur c24srtr Mar 20] won point in February: no other form: refused to race final outing. *E. A. Elliott*   c– §
h– §

PLACID MAN (IRE)   10 br.g. Un Desperado (FR) – Sparkling Gale (Strong Gale) [2003/4 c113p, h–: c20d* Mar 21] big, rangy gelding: lightly raced: won both completed starts in points in 2004: also successful both completed outings in steeplechases, though fortunate in 3-finisher hunter at Fontwell in March, 2 lengths behind Silence Reigns when left in front last: should stay beyond 2½m. *Ms A. E. Embiricos*   c116
h–

PLAISANCE (GER)   5 b.m. Monsun (GER) – Pariana (USA) (Bering) [2003/4 h87: 22dpu Mar 21] sturdy mare: modest form over hurdles in 2002/3: left J. Jenkins and off 11 months, beaten long way out in handicap at Fontwell: will prove best around 2m: acts on soft going. *A. M. Hales*   h–

PLANTAGANET (FR)   6 br.g. Cadoudal (FR) – Ever Young (FR) (Royal Charter (FR)) [2003/4 F89: 16g 19m5 Mar 4] useful-looking gelding: mid-division in 2 bumpers: much better effort over hurdles when fifth of 8 finishers to Heron's Ghyll in novice at Taunton. *Ian Williams*   h89

PLANTAGENET PRINCE   5 b.g. Lancastrian – Yuan Princess (Tender King) [2003/4 F18g Apr 22] fourth foal: half-brother to modest 21f hurdle winner Le Prince (by Le Moss): dam winning 2m hurdler/1¾m winner on Flat: well held in bumper on debut. *M. Scudamore*   F–

PLASTIC PADDY (IRE)   7 b.g. Beau Sher – Vultang Lady (Le Bavard (FR)) [2003/4 F105: 20dur 16d3 20sro Dec 26] rangy gelding: type to make a chaser: has reportedly been hobdayed: bumper winner: fair form when third to Oracle des Mottes in maiden at Chepstow on completed outing over hurdles: should stay beyond 2m: room for improvement in his jumping. *D. P. Keane*   h105

PLENTY   5 b.m. Terimon – Mrs Moneypenny (Relkino) [2003/4 F18v Jan 12] third foal: dam, poor novice hurdler, half-sister to fairly useful staying chaser Sneakapenny: no show in bumper on debut. *N. A. Gaselee*   F–

PLENTY COURAGE   10 ch.g. Gildoran – Fastlass (Celtic Cone) [2003/4 c68, h91: 22g3 22g4 24g4 22f3 22f3 21d4 20d6 21spu Dec 26] small gelding: poor handicap hurdler, on long losing run: should stay 3m: acts on any going: effective with/without cheekpieces: races prominently. *F. S. Storey*   c–
h81

PLENTY INN HAND   8 b.g. Alflora (IRE) – Shean Deas (Le Moss) [2003/4 h100?: c24gF c21gur c21mpu c26mpu Jul 18] sturdy gelding: third in novice on hurdling debut in 2002/3: no form since, including in points. *M. F. Harris*   c–
h–

PLUMIER (FR)   6 b.g. Beyssac (FR) – Plume Rose (FR) (Rose Laurel) [2003/4 h–, F–: c23vpu c19g2 c24v* c25gpu Apr 18] tall, useful-looking gelding: fair form over fences: won maiden at Lingfield in April, soon clear after leading thirteenth: let down by jumping final start: stays 3m: acts on heavy going: tongue tied last 3 outings: none too hearty. *Ms Bridget Nicholls*   c108
h–

PLURALIST (IRE)   8 b.g. Mujadil (USA) – Encore Une Fois (IRE) (Shirley Heights) [2003/4 17dpu 16d Jan 13] smallish gelding: poor hurdler in 2001/2: no encouragement on return: stays 21f: acts on firm and good to soft going: has had tongue tied. *A. P. Jones*   h–

PLUTOCRAT   8 b.g. Polar Falcon (USA) – Choire Mhor (Dominion) [2003/4 h117: 21d5 24d4 16s Jan 16] smallish, angular gelding: fairly useful handicap hurdler: not given hard time all 3 starts in 2003/4: effective at 2m, barely stays 3m: acts on good to firm and good to soft going (possibly not on softer): has good record at Musselburgh: usually patiently ridden. *L. Lungo*   h113 +

POACHER'S PADDY (IRE)   9 b.m. Jurado (USA) – Ross Maid (Random Shot) [2003/4 c19m* c28dpu May 30] fair pointer: won novice hunter at Exeter in May by 9 lengths from Kestick: probably amiss in valuable similar event at Stratford later in month: should stay beyond 19f: acts on good to firm going. *N. Poacher*   c94

POACHERS RUN (IRE) 9 b.m. Executive Perk – Rugged Run (Deep Run) [2003/4 c–, h84: 21m^pu 21g^4 Aug 8] angular mare: didn't take to chasing: poor handicap hurdler: stays 3m: acts on good to firm and heavy going: effective with or without blinkers/cheekpieces. *G. M. Moore* **c– h80**

POACHIN AGAIN (IRE) 7 b.g. Supreme Leader – Ariannrun (Deep Run) [2003/4 h109p. 16d^d 18d^4 16d^2 16s* 20d 16d Apr 13] strong, stocky gelding: fair hurdler: won maiden at Punchestown in February: bred to stay well beyond 2¼m: raced on going softer than good (acts on heavy). *A. L. T. Moore, Ireland* **h109**

POACHING (IRE) 6 b.g. Gone Fishin – Riveress (Dunphy) [2003/4 F–: F17m^6 Jul 22] well held in 3 bumpers. *Miss S. E. Forster* **F–**

POETRY AND JAZZ 5 b.g. Nomadic Way (USA) – Indian Crown (Welsh Captain) [2003/4 F16d^pu F17s^pu F16v F16m Feb 21] leggy gelding: first foal: dam maiden hurdler: no form in bumpers. *Dr P. Pritchard* **F–**

POGGENIP 5 b.m. Petoski – Princess Tria (Space King) [2003/4 F16g^3 Mar 17] second foal: dam winning pointer: third of 20 to Here's Johnny in bumper at Huntingdon on debut. *B. G. Powell* **F80**

POILU 6 ch.g. Fearless Action (USA) – Marielou (FR) (Carwhite) [2003/4 F16g^4 20s 20v 20d Feb 21] big, short-backed gelding: half-brother to 3 winners, including fair staying hurdler Dakota Girl (by Northern State) and 2½m hurdler Trading Trouble (by Petoski): dam, Flat winner in Belgium, sister to smart French performer up to 1½m Magistros: poor form in bumper at Newcastle on debut: well beaten in 3 novice hurdles. *J. M. Jefferson* **h– F73**

POINTALISM (IRE) 5 br.g. Roselier (FR) – Ballinahowna Dream (IRE) (Treasure Kay) [2003/4 19s^pu 21d^5 Mar 25] good-topped gelding: second foal: dam never ran: won maiden Irish point in 2003: little show in 2 novice hurdles. *Miss H. C. Knight* **h–**

POINT BARROW (IRE) 6 b.g. Arctic Lord – Credit Transfer (IRE) (Kemal (FR)) [2003/4 F16d* 19s^F 20g* 22s^5 20d^2 Apr 11] €37,000 4-y-o: good-topped gelding: first foal: dam, maiden hunter chaser, half-sister to dam of useful staying chaser Amble Speedy: won bumper at Leopardstown on debut in December: won maiden there in February on first completed start over hurdles: best effort when 3½ lengths second to easy winner Sadlers Wings in Grade 2 novice at Fairyhouse: should stay beyond 2½m. *P. Hughes, Ireland* **h126 F100**

POINT OF ORIGIN (IRE) 7 b.g. Caerleon (USA) – Aptostar (USA) (Fappiano (USA)) [2003/4 h–: c20s* c20s^pu c19g^pu c20d^pu Apr 24] smallish, lengthy gelding: 33/1-winner of handicap at Huntingdon on chasing debut in January: little other form: stays 2½m: acts on soft going: has had tongue tied, including last 2 starts. *C. C. Bealby* **c92 d h–**

POITIERS (FR) 5 b.g. Bering – Prusse (USA) (Ogygian (USA)) [2003/4 17g^5 18s^F 17s^4 18s* 16f* 21v^3 16d^3 17g 19g^3 16d^2 c17s^2 Apr 17] leggy ex-French gelding: third foal: half-brother to fair chaser around 2m Patterson and 8.5f winner Loving Smile (both by Sillery): dam maiden: fair hurdler: won claimer (claimed from J. Bertran de Balanda €18,000) at Auteuil in October and novice at Wincanton in November: 6 lengths second of 3 finishers to Atum Re in novice at Bangor on chasing debut: stays 21f: acts on any going: visored in Britain. *M. C. Pipe* **c103 h106**

POLAR CHAMP 11 b.g. Polar Falcon (USA) – Ceramic (USA) (Raja Baba (USA)) [2003/4 c132, h130: 27g^pu 27g c26d Mar 18] sturdy gelding: useful hurdler/chaser at best, left M. Pipe after second outing: won first 3 starts in points in 2004: set strong pace and soon beaten once headed eighteenth in Foxhunter at Cheltenham: stays 33f: acts on any going: blinkered twice, usually visored nowadays. *D. Pipe* **c– h–**

POLAR GUNNER 7 b.g. Gunner B – Polar Belle (Arctic Lord) [2003/4 h–, F69: 21m^4 Sep 5] good-topped gelding: well held over hurdles: has had tongue tied. *J. M. Jefferson* **h–**

POLAR PROSPECT 11 b.g. Polar Falcon (USA) – Littlemisstrouble (USA) (My Gallant (USA)) [2003/4 c21d^pu c24m^pu c20d Mar 25] workmanlike gelding: one-time smart hurdler/fairly useful chaser: no show in 3 hunters, left Mrs M. McGuinness after first: stays 2½m: acts on good to firm and heavy going: effective blinkered or not. *Miss Sarah George* **c– h–**

POLAR RED 7 ch.g. Polar Falcon (USA) – Sharp Top (Sharpo) [2003/4 h141: c16d^2 c19s* c16v* c17s^ur c20g^6 c20g^3 c19m* Apr 13] angular gelding: useful hurdler: successful 3 times over fences, in novices at Chepstow in December and February and Exeter, **c139 h–**

Chepstow On-Course Bookmakers Novices' Chase—
Polar Red (stripes) and Le Duc both make mistakes two out, Le Duc coming down

simple tasks last 2 occasions: better form in handicaps, including when third to Keltic Bard in amateur novice at Aintree: barely stays 2½m: acts on heavy and good to firm going: usually visored over hurdles. *M. C. Pipe*

POLAR SCOUT (IRE) 7 b.g. Arctic Lord – Baden (IRE) (Furry Glen) [2003/4 c21g⁵ c24s³ c22g* c24gᵘʳ c22g² 22g* Apr 10] IR £45,000 4-y-o: rather leggy ex-Irish gelding: second foal: half-brother to smart 2m hurdler/chaser Thisthatandtother (by Bob Back): dam fairly useful hurdler who stayed 19f: modest hurdler: sold out of T. Walsh's stable 16,000 gns Doncaster May Sales: won 16-runner novice handicap at Newton Abbot in April: similar form over fences: won handicap at Market Rasen in February: best up to 2¾m: acts on any going: tongue tied last 5 starts. *C. J. Mann*   c97 h96

POLAR SUMMIT (IRE) 8 b.g. Top of The World – Blackrath Beauty (Le Tricolore) [2003/4 c24sᶠ c25dᶠ Jan 7] rangy gelding: poor form on first of 2 starts over hurdles in 2001/2: not fluent and fell both outings in handicap chases on return. *N. A. Twiston-Davies*   c– h–

POLIANTAS (FR) 7 b.g. Rasi Brasak – Popie d'Ecorcei (FR) (Balsamo (FR)) [2003/4 c151, h–: c20g² Nov 15] leggy gelding: very smart chaser: ran well when 8 lengths second of 9 to Fondmort in valuable handicap at Cheltenham (collapsed and died after race): best around 2½m: acted on heavy and good to firm going. *P. F. Nicholls*   c155 h–

POLICASTRO 6 b.g. Anabaa (USA) – Belle Arrivee (Bustino) [2003/4 h–: 16mᵖᵘ May 5] maiden on Flat: pulled up both starts over hurdles. *Miss K. M. George*   h–

POLISH BARON (IRE) 7 b.g. Barathea (IRE) – Polish Mission (Polish Precedent (USA)) [2003/4 h84: 16g 16v³ 17d c20g⁴ c17g⁶ c16s* c24s³ Apr 21] close-coupled gelding: modest hurdler, claimed from J. White £5,000 on Flat after reappearance: modest form on chasing debut: won 3-finisher novice at Towcester in April from reluctant Circus Maximus, jumping erratically: stays 2½m: acts on any ground. *J. R. Cornwall*   c89 h88

POLISH CLOUD (FR) 7 gr.g. Bering – Batchelor's Button (FR) (Kenmare (FR)) [2003/4 h98: 16g² 16d³ 17s² 22d² 24d⁶ 21g 19g⁴ 20d* Apr 22] medium-sized gelding: fair handicap hurdler: largely creditable efforts in 2003/4, won conditional jockeys event at Perth in April: effective at 2m to 2¾m: acts on soft going, below form on good to firm: races prominently. *T. R. George*   h106

POLISHED   5 ch.g. Danzig Connection (USA) – Glitter (FR) (Reliance II) [2003/4   c85 +
h76: 17s^{pu} 17d 17v^2 c16v* c16s* c19g^{ur} Mar 5] leggy gelding: best effort over hurdles   h85
when second in selling handicap at Sedgefield in January: successful both completed
starts over fences, in handicaps at Newcastle (novice) and Sedgefield within 7 days in
February: raced mainly around 2m. acts on heavy going. *R. C. Guest*

POLISH LEGEND   5 b.g. Polish Precedent (USA) – Chita Rivera (Chief Singer)   h82
[2003/4 h67: 17s^4 16g^{pu} 17g^F 17m 17d^2 16d^3 Apr 8] poor maiden hurdler, left B. Baker
after reappearance: raced around 2m: acts on good to soft going, probably on firm: tried
blinkered: tongue tied last 4 starts. *B. R. Millman*

POLISH PADDY (IRE)   6 b.g. Priolo (USA) – Polish Widow (Polish Precedent   h–
(USA)) [2003/4 h87: 20s 22g^{pu} 24s^{pu} 26s^{pu} Jan 7] compact gelding: handicap hurdler: left
J. W. Mullins, no show in 2003/4: stays 25f: blinkered/visored. *A. G. Hobbs*

POLISH PILOT (IRE)   9 b.g. Polish Patriot (USA) – Va Toujours (Alzao (USA))   c74
[2003/4 c73, h–: c20m^3 c17d^3 c17g* c17g c16f^2 c17m^4 c16f^3 c16g^3 c16d c16g^4 c16d^4 h–
c17d^3 Apr 24] smallish gelding: poor hurdler/chaser: first win over fences in handicap at
Market Rasen in May: best around 2m: acts on any going: tried blinkered/tongue tied
earlier in career. *J. R. Cornwall*

POLITBURO   9 b.g. Presidium – Kitty Come Home (Monsanto (FR)) [2003/4 c72,   c–
h–: c17g^{pu} 16g^{pu} Jun 27] lengthy gelding: winning chaser/maiden hurdler, has lost his   h–
form: raced mainly around 2m: acts on firm ground: tried in cheekpieces. *N. J. Gifford*

POLITICAL CRUISE   6 b.g. Royal Fountain – Political Mill (Politico (USA))   h–
[2003/4 F–: 20d 20s 22g Mar 28] smallish gelding: little sign of ability: blinkered (gave
trouble in preliminaries) final start in 2002/3. *R. Nixon*

POLITICAL SOX   10 br.g. Mirror Boy – Political Mill (Politico (USA)) [2003/4 c–,   c–
h91: 24g^3 22g^3 24d^2 24g* 24d^4 17m^6 22g^2 24g^4 20d^5 24d 16s 20v^5 25g 22g 22g^4 24s^5 h98
17d^5 20d^2 Apr 22] compact gelding: modest handicap hurdler: won conditional jockeys
event at Perth in June: effective at testing 2m to 27f: acts on good to firm and heavy going:
tried blinkered/in cheekpieces: best around 2m. *R. Nixon*

POLLENSA BAY   5 b.g. Overbury (IRE) – Cloncoose (IRE) (Remainder Man) [2003/4   h89
F16m^4 F16m^6 F17m^2 16m^3 17d 21d^4 20g^{pu} 21g^6 24d^{pu} 20s^{pu} Apr 17] €11,000 3-y-o: F85
smallish gelding: sixth foal: half-brother to fairly useful chaser Cassia Heights (by Montelimar), stays 27f: dam, lightly raced in bumpers/over hurdles, half-sister to very smart
staying chaser Father Delaney: modest form in bumpers: easily best effort over hurdles
when fourth in maiden at Ludlow: should stay 3m: visored final outing. *S. A. Brookshaw*

POLLIGANA   8 b.g. Lugana Beach – Pollibrig (Politico (USA)) [2003/4 h85: 22m^3 c88
c26g^2 c26g^5 Apr 10] modest novice hurdler: similar form on first of 2 starts over fences: h86
stays 3¼m: acts on good to firm going. *V. R. A. Dartnall*

POLLY'S PRIDE   5 b.m. Syrtos – Polly Minor (Sunley Builds) [2003/4 F16s^{pu} Dec   F–
19] £1,300 3-y-o, £2,800 4-y-o: leggy mare: second foal: half-sister to 2m hurdle winner
Carly Bay (by Carlton): dam modest hurdler up to 2¾m: went wrong in bumper on debut.
C. L. Popham

POLO PONY (IRE)   12 b.g. The Noble Player (USA) – Mangan Lane (Le Moss)   c– x
[2003/4 c25d^{ur} Mar 11] sturdy gelding: winning hurdler/chaser: poor pointer nowadays: h–
thorough stayer: acts on soft and good to firm going: tried blinkered/in cheekpieces: often
let down by jumping. *Mrs K. D. Horan*

POLY AMANSHAA (IRE)   12 b. or br.g. Nashamaa – Mombones (Lord Gayle   c109 §
(USA)) [2003/4 c108§, h–: c20m^{pu} c20m^5 c21m^4 c20g* c20g* Nov 11] workmanlike   h–
gelding: fair handicap chaser: won twice at Huntingdon in November: stays 21f: acts on
firm and soft going: inconsistent. *M. C. Banks*

POLYANTHUS JONES   5 b.m. Sovereign Water (FR) – Cindie Girl (Orchestra)   F96
[2003/4 F16s F16g^2 Mar 4] 13,000 4-y-o: seventh foal: half-sister to several winners,
including fairly useful chaser Dorans Gold (by Gildoran), stays 3m: dam, fairly useful
hurdler, stayed 21f: much better effort in mares bumpers when 2 lengths second to
Candello at Ludlow. *H. D. Daly*

POLYPHON (FR)   6 b.g. Murmure (FR) – Petite Folie (Salmon Leap (USA)) [2003/4   c85
c20g^2 c21s^{pu} 20v^6 c16g^3 c17g Apr 5] fourth foal: dam maiden: modest form on second of   h74
2 starts in 4-y-o hurdles at Auteuil in 2001/2: left T. Trapenard, won first of 2 outings in

points in 2003: modest form in steeplechases, left Miss P. Robson after first start: likely
to prove best at 2m. *P. Monteith*

POLYPHONY (USA)   10 b.g. Cox's Ridge (USA) – Populi (USA) (Star Envoy   **c–**
(USA)) [2003/4 c–, h67: 20g⁵ 17g 17sᵖᵘ 22sᵖᵘ Jan 2] lengthy gelding: of little account   **h–**
nowadays: tried visored. *D. C. O'Brien*

POMPEII (IRE)   7 b.g. Salse (USA) – Before Dawn (USA) (Raise A Cup (USA))   **h83**
[2003/4 17g⁴ 17m* 17f² 16g 17d⁶ 17s 16s² 19d² 17sᵖᵘ 16g 16d Mar 22] neat gelding: poor
hurdler: left R. Thompson, won novice handicap at Market Rasen in September: effective
at 2m to 2½m: acts on firm and soft going: tongue tied once. *A. J. Lockwood*

PONTIUS   7 b.g. Terimon – Coole Pilate (Celtic Cone) [2003/4 c84x, h104: c22g*   **c104 x**
c21dᵘʳ May 30] tall, leggy gelding: fair hurdler/chaser: won handicap over fences at   **h–**
Kelso (much better round of jumping than usual) in May: stays 27f: raced on good going
or softer. *N. A. Twiston-Davies*

POONY HAW   5 b.m. Minster Son – Miss Brook (Meadowbrook) [2003/4 F16g 16dᵖᵘ   **h–**
24dᵖᵘ 18sᵖᵘ 20gᵖᵘ Jan 23] second foal: dam no sign of ability over hurdles: of little   **F–**
account: tried in cheekpieces/visor. *W. S. Coltherd*

POP GUN   5 ch.g. Pharly (FR) – Angel Fire (Nashwan (USA)) [2003/4 16m 20g³ 21mᵖᵘ   **h75**
Nov 13] sturdy gelding: fair on Flat (may prove best short of 2m), successful twice in
2003 for B. Hills: poor form first 2 starts in maiden hurdles. *Miss K. Marks*

POPPY'S PROGRESS   7 ch.m. Carlton (GER) – Countess Blakeney (Baron Blak-   **F–**
eney) [2003/4 F–: F16m May 26] lengthy mare: no form in 3 bumpers. *T. D. McCarthy*

PORAK (IRE)   7 ch.g. Perugino (USA) – Gayla Orchestra (Lord Gayle (USA))   **h–**
[2003/4 h116: 16m May 31] close-coupled gelding: fairly useful hurdler in 2002/3: not
fluent and never a factor only start in 2003/4: raced around 2m: acts on soft going (won
on good to firm on Flat). *G. L. Moore*

PORNIC (FR)   10 b.g. Shining Steel – Marie de Geneve (FR) (Nishapour (FR)) [2003/4   **c80 §**
c–§, h96§: 17d 16d⁵ 19g⁴ c20m² c17s⁶ c19g c20d c21d² c21g⁴ c20d* Apr 24] workman-   **h86 §**
like gelding: modest handicap hurdler: poor handicap chaser: found more for pressure
than usual when winning at Market Rasen: stays 21f: acts on good to firm and heavy
going: tried visored: unreliable. *A. Crook*

PORTANT FELLA   5 b.g. Greensmith – Jubilata (USA) (The Minstrel (CAN))   **h116**
[2003/4 16v⁴ 16f* 16m* 16m* 16f² 16g 16m 16m 16dᵇᵈ 16d Apr 13] rather leggy gelding:
fairly useful on Flat (stays 9.5f): fairly useful handicap hurdler: successful at Sligo,
Navan and Cork in summer: back to form when fourth at Punchestown in late-April: best
at 2m with emphasis on speed: acts on firm ground. *Ms J. Morgan, Ireland*

PORT DU SALUT (FR)   4 br.g. Garde Royale – Landevennec (FR) (Gairloch)   **h–**
[2003/4 F14g 16g Jan 17] good-bodied gelding: third foal: half-brother to 7f/9f winner in   **F–**
Italy by Bishop of Cashel: dam maiden: ninth of 17 in 3-y-o bumper at Warwick on debut:
not fluent when tailed off in juvenile hurdle. *A. Ennis*

PORTICHOL PRINCESS   4 b.f. Bluegrass Prince (IRE) – Barbrallen (Rambo   **h–**
Dancer (CAN)) [2003/4 16sᵖᵘ 16d 16s 17d Mar 15] little sign of ability on Flat and over
hurdles: tried tongue tied. *R. M. Stronge*

PORT MORENO (IRE)   4 b.g. Turtle Island (IRE) – Infra Blue (IRE) (Bluebird   **h93**
(USA)) [2003/4 17m 17g² Apr 3] modest on Flat (stays 1½m): blinkered, much better
effort over hurdles at Hereford when second in novice seller. *J. G. M. O'Shea*

POSH PEARL   9 b.m. Rakaposhi King – Rim of Pearl (Rymer) [2003/4 h91+: 20s²   **h98**
May 22] leggy mare: useful bumper performer in 2000/1: off nearly 2 years, modest form
when placed in mares novices both completed starts over hurdles: may prove best short
of 2½m. *Miss Venetia Williams*

POSH STICK   7 b.m. Rakaposhi King – Carat Stick (Gold Rod) [2003/4 h65, F–: 16g⁴   **h65**
16g⁵ 20m⁵ 20d⁵ Jul 2] sturdy mare: poor maiden hurdler: won point in April: stays 2½m:
acts on good to soft and good to firm going. *J. B. Walton*

POSITIVE PROFILE (IRE)   6 b.g. Definite Article – Leyete Gulf (IRE) (Slip   **h116**
Anchor) [2003/4 h83: 16g* 19g* 25d³ Dec 12] rather sparely-made gelding: fairly useful
hurdler: won novice at Kelso and handicap at Doncaster (flicked tail under pressure) in
November, beating Javelin 6 lengths in latter: barely stays 25f: acts on good to soft going:
carries head high. *P. C. Haslam*

POSSIBLE PARDON (NZ) 10 b.g. Iades (FR) – Wonderful Excuse (NZ) (Alibhai **c109 x** (NZ)) [2003/4 c119x: c26g⁶ c26g⁴ c24dᵖᵘ Dec 5] medium-sized gelding: fair handicap chaser: not at best in 2003/4, lame final start: should stay beyond 27f: acts on heavy going: blinkered: often less than fluent: takes plenty of driving. *P. J. Hobbs*

POTTS OF MAGIC 5 b.g. Classic Cliche (IRE) – Potter's Gale (IRE) (Strong Gale) **F71** [2003/4 F16d Mar 21] first foal: dam, useful hurdler/fairly useful chaser, effective at 2m to 21f: seventh in bumper at Stratford on debut. *R. Lee*

POTTSY'S JOY 7 b.g. Syrtos – Orange Spice (Orange Bay) [2003/4 F17d 16d⁵ 16d **h93** 19gᶠ 20d⁵ Mar 22] 3,800 4-y-o: workmanlike gelding: ninth foal: dam unraced, out of **F—** half-sister to dam of top-class staying chaser Spanish Steps: backward, well held in bumper on debut: modest form over hurdles: stays 2½m: raced only on good/good to soft going. *Mrs S. J. Smith*

POUGATCHEVA (FR) 5 ch.m. Epervier Bleu – Notabilite (FR) (No Pass No Sale) **h94** [2003/4 20s³ 16v* 17g⁴ 20m⁵ 22m⁵ 17d 16s³ 19s⁶ 19s* 21g⁴ 21d Mar 1] sparely-made mare: seventh foal: half-sister to fair hurdler/winning chaser Noisetine (by Mansonnien), stays 2¾m, and winning hurdler/chaser up to 19f Treize Mars (by Perrault): dam maiden half-sister to useful hurdler/chaser up to 2½m Saint Preuil, out of very smart chaser up to 29f Montecha: modest hurdler (trained in 2002/3 by G. Macaire): won mares novice at Uttoxeter in May and amateurs mares handicap at Hereford in February: stays 21f: acts on heavy going, seemingly not on good to firm. *Miss Venetia Williams*

POUNSLEY MILL (IRE) 11 b.g. Asir – Clonroche Abendego (Pauper) [2003/4 **c96** c20g* c19m³ c21s² Dec 30] sturdy gelding: maiden hurdler: modest handicap chaser: **h—** won at Fontwell in May on return from 2-year absence: stays 21f: acts on heavy and good to firm going. *N. J. Gifford*

POWDER CREEK (IRE) 7 b.g. Little Bighorn – Our Dorcet (Condorcet (FR)) **h96** [2003/4 F104: 20d³ 16s⁶ 16d 16d² 20d⁴ 16g³ Apr 5] well-made gelding: modest hurdler: won maiden at Wetherby in March, idling: stays 2½m: raced on good going or softer. *Mrs M. Reveley*

POWER ELITE (IRE) 4 gr.g. Linamix (FR) – Hawas (Mujtahid (USA)) [2003/4 **h133** 16s³ 16s* 16d* 16d³ Apr 13]

Some of Ireland's leading juvenile hurdlers did well on their visits to Britain, with Al Eile winning the Anniversary Hurdle at Aintree and Top Strategy finishing third in the Triumph Hurdle at Cheltenham. However, the pick of the Irish was Power Elite who was not seen out in Britain. He was an intended runner in the Triumph but failed to scope cleanly beforehand and didn't make the trip. When he did get the chance to take on the best juveniles on both sides of the Irish Sea, at Punchestown after the end of the season in Britain, he fluffed his lines. Power Elite started favourite for the Champion Four Year Old Hurdle, taking on the likes of Al Eile, Top Strategy and a four-strong raiding party from Britain headed by the Triumph winner Made In Japan, but a blunder at the first was a bad start and Power Elite was unable to recover from another mistake three out, eventually finishing only eighth behind another of the British challengers, Cherub.

Power Elite was a 45,000 guineas purchase from Andre Fabre's stable at the Newmarket Autumn Sales. He was a useful performer on the Flat, and won a seven-furlong listed race at Deauville as a two-year-old. He failed to add to that success at three, however, and showed signs of temperament, his trainer fitting him with cheekpieces and then blinkers, but to no avail. It looked as though Power Elite's quirks were going to get the better of him over hurdles too when he found little on his debut for his new stable at Gowran in January, finishing third in a twenty-runner juvenile maiden. That turned out to be quite a well-contested affair, because Nopekan and Quel Doun, fifth and second respectively at Gowran, chased home Power Elite on his next start when he won the Grade 2 Cashmans Juvenile Hurdle at Leopardstown in February. Power Elite did nothing wrong this time, quickening to lead on the run-in and winning comfortably despite being hampered by the third. Top Strategy was also in the field, and came out best at the weights, not far behind in fourth. It was Power Elite's next race which established his claims to being Ireland's top juvenile hurdler. He was again up against Top Strategy in the Tattersalls (Ireland) Derby Sale Juvenile Hurdle at Fairyhouse later in February but Top Strategy ran poorly, and it was the two hurdling debutants in the line-up who gave Power Elite most to do. Held up, Power Elite cruised up to the leaders between the last two flights and, after briefly hanging right, kept on well to beat stable-companion Wild Passion, formerly a useful Flat performer himself in Germany, by half a length, the pair eleven lengths clear of another German import Zeroberto. Forced to miss Cheltenham, Power Elite was returned to Fairyhouse in April to take on older rivals in the Menolly Homes Novices' Hurdle. He confirmed the improvement he had shown the time before in finishing two lengths third to the favourite Royal Alphabet, travelling as well as the winner for much of the way and taking a good hold, then keeping on after taking time to quicken.

		Mendez (gr 1981)	Bellypha
	Linamix (FR)		Miss Carina
	(gr 1987)	Lunadix (gr 1972)	Breton
Power Elite (IRE)			Lutine
(gr.g. 2000)		Mujtahid (ch 1988)	Woodman
	Hawas		Mesmerize
	(ch 1995)	Alyakkh (b 1990)	Sadler's Wells
			Al Bahathri

Power Elite ran in the colours of Khalid Abdulla on the Flat, though was a rarity among his owner's runners in not having also been bred by Juddmonte Farms. He had been purchased for IR 190,000 guineas as a yearling and comes from a family whose members for the most part have carried the colours of Hamdan Al Maktoum. Power Elite's great grandam is the Irish One Thousand Guineas winner Al Bahathri who has bred several at least useful performers in a lengthy stud career,

Mr D. P. Sharkey's "Power Elite"

none better than the latest Two Thousand Guineas winner Haafhd. Power Elite's grandam Alyakkh was more modest, winning a maiden at Brighton over a mile, but she has bred a couple of good winners herself. One was the filly Nafisah, second in the Ribblesdale, and, more importantly from a jumping perspective, the other is Mutakarrim, a fairly useful hurdler and winning chaser in the latest season for Dermot Weld. Mutakarrim is also a smart performer at up to a mile and three quarters on the Flat, and Weld also trained his sister, Power Elite's dam Hawas, who won a mile maiden at Limerick. After first foal Power Elite, Hawas has since produced three-year-old Khulasah (by Darshaan) and Alexander Capetown (by Fasliyev), each lightly-raced maidens at the time of writing for Dermot Weld and Barry Hills respectively. The lengthy, well-made Power Elite has his quirks but has taken well to hurdling and appeals as one of those among the leading juvenile hurdlers to continue to do well. He has raced on good ground or softer so far, and is likely to prove best at around two miles for the time being. *N. Meade, Ireland*

POWER FACTOR (IRE)   8 ch.g. Fayruz – Shragraddy Lass (IRE) (Jareer (USA)) **h–**
[2003/4 17s 16d 16m 16d⁵ 16d 18f⁵ 18m Sep 23] ex-Irish gelding: bad maiden hurdler, trained first 5 starts by T. Nagle Jr: tried in headgear: usually tongue tied. *P. Butler*

POWER HIT (USA)   8 b.g. Leo Castelli (USA) – Rajana (USA) (Rajab (USA)) **h–**
[2003/4 h–: 22gᵖᵘ Jun 21] compact gelding: seems not to retain any ability: usually blinkered/visored. *K. Bishop*

POWER UNIT   9 ch.g. Risk Me (FR) – Hazel Bee (Starch Reduced) [2003/4 c100, **c109 x**
h90: c16m* c16mᵘʳ c20mᵖᵘ c19g³ c17sᵖᵘ 16g* Apr 18] workmanlike gelding: fair chaser: **h109**
won handicap at Worcester in May: took advantage of lower mark over hurdles in novice handicap at Stratford: stays 19f: probably acts on any going: visored fifth start, effective with or without cheekpieces: usually let down by jumping over fences. *Mrs D. A. Hamer*

POYNDER PARK (IRE)   13 b.g. Mandalus – So Deep (Deep Run) [2003/4 c87: **c77**
c25g⁵ Apr 30] fair pointer: similar form at best in hunter chases: wears cheekpieces. *Mrs J. Williamson*

POYNTON HENRY (IRE)   8 b.g. Supreme Leader – Short Memories (Quisling) **c–**
[2003/4 c19d c22sᵖᵘ c26s⁴ c26dᶠ c23d c21gᵖᵘ Apr 10] lengthy gelding: winning hurdler: **h–**
didn't impress with jumping over fences after 2-year-absence. *R. H. Buckler*

PRAETORIAN GOLD   9 ch.g. Presidium – Chinese Princess (Sunny Way) [2003/4 **c83**
c20dᶠ c21m⁴ c21m⁴ c22d 24d c16fᵘʳ c25mᵖᵘ c24g c24gᵖᵘ 16s 20d Dec 14] good-topped **h–**
gelding: winning hurdler/maiden chaser: generally out of sorts in 2003/4: probably stays 21f: acts on any going: has worn cheekpieces/blinkers: has looked moody. *N. F. Glynn, Ireland*

PRAIRIE MINSTREL (USA)   10 b.g. Regal Intention (CAN) – Prairie Sky (USA) **c97 §**
(Gone West (USA)) [2003/4 c98, h–: c20gᶠ c20m* c24m³ c24m³ c20f* c20m² c17g³ c20m⁵ **h–**
c20gᵖᵘ Apr 18] sturdy, close-coupled gelding: modest handicap chaser: won at Worcester in November and Leicester in December: effective around 2m to 3m: acts on any going: wore cheekpieces after reappearance: didn't jump fluently last 3 starts: not one to trust. *R. Dickin*

PRANCING BLADE   11 b.g. Broadsword (USA) – Sparkling Cinders (Netherkelly) **c97**
[2003/4 c119, h–: c24g c26m* c31gᵖᵘ c20d⁶ c24m* c24m Mar 4] rather leggy gelding: **h–**
modest handicap chaser nowadays: won at Warwick in November and Ludlow (conditional jockeys) in February: stays 3¼m: acts on firm and good to soft going: lame final start: usually front runner. *N. A. Twiston-Davies*

PRATE BOX (IRE)   14 b.g. Ela-Mana-Mou – Prattle On (Ballymore) [2003/4 c–, h–: **c97**
c24g² c25m⁴ Mar 9] angular gelding: veteran chaser: fair in hunter chases nowadays: **h–**
probably stays 3m: acts on any going: sometimes let down by jumping. *F. A. Hutsby*

PRAYERFUL   5 b.m. Syrtos – Pure Formality (Forzando) [2003/4 h–: 26mᵖᵘ 16m⁶ **h81**
17m⁶ 21m⁴ 20g³ 22g 19v³ 16s 19g³ 19s² Apr 11] poor maiden hurdler: stays 19f: best effort on soft going: wore cheekpieces last 5 starts. *B. N. Doran*

PRECIOUS LUCY (FR)   5 gr.m. Kadrou (FR) – Teardrops Fall (FR) (Law Society **h–**
(USA)) [2003/4 22g 17g Apr 10] ex-French mare: third foal: half-sister to winning hurdlers around 2m Wonderfall and Star of Wonder (both by The Wonder): dam placed up to 1½m on Flat: twice-raced around 1½m on Flat at 3 yrs for R. Hobson: well beaten in 2 mares events over hurdles. *C. J. Down*

PRECIOUS MYSTERY (IRE) 4 ch.f. Titus Livius (FR) – Ascoli (Skyliner) [2003/4   **h99**
16s 16s* 16g⁴ 19g⁶ 22g⁶ Apr 22] leggy filly: fair on Flat (stays 1m), sold out of J. Nicol's
stable 16,000 gns Newmarket Autumn Sales: best effort over hurdles when winning
fillies juvenile at Fakenham in January: likely to prove best around 2m: acts on soft going.
A. King

PREDESTINE (FR) 4 ch.g. Signe Divin (USA) – Smyrna (FR) (Lightning (FR))   **h102**
[2003/4 16s³ 17s* 20v² 20sᵖᵘ Feb 14] tall ex-French gelding: fifth foal: half-brother to
winning hurdler around 2m Spoon River (by Spud): dam unraced, from family of smart
2m hurdler Shawiya: fair form over hurdles (ran twice in April 2003 for L. Manceau),
winning juvenile at Hereford in January: may prove best short of 2½m: changed hands
38,000 gns Doncaster May Sales. *K. C. Bailey*

PREMIER CHEVAL (USA) 5 ch.g. Irish River (FR) – Restikarada (FR) (Akarad   **h–**
(FR)) [2003/4 16dᵖᵘ 21dᵖᵘ 17sᵖᵘ Feb 17] sturdy gelding: modest maiden on Flat (probably
stays 1½m): no show in 3 novice hurdles. *R. Rowe*

PREMIER DRIVE (IRE) 11 ch.g. Black Minstrel – Ballyanihan (Le Moss) [2003/4   **c– x**
c111, h–: c20gᶠ c20gᶠ 20m 16d 19d⁶ 20vᵖᵘ c22gᵘʳ 20v⁶ 20s Apr 4] workmanlike gelding: **h91**
one-time fair hurdler/chaser: modest form at best over hurdles in 2003/4, failed to
complete over fences: should stay 3m: raced mainly on good going or softer (acts on
heavy): has had tongue tied. *G. M. Moore*

PREMIER ESTATE (IRE) 7 b.g. Satco (FR) – Kettleby (IRE) (Tale Quale) [2003/4   **h103**
h79: 22g* 22d* 20d 20v* Jan 12] tall gelding: much improved in handicap hurdles in
2003/4, winning at Fontwell in November, Exeter in December and Fontwell again in
January: likely to be suited by 3m+: raced on good going or softer (acts on heavy).
R. Rowe

PREMIER GENERATION (IRE) 11 b.g. Cadeaux Genereux – Bristle (Thatch   **c83**
(USA)) [2003/4 c100, h–: 17gᵖᵘ c20sᵖᵘ 17s⁶ 16d⁶ c16s c16d⁶ c16m⁵ Mar 9] leggy   **h–**
gelding: winning chaser: one-time useful hurdler: poor form in 2003/4: raced mainly
around 2m: acted on good to firm and heavy going: won with/without blinkers, wore
cheekpieces last 5 starts: tried tongue tied: dead. *Dr P. Pritchard*

PREMIUM FIRST (IRE) 5 ch.g. Naheez (USA) – Regular Rose (IRE) (Regular   **h93 p**
Guy) [2003/4 F16g³ F16s* 20s⁵ 21d⁶ Apr 12] medium-sized gelding: first foal: dam   **F96**
unraced: won last of 3 starts in maiden Irish points in 2003: bought 30,000 gns Doncaster
August Sales: better effort in bumpers (tended to hang on first occasion) when winning at
Wetherby in January by neck from Born Leader: shaped as if needing more of a test of
stamina in maiden hurdles at Folkestone and Huntingdon: likely to do better.
Mrs H. Dalton

PRESENCE OF MIND (IRE) 6 ch.g. Presenting – Blue Rose (IRE) (Good Thyne   **h91**
(USA)) [2003/4 F17s 19sᵖᵘ 24g² 22g⁴ Apr 13] €13,500 4-y-o: first foal: dam unraced: **F66**
eighth foal on debut: modest form at Exeter last 2 starts in novice hurdles: stays
3m. *Miss E. C. Lavelle*

PRESENT GLORY (IRE) 5 br.g. Presenting – Prudent Rose (IRE) (Strong Gale)   **F80**
[2003/4 F17g Apr 13] sixth foal: half-brother to winning hurdler up to 2¾m Phar Glory
(by Phardante) and poor chaser Tall Tale (by Tale Quale), stays 3½m: dam unraced half-
sister to useful 2m to 2¾m hurdler/chaser King Wah Glory: badly outpaced soon after
halfway when ninth of 15 in bumper at Exeter on debut. *C. Tinkler*

PRESENTING ROXY (IRE) 6 br.m. Presenting – Two Hills Folly (IRE) (Pollerton)   **F–**
[2003/4 F16d Nov 26] IR £1,650 3-y-o: small, sturdy mare: second foal: dam, runner-up
in 2½m hurdle, out of half-sister to smart chaser up to 25f Firions Law: no sign of ability
in Irish points and mares bumper. *G. A. Harker*

PRESENTINGTHECASE (IRE) 6 b.g. Presenting – Let The Hare Run (IRE) (Tale   **c–**
Quale) [2003/4 17s 22g 21d c16dᵘʳ Apr 12] good-topped gelding: third foal: half-brother   **h–**
to fair hurdler/fairly useful chaser Coursing Run (by Glacial Storm), stays 3m: dam
unraced half-sister to useful 3m hurdler Direct, from family of useful long-distance
chaser Laura's Beau: no form in 3 runs over hurdles: unseated third on chasing debut.
Jonjo O'Neill

PRESIDIO (GER) 9 b.g. Konigsstuhl (GER) – Pradera (GER) (Abary (GER)) [2003/4   **c–**
16m 19vᵖᵘ c16g c20d⁶ c21gᵖᵘ Apr 10] close-coupled gelding: maiden hurdler: no form in   **h–**
2003/4, including over fences. *N. J. Hawke*

PRESTON BROOK 7 b.g. Perpendicular – Tommys Dream (Le Bavard (FR)) [2003/4 c24s^F c25g^5 16s^4 22g^6 Apr 24] sturdy gelding: would have been third but for falling last in hunter chase at Huntingdon on reappearance: modest hurdler: stays 3m, effective at much shorter: raced on good going or softer (acts on heavy) *M. W. Easterby* — c82 h92

PRESUMPTUOUS 4 ch.g. Double Trigger (IRE) – T O O Mamma's (IRE) (Classic Secret (USA)) [2003/4 17d^2 16g* 16d^5 Apr 17] behind in three 7f maidens at 2 yrs for A. Berry: fair form in juvenile hurdles: won at Kelso in March by ½ length from Rayshan: pulled hard in steadily-run event final start: likely to stay beyond 17f. *Mrs S. J. Smith* — h106

PRETTY BOY BLUE 9 gr.g. Portogon – Nicola Lisa (Dumbarnie) [2003/4 24v^pu 17s 16s^pu 17m c16s^bd Mar 24] no sign of ability. *W. Davies* — c– h–

PRIAISY (IRE) 5 b.g. Priolo (USA) – Daisy Dobson (Gorytus (USA)) [2003/4 F17m^3 F16g Aug 23] IR 10,000F, 10,000Y, 10,500 2-y-o, 2,000 3-y-o: sixth foal: dam unraced half-sister to fairly useful staying hurdler Mushtaaq and dam of useful 2m to 21f hurdler Warm Spell: third in bumper at Sedgefield on debut: well held in strongly-run event at Worcester following month. *J. Wade* — F81

PRIDE OF FINEWOOD (IRE) 6 ch.g. Old Vic – Macamore Rose (Torus) [2003/4 F16g Mar 6] €20,000 4-y-o: fifth foal: half-brother to winning Irish pointer by Montelimar: dam, placed in bumpers, half-sister to useful jumpers Loving Around and Verrazano Bridge, out of sister to smart staying hurdler Rose Ravine: failed to settle when tenth of 18 in bumper at Doncaster on debut. *Noel T. Chance* — F82

PRIDE OF PENLEE 4 b.g. Pontevecchio Notte – Kindly Lady (Kind of Hush) [2003/4 F18s Feb 9] second foal: dam winning pointer: showed little in bumper on debut. *J. D. Frost* — F–

PRIDE OF PENNKER (IRE) 11 b.m. Glacial Storm (USA) – Quitrentina (Green Shoon) [2003/4 c60, h–: c16m^F c20m c25m^4 22m^pu c16g^3 c20m^pu c20f^4 c19m^pu Oct 2] lengthy mare: winning hurdler: bad maiden chaser: stays 2¾m: acts on firm and soft going. *G. A. Ham* — c– h–

PRIDE OF THE OAKS 4 b.f. Faustus (USA) – Annabel's Baby (IRE) (Alzao (USA)) [2003/4 F17g Mar 28] second foal: dam, winning selling hurdler, best around 2m: showed nothing in mares bumper on debut. *G. G. Margarson* — F–

PRIDEWOOD DOVE 5 b.m. Alderbrook – Flighty Dove (Cruise Missile) [2003/4 F16g Aug 23] second foal: dam, once-raced in bumpers, from family of Champion Hurdle winner Flakey Dove: showed more temperament than ability in bumper on debut (hung badly right first bend). *R. J. Price* — F–

PRIESTS BRIDGE (IRE) 8 ch.m. Mr Ditton – Paddys Gale (Strong Gale) [2003/4 h120, F106: 17g^4 Sep 13] sparely-made mare: fairly useful hurdler: shaped well over inadequate trip when fourth to Rigmarole in handicap at Bangor only start in 2003/4: likely to prove best at 3m+: raced on good going or softer (acts on heavy): front runner. *N. A. Twiston-Davies* — h118

PRIMA CASA 4 ch.f. First Trump – Welcome Home (Most Welcome) [2003/4 F16s F16g Mar 6] lengthy, unfurnished filly: second foal: dam 1½m winner: well beaten in 2 mares bumpers. *P. T. Dalton* — F–

PRIMATICCIO (IRE) 9 b.g. Priolo (USA) – Martinova (Martinmas) [2003/4 c111+, h–: c25m^pu Mar 4] progressed into useful hunter chaser in 2002: returning from 21-month absence, no show only start in 2003/4: stays 3½m: acts on firm going: tried visored/blinkered. *Ian Williams* — c– h–

PRIME ATTRACTION 7 gr.m. Primitive Rising (USA) – My Friend Melody (Sizzling Melody) [2003/4 h81, F93: 20m^F Oct 10] leggy mare: bumper winner: modest on Flat (stayed 2m): poor form on completed start over hurdles: dead. *W. M. Brisbourne* — h–

PRIME MINISTER 10 ch.g. Be My Chief (USA) – Classic Design (Busted) [2003/4 h70: 17g^5 17m^4 19m^5 May 31] angular gelding: poor maiden hurdler: stays 19f: acts on soft and good to firm going: usually races up with pace: has pulled hard/looked less than keen. *G. E. Jones* — h70

PRIMITIVE JEAN 5 b.m. Primitive Rising (USA) – Gemma Jean (Derek H) [2003/4 F16g 16d^pu Dec 29] sixth foal: dam never ran: showed nothing in bumper and novice hurdle. *C. W. Fairhurst* — h– F–

PRIMITIVE RITES 7 b.g. Primitive Rising (USA) – Sun Goddess (FR) (Deep Roots) [2003/4 c25s^pu Feb 7] fifth foal: half-brother to fair chaser Oban (by Scottish Reel), suited — c–

by good test of stamina: dam 1¼m and 1½m winner in France: lightly-raced winning pointer: never a threat on hunter chase debut. *M. J. Brown*

PRIMITIVE SATIN   9 ch.g. Primitive Rising (USA) – Satinanda (Leander) [2003/4 c89: c25g^F Mar 28] fair hunter chaser: fell second only start in 2003/4: stays 25f: acts on good to soft going: wears blinkers. *Mrs R. Tate*   **c–**

PRIMITIVE WAY   12 b.g. Primitive Rising (USA) – Potterway (Velvet Prince) [2003/4 c94: c25d^5 c25g^5 c25m* c27g² c27d^pu c24f³ c24s² c25g^5 c27g^6 Apr 16] sturdy gelding: modest chaser: won handicap at Hexham in October: stays 25f: acts on firm and soft going: wears blinkers/cheekpieces. *Miss S. E. Forster*   **c95**

PRIMROSE HILL   11 b.m. Lord David S (USA) – Country Carnival (Town And Country) [2003/4 21m Jun 18] of no account: temperamental. *Ms A. E. Embiricos*   **h– §**

PRINCE ADJAL (IRE)   4 b.g. Desert Prince (IRE) – Adjalisa (IRE) (Darshaan) [2003/4 16f* 16m 16f 16s² Dec 19] useful-looking gelding: no sign of ability on Flat: 33/1, soon clear when winning juvenile at Kelso on hurdling debut in October: best subsequent effort when second in juvenile seller at Uttoxeter: headstrong. *G. M. Moore*   **h90**

PRINCE AMONG MEN   7 b.g. Robellino (USA) – Forelino (USA) (Trempolino (USA)) [2003/4 h101: 16g³ 16m* 16g* 17m 16s⁵ Apr 21] angular gelding: fair handicap hurdler: won at Uttoxeter (ladies event, idled) in June and Perth in July: raced around 2m: acts on any going: effective visored or not: has found little. *N. G. Richards*   **h114**

PRINCE AURUM   9 ch.g. Mystiko (USA) – Jarin Rose (IRE) (Jareer (USA)) [2003/4 18v 17s Jan 22] first foal: dam little sign of ability: no show in 2 novice hurdles. *B. G. Powell*   **h–**

PRINCE DARKHAN (IRE)   8 b.g. Doyoun – Sovereign Dona (Sovereign Path) [2003/4 17g^pu Jul 4] maiden on Flat: showed nothing in 2 starts over hurdles 2 years apart. *G. A. Harker*   **h–**

PRINCE DE GALLES   11 b.g. Prince Des Coeurs (USA) – Royal Brush (King of Spain) [2003/4 c–, h84: 24v⁴ 24g³ 26m 24m⁴ 24m^pu Sep 30] angular gelding: poor handicap hurdler: best at 3m+: acts on any going: usually blinkered: ungenuine. *P. Bowen*   **c–**
h74 §

PRINCE DIMITRI   5 ch.g. Desert King (IRE) – Pinta (IRE) (Ahonoora) [2003/4 h108+: 16d^pu 16m 20m⁵ 16m 16d⁶ Jan 19] good-topped gelding: fair juvenile hurdler in 2002/3: no form in 2003/4: tried visored/in cheekpieces: has had tongue tied: one to avoid. *M. C. Pipe*   **h– §**

PRINCE DU SOLEIL (FR)   8 b.g. Cardoun (FR) – Revelry (FR) (Blakeney) [2003/4 16d⁵ Nov 13] poor and ungenuine on Flat (stays 1m) nowadays: second start over hurdles, pulled hard when fifth in maiden at Fakenham: will need sharp 2m. *J. R. Jenkins*   **h75**

PRINCE HOLING   4 ch.g. Halling (USA) – Ella Mon Amour (Ela-Mana-Mou) [2003/4 16s^pu Feb 7] angular gelding: half-brother to winning 2¾m hurdler Myosotis (by Don't Forget Me): fairly useful on Flat (stays 1½m), sold out of J. Gosden's stable 26,000 gns Newmarket Autumn Sales: not fluent and dropped away 3 out in juvenile on hurdling debut. *Miss Venetia Williams*   **h–**

PRINCE IVOR   4 b.g. Polar Falcon (USA) – Mistook (USA) (Phone Trick (USA)) [2003/4 16g^pu Mar 15] poor maiden on Flat (may prove best around 1m): showed little in juvenile on hurdling debut. *J. C. Fox*   **h–**

PRINCE MILLENNIUM   6 b.g. First Trump – Petit Point (IRE) (Petorius) [2003/4 17g Aug 25] poor maiden on Flat (stays 1¼m): tailed off in maiden on hurdling debut. *R. A. Fahey*   **h–**

PRINCE NASSEEM (GER)   7 b.h. Neshad (USA) – Penola (GER) (Acatenango (GER)) [2003/4 19d⁵ Dec 2] good-topped horse: successful twice in Germany (raced mainly around 1m) at 4 yrs, in frame most starts in 2002, well held in Britain: tailed off in novice on hurdling debut. *A. G. Juckes*   **h–**

PRINCE OF PERILS   10 b.g. Lord Bud – Kumari Peril (Rebel Prince) [2003/4 c25d^F 20v 17s⁶ 27d* Mar 16] winning pointer: fell in hunter chase in May: best effort over hurdles when winning selling handicap at Sedgefield: stays 27f: raced on going softer than good. *J. S. Haldane*   **c–**
h79

PRINCE OF PERSIA   4 b.g. Turtle Island (IRE) – Sianiski (Niniski (USA)) [2003/4 16g^F 16s⁶ 16g⁴ 16s⁴ 16d* 16d⁵ Apr 21] leggy, close-coupled gelding: modest maiden on Flat (should stay 1¼m), no show in 2003 for D. Nicholls/R. Hannon: fair juvenile hurdler: won seller (sold from R. C. Guest 13,000 gns) at Ludlow in April: raced at 2m: acts on good to soft going: wore cheekpieces last 2 starts. *R. S. Brookhouse*   **h97**

PRINCE OF PLEASURE (IRE) 10 b.g. Spanish Place (USA) – Oronocco Gift **c119** (Camden Town) [2003/4 c110, h105: c17f² 16m* c17g⁶ 16m c18f⁴ 17s 20v 20s c16d **h105** c25dᶠ Apr 11] good-topped gelding: fair hurdler: won novice at Limerick in July: fairly useful handicap chaser: won competitive event at Punchestown in late-April by 3 lengths from Winning Dream: effective at 2m to 2½m: probably acts on any ground, very best form on good or firmer. *D. Broad, Ireland*

PRINCE OF SAINTS (IRE) 13 ch.g. Boyne Valley – Sandy's Daughter (Raise You **c–** Ten) [2003/4 c25d⁵ May 22] sturdy gelding: veteran chaser: poor pointer nowadays: acts **h–** on soft going: blinkered. *Miss L. Ingram*

PRINCE OF SLANE 5 b.g. Prince Daniel (USA) – Singing Slane (Cree Song) [2003/4 **F84** F98: F17m⁵ F16m³ F17g⁴ Apr 24] best effort in bumpers when second on debut in late-2002/3: left C. Grant and off 10 months before final start. *G. A. Swinbank*

PRINCE OF TARA (IRE) 7 b.g. Prince of Birds (USA) – Fete Champetre (Welsh **h127** Pageant) [2003/4 20d⁶ 24d⁵ 24sᴾᵁ 24s³ 24v³ 24s² Feb 15] strong, workmanlike gelding: fairly useful hurdler, missed 2002/3: best efforts in 2003/4 when placed last 2 starts, third to Shivermetimber in handicap at Punchestown and second to Rosaker in Grade 2 at Navan: stays 3m: raced on good going or softer (acts on heavy). *Patrick O. Brady, Ireland*

PRINCE OF THE WOOD (IRE) 4 ch.g. Woodborough (USA) – Ard Dauphine **h85** (IRE) (Forest Wind (USA)) [2003/4 16m³ 16s⁵ 16s⁶ Dec 20] strong, close-coupled gelding: modest maiden on Flat (stays 11.6f) for D. Cosgrove: seemingly best effort in juvenile hurdles when fifth at Huntingdon in November. *A. Bailey*

PRINCE SANDROVITCH (IRE) 10 b.g. Camden Town – Devon Royale (Le **c–** Prince) [2003/4 c–, h–: c26dᴾᵁ c22v⁶ c25gᴾᵁ c26g⁶ Apr 22] winning hurdler/pointer: no **h–** form in steeplechases: tried in cheekpieces. *Mrs Jane Galpin*

PRINCE SHAAMAAL 6 b.g. Shaamit (IRE) – Princess Alaska (Northern State **h79** (USA)) [2003/4 h72+: 16m May 5] poor form over hurdles: will prove best around 2m. *K. Bell*

PRINCE SLAYER 8 b.g. Batshoof – Top Sovereign (High Top) [2003/4 h86: 16m **h82** 16m⁴ 16d⁶ 16d 16s 16d⁴ Apr 11] poor maiden hurdler: likely to prove best at 2m: acts on heavy going, probably on good to firm: has worn cheekpieces: none too consistent. *T. P. McGovern*

PRINCE SORINIERES (FR) 9 br.g. Valanjou (FR) – Somewhat Better (Rheingold) **c117 §** [2003/4 c116, h–: c23g² c25m³ c23m⁴ c24g⁶ c26mᴾᵁ Jul 14] workmanlike gelding: fairly **h–** useful handicap chaser: moody efforts last 2 starts (bled from nose final one): stays 25f: acts on soft and firm going: tried blinkered/visored: one to be wary of. *M. C. Pipe*

PRINCESS AIMEE 4 b.f. Wizard King – Off The Air (IRE) (Taufan (USA)) [2003/4 **h–** 16gᴾᵁ 18sᴾᵁ Jan 26] fourth foal: half-sister to fairly useful hurdler Jollyolly (by Environment Friend), stays 21f, and prolific 1m/11f winner in Italy by Contract Law: dam, modest 5f to 9.4f winner on Flat, pulled up all 3 starts over hurdles: showed nothing in 2 juvenile hurdles. *P. Bowen*

PRINCESS CLAUDIA (IRE) 6 b.m. Kahyasi – Shamarra (FR) (Zayyani) [2003/4 **h72** h83: 21s² 20m 20gᴾᵁ 22g⁴ 22m³ 22m4 17m 27f⁴ 22g³ Sep 6] small, leggy mare: poor maiden hurdler: probably stays 27f: acts on soft and firm going: sold 3,900 gns Doncaster October Sales. *M. F. Harris*

PRINCESSE GREC (FR) 6 b.m. Grand Tresor (FR) – Perimele (FR) (Mon Fils) **c70** [2003/4 c–, h78: c20m² c16m⁴ c21m³ c16d³ c21g² c23mᴾᵁ c18m⁴ c22g c17f³ c20sᶠ Dec **h–** 26] plain mare: poor maiden hurdler/chaser: probably stays 21f: acts on soft going, probably on good to firm. *Dr P. Pritchard*

PRINCESS FAITH 4 b.f. Polar Prince (IRE) – Crissem (IRE) (Thatching) [2003/4 **h–** 17m⁴ 16sᶠ Nov 18] half-sister to 17f hurdle winner Freya Alex (by Makbul): no form on Flat (sold out of R. Hollinshead's stable £1,400 Ascot June Sales) or over hurdles. *A. J. Chamberlain*

PRINCESS GILLIE 5 br.m. Prince Daniel (USA) – Gilmanscleuch (IRE) (Mandalus) **F–** [2003/4 F17d F16g Mar 13] fourth foal: half-sister to winning 25f chaser Minsgill Glen (by Minster Son): dam, poor maiden hurdler/chaser, half-sister to dam of very smart staying hurdler Splendid Thyne: showed little in 2 bumpers. *Mrs J. K. M. Oliver*

PRINCESS MAGDALENA 4 ch.f. Pennekamp (USA) – Reason To Dance (Dam-**h–** ister (USA)) [2003/4 16g 16dᴾᵁ 17g Apr 16] modest on Flat (stays 1¼m): no form over hurdles. *L. G. Cottrell*

PRINCESS STEPHANIE 6 b.m. Shaab – Waterloo Princess (IRE) (Le Moss) [2003/4 F–: F16m 17m 16m 19f³ 16d Nov 13] little sign of ability: tried visored. *M. J. Gingell*   h– F–

PRINCESS TESSA 8 b.m. King's Ride – Kathy Cook (Glenstal (USA)) [2003/4 21g³ Dec 18] modest form first 2 starts in bumpers in 2001/2: remote third in mares novice on hurdling debut: should stay at least 2½m. *N. A. Twiston-Davies*   h–

PRINCE ZAR (IRE) 4 b.g. Inzar (USA) – Salonniere (FR) (Bikala) [2003/4 16m⁵ 16m⁶ Oct 9] half-brother to fairly useful hurdler/chaser around 2m Kissair (by Most Welcome): modest maiden on Flat (stays 8.5f), sold out of C. Cox's stable 2,800 gns Doncaster August Sales: tongue tied, showed little in 2 juvenile hurdles: blinkered second outing. *A. M. Hales*   h–

PRIORY WOOD 8 ch.m. Gunner B – Penlea Lady (Leading Man) [2003/4 h–: 21sᵖᵘ c16s⁴ c19dᵖᵘ Jan 7] good-topped mare: won mares bumper on debut in 2001/2: disappointing since: has had tongue tied. *M. Sheppard*   c– h–

PRISTEEN SPY 7 b.g. Teenoso (USA) – Sikera Spy (Harvest Spirit) [2003/4 24sᵖᵘ 20d⁴ 17d May 28] second foal: dam, fairly useful staying chaser, half-sister to smart staying chaser Ardent Spy and useful 2½m to 25f chaser Ida's Delight: signs of only a little ability over hurdles: returned to pointing and won in March (twice) and April. *R. Ford*   h–

PRIVATE BENJAMIN 4 gr.g. Ridgewood Ben – Jilly Woo (Environment Friend) [2003/4 16m* 16f Oct 28] leggy gelding: modest on Flat (stays 1½m): won juvenile at Plumpton on hurdling debut: tailed off in similar event at Cheltenham month later: will prove best around 2m. *Jamie Poulton*   h92

PRIVATE PETE 11 ch.g. Gunner B – Vedra (IRE) (Carlingford Castle) [2003/4 c104: c26v³ May 21] sturdy gelding: fair hunter chaser: stays 25f: acts on soft going: often let down by jumping. *Lady Connell*   c89 x

PRIZE RING 5 ch.g. Bering – Spot Prize (USA) (Seattle Dancer (USA)) [2003/4 17m* 16g⁶ 17g* 17g 16g⁶ 17g⁴ Apr 12] modest on Flat (stays 1½m), sold from Mrs J. Ramsden 14,000 gns after winning seller in August: modest novice hurdler: won twice at Sedgefield in September: raced around 2m on good/good to firm going. *G. M. Moore*   h95

PRO BONO (IRE) 14 ch.g. Tale Quale – Quality Suite (Prince Hansel) [2003/4 c–§, h–: c25dᵖᵘ Apr 30] lengthy gelding: hunter chaser, retains little ability: tends to make mistakes. *M. G. Hazell*   c– h–

PROBUS LADY 7 ch.m. Good Times (ITY) – Decoyanne (Decoy Boy) [2003/4 h–: 22m 17d⁴ Jul 27] signs of only a little ability in novice hurdles. *C. J. Down*   h66

PROBUS LORD 9 b.g. Rough Stones – Decoyanne (Decoy Boy) [2003/4 h–: 27s² 24mF 26m² Jun 11] quite good-topped gelding: modest novice hurdler: stays 27f: acts on soft and good to firm going. *C. J. Down*   h93

PROCEDURE (USA) 8 b. or br.g. Strolling Along (USA) – Bold Courtesan (USA) (Bold Bidder) [2003/4 c87, h–: c21sᵖᵘ 16mᵖᵘ May 7] good-topped gelding: maiden hurdler/chaser, no form either start very early in season or in points in 2004: raced mainly around 2m: acts on soft ground: takes good hold. *J. A. B. Old*   c– h–

PROFILER (USA) 9 b.g. Capote (USA) – Magnificent Star (USA) (Silver Hawk (USA)) [2003/4 c–, h–: c24m 18d Dec 1] big, rangy gelding: winning hurdler/chaser, little form for long time: wears headgear: sketchy jumper: has looked reluctant. *Ferdy Murphy*   c– h–

PROFOWENS (IRE) 6 b.g. Welsh Term – Cutty Sark (Strong Gale) [2003/4 F16d F16v² F16g Feb 28] workmanlike gelding: eighth foal: half-brother to winning 2½m hurdler Sarcastic (by Lafontaine) and winning 2m chaser Newtown Native (by Be My Native): dam unraced half-sister to dam of useful staying chaser Amble Speedy: fair form in bumpers (off 9 months after debut), second at Newcastle in February. *P. Beaumont*   F89

PROGRESSIVE (IRE) 6 ch.g. Be My Native (USA) – Move Forward (Deep Run) [2003/4 F16s* Dec 26] half-brother to several winners, including fairly useful hurdler up to 3m Green Light (by Lafontaine) and fair bumper winner Tell The Country (by Good Thyne): dam, lightly-raced maiden, half-sister to useful hurdler up to 2½m Stag Hill: favourite, won bumper at Huntingdon on debut by 1¼ lengths from Before Dark, barely coming off the bridle: smart prospect. *Jonjo O'Neill*   F109 p

PROKOFIEV (USA) 8 br.g. Nureyev (USA) – Aviara (USA) (Cox's Ridge (USA)) [2003/4 c–§, h121§: c20g* c20g* c22gᵖᵘ c24mᵖᵘ c23g⁵ c22g* c24dᵖᵘ c24s Apr 17]   c113 § h– §

724

angular gelding: fairly useful hurdler: fair chaser: won novice and handicap at Bangor in October and novice handicap at Newbury in March: effective at 2½m to 25f: acts on good to firm and heavy going: blinkered: has had tongue tied: moody. *Jonjo O'Neill*

PROMINENT PROFILE (IRE) 11 ch.g. Mazaad – Nakuru (Mandalus) [2003/4 c96, h–. c17m² c22g^{ur} c20d* c16s^{bd} c20d² c18s² c24d* c24g c24g⁵ c24d² Apr 23] angular gelding: fairly useful handicap chaser: won at Aintree in November and Sandown in February: effective around 2m to 3m: acts on good to firm and heavy going: tried blinkered: front runner. *N. A. Twiston-Davies*   **c122 h–**

PROMISES 4 b.f. Nashwan (USA) – Balliasta (USA) (Lyphard (USA)) [2003/4 F12g F13g⁵ F17s Jan 20] 5,500 3-y-o: sister to fairly useful 7f (at 2 yrs)/1m (in France) winner Kilting who stayed 1¼m and half-sister to 2 winners, including fairly useful 2001 2-y-o 1m winner Blackthorn (by Deploy) who stays 1½m: dam, ran twice, half-sister to Prix du Jockey Club winner Sanglamore out of Ribblesdale winner Ballinderry: best effort in bumpers when fifth at Doncaster in November. *D. Shaw*   **F76**

PROMISING (FR) 6 ch.m. Ashkalani (IRE) – Sea Thunder (Salse (USA)) [2003/4 h66: 16g³ 17m⁵ 17m 19g⁴ Jul 31] poor maiden hurdler: likely to prove best around 2m: acts on good to firm and good to soft going: tongue tied: poor jumper: none too reliable. *M. C. Chapman*   **h70 x**

PROPER POSH 6 b.m. Rakaposhi King – Rim of Pearl (Rymer) [2003/4 F17s F16v 21d^{pu} 20d^{pu} Mar 22] angular mare: fourth foal: sister to useful bumper winner Posh Pearl: dam, poor maiden hurdler, half-sister to dam of top-class 2m chaser Pearlyman: little sign of ability. *Mrs H. Dalton*   **h– F–**

PROPER SQUIRE (USA) 7 b.g. Bien Bien (USA) – La Cumbre (Sadler's Wells (USA)) [2003/4 h116: c24m* c25g³ c26m² c26m^F c24m³ c32g³ c30g³ c33d^F Apr 17] sturdy gelding: fairly useful handicap hurdler: similar form over fences: won novice at Fakenham in May: good third to Twisted Logic in handicap at Exeter final completed start: stays 4m: acts on soft and good to firm going: tried blinkered/in cheekpieces: not a fluent jumper of fences. *C. J. Mann*   **c115 x h–**

PROPERTY ZONE 6 b.g. Cool Jazz – Prime Property (IRE) (Tirol) [2003/4 c–, h100: 16d^{pu} May 16] tall, leggy gelding: fell second only outing over fences: fair handicap hurdler: amiss only start in 2003/4: raced around 2m: acts on good to firm and heavy going: has found little. *C. Grant*   **c– h–**

PROTECTION MONEY 4 ch.g. Hector Protector (USA) – Three Piece (Jaazeiro (USA)) [2003/4 16d 16d^{ur} 16d⁵ 21g² Mar 17] sturdy, lengthy gelding: half-brother to useful hurdler around 2m Dance So Suite (by Shareef Dancer): fair maiden on Flat (best effort at 1m): improved effort over hurdles when second in 21f selling handicap at Huntingdon: sold 7,000 gns Doncaster May Sales. *Mrs M. Reveley*   **h81**

PROTECTOR 7 b.g. Be My Chief (USA) – Clicquot (Bold Lad (IRE)) [2003/4 16g May 2] workmanlike gelding: modest handicap hurdler in 2001/2: tailed off on return: tried blinkered. *C. J. Price*   **h–**

PROTOCOL (IRE) 10 b.g. Taufan (USA) – Ukraine's Affair (USA) (The Minstrel (CAN)) [2003/4 h86: 17g 17f⁵ 16m 22g 17g³ 22g 16s* 17g⁴ Mar 28] compact gelding: modest handicap hurdler: won seller at Fakenham in March: should stay 2½m: best efforts on good going or softer (acts on heavy): tried visored/in cheekpieces: tongue tied: none too consistent. *Mrs S. Lamyman*   **h88**

PROUD PEER (IRE) 6 ch.g. Mister Lord (USA) – Raffeen Pride (Shackleton) [2003/4 F84: F16g May 2] thrice-raced in bumpers, well held only start in 2003/4. *M. Pitman*   **F–**

PROVENCE DREAMER 7 b.g. Alflora (IRE) – Kilbragh Dreamer (IRE) (Decent Fellow) [2003/4 h85, F91: 20g^{pu} 19g 24m^{pu} Aug 1] well-made gelding: maiden hurdler, no form in 2003/4. *Jonjo O'Neill*   **h–**

PROVERBIAL GRAY 7 ro.m. Norton Challenger – Clove Bud (Beau Charmeur (FR)) [2003/4 h63: 16g² May 2] poor maiden hurdler: raced around 2m: acts on good to soft going. *D. R. Gandolfo*   **h63**

PROVOCATIVE (FR) 6 b. or br.g. Useful (FR) – All Blue (FR) (Noir Et Or) [2003/4 F102: 20d* 20g 20s* 24s³ 22g Mar 28] tall, quite good-topped gelding: fair novice hurdler: easily won at Carlisle in November and Ayr in December: disappointing other 3 starts, possibly amiss: stays 2½m: acts on soft going. *M. Todhunter*   **h111**

Martell Cordon Bleu Handicap Hurdle, Aintree—
Puck Out comes with a well-timed run; Demi Beau's fall at the last leaves Fundamental second

PRUDISH LASS   7 b.m. Warcraft (USA) – Bella Delite (Uncle Pokey) [2003/4 F–:   **h–**
19gpu May 1] no sign of ability in bumper or mares novice hurdle 3½ months apart: sold
£1,000 Ascot June Sales. *A. J. Lidderdale*

PUCK OUT (IRE)   6 ch.g. Topanoora – Prosaic Star (IRE) (Common Grounds)   **h130**
[2003/4 16d* 16d 16m² 16s² 16s 16d* Apr 3] leggy gelding: half-brother to 2 winners on
Flat: dam 2-y-o 1m winner: won only start in bumpers: useful hurdler: won minor event
at Roscommon in June and listed handicap at Aintree in April, ridden clear after leading
2 out when beating Fundamental 4 lengths at latter: not certain to stay beyond 2m: acts on
soft and good to firm going: held up: may have further improvement in him. *C. Roche,
Ireland*

PUCKS COURT   7 b.g. Nomadic Way (USA) – Miss Puck (Tepukei) [2003/4 F–:   **h–**
17d⁶ 20gpu 22dpu 21d⁶ Mar 30] no sign of ability. *I. A. Brown*

PUCKS WAY   5 b.g. Nomadic Way (USA) – Adventurous Lady (Roman Warrior)   **h–**
[2003/4 h–: 16g⁵ Nov 7] no show in 2 races over hurdles. *D. G. Bridgwater*

PUDLICOTT MILL (IRE)   5 b.g. Definite Article – Mimining (Tower Walk)   **h–**
[2003/4 h–: 23mF 20g 16gpu May 30] no sign of ability. *M. F. Harris*

PULHAM DOWNE   9 ch.g. Baron Blakeney – Dame Nellie (Dominion) [2003/4   **c–**
c19spu Apr 6] winning pointer, including in February: no show in hunter on steeplechasing debut. *Mrs A. L. Tory*

PUNCHY (IRE)   8 b.g. Freddie's Star – Baltimore Fox (IRE) (Arapahos (FR)) [2003/4   **c111**
22gpu 20s* 22m* 20mpu 24m⁵ 26g* c23f* c24f² c20f⁵ c25d⁶ c19s⁶ c24g⁶ Feb 19]   **h113**
lengthy, workmanlike gelding: fair handicap hurdler: made all at Bangor and Fontwell
within 5 days in May: successful in novices at Uttoxeter and Exeter in October first 2
starts over fences: below form after next outing: likely to prove best short of 3¼m: acts
on soft and firm going. *M. C. Pipe*

PUNTAL (FR)   8 b.g. Bering – Saveur (Ardross) [2003/4 c–, h142: c16f* c19g²   **c147**
c20g* c20g* c16d⁴ c16s* c20s⁵ c16gur c36dur c29m* Apr 24]   **h–**
    What a way to go. The legendary radio commentator and writer John Arlott
completed his last Test match broadcast, in the Centenary Test match at Lord's in
1980 between England and Australia, with the plain words 'And after Trevor
Bailey, it will be Christopher Martin-Jenkins.' Asked why he hadn't said something
'romantic', he reportedly replied 'What's more romantic than the clean break?'
Contrast that with the orgy of self-congratulation and heavy-hearted messages read

out from the viewers that marked the final broadcast of attheraces. The satellite and cable channel dedicated to horse racing closed at the end of March after the collapse of an original ten-year deal. Arena Leisure—which co-owned attheraces with BSkyB and Channel 4—recorded post-tax losses of £12.2m for 2003 following the demise of the attheraces media rights deal. By June, however, two new channels had been launched showing live racing, a revamped At The Races (Channel 4 withdrawing as a partner) and the rival Racing UK (owned by the racecourses and promoted as providing signed-up courses with an opportunity to control their own TV rights). Both were initially free, though Racing UK, which has nearly all the top tracks (with the notable exception of Ascot), announced plans to become a subscription-based service. It remains to be seen whether operating separately is financially viable for either Racing UK or ATR. One thing is certain: racing's need for dedicated daily TV coverage was clearly illustrated by a worrying fall in credit and internet betting turnover in April and May.

The withdrawal of attheraces from sponsorship of what was originally the Whitbread Gold Cup at Sandown had been announced at the end of October, a sign of the company's financial worries. The prospect of the Whitbread losing its historic title had first alarmed traditionalists when the brewing giant announced in the 1999/00 season that it was pulling out of racing, largely because the sport was not attracting enough young people, Whitbread's target audience. The longest-running sponsorship in British sport—the Whitbread Gold Cup was inaugurated in 1957—earned a reprieve, but it proved short-lived. The first of only two runnings of the attheraces Gold Cup took place in 2002 and, in the latest season, the race had another sponsor, the bookmaker Fred Done. Done has built a betting empire of around four hundred shops, offering bonuses to customers on selected multiple bets and operating concessions such as paying 'first past the post' if placings are changed, as well as paying on the official result. If Fred Done can get everybody in racing thinking of the 'Whitbread' as the 'Betfred' it will be another feather in his cap. Two name changes for one of the season's great staying handicap chases in so short a space of time runs the risk of some loss of identity for the race and it is to be hoped the latest sponsorship lasts considerably longer than that by attheraces.

Champion trainer Martin Pipe won the Whitbread Gold Cup only once but now has the distinction of saddling a winner under all three of its guises. He had

CiSTM Fulke Walwyn Novices' Chase, Newbury—Puntal gains a third win from four starts in the autumn; a total of only nine took him on in these races as the dry weather took its toll

first and second, Bounce Back and Dark Stranger, from six runners in the first attheraces Gold Cup and, after runner-up Stormez had done best of his five representatives in the intervening running, he landed the first Betfred Gold Cup with 25/1-shot Puntal. Pipe was again heavily represented, sending out seven of the eighteen runners, with stable-jockey Tony McCoy, successful on Bounce Back, riding Stormez for the second year running. McCoy was out of luck this time, Stormez unseating him at the third. A winner six times over hurdles in 2002/3, Puntal started the latest season as a novice over fences, though he had shown useful form over the larger obstacles without winning when trained in France. He got off the mark at the first time of asking in Britain, jumping fluently when landing the odds from three previous winners over two miles at Cheltenham in October. He had made it three out of four by the end of November, adding further successes in very small fields at Cheltenham and Newbury, stepped up to two and a half miles. Puntal's jumping wasn't so fluent,

Betfred Gold Cup Chase (Handicap), Sandown—
Puntal is clear at the last but only just holds on from Royal Auclair (noseband)

though, and in later races he began to look none too reliable into the bargain, sometimes taking plenty of driving. Victory in a novice chase at Ascot at the end of January, which owed a lot to a typically-determined McCoy ride, was his only one in five other starts before the Betfred Gold Cup. Puntal downed tools completely tried in a visor first time in the Scilly Isles Novices' Chase at Sandown, a week after his Ascot win, and failed to complete the course in the Arkle Trophy (for which he started at 50/1) or in the Grand National (150/1). Puntal was one of the surprises of the Aintree showpiece, however, going with plenty of zest and jumping well for claiming rider Danny Howard, still third when the pair parted company at the nineteenth. Howard had excelled on Dark Stranger when he was runner-up in the attheraces Gold Cup and Puntal gave him the biggest triumph of his career so far in the Betfred when holding off Royal Auclair, whom Pipe used to train, by a short head. In terms of quality, the latest edition must rank as one of the worst in the history of the race (the top weight ran off a BHB mark of only 147). But, for Puntal, it provided proof that he possesses a good deal more stamina than had previously been appreciated. Another tilt at the Grand National will almost certainly be on the cards in the next season.

		Bering (ch 1983)	Arctic Tern (ch 1973)	Sea Bird II
				Bubbling Beauty
Puntal (FR)			Beaune (ch 1974)	Lyphard
(b.g. 1996)				Barbra
		Saveur (b 1988)	Ardross (b 1976)	Run The Gantlet
				Le Melody
			Youthful (b 1980)	Green Dancer
				First Bloom

The medium-sized Puntal was bred in France, as were the first three in the Betfred Gold Cup, though Puntal himself was Flat-bred and won twice on the Flat when trained in Spain as a three-year-old. His sire Bering, responsible for the Two Thousand Guineas winner Pennekamp and the Poulains winner American Post, has not proved so strong an influence for stamina at stud as might have been expected from his racing record—he won the Prix du Jockey-Club and was runner-up in the Arc. However, Puntal's unraced dam Saveur was stoutly bred, by Ardross out of French mile-and-a-half-winner Youthful, who also bred two notable half-brothers to Saveur in Beneficial and Jeune who completed a family double in the King Edward VII Stakes and the Hardwicke Stakes at Royal Ascot in 1993. Jeune was sent to Australia, to be joined in 1997 by Saveur (who has had winners there by Barathea and Charnwood Forest) after Jeune had made an even bigger name for himself when winning the two-mile Melbourne Cup. Front-running Puntal acts on any going. He had his tongue tied down on his last four starts. *M. C. Pipe*

PUPPET KING 5 b.g. Mistertopogigo (IRE) – Bold Gift (Persian Bold) [2003/4 **h–** 16gᵖᵘ 16g Nov 15] half-brother to winning pointer by Aragon: modest maiden on Flat at 2 yrs for I. Balding, tailed off both starts in 2003: showed nothing in 2 outings over hurdles: sold 1,000 gns Doncaster November Sales. *A. C. Whillans*

PURE BRIEF (IRE) 7 b.g. Brief Truce (USA) – Epure (Bellypha) [2003/4 h86: 20m⁶ c21m^ur c21m⁶ c16mᵖᵘ Aug 25] angular gelding: poor hurdler: little show over fences: best around 2m: acts on good to firm going: blinkered/visored. *Mrs J. Candlish* c–
h–

PURE FAST BELLEVUE (FR) 7 ch.m. Start Fast (FR) – Si Pure (FR) (Pure Flight (USA)) [2003/4 aF16g 20sᶠ 19dᵖᵘ 18dᵖᵘ Mar 21] seventh foal: half-sister to 1¼m winner Milady Si (by The Quiet Man): dam maiden: no sign of ability: tried tongue tied. *Jean-Rene Auvray* h–
F–

PURE FUN (IRE) 7 b.g. Lord Americo – Rath Caola (Neltino) [2003/4 h107: 24m² 27g* 27g⁶ 24m⁵ c23m³ Aug 2] compact gelding: fair handicap hurdler: won at Stratford in May: not fluent and looked unwilling on chasing debut: stays 27f: best form on good going or firmer: has looked difficult ride. *P. J. Hobbs* c–
h107

PURE MISCHIEF (IRE) 5 b.g. Alhaarth (IRE) – Bellissi (IRE) (Bluebird (USA)) [2003/4 h86: 16g³ 22d 20g^ur Jul 3] angular gelding: poor hurdler: claimed from Miss J. Feilden £6,000 on reappearance: likely to prove best around 2m: acts on soft going: successful on Flat in April for W. M. Brisbourne. *M. Todhunter* h83

PURE PLATINUM (IRE) 6 gr.g. Roselier (FR) – Waterloo Ball (IRE) (Where To Dance (USA)) [2003/4 F16s³ 25sᵖᵘ 19g 21g Mar 5] IR £34,000 3-y-o, €65,000 4-y-o: medium-sized gelding: first foal: dam, fair hurdler/chaser who stayed 25f, out of half-sister to useful hurdler/chaser up to 25f Boyneside: third in bumper at Uttoxeter on debut, shaping like a stayer: no form in 3 races over hurdles. *Jonjo O'Neill* h–
F89

PURPLE PATCH 6 b.m. Afzal – My Purple Prose (Rymer) [2003/4 F16m F16d⁴ F17g² Apr 1] £2,000 4-y-o: small, leggy mare: sixth foal: dam fair 2m chaser: failed to complete in 2 points in 2003: fair form in bumpers, second at Taunton: will stay beyond 17f. *C. L. Popham* F88

PURRFECT PRINCE (IRE) 6 b.g. Commanche Run – Castle Leney (Mandalus) [2003/4 F16s F16v⁶ 20vᶠ 22gᵖᵘ 25dᵖᵘ Mar 19] €48,000 4-y-o: rangy gelding: sixth foal: brother to bumper winner Vicci Van Dame: dam unraced, from family of 1968 Cheltenham Gold Cup winner Fort Leney: modest form on second of 2 starts in bumpers at Uttoxeter: no form in novice hurdles, bled from nose fourth outing. *Jonjo O'Neill* h–
F77

PUTSOMETNBY (IRE) 8 ch.g. Phardante (FR) – Bobs My Uncle (Deep Run) [2003/4 c124x, h106: c24gᶠ Sep 17] sturdy, lengthy gelding: fair hurdler: fairly useful chaser: in contention when falling fatally 3 out in valuable handicap at Listowel: stayed 4m: acted on firm and soft going: tried blinkered: often let down by jumping over fences. *Jonjo O'Neill* c– x
h–

PYRRHIC 5 b.g. Salse (USA) – Bint Lariaaf (USA) (Diesis) [2003/4 17m⁵ 16m⁵ Sep 27] modest maiden on Flat (stays 1¼m): signs of only a little ability in 2 outings over hurdles, in cheekpieces on second occasion. *R. M. Flower* h–

PYTHAGORAS 7 ch.g. Kris – Tricorne (Green Desert (USA)) [2003/4 h71: 17g 16g c16m⁴ 16m c16m c16mᵖᵘ Jul 16] sturdy gelding: poor maiden hurdler: no worthwhile form in novice chases: unlikely to stay much beyond 2m: acts on good to firm and good to soft going: has worn cheekpieces. *M. Sheppard* c–
h–

Q

QABAS (USA) 4 b.g. Swain (IRE) – Classical Dance (CAN) (Regal Classic (CAN)) [2003/4 16s 16g⁶ 16g Apr 12] sturdy gelding: fair but ungenuine maiden on Flat (stays 11.7f), sold out of A. Stewart's stable 29,000 gns Newmarket Autumn Sales and gelded: poor form at best in juvenile hurdles. *P. R. Webber* h71

QUABMATIC 11 b.g. Pragmatic – Good Skills (Bustino) [2003/4 h101: 22sᵇᵈ 20v 19g³ 22d 19d⁵ 17s⁶ 19v³ 19g Feb 19] leggy gelding: modest handicap hurdler: stays 2½m: raced mainly on good going or softer (acts on heavy): tried blinkered, not since 1999/00: inconsistent. *K. Bishop* h97

QUADCO (IRE) 10 b.g. Be My Native (USA) – Anega (Run The Gantlet (USA)) [2003/4 c116, h113: 17s 16d^ur c17m² c17g³ c20m* c17m² c16dᵖᵘ Nov 16] leggy gelding: fair hurdler/chaser: easily landed odds in maiden over fences at Tipperary in October: stays 2½m: acts on firm and soft going (won bumper on heavy): tried blinkered: has found little. *P. A. Fahy, Ireland* c109
h102

QUAINTON HILLS 10 b.g. Gildoran – Spin Again (Royalty) [2003/4 c–, h–: c20g^{pu} c20s³ c22v* c25s^{ur} 23v c20g² c23m² Mar 2] medium-sized gelding: modest handicap chaser: won at Towcester in November: has form on good to firm going, goes well on soft/heavy: sketchy jumper. *D. R. Stoddart*   **c98 x** **h–**

QUALICUM (IRE) 5 br.g. Son of Sharp Shot (IRE) – Rugged Perk (IRE) (Executive Perk) [2003/4 F16m F16m F16m F17g⁶ 16d 21d^{pu} 22s Jan 20] €7,400 3-y-o: rangy gelding: first foal: dam unraced, from family of useful hurdler/chaser up to 2½m Admiral's Cup: little sign of ability: left J. S. Moore after fifth start (blinkered). *G. Brown*   **h–** **F–**

QUALITAIR PLEASURE 4 b.f. Slip Anchor – Qualitair Ridge (Indian Ridge) [2003/4 F16g F16g* Mar 13] third foal: half-sister to 1½m/13f winner Cyber Santa (by Celtic Swing) and fairly useful 1m winner Indian Welcome (by Most Welcome): dam poor half-sister to fairly useful chaser up to 21f Saskia's Hero: left debut effort well behind when winning 10-runner bumper at Ayr in March by ½ length from Aces Four. *J. Hetherton*   **F87**

QUALITY FIRST (IRE) 11 b.g. Un Desperado (FR) – Vipsania (General Ironside) [2003/4 c128, h106: c20g⁶ 20v c20g³ Apr 18] good-topped gelding: winning hurdler: fairly useful handicap chaser: probably best up to 21f: acts on heavy and good to firm going: ran respectably in cheekpieces final start: has refused to line up: untrustworthy. *Mrs H. Dalton*   **c117 §** **h– §**

QUANGO 12 b.g. Charmer – Quaranta (Hotfoot) [2003/4 c22g⁵ May 24] workmanlike gelding: one-time fairly useful hurdler/fair chaser: successful 3 times in points, including in 2003 (well held in hunter): best form around 2m: acts on good to firm and heavy going: has worn blinkers/cheekpieces. *Miss J. E. Foster*   **c64 §** **h–**

QUARTER MASTERS (IRE) 5 b.g. Mujadil (USA) – Kentucky Wildcat (Be My Guest (USA)) [2003/4 h84: 21g^{pu} 17d² c16d⁶ c19g^F c16g c21s² c20s² c20s^{ur} c21d⁶ Mar 30] lengthy gelding: modest hurdler: poor novice chaser: stays 21f: acts on soft going: wore cheekpieces second outing: often races prominently. *G. M. Moore*   **c82** **h88**

QUARTERSTAFF 10 b.g. Charmer – Quaranta (Hotfoot) [2003/4 c101, h–: c25g^F c24g⁵ c24g^F c24g² Apr 10] lengthy gelding: fair handicap chaser: fortunate to win at Kelso very early in season: ran well after 10-month absence final outing: stays 25f: raced mainly on good going: has been let down by jumping. *C. R. Wilson*   **c110**

QUATRAIN (IRE) 4 ch.g. Anshan – Gray's Ellergy (Oats) [2003/4 F12s⁴ F16s F16g Mar 6] good-topped gelding: third foal: dam, fair staying hurdler, half-sister to Tolworth Hurdle winner Hawkbarrow: best effort in bumpers when seventh of 19 in maiden at Huntingdon second start: likely to be suited by further than 2m. *D. R. Gandolfo*   **F86**

QUAZAR (IRE) 6 b.g. Inzar (USA) – Evictress (IRE) (Sharp Victor (USA)) [2003/4 h152: 16d* 16f² 20g² 16s⁴ 16g⁵ 20g⁴ 21g 20d Apr 3] strong, compact gelding: smart hurdler: won Grade 1 Emo Oil Champion Hurdle at Punchestown in May 2003: generally below best after next outing, only seventh of 9 in latest renewal of race when blinkered (wore cheekpieces previous start): effective at 2m to 2½m: acts on any going: tongue tied: has run in snatches: tends to idle. *Jonjo O'Neill*   **h153**

QUEDEX 8 b.g. Deploy – Alwal (Pharly (FR)) [2003/4 h94: 24m^{pu} May 15] smallish, angular gelding: modest hurdler: lost action only start in 2003/4: stays 19f: acts on good to firm and good to soft going: has worn cheekpieces. *R. J. Price*   **h–**

QUEEN OF JAZZ 7 b.m. Sovereign Water (FR) – When The Saints (Bay Express) [2003/4 F–: 16g⁴ 25d^{pu} 19g⁵ 20s^{pu} Apr 17] leggy mare: no form. *V. Y. Gethin*   **h–**

QUEEN OF LIGHT (IRE) 4 b.f. Ali-Royal (IRE) – Blaze of Light (Blakeney) [2003/4 16m 16d Nov 29] leggy filly: half-sister to fairly useful hurdler/chaser Purevalue (by Keefah), stays 25f: modest form on second of 3 starts in maidens on Flat: well beaten both outings over hurdles. *J. K. Magee, Ireland*   **h–**

QUEEN OF THE SOUTH 7 b.m. Cut The Mustard (IRE) – Kawarau Queen (Taufan (USA)) [2003/4 c16d³ c16d³ c17g^{pu} c17d^{pu} c16d^{pu} Apr 22] lengthy mare: fifth foal: half-sister to winning hurdler Robert The Bruce (by Distinct Native), stays 2½m: dam 1m winner: placed once from 2 starts in maiden points in 2002: well beaten only completed outing in steeplechases. *L. Lungo*   **c–**

QUEEN'S BANQUET 7 b.m. Glacial Storm (USA) – Culinary (Tower Walk) [2003/4 F85: 20g^{pu} Oct 27] modest form in bumpers: breathing problem on hurdling debut: has looked temperamental (hung badly right and ran out final start in 2002/3). *P. R. Webber*   **h–**

QUEENSBERRY 5 b.g. Up And At 'em – Princess Poquito (Hard Fought) [2003/4 16d⁶ 17s⁴ 21d 19g Mar 26] medium-sized gelding: half-brother to poor 2m hurdler Magic   **h92**

Box (by Magic Ring) and winning pointer by Emarati: fair but ungenuine on all-weather on Flat (stays 1½m), successful 3 times in 2003 for N. Littmoden/J. Reilly, claimed out of latter's stable £8,000 in December: easily best effort over hurdles when fourth of 20 in novice at Folkestone. *Miss L. J. Sheen*

QUEENS BRIGADE   12 b.g. K-Battery – Queen of Dara (Dara Monarch) [2003/4 24s* 16d² 19v² Feb 2] close-coupled gelding: poor handicap chaser in 2001/2: returned in good form over hurdles, winning 16-runner selling handicap at Taunton in December: better form after when second in handicaps at Ludlow and Exeter: effective at 2m to 3m: acts on any going: amateur ridden. *Miss V. A. Stephens* — **c–** **h82**

QUEENSLAND BAY   5 ch.m. Primitive Rising (USA) – Hysteria (Prince Bee) [2003/4 F–: F17m⁶ Oct 18] tall mare: little show in 3 bumpers. *T. D. Easterby* — **F–**

QUEEN SORAYA   6 b.m. Persian Bold – Fairlead (Slip Anchor) [2003/4 F16m* F16g* F16s F17d⁶ Apr 3] rather unfurnished mare: third foal: half-sister to fair hurdler Follow Me (by Keen), stays 3m: dam 1m winner: fairly useful in bumpers: won at Ludlow in November (maiden) and December (mares): much better effort after when sixth of 15 to Diamond Sal in Grade 2 at Aintree. *Miss H. C. Knight* — **F96**

QUEEN'S PAGEANT   10 ch.m. Risk Me (FR) – Mistral's Dancer (Shareef Dancer (USA)) [2003/4 h104§: 24m⁴ Aug 2] compact mare: fair handicap hurdler: below best only outing in 2003/4: stays 2½m: acts on soft going: wore cheekpieces last 3 starts: none too reliable: sold 1,800 gns Doncaster November Sales. *J. L. Spearing* — **h92 §**

QUEENSWAY (IRE)   12 b.g. Pennine Walk – Polaregina (FR) (Rex Magna (FR)) [2003/4 c70, h–: c16m³ c16g⁶ c16m³ c16gᶠ Aug 4] sturdy gelding: handicap chaser, modest at best: barely stayed 19f: acted on firm and good to soft going: tongue tied: dead. *R. M. Carson* — **c64** **h–**

QUEENS WOOD   5 br.m. Abzu – Fleur de Tal (Primitive Rising (USA)) [2003/4 F17g Oct 11] angular mare: first foal: dam, winning 2m hurdler, half-sister to useful 5f to 7f winner Blakeset: soon well behind in mares bumper on debut. *N. M. Babbage* — **F–**

QUEL BON CHOIX (FR)   6 b.g. Tel Quel (FR) – Special Marianna (FR) (Kaldoun (FR)) [2003/4 19gᵖᵘ 22gᵖᵘ Jul 26] leggy gelding: third in 3-y-o event, only run over fences: fair hurdler in 2001/2: little sign of retaining ability after over a year off: stays 2¾m: raced on good ground or softer. *M. C. Pipe* — **c–** **h–**

QUEL DOUN (FR)   4 br.g. Tel Quel (FR) – Dounasa (FR) (Kaldoun (FR)) [2003/4 16d² 16s² 16s³ 16d³ Feb 18] leggy gelding: modest maiden on Flat: placed all 4 starts in juvenile hurdles, 4½ lengths third of 11 to Power Elite in Grade 2 at Leopardstown third one. *W. P. Mullins, Ireland* — **h112**

QUEL REGAL (FR)   6 b.g. Comte du Bourg (FR) – Rigala (FR) (Roi Dagobert) [2003/4 20dᵖᵘ 16gᵖᵘ May 10] leggy gelding: little sign of ability, including in points: sold 850 gns Doncaster August Sales. *A. R. Dicken* — **h–**

QUEST FOR ROME   8 ch.g. Question of Pride – Unbeknown (Most Secret) [2003/4 21sᵖᵘ Jan 4] failed to complete in 4 maiden points in 2003 and in novice hurdle. *M. Appleby* — **h–**

QUETAL (IRE)   11 ch.g. Buckskin (FR) – Cantafleur (Cantab) [2003/4 c117, h–: c33d⁶ c25gᵖᵘ c26dᵖᵘ c25sᶠ Apr 11] rather sparely-made gelding: smart hunter chaser at best, no form in 2003/4: should stay beyond 3¼m: acts on soft and good to firm going, probably on heavy: tends to make mistakes. *Mrs Laura J. Young* — **c–** **h–**

QUICK   4 b.g. Kahyasi – Prompt (Old Vic) [2003/4 17m* 22f* 24m* 25s* 24g 22d* 24s⁴ 24g 24m³ 20m Apr 24] leggy gelding: lightly-raced maiden on Flat for R. Cowell: progressed into fairly useful hurdler, winning juvenile seller at Market Rasen and novice handicaps at Exeter, Taunton and Plumpton on first 4 outings and handicap at Sandown (beat Midnight Creek by 4 lengths) in March: good efforts next 3 starts: suited by 2¾m+: acts on firm and soft going: visored: usually races prominently. *M. C. Pipe* — **h128**

QUICK TO MOVE (IRE)   4 b.g. Night Shift (USA) – Corynida (USA) (Alleged (USA)) [2003/4 17m 17mᵖᵘ Aug 1] workmanlike gelding: poor maiden on Flat at 3 yrs, trained first 3 starts by Mrs J. Ramsden: no show in 2 juvenile hurdles. *C. N. Kellett* — **h–**

QUIDDITCH   4 b.f. Wizard King – Celtic Chimes (Celtic Cone) [2003/4 16dᵖᵘ Dec 15] fourth foal: dam won at 2m over hurdles: soundly beaten in maidens on Flat: didn't jump well when pulled up in juvenile on hurdling debut. *P. Bowen* — **h–**

QUID PRO QUO (FR)   5 b.g. Cadoudal (FR) – Luzenia (FR) (Armos) [2003/4 F17d⁴ F17s² F17s* F16g² Mar 25] lengthy gelding: sixth foal: brother to one-time useful chaser/ — **F103**

winning hurdler Luzcadou, best form around 2½m: dam, won 3 times at 2¼m over hurdles in France, half-sister to useful French chaser New Fort: fairly useful form in bumpers, winning maiden at Taunton in February by 5 lengths from Lord Killeshanra. *P. F. Nicholls*

QUIET DESPERATION   8 b.g. Supreme Leader – Wing On (Quayside) [2003/4   h–
22g^pu 17g 16d^pu 19g Dec 18] 27,000 4-y-o: ex-Irish gelding: half-brother to several winners, including useful 2m jumper Crack On (by Gunner B), fairly useful hurdler/chaser Captain Khedive (by Deep Run) and fair staying hurdler Richmond Lady (by Broadsword): dam unraced: no sign of ability in points/over hurdles, left K. Burke after hurdling debut: sold £1,800 Ascot February Sales. *J. D. Frost*

QUIET WATER (IRE)   8 br.g. Lord Americo – Sirana (Al Sirat (USA)) [2003/4 h98:   c105
18g 19m* 20m⁴ 21m* Jul 14] leggy gelding: fair handicap hurdler: won amateur event   h104
at Stratford in May: similar form when successful in 5-runner novice at Newton Abbot on chasing debut, beating Miss Cool 6 lengths: stays 21f: acts on soft and good to firm going. *P. J. Hobbs*

QUINCY'S PERK (IRE)   11 ch.g. Executive Perk – Quincy Bay (Buckskin (FR))   c91 ?
[2003/4 c21m⁴ c25g³ c24g² c24s^pu c24d² c21s* c24g^pu c21d^pu c24d^pu c24d^pu Apr 12]
lengthy gelding: maiden pointer: 25/1-winner of maiden chase at Sedgefield in February: no form after, blinkered final outing: stays 3m: acts on soft going. *C. T. Pogson*

QUINTRELL DOWNS   9 b.g. Efisio – Nineteenth of May (Homing) [2003/4 h93:   h–
17d^pu 19m^pu May 31] modest 2m hurdler: no encouragement in 2 handicaps early in 2003/4. *T. R. George*

QUITE REMARKABLE   5 b.g. Danzig Connection (USA) – Kathy Fair (IRE)   h83
(Nicholas Bill) [2003/4 17s 17d 16d Mar 24] fair but ungenuine on Flat (stays 1¼m): poor form on first of 3 starts over hurdles. *Ian Williams*

QUIZZICAL   6 ch.g. Indian Ridge – Mount Row (Alzao (USA)) [2003/4 h77: c24g^pu   c76
20m⁴ 22g^ur 17g² 24g³ 24m² 24m³ 21g c20s⁶ c17s c17s c20s^F c20s^pu Mar 20] smallish,   h84
angular gelding: poor maiden hurdler: showing form over fences only when falling 2 out in handicap at Navan: effective at 2m to 3m: acts on soft and good to firm going: tried in cheekpieces. *J. G. Carr, Ireland*

QUIZZLING (IRE)   6 b.g. Jurado (USA) – Monksville (Monksfield) [2003/4 F16g⁶   h73
19v⁶ 22g⁶ 24m Mar 4] 15,500 4-y-o: lengthy gelding: fifth foal: brother to winning 2m   F86
hurdler Nan Chero and half-brother to winning pointer by Strong Gale: dam, modest staying chaser, half-sister to useful staying chaser Loving Around and useful hurdler up to 2½m Verrazano Bridge: sixth of 20 in maiden bumper at Worcester on debut: poor form in novice hurdles. *B. J. M. Ryall*

R

RACING DEMON (IRE)   4 b.g. Old Vic – All Set (IRE) (Electric) [2003/4 F16d*   F105 p
Mar 28] third foal: dam unraced half-sister to top-class chaser up to 25f Merry Gale: looked good prospect when winning 15-runner bumper at Huntingdon on debut by 4 lengths from Reel Missile. *Miss H. C. Knight*

RACING SURVEYOR   9 b.m. Mazilier (USA) – Ruthenia (IRE) (Taufan (USA))   h–
[2003/4 16m^pu Oct 11] no sign of ability in sellers on Flat at 2 yrs or in novice hurdle. *H. Alexander*

RACONTEUR (IRE)   10 b.g. Top of The World – Blackrath Gem (Bargello) [2003/4   c–
c24s^pu May 2] IR 6,400 4-y-o: ex-Irish gelding: seventh foal: half-brother to 2 winners,   h–
notably useful hurdler/useful chaser Connor Macleod (by Torus), stayed 3m: dam twice-raced half-sister to useful chaser up to 3m Poll's Turn, dam of smart chaser/useful hurdler up to 3m Lanturn: winning pointer/hurdler: little form in steeplechases: sold out of J. Gleason's stable 3,000 gns (privately) Doncaster May (2002) Sales: best form around 2m: acts on heavy ground: tried blinkered. *G. D. Hanmer*

RADAR (IRE)   9 b.g. Petardia – Soignee (Night Shift (USA)) [2003/4 c106, h84: 17d²   c–
17d³ 16s² 17s² 20g⁴ Mar 13] angular gelding: fair hurdler/chaser: raced mainly around   h101
2m: acts on any going. *Miss S. E. Forster*

RADCLIFFE (IRE)   7 b.g. Supreme Leader – Marys Course (Crash Course) [2003/4   c98
h–, F96: 26g⁶ 16d² 20m³ 21g³ 18m² c22g⁵ c26s* c26g^F c28d⁴ c24d⁵ c24s⁶ c22m^pu   h92
c26d² Mar 15] rather leggy gelding: modest maiden hurdler: modest handicap chaser:

won 5-runner novice at Plumpton in November: suited by 3m+: acts on soft going, below
form all starts on firmer than good. *Miss Venetia Williams*

RADICAL JACK 7 b.g. Presidium – Luckifosome (Smackover) [2003/4 c–, h–:
c16vᵖᵘ o16gᵖᵘ Mar 5] of no account. *C. W. Fairhurst* — c–/h–

RADMORE SPIRIT 4 b.f. Whittingham (IRE) – Ruda (FR) (Free Round (USA))
[2003/4 F17s F17s Feb 3] stocky filly: sister to 2 winners, including modest hurdler
Mister Webb, stays 2¾m, and half-sister to 2 others, including fair stayer Kikam (by
Ardross): dam never ran: tailed off in bumpers and on Flat debut. *G. A. Ham* — F–

RAFFLES ROOSTER 12 ch.g. Galetto (FR) – Singapore Girl (FR) (Lyphard (USA))
[2003/4 c120x, h–: c25sᵖᵘ c24g⁵ c25gᵘʳ Mar 28] good-topped gelding: fairly useful
handicap chaser at best: left Miss V. Williams, little impact in 3 hunters in 2003/4: stays
3¼m: acts on good to firm and heavy going: often finds less than expected, and best with
exaggerated waiting tactics: often let down by jumping. *Miss L. Revell* — c68 x/h–

RAGDALE HALL (USA) 7 b.g. Bien Bien (USA) – Gift of Dance (USA) (Trempolino (USA)) [2003/4 h115: 16m⁶ 16g* 17m⁶ c16g* 17m⁵ c20m* c16f³ 16m⁴ 20m⁴ Apr
24] medium-sized gelding: fairly useful handicap hurdler: trained by P. Hobbs second to
seventh starts, winning at Stratford in June: successful first 2 starts over fences, in maiden
at Newton Abbot in August and novice at Perth in September, though hasn't convinced
with jumping: stays 2½m: acts on firm and good to soft going: tried blinkered: tried
tongue tied. *J. Joseph* — c101/h119

RAGING TORRENT 9 b.g. Meadowbrook – Charons Daughter (Another River)
[2003/4 c26g⁴ c21s Feb 24] fair pointer: much better effort in hunters when fourth in
maiden at Cartmel. *S. Waugh* — c80

RAGSTONE LAD 5 b.g. Zamindar (USA) – Thahabyah (USA) (Sheikh Albadou)
[2003/4 F16m 16sᵖᵘ 16sᵖᵘ Jan 16] £3,100 4-y-o: big gelding: first foal: dam 2-y-o 6f
winner: no sign of ability: headstrong. *M. A. Barnes* — h–/F–

RAGU 6 b.m. Contract Law (USA) – Marnworth (Funny Man) [2003/4 h88: 20m²
20m* 21d⁵ 21dᶠ 16v 24g 20dᵖᵘ Apr 12] leggy, unfurnished mare: modest hurdler: won
4-runner mares novice at Haydock in October: out of form last 3 starts, left F. Murphy
before final one: stays 21f: acts on good to firm and heavy going: tried cheekpieces.
M. J. Gingell — h90

RAHEEL (IRE) 4 ch.g. Barathea (IRE) – Tajawuz (Kris) [2003/4 17dᵖᵘ Nov 17] fair
on Flat (stays 1½m), successful in February: tongue tied, behind when pulled up in
juvenile maiden on hurdling debut. *P. Mitchell* — h–

RAHWAAN (IRE) 5 b.g. Darshaan – Fawaakeh (USA) (Lyphard (USA)) [2003/4
16g* Mar 10] good-topped gelding: useful stayer on Flat, successful on reappearance
in 2004: made all when beating Bourgeois by 2 lengths in 14-runner novice at Catterick
on hurdling debut: will stay beyond 2m: open to fair amount of improvement.
C. W. Fairhurst — h98 p

RAIKKONEN (IRE) 4 b.g. Lake Coniston (IRE) – Jour Ferie (IRE) (Taufan (USA))
[2003/4 16m² 16m³ 16s⁴ 16s⁴ 16s* 17g 16d Apr 12] smallish gelding: modest on Flat
(stays 9f), claimed out of A. Leahy's stable after winning (blinkered) in August: fairly
useful juvenile hurdler: won maiden at Gowran in February by length from Diego Garcia:
creditable eighth of 18 finishers to Made In Japan in Triumph Hurdle at Cheltenham next
time: raced around 2m: acts on soft and good to firm ground. *W. P. Mullins, Ireland* — h116

RAINBOW DANCE (IRE) 8 ch.g. Rainbows For Life (CAN) – Nishila (USA)
(Green Dancer (USA)) [2003/4 c93, h114: c20g² c20m⁴ c20mᶠ c23m⁴ 16m² c20f² c16gᵖᵘ
Oct 14] sturdy gelding: fair hurdler at best: modest maiden chaser: stays 25f: acts on any
going: usually blinkered: has had tongue tied, including last 4 starts: ungenuine. *Jonjo
O'Neill* — c103 d/h82 §

RAINBOW RIVER (IRE) 6 ch.g. Rainbows For Life (CAN) – Shrewd Girl (USA)
(Sagace (FR)) [2003/4 h104: 17g May 24] fair hurdler in 2002/3: last in handicap at
Cartmel only start in 2003/4: stays 21f: acts on good to firm ground. *M. C. Chapman* — h–

RAINBOWS AGLITTER 7 ch.g. Rainbows For Life (CAN) – Chalet Waldegg
(Monsanto (FR)) [2003/4 h112: 17g² 17g³ c16m* c20g² c19d² c20gᵖᵘ Dec 11] angular
gelding: fair handicap hurdler: 9/4-on, won 3-runner novice at Towcester on chasing
debut in October: better form when: runner-up in small fields next 2 starts: stays 21f: acts
on soft and good to firm going: edgy sort: held up: has found little. *D. R. Gandolfo* — c110/h112

RAINBOW STAR (FR) 10 b. or br.g. Saumarez – In The Star (FR) (In Fijar (USA))
[2003/4 c–§, h–§: c20mʳᵗʳ Feb 25] tall gelding: winning hurdler/maiden chaser: bought — c§§/h§§

RAI

out of Mrs P. Ford's stable £1,500 Ascot October Sales: usually blinkered/visored: has had tongue tied: thoroughly ungenuine. *Mrs Myfanwy Miles*

RAINBOW SUN 8 ch.g. Minster Son – Rilin (Ribston) [2003/4 h–: c19g^{pu} May 13] no form over jumps: has worn cheekpieces. *N. M. Babbage* c– h–

RAISE A MCGREGOR 8 br.g. Perpendicular – Gregory's Lady (Meldrum) [2003/4 h–: c20g^{pu} 20m c16m⁵ c16m⁴ c20m* c20m³ Sep 7] little form over hurdles: modest over fences, won novice handicap at Bangor in August: stays 2½m: acts on good to firm going. *Mrs S. J. Smith* c87 h–

RAISE A STORM (IRE) 7 b.g. Fourstars Allstar (USA) – Tipperary Tartan (Rarity) [2003/4 h–, F102: 16m^F 16g* 17f³ 16f⁴ Apr 10] good-topped gelding: fairly useful up to 2m on Flat: similar form over hurdles: would have won maiden at Tramore in May but for falling last: gained compensation in similar event at Sligo (final start for D. Wachman) in August, comfortably beating Palace Storm 20 lengths: stays 2½m: acts on firm and good to soft going. *Katherine Neilson, USA* h119

RAISE YOUR GLASS (IRE) 5 b. or br.g. Namaqualand (USA) – Toast And Honey (IRE) (Glow (USA)) [2003/4 F–: 16m^F 17g 17m⁵ 16m 16m³ 21g⁵ 20m* 20m 24g 20d⁵ Feb 23] sparely-made gelding: modest hurdler: won conditional jockeys selling handicap (sold from C. Thornton 5,400 gns) at Sedgefield and novice handicap at Carlisle (improved again when making virtually all) in October: trained ninth start only by N. Ewart: should stay beyond 21f: acts on good to firm and good to soft going: usually blinkered: reluctant to race fourth outing. *Miss V. Scott* h91

RAJAM 6 b.g. Sadler's Wells (USA) – Rafif (USA) (Riverman (USA)) [2003/4 16s³ 16g^F Mar 17] sturdy gelding: fairly useful on Flat (stays 1¾m) for D. Nicholls: third in novice at Kelso (better effort, beaten 7 lengths by Paddy The Piper) and maiden at Huntingdon over hurdles. *R. C. Guest* h102

RAKA KING 11 b.g. Rakaposhi King – Spartan Native (Native Bazaar) [2003/4 c25m^{pu} Jun 11] winning pointer: novice hurdler/steeplechaser, usually let down by jumping over fences. *J. A. T. de Giles* c– x h–

RAKALACKEY 6 br.g. Rakaposhi King – Celtic Slave (Celtic Cone) [2003/4 F95: 19g* 22s⁶ 21g* 20g 22g^{pu} Apr 18] medium-sized gelding: fairly useful form when winning novice hurdles at Market Rasen in November and Ludlow in February, beating Beau Supreme 2½ lengths in 18-runner event at latter despite hanging right under pressure and mistakes last 3: went wrong final outing: stays 21f: laboured effort on soft ground second start: possibly not straightforward. *H. D. Daly* h120

RAKASSA 6 ch.m. Ballet Royal (USA) – Shafayif (Ela-Mana-Mou) [2003/4 F78: 16m⁴ 20d⁴ 21g^F 19s³ 21d² 24s³ 21g* 22g⁴ 22d² 22g⁴ Mar 25] lengthy, plain mare: fair hurdler: won mares novice handicap at Kempton in February by ¾ length from Leith Hill Star: good fourth after in handicap at Fontwell and mares novice at Wincanton: stays 3m: acts on soft going. *H. J. Manners* h106

RAMBLEES HOLLY 6 ch.g. Alfie Dickins – Lucky Holly (General David) [2003/4 h83, F76: 21s⁴ 20g³ 24g³ 17m³ 16m⁵ 17g 21m* 21g² 19m 20f³ 20m⁵ 21g⁵ 17s 20s 22g Mar 28] angular gelding: modest hurdler: won at Sedgefield in May (novice) and July (handicap): probably stays easy 3m: acts on firm and soft going. *R. S. Wood* h86

RAMBLING MINSTER 6 b.g. Minster Son – Howcleuch (Buckskin (FR)) [2003/4 F17m² F17g³ F16g* F16s⁵ 19g² 16g⁶ Mar 27] 15,000 4-y-o: tall, good-topped gelding: first foal: dam fair staying chaser: fairly useful form in bumpers, landed odds at Hexham in November: good fifth to Refinement in 20-runner event at Ascot: promising second of 16 to eased Team Tassel in novice at Market Rasen on hurdling debut: considerably handled again (tended to hang) and moderate late progress when sixth in similar event at Newbury: will be suited by 2½m+: possibly not straightforward but open to improvement. *Mrs M. Reveley* h103 p F102

RAMON ALLONES (IRE) 6 br.g. Good Thyne (USA) – Cuban Vacation (Ovac (ITY)) [2003/4 F17m Oct 25] IR 4,900 3-y-o, 5,500 4-y-o: third foal: dam unraced half-sister to very smart chaser around 2½m The Outback Way: little sign of ability in points and bumper. *Mrs R. L. Elliot* F–

RAMPANT (IRE) 6 b.g. Pursuit of Love – Flourishing (IRE) (Trojan Fen) [2003/4 16s^{pu} Dec 26] half-brother to modest hurdler up to 3m Musally (by Muhtarram): fairly useful on Flat (stays 1½m) at 3 yrs, lightly raced and no form since: pulled up in seller on hurdling debut. *C. J. Teague* h–

RAND (NZ) 10 gr.g. Omnicorp (NZ) – Foreign Coin (NZ) (Amyntor (FR)) [2003/4 **c126 +** c18v* Apr 21] smallish, strong gelding: successful several times on Flat and over hurdles **h–** in New Zealand: also won once over hurdles in USA and once over fences (very valuable event) in Japan: reportedly fired and off over 2 years prior to winning minor event at Gowran on Irish debut, always prominent and beating Oh Be The Hokey 6 lengths: good fourth to Junior Fontaine in Punchestown 9 days later, jumping well and staying on strongly again late on: stays 3m: acts on any going. *N. Meade, Ireland*

RANDOLPH O'BRIEN (IRE) 4 b.g. Zaffaran (USA) – Gala's Pride (Gala Perform- **h86** ance) [2003/4 F12s⁵ F13v 17v² 17d⁴ Mar 10] good-topped gelding: fourth foal: dam, **F67** winning hurdler, stayed 2¾m: fifth of 11 on first of 2 starts in bumpers: modest form in juvenile hurdles at Exeter (hung left) and Bangor: bred to be suited by 2½m+. *N. A. Twiston-Davies*

RANDOM HARVEST (IRE) 15 br.g. Strong Gale – Bavello (Le Bavard (FR)) **c102** [2003/4 c118, h–: 24m 23m⁵ c25g c25d⁴ c24d⁵ c28d⁶ Mar 30] tall, leggy gelding: has **h99** been fired: winning hurdler: one-time smart handicap chaser, well into veteran stage: stays 3½m: acts on good to firm and heavy going: has won 7 times at Wetherby: none too reliable. *Mrs M. Reveley*

RANDOM PRECISION (IRE) 5 ch.g. Presenting – Rendezvous (Lorenzaccio) **h–** [2003/4 F18v² F16v 21gᵖᵘ 18d 16g⁵ Apr 4] lengthy gelding: eleventh foal: half-brother to **F84** fair hurdler/chaser Countess Verushka (by Strong Gale), stayed 25f, and winning 2½m hurdler Oneway (by Bob's Return): dam, placed over hurdles, half-sister to useful juvenile hurdler Tenth of October, from family of Lanzarote: 25 lengths second to Major Catch in maiden bumper at Fontwell on debut: little worthwhile form on last of 3 starts in novice hurdles: has looked temperamental (tried to run out second outing). *B. G. Powell*

RANDWICK ROAR (IRE) 5 b.g. Lord Americo – Le Bavellen (Le Bavard (FR)) **h118** [2003/4 F16d 24s 16s⁵ 16s* 16s⁶ 20d* Apr 12] tall gelding: fourth foal: half-brother to **F–** fair hurdler/fairly useful chaser Lord Who (by Mister Lord), stays 25f, and winning pointer by Good Thyne: dam winning pointer: well held in bumper on debut: progressive hurdler, winning maiden at Gowran in February and minor event at Fairyhouse in April: fairly useful form when beating Star of Bethlehem by length at latter: matched that effort when sixth of 8 to Sadlers Wings in Grade 1 novice at Punchestown in late-April: stays 2½m: acts on soft going. *P. M. J. Doyle, Ireland*

RANDY (GER) 6 gr.g. Neshad (USA) – Regal Beauty (GER) (Windwurf (GER)) **h59** [2003/4 h–: 17g⁴ 16m Jun 18] not fluent and no worthwhile form over hurdles. *M. C. Pipe*

RANEEN NASHWAN 8 b.g. Nashwan (USA) – Raneen Alwatar (Sadler's Wells **h84 §** (USA)) [2003/4 h83§: 19d⁶ 17g Sep 3] lengthy gelding: poor maiden hurdler: best around 2m: tried blinkered (raced freely): irresolute. *R. J. Baker*

RANELAGH GRAY (IRE) 7 gr.g. Roselier (FR) – Bea Marie (IRE) (King's Ride) **h101** [2003/4 h83, F83: 21g 17s* 16d² 16g 16s* Apr 11] leggy gelding: modest hurdler: won handicaps at Folkestone in January and Towcester in April: should stay beyond 17f: acts on soft going: races prominently. *Miss Venetia Williams*

RAOUL DUFY (USA) 4 gr.g. El Prado (IRE) – Parrish Empress (USA) (His Majesty **h–** (USA)) [2003/4 16d Jan 3] tall gelding: fair maiden on Flat (stays 9.4f) when trained by P. Cole: seemed less than willing when tailed-off last of 18 in juvenile at Sandown on hurdling debut. *P. J. Hobbs*

RAPID DEPLOYMENT 7 b.g. Deploy – City Times (IRE) (Last Tycoon) [2003/4 **h125** h118: 22d² 20s* Sep 20] compact gelding: fairly useful on Flat (probably stays 2¼m): fairly useful handicap hurdler: improved effort when beating Pay It Forward 2½ lengths at Listowel in September: needs further than 2m and stays 3m: acts on heavy going: sometimes let down by jumping. *P. Hughes, Ireland*

RAPIDE PLAISIR (IRE) 6 b.g. Grand Plaisir (IRE) – Royal Well (Henbit (USA)) **h114** [2003/4 16g* 20g³ 16g² Oct 6] IR £40,000 3-y-o: rather leggy gelding: brother to fairly useful hurdler/winning 2m chaser Royal Plaisir and half-brother to fairly useful hurdler/ useful chaser who stays 25f Royaltino: dam unraced, from family of high-class 2m jumpers Celtic Ryde and Noddys Ryde and smart staying hurdler/chaser Ryde Again: fair form on first of 3 starts in bumpers: similar form over hurdles: won maiden at Sligo in August: placed in novices at Tipperary and Roscommon: good fifth in competitive handicap at Punchestown in late-April: stays 2½m: not a fluent jumper. *M. Halford, Ireland*

RAPID LINER 11 b.g. Skyliner – Stellaris (Star Appeal) [2003/4 c–, h57: 22m Jun **c–** 29] bad maiden jumper: stays 21f: tried blinkered/tongue tied. *B. G. Powell* **h–**

RAPT (IRE) 6 b.g. Septieme Ciel (USA) – Dream Play (USA) (Blushing Groom (FR)) **h86**
[2003/4 h–: 17m⁶ 17g⁵ 16m* 16m⁵ 17g 16dᵖᵘ Apr 21] leggy gelding: poor on Flat nowadays: won seller at Stratford in October: little other form over hurdles: raced around 2m:
usually tongue tied. *M. A. Barnes*

RARCHNAMARA (IRE) 9 b.g. Commanche Run – Knollwood Court (Le Jean) **c– §**
[2003/4 c80, h–§: c25dᶠ c32d⁵ Mar 18] tall, leggy gelding: winning hurdler: generally let **h– §**
down by jumping over fences: stays 27f: raced mainly on good going or softer (acts on
soft): effective blinkered/visored or not: ungenuine (refused to go to start second intended
outing): sold 1,000 gns Doncaster May Sales. *Ferdy Murphy*

RARE PRESENCE (IRE) 5 b.g. Sadler's Wells (USA) – Celebrity Style (USA) **h75**
(Seeking The Gold (USA)) [2003/4 h79: 18g⁶ 24sᵖᵘ 22vᵖᵘ 20s 22d³ 22d Mar 21] leggy
gelding: poor maiden hurdler: stays 2¾m: acts on good to soft going: tried visored,
usually blinkered: tongue tied last 3 starts: possibly temperamental. *C. P. Morlock*

RARE QUALITY 6 b.m. Chaddleworth (IRE) – Pink Mex (Tickled Pink) [2003/4 **h80**
16m⁴ 16v 21d 21dᵖᵘ 17dᵖᵘ Mar 15] half-sister to useful hurdler/fairly useful chaser Tragic
Hero (by Tragic Role), stays 3m: poor maiden on Flat at 3 yrs for R. Guest: form over
hurdles only on debut. *N. J. Henderson*

RARE VINTAGE (IRE) 6 b.m. Germany (USA) – Tatlock (Paico) [2003/4 20gᵖᵘ **h–**
21gᵖᵘ 17d 20d⁴ Apr 7] good-topped mare: fifth live foal: half-sister to modest hurdler
King's Country (by King's Ride), stays 21f: dam, poor maiden Irish pointer, sister to
fairly useful hurdler who stayed 2½m Gods Fox: no form in novice hurdles.
Miss H. C. Knight

RASCELLA 9 gr.m. Scallywag – Blue Gift (Hasty Word) [2003/4 16g² 17d⁶ 16m⁴ 20m³ **h91**
20g⁴ 20g² Nov 19] angular mare: modest novice hurdler: stays 2½m: has found little.
Mrs S. J. Smith

RATHBAWN PRINCE (IRE) 12 ch.g. All Haste (USA) – Ellis Town (Camden **c99**
Town) [2003/4 c140, h–: c20dᵖᵘ c25d² c24g² Mar 5] good-bodied gelding: smart chaser/ **h–**
useful hurdler at best: left D. Hughes and off 9 months, runner-up in hunters at Wincanton
(promoted) and Newbury: stays 29f: acts on good to firm and heavy going: has worn
cheekpieces. *Miss H. C. Knight*

RATHGAR BEAU (IRE) 8 b. or br.g. Beau Sher – Salerina (Orchestra) [2003/4 **c145 x**
c145, h–: c16d³ c16m³ c16d² c16d² c17dᶠ c17s³ c16v² c20s*ᵈⁱˢ 17d c20s* c17d⁵ Apr 11] **h–**
useful-looking gelding: winning hurdler: smart chaser: first past post in Red Mills Chase
at Gowran (disqualified on technical grounds) in February and An Uaimh Chase at Navan
(led on on line to beat Strong Run) in March: ran really well when 2 lengths second to
Moscow Flyer in Grade 1 at Punchestown in late-April: stays 2½m: raced mainly on
going softer than good (acts on heavy): blinkered fourth/fifth starts: patiently ridden:
inclined to make the odd bad mistake: consistent. *E. Sheehy, Ireland*

RATHOWEN (IRE) 5 b.g. Good Thyne (USA) – Owenageera (IRE) (Riot Helmet) **F–**
[2003/4 F17d Apr 3] tall gelding: third foal: dam, placed in point, half-sister to very smart
staying chaser Everett: badly in need of experience when tailed off in Grade 2 bumper at
Aintree on debut. *J. I. A. Charlton*

RATLING 8 gr.g. Pittacus (USA) – Sedgewell Orchid (John de Coombe) [2003/4 21m⁴ **h–**
Oct 6] first foal: dam winning hurdler around 2m: showed nothing in maiden point and
novice hurdle. *J. F. Panvert*

RATTY'S BAND 10 ch.g. Gunner B – Arctic Ander (Leander) [2003/4 c16vᵖᵘ c16g² **c62**
c16dᵖᵘ Apr 22] poor maiden hurdler/chaser. *Mrs L. B. Normile* **h–**

RAVEN'S LAST 5 b.g. Sea Raven (IRE) – Lavenham's Last (Rymer) [2003/4 F16v* **F102**
F16s² Mar 13] sixth foal: half-brother to bumper/17f hurdle winner Gohh (by Alflora):
dam unraced half-sister to high-class staying chaser Cybrandian: won maiden Irish point
on debut in 2003: 11/8-on, won 12-runner bumper at Newcastle in February by 6 lengths
from Profowens with plenty in hand: beaten 1¾ lengths by Big Bone in similar event
there 5 weeks later. *R. T. Phillips*

RAVING LORD (IRE) 7 b.g. Lord Americo – Miss Kertina (IRE) (Orchestra) [2003/4 **h–**
h–, F83: 16g 16gᵘʳ Mar 12] no form over hurdles: has looked difficult ride. *J. P. Dodds*

RAW SILK 6 b.g. Rudimentary (USA) – Misty Silks (Scottish Reel) [2003/4 h98: **h106**
16m² 17g* 17m 16gᵖᵘ 17g⁶ Aug 23] good-bodied gelding: fair handicap hurdler: won at
Cartmel in May: ran poorly after: probably best around 2m: acts on any going: effective
in blinkers/cheekpieces or without: tried tongue tied. *M. Todhunter*

RAYBAAN (IRE)   5 b.g. Flying Spur (AUS) – Genetta (Green Desert (USA)) [2003/4   **h–**
h–: 17d⁶ 16d⁵ Mar 25] compact gelding: fair on Flat (stays easy 1½m), sold out of
S. Dow's stable £1,800 Ascot December Sales: no form over hurdles, including in seller.
Miss J. S. Davis

RAYGALE   7 b.g. Superpower – Little Missile (Ile de Bourbon (USA)) [2003/4 16v⁶   **h81**
20d 16v² 19dᵘʳ 26dᵖᵘ 19sᵖᵘ Apr 11] sturdy gelding: fair form in bumpers in 2001/2: form
over hurdles only when second to easy winner Tighten Your Belt in novice at Towcester:
sold 1,400 gns Doncaster May Sales. *K. C. Bailey*

RAYSHAN (IRE)   4 b.g. Darshaan – Rayseka (IRE) (Dancing Brave (USA)) [2003/4   **h113 p**
16g* 16g² Mar 28] dam from family of smart French hurdler Tiger Groom: useful on
Flat (stays 1¾m), successful in June, sold out of J. Oxx's stable 140,000 gns Newmarket
Autumn Sales: won juvenile at Musselburgh on hurdling debut by 11 lengths from Humid
Climate, taking while to assert: 10/3-on, ½-length second to Presumptuous in similar
event at Kelso following month: will be suited by greater test of stamina: should do better,
particularly if jumping improves. *J. Howard Johnson*

RAY SOURCE (IRE)   9 b.g. Lashkari – Salote (USA) (Forli (ARG)) [2003/4 22mᵖᵘ   **c98**
26m* c24g² c25m³ c24m* c25f⁵ c24m* Nov 21] leggy gelding: modest hurdler: second   **h93**
outing after long absence, won 5-runner handicap at Huntingdon in August: similar form
over fences, winning maiden at Chepstow in October and handicap at Ascot (blinkered)
in November in very small fields: stays 3¼m: acts on good to firm and heavy going. *Ian
Williams*

RAYWARE BOY (IRE)   8 b.g. Scenic – Amata (USA) (Nodouble (USA)) [2003/4   **h74 §**
h75§: 17g 20v³ 16g⁴ 16d⁵ 20d² 19d 16v⁵ 16gᵗʳ 19g⁴ 17gᵗʳ 20dᵗʳ Apr 12] sparely-made
gelding: poor hurdler: stays 2½m: acts on heavy and good to firm going: blinkered/
visored: sometimes reluctant/refuses to race: one to leave alone. *D. Shaw*

RAZZMATAZZ (IRE)   10 br.g. Camden Town – Sallys Wish (Proverb) [2003/4 h–:   **h–**
16m⁴ Oct 3] tall gelding: little form, very lightly raced nowadays. *J. Howard Johnson*

REACHFORTHESTARS   8 b.m. Royal Fountain – China's Way (USA) (Native   **c–**
Uproar (USA)) [2003/4 h–: 20sᵖᵘ 21sᵖᵘ 21sᵖᵘ c16gᵖᵘ Jan 15] leggy mare: of no account.   **h–**
J. Mackie

REACH THE CLOUDS (IRE)   12 b.g. Lord Americo – Dusky Stream (Paddy's   **c93 §**
Stream) [2003/4 c95, h–: c16d² c16m⁶ c17s* c16m³ c16g² c17sᵖᵘ c17sᶠ c16s⁶ c16d² 16d⁵   **h78**
Apr 11] good-topped gelding: modest handicap chaser: ended long losing run in 4-runner
event at Plumpton in November: first run over hurdles for 3 years final start: barely stays
2½m when conditions are testing: acts on heavy and good to firm going: blinkered twice:
probably best on left-handed course: usually finds little and not one to trust (very reluctant to race sixth outing). *John R. Upson*

READY TO RUMBLE (IRE)   9 ch.g. Phardante (FR) – My Only Hope (Brave   **c105**
Invader (USA)) [2003/4 c19d⁶ c20g⁴ c22gᵖᵘ Mar 5] sturdy gelding: fair hurdler in 2000/1:   **h–**
easily best effort over fences on return when fourth to Sir Talbot in novice at Leicester:
stays 3m: acts on soft going. *Noel T. Chance*

REAL CRACKER (IRE)   5 b.g. Lahib (USA) – Loreo (IRE) (Lord Chancellor   **h92 p**
(USA)) [2003/4 F17m* 19sᵖᵘ 16gᶠ Feb 25] €6,000 3-y-o: fourth foal: half-brother to   **F91**
2001 3-y-o winner in Turkey: dam unraced: won maiden bumper at Market Rasen in
May: seemed amiss on hurdling debut 7 months later: upsides leader when falling 3 out
in novice won by Gentle Beau at Ludlow. *Miss Venetia Williams*

REAL DEFINITION   5 br.g. Highest Honor (FR) – Segovia (Groom Dancer (USA))   **F94**
[2003/4 F16s⁴ F16s F16d* Mar 19] good-topped gelding: third foal: half-brother to useful
bumper/2m hurdle winner Govamix (by Linamix): dam 1¼m winner who stayed 1½m:
fair form in bumpers, winning 19-runner maiden at Warwick by ½ length from Continental. *D. J. Wintle*

REAL FIRE (IRE)   10 b.g. Astronef – Golden Arum (Home Guard (USA)) [2003/4   **c– §**
c–§, h65§: c16g⁴ c16g⁴ 22m³ 22g⁴ 26m⁵ Sep 28] small gelding: poor handicap hurdler: **h62 §**
maiden chaser: stays 2¾m: acts on heavy and good to firm going: usually wears headgear:
often tongue tied: irresolute. *R. Johnson*

REAL SHADY   7 b.g. Bob's Return (IRE) – Madam Margeaux (IRE) (Ardross) [2003/4   **h104**
h82: 16g* 16g² 20d² 23d⁶ 16d³ Jan 13] tall gelding: chasing sort: fair hurdler: won handicap at Hexham in November: likely to prove best up to 2½m: raced on good going or
softer (won bumper on soft): has raced freely. *M. W. Easterby*

REAL SHARP (IRE) 6 br.g. Son of Sharp Shot (IRE) – Lady By Chance (IRE) (Never **h–**
Got A Chance) [2003/4 h–, F72: 21m 20s Feb 12] well held all 5 starts over hurdles: tried
in blinkers. *S. E. H. Sherwood*

REAL VALUE (IRE) 13 b.g. Matching Pair – Silent Verb (Proverb) [2003/4 c109: **c–**
c24g³ c28gᵖᵘ c25dᵖᵘ Feb 17] sturdy gelding: veteran chaser: no form in hunters in 2003/4:
won 3-runner point in April: stays 3½m: acts on soft and good to firm going, probably on
heavy. *Mrs D. M. Grissell*

REASONABLE RESERVE (IRE) 7 ch.g. Fourstars Allstar (USA) – Alice **c– x**
O'Malley (The Parson) [2003/4 h81, F81: 24s 24m⁶ 24m* 24m* 24m* 24m³ c24m² 24fʳᵒ **h107**
c26gᵘʳ c24mᵘʳ Oct 22] ex-Irish gelding: left C. Swan after reappearance: much improved
over hurdles when winning novice and 2 handicaps at Worcester in summer: let down by
jumping over fences: will stay beyond 3m: acts on good to firm going: tried blinkered/in
cheekpieces: not a straightforward ride (ran out eighth outing). *B. G. Powell*

REBELLE 5 b. or br.g. Reprimand – Blushing Belle (Local Suitor (USA)) [2003/4 **h–**
22sᵖᵘ Dec 30] quite good-topped gelding: fair on Flat (stays 2m), sold out of I. Wood's
stable 4,000 gns Doncaster March (2003) Sales: breathing problem on hurdling debut.
P. Bowen

REBEL RAIDER (IRE) 5 b.g. Mujadil (USA) – Emily's Pride (Shirley Heights) **h90**
[2003/4 h–: 16m² 17g² 16m² Jul 16] modest form when runner-up all 3 completed starts
over hurdles. *B. N. Pollock*

REBEL RHYTHM 5 b.g. Robellino (USA) – Celt Song (IRE) (Unfuwain (USA)) **F108**
[2003/4 F16d* F17d³ F16d³ Apr 17] 6,000 4-y-o: good-bodied gelding: third foal: half-
brother to smart 6f/7f winner Princess Ellen (by Tirol): dam never ran: won 16-runner
bumper at Wetherby on debut in March most impressively by 17 lengths from Gay Oscar:
again showed useful form when third, to Diamond Sal in Grade 2 at Aintree and Wild
Cane Ridge at Ayr in April. *Mrs S. J. Smith*

The Fees R Us Syndicate's "Rebel Rhythm"

REBEL'S GIFT 11 b.g. Genuine Gift (CAN) – Princess Veronica (Rebel Prince) **c–**
[2003/4 c–, h–: 24g^{pu} May 10] leggy gelding: poor handicap hurdler, no form for long **h–**
time: visored once. *F. P. Murtagh*

RECOLETA 7 b.m. Ezzoud (IRE) – Hug Me (Shareef Dancer (USA)) [2003/4 16m^{pu} **h–**
16v^{pu} Nov 29] leggy mare: no form: tried blinkered/visored. *F. Jordan*

RECTORY (IRE) 5 b.g. Presenting – Billys Pet (Le Moss) [2003/4 F16s F16g Jan **F83**
24] ninth foal: half-brother to useful hurdler/chaser Ashwell Boy, stays 21f, and fair
hurdler up to 2½m Macaw-Bay (both by Strong Gale): dam unraced: mid-division in 2
bumpers. *Mrs S. J. Smith*

RED ADDICK (IRE) 5 gr.g. Grand Lodge (USA) – Glad's Night (IRE) (Sexton **h–**
Blake) [2003/4 16m 24g^{pu} Jun 11] no sign of ability on Flat or over hurdles: tried
blinkered. *Miss Suzy Smith*

RED AFGEM 7 ch.m. Afzal – Preacher's Gem (The Parson) [2003/4 F–: 21g^{pu} 24d **h–**
Apr 8] sturdy mare: no sign of ability. *Mrs S. M. Johnson*

RED ALERT MAN (IRE) 8 ch.g. Sharp Charter – Tukurua (Noalto) [2003/4 c74?, **c74 ?**
h–: c17s^3 c20s^4 c24m^2 c21g^3 24d^{pu} Apr 21] workmanlike gelding: poor chaser: maiden **h–**
hurdler: stays easy 21f: acts on heavy going: tried in cheekpieces, usually blinkered.
Mrs L. Williamson

REDBERRY HOLLY (IRE) 6 gr.m. Roselier (FR) – Solvia (IRE) (Persian Mews) **c–**
[2003/4 21d 21s 21s^{pu} c25d c26g^F c22s^4 c26d^3 Apr 11] IR £5,700 3-y-o: fourth foal: dam **h–**
unraced half-sister to dam of very smart chaser up to 21f Gales Cavalier: winning Irish
pointer: no form over hurdles or in steeplechases. *R. H. Buckler*

RED BLAZER (NZ) 11 ch.g. Omnicorp (NZ) – Gay Reef (Reform) [2003/4 16s^{pu} **c86**
c22d^6 c23g^6 c20d^2 c20s Feb 12] close-coupled gelding: winning hurdler, off 2 years **h–**
before reappearance: easily best effort over fences when second of 4 finishers in novice
handicap at Kempton: lame next time: stays 21f: acts on heavy going. *A. W. Carroll*

RED BLOODED (IRE) 7 b.g. River Falls – Volkova (Green Desert (USA)) [2003/4 **c–**
c–, h–: 20m^{pu} c17g^5 c18f^{pu} 21m^{pu} 16m Oct 6] leggy gelding: no form over jumps: tried **h–**
visored: usually tongue tied: sold £2,400 Ascot October Sales. *Mrs L. C. Jewell*

RED BOY (GER) 5 ch.h. Royal Abjar (USA) – Royal Wind (GER) (Windwurf (GER)) **h– p**
[2003/4 17s^{pu} Feb 17] successful once over 1m at 2 yrs for P. Rau in Germany, in frame 4
times on Flat in 2003: 16/1, better than result suggests in novice at Folkestone on hurdling
debut, weakening rapidly leaving back straight having jumped none too fluently: should
do better under less testing conditions. *M. Hofer, Germany*

RED BRAE 7 b.g. Rakaposhi King – Sayshar (Sayfar) [2003/4 h–: 20d 17d 16s c16g^5 **c74**
c16g^3 c25v^{bd} c24g c16s* c16d^5 c20d^{pu} Apr 18] lengthy gelding: little show over hurdles, **h–**
poor novice chaser: in cheekpieces, won handicap at Towcester in March: lame final
outing: form only around 2m: acts on soft going: tried blinkered, visored last 2 starts.
P. D. Niven

RED BROOK LAD 9 ch.g. Nomadic Way (USA) – Silently Yours (USA) (Silent **c113**
Screen (USA)) [2003/4 c104, h–: c21d* c25m* c20d* c26d^{pu} c19s Apr 6] leggy gelding: **h–**
useful hunter chaser: won hunters at Cheltenham (maiden) in April, Wincanton (novice)
in May and Sandown in February, beating Hermes III in good style by 11 lengths at
last-named: possibly amiss in Foxhunter at Cheltenham next time: stays 25f: acts on firm
and good to soft going: tried blinkered over hurdles: still prone to mistakes. *C. St V. Fox*

RED CANYON (IRE) 7 b.g. Zieten (USA) – Bayazida (Bustino) [2003/4 h92: 20m^4 **h95**
20m^3 20m^5 24m^6 22g^4 21d^2 20g^2 20m^3 22m^6 22m^F 20m^4 Oct 22] sturdy gelding: modest
handicap hurdler: effective at 2½m to 3m: acts on firm and good to soft going: tried
blinkered/visored. *A. G. Hobbs*

RED CHIEF (IRE) 4 b.g. Lahib (USA) – Karayb (IRE) (Last Tycoon) [2003/4 17d^5 **h83**
Mar 10] fair on Flat (stays 1m), sold out of M. Bell's stable 12,000 gns Newmarket
Autumn Sales: fifth in amateur juvenile maiden at Bangor on hurdling debut. *R. Lee*

RED CRYSTAL 6 b.m. Presidium – Crystallography (Primitive Rising (USA)) **h–**
[2003/4 19g^{pu} 21m^{pu} 17g^{pu} 25g^{pu} Jan 24] no form on Flat or in 4 starts over hurdles: tried
in cheekpieces: has pulled hard. *C. R. Wilson*

RED DAHLIA 7 b.m. Alflora (IRE) – Redgrave Devil (Tug of War) [2003/4 21g^4 **h–**
21d^F 16s^6 17d^{pu} Mar 3] ex-Irish mare: fourth foal: half-sister to 1¼m winner Red Piper
(by Emarati): dam, fairly useful hurdler/chaser, stayed 21f: poor form on second of 2

starts in bumpers: well beaten over hurdles, left Mrs J. Harrington prior to reappearance. *M. Pitman*

REDDE (IRE)   9 ch.g. Classic Memory – Stoney Broke (Pauper) [2003/4 h–: c23g^{pu} c23v* c26v^{pu} c20s⁴ 21g 24s⁶ c23s³ Apr 6] deep-girthed gelding: fairly useful hurdler in 2001/2: won weak maiden chase at Uttoxeter in May: off 6 months, little impact subsequently, including over hurdles: should stay 3¼m: acts on heavy going: blinkered twice, including at Uttoxeter: usually races prominently. *R. J. Smith*   **c101** **h–**

RED DEVIL ROBERT (IRE)   6 ch.g. Carroll House – Well Over (Over The River (FR)) [2003/4 20d² 24s³ 21g² 22g² Apr 18] good-topped gelding: seventh foal: half-brother to several winners, including smart staying chaser Lord of The River and fairly useful hurdler up to 19f Ruby Gale (both by Lord Americo) and useful hunter chaser Miners Melody (by Miner's Lamp): dam, won 3 points in Ireland, half-sister to useful staying chaser Moorcroft Boy: fifth in maiden Irish point on debut in 2003: placed all 4 starts over hurdles, again travelling well long way when second to El Vaquero in novice at Wincanton final outing: will probably prove best short of 3m. *P. F. Nicholls*   **h106**

RED EMPEROR   10 b.g. Emperor Fountain – Golden Curd (FR) (Nice Havrais (USA)) [2003/4 c90, h–: c20m³ c24d⁴ c24m³ 17d 25s 22d c22s c25m⁶ c24g 23d Apr 12] lengthy gelding: maiden hurdler/winning chaser: showed nothing in 2003/4: tried in headgear: has had tongue tied. *Dr P. Pritchard*   **c–** **h–**

REDEMPTION   9 b.g. Sanglamore (USA) – Ypha (USA) (Lyphard (USA)) [2003/4 c141, h–: c20f^{ur} c20g^{pu} c20g* c20s^{F} 21d* c16g^{ur} 20d⁵ 21g 24g 20g³ Apr 1] workmanlike gelding: smart handicap chaser: jumped better than usual when winning quite valuable event at Newbury readily by 9 lengths from Claymore: again running well when falling 2 out in valuable contest at Cheltenham next time: useful hurdler: won handicap at Cheltenham in January easily by 1¼ lengths from Monkerhostin: creditable third to Zibeline in listed handicap at Aintree final outing: stays 21f: acts on heavy and good to firm going: blinkered once (went in snatches): usually makes mistakes over fences. *N. A. Twiston-Davies*   **c142 x** **h135**

RED ENSIGN   7 ch.g. Lancastrian – Medway Queen (Pitpan) [2003/4 F–: 21v 22s 22v⁶ 22s⁵ 25s⁵ Mar 15] signs of only a little ability. *Mrs L. C. Jewell*   **h–**

RED FLYER (IRE)   5 br.g. Catrail (USA) – Marostica (ITY) (Stone) [2003/4 h94: 20m⁶ 16g² 16g⁵ 18g⁴ Nov 1] leggy, quite good-topped gelding: modest hurdler: best around 2m: acts on good to soft going. *P. C. Haslam*   **h94**

RED FOREST (IRE)   5 b.g. Charnwood Forest (IRE) – High Atlas (Shirley Heights) [2003/4 h–: 16d^{pu} Nov 15] smallish gelding: modest on Flat (stays 1½m): pulled up in 3 races over hurdles: tried tongue tied. *J. Mackie*   **h–**

George Stevens Handicap Hurdle, Cheltenham—
Redemption puts up a useful performance back over hurdles; Monkerhostin is in vain pursuit

Mr John Duggan & Mr Michael Purtill's "Redemption"

RED FRED 4 ch.g. Case Law – Mississipi Maid (All Systems Go) [2003/4 16gᵖᵘ Jul 26] regressive sprinter on Flat: pulled hard and made mistakes in juvenile on hurdling debut. *P. D. Evans*

h–

RED GENIE 6 ch.g. Primitive Rising (USA) – Marsden Rock (Tina's Pet) [2003/4 F85: 20d³ 16m⁵ 17g⁶ 16mᶠ 16m Sep 13] poor form over hurdles, sold out of R. C. Guest's stable 4,000 gns Doncaster May Sales after second start: has worn cheekpieces. *C. J. Gray*

h71

RED GOLD 10 ch.g. Sula Bula – Ruby Celebration (New Member) [2003/4 c–x, h–: c24d² c24sᵖᵘ c25d² c24vᵘʳ c24gᵖᵘ c24g³ c25sᵘʳ c23dᵖᵘ Apr 21] workmanlike gelding: poor maiden chaser: stays 25f: acts on heavy going: tried tongue tied: poor jumper. *Andrew Turnell*

c75 x
h–

REDGRAVE WOLF 11 ch.m. Little Wolf – Redgrave Rose (Tug of War) [2003/4 c70, h–: c25d⁶ c22g Nov 6] leggy, angular mare: maiden chaser: no show either start in 2003/4: stays 25f: acts on firm and soft going: well held both runs in blinkers. *K. Bishop*

c–
h–

RED GUARD 10 ch.g. Soviet Star (USA) – Zinzara (USA) (Stage Door Johnny (USA)) [2003/4 c117§, h–§: c25g⁵ c20m⁴ c24gᵖᵘ c22d² Apr 7] workmanlike gelding: fair handicap chaser: stays 25f: acts on firm and soft going: usually blinkered/in cheekpieces nowadays: best held up: often fails to go through with effort and not one to trust: sold 8,500 gns Doncaster May Sales. *N. J. Gifford*

c107 §
h– §

RED HALO 5 b.g. Be My Guest (USA) – Pray (IRE) (Priolo (USA)) [2003/4 h102: c16mᶠ Nov 25] angular gelding: successful first 3 starts in juvenile hurdles in 2002/3: fell fatally first on chasing debut: raced around 2m: acted on soft and good to firm going: usually front runner. *S. Kirk*

c–
h–

RED

RED HARE (NZ) 10 ch.g. Famous Star – Mutual Belle (NZ) (Western Bay (NZ)) **c– §**
[2003/4 c94§, h–§: c21g^{pu} c25m^{pu} Jun 11] compact gelding: winning hurdler/chaser: **h– §**
largely disappointing since winning over fences in October 2002, including in points:
stays 3m: probably acts on any going: tried blinkered/in cheekpieces: best left alone.
Miss K. Marks

RED HEATHER 7 b.m. Mistertopogigo (IRE) – That's Rich (Hot Spark) [2003/4 **h–**
16d^{pu} Dec 1] well beaten in sellers on Flat and in 2 outings over hurdles. *D. W. Whillans*

RED HOT ROBBIE 11 ch.g. Gildoran – Quarry Machine (Laurence O) [2003/4 h81: **h–**
22m^{pu} Aug 9] poor maiden hurdler: went lame for second successive start in August:
should stay 3m. *Mrs N. S. Sharpe*

RED HUSTLER (IRE) 8 ch.g. Husyan (USA) – Isoldes Tower (Balliol) [2003/4 c92, **c88**
h–: c16s^{4} c17s^{F} c19g c16s^{6} c22s^{2} c20g c20g^{pu} c21g Apr 12] workmanlike gelding: **h–**
modest handicap chaser: stays 2¾m: acts on soft and good to firm going: wore cheek-
pieces/visor last 5 starts: inconsistent: sold 900 gns Doncaster May Sales. *C. Grant*

RED KNIGHT (IRE) 6 b. or br.g. Goldmark (USA) – Dafwan (Nashwan (USA)) **F100**
[2003/4 F95+: F16d* Aug 3] rather unfurnished gelding: successful twice from 3 starts in
bumpers, including at Galway only start in 2003/4, beating Fatherofthebride 1½ lengths.
C. Roche, Ireland

RED LADY 8 b.g. Toulon – Winter Music (Young Emperor) [2003/4 17g^{6} 16s Dec **c–**
31] IR 20,000 4-y-o: fifth foal: half-brother to winning Irish pointer by Erin's Hope: dam **h–**
successful up to 3m over hurdles in Ireland: well held in novice hurdle (for Mrs
A. Naughton) and maiden chase. *P. D. McCreery, Ireland*

RED LION (FR) 7 ch.g. Lion Cavern (USA) – Mahogany River (Irish River (FR)) **h–**
[2003/4 h95: 16g 16d Dec 6] good-topped gelding: maiden hurdler: stays 21f: act on good
to firm and good to soft ground: tongue tied twice in 2002/3: sold 2,000 gns Doncaster
May Sales. *N. J. Henderson*

RED MAIL (USA) 6 b.g. Red Ransom (USA) – Seattle Byline (USA) (Slew City **c77**
Slew (USA)) [2003/4 c–, h–: c17g^{2} c17m^{4} c20g^{pu} May 24] workmanlike gelding: poor **h–**
maiden chaser: unlikely to stay much beyond 17f: acts on good to firm ground.
M. A. Barnes

RED MAN (IRE) 7 ch.g. Toulon – Jamie's Lady (Ashmore (FR)) [2003/4 h88: 20g^{2} **h106**
22f^{8} Oct 5] improved hurdler in 2003/4, second in maiden at Perth and won novice at
Kelso (jumped none too fluently): stays 2¾m: acts on firm going. *Mrs E. Slack*

RED MARSALA 6 b.g. Tragic Role (USA) – Southend Scallywag (Tina's Pet) **c–**
[2003/4 F–p: 20d^{pu} 19g^{F} 25s^{pu} 20v^{F} 16v^{6} 20s^{ur} c20d^{pu} c16d^{4} Mar 28] leggy gelding: no **h–**
form over hurdles or fences: wore blinkers/cheekpieces last 4 starts. *R. C. Guest*

RED MINSTER 7 b.g. Minster Son – Minty Muncher (Idiot's Delight) [2003/4 c87, **c–**
h–: c24g^{pu} c20g Apr 10] sturdy, lengthy gelding: no form over hurdles: modest chaser: **h–**
off a year, showed little in 2003/4: stays 2½m: acts on heavy going: usually wears cheekpieces. *R. C. Guest*

RED NATIVE (IRE) 8 b.g. Be My Native (USA) – Larry's Peach (Laurence O) **c?**
[2003/4 c25g^{F} Apr 4] rangy gelding: successful several times in points, including in **h–**
2-runner event in April: showed ability on hunter chase debut in novice at Wincanton
earlier in month, disputing second when falling 4 out: tried blinkered. *R. Barber*

RED NOSE LADY 7 b.m. Teenoso (USA) – Red Rambler (Rymer) [2003/4 h87§, **c– §**
F–: 20g^{5} 20d c25d^{pu} 16v^{5} 16v^{pu} 22v^{pu} 24v^{4} 24d Apr 21] lengthy mare: visored, no show **h82 §**
on chasing debut: poor maiden hurdler: stays 2½m: possibly best on soft/heavy going:
tried in cheekpieces: ungenuine. *J. M. Jefferson*

RED OASSIS 13 ch.g. Rymer – Heron's Mirage (Grey Mirage) [2003/4 c74, h–: **c63**
c16m^{4} c20s^{6} c20g^{5} c16d^{4} c19m^{6} Apr 13] compact gelding: poor handicap chaser: best at **h–**
2m: acts on heavy going. *M. J. M. Evans*

RED OR WHITE (IRE) 5 ch.g. Semillon – Sweet Chimes (Orchestra) [2003/4 **h112**
F16v^{5} F17g^{4} 16s 19g^{3} 20g* 20d^{2} 24s 19s^{2} 20s^{4} 20d 20s^{4} 20g Apr 11] half-brother to fair **F74**
hurdler/winning chaser Donnickmore (by Carmelite House), stays 2½m: dam placed over
1½m: poor form both starts in bumpers: fair hurdler: made all in novice at Wexford in
October: best effort when second in handicap at Punchestown in early-May: stays 2½m:
acts on soft and good to firm going. *W. P. Mullins, Ireland*

REDOUBLE 8 b.g. First Trump – Sunflower Seed (Mummy's Pet) [2003/4 h83§: 20m^{4} **h66 §**
20m^{5} 22f^{5} 22f^{5} 16m^{5} Oct 26] compact gelding: poor maiden hurdler: probably stays

2¾m: acts on firm and soft going: effective with or without headgear: has had tongue tied: not one to trust. *E. L. James*

RED PERK (IRE) 7 b.g. Executive Perk – Supreme View (Supreme Leader) [2003/4 h61+, F–: 25s^pu 20v^6 c25v^pu 24d^4 c32d^2 c26d^2 Apr 18] workmanlike gelding: poor maiden hurdler: best effor over fences when second in handicap at Carlisle final start: thorough stayer: acts on good to soft going: tried in cheekpieces. *R. C. Guest* **c87 h76**

RED RAJA 11 b.g. Persian Heights – Jenny Splendid (John Splendid) [2003/4 c–, h–: c16d^F c16g^pu 16s 20g^6 Mar 6] close-coupled gelding: winning hurdler/maiden chaser: retains very little ability: left C. Cox after second start: tried in cheekpieces. *Miss Victoria Roberts* **c– h–**

RED RAMONA 9 b.g. Rudimentary (USA) – Apply (Kings Lake (USA)) [2003/4 24m^rtr 17m Jun 21] leggy gelding: one-time useful stayer on Flat: has become thoroughly ungenuine, twice refusing to race over hurdles: one to leave well alone. *R. M. Stronge* **h§§**

RED RAMPAGE 9 b.g. King's Ride – Mighty Fly (Comedy Star (USA)) [2003/4 c101, h–: c24g^4 c24s^4 c25g^pu c27v^2 c24v^2 c27s^2 c26d^* c24g^3 c31d^2 Apr 22] good-topped gelding: fair handicap chaser: sold out of R. C. Guest's stable 13,500 gns Doncaster May Sales after second start: won at Carlisle in March stays 31f: acts on heavy and good to firm going: tried visored, usually blinkered: effective tongue tied or not: often front runner. *H. P. Hogarth* **c106 h–**

RED RETURN (IRE) 7 ch.g. Bob's Return (IRE) – Kerrie's Pearl (Proverb) [2003/4 F78: 24m^4 24m^pu 20g 22d Jan 1] modest form only on first of 4 starts in novice hurdles. *L. A. Dace* **h88**

RED ROVER 7 ch.m. Infantry – M I Babe (Celtic Cone) [2003/4 22g^5 24d^* 20d^pu 24d^6 24v Mar 21] sturdy mare: poor hurdler: off 5 months, won amateur handicap at Carlisle in November: better at 3m than shorter: raced on good going or softer: blinkered final start: joined P. Nolan. *Mrs M. Reveley* **h70**

RED RUFFLES (IRE) 5 b.g. Anshan – Rosie Ruffles (IRE) (Homo Sapien) [2003/4 F16d^* 16v^4 16v^2 19g^* 22g^2 Apr 18] unfurnished gelding: first foal: dam twice-raced half-sister to useful hurdler up to 3m Abbot of Furness: won bumper at Newbury on debut in November: fairly useful form over hurdles: won novice at Doncaster in March by 9 lengths from Jack Martin: will stay beyond 2¾m. *Noel T. Chance* **h116 F104**

REDSKIN RAIDER (IRE) 8 b.g. Commanche Run – Sheltered (IRE) (Strong Gale) [2003/4 c–, h–: c22g^ur c16d^4 c24d^F c24g^pu c25g^2 Apr 4] lengthy gelding: maiden hurdler: modest form both completed starts over fences: stays 25f: best effort on good to firm going. *T. R. George* **c93 h–**

RED SOCIALITE (IRE) 7 ch.g. Moscow Society (USA) – Dees Darling (IRE) (King Persian) [2003/4 h107p: c19g^4 Nov 4] tall, angular gelding: much improved over hurdles when winning maiden final start in 2002/3: last of 4 finishers to One Nation in maiden chase at Exeter only outing in 2003/4: stays 21f: acts on good to firm going. *D. R. Gandolfo* **c100 h–**

RED SOCIETY (IRE) 6 ch.g. Moscow Society (USA) – Allendara (IRE) (Phardante (FR)) [2003/4 20f^4 21g^3 20m^2 21g^3 23m^2 24g c16d^5 c21v^5 c21s^3 c16g c21d^* Mar 16] IR £6,500 3-y-o: angular gelding: third foal: dam unraced: poor form in bumpers: poor maiden hurdler: left E. Sheehy prior to reappearance: best effort over fences when winning novice at Sedgefield: stays 23f: acts on good to firm and good to soft going, probably on heavy: sometimes wears cheekpieces: sold 20,000 gns Doncaster May Sales. *Ferdy Murphy* **c100 h77**

REDSPIN (IRE) 4 ch.g. Spectrum (IRE) – Trendy Indian (IRE) (Indian Ridge) [2003/4 16m^2 16m^5 16g^2 16s 16s^5 Dec 13] angular gelding: fairly useful on Flat at 3 yrs for J. Hills: best effort in juvenile hurdles when second in maiden at Kempton on debut: raced at 2m, will stay further: acts on good to firm going: fair form at 1¾m+ on Flat in 2004. *J. S. Moore* **h98**

RED SQUARE DAWN 8 b.m. Derrylin – Raise The Dawn (Rymer) [2003/4 h68: 20g 22g 24g Jun 12] smallish mare: maiden hurdler, no form in 2003/4: usually blinkered/visored: prone to mistakes: has looked none too keen. *Mrs L. Williamson* **h–**

RED SQUARE KING 6 ch.g. Sure Blade (USA) – Patscilla (Squill (USA)) [2003/4 h–: 16g^pu c17g^5 c16m^pu Jun 11] little sign of ability: sold 1,600 gns Doncaster August Sales. *Mrs L. Williamson* **c– h–**

RED SQUARE LAD (IRE) 8 ch.g. Toulon – Tempestuous Girl (Tumble Wind) [2003/4 22g Nov 1] sixth foal: half-brother to winning 2m hurdler Layham Low (by **h–**

Mandalus): dam placed once over 2m on Flat in Ireland: pulled hard when well held in novice hurdle on debut. *Mrs L. Williamson*

RED SQUARE MAN (IRE) 9 b.g. Rashar (USA) – November Tide (Laurence O) [2003/4 h–§: 17m c16m c17m^{ur} 17d^{ur} 17m^6 21m^{pu} Sep 5] tall gelding: temperamental maiden: tried in cheekpieces: dead. *Mrs L. Williamson*   **c– §** **h– §**

RED SQUARE PRINCE (IRE) 8 b.g. Alphabatim (USA) – Dawn Rising (Le Moss) [2003/4 c26f^{pu} May 21] tall gelding: winning pointer, pulled up most starts in 2004: not fluent and soon tailed off in hunter chase (saddle reportedly slipped). *Mrs Alison Hickman*   **c–**

REDSTAR ATTRACTION 6 ch.g. Nalchik (USA) – Star Gal (Starch Reduced) [2003/4 F16d Jan 22] second foal: dam unraced: well held in bumper on debut. *W. M. Brisbourne*   **F–**

RED STORM 5 ch.m. Dancing Spree (USA) – Dam Certain (IRE) (Damister (USA)) [2003/4 17s^{pu} 16d^{pu} Mar 21] modest on all-weather on Flat (stays 11f): showed nothing in 2 novice hurdles, visored on second occasion. *J. R. Boyle*   **h–**

RED SUN 7 b.g. Foxhound (USA) – Superetta (Superlative) [2003/4 h108: 19g^3 19g^2 17f* 16g* 16m 16g 16d^5 16d^F Apr 3] small, leggy gelding: fairly useful handicap hurdler: successful in small fields at Hereford in May and Market Rasen and Uttoxeter in October (made all on last 2 occasions): stays 19f: acts on soft and firm going: tongue tied final start: consistent. *J. Mackie*   **h121**

RED TYRANT 6 b.g. Minster Son – By The Lake (Tyrant (USA)) [2003/4 h81, F87: 20m^3 20d^6 22g^{ro} 20m^4 May 27] lengthy gelding: poor form in novice hurdles: will probably stay beyond 2½m: acts on good to firm and good to soft gong: tried in cheek-pieces: sold 3,2000 gns Doncaster August Sales, no form in points in 2004. *R. C. Guest*   **c–** **h79**

REDVIC 4 b.g. Alhaatmi – Sweet Fortune (Dubassoff (USA)) [2003/4 19s^{pu} Apr 11] no form on Flat for Mrs N. Macauley: showed nothing on hurdling debut. *G. J. Smith*   **h–**

RED WILL DANAGHER (IRE) 7 b.g. Glacial Storm (USA) – Clodas Pet (IRE) (Andretti) [2003/4 h88§: 26g 22d^4 22g^2 24m Jun 7] workmanlike gelding: modest maiden hurdler: stays 2¾m: has shown signs of temperament. *John Allen*   **h85**

RED WILLIE 5 b.g. Master Willie – Ormania (FR) (Synefos (USA)) [2003/4 F16m F16d 19s^{pu} 19m^{pu} 17s^6 Mar 23] angular gelding: first foal: dam fairly useful hurdler around 2m: modest form on first of 2 starts in bumpers (hung right): no show in 3 outings over hurdles: downed tools in visor final start: pulls hard: needs treating with caution. *M. C. Pipe*   **h– §** **F80**

RED WIZARD 4 b.g. Wizard King – Drudwen (Sayf El Arab (USA)) [2003/4 16f* 16f^2 16m^3 16d Jan 10] workmanlike gelding: fairly useful at 2 yrs for W. O'Gorman, fair form on Flat in 2003: fair form over hurdles: won juvenile maiden at Ludlow in October: likely to prove best at 2m with emphasis on speed. *Jonjo O'Neill*   **h97**

REEFA'S MILL (IRE) 12 b.g. Astronef – Pharly's Myth (Pharly (FR)) [2003/4 17g^{pu} Aug 25] sturdy gelding: winning hurdler/maiden chaser: pulled up only start since 1998/9: often blinkered/visored. *B. P. J. Baugh*   **c–** **h–**

REEL DANCER 7 b.g. Minshaanshu Amad (USA) – Sister Rosarii (USA) (Proper-antes (USA)) [2003/4 h80: c19d^2 c19s^{pu} Dec 27] sturdy gelding: well beaten in 2 novice hurdles: fair form when second to Supreme Prince in maiden at Chepstow on chasing debut: ran poorly in novice there next time: stays 19f: raced on ground softer than good. *B. De Haan*   **c105** **h–**

REEL HANDSOME 12 ch.g. Handsome Sailor – Reel Chance (Proverb) [2003/4 c71: c20m^4 c17g^6 c21v^4 May 26] big, lengthy gelding: poor maiden chaser: stays 2¾m: acts on good to firm and heavy going: tongue tied. *C. T. Pogson*   **c–**

REEL MISSILE 5 b.g. Weld – Landsker Missile (Cruise Missile) [2003/4 F16g* F16d^2 Mar 28] 7,000 4-y-o: first foal: dam fairly useful hunter who stayed 21f: 100/1, won bumper at Doncaster on debut by 4 lengths from La Perrotine, finding plenty despite signs of greenness: again dictated pace when 4 lengths second to Racing Demon at Huntingdon later in month. *C. T. Pogson*   **F109**

REFINEMENT (IRE) 5 b.m. Oscar (IRE) – Maneree (Mandalus) [2003/4 F17g* F16s* F16g^2 Mar 17]   **F115**

When the favourite Refinement landed the Bangor Mares' Only Standard Open National Hunt Flat on her debut in October she was the first of what is likely to be many winners in Britain for her sire Oscar, who stands at Coolmore's Grange

Ascot Standard Open National Hunt Flat—Refinement is impressive

Stud. Although her second win, at Ascot ten weeks later, was the only other for Oscar's progeny in Britain in 2003/4, he was much more strongly represented in Ireland with several promising performers running for him, including Augherskea, third in the Grade 1 bumper at Punchestown, the Land Rover Bumper winner Arteea and the useful bumper winners Nowyouretalking and Oscar's Advance, as well as the fairly useful French jumper Knock Down, winner of a Group 3 event over fences at Auteuil in 2003. That Oscar will have plenty of winners is almost guaranteed by weight of numbers: in his first season at stud, 1998, he covered no fewer than three hundred and twenty-two mares, more than any other sire (the well-established Supreme Leader came next with two hundred and ninety-nine). Oscar has continued to cover huge books of mares, with well over two hundred and fifty visiting him in both 2002 and 2003. Before he had even had a runner, Oscar had sired over seven hundred foals, which represents an astonishing gamble for at least some of the breeders involved. Oscar's progeny have made an impact at the store sales as well. In 2002, a three-year-old half-brother to the Grade 1 bumper winner Supreme Developer made €100,000 at the Derby Sale and, named Bold Jack Donoghue, was a promising third in a bumper on his debut in February in the colours of Sue Magnier. At the same sale a year later, €165,000, the biggest sum at the sale (a fact used by Coolmore in their advertising), was paid for an Oscar three-year-old out of a half-sister to Morley Street and Granville Again, bought by Paul Shanahan reportedly on behalf of John Magnier. He has yet to race. The strategy behind promoting Oscar as a National Hunt stallion from the outset is pretty obvious: he is by Sadler's Wells but he has too stout a pedigree and a racing record that would not make much appeal to Flat breeders. A brother to the Derby runner-up Blue Stag, Oscar ran just four times, improving with each run and ending his career with a staying-on second in the 1997 Prix du Jockey Club. There isn't much evidence yet as to the durability or aptitude for jumping of Oscar's offspring, and it is possible they might take a while to mature, all the bumper performers mentioned earlier coming from his first rather than his second crop.

Refinement is, by a narrow margin, the highest rated of Oscar's bumper performers in 2003/4, by virtue of her second placing in the Champion Bumper at Cheltenham. She had won impressively at both Bangor and Ascot, showing useful form in a quite valuable event at the latter track, and started joint second favourite at Cheltenham at 7/1. Refinement was again held up going well and made good progress coming down the hill, but she couldn't match the pace of the winner Total Enjoyment into the straight, though keeping on towards the finish, two and a half lengths behind at the line. Coincidentally, Total Enjoyment is by another Coolmore stallion Flemensfirth, who was lightly raced on the Flat and who covered large books of mares before he'd had any runners.

		Sadler's Wells (b 1981)	Northern Dancer
	Oscar (IRE) (b 1994)		Fairy Bridge
		Snow Day (b 1978)	Reliance II
Refinement (IRE) (b.f. 1999)			Vindaria
		Mandalus (b 1974)	Mandamus
	Maneree (b 1987)		Laminate
		Damberee (ch 1975)	Deep Run
			Star O'Meath

In finishing second at Cheltenham, Refinement went one better than her dam Maneree, who was third to Montelado and Tiananmen Square in the inaugural running of the Champion (then Festival) Bumper. Maneree went on to show herself fairly useful over hurdles and fair over fences, with form at up to three miles. Like Maneree, Refinement races for Michael Tabor, who also owns her year-older half-brother Manners (by Topanoora), who made an impressive debut in a bumper at Haydock in November. There is little to say about the rest of this family in the recent past. Neither the grandam Damberee nor the third dam Star of Meath showed much ability and, apart from Maneree, can muster just a bumper winner and a winning pointer from their collective progeny. Refinement is nothing to look at, being very much on the small side, and may not be anything out of the ordinary over hurdles though she should be able to win a mares race or two at least. *Jonjo O'Neill*

REFLECTIVE WAY 11 ch.m. Mirror Boy – Craigie Way (Palm Track) [2003/4 c84, h–: c24g^{pu} c25g^5 c20g^2 c25g^{pu} c20s^3 c25v^F c25v^2 c20s^2 c27s^6 Feb 24] good-topped **c79** **h–**

mare: poor handicap chaser: stays 3¼m: acts on heavy going: has had tongue tied. *A. C. Whillans*

REFLEX BLUE   7 b.g. Ezzoud (IRE) – Briggsmaid (Elegant Air) [2003/4 h81§: 16m⁴ 17m¹ 16d* 16s⁵ 16d* 16s Feb 22] angular gelding: modest hurdler: won selling handicaps at Uttoxeter (conditional jockeys) in November and Ludlow in January: stays easy 21f: acts on firm and good to soft going, possibly not on softer: usually visored (wasn't at Uttoxeter): temperamental. *R. J. Price*   **h89 §**

REFLEX COURIER (IRE)   12 b.g. Over The River (FR) – Thornpark Lady (Mandalus) [2003/4 c91: c22g⁶ c21s* c24s⁵ c22s⁵ c22s⁴ Mar 7] good-bodied gelding: modest handicap chaser: won at Stratford in December: stays 25f: raced on good going or softer (acts on heavy). *John R. Upson*   **c88**

REGAL ACT (IRE)   8 ch.g. Montelimar (USA) – Portal Lady (Pals Passage) [2003/4 c20sᵖᵘ c20sᵇᵈ c16g³ Dec 19] angular ex-Irish gelding: half-brother to winning hurdler by Good Thyne: dam maiden: bumper winner: modest maiden hurdler: sold out of M. Purcell's stable €30,000 Goffs June Sale: no form over fences: stays 19f: raced on good ground or softer: tried tongue tied: sold 1,000 gns Doncaster May Sales. *C. J. Mann*   **c–** **h–**

REGAL ALI (IRE)   5 ch.g. Ali-Royal (IRE) – Depeche (FR) (Kings Lake (USA)) [2003/4 h–: 16g Apr 4] winning hurdler in Jersey, including twice in 2003/4: no form in Britain. *G. A. Ham*   **h?**

REGAL APPLAUSE   5 b.m. Royal Applause – Panchellita (USA) (Pancho Villa (USA)) [2003/4 h–: 16s 16m⁶ 16gᵖᵘ Apr 18] no worthwhile form over hurdles. *Mrs J. A. Ewer*   **h–**

REGAL BANDIT (IRE)   6 b.g. Un Desperado (FR) – Rainbow Alliance (IRE) (Golden Love) [2003/4 F17g⁵ F16g³ 22s 22d⁶ 21gᵖᵘ Mar 5] useful-looking gelding: will make a chaser: third foal: dam winning pointer: better effort in bumpers when third at Ludlow: caught the eye in novice at Wincanton on hurdling debut, better form when sixth in similar event there next time: reportedly lost action final start: will stay beyond 2¾m. *Miss H. C. Knight*   **h93 +** **F86**

REGAL CHANCE   11 b.g. Cisto (FR) – Regal Flutter (Henry The Seventh) [2003/4 c89, h–: c20d³ c20dᵖᵘ c19g⁴ Apr 16] good-bodied gelding: winning chaser, just poor form in 2003/4: stays 2½m: acts on heavy going. *A. King*   **c76** **h–**

REGAL CUSTOM   6 ch.g. Royal Vulcan – Rural Custom (Country Retreat) [2003/4 F18s F18s⁵ Feb 16] first foal: dam winning pointer: better effort in bumpers when fifth at Plumpton. *N. B. King*   **F72**

REGAL EMPRESS   6 b.m. Regal Embers (IRE) – Mis-E-Fishant (Sunyboy) [2003/4 F17g⁶ F17m F16m 16gᵖᵘ Feb 11] unfurnished mare: first foal: dam winning pointer: no form (trained by G. H. Jones on debut): wore hood and blinkers on hurdling debut. *C. J. Price*   **h–** **F–**

REGAL EXIT (FR)   8 ch.g. Exit To Nowhere (USA) – Regalante (Gairloch) [2003/4 c124, h120: c17g 16d* 16s c20g³ c19gᶠ 17d Mar 18] good-topped gelding: shows traces of stringhalt: fairly useful handicap hurdler/chaser: won over hurdles at Doncaster in December by 5 lengths from Noshinannikin: probably stays 21f: acts on good to firm and heavy going: has found little. *N. J. Henderson*   **c124** **h129**

REGAL HOLLY   9 b.m. Gildoran – Pusey Street (Native Bazaar) [2003/4 c115, h–: c24sᵖᵘ 24g⁴ 24s Feb 3] angular mare: fair hurdler: fairly useful chaser in 2003/4, possibly needed race on reappearance: stays 25f: raced on good going or softer over jumps (acts on heavy): blinkered. *C. J. Mann*   **c–** **h100**

REGAL JONES (IRE)   4 b.f. Sovereign Water (FR) – Juleit Jones (IRE) (Phardante (FR)) [2003/4 F18g aF16g Apr 4] leggy filly: second foal: dam winning 2m hurdler: showed nothing in 2 bumpers. *P. Butler*   **F–**

REGAL LIGHT   9 gr.g. Gran Alba (USA) – Light of Zion (Pieces of Eight) [2003/4 h–: c25gᵖᵘ May 1] strong gelding: little sign of ability. *J. C. Tuck*   **c–** **h–**

REGAL RIVER (IRE)   7 b.g. Over The River (FR) – My Friend Fashion (Laurence O) [2003/4 c93, h–: c25vᵘʳ c25vᵘʳ c29sᵖᵘ c27sᵖᵘ Feb 24] close-coupled gelding: modest handicap chaser: let down by jumping first 2 starts, amiss next 2: will prove best at 3m+: raced on good going or softer (acts on heavy). *John R. Upson*   **c–** **h–**

REGAL STATESMAN (NZ)   11 br.g. Vice Regal (NZ) – Hykit (NZ) (Swinging Junior) [2003/4 c–, h89§: 21m 22gᵖᵘ Mar 28] rangy gelding: winning hurdler, appears to retain little ability. *O. Brennan*   **c–** **h– §**

REGAL VINTAGE (USA)   4 ch.g. Kingmambo (USA) – Grapevine (IRE) (Sadler's   **h65**
Wells (USA)) [2003/4 16f^{pu} 16d 16f^4 19d 20s^{pu} Mar 13] little form on Flat: poor form
over hurdles: usually visored and tongue tied: has looked none too keen. *C. Grant*

REGAL VISION (IRE)   7 b.g. Emperor Jones (USA) – Shining Eyes (USA) (Mr   **c97 §**
Prospector (USA)) [2003/4 h97§: c21g^{ur} c21g* c21g^5 c21g^{ur} c21m c23m^{pu} c24f^2 c20f^6 **h– §**
20d 24s c24g c20m^2 c20d^4 c21s^{rtr} c19g^3 Apr 16] leggy gelding: winning hurdler: modest
chaser: won novice at Newton Abbot in June: sold out of C. Cox's stable 6,000 gns
Doncaster November Sales after eighth start: probably stays 3m: acts on firm going,
probably on soft: effective blinkered or not: one to steer clear of (refused to race once).
C. J. Mann

REGARDEZ-MOI   7 b.m. Distinctly North (USA) – Tomard (Thatching) [2003/4   **h53**
h62: 16g^5 22m^6 May 29] bad maiden hurdler: pulled up in point in March. *Miss M. Bragg*

REGAR (IRE)   12 b.g. Buckskin (FR) – Pass Thurn (Trimmingham) [2003/4 c82, h–:   **c76**
c25d^{pu} c16s c20m^5 c16d^2 c17m^4 c16m^3 c16g Aug 8] poor maiden chaser: tried blinkered: **h–**
has had tongue tied. *M. A. Barnes*

REGENTS WALK (IRE)   6 b.g. Phardante (FR) – Raw Courage (IRE) (The Parson)   **h101 p**
[2003/4 F91: 16m^6 Feb 21] sturdy gelding: third in bumper on debut in 2002/3: off 11
months, still looked green when sixth to Fool On The Hill in novice hurdle at Wincanton
(reportedly hung left) only start in 2003/4: should do better. *B. De Haan*

REGGAE RHYTHM (IRE)   10 b.g. Be My Native (USA) – Invery Lady (Sharpen   **c82**
Up) [2003/4 c–, h74: 16s c16d^2 c16s^{pu} 21d Apr 12] angular gelding: winning hurdler,   **h–**
on the downgrade: poor maiden chaser: stays 2½m: acts on heavy going: usually wears
cheekpieces: not a fluent jumper of fences. *R. N. Bevis*

REGGIE BUCK (USA)   10 b. or br.g. Alleged (USA) – Hello Memphis (USA)   **h92**
(Super Concorde (USA)) [2003/4 h94: 16d^3 16m^3 16g^2 May 29] angular gelding: modest
handicap hurdler: won at Hexham very early in season: best around 2m: acts on soft and
good to firm going: tried blinkered. *J. Mackie*

REGIMENTAL DANCE   4 b.f. Groom Dancer (USA) – Enlisted (IRE) (Sadler's   **h–**
Wells (USA)) [2003/4 17m^F Sep 27] modest on Flat (seemed to stay 1¼m): fell second on
hurdling debut: dead. *C. Grant*

REGISTANA (GER)   8 br.m. Tauchsport (EG) – Reklame (EG) (Immer (HUN))   **c?**
[2003/4 c19g^8 c28g* c19g^8 c34m^8 Oct 12] sister to 2 winners, including useful German
chaser Registano and half-sister to others: dam never ran: prolific winner over fences in
Italy and Czech Republic, unbeaten in 4 starts in 2003/4, at Merano in June (Grade 3
event) and August and Pardubice later in June and October: beat Maskul ¾ length in
Velka Pardubicka Ceske Pojistovny on last-named occasion: effective around 2½m to
4¼m. *C. Olehla, Czech Republic*

REIVERS MOON   5 b. or br.m. Midnight Legend – Here Comes Tibby (Royal   **h93**
Fountain) [2003/4 F83: 21s^2 20g 22f^3 22g^3 16d^3 20m^2 21v^3 20g^2 20d Feb 8] smallish,
leggy mare: modest novice hurdler: placed 7 of 9 starts in 2003/4: effective at 2m, will
stay 3m: acts on firm and good to soft going. *W. Amos*

Velka Pardubicka Ceske Pojistovny, Pardubice—the mare Registana leads over the Taxis;
Peter Gehm rides the winner for the third successive year, on a different horse each time

REIZIGER (FR)   8 gr.g. Balleroy (USA) – Dany Ohio (FR) (Script Ohio (USA))   **c125** [2003/4 16m⁴ 16s 17g c19s² c20g⁵ c20m² c20g⁴ c16d* c16d³ Mar 18] neat gelding: fairly   **h116** useful handicap hurdler/chaser: won over fences at Sandown in March by length from 3uper Noimai: barely stays 2½m: acts on heavy and good to firm going: usually held up: sometimes none too fluent. *P. J. Hobbs*

RELATIVE HERO (IRE)   4 ch.g. Entrepreneur – Aunty (FR) (Riverman (USA))   **h–** [2003/4 17d Nov 28] half-brother to 17f hurdle winner Padishah (by Kris): fair on Flat (stays 1m), sold out of H. Morrison's stable 12,000 gns Doncaster October Sales: always behind in juvenile on hurdling debut. *Miss S. J. Wilton*

RELIX (FR)   4 gr.g. Linamix (FR) – Resleona (Caerleon (USA)) [2003/4 17s 17dᵖᵘ 17g   **h–** Apr 12] ex-French gelding: dam sister to useful French hurdler Restless Carl: won once over 11f from 16 starts on Flat mainly in Provinces at 2/3 yrs for G. Henrot/H-A. Pantall: little show in 3 starts over hurdles. *Ferdy Murphy*

REMEMBRANCE   4 b.g. Sabrehill (USA) – Perfect Poppy (Shareef Dancer (USA))   **h–** [2003/4 16g 17d 16sᶠ Mar 19] fair maiden on Flat (stayed 1½m) for J. Eustace: tongue tied, showed little over hurdles: dead. *M. J. Gingell*

REMINISCENT (IRE)   5 b.g. Kahyasi – Eliza Orzeszkowa (IRE) (Polish Patriot   **h94** (USA)) [2003/4 17g² 20g⁵ Mar 8] fair on all-weather, modest on turf on Flat (stays 2m): modest form in maiden hurdles at Taunton and Fontwell. *R. F. Johnson Houghton*

RENALOO (IRE)   9 gr.g. Tremblant – Rare Flower (Decent Fellow) [2003/4 c85§,   **c– §** h–: c17sᵖᵘ 23m⁶ c22gᵖᵘ c16gᵖᵘ Mar 3] workmanlike gelding: maiden hurdler/winning   **h–** chaser, no form in 2003/4: probably best around 2m: acts on soft going: irresolute (reluctant to race on reappearance). *R. Rowe*

RENDARI (IRE)   9 b.g. Shardari – Reneagh (Prince Regent (FR)) [2003/4 20s 16vᵖᵘ   **h96** 17s 24g³ 26d* 23dᵖᵘ Apr 12] ex-Irish gelding: fourth foal: half-brother to winning pointer by Phardante: dam 2m hurdle winner, also successful on Flat: placed in points: bumper winner: modest hurdler: sold out of P. Cashman's stable 10,000 gns Doncaster August (2002) Sales: won handicap at Huntingdon in March: stays 3¼m: acts on good to soft going. *R. Ford*

RENDOVA   5 b.g. Darshaan – Mary Astor (FR) (Groom Dancer (USA)) [2003/4 F16g   **F86** F17d Apr 3] leggy gelding: fourth foal: half-brother to winner around 1m in Germany by Barathea: dam, won up to around 1½m on Flat in France, half-sister to dam of winning high-class 6f to 8.5f performer Lit de Justice and very smart 1½m colts Colonel Collins and Commander Collins: tenth of 24 to Secret Ploy in Grade 2 bumper at Newbury on debut: well beaten in similar event at Aintree. *A. M. Balding*

RENO   4 ch.f. Efisio – Los Alamos (Keen) [2003/4 16m² 16f² 16g³ 16d² 16v⁴ 17sᶠ 16g   **h88** 20s 17g³ Apr 12] smallish filly: modest maiden on Flat (stays 1¼m): modest juvenile hurdler: will prove best around 2m: acts on firm and soft going: tongue tied last 2 starts. *C. W. Thornton*

REN'S MAGIC   6 gr.g. Petong – Bath (Runnett) [2003/4 16d⁵ 16m² 16mᵖᵘ Oct 18]   **h86** close-coupled gelding: modest maiden on Flat (stays 1¾m): easily best effort in novice company over hurdles when second at Plumpton in September: visored following month. *J. R. Jenkins*

RENVYLE (IRE)   6 b. or br.g. Satco (FR) – Kara's Dream (IRE) (Bulldozer) [2003/4   **c108** F16f F17g* F16m² F17m⁴ 24d⁴ 21d 16s⁴ c20d* Mar 10] IR £25,000 3-y-o: close-coupled   **h98** gelding: second foal: dam placed in bumpers: finished second both starts in maiden Irish   **F100** points in 2003 (disqualified, rider failed to weigh in on first occasion): fairly useful form in bumpers, won at Newton Abbot (first run after leaving H. de Bromhead) in September: modest form in 3 starts over hurdles: fair form when winning novice handicap at Bangor on steeplechasing debut: should stay beyond 2½m. *Jonjo O'Neill*

RENZO (IRE)   11 b.g. Alzao (USA) – Watership (USA) (Foolish Pleasure (USA))   **h– §** [2003/4 h103§: 16s⁵ 16d Jan 13] good-topped gelding: winning hurdler, lost his way: likely to have stayed beyond 19f: acted on soft and good to firm ground: jumped none too fluently: ungenuine: dead. *John A. Harris*

REPUNZEL   9 b.m. Carlingford Castle – Hi-Rise Lady (Sunyboy) [2003/4 c84, h–:   **c84** c16mᵖᵘ c16s² c20d³ c16d c17dᵇᵈ c19s³ Mar 24] tall mare: poor hurdler/chaser: best   **h–** around 2m: unraced on firm going, acts on any other: all 3 wins at Plumpton: none too consistent. *N. A. Gaselee*

REQUESTOR   9 br.g. Distinctly North (USA) – Bebe Altesse (GER) (Alpenkonig   **h74** (GER)) [2003/4 h90: 16m² May 5] modest form when winning conditional jockeys selling handicap hurdle in 2002/3: again tongue tied, second in novice seller at Huntingdon following month: stays 2½m. *T. J. Fitzgerald*

RESCATOR (FR)   8 b.g. Saint Estephe (FR) – La Narquoise (FR) (Al Nasr (FR)) [2003/4 h84: 16d* 16m⁶ 20v 20s Apr 17] workmanlike gelding: winning pointer: poor hurdler: won seller at Hexham in May: stays 21f: acts on soft going, probably on good to firm: has looked temperamental. *Mrs S. J. Smith*   **h82**

RESCIND (IRE)   4 b.f. Revoque (IRE) – Sunlit Ride (Ahonoora) [2003/4 16g³ 16d⁴ Nov 23] modest maiden at 2 yrs, well held on Flat in 2003: better effort over hurdles when third in juvenile maiden at Huntingdon. *Jedd O'Keeffe*   **h78**

RESCINDO (IRE)   5 b.g. Revoque (IRE) – Mystic Dispute (IRE) (Magical Strike (USA)) [2003/4 h100: 16m⁴ 18m³ 17m⁴ 17m² 17m⁴ 19g² Jul 31] medium-sized gelding: fair maiden hurdler, in frame all 9 starts: stays 19f: acts on good to firm and good to soft going: visored after reappearance: sold 3,400 gns Doncaster August Sales, runner-up on completed start in points in 2004. *M. C. Pipe*   **h103**

RESEARCHER   5 ch.m. Cosmonaut – Rest (Dance In Time (CAN)) [2003/4 h93: 17g* 17g⁴ 16g⁶ 19g* 24g³ 17s* 21g 22d 21m Apr 15] lengthy mare: fair hurdler: won mares novices at Exeter very early in season and Doncaster in November and mares handicap at Exeter in January: effective at 2m to 3m: raced mainly on good going or softer (acts on soft): sometimes jumps poorly. *Miss Venetia Williams*   **h107**

RESEDA (GER)   5 b.m. Lavirco (GER) – Reklame (EG) (Immer (HUN)) [2003/4 F17g⁴ Apr 13] half-sister to several winners, including useful German chaser up to 25f Registano and Velka Pardubicka winner Registana (both by Tauchsport): dam never ran: fourth in bumper at Exeter on debut. *Ian Williams*   **F82**

RESILIENCE   4 b.f. Most Welcome – Abstone Queen (Presidium) [2003/4 16f⁵ Oct 5] sprint maiden on Flat, well held in 2003: not fluent and always behind in juvenile on hurdling debut. *B. Mactaggart*   **h–**

RESISTANCE (IRE)   7 br.g. Phardante (FR) – Shean Hill (IRE) (Bar Dexter (USA)) [2003/4 h84: 16dᵖᵘ Jan 13] lengthy gelding: poor maiden hurdler: raced freely when visored only start in 2003/4: seems to stay 19f: joined Mrs H. Dalton. *G. A. Ham*   **h–**

RESSOURCE (FR)   5 b.g. Broadway Flyer (USA) – Rayonne (Sadler's Wells (USA)) [2003/4 h89: 16s⁶ 18g² 17dᶠ 17s² 17s⁴ 17g³ 16d³ Apr 11] leggy gelding: modest maiden hurdler: raced around 2m: acts on heavy going: blinkered in 2003/4, also tried in eyeshields: ungenuine. *G. L. Moore*   **h85 §**

RESTLESS WIND (IRE)   12 b.g. Celio Rufo – Trulos (Three Dons) [2003/4 c109: c23dᵖᵘ c19s³ c24sᵖᵘ c24g c24g⁶ c24d* c24g² Apr 1] lengthy gelding: modest chaser: won minor event at Taunton in March: stays 25f: acts on soft and good to firm going: patiently ridden, and sometimes finds little: sold 3,500 gns Doncaster May Sales. *G. B. Balding*   **c94 §**

RETAIL THERAPY (IRE)   4 b.f. Bahhare (USA) – Elect (USA) (Vaguely Noble) [2003/4 16g* 16sᵖᵘ 16s 16g Mar 5] leggy filly: modest form on Flat (stays 1½m): form over hurdles only when winning juvenile maiden at Huntingdon in November. *M. A. Buckley*   **h83**

RETURNED UNPAID (IRE)   7 b.g. Actinium (FR) – Claregalway Lass (Ardross) [2003/4 20mᵖᵘ c26m⁴ c23d⁴ 26d³ 27fᵖᵘ c26m* c26mᶠ c26mᵖᵘ c25d³ c27v³ c20s Feb 11] IR 5,000 4-y-o, resold IR £4,000 4-y-o: workmanlike gelding: third foal: dam unraced, from family of useful hurdler up to 21f Buddy Marvel: poor form over hurdles: poor chaser: won maiden at Southwell in August: sold out of P. Blockley's stable 5,000 gns Doncaster October Sales after eighth start: stays 3¼m: acts on good to firm and heavy going: blinkered sixth to eighth outings: sometimes makes mistakes/looks difficult ride. *Mrs S. J. Smith*   **c75**   **h67**

RETURN TICKET   5 br.g. Bob's Return (IRE) – Mrs Jennifer (River Knight (FR)) [2003/4 F18g⁴ Apr 22] fourth foal: half-brother to 3 winning hurdlers, including smart stayer Splendid Thyne (by Good Thyne) and useful performer up to 25f His Nibs (by Alflora): dam, poor novice hurdler, from family of top-class staying chaser Brown Chamberlin: fourth in bumper at Fontwell on debut: will be suited by 2½m+. *R. T. Phillips*   **F76**

REVELINO (IRE)   5 b.g. Revoque (IRE) – Forelino (USA) (Trempolino (USA)) [2003/4 h73: 16d 17d³ 19d⁴ 16s 16g⁵ Apr 17] poor maiden hurdler: stays 19f: raced on good going or softer: finishes weakly. *Miss S. J. Wilton*   **h72**

REVERSE PACE (IRE)   7 b.g. Leading Counsel (USA) – Drumscap (IRE) (Remainder Man) [2003/4 F17d Nov 22] showed ability in 2 bumpers in 2001/2: left Mrs P. Sly and off nearly 20 months, well held in similar event only outing in 2003/4. *Mrs H. Dalton*   **F–**

REVERSE SWING   7 b.m. Charmer – Milly Kelly (Murrayfield) [2003/4 h77: 16g   **h–**
May 2] good-topped mare: poor 2m handicap hurdler: acts on good to soft going:
free-going sort. *Mrs H. Dalton*

REVERSO (FR)   4 h g Kaldounevees (FR) Sweet Racine (FR) (Dom Racine (FR))   **h–**
[2003/4 19v 21g^{pu} Mar 26] workmanlike gelding: eighth foal: half-brother to several
winners in France, including useful hurdler/chaser up to 19f Pontvallain (by Pampabird)
and useful chaser Turgot (by Turgeon), stays 2¾m: dam unraced half-sister to very smart
French jumper up to 2¾m Lute Antique: no sign of ability on Flat debut or in 2 races over
hurdles. *N. J. Hawke*

REVIEWER (IRE)   6 b.g. Sadler's Wells (USA) – Clandestina (USA) (Secretariat   **h111**
(USA)) [2003/4 h121: 22m 22d^3 21g 24d Mar 27] neat gelding: fair handicap hurdler:
stays 2¾m: acts on soft going. *C. M. Meade*

RHAPSODY IN BLUE (IRE)   9 b.g. Magical Strike (USA) – Palace Blue (IRE)   **c–**
(Dara Monarch) [2003/4 c70, h92: 20d^{pu} c24s^{pu} May 23] good-topped gelding: winning   **h–**
hurdler/maiden chaser: ran as if amiss both starts very early in season: stays 3m: acts on
any going: tongue tied. *R. Ford*

RHEINDROSS (IRE)   9 gr.g. Ala Hounak – Ardcarn Girl (Ardross) [2003/4 c111:   **c117**
c22s^2 c20d^2 c24d^{ur} c21g^4 c24s Mar 14] strong gelding: fairly useful handicap chaser:
might well have won fairly valuable event at Punchestown in late-April but for trouble in
running: stays 2¾m: acts on heavy ground: usually held up: refused to race once.
A. L. T. Moore, Ireland

RHETORIC (IRE)   5 b.g. Desert King (IRE) – Squaw Talk (USA) (Gulch (USA))   **h–**
[2003/4 h63: 16g 21m May 29] angular gelding: little form over hurdles: tongue tied
once. *D. G. Bridgwater*

RHINESTONE COWBOY (IRE)   8 b.g. Be My Native (USA) – Monumental   **h168 +**
Gesture (Head For Heights) [2003/4 h156p, F123: 20s* 16d^6 16s* 21g^3 20d*
Apr 3]
      One horse Tony McCoy won't have first call on as stable jockey at Jack-
daws Castle is Rhinestone Cowboy. The victories at Punchestown in late-April of
the stable's Cherub, in the Colm McEvoy Auctioneers Champion Four Year Old
Hurdle, and of Rhinestone Cowboy, in the Ballymore Properties Champion
Stayers' Hurdle, came the day after news broke that McCoy had been lured from

*Tote Placepot Handicap Hurdle, Haydock—the start of a productive campaign
for Rhinestone Cowboy and his amateur rider; Double Honour (left) is second*

Martin Pipe, ending the most successful partnership in the history of racing over jumps. Tony Dobbin rode Cherub, standing in for the injured Liam Cooper, and young amateur J. P. Magnier, unable to claim his 5-lb allowance because of the status and value of the race, was on Rhinestone Cowboy in a fascinating clash with stable-companion Iris's Gift, winner of the Stayers' Hurdle at Cheltenham and the Liverpool Hurdle (a race known as the Long Distance Hurdle and transferred from Ascot). Rhinestone Cowboy, over three miles for the first time, upset the odds laid on Iris's Gift by seven lengths, quickening to lead just before the last, after being waited with, and soon overcoming a mistake to finish well on top at the post.

Iris's Gift wasn't at his best at Punchestown but, with that horse now going chasing, Rhinestone Cowboy, who carries the colours of Sue Magnier, looks set to dominate the staying hurdle division with Baracouda in the next season. J. P. Magnier, the son of John and Sue Magnier, will keep the ride. Tactical inexperience found out Mr Magnier in the hotly-contested Coral Cup at the Cheltenham Festival but, apart from that, he did nothing wrong on Rhinestone Cowboy in the latest season and was said to have given his famous father his 'biggest thrill in racing' when winning the Martell Cognac Aintree Hurdle. Unable to claim, and up against Richard Johnson on Rooster Booster and Tony McCoy on Westender in a close finish, Mr Magnier got Rhinestone Cowboy up despite the horse twice being hampered in the closing stages.

Rhinestone Cowboy's victory over Iris's Gift wasn't his first. Rhinestone Cowboy had finished three places ahead when runner-up to Pizarro in the Champion Bumper at the 2002 Cheltenham Festival. Rhinestone Cowboy went down by a neck after twice being bumped by the winner, unlucky in the view of many not to

Agfa Hurdle, Sandown—
Rhinestone Cowboy bounces back from a poor run at Leopardstown; Garde Champetre is second

Martell Cognac Aintree Hurdle—
ground to make up at the last, with Rooster Booster (No.6), Intersky Falcon and Westender still to pass

get the race in the stewards room. Norman Williamson was Rhinestone Cowboy's jockey that day and became his regular partner during an exciting novice hurdle campaign in which four impressive victories in succession persuaded connections to have a tilt at the Champion Hurdle. Rhinestone Cowboy started favourite and finished third to Rooster Booster after blundering at the second and putting in a far from fluent round of jumping. When Williamson announced his retirement from the saddle on medical advice in October, the ride went—conditionally at first—to Mr Magnier. He had partnered Rhinestone Cowboy to victory over subsequent Champion Bumper winner Liberman (ridden by McCoy) on only his seventh ride under rules in the bumper at Cheltenham's Open meeting, a prelude to the horse's novice hurdling campaign.

When Mr Magnier teamed up again with Rhinestone Cowboy—in the Tote Placepot Handicap Hurdle at Haydock on his reappearance—he had raised his tally of bumper winners to eleven, plus one on the Flat, but had had only three rides over hurdles. Conceding plenty of weight all round, the patiently-ridden Rhinestone Cowboy didn't have to be asked a serious question, leading at the last and quickening away to win by eight lengths from Double Honour. With Rooster Booster beaten in the Bula Hurdle at Cheltenham later in the afternoon, Rhinestone Cowboy was promoted to ante-post favouritism for the Champion Hurdle. He lost that position after running too badly to be true when a short-priced favourite for the December Festival Hurdle, in which his rider couldn't claim, at Leopardstown just over a fortnight later. A trio of outsiders, led home by 66/1-shot Golden Cross, dominated the finish of an event in which Rhinestone Cowboy wasn't the only disappointment, Solerina and Back In Front below form in fourth and fifth and Hardy Eustace finishing last. Mr Magnier, by the way, showed commendable good sense in not unduly knocking Rhinestone Cowboy about once he realised he wasn't going to get a winning response, Rhinestone Cowboy beating only Hardy Eustace home.

Given a short break after returning 'quiet' from Ireland, Rhinestone Cowboy bounced back to form (Mr Magnier again unable to claim) with a convincing victory from the novice Garde Champetre in the Agfa Hurdle at Sandown in February. Mr Magnier gave a calm display both in and out of the saddle, the media also focussing on speculation that there might be a racecourse protest by a militant section of fans from Manchester United. The club's manager Alex Ferguson was embroiled in a well-publicised dispute at the time with John Magnier and Coolmore over the stallion rights to Rock of Gibraltar who had won seven consecutive Group 1 races on the Flat in Ferguson's colours. Magnier and J P McManus had staked a claim to ownership of Manchester United by increasing their shareholding since the Rock of Gibraltar dispute had arisen. As it turned out, disturbances the previous day at Hereford (where McManus had a runner) were not repeated at Sandown.

Ballymore Properties Champion Stayers Hurdle, Punchestown—a second Grade 1 success, at the chief expense of a below-par Iris's Gift (largely hidden); Rosaker takes third

Rhinestone Cowboy's Cheltenham Festival target wasn't finally decided until the week before. Talk of his possibly going for the Stayers' Hurdle came to nothing and the choice rested between the Champion Hurdle (if the going was soft) or shouldering top weight in the Coral Cup (if the going was good or good to firm). Set to carry 11-12 in the two-mile-five-furlong handicap, Rhinestone Cowboy faced having to break the weight-carrying record for the race. Seeing that he was racing off a BHB mark of 165, it seemed hardly justified to say—as the *Racing Post* did—that, in contesting the Coral Cup instead of the Champion Hurdle, Rhinestone Cowboy was having 'his sights lowered'. Rhinestone Cowboy's presence kept most of his rivals out of the weights, and his rider's then 7-lb allowance reduced his weight to 11-5, but he still faced a stiff task. The more prominently-ridden than usual Rhinestone Cowboy produced a top-class effort to finish third—his form on a par with Hardy Eustace's winning effort in the Champion Hurdle—and it isn't stretching things to say that he might well have won had his rider not let the first two get first run on him going to the last. Rhinestone Cowboy kept on strongly up the steep climb to the winning post but couldn't get on terms and went down by a length and a length and a quarter, to Monkerhostin and Court Shareef.

The second, third, fourth and fifth in the Champion Hurdle—Rooster Booster, Intersky Falcon, Foreman and Westender—were all in the line-up for the Aintree Hurdle two and a half weeks later, when Monkerhostin was among four Coral Cup runners who renewed rivalry with Rhinestone Cowboy. Even though his rider couldn't claim, Rhinestone Cowboy was still considerably better off with Monkerhostin and the other Coral Cup runners and he started 5/2 joint favourite with Rooster Booster, the pair followed by Monkerhostin at 5/1, Intersky Falcon and Foreman both at 8/1, then 14/1 bar in a field of eleven. Rhinestone Cowboy looked in tremendous shape, clearly none the worse for his Cheltenham exertions, and confirmed his status as one of the best hurdlers around. Waited with, he met trouble, both two out and after the last, before quickening in fine style on the run-in to win with something to spare by three quarters of a length and half a length from Rooster Booster and Westender, with Intersky Falcon a further half a length behind. Coupled with his follow-up victory at Punchestown shortly after the end of the British season, Rhinestone Cowboy's performances at Cheltenham and Aintree put him only a little behind Baracouda on form. Meetings between the pair might provide some interesting tactical battles since both are usually held up. Rhinestone Cowboy probably possesses the better turn of finishing speed and, in that respect, will be less beholden to a truly-run race. An end-to-end gallop over three miles is more likely to favour Baracouda. Fields for some of the top three-mile conditions hurdles can be on the small side and it will be interesting to see whether either camp decides to employ pacemakers to ensure races are run to suit.

Rhinestone Cowboy (IRE) (b.g. 1996)	Be My Native (USA) (br 1979)	Our Native (b or br 1970)	Exclusive Native
			Our Jackie
		Witchy Woman (ch 1972)	Strate Stuff
			Witchy Norma
	Monumental Gesture (b 1987)	Head For Heights (b 1981)	Shirley Heights
			Vivante
		Temporary Lull (ch 1980)	Super Concorde
			Magazine

Rhinestone Cowboy is a medium-sized, well-made gelding by Be My Native who is still very strongly represented, though he had no offspring younger than six by the end of the latest season. He died at Coolmore's Kilsheelan Stud in 1997. With his Coolmore connection, it is interesting that two of Be My Native's best offspring, Rhinestone Cowboy and dual Melling Chase winner Native Upman-

Mrs John Magnier's "Rhinestone Cowboy"

ship, race in the colours of Mrs Magnier who is more usually associated with top horses on the Flat. Many of Rhinestone Cowboy's relatives are best known for their Flat performances, but there have been some notable jumpers in the family too, including Triumph Hurdle winner Rare Holiday (also smart on the Flat) who is a half-brother to Rhinestone Cowboy's dam Monumental Gesture, herself a winner on the Flat and over hurdles. Further back, Rhinestone Cowboy's great grandam Magazine, who won the Coaching Club American Oaks, was closely related to the dam of dual Champion Chase winner Barnbrook Again. Rhinestone Cowboy has been raced only on good going or softer (acts on soft) and stays three miles. *Jonjo O'Neill*

RHOSSILI (IRE) 4 b.g. Perugino (USA) – Velinowski (Malinowski (USA)) [2003/4 17m Jul 19] workmanlike gelding: half-brother to winning 2m hurdler Tendresse (by Tender King): little form on Flat, trained at 2 yrs by Bob Jones: showed nothing on hurdling debut: joined Mrs L. Wadham. *John Allen*   h–

RHYTHMICALL (IRE) 7 b.g. In The Wings – Rhoman Ruby (IRE) (Rhoman Rule (USA)) [2003/4 16d Nov 26] fairly useful at one time on Flat: well behind in 2 races over hurdles 2 years apart. *B. S. Rothwell*   h–

RHYTHM KING 9 b.g. Rakaposhi King – Minim (Rymer) [2003/4 c–, h–: c19gF Apr 30] lengthy gelding: poor maiden hurdler: no form in steeplechases: successful 4 times in points between January and April: should stay 2½m: raced on good going or softer. *J. A. B. Old*   c–
h–

RICARDO 10 b.g. Sanglamore (USA) – Nurica (USA) (Nureyev (USA)) [2003/4 c129, h–: c16d² c17d³ c16sF 16s c17s⁵ Jan 18] good-topped gelding: useful hurdler at best, well held in Pierse Hurdle (Handicap) at Leopardstown fourth start: fairly useful maiden chaser: easily best effort in 2003/4 when second to Mossy Green in strongly-contested event at Naas: generally let down by jumping subsequently: best around 2m: raced on good going or softer (acts on heavy): tried blinkered/in cheekpieces. *Brian Nolan, Ireland*   c117 x
h–

RICCARTON 11 b.g. Nomination – Legendary Dancer (Shareef Dancer (USA)) [2003/4 c84, h76: c16m⁵ c16g² c16m⁴ Jul 14] leggy gelding: winning hurdler: poor maiden chaser: stays 19f: acts on any going: has had tongue tied. *D. C. Turner*   c84
h–

RICHIE'S DELIGHT (IRE) 11 br.g. Phardante (FR) – Johnstown Love (IRE) (Golden Love) [2003/4 c94, h96: c22g⁴ c20g⁶ c22g³ c23m⁵ 20m² 20mF 22g* 19m³ 19m³ c21gF 20m⁶ 20d⁴ 19d³ 21s Dec 26] well-made gelding: poor chaser nowadays: modest hurdler: won conditional jockeys selling handicap at Stratford in September: effective at 2½m to 2¾m: acts on soft and firm going: blinkered/in cheekpieces in 2003/4: not an easy ride. *J. A. Supple*   c82 §
h88 §

RICKHAM GLORY 6 b.g. Past Glories – Rickham Bay (Snow Warning) [2003/4 F–: F16m 19sur Feb 6] leggy gelding: no form in bumpers or selling hurdle: tried blinkered. *H. E. Haynes*   h–
F–

RICKO (NZ) 10 b.g. Defensive Play (USA) – Native Hawk (NZ) (War Hawk) [2003/4 c103, h–: c20mᵖᵘ May 10] workmanlike gelding: fair chaser: lame only outing in 2003/4: stays 21f: acts on soft and good to firm going: makes running. *B. G. Powell*   c–
h–

RICO HOMBRE (FR) 5 b.g. Cadoudal (FR) – Lady Carolina (FR) (Noir Et Or) [2003/4 F18s* Feb 9] fifth foal: half-brother to winning hurdler/chaser Messire Tango (by Fijar Tango), stays 21f, and winning 2¾m hurdler Semaphore (by Nikos), also both successful up to 13f on Flat: dam successful several times up to 1½m on Flat in France: favourite, overcame inexperience to win bumper at Fontwell on debut by neck from The Fridge. *N. J. Henderson*   F103 +

RIDAPOUR (IRE) 5 b.g. Kahyasi – Ridiyara (IRE) (Persian Bold) [2003/4 h81+: 16g 16m⁵ 20m⁵ 17m⁴ 20m 16m³ 16g⁵ 19s³ 19v* 22s⁵ 24sᵖᵘ Feb 22] medium-sized gelding: poor hurdler: won amateur handicap at Towcester in January: likely to prove better around 2½m than shorter: acts on good to firm and heavy going. *D. J. Wintle*   h80

RIDEAWAY ROSE (IRE) 8 b.m. King's Ride – Miss Rockaway (Le Moss) [2003/4 21sᵖᵘ 19m³ 24s⁵ 26s c19vᵖᵘ Feb 2] won last 2 starts in points in 2003: signs of only a little ability otherwise. *C. J. Down*   c–
h67

RIDERS REVENGE (IRE) 6 b.g. Norwich – Paico Ana (Paico) [2003/4 F86: F16vᵛ 19v³ Feb 2] sturdy ex-Irish gelding: fair form in bumpers: around 6 lengths third to Perfect Liaison in novice at Exeter on hurdling debut. *Miss Venetia Williams*   h88
F84

RIDE THE STORM (IRE)   7 ch.g. Glacial Storm (USA) – Reach Down (IRE)   **c119**
(Cheval) [2003/4 c22d⁶ c25f⁴ c20m c22m* c20sᵘʳ c22g² c24v* c25d* c28v³ c20vᵖᵘ Apr   **h–**
17] good-topped gelding: winning hurdler: fairly useful chaser: won handicaps at Thurles
in November, Limerick in December and Fairyhouse (beat Lord Who 20 lengths) in
January, last 2 within 5 days: good second to Liscannor Lad in valuable novice handicap
at Punchestown in late-April: stays 25f: acts on good to firm and heavy going.
E. J. O'Grady, Ireland

RIDGEWAY (IRE)   9 b.g. Indian Ridge – Regal Promise (Pitskelly) [2003/4 c101,   **c101**
h89: c20mᶠ c25g² c24g² c25m³ Mar 4] lengthy gelding: maiden hurdler: fairly useful   **h–**
hunter chaser, placed all 3 completed starts in 2003/4: stays 25f: acts on good to firm and
heavy going: usually wears cheekpieces. *Miss J. E. Foster*

RIFT VALLEY (IRE)   9 b.g. Good Thyne (USA) – Necochea (Julio Mariner) [2003/4   **c113**
h104: c23m* c23m* c23m² Jun 18] good-topped gelding: fair handicap hurdler: succes-   **h–**
sful first 2 starts over fences, in novices at Exeter (by 17 lengths from Stromness) in May
and Worcester (7/2-on) in June: distressed final outing: stays 3m: best on good going
or firmer (acts on firm): best in visor: front runner/races prominently: jumps right over
fences. *P. J. Hobbs*

RIGHT ON TARGET (IRE)   6 b.m. Presenting – Owenageera (IRE) (Riot Helmet)   **h–**
[2003/4 16sᵖᵘ 21sᵖᵘ Feb 10] €12,500 4-y-o: leggy mare: second foal: dam, placed in
point, half-sister to very smart staying chaser Everett: showed nothing in 2 novice
hurdles. *J. Howard Johnson*

RIGHT TO REPLY (IRE)   10 b. or br.g. Executive Perk – Sesheta (Tumble Wind)   **c109 +**
[2003/4 c24g* c25d³ c19sᵖᵘ Apr 6] big, good-topped gelding: lightly raced: fairly useful   **h–**
bumper winner/winning hurdler: won completed start in points in 2004 and 14-runner
hunter at Newbury in March, jumping ponderously early but making up considerable
amount of ground in straight to beat Rathbawn Prince 3½ lengths: soon struggling final
outing: stays 3m: acts on heavy going. *J. R. Scott*

RIGMAROLE   6 b.g. Fairy King (USA) – Cattermole (USA) (Roberto (USA))   **c101 p**
[2003/4 h120: c18g² 16m⁴ 17mᶠ 17mᶠ 17m* 17g* 16f² 16m* 16f⁴ 16m* 16s*   **h151**
16m* 16g 16m² Apr 23]
Racecourse Holdings Trust, which runs thirteen tracks including jumping's
two most important flagship courses Cheltenham and Aintree, published a blueprint in November for the future of jumping. It was presented as 'a starting point for
discussion' and addressed a potential crisis facing the sport against the backdrop of
a heralded 'explosion' in all-weather Flat racing during the winter months. The
paper contained a number of proposals, among the most important of which were
the 'absolutely essential' requirement for courses to produce going that is 'at least
good to firm' and the prime need for jumping to 'deliver competitive racing'. The
two are connected, of course, the paper openly acknowledging the need to make
jumping commercially appealing for betting, even to the extent of suggesting that
there 'might be merit' in reducing the number of jumps fixtures to increase the
average number of runners in a race (a third of all jump races in 2003 had fewer
than the eight runners desired by bookmakers). Another proposal was to reduce the

Greatwood Hurdle (Handicap), Cheltenham—a fourth handicap success of the season for Rigmarole;
he leads over the last from (left to right) Hasty Prince, Jaboune and Caracciola

Tote Bula Hurdle, Cheltenham—
Rigmarole (right) steps up in class and springs a surprise; (left to right) Davenport Milenium,
Spirit Leader and the grey Rooster Booster still have every chance at the last

number of races for the top horses (with a significant increase in prize money for the slimmed-down programme) and to introduce a £500,000 Grand Prix series for the top hurdlers and chasers who would earn points on a sliding scale based on performances in designated races. A related merit table could be used as part of the entry process for the season's championship races. Tempting the best jumpers to run more often will be difficult, but trainers should be encouraged by the tremendous progress of the hard-raced Rigmarole in the latest season.

When Rigmarole lined up for the Grade 2 Tote Bula Hurdle at Cheltenham in mid-December, he had already had ten races in the current season, one more than the combined total of his six opponents who included two making their seasonal reappearance—Champion Hurdle winner Rooster Booster and County Hurdle winner Spirit Leader. Rigmarole had been defying expectations for most of the season. After being beaten in a beginners chase at Fontwell in May, a little over a week into the new season, he had been put back over hurdles and kept on the go through the summer. After a couple of hiccups (falling when still travelling well in two races at Market Rasen), he won off a BHB mark of 120 at Newton Abbot in

Axminster Kingwell Hurdle, Wincanton—another upset, as odds-on Intersky Falcon is defeated

August, then followed up off a mark 9 lb higher at Bangor in mid-September. Rigmarole continued in really good form on the prevailing firm going in the autumn, adding a conditions event at Kempton and, off a BHB mark of 140, landing the valuable Greatwood Hurdle at Cheltenham in mid-November. Rigmarole had top weight of 11-12 in the Greatwood Hurdle and started at 33/1, but gave the impression that there could be still more improvement to come, held up (as usual) and making smooth headway to lead at the last to win from Caracciola and the hot favourite Hasty Prince.

Rigmarole was by now progressing through the ranks following the same route as Rooster Booster the previous year. Rooster Booster won the conditions event at Kempton and the Greatwood Hurdle before starting a short-priced fav- ourite and winning the Bula. Rigmarole, however, was a 25/1-shot in the Bula, but his remarkable season continued when he led on the run-in, after still being on the bridle when short of room going to the last, to win from Davenport Milenium and Hasty Prince, with Rooster Booster back in fifth. It seemed that Rigmarole would be turned out again a week later under top weight in the Ladbroke Hurdle at Ascot, for which he avoided a penalty. Punters who backed him ante-post were left poorer by his overnight defection which coincided with a run on stable-companion Sud Bleu (10/1 to 6/1) who came second to Thesis. The soft going and a feeling that Ascot might not suit Rigmarole were given as reasons for his late withdrawal and he wasn't seen out again until February. Rigmarole took advantage of a below-form effort from odds-on Intersky Falcon to extend his winning run in the Axminster Kingwell Hurdle at Wincanton, a performance which led to his starting 4/1 second

Mr & Mrs Mark Woodhouse's "Rigmarole"

favourite behind Rooster Booster in the Champion Hurdle. In truth, his form didn't quite warrant such a position in the market, and Rigmarole managed only eighth at Cheltenham, found to be slightly lame the next morning and withdrawn from the County Hurdle after the final forty-eight-hour declaration stage (leaving stable-companion Sporazene to win under top weight of 10-13, with most of the others running from out of the handicap). Rigmarole had his fourteenth and last race of the season in the Concept Hurdle at Sandown and wasn't discredited when second to Hasty Prince, with the Champion Hurdle fifth and third, Westender and Intersky Falcon, behind him.

Rigmarole (b.g. 1998)	Fairy King (USA) (b 1982)	Northern Dancer (b 1961)	Nearctic Natalma
		Fairy Bridge (b 1975)	Bold Reason Special
	Cattermole (USA) (ch 1989)	Roberto (b 1969)	Hail To Reason Bramalea
		Catty (b 1975)	Never Bend T. C. Kitten

The compact Rigmarole was a useful maiden for Pascal Bary in France when bought off the Flat at the end of his three-year-old days for 55,000 guineas at the Newmarket Autumn Sales. He won three times in his first season over hurdles but developed a tendency to finish weakly and hadn't won since the 2001/2 season before picking up the winning thread again at Newton Abbot. He is Flat-bred, his dam the useful French miler Cattermole being out of an American half-sister to the dams of such as Belmont Stakes winner Editor's Note, Johannesburg's sire the Grade 1 winner Hennessy, the Grade 1-winning two-year-old fillies Family Style and Lost Kitty and the very smart sprinter-miler Arkadian Hero. Cattermole's sister Caithness is the dam of the Sefton Novices' Hurdle winner Stromness, a fairly useful novice chaser in the latest season. Cattermole herself has bred several other winners, notably the smart French middle-distance stayer Spendent (by Generous). Rigmarole is best at two miles and is usually held up to make the best use of his turn of foot. He acts on soft and firm going and has his tongue tied. *P. F. Nicholls*

RIMOSA 9 b.m. Miner's Lamp – Crosa (Crozier) [2003/4 h74: 18g⁴ 17d² 16v⁵ Dec 26] **h72**
angular mare: poor maiden hurdler: raced mainly around 2m: acts on good to firm going, possibly not on heavy. *A. P. Jones*

RIMPTON BOY 9 gr.g. Interrex (CAN) – Ardelle Grey (Ardross) [2003/4 c21g* **c99** May 12] fair pointer, won in January: odds on, far from fluent and all out when winning **h–** novice hunter at Uttoxeter. *R. Barber*

RINCE RI (IRE) 11 ch.g. Orchestra – Mildred's Ball (Blue Refrain) [2003/4 c165, **c162** h117?: c25g² c20d³ c24dF c17s² c25d² c24d³ Feb 8] strong gelding: high-class chaser: **h–** generally creditable efforts in 2003/4, placed in 3 Grade 1 events, including when third to Beef Or Salmon in Punchestown Chase in December and Florida Pearl in Hennessy Cognac Gold Cup at Leopardstown in February: retried in blinkers when fourth of 6 to Beef Or Salmon in Punchestown Heineken Gold Cup in late-April: effective at 2½m and will stay beyond 25f: acts on heavy going, probably on good to firm: tried tongue tied earlier in career: reliable. *T. M. Walsh, Ireland*

RINCOOLA (IRE) 5 br.m. Warcraft (USA) – Very Tense (IRE) (Orchestra) [2003/4 **F–** F17g Mar 28] €1,000 4-y-o: first foal: dam unraced: well held in mares bumper at Market Rasen on debut. *J. S. Wainwright*

RINGAGOLD 5 ch.m. Karinga Bay – Miss Marigold (Norwick (USA)) [2003/4 F16gᵖᵘ **F– §** F17gᵖᵘ Apr 1] second foal: half-sister to fairly useful hurdler Goldbrook (by Alderbrook), stays 2½m: dam, winning hurdler/chaser who stayed 3m, half-sister to smart hunter What A Hand: looked temperamental in bumpers: refused to line up third intended start. *R. J. Hodges*

RING OF ROSES 5 b.m. Efisio – True Ring (High Top) [2003/4 F16g F17d Mar 11] **F–** seventh foal: sister to useful performer up to 1¼m Future Perfect and half-sister to 2 winners, including fairly useful hurdler around 2m Semi Circle (by Noble Patriarch): dam, well beaten both starts at 2 yrs, out of half-sister to very smart 2-y-o Circus Ring: well held in bumpers: tongue tied on debut. *M. W. Easterby*

RINGSIDE JACK 8 b.g. Batshoof – Celestine (Skyliner) [2003/4 17d⁴ 16s⁴ Mar 20] **h87** modest on Flat (stays 2m): better effort in novice hurdles when fourth of 18 to Navado at Market Rasen on debut. *C. W. Fairhurst*

RIO DIAMOND (IRE)　　8 ch.g. Montelimar (USA) – Timely Run (IRE) (Deep Run)　　**c113**
[2003/4 c24d² c24dᵖᵘ c24s* c28vᵖᵘ c24sᵖᵘ Mar 14] fair handicap chaser: best effort when
winning at Naas (has very good record there) in January, beating Graineuaile 3½ lengths:
stays 3m: acts on heavy going: tongue tied final start. *P. R. Lenihan, Ireland*

RIO REAL (IRE)　　8 b.g. Case Law – Fine Flame (Le Prince) [2003/4 h95*: 20m⁶ 16d　　**h73**
17d⁵ 16m⁴ Dec 10] good-topped gelding: fair hurdler at best: well below form in 2003/4,
in sellers last 2 starts: raced mainly around 2m: acts on soft and good to firm going:
blinkered/visored. *J. Mackie*

RIOTHAMUS (IRE)　　6 b.g. Supreme Leader – Kemchee (Kemal (FR)) [2003/4 F101:　　**h108**
24d* 20d² 20s³ 24s² 24m⁴ Apr 14] useful-looking gelding: bumper winner: fair novice
hurdler: won 7-runner event at Carlisle in November: outbattled when placed next 3
starts: stays 3m: acts on soft going, probably on good to firm. *Ferdy Murphy*

RIPCORD (IRE)　　6 b.g. Diesis – Native Twine (Be My Native (USA)) [2003/4 16g　　**h69**
Nov 11] temperamental maiden on Flat: never a threat when seventh of 14 in novice at
Huntingdon on hurdling debut. *Lady Herries*

RISING GENERATION (FR)　　7 ch.g. Risen Star (USA) – Queen's Victory (FR)　　**c– §**
(Carmarthen (FR)) [2003/4 c–§, h103§: 16s² 16g⁵ 21mᶠ 16d 17d⁵ 16d 17d* Apr 18]　　**h107 §**
winning chaser: fair handicap hurdler, below form after first start: stays 19f: acts on good
to firm and heavy going: often finds little. *N. G. Richards*

RISING TALISKER　　11 ch.m. Primitive Rising (USA) – Dialect (Connaught)　　**c–**
[2003/4 c25gᵖᵘ Mar 28] lengthy, angular mare: maiden hurdler/chaser: tried blinkered.　　**h–**
O. R. Dukes

RISK ACCESSOR (IRE)　　9 b.g. Commanche Run – Bellatollah (Bellman (FR))　　**c139**
[2003/4 c137, h–: 16v* c22s⁶ c18m* c20gᶠ c20s² c20g c36dᵘʳ c21m⁴ Apr 14] tall gelding:　　**h132**
useful hurdler/chaser: won minor events at Tipperary (hurdle) in July and Thurles (chase,
hard held) in October: ran well when second to Iris Royal in valuable handicap chase at
Cheltenham, looking likely to get up on run-in but losing momentum close home: still to
be asked for effort when falling 2 out in similar event there time before: effective at 2m to
2¾m: acts on good to firm and heavy going: has had tongue tied: effective held up or
ridden prominently (takes good hold): bold jumper, prone to odd bad mistake (badly hampered when unseating early in Grand National): often weak finisher. *C. Roche, Ireland*

RISK AND REWARD (IRE)　　6 b.m. Topanoora – Khaiylasha (IRE) (Kahyasi)　　**h–**
[2003/4 20g 16gᵖᵘ Nov 2] IR £22,000 3-y-o, €5,000 4-y-o: smallish ex-Irish mare:
second foal: half-sister to poor hurdler/modest chaser Classic Lash (by Classic Cheer),
stays 3m: dam unraced half-sister to smart hurdler up to 3m Khayrawani: poor form over
hurdles and in bumper, left C. Roche after 2002/3: blinkered final outing. *Jonjo O'Neill*

RISKER (USA)　　5 b.g. Gone West (USA) – Trampoli (USA) (Trempolino (USA))　　**h–**
[2003/4 h82: 16mᵇᵒ 20m 19gᵖᵘ 16vᵇᵒ 16s 19m 21gᵖᵘ Mar 17] smallish gelding: little show
over hurdles: tried blinkered. *J. Joseph*

RISKY REEF　　7 ch.g. Risk Me (FR) – Pas de Reef (Pas de Seul) [2003/4 h129: 16d⁴　　**h136**
16d⁴ 16g Feb 14] lengthy gelding: useful hurdler: off 6 months, good fourth to Back In
Front in Grade 2 at Punchestown second start: unable to sustain run after 2 out when
twelfth to Geos in very valuable handicap at Newbury: will prove best at 2m: raced on
good going or softer. *Andrew Lee, Ireland*

RISKY WAY　　8 b.g. Risk Me (FR) – Hot Sunday Sport (Star Appeal) [2003/4 c90,　　**c90 x**
h–: c16m⁵ c17gᵖᵘ c21g⁴ c17m⁶ 19m 17g⁴ 19m* 17g⁶ 16m 20g 19g c19g Mar 5] leggy,　　**h82**
close-coupled gelding: modest handicap chaser: poor handicap hurdler: lost form after
winning at Market Rasen in September: stays 2½m: acts on good to firm and good to soft
going: visored twice, has won with/without blinkers: often let down by jumping over
fences. *B. S. Rothwell*

RIVAL BIDDER　　7 ch.g. Arzanni – Beltalong (Belfort (FR)) [2003/4 16m* 16m² 16m*　　**h95**
16d 16vᵘʳ Jan 17] close-coupled gelding: modest hurdler: won maiden at Worcester (on
return after 2-year absence) in September and 3-runner novice at Haydock in October:
will stay beyond 2m. *Mrs S. J. Smith*

RIVAL (IRE)　　5 b.g. Desert Style (IRE) – Arab Scimetar (IRE) (Sure Blade (USA))　　**h–**
[2003/4 16g Feb 11] compact gelding: maiden on Flat, no form for long time: showed
nothing in seller on hurdling debut: sold £1,100 Ascot April Sales. *S. T. Lewis*

RIVELLI (IRE)　　5 b.m. Lure (USA) – Kama Tashoof (Mtoto) [2003/4 17dᵖᵘ Mar 27]　　**h–**
half-sister to winning hurdler around 2m Alchemystic (by In The Wings): maiden on Flat,

little form since 2002: soon tailed off after jumping slowly fourth in novice hurdle at Bangor. *B. R. Foster*

RIVENDELL 8 b.m. Saddlers' Hall (IRE) – Fairy Kingdom (Prince Sabo) [2003/4 16d^{pu} May 16] of little account on Flat: tongue tied, showed nothing on hurdling debut. *M. Wigham*   **h–**

RIVER ALDER 6 b.m. Alderbrook – River Pearl (Oats) [2003/4 20d* Apr 10] 2,600 4-y-o: second foal: half-sister to 2¾m hurdle winner Silken Pearls (by Leading Counsel): dam fair chaser up to 3m: won second of 2 starts in points in 2004: successful also in 15-runner novice at Carlisle on hurdling debut, kicking clear before 3 out and keeping on well despite mistakes to beat Monolith 4 lengths: may do better. *Miss S. E. Forster*   **h96 +**

RIVER AMORA (IRE) 9 b.g. Willie Joe (IRE) – That's Amora (Paddy's Stream) [2003/4 c74x, h–: c17d³ c20v² c20d⁵ Apr 24] stocky gelding: maiden hurdler: poor chaser: stays 21f: acts on any going: visored last 2 starts in 2002/3: prone to mistakes. *P. Butler*   **c66 x** **h–**

RIVER BAILIFF (IRE) 8 ch.g. Over The River (FR) – Rath Caola (Neltino) [2003/4 c77: c20d Feb 19] sturdy gelding: winning pointer: poor form in steeplechases: stays 3¼m: failed to settle only start in blinkers. *R. Gurney*   **c72**

RIVER BANN (USA) 7 ch.g. Irish River (FR) – Spiritual Star (USA) (Soviet Star (USA)) [2003/4 h89: 16f³ 16d⁵ 22g 20v⁵ 16d³ 19s* Feb 6] modest hurdler: 9/2, won 16-runner seller at Hereford (sold to join B. Leary 7,000 gns): stays 19f (tired badly over testing 2½m): acts on firm and soft going. *Mrs Jane Galpin*   **h94**

RIVER BUG (IRE) 10 ch.g. Over The River (FR) – Fiona's Wish (Wishing Star) [2003/4 c114: c29v⁵ c29d⁵ c28d⁶ c33d^{ur} c29d Mar 14] sturdy gelding: fair handicap chaser, below best in 2003/4: thorough stayer: acts on heavy going: blinkered: hard ride. *Jamie Poulton*   **c98 §**

RIVER CITY (IRE) 7 b.g. Norwich – Shuil Na Lee (IRE) (Phardante (FR)) [2003/4 h115: 16m* Apr 13] fairly useful hurdler: off a year, improved effort when winning well-contested handicap at Chepstow readily by 2½ lengths from Wakeup Smiling: should stay 2½m: acts on any going. *Noel T. Chance*   **h121 +**

RIVER CORA (IRE) 10 br.g. Over The River (FR) – Cora Swan (Tarqogan) [2003/4 c16d⁴ c22s⁴ c17d³ c20f^{ur} c22d² c24g² c19s^{ur} Sep 21] leggy gelding: fairly useful handicap chaser: good efforts when second to Wotsitooya in listed event at Galway and to Native Performance in valuable race at Listowel in September: fatally injured later in month: would have stayed beyond 3m: acted on good to firm and heavy going: tough and consistent. *W. P. Mullins, Ireland*   **c117** **h–**

RIVER COTTAGE 11 b.g. Henbit (USA) – Tamorina (Quayside) [2003/4 24d^{pu} c24g^{pu} Apr 18] half-brother to useful staying chasers Huntworth and Riverside Boy (both by Funny Man): dam unraced, out of half-sister to top-class staying chaser Spanish Steps: showed nothing in novice hurdle and maiden chase. *S. T. Lewis*   **c–** **h–**

RIVER DANTE (IRE) 7 ch.g. Phardante (FR) – Astral River (Over The River (FR)) [2003/4 c20g^F Mar 12] 9,000 5-y-o: fourth foal: half-brother to fairly useful chaser Fear Siuil (by Strong Gale): dam, winning hurdler/chaser, stayed 3m: won maiden point in 2003: towards rear when falling 4 out in maiden hunter at Leicester. *Miss L. Blackford*   **c–**

RIVER JOY (IRE) 6 b.g. Norwich – Vanessa's Palace (Quayside) [2003/4 F–: F17m May 14] lengthy gelding: well held in bumpers: tried tongue tied: dead. *Noel T. Chance*   **F–**

RIVER MARSHAL (IRE) 6 b.g. Synefos (USA) – Marshallstown (Callernish) [2003/4 F95: F16v³ 16s 19g³ 16d^{pu} Mar 28] workmanlike gelding: fair form when placed in bumpers (hung right only start in blinkers), bought out of M. Easterby's stable 12,500 gns Doncaster October Sales: easily best effort in novice hurdles when third to Juralan at Doncaster: sold 17,000 gns Doncaster May Sales. *S. Gollings*   **h88** **F81**

RIVER MERE 10 b.g. River God – Rupert's Daughter (Rupert Bear) [2003/4 h89?: 16m 16g⁴ 17g² 17m 17m⁵ 16d³ 17m* 16g⁶ Aug 23] workmanlike gelding: poor hurdler: got up close home in novice handicap at Bangor in August: best around 2m: acts on good to firm and good to soft going. *Mrs L. Williamson*   **h78**

RIVER MIST (IRE) 5 ch.m. Over The River (FR) – Minature Miss (Move Off) [2003/4 F73: F16g F16d⁵ F17d^{ro} 21d³ 20d³ Apr 10] modest form at best in bumpers: second and better effort over hurdles when third to River Alder in novice at Carlisle: likely to be suited by 3m. *D. Eddy*   **h83** **F83**

RIVER NESS 8 br.m. Buckskin (FR) – Stubbin Moor (Kinglet) [2003/4 c–, h102: 16g May 24] fair handicap hurdler at best: well beaten on chasing debut: won points in March/ April: stays 3m: raced on good going or softer (acts on heavy). *N. G. Richards* c–
h–

RIVER PARADISE (IRE) 8 ch.g. John French – Barbara Brook (Over The River (FR)) [2003/4 c20s³ c25dᵘʳ c26sᵖᵘ Jan 23] tall, lengthy gelding: runner-up in novice hurdle in 2001/2: no form in novice company over fences on return, though twice shaped as though retaining ability: stays 2½m: acts on good to firm going. *R. H. Alner* c– p
h–

RIVER PHANTOM (IRE) 5 b.g. Over The River (FR) – Cathilda (IRE) (Cataldi) [2003/4 F16g F16d⁴ Apr 21] €5,500 4-y-o: good-topped gelding: fifth foal: dam unraced half-sister to Supreme Novices' Hurdle winner Stranfield and to dam of useful 2½m chaser Multum In Parvo: better effort in bumpers when seventh of 21 to Spirit of New York at Newbury, coming from well off pace. *Ian Williams* F90

RIVER PILOT 10 b.g. Unfuwain (USA) – Cut Ahead (Kalaglow) [2003/4 c103, h–: c20dᵖᵘ c24gᶠ c24sᵖᵘ Jan 23] useful-looking gelding: fair handicap chaser in 2002/3: failed to complete all 3 starts after 10-month absence: stays 21f: acts on heavy and good to firm going: tongue tied last 2 outings: has found little. *C. J. Mann* c–
h–

RIVER PIRATE (IRE) 7 b.g. Un Desperado (FR) – Kigali (IRE) (Torus) [2003/4 h104, F97: 16m* 17m* 17g⁵ 21g 16g² 18d⁴ Apr 7] tall gelding: fair hurdler: won intermediate at Ludlow and novice at Hereford (odds on) in May: best efforts around 2m: acts on good to firm and heavy going: has found little. *N. J. Henderson* h106

RIVER QUOILE (IRE) 8 b.g. Terimon – Carrikins (Buckskin (FR)) [2003/4 22g⁴ 22d² 24g 24m c22s c20m⁵ c25f³ c24mᶠ 24f c24m³ c20gᶠ c24g³ c24dᶠ c24g⁴ c26d⁴ Mar 15] workmanlike ex-Irish gelding: first foal: dam, modest hurdler who stayed 2½m, half-sister to useful hurdler up to 21f Yellow Spring: winning pointer: modest maiden hurdler/ steeplechaser: left M. Cunningham after twelfth start: stays 25f: acts on firm and good to soft going: tried blinkered: has had jumping problems. *R. H. Alner* c88
h88

RIVER RAMBLER 5 ch.m. River Falls – Horsepower (Superpower) [2003/4 F–: F16d 16vᵖᵘ 17dᵖᵘ Mar 7] little sign of ability. *J. R. Norton* h–
F–

RIVER REINE (IRE) 5 br.m. Lahib (USA) – Talahari (IRE) (Roi Danzig (USA)) [2003/4 h–: 20mᵖᵘ 19f² 22g³ 23m⁵ 23s⁶ 18g⁴ Apr 22] quite good-topped mare: poor maiden hurdler: probably stays 2¾m. *R. H. Buckler* h85

RIVER RIDE (IRE) 10 b.g. King's Ride – Over The Village (IRE) (Over The River (FR)) [2003/4 16dᵖᵘ 17s 21mᵖᵘ 21m⁴ c21g⁶ Jul 28] signs of only a little ability. *C. J. Teague* c–
h–

RIVER RISING 10 br.g. Primitive Rising (USA) – Dragons Daughter (Mandrake Major) [2003/4 h–: c16d⁴ c16g⁶ c20mᵖᵘ c16mᶠ c16dᵖᵘ c16g⁶ c21vᵖᵘ Jan 13] long-backed gelding: poor maiden hurdler/chaser: wore cheekpieces/blinkers last 2 starts. *C. R. Wilson* c76 d
h–

RIVER SLAVE (IRE) 10 b. or br.g. Over The River (FR) – Sally Slave (Paddy's Stream) [2003/4 c85, h–: c20sᶠ c20dᵖᵘ c22vᵖᵘ Jan 12] lengthy gelding: maiden chaser: stays 25f: acts on heavy going. *T. R. George* c–
h–

RIVER STYX (IRE) 9 ch.g. Over The River (FR) – Money For Honey (New Brig) [2003/4 c80, h72: c16mᵖᵘ c16g³ c19m⁴ c26m⁵ Nov 3] workmanlike gelding: maiden hurdler: poor chaser: should stay 2½m: acts on firm and good to soft going: usually blinkered: tongue tied: has looked unwilling. *D. McCain* c77
h–

RIVER SURPRISE (IRE) 11 b.g. Over The River (FR) – Reelin Surprise (Royal Match) [2003/4 c–: c16dᵖᵘ c24m⁶ c24mᵖᵘ May 29] of no account. *Mike Lurcock* c–

RIVER TRAPPER (IRE) 5 b.g. Over The River (FR) – Mousa (Callernish) [2003/4 F16d³ F16g* Mar 27] has scope: third foal: dam placed in points: fairly useful form both starts in bumpers, winning 18-runner event at Newbury by ¾ length from Ungaro, travelling well, leading over 3f out and showing plenty of resolution: sort to do well over jumps. *Miss H. C. Knight* F95

RIVER TRIX (IRE) 10 b.g. Riverhead (USA) – Game Trix (Buckskin (FR)) [2003/4 c92, h–: c25g³ c20g* c26g³ c21mᶠ c24d⁵ c20dᴿ Apr 11] useful-looking gelding: modest chaser: left D. Caro after third start, M. Pipe after fourth: won maiden at Hexham in May and handicap at Plumpton (challenging when left clear last) in April: stays 3¼m: acts on good to soft and good to firm going: tried tongue tied. *M. Scudamore* c98
h–

RIVER WYE (IRE) 12 b.g. Jareer (USA) – Sun Gift (Guillaume Tell (USA)) [2003/4 c–, h–: c20g c24mᵖᵘ c19g⁴ c19s⁴ Mar 24] good-topped gelding: one-time useful chaser, c67 ?
h–

retains little ability: stays 2½m: acts on soft and good to firm going: blinkered third start: usually tongue tied. *G. H. Yardley*

ROADWORTHY (IRE) 7 b.m. Lord Americo – Henry Woman (IRE) (Mandalus) **h–** [2003/4 F16s 16v 16m Jun 14] IR £1,000 4-y-o: fourth foal: half-sister to winning pointer **F–** by Supreme Leader: dam unraced, out of sister to smart chaser up to 3m Royal Dipper and half-sister to very smart staying hurdler/useful chaser Henry Mann: well held in bumpers or over hurdles: won mares maiden point in April. *J. K. Magee, Ireland*

ROAR BLIZZARD (IRE) 6 b.h. Roar (USA) – Ragtime Rumble (USA) (Dixieland **h–** Band (USA)) [2003/4 17d 19d⁶ 16g Sep 7] successful over 1m and 9.5f on Flat in Germany at 3 yrs, in frame several times since, including in 2003 for P. Hirschberger: well held in 3 starts over hurdles, after several mistakes in seller at Uttoxeter on final one: has had tongue tied. *Frau A. Bodenhagen, Germany*

ROAR WITH ME 6 gr.m. Arzanni – Courtesy Call (Northfields (USA)) [2003/4 F16m **F–** Oct 10] half-sister to several winners, including fairly useful 2m hurdler/winning chaser Joshua Tree (by Hello Gorgeous): dam thrice-raced half-sister to smart 1976 2-y-o 5f performer Piney Ridge: seventh of 8 in bumper on debut. *M. A. Buckley*

ROBBER (IRE) 7 ch.g. Un Desperado (FR) – Christy's Girl (IRE) (Buckskin (FR)) **c80** [2003/4 h85: 22g c24g⁶ c25v³ c24d c29d³ c23d⁴ Apr 21] leggy gelding: poor maiden **h–** hurdler/chaser: probably stays 29f: unraced on firm going, acts on any other. *P. J. Hobbs*

ROBBIE CAN CAN 5 b.g. Robellino (USA) – Can Can Lady (Anshan) [2003/4 h90: **h97** 16m² 20m 16d² 16d³ Mar 12] leggy, close-coupled gelding: fair on Flat, (stays 2¼m), successful twice in February: modest hurdler: should be suited by further than 2m: acts on good to firm and heavy going. *A. W. Carroll*

ROBBIE ON TOUR (IRE) 5 b.g. Oscar (IRE) – Mystery Woman (Tula Rocket) **h–** [2003/4 17d 19s 19s Jan 22] ninth foal: half-brother to bumper winners by Marktingo and Roselier: dam won 2m hurdle: no form in 3 novice hurdles. *M. C. Pipe*

ROBBIE'S ADVENTURE 10 ch.g. Le Coq d'Or – Mendick Adventure (Mandrake **c64 x** Major) [2003/4 c66x, h–: c26gᵖᵘ c26d⁵ Apr 7] close-coupled gelding: poor chaser, often **h–** let down by jumping: sold out of D. Williams' stable £2,100 Ascot June Sales: won point in March: stays 3¼m: acts on heavy and good to firm going: often wears visor/cheek-pieces. *Miss Emma Wettern*

ROBBIE WILLIAMS 6 b.g. Missed Flight – Michelle's Ella (IRE) (Ela-Mana-Mou) **F–** [2003/4 F17g Oct 27] small gelding: first foal: dam no sign of ability on Flat: well held in bumper on debut. *P. M. Rich*

ROBBO 10 b.g. Robellino (USA) – Basha (USA) (Chief's Crown (USA)) [2003/4 **c129 §** c129§, h124§: 24m⁴ c26g³ c27dᶜᵒ c25d² c29d 24d³ c24d⁴ c20v³ c24s⁵ c33d² c24s⁴ c32g² **h114 §** c24g* c24d³ Apr 23] strong, close-coupled gelding: winning hurdler: fairly useful handi-cap chaser: won well-contested event at Carlisle in April by neck from Quarterstaff: stays 33f: acts on heavy going: effective with or without headgear: moody. *Mrs M. Reveley*

ROBERGERIE (IRE) 8 b.g. Robellino (USA) – Daisy Grey (Nordance (USA)) **c–** [2003/4 c22g⁵ c16m⁵ c25f c27m⁶ Jul 22] winning pointer: poor maiden hurdler/ **h–** steeplechaser: tried blinkered. *C. A. McBratney, Ireland*

ROBERT THE RASCAL 11 ch.g. Scottish Reel – Midnight Mary (Celtic Cone) **c–** [2003/4 c24s⁶ c21gᵖᵘ c23v⁴ c24dᵖᵘ Mar 10] poor maiden pointer: refused once. *Mrs C. M. James*

ROBERTY BOB (IRE) 9 ch.g. Bob Back (USA) – Inesdela (Wolver Hollow) [2003/4 **c119** c122, h84: c24s² c26v* May 26] good-topped gelding: maiden hurdler: fairly useful **h–** handicap chaser: made very hard work of landing odds in weakly-contested event at Uttoxeter: suited by 3m+: raced mainly on going softer than good (acts on heavy): sometimes jumps less than fluently: has raced lazily. *H. D. Daly*

ROBINS MEG 8 b.m. Skyliner – Home Dove (Homeboy) [2003/4 h–, F–: 21sᵖᵘ May **h–** 17] third in bumper on debut in 2001/2: no form since, including over hurdles. *M. E. Sowersby*

ROBINS PRIDE (IRE) 14 b.g. Treasure Hunter – Barney's Sister (Abednego) **c– §** [2003/4 c66§, h–§: c21v³ c20mᵖᵘ Feb 25] tall gelding: veteran chaser: stays 3m: acts on **h– §** any going: blinkered: unreliable. *C. L. Popham*

ROBSHAW 4 b.g. Robellino (USA) – Panorama (Shirley Heights) [2003/4 16dᵖᵘ Dec **h–** 27] modest maiden on Flat (stays 7f): showed little in juvenile on hurdling debut. *T. P. Tate*

ROBYN ALEXANDER (IRE)   6 ch.m. Sharifabad (IRE) – Flagship Ahoy (IRE) **c102**
(Accordion) [2003/4 h101+, F90: 16f² 16g² c16g² c21f* Nov 20] lengthy mare: fair **h111**
hurdler: didn't impress with jumping in 2 novice chases, though won mares event at
Wincanton: stays easy 21f: acts on firm and soft going. *P. F. Nicholls*

ROBYNS CHANCE   5 b.m. Overbury (IRE) – Caithness Dawn (Deep Run) [2003/4 **h–**
F16g F17s 19s^pu Feb 6] sixth foal: half-sister to winning hurdler/chaser The Hen Hut (by **F–**
Henbit), stays 21f: no form or ability, out of half-sister to dam of useful staying
chaser Dakyns Boy: no form in bumpers or selling hurdle (jumped badly).
Mrs A. M. Thorpe

ROBYN'S DELIGHT   5 b.m. Perpendicular – Woodram Delight (Idiot's Delight) **h–**
[2003/4 F16d 17s Feb 24] eighth foal: half-sister to fairly useful staying chaser Bank **F–**
Avenue (by Homo Sapien): dam unraced half-sister to dual Scottish National winner
Androma and useful staying chaser Bigsun: well held in bumper and novice hurdle.
M. A. Barnes

ROCABEE (IRE)   10 b.g. Phardante (FR) – Auling (Tarqogan) [2003/4 21v^pu 21s² **c–**
c23s^pu 22s c25s^pu c20g^pu Mar 1] rangy gelding: modest maiden hurdler: off over 4 years **h87 ?**
before reappearance: no form over fences: sold out of A. Chamberlain's stable £2,500
Ascot February Sales before final start: stays 21f: acts on soft and good to firm going:
tried blinkered. *N. B. King*

ROCHES FLEURIES (IRE)   4 b.f. Barathea (IRE) – Princess Caraboo (IRE) (Alzao **h–**
(USA)) [2003/4 16m Nov 3] little sign of ability on Flat or on hurdling debut: sold 2,200
gns Doncaster November Sales. *Andrew Turnell*

ROCKCLIFFE GOSSIP   12 ch.g. Phardante (FR) – Clonmello (Le Bavard (FR)) **c– §**
[2003/4 c105§, h–: c24g c24f⁶ c27s c26g⁵ c29d^pu Mar 14] lengthy gelding: fair handicap **h–**
chaser in 2002/3, no show in 2003/4: tried blinkered: lazy. *N. A. Twiston-Davies*

ROCK CONCERT   6 b.m. Bishop of Cashel – Summer Pageant (Chief's Crown **h–**
(USA)) [2003/4 17m^ur Aug 3] fair on all-weather, modest on turf on Flat (stays 1¼m):
unseated third on hurdling debut: rejoined I. McInnes. *J. S. Wainwright*

ROCKERFELLA LAD (IRE)   4 b.g. Danetime (IRE) – Soucaro (Rusticaro (FR)) **h65**
[2003/4 16d 16d 16s Jan 16] quite good-topped gelding: fair on Flat (stays 9f) for
K. Ryan: well held over hurdles. *M. Todhunter*

ROCKET BLEU (FR)   4 ch.g. Epervier Bleu – Egeria (FR) (Baly Rockette) [2003/4 **h92**
17m* 17s⁵ 16s* 16s⁴ Apr 4] good-topped gelding: fifth foal: half-brother to French
middle-distance winner Royal Rocket (by Garde Royale): dam won several times up to
1½m on Flat in France: modest juvenile hurdler: won at Carlisle (maiden) in October and
Newcastle in March: ran as if amiss final start. *N. G. Richards*

ROCKET RADAR   13 b.g. Vouchsafe – Courtney Pennant (Angus) [2003/4 c106: **c98**
c25g³ c24m² May 29] sturdy gelding: fair hunter chaser: stays 27f: acts on good to firm
and good to soft going: has had tongue tied. *Mrs J. Hughes*

ROCKET SHIP (IRE)   4 b.c. Pennekamp (USA) – Rock The Boat (Slip Anchor) **h109 p**
[2003/4 16d⁴ 16v² Jan 31] useful around 1¼m on Flat, sold out of R. Charlton's stable
85,000 gns Newmarket Autumn Sales: promising efforts in frame in juvenile hurdles at
Leopardstown (pulled hard) and Fairyhouse (2 lengths second to Alicudi): will improve
further back under less testing conditions. *N. Meade, Ireland*

ROCKFIELD LANE (IRE)   8 b. or br.g. Alhaarth (IRE) – Suir Surprise (Rusticaro **c–**
(FR)) [2003/4 h89, F80: 17g 17m⁶ c24m³ Jul 13] good-topped gelding: maiden hurdler, **h–**
badly out of sorts early in season, including in novice chase: tried visored: has pulled
hard/found little: sold £2,000 Ascot August Sales, runner-up in point in January for
J. Trice-Rolph. *G. F. Bridgwater*

ROCK GARDEN (IRE)   5 br.m. Bigstone (IRE) – Woodland Garden (Godswalk **h105**
(USA)) [2003/4 F96: 16d³ 20s³ 21d* 21g⁵ 21g⁵ Mar 27] smallish, angular mare: fair
hurdler: made all in mares maiden at Ludlow in January: stays easy 21f: acts on good to
soft going (best bumper effort on firm): ran creditably in blinkers final start: usually races
prominently: sold 20,000 gns Doncaster May Sales. *R. F. Johnson Houghton*

ROCKLEY BEACH (IRE)   5 b.g. Tidaro (USA) – Green Fairy (Green Shoon) **h–**
[2003/4 F16g⁶ F16s 22g^pu Apr 18] ninth foal: dam ran once: better effort in bumpers at **F87**
Ascot when sixth on debut: showed little in novice on hurdling debut. *V. R. A. Dartnall*

ROCK'N COLD (IRE)   6 b.g. Bigstone (IRE) – Unalaska (IRE) (High Estate) [2003/4 **c79**
h103: 19g³ c20g⁵ Jul 6] lengthy gelding: fair hurdler: none too fluent and tended to run in **h106**

snatches when fifth of 7 in novice at Market Rasen on chasing debut: stays 19f: acts on good to firm and heavy ground: tried visored, usually wears cheekpieces. *J. G. Given*

ROCK ROSE 11 b.m. Arctic Lord – Ovington Court (Prefairy) [2003/4 c77, h75: c20d⁶ c24mᵘʳ Mar 4] workmanlike mare: modest chaser: stays 3m: acts on good to firm and heavy going. *G. L. Davis* **c91** **h–**

ROCKSPRING HERO 8 b.g. Minster Son – Niel's Crystal (Indiaro) [2003/4 c18g⁵ c16g³ c24d⁴ c16s² c20s* c20v² 20d² c24sᶠ 24s Mar 27] fair maiden hurdler: fairly useful chaser: comfortably won handicap at Gowran in January: best effort when second to Tristernagh in similar event at Punchestown following month: effective at 2m to 3m: acts on heavy going. *John J. Walsh, Ireland* **c119** **h103**

ROCKSTOWN BOY (IRE) 6 b.g. Toulon – Palatine Lady (Pauper) [2003/4 F116: F16g⁶ 20s* 16d* 20d² 16mˢᵘ 16sᶠ Mar 14] **h137 p**
Rockstown Boy hasn't had the most fortunate of careers thus far in bumpers and over hurdles, but he has still managed to show himself a useful performer and, given the rub of the green, could well have a profitable time in 2004/5, particularly if sent over fences. Five outings in bumpers brought two victories, at Gowran on his debut in October 2002 and at Limerick the following March but, on his final appearance in bumpers, he might have won a much more prestigious prize with some luck in running, failing to get any sort of clear passage and finishing full of running when sixth to Royal Rosa in the Grade 1 event at the Punchestown Festival. It wasn't long before Rockstown Boy was sent over hurdles and within a month he had run three times, landing the odds in a maiden at Gowran and a novice at Tralee before being beaten in a novice at Cork, a mistake two out in a tactical race almost certainly crucial. Rockstown Boy was then given a break, off over three months before a pipeopener on the Flat and then an appearance in a Grade 3 novice at Tipperary. It looked a stronger race than those Rockstown Boy had contested in the summer but he was again sent off favourite. He didn't get a chance to show what he could do as he slipped up with a circuit to go. Worse, the fall kept him off until the spring when he returned in a handicap at Cork, in which he looked to have a stiff-looking mark. He still went off second favourite, though, and was poised just behind the winner She'll Be Lucky when he fell at the last. It is hard to say for certain whether or not Rockstown Boy would have won had he stood up, but either way that was a useful performance which was confirmed in a cracking renewal of the Evening Herald Champion Novices' Hurdle at Punchestown in late-April. No excuses were needed for finishing six lengths adrift of Brave Inca, though Rockstown Boy was ridden further off the pace than the three that finished ahead of him.

Rockstown Boy was kept on the go on the Flat after Punchestown, showing fair form and winning a maiden over a mile and three quarters in June. There may be more to come over hurdles, particularly stepped back up in trip. But physically the rangy, useful-looking Rockstown Boy impresses as the sort to do even better once he goes over fences. Rockstown Boy comes from the penultimate crop of Toulon and is out of the maiden pointer Palatine Lady. This is not a distinguished family, though the dam has bred two other winners, Bens Dilemma (by Torus), successful in a two-and-a-half-mile chase, and the nineteen-furlong bumper winner Quarter Marker (by Celio Rufo). Rockstown Boy's bumper wins came at two and a half miles and he is likely to stay three over jumps. The ground was good to firm when he slipped up at Tipperary but otherwise Rockstown Boy has raced on good going or softer. *C. Byrnes, Ireland*

ROCKWELDA 9 b.m. Weld – Hill's Rocket (Hill's Forecast) [2003/4 c22mᵖᵘ Aug 18] won maiden point in 2003: little worthwhile form otherwise, bought £1,800 Ascot June Sales: tried blinkered. *M. P. Muggeridge* **c–** **h–**

ROCKWELL ISLAND (IRE) 8 b. or br.g. Satco (FR) – Weather Oak (Pitskelly) [2003/4 16g c24d c22d c22s* c22d 24g 24m* c24g* c24d* c22dᵖᵘ c24dᶠ c29sᵖᵘ Nov 29] IR 12,500 4-y-o: sturdy gelding: fair hurdler/chaser: won over fences at Killarney (maiden) in July, Wexford (listed handicap) in October and Naas (novice) in November, eased to beat Rose Perk ¾ length for final success: also won handicap hurdle at Punchestown in October: stays 3m well: acts on soft and good to firm going: usually blinkered: tongue tied final outing. *Miss F. M. Crowley, Ireland* **c111** **h111**

Forbra Gold Challenge Cup (Handicap Chase), Ludlow—
course specialist Rodalko (right) defeats Cassia Heights to complete a hat-trick

RODALKO (FR) 6 b.g. Kadalko (FR) – Darling Rose (FR) (Rose Laurel) [2003/4 **c136** h102: c23m* c24m^F c24m* c24m* c24m* c24g^4 c33d^{pu} Apr 17] good-topped gelding: **h–** fair hurdler: much better over fences, showing useful form: successful first 4 completed starts, in maiden at Worcester and novice at Ludlow in November and handicaps at Ludlow in December and March (jumped well, beat Cassia Heights 7 lengths): probably found race coming too soon sixth outing: stays 3m: raced mainly on good/good to firm going over fences, won on good to soft over hurdles: races prominently. *O. Sherwood*

RODBER (USA) 8 ch.g. Rodrigo de Triano (USA) – Berceau (USA) (Alleged (USA)) **c113** [2003/4 h93, F95: 20s^4 24v^6 24v^6 c20s^2 c17g^2 c16s^2 c17d* c17g* c20g^{ur} c16g^3 Apr 16] **h78** poor maiden hurdler: much better over fences, successful in maiden at Bangor and novice at Market Rasen on consecutive days in March: excellent second to Junior Fontaine in handicap at Punchestown in late-April: best form around 2m: raced on good going or softer (acts on soft): has broken blood vessels. *Mrs L. B. Normile*

RODDY THE VET (IRE) 6 ch.g. Be My Native (USA) – Caronia (IRE) (Cardinal **c93** Flower) [2003/4 h91, F89: 21f^3 c20d^3 c22d^3 c23g^2 c24d^{pu} Feb 20] sturdy gelding: modest **h–** maiden hurdler/chaser: lame final outing: stays 23f: acts on good to soft going. *A. Ennis*

RODIAK 5 b.g. Distant Relative – Misty Silks (Scottish Reel) [2003/4 h81: 16g 16d^{pu} **h– §** 18s 16s Jan 4] poor maiden hurdler: no show in 2003/4: wears headgear: ungenuine. *P. R. Hedger*

RODOLFO 6 b.g. Tragic Role (USA) – Be Discreet (Junius (USA)) [2003/4 h98: 19m^2 **h99** 20g* 19s^6 Dec 29] tall gelding: has reportedly had 2 wind operations: best effort over hurdles (found little on reappearance) when winning maiden at Uttoxeter (reportedly made a noise) in November: stays 2½m when emphasis is on speed. *O. Sherwood*

RODY (IRE) 7 b. or br.g. Foxhound (USA) – Capable Kate (IRE) (Alzao (USA)) **h–** [2003/4 h–: 16g 19m^{pu} 16m Jun 18] no form over hurdles: runner-up twice in points in 2004, ran out 5 other starts. *I. R. Brown*

RO ERIDANI 4 b.f. Binary Star (USA) – Hat Hill (Roan Rocket) [2003/4 17g Apr 12] **h–** half-sister to several winners, including 2m hurdler Nore Hill (by Town And Country): modest maiden on Flat (stays 9f): sold out of T. Etherington's stable 850 gns Doncaster March Sales: well beaten in juvenile on hurdling debut. *Miss S. E. Forster*

RO GEMA RI 6 b.g. Perpendicular – Pretty Soon (Tina's Pet) [2003/4 F17g Apr 24] **F–** sixth known foal: half-brother to bumper winner Petite Flora and winning pointer both by Lord Bud: dam, 7f winner, possibly became ungenuine: always behind in bumper on debut. *T. D. Walford*

ROGERO 5 b.g. Presidium – Richesse (FR) (Faraway Son (USA)) [2003/4 F16g F16m **h–** F17m⁵ 19g\u1d56ᵘ 20f⁴ 22g Mar 28] half-brother to several winners, including fairly useful **F–** hurdler Rich Desire (by Grey Desire), stayed 25f: dam ran once: no worthwhile form. *R. E. Barr*

ROHAN 8 gr.g. Norton Challenger – Acushla Macree (Mansingh (USA)) [2003/4 h87: **h87** 19s⁴ 22d 20s⁴ 19g⁶ 19d² 19g Apr 1] sturdy gelding: modest maiden hurdler: should stay beyond 2½m: acts on soft and good to firm going: tried blinkered. *R. F. Johnson Houghton*

ROJABAA 5 b.g. Anabaa (USA) – Slava (USA) (Diesis) [2003/4 16m 17g 22g 17m⁵ **h–** 17d⁶ Dec 2] small gelding: modest on Flat (stays 1½m): well held over hurdles: blinkered and tongue tied second start. *W. G. M. Turner*

ROKY STAR (FR) 7 b.g. Start Fast (FR) – Rosydolie (FR) (Dhausli (FR)) [2003/4 **h88** h95: 17g⁶ 20v⁶ 21g⁴ Dec 6] modest maiden hurdler: probably stays 2¾m: acts on heavy ground: tried tongue tied: has finished weakly. *M. R. Bosley*

ROLEX FREE (ARG) 6 ch.g. Friul (ARG) – Karolera (ARG) (Kaljerry (ARG)) **c–** [2003/4 h–: 16s 20s 16g c17d\u1d56ᵘ 16d\u1d56ᵘ Apr 21] leggy gelding: won up to 1¼m on Flat in **h–** Argentina, fair form at best in Britain: little sign of ability over jumps: tried cheek-pieces/blinkers: has had tongue tied. *Mrs L. C. Taylor*

ROLFES DELIGHT 12 b.g. Rolfe (USA) – Idiot's Run (Idiot's Delight) [2003/4 **c84 §** c84§, h–: c25m* c24d\u1d56ᵘ Aug 7] workmanlike gelding: poor chaser: won selling handicap **h–** at Hereford in June: stays 25f: acts on firm going: tried tongue tied: inconsistent. *A. E. Jones*

ROLLER 8 b.g. Bluebird (USA) – Tight Spin (High Top) [2003/4 16m⁴ 16g⁶ 17g\u1d56ᵘ **h71** 16m\u1d56ᵘ Jul 16] half-brother to fair pointer Golden Star (by Salse): poor on Flat (stayed easy 1¼m): poor form over hurdles, blinkered after dead. *J. M. Bradley*

ROLLING MAUL (IRE) 9 b.g. Simply Great (FR) – Soyez Sage (FR) (Grundy) **c–** [2003/4 c–, h–: c24m³ May 7] rangy gelding: winning hurdler/maiden chaser: seems **h–** of little account nowadays: tried blinkered/visored: sold £3,800 Ascot June Sales. *Miss C. J. E. Caroe*

ROLLING TIDE (IRE) 8 b.g. Alphabatim (USA) – St Cristoph (The Parson) [2003/4 **h81 +** h–: 20f* Aug 25] angular gelding: lightly-raced hurdler: sold out of N. Henderson's stable 2,400 gns Doncaster August Sales: made all in weak claimer (claimed to join M. Hoad £3,000) at Fontwell only outing in 2003/4: stays 2½m: acts on firm and soft going: has pulled hard. *Evan Williams*

ROLLO (IRE) 6 gr.g. Roselier (FR) – Comeragh Queen (The Parson) [2003/4 F16v³ **F92** F16s F16d⁵ Mar 24] angular gelding: fifth foal: half-brother to 3m chase winner Dalligan (by Executive Perk): dam unraced half-sister to very smart chaser up to 3m Comeragh King and useful staying chaser Seskin Bridge: fair form when third in bumper at Ascot on debut: below that form in 2 similar events: sold 46,000 gns Doncaster May Sales. *M. G. Rimell*

ROLLSWOOD (USA) 4 ch.g. Diesis – Spit Curl (USA) (Northern Dancer) [2003/4 **F79** F12d F17s Feb 3] compact gelding: tenth foal: half-brother to several winners, including 1m winner Miss Kirsty (by Miswaki): dam US Grade 1 1¼m winner: modest form on first of 2 starts in bumpers: fifth over 1¼m on all-weather on Flat in late-February. *P. R. Hedger*

ROLL WITH IT (IRE) 11 b.g. Royal Fountain – Deirdre Elizabeth (Salluceva) **c–** [2003/4 c90, h–: c24s\u1d56ᵘ May 2] winning pointer: maiden hurdler/steeplechaser: blinkered **h–** once. *I. Anderson*

ROMAN ARK 6 br.g. Terimon – Larksmore (Royal Fountain) [2003/4 23d³ 20s² Mar **h96** 13] lengthy gelding: won bumper on debut in 2001/2: placed in novice hurdles at Wetherby and Newcastle on return. *J. M. Jefferson*

ROMAN CANDLE (IRE) 8 b.g. Sabrehill (USA) – Penny Banger (IRE) (Pennine **h74**
Walk) [2003/4 h80: 16m 16g³ 17m⁶ 16m⁴ 20m⁶ 16d⁴ Aug 7] lengthy, workmanlike
gelding: poor maiden hurdler: best given test of speed around 2m: acts on good to firm
going. *Mrs Lucinda Featherstone*

ROMAN CONSUL (IRE) 6 ch.g. Alphabatim (USA) – Stella Romana (Roman **h–**
Warrior) [2003/4 20sᵖᵘ Nov 29] €23,000 4-y-o: workmanlike gelding: looks a chaser:
eighth foal: brother to fairly useful hunter Alpha Romana, stays 21f: dam unraced, from
family of dual Scottish National winner Androma and useful staying chaser Bigsun: won
maiden Irish point in 2003: showed little in novice on hurdling debut. *Jonjo O'Neill*

ROMAN COURT (IRE) 6 b.g. Witness Box (USA) – Small Iron (General Ironside) **h87**
[2003/4 h80, F84: 26g 22m³ 22f³ 20m⁶ 22f³ 24m² 24d⁶ 24g³ 25d³ Apr 11] modest novice
hurdler: stays 25f: acts on firm and good to soft going. *R. H. Alner*

ROMAN HIDEAWAY (IRE) 6 b.g. Hernando (FR) – Vaison La Romaine (Arctic **h–**
Tern (USA)) [2003/4 16d Jan 10] half-brother to several winners over jumps, notably
useful hurdler Overstrand (by In The Wings), stays 2½m: fairly useful on Flat (stays 2m)
at 3 yrs for Sir Mark Prescott: well held in novice on hurdling debut. *J. A. B. Old*

ROMAN OUTLAW 12 gr.g. Alias Smith (USA) – Roman Moor (Owen Anthony) **c– x**
[2003/4 c95x, h–: c25gᵖᵘ c24sᶠ c28d⁶ 24d c24s c25vᵖᵘ Jan 26] strong, workmanlike **h–**
gelding: winning hurdler/chaser: no form in 2003/4: usually wears blinkers/cheekpieces:
sketchy jumper. *Mrs K. Walton*

ROMAN RAMPAGE 9 b.g. Perpendicular – Roman Moor (Owen Anthony) [2003/4 **h82**
24gᵖᵘ 24s 22s 27g⁴ Apr 22] medium-sized gelding: lightly-raced winning hurdler for
T. Easterby: poor form in 2003/4 after 2½-year absence: tried in cheekpieces.
Miss Z. C. Davison

ROMAN REBEL 5 ch.g. Primitive Rising (USA) – Roman Moor (Owen Anthony) **F89**
[2003/4 F16m F16v⁴ F17d F16s⁶ Mar 13] workmanlike gelding: fifth foal: brother to fair
hurdler Roman Uproar, stays 3m, and half-brother to 2½m hurdle winner Roman Rampage (by Perpendicular) and modest staying chaser Roman Outlaw (by Alias Smith): dam
poor novice hurdler: fair form in bumpers: will stay 2½m+. *Mrs K. Walton*

ROMAN RODNEY 7 b.g. Feelings (FR) – Pohet (Pongee) [2003/4 20v 20d Feb 21] **h–**
third foal: dam, winning hurdler, stayed 27f: little sign of ability in points and novice
hurdles. *G. M. Moore*

ROMANTIC AFFAIR (IRE) 7 ch.g. Persian Bold – Broken Romance (IRE) (Ela- **h89**
Mana-Mou) [2003/4 16d⁶ 16s⁶ 16d⁵ Mar 28] good-topped gelding: half-brother to
winning 2½m hurdler Legendary Lover (by Fairy King): smart on Flat (stays 2m) in 2001
for J. Dunlop: modest form in novice hurdles, jumping none too fluently: will stay beyond
2m. *Miss H. C. Knight*

ROMANTIC HERO (IRE) 8 b.g. Supreme Leader – Right Love (Golden Love) **c–**
[2003/4 c100, h–: c24dᵘʳ Nov 27] big, strong gelding: fair handicap chaser: stays 3m: acts **h–**
on soft going: effective blinkered or not: free-going sort, probably best allowed to stride
on. *N. A. Gaselee*

ROMANY CHAT 12 b.g. Backchat (USA) – Ranee's Song (True Song) [2003/4 c88: **c84**
c21d⁶ c25g⁴ c28gᵖᵘ May 31] good-topped gelding: modest hunter chaser: stays 25f: acts
on good to firm going. *Mrs Rosemary Gasson*

ROMANY DREAM 6 b.m. Nomadic Way (USA) – Half Asleep (Quiet Fling (USA)) **c–**
[2003/4 h–, F74: 21f⁴ 21g 24sᵖᵘ 17d c16d 21m Apr 14] leggy mare: little show over **h–**
hurdles or in handicap chase: usually blinkered. *R. Dickin*

ROMANY MOVE 10 b.g. Silly Prices – Go Gipsy (Move Off) [2003/4 c21sᶠ May 2] **c–**
compact gelding: little form over hurdles/in steeplechases: tried in cheekpieces: sold **h–**
£1,200 Ascot June Sales: won point in March. *Miss Maria D. Myco*

ROMA ROAD 8 b.g. Syrtos – Fair Cruise (Cruise Missile) [2003/4 F89: 16g 17m⁶ **h–**
22m⁵ May 31] lengthy gelding: fair form in bumpers: not fluent when well held in novice
company over hurdles. *R. J. Smith*

ROMEO JONES 5 bl.g. Roselier (FR) – Juleit Jones (IRE) (Phardante (FR)) [2003/4 **F–**
F16d Feb 2] leggy gelding: first foal: dam winning 2m hurdler: tailed off in bumper on
debut. *P. Butler*

ROMERO 8 b.g. Robellino (USA) – Casamurrae (Be My Guest (USA)) [2003/4 c112§, **c– §**
h103§: 16m 23m⁴ 22v⁵ 22d⁵ 18d⁶ Apr 7] compact gelding: winning hurdler/chaser: long **h88 §**
way below best in 2003/4: stays 2¾m: probably acts on any going: sometimes visored:

has had tongue tied: has won 4 times at Ascot: usually races prominently: ungenuine. *P. R. Chamings*

ROMIL STAR (GER)   7 b.g. Chief's Crown (USA) – Romelia (USA) (Woodman c–
(USA)) [2003/4 h88: 17s^{ur} 16g 21g^2 24m 21d* 25f^5 20g 21s^3 c21s^4 c19g^{pu} c16d Mar 30]   **h101**
sturdy gelding: fair handicap hurdler: left R. Wylie after second start: made all at Sedgefield in November: little show in maiden chases: stays 21f: acts on firm and soft going:
often wears cheekpieces: has had tongue tied: joined K. Burke. *G. M. Moore*

ROMNEY   7 ch.g. Timeless Times (USA) – Ewe Lamb (Free State) [2003/4 26g Mar   **h–**
6] small gelding: modest hurdler in 2001/2: tailed off in handicap on return: should stay
3m: acts on good to firm and heavy going. *Mrs P. Sly*

RONALD   5 ch.g. Karinga Bay – Hy Wilma (Jalmood (USA)) [2003/4 F17m Aug 25]   **F–**
fifth foal: half-brother to 1m winner Leonie Samual (by Safawan): dam, 2-y-o 6f winner,
out of Galtres Stakes winner Hymettus: well beaten in bumper on debut. *N. J. Hawke*

RONANS CHOICE (IRE)   11 b.g. Yashgan – Petite Port (IRE) (Decent Fellow)   **c99**
[2003/4 c–: c26d^2 c24g^{su} Apr 16] workmanlike gelding: winning chaser: won 2 points in
February: second in hunter at Fontwell late in month: stays 3¼m: acts on good to soft
ground: blinkered: tried tongue tied. *Miss Emma Oliver*

RONANS SONG (IRE)   9 b.g. Insan (USA) – Start Singing (IRE) (Orchestra) [2003/4   c–
20g^{pu} May 14] signs of some ability in points: lightly raced and little show over hurdles: **h–**
tried tongue tied: dead. *Mrs C. J. Kerr*

RONQUISTA D'OR   10 b.g. Ron's Victory (USA) – Gild The Lily (Ile de Bourbon   **h–**
(USA)) [2003/4 17g^{pu} 19m^{pu} Jun 11] poor on Flat: pulled up both starts over hurdles:
reportedly lame second occasion. *G. A. Ham*

ROOBIHOO (IRE)   5 b.g. Norwich – Griffinstown Lady (Over The River (FR))   **h89**
[2003/4 F88: F17m^6 20d^6 20s 20s^5 20v^3 22g^{pu} 20s^4 20s^4 20d* Apr 18] rangy gelding: **F77**
modest in bumpers: modest novice hurdler: won handicap at Carlisle: should stay beyond
2½m: acts on heavy going. *C. Grant*

ROOFING SPIRIT (IRE)   6 b.g. Beneficial – Vulcash (IRE) (Callernish) [2003/4   **h93**
F17g^2 16s^6 16d 16d^4 20s 16d^2 Mar 14] €11,000 4-y-o: quite good-topped gelding: **F97**
seventh foal: half-brother to fairly useful hurdler/chaser Silver Streak, stays 25f, and
modest 2m hurdler Chevet Girl (both by Roselier): dam unraced half-sister to smart
chaser up to 3m Kilkilowen and dam of high-class staying chaser Couldnt Be Better:
second in bumper at Newton Abbot on debut: modest form over hurdles: bred to be suited
by further than 2m: raced on good going or softer: has flashed tail under pressure.
D. P. Keane

ROOKERY LAD   6 b.g. Makbul – Wayzgoose (USA) (Diesis) [2003/4 h72, F–: 16m*   **h92**
16m^2 17m^2 17g^3 22g^2 20f^4 24d^{pu} 21d 20d* Apr 12] modest hurdler: won novice seller at
Huntingdon in May and handicap at Fakenham in April: effective at 2m to 2¾m: acts on
good to firm and good to soft going. *C. N. Kellett*

ROOKWITH (IRE)   4 b.g. Revoque (IRE) – Resume (IRE) (Lahib (USA)) [2003/4   **h97**
16s^3 16d^3 16d^4 Feb 8] fair on Flat (stays 9f), sold out of J. Bethell's stable 12,000 gns
Newmarket Autumn Sales: modest form in juvenile hurdles: visored final start.
T. G. McCourt, Ireland

ROOM TO ROOM GOLD (IRE)   8 b.g. Phardante (FR) – Kiwi Circle (Strong   **h113**
Gale) [2003/4 F16f^3 F17g^2 F16f^2 F16m* 16f^F 17f^2 Aug 30] IR 11,500 3-y-o, resold IR   **F92**
22,000 3-y-o: first foal: dam unraced sister to fairly useful hurdler/chaser up to 3m Storm
Gem: fair in bumpers, winning at Kilbeggan in August: won maiden there on hurdling
debut later in month: no match for Lowlander in novice at Tralee final start: raced mainly
around 2m: acts on firm going. *M. Halford, Ireland*

ROOSTER   9 b.g. Roi Danzig (USA) – Jussoli (Don) [2003/4 c71, h–: c20m^2 c21s^F **c84**
c21d^6 Apr 12] good-topped gelding: winning hurdler: modest form in hunter chases: **h–**
stays 21f: acts on good to firm and good to soft going. *Mrs Julie Read*

ROOSTER BOOSTER   10 gr.g. Riverwise (USA) – Came Cottage (Nearly A   **h166**
Hand) [2003/4 h170: 16s^5 16g^2 16s* 16g^2 16g^2 20d^2 Apr 3]
'Bookies face £25 million payout!' Never underestimate the capacity of the
big bookmakers to get the maximum free publicity out of impending or—much
more rarely—actual financial disaster. The headline this time was generated by the
prospect of the four main races at the 2004 Cheltenham Festival being won by the
quartet that had been successful in 2003. For only the third time since the Stayers'

Red Square Vodka Champion Hurdle Trial, Haydock—
Rooster Booster gains his sole victory of the season; Hasty Prince takes second

Hurdle was added to the Festival programme, all four of the title-holders were going to be there to defend their crown and, unlike the two previous occasions, all four went to Cheltenham in pole position. In 1983, none of the returning champions managed to retain their title—For Auction finished third in the Champion Hurdle, Crimson Embers and Silver Buck fourth in the Stayers' and the Gold Cup respectively and Rathgorman fifth in the Champion Chase, with all except Silver Buck starting favourite or joint favourite. On the second occasion, in 2003, the pair that started favourite, Best Mate and Baracouda (who disputed market leadership with Limestone Lad), both went on to further success, but Flagship Uberalles managed only fifth in the Champion Chase and Hors La Loi III refused to race in the Champion Hurdle.

2004 promised to be different and, for the bookies, expensive. Baracouda, Best Mate and the Champion Chase winner Moscow Flyer were all set to start odds on and the defending Champion Hurdle winner Rooster Booster probably ought to have been as well. Rooster Booster won the 2003 renewal in most emphatic fashion, by eleven lengths, and though he had won only once from five starts in the interim—in the Red Square Vodka Champion Hurdle Trial at Haydock in January —he had shown form in the Tote Gold Trophy in February which appeared every bit as good as his Champion-winning performance. At Newbury, he finished second in the Tote Gold Trophy for the third time. When runner-up to Landing Light in 2001 and Copeland in 2002, Rooster Booster was working his way up the handicap with a series of solid efforts in defeat. In 2004, he was right at the top of the tree, his presence in the biggest handicap hurdle of the season meaning half of his rivals were out of the weights and the nearest to him in the handicap was the 2003 Champion Hurdle runner-up Westender, who was set to receive 13 lb from Rooster Booster. That Rooster Booster failed only by a short head to hold the late challenge of Geos rightly earned him considerable praise, any doubts raised by his being beaten after travelling the best at the last mitigated by the fact that he might just have won had he jumped the flight more fluently.

So, Rooster Booster went to Cheltenham with form which put him just about as far in front of his rivals as Best Mate was in front of his, and the main question before the race was not whether Rooster Booster would win, but whether the pace would be strong enough to show him to best advantage. Lack of a true gallop was to blame for defeats when fifth to Rigmarole in the Bula Hurdle at Cheltenham on his reappearance, and the Christmas Hurdle at Kempton, in which he was supplied with a pacemaker who was ignored by Rooster Booster's jockey as well as by the rest of the field, and where Rooster Booster was beaten two and a half lengths by Intersky Falcon. When winning at Haydock, Rooster Booster's rider Richard Johnson unusually took up the running at the fourth, Rooster Booster's owner Terry Warner suggesting afterwards that if nothing else went on then Rooster Booster would again race prominently in the Champion. That proved not to be necessary with the largely-unconsidered Hardy Eustace setting the pace. The gallop wasn't so strong as ideal but, as Rooster Booster sliced through the field down the hill, all appeared well. As he landed alongside the ridden-along Hardy Eustace at the last, Rooster Booster appeared the likely winner, but Hardy Eustace was still not done with and, soon afterwards, Rooster Booster was off the bridle and patently not finding so much as his rival. Five lengths was the margin of defeat, the bookies twenty-five million stayed in the satchels and the writers and commentators went off in search of excuses. None was forthcoming from connections: Johnson felt the horse had not been good enough and so did trainer Philip Hobbs. 'He's run a brilliant race but was not good enough on the day,' said Hobbs. Perhaps no excuses, or reasons for defeat, were needed against a clearly much improved winner, especially as such as Intersky Falcon and Westender were firmly in their place behind him. As it turned out, the performances at Newbury and Cheltenham were the start of a sequence of defeats for Rooster Booster which must have been frustrating for both his connections and supporters.

Rooster Booster's next appearance was his third successive one in the Aintree Hurdle over two and a half miles. The trip had been put forward as a partial explanation for his fourth to Ilnamar on his first step out of handicap company in 2002, and also for a last-gasp defeat by Sacundai in 2003 (when Johnson's dropped whip also contributed). Third time lucky looked the apposite cliche as, in a steadily-run race, Rooster Booster led on the bridle at the last looking set for victory. Once again little was forthcoming off the bridle and Rhinestone Cowboy swept past to win by three quarters of a length. A blunder two out was offered as something of an excuse, while Johnson blamed himself for getting there too soon. Hobbs added that

Mr Terry Warner's "Rooster Booster"

Rooster Booster was 'one hundred percent genuine' but didn't need to hit the front too soon. A run of five second places in seven starts, with a pattern of weak responses off the bridle, was certainly beginning to raise the question of Rooster Booster's temperament.

Punchestown, and a rematch with Hardy Eustace in the Emo Oil Champion Hurdle, provided one final chance to balance the account. Punters hadn't lost faith, Rooster Booster starting favourite ahead of Hardy Eustace, and, in a race run at a much better gallop than at Cheltenham, everything appeared to be going to plan as the field approached the straight. Hardy Eustace was in front and finding plenty for pressure but Rooster Booster was just behind, poised to pounce. However, a quicker jump at the last began to swing things in Hardy Eustace's favour and, once again, Rooster Booster failed to respond so well as anticipated under pressure, going down by a length. It was a disappointing end to a spring campaign which promised much. In the end, the excuses ran out for Rooster Booster. The gallop, the trip, his jumping, the ride he received—none of these could be blamed—and in the end the only conclusion was that the horse had effectively beaten himself. Rooster Booster is unquestionably tough and consistent, with a clear excuse for the two occasions he has failed completely to give his running in five full campaigns over hurdles. Unlike some that find little off the bridle, Rooster Booster doesn't make it obvious that he's not putting it all in by, for example, hanging in behind or sticking his head in the air, and he isn't yet getting beaten by horses he definitely ought to beat—and yet it has to be stated that he can't be relied upon fully.

	Rooster Booster (gr.g. 1994)	Riverwise (USA) (b 1988)	Riverman (b 1969)	Never Bend
				River Lady
			Village Sass (1982)	Sassafras
				Village Beauty
		Came Cottage (gr 1980)	Nearly A Hand (ch 1974)	Busted
				Petite Chou
			Maybelle (gr 1965)	Perhapsburg
				Tinkling

The sparely-made Rooster Booster is likely to have a campaign aimed at a third Champion Hurdle bid and, as such, his programme more or less plans itself, particularly as he is effective on any ground he is likely to encounter. Whether, heading to the veteran stage, he can regain the winning touch that took him from the County Hurdle to the Champion in a glorious twelve-month period has to be doubted. Comedy of Errors is the only horse to have regained the Champion Hurdle crown, while only two eleven-year-olds, Hatton's Grace and Sea Pigeon, have won the race. There is little to add to previous details of Rooster Booster's pedigree. His bumper-winning brother Cockatoo Ridge showed modest form at up to three miles over hurdles without winning while the five-year-old Silkie Pekin made her debut without distinction in a bumper. For the name of the latest offspring by Riverwise out of their dam Came Cottage, the Mitchell family, who own the mare, have forsaken the feathery theme (others out of the mare are King Rooster and Madame Poulet). Perhaps with questions about Rooster Booster in mind she has been named Attitude. *P. J. Hobbs*

ROOSTER'S REUNION (IRE)   5 gr.g. Presenting – Court Town (Camden Town)   **h105 p**
[2003/4 F97+: 16d² 16d 16g* Mar 6] useful-looking gelding: off over 3 months, best effort over hurdles when comfortably winning novice at Huntingdon, cruising through to lead last and beat Captain Corelli by 2 lengths: open to further improvement. *D. R. Gandolfo*

ROPPONGI DANCER   5 b.m. Mtoto – Ice Chocolate (USA) (Icecapade (USA))   **h77 §**
[2003/4 h71: 17d³ 17m² 20m² 19m³ 16gᵖᵘ 16gᵖᵘ 19g⁵ 22gᵖᵘ 17gᵖᵘ Apr 24] small mare: poor maiden hurdler, left Mrs M. Reveley after reappearance: stays 2½m: acts on good to firm going: tongue tied after reappearance, also tried in visor/cheekpieces: ungenuine. *Mrs N. Macauley*

RORY SUNSET (IRE)   6 b.g. Lord Americo – Dunany Star (IRE) (Salluceva) [2003/4   **h108**
F19f³ F16f* F16m³ F16m² 16d³ 16s³ 16s² 16d² Apr 10] first foal: dam unraced, out of   **F107**
half-sister to useful chaser up to 2½m Ebony Star: useful form in bumpers: won at Down Royal in September: placed all 4 starts in maiden hurdles: should stay beyond 2m: acts on soft going, won bumper on firm. *C. F. Swan, Ireland*

Philips Electronics Lismullen Hurdle, Navan—
Rosaker is well clear going to the last, as Hardy Eustace makes a disappointing return

ROSADARE (IRE)   6 b.g. Roselier (FR) – Mosephine (IRE) (The Parson) [2003/4 **F105**
F18d F16s⁴ F16v* F20d² Mar 17] €13,000 4-y-o: first foal: dam lightly-raced sister to
useful hurdler up to 2¾m Gravity Gate: well-beaten third on second of 2 starts in points
in 2003: won bumper at Tramore in January: better form when second to That's An Idea
in 2½m event at Limerick final start: sold to join Miss K. Marks £60,000 Cheltenham
April Sales. *D. P. Murphy, Ireland*

ROSAKER (USA)   7 b.g. Pleasant Tap (USA) – Rose Crescent (USA) (Nijinsky **h153**
(CAN)) [2003/4 h129: 20d 20m* 20s² 24s* 24s* 21g Mar 17] leggy, rather sparely-made
gelding: smart hurdler: won Grade 2 Philips Electronics Lismullen Hurdle at Navan
(made all to beat Hardy Eustace by 8 lengths) in November, Grade 3 betfair.com Galmoy
Stayers Hurdle Trial at Gowran in January and Grade 2 McCabe Builders Ltd Boyne
Hurdle at Navan (beat Prince of Tara easily by 4 lengths) in February: excellent efforts
when second to Solerina in Grade 3 at Navan in December and third to Rhinestone
Cowboy in Grade 1 at Punchestown in late-April: stays 3m: acts on soft and good to firm
going. *N. Meade, Ireland*

ROSALEE ROYALE   12 ch.m. Out of Hand – Miss Ark Royal (Broadsword (USA)) **c–**
[2003/4 c–, h–: c19mᵖᵘ May 14] workmanlike mare: winning pointer, little sign of ability **h–**
otherwise. *Mrs S. Kittow*

ROSALYONS (IRE)   10 gr.g. Roselier (FR) – Coffee Shop (Bargello) [2003/4 c82, **c74 §**
h87: 22g 20d⁶ c30d² c25s⁵ c25sᵘʳ c16v⁴ c24vᵘʳ 27s 22g c32dᵖᵘ 20s Apr 4] leggy gelding: **h80 d**
has stringhalt: winning hurdler: poor maiden chaser, often let down by jumping: stays
3¾m: acts on heavy going: tried blinkered: lazy, and one to avoid. *Mrs H. O. Graham*

ROSARIAN (IRE)   7 b.g. Fourstars Allstar (USA) – Only A Rose (Glint of Gold) **h127**
[2003/4 h127: 24g* Nov 8] fairly useful hurdler: in cheekpieces, won handicap at Chepstow only start in 2003/4 by neck from Ballyvaddy, just holding on after going clear early
in straight (finished lame): will prove best at 3m+: acts on good to firm and heavy going:
visored (fell) once. *V. R. A. Dartnall*

ROSCHAL (IRE)   6 gr.g. Roselier (FR) – Sunday World (USA) (Solford (USA)) **h79**
[2003/4 F16m³ 20d⁵ 19g⁶ 19d⁶ 22m Mar 11] IR £13,000 3-y-o, €48,000 4-y-o: rather **F85**
unfurnished gelding: fifth foal: dam winning 2m hurdler: third in bumper at Sandown on
debut: poor form over hurdles: blinkered, no show in handicap (finished lame) final start:
should stay beyond 2½m. *P. J. Hobbs*

ROSCOE BURN   12 ch.g. Meadowbrook – Rosecko (White Speck) [2003/4 c24dᵖᵘ **c–**
Apr 18] modest pointer, successful in March: no show in maiden hunter chase.
Mrs K. Massie

ROSDARI (IRE)   7 b.g. Shardari – Tullahought (Jaazeiro (USA)) [2003/4 20m⁵ 20g⁵ **c–**
22g c26g⁴ c16m 24m⁶ Aug 1] IR 16,000 3-y-o: half-brother to fair 2m hurdler Frances **h–**
Street (by Be My Native) and winning pointer by Broken Hearted: dam, fair 2m to 2½m
hurdler, half-sister to prolific 2-y-o winner Spindrifter: placed twice from 6 starts in
maiden Irish points: bought 8,500 gns Doncaster May Sales: well beaten over hurdles and

in handicap chases (not fluent): tongue tied last 2 outings, also visored on first occasion. *M. C. Pipe*

ROSEBERRY ROSE   5 ch.m. Keen – Scotch Imp (Imperial Fling (USA)) [2003/4 F16g F16s F16g Mar 10] strong mare: fifth foal: dam fairly useful at 6f/7f: soundly beaten in bumpers. *M. E. Sowersby*   **F–**

ROSE BOWL BOY (IRE)   6 ch.g. Lahib (USA) – Danita (IRE) (Roi Danzig (USA)) [2003/4 F–: 16g 16g 21dᵖᵘ Mar 28] no sign of ability: sold out of C. Mann's stable 3,400 gns Doncaster November Sales before reappearance: tongue tied last 2 starts: sold 1,100 gns Doncaster May Sales. *B. N. Pollock*   **h–**

ROSE D'APRIL (FR)   7 gr.g. April Night (FR) – Rose de Hoc (FR) (Rose Laurel) [2003/4 h103: c16g⁶ c20d⁵ c21sᵘʳ Dec 26] rangy gelding: fair hurdler: no form over fences, though only just starting to weaken when unseating 2 out in maiden at Sedgefield: stays easy 2½m: acts on soft ground: tried in cheekpieces. *L. Lungo*   **c?** **h–**

ROSEGROVE ROOSTER   7 b.g. Henbit (USA) – Cornbelt (Oats) [2003/4 h–: 16gᵖᵘ May 2] little sign of ability in bumpers or over hurdles: runner-up twice in points in 2004. *D. J. Caro*   **h–**

ROSEMEAD TYE   8 b.m. Kasakov – Nouvelle Cuisine (Yawa) [2003/4 h–, F–: 16g 16m c17m³ c17m⁵ 17g c17g⁶ Aug 23] little sign of ability, trained until after reappearance by J. A. Moore: has had tongue tied: sold £2,200 Ascot October Sales. *D. W. Thompson*   **c–** **h–**

ROSE OF YORK (IRE)   4 b.f. Emarati (USA) – True Ring (High Top) [2003/4 16m 17d 18gᵘʳ 16d 21gᵖᵘ Feb 25] rather leggy filly: half-sister to 2 winning hurdlers, including Semi Circle (by Noble Patriarch), fairly useful around 2m: no show on Flat or over hurdles. *J. G. Portman*   **h–**

ROSE PALMA (FR)   6 gr. or ro.m. Great Palm (USA) – Rose Angevine (FR) (Master Thatch) [2003/4 c20sᵖᵘ c17g c26gᶠ Mar 1] leggy ex-French mare: second foal: half-sister to winning hurdler around 2m Rose Beryl (by Lost World): dam winning jumper up to around 2¾m: maiden hurdler: modest chaser, left T. Trapenard before reappearance: no show in 3 handicaps in Britain: stays 23f: raced on good ground or softer: tongue tied last 2 starts. *S. J. Gilmore*   **c–** **h–**

ROSE PERK (IRE)   8 b.m. Executive Perk – Timeless Rose (Bulldozer) [2003/4 c20m* c21m c24d² c20d* c18d³ c24dᵖᵘ c20s² c24s² c22sᵖᵘ c29dᶠ Apr 12] modest hurdler: fairly useful novice chaser: won at Clonmel (mares maiden) in September and Gowran in November: best efforts when runner-up seventh and eighth starts, behind Colnel Rayburn in quite valuable handicap at Navan on second occasion: stayed 3m: acted on good to firm and heavy going: tried tongue tied: front runner: dead. *E. Sheehy, Ireland*   **c115** **h–**

ROSES ARE WILD (IRE)   6 gr.m. Roselier (FR) – Wild Bramble (IRE) (Deep Run) [2003/4 F16m F16s 20s³ 19gᶠ Mar 9] small mare: fourth foal: dam won point and around 2½m over hurdles: pulled up in 2 mares maiden Irish points in 2003: bought 5,000 gns Doncaster August Sales: showed little in bumpers and mares novice hurdles. *Mrs B. K. Thomson*   **h–** **F–**

ROSETA PEARL (IRE)   8 gr.m. Roselier (FR) – Brown Pearl (Tap On Wood) [2003/4 c–: c26vᵖᵘ c25dᵖᵘ Jan 2] no form over fences: has had tongue tied. *Mrs S. Wall*   **c–**

ROSE TEA (IRE)   5 ro.m. Alhaarth (IRE) – Shakamiyn (Nishapour (FR)) [2003/4 21g* 20m 23m² 21m Apr 15] poor maiden on balance of form on Flat (should stay at least 1½m): modest form over hurdles: won weak events on first 2 starts, mares maiden at Southwell in September and novice at Hexham in October: stays 23f: joined Miss E. Lavelle. *N. A. Graham*   **h89**

ROSE TINA   7 b.m. Tina's Pet – Rosevear (IRE) (Contract Law (USA)) [2003/4 c90, h71: c19g³ c20mᶠ c19mʳᵒ c21g² c18m* c22g² c19f* c19m* c20gᶠ 20m³ Nov 8] leggy mare: poor maiden hurdler: fair chaser: won in small fields in maiden at Fontwell and novice and handicap at Towcester in autumn: stays 2¾m: best efforts on good going or firmer: free-going front runner: ran out third start. *B. G. Powell*   **c100** **h75 +**

ROSE TINTED   5 b.m. Spectrum (IRE) – Marie La Rose (FR) (Night Shift (USA)) [2003/4 16g 19f⁵ Nov 22] small, close-coupled mare: half-sister to winning hurdler/ chaser around 2m Contemporary Art (by Blushing Flame): modest maiden on Flat (stays 1½m): well held both starts over hurdles. *M. E. Sowersby*   **h–**

ROSETOWEN (IRE)   6 gr.g. Roselier (FR) – Railstown Cheeky (IRE) (Strong Gale) [2003/4 F17d 20d 20sᵖᵘ 22v Jan 12] IR £22,000 3-y-o: smallish gelding: third foal: brother to fair hurdler Cheeky Lady, stays 2½m: dam unraced: little show in bumper or novice hurdles: tongue tied final outing. *T. R. George*   **h–** **F–**

ROSIE REDMAN (IRE) 7 gr.m. Roselier (FR) – Carbia's Last (Palm Track) [2003/4 **c105**
h84: c25g³ c24d^co c25g* c22s* 20s* c25d* Apr 17] leggy mare: modest hurdler: won **h95**
novice handicap at Hexham in April: fair chaser: won novices at Market Rasen (handicap,
by distance) in December, Kelso (mares) in January and Ayr (handicap) in April: stays
25f: raced on good going or softer (acts on soft): front runner: game. *J. R. Turner*

ROSSCARBERY GREY (IRE) 6 gr.g. Gothland (FR) – Millroad (Buckskin (FR)) **h–**
[2003/4 F–: 22m^pu 20s^pu Jan 27] lengthy, angular gelding: no sign of ability. *S. T. Lewis*

ROSS GEE (IRE) 8 gr.g. Roselier (FR) – Miss Leader (Taufan (USA)) [2003/4 17d **c68**
20s c21v^pu c19g⁶ Feb 6] medium-sized ex-Irish gelding: fourth foal: dam unraced: **h–**
half-sister to smart 2-y-o Atall Atall: first form outside points when sixth in novice chase
at Catterick. *Mrs S. J. Smith*

ROSS LEADER (IRE) 7 b.g. Supreme Leader – Emmagreen (Green Shoon) [2003/4 **c92**
c24d^pu c24g⁵ c23s^pu c24d² Mar 27] IR £25,000 4-y-o: sixth foal: brother to winning
chaser around 2m Superb Leader and half-brother to winning 3m hurdler No Picnic (by
Be My Native): dam won at 2½m over hurdles in Ireland: won maiden Irish point on
debut in 2003: modest form in steeplechases. *Mrs Susan Nock*

ROSSLEA (IRE) 6 b.g. Roselier (FR) – Burren Gale (IRE) (Strong Gale) [2003/4 **c141**
h112+: c24d* c25d² c24d² c24d* c24g² Feb 21] good-topped gelding: fair maiden **h–**
hurdler: useful novice chaser: won at Bangor in November and Kempton in February,
beating Look Collonges 3 lengths at latter course: better form when second to Therealbandit at Cheltenham, Pizarro at Leopardstown and Our Vic at Ascot, last 2 graded
events: fell fatally at Punchestown in late-April: would have stayed beyond 25f: raced on
good going or softer: usually sound jumper. *Miss H. C. Knight*

ROSSMAY (IRE) 7 b.g. Kasmayo – Ross Rag (Ragapan) [2003/4 16m^pu 20g^pu 16m **c–**
c16m³ c19d^pu Jan 7] IR £2,600 4-y-o and £3,000 5-y-o: third foal: half-brother to fair hurdler/ **h–**
chaser Mister Ross (by Mister Lord), stayed 25f: dam unraced: no sign of ability: sold
500 gns Doncaster January Sales. *G. F. Bridgwater*

ROSS MINSTER (IRE) 10 br. or b.g. Roselier (FR) – Face To Face (The Parson) **c118**
[2003/4 c–, h–: c25s² c26v^pu c29d⁴ Mar 14] medium-sized gelding: fairly useful handicap **h–**

chaser: stays 4m: raced on good going or softer (acts on heavy): effective blinkered or not: usually races prominently: sometimes none too fluent: usually takes plenty of driving. *P. J. Hobbs*

ROSS MOFF (IRE)   11 b.g. Good Thyne (USA) – Miss Kamsy (Kambalda) [2003/1 c132x, h–: c17d² c29dᶠ Apr 12] good-topped gelding: useful chaser: reportedly had wind operation prior to creditable second to Native Scout in handicap at Fairyhouse in November: let down by jumping at same course and at Punchestown in April: needs good test at 2m, stays 25f: acts on good to firm and heavy going: usually tongue tied: makes mistakes. *A. J. Martin, Ireland*
`c132 x`
`h–`

ROSS PARK (IRE)   8 b.g. Roselier (FR) – La Christyana (IRE) (The Parson) [2003/4 h66: 19g Feb 6] poor maiden hurdler: stays 3m: acts on heavy ground: tried tongue tied. *J. Howard Johnson*
`h–`

ROSS RIVER   8 gr.g. Over The River (FR) – Solo Rose (Roselier (FR)) [2003/4 20d* 21g 20s⁵ Apr 17] lengthy, useful-looking gelding: sort to make a chaser: fourth in point on debut: won Powers Gold Label Point-To-Point Championship Final at Fairyhouse on first of 2 starts in bumpers in 2001/2, when trained by G. Stewart: very promising when over hurdles when winning novice at Chepstow in December very easily: not knocked about when well held in Grade 1 novice at Cheltenham over 3 months later, weakened quickly as if amiss final start: will stay 3m. *P. J. Hobbs*
`h122`

ROSTROPOVICH (IRE)   7 gr.g. Sadler's Wells (USA) – Infamy (Shirley Heights) [2003/4 h141: 24g³ 25m³ 16d 24d³ 24v 23s⁶ 25g 24g Apr 2] well-made gelding: useful hurdler: creditable third to Sacundai in Grade 2 at Leopardstown in December, laboured efforts when below form all 4 starts after: stays 3m well: acts on soft and good to firm going: usually wears cheekpieces nowadays (blinkered once): tongue tied: possibly been ridden up with pace: has hung left: none too genuine or consistent. *M. F. Morris, Ireland*
`h133 §`

ROTHKO (IRE)   6 b.g. Naheez (USA) – Dizzy Lady (IRE) (Sarab) [2003/4 19g 22gᵖᵘ 20dᵖᵘ Apr 10] sturdy gelding: fourth foal: dam lightly raced in bumpers: placed in 2 Irish points in 2003: looked green and showed ability in novice on hurdling debut, no encouragement both starts in similar events subsequently. *P. D. Niven*
`h–`

ROUGE BLANC (USA)   4 b.f. King of Kings (IRE) – Style N' Elegance (USA) (Alysheba (USA)) [2003/4 16d 16g 21d⁵ Mar 16] tall, leggy filly: fair on Flat (stays 2¼m) for P. McBride: well held over hurdles. *G. A. Harker*
`h–`

ROUGE ET NOIR   6 b.g. Hernando (FR) – Bayrouge (IRE) (Gorytus (USA)) [2003/4 F16g² F16s Nov 28] second foal: dam, useful hurdler/fairly useful chaser who stayed 25f, half-sister to useful staying chaser Duntree: promising second in bumper at Wetherby on debut: again carried head high when soundly beaten later in month. *Mrs M. Reveley*
`F90`

ROUGH TIGER (IRE)   11 ch.g. Glacial Storm (USA) – Mourne Trix (Golden Love) [2003/4 c94: c33d⁴ c20g³ May 24] fair point pointer: thrice-raced in hunters, easily best effort on first occasion: tried visored. *F. A. Hutsby*
`c71`

ROUND THE BEND   12 b.g. Revolutionary (USA) – No Love (Bustiki) [2003/4 c90: c21sᵖᵘ Mar 19] winning pointer: fair form both starts in hunter chases in 2002, well beaten on return. *Miss Louise Allan*
`c–`

ROUSING THUNDER   7 b.g. Theatrical – Moss (USA) (Woodman (USA)) [2003/4 16g⁵ 16g³ 16g⁵ 16g⁴ 21d³ Nov 11] modest on Flat (probably best up to 1¾m): poor form over hurdles: raced mainly at 2m: tried in cheekpieces: usually tongue tied: poor jumper: dead. *W. Storey*
`h69 x`

ROUTE ONE (IRE)   11 br.g. Welsh Term – Skylin (Skyliner) [2003/4 c92, h–: c16d³ c20m* c20d c16gᵖᵘ c20d⁴ Mar 25] rather sparely-made gelding: fair hunter chaser: won at Huntingdon (novice) in May and Leicester: stays easy 2½m: acts on good to firm and good to soft going: tried blinkered: best on right-handed tracks: sometimes let down by jumping. *D. Frankland*
`c91`
`h–`

ROUTE SIXTY SIX (IRE)   8 b.m. Brief Truce (USA) – Lyphards Goddess (IRE) (Lyphard's Special (USA)) [2003/4 c82, h–: 16m⁶ 16g⁵ 16d 16d⁴ 16g⁴ 16gᵖᵘ 17g⁵ 16g⁶ Apr 16] strong, compact mare: winning chaser (jumps none too fluently): modest handicap hurdler: best at sharp 2m: acts on good to soft going: wore cheekpieces last 4 outings. *Jedd O'Keeffe*
`c–`
`h91`

ROVESTAR   13 b.g. Le Solaret (FR) – Gilberts Choice (My Swanee) [2003/4 c–§, h–: c19gᵖᵘ Apr 30] sparely-made gelding: veteran chaser, very much on the downgrade (often takes little interest): usually blinkered, tried in cheekpieces. *C. L. Popham*
`c– §`
`h– §`

ROWLEY HILL   6 b.g. Karinga Bay – Scarlet Dymond (Rymer) [2003/4 F17d[4] 20d[6]   **h85** 25s[5] 24g Mar 6] 15,000 4-y-o: useful-looking gelding: fifth living foal: half-brother to   **F82** winning 3m hurdler Diamond Rose (by Ardross): dam, poor novice hurdler/winning chaser, stayed 25f: fourth in bumper on debut: easily best effort over hurdles when distant sixth to Trabolgan in maiden at Ascot: should stay beyond 2½m. *A. King*

ROYAL ALLEGIANCE   9 ch.g. Kris – Wilayif (USA) (Danzig (USA)) [2003/4 c–,   **c–** h–: c16d[6] c21g[4] c16g[6] c17m[4] c16d Dec 2] compact gelding: winning hurdler: of little   **h–** account nowadays: tried in headgear. *P. Wegmann*

ROYAL ALL STAR (IRE)   7 b.g. Fourstars Allstar (USA) – Riverhead (Quayside)   **h113** [2003/4 20m[4] 22g[2] 24d* 24s* 24d[F] Feb 21] 42,000 3-y-o: half-brother to winning 2½m hurdler Iada (by Accordion): dam, poor maiden, from family of top-class 2m to 21f chaser Katabatic: fair hurdler: won maiden at Gowran in December and handicap at Leopardstown in January, improved form when beating G V A Ireland by head at latter course: stayed 3m: acted on heavy going: tried blinkered: dead. *G. M. Lyons, Ireland*

ROYAL ALPHABET (IRE)   6 b.g. King's Theatre (IRE) – A-To-Z (IRE) (Ahon-   **h140** oora) [2003/4 F117: F16g[2] 16f* 16d* 16d* Apr 13]
     When the winners of the top two-mile novice hurdles at the Cheltenham Festival, Aintree and Fairyhouse met at Punchestown shortly after the end of the British season something had to give. Supreme Novices' Hurdle winner Brave Inca had won all four of his starts in 2003/4, Royal Shakespeare was making it three from three when winning the Top Novices' Hurdle at Aintree and Royal Alphabet was also on a four-timer over hurdles after victories at Punchestown, Thurles and in the Grade 2 Menolly Homes Novices' Hurdle at Fairyhouse. The trainers of all three sounded full of confidence beforehand but two were bound to be disappointed, if only slightly. In a thrilling race, Brave Inca beat Royal Shakespeare a short head and, though he was two and a half lengths further back in third, Royal Alphabet acquitted himself really well against two good novices, putting up a smart performance and leaving open the possibility of more to come.

Menolly Homes Novices' Hurdle, Fairyhouse—
Royal Alphabet pounces at the last as front-running Snapper Creek makes a mistake

After making his hurdling debut as early as September, impressing when winning a five-runner maiden hard held, Royal Alphabet wasn't seen again until March. He was entered for the Supreme Novices' but hadn't run up to expectations in the Champion Bumper the year before and missed Cheltenham. Royal Alphabet returned a week after Cheltenham to win an ordinary novice at odds on, scoring every bit as impressively as on his debut. Fairyhouse represented rather more of a test, with the top Irish-trained juvenile Power Elite in the field, but Royal Alphabet was again sent off odds on and won with plenty to spare, though not before giving his supporters a bit of a scare. Under a very confident ride, Royal Alphabet only got past the runaway leader Snapper Creek in the last fifty yards, winning by a length and a half with half a length back to Power Elite in third. Had he won at Punchestown, Royal Alphabet might well have tried to emulate his stable-companion Davenport Milenium who won both a Grade 1 novice hurdle and the Emo Oil Champion Hurdle at the Festival in 2002. As it was, Royal Alphabet was sent instead for a valuable mile-and-a-half handicap on the Flat at the end of May, in which he dead-heated, unfortunate not to win outright. He is likely to be campaigned as a potential Champion Hurdle candidate when he returns over hurdles, though he has a fair way to go to be up to that standard.

Royal Alphabet (IRE) (b.g. 1998)	King's Theatre (IRE) (b 1991)	Sadler's Wells (b 1981)	Northern Dancer / Fairy Bridge
		Regal Beauty (b or br 1981)	Princely Native / Dennis Belle
	A-To-Z (IRE) (b 1989)	Ahonoora (ch 1975)	Lorenzaccio / Helen Nichols
		Zenga (b 1982)	Try My Best / Dusky Evening

Ballylinch Stud's "Royal Alphabet"

Royal Alphabet has been entered at two and a half miles over hurdles and has form at two miles on the Flat, but it will be no surprise if he proves best at two miles over hurdles. There certainly isn't much in the way of stamina in his family. His dam A-To-Z won the Nell Gwyn Stakes and has produced a couple of fairly useful mile winners in Alphabet (by Saddlers' Hall) and Red Spell (by Soviet Star). A-To-Z is a sister to the dam of the Craven Stakes winner Hurricane Alan. There is one notable stayer in the family, Night In Town, a half-brother to the grandam Zenga and a useful performer for Ian Balding in the mid-'seventies. Another half-brother was the useful mile- to mile-and-a-half performer Spur On. Royal Alphabet, who is still rather unfurnished in appearance, has raced mainly on good or good to soft going over hurdles and in bumpers (where he showed smart form, finishing second to Royal Rosa in the Grade 1 at Punchestown in 2003), though it was firm when he won his maiden hurdle and his trainer reportedly regards him as likely to prove best on good or firmer. Royal Alphabet has worn a tongue strap in all his races over hurdles. *W. P. Mullins, Ireland*

ROYAL AMARETTO (IRE)   10 b.g. Fairy King (USA) – Melbourne Miss (Chaparral (FR)) [2003/4 17m² 16m⁴ Aug 2] formerly useful on Flat: fair hurdler: very lightly raced: unlikely to stay much beyond 17f: acts on good to firm going: effective tongue tied or not: front runner. *Mrs S. J. Smith*   **h109**

ROYAL ATALZA (FR)   7 gr.g. Saint Preuil (FR) – Crystalza (FR) (Crystal Palace (FR)) [2003/4 21s c20d⁶ 24s c21v* c19sᵖᵘ c36dᵖᵘ Apr 3] angular ex-French gelding: half-brother to 7 winners, including smart hurdler around 2½m Crylza Royal (by Northern Fashion) and smart staying hurdler Royal Rosa (by Garde Royale): dam poor half-sister to smart middle-distance colt Dom Alco: fairly useful hurdler: useful chaser: won handicap at Auteuil in November, final start for B. Barbier: pulled up both starts over fences in Britain (successful on Flat in February), in Grand National at Aintree on second occasion: stays 3m: acts on heavy going: has won with/without blinkers, wore cheekpieces at Aintree. *C. N. Allen*   **c134**
h121

ROYAL AUCLAIR (FR)   7 ch.g. Garde Royale – Carmonera (FR) (Carmont (FR)) [2003/4 c151, h–: c20s⁴ c21dᶠ c19g c20s⁴ c24g⁴ c25m² c24g² c24g³ c25g c29m² Apr 24] good-topped gelding: useful chaser: best efforts in 2003/4 when second, to Exit Swinger in listed event at Wincanton, Grey Abbey in handicap at Doncaster and Betfred Gold Cup (Handicap) at Sandown: failed by short head to catch Puntal at last-named: stays 29f: acts on good to firm and heavy going: blinkered third start: tongue tied. *P. F. Nicholls*   **c144**
h–

ROYAL BARGE   14 b.g. Nearly A Hand – April Airs (Grey Mirage) [2003/4 c101, h92: c21g Apr 1] good-topped gelding: winning hurdler/chaser: runner-up on second of 2 starts in points in 2004: never going with any fluency when well held in Fox Hunters' at Aintree: suited by 3m+: acts on any going: has jumped right. *G. Barber*   **c–**
h–

ROYAL BELUGA (USA)   7 b.g. Rahy (USA) – Navratilovna (USA) (Nureyev (USA)) [2003/4 c116, h89: 20m⁵ c20m⁴ c21dᵖᵘ c19d* c20s² c20g⁴ c24m⁴ c24gᵖᵘ Mar 16] smallish gelding: modest maiden hurdler (has hinted at temperament): fairly useful handicap chaser: made all at Doncaster in December: stays 21f: acts on good to firm and heavy going: tried visored/tongue tied: didn't seem to take to National fences at Aintree third start. *T. R. George*   **c117**
h–

ROYAL BLAZER (IRE)   4 b.g. Barathea (IRE) – Royale (IRE) (Royal Academy (USA)) [2003/4 16d⁴ 16d 16g 17s 16d 24] well held in 3 maidens on Flat: signs of some ability on first and third starts over hurdles. *C. Grant*   **h79**

ROYAL BUBBEL (IRE)   6 ch.m. Hubbly Bubbly (USA) – Last Royal (Kambalda) [2003/4 17g³ Apr 10] second foal: half-sister to winning pointer by Beau Sher: dam maiden pointer: won mares maiden Irish point in 2003: modest form when third in mares maiden at Newton Abbot on hurdling debut. *D. R. Gandolfo*   **h89**

ROYAL CASTLE (IRE)   10 b.g. Caerleon (USA) – Sun Princess (English Prince) [2003/4 h109: c21s* c21g* c24d⁴ c21g c21m² c22gᶠ c26mᵖᵘ 22s 24d⁵ c30gᵘʳ 25g Feb 6] workmanlike gelding: fair hurdler/chaser: won novice chases at Sedgefield and Cartmel in May: lost his form: stays 3m: acts on firm and good to soft going, probably on soft: blinkered twice. *Mrs K. Walton*   **c106 d**
h103 d

ROYAL CHARLIE   7 br.g. Royal Fountain – Cool View (Kinglet) [2003/4 F–: 20sᵖᵘ 16s Jan 16] no sign of ability. *Mrs R. L. Elliot*   **h–**

ROYAL CHINA (IRE)   6 b.g. Aristocracy – Luan Causca (Pampapaul) [2003/4 h83, F74: c17g⁴ c20m⁴ c21s² c20d³ c19dᶠ c20dᵖᵘ 21d Apr 12] leggy, unfurnished gelding: **c87 x**
h–

lightly-raced maiden hurdler: modest novice chaser, often let down by jumping: may prove best short of 2¾m: acts on soft and good to firm going: races freely. *Miss H. C. Knight*

ROYAL COUNTY BUCK (IRE)   9 b.g. Good Thyne (USA) – Little Quince (Laurence O) [2003/4 c80, h–: c25f* c23g⁴ 24d c25m* c24m³ c24m³ c32g² Nov 14] maiden hurdler: fair handicap chaser: won at Kilbeggan in June and September: took wrong course fifth outing: stays 4m: best form on good going or firmer (acts on firm): tongue tied. *A. J. Martin, Ireland*   **c104** **h–**

ROYAL CRIMSON   13 b.g. Danehill (USA) – Fine Honey (USA) (Drone (USA)) [2003/4 c68§, h–: c25m⁴ c24g⁴ Mar 12] lengthy gelding: poor hunter chaser: left Mrs F. Needham after first start: left alone in point in April: barely stays 3m: acts on soft and good to firm going: usually blinkered/visored: often looks less than keen. *Miss A. Armitage*   **c71 §** **h–**

ROYALE ACADOU (FR)   6 b. or br.m. Cadoudal (FR) – Girl Vamp (FR) (Kaldoun (FR)) [2003/4 18s c21sᵖᵘ c22sᵖᵘ 18v⁵ c18v⁶ c18m 18d³ 16d 18d c22g⁴ Apr 22] ex-French mare: eighth foal: sister to winning hurdler/chaser around 2m Royal Dikinson and half-sister to useful chaser Royal Predica (by Tip Moss), stays 25f: dam winning hurdler around 2m: once-raced on Flat: fair hurdler: maiden chaser: left B. Barbier, 3¾ lengths fourth of 7 in novice at Fontwell: should stay 3m: acts on heavy ground: has worn blinkers. *Miss L. J. Sheen*   **c88** **h110**

ROYALE ANGELA (FR)   12 ch.g. Garde Royale – Santa Angela (FR) (Son of Silver) [2003/4 c–, h–: 21gᵖᵘ 27gᵖᵘ Jun 3] neat gelding: has been hobdayed: thrice-raced novice chaser: veteran hurdler, no form since 2000/1: tried blinkered/visored. *C. Roberts*   **c–** **h–**

ROYALEETY (FR)   5 b.g. Garde Royale – La Grive (FR) (Pharly (FR)) [2003/4 h133: 18s c17s* c17s* c20s⁵ c19s* c22s c20sᶠ c16gᵖᵘ c16gᵘʳ Apr 16] leggy ex-French gelding: useful hurdler, raced exclusively at Auteuil, winning 6 of 13 starts: fairly useful chaser: won 4-y-o events at Enghien and Auteuil in September and Enghien (listed contest) in October: left T. Civel, failed to complete all 3 starts in Britain, though twice running creditably when departing in closing stages at Ayr: stays 2¾m: raced on good ground or softer: has had tongue tied. *Ian Williams*   **c133** **h122**

ROYAL EMPEROR (IRE)   8 gr.g. Roselier (FR) – Boreen Bro (Boreen (FR)) [2003/4 h152: 25m² c22d* c24gᶠ c25s* c24g² c25gᶠ Apr 2]   **c153** **h136 +**

   File the latest Royal & SunAlliance Novices' Chase as one of those big races whose outcome could have been different had one of the riders involved not dropped his whip at a crucial stage. Dominic Elsworth dropped his on the long run to the third last on Royal Emperor at Cheltenham. Any view about whether the loss of a whip makes the difference between defeat and victory is necessarily subjective. There are horses who give their all without their riders having recourse to the whip, and, for a few others, use of the whip can be counter-productive. When an incident occurs in one of the most important races of the season, however, there is bound to be debate. Richard Quinn's name usually comes to the fore whenever the subject of dropped whips arises. Quinn had his whip knocked out of his hand around a hundred yards out in the 1988 Irish Derby on Insan, who was beaten a short head by Kahyasi. Richard Johnson's loss of his whip just after the final flight in the 2003 Aintree Hurdle saw Sacundai get up to pip Rooster Booster on the post. Liam Cooper was forced to ride the closing stages of the latest Grand National with hands and heels after dropping his whip when Clan Royal blundered at the fifth last. Whether its loss cost his mount more than the three lengths he was beaten will be debated for some time, just as backers and connections of Astbury must have spent many an hour wondering whether the loss of Jimmy Bourke's whip in the 1971 National cost him more than the neck and two and a half lengths he was beaten into third behind Specify and Black Secret. Lester Piggott gave the stories of lost whips a novel twist when riding African Hope in the Grand Prix de Deauville in 1979 when he 'borrowed' one from rival Alain Lequeux after dropping his own. By all accounts, Piggott returned it with a polite 'thank you' after passing the post in second, but the stewards failed to see the funny side and gave him a twenty-day ban which kept him out of the St Leger, which was won, ironically, by Lequeux aboard Son of Love. Readers will doubtless be able to recall their own examples of similar incidents over the years.

Weatherbys Bank Towton Novices' Chase, Wetherby—Royal Emperor is out on his own

Back to Royal Emperor. He went down by a length and a quarter to Rule Supreme at Cheltenham, though those who feel that the loss of Elsworth's whip made no material difference to the outcome will argue that the winner finished very strongly and, if anything, was going away close home. It can, however, be pointed out with justification that Royal Emperor has found plenty under strong driving on occasions. This time, though, a serious error four fences from home was probably every bit as important a factor in Royal Emperor's defeat as the loss of Elsworth's whip. Added together, the two things made Royal Emperor a most unfortunate loser, the frustration felt by connections probably compounded by the fact that he had been beaten a short head by Inching Closer in the Pertemps Final at the 2003 Festival after making a hash of the final flight. Royal Emperor started 6/1 third favourite for the Royal & SunAlliance after three runs over fences. The first, which followed a second behind Gralmano in the West Yorkshire Hurdle at Wetherby, came in a beginners chase at Kelso in December. Royal Emperor strolled home a distance clear at 9/2-on and was stepped up sharply in class at Warwick the following month. With the progressive dual course winner D'Argent and promising types like Silver Knight, Rum Pointer and Ar Muin Na Muice in the line-up, the Roscoe Harvey Memorial Novices' Chase looked sure to prove a good test of Royal Emperor's potential over fences. Warwick's chase course features five fences in quick succession on the far side which are jumped in a little over thirty seconds at racing pace. D'Argent took them well as he made virtually all the running, but Royal Emperor tended to jump right as he hesitated on several occasions and looked likely to finish only second at best when making one mistake too many and coming down at the third last.

Connections reported that Royal Emperor returned from Warwick with a bruised foot, but he was back in action four weeks later, putting up a highly impressive performance in the Weatherbys Bank Towton Novices' Chase at Wetherby. His shorter-priced stable-companion Simply Supreme, fresh from a runaway course win, fell at halfway and his departure left Royal Emperor in front. Jumping much better than he had at Warwick and relishing the very soft ground, Royal Emperor saw off Native Emperor early in the straight and galloped on relentlessly to come home twenty lengths clear. It could be significant that a flaw in Royal Emperor's jumping technique has surfaced on good ground. The costly blunder which sent Elsworth up his neck at the fourth last in the Royal & SunAlliance Chase was not his first mistake in the race. The going was also good at Aintree for the Mildmay Novices' Chase. Royal Emperor was sent off the 5/2 favourite—Rule Supreme was an 8/1-chance on the same terms as at Cheltenham—and jumped soundly enough until he fell at the eleventh. Simply Supreme took advantage this time, coming home unchallenged in a race in which only four of the eleven starters completed the course. The tough and reliable Royal Emperor is a better horse than Simply Supreme at this stage and looks capable of making his mark in open company, provided his jumping becomes more reliable with experience.

Royal Emperor (IRE) (gr.g. 1996)	Roselier (FR) (gr 1973)	Misti IV (or b 1958)	Medium Mist
		Peace Rose (gr 1959)	Fastnet Rock La Paix
	Boreen Bro (b 1985)	Boreen (b 1968)	Tamerlane Scyllinda
		Miss Bro (br 1970)	Rigi Reynoldstown's Niece

The workmanlike Royal Emperor showed ability on firm ground early in his career, but has done nearly all his racing on good or softer since joining Sue Smith. His two Cheltenham runs show that he is fully effective on good ground granted a true gallop. However, his record in the mud is impressive and testing conditions may always show him to very best advantage. Wetherby's Charlie Hall Chase and the Hennessy Gold Cup at Newbury could figure on his agenda in the early part of the next season, while he has the breeding and racing character of a chaser who could really come into his own when he gets the chance to tackle three and a half miles or more. Royal Emperor's pedigree was fully analysed in last year's *Chasers & Hurdlers*, though it bears repeating that he comes from a family with strong links to various Grand Nationals. It would come as no surprise to see Royal Emperor strengthen the link over the next couple of seasons, though he also has the ability to figure in good handicaps at around three miles granted a suitably stiff test of stamina. *Mrs S. J. Smith*

ROYALENTERTAINMENT (IRE) 6 b. or br.m. King's Ride – Spring Fiddler (IRE) (Fidel) [2003/4 F17s* Jan 20] IR £8,800 3-y-o: first foal: half-sister to bumper winner Easter Present (by Presenting): dam unraced half-sister to fairly useful chaser up to 21f Cuban Question: won maiden bumper at Folkestone on debut by 4 lengths from Kiwi Babe. *J. R. Best* **F97**

ROYALE PEARL 4 gr.f. Cloudings (IRE) – Ivy Edith (Blakeney) [2003/4 17d³ 16s⁴ Jan 21] second foal: dam fairly useful 2m hurdler: poor on Flat (stays 1½m): better effort in juvenile hurdles when 16 lengths third to Pequenita at Folkestone, soon clear. *R. Ingram* **h79**

ROYAL FEELINGS 10 b.g. Feelings (FR) – Wedderburn (Royalty) [2003/4 c79, h–: c24g⁴ May 14] small gelding: poor maiden hurdler/chaser: should stay beyond 25f: acts on good to firm and good to soft going. *Mrs J. C. McGregor* **c– h–**

ROYAL FONTENAILLES (FR) 5 ch.g. Tel Quel (FR) – Sissi Fontenailles (FR) (Pampabird) [2003/4 16m⁶ Sep 13] ex-French gelding: fairly useful on Flat (stays 1½m), successful twice in Provinces, sold out of E. Libaud's stable €54,000 Goffs November (2002) Sale: weakened tamely after 4 out in maiden at Worcester on hurdling debut. *R. H. Buckler* **h–**

ROYAL GILLIE 7 br.m. Royal Fountain – Gilmanscleuch (IRE) (Mandalus) [2003/4 F–: F16m 16g Apr 5] no form in bumpers or novice hurdle. *Mrs J. K. M. Oliver* **h– F–**

ROYAL HECTOR (GER) 5 b.g. Hector Protector (USA) – Rudolfina (CAN) (Pleasant Colony (USA)) [2003/4 h102: 20m 16g 16m⁴ 17d⁴ 16s⁵ 20s⁵ 19g⁵ 19d⁴ 21d 20d Apr 21] good-topped gelding: modest maiden hurdler: stays 2½m: acts on soft and good to firm going. *A. G. Hobbs* **h89**

ROYAL INDULGENCE 4 b.g. Royal Applause – Silent Indulgence (USA) (Woodman (USA)) [2003/4 17g Sep 13] modest maiden on Flat (best at 6f/7f): 50/1, hampered **h–**

first and never a factor in juvenile at Bangor on hurdling debut: sold 1,000 gns Doncaster October Sales. *M. Dods*

ROYAL KATIDOKI (FR) 4 b.g. Rochesson (FR) – Miss Coco (FR) (Bay Comeau (FR)) [2003/4 18s² 16s² Feb 19] angular ex-French gelding: third foal: dam, winning chaser up to 2¾m, half-sister to smart French chaser up to 2¾m Royal Vergaland: runner-up over 13f only start on Flat: also second in juvenile hurdles at Auteuil (for B. Barbier) and Sandown, beaten length by Made In Japan in 7-runner event at latter: sure to win a race. *N. J. Henderson*   **h125**

ROYAL MAID (FR) 6 b.g. Bakharoff (USA) – Swimming Maid (FR) (Esprit du Nord (USA)) [2003/4 F16m³ F16m 16d² 19s³ 19d 17m Mar 9] fourth foal: half-brother to French 12.5f winner Swimming Blue (by Art Bleu): dam won 5 times up to 2m on Flat in France: modest form on first of 2 starts in bumpers: placed in sellers first 2 outings over hurdles (claimed from O. Sherwood £6,000 second occasion): ran poorly after: stays 19f. *J. G. M. O'Shea*   **h87** / **F83**

ROYAL NIECE (IRE) 5 b.m. Rakaposhi King – Sister Stephanie (IRE) (Phardante (FR)) [2003/4 F16s³ 17s Apr 6] first foal: dam, useful chaser who stayed 4¼m, sister to fairly useful chaser up to 3m The Carrig Rua: signs of ability in mares bumper at Towcester and novice hurdle at Exeter: will be suited by stiffer test of stamina. *D. J. Wintle*   **h72** / **F75**

ROYALOUTLOOK 7 br.g. Royal Fountain – Broad Outlook (Broadsword (USA)) [2003/4 h–, F74: 16f* Oct 18] poor form in bumpers: in cheekpieces, made all and left clear home turn when winning 2-finisher novice at Kelso on hurdling debut: should be suited by further than 2m. *G. A. Harker*   **h79**

ROYAL PARADISE (FR) 4 b.g. Cadoudal (FR) – Crystalza (FR) (Crystal Palace (FR)) [2003/4 F16s* F16g⁴ Mar 17] lengthy, angular gelding: half-brother to 7 winners, including smart hurdlers Crylza Royal (by Northern Fashion) and Royal Rosa (by Garde Royale) and useful chaser up to 3m Royal Atalza (by Saint Preuil): dam poor half-sister to smart middle-distance colt Dom Alco: 7/4, won 21-runner bumper at Sandown on debut in February by 3½ lengths from Here's Johnny: looked very well, better form when 8½ lengths fourth of 24 to Total Enjoyment in Champion Bumper at Cheltenham, under pressure quite long way out, not clear run approaching straight but keeping on well: will be suited by further: sold privately to join T. Foley. *F. Doumen, France*   **F115**

ROYAL PLUM 8 ch.g. Inchinor – Miss Plum (Ardross) [2003/4 h–§: c27d^R Mar 16] leggy gelding: winning hurdler: no form in points or hunter chase: stays 3¼m: acts on soft and good to firm going: usually visored/blinkered: ungenuine. *S. J. Robinson*   **c–** / **h– §**

ROYAL PREDICA (FR) 10 ch.g. Tip Moss (FR) – Girl Vamp (FR) (Kaldoun (FR)) [2003/4 c144, h–: c26g c24s^pu c20g⁵ c24g^F c29m Apr 24] leggy gelding: useful handicap chaser: well below form in 2003/4: stays 25f: acts on any going: formerly blinkered/visored: tongue tied: often let down by jumping. *M. C. Pipe*   **c121** / **h–**

ROYAL PRODIGY (USA) 5 ch.g. Royal Academy (USA) – Prospector's Queen (USA) (Mr Prospector (USA)) [2003/4 16m³ 17g³ 17g^pu 16g* 17m 16g⁶ 17f* 19f² 22s^pu 16g^F Apr 4] fair on Flat (stays 13f), successful 4 times in 2003: modest hurdler: won sellers at Stratford in July and Exeter (handicap) in September: left M. Pipe, showed little last 2 starts: stays 19f: acts on firm going: visored third outing: often looks temperamental. *R. J. Hodges*   **h86 §**

ROYAL RACKEEN 7 b.m. Rakaposhi King – Snippet (Ragstone) [2003/4 F16d 16d May 16] sister to winning staying hurdler/chaser The Eens and half-sister to winning 27f hurdler Snappit (by Billion): dam of little account: well held in bumper and novice selling hurdle: sold £2,000 Ascot June Sales. *D. McCain*   **h–** / **F–**

ROYAL REFERENCE 8 br.m. Royal Fountain – Cross Reference (Oats) [2003/4 17d 24d^pu c25v^pu Jan 17] lengthy mare: first foal: dam, no form over hurdles, half-sister to Stayers' Hurdle and Sun Alliance Chase winner A Kinsman: successful twice in points in 2002, runner-up on second of 2 starts in 2003: little show in novice hurdles/chase (lame). *J. E. Brockbank*   **c–** / **h–**

ROYAL ROCKET (IRE) 7 b.m. King's Ride – Carols Cracker (IRE) (Persian Mews) [2003/4 F75: 21d^pu 19d 21d^pu 24d Apr 8] no form over hurdles, looking less than keen third outing. *Miss Venetia Williams*   **h–**

ROYAL ROSA (FR) 5 ch.g. Garde Royale – Crystalza (FR) (Crystal Palace (FR)) [2003/4 F118: F16g* 24d* 23s² 20v* 23g* 24g² Apr 1]   **h147**

Andrea and Graham Wylie's decision not to insure any of their racehorses turned out to be successful as a money-saving measure. They might have seen it as an exercise in damage limitation where certain horses were concerned. Beauchamp

Red Square Vodka Prestige Novices' Hurdle, Haydock—
two smart novices: Royal Rosa and Fundamentalist

Gigi and Inching Closer, for example, failed to come anywhere near justifying the huge amounts that were paid for them at the Doncaster November Sales. Beauchamp Gigi, bought for 200,000 guineas after showing no more than fair form to win a bumper at Cork in October, made the racecourse only once in the Wylies' beige and black colours, finishing fourth in a mares bumper at Musselburgh, missing out by three quarters of a length on picking up third prize money of £426. Inching Closer was purchased as a Royal & SunAlliance Chase hope for 150,000 guineas, but produced his only worthwhile effort from four starts for new connections when winning a novice chase at Newcastle worth £2,886. Even Royal Rosa's prize money earnings of over £43,000 would have failed to cover the cost of the cheapest insurance quote for him, reportedly £45,000 a year. But Royal Rosa, a then-record 340,000-guinea purchase at the 2003 Doncaster May Sales, could hardly be described as having failed to come up to expectations. Far from it. He developed into one of the leading novice hurdlers of 2003/4 and his prospects of succeeding where Inching Closer failed, and developing into a leading contender for the Royal & SunAlliance Chase, might even prompt his owners to consider an insurance quote for the coming season.

Royal Rosa's achievements were somewhat overshadowed for much of the season by those of another of his owners' success stories, Inglis Drever, though there was no doubt which of the pair earned most plaudits for their efforts on the opening day of the Grand National meeting. While Inglis Drever had excuses when finishing only fourth in the two-and-a-half-mile novice, Royal Rosa lined up against seven more experienced rivals in the Liverpool Hurdle over an extended three miles. Royal Rosa made odds-on Iris's Gift work to supplement his Stayers' Hurdle win, always in touch and the only threat to the winner from three out, keeping on gamely and going down by two and a half lengths. The proximity of

ROY

Aine Dubh five lengths back in third suggests that the winner was nowhere near his best, and that Royal Rosa's effort was a little below the pick of Inglis Drever's form. But Royal Rosa's form would still have been good enough to win the Grade 1 Sefton Novices' Hurdle over the same course and distance the following day, a race in which his stable instead relied on Kasthari (in different ownership), who was pulled up. Royal Rosa had missed the Cheltenham Festival, with Inglis Drever representing connections in the Royal & SunAlliance Novices Hurdle, but he had earlier followed Iris's Gift when winning the Red Square Vodka Prestige Novices' Hurdle at Haydock at the end of February, when he beat Inglis Drever's Cheltenham conqueror Fundamentalist. Royal Rosa, unpenalised after landing weakly-contested novices at Hexham in December and Ayr in January, took up the running from Young Collier before three out and made his greater experience, and the receipt of 4 lb, count as he held off Fundamentalist by half a length. Favourite Diamant Noir was dropping away in third when falling at the last, leaving Special Rate to take that place, nineteen lengths behind Fundamentalist. Royal Rosa put up another notable performance for a novice at Haydock in between his wins at Hexham and Ayr, in the Premier Stayers' Hurdle, a race his connections had landed with Lord Transcend the previous season. The sound-jumping Royal Rosa went down by eight lengths to Sh Boom, giving best only approaching the last and finishing clear of the remainder.

			Never Bend
		Mill Reef	Milan Mill
	Garde Royale	(b 1968)	Sicambre
	(br 1980)	Royal Way	Right Away
Royal Rosa (FR)		(gr 1969)	Caro
(ch.g. 1999)		Crystal Palace	Hermieres
	Crystalza (FR)	(gr 1974)	Exbury
	(gr 1982)	Aldonza	La Bamba
		(b 1969)	

Andrea & Graham Wylie's "Royal Rosa"

The pedigree of Royal Rosa was covered in depth in last year's Annual. One notable development is that Royal Paradise (by Cadoudal) became the eighth winner produced by the dam Crystalza when winning a bumper at Sandown in February, before going on to show small form when fourth in the Champion Bumper at Cheltenham. Another of Royal Rosa's half-brothers, Royal Atalza (by Saint Preuil), showed useful form when winning a twenty-one-furlong handicap at Auteuil in November, then moved to the Newmarket yard of Conrad Allen, who gave him a most unorthodox Grand National preparation, Royal Atalza winning a mile-and-a-half maiden on fibresand at Wolverhampton before being pulled up at Aintree. Royal Rosa was trained before his big-money purchase by Nicky Henderson, for whom he won three of his four starts in bumpers, including the Paddy Power Champion INH Flat Race at Punchestown. The good-topped Royal Rosa should stay beyond three miles and has raced only on good going or softer. Although he didn't keep straight over the last three flights at Ayr, Royal Rosa generally jumps fluently and there is no reason why he shouldn't prove just as effective over fences. *J. Howard Johnson*

ROYAL SATIN (IRE)   6 b.g. Royal Academy (USA) – Satinette (Shirley Heights)   **h–**
[2003/4 16g^F 16g^{pu} Nov 12] little form on Flat, looks wayward: failed to complete in 2 starts over hurdles. *B. Mactaggart*

ROYAL SHAKESPEARE (FR)   5 b.g. King's Theatre (IRE) – Persian Walk   **h142**
(FR) (Persian Bold) [2003/4 17s* 19g* 16g* Apr 2]
Stratford might have been a more apt starting-point for Royal Shakespeare, but Sedgefield was the unlikely venue for the debut of what turned out to be one of the season's leading novice hurdlers. Royal Shakespeare was no stranger to competing at exotic locations though, having won at Abu Dhabi in a Flat campaign with Kiaran McLaughlin in the UAE before joining Steve Gollings' stable for 52,000 guineas at the Doncaster May Sales in 2003. Starting at 14/1, Royal Shakespeare made his hurdling debut a winning one, racing freely but jumping soundly before running out a seven-length winner from the favourite Mobasher. The first two met again in a more valuable novice hurdle at Doncaster in March, the runner-up this time meeting Royal Shakespeare on terms 5 lb better, but the result was the same. A better jump by Royal Shakespeare at the last sealed matters, and he had three lengths to spare over Mobasher this time, the first two finishing a distance clear of the remainder. Royal Shakespeare was therefore unexposed and unbeaten but some way behind the leading contenders on form, hence his odds of 25/1, when he took on the likes of the Imperial Cup runner-up Bold Bishop, the Supreme Novices' third Fleet Street and the six-time winner Albuhera in the Premier Convenience Stores Top Novices' Hurdle at Aintree. In the event, none of that trio

Premier Convenience Stores Top Novices' Hurdle, Aintree—
25/1-chance Royal Shakespeare wears down Contraband (rails) on the flat

ROY

ran up to their best while Royal Shakespeare found the necessary improvement to take full advantage. With favourite Bold Bishop having a pacemaker, there was a strong pace which suited Royal Shakespeare on his first run over a bare two miles. Able to be settled as a result, he then made headway in the straight, went second after two out and wore down Contraband inside the last hundred yards to win by a neck after the runner-up had fluffed the last. Fleet Street was another four lengths back in third, with Bold Bishop and Albuhera well held. Royal Shakespeare ran an even better race just after the end of the season in Britain when one of three British-trained runners (along with Dempsey and Overstrand) who contested the Evening Herald Champion Novices' Hurdle at Punchestown. Royal Shakespeare fared much the best of the three visitors and played his part in a thrilling finish with the Supreme Novices' winner Brave Inca. Travelling strongly behind the leaders, Royal Shakespeare went on three out and only just lost out by a short head after making the favourite pull out all the stops.

Royal Shakespeare (FR) (b.g. 1999)	King's Theatre (IRE) (b 1991)	Sadler's Wells (b 1981)	Northern Dancer / Fairy Bridge
		Regal Beauty (b or br 1981)	Princely Native / Dennis Belle
	Persian Walk (FR) (ch 1994)	Persian Bold (br 1975)	Bold Lad / Relkarunner
		Walk On Air (ch 1983)	Cure The Blues / Warsaw

Mr J. B. Webb's "Royal Shakespeare"

Royal Shakespeare is by the King George VI & Queen Elizabeth Stakes winner King's Theatre whose best jumpers also include Royal Alphabet, third behind Royal Shakespeare at Punchestown, and the ill-fated Grande Course de Haies d'Auteuil winner Nobody Told Me. Royal Shakespeare was bred with a Flat career in mind, however, and had a price-tag to match; he was sold for 200,000 guineas as a yearling and joined David Loder, then in charge of the Godolphin juveniles, though it wasn't until his four-year-old season that he finally reached the track, having by then been sent to Dubai. Royal Shakespeare's dam has had two other runners on the Flat so far, including the two-year-old seven-furlong winner Prince of Thebes (by Desert Prince). Royal Shakespeare also has a two-year-old brother named Safari Adventures. Their dam Persian Walk won her only two starts, both mile-and-a-half races at Nancy for Andre Fabre. Persian Walk is a half-sister to the smart French middle-distance performers Walkamia, Walking Around and Walk On Mix. The last-named of that trio subsequently became a smart novice hurdler in Ireland for Noel Meade. The grandam Walk On Air was second on her only start and was out of a mare who produced the family's most notable jumper World Citizen, successful in the Grande Course de Haies and also the winner of some good chases at Auteuil. This is also a family that will be familiar to followers of Flat racing. Among its recent members to excel is the very smart French stayer Westerner, a son of Walk On Air's Prix Vermeille-winning half-sister Walensee.

The useful-looking Royal Shakespeare gave his trainer just about his biggest success so far at Aintree. If Royal Shakespeare is to win more good races in open company, he will have to improve a fair bit more, though with only four races over hurdles under his belt further progress cannot be ruled out. Royal Shakespeare stays nineteen furlongs and he has raced only on good ground since his debut at Sedgefield on soft. *S. Gollings*

ROYALTINO (IRE) 12 b.g. Neltino – Royal Well (Royal Vulcan) [2003/4 c100, h–: c22s[pu] Feb 14] angular gelding: one-time fairly useful hurdler/useful chaser for F. Doumen: only completion since 3-year absence when second in hunter in 2003: stays 25f: acts on heavy going, probably on good to firm. *Miss T. McCurrich* — c– h–

ROYAL TWIST (USA) 4 ch.g. Royal Academy (USA) – Musical Twist (USA) (Woodman (USA)) [2003/4 16g[6] Nov 2] modest maiden at best on Flat (may prove best short of 1m), sold out of T. Tate's stable 1,800 gns Doncaster October Sales: none too fluent and never a threat in juvenile maiden on hurdling debut: sold 2,500 gns Doncaster January Sales. *J. S. Wainwright* — h–

ROYAL VARIETY (IRE) 6 gr.g. Roselier (FR) – Private Dancer (Deep Run) [2003/4 20s[3] Jan 6] €34,000 4-y-o: lengthy gelding: seventh foal: half-brother to bumper winners Kate Fisher and Murleys Cross (both by Over The River): dam, useful hurdler around 2m in Ireland, also won up to 2m on Flat: remote third of 11 finishers to Graphic Approach in novice hurdle at Wetherby on debut, steady progress without being knocked about in straight: likely to improve. *L. Lungo* — h89 p

ROYAL WHISPER 5 b.g. Prince of Birds (USA) – Hush It Up (Tina's Pet) [2003/4 F16g Mar 10] seventh foal: half-brother to smart 2m hurdler Shadow Leader (by Tragic Role) and to 2 modest winning sprinters: dam poor Flat maiden: well beaten in bumper on debut. *R. Ford* — F–

ROYMILLON (GER) 10 b.g. Milesius (USA) – Royal Slope (USA) (His Majesty (USA)) [2003/4 h76§: c23d[6] Apr 21] leggy gelding: poor handicap hurdler: off 17 months, well held on chasing debut: best at 3m+: acts on firm going: blinkered once: often gets behind. *D. J. Wintle* — c– § h– §

ROZNIC (FR) 6 b.g. Nikos – Rozamie (FR) (Azimut (FR)) [2003/4 F16d[3] F16g[4] F17d[3] Mar 27] IR £20,000 3-y-o: useful-looking gelding: fourth foal: half-brother to 2 winners, including Prolute (by Lute Antique), successful up to around 19f over jumps in France: dam won on Flat/over jumps in France: fairly useful form in bumpers, third of 18 to Pearly Bay in maiden at Bangor final start, switched over 1f out. *P. Winkworth* — F97

RUBBERDUBBER 4 b.g. Teenoso (USA) – True Clown (True Song) [2003/4 F16g* Mar 25] sixth foal: brother to fairly useful 2m chaser Percy Parkeeper and modest hurdler/chaser up to 25f Brambly Hedge: dam, winning chaser, stayed 3¼m: won 15-runner bumper at Wincanton on debut by 3½ lengths from Quid Pro Quo, taken wide after slow start and galloping on strongly without being hard ridden: promising. *C. R. Egerton* — F98 p

RUBY DANTE (IRE) 6 b.m. Ajraas (USA) – Phar Glen (IRE) (Phardante (FR)) **F79**
[2003/4 F17m F17m³ F16m Jul 23] first foal: dam unraced, out of half-sister to Sun
Alliance Hurdle winner Rebel Song: modest form on second of 3 starts in bumpers:
difficult ride: won mares maiden in April on second completed outing in points. *P. Bowen*

RUBY GALE (IRE) 8 b.g. Lord Americo – Well Over (Over The River (FR)) **c116**
[2003/4 c118, h–: 22g² 20d c21d² c21d² c21d³ c24g³ Feb 19] sturdy gelding: fairly useful **h123**
handicap hurdler: good second of 5 to Achilles Wings at Newton Abbott on reappearance:
similar form over fences, second in novices won by One Nation and Tucacas at Wincanton, would probably have won on second occasion but for mistake last: left in front 3
out but pulling himself up on run-in and headed final strides (lost a shoe) in similar event
at Taunton final outing: stays 2¾m: raced only on good/good to soft going: tongue tied
last 4 starts: room for improvement in jumping over fences. *P. F. Nicholls*

RUBY GLEN (IRE) 6 b.m. Insan (USA) – Le Glen (Le Bavard (FR)) [2003/4 F17s⁶ **h–**
18v 20s 18g Apr 22] fourth foal: half-sister to winning 2m hurdler Mr McDuff (by **F–**
Mandalus): dam twice-raced in bumpers: well beaten in varied events, including points.
B. G. Powell

RUBYLUV 5 ch.m. Rock Hopper – Hunting Cottage (Pyjama Hunt) [2003/4 F16s **F–**
F16v Feb 4] eighth foal: half-sister to French 1¼m and 15f winner Reine de La Chasse
(by Ti King): dam unraced half-sister to useful hurdler up to 2½m Charlie's Cottage and
fairly useful staying chaser Puck's Place: soundly beaten in 2 bumpers. *Miss S. E. Forster*

RUBY RAINNE 5 gr.m. Perugino (USA) – Lady Shikari (Kala Shikari) [2003/4 F16s **F–**
F17g Apr 1] sixth foal: closely related to fairly useful 1999 Irish 2-y-o 6f winner Harry's
Game (by Emperor Jones): dam unraced: well beaten in 2 bumpers. *A. P. Jones*

RUBY TOO 5 b.m. El Conquistador – Ruby Flame (Tudor Flame) [2003/4 F16f³ **F84**
aF16g* F16v⁴ F16g Mar 25] third foal: dam fair pointer: modest form in bumpers: won
on polytrack at Lingfield in December: flashed tail under pressure final outing.
J. W. Mullins

RUDETSKI 7 b.g. Rudimentary (USA) – Butosky (Busted) [2003/4 h83: 17g⁵ c16g² **c101**
c16m⁴ c16gᶠ c16d* Jan 19] lengthy gelding: poor form over hurdles: sold out of **h72**
M. Dods's stable 5,000 gns Doncaster August Sales after reappearance: tongue tied
second time, best effort over fences when winning novice handicap at Doncaster: raced
around 2m: acts on good to firm and good to soft going. *M. Sheppard*

RUDGE HILL 8 b.g. Almushmmir – Time After Time (High Award) [2003/4 c–: **c–**
17mᵖᵘ 20m 17g 22dᵖᵘ Jul 30] workmanlike gelding: no sign of ability. *S. C. Burrough* **h–**

RUDI KNIGHT 9 ch.g. Rudimentary (USA) – Fleeting Affair (Hotfoot) [2003/4 **c104 x**
c104, h–: c21s* c20d³ c20g* c22g⁶ Mar 26] angular gelding: one-time useful handicap **h–**
hurdler: generally not fluent in novice chases but successful at Newton Abbott and Market
Rasen early in season: off over 8 months before running poorly final start: stays 21f: acts
on heavy and good to firm going. *Miss Venetia Williams*

RUDI'S CHARM 7 b.g. Rudimentary (USA) – Irene's Charter (Persian Bold) **h–**
[2003/4 F78: 22g 22g Apr 18] modest form on first of 2 starts in bumpers: well held in 2
novice hurdles. *D. W. Thompson*

RUDOLF RASSENDYLL (IRE) 9 b.g. Supreme Leader – Chantel Rouge (Boreen **c110**
(FR)) [2003/4 c103, h101: c25dᵖᵘ c20g* c31d⁵ Apr 22] workmanlike gelding: winning **h– x**
hurdler: successful on 2 of 6 starts over fences, including in 17-runner handicap at
Carlisle in April after 11-month absence: failed to stay final outing: effective around 2½m
to 3m: acts on soft going. *Miss Venetia Williams*

RUE DU RIVOLI 6 ch.g. Rudimentary (USA) – Lovers Tryst (Castle Keep) [2003/4 **F76**
F18s⁴ F18v⁵ F16d Apr 12] good-topped gelding: fifth foal: dam 1¼m winner: failed to
see races out in bumpers, best effort on debut. *Lady Herries*

RUFIUS (IRE) 11 b.g. Celio Rufo – In View Lass (Tepukei) [2003/4 c99, h–: c25gᵖᵘ **c93**
c23m⁴ c20m* c20f⁵ c32gᵘʳ c25m⁴ c24sᵖᵘ c24g⁴ c24d Feb 2] workmanlike gelding: **h–**
modest handicap chaser: won at Huntingdon in October: stays 25f: acts on firm and soft
going: blinkered once (raced too freely): usually held up: has found little. *P. Kelsall*

RUGGED MAN (IRE) 6 b.g. Topanoora – The Grey (GER) (Pentathlon) [2003/4 **h86**
h90: 16g* 20sᵖᵘ 16m² 16f 16f⁵ 16f² Jul 13] modest hurdler: won maiden at Sligo on first
day of season: best around 2m: acts on soft and firm going: blinkered: has had tongue
tied. *J. G. Cosgrave, Ireland*

RUGGED RIVER (IRE) 9 b.g. Over The River (FR) – Early Dalus (IRE) (Mandalus) **c132**
[2003/4 c135: c28s² Nov 29] lengthy gelding: useful handicap chaser, lightly raced:

creditable second to impressive Artic Jack at Haydock, only outing in 2003/4: will stay beyond 3½m: acts on heavy going. *R. H. Alner*

RULE SUPREME (IRE) 8 b.g. Supreme Leader – Book of Rules (IRE) (Phardante (FR)) [2003/4 c135p, h–: c25g* c20s^{ur} c24g* c24g^3 c24s^3 c28v^2 c24g* c25g^{ur} c29m^5 Apr 24]   **c149 x h149**

If there had been any betting on runners who would fail to complete the course in the Royal & SunAlliance Chase at Cheltenham in March, one of the favourites would have been the horse who went on to win it. As most of his nine rivals struggled to cope with the stiff fences, 25/1-shot Rule Supreme, perversely, turned in one of his best rounds of jumping and became the second outsider in the last three years to capture the main championship event for staying novice chasers, the 2002 winner Hussard Collonges having started at 33/1. The fences are there to be jumped, of course, and all credit to Rule Supreme for negotiating all nineteen as well as he did, but, that said, he seemed a fortunate winner of what was just an average renewal of the Royal & SunAlliance and it is unlikely that he will be up to making an impact in weight-for-age championship events in open company. Tellingly, Rule Supreme's trainer was reported as saying after the race that the horse's jumping was likely to remain a problem—Rule Supreme did nothing to suggest otherwise when reverting to type on his next two starts—and that the Stayers' Hurdle could be the race he goes for at the next Cheltenham Festival.

That now looks a realistic target in the light of Rule Supreme's victory in the Grande Course de Haies d'Auteuil, which took place after the end of the British season. The principal hurdle race of the year in France, the Grande Course, run over an extended three miles and a furlong at Auteuil in June, featured a rematch between Rule Supreme and the two who had finished in front of him in the main trial race for the Grande Course, the Prix La Barka, namely Great Love and Nick-name; while extra interest was added by the presence of the top French chaser Kotkijet, attempting to become the first horse to win this race and the Grand Steeple-Chase de Paris in the same year. The pace was steady to past halfway and, with the ground not as soft as usual at Auteuil, it made for less of a test of stamina than might have been expected. The extra half mile made it a stiffer test than the La Barka, though, and that was very much in Rule Supreme's favour. Once again Rule Supreme jumped the French-style hurdles fluently and, having travelled well held up, was ridden to challenge two out and stayed on well to lead in the last hundred metres, winning going away by two lengths from Great Love, with Kotkijet a further two and a half lengths back in third. It was a second successive victory in the Grande Course de Haies for trainer Willie Mullins, who won it twelve months earlier with Nobody Told Me. Sadly, that mare had to be put down after breaking a

Royal & SunAlliance Chase, Cheltenham—Rule Supreme (left) leads the survivors home; Royal Emperor outlasts Our Vic for second, Calling Brave and Pizarro are riderless behind

Grande Course de Haies d'Auteuil—Rule Supreme (nearest camera) is produced with a well-timed run to defeat the grey Great Love and Kotkijet

leg in November. Nobody Told Me had been the first mare to win the Grande Course de Haies, and the first horse trained in Britain or Ireland to win it since Dawn Run triumphed for Mullins' father Paddy under brother Tony in 1984. Two years later, Dawn Run's magnificient career ended when she broke her neck bidding for a second Grande Course de Haies. Rule Supreme's victory was excellent reward for his trainer's enterprise, and there seems a chance the gelding will attempt to pick up more valuable prizes in France. Incidentally, Rule Supreme's jockey David Casey (also successful on Nobody Told Me) went on to win the other championship event on the card, the Prix Alain du Breil, on Mesange Royale.

That Rule Supreme's jumping was such a concern going into the Royal & SunAlliance Chase could not be put down to any lack of experience, as he had made eight appearances in chases and successfully negotiated one hundred and twenty-three fences, albeit in a haphazard manner on many occasions. To be fair to Rule Supreme, the only time he failed to complete the course was on his fourth chase start, when he unseated at the eighth. He won two races in that period. The first of them was a valuable novice handicap at Punchestown, a race run shortly after the end of the British 2002/3 season had ended and which was dealt with fully in the preceding edition of *Chasers & Hurdlers*; the second was a six-runner minor event at Thurles in December, when he justified favouritism by four and a half lengths from Never More. In his race immediately before Cheltenham, Rule Supreme ran very well in the Grand National Trial Handicap run over three and a half miles in very testing conditions at Punchestown, giving lumps of weight all round and going down by only three quarters of a length to Coq Hardi Diamond, the pair finishing well clear. Rule Supreme's form at Punchestown was as good as any produced by those who opposed him in the Royal & SunAlliance, though some of his less experienced rivals, notably Our Vic, looked open to greater improvement. Smart hurdler Our Vic, who had impressed when winning both his starts over fences, including the Reynoldstown Chase at Ascot, represented the Pipe stable whose other promising staying novice Therealbandit—saddled in the Gold Cup instead—was one of several notable absentees, along with such as D'Argent, Lord Sam, Nil Desperandum and Strong Flow. Our Vic started favourite at 11/8 with Pizarro, the winner of all three of his completed starts over fences, next in the betting at 9/2. The race was run at a sound pace, set by Rule Supreme's stable-companion Mossy Green who was pressed by Our Vic for much of the way, this pair stretching the field after six out where Rule Supreme, taken wide from the off, was towards the rear. Two fences later Calling Brave unseated his rider when disputing third with Royal Emperor, who also made a bad mistake there, and the shape of the contest underwent an even more significant change at the second last.

Mossy Green, disputing the lead with Our Vic, fell and brought down Pizarro who was staying on strongly just behind them, leaving Rule Supreme in third behind Our Vic and the rallying Royal Emperor. After looking one-paced coming down the hill, Rule Supreme was now making very good headway and soon joined issue. Three horses were virtually in line setting off up the run-in, but Our Vic, having not been that fluent, soon found his exertions taking their toll while Royal Emperor, whose rider had dropped his whip going to three out, was unable to stay on so well as Rule Supreme, who went on to beat him by a length and a quarter, with a further two lengths back to Our Vic. Any hopes that Rule Supreme's jumping problems were now behind him were soon dashed. On his next start he made several mistakes before unseating his rider at the eighth in the Mildmay Novices' Chase at Aintree; and three weeks later he continually lost ground at the fences on the final circuit of the Betfred Gold Cup at Sandown, in the circumstances doing quite well to finish fifth. Not long after that, Rule Supreme seemed to run above himself, despite his usual quota of mistakes, in finishing fifth to Beef Or Salmon in the Grade 1 Punchestown Heineken Gold Cup, though the chances are that he was flattered a little in a race which wasn't truly run.

Rule Supreme (IRE) (b.g. 1996)	Supreme Leader (b 1982)	Bustino (b 1971)	Busted Ship Yard
		Princess Zena (b 1975)	Habitat Guiding Light
	Book of Rules (IRE) (b 1989)	Phardante (b 1982)	Pharly Pallante
		Chapter Four (ch 1971)	Shackleton First Edition

The well-made Rule Supreme is the first foal out of the unraced Book of Rules, whose second and third foals, both by Good Thyne, raced for the first time in the latest season, Good Book achieving very little but Tynedale showing fair form

Mr John J. Fallon's "Rule Supreme"

in bumpers. Book of Rules is a half-sister to six winners, including the useful performers Book of Kells, Sarsfield The Man and Scribbler. Both Book of Kells and Scribbler were effective at three miles or more. The next dam Chapter Four, a fairly useful hurdler, is a daughter of the fortuitous novice chase winner First Edition, dam of the smart staying chaser Our Edition. Rule Supreme, who is suited by a good test of stamina, acts on heavy going and probably on good to firm. He looked in particularly good shape on several occasions in the latest season, though he did sweat at Sandown. *W. P. Mullins, Ireland*

RUM POINTER (IRE) 8 b.g. Turtle Island (IRE) – Osmunda (Mill Reef (USA)) [2003/4 h123: c20s[F] c24s[3] c24s* c24g[4] c22s* c22d* c24g[4] Mar 27] small gelding: fairly useful hurdler/novice chaser: won at Uttoxeter (by neck from Ar Muin Na Muice) in December, Haydock (beat Valleymore 2 lengths) in February and Towcester (facile task) in March: close fourth though looked held when fell 2 out in valuable handicap at Punchestown in late-April: stays 3m: raced on good going or softer (acts on heavy). *R. H. Buckler*   c127 h–

RUN ATIM 6 ch.g. Hatim (USA) – Run Pet Run (Deep Run) [2003/4 F16g[5] F16s Mar 13] second foal: dam fair but temperamental staying chaser: better effort in bumpers when around 10 lengths fifth of 16 to The Thunderer at Ascot, never nearer. *K. C. Bailey*   F89

RUNAWAY BISHOP (USA) 9 b. or br.g. Lear Fan (USA) – Valid Linda (USA) (Valid Appeal (USA)) [2003/4 c91, h84: c20s[4] c20d[4] c24s[F] 19v[5] 23v[5] c22s c24g* c19s* c25s* Apr 11] lengthy gelding: maiden hurdler: modest handicap chaser: successful at Huntingdon (first win for 4 years) and Towcester in March and completed hat-trick when returned to latter: effective at 19f (given a test) to 25f: acts on any going: effective blinkered/visored or not: often looks temperamental. *J. R. Cornwall*   c91 h70

RUNDETTO (IRE) 7 b.g. Warcraft (USA) – Deep Link (Deep Run) [2003/4 F17m F16m[pu] Jun 14] IR £6,500 4-y-o, 800 6-y-o: eighth foal: half-brother to bumper winner Mandalink (by Mandalus) and to 2 winning pointers: dam maiden chaser: no form in bumpers and points: sold £1,300 Ascot October Sales. *R. Bastiman*   F–

RUN FOR PADDY 8 b.g. Michelozzo (USA) – Deep Selection (IRE) (Deep Run) [2003/4 c140§, h–: c20m[pu] c21g c20s[4] c29d[pu] Apr 12] useful-looking gelding: useful hurdler/chaser on his day: well below best in 2003/4, left Mrs H. Dalton after reappearance: stays 25f: acts on soft and good to firm going: unreliable. *T. Hogan, Ireland*   c118 § h–

RUN FORREST (IRE) 7 ch.g. Forest Wind (USA) – Katie's Delight (Relko) [2003/4 16g[4] 16m[F] Sep 27] well held both completed outings over hurdles: dead. *Miss S. West*   h–

RUNNER BEAN 10 b. or br.g. Henbit (USA) – Bean Alainn (Candy Cane) [2003/4 c93x, h–: c16m[3] c16m* c17g c16s[3] c16s[3] c16m[2] c16s[2] c16m[3] c16m[4] c20d[F] Apr 8] lengthy gelding: modest handicap chaser: won at Huntingdon in May: creditable efforts when placed after: stays 2½m: acts on soft and good to firm going: blinkered once (reportedly bled): has carried head awkwardly: sketchy jumper. *R. Lee*   c94 x h–

RUNNING DE CERISY (FR) 10 ch.g. Lightning (FR) – Niloq (FR) (Nikos) [2003/4 c–x, h–: c19m[pu] c19m[pu] 16s[pu] 19g Apr 18] tall, lengthy gelding: winning hurdler/chaser: lightly raced and no form since 2001/2, left Miss S. Wilton after second start: tried blinkered/in cheekpieces: poor jumper of fences. *P. L. Clinton*   c– x h–

RUNNING FREE 10 b.g. Waajib – Selchis (Main Reef) [2003/4 c16m[pu] c25m[pu] Jun 20] good-topped gelding: maiden hurdler: no form over fences: tried blinkered/visored. *W. S. Cunningham*   c– h–

RUNNING MACHINE (IRE) 7 b.g. Classic Memory – Foxborough Lady (Crash Course) [2003/4 c100x, h96x: c26v[pu] c21d* c20g[5] c24g[3] c25s[5] c24g[4] c24d[2] Feb 20] lengthy, good sort: modest form when placed twice over hurdles: fair chaser: sold out of A. Hales's stable 18,000 gns Doncaster May Sales after reappearance: won novice handicap at Folkestone in December: stays 3m: raced on good going or softer: formerly tongue tied: poor jumper. *Miss Venetia Williams*   c106 x h–

RUNNING MOSS 12 ch.g. Le Moss – Run'n Fly (Deep Run) [2003/4 c107, h–: c25s[ur] c25s c22v[pu] Feb 5] lengthy gelding: fair handicap chaser: no form in 2003/4 after year's absence: stays 4m: raced on good going or softer (acts on heavy). *A. H. Mactaggart*   c– h–

RUNNING MUTE 10 b.g. Roscoe Blake – Rose Albertine (Record Token) [2003/4 c90: c22g[2] c20g* c24d[2] c20g[pu] Mar 12] modest chaser: won novice handicap at Perth in June: stays 3¼m: raced on good/good to soft ground. *Mrs S. H. Shirley-Beavan*   c98

RUNNING TIMES (USA)   7 b.g. Brocco (USA) – Concert Peace (USA) (Hold Your   c–
Peace (USA)) [2003/4 c–, h106: 16g 22m^{pu} 16m 22g^5 16m^6 Oct 26] workmanlike   h–
gelding: fair hurdler at best, out of form in 2003/4: no show in maiden chase, last on both
completed outings in points. has worn visor, including when successful. *H. J. Manners*

RUNNINGWITHTHEMOON   8 b.g. Homo Sapien – Ardeal (Ardross) [2003/4 h–,   c–
F–: 20m^6 21m^4 26g^3 c26d^{pu} Aug 11] bad maiden hurdler: little show on chasing debut: h60
won maiden point in April. *C. C. Bealby*

RUN OF KINGS (IRE)   6 b.g. King's Ride – Arctic Tartan (Deep Run) [2003/4 c24g^F c–
22g^5 21m Apr 14] IR £18,000 3-y-o, €25,000 4-y-o: tall, unfurnished gelding: fifth foal: h111 ?
half-brother to fair hurdlers around 2½m Townleyhall and My Man Dan (both by Phardante): dam, bumper winner, half-sister to top-class chaser Buck House: won maiden
Irish point on debut in 2003: fell fourth on steeplechasing debut: fair form both starts
over hurdles, though looked difficult ride, hanging left and carrying head awkwardly.
M. C. Pipe

RUN RIVER RUN   10 b.m. River God (USA) – Run Lady Run (General Ironside)   c–
[2003/4 c20d^F c26d^{pu} Mar 14] smallish mare: poor form in bumpers and over hurdles: h–
no form in points and hunter chases: blinkered both starts in 2003/4: joined B. Leary.
M. A. Hill

RUPUNUNI (IRE)   7 b.g. Fourstars Allstar (USA) – Pisa (Carlingford Castle) [2003/4   h117
16m^2 16s* 16m* 16f* 16d^6 16d^{pu} Apr 13] big, good-bodied gelding: fifth foal: dam
unraced half-sister to smart chaser up to 2½m Another Dolly: fairly useful hurdler:
successful in maiden at Listowel in September and Grade 3 novice at Tipperary (idled
when beating Felix The Great 2½ lengths) and intermediate at Cork (produced easily best
turn of foot when beating Commonchero a length) in October: off 4½ months, well below
form in graded novices at Fairyhouse and Punchestown in April: raced at 2m: successful
on soft going, better on firmer (acts on firm). *Francis Ennis, Ireland*

RUSH ABOUT (IRE)   5 ch.g. Kris – Rachrush (IRE) (Sadler's Wells (USA)) [2003/4   h–
17d^{pu} 19g^5 16m^{pu} 26g^{pu} 16d^{pu} Nov 15] fair maiden on Flat (stays 1½m), sold out of
H. Cecil's stable 12,000 gns Newmarket Autumn (2002) Sales: no form over hurdles,
looking none too keen in blinkers third start (claimed from Miss K. Marks £5,000): sold
£650 Ascot December Sales. *P. A. Blockley*

RUSHEN RAIDER   12 br.g. Reprimand – Travel Storm (Lord Gayle (USA)) [2003/4   h–
h70: 20s^{pu} 21s^{ur} Dec 26] leggy gelding: winning hurdler: lightly raced and little form
since 2001/2. *P. Needham*

RUSHING AGAIN   9 br.g. Rushmere – Saunders Grove (IRE) (Sunyboy) [2003/4 c–,   c–
h–: c20m^{pu} c21m^5 24m^{pu} 24m^6 c18m^5 c22g^{pu} Oct 5] workmanlike gelding: little   h–
worthwhile form over hurdles or in steeplechases: won point in March: tried blinkered.
Dr P. Pritchard

RUSINGA   6 gr.g. Homo Sapien – Royal Blaze (Scallywag) [2003/4 F18s F16g F16d   F–
Mar 19] 8,000 3-y-o: good-bodied gelding: fourth foal: half-brother to bumper winner
Princess Timon (by Terimon): dam unraced, out of half-sister to useful juvenile hurdler
The Grey Bomber (by Scallywag) and useful 2m to 3m+ hurdler/chaser Onapromise:
well held in 3 bumpers. *L. Wells*

RUSSIAN COMRADE (IRE)   8 b.g. Polish Patriot (USA) – Tikarna (FR) (Targo-   h109 d
wice (USA)) [2003/4 16d^2 16g 16d^{pu} 16m 16g Mar 4] leggy, close-coupled ex-Irish
gelding: half-brother to fairly useful hurdler/winning chaser Tidjani (by Alleged), stays
21f, and fair hurdler up to 19f Tirmizi (by Shahrastani): fair on Flat (stays 1½m): easily
best effort over hurdles when second in novice at Punchestown very early in season: left
W. J. Fitzpatrick, well beaten in Britain: raced at 2m: tried blinkered: temperamental.
J. C. Tuck

RUSSIAN COURT   8 b.g. Soviet Lad (USA) – Court Town (Camden Town) [2003/4   h98
h84: 16m^2 21m 16m^3 17d^4 16g^4 19d^5 17d 16s Feb 20] leggy gelding: modest handicap
hurdler: won at Bangor in November: best around 2m: acts on heavy and good to firm
going: tried in cheekpieces: headstrong. *S. E. H. Sherwood*

RUSSIAN GIGOLO (IRE)   7 b. or br.g. Toulon – Nanogan (Tarqogan) [2003/4 h97:   c116
20g^3 c21d* c20d* c25g^2 c20d^3 Feb 20] lengthy, workmanlike gelding: modest maiden   h91
hurdler: much better over fences, winning handicaps at Uttoxeter in November and
Bangor in December: creditable second to Magical Bailiwick in novice handicap at
Cheltenham fourth start, let down by jumping when last of 3 finishers final one: stays 25f:
acts on heavy going. *N. A. Twiston-Davies*

RUSSIAN LORD (IRE) 5 br.g. Topanoora – Russian Gale (IRE) (Strong Gale) **F79 p**
[2003/4 F16d Feb 2] strong, good sort: fourth foal: half-brother to useful hurdler/very
promising chaser Lord Sam (by Supreme Leader), stays 3m: dam won 3m chase in
Ireland: travelled strongly but very green once pace lifted when tenth of 17 in bumper at
Kempton on debut: likely to improve. *V. R. A. Dartnall*

RUSSIAN SKY 5 gr.g. Endoli (USA) – Anzarna (Zambrano) [2003/4 22m 24d^pu 16d **h71 ?**
17g^4 22g^4 22d Apr 5] leggy gelding: first live foal: dam winning pointer: poor form over
hurdles: should stay 3m. *Mrs H. O. Graham*

RUSSIAN STEPPES (IRE) 6 gr.g. Moscow Society (USA) – Pryana (Pry) [2003/4 **h65**
22s 21g^6 Feb 11] leggy gelding: seventh foal: dam placed in Irish bumper: poor form on
second of 2 starts over hurdles: will be suited by 3m+. *H. D. Daly*

RUST EN VREDE 5 b.g. Royal Applause – Souveniers (Relko) [2003/4 h81: 17g **h81**
17m^6 Jul 17] poor maiden hurdler: raced around 2m: acts on good to firm going: tried
visored: won on Flat in February and April. *D. Carroll*

RUSTIC CHARM (IRE) 4 b.f. Charnwood Forest (IRE) – Kabayil (Dancing Brave **h92**
(USA)) [2003/4 16d 17g^pu Apr 10] useful-looking filly: half-sister to fairly useful hurdler
Dancing Bay (by Suave Dancer), stays 21f: fair maiden on Flat (stays 1¼m) for D. Cox:
travelled comfortably in rear long way when ninth of 18 in juvenile at Sandown on
hurdling debut: blinkered, weakened quickly approaching straight having raced freely in
mares maiden at Newton Abbot next time. *C. R. Egerton*

RUSTIC REVELRY 11 b.g. Afzal – Country Festival (Town And Country) [2003/4 **c92**
c87, h–: c16d^2 c24m* c21m^3 May 21] tall gelding: fair hunter chaser: won at Huntingdon **h–**
in May: effective at 2m to 3m: acts on good to firm and good to soft going: blinkered.
R. H. York

RUTLAND CHANTRY (USA) 10 b.g. Dixieland Band (USA) – Christchurch **h80**
(FR) (So Blessed) [2003/4 17d^3 16s^ro Dec 26] smallish, good-bodied gelding: modest on
Flat (stays 1½m): lightly-raced winning hurdler, poor form on completed start in 2003/4:
raced around 2m: acts on heavy going. *S. Gollings*

RUTLEDGE RED (IRE) 8 gr.g. Roselier (FR) – Katebeaujolais (Politico (USA)) **c–**
[2003/4 h102: c21g^F c22f^ur Oct 5] tall gelding: fair hurdler: failed to complete both starts **h–**
over fences: will probably stay 3m: acts on soft and good to firm going. *J. M. Jefferson*

RYALUX (IRE) 11 b.g. Riverhead (USA) – Kings de Lema (IRE) (King's Ride) **c–**
[2003/4 c146, h–: 22g^6 c24d^5 Dec 13] lengthy gelding: winning hurdler: smart chaser: **h–**
won 2 handicaps at Ayr in 2002/3, notably Scottish Grand National: still short of peak
fitness, well beaten in face of very stiff task in Grade 2 at Haydock in December: reported
following month to have suffered leg injury and missed rest of season: stays 33f: probably
acts on any going: usually sound jumper: tremendously game and consistent. *A. Crook*

RYDERS STORM (USA) 5 b. or br.g. Dynaformer (USA) – Justicara (Rusticaro **c111**
(FR)) [2003/4 h101§: c17m^2 c16m^2 c16m^2 c16d^pu Dec 20] workmanlike gelding: fair **h– §**
hurdler/novice chaser: runner-up first 3 starts over fences, no match for very impressive
Thisthatandtother in Grade 2 at Cheltenham on third occasion: will probably stay 2½m:
raced mainly on good to firm going. *T. R. George*

RYDON LANE (IRE) 8 br.g. Toca Madera – Polocracy (IRE) (Aristocracy) [2003/4 **c–**
c–, h91: 24g^3 19g^2 22d^F 22g^4 24s^3 19g^4 19g* 19g^pu Apr 1] useful-looking gelding: fell **h93**
second on chasing debut: modest handicap hurdler: won at Exeter in March: ran as if
amiss following month: stays 3m: raced on good going or softer. *Mrs S. D. Williams*

RYE BROOK 7 b.g. Romany Rye – Nearly A Brook (Nearly A Hand) [2003/4 F16m* **h–**
F16m^2 22s^pu Dec 30] workmanlike gelding: best effort in bumpers (ran twice for **F81**
R. Hodges in 2001/2) when making all in very weak event at Chepstow in October: never
a factor in maiden on hurdling debut. *P. F. Nicholls*

RYE RUM (IRE) 13 br.g. Strong Gale – Eimers Pet (Paddy's Stream) [2003/4 c–§, **c– §**
h–: c20m^pu c25m Jun 20] small gelding: of no account nowadays: tried visored/blinkered: **h– §**
refused to race once. *J. W. F. Aynsley*

RYHALL (IRE) 4 b.f. Saddlers' Hall (IRE) – Loshian (IRE) (Montelimar (USA)) **F78**
[2003/4 F16s F16d^4 Mar 22] unfurnished filly: fourth foal: dam useful chaser up to
2m/12.5f to 2m winner: much better effort in bumpers when fourth at Wetherby.
T. D. Easterby

RYMINSTER 5 ch.g. Minster Son – Shultan (IRE) (Rymer) [2003/4 19g 18s 16g Mar **h–**
10] lengthy gelding: first foal: dam 2¼m chase winner: well held in novice hurdles.
J. Wade

RYMON   4 br.g. Terimon – Rythmic Rymer (Rymer) [2003/4 F13g F16g Mar 10] good-topped gelding: first foal: dam poor half-sister to useful hurdler up to 2½m Anabranch: well held in 2 bumpers. *J. M. Jefferson*   F—

S

SAAFEND ROCKET (IRE)   6 b.g. Distinctly North (USA) – Simple Annie (Simply   h106
Great (FR)) [2003/4 h74: 16m² 16g² 16m⁴ 16m* 17d* 16g* 16d⁶ 17d 16d⁴ 16d³ Apr 8]
leggy, sparely-made gelding: fair hurdler: won conditional jockeys seller at Ludlow (first start since leaving R. Lee) in November and handicaps at Hereford (amateur novice) and Ludlow in December: will prove best around 2m: unraced on extremes of going: free-going sort. *H. D. Daly*

SABADILLA (USA)   10 b.g. Sadler's Wells (USA) – Jasmina (USA) (Forli (ARG))   h120
[2003/4 h105: 16g* 17g 16g* 17s³ 16d* 16g⁶ 16mᵖᵘ 16d Apr 13] leggy gelding: fairly useful hurdler: won handicaps at Punchestown very early in season, Limerick in June and Guinness Galway Hurdle (beat Cloone River ¾ length) in July: best around 2m: acts on soft and good to firm going: lame seventh start: held up. *Patrick Michael Verling, Ireland*

SABI SAND   8 b.m. Minster Son – Radical Lady (Radical) [2003/4 c88, h–: c22vᵖᵘ   c—
c27sᵖᵘ c24vᵖᵘ c20sᵖᵘ Feb 11] lengthy, sparely-made mare: poor maiden hurdler: modest   h—
handicap chaser in 2002/3 for R. C. Guest, no form in 2003/4: formerly usually wore cheekpieces: tried tongue tied: usually sound jumper. *J. R. Turner*

SABREFLIGHT   4 ch.f. Sabrehill (USA) – Little Redwing (Be My Chief (USA))   F95
[2003/4 F16g³ F16s³ Mar 13] 6,000 3-y-o: leggy, rather unfurnished filly: third foal: half-sister to 6f winner in Germany by Dancing Spree: dam maiden: third in mares bumpers at Musselburgh in February and Sandown (valuable event, beaten 4¼ lengths by Marsh Run) in March. *R. A. Fahey*

SABY (FR)   6 b. or br.g. Sassanian (USA) – Valy Flett (FR) (Pietru (FR)) [2003/4 c108,   c86
h79: c19gᶠ 17g⁴ 19d c16g c16s⁴ 19g c18g⁶ c16d³ c16g³ c19gᵖᵘ Apr 16] tall gelding: poor   h71
maiden hurdler: modest maiden chaser: best around 2m: acts on heavy going. *P. J. Hobbs*

Guinness Galway Hurdle (Handicap)—
plenty in with a chance at the last; Sabadilla (left) is behind eventual fifth Crimson Flower
who has just been headed by runner-up Cloone River

SACHSENWALZER (GER)   6 ch.g. Top Waltz (FR) – Stairway To Heaven (GER)   **h81**
(Nebos (GER)) [2003/4 16g 16g⁵ 16v 16g⁵ 16s⁴ Mar 19] ex-German gelding: successful
up to 1m on Flat, including at Bremen in 2003 for U. Stoltefuss: poor form over hurdles:
likely to prove best at sharp 2m. *C. Grant*

SACREBLEU (FR)   5 b.g. Epervier Bleu – Sa Majeste (FR) (Garde Royale) [2003/4   **h98 ?**
16s⁴ 20sᵖᵘ 17sᵖᵘ Feb 11] strong, lengthy gelding: third foal: half-brother to 1m/11f winner
Saonoise (by Homme de Loi): dam lightly raced on Flat: fourth in novice hurdle at
Haydock on debut: breathing problem in 2 similar events: sold 2,200 gns Doncaster May
Sales. *M. Todhunter*

SACRIFICE   9 b.g. Arctic Lord – Kellyann (Jellaby) [2003/4 c99: c16d⁴ c20m⁴ c21gᵘʳ   **c93**
c20gᵖᵘ c19m⁶ c16m⁶ c21f³ c21d⁴ Nov 15] modest chaser: left T. Long after second start,
form after only when close third of 4 in handicap at Wincanton: stays 21f: acts on firm
going. *K. Bishop*

SACSAYHUAMAN   5 b.m. Halling (USA) – La Dolce Vita (Mazilier (USA)) [2003/4   **h–**
16gᶠ 16v 16s 16d Apr 12] fair maiden at best on Flat (stays 1m), well held in 2003, sold
out of R. Beckett's stable £1,350 Ascot July Sales: no form over hurdles. *D. W. Thompson*

SACUNDAI (IRE)   7 b.g. Hernando (FR) – Shahdiza (USA) (Blushing Groom   **h153**
(FR)) [2003/4 h159: 24g² 16d² 20d⁵ 24d* Dec 28]
        Sacundai was denied the opportunity to take on Baracouda and Iris's Gift in
the Stayers' Hurdle when a setback in training in January brought his third season
over hurdles to a premature end. At the time, Sacundai was a leading fancy for the
race, with only the aforementioned pair and Solerina at shorter odds in the ante-post
betting. It is believed that the problem with Sacundai wasn't very serious and that he
will be back in action in the next season, when, no doubt, the Stayers' Hurdle will be
his main objective once again. At least Sacundai isn't likely to have to contend with
Iris's Gift, who is to be sent chasing; with time on his side, Sacundai could be the one
to give Baracouda and Rhinestone Cowboy most to do. Sacundai had made great strides
in the 2002/3 season, and might well have shown further improvement in the latest one
given further opportunities. After returning from a six-month break, he was restricted
to just three races in a six-week period towards the end of the year, winning a Grade 2
event at Leopardstown on his last appearance.

woodiesdiy.com Christmas Hurdle, Leopardstown—Sacundai (left) heads Be My Belle at the second last

Sacundai won four races in succession in 2002/3, completing his four-timer in the Aintree Hurdle in which he beat that season's Champion Hurdle winner Rooster Booster by a head. A five-timer was denied him by Holy Orders in the Champion Stayers' Hurdle at Punchestown, which took place shortly after the end of the British 2002/3 season. Punchestown was also the scene of Sacundai's reappearance, though this time it was in the Grade 2 Morgiana Hurdle over a mile shorter. Sacundai has won five times at two miles but is suited by further nowadays, and in coming quite close to upsetting the odds laid on his stable-companion Back In Front he ran a race full of promise, all the more so given how weak he was in the market. Having worn down the leader Solerina after the last, Sacundai was caught in the last seventy yards, going down by a length and a half. Sacundai shared favouritism with Solerina when the pair re-opposed in the Hatton's Grace Hurdle over two and a half miles at Fairyhouse two weeks later, but he ran way below expectations, reportedly struck into, in finishing fifth behind that mare. Sacundai put that rare disappointing effort well behind him when returned to three miles on his next start, in the woodiesdiy.com Christmas Hurdle at Leopardstown. Sacundai's six opponents there were no more than useful and, sent off at evens, he didn't need to run up to his best to win, particularly with second favourite Florida Coast reportedly amiss. Always handy in a race run at a sound pace, Sacundai quickened clear after two out to win comfortably by seven lengths from Be My Belle. Incidentally, this was one of six winners at the Leopardstown Christmas fixture for Sacundai's rider Barry Geraghty, who not only went on to win the jockeys' championship in Ireland with one hundred and nine wins, but also became the first jockey to be voted Irish Sports Personality of the Year following a remarkably successful 2003, when he won the Grand National on Monty's Pass and rode five winners at the Cheltenham Festival.

Sacundai (IRE)
(b.g. 1997)

Hernando (FR)
(b 1990)

Shahdiza (USA)
(ch 1982)

Niniski
(b 1976)

Whakilyric
(b 1984)

Blushing Groom
(ch 1974)

Shahneez
(b 1977)

Nijinsky
Virginia Hills
Miswaki
Lyrism
Red God
Runaway Bride
St Paddy
Tazeem

Sacundai began his career with Pascal Bary in France, though he did most of his racing on the Flat in Italy, where he won a newcomers event at Milan. Three of his half-brothers also won in Italy, including useful hurdler Sallustro (by Shahrastani). Another, Shahdjat (by Vayrann), was a useful stayer on the Flat in Ireland and subsequently won a couple of three-mile novice hurdles for Kim Bailey's stable. Sacundai's dam and grandam, Shahdiza and Shahneez, were both owned by the Aga Khan. The dam Shahdiza was useful on the Flat, winning at up to thirteen furlongs, while Shahneez won at up to a mile and a quarter in France. The medium-sized Sacundai seems best at two and a half miles to three miles. He has won on good to firm going, but has raced mainly on good or softer and acts on heavy.
E. J. O'Grady, Ireland

SADDLER'S QUEST   7 b.g. Saddlers' Hall (IRE) – Seren Quest (Rainbow Quest (USA)) [2003/4 h73: 22d 19g 16m Oct 6] poor form over hurdles, lightly raced: claimed from C. Morlock £4,000 after winning on Flat in June after second start: raced too freely in blinkers final outing: sold to join A. Deakin 3,500 gns Doncaster January Sales. *J. White*   **h73**

SADIE JANE   4 b.f. Zahran (IRE) – So We Know (Daring March) [2003/4 17m[pu] Nov 27] no sign of ability on Flat or on hurdling debut. *J. M. Bradley*   **h–**

SADLER'S COVE (FR)   6 b.g. King's Theatre (IRE) – Mine d'Or (FR) (Posse (USA)) [2003/4 h–: 22g[pu] 16g[pu] May 18] compact gelding: no worthwhile form over hurdles (tried tongue tied), though successful twice up to 1¾m on Flat in 2003: sold £1,400 Ascot October Sales. *Mrs L. C. Jewell*   **h–**

SADLER'S REALM   11 b.g. Sadler's Wells (USA) – Rensaler (USA) (Stop The Music (USA)) [2003/4 c–, h–: 20d c19d* c19s[3] Apr 6] smallish, leggy gelding: has had leg problems: winning hurdler/chaser: left P. Hobbs and fit from points, won hunter at   **c96**
h–

Hereford in March: stays 2½m: raced on good going or softer (acts on heavy): often let down by jumping over fences, though not in hunters. *Ms S. J. Gordon*

SADLER'S ROCK (IRE)   6 b.g. Sadler's Wells (USA) – Triple Couronne (USA)   **h–**
(Riverman (USA)) [2003/4 16d^pu Nov 30] good-topped gelding: weakened closing stages after travelling well both starts in bumpers in 2001/2, much better effort when fourth to Lord Sam at Newbury on debut: showed ability but weakened as if amiss in maiden hurdle on return. *G. L. Moore*

SADLER'S SECRET (IRE)   9 b.g. Sadler's Wells (USA) – Athyka (USA) (Secret-   **c–**
ariat (USA)) [2003/4 c–, h105: 20m² 23m² 21g 20s* 19g³ 20v^pu 20d* Apr 21] workman-   **h115**
like gelding: fairly useful hurdler: won claimer at Haydock (claimed from A. Deakin £8,000) in November and handicap at Worcester (looked none too keen) in April: stays 27f: acts on any going: effective with or without headgear: has had tongue tied: bled from nose third start: not a fluent jumper: often goes in snatches. *G. J. Smith*

SADLER'S VIC   6 b.g. Old Vic – Lorna-Gail (Callernish) [2003/4 F16d Apr 12]   **F–**
£1,900 5-y-o, £3,200 6-y-o: leggy, plain gelding: first foal: dam, useful hurdler/fair novice chaser, stayed 3m: more temperament than ability in points: tailed off in bumper: sold 1,800 gns Doncaster May Sales. *A. J. Chamberlain*

SADLERS WINGS (IRE)   6 b.g. In The Wings – Anna Comnena (IRE) (Shareef   **h139**
Dancer (USA)) [2003/4 20d* 16s* 21g⁶ 20d* Apr 11]
     Willie Mullins had a couple of smart six-year-old novice hurdlers in his stable in the latest season, and, while he has kept them apart on the racecourse so far, it is possible they could meet in 2004/5. With Royal Alphabet raced solely at two miles to date and Sadlers Wings mainly at around two and a half, it might have been expected that their careers would continue on different paths, but Mullins believes that Sadlers Wings has the speed to make up into a Champion Hurdle contender. Whether Sadlers Wings is good enough to win a Champion Hurdle is another matter. He still has a great deal of improvement to make even if he does prove fully effective at two miles. Champion Hurdle winners Morley Street, Istabraq and Hardy Eustace also put up their best performances as a novice at distances beyond two miles, and they managed to bridge the gap, although the rating they achieved in their first season over hurdles was around 10 lb higher than the one allotted to Sadlers Wings.

Menolly Homes Champion Novices' Hurdle, Punchestown—useful Flat performer Sadlers Wings
makes it four out of five over hurdles, taking over from Kadiskar at the last

Hardy Eustace won the 2003 Royal & SunAlliance Novices' Hurdle, whereas Sadlers Wings met his first defeat as a hurdler in the latest running of that event at Cheltenham in March. A smart performer at up to a mile and three quarters on the Flat at his best, Sadlers Wings created such a highly favourable impression when winning a maiden at Punchestown in December and a minor event at Navan in February that only the unbeaten Inglis Drever started at shorter odds in the SunAlliance. In the event, Sadlers Wings managed only sixth behind Fundamentalist, beaten nine lengths, having run a rather puzzling race. In rear and appearing to be going none too well early on, Sadlers Wings was back on the bridle with a circuit to go and cruised into contention from the top of the hill before not finding anything like so much as expected when asked for his effort after two out. The performance cast doubts over Sadlers Wings's temperament. His trainer thought it possible that the tongue strap, which had also been fitted on his first two starts, had unsettled Sadlers Wings and, significantly, the horse raced without one on his next three starts. He won the first two of them without needing to run up to the form shown at Cheltenham, starting a short-priced favourite each time. In the Rathbarry & Glenview Studs Festival Novices' Hurdle, a Grade 2 event run at Fairyhouse in April, Sadlers Wings went with much more zest than at Cheltenham and asserted after two out to win by three and a half lengths from Point Barrow. Point Barrow was one of seven who opposed Sadlers Wings in the Menolly Homes Champion Novices' Hurdle at Punchestown which took place shortly after the end of the British season, most of the septet looking short of the standard usually required to win this Grade 1 event. Once again Sadlers Wings's winning margin was three and

Mr John J. Brennan's "Sadlers Wings"

a half lengths, Kadiskar taking second place this time but having little chance with Sadlers Wings who, waited with as usual, needed only to be shaken up to lead before the last. Sadlers Wings made his final appearance before his summer break in the Prix La Barka at Auteuil, running up to form in finishing fourth to Great Love, one place behind another Mullins runner Rule Supreme, who went on to win the Grande Course de Haies. It was, nonetheless, slightly disappointing that Sadlers Wings couldn't produce a better turn of foot at the end of a steadily-run race.

Sadlers Wings (IRE) (b.g. 1998)	In The Wings (b 1986)	Sadler's Wells (b 1981)	Northern Dancer Fairy Bridge
		High Hawk (b 1980)	Shirley Heights Sunbittern
	Anna Comnena (IRE) (b 1989)	Shareef Dancer (b 1980)	Northern Dancer Sweet Alliance
		Anna Paola (ch 1978)	Prince Ippi Antwerpen

Sadlers Wings, whose sire In The Wings was put down in April having been removed from covering duties earlier in the year due to laminitis, is the fifth foal of Anna Comnena, a maiden sister to the useful two-mile hurdler/chaser Atlaal and half-sister to the dams of Annus Mirabilis and Annaba. Anna Comnena looked a promising filly when runner-up in a mile-and-a-quarter maiden at Newmarket on her second start, but she disappointed over a mile and a half, a trip she should have stayed, on her next outing and wasn't seen out again. All eight of Anna Comnena's progeny to reach the racecourse are winners. They also include the useful four-year-old hurdler Analogy (by Bahhare), who stays three miles, the useful middle-distance fillies Abyaan (by Ela-Mana-Mou) and Anna Kareena (by Charnwood Forest); and another filly, Gipsy Anna (by Marju), who was a fairly useful winner of her only two starts, both over five furlongs at two. Sadlers Wings's grandam Anna Paola was the top filly at two and three in Germany and won the Preis der Diana, the German classic for middle-distance fillies. The lengthy, good-topped Sadlers Wings stays twenty-one furlongs but isn't short of speed and is likely to prove as effective at around two miles. So far, Sadlers Wings has raced only on good going or softer over hurdles and acts on soft. It is worth noting that he failed to run up to his best on the few occasions he encountered going firmer than good on the Flat. *W. P. Mullins, Ireland*

SAD MAD BAD (USA) 10 b.g. Sunny's Halo (CAN) – Quite Attractive (USA) (Well Decorated (USA)) [2003/4 c120d, h–: c25g⁵ c28dᵖᵘ c24g⁵ c27d* c27g² Apr 16] workmanlike gelding: one-time fairly useful handicap chaser: left Mrs M. Reveley prior to winning hunter at Sedgefield (hung right) in March and point in April: stays at least 29f (won 33f point): acts on good to firm and heavy going: effective blinkered/visored or not. *G. Tuer* **c100 h–**

SAFARI PARADISE (FR) 7 ch.g. Red Paradise – Safari Liz (USA) (Hawaii) [2003/4 c119, h109: 21g c24m³ 21s⁵ Dec 3] lengthy gelding: one-time useful maiden over fences in France: fair form at best over hurdles: tried visored/in cheekpieces: a thorough rogue. *M. C. Pipe* **c§§ h§§**

SAFE ENOUGH (IRE) 8 ch.g. Safety Catch (USA) – Godfreys Cross (IRE) (Fine Blade (USA)) [2003/4 h85: 21g² Apr 12] medium-sized gelding: modest hurdler, lightly raced: stays 21f: acts on soft and good to firm going. *N. J. Gifford* **h90**

SAFE ROUTE (USA) 6 b. or br.m. Farma Way (USA) – Taiki Victoria (IRE) (Caerleon (USA)) [2003/4 16m 20m³ 20s⁵ 18s* 16s 19s⁴ Jan 24] fairly useful hurdler: won minor event at Cork in January: excellent effort when very close third in conditional jockeys handicap at Punchestown in early-May: better at 2½m than shorter: acts on soft and good to firm going. *W. J. Austin, Ireland* **h118**

SAFE SHOT 5 b.g. Salse (USA) – Optaria (Song) [2003/4 h–: 16g 16g⁵ 20g³ 20gᵖᵘ 20sᵖᵘ Apr 21] leggy gelding: little form over hurdles: wore cheekpieces after reappearance. *Mrs J. C. McGregor* **h–**

SAFE TO BLUSH 6 gr.m. Blushing Flame (USA) – Safe Arrival (USA) (Shadeed (USA)) [2003/4 F16d⁶ F16m⁶ Apr 13] second foal: dam, placed over hurdles/in middle-distance maiden on Flat, closely related to smart middle-distance performer Icona and half-sister to very smart 2-y-o Cock Robin: modest form in bumpers at Stratford and Chepstow. *P. A. Pritchard* **F80**

SAJ

SAFFRON SUN 9 b.g. Landyap (USA) – Saffron Bun (Sit In The Corner (USA)) [2003/4 c106, h–: c20m² c24f⁴ c24m³ c25mᵖᵘ c23d³ c19s* c19sᵖᵘ c20d⁴ Apr 8] tall, workmanlike gelding: fair handicap chaser: won at Exeter (third course success) in January: stays 23f: acts on firm and soft going: sometimes makes mistakes. *J. D. Frost* — **c112 h–**

SAFI 9 b.g. Generous (IRE) – Jasarah (IRE) (Green Desert (USA)) [2003/4 c–, h–: c26d⁵ May 28] leggy gelding: poor hurdler/maiden chaser: probably best short of 3¼m: acts on firm and good to soft going: usually blinkered/tongue tied. *D. McCain Jnr* — **c77 h–**

SAGARDIAN (FR) 5 b.g. Mister Mat (FR) – Tipnik (FR) (Nikos) [2003/4 F16g⁵ 17d 16dᵖᵘ 16g 16v 24g⁵ Feb 18] €28,000 3-y-o: leggy, quite good-topped gelding: first foal: dam won twice at 15f over hurdles in France: fifth in bumper at Perth on debut: no form over hurdles: tried in cheekpieces. *L. Lungo* — **h– F78**

SAHHAR 11 ch.g. Sayf El Arab (USA) – Native Magic (Be My Native (USA)) [2003/4 h80: 19m² 16m⁵ 16m³ Jun 28] small gelding: has reportedly had leg problems: poor hurdler: barely stays 19f: acts on firm and good to soft going. *B. D. Leavy* — **h77**

SAILING THROUGH 4 b.g. Bahhare (USA) – Hopesay (Warning) [2003/4 16sᵖᵘ 16g 16g 17m⁵ Apr 14] leggy gelding: useful on Flat (stays 1¼m), sold out of T. Mills's stable 52,000 gns Newmarket Autumn Sales after refusing to enter stall in October: poor form over hurdles. *R. Dickin* — **h78**

SAILOR A'HOY 8 b.g. Handsome Sailor – Eye Sight (Roscoe Blake) [2003/4 17d 16sᵖᵘ 17d² Mar 15] compact gelding: poor maiden hurdler: best efforts around 2m, worth another try over further: acts on good to firm and good to soft going, probably on heavy. *M. Mullineaux* — **h83**

SAINT ALBERT 9 ch.g. Keen – Thimbalina (Salmon Leap (USA)) [2003/4 23sᵖᵘ Jan 21] sturdy gelding: thrice-raced and no form over hurdles: dead. *C. C. Bealby* — **h–**

SAINT-DECLAN (IRE) 11 b.g. Polykratis – Welsh Symphony (Welsh Saint) [2003/4 c16g⁵ Feb 8] ex-Irish gelding: poor maiden steeplechaser, trained by J. Codd prior to only start in 2003/4: stays 2½m: acts on firm and soft going: tried blinkered: formerly tongue tied. *Richard Mathias* — **c–**

SAINT ESTEBEN (FR) 5 b.g. Poliglote – Highest Tulip (FR) (Highest Honor (FR)) [2003/4 c16m² c16s² c21m² c19g³ Apr 1] leggy ex-French gelding: third foal: half-brother to winner in Italy by Bering: dam, winning middle-distance stayer, half-sister to smart French hurdler up to 21f Kim: 1½m winner on Flat: fairly useful hurdler for J. Bertran de Balanda: second in 3 novice chases, best efforts behind Look Collonges at Warwick and Well Chief at Taunton first 2 starts, carrying head bit awkwardly under pressure each time: disappointing last 2 outings, looking unenthusiastic when odds on in maiden at Taunton final one: best form around 2m: acts on heavy going, probably on good to firm. *P. F. Nicholls* — **c114 h–**

SAINTLY THOUGHTS (USA) 9 b. or br.g. St Jovite (USA) – Free Thinker (USA) (Shadeed (USA)) [2003/4 16m Jun 28] probably of little account nowadays. *C. J. Gray* — **h–**

SAINT REVERIEN (FR) 5 b.g. Silver Rainbow – La Briganderie (FR) (Noir Et Or) [2003/4 c20s³ c16dꟳ 19s 20d⁶ 17s Apr 6] rather leggy gelding: third foal: dam winning hurdler/chaser up to 2½m: twice-raced on Flat: fairly useful maiden hurdler/fair maiden chaser in France: left J. Bertran de Balanda after reappearance, failed to impress with temperament in Britain: stays 2½m: acts on heavy ground. *Ian Williams* — **c109 h–**

SAINT ROMBLE (FR) 7 b.g. Sassanian (USA) – Limatge (FR) (Trac) [2003/4 c92, h–: c16g* c19s⁴ c17s⁶ c18s³ c20g³ c21g² Mar 25] leggy gelding: winning hurdler in France: modest chaser: won minor event at Worcester in May: stays 19f: best efforts on good going or softer (acts on heavy). *P. J. Hobbs* — **c91 h–**

SAINTSAIRE (FR) 5 b.g. Apeldoorn (FR) – Pro Wonder (FR) (The Wonder (FR)) [2003/4 h125: 16d³ 16s³ 16g 16s 16d³ Apr 17] leggy, useful-looking gelding: useful handicap hurdler: contested valuable events in 2003/4, good efforts on first 3 starts, third to Tramantano in Gerry Feilden at Newbury and Thesis in Ladbroke at Ascot and around 3 lengths seventh to Geos in Tote Gold Trophy at Newbury (5 lb out of handicap): below form in Imperial Cup (not fluent) at Sandown and Scottish Champion Hurdle (Limited Handicap) at Ayr last 2 outings: will prove best around 2m: acts on soft going. *N. J. Henderson* — **h140**

SAJOMI RONA (IRE) 7 ch.g. Riberetto – Mauma Lady (IRE) (Le Moss) [2003/4 26mᵖᵘ 20m⁵ c21gꟳ c16gᵖᵘ c25v⁶ c21s c20s³ c25sᵘʳ Apr 4] sturdy gelding: won maiden point in 2003, little sign of ability otherwise (tried visored/blinkered/tongue tied): not a fluent jumper of fences. *A. Crook* — **c– x h–**

803

SALEEN (IRE) 4 b.f. Kahyasi – Sabrata (IRE) (Zino) [2003/4 F12g Nov 12] smallish   F–
filly: fourth foal: half-sister to fairly useful 2001 2-y-o 7f/7.5f winner Receivedwiththanx
(by Celtic Swing), later 1m/1¼m winner in Spain, and 7f seller winner Head Scratcher
(by Alhijaz): dam French 2-y-o 4.5f winner: well held in 3-y-o bumper and 1m maiden
on Flat debut in January. *P. D. Cundell*

SALFORD 9 ch.g. Salse (USA) – Bustellina (Busted) [2003/4 c85§, h–: c20g^pu c21d^6   c90 §
c21d^3 c22f^3 c20m^pu 21m^5 c24m* c25f* Oct 26] strong gelding: winning hurdler: modest   h–
handicap chaser: won weak races at Huntingdon and Wincanton (third course win) in
October: stays 25f: best on good going or firmer (acts on firm): tried visored: usually
races prominently: makes mistakes: unreliable. *N. J. Hawke*

SALFORD FLYER 8 b.g. Pharly (FR) – Edge of Darkness (Vaigly Great) [2003/4   h– §
21g^pu 16v Jan 31] leggy gelding: fairly useful juvenile hurdler in 1999/00: very lightly
raced since: sold out of D. Elsworth's stable 4,200 gns Newmarket Autumn (2001) Sales
and no encouragement both starts on return: ungenuine. *Jane Southcombe*

SALGRADO (NZ) 8 ch.g. Prince Salieri (AUS) – Musing (Music Maestro) [2003/4   h–
h77: 16g^su May 21] angular gelding: won twice up to 1¼m from 15 starts on Flat in New
Zealand: well held both completed starts in novice hurdles: dead. *Jonjo O'Neill*

SALHOOD 5 b.g. Capote (USA) – Princess Haifa (USA) (Mr Prospector (USA))   h118
[2003/4 F91: F16m* F17d 16s^2 16d* 16d* 16s^3 16d* 16g^4 Mar 6] big, leggy gelding: F96
won bumper at Chepstow in May: fairly useful novice hurdler: won at Leicester and
Doncaster in January, and handicap at Newcastle (by 1½ lengths from Powder Creek) in
February: raced around 2m: acts on soft going, bumper win on good to firm: usually races
prominently. *S. Gollings*

SALIM 7 b.g. Salse (USA) – Moviegoer (Pharly (FR)) [2003/4 h–: 16g^5 16g^pu 17m 17d   c–
16g^3 c23m^pu c20d^3 c16g c24d^5 Mar 15] angular gelding: modest on Flat (stays easy   h77
1¼m), sold out of G. L. Moore's stable £5,000 Ascot June Sales: poor maiden hurdler: no
form over fences: best around 2m: has had tongue tied. *Miss J. S. Davis*

SALINAS (GER) 5 b.g. Macanal (USA) – Santa Ana (GER) (Acatenango (GER))   h94
[2003/4 16g 16g^4 17g^3 16g 16s^3 17g Apr 3] good-topped gelding: successful 3 times over
7f at 2/3 yrs in Germany, unplaced all 6 starts in 2003 for P. Schiergen: modest novice
hurdler: left C. Von Der Recke after second start: raced around 2m on good and soft
ground. *M. F. Harris*

SALLIEMAK 6 b.m. Makbul – Glenbrook Fort (Fort Nayef) [2003/4 F–: F17m 17g   h–
24m Mar 4] well beaten in bumpers/novice hurdles: breathing problem second start.   F–
A. J. Wilson

SALLY LIGHTFOOT 10 ch.m. Derrylin – Vino Festa (Nebbiolo) [2003/4 20s^pu 21m   h–
May 29] close-coupled mare: poor maiden hurdler, no form on return from lengthy
absence: tried in cheekpieces. *P. T. Dalton*

SALLY SCALLY 12 ch.m. Scallywag – Petite Cone (Celtic Cone) [2003/4 c77, h–:   c63
c26g May 26] smallish mare: winning pointer, modest form at best in hunters: stays 25f: h–
acts on firm going, possibly unsuited by soft: blinkered once: takes good hold, and is a
weak finisher. *Miss T. Jackson*

SALLY'S PRIDE 7 gr.m. Norton Challenger – Another Scally (Scallywag) [2003/4   h–
F71: 20s^ur 16v^pu Jan 10] poor form in bumper in 2002/3: let down by jumping and didn't
look keen over hurdles. *W. Clay*

SALMON LADDER (USA) 12 b.g. Bering – Ballerina Princess (USA) (Mr   h78
Prospector (USA)) [2003/4 h90: 24d 20g^2 24m^6 Jul 7] poor maiden hurdler: stays 2½m:
acts on good to firm and heavy going: has had tongue tied. *A. J. Martin, Ireland*

SALOUP 6 b.m. Wolfhound (USA) – Sarcita (Primo Dominie) [2003/4 h–: 17s^F Dec   h88
29] leggy mare: modest form at best over hurdles: off 19 months, still to be asked for
maximum effort when falling heavily 2 out in handicap at Taunton only start in 2002/3:
likely to prove best at sharp 2m. *O. Sherwood*

SALT CELLAR (IRE) 5 b.g. Salse (USA) – Athene (IRE) (Rousillon (USA)) [2003/4   F85
F16d F16d^6 Mar 19] medium-sized gelding: fourth foal: brother to middle-distance stayer
Last Roman and half-brother to useful middle-distance stayer Side Saddle (by Saddlers'
Hall): dam, 1¼m winner, half-sister to high-class 2m hurdler/smart Flat stayer Landing
Light: sold unraced out of M. Tregoning's stable 5,000 gns Newmarket Autumn (2002)
Sales: better effort in bumpers when sixth at Warwick. *P. R. Webber*

SALVAGE 9 b.g. Kahyasi – Storm Weaver (USA) (Storm Bird (CAN)) [2003/4 c89,   c89
h–: c16g^2 c16m^2 c17g* c21m^5 c17d^2 c17s^3 c17g^3 c17g^3 c16d^2 Apr 22] angular gelding: h–

modest chaser: won handicap at Kelso in November: best around 2m: acts on heavy and good to firm going: has had tongue tied. *Mrs J. C. McGregor*

SALVO   13 ch.g. K-Battery – Saleander (Leander) [2003/4 22g 20m^pu c26g^5 Sep 3] leggy gelding: winning hurdler/chaser, no form after 18-month absence. *Miss M. Bragg*

c–
h–

SAM ADAMSON   9 br.g. Domitor (USA) – Sardine (Saritamer (USA)) [2003/4 h–: c21m* c16m^2 c20m^3 c21m* c24g^u c20g^2 c20m* c19m* c22g^pu Oct 5] sturdy gelding: fair chaser: won novice handicaps at Wincanton, Stratford, Worcester and Hereford in first half of season: lame final outing: stays 21f: acts on good to firm going: tongue tied: often makes mistakes. *J. W. Mullins*

c101
h–

SAMANDARA (FR)   4 b.f. Kris – Samneeza (USA) (Storm Bird (CAN)) [2003/4 16g^pu Feb 13] rather leggy ex-French filly: fifth foal: half-sister to fair hurdler/winning chaser Samapour (by Kahyasi), stays 2½m: dam, won up to 1½m, half-sister to smart French jumper Sprong and to dam of smart 2m to 2½m chaser Samakaan: fair on Flat (stays 11f), successful twice in 2003 for A. de Royer Dupre: ran no sort of race in juvenile on hurdling debut. *A. King*

h–

SAMAR QAND   5 b.m. Selkirk (USA) – Sit Alkul (USA) (Mr Prospector (USA)) [2003/4 21d^pu Apr 12] good-topped mare: poor maiden on Flat (stays 1½m): showed little in maiden on hurdling debut. *Julian Poulton*

h–

SAMBY   6 ch.g. Anshan – Mossy Fern (Le Moss) [2003/4 F99: 16d* 19g^2 19d* 24s^pu Jan 31] big, chunky gelding: will make a chaser: fairly useful form in novice hurdles: won at Towcester (not always fluent) in October and Doncaster (improved form, beat Jodante a distance) in December: upped in trip, weakened quickly 4 out in Grade 2 at latter course final start: should stay beyond 19f: acts on good to soft going (possibly not soft). *O. Sherwood*

h124

SAMMAGEFROMTENESSE (IRE)   7 b.g. Petardia – Canoora (Ahonoora) [2003/4 h75: 17g* 16d 16d 16m^6 16m^pu 16g 18s^pu Dec 29] angular gelding: poor handicap hurdler: won seller at Hereford in May: below form after: best around 2m with emphasis on speed: best efforts on good ground: tried blinkered/in cheekpieces: has had tongue tied: broke blood vessel final start: has looked far from keen: unreliable. *N. F. Glynn, Ireland*

h75 §

SAMON (GER)   7 ch.g. Monsun (GER) – Savanna (GER) (Sassafras (FR)) [2003/4 h139: c21g* c20m* c21g* Jun 12] angular gelding: useful handicap hurdler: landed odds in novice chases at Southwell (easily), Fontwell and Uttoxeter (simple task but unimpressive, jumping slowly and untidily throughout) early in season: stays 21f: acts on soft and good to firm going: usually races prominently. *M. C. Pipe*

c112
h–

SAM ROCKETT   11 b.g. Petong – Art Deco (Artaius (USA)) [2003/4 c–, h91§: 22g^6 27d 22g c23g^pu Aug 23] small gelding: modest handicap hurdler: maiden chaser: stays 27f: acts on firm going: usually blinkered: usually races at Newton Abbot: hard ride (tends to get behind). *P. J. Hobbs*

c– §
h85 §

SAMSAAM (IRE)   7 b.g. Sadler's Wells (USA) – Azyaa (Kris) [2003/4 h117: 20m* 17m^ur Jul 19] lengthy gelding: fairly useful handicap hurdler: easily landed odds at Uttoxeter in June: behind when hampered and unseated 2 out in quite valuable event at Market Rasen following month: stays 2½m: acts on good to firm going: blinkered/visored: tongue tied nowadays: has looked less than keen. *M. C. Pipe*

h121

SAMSON DES GALAS (FR)   6 b. or br.g. Agent Bleu (FR) – Sarema (FR) (Primo Dominie) [2003/4 F89: 16m^pu Apr 13] fourth foal: half-brother to winners around 9f by Lights Out and Luchiroverte: dam maiden: sixth in bumper in 2002/3: showed little in maiden hurdle over year later. *R. Ford*

h–

SAMUEL WILDERSPIN   12 b.g. Henbit (USA) – Littoral (Crash Course) [2003/4 c132, h–: c24g^5 c32g^4 c33d^5 c24s c26g^4 c26m^pu Apr 14] rangy gelding: fairly useful handicap chaser: looked unwilling when well below form last 3 starts: stays 33f: acts on heavy going, possibly not on good to firm: tongue tied: has broken blood vessels. *R. Lee*

c120 d
h–

SANDABAR   11 b.g. Green Desert (USA) – Children's Corner (FR) (Top Ville) [2003/4 16g^F 17m 16g^4 17d^3 Oct 29] leggy gelding: modest handicap hurdler in 2001/2: off 20 months before reappearance, then left N. Waggott: poor form last 3 starts: best around 2m: acts on firm and good to soft going: tongue tied. *G. A. Swinbank*

h74

SANDAL SAPHIRE   5 b.m. Danzig Connection (USA) – Mudflap (Slip Anchor) [2003/4 F17m^pu Jul 22] first foal: dam, 2-y-o 7f winner, from family of smart performer up to 12.5f Lord of Men: showed nothing in bumper on debut. *K. A. Ryan*

F–

SAN DIMAS (USA) 7 gr.g. Distant View (USA) – Chrystophard (USA) (Lypheor) [2003/4 h80: 22f* 22fF Oct 18] modest hurdler: won handicap at Kelso in October: fell first later in month: will stay 3m: acts on firm and good to soft going, possibly unsuited by soft/heavy: usually visored, tried blinkered/in cheekpieces. *R. Allan* **h92**

SANDRONE (IRE) 4 b.f. In Command (IRE) – Florinda (CAN) (Vice Regent (CAN)) [2003/4 17dpu Nov 17] fair maiden at 2 yrs, little encouragement in 3 starts on Flat in 2003: no show in juvenile on hurdling debut. *P. M. Phelan* **h–**

SANDS OF THYNE (IRE) 6 ch.g. Good Thyne (USA) – Yesterdays Gorby (IRE) (Strong Gale) [2003/4 F17m2 16g Nov 25] sturdy gelding: third foal: dam unraced sister to high-class staying chaser Sibton Abbey: neck second to Real Cracker in bumper at Market Rasen on debut: bled from nose when tailed off in novice hurdle. *Noel T. Chance* **h–** **F91**

SANDS RISING 7 b.g. Primitive Rising (USA) – Celtic Sands (Celtic Cone) [2003/4 h91: 22g2 20d* 20s 20v5 20s 20v3 20s Apr 4] sturdy gelding: modest hurdler: won novice at Carlisle in November: stays 3m: raced on good going or softer (acts on soft). *R. Johnson* **h97**

SANDY BAY (IRE) 5 b.g. Spectrum (IRE) – Karinski (USA) (Palace Music (USA)) [2003/4 17m5 Jul 19] angular gelding: no form on Flat for long time: showed nothing on hurdling debut: sold to join R. Allan 1,900 gns Doncaster November Sales. *M. W. Easterby* **h–**

SANDY DUFF 10 ch.g. Scottish Reel – Not Enough (Balinger) [2003/4 c–, h–: c16m6 May 29] tall, lengthy gelding: fairly useful 2m chaser in 2001/2 for P. Webber: lightly raced and no form in steeplechases since, though won points in March and April (2): acts on good to firm and heavy going: tried blinkered/visored: often shapes as if amiss. *J. D. Frost* **c–** **h–**

SANDYWELL GEORGE 9 ch.g. Zambrano – Farmcote Air (True Song) [2003/4 h–: 21f3 24v 20m2 24m5 20m2 20m2 20g3 20m2 20m3 19s* 22d 18s 22d Mar 21] good-topped gelding: modest hurdler: won amateur novice handicap at Warwick in December: seems to stay 3m: acts on soft and good to firm going: tongue tied. *L. P. Grassick* **h93**

SAN FRANCISCO 10 b.g. Aragon – Sirene Bleu Marine (USA) (Secreto (USA)) [2003/4 c82, h–: c22g c20s3 May 23] tall gelding: poor chaser: stays 2½m: acts on heavy going: effective tongue tied or not: races prominently: sold 3,000 gns Doncaster October Sales, runner-up 3 of 4 starts in points in 2004. *A. C. Whillans* **c66** **h–**

SANGATTE (IRE) 6 b.g. Un Desperado (FR) – Mad House (Kabour) [2003/4 F16d5 16dpu 16d Jan 10] rangy gelding: fourth foal: half-brother to winning 2¾m chaser Shanty Town (by Buckskin): dam, of little account, out of half-sister to smart hurdler/chaser up to 19f Denys Adventure: fifth in bumper at Uttoxeter on debut: again failed to see race out on hurdling debut, didn't jump with any fluency when well-held ninth of 14 in above-average novice at Ascot. *N. J. Henderson* **h88 ?** **F70**

SAN MARCO (IRE) 6 b.g. Brief Truce (USA) – Nuit Des Temps (Sadler's Wells (USA)) [2003/4 h–: 20d3 20g4 20m 16d3 20d3 c20f2 c23m4 c23gF Jan 13] poor maiden hurdler: similar form on completed starts over fences: stays 23f: probably acts on any going: wears cheekpieces: ungenuine. *Mrs P. Sly* **c80 §** **h80 §**

SAN MARINO (IRE) 8 b.g. Torus – Lousion (Lucifer (USA)) [2003/4 c67: 17gF May 1] winning pointer: poor form only completed start in steeplechases and hurdle. *Miss Venetia Williams* **c–** **h–**

SAN PEIRE (FR) 7 b.g. Cyborg (FR) – Shakapoura (FR) (Shakapour) [2003/4 h86+: 27s* 21g2 21s4 c27s* 27s5 27d5 Mar 30] modest hurdler, won handicap at Sedgefield in May: not always fluent when winning novice at same course in February on chasing debut: stays 27f: raced on good going or softer (acts on soft): tried in cheekpieces: not one to trust. *J. Howard Johnson* **c99** **h98 §**

SANTA LUCIA 8 b.m. Namaqualand (USA) – Villasanta (Corvaro (USA)) [2003/4 h93: 20g6 24m 20m3 20g* c21g3 c20m3 c25m3 c21s5 c21dF 16g3 Apr 16] sturdy mare: modest hurdler, won claimer at Perth (claimed from M. Dods £5,000) in July: poor novice chaser: seems best around 2½m: acts on good to firm and good to soft going: tried in cheekpieces: effective making running or held up. *Miss Lucinda V. Russell* **c83** **h97**

SANTELLA BOY (USA) 12 b.g. Turkoman (USA) – Dream Creek (USA) (The Minstrel (CAN)) [2003/4 c73, h–: 24mpu c24d3 c24gpu c21g3 Mar 25] leggy gelding: winning hurdler/chaser: no sign of retaining ability: formerly blinkered. *Miss C. Dyson* **c–** **h–**

betfair.com Novices' Chase, Aintree—Santenay has little trouble defeating three rivals after winning a walkover and a match on his two previous starts

SANTENAY (FR) 6 b.g. Mister Mat (FR) – Guigone (FR) (Esprit du Nord (USA)) **c138** [2003/4 h155: c16f² c19m² c16fʷᵒ c16m* c16d* c16sᶠ c16g* c20m³ c16d 16m⁶ Apr 23] **h141** tall gelding: useful novice chaser: successful at Kempton (walked over) in October, Sandown (match) and Aintree in November and Cheltenham (didn't find much but still beat Tikram 3 lengths) in December: very smart hurdler in 2002/3, just useful form when sixth of 8 to Hasty Prince in minor event at Sandown final outing: best around 2m: acts on firm and soft going: sold to race in USA 135,000 gns Doncaster May Sales. *P. F. Nicholls*

SANTIBURI LAD (IRE) 7 b.g. Namaqualand (USA) – Suggia (Alzao (USA)) **h68** [2003/4 20m³ 16f⁴ Oct 15] half-brother to fairly useful hurdler/chaser Fullopep (by Dunbeath), stays 3m: modest on Flat (stays 1¼m) for N. Tinkler: better effort over hurdles when third of 4 in weak novice at Hexham. *N. Wilson*

SANTI (FR) 6 b.g. Brief Truce (USA) – Sun River (IRE) (Last Tycoon) [2003/4 c19dᵖᵘ **c–** Mar 22] ex-French gelding: second foal: half-brother to French middle-distance winner **h–** Starting Line (by Poplar Bluff): dam ran twice: winning hurdler/chaser for J-P. Gallorini: last of 9 over 11f on Flat debut for G. Blasco in March 2003: pulled up in point and hunter chase in Britain: raced mainly around 2m: acts on soft ground: has won with/without blinkers. *Mrs K. J. Gilmore*

SAORSIE 6 b.g. Emperor Jones (USA) – Exclusive Lottery (Presidium) [2003/4 h93: **h98** 16g* 16m4 16v³ 17d⁴ 17gᵖᵘ 16g⁵ 17m³ 16m³ 17g² 16m² 17g² 16f 16g 16g 16g 16gᵇᵈ 17sᵖᵘ Mar 23] leggy gelding: modest handicap hurdler: won at Worcester in May and Newton Abbot in June: reportedly lost action final start: raced around 2m: acts on good to firm and good to soft going: tried blinkered (has looked awkward off bridle): held up. *J. C. Fox*

SAPOSCAT (IRE) 4 b.g. Groom Dancer (USA) – Dance of Joy (Shareef Dancer **h–** (USA)) [2003/4 16gᵖᵘ Apr 18] ex-Irish gelding: fair form on first of 2 starts around 7f at 2 yrs for Miss I. Oakes: bought £1,200 Ascot April (2003) Sales: showed little in novice on hurdling debut. *D. P. Keane*

SARAGANN (IRE) 9 b.g. Danehill (USA) – Sarliya (IRE) (Doyoun) [2003/4 c129, **c112 x** h127: c20f⁶ c20g⁵ c16m³ c16s* c16d⁵ c16mᵖᵘ c20s⁴ c16d⁴ Apr 22] leggy gelding: fairly **h–** useful hurdler/chaser in 2002/3: well below that level over fences in 2003/4 (usually let down by jumping), though won at Huntingdon in January: stays easy 2½m: acts on soft and good to firm going: tried blinkered. *P. J. Hobbs*

SARA MONICA (IRE) 7 ch.m. Moscow Society (USA) – Swift Trip (IRE) (Duky) **h90** [2003/4 F16d⁴ 16s 21v* 24v³ Mar 21] sturdy, lengthy mare: third foal: dam never ran: **F77**

fourth in bumper at Wetherby on debut: modest form over hurdles: won mares novice at Sedgefield in January: good third in novice handicap at Carlisle: stays 3m: acts on heavy going. *L. Lungo*

SARAS DELIGHT   12 b.g. Idiot's Delight – Lady Bess (Straight Lad) [2003/4 c–, h–: c25g^{ur} Apr 30] rangy gelding: winning chaser/pointer: stayed 25f: acted on soft going: dead. *Major General C. A. Ramsay*
   c86
   h–

SARASOTA (IRE)   9 b.g. Lord Americo – Ceoltoir Dubh (Black Minstrel) [2003/4 h–: 21m^5 May 5] angular gelding: poor maiden hurdler: probably stays 21f: acts on firm going. *P. Bowen*
   h80

SARATOV (GER)   5 b.g. Acatenango (GER) – Sovereign Touch (IRE) (Pennine Walk) [2003/4 h112p: 17d 16v^{pu} Jan 9] rather leggy gelding: shaped encouragingly on hurdling debut in 2002/3, every chance when falling last: no form in 2 starts on return. *Jonjo O'Neill*
   h–

SARENA PRIDE (IRE)   7 b.m. Persian Bold – Avidal Park (Horage) [2003/4 17g^3 Jun 28] fair on Flat (stays 1½m) for R. O'Sullivan: poor form over hurdles: caught the eye when third in maiden at Newton Abbot, though reportedly lame and not seen out again: likely to need sharp 2m: tried blinkered. *J. D. Frost*
   h84

SARGASSO SEA   7 gr.g. Greensmith – Sea Spice (Precipice Wood) [2003/4 F102: 16d^4 20s^3 22d c19g^{pu} Apr 1] strong gelding: type to make a chaser: fairly useful bumper winner: modest form in novice hurdles: badly hampered seventh on chasing debut: should stay beyond 2½m. *J. A. B. Old*
   c– p
   h99

SARIBA   5 b.m. Persian Bold – En Vacances (IRE) (Old Vic) [2003/4 19s^{pu} Jan 14] modest on Flat (stays 2¼m): showed nothing on hurdling debut. *A. Charlton*
   h–

SASPYS LAD   7 b.g. Faustus (USA) – Legendary Lady (Reprimand) [2003/4 h110: 16m^4 16m^2 16m^4 16g* 16v Jan 10] smallish gelding: fair handicap hurdler: won at Wetherby in November: suited by test of speed at 2m: has won on soft going, best form on good/good to firm. *W. M. Brisbourne*
   h110

SASSYROSE   5 b.m. Thowra (FR) – Atlantic Line (Capricorn Line) [2003/4 F17d F16m 20m^{pu} Jul 23] fifth foal: sister to useful handicap hurdler Thrower, stayed 2½m, and bumper winner Rupert Blues: dam unraced half-sister to useful 2m to 3m chaser Baluchi: no sign of ability. *B. G. Powell*
   h–
   F–

SATANAS (FR)   6 b.g. Dress Parade – Oiseau Noir (FR) (Rex Magna (FR)) [2003/4 h81: c17s^5 May 2] close-coupled gelding: poor form over hurdles: soundly beaten in novice handicap on chasing debut: probably failed to stay 25f: sold 3,100 gns Doncaster May Sales prior to showing little in points. *O. Sherwood*
   c–
   h–

SATCHMO (IRE)   12 b.g. Satco (FR) – Taradale (Torus) [2003/4 c127: c20d c22s c21g^4 Apr 1] big gelding, often impresses in appearance: useful chaser at best: left E. O'Grady to rejoin former yard, won point in March: also shaped as if retaining plenty of ability when fourth in Fox Hunters' at Aintree: effective at 2½m to 25f: acts on firm and soft going: races prominently: bold jumper. *Mrs D. M. Grissell*
   c106

SATCO EXPRESS (IRE)   8 b.g. Satco (FR) – Rosel Chris (Roselier (FR)) [2003/4 h132: c22g* c22d* c20d c24d^4 c24s^{pu} c24s* c32g c29d^F Apr 12] strong, well-made gelding: useful hurdler: similar level over fences, successful in maiden at Cork in November and Grade 3 novices at Punchestown later in month and Navan (again had to rally after being headed, beat Lord Who by length) in February: below form in valuable novice handicap at Punchestown in late-April: stays 3m, appeared not to stay 4m: raced on good going or softer (acts on soft): tried tongue tied: reportedly coughing fifth outing: front runner: tough and genuine. *E. Sheehy, Ireland*
   c130
   h–

SATCOSLAM (IRE)   9 b.g. Satco (FR) – Candy Slam (Candy Cane) [2003/4 c117, h–: c20v^6 c22d^{pu} c24f^6 c20d c24d^3 c24s^F Jan 24] tall gelding: fair handicap chaser: best around 3m nowadays: acts on heavy going: tried blinkered: inconsistent. *L. Whitmore, Ireland*
   c110
   h–

SATINEYEVA (FR)   5 b.m. Goldneyev (USA) – Sataga (FR) (Satingo) [2003/4 F16m Jun 28] fourth foal: dam, won 17f hurdle in France, half-sister to smart French hurdler/chaser up to 23f Afferco: achieved little in bumper on debut. *R. J. Baker*
   F–

SATIVA BAY   5 ch.g. Karinga Bay – Busy Mittens (Nearly A Hand) [2003/4 F16g F18v F16m F16s Mar 20] angular gelding: third foal: half-brother to modest hurdler/winning pointer Kentford Busy B (by Petoski), stays 2¾m, and winning hurdler/fair chaser Kentford Fern (by El Conquistador), stays 3¼m: dam, fairly useful hunter chaser, stayed 25f: best effort in bumpers when eighth of 18 at Wincanton third start. *J. W. Mullins*
   F84

SAY

SATOHA (IRE) 6 br.g. Zaffaran (USA) – Whackers World (Whistling Deer) [2003/4 **F100**
F16v³ F19s* Jan 24] IR £28,000 3-y-o: fifth foal: half-brother to fair chaser Pettree (by
King Persian), stays 3¼m: dam winning 2m hurdler: fairly useful form in 2 bumpers,
winning at Naas by 2 lengths from Tardenois. *F. Flood, Ireland*

SATSHOON (IRE) 11 b.g. Satco (FR) – Tudor Lady (Green Shoon) [2003/4 c126, **c126**
h93: 22g* 24s* 26d* 22m³ 24f* 24f^F 25f^d c25f³ c31g* c24d³ c24g³ Mar 12] tall, useful- **h108**
looking gelding: successful 4 times over hurdles in first half of season, in weak novices at
Exeter (amateurs), Perth and Cartmel in April/May and handicap at Exeter in September:
fairly useful chaser: won handicap at Ludlow in December: stays 31f: acts on any going:
blinkered: often races prominently: has looked temperamental. *P. F. Nicholls*

SAUCYNORWICH (IRE) 6 b.g. Norwich – Kelly Gales (IRE) (Strong Gale) **h92 ?**
[2003/4 F16m 20dᵖᵘ 20d 19g⁵ Feb 10] unfurnished gelding: fourth foal: dam unraced **F82 ?**
half-sister to smart staying chasers Calling Brave and Ottowa: runner-up twice from 4
starts in maiden Irish points in 2003: sold 15,000 gns Doncaster May Sales: eighth of 12
in bumper at Sandown: 100/1, seemingly easily best effort over hurdles when fifth in
novice at Market Rasen, close up to 3 out and possibly flattered. *J. G. Portman*

SAVANNAH MO (IRE) 9 ch.m. Husyan (USA) – Sweet Start (Candy Cane) [2003/4 **c–**
h79: c20g⁴ c21sᵖᵘ c22s^F c25v^F 27s⁶ 22g 24s Apr 21] leggy, lengthy mare: showed no apt- **h72**
itude for chasing: poor handicap hurdler: stays 3m: acts on heavy going. *J. N. R. Billinge*

SAWAH 4 gr.g. Linamix (FR) – Tarhhib (Danzig (USA)) [2003/4 F12g Nov 12] fourth **F–**
foal: dam, 7f winner, half-sister to high-class middle-distance performer Dancehall: sold
unraced out of J. Gosden's stable 9,000 gns Newmarket July Sales: well held in 3-y-o
bumper on debut: poor form on Flat subsequently. *D. Shaw*

SAXON KINGDOM 5 b.g. Petoski – Saxon Magic (Faustus (USA)) [2003/4 F16m **F–**
F17d Dec 17] first live foal: dam, winning hurdler, stayed 2½m: tailed off in 2 bumpers.
M. Bradstock

SAXON MILL 9 ch.g. Saxon Farm – Djellaba (Decoy Boy) [2003/4 h95§: 22dᵖᵘ 24d **h– §**
Mar 7] workmanlike gelding: modest hurdler in 2002/3, well held on completed start in
2003/4: stays 2½m: acts on heavy going: inconsistent. *Mrs P. Bickerton*

SAXON MIST 5 b.g. Slip Anchor – Ruby Venture (Ballad Rock) [2003/4 F16g⁶ Feb **F92**
28] 27,000 4-y-o: strong, close-coupled gelding: third foal: closely related to 1999 2-y-o
7f seller winner Rubys Reply (by Deploy): dam maiden who stayed 1¼m: sixth to Lord
Gale in bumper at Haydock on debut. *A. King*

SAXON VICTORY (USA) 9 b.g. Nicholas (USA) – Saxon Shore (USA) (Halo **c90 §**
(USA)) [2003/4 c24m⁵ c24sᵖᵘ Feb 12] workmanlike gelding: winning pointer: maiden **h– §**
steeplechaser: fifth in hunter at Huntingdon in May: stays 3m: acts on any going: tried
visored/blinkered: has had tongue tied: not a fluent jumper over fences: ungenuine. *Tim
Tarratt*

SAY AGAIN (IRE) 8 gr.g. Celio Rufo – Tricias Pet (Mandalus) [2003/4 c122, **c135 +**
h131: c16s^F c17s² c16f* c16g³ c17d³ Apr 11] **h–**
    The race now known as the Swordlestown Cup, the Grade 1 two-mile
novice chase at the Punchestown Festival, has a distinguished list of winners including Viking Flagship, Strong Platinum, Ventana Canyon, Direct Route, Tiutchev
and Moscow Flyer (Viking Flagship and Strong Platinum also won a valuable
handicap at the meeting in the days when the novice chase had only Grade 3 status).
The latest edition seemed to present odds-on Kicking King, the Arkle Trophy
runner-up, with a fairly straightforward opportunity. Approaching the second last,
however, 6/1-shot Say Again was moving best of the three still in contention and,
when narrow leader Colca Canyon fell and brought down Kicking King, Say Again
was left clear. Say Again had to survive a blunder of his own at the last before
coming home eleven lengths in front of Commonchero. Kicking King was running
as if feeling the effects of his campaign and wouldn't have run to within a stone of
his best form had he stood up. A useful hurdler, Say Again had won only one race
over fences before Punchestown, a beginners chase at Tralee at the end of August.
The Swordlestown Cup wasn't his first tilt at a Grade 1, however, as he had finished
fourth—beaten over twenty lengths—to Le Coudray in the Denny Gold Medal
Novices' Chase at Leopardstown in the 2002/3 season when he had mixed handicap
hurdling—his wins including the Galway Hurdle—and novice chasing. His best
effort over fences before Punchestown was third to Fadoudal du Cochet and Colca

809

Mr Sean Duggan's "Say Again"

Canyon in a good quality handicap at Fairyhouse in April, returning from a six-month absence.

The good-topped Say Again is by the now-deceased Gran Premio d'Italia and St Leger Italiano winner Celio Rufo out of the maiden hurdler Tricias Pet (also the dam of a winning pointer by Gallic Heir), who herself is out of a half-sister to the dam of the smart two-mile chaser Long Engagement. Say Again, who is sometimes let down by his jumping over fences, is best at around two miles. He acts on any going. *Paul Nolan, Ireland*

SAYEH (IRE) 12 b.g. Fools Holme (USA) – Piffle (Shirley Heights) [2003/4 17m⁵ 16f³ 21gᵖᵘ Nov 9] lengthy, sparely-made gelding: maiden chaser: fairly useful handicap hurdler for P. Bowen in 2001/2, long way below best on return: pulled up amiss between last 2 in handicap at Southwell: stays 2½m: acts on firm and soft going: has been reluctant to race. *Mrs D. Thomas*   c– h88

SAYOUN (IRE) 5 gr.g. Primo Dominie – Sarafia (Dalsaan) [2003/4 F16d F16d 16gᵖᵘ Apr 5] IR £5,000 2-y-o: fifth foal: half-brother to smart 7f/1m winner Saratan (by Tirol): dam, 7f winner, half-sister to smart French 7f/1m winner Safita, herself dam of smart miler Safawan: no sign of ability in bumpers and novice hurdle. *Mrs L. B. Normile*   h– F–

S B S BY JOVE 11 ch.g. Jupiter Island – Mill Shine (Milan) [2003/4 c23mᵖᵘ Apr 13] fairly useful pointer at best: pulled up in novice hunter chase. *Miss L. Blackford*   c–

SCALLOWAY (IRE) 4 b.g. Marju (IRE) – Zany (Junius (USA)) [2003/4 16m⁴ Aug 9] fair on Flat (stays 1¼m) for J. Osborne: pulled hard when fourth in juvenile at Stratford on hurdling debut. *D. J. Wintle*   h85

SCALLYBUCK (IRE)   12 br.g. Scallywag – Miss McNight (Master Buck) [2003/4 **c–** c96, h86: c17g⁵ c26m⁵ Jun 18] workmanlike gelding: winning chaser: showed little in 2 **h–** points in 2004: stays 25f: acts on any going: tried blinkered. *R. H. Buckler*

SCALLYWACE   10 br.g. Wace (USA) – Scally Jenks (Scallywag) [2003/4 c24d⁴ **c–** c23m⁵ c24sᶠ c23g c19dᵖᵘ c26gᵖᵘ Mar 10] workmanlike gelding: winning pointer: little sign of ability in steeplechases, breaking down final start. *T. R. Wall*

SCALLYWAGS RETURN   5 b.m. Bob's Return (IRE) – Bee-A-Scally (Scallywag) **F–** [2003/4 F16d Apr 23] first foal: dam pulled up both starts in points: failed to settle and always behind in bumper on debut. *Miss Lucinda V. Russell*

SCAMP   5 b.m. Selkirk (USA) – Cut And Run (Slip Anchor) [2003/4 F90: F16m² F17d **F90** Apr 3] leggy mare: fair bumper winner: sold out of H. Daly's stable 20,000 gns Doncaster May Sales after reappearance, ran no sort of race over 10 months later: free-going sort. *S. Gollings*

SCARAMOUCHE   4 b.c. Busy Flight – Laura Lye (IRE) (Carlingford Castle) [2003/4 **F92** F13v* F12d⁶ Jan 1] has scope: first foal: dam, untrustworthy 17f hurdle winner, out of half-sister to high-class hurdler up to 2½m Corporal Clinger: won 3-y-o bumper at Towcester on debut, beating Layasar by neck: failed to improve under less testing conditions when sixth to Secret Ploy in 4-y-o event at Cheltenham. *B. De Haan*

SCARBOROUGH FAIR (IRE)   7 b.g. Synefos (USA) – Hue 'n' Cry (IRE) (Denel **c105** (FR) [2003/4 h98: c25gᵖᵘ c25d* c25gᵖᵘ c25sᶠ Jan 6] rangy gelding: placed once from 4 **h–** starts over fences: form over fences only when winning novice handicap at Hexham in December on first outing after leaving J. O'Neill: will prove best at 3m+: raced on good going or softer: sold 3,500 gns Doncaster May Sales. *R. C. Guest*

SCARFACE   7 ch.g. Hernando (FR) – Scarlatine (IRE) (Alzao (USA)) [2003/4 h78: **h80** 20d² 22g³ 21g³ 20g⁵ Sep 13] poor maiden hurdler: stays 2¾m: races on good going or softer over hurdles: lame final start: races prominently. *A. G. Hobbs*

SCARLET DAWN (IRE)   6 b.m. Supreme Leader – Dawn Appeal (Deep Run) **F69 ?** [2003/4 F16m⁶ Sep 14] 7,500 4-y-o: third foal: half-sister to winning pointer by Montelimar: dam bumper winner: sixth in slowly-run bumper at Worcester on debut. *D. A. Rees*

SCARLET FANTASY   4 b.g. Rudimentary (USA) – Katie Scarlett (Lochnager) **h94** [2003/4 16gᵖᵘ 16mᵖᵘ 16gᵖᵘ 16s* 16v⁴ 16s⁵ 17g 16s* Apr 11] half-brother to bumper winner Coleham and 2m hurdle winner Tara Hall (both by Saddlers' Hall): modest maiden on Flat (should stay beyond 6f) for E. Wheeler: modest juvenile hurdler: won claimer at Chepstow in January and handicap at Towcester in April: will prove best around 2m: acts on heavy ground: pulled very hard/saddle slipped on hurdling debut, bled from nose third start. *P. A. Pritchard*

SCARLETTI (GER)   7 ch.g. Master Willie – Solidago (USA) (Decies) [2003/4 h110: **h110** 16g⁴ 17mᵖᵘ Jul 19] stocky gelding: fair hurdler: creditable fourth on first of 2 starts when blinkered in handicaps in 2003/4, thrice-raced on Flat for I. Semple subsequently: will prove best in strongly-run races around 2m: has won on soft going, best efforts on good/ good to firm: effective tongue tied or not: tends to pull hard/find little. *Jonjo O'Neill*

SCARTHY LAD (IRE)   6 ch.g. Magical Wonder (USA) – Grangeclare Rose (IRE) **h138** (Jaazeiro (USA)) [2003/4 h118p: 16d⁵ 20d³ 20s⁴ 16d³ Apr 12] tall, close-coupled gelding: useful hurdler: ran well despite failing to win in 2003/4, very good fifth of 9 to Hardy Eustace in Grade 1 at Punchestown in late-April: in frame earlier behind Solerina in Grade 1 at Fairyhouse and Grade 3 at Navan, and Dawn Invasion in minor event at Fairyhouse: stays 2½m, at least as effective at 2m: raced on good going or softer (acts on soft). *T. G. O'Leary, Ireland*

SCENIC LADY (IRE)   8 b.m. Scenic – Tu Tu Maori (IRE) (Kings Lake (USA)) **h77** [2003/4 17m⁴ Aug 3] fair on Flat up to 1½m: fourth in novice at Market Rasen on hurdling debut. *L. A. Dace*

SCENTED AIR   7 b.m. Lion Cavern (USA) – Jungle Rose (Shirley Heights) [2003/4 **h101** h93+: 16f* 17d⁵ May 17] lengthy, rather sparely-made mare: fair hurdler: won maiden handicap at Warwick in May: needs sharp 2m: has form on good to soft going, best efforts on good or firmer (acts on firm): not a fluent jumper. *J. D. Czerpak*

SCHOODIC POINT (IRE)   9 ch.g. Roselier (FR) – Madam Beau (Le Tricolore) **h83** [2003/4 21m³ 26gᵘʳ 24m² Aug 3] best effort over hurdles when second in novice at Market Rasen: saddle slipped previous outing: stays 3m: headstrong, and has looked thoroughly ungenuine in points. *Mrs S. J. Smith*

SCHOOLHOUSE WALK 6 b.g. Mistertopogigo (IRE) – Restandbejoyful (Taka-
chiho) [2003/4 F75: 21mᵖᵘ 24f⁵ 20f³ 19s* Apr 11] winning pointer, placed all 3 starts in
2004: best effort over hurdles (struck into on debut) when winning maiden at Towcester:
stays 19f. *M. E. Sowersby*   **h93 ?**

SCHUH SHINE (IRE) 7 gr.g. Roselier (FR) – Naar Chamali (Salmon Leap (USA))
[2003/4 23dᶠ 20sᵖᵘ 20v² 20d⁴ 24s² Apr 4] 12,500 4-y-o, resold IR £34,000 4-y-o: robust
gelding: type to make a chaser: fourth foal: brother to 2m hurdle winner/winning Irish
pointer True Rose: dam, lightly-raced maiden, half-sister to dam of useful hurdler up to
3m Out Ranking: best effort over hurdles when second to No Picnic in novice at Hexham
final start: will stay beyond 3m: sold 31,000 gns Doncaster May Sales. *L. Lungo*   **h103**

SCHWARTZHALLE (IRE) 7 ch.g. Magical Wonder (USA) – Liams Flash (IRE)
(Callernish) [2003/4 c128, h97: c20f² c24dᵖᵘ c20sᵖᵘ c17dᶠ Apr 11] workmanlike gelding:
winning hurdler: fairly useful chaser: creditable second of 3 to Splendour in Grade 3 at
Down Royal on reappearance: no show after: effective at 2m, probably stays 3m: acts on
any going. *D. Harvey, Ireland*   **c125**
h–

SCIPPIT 5 ch.g. Unfuwain (USA) – Scierpan (USA) (Sharpen Up) [2003/4 17g 17g⁴
16g³ 17g 16m³ 17m⁵ 16g⁴ 17g⁴ 16g⁵ 16f³ 16g⁵ 16m⁴ 16f² 16f² 16m³ 16g³ 16d⁴ 16d⁶ 16s
Dec 13] small, compact gelding: poor maiden hurdler: will prove best at 2m: acts on firm
going: has had tongue tied: races prominently: has finished weakly. *N. Waggott*   **h83**

SCOLT HEAD 5 b.g. Bal Harbour – Curlew Calling (IRE) (Pennine Walk) [2003/4
F16m² F17m F16s F16v Jan 17] sturdy gelding: third foal: half-brother to 2½m hurdle
winner Trevaisci (by Dilum): dam once-raced half-sister to smart stayer Dusky Warbler
and Dee Stakes winner Merry Merlin: form in bumpers only when second in weak event
at Hexham on debut: takes good hold. *M. W. Easterby*   **F82**

SCOOP THIRTY NINE 6 b.m. Petoski – Welsh Clover (Cruise Missile) [2003/4
h65: 17s³ 19g³ Mar 10] leggy mare: poor hurdler: will stay 2½m: acts on soft going.
Mrs E. Slack   **h81**

SCORNED (GER) 9 b.g. Selkirk (USA) – Spurned (USA) (Robellino (USA)) [2003/4
16v⁶ 16g² 16s* 17d Mar 18] tall, useful-looking gelding: fairly useful hurdler: very
lightly raced prior to 2003/4: improved effort when winning 23-runner Sunderlands
Imperial Cup Handicap at Sandown in March, always close up and rallying well to beat
Bold Bishop 4 lengths: 20 lb out of weights, well held in similar event at Cheltenham 5
days later (reportedly pulled a hamstring): will stay beyond 2m: raced on good going or
softer. *A. M. Balding*   **h126**

Sunderlands Imperial Cup Handicap Hurdle, Sandown—
Scorned (left) and Bold Bishop have the race between them over the last

Jobs TV 683 Handicap Chase, Kempton—
Scots Grey gets the better of Hand Inn Hand in a thrilling finish

SCOTCH CORNER (IRE) 6 b.g. Jurado (USA) – Quennie Mo Ghra (IRE) (Mandalus) [2003/4 F16g* 20d^{pu} 26s^{pu} Dec 26] €1,100 4-y-o: first foal: dam, placed in bumper, half-sister to fairly useful jumpers Badger's Wood, stays 3m, and Khan Kicker, stays 21f: ran 3 times in Irish points in 2003, winning maiden on completed start: favourite, won bumper at Wetherby in November: dropped away tamely in novice hurdles at Chepstow (reportedly lost action) and Huntingdon: should be suited by 2½m+. *N. A. Twiston-Davies*   **h–**
   F92

SCOTISH LAW (IRE) 6 ch.g. Case Law – Scotia Rose (Tap On Wood) [2003/4 h87: 19m³ 19m³ 19g² Jul 26] workmanlike gelding: modest on Flat (stays 1¼m): stays easy 21f: acts on good to firm going: visored: has pulled hard and unseated/bolted before start. *P. R. Chamings*   **h97**

SCOTMAIL BOY (IRE) 11 b.g. Over The River (FR) – Princess Paula (Smoggy) [2003/4 c96, h–: c24m⁴ c21d² c24d* c20d* c21g³ c29m^{pu} Apr 24] lengthy gelding: fairly useful handicap chaser: won at Sandown in December and Carlisle in February: third in race for second time when placed behind Cassia Heights in Topham Chase at Aintree in April: lame later in month: stays 27f: acts on good to firm and heavy going: tried blinkered/in cheekpieces: sound jumper. *J. Howard Johnson*   **c115**
   h–

SCOTMAIL LAD (IRE) 10 b.g. Ilium – Nicholas Ferry (Floriferous) [2003/4 c110, h–: c20g⁴ c16d* c17g² c20d⁶ c20s⁵ c16s⁵ c16s⁵ c21g Apr 12] leggy, workmanlike gelding: fairly useful handicap chaser: won at Sedgefield in November: creditable second at Market Rasen next time, well below form after (appeared to lose interest sixth start): effective at 2m to 3m: raced on good going or softer (acts on heavy): effective blinkered/visored or not: sold 8,500 gns Doncaster May Sales. *G. M. Moore*   **c115 d**
   h–

SCOTMAIL PARK 5 b.g. Presidium – Miss Tri Colour (Shavian) [2003/4 h–: 17d^F Nov 11] no form over hurdles: dead. *G. M. Moore*   **h–**

SCOTS GREY 9 gr.g. Terimon – Misowni (Niniski (USA)) [2003/4 c138, h–: c20g* c21g^F Apr 2] sturdy gelding: useful chaser: better than ever when winning handicap at Kempton in December by short head from Hand Inn Hand, pair well clear: close up and going well when fell heavily twelfth (Canal Turn) in Topham Chase at Aintree: may prove best up to 2½m: acts on any going: races prominently: usually sound jumper. *N. J. Henderson*   **c142**
   h–

SCOTTIE YORK 8 b.g. Noble Patriarch – Devon Dancer (Shareef Dancer (USA)) [2003/4 h–: 24g^{pu} Jan 7] tall gelding: well held all starts over hurdles, off 19 months before only one in 2003/4. *A. R. Dicken*   **h–**

SCOTTISH DANCE 7 ch.m. Bustino – Highland Lyric (Rymer) [2003/4 h93: 19s^{pu} Dec 20] angular mare: winning hurdler for N. Henderson, showed nothing only outing in 2003/4: better around 2½m than shorter: tried tongue tied. *Mrs D. A. Hamer*   **h–**

SCOTTISH MEMORIES (IRE)   8 ch.g. Houmayoun (FR) – Interj (Salmon Leap **h–**
(USA)) [2003/4 h145: 16d Nov 16] good-topped gelding: smart hurdler: won fairly
valuable event on Flat prior to well below-par seventh of 9 in Grade 2 at Punchestown
(reportedly coughed) only start in 2003/4: will prove best around 2m: acts on heavy
going: has had tongue tied. *N. Meade, Ireland*

SCOTTISH ROOTS   9 b.g. Roscoe Blake – Lothian Queen (Scorpio (FR)) [2003/4 **c83**
c–, h–: c21s³ c25sᵖᵘ Mar 7] angular gelding: no form in novice hurdles (tried blinkered): **h–**
winning pointer, including in April: better effort in novice hunters earlier when third at
Sedgefield: should stay 3m. *David M. Easterby*

SCOTTISH SONG   11 b.g. Niniski (USA) – Miss Saint-Cloud (Nonoalco (USA)) **h77**
[2003/4 h80: 20m⁴ 21m 24gᵖᵘ Jun 11] quite good-topped gelding: bumper winner: poor
maiden hurdler: should have stayed beyond 2½m: acted on firm and good to soft going:
dead. *Mrs M. Reveley*

SCOUNDREL   13 gr.g. Scallywag – Nicholcone (Celtic Cone) [2003/4 c26dᵖᵘ c20dᵖᵘ **c–**
c24sᵖᵘ Apr 17] sturdy gelding: winning hurdler: no longer of any account. *F. L. Matthews* **h–**

SCOWLIN BRIG   8 ch.g. Minster Son – Gideonscleuch (Beverley Boy) [2003/4 c61, **c–**
h–: c25dᵖᵘ c20m⁴ c24gᵖᵘ Jul 3] compact gelding: poor maiden chaser: tried blinkered. **h–**
F. P. Murtagh

SCRAMBLE (USA)   6 ch.g. Gulch (USA) – Syzygy (ARG) (Big Play (USA)) [2003/4 **h–**
17gᵖᵘ Sep 30] modest on Flat (stays 1¼m): tongue tied, little show in 2 starts over hurdles.
B. Ellison

SCRATCH THE DOVE   7 ch.m. Henbit (USA) – Coney Dove (Celtic Cone) [2003/4 **h97**
h91: 22d 19s² 17s² 16g 21m Apr 15] sturdy mare: modest handicap hurdler: stays 21f:
acts on soft and good to firm going. *C. J. Price*

SCRUMPY   5 b.g. Sir Harry Lewis (USA) – Superfina (USA) (Fluorescent Light **h–**
(USA)) [2003/4 F–: F16s 17s 19g⁶ 21d Apr 12] lengthy gelding: no sign of ability: tried **F–**
tongue tied. *S. E. H. Sherwood*

SCULPTOR   5 b.g. Salse (USA) – Classic Colleen (IRE) (Sadler's Wells (USA)) **h94 +**
[2003/4 h78: 16m² May 9] good-topped gelding: fair on Flat (should stay 1½m): much
better effort over hurdles when 1¼ lengths second to Goldbrook in novice at Wincanton:
likely to stay beyond 2m. *C. J. Mann*

SCURRY DANCER (FR)   8 b.g. Snurge – Fijar Dance (FR) (In Fijar (USA)) [2003/4 **c–**
c16dᵖᵘ c20g c20dᶠ c17g⁴ Apr 12] lengthy gelding: won novice hurdle in 2001/2 when **h–**
also third in novice on chasing debut: no form over fences on return: wore cheekpieces
third start: sold 2,100 gns Doncaster May Sales. *O. Sherwood*

SEABROOK LAD   13 b.g. Derrylin – Moll (Rugantino) [2003/4 c91x, h–: c26dᵖᵘ **c– x**
Mar 14] good-topped gelding: veteran hunter chaser: third on reappearance in points in **h–**
2004, showed little subsequently: stays 3m: acts on soft and good to firm going: tried in
cheekpieces: sketchy jumper. *Mrs F. Kehoe*

SEA COVE   4 b.f. Terimon – Regal Pursuit (IRE) (Roi Danzig (USA)) [2003/4 16m⁴ **h80**
16m⁵ 16s 17s Feb 10] first foal: dam winning 17f hurdler: best effort over hurdles when
fourth in juvenile at Haydock in November: first form on Flat when fourth over 1½m in
April. *J. M. Jefferson*

SEA DRIFTING   7 b.g. Slip Anchor – Theme (IRE) (Sadler's Wells (USA)) [2003/4 **c–**
c127, h–: 20m⁶ 24d⁶ c26g Dec 31] good-topped gelding: fairly useful hurdler/chaser at **h–**
best: no form in 2003/4: stays 3m: acts on firm and soft going, seemingly not on heavy:
tried in cheekpieces: joined Miss M. Rowland. *K. A. Morgan*

SEA FALCON (IRE)   5 ch.m. Synefos (USA) – Kasterlee (FR) (Stay For Lunch **F–**
(USA)) [2003/4 F16g F16g Feb 20] first foal: dam won twice over 1½m on Flat in France:
badly hampered start and always behind in mares bumper on debut. *M. J. Ryan*

SEAFORDE (IRE)   4 ch.g. Titus Livius (FR) – Rosy Affair (IRE) (Red Sunset) [2003/4 **h112**
16d⁵ 16d⁴ 16d* 16d* 16s⁶ 17g Mar 18] leggy gelding: half-brother to one-time useful
hurdler performer (by Mujadil), probably stays 2½m: fairly useful on Flat (stays 11f):
fairly useful juvenile hurdler: won at Clonmel in December and Thurles in January, beating Nopekan by head at latter course: raced around 2m on good going or softer: makes
running. *M. F. Morris, Ireland*

SEA GRASS (IRE)   6 b.g. Jolly Jake (NZ) – Furry Dream (Furry Glen) [2003/4 F16d **F–**
Mar 21] IR £5,000 3-y-o: sixth foal: dam placed once over hurdles: won maiden Irish
point in 2003: favourite, well held in bumper at Stratford. *N. A. Twiston-Davies*

SEA HAITCH EM 9 ch.g. Norton Challenger – One Way Circuit (Windjammer **c87**
(USA)) [2003/4 c87, h–: c21f* c24g^{pu} c20d^{pu} c24g^{pu} Apr 1] workmanlike gelding: won **h–**
both starts in points in 2003 and novice hunter at Folkestone (despite mistakes) in May:
no form after 9½-month absence: stays easy 21f: acts on firm and good to soft going.
V. J. Hughes

SEAHORSE GIRL 7 b,m Sea Raven (IRE) – Kakapo (Oats) [2003/4 F16m F16v **h–**
19s^6 Apr 11] 2,500 5-y-o: seventh foal: half-sister to winning 3m hurdler Maori Wisdom **F–**
(by Be My Native): dam unraced half-sister to quite useful staying hurdler Mynah Key:
well held in bumpers and maiden hurdle: pulled hard second start. *R. J. Smith*

SEA KNIGHT (IRE) 7 b.g. Beau Sher – Meaney (Delamain (USA)) [2003/4 20g^5 **h81**
24d^2 24d^6 20s 24d^3 Mar 11] lengthy gelding: poor maiden hurdler: stays 3m: raced on
good going or softer. *J. I. A. Charlton*

SEA LAUGHTER (IRE) 6 gr.m. Presenting – Bruna Rosa (Roselier (FR)) [2003/4 **F86**
F16m F16s^2 F17v^4 Mar 21] 3,000 4-y-o: big mare: fourth foal: dam maiden half-sister to
useful 2m hurdler Another Row: best effort in bumpers when second to Fairy Skin Maker
at Ayr in November: will stay beyond 2m. *J. N. R. Billinge*

SEA MAIZE 6 b.m. Sea Raven (IRE) – Dragons Daughter (Mandrake Major) [2003/4 **h65**
F–: F16d^6 21v 22d 24d^6 22g^5 22g^5 Apr 24] lengthy mare: signs of only a little ability in **F–**
bumpers and over hurdles: wore cheekpieces last 2 starts. *C. R. Wilson*

SEAN AT THE IVY (FR) 5 b.g. Nikos – Matelica (FR) (R B Chesne) [2003/4 F–: **h–**
F18m^4 16f^3 Oct 26] favourite but no show in 2 bumpers, reportedly showing action on **F–**
debut: tailed-off last of 3 in novice on hurdling debut, pulling very hard and jumping
erratically (had breathing problem): tongue tied on reappearance. *P. F. Nicholls*

SEANIETHESMUGGLER (IRE) 6 b.g. Balla Cove – Sharp Shauna (Sayyaf) **F92**
[2003/4 F16g^2 F16s F16d Jan 22] sixth foal: dam, maiden, stayed 7f: thrice-raced in Irish
points, winning completed start in 2003: best effort in bumpers when second at Warwick
in December. *S. Gollings*

SEAN'S MINSTREL (IRE) 11 gr.g. Black Minstrel – Gala Star (Gail Star) [2003/4 **c–**
c–: c27d^{ur} Mar 16] winning pointer: well beaten only completed outing in steeplechases.
Miss Tina Hammond

SEA OTTER (IRE) 7 b.g. King's Ride – Knockarctic (Quayside) [2003/4 F16d May **F–**
3] IR 42,000 3-y-o: half-brother to several winners, notably useful hurdler/very smart
staying chaser Ad Hoc (by Strong Gale): dam, winning Irish hurdler/novice chaser, out of
sister to top-class 2m chaser Buck House: tailed off in bumper on debut: sold 3,000 gns
Doncaster May Sales. *L. Lungo*

SEARCH AND DESTROY (USA) 6 b. or br.g. Sky Classic (CAN) – Hunt The **c118**
Thimble (USA) (Turn And Count (USA)) [2003/4 h102: c16m* c16m^2 c16m* c20m* **h103**
21m^2 c24f^6 c20f^3 c24g^3 c22g^3 Nov 16] useful-looking gelding: fair hurdler/fairly useful chaser: successful over fences in novice at Newcastle and handicaps at Wincanton
(novice) and Perth early in season: stays easy 2¾m: acts on good to firm and good to soft
going, possibly unsuited by soft: blinkered last 3 starts. *T. R. George*

SEASON EXPRESS 9 ch.g. Vital Season – Coach Rd Express (Pony Express) [2003/4 **c–**
h–: c23m^{pu} May 14] signs of only a little ability over hurdles: probably amiss on steeple- **h–**
chase debut. *C. L. Tizzard*

SEASQUILL (AUS) 9 bl.g. Squill (USA) – Sea Surge (AUS) (Rolle) [2003/4 h80: **c94**
c16f^2 c16m^2 c16m^4 c20f^3 c20m^4 c24g^F Jan 7] poor hurdler: modest form first 2 starts over **h–**
fences: best around 2m: acts on firm going: tends to find little. *Ferdy Murphy*

SEA SWALLOW 5 b.m. Sea Raven (IRE) – Denby Wood (Lord Bud) [2003/4 F16f **F–**
Sep 14] fourth foal: dam unraced, out of half-sister to very smart middle-distance colt
Town And Country: showed nothing in bumper or 1¼m maiden on Flat. *J. S. Wainwright*

SEA TERN 4 b.f. Emarati (USA) – Great Tern (Simply Great (FR)) [2003/4 16m^{pu} **h–**
Aug 9] no sign of ability on Flat or on hurdling debut. *N. M. Babbage*

SEATTLE ART (USA) 10 b.g. Seattle Slew (USA) – Artiste (Artaius (USA)) [2003/4 **c– §**
c83§, h–: 16g c24m^{pu} c20d^{pu} 16d^{pu} c22s c19s^{pu} Feb 22] strong gelding: maiden hurdler/ **h–**
winning chaser, no form in 2003/4: tried blinkered (raced too freely): ungenuine.
Dr P. Pritchard

SEATTLE EXPRESS 4 b.g. Salse (USA) – Seattle Ribbon (USA) (Seattle Dancer **h–**
(USA)) [2003/4 17g Aug 23] fair on Flat (stays 1¼m), claimed from D. Elsworth £10,000

after winning in August: looked reluctant when well held in juvenile at Cartmel on hurdling debut: sold 3,200 gns Newmarket Autumn Sales. *E. A. Elliott*

SEA URCHIN   11 b.g. Scallywag – Sailor's Shanty (Dubassoff (USA)) [2003/4 c–§:   **c73 §** c19m c26m³ c20m^pu c23m^pu Sep 14] modest pointer: little impact in steeplechases, left Mrs H. Wiegersma after second start. *C. J. Gray*

SECAM (POL)   5 gr.g. Alywar (USA) – Scytia (POL) (Euro Star) [2003/4 15g* 17g^pu   **h–** 19g⁵ 18g⁶ 16d Mar 21] successful 3 times over 1m on Flat and once over hurdles in Poland for G. Wroblewski: poor form on second of 2 starts on Flat in Britain: blinkered, soundly beaten in novice hurdle (pulled hard) in between. *Mrs P. Townsley*

SECOND AFFAIR (IRE)   7 b.m. Pursuit of Love – Startino (Bustino) [2003/4 16v^pu   **h–** 16f⁶ Feb 29] half-sister to poor chaser Advance East (by Polish Precedent) and fairly useful hunter Stoney Valley (by Caerleon), both of whom stayed 21f: fairly useful on Flat (stays 1½m) at 3/4 yrs for J. O'Keeffe: hinted at retaining a little ability both starts over hurdles. *Miss S. E. Hall*

SECOND PAIGE (IRE)   7 b.g. Nicolotte – My First Paige (IRE) (Runnett) [2003/4   **h108** 20v⁴ 20m³ 17m* 17g* 19m* 16g* 16f⁶ Oct 29] modest on Flat (stays 2m): fair hurdler: won novices at Cartmel (handicap), Sedgefield, Hereford and Perth (beat Breknen Le Noir 5 lengths) between July and September: stays 2½m: acts on heavy and good to firm going. *N. A. Graham*

SECOND PICK (IRE)   8 b.g. Doubletour (USA) – Wurli (Wolver Hollow) [2003/4   **c– §** c–§, h–§: c21g^pu c16m⁵ 16m Aug 8] smallish gelding: no form outside points: tempera-   **h– §** mental. *C. J. Gray*

SECRET CONQUEST   7 b.m. Secret Appeal – Mohibbah (USA) (Conquistador   **h–** Cielo (USA)) [2003/4 h76: 17g^pu 17m Oct 11] poor on Flat (barely stays 1m) in 2003: form over hurdles only on debut: has had tongue tied. *A. Crook*

SECRET DRINKER (IRE)   8 b.g. Husyan (USA) – Try Le Reste (IRE) (Le Moss)   **c82** [2003/4 c82, h–: c25s^ur c26d² c29s³ Jan 4] useful-looking gelding: winning hurdler: poor   **h–** novice chaser: stays 29f: raced on good going or softer (acts on soft): wears cheekpieces: has looked none too keen. *O. Sherwood*

SECRET NATIVE (IRE)   9 b.g. Be My Native (USA) – Rivers Secret (Young Man   **c109** (FR)) [2003/4 c16d* c24d⁴ c19d 23s^pu Feb 14] rangy, useful-looking gelding: fairly   **h–** useful handicap hurdler in 2001/2: fair chaser: won handicap at Gowran in November on return from 14-month absence: better form despite jumping none too fluently when fourth of 28 to World Wide Web in very valuable handicap at Leopardstown: poor efforts last 2 starts: effective at 2m to 3m: acts on good to firm and heavy going: effective tongue tied or not: hasn't always looked an easy ride. *T. J. Taaffe, Ireland*

SECRET ORDER   5 ch.m. Chocolat de Meguro (USA) – Kilkenny Gorge (Deep   **h–** Run) [2003/4 16s 20d^pu 21d⁶ Mar 16] lengthy mare: fifth foal: half-sister to winning 2¾m hurdler Corbie Lynn (by Jumbo Hirt): dam poor pointer: no show in 3 novice hurdles, trained by M. Barnes on debut. *W. S. Coltherd*

SECRET PLOY   4 b.g. Deploy – By Line (High Line) [2003/4 F12g* F12d*   **F122** F16g* Feb 14]

The series of so-called junior bumpers, which eventually comprised eight races between November 12th and January 1st (two others scheduled had to be abandoned), was as well subscribed as it had been when introduced in 2002/3, even though the first seven races were restricted to three-year-olds, and the final one to four-year-olds. The fact that the races are staged over distances between twelve and fourteen furlongs lends itself to attracting Flat-bred types, and very few of the runners who contested them look to have a long-term future over jumps. Of the eighty-eight horses who appeared in at least one of the races, only six achieved a Timeform bumper rating of 100 or higher and, among those few, only Locksmith and Secret Ploy went on to significantly better things later in the season. The former showed himself to be a useful novice hurdler, while Secret Ploy, who won the first and last races in the junior bumper series, put up the best performance of the season in a bumper when tried in open company.

Quite an attractive gelding, Secret Ploy impressed as having a bit more about him physically than most of his twenty-two opponents before his debut at Newbury, where he travelled well for a long way and drew clear with Into The Shadows before asserting close home to win by a length and a quarter, with Baby

Run eight lengths back in third. Into The Shadows and Baby Run reopposed Secret Ploy in another mile-and-a-half event at Cheltenham on New Year's Day, the shortest race ever staged on an official card there, and effectively the final of the series. Sent off favourite, Secret Ploy confirmed the placings, waited with, making his effort into the straight and getting the better of Baby Run by half a length, with Historic Place four lengths back in third, Locksmith and Into The Shadows the next to finish. The Grade 2 open bumper on Newbury's Tote Gold Trophy Card the following month provided a much sterner test for Secret Ploy, featuring seven other previous winners among the twenty-four runners, as well as a couple who had come second in good races on their debut. In a race run at a stronger pace and over a four-furlong longer trip than his first two, Secret Ploy eventually won impressively, though, after failing to settle early and losing his place a bit turning in, it took him most of the straight to get on top. Secret Ploy came with a run on the outside to lead a furlong out and ran on strongly to win by four lengths from Mount Clerigo, who held on to second by a short head from the staying-on Demarco, with the remainder well strung out. Secret Ploy received 10 lb from Mount Clerigo, and the pair put up performances which would have been good enough to give the mare Total Enjoyment, receiving 7 lb, a run for her money in the Champion Bumper. As it was, neither Secret Ploy nor Mount Clerigo went on to Cheltenham, both trainers reportedly fearing that race could have a detrimental effect on a young horse.

		Shirley Heights (b 1975)	Mill Reef
	Deploy (b 1987)		Hardiemma
Secret Ploy		Slightly Dangerous (b 1979)	Roberto
(b.g. 2000)			Where You Lead
		High Line (ch 1966)	High Hat
	By Line (b 1984)		Time Call
		Mount Hala (b 1977)	Mount Haga
			Nantahala

Secret Ploy might not have contested the Champion Bumper at Cheltenham in the latest season, but his year-older half-brother The Thunderer (by Terimon) did, cutting little ice in finishing only twentieth. The Thunderer had earlier shown fairly useful form when winning a bumper at Ascot a week after Secret Ploy's Newbury success. Secret Ploy's dam By Line has produced another couple of foals who have passed the post first, the fair six-furlong winner Press Ahead (by Precocious) and the poor jumper Hi Lily (by Jupiter Island), who was disqualified on technical grounds after landing a two-and-a-half-mile conditional jockeys handicap chase at Southwell in 2002/3. By Line was a headstrong sort who failed to win from a handful of attempts on the Flat, but she was a fair hurdler at up to nineteen furlongs. She has an unraced three-year-old by Silver Patriarch named Hiho Silver Lining. Secret Ploy's grandam Mount Hala was a half-sister to the 1977 Irish Oaks winner Olwyn, and shaped as if she would have stayed middle distances herself when gaining her only success in a nine-furlong minor event on soft ground at Hamilton. While it wouldn't be a surprise to see him campaigned over middle distances or further on the Flat, Secret Ploy, who took the eye before his last two outings, is reportedly set to embark on a hurdling campaign in 2004/5, and obviously has the ability to do very well, assuming he jumps proficiently. He has raced on good and good to soft going. *H. Morrison*

SECRET RACINE   5 b.m. Secret Appeal – Miss Racine (Dom Racine (FR)) [2003/4 F16f Sep 14] half-sister to winning hurdler Master Ofthe House (by Kind of Hush), stayed 2¾m: dam, won over 1m in Ireland, half-sister to fairly useful 2m to 27f hurdler Logamimo: well tailed off in bumper on debut. *I. A. Brown*   **F–**

SECRET'S OUT   8 b.g. Polish Precedent (USA) – Secret Obsession (USA) (Secretariat (USA)) [2003/4 h81: 17m³ 17m³ 16m⁵ 17mᵖᵘ 17m² 16m³ 17g 16d⁶ 16m² Nov 24] leggy gelding: long-standing poor maiden hurdler: left W. Clay after fifth start: best around 2m: acts on good to soft and good to firm going: effective visored or not. *W. M. Brisbourne*   **h81**

SECURON DANCER   6 b.m. Emperor Jones – Gena Ivor (USA) (Sir Ivor) [2003/4 h–: 17gᵖᵘ 17s Dec 16] no form in 3 starts over hurdles: dead. *R. Rowe*   **h–**

SEDGE (USA)   4 b.g. Lure (USA) – First Flyer (USA) (Riverman (USA)) [2003/4 F17g Apr 24] 2,200 3-y-o: first foal: dam, winner in USA, sister to smart US Grade 1 9f winner River Flyer and half-sister to smart US Grade 1 7f winner Victory Ride: never a factor in bumper on debut. *P. T. Midgley*   **F–**

SEEADOR   5 b.g. El Conquistador – Shepani (New Member) [2003/4 F16d F16d 17s⁵ Apr 6] workmanlike gelding: sixth foal: half-brother to useful hurdler See You Sometime (by Sharp Deal), stays 3¼m, and bumper winner Seem of Gold (by Gold Dust): dam, maiden Irish pointer, half-sister to Rendlesham Hurdle winner See Enough: well held in 2 bumpers: modest form when fifth of 13 in novice at Exeter on hurdling debut: will stay further. *J. W. Mullins*   **h86**
F–

SEEBALD (GER)   9 b.g. Mulberry (FR) – Spartina (USA) (Northern Baby (CAN)) [2003/4 c167, h–: c17g⁴ c16d⁶ c24gᵘʳ c24g c20g³ c16dᵘʳ c25g⁵ c21m* c16m Apr 24] leggy gelding: high-class chaser at best: generally let down by jumping in 2003/4, but still capable of smart form and won 8-runner Grade 2 Silver Trophy (Limited Handicap) at Cheltenham in April by ½ length from Tikram: should stay beyond 21f: acts on any going: visored once. *M. C. Pipe*   **c152 x**
h–

Faucets For Mira Showers Silver Trophy Chase (Limited Handicap), Cheltenham—
Seebald challenges Jakari two out; runner-up Tikram is jumping in third

SEEF 10 b.g. Slip Anchor – Compton Lady (USA) (Sovereign Dancer (USA)) [2003/4 c66 x
c75x, h–: c25g⁵ c26g⁵ Apr 22] compact gelding: poor chaser: well held in handicaps h–
afer year's absence: stays 3¼m: raced mainly on good going or firmer: sketchy jumper.
J. S. King

SEEKING SHELTER (IRE) 5 b.m. Glacial Storm (USA) – Seeking Gold (IRE) F–
(Lancastrian) [2003/4 F16d Apr 17] first foal: dam modest staying chaser: tailed off in
bumper on debut. *N. G. Richards*

SEE ME THERE 4 b.g. Busy Flight – See-A-Rose (Halyudh (USA)) [2003/4 F14g⁵ h–
F16d 17s⁴ Jan 20] useful-looking gelding: first foal: dam, placed twice from 3 starts in F81
points, half-sister to Rendlesham Hurdle winner See Enough: modest form in 2 bumpers:
showed little on hurdling debut: likely to be suited by further than 2m. *J. W. Mullins*

SEE MORE BUSINESS (IRE) 14 b.g. Seymour Hicks (FR) – Miss Redlands c–
(Dubassoff (USA)) [2003/4 c162, h–: c26d⁴ Dec 6] leggy, lengthy gelding: one of the best h–
chasers of his generation, successful in 1999 Cheltenham Gold Cup and King George VI
Chase in 1997 and 1999: retired after attempting to win Rehearsal Chase at Chepstow for
a fourth time: stayed 3¼m: acted on soft and good to firm going (ran poorly both starts on
heavy): usually blinkered: raced prominently. *P. F. Nicholls*

SEE MORE JOCK 6 b.g. Seymour Hicks (FR) – Metafan (Last Fandango) [2003/4 F89
F16m² F16m F16g F16d Apr 12] sturdy gelding: fifth foal: dam well beaten in bumper/
novice hurdle: refused both starts in maiden points: best effort in bumpers when 10
lengths second of 21 to Alpine Fox at Worcester: off 9 months, well held last 2 starts.
Dr J. R. J. Naylor

SEE MORE SNOW 7 b.g. Seymour Hicks (FR) – Snow Child (Mandrake Major) c71
[2003/4 h79: c20m² c17g⁵ 22m⁴ Dec 4] smallish gelding: poor maiden hurdler: achieved h77
little form in 2 races over fences: should stay 2½m: acts on good to soft going:
tried in headgear: has looked none too keen under pressure. *W. G. M. Turner*

SEEMORE SUNSHINE 7 br.g. Seymour Hicks (FR) – Temporary Affair (Mandalus) h–
[2003/4 22g 24sᵖᵘ 16d Apr 23] 1,200 5-y-o: fourth foal: half-brother to winning pointer
by Derrylin: dam poor novice hurdler/chaser: no sign of ability in maiden point or over
hurdles. *R. Johnson*

SEE MY GIRL 6 gr.m. Terimon – Nessfield (Tumble Wind) [2003/4 F–: 20d⁵ Dec 29] h72 ?
tall mare: well held in 2 bumpers: around 13 lengths fifth of 13 to Silver Samuel in novice
hurdle at Haydock. *K. A. Morgan*

SEE RED BILLDAN (IRE) 8 bl.g. Riverhead (USA) – Sweet Mayo (IRE) (Sexton c–
Blake) [2003/4 c21gᵖᵘ Mar 3] failed to complete in maiden points and hunter chase.
R. J. Lancaster

SEEYAAJ 4 b.g. Darshaan – Subya (Night Shift (USA)) [2003/4 16sᵖᵘ 16g 20s 16d⁴ h92
16g³ Apr 18] good-topped gelding: fairly useful on Flat (should stay 1½m), sold out of
A. Stewart's stable 16,000 gns Newmarket Autumn Sales: modest form last 2 starts over
hurdles. *Jonjo O'Neill*

SEE YOU AROUND 9 b.g. Sharp Deal – Seeborg (Lepanto (GER)) [2003/4 c91, h–: c80
c21s⁴ c21mᵖᵘ c26g² c24s⁴ c25v⁴ c26gᵖᵘ c24d² c26g⁴ Apr 12] compact gelding: poor h–
maiden chaser: left C. Tizzard after second start: stays 3¼m: acts on heavy going, possibly not on firmer than good: tried visored, effective blinkered or not: tongue tied last 2
outings. *J. W. Mullins*

SEE YOU SOMETIME 9 b.g. Sharp Deal – Shepani (New Member) [2003/4 h136: c124 +
c19s² c19s³ c20sᶠ c20g⁶ c25gᶠ Apr 2] medium-sized gelding: useful handicap hurdler: h–
highly tried all starts over fences, fairly useful form when second of 3 finishers to
Supreme Prince in Grade 2 novice at Ascot and sixth to Isio in very valuable handicap at
Newbury: effective around 2½m, probably stays 3¼m: acts on soft and good to firm
going (bumper form on heavy): genuine. *J. W. Mullins*

SEFTON BLAKE 10 b.g. Roscoe Blake – Rainbow Lady (Jaazeiro (USA)) [2003/4 c–
c–, h–: 20s⁴ 26gᵖᵘ May 26] workmanlike gelding: winning hurdler/chaser, lightly raced h70
and poor nowadays: lame final outing: stays 25f: acts on firm and soft going: tried
visored/blinkered: usually front runner. *R. D. Wylie*

SEFTON LODGE 5 b.g. Barathea (IRE) – Pine Needle (Kris) [2003/4 h–: 16mᵖᵘ h–
17dᵖᵘ 16dᵖᵘ Dec 12] modest maiden on Flat (raced mainly at 6f/7f), sold out of A. Reid's
stable £1,400 Ascot July Sales: no form over hurdles: tongue tied last 2 starts.
M. A. Barnes

SEGSBURY BELLE 9 b.m. Petoski – Rolling Dice (Balinger) [2003/4 21d^{pu} 16m^{pu} Feb 21] no form in bumpers or over hurdles. *Mrs G. Harvey*   h–

SEKWANA (POL) 5 b.m. Duke Valentino – Surmia (POL) (Demon Club (POL)) [2003/4 h–: 17g 18m^5 16m^{pu} 16s 22g^{pu} Apr 22] no form over hurdles: often wears cheekpieces/tongue strap. *Miss A. M. Newton-Smith*   h–

SELASSIE 5 ch.g. Alflora (IRE) – Zanditu (Presidium) [2003/4 F16v 17s^F Feb 6] first foal: dam unraced half-sister to useful staying hurdler Haile Derring: no show in bumper or novice hurdle. *M. Scudamore*   h– F–

SELBERRY 10 b.g. Selkirk (USA) – Choke Cherry (Connaught) [2003/4 17s^{pu} c16m^2 c16v^2 c17s^3 c21d^3 c16g^{bd} c18g c18g^5 Apr 22] good-bodied gelding: winning hurdler: fair handicap chaser: has form at 2½m, raced mainly around 2m: acts on heavy and good to firm going: visored once, blinkered nowadays: usually races up with pace. *E. L. James*   c106 d h–

SELBY ROAD (IRE) 5 b.g. Erins Isle – Motus (Anfield) [2003/4 F104: F16d^2 16s* Jul 28] fairly useful bumper winner: won 4-y-o novice at Galway on hurdling debut by 2½ lengths from Always: looked sure to improve but not seen out again. *C. Roche, Ireland*   h114

SELF DEFENSE 7 b.g. Warning – Dansara (Dancing Brave (USA)) [2003/4 h155: 16g* 20d^2 16d^4 16g 16g 16g* 17m^2 Apr 15] sturdy gelding: useful hurdler on balance of form: won Grade 2 Sharp Novices' Hurdle at Cheltenham (by short head from Albuhera) in November and novice at Newbury (simple task) in March: unable to match performance in race previous year when tenth in Champion Hurdle at Cheltenham fifth outing: probably as effective at 2½m as 2m: acts on heavy going, below form on good to firm final start: has looked none too keen: gelded after final start: joined P. Chamings. *Miss E. C. Lavelle*   h140

SELVAS (GER) 4 ch.g. Lomitas – Subia (GER) (Konigsstuhl (GER)) [2003/4 16s* Mar 20] successful twice around 11f on Flat in Germany for P. Schiergen, showing useful form: won 11-runner juvenile at Ascot on hurdling debut by 4 lengths from Croix de Guerre, patiently ridden and leading run-in: will stay beyond 2m: likely to progress. *Jonjo O'Neill*   h110 p

SEMI PRECIOUS (IRE) 6 ch.g. Semillon – Precious Petra (Bing II) [2003/4 F18s 21v^3 19s^5 20s 16s* 17s^3 Mar 23] €9,500 4-y-o, resold 10,000 4-y-o: plain gelding: half-brother to several winners, including fair chaser Precious Music (by Orchestra), stays 3m, and fair 2m hurdler Captains Bar (by Lochnager): dam winner on Flat and over hurdles: well held in maiden bumper on debut: poor novice hurdler: won 16-runner handicap at Huntingdon in January: should stay 2½m. *D. P. Keane*   h79 F–

Blue Chip Feeds Sharp Novices' Hurdle, Cheltenham—Self Defense (left) finally gets off the mark over hurdles; he leads narrowly from Contraband two out but Albuhera proves a bigger danger

SENNA DA SILVA 4 gr.f. Prince of Birds (USA) – Impulsive Decision (IRE) (Nomination) [2003/4 F12g 16g 17s⁶ 17v⁴ 16g⁴ Mar 10] £1,000 3-y-o: first foal: dam, 6f and 1m winner, out of half-sister to smart French performer up to 15f Sealy: well beaten in bumper on debut: form over hurdles only when fourth in selling handicap at Chepstow final start. *J. L. Flint*   **h69**
F—

SENNA (IRE) 4 b.g. Petardia – Saborinie (Prince Sabo) [2003/4 16gᵖᵘ Mar 5] leggy gelding: showed little on Flat and in juvenile hurdle: sold £1,400 Ascot April Sales. *P. D. Cundell*   **h—**

SENOR EDUARDO 7 gr.g. Terimon – Jasmin Path (Warpath) [2003/4 F77: 16d⁶ 16dᵖᵘ 17s 16g Mar 6] workmanlike gelding: modest in bumpers: first form over hurdles when catching the eye in mid-field in 16-runner novice handicap at Doncaster final start, not fluent on a few occasions but travelling strongly long way and not given at all a hard time: capable of better. *S. Gollings*   **h72 p**

SENOR GIGO 6 b.g. Mistertopogigo (IRE) – Lady Carol (Lord Gayle (USA)) [2003/4 F—: 16gᶠ 16f Feb 29] well held in bumpers and on completed outing over hurdles (pulled hard): trained on hurdling debut by N. Ewart. *Miss V. Scott*   **h—**

SENOR HURST 9 b.g. Young Senor (USA) – Broadhurst (Workboy) [2003/4 h—: 16g 17g⁵ c17d⁶ 16d³ 16s⁶ 16g³ 21g 16dᵖᵘ Apr 12] angular gelding: poor maiden hurdler: well held on chasing debut: raced mainly around 2m: acts on soft and good to firm going. *Mrs P. Sly*   **c—**
h67

SENOR SEDONA 5 b.g. Royal Vulcan – Star Shell (Queen's Hussar) [2003/4 F16v² F16g² Feb 21] brother to 3 winners, notably very smart chaser up to 3m Royal Mountbrowne, and half-brother to 2 others: dam never ran: fairly useful form when second in 2 bumpers at Ascot, beaten a length by Historic Place, having been hampered, and 3½ lengths by The Thunderer: swished tail under pressure on second occasion: likely to stay well. *N. J. Gifford*   **F95**

SENOR TORAN (USA) 4 b.g. Barathea (IRE) – Applaud (USA) (Rahy (USA)) [2003/4 16gᵘʳ Mar 15] modest maiden on Flat (stays 1¼m), sold out of P. Cole's stable £5,000 Ascot June Sales: unseated second on hurdling debut. *P. Burgoyne*   **h—**

SENTO (IRE) 6 ch.g. Persian Bold – Esclava (USA) (Nureyev (USA)) [2003/4 h103, F96: 22g⁴ 21m⁴ 22g³ Jul 26] good-topped gelding: fair hurdler: will stay 3m: acts on good to firm going. *A. King*   **h105**

SENZA SCRUPOLI 4 ch.g. Inchinor – Gravette (Kris) [2003/4 18vᵖᵘ 17d 16s 17d⁶ 16d² Apr 12] angular gelding: poor maiden on balance on Flat (stays 1¼m): blinkered, best effort over hurdles when second in selling handicap at Huntingdon. *M. D. Hammond*   **h64**

SEPTEMBER MOON 6 b.m. Bustino – Lunabelle (Idiot's Delight) [2003/4 h92+, F—: 26gᶠ 21m Apr 15] angular mare: form only when winning novice hurdle in 2002/3: will stay 3m: acts on good to firm going: wore cheekpieces final start (stiff task). *Mrs A. M. Thorpe*   **h—**

SEPTEMBER WHISPER 6 b.m. Country Classic – Marjimel (Backchat (USA)) [2003/4 F16mᵖᵘ Aug 2] first foal: dam poor maiden who stayed 1½m: showed nothing in bumper on debut. *Miss L. C. Siddall*   **F—**

SERAPH 4 ch.g. Vettori (IRE) – Dahlawise (IRE) (Caerleon (USA)) [2003/4 16fᵘʳ 16d 16g⁵ᵈ 17g Mar 28] poor on Flat (stays 1½m), won in January: signs of ability over hurdles only in seller on third outing (disqualified after taking wrong course). *John A. Harris*   **h—**

SEREN FACH (IRE) 6 b. or br.m. Fourstars Allstar (USA) – Caurieddator (Laurence O) [2003/4 F17m Oct 2] seventh foal: half-sister to bumper winner Supreme Wonder (by Supreme Leader): dam unraced, out of half-sister to smart chaser up to 3m Comeragh King and useful staying chaser Seskin Bridge: more signs of temperament than ability in maiden point and bumper: sold £900 Ascot November Sales. *Mrs D. A. Hamer*   **F—**

SERIOUS POSITION (IRE) 9 ch.g. Orchestra – Lady Temba (Callernish) [2003/4 h84: 22m* c20gᵖᵘ Oct 15] workmanlike gelding: off 11 months, finally got off mark over hurdles in 6-runner novice at Uttoxeter in October, making virtually all: every chance when going lame 4 out in novice handicap on chasing debut: stays 2¾m: acts on good to soft and good to firm going. *D. R. Stoddart*   **c—**
h84

SERPENTINE ROCK 4 ch.g. Hernando (FR) – Serpentara (Kris) [2003/4 F12g⁵ F17d⁵ F16s² Apr 4] tall, lengthy gelding: second foal: half-brother to 9.5f winner in Germany by Emperor Jones: dam maiden, from family of very smart middle-distance performer Sandmason: fair form in bumpers, second in maiden at Hexham in April. *Ferdy Murphy*   **F93**

SETTING SUN 11 ch.g. Generous (IRE) – Suntrap (USA) (Roberto (USA)) [2003/4 **h–**
h89: 19m^{pu} Aug 3] sturdy gelding: winning hurdler: went as if amiss only outing in
2003/4: stays 3m: acts on good to firm and good to soft going, probably on soft: usually
races up with pace. *N. Waggott*

SEVEN COLOURS 4 b.g. Spectrum (IRE) – Sinking Sun (Danehill (USA)) [2003/4 **F– p**
F16d Apr 12] stocky gelding: third foal: brother to 2000 2-y-o 7f winner Caspian: dam,
untrustworthy maiden who stayed 1¼m, half-sister to very smart hurdler up to 2½m
Sanmartino and very smart 1m to 1½m performer Urgent Request: shaped as though
needing experience when tenth of 18 in bumper at Huntingdon on debut. *Miss V. Scott*

SEVERN AIR 6 b.m. Alderbrook – Mariner's Air (Julio Mariner) [2003/4 F73: F16g^4 **h90**
17d^4 16d^2 19s 17d* 18d^6 16d^6 Apr 21] best effort in bumpers when fourth in maiden at **F89**
Worcester: modest novice hurdler: won mares event at Bangor in March: will prove best
around 2m: raced mainly on good to soft going. *J. L. Spearing*

SEVERN BELLE (IRE) 8 ch.m. Executive Perk – Our Siveen (Deep Run) [2003/4 **h–**
17g^4 20m^4 26g^6 Nov 9] sparely-made mare: little form over hurdles. *Mrs S. J. Smith*

SEVERN MAGIC 11 b.m. Buckley – La Margarite (Bonne Noel) [2003/4 c–: c24m^{ur} **c–**
Mar 4] fair pointer in 2002: well held completed start in hunter chases. *D. Thomas*

SHAADIVA 6 b.m. Shaamit (IRE) – Kristal Diva (Kris) [2003/4 h83, F67: 17g^3 16f* **h104**
20s* 21d^{pu} 21g^2 21g^{pu} Mar 27] good-topped mare: fair hurdler: won mares novices at
Wincanton (handicap) in November and Huntingdon in December: stays 21f: acts on firm
and soft going: has jumped none too fluently. *A. King*

SHAAMIT THE VAAMIT (IRE) 4 b.g. Shaamit (IRE) – Shocker (IRE) (Sabrehill **F–**
(USA)) [2003/4 F14d^5 Mar 22] first foal: dam 1m winner: well-held fifth of 14 in bumper
at Hereford on debut. *M. Scudamore*

SHADBOLT (NZ) 6 gr.g. Heroicity (AUS) – Another Day (NZ) (Open Day) [2003/4 **F–**
F16m F16s Dec 11] tall gelding: signs of only a little ability in 2 bumpers. *L. A. Dace*

SHADED (IRE) 10 b.g. Night Shift (USA) – Sarsaparilla (FR) (Shirley Heights) **c–**
[2003/4 c–, h–: 22m^4 17d 19d 17m c19g^6 19m^{pu} Mar 4] good-topped gelding: bad **h58**
hurdler: well beaten completed start over fences: stays easy 2¾m: acts on firm and good
to soft going. *D. J. Minty*

SHADE LUCKY 8 ch.g. Gildoran – Snowy Autumn (Deep Run) [2003/4 h–: 22g^{pu} **c–**
c23g^5 c23m^F Jun 7] workmanlike gelding: no form: tried blinkered. *B. J. M. Ryall* **h–**

SHADOW RIVER (IRE) 6 b.g. Over The River (FR) – Society Belle (Callernish) **F94**
[2003/4 F16d F18g^2 Apr 22] sixth foal: half-brother to smart hurdler up to 2½m
Davenport Milenium (by Insan) and bumper winner Little Buckie (by Miner's Lamp):
dam unraced half-sister to useful chaser up to 3m Sullane River (by Over The River):
better effort in bumpers when 11 lengths second to Just Classic at Fontwell: will be suited
by 2½m+. *P. J. Hobbs*

SHADY AFFAIR (IRE) 13 b.g. Black Minstrel – Golden Ice (Golden Love) [2003/4 **c–**
c–, h–: 20s^{pu} May 2] winning chaser: no form over hurdles: tried in cheekpieces. **h–**
R. N. Bevis

SHADY ANNE 6 ch.m. Derrylin – Juno Away (Strong Gale) [2003/4 h76, F96: 24s^5 **h78**
20d^4 16v^{pu} 26s^6 26d 20s Apr 17] smallish mare: bumper winner: poor novice hurdler:
stays 2½m: acts on soft going: wore cheekpieces last 2 starts. *F. Jordan*

SHADY EXCHANGE (IRE) 9 b.g. Le Bavard (FR) – Torus Light (Torus) [2003/4 **c–**
c22v^{pu} c26s^{pu} c24g^5 c25g^{pu} c24d^{pu} Apr 8] rather leggy gelding: winning pointer in 2002:
no form in steeplechases: wore cheekpieces/blinkers last 3 starts. *R. Lee*

SHADY GREY 6 gr.m. Minster Son – Yemaail (IRE) (Shaadi (USA)) [2003/4 F65: **h81**
20d 16g 16v^3 20s^2 21d^5 24s^4 Apr 21] poor novice hurdler: shaped like non-stayer over 3m
final start: sold 7,000 gns Doncaster May Sales. *Miss S. E. Forster*

SHADY MAN 6 b.g. Shaamit (IRE) – Miss Hardy (Formidable (USA)) [2003/4 h77: **h90**
20s^{pu} 17g* Apr 24] chunky gelding: modest hurdler: saddle slipped on reappearance:
improved form when winning selling handicap at Market Rasen 3 weeks later: raced
mainly around 2m: acts on heavy going. *Mrs S. J. Smith*

SHAFFISHAYES 12 ch.g. Clantime – Mischievous Miss (Niniski (USA)) [2003/4 **h91**
h80: 16g* 16g* 16g 16g 17g^2 16s^3 16v^6 20d* 19g Mar 5] lengthy gelding: has been
hobdayed: modest handicap hurdler: won at Perth (conditional jockeys seller) and Kelso
(novice) in May, and Musselburgh in February: stays 2½m: raced on good ground or
softer: held up, and sometimes finds little. *Mrs M. Reveley*

SHAFTS CHANCE (IRE)   7 br.m. Over The River (FR) – Lunar Approach (IRE) **c61 x**
(Mandalus) [2003/4 F16d⁵ F16m 18f c26m³ c25m⁴ c20gᶠ c20gᶠ Oct 15] ex-Irish mare: **h–**
first foal: dam, runner-up in Irish point, sister to useful 2m hurdler/chaser Adamant **F68**
Approach: little worthwhile form in bumpers, over hurdles or in steeplechases (let down
by jumping), left J. Flynn after third start: won mares maiden point in March: tried
blinkered. *C. R. Egerton*

SHAHBOOR (USA)   10 b.g. Zilzal (USA) – Iva Reputation (USA) (Sir Ivor) [2003/4 **c–**
c101, h–: c20m⁶ Oct 9] close-coupled gelding: fairly useful handicap hurdler: fair chaser: **h–**
stayed 2½m: acted on soft and good to firm going: dead. *Mrs P. Robeson*

SHAH (IRE)   11 b.g. King Persian – Gay And Sharp (Fine Blade (USA)) [2003/4 c82, **c77**
h–: c21mᵖᵘ c16s³ c16sᵖᵘ c20dᵖᵘ Jan 22] angular gelding: poor handicap chaser, lightly **h–**
raced: effective from 2m to 2½m: acts on firm and soft ground: blinkered (bled from
nose) final start. *P. Kelsall*

SHAKE EDDIE SHAKE (IRE)   7 b.g. Blues Traveller (IRE) – Fortune Teller (Troy) **c–**
[2003/4 h–: 16m c16dᵖᵘ Mar 15] sturdy gelding: little form over hurdles: showed nothing **h–**
on chasing debut: tried blinkered. *H. S. Howe*

SHAKWAA   5 ch.m. Lion Cavern (USA) – Shadha (USA) (Devil's Bag (USA)) [2003/4 **h83 ?**
h–: 17g 16g 21s 17d³ 20sᵖᵘ Apr 21] novice hurdler: easily best effort when third of 15 to
Moonlit Harbour at Carlisle, though possibly flattered in falsely-run race. *E. A. Elliott*

SHALAKO (USA)   6 ch.g. Kingmambo (USA) – Sporades (USA) (Vaguely Noble) **h122**
[2003/4 h110: 16m² 16m⁵ 20d⁴ 16d² 16s 21d⁴ 21g⁶ 16s⁶ 20g 16m Apr 13] angular
gelding: fairly useful handicap hurdler: below best after fourth outing: stays 2½m: acts on
good to firm going, probably on heavy: blinkered/visored last 3 starts. *P. J. Hobbs*

SHALBEBLUE (IRE)   7 b.g. Shalford (IRE) – Alberjas (IRE) (Sure Blade (USA)) **c–**
[2003/4 c96, h102: c16m⁶ 17g³ Sep 30] neat gelding: modest on Flat: fair hurdler: not **h102**
fluent and modest form at best over fences: raced mainly around 2m: acts on heavy and
good to firm going: blinkered/visored: no easy ride. *B. Ellison*

SHALLEE (IRE)   11 b.g. Good Thyne (USA) – Ferdia's Fancy (Proverb) [2003/4 **c114**
c24d* c24g³ Dec 4] winning hurdler: best effort over fences when winning maiden at **h–**
Cork in May by 25 lengths from Heroic: stays 3m: acts on good to firm and heavy going:
effective blinkered/tongue tied or not. *C. Byrnes, Ireland*

SHAMAN   7 b.g. Fraam – Magic Maggie (Beveled (USA)) [2003/4 h66: 17g⁵ 16m² **h100**
16g² 16d² 16d² 16s* 16sᵖᵘ Mar 15] modest up to 1½m on Flat: fair hurdler: won handicap
at Plumpton in January: will probably prove best around 2m: acts on soft and good to firm
going. *G. L. Moore*

SHAMAWAN (IRE)   9 b.g. Kris – Shamawna (IRE) (Darshaan) [2003/4 c143, h–: 20s⁵ **c–**
Feb 7] leggy gelding: useful handicap chaser: reportedly suffered fracture final start in **h99 +**
2002/3: modest maiden hurdler, shaped encouragingly on return from year's absence but
not seen again: stays 21f: acts on heavy going: tried tongue tied: takes good hold, and is
patiently ridden. *Jonjo O'Neill*

SHAMDIAN (IRE)   4 b.g. Indian Ridge – Shamadara (IRE) (Kahyasi) [2003/4 16d³ **h105**
16gᵖᵘ Jan 17] rather leggy ex-French gelding: fairly useful maiden up to 1¼m on Flat,
sold out of A. de Royer Dupre's stable €85,000 Goffs Arc Sale: encouraging third of
18 to Dickens in juvenile at Sandown on hurdling debut: went as if amiss in similar event
at Kempton 2 weeks later, weakening quickly on turn and pulled up before 2 out.
N. J. Henderson

SHAMEL   8 b.g. Unfuwain (USA) – Narjis (USA) (Blushing Groom (FR)) [2003/4 h–: **c–**
22d c16gᵖᵘ Mar 12] strong gelding: no form over jumps, even in points: left A. Price after **h–**
first outing: has had tongue tied. *S. Flook*

SHAMELESS   7 ch.g. Prince Daniel (USA) – Level Edge (Beveled (USA)) [2003/4 **h–**
h–: 17vᵖᵘ Jan 13] leggy gelding: no form over hurdles. *H. Alexander*

SHAMPOOED (IRE)   10 b.m. Law Society (USA) – White Caps (Shirley Heights) **c115**
[2003/4 c110, h–: 16f 19m³ c17g² c17g⁴ c20m* Jul 13] workmanlike mare: fair handicap **h99**
chaser: won at Stratford by neck from Flahive's First, all out to hold on after being left
clear 2 out: runs just occasionally over hurdles nowadays: barely stays 2½m: acts on
heavy and good to firm going: usually visored (ran poorly when blinkered): races prominently. *R. Dickin*

SHAMROCK   7 ch.m. Sanglamore (USA) – Rockfest (USA) (Stage Door Johnny **F83**
(USA)) [2003/4 F16g F17m³ May 24] modest form in bumpers, off 19 months before

reappearance: dictated slow pace when third to Real Cracker in maiden at Market Rasen. *Lady Herries*

SHAMSAN (IRE)   7 ch.g. Night Shift (USA) – Awayil (USA) (Woodman (USA)) [2003/4 c98, h116: 21m⁶ 16m⁴ 20m 20m² 16m² 20m² Oct 22] small, sturdy gelding: modest chaser: fair hurdler: left J. Joseph after first outing: stays easy 2½m: acts on firm and good to soft going: effective blinkered/tongue tied or not: has idled and usually held up. *P. J. Hobbs*   c– h101

SHAM SHARIF   7 b.m. Be My Chief (USA) – Syrian Queen (Slip Anchor) [2003/4 17mᵖᵘ 20mᵖᵘ 17g² 16m 17d² Jul 27] novice hurdler, runner-up twice at Newton Abbot in summer: tried visored, blinkered last 3 outings. *C. J. Down*   h82

SHANAVOHER (IRE)   12 ch.g. Phardante (FR) – Lane Baloo (Lucky Brief) [2003/4 c21m⁶ c25mᵖᵘ Jun 11] ex-Irish gelding: modest maiden hurdler/chaser at best: trained on reappearance by D. Phelan: stays 3m: acts on soft and good to firm going: has had tongue tied. *B. G. Powell*   c– h–

SHANESIA (IRE)   5 b.m. Erins Isle – Canadian Project (IRE) (Project Manager) [2003/4 h110: 20gᶠ 16d 16g³ 20m* Jan 22] fair hurdler: best effort when winning handicap at Naas in October: stays 2½m: acts on good to firm going: has had tongue tied. *Paul Nolan, Ireland*   h112

SHANKLY   9 b.g. King's Ride – Brandy Run (Deep Run) [2003/4 c25dᵘʳ May 3] rangy gelding: fair pointer, passed post first on 4 occasions in 2003: no form over hurdles/in steeplechases. *C. J. Barker*   c– x h– §

SHANNON LEADER (IRE)   6 b.h. Supreme Leader – Shannon Lass (Callernish) [2003/4 F16d* F16s F16d 16s⁴ Mar 20] sixth foal: brother to winning Irish pointer Theennisconnection and half-brother to winning 3m hurdler Shannon Light (by Electric): dam maiden half-sister to dam of smart 2m to 23f hurdler Lord Transcend: promising debut when winning bumper at Naas by 3½ lengths from Jackie Cullen: failed to progress in 2 similar events and a maiden hurdle: will stay at least 2½m. *Anthony Mullins, Ireland*   h97 F103

SHANNON LIGHT (IRE)   12 b. or br.g. Electric – Shannon Lass (Callernish) [2003/4 h95: 22s⁶ 22sᵖᵘ Feb 9] compact gelding: winning hurdler: off over 18 months, no show either start in 2003/4, went with no zest in cheekpieces on second occasion. *N. R. Mitchell*   h– §

SHANNON QUEST (IRE)   8 b. or br.g. Zaffaran (USA) – Carrick Shannon (Green Shoon) [2003/4 c86, h–: 22m² 20m² 24g 20m³ Jul 16] lengthy gelding: poor maiden hurdler/chaser: stays 2¾m: acts on soft and good to firm going: blinkered: sometimes let down by jumping over fences: tends to find little. *O. Sherwood*   c– h84 §

SHANNON'S PRIDE (IRE)   8 gr.g. Roselier (FR) – Spanish Flame (IRE) (Spanish Place (USA)) [2003/4 h113+: c20dᵖᵘ c21sᵖᵘ Dec 26] well-made gelding: fair hurdler: shaped as if something amiss both outings in novice chases: bred to stay at least 3m. *N. G. Richards*   c– h–

SHANNON WATER'S (IRE)   8 b.m. Moscow Society (USA) – Percy's Pet (Blakeney) [2003/4 c20d⁶ c20fᵖᵘ 26m* 25sᶠ Mar 15] successful twice in Irish points: left T. Begley and refitted with tongue strap, made all in weakly-contested novice handicap hurdle at Hereford in March: no form in steeplechases: stays 3¼m: acts on good to firm ground, possibly not on soft. *M. C. Pipe*   c– h83

SHARABAD (FR)   6 b.g. Ela-Mana-Mou – Sharbada (FR) (Kahyasi) [2003/4 F16s F16v F16d 20f³ 18g 16g Apr 5] second foal: dam, lightly-raced maiden, half-sister to Shardari: well beaten in bumpers: poor form on first of 3 starts over hurdles. *Mrs L. B. Normile*   h65 F–

SHARDAM (IRE)   7 b.g. Shardari – Knockea Hill (Buckskin (FR)) [2003/4 c131, h102: c25gᵘʳ c25g* c27g* c26gᵖᵘ c24g c24m⁴ c24g² c36dᵘʳ c29m Apr 24] tall, leggy gelding: fair hurdler: useful chaser: won intermediate at Kelso in May and listed handicap at Cheltenham (made all and unchallenged) in November: best efforts when in frame in valuable handicaps won by Marlborough at Kempton and Fork Lightning at Cheltenham: should stay beyond 27f: acts on soft and good to firm going: usually sound jumper (unseated third in Grand National). *N. A. Twiston-Davies*   c140 h–

SHARDANTE (IRE)   11 ch.g. Phardante (FR) – Shirabas (Karabas) [2003/4 c21m³ c25g* c25g⁵ c26d³ c25s* c25vᵘʳ c24gᵖᵘ Mar 6] workmanlike gelding: fairly useful handicap chaser, left J. M. Jefferson and off 2 years before reappearance: won at Aintree in October and Wetherby (beat Be Upstanding 20 lengths) in January: stays 3¼m: acts on soft and good to firm going. *Mrs S. J. Smith*   c119 h–

SHARED ACCOUNT (IRE)   10 b.g. Supreme Leader – Ribble Rabble (Deep Run)   **h105**
[2003/4 19s* 19f 20s 20s 24d⁵ 25g⁵ 27s 24d² 20d⁵ Mar 11] sturdy ex-Irish gelding: third
foal: brother to winning pointer Royal Leader: dam unraced: fair handicap hurdler: won
at Kilbeggan in May: sold out of F. Flood's stable 5,000 gns (privately) Doncaster
October Sales after fourth outing: stays 25f: acts on good to firm and heavy ground.
P. A. Blockley

SHARED EXPECTATION (IRE)   8 ch.g. Husyan (USA) – Calmount (IRE) (Cal-   **h–**
lernish) [2003/4 16s Jan 16] lengthy gelding: well held in bumper and novice hurdle over
2 years apart. *J. M. Jefferson*

SHARED-INTEREST   10 ch.m. Interrex (CAN) – La Campagnola (Hubble Bubble)   **c–**
[2003/4 h–; c19gᵖᵘ Apr 30] angular mare: no form outside points: has worn tongue strap.   **h–**
K. Bishop

SHAREEF (FR)   7 b.g. Port Lyautey (FR) – Saralik (Salse (USA)) [2003/4 c119, h98:   **c–**
c20s⁵ Dec 26] good-topped gelding: winning hurdler: fairly useful form when second   **h–**
first 2 starts in novice chases: well held only outing in 2003/4: will stay 3m: acts on good
to firm and good to soft going (won bumper on soft). *A. King*

SHARES (IRE)   4 b.g. Turtle Island (IRE) – Glendora (Glenstal (USA)) [2003/4 16s⁵   **h98 +**
18v⁵ 16g* Mar 6] fair maiden on Flat (will probably stay 1½m): fair form over hurdles at
Kelso, won 14-runner juvenile in March by 3 lengths from Unicorn Reward, travelling
smoothly into contention and staying on to lead run-in. *P. Monteith*

SHARMY (IRE)   8 b.g. Caerleon (USA) – Petticoat Lane (Ela-Mana-Mou) [2003/4   **c114**
h103: 16s³ c16g* c16d³ c16g* c16g³ Apr 18] close-coupled gelding: fair hurdler: quickly   **h111**
showed himself at least as good over fences, winning maiden at Ludlow in December and
handicap at Huntingdon in March, showing better turn of foot than sole remaining rival
Great Travel at latter: likely to prove best around 2m: acts on soft and good to firm going.
Ian Williams

SHARP AS CROESUS   4 b.f. Sesaro (USA) – Chushan Venture (Pursuit of Love)   **h–**
[2003/4 16mᵖᵘ Sep 27] modest form at best at 2 yrs (should stay 1m): pulled hard and
jumped poorly prior to pulled up with slipped saddle on hurdling debut. *J. R. Best*

SHARPASTRIZAM (NZ)   9 b.g. Try To Stop Me – Atristazam (NZ) (Zamazaan   **c97**
(FR)) [2003/4 c107, h–: c16m⁶ c16d⁴ c16m⁴ c17g⁵ c20d c16g* c16d³ c16s³ c17g⁵ c16m*   **h–**
c17g⁴ Apr 5] good-topped gelding: modest chaser: won handicap at Catterick in December and 4-runner minor event at Leicester in March: best around 2m: acts on good to
soft going, though all wins on good/good to firm: sound jumper. *P. Beaumont*

Open Trophy Handicap Chase, Cheltenham—Shardam is soon clear and makes all

SHARPATEN (IRE)   9 b.g. Scenic – Sloane Ranger (Sharpen Up) [2003/4 c–, h124: **c–** 16m 20d 20d 16g 16v 16s⁴ 16s* c16dᶠ Mar 13] leggy, angular gelding: winning chaser: **h106** one-time useful hurdler: nowhere near so good nowadays, though won claimer at Leicester in February: best form at 2m, should stay further: acts on good to firm and heavy going: has shown signs of temperament. *Ian Williams*

SHARP BELLINE (IRE)   7 b.g. Robellino (USA) – Moon Watch (Night Shift (USA)) **c92** [2003/4 h103: 22g⁴ 19g⁶ c24s⁵ c24sᵖᵘ c20d⁶ 27d Mar 30] small, close-coupled gelding: **h90** handicap hurdler, just modest form in 2003/4: modest form over fences, left John Harris after fourth start: best at 3m+: acts on firm and soft going: lazy. *Mrs S. J. Smith*

SHARP EXIT (IRE)   5 ch.g. Fourstars Allstar (USA) – Dipper's Gift (IRE) (Sallu- **F–** ceva) [2003/4 F17m Sep 27] fourth foal: dam unraced half-sister to smart staying chaser Royal Dipper and very smart staying hurdler/useful chaser Henry Mann: soon off bridle in rear in bumper on debut. *C. Grant*

SHARP HAND   8 ch.g. Handsome Sailor – Sharp Glance (IRE) (Deep Run) [2003/4 **h–** h69, F73: 17g May 1] big, plain gelding: poor novice hurdler: should stay 2½m. *J. G. M. O'Shea*

SHARP JACK (IRE)   6 b.g. Be My Native (USA) – Polly Sharp (Pollerton) [2003/4 **h77 +** F16s 20s⁵ Mar 13] €30,000 4-y-o: sixth foal: half-brother to winning pointer by Electric: **F80** dam, lightly raced in bumpers, half-sister to smart hurdler up to 2½m Tom Sharp: seventh of 10 in bumper at Huntingdon on debut: never a factor when fifth of 19 in novice hurdle at Newcastle. *R. T. Phillips*

SHARP RIGGING (IRE)   4 b.g. Son of Sharp Shot (IRE) – In The Rigging (USA) **h112** (Topsider (USA)) [2003/4 16s³ 17d* 16g* Apr 12] half-brother to fair 2m hurdler Chem's Truce (by Brief Truce): fair maiden on Flat (stays 1¼m), sold out of E. Dunlop's stable 7,500 gns Newmarket Autumn Sales: successful on last 2 of 3 starts in juvenile hurdles, in 12-runner events at Hereford (by 5 lengths from Wasted Talent) in March and Plumpton (by 10 lengths from Lord of Beauty): likely to prove best at 2m with emphasis on speed. *A. M. Hales*

SHARP SEAL   10 b.g. Broadsword (USA) – Little Beaver (Privy Seal) [2003/4 c78, **c71** h–: c21m³ c18m³ May 26] poor chaser: won maiden point in January: probably stays 3m: **h–** acts on firm and soft going. *M. Madgwick*

SHARP SINGLE (IRE)   8 b.m. Supreme Leader – Pollyville (Pollerton) [2003/4 h–: **c82** 20s⁴ 20d³ 20d⁵ c22s⁴ c20gᵖᵘ c17d⁵ c16d³ c16s Apr 4] workmanlike mare: poor maiden **h76** hurdler/chaser: stays 2½m: raced on good ground or softer. *P. Beaumont*

SHARP SPICE   8 b.m. Lugana Beach – Ewar Empress (IRE) (Persian Bold) [2003/4 **h64** 16sᵖᵘ 16m⁵ 16gᵇᵈ 16s⁴ 17vᵖᵘ 17sᵖᵘ Feb 1] poor on Flat (stays 1½m) in 2003 for D. Coakley: poor novice hurdler: pulled up at Pau last 2 starts. *D. L. Williams*

SHARP STEEL   9 ch.g. Beveled (USA) – Shift Over (USA) (Night Shift (USA)) **c92 x** [2003/4 c76, h81: c16mᶠ c16m³ c16m* c16s⁵ c17m² c16m⁴ c16m³ c19mᵖᵘ c17mᵘʳ c16m² **h–** c16mᶠ Nov 13] tall gelding: poor maiden hurdler: modest chaser: won novice handicap at Worcester in July: would have won similar event at Ludlow but for falling fatally 2 out: best around 2m: acted on good to soft and good to firm going: headstrong: often let down by jumping. *Miss S. J. Wilton*

SHARP'S THE WORD   5 b.g. Keen – Scally's Girl (Scallywag) [2003/4 F16d F16g **F–** Jan 24] seventh foal: half-brother to modest staying chaser Willubelong (by Move Off) and winning 21f hurdler Choir Belle (by Minster Son): dam never ran: behind in bumpers at Catterick. *C. Grant*

SHARVIE   7 b.g. Rock Hopper – Heresheis (Free State) [2003/4 h–: 19gᵖᵘ 19m⁵ 26g² **h65** 26m 24g⁵ 26sᵖᵘ Dec 20] close-coupled gelding: little form over hurdles: usually blink-ered/in cheekpieces. *C. J. Hemsley*

SHAYADI (IRE)   7 b.g. Kahyasi – Shayrdia (IRE) (Storm Bird (CAN)) [2003/4 16m* **h115** 16d* 16s 16d Apr 3] useful-looking gelding: fairly useful on Flat (stays 2m), sold out of M. Johnston's stable 5,500 gns Newmarket Autumn Sales: successful first 2 starts over hurdles, in seller at Leicester (well-backed favourite) and novice at Newcastle (beat Wet Lips 2 lengths) in December: little impact in 2 handicaps: will stay beyond 2m: tongue tied. *B. Ellison*

SHAYDEYLAYDEH (IRE)   5 b.m. Shaddad (USA) – Spirito Libro (USA) (Lear **h72 ?** Fan (USA)) [2003/4 h–: 20gᵘʳ 16s⁵ 17d⁶ 21s³ 19vᵖᵘ 23s⁵ 19s 24gᵖᵘ Feb 19] angular mare: little worthwhile form over hurdles: wore cheekpieces on debut. *Miss J. Feilden*

SHAYS LANE (IRE)   10 b.g. The Bart (USA) – Continuity Lass (Continuation) [2003/4 c–, h–: c25d³ c25g* c25m* c25sᵖᵘ c25sᵖᵘ c25g⁴ c26dᵖᵘ Apr 18] rangy gelding: modest chaser: won handicaps at Hexham in May and June (novice): well below form after break last 4 starts: should stay beyond 25f: acts on good to firm going: usually patiently ridden. *Ferdy Murphy*   **c88 h–**

SHAZAL   7 b.m. Afzal – Isolationist (Welsh Pageant) [2003/4 h63: 16d 16g² 16g* 18g 16sᵖᵘ Dec 26] smallish, leggy mare: poor hurdler: won mares handicap at Perth in June: should stay 2½m. *J. N. R. Billinge*   **h73**

SH BOOM   6 b.g. Alderbrook – Muznah (Royal And Regal (USA)) [2003/4 h141, F104: 24d² 21s² 24g* 23s* 24gᶠ 24g Apr 1] lengthy, useful-looking gelding: smart hurdler: further improvement in 2003/4, winning minor event at Cheltenham (by length from Crystal d'Ainay) in December and Grade 2 Commhoist Premier Stayers' Hurdle at Haydock (odds on, got on top between last 2 when beating Royal Rosa 8 lengths) in January: let down by jumping last 2 starts: stays 3m: raced on good going or softer (acts on heavy): usually held up. *Jonjo O'Neill*   **h149**

SHEER FRUSTRATION (IRE)   8 b.m. Montelimar (USA) – Deep Lass (Deep Run) [2003/4 20d³ 16m c20s³ c16s² c22s² Mar 28] workmanlike mare: fair handicap hurdler: placed all 3 starts over fences, second to Baily Mist in Grade 3 mares novice at Limerick in March: badly hampered in handicap at Punchestown month later: effective at 2m to 2¾m: acts on soft going (won bumper on good to firm): effective with or without cheek-pieces. *Paul Nolan, Ireland*   **c107 h110**

SHEER GENIUS (IRE)   8 br.g. Insan (USA) – Mulberry (IRE) (Denel (FR)) [2003/4 c16m² c24gᵖᵘ Jan 17] rangy gelding: useful hurdler: off over 20 months, flattered when beaten 2½ lengths by Santenay in 2-runner race at Sandown, second start in novice chases: stayed 3m: acted on soft and good to firm going: sometimes failed to impress with finishing effort: dead. *M. Pitman*   **c103 § h–**

SHEER GUTS (IRE)   5 b.g. Hamas (IRE) – Balakera (FR) (Lashkari) [2003/4 16g* 16mʳᵒ 16v* 16s 17dᵖᵘ 16s 16d 17g Mar 28] leggy gelding: fair on Flat (stays 1¼m) at 3 yrs for B. Hills, little show in 2003: won sellers at Towcester in November and December: no other form over hurdles, ran out in between: raced around 2m: acts on heavy going: blinkered third to sixth outings, also tried in cheekpieces: has worn tongue strap. *John A. Harris*   **h81 §**

Commhoist Premier Stayers' Hurdle, Haydock—
Sh Boom (left) and Royal Rosa jump the second last in unison

SHEILA MCKENZIE 7 b.m. Aragon – Lady Quachita (USA) (Sovereign Dancer (USA)) [2003/4 c–: c16g^{ur} Apr 3] winning pointer, including in February: yet to complete in hunter chases. *C. O. King* — **c–**

SHE'LL BE LUCKY (IRE) 6 ch.m. Arctic Cider (USA) – Johnnys Girl (Orchestra) [2003/4 20g^2 20g^5 20d^4 20s^4 18s^3 16s^3 16s 16s* 16g 16s* Mar 14] fair handicap hurdler: won at Limerick in December, Leopardstown (mares) in February and Cork in March: stays 2½m: acts on heavy going. *M. Hourigan, Ireland* — **h110**

SHELLIN HILL (IRE) 10 ch.g. Sharp Victor (USA) – Queenspay (Sandhurst Prince) [2003/4 c89d, h–: c16g^{pu} c20s c16m^5 c16d^3 c16d^6 c19m^4 c20d^5 Apr 21] strong, lengthy gelding: poor handicap chaser: best around 2m: acts on firm and soft going: wore cheek-pieces last 2 starts: has had tongue tied: none too hearty. *R. J. Price* — **c66 h–**

SHELU 6 b.g. Good Thyne (USA) – Nearly Married (Nearly A Hand) [2003/4 h88?, F–: c25g* Nov 7] good-bodied gelding: modest form at best over hurdles: favourite, stayed on dourly when winning maiden chase at Hexham only start in 2003/4: will stay beyond 25f: acts on heavy going: reportedly lame final outing in 2002/3. *Ferdy Murphy* — **c74 + h–**

SHEMDANI (IRE) 7 b.g. Unfuwain (USA) – Shemaka (IRE) (Nishapour (FR)) [2003/4 h118+: 16g Dec 27] leggy gelding: fairly useful hurdler: lame when well held in handicap only start in 2003/4: raced around 2m: acts on any going. *M. C. Pipe* — **h–**

SHEPHERDS REST (IRE) 12 b.g. Accordion – Mandy's Last (Krayyan) [2003/4 c103, h–: c26d^2 c24m^3 c26g^{pu} Sep 3] angular gelding: winning hurdler/chaser, very much on downgrade: stays 3¼m: acts on good to firm and heavy going: visored: often finds little. *C. P. Morlock* — **c83 h–**

SHERBET FIZZ (IRE) 8 b.m. Petardia – Skiddaw (USA) (Grey Dawn II) [2003/4 20m 22g^{pu} Aug 4] winning pointer: no show in 3 novice hurdles: tongue tied final outing. *C. Roberts* — **h–**

SHERBET LAD (IRE) 8 b.g. Cataldi – She's Foolish (IRE) (Callernish) [2003/4 h102: 24d 20v^{pu} May 21] workmanlike gelding: winning hurdler in 2002/3: something amiss in handicap in May: should stay beyond 2½m: acts on heavy going. *V. R. A. Dartnall* — **h–**

SHERFIELD LASS 6 b.m. Tina's Pet – Mindyerownbusiness (IRE (Roselier (FR)) [2003/4 F–: 19g^4 May 1] no sign of ability in mares bumper, mares novice hurdle and a point, sold 3,000 gns Doncaster May Sales before last-named event. *Mrs H. Dalton* — **h–**

SHERIFF'S FRIEND (IRE) 9 b. or br.g. Supreme Leader – Arctic Scale (IRE) (Strong Gale) [2003/4 c28d* c26d^{pu} Mar 18] sturdy gelding: fairly useful hunter chaser: won valuable novice hunter at Stratford in May: stiff task in Foxhunter at Cheltenham in March but unbeaten in 4 completed points in 2004: likely to stay beyond 3½m: acts on soft going: tried visored: has worn near-side pricker. *Mrs Jenny Gordon* — **c102 h–**

SHERKIN ISLAND (IRE) 6 b.g. Shernazar – Tullerolli (IRE) (Barbarolli (USA)) [2003/4 26s^4 24v* c18g* 23d Apr 12] IR 11,000 3-y-o: tall, useful-looking gelding: second foal: dam in frame once over 2m: runner-up on second of 2 starts in maiden Irish points in 2003: promising start in Britain, won novice hurdle at Uttoxeter in January and novice handicap chase at Newbury (by 1½ lengths from Acertack, jumping fluently and again idling run-in) in March: only seventh of 9 finishers in handicap back over hurdles final start: effective around 2m to 3m: open to improvement over fences. *Jonjo O'Neill* — **c109 p h96**

SHERWOOD ROSE (IRE) 8 gr.m. Mandalus – Cronlier (Roselier (FR)) [2003/4 h–: 16v^{pu} 16m 26s^{pu} 17s^6 c21s^6 c24g^{pu} c22s^{ur} 21d^{pu} Apr 8] sturdy mare: poor maiden hurdler: let down by jumping all 3 starts over fences. *K. C. Bailey* — **c– x h68**

SHERZABAD (IRE) 7 b. or br.g. Doyoun – Sheriya (USA) (Green Dancer (USA)) [2003/4 17s^{pu} Feb 3] modest on Flat (stays 1¾m) for H. Collingridge: showed nothing on hurdling debut. *Miss I. E. Craig* — **h–**

SHES ELITE (IRE) 6 b.m. Supreme Leader – Chic And Elite (Deep Run) [2003/4 F17d F17m Jun 21] first live foal: dam, winning hurdler/chaser, stayed 2½m: soundly beaten in 2 bumpers. *Jonjo O'Neill* — **F–**

SHE'S FLASH (IRE) 5 b.m. Woodborough (USA) – Beechwood Quest (IRE) (River Falls) [2003/4 16m 16d^F May 16] poor maiden on Flat: in cheekpieces, tailed off in novice seller on hurdling debut: failed to settle when blinkered next time. *J. A. Supple* — **h–**

SHE'S OUR NATIVE (IRE) 6 b.m. Be My Native (USA) – More Dash (IRE) (Strong Gale) [2003/4 F95: 16m^6 16m^2 16g 19s^{ur} 19s^2 19g 22g Apr 10] lengthy, rather unfurnished mare: modest novice hurdler: stays 19f: acts on soft going. *P. J. Hobbs* — **h87**

SHE'SSOMELADY (IRE)   5 b.m. Muroto – Designer (Celtic Cone) [2003/4 F17m   h–
17g 21s Nov 18] half-sister to poor 2m chaser Follow De Call (by Callernish) and to   F—
winning pointer by Rustingo: dam never ran: well held in bumper and novice hurdles.
R. J. Baker

SHIFTING MOON   12 b.g. Night Shift (USA) – Moonscape (Ribero) [2003/4 c–§,   c– §
h84§: 16v⁶ 22g² 22m* 24m Aug 1] compact gelding: poor handicap hurdler: won at   h74 §
Stratford in July: lame following month: possibly best up to 2¾m: acts on any going:
effective blinkered or not: tongue tied: unreliable. *F. Jordan*

SHIFTY SHAKOMALA (IRE)   7 b.g. Lord Americo – I'll Say She Is (Ashmore   F—
(FR)) [2003/4 F16mᵖᵘ May 26] €4,500 5-y-o: medium-sized gelding: fifth foal: brother
to 2½m chase winner Good Outlook and half-brother to fair 2m hurdle winner Tax
Exempt (by Be My Native) and 2½m bumper winner Five Alive O (by Alphabatim): dam
placed in point: lame in bumper on debut. *M. J. Ryan*

SHILLELAH LAW   8 ch.g. Weld – Compasita (Old Jocus) [2003/4 24m 20m 22m³   c–
c24mᵖᵘ Aug 9] third foal: dam unraced half-sister to useful but temperamental staying   h83
hurdler Vivaque: successful once from 5 starts in maiden Irish points: bought privately
3,000 gns Doncaster May Sales: form over hurdles and in steeplechase only when third
in novice hurdle at Stratford in July: subsequently ran out then well beaten in 2 points.
M. C. Pipe

SHILO (IRE)   10 ch.g. Roselier (FR) – Cathedral Street (Boreen Beag) [2003/4 c–:   c79 +
c22v⁴ c26s³ c25sᶠ Apr 11] compact gelding: lightly raced: fourth in novice chase at Towcester on reappearance, making running and possibly flattered: possibly had too much
use made of him when soundly beaten in maiden at Chepstow next time, fell heavily
fourth final outing. *Mrs Merrita Jones*

SHINING STRAND   5 ch.g. Karinga Bay – First Romance (Royalty) [2003/4 F16d²   F104
Nov 30] has scope: seventh foal: half-brother to several winners, including fairly useful
hurdler/useful chaser First Love (by Bustino), stays 3m: dam, winning 2m hurdler who
stayed 3m, daughter of half-sister to top-class staying chaser Spanish Steps: green, neck
second of 22 to Red Ruffles in bumper at Newbury on debut. *N. J. Henderson*

SHINING TYNE   10 b.g. Primitive Rising (USA) – Shining Bann (Bargello) [2003/4   c70 §
c91§, h–: c24d⁵ c24d⁴ c20s³ c20v² c33dᵖᵘ Feb 21] lengthy gelding: poor maiden chaser: h– §
stays 3m: probably acts on heavy going: blinkered after reappearance, wore cheekpieces
previously: tongue tied: ungenuine (has refused to race): joined S. Bell. *R. Johnson*

SHINY BAY (IRE)   11 ch.g. Glacial Storm (USA) – Raby (Pongee) [2003/4 c24sᵖᵘ   c– x
Apr 17] compact ex-Irish gelding: one-time fairly useful handicap hurdler: winning   h–
chaser, but often let down by jumping: won points in March and April (2): stays 2½m:
acts on any going. *Miss Jenny Garley*

SHIRAZI   6 b.g. Mtoto – Al Shadeedah (USA) (Nureyev (USA)) [2003/4 17d⁵ 17g*   h101
17m⁴ 16g 16d 17g Apr 3] leggy gelding: fairly useful on Flat (stays 1¼m) for J. Hills:
confirmed promise of hurdling debut when winning maiden at Newton Abbot in June:
disappointing subsequently: breathing problem fifth outing. *D. R. Gandolfo*

SHIVERMETIMBER (IRE)   6 b.m. Arctic Lord – Cherry Dancer (Monksfield)   h114
[2003/4 16g F20d* 20d⁴ 16d 18dᶠ 24d³ 22s² 22s² 20s² 22d* 24v* 24d 22s* 20d⁴ Apr 11]   F94
leggy mare: half-sister to winning hurdler/pointer Mardon (by Mandalus): dam bumper
winner: won bumper at Downpatrick in May: fair hurdler: won handicaps at Leopardstown in January and Punchestown in February and March, best effort when beating
Derawar by ½ length for final success: stays 3m: acts on heavy going. *F. Flood, Ireland*

SHOBROOKE MILL   11 ch.g. Shaab – Jubilee Leigh (Hubble Bubble) [2003/4 c87:   c– x
c21dᶠ c23m⁴ Apr 13] fairly useful pointer/maiden hunter chaser on his day: in frame
several times in points in 2004 but tailed off in novice hunter: stays 3¼m: acts on good to
firm going: none too consistent (often let down by jumping). *Mrs S. Prouse*

SHOCK'S PRIDE (IRE)   12 b.g. Glacial Storm (USA) – Ewood Park (Wishing Star)   c– §
[2003/4 c26sᵖᵘ Apr 29] pulled up in maiden hurdle for R. Tyner in 1998/9: modest pointer   h–
(has refused): no show in novice hunter on steeplechase debut. *Mrs S. Clarke*

SHOGOON (FR)   5 b.g. Rangoon (FR) – Touranlad (FR) (Tourangeau (FR)) [2003/4   c57
17d 20d 20v c24fᶠ c16g* c20dᶠ Apr 18] close-coupled ex-French gelding: third foal: dam   h–
maiden: second in juvenile hurdle at La Rochelle Chattelaillon on debut for J. M. Cana-
bate: well held in 3 novice hurdles in Britain, showing temperament on first occasion:
fortunate winner of 2-finisher maiden chase at Catterick in March. *M. D. Hammond*

AON Chase, Newbury—the visored Shooting Light
springs a surprise on his return from injury as Keen Leader (right) flops;
runner-up Irish Hussar is hidden by the winner while Royal Auclair (noseband) is soon to weaken

SHOLAY (IRE) 5 b.g. Bluebird (USA) – Splicing (Sharpo) [2003/4 16d 17s Feb 3] **h83**
sturdy gelding: poor form in novice hurdles at Leicester and Taunton: well held on Flat in
2004 after rejoining P. Mitchell. *N. A. Twiston-Davies*

SHOOTING LIGHT (IRE) 11 b.g. Shernazar – Church Light (Caerleon (USA)) **c150**
[2003/4 c149, h–: c24g* c24m^{pu} Feb 28] sturdy, workmanlike gelding: smart chaser: won **h–**
AON Chase at Newbury on reappearance by ¾ length from Irish Hussar, quickening into
clear lead 3 out but winning with little to spare: broke leg at Kempton later in month:
should have stayed beyond 3m: acted on soft and good to firm going: blinkered/visored.
M. C. Pipe

SHORT CHANGE (IRE) 5 b.g. Revoque (IRE) – Maafi Esm (Polish Precedent **h103**
(USA)) [2003/4 h98: 16m* 16m^6 16g Nov 30] workmanlike gelding: modest on Flat
(barely stays 1½m): fair handicap hurdler: easily best effort in 2003/4 when winning at
Warwick in November: raced around 2m: best on good going or firmer. *A. W. Carroll*

SHOSEN (IRE) 8 b.g. Persian Mews – Lugnagullagh (Pitpan) [2003/4 20v 24g^{pu} Feb **h–**
14] rangy, useful-looking gelding: has reportedly been fired: progressive form over
hurdles in 2001/2, little sign of retaining ability on return. *A. King*

SHOTACROSS THE BOW (IRE) 7 b.g. Warning – Nordica (Northfields (USA)) **h–**
[2003/4 16g^{pu} Mar 27] close-coupled gelding: fair on all-weather, poor on turf on Flat
(stays 1¼m) for M. Blanshard: poor form when in frame both starts over hurdles in
2001/2, showed little on return. *Mrs H. E. Rees*

SHOTGUN ANNIE 4 b.f. Double Trigger (IRE) – Coh Sho No (Old Vic) [2003/4 **F–**
F12s Nov 22] small, lengthy filly: first foal: dam, 21f hurdle winner who would have
stayed 3m+, also won at 15.4f on Flat, out of half-sister to smart French stayer Sought
Out: bit backward, well held in 3-y-o bumper on debut. *S. Dow*

SHOULTON (IRE) 7 br.g. Aristocracy – Jay Joy (Double-U-Jay) [2003/4 c–, h–, F–: **c96**
c24d^2 c24s^{co} c24d^F c26s^2 c24d^{ur} c24d^4 Mar 27] medium-sized gelding: well held over **h–**
hurdles: modest novice chaser: stays 3¼m: acts on soft going: sometimes let down by
jumping. *G. H. Yardley*

SHOWPIECE 6 b.g. Selkirk (USA) – Hawayah (IRE) (Shareef Dancer (USA)) [2003/4 **h133**
h107p: 16d* 18g^2 17g* 17m* 17m^2 16g Nov 14] rather leggy, useful-looking gelding:
useful novice hurdler: won at Aintree (flashed tail under pressure) in May and Newton
Abbot and Market Rasen (handicap, beat Ei Ei 6 lengths) in June: ran well when second
to Italian Counsel in another quite valuable handicap at Market Rasen in July: will prove
best around 2m: unraced on extremes of going over hurdles. *C. J. Mann*

SHRADEN EDITION 7 b.g. Tina's Pet – Star Edition (Leading Man) [2003/4 c24d^2 **c93**
c24s^{pu} Apr 17] second foal: dam ran once in point: lightly-raced winning pointer: second
in novice at Stratford on first of 2 starts in hunter chases. *P. A. Jones*

SHRILANKA (IRE) 8 b.m. Lashkari – Lady Nerak (Pitpan) [2003/4 c–, h67: c25g **c–**
May 13] sturdy mare: runner-up once from 3 starts in Irish points: poor form over hurdles: **h–**
well held in 2 steeplechases. *P. J. Hobbs*

SHU GAA (IRE) 11 ch.g. Salse (USA) – River Reem (USA) (Irish River (FR)) [2003/4 **c88**
c–, h–: c21m* c22g Mar 26] compact gelding: fair handicap chaser on his day, lightly **h–**
raced nowadays: dead-heated in weak hunter at Folkestone in May: stays 3m: acts on soft
and good to firm going: effective blinkered/visored or not: probably suited by strongly-
run race. *C. Goulding*

SHUHOOD (USA) 4 b.g. Kingmambo (USA) – Nifty (USA) (Roberto (USA)) [2003/4 **h114**
16g^3 16g Apr 1] close-coupled gelding: fairly useful on Flat (should stay 1½m), lightly
raced, sold out of E. Dunlop's stable 30,000 gns Newmarket Autumn Sales: similar level
of ability in Grade 2 juvenile hurdles won by Trouble At Bay at Kempton and Al Eile at
Aintree. *P. R. Webber*

SHUIL BACK (IRE) 7 b.m. Bob Back (USA) – Shuil Ar Aghaidh (The Parson) **h–**
[2003/4 h–: 22d May 3] third in bumper on debut in 2001/2: no form in 2 novice hurdles
since, jumping poorly. *A. J. Lidderdale*

SHUIL TSARINA (IRE) 6 b.m. King's Ride – Shuil Realt (IRE) (Jolly Jake (NZ)) **h–**
[2003/4 F77: F17g 20s Dec 11] rangy mare: has scope: modest form in bumpers: tailed **F76**
off in mares novice on hurdling debut: bred to stay well beyond 17f. *J. M. Jefferson*

SI CELIA 9 ch.m. Primitive Rising (USA) – Easterly Gael (Tudor Music) [2003/4 **c–**
c25d^6 May 3] sixth foal: half-sister to winning chaser Timanfaya (by Sparkling Boy),
stayed 3m: dam won on Flat and on all 6 completed starts over hurdles up to 2½m:
winning pointer: well held in maiden on hunter chase debut. *Mrs J. Williamson*

SIDEWINDER (IRE) 9 br.g. Jolly Jake (NZ) – Silk Empress (Young Emperor) **c68**
[2003/4 c18d 26m 29d c23f^2 c26m^4 Nov 3] winning Irish pointer: no form over hurdles: **h–**
poor form in steeplechases, leaving D. O'Connor after reappearance, L. Dace after third
start: possibly best short of 3¼m: acts on firm and soft going: tried blinkered/in cheekpieces: has had tongue tied. *M. C. Pipe*

SIENNA SUNSET (IRE) 5 ch.m. Spectrum (IRE) – Wasabi (IRE) (Polar Falcon **h74**
(USA)) [2003/4 17s 16g 16s^5 Mar 15] fair on Flat (stays 1¼m): poor form in novice
hurdles: may prove best at sharp 2m. *Mrs H. Dalton*

SIGMA DOTCOMM (IRE) 8 b.g. Safety Catch (USA) – Dream Academy (Town **c112**
And Country) [2003/4 c112, h–: c16d^{ur} c19d c28g^3 c29s^{pu} c24s^{pu} c21g Apr 2] good- **h–**
topped gelding: fair handicap chaser: left N. Meade after reappearance: form in 2003/4
only when third in valuable event at Cork in November: stays 3½m: raced on good going
or softer (acts on heavy): tried blinkered/in cheekpieces. *James Joseph Mangan, Ireland*

SIGNATURE TUNE (IRE) 5 b.g. Gothland (FR) – Divine Affair (IRE) (The Parson) **h–**
[2003/4 F16s F18v 18d^{ur} Apr 7] sixth foal: half-brother to useful hurdler up to around **F–**
2½m Concert Pianist (by Rakaposhi King): dam never ran: well held in 2 bumpers, and
when unseating 3 out in novice on hurdling debut. *P. Winkworth*

SIGNED AND DATED (USA) 5 b.g. Red Ransom (USA) – Libeccio (NZ) (Danza- **h– x**
tore (CAN)) [2003/4 h–x: 16g^6 20m^{pu} 20m 16g^{pu} Nov 7] workmanlike gelding: no
worthwhile form over hurdles: has worn cheekpieces: poor jumper. *Mrs E. Slack*

SIGN OF NIKE 6 b.h. Mistertopogigo (IRE) – Infanta Maria (King of Spain) [2003/4 **h–**
16g Aug 23] useful on Flat, successful 4 times up to 7f, placed in 2003: well held in
novice on hurdling debut. *C. Von Der Recke, Germany*

SIGWELLS CLUB BOY 4 b.g. Fayruz – Run With Pride (Mandrake Major) [2003/4 **h87**
17m^5 17m^3 16g^{6d} 16g^2 16s^4 16g^3 17g^2 18d Apr 6] angular gelding: fair at 2 yrs,
well below form on Flat in 2003: modest juvenile hurdler: left W. Turner after seventh
start: will prove best around 2m: acts on good to soft going: wore cheekpieces sixth/
seventh outings. *J. L. Flint*

SIJUJAMA (IRE) 9 b.g. Torus – Knights Bounty (IRE) (Henbit (USA)) [2003/4 c71, **c–**
h–: c16g^6 c16g^{pu} c23d^{pu} c25f^2 Oct 5] good-topped gelding: maiden hurdler/chaser: no **h–**
form in novice chases in first half of season: tried tongue tied: placed twice from 4 starts
in points in 2004. *Miss Lucinda V. Russell*

SIKANDER A AZAM 11 b.g. Arctic Lord – Shanlaragh (Gaberdine) [2003/4 c19s*   **c115**
c21g² Apr 1] sturdy gelding: fairly useful chaser: won hunter at Ascot in March: better   **h–**
form when second of 25 to Forest Gunner in Fox Hunters' at Aintree: stays 21f: acts on
soft and good to firm going: used to make running, patiently ridden nowadays: free-going
sort. *David M. Easterby*

SILCHESTER DREAM 6 ch.m. Karinga Bay – Raghill Hannah (Buckskin (FR))   **h–**
[2003/4 h–, F70: 21g 22g Apr 13] leggy mare: no form over hurdles. *C. G. Cox*

SILENCE REIGNS 10 b.g. Saddlers' Hall (IRE) – Rensaler (USA) (Stop The Music   **c118 x**
(USA)) [2003/4 c–, h–: c20d^(ur) c22g* c21g^(bd) Apr 1] sturdy gelding: fairly useful chaser,   **h–**
lightly raced: would probably have won hunter at Fontwell in March but for unseating
last: easily won similar event at Newbury later in month: not fluent and towards rear when
brought down Becher's in Fox Hunters' at Aintree final start: stays 2¾m: acts on good to
firm and good to soft going: blinkered last 2 starts: often let down by jumping over fences.
P. F. Nicholls

SILENT ACTION (USA) 12 b.g. Greinton – Heather Bee (USA) (Drone (USA))   **c69**
[2003/4 c–, h–: c21d c21f⁵ c25m⁵ c23m⁴ Jun 18] angular gelding: won 2 points in 2003:   **h–**
poor maiden hurdler/chaser, left Miss E. Grainger after second start: probably stays 3¼m:
acts on firm going: tongue tied. *N. A. Smith*

SILENT GUEST (IRE) 11 b.g. Don't Forget Me – Guest House (What A Guest)   **h63**
[2003/4 h–: 17g⁶ 17s⁴ Apr 6] leggy gelding: poor handicap hurdler: effective at 2m to 3m:
acts on firm and good to soft going, probably on firm. *J. D. Frost*

SILENT GUNNER 6 ch.g. Gunner B – Quiet Dawn (Lighter) [2003/4 F–: F17s³   **h–**
F18v 25d^(pu) 21d^(pu) Apr 12] workmanlike gelding: poor form in bumpers: showed little in 2   **F68**
races over hurdles. *J. S. King*

SILENT KEYS (SWE) 12 br.g. Eighty Eight Keys (USA) – Habilage (Horage)   **c?**
[2003/4 c21d c17g⁴ c21m^(pu) c18g⁶ c25g^(pu) c20m c24m^(pu) c26d⁶ Apr 7] winning hurdler: **h–**
raced on Flat/over fences since 1997, winning Swedish Grand National at Stromsholm
twice, including in June: left T. Oscarsson, showed very little in 3 hunters: stays 23f: acts
on soft and good to firm going: tried blinkered/tongue tied. *Mrs Alison Hickman*

SILENT SNIPE 11 ch.g. Jendali (USA) – Sasol (Bustino) [2003/4 c73, h–: c24m^(pu)   **c72**
c25g c25m³ c26m^(pu) 24m c27m² c25m³ c27g* c25d³ c27d* c23m² c29d² c27s³ c25d^(pu)   **h–**
c24g* c28d Mar 30] leggy gelding: no form over hurdles: poor handicap chaser: won in
small fields at Sedgefield in October and November and Musselburgh in January: stays
27f: acts on soft and good to firm going: tried tongue tied. *Miss L. C. Siddall*

SILENT SOUND (IRE) 8 b.g. Be My Guest (USA) – Whist Awhile (Caerleon (USA))   **c88 x**
[2003/4 h79: c18g^(pu) 16m 17d² 20m* 22g⁴ 18f⁶ 17m² 22g⁴ 16m⁵ c16g^(F4) c19g* c19s^(pu)   **h83**
c17s^(pu) Jan 4] poor hurdler, won seller at Worcester in August: modest chaser: won handicap at Taunton in December: let down by jumping both subsequent starts: stays 2½m:
acts on firm and good to soft going: tried visored, effective with or without cheekpieces.
C. L. Tizzard

SILENTTOUCHOFTIME (IRE) 6 b.m. Hymns On High – Ballinaboy Queen   **h–**
(IRE) (Black Minstrel) [2003/4 24s^(pu) 19d^(pu) Feb 15] sturdy mare: first foal: dam unraced:
showed nothing in 2 races over hurdles. *C. J. Down*

SILISTRA 5 gr.g. Sadler's Wells (USA) – Dundel (IRE) (Machiavellian (USA))   **h–**
[2003/4 20g 19s^(pu) Apr 4] of little account on Flat nowadays: showed nothing in 2 maiden
hurdles, wearing visor/cheekpieces. *Mrs L. C. Jewell*

SILKEN PEARLS 8 b.m. Leading Counsel (USA) – River Pearl (Oats) [2003/4 h72+,   **h–**
F92+: 20v^(pu) Mar 21] good-topped mare: won weak mares novice on hurdling debut in
2002/3: very disappointing in similar event and handicap since: will stay 3m: acts on
heavy going. *L. Lungo*

SILKEN THOMAS 9 b.g. King's Ride – Padykin (Bustino) [2003/4 c21m c21s^F Dec   **c– x**
30] tall, lengthy gelding: poor maiden hurdler/chaser, often let down by jumping over   **h–**
fences: has worn near-side pricker: has hinted at temperament. *N. J. Hawke*

SILKIE PEKIN 5 gr.m. Riverwise (USA) – Came Cottage (Nearly A Hand) [2003/4   **F–**
F16g Mar 25] seventh foal: sister to top-class 2m hurdler Rooster Booster and 2¼m
bumper winner Cockatoo Ridge: dam fairly useful pointer: well beaten in bumper on
debut. *N. R. Mitchell*

SILK SCREEN (IRE) 4 b.c. Barathea (IRE) – Sun Screen (Caerleon (USA)) [2003/4   **h124**
16d² 16s* 16s* Mar 27] good-topped colt: half-brother to one-time smart chaser/useful
hurdler Hill Society (by Law Society), stays 2½m: fairly useful on Flat (stays 1½m):

similar form over hurdles, winning juvenile maiden at Gowran in February and novice at Navan (by ½ length from Corrib Boy) in March: good fourth to Cherub in Grade 1 at Punchestown in late-April. *W. P. Mullins, Ireland*

SILK ST JOHN 10 b.g. Damister (USA) – Silk St James (Pas de Seul) [2003/4 h–: 16m^{pu} Jun 1] compact gelding: no longer of much account on Flat: lightly-raced maiden hurdler, showed little only start in 2003/4. *W. M. Brisbourne*   **h–**

SILK TRADER 9 b.g. Nomadic Way (USA) – Money Run (Deep Run) [2003/4 h109: 16g^6 16m 16m^{su} c19d^2* c19g^2 c19g^F 16s^3 16d* 18g^2 16m Apr 13] leggy gelding: won novice at Doncaster in December on chasing debut, left alone second, refusing tenth then remounted: second in similar event at Catterick next time: fair handicap hurdler: won amateur race at Sandown in March for third year running: stays easy 2½m: acts on heavy and good to firm going: tried tongue tied. *J. Mackie*   **c96** **h109**

SILKWOOD TOP (IRE) 5 b.g. Norwich – Brave Mum (Brave Invader (USA)) [2003/4 F17g^3 Apr 10] eighth foal: dam unraced: third in bumper at Newton Abbot on debut. *V. R. A. Dartnall*   **F86**

SILLY BOY 9 ch.g. Crested Lark – Sutton Lass (Politico (USA)) [2003/4 c–: c19g^{pu} May 1] lengthy, workmanlike gelding: no form in novice chases: winning pointer, including in April. *R. C. Harper*   **c–**

SILLY SARAH 4 b.f. Sovereign Water (FR) – Fortria's Delight (Idiot's Delight) [2003/4 F12g Nov 12] third foal: dam ran once: showed nothing in 3-y-o bumper on debut. *Mrs A. M. Thorpe*   **F–**

SILOGUE (IRE) 7 b. or br.g. Distinctly North (USA) – African Bloom (African Sky) [2003/4 h–: 16m 17g^6 17m 17g 20m 16g^3 17m^4 17m^3 17m^3 17m Sep 5] poor maiden hurdler around 2m: raced mainly on good/good to firm going: tried visored: sold 1,500 gns (privately) Doncaster November Sales, fourth in point in April. *O. Brennan*   **h66**

SILVA VENTURE (IRE) 7 b.m. Mandalus – Miss The Post (Bustino) [2003/4 h–, F–: 16d^2 16g 20m Jun 14] form only when fourth in novice hurdle at Hexham in April: let down by jumping in handicaps both subsequent starts: bred to be suited by 2½m+. *L. Lungo*   **h–**

SILVER BIRCH (IRE) 7 b.g. Clearly Bust – All Gone (Giolla Mear) [2003/4 h111: c25d^3 c26s* c25d^2 c32g^4 c25d^{pu} Apr 17] workmanlike gelding: fair hurdler: fairly useful novice chaser: won maiden at Chepstow in January: much better form next 2 starts, second to Fork Lightning at Wincanton and fourth to Native Emperor in valuable amateur event at Cheltenham: likely to prove best at 3m+: acts on heavy going: sound jumper. *P. F. Nicholls*   **c120** **h–**

SILVER BUZZARD (USA) 5 b. or br.g. Silver Hawk (USA) – Stellarina (USA) (Pleasant Colony (USA)) [2003/4 h108: 17s^2 16d^4 20m^4 Sep 7] workmanlike gelding: fair handicap hurdler: needs good test around 2m, stays 2¾m: best efforts on ground softer than good (acts on heavy): poor form in points in 2004. *Jonjo O'Neill*   **h109**

SILVER CHARMER 5 b.m. Charmer – Sea Dart (Air Trooper) [2003/4 h117?: 16m 19g^6 16d^6 22m 16g^{ur} 21m* Apr 15] close-coupled mare: fair handicap hurdler: best effort in 2003/4 when winning listed mares event at Cheltenham by 3 lengths from Kombinacja, doing well to come off pace and lead run-in: stays 21f: acts on good to firm and good to soft going. *H. S. Howe*   **h112**

SILVER CHARTER (USA) 5 b.g. Silver Hawk (USA) – Pride of Darby (USA) (Danzig (USA)) [2003/4 h82x: 20m c19s c17s^{ur} c20g^F 17s Mar 23] workmanlike gelding: modest juvenile hurdler in 2002/3: bought out of G. Balding's stable £6,500 Ascot June Sales: no show in 2003/4, including in novice chases: stays 19f: acts on good to firm and good to soft going: poor jumper. *H. S. Howe*   **c– x** **h– x**

SILVER CHEVALIER (IRE) 6 gr.g. Petong – Princess Eurolink (Be My Guest (USA)) [2003/4 h–: 17g 16m Jul 16] angular gelding: of little account: tried visored. *D. Burchell*   **h–**

SILVER CHIEFTAN (IRE) 6 gr.g. Be My Native (USA) – Mystery Rose (Roselier (FR)) [2003/4 F78: 17d^5 20s 19d^6 20d^F Apr 23] tall, angular gelding: easily best effort in novice hurdles when seventh of 10 finishers at Haydock second start. *P. J. Hobbs*   **h85**

SILVER COIN (IRE) 4 gr.g. Night Shift (USA) – Eurythmic (Pharly (FR)) [2003/4 16m 16d 16g^2 20d 16f* 16g^3 Mar 13] strong, useful-looking gelding: half-brother to winning 2m hurdler I Got Rhythm (by Lycius): fair on Flat (stays 1¾m): fair juvenile hurdler: won maiden at Musselburgh in February: should stay 2½m: acts on firm going. *T. D. Easterby*   **h95**

SILVER DAGGER 6 gr.g. Dr Devious (IRE) – La Belle Affair (USA) (Black Tie **h–**
Affair) [2003/4 16d 20s^F 17m 16g 21d^{pu} Apr 12] good-topped gelding: fairly useful 1m
and 1¼m winner on Flat at 3 yrs: maiden hurdler: little form in 2003/4, leaving C. Roche
after reappearance: best efforts at 2m: acts on soft going: sometimes tongue tied. *Jonjo
O'Neill*

SILVER DANCER (IRE) 8 gr.g. Roselier (FR) – Fancy Step (Step Together (USA)) **c–**
[2003/4 h–, F–: c16v^{ur} c22s⁶ c24d^{pu} c16s^{ur} c19m⁴ Apr 13] leggy gelding: of no account: **h–**
tried blinkered. *M. G. Rimell*

SILVER GHOST 5 gr.g. Alderbrook – Belmore Cloud (Baron Blakeney) [2003/4 **F–**
F16s F16d Mar 19] 14,500 3-y-o: good-topped gelding: first foal: dam, fair hurdler,
stayed 21f: well held in 2 bumpers, showing some ability on debut. *M. Bradstock*

SILVER GIFT 7 b.m. Rakaposhi King – Kellsboro Kate (Paddy's Stream) [2003/4 c–, **c–**
h88: 27g c23m^{ur} 26m² 24f³ 24m⁶ 24g⁴ 26s⁴ Nov 22] leggy mare: failed to complete in 2 **h91**
races over fences: poor handicap hurdler: stays 27f: acts on good to firm and good to soft
going, probably not on softer: held up: inconsistent. *G. Fierro*

SILVER GREY ANNIE 7 gr.m. Arzanni – Celtic Berry (Celtic Cone) [2003/4 20m^{ur} **h– x**
20d^{pu} Jul 2] no sign of ability, jumping badly both starts over hurdles. *F. P. Murtagh*

SILVER INNGOT (IRE) 5 gr.g. Gothland (FR) – Hotel Saltees (IRE) (Over The **h92**
River (FR)) [2003/4 19g⁵ 16d 18s 22g Apr 18] second foal: dam maiden hurdler/chaser
who stayed 3m: modest form in novice hurdles: bred to be suited by further than 19f.
R. H. Alner

SILVER JACK (IRE) 6 gr.g. Roselier (FR) – Consharon (IRE) (Strong Gale) [2003/4 **h84**
F86: 20d⁵ 24d⁴ 25s⁶ Jan 6] leggy gelding: fair form in bumper: travelled well long way in
3 starts over hurdles, poor form on first 2: may do better. *M. Todhunter*

SILVER KNIGHT 6 gr.g. Simply Great (FR) – Hysteria (Prince Bee) [2003/4 h118: **c125**
c24g² c25d* c20d² c25d* c24g³ c25s³ c25s² c25g² c25d³ Apr 17] tall, useful-looking **h–**
gelding: fairly useful hurdler: at least as good over fences: won twice at Wetherby,
maiden in November and novice in December: placed all other starts in 2003/4: will stay
beyond 25f: acts on heavy going: blinkered (found little) once: has hung left/looked
tricky ride: sound jumper of fences: tough. *T. D. Easterby*

SILVER LAKE (IRE) 10 gr.g. Roselier (FR) – Over The Pond (IRE) (Over The River **c–**
(FR)) [2003/4 c25d^{pu} c24g^{pu} Mar 5] workmanlike gelding: successful both starts over **h–**
hurdles: modest form in points in 2004, little encouragement in 2 hunters (left F. Jackson
after first of them): should be suited by 3m+. *S. Breen*

SILVER LOUIE (IRE) 4 gr.f. Titus Livius (FR) – Shakamiyn (Nishapour (FR)) **h–**
[2003/4 17m Nov 20] half-sister to modest hurdler Rose Tea (by Alhaarth), stays 23f:
temperamental maiden on Flat: well held in juvenile on hurdling debut. *G. B. Balding*

SILVER MAN 10 gr.g. Silver Owl – What An Experiance (Chance Meeting) [2003/4 **c–**
c–: c21g c26g^{pu} Jun 21] winning pointer: no form in steeplechases: has worn cheekpieces.
D. C. Turner

SILVER PROPHET (IRE) 5 gr.g. Idris (IRE) – Silver Heart (Yankee Gold) [2003/4 **h85 +**
16d 17s⁴ 16g* 17s Apr 6] leggy gelding: fairly useful on Flat (stays 11f): modest form
over hurdles: won maiden at Huntingdon in March: raced around 2m: tongue tied last 2
starts. *M. R. Bosley*

SILVER SAMUEL (NZ) 7 gr.g. Hula Town (NZ) – Offrande (NZ) (Decies) [2003/4 **c–**
c24g⁴ c24d^{pu} c20d 20d* 20v⁴ 21g⁵ 20g 25d^{pu} c24d^{pu} Apr 8] big, lengthy gelding: won **h95**
maiden point in 2003, no show in 4 steeplechases, tried in cheekpieces final start: modest
novice hurdler: 50/1-winner at Haydock in December: stays 2½m: acts on heavy going.
S. A. Brookshaw

SILVER SEDGE (IRE) 5 br.g. Aristocracy – Pollyfaster (Polyfoto) [2003/4 17d^F **h69**
Apr 10] €40,000 4-y-o: brother to several winners, including fair hurdler/chaser Mister
Drum, stayed 2½m: dam unraced: showed some ability prior to falling 2 out in novice
hurdle at Carlisle on debut. *J. Howard Johnson*

SILVER SLEEVE (IRE) 12 b.g. Taufan (USA) – Sable Coated (Caerleon (USA)) **c–**
[2003/4 c68, h57: 17d^{pu} 21m⁶ 17s⁵ 19v 16d⁴ 19v⁵ 17g 20d⁶ c19m c20d^{pu} Apr 21] rather **h–**
leggy gelding: bad handicap hurdler/maiden chaser: wears headgear: has had tongue tied.
Mrs H. M. Bridges

SILVER SQUIRREL (IRE) 4 b.f. Silver Wizard (USA) – Farah (Lead On Time (USA)) **h–**
[2003/4 F13g F16v 21d^{pu} Mar 16] leggy filly: third foal: dam once-raced half-sister to **F–**

high-class staying hurdler Anzum and high-class 2m hurdler Jazilah: soundly beaten in 2 bumpers and in mares novice on hurdling debut. *J. R. Turner*

SILVER STREAK (IRE) 10 gr.g. Roselier (FR) – Vulcan (IRE) (Callernish) [2003/4 c–, h–: c24g⁻ᵘʳ c24d⁵ c26m Apr 14] tall, good-topped gelding: winning hurdler/chaser, lightly raced and out of sorts since 2001/2. *N. J. Gifford*   **c–** **h–**

SILVERTOWN 9 b.g. Danehill (USA) – Docklands (USA) (Theatrical) [2003/4 h125p: 17mᵖᵘ 20vᵖᵘ Jan 17] sturdy, lengthy gelding: fairly useful handicap hurdler in 2002/3: successful twice on Flat in 2003 but pulled up both starts over hurdles in 2003/4: stays 2½m: seems best on good going or firmer: has reportedly had breathing problems (including final outing): usually makes running: has flashed tail. *L. Lungo*   **h–**

SIMBER HILL (IRE) 10 ch.g. Phardante (FR) – Princess Wager (Pollerton) [2003/4 c115, h–: c24d³ c24gᵖᵘ c24g² c23m⁴ c24g⁵ c24d⁴ c24g⁵ Apr 16] lengthy gelding: fair chaser: suited by 3m+: acts on good to firm and good to soft going: effective blinkered or not: has idled/found less than expected: not a fluent jumper. *P. J. Hobbs*   **c113 d** **h–**

SIMIOLA 5 b.m. Shaamit (IRE) – Brave Vanessa (USA) (Private Account (USA)) [2003/4 16gᵖᵘ 16mᵖᵘ 19m⁶ 17dᵖᵘ Dec 2] modest on Flat for G. L. Moore: well beaten over hurdles. *S. T. Lewis*   **h–**

SIMLET 9 b.g. Forzando – Besito (Wassl) [2003/4 24g³ 24mᵖᵘ 20d* 20g³ c19g³ c24g c21d³ c20g⁴ Apr 10] good-topped gelding: fair handicap hurdler: dead-heated at Newcastle in November: modest form in handicap chases: stays 3m: acts on firm and good to soft going: has won with and without cheekpieces/tongue strap. *E. W. Tuer*   **c98** **h107**

SIMON'S SEAT (USA) 5 ch.g. Woodman (USA) – Spire (USA) (Topsider (USA)) [2003/4 16d 21g⁶ Feb 28] leggy gelding: fair maiden on Flat (stays 2m), sold out of J. Toller's stable 13,000 gns Newmarket Autumn Sales: showed little in novice hurdles at Ascot and Kempton. *C. Drew*   **h–**

SIMON THE POACHER 5 br.g. Chaddleworth (IRE) – Lady Crusty (Golden Dipper) [2003/4 17g Apr 1] half-brother to poor hurdler Mike Simmons (by Ballacashtal), stays 21f: little form on Flat: pulled hard and blundered badly sixth when tailed off in maiden on hurdling debut. *L. P. Grassick*   **h–**

SIMOSKI 7 b.g. Petoski – Miss Simone (Ile de Bourbon (USA)) [2003/4 c–, h65: 16m 16m² 16m³ 17f⁵ Sep 30] smallish, angular gelding: unseated only outing over fences: poor maiden hurdler: stays 19f: acts on firm going. *N. A. Twiston-Davies*   **c–** **h72**

SIMOUN (IRE) 6 b.g. Monsun (GER) – Suivez (FR) (Fioravanti (USA)) [2003/4 16d⁵ 17s* 16s² 16g 20g⁶ 19g* Apr 16] compact gelding: smart on Flat (stays 11f) at 3 and 4 yrs for P. Schiergen, poor efforts both starts in 2003: fairly useful novice hurdler: easily won at Taunton in February and April: seemed to take little interest after mistake fourth when tailed off in Supreme Novices' Hurdle at Cheltenham fourth outing: best effort when never-nearer sixth of 23 to Zibeline in strongly-contested handicap at Aintree next time: stays 2½m: acts on soft going: tongue tied after hurdling debut. *M. C. Pipe*   **h123**

SIMPLY GIFTED 9 b.g. Simply Great (FR) – Souveniers (Relko) [2003/4 c16s* c16dᵘʳ c16g⁴ c20g* Apr 16] well-made gelding: useful hurdler/chaser: left T. Easterby and returned from long absence (has reportedly had wind operation) to win handicap chase at Chepstow in January: at least as good as ever when winning similar event at Ayr in April by neck from Turgeonev: creditable eighth to Prince of Pleasure at Punchestown later in month: stays 2½m: acts on heavy going, below best on good to firm: tried visored/blinkered, best efforts when not: sometimes jumps none too fluently. *Jonjo O'Neill*   **c135** **h–**

SIMPLY MYSTIC 4 ch.f. Simply Great (FR) – Mystic Memory (Ela-Mana-Mou) [2003/4 F13g³ F16d³ F16g² Mar 6] fourth foal: half-sister to fair bumper winner Flash of Memory (by Rock Hopper): dam, useful staying hurdler/2m winner on Flat, half-sister to useful staying hurdler/chaser Wain Mountain: modest form when placed in bumpers. *P. D. Niven*   **F84**

SIMPLY SILVER LADY 9 ch.m. Push On – Pentwd Mundy (Vital Season) [2003/4 c20mᵖᵘ Apr 28] lengthy mare: no sign of ability: has had tongue tied. *Mrs H. O. Graham*   **c–** **h–**

SIMPLY STUNNING 5 ch.m. Primitive Rising (USA) – Qurrat Al Ain (Wolver Hollow) [2003/4 F17g F17d 22vᵖᵘ Jan 24] good-topped mare: eighth foal: half-sister to top-class chaser Simply Dashing (by Simply Great), stayed 25f: dam 2m winner over hurdles: no form in bumpers or mares novice hurdle. *Jonjo O'Neill*   **h–** **F–**

SIMPLY SUPREME (IRE)   7 b.g. Supreme Leader – Some Gift (Avocat) [2003/4   **c138 +**
h125: c16g² c20d² c20s³ 23s⁴ c23v* c25sᶠ c25g* c33dᶠ Apr 17]   **h120**

     The standard of jumping among the season's leading staying novice chasers
often left a great deal to be desired, never more so than in the Martell Cognac
Sainsbury's Mildmay Novices' Chase at Aintree in April. Just four of the eleven
who set out completed the course, and far and away the best round was put in by the
winner Simply Supreme, who himself had fallen on his previous start and was to do
so again on his only subsequent one. What beforehand had looked a competitive
Grade 2 contest turned out to be anything but, the Mildmay field reduced to four
with almost a circuit remaining and eight of the nineteen fences still to be jumped.
The first and second in the Royal & SunAlliance Chase at Cheltenham were two of
those out of the race by this stage, Rule Supreme unseating his rider at the eighth
and Simply Supreme's stable-companion Royal Emperor, who started favourite,
falling at the eleventh. The narrow leader See You Sometime also came down at the
latter fence, leaving Simply Supreme in front. By the time the twelfth was reached,
the three stragglers, including second favourite D'Argent, had been pulled up and
Simply Supreme had gone clear of Double Honour, L'Aventure and Liberthine,
the result never in much doubt from thereon. Twenty lengths clear of his nearest
pursuer Double Honour two out, Simply Supreme tired a little late on as L'Aventure
stayed on into second but Simply Supreme still had a twelve-length advantage at
the line. It was Simply Supreme's second chase win. He had got off the mark in
similar style in a novice event at Wetherby in January, impressing with his jumping
as he made all to win by a distance from one other finisher. Further successes for
Simply Supreme seem assured, especially as his jumping is likely to become
consistently good as he gains further experience, and he could well pick up a
valuable staying handicap in due course, possibly one—knowing his owner—with
'National' somewhere in the title. Unfortunately, Simply Supreme got no further

Martell Cognac Sainsbury's Mildmay Novices' Chase, Aintree—
Simply Supreme (centre) for once gives his rivals a jumping lesson;
Royal Emperor (grey) and See You Sometime are both about to depart

than the first when given the chance and sent off joint favourite in the Scottish Grand National on his final start. The distance of four miles and a furlong, a mile further than he'd attempted previously, wouldn't have troubled Simply Supreme.

Simply Supreme (IRE) (b.g. 1997)	Supreme Leader (b 1982)	Bustino (b 1971)	Busted Ship Yard
		Princess Zena (b 1975)	Habitat Guiding Light
	Some Gift (ch 1982)	Avocat (ch 1969)	Relko Pourparler
		Royal Escort (br 1972)	Royal Highway Autumn Parade

Simply Supreme started off in bumpers in 2001/2, winning at Bangor, and went on to show himself a fairly useful novice hurdler the following season, winning twice at Haydock, and also at Kelso. He has already earned, in win and place money, almost four times the 22,000 guineas paid for him at the Doncaster May Sales in 2000. Simply Supreme is the eighth foal of the lightly-raced Some Gift, who gained her only placing when runner-up in a maiden hurdle at Tramore. Some Gift, a half-sister to the useful hunter chaser No Escort, has bred one other winner, Simply Supreme's brother Mega Deal, a fairly useful hurdler up to three miles for Aidan O'Brien. The next two mares on the bottom line, Royal Escort and Autumn Parade, also failed to win a race. Interestingly, Autumn Parade is also the great grandam of Simply Supreme's former stable-companion the high-class staying chaser The Last Fling, one of the best of the many winning jumpers to race in the colours of Simply Supreme's owner Trevor Hemmings. Simply Supreme, a front runner, has raced only on good ground or softer over jumps (he ran below form on good to firm in a Grade 2 bumper) and acts well on heavy. *Mrs S. J. Smith*

SINALCO (USA)   6 b.g. Quest For Fame – Sin Lucha (USA) (Northfields (USA)) [2003/4 F–: F16s 16d⁵ 24v⁴ 20vᵖᵘ Jan 31] no form in bumpers: apparently best effort over hurdles when fourth in novice hurdle at Uttoxeter in January. *Mrs L. B. Normile*   **h84 ?**
F–

SINDAPOUR (IRE)   6 b.g. Priolo (USA) – Sinntara (IRE) (Lashkari) [2003/4 16d* 21g 17s³ 22g³ Apr 18] half-brother to top-class middle-distance colt Sinndar (by Grand Lodge) and winning 2½m selling hurdler Sirinndi (by Shahrastani): fairly useful on Flat (stays 2½m): fair form over hurdles: odds on, won maiden at Plumpton in March: best subsequent effort when third to Almaydan in novice at Exeter third outing: didn't jump well other 2 appearances: should be suited by 2½m+. *M. C. Pipe*   **h114**

SINGLE SOURCING (IRE)   13 b.g. Good Thyne (USA) – Lady Albron (Royal Match) [2003/4 c–, h–: c25g² c25dᵖᵘ c30g* c24dᵖᵘ Jul 2] rangy gelding: modest handicap chaser: as good as ever when winning at Cartmel in June: stays 3¾m: acts on heavy going: has reportedly bled from nose, including first start. *A. C. Whillans*   **c96**
h–

SINGULARITY   4 b.g. Rudimentary (USA) – Lyrical Bid (USA) (Lyphard (USA)) [2003/4 19sᵖᵘ Apr 4] poor maiden on Flat (stays 7f) for W. Muir: always behind in maiden on hurdling debut. *K. F. Clutterbuck*   **h–**

SINK OR SWIM (IRE)   6 b.m. Big Sink Hope (USA) – Cragreagh VII (Damsire Unregistered) [2003/4 F16g⁴ F16m² F16f³ F16f⁴ 16m 16gᵖᵘ Nov 19] ex-Irish mare: first foal: dam never ran: maiden pointer: in frame all 4 starts in bumpers: little form over hurdles, leaving W. Flavin before final start. *J. J. Bridger*   **h–**
F85

SINTOS   6 b. or br.g. Syrtos – Sindur (Rolfe (USA)) [2003/4 F17g² F17s Nov 17] seventh foal: half-brother to modest hurdler Little Bud (by Lord Bud), stays 21f: dam poor on Flat/over jumps: soon off bridle when second of 5 in bumper at Folkestone on debut: well held there under more testing conditions 2 weeks later. *Miss A. M. Newton-Smith*   **F77**

SIP OF BRANDY (IRE)   11 ch.g. Sharp Charter – Manhattan Brandy (Frankincense) [2003/4 c93: c25dᵘʳ c25m² c22g⁶ c24d Apr 8] angular gelding: winning hunter chaser: form in 2004 only when second at Hereford in March: let down by jumping otherwise: stays 25f: acts on good to firm and heavy going: tried blinkered. *Miss J. Hughes*   **c83 x**

SIR ALFRED   5 b.g. Royal Academy (USA) – Magnificent Star (USA) (Silver Hawk (USA)) [2003/4 h94: 16m⁶ Aug 2] leggy gelding: modest hurdler: below best in handicap only start in 2003/4: will prove best with emphasis on speed around 2m: excitable sort (has been early to post). *A. King*   **h89**

SIR BOB (IRE)   12 br.g. Aristocracy – Wilden (Will Somers) [2003/4 c112, h–: c23g c25v³ c24m Apr 13] tall gelding: fair chaser: out of sorts in 2003/4: should stay beyond 3m: acts on heavy going: blinkered once: often none too fluent: lazy. *Mrs H. Dalton*   **c–** **h–**

SIR BRASTIAS   5 b.g. Shaamit (IRE) – Premier Night (Old Vic) [2003/4 16g² Mar 17] fairly useful on Flat (stays 13f) for S. Dow: shaped well when second in maiden at Huntingdon on hurdling debut, held up pulling hard and staying on well not knocked about: sure to improve. *K. C. Bailey*   **h84 p**

SIR CUMFERENCE   8 b.g. Sir Harry Lewis (USA) – Puki Puki (Roselier (FR)) [2003/4 c94: c24gᵖᵘ c24dᶠ Nov 15] rangy gelding: handicap chaser: favourite both outings in 2003/4 (breathing problem on reappearance), already weakening when falling twelfth final one: will prove best at 3m+: acts on good to firm going: usually sound jumper. *Miss H. C. Knight*   **c–**

SIR D'ORTON (FR)   8 ch.g. Beyssac (FR) – Prime Target (FR) (Ti King (FR)) [2003/4 c24sᵖᵘ c20g⁴ c26dᵖᵘ Jun 9] leggy gelding: maiden hurdler: fair handicap chaser: won points in January and March: effective at 2½m to 3¼m: raced mainly on going softer than good (acts on heavy): tried visored/blinkered: has found less than seemed likely. *P. F. Nicholls*   **c113** **h–**

SIR EDWARD BURROW (IRE)   6 b.g. Distinctly North (USA) – Alalja (IRE) (Entitled) [2003/4 h85+: 16m³ 20g³ May 15] strong, good-topped gelding: modest maiden hurdler: will stay beyond 2½m: acts on good to firm and good to soft going. *W. Storey*   **h92**

SIRERIC (IRE)   14 b.g. Asir – Twice Regal (Royal Prerogative) [2003/4 c97, h98: c25g³ 24g c30g³ c30dᵖᵘ Nov 29] leggy, angular gelding: modest handicap hurdler/chaser: stays 4m: acts on heavy going: front runner: very tough. *R. Johnson*   **c94** **h–**

SIR FROSTY   11 b.g. Arctic Lord – Snowy Autumn (Deep Run) [2003/4 c123: c29vᵖᵘ c30g c25g⁶ c33dᵖᵘ Apr 17] lengthy gelding: fairly useful handicap chaser, lightly raced: form in 2003/4 only when sixth to Lord of The River in valuable event at Aintree in April: stays 33f: acts on heavy going: tongue tied prior to second start. *B. J. M. Ryall*   **c115** **h–**

SIR GORDON   6 ch.g. Hatim (USA) – Sweet Colleen (Connaught) [2003/4 16sᵖᵘ Feb 22] half-brother to several winners, including fairly useful 2m hurdler Broctune Bay (by Midyan) and bumper performer Double Chimes (by Efisio): dam, winning 2m hurdler, half-sister to smart hurdler/useful chaser up to 21f Brave Hussar: showed nothing in novice hurdle on debut. *C. N. Kellett*   **h–**

SIR HARVY (IRE)   5 gr.g. Gothland (FR) – Promised Path (Hello Gorgeous (USA)) [2003/4 h1dᵖᵘ Oct 29] fifth foal: dam 11f winner: bled from nose in novice hurdle on debut. *M. Todhunter*   **h–**

SIR HOMO (IRE)   10 b.g. Homo Sapien – Deise Lady (Le Bavard (FR)) [2003/4 h–: 17m 17m² 16m² 16f² 20d 19d⁵ 17s 20s³ 17d Mar 30] poor maiden hurdler: effective at 2m, probably at 2½m: acts on any going: tried blinkered: usually finds little and not one to trust. *E. W. Tuer*   **h78 §**

SIRINNDI (IRE)   10 b.g. Shahrastani (USA) – Sinntara (IRE) (Lashkari) [2003/4 c–, h65: 20sᶠ May 2] small gelding: no show only start over fences: poor hurdler: stays 21f: acts on heavy going: has had tongue tied. *Miss K. Marks*   **c–** **h–**

SIRIUS LADY   4 b.f. Sir Harry Lewis (USA) – Intrepida (Fair Season) [2003/4 16mᵖᵘ Aug 9] well held in 3 maidens on Flat for A. Balding: tongue tied, no show on hurdling debut. *E. L. James*   **h–**

SIR MOUSE   8 gr.g. Phardante (FR) – Place Stephanie (IRE) (Hatim (USA)) [2003/4 h92: 23d* 26s 25sᵖᵘ 19d² 25g Feb 6] strong gelding: modest hurdler: won 5-runner novice at Fakenham in November: stays 23f: acts on heavy going: hard ride. *M. F. Harris*   **h91 §**

SIR MURPHY   11 ch.g. Brando – Bemas (Levanter) [2003/4 16m 24gᶠ Nov 8] workmanlike gelding: very lightly raced and no sign of ability: tried visored. *Mrs B. E. Matthews*   **h–**

SIR NIGHT (IRE)   4 b.g. Night Shift (USA) – Highly Respected (IRE) (High Estate) [2003/4 16g 16g⁴ 16g⁵ 17g* Apr 12] smallish gelding: fair at best on Flat (stays 1¼m), sold out of J. Bethell's stable 15,000 gns Newmarket Autumn Sales: improved effort over hurdles when winning juvenile at Sedgefield: not sure to stay much further than 17f. *Jedd O'Keeffe*   **h95**

SIR NORMAN   9 b.g. Arctic Lord – Moy Ran Lady (Black Minstrel) [2003/4 c98, h–: c16m² c17g* c20g c17m⁵ c16dᵖᵘ c20sᵖᵘ c17s⁵ c20g³ c19g c20g Apr 10] tall gelding: fair   **c101 d** **h–**

handicap chaser: won at Kelso in May: largely disappointing after: best up to 21f: acts on soft and good to firm going: usually tongue tied: usually bold-jumping front runner. *R. D. E. Woodhouse*

SIR OJ (IRE)   7 br.g. Be My Native (USA) – Fox Glen (Furry Glen) [2003/4 18s* 22d²   **h116** 22s⁴ 20d Apr 12] IR £9,000 4-y-o; half-brother to a winning pointer by Orchestra: dam, placed over hurdles, from family of Grand National winner Last Suspect: bumper winner: won maiden at Navan on hurdling debut in February: best effort when second to Florida Coast in minor event at Fairyhouse later in month: stays 2¾m: raced on going softer than good. *N. Meade, Ireland*

SIR PELINORE   9 b.g. Caerleon (USA) – Soemba (General Assembly (USA)) [2003/4   **h–** h–, F–: 21sᵖᵘ 22sᵖᵘ 16s 19d⁵ 26dᵖᵘ 19sᵖᵘ Apr 11] of little account: tongue tied on debut. *Mrs A. M. Woodrow*

SIR REMBRANDT (IRE)   8 b.g. Mandalus – Sue's A Lady (Le Moss) [2003/4   **c169** c138p, h–: c26gᶠ c26d* c29d² c25dᵖᵘ c24g⁶ c26g² Mar 18]   **h–**
      Preparations for Cheltenham don't come less trouble-free than that of Sir Rembrandt in the build-up to this year's Gold Cup. Two appearances in trial races for which he was fancied were dismal: he was pulled up early on the final circuit in the Pillar Property Chase at Cheltenham in January and three weeks later trailed in sixth of eight behind Shooting Light in the AON Chase at Newbury. Little wonder that after the latter event, trainer Robert Alner all but ruled Sir Rembrandt out of participation at the Festival. Sir Rembrandt's jumping was part of the problem, but he gave the impression of not being right in himself, so it came as something of a surprise a week before the Gold Cup when his trainer, having ruled out the stable's leading hope Kingscliff, reported that Sir Rembrandt, whose treatment reportedly included acupuncture, had come to himself in the month since Newbury and would after all take his chance at Cheltenham. 33/1-shot Sir Rembrandt made the most of the opportunity, making good progress on the final circuit in the Gold Cup to challenge down the hill, keeping on well after the last after being none too fluent two out, and, challenging wide, splitting the two others involved in the finish Best Mate and Harbour Pilot at the line, just half a length off the winner. The 2004 renewal wasn't by any stretch of the imagination a vintage Cheltenham Gold Cup but Sir Rembrandt acquitted himself really well and put up a top-class performance.

John Hughes Rehearsal Chase (Limited Handicap), Chepstow—Sir Rembrandt wins impressively

SIR

Earlier in the winter, before his troubles in the build-up to Cheltenham, Sir Rembrandt had been on offer at only half those odds, following a couple of excellent performances in valuable handicaps at Chepstow. After falling at the third in the Hennessy at Newbury on his reappearance, he was aimed at the John Hughes Rehearsal Chase a week later. He went off second favourite, though most eyes to begin with were on two others in the field of six, the favourite Keen Leader and the veteran See More Business. The spotlight by the end, though, was very much on Sir Rembrandt—he didn't have to come off the bridle at any stage and drew right away after the second last to beat the former Grand National winner Bindaree eight lengths; Keen Leader lost his rider around halfway and See More Business was a remote fourth. Sir Rembrandt was returned to Chepstow three weeks later for the Welsh National, in which he carried an 8-lb penalty for his Rehearsal success. This still meant he was 8 lb better off than he would have been had the BHB handicapper had the chance to reassess him but it still proved just too much to enable him to confirm placings with Bindaree. Sir Rembrandt went down by half a length, though had he not ploughed through five out, a blunder he did well to recover from at all, he might well have edged the victory. Sir Rembrandt's lack of experience (his first season over fences, in 2002/3, was limited to two outings due to a leg injury) might have played a part in his early jumping problems and it was encouraging for his future prospects that he avoided serious error in the Gold Cup.

		Mandamus (br 1960)	Petition
	Mandalus (b or br 1974)		Great Fun
Sir Rembrandt (IRE) (b.g. 1996)		Laminate (gr 1957)	Abernant
			Lamri
		Le Moss (ch 1975)	Le Levanstell
	Sue's A Lady (ch 1986)		Feemoss
		Warrior Queen (b 1964)	King's Bench
			Princess Antiope

Mr A. Hordle's "Sir Rembrandt"

SIS

Sir Rembrandt is a big, strong, lengthy gelding, altogether a grand stamp of a chaser, and the sort that might well make an Aintree horse one day. His pedigree, though, isn't exactly that of an old-fashioned jumper, for all that he's by Mandalus out of a bumper-winning Le Moss mare. His grandam Warrior Queen and third dam Princess Antiope were above average on the Flat, Warrior Queen fairly useful at two when winning at six furlongs and at three when successful at a mile and a quarter, Princess Antiope a useful performer at up to a mile. Warrior Queen produced numerous minor Flat winners, while Princess Antiope was a half-sister to the very smart miler Lord of Verona who won the Britannia Handicap at Royal Ascot. He later won over hurdles and finished second in a division of the Gloucestershire Hurdle before retiring to stud, where his progeny included the dam of another Gold Cup runner-up Rushing Wild. Sir Rembrandt is the fourth foal out of Sue's A Lady. Her other offspring include a couple of winning pointers and the useful hurdler/fairly useful chaser Audacter (by Strong Gale), who stayed three miles. Her latest runner Monsieur Monet (by Norwich) showed fairly useful form in winning a two-and-a-half-mile bumper late in 2003/4. Sir Rembrandt was well bought at only IR 9,000 guineas as a four-year-old. He will stay beyond three miles five furlongs and has raced only on good or good to soft going. *R. H. Alner*

SIR ROBBO (IRE) 10 b.g. Glacial Storm (USA) – Polly's Slipper (Pollerton) [2003/4 c92, h–: c25g5 c24g4 c25dpu c24m4 Feb 25] workmanlike gelding: winning chaser, little show in 2003/4: stays 3¼m: acts on good to firm and good to soft going (pulled up feelingly only start on firm): all 4 wins at Hereford. *N. A. Twiston-Davies* — c– h–

SIR ROWLAND HILL (IRE) 5 b.g. Kahyasi – Zaila (IRE) (Darshaan) [2003/4 F89: F16g3 20d4 20s 20v3 24gpu Feb 18] sturdy gelding: progressive form in bumpers: disappointing over hurdles after fourth of 8 in novice at Newcastle: should stay beyond 2½m: *Ferdy Murphy* — h89 F95

SIR STORM (IRE) 8 b.g. Ore – Yonder Bay (IRE) (Trimmingham) [2003/4 c108, h–: c16m* c20g c16m4 c16m2 c16d* c16d* c16v5 c16m c16d* c16d* Apr 22] lengthy gelding: fairly useful handicap chaser: had excellent season, winning at Perth in September, Wetherby in November, Haydock in December, Wetherby in March and Perth in April, best effort when beating Stamparland Hill 8 lengths at last-named: raced mainly around 2m: acts on heavy and good to firm going: wore cheekpieces last 5 starts: usually races prominently: sound jumper. *G. M. Moore* — c128 h–

SIR TALBOT 10 b.g. Ardross – Bermuda Lily (Dunbeath (USA)) [2003/4 20g3 24dpu 21d6 c16g2 c20g* c20g2 c20m4 c19d2 Mar 23] quite good-topped gelding: one-time smart hurdler: fair over hurdles and fences nowadays: won novice chase at Leicester in January by head from Old Marsh: good efforts when runner-up in similar events at Kempton and Exeter: should stay beyond 2½m: acts on good to firm going, probably on soft. *J. A. B. Old* — c115 h113

SIR TOBY (IRE) 11 bl.g. Strong Gale – Petite Deb (Cure The Blues (USA)) [2003/4 c112, h–: c20m5 c20g6 c20g2 c21s* Apr 12] rangy gelding: fair handicap chaser: won 4-finisher event at Fakenham: probably best short of 3m: acts on soft and good to firm going: usually sound jumper: races prominently. *R. Rowe* — c102 h–

SIR WALTER (IRE) 11 b.g. The Bart (USA) – Glenbalda (Kambalda) [2003/4 c73, h–: 16g4 17d3 20m 20m5 16m6 17d5 16spu 16s 16d 16d6 19m6 21g4 16d4 Apr 12] leggy gelding: less than fluent over fences, modest handicap hurdler, below form after second start: stays 19f: acts on good to firm and heavy going: has had tongue tied: has looked ungenuine. *A. G. Hobbs* — c– h94 d

SIR WILLIAMWALLACE (IRE) 11 br.g. Strong Gale – Kemchee (Kemal (FR)) [2003/4 c77d, h–: c24mpu May 10] lengthy gelding: poor chaser: stays 3¼m: acts on firm and good to soft going: has worn headgear: tried tongue tied. *D. L. Claydon* — c– h–

SISSINGHURST STORM (IRE) 6 b. or br.m. Good Thyne (USA) – Mrs Hill (Strong Gale) [2003/4 h69, F–: 16g 21s5 26s3 c20d4 c25m* c22s2 c21m3 Apr 15] poor maiden hurdler: of similar standard over fences, won mares novice at Hereford in March: likely to prove best at 3m+: acts on soft and good to firm going. *R. Dickin* — c80 h82

SISTER AMY 7 gr.m. Gods Solution – Amys Sister (Silly Prices) [2003/4 F–: 20dpu Apr 28] little show in varied events. *J. R. Turner* — h–

SISTER ANNA 6 br.m. Gildoran – Take The Veil (Monksfield) [2003/4 h66, F77: 20gF 16s5 23v2 21d6 22g* Apr 24] tall mare: modest hurdler: won handicap at Market Rasen in April: stays 23f: acts on heavy going. *T. D. Walford* — h89

841

SISTER CINNAMON 6 ch.m. Karinga Bay – Cinnamon Run (Deep Run) [2003/4 **F95** F16s[2] F17s[4] F16s* F16s Mar 13] 5,500 3-y-o: lengthy mare: fifth foal: half-sister to poor 2m hurdler Cinnamon Club (by Derrylin): dam fair 2m hurdler/chaser: fair form in bumpers, winning 16-runner mares event at Towcester in February by 21 lengths from Lady Dynamite: will be suited by further. *S. Gollings*

SISTER SUPERIOR (IRE) 9 b.m. Supreme Leader – Nicat (Wolver Hollow) **c–** [2003/4 c–, h92§: 20m May 7] good-topped mare: handicap hurdler: no worthwhile form **h– §** in 3 novice chases: stays 2¾m: acts on heavy going: hard ride. *S. Gollings*

SIX BELLS 8 b.m. Gildoran – Strikealightlady (Lighter) [2003/4 17m[pu] Aug 25] **h–** lengthy mare: poor maiden pointer: blinkered, no show in claimer on hurdling debut: sold £1,000 Ascot November Sales, resold £650 Ascot February Sales. *J. D. Frost*

SIX CLERKS (IRE) 11 b.g. Shadeed (USA) – Skidmore Girl (USA) (Vaguely Noble) **c76** [2003/4 c81, h–: c21s[F] c24g c24d[F] Mar 15] leggy gelding: poor maiden steeplechaser: **h–** stays 3m: acts on firm and good to soft going: blinkered once, wears visor/cheekpieces nowadays: has looked ungenuine. *Mrs S. M. Odell*

SIX OF ONE 6 b.g. Kahyasi – Ten To Six (Night Shift (USA)) [2003/4 h83: 16d[3] 17g[2] **h99** 20s[6] 18s[2] 20s[3] 21g 20d[4] 19g[2] Apr 16] useful-looking gelding: fair maiden hurdler: stays 2½m: acts on soft going. *R. Rowe*

SIXO (IRE) 7 gr.g. Roselier (FR) – Miss Mangaroo (Oats) [2003/4 F114: 16d* 20d[4] **h122** 21d[3] 20s 24g[6] Apr 2] leggy, close-coupled gelding: useful form in bumpers in 2002/3: odds on, all out to beat Gods Token ½ length in novice at Sandown in December on hurdling debut: generally disappointing after, ran better though went in snatches when just over 20 lengths sixth of 13 to Accipiter in Grade 1 novice at Aintree: stays 3m: raced on good ground or softer: usually front runner. *M. C. Pipe*

SIX PACK (IRE) 6 ch.g. Royal Abjar (USA) – Regal Entrance (Be My Guest (USA)) **c97** [2003/4 h–: 16f[3] 16g 17d[3] c16f[2] c16m* Dec 27] good-topped gelding: modest on Flat **h88** (stays 1¼m): poor form over hurdles: better in 2 starts over fences at Leicester, recovering from blunder 5 out and idling run-in when winning novice handicap in December: raced around 2m: possibly best on good ground or firmer. *Andrew Turnell*

SIX STAR 4 b.f. Desert Story (IRE) – Adriya (Vayrann) [2003/4 16g[2] 17d[4] 16s[6] 16d **h71** Jan 22] disappointing maiden on Flat: poor form over hurdles: barely stays 2m: left B. Duke before final start. *B. G. Powell*

SKENFRITH 5 b.g. Atraf – Hobbs Choice (Superpower) [2003/4 h86: 16g[2] 24d[5] 16g[2] **h86** 20g[5] 20m[3] 20d[3] 27d[2] 16d 19d 20v* 22g[4] 24g[6] Mar 13] modest hurdler: won 16-runner novice at Newcastle in February: effective at 2m to 27f: acts on good to firm and heavy going. *Miss S. E. Forster*

SKIDDAW ROSE (IRE) 8 gr.m. Terimon – Whimbrel (Dara Monarch) [2003/4 h66x: **c66** 16g[6] 16g[6] 16m[5] 20d[3] 17m 17m[4] 17g[4] 17g[5] c16f[6] c16f[2] c16m[ur] Oct 31] small mare: poor **h66 x** maiden hurdler: grossly flattered by proximity to Flame Creek when second of 3 in novice chase at Kelso: stays 2½m: acts on firm and good to soft ground: makes mistakes. *M. A. Barnes*

SKILLWISE 12 b.g. Buckley – Calametta (Oats) [2003/4 c–§, h–: c20m[4] c23d[5] c25d[pu] **c94 §** c27s[6] Dec 26] big, workmanlike gelding: handicap chaser, very little form since early- **h–** 2002: stays 3¼m: acts on good to firm and heavy going: blinkered once. *T. D. Easterby*

SKINSEY FINNEGAN (IRE) 10 b.g. Fresh Breeze (USA) – Rose of Solway (Der- **c90** ring Rose) [2003/4 c104: c20m[3] c26m[4] c22g[4] Oct 5] lengthy gelding: handicap chaser, not at best over unsuitable trips in 2003/4: best around 2m: acts on soft and good to firm going: wore cheekpieces in 2003/4: best efforts when tongue tied: has failed to impress with attitude. *C. A. Dwyer*

SKIORA 7 br.m. Petoski – Coral Delight (Idiot's Delight) [2003/4 h–§, F79: 16m[pu] **h– §** 16m 19s[pu] 17d 26m[5] 22g[pu] Mar 25] leggy, angular mare: of little account: tried blinkered, wore cheekpieces last 4 starts: temperamental. *A. J. Wilson*

SKIPPERS CLEUCH (IRE) 10 b.g. Be My Native (USA) – Cloughoola Lady **c139** (Black Minstrel) [2003/4 c109, h–: c25g[pu] c25d* c25d[2] c20v[pu] Jan 31] big, good-topped **h–** gelding: useful handicap chaser: improved efforts on completed starts in 2003/4, winning at Wetherby in December by 14 lengths from Tonoco: reportedly hung/lost action when running poorly final outing: stays 25f: raced on good going or softer (acts on heavy). *L. Lungo*

SKI SEAL   10 b.g. Petoski – Roving Seal (Privy Seal) [2003/4 c23s^{pu} c21d^{pu} c22g Apr 22] lightly-raced gelding: no form in novice company over fences, left B. Ryall before final outing: tried visored. *Miss V. A. Stephens*   c– h–

SKRAM   11 b.g. Rambo Dancer (CAN) – Skarberg (FR) (Noir Et Or) [2003/4 c–, h–: 20m^4 16g c21m ç17g Sep 6] leggy gelding: winning hurdler/chaser: no form in 2003/4: tried blinkered: has had tongue tied. *R. Dickin*   c– h–

SKYCAB (IRE)   12 b.g. Montelimar (USA) – Sams Money (Pry) [2003/4 c130, h–: c25g^3 c20g c24d^{ur} c25d c24d^5 c36d^{ur} c20g Apr 18] useful-looking gelding: useful handicap chaser: out of form after first outing, looked unwilling final one: stays 25f: acts on soft and good to firm going. *N. J. Gifford*   c133 d h–

SKYE BLUE (IRE)   7 b.g. Blues Traveller (IRE) – Hitopah (Bustino) [2003/4 16d^4 Mar 24] strong gelding: fair hurdler for N. Henderson in 2001/2: off 2 years and blinkered, well held in seller: should stay 2½m: acts on soft going. *B. J. Llewellyn*   h–

SKYLANDER   8 b.g. Thethingaboutitis (USA) – Mesembryanthemum (Warpath) [2003/4 h–, F76: 16g^6 20m^4 c19d^{pu} Jan 7] good-bodied gelding: poor form over hurdles: pulled up after hampered and mistake fourth on chasing debut: headstrong. *Mrs Merrita Jones*   c– h79

SKYLARKER (USA)   6 b.g. Sky Classic (CAN) – O My Darling (USA) (Mr Prospector (USA)) [2003/4 h74p: 16m^{pu} Mar 11] fairly useful on Flat (stays easy 1½m): only poor form in 3 starts over hurdles: pulls hard. *W. S. Kittow*   h–

SKY WARRIOR (FR)   6 b.g. Warrshan (USA) – Sky Bibi (FR) (Sky Lawyer (FR)) [2003/4 20g^6 19d c16s^4 c24s c21m^2 c20d Mar 27] medium-sized gelding: fifth foal: half-brother to winners up to 1m in France and Czech Republic: dam maiden: placed up to around 1½m on Flat: fair hurdler: successful 3 times over fences in French Provinces in 2002/3 for P. Monfort: best effort in Britain when length second of 4 finishers to Zaffamore in handicap chase at Wincanton: stays 21f: acts on heavy and good to firm going. *Evan Williams*   c118 h107

SLEDMERE (IRE)   9 ch.g. Shalford (IRE) – Jazirah (Main Reef) [2003/4 c–, h–: c25s^{pu} Mar 7] winning pointer: yet to complete in 4 starts in hunter chases: has had tongue tied. *George R. Moscrop*   c– h–

SLEEP BAL (FR)   5 b.g. Sleeping Car (FR) – Balle Six (FR) (Balsamo (FR)) [2003/4 20g^6 20d 16m Apr 23] angular gelding: third foal: half-brother to winning 17f hurdler Ptite Margotte (by Roi de Rome): dam unraced: trained by T. Trapenard, won 4-y-o hurdle at Enghien on debut in 2002/3: stiff tasks all 3 starts in Britain, possibly flattered when ninth of 11 to Rhinestone Cowboy in steadily-run Aintree Hurdle second one. *N. J. Henderson*   h145 ?

SLEEPING NIGHT (FR)   8 b.g. Sleeping Car (FR) – Doll Night (FR) (Karkour (FR)) [2003/4 24d^5 Nov 29] rather leggy gelding: one-time high-class chaser/useful hurdler: off 20 months reportedly due to leg injury, needed race when fifth of 8, tending to hang left, to Baracouda in Grade 2 hurdle at Newbury only start in 2003/4: stays 25f: acts on heavy going: has high head carriage. *P. F. Nicholls*   c– h120 +

SLEEPY RIVER (IRE)   13 ch.g. Over The River (FR) – Shreelane (Laurence O) [2003/4 c87d, h–: c24m 27s c27s^4 c24s^3 c25v^F Feb 5] compact gelding: poor handicap chaser nowadays: stays 3½m: acts on heavy going: has worn cheekpieces. *Miss Kate Milligan*   c66 h–

SLEIGHT   5 ch.m. Bob's Return (IRE) – Jolejester (Relkino) [2003/4 F80: 17d 21d Jan 22] modest form when fourth in 2 mares maiden bumpers: well held both starts over hurdles, raced too freely when upped in trip. *W. Jenks*   h70

SLINKY MALINKY   6 b.m. Alderbrook – Winnie The Witch (Leading Man) [2003/4 F16m F17g Sep 3] third foal: dam, useful hurdler/fairly useful chaser, stayed 27f: little show in 2 bumpers. *D. G. Bridgwater*   F–

SLIPPY HITHERAO   4 b.f. First Trump – Child Star (FR) (Bellypha) [2003/4 17d 16s^{pu} 16g Apr 12] poor maiden on Flat (stays 1½m): no show in 3 juvenile hurdles, left B. Johnson after debut. *Miss L. J. Sheen*   h–

SLIP THE RING   10 b.g. Belmez (USA) – Sixslip (USA) (Diesis) [2003/4 c–, h–: 20d^5 c26d^4 Mar 14] compact gelding: poor maiden hurdler: winning pointer: left Miss K. Marks, well-beaten fourth to Macgeorge in hunter at Warwick on completed start in steeplechases: stays 3m: acts on soft going: tried in cheekpieces. *P. Senter*   c80 + h–

SLOANE STREET (FR) 5 b.g. Sadler's Wells (USA) – Shy Danceuse (FR) (Groom **h97** Dancer (USA)) [2003/4 h77: 16m⁵ 16m² 21s² 24m² 24g* 24d⁵ 23dᵖᵘ Dec 29] close-coupled gelding: modest hurdler, left D. Caro after reappearance: won novice handicap at Doncaster in November: stayed 3m: acted on soft and good to firm going: tried visored (ran poorly): dead. *M. Scudamore*

SLYBOOTS (GER) 5 gr.g. Neshad (USA) – Shanice (USA) (Highland Park (USA)) **h90** [2003/4 24m 20m* 20m² 22m* 21m⁵ Oct 6] ex-German gelding: successful once over 12.5f from 13 starts on Flat: modest form over hurdles (left Frau P. Gehm after debut), winning novices at Worcester in July and Stratford (outbattled Lady Laureate in slowly-run 4-runner race) in August: should stay 3m: acts on good to firm going. *C. J. Mann*

SLY CELEBRITY (IRE) 7 ch.g. Fourstars Allstar (USA) – Over Slyguff (IRE) **F–** (Over The River (FR)) [2003/4 F16d May 3] IR 80,000 3-y-o: first foal: dam unraced half-sister to fairly useful staying chaser Act The Wag: showed nothing in bumper on debut: sold £1,700 Ascot June Sales. *J. A. B. Old*

SMALL AMOUNT 4 ch.f. Sir Harry Lewis (USA) – Pretty Scarce (Handsome Sailor) **F–** [2003/4 F14g F12m Dec 10] lengthy, angular filly: third foal: half-sister to untrustworthy 5f winner Sergeant Slipper (by Never So Bold): dam, little sign of ability, half-sister to one-time fairly useful 2m chaser Sandy Duff: well held in 3-y-o bumpers. *W. Jenks*

SMART GUY 12 ch.g. Gildoran – Talahache Bridge (New Brig) [2003/4 c72§, h–: c20g **c79 §** c22g* c22v c22s c20m c22d⁵ c18g⁶ Apr 22] workmanlike gelding: poor handicap chaser: **h–** form in 2003/4 only when winning at Fontwell in December, making virtually all: stays 3m: acts on any going: wears cheekpieces: prone to mistakes: unreliable. *Mrs L. C. Jewell*

SMART LORD 13 br.g. Arctic Lord – Lady Catcher (Free Boy) [2003/4 c64, h61: **c–** 17g 17m³ 16g c20m⁶ Dec 18] angular gelding: poor maiden hurdler/chaser: stays 21f: **h65** acts on firm and soft going: visored 6 starts: has had tongue tied. *M. R. Bosley*

SMART SAVANNAH 8 b.g. Primo Dominie – High Savannah (Rousillon (USA)) **h123** [2003/4 17s² 17d 16d* 16d* 16d* Apr 8] rather leggy gelding: fairly useful hurdler, off over 2 years before reappearance: much improved last 3 outings, winning handicaps at Stratford and Ludlow within 5 days in March and Ludlow in April, beating Forever Dream by 4 lengths on last occasion: probably best at 2m: acts on soft and good to firm going. *C. Tinkler*

SMART SCOT 5 ch.g. Selkirk (USA) – Amazing Bay (Mazilier (USA)) [2003/4 16m **h–** 16g 16s 16sᵖᵘ Dec 30] close-coupled gelding: modest on Flat (stays 1m), successful first 4 starts in 2004: no form over hurdles. *B. P. J. Baugh*

SMARTY BOOTS (IRE) 5 b.m. Arctic Lord – Solmus (IRE) (Sexton Blake) **F84** [2003/4 F16g⁶ F16d F16s⁶ F16g⁵ Feb 18] third foal: dam, placed in bumper, half-sister to smart staying chaser Glyde Court: modest form at best in mares bumpers. *A. M. Crow*

SMARTY (IRE) 11 b. or br.g. Royal Fountain – Cahernane Girl (Bargello) [2003/4 **c108** c–, h–: c24g⁴ c24g c36d⁶ c33d⁵ Apr 17] tall, close-coupled gelding: one-time useful **h–** handicap chaser: nothing like the force of old, remote sixth in Grand National at Aintree and fifth in Scottish National at Ayr: stays 3½m: acts on heavy and good to firm going: often wears headgear: sound jumper. *M. Pitman*

SMASHING TIME (USA) 6 b.m. Smart Strike (CAN) – Broken Peace (USA) **h60** (Devil's Bag (USA)) [2003/4 h–: 17m³ 24f 19d Dec 4] little show over hurdles. *M. C. Chapman*

SMEATHE'S RIDGE 6 b.g. Rakaposhi King – Mrs Barty (IRE) (King's Ride) **F–** [2003/4 F16g F16d Mar 19] good-topped gelding: first foal: dam ran 3 times: well held in bumpers. *J. A. B. Old*

SMETHERDS TOM 10 b.g. Dortino – Nellie's Joy VII (Damsire Unregistered) **c–** [2003/4 c–: c19g c21mᶠ c18m⁴ c21g⁵ c21g c21gᵖᵘ c16mᵘʳ c22m⁴ c18fᶠ Aug 22] workmanlike gelding: no worthwhile form in steeplechases: wore cheekpieces: dead. *N. R. Mitchell*

SMILE PLEEZE (IRE) 12 b.g. Naheez (USA) – Harkin Park (Pollerton) [2003/4 **c75 §** c86§, h–: c25d⁵ c28dᵖᵘ May 30] fair hunter chaser on his day but increasingly difficult **h–** ride: probably stays 3¼m: acts on soft going. *M. R. Daniell*

SMILING APPLAUSE 5 b.g. Royal Applause – Smilingatstrangers (Macmillion) **h–** [2003/4 19m⁴ 22g 21g Dec 6] half-brother to 23f hurdle winner Frankie Anson (by Anshan): well held on Flat and on 3 starts over hurdles: tried visored. *Mrs Barbara Waring*

SMITHLYN 7 b.g. Greensmith – Sunylyn (Sunyboy) [2003/4 F16g* F16d³ 21d² 20s⁴ **h89** Apr 21] 4,000 4-y-o: fifth foal: dam, fairly useful hunter chaser, sister to smart staying **F99** chaser Elmboy: fairly useful form in 2 bumpers, winning at Perth on debut in May: better effort in maiden hurdles when 14 lengths second of 17 to easy winner Fair Question at Huntingdon, despite making mistakes: will stay beyond 2¼. *K. C. Bailey*

SMITHS LANDING 7 b.g. Primitive Rising (USA) – Landing Power (Hill's Forecast) **h114** [2003/4 h112, F83: 20g* 20mᵖᵘ 20s* Apr 4] medium-sized gelding: fair hurdler: won handicaps at Wetherby (odds on in 4-runner race) in May and Hexham in April: off 9 months, beat Crystal Gift 3½ lengths in 16-runner event at latter: will stay beyond 2½m: acts on soft and good to firm going. *Mrs S. J. Smith*

SMITH'S PERK (IRE) 11 b.g. Executive Perk – Sister of Slane (The Parson) **c–** [2003/4 c–, h–: c18g May 5] tall gelding: no longer of any account: tongue tied. **h–** *Mrs L. C. Jewell*

SMOKESTACK (IRE) 8 b.g. Lord Americo – Chiminee Fly (Proverb) [2003/4 h94?: **h–** 16g 22gᵖᵘ Apr 10] sturdy gelding: maiden hurdler: showed little in 2 handicaps after year's absence: should stay 2½m: acts on soft going. *J. A. B. Old*

SMOKEY ROBOT (IRE) 11 b.g. Riberetto – Smokey Queen (Proverb) [2003/4 **c–** c24d Feb 19] rather sparely-made gelding: maiden hurdler/chaser, appears to retain no **h–** ability: often tongue tied. *D. S. Dennis*

SMOKIN GREY 4 gr.f. Terimon – Wollow Maid (Wollow) [2003/4 F14g⁴ F12m⁴ **F93** F16gʳᵗʳ F16s Mar 13] unfurnished filly: half-sister to several winners, including 2m hurdler Janglynvye (by Sharpo) and 7f/1m winner Reverand Thickness (by Prince Sabo): dam 1¼m winner: fourth in 3-y-o bumpers for G. Margarson: hampered and whipped round start third outing. *M. J. Gingell*

SMOOTHIE (IRE) 6 gr.g. Definite Article – Limpopo (Green Desert (USA)) [2003/4 **h76** 16d 17d 16d Mar 21] fair on Flat (stays 1½m), successful twice in 2003: poor form on first of 3 starts in novice hurdles. *Ian Williams*

SMOOTH PASSAGE 5 b.g. Suave Dancer (USA) – Flagship (Rainbow Quest **h–** (USA)) [2003/4 h–: 16m⁵ Jul 13] little form on Flat: well held both starts over hurdles, blinkered on second occasion. *J. Gallagher*

SMUDGE (IRE) 7 br.g. Be My Native (USA) – Crash Call (Crash Course) [2003/4 **c–** h93: 20g⁵ 20d³ c20dꟳ Apr 18] workmanlike gelding: modest form over hurdles: tongue **h98** tied, fell eighth on chasing debut: stays 2½m: raced only on good/good to soft going. *R. Ford*

SMUDGER SMITH 7 ch.g. Deploy – Parfait Amour (Clantime) [2003/4 16s⁶ 16d **c–** 23d 21v Jan 13] compact gelding: modest handicap hurdler in 2001/2: little impact **h–** following near 2-year absence, including on chasing debut: should stay 2½m: used to go well on soft/heavy going. *B. S. Rothwell*

SMYSLOV 6 b.g. Rainbow Quest (USA) – Vlaanderen (IRE) (In The Wings) [2003/4 **h–** h–: 16g Jun 12] fair form on Flat in 2003: lightly-raced novice hurdler: sold 5,500 gns Doncaster August Sales. *P. R. Webber*

SNAILS CASTLE (IRE) 5 b.g. Danehill (USA) – Bean Island (USA) (Afleet **h–** (CAN)) [2003/4 h86: 20f⁶ Sep 14] modest form on second of 2 outings in juvenile hurdles: let down by jumping only start in 2003/4. *E. W. Tuer*

SNAPPER CREEK (IRE) 8 b.g. Castle Keep – Vultang Lady (Le Bavard (FR)) **h123** [2003/4 16dᵇᵈ 16d⁴ 20s* 18x* 20d 16d² Apr 13] IR 5,000 4-y-o: good-topped gelding: fifth foal: half-brother to bumper winner Plastic Paddy (by Beau Sher) and winning 3m chaser Belharbour (by Lancastrian): dam unraced sister to dam of high-class staying chaser Couldnt Be Better and half-sister to smart chaser up to 3m Kilkilowen: pulled up only start in points: successful over hurdles when making all in weak maiden at Tramore in December and minor event at Punchestown (beat Euro Leader 7 lengths) in January: much better form when 1½ lengths second to Royal Alphabet in Grade 2 novice at Fairyhouse (allowed to build long lead) and when seventh of 13 to Brave Inca in Grade 1 novice at Punchestown later in April: bred to be suited by further than 2m: acts on heavy going. *J. A. Berry, Ireland*

SNIPE 6 ch.g. Anshan – Flexwing (Electric) [2003/4 F87: 20g 17d⁵ 16d⁴ 16d 17d⁴ 19g⁵ **h85** Mar 26] lengthy, angular gelding: modest novice hurdler: should stay 2½m: found little last 2 starts. *Ian Williams*

SNITTON WEST 8 b.g. Derrylin – Snitton (Rymer) [2003/4 c20mᵖᵘ May 15] fourth **c–** foal: half-brother to winning pointer by Little Wolf: dam, placed in points, half-sister to smart chaser up to 19f Snitton Lane: modest pointer, won 2-finisher maiden in March: showed nothing in hunter chase. *G. C. Evans*

SNOOPY LOOPY (IRE) 6 ch.g. Old Vic – Lovely Snoopy (IRE) (Phardante (FR)) **F108** [2003/4 F16d* Apr 12] IR 15,000 3-y-o: leggy gelding: seventh foal: half-brother to 2 winners by Royal Fountain, fairly useful hurdler/chaser Royal Snoopy, stays 27f, and winning hurdler Royal Signature, stays 21f: dam unraced half-sister to Aintree Bumper winner Black Mocassin out of useful Irish hurdler Lovely Bio: won both completed starts in Irish points in 2004: promising start in Britain when winning 18-runner bumper at Huntingdon by ¾ length from Into The Shadows: will stay at least 2½m. *Miss V. Scott*

SNOOTY ESKIMO (IRE) 12 ch.g. Aristocracy – Over The Arctic (Over The River **c66** (FR)) [2003/4 c20m c25g⁶ Mar 6] workmanlike gelding: fair pointer, won in February: **h–** long-standing maiden hurdler/steeplechaser. *W. T. Reed*

SNOWMORE 8 ch.m. Glacial Storm (USA) – Royal Typhoon (Royal Fountain) **h107** [2003/4 h107: 21g* May 18] angular mare: fair handicap hurdler: went lame run-in when winning at Southwell (third course success): stays 3m: acts on good to firm and heavy going: usually races prominently. *Mrs S. J. Smith*

SNOWY FORD (IRE) 7 b.g. Be My Native (USA) – Monalee Stream (Paddy's **c119** Stream) [2003/4 h117: 20g c17s* c20d³ c20d c24d c19d³ c22s c24s⁴ c20s* c20sF c20vR **h–** Apr 17] medium-sized gelding: fairly useful handicap hurdler: similar level over fences: won maiden at Killarney in May and minor event at Tramore (by 4½ lengths from Ollar Rose) in March: should stay beyond 2½m: acts on heavy going: effective blinkered or not: races prominently. *Paul Nolan, Ireland*

SNOWY (IRE) 6 gr.g. Pierre – Snowy Gunner (Gunner B) [2003/4 F16m 17s³ 20d **h97** 22g* 20d³ Apr 18] good-topped gelding: third foal: dam unraced: mid-field in bumper **F88** on debut: modest novice hurdler: won 16-runner event at Kelso in March by 14 lengths from Brave Lord: good third to Roobihoo in novice handicap at Carlisle: will stay 3m. *J. I. A. Charlton*

SOBRAON (IRE) 5 b.g. Topanoora – Anniepepp (IRE) (Montelimar (USA)) [2003/4 **F111** F17d³ F17d* Mar 11] £13,000 3-y-o: quite good-topped gelding: second foal: dam unraced, from family of top-class chaser up to 3m Bradbury Star: encouraging 2½ lengths third of 16 to Mount Clerigo in bumper at Aintree on debut: easily landed odds in 18-runner similar event at Carlisle 4 months later by 10 lengths from Hello Baby: type to make his presence felt in novice hurdles. *N. G. Richards*

SOCIETY AFFAIR 5 b.g. Moscow Society (USA) – Society News (Law Society **h98** (USA)) [2003/4 F16m³ F17m² 19g⁴ 20sⁿ 21d 20s⁵ 26g* 27d Apr 23] workmanlike **F93** gelding: fourth foal: half-brother to 3 winners by Be My Native, including 3m chaser Native Society: dam bumper winner: last of 3 finishers in maiden Irish point on debut in 2003: fair form when placed in 2 bumpers: upped in trip, best effort over hurdles when winning handicap at Huntingdon in March: stays 3¼m: not an easy ride (carries head high). *Jonjo O'Neill*

SOCIETY BUCK (IRE) 7 b.g. Moscow Society (USA) – Bucks Grove (IRE) **h108** (Buckskin (FR)) [2003/4 h71, F88: 17d³ 22s 22d² 22g* Apr 18] smallish, lengthy gelding: fair form over hurdles: improved again when winning novice at Stratford by ½ length from Red Ruffles, left in front after 3 out and battling on gamely: will stay 3m. *John Allen*

SO DAISY 6 b.m. Teenoso (USA) – La Margarite (Bonne Noel) [2003/4 F16m Apr 13] **F–** fourth foal: half-sister to winning pointers by Dalsaan and Buckley: dam lightly-raced novice hurdler up to 2½m: well beaten in bumper on debut. *C. J. Price*

SOHAPARA 9 ch.m. Arapahos (FR) – Mistress Boreen (Boreen (FR)) [2003/4 c24m² **c75 +** Apr 13] fairly useful pointer nowadays: completed 4-timer prior to 16 lengths second to **h–** Cherry Gold at Chepstow on hunter chase debut. *Miss J. E. Mathias*

SOHO FIELDS (IRE) 7 b.g. Good Thyne (USA) – Rosie Owen (IRE) (Roselier (FR)) **h93** [2003/4 h103: 16m³ May 5] leggy, useful-looking gelding: rather disappointing since winning novice hurdle on debut in 2002/3: should stay beyond 2m. *Miss H. C. Knight*

SOLAR DOVE 8 b.g. Jupiter Island – Celtic Dove (Celtic Cone) [2003/4 c20dᵖᵘ **c–** c24gF Feb 11] angular gelding: winning hurdler in 2000/1: no form since, including over **h–** fences: tried blinkered. *C. J. Price*

SOLAR SYSTEM (IRE) 7 b.g. Accordion – Fauvette (USA) (Youth (USA)) [2003/4 **c116** c20d³ c20d⁴ c16sᵘʳ c17sᵘʳ c20d* c24s c17s³ Mar 27] 10,000 3-y-o: half-brother to win- **h–** ning 2m hurdler Tempted (by Invited) and winning pointer by Boyne Valley: dam unraced: winning hurdler: won maiden chase at Fairyhouse in February: best effort when third to Nil Desperandum in similar event at Punchestown in November: effective around 2m to 3m: raced on going softer than good (acts on heavy). *T. J. Taaffe, Ireland*

SOL CHANCE   5 ch.g. Jupiter Island – Super Sol (Rolfe (USA)) [2003/4 F87: F16m⁴   **h79**
F16d 19g^pu 24d 19g Apr 24] rather unfurnished gelding: best effort in bumpers on debut: **F79**
little form in novice hurdles. *R. S. Brookhouse*

SOLDERSHIRE   7 b.g. Weld – Dishcloth (Fury Royal) [2003/4 h83?, F–: 21d⁵ Apr   **h–**
11] signs of ability only when third in novice hurdle at Fontwell in 2002/3. *S. Dow*

SOLERINA (IRE)   7 b.m. Toulon – Deep Peace (Deep Run) [2003/4 h146p, F87:   **h149**
16d³ 20d* 20s* 16d⁴ 19s* 24g⁴ Mar 18]

The tendon injury which forced Limestone Lad to miss the whole of the 2003/4 season also meant that the James Bowe team was reduced to three, leaving the five-year-younger Solerina to try to fill the gap as best she could. Like her illustrious stable-companion, Solerina is a tough and game front runner but, smart though she undoubtedly is, she is some way short of Limestone Lad in terms of ability and it is very much to her credit that this grand mare made such a good fist of the job. In what was her second season over hurdles, Solerina won three races, including the Hatton's Grace Hurdle at Fairyhouse and the Tara Hurdle at Navan, both of which had been won by Limestone Lad twelve months earlier, the former for a third time.

Solerina was one of the top novice hurdlers in Ireland in 2002/3, when her seven victories from eight starts included a defeat of Hardy Eustace in the Deloitte And Touche Novices' Hurdle at Leopardstown. Three of those victories came at a bare two miles, but that trip looked too short for her in 2003/4 and all her wins were gained at or close to two and a half miles. Solerina opened her account for the season in the Ballymore Properties Hatton's Grace Hurdle at the end of November. It was hardly a vintage renewal of this Grade 1 race and the betting suggested that it lay between Sacundai and Solerina who had finished second and third respectively when reappearing in the two-mile Morgiana Hurdle at Punchestown two weeks previously, the pair joint favourites at 7/4. With Sacundai running well below form, Solerina was left with a fairly straightforward task, even though Gary Hutchinson, who rode Solerina in all but her first and fourth starts in the latest season, was unable to claim his 3-lb allowance. She made all and ran on strongly to win by eight lengths from her stable-companion Florida Coast who, along with Sweet Kiln, also played his part in ensuring that Limestone Lad's absence wasn't so serious as it might have been for their small yard. Solerina's half-brother Florida Coast (by Florida Son) developed into a useful hurdler and won a minor event at Fairyhouse,

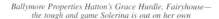

Ballymore Properties Hatton's Grace Hurdle, Fairyhouse—
the tough and game Solerina is out on her own

while the five-year-old Sweet Kiln, who is from the family of Limestone Lad, showed useful form in bumpers, winning at Naas and Navan.

Florida Coast was in opposition again when Solerina reappeared two weeks later in the Giltspur Scientific Tara Hurdle at Navan, along with Rosaker who had made all when beating Hardy Eustace in a Grade 2 event over the same course and distance on his previous start. Solerina started at 3/1-on and, in a manner so reminiscent of Limestone Lad, simply galloped her rivals into the ground, jumping well as she forced a good pace and having things sewn up by two out. Solerina won by seven lengths from Rosaker, with a further six lengths back to Florida Coast in third. Found wanting for finishing speed when fourth to Golden Cross in the Festival Hurdle over two miles at Leopardstown next time, Solerina regained the winning thread in a minor event at Naas in January. Starting at 4/1-on this time, Solerina didn't need to run up to her best to win very easily, by six lengths from Bob Justice. It was a good warm up for the Stayers' Hurdle at Cheltenham, which was to be Solerina's first run outside Ireland and her first over as far as three miles. Limestone Lad had come third to Baracouda and Iris's Gift in the 2003 Stayers' Hurdle (as well as second in 2000), and that pair, along with Crystal d'Ainay, finished ahead of Solerina in the latest edition. On ground less testing than she had encountered previously, Solerina didn't jump so well as usual and was soon beaten once headed two out. Three miles had promised to suit her well, and she is certainly worth another chance at the trip. Not surprisingly, Solerina was found wanting over two miles on good ground when contesting the Emo Oil Champion Hurdle at Punchestown in April, shortly after the end of the British season, Florida Coast representing the stable in the Champion Stayers' Hurdle.

			Top Ville		High Top
	Toulon		(b 1976)		Sega Ville
	(b 1988)		Green Rock		Mill Reef
Solerina (IRE)			(ch 1981)		Infra Green
(b.m. 1997)			Deep Run		Pampered King
	Deep Peace		(ch 1966)		Trial By Fire
	(ch 1984)		Bargy Music		Tudor Music
			(ch 1971)		Patsy Brown

Solerina is bred very much on jumping lines but had been given the opportunity to show what she is capable of on the Flat earlier in April. She responded by producing fairly useful performances to win both her starts, minor events over two miles at the Curragh and a mile and three quarters at Tipperary, earning herself an entry, albeit a very optimistic one, for the Irish St Leger in September. Solerina, bred by one of James Bowe's sons and owned by another, is out of the non-thoroughbred mare Deep Peace, whose only other offspring to reach the racecourse apart from Solerina and Florida Coast is Chester Pool. A sister to Florida Coast, Chester Pool failed to show much in the way of ability and was fatally injured on the last of three starts in bumpers in 1999. Deep Peace showed some ability over hurdles, gaining places at around two miles and indicating she probably stayed two and three quarters. The next two dams were both unraced. In appearance, Solerina could hardly be more different to the strong, lengthy Limestone Lad, being a small, leggy individual. She is likely to stay over hurdles, which she jumps well. If Limestone Lad fails to make it back to the racecourse in 2004/5, then Solerina should prove an able deputy for him once again. The pair have been a great credit to their connections. *James Bowe, Ireland*

SOLMORIN 6 b.m. Fraam – Reclusive (Sunley Builds) [2003/4 F17g Sep 3] third foal: sister to 8.5f winner Sheerness Essity and half-sister to 7f winner Solianna (by Beveled): dam unraced: behind in bumper (raced freely, withdrawn after bolting next intended outing) and maiden on Flat. *R. J. Baker* **F—**

SOL MUSIC 12 ch.g. Southern Music – Tyqueen (Tycoon II) [2003/4 c112, h–: c21s² c16g* c20m⁴ c20g³ c19s⁴ Apr 6] lengthy gelding: useful hunter chaser in 2003, won at Uttoxeter in May: well below best in 2004: stays 21f: acts on any going: front runner. *Mrs V. M. Graham* **c113 d h—**

SOLO DANCER 6 ch.m. Sayaarr (USA) – Oiseval (National Trust) [2003/4 h59x: 17g⁶ 19m⁵ 19m⁵ 19d⁵ 16s³ 21d* 22s 21d³ 22gᵖᵘ Apr 18] rather sparely-made mare: poor hurdler: won mares handicap at Plumpton in March: stays 21f: acts on soft going: wears cheekpieces. *Mrs H. M. Bridges* **h80**

SOLOMAN (IRE) 11 br.g. Mandalus – Solo Player (Blue Refrain) [2003/4 c25d^{pu} Feb 12] well-made gelding: fair handicap chaser in 2001/2: pulled up in 2 points and hunter chase: stays 3¼m: acts on soft and good to firm going. *Mrs Jane Galpin* — **c–ℎ–**

SOLVANG (IRE) 12 b.g. Carlingford Castle – Bramble Bird (Pitpan) [2003/4 c , h–: c20g⁴ c20d^{pu} c19s^{pu} Apr 6] smallish gelding: handicap chaser, retains little ability: usually tongue tied prior to 2003/4. *Mrs J. Marles* — **c70 ℎ–**

SOLVE IT SOBER (IRE) 10 b. or br.g. Carefree Dancer (USA) – Haunted Lady (Trimmingham) [2003/4 c24m^{ur} 20s^{pu} c19d^{pu} 19s 19g c19m² Apr 13] good-topped gelding: maiden hurdler: winning pointer in Ireland, left S. Slevin after steeplechasing debut: blinkered, 12 lengths second to Paddy The Optimist in selling handicap chase at Chepstow: usually tongue tied (wasn't at Chepstow). *S. G. Griffiths* — **c67 ℎ–**

SOLWAY BREEZE (IRE) 11 b.m. King's Ride – Spicey Cut (Cut Above) [2003/4 c–, h–: c25g c27v^{ur} c24s⁴ c20v³ c25s^{ur} c26d^{pu} Apr 18] modest chaser in 2001/2, little form since: stays 3¼m: acts on heavy going: tried blinkered. *Ms Liz Harrison* — **c– ℎ–**

SOLWAY DAWN 9 ch.m. Minster Son – Oh Dear (Paico) [2003/4 20g^{pu} 16g⁴ 16m 20d 24m³ 20d⁵ 24d^{pu} Nov 28] smallish mare: little form over hurdles. *Ms Liz Harrison* — **ℎ–**

SOLWAY DONAL (IRE) 11 b.m. Celio Rufo – Knockaville (Crozier) [2003/4 c–x, h–: c24m^{pu} c20m³ May 27] medium-sized mare: poor chaser: stays 25f: wore cheekpieces final outing: sketchy jumper. *Ms Liz Harrison* — **c71 x ℎ–**

SOLWAY GALE (IRE) 7 b.m. Husyan (USA) – Some Gale (Strong Gale) [2003/4 h–: 20m* 20m⁵ 21d⁴ c25d^{pu} c20m⁵ c24g³ c22s^F Jan 16] angular mare: poor hurdler: made all under good tactical ride in mares maiden at Carlisle in October: similar form on second of 2 completed starts over fences: stays 3m: acts on good to firm going. *Ms Liz Harrison* — **c73 ℎ73**

SOLWAY GORGE 8 ch.g. Jumbo Hirt (USA) – Kilkenny Gorge (Deep Run) [2003/4 h–, F–: c21v^{pu} c25v^{pu} 24d^{pu} Mar 11] sturdy, lengthy gelding: no sign of ability: tried blinkered. *Ms Liz Harrison* — **c– ℎ–**

SOLWAY LARKIN (IRE) 6 b.m. Supreme Leader – In Any Case (IRE) (Torus) [2003/4 F16d⁶ Apr 23] first foal: dam, disqualified 19f Irish hurdle winner, out of half-sister to useful hurdler up to 2¾m Firm Price: sixth of 16 in bumper at Perth on debut, twice carried head and looking green under pressure. *Ms Liz Harrison* — **F65**

SOLWAY MINSTREL 7 ch.g. Jumbo Hirt (USA) – Spicey Cut (Cut Above) [2003/4 F–: 24m³ 22g³ 24g² 24m⁴ 22g³ 24v⁵ 24s⁴ 27d* Apr 23] sturdy gelding: modest hurdler: improved form upped in trip when winning handicap at Perth on second run in 3 days: thorough stayer: acts on good to firm and heavy going. *Ms Liz Harrison* — **ℎ99**

SOLWAY PLAIN 10 b.g. King's Ride – Oh Dear (Paico) [2003/4 c– , h–: c25d^{pu} c20g² c20m^F Jun 14] winning pointer: best effort when second in maiden chase at Hexham: stayed 25f: acted on heavy going: wore cheekpieces last 2 outings: dead. *Ms Liz Harrison* — **c93 ℎ–**

SOLWAY QUEST 6 ch.m. Jumbo Hirt (USA) – Kilkenny Gorge (Deep Run) [2003/4 F17d 21d^{pu} 20d^{pu} 24s^{pu} Apr 21] fourth foal: sister to winning 2¾m hurdler Corbie Lynn: dam poor pointer: no form in bumper or novice hurdles. *Ms Liz Harrison* — **ℎ– F–**

SOLWAY RAIDER 6 ch.g. Jumbo Hirt (USA) – Lady Mag (Silver Season) [2003/4 F17d F17d Apr 18] lengthy gelding: half-brother to staying hurdler/chaser Solway Rose (by Minster Son): dam unraced half-sister to useful chaser up to 2½m Yangste-Kiang: well beaten in bumpers. *Ms Liz Harrison* — **F–**

SOLWAY ROSE 10 ch.m. Minster Son – Lady Mag (Silver Season) [2003/4 c95§, h–: c25g³ c25g c24s² c25v³ c26d⁴ Mar 11] small, lengthy mare: modest handicap chaser: best at 3m+: acts on heavy and good to firm going: races prominently. *Ms Liz Harrison* — **c87 § ℎ–**

SOMAYDA (IRE) 9 b.g. Last Tycoon – Flame of Tara (Artaius (USA)) [2003/4 h–: 16m Oct 18] leggy gelding: modest on Flat (stays 1½m) in 2003: no form over hurdles: tried tongue tied. *Miss Jacqueline S. Doyle* — **ℎ–**

SOME JUDGE 7 ch.g. Rakaposhi King – Si-Gaoith (Strong Gale) [2003/4 F17d⁶ F17d 16d⁶ 24s⁶ 20s 24s⁶ Apr 21] rather leggy ex-Irish gelding: sixth foal: dam unraced half-sister to fairly useful 3m hurdle winner Mount Hillary: fair form in bumpers, trained in 2001/2 by E. O'Grady: modest form over hurdles: should stay at least 2½m: room for improvement in his jumping. *Jonjo O'Neill* — **ℎ85 F95**

SOMEMANFORONEMAN (IRE) 10 b.g. Asir – Wintry Shower (Strong Gale) [2003/4 c–§, h95§: 22g 27d^{pu} c24d⁴ c30d^{ur} c25d^{pu} c25d^{pu} 26s Feb 12] rangy gelding: winning hurdler/one-time useful staying chaser, little form since 2001/2: tried in cheekpieces, usually blinkered: often makes mistakes: one to leave alone. *R. S. Brookhouse* — **c– § ℎ– §**

SOME OPERATOR (IRE) 10 b.g. Lord Americo – Rathvilly Flier (Peacock (FR)) **h86 x**
[2003/4 h84x: 21m 20g^pu 16m* 16g^pu Jun 27] sturdy gelding: modest hurdler: form early
in 2003/4 only when winning novice handicap at Stratford: best at 2m: acts on firm going:
headstrong, often forces pace: not a fluent jumper: inconsistent. *T. R. Wall*

SOMETHING DANDY (IRE) 11 b.g. Brush Aside (USA) – Hawthorn Dandy (Deep **c91**
Run) [2003/4 c93+, h111: c20m^5 c23m^4 20m c19m^2 c21m^3 c23s^3 c25m^ur Apr 13] **h–**
lengthy, angular gelding: winning hurdler: modest handicap chaser: effective at 19f to
3¼m: acts on firm and soft going. *J. A. B. Old*

SOMETHING GOLD (FR) 4 gr.g. Baby Turk – Exiled (USA) (Iron Ruler (USA)) **F103**
[2003/4 F16s* Mar 20] 32,000 3-y-o: eighth foal: brother to smart hurdler/chaser up to
25f in France/Italy Something Special and half-brother to several other winners: dam
won in US: fairly useful form when winning 21-runner bumper at Ascot on debut by ¾
length from The Fridge, pair clear, outpaced turning for home then showing plenty of
determination to lead final 1f: will stay at least 2½m. *M. Bradstock*

SOMETHING SMALL 4 br.g. Supreme Leader – Rachel C (IRE) (Phardante (FR)) **F86**
[2003/4 F17g^3 Apr 13] second foal: dam unraced half-sister to useful Irish chaser Master
Aristocrat VI: 5½ lengths third of 15 to Gaelic Music in bumper at Exeter on debut.
R. Waley-Cohen

SOME TRAINER (IRE) 8 b.g. Leading Counsel (USA) – Miss Polymer (Doulab **c75**
(USA)) [2003/4 c17g^2 c17g^4 20m^3 c17g^5 c21m^2 c20f 20g^2 c16m^5 c20m^3 c16g^2 c20s* **h80**
c20v^4 c20s Feb 1] rather sparely-made gelding: poor maiden hurdler: poor chaser: won
handicap at Down Royal in December: effective at 2m to 25f: acts on any going: wore
cheekpieces last 4 starts: tongue tied. *J. G. Cromwell, Ireland*

SOMEWIN (IRE) 4 b.f. Goldmark (USA) – Janet Oliphant (Red Sunset) [2003/4 **F85**
F16g^2 F16d* Feb 8] fourth foal: half-sister to 1m winner in Italy by Spectrum and winner
up to 9f in Scandinavia by Mujadil: dam maiden half-sister to high-class middle-distance
performer Amyndas: fair form in bumpers at Musselburgh, doing well to dead-heat with
Word Gets Around in 15-runner event having been held up in slowly-run race: sold to join
Miss K. Marks £20,000 Cheltenham April Sales. *R. A. Fahey*

SONEVAFUSHI (FR) 6 b.g. Ganges (USA) – For Kicks (FR) (Top Ville) [2003/4 **h126 §**
h119§: 16d^3 16g^2 16m 16m 25g^3 24s^4 21s^pu 20d^2 22s 20g^4 20d 21m Apr 14] leggy, useful-
looking gelding: fairly useful handicap hurdler: effective at 2m to 25f: acts on heavy and
good to firm going: usually blinkered: irresolute. *Miss Venetia Williams*

SONGINO (IRE) 8 ch.g. Perugino (USA) – Sonbere (Electric) [2003/4 16g^6 17g 20f **h63**
Jun 30] poor maiden hurdler: stays 2¾m: acts on good to firm going: tried blinkered.
James Clements, Ireland

SONIC SOUND 5 b.g. Cosmonaut – Sophiesue (Balidar) [2003/4 F16d Apr 12] **F–**
lengthy, rather unfurnished gelding: second foal: dam never ran: tailed off in bumper on
debut. *Miss C. J. E. Caroe*

SONNYANJOE (IRE) 6 b.g. Roselier (FR) – Carrabawn (Buckskin (FR)) [2003/4 **F104**
F16d^3 F20g^6 F16d F16s* F20d^4 F16d Apr 11] second foal: dam lightly-raced sister to
one-time useful hurdler Vanilla Man, stays 3m, and useful hurdler up to 21f Buckminster:
best effort in bumpers when winning 19-runner event at Down Royal in December by 20
lengths from Mr Murphy: will stay 3m. *T. Hogan, Ireland*

SONNY JIM 6 b.g. Timeless Times (USA) – Allesca (Alleging (USA)) [2003/4 h85: **h80**
21m 20m* 20m^ur 21g^m 20m 19g 19s^4 24s Dec 29] compact gelding: poor handicap
hurdler: won at Worcester in June: sold out of M. Usher's stable £5,800 Ascot October
Sales after fifth start: barely stays 21f: acts on any going: looked none too keen when tried
blinkered/visored. *N. G. Ayliffe*

SONO 7 b.g. Robellino (USA) – Sweet Holland (USA) (Alydar (USA)) [2003/4 16g^5 **h103**
16d^3 16d^3 16d^5 16g 20v^4 17s^6 16d^pu 20d^5 Apr 23] leggy, close-coupled gelding: half-
brother to winning hurdler/fair chaser Chalcedony (by Highest Honor), stays 2½m: fairly
useful on Flat (stays 1½m), successful 7 times in Germany: novice hurdler, fair form at
best: best efforts around 2m: acts on good to soft going: tried in cheekpieces: has jumped
less than fluently. *P. D. Niven*

SON OF A GUN 10 b.g. Gunner B – Sola Mia (Tolomeo) [2003/4 h84: 16m^6 26d^5 21m **c83 §**
c16m^5 c16m^2 c20m^4 c17m^3 c16f^4 c16m^pu c20g^F Nov 15] smallish, sturdy gelding: poor **h75 §**
hurdler/novice chaser: let down by temperament and/or jumping last 3 starts: best efforts
around 2m: probably acts on any going: ungenuine. *M. J. Polglase*

SON OF ANSHAN 11 b.g. Anshan – Anhaar (Ela-Mana-Mou) [2003/4 c103+, h–: **c96**
c24g^2 c25g^6 c27g* Apr 12] rangy, workmanlike gelding: fair hunter chaser: won 6-runner **h–**

event at Sedgefield: stays 27f: acts on heavy and good to firm going: tried blinkered: tongue tied. *G. Tuer*

SON OF FLIGHTY 6 b.g. Then Again – Record Flight (Record Token) [2003/4 **c–** 17m⁴ 26sᵖᵘ 17s 16mᵖᵘ 17s³ 17g Apr 13] good-topped gelding: third foal: dam, fair **h69 §** hurdler/modest chaser who stayed 25f, half-sister to useful staying chaser Toogood To Be True: no form on Flat: poor and temperamental maiden hurdler: no show on chasing debut. *R. J. Hodges*

SON OF ROSS 10 b.g. Minster Son – Nancy Ardross (Ardross) [2003/4 h–: c25gᵖᵘ **c–** c24mᵖᵘ c25m 24d 22m 21gᵘʳ 22g³ 20g 22f 21g² 24v 27d² Mar 16] tall, angular gelding: **h61** no form over fences: poor handicap hurdler: stays 27f: acts on firm and good to soft going: wears cheekpieces nowadays. *R. W. Thomson*

SON OF SNURGE (FR) 8 b.g. Snurge – Swift Spring (FR) (Bluebird (USA)) [2003/4 **h78 ?** h78?: 20m⁵ 24d³ 24g 26d³ 24m⁵ 20m 20m² 20g³ 24g³ 22m³ 21m³ 24g⁴ 20f⁵ 24g⁵ 24m² 20m⁴ 24m⁵ 27d⁵ 22g⁶ 20gᵖᵘ Nov 19] well-made gelding: poor maiden hurdler: stays 3m: acts on good to soft and good to firm going: tried blinkered, usually wears cheekpieces: tried tongue tied: sketchy jumper. *W. G. Young*

SOOTSIR 8 b.g. Baron Blakeney – Furry Bear (Rymer) [2003/4 c25dᵖᵘ Mar 23] modest **c–** pointer, successful in February: pulled up in hunter on steeplechasing debut. *Richard Hawker*

SOPHOMORE 10 b.g. Sanglamore (USA) – Livry (USA) (Lyphard (USA)) [2003/4 **h59** 17g 16d² 16s Dec 19] lengthy, rather sparely-made gelding: bad maiden hurdler: raced around 2m: acts on soft going. *John A. Harris*

SOPRANO LASS (IRE) 7 ch.m. Black Monday – Kam Country (IRE) (Kambalda) **c76 ?** [2003/4 F17v 21dᵖᵘ c23m² c25mᵘʳ c25dᵖᵘ c24g³ Apr 16] IR 1,400 3-y-o: sturdy mare: **h–** third foal: dam unraced half-sister to Sun Alliance Hurdle winner Rebel Song: won mares **F–** maiden on last of 3 starts in Irish points in 2003: signs of only a little ability otherwise. *J. G. Portman*

SORELY MISSED (IRE) 9 br.g. Yashgan – Well Honey (Al Sirat (USA)) [2003/4 **c–** c–, h–: c20gᵖᵘ Oct 15] well-made gelding: winning hurdler: no form since 2001/2, includ- **h–** ing over fences: tried visored/in cheekpieces. *R. Dickin*

SORRENTO KING 7 ch.g. First Trump – Star Face (African Sky) [2003/4 c93, h–: **c–** 20sᵖᵘ Apr 17] smallish gelding: modest hurdler/chaser: bought out of Mrs M. Reveley's **h–** stable 4,000 gns Doncaster August Sales: showed nothing on return from year off: blink- ered once. *C. N. Kellett*

SOSSUS VLEI 8 b.g. Inchinor – Sassalya (Sassafras (FR)) [2003/4 h102: c17d² c16d² **c105 §** c17s³ c24sᵘʳ c21d⁵ c20g² c20g² c18dᵘʳ Apr 7] medium-sized gelding: fair maiden hurdler: **h–** similar form over fences: stays 2½m: acts on soft ground: tends to carry head high, and not an easy ride. *P. Winkworth*

SO SURE (IRE) 4 b.g. Definite Article – Zorilla (Belmez (USA)) [2003/4 17gᵖᵘ 16f* **h98** 16f⁵ 16m² 16g² 16m 16s 17d⁴ 17m⁶ 17gᶠ 16g⁶ Apr 18] smallish gelding: fair on Flat (stays 1¼m): fair juvenile hurdler: won claimer (claimed from P. Haslam £4,000) at Towcester in October: will prove best at 2m with emphasis on speed: acts on firm and good to soft going: consistent. *J. G. M. O'Shea*

SO TEMPTED 5 br.m. So Factual (USA) – Bystrouska (Gorytus (USA)) [2003/4 **h–** F66: 16mᵖᵘ Oct 11] angular mare: signs of only a little ability in varied events. *N. Wilson*

SOUL (IRE) 7 b.g. Jurado (USA) – Pachamama (Glen Quaich) [2003/4 17d 17dᵖᵘ **c83 p** c16s² Jan 16] workmanlike ex-Irish gelding: fourth foal: half-brother to useful staying **h–** chaser Shanagarry and fair chaser up to 2½m Lord of The Dance (both by Mister Lord): dam won 2m hurdle, half-sister to useful 1¼m winner Nioulargo: modest hurdler: sold out of M. Morris' stable 19,000 gns Doncaster May Sales: shaped as if in need of run on reappearance, let down by jumping next time: tired badly after hitting 2 out when second in handicap at Huntingdon on chasing debut: stays 2½m: acts on heavy going: will prob- ably do better over fences. *C. J. Mann*

SOUL KING (IRE) 9 b.g. King's Ride – Soul Lucy (Lucifer (USA)) [2003/4 c25d³ **c91 ?** c25dᵖᵘ c25s⁴ Apr 11] workmanlike gelding: well held over hurdles: winning pointer: best **h–** effort in hunter chases when third at Towcester in March, though probably flattered: stays 25f: tried visored/tongue tied. *Michael Blake*

SOUND OF CHEERS 7 br.g. Zilzal (USA) – Martha Stevens (USA) (Super Concorde **c109** (USA)) [2003/4 c94, h–: c17m³ c16s² c17gᵘʳ c21s⁴ c19g⁶ c16g* c16s⁴ c16g c16s* c17g* **h–** Apr 5] good-topped gelding: winning hurdler: fair handicap chaser: won at Catterick (novice) in January, Newcastle in March and Kelso in April: stays 21f: acts on heavy going: tongue tied: has finished weakly/shaped as if amiss. *F. Kirby*

SOUNDS COOL 8 b.g. Savahra Sound – Lucky Candy (Lucky Wednesday) [2003/4 h75: c16g⁶ c16s⁴ 17g 17g³ 16m c17d³ c17gᶠ c17m⁶ c17g* Apr 12] leggy gelding: poor hurdler/chaser: left Mrs S. Smith and off 6 months, won selling handicap over fences at Plumpton in April: raced mainly around 2m: acts on soft and good to firm going: tried visored. *Mrs A. M. Thorpe* `c75` `h67`

SOUND SENSE 6 br.g. So Factual (USA) – Sight'n Sound (Chief Singer) [2003/4 c24mᵖᵘ Mar 4] poor pointer. *Mrs Laura J. Young* `c–`

SOUNDTRACK (IRE) 11 b.g. Orchestra – Misty Boosh (Tarboosh (USA)) [2003/4 c–, h–: c25m⁴ c24g⁵ c22g⁴ Jul 6] rangy gelding: fair handicap chaser: won point in March for G. Hanmer: best at 3m+: acts on any going: front runner: sometimes let down by jumping. *Miss Venetia Williams* `c101` `h–`

SOUTHAMPTON JOE (USA) 4 ch.g. Just A Cat (USA) – Maple Hill Jill (USA) (Executive Pride) [2003/4 16mᵘʳ 16g⁶ Apr 18] fair 6f/7f winner at 2 yrs, well beaten in 2003, sold out of A. Balding's stable 3,000 gns Doncaster October Sales: tailed off on completed start over hurdles. *J. G. M. O'Shea* `h–`

SOUTHBAY (IRE) 10 b.g. Montelimar (USA) – Herbal Lady (Good Thyne (USA)) [2003/4 c24d³ c25dᶠ Apr 11] lengthy gelding: maiden hurdler: modest chaser: placed on completed starts in points and handicaps in 2004: stays 3m: acts on good to firm and heavy ground: tried blinkered: has had tongue tied. *A. J. Martin, Ireland* `c93` `h–`

SOUTHBOUND (IRE) 5 ch.g. Zaffaran (USA) – Soxess (IRE) (Carlingford Castle) [2003/4 F17d Apr 18] €2,000 4-y-o: fourth foal: dam unraced: well held in bumper on debut. *J. Howard Johnson* `F–`

SOUTHERN BELIZE 10 ch.m. Southern Music – Belize (Tom Noddy) [2003/4 c19mᵖᵘ May 14] poor pointer. *Miss M. Ree* `c–`

SOUTHERNCROSSPATCH 13 ch.g. Ra Nova – Southern Bird (Shiny Tenth) [2003/4 c–, h87: 24m⁵ 21g⁶ 22m⁶ 26s³ 24s 26s* 24d⁶ 23gᵖᵘ 26g 24g³ Apr 1] strong, compact gelding: winning chaser: poor hurdler: first win for long time in minor event at Hereford in January: best at 3m+: probably acts on any going. *Mrs Barbara Waring* `c–` `h83`

SOUTHERNDOWN (IRE) 11 ch.g. Montelimar (USA) – Country Melody (IRE) (Orchestra) [2003/4 c92, h77: c25g c25mᵖᵘ c26m⁴ c23mᵖᵘ 26d* c23m⁴ c26m² 24m⁶ c30d⁵ 26s² c26s⁵ 24s⁴ c26g² c25d⁴ Mar 22] sparely-made gelding: poor hurdler/chaser: won seller over hurdles at Southwell in August: stays 3¾m: has form on heavy ground, best efforts under less testing conditions (acts on firm): tried blinkered/visored: usually makes mistakes over fences. *R. Lee* `c83 x` `h81`

SOUTHERN STAR (GER) 4 gr.g. Sternkoenig (IRE) – Sun Mate (IRE) (Miller's Mate) [2003/4 18v⁶ 16d² 16g Mar 10] in frame both starts around 1¼m on Flat in Germany at 3 yrs for P. Schiergen: best effort over hurdles when never-nearer second in juvenile maiden at Musselburgh in January: well held on Flat in April. *R. C. Guest* `h86`

SOUTHERN STAR (IRE) 9 ch.g. Montelimar (USA) – Flying Pegus (Beau Chapeau) [2003/4 c140, h–: c27g⁴ c33d³ c29g* c36dᵖᵘ Apr 3] `c144` `h–`

Southern Star has kept good company from day one. He beat a future Grand National winner on his debut in a bumper at Huntingdon and finished third to a future Gold Cup winner on his next start, in a similar event at Cheltenham. Southern Star had to go a lot longer, however, than either Bindaree or Best Mate before landing a big prize, but the wait was finally ended when he won one of the season's most valuable staying handicaps, the Tote Classic Chase, at Warwick in January. This was the first running of the race in its new guise, though to all intents and purposes it was a revamped version of what was long known as the Warwick National. For much of its history, at least on the occasions when it managed to survive the weather, the Warwick National was run over four miles and a furlong under Brooke Bond Oxo sponsorship. In its later years it had been shortened by half a mile and its conditions restricted to keep out the best staying chasers, the final running in 2000 going to Choisty. For the next two seasons it was replaced with the short-lived Warwickshire Gold Cup, worth twice as much as the old Warwick National and run over three and a quarter miles. The weather intervened again in 2003, and after another 'make-over' the Tote Classic Chase emerged in 2004, back at three miles five furlongs and with a first prize which was the equal of the

Tote Classic Chase (Handicap), Warwick—
Southern Star returns to his best, at the chief expense of Jurancon II

Hennessy Gold Cup and greater than the Welsh National. The 'new' race, incidentally, filled the gap which had been left by the scrapping of Sandown's well-established handicap run over the same trip in January, the Mildmay Cazalet Memorial Chase. A victim of the weather for the previous three seasons, that race was switched to Sandown's December fixture and, to less than universal approval, was renamed the williamhill.co.uk Marathon Chase.

The Tote Classic, open to all-comers, drew a field of twelve and, while there were a number of former big-race winners in the line-up, several were either out of form or no longer quite so good as they once were. Ad Hoc, Take Control and Ardent Scout, former winners of the Whitbread/attheraces Gold Cup, Scottish National and Becher Chase respectively all came into that category. Bindaree and Gunner Welburn, on the other hand, had shown their well-being more recently, though both had had gruelling races when gaining wins in the Welsh National and the Rowland Meyrick respectively just a couple of weeks earlier. Akarus, a faller when going well in the Welsh National, started favourite, ahead of the Irish-trained What Odds (out of the handicap) and top weight Behrajan, with Southern Star on 15/2.

Conditions were anything but testing at Warwick—the ground on the chase course was good—but the race was strongly run with the well-backed What Odds taking them along, and the pace took its toll on the runners by the finish. Southern Star travelled better than most and made good progress on the final circuit to lead six out as most of his rivals struggled. Only rank outsider Jurancon II was still in touch in the straight and he made his challenge at the last as Southern Star idled, but Southern Star found more again on the run-in to win by three and a half lengths, providing rider Graham Lee with another big-race win in what proved to be an excellent season for him. The rest of the field was a sorry sight. Behind Jurancon, What Odds was left a distant third when Bindaree fell at the last and Ardent Scout and Montifault were the only others to complete without mishap, though Bindaree was remounted for the sixth prize. Among those who didn't get round, Take Control and Behrajan both suffered fatal falls, the latter coming down two out when a tired third.

Somewhat surprisingly, Southern Star took his chance in the Grand National on his only outing after Warwick. He had shown little aptitude for the fences when the last to finish in the race the year before and showed even less liking for the experience twelve months on before being pulled up early on the second circuit. Southern Star's win at Warwick represented a return to his best form after a couple of just respectable efforts at Cheltenham on his first two outings. He was fourth to Shardam in the valuable staying handicap at the Open meeting in November, and then third to Bear On Board in the four-mile-one-furlong handicap on New Year's Day, just nine days before Warwick.

Southern Star (IRE) (ch.g. 1995)	Montelimar (USA) (b 1981)	Alleged (b 1974)	Hoist The Flag Princess Pout
		L'Extravagante (br 1973)	Le Fabuleux Fanfreluche
	Flying Pegus (br 1979)	Beau Chapeau (ch 1963)	High Hat Beau Co Co
		Romany Miss (b 1966)	Master Owen Scarlet Gypsy

Southern Star is much the best of four winners out of his dam Flying Pegus. The others are Beacon Flight (by Phardante), Chevalier Bayard and Trassey Bridge (both by Strong Gale), none of whom have stayed so well as Southern Star. His dam won a bumper and three hurdles (up to two and three quarter miles) in Ireland. The unraced grandam, Romany Miss, produced several other winners, notably Miss Nero, a smart staying hurdler who was twice placed in the Stayers' Hurdle at Cheltenham, and two brothers to Flying Pegus, the useful hurdler up to two and three quarter miles Mr Maguire and the useful two-and-a-half-mile chaser of the 'eighties Dunkirk. Romany Miss is also the grandam of the Irish Grand National runner-up Give Over. The big, lengthy Southern Star has always looked the type to do well over fences, but his Warwick win was his first success since early in his novice season in 2001/2. He stays beyond four miles and acts on both soft and good to firm ground, though he has had little racing on testing ground. *Miss H. C. Knight*

SOUTH WEST WON 6 b.g. Bedford (USA) – Wood Heath (Heres) [2003/4 F–: F18s⁶ 21s^pu 19s^pu 22g^pu Feb 22] sturdy gelding: no form: wore tongue strap and cheekpieces final start. *Miss S. West* h– F—

SOU'WESTER 4 b.g. Fleetwood (IRE) – Mayfair (Green Desert (USA)) [2003/4 17d⁶ 19s Feb 6] disappointing maiden on Flat, sold out of M. Tregoning's stable 5,000 gns Newmarket July Sales: well beaten both starts over hurdles, including in seller. *B. J. Llewellyn* h–

SOVEREIGN 10 b.m. Interrex (CAN) – Shiny Penny (Glint of Gold) [2003/4 h90: 20m⁴ 19m⁴ 22g³ 22g⁴ 22m³ 22g³ 22f² 24m* 22m³ 24f² 24f³ Oct 8] small mare: modest handicap hurdler: won at Fontwell (conditional jockeys) and Market Rasen in August: stays 3m: has form on soft going, races on good or firmer nowadays (acts on firm): tough and consistent. *J. F. Panvert* h99

SOVEREIGN GOLD 7 b.g. Rakaposhi King – Page of Gold (Goldhill) [2003/4 h–: 20s c21d^pu 22s Mar 23] good-topped gelding: signs of ability in 3 starts over hurdles: 2 bad mistakes on chasing debut. *D. R. Gandolfo* c– h71

SOVEREIGN'S GIFT 8 ch.m. Elegant Monarch – Cadeau d'Aragon (Aragon) [2003/4 h86: 17g² 17g* 22g³ Jun 21] workmanlike mare: modest hurdler: won weak mares novice at Newton Abbot in June: effective around 2m to 2¾m: acts on firm and good to soft going. *Mrs S. D. Williams* h86

SOVEREIGN STATE (IRE) 7 b.g. Soviet Lad (USA) – Portree (Slip Anchor) [2003/4 h78x: 16m⁵ 16g⁴ 17g³ 16m² 16m* 17m³ 17g* 16m* 16m 16m³ 16s 16g 16g⁴ Apr 18] modest hurdler, trained until after third start by J. A. Moore: won sellers at Fakenham (handicap) in May and Stratford (novice) in July, novice handicap at Cartmel in August and handicap at Worcester in September: best around 2m: acts on good to firm going: has won in visor/cheekpieces or without: usually races prominently. *D. W. Thompson* h96

SOVIET SOCIETY (IRE) 6 b.g. Moscow Society (USA) – Catchmenot (IRE) (Bluebird (USA)) [2003/4 F17s F16d Feb 2] fourth foal (all by Moscow Society): brother to 2½m hurdle winner Off The Boil: dam thrice-raced, out of half-sister to smart miler Eve's Error: fell in maiden Irish point on debut in 2003: second and seemingly better effort in bumpers when twelfth of 16 at Kempton. *Noel T. Chance* F81

SPACE CADET 8 b.g. Teenoso (USA) – Spaced Out (Space King) [2003/4 c24d^pu Apr 12] lengthy gelding: twice-raced pointer: soon tailed off in novice chase. *J. Rudge* c–

SPACE COWBOY (IRE) 4 b.c. Anabaa (USA) – Lady Moranbon (USA) (Trempolino (USA)) [2003/4 16s^F 16m² 16g⁵ 16g³ 16d³ Mar 1] useful-looking colt: fairly useful form when winning 1¼m maiden on Flat, sold out of Mrs A. Perrett's stable 35,000 gns Newmarket Autumn Sales: fair juvenile hurdler: blinkered last 2 starts. *G. L. Moore* h95

SPACE STAR 4 b.g. Cosmonaut – Sophiesue (Balidar) [2003/4 16s 16g 17g² Apr 16] compact gelding: modest form on Flat for J. Given: best effort in juvenile hurdles when h85 +

second to easy winner Fontanesi at Taunton, left with plenty to do: likely to prove best at 2m with emphasis on speed. *P. R. Webber*

SPAGHETTI JUNCTION   6 ch.m. Sir Harry Lewis (USA) – Up The Junction (IRE) (Treasure Kay) [2003/4 h100. 22d 22d 20d⁶ 21g³ Apr 12] sturdy mare: handicap hurdler, below best in 2003/4: stays 21f: acts on soft and good to firm going. *R. H. Alner*   **h90**

SPAINKRIS   5 b.g. Kris – Pennycairn (Last Tycoon) [2003/4 h98: 19g 16d 17s⁴ 19d 23s⁴ 17s⁶ 19g Mar 10] close-coupled gelding: winning hurdler: disappointing in handicaps in 2003/4: probably best around 2m: acts on heavy going: blinkered fourth start: sometimes races freely: has folded tamely. *A. Crook*   **h86**

SPANCHIL HILL   4 b.g. Sabrehill (USA) – War Shanty (Warrshan (USA)) [2003/4 16d 16s 16d⁶ 17g⁶ Mar 16] ex-Irish gelding: first foal: dam lightly-raced half-sister to very smart sprinter Bold Edge: well held in 4 starts over hurdles, trained first by C. McCarthy. *J. Howard Johnson*   **h–**

SPANDAU (NZ)   10 br.g. Fiesta Star (AUS) – Koru (NZ) (Diplomatic Agent (USA)) [2003/4 h73: 16g 17g* 18f⁵ 20g² 19m² 16g³ Oct 15] well-made gelding: poor handicap hurdler: won at Newton Abbot in August: stays 2½m: probably acts on any going: has worn cheekpieces/visor: none too reliable (threw race away fourth start). *J. C. Tuck*   **h80 §**

SPANISH ARCHER (IRE)   9 b.g. Spanish Place (USA) – Bow Gello (Bargello) [2003/4 c68: 19m⁶ 22mᵖᵘ May 29] tall, angular gelding: poor handicap chaser/maiden hurdler: stays 23f: acts on firm and good to soft going: tried blinkered/visored: has had tongue tied. *L. Waring*   **c–** **h–**

SPANISH POINT (IRE)   7 br.g. Un Desperado (FR) – Molly Murphy (IRE) (Phardante (FR)) [2003/4 22g³ c25g³ c22s⁵ c24d⁵ Feb 20] IR £16,000 4-y-o: rangy gelding: first foal: dam placed in Irish bumper: runner-up once from 3 starts in maiden Irish points in 2003: close third of 4 finishers in novice at Folkestone on hurdling debut: best effort over fences when 18 lengths third of 8 to Calling Brave in maiden at same course: stays 25f. *D. B. Feek*   **c102** **h93**

SPARKLING CASCADE (IRE)   12 b.m. Royal Fountain – Yukon Law (Goldhill) [2003/4 c81: c19g⁴ c20mᵖᵘ c21d⁵ Jul 30] lengthy mare: poor chaser: stays 3m: acts on good to firm and good to soft going. *A. G. Newcombe*   **c63**

SPARKLING JESS   5 b.m. Alderbrook – Tasmin Gayle (IRE) (Strong Gale) [2003/4 F–: 20s 22g Feb 22] angular mare: no sign of ability. *M. J. Roberts*   **h–**

SPARKLING LASS   10 gr.m. Nicholas Bill – Sparkling Time (USA) (Olden Times) [2003/4 c–, h–: c21mᵘʳ 22d⁵ 19m³ 19f⁵ 22g⁶ 22gᵖᵘ 19v Feb 2] angular mare: of no account nowadays: tried blinkered. *N. G. Ayliffe*   **c–** **h–**

SPARKLING SABRINA   4 b.f. Classic Cliche (IRE) – Sparkling Yasmin (Derring Rose) [2003/4 F12m F16v F16s Feb 20] rather unfurnished filly: first foal: dam, fairly useful hurdler, stayed 25f: well held in bumpers. *B. R. Millman*   **F–**

SPARKLING SPRING (IRE)   13 b.g. Strong Gale – Cherry Jubilee (Le Bavard (FR)) [2003/4 25d* Apr 11] smallish gelding: one-time fair chaser: prolific winning pointer: lightly raced over hurdles, won handicap at Plumpton on return from 11-month absence: stays 3½m: acts on any going. *Evan Williams*   **c–** **h86**

SPARKLING WATER (USA)   5 br. or b.h. Woodman (USA) – Shirley Valentine (Shirley Heights) [2003/4 16m³ 16m⁵ 17m⁴ 22f² 21m³ 18g⁶ Oct 5] close-coupled horse: half-brother to fair hurdler Achilles Wings (by Irish River), stays 2¾m: useful but unreliable on Flat (stays 1½m) at 3 yrs, sold out of H. Cecil's stable 20,000 gns Newmarket Autumn (2002) Sales, well held since: modest novice hurdler: stays easy 2¾m: acts on firm going: blinkered final outing. *D. L. Williams*   **h88**

SPECIAL AGENDA (IRE)   10 b.g. Torus – Easter Blade (IRE) (Fine Blade (USA)) [2003/4 c115x, h–: 16m² c16m⁴ c16d² c20gᵖᵘ c16m⁴ c17sᵖᵘ c16v⁴ c16s⁶ c16d Feb 15] useful-looking gelding: maiden hurdler: fair handicap chaser, well below form after third start: best around 2m: acts on heavy going: tried in cheekpieces/blinkers: tongue tied last 3 outings: usually let down by jumping: joined M. Evans. *C. J. Mann*   **c110 x** **h87**

SPECIAL BRANCH   4 ch.g. Woodborough (USA) – Sixslip (USA) (Diesis) [2003/4 17m³ 16d⁵ 16g⁶ 24g⁴ 20v⁴ Mar 21] medium-sized gelding: half-brother to bumper winner Point (by Polish Precedent) and winning pointer by Belmez: fair maiden on Flat (stays 1½m): modest novice hurdler: seems barely to stay 3m. *Jedd O'Keeffe*   **h93**

SPECIAL CONQUEST   6 b.g. El Conquistador – Kellys Special (Netherkelly) [2003/4 F97: F16s 20v³ 20s² 24g³ Mar 26] big, workmanlike gelding: won maiden   **h112** **F97**

bumper on debut in 2002/3: best effort in novice hurdles when 1¾ lengths second to Pass Me By at Haydock in February: should stay 3m: raced on good going or softer. *J. W. Mullins*

SPECIAL CONSTABLE 6 b. or br.g. Derrylin – Lavenham's Last (Rymer) [2003/4 h–, F–: 20g^{pu} 17g c24s^{pu} c20d³ c20v⁵ Apr 4] medium-sized gelding: no form: tongue tied last 4 outings. *B. I. Case* **c–** **h–**

SPECIALISM 6 ch.g. Spectrum (IRE) – Waft (USA) (Topsider (USA)) [2003/4 h–: 20g 16m 17m 20f⁶ 16m⁶ 16g^{pu} Oct 24] no form over hurdles. *M. J. Gingell* **h–**

SPECIAL PROMISE (IRE) 7 ch.g. Anjiz (USA) – Woodenitbenice (USA) (Nasty And Bold (USA)) [2003/4 20d Apr 10] unbeaten in 2 starts over hurdles as a novice (dead-heat on first occasion) in early-2001/2 for P. Haslam: last of 14 finishers in handicap at Carlisle on return. *P. Monteith* **h–**

SPECIAL RATE (IRE) 7 br.g. Grand Plaisir (IRE) – Clerical Artist (IRE) (The Parson) [2003/4 F16m² F16m* 20s² 20s* 22d* 23g³ Feb 28] IR £9,000 4-y-o: useful-looking gelding: second foal: dam unraced, from family of Amberleigh House: won at Navan in November on second of 2 starts in bumpers for J. Kiely: confirmed promise of hurdling debut when winning novices at Leicester in January and Wincanton in February, hanging left both times, beating Jollyolly 3½ lengths on second occasion: ran well in face of far stiffer task when 19½ lengths third of 6 to Royal Rosa in Grade 2 novice at Haydock: stays 23f: acts on soft going (won bumper on good to firm): type to do well in novice chases in 2004/5. *A. King* **h131** **F102**

SPECTACULAR HOPE 4 b.f. Marju (IRE) – Distant Music (Darshaan) [2003/4 16g^{ur} 18s^{pu} Jan 26] modest maiden on Flat (should stay further than 1m), sold out of R. Beckett's stable 7,500 gns Newmarket Autumn Sales: no show in 2 juvenile hurdles. *J. W. Mullins* **h–**

SPECTACULAR (IRE) 5 b.g. Spectrum (IRE) – Azra (IRE) (Danehill (USA)) [2003/4 16g⁵ 16s 16v 16g⁵ 16d⁵ Apr 22] ex-Irish gelding: fair on Flat (stays 9.5f, blinkered), sold out of J. Bolger's stable 11,000 gns Newmarket Autumn Sales: regressive form over hurdles. *F. P. Murtagh* **h81 d**

SPECTROMETER 7 ch.g. Rainbow Quest (USA) – Selection Board (Welsh Pageant) [2003/4 h143: 20g 22g⁴ Apr 16] leggy gelding: useful handicap hurdler in 2002/3 for P. Hobbs: trained by M. Johnston, successful on Flat in August: back to form when 7 lengths fourth of 7 finishers to Kivotos at Ayr: barely stays 3m: acts on firm and soft going: takes good hold and is held up: sometimes drifts left: consistent. *R. C. Guest* **h141**

SPECTROSCOPE (IRE) 5 b.g. Spectrum (IRE) – Paloma Bay (IRE) (Alzao (USA)) [2003/4 h137: 16g² 16d 20v^{pu} 20g 20d^{pu} Mar 20] compact gelding: useful hurdler, won JCB Triumph Hurdle at Cheltenham in 2002/3: very disappointing all 4 starts in handicaps, looked unwilling: should stay 2½m: raced mainly on good/good to soft ground over hurdles: best left alone. *Jonjo O'Neill* **h– §**

SPECTRUM STAR 4 b.g. Spectrum (IRE) – Persia (IRE) (Persian Bold) [2003/4 17g 16g^{pu} Sep 7] no form on Flat (for D. Ivory) or in 2 juvenile hurdles (not fluent). *F. P. Murtagh* **h–**

SPECULAR (AUS) 8 b.g. Danehill (USA) – Spyglass (NZ) (Sir Sian (NZ)) [2003/4 h?: 17s* 17g* 20g² 16s³ 16g 16d^{ur} Apr 17] smallish, strong gelding: formerly a leading hurdler in Australia: useful form both completed starts in Britain, 17 lengths third of 6 to Rooster Booster in Grade 2 at Haydock, carrying head awkwardly off bridle, and ninth of 13 finishers to Hardy Eustace in Champion Hurdle at Cheltenham: stays 2½m: raced on good going or softer. *Jonjo O'Neill* **h139**

SPECULATIVE 10 b.g. Suave Dancer (USA) – Gull Nook (Mill Reef (USA)) [2003/4 19v^{pu} Feb 2] of no account: tried blinkered. *J. W. Mullins* **h–**

SPEED BOARD (IRE) 12 b.g. Waajib – Pitty Pal (USA) (Caracolero (USA)) [2003/4 c79, h–: c25d^{pu} Feb 15] sturdy gelding: one-time fair hurdler/chaser, only poor nowadays: won 2-finisher point in March: stays 25f: unraced on firm going, acts on any other: blinkered. *Dennis Pugh* **c–** **h–**

SPEED KRIS (FR) 5 b.g. Belmez (USA) – Pandia (USA) (Affirmed (USA)) [2003/4 c17d⁵ 17g* 16s⁴ 16g 20s³ 22g 20s 16s² Apr 21] ex-French gelding: seventh foal: half-brother to 4 winners, including fairly useful hurdler/chaser up to 19f Diamona (by Diamond Shoal): dam, 1m and 11f winner, half-sister to smart miler Acteur Francais: 1½m winner on Flat: maiden chaser: won 4-y-o claiming hurdle at Montauban in October, final start for J-P. Totain: best effort in Britain when second to Westernmost in handicap at **c?** **h96**

Perth, seeming less than keen long way: stays 2½m: raced on good ground or softer: tried blinkered in France, visored last 4 starts. *Mrs S. C. Bradburne*

SPEED VENTURE 7 h.g. Owington – Jade Venture (Never So Bold) [2003/4 h92: 17s* 17d⁴ 17d⁴ 19g 17d 16d 17g^pu 20s* Apr 17] sparely-made gelding: modest handicap hurdler: won at Bangor at start and end of season: mostly well below form in between: probably best up to 2½m: raced on good going or softer (acts on heavy): usually visored, as effective when not: tongue tied: has found little. *J. Mackie* **h98**

SPEEDY RICHARD (IRE) 4 ch.g. Zaffaran (USA) – Chadandy (USA) (Fast Enough (USA)) [2003/4 F16d F16g Mar 7] second foal: dam unraced: mid-field in bumpers at Ludlow and Kempton. *M. Scudamore* **F–**

SPEEDY TAURUB (USA) 4 b.g. El Prado (IRE) – Off To Glory (USA) (Miswaki (USA)) [2003/4 F17g Apr 10] $33,000F, IR 60,000Y, 50,000 2-y-o, 3,000 3-y-o: fourth foal: half-brother to winner in Singapore by The Name's Jimmy: dam, placed in US, out of half-sister to very smart Italian performer up to 1½m Misil: tailed off in bumper on debut. *N. J. Hawke* **F–**

SPENDENT 8 ch.h. Generous (IRE) – Cattermole (USA) (Roberto (USA)) [2003/4 21g 18d Apr 7] tall, rather sparely-made horse: half-brother to smart 2m hurdler Rigmarole (by Fairy King): smart on Flat (stays 15f) in France at 3/4 yrs for P. Bary: sold 17,500 gns Newmarket December (2000) Sales, and has been to stud: well held in novice company over hurdles. *J. J. Sheehan* **h82 +**

SPENDID (IRE) 12 b.g. Tidaro (USA) – Spendapromise (Goldhill) [2003/4 c138, h145: 25m⁶ c26d² Dec 13] sturdy gelding: smart hurdler, needed race on reappearance: useful chaser: creditable 5 lengths second of 7 to Tyndarius in handicap at Doncaster: best at 3m+: acted on soft and firm going: blinkered once (pulled up): usually raced up with pace: usually less than fluent over fences: genuine and consistent: has been retired. *A. King* **c136 h118**

SPIDER BOY 7 b.g. Jupiter Island – Great Dilemma (Vaigly Great) [2003/4 F76?: 22d^pu 20m 21m³ 16m³ 25m⁴ Nov 3] workmanlike gelding: no form over hurdles. *Miss Z. C. Davison* **h–**

SPIDER MCCOY (USA) 4 ch.g. Irish River (FR) – Indy's Princess (USA) (A P Indy (USA)) [2003/4 16m^pu Aug 9] disappointing maiden on Flat: no show in juvenile on hurdling debut. *N. Tinkler* **h–**

SPIDER MUSIC 8 ch.g. Orchestra – Muffet's Spider (Rymer) [2003/4 h91: 22s 16v^pu 17g^pu Mar 16] sturdy gelding: novice hurdler, well held only completed outing in 2003/4: should stay 2½m: wore cheekpieces final start: sold 2,000 gns Doncaster May Sales. *N. G. Richards* **h–**

SPIKE AND DIVEL (IRE) 6 b.g. Zaffaran (USA) – Lady Go Marching (USA) (Go Marching (USA)) [2003/4 F16s² F16s⁴ 17s 16g 16d² Mar 21] 15,000 4-y-o, resold €28,000 4-y-o: ex-Irish gelding: half-brother to several winners, including fairly useful chaser Marching Marquis (by Aristocracy), stays 25f: dam won 3 times in US: in frame in bumpers at Listowel (for Ms M. Mullins) and Huntingdon: modest form in novice hurdles, off bridle long way out when second to easy winner Man From Highworth at Stratford: likely to be suited by a greater test of stamina. *Jonjo O'Neill* **h90 F90**

SPIKE JONES (NZ) 6 b.g. Colonel Collins (USA) – Gloss (NZ) (Kaapstad (NZ)) [2003/4 F16f⁴ F16m* 17d⁶ 16g^bd 16d 16d³ 16d⁵ Apr 8] medium-sized gelding: fair form in bumpers, landed odds in 4-runner event at Ludlow in November: best effort over hurdles when third in handicap at Stratford: raced around 2m: acts on good to soft going, won bumper on good to firm: room for improvement in his jumping. *Jonjo O'Neill* **h96 F92**

SPILAW (FR) 8 b.g. Sky Lawyer (FR) – Spinage (FR) (Village Star (FR)) [2003/4 c71, h–: c25g^pu c24g^F c26d^pu Mar 14] angular gelding: poor chaser: failed to complete in 2003/4, including in 2 hunters: stays 3¼m: acts on heavy going: blinkered once (less than keen). *John Allen* **c– h–**

SPINAROUND 6 br.g. Terimon – Re-Spin (Gildoran) [2003/4 h–, F77: 17g⁶ 17d 21v⁵ 17d² 16g⁶ 19s⁴ Apr 11] poor novice hurdler: should be suited by further than 17f: poor efforts on soft/heavy going. *N. A. Gaselee* **h84**

SPINOSA 6 br.m. Afzal – Rose Water (Waterfall) [2003/4 F–: 24g⁴ Jun 11] well held in varied events, including a point. *Mrs P. Sly* **h–**

SPIRIT LEADER (IRE) 8 b. or br.m. Supreme Leader – That's The Spirit (Mandalus) [2003/4 h143: 16s⁶ 16d² 16d⁴ Jan 25] smallish, sturdy mare: useful hurdler: creditable efforts in Grade 1 events at Leopardstown last 2 starts, 1½ lengths second of 7 to Golden **h144**

Cross then fourth of 8 to Foreman: missed Champion Hurdle reportedly due to being off colour: has form at 2½m, races mainly over shorter: acts on heavy going: held up: genuine and consistent. *Mrs J. Harrington, Ireland*

SPIRIT OF DESTINY 7 ch.m. Riverwise (USA) – Tearful Sarah (Rugantino) [2003/4 h–: 22g[pu] Mar 25] small mare: no sign of ability. *C. W. Mitchell*   **h–**

SPIRIT OF NEW YORK (IRE) 5 b.g. Topanoora – Fiona's Blue (Crash Course) [2003/4 F16g* Mar 6] €71,000 3-y-o: well-made gelding: sixth foal: half-brother to 3 winners, including smart hurdler/useful chaser up to 4m Native Emperor (by Be My Native): dam, lightly-raced Irish maiden jumper, half-sister to useful jumpers Treyford, Dis Train and Deep Heritage: well-backed 2/1 favourite, won 21-runner bumper at Newbury on debut by head from Itsa Legend, driven to close 2f out and all out after leading in final 1f: will stay beyond 2m. *Jonjo O'Neill*   **F100**

SPIRIT OFTHE GREEN (IRE) 6 b.g. Detroit Sam (FR) – Golden Hearted (Corvaro (USA)) [2003/4 F82?: aF16g 21s³ 21s⁵ 22s[pu] Feb 9] better effort in bumpers when fifth on debut: poor form first 2 starts over hurdles: likely to stay 3m: looked most ungenuine in blinkers final outing. *L. Wells*   **h69 §**   **F–**

SPIRITUAL DANCER (IRE) 9 b.g. King's Ride – Arctic Tartan (Deep Run) [2003/4 25s³ Dec 3] deep-girthed gelding: lightly-raced novice hurdler, modest form only start on return from 2-year absence: thorough stayer: acts on heavy going: has worn near-side pricker. *L. Wells*   **h88**

SPLASH AND DASH (IRE) 9 ch.g. Arcane (USA) – Quilty Rose (Buckskin (FR)) [2003/4 c103: c26g⁶ c26d[F] Apr 7] fairly useful hunter chaser: won point in March: stays 3m: acts on soft ground: not a fluent jumper. *Mrs S. J. Hickman*   **c88**

SPLASH OUT AGAIN 6 b.g. River Falls – Kajetana (FR) (Caro) [2003/4 17s 22g* 24m Apr 14] useful-looking gelding: half-brother to winning 2m hurdler K-Brigade (by Brigadier Gerard): fair on Flat (barely stays 2m): easily best effort over hurdles when winning 4-runner novice at Fontwell in March: possibly amiss next time: sold 18,000 gns Doncaster May Sales. *H. Morrison*   **h104**

SPLENDID TOUCH 4 b.f. Distinctly North (USA) – Soft Touch (GER) (Horst-Herbert) [2003/4 16m⁶ 16g Dec 4] ex-German filly: in frame twice around 7f on Flat, including in 2003 for T. Gibson: well beaten in juvenile hurdles, tongue tied and pulled hard on second occasion. *J. R. Jenkins*   **h–**

SPLENDOUR (IRE) 9 b.g. Broken Hearted – Black Trix (Peacock (FR)) [2003/4 c112, h115: c17d[F] c20d 16d c16g* c18m² c20f* c20d[F] c20s⁶ Dec 14] smallish, leggy gelding: fairly useful hurdler: progressed into useful chaser in 2003/4, won listed novice chase at Roscommon in October and 3-runner Grade 3 Killultagh Properties Ltd Chase at Down Royal in November: sometimes jumps none too fluently, bad mistake 3 out when sixth in valuable novice handicap at Punchestown in late-April: effective at 2m to 3m: has form on any going, possibly best on good or firmer. *Miss S. Cox, Ireland*   **c130**   **h–**

SPOKESMAN 10 b.g. Rudimentary (USA) – Ravaro (Raga Navarro (ITY)) [2003/4 c16d³ c20d[ur] c20d[pu] c17g Feb 10] workmanlike ex-Irish gelding: useful handicap hurdler at best: fair maiden chaser, left C. Roche before reappearance: let down by jumping in 2003/4: best around 2m: acts on good to firm and heavy going: held up (often finds little), and best with strong pace. *Jonjo O'Neill*   **c103 x**   **h–**

SPORAZENE (IRE) 5 gr.g. Cozzene (USA) – Sporades (USA) (Vaguely Noble) [2003/4 h138p: 16g* 16d² 16g³ 16g 17d* 20d Apr 3]   **h153**

Britain and Ireland are the only two major racing countries still using twenty-four-hour declarations. Almost every other major nation, including France, the United States, Hong Kong and South Africa, makes the final list of runners known a minimum of forty-eight hours beforehand. Punters in these countries are used to seeing information about meetings in their newspapers or in betting shops the day before racing. Trials with forty-eight-hour declarations have taken place for all-weather fixtures in Britain over the last two winters and the system is now permanently in use for all pattern races and major handicaps on the Flat and for all Grade 1 non-novice jump races and Grade 3 jumping handicaps, in addition, as before, for all Sunday meetings. The sooner the system is universally adopted the better.

Supporters of earlier declaration times have been pointing out for years that racing in Britain is missing the chance to promote itself to full effect in a crowded sporting calendar. The total readership of regional and local newspapers in Britain

exceeds that for the national dailies and clearly a way needs to be found to cater for those in this large audience who are being short-changed by the present system. While some of the larger-circulation evening papers—the Liverpool Echo, the Manchester Evening News and the London Evening Standard to name three—all carry overnight declared runners in at least their later editions, the current final declarations are published too late for the deadline for some evening newspapers and these either publish lists of five-day entries or publish nothing at all. The promotion of particular meetings can be done more effectively if the runners are known earlier, better promotion leading to increased interest, bigger racecourse attendances and higher betting turnover. The prosperity of racing is directly linked to the prosperity of the betting industry nowadays and anything that stimulates betting turnover has to be welcomed, provided there are no integrity issues for racing and no effect on the sport's public appeal.

The movement towards two-day declarations has not, however, come as a result of arguments put forward by long-standing supporters of the idea, but from a realisation of the benefits to be gained for British racing from the global market. High quality British racing is potentially a world brand leader—it is currently broadcast to sixteen countries in seven different time zones—and there is significant income, bringing considerable benefits, to be gained from international simulcasts. The United States, South Africa, France, Australia and Hong Kong all export their racing, and all ten meetings of the Dubai International Racing Carnival were broadcast to the States in 2004. The market is highly competitive and British racing needs to adopt the international standard for declarations to ensure, for example, that runners and form appear in local betting publications. The potential value of the international market for British racing with forty-eight-hour declarations has been estimated at around £30m over the next five years. None of the arguments used against early declarations is particularly convincing, not least the supposition that the going is less predictable two days before racing. Ground conditions can change in hours, let alone days, and this is a poor reason for objection, as is the argument that there will be more non-runners. It would, however, be wise to provide a disincentive for withdrawing horses, perhaps by sidelining them for at least a week afterwards.

Forty-eight-hour declarations received some adverse publicity after confusion was caused by the withdrawal of top weight Rigmarole from the Grade 3 Vincent O'Brien County Hurdle on the third day of the Cheltenham Festival. Rigmarole's withdrawal came after he was found to be slightly lame the morning after finishing a below-form eighth in the Champion Hurdle on the opening day. The Champion Hurdle took place after the Tuesday deadline for County Hurdle declarations and Rigmarole's trainer Paul Nicholls was referred to the stewards of the Jockey Club under Instruction H21 'Withdrawal of Top Weight'. The stewards found that Rigmarole had been correctly withdrawn on veterinary advice and did not refer the case to the Disciplinary Committee. Rigmarole was set to carry 11-12 in the County Hurdle and his withdrawal left stable-companion Sporazene heading the weights on 10-13, with only four others who came under orders racing from their correct marks. A maximum field of thirty was originally declared for the race and vets certificates were also produced for five of the six other defectors, including four others that had run earlier at the meeting. With the County Hurdle set to be run a day later in 2005, the specific problem in 2004 ought not to be repeated.

Rigmarole's withdrawal gave the handicap for the County Hurdle a lop-sided look and made it considerably less competitive than it should have been. Joint-favourite Sporazene, the horse with most to gain from Rigmarole's withdrawal, won the race but idled markedly after being four lengths clear early on the run-in and held off 50/1-shot Hawadeth (13 lb out of the handicap) only by half a length; of the others in the handicap proper, Copeland finished third, Benbyas sixth, Adamant Approach seventh and the never-dangerous In Contrast fifteenth. The British Horseracing Board promised a rethink and its Race Planning Committee subsequently recommended that no horse should be allowed to be declared as top weight in a big handicap 'if it has run in the preceding forty-eight hours or is already declared to run on the day of declaration.' However, it was later decided that a declaration should stand but the next horse down would be given the allotted top weight, with the highest rated horse set to carry an additional burden over and above that weight (for example, Rigmarole would have been allotted 12-11). The weights for the County Hurdle could have been raised if there had been a similar provision to that for the Grand National, for which the conditions allow for the raising of weights the day before the race, should any horse be notified a non-runner after the forty-eight-hour stage. Such a condition should apply to all handicaps with early declarations, in order to ensure they are as competitive as possible.

Sporazene's biggest success so far came in the IAWS Champion Four Year Old Hurdle at Punchestown in May, very early in the latest season. The form of Cheltenham's Triumph Hurdle and Aintree's Anniversary Hurdle was well represented and Sporazene's performance entitled him to be regarded as the best four-year-old hurdler in Britain and Ireland. The top four-year-old hurdlers often find things much tougher in open company in their second season and Sporazene proved fairly typical. He had to show a fair amount of improvement to bridge the gap between being a top juvenile and becoming a Champion Hurdle contender. He took his first step in a good renewal of the Gerry Feilden Hurdle, a limited handicap at Newbury designed for second-season hurdlers. Sporazene was let down by his jumping, going down by a neck to outsider Tramantano after two howlers, but he did enough to suggest he had prospects of making the transition to open company. His next assignment was the Christmas Hurdle at Kempton, up against the top two-mile hurdlers for the first time. Sporazene's jumping was generally fluent this time and he came a creditable third to the previous year's winner Intersky Falcon and the Champion Hurdle winner Rooster Booster. Sporazene met Rooster Booster on terms 15 lb better in a vintage renewal of the Tote Gold Trophy at Newbury in February, but he couldn't turn the tables, managing eighth, beaten little over four lengths, in the big field, with Rooster Booster finishing runner-up. It was hard to see Sporazene making an impact in the Champion Hurdle after this performance and connections chose wisely in targeting the County Hurdle instead. Sporazene took on the top hurdlers again on level terms in the Aintree Hurdle but he didn't look up to the task on form and wasn't sure to be suited by the longer trip either. He finished last of eleven behind Rhinestone Cowboy, a performance which might result in Sporazene's being campaigned over fences in the next season.

		Caro	Fortino II
	Cozzene (USA)	(gr 1967)	Chambord
	(gr 1980)	Ride The Trails	Prince John
Sporazene (IRE)		(b 1971)	Wildwook
(gr.g. 1999)		Vaguely Noble	Vienna
	Sporades (USA)	(b 1965)	Noble Lassie
	(ro 1989)	Stresa	Mill Reef
		(gr 1975)	Ileana

The tall, lengthy, angular Sporazene, who took the eye before most of his races in the latest season, has the size and scope to do well over fences, though he sometimes jumps hurdles none too fluently. Sporazene won over eleven furlongs on the Flat in France for Andre Fabre before joining his present stable, but most of the notable performers in his family—about whom details were given in last year's Annual—have shone at shorter distances. Sporazene is likely to prove best at around two miles over jumps, at least for the time being. He has been raced mainly on good going or softer, though was successful on his only outing on good to firm. *P. F. Nicholls*

SPORTING CHANCE   12 ch.g. Ikdam – Tumbling Ego (Abednego) [2003/4 c76, h–: c21dpu c24m6 c19spu c24g4 Apr 16] sturdy gelding: poor chaser: stays 3m: acts on firm going. *Ms J. Channon*   **c76 h–**

SPORTING HERO   4 b.g. Safawan – Cryptic Gold (Glint of Gold) [2003/4 F17d 16s3 17g Apr 12] seventh foal: half-brother to fairly useful hurdler Handy Money (by Imperial Frontier), stays 2½m, and Irish bumper winner Cryptic Myth (by Carlingford Castle): dam middle-distance maiden: well held in bumper on debut: poor form in juvenile hurdles at Newcastle and Sedgefield. *M. W. Easterby*   **h76 F–**

SPORTS EXPRESS   6 ch.m. Then Again – Lady St Lawrence (USA) (Bering) [2003/4 19g4 22spu 20s4 24g5 20d5 20d4 Apr 23] quite good-topped mare: modest novice hurdler: stays 2½m: acts on soft going. *Miss Lucinda V. Russell*   **h87**

SPORTSMAN (IRE)   5 b.g. Sri Pekan (USA) – Ardent Range (IRE) (Archway (IRE)) [2003/4 h90: 16v5 23v 22gur Apr 24] leggy gelding: novice hurdler, well below best both completed starts in 2003/4: should stay beyond 2m: acts on good to firm and good to soft going: blinkered since debut. *M. W. Easterby*   **h–**

SPOT IN TIME   4 b.f. Mtoto – Kelimutu (Top Ville) [2003/4 F17s3 F16g5 Feb 20] fifth foal: half-sister to useful 1m and 1¼m winner Whitefoot (by Be My Chief) and fairly useful 1¼m winner Ark Admiral (by Inchinor): dam middle-distance winner: 6½ lengths third to Royalentertainment in maiden at Folkestone, better effort in bumpers: tailed off in maiden on Flat: sold 6,800 gns Doncaster May Sales. *J. Pearce*   **F86**

SPOT THEDIFFERENCE (IRE)   11 b.g. Lafontaine (USA) – Spotted Choice (IRE) (Callernish) [2003/4 c116, h–: c33gur 16d 20d4 c32m2 c24d2 c26d5 c36d5 Apr 3] tall gelding: fairly useful chaser: easily best effort for long time when ½-length second to Jurancon II in valuable handicap at Uttoxeter in June: off bridle in rear much of way when remote fifth of 11 finishers to Amberleigh House in Grand National at Aintree: didn't   **c129 h93**

Quinns of Baltinglass Chase For The La Touche Cup, Punchestown—
the winner Spot Thedifference (No.15) safely clears the Big Double

SPR

have to be anywhere near best to win La Touche Cup (cross-country event) at Punchestown in late-April: stays very well: acts on good to firm and heavy ground: tried in blinkers/cheekpieces: probably best with strong handling nowadays. *E. Bolger, Ireland*

SPREAD THE DREAM   6 ch.g. Alflora (IRE) – Cauchemar (Hot Brandy) [2003/4 F93: 16s⁶ Jan 16] rather unfurnished gelding: second in bumper on debut in 2002/3: well-beaten sixth of 13 in novice hurdle at Huntingdon 10 months later. *N. J. Henderson*   h77

SPREAD THE WORD   12 b.m. Deploy – Apply (Kings Lake (USA)) [2003/4 c–, h–: c25m² c25f* c25d² c24m³ Nov 13] sparely-made mare: modest chaser: won 5-runner handicap at Towcester in October: will stay beyond 25f: acts on firm and good to soft going: tried visored. *J. G. Cann*   c91 h–

SPREE VISION   8 b.g. Suave Dancer (USA) – Regent's Folly (IRE) (Touching Wood (USA)) [2003/4 h95: 18g⁵ 16m⁵ 17s 17d⁶ 20g 17d³ 16g Apr 5] smallish gelding: poor handicap hurdler: stays easy 2½m: acts on heavy and good to firm going: has had tongue tied: sometimes finds little. *P. Monteith*   h82

SPREEWALD (GER)   5 b.g. Dulcero (USA) – Spartina (USA) (Northern Baby (CAN)) [2003/4 16m 16m² 17d 16d 17d 17s Mar 23] rather leggy gelding: half-brother to one-time high-class chaser Seebald (by Mulberry): won on Flat (stays 1¼m) at 3 yrs for P. Rau: poor novice hurdler: raced around 2m. *J. C. Tuck*   h78

SPRINGAWAY   5 ch.g. Minster Son – Galway Gal (Proverb) [2003/4 F16m⁶ F16g Jan 23] third foal: half-brother to winning 2½m chaser Mr Laggan (by Tina's Pet) and winning 3m hurdler Middleway (by Milieu): dam, winning hurdler, stayed 3m: achieved little in bumpers 7 months apart. *Miss Kate Milligan*   F–

SPRING BEE   4 b.f. Parthian Springs – First Bee (Gunner B) [2003/4 F13v 17s Jan 7] first foal: dam, poor hurdler, stayed 2½m: no sign of ability in bumper or juvenile hurdle. *T. R. Wall*   h– F–

SPRINGBOK ATTITUDE   7 b.g. Pharly (FR) – Tugra (FR) (Baby Turk) [2003/4 h62: 16gᵖᵘ 16mᵖᵘ 16dᵖᵘ Jan 22] smallish gelding: poor maiden hurdler: form only around 2m on firm/good to firm going: has had tongue tied. *B. Llewellyn*   h–

SPRINGBROOK GIRL   6 br.m. Alderbrook – Springaleak (Lafontaine (USA)) [2003/4 F16g³ F16d 20sᵖᵘ 19s 19d⁶ 22m⁶ 19g³ Apr 16] sturdy mare: fourth foal: dam useful chaser who stayed 25f: third of 7 on first of 2 outings in bumpers: poor novice hurdler: may prove best up to 2½m. *A. G. Hobbs*   h81 F67

SPRING DAWN   9 gr.g. Arzanni – Another Spring (Town Crier) [2003/4 h105: c16gᶠ c19dᵖᵘ 23s⁶ c24dᵖᵘ c20m⁶ c16d³ c16d³ Apr 12] workmanlike gelding: maiden hurdler/chaser, fair at best: form only around 2m: acts on soft going: tried in cheekpieces. *N. J. Henderson*   c100 h–

SPRING DOUBLE (IRE)   13 br.g. Seclude (USA) – Solar Jet (Mandalus) [2003/4 c–, h–: 27g³ c26g⁶ 24m Jul 23] leggy, close-coupled gelding: winning hurdler/chaser: fair pointer nowadays, successful in February and March: best at 3m+: acts on good to firm and heavy going: has worn blinkers/visor: jumps none too fluently, and has run in snatches. *N. A. Twiston-Davies*   c– h88

SPRINGER THE LAD   7 ch.g. Carlton (GER) – Also Kirsty (Twilight Alley) [2003/4 c–, h76: c24mᶠ 22g³ 21s* 21sᵖᵘ 22s 17d⁶ Mar 3] strong gelding: no show completed start in novice chases: poor hurdler: won novice claimer (claimed from D. Feek £5,000) at Plumpton in December: no form after: stays 2¾m: acts on soft going: blinkered 3 of last 4 starts. *Miss M. P. Bryant*   c– h76

SPRINGFIELD GILDA (IRE)   6 b.m. Gildoran – Ledee (Le Bavard (FR)) [2003/4 h–, F82: 17g⁴ 16m 16v³ Dec 26] modest form in bumpers: signs of only a little ability over hurdles: bred to need greater test of stamina. *S. Gollings*   h70

SPRINGFIELD SCALLY   11 ch.g. Scallywag – Ledee (Le Bavard (FR)) [2003/4 h132: 24g⁴ 24d⁴ 24d³ 25d 25d⁶ 23v³ 24g³ 24d⁵ Mar 27] quite good-topped gelding: fairly useful hurdler: stays 3¼m: acts on good to firm and heavy going: usually forces pace: tough. *S. Gollings*   h124

SPRINGFORD (IRE)   12 b.g. King's Ride – Tickenor Wood (Le Bavard (FR)) [2003/4 c–, h–: c24g² Apr 1] workmanlike gelding: fairly useful pointer: ran well when second to Kestick in hunter chase at Taunton: stays 25f: best form on good going. *Mrs Caroline Keevil*   c94 h–

SPRING GALE (IRE)   13 b.g. Strong Gale – Orospring (Tesoro Mio) [2003/4 c74§, h–: c25f³ May 21] rather leggy gelding: fair hunter chaser: stays 3½m: acts on soft and good to firm going: has worn blinkers: temperamental. *J. M. Turner*   c91 § h–

STA

SPRING GAMBLE (IRE) 5 b.g. Norwich – Aurora Run (IRE) (Cyrano de Bergerac) **h95**
[2003/4 F16f³ F17g⁴ F17d³ F16d³ 19g² 17s³ 16g⁴ 20s⁶ Apr 4] €8,000 3-y-o: third foal: **F90**
dam unraced: in frame all 4 starts in bumpers: modest form over hurdles: should stay
2½m: acts on soft going (bumper form on firm). *G. M. Moore*

SPRING GIFT 7 b.m. Slip Anchor – Belmez Melody (Belmez (USA)) [2003/4 16mᵖᵘ **h–**
16g 16g 17v Jan 13] sparely-made mare: poor maiden on Flat: no show over hurdles,
sold out of P. McEntee's stable £380 Ascot August Sales: has looked temperamental.
D. W. Thompson

SPRING GROVE (IRE) 9 b.g. Mandalus – Lucy Lorraine (IRE) (Buckskin (FR)) **c129**
[2003/4 c–, h–: 22g⁵ c16m* c17g⁴ c20d* c21d² c20g c24g³ c20g⁴ Apr 18] workmanlike **h105**
gelding: fair hurdler: fairly useful handicap chaser: won 6-runner events at Lingfield in
November and Warwick in December: creditable efforts when in frame after, third to Bee
An Bee at Newbury: effective at 2m to 3m: acts on heavy and good to firm going: has run
well when sweating and on toes: usually races prominently. *R. H. Alner*

SPRINGHILL 9 b.g. Relief Pitcher – Early Call (Kind of Hush) [2003/4 16d Apr 21] **h–**
strong gelding: fair maiden hurdler in 2001/2: seventh of 11 finishers in novice at Worcester on first outing since: stays 2½m: acts on good to soft going (won bumper on good to
firm). *Mrs Mary Hambro*

SPRING LOVER (FR) 5 b.g. Fijar Tango (FR) – Kailasa (FR) (R B Chesne) [2003/4 **c–**
16m 22g² 20d 16g 16d³ c23m⁴ c25sᶠ c25s⁵ Apr 11] smallish gelding: half-brother to fair **h95**
4-y-o hurdle winner Magic Sky (by Simon du Desert): placed twice around 9f from 3
starts on Flat: won juvenile chase at Pau in 2002/3 for J-P. Totain, let down by jumping
and little worthwhile form over fences in Britain: modest maiden hurdler: stays 2¾m:
acts on good to soft going: has finished weakly. *Miss Venetia Williams*

SPRING PURSUIT 8 b.g. Rudimentary (USA) – Pursuit of Truth (USA) (Irish River **h104**
(FR)) [2003/4 h81: 16d² 16d⁵ 16s⁵ 16g³ 16d* 17d⁴ 20s⁴ 16d⁴ 16g⁵ 16m⁵ 16g 17g⁶ 20d³
Apr 21] neat gelding: fair handicap hurdler: won 18-runner novice at Warwick in January:
creditable efforts most other starts, left R. Price after eighth one: stays 2½m: acts on soft
going. *E. G. Bevan*

SPRING ROCK 7 b.g. Rock Hopper – Shaft of Sunlight (Sparkler) [2003/4 F–: F16m **F–**
Jun 14] no form in bumpers or points: tried visored: sold 3,700 gns Doncaster August
Sales. *R. M. Whitaker*

SPRINGWOOD WHITE 10 gr.g. Sharkskin Suit (USA) – Kale Brig (New Brig) **c71**
[2003/4 c78: c20m⁵ c20m c25m³ Jun 20] poor chaser: placed in points in 2004: stays 25f:
acts on good to firm going: wears cheekpieces. *J. L. Gledson*

SPUD'S FANCY 5 ch.m. You My Chief – Adelbaran (FR) (No Pass No Sale) [2003/4 **F–**
F17g Oct 11] sturdy mare: third foal: half-sister to 2 winning pointers by Itsu: dam 1m
winner in France: tailed off in bumper on debut. *B. J. Llewellyn*

SPY BOY (IRE) 8 b.g. Balla Cove – Spy Girl (Tanfirion) [2003/4 c–, h–: c20d³ c26dᵖᵘ **c–**
Apr 7] leggy gelding: no longer of any account: has worn blinkers/visor. *Arun Green* **h–**

SQUANDAMANIA 11 b.g. Ela-Mana-Mou – Garden Pink (FR) (Bellypha) [2003/4 **h62**
h53: 20v² 24v⁶ 24d 20s² Mar 13] tall gelding: poor handicap hurdler: stays 2½m: acts on
heavy going: tried in headgear: all 4 wins at Sedgefield. *J. R. Norton*

SQUEEZE BOX (IRE) 5 b.m. Accordion – Spread Your Wings (IRE) (Decent **h74**
Fellow) [2003/4 F84: 16g 20g⁵ 20d 21d⁴ Mar 16] poor novice hurdler: tried in cheekpieces (raced freely): looked temperamental final outing. *J. Howard Johnson*

SQUEEZE (IRE) 6 b.g. Old Vic – Petaluma Pet (Callernish) [2003/4 F77: F17mᵖᵘ **F–**
Jun 21] twice-raced in bumpers, lame second start. *B. N. Pollock*

SQUIRTLE TURTLE 4 ch.g. Peintre Celebre (USA) – Hatton Gardens (Auction **h–**
Ring (USA)) [2003/4 17s Jan 20] half-brother to one-time fairly useful 2m hurdler Kew
Gardens (by Arazi): fair on Flat (stays 11f), successful in January: well held in juvenile
maiden on hurdling debut: likely to do better under less testing conditions. *P. F. I. Cole*

STACUMNY BRIDGE 6 b.g. Flying Spur (AUS) – Karoi (IRE) (Kafu) **h119**
[2003/4 h125, F99: 16g⁴ 16d² 16d* 20d Feb 21] good sort: will make a chaser: fairly
useful hurdler: didn't have to be at best to win minor event at Thurles in December: raced
mainly at 2m: acts on heavy going. *M. Halford, Ireland*

STAFFORD KING (IRE) 7 b.h. Nicolotte – Opening Day (Day Is Done) [2003/4 **h–**
h86: 16gᵖᵘ 16s Dec 20] workmanlike horse: novice hurdler, below form in 2 handicaps

863

after over year's absence: probably stays 25f: acts on soft and good to firm going.
J. G. M. O'Shea

STAGE AFFAIR (USA) 10 b. or br.g. Theatrical – Wooing (USA) (Stage Door Johnny (USA)) [2003/4 c127, h144: c16d* c17s³ 16d 16s Feb 14] tall gelding: highly tried first 2 starts over fences, easily won maiden at Punchestown in May when dropped in class: one-time very smart hurdler: last in graded events at Leopardstown and Gowran last 2 outings: raced around 2m: acts on good to firm and heavy going: tried blinkered: has had tongue tied. *D. K. Weld, Ireland* — **c117 h–**

STAGECOACHSAPPHIRE 6 b.g. Teenoso (USA) – Zajira (IRE) (Ela-Mana-Mou) [2003/4 F17d* F16g Mar 17] 6,000 4-y-o: well-made gelding: second foal: brother to winning 2½m hurdler Arijaz: dam, fair hurdler/chaser, stayed 2½m: fairly useful form when winning 19-runner conditional jockeys bumper at Carlisle on debut in February by 3½ lengths from The Outlier: pulled far too hard when well held in Champion Bumper at Cheltenham. *Mrs S. J. Smith* — **F99**

STAGE FRIENDLY (IRE) 5 ch.g. Old Vic – Just Affable (IRE) (Phardante (FR)) [2003/4 F16d⁵ F16s Dec 26] €13,000 4-y-o: first foal: dam unraced half-sister to smart chaser up to 2¾m Bells Life: poor form in bumpers, looking very much a stayer on debut. *N. A. Twiston-Davies* — **F72**

STAKEHOLDER (IRE) 6 ch.g. Priolo (USA) – Island Goddess (Godswalk (USA)) [2003/4 h–: 22g 26sᵖᵘ Jan 7] angular gelding: no form over hurdles: tried tongue tied: sold £1,400 Ascot February Sales. *M. Sheppard* — **h–**

STALKY DOVE 7 b.m. Homo Sapien – Sally's Dove (Celtic Cone) [2003/4 F74: F16d² 16dᵖᵘ May 16] modest form at best in bumpers: went off too quickly on hurdling debut. *W. M. Brisbourne* — **h– F76**

STALLONE 7 ch.g. Brief Truce (USA) – Bering Honneur (USA) (Bering) [2003/4 h81: 20mᵖᵘ Oct 25] fair on Flat (stays 1½m), successful 3 times in 2003: poor novice hurdler: likely to prove best around 2m: tongue tied on debut. *N. Wilson* — **h–**

STAMPARLAND HILL 9 b.g. Gildoran – Woodland Flower (Furry Glen) [2003/4 c–, h107: 17d⁵ 24d c16d² c16d² Apr 22] lengthy gelding: fair at best over hurdles: better over fences: jumped more fluently than usual when runner-up to Sir Storm in handicaps last 2 starts: stays 19f: raced on good ground or softer: free-going sort: sold 12,000 gns Doncaster May Sales. *J. M. Jefferson* — **c120 h–**

STANCE 5 b.g. Salse (USA) – De Stael (USA) (Nijinsky (CAN)) [2003/4 19s 17g⁴ 20g⁴ 18d* Apr 7] close-coupled gelding: useful on Flat at 3 yrs, winning over 1½m for H. Cecil: mostly disappointing in 2003, trained much of year in Spain: fair form over hurdles: trained by C. Von Der Recke on debut: won handicap at Fontwell by neck from Pardishar, despite hanging right: stays 2½m: acts on good to soft ground: joined G. L. Moore. *P. R. Hedger* — **h109**

STAND EASY (IRE) 11 b.g. Buckskin (FR) – Geeaway (Gala Performance) [2003/4 c101§, h83§: c26s* c26v* c24gᵖᵘ c25d⁶ Nov 23] tall gelding: maiden hurdler: fair chaser: won intermediate and novice at Uttoxeter in May: will stay beyond 3¼m: acts on heavy and good to firm going: has worn cheekpieces: often none too fluent over fences: temperamental. *J. R. Cornwall* — **c102 § h– §**

STANDING APPLAUSE (USA) 6 b. or br.g. Theatrical – Pent (USA) (Mr Prospector (USA)) [2003/4 h70: 22s 22g³ 22gᵖᵘ Apr 18] lightly-raced novice hurdler, easily best effort when close third in handicap at Newton Abbot: stays 2¾m: tongue tied. *Mrs A. J. Hamilton-Fairley* — **h84**

STANDING BLOOM 8 ch.m. Presidium – Rosie Cone (Celtic Cone) [2003/4 h92: 20sᵖᵘ 20m 23d c24s* c20g⁴ Feb 10] medium-sized mare: winning hurdler, no form in handicaps first 3 starts in 2003/4: modest form both outings over fences, won novice at Huntingdon in January: likely to stay beyond 3m: acts on heavy going, bumper form on good to firm. *Mrs P. Sly* — **c92 h–**

STANLEY PARK 6 ch.g. Bold Arrangement – Queen Buzzard (Buzzards Bay) [2003/4 h–, F–: 17s³ 16m⁴ 19f² Oct 5] workmanlike gelding: poor form over hurdles. *J. R. Weymes* — **h73**

STANMORE (IRE) 12 b.g. Aristocracy – Lady Go Marching (USA) (Go Marching (USA)) [2003/4 c103, h–: c24gᵖᵘ c22g⁶ c24m⁶ c21m* c24g³ c24m⁶ c22g⁶ c23m³ Nov 17] lengthy gelding: modest handicap chaser: won 5-runner event at Southwell in August: little other form in 2003/4: stays 3m: has won on soft going, races on firmer nowadays — **c95 h–**

(acts on firm): tried blinkered, wore cheekpieces final start: usually races prominently: sound jumper. *Mrs J. A. Saunders*

STANS MAN CAN   6 gr.g. Arzanni – Tais Toi (Vitiges (FR)) [2003/4 19v⁶ 25dᵖᵘ c24mᵖᵘ Apr 13] third foal: dam, middle-distance maiden on Flat, of little account over hurdles: showed nothing in novice hurdles or chase. *S. C. Burrough*   **c–** **h–**

STANTONS CHURCH   7 b.g. Homo Sapien – Valkyrie Reef (Miramar Reef) [2003/4 h80: 17g 19g c20gᵖᵘ Mar 12] temperamental maiden hurdler, left H. Daly after second outing: no show on steeplechase debut: runner-up in maiden point following month. *Mark Doyle*   **c– §** **h– §**

STANWAY   5 b.g. Presenting – Nicklup (Netherkelly) [2003/4 F17d² F16m⁴ aF16g² F16d³ 16s 20sᶠ 17s 22g⁶ Apr 18] close-coupled, workmanlike gelding: second foal: dam winning hurdler/fair staying chaser: in frame all 4 starts in bumpers: modest form last 2 outings over hurdles: should prove suited by 2½m+. *Mrs Mary Hambro*   **h86** **F87**

STAPLE SOUND   7 b.g. Alflora (IRE) – Loch Scavaig (IRE) (The Parson) [2003/4 h–, F–: 27sᵖᵘ 22m Jul 17] leggy gelding: of little account over hurdles: visored in 2003/4: runner-up in maiden point in March. *James Moffatt*   **h– §**

STARBUCK   10 b.g. Brush Aside (USA) – Clonmello (Le Bavard (FR)) [2003/4 c24f⁶ Feb 29] tall gelding: modest pointer: well beaten in hunter chase: should stay 3m. *Miss J. Fisher*   **c–** **h–**

STAR BUSTER (IRE)   6 b.g. Eurobus – Lucciola (FR) (Auction Ring (USA)) [2003/4 F17d Dec 2] €5,000 4-y-o, £4,400 5-y-o: workmanlike gelding: fifth foal: half-brother to winner up to 1m in Germany by Nashamaa: dam unraced: showed nothing in bumper on debut. *H. M. Kavanagh*   **F–**

STAR CATCHER (IRE)   8 b.g. Toulon – Paper Merchant (Hays) [2003/4 h–: 20mᵖᵘ Aug 8] no sign of ability: has had tongue tied. *B. G. Powell*   **h–**

STAR CHANGES   11 b.g. Derrylin – Sweet Linda (Saucy Kit) [2003/4 c24g May 31] fair pointer, won 3 times in 2004: outclassed in hunter chases. *A. Hollingsworth*   **c77** **h–**

STAR CLIPPER   7 b.h. Kris – Anne Bonny (Ajdal (USA)) [2003/4 c122, h113: c16d⁴ c20s* c24d² Nov 23] good sort: fairly useful hurdler/chaser: ran well when second to Cloudy Bays in Troytown Chase (Handicap) at Navan: made hard work of straight-forward task in minor event at Gowran 6 months earlier: stays 3m: acts on heavy going: has looked reluctant, including when blinkered. *N. Meade, Ireland*   **c118** **h–**

STAR COUNCEL (IRE)   8 b.m. Leading Counsel (USA) – Black Avenue (IRE) (Strong Gale) [2003/4 c–, h86: 21g⁵ 26g³ c17g⁵ c26m⁴ 23m 20d 20m 24d 23d* 24g³ 23s⁶ 16g 25g Feb 6] angular mare: maiden chaser: modest handicap hurdler: won at Haydock in December: stays 3¼m: acts on any going: tried blinkered: has worn cheekpieces, including last 5 starts. *B. S. Rothwell*   **c–** **h95**

STARELLO   5 b.m. Supreme Leader – Oubava (FR) (Groom Dancer (USA)) [2003/4 F18g⁶ F16d Mar 28] lengthy mare: fourth known foal: sister to bumper winner Candello and half-sister to French middle-distance winner Belle Oubava (by Linamix): dam, French middle-distance winner, half-sister to useful French hurdler Grand Patron and fairly useful hurdler/chaser around 2½m Litchanine: sixth of 8 in mares bumper at Fontwell on debut: tailed off next time. *N. J. Henderson*   **F81**

STAR JACK (FR)   9 b.g. Epervier Bleu – Little Point (FR) (Le Nain Jaune (FR)) [2003/4 c124, h–: 22g May 22] lengthy gelding: winning hurdler: fairly useful handicap chaser in 2002/3: effective at 2m (given test) to 2½m: unraced on firm going, acts on any other: wears cheekpieces: tongue tied: bold jumper. *T. J. Fitzgerald*   **c–** **h–**

STARLIGHT EXPRESS (FR)   4 b.f. Air Express (IRE) – Muramixa (FR) (Linamix (FR)) [2003/4 F12g⁴ F13d 17s 19g² 23s⁴ Apr 4] second foal: half-sister to 1¼m winner in Italy by Bahamian Bounty: dam won several times up to 1½m in France: better effort in bumpers when fourth of 23 to Secret Ploy in 3-y-o event at Newbury: progressive form in novice hurdles, travelled well long way when 11 lengths fourth to Lisa du Chenet in mares event at Lingfield: capable of better again, particularly when emphasis is less on stamina. *Miss E. C. Lavelle*   **h89 p** **F89**

STAR OF BETHLEHEM (IRE)   6 b. or br.g. Jolly Jake (NZ) – In Reverse (IRE) (Paico) [2003/4 18d* 16d³ 18s² 18d² 20d² Apr 12] IR £1,100 3-y-o: first foal: dam unraced, out of half-sister to useful 2m to 21f hurdler Don Valentino: successful on last of 3 starts in bumpers in 2002/3: fairly useful novice hurdler: won maiden at Fairyhouse in November and minor event at Punchestown (by ½ length from Major Burns) in early-   **h118**

May: largely creditable efforts in between: stays 2½m: acts on good to soft and good to firm going. *M. J. P. O'Brien, Ireland*

STAR OF GERMANY (IRE) 4 b.g. Germany (USA) – Twinkle Bright (USA) (Star   **h70** de Naskra (USA)) [2003/4 17m 16d 16s 16g⁴ 16g 20s⁴ Mar 13] no form in 3 starts on all-weather on Flat, sold out of T. Tate's stable 3,000 gns Doncaster May Sales: poor juvenile hurdler: stays 2½m: acts on soft going. *Ferdy Murphy*

STAR OF RAVEN 7 b.m. Sea Raven (IRE) – Lucy At The Minute (Silly Prices)   **c102** [2003/4 c78: c25s* c23g² Mar 12] winning pointer: second start in hunters when winning at Wetherby in February: similar form when second at Leicester (reportedly lost a shoe) month later: stays 25f: acts on soft going. *Joss Saville*

STAROSKI 7 b.m. Petoski – Olnistar (FR) (Balsamo (FR)) [2003/4 F17v⁵ Dec 1]   **F–** angular mare: modest form on 2 of 3 starts in bumpers in 2001/2 for C. Bealby: shaped as if run was needed in mares event on return. *Simon Earle*

STARPATH (NZ) 12 ch.g. Starjo (NZ) – Centa Belle (NZ) (Centurius) [2003/4 c33dᵖᵘ   **c–** Apr 30] sturdy gelding: fairly useful hunter chaser in 2001 for P. Nicholls: lightly raced and not so good since, pulled up at Cheltenham (for J. Boulter) in 2003 and in cross-country event at Punchestown in late-April: stays 33f: acts on heavy and good to firm going. *A. J. Martin, Ireland*

STAR PRIZE (IRE) 7 b.g. Fourstars Allstar (USA) – Dipper's Gift (IRE) (Salluceva)   **h98 p** [2003/4 F16g² 16s⁴ Feb 19] IR 30,000 3-y-o, 30,000 4-y-o: rather leggy gelding: third   **F88** foal: dam unraced half-sister to smart staying chaser Royal Dipper and very smart staying hurdler/useful chaser Henry Mann: shaped well when second in bumper at Worcester and when fourth in novice hurdle at Sandown: will stay beyond 2m: should improve. *N. J. Henderson*

STARS DELIGHT (IRE) 7 ch.g. Fourstars Allstar (USA) – Celtic Cygnet (Celtic   **h107** Cone) [2003/4 h104, F71: 21m² 19m³ May 31] workmanlike gelding: fair hurdler: creditable placed efforts in amateur handicaps at Huntingdon and Stratford in May: may prove best up to 21f: seems to act on any going: has found less than seemed likely. *G. L. Moore*

STAR SEVENTEEN 6 ch.m. Rock City – Westminster Waltz (Dance In Time (CAN))   **h–** [2003/4 h–: 17g Feb 19] no form over hurdles: has pulled hard. *Mrs N. S. Sharpe*

STARSHIPENTERPRISE 6 b.g. The Star of Orion VII – Lequest (Lepanto (GER))   **c–** [2003/4 21s⁶ c19g⁶ c24v⁵ c20gᵘʳ Apr 12] second foal: dam never ran: no sign of ability.   **h–** *L. Wells*

STARS'N'STRIPES (IRE) 6 b.g. Lord Americo – Drumdeels Star (IRE) (Le Bavard   **F–** (FR)) [2003/4 F17d Jun 9] fourth foal: half-brother to modest chaser Guid Willie Waught (by Montelimar), stays 2¾m: dam, won 2½m hurdle, half-sister to high-class hurdler/ top-class chaser up to 3m Bradbury Star: little show in bumper on debut. *W. W. Dennis*

STARS OUT TONIGHT (IRE) 7 b.g. Insan (USA) – Go And Tell (Kemal (FR))   **c133** [2003/4 c123, h–: c22g² c24gᵖᵘ Dec 27] rangy, good sort: useful chaser: good second to   **h–** Mighty Strong in handicap at Newbury on reappearance, bled from nose only other start in 2003/4: likely to prove better around 3m than shorter: yet to race on extremes of going: sold to join C. Bealby 32,000 gns Doncaster May Sales. *Miss H. C. Knight*

STAR TIME (IRE) 5 b.g. Fourstars Allstar (USA) – Punctual (Lead On Time (USA))   **h71 §** [2003/4 h–, F–: 16d 16d 22s³ 26mᵖᵘ 22sᵖᵘ Mar 23] good-bodied gelding: poor maiden hurdler: stays 2¾m: acts on soft going: visored last 3 outings, looked unwilling last 2. *M. Scudamore*

STARTING AGAIN 10 b.g. Petoski – Lynemore (Nearly A Hand) [2003/4 c–, h–:   **c107** c19dᵖᵘ c20dᶠ c20g⁶ c24m Mar 4] lengthy gelding: fair handicap chaser: form in 2003/4   **h–** only when sixth at Ludlow in February, off bridle some way out: stays 2¾m: acts on any going. *H. D. Daly*

STAR TROOPER (IRE) 8 b. or br.g. Brief Truce (USA) – Star Cream (Star Appeal)   **c81** [2003/4 h93: 16g 18g 16g³ 16f² 16f⁵ 20d* 18d³ 24d 16v 20d 20s⁵ 17s 20d c16d³ c21g⁶   **h88 §** Apr 12] modest handicap hurdler, won amateur event at Carlisle in November: poor form in 2 races over fences: stays 2½m: probably acts on any going: tried blinkered, usually wears cheekpieces: inconsistent, and has looked none too keen. *Miss S. E. Forster*

STAR WONDER 4 b.f. Syrtos – Galava (CAN) (Graustark) [2003/4 17mᵘʳ 16gᵖᵘ 16vᵖᵘ   **h–** 16s Jan 27] no form on Flat or over hurdles (tried to refuse on debut): tried blinkered. *B. N. Doran*

STARZAAN (IRE)   5 b.g. Darshaan – Stellina (IRE) (Caerleon (USA)) [2003/4   **h145 +**
h129+: 16g⁴ 22g² 16d⁴ 21s³ 25d³ 20g* 21g 20d⁵ 16m⁴ Apr 23]
        So, farewell then the showcase race. An admirable concept that, sadly, was
not well executed and ultimately failed for lack of support. The idea of highlighting
one particular race each day, worth at least £10,000, to maximise publicity and
boost turnover is fine in principle but the right races needed to be created. Instead,
races were chosen from those which were available—it could have been the Grand
National one day and a class F event at Plumpton the next. The National needs no
enhancement but focussing on races like the latter merely highlights the feeble
quality of that day's racing. The idea that punters would be more likely to bet on a
race simply because it had 'showcase' in the title was naive, and more work should
have been done to give showcase races a much clearer identity and a coherence they
never achieved. The major bookmakers stumped up the cash to boost the showcase
events on days when there weren't qualifying races, but they clearly began to feel
they were paying extra for the product but getting no obvious benefit. Initially,
showcase races were sponsored under the blanket banner of the bookmakers' 49s
numbers game, individual bookmakers then taking on the sponsorship before the
concept began to die a slow death when much of that was withdrawn, as bookmakers also dropped early prices on many of the races. The last 'showcase' race
was the Grade 2 National Spirit Hurdle in February, Fontwell's biggest race, but a
conditions race—though an excellent one on this occasion—run on a Sunday and
without terrestrial television coverage.
        The showcase concept stemmed from the report in 1997 of the BHB's Off-
Course Betting Development Group which emphasised the need to produce races
attractive to punters. The review group brought forward a number of sensible
proposals which also included the introduction of late flexibility in race timing to
ensure the most attractive events are televised, thereby making best use of an inval-
uable shop window for the sport. So far as many of the other ideas were concerned,
hardly any were properly implemented. There was a suspicion that, because some

Tote National Spirit Hurdle, Fontwell—Starzaan (sweating) jumps ahead of Vic Toto at the last

Mr Ben Arbib's "Starzaan"

of the ideas were opposed by factions within the sport, most of the report was just shelved as being too difficult. Among the ideas set out were: entries for the following Saturday's televised meetings available a week in advance (to enable broadcasters and Sunday papers to publise them more fully); introducing forty-eight-hour declarations for all Saturday TV meetings; making sure one of the Sunday fixtures was at a top course and that there was a race worth at least £20,000 every Sunday; experiments with Saturday morning fixtures; and the development of a plan to attract newcomers to betting on horse racing. Some headway is being made with forty-eight-hour declarations (discussed more fully in the essay on Sporazene), but there is no prospect of changes to the schedule for entries for big Saturday meetings, nor—judging by some of the winter scheduling—does there appear much hope of introducing quality and value criteria for Sunday fixtures. An experiment with Saturday morning fixtures is scheduled for the coming autumn.

It was ironic that the last 'showcase' race was sponsored by the Tote, whose chairman Peter Jones chaired the Off-Course Betting Development Group, just before succeeding Lord Wyatt at the Tote. The impetus for setting up the Group was concern over horseracing's loss or market share, which had fallen from 75% of off-course betting with bookmakers at the start of the 'nineties to around 70% by 1997. The figure has continued to fall and is now just over 60%, albeit 60% of a considerably larger pool, so perhaps the time is right for another review. The sport must address the dullness of so many of its race programmes, pandering to mediocrity seeming to be the only way racing is able to service its ever-expanding fixture list, particularly on the Flat. Some races nowadays, however, are so unappealing that they virtually invite discerning punters *not* to bet on them. In an age when the major bookmakers can earn publicity for paying out after two people taking part in a television programme were reported to have had a sexual encounter, those in charge of race planning need to get their act together and come up with fresh and imaginative race programmes to replace the tired ones that are too often palmed off on the betting public these days.

The National Spirit resulted in Starzaan's clear-cut victory from Vic Toto and was just reward for a series of good performances up to that point. Starzaan had improved on his juvenile efforts (including a good fourth in the Champion Four Year Old Hurdle at Punchestown in May) and shown his form over distances ranging from two miles to three miles one furlong. Running in a variety of handicaps and conditions events, Starzaan showed himself a smart hurdler. His only below-par effort came in the Coral Cup at Cheltenham on his next start after Fontwell, but he redeemed himself in good company on his last two outings. Starzaan was probably flattered when fifth to Rhinestone Cowboy after dictating the pace for a long way in the Aintree Hurdle, but he came a creditable fourth to Hasty Prince in the two-mile Concept Hurdle at Sandown, rallying late after losing his position when the pace quickened in a muddling race.

		Darshaan (br 1981)	Shirley Heights (b 1975)	Mill Reef Hardiemma
Starzaan (IRE) (b.g. 1999)			Delsy (br 1972)	Abdos Kelty
		Stellina (IRE) (b 1988)	Caerleon (b 1980)	Nijinsky Foreseer
			Mariella (b 1977)	Sir Gaylord Zambara

Starzaan is bred to stay well. His sire Darshaan is a strong influence for stamina and his dam, who won at a mile and a quarter as a two-year-old in France, is from the family of Sagaro who won the Gold Cup at Royal Ascot three times. Although he has shown form at two miles, there is little doubt that Starzaan is ideally suited by more of a test of stamina and is possibly best at around two and a half miles. The tall, angular Starzaan, who has the scope to make a chaser, acts on soft and good to firm going. *H. Morrison*

STASHEDAWAY (IRE)   7 b.m. Treasure Hunter – Mugs Away (Mugatpura) [2003/4 c82p, h118: 20g⁵ 20d² 16d³ c18d* c16d³ c20s² c21s² c20s* c20d³ c22s³ Mar 28] lengthy mare: fairly useful hurdler/chaser: won mares novice chases at Punchestown (listed) in December and Thurles (Grade 3, beat Rose Perk 11 lengths) in February: stays 21f: acts on soft going: consistent. *M. J. P. O'Brien, Ireland*   **c124 h124**

STATE EXPRESS   13 b.m. State Diplomacy (USA) – Roman Bonnet (Roman Warrior) [2003/4 c24mᵘʳ May 10] poor pointer: dead. *Mrs H. E. Oxendale*   **c–**

STATELEY LORD (IRE)   8 br. or b.g. Good Thyne (USA) – Sixfoursix (Balinger) [2003/4 c–, h–: 22mᵖᵘ Dec 4] workmanlike gelding: little sign of ability: usually tongue tied. *Miss E. C. Lavelle*   **c– h–**

STATE OF PLAY   4 b.g. Hernando (FR) – Kaprice (GER) (Windwurf (GER)) [2003/4 F16g F16d* Mar 25] rather leggy gelding: half-brother to 1m winner Komago (by Big Shuffle) and 6f/7f winner Ksara (by Most Welcome): dam 11f winner in Germany: shaped quite well when eighth of 24 to Secret Ploy in Grade 2 bumper at Newbury on debut: won steadily-run event at Ludlow following month by 4 lengths from Maljimar. *P. R. Webber*   **F94**

STATE POWER (IRE)   6 b.g. Sadler's Wells (USA) – Lady Liberty (NZ) (Noble Bijou (USA)) [2003/4 16g* 20m³ Jun 5] 8,000 2-y-o: brother to 2 winners, including fairly useful 1½m performer Majority Rule, and half-brother to smart 1996 2-y-o 7f/1m winner Equal Rights (by Royal Academy) and fairly useful 2½m hurdler Outer Limit (by Caerleon): dam Australian Group 1 1¼m winner: modest handicap hurdler: much improved when winning at Sligo in April: heavily backed, creditable third at Perth next time: stays easy 2½m: acts on good to firm going. *A. J. Martin, Ireland*   **h93**

STATIM   5 b.m. Marju (IRE) – Rapid Repeat (IRE) (Exactly Sharp (USA)) [2003/4 h111§: 16f² 16g* 18m* 20m* Oct 27] leggy mare: fair hurdler: won 4-y-o maiden at   **h111 §**

Listowel in September and mares novice at Punchestown and novice at Galway (flashed tail and cocked jaw) in October: stays 2½m: probably acts on any going: best in blinkers/cheekpieces: temperamental. *M. J. P. O'Brien, Ireland*

STATION ISLAND (IRE)   7 ch.g. Roselier (FR) – Sweet Tulip (Beau Chapeau) **h99**
[2003/4 F79: 23d² 21v² 25s^pu 22s⁵ 25g^F 24d⁴ 26g³ 26d* 27d* 24m⁶ Apr 14] close-coupled gelding: winning Irish pointer: modest hurdler: won handicaps at Hereford (conditional jockeys) and Sedgefield in March: stays 27f: raced mainly on good going or softer (acts on heavy): tongue tied last 6 starts: sweating when below form final outing. *J. Mackie*

STATLEY RAJ (IND)   5 b.g. Mtoto – Donna Star (Stately Don (USA)) [2003/4 F16s **h–**
F16d 16g^pu Apr 4] medium-sized gelding: fourth foal: brother to 9f winner in Czech **F83**
Republic and half-brother to smart French 1m to 1¼m winner Star of Akkar (by Distant Relative): dam third at 1m at 2 yrs in France: ninth of 19 in bumper at Huntingdon on debut: well held both subsequent starts, hurdling debut on second occasion. *R. Rowe*

STAVORDALE LAD (IRE)   6 b.g. Mister Lord (USA) – Ath Trasna (Amoristic **c111**
(USA)) [2003/4 c23g⁴ c25d² c23s^F Jan 20] 10,000 (privately) 4-y-o: fifth foal: half-brother to winning pointer by Royal Fountain: dam winning pointer: won both starts in points in 2003: best effort in steeplechases when second to Lords Best in maiden at Folkestone in January: stays 25f. *P. F. Nicholls*

ST BEE   9 br.g. St Ninian – Regal Bee (Royal Fountain) [2003/4 c–x, h–: c25d^pu c25g^ur **c– x**
c23g⁴ c25g c24f Feb 29] of little account outside points: often wears cheekpieces: sketchy **h–**
jumper of fences. *W. G. Reed*

ST CASSIEN (IRE)   4 b.g. Goldmark (USA) – Moonlight Partner (IRE) (Red Sunset) **h–**
[2003/4 16g^F Nov 2] showed little on Flat or on hurdling debut. *T. M. Jones*

STEEL BAND   6 b.g. Kris – Quaver (USA) (The Minstrel (CAN)) [2003/4 16d³ 16d² **h116**
16s⁴ 16s³ 16s* 16s² 16d⁵ 16d Apr 13] fairly useful handicap hurdler: won at Punchestown in February: best effort when second to She'll Be Lucky at Cork next time: best form at 2m: acts on heavy going. *Paul A. Roche, Ireland*

STEEL EDGE (IRE)   10 ch.g. Torus – Lasting Impression (Proverb) [2003/4 c–, h–: **c– x**
22g 24v^pu c20m^pu Jun 7] workmanlike gelding: no form over hurdles: modest maiden **h–**
chaser: lightly raced and let down by jumping since 2000/1. *Miss Venetia Williams*

STEEL MILL (IRE)   9 gr.g. Roselier (FR) – Chatmando (IRE) (Mandalus) [2003/4 **c87**
c–, h87: c22s² c24g⁵ c24g^F c25s* c25s^ur Apr 11] sturdy gelding: maiden hurdler: modest **h–**
chaser: 5 lb out of weights when winning handicap at Towcester in March: stays 25f: acts on soft and good to firm going. *D. J. Caro*

STEEL WARRIOR   7 ch.g. Michelozzo (USA) – Iskra Bay (IRE) (Un Desperado **F–**
(FR)) [2003/4 F16d⁶ aF16g Dec 13] first foal: dam unraced: well beaten in 2 bumpers. *J. S. Smith*

STEPASTRAY   7 gr.g. Alhijaz – Wandering Stranger (Petong) [2003/4 h–: 16d Nov **h–**
26] modest maiden on Flat (stays 1½m): no form in 2 novice hurdles. *R. E. Barr*

STEP ON EYRE (IRE)   14 b.g. Step Together (USA) – Jane Eyre (Master Buck) **c73 §**
[2003/4 c92§, h–: c34v³ c24d^pu Mar 10] big gelding: veteran chaser: won point in **h–**
February: stays 33f: acts on good to firm and heavy going: tried blinkered: usually jumps soundly: unreliable. *S. Wynne*

STEPPES   9 b.g. Jendali (USA) – Asoness (Laxton) [2003/4 c–, h68: c24m^ur c21s^pu **c–**
c21s^pu Apr 12] form only when winning weak maiden hurdle in 2002/3. *M. J. Gingell* **h–**

STEPPES OF GOLD (IRE)   7 b.g. Moscow Society (USA) – Trysting Place (He **h133**
Loves Me) [2003/4 F104p: 16s* 18s* 18g² 16g⁵ Apr 2] tall gelding: will make a chaser: useful novice hurdler: won at Haydock in December and Kelso in January: best efforts in Grade 2 events last 2 starts, second to Paddy The Piper at Kelso and fifth to Royal Shakespeare at Aintree (tended to carry head awkwardly), doing particularly well in latter given less emphasis on stamina: will stay beyond 2¼m: raced on good going or softer. *N. G. Richards*

STEP QUICK (IRE)   10 ch.g. All Haste (USA) – Little Steps (Step Together (USA)) **c85**
[2003/4 c94: c21s^pu c24g⁶ c21g⁴ c22g³ c22m* c25f² c20m² c20m³ Nov 24] tall, angular gelding: modest chaser: left W. Bryan after second start: won novice handicap at Market Rasen in October: stays 25f: acts on soft and firm going: wore cheekpieces final outing: none too fluent last 3 appearances. *P. Bowen*

STERLING DOT COM (IRE) 8 b.g. Roselier (FR) – Daddy's Folly (Le Moss) [2003/4 c88, h–: c24g³ c23g² c22d⁴ c25s³ c24g⁴ c29d⁵ c25m⁵ Apr 13] tall gelding: modest maiden chaser: should be suited by 3m+: acts on soft going: blinkered once: not a fluent jumper. *P. J. Hobbs* c97 x h–

STERN LEADER (IRE) 5 b.g. Supreme Leader – Strong Stern (IRE) (Lancastrian) [2003/4 F16v⁴ F16v⁴ 17g 21dᵖᵘ Mar 1] first foal: dam runner-up in point: much better effort in bumpers at Towcester when fourth on debut: no show in 2 races over hurdles. *D. J. Wintle* h– F81

STEVE FORD 15 gr.g. Another Realm – Sky Miss (Skymaster) [2003/4 c–, h–: c24gᶠ Apr 18] leggy gelding: winning hurdler/chaser, retains little ability. *Mrs S. S. Harbour* c– h–

STEVE THE FISH (IRE) 8 ch.g. Dry Dock – Country Clothing (Salluceva) [2003/4 c–, h–: 22s 24v* 24s c25dᴿ c24dᵖᵘ Mar 24] medium-sized gelding: has reportedly had breathing operation: modest hurdler: off 7 months, best effort when winning handicap at Towcester in November: no subsequent form, including on return to chasing: stays 3m well: raced on good going or softer (acts on heavy). *J. A. B. Old* c– h98

STEVIE DEE 10 ch.g. Emperor Fountain – Babe In The Wood (Athens Wood) [2003/4 c25sᵖᵘ Mar 1] angular gelding: winning hurdler: poor maiden hurdler: no show both starts in steeplechases: visored once. *R. A. Maletroit* c– h–

STEWART'S LAD 7 b.g. Well Beloved – Moneyacre (Veloski) [2003/4 h–: 20s⁵ 17s⁴ Feb 6] workmanlike gelding: modest maiden hurdler: should stay beyond 17f: acts on soft going. *B. D. Leavy* h90

STILL GOING ON 7 b.g. Prince Sabo – Floppie (FR) (Law Society (USA)) [2003/4 16d 16g² 16g² 16g 16d⁴ 16sᵖᵘ Jan 1] angular gelding: 7f winner on Flat: modest maiden hurdler: raced at 2m: acts on good to soft ground, probably on firm: wore cheekpieces fourth and final starts: tongue tied after reappearance. *Eoin Doyle, Ireland* h90

STILLMORE BUSINESS 13 ch.g. Don Enrico (USA) – Mill Miss (Typhoon) [2003/4 c19mᵖᵘ May 14] winning pointer: well beaten in steeplechases. *Mrs F. J. Walker* c–

STILL SPEEDY (IRE) 7 b.g. Toulon – Gorge (Mount Hagen (FR)) [2003/4 F83: F16m³ 16sᶠ 16m³ Apr 13] fair in bumpers: carried head particularly high and only poor form when third in maiden at Chepstow on completed start over hurdles: has pulled hard. *Noel T. Chance* h77 F87

STING LIKE A BEE (IRE) 5 b.g. Ali-Royal (IRE) – Hidden Agenda (FR) (Machiavellian (USA)) [2003/4 h73: 20g* 20gᶠ 16dᶠ 16sᵖᵘ 16s 20g Jan 7] small gelding: modest hurdler: won selling handicap at Hexham in November: running well when falling 3 out next time: no form over hurdles subsequently, though won on Flat after final start: stays 2½m: has had tongue tied. *J. S. Goldie* h85

STIRRED NOT SHAKEN (IRE) 5 b.g. Revoque (IRE) – Shakey (IRE) (Caerleon (USA)) [2003/4 17gᵖᵘ Feb 19] tailed off in 7f maiden at 2 yrs for Miss L. Siddall: showed nothing on hurdling debut. *Miss J. S. Davis* h–

STITTENHAM 5 b.g. Blushing Flame (USA) – Coronati (IRE) (Bluebird (USA)) [2003/4 F16f⁵ Sep 14] fourth foal: half-brother to 7f winner Grand Coronet (by Grand Lodge): dam, German 7f/1m winner, from family of top-class 1m to 1½m filly Salsabil: prominent until weakening markedly in straight as if amiss when fifth in bumper at Hexham on debut. *M. W. Easterby* F71

ST KILDA 7 b.m. Past Glories – Oiseval (National Trust) [2003/4 h70, F70: 21vᶠ 22s 16s³ 19s c22d⁴ Mar 21] poor maiden hurdler: well held in mares novice on chasing debut. *Mrs H. M. Bridges* c– h65

ST MARTINS (IRE) 6 b.g. Old Vic – Mardior (Martinmas) [2003/4 F16sᵖᵘ Dec 26] IR 500 3-y-o: third foal: dam 1m winner: showed nothing in bumper on debut. *Miss C. J. E. Caroe* F–

STOCK DOVE 6 ch.m. Deploy – Lady Stock (Crofter (USA)) [2003/4 F16d² F17v 16s Jan 6] small mare: fifth foal: half-sister to poor hurdlers Auk (by Absalom) and Hylia (by Sir Harry Lewis): dam 7f winner who stayed 1¼m: runner-up on first of 2 starts in bumpers: poor form when eighth of 25 in mares novice at Wetherby on hurdling debut, shaping as though further will suit. *Mrs P. Robeson* h66 F87 ?

STOCKERS PRIDE 9 b.g. Sula Bula – Fille de Soleil (Sunyboy) [2003/4 c–, h–: 24sᵖᵘ 22vᵖᵘ 26g Mar 6] winning hurdler in 2001/2: no form since, including over fences: tried blinkered. *P. R. Hedger* c– h–

STOCKS 'N SHARES 8 b.m. Jupiter Island – Norstock (Norwich (USA)) [2003/4 **c107**
h78, F73: 19g⁶ c16m* c16m³ c16d* c20s² c16m² 17s³ c19s* 17dᵘʳ c20g⁴ c20g⁴ Mar 12] **h83 +**
good-topped mare: poor maiden hurdler: fair novice chaser: won at Folkestone (maiden,
only finisher in match) in November, Hereford in December and Taunton in January, last
2 handicaps: stays 2½m: acts on soft and good to firm going: tongue tied: tough. *J. White*

STOKESIES BOY 4 b.c. Key of Luck (USA) – Lesley's Fashion (Dominion) **h73**
[2003/4 16g⁴ 17g 17g⁵ Apr 16] maiden up to 1m on Flat, modest form at best: poor form
2 of 3 starts in juvenile hurdles, pulling hard final one. *J. L. Spearing*

STOLEN HOURS (USA) 4 b. or br.c. Silver Deputy (CAN) – Fasta (USA) (Seattle **h88**
Song (USA)) [2003/4 16d⁴ 16g⁶ 16s⁵ 20s Feb 19] leggy colt: fair maiden on Flat (will
stay 2m), sold out of E. Dunlop's stable 26,000 gns Newmarket Autumn Sales: modest
form over hurdles: should be suited by further than 2m. *J. Akehurst*

STOLEN SONG 4 b.g. Sheikh Albadou – Sparky's Song (Electric) [2003/4 16g⁵ 16g² **h97**
16gᵖᵘ 16s 16d⁵ 16d* Mar 28] fair on Flat (stays 2m): easily best efforts in juvenile hurdles
when second at Warwick in December and when winning handicap at Huntingdon in
March: will stay beyond 2m: acts on good to soft going: blinkered second to fifth starts.
M. J. Ryan

STONE COLD 7 ch.g. Inchinor – Vaula (Henbit (USA)) [2003/4 c97, h–: c25g² c25dᵖᵘ **c99**
c24g⁶ c20g* c19f² c20d³ c20d⁵ c20g² c25dᵖᵘ Jan 15] angular gelding: modest handicap **h–**
chaser: won at Carlisle in November: stays 23f, effective at much shorter: acts on firm and
soft going: usually blinkered, wore cheekpieces (ran poorly) seventh outing: has failed to
impress with attitude. *T. D. Easterby*

STONE CRAIC 6 b. or br.g. Safawan – Stone Madness (Yukon Eric (CAN)) [2003/4 **F–**
F16d Mar 24] fourth foal: dam poor 2¾m hurdler: soon tailed off in bumper on debut.
Miss Z. C. Davison

STONED (IRE) 4 b.g. Bigstone (IRE) – Lady Celina (FR) (Crystal Palace (FR)) **h–**
[2003/4 F14g 17s 22gᵖᵘ Apr 18] 6,000 (privately) 3-y-o: good-topped gelding: half- **F–**
brother to winner up to 7.7f Binneas (by Roi Danzig) and to 3 winners abroad: dam
French 1¼m winner: backward, showed some ability in 3-y-o bumper on debut: little
promise in 2 novice hurdles, wearing cheekpieces final start. *L. Wells*

STONEHENGE (IRE) 7 b.g. Caerleon (USA) – Sharata (IRE) (Darshaan) [2003/4 **c–**
c–, h–: 21dᵖᵘ Apr 11] angular gelding: little form over fences: winning hurdler, showed **h–**
nothing only start in 2003/4: tried visored. *D. Burchell*

STONERAVINMAD 6 ch.g. Never So Bold – Premier Princess (Hard Fought) **c–**
[2003/4 h–: 22gᵘʳ c25f³ 25d⁵ Dec 27] little sign of ability. *Mrs E. Slack* **h–**

STONEYFORD BEN (IRE) 5 b.g. Beneficial – Rosie Rock (Swan's Rock) [2003/4 **F96**
F17s³ F16g³ F16d⁶ Mar 22] unfurnished gelding: third foal: brother to winning pointer/
2½m bumper winner Rosy Rockford: dam pulled up in 2 Irish points: won maiden Irish
point on debut in 2003: fairly useful form when third at Folkestone and Doncaster first 2
starts in bumpers. *S. Gollings*

STOPWATCH (IRE) 9 b.g. Lead On Time (USA) – Rose Bonbon (FR) (High Top) **c–**
[2003/4 c84, h73: c19gᵘʳ c18g⁵ c21g⁴ c20m⁴ c20g c18s⁶ 18g Mar 8] lengthy gelding: **h–**
handicap hurdler/maiden chaser, no form in 2003/4: stays easy 21f: acts on soft and good
to firm going (possibly not heavy): blinkered once, often wears cheekpieces. *Mrs
L. C. Jewell*

STORM A BREWING 8 ch.g. Glacial Storm (USA) – Southern Squaw (Buck- **h83**
skin (FR)) [2003/4 h68: 22d² May 16] angular gelding: best effort over hurdles when
second in novice at Stratford in May: stays 2¾m: sold £1,800 Ascot February Sales.
R. M. Stronge

STORM AHEAD (IRE) 10 b.g. Glacial Storm (USA) – Little Slip (Super Slip) **c–**
[2003/4 c–, h–: 21s⁴ c20g⁴ c25mᵘʳ Jun 20] maiden hurdler/steeplechaser, little worth- **h–**
while form since 2002: runner-up in point in February: stays 2½m: acts on soft going: has
worn cheekpieces: sometimes tongue tied. *A. Parker*

STORM CLEAR 5 b.h. Mujadil (USA) – Escape Path (Wolver Hollow) **h–**
[2003/4 16dᵖᵘ 17s 16s 16s 16d Mar 14] half-brother to fair hurdler/chaser around 2m Sea
Fisher (by Mulhollande): modest maiden on Flat (stays 1m) for R. Hannon: achieved little
over hurdles, tongue tied final start. *D. J. Wintle*

STORM DAMAGE (IRE) 12 b.g. Waajib – Connaught Lace (Connaught) [2003/4 **c– §**
c126§, h–: c24sᵖᵘ May 3] angular gelding: veteran chaser: stays 31f: acts on good to firm **h–**

and heavy going: effective with/without blinkers: often soon off bridle and not one to trust. *P. F. Nicholls*

STORMDANCER (IRE)   7 ch.g. Bluebird (USA) – Unspoiled (Tina's Pet) [2003/4   h–
h–: 23m May 7] workmanlike gelding: no form in novice hurdles: has worn cheekpieces.
Mrs Lucinda Featherstone

STORMEZ (FR)   7 b.g. Ezzoud (IRE) – Stormy Scene (USA) (Storm Bird (CAN))   c145
[2003/4 c151, h–: c27g² c26d³ 23s³ 25g c33d⁶ c29mᵘʳ Apr 24] smallish gelding: useful   h132
hurdler: creditable third in handicap at Haydock in February: smart chaser: best effort in
2003/4 when second to Shardam in listed handicap at Cheltenham on reappearance: best
at 3m+: unraced on firm going, acts on any other: tried visored: tongue tied: no easy ride
(tends to go in snatches/jump none too fluently). *M. C. Pipe*

STORMHILL STAG   12 b.g. Buckley – Sweet Sirenia (Al Sirat (USA)) [2003/4   c108 d
c110, h95: c23g⁴ c19d⁶ c25v* c19sᵘʳ c23g⁶ c21d⁴ c20g³ c23s⁶ c20dᵖᵘ Apr 21] leggy   h–
gelding: fair handicap chaser: off 7 months after first start, little form subsequently,
including when awarded amateur event at Towcester in December after passing post
well-beaten sixth: stays 3m, effective at much shorter: acts on good to firm and heavy
going: tried blinkered, including last 3 starts: has looked difficult ride. *R. Lee*

STORMING BACK   5 b.g. Bob Back (USA) – Prussian Storm (IRE) (Strong Gale)   F81
[2003/4 F16s⁵ F16g Mar 6] useful-looking gelding: second foal: dam, lightly-raced
jumper, sister to top-class 2m to 3¼m chaser Strong Promise: signs of ability despite
inexperience when fifth in bumper at Wetherby on debut: may have been amiss in similar
event at Newbury. *R. Waley-Cohen*

STORM OF GOLD (IRE)   11 b.g. Glacial Storm (USA) – Tipperary Tartan (Rarity)   c78 §
[2003/4 c103d, h–: c33d³ Apr 30] useful-looking gelding: winning hurdler/chaser: on   h–
downgrade, remote third in hunter at Cheltenham very early in season: stays 31f: acts on
soft going: tried blinkered/visored/in cheekpieces: not an easy ride. *D. L. Williams*

STORM PRINCE (IRE)   7 ch.g. Prince of Birds (USA) – Petersford Girl (IRE)   h102
(Taufan (USA)) [2003/4 h94: 17s³ 16s⁶ 19d 24s⁵ 22g⁵ 22m* 21d* 22g³ 22s Apr 6]
smallish gelding: fair handicap hurdler: won at Wincanton and Warwick within 4 days
in March, making most both times: stays 2¾m: acts on soft and good to firm going:
blinkered last 5 starts: tongue tied on reappearance. *J. L. Spearing*

STORM VALLEY (IRE)   12 b.g. Strong Gale – Windy Run (Deep Run) [2003/4 c–x,   c– x
h–: c25mᵖᵘ Jun 11] leggy gelding: winning chaser in 2001/2: let down by jumping and no   h–
form since: has had tongue tied. *T. R. Wall*

STORMY BEECH   8 b.g. Glacial Storm (USA) – Cheeny's Brig (New Brig) [2003/4   c88
h82: 16d 17s* 17g⁶ 21d³ 21d² 17d 16s 19d 16v c16s* c16d⁵ c20v c20dᵖᵘ Apr 23] angular   h88
gelding: modest handicap hurdler, won at Sedgefield in May: best effort over fences when
winning weak handicap at Carlisle in February: barely stays 21f: acts on heavy going:
tried in cheekpieces, effective blinkered or not: has had tongue tied: free-going sort: has
hung left. *R. Johnson*

STORMYFAIRWEATHER (IRE)   12 b.g. Strong Gale – Game Sunset (Menelek)   c–
[2003/4 c–, h–: c25dᵖᵘ c19d c24dᵘʳ c24dᵖᵘ Feb 2] small, angular gelding: very smart   h–
chaser at best: suffered leg injury and no sign of retaining ability. *N. J. Henderson*

STORMY SESSION   14 b.g. Celestial Storm (USA) – No Jazz (Jaazeiro (USA))   c–
[2003/4 c25mᵖᵘ Jun 11] lengthy, sparely-made gelding: veteran chaser, retains little   h–
ability: usually blinkered/visored: prone to mistakes. *M. F. Harris*

STORMY SKYE (IRE)   8 b.g. Bluebird (USA) – Canna (Caerleon (USA)) [2003/4   c100 §
c98§, h–§: c24mᵘʳ c24m* Nov 11] useful-looking gelding: fair hurdler/chaser: won   h– §
weak novice over fences at Lingfield, hanging left: stays 25f: acts on soft and good to
firm going, probably on heavy: usually blinkered: formerly tongue tied: ungenuine.
G. L. Moore

STORMY SUNRISE (IRE)   8 b.g. Glacial Storm (USA) – Commanche Maid   c–
(Commanche Run) [2003/4 c24g c33gˢᵘ c21g c20f c16g Mar 12] compact gelding: no   h–
worthwhile form outside points, leaving E. Bolger after fourth start: has had tongue tied.
Miss A. Armitage

ST PALAIS   5 b.m. Timeless Times (USA) – Crambella (IRE) (Red Sunset) [2003/4   h–
h68: 19g⁶ 16m May 5] bad maiden hurdler: third in points in February and March: sometimes wears cheekpieces/visor. *D. L. Williams*

Cheltenham Grand Annual Chase Challenge Cup (Handicap)—
St Pirran (right) and Ground Ball have the race between them at the last

ST PIRRAN (IRE) 9 b.g. Be My Native (USA) – Guess Twice (Deep Run) [2003/4 c20g⁶ c16d* c16sᶠ c16d* c16g³ c16m Apr 24] tall gelding: useful handicap chaser: won at Sandown in January and Cheltenham in March: in superb shape, beat Ground Ball 2½ lengths in Grand Annual Chase at latter, produced to lead run-in and idling: improved again when third to Tidour in another valuable event at Aintree in April: best around 2m: acts on soft going, stiff task on good to firm: tried blinkered: has broken blood vessel: free-going sort, usually patiently ridden. *P. F. Nicholls*   **c142 h–**

STRAIGHT EIGHT 5 b.g. Octagonal (NZ) – Kalymnia (GER) (Mondrian (GER)) [2003/4 17dᵇᵈ Nov 11] signs of only a little ability on Flat: brought down second on hurdling debut: dead. *T. D. Easterby*   **h–**

STRAIN THE REIN 9 b.g. Petoski – Valls d'Andorra (Free State) [2003/4 16m Oct 4] rangy, workmanlike gelding: bumper winner: extremely lightly raced over hurdles: tongue tied once. *M. C. Pipe*   **h–**

STRAIT TALKING (FR) 6 b.g. Bering – Servia (Le Marmot (FR)) [2003/4 c–, h87: 16m Jun 14] leggy gelding: fell heavily on chasing debut: modest hurdler: well held in handicap only start in 2003/4: likely to prove best around 2m: acts on soft and good to firm going: has worn cheekpieces. *Jedd O'Keeffe*   **c– h–**

STRATH FILLAN 6 b.m. Dolphin Street (FR) – Adarama (IRE) (Persian Bold) [2003/4 h–: 18m May 26] poor on Flat: little form over hurdles. *H. J. Collingridge*   **h–**

STRAWBERRY HILL (IRE) 10 b.g. Lancastrian – Tudor Lady (Green Shoon) [2003/4 h80: 17s⁵ 24m c17gᵖᵘ c24gᵖᵘ Jan 7] poor maiden hurdler: no form in 2003/4, including over fences, left Miss V. Scott before final start. *B. Mactaggart*   **c– h–**

STRAWMAN 7 b.g. Ela-Mana-Mou – Oatfield (Great Nephew) [2003/4 c78, h–: c21sᵖᵘ c25dᵖᵘ c23g c24gᵘʳ c16g* c17d⁴ c21s² c26g⁴ Apr 22] angular gelding: poor handicap chaser: won at Folkestone in March: stays 21f: acts on good to firm and heavy going: tried visored (including last 4 starts)/in cheekpieces: sometimes makes mistakes: unreliable. *C. N. Kellett*   **c78 h–**

STRAY RAVEN 5 b.g. Sea Raven (IRE) – Gone Astray (The Parson) [2003/4 F16s F16s Apr 4] second foal: dam, winning hurdler/pointer, half-sister to useful staying chaser Merry Master: soundly beaten in 2 bumpers. *J. B. Walton*   **F–**

STREAMSFORTH LAD (IRE)   7 b.g. Be My Native (USA) – Protrial (Proverb) **c–**
[2003/4 h87§, F88: c24m^{pu} May 5] good-topped gelding: disappointing maiden hurdler: **h– §**
showed nothing on chasing debut: looked temperamental in blinkers last 2 starts in
2002/3: one to treat with caution. *S. A. Brookshaw*

STREAMSTOWN (IRE)   10 b. or br.g. Rashar (USA) – Lady Torsil (Torus) [2003/4 **c–**
c–, h–: c24d^{pu} Dec 13] useful-looking gelding: useful handicap chaser in 2001/2: bit **h–**
backward and very stiff task on only second start since: should stay beyond 3½m: raced
mainly on good going or softer (acts on heavy): patiently ridden: tends to make odd
mistake. *Ferdy Murphy*

STRENUE (USA)   4 ch.g. Crafty Prospector (USA) – Shawgatny (USA) (Danzig **h– §**
Connection (USA)) [2003/4 16m 17g^{pu} 18m^{pu} 16g Mar 4] showed some ability at 2 yrs
for M. Channon: no form over hurdles: visored first 3 starts: has looked ungenuine.
M. C. Pipe

STREWTH   10 b.g. Cruise Missile – Storm Foot (Import) [2003/4 c79§, h–: c24s^5 May **c77**
2] fair pointer, not so good in hunter chases. *Mrs L. Pomfret* **h–**

STRICTLY SPEAKING (IRE)   7 b.g. Sri Pekan (USA) – Gaijin (Caerleon (USA)) **h82 §**
[2003/4 h92: 16g^4 20m^2 16m^5 Oct 4] medium-sized gelding: poor maiden hurdler: stays
2½m: acts on good to firm and good to soft going: lame final start: has looked ungenuine.
R. Brotherton

STRIKE BACK (IRE)   6 b.g. Bob Back (USA) – First Strike (IRE) (Magical Strike **h140**
(USA)) [2003/4 F16g* F16g^2 16g* 19d* 16d^3 20s^6 20d^2 20g^5 Apr 1] IR £22,000 3-y-o, **F108**
€44,000 4-y-o: useful-looking gelding: second foal: brother to bumper winner Rugged
Jacket: dam ran once: won bumper at Down Royal in May: progressive novice hurdler:
won at Roscommon in October and Naas in November: useful efforts when fifth to Garde
Champetre in Grade 2 at Aintree and second to Supreme Being in valuable handicap at
Punchestown in late-April: stays 2½m: acts on good to soft going (reportedly amiss on
soft): type to do well in novice chases in 2004/5. *Mrs J. Harrington, Ireland*

STROLLING   7 br.g. Alflora (IRE) – Emmabella (True Song) [2003/4 F16m Jun 1] **F71**
first foal: dam lightly-raced maiden pointer: seventh of 21 in bumper at Worcester on
debut. *A. Hollingsworth*

STROMNESS (USA)   7 ch.g. Trempolino (USA) – Caithness (USA) (Roberto **c116**
(USA)) [2003/4 h139: c23g^2 c23m^2 c23m* 25m^4 25g^4 c24d* c23m^F 25d^6 24g^4 25g Mar **h135**
16] compact gelding: has had several wind operations: fairly useful novice chaser: won at
Worcester in July and Doncaster (match) in December: useful hurdler: best effort in
2003/4 when fourth to Therealbandit in listed handicap at Cheltenham fourth start: stays
25f: acts on heavy and good to firm going: effective tongue tied or not: jumps fences less
than fluently. *A. King*

STRONG FLOW (IRE)   7 br.g. Over The River (FR) – Stormy Skies (Strong **c156 p**
Gale) [2003/4 h125p: c23g* c25g* c25g^f c21g* c26g* c24g* Dec 26] **h–**
    Out of sight, out of mind. While Best Mate and others grabbed the headlines
at the back-end of the season, a horse who had been one of the most talked about
midway through it no longer merited a mention. Instead of turning up at the
Cheltenham Festival to contest the Royal & SunAlliance Chase, or possibly even
the Gold Cup, Strong Flow was still recuperating from an injury sustained at
Kempton on Boxing Day, when gaining his fifth win from five completed starts
over fences. At that time Strong Flow, who on his previous start had put up a very
impressive performance in the Hennessy Cognac Gold Cup at Newbury, was clear
favourite for the Royal & SunAlliance and a most exciting prospect, and it is to be
hoped that he makes a full recovery and returns to action in the next season. If he
does, then Strong Flow will almost certainly prove himself a top-class staying
chaser, one of the more likely obstacles to a fourth Gold Cup for Best Mate.
    Strong Flow was sent off joint favourite for the Hennessy despite being very
short of experience. The winner of a maiden on his only start in Irish points and
successful at Taunton on the second of two outings in novice hurdles in 2002/3,
Strong Flow didn't begin his chasing career until May, less than seven months
before the Hennessy, and he turned up at Newbury with just four outings in chases
under his belt. Fluent jumping was a feature of Strong Flow's performances as he
easily brushed aside the opposition in novice events at Worcester and Newton
Abbot and in a valuable handicap at Kelso in between; and he hadn't put a foot
wrong prior to falling four out when looking set for victory in a three-runner novice
at Aintree. Apart from a single error, albeit a major one, Strong Flow's jumping

held up very well in a twenty-one-runner Hennessy field comprised largely of far more experienced rivals, a field which, unusually for this highly competitive handicap, included no established top- or high-class chasers and was dominated by second-season chasers, twelve of the runners coming from this group. Also unusual was the fact that, due to the dry weather, a larger number than usual were reappearing after a lay-off, seven having their first race of the season and another three running for the first time since June.

The weights were headed by the previous season's Royal & SunAlliance winner One Knight, but he fell at the first, bringing down Take The Stand, while Sir Rembrandt departed at the third and several others were also let down by their jumping, notably the other joint-favourite Irish Hussar. Strong Flow himself did well to survive his mistake at the ninth. Remarkably, it seemed to take very little out of him and he continued to travel strongly as one of the outsiders, Tom's Prize, set a good pace until the fifth last, where Barrow Drive took over. It wasn't long before the leader was swallowed up by Hedgehunter, Joss Naylor and Strong Flow, the race soon looking to concern only this trio. Hedgehunter was the first to give way, followed by Joss Naylor, and when Strong Flow was asked for extra after two out he quickly put the issue beyond doubt, quickening really well and drawing still further clear as he was kept up to his work. The winner passed the post with fourteen lengths to spare over Joss Naylor, with Take Control staying on late to deprive Hedgehunter of third place near the line. Other impressive Hennessy winners in recent years include One Man and Teeton Mill, the former off the same BHB mark as Strong Flow (140) and the latter off 139. Both went on to show themselves topclass chasers. Strong Flow is the first horse to win the Hennessy in his first season over fences; and he is now the only novice to have done so, the 2002 winner Be My Royal, who had tested positive for morphine, having been disqualified in January, though an appeal against that decision was heard in July, with no time specified for the result.

Despite speculation that he would soon be asked to take on the top established staying chasers, the Network Design Feltham Novices' Chase at Kempton,

Isle of Skye Handicap Chase, Kelso—
Strong Flow picks up the feature event on a valuable early-season card

*Hennessy Cognac Gold Cup Chase (Handicap), Newbury—a tremendous leap two out;
runner-up Joss Naylor and fourth Hedgehunter are left in the wake*

rather than the King George VI Chase on the same card, was the race chosen for
Strong Flow's next appearance, and his presence scared off most of the serious
opposition. Strong Flow was sent off at 11/4-on to account for just four rivals, the
pick of whom were Ballycassidy, the winner of seven races over fences including
when finishing alone in the race at Aintree in which Strong Flow fell, and the Irish
challenger Rule Supreme, successful on his two previous completed starts including in a valuable novice handicap at Punchestown. With Rule Supreme let down by
his jumping, it was left to the front-running Ballycassidy to take the fight to Strong
Flow, who had to work hard to peg him back after making very serious mistakes at
the second and the ninth, both of which he did well to survive. Strong Flow finally
got on top at the last and went on to win by eight lengths from Ballycassidy, who
was eased, with a further eight lengths back to Rule Supreme. It was a brave

Network Design Feltham Novices' Chase, Kempton—not one of Strong Flow's two serious mistakes

performance from Strong Flow, who at some stage in the race had cracked a bone in the knee of his near-fore. At the time he was clear favourite for the Royal & SunAlliance, a race which was won by Rule Supreme.

	Over The River (FR) (ch 1974)	Luthier (b or br 1965)	Klairon
			Flute Enchantee
Strong Flow (IRE) (br.g. 1997)		Medenine (b 1967)	Prudent II
			Ma Congaie
	Stormy Skies (br 1987)	Strong Gale (br 1975)	Lord Gayle
			Sterntau
		Perspex-Pride (br 1972)	Perspex
			Pride of Ednego

Strong Flow, whose sire Over The River has been responsible for the Cheltenham Gold Cup winners Cool Ground and Cool Dawn, is the second foal of Stormy Skies who managed only one placing in numerous starts over hurdles and fences, finishing runner-up in a maiden chase at Fairyhouse. On her next start Stormy Skies unseated her rider in the National Hunt Chase at Cheltenham. Stormy Skies, whose first foal Ballyconnell was fairly useful at up to three miles over fences in the latest season, is a sister to the fair chaser up to two and three quarter miles Perspex Gale and half-sister to two other winners, including the useful staying chaser Plenty Crack. Her dam, Perspex-Pride, won over hurdles and fences in Ireland. Strong Flow, a good sort in appearance, certainly isn't short of speed, but he stays three and a quarter miles well and should get further. Both of his runs over hurdles were on soft ground, whereas he has raced only on good going over fences. *P. F. Nicholls*

STRONG MAGIC (IRE)   12 br.g. Strong Gale – Baybush (Boreen (FR)) [2003/4 c96, h–: c24gpu c20mur c25f5 c24g3 c20g3 c24g2 c20s5 c24g4 c20s2 c21s3 c20s2 c24g* c24d5 c19s* c20g5 Apr 2] workmanlike gelding: modest chaser: won handicap at Ascot in February and minor event at Towcester in March: stays 25f: acts on soft and good to firm going: often makes running: none too consistent. *J. R. Cornwall*   **c95 h–**

STRONG PALADIN (IRE)   13 b.g. Strong Gale – Kalanshoe (Random Shot) [2003/4 c109, h–: c22m4 May 26] rangy gelding: fair handicap chaser: creditable fourth at Fontwell very early in season: stays 3¾m: acts on firm and soft going: has run creditably when sweating: sound jumper. *N. A. Gaselee*   **c104 h–**

STRONG PROJECT (IRE)   8 ch.g. Project Manager – Hurricane Girl (IRE) (Strong Gale) [2003/4 c95, h116: 20m3 22g* 20s3 24d6 24d2 24g3 22d Apr 12] workmanlike gelding: maiden chaser (needs to jump better): fairly useful hurdler: won minor event at Thurles in December: creditable placed efforts in handicaps at Naas and Aintree (third of 20 to His Nibs in valuable event) 2 starts prior to running poorly final one: stays 3m: acts on soft and good to firm going. *C. F. Swan, Ireland*   **c– h126**

STRONG RESOLVE (IRE)   8 gr.g. Roselier (FR) – Farmerette (Teofane) [2003/4 h87: c20g3 c25d2 c25s* c20spu c25v2 c25s2 c25g* c25g* c25d2 Apr 17] leggy gelding: modest hurdler: fairly useful chaser: won handicap at Ayr in December and novices at same course and Kelso in March: stays 25f: acts on heavy going: sound-jumping front runner: genuine. *Miss Lucinda V. Russell*   **c118 h–**

STRONG RUN (IRE)   11 b.g. Strong Gale – Arctic Run (Deep Run) [2003/4 c16v5 c16d* c16d5 c20s2 Mar 27] workmanlike gelding: smart chaser, missed 2002/3: made all in Grade 2 Paddy & Helen Cox Memorial Newlands Chase at Naas in February, beating Native Scout 2½ lengths: very good placed efforts in Grade 3 at Navan (short-headed by Rathgar Beau) in March and Grade 1 at Punchestown (third to Moscow Flyer) in late-April: stays 2½m: raced on good going or softer (acts on soft): tongue tied: carries head awkwardly under pressure. *N. Meade, Ireland*   **c145 h–**

STRONG TARTAN (IRE)   10 b.g. Strong Gale – Kemchee (Kemal (FR)) [2003/4 c89, h75: c22g3 c20m* c24d* c24g4 24g3 c21gpu c27g4 Apr 16] well-made gelding: maiden hurdler: fair chaser: won handicaps at Hexham in June and Perth in July: stays 27f, at least with emphasis on speed: acts on soft and good to firm going: wore cheek-pieces after reappearance, also tongue tied final start: sold 10,000 gns Doncaster May Sales. *A. Parker*   **c104 h78**

STRONG TEA (IRE)   13 b.g. Electric – Cutty Sark (Strong Gale) [2003/4 c25s2 Apr 11] fair pointer, successful in January: 25 lengths second of 5 finishers in hunter at Towcester on steeplechasing debut. *Miss S. Waugh*   **c76**

STRONGTROOPER (IRE)   9 b.g. Doubletour (USA) – Moss Gale (Strong Gale)   **c106**
[2003/4 c–, h–: c24g³ c25g² c22g* c22gᵘʳ c24g c24gᶠ c20f² c21gᵖᵘ Dec 16] big, angular   **h–**
gelding: fair handicap chaser: won at Market Rasen in June: stays 25f: acts on firm and
good to soft going: distressed final outing: has been led in. *O. Sherwood*

STRUGGLES GLORY (IRE)   13 b.g. Kamehameha (USA) – Another Struggle   **c–**
(Cheval) [2003/4 c28gᵖᵘ May 31] rangy gelding: useful handicap chaser in 2001/2: ran
no sort of race in valuable hunter at Stratford in May: won points in March and April:
stays 3½m: acts on good to soft and good to firm going: usually a good jumper.
D. C. Robinson

STURM UND DRANG   10 ch.g. Selkirk (USA) – Historiette (Chief's Crown (USA))   **c93**
[2003/4 c80, h88: 16m 16mᵖᵘ 17g² c16m³ c16d² c16m* c16g² c16m³ Sep 7] modest   **h88**
maiden hurdler: modest chaser: fortunate to win maiden at Newton Abbot in August: not
sure to stay much beyond 17f: acts on good to firm and good to soft going: ran well in
blinkers seventh start. *C. J. Down*

STUTTER   6 ch.g. Polish Precedent (USA) – Bright Spells (Salse (USA)) [2003/4   **h102**
16m⁴ 17g⁵ 17g 16g⁵ 16v⁵ 16s² 16d* 16s² 16s* Apr 4] sparely-made gelding: fair maiden
at best on Flat up to 1m: fair hurdler: won novice handicap at Thurles in February and
handicap at Tramore in April: will prove best around 2m: acts on soft going: tried in
cheekpieces: pulls hard. *J. G. Carr, Ireland*

STYLISH PRINCE   4 b.g. Polar Prince (IRE) – Simply Style (Bairn (USA)) [2003/4   **h–**
17mᵖᵘ Aug 1] half-brother to poor hurdler Weet And See (by Lochnager), stays 2½m: 5f
winner at 2 yrs, well beaten since: no show in juvenile on hurdling debut. *J. G. M. O'Shea*

SUAVEROF (IRE)   9 ch.g. Suave Dancer (USA) – Mild Intrigue (USA) (Sir Ivor)   **c–**
[2003/4 c24mᵖᵘ c25g c24dᵖᵘ Mar 27] fair hurdler in 2001/2: won point in May: tongue   **h–**
tied, little encouragement in varied company in steeplechases subsequently: stays 3m:
acts on good to firm ground: held up. *J. Rudge*

SUD BLEU (FR)   6 b.g. Pistolet Bleu (IRE) – Sudaka (FR) (Garde Royale) [2003/4   **h135**
h120§: 16g² 16s² 17d 16g 16s 21g 24g Apr 2] tall, useful-looking gelding: useful
handicap hurdler: formerly a weak finisher, and operated on for breathing problem after
final outing in 2002/3: better than ever when 2 lengths second to Thesis in Ladbroke
Hurdle at Ascot second start: best around 2m: raced on good going or softer: held up, and
suited by well-run race. *P. F. Nicholls*

Paddy & Helen Cox Memorial Newlands Chase, Naas—
Strong Run makes all and outpoints the Natives, Scout and Upmanship (centre)

SUDDEN SHOCK (GER) 9 b.g. Motley (USA) – Santalina (Relko) [2003/4 c129, h129: 25m c29d^{pu} Dec 6] useful-looking gelding: has had soft palate operation: smart hurdler at best, took little interest after fifth in Grade 2 at Wetherby on reappearance: won National Hunt Chase at Cheltenham in 2002/3, largely disappointing over fences otherwise (dismounted circuit out in listed handicap at Sandown in December): stays 4m: had form in France on heavy going, best efforts in Britain on good or firmer: ungenuine. *Jonjo O'Neill* — c– § h– §

SUGGEST 9 b.g. Midyan (USA) – Awham (USA) (Lear Fan (USA)) [2003/4 24m^{pu} 25f^2 24g 25g^4 27s 27f* 24s^{pu} 27d Mar 30] rather leggy gelding: poor handicap hurdler: won at Musselburgh in February: stays 27f: acts on any going: usually held up: inconsistent. *W. Storey* — h82

SULAGH RUN 10 b.g. Sula Bula – Brackagh Run (Deep Run) [2003/4 17d^{pu} 20m^6 Dec 16] seems of no account. *R. Nixon* — h–

SULLANE STORM (IRE) 9 b.g. Glacial Storm (USA) – Heather Point (Pollerton) [2003/4 c90: c25g^{pu} c26v^{pu} c24d^{pu} Nov 27] good-topped gelding: winning chaser: no form in handicaps in 2003/4, running moody race final outing: stays 3m: acts on good to firm and heavy ground: has reportedly bled: sometimes jumps none too fluently. *M. C. Pipe* — c–

SULLY SHUFFLES (IRE) 9 b.g. Broken Hearted – Green Legend (IRE) (Montekin) [2003/4 c24s^F 17d 23d^4 21v 20d^4 Feb 21] angular ex-Irish gelding: fair handicap hurdler: fell fifth on chasing debut, then left F. Flood: limited encouragement over hurdles next 3 starts, left M. Barnes prior to running well final outing: stays 3m: acts on good to firm and soft going. *M. Todhunter* — c– p h107

SULPHUR SPRINGS (IRE) 12 ch.g. Don't Forget Me – Short Wave (FR) (Trepan (FR)) [2003/4 c130, h–: c28g^{pu} c24g^{pu} c20g Apr 18] leggy gelding: one-time useful chaser: retains only a little ability: stays 3¼m: acts on soft and firm going: tongue tied: races prominently. *M. C. Pipe* — c– h–

SUM LEADER (IRE) 8 b.g. Leading Counsel (USA) – Greenodd (Green Shoon) [2003/4 h124: 20g c20g* c22s* c24d^4 c20s^5 Dec 14] lengthy gelding: fairly useful handicap hurdler: similar form over fences: successful in maiden at Ballinrobe and minor event at Galway in July, beating Beausheram 11 lengths at latter course: disappointing in novices next 2 starts, almost certainly flattered when third in Grade 3 novice at Punchestown (first start after leaving G. Keane, made running) in late-April: stays 3m: acts on good to firm and heavy going. *Miss Jane Thomas, Ireland* — c122 h–

SUMMER BOUNTY 8 b.g. Lugana Beach – Tender Moment (IRE) (Caerleon (USA)) [2003/4 h84: 16f* 16m^3 19m^2 16g^4 16g Dec 18] close-coupled gelding: fair on turf, modest on all-weather Flat (stays 1½m): poor hurdler: won handicap at Towcester in October: stays 19f when emphasis on speed: acts on firm and good to soft going: patiently ridden. *F. Jordan* — h84

SUMMER IN THE SUN (IRE) 10 ch.g. Shardari – Sacajawea (Tanfirion) [2003/4 c24s^{pu} May 2] modest pointer: no show in 2 hunter chases: tongue tied. *Mrs Edward Crow* — c–

SUMMER STOCK (USA) 6 b.g. Theatrical – Lake Placid (IRE) (Royal Academy (USA)) [2003/4 16m^3 16m^6 16d^3 16d^3 16d^3 Dec 12] smallish gelding: modest maiden on Flat (stays 11f): similar level over hurdles: raced at 2m: tongue tied. *J. A. Supple* — h88

SUMMERWOOD LILLEY 4 b.f. Tragic Role (USA) – Celtic Lilley (Celtic Cone) [2003/4 F18s^{pu} Feb 9] second foal: dam bad novice hurdler: showed nothing in bumper on debut. *M. R. Hoad* — F–

SUMTHYNE SPECIAL (IRE) 12 b.g. Good Thyne (USA) – Condonstown Rose (Giolla Mear) [2003/4 20d^{pu} 24d^{pu} 20v^{pu} 20d^4 Mar 11] strong, close-coupled gelding: mistakes in 2 outings over fences: fair hurdler in 2001/2: no show on return: stayed 3m: raced on going softer than good (acted on heavy): dead. *L. Lungo* — c– h–

SUMUT 5 b.g. Hamas (IRE) – Simaat (USA) (Mr Prospector (USA)) [2003/4 F77: 17g^6 Sep 30] signs of only a little ability in varied events. *G. A. Swinbank* — h–

SUN BIRD (IRE) 6 ch.g. Prince of Birds (USA) – Summer Fashion (Moorestyle) [2003/4 h101p: 16m^2 18g^3 May 22] smart stayer on Flat, second in Ebor and Cesarewitch in 2003: fair form over hurdles at Kelso, close third to Laouen in intermediate in May: will stay beyond 2¼m: probably capable of better. *R. Allan* — h112 p

SUNBURNT 10 b.g. Henbit (USA) – Sunshine Gal (Alto Volante) [2003/4 c24g^3 May 31] sturdy gelding: poor handicap chaser/maiden hurdler: sold out of R. Buckler's stable — c93 h–

£2,100 Ascot June (2002) Sales: did well in points in 2003 (successful twice) and creditable third in hunter at Stratford in May: stays 3m: acts on firm and soft going: has had tongue tied. *Miss J. Houldey*

SUN CAT (IRE) 4 br.g. Catrail (USA) – Susie Sunshine (IRE) (Waajib) [2003/4 16m²   **h108**
16d⁴ 19d⁵ 16s² 16g* 16g Apr 1] tall, good-topped gelding: poor maiden on Flat
(stays 1½m) for M. Polglase: fair juvenile hurdler: improved form when winning at
Ayr in March despite mistakes: seems ideally suited to sharp 2m: free-going sort.
Mrs S. J. Smith

SUNCZECH (IRE) 14 b.m. Sunyboy – Miss Prague (Mon Capitaine) [2003/4 c72:   **c68**
c21dᵖᵘ c23g⁴ Mar 12] winning pointer: poor maiden hunter chaser. *Mrs S. S. Harbour*

SUNDANCE SID (IRE) 8 b.g. Phardante (FR) – The Kid's Sister (Black Minstrel)   **c–**
[2003/4 h–: c16mᵖᵘ 16mᵖᵘ Jun 18] of little account: tried in visor: tongue tied final start.   **h–**
V. Y. Gethin

SUNDAWN LADY 6 b.m. Faustus (USA) – Game Domino (Derring Rose) [2003/4   **h75**
h78, F66: 22m⁶ 20m³ 22gᵖᵘ Nov 21] medium-sized mare: poor maiden hurdler: stays
2¾m: raced only on good/good to firm going over hurdles. *C. P. Morlock*

SUNDAY HABITS (IRE) 10 ch.g. Montelimar (USA) – Robertina (USA) (Roberto   **c83 §**
(USA)) [2003/4 c77: c26g² c25m² c24g² c26m² c26mᵇᵈ c24gᵖᵘ Jul 31] poor handicap
chaser: stays 3¼m: acts on good to firm going: tried in cheekpieces/visor: has had tongue
tied: one to treat with caution. *D. P. Keane*

SUNDAY RAIN (USA) 7 b.g. Summer Squall (USA) – Oxava (FR) (Antheus (USA))   **c112**
[2003/4 h100: 18g⁴ c17g³ c16g³ c16d* c20m* c20g⁴ c20m² c17g² c17gF Apr 5] well-   **h87**
made gelding: winning hurdler: fair chaser: won novices at Perth in July and Bangor in
August: stayed 2½m: acted on soft and good to firm going: blinkered once (ran poorly):
dead. *Miss Lucinda V. Russell*

SUNDAYS SARAH 6 b.m. Sea Raven (IRE) – Sundays Off (Dubassoff (USA))   **h–**
[2003/4 17m Jul 17] no sign of ability in seller on Flat (for J. O'Keeffe) or maiden hurdle.
M. A. Barnes

SUNDIAL 5 ch.m. Cadeaux Genereux – Ruby Setting (Gorytus (USA)) [2003/4 16mᵖᵘ   **h–**
Sep 13] disappointing maiden on Flat: showed nothing on hurdling debut. *A. E. Jones*

SUNGATES (IRE) 8 ch.g. Glacial Storm (USA) – Live It Up (Le Coq d'Or) [2003/4   **h105 +**
h77: 21d⁶ 22s* 26s 26g* Apr 3] lengthy gelding: fair hurdler: won novice at Folkestone
in January and conditional jockeys handicap at Hereford in April, improved again when
beating Normandy Sands by 1½ lengths in latter, idling after leading 2 out: stays 3¼m:
raced on good ground or softer: may do better still. *C. Tinkler*

SUN HILL 4 b.g. Robellino (USA) – Manhattan Sunset (USA) (El Gran Senor (USA))   **h–**
[2003/4 16sᵖᵘ Jan 14] sturdy gelding: fairly useful on all-weather on Flat (stays 2m),
successful 3 times early in 2004: no show in juvenile at Newbury on hurdling debut.
M. Blanshard

SUN KING 7 ch.g. Zilzal (USA) – Opus One (Slip Anchor) [2003/4 h96: 16m³ 16m²   **h97**
16d³ 16s³ 19g⁴ 16d 16g⁶ 24d 16d 20v Mar 21] leggy gelding: fair maiden on Flat: modest
handicap hurdler: well below form last 3 starts: stays easy 2½m: acts on soft and good to
firm going: usually patiently ridden. *Mrs M. Reveley*

SUN LARK 10 b.g. Crested Lark – Sunylyn (Sunyboy) [2003/4 c21fᵖᵘ May 21] modest   **c–**
pointer, won maiden in 2003: pulled up as if amiss in novice hunter chase at Folkestone.
A. D. Old

SUNLEY FUTURE (IRE) 5 b.g. Broken Hearted – The Wicked Chicken (IRE)   **F87**
(Saher) [2003/4 F16d F16d F16d F16d⁶ Apr 21] €28,000 3-y-o, €31,000 4-y-o: first foal: dam
modest 2m hurdler: favourite, eighth of 17 to Moorlands Return in bumper at Kempton
(galloped loose beforehand) on debut: disappointed after, hung right final start.
N. J. Henderson

SUNLIT BOY 12 ch.g. Ardross – Sunlit River (Roi Soleil) [2003/4 c–, h–: c16g c26d⁶   **c–**
c22vᵖᵘ Jan 12] rangy gelding: no longer of any account: tried blinkered/tongue tied.   **h–**
J. J. Bridger

SUNNE LORD (IRE) 7 b.g. Mister Lord (USA) – Happy Party (Invited (USA))   **h88**
[2003/4 h–, F76: 19s⁴ 22s⁵ 21d⁶ 20s⁴ 21dᵖᵘ Mar 14] useful-looking gelding: modest
maiden hurdler: lame final start: stays 21f: acts on soft going. *A. King*

SUNNYARJUN 6 ch.g. Afzal – Hush Tina (Tina's Pet) [2003/4 h–, F–: 16m 19d Jul   **h–**
30] workmanlike gelding: well held all starts: pulled hard. *J. C. Tuck*

SUNNYCLIFF 11 b.g. Dancing High – Nicolini (Nicholas Bill) [2003/4 c22m^{pu} c20g^{pu} c16m^4 c20g^{ur} c25g^6 c20m^6 c24g^{pu} Feb 18] big, strong gelding: poor chaser: stays 2½m: acts on good to firm and good to soft going: tongue tied. *Miss R. Brewis*   **c–**

SUNNYLAND 5 b.m. Sovereign Water (FR) – Quadrapol (Pollerton) [2003/4 F16s^4 F16d 19g^5 22g^5 24d Apr 8] lengthy, unfurnished mare: third foal: half-sister to fair hurdlers up to around 2½m Forever Dream and Brown Teddy (both by Afzal): dam bumper winner: much better effort in bumpers when fourth in mares event at Haydock: poor form in novice hurdles: stays 19f. *P. J. Hobbs*   **h79**
F81

SUNNY NATIVE (IRE) 7 ch.m. Be My Native (USA) – My Sunny South (Strong Gale) [2003/4 20f^2 20g^4 20m^2 22g 21m* 19g^5 Nov 30] quite good-topped ex-Irish mare: sister to fair hurdler/fairly useful chaser Cape Stormer, stays 3m: lightly-raced maiden on Flat: bumper winner: poor hurdler: left W. J. Burke after second start: odds on, fortunate to win 6-runner maiden at Ludlow in November, seemingly held when left clear 2 out: stays 21f: acts on firm ground: wore cheekpieces fourth outing, tongue tied last 3. *Mrs H. Dalton*   **h83**

SUNNYSIDE ROYALE (IRE) 5 b.g. Ali-Royal (IRE) – Kuwah (IRE) (Be My Guest (USA)) [2003/4 h65: 16dp^u 20d 25dp^u 20g^f 17s* 17s^5 16g^3 Mar 6] leggy, close-coupled gelding: modest on Flat (stays 1¾m): modest hurdler: 25/1-winner of novice handicap at Sedgefield in February: form only around 2m: acts on soft going: tongue tied. *R. Bastiman*   **h85**

SUNRAY 4 b.g. Spectrum (IRE) – Sharkashka (IRE) (Shardari) [2003/4 16g^4 17m^4 17g^3 16g^4 16m^2 16fp^u 16s* 17d^6 16s Feb 7] leggy gelding: trained by P. Cole, tailed off in maiden only start on Flat: bought 700 gns Doncaster May Sales: 40/1, won Grade 1 eLINIA Finale Juvenile Hurdle at Chepstow in December by 3 lengths from Mondul, closing rapidly from 2 out as leaders tired and probably flattered: had shown no better than fair form previously: will be suited by 2½m: acts on soft and good to firm going: tried visored. *Evan Williams*   **h118 ?**

SUNSET KING (USA) 4 b.c. King of Kings (IRE) – Sunset River (USA) (Northern Flagship (USA)) [2003/4 16g 16g 16d Mar 21] small colt: fair maiden on Flat (stays 1m), best form when trained by S. Kirk: well held over hurdles. *J. C. Fox*   **h–**

SUNSHAN 8 b.g. Anshan – Kyrenia Sunset (CYP) (Lucky Look (CYP)) [2003/4 c75: c19m^{pu} c16m^3 c16d^6 c16d^6 c16g^4 c24g* Apr 16] workmanlike gelding: has reportedly been tubed: poor chaser: left T. Long and off 10 months after reappearance: upped markedly in trip, won novice handicap at Taunton: stays 3m: acts on good to firm going: has had tongue tied. *R. J. Hodges*   **c82**

SUNSHINE BOY 8 b.g. Cadeaux Genereux – Sahara Baladee (USA) (Shadeed (USA)) [2003/4 h84: 21m^3 c20m Jun 7] workmanlike gelding: modest hurdler: favourite, well beaten in novice handicap at Worcester on chasing debut: stays 27f: best on good going or firmer (acts on firm): blinkered once: flashes tail under pressure. *Miss E. C. Lavelle*   **c–**
h91

SUPERB LEADER (IRE) 10 b.g. Supreme Leader – Emmagreen (Green Shoon) [2003/4 c102, h84: 20g^4 c24s^3 c20m^{pu} c20m^F c20d^2 c17s^4 c20m^4 c20d^5 Apr 8] useful-looking gelding: maiden hurdler: fair chaser: stays 3m: acts on heavy going: weak finisher: sold 4,500 gns Doncaster May Sales. *Miss Venetia Williams*   **c100 §**
h–

SUPER BLUE (IRE) 7 b.m. Supreme Leader – Tip Marie (IRE) (Celio Rufo) [2003/4 h–, F–: 19g 16m^5 Apr 13] no worthwhile form in bumpers or over hurdles. *Mrs S. D. Williams*   **h–**

SUPER BOSTON 4 b.g. Saddlers' Hall (IRE) – Nasowas (IRE) (Cardinal Flower) [2003/4 F16s F17s Feb 10] second foal: dam, modest maiden hurdler up to 2½m, from family of top-class hurdler Beech Road: tailed off in bumpers: blinkered second start. *R. D. E. Woodhouse*   **F–**

SUPERCHARMER 10 ch.g. Charmer – Surpassing (Superlative) [2003/4 c20m^{ur} c22g c20g Mar 12] fair pointer: has made little impact in hunter chases, usually let down by jumping: tried blinkered. *M. A. Humphreys*   **c–**
h–

SUPER FELLOW (IRE) 10 b.g. Shy Groom (USA) – Killough (Lord Gayle (USA)) [2003/4 c132?, h–: c24s c20m c19d^2 c24d c24s^3 c24d c24g c26m^4 Apr 14] angular gelding: fair handicap chaser: in-and-out form in 2003/4, ran creditably though looked tricky ride when fourth to Flying Trix at Cheltenham: stays 3¼m: acts on any going: tried in blinkers/cheekpieces, effective without: often tongue tied: joined C. Kellett. *D. P. Murphy, Ireland*   **c114**
h–

SUPERIOR WEAPON (IRE)   10 b.g. Riverhead (USA) – Ballytrustan Maid (IRE) **c84**
(Orchestra) [2003/4 c87: c20s⁵ c16g* c16s² c17g Apr 5] modest chaser, off 15 months
before reappearance: won handicap at Ayr in March: effective at 2m to easy 3m: acts on
soft and good to firm going: tongue tied. *Mrs A. Hamilton*

SUPER LUCKY (IRE)   8 b.m. Moscow Society (USA) – Ballela Maid (Boreen **c–**
(FR)) [2003/4 20d* 17g² 21g³ 24gᵖᵘ Aug 16] IR 4,200 4-y-o: fourth foal: sister to 2m **h80**
winner Moscow Maid: dam unraced sister to fairly useful staying chaser Patrico: placed
in bumpers: once-raced in steeplechases: winning pointer in 2003: poor hurdler: won
mares maiden at Perth in July: stays 21f (beaten long way out over 3m): acts on good to
soft ground: blinkered twice. *J. J. Lambe, Ireland*

SUPER NOMAD   9 b.g. Nomadic Way (USA) – Super Sue (Lochnager) [2003/4 **c119**
c118, h110: c16d³ c20d³ c16d² c20d³ c16s c19g² c16d² c21gᴿ c16m Apr 15] strong **h–**
gelding: winning hurdler: fairly useful handicap chaser: placed 9 of last 11 completed
starts over fences without winning, didn't take to course and refused twelfth in Topham at
Aintree: effective at 2m to 2½m: acts on heavy and good to firm going: ran badly only
outing in blinkers: has had tongue tied: sound jumper in main. *M. W. Easterby*

SUPER ROAD TRAIN   5 b.g. Petoski – Foehn Gale (IRE) (Strong Gale) [2003/4 **h91**
F91: 21s⁴ 25d 20dᶠ 21d² Apr 11] bumper winner: running best race in novice hurdles
when falling 2 out at Fontwell: wore cheekpieces second and third outings. *L. Wells*

SUPER RUN (IRE)   6 b.g. Supreme Leader – Arctic Run (Deep Run) [2003/4 F18d⁶ **h119**
18d* 20d² 22d⁵ Nov 12] brother to useful hurdler/smart chaser who stays 2½m Strong **F80**
Run and half-brother to 2 winning hurdlers: dam unraced: modest form in 2 bumpers:
won maiden at Downpatrick on hurdling debut in May: much better form when 3½
lengths second to Patrizio in novice at Clonmel in June: stays 2½m: raced solely on good
to soft going. *N. Meade, Ireland*

SUPER SAMMY   8 br.m. Mesleh – Super Sue (Lochnager) [2003/4 h92: c16g⁴ c17d² **c100**
c21sᵘʳ c19g³ c20dᶠ c20v⁵ 20s⁶ c17dᵖᵘ Apr 24] lengthy mare: modest hurdler: fair novice **h85**
chaser: best efforts first 2 starts: stays 2½m: raced mainly on good going or softer (acts on
heavy). *M. W. Easterby*

SUPER SATCO (IRE)   6 b.g. Satco (FR) – Brae (IRE) (Runnett) [2003/4 F82: F16g **h–**
F16f⁵ 21m⁵ Jul 22] unfurnished gelding: modest form on first of 4 starts in bumpers: **F71**
raced freely when tailed off in novice on hurdling debut: no form in maiden Irish points
(refused to race once) later in 2003. *J. J. Lambe, Ireland*

SUPER TIP (IRE)   6 b.g. Supreme Leader – Tip Marie (IRE) (Celio Rufo) [2003/4 **h–**
F16m⁵ F17d 16d 16d⁶ 18s 17d 23sᵖᵘ Apr 4] lengthy gelding: fourth foal: half-brother to **F85**
Irish bumper winner Quick Pick (by Alphabatim): dam unraced half-sister to useful
chasers Bold Argument, stayed 3¼m, and Camelot Knight, thorough stayer: better effort
in bumpers when fifth of 12 at Sandown: probably flattered when sixth in novice at
Wincanton, no other form over hurdles: tried in blinkers. *P. Winkworth*

SUPRALUNA   5 ch.m. Classic Cliche (IRE) – Spring Flyer (IRE) (Waajib) [2003/4 **h81 §**
F–: 17g² 16gᵘʳ 17d⁶ 20mᵖᵘ Aug 8] sturdy mare: form over hurdles only when second in
weak mares novice at Newton Abbot: wears eyeshields: looked very difficult ride final
outing. *M. C. Pipe*

SUPREME ARROW (IRE)   9 b.m. Supreme Leader – Clover Run (IRE) (Deep **c110**
Run) [2003/4 22m* 21m² c24g* c24s² 21g⁴ c20d⁵ Mar 15] workmanlike ex-Irish mare: **h118**
fairly useful handicap hurdler: left D. Wachman, improved form when winning at
Stratford and second at Kempton in October: fair handicap chaser: landed odds in
6-runner event at Huntingdon (mistakes in second half of race) in November: stays easy
3m: acts on soft and good to firm going: usually makes running. *Miss E. C. Lavelle*

SUPREME BEING (IRE)   7 b.g. Supreme Leader – Parsonetta (The Parson) [2003/4 **h108**
h104: 20d⁴ 22s Mar 14] fair handicap hurdler: back near best when winning fairly
valuable event at Punchestown in late-April: should be suited by further than 2½m: acts
on heavy going: effective blinkered or not, also tried in cheekpieces: none too consistent.
Michael Cunningham, Ireland

SUPREME BREEZE (IRE)   9 b.g. Supreme Leader – Merry Breeze (Strong Gale) **c94 §**
[2003/4 c90§, h–: c26g³ c27d⁴ c25gᵘʳ c24sᵖᵘ c20d³ c28d⁴ c20d⁶ Apr 18] small gelding: **h–**
modest maiden chaser: left F. Murphy after fourth start: stays 31f: raced on good going
or softer (acts on soft): tried in cheekpieces, effective blinkered or not: sketchy jumper:
ungenuine. *Mrs S. J. Smith*

SUPREME CATCH (IRE) 7 b.g. Supreme Leader – Lucky Trout (Beau Charmeur (FR)) [2003/4 c119, h–: c19g* c24s⁴ c19g² c20m⁶ Apr 23] workmanlike gelding: fairly useful handicap chaser: off 13 months, won at Ascot in January by 2½ lengths from Ei Ei: good efforts next 2 starts, staying-on second to Trouble Ahead at same course on second occasion: will stay beyond 3m: acts on heavy going: patiently ridden. *Miss H. C. Knight*   **c127 h–**

SUPREME DAWN (IRE) 7 b.g. Supreme Leader – Tudor Dawn (Deep Run) [2003/4 F85: F17s 16g² 21g³ 16dᶠ Jan 19] useful-looking gelding: fair form when in frame in bumpers: left A. Lidderdale, best effort over hurdles when head second to Kercabellec in novice at Warwick: should stay beyond 2m. *C. Tinkler*   **h106 F–**

SUPREME DESTINY (IRE) 6 b.g. Supreme Leader – Shuil Le Gaoth (IRE) (Strong Gale) [2003/4 F16s Nov 28] 34,000 4-y-o: second foal: half-brother to useful bumper winner Bob Le Gaoth (by Bob Back): dam unraced half-sister to very smart staying hurdler Shuil Ar Aghaidh and useful staying jumper Rawhide, from excellent family: kept on from rear when eighth of 17 to Fairy Skin Maker in maiden bumper at Ayr on debut: joined Miss V. Williams. *Miss V. Scott*   **F79**

SUPREME FORTUNE (IRE) 10 b.g. Supreme Leader – Lucylet (Kinglet) [2003/4 c97§, h110§: c17m⁵ 20sᵖᵘ Nov 29] close-coupled gelding: winning hurdler/chaser: ran poorly both starts in 2003/4: stays 21f: acts on heavy going, possibly not on good to firm: held up, and suited by well-run race: ungenuine. *Mrs M. Reveley*   **c– § h– §**

SUPREME HILL (IRE) 7 br.g. Supreme Leader – Regents Prancer (Prince Regent (FR)) [2003/4 h111: c24dᶠ c24dᶠ 22s⁵ Jan 2] workmanlike gelding: novice hurdler, fair at best: fell both starts over fences: should stay beyond 2½m: raced on going softer than good (acts on heavy). *C. J. Mann*   **c– h88**

SUPREME HOPE (USA) 5 b.g. Supreme Leader – Flaming Hope (IRE) (Callernish) [2003/4 F16m² Nov 24] second foal: dam, won over hurdles around 2m, half-sister to useful hurdler who stayed 23f Abbot of Furness: joint favourite, 3 lengths second of 7 to Queen Soraya in maiden bumper at Ludlow on debut. *H. D. Daly*   **F98**

SUPREME LASS (IRE) 8 b.m. Supreme Leader – Falas Lass (Belfalas) [2003/4 h–: 16f 17g³ 19f² 19g⁴ 21v² 20sᵖᵘ Feb 11] close-coupled mare: poor maiden hurdler: lame final outing: stays 21f: acts on any going. *G. M. Moore*   **h81**

SUPREME LEISURE (IRE) 7 b.g. Supreme Leader – Maid of Leisure (Le Moss) [2003/4 F16d² F16d* Jan 25] rangy gelding: second foal: half-brother to fair hurdler up to 2¾m Native Leisure (by Be My Native): dam winning pointer: fairly useful form in bumpers, ½-length second to The Rising Moon at Newbury in December and won slowly-run 9-runner event at Leopardstown in January by length from Mr McAuley: sold to join J. H. Johnson 50,000 gns Doncaster May Sales. *Noel T. Chance*   **F103**

SUPREMELY BRIGHT 7 b.m. Supreme Leader – Oh So Bright (Celtic Cone) [2003/4 F–: 16mᵖᵘ May 7] no sign of ability in bumpers and a selling hurdle. *M. J. Ryan*   **h–**

SUPREMELY RED (IRE) 7 b.g. Supreme Leader – Her Name Was Lola (Pitskelly) [2003/4 h82: 21gᵖᵘ Nov 9] medium-sized gelding: poor hurdler: raced mainly around 2¾m: acts on firm going: visored/blinkered last 5 starts: hard ride. *D. A. Rees*   **h–**

SUPREME OBSESSION (IRE) 6 br.g. Supreme Leader – Death Or Glory (Hasdrubal) [2003/4 F16g* Oct 26] seventh foal: brother to 2 winners, including fairly useful hurdler/chaser Super Dealer, stays 3¼m, and half-brother to winning pointer by Topanoora: dam unplaced in bumper and point: promising debut when winning bumper at Wexford by 2½ lengths from Rosnagowloge, but not seen out again. *W. P. Mullins, Ireland*   **F101**

SUPREME OPTIMIST (IRE) 7 b.g. Supreme Leader – Armagale (IRE) (Strong Gale) [2003/4 h95: 16s 21v Jan 13] workmanlike gelding: maiden hurdler: dropped out quickly in handicaps both starts in 2003/4: bred to stay 2½m: acts on heavy going: sold 3,000 gns Doncaster May Sales. *N. G. Richards*   **h–**

SUPREME PIPER (IRE) 6 b.g. Supreme Leader – Whistling Doe (Whistling Deer) [2003/4 F89, h104, F89: 19gᶠ 20dᶠ Apr 7] useful-looking gelding: chasing type: fairly useful form over hurdles: would probably have beaten Claymore in 7-runner handicap at Exeter on reappearance but for falling last: off 4 months, easily landed odds in novice at Fontwell: will stay 3m: acts on good to soft going. *P. J. Hobbs*   **h122**

SUPREME PRINCE (IRE) 7 b.g. Supreme Leader – Strong Serenade (IRE) (Strong Gale) [2003/4 h143: c23g² c19d* c19s* c24gᵖᵘ c23s² Apr 6] tall gelding: useful hurdler: fairly useful form over fences, won maiden at Chepstow (easily) and 4-runner Grade 2 Noel Novices' Chase at Ascot (by 2 lengths from See You Sometime, rallying   **c129 h–**

gamely) in December: odds on, laboured after hitting 3 out when 14 lengths second of 3 finishers to Biliverdin at Exeter final start: needs testing conditions around 2½m and stays 3m: raced on good ground or softer (acts on soft): needs to improve his jumping (mistakes when pulled up in Grade 1 at Cheltenham). *P. J. Hobbs*

SUPREME PRIORITY (IRE)   6 b.g. Supreme Leader – Kakemona (Kambalda) [2003/4 h74+, F90: 24m^{pu} 21f* 24s^{pu} 19g 22d 26g^4 Apr 3] lengthy gelding: poor hurdler: won seller (sold from J. O'Neill £6,750) at Towcester in October: stays 3¼m: probably acts on any going. *C. Roberts*   **h77**

SUPREME RETURN   5 b.g. Bob's Return (IRE) – Supreme Wonder (IRE) (Supreme Leader) [2003/4 F16v^5 F16g Mar 7] tall gelding with plenty of scope: second foal: dam, bumper winner, from family of smart chaser up to 3m Comeragh King and useful staying chaser Seskin Bridge: better effort in bumpers when 13½ lengths fifth of 17 to Historic Place at Ascot. *A. King*   **F83**

SUPREME RULLAH (IRE)   7 b.m. Supreme Leader – Trapper Jean (Orchestra) [2003/4 F18d 20s 20d 18d 20d^6 24s^{pu} Apr 21] fifth foal: half-sister to winning pointer by Good Thyne: dam unraced half-sister to very smart staying hurdler Trapper John: won maiden point in 2003: seventh of 14 in bumpers: poor form over hurdles: has had tongue tied. *I. R. Ferguson, Ireland*   **h68**
F—

SUPREME SERENADE (IRE)   5 b.m. Supreme Leader – Strong Serenade (IRE) (Strong Gale) [2003/4 F17s* 17g^2 17s* 19d^3 20s^2 21g^3 Mar 27] good-topped mare: fourth foal: sister to useful hurdler/novice chaser Supreme Prince and half-sister to winning 3m hurdler That's The Story (by Montelimar): dam bumper/2m hurdle winner: won bumper at Newton Abbot on debut in April: fair novice hurdler: won at Folkestone in December: threw race away when third to Kentford Grebe in valuable mares handicap at Newbury final start, hanging left under pressure: will stay 3m: raced on good going or softer: hard ride, and will be suited by exaggerated waiting tactics. *P. J. Hobbs*   **h111**
F103

SUPREME SILENCE (IRE)   7 b.g. Bluebird (USA) – Why So Silent (Mill Reef (USA)) [2003/4 c–§, h–§: 24g^{pu} c25s^{pu} c25s^2 c21s^{pu} c25g^{pu} Mar 28] angular gelding: winning hurdler: sold out of J. O'Keeffe's stable 1,150 gns Doncaster May Sales after first outing: won point in February: form in hunter chases only when second in 3-finisher novice (grossly flattered by proximity to winner Ababou) at Market Rasen: stays 25f: acts on soft going: tried blinkered/visored: tongue tied once: ungenuine. *Nick Kent*   **c80 §**
h– §

SUPREME'S LEGACY (IRE)   5 b.g. Supreme Leader – Lucylet (Kinglet) [2003/4 F17d^2 Nov 22] brother to ungenuine winning hurdler/chaser Supreme Fortune, stays 21f,   **F111**

and half-brother to fairly useful hunter chasers Garryspillane (by Royal Fountain) and Pharmistice (by Phardante): dam, fair hurdler, barely stayed 3m: 11/2, shaped well when 2 lengths second of 16 to Mount Clerigo in bumper at Aintree on debut. *Mrs M. Reveley*

SUREFAST 9 ch.g. Nearly A Hand – Meldon Lady (Ballymoss) [2003/4 c72, h75: c25v^pu c24m^pu c23d^5 c20v* c23d^2 Apr 21] stocky gelding: maiden hurdler: poor chaser: won conditional jockeys handicap at Lingfield in April: stays 3m: acts on heavy ground. *K. Bishop* **c82 h–**

SURE FUTURE 8 b.g. Kylian (USA) – Lady Ever-So-Sure (Malicious) [2003/4 h108+: 24d^2 22d^ur 25d^6 c22s^pu c19g c21d^6 c23d^6 c24v^3 c24m Apr 13] close-coupled gelding: fairly useful handicap hurdler: only modest form over fences (has been let down by jumping): probably better at 2¾m to 3m than shorter: acts on heavy and good to firm going: tried blinkered: tongue tied once: usually patiently ridden. *R. M. Stronge* **c94 h116**

SURPRISE GUNNER 14 b.g. Gunner B – Heckley Loch (Lochnager) [2003/4 19d^4 20d^6 22g^5 19v^ro c22s c24g^pu Mar 6] compact gelding: winning hurdler, retains little ability: no form over fences. *A. P. Jones* **c– h–**

SURPRISING 9 b.g. Primitive Rising (USA) – Ascot Lass (Touching Wood (USA)) [2003/4 c108, h132d: c24g* c28g^2 Nov 20] lengthy gelding: useful hurdler at best: left P. Hobbs, won 5-runner maiden chase at Carlisle on reappearance in November by short head from Silver Knight: better form when neck second to Fin Bec in handicap at Market Rasen: stays 3½m: acts on any going: formerly usually blinkered: held up: not an easy ride/has found little. *O. Sherwood* **c131 h–**

SURSUM CORDA 13 b.g. Idiot's Delight – Childhay (Roi Soleil) [2003/4 c96d, h–: c21s^F c16g^ur May 12] sturdy gelding: fair hunter chaser: normally sound jumper but failed to complete both starts early in 2003/4: barely stays 3m: acts on any going: usually tongue tied. *John Wall* **c– h–**

SUSIE BURY 5 b.m. Overbury (IRE) – Susie's Money (Seymour Hicks (FR)) [2003/4 F16s F16g Mar 4] sixth foal: half-sister to winning hurdler/modest chaser The Sawdust Kid (by River God), stays 3¼m, and winning 19f hurdler Manly Money (by Homo Sapien): dam unraced: no show in 2 bumpers. *S. A. Brookshaw* **F–**

SUSPENDID (IRE) 11 b.g. Yashgan – Spendapromise (Goldhill) [2003/4 c109, h–: c20g c21m^5 c20m* c21m c21m* c20f^pu Oct 29] sturdy gelding: fair handicap chaser: won at Worcester in June and Southwell in October: stays 21f: acts on good to firm and good to soft going: tried tongue tied: has broken blood vessels: unreliable. *R. Lee* **c110 § h–**

SUSSEX MIST 5 b.m. Phountzi (USA) – Dumerica (Yukon Eric (CAN)) [2003/4 F16g F16m Apr 13] seventh foal: dam unraced: well beaten in bumpers. *J. E. Long* **F–**

SUSY WELLS (IRE) 9 b.m. Masad (IRE) – My Best Susy (IRE) (Try My Best (USA)) [2003/4 16g 17d^pu 17g Apr 3] poor maiden on Flat, last raced at 5 yrs: no form in 3 starts over hurdles: has worn cheekpieces. *C. W. Moore* **h–**

SUTTON BALLAD 10 b.m. Emperor Fountain – Crescent Cottage (Cornuto) [2003/4 16m^pu May 5] third foal: dam poor maiden jumper: reportedly twisted pelvis on belated debut. *P. D. Purdy* **h–**

SUTTON LION 12 b.g. Lyphento (USA) – Crescent Cottage (Cornuto) [2003/4 19g^R Dec 18] first foal: dam poor maiden jumper: refused third in novice hurdle on belated debut. *P. D. Purdy* **h–**

SUZY SPITFIRE 6 ch.m. Afzal – Oatis Rose (Oats) [2003/4 F16m F17g 23m^pu Nov 11] good-bodied mare: first foal: dam, fair hurdler, stayed 3m: no form in 2 bumpers and novice hurdle. *B. G. Powell* **h– F–**

SWAN KNIGHT (USA) 8 b. or br.g. Sadler's Wells (USA) – Shannkara (IRE) (Akarad (FR)) [2003/4 h113: c17d^5 16v^5 16g^4 17d^4 c16s^F Feb 6] compact gelding: fair handicap hurdler: some promise on chasing debut: best at 2m with emphasis on speed: acts on good to firm and good to soft going. *R. A. Fahey* **c102 + h113**

SWANSEA BAY 8 b.g. Jurado (USA) – Slave's Bangle (Prince Rheingold) [2003/4 c126, h–: c23m* c24f* c25f* c24g* c24g Dec 26] **c149 h–**

After a spell in the doldrums the Peter Bowen stable was very much back on song in 2003/4. A total of thirty-eight wins equalled its previous best, set in 1997/8, while win prize money of £344,880 was almost double the previous highest amount, set in 1996/7 when its former stable stars Dreams End and Stately Home were in their prime. Bowen finished seventeenth in the table based on win and place prize money, a fine achievement given that, with the exception of Ginger McCain

who was responsible for Grand National winner Amberleigh House, he was operating with a string far smaller than any other trainer in the top twenty. The bulk of the victories came in an astonishing run of twenty-seven winners from around mid-September through to Boxing Day. The stable had a remarkable ratio of winners to runners of fifty-four per cent during this period, something which says much for Bowen's skill in placing his horses. It might seem surprising that Bowen hasn't attracted more horses, though the remoteness of his stables may be a factor—he trains in Pembrokeshire and his nearest course, as the crow flies at least, is Wexford.

Swansea Bay and Ballycassidy, along with Take The Stand, were the best horses in the yard and both did their trainer proud, winning eleven races between them. Swansea Bay provided the initial victory in what was to prove such a purple patch for his stable, returning from eight months off to win a handicap chase at Worcester which had been named after him. Swansea Bay had been successful in the same event twelve months earlier—one of six wins in his first season over fences—and at the same fixture in 2001 he had opened his account in a maiden hurdle. His record at Worcester now stands at five wins from five appearances. Not that Swansea Bay is a course specialist by any means, as he underlined by winning at Kempton, Wincanton and Haydock on his next three starts. Swansea Bay beat Peccadillo by two lengths in the Stan James Gold Cup at the first-named venue, and Gunther McBride by a length and three quarters when winning Wincanton's Badger Ales Chase, another race he was winning for a second year running, starting favourite both times. He was also narrowly preferred in the betting to the former top- and high-class chasers he met in the Edward Hanmer Memorial Chase, a limited handicap run at Haydock, even though he raced off a mark 21 lb higher than at the start of the season. Both Kingsmark, who had won the three previous runnings, and the 2002 Royal & SunAlliance Chase winner Hussard Collonges,

Edward Hanmer Memorial Chase (Limited Handicap), Haydock—
a tenth win in thirteen starts; Hussard Collonges is second

lacked a recent run, and a still-improving Swansea Bay proved too good for them at the weights. Swansea Bay came back on the bridle to lead after three out, then typically didn't do much in front, but still had five lengths to spare over Hussard Collonges at the line, Kingsmark having unseated his rider at the last when held in third. The form shown by Swansea Bay was smart, but it was still a long way short of that required to keep his winning run going on what proved to be his final start of the season, in the King George VI Chase at Kempton, despite his starting third favourite behind Jair du Cochet and First Gold. Not surprisingly, Swansea Bay wasn't up to the task and trailed home last of the seven finishers. Swansea Bay was then trained with the Grand National in mind but missed the race due to mucus on the lungs.

Swansea Bay (b.g. 1996)	Jurado (USA) (b 1983)	Alleged (b 1974)	Hoist The Flag L'Enjoleur
		Champagne Ginny (b 1977)	Seminole Girl
	Slave's Bangle (b 1983)	Prince Rheingold (b 1976)	Rheingold Hail To Vail
		La Campesina (b 1966)	Arctic Slave Diana's Rock

Swansea Bay is the sixth foal of Slave's Bangle and her fifth winner, following the fair hurdler and modest chaser up to two and a half miles Cittadino (by Good Thyne), the modest three-mile chaser Isle of Iona (by St Columbus), the useful chaser Gower-Slave (by Mandalus), winner of the 2001 John Hughes Trophy at Aintree, and the fair staying chaser Orswell Crest (by Crested Lark). Slave's Bangle, who showed little in bumpers and a maiden hurdle in Ireland, is a daughter of La Campesina, the winner of a two-mile maiden hurdle in Ireland and a half-sister to the useful staying hurdler Spaced Out. The next dam, Diana's Rock, is also the third dam of the 1998 Mumm Melling Chase winner Opera Hat. The lengthy Swansea Bay has raced only at around three miles over jumps, and mostly on good ground or firmer which suits him ideally. He acts well on firm. Before the latest season Swansea Bay, who has a tendency to idle in front, was often fitted with cheekpieces. *P. Bowen*

888

SWAZI PRINCE 5 b.g. Rakaposhi King – Swazi Princess (IRE) (Brush Aside (USA)) **F79**
[2003/4 F–: F16s³ F16s³ F17g Apr 10] sturdy gelding: modest form at best in bumpers.
N. A. Gaselee

SWEET AUBURN (IRE) 8 b. or br.g. Tidaro (USA) – Sweet View (King's Ride) **c82**
[2003/4 h–, F79: 16d⁵ 16m⁴ 16s 25s⁴ 23v⁴ 20v³ 24s⁴ 17gᵖᵘ c21d⁴ c25d⁵ c25g³ 20d⁶ Apr **h78**
23] sturdy gelding: poor maiden hurdler: similar form on first of 3 starts in steeplechases:
stays 25f: acts on heavy going, probably on good to firm: tried blinkered/in cheekpieces.
Mrs B. K. Thomson

SWEET BIRD (FR) 7 ch.g. Epervier Bleu – Sweet Virginia (FR) (Tapioca II) [2003/4 **h–**
h89: 24d⁴ 21g Apr 12] sturdy, lengthy gelding: lightly-raced maiden hurdler, modest form
at best: should stay 3m: acts on heavy going: tongue tied final start. *P. M. Phelan*

SWEET CHAMPAGNE 5 ch.m. Mazaad – Pink Sensation (Sagaro) [2003/4 21vᵖᵘ **h–**
16gᵖᵘ Mar 10] angular mare: half-sister to winning hurdler around 2m Sharp Sensation
(by Crofthall): well held in 3 maidens on Flat at 3 yrs: no show over hurdles. *G. A. Harker*

SWEET CHARIOT 5 b.g. Hatim (USA) – Evening Dusk (IRE) (Phardante (FR)) **F–**
[2003/4 F16g F17g Apr 13] first foal: dam no sign of ability over hurdles: well held in 2
bumpers. *B. G. Powell*

SWEET DIVERSION (IRE) 5 b.g. Carroll House – Serocco Wind (Roi Guillaume **h121**
(FR)) [2003/4 F90: F16m³ 16d³ 19s² 20g* 20s⁴ 21m⁴ Apr 14] sturdy gelding: placed **F87**
all 3 starts in bumpers: fairly useful novice hurdler: didn't need to be at best to win at
Fakenham in February: creditable fourth to Copsale Lad in quite valuable event at
Cheltenham final outing: stays 21f: acts on soft and good to firm going. *P. F. Nicholls*

SWEET KILN (IRE) 5 b.m. Beneficial – Miss Pollerton (IRE) (Pollerton) [2003/4 **F106 +**
F16s² F16d* F16s³ F16d³ Apr 11] second foal: dam, showed a little ability in bumpers,
half-sister to dam of Limestone Lad: progressive form in bumpers: won at Naas in
February and Navan (battled back to beat Granny Kellys Tart by short head) in March: set
good pace and stuck on really well when third to Geill Sli at Fairyhouse final start:
interesting prospect for novice hurdles in 2004/5. *James Bowe, Ireland*

SWEET MILLY 9 b.m. Milieu – Another Joyful (Rubor) [2003/4 h74: 16g⁴ 16gᵖᵘ **h68**
22gᵖᵘ Nov 12] poor maiden hurdler: raced mainly around 2m: acts on heavy going.
J. E. Dixon

SWEET MINUET 7 b.m. Minshaanshu Amad (USA) – Sweet N' Twenty (High Top) **h82**
[2003/4 h85: 22m⁴ May 26] lengthy mare: modest hurdler: stays 2¾m: acts on any going:
blinkered once in bumpers (tailed off). *M. Madgwick*

SWEET ROI (GER) 4 b.c. Roi Danzig (USA) – Sweet Royale (GER) (Garde **h79 p**
Royale) [2003/4 20s Feb 17] half-brother to winning 2m hurdler Sweet Brief (by Brief
Truce): successful once around 11f (for H. Blume) on Flat at 3 yrs in Germany: seems not
to stay when tenth of 16 in 2½m maiden at Folkestone (not fluent) on hurdling debut:
likely to do better granted less of a test of stamina. *M. Hofer, Germany*

SWEET SENSATION 9 ch.m. Carlingford Castle – Pink Sensation (Sagaro) [2003/4 **h–**
h–: 21sᵖᵘ 17d May 28] workmanlike gelding, rather sparely-made mare: no form over hurdles, failing
to impress with jumping and attitude: blinkered in 2003/4. *C. Grant*

SWEET SHOOTER 4 ch.f. Double Trigger (IRE) – Sweet N' Twenty (High Top) **F82**
[2003/4 F17s⁵ F18g⁵ F16g Mar 27] angular filly: fifth foal: half-sister to several winners,
including useful 2m hurdler Sweet Senorita (by Young Senor) and fair hurdler Twenty
Bucks (by Buckley), stays 2¾m: dam fairly useful and prolific winning hurdler up to
2½m/fair stayer on Flat: modest form first 2 starts in bumpers: will be suited by stiffer test
of stamina. *M. Madgwick*

SWIFT SETTLEMENT 5 br.m. King's Ride – Swift Conveyance (IRE) (Strong **F–**
Gale) [2003/4 F16s Apr 12] third foal: dam, modest 2m hurdler, from family of high-class
staying chaser Drumlargan: well beaten in mares bumper on debut. *J. Rudge*

SWIFT SWALLOW 6 ch.g. Missed Flight – Alhargah (Be My Guest (USA)) [2003/4 **F89**
F88: F16m⁶ F16g⁶ F16g² Mar 17] sturdy gelding: fair form in bumpers, second of 20 to
easy winner Here's Johnny at Huntingdon. *O. Brennan*

SWIFTWAY 10 ch.g. Anshan – Solemn Occasion (USA) (Secreto (USA)) [2003/4 **c–**
c22gᵖᵘ c26gᵖᵘ May 24] workmanlike gelding: one-time fair hurdler: third in novice on **h–**
chasing debut in April 2002: no encouragement on return: stays 3m: acts on soft and good
to firm going: tried blinkered. *Mrs E. Slack*

SWINCOMBE (IRE) 9 b.g. Good Thyne (USA) – Gladtogetit (Green Shoon) [2003/4 **c104 §**
c112: c24d^{pu} c25v^{2d} c23d^4 c24s^2 c26v^{pu} c29d c24g^{pu} Apr 1] fair handicap chaser: ran
poorly last 3 outings, appeared to take little interest when visored final one: stays 3¼m:
acts on heavy going. *R. H. Alner*

SWINGING SARAH 5 ch.m. Dr Devious (IRE) – Lupescu (Dixieland Band (USA)) **h–**
[2003/4 F17m F16g^5 F16d 16d 21v^{pu} Jan 13] small, sturdy mare: fourth foal: half-sister **F76**
to several winners, including fairly useful but unreliable hurdler Junkanoo (by Generous),
stays 23f, and 7f winner Lindissima (by Green Desert): dam useful 9f/1¼m winner:
modest form on first of 3 starts in bumpers: showed nothing in 2 novice hurdles. *N. Wilson*

SWING WEST (USA) 10 b.g. Gone West (USA) – Danlu (USA) (Danzig (USA)) **c– §**
[2003/4 c–, h–: c24d^{pu} c20s^5 c22g c24d^{pu} c21g^{pu} c26g^{pu} Apr 22] leggy ex-Irish gelding: **h–**
winning hurdler/chaser, has lost his way: left N. Glynn after fourth outing: tried in
cheekpieces, often blinkered: ungenuine. *A. E. Jones*

SWINKER 5 b.g. Roscoe Blake – Fly-Girl (Clantime) [2003/4 F16g 16g 21s^{pu} Feb 10] **h–**
1,900 (privately) 3-y-o: first foal: dam well beaten both starts on Flat: no show in bumper **F–**
or novice hurdles. *P. G. Atkinson*

SWORD LADY 6 b.m. Broadsword (USA) – Speckyfoureyes (Blue Cashmere) **h104**
[2003/4 F68: 16v* 16v^2 16d 19d^3 22v^3 21d* 21g Mar 27] leggy mare: fair hurdler: won mares
events at Towcester in November and March (odds on): will stay 3m: acts on heavy going.
Mrs S. D. Williams

SWORDPLAY 6 ch.g. Kris – Throw Away Line (Cragador) [2003/4 h122: 16g^5 16d **h130**
16f^2 16g 16m^2 16d Apr 13] leggy gelding: useful hurdler: easily best efforts in 2003/4
when second in intermediate at Punchestown and listed handicap at Galway in autumn:
will prove best at 2m: acts on firm and good to soft going: tried tongue tied.
M. J. P. O'Brien, Ireland

SYLPHIDE 9 b.m. Ballet Royal (USA) – Shafayif (Ela-Mana-Mou) [2003/4 c19m^4 **c90**
c26d* c26g^{ur} c26g^{pu} c20m^{pu} c23m^5 c24m^3 c26g^4 c19m^3 c22s^3 c25g c21s^2 c22d* Apr 7] **h–**
sparely-made mare: won 4 times in points in 2003: modest chaser: won maiden at Newton
Abbot in June and handicap at Fontwell in April: stays 3¼m: acts on good to firm and
heavy going: inconsistent. *H. J. Manners*

SYLVIAJAZZ 5 b.m. Alhijaz – Dispol Princess (IRE) (Cyrano de Bergerac) [2003/4 **h–**
h–: 16d May 16] probably of little account: tried in cheekpieces. *Miss J. Feilden*

SYLVIESBUCK (IRE) 7 b.g. Kasmayo – Sylvies Missiles (IRE) (Buckskin (FR)) **c96**
[2003/4 h86, F95: c21d^4 c20d^5 c25d^{ur} c27v* c23v^2 c27s^3 c27s^{ur} Feb 24] strong gelding: **h–**
novice hurdler: jumped more fluently than usual and easily best effort over fences when
winning novice handicap at Sedgefield in January: stays 27f: acts on heavy going:
blinkered final outing. *G. M. Moore*

SZEROKI BOR (POL) 5 b.g. In Camera (IRE) – Szuana (POL) (Five Star Camp **h102**
(USA)) [2003/4 16d 16d 17s^2 16d^2 Mar 1] Polish-bred gelding: trained by D. Kaluba,
successful from 6f to 2m on Flat in Poland: fair form over hurdles, runner-up in novice at
Folkestone and maiden at Plumpton: will stay beyond 2m. *M. Pitman*

T

TAAKID (USA) 9 b.g. Diesis – Tanwi (Vision (USA)) [2003/4 c91, h–: c17g* c20m **c105 +**
May 27] leggy, angular gelding: fair handicap chaser: off 7 months, best effort when
winning at Southwell in May by 19 lengths from Ceresfield: running well under penalty
when slipping on landing after 2 out at Hexham 9 days later: stays 21f: acts on good to
soft and good to firm ground: has had tongue tied. *Mrs S. J. Smith*

TABLE FOR FIVE 10 b.g. Sunley Builds – Prying Nell (Pry) [2003/4 26s Feb 12] **c– x**
tall gelding: jumped badly in 2 novice chases: won 2 points in 2003: one-time fair hurdler, **h–**
made most until 3 out in handicap at Huntingdon (wore cheekpieces) only outing in
2003/4: stays 3m: act on heavy going: has hung badly left/worn near-side pricker. *Miss
Victoria Roberts*

TACIN (IRE) 7 b.g. Supreme Leader – Nicat (Wolver Hollow) [2003/4 h112: 24d* **c–**
c24g^{pu} Nov 30] well-made gelding: fair form both completed starts over hurdles, won **h–**
maiden at Punchestown in May: losing place when mistake tenth in Grade 2 novice at
Newbury (lame) on steeplechase debut. *B. G. Powell*

TACOLINO (FR)   10 ch.g. Royal Charter (FR) – Tamilda (FR) (Rose Laurel) [2003/4 c102, h–: c16m c16m⁶ c20m* c20m* c17f† Sep 27] workmanlike gelding: fairly useful handicap chaser: much improved, successful on 4 of 7 starts for present stable, including at Worcester in June and Market Rasen later in June and September: led from fifth and just pushed out to beat Duke of Buckingham 3½ lengths in competitive race when completing hat-trick: effective at 2m to 2½m: acts on firm and good to soft ground, probably on heavy: tried blinkered: often tongue tied in Ireland. *O. Brennan*
c124 h–

TACO'S REVENGE   11 b.g. Henbit (USA) – Taco (High Season) [2003/4 c24mᵖᵘ May 7] tall gelding: pulled up in 2 chases 4 years apart. *M. D. McMillan*
c–

TACTFUL REMARK (USA)   8 ch.g. Lord At War (ARG) – Right Word (USA) (Verbatim (USA)) [2003/4 h124: 16m⁵ 17m* 16mᵖᵘ c16m* c16m⁴ Oct 4] angular gelding: fair hurdler: simple task when winning intermediate at Southwell in June: won novice at Worcester on chasing debut in September, despite not convincing with jumping: very disappointing in similar event 3 weeks later: raced around 2m: acts on soft and good to firm going: free-going sort, usually forces pace. *M. C. Pipe*
c96 h111

TADZIO   5 bl.g. Mtoto – Fresher (Fabulous Dancer (USA)) [2003/4 F–: F16m⁵ F16m 16mᶠ 20gᵘʳ 16gᶠ 16dᵖᵘ Nov 13] little show in bumpers (probably flattered on reappearance, subsequently sold out of P. Webber's stable 4,500 gns Doncaster May Sales): failed to complete all 4 starts over hurdles: pulls hard. *M. J. Gingell*
h– F–

TAFFRAIL   6 b.g. Slip Anchor – Tizona (Pharly (FR)) [2003/4 16d 16g 16g 16d Mar 24] strong gelding: useful at one time on Flat (best at 2m+), on downgrade, sold out of J. Dunlop's stable 11,000 gns Newmarket Autumn Sales: modest form at best in novice hurdles: will be suited by further than 2m. *D. Burchell*
h86

TAFFY DANCER   6 b.g. Emperor Jones (USA) – Ballerina Bay (Myjinski (USA)) [2003/4 20g² 24s⁵ 20s² 20g Mar 8] modest on Flat (stays 2¼m): fair form over hurdles when runner-up in novice at Fontwell and maiden at Folkestone: lost chance with bad mistake 4 out in maiden final start (finished lame). *H. Morrison*
h109

TAGAR (FR)   7 b.g. Fijar Tango (FR) – Fight For Arfact (Salmon Leap (USA)) [2003/4 h103: 16g⁴ c19g⁴ c16m* Sep 24] close-coupled gelding: fair maiden hurdler: sold out of N. Henderson's stable 4,600 gns Doncaster August Sales after chasing debut: won novice at Perth next time by 22 lengths from Salvage, not seen out again: best efforts at 2m: acts on good to firm and heavy going. *C. Grant*
c111 h100

TAHRIMA   5 b.m. Slip Anchor – Khandjar (Kris) [2003/4 F67+: F16d Nov 14] poor form on first of 2 starts in bumpers. *P. Monteith*
F–

TAI LASS   4 b. or br.f. Taipan (IRE) – Kerry's Oats (Derrylin) [2003/4 16g³ 16d³ 16s⁶ 16g² 16d² Mar 28] leggy filly: behind in 1¾m maiden on Flat: fair form when runner-up last 2 starts over hurdles: will stay beyond 2m: acts on good to soft going. *P. R. Hedger*
h105

TAILLEFER (FR)   8 b.g. Cyborg (FR) – Tourka (FR) (Rose Laurel) [2003/4 c–, h100: c20g May 17] tall, leggy gelding: has reportedly had wind operation: fair hurdler: winning chaser, no form over fences since 2000/1: stays 2¾m: raced on good ground or softer (acts on heavy): tried blinkered. *M. E. D. Francis*
c– h–

TAILS I WIN   5 b.g. Petoski – Spinayab (King of Spain) [2003/4 F–: F16g² F17g⁵ Nov 4] lengthy, plain, sparely-made gelding: form in bumpers only when second in poor race at Uttoxeter. *J. W. Mullins*
F73

TAIPO PRINCE (IRE)   4 b.g. Entrepreneur – Dedicated Lady (IRE) (Pennine Walk) [2003/4 17g 16g³ 16g⁶ 19g 16s³ Apr 4] modest maiden on Flat (stays 9.4f), sold out of A. Jarvis' stable 7,200 gns Doncaster August Sales: poor novice hurdler: likely to prove best around 2m. *Miss Kate Milligan*
h80

TAKAGI (IRE)   9 b.g. Husyan (USA) – Ballyclough Gale (Strong Gale) [2003/4 c138, h122: c25d⁴ c24d³ 24s⁵ c24s⁶ 24v c25d* c36dᵘʳ Apr 3] lengthy, useful-looking gelding: fairly useful handicap hurdler: useful chaser: blinkered, back to form when making all in 6-runner Grade 3 Bobbyjo Chase at Fairyhouse in February, beating Alexander Banquet 2½ lengths: visored, several mistakes before unseating fifteenth (the Chair) in Grand National at Aintree: well below best when twice in frame in cross-country events at Punchestown in late-April: should stay beyond 25f: acts on heavy going. *E. J. O'Grady, Ireland*
c139 h119

TAKEACHANCEONHIM   6 b.g. Dilum (USA) – Smilingatstrangers (Macmillion) [2003/4 F16m F16m⁶ Jul 23] second reported foal: half-brother to 23f hurdle winner Frankie Anson (by Anshan): dam fair stayer on Flat: poor form in 2 bumpers. *Mrs Barbara Waring*
F70

TAKE A RAIN CHECK (IRE)   7 b.m. Rainbows For Life (CAN) – Just A Second   h–
(Jimsun) [2003/4 h–: 16g⁵ 21sᵖᵘ 20s⁶ 20sᵖᵘ Jan 26] workmanlike mare: of no account:
tried in cheekpieces. *C. J. Drewe*

TAKE CONTROL (IRE)   10 b.g. Roselier (FR) – Frosty Fairy (Paddy's Stream)   c137 x
[2003/4 c130x, h–: c32m³ c26g³ c29dᵖᵘ c29gᶠ Jan 10] workmanlike gelding: useful   h–
handicap chaser: won Scottish Grand National at Ayr in 2002: third in valuable events at
Uttoxeter and Newbury (to Strong Flow in Hennessy) first 2 starts in 2003/4: stayed 33f:
acted on good to firm and heavy going: effective visored or not: often let down by
jumping: dead. *M. C. Pipe*

TAKE FIVE (IRE)   11 br.g. Satco (FR) – Shan's Moss (Le Moss) [2003/4 c19d*   c108
c24dᶠ 18sᶠ 19s³ 16s⁴ c20s⁵ c20dᶠ c18v⁴ Apr 21] tall, leggy gelding: fairly useful hurdler: h124
fair chaser: missed 2002/3: easily won handicap over fences at Naas on return in
November: fell next 2 starts, would have won minor event over hurdles at Cork but for
doing so last: effective around 2m to 3¼m: acts on heavy and good to firm going: usually
tongue tied in 2003/4: sometimes let down by jumping over fences. *J. E. Kiely, Ireland*

TAKE FLITE   7 b.g. Cadeaux Genereux – Green Seed (IRE) (Lead On Time (USA))   h123
[2003/4 h119: 16v⁴ 16m³ 16m⁴ 20s Nov 20] compact gelding: fairly useful on Flat
(stayed 1½m): fairly useful hurdler: good third to Intersky Falcon in Grade 1 at Tipperary
in October: below form in 2 handicaps subsequently: best at sharp 2m: acted on good to
firm and heavy going: held up: dead. *Anthony Mullins, Ireland*

TAKE HEED   8 b.g. Warning – Tunaria (USA) (Lyphard (USA)) [2003/4 h78: 17s⁴   h–
May 2] sturdy gelding: poor hurdler: will prove best around 2m: acts on good to firm and
good to soft going: tongue tied: tends to finish weakly. *K. A. Morgan*

TAKE THE ODDS (IRE)   8 gr.g. Roselier (FR) – Skinana (Buckskin (FR)) [2003/4   c–
c24mᶠ c22fᵖᵘ 23d³ Nov 13] sixth foal: brother to winning chaser up to 2½m Millbrook   h69 ?
Lad: dam unraced: won maiden Irish point on debut in 2003: little encouragement
in 2 steeplechases: less than fluent when third of 5 in novice hurdle at Fakenham.
G. Prodromou

TAKE THE STAND (IRE)   8 b.g. Witness Box (USA) – Denys Daughter (IRE)   c140
(Crash Course) [2003/4 c116, h–: c32mᶠ c26m* c23m² c24m* c26gᵇᵈ c25g* c29d⁴ c24sᶠ   h–

South-West Racing Club Handicap Chase, Exeter—
Take The Stand (right) and Arlas early on the final circuit

Jan 31] leggy gelding: useful handicap chaser: improved good deal further in 2003/4, won at Newton Abbot in July, Chepstow in October and Exeter in December, beating Over The Storm 6 lengths at last-named: far from discredited considering several mistakes when fourth of 15 to Bindaree in Welsh National at Chepstow, fell tenth in another valuable event final outing: should stay beyond 29f: acts on good to firm and good to soft ground. *P. Bowen*

TAKING (FR)   8 gr.g. Take Risks (FR) – Sonning (FR) (Moulin) [2003/4 c81x, h–: c16v^{pu} c19v^{F} c20s^{pu} c22g^{pu} Feb 10] leggy gelding: poor and error-prone handicap chaser: stays 21f: often blinkered nowadays: has had tongue tied. *C. N. Kellett*   **c– x** **h–**

TAKSINA   5 b.m. Wace (USA) – Quago (New Member) [2003/4 h–, F–: 17m 17s^{3} 22g^{5} 19s 21g c25m^{3} c22s^{F} c20g^{4} Apr 12] lengthy mare: signs of only a little ability. *R. H. Buckler*   **c–** **h–**

TALAMA LADY (IRE)   7 b.m. Persian Bold – Talama (FR) (Shakapour) [2003/4 F16d F16g^{6} 17d^{2} 17d^{pu} Apr 18] strong, close-coupled mare: successful first 2 starts in bumpers: off 2½ years, better effort in 2003/4 when sixth of 14 in mares event at Musselburgh: not fluent when 8 lengths second of 17 to King Solomon in novice at Bangor on hurdling debut: raced too freely next time. *G. A. Swinbank*   **h87** **F90**

TALARIVE (USA)   8 ch.g. Riverman (USA) – Estala (Be My Guest (USA)) [2003/4 h125: 16m^{3} 16s^{6} 16g^{6} 16g 16d 16s^{pu} 16v^{2} 20v 18v 16s Feb 7] smallish, sturdy gelding: fair handicap hurdler on his day: best efforts around 2m: acts on heavy going: wore cheekpieces seventh to ninth outings: unreliable. *P. D. Niven*   **h109 §**

TALBOT LAD   8 b.g. Weld – Greenacres Girl (Tycoon II) [2003/4 c83, h83: c19m^{2} c20g* c16m^{2} c18g* c20g^{F} c20d* Apr 8] leggy gelding: poor maiden hurdler: much improved over fences (reportedly had breathing operation after reappearance): won handicaps at Ludlow in January and April and Newbury (beat Motcomb Jam 1¼ lengths) in March, first 2 novice events: stays 2½m: acts on good to firm and heavy going: tongue tied. *S. A. Brookshaw*   **c115** **h–**

TALEBAN   9 b.g. Alleged (USA) – Triode (USA) (Sharpen Up) [2003/4 c21g^{2} c21g^{5} c21m^{2} c16f^{4} c25g^{3} Mar 10] smallish, angular gelding: one-time fair maiden hurdler: off 20 months, second to Virgin Soldier in novice company over fences at Sedgefield, flattered by proximity both times: stays 21f: acts on good to firm and good to soft going: tried blinkered/in cheekpieces. *J. Wade*   **c87** **h–**

TALE BRIDGE (IRE)   11 b.g. Tale Quale – Loobagh Bridge (River Beauty) [2003/4 c82, h–: c26s^{6} Apr 29] modest hunter chaser: stays 25f. *Mrs O. Bush*   **c–** **h–**

TALES OF BOUNTY (IRE)   9 b.g. Ela-Mana-Mou – Tales of Wisdom (Rousillon (USA)) [2003/4 c124, h114: 24m^{2} 22g^{6} c24g* c24s^{pu} Apr 17] lengthy, useful-looking gelding: fairly useful hurdler: fit from points (successful in February), won hunter chase at Sandown (for R. Barber) in March by 4 lengths from Act In Time: badly let down by jumping final outing: stays 3m: acts on soft and good to firm going: blinkered last 3 starts. *P. F. Nicholls*   **c106** **h121**

TALK ON CORNERS (IRE)   9 b.m. Alphabatim (USA) – Shannon Lass (Callernish) [2003/4 h–, F–: 19m 22g^{pu} Jun 21] of no account. *N. R. Mitchell*   **h–**

TALLAHASSEE (IRE)   6 ch.g. Moscow Society (USA) – Kemperstrat (The Parson) [2003/4 F16v F16s F16d Mar 22] strong gelding: third known foal: dam never ran: well beaten in 3 bumpers. *D. R. MacLeod*   **F–**

TALLDARK'N'ANDSOME   5 b.g. Efisio – Fleur du Val (Valiyar) [2003/4 16s^{2} Dec 3] half-brother to winning hurdler Cromer Pier (by Reprimand), stays 19f: fairly useful on Flat (should stay beyond 1¼m): encouraging 2 lengths second to Kadount in novice at Plumpton on hurdling debut: likely to prove best around 2m. *N. P. Littmoden*   **h101 p**

TALLOW BAY (IRE)   9 b.g. Glacial Storm (USA) – Minimum Choice (IRE) (Miner's Lamp) [2003/4 c99, h–: c20g c22v^{5} c25s^{pu} c24g^{5} c19s^{6} c20v^{6} Apr 4] sturdy gelding: winning chaser: little form in 2003/4: stays 3¼m: acts on heavy going: pulled up on firm: tried blinkered/in cheekpieces. *Mrs S. Wall*   **c–** **h–**

TALL TALE (IRE)   12 b.g. Tale Quale – Prudent Rose (IRE) (Strong Gale) [2003/4 c65§: c26m^{5} Jul 17] tall gelding: poor chaser: probably stays 3½m: acts on good to firm and heavy going: tried blinkered, usually wears visor/cheekpieces nowadays: has had tongue tied: ungenuine. *R. Johnson*   **c– §**

TAMANGO (FR)   7 gr.g. Klimt (FR) – Tipmosa (FR) (Tip Moss (FR)) [2003/4 c110, h112: c18g* c16m* c17g^{2} c17m^{3} c16m^{F} c17m* c16m^{4} Nov 1] leggy, lengthy gelding: fair hurdler: fairly useful chaser: won maiden at Fontwell and intermediate at Hereford   **c123** **h–**

(2/1-on in 5-runner race) in May and handicap at Stratford (by 21 lengths from Ceresfield in 4-runner event) in October: possibly best up to 19f: acts on good to firm and heavy going: blinkered fifth start (running creditably when falling last). *P. J. Hobbs*

TAMARINBLEU (FR) 4 b.g. Epervier Bleu – Tamainia (FR) (Lashkari) [2003/4 16s* 16s² 17v³ 17g 20g Apr 1] angular gelding: fourth foal: half-brother to fairly useful chaser/winning hurdler Tamarindor (by Noir Et Or), stays 23f: dam winning hurdler in France around 2m: easily won juvenile hurdle at Ascot in November on debut: better form when 7 lengths second to Trouble At Bay at Cheltenham: ran poorly 2 of last 3 outings, only third when 10/1-on on first occasion. *M. C. Pipe*   **h121**

TAMBO (IRE) 9 b.g. Shardari – Carmen Lady (Torus) [2003/4 c85, h–: c22m² c23m⁴ c21m* c21s* Mar 19] workmanlike gelding: fair handicap chaser: much improved in 2003/4, winning at Fontwell in May, Uttoxeter in September and Fakenham in March, narrow lead when left clear last in 3-finisher event at last-named: stays 2¾m: acts on soft and good to firm going: takes good hold and usually races prominently. *M. Bradstock*   **c112 h–**

TAM O'SHANTER 10 gr.g. Persian Bold – No More Rosies (Warpath) [2003/4 22g⁵ 24g⁴ Apr 1] neat gelding: poor chaser/modest hurdler early in 2001/2: better effort in selling handicap hurdles after 2½-year absence when fourth in conditional jockeys event at Taunton: stays 27f: acts on firm and soft going: visored (ran creditably) once: sometimes less than fluent. *J. G. M. O'Shea*   **c– h79**

TANAGER 9 ch.g. Carlingford Castle – Tangara (Town Crier) [2003/4 c23g³ Mar 12] workmanlike gelding: fair pointer, won in April: blinkered, weakened 2 out when third of 8 to Eastern Point in maiden hunter chase at Leicester. *Mrs K. Lawther*   **c77**

TANAJI 5 b.m. Marju (IRE) – Hamsaat (IRE) (Sadler's Wells (USA)) [2003/4 16vᵖᵘ Nov 29] fair on Flat (stays 1¼m): lost place quickly after fourth in mares novice at Towcester on hurdling debut: sold 5,500 gns Doncaster January Sales. *P. R. Webber*   **h–**

TANDAWIZI 7 b.m. Relief Pitcher – Arctic Ander (Leander) [2003/4 F16g⁶ May 15] half-sister to several winners, including fair chaser Relkander (by Relkino), stayed 3m: dam, fairly useful chaser from 2m to 3m, half-sister to useful staying chaser McGregor The Third: around 22 lengths sixth of 17 in bumper at Perth on debut. *Mrs L. B. Normile*   **F71**

TANGLIN BLAZE 10 ch.g. Southern Music – Wessex Flyer (Pony Express) [2003/4 16dᵖᵘ Mar 24] failed to complete in 3 maiden points in 2002: tailed off halfway in novice on hurdling debut. *A. J. Chamberlain*   **h–**

TANGO BOJANGLES 6 ch.m. Fraam – Hips'n Haws (IRE) (Thatching) [2003/4 F17d 21dᵖᵘ Mar 16] 600 4-y-o: third foal: dam lightly-raced maiden: half-sister to smart sprinter Eastern Purple: never better than mid-field in bumper at Carlisle on debut: showed nothing in mares novice hurdle 3 weeks later. *N. Wilson*   **h– F–**

TANGO ROYAL (FR) 8 gr.g. Royal Charter (FR) – Nazia (FR) (Zino) [2003/4 c–, h110: 16m* 17m⁴ 22d* 22g² c17g² c16s⁴ c20g² 20d c16dᵘʳ c16m* Apr 15] leggy gelding: fairly useful handicap hurdler: won at Stratford in May and Newton Abbot (4 ran) in July: useful handicap chaser: back to best when winning 15-runner event at Cheltenham in April by 6 lengths from New Bird: effective at 2m to 2¾m: acts on good to firm and heavy going: tongue tied: tends to make mistakes over fences. *M. C. Pipe*   **c136 x h122**

TANIKOS (FR) 5 b.g. Nikos – Tamana (USA) (Northern Baby (CAN)) [2003/4 h100+: 16g c19dF² c19d* c20s² c20d² c22g⁵ Mar 5] big, workmanlike gelding: winning hurdler: fair chaser: won maiden at Hereford in January: better form when second in novices to The Bandit at Plumpton and Flinders Chase at Sandown (headed post) next 2 starts: stays 2½m: acts on soft ground. *N. J. Henderson*   **c111 h–**

TANK BUSTER 4 b.g. Executive Perk – Macfarly (IRE) (Phardante (FR)) [2003/4 F16d⁶ Mar 11] good-topped gelding: first foal: dam placed in Irish points: backward, well beaten in bumper on debut. *Miss E. Hill*   **F–**

TANNERS COURT 7 b.g. Framlington Court – True Nell (Neltino) [2003/4 F88: 20v 20s⁴ 20d⁵ 21d⁵ 20g² 22d³ Mar 21] good-topped gelding: fair novice hurdler: good placed efforts in handicaps at Haydock and Stratford last 2 starts: stays 2¾m: acts on soft going: free-going sort. *Miss C. Dyson*   **h103**

TANNERS FRIEND 7 b.m. Environment Friend – Glenn's Slipper (Furry Glen) [2003/4 h–, F–: 16m 20d⁵ Dec 27] leggy mare: no form. *Miss C. Dyson*   **h–**

TANSHAN 9 ch.g. Anshan – Nafla (FR) (Arctic Tern (USA)) [2003/4 22sᵖᵘ 21gᵖᵘ Mar 17] compact gelding: very lightly-raced hurdler, no show since debut. *R. Rowe*   **h–**

TANTERARI (IRE) 6 b.g. Safety Catch (USA) – Cobblers Crest (IRE) (Step Together (USA)) [2003/4 F16d* c23^{vpu} c26s^F 24m^5 Mar 4] €3,600 4-y-o: second foal: dam ran twice in Irish bumpers: twice-raced in bumpers for D. Ahern, winning at Gowran in December: failed to complete both starts over fences. more encouragement when fifth of 14 to Willie John Daly in novice at Taunton on hurdling debut, travelling smoothly into contention but tiring before last: may prove best short of 3m. *M. C. Pipe* **c? h93 + f97**

TANTICO (IRE) 7 b.g. Lord Americo – Tanti's Last (Ardoon) [2003/4 F16f^4 F16m^5 17d Mar 27] ex-Irish gelding: fifth foal: half-brother to 2m hurdle winner Claramanda (by Mandalus) and bumper winner Levelander (by Commanche Run): dam unraced: fair form in bumpers: left A. Mullins, took good hold when well beaten in novice on hurdling debut: tongue tied last 2 starts in bumpers. *D. J. Wintle* **h– f88**

TARA-BROGAN 11 b.g. Jupiter Island – Princess Semele (Imperial Fling (USA)) [2003/4 c26m^2 c26m^2 Sep 27] rangy gelding: fairly useful chaser, lightly raced: off nearly 2 years prior to second in handicaps at Newton Abbot and Plumpton: stays 3¼m: acts on soft and firm going: usually races prominently: jumps soundly. *Ian Williams* **c118 h–**

TARA'S FLAME 4 ch.g. Blushing Flame (USA) – Lady Emm (Emarati (USA)) [2003/4 16d 16g^{pu} Jan 15] brother to fairly useful hurdler Polish Flame, stays 2½m: modest maiden on Flat (should be suited by 1½m+): favourite on second outing over hurdles, travelling strongly when going lame after 3 out in juvenile seller at Catterick. *Mrs M. Reveley* **h– p**

TARASHANI (IRE) 6 ch.g. Primo Dominie – Tarakana (USA) (Shahrastani (USA)) [2003/4 h73: 17m Sep 5] little sign of ability on Flat: poor maiden hurdler: in cheekpieces, lost action only outing in 2003/4: raced around 2m: acts on heavy going: tried visored. *B. Ellison* **h–**

TARBOLTON MOSS 9 b.m. Le Moss – Priceless Peril (Silly Prices) [2003/4 c107, h–: c25s* c25s c32g^{pu} 20d^6 c31d^{ur} Apr 22] modest hurdler: fair handicap chaser: won at Kelso in January: laboured efforts over fences after: best at 3m+: raced on good going or softer (acts on heavy): usually sound jumper. *M. Todhunter* **c108 h96**

TARBOUSH 7 b.g. Polish Precedent (USA) – Barboukh (Night Shift (USA)) [2003/4 h96+: 16g 16d 21d 16m 16g^4 16g* Apr 18] sturdy gelding: modest hurdler: won 8-runner novice at Wincanton in April: needs sharp 2m: headstrong/has found little. *B. G. Powell* **h96**

TARDAR (NZ) 8 br.g. Prince Ferdinand – La Magnifique (NZ) (Kampala) [2003/4 h121+: 20d 23s* 25g^F Mar 16] angular gelding: useful hurdler: upped in trip and 19 lb out of weights, much improved when winning 18-runner handicap at Haydock in February by 1¾ lengths from Iris's Gift: fell fatally 3 out in valuable handicap at Cheltenham: would have stayed beyond 23f: raced on good going or softer (acted on heavy): tried tongue tied. *Jonjo O'Neill* **h137**

TARENO (GER) 6 b.g. Saddlers' Hall (IRE) – Triclaria (GER) (Surumu (GER)) [2003/4 16g^{pu} Nov 11] smart on Flat (stayed 1½m) for P. Schiergen: broke down in novice hurdle: dead. *B. J. Curley* **h–**

TARN BECK (IRE) 5 b.m. Alderbrook – Skiddaw Samba (Viking (USA)) [2003/4 F17d^{pu} Feb 23] 1,000 3-y-o: first foal: dam poor 2m hurdler: lame on debut. *T. D. Walford* **F–**

TARONGO (FR) 6 b.g. Tel Quel (FR) – Rainbow Rainbow (Vision (USA)) [2003/4 c–, h–: c17g^5 c16m^3 c18m* c17d^{ur} c16d^2 c20d^F Apr 17] poor chaser: won selling handicap at Fontwell in May: not keen but in front when falling last at Plumpton final outing: stays 2½m: acts on good to firm and good to soft going: tried visored: often tongue tied. *Mrs L. C. Taylor* **c82 h–**

TARPON TALE (IRE) 7 b.g. Mujadil (USA) – Lady of The Mist (IRE) (Digamist (USA)) [2003/4 26m^5 c26g^{pu} c25m^4 22f^{ur} c23f^4 Oct 21] ex-Irish gelding: no form on Flat: poor maiden hurdler: little show over fences, including in points: stays 3¼m: acts on good to firm going: visored in 2003/4: one to leave alone. *M. C. Pipe* **c– § h65 §**

TARQUE (IRE) 4 b.g. Revoque (IRE) – Tarquinia (IRE) (In The Wings) [2003/4 16s^{ur} 18v^2 18s^{bd} 17s^2 16g* 17g^{hd} 16g^4 Apr 1] tall, lengthy gelding: second foal: half-brother to French 7.5f and 11f winner Polar Fleet (by Grand Lodge): dam unraced half-sister to useful staying hurdler Tamarpour and Dante Stakes winner Torjoun: lightly-raced maiden on Flat: fairly useful juvenile hurdler: won 17-runner event at Kempton in December by 11 lengths from After Eight, final start for F. Doumen: creditable fourth of 18 to Al Eile in Grade 2 at Aintree: fatally injured at Punchestown later in April: would have stayed beyond 2¼m: raced on good going or softer: tongue tied all starts in Britain/Ireland: free-going sort. *Miss Venetia Williams* **h122**

TARSKI 10 ch.g. Polish Precedent (USA) – Illusory (Kings Lake (USA)) [2003/4 h87: **h95**
16m 20m* 20m^pu 16m 22f² 24f⁴ 19f⁶ Oct 21] smallish gelding: modest handicap hurdler:
won seller at Worcester in July: probably best short of 3m: best form on good to firm/firm
going: usually blinkered/visored, has won when not. *W. S. Kittow*

TARXIEN 10 b.g. Kendor (FR) – Tanz (IRE) (Sadler's Wells (USA)) [2003/4 c150, **c141**
h–: c19d³ c21d^F 20d⁴ 23s 24g 24m⁶ Apr 15] strong, sturdy gelding: useful hurdler/chaser: **h128**
will stay beyond 3m: acts on good to firm and heavy going: tongue tied: not a fluent
jumper of fences. *M. C. Pipe*

TASKMASTER 7 b.g. Alflora (IRE) – Travail Girl (Forties Field (FR)) [2003/4 h105: **c–**
17g 19s⁴ 17d 16g c16d^pu Mar 24] big, rangy gelding: would have made winning debut **h–**
over hurdles in 2002/3 but for falling last: went as if having problems in 2003/4: always
behind on chasing debut: should be suited by further than 2m: sold 2,000 gns Doncaster
May Sales. *P. J. Hobbs*

TASNEEF (USA) 5 b.g. Gulch (USA) – Min Alhawa (USA) (Riverman (USA)) **h78**
[2003/4 17m³ 17s Dec 29] fair on Flat (stays 1¾m), successful in August: failed to see
race out both starts over hurdles. *T. D. McCarthy*

TA TA FOR NOW 7 b.g. Ezzoud (IRE) – Exit Laughing (Shaab) [2003/4 c83, h89: **c78 x**
c20g⁴ c25d⁵ c22g^F c24g c24g c25s^pu 20d^pu 19g 24s³ Apr 21] lengthy gelding: poor **h86**
hurdler/maiden chaser, left P. Beaumont before final start: stays 3m: acts on soft and
good to firm going: tried blinkered: usually let down by jumping over fences. *Mrs
S. C. Bradburne*

TATES AVENUE (IRE) 6 b.g. Zaffaran (USA) – Tate Divinity (IRE) (Tate Gallery **F67**
(USA)) [2003/4 F16v⁶ F16g Mar 15] well-made gelding: second foal: dam, lightly
raced on Flat, half-sister to dam of useful 2m hurdlers Bolino Star and More Dash Thancash: seventh of 8 finishers in maiden Irish point in 2003: poor form in 2 bumpers.
N. A. Twiston-Davies

TAW PARK 10 b.g. Inca Chief (USA) – Parklands Belle (Stanford) [2003/4 17d³ 17g* **h87**
Aug 4] modest hurdler, lightly raced: won steadily-run 4-runner claimer at Newton
Abbot, handed initiative when Governor Daniel hit last: will prove best around 2m.
R. J. Baker

TEAATRAL 10 b.g. Saddlers' Hall (IRE) – La Cabrilla (Carwhite) [2003/4 c–, h–: **c98 §**
c20m* c20g² c20g* c24g^R c25d^R 25d⁵ 16s³ 24g⁶ Feb 28] leggy, good-topped gelding: **h124 ?**
high-class hurdler at best, has deteriorated considerably: modest novice chaser: successful in weak events at Huntingdon in May and Market Rasen in June: refused 3 of 4 other
starts over fences: stays easy 3m: unraced on firm going, acts on any other: usually
blinkered: best efforts on right-handed courses: races prominently: temperamental.
C. R. Egerton

TEACH ALTRA (IRE) 7 b.g. Warcraft (USA) – Miss Pushover (Push On) [2003/4 **c–**
F17s c25d⁵ Feb 17] IR 8,500 4-y-o: ex-Irish gelding: eighth foal: half-brother to winning **F–**
3¼m chaser Heavenly Citizen and winning Irish pointer Push Gently (both by Ovac):
dam unraced half-sister to useful staying chaser Bold Agent: ninth of 14 in bumper at
Killarney (wore cheekpieces) for W. Burke: successful twice in points, in Irish maiden in
2003 and in January: well held in hunter chase at Folkestone. *M. J. Roberts*

TEALBY 7 b.m. Efisio – Al Raja (Kings Lake (USA)) [2003/4 h110: 16g⁵ 16d^pu 16s* **h110**
Jan 21] good-topped mare: fair hurdler: fortunate to win handicap at Fakenham, held in
second when left clear last: will prove best around 2m: acts on soft and good to firm
going. *Mrs L. Wadham*

TEAM CAPTAIN 10 ch.g. Teamster – Silly Sausage (Silly Answer) [2003/4 c99: **c99**
c25g^pu c20g^pu c25g* Apr 3] angular gelding: fair chaser: winning return from 10-month
absence in handicap at Hereford: stays 3½m: acts on firm and good to soft going, pulled
up on soft: has bled, including on second start. *C. J. Down*

TEAM TASSEL (IRE) 6 b.g. Be My Native (USA) – Alcmena's Last (Pauper) **h109 p**
[2003/4 19g* Feb 10] sixth foal: half-brother to winning hurdlers Gorman, at 2¾m, and
One Shot Sheehan (both by Lord Americo), around 2½m: dam never ran: third in maiden
Irish point in 2003: won 16-runner novice at Market Rasen on hurdling debut by 2 lengths
from Rambling Minster, leading after 2 out and quickly clear before being eased: likely
to stay beyond 19f: open to improvement. *M. C. Pipe*

TEA'S MAID 4 b.f. Wizard King – Come To Tea (IRE) (Be My Guest (USA)) [2003/4 **h78 ?**
16v^pu 16d³ 16g⁴ 16g Mar 13] half-sister to winning pointer by Henbit: well held on Flat
for J. Given: poor form in juvenile hurdles. *M. A. Barnes*

TEE-JAY (IRE)   8 ch.g. Un Desperado (FR) – N T Nad (Welsh Pageant) [2003/4 c88, h99: 24g* 20g* 20v 25gᵖᵘ 24d 20d⁴ Apr 10] workmanlike gelding: made mistakes over fences: fair handicap hurdler: won at Hexham in May and Southwell in December: stays 3m: raced mainly on good going or softer (acts on soft). *M. D, Hammond*   **c–ʜ107**

TEENAGER   4 b.f. Young Ern – Washita (Valiyar) [2003/4 F16d⁵ F17d Mar 27] sixth foal: half-sister to winner up to 1¾m Los Alamos (by Keen) and 1994 2-y-o 7f winner Last Roundup (by Good Times): dam poor maiden half-sister to high-class stayer Dakota and useful stayer Warpath: poor form on first of 2 outings in bumpers: sold 4,800 gns Doncaster January Sales in between. *P. Wegmann*   **F71**

TEENO ROSSI (IRE)   6 b.m. Teenoso (USA) – Mistress Ross (Impecunious) [2003/4 F16f⁴ F16s F17s F16s 21d 24sᵖᵘ Apr 4] 1,200 4-y-o: small, lightly-made mare: second foal: dam modest staying hurdler: signs of ability only in bumper at Hexham on debut. *J. R. Norton*   **h– F75 ?**

TEES COMPONENTS   9 b.g. Risk Me (FR) – Lady Warninglid (Ela-Mana-Mou) [2003/4 h141+: 22m* May 7] strong gelding: useful up to 2m on Flat, well held only outing in 2003: useful hurdler: 7/1-on, easily won intermediate at Kelso: stays 3m: acts on soft and good to firm going: tends to edge left under pressure. *Mrs M. Reveley*   **h120 +**

TEFI   6 ch.g. Efisio – Masuri Kabisa (USA) (Ascot Knight (CAN)) [2003/4 h–: 20gᵖᵘ 17g 17g Jun 11] modest on Flat (best form at 6f to 1m) in 2003: no form in 4 starts over hurdles: tongue tied in 2003/4. *S. R. Bowring*   **h–**

TELEMOSS (IRE)   10 b.g. Montelimar (USA) – Shan's Moss (Le Moss) [2003/4 c125p, h–: c20s³ c21dᵖᵘ Jan 24] useful-looking gelding: one-time smart hurdler: fairly useful chaser: off 10 months after reportedly suffering knee injury, travelled strongly to 2 out when third to Iris Royal in valuable handicap at Cheltenham: ran as if amiss there next time: stays 3m: acts on good to firm and heavy going. *N. G. Richards*   **c126 h–**

TELL HER OFF   4 b.f. Reprimand – My Valentina (Royal Academy (USA)) [2003/4 16m 16d 21d 19m 23s Apr 4] half-sister to winning hurdler around 2m Ashton Vale (by Ashkalani): poor maiden on Flat (ran below difficult ride): well held over hurdles, including in seller: wore cheekpieces last 3 starts. *Miss Victoria Roberts*   **h–**

TELL ME WHY (IRE)   8 b.g. Roselier (FR) – Clonarctic Slave (Sir Mordred) [2003/4 c110, h–: c24s² Feb 11] long good-topped gelding: fifth in novice hurdle on debut in 2001/2: fair form when runner-up in 2 novice chases over a year apart, jumping sketchily on second occasion: will stay beyond 3m: clearly difficult to train. *P. R. Webber*   **c106 h–**

TELL TALE (IRE)   12 b.g. Tale Quale – Loobagh Bridge (River Beauty) [2003/4 c28dᵖᵘ c23vᵖᵘ c24m² c26d⁶ c25g² c23m² Apr 13] fair hunter chaser: stays 25f: acts on good to firm going. *J. G. Cann*   **c94 +**

TELMAR FLYER   7 b.m. Neltino – Flying Mistress (Lear Jet) [2003/4 h–, F–: 16g⁵ 16f⁵ 16f⁵ 16dᵇᵈ 17sᵖᵘ Jan 2] lengthy mare: of little account, left J. Cullinan after second start: tongue tied last 3. *P. R. Webber*   **h–**

TEME VALLEY   10 br.g. Polish Precedent (USA) – Sudeley (Dancing Brave (USA)) [2003/4 h99§: 18g⁶ c16s⁵ 16m 16d 20m³ 17s* c16d* 17g* Apr 12] leggy gelding: fair handicap hurdler: won at Sedgefield in December and April (tenth course win), beating Untidy Daughter on both occasions: easily better effort over fences when successful in maiden at same course in March: stays easy 2½m: acts on soft and good to firm going, possibly not on heavy: effective tongue tied or not. *J. Howard Johnson*   **c88 + ʜ110**

TEMPER LAD (USA)   9 b.g. Riverman (USA) – Dokki (USA) (Northern Dancer) [2003/4 h82: 24s 21g⁵ 23s Apr 4] neat gelding: has had wind operation: poor hurdler nowadays, off 20 months prior to reappearance: stays 2¾m: acts on soft going, probably on firm: tried blinkered: tongue tied. *J. Joseph*   **h74**

TEMPLEBREEDY (IRE)   10 br.g. Torenaga – Points Review (Major Point) [2003/4 c20dᵖᵘ Mar 25] fair pointer, won in March: had too much use made of him in hunter chase at Ludlow. *Mrs Edward Crow*   **c–**

TEMPLE DOG (IRE)   8 ch.g. Un Desperado (FR) – Shower (Kings Lake (USA)) [2003/4 h122p: c20d³ c20v* c23vᵖᵘ 20d⁶ 24s Mar 20] workmanlike gelding: fairly useful hurdler: won novice chase at Uttoxeter in January, dismal efforts both other starts over fences: should stay beyond 2½m: raced on going softer than good (acts on heavy): blinkered last 2 starts: ungenuine: sold 12,000 gns Doncaster May Sales. *T. P. Tate*   **c110 § ʜ115 §**

TEMPLELUSK (IRE)   6 ch.g. Over The River (FR) – Leafy Moss (Le Moss) [2003/4 F16d* Dec 6] half-brother to fair staying chaser Jimmy The Lark and fair hurdler up to 3m Casey Jane (both by Mandalus): dam unraced: won maiden bumper at Punchestown   **F109 p**

TEM

on debut by 4 lengths from Afistfullofdollars, travelling strongly long way and shaken up to go clear over 1f out: bred to be suited by much further than 2m: good prospect. *W. P. Mullins, Ireland*

TEMPLE OF ARTEMIS 5 b.h. Spinning World (USA) – Casessa (USA) (Caro) **h–**
[2003/4 26g Nov 9] fairly useful 7f winner at 2 yrs in Ireland, left A. O'Brien after final 3-y-o start and well beaten since: tailed off in novice on hurdling debut. *P. A. Blockley*

TENDER TOUCH (IRE) 9 gr.m. Weldnaas (USA) – Moments Peace (Adonijah) **c73**
[2003/4 c63, h67: c16g² c16g c16m⁴ c17m* c20dᵘʳ c17m³ c21d² c17g⁴ c17g⁶ Sep 12] **h–**
leggy mare: winning hurdler: poor novice handicap chaser: won at Southwell in June: stays 19f: acts on heavy and good to firm going. *Miss Kate Milligan*

TENNANT CREEK (IRE) 6 b.g. Lord Americo – Coolstuff (Over The River (FR)) **h–**
[2003/4 F17m⁴ 22dᵖᵘ 18f⁴ Aug 22] IR £14,000 3-y-o: sixth foal: brother to one-time **F78**
fairly useful chaser up to 3m Yankie Lord: dam, winning Irish pointer, half-sister to useful staying chaser Imperial Black: left E. Hales, better effort in bumpers when fourth of 16 at Hereford: no show either start over hurdles. *Miss E. C. Lavelle*

TEN PAST SIX 12 ch.g. Kris – Tashinsky (USA) (Nijinsky (CAN)) [2003/4 20vᵖᵘ Jan **c–**
21] angular gelding: maiden hurdler: no form over fences: sometimes visored/blinkered. **h–**
R. C. Guest

TEN PRESSED MEN (FR) 4 b.g. Video Rock (FR) – Recolte d'Estruval (FR) **F95**
(Kouban (FR)) [2003/4 F16g³ F17d Apr 3] good-topped gelding: fifth foal: half-brother to bumper winner Lin d'Estruval (by Cadoudal) and 11f winner Grain d'Estruval (by Tropular): dam winner up to 11f on Flat, won around 2m over hurdles and fences in France: close third of 18 to Toemac in bumper at Kempton on debut: well held in Grade 2 at Aintree. *Jonjo O'Neill*

TENSHOOKMEN (IRE) 10 ch.g. Cardinal Flower – April Rise (Prominer) [2003/4 **c99**
c100: c22d c16d⁵ c20d c21d 22s⁶ c21g Apr 2] strong gelding: fair handicap chaser: **h–**
generally below form in 2003/4: well beaten only outing over hurdles: best form up to 2½m: acts on soft and good to firm going: tried blinkered. *W. F. Codd, Ireland*

TENSILE (IRE) 9 b.g. Tenby – Bonnie Isle (Pitcairn) [2003/4 c119, h128: 23m⁵ May **c–**
3] compact gelding: not fluent in novice chases but won twice in early-2002/3: fairly **h120**
useful handicap hurdler: not discredited when fifth to Persian Waters in quite valuable event at Haydock: stays 3m: acts on any going: has had tongue tied: held up. *P. J. Hobbs*

TENTSMUIR 8 b.m. Arctic Lord – Deep Pier (Deep Run) [2003/4 h72: 22g 24m² **h72**
20mᶠ 22dᵖᵘ 20g 24gᵖᵘ 27f⁵ Feb 29] sparely-made mare: poor novice hurdler: stays 3m: acts on good to firm going (won bumper on soft). *D. W. Whillans*

TEORBAN (POL) 5 b.g. Don Corleone – Tabaka (POL) (Pyjama Hunt) [2003/4 h80: **h90**
16m⁴ 21m³ 20m 20vᵖᵘ 21s³ 24vᵖᵘ 20s⁶ 26g⁶ Mar 6] fair on Flat, successful twice over 2m on all-weather in 2003: novice hurdler, apparently best effort when third in handicap at Huntingdon fifth start: stays 21f: acts on soft going: has looked hard ride. *M. Pitman*

TERDAD (USA) 11 ch.g. Lomond (USA) – Istiska (FR) (Irish River (FR)) [2003/4 **c– §**
c–§, h82§: 26g² 24g⁴ 24g² 22m² 26m³ 26m³ 24f² 27d² 24sᵖᵘ 21v⁶ 26s Feb 12] big, **h88 §**
rangy gelding: no form over fences: modest hurdler: on long losing run, though mostly creditable efforts in handicaps in 2003/4, left M. Chapman after fourth start: stays 27f, effective at much shorter: acts on any going: best in headgear: ungenuine. *J. G. Given*

TEREK (GER) 8 ch.g. Irish River (FR) – Turbaine (USA) (Trempolino (USA)) **c101**
[2003/4 h100: 17s⁴ 17m* 17m² 16d⁶ c20g⁴ c16mᵘʳ c16d* c18gᶠ Mar 27] leggy, close- **h100**
coupled gelding: fair hurdler: won maiden at Cartmel in July: easily best effort over fences when winning 7-runner maiden at Taunton in March: held when falling heavily 2 out final start: best around 2m: acts on soft and good to firm going: free-going sort. *R. T. Phillips*

TERIDOVE 7 b.g. Terimon – Flakey Dove (Oats) [2003/4 F–: 16mᵖᵘ Jun 1] no show **h–**
in bumpers or novice hurdle. *A. E. Price*

TERIMONS DAUGHTER 5 b.m. Terimon – Fun While It Lasts (Idiot's Delight) **F–**
[2003/4 F17m Oct 10] 5,200 4-y-o: medium-sized mare: first foal: dam, modest 2m novice hurdler, half-sister to useful staying chaser Sail By The Stars: well held in bumper on debut. *E. W. Tuer*

TERINO 8 b.g. Terimon – Ashmo (Ashmore (FR)) [2003/4 h–: 20gᶠ 20m May 26] **h–**
lengthy gelding: no form over hurdles: sold £1,300 Ascot October Sales: in frame in maiden points. *A. E. Jessop*

TERIVIC 4 br.g. Terimon – Ludoviciana (Oats) [2003/4 F16d³ F16d Mar 28] compact gelding: third foal: dam winning pointer: better effort in bumpers when 17 lengths third of 8 to The Sawyer at Towcester: pulls hard. *J. W. Payne* **F82**

TERMINOLOGY 6 gr.g. Terimon – Rhyming Moppet (Rymer) [2003/4 F16v¹ F16d⁴ Mar 19] 10,000 4-y-o: first foal: brother to bumper winner Ferimon: dam winning pointer: fourth both starts in bumpers, better effort when beaten 3 lengths by Real Definition in 19-runner maiden at Warwick on second occasion: bred to stay beyond 2m. *K. C. Bailey* **F88**

TERN INTERN (IRE) 5 b. or br.g. Dr Devious (IRE) – Arctic Bird (USA) (Storm Bird (CAN)) [2003/4 16m 16m Jun 18] of little account on Flat nowadays: jumped poorly and looked tricky ride over hurdles: tried in cheekpieces. *Miss J. Feilden* **h–**

TERRE DE JAVA (FR) 6 b.g. Cadoudal (FR) – Terre d'Argent (FR) (Count Ivor (USA)) [2003/4 20m² 20d 20d² 16d³ Apr 21] ex-French gelding: fourth foal: brother to 2¾m cross-contry chase winner Terre d'Ivoire: dam won twice over fences up to 2½m in France: fair novice hurdler, formerly trained by F. Rohaut: better suited by 2½m than 2m: acts on good to firm and heavy going. *Mrs H. Dalton* **h108**

TERRIBLE TENANT 5 gr.g. Terimon – Rent Day (Town And Country) [2003/4 20d 16dᵖᵘ Jan 17] good-topped gelding: first foal: dam, poor maiden hurdler/chaser who stayed 3m, sister to one-time useful chaser up to 3m The Land Agent: no show in 2 novice hurdles. *J. W. Mullins* **h–**

TESTIFY (IRE) 11 b.g. Montelimar (USA) – Test Drive (Crash Course) [2003/4 h117: 22g⁴ 22f Aug 30] fair handicap hurdler: much better effort in 2003/4 when fourth at Cork: stays 3m: has won on soft going, best efforts on good or firmer (acts on firm): tongue tied. *M. J. O'Connor, Ireland* **h114**

TEST OF FAITH 5 b.g. Weld – Gold Pigeon (IRE) (Goldhill) [2003/4 F16d Apr 23] first foal: dam poor staying chaser: behind in bumper on debut. *J. N. R. Billinge* **F–**

TEST OF FRIENDSHIP 7 br.g. Roselier (FR) – Grease Pot (Gala Performance) [2003/4 F16s 22sᵖᵘ c24d³ Mar 27] half-brother to winning hurdler/chaser Welsh Lustre (by Mandalus), stayed 3¼m: dam lightly-raced sister to smart staying chaser Greasepaint: no show in bumper or novice hurdle for I. Williams: led 4 out until approaching last when third of 5 finishers in novice at Bangor on chasing debut: will stay beyond 3m. *Mrs H. Dalton* **c87** **h–** **F–**

TEST OF LOYALTY 10 b.g. Niniski (USA) – River Chimes (Forlorn River) [2003/4 c83, h–: c20s⁵ c16mᵖᵘ c17g⁶ c16dᵖᵘ Nov 25] workmanlike gelding: winning chaser, no form in 2003/4: ideally suited by around 2m: acts on soft going. *J. N. R. Billinge* **c–** **h–**

TEST THE WATER (IRE) 10 ch.g. Maelstrom Lake – Baliana (CAN) (Riverman (USA)) [2003/4 17d⁶ 20m⁵ Jun 1] half-brother to winning staying hurdler Danzante (by Ajraas): poor and ungenuine on Flat (stays 1¼m) nowadays: no show in 2 novice hurdles: tried tongue tied. *Dr J. R. J. Naylor* **h–**

TETRAGON (IRE) 4 b.g. Octagonal (NZ) – Viva Verdi (IRE) (Green Desert (USA)) [2003/4 16m 16g⁴ 17m⁵ 16m⁴ 16s⁶ 16v 16gᵖᵘ Feb 18] compact gelding: fair on Flat (barely stays 1½m), claimed from K. Burke after winning in June: little show over hurdes: usually wears blinkers/cheekpieces and tongue strap. *Miss Lucinda V. Russell* **h–**

THAI LA 4 gr. or ro.g. Rashik – Bonyalua Mill (Chilibang) [2003/4 17gᵖᵘ 18g⁵ 16sᵖᵘ Dec 19] second foal: dam 6f winner: showed nothing in 3 starts over hurdles. *Mrs J. Candlish* **h–**

THALYS (GER) 6 bl.g. Gold And Ivory (USA) – Tachira (Faraway Times (USA)) [2003/4 h96: c16mᵖᵘ c17m⁶ c16m² c17g* c17m³ c19d* Feb 15] good-topped gelding: modest hurdler: similar standard over fences, won novice handicaps at Southwell in September and Hereford in February: sold out of Mrs H. Dalton's stable 8,000 gns Doncaster October Sales before latter: stays 19f: acts on good to firm and good to soft going: usually tongue tied prior to final start. *N. A. Graham* **c99** **h–**

THAMES (IRE) 6 b.g. Over The River (FR) – Aon Dochas (IRE) (Strong Gale) [2003/4 F96: 20d³ 24gᵖᵘ Apr 2] strong, lengthy gelding: better effort in bumpers in 2002/3 when fourth in Grade 2 at Aintree: 14½ lengths third of 10 to Inglis Drever in novice at same course on hurdling debut: very stiff task and sweating, tailed off when pulled up 3 out in Grade 1 novice there over 4 months later: likely to prove best at 2½m+. *N. J. Henderson* **h105**

THARI (USA) 7 b. or br.g. Silver Hawk (USA) – Magic Slipper (Habitat) [2003/4 c122, h–: c25g c22s c24gᶠ c29d Apr 12] good-topped gelding: one-time useful hurdler: **c125** **h–**

fairly useful chaser: form in 2003/4 only when seventh of 22 to Nearly A Moose in 2¾m Galway Plate in July: acts on heavy ground, probably on good to firm: tried blinkered: has had tongue tied. *N. Meade, Ireland*

THATCHERS LONGSHOT 7 ch.g. Gunner B – Formidable Lady (Formidable (USA)) [2003/4 F–: c24d⁵ c24s⁴ 20v c24g⁴ Feb 11] strong gelding: no form outside points. *S. A. Brookshaw* — c– h–

THATS ALL JAZZ 6 b.m. Prince Sabo – Gate of Heaven (Starry Night (USA)) [2003/4 16m 16sᵖᵘ Feb 12] poor and unreliable on Flat (stays easy 1m): no show in selling or claiming hurdles. *C. R. Dore* — h–

THAT'S AN IDEA (IRE) 6 b.g. Arctic Lord – Annsgrove Polly (IRE) (Pollerton) [2003/4 F18s⁵ F20d* Mar 17] second foal: dam ran twice: successful on second of 2 starts in points: useful form when winning bumpers at Clonmel in February and Limerick in March, made all and stayed on strongly to beat Rosadare 1½ lengths in 9-runner event at latter: will stay 3m: joined D. Wachman: promising. *Ms Margaret Mullins, Ireland* — F106

THATSFOREEL 11 b.g. Scottish Reel – That Space (Space King) [2003/4 c88: c25d⁴ Apr 30] fair pointer in 2003: winning hunter chaser: stays 25f: acts on good to soft going: tried blinkered: has looked ungenuine. *Miss Joanne Tremain* — c77

THE ALLEYCAT (IRE) 13 b.g. Tidaro (USA) – Allitess (Mugatpura) [2003/4 c83, h71: c16m³ c17g⁴ 22mᵖᵘ c21g² 19g c21g⁵ c16m⁶ c19m² c18g* c17g⁴ c16m⁶ c16m⁴ c20g⁴ c19mᵖᵘ Apr 13] maiden over hurdles: poor handicap chaser: won weak amateur event at Fontwell in November: stays easy 21f: raced mainly on good going or firmer (acts on firm): tried in cheekpieces: races prominently. *R. Ford* — c81 h–

THEATRE CALL (IRE) 6 b.g. Old Vic – Jennycomequick (Furry Glen) [2003/4 F85: F16g⁶ 22sᵖᵘ 16g 16s 22gᵖᵘ Apr 10] rather unfurnished gelding: fair form both outings in bumpers: little show over hurdles. *J. A. B. Old* — h84 ? F88

THEATRE GROOM (USA) 5 ch.g. Theatrical – Model Bride (USA) (Blushing Groom (FR)) [2003/4 F16m² F16m⁸ F17mᵖᵘ Aug 25] 27,000 4-y-o: seventh living foal: half-brother to 3 winners, including useful milers Arabride (by Unfuwain) and Mediterraneo (by Be My Guest), latter also successful over hurdles: dam unraced half-sister to smart miler Zaizafon, dam of Zafonic, and to dam of very smart middle-distance performers Reams of Verse and Elmaamul: promising start in bumpers, won 21-runner event at Worcester in August by ½ length from Dark Whisper, again edging left: went lame next time. *Mrs G. Harvey* — F99

THE BAILLIE (IRE) 5 b.g. Castle Keep – Regular Dolan (IRE) (Regular Guy) [2003/4 F17d⁵ Mar 27] fourth foal: dam unraced half-sister to useful chaser up to 3m Regular Time: around 10 lengths fifth of 18 to Pearly Bay in bumper at Bangor on debut. *C. R. Egerton* — F93

THE BAJAN BANDIT (IRE) 9 b.g. Commanche Run – Sunrise Highway VII (Damsire Unregistered) [2003/4 c129, h–: 23m 25dᵖᵘ 20v* 25gᵖᵘ Mar 16] medium-sized gelding: fairly useful chaser: useful handicap hurdler: easily won at Ayr in January, beating Crystal Gift 6 lengths: on heels of leaders when pulled up (for fourth time in last 6 starts) after 3 out in valuable event at Cheltenham (reportedly lost action): stays 2¾m: acts on heavy ground: sketchy jumper of fences. *L. Lungo* — c– h137

THE BANDIT (IRE) 7 b.g. Un Desperado (FR) – Sweet Friendship (Alleging (USA)) [2003/4 h88*: 22g 20m* 20g⁶ c20s* c20s* c20mᵖᵘ c20g² c20m³ Apr 23] useful-looking gelding: modest hurdler: improved form when winning handicap at Ascot easily in November: much better form again in novice chases, winning at Huntingdon (made all) in December and Plumpton in January: placed in handicaps last 2 starts, 5 lengths second to Keltic Bard in amateur event at Aintree and third of 4 to Biliverdin at Sandown: should stay beyond 2½m: acts on soft and good to firm going. *Miss E. C. Lavelle* — c128 h99 +

THE BARGE 11 b.g. Un Desperado (FR) – Marble Owen (Master Owen) [2003/4 c64, h–: c26gᵖᵘ May 18] poor novice chaser: stays 3¼m: acts on heavy ground, probably on good to firm: sometimes blinkered. *J. White* — c– h–

THE BAR MAID 6 b.m. Alderbrook – Corny Story (Oats) [2003/4 F17m F17m F16m⁶ 16g 21s² 22sᵖᵘ 21dᵖᵘ 21d² 23s 19s² Apr 11] 12,000 4-y-o: leggy mare: half-sister to several winners, including fairly useful chaser Cornet (by Coquelin), stayed 3m: dam, 11f winner, half-sister to useful French chaser up to 2¾m Timoleon and smart sprinter Petipa: little worthwhile form in bumpers: modest novice hurdler: stays 21f: acts on soft going: fee going sort. *Mrs G. Harvey* — h88 F70 ?

THE BATTLIN BISHOP 5 br.g. Bishop of Cashel – Angel Drummer (Dance In F–
Time (CAN)) [2003/4 F16d Apr 12] useful-looking gelding: half-brother to 3 minor
winners on Flat: dam, 2-y-o 7f winner, later successful over hurdles: last of 18 in bumper
on debut. *Ian Williams*

THE BAY BRIDGE (IRE) 5 b. or br.g. Over The River (FR) – Alamo Bay (Torenaga) F– p
[2003/4 F16s Mar 20] €13,500 4-y-o: fifth foal: dam of little account: looked to need
experience when well held in bumper at Ascot on debut: type to do better. *Miss
E. C. Lavelle*

THE BEANFIELD (IRE) 5 b.g. Good Thyne (USA) – Carry Me (IRE) (Lafontaine F–
(USA)) [2003/4 F18s Feb 16] first foal: dam never ran: tailed off in bumper on debut.
J. W. Mullins

THEBELLINNBROADWAY 4 b.f. El Conquistador – Ten Deep (Deep Run) F80
[2003/4 F17g⁴ Apr 10] fifth foal: dam, poor novice hurdler, barely stayed 3m: 17 lengths
fourth to Honan in 16-runner maiden bumper at Newton Abbot on debut. *S. C. Burrough*

THE BIG'UN 10 b.g. Green-Fingered – Lismore (Relkino) [2003/4 c84: c24m May c–
5] good-bodied gelding: lightly-raced novice chaser, poor on balance of form: stays 3m:
blinkered last 3 starts: often looks less than keen: sold £2,800 gns Ascot June Sales.
G. L. Moore

THE BIKER (IRE) 7 br.g. Arctic Lord – Glenravel (Lucifer (USA)) [2003/4 h123p: h–
21m 16dpu 16d 22d⁴ 16dᶠ 22sᵖᵘ 19g Apr 16] tall, workmanlike gelding: successful first 2
starts over hurdles: off a year, most disappointing in handicaps in 2003/4 (tried visored):
should stay beyond 17f: acts on heavy going: not a fluent jumper: sold 6,500 gns Doncaster May Sales. *M. C. Pipe*

THE BISCUIT 10 ch.m. Nomadic Way (USA) – Not To Worry (USA) (Steward) h–
[2003/4 h–: 20m⁴ 24g 20d 22g⁶ Mar 28] lightly raced and little sign of ability, flattered on
reappearance: often tongue tied. *B. Mactaggart*

THE BOMBERS MOON 11 br.g. Lord Bud – Oakington (Henry The Seventh) c–
[2003/4 c22g May 24] good-bodied gelding: no form outside points (won maiden in h–
2003). *Mrs C. H. Covell*

THE BONGO MAN (IRE) 11 b.g. Be My Native (USA) – Fight For It (Strong Gale) c91
[2003/4 c–, h95: 24m⁵ c18g c20s⁵ 20s c16vᵘʳ 20d 16d Apr 10] lengthy gelding: winning h82
hurdler/chaser, modest at best nowadays: left D. Wintle after first outing: stays 3m: acts
on any going: tried in cheekpieces: has had tongue tied. *Lindsay Woods, Ireland*

THE BOSUN 7 b.g. Charmer – Sailors Joy (Handsome Sailor) [2003/4 F76: F16m F–
F16m May 26] workmanlike gelding: poor in bumpers: tried tongue tied. *A. E. Jessop*

THE BOUNDER 14 b.g. Uncle Pokey – Young Romance (King's Troop) [2003/4 c–
c24gᶠ May 31] lengthy gelding: veteran chaser: modest pointer nowadays: stays 25f: acts h–
on firm and good to soft going: blinkered once: races prominently. *A. J. Tizzard*

THE BOYS IN GREEN (IRE) 7 b.g. Shernazar – Mursuma (Rarity) [2003/4 c85
h113p: F16s* 18d* 16d² 19dᵖᵘ 16d⁵ c21s c18d Feb 28] won bumper at Ballinrobe and h110
minor event over hurdles at Navan (beat Florida Coast 3 lengths) in May: came second to F94
Rockstown Boy in novice hurdle at Tralee third start, disappointing subsequently, including over fences: raced mainly around 2m, only on good to soft/soft going. *C. Roche,
Ireland*

THE BUNNY BOILER (IRE) 10 b.g. Tremblant – Danny's Charm (IRE) (Arapahos c– x
(FR)) [2003/4 c–x, h129: 20s c24sᵖᵘ c21g c36d Apr 3] tall, useful-looking gelding: fairly h–
useful hurdler/useful chaser at best, has completely lost his way: stays 4¼m: best on
going softer than good (acts on heavy): tried blinkered: often let down by jumping over
fences. *N. Meade, Ireland*

THE BUTTERWICK KID 11 ch.g. Interrex (CAN) – Ville Air (Town Crier) [2003/4 c101
c25d⁴ c25m* c22s³ c24s* c21g c24s³ Apr 17] neat gelding: fairly useful chaser h– §
nowadays: won in small fields at Wetherby in May and Newcastle (by 12 lengths from
Primitive Way) in March: stays 25f: acts on good to firm and heavy ground: usually
visored/blinkered. *T. P. Tate*

THE BYEDEIN (IRE) 7 b.m. Alflora (IRE) – Southern Squaw (Buckskin (FR)) c80
[2003/4 h72, F72: c21sᵖᵘ c22s³ Jan 16] poor maiden hurdler: much better effort over h–
fences when third in mares novice at Kelso: stays 3m: acts on soft going.
A. H. Mactaggart

THE CHAIN GANG 11 b.g. Baron Blakeney – Delvin Princess (Aglojo) [2003/4 c–
c25d^{pu} Apr 30] modest pointer, successful twice in 2003: little show in hunter chase.
N. Thomas

c–

THE COCKNEY KID (IRE) 9 ch.g. Glacial Storm (USA) – Rainbow Days (Sunyboy) [2003/4 19s^{pu} 17m Mar 9] very lightly raced over hurdles, no show in sellers in
2003/4. *N. A. Twiston-Davies*

h–

THE COLLECTOR (IRE) 5 ch.g. Forest Wind (USA) – Glowing Reeds (Kalaglow)
[2003/4 F16m⁴ F16v Feb 4] second foal: dam little worthwhile form on Flat: little show
in 2 bumpers, sold out of M. Pipe's stable 2,800 gns Doncaster November Sales after
debut. *N. P. McCormack*

F–

THE COUNT (FR) 5 b.g. Sillery (USA) – Dear Countess (FR) (Fabulous Dancer
(USA)) [2003/4 h–: 17g⁴ 17m⁴ 16m⁶ 17g^{rtr} Aug 25] poor maiden hurdler: refused to
race final outing (also difficult at start time before): headstrong: one to leave alone.
F. P. Murtagh

h65 §

THE CROOKED OAK 12 ch.g. Fearless Action (USA) – Life Goes On (Pharly (FR))
[2003/4 c–, h–: 24d^{pu} 24g^{pu} Aug 16] tall gelding: poor chaser/novice hurdler, lame final
outing: stays 25f. *K. S. Thomas*

c–
h–

THE CROPPY BOY 12 b.g. Arctic Lord – Deep Cut (Deep Run) [2003/4 c–x, h–:
24g⁶ 24m^{pu} Sep 14] angular gelding: of little account nowadays. *Mrs N. S. Sharpe*

c– x
h–

THE CULDEE (IRE) 8 ch.g. Phardante (FR) – Deep Inagh (Deep Run) [2003/4
h121: c16d c17s⁴ c16d c17s c20d⁴ c20s* Apr 4] stocky gelding: fairly useful handicap
hurdler at best: fair chaser: won handicap at Tramore in April: good fifth to Wotsitooya in
similar event at Punchestown later in month: stays 25f: acts on heavy going. *F. Flood,
Ireland*

c112
h–

THE DARK FLASHER (IRE) 7 b.g. Lucky Guest – Perpignan (Rousillon (USA))
[2003/4 h118: 16m 16d⁶ 16g⁵ c16g² c16m² c17g³ c16d⁶ c17s^{bd} c17s⁵ Dec 29] leggy
gelding: fair hurdler/maiden chaser: raced around 2m: acts on good to firm and heavy
going: often finds little. *C. F. Swan, Ireland*

c105
h113

THE DARK LORD (IRE) 7 b.g. Lord Americo – Khalkeys Shoon (Green Shoon)
[2003/4 h88: 20m* 21g^F 20g* 21g⁴ 19g³ 20s^F Mar 13] lengthy gelding: fair hurdler: won
maiden at Worcester (easily) in June and novice at Haydock in November: will stay 3m:
acts on good to firm going. *Mrs L. Wadham*

h114

THE DELL (IRE) 11 b.g. Denel (FR) – Rocks Rose (Little Buskins) [2003/4 c125,
h–: c25d^{ur} c22s³ May 12] well-made gelding: fairly useful handicap chaser: creditable
third to Dromhale Lady at Killarney in May, not seen out again: stays 25f: acts on good to
firm and heavy going: consistent. *Miss F. M. Crowley, Ireland*

c123
h–

THE DREAM LIVES ON (IRE) 8 ch.g. Phardante (FR) – Rare Dream (Pollerton)
[2003/4 22g⁴ 21v^{pu} Nov 23] no form in 3 races over hurdles, off 2 years before reappearance. *T. P. McGovern*

h–

THE EENS 12 b.g. Rakaposhi King – Snippet (Ragstone) [2003/4 c–, h–: c24g⁶ c22g⁵
c20s⁵ 19v^{pu} c24d^{pu} 27d^{pu} Mar 16] rather leggy, close-coupled gelding: winning hurdler/
chaser, retains little ability: tried in headgear. *D. McCain*

c–
h–

THE EXTRA MAN (IRE) 10 b.g. Sayaarr (USA) – Chez Georges (Welsh Saint)
[2003/4 c20s³ c20d² c24d⁶ c21d^F c20g* Mar 17] tall gelding: one-time fairly useful
handicap hurdler: fair novice chaser, off nearly 20 months prior to reappearance: won at
Huntingdon by short head from Sossus Vlei: stays 3m: acts on any going: blinkered:
usually makes running. *M. J. Ryan*

c107
h–

THE FAIRY FLAG (IRE) 6 ch.m. Inchinor – Good Reference (IRE) (Reference
Point) [2003/4 h–: 16g³ 16s 16d^{pu} Mar 18] neat mare: fair on Flat, won twice in 2003:
disappointing hurdler: not sure to stay much beyond 2m: acts on good to soft
going: tried blinkered, wore cheekpieces in 2003/4. *A. Bailey*

h83

THE FENMAN 6 b.g. Mazaad – Dalgorian (IRE) (Lancastrian) [2003/4 h77: 20g⁶
26s 21g⁵ 19g⁴ 19d³ Mar 22] leggy gelding: poor maiden hurdler: stays 21f: acts on soft
going: blinkered last 3 runs in 2002/3, wore cheekpieces last 3 in 2003/4. *R. J. Armson*

h63

THE FLYER (IRE) 7 b.g. Blues Traveller (IRE) – National Ballet (Shareef Dancer
(USA)) [2003/4 h109: 20m 20d 22d^{pu} 24d 22d⁶ 22g 24s⁵ Apr 17] leggy gelding: fair
handicap hurdler: generally well below best in 2003/4: stays 2¾m: acts on heavy going:
unbeaten in 3 starts at Hereford: not an easy ride. *Miss S. J. Wilton*

h103 d

Pertemps 'Fighting Fifth' Hurdle, Newcastle—The French Furze (left) finally gets his head in front after finishing second in the race three times; Geos will also overtake the flagging Intersky Falcon

THE FRENCH FURZE (IRE) 10 ch.g. Be My Guest (USA) – Exciting (Mill Reef (USA)) [2003/4 c106, h139: 16f 20m* 16d* 16s 23s⁵ 20d³ 21g 20d 16d⁴ Apr 17] leggy, close-coupled gelding: won first of 2 starts in novice chases at Sedgefield in 2002/3, tending to jump left: smart hurdler: won handicap at Ayr and Pertemps Fighting Fifth Hurdle at Newcastle (back to best to beat Geos ¾ length after leaders went for home too soon) in November: failed to make much of an impact subsequently: stays 21f: acts on heavy and good to firm going: has worn blinkers (jumped and hung markedly left when last tried in them): effective ridden from front or held up. *N. G. Richards*   c– h146

THE FRIDGE 6 ch.g. Karinga Bay – Sovereign Maiden (Nearly A Hand) [2003/4 F18s² F16s² Mar 20] 6,500 4-y-o: fourth foal: half-brother to winning pointer by Little Wolf: dam placed in point: fairly useful form when runner-up in bumpers at Fontwell and Ascot, clear of remainder when beaten ¾ length by Something Gold in 21-runner event at latter: will stay at least 2½m. *P. R. Webber*   F98

THE FROSTY FERRET (IRE) 6 b.g. Zaffaran (USA) – Frostbite (Prince Tenderfoot (USA)) [2003/4 F16g F17d 21d 17d³ Apr 18] 15,000 3-y-o: big gelding: has stringhalt: fifth foal: half-brother to fair Irish hurdler Dramatist (by Homo Sapien), stayed 21f, and fair hurdler up to 2½m Professor Cool (by Cataldi): dam unraced: modest form on second of 2 starts in bumpers: better effort over hurdles when 27 lengths third to Lucky Duck in novice at Carlisle: will prove better suited by 2½m than 2m. *J. M. Jefferson*   h83 F84

THE GALWAY MAN (IRE) 7 b.g. Zaffaran (USA) – Nestly River (IRE) (Over The River (FR)) [2003/4 F16g c18g c20d* c20s² c24sᵘʳ c20dꟳ Feb 22] rangy, good sort: useful bumper performer in 2001/2: lame only outing over hurdles: progressive form first 3 starts over fences, winning maiden at Clonmel in December: beaten ½ length by Colnel Rayburn in novice at Navan 6 days later: stays 2½m: acts on heavy going: remains open to improvement over fences. *Anthony Mullins, Ireland*   c120 p h– F–

THE GENE GENIE 9 b.g. Syrtos – Sally Maxwell (Roscoe Blake) [2003/4 c85, h94: 17g 16m² 16g 17s⁵ 16s* 16d⁴ 16v 16d 16m Feb 21] workmanlike gelding: not fluent both starts over fences: fair handicap hurdler: won conditional jockeys event at Wincanton (third course success) in January: best short of 2¾m: acts on good to firm and heavy going: tried visored: held up. *R. J. Hodges*   c– h100

THE GERRY MAN (IRE) 5 b.g. Arctic Lord – Soldeu Creek (IRE) (Buckskin (FR)) [2003/4 F16g Mar 17] second foal: dam unraced sister to useful staying chaser Buckboard Bounce: well held in bumper on debut. *D. J. Wintle*   F–

THE GINGER PRINCE 4 ch.g. Alderbrook – Chapel Haven (IRE) (King Persian) [2003/4 F16g Feb 28] compact gelding: fourth foal: dam no sign of ability on Flat or over hurdles: soundly beaten in bumper on debut. *D. McCain*   F–

THE GLEN 6 gr.g. Mtoto – Silver Singer (Pharly (FR)) [2003/4 17s 16d⁴ Mar 21] leggy gelding: fairly useful on Flat (stays 11f), sold out of M. Tompkins' stable 25,000 gns Newmarket Autumn Sales: better effort in novice hurdles when fourth at Stratford. *R. Lee*   h83

THE GRANBY (IRE) 10 b.g. Insan (USA) – Elteetee (Paddy's Stream) [2003/4 c–, h119: c25d² c25d² c24g^ur Apr 18] leggy gelding: fairly useful hurdler/chaser at best: bought out of Mrs M. Reveley's stable 12,000 gns Doncaster October Sales: won points in February and April: runner-up in hunters at Towcester and Exeter: stays 25f: acts on soft and good to firm going. *Miss H. M. Irving*　　c110 h–

THE GRAND DUKE (IRE) 6 ch.g. Moscow Society (USA) – In For It (IRE) (Tale Quale) [2003/4 F16g Dec 6] €20,000 4-y-o: fourth foal: brother to 2¼m hurdle winner Family Affair: dam unraced half-sister to fairly useful hurdlers Go For It, stayed 3m, and More of It, stayed 2½m: tailed-off last of 20 finishers in bumper on debut, tending to hang right. *P. R. Webber*　　F–

THE GREY BUTLER (IRE) 7 gr.g. Roselier (FR) – Georgic (Tumble Gold) [2003/4 F89: 21s² 22s* 22v 24g 21m Apr 14] workmanlike gelding: much improved when winning maiden hurdle at Stratford in December by 12 lengths from Willie John Daly: well held all 3 subsequent starts (reportedly lost shoe on first occasion): should be suited by 3m+: acts on soft ground. *B. De Haan*　　h125

THE GREY DYER (IRE) 10 gr.g. Roselier (FR) – Tawny Kate (IRE) (Crash Course) [2003/4 c116, h–: c24s^ro c25s6 Jan 6] lengthy, angular gelding: fairly useful handicap chaser: narrow advantage when rider mistakenly bypassed last at Haydock on reappearance: badly hampered and finished lame next time: stays 25f: raced mainly on going softer than good (acts on heavy): has found less than seemed likely. *L. Lungo*　　c119 h–

THE GREY GUNNER 7 gr.g. Paris of Troy – Aldington Annie (Baron Blakeney) [2003/4 F17m 20v^pu Jan 10] first foal: dam no sign of ability in 2 points or novice hurdle: showed nothing in bumper (trained by B. Baugh) and selling hurdle. *P. R. Johnson*　　h– F–

THE GUARANTOR (IRE) 7 b.g. Executive Perk – Chancy Gal (Al Sirat (USA)) [2003/4 F16f* F20m* 16d5 Aug 2] IR 40,000 3-y-o: half-brother to Amberleigh House (by Buckskin): dam modest maiden on Flat and over hurdles: successful twice from 3 starts in bumpers at Tipperary, beating Fatherofthebride on final occasion in July: reportedly pulled muscle on hurdling debut: should do better. *W. P. Mullins, Ireland*　　h76 p F100

THE GUINEA STAMP 5 b.g. Overbury (IRE) – Gagajulu (Al Hareb (USA)) [2003/4 h–, F–: 16g 21d5 22g 19d6 17g 20v5 20v6 Jan 21] of little account: has had tongue tied. *C. Grant*　　h– F–

THE HAIRY LEMON 4 b.g. Eagle Eyed (USA) – Angie's Darling (Milford) [2003/4 F13g F13v6 17s^pu 16s^ur 16d Mar 21] quite good-topped gelding: eighth foal: dam of little account: little sign of ability in bumpers or juvenile hurdles (none too fluent). *M. F. Harris*　　h– F–

THE HEARTY JOKER (IRE) 9 b.g. Broken Hearted – Furryway (Furry Glen) [2003/4 c72, h–: c21m^pu c20m5 c22m² c22g* c21m³ c22f⁴ c20m c19m^F c19m⁴ c22m⁴ c19d³ c20d c25g^pu c19d³ c19s Apr 6] lengthy gelding: modest chaser: 10 lb out of handicap when winning at Market Rasen in July: stays 2¾m: acts on firm and good to soft going: tried visored/blinkered: possibly best on right-handed tracks: usually makes running: unreliable. *B. G. Powell*　　c86 § h–

THE HIGHERHO 4 ch.g. Forzando – Own Free Will (Nicholas Bill) [2003/4 F17v5 Mar 21] sixth foal: half-brother to modest hurdler up to 2½m Duke of Perth (by Scottish Reel) and fair pointer Posh As You Like (by Rakaposhi King): dam 7f to 11f winner: fifth in bumper at Carlisle on debut. *M. W. Easterby*　　F77

THEICECREAMMAN (IRE) 7 ch.g. Glacial Storm (USA) – Miss Cornetto (IRE) (Parliament) [2003/4 h93, F89: 26m^pu 20v 17m⁴ 22m^F Jun 29] modest hurdler: little form in Britain: should have stayed beyond 2½m: acted on heavy going, possibly on good to firm: tried visored/blinkered: dead. *G. Prodromou*　　h–

THE INDISPENSABLE (IRE) 8 ch.g. College Chapel – Fanellan (Try My Best (USA)) [2003/4 21g² 17d 16s* Dec 13] compact gelding: fair hurdler: off 20 months prior to reappearance: won handicap at Lingfield in December: stays 21f: acts on soft and good to firm going. *Jonjo O'Neill*　　h104

THE JOKER (IRE) 6 ch.g. Montelimar (USA) – How Doudo (Oats) [2003/4 F101: 16m* 20f* 16m 16d* Nov 29] successful 3 out of 4 starts over hurdles, maiden at Sligo in August, novice at Hexham in September and handicap at Newcastle (amateurs, beat Bergamo 2½ lengths) in November: will be suited by 2½m+: probably acts on any going: capable of better still. *J. K. Magee, Ireland*　　h109 p

THE JOLLY BEGGAR (IRE) 6 gr.g. Jolly Jake (NZ) – Silk Empress (Young Emperor) [2003/4 F16s Mar 20] half-brother to several winners, including fairly useful　　F–

hurdler/fair chaser The Pickled Duke (by Duky), stays 25f, and fair chaser up to 2½m Quassimi (by Ahonoora): dam, unplaced in 4 races, closely related to disqualified 1978 Premio Regina Elena winner Romantic Love: well held in bumper on debut, tending to hang left. *Noel T. Chance*

THE KELT (IRE)   7 b.g. Leading Counsel (USA) – Casheral (Le Soleil) [2003/4 21d* Apr 12] sturdy ex-Irish gelding: little form on Flat or over hurdles for J. Hassett: much improved on return from lengthy absence when winning handicap at Huntingdon (tongue tied), hard driven to lead near line (jockey banned): will stay beyond 21f. *Eoin Doyle, Ireland*   **h89**

THE KEW TOUR (IRE)   8 ch.g. Un Desperado (FR) – Drivers Bureau (Proverb) [2003/4 h107: 24m⁴ c25m* c26gᶠ c25d² c22s³ c24g* c24g² Apr 10] big, workmanlike gelding: fair hurdler: similar standard over fences, won novices at Wetherby in October and Doncaster in March, beating Exstoto ½ length at latter: stays 25f: yet to race on extremes of going: front runner: has carried head high/swished tail. *Mrs S. J. Smith*   **c112 h–**

THE KING'S DOCTOR (IRE)   10 gr.g. Glacial Storm (USA) – Grandpa's River (Over The River (FR)) [2003/4 c16g^pu May 2] workmanlike gelding: lightly-raced maiden hurdler/chaser: jumped poorly only start in 2003/4: tried tongue tied. *J. D. Frost*   **c– h–**

THE KINGS FLING   8 b.g. Rakaposhi King – Poetic Light (Ardross) [2003/4 c25d⁴ Feb 17] fair pointer, successful in February: well-beaten fourth of 5 finishers in hunter chase. *James Richardson*   **c69**

THE KOP END (IRE)   6 b.g. Topanoora – Shermaya (FR) (Shardari) [2003/4 F16d 16d² 16d³ 16dᶠ 18d³ 16d³ Apr 13] first foal: dam once-raced half-sister to smart 1m to 1½m filly Sherarda and to dam of high-class miler Sendawar: fairly useful form at best in bumpers: fair hurdler: won conditional jockeys maiden at Downpatrick in March: raced around 2m on good to soft/soft going: effective tongue tied or not. *C. Roche, Ireland*   **h113 F94**

THE LAIRD'S ENTRY (IRE)   9 b.g. King's Ride – Balancing Act (Balinger) [2003/4 h–: c21s² c21v⁴ c16vᶠ c20g* Mar 12] big gelding: lightly-raced workmanlike hurdler: best effort over fences when winning novice at Ayr: stays 21f: acts on heavy going: front runner: jumps low: sold 3,500 gns Doncaster May Sales. *L. Lungo*   **c106 h–**

THE LAND AGENT   13 b.g. Town And Country – Notinhand (Nearly A Hand) [2003/4 c104, h–: c20g³ c21m⁶ c19m⁵ Sep 10] rangy gelding: fair handicap chaser nowadays: barely stays 25f: acts on heavy and good to firm going: has worn cheekpieces: bolted before final start. *J. W. Mullins*   **c104 h–**

THE LAST CAST   5 ch.g. Prince of Birds (USA) – Atan's Gem (USA) (Sharpen Up) [2003/4 h116: 16g 17d⁶ 21g* 20d Mar 20] workmanlike gelding: fairly useful handicap hurdler: won at Newbury in March by short head from Legal Lunch: stays 21f: raced on good going or softer (acts on heavy). *H. Morrison*   **h121**

THE LAST MOHICAN   5 b.g. Common Grounds – Arndilly (Robellino (USA)) [2003/4 h87: 18m³ 20g⁵ 20s⁴ 16d⁴ 16d⁶ 19d Mar 11] small gelding: poor maiden hurdler: probably stays 21f: acts on good to firm and good to soft going. *P. Howling*   **h74**

THE LEADER   11 b.g. Ardross – Leading Line (Leading Man) [2003/4 c92, h–: c16v* c17s³ c16d c16d⁶ c24m Apr 13] rangy gelding: modest handicap chaser: fortunate to win at Towcester in December: effective at 2m to 3¼m: raced on good going or softer (acts on heavy): often weak finisher: none too consistent. *P. R. Chamings*   **c92 h–**

THE LEAZES   5 b.g. Shaamit (IRE) – Air of Elegance (Elegant Air) [2003/4 F–: F17m F16g Jul 3] no sign of ability in bumpers: tried tongue tied: sold 3,500 gns Doncaster August Sales, pulled up in 2 points subsequently. *A. Dickman*   **F–**

THE LITTLE LAD (IRE)   8 b.g. Phardante (FR) – Lady Bar (Crash Course) [2003/4 20m² Aug 25] IR 14,000 3-y-o: ex-Irish gelding: first foal: half-brother to 2m hurdle winner Slainte (by Good Thyne): dam fairly useful hurdler/chaser up to 3m: maiden hurdler: sold out of C. Roche's stable 3,200 gns Doncaster September (2002) Sales: blinkered when second in conditional jockeys seller at Huntingdon only start in 2003/4: stays 2¾m: acts on good to firm and good to soft ground. *T. P. McGovern*   **h80**

THE LOCAL   4 b.g. Selkirk (USA) – Finger of Light (Green Desert (USA)) [2003/4 16d⁶ 16d 18s^pu 16s* 17d⁶ 16d² 16d⁵ 16g⁵ Apr 12] fair on Flat (stays 11.6f), sold out of M. Blanshard's stable £13,000 Ascot November Sales: modest juvenile hurdler: won conditional jockeys handicap at Plumpton in February: likely to prove best around 2m: acts on soft going: free-going front runner. *N. A. Gaselee*   **h89**

THELONIUS (IRE) 9 ch.g. Statoblest – Little Sega (FR) (Bellypha) [2003/4 16gᵖᵘ   h–
19g Apr 18] leggy gelding: fairly useful handicap hurdler in early-2001/2 for P. Hobbs:
some encouragement on second of 2 outings since: best at sharp 2m: acts on firm and
good to soft going: pulled hard and virtually ran off course on bend on reappearance.
C. J. Down

THE LORD OF MYSTERY (IRE) 6 b.g. Mister Lord (USA) – Cooline Mist (IRE)   h76
(Actinium (FR)) [2003/4 20d³ Apr 21] IR £4,200 4-y-o: third foal: dam unraced: pulled
up in 2 maiden points in 2003: third in maiden at Worcester on hurdling debut. *Mrs
H. Dalton*

THE LYME VOLUNTEER (IRE) 7 b.m. Zaffaran (USA) – Dooley O'Brien (The   c105
Parson) [2003/4 h105+, F–: c22g⁴ c22g² c23m³ c25s² Feb 6] useful-looking mare: fair   h–
hurdler: let down by jumping first 3 starts over fences, but better effort when second in
handicap at Hereford final outing: suited by 3m+: acts on heavy and good to firm going.
O. Sherwood

THE MAJOR (NZ) 11 ch.g. Try To Stop Me – Equation (NZ) (Palatable (USA))   c106 x
[2003/4 c114x: c20dᵖᵘ c20d⁵ c20v³ c17g⁶ c24g c21g Apr 2] tall gelding: fair chaser: stays
3m: best efforts on going softer than good (acts on heavy): idles, and best held up: makes
mistakes. *J. R. Cornwall*

THEMANFROMCARLISLE 8 br.g. Jupiter Island – Country Mistress (Town And   c92
Country) [2003/4 c–, h90: 21fᵖᵘ 18f⁴ 22m⁴ c20g* c16d⁴ Nov 11] tall gelding: winning   h–
hurdler, out of form first 3 starts: easily best effort in steeplechases when winning maiden
at Plumpton in October, final outing for M. Pitman: will probably stay 3m: acts on good
to firm going, pulled up on soft: has taken good hold: possibly best on left-handed tracks.
Mrs S. H. Shirley-Beavan

THE MASARETI KID (IRE) 7 b.g. Commanche Run – Little Crack (IRE) (Lan-   c–
castrian) [2003/4 h–, F93: 22g³ 17g³ 24m³ c25mᵖᵘ 22g* 23d² 22d² 27s³ 24vᵖᵘ 20d   h83
22gᵖᵘ Mar 6] workmanlike gelding: poor hurdler: left Miss V. Williams, won conditional
jockeys handicap at Kelso in November: stays 27f: acts on firm and soft going: has worn
cheekpieces (including when successful): sometimes fails to impress with attitude,
including on chasing debut. *G. A. Harker*

THE MERRY MASON (IRE) 8 b.g. Roselier (FR) – Busters Lodge (Antwerp City)   c87 §
[2003/4 h85: c25gᵖᵘ c25m² c27m⁴ c26mᵖᵘ c24g³ c24gᵖᵘ Feb 18] leggy, good-topped   h– §
gelding: modest hurdler/maiden chaser: suited by thorough test of stamina: acts on good
to firm going: lazy/carries head high, and needs treating with caution. *J. M. Jefferson*

THEME SONG (IRE) 5 b.g. Singspiel (IRE) – Glatisant (Rainbow Quest (USA))   F99
[2003/4 F16d⁶ F18m* Aug 9] close-coupled gelding: third foal: half-brother to 1998
2-y-o 6f winner Frappe (by Inchinor): dam, useful 6f and 7f winner who became not one
to trust implicitly, out of Nassau Stakes winner Dancing Rocks: much better effort in
bumpers when winning at Downpatrick in August by 15 lengths from Tullywood Queen:
useful form at 2m on Flat subsequently, winning twice from 4 starts. *Anthony Mullins,
Ireland*

THE MET MAN (IRE) 8 b.g. Executive Perk – Supplicate (Furry Glen) [2003/4   c– x
c26dᵘʳ Apr 23] second foal: dam won 2m hurdle: winning Irish pointer: mid-division in
bumper in early-2002/3: sold out of W. Burke's stable 2,600 gns Doncaster August (2002)
Sales: unseated both starts in points and hunter chase in Britain. *Michael Smith*

THE MIGHTY FLYNN 5 ch.g. Botanic (USA) – Owdbetts (IRE) (High Estate)   h–
[2003/4 F–: F17m 16g Jan 7] no show in bumpers and novice hurdle. *P. Monteith*   F–

THE MIGHTY SPARROW (IRE) 11 b.g. Montelimar (USA) – Tamer's Belle   c82
(Tamerlane) [2003/4 17gᵖᵘ 20m* c17d⁴ c21fᶠ c19m⁴ 16v 16d Feb 25] eighth foal: half-   h85
brother to bumper winner Miss Ivy (by Le Bavard): dam, winning hurdler, stayed 2½m:
poor hurdler from both completed outings over fences: modest hurdler: won weak handicap
at Uttoxeter in June: stays 2½m: acts on good to firm and good to soft going. *N. F. Glynn,
Ireland*

THE MINER 6 ch.g. Hatim (USA) – Glen Morvern (Carlingford Castle) [2003/4 F83:   h89
22mᵖᵘ 16d 16s 18v³ 22g⁶ 20s 20s³ Apr 21] well-made gelding: modest maiden hurdler:
probably stays 2½m: acts on heavy going. *Miss S. E. Forster*

THE MOG 5 b.g. Atraf – Safe Secret (Seclude (USA)) [2003/4 h64: 16gᵖᵘ 17g 19g   h70 §
16m² 21mᵖᵘ 16s⁴ 16d Apr 12] leggy gelding: modest on all-weather, poor on turf on Flat
(stays 7f): poor maiden hurdler: left S. Bowring after fifth start: will prove best at 2m:

acts on good to firm going: tried in cheekpieces: tongue tied: pulls hard: untrustworthy. *Miss M. E. Rowland*

THE MURATTI 6 b.g. Alflora (IRE) – Grayrose Double (Celtic Cone) [2003/4 F16g* F18s⁶ F16g Mar 6] 18,000 4-y-o: sixth foal: half-brother to bumper winner Grayrose Fleur (by Henbit): dam, winning hurdler who stayed 3m, out of half-sister to smart 2m to 3m chaser Clear Cut: fair form in bumpers: won at Warwick on debut in December by 2 lengths from Seaniethesmuggler. *D. J. Caro*   **F94**

THE NAMES BOND 6 b.g. Tragic Role (USA) – Artistic Licence (High Top) [2003/4 h89: 16g May 2] close-coupled gelding: modest maiden hurdler: probably best around 2m: acts on soft and good to firm going: usually races prominently. *Andrew Turnell*   **h–**

THE NEGOTIATOR 10 ch.g. Nebos (GER) – Baie Des Anges (Pas de Seul) [2003/4 c114, h–: c17s c16v³ c20fᵘʳ Feb 29] workmanlike gelding: handicap chaser: below best in 2003/4: stays 2¾m, at least as effective at shorter: has form on soft/heavy going, very best efforts under less testing conditions (acts on firm): has had tongue tied: usually races prominently. *M. A. Barnes*   **c94** **h–**

THE NELSON TOUCH 7 b.g. Past Glories – Kellys Special (Netherkelly) [2003/4 h–x: 21mᵖᵘ c23g³ c26dᵖᵘ Jun 9] shallow-girthed gelding: sketchy jumper and little worth-while form, though twice runner-up in points in March. *J. W. Mullins*   **c– x** **h– x**

THE NEWSMAN (IRE) 12 b.g. Homo Sapien – Miller Fall's (Stubbs Gazette) [2003/4 c106, h–: 18m* 18f* 18g² c20s* c20m⁴ c20g 18dᵖᵘ Apr 7] tall gelding: fair handicap hurdler: won at Fontwell in May and August (sixth course win, made all): fairly useful handicap chaser: better than ever when winning at Plumpton in November: well below form after (broke blood vessel final start): stays 21f: probably acts on any going: tried blinkered: held up: has found little. *G. Wareham*   **c121** **h101**

THE NOBLEMAN (USA) 8 b.g. Quiet American (USA) – Furajet (USA) (The Minstrel (USA)) [2003/4 c24m⁴ May 10] sturdy gelding: winning hurdler: well-held fourth of 6 in hunter chase at Huntingdon: won point in February: will probably prove best short of 3m: acts on any going. *Mrs M. Morris*   **c71** **h–**

THE NOBLE MOOR (IRE) 8 br.g. Euphemism – Who Says (IRE) (Amazing Bust) [2003/4 h–: 21sᵖᵘ May 2] tall gelding: of little account. *T. R. George*   **h–**

THE NOMAD 8 b.g. Nomadic Way (USA) – Bubbling (Tremblant) [2003/4 h108: c20d³ c17g² c16sᶠ c19g⁴ c25s⁵ c16d* c16s* c20g² Apr 24] workmanlike gelding: fair hurdler: similar form over fences: jumped soundly when winning maiden and novice at Hexham in spring: should stay at least 2¾m: acts on heavy and good to firm going: races prominently: has hung: has been let down by jumping. *M. W. Easterby*   **c110** **h–**

THE OCTOBER MAN 7 ch.g. Afzal – Florence May (Grange Melody) [2003/4 h71: 20m c20m⁵ c23gᵖᵘ Jan 27] compact gelding: signs of only a little ability: bred to stay well. *Jonjo O'Neill*   **c–** **h–**

THEORIST 4 b.g. Machiavellian (USA) – Clerio (Soviet Star (USA)) [2003/4 16sᵖᵘ 16gᶠ Feb 13] angular gelding: fair on Flat (should stay 1¼m), sold out of M. Johnston's stable 20,000 gns Doncaster August Sales: showed little in 2 juvenile hurdles, mistakes prior to falling on second occasion. *J. L. Spearing*   **h–**

THE OUTLIER (IRE) 6 br.g. Roselier (FR) – Shuil A Cuig (Quayside) [2003/4 F17d² F17v Mar 21] €32,000 4-y-o: fifth foal: half-brother to 2m hurdle winner Whithworth Ben (by Commanche Run): dam unraced half-sister to useful staying chaser Baronet (by Roselier), useful 2m hurdler Tartan Trader and dam of very smart hurdler Liss A Paoraigh: encouraging second to Stagecoachsapphire in conditional jockeys bumper at Carlisle on debut: well below that form under more testing conditions there next time. *Miss Venetia Williams*   **F96**

THE PALLETMAN 4 ch.g. Lion Cavern (USA) – Aquarela (Shirley Heights) [2003/4 17fᵖᵘ 16mᵖᵘ Oct 9] second foal: dam ran once: showed nothing in 2 juvenile hurdles. *M. F. Harris*   **h–**

THE PARISHIONER (IRE) 6 ch.g. Glacial Storm (USA) – Phairy Miracles (IRE) (Phardante (FR)) [2003/4 F16s F16s* 20s* 22s* 20d 22s³ Mar 27] €28,000 4-y-o: first foal: dam, winning chaser, stayed 3m: successful both outings in points in 2003: better effort in bumpers when winning at Limerick in December: successful first 2 starts over hurdles, in maiden at Cork in January and novice at Thurles (useful effort to beat Kim Fontaine ½ length) in February: disappointing favourite last 2 starts: will stay 3m: raced on good to soft/soft going. *M. Hourigan, Ireland*   **h130** **F94**

Betfair Open Bumper, Cheltenham—hat-trick-seeking The Posh Paddy leads into the straight

THE PARSONS DINGLE 9 ch.g. Le Moss – Not Enough (Balinger) [2003/4 c100, h–: 19m⁵ 21g⁴ 19s⁴ 17d⁶ 21g⁵ 22g c20d⁶ Apr 21] workmanlike gelding: winning chaser, well held final start: poor maiden hurdler, lost his form: best form around 2m: acts on heavy going (won bumper on good to firm). *T. P. Walshe*   **c– h80 d**

THE PECKER DUNN (IRE) 10 b.g. Be My Native (USA) – Riversdale Shadow (Kemal (FR)) [2003/4 22g⁴ 24s^pu 24s* Feb 22] strong gelding: lightly raced: modest hurdler: won handicap at Towcester: stays 3m: acts on soft going. *Mrs N. S. Sharpe*   **h85**

THE PENNYS DROPPED (IRE) 7 ch.g. Bob's Return (IRE) – Shuil Alainn (Levanter) [2003/4 h100, F95: c16g⁴ c22s^F c20s⁵ c25g⁵ c24s⁵ c24s^pu c22s^pu Mar 7] sturdy gelding: awarded novice hurdle in 2002/3 on technical grounds: disappointing over fences in 2003/4, went as if amiss last 2 starts: probably stays 25f: raced on good going or softer: tried tongue tied. *Jonjo O'Neill*   **c98 h–**

THE PHAIR CRIER (IRE) 9 ch.g. Phardante (FR) – Maul-More (Deep Run) [2003/4 h–: 20d³ 22s⁵ Nov 29] good-topped gelding: fairly useful hurdler: never nearer in handicaps at Hexham and Haydock: likely to prove best at 3m+: raced on good going or softer (acts on soft): sold 3,200 gns Doncaster May Sales. *L. Lungo*   **h115**

THE POSH NIPPER 5 b.g. Rakaposhi King – Jindabyne (Good Times (ITY)) [2003/4 F17d F16d Mar 19] leggy gelding: second foal: dam of little account: well held both starts in bumpers. *M. Mullineaux*   **F–**

THE POSH PADDY (IRE) 7 b. or br.g. Be My Native (USA) – Dizzy Dot (Bargello) [2003/4 F16f* F16m* F16m* 16d⁵ Dec 13] rather leggy gelding: half-brother to 4 winners around 2½m, including fairly useful hurdler/bumper winner Rye Fontaine (by Lafontaine): dam never ran: useful form in bumpers, winning listed event at Cheltenham in November by ½ length from Alpine Fox, making most: earlier won at Clonmel in June and Roscommon in August: only fifth in maiden at Fairyhouse on hurdling debut: raced at 2m: tongue tied on debut in 2002/3: likely to do better over hurdles. *Anthony Mullins, Ireland*   **h100 p F112**

THE PREACHER MAN (IRE) 9 b.g. Be My Native (USA) – Frankford Run (Deep Run) [2003/4 c–, h–: 20v c27s⁶ c21s 24d⁵ 24v Mar 21] winning pointer: lightly-raced maiden hurdler/chaser, showed little in 2003/4. *V. Thompson*   **c– h–**

THE PREMIER CAT (IRE) 8 b.g. Glacial Storm (USA) – Carraigaloe (Little Buskins) [2003/4 c138, h–: 24m c20s⁴ c26g^pu c24d^ur c22s³ 24d⁴ c24s Mar 14] tall gelding: fairly useful hurdler: useful chaser: best effort in 2003/4 when fourth to Edredon Bleu in Grade 2 at Clonmel (has won there 4 times) second outing: best at 2½m+: raced mainly on going softer than good (acts on heavy): usually sound-jumping front runner. *T. Cahill, Ireland*   **c132 h118**

THE PRINCE 10 b.g. Machiavellian (USA) – Mohican Girl (Dancing Brave (USA)) [2003/4 16m^pu Sep 27] well-made gelding: fairly useful on Flat (stays 9f): fairly useful   **h–**

hurdler in 2000/1: lost action only start in 2003/4: best at sharp 2m: acts on good to firm going: tongue tied: patiently ridden. *Ian Williams*

THE PROJECT 8 b.g. Prince of Darkness (IRE) – Kerry Calluna (Celtic Cone) **h–**
[2003/4 h–, F–: 22m^{pu} May 9] tall, lengthy, angular gelding: little sign of ability. *J. C. Fox*

THE PROOF 7 b.g. Rudimentary (USA) – Indubitable (Sharpo) [2003/4 h69?: 17d⁵ **h75**
17s^F Mar 23] lengthy, sparely-made gelding: very lightly raced over hurdles: dead. *G. B. Balding*

THE QUADS 12 b.g. Tinoco – Queen's Royale (Tobrouk (FR)) [2003/4 c128?, h–: **c–**
c33g³ 24m Aug 30] leggy gelding: veteran hurdler/chaser, seems to retain little ability: **h–**
blinkered: usually tongue tied. *Ferdy Murphy*

THE RAILWAY MAN (IRE) 5 b.g. Shernazar – Sparky Sue (IRE) (Strong Gale) **F103**
[2003/4 F16d³ F16s² Feb 8] €90,000 3-y-o: well-made gelding: fifth.foal: half-brother to winning 2m hurdler Native Craft (by Be My Native): dam unraced half-sister to top-class hurdler who stayed 3m Mole Board: placed in 2 bumpers at Leopardstown, length second to Malahide Marina on latter occasion. *A. L. T. Moore, Ireland*

THEREALBANDIT (IRE) 7 b.g. Torus – Sunrise Highway VII (Master Owen) **c155 +**
[2003/4 h107+: 22s² 27d* 22m* 22g* 25g* c25d* c21d* c25d^F c26g Mar 18] **h133 p**
A very different test awaited the seven-year-old Therealbandit at the Cheltenham Festival in March compared to the one which his two-year-older half-brother The Bajan Bandit had faced at the same age. The Bajan Bandit, still in his first season over hurdles, contested the Royal & SunAlliance Novices' Hurdle, whereas Therealbandit, switched to fences just three months earlier following a run of four straight wins over hurdles, took on Best Mate and company in the Cheltenham Gold Cup. Neither proved up to the task, The Bajan Bandit finishing tenth and Therealbandit, who started second favourite, trailing home seventh, a long way behind Best Mate, not quite so fluent as some on the second circuit and already struggling four from home.
Time was when horses lacking in chasing experience made a great impact on the Gold Cup. Golden Miller won his first at five and Fortina, Mont Tremblant and Mill House were all successful at six, Mont Tremblant after taking part in only four chases and Golden Miller and Mill House after only five. The seven-year-old Captain Christy, with six chases under his belt, won it in 1974, and was the last novice to do so. Of the six other novices to have contested the Gold Cup in the past decade, Dorans Pride fared much the best, finishing third in 1997. Beef Or Salmon, Danoli and Gloria Victis all fell, while Cyborgo was last of eight finishers and Unsinkable Boxer was pulled up. Cyborgo, Unsinkable Boxer and Gloria Victis were trained, like Therealbandit, by Martin Pipe, who must have had some mis-givings about Therealbandit's participation given the widespread, and, in our opinion, totally unjustified criticism which followed the death of Gloria Victis in the 2000 Gold Cup. The easier option with Therealbandit would have been to take on other novices in the Royal & SunAlliance Chase, for which he was ante-post favourite. Instead, Our Vic represented connections in that race, starting favourite and finishing third. Therealbandit, at his best, would probably have won the Royal & SunAlliance. However, he was clearly well below his best in the Gold Cup, possibly due to an interrupted preparation, and the chances are that Therealbandit wouldn't have been involved in the finish of the Royal & SunAlliance either. Despite their recent record, novices remain capable of making their mark in the Gold Cup—Gloria Victis was virtually disputing the lead with the winner Looks Like Trouble and runner-up Florida Pearl when he came down two out—and another Captain Christy will come along.
Therealbandit was successful in a handicap hurdle at Newton Abbot on the last of four starts in his first season and continued his improvement in his second, winning a handicap at Stratford, two novice events at Newton Abbot and the Lombard Properties Handicap Hurdle at Cheltenham, giving an impressive display, as well as showing useful form, on the last-named course in November. One month later Therealbandit was back at Cheltenham for his first run over fences and he could hardly have made a more promising start. Bar one mistake, Therealbandit's jumping was a joy to watch and, still pulling double as he took the lead running

Ian Williams' Owners Novices' Chase, Cheltenham—
Therealbandit continues his impressive start over fences

down the hill, he didn't have to come off the bridle to go clear, winning by eight lengths from Rosslea. Cheltenham was also the venue for his two other appearances over fences before the Gold Cup. In another novice chase, on New Year's Day, he was sent off at odds on to account for three rivals and did so with the minimum of fuss, again jumping well in the main and winning by twenty lengths from one of the two French-trained runners Massac. Just over three weeks later Massac's stable-companion Jair du Cochet was one of five much more experienced chasers, all of them at least very smart, who lined up against Therealbandit in the Pillar Property Chase. The race represented a very big step up in class for Therealbandit, but such was the impression he had created in his two runs over fences that he was sent off favourite. Therealbandit was held up and didn't jump quite so fluently this time around, though his only error of note came at the fourth last, where, unfortunately, he fell. He was moving up to the leader, and eventual winner, Jair du Cochet at the time, still travelling well, and even though the fall occurred too far from home to say precisely where Therealbandit would have finished, he had done enough to suggest that he was a chaser capable of very smart form at least. It is to be hoped he has plenty of opportunities in the next season to show just how good he is.

Therealbandit, bought as an unraced four-year-old for IR 18,000 guineas, is by the Irish St Leger second Torus, sire among others of the top-class chasers Bradbury Star and Mr Mulligan, the latter the winner of the Cheltenham Gold Cup in 1997. The dam, Sunrise Highway VII, is a non-thoroughbred mare whose sire is understood to be Master Owen and her dam said to be the unraced Hack On. Sunrise Highway VII does come from a useful family. Her third dam Blue Petrel is the grandam of the 1977 Whitbread winner Andy Pandy and 1982 Imperial Cup winner Holemoor Star; and her grandam Sagotox, successful herself on the Flat over a mile, over nine furlongs and over a mile and a half, is the grandam of the useful staying chaser King Ba Ba and the third dam of the 1997 Scottish National winner Belmont King. Sunrise Highway VII, who didn't appear on a racecourse until she was eight, was twice successful over two miles at Down Royal, in a bumper (at 20/1, by twenty lengths) in her first season and in a maiden on the Flat at the age of nine. Also in the frame (at up to two and a half miles) in five of her seven starts over hurdles, she had her last two outings at the age of twelve. The Bajan Bandit (by Commanche Run), who stays two and three quarter miles, is useful over hurdles and almost as good over fences; while Sunrise Highway VII's other winner

		Ribero (b 1965)	Ribot
	Torus (b 1976)		Libra
		Lighted Lamp (b 1967)	Sir Gaylord
Therealbandit (IRE) (b.g. 1997)			Chandelier
		Master Owen (b 1956)	Owen Tudor
	Sunrise Highway VII (b 1977)		Miss Maisie
		Hack On (br 1969)	Tarqogan
			Sagotox

Mr D. A. Johnson's "Therealbandit"

Hennessy Feeds (by Mazaad), still racing in Ireland at the age of eleven, was a fair hurdler/chaser at his best, one who stayed three miles well. Therealbandit is by no means short of stamina either and has won over as far as twenty-seven furlongs, though he is also effective at twenty-one furlongs. A tall, lengthy, rather sparely-made gelding, Therealbandit acts on soft and good to firm going. *M. C. Pipe*

THE REBEL LADY (IRE)   7 br.m. Mister Lord (USA) – Arborfield Brook (Over The River (FR)) [2003/4 h87+: c24g* c24spu c24gF c24d5 c24m* c25mpu Apr 13] tall mare: modest form over hurdles: fair form over fences, winning novices at Huntingdon (handicap) in November and Ludlow in February: usually ran as if amiss on other starts over fences (breathing problem second): stays 3m: acts on good to firm and good to soft going. *Miss H. C. Knight*   c100 h–

THE RECRUITER   4 gr.g. Danzig Connection (USA) – Tabeeba (Diesis) [2003/4 16spu Dec 20] poor maiden on Flat: always behind in juvenile on hurdling debut. *J. G. M. O'Shea*   h–

THE RED BOY (IRE)   10 ch.g. Boyne Valley – River Regent (Over The River (FR)) [2003/4 c21d5 Apr 12] fair point pointer, successful twice in January: never-dangerous fifth in novice hunter chase at Fakenham: will be suited by further than 21f. *C. Sporborg*   c88

THERE GOES WALLY   6 b.g. Lyphento (USA) – Dutch Majesty (Homing) [2003/4 F18s F16g 19spu 22gpu Apr 22] sixth foal: half-brother to fair hurdlers up to 3m Lets Go Dutch and Barton Nic (both by Nicholas Bill), latter also winning chaser: dam, won 2¼m hurdle, half-sister to useful stayer Double Dutch: no form in bumpers or over hurdles: tried in cheekpieces. *A. Ennis*   h– F–

THE RILE (IRE)   10 ch.g. Alphabatim (USA) – Donna Chimene (Royal Gunner) [2003/4 c116+, h101: 16s2 c25spu 24spu Mar 20] strong, lengthy gelding: fairly useful hurdler/chaser: form in 2003/4 only when second to Paperprophet in handicap over hurdles at Ayr on reappearance: should stay beyond 21f: raced mainly on going softer than good (acts on heavy): has won 3 times at Carlisle. *L. Lungo*   c– h115

THE RISING MOON (IRE)   5 br.g. Anshan – I'm So Happy (IRE) (Miner's Lamp) [2003/4 F16d* 21dpu Jan 10] €26,000 3-y-o: good-topped gelding: second foal: dam, winning pointer, half-sister to fairly useful hurdler/chaser up to 3m Kirmar: won maiden Irish point in 2003: favourite, won bumper at Newbury in December by ½ length from Supreme Leisure: shaped well in Grade 2 novice at Warwick on hurdling debut, still in touch when faltering 3 out: likely to do better. *Jonjo O'Neill*   h– p F103

THE RIVER JOKER (IRE)   8 ch.g. Over The River (FR) – Augustaeliza (IRE) (Callernish) [2003/4 h80: 24g2 24v2 25v* c25v* c25v2 24spu 26d Mar 28] lengthy, angular gelding: poor hurdler: modest form over fences, winning minor event at Towcester in December: thorough stayer: acts on heavy going: hard ride, and probably ungenuine. *John R. Upson*   c94 § h80 §

THE SAWDUST KID   10 ch.g. River God (USA) – Susie's Money (Seymour Hicks (FR)) [2003/4 c93, h–: c25mur c25m2 27g c26g2 c26gpu Aug 4] good-bodied gelding: winning hurdler: modest handicap chaser: stays 3¼m: acts on firm going, possibly not on softer than good: tried blinkered: sketchy jumper of fences. *R. H. Buckler*   c88 x h–

THE SAWYER (BEL)   4 ch.g. Fleetwood (IRE) – Green Land (BEL) (Hero's Honor (USA)) [2003/4 F16d* F16m2 Apr 13] €2,200 3-y-o: compact gelding: second foal: dam modest 1½m to 15f winner: won bumper at Towcester on debut in March: better form when second to From Dusk To Dawn at Chepstow, staying on strongly: will stay beyond 2m. *R. H. Buckler*   F105

THE SEA CLUB (IRE)   9 b.g. Be My Native (USA) – Furry Slipper (Furry Glen) [2003/4 c25gur Mar 28] lengthy gelding: signs of only a little ability over hurdles for H. Alexander in 2001: unseated first in hunter chase on return: third in point following month. *Andrew Nicholls*   c– h–

THE SECRETARY (IRE)   7 b.m. Shernazar – Exemplary Fashion (Master Owen) [2003/4 h75, F81: 17g 20m Jul 5] poor form over hurdles, leaving Mrs H. Dalton after reappearance: has had tongue tied. *E. J. O'Grady, Ireland*   h–

THESEUS (IRE)   8 b.g. Danehill (USA) – Graecia Magna (USA) (Private Account (USA)) [2003/4 c107, h–: c17g* c17d6 c16f* c16g3 c19s5 c16m3 c17m* Oct 12] useful-looking gelding: useful chaser: won handicaps at Killarney in July and Cork (amateurs) in August, and intermediate at Limerick (easily beat Fiery Ring 9 lengths) in October: best around 2m: acts on firm and soft going. *P. Hughes, Ireland*   c130 h–

THESIS (IRE)   6 ch.g. Definite Article – Chouette (Try My Best (USA)) [2003/4   **h138 +**
h110: 16g* 16g* 16m* 16g³ 16d³ 16s* Dec 20]

Geos was in his fifth season and having his eighteenth start over hurdles in
Britain and Ireland when winning the Tote Gold Trophy in February. But horses
like Geos are often vulnerable to opponents who are a little less exposed and, in
the latest season at least, it paid to look out for novices in the top handicap hurdles.
Scorned and Overstrand were making their handicap debut when winning
respectively the Imperial Cup (in which the first four home were all novices) and
William Hill Handicap Hurdle, Scorned running over hurdles for just the fourth
time, Overstrand for the seventh. Zibeline won the listed two-and-a-half-mile
handicap at Aintree on his seventh start, though he had been beaten twice previously in handicaps. At Cheltenham, there were near misses for G V A Ireland and
Alexanderthegreat in the Pertemps Final and Court Shareef in the Coral Cup.
Thesis gained the most valuable success by a novice, becoming the second novice
in succession to win the Ladbroke Hurdle at Ascot in December, Chauvinist having
triumphed the year before. Thesis was slightly more experienced over hurdles than
the trio mentioned, the Ladbroke Hurdle being his tenth appearance and his third in
a handicap, though, like Scorned, Overstrand and Zibeline, he had the great asset
for a race of this type of having bags of experience, as well as at least fairly useful
form, on the Flat.

Thesis started a 33/1 chance in a field of seventeen at Ascot, coming into
the race on the back of a disappointing run when favourite and only third to Perouse
at Cheltenham eight days previously. His problem that day, as on several other
occasions, had been his jumping, but on his form the time before, in a competitive
handicap at Newbury when he had finished a close third to the Ladbroke joint-
favourite Tom Paddington and another leading contender Sud Bleu, ten lengths
clear of the rest, he clearly had a much better chance than the market indicated. This
time it was Tom Paddington whose jumping let him down, but Sud Bleu again
played a major part. In a truly-run contest, both Thesis and Sud Bleu made ground
three out as the well-supported Saintsaire was sent for home, the trio having the
race to themselves in the straight. Thesis didn't get to the front until the run-in, beating Sud Bleu by two lengths, with a length and a quarter back to Saintsaire
and no fewer than sixteen to the fourth Monkerhostin. Although the majority of the
field came into the race in top form, subsequent events suggest that the first three
didn't show vast improvement on previous efforts and most of the rest simply
weren't near their best. Not that Thesis got the chance to show what he could do.
The Tote Gold Trophy looked the logical next step before possibly following
Chauvinist in contesting the Supreme Novices' at Cheltenham (Chauvinist, having
shown a similar level of ability, was good enough to finish third at the Festival) but
it was reported in January that Thesis had met with a setback and would miss the
rest of the season.

Ladbroke Hurdle (Handicap), Ascot—
Thesis (centre), Sud Bleu (left) and Saintsaire are in line over the last

The 1961 Partnership's "Thesis"

		Indian Ridge (ch 1985)	Ahonoora
			Hill Brow
	Definite Article (b 1992)	Summer Fashion (b 1985)	Moorestyle
Thesis (IRE) (ch.g. 1998)			My Candy
		Try My Best (b 1975)	Northern Dancer
	Chouette (b 1990)		Sex Appeal
		Bugle Sound (b 1977)	Bustino
			Melodina

Earlier, Thesis had won on his first three appearances in 2003/4, though the first two, in a maiden and novice at Worcester in May, were really the tail-end of his first campaign over hurdles. He returned in the autumn to win another novice, at Wetherby. Before going hurdling with his current stable, Thesis had shown fairly useful form on the Flat for Jamie Osborne, winning at a mile and at nine furlongs, before being sold for 27,000 guineas at the Newmarket Autumn (2002) Sales. It's slightly surprising that he didn't fetch more as a prospective jumper, as his family contains several that have done well over hurdles. The grandam Bugle Sound produced two useful hurdlers, Major Bugler, who won the Finesse Hurdle and was third in the Triumph, and Docklands Limo, who won the Cordon Bleu Handicap at Aintree and was second in the Swinton Handicap. The third dam Melodina was responsible for a much more celebrated performer in See You Then, who won the Champion Hurdle three years in succession from 1985. Melodina, herself placed in the Cheveley Park and Ribblesdale Stakes, also produced a notable Flat performer, the Oaks third Dubian who is the dam of the One Thousand Guineas and Sussex Stakes winner Sayyedati and also of the high-class middle-distance colt Golden Snake. Bugle Sound was also useful on the Flat, staying a mile and three quarters, but Thesis' dam Chouette was a poor maiden. Chouette has produced another fairly useful Flat performer, Territory (by Common Grounds), who stayed a mile. This isn't a family especially noted for stamina and Thesis is likely to prove best at around two miles. He acts on soft and good to firm going. The leggy Thesis may not yet be totally exposed over hurdles and could make an impact in more good handicaps when he returns. He won't, though, be contesting the Ladbroke at Ascot. With the course closed while major building work is carried out, the December meeting is being transferred to Windsor, marking the return of jump racing to the track, though Ladbrokes are to stage their race at Sandown's early-January fixture. *Miss Venetia Williams*

THE SISTER 7 b.m. Alflora (IRE) – Donna Farina (Little Buskins) [2003/4 h79: 24m* 24f² 20g³ 24g³ 22sᵖᵘ 24s⁴ Apr 17] leggy, workmanlike mare: modest hurdler: won maiden at Worcester in September: will stay beyond 3m: acts on firm and soft going. *Jonjo O'Neill* **h91**

THE SLEEPER 8 b.g. Perpendicular – Distant Cherry (General Ironside) [2003/4 h–, F–: 16m⁶ c20g⁵ c16m³ Oct 31] strong, workmanlike gelding: little worthwhile form over hurdles and fences. *H. P. Hogarth* **c– h–**

THE SPOONPLAYER (IRE) 5 b.g. Accordion – Jennie Dun (IRE) (Mandalus) [2003/4 F16d² Apr 13] €22,000 4-y-o: first foal: dam unraced: showed plenty of ability when 3 lengths second to Arteea in valuable bumper at Fairyhouse on debut. *Henry De Bromhead, Ireland* **F96**

THE STAGGERY BOY (IRE) 8 b.g. Shalford (IRE) – Murroe Star (Glenstal (USA)) [2003/4 c92, h–: c16g² c20m⁴ c16d* c16g* Jun 13] sturdy gelding: modest chaser: won handicaps at Newton Abbot within 5 days in June: possibly best around 2m: acts on good to firm and good to soft going: effective tongue tied or not: game. *M. R. Hoad* **c92 h–**

THE TALLET 6 ch.g. Alflora (IRE) – Bustle'em (IRE) (Burslem) [2003/4 h–: 16d⁶ 20d c21d⁶ c17dᵖᵘ c16g⁵ Jan 15] no sign of ability: tried blinkered. *D. McCain* **c– h–**

THE TALL GUY (IRE) 8 b. or br.g. Zaffaran (USA) – Mullangale (Strong Gale) [2003/4 c–, h91: c20f² c24g* c20m* c24d* c20g² c20dᵖᵘ Mar 14] tall gelding: modest hurdler: fair chaser: won novice handicaps at Newbury in November and Ludlow in December and January: effective at 2½m to 25f: acts on firm and good to soft going: tongue tied prior to 2003/4. *N. A. Twiston-Davies* **c103 h–**

THE TEUCHTER 5 b.g. First Trump – Barefoot Landing (USA) (Cozzene (USA)) [2003/4 h–: 19d⁶ 16s² 21s² 18sᵖᵘ 16s 25s³ Mar 15] medium-sized gelding: poor maiden hurdler: effective at 2m to 25f: acts on soft going: tried in cheekpieces/blinkers: ungenuine. *N. A. Dunger* **h75 §**

THE THREE BANDITS (IRE) 4 b.g. Accordion – Katie Baggage (IRE) (Brush Aside (USA)) [2003/4 24s 16gᵖᵘ 16d Mar 1] rather unfurnished gelding: second foal: dam unraced: showed little in 3 maiden hurdles. *M. C. Pipe* **h–**

THE THUNDERER 5 gr.g. Terimon – By Line (High Line) [2003/4 F16s F16g* F16g Mar 17] rather unfurnished gelding: fifth foal: half-brother to 2 winners, notably smart bumper winner Secret Ploy (by Deploy), and to disqualified 2½m chase winner Hi Lily (by Jupiter Island): dam, winning hurdler, stayed 19f: easily best effort in bumpers when winning at Ascot in February by 3½ lengths from Senor Sedona. *N. J. Henderson* **F99**

THE TILE BARON (IRE) 7 b.g. Little Bighorn – Elegant Miss (Prince Tenderfoot (USA)) [2003/4 h–: 22g* May 24] medium-sized gelding: upped in trip, first form over hurdles when winning novice handicap at Cartmel only start in 2003/4. *L. Lungo* **h79**

THE TINKER 9 b.g. Nomadic Way (USA) – Miss Tino (Relkino) [2003/4 c98x, h–: c20g³ c16g⁴ c16mᵘʳ c16f³ c17gᶠ c16m* c16g³ c20g c20g* c20g³ c16d³ Apr 22] fair chaser: won novices at Ayr in November and Musselburgh in January: effective at 2m to 2½m: acts on good to firm and good to soft going: often let down by jumping. *Mrs S. C. Bradburne* **c102 x h–**

THE TROJAN HORSE (IRE) 4 b.g. Ilium – Miss Cynthia (Dawn Review) [2003/4   **F–**
F16s Feb 20] tall, rather unfurnished gelding: sixth foal: half-brother to winning Irish
pointer by Strong Gale: dam unraced, from family of high-class 2m chaser I'm A Driver:
green, well held in bumper on debut. *Miss H. C. Knight*

THE VILLAGER (IRE) 8 br.g. Zaffaran (USA) – Kitty Wren (Warpath) [2003/4   **c123 +**
c127+, h117+: c21d⁵ c20g⁵ Feb 13] workmanlike gelding: fairly useful hurdler/chaser: **h–**
much better effort in handicaps over fences in 2003/4 when fifth to Hunters Tweed in
valuable event at Cheltenham on reappearance: will stay beyond 25f: acts on heavy
going, won bumper on good to firm: has worn tongue strap, including at Cheltenham.
M. Scudamore

THE VINTAGE DANCER (IRE) 8 b.g. Riberetto – Strong Swimmer (IRE) (Black   **c91**
Minstrel) [2003/4 c20g³ c21d³ Apr 12] winning pointer: better effort in hunter chases
when third in 21f novice at Fakenham. *Mrs Nicola Pollock*

THE WEAVER (FR) 5 ch.g. Villez (FR) – Miss Planette (FR) (Tip Moss (FR))   **F89**
[2003/4 F16d F16g* F17d³ Apr 18] 13,000 3-y-o: lengthy gelding: second foal: dam
placed over fences in France: fair form in bumpers: won at Catterick in March: again took
strong hold final start. *L. Lungo*

THE WELDER 10 b.g. Buckley – Crystal Run VII (Damsire Unregistered) [2003/4   **c– x**
c–, h–: c23g⁵ c23gᵖᵘ May 21] workmanlike gelding: little form over hurdles/in steeple-   **h–**
chases (makes mistakes): tried tongue tied. *V. Y. Gethin*

THE WHO SHALL (IRE) 6 b. or br.g. Warcraft (USA) – Pollerton Park (Pollerton)   **h–**
[2003/4 22dᵖᵘ Nov 27] sturdy ex-Irish gelding: seventh foal: half-brother to winning 25f
chaser Dalus Park (by Mandalus): dam unraced, from family of top-class jumpers Royal
Bond, Morley Street and Granville Again: signs of only a little ability over hurdles,
leaving C. Roche before only start in 2003/4. *Jonjo O'Neill*

THE WOODEN SPOON (IRE) 6 b.g. Old Vic – Amy's Gale (IRE) (Strong Gale)   **F90**
[2003/4 aF16g⁶ F18s³ Dec 3] IR £2,100 3-y-o: first foal: dam unraced, from family of
One Man: better effort in bumpers when third at Plumpton, benefiting from increased test
of stamina. *L. Wells*

THE WRITER (IRE) 11 b.g. Royal Fountain – Novelist (Quayside) [2003/4 c26d⁵   **c–**
Mar 14] close-coupled, rather lightly-made gelding: winning pointer: well held in hunter,   **h–**
first start in steeplechase since 2000: stays 27f: acts on good to soft going: blinkered once
(pulled up). *The Hon Mrs S. Sherwood*

THE YOUNG BISHOP (IRE) 7 b. or br.g. Be My Native (USA) – Gypsy Lass   **c111**
(King's Ride) [2003/4 c16s⁶ c16d⁴ c16d* Apr 8] tall, useful-looking gelding: second foal: **h–**
dam, fair hurdler/chaser, stayed 2¾m: winning hurdler: best effort over fences on return
from 2-year absence when easily winning maiden at Thurles by 5 lengths from Jackie
Cullen: stays 2½m: acts on soft going. *W. Harney, Ireland*

THIEVES'GLEN 6 b.g. Teenoso (USA) – Hollow Creek (Tarqogan) [2003/4 F97:   **h110 p**
25s⁵ 20dˢᵘ Jan 10] good sort: fairly useful form in bumpers: shaped very well when fifth
to Comply Or Die in Grade 2 novice at Cheltenham on hurdling debut, jumping fluently
in main and allowed to come home in own time after 3 out: under pressure in fourth when
clipped heels and fell home turn in novice at Ascot next time (reportedly returned lame
and likely to be off some time): bred to stay 2½m+: remains open to improvement.
H. Morrison

THISISYOURLIFE (IRE) 6 b.g. Lord Americo – Your Life (Le Bavard (FR))   **h94**
[2003/4 F17d² 16dᶠ 19m Mar 4] €42,000 4-y-o: compact gelding: fourth foal: half-   **F88**
brother to winning 3m hurdler Lifes A Flyer (by Roselier): dam, winning 3m chaser, from
family of Moscow Flyer: second in bumper at Hereford on debut: again showed promise
in novice hurdle at Wincanton, fading in third when falling last: poor effort in similar
event final start: pulls hard. *H. D. Daly*

THISTHATANDTOTHER (IRE) 8 b.g. Bob Back (USA) – Baden (IRE) (Furry   **c149**
Glen) [2003/4 h145: c17g* c16m* c16d* c16g² c16m* c16gᶠ c16g² c20d² Apr 17]   **h–**
 When 5/2 favourite Thisthatandtother crashed out of the Arkle at the second
fence, having already belted the first, he was failing for the third year in succession
to turn an impressive build-up into success at the Cheltenham Festival. In 2002 he
went into the Champion Bumper as one of the best of the home team, and ran well

Independent Newspaper November Novices' Chase, Cheltenham—
four of the five runners in the air together two out (left to right) Le Duc,
the winner Thisthatandtother, Atum Re and Ryders Storm

to make the frame behind Pizarro, Rhinestone Cowboy and Back In Front. But the following season, he managed only fifth in the Supreme Novices' Hurdle, for which he started second favourite on the strength of a win in the Tolworth Hurdle and a second to Rhinestone Cowboy in the Kingwell Hurdle. Thisthatandtother's preparation for the Arkle included success in two recognised trials, the Independent Newspaper November Novices' Chase at Cheltenham and the Henry VIII Novices' Chase at Sandown in December. Thisthatandtother's trainer Paul Nicholls had won the first-named with Azertyuiop the year before and with Fadalko in 1999, but the form Thisthatandtother showed wasn't enough to put him in the same league as that pair. The race developed into a sprint, which meant Thisthatandtother's margin of superiority was not what it might have been, though he jumped very accurately and quickened in impressive fashion to win by eleven lengths from Ryders Storm, to whom he was conceding 16 lb, with Atum Re just a short head back in third. Stable-companion Le Duc had been shaping up to be the main challenger among Thisthatandtother's four rivals, but could not recover after pecking badly two out.

The Henry VIII was, in contrast, run at a good pace and, though Thisthatandtother won by a smaller margin than at Cheltenham, he was every bit as dominant, though his jumping was not quite so fluent on Sandown's trappy circuit. Thisthatandtother travelled very well again, cruising to the front before the last and quickening away to beat Atum Re by four lengths. Thisthatandtother won two other very one-sided affairs before the Arkle. Only four completed when he coasted home on his chasing debut in a maiden at Bangor in October, while he was already well clear when left to beat Jahash by a distance after Kalca Mome departed at the last in a novice at Wincanton in February. Thisthatandtother's only defeat leading up to the Arkle came in the three-runner Wayward Lad Novices' Chase at Kempton

Henry VIII Novices' Chase, Sandown—Cheltenham placings are easily confirmed with Atum Re

three weeks after the Henry VIII. Thisthatandtother went down fairly and squarely by three and a half lengths to Caracciola, always looking likely to come off second best in a protracted tussle. Thisthatandtother didn't look quite so well beforehand as he had at Sandown and he was also reportedly found to be suffering from sore shins afterwards. Thisthatandtother's true merit as a chaser came into sharper focus after the Arkle, in the Maghull Novices' Chase at Aintree in April. He went down by two and a half lengths to Arkle winner Well Chief, showing himself to be a smart novice. The Nicholls string seemed mostly out of sorts by the time Thisthatandtother made his final appearance of the season in the Future Champion Novices' Chase at Ayr two weeks after Aintree, though the step up to two and a half miles probably also played a part in his finishing a below-par second to Keltic Bard.

		Roberto	Hail To Reason
	Bob Back (USA)	(b 1969)	Bramalea
	(br 1981)	Toter Back	Carry Back
Thisthatandtother (IRE)		(ch 1967)	Romantic Miss
(b.g. 1996)		Furry Glen	Wolver Hollow
	Baden (IRE)	(b 1971)	Cleftess
	(b 1988)	St Moritz	Linacre
		(b 1974)	Machete

Thisthatandtother also seemed to find his stamina stretched on his only run at two and a half miles over hurdles, and he is likely to prove ideally suited by the minimum trip. However, as stated in *Chasers & Hurdlers 2002/03*, he is bred to stay a bit further, considering his dam Baden was a fairly useful hurdler at up to nineteen furlongs in Ireland. Thisthatandtother's year-younger half-brother Polar Scout (Arctic Lord) is modest over hurdles and fences, winning a handicap in each sphere at around two and three quarter miles in the latest season. Thisthatandtother has shown himself every bit as good over fences as he was over hurdles and it is possible there may be more to come. His normally fluent jumping should stand him in good stead against more experienced opponents in handicaps, which will

918

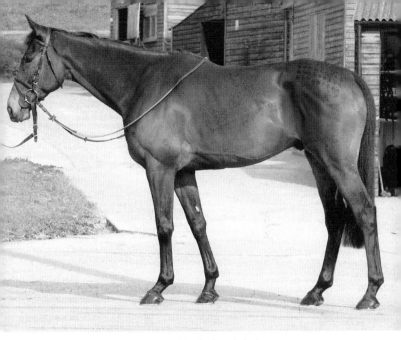

presumably be his target at the start of the 2004/5 campaign. The useful-looking Thisthatandtother acts on soft and good to firm going. *P. F. Nicholls*

THIS THYNE 8 b.m. Good Thyne (USA) – Dalkey Sound (Crash Course) [2003/4 h98: c20d c20s^F Dec 11] lengthy mare: fair hurdler: little encouragement in 2 starts over fences: suited by 2½m+: acts on good to firm and good to soft going: tried tongue tied. *Mrs M. Reveley*

c–
h–

THISTLECRAFT (IRE) 5 b.g. Warcraft (USA) – Thistletopper (Le Bavard (FR)) [2003/4 F16s* 20s^{pu} 20g^2 24g Mar 6] well-made gelding: seventh foal: half-brother to fairly useful hurdler/chaser Hilltopper, stays 2½m, and useful hunter chaser Keeper's Call (both by Mandalus): dam, maiden pointer, from family of useful staying chaser Roman Bar: won bumper at Huntingdon on debut in December: best effort in novice hurdles when 2½ lengths second to Sweet Diversion at Fakenham in February: appeared not to stay 3m final start: probably still capable of improvement over hurdles, but also type to do even better over fences. *C. C. Bealby*

h110 p
F91 +

THISTLE DO 6 b.g. College Chapel – Fishki (Niniski (USA)) [2003/4 h87d, F79: 20m^{pu} May 27] lengthy gelding: little worthwhile form over hurdles. *M. D. Hammond*

h–

THISTLEKICKER (IRE) 12 b.g. Mandalus – Miss Ranova (Giacometti) [2003/4 c–, h74: 16g^5 16m^6 16m 17g^3 16g^4 16f^4 21d Oct 29] leggy gelding: poor hurdler: needs sharp 2m on good going or firmer. *Mrs J. C. McGregor*

c–
h64

THIXENDALE 7 b.m. Reprimand – Havenwood Lady (Fair Season) [2003/4 F17m^5 F17d F17d c21s^{pu} Feb 24] eighth foal: half-sister to winning pointer Dalby Carr (by Henbit): dam unraced half-sister to fairly useful 2m chaser Maudlins Cross: no sign of ability in bumpers (for M. Easterby) or in hunter chase, though some encouragement in points. *Miss J. E. Foster*

c–
F–

TH'MOONS A BALLOON (IRE)   10 b.g. Euphemism – Gerti's Quay (Quayside)   **c89** [2003/4 c19m³ c26mᵖᵘ May 29] modest pointer: third in novice hunter at Exeter in May. *S. J. Partridge*

THOMO (IRE)   6 b.g. Faustus (USA) – Dawn O'Er Kells (IRE) (Pitskelly) [2003/4   **F–** F16d F16g Dec 6] third foal: dam unraced: well held in 2 bumpers. *P. M. Rich*

THORALBY   5 b.g. Son Pardo – Polish Lady (IRE) (Posen (USA)) [2003/4 20f⁴ 16g²   **h74** 17d 16d 17v Jan 13] angular gelding: no form at 2 yrs for C. Fairhurst: best effort over hurdles (poor form) when second in novice seller at Kelso in November: tried in cheekpieces. *M. Dods*

THORNBIRD LASS   8 b.m. Alflora (IRE) – Burling Moss (Le Moss) [2003/4 22gᵖᵘ   **h–** Mar 28] third foal: dam, maiden pointer, from family of Cheltenham Gold Cup and Grand National winner L'Escargot: showed nothing in novice hurdle on debut. *R. Johnson*

THORNTOUN HOLM   6 ch.g. Dancing Spree (USA) – Furry Friend (USA) (Bold   **h69** Bidder) [2003/4 F18f* F16f² F17f⁵ 19d⁴ Dec 11] 3,200 5-y-o: half-brother to several   **F85** winners, including 1990 2-y-o 6f winner Russian Mink (by L'Emigrant) and 1¼m winner who probably stayed 15f Thorntoun Estate (by Durgam): dam lightly-raced maiden: fair form in bumpers, winning weak event at Fontwell in August: poor form when fourth in seller on hurdling debut. *P. F. Nicholls*

THORPENESS (IRE)   5 b.g. Barathea (IRE) – Brisighella (IRE) (Al Hareb (USA))   **h–** [2003/4 h84: 20dᵖᵘ 22sᵖᵘ Jan 2] lightly-raced maiden hurdler, no form in 2003/4. *J. White*

THOR'S PHANTOM   11 ch.g. Weldnaas (USA) – La Carlotta (Ela-Mana-Mou)   **c73** [2003/4 c20d⁴ May 16] successful twice in points in 2003: fourth of 5 finishers in novice   **h–** hunter chase at Stratford. *Mrs F. J. Marriott*

THOSEWERETHEDAYS   11 b.g. Past Glories – Charlotte's Festival (Gala Perform-   **c135 +** ance) [2003/4 c127+, h–: 19g* c20vᶠ Jan 31] sturdy gelding: second start over hurdles   **h110 +** when winning novice at Catterick in December: useful chaser: would have won quite valuable handicap at Ayr but for falling last when well clear of Luzcadou: may prove best short of 3m: raced on good going or softer (acts on heavy): bold-jumping front runner. *Miss P. Robson*

THOUTMOSIS (USA)   5 ch.g. Woodman (USA) – Toujours Elle (USA) (Lyphard   **h100** (USA)) [2003/4 h98: 16g⁶ 17d³ 17d² 24g⁶ 22g⁶ Mar 12] fair handicap hurdler: should stay beyond 2¼m: raced only on good/good to soft ground. *L. Lungo*

THRASHING   9 b.g. Kahyasi – White-Wash (Final Straw) [2003/4 22m c21g³ 17d⁵   **c–** c16mᵖᵘ 24gᵖᵘ 24s 24g* Apr 1] smallish gelding: no show in 2 starts over fences: modest   **h90** hurdler, missed 2002/3: easily best effort in 2003/4 when winning conditional jockeys selling handicap at Taunton: stays 25f: best efforts on good going or firmer: tried in headgear: tongue tied. *A. E. Jones*

THREAD OF HONOUR (IRE)   7 gr.g. Roselier (FR) – Sharkezan (IRE) (Double   **h90** Schwartz) [2003/4 F93: 17d² 19s³ 21g Feb 11] good-topped gelding: modest form when placed in novice hurdles at Market Rasen and Hereford: possibly amiss final start: should stay beyond 19f. *Miss H. C. Knight*

THREE DAYS REIGN (IRE)   10 br.g. Camden Town – Little Treat (Miner's Lamp)   **c96** [2003/4 c75, h–: c20d² c20g* c23m² Jun 28] robust gelding: modest chaser: won   **h–** handicap at Worcester in May: stays 23f: acts on good to firm going, probably on good to soft: tried blinkered: sound jumper. *P. D. Cundell*

THREE EAGLES (USA)   7 ch.g. Eagle Eyed (USA) – Tertiary (USA) (Vaguely   **c110** Noble) [2003/4 h92: 20m c16m² c16m² c23mᶠ c24m* 21m* c23m² c21g² 21m² 24mᵖᵘ   **h110** 25g⁴ c26gᵘʳ c24g³ Dec 11] small gelding: fair hurdler/chaser: left D. Caro after second outing, M. Pipe after third: won handicaps over fences at Bangor and hurdles at Southwell in August: stays easy 3m: acts on any going, usually races on good or firmer: has bolted to post: usually forces pace (has lost interest when unable to dominate). *M. Scudamore*

THREE LIONS   7 ch.g. Jupiter Island – Super Sol (Rolfe (USA)) [2003/4 h90: 16m⁵   **h90 §** 19gᵖᵘ 16g⁶ 16s⁵ 18s³ 20s 23s 20s³ Apr 17] leggy gelding: modest handicap hurdler: stays 2½m: acts on soft going: tried in cheekpieces: temperamental. *R. S. Brookhouse*

THREE MIRRORS   4 b.g. Cloudings (IRE) – Aliuska (IRE) (Fijar Tango (FR))   **h116** [2003/4 16m 16s⁵ 16s* 16g⁵ Feb 29] tall gelding: half-brother to fairly useful 2m hurdler Altay (by Erins Isle): fairly useful juvenile hurdler: sweating badly, made all in maiden at Gowran in January, hanging badly left circuit out but finding plenty when beating Quel Doun 3½ lengths: creditable efforts at Leopardstown following month and Punchestown (sixth to Definate Spectacle) in late-April: usually tongue tied: successful on Flat in March. *Anthony Mullins, Ireland*

THREEPENNY BIT 6 b.m. Safawan – Tuppence In Clover (Petoski) [2003/4 F17m F17d 20s^{pu} 1 /g Apr 10] lengthy mare: first foal: dam unraced half-sister to very smart staying hurdler Simpson and useful hurdler Three Farthings: signs of some ability on first of 2 starts in bumpers: showed little in 2 races over hurdles, bled from nose on first occasion. *Mrs S. M. Johnson* **h F—**

THREE TIMES A LADY 4 b.f. Syrtos – Pure Formality (Forzando) [2003/4 F16s⁴ Apr 12] seventh foal: half-sister to 3 winners, including fair chaser Ritual (by Selkirk), stays 2½m: dam 2-y-o 6f winner, granddaughter of Irish Oaks winner Celina: beaten long way when fourth of 14 in mares bumper at Fakenham on debut. *D. W. Thompson* **F—**

THREEZEDZZ 6 ch.g. Emarati (USA) – Exotic Forest (Dominion) [2003/4 h98?: 16s⁴ 16g⁶ Apr 4] poor maiden hurdler: will need sharp 2m: free-going sort. *Mrs P. N. Dutfield* **h83**

THRILLING PROSPECT (IRE) 7 b.m. King's Ride – Bail Out (Quayside) [2003/4 F17d F17m⁶ 20d² 20s⁴ Apr 17] fifth foal: half-sister to Irish bumper winner Know Thyne (by Good Thyne): dam unraced sister to useful staying chaser Woodgate and half-sister to useful staying jumper Gola Cher: well held in 2 bumpers: modest form in novice company over hurdles: likely to stay beyond 2½m. *R. T. Phillips* **h88 F—**

THROUGH THE RYE 8 ch.g. Sabrehill (USA) – Baharlilys (Green Dancer (USA)) [2003/4 h131: c16f^F 16s 16v 16s* 16g 17d Mar 18] strong gelding: fell fourth on chasing debut: useful handicap hurdler: won at Wetherby in February by length from Avitta: below form otherwise in 2003/4: raced mainly around 2m on good going or softer (acts on heavy): tongue tied once: usually front runner. *G. A. Swinbank* **c– h131**

THROWALINE 8 b.g. Thowra (FR) – Stockline (Capricorn Line) [2003/4 h106: 24g^{pu} Sep 24] smallish gelding: fair hurdler: still in contention when pulled up approaching 3 out in handicap at Perth (struck into) only start in 2003/4: will prove as effective at 3m as shorter: acts on firm and soft ground. *P. J. Hobbs* **h–**

THUMPER (IRE) 6 b.g. Grand Lodge (USA) – Parkeen Princess (He Loves Me) [2003/4 h98: 16g* 16g3 20m^{pu} 20d^{pu} Apr 21] modest hurdler: won novice at Worcester in August: better form when third in similar event at Perth month later: blinkered second and third starts. *Jonjo O'Neill* **h98**

THUNDER CANYON (USA) 5 b. or br.g. Gulch (USA) – Naazeq (Nashwan (USA)) [2003/4 h92: 16g 17d4 16d4 16d6 22g4 21d4 Mar 19] poor maiden hurdler: left N. Richards after second start: stays 2½m: acts on soft and good to firm going: tried in cheekpieces. *Evan Williams* **h82**

THUNDERPOINT (IRE) 12 b.g. Glacial Storm (USA) – Urdite (FR) (Concertino (FR)) [2003/4 c75§, h–§: 20m* c20g^{ur} c21v2 c19m* c21g2 c20g4 20m2 c17g2 c24m* c24m4 c20g Mar 12] smallish, lengthy gelding: poor handicap hurdler/modest chaser: won over hurdles at Chepstow (seller) in May and handicaps over fences at Hereford in June and Stratford in August: stays 3m: acts on any going: usually blinkered, effective when not (also tried visored): has looked temperamental. *R. J. Price* **c98 h69**

THYNE FOR INTERSKY (IRE) 5 ch.g. Good Thyne (USA) – One Last Chance (Le Bavard (FR)) [2003/4 F17m* F17m* Oct 10] €18,000 3-y-o: sturdy gelding: second foal: dam bad maiden hurdler: favourite, won bumpers at Market Rasen in September and Carlisle in October, staying on strongly when beating Weston Rock 6 lengths at latter course. *Jonjo O'Neill* **F105**

THYNE WILL TELL (IRE) 9 ch.g. Good Thyne (USA) – Deep Khaletta (Deep Run) [2003/4 c137, h–: c20m^F c20m3 Jun 29] lengthy gelding: has reportedly suffered knee problems: fairly useful hurdler/useful chaser at best: has fallen 2 of last 4 starts and jumped with little confidence final one (reportedly finished lame): will stay 3m: acts on firm and good to soft going (won bumper on heavy): has broken blood vessels. *P. J. Hobbs* **c– h–**

TIANYI (IRE) 8 b.g. Mujadil (USA) – Skinity (Rarity) [2003/4 h77: 16m4 18m 22g^{pu} 16d3 18f4 20m4 c17m5 16m* 19f2 16d3 16g3 18s2 17s 16d6 Apr 11] angular gelding: no show on chasing debut (final outing for D. Caro): poor hurdler: won 3-runner handicap at Huntingdon in October: stays 19f: unraced on heavy going, acts on any other: usually blinkered/visored: often front runner. *M. Scudamore* **c– h84**

TICKER 6 b.g. Timeless Times (USA) – Lady Day (FR) (Lightning (FR)) [2003/4 16g^F Jun 27] fair on Flat (stays 1½m) at 4 yrs: won maiden hurdle at Naas in 2002/3 for **h108**

P. Roche: making progress from rear when falling fatally 3 out in handicap at Stratford. *P. J. Hobbs*

TICKTON FLYER 6 b.g. Sovereign Water (FR) – Contradictory (Reprimand) [2003/4 h98, F100: 20m² 24d* 17d Mar 7] dual bumper winner: modest form over hurdles: won novice at Hexham in May very easily: well held over inadequate trip 10 months later: stays 3m: acts on good to soft and good to firm going: blinkered last 2 starts: hasn't always looked an easy ride. *M. W. Easterby*   **h98**

TIDJANI (IRE) 12 b.g. Alleged (USA) – Tikarna (FR) (Targowice (USA)) [2003/4 17d⁴ 21s* 20vᵖᵘ 20v² c24sᵖᵘ Mar 21] sparely-made gelding: one-time fairly useful hurdler/fair chaser for C. Roche: fair form over hurdles in 2003/4: won handicap at Huntingdon in December: stays 21f: acts on heavy ground: tried blinkered. *Jonjo O'Neill*   **c–** **h102**

TIDOUR (FR) 8 b.g. Rahotep (FR) – Softway (FR) (Tyrant (USA)) [2003/4 c16s* c17s² c16v² c17s* c16gᶠ c16g* Apr 1]   **c145 +** **h–**

Tidour was off the track for two whole seasons—nine hundred and eighty-eight days to be precise—with a leg problem, but he was worth the wait, returning as one of the season's leading two-mile novice chasers. His first season of racing in 2000/1 had consisted of just three runs in bumpers and two in novice hurdles, ending with third place, at 50/1, in the Grade 2 two-mile novices' hurdle at Aintree's Grand National meeting. Three years later, he was back at Aintree, this time starting favourite for the Martell Cognac Red Rum Handicap Chase and bidding to keep up the good record of novices in the race. Dark'n Sharp and Golden Alpha had won the last two runnings, and Jungli had also been a novice when winning for Tidour's stable in 2000, a year after Paul Webber won the race for the first time with Flying Instructor. Golden Alpha was in the field again and one of Tidour's chief rivals, along with St Pirran and Ground Ball, the first two home in the Grand Annual at Cheltenham. With several front runners in the field the Red Rum Handicap was never going to turn into a muddling affair. Tidour's stable-companion Duke of Buckingham set a strong gallop, effectively acting as a pacemaker for the favourite. Surprisingly, Duke of Buckingham was still in front two out, but the patiently-ridden Tidour came to lead soon afterwards, asserting in really good style and passing the post nine lengths clear. Armaturk fared best of those who raced up with the pace, just emerging the best in a tight finish for the places ahead of St Pirran, Simply Gifted and Ei Ei. Tidour became the eighth novice

Martell Cognac Red Rum Handicap Chase, Aintree—the novice Tidour comes between Armaturk and the largely hidden Duke of Buckingham at the second last

to win the race in the last sixteen years, Prideaux Boy (1988), Feroda (1989), Arctic Kinsman (1996) and Down The Fell (1997) successful in addition to those already mentioned.

    Tidour earned favouritism at Aintree with a promising and much improved effort in the Arkle at Cheltenham a couple of weeks earlier. He was only a couple of lengths behind the leaders and still to be asked for his effort when falling two out, giving the impression he would have finished third behind Well Chief and Kicking King. Those well-run races on good ground at Cheltenham and Aintree were a far cry from the steadily-run novice chases in the mud which Tidour had been contesting during the winter. He caused a 25/1 surprise when winning on his return to action at Uttoxeter in December and was impressive when an easy winner at Plumpton in February on his last start before Cheltenham. He had finished second on his two starts in between, beaten just over a length both times, firstly behind Non So at Plumpton and then behind Kalca Mome at Haydock where his jumping had been rather indifferent in the straight.

Tidour (FR) (b.g. 1996)	Rahotep (FR) (b 1978)	Matahawk (br 1972)	Sea Hawk II
			Carromata
		La Masure (b 1965)	Net
			Miss Pink
	Softway (FR) (b 1980)	Tyrant (b 1966)	Bold Ruler
			Anadem
		Cialenga (b 1975)	Devon
			Rieka

    Tidour is by the high-class French middle-distance performer Rahotep, best known now as the sire of Jair du Cochet. Tidour's dam Softway had a frustrating career on the Flat, finishing second six times at up to a mile but failing to win. She finally got her head in front when sent hurdling, winning over a mile and three quarters at Enghien as a three-year-old. She also finished second on her only start over fences. Softway has bred two other winners by Rahotep, one on the Flat, but more notably Ramban, winner of the top French hurdle for three-year-olds, the Prix Cambaceres, in 1994. Tidour is also a half-brother to four other minor winners in France over jumps, two by Great Palm and one each by April Night and Our Account. There is little to be said about Tidour's family in the next generation or two, but, going back a bit, his great grandam is out of a half-sister to the dam of a top-class Prix du Jockey Club winner Le Fabuleux. The good-topped Tidour, still with just eleven starts behind him all told, may be capable of better over fences and there should be more handicaps to be won with him. He has so far been raced only at around two miles, though can be expected to stay a bit further. He looks well suited by being held up off a good pace and has done most of his racing on soft or heavy ground, though his last two runs showed he doesn't need the mud. *P. R. Webber*

TIDY (IRE)   4 b.c. Mujadil (USA) – Neat Shilling (IRE) (Bob Back (USA)) [2003/4   **h–** 16g^{pu} Feb 6] smallish colt: fairly useful on Flat (stays 7f), sold out of J. Osborne's stable 8,000 gns Newmarket Autumn Sales, successful in April: no aptitude for hurdling in juvenile on debut over jumps. *M. D. Hammond*

TIERKELY (IRE)   9 br.g. Yashgan – Island Dream (Lucifer (USA)) [2003/4 c24g^2 **c94** c27m* c21g* c26m^{pu} c28d^6 c24s Mar 21] IR 700 4-y-o: fifth foal: half-brother to winner in Italy by Broken Hearted: dam maiden who won last of 7 starts in Irish points in 2003: modest chaser: won novice in July and handicap in August, both at Sedgefield: no form after: stays 27f: acts on good to firm going. *J. J. Lambe, Ireland*

TIGER CRY (IRE)   6 b.g. Germany (USA) – Dream Academy (Town And Country)   **h122** [2003/4 F17g^4 16d^2 16s^2 16v^2 16g* 16d^2 Apr 13] €70,000 4-y-o: fifth foal: half-brother   **r94** to winning hurdler/fairly useful chaser who stays 3½m Sigma Dotcomm (by Safety Catch) and winning 17f hurdler Academy (by Archway): dam winning 2m hurdler: fourth in bumper on debut: fairly useful hurdler: won maiden at Leopardstown in February: very good second to Macs Joy in handicap at Fairyhouse in April: raced around 2m on good going or softer. *A. L. T. Moore, Ireland*

TIGER FROG (USA)   5 b.g. French Deputy (USA) – Woodyoubelieveit (USA)   **c70** (Woodman (USA)) [2003/4 h86: 16m 16f 16g 22g^5 23d 16g* 16s^5 20g^3 c21v c16g^2 19g^2 **h83** 16g^4 16d^6 16s^2 Apr 11] lengthy gelding: not fluent and poor form on second of 2 starts over fences inside 3 days: poor handicap hurdler: won seller at Catterick in December:

TIG

claimed from R. C. Guest £6,000 eleventh outing: stays 2½m: acts on soft going: tried in cheekpieces, usually blinkered: has had tongue tied. *J. Mackie*

TIGERLION (IRE) 6 b.g. Supreme Leader – Avida Dancer (Ballymore) [2003/4 **F114** F16s² Feb 7] rangy, good sort: will make a chaser: brother to useful chaser/fair hurdler Lord of The Turf, stays 3m, and fair 2m and 19f hurdle winner Back On The Lash, and half-brother to fairly useful 2½m hurdle winner Canary Wharf (by Accordion): dam unraced: progressive form in bumpers, won at Naas on debut in 2002/3: in frame behind No Complications at same course 11 months later and Geill Sli in Grade 1 at Punchestown in late-April: will stay beyond 2m: type to do well over jumps in 2004/5. *J. Bleahen, Ireland*

TIGERS LAIR (IRE) 5 b. or br.g. Accordion – Eadie (IRE) (Strong Gale) [2003/4 **F105** F16s⁴ F16g² F17d⁴ Apr 3] €92,000 3-y-o: leggy, rather unfurnished gelding: second foal: dam lightly raced in points: progressive form in bumpers, 5 lengths fourth of 15 to Diamond Sal in Grade 2 at Aintree final start. *Jonjo O'Neill*

TIGER TALK 8 ch.g. Sabrehill (USA) – Tebre (USA) (Sir Ivor (USA)) [2003/4 c74, c– h86: 17s² 17s 16gᵖᵘ 19g³ 17m 24g⁴ 21mᵖᵘ Jul 22] angular gelding: poor handicap hurdler/ h74 § maiden chaser: stays 19f: acts on heavy and good to firm going: tried in cheekpieces, often blinkered: unreliable: sold to join D. Pipe 4,200 gns Doncaster August Sales, modest form in points in 2004. *M. E. Sowersby*

TIGER TIPS LAD (IRE) 5 b.g. Zaffaran (USA) – Halens Match (IRE) (Matching h90 Pair) [2003/4 F16m F16d 22s⁶ 24s⁴ 16s² Mar 15] lengthy gelding: first foal: dam winning F83 Irish pointer: better effort in bumpers when seventh of 12 at Sandown on debut: dropped back in trip, best effort in novice hurdles when 3 lengths second to Nathos at Plumpton, settling better: should stay beyond 2m. *N. A. Twiston-Davies*

TIGER TOPS 5 ch.g. Sabrehill (USA) – Rose Chime (IRE) (Tirol) [2003/4 16sᵖᵘ Mar h– 19] fair on Flat (best at 1m): broke down on hurdling debut: dead. *J. A. Supple*

TIGER TYPHOON (IRE) 8 b.g. Cataldi – Churchtown Breeze (Tarqogan) [2003/4 c76 c–, h76: c17g⁴ c16g³ c16mᶠ May 15] strong gelding: maiden hurdler/chaser, poor form: h– should prove better at 2½m than 2m. *R. J. Hodges*

TIGHE CASTER 5 b.g. Makbul – Miss Fire (Gunner B) [2003/4 F18v³ F16s Mar 20] F83 first foal: dam unraced half-sister to fairly useful staying hurdler Shirley Grove: better effort in bumpers when seventh of 21 to Something Gold at Ascot, keeping on steadily. *P. R. Webber*

TIGHTEN YOUR BELT (IRE) 7 b.g. Phardante (FR) – Hi' Upham (Deep Run) h135 p [2003/4 F106: 16v* 16s* 21g Mar 17] useful-looking gelding: winning Irish pointer: useful bumper winner: successful first 2 starts in novice hurdles, both at Towcester, beating Raygale 17 lengths in January and Twenty Degrees 11 lengths in February: much better form when around 13 lengths seventh of 15 to Fundamentalist in Grade 1 novice at Cheltenham: will stay 3m: raced on good going or softer: hasn't finished improving, especially granted still greater test of stamina. *Miss Venetia Williams*

TIK-A-TAI (IRE) 9 b.g. Alphabatim (USA) – Carrig Ross (Lord Ha Ha) [2003/4 c– c118, h116: 20g² 21s² 16s* Jan 31] strong gelding: fairly useful chaser: of similar merit h126 over hurdles, best effort this season when winning handicap at Doncaster by 26 lengths from Sun Cat: stays 3m, effective at much shorter when conditions are testing: acts on soft going: prone to mistakes over fences. *O. Sherwood*

TIKRAM 7 ch.g. Lycius (USA) – Black Fighter (USA) (Secretariat (USA)) c143 [2003/4 h133: 16m³ c20g² c20g² c22s* c20s⁴ c20g* c20g* c21m² Apr 14] h134
Life has been anything but dull for Timmy Murphy since he moved from Ireland in 1995 to continue his career in Britain as conditional jockey to the Kim Bailey stable. He got off the mark on the Bailey-trained Quiet Amusement in the August of that year and further wins followed, but just over twelve months later Murphy lost his job, reportedly because of bad timekeeping, and there have been several other low points since, none more so than a three-month spell in prison in 2002, Murphy having been found guilty of indecent assault on an aircraft. That brought to an end a second spell as stable jockey to Paul Nicholls, but to his credit Murphy has gradually rebuilt his career and in 2004/5 he will find himself with another of jump racing's plum jobs, having been retained to ride the horses belonging to the champion jumps owner David Johnson following Tony McCoy's move from Martin Pipe to Jonjo O'Neill. Murphy probably won't be able to continue his association with Beef Or Salmon, the horse who, more than any other, helped put

924

Mildmay of Flete Challenge Cup Handicap Chase, Cheltenham—
Tikram (far left) comes late to deny Iznogoud; also in contention at the last are
(left to right) Fondmort, Kelrev, Polar Red and Inn Antique

the rider back in the spotlight. Still, with the likes of Our Vic, Therealbandit and Well Chief, plus a host of other promising individuals to look forward to riding, it isn't a problem that should occupy Murphy too much.

Watching Timmy Murphy in action nowadays, it is difficult to believe that early on in his career he should have fallen foul of the stewards so often as he did for improper use of the whip. His quiet, patient style coupled with the ability to get the best out of his mounts in a close finish without being overly-hard on them, is very much in contrast to how he sometimes used to approach the job of race-riding. Murphy also has the knack of persuading horses who look less than straightforward to race more sweetly, as he demonstrated to such good effect on Tikram in the Mildmay of Flete Challenge Cup at Cheltenham. Tikram is a horse who has a tendency to race lazily and usually takes plenty of driving, and Murphy looked as though he would have his work cut out to keep his mount up to the mark in such a competitive race, Tikram's first in open company over fences.

Judged on the form he had shown in his five previous starts over fences Tikram looked to have a stiffish task racing from 3 lb out of the weights in the Mildmay of Flete, though it was clear from his displays as a hurdler that he had the potential to give a good account of himself off a BHB mark of 133. In three full seasons' racing over hurdles Tikram developed into a useful handicapper, though won just twice from nineteen starts, and on his first start in the latest campaign he finished a good third off a mark of 132 in a well-contested handicap at Ascot. Tikram won two of his first five chases, landing the odds in a maiden and a novice at Fontwell, and he ran well at Cheltenham in two of the other three, when runner-up to Puntal and to Santenay.

The sixteen-runner Mildmay of Flete was a truly-run contest, which suited Tikram who was dropped out towards the rear from the off, Murphy cajoling him in the back straight then becoming more insistent as Tikram gradually began to improve his position. At the second last, Tikram, racing wide, still had eight horses in front of him and was over ten lengths adrift of the leader Iznogoud. Now Murphy began to get serious and Tikram, having finally warmed to his task, responded so well that he was almost on terms jumping the last. He took over from Iznogoud very soon after and continued to run on strongly to win by two and a half lengths from that horse, with top weight Fondmort a further length and a half behind in third. Tikram gave Murphy a second winner of the meeting following his success on the enigmatic Creon at 50/1 in the Pertemps Final.

The form shown by Tikram surpassed anything that he had achieved over hurdles, and he went on to better it on his only subsequent start, when returned to

925

Cheltenham to race off a mark 8 lb higher in a Grade 2 limited handicap. With Murphy taking the mount on Risk Accessor, the ride on Tikram went to Jamie Moore, who claimed the 3-lb allowance and had been on board when Tikram gained his second chase win. Moore, the son of Tikram's trainer, is one of the most promising young riders around and he looked to have brought Tikram with a run which would prove successful, only for Seebald to hold his challenge by half a length. Cheltenham does appear to bring out the best in Tikram, and the Paddy Power and Tripleprint Gold Cups look obvious early targets for him in the next season.

		Mr Prospector	Raise A Native
		(b 1970)	Gold Digger
	Lycius (USA)		
	(ch 1988)	Lypatia	Lyphard
Tikram		(b 1975)	Hypatia
(ch.g. 1997)		Secretariat	Bold Ruler
		(ch 1970)	Somethingroyal
	Black Fighter (USA)		
	(br 1987)	Faten	Northern Dancer
		(b 1978)	Treat Me Nobly

Tikram is bred very much on Flat-racing lines and has run on the Flat for present connections, including when twelfth in the Cesarewitch shortly before his latest jumping campaign got under way. By the very smart six-furlong to one-mile performer Lycius, Tikram is the sixth foal of Black Fighter who showed fairly useful form over a mile and a mile and a quarter as a three-year-old. Black Fighter was disqualified on three occasions for testing positive for a steroid, one of those disqualifications depriving her of her only win, in a maiden at Kempton. Black Fighter has done well at stud and her other winners include Tikram's full brothers Taming, a fairly useful performer both on the Flat and over hurdles, and Tramway, who showed smart form over middle distances; and close relatives Tracking (by Machiavellian) and Transit (by Lion Cavern), the former a useful nine-furlong winner and the latter a fair two-mile hurdler/chaser. Tikram's grandam Faten, who won over a mile and a half in France, is from the family of Be My Guest. Tikram, a tall gelding, stays two and three quarter miles and acts on any going. He was well held when tried once in a visor and once in blinkers over hurdles, pulling hard in the latter. Tikram might not be the most straightforward of horses to ride, but no jockey is going to pass up the opportunity to partner him. As well as being a useful performer, he is a most reliable one, too. *G. L. Moore*

TILLEY LANE (IRE) 7 b.g. Blues Traveller (IRE) – Divine Apsara (Godswalk (USA)) [2003/4 17d^pu Mar 27] half-brother to several winners, including fair 2m hurdler Wesperada (by Waajib): dam Irish 5f to 1m winner: breathing problem in novice hurdle on debut. *R. A. Fahey* — **h–**

TIMBERA (IRE) 10 b. or br.g. Commanche Run – Morry's Lady (The Parson) [2003/4 c135, h–: c24d^5 c24s^5 c21g^5 c29d^5 Apr 12] lengthy gelding: useful handicap chaser: usually runs with credit, fifth of 10 finishers to Granit d'Estruval in 29f Irish Grand National (won race previous year) at Fairyhouse and 2½ lengths second to Wotsitooya in valuable event at Punchestown in April: raced on good going or softer (acts on heavy): usually tongue tied: usually sound jumper: tends to idle but is genuine. *D. T. Hughes, Ireland* — **c139 h–**

TIMBERLEY 10 ch.g. Dancing High – Kimberley Rose (Monksfield) [2003/4 c21d^pu Oct 29] modest pointer, won maiden in 2003: tongue tied, showed nothing in maiden on steeplechasing debut. *Miss R. Brewis* — **c–**

TIME FOR ACTION (IRE) 12 b.g. Alzao (USA) – Beyond Words (Ballad Rock) [2003/4 21m^pu 17g 20g^2 17s^pu 19m Mar 4] small gelding: poor handicap hurdler nowadays: stays 2½m: acts on firm and soft going: tongue tied. *H. J. Evans* — **h74**

TIMELESS CHICK 7 ch.m. Timeless Times (USA) – Be My Bird (Be My Chief (USA)) [2003/4 h69: 21m^2 20m^4 Aug 2] angular mare: poor maiden hurdler: stays easy 2½m: acts on good to firm and good to soft going (well held on soft): blinkered once. *J. L. Spearing* — **h69**

TIME MARCHES ON 6 b.g. Timeless Times (USA) – Tees Gazette Girl (Kalaglow) [2003/4 h82: 16d Apr 28] leggy gelding: poor on Flat (stays 1½m): no better over hurdles. *Mrs M. Reveley* — **h–**

TIME N TIDE (IRE) 8 b.g. Namaqualand (USA) – Now Then (Sandford Lad) [2003/4 **h–§**
h115§: 26m^{pu} 26g^{pu} May 18] lengthy gelding: fairly useful hurdler at best, showed signs
of temperament: stayed 2½m: acted on soft and good to firm going: tried blinkered
(downed tools early): dead. *Jonjo O'Neill*

TIME OF FLIGHT (IRE)   11 ch.g. Over The River (FR) – Icy Lou (Bluerullah)   **c– §**
[2003/4 c102§, h–: c20v^{pu} c16s^{pu} Feb 11] compact gelding: winning hurdler: fairly useful   **h–**
handicap chaser at best, lightly raced and little form since 2001/2: should stay beyond
2½m: acts on good to firm and heavy going: has had tongue tied: has looked unwilling.
Mrs M. Reveley

TIMES PAST (IRE) 9 b.g. Commanche Run – Orient Moonbeam (Deep Run) [2003/4   **c66**
c89, h–: c20m^4 20g^5 24g^4 19s Dec 20] leggy gelding: winning pointer: twice-raced in   **h76**
steeplechases, trained by P. Jones on reappearance: novice hurdler, poor form in Britain:
stays 3m. *J. W. Unett*

TIME SPIN 4 b.g. Robellino (USA) – Chiltern Court (USA) (Topsider (USA)) [2003/4   **h91**
16d^6 16d^{pu} 18v^2 Feb 5] lightly-raced maiden on Flat (probably stays 1¼m): best effort in
juvenile hurdles when second to Dr Sharp at Kelso. *C. Grant*

TIME TO PARLEZ   13 b.g. Amboise – Image of War (Warpath) [2003/4 c73§, h–:   **c– §**
c25d^4 c25s^{pu} c26m^5 Nov 25] strong gelding: poor handicap chaser, no form in 2003/4:   **h–**
stays 3½m: all wins on soft/heavy going: blinkered once: moody. *C. J. Drewe*

TIME TO REFLECT (IRE)   5 ch.g. Anshan – Castlemitchle (IRE) (Roselier (FR))   **c–**
[2003/4 F18m* 17g^3 24g* 16g^2 20d 22d c25g^{pu} 22g 20s 21m^{pu} Apr 14] €9,000 3-y-o: **h96 d**
rather leggy gelding: third foal: dam unraced from family of good-class 2m jumpers   **F90**
Kesslin and Rathconrath: won weak maiden bumper at Plumpton on debut in October:
modest hurdler: won maiden at Chepstow in November: very disappointing after next
start, including over fences: effective at 2m to easy 3m: visored last 2 starts: ungenuine.
M. C. Pipe

TIME TO REGRET   4 b.g. Presidium – Scoffera (Scottish Reel) [2003/4 17g Aug 8]   **h–**
modest maiden on Flat (stays 9.3f): mistake 3 out and weakened quickly in straight in
juvenile at Sedgefield on hurdling debut. *J. J. Quinn*

TIME TO SHINE   5 b.m. Pivotal – Sweet Jaffa (Never So Bold) [2003/4 16m* 15s*   **h113**
19s^4 16v^2 16g* 20s^2 20g Apr 1] tall, leggy mare: fair on Flat (stays 2m): progressive in
first season over hurdles, won seller at Fakenham (for B. Johnson) in May and mares
novices at Folkestone (handicap) in January and Ascot (in command when left clear last
by fall of Lalagune) in February: out of depth final start: stays 2½m: acts on good to firm
and heavy going. *Miss L. J. Sheen*

TIME TO TELL   8 b.m. Keen – Meet Again (Lomond (USA)) [2003/4 h–, F77:   **c–**
c26g^{pu} May 5] no form in novice hurdles: lame on chasing debut. *B. G. Powell*   **h–**

TIMIDJAR (IRE)   11 b.g. Doyoun – Timissara (USA) (Shahrastani (USA)) [2003/4   **h68**
h70: 17g^2 17m^3 16m 17d^{pu} 16m^5 17g^6 19m Sep 10] neat gelding: poor handicap hurdler:
best around 2m: acts on firm and good to soft going: tried blinkered. *Mrs D. Thomas*

TIM'S THE MAN (IRE)   8 gr.g. Roselier (FR) – Pindas (Bargello) [2003/4 h96:   **c83**
c26g c20d^5 c19d^6 Jan 27] good-topped gelding: modest hurdler, prominent long way   **h–**
in handicap final start: poor form over fences, making mistakes: should stay beyond 19f:
raced on good going or softer: wore cheekpieces last 3 starts: sold 6,000 gns Doncaster
May Sales. *C. J. Mann*

TINA COOKE   8 gr.m. Tina's Pet – Up Cooke (Deep Run) [2003/4 h–: c16m^4 c17m^{pu} **c–**
c21g^{pu} 21g^5 c16s Apr 4] lengthy mare: little sign of ability. *Miss Kate Milligan*   **h–**

TINA THYNE (IRE)   10 b.m. Good Thyne (USA) – Tiny Tina (Deep Run) [2003/4   **c–**
h86: c20m^{pu} May 5] smallish, angular mare: modest hurdler: lame on chasing debut: stays   **h–**
27f: raced mainly on good going or softer (acts on heavy): tried blinkered/visored.
J. G. M. O'Shea

TINERANA HOUSE (IRE)   5 gr.g. Paris House – Tony Award (USA) (Kirtling)   **F–**
[2003/4 F16g F16m Jul 9] ex-Irish gelding: fourth foal: half-brother to 1½m winner Pearl
Anniversary (by Priolo): dam, minor sprint winner at 4 yrs in USA, half-sister to dam of
Breeders' Cup Classic winner Skywalker: failed to complete in 2 points: tailed off in
2 bumpers (trained on first occasion by K. J. Burke): sold £1,300 Ascot April Sales.
Miss C. J. E. Caroe

Ashleybank Investments Scottish Borders National (Handicap Chase), Kelso—
Tipsy Mouse caps an excellent novice campaign over fences,
just denying Robbo (cheekpieces) at the end of four miles

TINO (IRE)   8 ch.g. Torus – Delphic Thunder (Viking (USA)) [2003/4 c73, h–: c26g^{pu} c23m^{pu} c23m^{pu} c26m² c23f² c21m* c24m* c23m* c22g⁵ c24s Dec 29] sturdy gelding: poor handicap chaser: won events in small fields at Folkestone (conditional jockeys, for second year running), Ludlow (10 lb out of weights) and Leicester within 2 weeks in November: stays 3¼m: acts on firm going: tried blinkered. *J. S. King*   **c77**
h–

TINOVERITAS (FR)   6 b.g. Saint Estephe (FR) – Tinorosa (FR) (Concertino (FR)) [2003/4 F100: F16g* 17g³ 19m* 21g⁶ 16d³ 17s* Apr 6] big, rangy gelding: fairly useful in bumpers, won maiden at Worcester in May: fair novice hurdler: won at Newbury in December and Exeter in April, beating Breken Le Noir 2 lengths at latter: didn't impress with attitude in handicaps both starts in between: best efforts around 2m: acts on soft and good to firm going: not one to trust. *P. F. Nicholls*   **h114 §**
F104

TIN SYMPHONY   6 ch.m. Opera Ghost – Bronze Age (Celtic Cone) [2003/4 F81: 16d^{bd} 17s⁵ 16d² 17s⁶ Feb 6] novice hurdler, easily best effort when second to Tragic Ohio at Wincanton. *B. J. M. Ryall*   **h96**

TINTON MILL   5 b.m. Shambo – Mill Thyme (Thowra (FR)) [2003/4 F17g Apr 13] first foal: dam unreliable winning 2m hurdler: tailed off in bumper on debut. *Jane Southcombe*   **F–**

TIOGA GOLD (IRE)   5 b.g. Goldmark (USA) – Coffee Bean (Doulab (USA)) [2003/4 16m³ 19d 16f Feb 29] leggy gelding: modest on Flat (stays 1½m): 100/1, nearest finish when third of 8 to 20-length winner Thesis in novice at Wetherby on hurdling debut: well beaten both other starts. *L. R. James*   **h–**

TIOMAN (IRE)   5 b. or br.g. Dr Devious (IRE) – Tochar Ban (USA) (Assert) [2003/4 17s 16s⁶ 16g Mar 27] leggy gelding: half-brother to winning hurdler Albany (by Alhaarth), stays 3m: fairly useful on Flat (stays 2m), sold out of M. Jarvis' stable 6,000 gns Doncaster August Sales: well beaten in 3 outings over hurdles (whipped round start on debut). *Mrs Mary A. Meek*   **h–**

TIP KASH (FR)   7 ch.g. Kashtan (FR) – Tipas (FR) (Tip Moss (FR)) [2003/4 h106: 20m³ 22d⁴ 24d 20v^{pu} 16d^{pu} 21d c24d³ c21m Apr 15] angular gelding: fair handicap   **c–**
h102 d

hurdler: below form after second start, often shaping as if amiss (including on chasing debut): stays 2¾m: acts on soft going: has had tongue tied. *P. M. Phelan*

TIPP TOP LORD (IRE) 7 gr.g. Mister Lord (USA) – Dark Fluff (Mandalus) [2003/4   **c104 p** h–: c25d^{pu} c24d^3 c26s^2 c24v* c25d* c32g Mar 17] tall gelding: well beaten on hurdling   **h–** debut: fair form in steeplechases: won handicaps at Chepstow in February and Towcester (by 3 lengths from Ah Yeah) in March, prominent throughout each time: stiff task, ninth of 13 finishers to Royal Emperor in valuable amateur novice at Cheltenham: thorough stayer: raced on good ground or softer (acts on heavy): type to do well in staying handicaps in 2004/5. *N. A. Twiston-Davies*

TIPSY MOUSE (IRE) 8 ch.g. Roselier (FR) – Darjoy (Darantus) [2003/4 c–, h97:   **c122 +** c20g^2 c25g* c23g^2 c24s^2 c24d* c24v* c33d^F c32g* c33d^4 Apr 17] workmanlike gelding: **h–** modest maiden hurdler: much better over fences, winning handicaps (first 2 novices) at Hexham in May, Haydock in December and January and Kelso (beat Robbo a short head, pair clear, in Ashleybank Investments Scottish Borders National) in March: distant fourth behind Grey Abbey in Scottish Grand National at Ayr: thorough stayer: raced on good going or softer (acts on heavy): usually sound jumper. *Mrs S. J. Smith*

TIQUET 5 b.g. Bedford (USA) – Lady Kay-Lee (Cruise Missile) [2003/4 F16s 20s 24g^F **h82 ?** 21g^{pu} Mar 26] medium-sized gelding: first foal: dam poor maiden hurdler: signs of ability   **F–** only when eighth of 16 in maiden at Folkestone on hurdling debut. *N. J. Henderson*

TIRAILLEUR (IRE) 4 b.f. Eagle Eyed (USA) – Tiralle (IRE) (Tirol) [2003/4 17f^4 **h–** Sep 30] modest on Flat (stays 1¼m), successful twice in 2003: last of 4 finishers in weak juvenile maiden at Exeter on hurdling debut: sold to join Mrs P. Townsley £2,000 Ascot April Sales. *J. White*

TIRALDO (FR) 11 b.g. Royal Charter (FR) – Tamilda (FR) (Rose Laurel) [2003/4 c70,   **c–** h–: c30m^6 c25s c25d Feb 15] compact gelding: poor chaser: well beaten in hunters in   **h–** 2003/4, left A. Juckes after first outing: stays 25f: acts on heavy going: wears blinkers/ cheekpieces nowadays. *S. Flook*

TIRIKUMBA 8 ch.m. Le Moss – Ntombi (Trasi's Son) [2003/4 F95: 22m^2 21d 19d^3 **h93** 21g Mar 27] lengthy mare: bumper winner: modest form over hurdles, seventh to Kentford Grebe in valuable mares novice handicap at Newbury final start: will be suited by 3m+. *S. G. Griffiths*

TIRLEY GALE 12 b.g. Strong Gale – Mascara VII (Damsire Unregistered) [2003/4   **c82 §** c74§, h–: c24m^4 c25g May 24] big, rangy gelding: poor chaser: won 4-runner point in   **h–** April: stays 3m: acts on soft and good to firm going: temperamental. *J. S. Smith*

TIRLEY STORM 9 b.g. Tirley Gale – Random Select (Random Shot) [2003/4 c–,   **c79** h–: c21m* c20s^2 c21g c21m^3 c22g^2 c21g* c20g^2 c21d^3 c19s^6 Dec 29] rangy gelding: **h–** poor chaser: won handicaps at Fakenham in May and October: should stay 3m: acts on soft and good to firm going. *J. S. Smith*

TIS GROMIT 10 b.m. Bedford (USA) – Lac Royale (Lochnager) [2003/4 c70§, h–§:   **c77 §** c26s^{ur} c25v^d c24s^{pu} c29s^4 c26s^4 Jan 19] poor maiden hurdler/chaser: stays 29f: acts on   **h– §** soft going: tried blinkered, wore cheekpieces last 7 starts: ungenuine. *Miss S. West*

TISHO 8 ch.m. Sir Harry Lewis (USA) – Sister-In-Law (Legal Tender) [2003/4 h94,   **h110** F93: 16g^3 19m* 16m* 21d* 16d 21g 21m Apr 15] strong, rangy mare: chasing type: fair hurdler: won mares novices at Taunton in November and Leicester and Newbury (further improvement when beating Our Dream gamely by 2 lengths) following month: respectable eighth of 17 in competitive mares handicap at Cheltenham final start: will stay beyond 21f: acts on good to firm and good to soft going (won bumper on soft): free-going front runner. *P. R. Webber*

TISN'T EASY (IRE) 6 b.m. Mandalus – Gemini Gale (Strong Gale) [2003/4 F16f   **h93** F18m^2 F16d^5 18g 20s^6 16s^2 20g^3 16v* 20s^5 18d^3 22d* 20g Apr 11] 14,000 4-y-o: fifth   **F82** foal: sister to fairly useful hurdler/fair novice chaser Oliver Cromwell, stays 3m, and half-sister to fairly useful hurdler up to 19f Tidal Princess (by Good Thyne): dam, winning pointer, sister to useful hurdler up to 3m Basilea: modest hurdler: won bumpers: modest hurdler: won 18-runner maiden at Thurles in March: stays 2¾m: acts on soft going (bumper form on good to firm). *C. F. Swan, Ireland*

TITIAN FLAME (IRE) 4 ch.f. Titus Livius (FR) – Golden Choice (Midyan (USA))   **h82** [2003/4 17d^4 17s^5 16s^2 16m^{ur} 17g^6 Apr 10] fair on Flat (stays 1½m): poor form over hurdles, second in 16-runner mares novice at Plumpton. *Mrs P. N. Dutfield*

TIUTCHEV 11 b.g. Soviet Star (USA) – Cut Ahead (Kalaglow) [2003/4 c164, **c168**
h–: 20g[4] c20d[2] c24g[2] c19s[F] c16g[3] c25g* Apr 1] **h145**

Is he about to be overthrown? Martin Pipe has topped the jump trainers' table for so long that it might seem heretical to some to suggest that his dominance could be coming to an end, Pipe won the trainers' championship for a record ninth season in a row—he has been champion fourteen times in all—but his latest title was achieved against the odds. His greatest rival Paul Nicholls, who has now finished second in the table in each of the last six seasons, was odds on to take the title through most of the season.

Pipe reached a hundred winners on December 31st, well behind his schedule of recent seasons. He holds the record for the fastest hundred, set on November 3rd in the 2001/2 season, and had passed the century mark during November in each of the four previous seasons. Pipe lost his place to Nicholls at the top of the trainers' table before the turn of the year and only regained it in March. The Festival meetings at Cheltenham and Aintree saw fortunes change again, Pipe losing the lead at Cheltenham where Nicholls won four races, including the Queen Mother Champion Chase, to Pipe's two. The opening day at Aintree saw the lead change twice, Pipe going back to the top when Tiutchev won the Martell Cognac Cup, only for Nicholls to regain it when Garde Champetre won the Mersey Novices' Hurdle. Well Chief's victory in the Maghull Novices' Chase and, even more significantly, the £66,000 earned by Lord Atterbury when third in the Grand National meant that Pipe was back in front by the end of Aintree.

Pipe held on in a nip-and-tuck championship battle that provided acres of copy for the racing pages almost to the end of the campaign which Pipe concluded with three of the six jumping winners at Sandown's finale, including the featured Betfred Gold Cup which Puntal won by a short head from the Nicholls-trained Royal Auclair, a former inmate of Pond House. Pipe earned £2,263,718 in 1,2,3 prize money in the latest season, compared to £2,078,144 for Nicholls. But Pipe won the title with the lowest total of winners he has achieved in his last nine championships (except for the foot and mouth restricted season of 2000/1). Pipe's one hundred and seventy-five wins compares to his record total of two hundred

Martell Cognac Cup Chase, Aintree—
Tiutchev shows his effectiveness at around three miles;
First Gold (blinkers) and Hand Inn Hand take the places

The Liars Poker Partnership's "Tiutchev"

and forty-three, set in 1999/00 (he has saddled over two hundred winners on eight occasions). Pipe once said that he didn't believe in the jockeys' retainer system—'I think a stable jockey ought to be paying me for the guaranteed bucketful of winners every season.' One rival stable that does believe in the retainer system is Jackdaws Castle which has lured champion jockey Tony McCoy from Pipe, ending the most successful trainer-jockey partnership there has been in jump racing. With McCoy in place for the 2004/5 season, Jonjo O'Neill, third in the trainers' table in the latest season, seems set to be another formidable challenger for the trainers' title in the next season.

At the start of the latest season, Martin Pipe seemed to have high hopes for what he described as 'the most exciting team of youngsters I have ever had here.' But Pond House also did well with some of those who were at the veteran stage, including the ill-fated Shooting Light, successful in the AON Chase, and Tiutchev, the highest-rated horse in the yard who stood more racing than in the past and was placed in three Grade 1 events, in addition to winning the Grade 2 Martell Cognac Cup Chase. Pipe is the fourth trainer to handle Tiutchev over jumps and his record since joining Pipe in 2002/3 has reflected great credit on those who have handled him at Pond House. Nicky Henderson did very well with Tiutchev before Pipe, saddling him to win an Arkle Trophy, a Swordlestown Cup and an Ascot Chase, but Henderson found the horse difficult to get fit—'He's massive and we have to be careful with his legs'—and hard to keep at his peak. A susceptibility to colic has also restricted Tiutchev's appearances over the years and contributed to his form becoming a little inconsistent after his novice chasing days. Pipe, who installed closed-circuit television in Tiutchev's box to monitor his well-being more closely, seems to have cured Tiutchev's inconsistency.

Apart from falling when attemping a third win in the Ascot Chase at the end of January, Tiutchev was never out of the frame in the latest season, including when reappearing in the Tote Silver Trophy Handicap Hurdle at Chepstow in November, his first outing over hurdles since 1998/9 when David Nicholson trained him and he finished sixth in the Champion Hurdle. Tiutchev's first outing over fences in the latest season came in the two-and-a-half-mile Punchestown Chase in early-December when he went down by three and a half lengths to Beef Or Salmon in a high-class field, alongside the winner when clouting the last but for which he would have finished closer. Many thoroughbreds are more versatile than their trainers sometimes give them credit for and Pipe has run Tiutchev over a wider variety of distances than previous trainers, who campaigned him mostly as a two-miler. Tiutchev was a keeping-on third to Azertyuiop and Flagship Uberalles in the latest Queen Mother Champion Chase, but he showed himself equally effective at around three miles, at least when conditions aren't testing, probably running better than he has ever done when second to Edredon Bleu in the King George VI Chase and when confirming Kempton placings with the third and fourth, First Gold and Fondmort, in the Martell Cognac Cup. First Gold, twice a winner of the race, tried to make all at Aintree but Tiutchev, disputing second turning for home, took over before the last and ran on well to beat First Gold by three and a half lengths, with Ascot Chase winner Hand Inn Hand third and Fondmort fourth.

		Nureyev (b 1977)	Northern Dancer
	Soviet Star (USA) (b 1984)		Special
		Veruschka (b 1967)	Venture VII
Tiutchev (b.g. 1993)			Marie d'Anjou
		Kalaglow (gr 1978)	Kalamoun
	Cut Ahead (b 1986)		Rossitor
		Cut Loose (b 1979)	High Top
			Cutle

The rangy Tiutchev, who invariably impresses in appearance, is Flat bred and ran in three maidens as a three-year-old for Roger Charlton. He is by the sprinter-miler Soviet Star, but his dam, the mile-and-a-quarter-winner Cut Ahead, comes from a branch of the famous Felucca family which became noted for stamina. Tiutchev's grandam Cut Loose, herself a smart mile-and-a-quarter performer, is a sister to the St Leger winner Cut Above, as well as being a half-sister to Irish Two Thousand Guineas winner Sharp Edge. Tiutchev himself is a brother to the Ebor winner Far Ahead, who went on to show fairly useful form at up to two and a half miles over hurdles; the dam bred two other useful winning middle-distance stayers on the Flat, River Pilot (by Unfuwain), also fairly useful over hurdles and fair over fences at one time, and Borgia (by Machiavellian). Tiutchev has shown his form at two miles to twenty-five furlongs and acts on soft and good to firm going. He is usually a sound jumper. *M. C. Pipe*

TIVERTON TRYER 6 b.g. Gran Alba (USA) – Chester Belle (Ballacashtal (CAN)) [2003/4 F17m Jun 11] fourth foal: dam of little account: joint-favourite, showed nothing in bumper on debut. *N. A. Twiston-Davies*   **F–**

T'NIGHTSTHENIGHT 10 b.g. Scallywag – Misty Sky (Hot Brandy) [2003/4 c21gF Mar 12] maiden pointer. *Miss Liz Slattery*   **c–**

TOAD HALL 10 b.g. Henbit (USA) – Candlebright (Lighter) [2003/4 c–, h–: c16s6 c24mpu c20m3 c20m4 c16g3 c24mur Sep 24] lengthy gelding: winning hurdler: poor novice on balance of form over fences: stays 2½m: acts on good to firm going. *Mrs L. B. Normile*   **c63** **h–**

TOBEROE COMMOTION (IRE) 6 b.g. Great Commotion (USA) – Fionn Varragh (IRE) (Tender King) [2003/4 16m4 17g 17m6 17m 16d Apr 12] leggy, angular gelding: modest maiden on Flat (stays 1½m): poor form on hurdling debut: sold out of W. Muir's stable 4,500 gns Newmarket Autumn Sales, well beaten subsequently. *B. J. Llewellyn*   **h72 d**

TOBESURE (IRE) 10 b.g. Asir – Princess Citrus (IRE) (Auction Ring (USA)) **c92 x**
[2003/4 c–, h93: 22f² c25g* c25d² c25dᵖᵘ 24d³ᵈ 22g⁵ 24d² 22d³ 27d⁶ Apr 23] modest **h98**
hurdler/chaser: won novice handicap over fences at Hexham in November: stays 25f:
probably acts on any going: tongue tied once: sketchy jumper of fences. *J. I. A. Charlton*

TO-DAY TO-DAY (IRE) 11 b.g. Waajib – Balela (African Sky) [2003/4 c22g May **c–**
24] strong, lengthy gelding: winning hurdler/chaser: modest pointer in 2003: stays 25f: **h–**
acts on good to firm and heavy going: effective visored or not. *T. P. Tate*

TOD'S BROTHER 10 b.g. Gildoran – Versina (Leander) [2003/4 c24dᵖᵘ Mar 15] **c–**
fair pointer, won twice in April: not fluent and never a danger in hunter chase at Stratford.
Mrs D. M. Grissell

TOEJAM 11 ch.g. Move Off – Cheeky Pigeon (Brave Invader (USA)) [2003/4 h68: **h77**
17s² 17d⁵ 16d⁶ 20d 16g⁶ Mar 10] poor maiden hurdler: best around 2m: acts on soft
going. *R. E. Barr*

TOEMAC 5 b.g. Slip Anchor – Bobanlyn (IRE) (Dance of Life (USA)) [2003/4 F16s **F112**
F16m⁵ F16g* F17g* Apr 1] 12,000 4-y-o: smallish gelding: third foal: half-brother to
winning 2¾m hurdler Bobanvi (by Timeless Times) and 7.5f winner in Italy by Kris: dam
6f (at 2 yrs) to 1½m winner: progressive form in bumpers: won 18-runner event at
Kempton (by short head from Bishop's Bridge) in March and 14-runner event at Taunton,
ridden by 10-lb claimer when showing useful form at latter, making all to beat Purple
Patch by 14 lengths. *M. Bradstock*

TOHUNGA 9 b. or br.g. Rudimentary (USA) – Refinancing (USA) (Forli (ARG)) **c–**
[2003/4 22mᵖᵘ Jun 29] lengthy gelding: once-raced in steeplechases: novice hurdler, **h–**
modest form at best: lame only outing (tongue tied) in 2003/4. *C. Roberts*

TOI EXPRESS (IRE) 8 ch.g. Phardante (FR) – Toi Figures (Deep Run) [2003/4 c105, **c115**
h–: 19m* 19g² 19f* 17f* 16f* c16gᶠ c16m³ Nov 11] workmanlike gelding: fair chaser, **h112**
though prone to mistakes, would have won 4-runner handicap at Chepstow but for falling
last: successful earlier in season in novice hurdles in small fields at Newton Abbot, Exeter
(2) and Wincanton: stays 19f: acts on firm going, probably on good to soft. *P. J. Hobbs*

TOJONESKI 5 b.g. Emperor Jones (USA) – Sampower Lady (Rock City) [2003/4 **h–**
17gᵘʳ 16dᶠ Dec 27] poor on Flat (stays 1½m): failed to complete in 2 starts over hurdles,
well beaten when falling last in seller. *K. A. Morgan*

TOLCEA (IRE) 5 ch.g. Barathea (IRE) – Mosaique Bleue (Shirley Heights) [2003/4 **h–**
h–: 20g 17g⁶ 20m 20d Nov 2] well-made gelding: no form over hurdles. *W. Storey*

TOLEDO SUN 4 b.g. Zamindar (USA) – Shafir (IRE) (Shaadi (USA)) [2003/4 17s⁵ **h90**
17dᵖᵘ Mar 22] modest on Flat (stays 1½m): 20 lengths fifth of 20 to Fenix in novice at
Folkestone on hurdling debut: left H. Collingridge, hung badly left (reportedly lost a
shoe) when pulled up in juvenile at Hereford. *V. Smith*

TOLLBRAE (IRE) 7 gr.g. Supreme Leader – Miss Henrietta (IRE) (Step Together **c110 p**
(USA)) [2003/4 h98: 20d² c20s⁴ c16g² c20g* Apr 12] sturdy gelding: fair novice hurdler: **h107**
similar form over fences, easily landed odds by 12 lengths from Lucky Sinna in maiden
at Plumpton: stays 2½m: raced on good going or softer over jumps: sold to join J. H. Johnson 38,000 gns Doncaster May Sales: capable of better over fences. *N. J. Henderson*

TOM BARRY (IRE) 8 ch.g. Samhoi (USA) – Royal Custody (Reform) [2003/4 c21fᵖᵘ **c–**
May 21] poor maiden pointer: showed more temperament than ability in hunter chase.
K. D. Giles

TOMCAPPAGH (IRE) 13 br.g. Riberetto – Shuil Suas (Menelek) [2003/4 c86?: **c–**
c22mᵖᵘ May 26] lengthy gelding: poor handicap chaser, probably flattered only 2 completed starts since 2001/2: stays 3¼m: acts on heavy and good to firm going. *Mrs S. Wall*

TOM COBBLER (IRE) 10 ch.g. Zaffaran (USA) – Po Bo Pu (Pollerton) [2003/4 **c97 x**
c31f³ May 21] rather sparely-made gelding: winning hurdler/chaser, often let down by **h– §**
jumping/temperament: fair pointer nowadays, won in January and March (twice): stays
27f: acts on soft and good to firm going: tried blinkered. *Mrs C. S. Hall*

TOM COSTALOT (IRE) 9 gr.g. Black Minstrel – Hop Picker (USA) (Plugged **c116**
Nickle (USA)) [2003/4 c123, h–: c20mᵖᵘ c24g³ c21d² c20g⁶ c24sᵖᵘ Mar 20] good-topped **h–**
gelding: fairly useful handicap chaser: best effort in 2003/4 when second to Waterlaw at
Cheltenham: poor efforts last 2 starts: seems best around 2½m: acts on soft and good to
firm going: jumps soundly. *Mrs Susan Nock*

TOMENOSO 6 b.g. Teenoso (USA) – Guarded Expression (Siberian Express (USA)) **h110**
[2003/4 h97: 20v² 17m⁵ 20d⁵ 20d* Apr 10] lengthy gelding: fair handicap hurdler: im-

proved effort when winning 16-runner event at Carlisle on return from 5-month absence, kicking clear before 3 out: stays 21f: acts on heavy and good to firm going: front runner: genuine. *Mrs S. J. Smith*

TOMFOOLARY (IRE)   7 ch.g. Erins Isle – Liberty Bird (USA) (Danzatore (CAN)) [2003/4 h–: 16d 24sᵖᵘ c19dᵖᵘ 22gᵖᵘ Apr 4] lengthy gelding: no form over hurdles: jumped poorly on chasing debut. *J. A. B. Old*   **c–** **h–**

TOM JELLY   6 b.g. Elmaamul (USA) – Primitive Gift (Primitive Rising (USA)) [2003/4 F16s F16gᵖᵘ Jan 23] workmanlike gelding: fourth foal: half-brother to fair 7f/ 1m winner La Sylphide (by Rudimentary) and 6f winner in Macau by Then Again: dam, temperamental and lightly-raced maiden, half-sister to useful 2m hurdler Express Gift and one-time smart sprinter Indian Spark: no show in 2 bumpers. *A. Crook*   **F–**

TOMMY CARSON   9 b.g. Last Tycoon – Ivory Palm (USA) (Sir Ivor (USA)) [2003/4 c–, h–: c24g⁴ c20d* c24vᵖᵘ Apr 4] compact gelding: modest handicap chaser: won 5-runner event at Plumpton in March: effective at 2½m to 3m: acts on good to firm and heavy going: tried visored/blinkered, not since 1999/00: hard ride. *Jamie Poulton*   **c88** **h–**

TOMMY NUTTER (IRE)   4 b.g. Desert Style (IRE) – Ahakista (IRE) (Persian Bold) [2003/4 17m Aug 1] poor and unreliable maiden on Flat (best at 5f): well held in juvenile on hurdling debut. *R. Brotherton*   **h–**

TOMMY SPAR   4 b.g. Silver Owl – Lady of Mine (Cruise Missile) [2003/4 F16d Jan 22] second foal: dam winning chaser, stayed 23f: well held in bumper on debut. *P. Bowen*   **F–**

TOMMY TROOPER   9 ch.g. Infantry – Steady Saunter VII (Damsire Unregistered) [2003/4 c–, h96: 21g Jul 4] medium-sized gelding: let down by jumping both starts over fences: modest hurdler: found nothing only outing in 2003/4: should stay 2½m: acts on heavy going, bumper form on good to firm: tongue tied once. *Miss K. M. George*   **c–** **h–**

TOMORROWS TREASURE   4 ch.f. Bahamian Bounty – Yesterday's Song (Shirley Heights) [2003/4 F13g Nov 30] second foal: half-sister to 1m winner Audrey's Dilemma (by Piccolo): dam unraced, out of sister to useful stayer Parting Moment: well held in bumper on debut. *C. W. Fairhurst*   **F–**

TOM PADDINGTON   9 b.g. Rock Hopper – Mayfair Minx (St Columbus) [2003/4 16g* 16sᶠ 16g 24gᵖᵘ Feb 28] neat gelding: fairly useful on Flat (stayed 2¼m), better than ever in 2003: took well to hurdling as a juvenile in 1998/9 (broke down final start): won strongly-contested 18-runner handicap at Newbury on reappearance in November, travelling comfortably under restraint before coming through late to beat Sud Bleu 2½ lengths: broke down again in Grade 2 at Kempton: effective at well-run 2m, would have stayed further: reportedly retired. *H. Morrison*   **h133**

TOM PINCH (IRE)   15 b.g. Mandalus – Spanish Royale (Royal Buck) [2003/4 c68, h–: c21dᵖᵘ Apr 30] sturdy gelding: veteran chaser: stays 3m: acts on good to firm and heavy going: tried blinkered/tongue tied. *Mark Bennison*   **c–** **h–**

TOMS GONE GREY (IRE)   5 gr.g. Gothland (FR) – Cpv Lady (Le Moss) [2003/4 F16m 19m⁴ 20g 17s⁶ 19v 17d³ 19g³ 22g⁵ 22gᵖᵘ Apr 18] tall gelding: sixth foal: half-brother to winning pointer by Mandalus: dam twice-raced half-sister to useful chaser up to 25f Kumon Sunshine: seventh of 17 in bumper on debut: poor novice hurdler: should stay beyond 19f: acts on soft going. *R. H. Alner*   **h85** **F70**

TOMSK (IRE)   4 b.g. Definite Article – Merry Twinkle (Martinmas) [2003/4 16gᵖᵘ Dec 3] half-brother to fairly useful chaser up to 19f Smolensk (by Ela-Mana-Mou): no sign of ability on Flat or on hurdling debut. *A. Berry*   **h–**

TOM'S MAN   10 ch.g. Milieu – Lorna's Choice (Oats) [2003/4 c24gᵖᵘ Feb 18] workmanlike gelding: little form outside points: usually tongue tied. *G. F. White*   **c–** **h–**

TOM'S PRIZE   9 ch.g. Gunner B – Pandora's Prize (Royal Vulcan) [2003/4 c125, h–: c24dᵖᵘ 26g* c26g 25s² c24d⁴ 24g* c24s² Apr 17] plain gelding: fairly useful hurdler: won novices at Southwell in November and Newbury in March, beating Fountain Hill a length at latter: fairly useful handicap chaser: good second to Ivanoph at Bangor: stays 3¼m: acts on good to firm and heavy going: makes running/races prominently: usually jumps soundly: game. *J. L. Spearing*   **c123** **h127**

TOM'S RIVER (IRE)   12 ch.g. Over The River (FR) – Nesford (Walshford) [2003/4 c99x, h–: c19g³ c25g⁶ c25dᵖᵘ Feb 15] lengthy gelding: maiden hurdler: poor chaser nowadays: sold out of R. Hodges' stable £1,600 Ascot December Sales after second outing: stays 3¾m: acts on soft going: blinkered once: held up: often let down by jumping. *Chris Nenadich*   **c76 x** **h–**

TOMSWAY   5 b.g. Relief Pitcher – Thank Yourself (Le Bavard (FR)) [2003/4 20s^{pu}   **h–**
24g^{pu} 21d⁶ Apr 11] tall, angular gelding: fourth foal: dam, poor novice hurdler, from
family of useful staying hurdler/chaser So: showed nothing in 3 starts over hurdles.
Mrs P. A. Tetley

TOMWONTPAYALOT   5 gr.g. Overbury (IRE) – Alice Smith (Alias Smith (USA))   **h85 §**
[2003/4 F96: 16g² 19d^{pu} 16d^F 17g^{pu} 25d^{pu} Apr 11] good-topped gelding: second in
maiden at Uttoxeter on hurdling debut: failed to complete after, twice downing tools: bred
to be suited by further than 2m: best left alone. *M. C. Pipe*

TONI'S PET   4 b.g. Wizard King – Dannistar (Puissance) [2003/4 16g^{pu} Nov 2] poor   **h–**
maiden on Flat for various trainers: showed nothing on hurdling debut. *B. N. Pollock*

TONOCO   11 b.g. Teenoso (USA) – Lady Shoco (Montekin) [2003/4 c118, h–: c21d⁶   **c120**
c25d² c24d² c24s⁵ c24s³ Feb 14] tall, lengthy gelding: tubed: fairly useful handicap   **h–**
chaser: ran at least creditably in 2003/4, except on fourth outing: stays 25f: acts on good
to firm and heavy going: tried tongue tied: usually races prominently: sound jumper.
Mrs S. J. Smith

TONY'S TIME   10 b.g. Tina's Pet – Time Warp (Town And Country) [2003/4 c24m⁶   **c74 +**
May 7] fair pointer, successful 3 times in 2003: no show in steeplechases. *Mrs Sarah
Faulks*

TOOMEBRIDGE (IRE)   6 b.g. Warcraft (USA) – The Foalicule (Imperial Fling   **h97 p**
(USA)) [2003/4 19g² Apr 3] sixth foal: half-brother to winning Irish pointer by Mandalus: dam, poor maiden on Flat, half-sister to useful jumpers Homeson, stayed 3m, and
Hill's Pageant, best at 2m: won maiden Irish point in 2004: encouraging 2½ lengths
second to Trinket in maiden at Hereford on hurdling debut: will stay beyond 19f: open to
improvement. *J. S. King*

TOON SOCIETY (IRE)   6 b.g. Moscow Society (USA) – Sweet Defeet (Deep Run)   **h–**
[2003/4 F17m⁵ F16g⁶ 21f⁴ Oct 8] €51,000 4-y-o: fifth foal: dam, placed in bumpers,   **F80**
half-sister to fairly useful hurdlers Khan Kicker and Badger's Wood: better effort in
bumpers when fifth of 10 at Newton Abbot: tailed off in seller on hurdling debut:
blinkered last 2 starts: placed in points in February and March. *Jonjo O'Neill*

TOON TROOPER (IRE)   7 ch.g. Bob Back (USA) – Salmoncita (Salmon Leap   **h106**
(USA)) [2003/4 20d³ 23d 25s* 24v⁴ 24g^{pu} Feb 14] big, lengthy ex-Irish gelding: chasing
sort: third foal: dam, won around 2m over hurdles, half-sister to useful hurdler around
2½m Special Vintage: sixth in bumper at Punchestown on debut for E. O'Grady: fair form
when winning novice hurdle at Warwick in December by 4 lengths from Tom's Prize:
poor efforts on previous and next 2 starts: will stay beyond 25f: acts on soft going.
Jonjo O'Neill

TOO PHAR TO TOUCH   9 br.m. Wace (USA) – Carew Mill (Hubble Bubble)   **c–**
[2003/4 c20d^{pu} May 16] poor maiden pointer. *Miss F. Goldsworthy*

TOORAK (USA)   7 b.g. Irish River (FR) – Just Juliet (USA) (What A Pleasure (USA))   **h–**
[2003/4 h–: 16g 16m 17g^{pu} May 24] workmanlike gelding: maiden hurdler, no form since
2001/2: in frame in 2 points in February. *Mrs T. J. McInnes Skinner*

TOO TECHNICAL (IRE)   9 b.g. Archway (IRE) – Another Side (Bold Lad (IRE))   **h95**
[2003/4 h78: 20m* 19g* 22m^{pu} Aug 9] modest hurdler: won novice handicaps at Hexham
in June and Stratford in July: lame final outing: stays 2½m: acts on good to firm going
(won bumper on heavy): patiently ridden. *J. M. Jefferson*

TOPANBERRY (IRE)   5 ch.m. Topanoora – Mulberry (IRE) (Denel (FR)) [2003/4   **F90**
F16g² F16s Mar 13] rather leggy mare: third foal: half-sister to useful but untrustworthy
hurdler Sheer Genius (by Insan), stayed 3m: dam, maiden pointer, half-sister to smart
staying chaser Fiddling The Facts: ½-length second to Marsh Run in mares bumper at
Hexham on debut: well held in valuable similar event at Sandown: will stay beyond 2m.
N. G. Richards

TOP BUCK (IRE)   10 b.g. Top of The World – Orlita (Master Buck) [2003/4 c119p,   **c119**
h–: c20g³ c24g⁵ c20g^{ur} c20s^F Apr 21] tall, useful-looking gelding: winning hurdler: fairly   **h–**
useful chaser: let down by jumping in handicaps last 3 starts, yet to be asked for effort
when falling 4 out at Perth (wore cheekpieces): stays 2¾m: raced on good going or softer
(acts on soft). *K. C. Bailey*

TOP DOG (IRE)   5 b.g. Topanoora – Dun Oengus (IRE) (Strong Gale) [2003/4 F18g⁵   **F74**
Apr 22] €20,000 4-y-o: third foal: dam, 2½m hurdle winner, half-sister to dam of smart
chaser up to 2½m Strong Run (by Strong Gale): 29 lengths fifth of 13 to Itsmyboy in
bumper at Fontwell on debut. *L. Wells*

TOP

TOP GALE (IRE)   5 b.m. Topanoora – Amy's Gale (IRE) (Strong Gale) [2003/4 F17d   F–
May 17] 2,200 3-y-o: second foal: dam unraced, from family of One Man: well beaten in
mares bumper on debut. *R. Dickin*

TOP GUARD (IRE)   6 b.g. Topanoora – Garter Royale (IRE) (Garde Royale) [2003/4   h–
F16d 25g⁴ May 29] second foal: dam, placed at 1¼m to 1¾m in Ireland, closely related to   F–
smart Irish performer up to 9f Island Reef: little sign of ability. *E. U. Hales, Ireland*

TOP NOTCH   6 br.m. Alderbrook – Gaygo Lady (Gay Fandango) (USA)) [2003/4 F–:   h–
F16m F16m⁵ 16d⁵ 17s⁶ 16s Jan 6] rather unfurnished mare: modest in bumpers: well held   **F81**
in novice hurdles. *K. C. Bailey*

TOP OF THE AGENDA   5 b.g. Michelozzo (USA) – Expensive Lark (Sir Lark)   **F97**
[2003/4 F16m² Oct 10] third foal: half-brother to bumper winner Brush The Ark (by
Brush Aside): dam winning hunter chaser: shaped quite well when 9 lengths second of 8
to Before The Mast in bumper at Huntingdon on debut. *M. Pitman*

TOP OF THE CHARTS   8 b.g. Salse (USA) – Celebrity (Troy) [2003/4 c31fᵖᵘ May   c–
21] leggy gelding: poor maiden hurdler: no form in steeplechases: tried blinkered/   h–
visored. *Miss T. McCurrich*

TOP OF THE DEE   7 ch.m. Rakaposhi King – Lavenham's Last (Rymer) [2003/4   h–
h65: 16v³ 20mᵖᵘ 16g 20sᵖᵘ Apr 17] rangy mare: poor maiden hurdler: probably stays
2½m: acts on good to firm and heavy going: tongue tied last 3 outings in 2002/3.
Mrs L. Williamson

TOP OF THE LEFT   9 b. or br.g. Nomination – Diva Madonna (Chief Singer) [2003/4   c– p
h98p: 20d² 19d² c18sᶠ Jan 14] good-topped gelding: fair maiden hurdler, very lightly   **h105**
raced: in touch when falling 5 out in handicap at Newbury on chasing debut: stays 2½m:
raced on good to soft/soft going. *Jonjo O'Neill*

TOPOL (IRE)   6 br.g. Topanoora – Kislev (IRE) (Be My Guest (USA)) [2003/4 h78:   **c94**
c16d² c20d c16d⁶ c18g⁴ c16dᵖᵘ Apr 12] rangy gelding: poor form in novice hurdles: h–
modest novice chaser: free-going sort, may prove best around 2m. *Miss H. C. Knight*

TOP STOPPA   6 gr.g. Environment Friend – Orchid Valley (IRE) (Cyrano de Bergerac)   F–
[2003/4 F–: F16g Sep 25] pulled hard and well beaten in 2 bumpers a year apart.
Miss V. Scott

TOP STRATEGY (IRE)   4 b.g. Hernando (FR) – Sudden Stir (USA) (Woodman   **h132**
(USA)) [2003/4 16d 16s² 16d* 16v² 16s⁴ 16d 16d⁶ 17g³ Mar 18] useful-looking gelding:
first foal: dam once-raced, from family of high-class miler Be My Guest: won 1¼m
maiden on debut on Flat, sold out of D. Weld's stable €43,000 Goffs June Sale: useful
juvenile hurdler: won Grade 2 Denny Juvenile Hurdle at Leopardstown in December by

Mr W. J. Kane's "Top Strategy"

3½ lengths from Al Eile: 33/1, best effort when just over 2 lengths third of 18 finishers to Made In Japan in JCB Triumph Hurdle at Cheltenham: raced around 2m: blinkered after sixth outing: has looked none too keen, particularly in Grade 1 at Punchestown in late-April. *T. M. Walsh, Ireland*

TOP TENOR (IRE)   4 b.g. Sadler's Wells (USA) – Posta Vecchia (USA) (Rainbow Quest (USA)) [2003/4 17g Apr 12] fairly useful on Flat (stays 2m) at 3 yrs for J. Dunlop, poor form in 2004, claimed from B. Johnson £6,000 in March: well beaten in juvenile on hurdling debut. *V. Thompson*   **h–**

TOP THE BILL (IRE)   4 b.g. Topanoora – Rio Star (IRE) (Riot Helmet) [2003/4 F16d F16g F16d⁴ Feb 8] first foal: dam winning Irish pointer: 100/1, first form in bumpers when 6 lengths fourth of 15 behind dead-heaters Word Gets Around and Somewin at Musselburgh, dictating slow pace. *Mrs S. A. Watt*   **F84 ?**

TOP TREES   6 b.g. Charnwood Forest (IRE) – Low Line (High Line) [2003/4 h75: 16mᶠ 17mʳᵗʳ 17g³ 17fᵗ 19f³ 16g⁵ 19mᶠ Nov 27] modest and temperamental on Flat (stays 13f), successful in September: poor maiden hurdler: raced mainly around 2m: acts on firm going: in cheekpieces final outing: refused to race second start. *W. S. Kittow*   **h81 §**

TORCHE (IRE)   6 b.g. Taos (IRE) – Orchette (IRE) (Orchestra) [2003/4 F85: F17s 20g⁴ 20sʳᵗʳ 23d 25s⁴ 25s* 24s⁴ 25d³ Mar 14] strong gelding: fair form on first of 2 starts in bumpers (trained by D. Caro): fair hurdler: won 14-finisher maiden at Wetherby (beat Bacyan 4 lengths) in January: will stay beyond 25f: acts on soft going: visored last 3 starts: whipped round at start second outing over hurdles. *M. Scudamore*   **h101 F–**

TORDUFF BOY (IRE)   11 b.g. Yashgan – Couleurs Volants (Peacock (FR)) [2003/4 c131, h95: c20d* c20d⁴ c20g³ c22s Jul 30] workmanlike gelding: twice-raced over hurdles: useful handicap chaser: won quite valuable race at Punchestown in May 2003 for   **c131 h–**

second successive year: ran well subsequently only on next start: stays 29f: acts on soft and good to firm going: sometimes tongue tied. *Paul Nolan, Ireland*

TORDUFF EXPRESS (IRE) 13 b.g. Kambalda – Marhabtain (Touching Wood (USA)) [2003/4 c118, h–: c22s² c26d c21g⁵ Apr 1] rather leggy gelding: one-time useful chaser: well below best in 2003/4, fifth of 15 finishers to Forest Gunner in Fox Hunters' at Aintree (won race in 2002): stays 4m: acts on good to firm and heavy going: blinkered nowadays: has flashed tail under pressure, but is genuine. *P. F. Nicholls*   **c104 h–**

TOREO (FR) 10 ch.g. Bakharoff (USA) – Becerrada (FR) (Tip Moss (FR)) [2003/4 h–: 16g 22d Dec 1] sturdy, lengthy gelding: lightly-raced maiden hurdler: left J. Adam after first outing: tried tongue tied. *M. Todhunter*   **h–**

TOR HEAD 8 b.g. Then Again – Free Form (Glenstal (USA)) [2003/4 c21s² c25gᶠ c16d² c21gᵖᵘ Apr 12] 3,500 4-y-o: second foal: half-brother to winner in Denmark by Mistertopogigo: dam winning 2m hurdler: completed once in Irish points, winning maiden in 2003: runner-up in novice hunter at Sedgefield and maiden at Hexham on completed starts in steeplechases: lame final outing: should stay 3m: acts on soft going. *J. Howard Johnson*   **c89**

TORINGA ROSE 5 ch.m. Karinga Bay – Topsy Turvy (IRE) (Roselier (FR)) [2003/4 F17m Jul 14] first foal: dam no show in 2 bumpers: tailed off in bumper on debut. *R. H. York*   **F–**

TOROSAY (IRE) 6 b.g. Presenting – Mazuma (IRE) (Mazaad) [2003/4 F98: 20s⁵ 20v⁵ 24d⁵ Mar 18] fairly useful form in bumper on debut: well beaten in 3 novice hurdles, though not given hard time: will possibly be suited by less emphasis on stamina. *N. G. Richards*   **h–**

TORPICA 8 br.g. Be My Native (USA) – Irish Mint (Dusky Boy) [2003/4 c20dᵖᵘ c24vᶠ Apr 4] poor novice hurdler in 2002/1: let down by jumping both starts over fences: stays 25f: acts on soft going: tried blinkered. *P. Winkworth*   **c– h–**

TORRID KENTAVR (USA) 7 b.g. Trempolino (USA) – Torrid Tango (USA) (Green Dancer (USA)) [2003/4 c16s* c16m* 17g³ 16m* 16m² Oct 31] compact gelding: fair on Flat (stays 1½m), successful in April: won both starts over fences, novice at Sedgefield (made virtually all despite jumping right on occasions) in May and handicap at Perth (not fluent and 2 lengths down when Billie John fell last) in June: fairly useful handicap hurdler: won at Plumpton in September: improved again when second to Mister McGoldrick at Wetherby: likely to prove best around 2m: has won on soft going, best form under less testing conditions: free-going sort. *B. Ellison*   **c107 h118**

TORTUGA DREAM (IRE) 5 b.g. Turtle Island (IRE) – Tycoon's Catch (IRE) (Thatching) [2003/4 h–: 16g Dec 4] lengthy gelding: no show on Flat or over hurdles: tried visored. *A. Charlton*   **h–**

TORTUGAS (FR) 7 b.g. Subotica (FR) – Northern Whisper (FR) (Vacarme (USA)) [2003/4 c54§, h–§: 16m Jun 18] angular gelding: winning hurdler: little form since 2000/1 (let down by jumping over fences): visored once: ungenuine. *Mrs H. Dalton*   **c– § h– §**

TOSAWI (IRE) 8 b.g. Commanche Run – Deep Satisfaction (Deep Run) [2003/4 h100: c16gᶠ 19d 22dᵖᵘ 16s⁶ 17g* 16d⁴ 17s⁶ 19g³ Apr 13] good-topped gelding: fell first on chasing debut: modest handicap hurdler: won amateur event at Exeter in March: stays 21f: acts on heavy and good to firm going. *R. J. Hodges*   **c– h96**

TOSCANINI (GER) 8 b.g. Goofalik (USA) – Tosca Stella (GER) (Surumu (GER)) [2003/4 h89: 22s⁶ 20s³ May 22] useful-looking gelding: modest handicap hurdler: third in point in March: stays 2¾m: acts on heavy going: has looked difficult ride. *D. R. Gandolfo*   **h89**

TOSHEROON (IRE) 8 b.g. Good Thyne (USA) – Rare Currency (Rarity) [2003/4 h104p: 26mᵖᵘ May 5] useful-looking gelding: fell in maiden Irish point: twice-raced over hurdles in 2002/3, successful in novice on debut: ran as if amiss on return from 6-month absence. *A. M. Hales*   **h–**

TOTAL ENJOYMENT (IRE) 5 b.m. Flemensfirth (USA) – Oak Court (IRE) (Bustineto) [2003/4 F16d³ F16d* F16d* F16g* Mar 17]   **F118**

    The sex allowance for fillies and mares in Grade 1 and Grade 2 races over jumps was increased from 5 lb to 7 lb in the latest season (to be extended to all races in 2004/5), but the so-called 'weaker sex' still found it very tough going. Mares were represented in only three of the ten Grade 1 events at the latest Cheltenham

Weatherbys Champion Bumper (Standard Open National Hunt Flat), Cheltenham—
mares to the fore as Total Enjoyment wins from Refinement

Festival. Mariah Rollins and Perle de Puce failed to complete the course in the Supreme Novices' Hurdle and the smart Solerina managed just a respectable fourth in the Stayers' Hurdle. The three mares who contested a less than vintage renewal of the twenty-four-runner Weatherbys Champion Bumper collectively did much better. Total Enjoyment, Refinement and Blazing Liss all looked to have a good chance at the weights and were prominent in the betting behind 7/2 favourite Martinstown, in a field lacking the season's three highest-rated bumper horses up to that time, British-trained Secret Ploy and Mount Clerigo and Ireland's best performer Forty Licks who was too old to qualify. Martinstown didn't give his supporters much of a run for their money and Blazing Liss fell six furlongs out after clipping the heels of another runner. But Total Enjoyment and Refinement finished first and second, Total Enjoyment leading over three furlongs out and quickening in good style entering the home straight to win by two and a half lengths; Refinement finished five lengths ahead of third-placed Master Albert, who had been beaten by Martinstown on his previous start.

Total Enjoyment became only the second mare to win the Champion Bumper in its twelve runnings so far, following the third winner Mucklemeg, and she kept up the tremendous record of Irish-trained runners in the race, becoming the ninth Irish-trained winner. Total Enjoyment looked a good prospect when shaping well in third behind Blazing Liss on her debut at Punchestown in May and she won both her starts after a summer break. Already earmarked for Cheltenham, she won in good style at Fairyhouse in December and then showed how rapidly she was progressing when making nearly all to win by twenty-five lengths, recording a smart effort, at Leopardstown just after Christmas. She completed her preparation when reportedly working very well—for her Cheltenham jockey Jim Culloty—with Solerina after racing at Leopardstown at the end of February, a fixture where the host of Festival hopefuls working is almost of more interest than the racing itself. Total enjoyment summed up the reaction of members of the County Kerry-based winning syndicate who hoisted trainer Tom Cooper shoulder high as they performed an impromptu rendition of *The Rose of Tralee* in the Cheltenham winner's enclosure.

	Flemensfirth (USA) (b 1992)	Alleged (b 1974)	Hoist The Flag Princess Pout
Total Enjoyment (IRE) (b.f. 1999)		Etheldreda (ch 1985)	Diesis Royal Bund
	Oak Court (IRE) (b 1988)	Bustineto (b 1978)	Bustino Petipa
		Tourney's Girl (br 1981)	Yankee Gold Tourney

Whether the It Will Never Last Syndicate, which owns Total Enjoyment, also turns out to be appropriately named remains to be seen. Mucklemeg ran only three times after her win at Cheltenham, failing to win again. The leggy Total Enjoyment hasn't got a lot of scope for physical development and she looked less of a stayer than most of those behind her in the Champion Bumper. Her dam Oak Court was a fairly useful two-mile hurdler and Total Enjoyment looks likely to fare best at the minimum trip when she is sent over hurdles in the next season. Her half-brother Coogee Boy (by Executive Perk) is only a poor hurdler and gained his first success in a two-and-a-half-mile handicap at Wexford in October. The best horse produced by Total Enjoyment's immediate family before her was Oak Court's half-brother Feeling Grand, a fairly useful chaser effective at two to three miles. Total Enjoyment's sire the Prix Lupin winner Flemensfirth had the somewhat dubious distinction—according to figures in the *Return of Mares*—of being the most active sire of 2003, covering three hundred and ten mares under the Coolmore banner at The Beeches Stud in Ireland. Horses by Coolmore jumping stallions filled the first three places in the Champion Bumper. Refinement is by Oscar, the second most active sire of 2003, with three hundred and six mares, and the third Master Albert is by the now-deceased Supreme Leader who was the most active sire in 2001, covering three hundred and twenty-five mares. Being represented in huge numbers keeps the Coolmore stallions to the fore in the sires tables. Saturation coverage leads to a number—significant in some cases—of smart performers being produced, though, as with the offspring of all stallions, the indifferent or poor ones inevitably outnumber them by a considerable margin. *T. Cooper, Ireland*

TOTALLY SCOTTISH   8 b.g. Mtoto – Glenfinlass (Lomond (USA)) [2003/4 h117: 18g 20g³ 16g⁴ 19g³ 16d⁶ 20v⁵ 17d 20d 20d² 18g⁵ Mar 28] rather sparely-made gelding: maiden on Flat: fair hurdler: stays 2½m: acts on soft and good to firm going: blinkered/tongue tied on debut: held up: irresolute. *Mrs M. Reveley*   h106 §

TO THE FUTURE (IRE)   8 ch.g. Bob Back (USA) – Lady Graduate (IRE) (Le Bavard (FR)) [2003/4 c96, h–: c25g⁶ Apr 28] tall gelding: lightly raced: modest chaser: poor efforts very early in season: will stay beyond 3¼m: raced mainly on going softer than good (acts on heavy). *A. Parker*   c– h–

TOTLAND BAY (IRE)   8 br.g. Phardante (FR) – Seanaphobal Lady (Kambalda) [2003/4 h100: 22g⁴ c21dᵖᵘ 22g² 20m⁴ 22g³ 24m Sep 14] modest hurdler: largely disappointing in 2003/4, left J. Mullins before final start: not fluent on chasing debut: stays 2¾m: acts on firm going, seemingly not on softer than good: tried tongue tied. *B. D. Leavy*   c– h95

TOTO TALECA   7 b.m. Mtoto – Miss Taleca (Pharly (FR)) [2003/4 h–, F–: 17sᵖᵘ 17g 17m Jun 21] leggy mare: of little account: visored/tongue tied final start. *M. E. Sowersby*   h–

TOTO TOSCATO (FR)   10 b.g. Lesotho (USA) – Tosca de Bellouet (FR) (Olmeto) [2003/4 c24gᵖᵘ c25gᵖᵘ Apr 2] rangy gelding: one-time smart hurdler/chaser: off 4 years suffering tendon injury and pulled up both starts on return: stays 25f: acts on soft and good to firm going: has finished weakly. *M. C. Pipe*   c– h–

TOUCH CLOSER   7 b.g. Inchinor – Ryewater Dream (Touching Wood (USA)) [2003/4 h67: 17d 20d5 21s* 20g⁶ 16s² c20d5 22d* 20d³ Apr 22] angular gelding: fair hurdler: won handicaps at Sedgefield in December and Kelso (first start after leaving G. A. Swinbank, easily beat Lago 11 lengths) in April: modest form when fifth of 7 finishers in maiden at Carlisle on chasing debut: will stay 3m: acts on soft going. *Miss V. Scott*   c93 h106

TOUCH OF SPIRIT   5 b.m. Dancing Spree (USA) – Soft Touch (GER) (Horst-Herbert) [2003/4 16g 16gF Dec 5] lightly-raced maiden on Flat: no show in 2 novice hurdles. *J. R. Jenkins*   h–

TOUCH THE TAMBOUR (IRE)   7 b.g. Insan (USA) – Queen River (Over The River (FR)) [2003/4 F16dᵖᵘ Nov 26] IR £8,500 4-y-o: third foal: dam winning pointer: lame in bumper on debut. *P. R. Webber*   F–

TOULON CREST (IRE) 7 b.g. Toulon – Another Contact (Martin John) [2003/4 **c89**
c88?, F–: c20m^F c16m^3 c16m c17m^2 c17m^3 c16m^{pu} Dec 27] modest novice chaser: form
only around 2m on good to firm going: tried tongue tied in bumpers. *G. Prodromou*

TOULOUSE (IRE) 7 b.g. Toulon – Neasham (Nishapour (FR)) [2003/4 h109, F87: **c100**
c19d^F c20g^{pu} c21d^4 c18g^3 Mar 6] rangy gelding: fair hurdler: best effort over fences when **h–**
third in novice handicap at Newbury (several mistakes): should stay beyond 2¼m: acts
on soft going. *R. H. Alner*

TOULOUSE-LAUTREC (IRE) 8 ch.g. Toulon – Bucks Slave (Buckskin (FR)) **c107 x**
[2003/4 c112p, h–: c33d^{pu} c24s^2 c26v^{pu} Feb 7] tall gelding: fair chaser: made mistakes all **h–**
3 starts in 2003/4: should stay beyond 3m: raced on going softer than good (acts on
heavy). *T. R. George*

TOURNIQUET (IRE) 9 b.g. Torus – Treidlia (Mandalus) [2003/4 h98: 27s^{pu} c22v* **c102 +**
c25s^F Jan 20] strong gelding: regressive form over hurdles: off 8 months, won 2-finisher **h–**
novice at Towcester in December on steeplechasing debut: fell seventh next time: stays
25f: acts on heavy and good to firm going. *D. J. Caro*

TOWN CRIER (IRE) 9 br.g. Beau Sher – Ballymacarett (Menelek) [2003/4 h–: **h115**
16m* 17m^F 16d* Aug 7] tall gelding: lightly raced: won novice hurdles at Uttoxeter in
July and August, much improved when beating Conroy 10 lengths on second occasion:
should stay beyond 2m: acts on good to firm and good to soft going: seemed sure to
progress further, but clearly not easy to train and wasn't seen out again. *Mrs S. J. Smith*

TOWNS ENDER (IRE) 6 b.g. Zaffaran (USA) – Delway (Fidel) [2003/4 h–, F–: **c89 p**
17d^3 19m 22s^{pu} c16g^3 c19d^5 Feb 15] strong, lengthy gelding: best effort over hurdles **h87**
when third in novice at Bangor: similar form both starts over fences, shaping as if capable
of better each time, though isn't straightforward ride: should stay 2½m: tongue tied.
M. Scudamore

TOY BOY (IRE) 6 b.g. Un Desperado (FR) – Too Sharp (True Song) [2003/4 F–: 19m^5 **h88**
21g^{pu} 20s^{pu} Apr 17] rather unfurnished gelding: modest form when fifth to Tinoveritas in
novice hurdle at Newbury: went as if amiss all other starts, sweating and on toes next
time. *Miss H. C. Knight*

TRABOLGAN (IRE) 6 b.g. King's Ride – Derrella (Derrylin) [2003/4 F118: 16d^F **h125 p**
20d* 19s* 19g^{pu} Feb 10] rangy gelding: will make a chaser: runner-up in Champion
Bumper at Cheltenham final start in 2002/3: landed odds in maiden at Ascot (by 7 lengths
from Yardbird) in December and novice at Newbury in January on completed outings
over hurdles, jumping better and not having to come off bridle at latter: pulled up early
final start and later reported to have sustained knee injury, but remains open to improvement. *N. J. Henderson*

TRACK O' PROFIT (IRE) 12 ch.g. Kambalda – Teazle (Quayside) [2003/4 c99, **c–**
h–: c26m^{pu} May 29] medium-sized gelding: fairly useful hunter chaser: stayed 3¼m: **h–**
acted on firm and soft going: dead. *Miss S. Young*

TRADE OFF (IRE) 6 b.g. Roselier (FR) – Lady Owenette (IRE) (Salluceva) [2003/4 **c94**
F17g^4 16d 16d 19s^3 c24s^F c24g^5 c26d^{F2} Apr 11] €29,000 4-y-o: rather unfurnished **h90**
gelding: fifth foal: half-brother to one-time fairly useful hurdler/fair chaser Castle Owen **F82**
(by Castle Keep), stays 25f: dam unraced half-sister to fairly useful staying chaser The
Nigelstan: fourth in bumper at Newton Abbot on debut: best effort over hurdles when
third to Victory Gunner in novice at Taunton: fell on 2 of 3 starts over fences, held in
second when doing so at last (remounted) in handicap at Plumpton: stays 3¼m: acts on
soft going. *M. C. Pipe*

TRADING TROUBLE 7 b.g. Petoski – Marielou (FR) (Carwhite) [2003/4 c112, h–: **c83**
c16g^2 c20g^{ur} c20g^3 22m Jul 19] medium-sized gelding: fair hurdler/novice chaser, **h–**
long way below form early in 2003/4: stays 2½m: acts on heavy going: joined J. Wade.
J. M. Jefferson

TRADITIONAL (IRE) 8 ch.g. Erins Isle – Noorajo (IRE) (Ahonoora) [2003/4 h89: **c–**
c24m^{pu} c21m^5 c22m^{pu} c23g^{pu} c19d^4 c19s^{pu} c24g^{pu} Apr 16] close-coupled gelding: win- **h–**
ning hurdler: no form in steeplechases, left N. Hawke after third start: stays easy 3m: acts
on good to soft and good to firm going: usually wore blinkers/cheekpieces in 2003/4: has
looked none too keen. *Miss Chloe Newman*

TRAGIC DANCER 8 b.g. Tragic Role (USA) – Chantallee's Pride (Mansooj) [2003/4 **h75**
16g 16d 16s^5 17d^6 21d^{pu} Apr 11] lengthy gelding: fair at best on Flat (stays 1½m) at 2 and
3 years: poor form over hurdles. *D. J. Wintle*

Stan James Gerry Feilden Intermediate Hurdle (Limited Handicap), Newbury—
Tramantano takes advantage of Sporazene's last-flight blunder

TRAGIC OHIO 5 b.g. Tragic Role (USA) – Kiniohio (FR) (Script Ohio (USA)) **h122**
[2003/4 F102: 16d³ 17s* 18gᵖᵘ Mar 6] bumper winner: successful in novice hurdles at
Wincanton in January and Hereford in February, fairly useful form when beating Lough
Derg 24 lengths at latter: ran as though amiss in Grade 2 at Kelso: should stay beyond
17f: acts on soft going. *P. F. Nicholls*

TRAINED BYTHE BEST 6 b.m. Alderbrook – Princess Moodyshoe (Jalmood **h– §**
(USA)) [2003/4 h103§: 22dᵖᵘ Nov 27] leggy mare: fairly useful on Flat, tailed off last 3
starts in 2003: fair hurdler: stays 2½m: acts on good to soft going: visored only outing
(ran poorly) in 2003/4: ungenuine. *M. C. Pipe*

TRAMANTANO 5 b.g. Muhtarram (USA) – Hatta Breeze (Night Shift (USA)) [2003/4 **h140**
h121: 16m⁵ 22g² 16d* Nov 29] good-topped gelding: useful hurdler: off 6 months and
tongue strap left off, much improved when winning 8-runner Gerry Feilden Hurdle
(Intermediate Limited Handicap) at Newbury by neck from Sporazene, all out after
runner-up blundered last: raced mainly around 2m (remote second of 3 over 2¾m): acts
on good to firm and good to soft going. *N. A. Twiston-Davies*

TRANSATLANTIC (USA) 6 gr.g. Dumaani (USA) – Viendra (USA) (Raise A **h78**
Native) [2003/4 h77: 20m⁶ 16g² 17dᵖᵘ Dec 17] poor novice hurdler: headstrong, and
needs emphasis on speed at 2m. *H. D. Daly*

TRANSIT 5 b.g. Lion Cavern (USA) – Black Fighter (USA) (Secretariat (USA)) **c103 +**
[2003/4 h87+: 16g 21s³ 17d⁴ 16d⁴ 16sᵘʳ c16g² c17s* c21dᵖᵘ Mar 16] leggy gelding: **h89**
modest maiden hurdler: better form when winning handicap chase at Market Rasen in
March by 10 lengths from Venn Ottery, but not fluent all 3 starts over fences: best form
around 2m: acts on soft going: blinkered fifth start, in cheekpieces otherwise in 2003/4:
has looked less than keen. *B. Ellison*

TRANSLUCID (USA) 6 b.h. Woodman (USA) – Gossamer (USA) (Seattle Slew **c124**
(USA)) [2003/4 h114: 17g² 16f⁴ 16d⁶ c20g² c18g Mar 6] angular horse: fair hurdler: **h111 +**

easily best effort in 3 starts over fences when ½-length second to Jardin de Beaulieu in handicap at Kempton, making most but hanging right and caught close home: stays 2½m: acts on firm and soft going: free-going sort. *C. Von Der Recke, Germany*

TRAVELLER'S FAYRE (IRE) 5 b.g. Fayruz – The Way She Moves (North Stoke) **h–**
[2003/4 F17m F17d F16g 19g^{pu} 20v^{pu} 17s^F Feb 11] close-coupled gelding: brother to **F–**
several winners, including modest middle-distance performer, stays 2½m Fayrway Rhythm, and half-brother to others, including 1998 2-y-o 7f winner Welsh Governor (by Welsh Term): dam, little worthwhile form, from family of high-class middle-distance colt Master Willie: no form in bumpers or novice hurdles: tried tongue tied. *Mrs Dianne Sayer*

TRAVELLERS HEIR (IRE) 6 ch.g. Montelimar (USA) – Allaracket (IRE) (The **h109**
Parson) [2003/4 h90, F87: 20m^{pu} 16m* 17d* 17g 19g 16g⁴ Mar 15] stocky gelding: fair hurdler: made all in novices at Worcester (handicap) and Bangor in November: best form around 2m: acts on good to firm and good to soft going: sold to join Miss V. Williams 24,000 gns Doncaster May Sales. *H. D. Daly*

TRAVELLING BAND (IRE) 6 b.g. Blues Traveller (IRE) – Kind of Cute (Prince **h110**
Sabo) [2003/4 16s* 16s² 16g⁵ Dec 26] angular gelding: fairly useful on Flat (lightly raced, stays 1¼m): won novice at Haydock on hurdling debut in November: better form when second to Steppes of Gold in similar event there, tying up run-in having been left in front 2 out: likely to prove best at 2m with emphasis on speed. *A. M. Balding*

TRAVELLING WARRIOR 5 b.g. Emperor Fountain – Gipsy Princess (Prince **F84**
Daniel (USA)) [2003/4 F16m⁵ Aug 2] first foal: dam 7f winner: never-nearer fifth of 21 to Theatre Groom in bumper at Worcester on debut. *M. F. Harris*

TRAVELLO (GER) 4 b.c. Bakharoff (USA) – Travista (GER) (Days At Sea (USA)) **h95**
[2003/4 16g^{ur} 16d³ 16g⁴ 16s^{pu} Dec 13] rather unfurnished colt: in frame up to 1½m on Flat: unseated last in juvenile at Munich on hurdling debut for Frau J. Mayer: best effort when third in similar event at Wetherby, only outing for C. Von Der Recke. *M. F. Harris*

TRAVEL (POL) 4 gr.g. Freedom's Choice (USA) – Transylwania (POL) (Baby Bid **h–**
(USA)) [2003/4 17d 16s^{pu} 17s Jan 20] well-made gelding: successful twice around 6f in Poland at 2 yrs for M. Janikowski: lost all chance when jumping badly left 2 out in juvenile at Cheltenham on hurdling debut: no show both subsequent outings. *T. R. George*

TREASURED COIN 6 b.g. Overbury (IRE) – Slip A Coin (Slip Anchor) [2003/4 **h69**
h71: 21g⁴ Jul 28] leggy gelding: poor maiden hurdler: stays 2½m: acts on good to firm going. *P. Bowen*

TREASURE TRAIL 5 b.g. Millkom – Forever Shineing (Glint of Gold) [2003/4 16d* **h83**
16d 20g Dec 9] small, compact gelding: fairly useful on Flat (stays 2m): won maiden at Fakenham in November on hurdling debut by head from Montosari, getting up on line: failed to progress: should be suited by further than 2m. *S. Kirk*

TREBLE VISION (IRE) 10 ch.g. Down The Hatch – General Vision (General Iron- **h–**
side) [2003/4 24s^{pu} Apr 4] won maiden point in 2002, pulled all 3 starts since and on hurdling debut. *W. G. Young*

TREEN (IRE) 5 b.m. Charnwood Forest (IRE) – Legende d'Or (FR) (Diesis) [2003/4 **h55**
18m 16f⁴ Oct 9] no form on Flat: bad form on second of 2 starts over hurdles. *K. Burke, Ireland*

TREGASTEL (FR) 9 b.g. Tel Quel (FR) – Myrtlewood (FR) (Home Guard (USA)) **c121**
[2003/4 c22s³ c21s² c22g^{ur} c24d^{bd} Nov 27] ex-French gelding: placed around 1¾m on **h–**
Flat: fairly useful hurdler/chaser: claimed out of E. Chevalier du Fau's stable €19,000 after second in claiming chase at Auteuil in June: jumped better than on British debut and still to be asked for effort when brought down twelfth in handicap at Carlisle: stays 2¾m: raced on good ground or softer (acts on heavy). *R. Ford*

TREMALLT (IRE) 13 b.g. Henbit (USA) – Secret Romance (Gala Performance) **c124**
[2003/4 c110+, h94=: 22g⁴ c27d^F c24s² c24m^{pu} c25s^{ur} c25d² c20s² c24g⁴ c24s² c24d² **h102**
Apr 12] close-coupled gelding: winning hurdler: fairly useful handicap chaser: creditable efforts all completed outings in 2003/4: stays 25f: acts on heavy going, probably on good to firm: visored once: front runner: bold jumper, but still prone to odd error: tough. *T. R. George*

TREMEZZO 6 b.g. Mind Games – Rosa Van Fleet (Sallust) [2003/4 16g^F 17g^{pu} Apr **h–**
10] leggy gelding: modest juvenile hurdler in 2001/2: off 23 months, no show in 2 handi-caps on return: raced around 2m: acts on soft and good to firm ground: tongue tied since debut. *B. R. Millman*

943

TRENANCE 6 b.g. Alflora (IRE) – Carmel's Joy (IRE) (Carlingford Castle) [2003/4 **h88 ?**
F–: 20d^{pu} 24s^{pu} 16d^6 16d Apr 23] sturdy gelding: form only when sixth of 13 in novice
hurdle at Sandown, possibly flattered: bred to be suited by further than 2m. *T. R. George*

TRESOR DE MAI (FR) 10 ch.g. Grand Tresor (FR) – Lady Night (FR) (Pompon **c129 x**
Rouge) [2003/4 c150x, h–: c16g^5 c21f^3 c20g c24s^4 c19g^5 c24s c24s^5 Mar 20] sparely- **h–**
made gelding: one-time smart chaser, long way below best in 2003/4: stays 3m: acts on
heavy going: blinkered prior to 2001/2: sketchy jumper. *M. C. Pipe*

TRESOR PREZINIERE (FR) 6 b. or br.g. Grand Tresor (FR) – Rose de Martine **c108 x**
(FR) (The Quiet Man (FR)) [2003/4 c?, h?: 20m* 20g^3 22g^6 c19d^3 c20d^F c21d 20v^3 **h105**
c21m^6 c24d^F c26g^6 Apr 10] leggy gelding: fair chaser, often let down by jumping (tends
to go left): fair hurdler: won 4-runner novice at Chepstow in October: stays 2¾m: acts on
heavy and good to firm going: blinkered last 6 starts: has looked none too keen under
pressure. *P. J. Hobbs*

TRIBAL DANCER (IRE) 10 ch.g. Commanche Run – Cute Play (Salluceva) [2003/4 **c109**
c116, h112: c25g^F c24g^{pu} c26g^4 c24d^{pu} c29d^{pu} c24d^{pu} 22d 20v^{pu} 26g^2 c24m^3 26d^4 c24d* **h99**
Apr 12] leggy, close-coupled gelding: modest handicap hurdler: fair handicap chaser:
back near best when winning at Huntingdon, leading after 2 out and soon clear: stays
3¼m: acts on soft and good to firm going: too free when blinkered eighth start: sometimes
let down by jumping/attitude. *Miss Venetia Williams*

TRIBAL DISPUTE 7 b.g. Primitive Rising (USA) – Coral Princess (Imperial Fling **h–**
(USA)) [2003/4 h110, F–: 16d Mar 22] big, useful-looking gelding: will make a chaser:
fair hurdler: not knocked about when well held in handicap after 11-month absence,
only start in 2003/4: should prove as effective at 2½m as 2m: acts on heavy going.
T. D. Easterby

TRIBAL RUN (IRE) 9 ch.g. Be My Native (USA) – Queen's Run (IRE) (Deep Run) **c99**
[2003/4 c102, h–: c25s^6 c24v^3 c24s^2 Mar 20] fair chaser, off nearly a year before reap- **h–**
pearance: stays 3¾m: acts on heavy going: tongue tied: sold 5,000 gns Doncaster May
Sales. *C. Grant*

TRIBAL TRACT (IRE) 10 b.g. Alphabatim (USA) – Wiji Damar (Laurence O) **c–**
[2003/4 c–: c24s May 2] workmanlike gelding: winning pointer: novice steeplechaser,
little form since 2001/2 reappearance: stays 25f: acts on soft going: tried blinkered/tongue
tied. *P. H. Morris*

TRICKEY NICK 5 b.g. Nomadic Way (USA) – Nicky's Choice (Baron Blakeney) **F–**
[2003/4 F16g^{pu} Mar 15] second foal: dam well beaten in bumpers: no show in bumper on
debut. *B. N. Doran*

TRICKY THYNE (IRE) 5 b.g. Good Thyne (USA) – Cuban Vacation (Ovac (ITY)) **h–**
[2003/4 F17s 16d 19g 16d^{pu} Apr 21] 10,000 4-y-o: unfurnished gelding: fourth foal: dam **F–**
unraced half-sister to very smart chaser around 2½m The Outback Way: showed nothing
in bumper and over hurdles: tongue tied final outing. *R. Dickin*

TRICKY TREVOR (IRE) 11 b. or br.g. Arctic Lord – Chancer's Last (Foggy Bell) **c89**
[2003/4 c–, h–: c21m^2 c21g^F Mar 3] rangy gelding: novice steeplechaser: runner-up at **h–**
Folkestone on completed start in maiden hunters: fair pointer, successful twice in March:
best around 2½m: acts on firm and good to soft going: tried blinkered. *Mrs H. J. Cobb*

TRIGGER CASTLE 9 b.m. Henbit (USA) – Jane's Daughter (Pitpan) [2003/4 **c– x**
21m^{pu} c20m^{pu} c23m^{pu} Sep 14] 4,600 4-y-o: sixth foal: half-sister to fair staying chasers **h–**
River Don (by Over The River) and Mister Muddypaws (by Celtic Cone): dam, unplaced
in Irish bumpers and points, half-sister to useful hurdler up to 3m Trust The King: of little
account: trained first 2 starts by J. Wainwright. *P. T. Midgley*

TRIGGERLINO 4 b.f. Double Trigger (IRE) – Voolino (Relkino) [2003/4 F17s F16s **F72**
Feb 22] third foal: dam third on first of 2 starts over hurdles: poor form on first of 2 starts
in bumpers. *Miss Venetia Williams*

TRILLIONAIRE 6 ch.g. Dilum (USA) – Madam Trilby (Grundy) [2003/4 h74: 23g^4 **h77**
20m^3 24m 22g^6 24m^5 21s^{ur} 21s 22g Feb 10] smallish gelding: poor handicap hurdler:
barely stays 3m: acts on good to firm going: pulls hard. *Miss C. J. E. Caroe*

TRINKET (IRE) 6 b.g. Definite Article – Alamiya (IRE) (Doyoun) [2003/4 h100+, **h102**
F102: 19g* Apr 3] well-made gelding: fair hurdler: off 16 months, won maiden at
Hereford by 2½ lengths from Toombridge: stays 19f. *H. D. Daly*

TRIPLE GLORY (IRE) 5 b.m. Goldmark (USA) – Trebles (IRE) (Kenmare (FR)) **c–**
[2003/4 h74: 16d c19g c25g^{pu} Apr 4] angular mare: maiden hurdler: no form since second **h–**
start in 2002/3, including over fences. *Mrs P. N. Dutfield*

TRIPLE PLAY (IRE)   5 br.g. Tagula (IRE) – Shiyra (Darshaan) [2003/4 17d^{pu} 19g **h–** Apr 24] 5f winner at 2 yrs, poor on Flat since, left Don Enrico Incisa after final start in 2003: no encouragement in 2 novice hurdles. *Lady Susan Watson*

TRISONS STAR (IRE)   6 b.g. Roselier (FR) – Delkusha (Castle Keep) [2003/4 F16d² **F104** Apr 17] third foal: dam winning hurdler: failed to complete in 2 Irish points in 2003: 100/1, led to halfway when 1½ lengths second of 10 finishers to Wild Cane Ridge in bumper at Ayr on debut. *Mrs L. B. Normile*

TRISTANA   5 b.m. Efisio – Michelle's Ella (IRE) (Ela-Mana-Mou) [2003/4 F16s **F–** Feb 22] second foal: dam no sign of ability on Flat: tailed off in bumper on debut. *J. M. Bradley*

TRIUMPH OF DUBAI (IRE)   4 b.g. Eagle Eyed (USA) – Jack-N-Jilly (IRE) **h84** (Anita's Prince) [2003/4 16s⁶ 17m* 16m 16g³ᵈ Dec 18] poor on balance of form on Flat: best effort in juvenile hurdles when winning seller at Taunton in November: will prove best at sharp 2m. *J. S. Moore*

TRIVIAL (IRE)   12 b.m. Rakaposhi King – Miss Rubbish (Rubor) [2003/4 c–, h85: **c–** c20g⁵ 22d^{pu} May 28] quite good-topped mare: winning hurdler/pointer: well beaten on **h–** completed start in steeplechases: stays 3m: acts on good to firm and good to soft going. *J. E. Brockbank*

TROEDRHIWDALAR   7 b.m. Gunner B – Delladear (Sonnen Gold) [2003/4 h–, F–: **h–** 19g³ 20s⁶ 26m⁴ Jun 11] no form over hurdles: visored final outing. *Mrs D. A. Hamer*

TROJAN WOLF   9 ch.g. Wolfhound (USA) – Trojan Lady (USA) (Irish River (FR)) **h–** [2003/4 16m May 7] poor and unreliable on Flat (stays 1½m) nowadays: well beaten in seller on hurdling debut. *P. Howling*

TROODOS VALLEY (IRE)   5 b.g. Executive Perk – Valleymay (IRE) (King's **F92** Ride) [2003/4 F16v⁵ F16g² F16d Apr 21] 17,000 4-y-o: good-topped gelding: third foal: dam unraced sister to one-time useful hurdler/fairly useful chaser up to around 25f Valley Erne: best effort in bumpers when 8 lengths second of 16 to Gaelic Flight in maiden at Stratford: will be suited by further. *H. D. Daly*

TROOPER   10 b.g. Rock Hopper – Silica (USA) (Mr Prospector (USA)) [2003/4 c85§, **c85 §** h87§: c27s* 27s c25g^F c27d⁴ c27d² c27d⁴ c25g⁴ c27s c25d⁴ c30g^{bd} c27s⁴ c32d^{pu} Mar 18] **h– §** lengthy gelding: poor hurdler/chaser: won 5-runner handicap over fences at Sedgefield in May: stays 27f: acts on any going: visored/blinkered: ungenuine. *A. Crook*

TROOPER KIT   5 b.g. Petoski – Rolling Dice (Balinger) [2003/4 F18s^F F16d Nov **F–** 30] seventh foal: half-brother to modest chasers Pitchthedice (by Relief Pitcher), stays 3m, and DB My Son (by Gildoran), stays 2½m: dam, modest 2½m chaser, half-sister to smart hunter chaser Risk A Bet: more signs of temperament than ability in bumpers. *Mrs L. Richards*

TROUBLE AHEAD (IRE)   13 b.g. Cataldi – Why 'o' Why (Giolla Mear) [2003/4 **c122 x** c118x, h–: c16g* c16s³ c17g⁵ c20d^{pu} c16d⁵ c19g³ c19s c19g* c21m⁴ c20s^{pu} Apr 21] quite **h–** good-topped gelding: fairly useful handicap chaser: won at Perth in May and Ascot in February, beating Supreme Catch by 2½ lengths at latter: well below form most other starts in 2003/4: effective at 2m to 3m: acts on good to firm and heavy going: probably best on right-handed tracks: prone to mistakes. *Miss Venetia Williams*

TROUBLE AT BAY (IRE)   4 b.g. Slip Anchor – Fight Right (FR) (Crystal Glit- **h135** ters (USA)) [2003/4 16m⁴ 17m* 16m* 16s* 17d* 16g* 17g Mar 18]
The horse who headed the betting on the Triumph Hurdle five months before the race was due to be run, when still to jump a hurdle in public, was also favourite at the off. Unfortunately for his supporters, Trouble At Bay, as on his hurdling debut when fourth of ten at Kempton, failed to live up to expectations, still in touch with the leaders two out but dropping away to finish tenth behind Made In Japan. In between those runs Trouble At Bay was unbeaten in five appearances, and a reproduction of his best form would probably have been good enough to win what was a substandard renewal of the Triumph. He is the highest-rated juvenile hurdler to race in Britain or Ireland in this Annual.
Trouble At Bay, clearly having learnt a lot from his first run, easily landed the odds at Hereford and Wincanton on his second and third starts, before being stepped up in class. At Cheltenham in December he showed himself the best juvenile seen out in Britain and Ireland by that stage of the season, winning an eleven-runner event by seven lengths from Tamarinbleu with the remainder well

*Read The Racing Post Before You Bet Adonis Juvenile Novices' Hurdle, Kempton—
leading British-trained juvenile Trouble At Bay successfully concedes 7 lb to the grey Locksmith*

strung out, forging ahead after two out and still running on strongly at the end of a race run at a good pace in testing conditions. Trouble At Bay ran to a similar level when returned to Cheltenham the following month, though he was less impressive in a race which turned into something of a sprint from the second last. The patiently-ridden Trouble At Bay was shaken up to improve at the top of the hill, took control after the second last and was driven out to win by three quarters of a length and the same from the French challengers Meryl and Val du Don. Trouble At Bay's last run before the Cheltenham Festival came in the Grade 2 Adonis Juvenile Hurdle at Kempton at the end of February, a race run in the latest season under the cumbersome title of the Read The Racing Post Before You Bet Juvenile Novices' Hurdle. The event was won in 1999 and 2000 by Katarino and Snow Drop respectively, both of whom went on to justify favouritism in the Triumph. The latest renewal of the Adonis was weakened by the late withdrawals of Moulin Riche and Zimbabwe and by the poor showing of second favourite Mondul, but there was again plenty to like about the performance of Trouble At Bay, the favourite, in what was a true test under the conditions. Held up once again, Trouble At Bay came through to lead two out and ran on well to win by half a length from Locksmith who received 7 lb, the pair pulling nine lengths clear of third-placed Shuhood. There was an interesting postscript when winning jockey Robert Thornton declined an immediate post-race interview with a Channel 4 presenter walking alongside as Trouble At Bay returned to the unsaddling enclosure. Connections of Trouble At Bay evidently felt that Thornton should give his comments to them first. And who can blame them? Such 'instant' interviews rarely enlighten the viewer anyway and can be ill-timed as well as intrusive. One Channel 4 anchor sometimes ends such interviews with an exhortation to the jockey to 'enjoy the moment.' Wouldn't it be better if the jockey was actually allowed to do that and was given a little time to recover from his exertions and gather his thoughts?

946

Trouble At Bay, who finished second twice from five starts as a two-year-old, developed into a useful performer on the Flat at three, winning over a mile and a half at Newbury and Ascot. His dam, Fight Right, raced on the Flat in France, winning over a mile at two. Three of her earlier foals, Ken Fight (by Highest Honor), Royal Groom (by Al Nasr) and Suave Fighter (by Suave Dancer), also won on the Flat in France, with Royal Groom successful at fifteen furlongs over hurdles there, too. Another of Fight Right's foals is the useful Brigadier Jones (by Emperor Jones), a winner of a maiden at Southwell at two and later successful in the States; while her latest offspring to reach the racecourse, Saros (by Desert Sun), was a modest winner at around one mile on the Flat in 2004. Lyre de Saron, the grandam of Trouble At Bay, was placed numerous times without winning. She is a sister to the Prix de Malleret winner Luth de Saron out of the smart winner at up to a mile Rose de Saron. Trouble At Bay, a smallish, close-coupled gelding, has raced only at

		Shirley Heights	Mill Reef
	Slip Anchor	(b 1975)	Hardiemma
	(b 1982)	Sayonara	Birkhahn
Trouble At Bay (IRE)		(b 1965)	Suleika
(b.g. 2000)		Crystal Glitters	Blushing Groom
	Fight Right (FR)	(b 1980)	Tales To Tell
	(br 1987)	Lyre de Saron	Luthier
		(b 1975)	Rose de Saron

Mr Nigel Bunter's "Trouble At Bay"

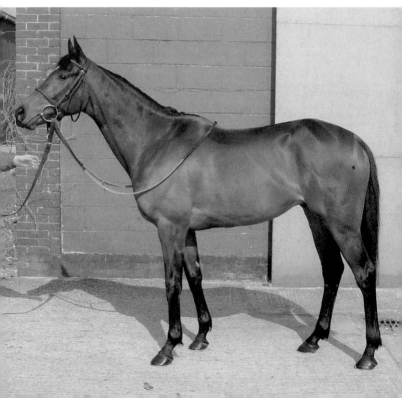

around two miles over hurdles, but will stay two and a half. He acts on soft and good to firm going. *A. King*

TROUBLEINALLENWOOD (IRE) 5 b.g. Big Sink Hope (USA) – Gometra (Lomond (USA)) [2003/4 F16m Apr 13] £1,000 4-y-o: first foal: dam behind in maidens on Flat: looked temperamental in maiden point on debut: well beaten in bumper 2 months later. *B. D. Leavy* **F–**

TROYSGREEN (IRE) 6 b.g. Warcraft (USA) – Moylena (Bustomi) [2003/4 h–§, F–: 20m^{pu} c25g^{ur} 24s^5 24m^4 20m Jun 14] of little account and temperamental to boot: tried blinkered. *P. D. Niven* **c– §**
h– §

TRUCKERS TAVERN (IRE) 9 ch.g. Phardante (FR) – Sweet Tulip (Beau Chapeau) [2003/4 c166, h–: 22s^4 c24d^2 c25d^F c25d^{ur} c26g^{pu} Mar 18] big, well-made gelding: excelled himself when second in 2003 Cheltenham Gold Cup: smart chaser on balance of form and prone to mistakes, all but came down third when 17 lengths second to Keen Leader in Grade 2 at Haydock reportedly had breathing problem when pulled up in Gold Cup final outing: suited by 3m+: raced on good going or softer (acts on heavy): tongue tied: effective held up or ridden from front. *Ferdy Murphy* **c154**
h120 +

TRUDI BAY 7 b.m. Terimon – Letterewe (Alias Smith (USA)) [2003/4 23s^{pu} Jan 21] fourth foal: dam temperamental winning 2m hurdler: showed nothing in amateur maiden hurdle on debut. *N. B. King* **h–**

TRUE BEAUTY (FR) 4 ch.f. Shernazar – Re-Release (Baptism) [2003/4 F16s^5 F16g^4 Mar 4] fourth foal: half-sister to fair hurdler Westmeath Flyer (by Deploy), stays 2½m: dam useful hurdler/fair chaser who stayed 21f: poor form in mares bumpers. *N. G. Richards* **F74**

TRUE BLUE VICTORY (IRE) 8 b.g. Catrail (USA) – Russian Ribbon (USA) (Nijinsky (CAN)) [2003/4 h127: c17s^2 c20s c18d* c17d c22d^3 c18d* c20s^3 c19d^5 c16s* c16d^4 Feb 22] leggy, useful-looking gelding: fairly useful hurdler: excellent first season over fences, showing useful form: won at Clonmel (maiden) in June, Punchestown (handicap) in December and Navan (Grade 2 novice, beat Jim 2½ lengths) in February: best form at 2m: raced on going softer than good (possibly not suited by heavy): blinkered last 2 starts: tongue tied prior to 2002/3. *T. M. Walsh, Ireland* **c135**
h–

TRUE CHIMES 13 ch.g. True Song – Ballytina (Rugantino) [2003/4 c21d^{pu} Apr 30] tall, good-topped gelding: winning pointer: not fluent and modest form at best in hunter chases. *Mrs J. Owen* **c– x**
h–

TRUE LOVER (GER) 7 b.g. Winged Love (IRE) – Truneba (GER) (Nebos (GER)) [2003/4 19s^5 16s 24g^2 21g* 22g* Apr 22] sturdy, close-coupled gelding: successful 6 times up to 2m on Flat in Scandinavia at 3 and 4 yrs for W. Neuroth: twice-raced over hurdles for E. Chevalier du Fau: much improved last 2 starts in Britain, winning 20-runner maiden at Newbury in March and 14-runner novice at Fontwell, taking strong hold and leading 3 out when beating Analogy 2½ lengths at latter: stays 3m. *J. W. Mullins* **h123**

TRUE NORTH (IRE) 9 b.g. Black Monday – Slip A Loop (The Parson) [2003/4 h114: 20v 25g Feb 6] workmanlike gelding: fair handicap hurdler: left L. Lungo, well held both starts in 2003/4: suited by 2¾m+: raced on good going or softer (acts on heavy). *D. R. MacLeod* **h–**

TRUE ROSE (IRE) 8 ch.m. Roselier (FR) – Naar Chamali (Salmon Leap (USA)) [2003/4 c78, h84: 21d^3 c20g^4 c16v^2 c21s^3 Feb 24] workmanlike mare: poor hurdler: modest novice steeplechaser, let down by jumping final outing: should stay beyond 2m: raced on good going or softer (acts on heavy): tongue tied last 2 starts. *J. R. Turner* **c88**
h78

TRUE TANNER 6 b.g. Lyphento (USA) – True Nell (Neltino) [2003/4 F16g F16d Mar 28] second foal: dam unraced, out of half-sister to top-class staying chaser Spartan Missile: well held in 2 bumpers. *Miss C. Dyson* **F–**

TRUICEAR 7 b.g. Petoski – Fit For A King (Royalty) [2003/4 c24g^{pu} Apr 1] sturdy gelding: little sign of ability in varied events (last of 3 finishers in maiden point in April): tried tongue tied. *L. Corcoran* **c–**
h–

TRUMP CARD 7 b.g. Distant Relative – Tell No Lies (High Line) [2003/4 h79, F98: 24m^4 16m^{pu} Sep 27] leggy gelding: bumper winner: poor form over hurdles: bought out of C. Swan's stable 8,500 gns Doncaster May Sales: fatally injured when running by mistake instead of stable-companion Investment Force at Plumpton: stayed 3m: acted on good to firm going: tried blinkered. *C. J. Mann* **h80**

TRUMPINGTON 6 ch.m. First Trump – Brockton Flame (Emarati (USA)) [2003/4 h85: 24g⁵ 23sᵖᵘ 24d Apr 21] modest maiden hurdler at best, no form in handicaps in 2003/4: stays 3m: acts on soft and good to firm going: wore cheekpieces final start: has hung/looked none too keen under pressure. *D. G. Bridgwater* **h–**

TRUSTED INSTINCT (IRE) 4 b.c. Polish Precedent (USA) – Trust In Luck (IRE) (Nashwan (USA)) [2003/4 16g 16mᵖᵘ Nov 8] fair on Flat (stays 1¼m), successful in September, sold out of D. Weld's stable €23,000 Goffs October Sale, well beaten in 2004: favourite, always behind and not knocked about (reportedly lame) in juvenile maiden at Huntingdon on hurdling debut: quickly pulled up before 2 out at Sandown week later. *C. A. Dwyer* **h–**

TRUSTING PADDY (IRE) 7 b.g. Synefos (USA) – Homefield Girl (IRE) (Rahotep (FR)) [2003/4 h82, F82: 17g⁵ 21mᵖᵘ c16mᶠ c20dᶠ 23s⁵ 20d⁶ Apr 21] lengthy gelding: poor maiden hurdler: fell both starts over fences, every chance in match for novice at Folkestone when doing so on chasing debut: stays 19f: acts on heavy going (bumper form on firm). *L. A. Dace* **c83** **h76**

TRUSTING TOM 9 b.g. Teamster – Florista (Oats) [2003/4 c104: c25g³ c26m* c28g² c25s⁵ c24d² c24sᵖᵘ c21sᵖᵘ Apr 12] sturdy gelding: fair handicap chaser: won at Southwell in November: poor efforts 3 of last 4 starts: stays 3½m: acts on soft and good to firm going: effective blinkered or not, wore cheekpieces last 3 starts: sold 15,000 gns Doncaster May Sales. *C. C. Bealby* **c112**

TRY ME AND SEE 10 ch.g. Rock City – Al Raja (Kings Lake (USA)) [2003/4 h–: c25gᵘʳ c25gᵘʳ c21g⁶ Apr 12] good-topped gelding: poor pointer: well held only completed start in steeplechases: tried tongue tied. *A. M. Crow* **c–** **h–**

TSAR PARTY (IRE) 7 b.g. Moscow Society (USA) – Full Choke (Shirley Heights) [2003/4 c19d⁵ c24dᶠ Apr 12] tall gelding: half-brother to fair hurdler/fairly useful chaser The Glow (by Glow), stayed 3m, and winner up to 9f in Italy by Nordico: dam, fair 2¼m winner on Flat: sister to smart but ungenuine 1½m filly Out of Shot: won 4-y-o maiden Irish point in 2001, well held in novice on steeplechase debut, but close up when falling thirteenth in similar event at Huntingdon. *Mrs Susan Nock* **c– p**

TSAR'S TWIST 5 b.g. Presidium – Kabs Twist (Kabour) [2003/4 F16g F17m F17m F17f⁴ 20m⁵ 17g 16g 22sᵖᵘ Mar 23] close-coupled gelding: second foal: brother to 2000 2-y-o 5.5f winner in Norway: dam unraced: seemed to show modest form 2 of 4 starts in bumpers: no form in novice company over hurdles: free-going sort: has given trouble in preliminaries. *Mrs S. Gardner* **h–** **r81 ?**

TSCHIERTSCHEN 4 ch.g. Master Willie – Smocking (Night Shift (USA)) [2003/4 F16d⁵ Mar 11] useful-looking gelding: third foal: dam poor maiden on Flat and over hurdles: green, well held in bumper on debut. *M. W. Easterby* **F–**

TSUKI (FR) 6 b.m. Perrault – Tsunami (FR) (Shafaraz (FR)) [2003/4 16v 16mᵖᵘ 16m⁶ 16vᵖᵘ 19s 16sᵖᵘ Dec 30] third foal: sister to 19f chase winner Chasca: dam won several times up to 1½m on Flat in France: last of 13 only outing on Flat in France at 3 yrs: no form over hurdles: tried blinkered. *S. J. Gilmore* **h–**

TSUNAMI 8 b.m. Beveled (USA) – Alvecote Lady (Touching Wood (USA)) [2003/4 c–, h79: 22dᵖᵘ 16s c20sᵖᵘ 20v⁷ 20s 21g 17g c24dᵖᵘ Apr 12] sparely-made mare: poor hurdler/maiden chaser: stays 21f: probably acts on any going: tried in headgear: has had tongue tied. *B. D. Leavy* **c–**

TUBBER ROADS (IRE) 11 b.g. Un Desperado (FR) – Node (Deep Run) [2003/4 c–: c21dᵖᵘ Apr 30] good-topped gelding: useful hunter chaser in 2002: pulled up lame amiss only 2 starts in hunters since (runner-up in points in 2004): stays 3m: best form on good to soft/soft going: often races up with pace. *M. G. Hazell* **c–**

TUBBER STREAMS (IRE) 7 b.g. Great Marquess – Much Obliged (Crash Course) [2003/4 20d Apr 21] IR 2,800 3-y-o: fifth foal: half-brother to winning pointers by Abednego and Classic Memory: dam placed in bumpers and over hurdles: winning pointer: mid-field in 12-runner bumper at Gowran: sold out of P. Lynch's stable 13,000 gns Doncaster May Sales: well beaten in maiden on hurdling debut. *R. T. Phillips* **h–**

TUCACAS (FR) 7 gr.m. Highest Honor (FR) – Three Well (FR) (Sicyos (USA)) [2003/4 h137: 22f⁴ c19d⁵ c19g* c21d* c21d⁵ c17d* 17m Apr 15] good-topped mare: useful hurdler: odds on, won novice chases in small fields at Exeter (mares) in December, Wincanton (fairly useful form when beating Ruby Gale 1½ lengths) in January and Plumpton in April: stays easy 2¾m: acts on any going: ran moody race in visor in 2002/3. *M. C. Pipe* **c118** **h129**

949

TUDOR BLONDE   13 ch.m. Pablond – Cottage Melody (Super Song) [2003/4 22m^pu   h–
May 29] of no account. *P. D. Purdy*

TUDOR COTTAGE   14 ch.g. Town And Country – Cottage Melody (Super Song)   h–
[2003/4 21m^pu May 5] very lightly raced and little sign of ability. *P. D. Purdy*

TUDOR KING (IRE)   10 br.g. Orchestra – Jane Bond (Good Bond) [2003/4 c82x,   c82 x
h65§: c25m^6 c22m^pu c21g^ur c21g* c21m^pu c26g^pu c20m^2 c21m^3 c25m* c20m^ur c24s Dec   h– §
29] rather sparely-made gelding: maiden hurdler: poor handicap chaser: won in small
fields at Southwell in July and Folkestone in November: stays easy 25f: acts on soft and
firm going: races prominently: often let down by jumping: inconsistent. *J. S. King*

TUDOR NATIVE   8 b.m. Distinct Native – Tudorfield Girl (Tudorville) [2003/4 h–:   h–
17d^pu 21v^pu Jan 13] lengthy mare: showed nothing in 3 novice hurdles. *A. Parker*

TUDOR NICKOLA   12 ch.m. Nicholas Bill – Cottage Melody (Super Song) [2003/4   h–
h–: 19m^pu 22g^pu Jun 3] lengthy, angular mare: of no account. *P. D. Purdy*

TUFTEX KING   7 b.g. Syrtos – More Laughter (Oats) [2003/4 h80d, F–: 22m^4 Jul 13]   h–
little form: tried blinkered: pulls hard: sold £2,500 Ascot August Sales. *Mrs S. Gardner*

TULLIMOSS (IRE)   9 b.m. Husyan (USA) – Ballynattin Moss (Le Moss) [2003/4   h75
h70: 16g^2 18g^6 20g^2 16s Dec 20] poor maiden hurdler: effective at 2m, should stay 3m:
acts on good to firm and heavy going: has had tongue tied. *J. N. R. Billinge*

TULLONS LANE   9 b.g. Riverwise (USA) – Pallanda (Pablond) [2003/4 c88, h–:   c77 x
c20g c20g^pu c19g^ur c22g^4 c21d* c21s^2 Jan 20] lengthy, angular gelding: poor handicap   h–
chaser: won amateur event at Folkestone in January: stays 2¾m: acts on heavy going:
often makes mistakes. *N. R. Mitchell*

TULLYNAGARDY   4 ch.g. Sabrehill (USA) – Moorefield Girl (IRE) (Gorytus   F–
(USA)) [2003/4 F13v F16d Apr 17] 9,000 3-y-o: fourth foal: half-brother to fair hurdler
up to 2½m Zsarabak (by Soviet Lad): dam fair staying hurdler: tailed off in bumpers.
J. M. Jefferson

TUMBLEWEED GLEN (IRE)   8 ch.g. Mukaddamah (USA) – Mistic Glen (IRE)   c–
(Mister Majestic) [2003/4 c82, h–x: c16m^pu c19g c20m^4 May 29] angular gelding: poor   h– x
maiden jumper: stays 2½m: acts on soft and good to firm going: sometimes blinkered
earlier in career. *P. Kelsall*

TUMBLING DICE (IRE)   5 b.g. King's Theatre (IRE) – Eva Fay (IRE) (Petong)   h110
[2003/4 16m 16d 16d 16d^2 16s^3 20s^5 22d^5 20s 20s* 20g^4 Apr 11] leggy gelding: fourth
foal: half-brother to 1½m winner Brisbane Road (by Blues Traveller): dam unraced half-
sister to top-class chaser Remittance Man and smart Italian middle-distance performer
Teach Dha Mhile: fair hurdler: won handicaps at Cork in January and Wexford in March:
stays 2¾m: acts on soft ground. *T. J. Taaffe, Ireland*

TUNES OF GLORY (IRE)   8 b.g. Symboli Heights (FR) – Coxtown Queen (IRE)   h112
(Corvaro (USA)) [2003/4 F16g* 22d 16f* 16g^F 16f^5 Sep 26] first foal: half-brother to   F93
winning 2½m chaser Adolphus (by Tidaro): dam unraced half-sister to useful staying
chaser Boraceva: won at Down Royal in May on last of 4 starts in bumpers: best effort
over hurdles when easily winning maiden at Sligo in July: raced mainly at 2m: acts on
firm going: tongue tied final start: sold only 1,200 gns Doncaster May Sales. *N. Meade,
Ireland*

TUPPENNY CODY (IRE)   5 b.g. Muroto – Alzena (Persian Bold) [2003/4 F16g*   h120
F16f* F16m^2 16g* 16m^4 16s^F 16g^F 16d^4 Mar 31] sixth foal: half-brother to bumper   F105
winners Fade To Black (by Shahanndeh) and Rachel's Swallow (by Castle Keep): dam,
maiden on Flat and over hurdles, half-sister to useful 2m hurdler Majestic Man: useful
bumper performer, successful at Sligo in August and Punchestown in September: fairly
useful hurdler: won maiden at Wexford in October: would have finished second to
Harchibald in handicap at Leopardstown seventh start but for falling last: raced at 2m:
acts on firm going: front runner. *Anthony Mullins, Ireland*

TURAATH (IRE)   8 b.g. Sadler's Wells (USA) – Diamond Field (USA) (Mr Prospector   h103 §
(USA)) [2003/4 h99: 22s 24m^ur 22d^2 21g^5 24s^pu 20g^F 20v^2 22g 24s Apr 17] stocky
gelding: fair handicap hurdler: left P. Hobbs after fifth start, D. Wintle after sixth: stays
2¾m: acts on good to firm and heavy going: usually wears headgear: tried tongue tied:
not an easy ride: unreliable. *A. J. Deakin*

TURBO (IRE)   5 b.g. Piccolo – By Arrangement (IRE) (Bold Arrangement) [2003/4   h105
h114: 16g Nov 30] close-coupled gelding: useful on Flat (stays 1½m), won November
Handicap in 2003: fair form over hurdles: will prove best with emphasis on speed at 2m:
tried blinkered/in cheekpieces. *G. B. Balding*

Tote Exacta Handicap Chase, Wetherby—Turgeonev gains a fourth course win

TURGEONEV (FR) 9 gr.g. Turgeon (USA) – County Kerry (FR) (Comrade In Arms) [2003/4 c144, h–: c20m* c16m6 c20s* c20g2 c20g5 c25g4 c20g2 Apr 16] tall gelding: smart handicap chaser: won at Wetherby in November and February (beat Tremallt 3 lengths): ran well after, particularly when second to Isio in very valuable event at Newbury in March and to Simply Gifted at Ayr in April: barely stays 25f: acts on any going: effective held up or ridden prominently: usually sound jumper. *T. D. Easterby*   **c154 h–**

TURKESTAN (FR) 7 b.g. Petit Loup (USA) – Turkeina (FR) (Kautokeino (FR)) [2003/4 16v 16g Mar 26] leggy, plain gelding: fairly useful hurdler in 2001/2: off nearly 2 years, well held in handicaps on return: raced mainly around 2m: acts on good to firm and heavy going. *M. C. Pipe*   **h–**

TURNED OUT NICE 6 b.m. Ezzoud (IRE) – Green Seed (IRE) (Lead On Time (USA)) [2003/4 h89: 16g5 20gpu Jun 22] modest form over hurdles at 2m: looked badly injured final start. *P. Beaumont*   **h86**

TURN OF PHRASE (IRE) 5 b.g. Cadeaux Genereux – Token Gesture (IRE) (Alzao (USA)) [2003/4 h100: 16m* 16d* 16g5 19gur 17d 19s4 20spu Apr 4] lengthy gelding: fair on Flat (stays 13f): fair handicap hurdler: won twice at Wetherby in May: likely to prove best around 2m: acts on good to firm and good to soft going: usually blinkered in 2003/4 (went with no zest when not final outing). *R. A. Fahey*   **h108**

TURTLEBACK (IRE) 6 b.g. Turtle Island (IRE) – Mimicry (Thatch (USA)) [2003/4 h129: 16s 16gF Feb 29] strong, well-made gelding: fairly useful hurdler: shaped quite well when mid-field in Pierse Hurdle at Leopardstown on reappearance: fell second next time: will prove best around 2m: raced on good going or softer (acts on heavy). *E. J. O'Grady, Ireland*   **h129**

TURTLE LOVE (IRE) 5 b.m. Turtle Island (IRE) – A Little Loving (He Loves Me) [2003/4 h67: 20m6 16m Jun 18] poor on Flat (stays 1¾m): poor maiden hurdler: best around 2m with emphasis on speed: blinkered, tried to refuse on debut. *K. A. Morgan*   **h–**

TURTLE QUEST (IRE) 5 b.g. Turtle Island (IRE) – Brooks' Quest (IRE) (Ahonoora) [2003/4 F16v F16g Jan 23] 19,000 3-y-o: fourth foal: half-brother to 2 winners   **F–**

by Night Shift, 5f winner Seychelles and 8.5f winner in Germany First Draw: dam disappointing Irish maiden: well tailed off in 2 bumpers. *J. M. Jefferson*

TURTLE RECALL (IRE)   5 b.g. Turtle Island (IRE) – Nora Yo Ya (Ahonoora)   h–
[2003/4 16d^{pu} 17s^{pu} 25d^{pu} 16d^{pu} Mar 28] workmanlike gelding: half-brother to 2 winning hurdlers around 2m: modest maiden on Flat (stays 1½m) at 3 yrs, sold out of P. Harris' stable 9,000 gns Newmarket Autumn (2002) Sales: showed nothing in novice hurdles. *F. Jordan*

TURTLE SOUP (IRE)   8 b.g. Turtle Island (IRE) – Lisa's Favourite (Gorytus (USA))   h133
[2003/4 22g^4 20d^3 21s* 21d^5 23s^3 20v^4 22s^5 Feb 7] medium-sized gelding: useful hurdler: improved in 2003/4 after 18-month absence, won handicap at Warwick in December by 14 lengths from Tik-A-Tai: creditable efforts last 3 starts, third to Sh Boom in Grade 2 at Haydock and fourth to Mythical King in valuable handicap at Ascot on first 2 occasions: stays 3m: acts on heavy going: races prominently: consistent. *T. R. George*

TUSCAN TEMPO   5 ch.g. Perugino (USA) – Fact of Time (Known Fact (USA))   h–
[2003/4 h–: 22g^{pu} Aug 12] workmanlike gelding: little worthwhile form over hurdles. *G. F. Edwards*

TUSK   4 ch.g. Fleetwood (IRE) – Farmer's Pet (Sharrood (USA)) [2003/4 16d^4 16g* h121
16s* 17g 16g Apr 1] strong, well-made gelding: half-brother to winning 2m hurdlers Fleet Street (by Wolfhound) and Never Can Tell (by Emarati): useful on Flat (stays 11f), successful 4 times in 2003, sold out of M. Channon's stable 55,000 gns Newmarket Autumn Sales: fairly useful juvenile hurdler: won at Kempton in January and Sandown (beat Cherub 1¼ lengths in 16-runner event) in February: bit disappointing after in graded events at Cheltenham and Aintree, pulling hard early and no danger after mistake sixth at latter: raced around 2m on good going or softer. *Miss H. C. Knight*

TUTTONS   6 ch.m. Whittingham (IRE) – Avonmouthsecretary (Town And Country)   F–
[2003/4 F17m F14d Mar 22] third foal: dam winning staying chaser: well held in 2 bumpers. *N. J. Hawke*

TUXEDO JUNCTION (NZ)   9 br.g. Little Brown Jug (NZ) – Just Kay (NZ) (St   c88
Puckle) [2003/4 c93+, h82: c21g^3 c19g^6 c21g^5 c19m^{pu} Apr 13] rather leggy gelding: poor   h–
maiden hurdler: modest handicap chaser: form in 2003/4 only on reappearance: stays 21f: acts on soft and good to firm going. *P. J. Hobbs*

TWELI   7 b.g. Deploy – Flying Fantasy (Habitat) [2003/4 h88, F84: 21g^{ur} 20d^{pu} 16s^6 h73
21s 20d^{pu} 17d^F 24g 20d^3 Apr 7] lengthy, sparely-made gelding: poor hurdler: stays 2½m: best form on good to firm going: wore blinkers/cheekpieces last 3 starts. *I. A. Wood*

TWENTY BUCKS   10 b.g. Buckley – Sweet N' Twenty (High Top) [2003/4 c17s^3 c92
c24d^{pu} c18g^5 c20d^F Apr 11] workmanlike gelding: modest novice chaser, off over 2 years   h–
prior to reappearance: should stay 3m: probably acts on any going: prone to mistakes over fences. *M. Madgwick*

TWENTY DEGREES   6 ch.g. Beveled (USA) – Sweet N' Twenty (High Top) [2003/4   h106
F18s* F16s^4 18s^4 16s^2 21g Mar 26] good-topped gelding: fourth foal: half-brother to 3   F103
winners, including useful 2m hurdler/winning chaser Sweet Senorita (by Young Senor) and fair hurdler Twenty Bucks (by Buckley), stays 2¾m: dam fairly useful and prolific winning hurdler up to 2½m/fair stayer on Flat: won bumper at Plumpton on debut in December: better form when fourth of 20 at Ascot: easily best effort over hurdles when fourth to Control Man in novice at Fontwell: should stay at least 2½m. *G. L. Moore*

TWENTYTWOSILVER (IRE)   4 ro.g. Emarati (USA) – St Louis Lady (Absalom)   h80
[2003/4 16m^F 16s^{pu} 16g^6 17s^F 17g^3 17g^3 Apr 16] leggy gelding: fair at best on Flat (likely to prove best up to 7f) for J. Osborne: modest juvenile hurdler: sold out of O. Sherwood's stable £5,600 Ascot February Sales after third outing, claimed from J. O'Shea £6,000 fifth start: will prove best around 2m. *N. J. Hawke*

TWICE AS GOOD (IRE)   10 b.g. Good Thyne (USA) – Twice As Fluffy (Pollerton)   c84
[2003/4 c87, h–: c24m^F c24d^{pu} c16d c20m^3 Dec 18] good-topped gelding: modest   h–
maiden hurdler/chaser at best: stays 25f: acts on good to firm and heavy going: wore cheekpieces final outing: sold 700 gns Doncaster May Sales. *K. C. Bailey*

TWISCOMBE   9 br.m. Arctic Lord – Flying Cherub (Osiris) [2003/4 h–: 19g^{pu} May   h–
1] sturdy mare: no sign of ability. *Mrs J. G. Retter*

TWISTED LOGIC (IRE)   11 b.g. Tremblant – Logical View (Mandalus) [2003/4   c124
c124, h–: 24g^5 c24m^3 c24f^3 c26g^3 c32g^6 c28d^3 c24s^3 c30g* c23s* Apr 6] smallish, sturdy   h–

gelding: maiden hurdler: fairly useful handicap chaser: won at Exeter in March and April, fifth course win when beating Athnowen 2 lengths in latter: stays 3¾m: acts on firm and soft going: blinkered once. *R. H. Alner*

TWIST OF FAITH (IRE)   5 b.g. Fresh Breeze (USA) – Merry And Bright (Beau   h–
Chapeau) [2003/4 F16s 21g Mar 26] rangy gelding: ninth foal: half-brother to winning   F–
pointer by Strong Gale: dam disqualified winning pointer: won maiden Irish point on
debut in 2003: bought 43,000 gns Doncaster May Sales: well held in bumper and maiden
hurdle. *N. J. Henderson*

TWO A PENNY   4 b.f. Classic Cliche (IRE) – Pennypot Bay (Suave Dancer (USA))   F–
[2003/4 F16g F16g F16d aF16g Apr 4] 1,200 3-y-o: sturdy filly: first foal: dam unraced: no
form in bumpers. *R. H. York*

TWO EWE   5 b.g. Endoli (USA) – Kelsey Lady (Pongee) [2003/4 16g Jan 7] fourth   h–
known foal: dam won on Flat and at 2m over hurdles: showed nothing in novice hurdle
on debut. *W. Storey*

TWO HUGE   6 gr.g. Norton Challenger – Rainy Miss (IRE) (Cheval) [2003/4 F–: 20m   h–
May 7] workmanlike gelding: well held in bumper and novice hurdle. *N. A. Twiston-
Davies*

TWO JACKS (IRE)   7 b.g. Fayruz – Kaya (GER) (Young Generation) [2003/4 16g^ro   h–
Apr 30] poor maiden on Flat (stays 7f): behind when ran out fifth on hurdling debut.
W. S. Cunningham

TWO OF DIAMONDS   10 b.g. Mr Fluorocarbon – Shelleys Rocky Gem (Kemal   c–
(FR)) [2003/4 c21m^pu May 21] third foal: dam unraced: of little account in points.
Miss R. Williams

TWO RIVERS (IRE)   5 b.g. Over The River (FR) – Clarin River (IRE) (Mandalus)   F–
[2003/4 F17m^pu F17s^5 F16v Jan 10] 5,000 4-y-o: first foal: dam unraced half-sister to
high-class staying chaser Harbour Pilot, from family of Grand National winner Monty's
Pass: no form in bumpers: hung badly left on debut. *Mrs J. Candlish*

TWOTENSFORAFIVE   11 b.g. Arctic Lord – Sister of Gold (The Parson) [2003/4   c85
c79, h–: c21g^2 c23m^pu c21d^3 20m^6 c20f^F c23m^pu Sep 7] angular gelding: poor chaser/   h73
novice hurdler: stays 3m: acts on good to firm and heavy going: blinkered once: sometimes let down by jumping. *S. C. Burrough*

TYNDARIUS (IRE)   13 b.g. Mandalus – Lady Rerico (Pamroy) [2003/4 c–, h–: c24m^6   c114
c22m^6 c24g c30g^6 c21g^3 c16m c25g^2 c20g* c22g^4 c24d* c26d* c28g^3 c25s^pu c24s^pu   h–
c25s^5 c25g^2 c32g^3 c24g^5 Apr 10] strong gelding: fair handicap chaser: won at Hexham
(conditional jockeys) and Uttoxeter in November and Doncaster in December: stays
3½m: acts on heavy going: blinkered once: held up. *J. Hetherton*

TYNEANDTHYNEAGAIN   9 b.g. Good Thyne (USA) – Radical Lady (Radical)   c144 x
[2003/4 c21m^2 c23d^2 c26d^pu c24g^2 c24s* c24s c33d* c24g^pu c33d^pu Apr 17]   h–
    Not many horses lose their maiden status over fences in a race worth as
much as £29,000. As if that weren't enough, Tyneandthyneagain gained his other
win in one worth £40,600. The races in question were two of the North's valuable
staying handicaps, the Skybet Chase at Doncaster (registered as and better known
as the Great Yorkshire) and the Tote Eider at Newcastle. The Skybet was only the
sixth chase of Tyneandthyneagain's career. A useful hurdler, he had made an in-
auspicious start to his chasing career in December 2001 and was promptly returned
to the smaller obstacles for the remainder of that season. Leg trouble then kept him
off the track for twenty months and, when he returned in the latest season, it was
for a second attempt at chasing, something that had long promised to be his forte.
Tyneandthyneagain finished second in all three of his completed starts before his
appearance in the Great Yorkshire; a novice at Southwell, a handicap at Wetherby
(carrying top weight) and a more valuable novice at Warwick. In his other outing,
in a handicap at Doncaster, he was pulled up, reportedly distressed. The Warwick
race demonstrated as well as any Tyneandthyneagain's chief characteristics as a
chaser: sketchy jumping and thorough stamina. Some deliberate jumps early on got
him well behind but he plugged on late to take a remote second behind another
smart novice D'Argent.
    The Great Yorkshire at Doncaster in January had been Tyneandthyneagain's
second preference on the day and he ran there only after the Singer & Friedlander

National Trial at Uttoxeter was abandoned. The bad weather had an impact at Doncaster as well and conditions there were more testing than usual, with a strong headwind in the straight in addition to soft ground, though that was all to the good so far as Tyneandthyneagain was concerned. His jumping was still not fluent, but ridden more prominently than usual he took up the running after the twelfth and smoothly pulled clear in the straight, winning eased down by six lengths, his lead three times that margin at the last. Fellow novice Magical Bailiwick took second, with the favourite Gottabe third. Tyneandthyneagain might have had to work harder had Jimmy Tennis not fallen when still going well five out. Oddly, Tyneandthyne-again was the second maiden over fences in a row to win the Great Yorkshire, Barryscourt Lad having been successful in 2003.

Tyneandthyneagain went up a stone in the weights after Doncaster, though that was not the reason for his poor showing at Haydock next time, when once again his jumping let him down. It was a different story just a week later at Newcastle, when Tyneandthyneagain faced nineteen rivals in a competitive Eider Chase, carrying top weight and starting at 28/1 (his Doncaster victim Magical Bailiwick was only an 8/1-chance). Tyneandthyneagain was fitted with cheekpieces for the first time and as at Doncaster was ridden more forcefully. After surviving a bad mistake with over a circuit to go, Tyneandthyneagain took a definite lead six out and saw out the four miles and a furlong really well, pulling away again between the last two fences after the placed horses tried to close. Eased close home, Tyneandthyneagain ran out the three-length winner from Robbo, with Magical Bailiwick third this time and Granit d'Estruval in fourth. The remaining finishers were well strung out. Wearing cheekpieces again, Tyneandthyneagain's jumping let him down once more in his two outings after Newcastle. He was pulled up after mistakes in both the National Hunt Handicap at Cheltenham and the Scottish National at Ayr where the return to four miles plus ought to have been in his favour. Given his lack of experience over fences and his sketchy jumping, Tyneandthyne-again did not make much appeal as a Grand National type, though he was declared to run before being withdrawn on the morning of the race. He had also been taken

Skybet Great Yorkshire Chase (Handicap), Doncaster—Tyneandthyneagain gains a first win over fences

Tote Eider (Handicap Chase), Newcastle—
cheekpieces and more forcing tactics help bring a second valuable staying prize

out of the Red Square Vodka Gold Cup at Haydock a week after the Eider, again because the ground was deemed unsuitable.

Tyneandthyneagain and the Cathcart winner Our Armageddon contributed to a highly successful first full season of training for Richard Guest. He had been assistant to permit holder Norman Mason for several seasons before officially taking over the licence in February 2003 and making a flying start. By the end of the following month, Guest had sent out fifteen winners, though three of those were disqualified during the latest season for testing positive to a banned substance. Becoming a fully-fledged trainer has not meant a complete break from the saddle. Guest had a handful of rides in the latest season with a view to partnering Red Striker (a brother to Red Marauder whom Guest had ridden to victory in the memorable 2001 National) at Aintree. However, with Tyneandthyneagain also an intended runner in the National, Guest was prevented from riding Red Striker under a newly-instigated integrity rule whereby trainers are forbidden to ride against other horses from their own yards. The rule had not been in force the year before when Guest had partnered the Henrietta Knight-trained Chives in the National whilst saddling two runners in the race, including Red Striker. In the event, Red Striker (who had not been out since the previous year's National) joined Tyneandthyneagain, who had been due to be ridden by regular partner Henry Oliver, on the sidelines at Aintree.

Tyneandthyneagain (b.g. 1995)	Good Thyne (USA) (br 1977)	Herbager (b 1956)	Vandale II
			Flagette
		Foreseer (b or br 1969)	Round Table
			Regal Gleam
	Radical Lady (b 1984)	Radical (b 1971)	Relko
			Won't Linger
		Peaceful Madrigal (ch 1970)	Blue Cliff
			Peaceful Blossom

Ground permitting, the lengthy Tyneandthyneagain could take his chance in the National one day, and if so would be following in the footsteps of his dam Radical Lady who completed, albeit well in rear, in Party Politics' year. She was a fine servant in the colours of Norman Mason at a more modest level, winning eleven chases with trainer George Moore. She also won a point in Ireland as a five-year-old. Radical Lady has bred two other winners for Mason so far, the modest staying chaser Sabi Sand (by Minster Son) and the fair hurdler Just The Jobe (by Roselier), successful at two miles and two and three quarter miles in the latest season. The grandam Peaceful Madrigal was unraced (she was a twin) and is out of Peaceful Blossom who won a maiden at Navan over a mile and a quarter. *R. C. Guest*

TYNEDALE (IRE) 5 b.g. Good Thyne (USA) – Book of Rules (IRE) (Phardante (FR)) [2003/4 F16m² F16g⁵ F17s³ Feb 10] €21,000 4-y-o: third foal: half-brother to smart hurdler/chaser Rule Supreme (by Supreme Leader), stays 29f: dam unraced half-sister to useful staying jumpers Scribbler and Sarsfield The Man: fair form in bumpers, third to Onyourheadbeit in maiden at Sedgefield: will be suited by greater test of stamina. *Mrs A. Hamilton* **F92**

TYRO'S BID 6 b.g. Greensmith – Two Hearts (Nearly A Hand) [2003/4 F17m⁴ F17m⁶ Aug 25] first foal: dam ran twice: modest form in 2 bumpers at Newton Abbot. *Jane Southcombe* **F84**

TYRRELLSPASS (IRE) 7 b.g. Alzao (USA) – Alpine Chime (IRE) (Tirol) [2003/4 h–: 17g⁵ 17m 17d³ 16gᵘʳ 16g² Mar 10] leggy gelding: first form over hurdles when second of 17 in selling handicap at Chepstow: raced around 2m: tongue tied last 3 starts. *J. D. Frost* **h66**

TYSOU (FR) 7 b.g. Ajdayt (USA) – Pretty Point (Crystal Glitters (USA)) [2003/4 c132+, h–: c16gᶠ c16s² c16d³ c16s c16m⁵ c16gᵖᵘ Apr 1] smallish, angular gelding: useful handicap chaser: creditable third to St Pirran at Sandown: below form after: best around 2m: acts on good to firm and good to soft going, seemingly not on softer: races freely: held up. *N. J. Henderson* **c131 h–**

U

ULAAN BAATAR (IRE) 7 b. or br.g. Jackson's Drift (USA) – Leinster Lady (IRE) (Lord Chancellor (USA)) [2003/4 F16m⁵ F16d* F16d² 20s* 20d⁶ Apr 11] first known foal: dam unraced: progressive form in bumpers: won 24-runner event at Cork in December and 2½ lengths second to Sweet Kiln at Naas in February: odds on, successful in 24-runner maiden at Cork on hurdling debut in March, beating Petertheknot comfortably by 3 lengths: stiff task when sixth of 11 to Sadlers Wings in Grade 2 novice at Fairyhouse: will stay beyond 2½m. *Mrs J. Harrington, Ireland* **h106 p F105**

ULSHAW 7 ch.g. Salse (USA) – Kintail (Kris) [2003/4 19sᵖᵘ 17s⁶ 21g 22d Mar 3] workmanlike gelding: modest on Flat (stays 21f), successful twice in 2003: poor form over hurdles. *B. J. Llewellyn* **h73 ?**

ULTRA MARINE (IRE) 4 b.c. Blues Traveller (IRE) – The Aspecto Girl (IRE) (Alzao (USA)) [2003/4 16d 16g Dec 3] compact colt: modest maiden on Flat (probably stays 1½m): well held in juvenile hurdles: blinkered second start. *J. S. Wainwright* **h74**

ULTRA PONTEM 12 b.m. Governor General – Rocquelle (Coquelin (USA)) [2003/4 c23mᵖᵘ c20m* c21g* c21d* Jul 27] sturdy mare: modest chaser: improved after nearly 2-year absence, winning handicaps at Worcester (novice) and Newton Abbot (2) in summer: stays 21f: acts on good to firm and good to soft ground. *S. C. Burrough* **c94 h–**

ULUNDI 9 b.g. Rainbow Quest (USA) – Flit (USA) (Lyphard (USA)) [2003/4 16g⁶ Dec 26] good-topped gelding: very smart on Flat at 7 yrs, lightly raced and well below best since (has reportedly undergone third wind operation): useful hurdler in 2001: tailed off in Grade 1 at Kempton, only outing over hurdles since: best over sharp 2m: acts on good to firm going (won bumper on good to soft). *P. R. Webber* **h–**

ULUSABA 8 b.g. Aflflora (IRE) – Mighty Fly (Comedy Star (USA)) [2003/4 c94, h98: c16m⁵ c20g³ c20g² c19m* c19d² c20s³ c20g⁶ Jan 23] neat gelding: modest handicap hurdler/chaser: sold out of R. C. Guest's stable 11,000 gns Doncaster May Sales after second start: easily won match over fences at Hereford in November: stays 2½m: acts on **c99 h–**

soft and good to firm going (no form on heavy): effective with or without headgear/tongue strap: not always fluent over fences. *Ferdy Murphy*

UMISTA (IRE) 5 b.m. Tagula (IRE) – Nishiki (USA) (Brogan (USA)) [2003/4 19g 16d^{pu} 19d^{pu} Feb 15] little form on Flat, sold out of M. Quinn's stable £700 Ascot August Sales: no show in 3 starts over hurdles. *A. S. T. Holdsworth* **h–**

UN AUTRE ESPERE 5 b.g. Golden Heights – Drummer's Dream (IRE) (Drumalis) [2003/4 17m^5 16f^4 16f 16f 16g Nov 5] poor on Flat (stays 7f): no form over hurdles. *T. R. Wall* **h–**

UNCLE BATTY 4 b.g. Bob Back (USA) – Aunt Sadie (Pursuit of Love) [2003/4 F16g^6 F16s Apr 4] 7,000 3-y-o: smallish gelding: first foal: dam, second over 5.7f at 2 yrs, out of half-sister to smart sprinter Monaassib: dictated pace long way when showing poor form in bumpers at Catterick and Hexham. *G. A. Harker* **F75**

UNCLE BERT (IRE) 14 b.g. Ovac (ITY) – Sweet Gum (USA) (Gummo) [2003/4 c85, h–: c21s^{pu} May 17] rangy gelding: modest handicap chaser: stays 21f: acts on any going. *Miss Lucinda V. Russell* **c–** **h–**

UNCLE MAX (IRE) 4 b.g. Victory Note (USA) – Sunset Park (IRE) (Red Sunset) [2003/4 16m^3 16m* 16g^4 16d^2 16s^{pu} 17d 24d 19g Mar 27] leggy, close-coupled gelding: fair maiden on Flat (stays easy 1½m) for J. Osborne: fair juvenile hurdler: won at Ascot in November: blinkered, jumped indifferently and looked less than hearty final outing: seems not to stay 3m: acts on good to firm and good to soft going. *N. A. Twiston-Davies* **h98**

UNCLE MICK (IRE) 9 b.g. Ikdam – Kandy Kate (Pry) [2003/4 c93, h113: c26g^4 c25m^2 c23d^2 c26m* c23m^3 c24m^4 c24f^2 c32g^4 c24s^3 c28d^5 Dec 31] medium-sized gelding: fair handicap hurdler: fairly useful chaser: made all in novice at Uttoxeter in September: at least creditable efforts all starts after, mostly in handicaps: stays 4m: acts on any going: effective visored or not: consistent. *C. L. Tizzard* **c116** **h–**

UNCLE SAM 5 ch.g. Superpower – Treasure Time (IRE) (Treasure Kay) [2003/4 17d^{pu} Dec 17] lengthy gelding: no sign of ability in 2 starts at 2 yrs or on hurdling debut. *M. Scudamore* **h–**

UNCLE TEDDY (IRE) 11 b.g. Arctic Cider (USA) – Ishtar (Dike (USA)) [2003/4 c93, h–: c21d^2 c24m^{pu} c22f^{pu} Aug 22] rather sparely-made gelding: modest chaser at best, seemingly difficult to keep sound: stays 25f: best form on good going or firmer (acts on firm): blinkered/visored over hurdles. *Miss E. C. Lavelle* **c81** **h–**

UNDENIABLE 6 b.g. Unfuwain (USA) – Shefoog (Kefaah (USA)) [2003/4 20g^F 20d 20g^2 19d 20v 20d^2 24d* Mar 7] strong, workmanlike gelding: fairly useful handicap hurdler, off 18 months before reappearance: better than ever last 2 starts, neck second to Hidden Bounty at Newcastle and won at Market Rasen by 5 lengths from Shared Account: stays 3m: acts on soft going: tongue tied once. *Mrs S. J. Smith* **h115**

UNDERLEY PARK (IRE) 10 ch.g. Aristocracy – Even Bunny VII (Damsire Unregistered) [2003/4 c–, h–: c26g* c26d^F 26m^2 24d c27v^{pu} 24d^{pu} c24v^4 c26d^{pu} Apr 18] medium-sized gelding: poor maiden hurdler: easily best effort in steeplechases when winning maiden hunt at Cartmel in May: stays 3¼m: acts on good to firm and heavy going: tried in cheekpieces: has been let down by jumping. *R. Ford* **c104 d** **h77**

UNDER THE SAND (IRE) 7 b.g. Turtle Island (IRE) – Occupation (Homing) [2003/4 h126: c16v^4 c16s c19d^F c22s^3 c23v^2 c25f* c25g* c22g^2 Apr 22] sturdy gelding: fairly useful handicap hurdler: fair novice chaser: won maiden at Wincanton in April: stayed 25f: acted on heavy going (possibly not on good to firm): dead. *P. J. Hobbs* **c107** **h–**

UNDER WRAPS (IRE) 10 b.g. In The Wings – Wrapping (Kris) [2003/4 c–, h–: c25g^{pu} c30d^{pu} c24s Jan 21] good-topped gelding: winning hurdler/chaser, no form since 2000/1: often blinkered, also tried in cheekpieces: ungenuine. *A. C. Whillans* **c–** **h–**

UNEVEN LINE 8 b.m. Jurado (USA) – Altovise (Black Minstrel) [2003/4 c21s^4 c21g^3 Apr 12] winning pointer: tongue tied, poor form both starts in steeplechases in 2003/4. *Miss S. E. Forster* **c76** **h–**

UNGARETTI (GER) 7 b.g. Law Society (USA) – Urena (GER) (Dschingis Khan) [2003/4 h96: 26g^4 24s^5 c26m^5 c22v^{pu} c24g^{pu} 26g^4 c29d^2 c24d^4 c26d* c23d^{pu} Apr 21] rangy gelding: modest handicap hurdler: best effort over fences when winning 3-finisher handicap at Plumpton in April, 3 lengths up when left well clear at last: stays 29f: acts on heavy going, possibly not on good to firm: tried blinkered: has had tongue tied. *Ian Williams* **c84** **h94**

Cheveley Park Stud's "Unleash"

UNGARO (FR) 5 b.g. Epervier Bleu – Harpyes (FR) (Quart de Vin (FR)) [2003/4 **F101** F16m* F16d F16g² Mar 27] small gelding: fourth foal: half-brother to fair hurdler around 2m Let's Fly (by Rose Laurel) and fairly useful chaser/fair hurdler Harkosa (by Nikos), stays 2¾m: dam, placed over jumps in France, half-sister to dam of useful chaser around 21f Dom Halma de Valta: fairly useful form in bumpers: won 18-runner event at Ayr on debut in November by ½ length from Master Sebastian: ¾-length second of 18 to River Trapper at Newbury. *Mrs M. Reveley*

UNICORN REWARD (IRE) 4 b.c. Turtle Island (IRE) – Kingdom Pearl (Statoblest) **h92** [2003/4 16g⁵ 16g⁴ 16g² 16g² Mar 13] smallish, sturdy colt: fairly useful on Flat at 3 yrs for R. Hannon, successful 4 times around 1m: modest form in novice and juvenile hurdles: likely to need sharp 2m. *M. D. Hammond*

UNION DEUX (FR) 5 ch.g. Nikos – Sanhia (FR) (Sanhedrin (USA)) [2003/4 16d **h80** 20s 24d⁴ 20s³ 20s³ Apr 4] unfurnished gelding: ninth foal: brother to fairly useful hurdler Nonantais, stays 2½m, and half-brother to winners in France, including fairly useful hurdler La Grande Ourse (by Mansonnien): dam won 3 times up to 1½m in France: poor novice hurdler: stays 3m: raced on going softer than good. *Ferdy Murphy*

UN JOUR A VASSY (FR) 9 b.g. Video Rock (FR) – Bayalika (FR) (Kashtan (FR)) **c127** [2003/4 c116, h–: c25m* c25m² c24g² c26mᵖᵘ c24f* c25f⁵ c22g⁴ c25g³ c25g³ Apr 2] **h–**

leggy gelding: fairly useful handicap chaser: won at Wincanton in May and Cheltenham (amateurs) in October: creditable efforts also when placed: stays 25f when emphasis is on speed: acts on firm and good to soft going. *P. F. Nicholls*

UNKNOWN WARRIOR   5 b.g. Mtoto – Ayodhya (IRE) (Astronef) [2003/4 F16m^{pu} **F–**
Jul 9] fifth foal: half-brother to several winners, including 2m hurdler Astronomer (by
Ardkinglass): dam, French 2-y-o 6f/7f winner, half-sister to useful Champion 4-y-o
Hurdle runner-up Dromod Hill: broke down on debut. *Mrs A. L. M. King*

UNLEASH (USA)   5 ch.g. Benny The Dip (USA) – Lemhi Go (USA) (Lemhi Gold   **h139 p**
(USA)) [2003/4 h126p: 16g* 16m^2 20g^2 Apr 1] leggy gelding: useful on Flat (stays 2m),
won Northumberland Plate in June: progressive hurdler: completed hat-trick in handicap
at Worcester in May: further improvement when second in similar company to Duke
of Earl at Chepstow and Zibeline in listed event at Aintree: better suited by 2½m than
2m and will stay further: acts on good to firm going: probably capable of better yet.
P. J. Hobbs

UNLIMITED FREE (IRE)   10 ch.g. Ile de Chypre – Merry Madness (Raise You Ten)   **c103**
[2003/4 c96, h–: c25d* c26d^3 c21g Apr 1] useful-looking gelding: fairly useful hunter   **h–**
chaser: won point and 5-finisher hunter at Folkestone (beat Galapiat du Mesnil 11
lengths) in February: not fluent and never a factor in Fox Hunters' at Aintree: stays 25f:
acts on soft and firm going: has jumped right. *Mrs S. Alner*

UNLOCKED (IRE)   6 b.g. Supreme Leader – Shunnagh Lass (IRE) (Buckskin (FR))   **c–**
[2003/4 19m^2 20d^2 19g^6 22d^5 24m^6 c19d^F Mar 23] 15,000 4-y-o: second foal: dam   **h105 d**
unraced: won second of 2 starts in maiden Irish points in 2003: bought 20,000 gns
Doncaster May Sales: fair form when second in novices first 2 starts over hurdles:
disappointing after, mistakes and well held when falling 3 out in novice on steeplechasing
debut: should stay at least 2¾m. *P. J. Hobbs*

UNMISTAKABLY (IRE)   7 gr.g. Roselier (FR) – Decent Debbie (Decent Fellow)   **c105 §**
[2003/4 18g* c17g^{ur} c20d^4 c24s^4 c23g^{pu} c24m^{ur} c25g^4 Apr 4] good-topped ex-Irish geld-   **h94 §**
ing: seventh foal: brother to 3 winners, including useful staying hurdler/chaser Berude
Not To: dam unraced half-sister to fairly useful staying hurdler Bankhead (by Roselier):
once-raced in bumpers: trained by T. Walsh, won maiden hurdle at Downpatrick in May:
running promising first race over fences when unseating 3 out in novice handicap at
Exeter: didn't go on, running poorly in blinkers final outing: should stay 3m: has gone in
snatches/found little: sold 9,500 gns Doncaster May Sales. *Ms Bridget Nicholls*

UNSHAKEN   10 b.h. Environment Friend – Reel Foyle (USA) (Irish River (FR))   **h–**
[2003/4 16m 16g Jan 15] fair on Flat (stays 1¼m), sold out of E. Alston's stable 800 gns
Doncaster October Sales: tailed off in 2 novice hurdles. *W. G. Young*

UNSIGNED (USA)   6 b. or br.g. Cozzene (USA) – Striata (USA) (Gone West (USA))   **h84**
[2003/4 h–: 17m^2 20m^4 21m^F 19m^5 Aug 30] poor form over hurdles: won at Worcester in
June: stays 2½m: acts on good to firm going: races freely. *R. H. Buckler*

UNTIDY DAUGHTER   5 b.m. Sabrehill (USA) – Branitska (Mummy's Pet) [2003/4   **h97**
h83: 17s^6 16g 21d^2 16d^6 17s^2 17s^2 16s^6 17g^2 Apr 12] lengthy mare: modest handicap
hurdler: won at Sedgefield in May, idling run-in: runner-up there on 4 occasions after:
stays 21f: acts on soft and good to firm going: wears cheekpieces: hasn't always impressed with attitude. *B. Ellison*

UNTWIST (IRE)   5 b.g. Un Desperado (FR) – Pearltwist (Roi Guillaume (FR)) [2003/4   **F–**
F18g Apr 22] fourth foal: dam fair Irish hurdler up to 3m: showed nothing in bumper on
debut. *D. R. Gandolfo*

UNUSUAL SUSPECT   5 b.g. Syrtos – Sally Maxwell (Roscoe Blake) [2003/4 aF16g   **F78**
F16s Feb 20] 9,000 4-y-o: good sort: sixth foal (all by Syrtos): brother to 2 winning
hurdlers, including Tilt And Turn, fair around 2m: dam placed in bumpers: modest form
in bumpers at Lingfield (on polytrack) and Sandown. *M. Pitman*

UP AT MIDNIGHT   4 b.f. Midnight Legend – Uplift (Bustino) [2003/4 F12s F12m^5 **h88**
17s^6 16s 16g^6 16d^6 Mar 28] compact filly: second live foal: dam, 2m winner on Flat, out   **F88**
of half-sister to useful 2m to 21f chaser Just Jasmine: much better effort in 3-y-o bumpers
when fifth in fillies event at Newbury: best effort in juvenile hurdles when around 25
lengths sixth of 22 to Numitas at Newbury fifth start: will be suited by greater test of
stamina. *R. Rowe*

UPGRADE   10 b.g. Be My Guest (USA) – Cantanta (Top Ville) [2003/4 c150§, h–§:   **c151**
c16m^2 c16s^2 c16g c16m* c21m^5 c16m^6 Apr 24] lengthy gelding: smart chaser: won   **h–**
7-runner handicap at Haydock in February by 2½ lengths from stable-companion Golden

Garswood Handicap Chase, Haydock—stable companions Upgrade and Golden Alpha fight out the finish

Alpha: ran creditably first 2 starts, below best last 2: effective at 2m to 21f: acts on soft and firm going: tried blinkered: often front runner: tends to idle: has looked temperamental (not so much in 2003/4). *M. C. Pipe*

UPHAM LORD (IRE)   11 b.g. Lord Americo – Top O The Mall (Don) [2003/4 c21g* c24d³ c26dᶠ c24s⁵ Apr 17] tall gelding: winning hurdler: prolific winning pointer, unbeaten in 8 starts in 2003: fairly useful hunter chaser: landed odds easily in uncompetitive event at Fakenham in February: effective at 2½m to easy 3m: acts on good to firm and heavy going: effective blinkered or not: front runner/races prominently. *P. Beaumont*   **c103 h–**

UPRIGHT IMA   5 b.m. Perpendicular – Ima Delight (Idiot's Delight) [2003/4 F80: F16d⁴ 20s⁶ 16v⁴ 16s 16g Mar 17] lengthy, angular mare: twice-raced in bumpers, last of 4 on reappearance: little worthwhile form over hurdles. *Mrs P. Sly*   **h63 F–**

UPSWING   7 b.g. Perpendicular – Moorfield Lady (Vicomte) [2003/4 h–: 16g 16g⁴ 16s 18s⁶ c16g³ 17g² Mar 16] tall gelding: modest novice hurdler: eye-catching third of 10 to Sound of Cheers in novice handicap at Catterick on chasing debut (final start for R. Johnson), jumping sketchily in rear but running on strongly after still being only seventh 2 out (found guilty of schooling in public): raced mainly around 2m: raced on good ground or softer. *S. B. Bell*   **c73 p h88**

UP THE GLEN (IRE)   10 b.g. Tale Quale – Etrenne (Happy New Year) [2003/4 h92: 20d* 20c0v⁴ 22s⁵ c24m³ Apr 13] angular gelding: modest hurdler: won selling handicap at Uttoxeter in May, final start for R. Phillips: better effort in novice chases when third of 7 to Fox In The Box at Chepstow: barely stays 27f: acts on good to firm and heavy ground. *A. W. Carroll*   **c98 h93**

UP THE SOUTHS (IRE)   6 ch.g. Aahsaylad – Siberian Princess (Northfields (USA)) [2003/4 24dᵖᵘ 16m 26mᵖᵘ 20mᵖᵘ Jul 16] sturdy ex-Irish gelding: half-brother to several winners, notably smart chaser Siberian Gale (by Strong Gale), stayed 3m: dam unraced half-sister to useful 2m hurdler Moody Man: no form over hurdles: left C. Roche after reappearance. *Jonjo O'Neill*   **h–**

UPTOWN LAD (IRE)   5 b.g. Definite Article – Shoka (FR) (Kaldoun (FR)) [2003/4 h81: 16m⁵ 20m³ 20d³ 17d* 17d* 16d 16s 18v* 16d 22g 18g⁴ 20d Apr 10] compact   **h105**

gelding: fair handicap hurdler: won at Carlisle in November, Market Rasen (fortunate) in December and Kelso (improved again when beating Kharak 12 lengths) in February: best short of 2½m: acts on heavy going: tongue tied. *R. Johnson*

UP YOUR STREET   9 b.m. Petoski – Air Streak (Air Trooper) [2003/4 h/6: 22g 26s Dec 20] sparely-made mare: maiden hurdler: stays 3¼m: acts on good to soft going. *C. Roberts*   **h–**

URBAN HYMN (IRE)   8 ch.g. College Chapel – Soltura (IRE) (Sadler's Wells (USA)) [2003/4 c87, h99: c21g* c21d2 Nov 25] close-coupled gelding: modest handicap hurdler: similar form over fences: won 5-runner maiden at Sedgefield in October: stays 21f: acts on heavy and good to firm going: blinkered once, wore cheekpieces in 2003/4. *Ferdy Murphy*   **c103**
h–

USK VALLEY (IRE)   9 b.g. Tenby – Penultimate (USA) (Roberto (USA)) [2003/4 c–, h–: 20g4 25s2 21vpu 24s 22g* c20d2 Apr 21] workmanlike gelding: poor hurdler: won selling handicap at Fontwell in March: only second completed start over fences when second to Khaladjistan in handicap at Worcester: stays 25f: acts on soft going. *P. R. Chamings*   **c75**
h85

<h1 style="text-align:center">V</h1>

VAGUE IDEA   11 gr.g. Tout Ensemble – Roodle Doodle (Rugantino) [2003/4 c94, h–: c26d* c26g2 c26d* 27d c24g c26gpu c32gpu c29spu c25vur Jan 9] twice-raced hurdler: modest chaser: won handicaps at Newton Abbot in June and July (having unseated after being badly hampered third in 3-runner event): no form after: stays 3¼m: acts on good to soft going. *O. J. Carter*   **c96**
h–

VAIGLY NORTH   6 b.m. Minshaanshu Amad (USA) – Straight Gold (Vaigly Great) [2003/4 h–, F74: 17g May 24] poor form in bumpers: no show in 2 starts over hurdles: sold £2,600 Ascot October Sales, pulled up both outings in points. *J. A. Moore*   **h–**

VAIN MINSTREL (IRE)   12 b.g. Royal Fountain – Minstrel Top (Black Minstrel) [2003/4 c23vF May 26] ex-Irish gelding: fair handicap chaser in 1999/00 for G. Cully: successful both completed starts in points in Britain, twice pulled up in 2004: stays 2½m: acts on heavy ground. *P. Jones*   **c–**

VALANCE (IRE)   4 br.g. Bahhare (USA) – Glowlamp (IRE) (Glow (USA)) [2003/4 16g* 16gF Nov 12] half-brother to poor hurdler Black Weasel (by Lahib), stayed 3m: fairly useful (stays 1¾m): won juvenile maiden at Huntingdon on hurdling debut in November: well held in second when falling last in race won by Lough Derg at Newbury 10 days later. *C. R. Egerton*   **h108**

VAL DE FLEURIE (GER)   9 b.m. Mondrian (GER) – Valbonne (Master Willie) [2003/4 17d* 19d* 16dpu 18F3 17g* 16gF 21g* 22m* 16f2 16g 20vpu 16m6 21g Mar 17] leggy mare: fairly useful hurdler: successful 5 times in first half of season following near 3-year absence, in minor event and 2 handicaps at Newton Abbot and handicaps at Sedgefield (made all) and Market Rasen (match): stays easy 2¾m: acts on firm and good to soft going. *J. G. M. O'Shea*   **h114**

VALDERRAMA   4 ch.g. Lahib (USA) – Silky Heights (IRE) (Head For Heights) [2003/4 F16m F17g Apr 10] third foal: half-brother to winning 2½m hurdler Winged Angel (by Prince Sabo): dam modest 11f and 1½m winner: no show in bumpers. *C. J. Down*   **F–**

VAL DU DON (FR)   4 b.c. Garde Royale – Vallee Normande (FR) (Bellypha) [2003/4 15s3 16s3 18s* 17d3 17d2 Jan 24] leggy colt: eighth foal: half-brother to several winners on Flat: dam maiden on Flat: won juvenile hurdle at Bordeaux in December: fairly useful form when placed in steadily-run events at Cheltenham last 2 starts, third to Trouble At Bay and second to Mondul in Grade 2, leading or disputing each time: will stay 2½m. *G. Macaire, France*   **h126**

VALERUN (IRE)   8 b.g. Commanche Run – Glenreigh Moss (Le Moss) [2003/4 20s 22d5 22g6 24f* 22f 22g2 22d Mar 12] lengthy, rather sparely-made ex-Irish gelding: brother to poor hurdler Moss Run, stays 3m: modest maiden on Flat: modest hurdler: won maiden at Kilbeggan in August: left T. Doyle after fifth outing: stays 3m: acts on firm going (won bumper on good to soft). *Miss E. C. Lavelle*   **h99**

VALEUREUX   6 ch.g. Cadeaux Genereux – La Strada (Niniski (USA)) [2003/4 h99: 16m* 17mF 16d2 17dpu 16v3 17d* 21d2 Mar 30] tall gelding: fair hurdler: won novices at   **h111**

Hexham (odds on) in October and Market Rasen (beat Alrida 10 lengths) in March: stays easy 21f: acts on heavy and good to firm going: has worn crossed noseband. *J. Hetherton*

VALFONIC   6 b.g. Zafonic (USA) – Valbra (Dancing Brave (USA)) [2003/4 h106d: 16m 19mᵖᵘ 19g Apr 1] winning 2m hurdler: no form since early-2002/3, left M. Pipe after second start: has been visored: usually tongue tied: ungenuine. *F. Jordan*   **h– §**

VALIGAN (IRE)   11 gr.g. Roselier (FR) – Wonderful Lilly (Prince Hansel) [2003/4 c–, h–: c26m⁴ c28gᵖᵘ 24vᵖᵘ Nov 29] sparely-made gelding: winning hurdler/chaser: bought out of T. Tate's stable 8,100 gns Doncaster August Sales: no sign of retaining ability in 2003/4: suited by 3m+: acts on heavy going: tried in headgear. *N. B. King*   **c– h–**

VALJEAN (IRE)   8 b.g. Alzao (USA) – Escape Path (Wolver Hollow) [2003/4 c59, h–: c19m c24gᵖᵘ Feb 11] medium-sized gelding: winning pointer: little other form: tried tongue tied. *Mrs Myfanwy Miles*   **c– h–**

VALLEY ERNE (IRE)   13 b.g. King's Ride – Erne Gold VII (Damsire Unregistered) [2003/4 c108x, h115: c25d³ c21g⁵ c27gᵖᵘ Apr 12] lengthy ex-Irish gelding: veteran hurdler/chaser: left M. Cunningham, little form in points or hunters after first outing: barely stays 25f: acts on heavy and good to firm going: often let down by jumping. *Norman Sanderson*   **c– h–**

VALLEY HENRY (IRE)   9 b.g. Step Together (USA) – Pineway VII (Damsire Unregistered) [2003/4 c172, h–: c25mᶠ c20s³ c24gᶠ c25dᵖᵘ c25g⁶ Apr 1] big, rangy gelding: top-class chaser at best, fourth in Cheltenham Gold Cup in 2002/3: respectable third of 6 to Jair du Cochet in Grade 2 Peterborough Chase at Huntingdon on final start for P. Nicholls, but generally let down by jumping in 2003/4: stays 3¼m: acts on soft and good to firm going. *J. Howard Johnson*   **c162 x h–**

VALLEYMORE (IRE)   8 br.g. Jolly Jake (NZ) – Glamorous Brush (IRE) (Brush Aside (USA)) [2003/4 h117p, h117p, F74: c20dᶠ c16s³ c20s³ c22s² c22mᵖᵘ c24dᵖᵘ Mar 27] lengthy gelding: fairly useful hurdler: fair novice chaser: left impression should have won when 2 lengths second of 6 to Rum Pointer at Haydock: reportedly broke blood vessel final outing: should be suited by 3m+: acts well on soft/heavy going, has run poorly on firmer than good. *S. A. Brookshaw*   **c110 h–**

VALLEY WARRIOR   7 b.g. Michelozzo (USA) – Mascara VII (Damsire Unregistered) [2003/4 F16sᵗᵗʳ 17s⁵ 20d⁵ 21dᵖᵘ Mar 28] lengthy gelding: fifth foal: brother to fairly useful hurdler Glen Warrior, stays 3m, and half-brother to winning 23f chaser Tirley Gale (by Strong Gale): dam winning hurdler/chaser in Ireland: withdrawn after getting loose on intended debut, refused to race in bumper 2 days later (unseated on way to post): fifth of 15 in novices first 2 starts over hurdles: should be suited by further than 2½m. *J. S. Smith*   **h86 F– §**

VALLICA   5 b.m. Bishop of Cashel – Vallauris (Faustus (USA)) [2003/4 19m⁵ 20m 16g 19s 16sᵖᵘ 19v 24g 21d 17d² Mar 27] workmanlike mare: well held in 2 maidens on Flat at 3 yrs: sold out of L. G. Cottrell's stable 1,000 gns Doncaster November (2002) Sales: seemingly much improved effort over hurdles when 1½ lengths second to Iambe de La See in mares claimer at Bangor, making lot of running. *Mrs A. M. Thorpe*   **h92 ?**

VALMAN (IRE)   8 b. or br.g. Valville (FR) – Omania (Runnett) [2003/4 c26sᵖᵘ c19gᵖᵘ c24gᵖᵘ c23mᵘʳ 24m³ Jul 16] winning pointer: little show over hurdles or in steeplechases, generally let down by jumping: has worn blinkers/visor: sold £4,000 Ascot August Sales. *C. J. Down*   **c89 x h–**

VALS WELL (IRE)   9 b.g. Be My Native (USA) – Castle-Lady (Little Buskins) [2003/4 c21mᵖᵘ c21d⁵ c22vᵖᵘ c26s 23sᵖᵘ Jan 21] no form outside points (won in 2003): blinkered last 2 starts. *G. Prodromou*   **c– h–**

VALTAR (FR)   4 b.f. Tot Ou Tard (IRE) – Valiance (FR) (Akarad (FR)) [2003/4 16s³ 16g Apr 1] angular filly: fifth foal: half-sister to fairly useful hurdler/chaser up to around 2½m Emivale (by L'Emigrant): dam 1½m winner: useful on Flat (stays 10.5f): shaped with promise when 4¾ lengths third to Selvas in juvenile at Ascot on hurdling debut, soon well clear jumping fluently: failed to settle ridden with more restraint when well held in Grade 2 juvenile at Aintree: tongue tied. *Y. Porzier, France*   **h100**

VALUABLE (IRE)   7 b.m. Jurado (USA) – Can't Afford It (IRE) (Glow (USA)) [2003/4 F–: 16m 20dᵖᵘ 16dᵖᵘ 16v 16dᵖᵘ Apr 22] of little account: has had tongue tied. *R. Johnson*   **h–**

VANDAL   4 b.g. Entrepreneur – Vax Star (Petong) [2003/4 17g⁶ 16d Apr 21] fair on Flat (should stay 1m), successful in August, sold out of J. Toller's stable 12,000 gns Newmarket Autumn Sales: off 6 months, shaped as if outing was needed when sixth of 11   **h73**

in juvenile at Market Rasen on hurdling debut: soundly beaten in stronger race next time. *Mrs L. Wadham*

VANDAS CHOICE (IRE) 6 b.g. Sadler's Wells (USA) – Morning Devotion (USA) **h117**
(Affirmed (USA)) [2003/4 h102, F86: 20g⁵ 16g* 16m* 16sᵖᵘ 20sᵖᵘ 16t³ 20d⁵ 20d⁴ Apr
22] stocky gelding: fairly useful handicap hurdler: won at Perth in September and Down
Royal (valuable event, beat Loughanelteen a length) in November: stays 2½m: acts on
good to firm and good to soft going: breathing problem fourth outing: has looked none
too easy ride. *Mrs L. B. Normile*

VAN DE VELDE 5 ch.g. Alhijaz – Lucky Flinders (Free State) [2003/4 h–: 21d⁶ 19sᵖᵘ **h80 ?**
Apr 11] little worthwhile form over hurdles, possibly flattered on reappearance.
P. A. Blockley

VANORMIX (FR) 5 gr.g. Linamix (FR) – Vadsa Honor (FR) (Highest Honor (FR)) **h117**
[2003/4 h120: 16g⁶ 17g 17g⁶ 17s* 21g⁴ 20d³ Mar 24] sturdy gelding: fairly useful handicap hurdler: won 6-runner event at Taunton in January, sent for home nearly a circuit out
and beating Smart Savannah 3 lengths: stays 21f: acts on heavy ground (not discredited
on good to firm): visored last 5 starts. *M. C. Pipe*

VATIRISK (FR) 7 gr.g. Take Risks (FR) – Vatipan (FR) (Trepan (FR)) [2003/4 h120: **c106**
20g c16dᶠ 16d⁵ c22s⁴ c22s³ c20fˢᵘ c22g⁴ c21m c20m* c17s⁵ 22d Apr 12] lengthy gelding: **h114**
fair handicap hurdler: similar form over fences, easily won maiden at Limerick in October: stays 2¾m: acts on soft and firm going: has worn blinkers (including at Limerick)/
cheekpieces: tried tongue tied. *E. J. O'Grady, Ireland*

VEILED DANCER (IRE) 11 b.m. Shareef Dancer (USA) – Fatal Distraction (Form- **c62**
idable (USA)) [2003/4 c71, h62: 24m⁵ 24vᵖᵘ c26g⁵ c23mᵖᵘ Jul 9] compact mare: poor **h69**
maiden hurdler/steeplechaser: broke down final outing: stays easy 3½m: acts on firm and
good to soft going. *A. S. T. Holdsworth*

VEINTE SIETE (USA) 4 ch.g. Trempolino (USA) – Satz (USA) (The Minstrel **h– §**
(CAN)) [2003/4 16mᵖᵘ Nov 1] modest maiden on Flat (should stay 1¼m) for J. Toller,
has refused to race: all but refused to do so and pulled up second on hurdling debut: one
to avoid. *P. R. Webber*

VELETA 5 b.m. Shaamit (IRE) – Keel Row (Relkino) [2003/4 F17m⁴ F17m³ Jun 18] **F83**
first foal: dam, modest 2m hurdler, half-sister to useful hurdler/fairly useful chaser
up to 2½m Easter Ross: modest form in bumpers at Market Rasen and Southwell.
N. J. Henderson

VELVET ROSE 10 ch.m. Cheyenne Dance (FR) – Privy Rose (Privy Seal) [2003/4 **h–**
26gᵖᵘ 22dᵖᵘ 24mᵖᵘ Jun 5] winning pointer: showed nothing over hurdles: dead. *Mrs
S. M. Johnson*

VENEGUERA (IRE) 11 b.g. Satco (FR) – Orlita (Master Buck) [2003/4 c–§, h90§: **c85 §**
21m* 21m³ 24g³ 24m⁶ 19d³ 20mᵖᵘ c24s³ c24g c24d⁵ Mar 28] lengthy gelding: **h92 §**
modest handicap hurdler: won amateur event at Huntingdon in May: modest form at best
over fences, well held last 3 starts: stays 3¼m: has form on any going, possibly not at best
on soft/heavy: sometimes blinkered earlier in career, wore cheekpieces in 2003/4: lazy
sort, often needs plenty of driving. *K. C. Bailey*

VENN OTTERY 9 b.g. Access Ski – Tom's Comedy (Comedy Star (USA)) **c148**
[2003/4 c–, h–: c20dᵖᵘ c16g³ 16d⁴ c16dᶠ c16g² c17gᵖᵘ c16g⁴ 20s⁶ c17gᵖᵘ c16g⁴ **h–**
c16s c16g* c16m* c17g* c17s² c16m* c16g⁵ c16g c16gᶠ c20dᵖᵘ Apr 17]
One of the abiding memories of the 2004 Cheltenham Festival is of Ruby
Walsh, on Azertyuiop, full of running, coming down the hill to two out in the Queen
Mother Champion Chase, looking behind to see with some astonishment Venn
Ottery going at least as well. It took some crediting for anyone with even a passing
knowledge of Venn Ottery or his octogenarian owner Oliver Carter, a man who
could teach Don Quixote a thing or two. Venn Ottery is making his fifth appearance
in *Chasers & Hurdlers*. He hasn't been worth a rating in previous editions and was
described in 2002/3 as 'of little account'. His appearance in the Champion Chase
wasn't his first at such an exalted level, though previously he had been regarded as
a danger more from the point of view of safety than in terms of ability. *Hunter
Chasers & Point To Pointers 2003* commented on one such appearance: 'Only
Oliver Carter would have the gall to run such a barmpot in a Grade 1 event at
Aintree.' In the latest season, before Venn Ottery's appearance in the Peterborough
Chase at Huntingdon, concern was voiced that he might get in Best Mate's way.

'Had no business being in the field' said *Timeform Perspective*. In his first twenty-three appearances outside of points, in many of them looking barely under control under assorted amateurs and claimers, Venn Ottery had nothing that could be described as worthwhile or reliable form to his name. He managed a couple of placed efforts in weakly-contested novice events at Newton Abbot in the summer of 2003 but that was questionable form.

Venn Ottery's twenty-third outing was typical—sent off at 100/1, last of nine finishers in a beginners chase at Uttoxeter. Up to that point Venn Ottery had been trained by his owner. For his next appearance, two months later, however, he was under the care of Paul Nicholls and it was from that point that something little short of a miracle began to take shape. Venn Ottery still looked as headstrong as ever but, in justifying good support in a weakly-contested maiden chase at Leicester, he began to reveal some of the ability which had lain hidden for so long. Handicap successes followed thick and fast, much too fast for the BHB handicapper to keep up with him. Venn Ottery won off a mark of 87 at Ludlow a week after Leicester, then had three outings off a mark fully 30 lb higher within the space of five days, winning on the bridle at Newbury and Hereford by twenty lengths and sixteen lengths respectively, but beaten at Market Rasen in between, reportedly suffering from a breathing problem. Venn Ottery had three things at Hereford which he didn't have at Market Rasen—firmish ground, a strong gallop and Ruby Walsh in the saddle. While the new trainer might have preferred another handicap outing next, Venn Ottery's owner was set on the Champion Chase, for which he had backed the horse to win at odds of 1,000/1 at the start of the year. The ground and the gallop at Cheltenham were likely to be in his favour but Walsh was clearly going to be required for Azertyuiop, whose form was fully four stone better. Denied Walsh and offered Joe Tizzard instead of Mick Fitzgerald (who was booked for Cenkos), the owner made his own arrangements, declaring the horse for Cheltenham with Timmy Murphy in the saddle, in the process forgetting to declare the tongue strap which, along with professional training, had been regarded as an important factor in Venn Ottery's progress. Matters became heated and an acrimonious split with Nicholls, which looked on the cards, appeared to have been avoided by the time the race took place. Going to two out the absence of neither Walsh, nor the tongue strap, seemed set to matter. Not for the first time, however, little was forthcoming off the bridle and Venn Ottery weakened in the straight, finishing fifth, twenty-three lengths behind Azertyuiop. That still represented one of the best novice performances of the season and would have seen Venn Ottery go very close had he run in the previous day's Arkle Chase. Venn Ottery hadn't been entered for that, though some of his other entries included the Cheltenham Gold Cup and the Betfred Gold Cup at Sandown. Thankfully, he didn't take up either of those engagements (his chances of staying three miles plus are virtually nil). Unfortunately, Venn Ottery failed to repeat his Champion Chase form, being well held in the Maghull Novices' Chase at Aintree and failing to complete when running on successive days at Ayr. Two outings without a tongue strap, back with his owner, very early in the new season were scarcely any more encouraging.

    Venn Ottery is by no means the first good horse connected with his idiosyncratic owner, who first took out a permit to train in the early-'sixties. Otter Way made his first appearance outside hunter chases in the 1976 Cheltenham Gold Cup and only weakened three out. Otter Way was by an unraced premium stallion out of an unregistered mare of unknown parentage and he won the Whitbread Gold Cup and the Horse And Hound Cup later in the season that he first contested the Gold Cup, winning the Horse And Hound for a second time at the age of fifteen. Carter's mare Ottery News also won a Horse And Hound Cup and was twice placed in the Whitbread. She would have contested the 1982 Grand Steeple-Chase de Paris but for going lame on the eve of the race. The fairly useful chaser Fishleigh Gamble, who also ran in the 1983 Goodwood Cup, was Carter's last runner in the Champion Chase, though the outcome was less than happy. Fishleigh Gamble belied odds of 100/1 for much of the way but fell fatally two out.

Venn Ottery (b.g. 1995)	Access Ski (b 1987)	Bustino (b 1971)	Busted
			Ship Yard
		Crimson Lake (b 1979)	Mill Reef
			Maroon
	Tom's Comedy (b 1980)	Comedy Star (b 1968)	Tom Fool
			Latin Walk
		Fleet Street Fifty (br 1971)	I Say
			True Dresden

Mr O. J. Carter's "Venn Ottery"

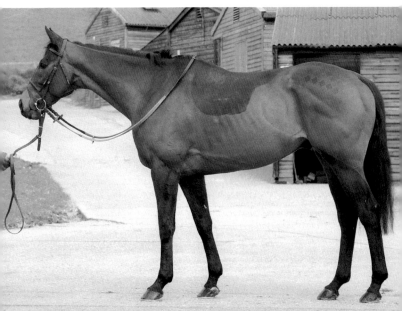

Venn Ottery is one of only two runners under rules by Access Ski, a useful out-and-out stayer on the Flat. Venn Ottery's dam Tom's Comedy is a half-sister to another smart West Country chaser Tom's Little Al, who stayed three miles just about well enough to win a forerunner of the Racing Post Chase at Kempton on firmish ground. Until he came along, this was a family noted more for ordinary sprinters than anything, although the second dam Fleet Street Fifty subsequently produced the fairly useful hurdler Tom's Little Bet, who finished third in the 1990 Sun Alliance Hurdle. The rangy Venn Ottery's prospects almost certainly rest with two things, the degree of success of a wind operation undergone in the summer and a return to Paul Nicholls' yard, or at least another professional stable—the owner has said the horse can go back to Nicholls 'any time Paul needs him'.

Until recently Carter rode out his own horses and he has said that were he eighty, and not five years older, he'd be able to manage Venn Ottery's training on his own. He also owns the Bishop's Court point-to-point course in Devon which he runs in inimitable fashion, though on one occasion his repeated public announcements about not dropping litter proved too much for some of the crowd and he reportedly ended the afternoon in one of the bins provided! *P. F. Nicholls*

VENTURE TO FLY (IRE)   10 ch.g. Roselier (FR) – Fly Run (Deep Run) [2003/4 c107, h–: 24g 23d 27s² 24s⁴ 27d Apr 23] sturdy gelding: fair form only completion over fences: fair handicap hurdler: stays 27f: raced on good going or softer (acts on heavy): sold 4,500 gns Doncaster May Sales. *N. G. Richards*   **c–ht107**

VERDE LUNA   12 b.g. Green Desert (USA) – Mamaluna (USA) (Roberto (USA)) [2003/4 c68, h–: 24gpu c23m⁵ c26gpu Aug 4] sparely-made gelding: winning hurdler/chaser: no form in 2003/4: blinkered/visored: has had tongue tied. *A. G. Hobbs*   **c–h–**

VERIDIAN   11 b.g. Green Desert (USA) – Alik (FR) (Targowice (USA)) [2003/4 c81, h116d: 16d c16spu Mar 24] compact gelding: winning hurdler, very much on downgrade: lightly raced and little form over fences (has had jumping problems): tried blinkered. *G. F. Bridgwater*   **c–h–**

VERO BEACH   8 ch.g. Nicholas Bill – My Moody Girl (IRE) (Alzao (USA)) [2003/4 h?: 27spu 24m Jun 28] workmanlike gelding: little sign of ability over hurdles: has looked hard ride: sold £2,700 Ascot August Sales, showed nothing in points in 2004. *Mrs S. D. Williams*   **h–**

VERROCCHIO (IRE)   4 b.g. Entrepreneur – Our Hope (Dancing Brave (USA)) [2003/4 16m⁴ 16d³ 16g³ 16v* 16d Feb 21] half-brother to fairly useful hurdler Derivative (by Erins Isle), stays 2¾m, and fair 2m hurdler Dochas Mor (by Project Manager): fair maiden on Flat (stays 2m): fair juvenile hurdler: won maiden at Tramore in January: creditable sixth to Star of Bethlehem in minor event at Punchestown in early-May: stays 2½m: acts on good to firm and heavy going. *W. P. Mullins, Ireland*   **h106**

VERSUS (GER)   4 gr.c. Highest Honor (FR) – Very Mighty (FR) (Niniski (USA)) [2003/4 17s² 16s³ 16s⁶ Mar 20] well-made colt: successful once over 1½m from 5 starts on Flat at 3 yrs in Germany for A. Kleinkorres: fair form when placed in juvenile hurdles at Folkestone and Sandown: took little interest final start: will be suited by greater test of stamina. *C. J. Mann*   **h102**

VERTEDANZ (IRE)   4 b.f. Sesaro (USA) – Blade of Grass (Kris) [2003/4 16dpu Jan 8] modest maiden on Flat (stays 1¼m), left F. Ennis early in 2003: showed nothing on hurdling debut. *Miss I. E. Craig*   **h–**

VERT ESPERE   11 ch.g. Green Adventure (USA) – Celtic Dream (Celtic Cone) [2003/4 h99: c17gur 21f⁴ 20v⁵ May 21] big, workmanlike gelding: unseated third on chasing debut: modest handicap hurdler: stays 3m: probably acts on any going. *Mrs J. Candlish*   **c–h88**

VERY EXCLUSIVE (USA)   5 b.g. Royal Academy (USA) – Exclusive Davis (USA) (Our Native (USA)) [2003/4 16mpu Jul 13] poor maiden on Flat (stays easy 1½m): in cheekpieces, no show in novice seller on hurdling debut. *R. M. H. Cowell*   **h–**

VERY OPTIMISTIC (IRE)   6 b.g. Un Desperado (FR) – Bright Future (IRE) (Satco (FR)) [2003/4 F102p: 20s* 16d* 21g Mar 17] rather unfurnished gelding: won first 3 starts, bumper in 2002/3 and 2 novice hurdles at Haydock in December, beating Accipiter 2 lengths on final occasion: eighth of 15 behind Fundamentalist in Grade 1 novice at Cheltenham final outing: probably hasn't finished improving. *Jonjo O'Neill*   **h129 p**

VERY TASTY (IRE)   7 ch.g. Be My Native (USA) – Jasmine Melody (Jasmine Star)   **h–**
[2003/4 h–: 20s^{pu} Mar 13] no sign of ability. *Mrs Dianne Sayer*

VERY VERY NOBLE (IRE)   10 ch.g. Aristocracy – Hills Angel (IRE) (Salluceva)   **c108**
[2003/4 c?1g* c21d^F c21d^F c21m^5 c24d^{pu} Mar 13] lengthy gelding: fair handicap chaser: off 2
years, made all at Folkestone in December: stays 25f: acts on soft going: tongue tied:
front runner: sold only 900 gns Doncaster May Sales. *A. M. Hales*

VICARS DESTINY   6 b.m. Sir Harry Lewis (USA) – Church Leap (Pollerton)   **h111**
[2003/4 h93, F92: 19g^4 21g^2 23m 16g^{ur} 19d^4 19g^{ur} 20v^5 20v* 20s^5 20d 24g^2 21m Apr 15]
leggy mare: fair handicap hurdler: won at Market Rasen in December and Wetherby in
January: stays 3m: acts on heavy going: wore cheekpieces last 8 starts: has been let down
by jumping. *Mrs S. Lamyman*

VICAR'S LAD   8 b.g. Terimon – Proverbial Rose (Proverb) [2003/4 h68, F85: 22g^2 **h101**
20d^5 25s^5 22s^6 Mar 23] tall, leggy gelding: fair form over hurdles first 2 starts in 2003/4:
should stay beyond 2¾m: pulled hard final outing. *N. A. Twiston-Davies*

VICENTIO   5 br.g. Vettori (IRE) – Smah (Mtoto) [2003/4 F81: 17d 16g^2 17g^4 16s^F **h72**
16s^5 20s^{ur} 19g 20s^6 21g^{pu} Apr 12] smallish, workmanlike gelding: poor novice hurdler:
raced mainly around 2m. *T. J. Fitzgerald*

VICIANA   5 b.m. Sir Harry Lewis (USA) – Ludoviciana (Oats) [2003/4 F16m^2 F16m   **h99**
aF16g^3 19g^F 19s^2 Apr 4] good-topped mare: second foal: dam winning pointer: modest   **F84**
form in bumpers and over hurdles. *J. W. Payne*

VICOMTE THOMAS (FR)   4 b.g. Highest Honor (FR) – Vigorine (FR) (Shakapour)   **h–**
[2003/4 F14g 17s 17s^5 19d Feb 15] 6,800 3-y-o: medium-sized gelding: brother to use-   **F–**
ful middle-distance performer Vicomtesse Mag (by Highest Honor) and half-brother to
several winners: dam French 1m to 1½m winner: no sign of ability: tried in cheekpieces/
blinkers. *R. Dickin*

VIC PLUM (IRE)   6 b. or br.m. Lord Americo – Naujella (Malinowski (USA))   **h–**
[2003/4 F–: 17d^{pu} May 28] seems of no account. *W. G. Young*

VIC'S BRUSH (IRE)   12 b.g. Brush Aside (USA) – Fair Vic (Fair Turn) [2003/4   **c–**
c26m^{pu} May 29] ex-Irish gelding: bought 700 gns Doncaster September (2002) Sales: **h–**
won twice in points in Britain in 2003, little sign of ability otherwise (jumped poorly in
hunter chase). *G. Chambers*

VICTORIA RYAN (IRE)   6 b.m. Good Thyne (USA) – No Not (Ovac (ITY)) [2003/4   **h–**
F–: 21v^{pu} 22d^{pu} Mar 7] sparely-made mare: no sign of ability. *J. R. Norton*

VICTORIA'S BOY (IRE)   11 b.g. Denel (FR) – Cloghroe Lady (Hardboy) [2003/4   **c93**
c75, h–: c26d* May 28] strong gelding: fair hunter chaser: won at Cartmel in May and   **h–**
point in February: stays 3¼m: acts on soft and good to firm ground: tried blinkered.
J. J. Coates

VICTORY BELL   6 b.g. Komaite (USA) – Shikabell (Kala Shikari) [2003/4 F18s   **h–**
F17s^6 F16s 20s^{ur} 21d Apr 12] sturdy gelding: third foal: dam winning 2m hurdler: little   **F–**
sign of ability, unseating after trying to refuse first on hurdling debut. *A. P. Jones*

VICTORY GUNNER (IRE)   6 ch.g. Old Vic – Gunner B Sharp (Gunner B) [2003/4   **h101**
F99: 22d^5 20d^{pu} 19s* 22s 19g* 24s^2 24m Apr 14] medium-sized gelding: fair hurdler:
won twice at Taunton, novice in December and handicap in February: stays 3m: acts on
soft ground, possibly not good to firm. *C. Roberts*

VICTORY ROLL   8 b.g. In The Wings – Persian Victory (IRE) (Persian Bold) [2003/4   **c105 ?**
h96: c17s^5 c20g c20g^F Feb 13] close-coupled gelding: winning hurdler: running best race   **h–**
in novice chases when falling 3 out (had jumped better until then) at Kempton final start,
still in lead at time: raced mainly around 2m on going softer than good (acts on heavy):
visored once. *Miss E. C. Lavelle*

VICTORY SIGN (IRE)   4 b.g. Forzando – Mo Ceri (Kampala) [2003/4 18g^3 16s^4 **h77**
16s^4 16g^2 Apr 12] half-brother to modest 2m hurdler Mazilla (by Mazilier): fair on Flat
(stays 1½m) for K. Burke: poor form in juvenile hurdles: wore cheekpieces after debut:
carries head awkwardly. *Miss M. P. Bryant*

VIC TOTO (FR)   7 b.g. Kaid Pous (FR) – Koberta (FR) (Don Roberto (USA)) [2003/4   **h147**
h156: 19s^4 20s 24s^4 20s^3 20g^2 Feb 22] leggy, angular gelding: smart hurdler: placed in
Grade 2 events at Auteuil (third to Great Love) in November and Fontwell (second to

Starzaan) in February: stays 25f: acts on heavy going: best ridden prominently: genuine. *F. Doumen, France*

VIC VILLE (IRE)   5 b.g. Old Vic – N T Nad (Welsh Pageant) [2003/4 F16d⁵ F16s*   **h115** 16s* 16s* 18s 20d Apr 11] well-made gelding: sixth living foal: half-brother to fair   **F102** hurdlers Robber Baron, successful at 19f, and Tee-Jay (both by Un Desperado), stays 3m: dam unraced: won at Naas in January on second of 2 starts in bumpers: successful later in month on first 2 starts over hurdles, minor event at Cork and novice at Naas, in latter beating Cupla Cairde gamely by a head: well held subsequently: should stay at least 2½m. *M. Hourigan, Ireland*

VIDI CAESAR (NZ)   9 b.g. Racing Is Fun (USA) – Vidi Vici (NZ) (Roman Empire)   **c86** [2003/4 h77: 17g³ c20mᵖᵘ c17g⁶ 20g c17m² c21d⁵ c17d² c20s³ c20d⁵ c16g⁴ c20sᵘʳ c24g⁵   **h88** c20m⁴ c16g Mar 13] sturdy gelding: modest maiden hurdler/chaser: stays 2½m: acts on soft and good to firm going: wore cheekpieces/blinkers last 8 starts: has looked ungenuine: sold 3,800 gns Doncaster May Sales. *R. C. Guest*

VI ET VIRTITE   5 b.m. Dancing Spree (USA) – Princess Scully (Weld) [2003/4   **h–** 20gᵖᵘ 16gᵖᵘ Nov 12] well beaten on Flat for Mrs A. Dobloug Talbot in Norway: no aptitude for hurdling: tried tongue tied. *R. C. Guest*

VIGOUREUX (FR)   5 b.g. Villez (USA) – Rouge Folie (FR) (Agent Bleu (FR))   **h96** [2003/4 h94: 16m⁴ 16g⁴ 16s⁶ 21d 16d 16d Apr 8] winning hurdler in France: modest form in Britain: raced mainly at 2m: acts on good to firm and heavy going. *S. Gollings*

VIGZOL   6 br.g. Relief Pitcher – Hammerhill (Grisaille) [2003/4 F17m 24s 18s Feb 9]   **h–** fifth known foal: half-brother to winning pointer Cold Feet (by Arctic Lord): dam   **F–** winning pointer: well held in bumper and 2 races over hurdles, whipping round start on debut. *R. J. King*

VIKING BUOY (IRE)   12 ch.g. Pimpernels Tune – Clare's Crystal (Tekoah) [2003/4   **c–** c–, h68: 20m May 7] tall gelding: winning hurdler/chaser, retains little ability: tried   **h–** blinkered. *Mrs P. Townsley*

VILLA   8 b.g. Jupiter Island – Spoonhill Wood (Celtic Cone) [2003/4 F110: 24s⁵ 21g⁵   **h93** 21g Mar 26] good-topped gelding: useful bumper winner: just modest form at best over hurdles: should be suited by 3m+: visored (weakened as if amiss) on hurdling debut: looked none too keen final start. *M. C. Pipe*

VILLAGE KING (IRE)   11 b.g. Roi Danzig (USA) – Honorine (USA) (Blushing   **c137** Groom (FR)) [2003/4 c137§, h–: c24m² Oct 4] good-bodied gelding: useful handicap   **h–** chaser: creditable second to Take The Stand at Chepstow only start in 2003/4: probably stays 3½m: acts on heavy and good to firm going: blinkered once (ran creditably): sometimes takes little interest. *P. J. Hobbs*

VILLAIR (IRE)   9 b.g. Valville (FR) – Brackenair (Fairbairn) [2003/4 c92, h74: c20s⁴   **c104** c19v³ c22v² c26s³ c24s⁴ c29d* c26g* c31d³ Apr 22] long-backed gelding: winning   **h–** hurdler: fair handicap chaser: won at Warwick in March and Newton Abbot in April: thorough stayer: raced on good going or softer: successful with and without blinkers: often looks hard ride. *C. J. Mann*

VILLON (IRE)   5 b.g. Topanoora – Deep Adventure (Deep Run) [2003/4 F17d*   **F115 p** Apr 18]
    Those racegoers who stayed on after teatime to watch the last of eight races, on a run-of-the-mill card at Carlisle's Sunday fixture in April, were rewarded with a performance from the winner which made the wait well worthwhile. There was little to suggest beforehand that the second division of the bumper would turn out to be of a significantly higher standard than the first, which had been won by two lengths by Elfkirk, a five-year-old mare making her debut. Yet in winning his division by eighteen lengths, another newcomer Villon, set to carry 5 lb more than Elfkirk, covered the distance of two miles and a furlong in a time more than seven seconds faster and, by our reckoning, achieved a level of form some two stone in advance of that shown by Elfkirk. Villon comes from a stable with an excellent record in bumpers and went off a well-backed favourite, so clearly he had been catching the eye at home. His supporters could have had few anxious moments. Villon travelled supremely well and drew clear with another debutant, the second favourite Blairgowrie, over three furlongs out, sprinting clear of that rival when

shaken up approaching the final furlong. It was a most impressive display. Third-placed Lord Rodney, also running for the first time, finished thirty-two lengths behind Villon, with a further seven lengths back to the fourth Classic Capers, who had shown fairly useful form on both of his previous starts, including a win at Ayr. Few winners achieve such a high level of form in a bumper first time up, and Villon is clearly an excellent prospect. It will take a good one to beat him if he is kept to bumpers while still qualified to run in them; and he is also the type to run up a sequence when he goes over hurdles, as his trainer is unlikely to deviate from his usual policy of keeping his young hurdlers in low-grade races while they learn their trade. Villon, who made €34,000 at the Derby Sale in 2002, fetched 45,000 guineas at the Doncaster May Sales the following year. He is the seventh winner out of the unraced Deep Adventure, the pick of the rest probably the fair hurdlers Deep C Diva and Windgap Hill (both by Supreme Leader), and My Sunny Glen (by Furry Glen). Deep C Diva and My Sunny Glen both stayed two and three quarter miles, while Windgap Hill put up easily her best effort over two miles. Deep Adventure herself is a half-sister to several winners, notably the 1973 Arkle Chase winner Denys Adventure and useful two-mile hurdler Miss Boon. Villon is by the very smart performer at up to a mile and a half Topanoora and should stay at least two and a half miles. *L. Lungo*

VILPRANO 13 b.g. Ra Nova – Village Princess (Rolfe (USA)) [2003/4 h107d: 24g⁶ 26g* 24g 27g⁵ Jul 28] smallish, leggy gelding: modest handicap hurdler: won at Cartmel in May: was best at 3m+: acted on any going: won with/without visor, tried in cheekpieces: difficult ride, usually soon off bridle: dead. *James Moffatt*   **h86**

VINCENT VAN GOGH (IRE) 9 b.g. Executive Perk – Rare Picture (Pollerton) [2003/4 c98, h–: c21d³ c25s⁴ c25s⁶ Jan 22] tall gelding: modest handicap chaser: stays 3m: acts on firm and soft going: no form on left-handed courses (has won 3 times at Taunton): often none too fluent: has failed to impress with attitude. *R. J. Hodges*   **c95 h–**

VIN DU PAYS 4 b.g. Alzao (USA) – Royale Rose (FR) (Bering) [2003/4 17s Jan 22] fair on all-weather, modest on turf on Flat (stays 2m): well held in novice on hurdling debut. *M. Blanshard*   **h–**

VINGIS PARK (IRE) 6 b.g. Old Vic – Lady Glenbank (Tarboosh (USA)) [2003/4 F17s² F17d F16s² 24s⁴ 22g³ 18d² Mar 21] IR £9,500 3-y-o: sixth foal: half-brother to winning pointer by Montelimar: dam won 5 times up to 17f on Flat: second in bumpers at Newton Abbot (useful form when 1¼ lengths behind Supreme Serenade) and Huntingdon: fair form in novice hurdles: stays 2¾m (probably had too much use made of him over 3m): tongue tied last 2 starts: front runner. *V. R. A. Dartnall*   **h105 F105**

VINO TINTO (IRE) 10 b.g. Glacial Storm (USA) – Pure Spec (Fine Blade (USA)) [2003/4 c91, h–: c21s* May 2] tall gelding: fair hunter chaser: won at Sedgefield in May, idling close home: stays 25f: raced on good going or softer (acts on heavy): tried blinkered: tongue tied once: has carried head high under pressure. *Mrs C. M. Mulhall*   **c94 h–**

VINTAGE PREMIUM 7 b.g. Forzando – Julia Domna (Dominion) [2003/4 16g² 16d³ 16g⁵ Feb 14] leggy gelding: smart on Flat (stayed 11f): shaped promisingly twice from 3 starts in novice hurdles, fifth to Albuhera at Newbury (still going well when badly hampered 4 out) final one: found little in between: dead. *R. A. Fahey*   **h111**

VIOLENT 6 b.m. Deploy – Gentle Irony (Mazilier (USA)) [2003/4 h–: 16sᵖᵘ 23m⁵ 21s⁶ Dec 3] no form over hurdles. *Miss A. M. Newton-Smith*   **h–**

VIRAC LAD (IRE) 10 b.g. Brush Aside (USA) – Garryduff Lass (Green Shoon) [2003/4 c24mᵖᵘ May 26] of little account. *Miss G. Browne*   **c– h–**

VIRGIN SOLDIER (IRE) 8 ch.g. Waajib – Never Been Chaste (Posse (USA)) [2003/4 h126: c16mᶠ c16mᵘʳ c21g* c16g* c21m* 16f⁵ c25m* c24f⁴ 18g⁶ Mar 28] angular gelding: fairly useful handicap hurdler: successful first 4 completed outings over fences in maiden and novices at Sedgefield and handicap at Market Rasen (2 ran) between July and October: effective at 2m to easy 25f: acts on firm and good to soft going. *G. A. Swinbank*   **c121 h116**

VISCOUNT BANKES 6 ch.g. Clantime – Bee Dee Dancer (Ballacashtal (CAN)) [2003/4 h–: c19d² c16g² Apr 3] won 2½m maiden point in January: poor form when second in 2 hunter chases. *Mrs Rosemary Gasson*   **c74 h–**

VISIBILITY (FR) 5 gr.g. Linamix (FR) – Visor (USA) (Mr Prospector (USA))   **h129 §**
[2003/4 h117: 16m* 16m^{pu} 16s^5 16g 16g Mar 26] tall, leggy, angular gelding: fairly
useful handicap hurdler: improved form when winning at Ascot in November by 3½
lengths from Shalako, despite jumping far from fluently: failed to repeat effort, generally
failing to impress with attitude: raced around 2m: acts on soft and good to firm going:
visored last 3 starts. *M. C. Pipe*

VISITATION 6 b.m. Bishop of Cashel – Golden Envoy (USA) (Dayjur (USA))   **h–**
[2003/4 20g^{pu} 16m^{pu} 17g^{pu} Jul 28] poor on turf, modest on all-weather on Flat (stays 11f),
left K. Ryan after final start in 2002: showed nothing in novice company over hurdles on
return: tried blinkered: sold 600 gns Doncaster January Sales. *Mrs J. C. McGregor*

VISTA VERDE 6 b.g. Alflora (IRE) – Legata (IRE) (Orchestra) [2003/4 F16g F16s^6 **h106**
22s^5 24g^3 24g^5 Mar 26] €14,000 4-y-o: useful-looking gelding: third foal: half-brother to   **F95**
winning pointer by Derrylin: dam well held in bumpers and over hurdles: fair form on
second of 2 starts in bumpers: fair novice hurdler: will prove suited by good test of
stamina. *A. King*

VITAL HESITATION 12 br.m. Vital Season – Jim's Darleen (Jimsun) [2003/4 c21f^{pu} **c–**
May 21] poor pointer. *M. H. Wood*

VITELLI 4 b.g. Vettori (IRE) – Mourne Trix (Golden Love) [2003/4 F13g^2 F13v   **F94**
F16g^2 F16d^3 Mar 28] lengthy gelding: tenth foal: half-brother to 2¼m hurdle winner
Good Thyne Guy (by Good Thyne) and fair pointer by Glacial Storm: dam unraced: fair
form when placed in bumpers. *G. A. Swinbank*

VITELUCY 5 b.m. Vettori (IRE) – Classic Line (Last Tycoon) [2003/4 h80: 20m*   **h85**
20m^{ur} 24m^4 22m^3 20g Oct 27] smallish mare: modest hurdler: won novice at Worcester
in August: stays 2¾m: acts on good to firm going. *Miss S. J. Wilton*

VITO ANDOLINI 6 br.g. Faustus (USA) – Sunshine Gal (Alto Volante) [2003/4   **h–**
F17g 19s 19s^{pu} 22v^{pu} Jan 12] 4,000 4-y-o, 3,000 5-y-o: half-brother to 3 winners, includ-   **F–**
ing fair hurdler Weather Wise (by Town And Country), stays 3¼m, and winning 2m
chaser Sunburnt (by Henbit): dam, winning hurdler who stayed 25f, also 1¼m to 2m
winner on Flat: no sign of ability: blinkered final outing. *Mrs Jane Galpin*

VIVA BINGO (IRE) 8 ch.g. Phardante (FR) – Kitty Frisk (Prince Tenderfoot (USA))   **c–**
[2003/4 h–, F83: c16g^R 16m 20d^{pu} Apr 7] angular gelding: no form over jumps, including   **h–**
points: tried blinkered. *C. L. Popham*

VIVA FOREVER (FR) 5 br.m. Lando (GER) – Very Mighty (FR) (Niniski (USA))   **h–**
[2003/4 17g^5 19g Nov 12] lengthy ex-German mare: successful twice around 11f from 7
starts on Flat at 3 yrs for A. Wohler: achieved little in 2 novice hurdles. *A. M. Hales*

VIVALDI ROSE (IRE) 9 b.m. Cataldi – Peaceful Rose (Roselier (FR)) [2003/4 c–,   **c–**
h62: 16g 16m May 27] signs of only a little ability, including in points: tried visored/in   **h–**
cheekpieces. *L. Lungo*

VIVANTE (IRE) 6 b.m. Toulon – Splendidly Gay (Lord Gayle (USA)) [2003/4 F16g   **F–**
F16g Mar 6] €5,200 4-y-o: smallish mare: seventh foal: half-sister to 7f winner Double-D
(by Fools Holme) and Irish 1½m winner Thatch Island (by Burslem): dam 1¼m and 1¾m
winner: well held in 2 bumpers. *A. J. Wilson*

VIVID IMAGINATION (IRE) 5 b.g. Moonax (IRE) – Sezu (IRE) (Mister Lord   **h– p**
(USA)) [2003/4 22g^4 Aug 4] second foal: dam, runner-up in maiden Irish point, from
family of smart staying hurdler Merry Masquerade: third in maiden Irish point: jumped
none too fluently when well held in novice on hurdling debut (should improve): unbeaten
on completed starts in points in 2004 for D. Pipe. *M. C. Pipe*

VIZULIZE 5 b.m. Robellino (USA) – Euridice (IRE) (Woodman (USA)) [2003/4 16v^{pu} **h–**
17d^{pu} Dec 17] modest maiden on Flat (stays 1½m, races freely): pulled up both starts in
novice hurdles. *A. W. Carroll*

VODKA BLEU (FR) 5 b.g. Pistolet Bleu (IRE) – Viva Vodka (FR) (Crystal Glitters   **h118**
(USA)) [2003/4 F103: 19g^3 16s^2 16d^5 22d 20v^5 24m^3 Apr 14] lengthy, unfurnished gelding:
fairly useful novice hurdler: visored, improved form when 2¼ lengths third to My Line in
handicap at Cheltenham final start, making most but tying up badly run-in: probably stays
3m: acts on good to firm and heavy going. *M. C. Pipe*

VODKA INFERNO (IRE) 7 ch.g. Moscow Society (USA) – Corrie Lough (IRE)   **h78**
(The Parson) [2003/4 h–, F87: 24d^2 24g^2 24m^4 Aug 1] medium-sized gelding: poor form

over hurdles, racing freely in blinkers final start: should stay beyond 3m: acts on good to firm and good to soft going: jumps none too fluently. *C. R. Egerton*

VOLANO (FR)   6 b.g. Pistolet Bleu (IRE) – Vouivre (FR) (Matahawk) [2003/4 h119: 20d 16d⁵ 16mᵖᵘ 16m* 19mᵖᵘ Oct 18] small, well-made gelding: fairly useful handicap hurdler: back to best when winning at Huntingdon in October, not extended to beat Hot Shots 5 lengths: lame start either side: likely to prove best around 2m: acts on soft and good to firm going. *N. J. Henderson*   **h121**

VOLCANO SNOW   4 ch.f. Zilzal (USA) – Ash Glade (Nashwan (USA)) [2003/4 F16d⁴ F16g⁵ 16s² 17g⁴ Apr 10] 6,000 3-y-o: angular filly: third foal: half-sister to useful 6f winner Magic Glade (by Magic Ring): dam unraced close relative to very smart middle-distance performer/useful 2m hurdler Ulundi and half-sister to 1000 Guineas winner Wince: fair form in 2 bumpers: left C. Von Der Recke, in frame in juvenile at Newcastle and mares maiden at Newton Abbot both starts over hurdles. *M. F. Harris*   **h83 F85**

VULCAN LANE (NZ)   7 ch.g. Star Way – Smudged (NZ) (Nassipour (USA)) [2003/4 h73: 16g 16f² 17gᵖᵘ 21g 17d³ c16dᵘʳ 16s⁵ 17g* c16g⁴ c16d 17s c16d Feb 15] compact gelding: poor hurdler: won selling handicap at Market Rasen in December: similar form over fences (unseated after trying to refuse chasing début): raced mainly around 2m: probably acts on any going: blinkered/in cheekpieces last 8 outings. *R. C. Guest*   **c72 h75**

VULCAN'S ASH   5 ch.g. Royal Vulcan – Ashraf (Gold Song) [2003/4 F16d aF16g Dec 13] first foal: dam well beaten on Flat: showed nothing in 2 bumpers. *S. J. Gilmore*   **F–**

W

WAGES   4 b.g. Lake Coniston (IRE) – Green Divot (Green Desert (USA)) [2003/4 16m³ 16s⁶ 16g 17g 16g Apr 18] lengthy gelding: fair on Flat (stays 7f): modest juvenile hurdler: likely to need sharp 2m. *P. M. Phelan*   **h93**

WAGGY (IRE)   8 b.g. Cataldi – Energance (IRE) (Salmon Leap (USA)) [2003/4 h–, F82: 25sᵖᵘ 19dᶠ Jan 19] no sign of ability in novice hurdles. *S. E. H. Sherwood*   **h– F–**

WAGNER (IRE)   7 b. or br.g. Lure (USA) – Tapaculo (Tap On Wood) [2003/4 h102: 27d³ 22g* 20m² c20m* c23d* c21gᶠ c24m c20g² c24g⁶ Mar 16] workmanlike gelding: fairly useful handicap hurdler: won unconvincingly at Newton Abbot in June: impressive start to chasing career when winning novices at Market Rasen in July and Uttoxeter in August: best effort when second to Mighty Strong in handicap at Newbury in November: best at 2½m+: acts on good to firm and heavy going: effective tongue tied or not. *Jonjo O'Neill*   **c126 h114 +**

WAHIBA SANDS   11 b.g. Pharly (FR) – Lovely Noor (USA) (Fappiano (USA)) [2003/4 c147, h–: c21fᶠ c17g² c16g⁴ c16m⁴ c16s³ c16d² c16g c17g³ c20g c16d c21gᵖᵘ c16m⁶ c16m Apr 24] tall, useful-looking gelding: useful chaser, in-and-out form in 2003/4: stays 21f: acts on heavy and good to firm going: wore visor last 8 starts, tried in one before and in cheekpieces: has raced lazily. *M. C. Pipe*   **c144 h–**

WAIMEA BAY   5 b.m. Karinga Bay – Smart In Sable (Roscoe Blake) [2003/4 F?: F16m 16d⁴ 17s⁴ 17g⁵ 16g⁵ 18g³ Apr 22] poor form in bumpers: modest novice hurdler: should prove best around 2m: has pulled hard. *P. R. Hedger*   **h92 F–**

WAINAK (USA)   6 b.g. Silver Hawk – Cask (Be My Chief (USA)) [2003/4 h88: 22m³ May 7] close-coupled gelding: modest maiden hurdler, well below best only start in 2003/4: stays 2½m: acts on good to firm going: often wears headgear: looks increasingly hard ride. *Miss Lucinda V. Russell*   **h72**

WAINDALE FLYER   5 ch.g. Abzu – Mellouise (Handsome Sailor) [2003/4 F17g Apr 24] second foal: brother to bumper winner/modest novice hurdler up to 2½m Abzuvian: dam little form in 3 bumpers or seller on Flat: well beaten in bumper on début. *J. R. Norton*   **F–**

WAIN MOUNTAIN   8 b.g. Unfuwain (USA) – Mountain Memory (High Top) [2003/4 c130, h–: c19d³ c25v² c24v² c28mᵖᵘ Feb 28] good-topped gelding: useful handicap chaser: creditable placed efforts first 3 starts in 2003/4, again veering left when second to Tipsy Mouse at Haydock on final occasion: stays 3¼m: acts on heavy going, possibly unsuited by good to firm: tends to flash tail under pressure. *J. A. B. Old*   **c132 h–**

WAIT FOR THE WILL (USA) 8 ch.g. Seeking The Gold (USA) – You'd Be **h118**
Surprised (USA) (Blushing Groom (FR)) [2003/4 h118: 17m* 17d² 16m⁴ Oct 4] tall
gelding: useful on Flat (stays 1¾m): : fairly useful hurdler: easily won novice at Newton
Abbot in May, beating Mirant 6 lengths: raced around 2m: acts on good to firm and good
to soft going: blinkered. *G. L. Moore*

WAIT FOR THIS (IRE) 9 b.g. Torus – Bar You Try (Bargello) [2003/4 c84, h–: 22fᵖᵘ **c–**
22mpᵘ 24gᵖᵘ Nov 6] winning hurdler/chaser, little form since 2001/2: tried blinkered **h–**
(looked none too keen)/tongue tied. *C. J. Down*

WAKEUP SMILING (IRE) 6 b.g. Norwich – Blackmiller Lady (Bonne Noel) **h120**
[2003/4 F92: 16g 21vᵖᵘ 19m⁴ 20d 16g* 19g* 16m² Apr 13] fairly useful hurdler: won 2
novice handicaps at Newbury in March, conditional jockeys event on second occasion:
much improved when second to River City in well-contested handicap at Chepstow final
start: stays 19f: acts on good to firm going: visored second outing: has flashed tail.
Miss E. C. Lavelle

WALCOT LAD (IRE) 8 b.g. Jurado (USA) – Butty Miss (Menelek) [2003/4 c70?: **c74**
21sᵖᵘ 16d⁶ 20g⁴ c20g³ c22v⁴ c21s⁴ c18s* c18s⁴ c25g c21s³ c20v³ c20d³ c26g³ Apr 22] **h–**
maiden hurdler: poor handicap chaser: won novice at Fontwell in January: stays 3¼m:
acts on good to firm and heavy going: wears headgear. *A. Ennis*

WALK OVER (IRE) 6 b.g. Welsh Term – Black-Crash (Crash Course) [2003/4 F16g³ **c–**
F16d⁵ 24dᵖᵘ 16s* 20dᵖᵘ 22d³ c18d Apr 12] IR £29,000 3-y-o: brother to useful hurdler up **h110**
to 2½m Wither Or Which and half-brother to fairly useful hurdler Total Confusion (by **F91**
Pollerton), stayed 3m, and to dam of top-class staying chaser Alexander Banquet: fair
form in 2 bumpers: fair hurdler: won maiden at Punchestown in January: third of 5 to
Florida Coast in minor event at Fairyhouse in February: well held in maiden on chasing
debut: should stay 3m: acts on soft going. *F. Flood, Ireland*

WALLY WONDER (IRE) 6 ch.g. Magical Wonder (USA) – Sally Gap (Sallust) **c–**
[2003/4 20s 20sᵖᵘ c20g c17d c20f 17d 16s 16d 16sᵖᵘ 20sᵖᵘ Apr 4] close-coupled ex-Irish **h–**
gelding: twice-raced on Flat: bumper winner: maiden hurdler/chaser, badly out of sorts in
2003/4: sold out of T. Kidd's stable €8,000 Goffs October Sale after fifth start, left
R. C. Guest after ninth: tried blinkered. *R. Bastiman*

WALSINGHAM (IRE) 6 b.g. Presenting – Let's Compromise (No Argument) **h–**
[2003/4 20sᵖᵘ 21d 21d 16s Feb 19] good-topped gelding: half-brother to several winners,
notably top-class 2m to 3¼m chaser Strong Promise (by Strong Gale): dam, winning
hurdler, from family of high-class staying chaser Contradeal: signs of only a little ability
over hurdles. *P. J. Hobbs*

WALTER PLINGE 8 b.g. Theatrical Charmer – Carousel Zingira (Reesh) [2003/4 **c–**
c68, h68: 20v 22mpᵘ 19d 21d Mar 19] compact gelding: poor form on first of 2 starts over **h–**
fences: poor hurdler: no form in 2003/4: stays 21f: acts on good to firm and good to soft
going (seems unsuited by heavy): tongue tied. *A. G. Juckes*

WALTER'S DESTINY 12 ch.g. White Prince (USA) – Tearful Sarah (Rugantino) **c97 §**
[2003/4 c103§, h–: c23g c25m³ c25m⁶ c25g⁵ c25d³ c25s³ c24g c30g c25g⁶ c25m⁶ Apr **h–**
13] lengthy gelding: modest handicap chaser: probably stays 3¾m: acts on good to firm
and heavy going: lazy and unreliable (worth try in headgear). *C. W. Mitchell*

WALTZING ALONG (IRE) 6 b.g. Presenting – Clyduffe Fairy (Belfalas) [2003/4 **h–**
F88: 16g 20d 17d Apr 10] lengthy gelding: in frame in 2 bumpers in 2002/3: well held in
novice company over hurdles, not knocked about first 2 starts: should stay beyond 2m.
L. Lungo

WAM 4 b.g. Distinctly North (USA) – Valise (Salse (USA)) [2003/4 F12g Nov 12] sturdy **F–**
gelding: third foal: dam, sprint maiden, half-sister to useful performer up to 1½m Billy
Bushwacker: well held in 3-y-o bumper on debut. *Mrs M. Reveley*

WANDERING LIGHT (IRE) 15 b.g. Royal Fountain – Pleaseme (Javelot) [2003/4 **c–**
c24gpᵘ c34vpᵘ May 21] sturdy gelding: veteran staying chaser: on downgrade, though **h–**
won 2 points in April: raced on good ground or softer (acts on heavy). *R. B. Francis*

WANNA SHOUT 6 b.m. Missed Flight – Lulu (Polar Falcon (USA)) [2003/4 h–: 16f⁶ **h–**
19sᵖᵘ Jan 7] rather leggy mare: no form over hurdles: tried in blinkers/cheekpieces: successful over 1m (stays 1¼m) on Flat in February and March. *R. Dickin*

WANSBECK 11 b.g. Dancing High – Mother Machree (Bing II) [2003/4 24sᵖᵘ Apr 4] **h–**
half-brother to temperamental winning staying chaser Donovans Reef (by Cool Guy) and

fair chaser Miss Mattie Ross (by Milieu), stays 25f: dam unraced: showed nothing in novice hurdle on belated debut. *S. B. Bell*

WANSFORD LADY   8 b.m. Michelozzo (USA) – Marnie's Girl (Crooner) [2003/4 17g 24g Mar 10] poor and lightly-raced maiden on Flat: well beaten in 3 novice hurdles: tried tongue tied: effectively refused to race final start. *A. P. Jones*   **h– §**

WAREYTH (USA)   5 b. or br.g. Shuailaan (USA) – Bahr Alsalaam (USA) (Riverman (USA)) [2003/4 h–: 18g May 5] tall gelding: no form over hurdles. *R. H. Buckler*   **h–**

WARMINGHAMSHARPISH   7 b.m. Nalchik (USA) – Tilstock Maid (Rolfe (USA)) [2003/4 F87: 16g* 17g* Jul 28] fair bumper winner: successful both starts over hurdles, in intermediate at Ludlow (despite wandering) in May and mares novice at Sedgefield in July: again pulled hard in latter: will prove best around 2m: sold 7,500 gns Doncaster October Sales. *W. M. Brisbourne*   **h87**

WAR OF ATTRITION (IRE)   5 br.g. Presenting – Una Juna (IRE) (Good Thyne (USA)) [2003/4 16d² 16g 16d* 16s* 20s 16g² Mar 16]   **h147**

As a runner-up in the Supreme Novices' Hurdle, War of Attrition almost has more to live up to in future than the winner Brave Inca. Among those to fill the runners-up spot in the last ten years have been Pridwell, Ventana Canyon, Princeful, His Song, Best Mate, Westender and Kicking King. The quartet that went over fences the following season all won a top novice chase of some description, His Song and Kicking King winning the Arkle at Leopardstown, Ventana Canyon the Cheltenham version and Best Mate the Scilly Isles Novices' Chase. His Song also won the Denny Gold Medal Novices' Chase and it's not hard to envisage War of Attrition having similar targets in the coming season. His Song, for his biggest successes, and War of Attrition were trained by Michael 'Mouse' Morris, both being grand chasing types in appearance (War of Attrition is strong and sturdy) who started off in the pointing field, though they enjoyed contrasting campaigns over hurdles. His Song won four of his six starts, including the Grade 1 at Punchestown in April, and contested the AIG Europe Champion Hurdle at Leopardstown on just his fourth outing, finishing second to Istabraq. He started favourite at Cheltenham, where he finished second to French Ballerina. In contrast, War of Attrition took nothing like the same high profile route to the Supreme and was sent off a 33/1 chance. He ran five times in little over two months from the start of November, winning a maiden at Punchestown and a minor event at Navan, in the latter accounting for Macs Joy, not then in the useful form he showed in handicaps later on. Both of War of Attrition's wins came over two miles, with plenty of use made of him. He seemed sure to benefit from a step up in trip in a Grade 3 at Naas in January but trailed in last of seven, later reported to have mucus in his lungs. War of Attrition was ridden with more restraint in the Supreme Novices' Hurdle, taking a good hold and making smooth headway before the third last, leading and quickening at the next and edged out by Brave Inca only near the line, beaten a neck by the winner and seven lengths clear of the third Fleet Street.

War of Attrition (IRE) (br.g. 1999)	Presenting (br 1992)	Mtoto (b 1983)	Busted / Amazer
		D'Azy (b 1984)	Persian Bold / Belle Viking
	Una Juna (IRE) (b 1992)	Good Thyne (br 1977)	Herbager / Foreseer
		An Bothar Dubh (br 1986)	Strong Gale / Tullow Performance

War of Attrition comes from the second crop of the Derby third Presenting. The sire was heavily represented in both Britain and Ireland in the latest season, though just eighteen of eighty-two individual runners managed to pick up a race. Apart from War of Attrition, the best of the other runners include the useful bumper winner Marsh Run, the fairly useful hurdlers Fairwood Present and Well Presented, and the National Hunt Chase third Drombeag. Although a two-year-old over six furlongs provided Presenting with his first winner as a sire, his progeny in general display plenty of stamina, so it is possible War of Attrition may do even better over longer trips. There's stamina on the distaff side of War of Attrition's pedigree as well. His dam Una Juna is a sister to the fairly useful staying chaser Max Pride, while his grandam An Bothar Dubh, a winning hurdler, is a sister to the fairly useful staying hurdler and fair chaser Crank Shaft. Others out of the third dam Tullow Performance are the fairly useful hurdler at up to three miles Cuilin Bui and Rosceen Bui, a maiden and the dam of the useful hurdler/chaser Emotional Moment. War of Attrition is the first foal of his dam, the second being Fighting Chance (by Germany), a promising third in a bumper at Newbury on his debut in March. Una Juna ran just once, in a point, though her appearance there wasn't so eventful as War of Attrition's only start in that sphere. Contesting a two-and-a-half-mile maiden in March 2003 he was clear and cantering when falling at the last, his rider Robert Widger breaking his leg. *M. F. Morris, Ireland*

WARRENS CASTLE (IRE) 7 b.g. Fourstars Allstar (USA) – Jerusalem Cruiser (IRE) (Electric) [2003/4 20d⁵ 20m* Jul 11] first foal: dam bumper winner: fair form in bumpers: successful twice from 3 starts over hurdles, winning intermediate at Navan in July easily by 8 lengths from Taranges: will stay beyond 2½m: acts on good to firm going. *W. P. Mullins, Ireland* — **h113**

WARRLIN 10 b.g. Warrshan (USA) – Lahin (Rainbow Quest (USA)) [2003/4 c97, h–: 19d 20s 19g⁶ 24dᵖᵘ 22g Apr 24] sparely-made gelding: winning hurdler/chaser: modest form at best over hurdles in 2003/4: barely stays 25f: acts on any going. *C. W. Fairhurst* — **c–**, **h87**

WARTON CRAG 8 b.g. Tina's Pet – Majestic Form (IRE) (Double Schwartz) [2003/4 h–: 20dᵖᵘ 21d Mar 30] sturdy gelding: of no account. *James Moffatt* — **h–**

WARTORN (IRE) 9 b.g. Warcraft (USA) – Alice Minkthorn (Party Mink) [2003/4 h95: 22g² 24m² 21g⁶ 24sᵖᵘ 22s³ Apr 6] workmanlike gelding: modest handicap hurdler: stays 3m: acts on good to firm and heavy going. *J. S. King* — **h96**

WAR TUNE 8 b.g. Warrshan (USA) – Keen Melody (USA) (Sharpen Up) [2003/4 c–, h88: 20s³ c22s* Mar 7] workmanlike gelding: modest hurdler: left B. Leavy and off 20 months, good third in handicap at Huntingdon on reappearance: second start over fences when winning handicap at Market Rasen, idling: likely to stay 3m: acts on soft and good to firm going: swishes tail under pressure. *Ian Williams* — **c100**, **h–**

WAS A DRIVE (IRE) 10 b.g. Yashgan – Alan's Rosalinda (Prefairy) [2003/4 c–, c20m⁶ c20m⁴ 22d c21v c20s⁶ c20d⁶ c25s³ Apr 4] good-topped gelding: well held in novice on hurdling debut: poor handicap chaser: stays 2½m: acts on heavy going: tried in cheekpieces/blinkers. *Miss Kate Milligan* — **c68**, **h–**

WASSL STREET (IRE) 12 b.g. Dancing Brave (USA) – One Way Street (Habitat) [2003/4 c–, h–: c20mᵖᵘ c25vᵖᵘ c23g c24vᵖᵘ 16sᵖᵘ 26g Mar 6] angular gelding: winning hurdler/chaser, no sign of retaining ability: tried blinkered/visored: tongue tied. *R. Lee* — **c–**, **h–**

WASTED TALENT (IRE) 4 b.f. Sesaro (USA) – Miss Garuda (Persian Bold) [2003/4 16g² 17d² 17g² 18g* Apr 22] leggy filly: half-sister to fair hurdler Pampered Guest (by Be My Guest), stays 2¾m: fairly useful on Flat (stays 1½m): runner-up first 3 starts over hurdles: won mares maiden at Fontwell easily by 12 lengths from Cherokee Bay: likely to stay 2½m: wore cheekpieces/blinkers after hurdling debut: free-going sort: races prominently. *J. G. Portman* — **h112**

WATCHFUL WITNESS 4 ch.c. In The Wings – Eternal (Kris) [2003/4 16s⁴ 16s* 16s⁴ 16d⁶ Mar 19] smallish colt: sixth foal: half-brother to 3 winners, including fairly useful middle-distance winner Wadi (by Green Desert): dam once-raced half-sister to Derby winner Quest For Fame: sold unraced out of A. Fabre's stable 8,500 gns Newmarket July Sales: best effort in juvenile hurdles when fourth at Ascot on debut: failed to impress with attitude subsequently, hard pressed to win weakly-contested event at Plumpton in January: will stay beyond 2m: blinkered third outing: sold to join Dr J. Naylor £9,000 Ascot April Sales. *G. L. Moore* — **h94**

WATCH IT 6 b.g. Sea Raven (IRE) – Magic Penny (Sharrood (USA)) [2003/4 F78: 17d Nov 27] tall gelding: modest form in bumpers: well held in novice on hurdling debut: free-going sort. *M. Todhunter* — **h–**

WATCH THE DOVE 7 b.g. Afzal – Spot The Dove (Riberetto) [2003/4 h90: 27s⁵ 25f² 24g² 19d c20v² c23vᵖᵘ c24gᶠ c24m³ c21mᶠ c22d⁴ Apr 7] angular gelding: modest maiden hurdler: generally let down by jumping over fences, best effort when third in novice at Taunton in March: stays 25f: acts on any going: tried in visor/cheekpieces. *C. L. Tizzard* — **c91 x**, **h98**

WATCHYOURBACK (NZ) 10 ch.g. Watchman (NZ) – English Lass (NZ) (English Harbour) [2003/4 c82, h–: c25s³ Mar 7] winning hurdler: fair pointer, successful in April: below that form in steeplechases: stays 3¼m: acts on good to firm and good to soft going: visored and tongue tied. *M. Trou*

c–
h–

WATERBERG (IRE) 9 b.g. Sadler's Wells (USA) – Pretoria (Habitat) [2003/4 c98, h–: c20g² c24g^ur c24g* c24g* c24m² c24g^pu Oct 11] smallish, workmanlike gelding: winning hurdler: fairly useful handicap chaser: improved at Stratford in June and July (beat Simber Hill 6 lengths): lame final outing: stays 3m: acts on good to firm and heavy going: tried blinkered: has bled from nose: patiently ridden. *H. D. Daly*

c117
h–

WATERHALL 11 b.g. River God (USA) – Tuneful Queen (Queen's Hussar) [2003/4 c–, h69: 21m⁴ 20m^pu May 26] workmanlike gelding: poor maiden hurdler, no form either start very early in season. *J. M. P. Eustace*

c–
h–

WATER KING (USA) 5 b.g. Irish River (FR) – Brookshield Baby (IRE) (Sadler's Wells (USA)) [2003/4 h84: 17g⁶ 16g 16g⁵ 16d* 16d² 20s 19g⁴ Mar 5] modest hurdler: won selling handicap at Fakenham in November: stays 19f: acts on soft going: has been led to post: withdrawn after refusing to line up in April. *G. Brown*

h88

WATERLAW (IRE) 10 b.g. Kahyasi – Shuss (USA) (Princely Native (USA)) [2003/4 c19d^pu c21d* c21d* c21d^pu Jan 17] angular gelding: improved chaser in 2003/4 (often let down by jumping in 2001/2 for E. Stanners), winning handicaps at Wincanton in December and Cheltenham (made all) in January: stays 21f: acts on firm and good to soft going: tongue tied. *M. C. Pipe*

c107
h–

WATERLILY (IRE) 5 b.m. Revoque (IRE) – Cochineal (USA) (Vaguely Noble) [2003/4 F92p: 16d 16d³ 16d* 16s³ 16g³ 16d³ Mar 17] fairly useful hurdler: won maiden at Leopardstown in December by 3½ lengths from Hardy Duckett: easily best effort afterwards when third of 17 to Nopekan in minor event on same course on fifth start: raced at 2m (will stay further): acts on good to soft going, won bumper on good to firm. *Mrs J. Harrington, Ireland*

h117

WATERLINER 5 b.m. Merdon Melody – Double Touch (FR) (Nonoalco (USA)) [2003/4 16m 16m⁶ 18m³ 16m Oct 6] poor maiden up to 7f at 2 yrs for P. D. Evans: showed little over hurdles or in points. *P. S. McEntee*

h–

WATERMOUSE 4 b.g. Alhaarth (IRE) – Heavenly Waters (Celestial Storm (USA)) [2003/4 16g⁶ 16s* Nov 18] poor maiden on Flat (should stay at least 1m): similar form over hurdles, winning novice seller at Towcester. *R. Dickin*

h69

WATER NYMPH (IRE) 4 ch.f. Be My Guest (USA) – Justitia (Dunbeath (USA)) [2003/4 17d^pu 21d^pu Apr 12] rather leggy filly: half-sister to several winners, notably high-class hurdler/top-class chaser Bacchanal (by Bob Back), stayed 3m: no sign of ability on Flat (for B. McMahon) or over hurdles. *N. J. Henderson*

h–

WATER QUIRL (GER) 5 ch.h. Dr Devious (IRE) – Water Quest (IRE) (Rainbow Quest (USA)) [2003/4 16g* 17d^f 16g^pu c17d⁴ c16m* Nov 25] leggy horse: successful 3 times up to around 1½m on Flat for A. Schutz, including in 2003: won 4-y-o hurdle at Bremen in July and 4-y-o novice chase at Warwick in November, beating L'Aventure 9 lengths at latter course: raced around 2m. *C. Von Der Recke, Germany*

c125
h?

WATER SPORTS (IRE) 6 b.m. Marju (IRE) – Water Splash (USA) (Little Current (USA)) [2003/4 h69: 24g* 20d* 20d* 22s 20d 24d^pu 24g* 24g 22d^pu 26d^pu Mar 22] smallish, lengthy mare: modest hurdler: won handicaps at Uttoxeter (mares novice), Fakenham (amateurs) and Newcastle in November and at Taunton (mares amateurs) in February: stays 3m: raced only on good going or softer: effective blinkered or not: often makes mistakes. *N. A. Twiston-Davies*

h101

WATERSPRAY (AUS) 6 ch.g. Lake Coniston (IRE) – Forain (NZ) (Nassipour (USA)) [2003/4 h93: 16m 17d⁶ 17g⁴ 16m³ 17f* 16g² 16m² 16m⁴ Nov 17] small, angular gelding: modest handicap hurdler: won at Exeter in September: raced mainly around 2m: best efforts on good going or firmer. *J. L. Spearing*

h97

WATSON LAKE (IRE) 6 b.g. Be My Native (USA) – Magneeto (IRE) (Brush Aside (USA)) [2003/4 F110: 19d² 18d² 18s* 20d* 18s⁶ Feb 8] tall, good sort: useful bumper winner: progressed to similar level over hurdles, easily winning maiden at Navan in December and Grade 3 Golden Cygnet Novices' Hurdle at Leopardstown (readily beat Away Home 4 lengths) in January: reportedly had epiglottal entrapment when sixth of 7 in Grade 1 novice at latter course in February: will stay beyond 2½m: acts on heavy going,

h133

Mr John Corr's "Watson Lake"

disappointing on good in Grade 1 novice at Punchestown in late-April: free-going sort.
N. Meade, Ireland

WAVERLEY ROAD 7 ch.g. Pelder (IRE) – Lillicara (FR) (Caracolero (USA)) **h97**
[2003/4 19s⁵ 16v⁵ 16g⁵ 18d⁴ Apr 7] close-coupled gelding: half-brother to 3 winners over jumps, including fair hurdler Rowlandsons Gems (by Enchantment), stayed 21f: modest on Flat (stays 2m): similar form in novice hurdles: likely to be suited by 2½m+.
M. Madgwick

WAVE ROCK 9 br.g. Tragic Role (USA) – Moonscape (Ribero) [2003/4 c134, h120: **c130 d**
c20m² c20d⁵ c20f⁴ c20g c19d⁶ c21d³ c18s⁴ c19g c24g Mar 27] neat gelding: useful **h–**
handicap chaser at best: creditable second at Worcester in May, badly out of sorts after: stays at least 2½m: acts on heavy and good to firm going: usually blinkered (not last 4 starts): has hung left/carried head awkwardly. *P. J. Hobbs*

WAYDALE HILL 5 ch.m. Minster Son – Buckby Folly (Netherkelly) [2003/4 F16d **F73**
F16s⁶ Apr 4] 6,000 4-y-o: sixth foal: half-sister to fairly useful hurdler/useful chaser Buckby Lane (by Nomadic Way), stays 21f, and modest chaser Guilsborough Gorse (by Past Glories), stays 25f: dam, winning hurdler, suited by 2½m: better effort in bumpers when never-nearer sixth at Hexham. *T. D. Walford*

WAYNESWORLD (IRE) 6 b.g. Petoski – Mariners Mirror (Julio Mariner) [2003/4 **c84 ?**
h–, F78: 20d³ 21vᵖᵘ 20dᵖᵘ 22d c20sᶠ c19d² c24vᵖᵘ Apr 4] smallish gelding: poor maiden **h–**
hurdler/chaser: should stay beyond 2½m: raced on good going or softer. *M. Scudamore*

WAYWARD BUTTONS 10 b.g. Nomadic Way (USA) – Lady Buttons (New Brig) **c78 §**
[2003/4 c98§, h–: c16g May 10] winning chaser: typically found little in handicap at **h– §**
Hexham very early in season: stays 25f: acts on good to soft going: has had tongue tied.
M. Todhunter

WAYWARD MELODY 4 b.f. Merdon Melody – Dubitable (Formidable (USA)) **h83**
[2003/4 18f⁴ 16g³ 18m* 16m⁶ 16f⁵ 20m 20m⁴ 19dʳᵒ 20d* Apr 7] good-topped filly: poor
maiden on Flat: modest juvenile hurdler: won at Fontwell in September (fortunate) and
April (selling handicap, having left S. Dow): stays 2½m: acts on good to firm and good to
soft going: difficult ride (ran out eighth start). *G. L. Moore*

WEARERICH 7 ch.m. Alflora (IRE) – Weareagrandmother (Prince Tenderfoot **h–**
(USA)) [2003/4 F–: 19dᵘʳ 20sᵖᵘ 21dᵖᵘ Jan 22] workmanlike mare: little sign of ability.
P. M. Rich

WEAVER GEORGE (IRE) 14 b.g. Flash of Steel – Nephrite (Godswalk (USA)) **c110 d**
[2003/4 c113, h–: c22m⁵ c24gᵘʳ c20g² c25g² c24d⁵ c25g² c20s⁴ c25sᵇᵈ c30g⁶ c24vᵖᵘ c27s **h–**
c24s³ c24s⁵ c21dᵖᵘ c26d⁴ Apr 18] leggy gelding: winning hurdler: handicap chaser, on
the downgrade: better at 3m+ than shorter: acts on any going: tried visored/blinkered,
usually wears cheekpieces: has won 6 times at Sedgefield and 4 times at Kelso: usually
comes from off pace. *W. Storey*

WEAVER OF DREAMS (IRE) 4 b.g. Victory Note (USA) – Daziyra (IRE) **h–**
(Doyoun) [2003/4 17g Apr 12] little form on Flat: well held in juvenile on hurdling debut.
G. A. Swinbank

WEAVERS CHOICE 11 ch.g. Sunley Builds – Wedding Song (True Song) [2003/4 **c–**
c–: c24sᵖᵘ Feb 12] fair pointer: largely well below that form in hunter chases. *Mrs Joan
Tice*

WEB MASTER (FR) 6 b.g. Arctic Tern (USA) – Inesperada (Cariellor (FR)) [2003/4 **h93**
F93?: F16d 24d⁵ 24d 25s 24v³ 27s* 24s³ 27d⁵ Apr 23] leggy gelding: best effort in **F–**
bumpers on debut in 2002/3: modest hurdler: won handicap at Sedgefield in February:
stays 27f: acts on soft going. *C. Grant*

WEB PERCEPTIONS (USA) 4 ch.c. Distant View (USA) – Squaw Time (USA) **h120**
(Lord At War (ARG)) [2003/4 16m* 16m* 16f* 16g² 16s³ 16g 17g Mar 18] good-topped
colt: fairly useful on Flat (stays 1¾m), claimed from P. Cole £40,000 in September: fairly
useful juvenile hurdler: won at Huntingdon in September and Chepstow and Cheltenham
in October, beating After Eight by neck for final win: tailed off in graded events at
Kempton and Cheltenham last 2 starts: blinkered and tongue tied. *M. F. Harris*

WEDGER'S WAY (IRE) 7 ch.g. Glacial Storm (USA) – Officer's Lady (General **c74**
Ironside) [2003/4 c22m² 24m³ Sep 14] sixth foal: half-brother to winning Irish pointer In **h75**
Your Interest (by Buckskin): dam unraced half-sister to smart Irish chaser Buck Rogers:
won maiden Irish point in 2003: poor form when placed in maiden chase at Fontwell and
maiden hurdle at Worcester: sold 2,000 gns Doncaster May Sales. *Mrs H. Dalton*

WEE DANNY (IRE) 7 b.g. Mandalus – Bonne Bouche (Bonne Noel) [2003/4 h70: **h101**
21m⁶ 24m³ 24m² 27d* 24g* 26m* 24f* 24m 21d 27g⁵ Apr 22] workmanlike gelding:
modest handicap hurdler: won at Newton Abbot in July, Worcester (conditional jockeys
novice) in August, Hereford in September and Exeter in October: stays 27f: acts on firm
and good to soft going: races prominently: genuine. *L. A. Dace*

WEE RIVER (IRE) 15 b.g. Over The River (FR) – Mahe Reef (Be Friendly) [2003/4 **c–**
c17g⁵ c20g³ 20dᵖᵘ c16s⁵ c20m⁴ c20g c17sᶠ c24g c20f⁴ c16g Mar 13] sturdy gelding: **h–**
veteran chaser, retains little ability. *J. Barclay*

WEE WILLOW 10 b.m. Minster Son – Peak Princess (Charlottown) [2003/4 h60: **h79**
27s² 21d* 20d 24gᶠ 24v² 24g⁴ 27d² 24sᵖᵘ Apr 21] smallish mare: poor hurdler: won mares
handicap at Sedgefield in November: best at 3m+: acts on heavy going: often front runner.
D. W. Whillans

WELBURN LADY 5 b.m. Primitive Rising (USA) – Tommys Dream (Le Bavard **F–**
(FR)) [2003/4 F17m F17g Oct 11] angular mare: seventh foal: half-sister to winning 2½m
hurdler Preston Brook (by Perpendicular): dam, fair hurdler, successful from 2m to 25f:
no sign of ability in 2 bumpers, tongue tied on debut: joined D. Easterby. *G. P. Kelly*

WELCOME ARCHIE 4 ch.g. Most Welcome – Indefinite Article (IRE) (Indian **F–**
Ridge) [2003/4 F13g Nov 30] 7,000Y, 2,200 3-y-o: smallish, lengthy gelding: third foal:
half-brother to 5f/6f winner Branston Pickle (by Piccolo) and 1¾m seller winner Branston Nell (by Classic Cliche): dam unraced sister to very smart Irish performer up to

1½m Definite Article and half-sister to smart stayer/promising hurdler Sun Bird: showed nothing in bumper on debut. *J. S. Haldane*

WELCOME NEWS   6 ch.m. Bob Back (USA) – Rosie O'Keeffe (IRE) (Royal Fountain) [2003/4 F–: F17m Jun 21] well held in 2 bumpers (tried tongue tied): won point in February. *Mrs H. Dalton*   **F—**

WELCOME TO UNOS   7 ch.g. Exit To Nowhere (USA) – Royal Loft (Homing)   **h110 §** [2003/4 h99: 16g 17g⁴ 16g* 16g³ 17g 20m* 24pu Apr 17] sturdy gelding: fair hurdler: won handicaps at Stratford (novice, first start after leaving Mrs M. Reveley) in October and Leicester in December: stays 2½m: acts on good to firm and heavy going: visored last 3 starts: often jumps less than fluently: probably ungenuine. *M. C. Pipe*

WELDMAN   5 b.g. Weld – Manettia (IRE) (Mandalus) [2003/4 F16g⁴ F16g⁶ 18s 19g   **h—** 16s Mar 20] lengthy, quite good-topped gelding: second foal: half-brother to bumper   **F85** winner Minster Missile (by Minster Son): dam, modest hurdler, stayed 27f: fourth in bumper on debut: well held all subsequent starts, last 3 over hurdles: should be suited by further than 2m. *Mrs M. Reveley*

WELL CHIEF (GER)   5 ch.g. Night Shift (USA) – Wellesiena (GER) (Scenic)   **c150 p** [2003/4 h134: 16f* 16d⁵ c16s* c16g* c16g* Apr 3]   **h142**
  Nothing, it seems, stops Tony McCoy who won his ninth jockeys' championship to surpass the record he had held jointly with Peter Scudamore, champion eight times between 1981/2 and 1991/2. McCoy's contemporary Richard Johnson rode one hundred and eighty-six winners in the latest season, a number surpassed only once by Scudamore during his reign as champion, and he must be wondering what he has to do to win the title. Johnson has been second to McCoy in each of the last seven seasons and in the latest one he moved into fourth place, behind McCoy, three-times champion Richard Dunwoody and Scudamore, in the all-time jump jockeys' list in Britain. Johnson's total in the latest season was his best to date, but McCoy beat him by twenty-three despite being sidelined for two months after

Irish Independent Arkle Challenge Trophy Chase, Cheltenham—
Well Chief (right) wins on just his second start over fences;
Kicking King (left) and Mister McGoldrick also hold every chance two out

breaking his right arm at Worcester in June and suffering complications. McCoy was eighteen behind Johnson when he returned to action towards the end of August. He still reached the hundred-winner mark for the season on the final day of Cheltenham's Open meeting in November, Johnson's lead by then down to half a dozen. McCoy was back in front by early December and Johnson wasn't able to close when McCoy was harshly suspended for five days for misuse of the whip when trying to cajole a reluctant Deano's Beeno to jump off in the Spa Hurdle at Cheltenham on New Year's Eve (described in more detail in the essay on Crystal d'Ainay). McCoy passed another landmark in his prodigious career when winning on Magical Bailiwick at Wincanton on a bleak January afternoon, a victory which made him the first jump jockey to reach 2,000 winners. McCoy had another spell on the sidelines after breaking a cheekbone in three places in a fall at Plumpton a month before the Cheltenham Festival. Astonishingly, he was back in action only nine days later, still two ahead of Johnson in the title race, and was soon in full cry again, riding twenty-seven winners from seventy-one mounts inside the space of three weeks leading up to the Festival.

McCoy's only victory at the three-day Cheltenham Festival—which is, as planned, being extended to four in the next season—came on the five-year-old Well Chief in the Arkle Challenge Trophy on the opening day. Front-running Well Chief had gone down by a head in the Triumph Hurdle twelve months earlier, after which he had come third in the Anniversary Hurdle at Aintree. He was still being talked of as a possible Champion Hurdle candidate at the turn of the year after showing further improvement to win the K J Pike & Sons Elite Hurdle, a Grade 2 limited handicap at Wincanton in November, and then running respectably under top weight in the Gerry Feilden Hurdle at Newbury later in the month. Well Chief entered the betting on the Arkle at the end of January after reports of encouraging schooling sessions over fences. It is by no means unusual for a Pipe-trained novice chaser to be sent to the Cheltenham Festival with little experience of jumping fences in public. When Pipe won the Arkle with another five-year-old, Champleve, for example, he had run only twice over fences, winning novices at Lingfield and

Mr D. A. Johnson's "Well Chief"

Ascot, after being switched from hurdling as late as February (the same connections' Wahiba Sands made his chasing debut in the 2000 Arkle, sent off second favourite). Well Chief had been due to make his chasing debut at Warwick at the end of January but the meeting was abandoned because of frost. His only outing over fences before Cheltenham came in a novice event at Taunton in early-February when he made a winning start, leading on the bridle after four out after proving a little intractable held up, and jumping none too fluently at times as a result. Well Chief had to be pushed along after hitting the last, winning by three lengths from Saint Esteben.

Well Chief started at 9/1 in the Irish Independent Arkle Challenge Trophy, fifth choice among the sixteen runners, in a market dominated by Thisthatandtother, who had won four of his five starts over fences, and Irish-trained Kicking King whose chasing experience extended to four races and included a victory in the Arkle at Leopardstown. Well Chief belied his inexperience, making the most of the 4-lb allowance five-year-olds receive over fences, to beat Kicking King in a thrilling finish. Again ridden with considerably more restraint than over hurdles, Well Chief stuck to the inside all the way, jumping soundly in the main, until moving through and taking the lead at the second last. Kicking King's supporters were given hope when Well Chief got in too close to the last, but Well Chief pulled out extra up the steep climb to the finish to win by a length, with another five-year-old, 25/1-shot Le Duc, seven lengths further back in third. Only half the runners completed the course, Thisthatandtother falling at the second, Tidour coming down two out when still going well enough to suggest he would have finished third, and Mister McGoldrick well held in fourth when blundering and unseating his rider at the last.

The Arkle field was by no means a vintage one and Well Chief's form at Cheltenham was some way below that shown by the last two Arkle winners, Moscow Flyer and Azertyuiop. Well Chief didn't have to improve on his Arkle form to follow up in the Martell Cognac Maghull Novices' Chase at Aintree two and a half weeks later. Thisthatandtother got the chance to show what he could do this time, and Well Chief beat him by two and a half lengths, with Mister McGoldrick five lengths further away in third. Again patiently ridden, and jumping soundly in the main, Well Chief quickened between the last two fences and won in good style. He was the third successive five-year-old to win the Maghull, following Armaturk and Le Roi Miguel, whose records in their second season over fences indicate how difficult it can be for good novices of their age when they lose the weight allowance. Well Chief has a lot of improvement to make in any case if he is to develop into a serious challenger to Moscow Flyer and Azertyuiop in the two-mile championship events. Well Chief's Arkle victory was the third in seven years—Or Royal preceded Champleve—for the owner/trainer/jockey combination of David Johnson, Martin Pipe and Tony McCoy, all of whom headed their respective tables at the end of the season, Johnson for the fourth time and Pipe for the fourteenth. The Johnson-owned horses will be ridden mostly by Timmy Murphy in the next season, following McCoy's decision to accept a retainer as stable jockey to Jonjo O'Neill at Jackdaws Castle.

			Northern Dancer	Nearctic
Well Chief (GER)	Night Shift (USA)		(b 1961)	Natalma
(ch.g. 1999)	(b 1980)		Ciboulette	Chop Chop
			(b 1961)	Windy Answer
			Scenic	Sadler's Wells
	Wellesiena (GER)		(b 1986)	Idyllic
	(b 1994)		Weltkrone	Lord Udo
			(ch 1982)	Weltdame

The angular Well Chief isn't an obvious chaser on looks, lacking in size and substance, which matters not a jot now that he has shown the ability. He was imported by his present stable from Germany (where he won in listed company on the Flat) and is the first foal of Wellesiena who didn't win a race but was placed in a listed trial for the Preis der Diana. Well Chief's sire, the Coolmore-based Night Shift, is still active at the age of twenty-four and is principally a Flat sire. Well Chief travels strongly in his races and is likely to prove best at around two miles. He has won on soft going but has shown his best form on good going or firmer, conditions which place the emphasis on speed. Still lightly raced, he should be capable of further improvement over fences. *M. C. Pipe*

WELLFRANKO (IRE) 9 b.g. Camden Town – Electana (Electrify) [2003/4 h–: 16g^F 16f^5 16d Apr 11] small, angular gelding: winning hurdler, no form since 2001/2. *Miss Z. C. Davison* **h–**

WELL GONE 7 b.g. Sanglamore (USA) – Well Away (IRE) (Sadler's Wells (USA)) [2003/4 F16g F17m* 20d^3 19m^pu 16g^3 Sep 6] heavy-topped gelding: easily best effort in bumpers when winning at Newton Abbot in July: reportedly distressed in novice on hurdling debut and failed to see race out both subsequent starts. *Ian Williams* **h72 ?** **F87**

WELLIE (IRE) 11 b.g. Aristocracy – Sweet View (King's Ride) [2003/4 c85x, h–: c20m² c20m² c18f^ur Aug 22] tall gelding: modest chaser: stays 2½m: acts on good to firm and good to soft ground: front runner: tends to pull hard/make mistakes. *S. J. Gilmore* **c92 x** **h–**

WE'LL MAKE IT (IRE) 6 b.g. Spectrum (IRE) – Walliser (Niniski (USA)) [2003/4 h101§: 21f² 20m* Nov 8] angular gelding: fair hurdler: won conditional jockeys handicap at Sandown on return from 6-month absence: stays 21f: acts on soft and firm going: usually blinkered: irresolute. *G. L. Moore* **h104 §**

WELL PRESENTED (IRE) 6 ch.g. Presenting – Casualty Madame (Buckskin (FR)) [2003/4 F20g³ F18m* 22m* 22s⁴ 24d⁴ 22d² Apr 12] workmanlike gelding: fourth foal: dam unraced, out of half-sister to high-class 2m chaser Little Bay: won comfortably at Tipperary in October on second of 2 starts in bumpers: progressive hurdler: won maiden at Down Royal in November despite hanging left: good efforts in frame in handicaps at Fairyhouse (2) and Punchestown in February and April, keeping-on third of 28 to Hurry Bob in strongly-contested event at latter course: stays 3m. *Mrs J. Harrington, Ireland* **h123** **F103**

WELL SAID SAM 8 b.g. Weld – Auto Sam (Even Say) [2003/4 c25g^{pu} Mar 28] pulled   **c–**
up in maiden point on debut and in hunter chase: runner-up twice in April returned to
pointing. *P. C. Handley*

WELSH AND WYLDE (IRE) 4 b.g. Anita's Prince – Waikiki (GER) (Zampano   **h82**
(GER)) [2003/4 16d⁶ 16d² Apr 8] modest maiden on Flat (stays 8.5f): better effort in
selling hurdles when second at Ludlow, pulling hard: likely to prove best at sharp 2m.
B. Palling

WELSH CRYSTAL 5 gr.m. Muqadar (USA) – Rupert's Daughter (Rupert Bear)   **F72 ?**
[2003/4 F18f⁶ F16m³ F17d F16s Dec 26] leggy mare: third known foal: half-sister to
winning 17f hurdler River Mere (by River God): dam novice selling hurdler: signs of
only a little ability in bumpers. *Mrs L. Williamson*

WELSH DREAM 7 b.g. Mtoto – Morgannwg (IRE) (Simply Great (FR)) [2003/4   **h97 +**
h88+: 17d* May 28] useful-looking gelding: modest form in maiden hurdles, won at
Cartmel only start in 2003/4: will stay beyond 17f: acts on good to soft going.
Miss S. E. Forster

WELSH GOLD 5 ch.g. Zafonic (USA) – Trying For Gold (USA) (Northern Baby   **h–**
(CAN)) [2003/4 F16m F17m 16d^{pu} 20m⁶ Nov 9] eighth foal: half-brother to 3 at least   **F–**
useful winners, including smart 1m to 13.3f winner Phantom Gold and 8.5f US Grade 3
event/1¼m winner Fictitious (both by Machiavellian): dam, 1½m winner, out of Ribblesdale winner Expansive: sold unraced out of R. Charlton's stable 16,000 gns Doncaster
January (2003) Sales: no form in bumpers or novice hurdles. *S. T. Lewis*

WELSH MAIN 7 br.g. Zafonic (USA) – Welsh Daylight (Welsh Pageant) [2003/4   **h106**
h116: 16g 20d 16g 16g² 16d⁶ 16s Apr 21] sturdy gelding: fair handicap hurdler: raced
mainly at 2m: acts on good to firm and good to soft going. *F. Jordan*

WELSH WHISPER 5 b.m. Overbury (IRE) – Grugiar (Red Sunset) [2003/4 F17m^F   **F–**
Sep 10] fourth foal: half-sister to 1½m/1¾m winner Barti-Ddu (by Mister Majestic) and
7f winner Croeso Adref (by Most Welcome): dam, ran 3 times at 2 yrs, out of half-sister
to Park Hill winner Cursorial: well held when collapsing final 1f in bumper on debut:
poor form up to 1m on Flat subsequently. *S. A. Brookshaw*

WEMYSS QUEST 9 b.g. Rainbow Quest (USA) – Wemyss Bight (Dancing Brave   **c108 d**
(USA)) [2003/4 c89p, h–: c23m* c20m⁵ c24m^{pu} c26m⁴ c24f^{pu} Oct 25] quite good-topped   **h–**
gelding: fair hurdler/chaser: made virtually all when winning handicap over fences at
Worcester in June: very disappointing subsequently: stays 25f: acts on firm and good to
soft going (below par on soft/heavy): sometimes tongue tied: rejoined F. Murphy. *Miss
Venetia Williams*

WENSLEY BLUE (IRE) 5 b.g. Blues Traveller (IRE) – Almasa (Faustus (USA))   **h79**
[2003/4 h77: 20d* Apr 28] big, good-topped gelding: poor form over hurdles, winning
novice seller (sold 5,500 gns) at Hexham very early in season: showed little in points
subsequently: stays 2½m: acts on good to soft ground. *P. C. Haslam*

WERE NOT STOPPIN 9 b.g. Mystiko (USA) – Power Take Off (Aragon) [2003/4   **h83**
h80: 16d⁴ 16g³ 17g Mar 28] good-topped gelding: poor hurdler: stays 19f: acts on firm
and good to soft ground. *R. Bastiman*

WESLEY'S LAD (IRE) 10 b. or br.g. Classic Secret (USA) – Galouga (FR) (Lou   **h85**
Piguet (FR)) [2003/4 h94: 16s 16s⁴ 17d 24s^{pu} 20d^{pu} 16g^F 16s^{pu} Apr 11] tall gelding:
handicap hurdler, form in 2003/4 only on second start: stays 2½m: acts on soft and good
to firm going. *D. Burchell*

WESSEX (USA) 4 ch.g. Gone West (USA) – Satin Velvet (USA) (El Gran Senor   **h–**
(USA)) [2003/4 16d^{pu} Feb 8] fairly useful on Flat (stays 1m), sold out of M. Johnston's
stable only 5,000 gns Doncaster October Sales: tongue tied, had breathing problem in
juvenile on hurdling debut. *James Moffatt*

WEST ASIDE (IRE) 10 b.g. Brush Aside (USA) – Chancy Belle (Le Bavard (FR))   **c–**
[2003/4 c–, h–: c25s⁶ c25v^{pu} c26d^{pu} c26d^{pu} c25d^{pu} 22g 25s^{pu} 21d⁴ Apr 11] little form: **h–**
tried blinkered/tongue tied. *T. P. McGovern*

WESTBOURNE (IRE) 6 b.m. King's Ride – Give Me Hope (IRE) (Be My Native   **F–**
(USA)) [2003/4 F16g F17g⁶ Apr 1] 2,000 4-y-o, resold 12,500 4-y-o: third foal: dam, 11f
winner, sister to useful 2m hurdler Be My Hope: well held in 2 bumpers. *A. King*

WESTCOAST 13 b.g. Handsome Sailor – Pichon (Formidable (USA)) [2003/4 c24m   **c–**
May 29] small gelding: winning hurdler: poor form in points: showed nothing in hunter   **h–**
chase: usually blinkered over hurdles. *Miss Joanne Priest*

WEST COASTER (IRE)   6 gr.g. Be My Native (USA) – Donegal Grey (IRE)   **h–**
(Roselier (FR)) [2003/4 h89: 20g⁴ 21s 21d Apr 8] lengthy, good-topped gelding: maiden
hurdler: well held in 2003/4. *Miss H. C. Knight*

WESTENDER (FR)   8 b.g. In The Wings – Trude (GER) (Windwurf (GER)) [2003/4   **h158**
h159: 16dᵖᵘ 16g⁶ 16g⁵ 20d³ 16m³ Apr 23] tall, close-coupled gelding: very smart hurdler:
at least respectable efforts when sixth to Geos in very valuable handicap at Newbury, fifth
to Hardy Eustace in Champion Hurdle at Cheltenham and third to Rhinestone Cowboy in
Aintree Hurdle second to fourth starts: stays 2½m when conditions aren't testing: acts on
good to firm and good to soft going, probably on heavy: blinkered: reportedly distressed
on reappearance: has looked none too keen. *M. C. Pipe*

WESTERN BLUEBIRD (IRE)   6 b.g. Bluebird (USA) – Arrastra (Bustino) [2003/4   **h67**
h–: 19g 20m* 22m⁵ 21gᵖᵘ 18d⁶ Dec 1] leggy gelding: poor hurdler: won conditional
jockeys selling handicap at Hexham in June: stays 2½m: acts on good to firm going:
possibly best in cheekpieces. *Miss Kate Milligan*

WESTERN CHIEF (IRE)   10 b.h. Caerleon (USA) – Go Honey Go (General   **c–**
Assembly (USA)) [2003/4 c90, h–: 20vᵖᵘ Jan 24] angular horse: modest handicap chaser: **h–**
winning hurdler: out of depth at Pau only start in 2003/4: stays 3¼m: acts on firm and
good to soft going: tried visored: tongue tied. *D. L. Williams*

WESTERN FORT (IRE)   14 ch.g. Saher – Moon Away (Mount Hagen (FR)) [2003/4   **c– x**
c23f³ c23m³ c25m⁴ c23gᵖᵘ Dec 5] fair pointer: showed nothing on return to steeplechasing: poor jumper. *P. R. Rodford*

WESTERN (IRE)   4 ch.g. Gone West (USA) – Madame Est Sortie (FR) (Longleat   **h–**
(USA)) [2003/4 16sᵖᵘ Mar 20] fairly useful on Flat (stays 2m): prominent to sixth in
juvenile at Ascot on hurdling debut. *J. Akehurst*

WESTERNMOST   6 b.g. Most Welcome – Dakota Girl (Northern State (USA))   **h92**
[2003/4 h103: 16g 17d 16s⁵ 23d 21v 16s* Apr 21] workmanlike gelding: modest
handicap hurdler: won at Perth in April: stays easy 21f: acts on heavy and good to firm
going: tried in cheekpieces. *M. Todhunter*

WESTERN RIDGE (FR)   7 b.g. Darshaan – Helvellyn (USA) (Gone West (USA))   **h105**
[2003/4 h72p: 16m² 20d⁵ 17m* 17g⁵ 17m* 16g* 17m² 16m⁴ 16f³ Oct 29] close-coupled
gelding: fair handicap hurdler: won at Newton Abbot in May and July and Stratford later
in July: best around 2m on good going or firmer: patiently ridden. *B. J. Llewellyn*

WESTERN VIEW (IRE)   12 br.g. Montelimar (USA) – Regency View (Royal High-   **c113**
way) [2003/4 c20d³ c24d* c20vᶠ c19d c24d⁵ c29sᵖᵘ Nov 29] compact gelding: fair   **h–**
handicap chaser: won at Clonmel in June: stays 25f: acts on heavy and good to firm going.
Cecil Ross, Ireland

WESTERTON (IRE)   11 b.g. Glacial Storm (USA) – Killiney Rose (Buckskin (FR))   **c92**
[2003/4 c92, h–: c25dᵖᵘ c25g* c20dᵖᵘ Feb 19] workmanlike gelding: fair hunter chaser: **h–**
won at Kelso in May: stays 25f: acts on heavy going: has been let down by jumping.
F. A. Hutsby

WESTFIELD JOHN   9 ch.g. Little Wolf – Moonbreaker (Twilight Alley) [2003/4   **c90**
c–, h–: c26f² c21dᵖᵘ Apr 12] big, workmanlike gelding: fair pointer/maiden hunter   **h–**
chaser: won 2 points in March: stays 3¼m: acts on firm going: blinkered final start.
J. M. Turner

WESTGATE RUN   7 b.m. Emperor Jones (USA) – Glowing Reference (Reference   **h91**
Point) [2003/4 h87: 16g³ 16g³ 16m² 16g² 16g Jul 3] leggy mare: modest hurdler: stays
21f: acts on good to firm going: sold 9,000 gns Doncaster August Sales. *R. A. Fahey*

WESTMEATH FLYER   9 b.g. Deploy – Re-Release (Baptism) [2003/4 16s⁵ 16sᶠ   **c–**
Jan 16] sturdy gelding: runner-up on completed start in novice chases: fair handicap   **h107**
hurdler: off nearly 2 years before reappearance: stays 2½m: raced on going softer than
good (acts on heavy): consistent. *N. G. Richards*

WESTMORLAND (IRE)   8 b.g. Phardante (FR) – Ticking Over (IRE) (Decent   **c–**
Fellow) [2003/4 h98+: c20dᶠ Mar 11] good-topped gelding: fair hurdler: off 22 months   **h–**
and better for race, towards rear when falling ninth in maiden at Carlisle on chasing
debut: will prove best at 3m. *R. MacLeod*

WESTON ROCK   5 b.g. Double Eclipse (IRE) – Mossberry Fair (Mossberry) [2003/4   **h96**
F74: F17m² F16g⁵ F16s³ 20s⁴ 16d⁵ 19g³ 24d Mar 10] angular gelding: fair form in   **F92**
bumpers: modest novice hurdler: will prove better around 3m than shorter: raced on good
going or softer over hurdles (ran well on good to firm in bumper). *T. D. Walford*

WEST PACES (IRE) 10 br.g. Lord Americo – Spanish Royale (Royal Buck) [2003/4 c94, h–: c25g⁴ c25m³ May 26] winning Irish pointer: modest maiden chaser: stays 25f: acts on good to firm ground: not a fluent jumper. *G. B. Balding* **c95**
h–

WEST PAL (IRE) 10 ch.g. Lancastrian – Buck And Roll (Buckskin (FR)) [2003/4 c26m* c24g² c26d² c26fᵖᵘ c25d⁶ c25g⁴ c24gᶠ Apr 18] workmanlike ex-Irish gelding: once-raced over hurdles: won point in 2003: won maiden at Southwell in July on return to steeplechasing: left R. York after fourth outing, no subsequent form: stays 3¼m: acts on good to firm and good to soft going. *Mrs S. J. Humphrey* **c85 §**
h–

WEST POINT 7 ch.g. Unfuwain (USA) – Western Reel (USA) (Gone West (USA)) [2003/4 F16d F17d 17d Dec 17] lengthy gelding: won bumper on debut in 2000/1: lightly raced and no form since, including on hurdling debut. *Mrs L. Williamson* **h–**
F–

WETHAAB (USA) 7 b.g. Pleasant Colony (USA) – Binntastic (USA) (Lyphard's Wish (FR)) [2003/4 16mᵖᵘ May 27] compact gelding: poor on Flat: no form over hurdles: tried in cheekpieces: tongue tied once. *Miss A. Stokell* **h–**

WET LIPS (AUS) 6 ch.g. Grand Lodge (USA) – Kissing (AUS) (Somalia (AUS)) [2003/4 17d³ 16dᶠ 16d² 20g² 16f* 16g³ Mar 7] leggy gelding: successful twice around 1m on Flat in Australia: fair hurdler: won handicap at Musselburgh in February: effective at 2m to 2½m: acts on firm and good to soft going: wore cheekpieces last 2 starts. *R. C. Guest* **h106**

WEXFORD (IRE) 10 ch.g. Be My Native (USA) – Mizuna (Ballymore) [2003/4 c25gᵖᵘ Apr 30] ex-Irish gelding: one-time modest maiden hurdler: sold out of N. Meade's stable 3,200 gns Doncaster May (2002) Sales: retains no ability: tried blinkered/in cheekpieces: has had tongue tied. *Miss S. K. Lamb* **c–**
h–

WHALEEF 6 b.g. Darshaan – Wilayif (USA) (Danzig (USA)) [2003/4 h–: 17m* 16g* 17g⁵ 17g* 16f 16g³ Nov 11] good-topped gelding: fair hurdler: won weakly-contested novices at Bangor and Perth in August and handicap at Bangor in October: will prove best around 2m: acts on good to firm going. *P. R. Webber* **h103**

WHATACHARLIE 10 b.g. Nicholas Bill – Zulu Dancer (Sula Bula) [2003/4 c–: 22m⁵ May 15] sturdy gelding: has reportedly been tubed: winning pointer, no form otherwise: has had tongue tied. *D. P. Keane* **c–**
h–

WHAT A FIDDLER (IRE) 11 ch.g. Orchestra – Crowenstown Miss (Over The River (FR)) [2003/4 c91, h–: c25dᵖᵘ c25g³ May 21] fair hunter chaser: stays 3¼m: acts on heavy going. *J. S. Haldane* **c88**
h–

WHAT A MONDAY 6 b.g. Beveled (USA) – Raise Memories (Skyliner) [2003/4 F92: F17d⁴ 16d Dec 29] lengthy, angular gelding: fair bumper winner: first start for 7 months, never-nearer seventh in novice at Newbury on hurdling debut: will probably do better. *K. Bell* **h101 p**
F92

WHAT A RACKET 5 b.m. Beveled (USA) – Bunny Gee (Last Tycoon) [2003/4 16g 16mᵖᵘ Nov 13] poor maiden on Flat at 3 yrs for D. ffrench Davis: no form in 2 races over hurdles, wearing headgear. *Mrs D. A. Hamer* **h–**

WHATAREYOUHAVING 8 b.g. Derrylin – Simple Mind (Decent Fellow) [2003/4 c–, h113: 20d 19d⁴ 22d⁴ Apr 12] leggy gelding: no show on chasing debut: fair handicap hurdler: stays 3m: raced on good going or softer (acts on heavy). *Henry De Bromhead, Ireland* **c–**
h112

WHATASHOCK 9 b.g. Never So Bold – Lady Electric (Electric) [2003/4 c–: c19s⁴ c21d⁴ c19m³ Apr 13] medium-sized gelding: won all 4 completed starts in points in 2002: poor form in novice chases: often folds tamely. *A. King* **c78**

WHATASUCKER (IRE) 10 ch.g. Meneval (USA) – Tuney Blade (Fine Blade (USA)) [2003/4 c24sᶠ 26g Feb 25] poor maiden pointer: tried in cheekpieces. *B. D. Leavy* **c–**
h–

WHATATOUCH (IRE) 7 b.g. Be My Native (USA) – Verbana (Space King) [2003/4 c25g² c24d* c25fᵖᵘ c29s⁵ c24s* c24d Dec 27] useful-looking gelding: has reportedly had wind operation: fair handicap chaser: won at Navan in May and December, making all when beating Golden Storm 4 lengths on second occasion: stays 25f: acts on heavy going: usually blinkered and tongue tied. *N. Meade, Ireland* **c113**
h–

WHAT A WONDER (IRE) 9 gr.g. Roselier (FR) – Lady Abednego VII (Damsire Unregistered) [2003/4 c83§, h102§: c28d⁴ c25vᶠ c27sᵖᵘ Dec 26] lengthy gelding: winning hurdler: poor maiden chaser, usually let down by jumping: should stay beyond 25f: acts on heavy and good to firm going: blinkered: temperamental. *Ferdy Murphy* **c– §**
h– §

WHATCHOWILLIE (IRE) 10 br.g. Un Desperado (FR) – Hooch (Warpath) [2003/4 c24m⁵ May 7] IR 10,000 4-y-o: ex-Irish gelding: fourth foal: dam maiden hurdler: **c82**
h–

winning hurdler: left Miss F. Crowley, successful in 2 points in 2003: little show in cheek-pieces: stays 3m: acts on good to firm and soft ground: blinkered once. *M. A. Kemp*

WHAT DO'IN (IRE) 6 b. or br.g. Good Thyne (USA) – Della Wee (IRE) (Fidel) **F96** [2003/4 F16g⁴ F16m⁴ Nov 16] €6,500 4-y-o: quite good-topped gelding: first foal: dam, bumper winner, sister to useful 2m hurdlers Helynsar and Eddie Wee: won maiden Irish point on debut in 2003: won bumper at Perth in good style, galloping on well to beat Emperor's Monarch 9 lengths: similar form when fourth to The Posh Paddy in listed event at Cheltenham (lost action) 2 months later. *N. A. Twiston-Davies*

WHATDO YOU WANT (IRE) 4 b.f. Spectrum (IRE) – Soviet Pretender (USA) **F–** (Alleged (USA)) [2003/4 F16s F17d Apr 18] tall filly: third foal: half-sister to fairly useful 2m hurdler Talking Tactics (by Bigstone): dam unraced daughter of useful 7f performer Russian Royal: well held in bumpers: tried tongue tied. *M. W. Easterby*

WHAT IF (IRE) 7 b.g. Lord Americo – Romany River (Over The River (FR)) [2003/4 **h99** 16m⁵ 16g² 16m⁴ 20d Nov 12] fourth foal: brother to useful hurdler/chaser Give Over, stays 29f, and bumper winner Call Kate: dam unraced half-sister to smart staying hurdler Miss Nero and useful chaser up to 2½m Dunkirk: won maiden point in 2002: third in 2 bumpers at Down Royal: modest form when in frame in novice hurdles: should stay at least 2½m: acts on good to firm going (bumper form on soft). *I. Buchanan, Ireland*

WHAT ODDS (IRE) 8 b.g. Torus – Merrywell (Mugatpura) [2003/4 c112p: c25g* **c122** c29s* c29g³ c28vᵖᵘ c33dᵖᵘ c28dᵖᵘ c29d Apr 12] strong gelding: fairly useful chaser: won hunter at Punchestown in April and handicap at Fairyhouse in November: lost form after next start, reported to be clinically abnormal sixth outing: should stay beyond 29f: acts on soft going: usually front runner. *T. K. Geraghty, Ireland*

WHAT'S A FILLY 4 b.f. Bob's Return (IRE) – Pearly-B (IRE) (Gunner B) [2003/4 **F–** F16s F16g Feb 18] 2,700 3-y-o: fifth foal: dam unraced, from family of outstanding 2m chaser Pearlyman: soundly beaten in 2 mares bumpers. *R. C. Guest*

WHATS GOOD (IRE) 6 b. or br.g. Religiously (USA) – Islet Time (Burslem) **F–** [2003/4 F17d F16d Mar 28] sturdy gelding: fifth foal: half-brother to 1m to 1¼m winner in Germany by Erins Isle: dam won up to 11f on Flat: tailed off in bumpers. *K. C. Bailey*

WHAT'S THE COUNT 8 gr.g. Theatrical Charmer – Yankee Silver (Yankee Gold) **c91** [2003/4 h98: 20m c20s³ c20g³ Apr 12] lengthy gelding: modest maiden hurdler: similar **h–** form both starts over fences: stays 2¾m: acts on heavy ground (seems unsuited by firmer than good): often tongue tied: free-going sort. *B. R. Johnson*

WHAT'S UP BOYS (IRE) 10 gr.g. Supreme Leader – Maryville Bick (Malacate **c123** (USA)) [2003/4 c–, h–: c25m⁴ c36dᵇᵈ c29mᵖᵘ Apr 24] leggy, lengthy gelding: high-class **h–** chaser in 2001/2: lightly raced since, well below best only completed start in 2003/4: stays 4½m: acts on good to firm and heavy going: effective blinkered or not: has gone in snatches: jumps none too fluently. *P. J. Hobbs*

WHAT YOU KNOW (IRE) 10 b.g. Be My Guest (USA) – Flamme d'Amour (Gift **h80 §** Card (FR)) [2003/4 h76§: 17g² 22g² 20gᵖᵘ 21f* 24g⁴ 24m⁶ Nov 24] angular gelding: poor hurdler: won minor event at Ludlow in October: stays 3m: acts on firm going: tried blinkered/visored: has had tongue tied: has been reluctant to race: not one to trust. *Mrs D. A. Hamer*

WHEREAREYOUNOW (IRE) 7 ch.g. Mister Lord (USA) – Angie's Delight **c133** (London Gazette) [2003/4 c132, h107: c20m* c24g* c21d³ c25d⁴ c21d* c21d c20g c21gᶠ **h–** c24s² Apr 21] workmanlike gelding: useful chaser: won novices in small fields at Strat-

Unicoin Homes Chase (Handicap), Cheltenham—Whereareyounow is clear of Spring Grove two out

ford in October and Cheltenham in November and quite valuable handicap at Cheltenham (by 7 lengths from Spring Grove) in January: effective at 2½m to 25f: very best efforts on going softer than good (acts on heavy): sound jumper: usually races prominently. *N. A. Twiston-Davies*

WHERE NOW (IRE) 8 b.g. Cataldi – Its A Honey (Raise You Ten) [2003/4 c16s⁵ c22sᵘʳ c20s⁴ c24d³ Apr 10] IR 10,000 4-y-o: tall gelding: sixth foal: half-brother to 2½m bumper winner Stillbyherself (by Le Bavard): dam unplaced in bumpers: winning hurdler: fairly useful chaser: won maiden at Punchestown in February: good fourth to Camden Tanner in novice there in March: stays 3m: acts on soft ground: tried blinkered. *J. Queally, Ireland* — c115 h–

WHERE'S TRIGGER 4 ch.g. Aristocracy – Queens Connection (Bay Express) [2003/4 F16m Apr 13] fifth foal: half-brother to modest 2m hurdler Queens Consul (by Kalaglow) and useful bumper winner/modest hurdler Bypharbeanri (by Phardante): dam ran 3 times at 2 yrs: ninth of 14 in conditional jockeys bumper at Chepstow on debut. *N. A. Twiston-Davies* — F–

WHETHER THE STORM (IRE) 8 b.g. Glacial Storm (USA) – Minimum Choice (IRE) (Miner's Lamp) [2003/4 c93, h–: c24d* c25g³ Apr 4] strong gelding: lightly raced: winning hurdler: left Miss H. Knight, won first of 2 starts in points and hunter chase at Bangor in March by short head from Heidi III: stays 3m: raced on good going or softer. *Miss I. E. Craig* — c92 h–

WHISPERED SECRET (GER) 5 b.g. Selkirk (USA) – Wells Whisper (FR) (Sadler's Wells (USA)) [2003/4 16d⁴ 17d³ 16dᵖᵘ 16g² Apr 18] rather leggy gelding: successful 3 times from 7f to 1¼m on Flat in Germany for P. Schiergen, including in 2003: left R. C. Guest, easily best effort over hurdles when ½-length second to Power Unit in novice handicap at Stratford: will prove best given test of speed around 2m: headstrong. *M. C. Pipe* — h115

WHISPERING HOLLY 5 b.g. Holly Buoy – Stuart's Gem (Meldrum) [2003/4 F–: F17g F17m F16g 16s 24s⁶ Apr 4] no sign of ability. *R. S. Wood* — h– F–

WHISPERING JOHN (IRE) 8 b.g. Grand Plaisir (IRE) – London Anne (London Bells (CAN)) [2003/4 c–, h104: c23g⁴ Dec 5] rangy gelding: fair form at best in novice hurdles: similar form when around 4 lengths fourth of 5 finishers in novice handicap at Exeter (finished lame) on completed start in steeplechases: stays 23f. *Ms Bridget Nicholls* — c101 h–

WHISPERING MOOR 5 br.g. Terimon – Larksmore (Royal Fountain) [2003/4 F16v⁶ F16s F16d⁴ Apr 23] third foal: brother to bumper winner Roman Ark: dam, modest chaser, stayed very well: easily best effort in bumpers when 23¼ lengths fourth of 16 to Eggmount at Perth. *N. W. Alexander* — F86

WHISPERING STORM (IRE) 6 br.g. Good Thyne (USA) – Ballybride Gale (IRE) (Strong Gale) [2003/4 F17s F16g⁵ Mar 25] 19,000 4-y-o: third foal: half-brother to fair hurdler/chaser up to 2¾m Dantie Boy (by Phardante): dam unraced: better effort in bumpers 11 months apart when 14¼ lengths fifth of 15 to Rubberdubber at Wincanton. *A. King* — F85

WHIST DRIVE 4 ch.g. First Trump – Fine Quill (Unfuwain (USA)) [2003/4 17d⁶ 16m³ 16d⁴ 18s³ 16s⁴ Mar 20] fair maiden on Flat (stays 1¾m), left J. Dunlop after final 3-y-o start: fair juvenile hurdler: will stay 2½m: acts on soft going, probably on good to firm. *Mrs N. Smith* — h100

WHISTLING SONG 9 ch.m. True Song – Sancal (Whistlefield) [2003/4 c–: c20s⁴ c19m³ May 26] lightly raced and little form over fences. *R. Dickin* — c–

WHITASIDE (IRE) 10 b. or br.g. Brush Aside (USA) – Flying Silver (Master Buck) [2003/4 h97: 20gᵖᵘ May 24] modest hurdler: reportedly lost shoe and his action only outing in 2003/4: likely to stay beyond 21f: sold 1,200 gns Doncaster May Sales. *Mrs S. J. Smith* — h–

WHITE DOVE (FR) 6 b.m. Beaudelaire (USA) – Hermine And Pearls (FR) (Shirley Heights) [2003/4 h65: 16d² c16d* c16g⁶ c20d⁶ Apr 24] poor maiden hurdler: similar form when winning handicap at Hereford on chasing debut in February: likely to prove best around 2m: acts on good to soft going. *Ian Williams* — c81 h80

WHITE PARK BAY (IRE) 4 b.f. Blues Traveller (IRE) – Valiant Friend (USA) (Shahrastani (USA)) [2003/4 17d Mar 27] modest maiden on Flat (stays 1½m): tailed off in mares claimer on hurdling debut. *J. Gallagher* — h–

WHITESTONE 8 b.m. Sula Bula – Flying Cherub (Osiris) [2003/4 21dᵖᵘ 21d 16mᵖᵘ Apr 13] no sign of ability: hung badly right on reappearance. *Mrs J. G. Retter* — h–

WHITFIELD WARRIOR 6 ch.g. Husyan (USA) – Valentines Day (Doctor **h–**
Pangloss) [2003/4 F92: 21v^{pu} 20d^{pu} 17d Apr 10] workmanlike gelding: fourth in bumper
on debut: no form in 3 novice hurdles. *J. R. Turner*

WHITFORD DON (IRE) 6 b.g. Accordion – Whitford Breeze (Le Bavard (FR)) **h109**
[2003/4 19d^{ur} 22s^2 24v^3 24g* Mar 6] well-made gelding: will make a chaser: fourth foal:
half-brother to winning Irish pointer by Over The River: dam Irish 2m hurdle winner:
improved form over hurdles when winning well-run novice at Newbury by neck from
Farnaheezview, staying on dourly to lead near finish: will stay long distances.
P. F. Nicholls

WHITLEY GRANGE BOY 11 b.g. Hubbly Bubbly (USA) – Choir (High Top) **c–**
[2003/4 c72?, h–: c25g May 24] tall gelding: winning hurdler: signs of only a little ability **h–**
over fences. *A. J. Lockwood*

WHITTON PARK 4 b.g. Sillery (USA) – Lady Golconda (FR) (Kendor (FR)) **h100**
[2003/4 16s 16d^{bd} 17s^4 Jan 20] ex-French gelding: third foal: half-brother to useful 5f to
7f winner Lady Vettori (by Vettori): dam never ran: successful twice up to 9f on Flat,
including in 2003, left F. Rohaut in August: running best race in 3 starts over hurdles
when brought down last in novice won by Grande Jete at Wincanton, disputing third at
time: will prove best with emphasis on speed at 2m. *P. F. Nicholls*

WHO CARES WINS 8 ch.g. Kris – Anne Bonny (Ajdal (USA)) [2003/4 h94: 21g^{pu} **h100**
22g^5 19d* 20d^2 22v^{pu} 20d^4 20s^3 23g^{pu} 16d^3 20s^2 Apr 17] sparely-made gelding: modest
handicap hurdler: won at Towcester (amateurs) in October: in-and-out form after: stays
2¾m: acts on soft and good to firm going: wore cheekpieces last 2 starts. *J. R. Jenkins*

WHO DARES WINS 11 b.g. Kala Shikari – Sarah's Venture (Averof) [2003/4 c88d, **c91**
h–: c25s^4 c27d^3 c27g^3 Apr 12] tall gelding: maiden hurdler: modest chaser, in frame in **h–**
hunters in 2003/4: dour stayer: acts on heavy going: tried blinkered/in cheekpieces.
Ms S. Duell

WHOSE LINE IS IT 6 gr.g. Sharp Deal – Madame Ruby (FR) (Homing) [2003/4 **h–**
F88: F16g 17g 24s Feb 3] angular gelding: modest form in bumpers: tailed off in 2 novice **F81**
hurdles. *N. J. Hawke*

WHY THE BIG PAWS 6 ch.m. Minster Son – Springdale Hall (USA) (Bates Motel **h–**
(USA)) [2003/4 17d^F Apr 18] fifth foal: dam winning 17f hurdler: fell first in novice
hurdle on debut. *R. C. Guest*

WHY THE LONG FACE (NZ) 7 ch.g. Grosvenor (NZ) – My Charm (NZ) (My **h105**
Friend Paul (USA)) [2003/4 21d 16v^5 21s* 20d 20g^5 17g^5 Apr 12] leggy gelding: won
1m maiden (at 6 yrs) from 20 starts on Flat in New Zealand: fair form over hurdles: won
novice at Sedgefield in November: stays 21f: acts on soft going. *R. C. Guest*

WIBBLEY WOBBLEY 12 b.g. Arctic Lord – Burrow Star (Four Burrow) [2003/4 **c77**
c24m^5 May 7] fair pointer: well held in 2 novice hunter chases. *T. Ellis*

WICHWAY NOW (IRE) 5 b.g. Norwich – Proverb's Way (Proverb) [2003/4 F16g^4 **F92**
F18g^3 Apr 22] lengthy, unfurnished gelding: seventh foal: half-brother to winning 2¾m
chaser Waydante (by Phardante): dam well beaten in points: fair form when in frame in
bumpers at Kempton and Fontwell. *Miss E. C. Lavelle*

WICKED WEASEL (IRE) 6 b.g. Religiously (USA) – Just A Maid (Rarity) [2003/4 **F99**
F17d* Dec 17] €41,000 4-y-o: lengthy gelding: fifth foal: half-brother to winning pointer
by Over The River: dam maiden: 40/1, won 17-runner bumper at Bangor on debut by 4
lengths from Looksharp Lad. *K. C. Bailey*

WIDEMOUTH BAY (IRE) 6 br.g. Be My Native (USA) – Lisaleen River (Over The **h112**
River (FR)) [2003/4 F117: 17g* 16d 21g^4 22g^6 Apr 18] lengthy, rather unfurnished
gelding: smart bumper performer: won at Exeter on reappearance in November, but disappointing overall in novice hurdles, running as if amiss last 2 outings: should stay at least
2½m. *P. J. Hobbs*

WIGMO PRINCESS 5 ch.m. Factual (USA) – Queen of Shannon (IRE) (Nordico **h56**
(USA)) [2003/4 17d 17s 16v 17g^4 16d^F Mar 21] poor on Flat (stays 9.4f), sold out of
A. Carroll's stable £2,100 Ascot October Sales: little form over hurdles. *S. C. Burrough*

WILBERFORCE 7 ch.g. Elegant Monarch – Eskimo Slave (New Member) [2003/4 **c–**
c19d^5 c23s^{pu} c25d^4 c25d^{pu} Mar 11] lengthy gelding: eighth foal: half-brother to winning pointer by Gold Dust: dam unraced half-sister to high-class chaser up to 3m Weather
The Storm: won first of 3 starts in points in 2002: showed little in 4 steeplechases.
N. J. Henderson

WILD ABOUT HARRY   7 ch.g. Romany Rye – Shylyn (Hay Chas) [2003/4 F91:   **h–**
 F16g 16s 20v 20s 22g^pu 22d Apr 5] workmanlike gelding: form only in bumper on debut.   **F–**
 A. R. Dicken

WILD CANE RIDGE (IRE)   5 gr.g. Roselier (FR) – Shuil Na Lee (IRE) (Phardante   **F113**
 (FR)) [2003/4 F17v* F16d* Apr 17] second foal: half-brother to fairly useful 2m hurdler
 River City (by Norwich): dam unraced, out of useful staying hurdler Gortnalee, from <br> excellent jumping family: made most promising start in bumpers, winning 11-runner <br> events at Carlisle in March and Ayr, useful form when beating Trisons Star 1½ lengths at <br> latter, always prominent and getting on top approaching final 1f: will stay at least 2½m: <br> sure to make an impact in novice hurdles in 2004/5. *L. Lungo*

WILD EDGAR (IRE)   7 ch.g. Invited (USA) – Ou La La (IRE) (Be My Native (USA))   **F–**
 [2003/4 F16g^su May 15] first foal: dam unraced, from family of Captain Christy: success-
 ful twice in points, in Irish maiden in 2002 and in 3-finisher event in February: rear when <br> slipped up in bumper. *Miss Lucinda V. Russell*

WILDFIELD RUFO (IRE)   9 b.g. Celio Rufo – Jersey Girl (Hardboy) [2003/4 c–,   **c100 x**
 h103: 25g* 21m^pu 24d* c24v^2 c31d^pu Apr 22] rangy gelding: fair hurdler: won 4-runner   **h113**
 intermediate at Wetherby in May and handicap at Newcastle (beat Great As Gold by short <br> head) in December: similar form over fences, but often let down by jumping and laboured <br> efforts last 2 starts: stays 25f: acts on heavy and good to firm going. *Mrs K. Walton*

WILD KNIGHT (IRE)   7 b.g. Jurado (USA) – Knight's Maid (Giolla Mear) [2003/4   **c108 x**
 h105, F94: c19g^3 c21m* c20g^pu c21d^ur c21m^ur c22g^pu c21m^3 Mar 11] medium-sized   **h–**
 gelding: fair chaser/maiden hurdler: won novice at Wincanton in December: stays easy
 21f: acts on good to firm going: takes strong hold: not a fluent jumper of fences: of <br> suspect temperament. *P. F. Nicholls*

WILD OATS   6 b.g. Primitive Rising (USA) – Miss Nosey Oats (Oats) [2003/4 F17s   **h96**
 F17m^6 19g* 24s^pu 21g 22s^pu 22g Apr 18] 12,000 4-y-o, resold €30,000 4-y-o: medium-   **F83**
 sized gelding: second foal: dam, modest staying hurdler, sister to Cheltenham Gold Cup <br> winner Master Oats: modest form on second of 2 starts in bumpers: won novice at Exeter <br> in November on hurdling debut: no form after in handicaps: should stay beyond 19f.
 P. J. Hobbs

WILD PASSION (GER)   4 b.g. Acatenango (GER) – White On Red (GER) (Konigs-   **h123 p**
 stuhl (GER)) [2003/4 16d^2 17g^F Mar 18] tall, leggy ex-German gelding: half-brother to <br> winning 2m hurdler Wild Power (by Turtle Island): useful on Flat (stays 1¾m), successful <br> twice from 7 starts at 3 yrs for R. Suerland: fairly useful form when ½-length second of
 10 to Power Elite in Grade 3 juvenile at Fairyhouse on hurdling debut: fell second in
 Triumph Hurdle at Cheltenham month later: sure to improve and win over hurdles.
 N. Meade, Ireland

WILD POWER (GER)   6 br.g. Turtle Island (IRE) – White On Red (GER) (Konigs-   **c–**
 stuhl (GER)) [2003/4 16m^4 16m^5 20m^6 16m^3 16m* 16g^6 17m^2 16g^5 Mar 25] ex-German   **h96**
 gelding: successful once over 9f from 13 starts on Flat: fourth of 7 on chasing debut and <br> in frame on 5 of 6 starts over hurdles in Germany: left C. Von Der Recke before reappear-
 ance: made nearly all when winning ladies handicap hurdle at Stratford in October: better <br> form last 2 starts, neck second to Imtihan in conditional jockeys handicap at Taunton on <br> first occasion, running on strongly under very tender handling having been left with <br> plenty to do: will prove best at 2m with emphasis on speed. *Ian Williams*

WILD ROMANCE (IRE)   9 b.g. Accordion – Mandy's Last (Krayyan) [2003/4   **h98**
 h110: 16m 16g^4 20m^4 23d^2 22d 20v^pu Feb 7] smallish gelding: modest handicap hurdler: <br> effective at 2m to 23f: acts on good to firm and heavy going: wore cheekpieces last 4 <br> starts: has run well when sweating. *D. J. Wintle*

WILD SPICE (IRE)   9 b.g. Mandalus – Curry Lunch (Pry) [2003/4 c107, h112: c26g^3   **c98**
 c23g^2 c26d^ur c32m^ro c26m^5 c23m* c26d* Aug 11] smallish gelding: winning hurdler: **h–**
 modest novice chaser: won weakly-contested events at Worcester (maiden, fortunate) and
 Southwell (several bad mistakes) in space of 10 days: stays 27f: best form on good going <br> or softer (acts on heavy): often let down by jumping. *Miss Venetia Williams*

WILD TIDE   5 b.m. Runnett – Polly Two (Reesh) [2003/4 F16d F16s Apr 12] second   **F–**
 foal: dam bad maiden hurdler: soundly beaten in 2 bumpers. *D. W. Thompson*

WILD WALTER (GER)   5 b.h. Leone (GER) – Welena (GER) (Nebos (GER))   **h83 +**
 [2003/4 16g^3 16d^4 22s^4 Dec 16] maiden on Flat: in frame all 3 starts over hurdles, tiring <br> badly after 2 out when fourth to Bohemian Boy in 2¾m maiden at Folkestone: joined
 S. Smrczek. *Frau A. Bertram, Germany*

WILFIE WILD 8 b.g. Nomadic Way (USA) – Wild Child (Grey Ghost) [2003/4 c–: c26g May 26] modest pointer: second start in hunter chases when seventh in maiden at Cartmel. *Mrs Lynne Ward*   **c76**

WILFRAM 7 b.g. Fraam – Ming Blue (Primo Dominie) [2003/4 h77: 20m⁶ 20m Aug 2] poor maiden hurdler: stays 2¾m: wears headgear: has failed to impress with attitude. *J. M. Bradley*   **h73**

WILL HE WISH 8 b.g. Winning Gallery – More To Life (Northern Tempest (USA)) [2003/4 16m⁶ May 5] useful on Flat, successful 5 times over 6f and 7f in 2003: well beaten both starts over hurdles, including in seller: tried tongue tied. *S. Gollings*   **h–**

WILLIAM LIONHEART 10 b.g. Henbit (USA) – Come To Tea (IRE) (Be My Guest (USA)) [2003/4 c65, h–: c23g⁶ c25g⁶ c18m May 26] sturdy gelding: little form outside points (won twice in April). *Mrs Jane Galpin*   **c–** **h–**

WILLIE JOHN DALY (IRE) 7 b.g. Mister Lord (USA) – Murphy's Lady (IRE) (Over The River (FR)) [2003/4 F100: 20s² 20d⁴ 22s² 24d² 24g³ 24m* 24gᶠ 27dᵖᵘ Apr 23] leggy gelding: winning Irish pointer: bumper winner: fairly useful novice hurdler: left D. Coffey after second start: won at Fontwell in January and Taunton (made all to beat Blue Business 10 lengths) in March: good efforts both outings in between, shaped as if amiss final one: should stay beyond 3m: acts on good to firm and heavy going: jumps none too fluently. *P. J. Hobbs*   **h119**

WILLIE MAKEIT (IRE) 14 b.g. Coquelin (USA) – Turbina (Tudor Melody) [2003/4 c–, h–: c21m⁴ May 21] rather sparely-made gelding: veteran hunter chaser, retains little ability: tried blinkered. *Mrs A. L. Tory*   **c67** **h–**

WILLIEMIND 4 b.g. Mind Games – No Exchange (Master Willie) [2003/4 16mᵖᵘ 16gᵖᵘ Nov 11] 2,600Y, resold 3,000Y: third foal: dam ran 3 times: pulled up in 2 juvenile hurdles. *Mrs Lucinda Featherstone*   **h–**

WILLIE THE FISH (IRE) 7 b.g. King's Ride – Bricon Lady (Proverb) [2003/4 25sᶠ 24dᶠ Mar 11] IR 18,500 3-y-o, IR 32,000 4-y-o: big gelding: seventh foal: brother to useful hurdler King of Kerry who stayed 3m: dam lightly raced in points: fell both starts over hurdles, though clear signs of ability in novice won by Chabrimal Minster at Carlisle on second occasion, keeping on in fourth when coming down 3 out. *J. M. Jefferson*   **h85**

WILL OF THE PEOPLE (IRE) 9 b.g. Supreme Leader – Another Partner (Le Bavard (FR)) [2003/4 20s² 21s 24d² 24d³ Mar 27] well-made gelding: lightly raced over hurdles, fair form when placed in handicaps in 2003/4: stays 3m: acts on soft going, probably on good to firm: races prominently. *M. C. Pipe*   **h113**

WILLOW RUN (NZ) 10 b.g. Conquistarose (USA) – Crazy Lady (NZ) (One Pound Sterling) [2003/4 h73§: 16m⁶ 16g 16gᶠ 19gᵖᵘ Jun 11] medium-sized gelding: poor hurdler: 4 lengths clear when fell last in conditional jockeys selling handicap at Perth: raced mainly around 2m: acts on soft and good to firm going: tried blinkered/in cheekpieces: has had tongue tied: unreliable. *B. Ellison*   **h73 §**

WILLOWS GATE 6 b.h. Petoski – Croix Val Mer (Deep Run) [2003/4 F16g⁵ Dec 6] third foal: dam poor novice hurdler: 4½ lengths fifth of 21 to The Muratti in bumper at Warwick on debut. *P. R. Webber*   **F89**

WILLOWS ROULETTE 12 b.g. High Season – Willows Casino (Olympic Casino) [2003/4 c21gᵖᵘ c23mᵖᵘ c23mᶠ c21dᵘʳ Aug 11] leggy gelding: poor handicap chaser in first half of 2001/2: sign of retaining ability: blinkered once. *A. G. Hobbs*   **c–** **h–**

WILL'SILLYSHANKERS 9 b.g. Silly Prices – Hannah's Song (Saintly Song) [2003/4 h–: c23fᵖᵘ c26s⁴ Jan 23] quite good-topped gelding: little sign of ability: tried visored. *Mrs E. B. Scott*   **c–** **h–**

WILL TELL 6 b.g. Rainbow Quest (USA) – Guillem (USA) (Nijinsky (CAN)) [2003/4 F93: F16m 17d³ Aug 11] tall gelding: fair form when fourth in bumper in 2002/3: shaped as if amiss after travelling strongly long way both starts since, remote third of 5 finishers in novice at Southwell on hurdling debut. *Mrs S. J. Smith*   **h–** **F–**

WILLY WILLY 11 ch.g. Master Willie – Monsoon (Royal Palace) [2003/4 c–, h80: c18m 20m c23mᵖᵘ 21mᵖᵘ Sep 27] tall, angular gelding: winning hurdler/chaser, no form in 2003/4: stays easy 21f: acts on firm going: blinkered final outing: free-going front runner: sold £1,000 Ascot October Sales. *G. Brown*   **c–** **h–**

WILLYWONT HE 5 b.g. Bollin William – Scalby Clipper (Sir Mago) [2003/4 F16m F17f³ F17m⁴ F17d⁶ Apr 18] fourth foal: dam lightly-raced daughter of useful hunter chaser Lady Annapurna: signs of ability in bumpers, possibly flattered. *P. T. Midgley*   **F79 ?**

WIMBLEDONIAN 5 b.m. Sir Harry Lewis (USA) – Ardent Love (IRE) (Ardross) [2003/4 F17m 20s⁴ 22d* Mar 3] first foal: dam, modest staying hurdler, sister to very smart but temperamental staying hurdler Burgoyne: favourite, tailed off in maiden bumper on debut: modest form in mares novice hurdles, won at Folkestone by 1½ lengths from Rakassa: will stay 3m. *R. T. Phillips* **h86 F—**

WIN ALOT 6 b.g. Aragon – Having Fun (Hard Fought) [2003/4 h76: 19m² 17f⁴ 17d⁵ 16s 19g⁶ 16s 19dᵇᵈ Jan 19] sturdy gelding: won on Flat in June: poor handicap hurdler, lost his form: probably stays 3m: acts on firm going, possibly not on softer than good: has hinted at temperament. *M. C. Chapman* **h84**

WINDFOLA 5 b.m. Sovereign Water (FR) – Sainte Martine (Martinmas) [2003/4 F68: F17g 19f⁵ 20s⁴ 16vᵖᵘ 16s 21s⁵ 19g⁶ 25dᵖᵘ Mar 22] leggy mare: poor in bumpers and over hurdles: tried blinkered. *R. D. E. Woodhouse* **h69 F—**

WINDHUND (GER) 4 ch.g. Surako (GER) – Windblume (GER) (Nebos (GER)) [2003/4 16sᵖᵘ Jan 14] tall gelding: unplaced in 3 races up to around 11f on Flat in Germany for U. Suter: showed little on hurdling debut. *C. Von Der Recke, Germany* **h—**

WINDING RIVER (IRE) 7 b.g. Montelimar (USA) – Bellora (IRE) (Over The River (FR)) [2003/4 25s³ c24s⁴ Jan 21] tall, useful-looking gelding: second foal: dam unraced sister to useful chaser up to 3m Sullane River and half-sister to dam of smart hurdler up to 2½m Davenport Milenium: won maiden on last of 3 starts in Irish points in 2003: bought 70,000 gns Doncaster May Sales: favourite, some promise when in frame in maiden hurdle won by Torche at Wetherby and novice chase won by Harrycone Lewis at Fakenham: should do better, though likely to need galloping track. *C. R. Egerton* **c93 p h95 p**

WINDROSS 12 b.g. Ardross – Dans Le Vent (Pollerton) [2003/4 c–, h–: c24sᵖᵘ c24d* c25g c26g⁵ c24dᵖᵘ c21g Apr 2] rangy gelding: fairly useful handicap chaser on his day: won at Stratford in May: stays 25f: acts on soft and good to firm going: usually waited with: inconsistent. *A. King* **c123 h—**

WINDSOR BEAUTY (IRE) 6 b. or br.g. Woods of Windsor (USA) – Tumble Dale (Tumble Wind) [2003/4 16g 22dᵖᵘ Jan 1] workmanlike gelding: little form over hurdles. *R. Rowe* **h—**

WINDSOR BOY (IRE) 7 b.g. Mtoto – Fragrant Belle (USA) (Al Nasr (FR)) [2003/4 16g 17s* 16g 16m⁴ 16m⁴ 16m⁵ Nov 8] fair on Flat (stays 1¾m) in 2003, won in June: fairly useful handicap hurdler: won at Killarney in July and Galway (8-runner listed event, beat Swordplay 2 lengths) in October: best around 2m: acts on soft and good to firm going. *E. J. O'Grady, Ireland* **h117**

WINGED ANGEL 7 ch.g. Prince Sabo – Silky Heights (IRE) (Head For Heights) [2003/4 h95: 17sᵖᵘ 16v 17sᵖᵘ Feb 10] modest hurdler at best, difficult to keep sound: better at 2½m than shorter: acts on good to soft going: held up. *L. Lungo* **h—**

WINGED HUSSAR 11 b.g. In The Wings – Akila (FR) (Top Ville) [2003/4 c94§, h101§: c21s² c20s* c21d³ Nov 15] lengthy gelding: fair maiden hurdler: similar form over fences, won weak novice handicap at Bangor in May: stays 2½m: raced on good going or softer (acts on soft): ungenuine. *D. R. Gandolfo* **c99 § h– §**

WINGED LADY (GER) 5 b.m. Winged Love (IRE) – Wonderful Lady (GER) (Surumu (GER)) [2003/4 h–: 16mᶠ 16m 16m⁴ 16g 21g⁴ Feb 25] little form over hurdles. *A. G. Juckes* **h66**

WINGS OF HOPE (IRE) 8 b.g. Treasure Hunter – She's Got Wings (Bulldozer) [2003/4 h87§: 20m 22mᵇᵈ 20gᵖᵘ Aug 23] close-coupled, quite good-topped gelding: winning hurdler, has lost his way: tried blinkered: irresolute. *C. J. Hemsley* **h– §**

WINNIE THE POOH 10 br.g. Landyap (USA) – Moorland Nell (Neltino) [2003/4 c–, h78: c16dᵖᵘ 19m⁴ Aug 25] maiden hurdler: no form in steeplechases (placed in maiden points in 2004): has worn cheekpieces. *J. D. Frost* **c— h—**

WINNIE WILD 7 b.m. Primitive Rising (USA) – Wild Child (Grey Ghost) [2003/4 25sᵖᵘ 21v⁶ 25gᵖᵘ Jan 24] lengthy mare: third foal: sister and half-sister to winning pointers: dam modest hunter chaser: no sign of ability in points or over hurdles. *Miss T. Jackson* **h—**

WINNING DREAM (IRE) 10 b.g. Hollow Hand – Lottosprite (IRE) (Sandalay) [2003/4 c126: 16d⁴ c20s³ Mar 27] strong gelding: useful chaser: ran well when placed behind Rathgar Beau in Grade 3 at Navan and Prince of Pleasure in valuable handicap at Punchestown month later: fair form when fourth in novice on hurdling debut, first start for over 10 months: effective around 2m and stays easy 29f: acts on soft going. *Oliver McKiernan, Ireland* **c134 h102**

WINNING LEADER (IRE)   8 b.g. Supreme Leader – Cromogue Lady (Golden **c–**
Love) [2003/4 c24g^{pu} Mar 12] strong gelding: brother to fair 2½m and 2¾m hurdle
winner Little Fencote and half-brother to winning pointer: dam, winning pointer, sister
to useful chaser up to 3m Gold Bearer and to dam of smart 2m chaser Golden Alpha:
won maiden Irish point in 2003: showed nothing in amateur chase at Sandown.
Miss L. Blackford

WINSLEY   6 gr.g. Sula Bula – Dissolve (Sharrood (USA)) [2003/4 F17g* F17d 21d* **h98**
21g³ 22d 24d⁴ 19g⁴ Apr 24] good-topped gelding: first foal: dam, winning hurdler who **F87**
stayed 2¾m, half-sister to useful filly up to 9f Karla Wyller: easily better effort in
bumpers (hung badly right only outing on left-handed course next time) when winning
5-runner event at Folkestone on debut in November: fair form over hurdles: won maiden
at Ludlow in January, despite drifting right: best effort when third of 18 to Rakalackey in
novice at same course: should stay beyond 21f: raced on good/good to soft going: wore
cheekpieces final start. *O. Sherwood*

WINSOME WINNIE   9 b.m. Teamster – G W Supermare (Rymer) [2003/4 24s^{pu} Jan **h–**
20] lightly-raced novice hurdler. *M. J. Weeden*

WINTER GALE (IRE)   12 b. or br.g. Strong Gale – Winter Fox (Martinmas) [2003/4 **c86**
c73, h–: c24m² c25d^{pu} May 22] lengthy gelding: fair hunter chaser, won point in April: **h–**
stays 25f: acts on good to firm and good to soft going: blinkered once in bumpers.
Mrs G. B. Walford

WINTER GARDEN   10 ch.g. Old Vic – Winter Queen (Welsh Pageant) [2003/4 c–, **c92 §**
h93: c16g³ c17m² c16g³ c16m² c20m² c16g² c17d^{F} c20s^{pu} 24g c16g c16g² c25g² c20d⁵
Apr 18] modest hurdler/novice chaser: stays 21f: acts on heavy and good to firm going:
tried blinkered, usually wears cheekpieces: has had tongue tied: difficult to win with.
Miss Lucinda V. Russell

WINTER MAN (IRE)   10 b.g. Aristocracy – Jane Eyre (Master Buck) [2003/4 c20g^{pu} **c–**
19g c16d Dec 17] tall ex-Irish gelding: fair hurdler at one time, no form since first start in **h–**
2002/3, including over fences: left C. McCarthy after reappearance: should stay at least
2½m: probably acts on heavy going: tried tongue tied. *J. Howard Johnson*

WINTER STAR   4 b.g. Overbury (IRE) – Pepper Star (IRE) (Salt Dome (USA)) **F–**
[2003/4 F16d F16d Apr 12] €30,000 3-y-o: leggy, unfurnished gelding: sixth foal: half-
brother to 1¼m winner Gunboat Diplomacy (by Mtoto): dam unraced half-sister to
Champion Hurdle winner Kribensis: well held in bumpers. *Miss Venetia Williams*

WINTERTIDE   8 b.g. Mtoto – Winter Queen (Welsh Pageant) [2003/4 h110: 20g* **h121**
20m⁴ 21f^{F} 22f* 25s⁴ 24g² 24m* Apr 15] angular gelding: fairly useful hurdler: won
maiden at Worcester in August, novice at Wincanton (5-runner event with plenty in hand)
in November and handicap at Cheltenham (beat Colourful Life 1¼ lengths) in April: stays
25f: unraced on heavy going, acts on any other: not a fluent jumper. *C. J. Mann*

WINTER WHISPER (IRE)   9 b.g. Jurado (USA) – Princess Annabelle (English **c84**
Prince) [2003/4 c84, h–: c20f³ May 10] medium-sized gelding: modest hunter chaser: **h–**
stays 2½m: acts on any ground: usually tongue tied. *Mrs S. E. Busby*

WIN THE TOSS   12 b.g. Idiot's Delight – Mayfield (USA) (Alleged (USA)) [2003/4 **c65**
c69, h–: c16d⁵ c20m⁶ 17g c20d^{pu} Feb 19] leggy, angular gelding: winning hurdle/novice **h–**
steeplechaser: modest pointer: best up to 2½m: acts on any going: tried blinkered: tongue
tied twice. *P. York*

WISEGUY (IRE)   5 b.g. Darshaan – Bibliotheque (USA) (Woodman (USA)) [2003/4 **h94**
16g 17d^{F} 20s^{pu} Apr 21] fairly useful maiden on Flat (stays 1½m), sold out of
M. Tregoning's stable 75,000 gns Newmarket Autumn Sales: running best race in 3 starts
over hurdles when falling 2 out in novice at Carlisle, in front and looking likely winner at
time: failed to stay next time: free-going sort. *J. Howard Johnson*

WISE KING   14 b.g. Rakaposhi King – Sunwise (Roi Soleil) [2003/4 c115, h–: c24d⁴ **c110**
c26d⁴ c20m² c20m^{F} Dec 27] lengthy gelding: fair handicap chaser: stays 3m: acts on soft **h–**
and good to firm going. *J. A. B. Old*

WISE MAN (IRE)   9 ch.g. Mister Lord (USA) – Ballinlonig Star (Black Minstrel) **c126**
[2003/4 c–, h100: c21s* c25v* c25s* c22g^{pu} c20v* c25d^{pu} Apr 17] modest maiden hur- **h–**
dler: fairly useful chaser: much improved in 2003/4, winning maiden at Ayr (fortunate) in
December, novice at Kelso and handicap at Ayr in February and novice at Carlisle in
March: ran as if amiss both other starts: stays 25f: yet to race on firm going, acts on any
other: has had tongue tied. *N. W. Alexander*

WISE REFLECTION (IRE)   10 b.g. Detroit Sam (FR) – Hester Ann (Proverb) **c–**
[2003/4 c24g^{pu} Nov 2] tall, leggy gelding: fair hurdler/novice chaser in 2001/2 for **h–**
A. King: only start since, in second when pulled up lame after 3 out in novice handicap
chase at Huntingdon: stays 3m: acts on good to firm and good to soft going (possibly not
softer): tried tongue tied. *N. J. Gifford*

WISE TALE   5 b.g. Nashwan (USA) – Wilayif (USA) (Danzig (USA)) [2003/4 h74: **h84 §**
17m^4 22m 16f^4 17m 17m^2 16m Oct 23] sturdy gelding: fair but inconsistent maiden up to
1¾m on Flat: poor maiden hurdler, just as in and out: raced mainly around 2m: acts on
firm going: often visored: has failed to impress with attitude. *P. D. Niven*

WISHFUL VALENTINE   8 ch.g. Riverwise (USA) – Wishful Dream (Crawter) **h70**
[2003/4 h–: 16m^6 May 9] sturdy, plain gelding: first form over hurdles when sixth of 14
in novice at Wincanton. *C. W. Mitchell*

WITCH'S BREW   7 b.m. Simply Great (FR) – New Broom (IRE) (Brush Aside **h94**
(USA)) [2003/4 h94: 19d 16g^3 16s^{pu} 16g Feb 18] lengthy mare: modest handicap hurdler:
stays 2½m: acts on heavy going. *T. D. Easterby*

WITH A DASH   6 ch.g. Afzal – Oh So Ripe (Deep Run) [2003/4 F–: 21g 25d^{pu} Mar **h–**
14] workmanlike gelding: no form in bumper or novice hurdles. *N. A. Twiston-Davies*

WITHOUT A DOUBT   5 b.g. Singspiel (IRE) – El Rabab (USA) (Roberto (USA)) **F101**
[2003/4 F89: F16m^2 F16d^6 F17d Apr 3] leggy gelding: placed twice from 5 starts in
bumpers: better form when around 9 lengths eighth of 15 to Diamond Sal in Grade 2 at
Aintree. *M. Pitman*

WITHOUT PRETENSE (USA)   6 b.g. St Jovite (USA) – Spark of Success (USA) **h–**
(Topsider (USA)) [2003/4 h63: 17d 17s^{pu} 22g^{pu} Apr 18] little form over hurdles.
N. G. Ayliffe

WITHOUT WORDS   6 ch.m. Lion Cavern (USA) – Sans Escale (USA) (Diesis) **h–**
[2003/4 16v^6 16m^{pu} Jun 1] modest maiden on Flat (barely stays 1¼m): no show in 2
novice hurdles: sold 1,000 gns Doncaster November Sales. *W. M. Brisbourne*

WITHTHELADS (IRE)   6 b.g. Tidaro (USA) – Quayside Charm (Quayside) [2003/4 **h91**
F16m^4 F16d^2 24s^{pu} 20s 18s^6 21d^4 22d^5 21g* Apr 12] leggy, angular gelding: brother to **F85**
poor staying chaser Deel Quay and half-brother to bumper winner by Salluceva: dam
bumper winner: won maiden on last of 3 starts in Irish points in 2003: bought 8,000 gns
Doncaster May Sales: in frame in 2 bumpers: modest hurdler: blinkered, won handicap at
Plumpton: should stay beyond 21f: acts on good to soft going (bumper form on good to
firm). *L. Wells*

WITNESS TIME (IRE)   8 b.g. Witness Box (USA) – Lisnacoilla (Beau Chapeau) **c–**
[2003/4 h93: 24s^{pu} c19d^{pu} c26s^{pu} Jan 23] strong, workmanlike gelding: winning hurdler: **h–**
no form in 2003/4, including over fences: suited by 3m+: acts on heavy going.
B. J. Eckley

WITNEY O'GRADY (IRE)   11 ch.g. Ring of Ford – C B M Girl (Diamonds Are **c–**
Trump (USA)) [2003/4 h–: c21g^{pu} Jun 12] strong, lengthy gelding: little show outside **h–**
points. *Miss L. V. Davis*

WITTERING   5 b.m. Keen – Club Elite (Salse (USA)) [2003/4 F16s F17g^{pu} Apr 1] **F–**
first foal: dam staying maiden: showed nothing in 2 bumpers. *J. G. M. O'Shea*

WIZARD OF EDGE   4 b.g. Wizard King – Forever Shineing (Glint of Gold) [2003/4 **h88**
16s 16g 16d^4 Mar 21] workmanlike gelding: half-brother to winning 2m hurdler Treasure
Trail (by Millkom): fair maiden on Flat (should stay 1¼m+): modest form in juvenile
hurdles, around 22 lengths fourth to De Blanc at Stratford. *G. B. Balding*

WIZARD OF THE WEST   4 b.g. Wizard King – Rose Burton (Lucky Wednesday) **h–**
[2003/4 16g^F 16g 18s^{pu} Jan 26] medium-sized gelding: fair maiden at best on Flat (stays
9.4f): no form in juvenile hurdles. *Miss S. West*

WIZARD O' WASS   6 ch.g. Imp Society (USA) – Sabeel (Local Suitor (USA)) **h–**
[2003/4 F–: 16d^{pu} 16d 18s Jan 16] workmanlike gelding: no form: tried visored.
J. R. Turner

WIZARDTREE   5 ch.g. Presidium – Snow Tree (Welsh Pageant) [2003/4 F–: F16g^{pu} **F–**
May 2] plain gelding: no show in 2 bumpers. *R. S. Brookhouse*

WOMAN   6 b.m. Homo Sapien – La Princesse (Le Bavard (FR)) [2003/4 F–: F17m^6 **h–**
17g^{pu} 16m^F 19g^{ur} 19s^6 18g^{pu} Apr 22] leggy mare: of little account. *H. J. Manners* **F–**

WONDER BROOK 4 b.f. Alderbrook – Wordy's Wonder (Welsh Captain) [2003/4   **F—**
F16g⁶ F16s Apr 12] first foal: dam, modest hurdler, stayed 2½m: tailed off in bumpers.
Mrs C. A. Dunnett

WONDERFUL MAN 8 ch.g. Magical Wonder (USA) – Gleeful (Sayf El Arab (USA))   **c—**
[2003/4 h80: 16d c17mᵘʳ 16g⁵ 17m 16m⁶ Aug 9] good-topped gelding: maiden hurdler,   **h—**
no form in 2003/4: unseated sixth on chasing debut: raced around 2m: acts on good to
firm and good to soft going: tried in cheekpieces. *R. D. E. Woodhouse*

WONDERFUL REMARK 8 b.m. Golden Heights – Queen of Dreams (Ti King   **c— §**
(FR)) [2003/4 h–§, F–: 20mᵖᵘ 19gᵖᵘ 17m c17dᵖᵘ Aug 11] of little account and tempera-   **h— §**
mental to boot: tried in blinkers/cheekpieces. *P. T. Dalton*

WONDER WEASEL (IRE) 11 b.g. Lancastrian – The She Weasel (Gulf Pearl)   **c116**
[2003/4 c136, h–: 21g⁵ c27dᶠ c29dᵖᵘ c25vᵖᵘ c24s c29d³ c32g c36dᵖᵘ Apr 3] sturdy geld-   **h—**
ing: useful handicap chaser at best: disappointing in 2003/4: twice-raced over hurdles,
well held in handicap on reappearance: stays 3½m: acts on heavy and good to firm going:
usually wears headgear: sold 12,500 gns Doncaster May Sales. *K. C. Bailey*

WONDER WINGS 7 ch.g. Lir – Ginger Wings (Ginger Boy) [2003/4 F74: F16m   **h—**
20m Jun 7] poor form on first of 2 starts in bumpers: last of 9 finishers in maiden on   **F—**
hurdling debut. *G. L. Moore*

WONTCOSTALOTBUT 10 b.m. Nicholas Bill – Brave Maiden (Three Legs)   **c—**
[2003/4 c101, h109: 26g² 27g⁵ 25g³ c30sᵖᵘ 24d c25sᵖᵘ Dec 20] smallish mare: fair   **h104**
hurdler/chaser: back in cheekpieces, in front when going lame final outing: should stay
beyond 3¼m: acts on good to firm and heavy going: tried visored. *B. De Haan*

WON TOO PHAR (IRE) 8 b.g. Phardante (FR) – Townandcountrygirl (Buckskin   **c—**
(FR)) [2003/4 21g⁴ c24mᵖᵘ c20s⁶ Dec 3] third foal: dam ran twice: failed to complete in 2   **h—**
Irish points in 2002: no show in novice hurdle or steeplechases. *G. L. Moore*

WOOD BE KING 5 b.h. Prince Sabo – Sylvan Dancer (IRE) (Dancing Dissident   **h—**
(USA)) [2003/4 16mᵖᵘ May 10] of no account on Flat: no show on hurdling debut.
A. P. James

WOOD COLONY (USA) 6 b.g. Woodman (USA) – Promenade Colony (USA)   **h—**
(Pleasant Colony (USA)) [2003/4 16d Nov 27] rather leggy gelding: lightly raced on Flat,
best effort on debut at 3 yrs: looked unwilling on hurdling debut. *M. F. Harris*

WOODLANDS BEAU (IRE) 12 b.g. Beau Sher – Never Intended (Sayyaf) [2003/4   **c98 x**
c85x: c33d² c25m³ c31f² c26dᶠ Mar 18] workmanlike gelding: modest chaser: stays 31f:
acts on any going: usually blinkered/visored: sketchy jumper. *Mrs S. Alner*

WOODLANDS GENPOWER (IRE) 6 gr.g. Roselier (FR) – Cherished Princess   **F111**
(IRE) (Kemal (FR)) [2003/4 F17d* F16d* F16s³ F16s³ F16g Mar 17] quite good-topped
gelding: third foal: dam, winning Irish pointer, half-sister to fairly useful staying chaser
Cherry Field: useful in bumpers: made all at Newton Abbot in June and Chepstow in
November: better form when third to Noplanofaction in Grade 2 at Chepstow and Royal
Paradise in 21-runner event at Sandown: well held in Champion Bumper at Cheltenham:
will be well suited by 2½m+ over jumps. *P. A. Pritchard*

WOODLANDS LASS 8 ch.m. Nearly A Hand – Maranzi (Jimmy Reppin) [2003/4   **h—**
21s⁴ 25sᶠ 20dᵖᵘ 24gᵖᵘ Apr 1] smallish mare: no form: has had tongue tied. *P. A. Pritchard*

WOODLAND WARRIOR 7 b.g. Lyphento (USA) – Dutch Majesty (Homing)   **h—**
[2003/4 24g Apr 1] little form over hurdles: fell in 3 points in 2004: tried visored.
C. Roberts

WOOD STREET (IRE) 5 b.g. Eagle Eyed (USA) – San-Catrinia (IRE) (Knesset   **h82**
(USA)) [2003/4 16m 16m 16m² 16dᵖᵘ 17d 17gᵖᵘ Apr 10] fair on Flat (stays 8.5f) at 3 yrs:
poor novice hurdler: sold out of Mrs A. Bowlby's stable £5,600 Ascot July Sales after
second start: best given test of speed at 2m: pulls hard. *R. J. Baker*

WOODYBETHEONE 4 b.g. Wolfhound (USA) – Princesse Zelda (FR) (Defensive   **h98**
Play (USA)) [2003/4 17m³ 18f² 18mᵖᵘ Sep 23] disappointing maiden on Flat for
R. Hannon: placed in juvenile hurdles at Bangor and Fontwell, helping force good pace
when 5 lengths second of 7 to Analogy at latter: in cheekpieces, clear when swerved
markedly right and pulled up lame run-in in similar event back at Fontwell. *O. Sherwood*

WORD GETS AROUND (IRE) 6 b.g. King's Ride – Kate Fisher (IRE) (Over The   **F95**
River (FR)) [2003/4 F16m³ F16s⁴ F16g* F16d* Feb 8] €36,000 4-y-o: has scope: first
foal: half-brother to winning pointer by Anshan: dam, bumper winner, out of useful
hurdler around 2m Private Dancer: fair form in bumpers: won conditional jockeys event

at Catterick in January and 15-runner contest at Musselburgh, always to fore in slowly-run race at latter and joined line by Somewin. *L. Lungo*

WORDS AND DEEDS (USA)   5 ch.g. Shadeed (USA) – Millfit (USA) (Blushing Groom (FR)) [2003/4 16g² 16g⁵ Jul 3] half-brother to one-time fair hurdler/winning chaser Quiet Millfit (by Quiet American), stays 3m: modest maiden on Flat (stays 1½m): better effort in novice hurdles at Perth when 5 lengths second of 7 to Allude. *R. A. Fahey*   **h87**

WORKAWAY   8 b.g. Alflora (IRE) – Annicombe Run (Deep Run) [2003/4 h86: c16gᶠ c17d* c16gᵖᵘ 20d⁴ c16gᵖᵘ c20f³ c17gᵖᵘ Apr 5] modest handicap hurdler: easily best effort over fences when winning novice handicap at Kelso in December: stays 2½m: acts on good to firm and heavy going: free-going sort: has broken blood vessels. *A. Parker*   **c96**
h86

WORKING GIRL   7 b.m. Morpeth – Workamiracle (Teamwork) [2003/4 h60, F–: 22mᵖᵘ 19v 17s³ Mar 23] poor maiden hurdler: stays 19f. *J. D. Frost*   **h72**

WORLABY DALE   8 b.g. Terimon – Restandbethankful (Random Shot) [2003/4 16s⁴ 17d⁴ 20dᶠ Mar 22] modest staying maiden on Flat: modest form in novice company over hurdles: likely to prove best at 2½m than shorter. *Mrs S. Lamyman*   **h93**

WORLD VISION (IRE)   7 ch.g. Denel (FR) – Dusty Lane (IRE) (Electric) [2003/4 h–, F90: 24m⁴ 24d* 24g³ 22s 27s³ 27d⁴ Mar 30] big, leggy gelding: fell in maiden Irish point in 2002: modest hurdler: won 4-runner novice at Newcastle in November: stays 27f: acts on soft and good to firm going: wore cheekpieces last 2 starts: has finished weakly. *Ferdy Murphy*   **h92**

WORLD WIDE WEB (IRE)   8 b.g. Be My Native (USA) – Meldrum Lass (Buckskin (FR)) [2003/4 c99, h123+: c20s* c19d² c24d* c28mᵖᵘ Feb 28]   **c128**
h–

Best Mate was not the only British-trained chaser to bring back a good prize from Leopardstown's Christmas meeting. On the eve of Best Mate's win in the Ericsson Chase, World Wide Web won only a marginally less valuable prize in the Paddy Power Handicap. Second in value among Ireland's handicap chases to the Irish National, the Paddy Power was worth nearly £68,000 to the winner, a good sum by any standards, but particularly for a horse who was running off a Turf Club mark of just 111. With other options around Christmas time in both Britain and Ireland for the top chasers, the Paddy Power is framed specifically for those who are not much better than useful handicappers, with a rating limit of 140. Coupled with the prize money on offer, a large and competitive field for the race is virtually always assured, never more so than for the latest running when twenty-eight went to post. Five British-trained runners took part—all of them trained by Jonjo O'Neill. World Wide Web was joined by stable-companions Dark Room, Creon, Canon Barney and Ballylusky, all bar the last-named, like World Wide Web, carrying the colours of J. P. McManus. McManus was additionally represented by Irish-trained Take Five and Farinel. The weights were headed by Timbera, making his first appearance since winning the Irish National in the spring, and the Hennessy Gold Cup also-ran The Premier Cat. World Wide Web, on the other hand, had just 10-1 and was the subject of strong support, going off the 8/1 favourite, ahead of Ballylusky and the 2001 winner I Can Imagine on 9/1.

The 'McManus six' were reduced to five when Take Five was one of the early casualties, along with Ballylusky. For most of the race, a winner in the green and orange hoops looked unlikely, with none of the McManus team in a prominent role. That included World Wide Web, off the bridle before halfway and still well down the field with a mile to run. However, the favourite got going in the latter stages and, challenging after two out, soon led before going right away on the run-in with only a loose horse for company. The recent Punchestown winner Kymandjen was nine lengths back in second, just ahead of Satcoslam, runner-up the year before. Jonjo O'Neill's two other finishers, Creon and Dark Room, came well down the field. World Wide Web was the second British-trained winner of the Paddy Power after the Paul Nicholls-trained Calling Wild in 1998.

The Paddy Power Handicap provided World Wide Web with his second win at Leopardstown's Christmas meeting. Three years earlier he won a bumper there when trained in Ireland by John Mulhern. He was an improved performer over hurdles in 2002/3, his first season with Jonjo O'Neill, but finished last on two of his three outings over fences, albeit shaping rather better than the result suggested each time. Although still a novice, World Wide Web was put straight into handicap

Paddy Power Handicap Chase, Leopardstown—World Wide Web leads Kymandjem over the last

company on his return in the latest season, winning at Huntingdon with a much more assured display of jumping than he had given on his final start the previous season. He then came up against another unexposed type when second to Lord Maizey at Chepstow. The Welsh National had been World Wide Web's next intended outing but, when it became apparent that he would not get into the handicap proper, he was rerouted to Leopardstown. World Wide Web ran only once after the Paddy Power Handicap, starting joint favourite for the even more valuable Red Square Vodka Gold Cup at Haydock off a mark 15 lb higher. He was never going well under the firmer conditions, and was pulled up after completely losing his place, reportedly returning distressed.

World Wide Web comes from a better family than the racing and breeding records of his immediate relatives would suggest. His dam was unraced and the next two dams 'ran a few times over hurdles' as the sales catalogues put it. However, his great grandam Icydora (who in fact ran over fences as well) was a sister to the useful staying chaser Glenkiln and the 1969 Irish National winner Sweet Dreams, herself dam of the Sun Alliance Chase second Sweet September and grandam of the Grand National runner-up Romany King. Among other noteworthy family members are the Irish National runner-up Seskin Bridge, the smart chasers Credo's Daughter and Comeragh King and the Tote Gold Trophy winner King Credo. World Wide Web, an IR 7,800-guinea yearling, is a brother to a winning pointer in Ireland and a half-brother to Meldrum Star (by Fourstars Allstar), a fair winner over hurdles in the latest season.

World Wide Web (IRE) (b.g. 1996)	Be My Native (USA) (br 1979)	Our Native (b or br 1970)	Exclusive Native
			Our Jackie
		Witchy Woman (ch 1972)	Strate Stuff
			Witchy Norma
	Meldrum Lass (b 1987)	Buckskin (b 1973)	Yelapa
			Bete A Bon Dieu
		Mervins (b 1974)	Foggy Bell
			Icydora

A tall, good sort, who has always looked the type to make a chaser, World Wide Web should prove suited by further than three miles. Lightly raced over fences and unexposed over long distances, there is a chance that the best is still to be seen of World Wide Web. He would need to improve just to stand a chance of making the field for the Grand National, and he could be a Welsh National type in the meantime. He has raced almost exclusively on soft or good to soft ground, though has yet to race on heavy. The Paddy Power was not the only race in which World Wide Web has looked not the most straightforward of rides; he left himself with a fair bit to do on his first two starts of the season as well. World Wide Web ran well on his only start in blinkers in Ireland earlier in his career and might benefit from being fitted with headgear again. *Jonjo O'Neill*

WORTHY MAN   7 b.g. Homo Sapien – Marnworth (Funny Man) [2003/4 F–: 16m   c–
17g⁵ Jun 13] rangy gelding: no form, including in points: sold £1,900 Ascot February   h–
Sales. *T. R. George*

WOTAN (FR)   5 ch.g. Beaudelaire (USA) – Woglinde (USA) (Sunny's Halo (CAN))   h–
[2003/4 16vᵖᵘ Nov 23] little form on Flat: showed nothing on hurdling debut: sold £2,500
Ascot February Sales. *Miss I. E. Craig*

WOT NO CASH   12 gr.g. Ballacashtal (CAN) – Madame Non (My Swanee) [2003/4   c74
c65, h–: c20f⁴ c19m⁴ c17m² c19m* c16m³ c18gᶠ c20gᶠ c19g⁶ c16d³ c17gᵖᵘ Apr 12]   h–
lengthy gelding: poor handicap chaser: won seller at Chepstow in October: stays 19f: acts
on soft and firm going: inconsistent. *R. C. Harper*

WOTSITOOYA (IRE)   12 b.g. Rashar (USA) – Droppey Loops (Over The River   c125
(FR)) [2003/4 c113, h106: c25d² c24gᵖᵘ c23g⁶ c22s c22d* c24mᵈ 22d³ c24d Nov 23]   h112
lengthy gelding: fair hurdler: fairly useful handicap chaser: won listed event at Galway in
September and Castlemartin Stud Pat Taaffe Handicap Chase at Punchestown (after 5
months off, beat Timbera 2½ lengths) in late-April: unlucky at Limerick sixth start (in
front when taking wrong course): stays 29f: acts on good to firm and heavy going: has
worn cheekpieces: easily best efforts going right-handed. *M. J. P. O'Brien, Ireland*

WOULDN'T YOU AGREE (IRE)   8 ch.g. Toulon – Mention of Money (Le Bavard   c110
(FR)) [2003/4 h122, F106: 20d c22d* c20f² c22s⁶ c16v* c16d⁶ c16sᶠ c16d Feb 20] tall   h–
ex-Irish gelding: fairly useful hurdler: fair chaser: won maiden at Tralee in June and, on
first start after leaving C. Roche, novice at Towcester in November: let down by jumping
and/or attitude last 2 outings: effective at testing 2m to 2¾m: probably acts on any going:
effective tongue tied or not. *Jonjo O'Neill*

WOULD YOU BELIEVE   8 gr.g. Derrylin – Ramelton (Precipice Wood) [2003/4   c112
c109: c22v² c26vᵘʳ c25sᶠ c22s³ Mar 24] fair maiden steeplechaser: let down by jumping
after reappearance, hung right final outing: stays 3m: raced on good going or softer (acts
on heavy). *K. C. Bailey*

WOZZECK   4 b.g. Groom Dancer (USA) – Opera Lover (IRE) (Sadler's Wells (USA))   h83
[2003/4 16dᶠ 17s 16s Feb 16] angular gelding: half-brother to fairly useful 2m hurdler
Diva (by Exit To Nowhere): fair maiden on Flat (stays 1¼m), sold out of J. Fanshawe's
stable 20,000 gns Newmarket Autumn Sales: signs of ability over hurdles only on
hurdling debut: jumped poorly in cheekpieces final start. *R. H. Buckler*

WRAGS TO RICHES (IRE)   7 b.g. Tremblant – Clonea Lady (IRE) (Lord Ha Ha)   h94
[2003/4 F101: F17g³ 17d⁵ 16v³ 18v² 20sᵖᵘ 22d 17s Apr 6] raced 4 times in bumpers, well   F83
below best on reappearance: modest novice hurdler: should stay at least 2½m: raced on
good going or softer (acts on heavy). *J. D. Frost*

WRANGEL (FR)   10 ch.g. Tropular – Swedish Princess (Manado) [2003/4 c–, h83:   c–
c17g⁴ 17m* 18gᵖᵘ 17s Dec 29] good-topped gelding: well held only completed start over   h79
fences: poor hurdler: won selling handicap at Southwell in October: raced mainly around
2m: acts on soft and good to firm going: wore cheekpieces final outing (well beaten).
B. J. Llewellyn

WREFORD LAKE   4 ch.g. Karinga Bay – Sporting Annie (Teamster) [2003/4 F17g   F–
Apr 10] first foal: dam, showed little over hurdles, half-sister to fairly useful staying
hurdler/chaser The Bakewell Boy: never a factor in maiden bumper on debut. *J. D. Frost*

WRENS ISLAND (IRE)   10 br.g. Yashgan – Tipiton (Balboa) [2003/4 c102: c24m   c100
c23m² c24g Jun 27] well-made gelding: fair handicap chaser: stays 3m: best efforts on
good to firm going: often a front runner: inconsistent. *R. Dickin*

WRONG IMPRESSION (IRE)   6 b.m. Executive Perk – Adare Boreen (Boreen   h–
(FR)) [2003/4 F16g 16fᶠ 16g Nov 15] small mare: sixth foal: half-sister to fair hurdler   F–
around 2m Mr Wong (by Be My Native): dam unraced half-sister to high-class staying
hurdler Pragada: well held in bumper on debut: always behind after whipping round at
start on completed outing over hurdles. *Miss Lucinda V. Russell*

WUCHOWSEN (IRE)   6 b.m. King's Ride – Our Sioux (IRE) (Jolly Jake (NZ))   F–
[2003/4 F17g F16d F16s Jan 21] lengthy mare: second foal: half-sister to bumper winner
Dewasentah (by Supreme Leader): dam unraced half-sister to useful hurdler/chaser up to
25f Kings Measure (by King's Ride): well held in mares bumpers. *J. M. Jefferson*

WUN CHAI (IRE)   5 b.g. King's Theatre (IRE) – Flower From Heaven (Baptism)   h91
[2003/4 h84: 17s⁴ 16m 19s² 19d 19g 19m⁴ 17s 19g* Apr 16] modest handicap hurdler:
left F. Jordan after reappearance: made virtually all when winning at Taunton: stays 19f:
acts on soft and good to firm ground: blinkered last 3 outings. *R. J. Baker*

WUXI VENTURE   9 b.g. Wolfhound (USA) – Push A Button (Bold Lad (IRE)) **c106**
[2003/4 h110: 17m c16g^{pu} c19g* c20g^2 c16s^5 c16d^4 c16d^6 c16d^{ur} Mar 22] small, sturdy **h–**
gelding: fair hurdler: similar form over fences, won maiden at Catterick in January: stays
easy 19f: acts on soft going: patiently ridden. *R. A. Fahey*

WYLDE WINTER (IRE)   6 b.g. Fourstars Allstar (USA) – Wintry Shower (Strong **h–**
Gale) [2003/4 16g 16d^{pu} 16s^{pu} 20f^{pu} 16g Mar 10] €16,000 4-y-o: sturdy ex-Irish gelding:
fourth foal: half-brother to 3 winners, including one-time useful chaser/winning hurdler
Somemanforoneman (by Asir), stays 3m, and fairly useful hurdler/chaser Woodenbridge
Natif (by Be My Guest), stays 25f: dam, winning chaser, sister to smart staying chaser
Wylde Hide: no sign of ability: sold out of T. Carberry's stable 1,800 gns Doncaster May
Sales after first start: tongue tied last 3 outings. *P. Spottiswood*

WYNBURY FLYER   9 ch.g. Risk Me (FR) – Woolcana (Some Hand) [2003/4 c–, h–: **c80**
c16d^3 c16g^2 c16s^2 c16s^6 c16g^5 c16s^{pu} Mar 20] workmanlike gelding: poor handicap **h–**
chaser: stays 2½m: acts on heavy going. *Ferdy Murphy*

WYN DIXIE (IRE)   5 b.g. Great Commotion (USA) – Duchess Affair (IRE) (Digamist **h93**
(USA)) [2003/4 16g^2 17g^3 16d^6 16d 17g Dec 31] sparely-made gelding: first foal: dam
runner-up around 2m over hurdles in Ireland: modest novice hurdler: will prove best at
2m with emphasis on speed: joined P. Monteith. *M. C. Pipe*

WYNYARD DANCER   10 b.m. Minster Son – The White Lion (Flying Tyke) [2003/4 **c–**
c80, h–: c21s^F May 2] modest pointer/winning hunter chaser: stays 3m: acts on good to **h–**
firm going: tried in cheekpieces. *Miss T. Jackson*

X

XAIPETE (IRE)   12 b.g. Jolly Jake (NZ) – Rolfete (USA) (Tom Rolfe) [2003/4 c116, **c116**
h94: 18g^3 c20m^3 c17g^5 c17g^3 20m* c20m 16g^3 20m^3 20g^4 c17m^F 16g* 17g^2 16f^3 c21m^4 **h104**
c20g^2 c22g^{ur} 19g^3 c21d^2 c21s^3 c21g^3 c20s^2 Apr 21] useful-looking gelding: fair hurdler/
chaser, rarely out of the frame: won over hurdles at Worcester (handicap) in July and
Perth (claimer) in September: stays 21f: acts on any going: held up: tough and consistent.
R. C. Guest

XELLANCE (IRE)   7 b.g. Be My Guest (USA) – Excellent Alibi (USA) (Exceller **h121**
(USA)) [2003/4 h88: 21m^4 20g 20m^2 22g^3 22m^2 20m^2 22g* 22g* 19m* 20m^2 24m^2 24f^2
21m* 20m^2 Apr 24] angular gelding: had excellent season and developed into fairly
useful hurdler: won 2 novices at Newton Abbot and handicap at Market Rasen in August

Mitie Group Handicap Hurdle, Cheltenham—Xellance heads Dangerously Good at the last

and handicap at Cheltenham in April: again ran well when length second to Korelo in quite valuable handicap at Sandown final outing: stays easy 3m: raced mainly on good going or firmer (acts on firm): tough and reliable. *P. J. Hobbs*

XENOPHON (IRE) 8 b.g. Toulon – Fureen (Furry Glen) [2003/4 h145p: c20s³ c17dᶠ c20s³ c21d⁵ c29dᶠ Apr 12] lengthy gelding: most progressive handicap hurdler in 2002/3, won Pierse Hurdle at Leopardstown and Coral Cup at Cheltenham: not fluent over fences, best effort when fifth of 9 to Pizarro in Grade 1 novice at Leopardstown: fell fatally in Irish Grand National: stayed 21f: acted on heavy going: usually waited with. *A. J. Martin, Ireland* — **c128 h–**

XIXITA 4 ch.f. Fleetwood (IRE) – Conquista (Aragon) [2003/4 16g 16d 19sᵖᵘ Apr 11] poor maiden on Flat (stays 1¾m): little show over hurdles, probably flattered second start. *Dr J. D. Scargill* — **h–**

XTRA 6 b.g. Sadler's Wells (USA) – Oriental Mystique (Kris) [2003/4 h89: 16dᵖᵘ Dec 19] angular gelding: smart at one time on Flat: third in novice on hurdling debut: pulled up early in Grade 2 at Ascot 11 months later: dead. *J. A. B. Old* — **h–**

XYPHOR SEEKER (IRE) 4 b.g. Moonax (IRE) – Vera Dodd (IRE) (Riot Helmet) [2003/4 F16g Mar 15] fourth foal: half-brother to bumper winner Ball O Malt (by Star Seeker): dam unraced: seventh of 16 in maiden bumper at Stratford on debut, patiently ridden and not knocked about. *R. H. Alner* — **F75**

Y

YAIYNA TANGO (FR) 9 br.g. Fijar Tango (FR) – Yaiyna (FR) (Lashkari) [2003/4 23d⁶ 19g⁵ 24sᵖᵘ Mar 20] useful-looking gelding: lightly-raced novice hurdler, fair form at best: no show in 2003/4 after 3-year absence: tried in cheekpieces. *R. Ford* — **h–**

YANKEE CROSSING (IRE) 6 b.g. Lord Americo – Ath Leathan (Royal Vulcan) [2003/4 F–: 20d Nov 22] close-coupled gelding: well beaten in 2 bumpers and novice hurdle. *Jonjo O'Neill* — **h–**

YANKEE JAMIE (IRE) 10 b.g. Strong Gale – Sparkling Opera (Orchestra) [2003/4 c114p, h101+: 24g⁵ 21v 24dᵖᵘ 22d⁶ 27dᵖᵘ Apr 23] lengthy, angular gelding: progressive over fences, successful 2 of 3 starts: modest handicap hurdler, not given hard time more than once in 2003/4: stays 25f: acts on soft going: reportedly suffers breathing problems. *L. Lungo* — **c– h97**

YANKIE LORD (IRE) 12 b.g. Lord Americo – Coolstuff (Over The River (FR)) [2003/4 c91x: c20s⁴ c20m³ c16m³ c17gᵘʳ c20g⁴ c24gᶠ Feb 18] rangy gelding: modest handicap chaser: effective at 2m to 3m: acts on good to firm and heavy going: usually races up with pace: error prone. *Mrs J. C. McGregor* — **c87 x**

YANN'S (FR) 8 b.g. Hellios (USA) – Listen Gyp (USA) (Advocator) [2003/4 c124, h102: c23g³ c20d⁶ c24s⁶ Apr 17] lengthy, angular gelding: fair hurdler: fairly useful chaser: below form in handicaps both starts after 11-month absence: stays 25f: acts on heavy going: tends to swish tail: usually sound jumper. *R. T. Phillips* — **c118 h–**

YARDBIRD (IRE) 5 b.g. Moonax (IRE) – Princess Lizzie (IRE) (Homo Sapien) [2003/4 F93: 17g⁴ 16d⁴ 20d² 21g⁵ 24g* 21g 22g* Apr 13] medium-sized gelding: fair novice hurdler: won at Ascot in February and Exeter in April, beating On Les Aura 3½ lengths with something in hand at latter: will prove best at 3m+: unraced on extremes of going. *Miss H. C. Knight* — **h115**

YASSAR (IRE) 9 b.g. Yashgan – Go Hunting (IRE) (Abednego) [2003/4 c24d² c20d 24vᵖᵘ c20d² Mar 19] ex-Irish gelding: second foal: dam unraced half-sister to dams of top-class staying chaser The Grey Monk and very smart staying chaser Grey Abbey: winning pointer: best effort in 4 steeplechases when second in maiden hunter at Navan: left P. Heffernan after next outing: prominent long way on hurdling debut: stays 3m. *D. J. Wintle* — **c89 h–**

YELLOW RIVER (IRE) 4 b.g. Sesaro (USA) – Amtico (Bairn (USA)) [2003/4 16sᵖᵘ 16gᵖᵘ Apr 18] modest on all-weather on Flat (stays 9.4f), no form on turf: no show either outing over hurdles: tried in cheekpieces. *R. Curtis* — **h–**

YELLOW SKY 6 b.m. Gildoran – Summer Sky (Skyliner) [2003/4 h–, F–: 16sᵖᵘ 16d 16sᵖᵘ 19gᵗʳ Mar 15] of no account and temperamental to boot: has had tongue tied. *K. G. Wingrove* — **h– §**

YELLOW SOIL STAR (IRE) 5 b.m. Perugino (USA) – Standing Ovation (Godswalk (USA)) [2003/4 16f 17g^6 16g 17g Aug 23] half-sister to useful 2m hurdler Crowded House and fair 2m hurdler/poor chaser Grand Applause (both by Mazaad): poor maiden on Flat: maiden hurdler, modest at best: well beaten in 2003/4, left V. Bowens after reappearance: raced around 2m: acts on good to firm and heavy ground: blinkered final outing. *J. J. Lambe, Ireland*　　h– §

YEOMAN'S POINT (IRE) 8 b.g. Sadler's Wells (USA) – Truly Bound (USA) (In Reality) [2003/4 h133: c16d^4 c20s* c19s^2 c21s^5 c24s^6 Feb 15] good-topped gelding: useful handicap hurdler: fairly useful form over fences, winning down at Navan in December: held in close third when bad mistake last in Grade 3 novice won by Emotional Moment at Leopardstown fourth start, also let down by jumping at Navan in February and Punchestown in late-April: stays 25f: acts on soft going: tried blinkered/in cheekpieces: has had tongue tied. *C. Roche, Ireland*　　c127 h–

YER 'UMBLE (IRE) 13 b.g. Lafontaine (USA) – Miners Girl (Miner's Lamp) [2003/4 c–, h–: c26g^{pu} May 18] stocky gelding: winning hurdler/chaser, retains little ability: tried blinkered/visored. *J. K. Cresswell*　　c– h–

YESYES (IRE) 9 b.g. Supreme Leader – Barton Bay (IRE) (Kambalda) [2003/4 c–, h96: 18d Apr 7] lightly raced: showed little in hunter chase on debut in 2002/3: form over hurdles only when winning novice later in season. *Miss E. C. Lavelle*　　c– h–

YOGI (IRE) 8 ch.g. Glacial Storm (USA) – Good Performance VII (Damsire Unregistered) [2003/4 h114: 20g 20s* 16d 24s^2 22s^2 24g^6 Mar 18] leggy gelding: useful hurdler: won handicap at Clonmel in November: generally ran well afterwards, much improved last 2 starts, second to Baracouda in valuable handicap at Sandown in February and sixth to Iris's Gift in Stayers' Hurdle at Cheltenham in March: ideally suited by 2½m+: acts on heavy going: below form all starts in blinkers: races prominently. *Thomas Foley, Ireland*　　h142

YORKIE 5 b.g. Aragon – Light The Way (Nicholas Bill) [2003/4 17g^{pu} Sep 30] half-brother to useful hurdler around 2m Benbyas (by Rambo Dancer): fair on Flat (stays 1m), sold to join P. Blockley 8,400 gns after successful in March: tongue tied, showed little in novice on hurdling debut. *D. Carroll*　　h–

YORKIE MORGANS 8 b.g. Manhal – Placid Fury (Sovereign King) [2003/4 h–, F–: 20m^{pu} 16s^{pu} Dec 30] no sign of ability: headstrong. *Mrs D. A. Hamer*　　h–

YORK RITE (AUS) 8 ch.g. Grand Lodge (USA) – Amazaan (NZ) (Zamazaan (FR)) [2003/4 h66: c16m^{pu} 24m* 21m^4 c23m^2 20f^3 20g 19m^5 22f^6 Oct 5] strong gelding: better effort over fences (saddle slipped on debut) when second in handicap at Worcester in September: poor handicap hurdler: won conditional jockeys event at Bangor in August: stays 3m: acts on firm and good to soft going: blinkered/in cheekpieces and tongue tied after reappearance. *R. C. Guest*　　c72 h72

YORKSHIRE (IRE) 10 ch.g. Generous (IRE) – Ausherra (USA) (Diesis) [2003/4 c–, h124§: c20m^F c24g^F 20v^{pu} 24g 20g 16g^F Mar 10] workmanlike gelding: no form over fences: fairly useful hurdler on his day: stayed 2½m: best form on good/good to firm going: tried blinkered/visored: free-going sort: sometimes failed to impress with attitude: dead. *D. L. Williams*　　c– h112 §

YOU GOT ME 5 gr.g. First Trump – Simply Sooty (Absalom) [2003/4 16m Apr 13] fair maiden up to 1m at 2 yrs for R. Hannon: tailed off in maiden on hurdling debut. *Evan Williams*　　h–

YOULBESOLUCKY (IRE) 5 b.g. Accordion – Gaye Humour (IRE) (Montelimar (USA)) [2003/4 F16d Mar 19] €110,000 3-y-o: first foal: dam unraced half-sister to one-time high-class chaser Kingsmark, from family of top-class 2m to 3m hurdler Gaye Brief and very smart staying jumper Gaye Chance: favourite, seventh of 19 in bumper at Warwick on debut, shaping as if needing much stiffer test of stamina. *Jonjo O'Neill*　　F84

YOU NEED LUCK (IRE) 4 b.g. Key of Luck (USA) – Cathy Garcia (IRE) (Be My Guest (USA)) [2003/4 16m 16m^3 16m^2 16d^4 16s^3 16d^5 16g^5 16d^5 Apr 12] half-brother to modest 2m hurdler The Walrus (by Sri Pekan): lightly-raced maiden up to 1¼m on Flat (fair form): fairly useful juvenile hurdler: won maiden at Navan in November: respectable fifth to Essex at Fairyhouse final start: acts on good to firm and soft ground. *Mrs J. Harrington, Ireland*　　h114

YOU NEVER NO (IRE) 4 b.g. Eagle Eyed (USA) – Nordic Doll (IRE) (Royal Academy (USA)) [2003/4 17m 16m 16g^5 16m^4 16f 16s Apr 4] fair maiden on Flat (stays 8.5f): poor form over hurdles: left E. O'Neill before final start: will prove best around　　h79

2m: tried blinkered and tongue tied: sometimes doesn't impress with finishing effort. *Paul A. Roche, Ireland*

YOUNG AMERICAN (IRE) 8 br.g. Hamas (IRE) – Banana Peel (Green Dancer h–
(USA)) [2003/4 h117: 24d Mar 10] useful-looking gelding: fairly useful handicap
hurdler: off a year (reportedly lame final outing in 2002/3) prior to well below form only
start in 2003/4: stays 3m, at least when conditions aren't testing: acts on good to firm and
heavy going: tried blinkered: races prominently. *Jonjo O'Neill*

YOUNGBLOOD (IRE) 4 b.g. Perugino (USA) – Arctic Splendour (USA) (Arctic h106
Tern (USA)) [2003/4 16d 16d² 16s* 16v⁵ 16s Feb 8] small, angular gelding: modest 1m
winner on Flat: fair juvenile hurdler: won maiden at Naas in January: likely to prove best
at 2m: raced on going softer than good: may prove best on left-handed tracks. *H. Rogers, Ireland*

YOUNG BOUNDER (FR) 5 b. or br.g. Septieme Ciel (USA) – Far But Near (USA) h–
(Far North (CAN)) [2003/4 F–: F17d 16g Feb 14] unfurnished gelding: well held in 2 F–
bumpers and novice hurdle. *N. A. Twiston-Davies*

YOUNG BUCK (IRE) 10 ch.g. Glacial Storm (USA) – Lady Buck (Pollerton) [2003/4 c–
c–, h106: 21mᵖᵘ 20mᵖᵘ 20mᵖᵘ Aug 2] medium-sized gelding: no form in 3 starts over fen- h–
ces: winning hurdler, no form in 2003/4: blinkered/visored and tongue tied. *A. G. Juckes*

YOUNG BUTT 11 ch.g. Bold Owl – Cymbal (Ribero) [2003/4 h65: 17g⁶ May 1] h62
sparely-made gelding: poor maiden hurdler: best around 2m: acts on good to firm and
good to soft going: blinkered. *L. A. Dace*

YOUNG CHEVALIER 7 b.g. Alflora (IRE) – Mrs Teasdale (Idiot's Delight) [2003/4 c100
c–, h–: c22d² c16v⁶ c16g* c16g* c17g⁶ Apr 5] rangy gelding: little sign of ability over h–
hurdles: left J. Adam and improved form over fences in 2003/4, winning handicaps at
Doncaster (novice) and Carlisle within 7 days in March: best form around 2m on good/
good to soft going. *M. Todhunter*

YOUNG CLAUDE 7 b.g. Le Moss – Deirdres Dream (The Parson) [2003/4 h81: c–
24sᵖᵘ c24dᵖᵘ c24sᵖᵘ 25d² 25g c24s⁴ c32dᵖᵘ c25dᵖᵘ Mar 22] tall gelding: poor maiden h84
hurdler: no form over fences: needs 3m+: acts on soft going: blinkered last 5 starts: has
looked quirky. *P. Beaumont*

YOUNG COLLIER 5 b.g. Vettori (IRE) – Cockatoo Island (High Top) [2003/4 19s* h109
23g⁴ 24g Mar 26] tall, useful-looking gelding: has scope: half-brother to 1996 Champion
Hurdle winner/winning chaser Collier Bay (by Green Desert): fair on Flat (will stay
beyond 2m) for Sir Mark Prescott: won novice at Newbury on hurdling debut in January:
stiff task when fourth to Royal Rosa in Grade 2 novice at Haydock next time, but again
well held in non-graded contest at Newbury final start. *J. A. B. Old*

YOUNG DANCER (IRE) 6 b.g. Eurobus – Misquested (Lord Ha Ha) [2003/4 F91: h106 p
16d 16vᶠ 19dᵖᵘ 17g² Apr 10] good-topped gelding: fair maiden hurdler: should stay
beyond 17f. *V. R. A. Dartnall*

YOUNG DEVEREAUX (IRE) 11 b. or br.g. Lord Americo – Miss Iverk (Torus) c138 ?
[2003/4 c154, h–: c16g c21d 16d³ Mar 25] rangy, good-looking gelding: lightly raced h–
(has had leg trouble and been fired): winning hurdler: smart chaser in 2002/3: off 11
months, better effort in valuable handicaps in 2003/4 when eighth to Hunters Tweed at
Cheltenham second outing: stays 2½m: raced on good going or softer (acts on heavy).
P. F. Nicholls

YOUNG GARRICK (IRE) 6 b.g. Old Vic – Youngandfair (IRE) (Phardante (FR)) h–
[2003/4 F16g 19sᵖᵘ Apr 4] IR £17,000 3-y-o: rather leggy gelding: first foal: dam F–
lightly-raced hurdler/pointer: showed nothing in bumper/maiden hurdle. *P. R. Webber*

YOUNG HARRY 6 b.g. Karinga Bay – Heathfield Gale (Strong Gale) [2003/4 F17g F–
Apr 13] second foal: dam, fair hurdler, stayed 2¾m: showed more temperament than
ability in points in 2004, and hung badly left late on when behind in bumper. *M. C. Pipe*

YOUNG LIRRUP 6 ch.g. Lir – Blue-Bird Express (Pony Express) [2003/4 F68: F–
F17m May 14] compact gelding: signs of just a little ability in bumpers: fatally injured in
point. *W. S. Kittow*

YOUNG MONASH (IRE) 6 b.g. General Monash (USA) – Sound Pet (Runnett) h–
[2003/4 21sᵖᵘ Feb 10] poor sprint maiden on Flat: no show in 2 starts over hurdles.
A. C. Wilson

YOUNG OWEN 6 b.g. Balnibarbi – Polly Potter (Pollerton) [2003/4 h71: 16f 16m³ h70
16g³ 18d 16sᶠ Dec 19] rather leggy gelding: fair maiden on Flat (should stay 1½m) for

R. Fahey: poor maiden hurdler: raced around 2m: acts on soft and good to firm going. *Mrs L. B. Normile*

YOUNG RAB 9 b.g. Nomadic Way (USA) – Penny Pink (Spartan General) [2003/4 c20g⁵ May 15] compact gelding: poor pointer: has had tongue tied. *M. J. Brown* — **c– h–**

YOUNG SCOTTON 4 b.g. Cadeaux Genereux – Broken Wave (Bustino) [2003/4 F16v* F16d* F17d² Apr 3] 10,000Y: leggy gelding: half-brother to several winners, including French 1¼m winner Bressay (by Nureyev) and fairly useful hurdler/chaser Levallois (by Trempolino), stays 21f: dam, won up to 15f in Britain/France, out of Oaks third Britannia's Rule: successful at Wetherby in January and Musselburgh in February first 2 starts in bumpers: better form when ½-length second to Diamond Sal in Grade 2 at Aintree: sold to join J. H. Johnson 100,000 gns Doncaster May Sales. *K. A. Ryan* — **F109**

YOUNG SPARTACUS 11 b.g. Teenoso (USA) – Celtic Slave (Celtic Cone) [2003/4 c154, h–: c25g⁴ c20g⁴ c20s Dec 13] strong gelding: smart chaser: below form in valuable handicaps at Cheltenham both starts after 6½ months off: reportedly suffered recurrence of leg injury and not seen out again: barely stays 25f: acts on heavy going: jumps right. *H. D. Daly* — **c135 h–**

YOUNG TOMO (IRE) 12 b.g. Lafontaine (USA) – Siege Queen (Tarqogan) [2003/4 c–, h–: c25dᵖᵘ Mar 11] sturdy gelding: modest handicap chaser in 2001/2: no form since: blinkered: front runner. *Miss C. J. Goodall* — **c– h–**

YOUNG TOT (IRE) 6 b.g. Torus – Lady-K (IRE) (Rock Chanteur) [2003/4 F16g F16s 19g 16g 20d³ 22dᵖᵘ Apr 5] first foal: dam unraced half-sister to 2¾m hurdle winner Poynton Henry: poor form on first of 2 starts in bumpers: easily best effort over hurdles when third in maiden at Wetherby in March, making most to 2 out. *Mrs A. Duffield* — **h90 F74**

YOUNG WHACK (IRE) 10 br.g. Phardante (FR) – Flash Parade (Boreen (FR)) [2003/4 c116, h111: c16m³ c20g* c20d⁶ c21g⁵ c20gF Apr 16] big, good sort: winning hurdler: fairly useful handicap chaser: won at Ayr in November by 5 lengths from Carrick Troop, making running: best subsequent effort when fifth to Cassia Heights in Topham Chase at Aintree (finished distressed) in April: effective at 2½m to 3m: acts on soft and firm going: has had tongue tied: sold 15,000 gns Doncaster May Sales. *J. Howard Johnson* — **c123 h–**

YOU OWE ME (IRE) 7 b.g. Jurado (USA) – Bodyline (Crash Course) [2003/4 20g³ 21g* 20s* Dec 26] good-topped gelding: will make a chaser: second foal: half-brother to useful chaser Terao (by Furry Glen), stayed 3m: dam unraced, out of smart chaser up to 2½m Grangewood Girl: won maiden Irish point in 2003: progressive hurdler: won maiden at Warwick and novice at Uttoxeter in December, making all or most each time: beat Joes Edge 5 lengths at latter course: will stay beyond 21f: type to improve further. *N. A. Twiston-Davies* — **h115 p**

YOUPEEVEECEE (IRE) 8 b.g. Little Bighorn – Godlike (Godswalk (USA)) [2003/4 h87: c25dᵖᵘ c20sᵖᵘ Dec 19] workmanlike gelding: modest form over hurdles: visored, showed little both starts over fences: not an easy ride: sold to join Miss L. Davis 1,200 gns Doncaster January Sales. *Mrs J. Candlish* — **c– h–**

YOUR ADVANTAGE (IRE) 4 b.g. Septieme Ciel (USA) – Freedom Flame (Darshaan) [2003/4 16gᵖᵘ 16s 16d 16g 16d* 16dᵖᵘ 16gᵖᵘ Apr 2] good-topped ex-French gelding: successful 3 times (useful form) up to 1¼m on Flat in France, including in handicap in July, final start for R. Gibson: best effort over hurdles (reportedly distressed on debut) when winning juvenile handicap at Warwick in March: still going strongly in lead when rider took wrong course before 3 out in handicap at Ludlow 6 days later: acted as pacemaker final start: will prove best around 2m: possibly ideally suited by going softer than good: blinkered last 3 outings. *Jonjo O'Neill* — **h98**

YOUR A GASSMAN (IRE) 6 b.g. King's Ride – Nish Bar (Callernish) [2003/4 F100: F17g² 18s 19g² 21d² 20s² Apr 21] tall, useful-looking gelding: confirmed debut promise when impressively winning bumper at Southwell in May: fair form over hurdles, runner-up in novices and maiden last 3 starts: will stay beyond 21f: raced on good going or softer. *Ferdy Murphy* — **h109 F107**

YOUR ALMOST THERE (IRE) 8 br.g. Phardante (FR) – Your Nearly There (Deep Run) [2003/4 17s⁵ 16d⁶ c17sF 16d⁶ 22d² 19s² 16s* 20d 16s 16d² 20d Apr 12] won point on debut in 2002: fell fourth in maiden chase: fairly useful hurdler: made all in maiden at Punchestown in February: ran well when second to Royal Alphabet in novice at Thurles in March: best form at 2m, should stay further: raced only on good to soft/soft ground. *Michael John Phillips, Ireland* — **c– p h115**

YOU'RE A DIAMOND 6 ch.m. Superlative – Diamond Tip (Homing) [2003/4 F–: h–
17g[pu] 17g[pu] Jul 4] of no account. *T. P. Walshe*

YOU'RE AGOODUN 12 ch.g. Derrylin – Jennie Pat (Rymer) [2003/4 c144x, h–: c127 x
c24s³ c28m⁵ c24g⁶ Mar 16] medium-sized gelding: useful handicap chaser in 2002/3: h–
well below best in 2003/4: stays 3½m: acts on heavy and good to firm going: used to wear
blinkers, visored nowadays: often let down by jumping. *M. C. Pipe*

YOU'RE SPECIAL (USA) 7 b.g. Northern Flagship (USA) – Pillow Mint (USA) c125
(Stage Door Johnny (USA)) [2003/4 c101, h–: c20d* c26g* c20m* c25m² c25d⁵ c16g² h–
c20d² c20d² Dec 29] strong, close-coupled gelding: fair hurdler: fairly useful novice
chaser: won at Aintree and Cartmel in May and Hexham in June: runner-up 4 of 5 subsequent starts: effective at 2m to 3¼m: acts on soft and good to firm going: tried tongue tied
(has reportedly choked): front runner: very sound jumper: consistent. *P. C. Haslam*

YOU'RE THE MAN (IRE) 7 b.g. Lapierre – Another Advantage (IRE) (Roselier c–
(FR)) [2003/4 F16g⁶ 20g 20m⁵ 19g 24m[pu] 24d² 20d c20s[pu] 24d* 24v 24s[pu] Apr 21] h71
lengthy gelding: modest form on second of 2 starts in bumpers: showed little on chasing F–
debut: poor hurdler: won handicap at Hexham in March: will prove best at 3m+: acts on
good to soft going: wore cheekpieces 2 starts prior to seeming reluctant in blinkers on
final one. *Mrs Dianne Sayer*

YOURMAN (IRE) 4 b.g. Shernazar – Lantern Lover (Be My Native (USA)) [2003/4 h74
16m 16m⁵ 17s 16s[pu] Feb 16] half-brother to 6 winners, including fair hurdler up to 3m
Burnt Out (by Anshan) and German listed hurdle winner Louis (by Ordos): dam bumper
winner: poor form on second of 4 starts in juvenile hurdles: never a factor and not
knocked about third appearance (trainer fined, jockey and horse banned): looked less than
straightforward final outing. *M. C. Pipe*

YOUR MY ANGEL (IRE) 8 b.m. Commanche Run – Marshtown Fair (IRE) (Cam- h71
den Town) [2003/4 h67: 20g⁶ 20g⁴ 26g[ur] 26m⁴ Jul 18] winning Irish pointer: poor maiden
hurdler: stays 3¼m: raced on good/good to firm going. *Ferdy Murphy*

YOUR SO COOL 7 ch.g. Karinga Bay – Laurel Diver (Celtic Cone) [2003/4 h101: h119
21s² 24s* Feb 3] sturdy gelding: thrice-raced hurdler, improved effort when winning
novice at Taunton in February by ¾ length from Onwardsandupwards, pair clear, strong
run to lead close home: will prove best at 3m+: raced only on soft/heavy going: visored at
Taunton, blinkered other 2 starts. *M. C. Pipe*

YUKON (IRE) 6 b.g. Namaqualand (USA) – Redwood Hut (Miswaki (USA)) [2003/4 h112
16d* 16g* 20d 20s Jan 3] fair on Flat (stays 2¼m): fair handicap hurdler: won at Cork
in June and July: stays 2½m: acts on any going: has had tongue tied. *Patrick Mullins,
Ireland*

YVANOVITCH (FR) 6 b.g. Kaldounevees (FR) – County Kerry (FR) (Comrade In c100
Arms) [2003/4 h92+: c18g⁵ c16m³ c21d[F] c18s² 20g⁶ Feb 28] big, strong gelding: maiden h–
hurdler: fair novice chaser: raced mainly around 2m: acts on soft and good to firm going.
Mrs L. C. Taylor

Z

ZAAJER (USA) 8 ch.g. Silver Hawk (USA) – Crown Quest (USA) (Chief's Crown h–
(USA)) [2003/4 h–: 20m Jun 1] sturdy gelding: lightly-raced maiden hurdler, well held in
handicap only start in 2003/4. *Miss G. Browne*

ZABADI (IRE) 12 b.g. Shahrastani (USA) – Zerzaya (Beldale Flutter (USA)) [2003/4 c– §
c–, h–: c21g[pu] c17g[pu] c21d[pu] c19m[pu] Sep 10] rangy gelding: winning chaser), retains no h–
ability: tried blinkered: often a weak finisher. *Miss Venetia Williams*

ZABRISKIE POINT 5 b.m. Overbury (IRE) – Brownhill Lass (Sunyboy) [2003/4 h–
F–: F16g 24d[pu] 20v 24s 24g[F] 24s[pu] Apr 21] no sign of ability: left R. Allan after second F–
start, wore blinkers last 2. *Mrs J. C. McGregor*

ZACOPANI (IRE) 12 b.g. Lafontaine (USA) – Take A Dare (Pragmatic) [2003/4 c–, c–
h–: 24m[pu] May 27] lengthy gelding: winning hurdler/chaser: largely out of sorts since h–
2000/1: blinkered/visored. *R. Ford*

ZAFARABAD (IRE) 10 gr.g. Shernazar – Zarafa (Blushing Groom (FR)) [2003/4 c122 §
c138⁵, h–: c22s c24f⁵ c20m³ c25f² c23f[su] c23g Feb 18] sturdy gelding: fairly useful h–
handicap chaser nowadays: stays 3m: acts on firm and soft going: blinkered: races mostly

on right-handed tracks: usually races up with pace: has tendency to sulk and not one to trust. *P. J. Hobbs*

ZAFFAMORE (IRE) 8 ch.g. Zaffaran (USA) – Furmore (Furry Glen) [2003/4 c123, h–: c22d⁴ c24m⁴ c20g* c20g² c21m* c20m⁴ Apr 23] strong gelding: fairly useful handicap chaser: won at Kempton in January and Wincanton (beat Sky Warrior by length) in March: should stay 3m: acts on good to firm and good to soft going. *Miss H. C. Knight*   c127 h–

ZAFFARAN EXPRESS (IRE) 5 b.m. Zaffaran (USA) – Majestic Run (Deep Run) [2003/4 F16d⁵ Apr 17] fifth foal: sister to fairly useful hurdler Glenmoss Tara and fair hurdler Zaffaran Run, both of whom stay 21f: dam won poor 17f novice hurdle: distant fifth in bumper at Ayr on debut. *N. G. Richards*   F71

ZAFFRE (IRE) 5 gr.m. Mtoto – Zeferina (IRE) (Sadler's Wells (USA)) [2003/4 F16m* aF16g F17v F17m Apr 15] 800 3-y-o: big mare: first foal: half-sister to fairly useful juvenile hurdler Zimbabwe (by Kahyasi): dam, second only start in 9f Irish maiden at 2 yrs, out of smart Irish 9f and 11f winner Zafadola, also third in Irish St Leger: fair form in bumpers: won mares event at Warwick on debut in November. *Miss Z. C. Davison*   F86

ZAFFRE NOIR (IRE) 8 b.g. Zaffaran (USA) – Massinetta (Bold Lad (IRE)) [2003/4 h–: 16s⁶ 20s⁵ 21g 24dᵘʳ 24g c22sᵖᵘ c24d³ c24g⁶ Apr 18] tall, lengthy gelding: one-time fair hurdler: off 19 months, well below form in handicaps in 2003/4: best effort over fences when third in novice at Huntingdon: stays 3m: acts on any going: races prominently: rejoined M. Pitman. *T. D. McCarthy*   c98 h98

ZAGGY LANE 12 b.g. Prince of Peace – Meldon Lady (Ballymoss) [2003/4 c115d, h–: c24s⁶ c25m c24s c27s c25v⁵ Feb 2] workmanlike gelding: handicap chaser: disappointing in 2003/4, trained by S. Burrough on reappearance: best at 3m+: acts on good to firm and heavy going: blinkered once. *P. R. Rodford*   c95 d h–

ZAHAALIE (USA) 12 ch.g. Zilzal (USA) – Bambee T T (USA) (Better Bee) [2003/4 c–, h–: 20s³ 21m⁴ 20g 16d⁶ Jan 13] small gelding: poor hurdler: stays 3m: acts on firm and heavy going: blinkered once. *J. A. Pickering*   c– h74

ZALEEM (IRE) 7 b.g. Kahyasi – Zallaka (IRE) (Shardari) [2003/4 h–: 17dᵖᵘ May 17] fair form at best in bumpers in 2001/2: no show in 2 novice hurdles: tried visored. *Mrs J. Candlish*   h–

ZAMBEZI RIVER 5 ch.g. Zamindar (USA) – Double River (USA) (Irish River (FR)) [2003/4 F16mᵖᵘ Sep 13] 11,000 3-y-o: ninth foal: half-brother to several winners, including fairly useful sprinters Fly More (by Lycius) and So Intrepid (by Never So Bold): dam, French 6f/7f winner, half-sister to Royal Lodge winner Digression: showed little in bumper, maiden hurdle and on Flat. *J. M. Bradley*   h– F–

ZAMNAH (IRE) 6 ch.m. Naheez (USA) – Shazam (IRE) (Magical Strike (USA)) [2003/4 18g 20s⁶ 16m* 16d* 19f* 16d 16f 24m 20m 20d 19d Mar 7] smallish mare: fair handicap hurdler: won at Wexford in May and twice at Kilbeggan in June: form subsequently only on ninth start: stays 2½m: probably acts on any going: tried blinkered. *Frederick John Bowles, Ireland*   h112

ZAN LO (IRE) 4 ch.f. Grand Lodge (USA) – Zanella (IRE) (Nordico (USA)) [2003/4 16s Jan 27] leggy filly: half-sister to winning 17f hurdler Monsal Dale (by Desert King): won around 1½m on Flat in September: sold out of A. de Royer Dupre's stable 6,500 gns Doncaster December Sales: well beaten in mares novice hurdle and minor event on Flat in Britain. *B. S. Rothwell*   h–

ZANOORA (IRE) 6 br.m. Topanoora – Zagliarelle (FR) (Rose Laurel) [2003/4 F16g F16s F16d Mar 14] fifth foal: half-sister to poor hurdler Katy The Duck (by Over The River), stays 21f: dam soundly beaten in 2 maidens in Ireland: well beaten in 3 bumpers. *R. J. Price*   F–

ZANTANA BOY (IRE) 6 ch.g. Zaffaran (USA) – Ardtana (IRE) (Cidrax (FR)) [2003/4 F–: F16g 20m⁵ 16gᵖᵘ 17gᶠ 24d⁴ c16d⁴ c25dᵘʳ 19vᵖᵘ c18s⁴ c19s⁶ c16m³ c16d⁵ Mar 19] leggy gelding: no worthwhile form in bumpers or over hurdles: poor maiden chaser: form only around 2m: acts on soft and good to firm going: tried blinkered. *M. Scudamore*   c67 h– F–

ZAPATA HIGHWAY 7 ch.g. Bold Arrangement – Trailing Rose (Undulate (USA)) [2003/4 h–: 16gᵖᵘ 20dᵖᵘ 16vʳᵒ 17s Feb 10] good-topped gelding: no form over hurdles. *Mrs M. Reveley*   h–

ZARAKASH (IRE) 4 b.g. Darshaan – Zarannda (IRE) (Last Tycoon) [2003/4 16g 17d Apr 10] smallish gelding: fairly useful form when winning over 1¼m on Flat debut in August: sold out of J. Oxx's stable 30,000 gns Newmarket Autumn Sales: jumped   h– p

ZAR

better than on hurdling debut when eighth of 16 in novice at Carlisle, strong hold held up and not given hard race: likely to prove capable of better. *Jonjo O'Neill*

ZARBARI (IRE) 5 b.g. Kahyasi – Zarlana (IRE) (Darshaan) [2003/4 F–: 16g^pu May 10] tongue tied, no sign of ability in bumper and novice hurdle. *D. McCain*   **h–**

ZARZA BAY (IRE) 5 b.g. Hamas (IRE) – Frill (Henbit (USA)) [2003/4 h73: 20m May 26] good-topped gelding: modest but temperamental on Flat (stays 1¾m): poor form on first of 2 starts over hurdles. *R. M. Stronge*   **h–**

ZAWOYSKI (IRE) 7 b.g. Posen (USA) – Cri Basque (Gay Fandango (USA)) [2003/4 17g^pu 16g^pu Feb 21] compact ex-Irish gelding: 1¼m winner on Flat at 3 yrs: fair hurdler in 2001/2, aided by E. O'Grady's stable IR £1,100 Goffs October (2001) Sale: looked less than keen in 2 handicaps on return. *Jonjo O'Neill*   **h– §**

ZAWRAK (IRE) 5 ch.g. Zafonic (USA) – Gharam (USA) (Green Dancer (USA)) [2003/4 17d^pu Mar 7] useful at one time on Flat (stays 1¼m), modest nowadays: no show on hurdling debut (led in). *I. W. McInnes*   **h–**

ZELENSKY (IRE) 5 b.g. Danehill Dancer (IRE) – Malt Leaf (IRE) (Nearly A Nose (USA)) [2003/4 h–: 16d 16s 16g^5 19m 16s^bd Mar 19] rather leggy gelding: no worthwhile form over hurdles. *G. Brown*   **h–**

ZEN (IRE) 9 b.g. Shernazar – Mary Mary (Moulton) [2003/4 c25g^6 c25d^pu c22s^pu c24d^pu c26d^pu 20d Apr 21] sturdy gelding: modest form in novice hurdles in 2001/2: failed to take to fences, and no promise back over hurdles: has looked hard ride. *T. P. McGovern*   **c– x** **h–**

ZEROBERTO (IRE) 4 ch.g. Definite Article – Blazing Soul (IRE) (Common Grounds) [2003/4 16d^3 Feb 21] successful once (at 3 yrs, over 11f) from 4 starts on Flat in Germany for U. Suter: promising third to Power Elite in Grade 3 juvenile at Fairyhouse on hurdling debut: will improve. *D. K. Weld, Ireland*   **h112 p**

ZERO RISK (IRE) 8 ch.g. Insan (USA) – Serenade Run (Deep Run) [2003/4 16d^4 20s* 21g^2 23v^ur 24g^F 22d Mar 12] rather sparely-made gelding: fair handicap hurdler: off more than 2 years before reappearance: won at Fontwell in December: folded tamely final start: stays 21f: raced mainly on good going or softer (won bumper on heavy): has had tongue tied: front runner. *L. Wells*   **h110**

ZETA'S RIVER (IRE) 6 ch.g. Over The River (FR) – Laurebon (Laurence O) [2003/4 c17g^ur c19g^2 Nov 4] sturdy gelding: eighth foal: brother to winning pointer: dam, won 2m hurdle in Ireland, half-sister to dam of smart staying chaser Zeta's Lad (by Over The River): well clear of remainder when head second to One Nation at Exeter on completed start in maiden chases: will stay beyond 19f. *M. C. Pipe*   **c122**

ZIBELINE (IRE) 7 b.g. Cadeaux Genereux – Zia (USA) (Shareef Dancer (USA)) [2003/4 21g* 17g^3 16g^4 16d^5 16m^4 16g 20g* Apr 1]   **h133 p**

The decision to try Zibeline over hurdles following his move from Rod Millman's stable midway through his fifth season on the Flat paid off handsomely. Zibeline, without a win for over two years, landed the odds in a novice event at Sedgefield in September on his hurdling debut and ended the season with a victory in a valuable handicap at Aintree in April. Zibeline was a useful performer at up to two and a quarter miles on the Flat and finished third in the Northumberland Plate on his penultimate start for his previous trainer. He reached a similar level of form over hurdles on his sixth outing. A 100/1-shot for the Supreme Novices' Hurdle at Cheltenham, he finished ninth of nineteen to Brave Inca, poised to make his effort, seemingly going better than most, when pecking two out, after which he was quickly beaten. Judged on that run, Zibeline looked the pick of the weights in the twenty-three-runner Martell Cognac Beefeaters Restaurants Handicap at Aintree, and he didn't need to show improved form to win it. However, given the manner of his victory it will be surprising if there's isn't even better to come from Zibeline. Dropped out in a race run at no more than a fair pace, when the field had walked across the start line, Zibeline missed the trouble on the turn out of the back straight, was travelling best as he made headway going to three out and then quickened impressively to get the best of Unleash on the run-in. He won by three lengths from Unleash who, incidentally, had won the aforementioned Northumberland Plate. By the top-class sprinter Cadeaux Genereux out of the fairly useful mile-and-a-half winner Zia, Zibeline was with Clive Brittain for his first two seasons on the Flat, joining Millman after being sold for 32,000 guineas at the Newmarket

Martell Cognac Beefeater Restaurants Handicap Hurdle, Aintree—
Zibeline (left) confirms himself on the upgrade as he collars Unleash and Redemption

Autumn Sales in 2000. Zibeline is now with Brian Ellison who has reportedly already schooled him over fences and is likely to send him chasing in the next season. The leggy Zibeline, by no means an obvious chasing type on looks, stays two and a half miles, though he will prove just as effective in strongly-run races over two. He has done the majority of his racing over hurdles on good ground—he acts on firm going but probably not on soft on the Flat. Zibeline sometimes wore blinkers or cheekpieces on the Flat and was blinkered on his last five starts over hurdles. *B. Ellison*

ZIET D'ALSACE (FR) 4 b.f. Zieten (USA) – Providenc Mill (FR) (French Stress   **h69**
(USA)) [2003/4 16m⁵ 16d⁶ Nov 23] leggy, lengthy filly: modest on Flat (stays 1m): poor
form on first of 2 starts in juvenile hurdles. *A. W. Carroll*

ZIGALI 5 b.g. Zilzal (USA) – Alilisa (USA) (Alydar (USA)) [2003/4 16dᵖᵘ 16dᵘʳ 16dᵖᵘ   **h–**
Jan 13] tall, narrow gelding: poor maiden up to 2m on Flat: showed nothing in novice
hurdles. *John A. Harris*

ZIGGY'S WAY 9 b.g. Teenoso (USA) – Onaway (Commanche Run) [2003/4 c–, h–:   **c91**
c20d* c22g⁵ c23d³ Apr 21] sturdy, lengthy gelding: poor maiden hurdler: modest chaser: **h–**
first run for 13 months, 33/1-winner of maiden at Warwick in March: barely stays 23f:
acts on good to soft going. *Mrs A. Barclay*

ZIGGY ZEN 5 b.g. Muhtarram (USA) – Springs Welcome (Blakeney) [2003/4 21g*   **h118**
21gᵘʳ Feb 11] small, close-coupled gelding: fair on Flat (stays 2m), sold out of C. Cyzer's
stable 12,000 gns Newmarket July Sales: 25/1, won novice at Kempton on hurdling debut
by 6 lengths from Overstrand, pair clear: sweating, running well below that form when
unseating last in similar event at Ludlow following month. *C. J. Mann*

ZILARATOR (USA) 8 b.g. Zilzal (USA) – Allegedly (USA) (Sir Ivor (USA)) [2003/4 h107§: 19m^{pu} May 14] good-topped gelding: useful on Flat: maiden hurdler: increasingly let down by jumping and temperament: tried blinkered: dead. *P. J. Hobbs*   **h§§**

ZIMBABWE 4 b.g. Kahyasi – Zeferina (IRE) (Sadler's Wells (USA)) [2003/4 16s^2 17d^4 18s* 17g 17m^2 Apr 14] sturdy gelding: useful on Flat (stays 2m), sold out of J. Oxx's stable €125,000 Goffs October Sale after winning Irish Cesarewitch: fairly useful juvenile hurdler: easily won at Fontwell in January: sent for home too far out when second to Lough Derg at Cheltenham final start: will stay beyond 2¼m: acts on soft ground. *G. L. Moore*   **h118 +**

ZOFFANY (IRE) 7 b.g. Synefos (USA) – Shining Green (Green Shoon) [2003/4 h101: c17g^2 c16g^3 Nov 19] lengthy gelding: successful on first of 2 starts in novice hurdles: fair form when placed both starts in maiden chases: carrying head awkwardly and not finding so much as might have been expected at Hexham on second occasion. *M. Todhunter*   **c103 h–**

ZOLTANO (GER) 6 b.g. In The Wings – Zarella (GER) (Anatas) [2003/4 h110: 17d^5 22s^6 20s^5 Mar 20] workmanlike gelding: modest maiden hurdler: should stay beyond 2m: raced on going softer than good (acts on heavy): won on Flat in April. *M. Todhunter*   **h89**

ZONERGEM 6 ch.g. Zafonic (USA) – Anasazi (IRE) (Sadler's Wells (USA)) [2003/4 16g^2 Nov 11] useful if quirky on Flat (stays 1¼m): second to Dancer Life in novice at Huntingdon on hurdling debut: should improve. *Lady Herries*   **h104 p**

ZORALO (IRE) 8 gr.g. Toulon – Another Yankee (Le Moss) [2003/4 c21g^{pu} Aug 12] very lightly raced and no sign of ability: sold out of J. H. Johnson's stable 2,200 gns Doncaster May Sales before reappearance. *D. C. Turner*   **c– h–**

ZORRO REAL 7 b.g. Rakaposhi King – Sharp Vixen (Laurence O) [2003/4 22g^{pu} Apr 22] workmanlike gelding: no sign of ability in bumper or novice hurdle. *R. Rowe*   **h–**

ZSARABAK 7 br.g. Soviet Lad (USA) – Moorefield Girl (IRE) (Gorytus (USA)) [2003/4 c77, h106: c20d^3 c20g^4 c16g^3 c17m^F c17m c16g^4 c20m^3 Aug 16] close-coupled gelding: fair handicap hurdler: poor maiden chaser: barely stays 2½m: best efforts on good/good to firm going: effective visored or not: tried tongue tied (has reportedly gurgled): reportedly broke blood vessel second start. *P. D. Niven*   **c84 h–**

ZUM SEE (IRE) 5 ch.g. Perugino (USA) – Drew (IRE) (Double Schwartz) [2003/4 F16g 16d* 16m 16s^2 16d* 16g Mar 16] well-made gelding: will make a chaser: second foal: dam unraced, out of half-sister to disqualified Irish Oaks winner Sorbus: best effort in bumpers (didn't look easy ride final start) when winning at Punchestown in 2002/3: fairly useful form over hurdles: won maiden at Naas in November and novice there (beat Corrib Boy cheekily by 2 lengths) in March: looked none too cooperative when well held in Grade 1 novices at Cheltenham in March and Punchestown in late-April: raced at 2m: possibly needs going softer than good (yet to race on heavy). *N. Meade, Ireland*   **h126**

ZURS (IRE) 11 b.g. Tirol – Needy (High Top) [2003/4 c–, h107: 16g^5 21g^{pu} 16m^{pu} 16m Jun 28] leggy gelding: fell only start over fences: handicap hurdler: generally out of form in 2003/4: best around 2m: acts on good to firm going, probably on soft: visored final start. *H. J. Collingridge*   **c– h–**

ZYGOMATIC 6 ch.g. Risk Me (FR) – Give Me A Day (Lucky Wednesday) [2003/4 h62, F85: 21s^6 17m^3 20m* Aug 16] sturdy gelding: 5/1 from 10/1, much improved over hurdles when winning maiden at Bangor in August: stays 2½m: seems suited by good going or firmer. *R. F. Fisher*   **h83**

ERRATA & ADDENDA

'Chasers & Hurdlers 1979/80' &
'Chasers & Hurdlers 1980/81'

Kilkilwell dam Kilkilave not Kilkilane

'Chasers & Hurdlers 1995/96'

Chassange (Fr) second foal: brother to winning chaser: dam maiden, not as stated

'Chasers & Hurdlers 1996/97'

Kingswood Imperial dam winning hurdler/useful chaser, successful up to 25f, not as stated

'Chasers & Hurdlers 1999/00'

Adalie dam winning hurdler/useful chaser, successful up to 25f, not as stated

Cassia Heights dam half-sister not out of half-sister to Father Delaney

Go Boldly (Ire) bay not chestnut

'Chasers & Hurdlers 2001/02'

Sleepytime Tim dam half-sister not out of half-sister to Father Delaney

'Chasers & Hurdlers 2002/03'

P20 Note Enquiries relating to morphine cases are still ongoing; a full list of horses disqualified will appear in 'Chasers & Hurdlers 2004/05'

Mon Villez (Fr) trained first 3 starts by J. Peromingo

Muscadin has no (FR) suffix

PROMISING HORSES

British-trained horses in *Chasers & Hurdlers* thought capable of noteworthy improvement are listed under the trainers for whom they last ran.

R. ALLAN
Sun Bird (IRE) 6 ch.g   h112p

R. H. ALNER
Fox In The Box 7 b.g   h— c113p
Kingscliff (IRE) 7 b.g   c157p
River Paradise (IRE) 8 ch.g   h— c—p

K. C. BAILEY
Front Rank (IRE) 4 b.c   h92p
Fulgere (IRE) 6 b.g   h—p F70
Get Up And Go Go (IRE) 7 ch.g   h90p
Onyourheadbeit (IRE) 6 b.g   h86p F98
Sir Brastias 5 b.g   h84p

A. M. BALDING
Distant Prospect (IRE) 7 b.g   h120p

G. B. BALDING
Ballyvaddy (IRE) 8 gr.g   h125 c94p

C. C. BEALBY
Thistlecraft (IRE) 5 b.g   h110p F91+

P. BEAUMONT
Jodante (IRE) 7 ch.g   h89 c95p

K. BELL
What A Monday 6 b.g   h101p F92

S. B. BELL
Upswing 7 b.g   h88 c73p

P. BOWEN
Hirvine (FR) 6 ch.g   h123p
It's Definite (IRE) 5 b.g   h—p

R. H. BUCKLER
Father D (IRE) 9 b.g   h— c—p
Keepthedreamalive 6 gr.g   h103p F97

NOEL T. CHANCE
Flame Creek (IRE) 8 b.g   h149 c114p
Irish Flight (IRE) 7 ch.g   h90p F89
Kingscote Thunder (IRE) 7 b.g   h—p F99
Murphy's Cardinal (IRE) 8 b.g   h— c118p

C. G. COX
Noble Baron 8 gr.g   h118 c—p

MRS H. DALTON
Mount Cook (FR) 4 b.g   h95p
Premium First (IRE) 5 ch.g   h93p F96

H. D. DALY
Far To Fall (IRE) 6 br.g   h107p

V. R. A. DARTNALL
Lord Sam (IRE) 8 b.g   h— c150p
Russian Lord (IRE) 5 br.g   F79p
Young Dancer (IRE) 6 b.g   h106p

C. R. EGERTON
It's Just Harry 7 b.g   h107p
Rubberdubber 4 b.g   F98p
Winding River (IRE) 7 b.g   h95p c93p

B. ELLISON
Zibeline (IRE) 7 b.g   h133p

A. ENNIS
Beare Necessities (IRE) 5 ch.g   h88p

R. A. FAHEY
Alrida (IRE) 5 b.g   h94p
Classical Ben 6 ch.g   h84p F99
Exstoto 7 b.g   h109 c112p

C. W. FAIRHURST
Rahwaan (IRE) 5 b.g   h98p

J. D. FROST
Grey Brother 6 gr.g   h117p

D. R. GANDOLFO
Rooster's Reunion (IRE) 5 gr.g   h105p

T. R. GEORGE
Alpine Fox 7 b.g   h116p F111

N. J. GIFFORD
Joly Bey 7 ch.g   h128p c147

S. GOLLINGS
Senor Eduardo 3 gr.g   h72p

C. GRANT
Cruise Leader (IRE) 9 b.g   h— c120p

B. DE HAAN
Regents Walk (IRE) 6 b.g   h101p

M. D. HAMMOND
Green 'n' Gold 4 b.f   h87p

N. J. HENDERSON
Alpha Gioconda (IRE) 7 b.g   h—p
Candello 6 b.m   F98p
Chauvinist (IRE) 9 b.g   h— c121p
King Player (IRE) 7 b.g   h—p
Liberthine (FR) 5 b.m   h— c107p
Magic Mistress 5 b.m   h117p
Nas Na Riogh (IRE) 5 b.m   h114 c110p
Non So (FR) 6 b.g   h— c125p
Star Prize (IRE) 7 b.g   h98p F88
Tollbrae (IRE) 7 gr.g   h107 c110p
Trabolgan (IRE) 6 b.g   h125p

LADY HERRIES
Zonergem 6 ch.g   h104p

P. J. HOBBS
Made In Japan (JPN) 4 b.g   h134p
Unleash (USA) 5 ch.g   h139p

J. M. JEFFERSON
Elvis Returns 6 b.g   h99p F82

J. HOWARD JOHNSON
Flownaway 5 b.g   h104p
Giuliani 4 b.g   h83p
Lord Transcend (IRE) 7 gr.g   h— c117P
Rayshan (IRE) 4 b.g   h113p

A. KING
Nyrche (FR) 4 b.g h115p

J. S. KING
Toombridge (IRE) 6 b.g h97p

MISS H. C. KNIGHT
Captain Flinders (IRE) 7 b.g h109p
Harringay 4 b.f F85p
Maljimar (IRE) 4 b.g F90p
Racing Demon (IRE) 4 b.g F105p

MISS E. C. LAVELLE
Barfleur (IRE) 4 b.f F82p
Cloudy Grey (IRE) 7 gr.g h138p
Starlight Express (FR) 4 b.f h89p F89
The Bay Bridge (IRE) 5 b.g F—p

N. P. LITTMODEN
Halland 6 ch.g h93p
Talldark'n'andsome 5 b.g h101p

L. LUNGO
Armaguedon (FR) 6 b.g h111p
Brooklyn Breeze (IRE) 7 b.g h— c131p
Only Once 9 b.g h91p c—
Paddy The Piper (IRE) 7 b.g h134p
Royal Variety (IRE) 6 gr.g h89p
Villon (IRE) 5 b.g F115p

C. J. MANN
Afro Man 6 b.g h99p
Soul (IRE) 7 b.g h— c83p

T. P. MCGOVERN
Injunear (IRE) 6 ch.g h78p

G. L. MOORE
Kashimo (GER) 5 br.h h99p

H. MORRISON
Marble Arch 8 b.g h— c—p
Thieves'glen 6 b.g h110p

P. F. NICHOLLS
Ask The Gatherer (IRE) 6 b.g h109p F94
Azzemour (FR) 5 ch.g F85p
Chamoss Royale (FR) 4 ch.f h119p
Fair Prospect 8 b.g h112 c115p
Kadam (IRE) 4 b.g h80p
L'Ange Au Ciel (FR) 5 b.g h— c117p
Northern Edition (IRE) 7 br.g c102p
Rigmarole 6 b.g h151 c101p
Strong Flow (IRE) 7 br.g h— c156p

MRS SUSAN NOCK
Tsar Party (IRE) 7 b.g c—p

JONJO O'NEILL
Ar Muin Na Muice (IRE) 8 ch.m h139 c118p
Blood Sub (IRE) 7 b.g h— c—p
Claude Greengrass 8 ch.g h105 c91p
Drombeag (IRE) 6 b.g c124p
Lingo (IRE) 5 b.g h144p
Manners (IRE) 6 b.g F90P
Montevideo 4 b.g h106p
Progressive (IRE) 6 ch.g F109p
Selvas (GER) 4 ch.g h110p
Sherkin Island (IRE) 6 b.g h96 c109p
The Rising Moon (IRE) 5 br.g h—p F103
Top of The Left 9 b.g h105 c—p

Very Optimistic (IRE) 6 b.g h129p
Zarakash (IRE) 4 b.g h—p

J. A. B. OLD
Dunshaughlin (IRE) 7 b.g h83p F87
Sargasso Sea 7 gr.g h99 c—p

J. A. OSBORNE
Electrique (IRE) 4 b.g h103p

R. T. PHILLIPS
General Gossip (IRE) 8 b.g h93 c—p

D. PIPE
Oneminutetofive 7 b.g c116p

M. C. PIPE
Copeland 9 b.g h144 c101p
Don Fernando 5 b.h h133 c109p
Janus du Cochet (FR) 7 b.g h— c114p
Legatus (IRE) 7 ch.g c95p
Lord Payne (IRE) 6 b.g h100p
Manx Royal (FR) 5 b.g h—p
Milord Lescribaa (FR) 4 b.g h114p
Our Vic (IRE) 6 b.g h146p c150p
Over The Creek 5 br.g h102p
Team Tassel (IRE) 6 b.g h109p
Therealbandit (IRE) 7 b.g h133p c155+
Vivid Imagination (IRE) 5 b.g h—p
Well Chief (GER) 5 ch.g h142 c150p

M. PITMAN
Patriarch (IRE) 8 b.g h— c102p

B. G. POWELL
Colnside Brook 5 br.m h89p F85
Linens Flame 5 ch.g h84p

MRS M. REVELEY
Birdwatch 6 b.g h—p F93
Dara Capall (IRE) 4 b.g F84p
Our Dream (IRE) 5 b.m h97p F81
Rambling Minster 6 b.g h103p F102
Tara's Flame 4 ch.g h—p

R. ROWE
Amber Starlight 6 b.m h81p

K. A. RYAN
Joe Cooley (IRE) 4 b.g F80p

MISS V. SCOTT
Seven Colours 4 b.g F—p

M. SCUDAMORE
Towns Ender (IRE) 6 b.g h87 c89p

S. E. H. SHERWOOD
Oakley Gold 6 ch.m F77p

MRS S. J. SMITH
Cardington 5 b.g h98p F95

C. TINKLER
Northaw Lad (IRE) 6 ch.g h96p F98

M. TODHUNTER
Sully Shuffles (IRE) 9 b.g h107 c—p

N. A. TWISTON-DAVIES
Blue Dance 5 b.g h—p
Fundamentalist (IRE) 6 b.g h147p
Lord Maizey (IRE) 7 b.g c136p

1009

Tipp Top Lord (IRE) 7 gr.g   h— c104p
You Owe Me (IRE) 7 b.g   h115p

P. R. WEBBER
Buckby Lane 8 b.g   h— c131p
Opal Ridge 7 ch.g   c82p

IAN WILLIAMS
Hors La Loi (FR) 8 ch.g   h115 c101p

NICK WILLIAMS
Philson Run (IRE) 8 b.g   c107p

MISS VENETIA WILLIAMS
Golden Reward (SAF) 6 ro.g   h94p
Lazerito (IRE) 6 b.g   h110p F97
Real Cracker (IRE) 5 b.g   h92p F91
Tighten Your Belt (IRE) 7 b.g   h135p

SELECTED BIG RACES 2003/04

Prize money for racing abroad has been converted to £ sterling at the exchange rate current at the time of the race. The figures are correct to the nearest £.

HAYDOCK Saturday, May 3   GOOD to FIRM

1 **Merewood Homes Swinton Hcap Hdle (Gr 3) (A) (150) (4yo+)**   2m (8)
£40,600

ALTAY *RAFahey* 6-9-11[124] PWhelan[3]	13/2	1
PATSY VEALE (IRE) *JQueally,Ireland* 8-10-2[126] JCulloty	7/1	½ 2
IN CONTRAST (IRE) *PJHobbs* 7-11-12[150] RJohnson	10/1	¾ 3
Gralmano (IRE) *KARyan* 8-10-10[134] GLee	12/1	½ 4
Tramantano *NATwiston-Davies* 4-10-0[128] (t) CLlewellyn	20/1	1½ 5
Cita Verda (FR) *PMonteith* 5-10-0[124] KRenwick	14/1	½ 6
Colourful Life (IRE) *MrsMReveley* 7-10-0[124] (s) AJDempsey	20/1	1¾ 7
Loop The Loup *MrsMReveley* 7-10-2[129] (b) PAspell[3]	16/1	nk 8
Edmo Heights *TDEasterby* 7-10-0[124] DO'Meara	33/1	2 9
Brooklyn's Gold (USA) *IanWilliams* 8-9-9[126] JamesDavies[7]	12/1	3 10
Laouen (FR) *LLungo* 5-10-7[131] ADobbin	11/2	nk 11
Moratorium (USA) *NMeade,Ireland* 8-10-0[124] NWilliamson	9/1	5 12
The Dark Flasher (USA) *CFSwan,Ireland* 6-10-0[124] DJCasey	20/1	22 13
Man O'Mystery (USA) *PRWebber* 6-10-6[130] TDoyle	9/2f	rtr

Mr R. M. Jeffs & Mr J. Potter 14ran 3m36.90

UTTOXETER Sunday, Jun 29   GOOD to FIRM

2 **Britannia Building Society English Summer National (Hcap Chase)**   4m110y (24)
(B) 0-140(138) (5yo+) £34,800

JURANCON II (FR) *MCPipe* 6-10-10[122] RGreene	9/1	1
SPOT THEDIFFERENCE (IRE) *EBolger,Ireland* 10-10-12[124] DJCasey	12/1	½ 2
TAKE CONTROL (IRE) *MCPipe* 9-11-7[133] (v) TScudamore	9/1	4 3
General Claremont (IRE) *PFNicholls* 10-10-8[120] RWalsh	7/2f	12 4
Pettree (IRE) *NATwiston-Davies* 9-10-0[112] CLlewellyn	25/1	8 5
Berlin Blue *RMStronge* 10-10-4[116] JTizzard	8/1	8 6
Bold King (FR) *IanWilliams* 8-9-11[112] WHutchinson[3]	25/1	13 7
Take The Stand (IRE) *PBowen* 7-10-2[114] SDurack	12/1	f
Wild Spice (IRE) *MissVenetiaWilliams* 8-9-9[112] AO'Keeffe[5]	20/1	ro
Enrique (GER) *PJHobbs* 8-11-12[138] RJohnson	5/1	pu
Lanmire Tower (IRE) *SGollings* 9-10-6[118] (b) ADobbin	16/1	pu
Our Jolly Swagman *JWMullins* 8-10-5[117] (v) AThornton	8/1	pu
Pessimistic Dick *HMorrison* 10-10-0[112] JAMcCarthy	16/1	pu

Mr D. A. Johnson 13ran 8m13.66

MARKET RASEN Saturday, Jul 19   GOOD to FIRM

3 **Tote Scoop6 Summer Plate (Hcap Chase) (B) 0-145(140) (5yo+)**   2½m (15)
£40,600

BALLYCASSIDY (IRE) *PBowen* 7-10-13[127] BJGeraghty	11/2jf	1
EI EI *MCChapman* 8-11-9[140] LVickers[3]	14/1	6 2
IL CAPITANO *PFNicholls* 6-10-13[127] RWalsh	10/1	4 3
Goldstreet (IRE) *JosephCrowley,Ireland* 6-10-7[121] (b) TJMurphy	10/1	hd 4
Cobbet (CHR) *TRGeorge* 7-10-9[123] JMMaguire	7/1	1 5
Banjo Hill *MissECLavelle* 9-10-2[116] BFenton	10/1	1¾ 6
Xaipete (IRE) *RCGuest* 11-10-0[114] HOliver	20/1	nk 7
Chicuelo (FR) *MCPipe* 7-11-10[138] (v) TScudamore	10/1	6 8
Duke of Buckingham (IRE) *PRWebber* 7-10-6[120] TDoyle	11/2jf	1¼ 9
Fiery Ring (IRE) *JRHFowler,Ireland* 8-10-11[125] CO'Dwyer	20/1	dist 10
Brother Joe (NZ) *PJHobbs* 9-11-4[132] RJohnson	8/1	f
Ichi Beau (IRE) *FerdyMurphy* 9-10-11[125] (t) DNRussell	14/1	bd
Kaki Crazy (FR) *ERetter* 8-10-4[125] (b) MissSGaisford[7]	20/1	pu
Batswing *BEllison* 8-10-8[122] VTKeane	14/1	pu
Lisdante (IRE) *MrsSJSmith* 10-10-0[114] DSElsworth	33/1	pu

Mr R. Owen 15ran 4m48.88

GALWAY Wednesday, Jul 30   SOFT

4 **The Hewlett-Packard Galway Plate (Gr A Hcap Chase) (147) (4yo+)**   2¾m (14)
£65,018

NEARLY A MOOSE (IRE) *PatrickMullins* 7-10-1[123] (t) RMPower[3]	25/1	1
KADOUN (IRE) *MJPO'Brien* 6-10-9[133] (s) MrDWCullen[5]	10/1	4 2
GLYNN DINGLE (IRE) *AJMartin* 10-10-3[122] GLee	16/1	½ 3

BACK ON TOP (IRE) *JLHassett* 9-10-11[130] JRBarry .... 10/3f   nk 4
Ansar (IRE) *DKWeld* 7-10-7[126] DJCasey .... 12/1   ½ 5
Risk Accessor (IRE) *CRoche* 8-11-0[133] RWalsh.. 15/2   6
Thari (USA) *NMeade* 6-10-4[123] PCarberry 20/1   7
Go Roger Go (IRE) *EJO'Grady* 11-11-10[143] NWilliamson 16/1   8
Kirmar (IRE) *PAFahy* 9-10-1[120] JLCullen 20/1   9
Lord of The Turf (IRE) *JBleahen* 10-10-11[130] BJGeraghty 8/1   10
Wotsitooya (IRE) *MJPO'Brien* 11-9-11[116] (s) GCotter............................. 25/1   11
3 Ballycassidy (IRE) *PBowen,GB* 7-11-4[137] AThornton 12/1   12
Zafarabad (IRE) *PJHobbs,GB* 9-11-0[133] (b) KAKelly 33/1   13
Torduff Boy (IRE) *PaulNolan* 10-10-7[133] (t) MrDerekO'Connor[7] 16/1   14
Fnan *NMeade* 7-10-2[124] GTHutchinson[3] 33/1   15
Cregg House (IRE) *SDonohoe* 8-10-2[126] (b) MFMooney[5] 50/1   16
Knife Edge (USA) *MJPO'Brien* 8-12-0[147] CO'Dwyer 33/1   17
3 Goldstreet (IRE) *JosephCrowley* 6-10-4[123] (b) JCulloty 25/1   18
Michael Mor (IRE) *NMeade* 9-10-10[129] (s) TJMurphy............................. 25/1   19
Ceoil Agus Craic (IRE) *MGHolden* 12-9-11[119] MDGrant[3] .... 50/1   ur
Garvivonnian (IRE) *EdwardPMitchell* 8-11-5[138] TPTreacy .... 33/1   pu
Heart Midoltian (FR) *SNeville* 6-11-1[134] (t) DNRussell........................... 25/1   pu

Mr Michael J. McGinley 22ran 5m37.81

GALWAY Thursday, Jul 31   GOOD to SOFT

5   **Guinness Galway Hdle (Hcap) (Gr A) (150) (4yo+)** £73,209   2m (9)

SABADILLA (USA) *PatrickMichaelVerling* 9-9-7[115] PMVerling 14/1   1
CLOONE RIVER (IRE) *PaulNolan* 7-9-9[117] TJMurphy .... 8/1   ¾ 2
LAFAYETTE (IRE) *RJOsborne* 5-9-9[117] JRBarry 20/1   1½ 3
COLUMBA (IRE) *DTHughes* 7-9-6[121] PWFlood[7]..................................... 16/1   1 4
Crimson Flower (IRE) *JMorrison* 8-9-7[115] WSlattery 16/1   1½ 5
1 The Dark Flasher (IRE) *CFSwan* 6-9-9[117] BHarding............................... 20/1   6
Kickham (IRE) *EJO'Grady* 7-10-0[122] NWilliamson 12/1   7
Gemini Guest (IRE) *PHughes* 7-9-2[115] SCurling[5]................................. 14/1   8
Mutakarrim *DKWeld* 6-10-12[134] (b) BJGeraghty 12/1   9
King's Opera (IRE) *MJGrassick* 5-10-1[123] RWalsh 11/1   10
Carlesimo (IRE) *NMeade* 5-10-2[124] GLee... 25/1   11
Puck Out (IRE) *CRoche* 5-10-0[122] DJCasey 10/3f   12
Dashing Home (IRE) *NMeade* 4-10-1[125] PCarberry 16/1   13
Janidou (FR) *ALTMoore* 7-9-2[115] MrNPMadden[5] 20/1   14
Junior Fontaine (FR) *ALTMoore* 6-9-8[119] DJHoward[3] 16/1   15
Splendour (IRE) *MissSCox* 8-9-5[116] WSlattery 25/1   16
Auetaler (GER) *EMcNamara* 9-9-11[122] (b) APLane[3] 50/1   17
Aye Aye Popeye (IRE) *MrsJHarrington* 5-9-9[117] GCotter........................ 20/1   18
Grimes *CRoche* 10-12-0[150] CO'Dwyer 33/1   19
Zamnah (IRE) *FrederickJohnBowles* 5-9-7[118] JPElliott[3] 25/1   20
Liscahill Hill (IRE) *DLoughnane* 12-9-5[116] RGeraghty[3] 25/1   21
Swordplay *MJPO'Brien* 5-10-8[130] DNRussell.. 25/1   22
Ansari (IRE) *PatrickOBrady* 6-9-4[117] AJDonoghue[5] 40/1   23
Quadco (IRE) *PAFahy* 9-9-4[115] (b) GTHutchinson[3]............................... 25/1   ur

Mr W. Coleman 24ran 3m51.01

LISTOWEL Wednesday, Sep 17   GOOD

6   **Guinness Kerry National Hcap Chase (Gr A) (152) (4yo+)** £63,644   3m (17)

NATIVE PERFORMANCE (IRE) *MHourigan* 8-9-7[117] TJMurphy............... 8/1   1
RIVER CORA (IRE) *WPMullins* 9-9-7[117] JRBarry .... 12/1   nk 2
JUST IN DEBT (IRE) *PMJDoyle* 7-10-7[131] DNRussell............................. 10/1   3 3
COLONEL BRADLEY (IRE) *CFSwan* 9-9-10[120] DJCasey 11/2f   15 4
Killultagh Storm (IRE) *WPMullins* 9-10-11[140] (s) MrJJCodd[5] 20/1   1 5
Danaeve (IRE) *GKeane* 8-9-4[117] MDGrant[3] 20/1   6
Monty's Pass (IRE) *JamesJosephMangan* 10-12-0[152] BJGeraghty 7/1   7
Give Over (IRE) *EUHales* 10-11-0[138] (s) CO'Dwyer.............................. 20/1   8
4 Garvivonnian (IRE) *EdwardPMitchell* 8-10-11[135] TPTreacy 25/1   9
Putsometnby (IRE) *JonjoO'Neill,GB* 7-10-1[125] (b) LCooper.................... 13/2   f
4 Thari (USA) *NMeade* 6-9-8[123] MrNPMadden[5] .... 12/1   f
Moscow Express (IRE) *MissFMCrowley* 11-11-3[144] (b) KHadnett[3].............. 16/1   ur
4 Glynn Dingle (IRE) *AJMartin* 10-10-3[127] SDurack .... 8/1   ur
Cloudy Bays (IRE) *CByrnes* 6-9-7[117] PMVerling .... 7/1   ur
Montayral (FR) *PHughes* 6-10-1[125] JCulloty .... 16/1   pu
Ballyconnell (IRE) *DKWeld* 7-9-7[117] GCotter.. 10/1   pu
Dantes Bank (IRE) *AnnetteMcMahon* 11-9-5[118] (t) RGeraghty[3].................. 33/1   pu

Mr Donal O'Connor 17ran 5m50.20

MERANO Sunday, Sep 28   GOOD to SOFT

7   LXIV Gran Premio Merano Forst (4yo+) £122,200   3m1f (24)

TEMPO D'OR (FR) *GMacaire,France* 5-10-11 BGicquel	38/10		1
GOLD GENERATOR (IRE) *PFavero,Italy* 5-10-11 LJack		17	2
GAEL D'ANGRON (FR) *YFertillet,France* 9-10-9 DBerra		nk	3
Irish Dude (ITY) *FColleo* 6-10-11 LdeMaria		15	4
Barito (GER) *CVonDerRecke,Germany* 6-10-9 DFuhrmann		3½	5
Constantino (RE (ITY) *EdeLaMotte* 10-10-9 PChevalier		4	6
Daisy d'Angron (FR) *YFertillet,France* 12-10-9 PBrechet		9	7
Galant Moss (FR) *CAubert,France* 9-10-11 CGombeau		8	
Almanzor (POL) *HRadek,CzechRep* 7-10-11 MStromsky		f	
Siberius (GER) *MHofer,Germany* 5-10-11 PGehm		f	
Azulejo (FR) *JOrtet,France* 5-10-13 CPieux		pu	
Platinum (ITY) *FColleo* 5-10-9 ARenzi		pu	
Present Bleu (FR) *EdeLaMotte* 8-11-12 CMonjon		pu	

Mrs F. Montauban 13ran Time not taken

TIPPERARY Sunday, Oct 5   GOOD to FIRM

8   John James McManus Memorial Hdle (Gr 1) (4yo+) £44,828   2m (11)

INTERSKY FALCON *JonjoO'Neill,GB* 6-11-12 (b) LCooper	8/13f		1
BACK IN FRONT (IRE) *EJO'Grady* 6-11-12 NWilliamson	6/4	12	2
TAKE FLITE *AnthonyMullins* 6-11-12 JCulloty	25/1	6	3
Harchibald (FR) *NMeade* 4-11-7 PCarberry	20/1	sh	4
Doonaree (IRE) *THogan* 7-11-12 (t) BJGeraghty	25/1	25	5
5 Sabadilla (USA) *PatrickMichaelVerling* 9-11-12 PMVerling	16/1	pu	

Interskyracing com 6ran 3m44.20

WINCANTON Sunday, Oct 26   FIRM

9   Fieldspring Desert Orchid Chase (Ltd Hcap) (Gr 2) (A) (165) (5yo+)   2m5f (17)
£21,700

EDREDON BLEU (FR) *MissHCKnight* 11-11-10[165] (t) JCulloty	6/5f		1
EXIT SWINGER *PFNicholls* 8-10-1[145] ChristianWilliams[3]	7/2	15	2
TRESOR DE MAI (FR) *MCPipe* 9-10-9[150] RGreene	13/2	dist	3
Noble Comic *CLTizzard* 12-9-13[145] JamesDavies[5]	100/1	8	4
Wahiba Sands *MCPipe* 10-9-13[145] JEMoore[5]	3/1	f	

Mr Jim Lewis 5ran 4m59.00

WETHERBY Saturday, Nov 1   GOOD to FIRM

10   Bet365 Charlie Hall Chase (Gr 2) (A) (5yo+) £34,800   3m1f (18)

BALLYBOUGH RASHER (IRE) *JHowardJohnson* 8-11-0 GLee	40/1		1
MARLBOROUGH (IRE) *NJHenderson* 11-11-0 MAFitzgerald	11/4	6	2
BARROW DRIVE *AnthonyMullins,Ireland* 7-11-10 (t) JCulloty	8/1	16	3
Jungle Jinks (IRE) *GMMoore* 8-11-2 RGarritty	14/1	4	4
Alcapone (IRE) *MFMorris,Ireland* 9-11-10 GCotter	20/1	12	5
Valley Henry (IRE) *PFNicholls* 8-11-10 BJGeraghty	4/5f	f	

Comtake-Welding Engineering Specialists 6ran 6m06.65

EXETER Tuesday, Nov 4   GOOD

11   William Hill Haldon Gold Cup Chase (Ltd Hcap) (Gr 2) (A) (165)   2m1f110y (12)
(5yo+) £29,000

9 EDREDON BLEU (FR) *MissHCKnight* 11-11-10[165] (t) JCulloty	7/2		1
9 WAHIBA SANDS *MCPipe* 10-10-4[145] RGreene	20/1	2½	2
KADARANN (IRE) *PFNicholls* 6-11-5[160] JTizzard	6/1	2	3
Seebald (GER) *MCPipe* 8-11-8[163] APMcCoy	11/4	12	4
Castle Prince (IRE) *RJHodges* 9-10-4[145] TJMurphy	100/1	13	5
Dual Star (IRE) *LWaring* 8-10-4[145] (t) XAizpuru	300/1	27	6
Azertyuiop (FR) *PFNicholls* 6-11-6[161] MAFitzgerald	5/4f	ur	

Mr Jim Lewis 7ran 4m08.32

WINCANTON Saturday, Nov 8   FIRM

12   K J Pike & Sons Elite Hdle (Ltd Hcap) (Gr 2) (A) (152) (4yo+)   2m (8)
£18,600

WELL CHIEF (GER) *MCPipe* 4-10-5[138] JEMoore[5]	5/2		1
QUAZAR (IRE) *JonjoO'Neill* 5-11-10[152] (t) ADobbin	15/8f	1¾	2
CASTLESHANE (IRE) *SGollings* 6-10-4[132] JCulloty	9/2	6	3
Rigmarole *PFNicholls* 5-10-5[140] (t) NCarter[7]	3/1	16	4

Mr D. A. Johnson 4ran 3m27.74

AUTEUIL Sunday, Nov 9   SOFT

13   Prix La Haye Jousselin (Gr 1) (5yo+) £84,760   3m3f110y

BATMAN SENORA (FR) *IanWilliams,GB* 7-10-8 (b) CGombeau	15/1		1

1013

ROUGENOIR (FR) *RELecomte,France* 10-10-8 (b) HServeau 1½ 2
KILEFOU D'AIRY (FR) *JOrtet,France* 5-10-3 CPieux 1½ 3
Urga (FR) *GChaignon,France* 12-10-8 MrPBrechet.. 4 4
Sun Storm (FR) *TCivel,France* 6-10-8 BThelier.. 2 5
Scandor (FR) *FDanloux,France* 9-10-8 SBeaumard 15 6
Idole Des Fontaines (FR) *CDiard,France* 7-10-8 (b) SZuliani...................... ½ 7
Cerilly (FR) *JBertrandeBalanda,France* 6-10-8 LMetais.............................. 15 8
Sunny Flight (FR) *AChaille-Chaille,France* 9-10-8 PSourzac .... f
Hespoir d'Aurelie (FR) *MRolland,France* 8-10-8 PChevalier .... f
Kotkijet (FR) *J-PGallorini,France* 8-10-8 TMajorcryk .... f
Kotkita (FR) *BSecly,France* 5-9-13 JacquesRicou .... f
Paladin (FR) *JOrtet,France* 8-10-8 (b) AKondrat... pu
Mr G. Polinski 13ran 7m02.00

CHELTENHAM Saturday, Nov 15   GOOD (Old Course)

14   **Lombard Properties Hcap Hdle (L) (A) (149) (4yo+)** £23,200   3m1f110y (13)

THEREALBANDIT (IRE) *MCPipe* 6-10-4[127] APMcCoy 11/10f   1
AMBRY *MrsSJSmith* 6-10-0[123] DSElsworth.. 16/1   7 2
SONEVAFUSHI (IRE) *MissVenetiaWilliams* 5-10-0[123] (b) RJohnson 16/1   2½ 3
Stromness (USA) *AKing* 6-11-4[141] (t) RThornton .... 6/1   ½ 4
Blue Ride (IRE) *PFNicholls* 6-10-9[132] RWalsh 3/1   3 5
1 Gralmano (IRE) *KARyan* 8-11-5[149] MSeston[7]... 7/1   2½ 6
Ennel Boy (IRE) *NMBabbage* 10-10-0[123] TJMurphy 25/1   13 7
Good Lord Murphy (IRE) *DrPPritchard* 11-9-7[123] WKennedy[7]................ 100/1   19 8
Mr D. A. Johnson 8ran 6m22.44

15   **Paddy Power Gold Cup Chase (Hcap) (Gr 3) (A) (163) (5yo+)**   2½m110y (15)
£63,800

FONDMORT (FR) *NJHenderson* 7-10-13[150] MAFitzgerald 3/1f   1
POLIANTAS (FR) *PFNicholls* 6-11-0[151] RWalsh... 7/2   8 2
3 EI EI *MCChapman* 8-10-2[142] LVickers[3]... 33/1   15 3
Young Spartacus *HDDaly* 10-10-13[150] RJohnson 11/2   6 4
Cyfor Malta (FR) *MCPipe* 10-11-12[163] RGreene 10/1   4 5
9 Exit Swinger (FR) *PFNicholls* 8-10-2[142] ChristianWilliams[3] .... 16/1   dist 6
It Takes Time (IRE) *MCPipe* 9-10-10[147] APMcCoy .... 4/1   f
4 Risk Accessor (IRE) *CRoche,Ireland* 6-10-0[137] TJMurphy .... 8/1   f
Redemption *NATwiston-Davies* 8-10-0[137] CLlewellyn................................ 16/1   pu
Mr W. J. Brown 9ran 5m02.26

16   **Open Trophy Hcap Chase (L) (A) (154) (5yo+)** £29,000   3m3f110y (21)

SHARDAM (IRE) *NATwiston-Davies* 6-10-2[130] CLlewellyn....................... 9/2   1
STORMEZ (FR) *MCPipe* 6-11-7[149] RJohnson.. 7/2jf   8 2
6 MONTAYRAL (FR) *PHughes,Ireland* 6-10-1[129] SDurack .... 12/1   ½ 3
Southern Star (IRE) *MissHCKnight* 8-10-6[134] JCulloty .... 11/2   ½ 4
Lord Noelie (IRE) *MsBridgetNicholls* 10-11-9[151] JTizzard 12/1   4 5
Ad Hoc (IRE) *PFNicholls* 9-11-12[154] RWalsh 13/2   6 6
2 Enrique (GER) *PJHobbs* 8-11-3[145] RJohnson .... 10/1   pu
Carbury Cross (IRE) *JonjoO'Neill* 9-10-7[135] LCooper .... 7/2jf   pu
Mr Howard Parker 8ran 7m01.01

CHELTENHAM Sunday, Nov 16   GOOD to FIRM (Old Course)

17   **Independent Newspaper November Nov Chase (Gr 2) (A) (4yo+)**   2m (12)
£20,825

THISTHATANDTOTHER (IRE) *PFNicholls* 7-11-9 RWalsh 8/13f   1
RYDERS STORM (USA) *TRGeorge* 4-10-7 TJMurphy............................... 20/1   11 2
ATUM RE (IRE) *PRWebber* 6-11-11 TDoyle.. 7/1   sh 3
Le Duc (FR) *PFNicholls* 4-10-7 JTizzard.. 3/1   6 4
Forrestfield (IRE) *JEMulhern,Ireland* 9-11-11 RJohnson 16/1   19 5
Mr C. G. Roach 5ran 3m59.83

18   **Greatwood Hdle (Hcap) (A) (140) (4yo+)** £29,000   2m110y (8)

12 RIGMAROLE *PFNicholls* 5-11-12[140] (t) RWalsh.. 33/1   1
CARACCIOLA (GER) *NJHenderson* 6-10-11[125] MAFitzgerald................... 5/1   1¼ 2
HASTY PRINCE *JonjoO'Neill* 5-11-9[137] LCooper .... 11/10f   ½ 3
Jaboune (FR) *AKing* 6-10-13[130] WHutchinson[3] 20/1   6 4
Shalako (USA) *PJHobbs* 5-10-7[121] RJohnson .... 10/1   ½ 5
1 Altay *RAFahey* 6-11-0[131] PWhelan[3] 14/1   8 6
Do L'Enfant d'Eau (FR) *PJHobbs* 4-11-5[133] SDurack 50/1   14 7
Lewis Island (IRE) *NATwiston-Davies* 4-10-7[121] CLlewellyn 12/1   4 8
Gone Far (USA) *MCPipe* 6-11-2[130] RGreene.. 10/1   f
Visibility (FR) *MCPipe* 4-11-5[133] APMcCoy .... 7/1   pu
Mr & Mrs Mark Woodhouse 10ran 3m52.99

HAYDOCK Sunday, Nov 16   GOOD

19   Edward Hanmer Memorial Chase (Ltd Hcap) (Gr 2) (A) (163)   3m (18)
      (5yo+) £32,750

      SWANSEA BAY *PBowen* 7-10-7[146] AThornton 6/4f   1
      HUSSARD COLLONGES (FR) *PReaumont* 8-11-6[159] RGarritty 2/1   5 2
      KINGSMARK (IRE) *MTodhunter* 10-11-10[163] DRDennis .... 15/8   dist 3

      Mr Peter Bowling 3ran 6m11.21

PUNCHESTOWN Sunday, Nov 16   GOOD to SOFT

20   Mongey Communications Morgiana Hdle (Gr 2) (4yo+) £21,069   2m (9)

   8 BACK IN FRONT (IRE) *EJO'Grady* 6-11-11 BJGeraghty........................... 4/5f   1
      SACUNDAI (IRE) *EJO'Grady* 6-12-0 MDGrant 12/1   1½ 2
      SOLERINA (IRE) *JamesBowe* 6-11-6 DJCasey 5/1   1 3
      Risky Reef *AndrewLee* 6-11-9 JRBarry 20/1   2 4
      Scarthy Lad (IRE) *TGO'Leary* 5-11-3 CO'Dwyer 14/1   3½ 5
      Hunters Bar (IRE) *TimothyDoyle* 7-10-12 (t) IJPower......................... 66/1   6
      Scottish Memories (IRE) *NMeade* 7-12-0 PCarberry............................. 7/2   7
      Balapour (IRE) *PatrickOBrady* 5-11-9 (t) JLCullen 25/1   8
      Rostropovich (IRE) *MFMorris* 6-11-9 (b+t) GCotter............................ 20/1   9

      Mr D. Cox 9ran 3m50.40

CLONMEL Thursday, Nov 20   SOFT

21   Clonmel Oil Chase (Gr 2) (5yo+) £27,273   2½m (14)

  11 EDREDON BLEU (FR) *MissHCKnight,GB* 11-11-12 (t) JCulloty 2/1   1
      ARCTIC COPPER (IRE) *NMeade* 9-11-10 (s) PCarberry .... 10/1   hd 2
      BEEF OR SALMON (IRE) *MHourigan* 7-11-8 TJMurphy......................... 4/5f   1 3
      The Premier Cat (IRE) *TCahill* 7-11-4 JRBarry.................................... 12/1   3½ 4
  10 Alcapone (IRE) *MFMorris* 9-11-12 GCotter.. 12/1   4½ 5
   6 Garvivonnian (IRE) *EdwardPMitchell* 8-11-4 TPTreacy 50/1   6
      Intelligent (IRE) *MrsJHarrington* 7-11-6 BJGeraghty 16/1   7
      Charging (IRE) *JohnJosephMurphy* 7-11-1 JLCullen 200/1   8
      Boss Murphy (IRE) *PO'Keeffe* 9-11-5 KHadnett..................................100/1   9
      Whithworth Ben (IRE) *SJMahon* 7-11-1 IJPower................................. 66/1   f

      Mr Jim Lewis 10ran 5m07.60

AINTREE Saturday, Nov 22   GOOD to SOFT

22   betfair.com Hcap Hdle (B) (138) (4yo+) £13,443   3m110y (13)

      CALLING BRAVE (IRE) *NJHenderson* 7-11-1[127] MAFitzgerald 11/4f   1
      SH BOOM *JonjoO'Neill* 5-11-12[138] LCooper...................................... 7/2   5 2
      CILL CHURNAIN (IRE) *MrsSJSmith* 10-11-4[130] DSElsworth................... 12/1   5 3
      Springfield Scally *SGollings* 10-11-4[130] GLee .... 11/1   ½ 4
      Hugo de Perro (FR) *PMonteith* 8-11-7[133] KRenwick........................... 33/1   ¾ 5
      October Mist (IRE) *MrsMReveley* 9-11-7[136] PAspell[3] 6/1   10 6
      Forest Ivory (NZ) *DrPPritchard* 12-10-0[112] PaulMoloney 200/1   27 7
      Monolith *LLungo* 5-10-3[115] ADobbin... 5/1   dist 8
      General Duroc (IRE) *RTPhillips* 7-10-6[118] JMogford .... 14/1   pu
      Ballinclay King (IRE) *FerdyMurphy* 9-11-8[134] DNRussell..................... 12/1   pu

      Sir Robert Ogden 10ran 6m17.36

ASCOT Saturday, Nov 22   GOOD to SOFT

23   coral.co.uk Hcap Chase (B) 0-140(137) (5yo+) £13,702   3m110y (20)

      KINGSCLIFF (IRE) *RHAlner* 6-11-5[130] AThornton 5/6f   1
      HORUS (IRE) *MCPipe* 8-11-12[137] APMcCoy 6/1   17 2
      EXIT TO WAVE (FR) *PFNicholls* 7-11-9[134] RWalsh 6/1   1 3
      Indian Chance *DrJRJNaylor* 9-9-11[111] RWalford[3]........................... 16/1   24 4
      Silver Streak (IRE) *NJGifford* 9-11-1[126] LAspell.............................. 20/1   8 5
      Bramblehill Duke (IRE) *MissVenetiaWilliams* 11-10-8[126] SThomas[7] 12/1   30 6
      Druid's Glen (IRE) *JonjoO'Neill* 7-11-6[134] TSiddall[3]....................... 10/1   pu

      Mr A. J. Sendell 7ran 6m36.61

24   First National Gold Cup Chase (Limited Int Hcap) (Gr 2) (A) (157)   2m3f110y (16)
      (5yo+) £37,200

      IRIS ROYAL (FR) *NJHenderson* 7-10-4[137] MFoley 13/2   1
      LE ROI MIGUEL (FR) *PFNicholls* 5-11-10[157] RWalsh 10/3   1¾ 2
      TARXIEN *MCPipe* 9-11-1[148] (t) APMcCoy 9/4f   10 3
      Ibal (FR) *MrsNSmith* 7-10-7[140] LAspell.. 6/1   dist 4
      Farmer Jack *PJHobbs* 7-10-13[146] RJohnson...................................... 3/1   pu

      Sir Robert Ogden 5ran 5m11.54

HUNTINGDON Saturday, Nov 22   SOFT

25   Tote Peterborough Chase (Gr 2) (A) (5yo+) £29,000   2½m110y (16)

	JAIR DU COCHET (FR) *GMacaire,France* 6-11-5 JacquesRicou	10/3		1
	BEST MATE (IRE) *MissHCKnight* 8-11-10 JCulloty	8/13f	8	2
10	VALLEY HENRY (IRE) *PFNicholls* 8-11-10 JTizzard	7/1	1¾	3
	La Landiere (FR) *RTPhillips* 8-11-3 WMarston	9/1	dist	4
	Strong Magic (IRE) *JRCornwall* 11-11-0 RHobson	200/1	12	5
	Venn Ottery *OJCarter* 8-11-0 PHide	500/1	dist	6

Mrs F. Montauban 6ran 5m23.01

NAAS Saturday, Nov 22   GOOD to SOFT

26   Woodlands Park 100 Poplar Square Chase (Gr 3) (5yo+) £14,545   2m (10)

4	KADOUN (IRE) *MJPO'Brien* 6-11-3 MrDWCullen[5]	13/2		1
	RATHGAR BEAU (IRE) *ESheehy* 7-11-8 BJGeraghty	13/8f	½	2
	GROUND BALL (IRE) *CFSwan* 6-11-3 DJCasey	5/1	½	3
	Beachcomber Bay (IRE) *NMeade* 8-11-8 PCarberry	6/1	10	4
	Adamant Approach (IRE) *WPMullins* 9-11-5 JRBarry	9/4	10	5

Mr John P. McManus 5ran 4m10.20

AINTREE Sunday, Nov 23   GOOD to SOFT

27   Freephone Stanley Children In Need Hcap Hdle (C) 0-130(130)   2½m (11)
(4yo+) £12,870

	MUGHAS (IRE) *AKing* 4-11-5[126] WHutchinson[3]	16/1		1
	CRYSTAL D'AINAY (FR) *AKing* 4-11-12[130] RThornton	12/1	2	2
	HAND INN HAND *HDDaly* 7-11-10[128] RJohnson	9/4f	1¼	3
	KIVOTOS (USA) *ACWhillans* 5-10-1[105] KRenwick	20/1	10	4
1	Loop The Loup *MrsMReveley* 7-11-7[128] (s) PAspell[3]	16/1	1½	5
	East Tycoon (IRE) *JonjoO'Neill* 4-11-6[124] LCooper	9/2	hd	6
	Marked Man (IRE) *RLee* 7-10-7[111] TDoyle	20/1	nk	7
1	Colourful Life (IRE) *MrsMReveley* 7-11-5[123] AJDempsey	12/1	5	8
	The Flyer (IRE) *MissSJWilton* 6-10-13[117] NFehily	66/1	5	9
	Another Dude (IRE) *JHowardJohnson* 6-10-9[113] GLee	9/1	1¾	10
	Mythical King (IRE) *RLee* 6-10-12[119] AO'Keeffe[3]	33/1	5	11
	Fortunate Dave (USA) *IanWilliams* 4-10-1[105] PaulMoloney	25/1	5	12
	Barresbo *ACWhillans* 9-10-9[118] IJardine[5]	66/1	5	13
	Sharpaten (IRE) *IanWilliams* 8-11-2[120] DRDennis	33/1	17	14
	Undeniable *MrsSJSmith* 5-10-4[108] DSElsworth	9/1	4	15
	Bustling Rio (IRE) *PCHaslam* 7-10-11[118] NHannity[3]	33/1	2½	16
	Haydens Field *PMRich* 9-11-2[127] MCook[7]	25/1	12	17
	Inn Antique (FR) *FerdyMurphy* 7-11-1[124] JamesDavies[5]	33/1		pu

B. Winfield, C. Fenton & A. Longman 18ran 4m58.81

28   Tote Becher Chase (Hcap) (B) (138) (5yo+) £46,500   3m3f (Nat.) (21)

	CLAN ROYAL (FR) *JonjoO'Neill* 8-10-12[126] LCooper	11/2		1
	AMBERLEIGH HOUSE (IRE) *DMcCain* 11-11-5[133] GLee	8/1	sh	2
	ARDENT SCOUT *MrsSJSmith* 11-11-4[132] DSElsworth	5/1f	dist	3
	Moor Lane *AMBalding* 11-11-1[129] ADobbin	14/1	dist	4
	Bindaree (IRE) *NATwiston-Davies* 9-11-10[138] CLlewellyn	15/2		f
	Wonder Weasel (IRE) *KCBailey* 10-11-6[134] (s) JPMcNamara	14/1		f
	Tremallt (IRE) *TRGeorge* 12-10-9[123] JMMaguire	16/1		f
	Robbo *MrsMReveley* 11-11-1[129] (s) AJDempsey	25/1		co
16	Carbury Cross (IRE) *JonjoO'Neill* 9-11-7[135] (b) RMcGrath	16/1		ur
	Eau de Cologne *BGPowell* 11-10-11[130] (b) JamesDavies[5]	25/1		ur
	Granit d'Estruval (FR) *FerdyMurphy* 9-10-8[125] PAspell[3]	12/1		ur
2	Pessimistic Dick *HMorrison* 10-10-0[114] PaulMoloney	100/1		ur
	Maximize (IRE) *MCPipe* 9-11-2[130] (v) RGreene	11/1		pu
	Good Shuil (IRE) *CJMann* 8-11-1[129] NFehily	33/1		pu
	Good Vintage (IRE) *NMeade,Ireland* 8-10-7[121] BHarding	12/1		pu

Mr John P. McManus 15ran 7m01.63

NAVAN Sunday, Nov 23   GOOD to SOFT

29   Pierse Contracting Troytown Hcap Chase (Gr A) 0-150(142) (4yo+)   3m (17)
£36,364

6	CLOUDY BAYS (IRE) *CByrnes* 6-10-2[119] (s) RGeraghty[3]	3/1f		1
	STAR CLIPPER *NMeade* 6-10-5[119] TJMurphy	14/1	25	2
	TAKAGI (IRE) *EJO'Grady* 8-12-0[142] BJGeraghty	14/1	3½	3
	GOLDEN STORM (IRE) *JosephCrowley* 6-10-0[121] (b) JMAllen[7]	12/1	10	4
	Western View (IRE) *CecilRoss* 11-10-8[122] BMCash	20/1	3½	5
	Nomadic *NMeade* 9-10-11[125] CO'Dwyer	14/1		6
	Cherry Hunter (IRE) *JTRDreaper* 7-9-9[116] RCColgan[7]	10/1		7
	Super Fellow (IRE) *DPMurphy* 9-9-10[117] (t) MrCMotherway[7]	22/1		8

1016

    4 Cregg House (IRE) *SDonohoe* 8-10-3[124] DFO'Regan[7] 25/1   9
      Coq Hardi Diamond (IRE) *NMeade* 9-9-13[116] GTHutchinson[3] 14/1   10
      I'vehadit (IRE) *DTHughes* 9-10-8[127] MrRLoughran[5] 11/1   11
    4 Wotsitooya (IRE) *MJPO'Brien* 11-10-2[121] MrDWCullen[5] 7/1   12
    6 Glynn Dingle (IRE) *AJMartin* 10-10-13[127] WSlattery 14/1   13
      Rockwell Island (IRE) *MissFMCrowley* 7-10-3[120] (b) IJPower[5] .... 14/1   f
      Come In Moscow (IRE) *JohnJosephMurphy* 7-9-7[114] WOCallaghan[7] .... 33/1   f
      Schwartzhalle (IRE) *DHarvey* 6-10-13[130] MFMooney[3] .... 11/1   pu
      This Is Serious (IRE) *CFSwan* 9-11-2[130] DJCasey .... 7/1   pu
      Dutsdale Dancer (IRE) *AJWhelan* 9-10-9[126] DJHoward[3] .... 16/1   pu
      Killultagh Thunder (IRE) *WPMullins* 7-10-0[114] JRBarry .... 10/1   pu

    Cloudy Bay Syndicate 19ran 6m10.60

NEWBURY Saturday, Nov 29   Chase course: GOOD, Hurdles course: GOOD to SOFT

30 Ballymore Properties Long Distance Hdle (Gr 2) (A) (4yo+) £23,200   3m110y (13)

      BARACOUDA (FR) *FDoumen,France* 8-11-8 TDoumen 4/9f   1
      DEANO'S BEENO *MCPipe* 11-11-8 APMcCoy 4/1   7 2
    22 SPRINGFIELD SCALLY *SGollings* 10-11-0 JCulloty 33/1   10 3
      Count Campioni (IRE) *MPitman* 9-11-0 TJMurphy 50/1   3 4
      Sleeping Night (FR) *PFNicholls* 7-11-0 RWalsh 7/1   1 5
      Sea Drifting *KAMorgan* 6-11-0 PJBrennan 100/1   29 6
      Happy Hussar (IRE) *DrPPritchard* 10-11-0 DrPPritchard 300/1   11 7
      Sir Talbot *JABOld* 9-11-0 LAspell .... 33/1   pu

    Mr John P. McManus 8ran 5m58.34

31 Hennessy Cognac Gold Cup Chase (Showcase Hcap) (Gr 3) (A)   3¼m110y (21)
   (152) (5yo+) £63,800

      STRONG FLOW (IRE) *PFNicholls* 6-11-0[140] RWalsh.................................... 5/1jf   1
      JOSS NAYLOR (IRE) *JonjoO'Neill* 8-10-9[135] BJGeraghty 6/1   14 2
    2 TAKE CONTROL (IRE) *MCPipe* 9-10-9[135] (v) APMcCoy 25/1   1½ 3
      HEDGEHUNTER (IRE) *WPMullins,Ireland* 7-10-4[130] DJCasey 9/1   1¼ 4
      Merchants Friend (IRE) *CJMann* 8-10-3[129] NFehily 66/1   10 5
    10 Barrow Drive *AnthonyMullins,Ireland* 7-11-2[142] (t) JCulloty 20/1   26 6
    6 Native Performance (IRE) *MHourigan,Ireland* 8-10-0[126] TJMurphy 40/1   5 7
      Tom's Prize *JLSpearing* 8-10-1[127] LAspell .... 50/1   nk 8
      Iznogoud (FR) *MCPipe* 7-10-13[142] MrGordonElliott[3] 100/1   5 9
      Royal Predica (FR) *MCPipe* 9-11-0[143] (t) JEMoore[3] 66/1   11 10
      One Knight (IRE) *PJHobbs* 7-11-12[152] RJohnson .... 12/1   f
      Sir Rembrandt (IRE) *RHAlner* 7-11-3[143] AThornton .... 12/1   f
    2 Take The Stand (IRE) *PBowen* 7-10-5[131] SDurack .... 33/1   bd
      Irish Hussar (IRE) *NJHenderson* 7-11-4[144] MAFitzgerald............................ 5/1jf   pu
      Arlas (FR) *MCPipe* 8-11-2[142] TScudamore .... 100/1   pu
      Be My Belle (IRE) *SJTreacy,Ireland* 7-11-0[140] JPMcNamara .... 50/1   pu
    21 The Premier Cat (IRE) *TCahill,Ireland* 7-10-13[139] JRBarry .... 10/1   pu
      Gunther McBride (IRE) *PJHobbs* 8-10-10[136] TDoyle .... 20/1   pu
    16 Shardam (IRE) *NATwiston-Davies* 6-10-10[136] CLlewellyn............................ 9/1   pu
    10 Jungle Jinks (IRE) *GMMoore* 8-10-6[132] ARoss .... 25/1   pu
      Cruise The Fairway (IRE) *BGPowell* 7-10-4[130] PHide .... 66/1   pu

    Mr B. C. Marshall 21ran 6m36.94

32 Stan James Gerry Feilden Int Hdle (Ltd Hcap) (L) (A) 0-145(142)   2m110y (8)
   (4yo+) £14,500

    1 TRAMANTANO *NATwiston-Davies* 4-10-12[130] CLlewellyn 16/1   1
      SPORAZENE (IRE) *PFNicholls* 4-11-8[140] RWalsh .... 2/1f   nk 2
      SAINTSAIRE (IRE) *NJHenderson* 4-10-9[127] MAFitzgerald 5/2   5 3
    18 Do L'Enfant d'Eau (FR) *PJHobbs* 4-11-0[132] SDurack 40/1   11 4
    12 Well Chief (GER) *MCPipe* 4-11-10[142] APMcCoy 9/2   1½ 5
      Nawamees (IRE) *GLMoore* 5-10-4[122] TJMurphy 20/1   5 6
      Spectroscope (IRE) *JonjoO'Neill* 4-11-7[139] BJGeraghty .... 10/1   dist 7
      Limerick Boy (GER) *MissVenetiaWilliams* 5-11-8[140] AThornton .... 6/1   pu

    Mr H. R. Mould 8ran 4m01.40

NEWCASTLE Saturday, Nov 29   GOOD to SOFT

33 Pertemps 'Fighting Fifth' Hdle (Gr 2) (A) (4yo+) £26,100   2m (9)

      THE FRENCH FURZE (IRE) *NGRichards* 9-11-0 BHarding 25/1   1
      GEOS (FR) *NJHenderson* 8-11-0 MFoley .... 8/1   ¾ 2
    8 INTERSKY FALCON *JonjoO'Neill* 6-11-8 (b) LCooper................................... 1/2f   2½ 3
      Latalomne (USA) *BEllison* 9-11-0 (b) JCrowley.. 50/1   14 4
      Ontos (GER) *MissVScott* 7-11-0 ACCoyle 150/1   13 5
      Mister McGoldrick *MrsSJSmith* 6-11-0 PWhelan 16/1   18 6
      Teme Valley *JHowardJohnson* 9-11-0 PBuchanan 250/1   1½ 7

Westender (FR) *MCPipe* 7-11-0 (b) RGreene .... 7/2   pu

Mr Jim Ennis 8ran 3m52.89

FAIRYHOUSE Saturday, Nov 29   SOFT

34   **betfair.com Juv 3-Y-O Hdle (3yo)** £15,909   2m (10)

IMAZULUTOO (IRE) *MrsJHarrington* 3-10-6 MPWalsh[7]		6/1	1
TOP STRATEGY (IRE) *TMWalsh* 3-10-6 GTHutchinson[3]		6/1	1½ 2
YOU NEED LUCK (IRE) *MrsJHarrington* 3-10-2 ADLeigh[7]		7/1	4 3
Raikkonen (IRE) *WPMullins* 3-10-9 TPTreacy		10/1	3½ 4
Berkeley Note (IRE) *MHalford* 3-10-4 PCarberry		4/1f	½ 5
Golden Triangle (IRE) *PatrickCarey* 3-10-1 MDGrant[3]		20/1	6
Streets of Steel (IRE) *MissJaneThomas* 3-10-6 SPMcCann[3]		33/1	7
Monjoyau (FR) *EJO'Grady* 3-10-9 CO'Dwyer		6/1	8
Learn To Dance (USA) *PatrickMullins* 3-10-9 GCotter		14/1	9
Blue Corrig (IRE) *JosephCrowley* 3-10-9 (b) JLCullen		6/1	10
Guilt *DTHughes* 3-10-2 PWFlood[7]		16/1	11
Lucky Slipper (IRE) *ThomasCarmody* 3-10-1 APLane[3]		33/1	12
Smoking Barrels *PJFlynn* 3-10-4 SFitzgerald[5]		33/1	13
Loyal (GER) *PHughes* 3-10-6 IJPower[3]		20/1	14
Bobington (IRE) *AJMartin* 3-10-9 WSlattery		20/1	15
Spanchil Hill *CMcCarthy* 3-10-2 DFO'Regan[3]		33/1	16
Drift Away (USA) *JJLambe* 3-10-3 KHadnett[3]		12/1	17
Happenstance (IRE) *MHourigan* 3-10-9 JECasey		25/1	18
Chloe's Pride (IRE) *MVManning* 3-9-13 (t) OKelly[5]		50/1	ur
Bermaho (IRE) *GMLyons* 3-10-6 JPElliott[3]		14/1	pu
Loudspeaker (USA) *PHughes* 3-10-6 LAHurley[3]		25/1	pu
Queen Meabh (IRE) *DHassett* 3-10-4 PACarberry		50/1	pu

Mr E. Salmon 22ran 4m12.40

35   **Moynalvey GFC (Pro-Am) INH Flat (4yo+)** £5,790   2m

MARTINSTOWN (IRE) *CRoche* 4-11-2 MrPRoche[7]		1/1f	1
MASTER ALBERT (IRE) *DWachman* 5-11-7 MrJPMagnier[7]		5/1	4½ 2
AWAY HOME (IRE) *MJPO'Brien* 5-11-11 MrDWCullen[3]		9/1	nk 3
Another Native (IRE) *FFlood* 5-11-0 MrDMacAuley[7]		20/1	2½ 4
Golden Alliance (IRE) *ColmAMurphy* 5-10-9 MrJPFortune[7]		10/1	7 5
Millview Rose (IRE) *AlanLucey* 6-11-2 MrJGSheehan[7]		12/1	6
Desperado Queen (IRE) *LWDoran* 5-11-2 MissTDoran[7]		16/1	7
The Parishioner (IRE) *MHourigan* 5-11-2 MrROHarding[5]		10/1	8
Buddess (IRE) *ThomasCarberry* 6-10-9 MissNCarberry[7]		20/1	9
Corrycroar (IRE) *DPKelly* 5-11-0 MsRTiernan[7]		25/1	10
De Jure (IRE) *NMeade* 4-11-4 MrNPMadden[5]		11/2	11
Andreas Pet (IRE) *PAFahy* 5-10-9 (t) MrTCarroll[7]		20/1	12
Intergalactic (IRE) *DTHughes* 4-10-9 MrRMHennessy[7]		20/1	13
The Spacer (IRE) *MHourigan* 5-11-0 MrJWFarrelly[7]		20/1	14
The French Actor (IRE) *WAMurphy* 5-11-7 MrJPDempsey		33/1	15

Mr John P. McManus 15ran 4m07.50

NEWBURY Sunday, Nov 30   GOOD

36   **stanjamesuk.com Worcester Nov Chase (Gr 2) (A) (5yo+)** £23,450   3m (18)

4	BALLYCASSIDY (IRE) *PBowen* 7-11-9 RJohnson	2/1	1
	NATIVE EMPEROR *JonjoO'Neill* 7-11-2 LCooper	15/8f	hd 2
	CELESTIAL GOLD (IRE) *MCPipe* 5-11-1 APMcCoy	7/2	dist 3
	Gielgud *PRWebber* 6-11-2 (t) MAFitzgerald	16/1	pu
	High Cotton (IRE) *DRCElsworth* 8-11-2 AThornton	20/1	pu
	Tacin (IRE) *BGPowell* 6-11-2 JTizzard	11/1	pu

Mr R. Owen 6ran 5m58.63

FAIRYHOUSE Sunday, Nov 30   GOOD TO SOFT

37   **Boylesports Royal Bond Nov Hdle (Gr 1) (4yo+)** £31,818   2m (10)

NEWMILL (IRE) *TGO'Leary* 5-11-12 GCotter		13/2	1
MARIAH ROLLINS (IRE) *PAFahy* 5-11-7 DJCasey		14/1	¾ 2
STRIKE BACK (IRE) *MrsJHarrington* 5-11-12 BJGeraghty		3/1f	12 3
Always *NMeade* 4-11-7 PCarberry		14/1	1 4
Accordion Etoile (IRE) *PaulNolan* 4-11-7 JLCullen		9/2	2½ 5
Rupununi (IRE) *FrancisEnnis* 6-11-12 TJMurphy		9/1	6
Clounties Hill (IRE) *WPMullins* 6-11-12 (s+t) RWalsh		14/1	7
Field Marshal (IRE) *EJO'Grady* 5-11-12 DNRussell		10/1	8
Kim Fontaine (FR) *WPMullins* 5-11-7 MrJJCodd		10/1	9
Back Nine (IRE) *ALTMoore* 6-11-12 CO'Dwyer		5/1	10
Kelly's Craft (IRE) *WPMullins* 6-11-12 (t) JRBarry		33/1	11
Dyrick Daybreak (IRE) *DavidAKiely* 4-11-2 (t) KHadnett		12/1	f

Mrs Mary T. Hayes 12ran 3m51.93

38   **Pierse Group Drinmore Nov Chase (Gr 1) (5yo+)** £34,091   2½m (16)

NIL DESPERANDUM (IRE) *MissFMCrowley* 6-11-12 RWalsh 11/4   1
CATALPA CARGO (IRE) *CRoche* 9-11-12 CO'Dwyer 14/1 14 2
BALLYAMBER (IRE) *WPMullins* 8-11-12 DNRussell............................... 16/1   1 3
Satco Express (IRE) *ESheehy* 7-11-12 JRBarry 9/2 1½ 4
Anxious Moments (IRE) *CFSwan* 8-11-12 DJCasey 8/1   7 5
Hi Cloy (IRE) *MHourigan* 6-11-12 TJMurphy 8/1   6
Mullacash (IRE) *NMeade* 5-11-9 PCarberry 20/1   7
  5 Splendour (IRE) *MissSCox* 8-11-12 JLCullen .... 14/1   f
Golfeur (IRE) *JTRDreaper* 9-11-12 GCotter.. 50/1   pu
Pizarro (IRE) *EJO'Grady* 6-11-12 BJGeraghty...................................... 7/4f   pu

Mr M. L. Shone 10ran 5m08.35

39   **Ballymore Properties Hatton's Grace Hdle (Gr 1) (4yo+)** £34,091   2½m (12)

 20 SOLERINA (IRE) *JamesBowe* 6-11-7 GTHutchinson 7/4jf   1
FLORIDA COAST (IRE) *JamesBowe* 8-11-12 PCarberry 33/1   8 2
 20 SCARTHY LAD (IRE) *TGO'Leary* 6-11-12 CO'Dwyer 8/1   5 3
Davenport Milenium (IRE) *WPMullins* 7-11-12 RWalsh........................ 12/1 hd 4
 20 Sacundai (IRE) *EJO'Grady* 6-11-12 BJGeraghty 7/4jf 11 5
Prince of Tara (IRE) *SJMahon* 6-11-12 IJPower 50/1   6
Holy Orders (IRE) *WPMullins* 6-11-12 (b) JRBarry 12/1   7
Pay It Forward *MrsJHarrington* 5-11-12 TJMurphy 25/1   8
Aine Dubh (IRE) *KevinFO'Donnell* 6-11-7 SCurling 33/1   9
Fota Island (IRE) *MFMorris* 7-11-12 DJCasey .... 10/1   f

Mr John P. Bowe 10ran 4m51.29

SANDOWN Friday, Dec 5   GOOD to SOFT

40   **William Hill Winter Nov Hdle (Gr 2) (A) (4yo+)** £14,500   2½m110y (10)

INGLIS DREVER *JHowardJohnson* 4-11-7 GLee 5/2   1
SELF DEFENSE *MissECLavelle* 6-11-7 FKeniry............................... 6/4f   7 2
CONTROL MAN (IRE) *MCPipe* 5-11-0 APMcCoy 5/2 16 3
Mister Flint *PJHobbs* 5-11-0 PFlynn 22/1 3½ 4
Green Belt Flyer (IRE) *MrsJHarrington,Ireland* 5-11-4 RMPower 14/1 12 5
Father Abraham (IRE) *JAkehurst* 5-11-4 SDurack .... 66/1 dist 6
Dooberry Firkin *MrsSGardner* 5-10-7 JCulloty 150/1 22 7

Andrea & Graham Wylie 7ran 5m02.80

CHEPSTOW Saturday, Dec 6   GOOD to SOFT

41   **John Hughes Rehearsal Chase (Ltd Hcap) (L) (A) (162) (5yo+)**   3¼m110y (22)
    £23,800

 31 SIR REMBRANDT (IRE) *RHAlner* 7-10-5[143] AThornton.............................. 9/4   1
 28 BINDAREE (IRE) *NATwiston-Davies* 9-10-4[142] CLlewellyn 7/1   8 2
 16 STORMEZ (FR) *MCPipe* 6-10-8[149] (t) JEMoore[3] .... 7/1 dist 3
See More Business (IRE) *PFNicholls* 13-11-10[162] JTizzard 13/2 24 4
Blazing Batman *DrPPritchard* 10-9-13[142] DrPPritchard[5] .... 250/1 dist 5
Keen Leader (IRE) *JonjoO'Neill* 7-11-4[156] LCooper .... 6/4f   ur

Mr A. Hordle 6ran 6m52.28

SANDOWN Saturday, Dec 6   GOOD to SOFT

42   **Henry VIII Nov Chase (Gr 2) (A) (4yo+)** £17,400   2m (13)

 17 THISTHATANDTOTHER (IRE) *PFNicholls* 7-11-10 RWalsh............. 4/7f   1
 17 ATUM RE (IRE) *PRWebber* 6-11-10 MFoley 33/1   4 2
CHAUVINIST (IRE) *NJHenderson* 8-11-4 MAFitzgerald 9/2   5 3
Puntal (FR) *MCPipe* 7-11-10 APMcCoy 5/1   2 4
 18 Jaboune (FR) *AKing* 6-11-4 RJohnson.. 20/1   3 5
Translucid (USA) *CVonDerRecke,Germany* 5-11-4 TScudamore 66/1   7 6
Master Rex *BDeHaan* 8-11-4 RFlavin.. 50/1   pu

Mr C. G. Roach 7ran 3m58.34

43   **William Hill - Tingle Creek Trophy Chase (Gr 1) (A) (5yo+)** £58,000   2m (13)

MOSCOW FLYER (IRE) *MrsJHarrington,Ireland* 9-11-7 BJGeraghty......... 6/4f   1
 11 AZERTYUIOP (FR) *PFNicholls* 6-11-7 RWalsh 2/1   4 2
FLAGSHIP UBERALLES (IRE) *PJHobbs* 9-11-7 RJohnson 16/1   7 3
 24 Le Roi Miguel (FR) *PFNicholls* 5-11-7 MAFitzgerald.......................... 11/2 3½ 4
Cenkos (FR) *PFNicholls* 9-11-7 TJMurphy .... 8/1 ¾ 5
 11 Seebald (GER) *MCPipe* 8-11-7 APMcCoy 14/1 11 6
Eskleybrook *NATwiston-Davies* 10-11-7 RBiddlecombe .... 100/1 dist 7

Mr Brian Kearney 7ran 3m55.70

44   **William Hill Hcap Hdle (L) (A) 0-140(140) (4yo+)** £29,000   2m110y (8)

OVERSTRAND (IRE) *MrsMReveley* 4-10-6[120] RWalsh 9/1   1

OUR VIC (IRE) *MCPipe* 5-11-12[140] APMcCoy 3/1f 5 2
MONKERHOSTIN (FR) *PJHobbs* 6-11-8[136] RJohnson 16/1 4 3
Starzaan (IRE) *HMorrison* 4-11-10[138] TJMurphy 10/1 1¼ 4
Isio (FR) *NJHenderson* 7-11-2[130] MAFitzgerald 7/1 5 5
Yogi (IRE) *ThomasFoley,Ireland* 7-11-2[130] GCotter 33/1 2½ 6
5 Aye Aye Popeye (IRE) *MrsJHarrington,Ireland* 5-10-2[116] (b) MFoley 10/1 7 7
Mistanoora *NATwiston-Davies* 4-11-2[135] (b) RBiddlecombe[5] 25/1 6 8
27 East Tycoon (IRE) *JonjoO'Neill* 4-10-10[124] (b) BJGeraghty 4/1 4 9
Never (FR) *FDoumen,France* 6-11-12[140] TDoumen 6/1 7 10
Cotopaxi (IRE) *MissVenetiaWilliams* 7-10-11[128] AO'Keeffe[3] 50/1 8 11
The Biker (IRE) *MCPipe* 6-10-13[127] TScudamore .... 50/1 pu
Fortune Island (IRE) *MCPipe* 4-10-5[119] (v) BFenton .... 16/1 pu
27 Another Dude (IRE) *JHowardJohnson* 6-10-0[114] GLee .... 12/1 pu

F. F. Racing Services Partnership IV 14ran 4m02.05

PUNCHESTOWN Sunday, Dec 7   GOOD to SOFT

45 **John Durkan Memorial Punchestown Chase (Gr 1) (5yo+) £40,909**   2½m (13)

21 BEEF OR SALMON (IRE) *MHourigan* 7-11-12 TJMurphy 4/5f 1
TIUTCHEV *MCPipe,GB* 10-11-12 APMcCoy 11/2 3½ 2
RINCE RI (IRE) *TMWalsh* 10-11-12 RWalsh 14/1 2½ 3
Le Coudray (FR) *CRoche* 9-11-12 (t) BJGeraghty 10/1 10 4
Native Upmanship (IRE) *ALTMoore* 10-11-12 CO'Dwyer 3/1 2½ 5
4 Knife Edge (USA) *MJPO'Brien* 8-11-12 DNRussell 20/1 6
21 Arctic Copper (IRE) *NMeade* 9-11-12 (s) MAFitzgerald 25/1 7

Mr B. J. Craig 7ran 5m11.00

CHELTENHAM Friday, Dec 12   GOOD to SOFT (Old Course)

46 **Ian Williams' Owners Nov Chase (B) (5yo+) £12,586**   3m1f110y (18)

14 THEREALBANDIT (IRE) *MCPipe* 6-11-0 APMcCoy 11/10f 1
ROSSLEA (IRE) *MissHCKnight* 5-11-5 JCulloty 3/1 8 2
CHICAGO BULLS (IRE) *AKing* 5-11-0 RThornton .... 12/1 ¾ 3
Wheareareyounow (IRE) *NATwiston-Davies* 6-11-8 CLlewellyn 5/1 8 4
Dear Deal *CLTizzard* 10-11-8 JTizzard .... 14/1 dist 5
Punchy (IRE) *MCPipe* 7-11-8 RGreene 66/1 8 6
No Sam No *SCBurrough* 5-11-0 PFlynn .... 100/1 dist 7
Goodtime George (IRE) *MPitman* 10-11-5 TJMurphy .... 14/1 pu
Another Moose (IRE) *MissECLavelle* 8-11-0 BFenton .... 33/1 pu

Mr D. A. Johnson 9ran 6m44.66

47 **Tripleprint Chase (Hcap) (B) (158) (5yo+) £23,200**   3m1f110y (19)

23 KINGSCLIFF (IRE) *RHAlner* 6-11-2[148] AThornton 4/7f 1
HAUT CERCY (FR) *HDDaly* 8-10-5[137] RJohnson 7/1 6 2
10 MARLBOROUGH (IRE) *NJHenderson* 11-11-9[155] MAFitzgerald 8/1 6 3
16 Lord Noelie (IRE) *MsBridgetNicholls* 10-11-1[147] JTizzard 12/1 11 4
23 Exit To Wave (FR) *PFNicholls* 7-10-2[134] RWalsh .... 11/1 ½ 5
15 Cyfor Malta (FR) *MCPipe* 10-11-12[158] APMcCoy 20/1 12 6
Master Tern (USA) *JonjoO'Neill* 8-10-4[136] ADobbin 25/1 10 7

Mr A. J. Sendell 7ran 6m46.00

CHELTENHAM Saturday, Dec 13   SOFT (Old Course)

48 **Jet UK "Reelkeel" Hdle (B) (4yo+) £12,122**   2m5f (10)

27 CRYSTAL D'AINAY (FR) *AKing* 4-10-12 RThornton 2/1f 1
22 SH BOOM *JonjoO'Neill* 5-10-12 APMcCoy 9/4 1 2
44 STARZAAN (IRE) *HMorrison* 4-10-12 RWalsh 4/1 8 3
32 Do L'Enfant d'Eau (FR) *PJHobbs* 4-11-1 RJohnson 25/1 14 4
Glenmoss Tara (IRE) *NGRichards* 5-10-7 ADobbin 8/1 6 5
Patriarch Express *GAHarker* 6-10-12 NHannity 8/1 2 6
Gigs Bounty *MPitman* 5-10-12 TJMurphy .... 100/1 dist 7

Mr Tony Fisher & Mrs Jeni Fisher 7ran 5m19.26

49 **Tripleprint Gold Cup (Hcap Chase) (Gr 3) (A) (155) (5yo+) £58,000**   2½m110y (15)

24 IRIS ROYAL (FR) *NJHenderson* 7-10-13[142] MAFitzgerald 7/1 1
15 RISK ACCESSOR (IRE) *CRoche,Ireland* 10-10-8[137] (t) TJMurphy .... 10/1 hd 2
TELEMOSS (IRE) *NGRichards* 9-10-6[135] ADobbin 5/1 13 3
ROYAL AUCLAIR (FR) *PFNicholls* 6-11-1[147] (t) ChristianWilliams[3] 33/1 1½ 4
15 It Takes Time (IRE) *MCPipe* 9-11-4[147] APMcCoy 10/1 12 5
Armaturk (FR) *PFNicholls* 6-11-0[146] RPMcNally[3] 100/1 8 6
22 Ballinclay King (IRE) *FerdyMurphy* 9-10-11[143] NMulholland[3] 20/1 6 7
26 Kadoun (FR) *MJPO'Brien,Ireland* 6-10-8[142] (v) MrDWCullen[5] 10/1 5 8
15 Young Spartacus *HDDaly* 10-11-5[148] MBradburne 14/1 6 9
15 Ei Ei *MCChapman* 8-10-8[140] LVickers[3] 100/1 10 10

26 Adamant Approach (IRE) *WPMullins,Ireland* 9-11-2[145] RWalsh .... 20/1 ¾ 11
15 Redemption *NATwiston-Davies* 8-10-13[142] WMarston................................ 10/1 f
   Indian Scout (IRE) *BDeHaan* 8-9-9[129] JamesDavies[5] .... 14/1 f
27 Hand Inn Hand *HDDaly* 7-11-2[145] RJohnson................................... 7/2f bd
   Foly Pleasant (FR) *MissHCKnight* 9-11-12[155] (t) RThornton .... 40/1 pu
43 Eskleybrook *NATwiston-Davies* 10-11-1[149] P.Biddlecombe[5] .... 200/1 pu
   Banker Count *MissVenetiaWilliams* 11-10-5[141] SThomas[7]..................... 66/1 pu

   Sir Robert Ogden 17ran 5m15.44

50 Tote Bula Hdle (Gr 2) (A) (4yo+) £43,500   2m110y (8)
18 RIGMAROLE *PFNicholls* 5-11-4 (t) RThornton 25/1 1
39 DAVENPORT MILENIUM (IRE) *WPMullins,Ireland* 7-11-0 RWalsh 11/1 1 2
18 HASTY PRINCE *JonjoO'Neill* 5-11-0 APMcCoy 10/1 1¾ 3
   Flame Creek (IRE) *NoelTChance* 5-11-8 SDurack 20/1 1 4
   Rooster Booster *PJHobbs* 9-11-8 RJohnson 8/13f 1¼ 5
   Spirit Leader (IRE) *MrsJHarrington,Ireland* 7-10-11 MAFitzgerald .... 4/1 hd 6
33 The French Furze (IRE) *NGRichards* 9-11-8 ADobbin............................... 33/1 20 7

   Mr & Mrs Mark Woodhouse 7ran 4m10.16

51 Tripleprint Bristol Nov Hdle (Gr 2) (A) (4yo+) £17,400   3m1f110y (13)
   COMPLY OR DIE (IRE) *MCPipe* 4-11-4 APMcCoy 2/1f 1
   PHAR FROM FROSTY (IRE) *CREgerton* 6-11-4 ATinkler 9/2 3 2
   CHAMPAGNE HARRY *NATwiston-Davies* 5-11-7 RBiddlecombe................. 8/1 10 3
   Wintertide *CJMann* 7-11-7 DCrosse 8/1 2 4
   Thieves'glen *HMorrison* 5-11-0 TJMurphy... 9/1 ½ 5
   Keepers Mead (IRE) *RHAlner* 5-11-4 RWalford 33/1 18 6
   Red Emperor *DrPPritchard* 9-11-0 DrPPritchard .... 200/1 dist 7
   Bosham Mill *JonjoO'Neill* 5-11-4 ADobbin .... 11/4 pu
   Forbearing (IRE) *MCPipe* 6-11-0 TBalfour... 150/1 pu

   Mr D. A. Johnson 9ran 6m42.05

   HAYDOCK Saturday, Dec 13   SOFT

52 Tote Placepot Hcap Hdle (B) (157) (4yo+) £20,153   2½m (10)
   RHINESTONE COWBOY (IRE) *JonjoO'Neill* 7-11-5[157] MrJPMagnier[7] 5/6f 1
   DOUBLE HONOUR (FR) *PJHobbs* 5-10-2[133] PFlynn 11/4 8 2
27 LOOP THE LOUP *MrsMReveley* 7-9-7[131] (v) MrONelmes[7] 16/1 2½ 3
   Newhall (IRE) *FFlood,Ireland* 5-10-0[131] FJFlood 11/2 2 4
   Fred's In The Know *NWaggott* 8-10-1[137] ACCoyle[5] 50/1 21 5
   Bunkum *RLee* 5-9-11[131] AO'Keeffe[3] .... 22/1 dist 6
   Luzcadou (FR) *FerdyMurphy* 10-9-7[131] (b) CSharkey[7] .... 50/1 f
22 Hugo de Perro (FR) *PMonteith* 8-10-1[132] KRenwick............................. 20/1 rtr

   Mrs John Magnier 8ran 5m03.14

53 Tommy Whittle Chase (Gr 2) (A) (5yo+) £34,800   3m (18)
41 KEEN LEADER (IRE) *JonjoO'Neill* 7-11-5 BJGeraghty............................ 5/4f 1
   TRUCKERS TAVERN (IRE) *FerdyMurphy* 8-11-6 (t) DNRussell 11/2 17 2
19 HUSSARD COLLONGES (FR) *PBeaumont* 8-11-0 RGarritty 11/4 10 3
   Chives (IRE) *MissHCKnight* 8-11-0 JCulloty 6/1 17 4
   Ryalux (IRE) *ACrook* 10-11-6 RMcGrath .... 33/1 dist 5
19 Kingsmark (IRE) *MTodhunter* 10-11-6 DRDennis 11/1 21 6
   Streamstown (IRE) *FerdyMurphy* 9-11-0 CSharkey .... 100/1 pu

   Mrs Stewart Catherwood 7ran 6m19.40

   LINGFIELD Saturday, Dec 13   SOFT

54 Join The Sun Punters On 0800 900 8602 December Nov Chase   3m (18)
(Gr 2) (A) (5yo+) £14,500
   LORD SAM (IRE) *VRADartnall* 7-11-4 AThornton 8/13f 1
36 NATIVE EMPEROR *JonjoO'Neill* 7-11-0 TSiddall 11/4 1½ 2
   RUM POINTER (IRE) *RHBuckler* 7-11-0 BHitchcott................................ 8/1 12 3
   Muck Savage *CJMann* 6-11-4 NFehily .... 10/1 dist 4
   Garolsa (FR) *CLTizzard* 9-11-4 JTizzard .... 25/1 dist 5
   Flecthefawna (IRE) *LADace* 7-11-0 OKozak 66/1 27 6

   Plain Peeps 6ran 6m44.50

   CORK Sunday, Dec 14   GOOD to SOFT

55 O'Connell Warehousing Hilly Way Chase (Gr 2) (5yo+) £22,887   2m (11)
45 BEEF OR SALMON (IRE) *MHourigan* 7-11-12 TJMurphy......................... 2/5f 1
26 RATHGAR BEAU (IRE) *ESheehy* 7-11-7 (b) JRBarry 6/1 3½ 2
45 KNIFE EDGE (USA) *MJPO'Brien* 8-11-12 (s) MrDWCullen...................... 6/1 4½ 3
 6 Killultagh Storm (IRE) *WPMullins* 9-11-7 (s) RWalsh 8/1 4 4

   Mr B. J. Craig 4ran 3m59.40

1021

56 **Fermoy Nov Chase (4yo+)** £9,155   2m (11)

MOSSY GREEN (IRE) *WPMullins* 9-11-12 RWalsh 5/4f   1
38 HI CLOY (IRE) *MHourigan* 6-11-5 TJMurphy .... 4/1   ¾ 2
CAISHILL (IRE) *JosephCrowley* 4-11-1 JRBarry 10/1   7 3
Commonchero (IRE) *MJPO'Brien* 6-11-2 MrDWCullen[3] 6/1   25 4
Le Frere (IRE) *PJStokes* 8-11-2 DCrosse[3] 33/1   1½ 5
Urlan Castle (IRE) *PRLenihan* 6-11-2 SMMcGovern[3] 50/1   6
The Culdee (IRE) *FFlood* 7-11-5 KWhelan 16/1   7
Johnyyouronlyjoken (IRE) *NFGlynn* 7-11-5 WSlattery 33/1   8
Take The Oath (IRE) *MHourigan* 6-11-6 PGHourigan.................... 20/1   9
Bowling Green (IRE) *PRLenihan* 7-11-2 PJCrowley[3] 20/1   10
Ardragoal (IRE) *CByrnes* 5-10-9 DJHoward[3] 25/1   11
Camden Tanner (IRE) *RobertTyner* 7-11-12 DNRussell .... 3/1   f
Annshoon (IRE) *MGHolden* 8-11-4 MDGrant[3] .... 16/1   f
Future Strike (IRE) *JLHassett* 6-11-5 PACarberry .... 14/1   f
Touch Supreme (IRE) *JEKiely* 7-11-2 IJPower[3] .... 14/1   ur

Greenstar Syndicate 15ran 4m02.40

NAVAN Sunday, Dec 14   SOFT

57 **Barry & Sandra Kelly Memorial Nov Hdle (Gr 2) (4yo+)** £32,042   2½m (11)

37 NEWMILL (IRE) *TGO'Leary* 5-11-12 BJGeraghty 5/2   1
KILDARE (IRE) *DTHughes* 6-11-5 DJCasey 3/1   8 2
KADISKAR (IRE) *CRoche* 5-11-8 (t) CO'Dwyer 6/4f   3½ 3
37 Always *NMeade* 4-11-0 MAFitzgerald 10/1   9 4
Fairwood Present (IRE) *PJRothwell* 5-11-5 JLCullen...................... 8/1   ¾ 5

Mrs Mary T. Hayes 5ran 4m54.80

58 **Giltspur Scientific Tara Hdle (Gr 3) (4yo+)** £18,310   2½m (11)

39 SOLERINA (IRE) *JamesBowe* 6-11-4 GTHutchinson[3] 1/3f   1
ROSAKER (USA) *NMeade* 6-11-10 BJGeraghty 6/1   7 2
39 FLORIDA COAST (IRE) *JamesBowe* 8-10-9 DFO'Regan[7] 8/1   6 3
39 Scarthy Lad (IRE) *TGO'Leary* 5-11-5 CO'Dwyer 10/1   4½ 4
Leinster (IRE) *DTHughes* 6-11-10 DJCasey 20/1   1½ 5
Mutineer (IRE) *DTHughes* 4-10-12 (t) PWFlood[7] 33/1   6
Jack High (IRE) *TMWalsh* 8-11-8 GCotter..................................... 12/1   7
The Bunny Boiler (IRE) *NMeade* 9-11-1 PCStringer[7] 33/1   8
General Cloney (IRE) *SDonohoe* 7-11-2 MAFitzgerald 50/1   9

Mr John P. Bowe 9ran 4m52.40

59 **Bar-One Racing Hcap Hdle 0-130(130) (4yo+)** £10,299   2m (10)

BRAVE INCA (IRE) *ColmAMurphy* 5-10-3[105] BMCash................ 5/4f   1
GEORGES GIRL (IRE) *FFlood* 5-11-2[118] FJFlood........................ 12/1   4 2
SNOB WELLS (IRE) *NMeade* 6-10-0[109] PCStringer[7] 8/1   4 3
Oh Be The Hokey (IRE) *CFSwan* 5-10-7[109] DJCasey................. 6/1   1½ 4
Shaunas Vision (IRE) *MHalford* 4-9-9[100] APLane[3] 9/1   4½ 5
Joe Hill (IRE) *OliverFinnegan* 7-9-7[95] GCotter......................... 10/1   6
Native Stag (IRE) *PAFahy* 5-10-7[109] PWFlood........................... 12/1   7
Fadoudal du Cochet (FR) *ALTMoore* 10-11-9[130] MrJDMoore[5] ... 16/1   8
5 Columba (IRE) *DTHughes* 7-10-13[122] PWFlood[7] 14/1   9
5 Ansari (IRE) *PatrickOBrady* 6-10-8[113] MFMooney[3] 14/1   10
Phariwarmer (IRE) *ALTMoore* 9-11-0[116] CO'Dwyer 16/1   11
Maggies Mare (IRE) *RMcGlinchey* 5-9-0[95] DKane[7] 50/1   12
Samawi (IRE) *MrsAMO'Shea* 5-9-4[95] (b) AO'Shea[3] 20/1   13
Henry Afrika (IRE) *DGMcArdle* 5-9-13[104] MMcCann[3] 25/1   14
29 Dutsdale Dancer (IRE) *AJWhelan* 9-11-2[118] MAFitzgerald.......... 16/1   15

Novices Syndicate 15ran 3m59.90

ASCOT Friday, Dec 19   GOOD to SOFT

60 **Cantor Sport Long Walk Hdle (Gr 1) (A) (4yo+)** £40,600   3m1f110y (14)

30 BARACOUDA (FR) *FDoumen,France* 8-11-7 TDoumen............... 2/7f   1
MR COOL *MCPipe* 9-11-7 TScudamore 10/1   30 2
30 DEANO'S BEENO *MCPipe* 11-11-7 (b) APMcCoy 7/1   5 3
Beyond Control (IRE) *CLTizzard* 8-11-7 JTizzard 33/1   14 4
Teaatral (IRE) *CREgerton* 9-11-7 RJohnson................................ 40/1   21 5
30 Springfield Scally *SGollings* 10-11-7 JCulloty 50/1   27 6

Mr John P. McManus 6ran 6m19.89

61 **Scanmoor Construction Kennel Gate Nov Hdle (Gr 2) (A) (4yo+)**   2m110y (9)
£14,500

PERLE DE PUCE (FR) *NJHenderson* 4-11-0 MAFitzgerald............. 33/1   1
LINGO (IRE) *JonjoO'Neill* 4-11-7 LCooper................................... 13/2   1¼ 2
ERIC'S CHARM (FR) *OSherwood* 5-11-4 APMcCoy 11/2   5 3

```
40  Self Defense MissECLavelle 6-11-7 FKeniry ............................................. 11/4    2  4
    Albuhera (IRE) PFNicholls 5-11-7 (t) RWalsh ...................................... 9/4f  3½ 5
    Liberty Seeker (FR) GASwinbank 4-11-0 PWhelan ............................... 33/1   13  6
    Loup (FR) JRFanshawe 4-11-0 ADobbin ............................................... 16/1  2½ 7
    Widemouth Bay (IRE) PJHobbs 5-11-4 RJohnson ................................. 5/1  1½ 8
    Tomfoolary (IRE) JABOld 6-11-0 MBradburne ...................................... 100/1  dist 9
    Xtra JABOld 5-11-0 LAspell ................................................................ 33/1    pu
```

Mr Robert Waley-Cohen 10ran 4m02.56

UTTOXETER Friday, Dec 19   SOFT

62 St Modwen Properties Beginners' Chase (E) (5yo+) £3,426   2m (12)
```
    TIDOUR (FR) PRWebber 7-11-0 TDoyle ................................................ 25/1    1
    GREEN IDEAL FerdyMurphy 5-10-11 NMulholland[3] .......................... 33/1  2½ 2
    HEY REF (IRE) JonjoO'Neill 6-11-0 BJGeraghty ............................... 9/4  sh 3
    Gotham (FR) RHAlner 6-10-11 MAWalford[3] ...................................... 12/1  7  4
    Keltic Bard CJMann 6-11-0 NFehily .................................................. 11/8f  3  5
    Haditovski JMackie 7-11-0 (v) GLee................................................. 7/1   2  6
    Under The Sand (IRE) PJHobbs 6-11-0 PFlynn ................................. 33/1  9  7
    Jack of Spades (IRE) RDickin 7-11-0 DRDennis .............................. 66/1  1¼ 8
 25 Venn Ottery OJCarter 8-11-0 RGreene .............................................. 100/1  22  9
    Celtic Star (IRE) MissKMGeorge 5-11-0 SDurack.............................. 10/1    ur
    Just A Touch PWinkworth 7-11-0 PHide .............................................. 66/1    pu
```

Mrs M. Fisher 11ran 4m11.88

ASCOT Saturday, Dec 20   SOFT

63 cantorsport.co.uk Silver Cup (Hcap Chase) (L) (A) (158) (5yo+)   3m110y (20)
£29,000
```
 23 HORUS (IRE) MCPipe 8-10-1[136] JEMoore[3] .................................... 11/2    1
    BEHRAJAN (IRE) HDDaly 8-11-12[158] RJohnson............................... 11/4f  1½ 2
 46 DEAR DEAL CLTizzard 10-10-0[132] (t) JTizzard ............................... 20/1  25  3
  9 Tresor de Mai (FR) MCPipe 9-10-5[137] RGreene ............................. 12/1  1¾ 4
    Impek (FR) MissHCKnight 7-11-11[157] JCullotty ............................... 7/2   8  5
 16 Ad Hoc (IRE) PFNicholls 9-11-6[152] RWalsh ................................... 4/1  nk 6
 31 Royal Predica (FR) MCPipe 9-10-6[138] (t) ADobbin ........................ 25/1    pu
 31 Iznogoud (FR) MCPipe 7-10-5[137] APMcCoy .................................. 7/1    pu
```

Mr B. A. Kilpatrick 8ran 6m36.59

64 Ladbroke Hdle (Hcap) (L) (A) 0-150(137) (4yo+) £58,000   2m110y (9)
```
    THESIS (IRE) MissVenetiaWilliams 5-11-2[127] BJCrowley ................. 33/1    1
    SUD BLEU (FR) PFNicholls 5-11-1[126] RWalsh ............................... 7/1   2  2
 32 SAINTSAIRE (FR) NJHenderson 4-11-2[127] MAFitzgerald ................ 7/1  1¼ 3
 44 MONKERHOSTIN (FR) PJHobbs 6-11-12[137] RJohnson.................. 33/1  16  4
 18 Visibility (FR) MCPipe 4-11-7[132] (v) APMcCoy .............................. 25/1  6  5
  1 Cita Verda (FR) PMonteith 5-11-0[125] KRenwick ........................... 25/1  8  6
 44 Overstrand (IRE) MrsMReveley 4-11-7[132] BJGeraghty .................. 9/2jf  3  7
 18 Shalako (USA) PJHobbs 5-10-9[120] PFlynn ................................... 12/1  ¾ 8
    Reiziger (FR) PJHobbs 7-10-6[122] ATinkler[5] ................................. 40/1  ½ 9
    Benbyas DCarroll 6-11-3[135] JLevins[7] .......................................... 33/1  3½ 10
    Pirandello (IRE) KCBailey 5-10-9[120] JPMcNamara ....................... 16/1  5  11
  5 Puck Out (IRE) CRoche,Ireland 5-11-2[127] DJCasey ..................... 12/1  5  12
    Regal Exit (FR) NJHenderson 7-11-10[135] MFoley .......................... 33/1  6  13
    Tom Paddington HMorrison 8-11-6[131] JCullotty .............................. 9/2jf    f
  1 Man O'Mystery (USA) PRWebber 6-11-6[131] TDoyle ....................... 10/1    pu
    Over The First (IRE) CFSwan,Ireland 8-11-5[130] SDurack ............... 25/1    pu
    Vandas Choice (IRE) MrsLBNormile 5-11-0[125] ADobbin ................ 20/1    pu
```

The 1961 Partnership 17ran 4m08.66

KEMPTON Friday, Dec 26   GOOD

65 Network Design Feltham Nov Chase (Gr 1) (A) (5yo+) £36,850   3m (19)
```
 31 STRONG FLOW (IRE) PFNicholls 6-11-7 RWalsh ............................. 4/11f    1
 36 BALLYCASSIDY (IRE) PBowen 7-11-7 RJohnson ............................. 6/1   8  2
    RULE SUPREME (IRE) WPMullins,Ireland 7-11-7 APMcCoy ............ 7/1   8  3
    Yorkshire (IRE) DLWilliams 9-11-7 MrJDiment ................................. 100/1    f
    Kings Castle (IRE) RJHodges 8-11-7 MAFitzgerald ......................... 25/1    pu
```

Mr B. C. Marshall 5ran 5m57.10

66 jobs@pertemps City Christmas Hdle (Gr 1) (A) (4yo+) £46,400   2m (8)
```
 33 INTERSKY FALCON JonjoO'Neill 6-11-7 (b) LCooper........................ 11/4    1
 50 ROOSTER BOOSTER PJHobbs 9-11-7 RJohnson ............................ 7/4f  2½ 2
 32 SPORAZENE (IRE) PFNicholls 4-11-7 RWalsh ................................. 5/2  1¾ 3
    Foreman (GER) TDoumen,France 5-11-7 (b) TDoumen ................... 7/1  2½ 4
```

1	Brooklyn's Gold (USA) *IanWilliams* 8-11-7 PaulMoloney	100/1	10	5
	Ulundi *PRWebber* 8-11-7 TDoyle	16/1	dist	6

Interskyracing.com & Mrs Jonjo O'Neill 6ran 3m46.32

67   Pertemps King George VI Chase (Gr 1) (A) (5yo+) £92,800   3m (19)

21	EDREDON BLEU (FR) *MissHCKnight* 11-11-10 (t) JCulloty	25/1		1
45	TIUTCHEV *MCPipe* 10-11-10 APMcCoy	20/1	1¼	2
	FIRST GOLD (FR) *FDoumen,France* 10-11-10 (b) TDoumen	11/4	1	3
15	Fondmort (FR) *NJHenderson* 7-11-10 MAFitzgerald	10/1	5	4
47	Marlborough (IRE) *NJHenderson* 11-11-10 LCooper	25/1	24	5
25	La Landiere (FR) *RTPhillips* 8-11-3 RJohnson	16/1	20	6
19	Swansea Bay *PBowen* 7-11-10 AThornton	7/1	20	7
43	Le Roi Miguel (FR) *PFNicholls* 5-11-10 RWalsh	20/1		f
25	Valley Henry (IRE) *JHowardJohnson* 8-11-10 GLee	11/1		f
43	Seebald (GER) *MCPipe* 8-11-10 PaulMoloney	66/1		ur
49	It Takes Time (IRE) *MCPipe* 9-11-10 RGreene	50/1		pu
25	Jair du Cochet (FR) *GMacaire,France* 6-11-10 JacquesRicou	2/1f		pu

Mr Jim Lewis 12ran 5m55.21

LEOPARDSTOWN Friday, Dec 26   GOOD to SOFT

68   Denny Juv Hdle (Gr 2) (3yo) £22,727   2m (8)

34	TOP STRATEGY (IRE) *TMWalsh* 3-10-9 GTHutchinson	4/1		1
	AL EILE (IRE) *JQueally* 3-10-9 JRBarry	7/2f	3½	2
34	BERKELEY NOTE (IRE) *MHalford* 3-10-4 APLane	10/1	9	3
	Nopekan (IRE) *PatrickMullins* 3-10-9 RMPower	10/1	1	4
34	Blue Corrig (IRE) *JosephCrowley* 3-10-9 (b) JLCullen	10/1	4½	5
	Gone Dancing (IRE) *FFlood* 3-10-9 FJFlood	33/1		6
34	Bermaho (IRE) *GMLyons* 3-10-9 (b) PGMurphy	14/1		7
	Whatadifference (USA) *MBrowne* 3-10-9 CO'Dwyer	14/1		8
	Nassaro (IRE) *MHalford* 3-10-9 DTEvans	20/1		9
	Silvergino (IRE) *DWachman* 3-10-9 DJCasey	9/1		10
	Love On Request *TGMcCourt* 3-10-4 PWFlood	20/1		11
	Pantarez (FR) *DWachman* 3-10-9 MDGrant	6/1		12
34	Golden Triangle (IRE) *PatrickCarey* 3-10-4 SCurling	14/1		13
	Amid The Chaos (IRE) *DKWeld* 3-10-9 PCarberry	13/2		14

Mr W. J. Kane 14ran 4m12.80

69   Denny Gold Medal Nov Chase (Gr 1) (4yo+) £45,455   2m1f (11)

	CENTRAL HOUSE *DTHughes* 6-11-12 PCarberry	9/4f		1
38	ANXIOUS MOMENTS (IRE) *CFSwan* 8-11-12 DJCasey	6/1	25	2
	RICARDO *BrianNolan* 9-11-12 JRBarry	8/1	20	3
56	Caishill (IRE) *JosephCrowley* 4-11-1 (b) JLCullen	16/1	20	4
	In The Forge *MHalford* 6-11-12 (t) APLane	16/1		f
5	Mutakarrim *DKWeld* 6-11-12 (b) DTEvans	10/1		f
	Xenophon *AJMartin* 7-11-12 CO'Dwyer	7/2		f
	Kicking King (IRE) *TJTaaffe* 5-11-10 BJGeraghty	11/4		f

Mr John F. Kenny 8ran 4m19.90

CHEPSTOW Saturday, Dec 27   GOOD to SOFT

70   Coral Welsh National (Hcap Chase) (Gr 3) (A) (155) (5yo+) £47,600   3m5f110y (22)

41	BINDAREE (IRE) *NATwiston-Davies* 9-10-9[138] CLlewellyn	10/1		1
41	SIR REMBRANDT (IRE) *RHAlner* 7-11-4[147] AThornton	2/1f	½	2
31	HEDGEHUNTER (IRE) *WPMullins,Ireland* 7-10-2[131] RWalsh	7/2	22	3
31	Take The Stand *PBowen* 7-10-6[135] SDurack	12/1	10	4
2	Jurancon II (FR) *MCPipe* 6-10-1[130] RGreene	40/1	dist	5
	Akarus (FR) *MCPipe* 8-10-3[135] JEMoore[3]	18/1		f
	Kemal's Council (IRE) *JonjoO'Neill* 7-10-0[129] (b) MFoley	66/1		f
	Kings Mistral (IRE) *PRChamings* 10-10-0[129] RJohnson	20/1		f
53	Chives (IRE) *MissHCKnight* 8-11-12[155] JCulloty	16/1		pu
	Bounce Back (USA) *MCPipe* 7-10-11[140] TScudamore	33/1		pu
31	Take Control (IRE) *MCPipe* 9-10-6[135] (v) APMcCoy	10/1		pu
28	Wonder Weasel (IRE) *KCBailey* 10-10-5[134] (s) JPMcNamara	25/1		pu
	Mr Woodentop (IRE) *LLungo* 7-10-0[129] ADobbin	9/1		pu
	Jeremy Spider *CLTizzard* 10-9-9[129] SThomas[5]	20/1		pu

Mr H. R. Mould 14ran 7m49.76

KEMPTON Saturday, Dec 27   GOOD

71   jobs@pertemps Wayward Lad Nov Chase (B) (4yo+) £10,495   2m (13)

18	CARACCIOLA (GER) *NJHenderson* 6-11-8 MAFitzgerald	5/2		1
42	THISTHATANDTOTHER (IRE) *PFNicholls* 7-11-8 JTizzard	4/11f	3½	2
	MYLO (GER) *CVonDerRecke,Germany* 4-10-5 BJCrowley	25/1	dist	3

Mr P. J. D. Pottinger 3ran 3m50.95

WETHERBY Saturday, Dec 27   GOOD to SOFT

72   **skybet.com Rowland Meyrick Hcap Chase (L) (A) (162) (5yo+)**   3m1f (18)
£17,850

	GUNNER WELBURN *AMBalding* 11-10-0[136] RMcGrath	10/1	1
	SKIPPERS CLEUCH (IRE) *LLungo* 9-10-0[136] BHarding	7/2	4 2
	ARTIC JACK (FR) *MrsSJSmith* 7-10-8[144] DSElsworth	5/2f	dist 3
	A Piece of Cake (IRE) *MrsMReveley* 10-10-5[141] AJDempsey	16/1	4 4
	Hugo de Grez (FR) *AParker* 8-10-0[136] GLee	16/1	11 5
53	Truckers Tavern (IRE) *FerdyMurphy* 8-11-12[162] (t) DNRussell	5/1	f
53	Hussard Collonges (FR) *PBeaumont* 8-11-4[154] RGarritty	9/2	f
31	Jungle Jinks (IRE) *GMMoore* 8-10-0[136] WMarston	14/1	pu

W. A. Ritson/D. H. Hall 8ran 6m39.26

LEOPARDSTOWN Saturday, Dec 27   GOOD to SOFT

73   **paddypower.com Future Champions Nov Hdle (Gr 2) (4yo+)**   2m (8)
£22,727

37	MARIAH ROLLINS (IRE) *PAFahy* 5-10-13 DJCasey	4/1	1
57	NEWMILL (IRE) *TGO'Leary* 5-11-12 BJGeraghty	9/4	8 2
	MARK THE MAN (IRE) *NMeade* 6-11-4 PCarberry	2/1f	14 3
	Kahuna (IRE) *ESheehy* 6-11-4 JRBarry	6/1	¾ 4
	C'Est Fantastique (IRE) *MJPO'Brien* 6-10-13 (s+t) DJHoward	20/1	¾ 5
40	Green Belt Flyer (IRE) *MrsJHarrington* 5-11-4 RMPower	7/1	6

Gone West Racing Syndicate 6ran 4m02.52

74   **Paddy Power Dial-A-Bet Chase (Gr 2) (5yo+)** £22,727   2m1f (11)

43	MOSCOW FLYER (IRE) *MrsJHarrington* 9-11-12 BJGeraghty	2/7f	1
	NATIVE SCOUT (IRE) *DHassett* 7-11-7 (t) DJHoward	8/1	5 2
55	KNIFE EDGE (USA) *MJPO'Brien* 8-11-12 (s) LCooper	14/1	6 3
55	Killultagh Storm (IRE) *WPMullins* 9-11-7 (s) DJCasey	16/1	1 4
	No Need For Alarm *KBurke* 8-11-2 MrDerekO'Connor	20/1	dist 5
55	Rathgar Beau (IRE) *ESheehy* 7-11-7 (b) JRBarry	8/1	f

Mr Brian Kearney 6ran 4m18.50

75   **Paddy Power Hcap Chase 0-140(138) (5yo+)** £67,972   3m (17)

	WORLD WIDE WEB (IRE) *JonjoO'Neill,GB* 7-10-1[111] LCooper	8/1f	1
	KYMANDJEN (IRE) *PaulNolan* 6-10-5[118] RMPower[3]	25/1	9 2
	SATCOSLAM (IRE) *LWhitmore* 8-9-4[107] PWFlood[7]	33/1	hd 3
	SECRET NATIVE (IRE) *TJTaaffe* 8-9-10[109] SMMcGovern[3]	16/1	4½ 4
	Timbera (IRE) *DTHughes* 9-11-9[138] (t) MrRLoughran[5]	16/1	sh 5
	Farinel *ALTMoore* 7-9-0[103] MPWalsh[7]	20/1	6
	Snowy Ford (IRE) *PaulNolan* 6-10-7[117] JLCullen	10/1	7
	Newratking (IRE) *CByrnes* 7-9-4[103] LAHurley[3]	20/1	8
	Hume Castle (IRE) *MrsJHarrington* 7-9-11[107] TPTreacy	25/1	9
29	Golden Storm (IRE) *JosephCrowley* 6-10-5[122] (b) JMAllen[7]	25/1	10
	Jenniferjo (IRE) *PAFahy* 6-10-11[124] RGeraghty[3]	20/1	11
29	Come In Moscow (IRE) *JohnJosephMurphy* 7-9-1[104] WOCallaghan[7]	50/1	12
21	Garvivonnian (IRE) *EdwardPMitchell* 8-11-4[131] APLane[3]	50/1	13
29	Super Fellow (IRE) *DPMurphy* 9-9-13[116] (b) MrCMotherway[7]	33/1	14
	Creon *JonjoO'Neill,GB* 8-9-2[103] PGMurphy[5]	20/1	15
	I Can Imagine (IRE) *RobertTyner* 8-10-3[116] (t) MFMooney[3]	9/1	16
	Dark Room (IRE) *JonjoO'Neill,GB* 6-10-7[117] BJGeraghty	14/1	17
29	Coq Hardi Diamond (IRE) *NMeade* 9-10-6[116] PCarberry	16/1	18
	Whatatouch (IRE) *NMeade* 6-10-1[114] (b+t) GTHutchinson[3]	20/1	19
	Mystic Lord (IRE) *NMeade* 6-10-2[117] (t) MrNPMadden[5]	25/1	20
31	The Premier Cat (IRE) *TCahill* 7-11-7[138] MrMACahill[7]	20/1	ur
	Take Five (IRE) *JEKiely* 10-10-4[114] (t) CO'Dwyer	10/1	f
	Ballylusky (IRE) *JonjoO'Neill,GB* 6-9-10[106] GCotter	9/1	f
	Rheindross (IRE) *ALTMoore* 8-9-11[110] DJHoward[3]	20/1	ur
26	Beachcomber Bay (IRE) *NMeade* 8-11-8[135] IJPower[3]	33/1	pu
	Rose Perk (IRE) *ESheehy* 7-10-1[114] SGMcDermott[3]	33/1	pu
	Canon Barney (IRE) *JonjoO'Neill,GB* 8-10-1[111] DJCasey	20/1	pu
	Rio Diamond (IRE) *PRLenihan* 7-9-10[106] JRBarry	12/1	pu

Mr John P. McManus 28ran 6m18.45

LEOPARDSTOWN Sunday, Dec 28   GOOD to SOFT

76   **William Neville & Sons Nov Chase (Gr 1) (5yo+)** £34,091   3m (17)

38	PIZARRO (IRE) *EJO'Grady* 6-11-10 BJGeraghty	4/1	1
46	ROSSLEA (IRE) *MissHCKnight,GB* 5-11-8 JCulloty	9/2	9 2
56	HI CLOY (IRE) *MHourigan* 6-11-10 TJMurphy	10/1	1½ 3
38	Satco Express (IRE) *ESheehy* 7-11-10 JRBarry	4/1	3 4
	Colnel Rayburn (IRE) *PaulNolan* 7-11-10 JLCullen	13/2	dist 5

1025

Bizet (IRE) *AJMartin* 7-11-10 CO'Dwyer.. 16/1   f
Emotional Moment (IRE) *TJTaaffe* 8-11-10 DJCasey.................................. 5/2f   f
Tell Me See (IRE) *JohnMichaelBurke* 7-11-5 MrJMBurke .... 25/1   f
Mr Edward Wallace 8ran 6m24.15

77 **woodiesdiy.com Christmas Hdle (Gr 2) (4yo+)** £22,727   3m (12)

39	SACUNDAI (IRE) *EJO'Grady* 6-11-11 BJGeraghty	1/1f	1
31	BE MY BELLE (IRE) *SJTreacy* 7-11-2 TJMurphy	10/1	7 2
20	ROSTROPOVICH (IRE) *MFMorris* 6-11-7 (s+t) APMcCoy	6/1	1 3
	Bob Justice (IRE) *TMWalsh* 7-11-4 RWalsh	10/1	1 4
39	Prince of Tara (IRE) *PatrickOBrady* 6-11-4 JLCullen	25/1	8 5
	Strong Project (IRE) *CFSwan* 7-11-7 DJCasey	20/1	6
58	Florida Coast (IRE) *JamesBowe* 8-11-4 PCarberry	11/4	pu

Malm Syndicate 7ran 6m03.78

78 **Ericsson Chase (Gr 1) (5yo+)** £68,182   3m (17)

25	BEST MATE (IRE) *MissHCKnight,GB* 8-11-12 JCulloty	8/11f	1
45	LE COUDRAY (FR) *CRoche* 9-11-12 (t) BJGeraghty	14/1	9 2
55	BEEF OR SALMON (IRE) *MHourigan* 7-11-12 TJMurphy	2/1	4 3
	Colonel Braxton (IRE) *DTHughes* 8-11-12 APMcCoy	16/1	14 4
21	Alcapone (IRE) *MFMorris* 9-11-12 GCotter	100/1	13 5
	Alexander Banquet (IRE) *WPMullins* 11-11-12 DJCasey	40/1	6
13	Batman Senora (FR) *IanWilliams,GB* 7-11-12 (b) PaulMoloney	20/1	f
45	Rince Ri (IRE) *TMWalsh* 10-11-12 RWalsh	11/1	f

Mr Jim Lewis 8ran 6m21.04

79 **Star Racegoers Club INH Flat (5, 6 and 7yo)** £6,755   2½m

	FORTY LICKS (IRE) *EJO'Grady* 6-11-7 MrJPMagnier[7]	11/10f	1
	PETERTHEKNOT (IRE) *PatrickSinnott* 5-11-4 MrJJCodd[3]	4/1	10 2
	MACE WINDU (IRE) *TimothyDoyle* 5-11-2 MrDerekO'Connor[5]	8/1	11 3
	Laureldean (IRE) *SJTreacy* 5-12-0 MrAFitzgerald	10/3	25 4
	Theennisconnection (IRE) *JohnBrassil* 6-11-4 MrDWCullen[3]	8/1	dist 5
	Lorna's Lady (IRE) *DTHughes* 7-10-11 MrRLoughran[5]	10/1	6

Mrs Paul Shanahan 6ran 5m07.60

NEWBURY Monday, Dec 29 GOOD to SOFT

80 **Stan James Challow Nov Hdle (Gr 1) (A) (4yo+)** £20,300   2m5f (11)

	CORNISH REBEL (IRE) *PFNicholls* 6-11-7 RWalsh	5/2jf	1
	BIG MOMENT *MrsAJPerrett* 5-11-7 LAspell	11/2	½ 2
	GREY REPORT (IRE) *PJHobbs* 6-11-7 RJohnson	10/1	16 3
40	Control Man (IRE) *MCPipe* 5-11-7 APMcCoy	14/1	11 4
	Mon Villez (FR) *NJHenderson* 4-11-7 MAFitzgerald	4/1	13 5
	Distant Prospect (IRE) *AMBalding* 6-11-7 TJMurphy	5/2jf	11 6

Mr C. G. Roach 6ran 5m05.12

LEOPARDSTOWN Monday, Dec 29 GOOD to SOFT

81 **Bewleys Hotels December Festival Hdle (Gr 1) (4yo+)** £36,364   2m (8)

	GOLDEN CROSS (IRE) *MHalford* 4-11-7 (s) APLane	66/1	1
50	SPIRIT LEADER (IRE) *MrsJHarrington* 7-11-7 DJCasey	11/1	1½ 2
50	FLAME CREEK (IRE) *NoelTChance,GB* 7-11-12 SDurack	14/1	¾ 3
58	Solerina (IRE) *JamesBowe* 6-11-7 PCarberry	5/1	3 4
20	Back In Front (IRE) *EJO'Grady* 6-11-12 BJGeraghty	5/2	sh 5
52	Rhinestone Cowboy (IRE) *JonjoO'Neill,GB* 7-11-12 MrJPMagnier	11/10f	6
	Hardy Eustace (IRE) *DTHughes* 6-11-12 CO'Dwyer	20/1	7

Exors of Late Mrs H. Johnson 7ran 3m46.40

82 **Cill Dara Security INH Flat (4yo+)** £6,755   2m

	TOTAL ENJOYMENT (IRE) *TCooper* 4-10-11 MrDCO'Connor[7]	6/4	1
	IN THE MORNING (IRE) *CRoche* 4-10-9 MrPRoche[7]	8/1	25 2
	FARRANFORE (IRE) *EJO'Grady* 5-11-0 MrJPMagnier[7]	8/11f	½ 3
	Smart View (IRE) *MrsSandraMcCarthy* 5-11-2 (t) MrAPCrowe	20/1	7 4
	Barrow Bridge (IRE) *PHughes* 5-10-11 MrNPMadden[5]	14/1	hd 5
	Church Hill Girl (IRE) *SSlevin* 4-10-9 MrMTSlevin[7]	40/1	6

It Will Never Last Syndicate 6ran 3m48.30

CHELTENHAM Wednesday, Dec 31 GOOD (New Course)

83 **Unicoin New Homes Spa Hdle (B) (4yo+)** £12,412   3m (12)

48	SH BOOM *JonjoO'Neill* 5-11-0 LCooper	2/1	1
48	CRYSTAL D'AINAY (FR) *AKing* 4-11-4 RThornton	11/8f	1 2
30	COUNT CAMPIONI (IRE) *MPitman* 9-11-0 TJMurphy	12/1	9 3
60	Deano's Beeno *MCPipe* 11-11-8 (b) APMcCoy	9/2	2 4
51	Champagne Harry *NATwiston-Davies* 5-11-8 CLlewellyn	20/1	½ 5

| 22 | Forest Ivory (NZ) *DrPPritchard* 12-11-0 DrPPritchard | 250/1 | dist 6 |

T. G. K. Construction Ltd 6ran 5m58.63

CHELTENHAM Thursday, Jan 1   GOOD to SOFT

84   Unicoin Homes Chase (Hcap) (B) (153) (5yo+) £23,200   2m5f (17)

46	WHEREAREYOUNOW (IRE) *NATwiston-Davies* 7 10-1[120] CLlewellyn	11/2	1
	SPRING GROVE (IRE) *RHAlner* 9-10-3[130] AThornton	9/1	7 2
49	FOLY PLEASANT (FR) *MissHCKnight* 10-11-9[150] (t) JCulloty	20/1	1¼ 3
49	Armaturk (FR) *PFNicholls* 7-10-11[141] (t) RPMcNally[3]	20/1	3½ 4
	Jakari (FR) *HDDaly* 7-10-11[138] RJohnson	7/2f	dist 5
49	Ballinclay King (IRE) *FerdyMurphy* 10-11-1[142] DNRussell	18/1	10 6
49	Royal Auclair (FR) *PFNicholls* 7-11-6[147] (t) RWalsh	6/1	f
24	Tarxien *MCPipe* 10-11-6[147] (t) APMcCoy	5/1	f
49	Iris Royal (FR) *NJHenderson* 8-11-12[153] MAFitzgerald	9/2	pu

Mr H. R. Mould 9ran 5m19.32

85   Steel Plate Trial Juv Nov Hdle (B) (4yo) £9,613   2m1f (8)

	TROUBLE AT BAY (IRE) *AKing* 4-11-7 RThornton	5/6f	1
	MERYL (FR) *GMacaire,France* 4-11-0 BGicquel	25/1	¾ 2
	VAL DU DON (FR) *GMacaire,France* 4-11-7 JacquesRicou	9/1	¾ 3
	Zimbabwe *GLMoore* 4-11-0 JEMoore	7/2	3 4
	Downthereforddancin (IRE) *MCPipe* 4-11-4 (v) TScudamore	33/1	6 5
	Pilca (FR) *MCPipe* 4-11-7 RegisSchmidlin	100/1	19 6
	Travel (POL) *TRGeorge* 4-11-0 PaulMoloney	50/1	8 7
	Betterware Boy *PMPhelan* 4-11-0 DNRussell	100/1	2½ 8
	Major Speculation (IRE) *MCPipe* 4-11-7 APMcCoy	11/2	5 9

Mr Nigel Bunter 9ran 4m19.02

SANDOWN Saturday, Jan 3   GOOD to SOFT

86   Ladbrokes On attheraces - Press Red To Bet Nov Chase (C) (6yo+) 2½m110y (17)
£10,372

22	CALLING BRAVE (IRE) *NJHenderson* 8-11-5 MAFitzgerald	5/6f	1
	PATRICKSNINETEENTH (IRE) *PRWebber* 7-11-0 TDoyle	5/1	¾ 2
	MISTER BANJO (FR) *PFNicholls* 8-11-5 RWalsh	2/1	27 3

Sir Robert Ogden 3ran 5m20.08

87   ladbrokes.com Tolworth Hdle (Gr 1) (A) (4yo+) £27,900   2m110y (8)

61	LINGO (IRE) *JonjoO'Neill* 5-11-7 LCooper	5/4f	1
	GARDE CHAMPETRE (FR) *PFNicholls* 5-11-7 RWalsh	14/1	1½ 2
	BOURBON MANHATTAN (FR) *AKing* 6-11-7 RThornton	9/4	14 3
	Marrakech (IRE) *MrsNSmith* 7-11-0 LAspell	25/1	dist 4
61	Perle de Puce (FR) *NJHenderson* 5-11-0 MAFitzgerald	3/1	f

Mr John P. McManus 5ran 4m02.45

ASCOT Saturday, Jan 10   Chase course: GOOD, Hurdles course: GOOD to SOFT

88   thespinroom.com Nov Hdle (D) (5yo+) £5,356   2m110y (9)

	CLOUDY GREY (IRE) *MissECLavelle* 7-11-0 BFenton	10/3	1
	LE PASSING (FR) *PFNicholls* 5-11-10 RWalsh	13/8f	6 2
	DANGEROUSLY GOOD *GLMoore* 6-11-0 (b) BJGeraghty	16/1	7 3
	Nathos (GER) *CJMann* 7-11-10 NFehily	12/1	8 4
	Mister Mustard (IRE) *IanWilliams* 7-11-0 DRDennis	3/1	3 5
	Labelthou (FR) *FJordan* 5-10-4 SThomas[5]	50/1	1¾ 6
	Szeroki Bor (POL) *MPitman* 5-11-0 JCulloty	50/1	5 7
	Silver Prophet (IRE) *MRBosley* 5-11-0 SCurran	100/1	sh 8
	Sangatte (IRE) *NJHenderson* 6-11-0 MAFitzgerald	33/1	14 9
	Simon's Seat (USA) *CDrew* 5-10-9 BrianMurphy[5]	100/1	¾ 10
	Alsyati *DBurchell* 4-11-0 ASchole[7]	100/1	13 11
	Ehab (IRE) *GLMoore* 5-11-0 MBatchelor	66/1	9 12
	Roman Hideaway (IRE) *JABOld* 6-11-0 LAspell	33/1	6 13
	Montosari *PMitchell* 5-11-0 TScudamore	100/1	11 14

Mrs J. R. Lavelle & Mrs A. Hepworth 14ran 4m07.12

89   Victor Chandler Chase (Hcap) (Gr 2) (A) (168) (5yo+) £69,600   2m (12)

44	ISIO (FR) *NJHenderson* 8-10-5[149] MAFitzgerald	4/1	1
43	AZERTYUIOP (FR) *PFNicholls* 7-11-10[168] RWalsh	7/2f	nk 2
	GOT ONE TOO (FR) *NJHenderson* 7-10-4[148] BFenton	33/1	9 3
74	Native Scout (IRE) *DHassett,Ireland* 8-10-4[148] (t) BJGeraghty	4/1	4 4
	Hot Shots (FR) *MPitman* 9-10-4[148] JCulloty	16/1	2 5
	Bleu Superbe (FR) *MissVenetiaWilliams* 9-9-13[148] SThomas[5]	66/1	8 6
11	Wahiba Sands *MCPipe* 11-10-4[148] (v) RGreene	33/1	2½ 7
	Upgrade *MCPipe* 10-10-4[148] NFehily	25/1	4 8
	Palarshan (FR) *HDDaly* 6-10-4[148] MBradburne	7/1	½ 9

1027

	74	Killultagh Storm (IRE) *WPMullins,Ireland* 10-10-1[148] (s) DCrosse[3]	33/1	½ 10
24		Farmer Jack *PJHobbs* 8-10-4[148] PFlynn	16/1	sh 11
		Young Devereaux (IRE) *PFNicholls* 11-10-4[151] RPMcNally[3]	10/1	dist 12
49		Redemption *NATwiston-Davies* 9-10-4[148] TScudamore	9/1	ur

Sir Peter And Lady Gibbings 13ran 3m51.91

HAYDOCK Saturday, Jan 10   SOFT

90   Commhoist Premier Stayers' Hdle (Gr 2) (A) (5yo+) £23,200   2m7f110y (12)

	83	SH BOOM *JonjoO'Neill* 6-11-4 LCooper	1/2f	1
		ROYAL ROSA (FR) *JHowardJohnson* 5-11-0 ADobbin	4/1	8 2
		TURTLE SOUP (IRE) *TRGeorge* 8-11-0 JMMaguire	11/1	6 3
		Simply Supreme (IRE) *MrsSJSmith* 7-11-0 DSElsworth	20/1	16 4
50		The French Furze *NGRichards* 10-11-8 BHarding	16/1	10 5
		Star Councel (IRE) *BSRothwell* 8-10-7 (s) AJDempsey	66/1	9 6
14		Good Lord Murphy (IRE) *DrPPritchard* 12-11-0 WKennedy	200/1	24 7
		Crazy Horse (IRE) *LLungo* 11-11-0 BGibson	16/1	pu

T. G. K. Construction Ltd 8ran 6m04.14

91   Peter Marsh Chase (Ltd Hcap) (Gr 2) (A) (160) (5yo+) £37,200   3m (18)

	72	ARTIC JACK (FR) *MrsSJSmith* 8-10-6[142] DSElsworth	6/1	1
47		KINGSCLIFF (IRE) *RHAlner* 7-11-10[160] AThornton	4/7f	13 2
		YOU'RE AGOODUN *MCPipe* 12-10-9[145] (v) RJohnson	8/1	18 3
		Ebony Light (IRE) *DMcCain* 8-10-4[140] BHarding	40/1	nk 4
63		Horus (IRE) *MCPipe* 9-10-3[142] JEMoore[3]	5/1	ur

Mr Trevor Hemmings 5ran 6m20.19

92   Red Square Vodka Champion Hdle Trial (Gr 2) (A) (4yo+) £23,200   2m (8)

	66	ROOSTER BOOSTER *PJHobbs* 10-11-13 RJohnson	5/4f	1
50		HASTY PRINCE *JonjoO'Neill* 6-11-5 ADobbin	9/2	7 2
		SPECULAR (AUS) *JonjoO'Neill* 8-11-9 LCooper	13/8	10 3
		Copeland *MCPipe* 9-11-5 (v) JEMoore	16/1	dist 4
		Fifth Generation (IRE) *DrPPritchard* 14-11-5 DrPPritchard	250/1	9 5
		Tetragon (IRE) *MissLucindaVRussell* 4-10-7 (s+t) MrTGreenall	250/1	dist 6

Mr Terry Warner 6ran 3m53.41

WARWICK Saturday, Jan 10   Chase course: GOOD, Hurdles course: GOOD to SOFT

93   Roscoe Harvey Memorial Nov Chase (B) (5yo+) £14,040   3m110y (18)

		D'ARGENT (IRE) *AKing* 7-11-10 RThornton	5/1	1
		TYNEANDTHYNEAGAIN *RCGuest* 9-11-3 HOliver	18/1	26 2
		SILVER KNIGHT *TDEasterby* 6-11-10 RGarritty	15/2	1¾ 3
54		Rum Pointer (IRE) *RHBuckler* 8-11-7 BHitchcott	18/1	16 4
		Ross Leader (IRE) *MrsSusanNock* 7-11-3 CLlewellyn	150/1	15 5
		Royal Emperor (IRE) *MrsSJSmith* 8-11-7 WMarston	1/1f	f
		Ar Muin Na Muice (IRE) *JonjoO'Neill* 8-10-12 SDurack	4/1	f

Mr Nigel Bunter 7ran 6m11.43

94   Pertemps Leamington Nov Hdle (Gr 2) (A) (4yo+) £20,300   2m5f (11)

	40	INGLIS DREVER *JHowardJohnson* 5-11-12 GLee	8/15f	1
61		ERIC'S CHARM (FR) *OSherwood* 6-11-10 APMcCoy	4/1	17 2
		HE'S THE BOSS (IRE) *RHBuckler* 7-11-10 BHitchcott	9/1	10 3
		Lik Wood Power (NZ) *RCGuest* 7-11-6 HOliver	66/1	dist 4
		Distant Thunder (IRE) *RHAlner* 6-11-10 RThornton	25/1	f
		The Rising Moon (IRE) *JonjoO'Neill* 5-11-6 SDurack	12/1	pu

Andrea & Graham Wylie 6ran 5m07.70

95   Tote Classic Chase (Hcap) (L) (A) (158) (6yo+) £63,800   3m5f (22)

	16	SOUTHERN STAR (IRE) *MissHCKnight* 9-10-1[133] GLee	15/2	1
70		JURANCON II (FR) *MCPipe* 7-9-9[132] JPElliott[5]	50/1	3½ 2
		WHAT ODDS (IRE) *TKGeraghty,Ireland* 8-10-0[132] DNRussell	7/2	dist 3
28		Ardent Scout *MrsSJSmith* 12-10-0[132] WMarston	20/1	13 4
		Montifault (FR) *PFNicholls* 9-10-3[135] JTizzard	25/1	dist 5
70		Bindaree (IRE) *NATwiston-Davies* 10-10-10[142] CLlewellyn	8/1	dist 6
63		Behrajan (IRE) *HDDaly* 9-11-9[158] JPByrne[3]	11/2	f
63		Ad Hoc (IRE) *PFNicholls* 10-11-6[152] RThornton	25/1	f
70		Take Control (IRE) *MCPipe* 10-10-3[135] (v) PaulMoloney	28/1	f
72		Gunner Welburn *AMBalding* 12-10-10[142] McGrath	16/1	pu
28		Carbury Cross (IRE) *JonjoO'Neill* 10-10-0[132] (b) SDurack	28/1	pu
70		Akarus (FR) *MCPipe* 9-10-3[135] APMcCoy	5/2f	pu

Mr Trevor Hemmings 12ran 7m16.14

LEOPARDSTOWN Sunday, Jan 11   SOFT

96   Pierse Leopardstown Hcap Chase (159) (5yo+) £45,775   3m (17)

| | 29 | CLOUDY BAYS (IRE) *CByrnes* 7-10-1[135] (s) RGeraghty[3] | 3/1jf | 1 |

77	BE MY BELLE (IRE) *SJTreacy* 8-10-7[138] TJMurphy	9/2	14	2
	NATIVE JACK (IRE) *ALTMoore* 10-10-0[131] PCarberry	7/1	20	3
	Assessed (IRE) *WPMullins* 10-10-3[134] JRBarry	20/1	11	4
75	Timbera (IRE) *DTHughes* 10-10-7[138] JCulloty	3/1jf	7	5
78	Alexander Banquet (IRE) *WPMullins* 11-12-0[159] RWalsh	20/1		6
	More Than A Stroll (IRE) *ALTMoore* 12-11-3[148] (t) CO'Dwyer	20/1		f
78	Alcapone (IRF) *MFMorris* 10 10-13[111] GCotter	20/1		pu
	Silver Steel *CRoche* 9-10-0[131] DJCasey	6/1		pu

Cloudy Bay Syndicate 9ran 6m35.52

97 Pierse Hdle (Extended Hcap) 0-140(129) (4yo+) £55,387   2m (8)

	DROMLEASE EXPRESS (IRE) *CByrnes* 6-10-4[116] JMAllen[7]	6/1jf		1
	MACS JOY (IRE) *MrsJHarrington* 5-9-12[110] ADLeigh[7]	14/1	3½	2
59	GEORGES GIRL (IRE) *FFlood* 6-11-5[124] FJFlood	7/1	sh	3
	STEEL BAND *PaulARoche* 6-9-7[101] GTHutchinson[3]	20/1	11	4
	Arch Stanton (IRE) *WPMullins* 6-11-6[125] RWalsh	10/1	1	5
	Albatros (FR) *EJO'Grady* 7-11-2[121] MDGrant	25/1		6
	Doire-Chrinn (IRE) *DPKelly* 8-9-7[101] APLane[3]	50/1		7
59	Oh Be The Hokey (IRE) *CFSwan* 6-10-4[109] DJCasey	10/1		8
	Turtleback (IRE) *EJO'Grady* 6-11-10[129] CO'Dwyer	25/1		9
	Cronin's Boy *ESheehy* 10-10-5[113] (t) RMPower[3]	33/1		10
	Safe Route (USA) *WJAustin* 6-10-3[111] LAHurley[3]	20/1		11
59	Columba (IRE) *DTHughes* 8-11-2[121] JCulloty	14/1		12
	Beechcourt *MJPO'Brien* 7-10-12[117] PCarberry	6/1jf		13
69	Ricardo *BrianNolan* 10-11-0[119] (s) JRBarry	20/1		14
	Loughanelteen (IRE) *PJRothwell* 6-9-10[106] AJDonoghue[5]	9/1		15
	Newlands Girl (IRE) *MJPO'Brien* 5-11-2[128] TGMRyan[7]	10/1		16
	Larkhill Jo (IRE) *BrianNolan* 7-10-7[115] IJPower[3]	25/1		17
	Right Job (IRE) *PJFlynn* 9-10-13[118] BJGeraghty	14/1		18
37	Dyrick Daybreak (IRE) *DavidAKiely* 5-10-9[114] TJMurphy	14/1		rtr

RDS Syndicate 19ran 3m58.77

KEMPTON Saturday, Jan 17   GOOD

98 britishhorseracing.com Nov Chase (C) (5yo+) £8,736   3m (19)

54	LORD SAM (IRE) *VRADartnall* 8-11-11 JCulloty	4/11f		1
	FORK LIGHTNING (IRE) *AKing* 8-11-8 RThornton	3/1	1¼	2
	MISTER PEARLY *JWMullins* 7-10-12 (t) RYoung[5]	100/1	dist	3
	Erris Express (IRE) *JRJenkins* 6-11-3 JPMcNamara	100/1		f
	Sheer Genius *MPitman* 8-11-3 SDurack	20/1		pu

Plain Peeps 5ran 6m00.15

99 Tote Scoop6 Lanzarote Hdle (Hcap) (B) 0-145(140) (4yo+) £29,000   2m (8)

32	LIMERICK BOY (GER) *MissVenetiaWilliams* 6-11-7[140] SThomas[5]	10/1		1
	PEROUSE *PFNicholls* 6-11-9[137] (t) RWalsh	7/2f	nk	2
	GREENHOPE (IRE) *NJHenderson* 6-11-1[129] MAFitzgerald	5/1	9	3
	Swan Knight (USA) *RAFahey* 8-9-11[114] DO'Meara[3]	16/1	1¼	4
	Hawadeth *VRADartnall* 9-10-11[125] JCulloty	5/1	1¾	5
	Idaho d'Ox (FR) *MCPipe* 8-10-9[123] TScudamore	50/1	sh	6
18	Altay *RAFahey* 7-10-13[130] PWhelan[3]	7/1	1¾	7
	Kadount (FR) *AKing* 6-11-4[132] RThornton	11/2	3½	8
	Golden Alpha (IRE) *MCPipe* 6-10-1[131] JMoore[3]	16/1	2½	9
	Majlis (IRE) *TRGeorge* 7-10-2[116] (b) PaulMoloney	14/1	19	10
64	Pirandello (IRE) *KCBailey* 6-10-8[122] JPMcNamara	16/1		f

Favourites Racing 11ran 3m48.60

FAIRYHOUSE Sunday, Jan 18   SOFT

100 Normans Grove Chase (Gr 3) (5yo+) £14,444   2m1f (13)

	FLORIDA PEARL (IRE) *WPMullins* 12-11-12 RJohnson	8/1		1
78	RINCE RI (IRE) *TMWalsh* 11-11-12 RWalsh	11/2	2	2
74	RATHGAR BEAU (IRE) *ESheehy* 8-11-8 JRBarry	3/1f	7	3
74	Knife Edge (USA) *MJPO'Brien* 9-11-12 (s) CO'Dwyer	10/3	2½	4
75	Beachcomber Bay (IRE) *NMeade* 9-11-8 DNRussell	20/1	4	5
	Davids Lad (IRE) *AJMartin* 10-11-8 ADobbin	12/1		6
45	Arctic Copper (IRE) *NMeade* 10-11-10 (s) TPTreacy	5/1		7
96	More Than A Stroll (IRE) *ALTMoore* 12-11-12 (t) BMCash	20/1		8
59	Dutsdale Dancer (IRE) *AJWhelan* 11-11-5 (t) GCotter	14/1		pu

Mrs Violet O'Leary 9ran 4m28.31

GOWRAN PARK Thursday, Jan 22   SOFT

101 Goulding Thyestes Hcap Chase (155) (5yo+) £33,621   3m (16)

70	HEDGEHUNTER (IRE) *WPMullins* 8-10-2[129] DJCasey	10/3f		1

29 I'VEHADIT (IRE) *DTHughes* 10-9-7^{127} PWFlood^7 .... 14/1   8 2
65 RULE SUPREME (IRE) *WPMullins* 8-10-13^{140} DNRussell 7/1   3½ 3
96 Native Jack (IRE) *ALTMoore* 10-10-0^{130} DJHoward^3 .... 8/1   hd 4
96 Be My Belle (IRE) *SJTreacy* 8-10-12^{139} TJMurphy 7/2   11 5
29 Takagi (IRE) *EJO'Grady* 9-11-1^{142} BJGeraghty 7/2   6
96 Alexander Banquet (IRE) *WPMullins* 11-12-0^{155} CO'Dwyer...................... 20/1   7
58 The Bunny Boiler (IRE) *NMeade* 10-10-13^{140} (b) PCarberry .... 16/1   pu
76 Satco Express (IRE) *ESheehy* 8-10-1^{128} JRBarry .... 6/1   pu
Sigma Dotcomm (IRE) *JamesJosephMangan* 8-9-11^{127} (s) LAHurley^3 .... 50/1   pu
Mr Trevor Hemmings 10ran 6m17.52

CHELTENHAM Saturday, Jan 24   GOOD to SOFT

102   **Wragge & Co Finesse Juv Nov Hdle (Gr 2) (A) (4yo) £17,400**   2m1f (8)

      MONDUL (GER) *MFHarris* 4-11-8 OMcPhail 11/2   1
85 VAL DU DON (FR) *GMacaire,France* 4-11-8 JacquesRicou 12/1   1¼ 2
85 MERYL (FR) *GMacaire,France* 4-11-0 RWalsh 9/2   2 3
      Howle Hill (IRE) *AKing* 4-11-8 RJohnson 7/2jf   5 4
      Lough Derg (FR) *MCPipe* 4-11-8 APMcCoy................................... 7/2jf   5 5
      Sunray *EvanWilliams* 4-11-8 AThornton.. 20/1   4 6
      A Toi A Moi (FR) *MissVenetiaWilliams* 4-11-0 SThomas........................... 25/1   4 7
      Dalaram (IRE) *JHowardJohnson* 4-11-0 (t) GLee 16/1   16 8
34 Guilt *DTHughes,Ireland* 4-11-8 (t) CO'Dwyer 11/2   5 9
      Uncle Max (IRE) *NATwiston-Davies* 4-11-4 CLlewellyn 100/1   10 10
Let's Live Racing 10ran 4m19.31

103   **Byrne Bros Cleeve Hdle (Gr 2) (A) (5yo+) £29,000**   2½m110y (10)

83 CRYSTAL D'AINAY (FR) *AKing* 5-11-4 JAMcCarthy 1/1f   1
81 HARDY EUSTACE (IRE) *DTHughes,Ireland* 7-11-4 CO'Dwyer 3/1   3 2
90 THE FRENCH FURZE (IRE) *NGRichards* 10-11-8 ADobbin..................... 22/1   15 3
84 Tarxien *MCPipe* 10-11-0 (t) APMcCoy.. 10/1   13 4
89 Redemption *NATwiston-Davies* 9-11-0 CLlewellyn 5/1   5 5
      Grey Abbey (IRE) *JHowardJohnson* 10-11-0 GLee 40/1   2½ 6
Mr Tony Fisher & Mrs Jeni Fisher 6ran 5m00.91

104   **Pillar Property Chase (Gr 2) (A) (6yo+) £62,400**   3m1f110y (21)

67 JAIR DU COCHET (FR) *GMacaire,France* 7-11-10 JacquesRicou 11/4   1
100 RINCE RI (IRE) *TMWalsh,Ireland* 11-11-10 RWalsh 14/1   12 2
46 Therealbandit (IRE) *MCPipe* 7-11-3 APMcCoy.. 2/1f   f
72 Truckers Tavern (IRE) *FerdyMurphy* 9-11-6 (t) ADobbin............................ 13/2   ur
67 Valley Henry (IRE) *JHowardJohnson* 9-11-10 GLee .... 10/1   pu
70 Sir Rembrandt (IRE) *RHAlner* 8-11-6 AThornton .... 7/2   pu
Mrs F. Montauban 6ran 6m38.43

105   **Ladbroke Trophy Chase (Hcap) (L) (A) (155) (5yo+) £23,200**   2m5f (17)

      HUNTERS TWEED *PBeaumont* 8-10-3^{132} GLee 14/1   1
      KELREV (FR) *MissVenetiaWilliams* 6-9-12^{132} SThomas^5.......................... 9/1   8 2
67 LA LANDIERE (FR) *RTPhillips* 9-11-8^{151} RJohnson 11/1   1¾ 3
3 Chicuelo (FR) *MCPipe* 8-10-9^{141} (v) JEMoore^3 .... 66/1   3½ 4
      The Villager (IRE) *MScudamore* 8-10-0^{129} (t) TScudamore .... 14/1   hd 5
91 Horus (IRE) *MCPipe* 10-10-13^{142} GLee 11/2   3 6
84 Whereareyounow (IRE) *NATwiston-Davies* 7-10-9^{138} CLlewellyn .... 10/3f   nk 7
89 Young Devereaux (IRE) *PFNicholls* 11-6^{149} RWalsh 20/1   3 8
47 Master Tern (USA) *JonjoO'Neill* 9-10-4^{133} CO'Dwyer 16/1   3½ 9
84 Ballinclay King (IRE) *FerdyMurphy* 10-10-11^{140} TJMurphy 50/1   7 10
49 Hand Inn Hand *HDDaly* 8-11-7^{150} MBradburne .... 6/1   f
63 Impek (FR) *MissHCKnight* 8-11-12^{155} JCulloty .... 11/1   ur
49 Telemoss (IRE) *NGRichards* 10-10-7^{136} ADobbin .... 6/1   pu
Mr Trevor Hemmings 13ran 5m26.57

LEOPARDSTOWN Sunday, Jan 25   GOOD to SOFT

106   **Baileys Arkle Perpetual Challenge Cup Nov Chase (Gr 1) (5yo+)**   2m1f (11)
      £35,862

69 KICKING KING (IRE) *TJTaaffe* 6-11-12 BJGeraghty 11/10f   1
69 CENTRAL HOUSE *DTHughes* 7-11-12 TJMurphy 3/1   3½ 2
      COLCA CANYON (IRE) *MrsJHarrington* 7-11-12 RMPower 25/1   2½ 3
56 Mossy Green (IRE) *WPMullins* 10-11-12 RWalsh .... 6/1   nk 4
      Direct Bearing (IRE) *DKWeld* 7-11-12 DJCasey..................................... 6/1   11 5
38 Ballyamber (IRE) *WPMullins* 9-11-12 JRBarry 33/1   6
56 Commonchero (IRE) *MJPO'Brien* 7-11-12 DNRussell 12/1   7
Mr Conor Clarkson 7ran 4m18.73

107   **AIG Europe Champion Hdle (Gr 1) (4yo+) £62,241**   2m (8)

66 FOREMAN (GER) *TDoumen,France* 6-11-10 (b) TDoumen........................ 8/1   1

97	GEORGES GIRL (IRE) *FFlood* 6-11-5 FJFlood	25/1	hd 2
39	FOTA ISLAND (IRE) *MFMorris* 8-11-5 DJCasey	20/1	1½ 3
81	Spirit Leader (IRE) *MrsJHarrington* 8-11-5 BJGeraghty	5/2f	hd 4
50	Davenport Milenium (IRE) *WPMullins* 8-11-10 RWalsh	3/1	1 5
81	Flame Creek (IRE) *NoelTChance,GB* 8-11-10 SDurack	4/1	6
81	Golden Cross (IRE) *MHalford* 5-11-6 (s) APLane,,,,,,,,	5/1	7
	Stage Affair (USA) *DKWeld* 10-11-10 (b) DTEvans	33/1	8

Mr John P. McManus 8ran 3m51.66

ASCOT Saturday, Jan 31 SOFT

108 Servo Computer Services' Ascot Chase (Gr 1) (A) (5yo+) £59,500 2m3f110y (16)

105	HAND INN HAND *HDDaly* 8-11-7 MBradburne	15/2	1
105	IMPEK (FR) *MissHCKnight* 8-11-7 JCulloty	9/1	4 2
	SEE YOU SOMETIME *JWMullins* 9-11-7 AThornton	33/1	dist 3
67	Le Roi Miguel (FR) *PFNicholls* 6-11-7 (t) RWalsh	4/1	dist 4
67	Fondmort (FR) *NJHenderson* 8-11-7 MAFitzgerald	4/1	dist 5
67	Tiutchev *MCPipe* 11-11-7 APMcCoy	6/4f	f
	Royal Atalza (FR) *CNAllen* 7-11-7 (b) PaulMoloney	20/1	pu

Patrick Burling Developments Ltd 7ran 5m07.33

DONCASTER Saturday, Jan 31 SOFT

109 Skybet Great Yorkshire Chase (Hcap) (L) (A) 0-145(138) (5yo+) 3m (18)
£29,000

93	TYNEANDTHYNEAGAIN *RCGuest* 9-10-4[123] HOliver	7/1	1
	MAGICAL BAILIWICK (IRE) *MCPipe* 8-10-0[122] JEMoore[3]	5/1	6 2
81	GOTTABE *MrsSJSmith* 11-9-7[119] JRRyan[7]	4/1f	2½ 3
	Carryonharry (IRE) *MCPipe* 10-10-5[127] GSupple[3]	16/1	20 4
	Tonoco *MrsSJSmith* 11-10-2[121] WMarston	8/1	dist 5
	Montreal (IRE) *MCPipe* 7-9-13[123] JPElliott[5]	25/1	dist 6
70	Take The Stand (IRE) *PBowen* 8-11-5[138] SDurack	12/1	f
	Jimmy Tennis (IRE) *MissVenetiaWilliams* 7-10-6[125] BJCrowley	5/1	f
	Jaloux d'Estruval (FR) *MrsLCTaylor* 7-10-5[124] TDoyle	5/1	f
95	Montifault (FR) *PFNicholls* 9-10-13[132] (t) JTizzard	14/1	pu
	Tyndarius (IRE) *JHetherton* 13-9-11[119] PWhelan[3]	40/1	pu

Mr N. B. Mason 11ran 6m35.50

SANDOWN Saturday, Feb 7 SOFT

110 Agfa Hdle (L) (A) (5yo+) £15,500 2m110y (8)

81	RHINESTONE COWBOY (IRE) *JonjoO'Neill* 8-11-8 MrJPMagnier	2/5f	1
87	GARDE CHAMPETRE (FR) *PFNicholls* 5-11-0 RWalsh	4/1	2 2
60	TEAATRAL *CREgerton* 10-11-0 APMcCoy	20/1	15 3
12	Quazar (IRE) *JonjoO'Neill* 6-11-8 (t) LCooper	15/2	1½ 4
92	Fifth Generation (IRE) *DrPPritchard* 14-11-0 DrPPritchard	300/1	30 5

Mrs John Magnier 5ran 4m11.21

111 Tote Scilly Isles Nov Chase (Gr 1) (A) (5yo+) £32,725 2½m110y (17)

86	PATRICKSNINETEENTH (IRE) *PRWebber* 7-11-6 TDoyle	7/2	1
	L'AVENTURE (FR) *PFNicholls* 5-10-5 (b+t) RPMcNally	6/1	6 2
	ONE NATION (IRE) *MissHCKnight* 9-11-6 JCulloty	16/1	14 3
	Tikram *GLMoore* 7-11-6 JEMoore	14/1	7 4
42	Puntal (FR) *MCPipe* 8-11-6 (v+t) APMcCoy	7/2	30 5
108	See You Sometime *JWMullins* 9-11-6 MAFitzgerald	14/1	f
	Ladalko (FR) *PFNicholls* 5-10-12 RWalsh	2/1f	f

The Large G & T Partnership 7ran 5m26.09

112 Tote Scoop6 Sandown Hdle (Hcap) (Gr 3) (A) (170) (4yo+) £34,800 2¾m (11)

60	BARACOUDA (FR) *FDoumen,France* 9-11-12[170] TDoumen	8/15f	1
44	YOGI (IRE) *ThomasFoley,Ireland* 8-10-0[144] GCotter	25/1	2 2
	ALEXANDERTHEGREAT (IRE) *PFNicholls* 6-10-1[145] RWalsh	25/1	½ 3
44	Mistanoora *NATwiston-Davies* 5-10-0[144] (b) CLlewellyn	11/2	8 4
90	Turtle Soup (IRE) *TRGeorge* 8-10-0[144] RJohnson	12/1	2½ 5
	Carlovent (FR) *MCPipe* 9-9-11[144] (v) JEMoore[3]	40/1	17 6
14	Sonevafushi (FR) *MissVenetiaWilliams* 6-9-9[144] (b) SThomas[5]	33/1	4 7
105	Chicuelo (FR) *MCPipe* 8-9-9[144] (v) JPElliott[5]	40/1	5 8
75	Ballylusky (IRE) *JonjoO'Neill* 7-10-0[144] LCooper	9/1	7 9

Mr John P. McManus 9ran 5m38.01

113 Agfa Diamond Hcap Chase (B) 0-145(134) (5yo+) £29,000 3m110y (22)

70	KINGS MISTRAL (IRE) *PRChamings* 11-11-0[122] RJohnson	11/2	1
	DESAILLY *GBBalding* 10-10-12[120] MBradburne	8/1	½ 2
47	EXIT TO WAVE (FR) *PFNicholls* 8-11-12[134] RWalsh	14/1	12 3
	SUPREME CATCH (IRE) *MissHCKnight* 7-11-6[128] JCulloty	7/1	hd 4

31	Merchants Friend (IRE) *CJMann* 9-11-7[129] (s) NFehily	14/1	1 5
	Infrasonique (FR) *MrsLCTaylor* 8-10-12[120] JAMcCarthy	14/1	2 6
49	Banker Count *MissVenetiaWilliams* 12-11-5[132] SThomas[5]	50/1	½ 7
	Hersov (FR) *NJHenderson* 8-11-3[125] CLlewellyn	5/1f	8 8
	Sky Warrior (FR) *EvanWilliams* 6-10-11[119] LAspell	40/1	2½ 9
	Ballybrophy (IRE) *SEHSherwood* 9-11-4[126] (v) BFenton	10/1	5 10
63	Tresor de Mai (FR) *MCPipe* 10-11-9[131] RGreene	33/1	3½ 11
	Imperial de Thaix (FR) *MCPipe* 8-10-4[117] (t) JPElliott[5]	16/1	6 12
75	Canon Barney (IRE) *JonjoO'Neill* 9-10-4[112] GLee	16/1	3 13
105	Master Tern (USA) *JonjoO'Neill* 9-11-9[131] LCooper	20/1	1¾ 14
	Blowing Wind (FR) *MCPipe* 11-11-0[122] APMcCoy	20/1	ref
109	Jaloux d'Estruval (FR) *MrsLCTaylor* 7-10-11[124] RYoung[5]	12/1	ur

Mr R. V. Shaw 16ran 6m34.78

WETHERBY Saturday, Feb 7   SOFT

114   Weatherbys Bank Towton Nov Chase (Gr 2) (A) (5yo+) £20,825   3m1f (16)

93	ROYAL EMPEROR (IRE) *MrsSJSmith* 8-11-4 DSElsworth	3/1	1
54	NATIVE EMPEROR *JonjoO'Neill* 8-11-4 RMcGrath	10/3	20 2
93	SILVER KNIGHT *TDEasterby* 6-11-4 RGarritty	8/1	24 3
	Bee An Bee (IRE) *TRGeorge* 7-11-4 JMMaguire	11/1	18 4
	Ossmoses (IRE) *DMForster* 7-11-4 DRDennis	100/1	24 5
90	Simply Supreme (IRE) *MrsSJSmith* 7-11-4 WMarston	2/1f	f
65	Ballycassidy (IRE) *PBowen* 8-11-11 ADobbin	6/1	pu

Widpop Wanderers 7ran 6m28.00

LEOPARDSTOWN Sunday, Feb 8
Chase course: GOOD to SOFT, Hurdles course: SOFT

115   Cashmans Juv Hdle (Gr 2) (4yo) £24,357   2m (8)

	POWER ELITE (IRE) *NMeade* 4-11-0 PCarberry	8/1	1
68	NOPEKAN (IRE) *PatrickMullins* 4-11-0 RMPower	16/1	1½ 2
	QUEL DOUN (FR) *WPMullins* 4-11-0 JRBarry	12/1	3 3
68	Top Strategy (IRE) *TMWalsh* 4-11-6 RWalsh	11/10f	hd 4
102	Guilt *DTHughes* 4-11-0 (t) BJGeraghty	11/1	5 5
	Seaforde (IRE) *MFMorris* 4-11-0 CO'Dwyer	10/1	6
	Cupla Cairde *DTHughes* 4-11-3 JCulloty	8/1	7
	Eimear's Pride (IRE) *PAFahy* 4-11-0 GCotter	33/1	8
	Tacitus (IRE) *DTHughes* 4-11-0 TJMurphy	14/1	9
	Hasanpour (IRE) *CFSwan* 4-11-0 DJCasey	9/2	10
	Youngblood (IRE) *HRogers* 4-11-0 PACarberry	14/1	11

Mr D. P. Sharkey 11ran 4m04.76

116   Deloitte Nov Hdle (Gr 1) (5yo+) £35,374   2¼m (9)

59	BRAVE INCA (IRE) *ColmAMurphy* 6-11-10 BMCash	13/2	1
73	NEWMILL (IRE) *TGO'Leary* 6-11-10 BJGeraghty	11/2	¾ 2
73	MARIAH ROLLINS (IRE) *PAFahy* 6-11-5 DJCasey	7/2	5 3
97	Arch Stanton (IRE) *WPMullins* 6-11-10 RWalsh	14/1	nk 4
37	Kim Fontaine (IRE) *WPMullins* 6-11-10 DNRussell	16/1	½ 5
	Watson Lake (IRE) *NMeade* 6-11-10 PCarberry	9/10f	6
	Vic Ville (IRE) *MHourigan* 5-11-7 TJMurphy	14/1	7

Novices Syndicate 7ran 4m31.38

117   Dr P. J. Moriarty Nov Chase (Gr 1) (5yo+) £48,639   2m5f (14)

76	PIZARRO (IRE) *EJO'Grady* 7-11-12 BJGeraghty	1/1f	1
106	MOSSY GREEN (IRE) *WPMullins* 10-11-12 RWalsh	13/2	hd 2
76	HI CLOY (IRE) *MHourigan* 7-11-12 TJMurphy	12/1	2½ 3
	Boneyarrow (IRE) *WPMullins* 8-11-12 DJCasey	7/1	4 4
69	Xenophon (IRE) *AJMartin* 8-11-12 PCarberry	6/1	10 5
106	Direct Bearing (IRE) *DKWeld* 7-11-12 JCulloty	12/1	6
56	Camden Tanner (IRE) *RobertTyner* 8-11-12 DNRussell	7/1	7
39	Pay It Forward *MrsJHarrington* 6-11-12 RMPower	20/1	8
	Carneys Cross (IRE) *SJTreacy* 6-11-12 MDGrant	25/1	9

Mr Edward Wallace 9ran 5m35.26

118   Hennessy Cognac Gold Cup (Gr 1) (5yo+) £63,197   3m (17)

100	FLORIDA PEARL (IRE) *WPMullins* 12-11-12 RJohnson	5/1	1
78	LE COUDRAY (FR) *CRoche* 10-11-12 (t) BJGeraghty	15/8f	3 2
104	RINCE AN OIL (IRE) *TMWalsh* 11-11-12 RWalsh	4/1	6 3
101	Alexander Banquet (IRE) *WPMullins* 11-11-12 DJCasey	33/1	1½ 4
96	Cloudy Bays (IRE) *CByrnes* 7-11-12 (s) RGeraghty	6/1	dist 5
101	Be My Belle (IRE) *SJTreacy* 8-11-7 TJMurphy	40/1	6
	Harbour Pilot (IRE) *NMeade* 9-11-12 (b) PCarberry	7/2	ur

Mrs Violet O'Leary 7ran 6m21.62

HAYDOCK Saturday, Feb 14 SOFT

119 Pertemps Hcap Hdle (Qual) (B) (167) (5yo+) £12,870 2m7f110y (12)

	TARDAR (NZ) *JonjoO'Neill* 8-9-9^{143} ECooper^{7}	16/1		1
	IRIS'S GIFT *JonjoO'Neill* 7-11-12^{167} BJGeraghty	7/4f	1¾	2
41	STORMEZ (FR) *MCPipe* 7-10-0^{141} (t) TScudamore	16/1	1¾	3
	BREWSTER (IRE) *IanWilliams* 7-9-11^{141} JamesDavies^{3}	66/1	3	4
93	Ar Muin Na Muice (IRE) *JonjoO'Neill* 8-10-0^{141} TSiddall	10/1	16	5
77	Rostropovich (IRE) *MFMorris,Ireland* 7-10-0^{141} (s+t) PFlynn	12/1	5	6
103	Tarxien *MCPipe* 10-9-11^{141} (t) GSupple^{3}	33/1	2	7
	Kadara (IRE) *RHAlner* 5-9-11^{141} RWalford^{3}	12/1	sh	8
	Personal Assurance *JonjoO'Neill* 7-9-9^{141} TJPhelan^{5}	50/1	3½	9
46	Another Moose (IRE) *MissECLavelle* 9-10-0^{141} BFenton	25/1	1¼	10
112	Alexanderthegreat (IRE) *PFNicholls* 6-9-13^{147} MrNWilliams^{7}	5/1	hd	11
	Misty Class (IRE) *MrsSJSmith* 12-9-5^{142} PMadden^{10}	66/1	21	12
	Inching Closer *JHowardJohnson* 7-10-1^{142} (b) GLee	12/1	5	13
	Krack de L'Isle (FR) *ACWhillans* 6-10-1^{142} MBradburne	50/1	14	14
	Hidden Bounty (IRE) *MrsMReveley* 8-10-0^{141} AJDempsey	25/1		f
94	Distant Thunder (IRE) *RHAlner* 6-10-0^{141} JCulloty	9/1		pu
75	Secret Native (IRE) *TJTaaffe,Ireland* 9-9-9^{141} SMMcGovern^{5}	66/1		pu
	Eluna *IanWilliams* 6-10-0^{141} (t) WMarston	66/1		pu

Ray & Sue Dodd Partnership 18ran 6m07.86

NEWBURY Saturday, Feb 14 GOOD

120 Tote Gold Trophy Hdle (Hcap) (Gr 3) (A) (166) (4yo+) £72,500 2m110y (8)

33	GEOS (FR) *NJHenderson* 9-10-9^{149} MFoley	16/1		1
92	ROOSTER BOOSTER *PJHobbs* 10-11-12^{166} RJohnson	9/2f	sh	2
64	MONKERHOSTIN (FR) *PJHobbs* 7-10-2^{142} CLlewellyn	20/1	1¼	3
27	MUGHAS (IRE) *AKing* 5-9-13^{142} WHutchinson^{3}	16/1	½	4
110	Quazar (IRE) *JonjoO'Neill* 6-10-12^{152} (t) NFehily	50/1	sh	5
33	Westender (FR) *MCPipe* 8-10-13^{153} (b) APMcCoy	16/1	nk	6
64	Saintsaire (FR) *NJHenderson* 5-9-11^{140} ATinkler^{3}	25/1	1	7
66	Sporazene (IRE) *PFNicholls* 5-10-11^{151} RWalsh	6/1	1¼	8
64	Man O'Mystery (USA) *PRWebber* 7-10-0^{140} TDoyle	40/1	3	9
61	Self Defense *MissECLavelle* 7-10-9^{149} FKeniry	20/1	1¼	10
17	Le Duc (FR) *PFNicholls* 5-10-0^{140} JTizzard	33/1	1¾	11
20	Risky Reef *AndrewLee,Ireland* 7-10-0^{140} LAspell	11/1	9	12
	Goldbrook *RJHodges* 6-9-12^{143} AHoneyball^{5}	150/1	2	13
64	Sud Bleu (FR) *PFNicholls* 6-10-0^{140} RPMcNally	50/1	hd	14
92	Hasty Prince *JonjoO'Neill* 6-10-11^{151} LCooper	11/1	3½	15
44	Never (FR) *JonjoO'Neill* 7-9-6^{142} WJones^{10}	25/1	2½	16
64	Visibility (FR) *MCPipe* 5-9-9^{140} (v) JPElliott^{5}	100/1	1¾	17
	Contraband *MCPipe* 6-9-7^{140} TJMalone^{7}	50/1	2	18
64	Tom Paddington *HMorrison* 9-10-0^{140} TJMurphy	10/1	2½	19
92	Copeland *MCPipe* 9-10-7^{147} (v) RGreene	66/1	3½	20
	Through The Rye *GASwinbank* 8-9-11^{140} DCrosse^{3}	40/1	3½	21
64	Benbyas *DCarroll* 7-10-1^{144} PJBrennan^{3}	33/1	4	22
33	Latalomne (USA) *MCPipe* 10-9-11^{140} (v) JEMoore^{3}	66/1	nk	23
	Italian Counsel (IRE) *LADace* 7-9-7^{140} DLaverty^{7}	150/1	24	24
99	Limerick Boy (GER) *MissVenetiaWilliams* 6-10-3^{148} SThomas^{5}	13/2		ur

Thurloe Finsbury 25ran 3m48.52

121 AON Chase (Gr 2) (A) (6yo+) £40,600 3m (18)

	SHOOTING LIGHT (IRE) *MCPipe* 11-11-0 (v) RJohnson	33/1		1
31	IRISH HUSSAR (IRE) *NJHenderson* 8-11-5 MFoley	13/2	¾	2
53	KEEN LEADER (IRE) *JonjoO'Neill* 8-11-10 LCooper	10/11f	nk	3
84	Royal Auclair (FR) *PFNicholls* 7-11-0 (t) RWalsh	25/1	12	4
105	Horus (IRE) *MCPipe* 9-11-6 JEMoore	25/1	15	5
104	Sir Rembrandt (IRE) *RHAlner* 8-11-6 TJMurphy	4/1	4	6
67	Seebald (GER) *MCPipe* 9-11-6 APMcCoy	8/1	3	7
31	Shardam (IRE) *NATwiston-Davies* 7-11-6 CLlewellyn	16/1	1¼	8

J. M. Brown & M. J. Blackburn 8ran 5m56.70

122 AON Standard Open NHF (Gr 2) (A) (4, 5 and 6yo) £12,000 2m110y

	SECRET PLOY *HMorrison* 4-11-0 TJMurphy	11/2		1
	MOUNT CLERIGO (IRE) *VRADartnall* 6-11-7 AntonyEvans^{3}	9/1	4	2
	DEMARCO (IRE) *NJHenderson* 6-11-3 MFoley	9/2f	sh	3
	Bob Bob Bobbin *CLTizzard* 5-11-3 JTizzard	12/1	5	4
	Baby Run (FR) *NATwiston-Davies* 4-10-11 CLlewellyn	8/1	6	5
	Celtic Son (FR) *MCPipe* 5-11-7 APMcCoy	7/1	5	6
	Corrib Eclipse *JamiePoulton* 5-11-2 CBolger^{5}	14/1	5	7
	State of Play *PRWebber* 4-10-7 TDoyle	25/1	4	8
	He's The Guv'nor (IRE) *RHBuckler* 5-10-12 AHoneyball^{5}	66/1	sh	9

Rendova *AMBalding* 5-11-3 RJohnson 20/1   2 10
Blushing Bull *PFNicholls* 5-11-3 RWalsh 7/1   1½ 11
Grand Opinion (IRE) *BWDuke* 5-10-10 MrAshleePrice[7] 33/1   2½ 12
Looksharp Lad (IRE) *MrsAJBowlby* 6-11-0 JEMoore[3] 25/1   3½ 13
Finely Tuned (IRE) *MPitman* 5-11-3 NFehily 20/1   1 14
Ballyalbany (IRE) *MrsSusanNock* 6-11-3 SStronge 20/1   2 15
Miss Fahrenheit (IRE) *CRoberts* 5-11-0 JMogford .... 100/1   ¾ 16
Smeathe's Ridge *JABOld* 6-11-3 LAspell 100/1   10 17
Cossack Dancer (IRE) *MBradstock* 6-11-3 MBatchelor 20/1   3 18
Pink Eclipse *CRoberts* 4-10-0 RGreene 100/1   5 19
Vivante (IRE) *AJWilson* 6-10-10 VSlattery 100/1   2½ 20
Alexander Musical (IRE) *STLewis* 6-11-3 JMMaguire 100/1   8 21
Carpenters Boy *MrsAMThorpe* 4-10-4 WHutchinson[3] 100/1   22 22
Kitski (FR) *SGollings* 6-11-7 (b) RThornton 50/1   3½ 23
Mardello *NJHenderson* 6-10-11 ATinkler[3] 33/1   2 24

Mr A. M. Carding 24ran 3m52.23

GOWRAN PARK Saturday, Feb 14   SOFT

123 Red Mills Trial Hdle (Gr 2) (4yo+) £26,938   2m (8)

107	GEORGES GIRL (IRE) *FFlood* 6-10-12 FJFlood	11/8f	1
103	HARDY EUSTACE (IRE) *DTHughes* 7-11-11 CO'Dwyer	2/1	sh 2
77	BOB JUSTICE (IRE) *TMWalsh* 8-11-3 GCotter	12/1	10 3
39	Aine Dubh (IRE) *KevinFO'Donnell* 7-11-11 SCurling	25/1	2 4
76	Emotional Moment (IRE) *TJTaaffe* 7-11-9 DJCasey	8/1	1½ 5
49	Adamant Approach (IRE) *WPMullins* 10-11-3 JRBarry	9/1	.6
20	Balapour (IRE) *PatrickOBrady* 6-11-6 (t) JLCullen	25/1	7
	Goss *MJPO'Brien* 7-11-3 DNRussell	16/1	8
107	Stage Affair (USA) *DKWeld* 10-11-6 (b) DTEvans	12/1	9

Mr Glenn W. D. Martin 9ran 3m55.90

NAVAN Sunday, Feb 15   SOFT

124 Camlin (Pro-Am) INH Flat (4yo+) £7,625   2m

79	FORTY LICKS (IRE) *EJO'Grady* 7-12-2 MrJPMagnier[5]	6/4jf	1
	HOMER WELLS (IRE) *WPMullins* 6-12-1 MrJJCodd[3]	10/3	1 2
	MAN ABOUT TOWN (IRE) *TJTaaffe* 5-11-10 MrKEPower[5]	6/4jf	8 3
	Ardyne Bridge (IRE) *JohnJosephMurphy* 6-11-11 MrAJMcNamara[7] ..	12/1	1½ 4
	Church Island (IRE) *MHourigan* 5-11-5 MrNPMadden[3]	10/1	3½ 5
	Bilateralagreement (IRE) *GTHourigan* 6-11-4 JFLevins[7]	20/1	6
	Magic Mark *FFlood* 6-11-11 MrJPDempsey	16/1	7
	Drumlane Pal (IRE) *DesmondMcDonogh* 5-11-1 MissSMcDonogh[7]	25/1	8
	Deasun (FR) *JJLambe* 6-11-4 MrDanielKeenan[7]	25/1	9

Mrs Paul Shanahan 9ran 4m05.89

ASCOT Saturday, Feb 21   GOOD

125 Amlin Plus Reynoldstown Nov Chase (Gr 2) (A) (5yo+) £20,825   3m110y (20)

44	OUR VIC (IRE) *PFNicholls* 6-11-4 TJMurphy	11/10f	1
76	ROSSLEA (IRE) *MissHCKnight* 6-11-4 JCulloty	3/1	6 2
52	DOUBLE HONOUR (FR) *PJHobbs* 6-11-4 PFlynn	6/1	1½ 3
111	L'Aventure (FR) *PFNicholls* 5-10-0 (b+t) RPMcNally	4/1	5 4
	Buzybakson (IRE) *JRCornwall* 7-11-4 RHobson	100/1	dist 5
	Better Days (IRE) *MrsSJSmith* 8-11-8 DSElsworth	20/1	pu

Mr D. A. Johnson 6ran 6m16.13

NEWCASTLE Saturday, Feb 21   GOOD to SOFT

126 Tote Eider (Hcap Chase) (B) 0-150(137) (5yo+) £40,600   4m1f (25)

109	TYNEANDTHYNEAGAIN *RCGuest* 9-11-12[137] (s) HOliver	28/1	1
28	ROBBO *MrsMReveley* 10-9-13[115] FKing[5]	18/1	3 2
109	MAGICAL BAILIWICK (IRE) *MCPipe* 8-10-8[122] JEMoore[3]	8/1	nk 3
28	GRANIT D'ESTRUVAL (FR) *FerdyMurphy* 10-10-8[119] AJDempsey ...	33/1	8 4
	Harlov *AParker* 9-10-0[111] (s) RMcGrath	11/2	15 5
	Lord Jack *NGRichards* 8-11-0[125] (t) BHarding	20/1	8 6
109	Carryonharry (IRE) *MCPipe* 10-10-10[124] (v) GSupple[3]	25/1	15 7
	Briar Rose (IRE) *NMLEwart* 9-10-0[111] FKeniry	100/1	11 8
28	Maximize (IRE) *MCPipe* 10-11-5[130] RGreene	16/1	6 9
95	Ardent Scout *MrsSJSmith* 12-10-11[129] JRRyan[7]	14/1	11 10
	Tipsy Mouse (IRE) *MrsSJSmith* 8-10-0[111] WMarston	6/1	f
52	Luzcadou (FR) *FerdyMurphy* 11-10-8[119] (v) ARoss	50/1	bd
	River Bug (IRE) *JamiePoulton* 10-9-9[111] (b) CBolger[5]	40/1	ur
	Fasgo (IRE) *PFNicholls* 9-11-2[127] JTizzard	9/2f	pu
95	What Odds (IRE) *TKGeraghty,Ireland* 8-10-12[126] RGeraghty[3] ..	12/1	pu
	Only Once *LLungo* 9-11-0[125] ADobbin	11/1	pu

75	Dark Room (IRE) *JonjoO'Neill* 7-10-8[119] CO'Dwyer	25/1	pu
	Dionn Righ (IRE) *JHowardJohnson* 9-10-0[111] (s+t) GLee	50/1	pu
	Nativetrial (IRE) *CJMann* 9-9-11[111] (b+t) DCrosse[3]	50/1	pu
	Shining Tyne *RJohnson* 10-10-0[111] (b+t) KJohnson	200/1	pu

Mr N. B. Mason 20ran 8m43.45

WINCANTON Saturday, Feb 21   GOOD to FIRM

127 Axminster Kingwell Hdle (Gr 2) (A) (4yo+) £34,800   2m (8)

50	RIGMAROLE *PFNicholls* 6-11-10 (t) RWalsh	3/1	1
66	INTERSKY FALCON *JonjoO'Neill* 7-11-10 (b) LCooper	8/13f	3½ 2
	GRAVE DOUBTS *KBishop* 8-11-2 (t) BFenton	20/1	9 3
	Zibeline (IRE) *BEllison* 7-11-2 (b) RJohnson	50/1	11 4
110	Fifth Generation (IRE) *DrPPritchard* 14-11-2 DrPPritchard	500/1	5 5
	Val de Fleurie (GER) *JGMO'Shea* 9-10-9 GRichards	200/1	7 6
	The Gene Genie *RJHodges* 9-11-2 AHoneyball	300/1	17 7
99	Perouse *PFNicholls* 6-11-2 (t) RThornton	13/2	7 8

Mr & Mrs Mark Woodhouse 8ran 3m33.92

FAIRYHOUSE Saturday, Feb 21   GOOD to SOFT

128 Tattersalls (Ireland) Derby Sale Juv Hdle (Gr 3) (4yo) £15,395   2m (9)

115	POWER ELITE (IRE) *NMeade* 4-11-6 PCarberry	7/4f	1
	WILD PASSION (GER) *NMeade* 4-10-8 IJPower[3]	12/1	½ 2
	ZEROBERTO (IRE) *DKWeld* 4-10-11 DTEvans	16/1	11 3
	Callow Lake (IRE) *DWachman* 4-10-11 MDGrant	7/2	2 4
34	You Need Luck (IRE) *MrsJHarrington* 4-10-11 BJGeraghty	7/1	3 5
	Corrib Boy (IRE) *JosephCrowley* 4-10-11 GCotter	14/1	6
68	Blue Corrig (IRE) *JosephCrowley* 4-10-6 JMAllen[5]	9/1	7
	Verrocchio (IRE) *WPMullins* 4-10-11 DJCasey	8/1	8
115	Top Strategy (IRE) *TMWalsh* 4-11-3 GTHutchinson[3]	9/2	9
	Monroe Gold *CWilkinson* 4-10-6 SCurling[5]	66/1	10

Mr D. P. Sharkey 10ran 3m58.48

FONTWELL Sunday, Feb 22

129 Tote National Spirit Hdle (Gr 2) (A) (4yo+) £29,000   2½m (10)

48	STARZAAN (IRE) *HMorrison* 5-11-4 TJMurphy	5/1	1
	VIC TOTO (FR) *FDoumen,France* 7-11-12 TDoumen	7/1	6 2
80	BIG MOMENT *MrsAJPerrett* 6-11-4 LAspell	7/4f	2½ 3
120	Quazar (IRE) *JonjoO'Neill* 6-11-4 (t) ADobbin	9/2	15 4
1	In Contrast (IRE) *PJHobbs* 8-11-8 RJohnson	11/2	7 5
	Sleep Bal (FR) *NJHenderson* 5-11-8 SStronge	25/1	2½ 6
60	Mr Cool *MCPipe* 10-11-12 RGreene	16/1	7 7
65	Yorkshire (IRE) *DLWilliams* 10-11-4 DCrosse	100/1	dist 8
	Jollyolly *PBowen* 5-11-6 (s) GLee	11/1	pu

Mr Ben Arbib 9ran 4m41.34

NAAS Sunday, Feb 22   GOOD to SOFT

130 betfair.com Johnstown Nov Hdle (Gr 2) (4yo+) £23,093   2½m (11)

116	NEWMILL (IRE) *TGO'Leary* 6-11-12 BJGeraghty	1/2f	1
	INEXORABLE (IRE) *DWachman* 6-11-10 MDGrant	4/1	4½ 2
	MOSCOW COURT (IRE) *MrsJHarrington* 6-11-5 TPTreacy	8/1	1 3
	Hardy Duckett (IRE) *DTHughes* 5-11-2 PCarberry	5/1	1 4
	Harithabad (FR) *MrsOliviaByrne* 9-11-5 GTHutchinson	16/1	dist 5

Mrs Mary T. Hayes 5ran 4m44.98

HAYDOCK Saturday, Feb 28   Chase course: GOOD to FIRM, Hurdles course: GOOD

131 Red Square Vodka Prestige Nov Hdle (Gr 2) (A) (4yo+) £17,850   2m7f110y (12)

90	ROYAL ROSA (FR) *JHowardJohnson* 5-11-4 GLee	9/4	1
	FUNDAMENTALIST (IRE) *NATwiston-Davies* 6-11-8 CLlewellyn	9/4	½ 2
	SPECIAL RATE (IRE) *AKing* 7-11-11 JAMcCarthy	12/1	19 3
	Young Collier *JABOld* 5-11-4 LAspell	16/1	19 4
	Mantles Pride *DrPPritchard* 9-11-4 DrPPritchard	300/1	dist 5
	Diamant Noir *JonjoO'Neill* 6-11-4 LCooper	2/1f	f

Andrea & Graham Wylie 6ran 5m46.15

132 Red Square Vodka Gold Cup Chase (Hcap) (Gr 3) (A) (151) (5yo+) £69,600   3½m110y (22)

95	JURANCON II (FR) *MCPipe* 7-10-6[136] JPElliott[5]	10/1	1
	BEAR ON BOARD (IRE) *AKing* 9-10-5[130] JAMcCarthy	9/2	15 2
91	ARTIC JACK (FR) *MrsSJSmith* 8-11-12[151] DSElsworth	5/1	21 3
91	Ebony Light (IRE) *DMcCain* 8-10-1[126] BHarding	33/1	3½ 4
91	You're Agoodun *MCPipe* 12-10-6[138] (v) TJMalone[7]	12/1	nk 5

1035

```
 113  Exit To Wave (FR) PFNicholls 8-10-8¹³³ JTizzard .............................. 11/1    ¾ 6
   6  Just In Debt (IRE) MTodhunter 8-10-9¹³⁴ GLee ................................ 40/1      pu
      Joe Blake (IRE) LLungo 9-10-7¹³² RMcGrath .................................. 4/1jf     pu
      Wain Mountain JABOld 8-10-5¹³⁰ LAspell ...................................... 12/1      pu
  75  World Wide Web (IRE) JonjoO'Neill 8-10-1¹²⁶ LCooper............................ 4/1jf   pu
      Mr D. A. Johnson 10ran 7m00.23
```

KEMPTON Saturday, Feb 28   Chase course: GOOD to FIRM, Hurdles course: GOOD

133 **betfair.com Rendlesham Hdle (Gr 2) (A) (4yo+) £23,200**   3m110y (11)

```
 120  MONKERHOSTIN (FR) PJHobbs 7-11-4 RJohnson ............................. 3/1f      1
 112  MISTANOORA NATwiston-Davies 5-11-4 (b) RBiddlecombe .................. 7/2     4 2
  83  DEANO'S BEENO MCPipe 12-11-12 APMcCoy ................................. 11/2    4 3
  80  Mon Villez (FR) NJHenderson 5-11-8 RWalsh ............................... 5/1     nk 4
 119  Kadara (IRE) RHAlner 5-10-11 JPMcNamara................................. 12/1    ½ 5
 110  Teaatral CREgerton 10-11-4 RThornton .................................... 20/1    26 6
 119  Another Moose (IRE) MissECLavelle 9-11-4 BFenton ...................... 33/1      f
 120  Tom Paddington HMorrison 9-11-4 JCulloty ................................ 5/1     pu
      Mr M. G. St Quinton 8ran 5m55.19
```

134 **Read The Racing Post Before You Bet Adonis Juv Nov Hdle**   2m (8)
     (Adonis) (Gr 2) (A) (4yo) £17,400

```
  85  TROUBLE AT BAY (IRE) AKing 4-11-5 RThornton........................... 5/2f      1
      LOCKSMITH MCPipe 4-10-12 APMcCoy .................................... 11/2    ½ 2
      SHUHOOD (USA) PRWebber 4-10-12 TDoyle ............................... 25/1    9 3
      Chockdee (FR) PFNicholls 4-10-12 RWalsh ............................... 8/1     ¾ 4
 102  Mondul (GER) MFHarris 4-11-5 OMcPhail ................................. 11/4    2 5
      Analogy (IRE) CJMann 4-10-12 DCrosse ................................. 28/1    1¼ 6
      Kjetil (USA) PFNicholls 4-10-12 ChristianWilliams ..................... 11/1    10 7
      Web Perceptions (USA) MFHarris 4-11-5 (b+t) RJohnson ............... 9/1     dist 8
      Flying Wanda PFNicholls 4-10-5 SThomas ............................... 14/1    ur
      Mr Nigel Bunter 9ran 3m46.58
```

135 **Racing Post Chase (Hcap) (Gr 3) (A) (150) (5yo+) £58,000**   3m (19)

```
  67  MARLBOROUGH (IRE) NJHenderson 12-11-12¹⁵⁰ RWalsh ................. 8/1       1
  31  GUNTHER MCBRIDE (IRE) PJHobbs 9-10-8¹³² RJohnson................. 4/1     4 2
  63  IZNOGOUD (FR) MCPipe 8-10-6¹³⁰ RGreene............................... 7/1     2 3
 121  Shardam (IRE) NATwiston-Davies 7-11-2¹⁴⁰ JGoldstein................. 20/1    2 4
 112  Chicuelo (FR) MCPipe 8-10-13¹⁴⁰ (v) GSupple³ ....................... 25/1    14 5
 109  Jimmy Tennis (FR) MissVenetiaWilliams 7-9-10¹²⁵ SThomas⁵............ 3/1f    6 6
 121  Horus (IRE) MCPipe 9-11-0¹⁴¹ JEMoore³................................. 20/1    ur
 121  Shooting Light (IRE) MCPipe 11-11-12¹⁵⁰ (v) APMcCoy ............... 13/2    pu
 105  Hunters Tweed PBeaumont 8-11-3¹⁴¹ RGarritty.......................... 11/2    pu
      Perfect Fellow MissHCKnight 10-10-6¹³⁰ JCulloty ....................... 20/1    pu
      Itsonlyme (IRE) MissVenetiaWilliams 11-10-3¹²⁷ TDoyle ............... 25/1    pu
      Sir Robert Ogden 11ran 5m49.70
```

136 **racingpostpix.co.uk Pendil Nov Chase (Gr 2) (A) (5yo+) £21,700**   2½m110y (17)

```
  86  CALLING BRAVE (IRE) NJHenderson 8-11-7 APMcCoy ................... 1/1f      1
  42  ATUM RE (IRE) PRWebber 7-11-7 RJohnson.............................. 7/1     11 2
      SANTENAY (FR) PFNicholls 6-11-10 RWalsh ............................. 11/4    1½ 3
  30  Sir Talbot JABOld 10-11-3 JPMcNamara ................................. 16/1    dist 4
      The Bandit (IRE) MissECLavelle 7-11-3 JCulloty ....................... 11/2    pu
      Sir Robert Ogden 5ran 4m57.74
```

KELSO Saturday, Mar 6   GOOD

137 **Tote Exacta Premier Kelso Hdle (Nov) (Gr 2) (A) (4yo+) £17,400**   2¼m (10)

```
      PADDY THE PIPER (IRE) LLungo 7-11-2 ADobbin ....................... 5/1       1
      STEPPES OF GOLD (IRE) NGRichards 7-11-6 BHarding................. 3/1     1¾ 2
  48  PATRIARCH EXPRESS GAHarker 7-11-6 NHannity....................... 33/1    8 3
      Chivalry JHowardJohnson 5-11-9 GLee ................................. 9/4f    11 4
      Kentucky Blue (IRE) TDEasterby 4-10-12 RGarritty ................... 33/1    2½ 5
      Collier Hill GASwinbank 6-11-2 JCrowley ............................... 14/1    7 6
      Feel The Pride (IRE) JonjoO'Neill 6-11-2 (b) TSiddall................. 16/1    26 7
      After Galway (IRE) MissVScott 8-11-2 HOliver .......................... 50/1    30 8
      Sharabad (FR) MrsLBNormile 6-11-2 NMulholland ..................... 200/1   13 9
      Dr Sharp (IRE) TPTate 4-10-8 RMcGrath ............................... 20/1    ur
      Tragic Ohio PFNicholls 5-11-2 JTizzard ................................ 4/1     pu
      Mr & Mrs Raymond Anderson Green 11ran 4m20.90
```

NEWBURY Saturday, Mar 6   GOOD

138 **Vodafone Gold Cup Hcap Chase (B) (163) (5yo+) £61,202**   2½m (16)

```
  89  ISIO (FR) NJHenderson 8-11-4¹⁵⁵ BJGeraghty.......................... 11/2      1
```

	TURGEONEV (FR) *TDEasterby* 9-10-8[148] DO`Meara[3]	20/1	4 2
121	SEEBALD (GER) *MCPipe* 9-10-13[153] JEMoore[3]	25/1	6 3
108	Hand Inn Hand *HDDaly* 8-11-8[159] MBradburne	13/2	2 4
	Joly Bey (FR) *NJGifford* 7-10-7[147] MrDHDunsdon[3]	8/1	5 5
111	See You Sometime *JWMullins* 9-10-0[137] BFenton	50/1	5 6
105	Kelrev (FR) *MissVenetiaWilliams* 6-9-9[137] SThomas[3]	14/1	1 7
89	Farmer Jack *PJHobbs* 8-10-12[149] JCulloty	8/1	5 8
49	Risk Accessor (IRE) *CRoche,Ireland* 9-10-9[146] TJMurphy	6/1	2 9
84	Spring Grove (IRE) *RHAlner* 9-9-11[137] RWalford[3]	100/1	4 10
15	Exit Swinger (FR) *PFNicholls* 9-10-2[139] RWalsh	5/1f	9 11
89	Wahiba Sands *MCPipe* 11-9-11[139] (v) JPElliott[5]	33/1	19 12
11	Kadarann (IRE) *PFNicholls* 7-11-12[163] RThornton	25/1	pu
47	Cyfor Malta (FR) *MCPipe* 11-11-0[151] APMcCoy	16/1	pu
	Europa *TPTate* 8-10-3[140] JMMaguire	14/1	pu

Sir Peter And Lady Gibbings 15ran 4m58.29

SANDOWN Saturday, Mar 13   SOFT

139 **European Breeders Fund Sunderlands NH Nov Hcap Hdle Final (Gr 3) (A) (135) (4, 5, 6 and 7yo)** £34,800   2½m110y (9)

80	CONTROL MAN (IRE) *MCPipe* 6-10-11[120] (v) APMcCoy	8/1	1
94	ERIC'S CHARM (FR) *OSherwood* 6-11-12[135] BJGeraghty	8/1	2½ 2
	HOLLAND PARK (IRE) *MrsSDWilliams* 7-10-9[118] CLlewellyn	10/1	15 3
	SWEET DIVERSION (IRE) *PFNicholls* 5-10-12[121] JTizzard	25/1	3½ 4
	Accipiter *GBBalding* 5-11-1[129] TBest[5]	11/2f	¾ 5
	Bramlynn Brook (FR) *MissVenetiaWilliams* 6-9-10[110] SThomas[5]	12/1	hd 6
	Copsale Lad *NJHenderson* 7-10-8[117] RJohnson	7/1	7 7
	Sixo (IRE) *MCPipe* 7-10-13[122] TScudamore	33/1	hd 8
	Mount Karinga *PFNicholls* 6-11-3[126] RWalsh	6/1	2½ 9
	Joes Edge (IRE) *MissVenetiaWilliams* 7-10-8[120] AO`Keeffe[3]	20/1	5 10
	Moonlit Harbour *MWEasterby* 5-10-11[120] TJMurphy	33/1	dist 11
	Time To Reflect (IRE) *MCPipe* 5-9-11[100] (v) JEMoore[3]	100/1	6 12
	Lotier (FR) *MrsLCTaylor* 5-10-13[122] MBradburne	20/1	f
	El Vaquero (IRE) *MissHCKnight* 6-10-12[121] JCulloty	12/1	f
	The Dark Lord (IRE) *MrsLWadham* 7-10-4[113] LAspell	16/1	f
	Manly Money *PFNicholls* 6-10-3[115] ChristianWilliams[3]	16/1	pu

Mr D. A. Johnson 16ran 5m12.87

140 **Sunderlands Imperial Cup Hcap Hdle (B) 0-150(141) (4yo+)** £29,000   2m110y (8)

	SCORNED (GER) *AMBalding* 9-10-3[118] BFenton	14/1	1
	BOLD BISHOP (IRE) *JonjoO`Neill* 7-11-6[135] BJGeraghty	8/1	4 2
	FENIX (IRE) *MrsLWadham* 5-10-5[120] LAspell	16/1	3½ 3
120	GOLDBROOK *RJHodges* 6-10-8[123] JTizzard	33/1	6 4
	Gin Palace (IRE) *GLMoore* 6-10-13[131] JEMoore[3]	10/1	½ 5
64	Shalako (USA) *PJHobbs* 6-10-8[123] (b) PFlynn	33/1	1¼ 6
120	Saintsaire (FR) *NJHenderson* 5-11-12[141] MAFitzgerald	14/1	6 7
120	Italian Counsel (IRE) *LADace* 7-9-13[121] DLaverty[7]	66/1	½ 8
	Desert Air (JPN) *MCPipe* 5-10-9[124] (v+t) APMcCoy	12/1	3 9
64	Overstrand (IRE) *MrsMReveley* 5-11-2[131] AThornton	20/1	1 10
	Breknen Le Noir (FR) *PJHobbs* 6-10-5[120] (b) RJohnson	12/1	2 11
89	Hot Shots (FR) *MPitman* 9-10-5[120] TJMurphy	13/2f	sh 12
	Grand Finale (IRE) *MissVenetiaWilliams* 7-10-5[125] SThomas[5]	12/1	1 13
120	Sud Bleu (FR) *PFNicholls* 6-11-6[135] RWalsh	33/1	3 14
120	Never (FR) *JonjoO`Neill* 7-11-6[135] LCooper	10/1	4 15
	Ilabon (FR) *MCPipe* 8-10-0[120] JPElliott[5]	16/1	3½ 16
99	Idaho d`Ox (FR) *MCPipe* 8-10-9[127] GSupple[3]	40/1	dist 17
	Dancing Bay *NJHenderson* 7-10-12[130] ATinkler[3]	40/1	1¾ 18
99	Kadount (FR) *AKing* 6-11-1[130] RThornton	25/1	pu
18	Gone Far (USA) *MCPipe* 7-10-10[125] (v) TScudamore	33/1	pu
	Bernardon (GER) *RCGuest* 8-10-8[123] HOliver	20/1	pu
	Beat The Heat (IRE) *JeddO`Keeffe* 6-10-5[120] JCulloty	66/1	pu
	Friedhelmo (GER) *RAFahey* 8-10-0[118] PWhelan[3]	66/1	pu

Kingsclere Stud 23ran 4m09.05

141 **EBF/Doncaster Bloodstock Sales Mares' Only Standard Open NHF Final (L) (A) (4, 5, 6 and 7yo f+m)** £14,500   2m110y

	MARSH RUN *MWEasterby* 5-11-0 MrTGreenall[7]	66/1	1
	KINGS BAY *HMorrison* 5-11-4 TJMurphy	9/2	¾ 2
	SABREFLIGHT *RAFahey* 4-10-3 PWhelan[3]	16/1	3½ 3
	Countess Point *CLTizzard* 6-11-4 JTizzard	16/1	nk 4
	Diamond Sal *MrsMReveley* 6-11-0 RWalsh	16/1	4 5
	First Harmony *MBrittain* 5-11-7 AThornton	25/1	nk 6
	Sister Cinnamon *SGollings* 6-11-4 RThornton	25/1	8 7

	Golden Bay *GBBalding* 5-10-13 TBest[5]	25/1	1 8
	Queen Soraya *MissHCKnight* 6-11-7 JCulloty	14/1	14 9
	Averse (USA) *NGRichards* 5-11-0 BJGeraghty	6/1	2 10
	Topanberry (IRE) *NGRichards* 5-11-0 CLlewellyn	25/1	3½ 11
	Lady of Fortune (IRE) *NJHenderson* 5-11-4 MAFitzgerald	9/4f	2½ 12
	Emerald Express *PRWebber* 5-11-0 TDoyle	33/1	9 13
	Having A Party *JMackie* 6-11-4 PaulMoloney	33/1	18 14
	Lady Racquet (IRE) *MrsAJBowlby* 5-11-0 BFenton	66/1	22 15
	Maryland (IRE) *OBrennan* 7-11-4 NFehily	66/1	nk 16
	Arctic Moss (IRE) *GASwinbank* 5-11-4 JCrowley	14/1	27 17
122	Mardello *NJHenderson* 6-11-1 ATinkler[3]	50/1	dist 18
	Smokin Grey *MJGingell* 4-10-6 SFox	66/1	dist 19

Mrs M. E. Curtis 19ran 4m14.53

CHELTENHAM Tuesday, Mar 16   GOOD (Old Course)

142 **Letheby & Christopher Supreme Nov Hdle (Gr 1) (A) (4yo+)**   2m110y (8)
£58,000

116	BRAVE INCA (IRE) *ColmAMurphy,Ireland* 6-11-7 BMCash	7/2f	1
	WAR OF ATTRITION (IRE) *MFMorris,Ireland* 5-11-7 CO'Dwyer	33/1	nk 2
	FLEET STREET *NJHenderson* 5-11-7 ATinkler	20/1	7 3
	Cardenas (GER) *CREgerton* 5-11-7 JAMcCarthy	14/1	1¼ 4
110	Garde Champetre (FR) *PFNicholls* 5-11-7 TJMurphy	11/1	½ 5
116	Arch Stanton (IRE) *WPMullins,Ireland* 6-11-7 JRBarry	33/1	3½ 6
134	Locksmith *MCPipe* 4-11-0 APMcCoy	20/1	1¼ 7
87	Bourbon Manhattan *AKing* 6-11-7 RThornton	20/1	1 8
127	Zibeline (IRE) *BEllison* 7-11-7 (b) GLee	100/1	¾ 9
61	Albuhera (IRE) *PFNicholls* 6-11-7 (t) RWalsh	5/1	2 10
	Lacdoudal (FR) *PJHobbs* 5-11-7 RJohnson	16/1	22 11
	Zum See (IRE) *NMeade,Ireland* 5-11-7 PCarberry	16/1	6 12
	Euro Leader (IRE) *WPMullins,Ireland* 6-11-7 DNRussell	66/1	1¾ 13
	Simoun (IRE) *MCPipe* 6-11-7 (t) RGreene	66/1	21 14
	John Oliver (IRE) *EJO'Grady,Ireland* 6-11-7 BJGeraghty	25/1	5 15
116	Mariah Rollins (IRE) *PAFahy,Ireland* 6-11-0 DJCasey	7/1	ur
	Dictum (GER) *MrsSusanNock* 6-11-7 JCulloty	25/1	pu
	Island Stream (IRE) *JRJenkins* 5-11-7 WMarston	200/1	pu
87	Perle de Puce (FR) *NJHenderson* 5-11-0 MAFitzgerald	8/1	pu

Novices Syndicate 19ran 3m55.81

143 **Irish Independent Arkle Challenge Trophy Chase (Gr 1) (A) (5yo+)**   2m (12)
£81,200

32	WELL CHIEF (GER) *MCPipe* 5-11-3 APMcCoy	9/1	1
106	KICKING KING (IRE) *TJTaaffe,Ireland* 6-11-7 BJGeraghty	7/2	1 2
120	LE DUC (FR) *PFNicholls* 5-11-3 JTizzard	7/3	7 3
	Jahash *AKing* 6-11-7 RThornton	150/1	10 4
106	Colca Canyon (IRE) *MrsJHarrington,Ireland* 7-11-7 RMPower	16/1	6 5
	John James (IRE) *JHScott,Ireland* 8-11-7 KWhelan	100/1	4 6
62	Keltic Bard *CJMann* 7-11-7 NFehily	25/1	8 7
71	Caracciola (GER) *NJHenderson* 7-11-7 MAFitzgerald	15/2	14 8
71	Thisthatandtother (IRE) *PFNicholls* 8-11-7 RWalsh	5/2f	f
62	Tidour (FR) *PRWebber* 8-11-7 TDoyle	33/1	f
106	Central House *DTHughes,Ireland* 7-11-7 PCarberry	11/1	ur
33	Mister McGoldrick *MrsSJSmith* 7-11-7 DSElsworth	50/1	ur
111	Puntal (FR) *MCPipe* 8-11-7 (t) TJMurphy	50/1	ur
	Our Armageddon (NZ) *RCGuest* 5-11-7 LMcGrath	17/2	pu
	Palua *MissECLavelle* 7-11-7 BFenton	25/1	pu
	Royaleety (FR) *IanWilliams* 5-11-3 PaulMoloney	33/1	pu

Mr D. A. Johnson 16ran 3m55.86

144 **Smurfit Champion Hdle Challenge Trophy (Gr 1) (A) (4yo+)**   2m110y (8)
£174,000

123	HARDY EUSTACE (IRE) *DTHughes,Ireland* 7-11-10 (b) CO'Dwyer	33/1	1
120	ROOSTER BOOSTER *PJHobbs* 10-11-10 RJohnson	11/8f	5 2
127	INTERSKY FALCON *JonjoO'Neill* 7-11-10 (b+t) LCooper	8/1	4 3
107	Foreman (GER) *TDoumen,France* 6-11-10 (b) TDoumen	10/1	1¼ 4
120	Westender (FR) *MCPipe* 8-11-10 (b) APMcCoy	16/1	nk 5
107	Fota Island (IRE) *MFMorris,Ireland* 8-11-10 (b) DJCasey	50/1	3 6
107	Golden Cross (IRE) *MHalford,Ireland* 5-11-10 (s) PCarberry	40/1	6 7
127	Rigmarole *PFNicholls* 6-11-10 (t) RWalsh	4/1	2½ 8
92	Specular (AUS) *JonjoO'Neill* 8-11-10 BJGeraghty	14/1	4 9
120	Self Defense *MissECLavelle* 7-11-10 FKeniry	66/1	sh 10
120	Hasty Prince *JonjoO'Neill* 6-11-10 ADobbin	50/1	¾ 11
120	Limerick Boy (GER) *MissVenetiaWilliams* 6-11-10 SThomas	16/1	1 12

107 Davenport Milenium (IRE) *WPMullins,Ireland* 8-11-10 TJMurphy 25/1 1½ 13
120 Geos (FR) *NJHenderson* 9-11-10 MAFitzgerald .... 20/1 pu

Mr Laurence Byrne 14ran 3m54.43

145 **William Hill NH Hcap Chase (Gr 3) (A) (157) (5yo+) £46,400** 3m110y (19)

98 FORK LIGHTNING (IRE) *AKing* 8-10-5[130] RThornton 7/1 1
135 SHARDAM (IRE) *NATwiston-Davies* 7-10-7[138] CLlewellyn 11/2 2 2
121 ROYAL AUCLAIR (FR) *PFNicholls* 7-10-9[140] (t) RWalsh 7/1 9 3
Kelami (FR) *FDoumen,France* 6-10-5[136] TDoumen 11/2 1¾ 4
135 Chicuelo (FR) *MCPipe* 8-10-7[138] (v) APMcCoy 16/1 5 5
132 You're Agoodun *MCPipe* 12-9-11[135] (v) TJMalone[7] 25/1 6 6
113 Master Tern (USA) *JonjoO'Neill* 9-10-0[131] (s) ADobbin 10/1 3½ 7
47 Haut Cercy (FR) *HDDaly* 9-10-9[140] RJohnson 10/3f 12 8
Dark Stranger (FR) *MCPipe* 13-10-0[131] (b) PCarberry .... 50/1 dist 9
135 Marlborough (IRE) *NJHenderson* 12-11-12[157] MAFitzgerald .... 10/1 pu
126 Tyneandthyneagain *RCGuest* 9-11-1[146] (s) HOliver .... 20/1 pu

Mr & Mrs F. C. Welch 11ran 6m12.34

146 **Fulke Walwyn Kim Muir Challenge Cup Hcap Chase (Amat) (B)** 3m110y (19)
0-140(142) (5yo+) £29,000

126 MAXIMIZE (IRE) *MCPipe* 10-10-6[127] MrDEdwards[7] 40/1 1
113 MERCHANTS FRIEND (IRE) *CJMann* 9-10-11[125] (s) MrPCashman 20/1 1 2
IBIS ROCHELAIS (FR) *AEnnis* 8-10-4[121] MrTGreenall[3] 7/1f 9 3
DOMINIKUS *FerdyMurphy* 7-10-1[120] KMercer[5] 20/1 10 4
Jasmin Guichois (FR) *MissVenetiaWilliams* 7-10-1[120] MrNWilliams[5] 10/1 3 5
Wagner (IRE) *JonjoO'Neill* 7-10-8[125] MrRHarding[3] 12/1 20 6
Super Fellow (IRE) *DPMurphy,Ireland* 10-9-9[114] (s+t)
MrColinMotherway[5] 40/1 6 7
Prominent Profile (IRE) *NATwiston-Davies* 11-10-9[123] MrRWidger 14/1 1¼ 8
109 Montifault (FR) *PFNicholls* 9-11-2[130] MrDerekO'Connor .... 20/1 ¾ 9
6 Ballyconnell (IRE) *MissVenetiaWilliams* 8-10-7[121] MrBRHamilton........ 12/1 28 10
Innox (FR) *FDoumen,France* 8-11-8[136] (b) MrDHDunsdon............... 9/1 f
63 Royal Predica (FR) *MCPipe* 10-11-2[130] (t) MrGordonElliott .... 14/1 f
Jasmin d'Oudairies (FR) *WPMullins,Ireland* 7-10-7[121] MrJJCodd.............. 25/1 f
135 Horus (FR) *MCPipe* 9-12-0[142] MrAFarrant .... 12/1 pu
Toto Toscato (FR) *MCPipe* 10-10-9[130] MrGWeatherley[7] .... 8/1 pu
Sulphur Springs (IRE) *MCPipe* 12-10-3[124] (t) MrBKing[7] .... 66/1 pu
Jardin de Beaulieu (FR) *IanWilliams* 7-10-9[123] (s) MrAPCrowe............ 40/1 pu
2 Lanmire Tower (IRE) *SGollings* 10-10-4[118] (b) MrAFitzgerald .... 66/1 pu
109 Montreal (FR) *MCPipe* 7-10-4[118] MrLJefford.................................... 33/1 pu
Royal Beluga (USA) *TRGeorge* 7-10-4[118] MrNPMadden .... 40/1 pu
Mondial Jack (FR) *MCPipe* 5-9-10[125] TJMalone[5] .... 10/1 pu
36 Gielgud *PRWebber* 7-10-1[118] (t) MrSMorris[3] .... 66/1 pu

Mr D. A. Johnson 22ran 6m17.53

147 **Pertemps Final (Hcap Hdle) (L) (A) (146) (5yo+) £34,800** 3m1f110y (13)

75 CREON *JonjoO'Neill* 9-10-0[120] (s) TJMurphy 50/1 1
G V A IRELAND (IRE) *FFlood,Ireland* 6-10-5[125] FJFlood....................... 14/1 ½ 2
119 ALEXANDERTHEGREAT (IRE) *PFNicholls* 6-11-6[140] RWalsh 25/1 1 3
HIS NIBS (IRE) *MissVenetiaWilliams* 7-10-8[128] RJohnson.................... 25/1 ½ 4
119 Ar Muin Na Muice (IRE) *JonjoO'Neill* 8-11-6[140] BJGeraghty 10/1 1¼ 5
58 Mutineer (IRE) *DTHughes,Ireland* 5-10-11[131] (b+t) PCarberry.............. 33/1 1½ 6
Keepatem (IRE) *MFMorris,Ireland* 8-10-7[127] DJCasey...................... 4/1f 1 7
119 Personal Assurance *JonjoO'Neill* 7-10-4[124] LCooper 33/1 2 8
4 Back On Top (IRE) *JLHassett,Ireland* 10-10-7[127] CO'Dwyer.............. 14/1 2½ 9
133 Mistanoora *NATwiston-Davies* 5-11-8[142] (t) CLlewellyn .... 9/1 nk 10
119 Brewster (IRE) *IanWilliams* 7-11-0[137] JamesDavies[3].......................... 33/1 11 11
113 Imperial de Thaix (FR) *MCPipe* 8-9-7[120] (t) TJMalone[7] .... 25/1 sh 12
14 Stromness (USA) *AKing* 7-11-4[138] RThornton 40/1 1 13
119 Inching Closer *JHowardJohnson* 7-11-6[140] GLee .... 33/1 ½ 14
119 Rostropovich (IRE) *MFMorris,Ireland* 7-11-5[139] (s+t) PFlynn 40/1 10 15
Derivative (IRE) *MissVenetiaWilliams* 7-10-7[127] SThomas[3] 20/1 1¼ 16
Columbus (IRE) *MrsJCandlish* 7-10-0[120] (v) SDurack................... 100/1 15 17
Homeleigh Mooncoin *MrsLWadham* 9-10-0[120] LAspell 66/1 29 18
Freetown (IRE) *LLungo* 8-11-11[145] MAFitzgerald 33/1 2½ 19
119 Stormez (FR) *MCPipe* 7-11-6[140] (t) APMcCoy................................. 7/1 dist 20
119 Tardar (NZ) *JonjoO'Neill* 8-11-5[146] ECooper[7] .... 25/1 f
The Bajan Bandit (IRE) *LLungo* 9-11-6[140] ADobbin.......................... 25/1 pu
113 Carlovent (FR) *MCPipe* 9-10-9[129] (v) TScudamore.......................... 66/1 pu
119 Hidden Bounty (IRE) *MrsMReveley* 8-10-2[122] AJDempsey .... 7/1 pu

Mr John P. McManus 24ran 6m16.25

CHELTENHAM Wednesday, Mar 17   GOOD (Old Course)

148   Royal & SunAlliance Nov Hdle (Gr 1) (A) (4yo+) £58,000   2m5f (10)

131	FUNDAMENTALIST (IRE) *NATwiston-Davies* 6-11-7 CLlewellyn	12/1		1
94	INGLIS DREVER *JHowardJohnson* 5-11-7 GLee	7/4f	½	2
80	GREY REPORT (IRE) *PJHobbs* 7-11-7 RJohnson	25/1	4	3
51	Comply Or Die (IRE) *MCPipe* 5-11-7 TJMurphy	33/1	nk	4
129	Big Moment *MrsAJPerrett* 6-11-7 LAspell	11/1	4	5
	Sadlers Wings (IRE) *WPMullins,Ireland* 6-11-7 (t) RWalsh	9/2	nk	6
	Tighten Your Belt (IRE) *MissVenetiaWilliams* 7-11-7 SThomas	28/1	4	7
	Very Optimistic (IRE) *JonjoO'Neill* 6-11-7 BJGeraghty	9/2	7	8
83	Champagne Harry *NATwiston-Davies* 6-11-7 AntonyEvans	100/1	1	9
	Ammonias (GER) *CJMann* 5-11-7 NFehily	100/1	15	10
	Ross River *PJHobbs* 8-11-7 PFlynn	25/1	18	11
	King Solomon (FR) *MissVenetiaWilliams* 5-11-7 (t) ADobbin	100/1	11	12
	Sindapour (IRE) *MCPipe* 6-11-7 APMcCoy	12/1	3	13
	Fontanesi (IRE) *MCPipe* 4-10-13 RGreene	200/1	11	14
	Yardbird (IRE) *MissHCKnight* 5-11-7 JCulloty	100/1	dist	15

Gripen 15ran 5m01.89

149   Royal & SunAlliance Chase (Gr 1) (A) (5yo+) £81,200   3m110y (19)

101	RULE SUPREME (IRE) *WPMullins,Ireland* 8-11-4 DJCasey	25/1		1
114	ROYAL EMPEROR (IRE) *MrsSJSmith* 8-11-4 DSElsworth	6/1	1¼	2
125	OUR VIC (IRE) *MCPipe* 6-11-4 APMcCoy	11/8f	2	3
111	Patricksnineteenth (IRE) *PRWebber* 7-11-4 TDoyle	14/1	13	4
	Historic (IRE) *TRGeorge* 8-11-4 JMMaguire	33/1	19	5
	Liscannor Lad (IRE) *DTHughes,Ireland* 6-11-4 PCarberry	150/1	23	6
117	Mossy Green (IRE) *WPMullins,Ireland* 10-11-4 RWalsh	20/1		f
117	Pizarro (IRE) *EJO'Grady,Ireland* 7-11-4 BJGeraghty	9/2		bd
136	Calling Brave (IRE) *NJHenderson* 8-11-4 MAFitzgerald	8/1		ur
	Supreme Prince (IRE) *PJHobbs* 7-11-4 PFlynn	20/1		pu

Mr John P. Lynch 10ran 6m09.58

150   Queen Mother Champion Chase (Gr 1) (A) (5yo+) £145,000   2m (12)

89	AZERTYUIOP (FR) *PFNicholls* 7-11-10 RWalsh	15/8		1
43	FLAGSHIP UBERALLES (IRE) *PJHobbs* 10-11-10 RJohnson	14/1	9	2
108	TIUTCHEV (IRE) *NJHenderson* 11-11-10 APMcCoy	16/1	1½	3
43	Cenkos (FR) *PFNicholls* 10-11-10 MAFitzgerald	16/1	2½	4
62	Venn Ottery *PFNicholls* 9-11-10 TJMurphy	33/1	10	5
49	Ei Ei *MCChapman* 9-11-10 LVickers	100/1	12	6
49	Eskleybrook *VYGethin* 11-11-10 (s) MBradburne	200/1	10	7
74	Moscow Flyer (IRE) *MrsJHarrington,Ireland* 10-11-10 BJGeraghty	5/6f		ur

Mr J. Hales 8ran 3m53.81

151   Coral Cup (Hcap Hdle) (Gr 3) (A) (165) (5yo+) £43,500   2m5f (10)

133	MONKERHOSTIN (FR) *PJHobbs* 7-10-8[147] RJohnson	13/2		1
	COURT SHAREEF *RJPrice* 9-9-11[139] WHutchinson[3]	200/1	1	2
110	RHINESTONE COWBOY (IRE) *JonjoO'Neill* 8-11-5[165] MrJPMagnier[7]	5/1f	1¼	3
120	MUGHAS (IRE) *AKing* 5-10-5[144] RThornton	11/2	2½	4
123	Emotional Moment (IRE) *TJTaaffe,Ireland* 7-10-0[139] DJCasey	12/1	3	5
123	Aine Dubh (IRE) *KevinFO'Donnell,Ireland* 7-10-0[139] JAmcCarthy	100/1	sh	6
	Korelo (FR) *MCPipe* 6-10-0[139] RGreene	33/1	2½	7
103	The French Furze (IRE) *NGRichards* 10-10-6[145] BHarding	33/1	½	8
129	Quazar (IRE) *JonjoO'Neill* 6-11-1[154] (t) ADobbin	25/1	5	9
140	Sud Bleu (IRE) *PFNicholls* 6-10-1[140] RWalsh	50/1	nk	10
58	Rosaker (USA) *NMeade,Ireland* 7-10-9[148] PCarberry	7/1	1	11
	Ollie Magern *NATwiston-Davies* 6-9-11[139] AntonyEvans[3]	66/1	1¼	12
	Claymore (IRE) *OSherwood* 8-10-2[141] LAspell	33/1	2½	13
	Galileo (POL) *TRGeorge* 8-10-4[143] JMMaguire	33/1	½	14
84	Foly Pleasant (FR) *MissHCKnight* 10-9-12[140] (t) SThomas[3]	25/1	1	15
	Bow Strada *PJHobbs* 7-10-0[139] SDurack	100/1	1¾	16
103	Redemption *NATwiston-Davies* 9-10-0[139] CLlewellyn	16/1	4	17
129	Starzaan (IRE) *HMorrison* 5-10-11[150] TJMurphy	20/1	½	18
	Reviewer (IRE) *CMMeade* 6-9-9[139] TJPhelan[5]	200/1	1	19
	Inca Trail (IRE) *MissHCKnight* 8-10-0[139] (t) JCulloty	16/1	2½	20
	Joshua's Bay *JRJenkins* 6-10-0[139] GLee	200/1	11	21
	Anatar (IRE) *MCPipe* 6-9-9[139] JPElliott[5]	200/1	1¾	22
	Almaravide (GER) *MBradstock* 8-10-0[139] MBatchelor	100/1	nk	23
120	Contraband (IRE) *MCPipe* 6-9-11[139] JamesDavies[3]	100/1	3½	24
127	Val de Fleurie (GER) *JGMO'Shea* 9-9-11[139] DCrosse[3]	200/1	½	25
133	Mon Villez (FR) *NJHenderson* 5-10-0[142] ATinkler[3]	33/1	1¼	26
97	Dromlease Express (IRE) *CByrnes,Ireland* 6-10-0[139] JRBarry	12/1	½	27

Mr M. G. St Quinton 27ran 4m59.30

1040

152   NH Chase Challenge Cup (Amat Nov Chase) (B) (5yo+) £29,000   4m (24)

114	NATIVE EMPEROR *JonjoO'Neill* 8-11-11 MrRWidger	5/1jf	1
36	CELESTIAL GOLD (IRE) *MCPipe* 6-11-11 MrAFarrant	33/1	1¾ 2
	DROMBEAG (IRE) *JonjoO'Neill* 6-11-7 MrJTMcNamara	8/1	6 3
	Silver Birch (IRE) *PFNicholls* 7-11-11 MrDerekO'Connor	5/1jf	11 4
	Abbeytown (IRE) *KRiordan,Ireland* 7-11-7 MrDWCullen	25/1	nk 5
63	Dear Deal *CLTizzard* 11-12-0 MrNRMitchell	20/1	½ 6
86	Mister Banjo (FR) *PFNicholls* 8-11-11 MrRBurton	12/1	1½ 7
101	Satco Express (IRE) *ESheehy,Ireland* 8-12-0 MrMDarcy	7/1	3 8
	Tipp Top Lord (IRE) *NATwiston-Davies* 7-12-0 MrRStephens	20/1	19 9
	Multeen River (IRE) *JonjoO'Neill* 8-12-0 MrAPCrowe	33/1	1½ 10
	Go White Lightning (IRE) *MBradstock* 9-11-7 MrMJO'Connor	50/1	10 11
	Madam's Man *NATwiston-Davies* 8-11-11 MrMGoldstein	66/1	16 12
	Montemoss (IRE) *MGRimell* 7-11-7 MrMRimell	50/1	1¼ 13
126	Magical Bailiwick (IRE) *MCPipe* 8-12-0 (v) MrGShenkin	12/1	f
	Hawk's Landing (IRE) *JonjoO'Neill* 7-11-11 MrKEPower	10/1	f
	Atlastaboy (IRE) *TRGeorge* 8-11-11 MrGordonElliott	33/1	ur
	Billywill (IRE) *JWMullins* 10-11-11 (t) MrAFitzgerald	100/1	pu
	Boy's Hurrah (IRE) *JHowardJohnson* 8-11-11 MrPYork	20/1	pu
	Guard Duty *MCPipe* 7-11-11 (v+t) TJMalone	50/1	pu
	Intrepid Mogal *NJPomfret* 7-11-11 MrSMorris	200/1	pu
	Major Benefit (IRE) *MissKMarks* 7-11-11 MrMKeel	100/1	pu
	Northern Edition (IRE) *PFNicholls* 7-11-11 MrNWilliams	25/1	pu

J. C., J. R. and S. R. Hitchins 22ran 8m12.26

153   Mildmay of Flete Challenge Cup Hcap Chase (Gr 3) (A) (159) 2½m110y (15)
(5yo+) £43,500

111	TIKRAM *GLMoore* 7-10-0[133] TJMurphy	12/1	1
135	IZNOGOUD (FR) *MCPipe* 8-10-3[136] APMcCoy	9/2f	2½ 2
108	FONDMORT (FR) *NJHenderson* 8-11-2[159] MAFitzgerald	9/1	1½ 3
138	KELREV (FR) *MissVenetiaWilliams* 6-9-11[133] SThomas[3]	16/1	2 4
138	Turgeonev (FR) *TDEasterby* 9-10-12[148] DO'Meara[3]	10/1	¾ 5
	Polar Red *MCPipe* 7-10-7[140] TScudamore	20/1	1 6
27	Inn Antique (FR) *FerdyMurphy* 8-10-0[133] GLee	50/1	2½ 7
105	Whereareyounow (IRE) *NATwiston-Davies* 7-10-4[137] CLlewellyn	5/1	4 8
	Mighty Strong *NJHenderson* 10-9-13[135] ATinkler[3]	25/1	7 9
31	Barrow Drive *AnthonyMullins,Ireland* 8-10-11[144] (t) BJGeraghty	12/1	3½ 10
	The Newsman (IRE) *GWareham* 12-10-0[133] LAspell	66/1	5 11
138	Farmer Jack *PJHobbs* 8-11-2[149] AThornton	20/1	sh 12
84	Jakari (FR) *HDDaly* 7-10-12[145] RJohnson	8/1	7 13
135	Hunters Tweed *PBeaumont* 8-10-8[141] RGarritty	14/1	pu
147	Back On Top (IRE) *JLHassett,Ireland* 10-10-0[133] JRBarry	16/1	pu
	Byron Lamb *NGRichards* 7-10-0[133] ADobbin	33/1	pu

Mike Charlton And Rodger Sargent 16ran 4m59.90

154   Weatherbys Champion Bumper (Standard Open NHF) (Gr 1) (A)   2m110y
(4, 5 and 6yo) £23,200

82	TOTAL ENJOYMENT (IRE) *TCooper,Ireland* 5-10-12 JCulloty	7/1	1
	REFINEMENT (IRE) *JonjoO'Neill* 5-10-12 MAFitzgerald	7/1	2½ 2
35	MASTER ALBERT (IRE) *DWachman,Ireland* 6-10-12 MrJPMagnier[7]	50/1	5 3
	Royal Paradise (FR) *FDoumen,France* 4-10-12 TDoumen	16/1	1 4
	Mr McAuley (IRE) *MHalford,Ireland* 6-11-5 PCarberry	8/1	1½ 5
	Knocknabooly (IRE) *WPMullins,Ireland* 5-11-5 RWalsh	9/1	1 6
	Only Vintage (USA) *MHourigan,Ireland* 4-10-12 TJMurphy	50/1	¾ 7
	Itsa Legend *AKing* 5-11-5 RThornton	33/1	5 8
122	Demarco (IRE) *NJHenderson* 6-11-5 MAFitzgerald	33/1	1 9
122	Corrib Eclipse *JamiePoulton* 5-11-0 CBolger[5]	66/1	3½ 10
	Lord Gale (IRE) *NATwiston-Davies* 6-11-5 CLlewellyn	50/1	1½ 11
	Gayle Abated (IRE) *WPMullins,Ireland* 5-11-5 RJohnson	33/1	2½ 12
	Major Vernon (IRE) *WPMullins,Ireland* 5-11-2 MrJJCodd[3]	20/1	hd 13
35	Martinstown (IRE) *CRoche,Ireland* 5-11-5 FMBerry	7/2f	3½ 14
	Brassie *RMBeckett* 5-11-5 TDoyle	100/1	3½ 15
	Our Ben *WPMullins,Ireland* 5-11-5 APMcCoy	16/1	4 16
	Woodlands Genpower (IRE) *PAPritchard* 6-11-5 MBradburne	33/1	5 17
122	Celtic Son (FR) *MCPipe* 5-11-5 RGreene	33/1	3½ 18
	See More Jock *DrJRJNaylor* 6-11-5 AThornton	100/1	10 19
	The Thunderer *NJHenderson* 5-11-5 RHughes	20/1	13 20
	Millenaire (FR) *JonjoO'Neill* 5-11-5 LCooper	20/1	21 21
	Stagecoachsapphire *MrsSJSmith* 6-11-5 DSElsworth	100/1	3½ 22
	Blazing Liss (IRE) *JEKiely,Ireland* 5-10-7 MrDerekO'Connor[5]	8/1	f
122	Granny Kellys Tart (IRE) *WPMullins,Ireland* 6-11-5 DJCasey	33/1	ro

It Will Never Last Syndicate 24ran 3m48.30

1041

CHELTENHAM Thursday, Mar 18
First 3 Races: GOOD (New Course), Remainder: GOOD to SOFT

155 JCB Triumph Hdle (Gr 1) (A) (4yo) £58,000   2m1f (8)

	MADE IN JAPAN (JPN) *PJHobbs* 4-11-0 RJohnson	20/1	1
	CHIEF YEOMAN *MissVenetiaWilliams* 4-11-0 ADobbin	40/1	2 2
128	TOP STRATEGY (IRE) *TMWalsh,Ireland* 4-11-0 (b) RWalsh	33/1	nk 3
	Cherub (GER) *JonjoO'Neill* 4-11-0 (t) LCooper	16/1	1¼ 4
102	Howle Hill (IRE) *AKing* 4-11-0 WHutchinson	25/1	4 5
	Adopted Hero (IRE) *GLMoore* 4-11-0 APMcCoy	7/1	7 6
	Moulin Riche (FR) *FDoumen,France* 4-11-0 (b) TDoumen	10/1	1½ 7
34	Raikkonen (IRE) *WPMullins,Ireland* 4-11-0 DNRussell	66/1	2½ 8
	Tamarinbleu (FR) *MCPipe* 4-11-0 RGreene	33/1	1¼ 9
134	Trouble At Bay (IRE) *AKing* 4-11-0 RThornton	5/1f	5 10
	Border Tale *CWeedon* 4-11-0 CLlewellyn	100/1	1¼ 11
	Tusk *MissHCKnight* 4-11-0 JCulloty	6/1	1¼ 12
134	Mondul (GER) *MFHarris* 4-11-0 OMcPhail	16/1	7 13
85	Zimbabwe *GLMoore* 4-11-0 JEMoore	12/1	1¼ 14
68	Al Eile (IRE) *JQueally,Ireland* 4-11-0 TJMurphy	16/1	3½ 15
115	Seaforde (IRE) *MFMorris,Ireland* 4-11-0 CO'Dwyer	100/1	7 16
134	Analogy (IRE) *CJMann* 4-11-0 (b) NFehily	100/1	16 17
134	Web Perceptions (USA) *MFHarris* 4-11-0 (b+t) BHitchcott	66/1	3 18
128	Wild Passion (GER) *NMeade,Ireland* 4-11-0 PCarberry	12/1	f
85	Major Speculation (IRE) *MCPipe* 4-11-0 (v) TScudamore	200/1	bd
	Tarque (IRE) *MissVenetiaWilliams* 4-11-0 (t) SThomas	14/1	bd
	Edmo Yewkay (IRE) *TDEasterby* 4-11-0 RGarritty	50/1	pu
115	Hasanpour (IRE) *CFSwan,Ireland* 4-11-0 DJCasey	16/1	pu

Mr Terry Evans 23ran 4m05.28

156 bonussprint.com Stayers' Hdle (Gr 1) (A) (4yo+) £81,200   3m (12)

119	IRIS'S GIFT *JonjoO'Neill* 7-11-10 BJGeraghty	9/2	1
112	BARACOUDA (FR) *FDoumen,France* 9-11-10 TDoumen	8/11f	1½ 2
103	CRYSTAL D'AINAY (FR) *AKing* 5-11-10 RThornton	8/1	13 3
81	Solerina (IRE) *JamesBowe,Ireland* 7-11-3 GTHutchinson	14/1	13 4
39	Holy Orders (IRE) *WPMullins,Ireland* 7-11-10 (b) RWalsh	33/1	4 5
112	Yogi (IRE) *ThomasFoley,Ireland* 8-11-10 GCotter	66/1	3½ 6
119	Tarxien *MCPipe* 10-11-10 (t) JEMoore	150/1	1½ 7
14	Gralmano (IRE) *KARyan* 9-11-10 GLee	150/1	dist 8
151	Redemption *NATwiston-Davies* 9-11-10 CLlewellyn	150/1	19 9
90	Sh Boom *JonjoO'Neill* 6-11-10 LCooper	9/1	f

Mr Robert Lester 10ran 5m49.80

157 totesport Cheltenham Gold Cup Chase (Gr 1) (A) (5yo+) £203,000   3¼m110y (22)

78	BEST MATE (IRE) *MissHCKnight* 9-11-10 JCulloty	8/11f	1
121	SIR REMBRANDT (IRE) *RHAlner* 8-11-10 AThornton	33/1	½ 2
118	HARBOUR PILOT (IRE) *NMeade,Ireland* 9-11-10 (b) PCarberry	20/1	1¼ 3
78	Beef Or Salmon (IRE) *MHourigan,Ireland* 8-11-10 TJMurphy	10/1	1¾ 4
67	First Gold (FR) *FDoumen,France* 11-11-10 (b) TDoumen	12/1	10 5
121	Keen Leader (IRE) *JonjoO'Neill* 8-11-10 BJGeraghty	10/1	dist 6
104	Therealbandit (IRE) *MCPipe* 7-11-10 APMcCoy	15/2	4 7
118	Alexander Banquet (IRE) *WPMullins,Ireland* 11-11-10 RWalsh	80/1	3 8
121	Irish Hussar (IRE) *NJHenderson* 8-11-10 MAFitzgerald	16/1	pu
104	Truckers Tavern (IRE) *FerdyMurphy* 9-11-10 (b) ADobbin	22/1	pu

Mr Jim Lewis 10ran 6m42.49

158 Christie's Foxhunt Chase Challenge Cup (B) (5yo+) £23,200   3¼m110y (22)

	EARTHMOVER (IRE) *PFNicholls* 13-12-0 MissAGoschen	14/1	1
	NEVER COMPROMISE (IRE) *TMWalsh,Ireland* 9-12-0 MrAPCrowe	9/2	4 2
	COUNTY DERRY *JRScott* 11-12-0 (s) MrNHarris	16/1	12 3
	Oneminutetofive *DPipe* 7-12-0 MrGordonElliott	12/1	6 4
2	Spot Thedifference (IRE) *EBolger,Ireland* 11-12-0 MrJTMcNamara	8/1	14 5
	Irbee *PFNicholls* 12-12-0 (b) MissCTizzard	100/1	10 6
	Bright Approach (IRE) *MrsOBush* 11-12-0 MissPGundry	14/1	14 7
	Torduff Express (IRE) *PFNicholls* 11-12-0 (b) MrNWilliams	33/1	10 8
	Mullensgrove *DLowe* 10-12-0 MissSPhizacklea	100/1	5 9
	Polar Champ *DPipe* 11-12-0 (v) TJMalone	25/1	2 10
	Always On The Line (IRE) *RBarber* 10-12-0 MrAMerriam	50/1	f
	Arctic Times (IRE) *EugeneMO'Sullivan,Ireland* 8-12-0 MrWMO'Sullivan.	14/1	f
	Upham Lord (IRE) *PBeaumont* 11-12-0 MrGBrewer	33/1	f
	Woodlands Beau (IRE) *MrsSAlner* 12-12-0 (b) MrTJDreaper	200/1	f
	Bosuns Mate *MKeighley* 11-12-0 (b) MrsBKeighley	100/1	ur
	Geordies Express *GTBewley* 12-12-0 MrDJewett	100/1	ur
	Omni Cosmo Touch (USA) *JossSaville* 8-12-0 MrNSaville	50/1	ur

Castle Weir (IRE) *WPMullins,Ireland* 7-12-0 MrJJCodd .... 33/1   pu
Charlie Strong (IRE) *RKelvin-Hughes* 11-12-0 MrACharles-Jones .... 66/1   pu
Game Gunner *MissBLewis* 12-12-0 MissCStucley .... 50/1   pu
Lord Atterbury (IRE) *DPipe* 8-12-0 MrAFarrant .... 3/1f   pu
Quetal (IRE) *MrsLauraJYoung* 11-12-0 MrJamesYoung .... 50/1   pu
Red Brook Lad *CStVFox* 9-12-0 MrNRMitchell .... 14/1   pu
Sheriff's Friend (IRE) *MrsJennyGordon* 9-12-0 MrCGordon .... 20/1   pu

Mr R. M. Penny 24ran 6m57.15

159   **Cheltenham Grand Annual Chase Challenge Cup (Hcap) (Gr 3) (A)**   2m110y (14)
    (153) (5yo+) £43,500

	ST PIRRAN (FR) *PFNicholls* 9-10-1[130] RWalsh 4/1f	1
26	GROUND BALL (IRE) *CFSwan,Ireland* 7-10-5[134] DJCasey 10/1	2½ 2
64	REIZIGER (FR) *PJHobbs* 8-9-11[129] PJBrennan[3] 33/1	7 3
	NO VISIBILITY (IRE) *RHAlner* 9-10-0[129] TJMurphy 14/1	9 4
	Strong Run (IRE) *NMeade,Ireland* 11-11-2[145] (t) PCarberry 16/1	6 5
	Old Marsh (IRE) *MissVenetiaWilliams* 8-11-9[129] (t) SThomas[3] 28/1	1 6
	Korakor (FR) *IanWilliams* 10-10-0[129] DDennis 66/1	5 7
136	Santenay (FR) *PFNicholls* 6-10-8[137] JTizzard 8/1	2 8
138	Wahiba Sands *MCPipe* 11-10-10[139] (v) JCulloty 33/1	2½ 9
89	Palarshan (FR) *HDDaly* 6-11-4[147] RJohnson 15/2	½ 10
120	Latalomne (USA) *MCPipe* 10-10-6[138] (v) JEMoore[3] 14/1	6 11
89	Got One Too (FR) *NJHenderson* 7-11-3[146] MAFitzgerald 8/1	16 12
	Kandjar d'Allier (FR) *MFHarris* 6-10-3[132] BHitchcott 100/1	18 13
	Noshinannikin *MrsSJSmith* 10-10-0[129] DSElsworth 50/1	2 14
59	Fadoudal du Cochet (FR) *ALTMoore,Ireland* 11-10-8[137] (s) CO'Dwyer 25/1	f
	Jungli (IRE) *PRWebber* 11-10-0[129] JAMcCarthy 50/1	f
	Hit And Run (FR) *MCPipe* 9-10-0[129] (v) TScudamore 50/1	bd
138	Seebald (GER) *MCPipe* 9-11-10[153] APMcCoy 12/1	ur
	Tango Royal (FR) *MCPipe* 8-10-3[132] (t) RGreene 50/1	ur
	Simply Gifted *JonjoO'Neill* 9-10-1[130] (v) GLee 10/1	ur
24	Ibal (FR) *MrsNSmith* 8-10-1[130] LAspell 50/1	pu

Mr C. G. Roach 21ran 4m06.21

160   **Cathcart Challenge Cup Chase (Gr 2) (A) (5yo+) £46,400**   2m5f (17)

143	OUR ARMAGEDDON (NZ) *RCGuest* 7-11-5 LMcGrath 9/1	1
84	IRIS ROYAL (FR) *NJHenderson* 8-11-5 MAFitzgerald 11/4	2½ 2
108	IMPEK (FR) *MissHCKnight* 8-11-9 JCulloty 3/1	11 3
	Hazeljack *AJWhiting* 9-11-0 JamesDavies 100/1	23 4
	Don Fernando *MCPipe* 5-10-9 APMcCoy 11/2	5 5
105	La Landiere (FR) *RTPhillips* 9-11-2 RJohnson 5/2f	16 6
	Penthouse Minstrel *RJHodges* 10-11-0 (v) RGreene 100/1	¾ 7

Mr Leslie Garrett 7ran 5m18.56

161   **Vincent O'Brien County Hcap Hdle (Gr 3) (A) (151) (5yo+) £37,700**   2m1f (8)

120	SPORAZENE (IRE) *PFNicholls* 5-10-13[151] RWalsh 7/1jf	1
99	HAWADETH *VRADartnall* 9-9-7[138] (s) TJMalone[7] 50/1	½ 2
120	COPELAND *MCPipe* 9-10-1[142] (v) JEMoore[3] 25/1	1½ 3
123	BALAPOUR (IRE) *PatrickOBrady,Ireland* 6-10-0[138] (t) CLlewellyn 12/1	nk 4
8	Harchibald (FR) *NMeade,Ireland* 5-10-8[138] PCarberry 7/1jf	nk 5
120	Benbyas *DCarroll* 7-10-1[142] PJBrennan[3] 33/1	8 6
123	Adamant Approach (IRE) *WPMullins,Ireland* 10-10-2[140] DJCasey 8/1	6 7
99	Greenhope (IRE) *NJHenderson* 6-9-11[138] ATinkler[3] 33/1	sh 8
127	Grave Doubts *KBishop* 8-10-0[138] (t) RGreene 14/1	1¾ 9
120	Man O'Mystery (USA) *PRWebber* 7-10-0[138] TDoyle 25/1	1½ 10
52	Newhall (IRE) *FFlood,Ireland* 6-10-0[138] FJFlood 14/1	1¾ 11
120	Through The Rye *GASwinbank* 8-10-0[138] JCrowley 33/1	1¼ 12
64	Regal Exit (FR) *NJHenderson* 8-10-0[138] PFlynn 50/1	½ 13
140	Scorned (GER) *AMBalding* 9-10-0[138] JAMcCarthy 20/1	2 14
129	In Contrast (IRE) *PJHobbs* 8-10-12[150] RJohnson 12/1	1½ 15
140	Idaho d'Ox (FR) *MCPipe* 8-9-9[138] JPElliott[5] 66/1	1¾ 16
	Barton Nic *DPKeane* 11-10-0[138] (b) GLee 100/1	4 17
88	Le Passing (FR) *PFNicholls* 5-10-0[138] JTizzard 10/1	3 18
100	Rathgar Beau (IRE) *ESheehy,Ireland* 8-10-0[138] JRBarry 16/1	11 19
	Lilium de Cotte (FR) *NJHenderson* 5-10-0[138] TJMurphy 8/1	4 20
	Bound *MrsLWadham* 6-10-0[138] LAspell 33/1	5 21
	Demi Beau *CJMann* 6-10-1[139] NFehily 14/1	1 22
	Downpour (USA) *IanWilliams* 6-10-0[138] DRDennis 66/1	3½ 23

Ged Mason & David Jackson 23ran 4m03.67

162   Martell Cognac Laurel Pub Company Liverpool Long Distance Hdle (Gr 2) (A) (4yo+) £29,000   3m110y (13)

156	IRIS'S GIFT *JonjoO'Neill* 7-11-10 BJGeraghty	4/7f		1
131	ROYAL ROSA (FR) *JHowardJohnson* 5-11-6 GLee	11/1	2½	2
151	AINE DUBH (IRE) *KevinFO'Donnell,Ireland* 7-10-13 (t) JAMcCarthy	80/1	5	3
156	Crystal d'Ainay (FR) *AKing* 5-11-10 RThornton	12/1	1	4
144	Hasty Prince *JonjoO'Neill* 6-11-2 ADobbin	25/1	1	5
156	Holy Orders (IRE) *WPMullins,Ireland* 7-11-10 (b) RWalsh	25/1	½	6
156	Sh Boom *JonjoO'Neill* 6-11-10 LCooper	5/1	11	7
133	Deano's Beeno *MCPipe* 12-11-10 APMcCoy	33/1	27	8

Mr Robert Lester 8ran 6m12.93

163   Martell Cognac Cup Chase (Gr 2) (A) (5yo+) £87,000   3m1f (19)

150	TIUTCHEV *MCPipe* 11-11-12 APMcCoy	11/2		1
157	FIRST GOLD (FR) *FDoumen,France* 11-11-12 (b) TDoumen	6/4f	3½	2
138	HAND INN HAND *HDDaly* 8-11-12 MBradburne	6/1	3½	3
153	Fondmort (FR) *NJHenderson* 8-11-8 MAFitzgerald	15/2	3	4
159	Seebald (GER) *MCPipe* 9-11-8 RGreene	20/1	14	5
104	Valley Henry (IRE) *JHowardJohnson* 9-11-12 GLee	5/1	1½	6
	Glenelly Gale (IRE) *ALTMoore,Ireland* 10-11-12 CO'Dwyer	33/1	20	7
138	Cyfor Malta (FR) *MCPipe* 11-11-8 TJMurphy	33/1		pu

The Liars Poker Partnership 8ran 6m19.56

164   Unwins Wine Group Anniversary 4-Y-O Nov Hdle (Gr 2) (A) (4yo) £63,800   2m110y (9)

155	AL EILE (IRE) *JQueally,Ireland* 4-11-0 TJMurphy	25/1		1
155	MADE IN JAPAN (JPN) *PJHobbs* 4-11-4 RJohnson	7/1	¾	2
	MY WILL (FR) *PFNicholls* 4-11-0 RWalsh	10/1	6	3
155	Tarque (IRE) *MissVenetiaWilliams* 4-11-0 (t) SThomas	11/1	1¾	4
115	Nopekan (IRE) *PatrickMullins,Ireland* 4-11-0 BJGeraghty	14/1	¾	5
	King Revo (IRE) *PCHaslam* 4-11-0 AThornton	8/1	2	6
134	Shuhood (USA) *PRWebber* 4-11-0 TDoyle	20/1	7	7
155	Tusk *MissHCKnight* 4-11-0 JCulloty	12/1	nk	8
155	Cherub (GER) *JonjoO'Neill* 4-11-0 LCooper	9/1	hd	9
155	Howle Hill (IRE) *AKing* 4-11-4 RThornton	7/1	3½	10
155	Adopted Hero (IRE) *GLMoore* 4-11-0 APMcCoy	6/1f	2	11
	Arimero (GER) *CFSwan,Ireland* 4-11-0 DJCasey	100/1	2½	12
	Valtar (FR) *YPorzier,France* 4-10-7 (t) TDoumen	16/1	6	13
	More Rainbows (IRE) *NMeade,Ireland* 4-11-0 PCarberry	20/1	9	14
	Sun Cat (IRE) *MrsSJSmith* 4-11-0 DSElsworth	100/1	hd	15
	Mezereon *DCarroll* 4-10-7 AntonyEvans	100/1	2	16
102	Dalaram (IRE) *JHowardJohnson* 4-11-0 (t) GLee	25/1	8	17
	Humid Climate *RAFahey* 4-11-0 DO'Meara	100/1		pu

Mr M. A. Ryan 18ran 3m59.01

165   Martell Cognac Red Rum Hcap Chase (Gr 3) (A) (148) (5yo+) £37,700   2m (12)

143	TIDOUR (FR) *PRWebber* 8-10-11[135] TDoyle	5/1f		1
84	ARMATURK (FR) *PFNicholls* 7-11-10[148] (t) RPMcNally	16/1	9	2
159	ST PIRRAN (IRE) *PFNicholls* 9-11-3[141] RWalsh	6/1	sh	3
159	Simply Gifted *JonjoO'Neill* 9-10-6[130] LCooper	10/1	nk	4
150	Ei Ei *MCChapman* 9-10-10[137] LVickers[3]	33/1	hd	5
3	Duke of Buckingham (IRE) *PRWebber* 8-10-9[133] CO'Dwyer	12/1	5	6
99	Golden Alpha (IRE) *MCPipe* 10-11-10[148] APMcCoy	6/1	13	7
159	Ground Ball (IRE) *CFSwan,Ireland* 7-11-5[143] DJCasey	7/1	½	8
159	Old Marsh (IRE) *MissVenetiaWilliams* 8-10-0[122] (t) RMcGrath	16/1	2½	9
159	Latalomne (USA) *MCPipe* 10-10-9[133] RGreene	33/1	1	10
	Jurado Express (IRE) *ALTMoore,Ireland* 8-10-3[127] PCarberry	12/1	22	11
89	Bleu Superbe (FR) *MissVenetiaWilliams* 9-10-12[139] SThomas[3]	25/1		pu
	Log On Intersky (IRE) *JHowardJohnson* 8-10-12[136] GLee	33/1		pu
	Tysou (FR) *NJHenderson* 7-10-7[131] MAFitzgerald	12/1		pu

Mrs M. Fisher 14ran 3m49.93

166   Martell Cognac Beefeater Restaurants Hcap Hdle (L) (A) (144) (4yo+) £23,200   2½m (11)

142	ZIBELINE (IRE) *BEllison* 7-10-6[124] (b) GLee	12/1		1
	UNLEASH (USA) *PJHobbs* 5-11-3[135] RJohnson	5/1jf	3	2
156	REDEMPTION *NATwiston-Davies* 9-11-5[137] CLlewellyn	12/1	7	3
27	COLOURFUL LIFE (IRE) *MrsMReveley* 8-10-3[121] RWalsh	11/1	¾	4
	Lotus Des Pictons (FR) *MCPipe* 5-9-12[123] TJMalone[7]	25/1	½	5
142	Simoun (IRE) *MCPipe* 6-10-8[126] (t) PCarberry	66/1	sh	6

27	Mythical King (IRE) *RLee* 7-10-5[123] TDoyle	100/1	3½ 7
88	Nathos (GER) *CJMann* 7-9-11[122] SJCraine[7]	25/1	1½ 8
	Old Flame (IRE) *CFSwan,Ireland* 5-10-5[123] DJCasey	12/1	3 9
161	Copeland *MCPipe* 9-11-8[140] (v) RGreene	25/1	4 10
	Penny Pictures (IRE) *MCPipe* 5-9-11[118] RJHoward[3]	66/1	½ 11
	Just In Time *PJHobbs* 9-10-1[126] MrRStephens[7]	66/1	2 12
140	Dancing Bay *NJHenderson* 7-11-0[132] MAFitzgerald	16/1	nk 13
	Spectrometer *RCGuest* 7-11-12[144] HOliver	16/1	hd 14
	Golden Rambler (IRE) *JonjoO'Neill* 8-10-2[120] LCooper	20/1	15 15
140	Gin Palace (IRE) *GLMoore* 6-10-13[131] TJMurphy	5/1jf	1¾ 16
140	Gone Far (USA) *MCPipe* 7-10-6[124] (v) TScudamore	20/1	5 17
	Don't Sioux Me (IRE) *CRDore* 6-9-12[119] (t) SThomas[3]	66/1	5 18
151	Korelo (FR) *MCPipe* 6-11-5[137] (v) APMcCoy	14/1	2½ 19
140	Shalako (USA) *PJHobbs* 6-10-5[123] (b) AThornton	16/1	8 20
90	Crazy Horse (IRE) *LLungo* 11-11-8[140] ADobbin	33/1	¾ 21
161	Bound *MrsLWadham* 6-10-10[128] LAspell	33/1	5 22
151	Inca Trail (IRE) *MissHCKnight* 8-11-2[134] (t) JCulloty	16/1	25 23

Mr Ashley Carr 23ran 4m55.53

167 **Martell Cognac Makro Mersey Nov Hdle (Gr 2) (A) (4yo+)** £29,000   2½m (11)

142	GARDE CHAMPETRE (FR) *PFNicholls* 5-11-0 RWalsh	9/2	1
	MONET'S GARDEN (IRE) *NGRichards* 6-11-0 ADobbin	7/1	1¼ 2
151	COURT SHAREEF *RJPrice* 9-11-3 JCulloty	16/1	hd 3
148	Inglis Drever *JHowardJohnson* 5-11-8 GLee	11/8f	½ 4
37	Strike Back (IRE) *MrsJHarrington,Ireland* 6-11-3 BJGeraghty	10/1	1¼ 5
	Numitas (GER) *PJHobbs* 4-10-7 (b) RJohnson	12/1	11 6
142	Cardenas (GER) *CREgerton* 5-11-8 JAMcCarthy	14/1	½ 7
	Rakalackey *HDDaly* 6-11-0 RThornton	33/1	5 8
119	Distant Thunder (IRE) *RHAlner* 6-11-0 AThornton	50/1	9 9
	Leche Bottes (FR) *MCPipe* 5-11-0 RGreene	100/1	6 10
142	Perle de Puce (FR) *NJHenderson* 5-11-1 (s) MAFitzgerald	33/1	nk 11
	Time To Shine *MissLJSheen* 5-10-7 LAspell	66/1	5 12
155	Tamarinbleu (FR) *MCPipe* 4-10-7 APMcCoy	33/1	6 13

Million in Mind Partnership 13ran 4m54.37

AINTREE Friday, Apr 2   GOOD

168 **Martell Cognac Ember Inns Hcap Chase (B) (150) (5yo+)** £23,200   3m1f (19)

	LORD OF THE RIVER (IRE) *NJHenderson* 12-10-0[124] PCarberry	9/1	1
	MIDLAND FLAME (IRE) *MissHCKnight* 9-10-5[129] JCulloty	9/2	7 2
	UN JOUR A VASSY (FR) *PFNicholls* 9-10-0[124] RPMcNally	20/1	2½ 3
153	Turgeonev (FR) *TDEasterby* 9-11-9[150] DO'Meara[3]	25/1	2½ 4
135	Gunther McBride (IRE) *PJHobbs* 9-10-9[133] RJohnson	4/1f	12 5
	Sir Frosty *BJMRyall* 11-10-0[124] TJMurphy	66/1	sh 6
145	Royal Auclair (FR) *PFNicholls* 7-11-1[139] (t) RWalsh	8/1	9 7
146	Mondial Jack (FR) *MCPipe* 5-10-0[133] RGreene	25/1	½ 8
153	Hunters Tweed *PBeaumont* 8-11-0[138] RGarritty	25/1	dist 9
	Mercato (FR) *JRBest* 8-9-12[125] SThomas[3]	11/1	f
72	Hugo de Grez (FR) *AParker* 9-10-6[130] RMcGrath	66/1	pu
146	Merchants Friend (IRE) *CJMann* 9-10-6[130] (s) NFehily	8/1	pu
145	Master Tern (USA) *JonjoO'Neill* 9-10-2[126] (s) ADobbin	15/2	pu
146	Toto Toscato (FR) *MCPipe* 10-10-1[125] TScudamore	20/1	pu

Mr B. T. Stewart-Brown 14ran 6m21.22

169 **Premier Convenience Stores Top Nov Hdle (Gr 2) (A) (4yo+)** £29,000   2m110y (9)

	ROYAL SHAKESPEARE (FR) *SGollings* 5-11-3 RThornton	25/1	1
151	CONTRABAND *MCPipe* 6-11-3 APMcCoy	14/1	nk 2
142	FLEET STREET *NJHenderson* 5-11-0 MAFitzgerald	4/1	4 3
	Fool On The Hill *PJHobbs* 7-11-0 RJohnson	20/1	1½ 4
137	Steppes of Gold (IRE) *NGRichards* 7-11-0 BHarding	11/2	¾ 5
140	Bold Bishop (IRE) *JonjoO'Neill* 7-11-0 BJGeraghty	15/8f	7 6
142	Albuhera (IRE) *PFNicholls* 6-11-5 (t) RWalsh	9/1	4 7
	Dad's Elect (GER) *CJMann* 5-11-5 NFehily	40/1	19 8
	Green Tango *HDDaly* 5-11-0 MBradburne	8/1	12 9
	Man From Highworth *HJManners* 5-11-0 MrJAJenkins	150/1	dist 10
	My Last Bean (IRE) *BSmart* 7-11-3 TScudamore	100/1	pu
	Your Advantage (IRE) *JonjoO'Neill* 4-10-8 (b) TSiddall	100/1	pu

Mr J. B. Webb 12ran 3m57.74

170 **Martell Cognac Melling Chase (Gr 1) (A) (5yo+)** £87,000   2½m (16)

150	MOSCOW FLYER (IRE) *MrsJHarrington,Ireland* 10-11-10 BJGeraghty	1/1f	1
138	ISIO (FR) *NJHenderson* 8-11-10 MAFitzgerald	4/1	6 2

45	NATIVE UPMANSHIP (IRE) *ALTMoore,Ireland* 11-11-10 CO'Dwyer	5/1	13 3
150	Cenkos (FR) *PFNicholls* 10-11-10 JTizzard	33/1	1¼ 4
25	Strong Magic (IRE) *JRCornwall* 12-11-10 ARoss	200/1	dist 5
108	Le Roi Miguel (FR) *PFNicholls* 6-11-10 RWalsh	6/1	f
150	Flagship Uberalles (IRE) *PJHobbs* 10-11-10 RJohnson	16/1	pu

Mr Brian Kearney 7ran 5m02.39

171 Martell Cognac Topham Chase (Hcap) (B) 0-150(141) (5yo+)   2m5f110y (Nat.) (18)
£40,600

	CASSIA HEIGHTS *SABrookshaw* 9-10-0[115] (t) JCulloty	33/1	1
	LONGSHANKS *KCBailey* 7-10-5[120] JPMcNamara	10/1	1 2
	SCOTMAIL BOY (IRE) *JHowardJohnson* 11-10-1[116] GLee	14/1	¾ 3
	FLINDERS CHASE *CJMann* 9-10-5[120] NFehily	66/1	¾ 4
	Young Whack (IRE) *JHowardJohnson* 10-10-9[124] RMcGrath	33/1	1¾ 5
146	Montifault (FR) *PFNicholls* 9-10-10[125] (t) RWalsh	16/1	4 6
	Windross *AKing* 12-10-8[123] RThornton	50/1	2½ 7
125	Better Days (IRE) *MrsSJSmith* 8-11-3[132] DSElsworth	16/1	½ 8
41	Blazing Batman *DrPPritchard* 11-9-9[115] DrPPritchard[5]	100/1	4 9
	Chergan (IRE) *MrsSCBradburne* 11-10-0[125] MBradburne	25/1	19 10
	The Major (NZ) *JRCornwall* 11-10-0[115] ARoss	100/1	4 11
	Tenshookmen (IRE) *WFCodd,Ireland* 10-10-0[115] JRBarry	100/1	23 12
101	Sigma Dotcomm (IRE) *JamesJosephMangan,Ireland* 8-10-0[115] GCotter	100/1	5 13
	Il'athou (FR) *SEHSherwood* 8-11-10[139] TJMurphy	33/1	dist 14
	Scots Grey *NJHenderson* 9-11-12[141] MAFitzgerald	8/1	f
138	Joly Bey (FR) *NJGifford* 7-11-8[140] MrDHDunsdon[3]	5/1f	f
153	Iznogoud (FR) *MCPipe* 8-11-11[140] APMcCoy	7/1	f
7	Barito (GER) *CVonDerRecke,Germany* 7-10-13[128] PCarberry	16/1	f
159	Korakor (FR) *IanWilliams* 10-10-7[122] ADobbin	16/1	f
126	Dark Room (IRE) *JonjoO'Neill* 7-10-4[119] LCooper	12/1	f
	Aelred *RJohnson* 11-10-3[118] (s) KJohnson	66/1	f
153	Whereareyounow (IRE) *NATwiston-Davies* 7-11-6[135] CLlewellyn	12/1	f
4	Heart Midoltian (FR) *SNeville,Ireland* 7-11-1[130] (t) JCullen	33/1	ur
	Native Beat (IRE) *JRHFowler,Ireland* 9-9-7[115] MissDDuggan[7]	50/1	ur
	Grangewick Flight *NWilson* 10-10-0[120] GCarenza[5]	100/1	bd
	Hermes III (FR) *MWEasterby* 11-10-3[135] MrTGreenall[7]	25/1	bd
	Super Nomad *MWEasterby* 9-10-6[121] AJDempsey	50/1	ref
	Mr Bossman (FR) *RCGuest* 11-10-8[123] (s+t) HOliver	16/1	pu
159	Wahiba Sands *MCPipe* 11-11-5[134] (v) RGreene	33/1	pu

Mr B. Ridge & Mr D. Hewitt 29ran 5m30.53

172 Martell Cognac Sefton Nov Hdle (Gr 1) (A) (4yo+) £46,400   3m110y (13)

139	ACCIPITER *GBBalding* 5-11-4 TBest	14/1	1
148	GREY REPORT (IRE) *PJHobbs* 7-11-4 RJohnson	11/2	¾ 2
148	CHAMPAGNE HARRY *NATwiston-Davies* 7-11-4 DNRussell	20/1	13 3
139	Eric's Charm (FR) *OSherwood* 6-11-4 BJGeraghty	6/1	6 4
137	Patriarch Express *GAHarker* 7-11-4 NHannity	66/1	nk 5
139	Sixo (IRE) *MCPipe* 7-11-4 TScudamore	50/1	1¼ 6
	Quick *MCPipe* 4-10-10 (v) PCarberry	50/1	3½ 7
80	Cornish Rebel (FR) *PFNicholls* 7-11-4 RWalsh	5/4f	13 8
	Carapuce (FR) *LLungo* 5-11-4 ADobbin	33/1	pu
139	Control Man (IRE) *MCPipe* 6-11-4 (v) APMcCoy	9/1	pu
	Kasthari (IRE) *JHowardJohnson* 5-11-4 GLee	12/1	pu
	Manx Royal (FR) *MCPipe* 5-11-4 RGreene	66/1	pu
	Thames (IRE) *NJHenderson* 6-11-4 TJMurphy	33/1	pu

Miss B. Swire 13ran 6m03.39

173 Martell Cognac Sainsbury's Mildmay Nov Chase (Gr 2) (A) (5yo+)   3m1f (19)
£43,500

114	SIMPLY SUPREME (IRE) *MrsSJSmith* 7-11-2 RMcGrath	13/2	1
125	L'AVENTURE (FR) *PFNicholls* 5-10-0 (b+t) RPMcNally	16/1	12 2
125	DOUBLE HONOUR (FR) *PJHobbs* 6-11-2 RJohnson	9/1	25 3
	Liberthine (FR) *NJHenderson* 5-10-0 PCarberry	13/2	dist 4
149	Royal Emperor (IRE) *MrsSJSmith* 8-11-9 DSElsworth	5/2f	f
	Early Edition *PFNicholls* 8-11-2 (t) RWalsh	20/1	f
138	See You Sometime *JWMullins* 9-11-2 JTizzard	16/1	f
149	Rule Supreme (IRE) *WPMullins,Ireland* 8-11-9 DJCasey	8/1	ur
93	D'Argent (IRE) *AKing* 7-11-7 RThornton	5/1	pu
125	Buzybakson (IRE) *JRCornwall* 7-11-2 ARoss	200/1	pu
111	One Nation (IRE) *MissHCKnight* 9-11-2 JCulloty	25/1	pu

Mr Trevor Hemmings 11ran 6m22.06

174 Martell Cognac Somerfield Hcap Hdle (L) (A) (146) (5yo+) £23,200   3m110y (12)

147	HIS NIBS (IRE) *MissVenetiaWilliams* 7-10-10[130] JTizzard	14/1	1

147	KEEPATEM (IRE) *MFMorris,Ireland* 8-10-7[127] DJCasey	17/2	2 2
77	STRONG PROJECT (IRE) *CFSwan,Ireland* 8-10-8[128] PCarberry	14/1	1½ 3
	LEGAL LUNCH (USA) *WKGoldsworthy* 9-10-0[119] GLee	14/1	1¾ 4
151	Ollie Magern *NATwiston-Davies* 6-10-8[128] TScudamore	10/1	½ 5
151	Galileo (POL) *TRGeorge* 8-11-6[140] (b) JMMaguire	33/1	3 6
151	Emotional Moment (IRE) *TJTaaffe,Ireland* 7-11-4[138] BJGeraghty	7/1	5 7
140	Ilabon (FR) *MCPipe* 8-10-0[120] RGreene	50/1	2½ 8
147	Carlovent (FR) *MCPipe* 9-10-5[125] (v) APMcCoy	14/1	½ 9
151	Mughas (IRE) *AKing* 5-11-12[146] RThornton	11/1	1¼ 10
	Lorgnette *RHAlner* 10-9-11[120] RWalford[3]	33/1	4 11
147	Rostropovich (IRE) *MFMorris,Ireland* 7-11-1[135] (t) PFlynn	25/1	3½ 12
147	Derivative (IRE) *MissVenetiaWilliams* 6-10-8[128] AThornton	25/1	9 13
	Master Trix (IRE) *MPitman* 7-10-1[121] TJMurphy	10/1	23 14
	Glacial Sunset (IRE) *CTinkler* 9-10-8[128] JCulloty	25/1	7 15
151	Sud Bleu (FR) *PFNicholls* 6-11-1[135] RPMcNally	20/1	dist 16
	Willie John Daly (IRE) *PJHobbs* 7-10-5[125] RJohnson	6/1f	f
151	Claymore (IRE) *OSherwood* 8-11-7[141] LAspell	40/1	bd
151	Bow Strada *PJHobbs* 7-11-1[135] SDurack	66/1	bd
147	Personal Assurance *JonjoO'Neill* 7-10-3[123] LCooper	20/1	pu

Mr John Galvanoni 20ran 6m04.66

AINTREE Saturday, Apr 3
Hurdles and Grand National Course: GOOD to SOFT, Mildmay Chase Course: GOOD

175 Martell Cordon Bleu Hcap Hdle (L) (A) (148) (5yo+) £26,100 — 2m110y (9)

64	PUCK OUT (IRE) *CRoche,Ireland* 6-9-10[125] MPWalsh[7]	10/1	1
	FUNDAMENTAL *JonjoO'Neill* 5-10-1[123] LCooper	4/1f	4 2
	JACK DAWSON (IRE) *JohnBerry* 7-10-0[122] JCulloty	25/1	4 3
161	GREENHOPE (IRE) *NJHenderson* 6-10-7[129] MAFitzgerald	11/1	nk 4
161	In Contrast (IRE) *PJHobbs* 8-11-11[147] RJohnson	12/1	6 5
42	Jaboune (FR) *AKing* 7-10-8[130] WMarston	20/1	13 6
144	Limerick Boy (GER) *MissVenetiaWilliams* 6-11-12[148] ADobbin	9/1	4 7
140	Desert Air (JPN) *MCPipe* 5-10-2[124] (v+t) RGreene	20/1	½ 8
	Nowell House *MWEasterby* 8-9-13[128] MrTGreenall[7]	16/1	2 9
	Shayadi (IRE) *BEllison* 7-9-7[122] (t) SJCraine[7]	25/1	2½ 10
	Anno Jubilo (GER) *CFSwan,Ireland* 7-10-1[123] DJCasey	33/1	12 11
140	Italian Counsel (IRE) *LADace* 7-9-7[122] DLaverty[7]	50/1	24 12
161	Demi Beau *CJMann* 6-10-9[131] NFehily	25/1	f
	Red Sun *JMackie* 7-9-12[123] (t) LVickers[3]	80/1	f
148	King Solomon (FR) *MissVenetiaWilliams* 5-10-0[122] (t) RMcGrath	8/1	bd
	Portant Fella *MsJMorgan,Ireland* 5-10-0[122] PCarberry	14/1	bd
44	Another Dude (IRE) *JHowardJohnson* 7-10-0[122] GLee	20/1	pu
161	Man O'Mystery (USA) *PRWebber* 7-11-0[136] BJGeraghty	10/1	pu
161	Idaho d'Ox (FR) *MCPipe* 8-10-4[126] APMcCoy	25/1	pu

Mr John P. McManus 19ran 4m01.57

176 Martell Cognac Maghull Nov Chase (Gr 1) (A) (5yo+) £58,000 — 2m (12)

143	WELL CHIEF (GER) *MCPipe* 5-11-1 APMcCoy	15/8f	1
143	THISTHATANDTOTHER (IRE) *PFNicholls* 8-11-4 JTizzard	2/1	2½ 2
143	MISTER MCGOLDRICK *MrsSJSmith* 7-11-4 DSElsworth	12/1	5 3
	Bonus Bridge (IRE) *HDDaly* 9-11-4 MBradburne	25/1	7 4
	Emperors Guest *PatrickMullins,Ireland* 6-11-4 RMPower	50/1	1½ 5
143	Palua *MissECLavelle* 7-11-4 JAMcCarthy	25/1	hd 6
150	Venn Ottery *PFNicholls* 9-11-4 (t) TJMurphy	6/1	13 7
	No Shenanigans (IRE) *NJHenderson* 7-11-4 MAFitzgerald	25/1	17 8
	Kalca Mome (FR) *PJHobbs* 6-11-4 RJohnson	16/1	½ 9
	Nev Brown (IRE) *NATwiston-Davies* 8-11-4 CLlewellyn	100/1	pu

Mr D. A. Johnson 10ran 3m55.42

177 Martell Cognac Aintree Hdle (Gr 1) (A) (4yo+) £87,000 — 2½m (11)

151	RHINESTONE COWBOY (IRE) *JonjoO'Neill* 8-11-7 MrJPMagnier	5/2jf	1
144	ROOSTER BOOSTER *PJHobbs* 10-11-7 RJohnson	5/2jf	¾ 2
144	WESTENDER (FR) *MCPipe* 8-11-7 (b) APMcCoy	25/1	½ 3
144	Intersky Falcon *JonjoO'Neill* 7-11-7 (b+t) LCooper	8/1	½ 4
151	Starzaan (IRE) *HMorrison* 5-11-7 TJMurphy	50/1	2½ 5
151	Monkerhostin (FR) *PJHobbs* 7-11-7 CLlewellyn	5/1	3½ 6
144	Foreman (GER) *TDoumen,France* 6-11-7 (b) TDoumen	8/1	7 7
151	Quazar (IRE) *JonjoO'Neill* 6-11-7 (s+t) ADobbin	33/1	½ 8
129	Sleep Bal (FR) *NJHenderson* 5-11-7 MAFitzgerald	150/1	½ 9
151	The French Furze (IRE) *NGRichards* 10-11-7 GLee	100/1	1¼ 10
161	Sporazene (IRE) *PFNicholls* 5-11-7 JTizzard	14/1	1¾ 11

Mrs John Magnier 11ran 4m56.85

178   **Martell Cognac Grand National Chase (Hcap) (Gr 3) (A) 0-110(155)**   4½m (30)
       (6yo+) £348,000

28	AMBERLEIGH HOUSE (IRE) *DMcCain* 12-10-10[139] GLee	16/1	1
28	CLAN ROYAL (FR) *JonjoO'Neill* 9-10-5[134] LCooper	10/1cf	3 2
158	LORD ATTERBURY (IRE) *MCPipe* 8-10-1[130] MBradburne	40/1	2 3
6	MONTY'S PASS (IRE) *JamesJosephMangan,Ireland* 11-11-10[153]		29 4
	BJGeraghty	20/1	
158	Spot Thedifference (IRE) *EBolger,Ireland* 11-10-4[133] RMcGrath	50/1	1 5
	Smarty (IRE) *MPitman* 11-10-0[129] ATinkler	100/1	3½ 6
126	Ardent Scout *MrsSJSmith* 12-10-3[132] WMarston	50/1	17 7
132	Bear On Board (IRE) *AKing* 9-10-1[130] RThornton	14/1	8 8
53	Kingsmark (IRE) *MTodhunter* 11-11-7[150] MAFitzgerald	66/1	18 9
101	The Bunny Boiler (IRE) *NMeade,Ireland* 10-10-8[137] RGeraghty	33/1	nk 10
100	Davids Lad (IRE) *AJMartin,Ireland* 10-11-4[147] TJMurphy	12/1	dist 11
118	Le Coudray (FR) *CRoche,Ireland* 10-11-12[155] (t) CO'Dwyer	28/1	f
157	Alexander Banquet (IRE) *WPMullins,Ireland* 11-11-8[151] JRBarry	100/1	f
132	Artic Jack (FR) *MrsSJSmith* 8-11-7[150] DSElsworth	20/1	f
101	Hedgehunter (IRE) *WPMullins,Ireland* 8-10-12[141] DJCasey	11/1	f
132	Jurancon II (FR) *MCPipe* 7-10-7[136] APMcCoy	10/1cf	f
95	Akarus (FR) *MCPipe* 9-10-4[133] RGreene	33/1	f
70	Bounce Back (USA) *MCPipe* 8-10-4[133] (b) AThornton	50/1	f
146	Montreal (FR) *MCPipe* 7-10-0[129] JPElliott	200/1	f
126	Luzcadou (FR) *FerdyMurphy* 11-10-0[129] (b) BHarding	200/1	f
	What's Up Boys (IRE) *PJHobbs* 9-11-9[152] (b) RJohnson	25/1	bd
113	Blowing Wind (FR) *MCPipe* 11-10-1[130] JAMcCarthy	33/1	ref
23	Bramblehill Duke (IRE) *MissVenetiaWilliams* 12-10-0[129] JamesDavies	200/1	ref
132	Just In Debt (IRE) *MTodhunter* 8-10-5[134] JCulloty	33/1	ur
145	Kelami (FR) *FDoumen,France* 6-10-7[136] (t) TDoumen	66/1	ur
	Skycab (IRE) *NJGifford* 12-10-1[130] LAspell	200/1	ur
95	Bindaree (IRE) *NATwiston-Davies* 10-11-4[147] CLlewellyn	10/1cf	ur
138	Risk Accessor (IRE) *CRoche,Ireland* 9-11-4[147] SDurack	66/1	ur
143	Puntal (FR) *MCPipe* 8-10-13[142] (t) DJHoward	150/1	ur
145	Shardam (IRE) *NATwiston-Davies* 7-10-11[140] TScudamore	18/1	ur
101	Takagi (IRE) *EJO'Grady,Ireland* 9-10-11[140] (v) DNRussell	25/1	ur
96	Alcapone (IRE) *MFMorris,Ireland* 10-11-0[143] NFehily	80/1	pu
95	Southern Star (IRE) *MissHCKnight* 9-10-13[142] JTizzard	25/1	pu
31	Joss Naylor (IRE) *JonjoO'Neill* 9-10-11[140] PCarberry	10/1cf	pu
95	Gunner Welburn *AMBalding* 12-10-8[137] ADobbin	22/1	pu
108	Royal Atalza (FR) *CNAllen* 7-10-6[135] (s) PaulMoloney	100/1	pu
132	Exit To Wave (FR) *RPNicholls* 8-10-5[134] RPMcNally	50/1	pu
	Mantles Prince *AGJuckes* 10-10-1[130] (v) OMcPhail	250/1	pu
70	Wonder Weasel (IRE) *KCBailey* 11-10-6[135] (s) JPMcNamara	200/1	pu

    Halewood International Ltd 39ran 9m20.22

179   **Martell Cognac Nov Hcap Chase (Amat) (B) (142) (5yo+) £19,256**   2½m (16)

143	KELTIC BARD *CJMann* 7-11-1[131] MrDHDunsdon	12/1	1
136	THE BANDIT (IRE) *MissECLavelle* 7-11-9[125] MrRWidger	16/1	5 2
153	POLAR RED *MCPipe* 7-11-4[139] TJMalone[5]	7/1	4 3
160	Our Armageddon (NZ) *RCGuest* 7-11-9[142] MrDJewett[3]	9/4f	2½ 4
	Mounsey Castle *PJHobbs* 7-10-0[121] MrRStephens[5]	10/1	30 5
	Benrajah (IRE) *MTodhunter* 7-9-9[116] KMercer[5]	16/1	19 6
	Cyanara *DrPPritchard* 8-10-0[116] DrPPritchard	100/1	dist 7
	Talbot Lad *SABrookshaw* 8-10-0[116] (t) MrNPMadden	10/1	f
	Black Frost (IRE) *MrsSJSmith* 8-10-12[134] MrJJCodd	9/1	ur
	Rodber (USA) *MrsLBNormile* 8-10-6[122] MrRLoughran	20/1	ur
	Hehasalife (IRE) *MrsHDalton* 7-10-0[119] MrTGreenall[3]	40/1	ur
	Pharpost (IRE) *MissVenetiaWilliams* 9-9-8[117] (b) MrDJacob[7]	50/1	ur
143	Le Duc (FR) *PFNicholls* 5-11-0[137] MrNWilliams[3]	5/1	pu
146	Jardin de Beaulieu (FR) *IanWilliams* 7-10-5[121] (b) MrAPCrowe	20/1	pu

    M. Rowland, M. Collins & P. Cox 14ran 5m02.87

    FAIRYHOUSE Sunday, Apr 11   GOOD to SOFT

180   **Rathbarry & Glenview Studs Festival Nov Hdle (Gr 2) (4yo+)**   2½m (11)
       £20,694

148	SADLERS WINGS (IRE) *WPMullins* 6-11-5 DJCasey	1/1f	1
	POINT BARROW (IRE) *PHughes* 6-11-5 JCulloty	14/1	3½ 2
57	FAIRWOOD PRESENT (IRE) *PJRothwell* 6-11-5 BMCash	20/1	6 3
57	Always *NMeade* 5-11-4 PCarberry	16/1	9 4
147	G V A Ireland (IRE) *FFlood* 6-11-5 FJFlood	11/2	13 5
	Ulaan Baatar (IRE) *MrsJHarrington* 7-11-5 BJGeraghty	7/1	6
	Deep Return (IRE) *NMeade* 7-11-5 JJPower	16/1	7
116	Vic Ville (IRE) *MHourigan* 5-11-4 CO'Dwyer	16/1	8

128 Corrib Boy (IRE) *JosephCrowley* 4-10-9 JRBarry 10/1   9
      Hard Winter (IRE) *DTHughes* 7-11-5 PWFlood 7/1   10
130 Moscow Court (IRE) *MrsJHarrington* 6-11-5 TPTreacy .... 12/1   pu
      Mr John J. Brennan 11ran 4m56.20

181 Power Home Dan Moore Memorial Hcap Chase (149) (4yo+)   2m1f (13)
      £30,179
159 FADOUDAL DU COCHET (FR) *ALTMoore* 11-11-2[137] CO'Dwyer 12/1   1
143 COLCA CANYON (IRE) *MrsJHarrington* 7-10-12[133] BJGeraghty 3/1f 1 2
      SAY AGAIN (IRE) *PaulNolan* 8-10-7[128] JLCullen 10/1 1½ 3
 89 Native Scout (IRE) *DHassett* 8-12-0[149] (t) DNRussell 9/2 4½ 4
161 Rathgar Beau (IRE) *ESheehy* 8-11-11[146] JRBarry 6/1 1½ 5
  4 Michael Mor (IRE) *NMeade* 10-10-7[128] IJPower 10/1   6
100 Beachcomber Bay (IRE) *NMeade* 9-10-11[132] PCarberry 16/1   7
 89 Killultagh Storm (IRE) *WPMullins* 10-11-7[142] (s) JCulloty........................... 16/1   8
  3 Fiery Ring (IRE) *JRHFowler* 9-10-9[130] RGeraghty 16/1   9
106 Ballyamber (IRE) *WPMullins* 9-10-10[131] DJCasey .... 5/1   f
 29 Schwartzhalle (IRE) *DHarvey* 7-10-6[130] MFMooney[3]................................... 25/1   f
      Sir Anthony O'Reilly 11ran 4m18.30

FAIRYHOUSE Monday, Apr 12   GOOD to SOFT

182 Powers Gold Label Irish Grand National (Hcap) (149) (5yo+)   3m5f (23)
      £74,224
126 GRANIT D'ESTRUVAL (FR) *FerdyMurphy,GB* 10-10-0[121] BHarding 33/1   1
      MARCUS DU BERLAIS (FR) *ALTMoore* 7-9-11[121] DJHoward[3]................. 20/1 ½ 2
 75 GOLDEN STORM (IRE) *JosephCrowley* 7-9-9[121] (b) JMAllen[5] 25/1 2½ 3
101 NATIVE JACK (IRE) *ALTMoore* 10-11-4[139] CO'Dwyer 12/1 1½ 4
 96 Timbera (IRE) *DTHughes* 10-11-2[137] (t) JCulloty 11/1 3 5
 16 Montayral (FR) *PHughes* 7-10-12[133] SDurack 14/1   6
 75 Garvivonnian (IRE) *EdwardPMitchell* 9-10-6[130] LAHurley[3] 40/1   7
 49 Kadoun (IRE) *MJPO'Brien* 7-11-4[142] MrDWCullen[3]................................. 16/1   8
126 What Odds (IRE) *TKGeraghty* 8-10-1[122] RGeraghty 20/1   9
  6 Thari (USA) *NMeade* 7-10-1[122] PCarberry 25/1   10
      Ross Moff (IRE) *AJMartin* 11-10-10[131] (t) RPMcNally .... 20/1   f
171 Heart Midoltian (FR) *SNeville* 7-10-9[130] (t) IJPower .... 50/1   f
152 Satco Express (IRE) *ESheehy* 8-10-9[130] (t) JRBarry .... 12/1   f
117 Xenophon (IRE) *AJMartin* 8-10-9[130] DNRussell .... 12/1   f
 76 Colnel Rayburn (IRE) *PaulNolan* 8-10-8[129] (s) JLCullen.............................. 14/1   f
      Munster (IRE) *ALTMoore* 7-10-3[124] (t) MDGrant .... 33/1   f
158 Never Compromise (IRE) *TMWalsh* 9-9-13[123] GTHutchinson[3]...................... 11/1   f
 75 Rose Perk (IRE) *ESheehy* 8-9-7[121] PWFlood[7]....................................... 66/1   f
 29 Killultagh Thunder (IRE) *WPMullins* 8-9-9[121] SCurling[5].......................... 50/1   f
 28 Good Vintage (IRE) *NMeade* 9-9-9[121] DFO'Regan[5].................................. 50/1   ref
178 Artic Jack (FR) *MrsSJSmith,GB* 8-12-0[149] RMMcGrath .... 20/1   pu
153 Back On Top (IRE) *JLHassett* 10-10-11[132] MrJTMcNamara .... 20/1   pu
117 Direct Bearing (IRE) *DKWeld* 7-10-8[129] BJGeraghty................................. 9/1jf   pu
 75 Hume Castle (IRE) *MrsJHarrington* 8-10-2[126] RMPower[3].......................... 9/1jf   pu
 31 Native Performance (IRE) *MHourigan* 9-9-10[124] MrRMMoran[7] .... 50/1   pu
      Run For Paddy *THogan* 8-10-1[125] KHadnett[3] .... 66/1   pu
  6 Colonel Bradley (IRE) *CFSwan* 10-10-0[121] MrAPCrowe .... 28/1   pu
      Lanmire Glen (IRE) *FFlood* 7-10-0[121] TPTreacy..................................... 16/1   pu
      Mr W. J. Gott 28ran 7m46.09

FAIRYHOUSE Tuesday, Apr 13   GOOD to SOFT

183 Menolly Homes Nov Hdle (Gr 2) (4yo+) £25,697   2m (9)
      ROYAL ALPHABET (IRE) *WPMullins* 6-11-4 (t) DJCasey...................... 8/11f   1
      SNAPPER CREEK (IRE) *JABerry* 8-11-4 GTHutchinson 20/1 1½ 2
128 POWER ELITE (IRE) *NMeade* 4-11-2 PCarberry................................... 4/1 ½ 3
 73 Green Belt Flyer (IRE) *MrsJHarrington* 6-11-4 RMPower[3].......................... 7/1 4½ 4
      Common World (USA) *NMeade* 5-11-3 IJPower 9/1 13 5
      Boleyknowsbest (IRE) *RPBurns* 6-11-4 JRBarry 25/1   6
      Pedina (IRE) *GMLyons* 6-11-4 CO'Dwyer 16/1   7
      Akhtari (IRE) *DTHughes* 4-10-10 BJGeraghty .... 9/1   f
 37 Rupununi (IRE) *FrancisEnnis* 7-11-7 TJMurphy .... 16/1   pu
      Ballylinch Stud 9ran 3m59.06

184 Powers Gold Cup (Gr 1) (5yo+) £38,487   2½m (16)
117 HI CLOY (IRE) *MHourigan* 7-11-9 TJMurphy 7/1   1
143 KICKING KING (IRE) *TJTaaffe* 6-11-9 BJGeraghty .... 9/4f ½ 2
 38 NIL DESPERANDUM (IRE) *MissFMCrowley* 7-11-9 JRBarry 3/1 6 3
143 Central House *DTHughes* 7-11-9 PCarberry 3/1 6 4
143 John James (IRE) *JHScott* 8-11-9 KWhelan 20/1 9 5

| 149 | Mossy Green (IRE) *WPMullins* 10-11-9 DJCasey | 6/1 | f |

Mrs S. McCloy 6ran 5m08.13

185 Menolly Homes Hcap Hdle (131) (4yo+) £42,763 2m (9)

97	MACS JOY (IRE) *MrsJHarrington* 5-11-0[122] BJGeraghty	7/2f	1
	TIGER CRY (IRE) *ALTMoore* 6-10-8[116] DJCasey	12/1	1½ 2
	THE KOP END (IRE) *CRoche* 6-9-12[111] MPWalsh[5]	10/1	4 3
97	LOUGHANELTEEN (IRE) *PJRothwell* 6-9-5[106] MissNCarberry[7]	12/1	1½ 4
59	Native Stag (IRE) *PAFahy* 6-9-4[101] LAHurley[3]	33/1	1 5
	King Carew (IRE) *MHourigan* 6-10-8[116] TJMurphy	14/1	6
	Francys Fancy (IRE) *MissFMCrowley* 7-10-1[109] JRBarry	16/1	7
58	General Cloney (IRE) *SDonohoe* 8-10-13[121] RMcGrath	20/1	8
97	Steel Band *PaulARoche* 6-9-13[114] MrDRoche[7]	14/1	9
3	Ichi Beau (IRE) *AJMartin* 10-10-1[109] (t) BHarding	25/1	10
	Felix The Great (IRE) *MHalford* 6-10-3[118] JPEnnis[7]	14/1	11
5	Dashing Home (IRE) *NMeade* 5-11-0[122] PCarberry	5/1	12
37	Kelly's Craft (IRE) *WPMullins* 7-9-13[110] MrNPMadden[3]	20/1	13
	Johnjoe's Express (IRE) *MHourigan* 7-9-10[104] JECasey	16/1	14
175	Portant Fella *MsJMorgan* 5-10-6[114] RGeraghty	12/1	15
44	Aye Aye Popeye (IRE) *MrsJHarrington* 6-10-3[116] (b) TPTreacy[5]	14/1	16
	Poachin Again (IRE) *ALTMoore* 7-10-7[115] CO'Dwyer	16/1	17
	Kniaz (FR) *AJMartin* 6-10-1[109] KWhelan	14/1	18
5	Swordplay *MJPO'Brien* 6-11-6[131] MrDWCullen[3]	20/1	19
97	Right Job (IRE) *PJFlynn* 9-10-3[114] RMPower[5]	20/1	20
8	Sabadilla (USA) *PatrickMichaelVerling* 10-11-2[124] PMVerling	20/1	21
	Rob The Five (IRE) *ALTMoore* 7-10-0[111] DJHoward[3]	25/1	22
	Ultimate Accolade (IRE) *WPMullins* 8-10-8[116] DNRussell	16/1	23
	High Prospect (IRE) *PaulNolan* 6-9-13[110] (t) GTHutchinson[3]	12/1	24
5	Crimson Flower (IRE) *JMorrison* 9-10-4[117] JMAllen[5]	16/1	25
	Grinkov (IRE) *PHughes* 9-11-2[124] BMCash	25/1	f
164	More Rainbows (IRE) *NMeade* 4-10-8[116] IJPower	20/1	f

Mac's J. Racing Syndicate 27ran 3m57.02

186 Goffs Land Rover Bumper (4 and 5yo) £25,888 2m

	ARTEEA (IRE) *MHourigan* 5-11-0 MrMJO'Hare[7]	16/1	1
	THE SPOONPLAYER (IRE) *HenryDeBromhead* 5-11-7 MrAPCrowe	16/1	3 2
	RING OF BEARA (IRE) *RobertTyner* 4-10-7 MrDMurphy[7]	20/1	4 3
	Environment Gunner *LYoung* 4-11-0 MrPFenton	12/1	2½ 4
	Panthers Run *JosephCrowley* 4-10-9 MrKEPower[5]	11/2	1 5
	Arches Bar (IRE) *MrsJHarrington* 4-10-7 MrRO'Sullivan[7]	12/1	6
	Legendsofthefall (IRE) *MichaelCunningham* 5-10-12 MrJPMagnier[5]	10/1	7
	Kings Advocate (IRE) *TJTaaffe* 4-10-11 MrJJCodd[3]	8/1	8
	Ballyguider Bridge (IRE) *CFSwan* 4-10-2 MrLPFlynn[7]	12/1	9
	Golden Exchange (IRE) *DWachman* 4-11-0 MrAKWyse	6/1	10
	Fair Touch (IRE) *LWhitmore* 5-11-0 (t) MrRMMoran[7]	20/1	11
	Sirius Storm (IRE) *PaulNolan* 4-11-0 MrAFitzgerald	12/1	12
	Freddie Foster (IRE) *NMeade* 5-11-4 MrNPMadden[3]	5/2f	13
	Hardy Oliver (IRE) *DTHughes* 5-11-2 MrRLoughran[5]	8/1	14
	Heart N Hope (IRE) *JohnAWhite* 5-10-13 MrDWCullen[3]	33/1	15
	Teddie (IRE) *ThomasFoley* 4-10-9 MissAFoley[5]	25/1	16
	Kildare Minor (IRE) *DTHughes* 5-11-0 MrRMHennessy[7]	10/1	17
	We Got Him (IRE) *RobertTyner* 4-10-7 MrCJSweeney[7]	14/1	18
	Chase A Dream (IRE) *PaulNolan* 4-10-2 MrAJMcNamara[7]	20/1	19
	Fergus Vale (IRE) *JosephCrowley* 5-11-0 MrJTCarroll[7]	16/1	20
	Rugar (IRE) *TJKidd* 5-11-7 MrPFahey	25/1	21
	Umrigar Lord (IRE) *MichaelButler* 5-11-2 MrGJPower[5]	20/1	22
	Bob Dolphin (IRE) *MichaelKavanagh* 5-11-2 MrMMDarcy[5]	50/1	pu

Mr Michael O'Flaherty 23ran 3m54.70

CHELTENHAM Wednesday, Apr 14 GOOD to FIRM (New Course)

187 Telectronics Systems NH Auc Nov Hdle (B) (5, 6 and 7yo) £17,400 2m5f110y (10)

139	COPSALE LAD *NJHenderson* 7-10-6 MAFitzgerald	9/2	1
172	GREY REPORT (IRE) *PJHobbs* 7-12-0 RJohnson	13/8f	½ 2
147	BREWSTER (IRE) *IanWilliams* 7-11-4 PaulMoloney	9/1	2 3
139	Sweet Diversion (IRE) *PFNicholls* 5-11-3 JTizzard	8/1	8 4
	Ashley Brook *KBishop* 6-10-10 RGreene	4/1	1¾ 5
	Easibrook Jane *CLTizzard* 6-10-7 AThornton	40/1	1¼ 6
	Karinga City *ERetter* 7-10-6 MissSGaisford	33/1	1½ 7
	Run of Kings (IRE) *MCPipe* 6-11-4 APMcCoy	33/1	9 8
	Flaming Cheek *AGBlackmore* 6-10-6 CHonour	100/1	14 9
	Romany Dream *RDickin* 6-10-4 (b) BHitchcott	150/1	26 10

139 Time To Reflect (IRE) *MCPipe* 5-10-9 (v) JEMoore .... 40/1   pu
Swallow Partnership 11ran 5m05.05

188   **Faucets For Mira Showers Silver Trophy Chase (Ltd Hcap) (Gr 2)**   2m5f (17)
    (A) (161) (5yo+) £29,000

163	SEEBALD (GER) *MCPipe* 9-10-13[150] APMcCoy	13/2		1
153	TIKRAM *GLMoore* 7-10-1[141] JEMoore[3]	7/2f	½	2
153	JAKARI (FR) *HDDaly* 7-10-5[142] RJohnson	15/2	3	3
178	Risk Accessor (IRE) *CRoche,Ireland* 9-10-8[145] TJMurphy	4/1	9	4
89	Upgrade *MCPipe* 10-11-3[154] JCulloty	14/1	14	5
170	Le Roi Miguel (FR) *PFNicholls* 6-11-7[158] BJGeraghty	11/2	27	6
163	Cyfor Malta (FR) *MCPipe* 11-10-9[146] RGreene	33/1	13	7
163	Fondmort (FR) *NJHenderson* 8-11-10[161] MAFitzgerald	5/1		f

The Macca & Growler Partnership 8ran 5m02.23

NAKAYAMA Saturday, Apr 17   FIRM

189   **Nakayama Grand Jump Chase (Gr 1) (4yo+)** £414,330   2½m55y

BLANDICES (JPN) *TFujiwara* 7-10-3 TOehara	2.9/1		1
MERCI TAKA O (JPN) *KTake* 5-10-3 KIdetsu		5	2
MEJIRO ORMOND (JPN) *HOtonashi* 6-10-3 MHayashi		ds	3
Gilded Age (JPN) *SMatsumoto* 7-10-3 TFoley		nk	4
Daiwa Dur (JPN) *IShimada* 8-10-3 TTanaka		1½	5
Meiner Oper (JPN) *SYano* 5-10-3 TMunakata		3½	6
Yamato Forza (JPN) *NTanaka* 5-10-3 NKado		½	7
Oway (FR) *JOrtet,France* 6-10-3 FBarrao		¾	8
Oliverdance (NZ) *JWheeler,NewZealand* 8-10-3 BScott		ds	9
Neriette *J-PTotain,France* 5-9-13 TMajorcryk		ds	10
Jupiterienne (JPN) *YGoto* 9-10-3 STajima		2	11
Fusaichi Jihad (JPN) *TIwato* 7-10-3 NHamanoya			pu
Meiner Universe (JPN) *HGohara* 5-10-3 THokari			pu
Misty Weather (AUS) *MTrinder,Australia* 7-10-3 ATrinder			pu
Nicobury (NZ) *GBarlow,NewZealand* 7-10-3 RochelleLocket			pu

Sunday Racing Co Ltd 15ran Time not taken

AYR Saturday, Apr 17   GOOD to SOFT

190   **Ashleybank Investments Future Champion Nov Chase (Gr 2) (A)**   2½m (17)
    (5yo+) £20,825

179	KELTIC BARD *CJMann* 7-11-10 NFehily	9/4		1
176	THISTHATANDTOTHER (IRE) *PFNicholls* 8-11-10 JTizzard	6/4f	7	2
171	BETTER DAYS (IRE) *MrsSJSmith* 8-11-7 RMcGrath	25/1	25	3
	King of The Castle (IRE) *BMactaggart* 9-11-3 GLee	100/1	12	4
143	Jahash *AKing* 6-11-3 RThornton	9/1	13	5
176	Mister McGoldrick *MrsSJSmith* 7-11-7 DSElsworth	5/1		f
176	Venn Ottery *PFNicholls* 9-11-7 (t) MAFitzgerald	16/1		pu

M. Rowland, M. Collins & P. Cox 7ran 5m07.90

191   **Gala Casinos Daily Record Scottish Grand National Hcap Chase**   4m1f (26)
    (Gr 3) (A) (148) (5yo+) £69,600

103	GREY ABBEY (IRE) *JHowardJohnson* 10-11-12[148] GLee	12/1		1
	KERRY LADS (IRE) *MissLucindaVRussell* 9-10-0[122] (s) KRenwick	33/1	dist	2
146	MAXIMIZE (IRE) *MCPipe* 10-10-9[134] JEMoore[3]	28/1	1	3
126	TIPSY MOUSE (IRE) *MrsSJSmith* 8-10-1[123] DSElsworth	15/2	4	4
178	Smarty (IRE) *MPitman* 11-9-11[122] ATinkler[3]	66/1	6	5
147	Stormez (FR) *MCPipe* 7-11-10[146] (t) APMcCoy	12/1	14	6
113	Ballybrophy (IRE) *SEHSherwood* 9-10-3[125] (b) TDoyle	40/1	7	7
126	Carryonharry (IRE) *MCPipe* 10-9-11[122] (v) GSupple[3]	80/1	11	8
178	Exit To Wave (FR) *PFNicholls* 8-10-8[130] (t) RPMcNally	50/1	9	9
182	Granit d'Estruval (FR) *FerdyMurphy* 10-10-0[122] BHarding	25/1		f
	Proper Squire (USA) *CJMann* 7-10-2[124] NFehily	50/1		f
	Eyze (IRE) *BMactaggart* 8-9-7[122] PBuchanan[7]	200/1		f
173	Simply Supreme (IRE) *MrsSJSmith* 7-10-6[128] RMcGrath	7/1jf		f
178	Luzcadou (FR) *FerdyMurphy* 11-9-7[122] (b) KMercer[7]	150/1		pu
47	Lord Noelie (IRE) *MsBridgetNicholls* 11-11-9[145] JTizzard	28/1		pu
168	Sir Frosty *BJMRyall* 11-10-0[122] SDurack	50/1		pu
	Mini Sensation (IRE) *JonjoO'Neill* 11-11-8[144] BJGeraghty	28/1		pu
145	Chicuelo (FR) *MCPipe* 8-11-0[136] (v) RGreene	66/1		pu
152	Mister Banjo (FR) *PFNicholls* 8-10-10[132] RThornton	33/1		pu
113	Desailly *GBBalding* 10-10-5[127] MBradburne	9/1		pu
168	Mercato (FR) *JRBest* 8-9-12[123] SThomas[3]	25/1		pu
152	Native Emperor *JonjoO'Neill* 7-10-6[128] LCooper	7/1jf		pu
145	Tyneandthyneagain *RCGuest* 9-11-10[146] (s) HOliver	14/1		pu
168	Midland Flame (IRE) *MissHCKnight* 9-10-7[129] JCulloty	16/1		pu

```
  70  Mr Woodenton (IRE) LLungo 8-10-7¹²⁹ ADobbin ...................................... 50/1      pu
 178  Just In Debt (IRE) MTodhunter 8-10-6¹²⁸ DNRussell................................. 33/1      pu
 113  Hersov (IRE) NJHenderson 8-10-4¹²⁶ (b) MAFitzgerald.............................. 16/1      pu
      Rodalko (FR) OSherwood 6-10-8¹³⁰ JAMcCarthy ................................... 20/1      pu
```

Ken Roper,Elinor M. Roper,Norman Furness 28ran 8m35.68

192 Samsung Electronics Scottish Champion Hdle (Ltd Hcap) (Gr 2)   2m (9)
(A) (147) (4yo+) £23,200

```
 166  COPELAND MCPipe 9-10-1¹⁴¹ (v) JEMoore³ ........................................... 8/1      1
 161  BENBYAS DCarroll 7-10-1¹⁴¹ PJBrennan³ ......................................... 7/2jf    5  2
 140  SAINTSAIRE (FR) NJHenderson 5-10-4¹⁴¹ MAFitzgerald .................... 7/2jf   10  3
 177  The French Furze (IRE) NGRichards 10-10-6¹⁴³ BHarding ................... 14/1    8  4
      Imtihan (IRE) SCBurrough 5-10-4¹⁴¹ RGreene ..................................... 66/1    8  5
 167  Court Shareef RJPrice 9-10-5¹⁴⁵ WHutchinson³ ................................. 10/1   nk  6
 175  Limerick Boy (GER) MissVenetiaWilliams 6-10-7¹⁴⁷ SThomas³................. 7/1      f
 144  Specular (AUS) JonjoO'Neill 8-10-10¹⁴⁷ BJGeraghty ........................... 4/1     ur
 127  Perouse PFNicholls 6-10-6¹⁴³ (t) JTizzard ......................................... 9/1     pu
 175  Man O'Mystery (USA) PRWebber 7-10-4¹⁴¹ TDoyle ............................ 20/1     pu
```

Professor D.B.A.Silk & Mrs Heather Silk 10ran 3m43.29

CARLISLE Sunday, Apr 18   GOOD to SOFT

193 News & Star Int Open NHF (H) (DII) (4, 5 and 6yo) £2,078   2m1f

```
      VILLON (IRE) LLungo 5-11-4 ADobbin............................................... 6/4f      1
      BLAIRGOWRIE (IRE) JHowardJohnson 5-11-4 GLee ..................... 9/2    18  2
      LORD RODNEY (IRE) PBeaumont 5-11-4 RGarritty ......................... 16/1   14  3
      Classic Capers JMJefferson 5-11-6 FKing⁵ ......................................... 5/1    7  4
      Hello Baby ACWhillans 4-10-13 JCrowley ...................................... 5/1    6  5
      Willywont He PTMidgley 5-11-4 VTKeane ...................................... 25/1    6  6
      Mucky Mabel (IRE) PDNiven 5-10-10 DO'Meara³ ......................... 50/1    4  7
      Lady Godson BMactaggart 5-10-13 AJDempsey................................ 100/1   ¾  8
      Ice Rain (IRE) TPTate 4-10-13 JMMaguire ..................................... 16/1   27  9
      Freindlypersuasion MrsADuffield 4-10-10 CRafter³......................... 33/1  dist 10
      Cheeky Boy Danny RDEWoodhouse 6-10-8 DHarold¹⁰ ................. 100/1    7 11
      Solway Raider MsLizHarrison 6-10-11 GBerridge⁷.......................... 100/1   11 12
      Eltringham CRWilson 4-10-11 DCCostello⁷ .................................. 100/1  dist 13
```

Mr R. A. Bartlett 13ran 4m19.16

SANDOWN Friday, Apr 23   GOOD to FIRM

194 Concept Hdle (B) (4yo+) £40,600   2m110y (8)

```
 162  HASTY PRINCE JonjoO'Neill 6-11-4 BJGeraghty............................ 10/1      1
 144  RIGMAROLE PFNicholls 6-11-10 (t) RThornton ............................. 6/1   10  2
 177  WESTENDER (FR) MCPipe 8-11-4 (b) APMcCoy ......................... 11/4jf   hd  3
 177  Starzaan (IRE) HMorrison 5-11-10 TJMurphy ................................ 9/1    ½  4
 177  Intersky Falcon JonjoO'Neill 7-11-10 (b+t) LCooper...................... 11/4jf   1  5
 159  Santenay (FR) PFNicholls 6-11-8 JTizzard ...................................... 14/1   1½  6
 144  Geos (FR) NJHenderson 9-11-8 MAFitzgerald ................................. 13/2    7  7
 177  Sleep Bal (FR) NJHenderson 5-11-8 ATinkler ................................ 33/1   ¾  8
```

F. F. Racing Services P'ship III 8ran 3m50.80

SANDOWN Saturday, Apr 24   GOOD to FIRM

195 Queen Elizabeth The Queen Mother Celebration Chase   2m (13)
(Sponsored By Betfred) (B) (5yo+) £58,000

```
 170  CENKOS PFNicholls 10-11-10 BJGeraghty ...................................... 9/2      1
 160  IMPEK (FR) MissHCKnight 8-11-6 JCulloty...................................... 4/1   1½  2
 159  GOT ONE TOO (FR) NJHenderson 7-11-6 MAFitzgerald .................. 14/1    5  3
 165  Duke of Buckingham (IRE) PRWebber 8-11-6 TDoyle ....................... 14/1    8  4
 140  Hot Shots (FR) MPitman 9-11-6 TJMurphy ...................................... 7/1   2½  5
 188  Upgrade MCPipe 10-11-6 TScudamore ............................................. 20/1   ½  6
 188  Seebald (GER) MCPipe 9-11-6 APMcCoy ....................................... 7/2f    7  7
 165  St Pirran (IRE) PFNicholls 9-11-6 GLee......................................... 8/1   sh  8
 171  Wahiba Sands MCPipe 11-11-6 (v) JEMoore .................................. 33/1   3½  9
 163  Glenelly Gale (IRE) ALTMoore,Ireland 11-11-10 CO'Dwyer........... 25/1   18 10
 150  Eskleybrook VYGethin 11-11-6 (s) MBradburne .............................. 66/1     pu
```

Mrs J. Stewart 11ran 3m45.74

196 Betfred Gold Cup Chase (Hcap) (Gr 3) (A) (147) (5yo+) £87,000   3m5f110y (24)

```
 178  PUNTAL MCPipe 8-11-4¹⁴² (t) DJHoward³......................................... 25/1      1
 168  ROYAL AUCLAIR (FR) PFNicholls 7-11-1¹³⁹ (t) ChristianWilliams³.... 33/1   sh  2
 182  MONTAYRAL (FR) PHughes,Ireland 7-10-12¹³³ JCulloty ..................... 10/1  2½  3
 113  KINGS MISTRAL (IRE) PRChamings 11-10-10¹³¹ BJGeraghty............ 9/1    4  4
 173  Rule Supreme (IRE) WPMullins,Ireland 8-11-10¹⁴⁵ DJCasey.............. 10/1    7  5
```

171	Iznogoud (FR) *MCPipe* 8-11-1[136] TJMurphy	12/1	5 6
146	Royal Predica (FR) *MCPipe* 10-10-9[130] (t) RGreene	33/1	sh 7
191	Carryonharry (IRE) *MCPipe* 10-9-11[121] (v) GSupple[3]	66/1	½ 8
147	Imperial de Thaix (FR) *MCPipe* 8-9-7[121] (v+t) TJMalone[7]	50/1	1 9
126	Fasgo (IRE) *PFNicholls* 9-10-6[127] JTizzard	9/1	4 10
178	Bounce Back (USA) *MCPipe* 8-10-9[133] JEMoore[3]	12/1	7 11
	Lord 'n' Master (IRE) *RRowe* 8-10-0[121] TDoyle	25/1	2½ 12
178	Shardam (IRE) *NATwistwin-Davies* 7-11-3[138] CLlewellyn	6/1jf	12 13
	Multi Talented (IRE) *LWells* 8-9-12[121] (b) CBolger[5]	50/1	16 14
191	Stormez (FR) *MCPipe* 7-11-11[146] (v+t) APMcCoy	14/1	ur
178	What's Up Boys (IRE) *PJHobbs* 10-11-12[147] (b) RJohnson	16/1	pu
145	Haut Cercy (FR) *HDDaly* 9-11-5[140] MBradburne	8/1	pu
171	Scotmail Boy (IRE) *JHowardJohnson* 11-10-0[121] GLee	6/1jf	pu

Mr Terry Neill 18ran 7m20.23

AUTEUIL Saturday, Apr 24   SOFT

197 Prix Amadou (Gr 2) (4yo) £45,000   2m3f110y (12)

	MAIA ERIA (FR) *YPorzier,France* 4-10-6 CPieux	6/10f	1
155	MONDUL (GER) *MFHarris,GB* 4-10-3 OMcPhail		15 2
	KAUTO STAR (FR) *SFoucher,France* 4-10-6 JGuiheneuf		4 3
	Kizit Lo (FR) *RCaget,France* 4-10-3 CSanterne		4 4
	River Charm (FR) *GCherel,France* 4-10-10 PMarsac		5 5
	Kitka (FR) *BSecly,France* 4-9-11 MJulien		½ 6
	Pop Art (FR) *CAubert,France* 4-10-3 LMetais		¾ 7
	Key West Road (FR) *TTrapenard,France* 4-9-13 AKondrat		20 8

Mr J. P. Dubois 8ran 4m48.03

PUNCHESTOWN Tuesday, Apr 27   GOOD

198 Ellier Developments Nov Chase (Gr 3) (5yo+) £18,569   2½m (14)

	LORD SAM (IRE) *VRADartnall,GB* 8-11-3 JCulloty	5/4f	1
	HI CLOY (IRE) *MHourigan* 7-11-10 TJMurphy	5/2	nk 2
	SUM LEADER (IRE) *MissJaneThomas* 8-11-3 BJGeraghty	20/1	8 3
	Nil Desperandum (IRE) *MissFMCrowley* 7-11-10 RWalsh	9/4	1½ 4

Plain Peeps 4ran 5m13.11

199 betdaq.com Champion Chase (Gr 1) (5yo+) £62,591   2m (11)

	MOSCOW FLYER (IRE) *MrsJHarrington* 10-11-12 BJGeraghty	4/11f	1
	RATHGAR BEAU (IRE) *ESheehy* 8-11-12 JRBarry	12/1	2 2
	STRONG RUN (IRE) *NMeade* 11-11-12 (t) PCarberry	8/1	6 3
	Native Upmanship (IRE) *ALTMoore* 11-11-12 CO'Dwyer	7/1	8 4
	Killultagh Storm (IRE) *WPMullins* 10-11-12 (s) RWalsh	33/1	3½ 5
	Alcapone (IRE) *MFMorris* 10-11-12 JCulloty	16/1	6
	Native Scout (IRE) *DHassett* 8-11-12 (t) DNRussell	10/1	ur

Mr Brian Kearney 7ran 4m07.24

200 Evening Herald Champion Nov Hdle (Gr 1) (5yo+) £35,369   2m (9)

	BRAVE INCA (IRE) *ColmAMurphy* 6-11-12 BMCash	2/1f	1
	ROYAL SHAKESPEARE (FR) *SGollings,GB* 5-11-11 BJGeraghty	8/1	sh 2
	ROYAL ALPHABET (IRE) *WPMullins* 6-11-12 (t) RWalsh	4/1	2½ 3
	Rockstown Boy (IRE) *CByrnes* 6-11-12 DNRussell	10/1	3½ 4
	Kahuna (IRE) *ESheehy* 7-11-12 JRBarry	25/1	9 5
	Dawn Invasion (IRE) *AnthonyMullins* 5-11-11 DJCasey	7/1	6
	Snapper Creek (IRE) *JABerry* 8-11-12 GTHutchinson	20/1	7
	La Mandragola *RJOsborne* 7-11-12 MrDPMaher	50/1	8
	Dempsey (IRE) *MPitman,GB* 6-11-12 TJMurphy	12/1	9
	Common World (USA) *NMeade* 5-11-11 IJPower	25/1	10
	Zum See (IRE) *NMeade* 5-11-11 PCarberry	12/1	11
	Rupununi (IRE) *FrancisEnnis* 7-11-12 JCulloty	33/1	12
	Overstrand (IRE) *MrsMReveley,GB* 5-11-11 CO'Dwyer	20/1	pu

Novices Syndicate 13ran 3m47.95

PUNCHESTOWN Wednesday, Apr 28   GOOD

201 Punchestown Heineken Gold Cup (Gr 1) (5yo+) £72,483   3m1f (17)

	BEEF OR SALMON (IRE) *MHourigan* 8-11-12 TJMurphy	5/4f	1
	HARBOUR PILOT (IRE) *NMeade* 9-11-12 (b) PCarberry	3/1	4 2
	FIRST GOLD (FR) *FDoumen,France* 11-11-12 (b) TDoumen	5/2	2½ 3
	Rince Ri (IRE) *TMWalsh* 11-11-12 (b) RWalsh	9/1	7 4
	Rule Supreme (IRE) *WPMullins* 8-11-12 DJCasey	20/1	2½ 5
	Come In Moscow (IRE) *JohnJosephMurphy* 8-11-7 MrAJMcNamara	100/1	6

Mr B. J. Craig 6ran 6m17.02

202 Paddy Power Champion INH Flat (Gr 1) (4yo+ m) £26,215   2m

	GEILL SLI (IRE) *NMeade* 6-12-0 MrAPCrowe	11/1	1

BLAZING LISS (IRE) *JEKiely* 5-11-8 MrDerekO'Connor.......................... 6/4f 1½ 2
AUGHERSKEA (IRE) *NMeade* 5-11-8 MrNPMadden .... 13/2 ¾ 3
Tigerlion (IRE) *JBleahen* 6-12-0 MrMDarcy...................................... 12/1 1 4
Green Peach (IRE) *WPMullins* 6-12-0 MrJANash................................ 14/1 8 5
Gollum (IRE) *EGriffin* 4-11-6 MrRMMoran....................................... 16/1 6
Ardsallagh's Lark (IRE) *MichaelCGriffin* 5-11-8 MrPTobin 33/1 7
Arteea (IRE) *MHourigan* 5-11-13 MrMJO'Hare................................... 12/1 8
Another Superman (IRE) *PaulARoche* 5-11-13 MrDRoche................... 50/1 9
Sidalcea (IRE) *EJO'Grady* 5-11-8 MrPFenton..................................... 16/1 10
Foxton Brook (IRE) *NJHenderson,GB* 5-11-13 MrAFitzgerald 12/1 11
Knocknabooly (IRE) *WPMullins* 5-11-13 MrJJCodd........................... 4/1 12
Ambition Royal (FR) *MrsLBNormile,GB* 4-11-6 MrRHFowler 40/1 13
Mrs B. M. McKinney 13ran 3m43.75

PUNCHESTOWN Thursday, Apr 29 GOOD

203 Colm McEvoy Auctioneers Champion 4yo Hdle (Gr 1) (4yo)   2m (9)
£45,772

CHERUB (GER) *JonjoO'Neill,GB* 4-11-0 (t) ADobbin 14/1 1
MADE IN JAPAN (JPN) *PJHobbs,GB* 4-11-0 RJohnson.......................... 9/2 sh 2
ESSEX (IRE) *MJPO'Brien* 4-11-0 (s) DNRussell 4/1 1 3
Silk Screen (IRE) *WPMullins* 4-11-0 DJCasey 16/1 2 4
Nopekan (IRE) *ThomasMullins* 4-11-0 CO'Dwyer.............................. 20/1 2 5
Diego Garcia (IRE) *WPMullins* 4-11-0 JRBarry 25/1 6
More Rainbows (IRE) *NMeade* 4-11-0 IJPower................................... 50/1 7
Power Elite (IRE) *NMeade* 4-11-0 PCarberry 10/3f 8
Al Eile (IRE) *JQueally* 4-11-0 JCulloty... 8/1 9
My Will (FR) *PFNicholls,GB* 4-11-0 BJGeraghty 12/1 10
Top Strategy (IRE) *TMWalsh* 4-11-0 (b) RWalsh................................ 8/1 11
Cupla Cairde *DTHughes* 4-11-0 (b) MAFitzgerald 25/1 12
Tarque (IRE) *MissVenetiaWilliams,GB* 4-11-0 (t) SThomas .... 14/1 su
Atlantic Joinery Limited 13ran 3m51.43

204 Swordlestown Cup Nov Chase (Gr 1) (5yo+) £35,369   2m (11)

SAY AGAIN (IRE) *PaulNolan* 8-11-12 JLCullen 6/1 1
COMMONCHERO (IRE) *MJPO'Brien* 7-11-12 PCarberry 8/1 11 2
EMPERORS GUEST *ThomasMullins* 6-11-12 DJCasey 12/1 20 3
Colca Canyon (IRE) *MrsJHarrington* 7-11-12 RMPower .... 4/1 f
Kicking King (IRE) *TJTaaffe* 6-11-12 BJGeraghty .... 8/11f bd
Mr Sean Duggan 5ran 4m06.56

205 Ballymore Properties Champion Stayers Hdle (Gr 1) (4yo+) £52,013   3m (14)

RHINESTONE COWBOY (IRE) *JonjoO'Neill,GB* 8-11-12 MrJPMagnier.... 5/2 1
IRIS'S GIFT *JonjoO'Neill,GB* 7-11-12 BJGeraghty............................ 8/13f 7 2
ROSAKER (USA) *NMeade* 7-11-12 PCarberry 14/1 8 3
Holy Orders (IRE) *WPMullins* 7-11-12 (b) RWalsh........................... 10/1 20 4
Bob Justice (IRE) *TMWalsh* 8-11-12 GCotter .... 66/1 ½ 5
Florida Coast (IRE) *JamesBowe* 9-11-12 JFLevins.............................. 25/1 6
Mon Villez (FR) *NJHenderson,GB* 5-11-10 MAFitzgerald 40/1 7
Sunny Flight (FR) *AChaille-Chaille,France* 10-11-12 (b) PSourzac.......... 40/1 8
Mrs John Magnier 8ran 5m48.61

206 Castlemartin Stud Pat Taaffe Hcap Chase 0-145(139) (5yo+) £24,030   3m1f (17)

WOTSITOOYA (IRE) *MJPO'Brien* 12-10-6[121] DNRussell 10/1 1
TIMBERA (IRE) *DTHughes* 10-11-8[137] (t) JCulloty 9/2f 2½ 2
HUME CASTLE (IRE) *MrsJHarrington* 8-10-11[126] (t) BJGeraghty .... 10/1 hd 3
Golden Storm (IRE) *JosephCrowley* 7-10-3[123] (b) JMAllen[5] .... 8/1 hd 4
The Culdee (IRE) *FFlood* 8-9-7[111] GTHutchinson[3] 9/1 1 5
Killultagh Thunder (IRE) *WPMullins* 8-9-10[111] JRBarry..................... 25/1 6
Glynn Dingle (IRE) *AJMartin* 11-10-10[125] CO'Dwyer........................ 14/1 7
199 Killultagh Storm (IRE) *WPMullins* 10-11-10[139] RWalsh................. 20/1 8
Bramblehill Duke (IRE) *MissVenetiaWilliams,GB* 12-9-12[116] SThomas[3]...... 25/1 9
Thari (USA) *NMeade* 7-10-7[122] (b+t) PCarberry 14/1 10
Farinel *ALTMoore* 8-9-10[111] DJCasey 6/1 11
Lord of The River (IRE) *NJHenderson,GB* 12-11-6[135] MAFitzgerald 7/1 12
Cassia Heights *SABrookshaw,GB* 9-10-6[121] (b) MDGrant.................. 10/1 13
Native Performance (IRE) *MHourigan* 9-10-8[123] TJMurphy................. 16/1 pu
Sigma Dotcomm (IRE) *JamesJosephMangan* 8-9-10[111] GCotter .... 25/1 pu
Mrs Christopher Cullen 15ran 6m20.97

PUNCHESTOWN Friday, Apr 30 GOOD

207 Emo Oil Champion Hdle (Gr 1) (5yo+) £64,430   2m (9)

HARDY EUSTACE (IRE) *DTHughes* 7-11-12 (b) CO'Dwyer..................... 3/1 1

1054

ROOSTER BOOSTER *PJHobbs,GB* 10-11-12 RJohnson 13/8f   1 2
FOTA ISLAND (IRE) *MFMorris* 8-11-12 DJCasey 16/1   3 3
Harchibald (FR) *NMeade* 5-11-11 PCarberry .... 12/1 hd 4
Scarthy Lad (IRE) *TGO'Leary* 6-11-12 JCulloty .... 33/1 ö 5
Solerina (IRE) *JamesBowe* 7-11-7 GTHutchinson ....,,. 12/1   6
Quazar (IRE) *JonjoO'Neill,GB* 6-11-12 (h+t) MAFltzgerald 20/1   7
Georges Girl (IRE) *FFlood* 6-11-7 IJFlood 7/1   8
Hasty Prince *JonjoO'Neill,GB* 6-11-12 BJGeraghty 7/1   9

Mr Laurence Byrne 9ran 3m44.17

208   **Sharp Minds Betfair Nov Hcap Chase (137) (5yo+)** £37,450   3m1f (17)

LISCANNOR LAD (IRE) *DTHughes* 6-9-10[116] PWFlood[7] 14/1   1
RIDE THE STORM (IRE) *EJO'Grady* 7-10-3[116] MDGrant 16/1 1½ 2
ALBRIGHTON *NMeade* 9-10-3[116] PCarberry 25/1   2 3
Strong Resolve (IRE) *MissLucindaRussell,GB* 8-9-10[116] PBuchanan[7] 14/1   7 4
Joueur d'Estruval (FR) *WPMullins* 9-10-13[126] RWalsh .... 7/1   sh 5
Splendour (IRE) *MissSCox* 9-10-12[125] GCotter 25/1   6
Kymandjen (IRE) *PaulNolan* 7-10-11[124] JLCullen 8/1   7
Emotional Moment (IRE) *TJTaaffe* 7-11-10[137] BJGeraghty .... 12/1   f
Rosslea (IRE) *MissHCKnight,GB* 6-11-8[135] JCulloty .... 3/1f   f
Rum Pointer (IRE) *RHBuckler,GB* 8-10-12[125] JRBarry .... 16/1   f
Yeoman's Point (IRE) *CRoche* 8-11-0[127] (s+t) CO'Dwyer .... 12/1   ur
Satco Express (IRE) *ESheehy* 8-11-3[130] JRBarry .... 14/1   pu
Mounsey Castle *PJHobbs,GB* 7-10-7[120] RJohnson .... 20/1   pu
Colonel Bradley (IRE) *CFSwan* 10-10-6[119] DJCasey .... 16/1   pu
Where Now (IRE) *JQueally* 8-10-3[116] TJMurphy .... 14/1   pu

Mr C. P. O'Brien 15ran 6m16.16

209   **Menolly Homes Champion Nov Hdle (Gr 1) (4yo+)** £37,450   2½m (14)

SADLERS WINGS (IRE) *WPMullins* 6-11-12 RWalsh 4/5f   1
KADISKAR (IRE) *CRoche* 6-11-12 (t) CO'Dwyer 10/1 3½ 2
KILDARE (IRE) *DTHughes* 7-11-12 (b) BJGeraghty .... 16/1   sh 3
Be Fair *DECantillon,GB* 6-11-12 JCulloty .... 10/1 hd 4
Point Barrow (IRE) *PHughes* 6-11-12 TJMurphy 12/1 1½ 5
Randwick Roar (IRE) *PMJDoyle* 5-11-11 DNRussell 25/1   6
Watson Lake (IRE) *NMeade* 6-11-12 PCarberry 10/3   7
Fairwood Present (IRE) *PJRothwell* 6-11-12 BMCash 20/1   8

Mr John J. Brennan 8ran 4m48.10

AUTEUIL Sunday, May 30   SOFT

210   **Hipcover Gras Savoye - Prix La Barka (Gr 2) (5yo+)** £45,302   2m5f110y (14)

     GREAT LOVE (FR) *PBoisgontier,France* 6-10-8 LMetais 59/10   1
     NICKNAME (FR) *J-PGallorini,France* 5-10-10 TMajorcryk .... 4/5   nk 2
201 RULE SUPREME (IRE) *WPMullins,Ireland* 8-10-3 DJCasey 41/1   4 3
209 Sadlers Wings (IRE) *WPMullins,Ireland* 6-10-6 RWalsh....................... 6/1   ½ 4
     Ennemi d'Etat (FR) *MRolland,France* 5-10-6 PChevalier....................... 5/1   3 5
     Phonidal (FR) *MRolland,France* 8-10-6 (b) FBenech........................... 29/1   ¾ 6
     Saute Au Bois (FR) *ELeenders,France* 10-10-7 (b) MrGLeenders 31/1 15 7
208 Joueur d'Estruval (FR) *WPMullins,Ireland* 7-10-3 CPieux..................... 16/1   3 8
     Royal Speed (FR) *BBarbier,France* 5-10-1 CGombeau......................... 18/1   pu

Mrs Remy Picamau 9ran 5m18.41

211   **Gras Savoye Cinema - Prix Ferdinand Dufaure (Gr 1) (4yo)** £66,443 2½m110y (18)

CYRLIGHT (FR) *AChaille-Chaille,France* 4-10-6 PSourzac 3/10   1
MYSOKO (FR) *J-PGallorini,France* 4-10-6 SLeloup............................. 43/1 15 2
PSYCHEE DU BERLAIS (FR) *FMCottin,France* 4-10-1 (s) TMajorcryk 11/1 10 3
Star Glory (FR) *SFoucher,France* 4-10-6 (b) JGuiheneuf...................... 54/1 11½ 4
Feroe (FR) *TTrapenard,France* 4-10-1 (s) BChameraud 71/1   4 5
Bica (FR) *GMacaire,France* 4-10-6 BGicquel.................................... 9/1   2½ 6
Barramundi (FR) *GCherel,France* 4-10-6 PMarsac .... 74/1   ¾ 7
Mossburn (FR) *GCherel,France* 4-10-6 (b) CPieux.............................. 15/1   8 8
True Mariner (FR) *SBerard,France* 4-10-6 NMilliere............................ 101/1 15 9
Sybellius d'Artaix (FR) *J-PGallorini,France* 4-10-6 (s) LMetais 12/1 10 10
Lyfos du Charmil (FR) *GCherel,France* 4-10-6 SDehez .... 92/1   f
Baby du Rheu (FR) *PRago,France* 4-10-6 (b) CGombeau........................ 23/1   pu
Loin de Moi (FR) *TTrapenard,France* 4-10-1 AKondrat........................ 45/1   pu

Mr S. Mulryan 13ran 5m09.50

212   **Gras Savoye Grand Steeple-Chase de Paris (Gr 1) (5yo+)** £163,087   3m5f (23)

KOTKIJET (FR) *J-PGallorini,France* 8-10-8 TMajorcryk 1/2f   1
KAMILLO (FR) *FMCottin,France* 6-10-8 (t) DJCasey............................ 116/1 10 2
MAJADAL (FR) *GCherel,France* 6-10-8 PMarsac 83/1   2 3

Sun Storm (FR) *TCivel,France* 7-10-8 (s+t) BThelier 112/1   8 4
Turgot (FR) *JBertrandeBalanda,France* 7-10-8 PChevalier 23/1   3 5
Batman Senora (FR) *IanWilliams,GB* 8-10-8 (b) CGombeau 17/2   4 6
Urga (FR) *GChaignon,France* 13-10-8 XClaude 53/1   2 7
Pilitch (FR) *YPorzier,France* 6-10-8 DMongeard 87/1 15 8
Jerico Vallis (FR) *JBertrandeBalanda,France* 7-10-8 LMetais .... 11/1   f
Joseille (FR) *ELeenders,France* 7-10-8 (t) MrGLeenders .... 44/1   f
Rougenoir (FR) *RELecomte,France* 11-10-8 HServeau .... 45/1   pu
Samson (FR) *MmeLAudon,France* 7-10-8 BDelo .... 42/1   pu
Turkish Junior (FR) *J-PGallorini,France* 7-10-8 CCheminaud .... 28/1   pu
Jingle Rose (FR) *TTrapenard,France* 7-10-8 (t) BGicquel .... 25/1   pu
Montayral (FR) *PHughes,Ireland* 7-10-8 RWalsh .... 31/1   pu
Kilefou d'Airy (FR) *JOrtet,France* 6-10-8 CPieux .... 9/1   pu

Exors of the late Daniel Wildenstein 16ran 7m21.52

AUTEUIL Saturday, Jun 19   GOOD to SOFT

213   **Grande Course de Haies d'Auteuil (Gr 1) (5yo+)** £81,954   3m1f110y (16)

210 RULE SUPREME (IRE) *WPMullins,Ireland* 8-10-8 DJCasey 14/1   1
210 GREAT LOVE (FR) *PBoisgontier,France* 6-10-8 LMetais 8/1   2 2
212 KOTKIJET (FR) *J-PGallorini,France* 9-10-8 TMajorcryk 4/10f 2½ 3
210 Nickname (FR) *J-PGallorini,France* 5-10-3 CPieux 17/4 2½ 4
    Cerilly (FR) *JBertrandeBalanda,France* 7-10-8 OSauvaget 30/1   3 5
210 Phonidal (FR) *MRolland,France* 8-10-8 (b) PChevalier 27/1 10 6
212 Batman Senora (FR) *IanWilliams,GB* 8-10-8 (b) CGombeau 11/1   5 7

Mr John J. Fallon 7ran 6m20.20

214   **Prix Alain du Breil - Course de Haies d'Ete Des Quatre Ans (4yo)**   2m3f110y (12)
    £62,583

    MESANGE ROYALE (FR) *FMCottin,France* 4-10-1 DJCasey 17/1   1
    MA ROYALE (FR) *MRolland,France* 4-10-1 PChevalier .... 13/1   ½ 2
    MAIA ERIA (FR) *YPorzier,France* 4-10-1 CPieux 1/1f 2½ 3
    River Charm (FR) *GCherel,France* 4-10-6 YRougegrez 17/2   3 4
    Kizit Lo (FR) *RCaget,France* 4-10-6 (b) CSanterne 71/1   3 5
    Liverpool Echo (FR) *SWattel,France* 4-10-6 LGerard 55/1   6 6
211 Star Glory (FR) *SFoucher,France* 4-10-6 (b) JGuiheneuf....................... 13/1 1½ 7
    Enzo du Berlais (FR) *J-PGallorini,France* 4-10-6 TMajorcryk 13/2 1½ 8
    Mister Gyor (FR) *BBarbier,France* 4-10-6 CGombeau 17/1   5 9
    Mondul (GER) *MFHarris,GB* 4-10-6 OMcPhail................................. 11/2   pu
211 Loin de Moi (FR) *TTrapenard,France* 4-10-1 AKondrat....................... 33/1   pu
    Negresse de Cuta (FR) *MlleA-SMadelaine,France* 4-10-1 MJulien .... 78/1   pu

Ecurie Vallin 10ran 4m39.96

INDEX TO SELECTED BIG RACES

1059

Pessimistic Dick c2[pu], c28[ur]
Pethertheknot (IRE) F79[2]
Pettree (IRE) c2[5]
Phar From Frosty (IRE) 51[2]
Phariwarmer (IRE) 59
Pharpost (IRE) c179[ur]
Phonidal (FR) 210[6], 213[6]
Pilca (FR) 85[6]
Pilitch (FR) c212
Pink Eclipse F122
Pirandello (IRE) 64, 99[F]
Pizarro (FR) c38[pu], c76*, c117*, c149[bd]
Poachin Again (IRE) 185
Point Barrow (IRE) 180[2], 209[5]
Polar Champ c158
Polar Red c153[6], c179[3]
Poliantas (FR) c15[2]
Pop Art (FR) 197
Portant Fella 175[bd], 185
Power Elite (IRE) 115*, 128*, 183[3], 203
Prince of Tara (IRE) 39[6], 77[5]
Prominent Profile (IRE) c146
Proper Squire (USA) c191[F]
Psychee du Berlais (FR) c211[3]
Puck Out (IRE) 5, 64, 175*
Punchy (IRE) c46[6]
Puntal (FR) c42[4], c111[5], c143[ur], c178[ur], c196*
Putsometnby (IRE) c6[F]

Quadco (IRE) 5[ur]
Quazar (IRE) 12[2], 110[4], 120[5], 129[4], 151, 177, 207
Queen Meabh (IRE) 34[pu]
Queen Soraya F141
Quel Doun (FR) 115[3]
Quetal (IRE) c158[pu]
Quick 172

Raikkonen (IRE) 34[4], 155
Rakalackey 167
Randwick Roar (IRE) 209[6]
Rathgar Beau (IRE) c26[2], c55[2], c74[F], c100[3], 161, c181[5], c199[2]
Red Brook Lad c158[pu]
Red Emperor 51
Redemption c15[pu], c49[F], c89[ur], 103[5], 151, 156, 166[3]
Red Sun 175[F]
Refinement (IRE) F154[2]
Regal Exit (FR) 64, 161
Reizieger (FR) 64, c159[3]
Rendova F122
Reviewer (IRE) 151
Rheindross (IRE) c75[ur]
Rhinestone Cowboy (IRE) 52*, 81[6], 110*, 151[3], 177*, 205*
Ricardo c69[3], 97
Ride The Storm (IRE) c208[2]
Right Job (IRE) 97, 185
Rigmarole 12[4], 18*, 50*, 127*, 144, 194[2]
Rince Ri (IRE) c45[3], c78[F], c100[2], c104[2], c118[3], c201[4]
Ring of Beara (IRE) F186[3]
Rio Diamond (IRE) c75[pu]
Risk Accessor (IRE) c4[6], c15[F], c49[2], c138, c178[ur], c188[4]
Risky Reef 20[4], 120

River Bug (IRE) c126[ur]
River Charm (FR) 197[5], 214[4]
River Cora (IRE) c6[2]
Robbo c28[co], c126[2]
Rob The Five (IRE) 185
Rockstown Boy (IRE) 200[4]
Rockwell Island (IRE) c29[F]
Rodalko (FR) c191[pu]
Rodber (USA) c179[ur]
Roman Hideaway (IRE) 88
Romany Dream 187
Rooster Booster 50[5], 66[2], 92*, 120[2], 144[2], 177[2], 207[2]
Rosaker (USA) 58[2], 151, 205[3]
Rose Perk (IRE) c75[pu], c182[F]
Ross Leader (IRE) c93[5]
Rosslea (IRE) c46[2], c76[2], c125[2], c208[F]
Ross Moff (IRE) c182[F]
Ross River 148
Rostropovich (IRE) 20, 77[3], 119[6], 147, 174
Rougenoir (IRE) c13[2], c212[pu]
Royal Alphabet (IRE) 183*, 200[3]
Royal Atalza (FR) c108[pu], c178[pu]
Royal Auclair (FR) c49[4], c84[F], c121[4], c145[3], c168, c196[2]
Royal Beluga (USA) c146[pu]
Royaleety (FR) c143[pu]
Royal Emperor (FR) c93[F], c114*, c149[2], c173[F]
Royal Paradise (FR) F154[4]
Royal Predica (FR) c31, c63[pu], c146[F], c196
Royal Rosa (FR) 90[2], 131*, 162[2]
Royal Shakespeare (FR) 169*, 200[2]
Royal Speed (FR) 210[pu]
Rugar (FR) F186
Rule Supreme (IRE) c65[3], c101[3], c149*, c173[ur], c196[5], c201[5], 210[3], 213*
Rum Pointer (IRE) c54[3], c93[4], c208[F]
Run For Paddy c182[pu]
Run of Kings (IRE) 187
Rupununi (IRE) 37[6], 183[pu], 200
Ryalux (IRE) c53[5]
Ryders Storm (USA) c17[2]

Sabadilla (USA) 5*, 8[pu], 185
Sabreflight F141[3]
Sacundai (IRE) 20[2], 39[5], 77*
Sadlers Wings (IRE) 148[6], 180*, 209*, 210[4]
Safe Route (USA) 97
Saintsaire (FR) 32[3], 64[3], 120, 140, 192[3]
Samawi (IRE) 59
Samson (FR) c212[pu]
Sangatte (IRE) 88
Santenay (FR) c136[3], c159, 194[6]
Satco Express (IRE) c38[4], c76[4], c101[pu], c152, c182[F], c208[pu]
Satcoslam (IRE) c75[3]
Saute Au Bois (FR) 210

Say Again (IRE) c181[3], c204*
Scandor (FR) c13[6]
Scarthy Lad (IRE) 205, 39[3], 58[4], 207[5]
Schwartzhalle (IRE) c29[pu], c181[F]
Scorned (GER) 140*, 161
Scotmail Boy (IRE) c171[3], c196[pu]
Scots Grey c171[F]
Scottish Memories (IRE) 20
Sea Drifting 30[6]
Seaforde (IRE) 115[6], 155
Secret Native (IRE) c75[4], 119[pu]
Secret Ploy F122*
Seebald (GER) c11[4], c43[6], c67[ur], c121, c138[3], c159[ur], c163[5], c188*, c195
See More Business (IRE) c41[4]
See More Jock F154
See You Sometime c108[3], c111[F], c138[6], c173[F]
Self Defense 40[2], 61[4], 120, 144
Shalako (USA) 18[5], 64, 140[6], 166
Sharabad (FR) 137
Shardam (IRE) c16*, c31[pu], c121, c135[4], c145[2], c178[ur], c196
Sharpaten (IRE) 27
Shaunas Vision (IRE) 59[5]
Shayadi (IRE) 175
Sh Boom 22[2], 48[2], 83*, 90*, 156[F], 162
Sheer Genius (IRE) c98[pu]
Sheriff's Friend (IRE) c158[pu]
Shining Tyne c126[pu]
Shooting Light (IRE) c121*, c135[pu]
Shuhood (USA) 134[3], 164
Sidalcea (IRE) F202
Sigma Dotcomm (IRE) c101[pu], c171, c206[pu]
Silk Screen (IRE) 203[4]
Silver Birch (IRE) c152[4]
Silvergino (IRE) 68
Silver Knight c93[3], c114[3]
Silver Prophet (IRE) 88
Silver Steel c96[pu]
Silver Streak (IRE) c23[5]
Simon's Seat (USA) 88
Simoun (IRE) 142, 166[6]
Simply Gifted c159[ur], c165[4]
Simply Supreme (IRE) 90[4], c114[F], c173*, c191[F]
Sindapour (IRE) 148
Sir Frosty c168[6], c191[pu]
Sirius Storm (IRE) F186
Sir Rembrandt (IRE) c31[F], c41*, c70[2], c104[pu], c121[6], c157[2]
Sir Talbot 30[pu], c136[4]
Sister Cinnamon F141
Sixo (IRE) 139, 172[6]
Skippers Cleuch (IRE) c72[2]
Skycab (IRE) c178[ur]
Sky Warrior (FR) c113
Sleep Bal (FR) 129[6], 177, 194
Sleeping Night (FR) 30[5]
Smart View (IRE) F82[4]

1063

TIMEFORM 'TOP HORSES IN FRANCE'

There were three top-class chasers trained in France in 2003/4, and the exploits of two of them, **First Gold** and the ill-fated **Jair du Cochet**, hardly need dwelling on here as they will already be more familiar to racegoers in Britain than to those in their own country. Both made only fleeting appearances in France in recent seasons, essentially to warm up for campaigns this side of the Channel. That left **Kotkijet**, who returned from a two-year absence, to dominate the major chases at Auteuil. Wins in the Prix Heros XII and Prix George Courtois in the autumn, and then the Prix Ingre in May, were all gained in imposing fashion before a second success, three years after his first, in the Grand Steeple-Chase de Paris. That too was won most impressively, by ten lengths with any amount in hand, over a field which was stronger on quantity than quality. Kotkijet's supremacy at Auteuil could either encourage connections to stick with what he does best, as more big prizes there look at his mercy, or maybe it will spur them on to seek a new challenge in Britain. Those closest to Kotkijet gave out mixed messages during the latest season about the likelihood of his running abroad, though he'd obviously be a fascinating rival to the top chasers in the British Isles.

Nine-year-old Kotkijet is quite old by French standards, but it says something for the lack of quality among the top chasers that two even older veterans of Auteuil, eleven-year-old **Rougenoir** and thirteen-year-old **Urga** were still among the best of the rest over fences. Rougenoir won a second Prix Troytown at March (before Kotkijet had returned from the winter break), while Urga was thereabouts in several good chases as usual, including when making the frame in the top chase in the autumn, the Prix La Haye Jousselin, and in the Prix Murat in the spring. Both horses had been placed in the Grand Steeple-Chase in years past but neither figured in the latest edition, Urga contesting the race for the sixth time. Incidentally, the 2003 Grand Steeple-Chase winner **Line Marine** appeared just twice subsequently in the latest season, both times over hurdles; she had been a late withdrawal from the Prix Heros XII in the autumn.

There is no shortage of younger blood among the other leading chasers aged five or older, though they all have considerable progress to make to trouble an in-form Kotkijet in the short term. Kotkijet's stablemate, the front-running **Turkish Junior**, actually gained a shock win over him in the Prix Murat in April, though the long odds-on favourite returned bleeding from the nose and without a shoe on that occasion. Runner-up in the George Courtois and fourth in the Ingre, Turkish Junior ran poorly in the Grand Steeple-Chase when more patiently ridden to see out the longer trip. **Kilefou d'Airy**

Prix des Drags, Auteuil—winner Mister Mic and runner-up Majadal at an open ditch in this consolation prize for the Grand Steeple-Chase de Paris

Prix Maurice Gillois, Auteuil—the top chase for four-year-olds of the autumn; eventual winner Ladykish (centre) is preceded by Hautclan in the early stages

looked to have good place chances in the Grand Steeple-Chase but was another to run poorly. He had gained a pattern-race success in the Prix Robert de Clermont-Tonnerre in February when making his fitness count from a successful campaign at Pau during the winter, his best effort having come when failing by a nose successfully to give 10 kg to the mare Neriette in the Grand Prix there. The best impression among the beaten horses in the Grand Steeple-Chase was made by **Jerico Vallis** who paid for trying to go with Kotkijet on the final circuit before falling at the last when a tired fourth. He had injured himself in the race the year before but, on his second run back, was a good third in the Prix Ingre in May. **Mister Mic** did not contest the Grand Steeple-Chase but he put up his best effort to win the following month's consolation event, the Prix des Drags, by ten lengths from the Grand Steeple-Chase third **Majadal**. The Grand Steeple-Chase runner-up **Kamillo**, who had been just a fair novice when trained in Ireland, was unable to repeat that form in the Drags, supporting the view that he had been flattered in the big race.

The best prospect among the older chasers could be the Guillaume Macaire-trained five-year-old **Prince des Ifs**. He improved rapidly in the autumn, winning two Group 3 chases for four-year-olds, the Prix Edmond Barrachin and the Prix Orcada, only to disappoint in the Group 1 chase for that age-group, the Prix Maurice Gillois. He is being rested in 2004 (when he would have had to take on the established chasers), but with a career record of eight wins from eleven starts he is an interesting longer-term prospect. The Maurice Gillois winner **Ladykish** (earlier runner-up to Prince des Ifs in both his Group 3 wins) is also potentially interesting from a British point of view, being trained by Francois Doumen. This sister to Turkish Junior had her attentions switched back to hurdles after the turn of the year and showed form nearly as good over the smaller obstacles.

Of the other leading chasers, **Northerntown** did not compete at Auteuil but was seen to good effect at Enghien where he won the track's Grand Steeple-Chase in October and added the big hurdle race there, the Prix Leopold d'Orsetti, a month later. **Ty Benjam** put up a good effort when giving plenty of weight and a beating to Northerntown at Enghien earlier in the autumn but failed to repeat the form subsequently. Guillaume Macaire's foreign successes were not confined to Britain, as he saddled Tempo d'Or, rated 124+ over hurdles when last seen in Britain in 2001/2, to win Italy's most prestigious chase,

Gran Premio di Merano Forst—Tempo d'Or secures another big win outside France for Guillaume Macaire's stable in Italy's most important chase

the Gran Premio di Merano. Before leaving the older chasers, mention should also go to **Jingle Rose** who won France's most valuable handicap chase, the Prix du President de La Republique in April. The winner had come a long way since his last outing in Britain when winning a selling hurdle at Stratford for Philip Hobbs in 2001.

Baracouda stood out as the top French-trained hurdler, though he too needs no introduction this side of the Channel where he has raced exclusively since March 2001. **Foreman**, who joined him in J. P. McManus ownership in the latest season, also put up his best efforts in the British Isles, following a couple of appearances at Enghien which brought a win in a listed contest and a fall at the last in the Leopold d'Orsetti won by Northerntown.

For the second year running, the Grande Course de Haies d'Auteuil went to an Irish-trained horse, with the Willie Mullins-trained Rule Supreme succeeding ill-fated stable-companion Nobody Told Me on the roll of honour, taking advantage of the best local hurdlers' proving no better than smart. The Grande Course de Haies runner-up **Great Love** had just about the most consistent record in the top hurdles all through the season, with wins in the Prix Leon Olry-Roederer in the autumn from the revitalised eleven-year-old **El Fuego**, and in the Prix La Barka in May. Great Love had a tough rival after the turn of the year however in the form of **Nickname** who had won the top autumn race for four-year-olds, the Prix Renaud du Vivier. Nickname came out on top in meetings with Great Love in both the Prix Hypothese and (on worse terms) the Prix Leon Rambaud, but lost out narrowly when giving Great Love weight in the slowly-run Prix La Barka. The weights were back in Nickname's favour in the Grande Course de Haies but he was unable to take advantage, finishing fourth though not necessarily beaten by the longer trip. Odds-on favourite for the Grande Course de Haies was Nickname's stable-companion Kotkijet, attempting to become the first winner of Auteuil's top chase and hurdle in the same year, but he was unable to dominate in the same fashion as he had over fences and finished third.

Hipcover Gras Savoye-Prix La Barka, Auteuil—the grey Great Love and Nickname (second left) jump the last in the main trial for the Grande Course de Haies d'Auteuil; only a neck separates them at the line

Prix Carmarthen, Auteuil—the grey Nom d'Une Pipe takes the last in this Group 3 hurdle with eventual fourth Grand Match; the mares Karly Flight (noseband) and Arielle (second right) fill the places

The placed horses from the 2003 Grande Course de Haies, **Karly Flight** and **Katiki**, were not around for the 2004 renewal, though for very different reasons. The 2003 runner-up Karly Flight also finished second in all three of her races in the autumn, behind **Gold Magic** in the Prix de Compiegne and Nickname's half-brother **Nom d'Une Pipe** in the Prix Carmarthen (both unsatisfactory races) and behind the mercurial Katiki in the Grand Prix d'Automne. The mare Karly Flight was subsequently retired to stud, whereas Katiki was given his marching orders by the authorities. He put his best foot forward under a good ride to win the Grand Prix d'Automne but disgraced himself by refusing to race on his three other appearances. Gold Magic and Nom d'Une Pipe were others who failed to reappear after the turn of the year, though the latter did finish second in the Leopold d'Orsetti at Enghien. **Vic Toto** was another absentee in the spring, at least in France, though he was second in the National Spirit Hurdle at Fontwell on his final outing. Vic Toto seemed to have lost some of his old dash but generally ran respectably in all the big hurdles in the autumn, ending with a third place in the Leon Olry-Roederer. There were no progressive types among the leading hurdlers, but one who would not have to improve too much to win a good race is **Ennemi d'Etat**. A five-year-old with just eight races over hurdles behind him, he quickened impressively to beat Nickname in the Prix Pierre de Lassus in the autumn and split Nickname and Great Love when second in both the Hypothese and Leon Rambaud in the spring before finishing fifth in the Prix La Barka.

One horse dominated the chases for three/four-year-olds and that was the unbeaten **Cyrlight**. Not only did he win all five of the pattern races in that category up until the end of May, he won each impressively with plenty to spare by an average of nine lengths. His three wins over fences before the turn of the year included the Prix Congress, the most important chase for three-year-olds, and he reinforced his dominance with pattern-race successes in the spring in the Prix Duc d'Anjou, Fleuret, Jean Stern and Ferdinand Dufaure. He saved his biggest winning margin for the last-named race, a Group 1 event which he won by fifteen lengths from **Mysoko**. It is hard to see anything beating him in the remaining chases for four-year-olds in the autumn, while the King George VI Chase at Kempton has had its conditions altered (four-year-olds were previously ineligible) to allow him the option of taking part. Cyrlight made most of the running in his races, jumping accurately in the main although with a tendency to go right at times, and he looks a most exciting prospect. The rest of the four-year-old chasers were some way behind Cyrlight, though that didn't stop a number of them taking him on more than once. The Guillaume Macaire-trained **Positive Thinking** had one of the most consistent records against Cyrlight, finishing second in the Duc d'Anjou and Fleuret, and fourth in the Jean Stern. **Ecolomaniac** has yet to be tested against Cyrlight, but he could prove one of his more interesting rivals in the autumn as he has won both his chases at Auteuil and looks capable of better still.

For most of the season, it looked as though the juvenile hurdlers had a leader every bit as dominant as Cyrlight was over fences. The front-running filly **Maia Eria** is still entitled to be considered the best of her generation over hurdles judged on her performances in the spring, though two subsequent defeats dented her record and it will be interesting to see if she can return to her best in the autumn. Her style of racing—soon establishing a clear lead—gave rise to doubts that she might have been flattered to win Auteuil's pattern races for three-year-old hurdlers, the Prix Georges de Talhouet-Roy and the Prix Cambaceres, so easily, but she ran her rivals ragged again with even better performances in the spring. A fifteen-length win in the Prix de Pepinvast was followed by a victory over the British-trained Mondul by the same margin in the Prix Amadou. She was reportedly in season when only fifth in the Prix de Longchamp next time but seemed to have no excuses when third behind two other fillies, **Mesange Royale** and **Ma Royale**, in the Group 1 Prix Alain du Breil in June. Mesange Royale had finished behind Maia Eria on no fewer than five occasions earlier in the season. The Prix de Longchamp winner **Kauto Star** (who has since joined a British stable) was another who had become used to finishing behind Maia Eria, though he had shown promise when second to her in the Prix Cambaceres in the autumn. The other juvenile hurdler of note was **River Charm** who raced in the same ownership as Maia Eria. River Charm beat her into second place in the Prix Jacques d'Indy in March (with Kauto Star third), but River Charm was very much second best in both the Prix de Pepinvast and Prix de Longchamp and then fourth in the Alain du Breil.

This is the first review of the French jumping season in *Chasers & Hurdlers*, written at a time when links between French and Anglo-Irish form have probably never been stronger. British owners' and trainers' appetite for young French-bred horses is still as great as ever, with the likes of **Royaleety**, Perle de Puce and My Will among the better French recruits to British stables in the latest season. Challengers from Francois Doumen and Guillaume Macaire are now commonplace, and there are signs of other French trainers taking an interest in running jumpers in the British Isles. Maia Eria's trainer, Yann Porzier, ran the juvenile Valtar at Aintree, while Cyrlight's trainer, Arnaud Chaille-Chaille, sent **Sunny Flight** to Punchestown. Additionally, Jean-Paul Gallorini has announced his intention to campaign Nickname in Britain. There are indications, too, that British and Irish trainers are realising the potential for picking up good money at Auteuil. Juvenile hurdler Mondul (Milton Harris) was placed in two pattern races there, while the victory of chaser Batman Senora (Ian Williams) in the Group 1 Prix La Haye Jousselin was a notable achievement for a British yard. Also, Willie Mullins has shown on two occasions now, with Nobody Told Me and Rule Supreme, that the top French hurdling prize can be won with horses who were not even established as leading hurdlers in the British Isles. At present, the important races at Auteuil are spread through the autumn or spring/

Gras Savoye Vie Et Avenir-Prix de Longchamp, Auteuil—Kauto Star inflicts a shock defeat on top juvenile hurdler Maia Eria who fades into fifth after the last

early-summer, though, in an interesting development, the French authorities are planning in future to concentrate several important races into a whole weekend of high-class jumping at Autcuil in the autumn, built around the Prix La Haye Jousselin. The creation of such a 'mini-festival' meeting could act as a welcome incentive for more British and Irish trainers to send horses to compete at Auteuil.

Chasers (5yo+)
170	*Jair du Cochet 7
167	Kotkijet 9
165	*First Gold 11
148	Ty Benjam 8
148§	Rougenoir 11
145	Kilefou d'Airy 6
144	Prince des Ifs 5
144	Turkish Junior 7
143	Jerico Vallis 7
143	Urga 13
142	Princelou 7
141	Mister Mic 7
141	Northerntown 8
141	Sun Storm 7
140	Ice Mood 5
139	Azulejo 6
139	Paladin 9
138	Exit Sud 8
138	Saint Realise 7
137	Garde d'Estruval 10
137	Grand Canal 8
137	Joseille 7
137	Scandor 10
137?	Kamillo 6
136	Majadal 6
136§	*Innox 8
135	Idole des Fontaines 8
135	Ladykish (f) 5
135	Turgot 7
134	Choum 9
134	Green Turf 6
134	Holy Joe 7
134	Kotkita (f) 6
134	Royal Beaufort 6
133	Echo des Mottes 12
133	Royaleety 5
132	Dustar 9
132	Eperson 6
132	Hespoir d'Aurelie 9
132	Ilians de Juilley 10
132	Oway 6
132	Pilitch 6
132	Samson 7
132	Solarius 7
131p	Domirome 6
131	Belle de Juilley (f) 9
131	Hautclan 5
131	Jingle Rose 7
131	Loumie (f) 5
131	Yanau Lapin 5
131?	Roscoff 7
130	Dom Halma de Valta 8
130	Dourakine 7

130	Gypso de Lyse 10
130	*Kelami 6
130	Sphinx du Berlais 5

Hurdlers (5yo+)
171	*Baracouda 9
155	*Foreman 6
154§	Katiki 7
148+	Karly Flight (f) 6
147	Great Love 6
147	Nickname 5
147	*Vic Toto 7
145	El Fuego 12
145	Gold Magic 6
145	Kotkijet 9
144	Northerntown 8
143	Nom d'Une Pipe 7
141	Cerilly 7
139	Ilians de Juilley 10
138	Cielago 5
138	Ennemi d'Etat 5
138	Phonidal 8
137	Arielle (f) 8
137	Holy Joe 7
137	Ilare 8
136	Kimbi 7
136	Saute Au Bois 10
135	Grand Match 6
135	Mandrin des Aigles 7
134	Baleare (f) 6
134	Jameson du Berlais 5
134	Sphinx du Berlais 5
134	Stodoun 8
134	Turnium 9
133	El Paradiso 7
133	Klevin 6
133	Paladin 9
133	Royal Speed 5
133	Saint Realise 7
133	Solarius 7
133	Sunny Flight 10
133?	Oundle Scoundrel 5
132	Cheler 5
132	Dark Steel 6
132	Loumie (f) 5
132	Lycaon de Vauzelle 5
132	Oudry 7
131	Jivago 5
131	Katoune (f) 5
131	Knock Down (f) 5
131	Ladykish (f) 5
131§	Rougenoir 11
130+	Choum 9
130+	Line Marine (f) 7
130	Ipso Vallis 8
130	Kilefou d'Airy 6

130	Royal Bric 9

Chasers (4yo)
143p	Cyrlight
128	Mysoko
124	Loin de Moi (f)
123p	Ecolomaniac
122	Mesange Royale (f)
121	Aaly Star
121	Bica
120	Positive Thinking
119	Fiumincino
119p	Turlyr
118	Mosaka d'Airy (f)
118	River Dance
118	Star Glory
117	Nagging
117	Zonza
116	Mouskanan
116	Rigoureux
116	Sybellius d'Artaix
115	Baby du Rheu
115	Bento
115	Feroe
115	Manguier

Hurdlers (4yo)
143	Maia Eria (f)
136	Kauto Star
131	Ma Royale (f)
131	Mesange Royale (f)
131	River Charm
128	Kizit Lo
127	Geronito
126	*Val du Don
125	Fast Tempo
124	Il Manifico
124	Le Broadway
124	Le Seychellois
124	Psychee du Berlais (f)
123	Enzo du Berlais
122	Cap Falcon
122	Liverpool Echo
122	Prince Dayan
122	*Tarque
121	Aubane (f)
121	Nagging
121	Star Glory
120	Baby du Rheu
120	Centaure du Clos
120	Descent Destiny
120	Loin de Moi (f)
120	Pop Art

NB Horses marked with an * achieved their best performance in GB or Ireland, otherwise ratings relate to performances in France between September 2003 and June 2004.

There are essays in the main body of the book on Jair du Cochet, Kotkijet, Baracouda, Foreman, Cyrlight and Maia Eria

INDEX TO PHOTOGRAPHS

PORTRAITS & SNAPSHOTS

RACE PHOTOGRAPHS

Red Square Vodka 'Fixed Brush' Novices' Hurdle Final Bonus Race (Handicap) (Haydock)	*Alec Russell*	549
Red Square Vodka Gold Cup Chase (Handicap) (Haydock)	*Alec Russell*	478
Red Square Vodka Prestige Novices' Hurdle (Haydock)	*Alec Russell*	785
Rocom Handicap Hurdle (Wetherby)	*Alec Russell*	171
Roscoe Harvey Memorial Novices' Chase (Warwick)	*George Selwyn*	244
Royal & SunAlliance Chase (Cheltenham)	*John Grossick*	791
Royal & SunAlliance Novices' Hurdle (Cheltenham)	*Ed Byrne*	335
Royal British Legion Poppy Appeal Persian War Novices' Hurdle (Chepstow)	*Ed Byrne*	188
Servo Computer Services' Ascot Chase	*Ed Byrne*	387
Sharp Minds Betfair Novice Handicap Chase (Punchestown)	*Caroline Norris*	540
skybet.com Mansion House Handicap Chase (Doncaster)	*Alec Russell*	74
skybet.com River Don Novices' Hurdle (Doncaster)	*Alec Russell*	255
skybet.com Rowland Meyrick Handicap Chase (Wetherby)	*Alec Russell*	383
Skybet Great Yorkshire Chase (Handicap) (Alec Russell)	*Alec Russell*	954
skybetvegas.com Castleford Chase (Wetherby)	*Alec Russell*	484
Smurfit Champion Hurdle Challenge Trophy (Cheltenham)	*George Selwyn*	392
Smurfit Champion Hurdle Challenge Trophy (Cheltenham)	*Bill Selwyn*	393
South-West Racing Club Handicap Chase (Exeter)	*Bill Selwyn*	892
Stan James Challow Novices' Hurdle (Newbury)	*Ed Byrne*	222
Stan James Gerry Feilden Intermediate Hurdle (Limited Handicap) (Newbury)	*George Selwyn*	942
stanjamesuk.com Worcester Novices' Chase (Newbury)	*George Selwyn*	96
Stan James Win A Racehorse Gold Cup (Handicap Chase) (Kempton)	*W. Everitt*	887
Stewart Tory Memorial Trophy Hunters' Chase (Wincanton)	*Ed Byrne*	707
Sunderlands Imperial Cup Handicap Hurdle (Sandown)	*George Selwyn*	812
Telectronics Systems 'National Hunt' Auction Novices' Hurdle (Cheltenham)	*George Selwyn*	220
The Hewlett-Packard Galway Plate (Handicap Chase)	*Caroline Norris*	655
Thyson Technology 10th Anniversary Handicap Hurdle (Haydock)	*Alec Russell*	693
Timeform Novices' Handicap Chase (Cheltenham)	*Ed Byrne*	97
Tommy Whittle Chase (Haydock)	*Alec Russell*	490
Tote Becher Chase (Handicap) (Aintree)	*Alec Russell*	201
Tote Bula Hurdle (Cheltenham)	*Ed Byrne*	758
Tote Classic Chase (Handicap) (Warwick)	*George Selwyn*	853
Tote Eider (Handicap Chase) (Newcastle)	*Alec Russell*	955
Tote Exacta Handicap Chase (Wetherby)	*Alec Russell*	951
Tote Exacta Premier Kelso Hurdle (Novices')	*John Grossick*	690
Tote Gold Trophy Hurdle (Handicap) (Newbury)	*George Selwyn*	350
Tote National Spirit Hurdle (Fontwell)	*Ed Byrne*	867
Tote Peterborough Chase (Huntingdon)	*Ed Byrne*	461
Tote Placepot Handicap Hurdle (Haydock)	*Alec Russell*	751
Tote Scilly Isles Novices' Chase (Sandown)	*Bill Selwyn*	696
Tote Scoop6 Lanzarote Hurdle (Handicap) (Kempton)	*Bill Selwyn*	536
Tote Scoop6 Sandown Hurdle (Handicap)	*George Selwyn*	102
Tote Scoop6 Summer Plate (Handicap Chase) (Market Rasen)	*Alec Russell*	95
totesport Cheltenham Gold Cup Chase	*Bill Selwyn*	125
totesport Cheltenham Gold Cup Chase	*George Selwyn*	126
totesport Cheltenham Gold Cup Chase	*Bill Selwyn*	127
Tripleprint Chase (Handicap) (Cheltenham)	*Ed Byrne*	506
Tripleprint Gold Cup (Handicap Chase) (Cheltenham)	*Ed Byrne*	444
Unicoin Homes Chase (Handicap) (Cheltenham)	*Ed Byrne*	985
Unwins Wine Group Anniversary 4-Y-O Novices' Hurdle (Aintree)	*Alec Russell*	42
Velka Pardubicka Ceske Pojistovny (Pardubice)	*Bill Selwyn*	748
Victor Chandler Chase (Handicap) (Ascot)	*Bill Selwyn*	450
Victor Chandler Get More Back Lightning Novices' Chase (Ascot)	*W. Everitt*	92
Vincent O'Brien County Handicap Hurdle (Cheltenham)	*George Selwyn*	859
Vodafone Gold Cup Handicap Chase (Newbury)	*Ed Byrne*	451
Vodafone Handicap Chase (Newbury)	*Ed Byrne*	597
Vodafone Handicap Chase (Newbury)	*Ed Byrne*	964
Vodafone Handicap Hurdle (Newbury)	*Ed Byrne*	334
Weatherbys Bank Towton Novices' Chase (Wetherby)	*Alec Russell*	782

CHAMPIONS FROM THE 'CHASERS & HURDLERS' SERIES

Best Two-Mile Chaser

75/76	Lough Inagh	167	90/91	Desert Orchid	178
76/77	Skymas	156	91/92	Remittance Man	173
77/78	Tingle Creek	154	92/93	Katabatic	161 ?
78/79	Siberian Sun	151	93/94	Viking Flagship	166
79/80	I'm A Driver	163	94/95	Viking Flagship	169
80/81	Anaglogs Daughter	171	95/96	Klairon Davis	177
81/82	Rathgorman	170	96/97	Martha's Son	177
82/83	Badsworth Boy	179	97/98	One Man	176
83/84	Badsworth Boy	177	98/99	Direct Route	166
84/85	Bobsline	164 +	99/00	Flagship Uberalles	176
85/86	Dawn Run	167	00/01	Flagship Uberalles	175
86/87	Pearlyman	171	01/02	Flagship Uberalles	170
87/88	Pearlyman	174	02/03	Moscow Flyer	170 p
88/89	Desert Orchid	182	03/04	Moscow Flyer	183
89/90	Desert Orchid	187			

Best Staying Chaser

75/76	Captain Christy	182	90/91	Desert Orchid	178
76/77	Bannow Rambler	163	91/92	Carvill's Hill	182
77/78	Midnight Court	164	92/93	Jodami	174 p
78/79	Gay Spartan	166	93/94	The Fellow	171
79/80	Silver Buck	171	94/95	Master Oats	183
80/81	Little Owl	176	95/96	One Man	179
81/82	Silver Buck	175	96/97	One Man	176
82/83	Bregawn	177	97/98	Cool Dawn	173
83/84	Burrough Hill Lad	175	98/99	Suny Bay	176
	Wayward Lad	175	99/00	See More Business	182
84/85	Burrough Hill Lad	184	00/01	First Gold	180
85/86	Burrough Hill Lad	183	01/02	Best Mate	173
86/87	Desert Orchid	177		Florida Pearl	173
87/88	Desert Orchid	177	02/03	Best Mate	182
88/89	Desert Orchid	182	03/04	Best Mate	176 +
89/90	Desert Orchid	187			

Best Novice Chaser

75/76	Bannow Rambler	152 p	90/91	Remittance Man	153 p
76/77	Tree Tangle	159 §	91/92	Miinnehoma	152 p
77/78	The Dealer	145	92/93	Sybillin	156
78/79	Silver Buck	151	93/94	Monsieur Le Cure	156 p
79/80	Anaglogs Daughter	156	94/95	Brief Gale	159
80/81	Clayside	145	95/96	Mr Mulligan	154
81/82	Brown Chamberlin	147 p	96/97	Strong Promise	171 +
82/83	Righthand Man	150	97/98	Escartefigue	171 p
83/84	Bobsline	161 p	98/99	Nick Dundee	164 +
84/85	Drumadowney	159	99/00	Gloria Victis	172
85/86	Pearlyman	150	00/01	Bacchanal	161 p
86/87	Kildimo	151 p		Shotgun Willy	161
87/88	Danish Flight	156 p	01/02	Moscow Flyer	159 p
88/89	Carvill's Hill	169 p	02/03	Beef Or Salmon	165 p
89/90	Celtic Shot	152 p	03/04	Strong Flow	156 p

Best Two-Mile Hurdler

75/76	Night Nurse	178	90/91	Morley Street	174
76/77	Night Nurse	182	91/92	Granville Again	165 p
77/78	Monksfield	177	92/93	Mighty Mogul	170
78/79	Monksfield	180	93/94	Danoli	172 p
79/80	Sea Pigeon	175	94/95	Alderbrook	174 p
80/81	Sea Pigeon	175	95/96	Alderbrook	174
81/82	For Auction	174	96/97	Make A Stand	165
82/83	Gaye Brief	175	97/98	Istabraq	172 +
83/84	Dawn Run	173	98/99	Istabraq	177 +
84/85	Browne's Gazette	172	99/00	Istabraq	180
85/86	See You Then	173	00/01	Istabraq	180
86/87	See You Then	173	01/02	Limestone Lad	167
87/88	Celtic Shot	170	02/03	Rooster Booster	170
88/89	Beech Road	172	03/04	Hardy Eustace	167
89/90	Kribensis	169			

Best Staying Hurdler

75/76	Comedy of Errors	170	77/78	Monksfield	177
76/77	Night Nurse	182	78/79	Monksfield	180

79/80	Pollardstown	**167**	92/93	Sweet Duke	**161**
80/81	Daring Run	**171** +	93/94	Sweet Glow	**162**
81/82	Daring Run	**171**	94/95	Dorans Pride	**167**
82/83	Gaye Brief	**175**	95/96	Pleasure Shared	**163** p
83/84	Dawn Run	**173**	96/97	Paddy's Return	**164**
84/85	Bajan Sunshine	**162**	97/98	Paddy's Return	**168**
85/86	Gaye Brief	**167**	98/99	Deano's Beeno	**165**
86/87	Galmoy	**165**		Princeful	**165**
87/88	Galmoy	**160**	99/00	Limestone Lad	**177**
88/89	Rustle	**169**	00/01	Le Sauvignon	**178**
89/90	Trapper John	**159**	01/02	Baracouda	**169** +
90/91	King's Curate	**164**	02/03	Baracouda	**175**
91/92	Nomadic Way	**162**	03/04	Iris's Gift	**172**

Best Novice Hurdler

75/76	Grand Canyon	**159**	89/90	Regal Ambition	**151**
76/77	Outpoint	**154**	90/91	Ruling	**167**
77/78	Golden Cygnet	**176**	91/92	Royal Gait	**164** p
78/79	Venture To Cognac	**162**	92/93	Montelado	**150** P
79/80	Slaney Idol	**143**	93/94	Danoli	**172** p
80/81	Dunaree	**159**	94/95	Alderbrook	**174** p
81/82	Angelo Salvini	**149**	95/96	Pleasure Shared	**163** p
82/83	Dawn Run	**168**	96/97	Make A Stand	**165**
83/84	Desert Orchid	**158**	97/98	French Holly	**151** P
84/85	Asir	**148** p	98/99	Barton	**153** p
85/86	River Ceiriog	**158** p	99/00	Monsignor	**158** p
86/87	The West Awake	**153** p	00/01	Baracouda	**172**
87/88	Carvill's Hill	**157** p	01/02	Intersky Falcon	**152** p
88/89	Sondrio	**152** p	02/03	Iris's Gift	**172**
	Wishlon	**152** +	03/04	Inglis Drever	**152**

Best Juvenile Hurdler

75/76	Valmony	**157**	90/91	Oh So Risky	**149** p
76/77	Meladon	**149**	91/92	Staunch Friend	**151** p
77/78	Major Thompson	**144**	92/93	Shawiya	**141** p
78/79	Pollardstown	**141**	93/94	Mysilv	**144** p
79/80	Hill of Slane	**144**	94/95	Kissair	**143** p
80/81	Broadsword	**144**	95/96	Escartefigue	**159**
81/82	Shiny Copper	**141**	96/97	Grimes	**138** p
82/83	Sabin du Loir	**147** p	97/98	Deep Water	**149** p
83/84	Northern Game	**142**	98/99	Hors La Loi III	**162** p
84/85	Out of The Gloom	**151**	99/00	Grand Seigneur	**148** p
85/86	Dark Raven	**153** p	00/01	Jair du Cochet	**163**
86/87	Aldino	**154**	01/02	Scolardy	**147**
87/88	Kribensis	**143** p	02/03	Nickname	**142**
88/89	Royal Derbi	**144**	03/04	Maia Eria	**143**
89/90	Sybillin	**138**			

Best National Hunt Flat Race Performer

93/94	Aries Girl	**123**	99/00	Quadco	**129**
94/95	Dato Star	**120**	00/01	The Bajan Bandit	**128**
95/96	Wither Or Which	**122**	01/02	Pizarro	**123**
96/97	Florida Pearl	**124**		Rhinestone Cowboy	**123**
97/98	Alexander Banquet	**126**	02/03	Rhinestone Cowboy	**123**
98/99	Monsignor	**122**	03/04	Secret Ploy	**122**

Best Hunter Chaser

75/76	Otter Way	**143**	91/92	Rushing Wild	**127** p
76/77	Under Way	**124**	92/93	Double Silk	**122** p
77/78	Spartan Missile	**133**	93/94	Double Silk	**130** p
78/79	Spartan Missile	**133** +		Elegant Lord	**130** p
79/80	Rolls Rambler	**132**	94/95	Fantus	**139** p
80/81	Spartan Missile	**169**	95/96	Elegant Lord	**138** p
81/82	Compton Lad	**142**	96/97	Celtic Abbey	**136** p
82/83	Eliogarty	**147**		Fantus	**136**
83/84	Venture To Cognac	**149**	97/98	Earthmover	**140** p
84/85	Further Thought	**141**	98/99	Castle Mane	**148** p
85/86	Ah Whisht	**148**	99/00	Cavalero	**142**
86/87	Observe	**146**	00/01	Sheltering	**136**
87/88	Certain Light	**147**	01/02	Torduff Express	**130**
88/89	Call Collect	**142** p	02/03	Kingscliff	**137** P
89/90	Mystic Music	**143**	03/04	Earthmover	**133**
90/91	Mystic Music	**143** ?			

HIGHEST TIMEFORM RATINGS

Chasers & Hurdlers 1975/76 was the first in the Timeform annual series but the jumping edition of the weekly Timeform Black Book has been published since the early-'sixties. The following 'annual' ratings are the highest achieved since that time (Timeform ratings for the leading French jumpers were not published regularly until the 'nineties).

Chasers
212   Arkle
210   Flyingbolt
191   Mill House
187   Desert Orchid
186   Dunkirk
184   Burrough Hill Lad
183   Master Oats, Moscow Flyer
182   Azertyuiop, Best Mate, Captain Christy, Carvill's Hill,
       See More Business
180   First Gold
179   Badsworth Boy, Fortria, One Man
178   Imperial Call, Pendil
177   Bregawn, Kinloch Brae, Klairon Davis, Martha's Son, The Dikler
176   Buona notte, Little Owl, Looks Like Trouble, Suny Bay, Titus Oates
175   Brown Lad, Flagship Uberalles, L'Escargot, Night Nurse,
       Rough Quest, Silver Buck, Wayward Lad
174   Barnbrook Again, Bula, Jodami, Pearlyman
173   Al Capone II, Blazing Walker, Captain John, Cool Dawn,
       Cyfor Malta, Florida Pearl, Remittance Man, Teeton Mill
172   Barton Bank, Bradbury Star, Brown Chamberlin, Crisp, Gloria Victis,
       Go Ballistic, Katabatic, Rushing Wild, Strong Promise, Valley Henry,
       Valley Henry, Viking Flagship

Hurdlers
182   Night Nurse
180   Istabraq, Monksfield
179   Persian War
178   Comedy of Errors, Le Sauvignon
177   Lanzarote, Limestone Lad
176   Bird's Nest, Bula, Golden Cygnet
175   Baracouda, Deano's Beeno, Gaye Brief, Salmon Spray, Sea Pigeon
174   Alderbrook, Dramatist, For Auction, Magic Court, Morley Street
173   Dato Star, Dawn Run, Mon Romain, See You Then
172   Anzio, Bannow Rambler, Beech Road, Boreen Prince,
       Browne's Gazette, Danoli, Flatterer, Iris's Gift, Prideaux Boy
171   Barnbrook Again, Canasta Lad, Captain Christy, Celtic Gold, Chorus,
       Daring Run, Le Coudray, Moyne Royal, Pollardstown

The following ratings for horses in the pre-Timeform era, compiled by Randall and Morris for 'A Century of Champions', were used by Timeform for an exhibit in Cheltenham's Hall of Fame:

190   Easter Hero
188   Golden Miller
183   Pas Seul, Prince Regent
176   Sir Ken

REVOLUTIONISE YOUR RACING @
timeform.com

Timeform Race Cards for every meeting available for immediate download for £5.50 per meeting!

Timeform Daily Form Guide, exclusive to our internet site, provides ratings and commentaries for any individual race for only £1.50!

Horse Enquiry facility lets you see the up-to-date commentary, rating and Perspective history for any horse on the Timeform database for 50p!

Bonus Credits when you deposit £50 or more!

Before you bet know what we know!

Timeform, 19 Timeform House, Halifax, West Yorkshire HX1 1XF